The Literary Experience

Bruce Beiderwell
University of California, Los Angeles

Jeffrey M. Wheeler
Long Beach City College

THOMSON
WADSWORTH™

Australia • Brazil • Canada • Mexico • Singapore
Spain • United Kingdom • United States

THOMSON

WADSWORTH ™

The Literary Experience
Bruce Beiderwell/Jeffrey M. Wheeler

Publisher: *Lyn Uhl*
Senior Acquisitions Editor: *Aron Keesbury*
Development Editor: *Marita Sermolins*
Editorial Assistant: *Kristen Albertsen*
Technology Project Manager: *Joe Gallagher*
Marketing Manager: *Kate Edwards*
Marketing Assistant: *Kate Remsberg*
Marketing Communications Manager:
   Patrick Rooney
Signing Representative: *Bill Brisick*
Senior Content Project Manager:
   Samantha Ross

Print Buyer: *Betsy Donaghey*
Permissions Editor: *Ron Montgomery*
Permissions Researcher: *Marcy Lunetta*
Text Designer: *Garry Harman*
Photo Manager: *Sheri Blaney*
Photo Researcher: *Francelle Carapetyan*
Cover Designer: *Cabbage Design Company*
Cover Printer: *Phoenix Color*
Compositor/Production Service:
   Newgen–Austin
Printer: *RR Donnelly, Crawfordsville*

Library of Congress Control Number:
2006932324

ISBN-13 978-1-4130-1917-9

ISBN-10 1-4130-1917-X

Thomson Higher Education
25 Thomson Place
Boston, MA 02210-1202
USA

For more information about our products,
contact us at:
Thomson Learning Academic Resource Center
1-800-423-0563

For permission to use material from this text
or product, submit a request online at
http://www.thomsonrights.com
Any additional questions about permissions
can be submitted by e-mail to
thomsonrights@thomson.com

Credits appear on pages 1809–1825, which
constitute a continuation of the copyright page.

Brief Contents

Introduction to the Elements of Literature xxxiii
*How Do We Know What Terms to Use When We Talk about
Our Experiences with Literature?*

1 | **Scene, Episode, and Plot** 1
What Happened, and Why Do We Care?

2 | **Character** 115
Who Is Involved, and Why Does It Matter?

3 | **Theme** 195
What Does This Text Mean?
Is There One Right Way to Read This Text?

4 | **Point of View** 282
How Do We Know What We Know about What Happened?

5 | **Setting** 399
Where and When Does This Action Take Place?
Why Does It Make a Difference?

6 | **Rhythm, Pace, and Rhyme** 508
How Do Sounds Move?

7 | **Images** 630
How Do We Experience Sensations in a Written Text?

8 | **Coherence** 713
Is There a Pattern Here?
How Does This Fit Together?

9 | Interruption   787
Where Did That Come From?
Why Is This Here?

10 | Tone   1006
Did I Hear That Right?

11 | Word Choice   1077
Why This Word and Not Another?

12 | Allegory   1194
Is This Supposed to Mean Something Else, Too?

13 | Symbolism   1252
How Do I Know When an Event or an Image Is Supposed to Stand for Something Else?

14 | Context   1392
What Outside Information Do We Really Need to Know to Understand the Text?

15 | Allusions   1474
In Order to Understand This Text, Is There Something Else That I Am Supposed to Have Read?

16 | Genre   1582
How Do Our Expectations Impact Our Literary Experience?
How Are Those Expectations Formed?

17 | The Production and Reproduction of Texts   1674
How Does Retelling and Revising Impact My Experience of a Text?
How Can Literary Theory Clarify What Constitutes That Experience?

18 | An Orientation to Research   1695
Why Should I Use Sources?
How Do We Find Them?
What Material Do I Document?

Contents

Preface   xxv

Introduction to the Elements of Literature   xxxiii
How Do We Know What Terms to Use When We Talk about
Our Experience with Literature?

Developing a Flexible Critical Vocabulary   xxxiv
Critical Writing as Conversation   xxxv
Critical Writing as an Extension of Reading   xxxvii
  Langston Hughes, Harlem *[poem]*   xxxvii

1 | Scene, Episode, and Plot
What Happened, and Why Do We Care?   1

  Edouard Boubat, Rendez-vous at the Café La Vache Noire *[image]*   2
Incident, Scene, and Sequence   2
  Experiencing Literature through Plot   3
    Robert Pinsky, Poem with Lines in Any Order *[poem]*   4
    Wislawa Szymborska, ABC *[poem]*   5
Episode, Impression, and Fragment   5
  Claude Monet, Portal of Rouen Cathedral in Morning
    Light *[image]*   7
  Experiencing Literature through Impression and Episode   7
    Stephen Crane, An Episode of War *[fiction]*   8
Tension, Release, and Resolution   11
Multiple and Reflexive Plots   13
  Memento *[film]*   14
  A NOTE TO STUDENT WRITERS: *Critical Reading and Understanding*   14
  Marge Piercy, Unlearning to not speak *[poem]*   15
Modeling Critical Analysis: Jamaica Kincaid, Girl *[fiction]*   16
  Jamaica Kincaid, Girl *[fiction]*   16

Anthology

Detective Work: Figuring Plot   18

FICTION   **Arthur Conan Doyle**, A Scandal in Bohemia   20
Don Lee, The Price of Eggs in China   39

POETRY   **Emily Dickinson**, [A Route of Evanescence]   59
Emily Dickinson, [I like to see it lap the Miles—]   60
E. A. Robinson, Richard Cory   60
Robert Frost, Stopping by Woods on a Snowy Evening   61
William Stafford, Traveling through the Dark   62
Kevin Young, The Set-up   62
Kevin Young, The Chase   64
Aron Keesbury, On the Robbery across the Street   65
Muriel Rukeyser, Myth   66

DRAMA   **Sophocles**, Oedipus the King   67

2 | Character
Who Is Involved, and Why Does It Matter?   115

Building Character   116
Experiencing Literature through Character   117
Michael Chabon, *from* The Amazing Adventures of Kavalier &
Clay [fiction]   117
Presenting Character   120
A NOTE TO STUDENT WRITERS: *Leading Questions   121*
Picturing Character   121
Experiencing Film and Literature through Character   122
Gone with the Wind [film]   123
Hattie McDaniel accepting her Academy Award at
the Coconut Grove [image]   124
Rita Dove, Hattie McDaniel Arrives at the Coconut
Grove [poem]   124
Feeling for Character   126
Experiencing Literature through Character   126
Cathy Song, Picture Bride [poem]   127
Robert Hayden, Those Winter Sundays [poem]   128
Character and Function   129
Judith Ortiz Cofer, My Father in the Navy:
A Childhood Memory [poem]   130
Modeling Critical Analysis: Jamaica Kincaid, Girl *[fiction]*   131

Anthology

Power Plays: Characterizing Relationships   132

FICTION   **Alice Munro**, How I Met My Husband   134
Luigi Pirandello, The Soft Touch of Grass   148
Alice Walker, Everyday Use   152

POETRY   **Edgar Lee Masters**, Elsa Wertman   160
Edgar Lee Masters, Hamilton Greene   161
Robert Frost, Home Burial   161
Audre Lorde, Now That I Am Forever with Child   165
Eavan Boland, The Pomegranate   165
Sylvia Plath, Daddy   167
Quincy Troupe, Poem for My Father   170
Kitty Tsui, A Chinese Banquet   171
Billy Collins, Lanyard   173
E. A. Robinson, The Mill   174
Liz Rosenberg, 1:53 A.M.   175
Gwendolyn Brooks, Sadie and Maud   176
Seamus Heaney, Mid-Term Break   176
Michael Lassell, How to Watch Your Brother Die   177
Adrienne Rich, Aunt Jennifer's Tigers   180
Gary Soto, Black Hair   181

DRAMA   **Anton Chekhov**, The Proposal: A Jest in One Act   182

3 | Theme
What Does This Text Mean?
Is There One Right Way to Read This Text?   195

Theme and Thesis   196
Theme and Moral   197
Charles Perrault, Little Red Riding Hood [fiction]   198
James Thurber, The Girl and the Wolf [fiction]   201
Calvin Coolidge [image]   201
MGM Lion [image]   201
Girl Devoured by Wolf [fiction]   202
Experiencing Literature through Theme   202
Marge Piercy, A Work of Artifice [poem]   203
Multiple Themes in a Single Work   204
Experiencing Literature through Theme   205
Maxine Hong Kingston, The Wild Man of the Green
Swamp [fiction]   205

When the Message Is Unwanted   208

   Triumph of the Will *[film]*   209

   A NOTE TO STUDENT WRITERS: *Discovering What You Want to Say*   210

Modeling Critical Analysis: Jamaica Kincaid, Girl *[fiction]*   211

Anthology

Exploring Boundaries: Interpreting Theme   213

FICTION   **Luisa Valenzuela**, The Censors   214

   Flannery O'Connor, A Good Man Is Hard To Find   217

POETRY   **John Keats**, La Belle Dame sans Merci: A Ballad   230

   Edna St. Vincent Millay, [Women have loved before as
      I love now]   232

   Elizabeth Bishop, Casabianca   232

   Ted Hughes, Lovesong   233

   Carolyn Forché, The Colonel   234

   William Butler Yeats, Leda and the Swan   235

   D. H. Lawrence, Snake   236

   Richard Wilbur, A Fable   238

   Linda Pastan, Ethics   239

DRAMA   **Christopher Marlowe**, Doctor Faustus   240

4 | Point of View
How Do We Know What We Know about What Happened?   282

Perspective   282

   Albrecht Dürer, Working on Perspective *[image]*   283

   Masaccio, Trinity *[image]*   284

   Plan and elevation of Masaccio's *Trinity [image]*   285

   Dorothy Parker, Penelope *[poem]*   285

   A NOTE TO STUDENT WRITERS: *Distinguishing Author from Speaker*   286

The Narrative Eye   286

   Caspar David Friedrich, Wanderer above the Sea of Fog *[image]*   287

   Caspar David Friedrich, Woman in the Morning Light *[image]*   287

Reliable and Unreliable Narrators   288

Third-Person Narrators   **288**

   Charles Dickens, *from* A Christmas Carol *[fiction]*   288

First-Person Narrators   **290**

   Experiencing Literature through Point of View   291

      Wendell Berry, The Vacation *[poem]*   291

Film Focus and Angles   292
   The Magnicent Ambersons *[film]*   293
   Citizen Kane *[film]*   293
   Trapped *[film]*   294
   Nosferatu *[film]*   294
   Henry Taylor, After a Movie *[poem]*   295
   Experiencing Film through Point of View   296
      Rear Window *[film]*   297

Shifting Perspectives   298
   Stevie Smith, Not Waving but Drowning *[poem]*   299
   Experiencing Literature through Perspective   300
      Charles Sheeler, River Rouge Plant Stamping Press *[image]*   300
      Philip Levine, Photography 2 *[poem]*   300
      Frank X. Gaspar, It Is the Nature of the Wing *[poem]*   302

Modeling Critical Analysis: Robert Browning,
   My Last Duchess *[poem]*   303
   Robert Browning, My Last Duchess *[poem]*   303

Anthology

Trust and Doubt: A Matter of Point of View   306
FICTION   **Ann Beattie**, Janus   306
   Kate Chopin, The Story of an Hour   311
   Charlotte Perkins Gilman, The Yellow Wallpaper   314
POETRY   **Helane Levine Keating**, My Last Duke   327
   William Carlos Williams, This Is Just to Say   328
   Erica-Lynn Gambino, This Is Just to Say   329
   Elizabeth Bishop, The Fish   330
   Edna St. Vincent Millay, Childhood Is the Kingdom Where
      Nobody Dies   332
   Charles Simic, Prodigy   333
   John Donne, The Good-Morrow   334
   Adrienne Rich, Living in Sin   335
   W. S. Merwin, Separation   336
   H. D. Helen   336
   Sylvia Plath, The Applicant   337
   Sylvia Plath, Mirror   338
   Robert Morgan, Working in the Rain   339
DRAMA   **William Shakespeare**, Much Ado about Nothing   340

5 | Setting
Where and When Does This Action Take Place?
Why Does it Make a Difference?   399

Place and Time   399
   Greetings from Fargo postcard [image]   400
   A NOTE TO STUDENT WRITERS: *Descriptive Summaries*   401
   Experiencing Literature through Setting   401
      Denise Levertov, February Evening in New York [poem]   402
      Theodore Dreiser, *from* Sister Carrie [fiction]   403
      Department store interior [image]   404
The Role of Physical Objects   405
   Kazuo Ishiguro, *from* Remains of the Day [fiction]   405
Imaginary Places   408
   Experiencing Film through Setting   409
      Amélie [film]   410
      Babe: Pig in the City [film]   411
   A NOTE TO STUDENT WRITERS: *Paying Attention to Details*   412
Modeling Critical Analysis: Robert Browning,
   My Last Duchess [poem]   412

Anthology

From Gothic Space to Recognizable Place: Creating Setting   414
               Giovanni Piranesi, *from* Imaginary Prisons [image]   414
FICTION   **James Joyce**, Araby   415
               Edgar Allan Poe, The Fall of the House of Usher   420
POETRY   **Samuel Taylor Coleridge**, Kubla Khan: or, a Vision in a Dream   436
               Edgar Allan Poe, The Raven   437
               Christina Rossetti, Cobwebs   440
               Oscar Wilde, The Harlot's House   441
               Dudley Randall, Ballad of Birmingham   442
               Joy Harjo, New Orleans   444
               Joy Harjo, The Woman Hanging from the Thirteenth
                  Floor Window   446
               Gary Soto, Braly Street   448
               Gary Soto, Kearney Park   450
               Ginger Andrews, Rolls-Royce Dreams   451
               Barbara Ras, Childhood   452
               Chitra Banerjee Divakaruni, Indian Movie, New Jersey   453
               B. H. Fairchild, The *Dumka*   454
DRAMA   **Tennessee Williams**, The Glass Menagerie   455

6 | Rhythm, Pace, and Rhyme
How Do Sounds Move? 508

Filmic Rhythm 509
   Experiencing Film through Rhythm 510
      Jaws *[film]* 510
Poetic Rhythm 511
   Experiencing Literature through Rhythm 513
      Herman Melville, The Maldive Shark *[poem]* 514
      William Blake, Nurse's Song *[poem]* 514
The Rhythm of Pauses 517
   Experiencing Literature through Rhythm 517
      Samuel Johnson, On the Death of Dr. Robert Levet *[poem]* 518
      Ben Jonson, On My First Son *[poem]* 520
   A NOTE TO STUDENT WRITERS: *Commanding Attention* 520
The Rhythm of Sounds 521
   Experiencing Literature through Rhythm and Rhyme 522
      Randall Jarrell, The Death of the Ball Turret Gunner *[poem]* 523
      Robert Frost, Fire and Ice *[poem]* 524
Modeling Critical Analysis: Robert Browning,
My Last Duchess *[poem]* 524

Anthology

Innocence and Experience: Rhythm and Meaning 525

FICTION **James Baldwin**, Sonny's Blues 527
         Ursula K. Le Guin, The Ones Who Walk Away from Omelas 553
         Susan Minot, Lust 559
POETRY   **William Blake**, The Lamb 567
         William Blake, The Chimney Sweeper (Innocence) 568
         William Blake, Holy Thursday (Innocence) 569
         William Blake, The Tyger 569
         William Blake, The Chimney Sweeper (Experience) 570
         William Blake, Holy Thursday (Experience) 570
         Theodore Roethke, My Papa's Waltz 571
         Theodore Roethke, The Waking 572
         Langston Hughes, Dream Boogie 573
         Langston Hughes, The Negro Speaks of Rivers 573
         Gwendolyn Brooks, We Real Cool 574
         Countee Cullen, Incident 575
         Denise Levertov, In Mind 575
         Sharon Olds, I Go Back to May 1937 576
         Sharon Olds, The Death of Marilyn Monroe 577
DRAMA   **Suzan-Lori Parks**, Topdog/Underdog 578

7 | Images
  How Do We Experience Sensations in a Written Text?   630

Creating Pictures with Words   631
   William Carlos Williams, The Red Wheelbarrow *[poem]*   631
   Czeslaw Milosz, Watering Can *[poem]*   632
   Sailboat *[image]*   633
   Georges Seurat, Entrance to the Harbor *[image]*   633
   Experiencing Literature through Imagery   634
      Wislawa Szymborska, The Courtesy of the Blind *[poem]*   634

Registering Taste and Smell   636
   Sideways *[film]*   636
   Experiencing Literature through Images   637
      Salman Rushdie, On Leavened Bread *[prose]*   637
      Nun with Bread *[image]*   638

Interaction of the Senses   639
   John Milton, *from* Paradise Lost *[poem]*   640
   Gangs of New York *[film]*   642
   Lost in Translation *[film]*   642
   Experiencing Literature through Images   643
      Richard Wilbur, A Fire-Truck *[poem]*   643

Interaction of Words and Pictures   645
   Michael Ondaatje, King Kong Meets Wallace Stevens *[poem]*   645
   Wallace Stevens *[image]*   646
   King Kong *[film]*   647
   Experiencing Literature through Images   647
      Yosa Buson, Hokku Poems in Four Seasons *[poem]*   648
   A NOTE TO STUDENT WRITERS: *Using Specific Detail*   652

Modeling Critical Analysis: T. S. Eliot, The Love Song of
   J. Alfred Prufrock *[poem]*   652
   T. S. Eliot, The Love Song of J. Alfred Prufrock *[poem]*   653

Anthology

Home and Away: Personalizing Images   657
FICTION   **Alice Munro**, Boys and Girls   659
          Haruki Murakami, UFO in Kushiro   671
POETRY   **William Blake**, London   684
          William Wordsworth, London, 1802   684
          William Wordsworth, Composed upon Westminster Bridge,
             September 3, 1802   685

William Wordsworth, The World Is Too Much with Us   686
William Wordsworth, [I wandered lonely as a cloud]   686
Emily Dickinson, [There's a certain Slant of light]   687
Robert Frost, Birches   688
Robert Frost, Acquainted with the Night   689
Ezra Pound, In a Station of the Metro   690
Wallace Stevens, The Snow Man   690
Wallace Stevens, Thirteen Ways of Looking at a Blackbird   691
e. e. cummings, in Just-   693
Maya Angelou, Harlem Hopscotch   694
Richard Wilbur, April 5, 1974   695
Mary Oliver, Spring   695
Mary Oliver, Ghosts   697
Derek Walcott, Dry Season   699
DRAMA   **Susan Glaspell,** Trifles   699

8 | Coherence
Is There a Pattern Here?
How Does This Fit Together?   713

Nick Hornby, *from* High Fidelity *[fiction]*   713
High Fidelity *[film]*   714
Design and Shape   715
George Herbert, Easter Wings *[poem]*   716
Thomas Hardy, The Convergence of the Twain *[poem]*   717
Traditional Structures   718
Sonnet chart *[image]*   720
Experiencing Literature through Form   721
William Wordsworth, Nuns Fret Not *[poem]*   722
Edna St. Vincent Millay, I, Being Born a Woman
and Distressed *[poem]*   722
Robert Frost, Design *[poem]*   723
Dylan Thomas, Do Not Go Gentle into That Good
Night *[poem]*   724
A NOTE TO STUDENT WRITERS: *Complicating a Thesis*   725
Coherence without Traditional or Fixed Structure   726
Philip Levine, The Simple Truth *[poem]*   726
Modeling Critical Analysis: T. S. Eliot, The Love Song of
J. Alfred Prufrock *[poem]*   729

Anthology

Rituals and Routines: Structuring for Coherence   730

FICTION   **Charles W. Chesnutt**, Wife of His Youth   733
John Updike, A&P   742
Jonathan Safran Foer, The Very Rigid Search   748

POETRY   **William Cullen Bryant**, To Cole, the Painter,
Departing for Europe   769
Joe Kane, The Boy Who Nearly Won the Texaco Art
Competition   769
Elizabeth Bishop, Manners for a Child of 1918   770
Phillis Wheatley, On Being Brought from Africa to America   771
Robert Frost, The Road Not Taken   772
Thomas Lux, The Swimming Pool   773
Lawrence Ferlinghetti, Constantly risking absurdity   774
Allen Ginsberg, Supermarket in California   775
Richard Wilbur, A Sketch   776
Miller Williams, Thinking about Bill, Dead of AIDS   777

DRAMA   **David Ives**, Sure Thing   778

9 | Interruption
Where Did That Come From?
Why Is This Here?   787

Interrupting the Fictional Frame   787
The Princess Bride [film]   788
Experiencing Literature through Interruption   789
Douglas Adams, *from* The Hitchhiker's Guide to the
Galaxy [fiction]   790

Structural Interruptions   792
William Butler Yeats, The Folly of Being Comforted [poem]   792
Mary Oliver, Bone Poem [poem]   793
Experiencing Film through Interruption   794
Pulp Fiction [film]   795

Juxtaposition   795
Margaret Bourke-White, At the Time of the Louisville
Flood [image]   796
Experiencing Literature through Juxtaposition   797
Ted Kooser, Tattoo [poem]   798

Montage   798
    Experiencing Film through Juxtaposition   799
      Roger and Me *[film]*   800
    A NOTE TO STUDENT WRITERS: *Making Comparisons Relevant*   801
Modeling Critical Analysis: T. S. Eliot, The Love Song of
    J. Alfred Prufrock *[poem]*   802

Anthology

Framing, Mapping, and Exploration: Placing Interruption   805

FICTION   **Jorges Luis Borges,** The Garden of Forking Paths   806
          Joseph Conrad, The Secret Sharer   814
          Eudora Welty, A Worn Path   847
          Raymond Carver, Cathedral   854

POETRY   **Elizabeth Bishop,** Brazil, January, 1502   867
          Louise Bogan, Cartography   868
          Sharon Olds, Topography   869
          Langston Hughes, Theme for English B   870
          Laura Riding, The Map of Places   871
          Richard Wilbur, Worlds   871
          Samuel Taylor Coleridge, The Rime of the Ancient Mariner   872
          Alfred, Lord Tennyson, Ulysses   890
          Emily Dickinson, [The Brain—is wider than the Sky—]   892
          Emily Dickinson, [I never saw a Moor—]   893
          Emily Dickinson, [Tell all the Truth but tell it slant—]   893
          Emily Dickinson, [To make a prairie it takes a clover
            and one bee]   893
          John Donne, The Sun Rising   894
          John Donne, A Valediction: Forbidding Mourning   895

DRAMA   **William Shakespeare,** Hamlet   896

10 | Tone
    Did I Hear That Right?   1006

Hearing Right   1007
    Margaret Atwood, you fit into me *[poem]*   1007
    Experiencing Literature through Tone   1008
      Dorothy Parker, One Perfect Rose *[poem]*   1008
      Dorothy Parker, Thought for a Sunshiny Morning *[poem]*   1009
      John Donne, The Flea *[poem]*   1009
Mixing and Balancing Opposing Tones   1010
    Ted Kooser, A Letter from Aunt Belle *[poem]*   1011
    Experiencing Literature through Tone   1012
      Zora Neale Hurston, *from* Mules and Men *[fiction]*   1013

Irony and Introspection   1015
   Margaret Atwood, Siren Song *[poem]*   1015
   Chinua Achebe, Dead Men's Path *[fiction]*   1016
   Czeslaw Milosz, If There Is No God *[poem]*   1019
   A NOTE TO STUDENT WRITERS: *Signaling Your Own Understanding
      of Tonal Shifts*   1020
Modeling Critical Analysis: Joel Coen and Ethan Coen, O Brother,
   Where Art Thou? *[film]*   1020
   Margaret Bourke-White, Guard with a shotgun *[image]*   1021
   O Brother, Where Art Thou? *[film]*   1022

Anthology

Caught Between Laughter and Tears: Considering Tone in Analysis   1023
FICTION   **Katherine Mansfield**, A Dill Pickle   1025
      Herman Melville, Bartleby, the Scrivener   1031
POETRY   **Billy Collins**, I Chop Some Parsley While Listening to Art Blakey's
      Version of "Three Blind Mice"   1060
      W. H. Auden, Musée des Beaux Arts   1062
      Elizabeth Bishop, One Art   1062
      Quincy Troupe, Untitled   1063
      Sherman Alexie, Defending Walt Whitman   1064
      Ted Kooser, A Hairnet with Stars   1066
      Yusef Komunyakaa, A Break from the Bush   1067
      Lisel Mueller, Not Only the Eskimos   1068
DRAMA   **Christopher Durang** and **Wendy Wasserstein**, Medea   1070

11 | Word Choice
   Why This Word and Not Another?   1077

Precision and Playfulness   1078
   Erasmus, *from* De Duplici Copia Verborum et Rerum *[poem]*   1079
   Experiencing Film and Literature through Diction   1080
      Moulin Rouge *[film]*   1081
Beyond Summary   1083
   William Shakespeare, Sonnets (From fairest creatures we desire increase;
      When forty winters shall beseige thy brow; Look in thy glass, and tell
      the face thou viewest; Lo! in the orient when the gracious light; Music
      to hear, why hear'st thou music sadly?; Is it for fear to wet a widow's eye;
      Shall I compare thee to a summer's day?) *[poems]*   1084–1088
   A NOTE TO STUDENT WRITERS: *On the Paraphrase   1088*

Definition and Usage   1089
    Billy Collins, Thesaurus *[poem]*   1089
    Oxford English Dictionary, Love *[prose]*   1090
    Experiencing Literature through Word Choice   1092
        Robert Sward, For Gloria on Her 60th Birthday, or Looking for
        Love in Merriam-Webster *[poem]*   1092

Critically Reflecting on Words   1093
    Lewis Shiner, *from* The Turkey City Lexicon: A Primer for Science
    Fiction Workshops   1093
    Bulwer-Lytton Contest Winners   1094

Modeling Critical Analysis: Joel Coen and Ethan Coen,
O Brother Where Art Thou? *[film]*   1095

Anthology

Romantic Love: Expressing the Exact Emotion   1097
FICTION   **Raymond Carver**, What We Talk about When We Talk
        about Love   1098
        Edith Wharton, Roman Fever   1108
POETRY   **Anonymous**, My Love in Her Attire   1119
        John Donne, Elegy 19: To His Mistress Going to Bed   1119
        John Fletcher, [Take, oh take those lips away]   1121
        Anonymous, Western Wind   1121
        Henry Howard, Earl of Surrey, [Love that doth reign and live
        within my thought]   1122
        Thomas Wyatt, [The long love that in my heart doth harbor]   1122
        e. e. cummings, Spring is like a perhaps hand   1123
        e. e. cummings, since feeling is first   1124
        Emily Dickinson, [Wild Nights—Wild Nights!]   1124
        Galway Kinnell, Shelley   1125
        Robert Burns, A Red, Red Rose   1126
        Edna St. Vincent Millay, What Lips My Lips Have Kissed   1127
        Denise Levertov, The Ache of Marriage   1127
        Denise Levertov, Divorcing   1128
        Christopher Marlowe, The Passionate Shepherd to His Love   1128
        Sir Walter Ralegh, The Nymph's Reply to the Shepherd   1129
        Andrew Marvell, To His Coy Mistress   1130
        Elizabeth Barrett Browning, [How do I love thee? Let me
        count the ways.]   1131
        Elizabeth Barrett Browning, [When our two souls stand up]   1132
        Robert Browning, Meeting at Night   1132
        Robert Browning, Parting at Morning   1133
DRAMA   **Henrik Ibsen**, A Doll's House   1133

12 | Allegory
Is This Supposed to Mean Something Else, Too? *1194*

Learning through Likeness   1195
Gertrude Crampton, *from* Tootle *[fiction]*   1195
Front cover of Tootle *[image]*   1196
A NOTE TO STUDENT WRITERS: *Using Analogies in Arguments*   *1197*
Experiencing Literature through Allegory   *1198*
Aesop, The Crow and the Pitcher *[fiction]*   1198
Walter Crane, Aesop's "The Crow and
the Pitcher" *[image]*   1199
Emily Dickinson, [Eden is that old-fashioned House] *[poem]*   1199
Embodying Timeless Qualities   1200
Engraving of Statue of Justice holding the scales *[image]*   1200
Dosso Dossi, Allegory of Fortune *[image]*   1201
Billy Collins, The Death of Allegory *[poem]*   1202
Reading Allegory   1203
Plato, The Allegory of the Cave *[prose]*   1204
Experiencing Film through Allegory   *1207*
The Matrix *[film]*   1208
Modeling Critical Analysis: João Guimarães Rosa,
The Third Bank of the River *[fiction]*   1209
João Guimarães Rosa, The Third Bank of the River *[fiction]*   1209

Anthology

The Quest for Truth: Reading Allegory   1214
FICTION   **Nathaniel Hawthorne,** Young Goodman Brown   1216
POETRY   **Lewis Carroll,** Jabberwocky   1227
Sir John Tenniel, The Jabberwocky *[image]*   1228
Edmund Spenser, *from* The Faerie Queene   1228
Richard Corbett, The Fairies Farewell   1231
Robert Browning, Porphyria's Lover   1233
John Donne, Batter My Heart, Three-Personed God   1235
John Donne, The Canonization   1235
John Donne, Death, Be Not Proud   1237
Emily Dickinson, [Because I could not stop for Death—]   1237
Gerard Manley Hopkins, Pied Beauty   1238
Gerard Manley Hopkins, The Windhover   1239
Ogden Nash, Kind of an Ode to Duty   1239
Amiri Baraka, In Memory of Radio   1240
Anne Carson, TV Men: Lazarus   1242
DRAMA   **Jane Martin,** Beauty   1245

13 | Symbolism
How Do I Know When an Event or an Image Is Supposed to Stand for Something Else? 1252

Figurative Language 1254
Experiencing Literature through Symbols 1256
Mary Jo Salter, Home Movies: A Sort of Ode [poem] 1256
Recognizing Symbols 1258
What does an apple symbolize? [images] 1259–1260
Gary Soto, Oranges [poem] 1261
Allegory and Symbol 1262
Experiencing Literature through Symbolism 1263
Nathaniel Hawthorne, from Young Goodman Brown [fiction] 1263
A NOTE TO STUDENT WRITERS: Justifying a Symbolic Reading 1265
Modeling Critical Analysis: João Guimarães Rosa,
The Third Bank of the River [fiction] 1265

Anthology

Building and Undoing Community: Taking Part in Symbolism 1266
FICTION **Gabriel García Márquez,** A Very Old Man with Enormous Wings 1269
Gabriel García Márquez, The Handsomest Drowned Man in the World: A Tale for Children 1275
Jhumpa Lahiri, This Blessed House 1279
Shirley Jackson, The Lottery 1293
POETRY **Matthew Arnold,** Dover Beach 1301
Jimmy Santiago Baca, Green Chile 1302
e. e. cummings, [anyone lived in a pretty how town] 1304
Emily Dickinson, [The Soul selects her own Society—] 1305
Seamus Heaney, Valediction 1305
Peter Meinke, Sunday at the Apple Market 1306
Sharon Olds, The Possessive 1307
Alice Walker, Women 1307
Walt Whitman, There Was a Child Went Forth 1308
William Carlos Williams, At the Ball Game 1310
William Butler Yeats, The Wild Swans at Coole 1311
Elizabeth Bishop, Pink Dog 1312
Emma Lazarus, The New Colossus 1314
DRAMA **Arthur Miller,** Death of a Salesman 1314

14 | Context
*What Outside Information Do We Really Need to Know to
Understand the Text?*   1392

How Does New Knowledge Influence Our Experience
of Old Texts?   1393
Alfred, Lord Tennyson, The Charge of the Light Brigade *[poem]*   1393
Apocalypse Now *[film]*   1396
How Is Knowledge "Outside" the Text Helpful?   1397
Czeslaw Milosz, A Song on the End of the World *[poem]*   1397
Experiencing Literature in Context   1398
Czeslaw Milosz, Christopher Robin *[poem]*   1399
Do We Need to Know *Everything* in Order to Understand?   1400
The Maltese Falcon *[film]*   1401
Experiencing Art in Context   1402
Gustave Caillebotte, Young Man at His Window *[image]*   1403
What if Substantial Outside Knowledge Is Essential?   1404
Herman Melville, The House-Top *[poem]*   1404
A NOTE TO STUDENT WRITERS: *Using Electronic and Printed
Sources for Research*   1407

Modeling Critical Analysis: João Guimarães Rosa,
The Third Bank of the River *[fiction]*   1408

Anthology

Language and War: Considering Context in Analysis   1410
FICTION   **Ernest Hemingway,** Soldier's Home   1412
Tim O'Brien, The Things They Carried   1419
Tillie Olsen, I Stand Here Ironing   1434
POETRY   **Herman Melville,** A Utilitarian View of the Monitor's Fight   1441
Herbert Read, The Execution of Cornelius Vane   1442
Stephen Crane, There Was a Crimson Clash of War   1446
e. e. cummings, [i sing of Olaf glad and big]   1447
Richard Eberhart, The Fury of Aerial Bombardment   1448
Edgar A. Guest, The Things That Make a Soldier Great   1449
Sir Henry Newbolt, Vitaï Lampada   1450
Wilfred Owen, Anthem for Doomed Youth   1451
Wilfred Owen, Dulce et Decorum Est   1452
Carl Sandburg, Grass   1453
Siegfried Sassoon, The Rear-Guard   1453
Siegfried Sassoon, Repression of War Experience   1454
Anne Sexton, Courage   1455
Alice Moore Dunbar-Nelson, I Sit and Sew   1457

Yusef Komunyakaa, Facing It   1458
Judith Ortiz Cofer, The Changeling   1459
Mary Jo Salter, Welcome to Hiroshima   1460
Wislawa Szymborska, The End and the Beginning   1461
Wislawa Szymborska, Monologue of a Dog Ensnared
   in History   1463
Adrienne Rich, For the Record   1465
DRAMA   **Gina Victoria Shaffer,** War Spelled Backwards   1466

15 | Allusions
   *In Order to Understand This Text, Is There Something Else
   I Am Supposed to Have Read?   1474*

Creating Community   1475
   Experiencing Literature through Allusions   1477
      Charles Simic, My Weariness of Epic Proportions [poem]   1477
Revisiting and Renewal   1478
   Dick Barnes, Up Home Where I Come From [poem]   1479
   Leonardo da Vinci, The Last Supper [image]   1480
   William Wordsworth, My Heart Leaps Up [poem]   1481
   Experiencing Film through Allusions   1481
      Saturday Night Fever [film]   1482
      Pulp Fiction [film]   1482
Identifying and Responding to Allusions   1484
   A NOTE TO STUDENT WRITERS: *Reference versus Allusion*   1486
Modeling Critical Analysis: Tom Stoppard, The Fifteen Minute
   Hamlet [drama]   1486
   Tom Stoppard, The Fifteen Minute Hamlet [drama]   1487

Anthology

The Myth of Cheating Death: Keeping Literature Alive with Allusion   1497
FICTION   **Joyce Carol Oates,** Where Are You Going, Where Have
      You Been?   1498
      William Faulkner, A Rose for Emily   1512
POETRY   **Percy Bysshe Shelley,** Ozymandias   1520
      Sharon McCartney, After the Chuck Jones Tribute
         on Teletoon   1521
      Robert Duncan, Persephone   1522
      Sylvia Plath, Two Sisters of Persephone   1523
      John Keats, Ode on a Grecian Urn   1524
      John Keats, [When I have fears that I may cease to be]   1526

John Keats, On First Looking into Chapman's Homer   1527
Amy Clampitt, The Dakota   1527
Alfred, Lord Tennyson, The Lady of Shalott   1528
William Butler Yeats, Sailing to Byzantium   1533
Czeslaw Milosz, Orpheus and Eurydice   1534
Rainer Maria Rilke, Orpheus, Eurydice, Hermes   1536
Jorie Graham, Orpheus and Eurydice   1539
H. D., Eurydice   1541
Adrienne Rich, I Dream I'm the Death of Orpheus   1545
Robert Pinsky, Keyboard   1546
DRAMA   **Mary Zimmerman**, Metamorphoses   1547

16 | Genre
How Do Our Expectations Impact Our Literary Experience?
How Are Those Expectations Formed?   1582

What Is Genre?   1583
Conventions   1584
  Experiencing Literature through Genre   1585
    Mrs. J. H. Riddell, *from* Nut Bush Farm *[fiction]*   1585
Disruptions   1586
  Experiencing Literature through Genre   1587
    William Shakespeare, *from* Macbeth *[drama]*   1588
Displacement and Parody   1589
  Publicity poster for Buffy the Vampire Slayer *[image]*   1589
    Mark Twain, Ode to Stephen Dowling Bots, Dec'd *[poem]*   1591
Genre and Popular Culture   1592
  Boys dressed as cowboys *[images]*   1593
  Experiencing Film through Genre   1593
    Shane *[film]*   1594
    Unforgiven *[film]*   1595
  A NOTE TO STUDENT WRITERS: *Moving beyond Formulaic Writing   1596*
Modeling Critical Analysis: Tom Stoppard, The Fifteen Minute
  Hamlet *[drama]*   1597

Anthology

Honoring the Dead and Dignifying Death: Tracing Genre   1598
FICTION   **Katherine Anne Porter**, The Jilting of Granny Weatherall   1601
    Margaret Atwood, Happy Endings   1609

POETRY   **John Milton**, Lycidas   1612

Walt Whitman, When Lilacs Last in the Dooryard Bloom'd   1617

Gwendolyn Brooks, De Witt Williams on His Way to Lincoln Cemetery   1624

Allen Tate, Ode to the Confederate Dead   1625

Robert Lowell, For the Union Dead   1628

John Keats, Ode to Autumn   1630

Anne Bradstreet, In Memory of My Dear Grandchild, Elizabeth Bradstreet, Who Deceased August 1665, Being a Year and Half Old   1631

Anne Bradstreet, Here Followes Some Verses upon the Burning of Our House, July 10, 1666   1632

Chidiock Tichborne, Elegy Written with His Own Hand in the Tower before His Execution   1633

Theodore Roethke, Elegy for Jane   1634

Seamus Heaney, Punishment   1635

Louise Erdrich, Dear John Wayne   1637

Langston Hughes, Night Funeral in Harlem   1638

Emily Dickinson, [I like a look of Agony]   1640

Emily Dickinson, [After great pain, a formal feeling comes—]   1640

Rudyard Kipling, The Power of the Dog   1641

John Updike, Dog's Death   1642

DRAMA   **Sophocles**, Antigone   1643

17 | The Production and Reproduction of Texts

How Does Retelling and Revising Impact My Experience of a Text?

How Can Literary Theory Clarify What Constitutes That Experience?   *1674*

Texts and Technology   1675

Textual Form and Conditions of Production   1676

   Experiencing Literature through Issues of Production   1677

     William Blake, A Poison Tree [image]   1678

An Orientation to Contemporary Critical Theory   1679

   New criticism and auteur theory   1679

   Deconstruction   1680

   New historicism and other historically grounded approaches   1681

Why We Study the Texts We Study   1682

   Experiencing Literature through Theory   1683

     from Major Writers of America [prose]   1683

     from Heath Anthology of American Literature [prose]   1684

A NOTE TO STUDENT WRITERS: *Using Theory to Develop Critical Analysis* 1684

Abridging, Revising, and Repackaging Text 1685
Oliver Twist *[image]* 1686
Oliver Twist *[film]* 1687
Experiencing Literature through Issues of Production and Reproduction of Texts 1688
Mark Twain, *from* Adventures of Huckleberry Finn *[fiction]* 1688

Translations, Subtitles, and Dubbing 1689
from Lost in Translation *[screenplay]* 1690

Modeling Critical Analysis: *Tom Stoppard,* The Fifteen Minute Hamlet *[drama]* 1691

18 | An Orientation to Research
Why Should I Use Sources?
How Do I Use Them?
What Material Do I Document? 1695

Why We Use Sources 1696
Shaping a Topic 1698
How to Find Sources 1699
Giving Appropriate Credit: The Issue of Plagiarism 1703
David Sumner (Jones), Someone Forgotten (plagiarized) *[poem]* 1703
Neal Bowers, Ten-Year Elegy *[poem]* 1704
Experiencing Literature through Considerations of Plagiarism 1706
Plutarch, *from* Lives of the Noble Grecians and Romans *[prose]* 1706
William Shakespeare, *from* Julius Caesar 1707

Integrating Sources into Writing: What We Document 1709
Quotation, paraphrase, and summary 1710
Distinct insights and common observations 1712
Common knowledge 1712

How to Cite 1713
Parenthetical references in the text 1713
The Works Cited list 1714

Appendix A: Student Model Essay Collection 1721
Appendix B: Collection of Poet Biographies 1741
Appendix C: Alternate Contents by Genre 1779
Glossary 1791
Credits 1809
Index of First Lines of Poetry 1827
Index of Authors and Titles 1833

Preface

LITERARY ANALYSIS THAT GROWS FROM THE STUDENT'S READING EXPERIENCE

Books about literature sometimes create barriers to the very subject they intend to explore. The "about" may suggest that there is some special knowledge separate from the primary texts and the immediate experience of those texts that is somehow supposed to be mastered. The result is both disheartening and familiar. Students, for example, will sometimes say they love to read but that they hate to write about what they have read. Or they might resist "talking about" what they've read because talk seems somehow removed from whatever they've felt as they read. Literary study quickly becomes centered on definitions, on correct answers, on knowledge that can often be acquired without even reading a literary text (how many students have written on, say, *Great Expectations* after reviewing only a study guide to that novel?). *The Literary Experience* starts by recognizing that the experience of a text comes first. Critical questions, terminology, and theory are introduced not as the "real subject" (the things that will be on the test), but as means to deepen and clarify the reading of a text.

AN ORGANIZATION BASED ON INTERPRETIVE QUESTIONS OF INCREASING COMPLEXITY

In *The Literary Experience*, you will find literary selections and discussion of literary elements grouped in a way that facilitates the discussion that leads to thoughtful writing about the texts. The organization is both organic and progressive: while every chapter contains fiction, poetry, and drama, the opening chapters address the sorts of basic questions and essential elements that one encounters in nearly any text (questions of story, character, theme, and so on). These are elements that we need to identify in order to make sense of a text. From there, the book moves to elements involved in constructing a text (like coherence, interruption, symbol). These elements emphasize the rhetorical impact of the text, the relationship between the text's structure and an audience's reaction to that structure. The final chapters move to matters outside of the text (context, genre) to help us to think about how we experience any text not just as an isolated encounter but also as part of a larger culture. The thematic anthologies that accompany each chapter reinforce the element highlighted without narrowly tagging any particular work to that element. Instructors will, then, find considerable flexibility in constructing their own course.

A CRITICAL VOCABULARY THAT SPRINGS FROM A STUDENT'S OWN EXPERIENCE

Every chapter opens with framing questions that have been carefully crafted to show students they already ask crucial questions themselves—if not about literature, then about the things in life upon which literature is built. Rather than focusing discussions narrowly on the formal elements, the chapters address feelings, thoughts, and problems that arise from an active engagement with a text. The questions that lead into the chapter discussions serve as a starting place that is grounded in a meaningful and concrete critical issue.

The Literary Experience, then, leads students to encounter new words in familiar contexts. As teachers, we all seek to help students acquire a vocabulary that extends and deepens their understanding. Understanding a specialized word involves using it in ways that can lead one to a more engaged, nuanced, and powerful reading. Furthermore, command of such a word gives one the power to articulate the sorts of complex intellectual and emotional responses that works of art engender. For instance, the discussion of rhythm leads a student to consider the effect of silence in the film *Jaws*, the uses of pauses in poetry, and the motion created by language choices in prose. Such an active and thoroughly internalized acquisition of key words is consistent with a process oriented approach to reading and writing. No literature class is ever definitive. Often a student finds a class most fulfilling by leaving with a reading list longer than the one that completed the term. But perhaps the student achieves a bigger sense of what literary experiences might mean. For example, the student may begin to look at a painting or a television show in new and enlivening ways by bringing knowledge from the classroom back to what lies outside.

LITERARY ELEMENTS: TEACHING ACROSS GENRES

The most common textbook arrangement for an introductory literature class has three main divisions: fiction, poetry, and drama. They do contain most of the elements that *The Literary Experience* includes, but because they emphasize an element like plot in a story, rhythm in a poem, or setting in a play, they may suggest that any one element operates exclusively in a single genre. By isolating poetry in concentrated units, for example, students may be led to respond to a poem only in the constricting, artificial context of other poems. Furthermore, what is gained in such a study may be unnecessarily contained by the "poetry unit." It is useful to remember that the pleasures of rhythm are available to children long before they are able to read and long, long before they think of poetry as a "genre." Similarly, issues of plot or character do not arise only in the study of prose fiction. And setting is hardly a concern specific to the theater.

We mix genres to make the teaching of literature consistent with actual literary experience. After all, we read to explore feelings and ideas; we make connections among ideas without the constraints of genre; we do not seek to understand formal elements for their own sake. A reader's experience of a poem may be enhanced by reading a story that influenced it, by remembering a film that explores a similar theme, by looking at a painting that was produced at the same time, or by seeing a photograph that captures the poem's setting. Our mixing does more than simply create a superficial variety; it deepens our literary experience by enabling us to draw connections among genres instead of creating the impression that each genre is distinct and has its own set of literary terms.

The literary elements that we discuss spring from the interpretive questions that students ask about any text, beginning with plot: What is happening and why do we care? Of course, organizing this book around "elements" as opposed to genres suggests its own kind of arbitrariness. We've been careful to cross-reference elements within chapters in order to emphasize that a response to any given text (and the writing that it generates) isn't bound by a chapter heading. The recurring elements emphasize the fact that this critical vocabulary is not some arbitrary list; it enables us to develop deeper analysis. The *Making Connections* boxes in each chapter break through the problems that often arise from an "elements of" approach to teaching literature. The look ahead/ look back nature of this feature explicitly crosses from the consideration of the chapter's featured element to specific aspects of the critical discussions carried on in other chapters.

READING IS WRITING/WRITING IS READING

The Literary Experience emphasizes the importance of the student's writing throughout. Writing is presented as a means to explore and discover—as an extension of reading, not an assignment tagged on to reading. Students need to understand that their writing is important for something more than assessment. Since we believe that writing can be a means to deepen understanding, we do not divide "understanding" and "reading" from the activity of writing. All are part of a coherent, rich experience. Therefore, there is no large "writing about literature" section standing entirely separate from the rest of the text at the beginning or the end. Woven throughout are brief discussions that underscore what is ever present: an understanding of writing's centrality. For example, each chapter contains

- A *Note to Student Writers* that draws lessons from literary texts or the study of literary texts that can be applied to critical writing. Some of these notes offer specific generative suggestions (what kinds of questions prompt the development of ideas or the definition of a thesis?); some explain the logic of common conventions (why use the present tense when recounting the action of a narrative); some call attention to crucial rhetorical features that critical writers must master (how does one acknowledge a position and then turn strongly against it?).

- *Experiencing Literature* sections through which we demonstrate for students how they might interact with a piece of literature and what sorts of questions they can ask about a particular element as they engage a text.

- *Modeling Critical Analysis* section that ends every chapter and serves to show students how to incorporate what they have learned in the chapter and previous chapters, as well as show them how to translate their critical reading into writing.

- Discussion questions and writing prompts that both close each chapter and appear at the end of each anthology selection. The initial more broadly based questions are intended to help students understand how they can ask certain questions of most texts about the element featured. The questions that center on specific texts will help students prompt productive re-reading as well as lively discussion and writing.

CONNECTING LITERATURE TO THE ELEMENTS OF LITERATURE

Every chapter closes with an anthology of selected literature readings carefully chosen as useful examples of the element at hand. Topics for each anthology have been crafted to reflect a theme that complements the element. For instance, Chapter 1 on plot features an anthology titled *Detective Work: Figuring Plot* which highlights how a theme—Detective Work—can also serve to show how an element works in literature—a detective seeks to figure out what is going on, just as a reader reads to find out what was happened and functions as a detective. The anthology is contextualized by a short introductory essay that gives students a frame of reference for approaching the texts included. While these reading clusters are designed to work in relation to the chapter's focus, the thematic grouping allows instructors considerable flexibility. Those, for example, who prefer to organize their course thematically have opportunities to do so. With over 60 short stories, 298 poems, and 17 plays, *The Literary Experience* offers choices for every instructor. Included is a balance of new, modern, award-winning writers (like Pulitzer Prize winner Jhumpa Lahiri, MacArthur "genius grant" recipient Mary Zimmerman, and poet laureate Ted Kooser) coupled with established favorites (like Emily Dickinson, Arthur Miller, and James Baldwin). Of course, there's no way to represent literature—no matter how big the anthology. So *The Literary Experience* is built to give students the means to approach literature *outside* the book, now and in the future. For this reason, the concern is less about presenting "the right" selections, and more about giving students the tools they need to work with any complex and rewarding text.

SUPPLEMENTS

In order to further engage students in literature, *The Wadsworth Original Film Series* is available to be packaged with *The Literary Experience*. This DVD includes 3 short films, including Eudora Welty's "A Worn Path," John Updike's "A&P" and Raymond Carver's "Cathedral." This DVD also includes interviews with the authors themselves. In addition to the *Wadsworth Original Film Series* DVD, three films are also available on DVD or VHS to be packaged with *The Literary Experience*. These separate DVDs contain Alice Walker's "Everyday Use," Langston Hughes "Salvation," or Tillie Olson's "I Stand Here Ironing." Each adaptation is followed by author interviews. For students who have difficulty comprehending written text, these films provide one approach to five stories included in this book. Some instructors may find the films to be a useful conversation-starter.

Instructor's Manual

To aid in the task of teaching with this text, the *Instructor's Manual* is an all-in-one resource containing a brief introduction to each chapter that examines the literature examples, images, and film references used to further explain how the featured pieces work within the element, as well as what other pieces in the book exemplify that element; "Cultural Context" for every literature piece appearing in the anthologies; a "Discussion" section, with at least a paragraph about how the work fits into the element and one about how it fits into the theme, how the piece relates to other elements and themes in the book; an expansion of the questions that are currently in the book, and how the piece would work with the "Experiencing Literature through Writing" questions; and sample syllabi created by authors Bruce Beiderwell and Jeffrey Wheeler. In addition, the *Instructor's Manual* contains a bonus resource in "A Guide to Using Film"—a detailed chapter-by-chapter guide to give instructors advice of how to use film references currently in the book, along with new films, coupled with in-depth summaries and specific scene suggestions, to be used in the classroom. All the films are tied to in-class discussion questions and writing prompts to engage students' interests.

ACKNOWLEDGMENTS

A book this thick requires the work of many more people than we could ever list on a title page or even here in the acknowledgements. The following reviewers have looked at different incarnations of the chapters that you find here. Their careful reading, insightful questions, and generous advice have made the book more useful and more teachable.

Donald Andrews, *Chattanooga State Technical Community College*
Melissa Barth, *Appalachian State University*
Joseph Bathanti, *Appalachian State University*
Janet Beck, *Appalachian State University*
Betty Bettacchi, *Collin County Community College*
Jacqueline Blackwell, *Thomas Nelson Community College*
Amy Brazillier, *Red Rocks Community College*
Barbara L. Brown, *San Jacinto College Central*
Glenda Bryant, *South Plains College, Levelland*
Larry Carlson, *College of Charleston*
Laura Carroll, *Abilene Christian University*
Patricia Cearley, *South Plains College, Levelland*
Karen Chaffee, *Ulster County Community College*
Helen Chester, *Milwaukee Area Technical College*
Sherry Chisamore, *Ulster County Community College*

Basil Clark, *Saginaw Valley State University*
Mike Compton, *University of Memphis*
Denise Coulter, *Atlantic Cape Community College*
Christy Desmet, *University of Georgia*
Tammy DiBenedetto, *Riverside Community College*
Scott Douglass, *Chattanooga State Technical Community College*
Joy M. Eichner-Lynch, *Contra Costa College*
Jo Nell Farrar, *San Jacinto College*
Jane Focht-Hansen, *San Antonio College*
DeLisa Ging, *Northern Oklahoma College*
Diana Gingo, *University of Texas, Dallas*
Paul Goodin, *Northern Kentucky University*
Gary Harrington, *Salisbury University*
Dawn Hayward, *Delaware County Community College*
Ana Hernandez, *Miami Dade Community College*
Gillian R. Hettinger, *William Paterson University*
Kathy Houghton, *Erie Community College*
Rebecca Housel, *Rochester Institute of Technology*
David Johansson, *Brevard Community College*
Ken Johnson, *Georgia Perimeter College*
Jan McArthur, *Delgado Community College*
Miles McCrimmon, *J. Sargeant Reynolds Community College*
Linda McGann, *South Plains College, Levelland*
Thomas Gerard McNamee, *Eastern Oregon University*
Richard Middleton-Kaplan, *Harper College*
Rod Val Moore, *Los Angeles Valley College*
Michael Morris, *Eastfield College*
Mona Narain, *University of Texas, San Antonio*
Jeffrey N. Nelson, *University of Alabama, Huntsville*
Chris Partida, *North Harris Community College*
Peggy Peden, *Nashville State Community College*
Jan Prewitt, *Emporia State University*
Geri Rhodes, *Albuquerque TVI Community College*
Richard Rosol, *Quinnipiac University*
Steve Sansom, *North Harris Community College*
Cary Ser, *Miami Dade Community College*
Michael Sollars, *Texas Southern University*
Donald R. Stinson, *Northern Oklahoma College*
Constance Strickland, *Wesley College*
Raven Sweet, *University of Memphis*
Andrea Kaston Tange, *Eastern Michigan University*
Tom Treffinger, *Greenville Technical College*
Edward P. Walkiewicz, *Oklahoma State University, Stillwater*
Mark Woods, *Jefferson Community College*

Also special thanks to the following for their guidance:

Wilson Chen, *Benedictine University*
Suzy Holstein, *Michigan Technological University*
Dennis Lynch, *Michigan Technological University*
Thomas Lochhaas, *University of California, Los Angeles*
Linda Venis, *University of California, Los Angeles*
Shari Zimmerman, *Hofstra University*

We'd like to thank in particular Diana Gingo of the University of Texas, Dallas, who has offered thoughtful responses throughout our writing process and who has written the Film Guide for the book.

Much of our inspiration comes from the lively and informed conversations that we have had with the faculty at UCLA's Writing Programs and in the English Department at Long Beach City College. Good colleagues make for good teaching. Special thanks to Teddi Chichester, George Gadda, Sonia Maasik, Gina Shaffer, Velvet Pearson, Hiro Sasaki, Frank Gaspar, and Ron DiCostanzo.

It has been a great pleasure to work with the entire Thomson Wadsworth team on this project. Bill Brisick encouraged us to submit our proposal for a "very short book" teaching students to write about literature. Aron Keesbury, Senior Acquisitions Editor, liked that proposal but didn't let a positive first reading stop him from pressing for something better; he helped mold *The Literary Experience* into a very different and much more ambitious book than we originally envisioned it would be. Development Editor Marita Sermolins has guided the production of the book, looked at every draft, chased after every permission, and helped us to keep track of all of the pieces of this huge enterprise. Samantha Ross has led a group that has done far more than just check for typos in the manuscript. Francelle Carapetyan, Marcus Desmond Harmon, Marcy Lunetta, and Mary Keith Trawick have all helped Samantha make a book out of a manuscript. Bill Coyle of Salem State College has written the author headnotes. And Jessie Swigger of the University of Texas, Austin, has authored the instructor's manual. All of their good work in the final stages of the process built upon the efforts of those who have helped us get started and continue through to the end. Kate Edwards has taken our text and shown how it is marketable. Guided by their comments, we have rewritten and rethought the project; any remaining mistakes can only be the result of our own oversight.

Throughout the process, we have aimed to make a book worthy of the good students in our lives: Samuel Beiderwell, Renata Gusmão-Garcia, Chloe Wheeler, and Blake Wheeler. Finally, we must thank those who have lived with this project as it has developed: Ivna Gusmão and Laura Scavuzzo Wheeler They have heard about each proposal, each phone call, every review, and been our first editors and proofreaders. Their support is deeply appreciated.

Introduction to the Elements of Literature

How Do We Know What Terms to Use When We Talk about Our Experience with Literature?

THEODOTUS: The fire has spread from your ships. The first of the seven
    wonders of the world perishes. The library of Alexandria is in flames.
CAESAR: Is that all?
THEODOTUS (*unable to believe his senses*): All! Caesar: will you go down to
    posterity as a barbarous soldier too ignorant to know the value of
    books?
CAESAR: Theodotus, I am an author myself; and I tell you it is better that
    the Egyptians should live their lives than dream them away with the
    help of books.

(*Caesar and Cleopatra*, George Bernard Shaw)

As unlikely as it might seem the conversations that we have about literature—the very words we use to approach texts—are profoundly influenced by
historical chance. Consider, for example, the book that has been among the
most influential works of literary criticism in western civilization: Aristotle's
Poetics. The version of that work that survives is only a partial discussion. It is
possible we should blame Julius Caesar for what is missing: Caesar, in the
midst of his affair with Cleopatra, is reputed to have ordered his troops to set a
strategic fire in the port of Alexandria that spread to Alexandria's great library
and destroyed its collection. One of the books that may have been in that
library was the only surviving copy of Aristotle's treatise on comedy. Scholars

since have bemoaned the loss of such an important text. If that treatise had survived, the shape of literary studies might be very different today.

What if Caesar had ordered his men to be more careful with their torches? We might privilege Aristophanes instead of Sophocles. Students might be more likely to read *Much Ado about Nothing* than *Hamlet*. But of course we do *not* have Aristotle's seminal text on comedy and we manage pretty well without it. We sometimes try out the terms that Aristotle uses for tragedy to see which are most useful in the discussion of comedy. We still talk about character and plot, but we modify the discussion for this other genre. In his discussion of tragedy, Aristotle suggests that in comedy character is more important than plot, but it is up to us to continue the discussion, to make sense of that claim with our own examples. And then we can try out the same terms as they might relate to fiction or poetry or film.

The methodical approach Aristotle uses to examine dramatic productions is the same approach he takes to examine natural organisms, social structures, and philosophical systems. For Aristotle, everything in the world can be treated as a text to read. By classifying the parts of the thing that he is examining, he establishes a method of presenting his own perspective and of advancing his own argument. But by establishing distinct and well-defined categories, he sets up a system that others can use. Essentially, Aristotle establishes the groundwork for conversations that will follow. His clear definitions of the parts of drama give us a vocabulary to talk about what we have seen. More than two thousand years after he set up these categories, most discussions of drama still refer to and build upon Aristotle's vocabulary.

DEVELOPING A FLEXIBLE CRITICAL VOCABULARY

The advantage of a specialized vocabulary is that it helps us to identify parts of a whole with precision. In the study of anatomy, for instance, it is important to be able to distinguish among the various internal organs; the lungs, heart, and liver may all work together but they serve very different functions. Creating a vocabulary makes it possible to see and to discuss the intricacies of a subject. But the vocabulary isn't the thing itself; it is a tool that helps us understand the thing—the object of our study.

Because Aristotle gave us an especially rich and useful vocabulary, we often look for complications and moments of discovery when we begin to analyze drama, just as we locate the heart and lungs when we think about anatomy. But having such a perceptive guide may blind us to other aspects of the drama. We might find the parts of the play that Aristotle points out because we have words to describe them; we might miss parts of the play that Aristotle's vocabulary doesn't address. Still, we can argue that the loss of Aristotle's treatise on comedy, though unfortunate, helps us to push the boundaries that his terms set for us. As we establish definitions for the elements of comedy, we develop a process to identify the elements of any other sort of expressive art that we might want to discuss.

In this book, we foreground the process through which we establish and define elements of literary texts and the literary experience. Because Aristotle's text is so old and well established, it is easy to think about his elements of poetics as absolute and complete rather than arbitrary and useful. But systems only come alive when we realize they are both arbitrary *and* useful. The words that Aristotle uses to describe the elements of drama are the ones we begin with when we describe any expressive art, yet when we discuss poetry, for example, we discover that we need to adapt, elaborate, and invent. As we describe "new" elements, we develop a fuller vocabulary to describe general elements like word choice or rhythm. To understand that each of these elements is a tool for articulating the complex ideas presented in expressive arts, we find it helpful to break the traditional boundaries of genre. Using a symbol like a flag, for instance, to represent something other than itself (a country, a cause, patriotism, warmongering) is something that we often discuss when we study poetry because attention to the use of individual words is generally part of the discipline that we teach when we teach poetry. In reality, though, all forms of expressive arts use symbols. In fact, all of these genres share a set of common elements. By examining that single element across genres, a student can learn to manipulate that term more effectively and to use that term outside of the confines of this textbook.

The goal of this book is to help each of you to engage with Aristotle and with anyone else who has ever been interested in discussing their experience with a work of art. Furthermore, it seeks to enable you to express yourself when you read a book or see a film that moves you in some way. When you contribute to this discussion, others should be able to pick up the threads of your ideas to continue weaving further discussions. So we want you to acquire a critical vocabulary that helps you read, respond, and communicate something important about texts, a vocabulary that also enables others to respond to your reading. But we don't want to reduce literary study to a vocabulary lesson; we want you to discover and test the value of particular words as you experience a poem, play, story, or film.

CRITICAL WRITING AS CONVERSATION

Aristotle's approach to literature hasn't had such influence simply for abstract reasons: as we have suggested, his criticism has enabled people to communicate effectively about how they respond to literary texts. Imagine for a moment a fairly typical movie-going experience. Assume that you've gone with a friend to see a campus screening of Paul Haggis's *Crash*. As the final credits come to a close and you begin to move toward the exit, a conversation might begin with a basic question: "Did you like it?" This is an easy discussion to start, and also an easy one to end if the answer is simply "yes" or "no." But that will not likely be enough. If you hated the movie, you might say, "The characters were all just walking stereotypes that got jumbled together in a bunch of impossible coincidences." If you liked it, you might respond, "All the coincidences made me think about the stereotypes that exist in real life and affect how we think and act." Either way, you are beginning to establish criteria for your discussion. You suggest that to meet your standards a good film must adhere to a certain order, must fairly represent or comment upon life, or must purposefully employ familiar elements (of plot, of character, of structure, and so on).

Now imagine you stop at a coffee shop on campus and you find a group of friends seated around a table who have just seen the same movie. You join them and discover that they are in the midst of their own discussion about *Crash*. You probably do more listening at first than speaking; after all, you need to know what ground they've covered and what direction they've taken. But at some point, you find an opportunity to fit your own opinions into the public conversation. One of the people at the table found the film boring and shallow: "All the twists and turns of the story make it seem complicated, but when you get right down to it the only thing the film gives us is a bunch of clichés about tolerance." You catch at that complaint because it allows you to pick up on and contribute something of your own to the conversation:

> Yeah, this film ran through just about every stereotype around and strung together an unbelievable string of events. But somehow the whole thing seemed new to me. The energy was different—more than just "don't make stupid assumptions about people." The film kept me off-balance. I wasn't always sure where I was supposed to stand in relation to even some of the obvious stereotypes. It all got me to thinking about how hard it is to tell the difference between revealing racism and reinforcing it.

Note that our imagined talk has moved to a point. If you are challenged to back up your interpretation, you will do so by reference to the film. We have moved beyond simply liking or disliking. We are contextualizing, putting the film into categories based on our previous experience in film and in other studies. As we call up these familiar categories, we are able to conduct further analysis and continue the conversation.

Our imagined coffee shop meeting links conversations with reading and writing. The talk recounted in the sample dialogue just above represents a process of thinking through the literary experience. Note how these few sentences begin to define and follow a point as one would do in a paper. The passage even displays some of the rhetorical gestures common in writing; note, for example, that the speaker opens with a concession and then moves to a counterpoint that carries through to the end. The key term for both conversation and composition is *process*. As you discuss *Crash* (or any other work of art) with your friends, you will likely learn something. You'll clarify–indeed–discover ideas. You'll test arguments and, when you find them weak, you'll revise or discard them.

CRITICAL WRITING AS AN EXTENSION OF READING

Critical writing is often seen as merely an assignment—something to "get through" not something to grow from. But once we understand how writing takes a place as part of a whole literary experience we can begin to make writing seem less alien. Writing (like conversation) grows from alert, engaged, informed, and active reading. Literary texts ask—even demand—such a powerful idea of reading. Consider what occurs (what you feel, what you think) as you read the following short poem

Langston Hughes (1902–1967)

Harlem (1951)

What happens to a dream deferred?

Does it dry up
like a raisin in the sun?
Or fester like a sore—
And then run?
Does it stink like rotten meat?
Or crust and sugar over—
like a syrupy sweet?

Maybe it just sags
like a heavy load.

Or does it explode?

There is no script for your response to this (or any) poem. You might feel anger or frustration; you might sympathize with the speaker or want to argue with him. You might be confused by the questions posed. "Harlem" prompts us to describe, question, interpret, and feel. And whatever line of thought we follow, we search for words to clarify and deepen the experience. At some point, if we wish to move forward, we make writing part of our reading. In brief notes, journal entries, or exchanges over e-mail with other readers we actively seek words that register our sense of the text. Critical writing, then, emerges from active reading; indeed, it is part of active reading.

We can apply the same notions to our experience of any work of art. We hear, we see, we feel, we think—we experience. We try to explain and enrich our experience of a text through our own words. When we appreciate this connection between *our* reading and *our* writing (our viewing and our writing, our seeing and our writing, our listening and our writing) we can begin to appreciate what is involved in the discipline of literary criticism and how rewarding that discipline can be. Reading, after all, isn't just a matter of decoding letters on a page. At the broadest level, reading prompts reflection, interpretation, and discussion. We read a poem or a story of course, but we also read the look on a friend's face in a moment of crisis. We read paintings or a piece of music. We read movies. We receive complex signals in everyday life from various sorts of "texts"; we sort them out, give them shape, and set them in context of related signals. Things we read become a living part of our experience. The act of reading and writing are vitally connected: *to write about a work of art is to extend the very process that characterizes our reading.*

If we think of writing as an activity through which we gain understanding and deepen experience, we can realize a broad vision of what it means to write critically. We can appreciate the great importance of a narrowly specialized vocabulary. We can see how writing together with reading becomes a single creative process. Writing sharpens and enriches reading. Writing helps us see things we might have missed. Writing leads to discovery. *The Literary Experience* will consistently link critical writing, critical reading, and critical conversation. It will help you to write by helping you read more perceptively. It will help you to read by engaging you as a writer.

The Literary Experience

1

Scene, Episode, and Plot

What Happened, and Why Do We Care?

At some level, we're all storytellers. We have a need and a desire to give meaning to the raw experience of our lives by selecting and arranging details. When we recount something that happens to us, we're likely to leave out things that don't quite fit. We may even slightly modify what did happen in order to achieve a truth or power that goes beyond plain facts. We're attentive to dramatic design. We lead into our stories, build to a point of crisis, and finish forcefully. Our motives for crafting stories are complex and varied. We might want to give a satisfying close to a difficult period of our lives so that we can "move on"; in this respect, we are often the audience for our own stories. On other occasions, we want to make sure actions add up to some clear message or moral for the person we're speaking to (think of a parent telling a child a story that begins, "When I was your age . . . "). There is also a great pleasure in putting a string of events together so that those events become a unified story—a skillfully constructed work of art.

The drive to give artistic shape to experience is so strong that it often works with very little prompting. Much conversation involves exchanging stories. We listen to a friend tell a story and then tell another in response. Our intense need for—as well as our deep pleasure in—stories shows in the fact that we build them from the slightest bits of raw material that come our way: a small incident at work, a disagreement with a friend, an observed odd behavior of a stranger in line at a convenience store. We can even work something up from a single image. In fact, we often do work from something that small. A photograph, for example, captures feelings of a particular moment, but that moment often suggests to our imaginations a time before and a time after. We'll often build a narrative from the evidence a single picture provides, despite the obvious limitations of that

Edouard Boubat, *Rendez-vous at the Café La Vache Noire*, Paris (1957)

evidence. This building involves both our creative and our critical intelligence. We assess how details fit together to suggest actions that surround the picture. For example, look closely at the photograph above.

It's quite possible to tell a very brief story "around" Boubat's photograph *Rendez-vous at the Café La Vache Noire*. Some obvious questions may come quickly to mind that force us to respond in terms of narrative. What has brought the woman to the café? What is happening at the moment caught by the camera? What will unfold? How does the story end? We can't, of course, *know* the answers, but Boubat's photograph offers specific features that prompt us to speculate. Consider, for example, the woman's expression and body language. She looks out to the street with perhaps both expectation and anxiety. She seems uncomfortable waiting; she holds her purse with both hands. Notice, too, that behind her at the bar are only men. Reflected in the glass is the world before her that lies outside. What story do you make from such observations?

INCIDENT, SCENE, AND SEQUENCE

In the brief discussion of Boubat's photograph, we have touched upon the notions of incident and scene. **Incident** suggests a specific, small action. **Scene** is closely related to but more expansive than incident. In a dramatic work, a scene might be understood simply as the entrance and/or exit of important characters from the stage. A scene may also be defined by mood (a crying scene, a comic scene, a revenge scene), function (a transitional scene, an expository scene, an anticipatory scene), or even place (an outdoor scene, a bedroom scene, a courtyard scene). But the term is usually employed more broadly still and is not limited to dramatic productions. A scene may be thought of as a coherent action within a larger structure of action. In this sense, a scene should convey a particular conflict that is subordinate to some larger conflict.

Incidents and scenes (if left to stand alone) are fragments. They are the bits and pieces that can be arranged to build a plot. **Plot** refers to the meaningful fabric of action. It suggests structure. At the most basic level, this means that a plot has a beginning, middle, and end; it represents a whole action. More specifically, an author provides **exposition** (context), then conveys **rising action** (action that leads to a decisive point), a **climax** (the decisive point), **falling action**, and **resolution** or **denouement** (a French word meaning "the untying of a knot"). Plots, then, are usually highly crafted actions. The **sequence** of scenes that make up a plot is not a random sequence or a mere series of conflicts. It's a carefully laid out set of scenes that grow from **conflict** and make sense together. Perhaps one action causes another, or relates thematically to another, or counterpoints another. The author's careful arrangement of action in plot may be especially evident in **foreshadowing** (preparing the reader for action that is to come) and **flashback** (a return to past action). Both of these strategies illustrate how plot requires that we think of scenes in relation to one another.

Experiencing Literature through Plot

To sharpen our sense of plot's importance and *meaning*, we'll examine two brief pieces that upset or cut short our expectations. The two poems that follow ask us to consider what meaning we draw from plots by refusing to give us any plot in the usual sense. Both ask us to be self-conscious about the degree to which we actively shape stories. Can any significant piece of life be contained by a well-thought-out story? Can we assign a beginning, middle, and end to experience? Are lives as neat as that? Do we (as natural storytellers) impose order on chaos? If so, are stories a way to make experience significant? Robert Pinsky's "Poem with Lines in Any Order" centers us on these problems. Pinsky makes us think about many things, including our own active, participatory role in giving shape and meaning to events. Are we all plot makers in a world that has no master plot?

Robert Pinsky (1940–)

Poem with Lines in Any Order (2004)

Sonny said, *Then he shouldn't have given Molly the two more babies.*
Dave's sister and her husband adopted the baby, and that was Babe.
You can't live in the past.
Sure he was a tough guy but he was no hero.
Sonny and Toots went to live for a while with the Braegers.   5
It was a time when it seemed like everybody had a nickname.
Nobody can live in the future.
When Rose died having Babe, Dave came after the doctor with a gun.
Toots said, *What would you expect, he was a young man and there she was.*
Sonny still a kid himself when Dave moved out on Molly.   10
The family gave him Rose's cousin Molly to marry so she could raise the
    children.
There's no way to just live in the present.
In their eighties Toots and Sonny still arguing about their father.
Dave living above the bar with Della and half the family.

The first thing most readers do once they finish this poem is to go back and
play with the sequence of lines to make something more satisfying. But is this
what Pinsky is asking for? His title might encourage us to take the lines (and
the experiences they represent) as truly random. Is it possible that Pinsky is
asking us to accept chaos and reflect upon our tendencies to give events a beginning, middle, and end? Or perhaps he is suggesting that plots can be split into as many shapes as there are people to give them shape. Then again, maybe these lines aren't really random at all. There is a thread woven through the poem that makes us think about how we relate (or fail to relate) story to actual experience: "You can't live in the past" (line 3);

Making Connections

Szymborska's "ABC" and Pinsky's "Poem with Lines in Any Order" also inevitably raise questions about "character." Who are the characters here? Our sense of character arises largely out of seeing characters behave in the context of meaningfully ordered events. As you read about character in Chapter 2, think back on these two poems and ask yourself how much your sense of character depends upon plot.

"Nobody can live in the future" (line 7); "There's no way to just live in the
present" (line 12). That is, there is no way to live if we accept everything as a
jumbled mess of random signals and fail to give shape and meaning to the
events that happen around us: we seek some order in order to live.

Wislawa Szymborska also deftly toys with notions of sequence in "ABC"— a poem that reminds us of how artificial and arbitrary our storytelling can be. Szymborska doesn't present lines "in any order" as Pinsky does. By making the order unfold in alphabetical sequence, she leaves us struck by a sense of arbitrariness; the sequence is played out on a grid that has no necessary or organic relationship to experience. Szymborska is also blunt in marking off the limits of what we know or can know. If, like the narrators of the poem, we can't "find out" about things that are important to us, can we create richly interwoven plots? Can we find meaning?

Wislawa Szymborska (1923–)

ABC (2004, trans. Stanislaw Baranczak and Clare Cavanagh)

I'll never find out now
what A. thought of me.
If B. ever forgave me in the end.
Why C. pretended everything was fine.
What part D. played in E.'s silence.   5
What F. had been expecting, if anything.
Why G. forgot when she knew perfectly well.
What H. had to hide.
What I. wanted to add.
If my being around   10
meant anything
to J. and K. and the rest of the alphabet.

EPISODE, IMPRESSION, AND FRAGMENT

Some important thematic implications of a fully developed, carefully designed plot are challenged by writers with simple strategies of abbreviation. If a writer thinks that the real world can't be captured within a traditional plot, then some reduced form of narration becomes an attractive choice. An **episode** suggests a single, continuous, and brief action that stands alone. An episode within a large story or novel refers to a specific action that could be detached from the larger plot. Some novels are built from a string of episodes. This tumbled-out-one-thing-after-another sequence of actions constitutes an **episodic narrative** or an **episodic novel**. Episodic narratives tend to be open rather than closed. An **open ending** is one that leaves essential matters largely unresolved. Mark Twain's *Adventures of Huckleberry Finn* nicely illustrates an episodic, open narrative.

Huck recounts a string of adventures and at the end "lights out" to the territory ahead for what will be further adventures. Any sequel (and Twain did write one for Huck) will add episodes but will never "wrap up" Huck's experience. The reader may be left unsure about what happens to important characters, or what significance to draw from the action, or how "whole" the action was. A **closed ending** more aggressively wraps up the various strands of action. It communicates a relatively final conclusion. Popular detective stories are probably the clearest example of strongly closed fictions.

An episode can be thought of as a means to purposefully abbreviate plot. Plot, as we've mentioned, involves both writer and reader in a careful putting together of incidents and scenes. It challenges us to find patterns, discover relationships, and distinguish primary from secondary. Some modern writers, wary of the control implied by fully developed plots (as some painters are wary of fully realized representations of objects), deliberately cut stories short; they may feel that the **fragment** they offer readers more honestly represents the confusing, unstable world in which we live. Or at least they believe that the fragment more accurately registers the way we experience life. A deliberate emphasis on episode as opposed to plot is related to the notion of an **impression**. It's useful to think about what we mean by that word and by impressionism or impressionist. An impression brings us back to the immediate feeling created by a picture or a painting.

When critics first labeled the painter Claude Monet an "impressionist," they were not praising him. Many early viewers thought that Monet failed to make complete sense of—or achieve an ideal vision of—the subjects he painted. For example, some critics complained that Monet diminished his subjects by attending so closely to the particular qualities of light (conditioned by weather, the time of day, the season) that surrounded the subjects. In regard to Monet's *Portal of Rouen Cathedral in Morning Light* (p. 7), one criticism may have been: "Why is he painting the fog when he should be painting the church?" We could imagine Monet answering, "Because it was foggy on the day that I sat before the church" or "Fog is the main thing I saw when I painted that day" or "Because I wished to capture the ephemeral nature of fog." Monet might have asked his own questions in response to the complaint: "Why should I paint something that supposedly lies behind what I *actually see* at a particular moment? Why do you assume the church and not the fog is the real subject of my painting?"

There is an important idea here that relates very much to the vision of artists working with other materials (words, film, sound). An impression is of the moment. It is bound by time, subject to changing conditions. An impression is essentially subjective. It registers what an individual saw or felt at a single point in time. It is a sensation—something seen, felt, smelled. An impression is not a statement or an ideal; nor is it an absolute, fixed eternal truth. It is not a generalization. An impression is *not* a plot.

Claude Monet, *Portal of Rouen Cathedral in Morning Light* (1894)

Experiencing Literature through Impression and Episode

What Monet was doing with paint meshes with what Stephen Crane often-times did with words. Crane didn't believe that the world he knew allowed for long, carefully wrought, richly plotted fictions. He worked in short forms and often deliberately reduced his sense of scale. He registered impressions through the experiences of individual characters and believed that those subjective impressions were as close as he could get to "truth." The title of the story that follows deliberately announces his sense of limits. Crane uses the indefinite article *an*, not the definite article *the*. He promises to deliver a single fragment of experience, one bit from many that could have been selected. He also explicitly presents an "episode." We don't expect great length. We don't expect a complex weaving together of incidents. Because of his title, we don't seek to make this one episode more than a particular episode that occurs at a particular time and place. The life of the main character before the episode or after isn't really Crane's interest. Yet the shock of loss one feels upon reading this work is sufficient to justify it as art.

Stephen Crane (1871–1900)

An Episode of War (1899)

The lieutenant's rubber blanket lay on the ground, and upon it he had poured the company's supply of coffee. Corporals and other representatives of the grimy and hot-throated men who lined the breastwork had come for each squad's portion.

The lieutenant was frowning and serious at this task of division. His lips pursed as he drew with his sword various crevices in the heap, until brown squares of coffee, astoundingly equal in size, appeared on the blanket. He was on the verge of a great triumph in mathematics, and the corporals were thronging forward, each to reap a little square, when suddenly the lieutenant cried out and looked quickly at a man near him as if he suspected it was a case of personal assault. The others cried out also when they saw blood upon the lieutenant's sleeve.

He had winced like a man stung, swayed dangerously, and then straightened. The sound of his hoarse breathing was plainly audible. He looked sadly, mystically, over the breastwork at the green face of a wood, where now were many puffs of white smoke. During this moment the men about him gazed statue-like and silent, astonished and awed by this catastrophe which happened when catastrophes were not expected—when they had leisure to observe it.

As the lieutenant stared at the wood, they too swung their heads, so that for another instant all hands, still silent, contemplated the distant forest as if their minds were fixed upon the mystery of a bullet's journey.

The officer had, of course, been compelled to take his sword into his left hand. He did not hold it by the hilt. He gripped it at the middle of the blade, awkwardly. Turning his eyes from the wood, he looked at the sword as he held it there, and seemed puzzled as to what to do with it. In short, this weapon had all of a sudden become a strange thing to him. He looked at it in a kind of stupefaction, as if he had been endowed with a trident, a scepter, or a spade.

Finally he tried to sheathe it. To sheathe a sword held by the left hand, at the middle of the blade, in a scabbard hung at the left hip, is a feat worthy of a sawdust ring. This wounded officer engaged in a desperate struggle with the sword and the wobbling scabbard, and during the time of it he breathed like a wrestler.

But at this instant the men, spectators, awoke from their stone-like poses and crowded forward sympathetically. The orderly-sergeant took the sword and tenderly placed it in the scabbard. At the time, he leaned nervously backward, and did not allow even his finger to brush the body of the lieutenant. A wound gives strange dignity to him who bears it. Well men shy from this new and terrible majesty. It is as if the wounded man's hand is upon the curtain which hangs before the revelations of all existence—the meaning of ants, potentates, wars, cities, sunshine, snow, a feather dropped from a bird's wing; and the power of it sheds radiance upon a bloody form, and makes the other men understand sometimes that they are little. His comrades look at him with large eyes thoughtfully. Moreover, they fear vaguely that the weight of a finger upon him might send him headlong, precipitate the tragedy, hurl him at once into the dim, gray unknown. And so the orderly-sergeant, while sheathing the sword, leaned nervously backward.

There were others who proffered assistance. One timidly presented his shoulder and asked the lieutenant if he cared to lean upon it, but the latter waved him away mournfully. He wore the look of one who knows he is the victim of a terrible disease and understands his helplessness. He again stared over the breastwork at the forest, and then, turning, went slowly rearward. He held his right wrist tenderly in his left hand as if the wounded arm was made of brittle glass.

And the men in silence stared at the woods, then at the departing lieutenant; then at the wood, then at the lieutenant.

As the wounded officer passed from the line of battle, he was enabled to see many things which as a participant in the fight were unknown to him. He saw a general on a black horse gazing over the lines of blue infantry at the green woods which veiled his problems. An aide galloped furiously, dragged his horse suddenly to a halt, saluted, and presented a paper. It was, for a wonder, precisely like an historical painting.

To the rear of the general and his staff a group, composed of a bugler, two or three orderlies, and the bearer of the corps standard, all upon maniacal horses, were working like slaves to hold their ground, preserve their respectful interval, while the shells boomed in the air about them, and caused their chargers to make furious quivering leaps.

A battery, a tumultuous and shining mass, was swirling toward the right. The wild thud of hoofs, the cries of the riders, shouting blame and praise, menace and encouragement, and, last, the roar of the wheels, the slant of the glistening guns, brought the lieutenant to an intent pause. The battery swept in curves that stirred the heart; it made halts as dramatic as the crash of a wave on the rocks, and when it fled onward this aggregation of wheels, levers, motors had a beautiful unity, as if it were a missile. The sound of it was a war chorus that reached into the depths of man's emotion.

The lieutenant, still holding his arm as if it were of glass, stood watching this battery until all detail of it were lost, save the figures of the riders, which rose and fell and waved lashes over the black mass.

Later, he turned his eyes toward the battle, where the shooting sometimes crackled like bush-fires, sometimes sputtered with exasperating irregularity, and sometimes reverberated like the thunder. He saw the smoke rolling upward and saw crowds of men who ran and cheered, or stood and blazed away at the inscrutable distance.

He came upon some stragglers, and they told him how to find the field hospital. They described its exact location. In fact, these men, no longer having part in the battle, knew more of it than the others. They told the performance of every corps, every division, the opinion of every general. The lieutenant, carrying his wounded arm rearward, looked upon them with wonder.

At the roadside a brigade was making coffee and buzzing with talk like a girl's boarding school. Several officers came out to him and inquired concerning things of which he knew nothing. One, seeing his arm, began to scold. "Why, man, that's no way to do. You want to fix that thing." He appropriated the lieutenant and the lieutenant's wound. He cut the sleeve and laid bare the arm, every nerve of which softly fluttered under his touch. He bound his handkerchief over the wound, scolding away in the meantime. His tone allowed one to think that he was in the habit of being wounded every day. The lieutenant hung his head, feeling, in this presence, that he did not know how to be correctly wounded.

The low white tents of the hospital were grouped around an old schoolhouse. There was here a singular commotion. In the foreground two ambulances interlocked wheels in the deep mud. The drivers were tossing the blame of it back and forth, gesticulating and berating, while from the ambulances, both crammed with wounded, there came an occasional groan. An interminable crowd of bandaged men were coming and going. Great numbers sat under the trees nursing heads or arms or legs. There was a dispute of some kind raging on the steps of the schoolhouse. Sitting with his back against a tree a man with a face as gray as a new army blanket was serenely smoking a corncob pipe. The lieutenant wished to rush forward and inform him that he was dying.

A busy surgeon was passing near the lieutenant. "Good morning," he said, with a friendly smile. Then he caught sight of the lieutenant's arm, and his face at once changed. "Well, let's have a look at it." He seemed possessed suddenly of a great contempt for the lieutenant. This wound evidently placed the latter on a very low social plane. The doctor cried out impatiently: "What mutton-head had tied it up that way anyhow?"

The lieutenant answered, "Oh a man."

When the wound was disclosed the doctor fingered it disdainfully. "Humph," he said. "You come along with me and I'll 'tend to you." His voice contained the same scorn as if he were saying: "You will have to go to jail."

The lieutenant had been very meek, but now his face flushed, and he looked into the doctor's eyes. "I guess I won't have it amputated," he said.

"Nonsense, man!" Nonsense! Nonsense!" cried the doctor. "Come along, now. I won't amputate it. Come along. Don't be a baby."

"Let go of me," said the lieutenant, holding back wrathfully, his glance fixed upon the door of the old school house, as sinister to him as the portals of death.

And this is the story of how the lieutenant lost his arm. When he reached home, his sisters, his mother, his wife, sobbed for a long time at the sight of the flat sleeve. "Oh, well," he said, standing shamefaced amid these tears, "I don't suppose it matters so much as all that." ∎

The main action of Crane's "An Episode of War" occurs out of the blue. The soldiers are *not* in the midst of battle. They are in the midst of the most mundane of activities: rationing out the company's supply of coffee. The bullet comes as a surprise. The men don't spring into action in response. They gawk, feel awkward, seem a little awed that one among them has been injured. The wounding doesn't fit into a larger action—it is a random event, a horrifying reminder that danger is ever present and that the most momentous events are not scripted. Life matching up with art seems almost ridiculously accidental: "An aide galloped furiously, dragged his horse suddenly to a halt, saluted, and presented a paper. It was, for a wonder, precisely like an historical painting." It seems appropriate that Crane leaves his story open at the end. We have a strong impression of the moment he returns home, but a limited sense of how that moment will be played out in his family life ahead. By not attempting to strongly close the story, Crane suggests the most solid truths are limited ones.

TENSION, RELEASE, AND RESOLUTION

At some level, a grandly plotted story is like a great musical piece: it builds **tension**, releases tension, and achieves resolution. To put it another way, plots prompt us to think of (and feel) oppositions and alternatives. Will he stay or run? Will she tell or remain silent? Do they know, or are they still unaware of what is unfolding? The tension created and sustained by such questions produces a momentum that requires release. Tension and release (as we've suggested earlier) also lead to the desire for resolution: we want things more or less pulled together in most stories. The careful working together of various strands may lend a narrative great emotional force. Plots involve us in actions and in the fates of characters; plots encourage us to keep turning the pages. Plot can also help communicate a compelling worldview by giving larger shape, meaning, or purpose to action. But short of such grand effects, plot offers the sheer pleasure of artful management. We appreciate the craft involved in a well-made story.

Arthur Conan Doyle's Sherlock Holmes stories have long offered readers pleasure in the plot. Michael Chabon, a contemporary novelist, writes in the essay "The Game's Afoot" that "Conan Doyle found a way to fold several stories, and the proper means of telling them, over and over into a tightly compacted frame, with a proportionate gain in narrative power. [The Sherlock Holmes stories] are storytelling engines, steam driven, brass-fitted, but among the most efficient narrative apparatuses the world has ever seen. After all these years, they still run remarkably well."° "A Scandal in Bohemia" (p. 21) is one of these smooth-running engines. As you read the story, consider the distinction Holmes makes between "seeing" and "observing." For him, seeing is a mere matter of physical perception. Observing, though, is making sure that what we see registers fully. It is a neat distinction for a detective and one that also works well for a student of literature.

Doyle's "A Scandal in Bohemia" gives us an especially good chance to consider the point Chabon makes about Doyle's folding several stories together. The "folding" is what distinguishes a plot from a mere string of events. We're left with a strong sense of unity and closure with the Doyle story, because all the parts mesh so well. As Chabon points out, the meshing is so fine that we might not notice that Doyle has several stories working together. The King initially tells a story to Holmes: Irene Adler has a compromising picture that may influence world events. Holmes later tells a story to Watson: The detective went in disguise to Adler's neighborhood and became a participant in her elopement and marriage to Godfrey Norton. Watson recounts to us the trick Holmes pulls to uncover the picture's hiding place (after Holmes had spelled out to Watson what was to occur): the false injury, the smoke bomb, the cry of fire. Irene Adler tells a story to Holmes in her remaining letter: She was (despite forewarnings) taken in by him but saw through his deception just in time. And Watson again reports to us on how Holmes and the King respond to Adler's poise. All of these stories work together to give us a sense of a unified action that begins, builds, and closes. We have one plot woven of many incidents told from multiple perspectives and aimed at (seemingly) different audiences. Observing all of this complexity in "A Scandal in Bohemia" prepares us well for how subtly plots may operate.

° *The New York Review of Books* (vol. LII, no. 3; February 24, 2005, p. 14)

MULTIPLE AND REFLEXIVE PLOTS

The layers that make up a Sherlock Holmes story suggest a number of fresh possibilities for constructing plots. The layers can be more than an efficient engine; they can suggest the complex textures of "real" life. And the layers do not need to add up to a unified story or a simple chronological plot (in which action links to action in clear sequence, like beads on a string). We often discover that as a single work unfolds, we process multiple stories or **multiple plots**. We get a sense in many narratives that plots are there for us to discover, to construct. A cliché such as "there are always two sides to a story" becomes inadequate because we realize that two sides are hardly enough to account for the complexity we routinely contend with in both life and art. We're often prompted to consider how one story becomes something quite different if we simply shift a point of emphasis. A **subplot** (that is, a subordinate or secondary plot) might give us insight into what happens in the major action it parallels. A subplot might also flesh out for us some aspect of character. In *Hamlet*, for example, we might consider the tensions between Laertes and Hamlet as forming an instructive subplot to the conflict that unfolds between Hamlet and Claudius.

Many writers, particularly more recent writers, convey a high degree of self-consciousness in their work. That is, they are aware of, as well as interested in, the philosophical, psychological, and dramatic potential inherent in plot. Such self-consciousness can become a kind of strategy; readers are reminded as they read to think about the plot as a plot. We sometimes call such plots **reflexive plots**; the way in which a story is constructed becomes the very thing we are forced to think about, to reflect upon.

Memento (2000), a film directed by Christopher Nolan, is an exceptionally good example of a **reflexive** or **self-conscious narrative**. Nolan (who adapted the film from "Memento Mori," a short story by his brother, Jonathan Nolan) literally runs his plot backward. The main character—Leonard Shelby (played by Guy Pearce)—is a man who has no short-term memory as a result of a blow to his head. He remembers who he is (his name, his family, his life before his injury) but cannot hold in his mind the simplest moment-to-moment experiences. Leonard forgets not only his keys but his car. He forgets people he has met within minutes of leaving their presence; he forgets where he lives or how he got to whatever place he happens to be; he forgets why he is doing what he is doing; and he forgets very quickly what he has just done.

Nolan gives us the last action first—a brutal killing—and then moves backward to help us understand how and why things came to that end. Shelby, despite his forgetfulness, is motivated by revenge. He seeks to kill the man who raped and murdered his wife and who took his memory. His detective work, though, can move forward only through a painstaking process of note taking. Because he cannot remember any clue he uncovers, he must write

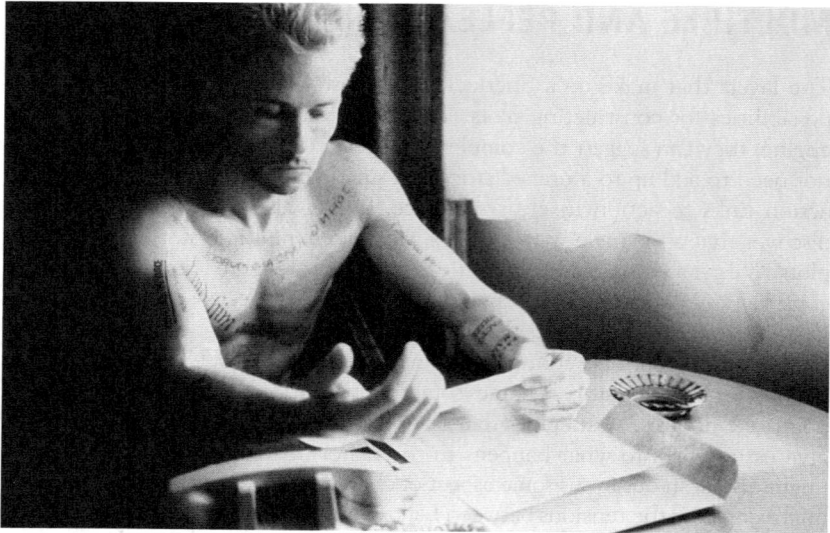

In *Memento* (2000), Leonard Shelby (Guy Pearce) develops a system of using notes, Polaroid pictures, and tattoos to help him remember crucial information.

down everything. He even tattoos crucial information on his own skin. And of course, once he consults his notes, the situations that prompted the writing have been forgotten. By telling the story in this fashion, Nolan demands that the viewers put many of the pieces together for themselves. He also makes us aware that the main character has fashioned a rather different plot than the actual truth. We're then left to think about truth, limits, motives, not just "what" happens but why "what" happened. In a sense, the plot in this case is the meaning or theme of the story.

A Note to Student Writers: Critical Reading and Understanding

The impulse to tell stories isn't all that different from the impulse to talk and write about the stories we encounter as readers and viewers. Critical reading isn't just passively absorbing a story; it involves participating in the creation of the story as it unfolds. As we read, we anticipate events and link incidents. We discuss, interpret, and evaluate. Sometimes we question, complain, and even "fix" the story. When we begin to write in response to literature, we press such impulses forward more forcefully still. In some ways, critical writing becomes its own kind of narrative. To analyze is to break something into pieces so that we can understand how it all fits together. A critical essay involves this breaking down and fitting together. Writing a critical essay makes a story *ours*. The process of writing critically forces us to understand what happens and why.

One seemingly simple thing you can do to get a grip on essential features of a text is to summarize the action that unfolds in a work you are reading. You'll find it is often a helpful exercise. Summary forces you to read closely and shrink the text to the barest essentials. Such a basic recounting can oftentimes open up what might seem puzzling works. Even when we don't think of a work primarily in terms of events, there is usually some core action that we must understand. For example, Marge Piercy's "Unlearning to not speak" is a short poem that relates types of incidents that don't necessarily add up to a fully realized story. The poem's total effect might seem to convey a mood (desperation and anger) and an appeal (speak up!). But neither the mood nor the appeal will make much sense if we can't recount what happens in the poem.

Marge Piercy (1936–)

Unlearning to not speak (1973)

Blizzards of paper
in slow motion
sift through her.
In nightmares she suddenly recalls
a class she signed up for   5
but forgot to attend.
Now it is too late.
Now it is time for finals:
losers will be shot.
Phrases of men who lectured her   10
drift and rustle in piles:
Why don't you speak up?
Why are you shouting?
You have the wrong answer,
wrong line, wrong face.   15
They tell her she is womb-man,
babymachine, mirror image, toy
earth mother and penis-poor,
a dish of synthetic strawberry ice cream
rapidly melting.   20
She grunts to a halt.
She must learn again to speak
starting with I
starting with We
starting as the infant does   25
with her own true hunger
and pleasure
and rage.

The nightmares referred to in the fourth line set up a succession of incidents that create a category of experience that is more than a single action. But Piercy gives us many particulars to work with. The girl in the poem feels desperate, unconfident, overpowered by the stern male authorities who teach not so much a subject as a set of attitudes about status and gender. We get quick hints of larger incidents that we need to flesh out for ourselves. A girl is thrown on the defensive by the instructor's questions. Why is it so difficult for her to respond? We can imagine a situation in which the questions are not fair, not even real. The questions don't arise from a subject or an intellectual problem; they arise from an established prejudice. The problem is being a girl. In the minds of the male teachers, the girl is too shy, too dumb, too pushy, too weak, too whatever. As the poem progresses, we learn that she has been disempowered by this education. Piercy suggests that by getting back to something that predates her education, some more elemental sense of personal need, desire, and identity, the girl can "unlearn to not speak." The poem's most basic action might be summarized as follows: The girl's male teachers routinely put her down in class until finally she realizes, out of frustration, anger, need, and joy, that she must stand up to speak her own mind.

MODELING CRITICAL ANALYSIS: JAMAICA KINCAID, GIRL

Jamaica Kincaid's "Girl" hardly seems to have a plot. Plots are, after all, made up of incidents and scenes that work together. A plot isn't a list of observations but a carefully arranged sequence of events. "Girl," for the most part seems to "list" demands an older woman (a mother?) makes on a young girl: do this, don't do that, do things this way, don't do things that way. And "Girl" packs everything into one very long sentence. How can a single sentence, however long, develop a plot?

Jamaica Kincaid (1949–)

Girl (1983)

Wash the white clothes on Monday and put them on the stone heap; wash the color clothes on Tuesday and put them on the clothesline to dry; don't walk barehead in the hot sun; cook pumpkin fritters in very hot sweet oil; soak your little cloths right after you take them off; when buying cotton to make yourself a nice blouse, be sure that it doesn't have gum on it, because that way it won't hold up well after a wash; soak salt fish overnight before you cook it; is it true that you sing benna in Sunday school?; always eat your food in such a way that it won't turn someone else's stomach; on Sundays try to walk like a lady and not like the slut you are so bent on becoming; don't sing benna in Sunday school; you mustn't speak to wharf-rat boys, not even to give directions; don't eat fruits on the street—flies will follow you; *but I don't sing benna on Sundays at all and never in Sunday school*; this is how to sew on a button; this is how to make a buttonhole for the button you have just sewed on; this is how to hem a dress when you see the hem coming down and so to prevent yourself from looking like the slut I know you are so bent on becoming; this is how you iron your father's khaki shirt so that it doesn't have a crease; this is how you iron your father's khaki pants so that they don't have a crease; this is how you grow okra—far from the house, because okra tree harbors red ants; when you are growing dasheen, make sure it gets plenty of water or else it makes your throat itch when you are eating it; this is how you sweep a corner; this is how you sweep a whole house; this is how you sweep a yard; this is how you smile to someone you don't like too much; this is how you smile to someone you don't like at all; this is how you smile to someone you like completely; this is how you set a table for tea; this is how you set a table for dinner; this is how you set a table for dinner with an important guest; this is how you set a table for lunch; this is how you set a table for breakfast; this is how to behave in the presence of men who don't know you very well, and this way they won't recognize immediately the slut I have warned you against becoming; be sure to wash every day, even if it is with your own spit; don't squat down to play marbles— you are not a boy, you know; don't pick people's flowers—you might catch something; don't throw stones at blackbirds, because it might not be a blackbird at all; this is how to make a bread pudding; this is how to make doukona; this is how to make pepper pot; this is how to make a good medicine for a cold; this is how to make a good medicine to throw away a child before it even becomes a child; this is how to catch a fish; this is how to throw back a fish you don't like, and that way something bad won't fall on you; this is how to bully a man; this is how a man bullies you; this is how to love a man, and if this doesn't work there are other ways, and if they don't work don't feel too bad about giving up; this is how to spit up in the air if you feel like it, and this is how to move quick so that it doesn't fall on you; this is how to make ends meet; always squeeze bread to make sure it's fresh; *but what if the baker won't let me feel the bread?*; you mean to say that after all you are really going to be the kind of woman who the baker won't let near the bread? ∎

It is useful to think of the many stories, the many plots, suggested by Kincaid's list of impressions, memories, and incidents. Kincaid triggers multiple associa-tions about growing up that readers can fill in, indeed must fill in. She, like Marge Piercy in "Unlearning to not speak" (p. 15), seems to depend upon the reader's ability to elaborate upon the smallest hints and create full scenes, or even stories. We can imagine how thickly textured the girl's life is with reprimands. For example, if she joins other children for a game of marbles, she can be scolded for squatting like a boy. Such gender lessons, of course, are part of larger assumptions about status and power. The girl is not a boy and must always remember what that fact means. It means that any sign of independence quickly becomes a marker of moral or social inadequacy. It means that the girl must control signs because she controls little else: how to "behave in the presence of men," how to hide who she is, "how to make a good medicine to throw away a child before it even becomes a child."

Kincaid, again like Piercy, gives readers some means to structure the whole. If we look at "Girl" carefully, we'll note some important interruptions and repetitions. On two occasions, we have a break in the voice—the person on the receiving end of all the instructions speaks for herself. The first time this happens (about a third of the way into the piece), the woman steams ahead without a pause. The girl has spoken, but the woman hasn't listened or hasn't thought any back talk is worth responding to. The second break (marked by italics, as the first is) occurs at the end of the piece. Here the girl questions the real-world application of the advice: "*what if the baker won't let me feel the bread.*" The older woman's response returns again to the strategy of diminishment that has been part of the whole story: What kind of woman is this girl bent on becoming? The older woman sees nothing but bad ahead, but readers are more likely to imagine the girl's youthful independence more than any presumed natural deficiency.

Using Plot to Focus Writing and Discussion

- What happens over the course of the text?
- How do things change from the opening scene?
- What events lead to this conclusion?
- Is this a conclusion that you expected? What led you to this expectation? What details in the opening of the text shape your expectations?
- Why do events unfold here in the order that they do? Is this a chronological account of events, or is there some other ordering principle?
- Are there events that we do not learn about? How are these undiscovered details significant?
- How has the author made this story interesting?

Anthology

DETECTIVE WORK: FIGURING PLOT

Detective work is, among other things, a professional activity. In "A Scandal in Bohemia" Sherlock Holmes is presented a problem and is asked to solve it for a fee. We would like, in this anthology, to apply the notion of detective work to your role as an active, engaged reader. Although we include Doyle's classic detective story along with modern variants of the form, we haven't restricted the following readings to a specific type of story. We'd like to use the image and activity of the detective to suggest something larger: we're using the activity of the detective to suggest a way of reading and writing.

Doyle has his detective draw a distinction between "seeing" and "observing." For Holmes, "seeing" is a purely physical act; Watson sees as well as Holmes. "Observing" takes the physical sensations the eye processes and subjects those sensations to reflection and analysis in relation to other available experience or information. We often think of "evidence" as some tangible thing, but we need to remember that *proving* is an intellectual activity. A hammer is just a hammer; it becomes evidence only if one can place the hammer in context of a complex body of information and make it serve to support an interpretation.

Don Lee's "The Price of Eggs in China" is a detective story with some element of the whodunit. But that seems only a slight element. "The Price of Eggs in China" is also a love story, a revenge story, a psychological study, a reflection upon art and the creative process. It's all of these things because it invites us to think about not just the story that Don Lee tells but also the stories that the different characters construct. As in the film *Memento*, we're left to question the "truth" of the various stories as well as the motives that lie behind the telling. We need to observe, in the Holmesian sense of the word, all the available material. We need to see details as clues to meaning. The fact that Dean, one of the main characters in "The Price of Eggs in China," is an avid reader of detective stories contributes to the self-conscious feel of the whole story. Dean becomes, quite literally, a plotter; he sets up evidence so that it will be read in a particular way. And of course, the three main characters (Dean, Caroline, and Marcella) are all artists. Perhaps Lee is suggesting that artists are inevitably plotters. Or to put it a slightly different way, maybe we all have to engage life as detectives encountering deep and dangerous mysteries.

Poems, too, involve narrative. Events unfold in a carefully (if minutely) plotted manner. But even when plot is not an issue, you'll need to pay close attention to what we might call "the facts" of a specific case. For example, you'll need to keep the seeing/observing distinction in mind as you read Emily Dickinson's "I like to see it lap the Miles—" and "A Route of Evanescence." If these two poems seem puzzling, the reason is that they are puzzles—or what are called **riddle poems**. Dickinson gives us descriptions without ever directly telling us what she is describing. We're left to identify the missing subject. Dickinson's playful poetic game suggests that she sees readers as having an important role. In some ways, we might think of ourselves as co-creating these poems with Dickinson. All the pieces in each poem will snap together as a coherent work of art only when we identify the subject Dickinson has left unnamed.

Few people think first of detective work in regard to *Oedipus the King*. But this play certainly builds on riddles solved and, more crucially, unsolved. The inability of Oedipus to appreciate the deepest mysteries of his own life moves the tragedy forward. Sophocles plots the action in a way that engages us in the forces that undo his protagonist. You'll note in this case a clear distinction between story and plot. The plot of the play centers on the quest to discover who murdered King Laius of Thebes. The story of Oedipus begins before his birth, with the prophecy that a son of Jocasta and Laius will kill the father. The story continues with the birth of Oedipus; the order for his death; the smuggling of the infant away from danger; his growth to adulthood as (he believes) the son of the King and Queen of Corinth; his departure from Corinth upon learning of the prophecy; his violent encounter with a group of travelers that (unknown to him) fulfills the prophecy; his return to Thebes; his solving of the riddle; his coronation as King; his marriage to Jocasta; his long reign; his investigation into the long-unsolved murder of Laius; his discovery of the truth; his self-blinding and banishment.

We could go on, because this story continues into the next generation (as you'll see when you read *Antigone*). But the way we've just related the events in the story does not match well the way that Sophocles arranges (that is, plots) actions. The play *Oedipus the King* begins very near the end of the long list of events that we noted. Much that is crucial to the story has no part in the action of the play itself (although everything listed can operate as a knowledge base the audience brings to the theater). The plot of *Oedipus the King* moves both forward and backward in time and allows us to experience the whole action in ways a reductive story line cannot communicate. The address Oedipus offers his citizens/supplicants to open the play establishes for the audience Oedipus as King. He is at the height of his powers, a proud and respected monarch. The forces that conspire to undo him have collected over his whole life but will be unleashed only in the compressed few hours of life to follow. We get, then, an intense experience of how complex events may link to bring about the fall of a noble subject. The plot of *Oedipus the King* puts us in the role of a seeker— looking for clues to meaning and significance. When we closely engage with a work of art, that role seems unavoidable. In the readings that follow, you can test a hypothesis: Reading is always a form of detective work.

FICTION

Arthur Conan Doyle (1859–1930)

Arthur Conan Doyle is one of the most widely read authors in English, and his character Sherlock Homes one of the most recognized characters in English literature. Born in Edinburgh, Scotland, Doyle worked as a physician before becoming a professional writer, and he returned to this profession during the Boer War (1899–1902) when he served as a field surgeon. Doyle wrote every kind of literature, from poetry to books on spiritualism to a political pamphlet in defense of British conduct during the Boer War (for which he was knighted). But his detective fiction is the work for which he is chiefly remembered. The character of Sherlock Homes, the utterly rational detective, has remained popular up to the present day and has been the subject of numerous books, plays, films, and television shows. Though Doyle once killed the character off, Holmes's enormous popularity (and the attendant money) made him reconsider.

A Scandal in Bohemia (1891)

To Sherlock Holmes she is always *the* woman. I have seldom heard him mention her under any other name. In his eyes she eclipses and predominates the whole of her sex. It was not that he felt any emotion akin to love for Irene Adler. All emotions, and that one particularly, were abhorrent to his cold, precise but admirably balanced mind. He was, I take it, the most perfect reasoning and observing machine that the world has seen, but as a lover he would have placed himself in a false position. He never spoke of the softer passions, save with a gibe and a sneer. They were admirable things for the observer—excellent for drawing the veil from men's motives and actions. But for the trained reasoner to admit such intrusions into his own delicate and finely adjusted temperament was to introduce a distracting factor which might throw a doubt upon all his mental results. Grit in a sensitive instrument, or a crack in one of his own high-power lenses, would not be more disturbing than a strong emotion in a nature such as his. And yet there was but one woman to him, and that woman was the late Irene Adler, of dubious and questionable memory.

I had seen little of Holmes lately. My marriage had drifted us away from each other. My own complete happiness, and the home-centred interests which rise up around the man who first finds himself master of his own establishment, were sufficient to absorb all my attention, while Holmes, who loathed every form of society with his whole Bohemian soul, remained in our lodgings in Baker Street, buried among his old books, and alternating from week to week between cocaine and ambition, the drowsiness of the drug, and the fierce energy of his own keen nature. He was still, as ever, deeply attracted by the study of crime, and occupied his immense faculties and extraordinary powers of observation in following out those clues, and clearing up those mysteries which had been abandoned as hopeless by the official police. From time to time I heard some vague account of his doings: of his summons to Odessa in the case of the Trepoff murder, of his clearing up of the singular tragedy of the Atkinson brothers at Trincomalee, and finally of the mission which he had accomplished so delicately and successfully for the reigning family of Holland. Beyond these signs of his activity, however, which I merely shared with all the readers of the daily press, I knew little of my former friend and companion.

One night—it was on the twentieth of March, 1888—I was returning from a journey to a patient (for I had now returned to civil practice), when my way led me through Baker Street. As I passed the well-remembered door, which must always be associated in my mind with my wooing, and with the dark incidents of the *Study in Scarlet*, I was seized with a keen desire to see Holmes again, and to know how he was employing his extraordinary powers. His rooms were brilliantly lit, and, even as I looked up, I saw his tall, spare figure pass twice in a dark silhouette against the blind. He was pacing the room swiftly, eagerly, with his head sunk upon his chest and his hands clasped behind him. To me, who knew his every mood and habit, his attitude and manner told their own story. He was at work again. He had risen out of his drug-created dreams and was hot upon the scent of some new problem. I rang the bell and was shown up to the chamber which had formerly been in part my own.

His manner was not effusive. It seldom was; but he was glad, I think, to see me. With hardly a word spoken, but with a kindly eye, he waved me to an armchair, threw across his case of cigars, and indicated a spirit case and a gasogene in the corner. Then he stood before the fire and looked me over in his singular introspective fashion.

"Wedlock suits you," he remarked. "I think, Watson, that you have put   5 on seven and a half pounds since I saw you."

"Seven!" I answered.

"Indeed, I should have thought a little more. Just a trifle more, I fancy, Watson. And in practice again, I observe. You did not tell me that you intended to go into harness."

"Then, how do you know?"

"I see it, I deduce it. How do I know that you have been getting yourself very wet lately, and that you have a most clumsy and careless servant girl?"

"My dear Holmes," said I, "this is too much. You would certainly have   10 been burned, had you lived a few centuries ago. It is true that I had a country walk on Thursday and came home in a dreadful mess, but as I have changed my clothes I can't imagine how you deduce it. As to Mary Jane, she is incorrigible, and my wife has given her notice; but there, again, I fail to see how you work it out."

He chuckled to himself and rubbed his long, nervous hands together.

"It is simplicity itself," said he; "my eyes tell me that on the inside of your left shoe, just where the firelight strikes it, the leather is scored by six almost parallel cuts. Obviously they have been caused by someone who has very carelessly scraped round the edges of the sole in order to remove crusted mud from it. Hence, you see, my double deduction that you had been out in vile weather, and that you had a particularly malignant boot-slitting specimen of the London slavery. As to your practice, if a gentleman walks into my rooms smelling of iodoform, with a black mark of nitrate of silver upon his right forefinger, and a bulge on the right side of his top-hat to show where he has secreted his stethoscope, I must be dull, indeed, if I do not pronounce him to be an active member of the medical profession."

I could not help laughing at the ease with which he explained his process of deduction. "When I hear you give your reasons," I remarked, "the thing always appears to me to be so ridiculously simple that I could easily do it myself, though at each successive instance of your reasoning I am baffled until you explain your process. And yet I believe that my eyes are as good as yours."

"Quite so," he answered, lighting a cigarette, and throwing himself down into an armchair. "You see, but you do not observe. The distinction is clear. For example, you have frequently seen the steps which lead up from the hall to this room."

"Frequently."   15

"How often?"

"Well, some hundreds of times."

"Then how many are there?"

"How many? I don't know."

"Quite so! You have not observed. And yet you have seen. That is just my   20
point. Now, I know that there are seventeen steps, because I have both seen and observed. By the way, since you are interested in these little problems, and since you are good enough to chronicle one or two of my trifling experiences, you may be interested in this." He threw over a sheet of thick, pink-tinted note-paper which had been lying open upon the table. "It came by the last post," said he. "Read it aloud."

The note was undated, and without either signature or address.

There will call upon you to-night, at a quarter to eight o'clock [it said], a gentleman who desires to consult you upon a matter of the very deepest moment. Your recent services to one of the royal houses of Europe have shown that you are one who may safely be trusted with matters which are of an importance which can hardly be exaggerated. This account of you we have from all quarters received. Be in your chamber then at that hour, and do not take it amiss if your visitor wears a mask.

"This is indeed a mystery," I remarked. "What do you imagine that it means?"

"I have no data yet. It is a capital mistake to theorize before one has data. Insensibly one begins to twist facts to suit theories, instead of theories to suit facts. But the note itself. What do you deduce from it?"

I carefully examined the writing, and the paper upon which it was written.

"The man who wrote it was presumably well to do," I remarked, endeavouring to imitate my companion's processes. "Such paper could not be bought under half a crown a packet. It is peculiarly strong and stiff."

"Peculiar—that is the very word," said Holmes. "It is not an English paper at all. Hold it up to the light."

I did so, and saw a large "E" with a small "g," a "P," and a large "G" with a small "t" woven into the texture of the paper.

"What do you make of that?" asked Holmes.

"The name of the maker, no doubt; or his monogram, rather."

"Not at all. The 'G' with the small 't' stands for 'Gesellschaft,' which is the German for 'Company.' It is a customary contraction like our 'Co.' 'P,' of course, stands for 'Papier.' Now for the 'Eg.' Let us glance at our Continental Gazetteer." He took down a heavy brown volume from his shelves. "Eglow, Eglonitz—here we are, Egria. It is in a German-speaking country—in Bohemia, not far from Carlsbad. 'Remarkable as being the scene of the death of Wallenstein, and for its numerous glass-factories and paper-mills.' Ha, ha, my boy, what do you make of that?" His eyes sparkled, and he sent up a great blue triumphant cloud from his cigarette.

"The paper was made in Bohemia," I said.

"Precisely. And the man who wrote the note is a German. Do you note the peculiar construction of the sentence—'This account of you we have from all quarters received.' A Frenchman or Russian could not have written that. It is the German who is so uncourteous to his verbs. It only remains, therefore, to discover what is wanted by this German who writes upon Bohemian paper and prefers wearing a mask to showing his face. And here he comes, if I am not mistaken, to resolve all our doubts."

As he spoke there was the sharp sound of horses' hoofs and grating wheels against the curb, followed by a sharp pull at the bell. Holmes whistled.

"A pair, by the sound," said he. "Yes," he continued, glancing out of the window. "A nice little brougham and a pair of beauties. A hundred and fifty guineas apiece. There's money in this case, Watson, if there is nothing else."

"I think that I had better go, Holmes."

"Not a bit, Doctor. Stay where you are. I am lost without my Boswell. And this promises to be interesting. It would be a pity to miss it."

"But your client——"

"Never mind him. I may want your help, and so may he. Here he comes. Sit down in that armchair, Doctor, and give us your best attention."

A slow and heavy step, which had been heard upon the stairs and in the passage, paused immediately outside the door. Then there was a loud and authoritative tap.

"Come in!" said Holmes.   40

A man entered who could hardly have been less than six feet six inches
in height, with the chest and limbs of a Hercules. His dress was rich with a
richness which would, in England, be looked upon as akin to bad taste.
Heavy bands of astrakhan were slashed across the sleeves and fronts of his
double-breasted coat, while the deep blue cloak which was thrown over
his shoulders was lined with flame-coloured silk and secured at the neck with a
brooch which consisted of a single flaming beryl. Boots which extended
halfway up his calves, and which were trimmed at the tops with rich brown
fur, completed the impression of barbaric opulence which was suggested by
his whole appearance. He carried a broad-brimmed hat in his hand, while
he wore across the upper part of his face, extending down past the cheekbones, a black vizard mask, which he had apparently adjusted that very
moment, for his hand was still raised to it as he entered. From the lower part of
the face he appeared to be a man of strong character, with a thick, hanging lip,
and a long, straight chin suggestive of resolution pushed to the length of
obstinacy.

"You had my note?" he asked with a deep harsh voice and a strongly
marked German accent. "I told you that I would call." He looked from one to
the other of us, as if uncertain which to address.

"Pray take a seat," said Holmes. "This is my friend and colleague, Dr.
Watson, who is occasionally good enough to help me in my cases. Whom
have I the honour to address?"

"You may address me as the Count Von Kramm, a Bohemian nobleman. I
understand that this gentleman, your friend, is a man of honour and discretion, whom I may trust with a matter of the most extreme importance. If not, I
should much prefer to communicate with you alone."

I rose to go, but Holmes caught me by the wrist and pushed me back into   45
my chair. "It is both, or none," said he. "You may say before this gentleman
anything which you may say to me."

The Count shrugged his broad shoulders. "Then I must begin," said he,
"by binding you both to absolute secrecy for two years; at the end of that time
the matter will be of no importance. At present it is not too much to say that
it is of such weight it may have an influence upon European history."

"I promise," said Holmes.

"And I."

"You will excuse this mask," continued our strange visitor. "The august
person who employs me wishes his agent to be unknown to you, and I may
confess at once that the title by which I have just called myself is not exactly
my own."

"I was aware of it," said Holmes drily.   50

"The circumstances are of great delicacy, and every precaution has to
be taken to quench what might grow to be an immense scandal and

seriously compromise one of the reigning families of Europe. To speak plainly, the matter implicates the great House of Ormstein, hereditary kings of Bohemia."

"I was also aware of that," murmured Holmes, settling himself down in his armchair and closing his eyes.

Our visitor glanced with some apparent surprise at the languid, lounging figure of the man who had been no doubt depicted to him as the most incisive reasoner and most energetic agent in Europe. Holmes slowly reopened his eyes and looked impatiently at his gigantic client.

"If your Majesty would condescend to state your case," he remarked, "I should be better able to advise you."

The man sprang from his chair and paced up and down the room in uncontrollable agitation. Then, with a gesture of desperation, he tore the mask from his face and hurled it upon the ground. "You are right," he cried; "I am the King. Why should I attempt to conceal it?"

"Why, indeed?" murmured Holmes. "Your Majesty had not spoken before I was aware that I was addressing Wilhelm Gottsreich Sigismond von Ormstein, Grand Duke of Cassel-Felstein, and hereditary King of Bohemia."

"But you can understand," said our strange visitor, sitting down once more and passing his hand over his high white forehead, "you can understand that I am not accustomed to doing such business in my own person. Yet the matter was so delicate that I could not confide it to an agent without putting myself in his power. I have come incognito from Prague for the purpose of consulting you."

"Then, pray consult," said Holmes, shutting his eyes once more.

"The facts are briefly these: Some five years ago, during a lengthy visit to Warsaw, I made the acquaintance of the well-known adventuress, Irene Adler. The name is no doubt familiar to you."

"Kindly look her up in my index, Doctor," murmured Holmes without opening his eyes. For many years he had adopted a system of docketing all paragraphs concerning men and things, so that it was difficult to name a subject or a person on which he could not at once furnish information. In this case I found her biography sandwiched in between that of a Hebrew rabbi and that of a staff-commander who had written a monograph upon the deep-sea fishes.

"Let me see!" said Holmes. "Hum! Born in New Jersey in the year 1858. Contralto—hum! La Scala, hum! Prima donna Imperial Opera of Warsaw— yes! Retired from operatic stage—ha! Living in London—quite so! Your Majesty, as I understand, became entangled with this young person, wrote her some compromising letters, and is now desirous of getting those letters back."

"Precisely so. But how——"

"Was there a secret marriage?"

"None."

"No legal papers or certificates?"

"None."

"Then I fail to follow your Majesty. If this young person should produce her letters for blackmailing or other purposes, how is she to prove their authenticity?"

"There is the writing."

"Pooh, pooh! Forgery."

"My private note-paper." 70

"Stolen."

"My own seal."

"Imitated."

"My photograph."

"Bought." 75

"We were both in the photograph."

"Oh, dear! That is very bad! Your Majesty has indeed committed an indiscretion."

"I was mad—insane."

"You have compromised yourself seriously."

"I was only Crown Prince then. I was young. I am but thirty now." 80

"It must be recovered."

"We have tried and failed."

"Your Majesty must pay. It must be bought."

"She will not sell."

"Stolen, then." 85

"Five attempts have been made. Twice burglars in my pay ransacked her house. Once we diverted her luggage when she traveled. Twice she has been waylaid. There has been no result."

"No sign of it?"

"Absolutely none."

Holmes laughed. "It is quite a pretty little problem," said he.

"But a very serious one to me," returned the King reproachfully. 90

"Very, indeed. And what does she propose to do with the photograph?"

"To ruin me."

"But how?"

"I am about to be married."

"So I have heard." 95

"To Clotilde Lothman von Saxe-Meningen, second daughter of the King of Scandinavia. You may know the strict principles of her family. She is herself the very soul of delicacy. A shadow of a doubt as to my conduct would bring the matter to an end."

"And Irene Adler?"

"Threatens to send them the photograph. And she will do it. I know that she will do it. You do not know her, but she has a soul of steel. She has the face of the most beautiful of women, and the mind of the most resolute of men.

Rather than I should marry another woman, there are no lengths to which she would not go—none."

"You are sure that she has not sent it yet?"

"I am sure."

"And why?"

"Because she has said that she would send it on the day when the betrothal was publicly proclaimed. That will be next Monday."

"Oh, then we have three days yet," said Holmes with a yawn. "That is very fortunate, as I have one or two matters of importance to look into just at present. Your Majesty will, of course, stay in London for the present?"

"Certainly. You will find me at the Langham under the name of the Count Von Kramm."

"Then I shall drop you a line to let you know how we progress."

"Pray do so. I shall be all anxiety."

"Then, as to money?"

"You have carte blanche."

"Absolutely?"

"I tell you that I would give one of the provinces of my kingdom to have that photograph."

"And for present expenses?"

The King took a heavy chamois leather bag from under his cloak and laid it on the table.

"There are three hundred pounds in gold and seven hundred in notes," he said.

Holmes scribbled a receipt upon a sheet of his note-book and handed it to him.

"And Mademoiselle's address?" he asked.

"Is Briony Lodge, Serpentine Avenue, St. John's Wood."

Holmes took a note of it. "One other question," said he. "Was the photograph a cabinet?"

"It was."

"Then, good-night, your Majesty, and I trust that we shall soon have some good news for you. And good-night, Watson," he added, as the wheels of the royal brougham rolled down the street. "If you will be good enough to call to-morrow afternoon at three o'clock I should like to chat this little matter over with you."

2

At three o'clock precisely I was at Baker Street, but Holmes had not yet returned. The landlady informed me that he had left the house shortly after eight o'clock in the morning. I sat down beside the fire, however, with the intention of awaiting him, however long he might be. I was already deeply interested in his inquiry, for, though it was surrounded by none of the grim and strange features which were associated with the two crimes which I have already recorded, still, the nature of the case and the exalted station of his client gave it a character of its own. Indeed, apart from the nature of the investigation which my friend had on hand, there was something in his masterly grasp of a situation, and his keen, incisive reasoning, which made it a pleasure to me to study his system of work, and to follow the quick, subtle methods by which he disentangled the most inextricable mysteries. So accustomed was I to his invariable success that the very possibility of his failing had ceased to enter into my head.

It was close upon four before the door opened, and a drunken-looking groom, ill-kempt and side-whiskered, with an inflamed face and disreputable clothes, walked into the room. Accustomed as I was to my friend's amazing powers in the use of disguises, I had to look three times before I was certain that it was indeed he. With a nod he vanished into the bedroom, whence he emerged in five minutes tweed-suited and respectable, as of old. Putting his hands into his pockets, he stretched out his legs in front of the fire and laughed heartily for some minutes.

"Well, really!" he cried, and then he choked and laughed again until he was obliged to lie back, limp and helpless, in the chair.

"What is it?"

"It's quite too funny. I am sure you could never guess how I employed my morning, or what I ended by doing."

"I can't imagine. I suppose that you have been watching the habits, and perhaps the house, of Miss Irene Adler." 125

"Quite so; but the sequel was rather unusual. I will tell you, however. I left the house a little after eight o'clock this morning in the character of a groom out of work. There is a wonderful sympathy and freemasonry among horsy men. Be one of them, and you will know all that there is to know. I soon found Briony Lodge. It is a *bijou* villa, with a garden at the back, but built out in front right up to the road, two stories. Chubb lock to the door. Large sitting-room on the right side, well furnished, with long windows almost to the floor, and those preposterous English window fasteners which a child could open. Behind there was nothing remarkable, save that the passage window could be reached from the top of the coach-house. I walked round it and examined it closely from every point of view, but without noting anything else of interest.

"I then lounged down the street and found, as I expected, that there was a mews in a lane which runs down by one wall of the garden. I lent the ostlers a hand in rubbing down their horses, and received in exchange twopence, a glass of half and half, two fills of shag tobacco, and as much information as I could desire about Miss Adler, to say nothing of half a dozen other people in the neighbourhood in whom I was not in the least interested, but whose biographies I was compelled to listen to."

"And what of Irene Adler?" I asked.

"Oh, she has turned all the men's heads down in that part. She is the daintiest thing under a bonnet on this planet. So say the Serpentine-mews, to a man. She lives quietly, sings at concerts, drives out at five every day, and returns at seven sharp for dinner. Seldom goes out at other times, except when she sings. Has only one male visitor, but a good deal of him. He is dark, handsome, and dashing, never calls less than once a day, and often twice. He is a Mr. Godfrey Norton, of the Inner Temple. See the advantages of a cabman as a confidant. They had driven him home a dozen times from Serpentine-mews, and knew all about him. When I had listened to all they had to tell, I began to walk up and down near Briony Lodge once more, and to think over my plan of campaign.

"This Godfrey Norton was evidently an important factor in the matter. He was a lawyer. That sounded ominous. What was the relation between them, and what the object of his repeated visits? Was she his client, his friend, or his mistress? If the former, she had probably transferred the photograph to his keeping. If the latter, it was less likely. On the issue of this question depended whether I should continue my work at Briony Lodge, or turn my attention to the gentleman's chambers in the Temple. It was a delicate point, and it widened the field of my inquiry. I fear that I bore you with these details, but I have to let you see my little difficulties, if you are to understand the situation."

"I am following you closely," I answered.

"I was still balancing the matter in my mind when a hansom cab drove up to Briony Lodge, and a gentleman sprang out. He was a remarkably handsome man, dark, aquiline, and moustached—evidently the man of whom I had heard. He appeared to be in a great hurry, shouted to the cabman to wait, and brushed past the maid who opened the door with the air of a man who was thoroughly at home.

"He was in the house about half an hour, and I could catch glimpses of him in the windows of the sitting-room, pacing up and down, talking excitedly, and waving his arms. Of her I could see nothing. Presently he emerged, looking even more flurried than before. As he stepped up to the cab, he pulled a gold watch from his pocket and looked at it earnestly, 'Drive like the devil,' he shouted, 'first to Gross & Hankey's in Regent Street, and then to the Church of St. Monica in the Edgeware Road. Half a guinea if you do it in twenty minutes!'

"Away they went, and I was just wondering whether I should not do well to follow them when up the lane came a neat little landau, the coachman with his coat only half-buttoned, and his tie under his ear, while all the tags of his harness were sticking out of the buckles. It hadn't pulled up before she shot out of the hall door and into it. I only caught a glimpse of

her at the moment, but she was a lovely woman, with a face that a man might
die for.

"'The Church of St. Monica, John,' she cried, 'and half a sovereign if you   135
reach it in twenty minutes.'

"This was quite too good to lose, Watson. I was just balancing whether I
should run for it, or whether I should perch behind her landau when a cab
came through the street. The driver looked twice at such a shabby fare, but I
jumped in before he could object. 'The Church of St. Monica,' said I, 'and half
a sovereign if you reach it in twenty minutes.' It was twenty-five minutes to
twelve, and of course it was clear enough what was in the wind.

"My cabby drove fast. I don't think I ever drove faster, but the others were
there before us. The cab and the landau with their steaming horses were in
front of the door when I arrived. I paid the man and hurried into the church.
There was not a soul there save the two whom I had followed and a surpliced
clergyman, who seemed to be expostulating with them. They were all three
standing in a knot in front of the altar. I lounged up the side aisle like any
other idler who has dropped into a church. Suddenly, to my surprise, the three
at the altar faced round to me, and Godfrey Norton came running as hard as
he could towards me.

"'Thank God,' he cried. 'You'll do. Come! Come!'

"'What then?' I asked.

"'Come, man, come, only three minutes, or it won't be legal.'   140

"I was half-dragged up to the altar, and before I knew where I was I
found myself mumbling responses which were whispered in my ear, and
vouching for things of which I knew nothing, and generally assisting in
the secure tying up of Irene Adler, spinster, to Godfrey Norton, bachelor.
It was all done in an instant, and there was the gentleman thanking me on
the one side and the lady on the other, while the clergyman beamed on
me in front. It was the most preposterous position in which I ever found
myself in my life, and it was the thought of it that started me laughing just
now. It seems that there had been some informality about their license, that
the clergyman absolutely refused to marry them without a witness of
some sort, and that my lucky appearance saved the bridegroom from having to
sally out into the streets in search of a best man. The bride gave me a
sovereign, and I mean to wear it on my watch-chain in memory of the
occasion."

"This is a very unexpected turn of affairs," said I; "and what then?"

"Well, I found my plans very seriously menaced. It looked as if the pair
might take an immediate departure, and so necessitate very prompt and
energetic measures on my part. At the church door, however, they separated,
he driving back to the Temple, and she to her own house. 'I shall drive out
in the park at five as usual,' she said as she left him. I heard no more. They

drove away in different directions, and I went off to make my own arrangements."

"Which are?"

"Some cold beef and a glass of beer," he answered, ringing the bell. "I have been too busy to think of food, and I am likely to be busier still this evening. By the way, Doctor, I shall want your coöperation."

"I shall be delighted."

"You don't mind breaking the law?"

"Not in the least."

"Nor running a chance of arrest?"

"Not in a good cause."

"Oh, the cause is excellent!"

"Then I am your man."

"I was sure that I might rely on you."

"But what is it you wish?"

"When Mrs. Turner has brought in the tray I will make it clear to you. Now," he said as he turned hungrily on the simple fare that our landlady had provided, "I must discuss it while I eat, for I have not much time. It is nearly five now. In two hours we must be on the scene of action. Miss Irene, or Madame, rather, returns from her drive at seven. We must be at Briony Lodge to meet her."

"And what then?"

"You must leave that to me. I have already arranged what is to occur. There is only one point on which I must insist. You must not interfere, come what may. You understand?"

"I am to be neutral?"

"To do nothing whatever. There will probably be some small unpleasantness. Do not join in it. It will end in my being conveyed into the house. Four or five minutes afterwards the sitting-room window will open. You are to station yourself close to that open window."

"Yes."

"You are to watch me, for I will be visible to you."

"Yes."

"And when I raise my hand—so—you will throw into the room what I give you to throw, and will, at the same time, raise the cry of fire. You quite follow me?"

"Entirely."

"It is nothing very formidable," he said, taking a long cigar-shaped roll from his pocket. "It is an ordinary plumber's smoke-rocket, fitted with a cap at either end to make it self-lighting. Your task is confined to that. When you raise your cry of fire, it will be taken up by quite a number of people. You may then walk to the end of the street, and I will rejoin you in ten minutes. I hope that I have made myself clear?"

"I am to remain neutral, to get near the window, to watch you, and at the signal to throw in this object, then to raise the cry of fire, and to wait you at the corner of the street."

"Precisely."

"Then you may entirely rely on me."

"That is excellent. I think, perhaps, it is almost time that I prepare for the new role I have to play."

He disappeared into his bedroom and returned in a few minutes in the character of an amiable and simple-minded Nonconformist clergyman. His broad black hat, his baggy trousers, his white tie, his sympathetic smile, and general look of peering and benevolent curiosity were such as Mr. John Hare alone could have equalled. It was not merely that Holmes changed his costume. His expression, his manner, his very soul seemed to vary with every fresh part that he assumed. The stage lost a fine actor, even as science lost an acute reasoner, when he became a specialist in crime.   170

It was a quarter past six when we left Baker Street, and it still wanted ten minutes to the hour when we found ourselves in Serpentine Avenue. It was already dusk, and the lamps were just being lighted as we paced up and down in front of Briony Lodge, waiting for the coming of its occupant. The house was just such as I had pictured it from Sherlock Holmes's succinct description, but the locality appeared to be less private than I expected. On the contrary, for a small street in a quiet neighbourhood, it was remarkably animated. There was a group of shabbily dressed men smoking and laughing in a corner, a scissors-grinder with his wheel, two guardsmen who were flirting with a nurse-girl, and several well-dressed young men who were lounging up and down with cigars in their mouths.

"You see," remarked Holmes, as we paced to and fro in front of the house, "this marriage rather simplifies matters. The photograph becomes a double-edged weapon now. The chances are that she would be as averse to its being seen by Mr. Godfrey Norton, as our client is to its coming to the eyes of his princess. Now the question is, Where are we to find the photograph?"

"Where, indeed?"

"It is most unlikely that she carries it about with her. It is cabinet size. Too large for easy concealment about a woman's dress. She knows that the King is capable of having her waylaid and searched. Two attempts of the sort have already been made. We may take it, then, that she does not carry it about with her."

"Where, then?"   175

"Her banker or her lawyer. There is that double possibility. But I am inclined to think neither. Women are naturally secretive, and they like to do their own secreting. Why should she hand it over to anyone else? She could trust her own guardianship, but she could not tell what indirect or political influence might be brought to bear upon a business man. Besides, remember that she had resolved to use it within a few days. It must be where she can lay her hands upon it. It must be in her own house."

"But it has twice been burgled."

"Pshaw! They did not know how to look."

"But how will you look?"

"I will not look."

"What then?"

"I will get her to show me."

"But she will refuse."

"She will not be able to. But I hear the rumble of wheels. It is her carriage. Now carry out my orders to the letter."

As he spoke the gleam of the side-lights of a carriage came round the curve of the avenue. It was a smart little landau which rattled up to the door of Briony Lodge. As it pulled up, one of the loafing men at the corner dashed forward to open the door in the hope of earning a copper, but was elbowed away by another loafer, who had rushed up with the same intention. A fierce quarrel broke out, which was increased by the two guardsmen, who took sides with one of the loungers, and by the scissors-grinder, who was equally hot upon the other side. A blow was struck, and in an instant the lady, who had stepped from her carriage, was the centre of a little knot of flushed and struggling men, who struck savagely at each other with their fists and sticks. Holmes dashed into the crowd to protect the lady; but just as he reached her he gave a cry and dropped to the ground, with the blood running freely down his face. At his fall the guardsmen took to their heels in one direction and the loungers in the other, while a number of better-dressed people, who had watched the scuffle without taking part in it, crowded in to help the lady and to attend to the injured man. Irene Adler, as I will still call her, had hurried up the steps; but she stood at the top with her superb figure outlined against the lights of the hall, looking back into the street.

"Is the poor gentleman much hurt?" she asked.

"He is dead," cried several voices.

"No, no, there's life in him!" shouted another. "But he'll be gone before you can get him to hospital."

"He's a brave fellow," said a woman. "They would have had the lady's purse and watch if it hadn't been for him. They were a gang, and a rough one, too. Ah, he's breathing now."

"He can't lie in the street. May we bring him in, marm?"

"Surely. Bring him into the sitting-room. There is a comfortable sofa. This way, please!"

Slowly and solemnly he was borne into Briony Lodge and laid out in the principal room, while I still observed the proceedings from my post by the window. The lamps had been lit, but the blinds had not been drawn, so that I could see Holmes as he lay upon the couch. I do not know whether he was seized with compunction at that moment for the part he was playing, but I know that I never felt more heartily ashamed of myself in my life than when I saw the beautiful creature against whom I was conspiring, or the grace and kindliness with which she waited upon the injured man. And yet it would be the blackest treachery to Holmes to draw back now from the part which he had intrusted to me. I hardened my heart, and took the smoke-rocket from under my ulster. After all, I thought, we are not injuring her. We are but preventing her from injuring another.

Holmes had sat up upon the couch, and I saw him motion like a man who is in need of air. A maid rushed across and threw open the window. At the same instant I saw him raise his hand, and at the signal I tossed my rocket into the room with a cry of "Fire!" The word was no sooner out of my mouth than the whole crowd of spectators, well dressed and ill—gentlemen, ostlers, and servant-maids—joined in a general shriek of "Fire!" Thick clouds of smoke curled through the room and out at the open window. I caught a glimpse of rushing figures, and a moment later the voice of Holmes from within assuring them that it was a false alarm. Slipping through the shouting crowd I made my way to the corner of the street, and in ten minutes was rejoiced to find my friend's arm in mine, and to get away from the scene of uproar. He walked swiftly and in silence for some few minutes until we had turned down one of the quiet streets which lead towards the Edgeware Road.

"You did it very nicely, Doctor," he remarked. "Nothing could have been better. It is all right."

"You have the photograph?"   195

"I know where it is."

"And how did you find out?"

"She showed me, as I told you she would."

"I am still in the dark."

"I do not wish to make a mystery," said he, laughing. "The matter was   200
perfectly simple. You, of course, saw that everyone in the street was an accomplice. They were all engaged for the evening."

"I guessed as much."

"Then, when the row broke out, I had a little moist red paint in the palm of my hand. I rushed forward, fell down, clapped my hand to my face, and became a piteous spectacle. It is an old trick."

"That also I could fathom."

"Then they carried me in. She was bound to have me in. What else could she do? And into her sitting-room, which was the very room which I suspected. It lay between that and her bedroom, and I was determined to see which. They laid me on a couch, I motioned for air, they were compelled to open the window, and you had your chance."

"How did that help you?"   205

"It was all-important. When a woman thinks that her house is on fire, her instinct is at once to rush to the thing which she values most. It is a perfectly over-powering impulse, and I have more than once taken advantage of it. In the case of the Darlington substitution scandal it was of use to me, and also in the Arnsworth Castle business. A married woman grabs at her baby; an unmarried one reaches for her jewel-box. Now it was clear to me that our lady of to-day had nothing in the house more precious to her than what we are in quest of. She would rush to secure it. The alarm of fire was admirably done. The smoke and shouting were enough to shake nerves of steel. She responded beautifully. The photograph is in a recess behind a sliding panel just above the right bell-pull. She was there in an instant, and I caught a glimpse of it as she half-drew it out. When I cried out that it was a false alarm, she replaced it, glanced at the rocket, rushed from the room, and I have not seen her since. I rose, and, making my excuses, escaped from the house. I hesitated whether to attempt to secure the photograph at once; but the coachman had come in, and as he was watching me narrowly it seemed safer to wait. A little over-precipitance may ruin all."

"And now?" I asked.

"Our quest is practically finished. I shall call with the King to-morrow, and with you, if you care to come with us. We will be shown into the sitting-room to wait for the lady, but it is probable that when she comes she may find neither us nor the photograph. It might be a satisfaction to his Majesty to regain it with his own hands."

"And when will you call?"

"At eight in the morning. She will not be up, so that we shall have a clear field. Besides, we must be prompt, for this marriage may mean a complete change in her life and habits. I must wire to the King without delay."

We had reached Baker Street and had stopped at the door. He was searching his pockets for the key when someone passing said:

"Good-night, Mister Sherlock Holmes."

There were several people on the pavement at the time, but the greeting appeared to come from a slim youth in an ulster who had hurried by.

"I've heard that voice before," said Holmes, staring down the dimly lit street. "Now, I wonder who the deuce that could have been."

3

I slept at Baker Street that night, and we were engaged upon our toast and coffee in the morning when the King of Bohemia rushed into the room.

"You have really got it!" he cried, grasping Sherlock Holmes by either shoulder and looking eagerly into his face.

"Not yet."

"But you have hopes?"

"I have hopes."

"Then, come. I am all impatience to be gone."   220
"We must have a cab."
"No, my brougham is waiting."
"Then that will simplify matters." We descended and started off once
more for Briony Lodge.
"Irene Adler is married," remarked Holmes.
"Married! When?"   225
"Yesterday."
"But to whom?"
"To an English lawyer named Norton."
"But she could not love him."
"I am in hopes that she does."   230
"And why in hopes?"
"Because it would spare your Majesty all fear of future annoyance. If the
lady loves her husband, she does not love your Majesty. If she does not love
your Majesty, there is no reason why she should interfere with your Majesty's
plan."
"It is true. And yet——Well! I wish she had been of my own station!
What a queen she would have made!" He relapsed into a moody silence,
which was not broken until we drew up in Serpentine Avenue.
    The door of Briony Lodge was open, and an elderly woman stood upon
the steps. She watched us with a sardonic eye as we stepped from the
brougham.
"Mr. Sherlock Holmes, I believe?" said she.   235
"I am Mr. Holmes," answered my companion, looking at her with a
questioning and rather startled gaze.
"Indeed! My mistress told me that you were likely to call. She left this
morning with her husband by the 5:15 train from Charing Cross for the
Continent."
"What!" Sherlock Holmes staggered back, white with chagrin and surprise. "Do you mean that she has left England?"
"Never to return."
"And the papers?" asked the King hoarsely. "All is lost."   240
"We shall see." He pushed past the servant and rushed into the
drawing-room, followed by the King and myself. The furniture was scattered about in every direction, with dismantled shelves and open drawers,
as if the lady had hurriedly ransacked them before her flight. Holmes
rushed at the bell-pull, tore back a small sliding shutter, and, plunging in
his hand, pulled out a photograph and a letter. The photograph was of
Irene Adler herself in evening dress, the letter was superscribed to "Sherlock Holmes, Esq. To be left till called for." My friend tore it open, and
we all three read it together. It was dated at midnight of the preceding
night and ran in this way:

My Dear Mr. Sherlock Holmes:
You really did it very well. You took me in completely. Until after the alarm of fire, I had not a suspicion. But then, when I found how I had betrayed myself, I began to think. I had been warned against you months ago. I had been told that if the King employed an agent it would certainly be you. And your address had been given me. Yet, with all this, you made me reveal what you wanted to know. Even after I became suspicious, I found it hard to think evil of such a dear, kind old clergyman. But, you know, I have been trained as an actress myself. Male costume is nothing new to me. I often take advantage of the freedom which it gives. I sent John, the coachman, to watch you, ran upstairs, got into my walking-clothes, as I call them, and came down just as you departed.
Well, I followed you to your door, and so made sure that I was really an object of interest to the celebrated Mr. Sherlock Holmes. Then I, rather imprudently, wished you good-night, and started for the Temple to see my husband.
We both thought the best resource was flight, when pursued by so formidable an antagonist; so you will find the nest empty when you call to-morrow. As to the photograph, your client may rest in peace. I love and am loved by a better man than he. The King may do what he will without hindrance from one whom he has cruelly wronged. I keep it only to safeguard myself, and to preserve a weapon which will always secure me from any steps which he might take in the future. I leave a photograph which he might care to possess; and I remain, dear Mr. Sherlock Holmes,

Very truly yours,

Irene Norton, *née* Adler.

"What a woman—oh, what a woman!" cried the King of Bohemia, when we had all three read this epistle. "Did I not tell you how quick and resolute she was? Would she not have made an admirable queen? Is it not a pity that she was not on my level?"

"From what I have seen of the lady she seems indeed to be on a very different level to your Majesty," said Holmes coldly. "I am sorry that I have not been able to bring your Majesty's business to a more successful conclusion."

"On the contrary, my dear sir," cried the King; "nothing could be more successful. I know that her word is inviolate. The photograph is now as safe as if it were in the fire."

"I am glad to hear your Majesty say so."

"I am immensely indebted to you. Pray tell me in what way I can reward you. This ring——" He slipped an emerald snake ring from his finger and held it out upon the palm of his hand.

"Your Majesty has something which I should value even more highly," said Holmes.

"You have but to name it."

"This photograph!"

The King stared at him in amazement.   250

"Irene's photograph!" he cried. "Certainly, if you wish it."

"I thank your Majesty. Then there is no more to be done in the matter. I have the honour to wish you a very good-morning." He bowed, and, turning away without observing the hand which the King had stretched out to him, he set off in my company for his chambers.

And that was how a great scandal threatened to affect the kingdom of Bohemia, and how the best plans of Mr. Sherlock Holmes were beaten by a woman's wit. He used to make merry over the cleverness of women, but I have not heard him do it of late. And when he speaks of Irene Adler, or when he refers to her photograph, it is always under the honourable title of *the* woman.

- List the insignificant details that Holmes finds significant in this story.
- How does Watson report the events that he is describing? Evaluate Watson's strength as a detective in his own right.
- What is the "scandal" that Holmes has been hired to deflect?
- Why is it significant that Holmes always refers to Irene Adler as "the" woman?

Don Lee (1959–)

Don Lee, a third-generation Korean American, was born in Tokyo, Japan, where Lee's father was serving in the American foreign service. The family then moved to a military base in Seoul, South Korea, before returning to Japan during Lee's teenage years. Lee attended the University of California Los Angeles and majored in engineering, but while there he decided to become a writer instead. It is perhaps not surprising, given his background, that the work he has published so far has been preoccupied with questions of identity. Lee has received a number of awards for his writing, which includes a book of short stories, *Yellow*, and a novel, *Country of Origin*. He has taught at Emerson College, and since 1988 he has edited *Ploughshares*, the school's literary journal.

The Price of Eggs in China (2001)

It was noon when Dean Kaneshiro arrived at Oriental Hair Poet No. 2's house, and as she opened the door, she said, blinking, "Hello. Come in. I'm sorry. I'm not quite awake."

He carried his measuring rig through the living room, noting the red birch floor, the authentic Stickley, the Nakashima table, the Maloof credenza—good craftsmanship, carefully selected, this poet, Marcella Ahn, was a woman who knew wood.

"When you called," she said in her study, "I'd almost forgotten. It's been over two years! I hope I wasn't too difficult to track down."

Immediately Dean was annoyed. When she had ordered the chair, he had been clear about his backlog, and today was the exact date he'd given her for the fitting. And she *had* been difficult to track down, despite his request, two years ago, that she notify him of any changes of address. Her telephone number in San Francisco had been disconnected, and he had had to find her book in the library, then call her publisher in New York, then her agent, only to learn that Marcella Ahn had moved an hour south of San Francisco to the very town, Rosarita Bay, where he himself lived. Never mind that he should have figured this out, having overheard rumors of yet another Asian poet in town with spectacular long hair, rumors which had prompted the references to her and Caroline Yip, his girlfriend of eight months, as the Oriental Hair Poets.

He adjusted his rig. Marcella Ahn was thin and tall, but most of her   5
height was in her torso, not her legs—typical of Koreans. She wore tight midnight-blue velvet pants, lace-up black boots, and a flouncy white Victorian blouse, her tiny waist cinched by a thick leather belt.

"Sit, please," he said. She settled into the measuring rig. He walked around her twice, then said, "Stand up, please." After she got up, he fine-tuned the back supports and armrests and shortened the legs. "Again, please."

She sat down. "Oh, that's much better, infinitely better," she said. "You can do that just by looking?"

Now came the part that Dean always hated. He could use the rig to custom-fit his chairs for every part of the body except for one. "Could you turn around, please?"

"Sorry?"

"Could you turn around? For the saddling of the seat?"   10

Marcella Ahn's eyes lighted, and the whitewash of her foundation and powder was suddenly broken by the mischievous curl of her lips, which were painted a deep claret. "You mean you want to examine . . . my *buttocks?*"

He could feel sweat popping on his forehead. "Please."

Still smirking, she raised her arms, the ruffled cuffs of her blouse dropping away, followed by the jangling release of two dozen silver bracelets on each wrist. There were silver rings on nearly every digit, too, and with her exquisitely lacquered fingers, she slowly gathered her hair—straight and lambent and hanging to midthigh—and raked it over one shoulder so it lay over her breast. Then she pivoted on her toe, turned around, and daintily lifted the tail of her blouse to expose her butt.

He squatted behind her and stared at it for a full ten seconds. It was a good butt, a firm, StairMastered butt, a shapely, surprisingly protuberant butt.

She peeked over her shoulder. "Need me to bend over a little?" she   15
asked.

He bounced up and moved across the room and pretended to jot down
some notes, then looked around. More classic modern furniture, very expensive. And the place was neat, obsessive-compulsive neat. He pointed to her
desk. "You'll be using the chair here?"

"Yes."

"To do your writing?"

"Uh-huh."

"I'll watch you, then. For twenty minutes, please."   20

"What? Right now?"

"It'll help me to see you work, how you sit, maybe slouch."

"It's not that simple," she said.

"No?"

"Of course not. Poets can't write on demand. You know nothing about   25
poetry, do you?"

"No, I don't," Dean said. All he ever read, in fact, were mystery novels.
He went through three or four of them a week—anything with a crime, an
investigation. He was now so familiar with forensic techniques, he could
predict almost any plot twist, but his head still swam in delight at the first hint
of a frame-up or double-cross.

He glanced out the window. Marcella Ahn lived off Skyview Ridge Road,
which crested the rolling foothills, and she had one of the few panoramic
views of Rosarita Bay—the harbor to the north, the marsh to the south, the
town in the middle, and, everywhere beyond, the vast Pacific.

Marcella Ahn had her hands on her hips. "And I don't slouch," she
said.

Eventually he did convince her to sit in her present desk chair, an ugly
vinyl contraption with pneumatic levers and bulky ergonomic pads. She
opened a bound notebook and uncapped a fountain pen, and hovered over the
blank page for what seemed like a long time. Then she abruptly set everything
aside and booted up her laptop computer. "What do you do with clients who
aren't within driving distance?"

"I ask for a videotape, and I talk to their tailor. Try to work, please.   30
Then I'll be out of your way."

"I feel so silly."

"Just pretend I'm not here," he said.

Marcella Ahn continued to stare at the computer screen. She shifted,
crossed her legs, and tucked them underneath her. Finally, she set her fingers
on the keys and tapped out three words—all she could manage, apparently.
She exhaled heavily. "When will the chair be ready?"

"I'll start on it next month, on April twentieth, then three weeks, so May
eleventh," he told her, though he required only half that time. He liked to

plan for contingencies, and he knew his customers wanted to believe—
especially with the prices they were paying—that it took him longer to make
the chairs.

"Can I visit your studio?" she asked.   35

"No, you cannot."

"Ah, you see, you can dish it—"

"It would be very inconvenient."

"For twenty minutes."

"Please don't," he said.   40

"Seriously. I can't swing by for a couple of minutes?"

"No."

Marcella Ahn let out a dismissive puff. "Artists," she said.

Oriental Hair Poet No. 1 was a slob. Caroline Yip lived in an apartment above
the R. B. Feed & Hardware store, one small room with a Pullman kitchen, a
cramped bathroom, and no closets. Her only furnishings were a futon, a boom
box, and a coffee table, and the floor was littered with clothes, CDs, shoes,
books, newspapers, bills, and magazines. There was a thick layer of grease on
the stovetop, dust and hair and curdled food on every other surface, and the
bathroom was clogged with sixty-two bottles of shampoo and conditioner,
some half-filled, most of them empty.

Dean had stayed in the apartment only once—the first time they had   45
slept together. He had lain naked on her futon, and Caroline had inspected
his erection, baldly surveying it from different angles. "Your penis looks like a
fire hydrant," she had said. "Everything about you is short, squat, and thick."
It was true. Dean was an avid weightlifter, not an ounce of fat on him, but his
musculature was broad and tumescent, absent of definition. His forearms were
pickle jars, almost as big as his thighs, and his crewcutted head sat on his
shoulders without the relief of a neck. "What am I doing with you?" Caroline
said. "This is what it's come down to, this is how far I've sunk. I'm about to
fuck a Nipponese fire hydrant with the verbal capacity of tap water."

There were other peculiarities. She didn't sleep well, although she had
done almost everything possible short of psychotherapy—which she didn't
believe in—to alleviate her insomnia and insistent stress: acupuncture, herbs,
yoga, homeopathy, tai chi. She ran five miles a day, and she meditated for
twenty minutes each morning and evening, beginning her sessions by trying
to relax her face, stretching and contorting it, mouth yowling open, eyes
bulging—it was a horrific sight.

Even when she did sleep, it was fitful. Because she ground her teeth, she
wore a plastic mouthpiece to bed, and she bit down so hard on it during the
night, she left black spots where her fillings were positioned. She had nightmares, a recurring nightmare, of headless baby chickens chasing after her,
hundreds of decapitated little chicks tittering in rabid pursuit.

The nightmares, however, didn't stop her from eating chicken, or any-
thing else, for that matter. She was a waif, five-two, barely a hundred pounds.
Her hair—luxuriant, butt-length, and naturally kinky, a rarity among
Asians—seemed to weigh more than she did. Yet she had a ravenous appetite.
She was constantly asking for seconds, picking off Dean's plate. "Where does
it all go?" he asked over dinner one night, a month into their courtship.

"What?"

"The food."   50

"I have a very fast metabolism. You're not going to finish that?"

He scraped the rest of his portion into her bowl, and he watched her eat.
He had surprised himself by how fond he'd become of her. He was a disciplined man, one with solitary and fastidious habits, yet Caroline's idiosyn-
crasies were endearing to him. Maybe this was the true measure of love,
he thought—when you willingly tolerate behavior that, in anyone else,
would be annoying, even abhorrent to you. Without thinking, he blurted out,
"I love you."

"Yikes," Caroline said. She put her chopsticks down and wiped her
mouth. "You are the sweetest man I know, Dean. But I worry about you.
You're so innocent. Didn't anyone let you out of the house when you were
young? Don't you know you're not supposed to say things like that so
soon?"

"Do you love me?"

She sighed. "I don't right now," she said. Then she laid her hands on   55
top of his head and shook it. "But I think I will. Okay, you big boob?"

It took her two more months to say that she might, maybe, be a little bit
in love with him, too. "Despite everything, I guess I'm still a romantic," she
said. "I will never learn."

They were both reclusive by nature, and most of the time were content
to sequester themselves in Dean's house, which was tucked in a canyon in
the coastal mountains. They watched videos, read, cooked Japanese dishes:
tonkatsu, oyako donburi, tempura, unagi. It was a quiet life, free of catastrophe,
and it had lulled Dean into thinking that there would be no harm in telling
her about his encounter with Oriental Hair Poet No. 2.

"That cunt!" Caroline said. "That conniving Korean cunt! She's moved
here on purpose!"

It was all she could talk about for three days. Caroline Yip and Marcella
Ahn, it turned out, had a history. They had both lived in Cambridge, Massachusetts, in their twenties, and for several years they had been the best of
friends—inseparable, really. But then their first books came out at the same
time, Marcella's from a major New York publisher, Caroline's from a small,
albeit respected press. Both had very similar jacket photos, the two women
looking solemn and precious, hair flowing in full regalia. An unfortunate
coincidence. Critics couldn't resist reviewing them together, mocking the

pair, even then, as "The Oriental Hair Poets," "The Braids of the East," and "The New Asian Poe-tresses."

But Marcella came away from these barbs relatively unscathed. Her 60
book, *Speak to Desire*, was taken seriously, compared to Marianne Moore and Emily Dickinson. Her poetry was highly erudite, usually beginning with mundane observations about birds or plant life, then slipping into long, abstract meditations on entropy and inertia, the Bible, evolution, and death, punctuated by the briefest mention of personal deprivations—anorexia, depression, abandonment. Or so the critics said. Dean still had the book from the library, but he couldn't make heads or tails of it.

In contrast, Caroline's book, *Chicks of Chinese Descent*, had been skewered. She wrote in a slangy, contemporary voice, full of topical, pop culture allusions. She wrote about masturbation and Marilyn Monroe, about tampons and *moo goo gai pan*, about alien babies and chickens possessed by the devil. She was roundly dispatched as a mediocre talent.

Worse, Caroline said, was what happened afterward. Marcella began to thwart her at every turn. Teaching jobs, coveted magazine publications, awards, residencies, fellowships—everything Caroline applied for, Marcella got. It didn't hurt that Marcella was a shameless schmoozer, flirting and networking with anyone who might be of use. Yet, the fact was, Marcella was rich. Her father was a shipping tycoon, and she had a trust fund in the millions. She didn't need any of these pitifully small sinecures which would have meant a livelihood to Caroline, and it became obvious that the only reason Marcella was pursuing them at all was to taunt her.

"She's a vulture, a vampire," Caroline told Dean. "You know she won't go out in the light of day? She stays up until four, five in the morning and doesn't wake up until past noon."

And then there was the matter of Evan Paviromo, the English-Italian editor of a literary journal whom Caroline had dated for seven years, waiting patiently for them to get married and have children. He broke it off one day without explanation. She dogged him. Why? Why was he ending it? She refused to let him go without some sort of answer. Finally he complied. "It's something Marcella said," he admitted.

At first Caroline feared they were having an affair, but the truth was 65
more vicious. "Marcella told me she admired me," Evan said, "that I was far more generous than she could ever be. She said she just wouldn't be able to stay with someone whose work she didn't really respect. I thought about that, and I decided I'm not that generous. It's something that would eat away at me, that's bothered me all along. It's something I can't abide."

Caroline fled to California, eventually landing in Rosarita Bay. She completely disengaged herself from the poetry world. She was still writing every day, excruciating as it was for her, but she had not attempted to publish anything in six years. She was thirty-seven now, and a waitress—the breakfast

shift at a diner, the dinner shift at a barbecue joint. Her feet had grown a
full size from standing so much, and she was broke. But she had started to feel
like her old self again, healthier, more relaxed, sleeping better. Dean had a
lot to do with it, she said. She was happy—or as happy as it was possible for a
poet to be. Until now. Until Marcella Ahn suddenly arrived.

"She's come to torment me," Caroline said. "Why else would she move to
Rosarita Bay?"

"It's not such a bad place to live."

"Oh, please."

Dean supposed she was right. On the surface, Rosarita Bay looked   70
like a nice seaside town, a rural sanctuary between San Francisco and
Santa Cruz. It billed itself as the pumpkin capital of the world, and it had a
Main Street lined with gas street lamps and old-time, clapboarded, saltbox
shops and restaurants. Secluded and quiet, it felt like genuine small-town
America, and most of the eight thousand residents preferred it that way,
voting down every development plan that came down the pike.

Yet the things that gave Rosarita Bay its charm were also killing it. There
were only two roads into town, Highway 1 on the coast and Highway 71
through the San Vicente Mountains, both of them just two lanes and prone to
landslides. The fishing and farming industries were drying up, there were no
new jobs, and, for those who worked in San Francisco or "over the hill" in San
Vicente, it was a murderous, traffic-choked commute. The weather was also
terrible, rain-soaked and wave-battered in the winter, wind-beaten in the
spring, and fog-shrouded all summer long, leaving basically two good
months—September and October.

In theory quaint and pretty, Rosarita Bay was actually a no-man's-land,
a sleepy, slightly seedy backwater with the gray air of anonymity. People
stuck to themselves, as if shied by failure and missed opportunities. You could
get lost here, forgotten. It was, when all was said and done, a place of exile.
It was not a place for a wealthy, jet-setting artiste and bon vivant like
Marcella Ahn. But to come here because of Caroline? No. Dean could not
believe it.

"How could she have even known you were here?" he asked Caroline.
"You said you're not in touch with any of those people anymore."

"She probably hired a detective."

"Come on."   75

"You don't understand. I suppose you think if anyone's looking for
revenge, it'd be me, that I can't be a threat to her because I'm such a loser."

"I wish you'd stop putting yourself down all the time. You're not a loser."

"Yes, I am. You're just too polite to say so. You're so fucking Japanese."

Early on, she had given him her book to read, and he had told her he liked
it. But when pressed, he'd had to admit that he didn't really understand the
poems. He was not an educated man, he had said.

"You pass yourself off as this simple chairmaker," Caroline said. "You 80
were practically monosyllabic when we began seeing each other. But I know
you're not the gallunk you make yourself out to be."

"I think you're talented. I think you're very talented." How could he
explain it to her? Something had happened as he'd read her book. The poems,
confusing as they were, had made his skin prickle, his throat thicken, random
images and words—*kiwi, quiver, belly, maw*—wiggling into his head and taking
residence.

"Are you attracted to her?" Caroline asked.

"What?"

"You're not going to make the chair for her, are you?"

"I have to." 85

"You don't have a contract."

"No, but—"

"You still think it's all a coincidence."

"She ordered the chair *sixteen months* before I met you."

"You see how devious she is?" 90

Dean couldn't help himself. He laughed.

"She has some sick bond to me," Caroline said. "In all this time, she
hasn't published another book, either. She *needs* me. She *needs* my misery.
You think I'm being hysterical, but you wait."

It began with candy and flowers, left anonymously behind the hardware store,
on the stairs that led up to Caroline's apartment. Dean had not sent them.

"It's her," Caroline said.

The gifts continued, every week or so, then every few days. Chocolates, 95
carnations, stuffed animals, scarves, hairbrushes, barrettes, lingerie. Caroline,
increasingly anxious, moved in with Dean, and quickly came down with a
horrendous cold.

Hourly he would check on her, administering juice, echinacea, or anti-
histamines, then would go back to the refuge of his workshop. It was where he
was most comfortable—alone with his tools and wood, making chairs that
would last hundreds of years. He made only armchairs now, one chair, over
and over, the Kaneshiro Chair. Each one was fashioned out of a single board of
keyaki, Japanese zelkova, and was completely handmade. From the logging to
the tung oil finish, the wood never touched a power tool. All of Dean's saws
and chisels and planes were hand-forged in Japan, and he shunned vises and
clamps of any kind, sometimes holding pieces between his feet to work on
them.

On first sight, the chair's design wasn't that special—blocky right angles,
thick Mission-style slats—but its beauty lay in the craftsmanship. Dean used
no nails or screws, no dowels or even glue. Everything was put together by
joints, forty-four delicate, intricate joints, modeled after a traditional method

of Japanese joinery dating to the seventeenth century, called *sashimono*. Once coupled, the joints were tenaciously, permanently locked. They would never budge, they would never so much as squeak.

What's more, every surface was finished with a hand plane. Dean would not deign to have sandpaper in his shop. He had apprenticed for four years with a master carpenter in the city of Matsumoto, in Nagano prefecture, spending the first six months just learning how to sharpen his tools. When he returned to California, he could pull a block plane over a board and produce a continuous twelve-foot-long shaving, without a single skip or dig, that was less than a tenth of a millimeter thick—so thin you could read a newspaper through it.

Dean aimed for perfection with each chair. With the first kerf of his *dozuki* saw, with the initial chip of a chisel, he was committed to the truth of the cut. Tradition dictated that any errors could not be repaired, but had to remain untouched to remind the woodworker of his humble nature. More and more, Dean liked to challenge himself. He no longer used a level, square, or marking gauge, relying on his eye, and soon he planned to dispense with rulers altogether, maybe even with pencils and chalk. He wanted to get to the point where he could make a Kaneshiro Chair blindfolded.

But he had a problem. Japanese zelkova, the one- to two-thousand-year-old variety he needed, was rare and very expensive—amounting to over $150 a pound. There were only three traditional woodcutters left in Japan, and Dean's sawyer, Hayashi Kota, was sixty-nine. Hayashi-san's intuition was irreplaceable. So much of the work was in reading the trees and determining where to begin sawing to reveal the best figuring and grain—like cutting diamonds. Afraid the sawyer might die soon, Dean had begun stockpiling wood five years ago. In his lumber shed, which was climate-controlled to keep the wood at a steady thirty-seven percent humidity, was about two hundred thousand dollars' worth of zelkova. Hayashi-san cut the logs through and through and air-dried them in Japan for a year, and after two weeks of kiln heat, the boards were shipped to Dean, who stacked them on end in *boule* order. When he went into the shed to select a new board, he was always overcome by the beauty of the wood, the smell of it. He'd run his hand over the boards—hardly a check or crack on them—and would want to weep.

Given the expense of the wood and the precision his chairs required, anyone seeing Dean in his shop would have been shocked by the rapidity with which he worked. He never hesitated. He *attacked* the wood, chips flying, shavings whirling into the air, sawdust piling at his feet. He could sustain this ferocity for hours, never letting his concentration flag. No wonder, then, that it took him a few moments to hear the knocking on the door late that afternoon. It took him even longer to comprehend why anyone would be disturbing him in his workshop, his *sanctum sanctorum*.

Caroline swung open the door and stepped inside, looking none too happy. "You have a visitor," she said.

Marcella Ahn sidled past her. "Hello!"

Dean almost dropped his *ryoba* saw.

"Is that my chair?" she asked, pointing to the stack of two-by-twos on   105
his bench. "I know, I know, you told me not to come, but I had to. You won't
hold it against me, will you?"

Without warning, Caroline let out a violent sneeze, her hair whiplashing
forward.

"Bless you," Dean and Marcella said at the same time.

Caroline snorted up a long string of snot, glaring at Oriental Hair Poet
No. 2. They were a study in contrasts, Marcella once again decked out as an
Edwardian whore: a corset and bodice, miniskirt and high heels, full makeup,
hair glistening. Caroline was wearing her usual threadbare cardigan and
flannel shirt, pajama bottoms, and flip-flops. She hadn't bathed in two days,
sick in bed the entire time.

"When you get over this cold," Marcella said to her, "we'll have to get
together and catch up. I just can't get over seeing you here."

"It *is* incredible, isn't it?" Caroline said. "It must defy all the laws of   110
probability." She walked to the wall and lifted a mortise chisel from the rack.
"The chances of your moving here, when you could live anywhere in the
world, it's probably more likely for me to shit an egg for breakfast. Why *did* you
move here?"

"Pure chance," Marcella told her cheerily. "I happened to stop for coffee
on my way to Aptos, and I saw one of those real estate circulars for this house. It
looked like an unbelievable bargain. Beautiful woodwork. I thought, What the
hell, I might as well see it while I'm here. I was tired of living in cities."

"What have you been doing since you got to town? Buying lots of gifts?"

Dean watched her dig the chisel blade into a piece of scrap. He wished
she would put the chisel down. It was very sharp.

Marcella appeared confused. "Gifts? No. Well, unless you count Mr.
Kaneshiro's chair as a gift. To myself. You don't have a finished one here?
I've actually never seen one except in the Museum of Modern Art."

"Sorry," he told her, nervous now, hoping it would slip by Caroline.   115
But it did not. "The Museum of Modern Art?" she asked. "In New York?"

Marcella nodded. She absently flicked her hair back with her hand,
and one of her bracelets flew off her wrist, pinging against the window and
landing on some wood chips.

Caroline speared it up with the chisel and dangled it in front of Marcella,
who slid it off somewhat apprehensively. Caroline then turned to Dean. "Your
chairs are in the Museum of Modern Art in New York?"

He shrugged. "Just one."

"You didn't know?" Marcella asked Caroline, plainly pleased she   120
didn't. "Your boyfriend's quite famous."

"How famous?"

"I would like to get back to work now," Dean said.

"He's in Cooper-Hewitt's permanent collection, the M.F.A. in Boston, the American Craft Museum."

"I need to work, please."

"Don't you have a piece in the White House?"   125

"Time is late, please."

"Can I ask you some questions about your process?"

"No." He grabbed the chisel out of Caroline's hand before she could react and ushered Marcella Ahn to the door. "Okay, thank you. Goodbye."

"Caroline, when do you want to get together? Maybe for tea?"

"She'll call you," Dean said, blocking her way back inside.   130

"You'll give her my number?"

"Yes, yes, thank you," he said, and shut the door.

Caroline was sitting on his planing bench, looking gaunt and exhausted. Through the window behind her, Dean saw it was nearing dusk, the wind calming down, the trees quiet. Marcella Ahn was out of view, but he could hear her starting her car, then driving away. He sat down next to Caroline and rubbed her back. "You should go back to bed. Are you hungry? I could make you something."

"Is there anything else about you I should know? Maybe you've taught at Yale or been on the Pulitzer committee? Maybe you've won a few genius grants?"

He wagged his head. "Just one."   135

"What?"

He told her everything. Earlier in his career, he had done mostly conceptual woodwork, more sculpture than furniture. His father was indeed a fifth-generation Japanese carpenter, as he'd told her, but Dean had broken with tradition, leaving his family's cabinetmaking business in San Luis Obispo to study studio furniture at the Rhode Island School of Design. After graduating, he had moved to New York, where he was quickly declared a phenomenon, a development that baffled him. People talked about his work with terms like "verticality" and "negation of ego" and "primal tension," and they might as well have been speaking Farsi. He rode it for all it was worth, selling pieces at a record clip. But eventually, he became bored. He didn't experience any of the rivalries that Caroline had, nor was he too bothered by the egos and fatuity that abounded in the art world. He just didn't believe in what he was doing anymore, particularly after his father died of a sudden stroke. Dean wanted to return to the pure craftsmanship and functionality of woodworking, building something people could actually *use*. So he dropped everything to apprentice in Japan. Afterward, he distilled all of his knowledge into the Kaneshiro Chair, which was regarded as significant a landmark as Frank Lloyd Wright's Willits Chair. Ironically, his work was celebrated anew. He received a five-year genius grant that paid him an annual $50,000, all of which he had put into hoarding the zelkova in his shed.

"How much do you get a chair?" Caroline asked.

"Ten thousand."

"God, you're only thirty-eight."

"It's an inflated market."   140

"And you never thought to tell me any of this in the eight months we've been going out? I thought you were barely getting by. You live in this crappy little house with cheap furniture, your pickup is ten years old, you never take vacations. I thought it was because you weren't very savvy about your business, making one chair at a time, no advertising or catalogue or anything, no store lines. I thought you were *clueless*."

"It's not important."

"Not important? Are you insane? Not important? It changes everything."

"Why?"   145

"You know why, or you wouldn't have kept this secret from me."

"It was an accident. I didn't set out to be famous. It just happened. I'm ashamed of it."

"You should be. You're either pathologically modest, or you were afraid I'd be repelled by how successful you are, compared to me. But you should have told me."

"I just make chairs now," Dean said. "I'm just like you with your poetry. I work hard like you. I don't do it for the money or the fame or to be popular with the critics."

"It's just incidental that you've gotten all of those things without even trying."

"Let's go in the house. I'll make you dinner."   150

"No. I have to go home. I can't be with you anymore."

"Caroline, please."

"You must think I'm pathetic, you must pity me," she said. "You're not like me at all. You're just like Marcella."

They had had fights before, puzzling affairs where she would walk out in a huff, incensed by an innocuous remark he'd made, a mysterious gaffe he'd committed. A day or two would go by, then she would talk to him, peevishly at first, ultimately relenting after she had dressed him down with a pointed lecture on his need to be more sensitive, more supportive, more complimentary, more assertive, more emotive, more sympathetic, above all, more *communicative*. Dean would listen without protest, and, newly educated and humbled, he would always be taken back. But not this time. This time was different. On the telephone the next day, Caroline was cool and resolute—no whining or nagging, no histrionics or ultimatums or room for negotiation. "It's over, Dean," she said.

The following afternoon, he went to her apartment with a gallon of   155
miso soup. "For your cold," he said.

She looked down at the tub in his hands. "I'm fine now. I don't need the soup. The cold's gone."

They were standing outside on the stairway landing. "You're not going to let me in?" he asked.

"Dean, didn't you hear what I said yesterday?"

"Just tell me how I should change. I'll change."

"It's not like that."   160

"What's it like, then? Tell me what you want me to do."

"Nothing," she said. "You can't fix this. Don't come by again, don't call, okay? It'll be easier if we just break it off clean."

He tried to leave her alone, but none of it made any sense to him. Why was she ending it? What had he done wrong? It had to be one of her mood swings, a little hormonal blip, a temporary synaptic disruption, all of which he'd witnessed and weathered before. It had to be more about Marcella Ahn than him. She couldn't really be serious. The best course of action seemed to be to wait it out, while at the same time being solicitous and attentive. So he called—not *too* frequently, maybe once a day or so—and since she wouldn't pick up her phone, he left messages: "I just wanted to see how you're doing. I miss you." He drove to her apartment and knocked on her door, and since she wouldn't answer it, he left care packages: macadamia nuts, coffee, cream, filters, toilet paper, sodas, granola bars, springwater, toothpaste—the everyday staples she always forgot to buy.

Five days passed, and she didn't appear to be weakening. A little desperate, he decided to go to Rae's Diner. When Caroline came out of the kitchen and saw him sitting in her station, she didn't seem surprised, but she was angry. She wouldn't acknowledge him, wouldn't come to his table. After twenty minutes, Dean flagged down Rae, the owner. "Could you tell Caroline to take my order?" he asked.

Rae, a lanky, middle-aged brunette with a fierce sunlamp tan, studied   165
him, then Caroline. "If you two are having a fight, I'm not going to be in the middle of it. You want to stay, you'll have to pay."

"That's what I'm trying to do. She won't take my order."

"Why don't you just move to another station?"

"There aren't any other tables."

"The counter, then."

"I'm a paying customer, I should be able to sit where I want."   170

Rae shook her head. "Any screaming, one little commotion, and you're out of here. And no dawdling over a cup of coffee, either. The minute your table's cleared, you go."

She had a brief conference with Caroline, who began arguing with her, but in the end Rae won out, and Caroline marched over to Dean's table. She didn't look well—pale and baggy-eyed. She wasn't sleeping or eating much, it was clear. He tried to make pleasantries. "How have you been?" he asked her.

She would not say a word, much less look at him. She waited for his order, ballpoint poised over her pad. A few minutes later, when his food was ready, she clattered the plate in front of him and walked away. When he raised his coffee cup for a refill, she slopped the pot, spilling coffee over the brim, almost scorching his crotch. He left her a generous tip.

He came to a similar arrangement with the manager of Da Bones, the barbecue restaurant where Caroline worked nights—as long as he paid, he could stay. He ate meals at every one of Caroline's shifts for a week, at the end of which he had gained eight pounds and was popping antacids as if they were gumballs. It was greasy, artery-busting food. A typical breakfast now consisted of six eggs over easy, sausage, hash browns, blueberry flapjacks, coffee, orange juice, biscuits, and milk gravy. Dinner was the hungry man combo—beef brisket, half a rack of baby backs, kielbasa, blackened chicken, rice, beans, slaw, and cornbread—accompanied by a side of mashed and two plates of conch fritters. But it was worth it. Caroline's resolve, he could tell, was beginning to crack (although the same could be said about her health; she looked awful). One night, as he asked for his fifth glass of water, she actually said something. She said, "You are getting to be a real pain in the ass," and she almost smiled. He was getting to her.

But two days later, he received a strange summons. A sergeant from the sheriff's office, Gene Becklund, requested he come down for a talk concerning Caroline. Mystified, Dean drove over to the sheriff's office on Highway 1 and was escorted into an interrogation room. Gene Becklund was a tall, soft-spoken man with prematurely gray hair. He opened the conversation by saying, "You've been going over to your ex-girlfriend's apartment a lot, dropping off little presents? Even though she told you not to call or visit?"

Unsettled, Dean nodded yes. 175

"You've also been bothering her at her workplace nearly every day?"

"'Bothering'?"

"And you've been leaving a lot of messages on her machine, haven't you?"

"We haven't really broken up," Dean said. "We're just having a fight."

"Uh-huh." 180

"I'm not harassing her or anything."

"Okay."

"Did she say I was harassing her?"

"Why don't we listen to something," Becklund said, and turned on a cassette player. On the tape was a garbled, robotic, unidentifiable voice, reciting the vile, evil things that would be done to Caroline—anal penetration, disembowelment. "You think you can treat people the way you've treated me, Miss Mighty High?" the voice said. "Think again. I'm going to enjoy watching you die."

"Jesus," Dean said. 185

Becklund clicked off the tape. "That's just a sample. There have been other calls—very ugly. The voice is disguised. It's hard to even know whether it's a man or a woman."

"The caller used a voice changer."

"You're familiar with them?"

"I read a lot of crime novels."

"I was surprised how cheap the things are. You can get them off the Internet," Becklund said. "The calls were made from various pay phones, mostly between two and four in the morning. Ms. Yip asked the phone company to begin tracing incoming calls a couple of weeks ago. We can trace where they're being made, but not who's making them." Almost as an afterthought, he asked, "You're not making them, are you?"

"No. Is that what Caroline thinks?"

"Here's what I never understand. She *should* think that, everything in my experience says so, but she doesn't. She thinks it's this woman, Marcella Ahn. I've talked to her, too, but she claims she's only left a couple of messages to invite Ms. Yip to tea, and to see if she would do a poetry reading with her at Beryl's Bookstore."

Dean had never really believed it was Marcella Ahn who was leaving the gifts. Maybe an enamored restaurant customer, or the pimply clerk in the hardware store, but not Marcella. Now he reconsidered. "Maybe it's not all a coincidence," he said. "Maybe it is her." Suddenly it almost made sense. "I think it might really be her."

"Maybe," Becklund said. "But my money's on you. Unfortunately, I can't get a restraining order issued without Ms. Yip's cooperation. But I can do this. I can tell you that all the things you did before—the presents, the calls, the workplace visits—weren't prosecutable under the anti-stalking laws until you made a physical threat. You crossed the line with the physical threat. From now on, you make one little slip-up, I can arrest you." He tapped the tabletop with his fingertip. "I suggest you stay away from her."

Dean ignored Becklund. He was frightened for Caroline, and he would do all he could to protect her. The next morning, he waited across the street from the diner for Caroline's shift to finish. When she came outside, he didn't recognize her at first. She had cut off all her hair.

She was walking briskly, carrying a Styrofoam food container, and he had to sprint to catch up to her. "Caroline, please talk to me," he said. "Will you talk to me? Sergeant Becklund told me about the messages."

She stopped but did not turn around. As he stepped in front of her, he saw she was crying. Her hair was shorn to no more than an inch, matted in clumps and tufts, exposing scalp in some places. Evidently she had chopped it off herself in a fit of self-immolation. "Oh, baby," he said, "what have you done?"

She dropped the container, splattering egg salad onto the sidewalk, and collapsed into him. "Do you believe me now?" she asked. "Do you believe it's her?"

"Yes. I do."

"What makes one person want to destroy another?" she asked. "For   200
what? The pettiness, the backstabbing, the meanness—what's the point? Is it fun? She has everything. What more does she want? Why is she doing this to me?"

Dean held her. "I don't know."

"It's such a terrible world, Dean. You can't trust anyone. No matter where you go, there's always someone wishing you ill will. You think they're your friends, and then they're smearing you, trying to ruin you. I can't take this anymore. Why can't she just go away? Can't you make her go away?"

"Is that what you want?"

"Yes," Caroline said.

It was all Dean needed to hear. He took her to his house, put her to bed,   205
and got to work.

It didn't take long to learn her routine. Caroline had been right: Marcella Ahn never left her house until near sunset, when she would go to the newly renovated Y.M.C.A. to attend a cardioboxing class, topped off with half an hour on the StairMaster. She usually didn't shower at the Y, but would go straight home in her workout clothes. At nine or so, she might emerge and drive to Beryl's Bookstore & Café in town for a magazine and a cappuccino. Once, she went to the Moonside Trading Post for a video. Another time, the Safeway on Highway 71 at two A.M. She had one guest, a male, dressed in a suit, an O.B./G.Y.N. at a San Francisco hospital, according to the parking sticker on his BMW. He spent the night. She didn't go anywhere near Caroline's apartment or make any clandestine calls from pay phones.

Dean didn't try to conceal his stakeouts from Caroline, but he misled her into thinking he wanted to catch Marcella in the act. He had no such expectations. By this time, Marcella had to know that she was—however removed—a suspect, that she might be watched. Dean had an entirely different agenda.

One afternoon, he interrupted his surveillance to go to a spy hobbyist shop in San Francisco. He had found it through the Internet on the Rosarita Bay Library computer—Sergeant Becklund had given him the idea. At the store, he bought a lock pick set, $34.95, and a portable voice changer, $29.95. (The clerk also tried to sell him a 200,000-volt stun gun, on sale for $119.95.) Dean paid cash—no credit card records or bank statements to implicate him later.

In the dead of night, he made a call from a pay phone in the neighboring town of Miramar to his own answering machine, imitating the taunts he'd

heard in the sheriff's office with the voice changer. "Hey, Jap boyfriend, you're
back together with her, are you? Well, fear not, I know where you live." Before
leaving the house, he had switched off his telephone's ringer and turned down
the volume on the answering machine. He didn't want to scare Caroline, even
though she was likely asleep, knocked out by the sleeping pills prescribed by a
doctor he'd taken her to see at the town clinic. Still, in the morning, he had
no choice but to play the message for her. Otherwise, she wouldn't have called
Becklund in a panic, imploring him to arrest Marcella Ahn. "She's insane,"
Caroline told him. "She's trying to drive me crazy. She's going to try to kill
me. You have to do something."

Becklund came to Dean's house, listened to the tape, and appeared to   210
have a change of heart. Dean and Caroline had reconciled. There was no
reason to suspect him anymore. Becklund had to look elsewhere. "Keep your
doors and windows locked," he told Dean.

After that, the only question was when. It couldn't be too soon, but each
day of waiting became more torturous.

The following Wednesday, before her dinner shift, he drove Caroline to
Rummy Creek and parked on the headlands overlooking the ocean. It was
another miserable, gray, windy day, Dean's truck buffeted by gusts. Rummy
Creek was world famous for its big waves, and there was supposed to be a
monster swell approaching, but the water was flat, a clump of surfers in the
distance bobbing gently on the surface like kelp.

"There haven't been any phone calls all week," Caroline said inside his
truck.

"I know. Maybe she's decided to stop."

"No," Caroline said, "she'd never stop. Something's going to happen. I   215
can feel it. I'm scared, Dean."

He dropped her off at Da Bones, then drove up Skyview Ridge Road
and nestled in the woods outside Marcella's house. On schedule, she left for
the Y.M.C.A. at six p.m. After a few minutes, he strolled to the door as
casually as possible. She didn't have a neighbor within a quarter mile, but
he worried about the unforeseen—the gynecologist lover, a UPS delivery,
Becklund deciding belatedly to serve a restraining order. Wearing latex
surgical gloves, Dean inserted a lock pick and tension bar into the keyhole
on the front door. The deadbolt opened within twenty seconds. Thankfully
she had not installed an alarm system yet. He took off his shoes and walked
through the kitchen into the garage. This was the biggest variable in his plan.
If he didn't find what he needed there, none of it would work. But to his relief,
Marcella Ahn had several cans of motor oil on the shelf, as well as some
barbecue lighter fluid—it wasn't gasoline, but it would do. In the recycle bin,
there were four empty bottles of pinot grigio. In the kitchen, a funnel and a
dishrag. He poured one part motor oil and one part lighter fluid into a bottle, a
Molotov cocktail recipe provided by the Internet. In her bedroom, he pulled
several strands of hair from her brush, pocketed one of her bracelets, and

grabbed a pair of platform-heeled boots from her closet. Then he was out, and he sped to his house in Vasquez Canyon. All he had to do was press in some bootprints in the dirt in front of the lumber shed, but he was running out of time. He drove back to Marcella's, hurriedly washed the soles of the boots in the kitchen sink, careful to leave a little mud, replaced the boots in the closet, checked through the house, and locked up. Then he went to Santa Cruz and tossed the lock pick set and voice changer into a dumpster.

He did nothing more until three A.M. By then, Caroline was unconscious from the sleeping pills. Dean drove to Marcella Ahn's again. He had to make sure she was home, and alone. He walked around her house, peeking into the windows. She was in her study, sitting at her desk in front of her laptop computer. She had her head in her hands, and she seemed to be quietly weeping. Dean was overcome with misgivings for a moment. He had to remind himself that she was at fault here, that she deserved what was coming to her.

He returned to his own property. Barefoot and wearing only the latex gloves and his underwear, he snagged the strands of Marcella's hair along the doorframe of the lumber shed. He threw the bracelet toward the driveway. He twisted the dishrag into the mouth of the wine bottle, then tilted it from side to side to mix the fluids and soak the rag. He started to flick his lighter, but then hesitated, once more stalled by doubt. Were those mystery novels he read really that accurate? Would the Hair & Fiber and Latent Prints teams be deceived at all? Was he being a fool—a complete amateur who would be ferreted out with ease? He didn't know. All he knew was that he loved Caroline, and he had to take this risk for her. If something wasn't done, he was certain he would lose her. He lit the rag and smashed the bottle against the first stack of zelkova inside the shed. The fire exploded up the boards. He shut the door and ran back into the house and climbed into bed beside Caroline. In a matter of seconds, the smoke detectors went off. The shed was wired to the house, and the alarm in the hallway rang loud enough to wake Caroline. "What's going on?" she asked.

Dean peered out the window. "I think there's a fire," he said. He pulled on his pants and shoes and ran to the shed. When he kicked open the door, the heat blew him back. Flames had already engulfed three *boules* of wood, the smoke was thick and black, the fire was spreading. Something had gone wrong. The sprinkler system—his expensive, state-of-the-art, dry-pipe sprinkler system—had not activated. He had not planned to sacrifice this much wood, one or two stacks at most, and now he was in danger of losing the entire shed.

There was no investigation, per se. Two deputies took photographs and 220 checked for fingerprints, but that was about all. Dean asked Becklund, "Aren't you going to call the crime lab unit?" and Becklund said, "This is it."

It was simple enough for the fire department to determine that it was arson, but not who set it. The insurance claims adjuster was equally lackadaisical. Within a few days, he signed off for Dean to receive a $75,000 check. Dean and Caroline had kept the blaze contained with extinguishers and garden hoses for the twenty-two minutes it took for the fire trucks to arrive, but nearly half of Dean's wood supply had been consumed, the rest damaged by smoke and water.

No charges were filed against Marcella Ahn. After talking to Becklund and a San Vicente County assistant district attorney, though, she agreed—on the advice of counsel—to move out of Rosarita Bay, which was hardly a great inconvenience for her, since she owned five other houses and condos. Caroline never heard from her again, and, as far as they knew, she never published another book—a one-hit wonder.

Caroline, on the other hand, finally submitted her second book to a publisher. Dean was relentless about making her do so. The book was accepted right away, and when it came out, it caused a brief sensation. Great reviews. Awards and fellowships. Dozens of requests for readings and appearances. Caroline couldn't be bothered. By then, she and Dean had had their first baby, a girl, Anna, and Caroline wanted more children, a baker's dozen if possible. She was transformed. No more nightmares, and she could nap standing up (house-keeping remained elusive). In relation to motherhood, to the larger joys and tragedies that befell people, the poetry world suddenly seemed silly, insignificant. She would continue to write, but only, she said, when she had the time and will. Of course, she ended up producing more than ever.

Marcella Ahn's chair was the last Dean made from the pristine zelkova. He would dry and clean up the boards that were salvageable, and when he exhausted that supply, he would switch to English walnut, a nice wood—pretty, durable, available.

He delivered the chair to Marcella just before she left town, on May 11, as 225 scheduled. She was surprised to see him and the chair, but a promise was a promise. He had never failed to deliver an order, and she had prepaid for half of it.

He set the chair down in the living room—crowded with boxes and crates—and she sat in it. "My God," she said, "I didn't know it would be this comfortable. I could sit here all day."

"I'd like to ask you for a favor," Dean said as she wrote out a check for him. He held an envelope in his hand.

"A favor?"

"Yes. I'd like you to read Caroline's new poems and tell me if they're good."

"You must be joking. After everything she's done?"   230

"I don't know poetry. You're the only one who can tell me. I need to know."

"Do you realize I could have been sent to state prison for two years? For a crime I didn't commit?"

"It would've never gone to trial. You would've gotten a plea bargain—a suspended sentence and probation."

"How do you know?" Marcella asked. "Your girlfriend is seriously deranged. I only wanted to be her friend, and she devised this insidious plot to frame me and run me out of town. She's diabolical."

"You stalked her."   235

"I did no such thing. Don't you get it? She faked it. She set me up. *She* was the stalker. Hasn't that occurred to you? Hasn't that gotten through that thick, dim-witted skull of yours? She burned your *wood*."

"You're lying. You're very clever, but I don't believe you," Dean said. And he didn't, although she made him think for a second. He pulled out the book manuscript from the envelope. "Are you going to read the poems or not?"

"No."

"Aren't you curious what she's been doing for the past six years?" Dean asked. "Isn't this what you came here to find out?"

Marcella slowly hooked her hair behind her ears and took her time to   240
respond. "Give it to me," she finally said.

For the next half hour, she sat in his chair in the living room, flipping through the seventy-one pages, and Dean watched her. Her expression was unyielding and contemptuous at first, then it went utterly slack, then taut again. She breathed quickly through her nose, her jaw clamped, her eyes blinked.

"Are they good?" Dean asked when she finished.

She handed the manuscript back to him. "They're pedestrian. They're clunky. There's no music to the language."

"They're good," Dean told her.

"I didn't say that."   245

"You don't have to. I saw it in your face." He walked to the door and let himself out.

"I didn't say they were good!" Marcella Ahn screamed after him. "Do you hear me? I didn't say that. I didn't say they were good!"

Dean never told Caroline about his last visit with Marcella Ahn, nor did he ever ask her about the stalking, although he was tempted at times. One spring afternoon, they were outside on his deck, Caroline leaning back in the rocker he'd made for her, her eyes closed to the sun, Anna asleep in her lap. It had rained heavily that winter, and the eucalyptus and pine surrounding the house were now in full leaf. They sat silently and listened to the wind bending through the trees. He had rarely seen her so relaxed.

Anna, still asleep, lolled her head, her lips pecking the air in steady rhythm—an infant soliloquy.

"Caroline," he said.   250

"Hm?"

"What do you think she's dreaming about?"

Caroline looked down at Anna. "Your guess is as good as mine," she said. "Maybe she has a secret. Can babies have secrets?" She ran her hand through her hair, which she had kept short, and she smiled at Dean.

Was it possible that Caroline had fabricated everything about Marcella Ahn? He did not want to know. She would, in turn, never question him about the fire. The truth wouldn't have mattered. They had each done what was necessary to be with the other. Such was the price of love among artists, such was the price of devotion.

- What is the conflict between Caroline and Marcella?
- Why do Dean and Caroline fight?
- Why is it important to the story that Dean reads a lot of crime novels?
- What are the different sorts of craftsmanship that we learn about in this story? Find specific details that illustrate achievement in each of these crafts. How are the values within the different crafts different from the values of other crafts described here?
- What is the crime in this story? What is the mystery? How does this story seem more open, or less closed, than the Sherlock Holmes story?

POETRY

Emily Dickinson (1830–1886)

[A Route of Evanescence] (1879)

A Route of Evanescence°
With a revolving Wheel—
A Resonance of Emerald—
A Rush of Cochineal°
And every Blossom on the Bush   5
Adjusts its tumbled Head—
The mail from Tunis, probably,
An easy Morning's Ride—

---

1. Evanescence: the tendency to vanish away. 4. Cochineal: a brilliant scarlet dye

Emily Dickinson (1830–1886)

[I like to see it lap the Miles—] (1862)

I like to see it lap the Miles—
And lick the Valleys up—
And stop to feed itself at Tanks—
And then—prodigious step

Around a Pile of Mountains—   5
And supercilious peer
In Shanties—by the sides of Roads—
And then a Quarry pare

To fit its sides
And crawl between   10
Complaining all the while
In horrid—hooting stanza—
Then chase itself down Hill—

And neigh like Boanerges—
Then—prompter than a Star   15
Stop—docile and omnipotent
At its own stable door—

- In these two poems, Dickinson offers us two different riddles. When we look closely at each of the details she has listed, what figure does she describe in each poem?
- In "A Route of Evanescence," the detail about "the mail from Tunis" appears not to fit with the other details. How can you account for the detail? Is there any similar detail in "I like to see it lap the Miles—"?

E. A. Robinson (1869–1935)

Richard Cory (1897)

Whenever Richard Cory went down town,
We people on the pavement looked at him:
He was a gentleman from sole to crown,
Clean favored, and imperially slim.

And he was always quietly arrayed,   5
And he was always human when he talked;
But still he fluttered pulses when he said,
"Good-morning," and he glittered when he walked.

And he was rich—yes, richer than a king—
And admirably schooled in every grace: 10
In fine, we thought that he was everything
To make us wish that we were in his place.

So on we worked, and waited for the light,
And went without the meat, and cursed the bread;
And Richard Cory, one calm summer night,   15
Went home and put a bullet through his head.

■ How does the final line of the poem challenge the appearances that the town
   has long accepted?

■ What were Cory's greatest strengths? How does their presentation in the
   poem create a dramatic impact?

Robert Frost (1874–1963)

Stopping by Woods on a Snowy Evening (1923)

Whose woods these are I think I know.
His house is in the village, though;
He will not see me stopping here
To watch his woods fill up with snow.

My little horse must think it queer   5
To stop without a farmhouse near
Between the woods and frozen lake
The darkest evening of the year.

He gives his harness bells a shake
To ask if there is some mistake.   10
The only other sound's the sweep
Of easy wind and downy flake.

The woods are lovely, dark and deep,
But I have promises to keep,
And miles to go before I sleep,   15
And miles to go before I sleep.

William Stafford (1914–1993)

Traveling through the Dark (1962)

Traveling through the dark I found a deer
dead on the edge of the Wilson River road.
It is usually best to roll them into the canyon:
that road is narrow; to swerve might make more dead.

By glow of the tail-light I stumbled back of the car   5
and stood by the heap, a doe, a recent killing;
she had stiffened already, almost cold.
I dragged her off; she was large in the belly.

My fingers touching her side brought me the reason—
her side was warm; her fawn lay there waiting,   10
alive, still, never to be born.

Beside that mountain road I hesitated.
The car aimed ahead its lowered parking lights;
under the hood purred the steady engine.
I stood in the glare of the warm exhaust turning red;   15
around our group I could hear the wilderness listen

I thought hard for us all—my only swerving—
then pushed her over the edge into the river.

■ In Frost's and Stafford's poems, the narrators describe a pause in their usual
routines. What are those routines? How does each decide to go on?

Kevin Young (1970–)

The Set-Up (2005)

Snake oil sales
  were slow. So I hung

out my shingle on
  a shadow.

Desk-drawer liquor   5

A dead man's loan. Soon
  chinless stoolies

slunk & doorjambed—
  ratted

that she ain't no   10
  good, that she wears a watch

on both wrists. Too
  many midnights.

Evidence mounting like butterflies

Still I made them informants   15
  for phonies, phoned

to hear her breath.
  She was faith

enough to believe.
  She's a peach. A pistol.   20

I waived my fee

I left my agency

Came home to rooms ran-
  sacked, tossed

by invisible hands.   25
  Hip flask. Blackjacked.

Swig,
  mickey slip, slug.

I woke doubled & crossed

Drug, ferried   30
  through whisky alleys

Bruisers, suicide doors

The crooked chief interrogated
  me about her body

She's no more mine, no eye   35
  witness, nor alibi

No one will attest she ever
   did exist.

I was her autumn guy

By the wharf was left   40
   waterlogged & wise

My dogs dead
   tired, I humped it

home, humming gumshoe blues.

Kevin Young (1970–)

The Chase (2005)

I didn't have a rat's chance.
   Soon as she walked in in

That skin of hers
   violins began. You could half hear

The typewriters jabber   5
   as she jawed on: *fee, find, me,*

poor, please.
   Shadows & smiles, she was.

Strong scent of before-rain

Her pinstripe two-lane   10
   legs, her blackmail menthol.

She had all the negatives

Hidden safe
   & would not reveal the place.

Before you could say   15
   denouement, I was on her case—

Slant hat, broad
   back, my entrenched coat

Of fog. Fleabags,
   neon blinds undrawn—   20

The foreshadows fell on her face.

All night I tailed, staked
  the joint. Found

Her with the butler
  playing patty-cake.   25

Baker's man. She nurse
  him like beer

Till dawn. Doozy.
  Was from her woozy,

My eyes wet.   30
  Binocular mist.

I took two to the chest

Was all
  rain, her blurring face

Her snuffed, stubbed-out   35
  lipstuck cigarette.

- ■ The narrator speaking here is a detective from the noir tradition of film and fiction. How do we learn this?
- ■ What sort of atmosphere do the short lines and the details presented here convey?

Aron Keesbury (1971–)

On the Robbery across the Street (1998)

(*An eyewitness to the Brinks heist*)

I tell them, look. Sure, I was around.
The tenant from four
come down to the store
that night to see can he get a cat.

Tony or Jimmy, his name is.   5
Henry maybe. Mike? Joe?

Maybe Jimmy. Look, I don't know
but he's a nice boy anyway. Wears specs,

you know. He come down
asks me, says can I get a cat   10
upstairs? I says sure. Keep that
sandy crap out of the drains, though—

clogs them all up, you know.
Then I got to get all new pipes.
So he runs upstairs. He's all hyped   15
up like I ain't seen the cat he's got

already. Maybe two,
three weeks he's got a cat up there.
These kids. Jazzing all around, I swear,
think they can get away with murder.   20

But he's a nice boy and I tell the cops,
I say, look. I been in this store here
for thirty-seven years.
Thirty-seven years in this store.

I tell them sure. I say, look.   25
I was here, I was around
that night. I been in this town
thirty-seven years.
And I don't see nothing.

■ What details in the poem give us information about the 1950 Brinks robbery in Boston?

■ This robbery in which nearly $3 million was stolen was famously difficult to solve. How does this poem illustrate that aspect of the heist?

Muriel Rukeyser (1913–1980)

Myth (1973)

Long afterward, Oedipus, old and blinded, walked the
roads.   He smelled a familiar smell.   It was
the Sphinx.   Oedipus said, "I want to ask one question.

Why didn't I recognize my mother?"   "You gave the
wrong answer," said the Sphinx.   "But that was what   5
made everything possible," said Oedipus.   "No," she said.
"When I asked, What walks on four legs in the morning,
two at noon, and three in the evening, you answered,
Man.   You didn't say anything about woman."
"When you say Man," said Oedipus, "you include women   10
too. Everyone knows that."   She said, "That's what
you think."

■ How is "You gave the wrong answer" stunning to both Oedipus and to those
of us who are familiar with his story?

■ How does Rukeyser's final line bring a modern sensibility to the Oedipus myth?

DRAMA

Sophocles (497 B.C.–406 B.C.)

Because ancient biographies are so often unreliable, it is difficult to know much
about Sophocles with any certainty. Literary historians generally accept, however,
that he was the son of a businessman; he was a gifted singer; his first victory in
the principal dramatic festival, the Greater Dionysia, occurred in 468 BC; and he
never won less than second prize and came in first on at least eighteen occasions.
He also served as treasurer, senator, and general in Athens. His plays that have
survived to the present day, including *Oedipus Rex* (*Oedipus the King*) and
Antigone, are among the undisputed classics of world literature.

Oedipus the King (ca. 430 BC, trans. Robert Fagles)

CHARACTERS

OEDIPUS, *king of Thebes*
A PRIEST *of Zeus*
CREON, *brother of Jocasta*
A CHORUS *of Theban citizens and their* LEADER
TIRESIAS, *a blind prophet*
JOCASTA, *the queen, wife of Oedipus*
A MESSENGER *from Corinth*

A SHEPHERD
A MESSENGER *from inside the palace*
ANTIGONE, ISMENE, *daughters of Oedipus and Jocasta*
GUARDS *and* ATTENDANTS
PRIESTS *of Thebes*

TIME AND SCENE: *The royal house of Thebes. Double doors dominate the facade; a
stone altar stands at the center of the stage.*

Many years have passed since OEDIPUS *solved the riddle of the Sphinx and ascended
the throne of Thebes, and now a plague has struck the city. A procession of priests
enters; suppliants, broken and despondent, they carry branches wound in wool and
lay them on the altar.*
The doors open. Guards assemble. OEDIPUS *comes forward, majestic but for a
telltale limp, and slowly views the condition of his people.*

OEDIPUS: Oh my children, the new blood of ancient Thebes,
   why are you here? Huddling at my altar,
   praying before me, your branches wound in wool.
   Our city reeks with the smoke of burning incense,
   rings with cries for the Healer and wailing for the dead.   5
   I thought it wrong, my children, to hear the truth
   from others, messengers. Here I am myself—
   you all know me, the world knows my fame:
   I am Oedipus.
   (Helping a PRIEST *to his feet.)*
                    Speak up, old man. Your years,
   your dignity—you should speak for the others.   10
   Why here and kneeling, what preys upon you so?
   Some sudden fear? some strong desire?
   You can trust me; I am ready to help,
   I'll do anything. I would be blind to misery
   not to pity my people kneeling at my feet.   15
PRIEST: Oh Oedipus, king of the land, our greatest power!
   You see us before you, men of all ages
   clinging to your altars. Here are boys,
   still too weak to fly from the nest,
   and here the old, bowed down with the years,   20
   the holy ones—a priest of Zeus myself—and here
   the picked, unmarried men, the young hope of Thebes.
   And all the rest, your great family gathers now,
   branches wreathed, massing in the squares,
   kneeling before the two temples of queen Athena   25
   or the river-shrine where the embers glow and die

and Apollo sees the future in the ashes.
                                      Our city—
look around you, see with your own eyes—
our ship pitches wildly, cannot lift her head
from the depths, the red waves of death . . .   30
Thebes is dying. A blight on the fresh crops
and the rich pastures, cattle sicken and die,
and the women die in labor, children stillborn,
and the plague, the fiery god of fever hurls down
on the city, his lightning slashing through us—   35
raging plague in all its vengeance, devastating
the house of Cadmus! And Black Death luxuriates
in the raw, wailing miseries of Thebes.

Now we pray to you. You cannot equal the gods,
your children know that, bending at your altar.   40
But we do rate you first of men,
both in the common crises of our lives
and face-to-face encounters with the gods.
You freed us from the Sphinx; you came to Thebes
and cut us loose from the bloody tribute we had paid   45
that harsh, brutal singer. We taught you nothing,
no skill, no extra knowledge, still you triumphed.
A god was with you, so they say, and we believe it—
you lifted up our lives.
                        So now again,
Oedipus, king, we bend to you, your power—   50
we implore you, all of us on our knees:
find us strength, rescue! Perhaps you've heard
the voice of a god or something from other men,
Oedipus . . . what do you know?
The man of experience—you see it every day—   55
his plans will work in a crisis, his first of all.
Act now—we beg you, best of men, raise up our city!
Act, defend yourself, your former glory!
Your country calls you savior now
for your zeal, your action years ago.   60
Never let us remember of your reign:
you helped us stand, only to fall once more.
Oh raise up our city, set us on our feet.
The omens were good that day you brought us joy—
be the same man today!   65
Rule our land, you know you have the power,

but rule a land of the living, not a wasteland.
Ship and towered city are nothing, stripped of men
alive within it, living all as one.

OEDIPUS: My children,
    I pity you. I see—how could I fail to see   70
    what longings bring you here? Well I know
    you are sick to death, all of you,
    but sick as you are, not one is sick as I.
    Your pain strikes each of you alone, each
    in the confines of himself, no other. But my spirit   75
    grieves for the city, for myself and all of you.
    I wasn't asleep, dreaming. You haven't wakened me—
    I've wept through the nights, you must know that,
    groping, laboring over many paths of thought.
    After a painful search I found one cure: 80
    I acted at once. I sent Creon,
    my wife's own brother, to Delphi—
    Apollo the Prophet's oracle—to learn
    what I might do or say to save our city.

    Today's the day. When I count the days gone by   85
    it torments me . . . what is he doing?
    Strange, he's late, he's gone too long.
    But once he returns, then, then I'll be a traitor
    if I do not do all the god makes clear.

PRIEST: Timely words. The men over there   90
    are signaling—Creon's just arriving.

OEDIPUS *(Sighting* CREON, *then turning to the altar.)*: Lord Apollo,
    let him come with a lucky word of rescue,
    shining like his eyes!

PRIEST: Welcome news, I think—he's crowned, look,
    and the laurel wreath is bright with berries.   95

OEDIPUS: We'll soon see. He's close enough to hear—
    (Enter CREON *from the side; his face is shaded with a wreath.)*
    Creon, prince, my kinsman, what do you bring us?
    What message from the god?

CREON: Good news.
    I tell you even the hardest things to bear,
    if they should turn out well, all would be well.   100

OEDIPUS: Of course, but what were the god's *words?* There's no hope
    and nothing to fear in what you've said so far.

CREON: if you want my report in the presence of these . . .
    (Pointing to the PRIESTS *while drawing* OEDIPUS *toward the palace.)*

I'm ready now, or we might go inside.

OEDIPUS: Speak out,
    speak to us all. I grieve for these, my people,   105
    far more than I fear for my own life.

CREON: Very well,
    I will tell you what I heard from the god.
    Apollo commands us—he was quite clear—
    "Drive the corruption from the land,
    don't harbor it any longer, past all cure,   110
    don't nurse it in your soil—root it out!"

OEDIPUS: How can we cleanse ourselves—what rites?
    What's the source of the trouble?

CREON: Banish the man, or pay back blood with blood.
    Murder sets the plague-storm on the city.   115

OEDIPUS: Whose murder?
    Whose fate does Apollo bring to light?

CREON: Our leader,
    my lord, was once a man named Laius,
    before you came and put us straight on course.

OEDIPUS: I know—
    or so I've heard. I never saw the man myself.

CREON: Well, he was killed, and Apollo commands us now—   120
    he could not be more clear,
    "Pay the killers back—whoever is responsible."

OEDIPUS: Where on earth are they? Where to find it now,
    the trail of the ancient guilt so hard to trace?

CREON: "Here in Thebes," he said.   125
    Whatever is sought for can be caught, you know,
    whatever is neglected slips away.

OEDIPUS: But where,
    in the palace, the fields or foreign soil,
    where did Laius meet his bloody death?

CREON: He went to consult an oracle, he said,   130
    and he set out and never came home again.

OEDIPUS: No messenger, no fellow-traveler saw what happened?
    Someone to cross-examine?

CREON: No,
    they were all killed but one. He escaped,
    terrified, he could tell us nothing clearly,   135
    nothing of what he saw—just one thing.

OEDIPUS: What's that?
    One thing could hold the key to it all,
    a small beginning gives us grounds for hope.

CREON: He said thieves attacked them—a whole band,
     not single-handed, cut King Laius down.   140
OEDIPUS: A thief,
     so daring, wild, he'd kill a king? Impossible,
     unless conspirators paid him off in Thebes.
CREON: We suspected as much. But with Laius dead
     no leader appeared to help us in our troubles.
OEDIPUS: Trouble? Your *king* was murdered—royal blood!   145
     What stopped you from tracking down the killer
     then and there?
CREON: The singing, riddling Sphinx.
     She . . . persuaded us to let the mystery go
     and concentrate on what lay at our feet.
OEDIPUS: No,
     I'll start again—I'll bring it all to light myself!   150
     Apollo is right, and so are you, Creon,
     to turn our attention back to the murdered man.
     Now you have *me* to fight for you, you'll see:
     I am the land's avenger by all rights
     and Apollo's champion too.   155
     But not to assist some distant kinsman, no,
     for my own sake I'll rid us of this corruption.
     Whoever killed the king may decide to kill me too,
     with the same violent hand—by avenging Laius
     I defend myself.   160
     (*To the* PRIESTS.)
                         Quickly, my children.
     Up from the steps, take up your branches now.
     (*To the* GUARDS.)
     One of you summon the city here before us,
     tell them I'll do everything. God help us,
     we will see our triumph—or our fall.
(OEDIPUS *and* CREON *enter the palace, followed by the* GUARDS.)
PRIEST: Rise, my sons. The kindness we came for   165
     Oedipus volunteers himself.
     Apollo has sent his word, his oracle—
     Come down, Apollo, save us, stop the plague.
(*The* PRIESTS *rise, remove their branches, and exit to the side. Enter a* CHORUS,
the citizens of Thebes, who have not heard the news that CREON *brings. They
march around the altar, chanting.*)
CHORUS: Zeus!
     Great welcome voice of Zeus, what do you bring?

What word from the gold vaults of Delphi   170
comes to brilliant Thebes? I'm racked with terror—
      terror shakes my heart
and I cry your wild cries, Apollo, Healer of Delos
I worship you in dread . . . what now, what is your price?
some new sacrifice? some ancient rite from the past   175
come round again each spring?—
    what will you bring birth?
Tell me, child of golden Hope
  warm voice that never dies!

You are the first I call, daughter of Zeus   180
deathless Athena—I call your sister Artemis,
heart of the market place enthroned in glory,
      guardian of our earth—
I call Apollo astride the thunderheads of heaven—
O triple shield against death, shine before me now!   185
If ever, once in the past, you stopped some ruin
launched against our walls
    you hurled the flame of pain
far, far from Thebes—you gods
  come now, come down once more!   190
       No, no
the miseries numberless, grief on grief, no end—
too much to bear, we are all dying
O my people . . .
  Thebes like a great army dying
and there is no sword of thought to save us, no   195
and the fruits of our famous earth, they will not ripen
no and the women cannot scream their pangs to birth—
screams for the Healer, children dead in the womb
  and life on life goes down
     you can watch them go   200
  like seabirds winging west, outracing the day's fire
down the horizon, irresistibly
   streaking on to the shores of Evening
       Death
so many deaths, numberless deaths on deaths, no end—
Thebes is dying, look, her children   205
stripped of pity . . .
  generations strewn on the ground
unburied, unwept, the dead spreading death

and the young wives and gray-haired mothers with them
cling to the altars, trailing in from all over the city—   210
Thebes, city of death, one long cortege
            and the suffering rises
                        wails for mercy rise
            and the wild hymn for the Healer blazes out
clashing with our sobs our cries of mourning—   215
            O golden daughter of god, send rescue
            radiant as the kindness in your eyes!
Drive him back!—the fever, the god of death
                        that raging god of war
not armored in bronze, not shielded now, he burns me,   220
battle cries in the onslaught burning on—
O rout him from our borders!
Sail him, blast him out to the Sea-queen's chamber
                        the black Atlantic gulfs
            or the northern harbor, death to all   225
where the Thracian surf comes crashing.
Now what the night spares he comes by day and kills—
the god of death.

                        O lord of the stormcloud,
you who twirl the lightning, Zeus, Father,
thunder Death to nothing!   230

Apollo, lord of the light, I beg you—
            whip your longbow's golden cord
showering arrows on our enemies—shafts of power
champions strong before us rushing on!

Artemis, Huntress,   235
torches flaring over the eastern ridges—
                        ride Death down in pain!

God of the headdress gleaming gold, I cry to you—
your name and ours are one, Dionysus—
            come with your face aflame with wine   240
                        your raving women's cries
            your army on the march! Come with the lightning
come with torches blazing, eyes ablaze with glory!
Burn that god of death that all gods hate!
(OEDIPUS *enters from the palace to address the* CHORUS, *as if addressing the
entire city of Thebes.*)

OEDIPUS: You pray to the gods? Let me grant your prayers.   245
   Come, listen to me—do what the plague demands:
   you'll find relief and lift your head from the depths.

   I will speak out now as a stranger to the story,
   a stranger to the crime. If I'd been present then,
   there would have been no mystery, no long hunt   250
   without a clue in hand. So now, counted
   a native Theban years after the murder,
   to all of Thebes I make this proclamation:
   if any one of you knows who murdered Laius,
   the son of Labdacus, I order him to reveal   255
   the whole truth to me. Nothing to fear,
   even if he must denounce himself,
   let him speak up
   and so escape the brunt of the charge—
   he will suffer no unbearable punishment   260
   nothing worse than exile, totally unharmed.
   (OEDIPUS *pauses, waiting for a reply.*)
                                                    Next,
   if anyone knows the murderer is a stranger,
   a man from alien soil, come, speak up.
   I will give him a handsome reward, and lay up
   gratitude in my heart for him besides.   265
   (*Silence again, no reply.*)
   But if you keep silent, if anyone panicking,
   trying to shield himself or friend or kin,
   rejects my offer, then hear what I will do.
   I order you, every citizen of the state
   where I hold throne and power: banish this man—   270
   whoever he may be—never shelter him, never
   speak a word to him, never make him partner
   to your prayers, your victims burned to the gods.
   Never let the holy water touch his hands.
   Drive him out, each of you, from every home.   275
   He is the plague, the heart of our corruption,
   as Apollo's oracle has revealed to me
   just now. So I honor my obligations:
   I fight for the god and for the murdered man.

   Now my curse on the murderer. Whoever he is,   280
   a lone man unknown in his crime
   or one among many, let that man drag out

his life in agony, step by painful step—
I curse myself as well . . . if by any chance
he proves to be an intimate of our house,   285
here at my hearth, with my full knowledge,
may the curse I just called down on him strike me!

These are your orders: perform them to the last.
I command you, for my sake, for Apollo's, for this country
blasted root and branch by the angry heavens.   290
Even if god had never urged you on to act,
how could you leave the crime uncleansed so long?
A man so noble—your king, brought down in blood—
you should have searched. But I am the king now,
I hold the throne that he held then, possess his bed   295
and a wife who shares our seed . . . why, our seed
might be the same, children born of the same mother
might have created blood-bonds between us
if his hope of offspring hadn't met disaster—
but fate swooped at his head and cut him short.   300
So I will fight for him as if he were my father,
stop at nothing, search the world
to lay my hands on the man who shed his blood,
the son of Labdacus descended of Polydorus,
Cadmus of old and Agenor, founder of the line: 305
their power and mine are one.
                                    Oh dear gods,
my curse on those who disobey these orders!
Let no crops grow out of the earth for them—
shrivel their women, kill their sons,
burn them to nothing in this plague   310
that hits us now, or something even worse.
But you, loyal men of Thebes who approve my actions,
may our champion, Justice, may all the gods
be with us, fight beside us to the end!

LEADER: In the grip of your curse, my king, I swear   315
    I'm not the murderer, cannot point him out.
    As for the search, Apollo pressed it on us—
    he should name the killer.

OEDIPUS: Quite right,
    but to force the gods to act against their will—
    no man has the power.   320

LEADER: Then if I might mention
    the next best thing . . .

OEDIPUS: The third best too—
    don't hold back, say it.
LEADER: I still believe . . .
    Lord Tiresias sees with the eyes of Lord Apollo.
    Anyone searching for the truth, my king,
    might learn it from the prophet, clear as day.   325
OEDIPUS: I've not been slow with that. On Creon's cue
    I sent the escorts, twice, within the hour.
    I'm surprised he isn't here.
LEADER: We need him—
    without him we have nothing but old, useless rumors.
OEDIPUS: Which rumors? I'll search out every word.   330
LEADER: Laius was killed, they say, by certain travelers.
OEDIPUS: I know—but no one can find the murderer.
LEADER: If the man has a trace of fear in him
    he won't stay silent long,
    not with your curses ringing in his ears.   335
OEDIPUS: He didn't flinch at murder,
    he'll never flinch at words.
(*Enter* TIRESIAS, *the blind prophet, led by a boy with escorts in attendance.*
He remains at a distance.)
LEADER: Here is the one who will convict him, look,
    they bring him on at last, the seer, the man of god.
    The truth lives inside him, him alone.   340
OEDIPUS: O Tiresias,
    master of all the mysteries of our life,
    all you teach and all you dare not tell,
    signs in the heavens, signs that walk the earth!
    Blind as you are, you can feel all the more
    what sickness haunts our city. You, my lord,   345
    are the one shield, the one savior we can find.

    We asked Apollo—perhaps the messengers
    haven't told you—he sent his answer back:
    "Relief from the plague can only come one way.
    Uncover the murderers of Laius,   350
    put them to death or drive them into exile."
    So I beg you, grudge us nothing now, no voice,
    no message plucked from the birds, the embers
    or the other mantic ways within your grasp.
    Rescue yourself, your city, rescue me—   355
    rescue everything infected by the dead.
    We are in your hands. For a man to help others

with all his gifts and native strength:
that is the noblest work.

TIRESIAS: How terrible—to see the truth
when the truth is only pain to him who sees!   360
I knew it well, but I put it from my mind,
else I never would have come.

OEDIPUS: What's this? Why so grim, so dire?

TIRESIAS: Just send me home. You bear your burdens,
I'll bear mine. It's better that way,   365
please believe me.

OEDIPUS: Strange response—unlawful,
unfriendly too to the state that bred and raised you;
you're withholding the word of god.

TIRESIAS: I fail to see
that your own words are so well-timed.
I'd rather not have the same thing said of me . . .   370

OEDIPUS: For the love of god, don't turn away,
not if you know something. We beg you,
all of us on our knees.

TIRESIAS: None of you knows—
and I will never reveal my dreadful secrets,
not to say your own.   375

OEDIPUS: What? You know and you won't tell?
You're bent on betraying us, destroying Thebes?

TIRESIAS: I'd rather not cause pain for you or me.
So why this . . . useless interrogation?
You'll get nothing from me.   380

OEDIPUS: Nothing! You,
you scum of the earth, you'd enrage a heart of stone!
You won't talk? Nothing moves you?
Out with it, once and for all!

TIRESIAS: You criticize my temper . . . unaware
of the one *you* live with, you revile me.   385

OEDIPUS: Who could restrain his anger hearing you?
What outrage—you spurn the city!

TIRESIAS: What will come will come.
Even if I shroud it all in silence.

OEDIPUS: What will come? You're bound to *tell* me that.   390

TIRESIAS: I'll say no more. Do as you like, build your anger
to whatever pitch you please, rage your worst—

OEDIPUS: Oh I'll let loose, I have such fury in me—
now I see it all. You helped hatch the plot,
you did the work, yes, short of killing him   395

with your own hands—and given eyes I'd say
you did the killing single-handed!
TIRESIAS: Is that so!
 I charge you, then, submit to that decree
 you just laid down: from this day onward
 speak to no one, not these citizens, not myself.   400
 You are the curse, the corruption of the land!
OEDIPUS: You, shameless—
 aren't you appalled to start up such a story?
 You think you can get away with this?
TIRESIAS: I have already.
 The truth with all its power lives inside me.   405
OEDIPUS: Who primed you for this? Not your prophet's trade.
TIRESIAS: You did, you forced me, twisted it out of me.
OEDIPUS: What? Say it again—I'll understand it better.
TIRESIAS: Didn't you understand, just now?
 Or are you tempting me to talk?   410
OEDIPUS: No, I can't say I grasped your meaning.
 Out with it, again!
TIRESIAS: I say you are the murderer you hunt.
OEDIPUS: That obscenity, twice—by god, you'll pay.
TIRESIAS: Shall I say more, so you can really rage?   415
OEDIPUS: Much as you want. Your words are nothing—
 futile.
TIRESIAS: You cannot imagine . . . I tell you,
 you and your loved ones live together in infamy,
 you cannot see how far you've gone in guilt.
OEDIPUS: You think you can keep this up and never suffer? 420
TIRESIAS: Indeed, if the truth has any power.
OEDIPUS: It does
 but not for you, old man. You've lost your power,
 stone-blind, stone-deaf—senses, eyes blind as stone!
TIRESIAS: I pity you, flinging at me the very insults
 each man here will fling at you so soon.   425
OEDIPUS: Blind,
 lost in the night, endless night that nursed you!
 You can't hurt me or anyone else who sees the light—
 you can never touch me.
TIRESIAS: True, it is not your fate
 to fall at my hands. Apollo is quite enough,
 and he will take some pains to work this out.   430
OEDIPUS: Creon! Is this conspiracy his or yours?
TIRESIAS: Creon is not your downfall, no, you are your own.

OEDIPUS: O power—
      wealth and empire, skill outstripping skill
      in the heady rivalries of life,
      what envy lurks inside you! Just for this,   435
      the crown the city gave me—I never sought it,
      they laid it in my hands—for this alone, Creon,
      the soul of trust, my loyal friend from the start
      steals against me . . . so hungry to overthrow me
      he sets this wizard on me, this scheming quack,   440
      this fortune-teller peddling lies, eyes peeled
      for his own profit—seer blind in his craft!

      Come here, you pious fraud. Tell me,
      when did you ever prove yourself a prophet?
      When the Sphinx, that chanting Fury kept her deathwatch here,   445
      why silent then, not a word to set our people free?
      There was a riddle, not for some passer-by to solve—
      it cried out for a prophet. Where were you?
      Did you rise to the crisis? Not a word,
      you and your birds, your gods—nothing.   450
      No, but I came by, Oedipus the ignorant,
      I stopped the Sphinx! With no help from the birds,
      the flight of my own intelligence hit the mark.

      And this is the man you'd try to overthrow?
      You think you'll stand by Creon when he's king?   455
      You and the great mastermind—
      you'll pay in tears, I promise you, for this,
      this witch-hunt. If you didn't look so senile
      the lash would teach you what your scheming means!
LEADER: I'd suggest his words were spoken in anger,   460
      Oedipus . . . yours too, and it isn't what we need.
      The best solution to the oracle, the riddle
      posed by god—we should look for that.
TIRESIAS: You are the king no doubt, but in one respect,
      at least, I am your equal: the right to reply.   465
      I claim that privilege too.
      I am not your slave. I serve Apollo.
      I don't need Creon to speak for me in public.
                                                               So,
      you mock my blindness? Let me tell you this.
      You with your precious eyes,   470
      you're blind to the corruption of your life,
      to the house you live in, those you live with—

who *are* your parents? Do you know? All unknowing
you are the scourge of your own flesh and blood,
the dead below the earth and the living here above,   475
and the double lash of your mother and your father's curse
will whip you from this land one day, their footfall
treading you down in terror, darkness shrouding
your eyes that now can see the light!
                                        Soon, soon
you'll scream aloud—what haven won't reverberate?   480
What rock of Cithaeron won't scream back in echo?
That day you learn the truth about your marriage,
the wedding-march that sang you into your halls,
the lusty voyage home to the fatal harbor!
And a crowd of other horrors you'd never dream   485
will level you with yourself and all your children.

There. Now smear us with insults—Creon, myself
and every word I've said. No man will ever
be rooted from the earth as brutally as you.
OEDIPUS: Enough! Such filth from him? Insufferable—   490
    what, still alive? Get out—
    faster, back where you came from—vanish!
TIRESIAS: I'd never have come if you hadn't called me here.
OEDIPUS: If I thought you'd blurt out such absurdities,
    you'd have died waiting before I'd had you summoned.   495
TIRESIAS: Absurd, am I? To you, not to your parents:
    the ones who bore you found me sane enough.
OEDIPUS: Parents—who? Wait . . . who is my father?
TIRESIAS: This day will bring your birth and your destruction.
OEDIPUS: Riddles—all you can say are riddles, murk and darkness.   500
TIRESIAS: Ah, but aren't you the best man alive at solving riddles?
OEDIPUS: Mock me for that, go on, and you'll reveal my greatness.
TIRESIAS: Your great good fortune, true, it was your ruin.
OEDIPUS: Not if I saved the city—what do I care?
TIRESIAS: Well then, I'll be going.   505
    (To his ATTENDANT.*)*
                            Take me home, boy.
OEDIPUS: Yes, take him away. You're a nuisance here.
    Out of the way, the irritation's gone.
    (Turning his back on TIRESIAS, *moving toward the palace.)*
TIRESIAS: I will go,
    once I have said what I came here to say.
    I'll never shrink from the anger in your eyes—
    you can't destroy me. Listen to me closely: 510

the man you've sought so long, proclaiming,
cursing up and down, the murderer of Laius—
he is here. A stranger,
you may think, who lives among you,
he soon will be revealed a native Theban   515
but he will take no joy in the revelation.
Blind who now has eyes, beggar who now is rich,
he will grope his way toward a foreign soil,
a stick tapping before him step by step.
(OEDIPUS *enters the palace.*)
Revealed at last, brother and father both   520
to the children he embraces, to his mother
son and husband both—he sowed the loins
his father sowed, he spilled his father's blood!

Go in and reflect on that, solve that.
And if you find I've lied   525
from this day onward call the prophet blind.
(TIRESIAS *and the boy exit to the side.*)
CHORUS: Who—
who is the man the voice of god denounces
        resounding out of the rocky gorge of Delphi?
The horror too dark to tell,
whose ruthless bloody hands have done the work?   530
His time has come to fly
        to outrace the stallions of the storm
                        his feet a streak of speed—
Cased in armor, Apollo son of the Father
lunges on him, lightning-bolts afire!   535
And the grim unerring Furies
            closing for the kill.
                            Look,
the word of god has just come blazing
flashing off Parnassus' snowy heights!
        That man who left no trace—   540
after him, hunt him down with all our strength!
Now under bristling timber
        up through rocks and caves he stalks
                like the wild mountain bull—
cut off from men, each step an agony, frenzied, racing blind   545
but he cannot outrace the dread voices of Delphi
ringing out of the heart of Earth,
        the dark wings beating around him shrieking doom

the doom that never dies, the terror—

The skilled prophet scans the birds and shatters me with terror!   550
I can't accept him, can't deny him, don't know what to say,
I'm lost, and the wings of dark foreboding beating—
I cannot see what's come, what's still to come . . .
and what could breed a blood feud between
          Laius' house and the son of Polybus?   555
I know of nothing, not in the past and not now,
no charge to bring against our king, no cause
to attack his fame that rings throughout Thebes—
          not without proof—not for the ghost of Laius,
          not to avenge a murder gone without a trace.   560

Zeus and Apollo know, they know, the great masters
          of all the dark and depth of human life.
But whether a mere man can know the truth,
whether a seer can fathom more than I—
there is no test, no certain proof   565
          though matching skill for skill
a man can outstrip a rival. No, not till I see
these charges proved will I side with his accusers.
We saw him then, when the she-hawk swept against him,
saw with our own eyes his skill, his brilliant triumph—   570
          there was the test—he was the joy of Thebes!
          Never will I convict my king, never in my heart.
(Enter CREON *from the side.)*
CREON: My fellow-citizens, I hear King Oedipus
levels terrible charges at me. I had to come.
I resent it deeply. If, in the present crisis,   575
he thinks he suffers any abuse from me,
anything I've done or said that offers him
the slightest injury, why, I've no desire
to linger out this life, my reputation a shambles.
The damage I'd face from such an accusation   580
is nothing simple. No, there's nothing worse:
branded a traitor in the city, a traitor
to all of you and my good friends.
LEADER: True,
but a slur might have been forced out of him,
by anger perhaps, not any firm conviction.   585
CREON: The charge was made in public, wasn't it?
I put the prophet up to spreading lies?

LEADER: Such things were said...
    I don't know with what intent, if any.
CREON: Was his glance steady, his mind right   590
    when the charge was brought against me?
LEADER: I really couldn't say. I never look
    to judge the ones in power.
(*The doors open.* OEDIPUS *enters.*)
                                        Wait,
    here's Oedipus now.
OEDIPUS: You—here? You have the gall
    to show your face before the palace gates?   595
    You, plotting to kill me, kill the king—
    I see it all, the marauding thief himself
    scheming to steal my crown and power!
                                    Tell me,
    in god's name, what did you take me for,
    coward or fool, when you spun out your plot?   600
    Your treachery—you think I'd never detect it
    creeping against me in the dark? Or sensing it,
    not defend myself? Aren't you the fool,
    you and your high adventure. Lacking numbers,
    powerful friends, out for the big game of empire—   605
    you need riches, armies to bring that quarry down!
CREON: Are you quite finished? It's your turn to listen
    for just as long as you've... instructed me.
    Hear me out, then judge me on the facts.
OEDIPUS: You've a wicked way with words, Creon,   610
    but I'll be slow to learn—from you.
    I find you a menace, a great burden to me.
CREON: Just one thing, hear me out in this.
OEDIPUS: Just one thing,
    don't tell me you're not the enemy, the traitor.
CREON: Look, if you think crude, mindless stubbornness   615
    such a gift, you've lost your sense of balance.
OEDIPUS: If you think you can abuse a kinsman,
    then escape the penalty, you're insane.
CREON: Fair enough, I grant you. But this injury
    you say I've done you, what is it?   620
OEDIPUS: Did you induce me, yes or no,
    to send for that sanctimonious prophet?
CREON: I did. And I'd do the same again.
OEDIPUS: All right then, tell me, how long is it now
    since Laius...   625

CREON: Laius—what did *he* do?
OEDIPUS: Vanished,
   swept from sight, murdered in his tracks.
CREON: The count of the years would run you far back . . .
OEDIPUS: And that far back, was the prophet at his trade?
CREON: Skilled as he is today, and just as honored.
OEDIPUS: Did he ever refer to me then, at that time?   630
CREON: No,
   never, at least, when I was in his presence.
OEDIPUS: But you did investigate the murder, didn't you?
CREON: We did our best, of course, discovered nothing.
OEDIPUS: But the great seer never accused me then—why not?
CREON: I don't know. And when I don't, *I* keep quiet.   635
OEDIPUS: You do know this, you'd tell it too—
   if you had a shred of decency.
CREON: What?
   If I know, I won't hold back.
OEDIPUS: Simply this:
   If the two of you had never put heads together,
   we'd never have heard about *my* killing Laius.   640
CREON: if that's what he says . . . well, you know best.
   But now I have a right to learn from you
   as you just learned from me.
OEDIPUS: Learn your fill,
   you never will convict me of the murder.
CREON: Tell me, you're married to my sister, aren't you?   645
OEDIPUS: A genuine discovery—there's no denying that.
CREON: And you rule the land with her, with equal power?
OEDIPUS: She receives from me whatever she desires.
CREON: And I am the third, all of us are equals?
OEDIPUS: Yes, and it's there you show your stripes—   650
   you betray a kinsman.
CREON: Not at all.
   Not if you see things calmly, rationally,
   as I do. Look at it this way first:
   who in his right mind would rather rule
   and live in anxiety than sleep in peace?   655
   Particularly if he enjoys the same authority.
   Not I, I'm not the man to yearn for kingship,
   not with a king's power in my hands. Who would?
   No one with any sense of self-control.
   Now, as it is, you offer me all I need,   660
   not a fear in the world. But if I wore the crown . . .

there'd he many painful duties to perform,
hardly to my taste.
How could kingship
please me more than influence, power
without a qualm? I'm not that deluded yet,   665
to reach for anything but privilege outright,
profit free and clear.
Now all men sing my praises, all salute me,
now all who request your favors curry mine.
I'm their best hope: success rests in me.   670
Why give up that, I ask you, and borrow trouble?
A man of sense, someone who sees things clearly
would never resort to treason.
No, I've no lust for conspiracy in me,
nor could I ever suffer one who does.   675

Do you want proof? Go to Delphi yourself,
examine the oracle and see if I've reported
the message word-for-word. This too:
if you detect that I and the clairvoyant
have plotted anything in common, arrest me,   680
execute me. Not on the strength of one vote,
two in this case, mine as well as yours.
But don't convict me on sheer unverified surmise.

How wrong it is to take the good for bad,
purely at random, or take the bad for good.   685
But reject a friend, a kinsman? I would as soon
tear out the life within us, priceless life itself.
You'll learn this well, without fail, in time.
Time alone can bring the just man to light;
the criminal you can spot in one short day.   690
LEADER: Good advice,
my lord, for anyone who wants to avoid disaster.
Those who jump to conclusions may be wrong.
OEDIPUS: When my enemy moves against me quickly,
plots in secret, I move quickly too, I must,
I plot and pay him back. Relax my guard a moment,   695
waiting his next move—he wins his objective,
I lose mine.
CREON: What do you want?
You want me banished?
OEDIPUS: No, I want you dead.

CREON: Just to show how ugly a grudge can . . .

OEDIPUS: So,
    still stubborn? you don't think I'm serious?   700

CREON: I think you're insane.

OEDIPUS: Quite sane—in my behalf.

CREON: Not just as much in mine?

OEDIPUS: You—my mortal enemy?

CREON: What if you're wholly wrong?

OEDIPUS: No matter—I must rule.

CREON: Not if you rule unjustly.

OEDIPUS: Hear him, Thebes, my city!

CREON: My city too, not yours alone!   705

LEADER: Please, my lords.

    (*Enter* JOCASTA *from the palace.*)

                    Look, Jocasta's coming,
    and just in time too. With her help
    you must put this fighting of yours to rest.

JOCASTA: Have you no sense? Poor misguided men,
    such shouting—why this public outburst?   710
    Aren't you ashamed, with the land so sick,
    to stir up private quarrels?
    (*To* OEDIPUS)
    Into the palace now. And Creon, you go home.
    Why make such a furor over nothing?

CREON: My sister, it's dreadful . . . Oedipus, your husband,   715
    he's bent on a choice of punishments for me,
    banishment from the fatherland or death.

OEDIPUS: Precisely. I caught him in the act, Jocasta,
    plotting, about to stab me in the back.

CREON: Never—curse me, let me die and be damned   720
    if I've done you any wrong you charge me with.

JOCASTA: Oh god, believe it, Oedipus,
    honor the solemn oath he swears to heaven.
    Do it for me, for the sake of all your people.
(*The* CHORUS *begins to chant.*)

CHORUS: Believe it, be sensible   725
            give way, my king, I beg you!

OEDIPUS: What do you want from me, concessions?

CHORUS: Respect him—he's been no fool in the past
    and now he's strong with the oath he swears to god.

OEDIPUS: You know what you're asking?   730

CHORUS: I do.

OEDIPUS: Then out with it!

CHORUS: The man's your friend, your kin, he's under oath—
    don't cast him out, disgraced
    branded with guilt on the strength of hearsay only.
OEDIPUS: Know full well, if that's what you want
    you want me dead or banished from the land.   735
CHORUS: Never—
    no, by the blazing Sun, first god of the heavens!
        Stripped of the gods, stripped of loved ones,
    let me die by inches if that ever crossed my mind.
    But the heart inside me sickens, dies as the land dies
    and now on top of the old griefs you pile this,   740
    your fury—both of you!
OEDIPUS: Then let him go,
    even if it does lead to my ruin, my death
    or my disgrace, driven from Thebes for life.
    It's you, not him I pity—your words move me.
    He, wherever he goes, my hate goes with him.   745
CREON: Look at you, sullen in yielding, brutal in your rage—
    you'll go too far. It's perfect justice:
    natures like yours are hardest on themselves.
OEDIPUS: Then leave me alone—get out!
CREON: I'm going.
    You're wrong, so wrong. These men know I'm right.   750
(*Exit to the side. The* CHORUS *turns to* JOCASTA.)
CHORUS: Why do you hesitate, my lady
            why not help him in?
JOCASTA: Tell me what's happened first.
CHORUS: Loose, ignorant talk started dark suspicions
    and a sense of injustice cut deeply too.   755
JOCASTA: On both sides?
CHORUS: Oh yes.
JOCASTA: What did they say?
CHORUS: Enough, please, enough! The land's so racked already
    or so it seems to me . . .
    End the trouble here, just where they left it.
OEDIPUS: You see what comes of your good intentions now?   760
    And all because you tried to blunt my anger.
CHORUS: My king,
    I've said it once, I'll say it time and again—
        I'd be insane, you know it,
    senseless, ever to turn my back on you.
    You who set our beloved land—storm-tossed, shattered—   765
    straight on course. Now again, good helmsman,

steer us through the storm!
(The CHORUS *draws away, leaving* OEDIPUS *and* JOCASTA *side by side.)*

JOCASTA: For the love of god,
    Oedipus, tell me too, what is it?
    Why this rage? You're so unbending.

OEDIPUS: I will tell you. I respect you, Jocasta,   770
    much more than these . . .
    (Glancing at the CHORUS.*)*
    Creon's to blame, Creon schemes against me.

JOCASTA: Tell me clearly, how did the quarrel start?

OEDIPUS: He says I murdered Laius—I am guilty.

JOCASTA: How does he know? Some secret knowledge   775
    or simple hearsay?

OEDIPUS: Oh, he sent his prophet in
    to do his dirty work. You know Creon,
    Creon keeps his own lips clean.

JOCASTA: A prophet?
    Well then, free yourself of every charge!
    Listen to me and learn some peace of mind: 780
    no skill in the world,
    nothing human can penetrate the future.
    Here is proof, quick and to the point.
    An oracle came to Laius one fine day
    (I won't say from Apollo himself   785
    but his underlings, his priests) and it said
    that doom would strike him down at the hands of a son,
    our son, to be born of our own flesh and blood. But Laius,
    so the report goes at least, was killed by strangers,
    thieves, at a place where three roads meet . . . my son—   790
    he wasn't three days old and the boy's father
    fastened his ankles, had a henchman fling him away
    on a barren, trackless mountain.
                    There, you see?
    Apollo brought neither thing to pass. My baby
    no more murdered his father than Laius suffered—   795
    his wildest fear—death at his own son's hands.
    That's how the seers and their revelations
    mapped out the future. Brush them from your mind.
    Whatever the god needs and seeks
    he'll bring to light himself, with ease.   800

OEDIPUS: Strange,
    hearing you just now . . . my mind wandered,
    my thoughts racing back and forth.

JOCASTA: What do you mean? Why so anxious, startled?

OEDIPUS: I thought I heard you say that Laius
  was cut down at a place where three roads meet. 805

JOCASTA: That was the story. It hasn't died out yet.

OEDIPUS: Where did this thing happen? Be precise.

JOCASTA: A place called Phocis, where two branching roads,
  one from Daulia, one from Delphi,
  come together—a crossroads. 810

OEDIPUS: When? How long ago?

JOCASTA: The heralds no sooner reported Laius dead
  than you appeared and they hailed you king of Thebes.

OEDIPUS: My god, my god—what have you planned to do to me?

JOCASTA: What, Oedipus? What haunts you so? 815

OEDIPUS: Not yet.
  Laius—how did he look? Describe him.
  Had he reached his prime?

JOCASTA: He was swarthy,
  and the gray had just begun to streak his temples,
  and his build . . . wasn't far from yours.

OEDIPUS: Oh no no,
  I think I've just called down a dreadful curse 820
  upon myself—I simply didn't know!

JOCASTA: What are you saying? I shudder to look at you.

OEDIPUS: I have a terrible fear the blind seer can see.
  I'll know in a moment. One thing more—

JOCASTA: Anything,
  afraid as I am—ask, I'll answer, all I can. 825

OEDIPUS: Did he go with a light or heavy escort,
  several men-at-arms, like a lord, a king?

JOCASTA: There were five in the party, a herald among them,
  and a single wagon carrying Laius.

OEDIPUS: Ai—
  now I can see it all, clear as day. 830
  Who told you all this at the time, Jocasta?

JOCASTA: A servant who reached home, the lone survivor.

OEDIPUS: So, could he still be in the palace—even now?

JOCASTA: No indeed. Soon as he returned from the scene
  and saw you on the throne with Laius dead and gone, 835
  he knelt and clutched my hand, pleading with me
  to send him into the hinterlands, to pasture,
  far as possible, out of sight of Thebes.
  I sent him away. Slave though he was,
  he'd earned that favor—and much more. 840

OEDIPUS: Can we bring him back, quickly?
JOCASTA: Easily. Why do you want him so?
OEDIPUS: I'm afraid,
    Jocasta, I have said too much already.
    That man—I've got to see him.
JOCASTA: Then he'll come.
    But even I have a right, I'd like to think,   845
    to know what's torturing you, my lord.
OEDIPUS: And so you shall—I can hold nothing back from you,
    now I've reached this pitch of dark foreboding.
    Who means more to me than you? Tell me,
    whom would I turn toward but you   850
    as I go through all this?

    My father was Polybus, king of Corinth.
    My mother, a Dorian, Merope. And I was held
    the prince of the realm among the people there,
    till something struck me out of nowhere,   855
    something strange . . . worth remarking perhaps,
    hardly worth the anxiety I gave it.
    Some man at a banquet who had drunk too much
    shouted out—he was far gone, mind you—
    that I am not my father's son. Fighting words!   860
    I barely restrained myself that day
    but early the next I went to mother and father,
    questioned them closely, and they were enraged
    at the accusation and the fool who let it fly.
    So as for my parents I was satisfied,   865
    but still this thing kept gnawing at me,
    the slander spread—I had to make my move.
                                And so,
    unknown to mother and father I set out for Delphi,
    and the god Apollo spurned me, sent me away
    denied the facts I came for,   870
    but first he flashed before my eyes a future
    great with pain, terror, disaster—I can hear him cry,
    "You are fated to couple with your mother, you will bring
    a breed of children into the light no man can bear to see—
    you will kill your father, the one who gave you life!"   875
    I heard all that and ran. I abandoned Corinth,
    from that day on I gauged its landfall only
    by the stars, running, always running
    toward some place where I would never see

the shame of all those oracles come true.   880
And as I fled I reached that very spot
where the great king, you say, met his death.
Now, Jocasta, I will tell you all.
Making my way toward this triple crossroad
I began to see a herald, then a brace of colts   885
drawing a wagon, and mounted on the bench . . . a man,
just as you've described him, coming face-to-face,
and the one in the lead and the old man himself
were about to thrust me off the road—brute force—
and the one shouldering me aside, the driver,   890
I strike him in anger!—and the old man, watching me
coming up along his wheels—he brings down
his prod, two prongs straight at my head!
I paid him back with interest!
Short work, by god—with one blow of the staff   895
in this right hand I knock him out of his high seat,
roll him out of the wagon, sprawling headlong—
I killed them all—every mother's son!

Oh, but if there is any blood-tie
between Laius and this stranger . . .   900
what man alive more miserable than I?
More hated by the gods? *I* am the man
no alien, no citizen welcomes to his house,
law forbids it—not a word to me in public,
driven out of every hearth and home.   905
And all these curses I—no one but I
brought down these piling curses on myself!
And you, his wife, I've touched your body with these,
the hands that killed your husband cover you with blood.

Wasn't I born for torment? Look me in the eyes!   910
I am abomination—heart and soul!
I must be exiled, and even in exile
never see my parents, never set foot
on native earth again. Else I'm doomed
to couple with my mother and cut my father down . . .   915
Polybus who reared me, gave me life.
                              But why, why?
Wouldn't a man of judgment say—and wouldn't he be right—
some savage power has brought this down upon my head?
Oh no, not that, you pure and awesome gods,
never let me see that day! Let me slip   920

from the world of men, vanish without a trace
before I see myself stained with such corruption,
stained to the heart.
LEADER: My lord, you fill our hearts with fear.
But at least until you question the witness,   925
do take hope.
OEDIPUS: Exactly. He is my last hope—
I'm waiting for the shepherd. He is crucial.
JOCASTA: And once he appears, what then? Why so urgent?
OEDIPUS: I'll tell you. If it turns out that his story
matches yours, I've escaped the worst.   930
JOCASTA: What did I say? What struck you so?
OEDIPUS: You said *thieves*—
he told you a whole band of them murdered Laius.
So, if he still holds to the same number,
I cannot be the killer. One can't equal many.
But if he refers to one man, one alone,   935
clearly the scales come down on me:
I am guilty.
JOCASTA: Impossible. Trust me,
I told you precisely what he said,
and he can't retract it now;
the whole city heard it, not just I.   940
And even if he should vary his first report
by one man more or less, still, my lord,
he could never make the murder of Laius
truly fit the prophecy. Apollo was explicit:
my son was doomed to kill my husband . . . my son,   945
poor defenseless thing, he never had a chance
to kill his father. They destroyed him first.

So much for prophecy. It's neither here nor there.
From this day on, I wouldn't look right or left.
OEDIPUS: True, true. Still, that shepherd,   950
someone fetch him—now!
JOCASTA: I'll send at once. But do let's go inside.
I'd never displease you, least of all in this.
(OEDIPUS *and* JOCASTA *enter the palace.*)
CHORUS: Destiny guide me always
Destiny find me filled with reverence   955
          pure in word and deed.
Great laws tower above us, reared on high
born for the brilliant vault of heaven—
          Olympian sky their only father,

nothing mortal, no man gave them birth,   960
their memory deathless, never lost in sleep:
within them lives a mighty god, the god does not grow old.

Pride breeds the tyrant
violent pride, gorging, crammed to bursting
    with all that is overripe and rich with ruin—   965
clawing up to the heights, headlong pride
crashes down the abyss—sheer doom!
    No footing helps, all foothold lost and gone,
But the healthy strife that makes the city strong
I pray that god will never end that wrestling: 970
god, my champion, I will never let you go.

But if any man comes striding, high and mighty
    in all he says and does,
no fear of justice, no reverence
for the temples of the gods—   975
    let a rough doom tear him down,
repay his pride, breakneck, ruinous pride!
If he cannot reap his profits fairly
    cannot restrain himself from outrage—
mad, laying hands on the holy things untouchable!   980

Can such a man, so desperate, still boast
    he can save his life from the flashing bolts of god?
      If all such violence goes with honor now
        why join the sacred dance?

Never again will I go reverent to Delphi,   985
    the inviolate heart of Earth
or Apollo's ancient oracle at Abae
or Olympia of the fires—
    unless these prophecies all come true
for all mankind to point toward in wonder.   990
King of kings, if you deserve your titles
    Zeus, remember, never forget!
You and your deathless, everlasting reign.

    They are dying, the old oracles sent to Laius,
    now our masters strike them off the rolls.   995
      Nowhere Apollo's golden glory now—
        the gods, the gods go down.
(Enter JOCASTA *from the palace, carrying a suppliant's branch wound in wool.)*

JOCASTA: Lords of the realm, it occurred to me,
just now, to visit the temples of the gods,
so I have my branch in hand and incense too. 1000

Oedipus is beside himself. Racked with anguish,
no longer a man of sense, he won't admit
the latest prophecies are hollow as the old—
he's at the mercy of every passing voice
if the voice tells of terror. 1005
I urge him gently, nothing seems to help,
so I turn to you, Apollo, you are nearest.
(*Placing her branch on the altar, while an old herdsman enters from the
side, not the one just summoned by the king but an unexpected* MESSENGER
from Corinth.)
I come with prayers and offerings . . . I beg you,
cleanse us, set us free of defilement!
Look at us, passengers in the grip of fear, 1010
watching the pilot of the vessel go to pieces.

MESSENGER (*Approaching* JOCASTA *and the* CHORUS.):
Strangers, please, I wonder if you could lead us
to the palace of the king . . . I think it's Oedipus.
Better, the man himself—you know where he is?

LEADER: This is his palace, stranger. He's inside. 1015
But here is his queen, his wife and mother
of his children.

MESSENGER: Blessings on you, noble queen,
queen of Oedipus crowned with all your family—
blessings on you always!

JOCASTA: And the same to you, stranger, you deserve it . . . 1020
such a greeting. But what have you come for?
Have you brought us news?

MESSENGER: Wonderful news—
for the house, my lady, for your husband too.

JOCASTA: Really, what? Who sent you?

MESSENGER: Corinth.
I'll give you the message in a moment. 1025
You'll be glad of it—how could you help it?—
though it costs a little sorrow in the bargain.

JOCASTA: What can it be, with such a double edge?

MESSENGER: The people there, they want to make your Oedipus
king of Corinth, so they're saying now. 1030

JOCASTA: Why? Isn't old Polybus still in power?

MESSENGER: No more. Death has got him in the tomb.

JOCASTA: What are you saying? Polybus, dead?—dead?

MESSENGER: If not,
    if I'm not telling the truth, strike me dead too.
JOCASTA *(To a* SERVANT.*)*:
    Quickly, go to your master, tell him this!   1035

    You prophecies of the gods, where are you now?
    This is the man that Oedipus feared for years,
    he fled him, not to kill him—and now he's dead,
    quite by chance, a normal, natural death,
    not murdered by his son.   1040
OEDIPUS *(Emerging from the palace.)*:
                         Dearest,
    what now? Why call me from the palace?
JOCASTA *(Bringing the* MESSENGER *closer.)*:
    Listen to *him*, see for yourself what all
    those awful prophecies of god have come to.
OEDIPUS: And who is he? What can he have for me?
JOCASTA: He's from Corinth, he's come to tell you   1045
    your father is no more—Polybus—he's dead!
OEDIPUS *(Wheeling on the* MESSENGER.*)*:
    What? Let me have it from your lips.
MESSENGER: Well,
    if that's what you want first, then here it is:
    make no mistake, Polybus is dead and gone.
OEDIPUS: How—murder? sickness?—what? what killed him?   1050
MESSENGER: A light tip of the scales can put old bones to rest.
OEDIPUS: Sickness then—poor man, it wore him down.
MESSENGER: That,
    and the long count of years he'd measured out.
OEDIPUS: So!
    Jocasta, why, why look to the Prophet's hearth,
    the fires of the future? Why scan the birds   1055
    that scream above our heads? They winged me on
    to the murder of my father, did they? That was my doom?
    Well look, he's dead and buried, hidden under the earth,
    and here I am in Thebes, I never put hand to sword—
    unless some longing for me wasted him away,   1060
    then in a sense you'd say I caused his death.
    But now, all those prophecies I feared—Polybus
    packs them off to sleep with him in hell!
    They're nothing, worthless.
JOCASTA: There.
    Didn't I tell you from the start?   1065
OEDIPUS: So you did. I was lost in fear.

JOCASTA: No more, sweep it from your mind forever.

OEDIPUS: But my mother's bed, surely I must fear—

JOCASTA: Fear?
     What should a man fear? It's all chance,
     chance rules our lives. Not a man on earth   1070
     can see a day ahead, groping through the dark.
     Better to live at random, best we can.
     And as for this marriage with your mother—
     have no fear. Many a man before you,
     in his dreams, has shared his mother's bed.   1075
     Take such things for shadows, nothing at all—
     Live, Oedipus,
     as if there's no tomorrow!

OEDIPUS: Brave words,
     and you'd persuade me if mother weren't alive.
     But mother lives, so for all your reassurances   1080
     I live in fear, I must.

JOCASTA: But your father's death,
     that, at least, is a great blessing, joy to the eyes!

OEDIPUS: Great, I know . . . but I fear *her*—she's still alive.

MESSENGER: Wait, who is this woman, makes you so afraid?

OEDIPUS: Merope, old man. The wife of Polybus.   1085

MESSENGER: The queen? What's there to fear in her?

OEDIPUS: A dreadful prophecy, stranger, sent by the gods.

MESSENGER: Tell me, could you? Unless it's forbidden
     other ears to hear.

OEDIPUS: Not at all.
     Apollo told me once—it is my fate—   1090
     I must make love with my own mother,
     shed my father's blood with my own hands.
     So for years I've given Corinth a wide berth,
     and it's been my good fortune too. But still,
     to see one's parents and look into their eyes   1095
     is the greatest joy I know.

MESSENGER: You're afraid of that?
     That kept you out of Corinth?

OEDIPUS: My *father*, old man—
     so I wouldn't kill my father.

MESSENGER: So that's it.
     Well then, seeing I came with such good will, my king,
     why don't I rid you of that old worry now?   1100

OEDIPUS: What a rich reward you'd have for that.

MESSENGER: What do you think I came for, majesty?
     So you'd come home and I'd be better off.

OEDIPUS: Never, I will never go near my parents.

MESSENGER: My boy, it's clear, you don't know what you're doing. 1105

OEDIPUS: What do you mean, old man? For god's sake, explain.

MESSENGER: If you ran from *them*, always dodging home . . .

OEDIPUS: Always, terrified Apollo's oracle might come true—

MESSENGER: And you'd be covered with guilt, from both your parents.

OEDIPUS: That's right, old man, that fear is always with me. 1110

MESSENGER: Don't you know? You've really nothing to fear.

OEDIPUS: But why? If I'm their son—Merope, Polybus?

MESSENGER: Polybus was nothing to you, that's why, not in blood.

OEDIPUS: What are you saying—Polybus was not my father?

MESSENGER: No more than I am. He and I are equals. 1115

OEDIPUS: My father—
  how can my father equal nothing? You're nothing to me!

MESSENGER: Neither was he, no more your father than I am.

OEDIPUS: Then why did he call me his son?

MESSENGER: You were a gift,
  years ago—know for a fact he took you
  from my hands. 1120

OEDIPUS: No, from another's hands?
  Then how could he love me so? He loved me, deeply . . .

MESSENGER: True, and his early years without a child
  made him love you all the more.

OEDIPUS: And you, did you . . .
  buy me? find me by accident?

MESSENGER: I stumbled on you,
  down the woody flanks of Mount Cithaeron. 1125

OEDIPUS: So close,
  what were you doing here, just passing through?

MESSENGER: Watching over my flocks, grazing them on the slopes.

OEDIPUS: A herdsman, were you? A vagabond, scraping for wages?

MESSENGER: Your savior too, my son, in your worst hour.

OEDIPUS: Oh—
  when you picked me up, was I in pain? What exactly? 1130

MESSENGER: Your ankles . . . they tell the story. Look at them.

OEDIPUS: Why remind me of that, that old affliction?

MESSENGER: Your ankles were pinned together; I set you free.

OEDIPUS: That dreadful mark—I've had it from the cradle.

MESSENGER: And you got your name from that misfortune too, 1135
  the name's still with you.

OEDIPUS: Dear god, who did it?—
  mother? father? Tell me.

MESSENGER: I don't know.

The one who gave you to me, he'd know more.
OEDIPUS: What? You took me from someone else?
You didn't find me yourself? 1140
MESSENGER: No sir,
another shepherd passed you on to me.
OEDIPUS: Who? Do you know? Describe him.
MESSENGER: He called himself a servant of . . .
if I remember rightly—Laius.
(JOCASTA *turns sharply*.)
OEDIPUS: The king of the land who ruled here long ago? 1145
MESSENGER: That's the one. That herdsman was *his* man.
OEDIPUS: Is he still alive? Can I see him?
MESSENGER: They'd know best, the people of these parts.
(OEDIPUS *and the* MESSENGER *turn to the* CHORUS.)
OEDIPUS: Does anyone know that herdsman,
the one he mentioned? Anyone seen him 1150
in the fields, in town? Out with it!
The time has come to reveal this once for all.
LEADER: I think he's the very shepherd you wanted to see,
a moment ago. But the queen, Jocasta,
she's the one to say. 1155
OEDIPUS: Jocasta,
you remember the man we just sent for?
Is *that* the one he means?
JOCASTA: That man . . .
why ask? Old shepherd, talk, empty nonsense,
don't give it another thought, don't even think—
OEDIPUS: What—give up now, with a clue like this? 1160
Fail to solve the mystery of my birth?
Not for all the world!
JOCASTA: Stop—in the name of god,
if you love your own life, call off this search!
My suffering is enough.
OEDIPUS: Courage!
Even if my mother turns out to be a slave, 1165
and I a slave, three generations back,
you would not seem common.
JOCASTA: Oh no,
listen to me, I beg you, don't do this.
OEDIPUS: Listen to you? No more, I must know it all,
see the truth at last. 1170
JOCASTA: No, please—
for your sake—I want the best for you!

OEDIPUS: Your best is more than I can bear.

JOCASTA: You're doomed—
     may you never fathom who you are!

OEDIPUS *(To a servant.)*
     Hurry, fetch me the herdsman, now!
     Leave her to glory in her royal birth.   1175

JOCASTA: Aieeeeee—
                         man of agony—
     that is the only name I have for you,
     that, no other—ever, ever, ever!

(Flinging [herself] through the palace doors, A long, tense silence follows.)

LEADER: Where's she gone, Oedipus?
     Rushing off, such wild grief...   1180
     I'm afraid that from this silence
     something monstrous may come bursting forth.

OEDIPUS: Let it burst! Whatever will, whatever must!
     I must know my birth, no matter how common
     it may be—must see my origins face-to-face.   1185
     She perhaps, she with her woman's pride
     may well be mortified by my birth,
     but I, I count myself the son of Chance,
     the great goddess, giver of all good things—
     I'll never see myself disgraced. She is my mother!   1190
     And the moons have marked me out, my blood-brothers,
     one moon on the wane, the next moon great with power.
     That is my blood, my nature—I will never betray it,
     never fail to search and learn my birth!

CHORUS: Yes—if I am a true prophet   1195
                    if I can grasp the truth,
             by the boundless skies of Olympus,
     at the full moon of tomorrow, Mount Cithaeron
     you will know how Oedipus glories in you—
     you, his birthplace, nurse, his mountain-mother!   1200
     And we will sing you, dancing out your praise—
     you lift our monarch's heart!
          Apollo, Apollo, god of the wild cry
                    may our dancing please you!
                                           Oedipus—
                    son, dear child, who bore you?   1205
     Who of the nymphs who seem to live forever
     mated with Pan, the mountain-striding Father?
     Who was your mother? who, some bride of Apollo
     the god who loves the pastures spreading toward the sun?

Or was it Hermes, king of the lightning ridges?   1210
Or Dionysus, lord of frenzy, lord of the barren peaks—
did he seize you in his hands, dearest of all his lucky finds?—
    found by the nymphs, their warm eyes dancing, gift
to the lord who loves them dancing out his joy!
(OEDIPUS *strains to see a figure coming from the distance. Attended by palace*
guards, an old SHEPHERD *enters slowly, reluctant to approach the king.*)
OEDIPUS: I never met the man, my friends . . . still,   1215
    if I had to guess, I'd say that's the shepherd,
    the very one we've looked for all along.
    Brothers in old age, two of a kind,
    he and our guest here. At any rate
    the ones who bring him in are my own men,   1220
    I recognize them,
    (*Turning to the* LEADER.)
                    But you know more than I,
    you should, you've seen the man before.
LEADER: I know him, definitely. One of Laius' men,
    a trusty shepherd, if there ever was one.
OEDIPUS: You, I ask you first, stranger,   1225
    you from Corinth—is this the one you mean?
MESSENGER: You're looking at him. He's your man.
OEDIPUS (*To the* SHEPHERD.):
    You, old man, come over here—
    look at me. Answer all my questions.
    Did you ever serve King Laius?   1230
SHEPHERD: So I did . . .
    a slave, not bought on the block though,
    born and reared in the palace.
OEDIPUS: Your duties, your kind of work?
SHEPHERD: Herding the flocks, the better part of my life.
OEDIPUS: Where, mostly? Where did you do your grazing?   1235
SHEPHERD: Well,
    Cithaeron sometimes, or the foothills round about.
OEDIPUS: This man—you know him? ever see him there?
SHEPHERD (*Confused, glancing from the* MESSENGER *to the King.*):
    Doing what—what man do you mean?
OEDIPUS (*Pointing to the* MESSENGER.):
    This one here—ever have dealings with him?
SHEPHERD: Not so I could say, but give me a chance,   1240
    my memory's bad . . .
MESSENGER: No wonder he doesn't know me, master.
    But let me refresh his memory for him.

I'm sure he recalls old times we had
on the slopes of Mount Cithaeron;   1245
he and I, grazing our flocks, he with two
and I with one—we both struck up together,
three whole seasons, six months at a stretch
from spring to the rising of Arcturus in the fall,
then with winter coming on I'd drive my herds   1250
to my own pens, and back he'd go with his
to Laius' folds.
(*To the* SHEPHERD.)
              Now that's how it was,
wasn't it—yes or no?
SHEPHERD: Yes, I suppose . . .
it's all so long ago.
MESSENGER: Come, tell me,
you gave me a child back then, a boy, remember?   1255
A little fellow to rear, my very own.
SHEPHERD: What? Why rake up that again?
MESSENGER: Look, here he is, my fine old friend—
the same man who was just a baby then.
SHEPHERD: Damn you, shut your mouth—quiet!   1260
OEDIPUS: Don't lash out at him, old man—
you need lashing more than he does.
SHEPHERD: Why,
master, majesty—what have I done wrong?
OEDIPUS: You won't answer his question about the boy.
SHEPHERD: He's talking nonsense, wasting his breath.   1265
OEDIPUS: So, you won't talk willingly—
then you'll talk with pain.
(*The guards seize the* SHEPHERD.)
SHEPHERD: No, dear god, don't torture an old man!
OEDIPUS: Twist his arms back, quickly!
SHEPHERD: God help us, why?—
what more do you need to know?   1270
OEDIPUS: Did you give him that child? He's asking.
SHEPHERD: I did . . . I wish to god I'd died that day.
OEDIPUS: You've got your wish if you don't tell the truth.
SHEPHERD: The more I tell, the worse the death I'll die.
OEDIPUS: Our friend here wants to stretch things out, does he?   1275
(*Motioning to his men for torture.*)
SHEPHERD: No, no, I gave it to him—I just said so.
OEDIPUS: Where did you get it? Your house? Someone else's?
SHEPHERD: It wasn't mine, no, I got it from . . . someone.

OEDIPUS: Which one of them?
(*Looking at the citizens.*)
Whose house?
SHEPHERD: No—
god's sake, master, no more questions!   1280
OEDIPUS: You're a dead man if I have to ask again.
SHEPHERD: Then—the child came from the house . . .
of Laius.
OEDIPUS: A slave? or born of his own blood?
SHEPHERD: Oh no,
I'm right at the edge, the horrible truth—I've got to say it!
OEDIPUS: And I'm at the edge of hearing horrors, yes, but I must hear! 1285
SHEPHERD: All right! His son, they said it was—his son!
But the one inside, your wife,
she'd tell it best.
OEDIPUS: My wife—
she gave it to you?   1290
SHEPHERD: Yes, yes, my king.
OEDIPUS: Why, what for?
SHEPHERD: To kill it.
OEDIPUS: Her own child,
how could she?   1295
SHEPHERD: She was afraid—
frightening prophecies.
OEDIPUS: What?
SHEPHERD: They said—
he'd kill his parents.
OEDIPUS: But you gave him to this old man—why?   1300
SHEPHERD: I pitied the little baby, master,
hoped he'd take him off to his own country,
far away, but he saved him for this, this fate.
If you are the man he says you are, believe me,
you were born for pain.   1305
OEDIPUS: O god—
all come true, all burst to light!
O light—now let me look my last on you!
I stand revealed at last—
cursed in my birth, cursed in marriage,
cursed in the lives I cut down with these hands!   1310
(*Rushing through the doors with a great cry. The Corinthian* MESSENGER,
the SHEPHERD, *and attendants exit slowly to the side.*)
CHORUS: O the generations of men
the dying generations—adding the total

of all your lives I find they come to nothing...
                    does there exist, is there a man on earth
who seizes more joy than just a dream, a vision?   1315
And the vision no sooner dawns than dies
blazing into oblivion.

You are my great example, you, your life,
your destiny, Oedipus, man of misery—
I count no man blest.   1320
                    You outranged all men!
            Bending your bow to the breaking-point
you captured priceless glory, O dear god,
and the Sphinx came crashing down,
                    the virgin, claws hooked
like a bird of omen singing, shrieking death—   1325
like a fortress reared in the face of death
you rose and saved our land.

From that day on we called you king
we crowned you with honors, Oedipus, towering over all—
mighty king of the seven gates of Thebes.   1330

But now to hear your story—is there a man more agonized?
More wed to pain and frenzy? Not a man on earth,
the joy of your life ground down to nothing
O Oedipus, name for the ages—
            one and the same wide harbor served you   1335
                    son and father both
son and father came to rest in the same bridal chamber.
How, how could the furrows your father plowed
bear you, your agony, harrowing on
in silence O so long?   1340

                    But now for all your power
Time, all-seeing Time has dragged you to the light,
judged your marriage monstrous from the start—
the son and the father tangling, both one—
O child of Laius, would to god
        I'd never seen you, never never!   1345
            Now I weep like a man who wails the dead
and the dirge comes pouring forth with all my heart!
I tell you the truth, you gave me life
my breath leapt up in you

and now you bring down night upon my eyes.   1350
(*Enter a* MESSENGER *from the palace.*)
MESSENGER: Men of Thebes, always the first in honor,
     what horrors you will hear, what you will see,
     what a heavy weight of sorrow you will shoulder . . .
     if you are true to your birth, if you still have
     some feeling for the royal house of Thebes.   1355
     I tell you neither the waters of the Danube
     nor the Nile can wash this palace clean.
     Such things it hides, it soon will bring to light—
     terrible things, and none done blindly now,
     all done with a will. The pains   1360
     we inflict upon ourselves hurt most of all.
LEADER: God knows we have pains enough already.
     What can you add to them?
MESSENGER: The queen is dead.
LEADER: Poor lady—how?
MESSENGER: By her own hand. But you are spared the worst,   1365
     you never had to watch . . . I saw it all,
     and with all the memory that's in me
     you will learn what that poor woman suffered.

     Once she'd broken in through the gates,
     dashing past us, frantic, whipped to fury,   1370
     ripping her hair out with both hands—
     straight to her rooms she rushed, flinging herself
     across the bridal-bed, doors slamming behind her—
     once inside, she wailed for Laius, dead so long,
     remembering how she bore his child long ago,   1375
     the life that rose up to destroy him, leaving
     its mother to mother living creatures
     with the very son she'd borne.
     Oh how she wept, mourning the marriage-bed
     where she let loose that double brood—monsters—   1380
     husband by her husband, children by her child.
                                             And then—
     but how she died is more than I can say. Suddenly
     Oedipus burst in, screaming, he stunned us so
     we couldn't watch her agony to the end,
     our eyes were fixed on him. Circling   1385
     like a maddened beast, stalking, here, there
     crying out to us—
                       Give him a sword! His wife,

no wife, his mother, where can he find the mother earth
that cropped two crops at once, himself and all his children?
He was raging—one of the dark powers pointing the way,   1390
none of us mortals crowding around him, no,
with a great shattering cry—someone, something leading him on—
he hurled at the twin doors and bending the bolts back
out of their sockets, crashed through the chamber.
And there we saw the woman hanging by the neck,   1395
cradled high in a woven noose, spinning,
swinging back and forth. And when he saw her,
giving a low, wrenching sob that broke our hearts,
slipping the halter from her throat, he eased her down,
in a slow embrace he laid her down, poor thing . . .   1400
then, what came next, what horror we beheld!

He rips off her brooches, the long gold pins
holding her robes—and lifting them high,
looking straight up into the points,
he digs them down the sockets of his eyes, crying, "You,   1405
you'll see no more the pain I suffered, all the pain I caused!
Too long you looked on the ones you never should have seen,
blind to the ones you longed to see, to know! Blind
from this hour on! Blind in the darkness—blind!"
His voice like a dirge, rising, over and over   1410
raising the pins, raking them down his eyes.
And at each stroke blood spurts from the roots,
splashing his beard, a swirl of it, nerves and clots—
black hail of blood pulsing, gushing down.

These are the griefs that burst upon them both,   1415
coupling man and woman. The joy they had so lately,
the fortune of their old ancestral house
was deep joy indeed. Now, in this one day,
wailing, madness and doom, death, disgrace,
all the griefs in the world that you can name,   1420
all are theirs forever.
LEADER: Oh poor man, the misery—
has he any rest from pain now?
(*A voice within, in torment.*)
MESSENGER: He's shouting,
"Loose the bolts, someone, show me to all of Thebes!
My father's murderer, my mother's—"
No, I can't repeat it, it's unholy.   1425

Now he'll tear himself from his native earth,
not linger, curse the house with his own curse.
But he needs strength, and a guide to lead him on.
This is sickness more than he can bear.
(*The palace doors open.*)
                         Look,
he'll show you himself. The great doors are opening—   1430
you are about to see a sight, a horror
even his mortal enemy would pity.
(*Enter* OEDIPUS, *blinded, led by a boy. He stands at the palace steps,
as if surveying his people once again.*)
CHORUS: O the terror—
the suffering, for all the world to see,
the worst terror that ever met my eyes.
What madness swept over you? What god,   1435
what dark power leapt beyond all bounds,
beyond belief, to crush your wretched life?—
godforsaken, cursed by the gods!
I pity you but I can't bear to look.
I've much to ask, so much to learn,   1440
so much fascinates my eyes,
but you . . . I shudder at the sight.
OEDIPUS: Oh, Ohhh—
the agony! I am agony—
where am I going? where on earth?
        where does all this agony hurl me?   1445
where's my voice?—
        winging, swept away on a dark tide—
My destiny, my dark power, what a leap you made!
CHORUS: To the depths of terror, too dark to hear, to see.
OEDIPUS: Dark, horror of darkness   1450
my darkness, drowning, swirling around me
crashing wave on wave—unspeakable, irresistible
        headwind, fatal harbor! Oh again,
the misery, all at once, over and over
the stabbing daggers, stab of memory   1455
raking me insane.
CHORUS: No wonder you suffer
twice over, the pain of your wounds,
the lasting grief of pain.
OEDIPUS: Dear friend, still here?
Standing by me, still with a care for me,
the blind man? Such compassion,   1460

loyal to the last. Oh it's you,
I know you're here, dark as it is
I'd know you anywhere, your voice—
it's yours, clearly yours.

CHORUS: Dreadful, what you've done . . .
how could you bear it, gouging out your eyes?   1465
What superhuman power drove you on?

OEDIPUS: Apollo, friends, Apollo—
he ordained my agonies—these, my pains on pains!
But the hand that struck my eyes was mine,
mine alone—no one else—   1470
          I did it all myself!
What good were eyes to me?
Nothing I could see could bring me joy.

CHORUS: No, no, exactly as you say.

OEDIPUS: What can I ever see?
     What love, what call of the heart   1475
can touch my ears with joy? Nothing, friends.
     Take me away, far, far from Thebes,
       quickly, cast me away, my friends—
this great murderous ruin, this man cursed to heaven,
the man the deathless gods hate most of all!   1480

CHORUS: Pitiful, you suffer so, you understand so much . . .
I wish you'd never known.

OEDIPUS: Die, die—
whoever he was that day in the wilds
who cut my ankles free of the ruthless pins,
he pulled me clear of death, he saved my life   1485
for this, this kindness—
       Curse him, kill him!
If I'd died then, I'd never have dragged myself,
my loved ones through such hell.

CHORUS: Oh if only . . . would to god.   1490

OEDIPUS: I'd never have come to this,
my father's murderer—never been branded
mother's husband, all men see me now! Now,
     loathed by the gods, son of the mother I defiled
       coupling in my father's bed, spawning lives in the loins
that spawned my wretched life. What grief can crown this grief?   1495
       It's mine alone, my destiny—I am Oedipus!

CHORUS: How can I say you've chosen for the best?
Better to die than be alive and blind.

OEDIPUS: What I did was best—don't lecture me,
no more advice. I, with *my* eyes,   1500
how could I look my father in the eyes
when I go down to death? Or mother, so abused . . .
I've done such things to the two of them,
crimes too huge for hanging.
                              Worse yet,
the sight of my children, born as they were born,   1505
how could I long to look into their eyes?
No, not with these eyes of mine, never.
Not this city either, her high towers,
the sacred glittering images of her gods—
I am misery! I, her best son, reared   1510
as no other son of Thebes was ever reared,
I've stripped myself, I gave the command myself.
All men must cast away the great blasphemer,
the curse now brought to light by the gods,
the son of Laius—I, my father's son!   1515

Now I've exposed my guilt, horrendous guilt,
could I train a level glance on you, my countrymen?
Impossible! No, if I could just block off my ears,
the springs of hearing, I would stop at nothing—
I'd wall up my loathsome body like a prison,   1520
blind to the sound of life, not just the sight.
Oblivion—a blessing . . .
for the mind to dwell a world away from pain.

O Cithaeron, why did you give me shelter?
Why didn't you take me, crush my life out on the spot?   1525

I'd never have revealed my birth to all mankind.
O Polybus, Corinth, the old house of my fathers,
so I believed—what a handsome prince you raised—
under the skin, what sickness to the core.
Look at me! Born of outrage, outrage to the core.   1530

O triple roads—it all comes back, the secret,
dark ravine, and the oaks closing in
where the three roads join . . .
You drank my father's blood, my own blood
spilled by my own hands—you still remember me?   1535

What things you saw me do? Then I came here
and did them all once more!
                          Marriages! O marriage,
you gave me birth, and once you brought me into the world
you brought my sperm rising back, springing to light
fathers, brothers, sons—one deadly breed—   1540
brides, wives, mothers, The blackest things
a man can do, I have done them all!
                          No more—
it's wrong to name what's wrong to do. Quickly,
for the love of god, hide me somewhere,
kill me, hurl me into the sea   1545
where you can never look on me again.
(Beckoning to the CHORUS *as they shrink away.)*
                          Closer,
it's all right. Touch the man of sorrow.
Do. Don't be afraid. My troubles are mine
and I am the only man alive who can sustain them.
(Enter CREON *from the palace, attended by palace* GUARDS.*)*
LEADER: Put your requests to Creon. Here he is,   1550
    just when we need him. He'll have a plan, he'll act.
    Now that he's the sole defense of the country
    in your place.
OEDIPUS: Oh no, what can I say to him?
    How can I ever hope to win his trust?
    I wronged him so, just now, in every way.   1555
    You must see that—I was so wrong, so wrong.
CREON: I haven't come to mock you, Oedipus,
    or to criticize your former failings.
    (Turning to the GUARDS.*)*
                          You there,
    have you lost all respect for human feeling?
    At least revere the Sun, the holy fire   1560
    that keeps us all alive. Never expose a thing
    of guilt and holy dread so great it appalls
    the earth, the rain from heaven, the light of day!
    Get him into the halls—quickly as you can.
    Piety demands no less. Kindred alone   1565
    should see a kinsman's shame. This is obscene.
OEDIPUS: Please, in god's name . . . you wipe my fears away,
    coming so generously to me, the worst of men.
    Do one thing more, for your sake, not mine.
CREON: What do you want? Why so insistent?   1570

OEDIPUS: Drive me out of the land at once, far from sight,
    where I can never hear a human voice.
CREON: I'd have done that already, I promise you.
    First I wanted the god to clarify my duties.
OEDIPUS: The god? His command was clear, every word: 1575
    death for the father-killer, the curse—
    he said destroy me!
CREON: So he did. Still, in such a crisis
    it's better to ask precisely what to do.
OEDIPUS: You'd ask the oracle about a man like me?   1580
CREON: By all means. And this time, I assume,
    even you will obey the god's decrees.
OEDIPUS: I will,
    I will. And you, I command you—I beg you . . .
    the woman inside, bury her as you see fit.
    It's the only decent thing,   1585
    to give your own the last rites. As for me,
    never condemn the city of my fathers
    to house my body, not while I'm alive, no,
    let me live on the mountains, on Cithaeron,
    my favorite haunt, I have made it famous,   1590
    Mother and father marked out that rock
    to be my everlasting tomb—buried alive.
    Let me die there, where they tried to kill me.
    Oh but this I know: no sickness can destroy me,
    nothing can. I would never have been saved   1595
    from death—I have been saved
    for something great and terrible, something strange.
    Well let my destiny come and take me on its way!

    About my children, Creon, the boys at least,
    don't burden yourself. They're men;   1600
    wherever they go, they'll find the means to live.
    But my two daughters, my poor helpless girls,
    clustering at our table, never without me
    hovering near them . . . whatever I touched,
    they always had their share. Take care of them,   1605
    I beg you. Wait, better—permit me, would you?
    Just to touch them with my hands and take
    our fill of tears. Please . . . my king.
    Grant it, with all your noble heart.
    If I could hold them, just once, I'd think   1610
    I had them with me, like the early days

when I could see their eyes.

(ANTIGONE *and* ISMENE, *two small children, are led in from the palace by a nurse.*)
       What's that?

O god! Do I really hear you sobbing?—
my two children. Creon, you've pitied me?
Sent me my darling girls, my own flesh and blood!   1615
Am I right?

CREON: Yes, it's my doing.
I know the joy they gave you all these years,
the joy you must feel now.

OEDIPUS: Bless you, Creon!
May god watch over you for this kindness,
better than he ever guarded me.   1620
       Children, where are you?
Here, come quickly—

(*Groping for* ANTIGONE *and* ISMENE, *who approach their father cautiously,
then embrace him.*)
      Come to these hands of mine,
your brother's hands, your own father's hands
that served his once bright eyes so well—
that made them blind. Seeing nothing, children,
knowing nothing, I became your father,   1625
I fathered you in the soil that gave me life.

How I weep for you—I cannot see you now . . .
just thinking of all your days to come, the bitterness,
the life that rough mankind will thrust upon you.
Where are the public gatherings you can join,   1630
the banquets of the clans? Home you'll come,
in tears, cut off from the sight of it all,
the brilliant rites unfinished.
And when you reach perfection, ripe for marriage,
who will he be, my dear ones? Risking all   1635
to shoulder the curse that weighs down my parents,
yes and you too—that wounds us all together.
What more misery could you want?
Your father killed his father, sowed his mother,
one, one and the selfsame womb sprang you—   1640
he cropped the very roots of his existence.
Such disgrace, and you must bear it all!
Who will marry you then? Not a man on earth.
Your doom is clear: you'll wither away to nothing,
single, without a child.   1645

(*Turning to* CREON.)

                    Oh Creon,
you are the only father they have now . . .
we who brought them into the world
are gone, both gone at a stroke—
Don't let them go begging, abandoned,
women without men. Your own flesh and blood!   1650
Never bring them down to the level of my pains.
Pity them. Look at them, so young, so vulnerable,
shorn of everything—you're their only hope.
Promise me, noble Creon, touch my hand.
(*Reaching toward* CREON, *who draws back.*)
You, little ones, if you were old enough   1655
to understand, there is much I'd tell you.
Now, as it is, I'd have you say a prayer.
Pray for life, my children,
live where you are free to grow and season.
Pray god you find a better life than mine,   1660
the father who begot you.
CREON: Enough.
    You've wept enough. Into the palace now.
OEDIPUS: I must, but I find it very hard.
CREON: Time is the great healer, you will see.
OEDIPUS: I am going—you know on what condition?   1665
CREON: Tell me. I'm listening.
OEDIPUS: Drive me out of Thebes, in exile.
CREON: Not I. Only the gods can give you that.
OEDIPUS: Surely the gods hate me so much—
CREON: You'll get your wish at once.   1670
OEDIPUS: You consent?
CREON: I try to say what I mean; it's my habit.
OEDIPUS: Then take me away. It's time.
CREON: Come along, let go of the children.
OEDIPUS: No—
    don't take them away from me, not now! No no no!
    (*Clutching his daughters as the* GUARDS *wrench them loose and take them
    through the palace doors.*)
CREON: Still the king, the master of all things?   1675
    No more: here your power ends.
    None of your power follows you through life.
(*Exit* OEDIPUS *and* CREON *to the palace. The* CHORUS *comes forward to
address the audience directly.*)
CHORUS: People of Thebes, my countrymen, look on Oedipus.
    He solved the famous riddle with his brilliance,
    he rose to power, a man beyond all power.   1680

Who could behold his greatness without envy?
Now what a black sea of terror has overwhelmed him.
Now as we keep our watch and wait the final day,
count no man happy till he dies, free of pain at last.
(*Exit in procession.*)

- How does Oedipus act as a detective? What crime is it that he is trying to solve? How does he collect clues to help him learn the truth about this past event?

- When does the action of this play take place? How does Sophocles introduce historical information into the plot?

- When does Jocasta realize the truth about her situation?

- How does Oedipus learn about his true history? Describe the specific scene where this information is broken to him.

- How does Oedipus fulfill his initial promise to the town of Thebes once he has learned the truth about his own identity?

Experiencing Literature through Writing

1. Select a single work from this chapter. As you consider what happened in that text, explain why the progress of events is interesting. As you write about the plot, don't just summarize. Begin by describing a specific incident that seems surprising or unusual within the story. Explain why it stands out in this way. Then, think about whether the surrounding events prepare us adequately for this aspect of the plot. Most important, explain why this aspect of the plot is significant to our understanding of the larger text.

2. The readings in this chapter focus on the role of detection. Discuss a single work from the chapter. Explore the ways in which that particular text is a detective story. How does this larger label help us give significance to the work in question?

3. The readings in this chapter appear under the title "Detective Work." Pick one work from this chapter, and discuss the ways in which it is inappropriate to label it as a detective story. Explain why it is interesting to make this distinction.

2 Character

Who Is Involved, and Why Does It Matter?

In Paul Thomas Anderson's film *Punch Drunk Love* (2002), the main character, Barry Egan (Adam Sandler), pulls aside his brother-in-law, Walter, at a family party. Barry wants to know if it's "normal" to break spontaneously and uncontrollably into tears. Walter responds awkwardly by asking Barry if there is "something wrong" or if these feelings just match the inner experience of "other people." Barry answers in a blank monotone: "I don't know if there is anything wrong because I don't know how other people are." It's a powerful moment in the film because it captures a sense of helpless loneliness, of profound disconnection. At some level, we recognize the uncomfortable truth that none of us knows for certain how other people are (how they feel or why they act as they do). And that fact suggests the frightening thought that none of us really *knows* other people.

It's a thought everyone confronts and almost no one fully accepts. We stubbornly seek to break from the boundaries of self and understand people around us. We can surely listen more openly and attentively than Walter does to Barry. We observe mannerisms and vocal tones. We "put ourselves in another person's shoes." We think about how our individual experience fits larger patterns of behavior. We use our own experience and our own feelings as a checkpoint against what we see in others. All of these efforts to realize how "other people are" demand much of our imaginative intelligence; we exercise close observation, shrewd analysis, and patient reflection. Such exercise reminds us that literary experience *is* experience; to put it another way, there is no need to distinguish literary experience from "life experience." Our fascination with stories is strongly rooted in our everyday desire to know people, to understand the motives that underlie action or to grasp the feelings that show in words and gestures. If we lose a belief in the possibility of such knowledge, we go blank, like poor Barry.

BUILDING CHARACTER

In describing their own creative process, some writers make character (quite simply, people or figures in a story) a primary force. Vividly imagined characters can, in effect, speak to the writers who create them. A turn in a plot might result from an author's sense that a main character demanded that turn. Did Caroline Yip in Don Lee's "The Price of Eggs in China" (p. 39) leave her lover, Dean, simply because the author needed to create a fight between the two that would set up their later actions? Or was Lee compelled to let Caroline leave because the insecure Caroline he had come to know could not stay with a man she learns is a tremendously successful artist—not the moderately accomplished craftsman she had thought he was? To put it another way, did Lee's characters emerge from the story, or did the story emerge from the characters?

We would need to ask Don Lee about his writing process, but it's certainly clear that characters can come alive for authors as well as readers. Experiencing a literary text, whether we are reading it or writing it, involves a close engagement with characters outside ourselves. This experience makes our world bigger. If we do not (as readers or writers) conceive of characters as people we can know, these characters will seem artificial, unconvincing, and uninteresting.

Of course, we must also imagine situations (usually points of conflict) that define characters. Usually, those situations involve some clear point of conflict. In fact, the word **protagonist** (the main or leading character) comes from the Greek for "the first one to battle." If the battle is against another character, the opponent is the **antagonist**. These words, because they capture a crucial defining tension are in some ways more useful than terms such as *main* and *secondary character*. It's also important to remember that although a protagonist is usually the hero or heroine and the antagonist may be a villain, the terms are not synonymous, for a hero or heroine may not be the central actor in a narrative; we could easily imagine a story with both a hero and a heroine, but not a story with two protagonists. **Hero** and **heroine** also introduce in common usage positive moral or social qualities (just as *villain* suggests evil or malice). *Protagonist* and *antagonist*, strictly speaking, center us on how characters function in a narrative action, not how they affirm the author's values.

Experiencing Literature through Character

Michael Chabon's highly regarded novel *The Amazing Adventures of Kavalier & Clay* gives us two vividly realized characters who need to create a character of their own. Sammy and Joe (Chabon's main characters) have a contract to produce a comic book; in the following scene, they begin, understandably enough, by trying to imagine a new superpower upon which to build a new superhero. But this line of thinking goes nowhere: Sammy and Joe get stuck on the wrong questions. Only when they change their approach to building character does their project come alive.

Michael Chabon (1963–)

from The Amazing Adventures of Kavalier & Clay (2000)

"Who is he," Joe said.

"Who is he, and what does he do?"

"He flies."

Sammy shook his head. "Superman flies."

"So ours does not?"

"I just think I'd ... "

"To be original."

"If we can. Try to do it without flying, at least. No flying, no strength of a hundred men, no bulletproof skin."

"Okay," Joe said. The humming seemed to recede a little. "And some others, they do what?"

"Well, Batman—"

"He flies, like a bat."

"No, he doesn't fly."

"But he is blind."

"No, he only dresses like a bat. He has no batlike qualities at all. He uses only his fists."

"That sounds dull."

"Actually, it's spooky. You'd like it."

"Maybe another animal."

"Uh, well, yeah. Okay. A hawk. Hawkman."

"Hawk, yes, okay. But that one must fly."

"Yeah, you're right. Scratch the bird family. The, uh, the Fox. The Shark."

"A swimming one."

"Maybe a swimming one. Actually, no, I know a guy works in the Chesler shop, he said they're already doing a guy who swims. For Timely."

"A lion?"

"Lion. The Lion. Lionman."

"He could be strong. He roars very loud."

"He has a super roar."

"It strikes fear."

"It breaks dishes."

"The bad guys go deaf."

They laughed. Joe stopped laughing.

"I think we have to be serious," he said.

"You're right," said Sammy. "The Lion, I don't know. Lions are lazy. How about the Tiger. Tigerman. No, no. Tigers are killers. Shit. Let's see."

They began to go through the rolls of the animal kingdom, concentrating naturally on the predators: Catman, Wolfman, the Owl, the Panther, the Black Bear. They considered the primates: the Monkey, Gorillaman, the Gibbon, the Ape, the Mandrill with his multicolored wonder ass that he used to bedazzle opponents.

"Be serious," Joe chided again.

"I'm sorry, I'm sorry. Look, forget animals. Everybody's going to be thinking of animals. In two months, I'm telling you, by the time our guy hits the stands, there's going to be guys running around dressed like every damn animal in the zoo. Birds. Bugs. Underwater guys. And I'll bet you anything there's going to be five guys who are really strong, and invulnerable, and can fly."

"If he goes as fast as the light," Joe suggested.

"Yeah, I guess it's good to be fast."

"Or if he can make a thing burn up. If he can—listen! If he can, you know. Shoot the fire, with his eyes!"

"His eyeballs would melt."

"Then with his hands. Or, yes, he turns into a fire!"

"Timely's doing that already, too. They got the fire guy and the water guy."

"He turns into *ice*. He makes the ice everywhere."

"Crushed or cubes?"

"Not good?"

Sammy shook his head. "Ice," he said. "I don't see a lot of stories in ice."

"He turns into electricity?" Joe tried. "He turns into acid?"

"He turns into gravy. He turns into an enormous hat. Look, stop. Stop. Just stop."

They stopped in the middle of the sidewalk, between Sixth and Seventh avenues, and that was when Sam Clay experienced a moment of global vision, one which he would afterward come to view as the one undeniable brush against the diaphanous, dollar-colored hem of the Angel of New York to be vouchsafed to him in his lifetime.

"This is not the question," he said. "If he's like a cat or a spider or a fucking wolverine, if he's huge, if he's tiny, if he can shoot flames or ice or death rays or Vat 69, if he turns into fire or water or stone or India rubber. He could be a Martian, he could be a ghost, he could be a god or a demon or a wizard or monster. Okay? It doesn't *matter*, because right now, see, at this very moment, we have a bandwagon rolling. I'm telling you. Every little skinny guy like me in New York who believes there's life on Alpha Centauri and got the shit kicked out of him in school and can smell a dollar is out there right this minute trying to jump into it, walking around with a pencil in his shirt pocket, saying, 'He's like a falcon, no, he's like a tornado, no, he's like a goddamned wiener dog.' Okay?"

"Okay."

"And no matter what we come up with, and how we dress him, some other character with the same shtick, with the same style of boots and the same little doodad on his chest, is already out there, or is coming out tomorrow, or is going to be knocked off from our guy inside a week and a half."

Joe listened patiently, awaiting the point of this peroration, but Sammy seemed to have lost the thread. Joe followed his cousin's gaze along the sidewalk but saw only a pair of what looked to be British sailors lighting their cigarettes off a single shielded match.

"So . . . " Sammy said. "So . . . "

"So that is not the question." Joe prompted.

"That's what I'm saying."

"Continue."

They kept walking.

"How? is not the question. What? is not the question," Sammy said.

"The question is why."

"The question is *why*."

"Why," Joe repeated.

"Why is he doing it?"

"Doing what?"

"Dressing up like a monkey or an ice cube or a can of fucking corn."

"To fight crime, isn't it?"

"Well, yes, to fight crime. To fight evil. But that's all any of these guys are doing. That's as far as they ever go. They just . . . you know, it's the right thing to do, so they do it. How interesting is that?"

"I see."

"Only Batman, you know . . . see, yeah, that's good. That's what makes Batman good, and not dull at all, even though he's just a guy who dresses up like a bat and beats people up."

"What is the reason for Batman? The why?"

"His parents were killed, see? In cold blood. Right in front of his eyes, when he was a kid. By a robber."

"It's revenge."

"That's interesting." Sammy said. "See?"

"And he was driven mad."

"Well . . ."

"And that's why he puts on bat's clothes."

"Actually, they don't go as far as to say that," Sammy said. "But I guess it's there between the lines."

"So we need to figure out what is the why."

"What is the why?" Sammy agreed. ∎

Chabon does double duty in this wonderfully vivid scene. He's telling us something about the creation of character; he's letting us into a secret of his art. Building character isn't about mere features or characteristics; it's about the underlying *why* that makes the choice of features or characteristics apt. To use Chabon's (or Sammy's) own example, Batman isn't a compelling, dark, and menacing hero simply because black bat suits and ominous stares are cool, but because this character's outfit and bearing express the barely controlled rage that resides within him. The *what* (the bat) builds from the *why* (a brutalizing childhood experience). Maybe Christopher Nolan, the director of *Memento*, read Chabon's book: in the latest movie version of the Batman story, Nolan makes *why* the film's premise. The film's title underscores the point: *Batman Begins*. Nolan has been quoted as saying that Batman was interesting largely because he isn't, in the usual sense, a superhero; he's just a "guy who does a lot of push-ups." But what is really interesting is that he is driven to do those push-ups. The motivation—the why—is generative. Nolan, like Sammy, believes the beginning provides the why that gives emotional substance to the costumes and toys that took over some of the earlier, less successful versions of the character.

PRESENTING CHARACTER

Chabon has a second thing going in the previous excerpt: he is building two richly imagined and freshly presented new characters—Sammy and Joe. Chabon's method of **characterization** (the technique of creating a sense of character) seems almost invisible; it is as if he simply allows the characters to present themselves. Sammy and Joe come alive primarily from **dialogue**; we hear them speak and observe them interacting. Chabon resists, for the most part, the temptation to swoop in like some authorial superhero and tell us everything about these characters directly. We're allowed to listen in and observe things for ourselves, much as we do when we watch a play. We might notice that Sammy consistently takes the lead in the conversation. He's the one dissatisfied with the usual run of superheroes. He's the one who, in his frustration of not breaking from the superficial formulas, presses boring ideas to ridiculous conclusions (for example, Lionman's "super roar" breaks dishes). Sammy is the one who is more drenched in comic-book lore and knowledge of comic-book competitors. Sammy fills Joe in on the essentials about Batman. He knows what's going on in the business—what the rivals are working on. He is also the one who first grasps the basic problem. Sammy realizes that they need to change the question. Joe speaks less, but Chabon manages to make him come alive too. Joe may not be brilliant, but he is persistent (he's the one who keeps bringing Sammy back by telling him to "be serious"). And he is smart enough to listen to his cousin and not allow the flash of insight to get away. He prods him just as it seems that Sammy's moment of inspiration dims. He even first comes up with the crucial word *why*, even if he doesn't fully grasp its importance.

A Note to Student Writers: Leading Questions

Sammy's insight is one that critical writers would do well to consider. A "what" question could be a good starting place for description and summary, but "whats" don't lead easily into analysis. "Why" questions lead more powerfully into developing ideas. They help us think through distinctions, explain impressions, and support assertions. So when you feel stuck on "what," try formulating critical questions around "why" and see if those questions help you press your ideas forward. And although Sammy insists that "how," like "what," is "not the question," critical writers may generate a great deal from "how" questions that turn attention to the artist's craft as opposed to the character's behavior.

PICTURING CHARACTER

Listening in on a conversation, catching a tone of voice or a turn of phrase, helps us know Sammy and Joe. But we can see character emerge as a physical presence and through gestures as well. We interpret character from a dense

Making Connections

Consider how we often read character in everyday life through specific observation of things the person owns or buys. For example, we might speculate about the person in front of us at the grocery store on the basis of items that person has in the shopping cart. If we notice that same person a few minutes later in the parking lot, our first impression might be reinforced or revised by the car the person drives. Writers manage such impressions very carefully. Remember that they are really the ones who choose the groceries and the cars for their characters.

fabric of visual clues: clothes, posture, facial expressions, physical size, age, and so on. We must also consider how those clues fit with other elements within our field of vision. Where is a scene taking place? What seems to be the situation? How do the characters interact? In Anton Chekhov's short play *The Proposal* (p. 182), we learn a great deal about character through nonverbal signals. For example, Lomov's physical complaints (his grand fainting scene, his nervous recourse to the water pitcher) define his character as clearly as any dialogue.

Experiencing Film and Literature through Character

The film still shown here from *Gone with the Wind* (1939) catches a moment when Mammy (played by Hattie McDaniel) is helping the heroine, Scarlett O'Hara (Vivien Leigh), dress. It's a picture loaded with information that helps us understand character. Of course, there is the obvious: Mammy is a servant (a slave actually, although we wouldn't necessarily know that if we had only this photograph). Scarlett is the served. Mammy is black; Scarlett, white. Mammy is enormous; Scarlett, trim. The clothes accent the size differences: Mammy's bluntly cut and buttoned-up housemaid's uniform contrasts sharply with Scarlett's elaborate yet delicate underclothes. The size difference is underscored further by the fact that Mammy is tightening a corset on the already very slender Scarlett. There can't be any doubt who has been sent the gift on the bed, or who sleeps in the bed. Scarlett quite literally owns this world.

The various bits of information from the photograph, along with the most minimal background information (the names of the two characters and knowledge that the scene is set in the pre-Civil War South), might lead us to fairly simple insights about these characters if it weren't for some more subtle signals. However subservient Mammy must ultimately be, subservience isn't what comes through here. Mammy is talking in an animated manner and Scarlett is listening, even though she hardly seems happy with what she is hearing. Furthermore, Hattie McDaniel's Mammy is not just big—she's substantial. She fills more than a large physical space within the frame. She expresses authority and strength. Scarlett, for her part, is hardly compliant. Vivien Leigh communicates Scarlett's impetuous willfulness. The way she

Vivien Leigh and Hattie McDaniel in *Gone with the Wind* (1939)

holds the bedpost against Mammy's tug on her corset strings suggests the forceful push/pull nature of her complex relationship with human "property."

The role that Hattie McDaniel played was, at the time of the film in 1939, one of a very narrow range of roles available for black actresses. That contemporary social reality lends further, troubling dimensions to the picture. McDaniel was to become the target of some who felt that her portrayal too expertly realized the essentially racist vision of the book and film. It's certainly a sad note that no black actor or actress from the film could attend the premiere in Atlanta, Georgia, with the rest of the principal actors. And to enlarge the affront, McDaniel's photograph was deleted from a publicity program to be distributed at that grand event (her prominence in that program insulted some local officials). Yet she won an Academy Award for her portrayal of Mammy (a first for an African American); she also had the satisfaction of knowing that playing a servant paid much better than actually working as one (McDaniel was a maid not long before coming to Hollywood).

The complexities of the situation that Hattie McDaniel finds herself in provide the African American poet Rita Dove a rich study in character. What does it feel like to be oversized but invisible? An award winner who cannot be a "star"? An actress who must play only the limited roles she has

Hattie McDaniel accepting her Academy Award
at the Coconut Grove in 1940

tried to escape with mixed success in life? The poem "Hattie McDaniel
Arrives at the Coconut Grove" pictures the night of the Academy Awards
in 1940 with greater complexity than the photograph of Hattie McDaniel
could possibly capture. We see in Dove's poem a method of characterization
that builds from the outside (from what we see around the character, not
from what the character says). We get only one line from McDaniel herself
amid much description; Dove sets the scene and helps us see McDaniel the
actress dressed very unlike Mammy the film character. We also get some
relevant cultural, historical, and biographical information. Finally, we get
the poet's reflections on Hattie McDaniel: questions, speculation, identification, and finally, judgment.

Rita Dove (1952–)

Hattie McDaniel Arrives at
the Coconut Grove (2004)

late, in aqua and ermine, gardenias
scaling her left sleeve in a spasm of scent,
her gloves white, her smile chastened, purse giddy
with stars and rhinestones clipped to her brilliantined hair,
on her free arm that fine Negro   5
Mr. Wonderful Smith.

It's the day that isn't, February 29th,
at the end of the shortest month of the year—
and the shittiest, too, everywhere

except Hollywood, California,   10
where the maid can wear mink and still be a maid,
bobbing her bandaged head and cursing
the white folks under her breath as she smiles
and shoos their silly daughters
in from the night dew . . . What can she be   15
thinking of, striding into the ballroom
where no black face has ever showed itself
except above a serving tray?

Hi-Hat Hattie, Mama Mac, Her Haughtiness,
the "little lady" from Showboat whose name   20
Bing forgot, Beulah & Bertha & Malena
& Carrie & Violet & Cynthia & Fidelia,
one half of the Dark Barrymores—
dear Mammy we can't help but hug you crawl into
your generous lap tease you   25
with arch innuendo so we can feel that
much more wicked and youthful
and sleek but oh what

we forgot: the four husbands, the phantom
pregnancy, your famous parties, your celebrated   30
ice box cake. Your giggle above the red petticoat's rustle,
black girl and white girl walking hand in hand
down the railroad tracks
in Kansas City, six years old.
The man who advised you, now   35
that you were famous, to "begin eliminating"
your more "common" acquaintances
and your reply (catching him square
in the eye): "That's a good idea.
I'll start right now by eliminating you."   40

Is she or isn't she? Three million dishes,
a truckload of aprons and headrags later, and here
you are: poised, between husbands
and factions, no corset wide enough
to hold you in, your face a dark moon split   45
by that spontaneous smile—your trademark,
your curse. No matter, Hattie: it's a long, beautiful walk
into that flower-smothered standing ovation,

so go on
and make them wait.   50

Dove's final lines suggest a deep appreciation and sympathy for Hattie McDaniel. The great smile was both a "trademark" and a "curse." But Dove's speaker doesn't end on that note of ambivalence. Hattie is to enjoy her moment, and Dove wants the reader to enjoy it with her.

FEELING FOR CHARACTER

The desire to know something about others isn't built on an abstract curiosity. We must *want* to know about a character. A character must matter to us. If Sammy felt that the *why* of Batman didn't justify the *what*, he would likely have found the character unbalanced (too violent) or just plain silly (bat suits and bat gadgets). He wouldn't think of Batman as a creative touchstone. Of course, we don't usually need to accept the kind of unlikely *what* that comes with a superhero. Most artists build from more mundane materials; many artists work from subjects quite literally close to home: family, friends, jobs, and so on. The simplest *whys* can lead to a rich and deeply involving sense of character: Why did she ask him to lunch? Why did he behave so coldly? Why did they eat so little? Why did she insist on paying the bill?

Experiencing Literature through Character

Concern for character often grows from immediate personal concerns. Cathy Song in the poem "Picture Bride" reflects on the distant past of a grandmother. How can the younger woman, the poem's speaker, connect with a grandmother over time and dramatically changed circumstances? How does the old woman encompass for the speaker a still-living history? Why is it important to rescue a sense of the older woman's past? Everything in the poem is driven by a powerful sense of **identification**. The grandmother was a year younger than the poet when she moved from home to a new land and an arranged marriage. The poet realizes the profundity of that move. She sorts through her own feelings, her own situation, and wonders how that young woman (that young woman who became the old woman who is the poet's grandmother) must have felt when she—at the poet's age—came to an unfamiliar land and looked in the face of a stranger she knew was to be her husband? This act of imagining also lends weight to the poem's speaker. It is not just the grandmother whom we meet in this poem. The speaker becomes a character as well.

Cathy Song (1955–)

Picture Bride (1983)

She was a year younger
than I,
twenty-three when she left Korea.
Did she simply close
the door of her father's house   5
and walk away. And
was it a long way
through the tailor shops of Pusan
to the wharf where the boat
waited to take her to an island   10
whose name she had only recently learned,
on whose shore
a man waited,
turning her photograph
to the light when the lanterns   15
in the camp outside
Waialua Sugar Mill were lit
and the inside of his room
grew luminous
from the wings of moths   20
migrating out of the cane stalks?
What things did my grandmother
take with her? And when
she arrived to look
into the face of the stranger   25
who was her husband,
thirteen years older than she,
did she politely untie
the silk bow of her jacket,
her tent-shaped dress   30
filling with the dry wind
that blew from the surrounding fields
where the men were burning cane?

Song suggests the character of both the grandmother and the granddaughter
through questions. Perhaps she cannot cross a gulf between past and present
with flat statements. Too much specific knowledge has been lost over the years;
the grandmother's youth has become too distant. But enough detail remains to

give substance to the questions. And the speaker of the poem can identify closely because the speaker is what the grandmother once was: a young woman.

Robert Hayden also reflects on family in "Those Winter Sundays." His speaker concretely remembers his father and doesn't need to imagine or project from bits of information others have collected. Nor does he ask questions about what his father felt or who he was; his knowledge is limited but firm. Hayden tells a brief story that unfolds a sense of a quiet, uncomplaining man who expresses feelings through hard work and everyday acts of attention. The picture of the father comes through clearly. We get a sketch of a character who is defined by his steadiness. At the end we're left thinking of the second character in the poem. The question that rounds off Hayden's poem is self-reflective. It causes us to think of the son who only as an adult begins to appreciate the depth of his father's love.

Robert Hayden (1913–1980)

Those Winter Sundays (1966)

Sundays too my father got up early
and put his clothes on in the blueback cold,
then with cracked hands that ached
from labor in the weekday weather made
banked fires blaze. No one ever thanked him.   5

I'd wake and hear the cold splintering, breaking.
When the rooms were warm, he'd call,
and slowly I would rise and dress,
fearing the chronic angers of that house,
Speaking indifferently to him,   10
who had driven out the cold
and polished my good shoes as well.
What did I know, what did I know
of love's austere and lonely offices?

The father and son in Hayden's poem introduce in miniature a broad distinction critics often make between character types in novels and plays: static and dynamic. **Static characters** do not change in the course of the story; **dynamic characters** do change. It is useful to further distinguish character types within these categories. Some static characters become objects of criticism; they foolishly resist what seems an appropriate or necessary change. Hayden's father is not this sort of static character. He is unchanging in a way that suggests steadiness, firmness of purpose, clarity of essential values. The father's static quality results from the unrelentingly hard world he must deal with; it's not a personality defect. Some dynamic characters change as a result of specific knowledge; they simply adjust behavior on the basis of new information. Other dynamic characters change at the deepest level of being; they undergo a revolution in their way of seeing and approaching the world. "Those Winter Sundays" is too brief a piece to communicate a full sense of what knowledge the son comes to, but it does suggest a profound insight on the nature of mature love that could hardly leave the son unchanged.

CHARACTER AND FUNCTION

So far, we've discussed character in terms of knowing or understanding others. We've used words like *motivation*, *sympathy*, and *identification*. The assumption is that we engage with characters as we engage with people. But we need to acknowledge that characters in literary texts serve a wide range of functions; they are not always in a work for us to "know" as we might hope to know a person.

Many people take the lead of the novelist E. M. Forster and distinguish between **round characters** and **flat characters**. Round characters (according to Forster) possess a complex psychology—layers of complex and perhaps even conflicting motivations. Flat characters are one-dimensional; they may possess a vivid trait but not a substantial identity. These terms can sometimes be useful in making broad distinctions among character types, but *round* and *flat* will be misleading words if we use them to signal a fixed artistic value. It would be a mistake, for example, to assume that round characters are "well drawn" and flat characters are "poorly conceived."

Characters must always be viewed in relation to a whole work. We don't ask only who they are but how they function. For example, we recognize many characters for roles that have become familiar over innumerable works (the shady gambler, the annoying little brother, the meddlesome mother-in-law). Such **stock characters** (the flattest of the flat) do not demand much of us, nor do they leave us with a feeling that we've enlarged our range of experience. But this is not to say that they are, from an artistic standpoint, failures. In such cases, the character's complexity is not the issue; what matters is, does the character fit within a plan for the whole? A stock character might be used to help move a plot forward or perhaps provide a bit of information necessary for a larger purpose. Some simple characters serve to bring out qualities in major characters; they act as **foils** that show off the relatively complex dimensions others possess.

More important still, we must remember that psychological insight isn't the only means to depth or the only type of depth. Some characters embody ideas (or ideals) more than recognizable behaviors. They may seem more satiric than realistic, more fanciful than grounded, more mythic than human. Distinctions such as these are about kind, not quality. A flat character may actually allow us (in some works at least) to access profound feelings. Occasionally, the character's supposed "narrowness" or one-dimensionality may be better described as intensely concentrated.

The father in Judith Ortiz Cofer's "My Father in the Navy: A Childhood Memory" isn't "real" in the same sense that a fully realized independent character is real. In the mind of the speaker, the father possesses no psychological depth or even independent existence. In this poem, that is hardly a problem, for the speaker's father, the angel who appears magically to herald a new day, helps us appreciate the longings of the child—the child's desire for a family's wholeness, for a strongly reassuring presence. The father is beautifully realized, not as a person but as an image a child holds. If the poet chose to give him "depth," the poem's subject would shift: it would no longer be the same intensely felt "childhood memory."

Judith Ortiz Cofer (1952–)

My Father in the Navy: A Childhood Memory (1987)

Stiff and immaculate
in the white cloth of his uniform
and a round cap on his head like a halo,
he was an apparition on leave from a shadow-world
and only flesh and blood when he rose from below   5
the waterline where he kept watch over the engines
and dials making sure the ship parted the waters
on a straight course.
Mother, brother and I kept vigil
on the nights and dawns of his arrivals,   10
watching the corner beyond the neon sign of a quasar
for the flash of white our father like an angel
heralding a new day.
His homecomings were the verses
we composed over the years making up   15
the siren's song that kept him coming back
from the bellies of iron whales
and into our nights
like the evening prayer.

The character who is most "rounded" here is the speaker. We feel and understand the rich desire of the child for the father. We can also appreciate the great power that the child feels the father possesses. If we complain that Cofer has not developed the father's character, we've missed what Cofer *has* accomplished in the character of the daughter.

MODELING CRITICAL ANALYSIS: JAMAICA KINCAID, GIRL

We mentioned in the previous chapter that Jamaica Kincaid's "Girl" (p. 16) defies any easy discussion of plot; it would seem that the story is more purely a character sketch. But a moment's reflection raises interesting critical issues. The title directs us to the girl as a point of focus, as the main character. But the story itself is almost entirely delivered by the woman who orders and instructs the girl. Only two short lines are spoken directly by the girl. Much of what we actually read isn't about the girl at all but about behaviors and duties that are pressed upon her. How is it that her character emerges? Is the girl the main character?

Kincaid from the very start opens with commands. Having the speaker aggressively load on obligations puts the reader, in effect, in the same position as the girl: we are at the receiving end of all the orders. One result is that we can sympathize with the girl. We can feel the weight of being a girl in a culture that is both demanding and restrictive of girls. A sense of character then emerges not from a look inside the girl or from the girl's words but from a visceral understanding of how outside forces (social rules, customs, and expectations) control the girl's experience of the world.

It is in that context that we may see her brief interruptions as admirable—perhaps even heroic. The main speaker projects an identity upon the girl, but the girl resists. She doesn't, she objects, sing *"benna on Sundays"*; she does question an order that does not match her own understanding of the way the world works. Of course, the question she asks at the story's end—*"what if the baker won't let me feel the bread"*—is quickly thrown back against her: "you mean . . . you are really going to be the kind of woman who the baker won't let near the bread?" This question rhetorically functions more as an accusation or as a judgment upon the girl. But as strongly as we might feel its sting, we hold steady and have some reason to think the girl will too. The girl is one who claims some sense of self against the identity put upon her from the outside.

It's also important to note that the girl is not the only character we get to know. The older woman who acts as mentor, boss, judge, and mother has internalized the many lessons that she gives so readily. The fact that she knows how to wash, sew, plant, cook, nurse, iron, and so on suggests that hers has been a life spent doing things for others. But she hasn't accepted a life lived wholly at the whims of those more powerful than she. She knows how to use the few powers she has: "this is how you smile to someone you don't like too much; this is how you smile to someone you don't like at all; this is how you smile to someone you like completely." She knows how to "bully" a man and how it can happen that a man bullies her. She is a character who has managed to achieve some independence in a highly restricted world. For example, near the end, she tells the girl how to love a man but also tells her to not feel too bad if those instructions don't work. It seems that the woman acknowledges limitations built into her society but finds ways to circumvent some of those limitations. And it seems she wants the girl to have that survivor's knowledge too.

Using Character to Focus Writing and Discussion

- Who are the characters in the story?
- How is each introduced? What are their names?
- What are their physical characteristics? What are their personalities?
- What details help us identify a particular character even when that character is not identified by name?
- Which characters (if any) are better developed than other characters in the text?
- What changes (if any) do we see in the characters?
- What contrasts or tensions, if any, do we see among characters?
- Which character gains our sympathy or support within the narrative? Does this sympathy lead us to feel unsympathetic for any other character?
- How do the characters function within the narrative? How important is any single character to moving the plot forward? How important is any single character to our knowledge of other characters within the narrative?
- How does any single character exhibit a value system that influences the ways that we receive the narrative?

Anthology

POWER PLAYS: CHARACTERIZING RELATIONSHIPS

Characters in literature or life never have a completely independent existence. We see characters/people in context of relations with others. In the most basic terms, we see character shaped by conflict. Often, characters emerge clearly in defining moments of opposition. How does the Hattie

McDaniel of Rita Dove's poem (p. 124) respond to those who presume themselves to be socially superior? How does she carry the burden of being the first African American to be at the Coconut Grove as an honored guest? How does the narrator of Cathy Song's "Picture Bride" (p. 127) present the forces that entrap her grandmother? How might the conflict the grandmother must address help us understand the narrator's own immediate personal concerns?

The readings here concentrate attention on conflicts that arise from family life. The dense and subtle interactions that occur within a family provide artists great opportunities for development of character. For example, in "Everyday Use" Alice Walker presents a power struggle among members of a family that leads to a sudden and dramatic shift in power. Dee (the educated daughter, the "pretty one") assumes an authority that is in many ways validated by the world beyond home. Dee has left her past and makes both her sister, Maggie, and her mother feel diminished by the fact that they stayed "behind." Notice how the mother at first tries to imagine herself as different (a slim woman on a TV show) so that she could better relate to Dee. The mother eventually comes to realize that Dee has lost something important by leaving; this insight allows her to stand up to Dee. She reclaims power for herself and Maggie through her sense that they are the ones who sustain a living family history.

The characters of Anton Chekhov's *The Proposal* are silly; they face nothing more than the trivial problems of their own making. Indeed, the conflict that first separates the would-be lovers need not be a conflict at all. Any disagreement over land claims would entirely disappear if the two would simply agree to do what they both want to do—get married. But silliness can be placed in a serious enough context. The characters in Chekhov's plays typically struggle with the loss of familiar social roles as well as the difficulties of defining new ones. Chekhov's characters don't achieve powerful moments of insight or take decisive and effective action in response to crises; that lack of force results from the nature of the disintegrating social and economic world in which they act. As the characters attack each other, call names, dispute pretensions, question family honor, and challenge integrity, we begin to see how worn the surface of upper-crust czarist Russian society has become. The society of Chekhov's play simply isn't stable enough or healthy enough to allow people to achieve the vibrant selfhood that the mother in "Everyday Use" discovers.

The poems here provide many additional angles on family life and probe richly varied feelings. Robert Frost's "Home Burial" dramatizes the shattering effects of the death of a child. We see unfold in subtle gestures how the surviving parents are painfully separated by their differing ways of responding to tragedy. Edgar Lee Masters probes the power of secrets and the pressures of reputation. His short poems quickly sketch a master emotion (fear, resentment, regret, and so on) that brings individual characters alive from the graveyard. Sylvia Plath dives deeply into childhood pains that do not relent in adulthood. She becomes the main character of her own poetry. In all of the readings that follow, characters emerge for us to know. They engage us in a broad yet intense human experience.

FICTION

Alice Munro (1931–)

> Award-winning short story writer Alice Munro was born in Ontario, Canada. She received her BA from the University of Western Ontario in 1952. Munro was artist-in-residence at the University of Western Ontario from 1974 to 1975 and at the University of British Columbia in 1980. She has received numerous awards for her writing, including the Governor General's Literary Award for *Dance of the Happy Shades* (1969), *Who Do You Think You Are?: Stories* (1978), *The Beggar Maid: Stories of Flo and Rose* (1979), and *The Progress of Love* (1987). Her collection of stories, *Runaway*, was published in October 2004. In 2005, Munro was honored for her lifetime achievement by the National Arts Club, which presented her with the Medal of Honor for Literature.

How I Met My Husband (1974)

We heard the plane come over at noon, roaring through the radio news, and we were sure it was going to hit the house, so we all ran out into the yard. We saw it come in over the treetops, all red and silver, the first close-up plane I ever saw. Mrs. Peebles screamed.

"Crash landing," their little boy said. Joey was his name.

"It's okay," said Dr. Peebles. "He knows what he's doing." Dr. Peebles was only an animal doctor, but had a calming way of talking, like any doctor.

This was my first job—working for Dr. and Mrs. Peebles, who had bought an old house out on the Fifth Line, about five miles out of town. It was just when the trend was starting of town people buying up old farms, not to work them but to live on them.

We watched the plane land across the road, where the fairgrounds used to be. It did make a good landing field, nice and level for the old race track, and the barns and display sheds torn down now for scrap lumber so there was nothing in the way. Even the old grandstand bays had burned.   5

"All right," said Mrs. Peebles, snappy as she always was when she got over her nerves. "Let's go back in the house. Let's not stand here gawking like a set of farmers."

She didn't say that to hurt my feelings. It never occurred to her.

I was just setting the dessert down when Loretta Bird arrived, out of breath, at the screen door.

"I thought it was going to crash into the house and kill youse all!"

She lived on the next place and the Peebleses thought she was a country-woman, they didn't know the difference. She and her husband didn't farm, he worked on the roads and had a bad name for drinking. They had seven children and couldn't get credit at the HiWay Grocery. The Peebleses made her welcome, not knowing any better, as I say, and offered her dessert.

Dessert was never anything to write home about, at their place. A dish of Jell-O or sliced bananas or fruit out of a tin. "Have a house without a pie, be ashamed until you die," my mother used to say, but Mrs. Peebles operated differently.

Loretta Bird saw me getting the can of peaches.

"Oh, never mind," she said. "I haven't got the right kind of a stomach to trust what comes out of those tins, I can only eat home canning."

I could have slapped her. I bet she never put down fruit in her life.

"I know what he's landed here for," she said. "He's got permission to use the fairgrounds and take people up for rides. It costs a dollar. It's the same fellow who was over at Palmerston last week and was up the lakeshore before that. I wouldn't go up, if you paid me."

"I'd jump at the chance," Dr. Peebles said. "I'd like to see this neighborhood from the air."

Mrs. Peebles said she would just as soon see it from the ground. Joey said he wanted to go and Heather did, too. Joey was nine and Heather was seven.

"Would you, Edie?" Heather said.

I said I didn't know. I was scared, but I never admitted that, especially in front of children I was taking care of.

"People are going to be coming out here in their cars raising dust and trampling your property, if I was you I would complain," Loretta said. She hooked her legs around the chair rung and I knew we were in for a lengthy visit. After Dr. Peebles went back to his office or out on his next call and Mrs. Peebles went for her nap, she would hang around me while I was trying to do the dishes. She would pass remarks about the Peebleses in their own house.

"She wouldn't find time to lay down in the middle of the day, if she had seven kids like I got."

She asked me did they fight and did they keep things in the dresser drawer not to have babies with. She said it was a sin if they did. I pretended I didn't know what she was talking about.

I was fifteen and away from home for the first time. My parents had made the effort and sent me to high school for a year, but I didn't like it. I was shy of strangers and the work was hard, they didn't make it nice for you or explain the way they do now. At the end of the year the averages were published in

10

15

20

the paper, and mine came out at the very bottom, 37 percent. My father said that's enough and I didn't blame him. The last thing I wanted, anyway, was to go on and end up teaching school. It happened the very day the paper came out with my disgrace in it, Dr. Peebles was staying at our place for dinner, having just helped one of our cows have twins, and he said I looked smart to him and his wife was looking for a girl to help. He said she felt tied down, with the two children, out in the country. I guess she would, my mother said, being polite, though I could tell from her face she was wondering what on earth it would be like to have only two children and no barn work, and then to be complaining.

When I went home I would describe to them the work I had to do, and it made everybody laugh. Mrs. Peebles had an automatic washer and dryer, the first I ever saw. I have had those in my own home for such a long time now it's hard to remember how much of a miracle it was to me, not having to struggle with the wringer and hang up and haul down. Let alone not having to heat water. Then there was practically no baking. Mrs. Peebles said she couldn't make pie crust, the most amazing thing I ever heard a woman admit. I could, of course, and I could make light biscuits and a white cake and dark cake, but they didn't want it, she said they watched their figures. The only thing I didn't like about working there, in fact, was feeling half hungry a lot of the time. I used to bring back a box of doughnuts made out at home, and hide them under my bed. The children found out, and I didn't mind sharing, but I thought I better bind them to secrecy.

The day after the plane landed Mrs. Peebles put both children in the car and drove over to Chesley, to get their hair cut. There was a good woman then at Chesley for doing hair. She got hers done at the same place, Mrs. Peebles did, and that meant they would be gone a good while. She had to pick a day Dr. Peebles wasn't going out into the country, she didn't have her own car. Cars were still in short supply then, after the war.

I loved being left in the house alone, to do my work at leisure. The kitchen was all white and bright yellow, with fluorescent lights. That was before they ever thought of making the appliances all different colors and doing the cupboards like dark old wood and hiding the lighting. I loved light. I loved the double sink. So would anybody new-come from washing dishes in a dishpan with a rag-plugged hole on an oilcloth-covered table by light of a coal-oil lamp. I kept everything shining.

The bathroom too. I had a bath in there once a week. They wouldn't have minded if I took one oftener, but to me it seemed like asking too much, or maybe risking making it less wonderful. The basin and the tub and the toilet were all pink, and there were glass doors with flamingoes painted on them, to shut off the tub. The light had a rosy cast and the mat sank under your feet like snow, except that it was warm. The mirror was three-way. With the mirror all steamed up and the air like a perfume cloud, from things

I was allowed to use, I stood up on the side of the tub and admired myself naked, from three directions. Sometimes I thought about the way we lived out at home and the way we lived here and how one way was so hard to imagine when you were living the other way. But I thought it was still a lot easier, living the way we lived at home, to picture something like this, the painted flamingoes and the warmth and the soft mat, than it was anybody knowing only things like this to picture how it was the other way. And why was that?

I was through my jobs in no time, and had the vegetables peeled for supper and sitting in cold water besides. Then I went into Mrs. Peebles' bedroom. I had been in there plenty of times, cleaning, and I always took a good look in her closet, at the clothes she had hanging there. I wouldn't have looked in her drawers, but a closet is open to anybody. That's a lie. I would have looked in drawers, but I would have felt worse doing it and been more scared she could tell.

Some clothes in her closet she wore all the time, I was quite familiar with them. Others she never put on, they were pushed to the back. I was disappointed to see no wedding dress. But there was one long dress I could just see the skirt of, and I was hungering to see the rest. Now I took note of where it hung and lifted it out. It was satin, a lovely weight on my arm, light bluish-green in color, almost silvery. It had a fitted, pointed waist and a full skirt and an off-the-shoulder fold hiding the little sleeves.

Next thing was easy. I got out of my own things and slipped it on. I was slimmer at fifteen than anybody would believe who knows me now and the fit was beautiful. I didn't, of course, have a strapless bra on, which was what it needed, I just had to slide my straps down my arms under the material. Then I tried pinning up my hair, to get the effect. One thing led to another. I put on rouge and lipstick and eyebrow pencil from her dresser. The heat of the day and the weight of the satin and all the excitement made me thirsty, and I went out to the kitchen, got-up as I was, to get a glass of ginger ale with ice cubes from the refrigerator. The Peebleses drank ginger ale, or fruit drinks, all day, like water, and I was getting so I did too. Also there was no limit on ice cubes, which I was so fond of I would even put them in a glass of milk. 30

I turned from putting the ice tray back and saw a man watching me through the screen. It was the luckiest thing in the world I didn't spill the ginger ale down the front of me then and there.

"I never meant to scare you. I knocked but you were getting the ice out, you didn't hear me."

I couldn't see what he looked like, he was dark the way somebody is pressed up against a screen door with the bright daylight behind them. I only knew he wasn't from around here.

"I'm from the plane over there. My name is Chris Watters and what I was wondering was if I could use that pump."

There was a pump in the yard. That was the way the people used to get their water. Now I noticed he was carrying a pail.

"You're welcome," I said. "I can get it from the tap and save you pumping." I guess I wanted him to know we had piped water, didn't pump ourselves.

"I don't mind the exercise." He didn't move, though, and finally he said, "Were you going to a dance?"

Seeing a stranger there had made me entirely forget how I was dressed.

"Or is that the way ladies around here generally get dressed up in the afternoon?"

I didn't know how to joke back then. I was too embarrassed.

"You live here? Are you the lady of the house?"

"I'm the hired girl."

Some people change when they find that out, their whole way of looking at you and speaking to you changes, but his didn't.

"Well, I just wanted to tell you you look very nice. I was so surprised when I looked in the door and saw you. Just because you looked so nice and beautiful."

I wasn't even old enough then to realize how out of the common it is, for a man to say something like that to a woman, or somebody he is treating like a woman. For a man to say a word like *beautiful*. I wasn't old enough to realize or to say anything back, or in fact to do anything but wish he would go away. Not that I didn't like him, but just that it upset me so, having him look at me, and me trying to think of something to say.

He must have understood. He said good-bye, and thanked me, and went and started filling his pail from the pump. I stood behind the Venetian blinds in the dining room, watching him. When he had gone, I went into the bedroom and took the dress off and put it back in the same place. I dressed in my own clothes and took my hair down and washed my face, wiping it on Kleenex, which I threw in the wastebasket.

The Peebleses asked me what kind of man he was. Young, middle-aged, short, tall? I couldn't say.

"Good-looking?" Dr. Peebles teased me.

I couldn't think a thing but that he would be coming to get his water again, he would be talking to Dr. or Mrs. Peebles, making friends with them, and he would mention seeing me that first afternoon, dressed up. Why not mention it? He would think it was funny. And no idea of the trouble it would get me into.

After supper the Peebleses drove into town to go to a movie. She wanted to go somewhere with her hair fresh done. I sat in my bright kitchen wondering what to do, knowing I would never sleep. Mrs. Peebles might not fire me, when she found out, but it would give her a different feeling about me altogether. This was the first place I ever worked but I already had picked up things about the way people feel when you are working for them. They like to think you aren't curious. Not just that you aren't dishonest, that isn't enough. They like to feel you don't notice things, that you don't think or wonder about anything but what they liked to eat and how they liked things ironed, and so on. I don't mean they weren't kind to me, because they were. They had me eat my meals with them (to tell the truth I expected to, I didn't know there were families who don't) and sometimes they took me along in the car. But all the same.

I went up and checked on the children being asleep and then I went out. I had to do it. I crossed the road and went in the old fairgrounds gate. The plane looked unnatural sitting there, and shining with the moon. Off at the far side of the fairgrounds, where the bush was taking over, I saw his tent.

He was sitting outside it smoking a cigarette. He saw me coming.

"Hello, were you looking for a plane ride? I don't start taking people up till tomorrow." Then he looked again and said, "Oh, it's you. I didn't know you without your long dress on."

My heart was knocking away, my tongue was dried up. I had to say something. But I couldn't. My throat was closed and I was like a deaf-and-dumb.

"Did you want a ride? Sit down. Have a cigarette." 55

I couldn't even shake my head to say no, so he gave me one.

"Put it in your mouth or I can't light it. It's a good thing I'm used to shy ladies."

I did. It wasn't the first time I had smoked a cigarette, actually. My girlfriend out home, Muriel Lowe, used to steal them from her brother.

"Look at your hand shaking. Did you just want to have a chat, or what?"

In one burst I said, "I wisht you wouldn't say anything about that dress." 60

"What dress? Oh, the long dress."

"It's Mrs. Peebles'."

"Whose? Oh, the lady you work for? Is that it? She wasn't home so you got dressed up in her dress, eh? You got dressed up and played queen. I don't blame you. You're not smoking the cigarette right. Don't just puff. Draw it in. Did anybody ever show you how to inhale? Are you scared I'll tell on you? Is that it?"

I was so ashamed at having to ask him to connive this way I couldn't nod. I just looked at him and he saw *yes*.

"Well I won't. I won't in the slightest way mention it or embarrass you. I 65 give you my word of honor."

Then he changed the subject, to help me out, seeing I couldn't even thank him.

"What do you think of this sign?"

It was a board sign lying practically at my feet.

SEE THE WORLD FROM THE SKY. ADULTS $1.00, CHILDREN 50¢. QUALIFIED PILOT.

"My old sign was getting pretty beat up, I thought I'd make a new one. That's what I've been doing with my time today."

The lettering wasn't all that handsome, I thought. I could have done a better one in half an hour.

"I'm not an expert at sign making."

"It's very good," I said.

"I don't need it for publicity, word of mouth is usually enough. I turned away two carloads tonight. I felt like taking it easy. I didn't tell them ladies were dropping in to visit me."

Now I remembered the children and I was scared again, in case one of them had waked up and called me and I wasn't there.

"Do you have to go so soon?"

I remembered some manners. "Thank you for the cigarette."

"Don't forget. You have my word of honor."

I tore off across the fairgrounds, scared I'd see the car heading home from town. My sense of time was mixed up, I didn't know how long I'd been out of the house. But it was all right, it wasn't late, the children were asleep. I got in bed myself and lay thinking what a lucky end to the day, after all, and among things to be grateful for I could be grateful Loretta Bird hadn't been the one who caught me.

The yard and borders didn't get trampled, it wasn't as bad as that. All the same it seemed very public, around the house. The sign was on the fairgrounds gate. People came mostly after supper but a good many in the afternoon, too. The Bird children all came without fifty cents between them and hung on the gate. We got used to the excitement of the plane coming in and taking off, it wasn't excitement anymore. I never went over, after that one time, but would see him when he came to get his water. I would be out on the steps doing sitting-down work, like preparing vegetables, if I could.

"Why don't you come over? I'll take you up in my plane."

"I'm saving my money," I said, because I couldn't think of anything else.

"For what? For getting married?"

I shook my head.

"I'll take you up for free if you come sometime when it's slack. I thought you would come, and have another cigarette."

I made a face to hush him, because you never could tell when the children would be sneaking around the porch, or Mrs. Peebles herself listening in the house. Sometimes she came out and had a conversation with him. He told her things he hadn't bothered to tell me. But then I hadn't thought to ask. He told her he had been in the war, that was where he learned to fly a plane, and now he couldn't settle down to ordinary life, this was what he liked. She said she couldn't imagine anybody liking such a thing. Though sometimes, she said, she was almost bored enough to try anything herself, she wasn't brought up to living in the country. It's all my husband's idea, she said. This was news to me.

"Maybe you ought to give flying lessons," she said.

"Would you take them?"

She just laughed.

Sunday was a busy flying day in spite of it being preached against from   90
two pulpits. We were all sitting out watching. Joey and Heather were over on the fence with the Bird kids. Their father had said they could go, after their mother saying all week they couldn't.

A car came down the road past the parked cars and pulled up right in the drive. It was Loretta Bird who got out, all importance, and on the driver's side another woman got out, more sedately. She was wearing sunglasses.

"This is a lady looking for the man that flies the plane," Loretta Bird said. "I heard her inquire in the hotel coffee shop where I was having a Coke and I brought her out."

"I'm sorry to bother you," the lady said. "I'm Alice Kelling, Mr. Watters' fiancée."

This Alice Kelling had on a pair of brown and white checked slacks and a yellow top. Her bust looked to me rather low and bumpy. She had a worried face. Her hair had had a permanent, but had grown out, and she wore a yellow band to keep it off her face. Nothing in the least pretty or even young-looking about her. But you could tell from how she talked she was from the city, or educated, or both.

Dr. Peebles stood up and introduced himself and his wife and me and   95
asked her to be seated.

"He's up in the air right now, but you're welcome to sit and wait. He gets his water here and he hasn't been yet. He'll probably take his break about five."

"That is him, then?" said Alice Kelling, wrinkling and straining at the sky.

"He's not in the habit of running out on you, taking a different name?" Dr. Peebles laughed. He was the one, not his wife, to offer iced tea. Then she sent me into the kitchen to fix it. She smiled. She was wearing sunglasses too.

"He never mentioned his fiancée," she said.

I loved fixing iced tea with lots of ice and slices of lemon in tall glasses. I   100
ought to have mentioned before, Dr. Peebles was an abstainer, at least around the house, or I wouldn't have been allowed to take the place. I had to fix a glass for Loretta Bird too, though it galled me, and when I went out she had settled in my lawn chair, leaving me the steps.

"I knew you was a nurse when I first heard you in that coffee shop."

"How would you know a thing like that?"

"I get my hunches about people. Was that how you met him, nursing?"

"Chris? Well yes. Yes, it was."

"Oh, were you overseas?" said Mrs. Peebles.

"No, it was before he went overseas. I nursed him when he was stationed at Centralia and had a ruptured appendix. We got engaged and then he went overseas. My, this is refreshing, after a long drive."

"He'll be glad to see you," Dr. Peebles said. "It's a rackety kind of life, isn't it, not staying one place long enough to really make friends."

"Youse've had a long engagement," Loretta Bird said.

Alice Kelling passed that over. "I was going to get a room at the hotel, but when I was offered directions I came on out. Do you think I could phone them?"

"No need," Dr. Peebles said. "You're five miles away from him if you stay at the hotel. Here, you're right across the road. Stay with us. We've got rooms on rooms, look at this big house."

Asking people to stay, just like that, is certainly a country thing, and maybe seemed natural to him now, but not to Mrs. Peebles, from the way she said, oh yes, we have plenty of room. Or to Alice Kelling, who kept protesting, but let herself be worn down. I got the feeling it was a temptation to her, to be that close. I was trying for a look at her ring. Her nails were painted red, her fingers were freckled and wrinkled. It was a tiny stone. Muriel Lowe's cousin had one twice as big.

Chris came to get his water, late in the afternoon just as Dr. Peebles had predicted. He must have recognized the car from a way off. He came smiling.

"Here I am chasing after you to see what you're up to," called Alice Kelling. She got up and went to meet him and they kissed, just touched, in front of us.

"You're going to spend a lot on gas that way," Chris said.

Dr. Peebles invited Chris to stay for supper, since he had already put up the sign that said: NO MORE RIDES TILL 7 P.M. Mrs. Peebles wanted it served in the yard, in spite of the bugs. One thing strange to anybody from the country is this eating outside. I had made a potato salad earlier and she had made a jellied salad, that was one thing she could do, so it was just a matter of getting those out, and some sliced meat and cucumbers and fresh leaf lettuce. Loretta Bird hung around for some time saying, "Oh, well, I guess I better get home to those yappers," and, "It's so nice just sitting here, I sure hate to get up," but nobody invited her, I was relieved to see, and finally she had to go.

That night after rides were finished Alice Kelling and Chris went off somewhere in her car. I lay awake till they got back. When I saw the car lights sweep my ceiling I got up to look down on them through the slats of my blind. I don't know what I thought I was going to see. Muriel Lowe and I used to sleep on her front veranda and watch her sister and her sister's boy friend saying good night. Afterward we couldn't get to sleep, for longing for somebody to kiss us and rub up against us and we would talk about suppose you were out in a boat with a boy and he wouldn't bring you in to shore unless you did it, or what if somebody got you trapped in a barn, you would have to, wouldn't you, it wouldn't be your fault. Muriel said her two girl cousins used to try with a toilet paper roll that one of them was a boy. We wouldn't do anything like that; just lay and wondered.

All that happened was that Chris got out of the car on one side and she got out on the other and they walked off separately—him toward the fairgrounds and her toward the house. I got back in bed and imagined about me coming home with him, not like that.

Next morning Alice Kelling got up late and I fixed a grapefruit for her the way I had learned and Mrs. Peebles sat down with her to visit and have another cup of coffee. Mrs. Peebles seemed pleased enough now, having company. Alice Kelling said she guessed she better get used to putting in a day just watching Chris take off and come down, and Mrs. Peebles said she didn't know if she should suggest it because Alice Kelling was the one with the car, but the lake was only twenty-five miles away and what a good day for a picnic.

Alice Kelling took her up on the idea and by eleven o'clock they were in the car, with Joey and Heather and a sandwich lunch I had made. The only thing was that Chris hadn't come down, and she wanted to tell him where they were going.

"Edie'll go over and tell him," Mrs. Peebles said. "There's no problem." 120
Alice Kelling wrinkled her face and agreed.

"Be sure and tell him we'll be back by five!"

I didn't see that he would be concerned about knowing this right away, and I thought of him eating whatever he ate over there, alone, cooking on his camp stove, so I got to work and mixed up a crumb cake and baked it, in between the other work I had to do; then, when it was a bit cooled, wrapped it in a tea towel. I didn't do anything to myself but take off my apron and comb my hair. I would like to have put some makeup on, but I was too afraid it would remind him of the way he first saw me, and that would humiliate me all over again.

He had come and put another sign on the gate: NO RIDES THIS P.M. APOLOGIES. I worried that he wasn't feeling well. No sign of him outside and the tent flap was down. I knocked on the pole.

"Come in," he said, in a voice that would just as soon have said *Stay out.* 125
I lifted the flap.

"Oh, it's you. I'm sorry. I didn't know it was you."

He had been just sitting on the side of the bed, smoking. Why not at least sit and smoke in the fresh air?

"I brought a cake and hope you're not sick," I said.

"Why would I be sick? Oh—that sign. That's all right. I'm just tired of 130 talking to people. I don't mean you. Have a seat." He pinned back the tent flap. "Get some fresh air in here."

I sat on the edge of the bed, there was no place else. It was one of those fold-up cots, really: I remembered and gave him his fiancée's message.

He ate some of the cake. "Good."

"Put the rest away for when you're hungry later."

"I'll tell you a secret. I won't be around here much longer."

"Are you getting married?"

"Ha ha. What time did you say they'd be back?"

"Five o'clock."

"Well, by that time this place will have seen the last of me. A plane can get further than a car." He unwrapped the cake and ate another piece of it, absent-mindedly.

"Now you'll be thirsty."

"There's some water in the pail."

"It won't be very cold. I could bring some fresh. I could bring some ice from the refrigerator."

"No," he said. "I don't want you to go. I want a nice long time of saying good-bye to you."

He put the cake away carefully and sat beside me and started those little kisses, so soft, I can't ever let myself think about them, such kindness in his face and lovely kisses, all over my eyelids and neck and ears, all over, then me kissing back as well as I could (I had only kissed a boy on a dare before, and kissed my own arms for practice) and we lay back on the cot and pressed together, just gently, and he did some other things, not bad things or not in a bad way. It was lovely in the tent, that smell of grass and hot tent cloth with the sun beating down on it, and he said, "I wouldn't do you any harm for the world." Once, when he had rolled on top of me and we were sort of rocking together on the cot, he said softly, "Oh, no," and freed himself and jumped up and got the water pail. He splashed some of it on his neck and face, and the little bit left, on me lying there.

"That's to cool us off, miss."

When we said good-bye I wasn't at all sad, because he held my face and said "I'm going to write you a letter. I'll tell you where I am and maybe you can come and see me. Would you like that? Okay then. You wait." I was really glad I think to get away from him, it was like he was piling presents on me I couldn't get the pleasure of till I considered them alone.

No consternation at first about the plane being gone. They thought he had taken somebody up, and I didn't enlighten them. Dr. Peebles had phoned he had to go to the country, so there was just us having supper, and then Loretta Bird thrusting her head in the door and saying, "I see he's took off."

"What?" said Alice Kelling, and pushed back her chair.

"The kids come and told me this afternoon he was taking down his tent. Did he think he'd run through all the business there was around here? He didn't take off without letting you know, did he?"

"He'll send me word," Alice Kelling said. "He'll probably phone tonight. He's terribly restless, since the war."

"Edie, he didn't mention to you, did he?" Mrs. Peebles said, "When you took over the message?"   150

"Yes," I said. So far so true.

"Well why didn't you say?" All of them were looking at me. "Did he say where he was going?"

"He said he might try Bayfield," I said. What made me tell such a lie? I didn't intend it.

"Bayfield, how far is that?" said Alice Kelling.

Mrs. Peebles said, "Thirty, thirty-five miles."   155

"That's not far. Oh, well, that's really not far at all. It's on the lake, isn't it?"

You'd think I'd be ashamed of myself, setting her on the wrong track. I did it to give him more time, whatever time he needed. I lied for him, and also, I have to admit, for me. Women should stick together and not do things like that. I see that now, but didn't then. I never thought of myself as being in any way like her, or coming to the same troubles, ever.

She hadn't taken her eyes off me. I thought she suspected my lie.

"When did he mention this to you?"

"Earlier."   160

"When you were over at the plane?"

"Yes."

"You must've stayed and had a chat." She smiled at me, not a nice smile. "You must've stayed and had a little visit with him."

"I took a cake," I said, thinking that telling some truth would spare me telling the rest.

"We didn't have a cake," said Mrs. Peebles rather sharply.   165

"I baked one."

Alice Kelling said, "That was very friendly of you."

"Did you get permission," said Loretta Bird. "You never know what these girls'll do next," she said. "It's not they mean harm so much, as they're ignorant."

"The cake is neither here nor there," Mrs. Peebles broke in. "Edie, I wasn't aware you knew Chris that well."

I didn't know what to say.   170

"I'm not surprised," Alice Kelling said in a high voice. "I knew by the look of her as soon as I saw her. We get them at the hospital all the time." She looked hard at me with her stretched smile. "Having their babies. We have to put them in a special ward because of their diseases. Little country tramps. Fourteen and fifteen years old. You should see the babies they have, too."

"There was a bad woman here in town had a baby that pus was running out of its eyes," Loretta Bird put in.

"Wait a minute," said Mrs. Peebles. "What is this talk? Edie. What about you and Mr. Watters? Were you intimate with him?"

"Yes," I said. I was thinking of us lying on the cot and kissing, wasn't that intimate? And I would never deny it.

They were all one minute quiet, even Loretta Bird.

"Well," said Mrs. Peebles. "I am surprised. I think I need a cigarette. This is the first of any such tendencies I've seen in her," she said, speaking to Alice Kelling, but Alice Kelling was looking at me.

"Loose little bitch." Tears ran down her face. "Loose little bitch, aren't you? I knew as soon as I saw you. Men despise girls like you. He just made use of you and went off, you know that, don't you? Girls like you are just nothing, they're just public conveniences, just filthy little rags!"

"Oh, now," said Mrs. Peebles.

"Filthy," Alice Kelling sobbed. "Filthy little rags!"

"Don't get yourself upset," Loretta Bird said. She was swollen up with pleasure at being in on this scene. "Men are all the same."

"Edie, I'm very surprised," Mrs. Peebles said. "I thought your parents were so strict. You don't want to have a baby, do you?"

I'm still ashamed of what happened next. I lost control, just like a six-year-old, I started howling. "You don't get a baby from just doing that!"

"You see. Some of them are that ignorant," Loretta Bird said.

But Mrs. Peebles jumped up and caught my arms and shook me.

"Calm down. Don't get hysterical. Calm down. Stop crying. Listen to me. Listen. I'm wondering, if you know what being intimate means. Now tell me. What did you think it meant?"

"Kissing," I howled.

She let go. "Oh, Edie. Stop it. Don't be silly. It's all right. It's all a mis-understanding. Being intimate means a lot more than that. Oh, I *wondered*."

"She's trying to cover up, now," said Alice Kelling. "Yes. She's not so stupid. She sees she got herself in trouble."

"I believe her," Mrs. Peebles said. "This is an awful scene."

"Well there is one way to find out," said Alice Kelling, getting up. "After all, I am a nurse."

Mrs. Peebles drew a breath and said, "No. No. Go to your room, Edie. And stop that noise. This is too disgusting."

I heard the car start in a little while. I tried to stop crying, pulling back each wave as it started over me. Finally I succeeded, and lay heaving on the bed.

Mrs. Peebles came and stood in the doorway.

"She's gone," she said. "That Bird woman too. Of course, you know you should never have gone near that man and that is the cause of all this trouble. I have a headache. As soon as you can, go and wash your face in cold water and get at the dishes and we will not say any more about this."

Nor we didn't. I didn't figure out till years later the extent of what I had been saved from. Mrs. Peebles was not very friendly to me afterward, but she was fair. Not very friendly is the wrong way of describing what she was. She had never been very friendly. It was just that now she had to see me all the time and it got on her nerves, a little.

As for me, I put it all out of my mind like a bad dream and concentrated on waiting for my letter. The mail came every day except Sunday, between one-thirty and two in the afternoon, a good time for me because Mrs. Peebles was always having her nap. I would get the kitchen all cleaned and then go up to the mailbox and sit in the grass, waiting. I was perfectly happy, waiting, I forgot all about Alice Kelling and her misery and awful talk and Mrs. Peebles and her chilliness and the embarrassment of whether she told Dr. Peebles and the face of Loretta Bird, getting her fill of other people's troubles. I was always smiling when the mailman got there, and continued smiling even after he gave me the mail and I saw today wasn't the day. The mailman was a Carmichael. I knew by his face because there are a lot of Carmichaels living out by us and so many of them have a sort of sticking-out top lip. So I asked his name (he was a young man, shy, but good-humored, anybody could ask him anything) and then I said, "I knew by your face!" He was pleased by that and always glad to see me and got a little less shy. "You've got the smile I've been waiting on all day!" he used to holler out the car window.

It never crossed my mind for a long time a letter might not come. I believed in it coming just like I believed the sun would rise in the morning. I just put off my hope from day to day, and there was the goldenrod out around the mailbox and the children gone back to school, and the leaves turning, and I was wearing a sweater when I went to wait. One day walking back with the hydro bill stuck in my hand, that was all, looking across at the fairgrounds with the full-blown milkweed and dark teasels, so much like fall, it just struck me: *No letter was ever going to come.* It was an impossible idea to get used to. No, not impossible. If I thought about Chris's face when he said he was going to write to me, it was impossible, but if I forgot that and thought about the actual tin mailbox, empty, it was plain and true. I kept on going to meet the mail, but my heart was heavy now like a lump of lead. I only smiled because I thought of the mailman counting on it, and he didn't have an easy life, with the winter driving ahead.

Till it came to me one day there were women doing this with their lives all over. There were women just waiting and waiting by mailboxes for one letter or another. I imagined me making this journey day after day and year after year, and my hair starting to go gray, and I thought, I was never made to go on like that. So I stopped meeting the mail. If there were women all through life waiting, and women busy and not waiting, I knew which I had to be. Even though there might be things the second kind of women have to pass up and never know about, it still is better.

I was surprised when the mailman phoned the Peebleses' place in the evening and asked for me. He said he missed me. He asked if I would like to go to Goderich, where some well-known movie was on, I forget now what. So I said yes, and I went out with him for two years and he asked me to marry him, and we were engaged a year more while I got my things together, and then we did marry. He always tells the children the story of how I went after him by sitting by the mailbox every day, and naturally I laugh and let him, because I like for people to think what pleases them and makes them happy.

- As readers, we know more about Edie than the other characters in the story know. Find a specific scene in which this extra knowledge is important, and explain its significance.
- Does the narrator use any consistent strategies to describe Chris in this story? How does Edie's presentation of Chris compare with that of any of the other characters she encounters?
- What are Edie's relations with her employers? How does this relationship help define Edie's character?
- How did Edie meet her husband?
- To what extent is the title of this work an appropriate description of the story it contains?

Luigi Pirandello (1867–1936)

Luigi Pirandello, born in Sicily and a precocious child, demonstrated an early interest in, and talent for, literature and staged his first play at the age of twelve. After he married and started a family, Pirandello was forced to take a teaching job to supplement his income. His economic situation worsened further when his father, a wealthy sulfur merchant, lost his fortune as the result of a flood. Rather than crush the writer, economic pressures spurred him on and led him to a degree of popular success as a novelist. Pirandello is best remembered for his dramatic works, which, with their formal experimentation and preoccupation with existential questions, helped establish the conventions of modernist drama. His most famous work, because most technically innovative, is *Six Characters in Search of an Author*, in which the rehearsal for a play is interrupted by characters from another play.

The Soft Touch of Grass (1959, trans. Lily Duplaix)

They went into the next room, where he was sleeping in a big chair, to ask if he wanted to look at her for the last time before the lid was put on the coffin.

"It's dark. What time is it?" he asked.

It was nine-thirty in the morning, but the day was overcast and the light dim. The funeral had been set for ten o'clock.

Signor Pardi stared up at them with dull eyes. It hardly seemed possible that he could have slept so long and well all night. He was still numb with sleep and the sorrow of these last days. He would have liked to cover his face with his hands to shut out the faces of his neighbors grouped about his chair in the thin light; but sleep had weighted his body like lead, and although there was a tingling in his toes urging him to rise, it quickly went away. Should he still give way to his grief? He happened to say aloud, "Always . . ." but he said it like someone settling himself under the covers to go back to sleep. They all looked at him questioningly. Always what?

Always dark, even in the daytime, he had wanted to say, but it made no   5
sense. The day after her death, the day of her funeral, he would always remember this wan light and his deep sleep, too, with her lying dead in the next room. Perhaps the windows . . .

"The windows?"

Yes, they were still closed. They had not been opened during the night, and the warm glow of those big dripping candles lingered. The bed had been taken away and she was there in her padded casket, rigid and ashen against the creamy satin.

No. Enough. He had seen her.

He closed his eyes, for they burned from all the crying he had done these past few days. Enough. He had slept and everything had been washed away with that sleep. Now he was relaxed, with a sense of sorrowful emptiness. Let the casket be closed and carried away with all it held of his past life.

But since she was still there . . .   10

He jumped to his feet and tottered. They caught him and, with eyes still closed, he allowed himself to be led to the open casket. When he opened his eyes and saw her, he called her by name, her name that lived for him alone, the name in which he saw her and knew her in all the fullness of the life they had shared together. He glared resentfully at the others daring to stare at her lying still in death. What did they know about her? They could not even imagine what it meant to him to be deprived of her. He felt like screaming, and it must have been apparent, for his son hurried over to take him away. He was quick to see the meaning of this and felt a chill as though he were stripped bare. For shame—those foolish ideas up to the very last, even after his night-long sleep. Now they must hurry so as not to keep the friends waiting who had come to follow the coffin to the church.

"Come on, Papa. Be reasonable."

With angry, piteous eyes, the bereaved man turned back to his big chair.

Reasonable, yes; it was useless to cry out the anguish that welled within him and that could never be expressed by words or deeds. For a husband who is

left a widower at a certain age, a man still yearning for his wife, can the loss be
the same as that of a son for whom—at a certain point—it is almost timely to
be left an orphan? Timely, since he was on the point of getting married and
would, as soon as the three months' mourning were passed, now that he had
the added excuse that it was better for both of them to have a woman to look
after the house.

"Pardi! Pardi!" they shouted from the entrance hall.

His chill became more intense when he understood clearly for the first
time that they were not calling him but his son. From now on their surname
would belong more to his son than to him. And he, like a fool, had gone in
there to cry out the living name of his mate, like a profanation. For shame!
Yes, useless, foolish ideas, he now realized, after that long sleep which had
washed him clean of everything.

Now the one vital thing to keep him going was his curiosity as to how
their new home would be arranged. Where, for example, were they going to
have him sleep? The big double bed had been removed. Would he have a
small bed? he wondered. Yes, probably his son's single bed. Now he would
have the small bed. And his son would soon be lying in a big bed, his wife
beside him within arm's reach. He, alone, in his little bed, would stretch out
his arms into thin air.

He felt torpid, perplexed, with a sensation of emptiness inside and all
around him. His body was numb from sitting so long. If he tried now to get up he
felt sure that he would rise light as a feather in all that emptiness, now that his
life was reduced to nothing. There was hardly any difference between himself
and the big chair. Yet that chair appeared secure on its four legs, whereas he no
longer knew where his feet and legs belonged nor what to do with his hands.
What did he care about his life? He did not care particularly about the lives of
others, either. Yet as he was still alive he must go on. Begin again—some sort of
life which he could not yet conceive and which he certainly would never have
contemplated if things had not changed in his own world. Now, deposed like this
all of a sudden, not old and yet no longer young . . .

He smiled and shrugged his shoulders. For his son, all at once, he had
become a child. But after all, as everyone knows, fathers are children to their
grown sons who are full of worldly ambition and have successfully outdis-
tanced them in positions of importance. They keep their fathers in idleness to
repay all they have received when they themselves were small, and their
fathers in turn become young again.

The single bed . . .

But they did not even give him the little room where his son had slept.
Instead, they said, he would feel more independent in another, almost
hidden on the courtyard; he would feel free there to do as he liked. They
refurnished it with all the best pieces, so it would not occur to anyone that

it had once been a servant's room. After the marriage, all the front rooms were pretentiously decorated and newly furnished, even to the luxury of carpets. Not a trace remained of the way the old house had looked. Even with his own furniture relegated to that little dark room, out of the mainstream of the young people's existence, he did not feel at home. Yet, oddly enough, he did not resent the disregard he seemed to have reaped along with the old furniture, because he admired the new rooms and was satisfied with his son's success.

But there was another deeper reason, not too clear as yet, a promise of another life, all shining and colorful, which was erasing the memory of the old one. He even drew a secret hope from it that a new life might begin for him too. Unconsciously, he sensed the luminous opening of a door at his back whence he might escape at the right moment, easy enough now that no one bothered about him, leaving him as if on holiday in the sanctuary of his little room "to do as he pleased." He felt lighter than air. His eyes had a gleam in them that colored everything, leading him from marvel to marvel, as though he really were a child again. He had the eyes of a child—lively and open wide on a world which was still new.

He took the habit of going out early in the morning to begin his holiday which was to last as long as his life lasted. Relieved of all responsibilities, he agreed to pay his son so much every month out of his pension for his maintenance. It was very little. Though he needed nothing, his son thought he should keep some money for himself to satisfy any need he might have. But need for what? He was satisfied now just to look on at life.

Having shaken off the weight of experience, he no longer knew how to get along with oldsters. He avoided them. And the younger people considered him too old, so he went to the park where the children played.

That was how he started his new life—in the meadow among the children in the grass. What an exhilarating scent the grass had, and so fresh where it grew thick and high. The children played hide-and-seek there. The constant trickle of some hidden stream outpurled the rustle of the leaves. Forgetting their game, the children pulled off their shoes and stockings. What a delicious feeling to sink into all that freshness of soft new grass with bare feet!

He took off one shoe and was stealthily removing the other when a young girl appeared before him, her face flaming. "You pig!" she cried, her eyes flashing.

Her dress was caught up in front on a bush, and she quickly pulled it down over her legs, because he was looking up at her from where he sat on the ground.

He was stunned. What had she imagined? Already she had disappeared. He had wanted to enjoy the children's innocent fun. Bending down, he put his two hands over his hard, bare feet. What had she seen wrong? Was he too old to share a child's delight in going barefoot in the grass? Must one

25

immediately think evil because he was old? Ah, he knew that he could change in a flash from being a child to becoming a man again, if he must. He was still a man, after all, but he didn't want to think about it. He refused to think about it. It was really as a child that he had taken off his shoes. How wrong it was of that wretched girl to insult him like that! He threw himself face down on the grass. All his grief, his loss, his daily loneliness had brought about this gesture, interpreted now in the light of vulgar malice. His gorge rose in disgust and bitterness. Stupid girl! If he had wanted that— even his son admitted he might have "some desires"—he had plenty of money in his pocket for such needs.

Indignant, he pulled himself upright. Shame-facedly, with trembling hands, he put on his shoes again. All the blood had gone to his head and the pulse now beat hot behind his eyes. Yes, he knew where to go for that. He knew.

Calmer now, he got up and went back to the house. In the welter of furniture which seemed to have been placed there on purpose to drive him mad, he threw himself on the bed and turned his face to the wall.

■ How does his new apartment reflect the changes that Pardi encounters in his life?
■ What it is that he has done that others consider to be unreasonable?
■ Why is it significant that his new life starts around children?
■ What does he do wrong?
■ What details in the story help create sympathy for the main character?

Alice Walker (1944–)

Alice Walker was born in Eatonton, Georgia. She enrolled at Spelman College in Atlanta, Georgia, in 1961 and transferred to Sarah Lawrence College in New York in 1963. After receiving her BA from Sarah Lawrence in 1965, Walker moved to Mississippi to teach and promote civil rights. Her career also includes cofounding a publishing company and writing poetry, essays, short stories, novels, and literary criticism. Walker's Southern roots and womanist beliefs have greatly influenced her writing. Her works often take place in rural settings and explore the historical and present-day struggles of African Americans, particularly African American women. Walker has received many awards for her work, including the 1974 American Academy and Institute of Arts and Letters Award for *In Love and Trouble: Stories of Black Women* (1973) and both the 1983 Pulitzer Prize and 1983 National Book Award for her fifth novel, *The Color Purple* (1982).

Everyday Use (1973)

for your grandmama

I will wait for her in the yard that Maggie and I made so clean and wavy yesterday afternoon. A yard like this is more comfortable than most people know. It is not just a yard. It is like an extended living room. When the hard clay is swept clean as a floor and the fine sand around the edges lined with tiny, irregular grooves, anyone can come and sit and look up into the elm tree and wait for the breezes that never come inside the house.

Maggie will be nervous until after her sister goes: she will stand hopelessly in corners, homely and ashamed of the burn scars down her arms and legs, eyeing her sister with a mixture of envy and awe. She thinks her sister has held life always in the palm of one hand, that "no" is a word the world never learned to say to her.

You've no doubt seen those TV shows where the child who has "made it" is confronted, as a surprise, by her own mother and father, tottering in weakly from backstage. (A pleasant surprise, of course: What would they do if parent and child came on the show only to curse out and insult each other?) On TV mother and child embrace and smile into each other's faces. Sometimes the mother and father weep, the child wraps them in her arms and leans across the table to tell how she would not have made it without their help. I have seen these programs.

Sometimes I dream a dream in which Dee and I are suddenly brought together on a TV program of this sort. Out of a dark and soft-seated limousine I am ushered into a bright room filled with many people. There I meet a smiling, gray, sporty man like Johnny Carson who shakes my hand and tells me what a fine girl I have. Then we are on the stage and Dee is embracing me with tears in her eyes. She pins on my dress a large orchid, even though she has told me once that she thinks orchids are tacky flowers.

In real life I am a large, big-boned woman with rough, man-working hands. In the winter I wear flannel nightgowns to bed and overalls during the day. I can kill and clean a hog as mercilessly as a man. My fat keeps me hot in zero weather. I can work outside all day, breaking ice to get water for washing; I can eat pork liver cooked over the open fire minutes after it comes steaming from the hog. One winter I knocked a bull calf straight in the brain between the eyes with a sledge hammer and had the meat hung up to chill before nightfall. But of course all this does not show on television. I am the way my daughter would want me to be: a hundred pounds lighter, my skin like an uncooked barley pancake. My hair glistens in the hot bright lights. Johnny Carson has much to do to keep up with my quick and witty tongue.

5

But that is a mistake. I know even before I wake up. Who ever knew a Johnson with a quick tongue? Who can even imagine me looking a strange white man in the eye? It seems to me I have talked to them always with one foot raised in flight, with my head turned in whichever way is farthest from them. Dee, though. She would always look anyone in the eye. Hesitation was no part of her nature.

"How do I look, Mama?" Maggie says, showing just enough of her thin body enveloped in pink skirt and red blouse for me to know she's there, almost hidden by the door.

"Come out into the yard," I say.

Have you ever seen a lame animal, perhaps a dog run over by some careless person rich enough to own a car, sidle up to someone who is ignorant enough to be kind to him? That is the way my Maggie walks. She has been like this, chin on chest, eyes on ground, feet in shuffle, ever since the fire that burned the other house to the ground.

Dee is lighter than Maggie, with nicer hair and a fuller figure. She's a woman now, though sometimes I forget. How long ago was it that the other house burned? Ten, twelve years? Sometimes I can still hear the flames and feel Maggie's arms sticking to me, her hair smoking and her dress falling off her in little black papery flakes. Her eyes seemed stretched open, blazed open by the flames reflected in them. And Dee. I see her standing off under the sweet gum tree she used to dig gum out of; a look of concentration on her face as she watched the last dingy gray board of the house fall in toward the red-hot brick chimney. Why don't you do a dance around the ashes? I'd wanted to ask her. She had hated the house that much.

I used to think she hated Maggie, too. But that was before we raised the money, the church and me, to send her to Augusta to school. She used to read to us without pity; forcing words, lies, other folks' habits, whole lives upon us two, sitting trapped and ignorant underneath her voice. She washed us in a river of make-believe, burned us with a lot of knowledge we didn't necessarily need to know. Pressed us to her with the serious way she read, to shove us away at just the moment, like dimwits, we seemed about to understand.

Dee wanted nice things. A yellow organdy dress to wear to her graduation from high school; black pumps to match a green suit she'd made from an old suit somebody gave me. She was determined to stare down any disaster in her efforts. Her eyelids would not flicker for minutes at a time. Often I fought off the temptation to shake her. At sixteen she had a style of her own: and knew what style was.

I never had an education myself. After second grade the school was closed down. Don't ask me why: in 1927 colored asked fewer questions than they do now. Sometimes Maggie reads to me. She stumbles along good-naturedly but can't see well. She knows she is not bright. Like good looks and money, quickness passed her by. She will marry John Thomas (who has mossy teeth in an earnest face) and then I'll be free to sit here and I guess just sing church songs to myself. Although I never was a good singer. Never could carry a tune. I was always better at a man's job. I used to love to milk till I was hooked in the side in '49. Cows are soothing and slow and don't bother you, unless you try to milk them the wrong way.

I have deliberately turned my back on the house. It is three rooms, just like the one that burned, except the roof is tin; they don't make shingle roofs any more. There are no real windows, just some holes cut in the sides, like the portholes in a ship, but not round and not square, with rawhide holding the shutters up on the outside. This house is in a pasture, too, like the other one. No doubt when Dee sees it she will want to tear it down. She wrote me once that no matter where we "choose" to live, she will manage to come see us. But she will never bring her friends. Maggie and I thought about this and Maggie asked me, "Mama, when did Dee ever *have* any friends?"

She had a few. Furtive boys in pink shirts hanging about on washday after   15
school. Nervous girls who never laughed. Impressed with her they worshiped the well-turned phrase, the cute shape, the scalding humor that erupted like bubbles in lye. She read to them.

When she was courting Jimmy T she didn't have much time to pay to us, but turned all her faultfinding power on him. He *flew* to marry a cheap gal from a family of ignorant flashy people. She hardly had time to recompose herself.

When she comes I will meet—but there they are!

Maggie attempts to make a dash for the house, in her shuffling way, but I stay her with my hand. "Come back here," I say. And she stops and tries to dig a well in the sand with her toe.

It is hard to see them clearly through the strong sun. But even the first glimpse of leg out of the car tells me it is Dee. Her feet were always neat-looking, as if God himself had shaped them with a certain style. From the other side of the car comes a short, stocky man. Hair is all over his head a foot long and hanging from his chin like a kinky mule tail. I hear Maggie suck in her breath. "Uhnnnh," is what it sounds like. Like when you see the wriggling end of a snake just in front of your foot on the road. "Uhnnnh."

Dee next. A dress down to the ground, in this hot weather. A dress so   20
loud it hurts my eyes. There are yellows and oranges enough to throw back the light of the sun. I feel my whole face warming from the heat waves it throws out. Earrings gold, too, and hanging down to her shoulders. Bracelets dangling and making noises when she moves her arm up to shake the folds of

the dress out of her armpits. The dress is loose and flows, and as she walks closer, I like it. I hear Maggie go "Uhnnnh" again. It is her sister's hair. It stands straight up like the wool on a sheep. It is black as night and around the edges are two long pigtails that rope about like small lizards disappearing behind her ears.

"Wa-su-zo-Tean-o!" she says, coming on in that gliding way the dress makes her move. The short stocky fellow with the hair to his navel is all grinning and he follows up with "Asalamalakim, my mother and sister!" He moves to hug Maggie but she falls back, right up against the back of my chair. I feel her trembling there and when I look up I see the perspiration falling off her chin.

"Don't get up," says Dee. Since I am stout it takes something of a push. You can see me trying to move a second or two before I make it. She turns, showing white heels through her sandals, and goes back to the car. Out she peeks next with a Polaroid. She stoops down quickly and lines up picture after picture of me sitting there in front of the house with Maggie cowering behind me. She never takes a shot without making sure the house is included. When a cow comes nibbling around the edge of the yard she snaps it and me and Maggie *and* the house. Then she puts the Polaroid in the back seat of the car, and comes up and kisses me on the forehead.

Meanwhile Asalamalakim is going through the motions with Maggie's hand. Maggie's hand is as limp as a fish, and probably as cold, despite the sweat, and she keeps trying to pull it back. It looks like Asalamalakim wants to shake hands but wants to do it fancy. Or maybe he don't know how people shake hands. Anyhow, he soon gives up on Maggie.

"Well," I say. "Dee."

"No, Mama," she says. "Not 'Dee,' Wangero Leewanika Kemanjo!"

"What happened to 'Dee'?" I wanted to know.

"She's dead," Wangero said. "I couldn't bear it any longer being named after the people who oppress me."

"You know as well as me you was named after your aunt Dicie," I said. Dicie is my sister. She named Dee. We called her "Big Dee" after Dee was born.

"But who was *she* named after?" asked Wangero.

"I guess after Grandma Dee," I said.

"And who was she named after?" asked Wangero.

"Her mother," I said, and saw Wangero was getting tired. "That's about as far back as I can trace it," I said. Though, in fact, I probably could have carried it back beyond the Civil War through the branches.

"Well," said Asalamalakim, "there you are."

"Uhnnnh," I heard Maggie say.

"There I was not," I said, "before 'Dicie' cropped up in our family, so why should I try to trace it that far back?"

He just stood there grinning, looking down on me like somebody inspecting a Model A car. Every once in a while he and Wangero sent eye signals over my head.

"How do you pronounce this name?" I asked.

"You don't have to call me by it if you don't want to," said Wangero.

"Why shouldn't I?" I asked. "If that's what you want us to call you, we'll call you."

"I know it might sound awkward at first," said Wangero.   40

"I'll get used to it," I said. "Ream it out again."

Well, soon we got the name out of the way. Asalamalakim had a name twice as long and three times as hard. After I tripped over it two or three times he told me to just call him Hakim-a-barber. I wanted to ask him was he a barber, but I didn't really think he was, so I didn't ask.

"You must belong to those beef-cattle peoples down the road," I said. They said "Asalamalakim" when they met you, too, but they didn't shake hands. Always too busy: feeding the cattle, fixing the fences, putting up salt-lick shelters, throwing down hay. When the white folks poisoned some of the herd the men stayed up all night with rifles in their hands. I walked a mile and a half just to see the sight.

Hakim-a-barber said, "I accept some of their doctrines, but farming and raising cattle is not my style." (They didn't tell me, and I didn't ask, whether Wangero (Dee) had really gone and married him.)

We sat down to eat and right away he said he didn't eat collards and   45
pork was unclean. Wangero, though, went on through the chitlins and corn bread, the greens and everything else. She talked a blue streak over the sweet potatoes. Everything delighted her. Even the fact that we still used the benches her daddy made for the table when we couldn't afford to buy chairs.

"Oh, Mama!" she cried. Then turned to Hakim-a-barber. "I never knew how lovely these benches are. You can feel the rump prints," she said, running her hands underneath her and along the bench. Then she gave a sigh and her hand closed over Grandma Dee's butter dish. "That's it!" she said. "I knew there was something I wanted to ask you if could have." She jumped up from the table and went over in the corner where the churn stood, the milk in it clabber by now. She looked at the churn and looked at it.

"This churn top is what I need," she said. "Didn't Uncle Buddy whittle it out of a tree you all used to have?"

"Yes," I said.

"Uh huh," she said happily. "And I want the dasher, too."

"Uncle Buddy whittle that, too?" asked the barber.   50

Dee (Wangero) looked up at me.

"Aunt Dee's first husband whittled the dash," said Maggie so low you almost couldn't hear her. "His name was Henry, but they called him Stash."

"Maggie's brain is like an elephant's," Wangero said, laughing. "I can use the churn top as a centerpiece for the alcove table," she said, sliding a plate over the churn, "and I'll think of something artistic to do with the dasher."

When she finished wrapping the dasher the handle stuck out. I took it for a moment in my hands. You didn't even have to look close to see where hands pushing the dasher up and down to make butter had left a kind of sink in the wood. In fact, there were a lot of small sinks; you could see where thumbs and fingers had sunk into the wood. It was beautiful light yellow wood, from a tree that grew in the yard where Big Dee and Stash had lived.

After dinner Dee (Wangero) went to the trunk at the foot of my bed and started rifling through it. Maggie hung back in the kitchen over the dishpan. Out came Wangero with two quilts. They had been pieced by Grandma Dee and then Big Dee and me had hung them on the quilt frames on the front porch and quilted them. One was in the Lone Star pattern. The other was Walk Around the Mountain. In both of them were scraps of dresses Grandma Dee had worn fifty and more years ago. Bits and pieces of Grandpa Jarrell's Paisley shirts. And one teeny faded blue piece, about the size of a penny matchbox, that was from Great Grandpa Ezra's uniform that he wore in the Civil War.

"Mama," Wangero said sweet as a bird. "Can I have these old quilts?"

I heard something fall in the kitchen, and a minute later the kitchen door slammed.

"Why don't you take one or two of the others?" I asked. "These old things was just done by me and Big Dee from some tops your grandma pieced before she died."

"No," said Wangero. "I don't want those. They are stitched around the borders by machine."

"That'll make them last better," I said.

"That's not the point," said Wangero. "These are all pieces of dresses Grandma used to wear. She did all this stitching by hand. Imagine!" She held the quilts securely in her arms, stroking them.

"Some of the pieces, like those lavender ones, come from old clothes her mother handed down to her," I said, moving up to touch the quilts. Dee (Wangero) moved back just enough so that I couldn't reach the quilts. They already belonged to her.

"Imagine!" she breathed again, clutching them closely to her bosom.

"The truth is," I said, "I promised to give them quilts to Maggie, for when she marries John Thomas."

She gasped like a bee had stung her.

"Maggie can't appreciate these quilts!" she said. "She'd probably be backward enough to put them to everyday use."

"I reckon she would," I said. "God knows I been saving 'em for long enough with nobody using 'em. I hope she will!" I didn't want to bring up how I had offered Dee (Wangero) a quilt when she went away to college. Then she had told me they were old-fashioned, out of style.

"But they're *priceless*!" she was saying now, furiously; for she has a temper. "Maggie would put them on the bed and in five years they'd be in rags. Less than that!"

"She can always make some more," I said. "Maggie knows how to quilt."

Dee (Wangero) looked at me with hatred. "You just will not understand.   70
The point is these quilts, *these* quilts!"

"Well," I said, stumped. "What would *you* do with them?"

"Hang them," she said. As if that was the only thing you *could* do with quilts.

Maggie by now was standing in the door. I could almost hear the sound her feet made as they scraped over each other.

"She can have them, Mama," she said, like somebody used to never winning anything, or having anything reserved for her. "I can 'member Grandma Dee without the quilts."

I looked at her hard. She had filled her bottom lip with checkerberry snuff   75
and it gave her face a kind of dopey, hangdog look. It was Grandma Dee and Big Dee who taught her how to quilt herself. She stood there with her scarred hands hidden in the folds of her skirt. She looked at her sister with something like fear but she wasn't mad at her. This was Maggie's portion. This was the way she knew God to work.

When I looked at her like that something hit me in the top of my head and ran down to the soles of my feet. Just like when I'm in church and the spirit of God touches me and I get happy and shout. I did something I never had done before: hugged Maggie to me, then dragged her on into the room, snatched the quilts out of Miss Wangero's hands and dumped them into Maggie's lap. Maggie just sat there on my bed with her mouth open.

"Take one or two of the others," I said to Dee.

But she turned without a word and went out to Hakim-a-barber.

"You just don't understand," she said, as Maggie and I came out to the car.

"What don't I understand?" I wanted to know.   80

"Your heritage," she said. And then she turned to Maggie, kissed her, and said, "You ought to try to make something of yourself, too, Maggie. It's really a new day for us. But from the way you and Mama still live you'd never know it."

She put on some sunglasses that hid everything above the tip of her nose and her chin.

Maggie smiled; maybe at the sunglasses. But a real smile, not scared. After we watched the car dust settle I asked Maggie to bring me a dip of snuff. And then the two of us sat there just enjoying, until it was time to go in the house and go to bed.

- Go back to the first two paragraphs of this story. Notice that they are written in the future tense. How do these paragraphs set up the story that follows?
- Look at the description of how Maggie walks. What details do we learn about her relationship to the narrator?
- What does the narrator tell us about her own background?
- How does Dee's new name, Wangero Leewanika Kemanjo, define her character within this story?
- How does the exchange with the quilt address Dee's claim that her mother and sister "just don't understand" their heritage?

POETRY

Edgar Lee Masters (1869–1950)

Elsa Wertman (1915)

I was a peasant girl from Germany,
Blue-eyed, rosy, happy and strong.
And the first place I worked was at Thomas Greene's.
On a summer's day when she was away
He stole into the kitchen and took me   5
Right in his arms and kissed me on my throat,
I turning my head.   Then neither of us
Seemed to know what happened.
And I cried for what would become of me.
And cried and cried as my secret began to show.   10
One day Mrs. Greene said she understood,
And would make no trouble for me,
And, being childless, would adopt it.
(He had given her a farm to be still.)
So she hid in the house and sent out rumors,   15
As if it were going to happen to her.
And all went well and the child was born—They were so kind to me.
Later I married Gus Wertman, and years passed.
But—at political rallies when sitters-by thought I was crying
At the eloquence of Hamilton Greene—   20
That was not it.

No!   I wanted to say:
That's my son!   That's my son!

Edgar Lee Masters (1869–1950)

Hamilton Greene (1915)

I was the only child of Frances Harris of Virginia
And Thomas Greene of Kentucky,
Of valiant and honorable blood both.
To them I owe all that I became,
Judge, member of Congress, leader in the State.   5
From my mother I inherited
Vivacity, fancy, language;
From my father will, judgment, logic.
All honor to them
For what service I was to the people!   10

■ These two poems come from a collection in which Masters imagines the lives of people buried together in a fictional small-town cemetery. They each speak about their lives with an honesty that they could not have employed during their lives. How is it possible for both of the characters in this particular pairing to be honest yet to offer such different accounts of the same story?

Robert Frost (1874–1963)

Home Burial (1914)

He saw her from the bottom of the stairs
Before she saw him. She was starting down,
Looking back over her shoulder at some fear.
She took a doubtful step and then undid it
To raise herself and look again. He spoke   5
Advancing toward her: "What is it you see
From up there always—for I want to know."
She turned and sank upon her skirts at that,
And her face changed from terrified to dull.
He said to gain time: "What is it you see,"   10
Mounting until she cowered under him.
"I will find out now—you must tell me, dear."
She, in her place, refused him any help

With the least stiffening of her neck and silence.
She let him look, sure that he wouldn't see,   15
Blind creature; and awhile he didn't see.
But at last he murmured, "Oh," and again, "Oh."

"What is it—what?" she said.
                    "Just that I see."

"You don't," she challenged. "Tell me what it is."

"The wonder is I didn't see at once.   20
I never noticed it from here before.
I must be wonted to it—that's the reason.
The little graveyard where my people are!
So small the window frames the whole of it.
Not so much larger than a bedroom, is it?   25
There are three stones of slate and one of marble,
Broad-shouldered little slabs there in the sunlight
On the sidehill. We haven't to mind *those*.
But I understand; it is not the stones,
But the child's mound—"   30

                    "Don't, don't, don't, don't," she cried.

She withdrew, shrinking from beneath his arm
That rested on the banister, and slid downstairs;
And turned on him with such a daunting look,
He said twice over before he knew himself:
"Can't a man speak of his own child he's lost?"   35

"Not you!—Oh, where's my hat? Oh, I don't need it!
I must get out of here, I must get air.
I don't know rightly whether any man can"

"Amy! Don't go to someone else this time.
Listen to me. I won't come down the stairs."   40
He sat and fixed his chin between his fists.
"There's something I should like to ask you, dear."

"You don't know how to ask it."
                    "Help me, then."

Her fingers moved the latch for all reply.
"My words are nearly always an offense.   45

I don't know how to speak of anything
So as to please you. But I might be taught,
I should suppose. I can't say I see how.
A man must partly give up being a man
With women-folk. We could have some arrangement   50
By which I'd bind myself to keep hands off
Anything special you're a-mind to name.
Though I don't like such things 'twixt those that love.
Two that don't love can't live together without them.
But two that do can't live together with them."   55
She moved the latch a little, "Don't—don't go.
Don't carry it to someone else this time.
Tell me about it if it's something human.
Let me into your grief. I'm not so much
Unlike other folks as your standing there   60
Apart would make me out. Give me my chance.
I do think, though, you overdo it a little.
What was it brought you up to think it the thing
To take your mother-loss of a first child
So inconsolably—in the face of love.   65
You'd think his memory might be satisfied—"

"There you go sneering now!"

                     "I'm not, I'm not!
You make me angry. I'll come down to you.
God, what a woman! And it's come to this,
A man can't speak of his own child that's dead."   70

"You can't because you don't know how to speak.
If you had any feelings, you that dug
With your own hand—how could you?—his little grave;
I saw you from that very window there,
Making the gravel leap and leap in air,   75
Leap up, like that, like that, and land so lightly
And roll back down the mound beside the hole.
I thought, Who is that man? I didn't know you.
And I crept down the stairs and up the stairs
To look again, and still your spade kept lifting.   80
Then you came in. I heard your rumbling voice
Out in the kitchen, and I don't know why,
But I went near to see with my own eyes.
You could sit there with the stains on your shoes

Of the fresh earth from your own baby's grave   85
And talk about your everyday concerns.
You had stood the spade up against the wall
Outside there in the entry, for I saw it."

"I shall laugh the worst laugh I ever laughed.
I'm cursed. God, if I don't believe I'm cursed."   90

I cant repeat the very words you were saying:
'Three foggy mornings and one rainy day
Will rot the best birch fence a man can build.'
Think of it, talk like that at such a time!
What had how long it takes a birch to rot   95
To do with what was in the darkened parlor?
You *couldn't* care! The nearest friends can go
With anyone to death, comes so far short
They might as well not try to go at all.
No, from the time when one is sick to death,   100
One is alone, and he dies more alone.
Friends make pretense of following to the grave,
But before one is in it, their minds are turned
And making the best of their way back to life
And living people, and things they understand.   105
But the world's evil. I won't have grief so
If I can change it. Oh, I won't, I won't!"

"There, you have said it all and you feel better.
You won't go now. You're crying. Close the door.
The heart's gone out of it: why keep it up?   110
Amy! There's someone coming down the road!"

"*You*—oh, you think the talk is all. I must go—
Somewhere out of this house. How can I make you—"

"If—you—do!" She was opening the door wider.
"Where do you mean to go? First tell me that.   115
I'll follow and bring you back by force. I *will!*—"

■ Who are the two characters who are speaking to each other in this poem?
How are they related? Where do they disagree? Why is discussion of a rotting
birch fence significant to their conversation? What are they really talking
about?

Audre Lorde (1934–1992)

Now That I Am Forever with Child (1963)

How the days went
while you were blooming within me
I remember   each upon each
the swelling changed planes of my body

how you first fluttered   then jumped   5
and I thought it was my heart.

How the days wound down
and the turning of winter
I recall   you
growing heavy against the wind.   10
I thought now her hands
are formed her hair
has started to curl
now her teeth are done
now she sneezes.   15
Then the seed opened
I bore you one morning
just before spring
my head rang like a fiery piston
my legs were towers between which   20
a new world was passing.

Since then
I can only distinguish
one thread within running hours
you   flowing through selves   25
toward You.

■ How is "I thought it was my heart" significant to the relationship that the
narrator describes?

Eavan Boland (1944–)

The Pomegranate (1994)

The only legend I have ever loved is
The story of a daughter lost in hell.

And found and rescued there.
Love and blackmail are the gist of it.
Ceres and Persephone the names.   5
And the best thing about the legend is
I can enter it anywhere. And have.
As a child in exile in
A city of fogs and strange consonants,
I read it first and at first I was   10
An exiled child in the crackling dusk of
The underworld, the stars blighted. Later
I walked out in a summer twilight
Searching for my daughter at bedtime.
When she came running I was ready   15
To make any bargain to keep her.
I carried her back past whitebeams
And wasps and honey-scented buddleias.
But I was Ceres then and I knew
Winter was in store for every leaf   20
On every tree on that road.
Was inescapable for each one we passed.
And for me.

            It is winter
And the stars are hidden.
I climb the stairs and stand where I can see   25
My child asleep beside her teen magazines,
Her can of Coke, her plate of uncut fruit.
The pomegranate! How did I forget it?
She could have come home and been safe
And ended the story and all   30
Our heartbroken searching but she reached
Out a hand and plucked a pomegranate.
She put out her hand and pulled down
The French sound for apple and
The noise of stone and the proof   35
That even in the place of death,
At the heart of legend, in the midst
Of rocks full of unshed tears
Ready to be diamonds by the time
The story was told, a child can be   40
Hungry. I could warn her. There is still a chance.
The rain is cold. The road is flint-coloured.

The suburb has cars and cable television.
The veiled stars are above ground.
It is another world. But what else   45
Can a mother give her daughter but such
Beautiful rifts in time?
If I defer the grief I will diminish the gift.
The legend will be hers as well as mine.
She will enter it. As I have.   50
She will wake up. She will hold
the papery, flushed skin in her hand.
And to her lips. I will say nothing.

■ Ceres was the goddess of the earth and harvest. Her daughter, Persephone,
was kidnapped by Hades, the god of the underworld. When her mother came to
rescue her, Persephone could not leave because she had eaten a pomegranate
seed there. Ceres and Hades agreed to share Persephone, each for half of the
year. When she is in the underworld, the earth goes dormant with fall and
winter. How does the story of Persephone describe the relationship between
this mother and her daughter?

Sylvia Plath (1932–1963)

Daddy (1962)

You do not do, you do not do
Any more, black shoe
In which I have lived like a foot
For thirty years, poor and white,
Barely daring to breathe or Achoo.   5

Daddy, I have had to kill you.
You died before I had time—
Marble-heavy, a bag full of God,
Ghastly statue with one gray toe
Big as a Frisco seal   10

And a head in the freakish Atlantic
Where it pours bean green over blue
In the waters off the beautiful Nauset.

I used to pray to recover you.
Ach, du.   15

In the German tongue, in the Polish town
Scraped flat by the roller
Of wars, wars, wars.
But the name of the town is common.
My Polack friend   20

Says there are a dozen or two.
So I never could tell where you
Put your foot, your root,
I never could talk to you.
The tongue stuck in my jaw.   25

It stuck in a barb wire snare.
Ich, ich, ich, ich,
I could hardly speak.
I thought every German was you.
And the language obscene   30

An engine, an engine,
Chuffing me off like a Jew.
A Jew to Dachau, Auschwitz, Belsen.
I began to talk like a Jew.
I think I may well be a Jew.   35

The snows of the Tyrol, the clear beer of Vienna
Are not very pure or true.
With my gypsy ancestress and my weird luck
And my Taroc pack and my Taroc pack
I may be a bit of a Jew.   40

I have always been scared of you,
With your Luftwaffe, your gobbledygoo.
And your neat mustache
And your Aryan eye, bright blue.
Panzer-man, panzer-man, O You—   45

Not God but a swastika
So black no sky could squeak through.
Every woman adores a Fascist,

The boot in the face, the brute
Brute heart of a brute like you.   50

You stand at the blackboard, daddy,
In the picture I have of you,
A cleft in your chin instead of your foot
But no less a devil for that, no not
Any less the black man who   55

Bit my pretty red heart in two.
I was ten when they buried you.
At twenty I tried to die
And get back, back, back to you.
I thought even the bones would do.   60

But they pulled me out of the sack,
And they stuck me together with glue.
And then I knew what to do.
I made a model of you,
A man in black with a Meinkampf look   65

And a love of the rack and the screw.
And I said I do, I do.
So daddy, I'm finally through.
The black telephone's off at the root,
The voices just can't worm through.   70

If I've killed one man, I've killed two—
The vampire who said he was you
And drank my blood for a year,
Seven years, if you want to know.
Daddy, you can lie back now.   75

There's a stake in your fat black heart
And the villagers never liked you.
They are dancing and stamping on you.
They always knew it was you.
Daddy, daddy, you bastard, I'm through.   80

■ Why does she need to kill Daddy? What is her relationship with her father?
■ How does a review of his heritage help her put the "stake in your fat black heart" (line 76)?

Quincy Troupe (1939–)

Poem for My Father (2002)

for Quincy Troupe, Sr.

father, it was an honor to be there, in the dugout
with you, the glory of great black men swinging their lives
as bats, at tiny white balls
burning in at unbelievable speeds, riding up & in & out
a curve breaking down wicked, like a ball falling off a table   5
moving away, snaking down, screwing its stitched magic
into chitlin circuit air, its comma seams spinning
again toward breakdown, dipping, like a hipster
bebopping a knee-dip stride in the charlie parker forties
wrist curling like a swan's neck   10
behind a "slick" black back
cupping an invisible ball of dreams

& you there, father, regal as an african, obeah man
sculpted out of wood from a sacred tree, of no name, no place, origin
thick branches branching down, into cherokee & someplace else lost   15
way back in africa, the sap running dry
crossing from north carolina into georgia, inside grandmother mary's
womb, where your mother had you in the violence of that red soil
ink blotter news, gone now, into blood graves
of american blues, sponging rococo   20
truth long gone as dinosaurs
the agent-oranged landscape of former names
absent of african polysyllables, dry husk, consonants there
now, in their place, names, flat, as polluted rivers
& that guitar string smile always snaking across   25
some virulent, american, redneck's face
scorching, like atomic heat, mushrooming over nagasaki
& hiroshima, the fever blistered shadows of it all
inked, as etchings, into sizzling concrete
but, you, there, father, through it all, a yardbird solo   30
riffing on bat & ball glory, breaking down the fabricated myths
of white major league legends, of who was better than who
beating them at their own crap
game, with killer bats, as bud powell swung his silence into beauty
of a josh gibson home run, skittering across piano keys of bleachers   35
shattering all manufactured legends up there in lights
struck out white knights, on the risky edge of amazement

awe, the miraculous truth sluicing through
steeped & disguised in the blues
confluencing, like the point at the cross   40
when a fastball hides itself in a slider, curve
breaking down & away in a wicked, sly grin
curved & posed as an ass-scratching uncle tom, who
like old satchel paige delivering his famed hesitation pitch
before coming back with a hard, high, fast one, is slicker   45
sliding, & quicker than a professional hitman—
the deadliness of it all, the sudden strike
like that of the "brown bomber's" crossing right
of sugar ray robinson's, lightning, cobra bite

& you, there, father, through it all, catching rhythms   50
of chono pozo balls, drumming like conga beats into your catcher's mitt
hard & fast as "cool papa" bell jumping into bed
before the lights went out

of the old negro baseball league, a promise, you were
father, a harbinger, of shock waves, soon come   55

■ How does the father symbolize the son's relation with the historical oppression of his race?

■ In what ways does the poem indicate that the "old negro baseball league" is a promise "of shock waves" soon to come?

Kitty Tsui (1953–)

A Chinese Banquet (1994)

for the one who was not invited

it was not a very formal affair but
all the women over twelve
wore long gowns and a corsage,
except for me.

it was not a very formal affair, just   5
the family getting together,
poa poa, kuw fu without *kuw mow*
(her excuse this year is a headache).

aunts and uncles and cousins,
the grandson who is a dentist, 10
the one who drives a mercedes benz,
sitting down for shark's fin soup

they talk about buying a house and
taking a two-week vacation in beijing.
i suck on shrimp and squab, 15
dreaming of the cloudscape in your eyes.

my mother, her voice beaded with sarcasm:
you're twenty-six and not getting younger.
it's about time you got a decent job.
she no longer asks when i'm getting married. 20

you're twenty-six and not getting younger.
what are you doing with your life?
you've got to make a living.
why don't you study computer programming?

she no longer asks when i'm getting married. 25
one day, wanting desperately to
bridge the boundaries that separate us,
wanting desperately to touch her,

tell her: mother, I'm gay,
mother i'm gay and so happy with her. 30
but she will not listen,
she shakes her head.

she sits across from me,
emotions invading her face.
her eyes are wet but 35
she will not let tears fall.

mother, i say,
you love a man.
i love a woman.
it is not what she wants to hear. 40

aunts and uncles and cousins,
very much a family affair.
but you are not invited,
being neither my husband nor my wife.

aunts and uncles and cousins   45
eating longevity noodles
fragrant with ham inquire:
sold that old car of yours yet?

i want to tell them: my back is healing,
i dream of dragons and water.   50
my home is in her arms,
our bedroom ceiling the wide open sky.

■ How do repeated phrases and images help establish characters within this poem?
■ How does the description of the banquet change the second time we read it?

Billy Collins (1941–)

Lanyard (2005)

The other day I was ricocheting slowly
off the blue walls of this room,
bouncing from typewriter to piano,
from bookshelf to an envelope lying on the floor,
when I found myself in the L section of the dictionary   5
where my eyes fell upon the word *lanyard*.

No cookie nibbled by a French novelist
could send one more suddenly into the past—
a past where I sat at a workbench at a camp
by a deep Adirondack lake   10
learning how to braid thin plastic strips
into a lanyard, a gift for my mother.

I had never seen anyone use a lanyard
or wear one, if that's what you did with them,
but that did not keep me from crossing   15
strand over strand again and again
until I had made a boxy
red and white lanyard for my mother.

She gave me life and milk from her breasts,
and I gave her a lanyard.   20
She nursed me in many a sick room,
lifted spoons of medicine to my lips,

laid cold face-cloths on my forehead,
and then led me out into the airy light

and taught me to walk and swim,   25
and I, in turn, presented her with a lanyard.
Here are thousands of meals, she said,
and here is clothing and a good education.
And here is your lanyard, I replied,
which I made with a little help from a counselor.   30

Here is a breathing body and a beating heart,
strong legs, bones and teeth,
and two clear eyes to read the world, she whispered,
and here, I said, is the lanyard I made at camp.
And here, I wish to say to her now,   35
is a smaller gift—not the archaic truth

that you can never repay your mother,
but the rueful admission that when she took
the two-tone lanyard from my hands,
I was as sure as a boy could be   40
that this useless, worthless thing I wove
out of boredom would be enough to make us even.

■ How does the absurdity of the lanyard allow the poet to move beyond the "worn truth / that you can never repay your mother"?

E. A. Robinson (1869–1935)

The Mill (1919)

The miller's wife had waited long,
   The tea was cold, the fire was dead;
And there might yet be nothing wrong
   In how he went and what he said:
"There are no millers any more,"   5
   Was all that she had heard him say;
And he had lingered at the door
   So long that it seemed yesterday.

Sick with a fear that had no form
   She knew that she was there at last;   10

And in the mill there was a warm
  And mealy fragrance of the past.
What else there was would only seem
  To say again what he had meant;
And what was hanging from a beam   15
  Would not have heeded where she went.

And if she thought it followed her,
  She may have reasoned in the dark
That one way of the few there were
  Would hide her and would leave no mark: 20
Black water, smooth above the weir
  Like starry velvet in the night,
Though ruffled once, would soon appear
  The same as ever to the sight.

- What does it mean to the miller's wife that "There are no millers any more"?
- What is the meaning of "one way of the few there were / Would hide her and would leave no mark"?

Liz Rosenberg (1954–)

1:53 A.M. (2004)

There's a thin film of March snow on the street—
like the skin on a cup of milk—
and I get to lie down
again, I get to lie down
beside this great, blond, muscled light.   5
David has left a lamp on so I can read myself to peace.
But he is my great ease, my slumbering moon—
our son orbiting
in dreams across the hall,
and our daughter, spinning much farther out,   10
runs into her Chinese orphanage
in the bright middle of the afternoon.

- How does the poem use the solar system to indicate the relations within the family?

Gwendolyn Brooks (1917–2000)

Sadie and Maud (1945)

Maud went to college.
Sadie stayed at home.
Sadie scraped life
With a fine-tooth comb.

She didn't leave a tangle in.   5
Her comb found every strand.
Sadie was one of the livingest chits
In all the land.

Sadie bore two babies
Under her maiden name.   10
Maud and Ma and Papa
Nearly died of shame.

When Sadie said her last so-long
Her girls struck out from home.
(Sadie had left as heritage   15
Her fine-tooth comb.)

Maud, who went to college,
Is a thin brown mouse.
She is living all alone
In this old house.   20

■ How does Brooks contrast the sisters? Which one appears to have done better in this narrative?
■ What is the significance of the "fine-tooth comb"?

Seamus Heaney (1939–)

Mid-Term Break (1966)

I sat all morning in the college sick bay
Counting bells knelling classes to a close.
At two o'clock our neighbors drove me home.

In the porch I met my father crying—
He had always taken funerals in his stride—   5
And Big Jim Evans saying it was a hard blow.

The baby cooed and laughed and rocked the pram
When I came in, and I was embarrassed
By old men standing up to shake my hand

And tell me they were "sorry for my trouble,"   10
Whispers informed strangers I was the eldest,
Away at school, as my mother held my hand

In hers and coughed out angry tearless sighs.
At ten o'clock the ambulance arrived
With the corpse, stanched and bandaged by the nurses.   15

Next morning I went up into the room. Snowdrops
And candles soothed the bedside; I saw him
For the first time in six weeks. Paler now,

Wearing a poppy bruise on his left temple,
He lay in the four foot box as in his cot.   20
No gaudy scars, the bumper knocked him clear.

A four foot box, a foot for every year.

- What happened to the speaker's brother?
- Trace the details that the narrator offers about each of the other members of
  his family.

Michael Lassell (1947–)

How to Watch Your Brother Die (1985)

For Carl Morse

When the call comes, be calm.
Say to your wife, "My brother is dying. I have to fly
to California."
Try not to be too shocked that he already looks like

a cadaver.   5
Say to the young man sitting by your brother's side,
"I'm his brother."
Try not to be shocked when the young man says,
"I'm his lover. Thanks for coming."

Listen to the doctor with a steel face on.   10
Sign the necessary forms.
Tell the doctor you will take care of everything.
Wonder why doctors are so remote.

Watch the lover's eyes as they stare into
your brother's eyes as they stare into   15
space.
Wonder what they see there.
Remember the time he was jealous and
opened your eyebrow with a sharp stick.
Forgive him out loud   20
even if he can't
understand you.
Realize the scar will be
all that's left of him.

Over coffee in the hospital cafeteria   25
say to the lover, "You're an extremely good-looking
young man."
Hear him say,
"I never thought I was good enough looking to
deserve your brother."   30

Watch the tears well up in his eyes. Say,
"I'm sorry. I don't know what it means to be
the lover of another man."
Hear him say,
"It's just like a wife, only the commitment is   35
deeper because the odds against you are so much
greater."
Say nothing, but
take his hand like a brother's.

Drive to Mexico for unproven drugs that might   40
help him live longer.

Explain what they are to the border guard.
Fill with rage when he informs you,
"You can't bring those across."
Begin to grow loud.   45
Feel the lover's hand on your arm
restraining you. See in the guard's eye
how much a man can hate another man.
Say to the lover, "How can you stand it?"
Hear him say, "You get used to it."   50
Think of one of your children getting used to
another man's hatred.

Call your wife on the telephone. Tell her,
"He hasn't much time.
I'll be home soon." Before you hang up say,   55
"How could anyone's commitment be deeper than
a husband and wife?" Hear her say,
"Please. I don't want to know the details."

When he slips into an irrevocable coma,
hold his lover in your arms while he sobs,   60
no longer strong. Wonder how much longer
you will be able to be strong.
Feel how it feels to hold a man in your arms
whose arms are used to holding men.
Offer God anything to bring your brother back.   65
Know you have nothing God could possibly want.
Curse God, but do not
abandon Him.

Stare at the face of the funeral director
when he tells you he will not   70
embalm the body for fear of
contamination. Let him see in your eyes
how much a man can hate another man.

Stand beside a casket covered in flowers,
white flowers. Say,   75
"Thank you for coming," to each of the several
hundred men
who file past in tears, some of them
holding hands. Know that your brother's life
was not what you imagined. Overhear two   80

mourners say, "I wonder who'll be next?" and
"I don't care anymore,
as long as it isn't you."

Arrange to take an early flight home.
His lover will drive you to the airport.   85
When your flight is announced say,
awkwardly, "If I can do anything, please
let me know." Do not flinch when he says,
"Forgive yourself for not wanting to know him
after he told you. He did."   90
Stop and let it soak in. Say,
"He forgave me, or he knew himself?"
"Both," the lover will say, not knowing what else
to do. Hold him like a brother while he
kisses you on the cheek. Think that   95
you haven't been kissed by a man since
your father died. Think,
"This is no moment not to be strong."

Fly first class and drink Scotch. Stroke
your split eyebrow with a finger and   100
think of your brother alive. Smile
at the memory and think
how your children will feel in your arms,
warm and friendly and without challenge.

- What impact does the scar have upon the narrator?
- Find the moments in the poem where the narrator contrasts his growing
  understanding of both love and hate.

Adrienne Rich (1929–)

Aunt Jennifer's Tigers (1951)

Aunt Jennifer's tigers prance across a screen,
Bright topaz denizens of a world of green.
They do not fear the men beneath the tree;
They pace in sleek chivalric certainty.

Aunt Jennifer's fingers fluttering through her wool   5
Find even the ivory needle hard to pull.

The massive weight of Uncle's wedding band
Sits heavily upon Aunt Jennifer's hand.

When Aunt is dead, her terrified hands will lie
Still ringed with ordeals she was mastered by.   10
The tigers in the panel that she made
Will go on prancing, proud and unafraid.

▦ How do the wedding band and the tigers symbolize two contrasting elements
of Aunt Jennifer's life?

Gary Soto (1952–)

Black Hair (1985)

At eight I was brilliant with my body.
In July, that ring of heat
We all jumped through, I sat in the bleachers
Of Romain Playground, in the lengthening
Shade that rose from our dirty feet.   5
The game before us was more than baseball.
It was a figure—Hector Moreno
Quick and hard with turned muscles,
His crouch the one I assumed before an altar
Of worn baseball cards, in my room.   10

I came here because I was Mexican, a stick
Of brown light in love with those
Who could do it—the triple and hard slide,
The gloves eating balls into double plays.
What could I do with 50 pounds, my shyness,   15
My black torch of hair, about to go out?
Father was dead, his face no longer
Hanging over the table or our sleep,
And mother was the terror of mouths
Twisting hurt by butter knives.   20
In the bleachers I was brilliant with my body,
Waving players in and stomping my feet,
Growing sweaty in the presence of white shirts.
I chewed sunflower seeds. I drank water
And bit my arm through the late innings.   25

When Hector lined balls into deep
Center, in my mind I rounded the bases
With him, my face flared, my hair lifting
Beautifully, because we were coming home
To the arms of brown people.   30

■ What sort of role model does Hector provide for the narrator?
■ Why is the poem titled "Black Hair"?

DRAMA

Anton Chekhov (1860–1904)

Anton Chekhov was born in Taganrog, Russia. As a teenager, he attended local schools while working to help support his family. While studying medicine at Moscow University, Chekhov continued to provide for his family by doing freelance work writing short, humorous vignettes of contemporary Russian life. After eight years of such writing, Chekhov began submitting serious pieces to *Petersburgskaya gazeta* (*The Petersburg Gazette*). Though Chekhov received much criticism for his refusal to provide instruction or moral guidance through his writings, he continued to portray real characters and actions rather than idealizations in his works. In 1887, Chekhov's first play, *Ivanov*, was performed at the Korsh Theatre in Moscow; he eventually wrote twelve more plays. He is often referred to as the father of both the modern short story and the modern play, and works such as *The Cherry Orchard* and *Uncle Vanya* are regarded as classics of world literature.

The Proposal : A Jest in One Act

(1888, trans. Elisaveta Fen)

CHARACTERS

CHOOBUKOV, *Stepan Stepanovich, a landowner*
NATALYIA STEPANOVNA (NATASHA), *his daughter, aged twenty-five*
LOMOV, *Ivan Vassilievich, a landowner and neighbor of Choobukov, a healthy, well-nourished but hypochondriacal person*

SCENE: *The action takes place on the estate of Choobukov*

The drawing-room in Choobukov's house. CHOOBUKOV *and* LOMOV; *the latter enters wearing evening dress and white gloves.*

CHOOBUKOV (*going to meet him*): My dearest friend, fancy seeing you! Ivan Vassilievich! I'm so glad! (*Shakes hands.*) Well, this is a real surprise, dear old boy! . . . How are you?

LOMOV: Thank you. And how are you, pray?

CHOOBUKOV: We're getting on reasonably well, my cherub—thanks to your prayers and all that . . . . Please do sit down . . . . You know it's too bad of you to forget your neighbors, old fellow. But, my dear friend, why all this formality? Tails, gloves, and all the rest of it! Are you going visiting, or what, dear boy?

LOMOV: No, I've only come to see you, my dear Stepan Stepanovich.

CHOOBUKOV: Then why wear tails, dear boy? As though you were making a formal call on New Year's day!   5

LOMOV: The fact is, you see . . . . (*Takes his arm.*) I've come to ask a favor of you, my dear Stepan Stepanovich—if I'm not causing too much trouble. I've taken the liberty of seeking your help more than once in the past, and you've always, so to speak . . . . But forgive me, I'm in such a state . . . . I'll take a drink of water, my dear Stepan Stepanovich. (*Drinks water.*)

CHOOBUKOV (*aside*): He's come to ask for money! I shan't give him any! (*To* LOMOV.) What's the matter, my dear young fellow?

LOMOV: You see, my dear Stepanych . . . . Forgive me, Stepan, my dear . . . . I mean I'm in such a state of nerves—as you can see . . . . In short, you're the only man who can possibly help me, though, of course, I haven't done anything to deserve it, and . . . and I have no right to count on your assistance . . . .

CHOOBUKOV: Oh, don't spin it out, dear boy! Out with it! Well?

LOMOV: Yes, yes . . . . I'll tell you straight away . . . . The fact is that I've come to ask for the hand of your daughter, Natalyia Stepanovna.   10

CHOOBUKOV (*joyfully*): Ivan Vassilievich! My dearest friend! Say it again—I didn't quite hear you!

LOMOV: I have the honor to ask . . .

CHOOBUKOV (*interrupting him*): My dearest chap! . . . . I am so very glad, and so forth . . . . Yes, indeed—and all that sort of thing. (*Embraces and kisses him.*) I've wished it for a long time. It always has been my wish. (*Sheds a tear.*) I've always loved you as if you were my own son, my dearest fellow! May God grant you love and sweet concord, and all the rest of it. As for myself, I've always wished . . . . But why am I standing here like an idiot? I'm stunned with joy, simply stunned! Oh, with all my heart . . . . I'll go and call Natasha, and so on . . . .

LOMOV (*moved*): My dear Stepan Stepanych, what do you think she'll say? May I count on her consenting?

CHOOBUKOV: She not consent to it?—and you such a good-looker, too! I bet she's up to her ears in love with you, and so forth . . . . I'll tell her straight away! (*Goes out.*)

LOMOV (*alone*): I'm cold . . . . I'm trembling all over as if I were going in for an examination. The main thing is to make up your mind. If you think too long, keep talking and hesitating and waiting for the ideal woman or for real true love, you'll never get married. Brr! . . . I'm cold! Natalyia Stepanovna is an excellent housekeeper, educated, not bad-looking . . . . What more do I want? But I'm in such a state that I'm beginning to have noises in my head . . . . (*Drinks water.*) Yet I mustn't stay single. In the first place, I'm thirty-five already—a critical age, so to speak. Secondly, I must have an ordered, regular life . . . I've got a heart disease, with continual palpitations . . . . I flare up so easily, and I'm always getting terribly agitated . . . . Even now my lips are trembling and my right eyelid's twitching . . . . But the worst thing is my sleep. No sooner do I get into bed and start dropping off to sleep than something stabs me in my left side. Stab! and it goes right through my shoulder to my head . . . . I jump up like a madman, walk about for a bit and lie down again . . . . But directly I start dozing off, there it goes again in my side—stab! And the same thing happens twenty times over . . . .

(*Enter* NATALYIA.)

NATALYIA: Oh, so it's you! And Papa said: go along, there's a customer come for the goods. How do you do, Ivan Vassilievich?

LOMOV: How do you do, my dear Natalyia Stepanovna?

NATALYIA: Excuse my wearing this apron and not being properly dressed. We're shelling peas for drying. Why haven't you been to see us for so long? Do sit down . . . .

(*They sit down.*)

Will you have some lunch?

LOMOV: No, thank you, I've already had lunch.

NATALYIA: Won't you smoke? Here are some matches . . . . It's a magnificent day, but yesterday it rained so hard that the men did nothing all day. How many ricks did you manage to get in? Would you believe it, I was so set on getting it done that I had the whole meadow cut, and now I almost feel sorry—I'm afraid the hay may rot. It might have been better to wait. But what's all this? I believe you're wearing tails! This is something new! Are you going to a ball or something? By the way, you've changed—you're better looking! . . . But really, why are you dressed up like this?

LOMOV (*in agitation*): You see, dear Natalyia Stepanovna . . . . The fact is that I've decided to ask you to . . . listen to me . . . . Naturally, you'll be surprised, possibly even angry, but I . . . . (*Aside.*) How dreadfully cold it is!

NATALYIA: What is it then? (*A pause.*) Well?

LOMOV: I'll try to be brief. You are aware, of course, my dear Natalyia Stepanovna, that I've had the honor of knowing your family a long time—from my very childhood, in fact. My late aunt and her husband—from whom, as you know, I inherited the estate—always entertained a profound respect for your father and your late mother. The family of the Lomovs and the family of the Choobukovs have always been on the friendliest and, one might almost say, on intimate terms. Besides, as you are aware, my land is in close proximity to yours. Perhaps you will recollect that my Volovyi meadows lie alongside your birch wood.

NATALYIA: Excuse me, but I must interrupt you there. You say "my" Volovyi   25
meadows . . . . But are they really yours?

LOMOV: Yes, mine . . . .

NATALYIA: Well, what next! The Volovyi meadows are ours, not yours!

LOMOV: No, they're mine, dear Natalyia Stepanovna.

NATALYIA: That's news to me. How do they come to be yours?

LOMOV: What do you mean, how? I'm speaking of the Volovyi meadows that   30
lie like a wedge between your birch wood and the Burnt Swamp.

NATALYIA: But yes, of course . . . . They're ours.

LOMOV: No, you're mistaken, my dear Natalyia Stepanovna, they are mine.

NATALYIA: Do come to your senses, Ivan Vassilievich! How long have they
been yours?

LOMOV: What do you mean by "how long"? As long as I can remember—
they've always been ours.

NATALYIA: Well, there you must excuse me for disagreeing   35

LOMOV: You can see it in the documents, my dear Natalyia Stepanovna. It's
true that the Volovyi meadows were a matter of dispute at one time, but
now everyone knows that they're mine. There's really no need to argue
about it. If I may explain—my aunt's grandmother handed over those
meadows to your great grandfather's peasants for their use, rent free, for
an indefinite period, in return for their firing her bricks. Your great
grandfather's peasants used the meadows rent free for forty years or so and
got accustomed to looking upon them as their own . . . and then when the
settlement was made after the emancipation . . . .

NATALYIA: But it wasn't at all as you say! Both my grandfather and my great
grandfather considered that their land reached to the Burnt Swamp—so
the Volovyi meadows must have been ours. So why argue about it? I can't
understand you. It's really rather annoying!

LOMOV: I'll show you the documents, Natalyia Stepanovna!

NATALYIA: No, you must be just joking, or trying to tease me . . . . What a
surprise indeed! We've owned the land for something like three hundred
years, and now suddenly someone declares that the land isn't ours! Forgive me, Ivan Vassilievich, but I just can't believe my own ears . . . . I set

no value on those meadows. They're not more than fifteen acres, and they're only worth about three hundred rubles, but it's the injustice of it that disgusts me! You can say what you like, but I can't tolerate injustice.

LOMOV: Do hear me out, I implore you! Your father's grandfather's peasants, as I've already had the honor of telling you, fired bricks for my aunt's grandmother. My aunt's grandmother, wishing to do something for them . . . .

NATALYIA: Grandfather, grandmother, aunt . . . I don't understand anything about it! The meadows are ours, that's all!

LOMOV: They're mine!

NATALYIA: They're ours! You can go on trying to prove it for two days, you can put on fifteen dress suits if you like, but they're still ours, ours, ours! . . . I don't want what's yours, but I have no desire to lose what's mine . . . . You can please yourself!

LOMOV: I don't want the meadows, Natalyia Stepanovna, but it's a matter of principle. If you wish, I'll give them to you as a present.

NATALYIA: But I'm the one who could make a present of them to you—because they're mine! . . . All this is very strange, Ivan Vassilievich, to say the least of it! Till now we've always regarded you as a good neighbor, a friend of ours. Last year we lent you our threshing machine, and because of that we had to finish threshing our own corn in November. And now you're treating us as if we were gypsies! You're making me a present of my own land! Forgive me, but this isn't neighborly conduct! To my mind it's almost impertinent, if you want to know . . . .

LOMOV: You mean to say then that I'm a usurper? I've never stolen other people's land, Madam, and I won't allow anyone to accuse me of it . . . . (*Goes rapidly to the decanter and drinks water.*) The Volovyi meadows are mine!

NATALYIA: That's not true, they're ours!

LOMOV: They're mine!

NATALYIA: It isn't true! I'll prove it to you! I'll send my men to mow those meadows today.

LOMOV: What's that?

NATALYIA: My men will be working there today!

LOMOV: I'll kick them out!

NATALYIA: You daren't do that!

LOMOV (*clutches at his heart*): The Volovyi meadows are mine! Don't you understand that? Mine!

NATALYIA: Don't shout, please! You can shout and choke with rage when you're at home, but please don't overstep the mark here!

LOMOV: If it weren't for these dreadful agonizing palpitations, Madam—if it weren't for the throbbing in my temples, I should speak to you very differently! (*Shouts.*) The Volovyi meadows are mine!

NATALYIA: Ours!

LOMOV: Mine!

NATALYIA: Ours!

LOMOV: Mine!   60

(*Enter* CHOOBUKOV.)

CHOOBUKOV: What's all this? What are you shouting about?

NATALYIA: Papa, please explain to this gentleman: to whom do the Volovyi meadows belong—to him or to us?

CHOOBUKOV (*to* LOMOV): The meadows are ours, dear chap.

LOMOV: But forgive me, Stepan Stepanych, how do they come to be yours? At least you might be reasonable! My aunt's grandmother gave over the meadows to your grandfather's peasants for temporary use without payment. The peasants had the use of the land for forty years and got accustomed to regarding it as their own. But when the settlement was made . . . .

CHOOBUKOV: Pardon me, my dear friend . . . . You forget that it was just   65
because there was a dispute and so on about these meadows that the peasants didn't pay rent to your grandmother, and all the rest of it . . . . And now every dog knows that they're ours—yes, really! You can't have seen the plans!

LOMOV: But I'll prove to you they're mine!

CHOOBUKOV: You won't prove it, my dear man.

LOMOV: Yes, I will!

CHOOBUKOV: But why shout, my dear boy? You won't prove anything by shouting! I don't want what is yours, but I've no intention of letting go of what's mine. Why should I? If it comes to that, my dear friend—if you're thinking of starting a dispute about the meadows and all the rest of it, I'd sooner make a present of them to the peasants than to you. So that's that!

LOMOV: I don't understand this! What right have you to give away someone   70
else's property?

CHOOBUKOV: Permit me to decide whether I have the right or not! And really, young man, I'm not used to being spoken to in that tone, and so forth . . . . I'm twice your age, young man, and I beg you to speak to me without getting excited, and all that . . . .

LOMOV: No, you're simply taking me for a fool and laughing at me! You call my land yours, and then you expect me to stay cool and talk to you in the ordinary way. Good neighbors don't behave in this way, Stepan Stepanych! You're not a neighbor, you're a usurper!

CHOOBUKOV: What's that? What did you say?

NATALYIA: Papa, send the men to mow the meadows at once!

CHOOBUKOV (*to* LOMOV): What was it you said, sir?   75

NATALYIA: The Volovyi meadows are ours, and I won't give them up! I won't, I won't!

LOMOV: We shall see about that! I'll prove to you in court that they're mine.

CHOOBUKOV: In court? You take it to court, sir, and all the rest of it! You do it! I know you—you've really just been waiting for a chance to go to law, and all that. It comes natural to you—this petty niggling. Your family always had a weakness for litigation. All of them!

LOMOV: Please don't insult my family! The Lomovs have all been honest men, and not one of them has ever been on trial for embezzling money like your uncle!

CHOOBUKOV: Every member of Lomov family has been mad!

NATALYIA: Every one of them—everyone!

CHOOBUKOV: Your grandfather was a dipsomaniac, and your youngest aunt, Nastasyia Mihailovna—it's a fact—ran away with an architect, and all the rest of it . . . .

LOMOV: And your mother was deformed! *(Clutches at his heart.)* This shooting pain in my side! . . . The blood's gone to my head . . . . Holy Fathers! Water!

CHOOBUKOV: Your father was a gambler and a glutton!

NATALYIA: Your aunt was a scandal-monger—and a rare one at that!

LOMOV: My left leg's paralyzed . . . . And you're an intriguer . . . . Oh, my heart! . . . And it's an open secret that before the elections you . . . . There are flashes in front of my eyes . . . . Where's my hat? . . .

NATALYIA: It's mean! It's dishonest! It's perfectly vile!

CHOOBUKOV: And you're just a malicious, double-faced, mean fellow! Yes, you are!

LOMOV: Here it is, my hat . . . . My heart . . . . Which way do I go? Where's the door? Oh! I believe I'm dying . . . . I've lost the use of my leg . . . . *(Walks to the door.)*

CHOOBUKOV *(calling after him):* I forbid you to set foot in my house again!

NATALYIA: Take it to court! We shall see!

(LOMOV goes out staggering.)

CHOOBUKOV: The devil take him! *(Walks about in agitation.)*

NATALYIA: Have you ever seen such a cad? Trust good neighbors after that!

CHOOBUKOV: The ridiculous scarecrow! The scoundrel!

NATALYIA: The monster! Grabs other people's land, then dares to abuse them into the bargain!

CHOOBUKOV: And this ridiculous freak, this eyesore—yes, he has the impertinence to come here and make a proposal and all the rest of it! Would you believe it? A proposal!

NATALYIA: What proposal?

CHOOBUKOV: Yes, just fancy! He came to propose to you.

NATALYIA: To propose? To me? But why didn't you tell me that before?

CHOOBUKOV: That's why he got himself up in his tail-coat. The sausage! The shrimp! 100

NATALYIA: To me? A proposal? Oh! *(Drops into a chair and moans.)* Bring him back! Bring him back! Oh, bring him back!

CHOOBUKOV: Bring whom back?

NATALYIA: Be quick, be quick! I feel faint! Bring him back! *(Shrieks hysterically.)*

CHOOBUKOV: What is it? What do you want? *(Clutches at his head.)* What misery! I'll shoot myself! I'll hang myself! They've worn me out!

NATALYIA: I'm dying! Bring him back! 105

CHOOBUKOV: Phew! Directly. Don't howl. *(Runs out.)*

NATALYIA *(alone, moans)*: What have we done! Bring him back! Bring him back!

CHOOBUKOV *(runs in)*: He's coming directly, and all the rest of it. Damnation take him! Ugh! You can talk to him yourself; I don't want to, and that's that!

NATALYIA *(moans)*: Bring him back!

CHOOBUKOV *(shouts)*: He's coming, I tell you! What a job it is, O Lord, to be a 110 grown-up daughter's father. I'll cut my throat! Yes, indeed, I'll cut my throat! We've abused the man, we've insulted him, we've kicked him out, and it was all your doing—your doing!

NATALYIA: No, it was yours!

CHOOBUKOV: So now it's my fault! What next!

(Enter LOMOV.)

LOMOV *(exhausted)*: These dreadful palpitations.... My leg feels numb... a shooting pain in my side....

NATALYIA: Forgive us, we were rather hasty, Ivan Vassilievich.... I remember now: the Volovyi meadows really are yours.

LOMOV: My heart's going at a terrific rate. The meadows are mine.... Both 115 my eyelids are twitching....

NATALYIA: Yes, they're yours, yours.... Sit down....
(They sit down.)
We were wrong.

LOMOV: To me it's a matter of principle.... I don't value the land, but I value the principle....

NATALYIA: That's it, the principle.... Let's talk about something else.

LOMOV: Especially as I have proof. My aunt's grandmother gave over to your father's grandfather's peasants....

NATALYIA: Enough, enough about that.... *(Aside.)* I don't know how to 120 begin.... *(To him.)* Will you soon be going shooting?

LOMOV: I expect to go grouse shooting after the harvest, dear Natalyia Stepanovna . . . . Oh, did you hear? Just fancy—what bad luck I've had! My Tryer—you know him—he's gone lame.

NATALYIA: What a pity! What was the cause of it?

LOMOV: I don't know . . . . He may have dislocated his paw, or he may have been bitten by other dogs . . . . (*Sighs.*) My best dog, to say nothing of the money! You know, I paid Mironov a hundred and twenty-five rubles for him.

NATALYIA: You paid too much, Ivan Vassilievich.

LOMOV: Well, I think it was very cheap. He's a marvelous dog!

NATALYIA: Papa paid eighty-five rubles for his Flyer, and Flyer is better than your Tryer by far.

LOMOV: Flyer better than Tryer? Come, come! (*Laughs.*) Flyer better than Tryer!

NATALYIA: Of course, he's better! It's true that Flyer's young—he's hardly a full-grown dog yet—but for points and cleverness even Volchanyetsky hasn't got a better one.

LOMOV: Excuse me, Natalyia Stepanovna, but you forget that he's got a pug-jaw, and a dog with pug-jaw can never grip properly.

NATALYIA: A pug-jaw? That's the first I've heard of it.

LOMOV: I assure you, his lower jaw is shorter than the upper one.

NATALYIA: Why, did you measure it?

LOMOV: Yes. He's all right for coursing, of course, but when it comes to gripping, he's hardly good enough.

NATALYIA: In the first place our Flyer is a pedigree dog—he's the son of Harness and Chisel—whereas your Tryer's coat has got such a mixture of colors that you'd never guess what kind he is. Then he's as old and ugly as an old hack . . . .

LOMOV: He's old, but I wouldn't take five of your Flyers for him . . . . I wouldn't think of it! Tryer is a real dog, but Flyer . . . it's absurd to go on arguing . . . . Every sportsman has any number of dogs like your Flyer. Twenty-five rubles would be a lot to pay for him.

NATALYIA: There's some demon of contradiction in you today, Ivan Vassi-lievich. First you pretend that the meadows are yours, and now you're saying that Tryer is better than Flyer. I don't like it when people say what they don't really believe. After all, you know perfectly well that Flyer is a hundred times better than your . . . . well, your stupid Tryer. So why say the opposite?

LOMOV: I can see, Natalyia Stepanovna, that you think I'm either blind or a fool. Won't you understand that your Flyer has a pug-jaw?

NATALYIA: That isn't true.

LOMOV: He has a pug-jaw.

NATALYIA (*shouts*): It's not true! . . .   140

LOMOV: What are you shouting for, Madam?

NATALYIA: Why are you talking nonsense? This is quite revolting! It's time
your Tryer was shot, and you're comparing him to Flyer!

LOMOV: Excuse me, I can't continue this argument. I have palpitations.

NATALYIA: I've noticed that the people who understand least about shooting
are the ones who argue most about it.

LOMOV: Madam, please be silent . . . . My heart's bursting . . . . (*Shouts.*) Be quiet!   145

NATALYIA: I won't be quiet till you admit that Flyer is a hundred times better
than your Tryer.

LOMOV: He's a hundred times worse! It's time he was dead, your Flyer! Oh, my
head . . . my eyes . . . my shoulder!

NATALYIA: As for your idiot Tryer—I don't need to wish him dead: he's half-
dead already!

LOMOV (*weeping*): Be quiet! My heart's going to burst.

NATALYIA: I won't be quiet!   150

(*Enter* CHOOBUKOV.)

CHOOBUKOV: Now what is it?

NATALYIA: Papa, tell us frankly, on your honor: which dog's the better—our
Flyer or his Tryer?

LOMOV: Stepan Stepanych, I implore you, tell us just one thing: has your Flyer
got a pug-jaw, or hasn't he? Yes or no?

CHOOBUKOV: Well, what if he has? As if it mattered! Anyway, there's no
better dog in the whole district, and all that.

LOMOV: But my Tryer is better, isn't he? On your honor!   155

CHOOBUKOV: Don't get excited, my dear boy . . . . Let me explain . . . . Your
Tryer, of course, has his good points . . . . He's a good breed, he's got strong
legs, he's well built and all the rest of it. But if you really want to know,
my dear friend, the dog has two serious faults: he's old and he's snub-
nosed.

LOMOV: Excuse me, I've got palpitations . . . . Let us look at the facts . . . .
Perhaps you'll remember that when we hunted in the Maruskin fields my
Tryer kept up with the Count's Spotter, while your Flyer was a good half-
mile behind.

CHOOBUKOV: He dropped behind because the Count's huntsman hit him with
his whip.

LOMOV: He deserved it. All the other dogs were chasing the fox, but Flyer
started worrying the sheep.

CHOOBUKOV: That's not true! . . . My dear friend, I lose my temper easily, so I   160
do beg you, let's drop this argument. The man hit him because people are
always jealous of other people's dogs . . . . Yes, everyone hates the other
man's dog! And you, sir, are not innocent of that either! Yes! For

instance, as soon as you notice that someone's dog is better than your Tryer, you immediately start something or other . . . and all the rest of it . . . . You see, I remember everything!

LOMOV: So do I!

CHOOBUKOV (*mimics him*): So do I! And what is it you remember?

LOMOV: Palpitations . . . . My leg's paralyzed . . . . I can't . . . .

NATALYIA (*mimics him*): Palpitations . . . . What sort of a sportsman are you? You ought to be lying on the stove in the kitchen squashing blackbeetles instead of hunting foxes! Palpitations indeed!

CHOOBUKOV: Yes, honestly, hunting's not your line at all! With your palpitations and all that, you'd be better at home than sitting on horseback being jolted about. It wouldn't matter if you really hunted, but you only go out so that you can argue, or get in the way of other people's dogs, and all the rest of it . . . . I get angry easily, so let's stop this conversation. You're just not a sportsman, and that's all there is to it.

LOMOV: What about you—are you a sportsman? You only go out hunting to make up to the Count, and intrigue against other people . . . . Oh, my heart! You're an intriguer!

CHOOBUKOV: What! I—an intriguer? (*Shouts.*) Be silent!

LOMOV: Intriguer!

CHOOBUKOV: Milksop! Puppy!

LOMOV: You old rat! Hypocrite!

CHOOBUKOV: Hold your tongue, or I'll shoot you with a dirty gun like a partridge! Windbag!

LOMOV: Everyone knows—oh, my heart!—that your wife used to beat you! . . . My leg . . . my head . . . in front of my eyes . . . . I'm going to fall down . . . . I'm falling . . . .

CHOOBUKOV: And your housekeeper has got you under her thumb!

LOMOV: Oh! oh! oh! . . . My heart's burst! My shoulder's gone . . . . Where's my shoulder? . . . I'm dying! (*Drops into an armchair.*) A doctor! (*Faints.*)

CHOOBUKOV: Milksop! Puppy! Windbag! I'm feeling faint. (*Drinks water.*) Faint!

NATALYIA: A sportsman indeed! You don't even know how to sit on a horse! (*To her father.*) Papa! What's the matter with him? Papa! Look, Papa! (*Shrieks.*) Ivan Vassilievich! He's dead.

CHOOBUKOV: I feel faint! . . . I'm suffocating! Give me air!

NATALYIA: He's dead! (*Shakes* LOMOV *by the sleeve.*) Ivan Vassilych! Ivan Vassilych! What have we done! He's dead! (*Drops into an armchair,*) Doctor, doctor! (*Sobs and laughs hysterically*)

CHOOBUKOV: What now? What's the matter? What do you want?

NATALYIA (*moans*): He's dead! . . . Dead!

CHOOBUKOV: Who's dead? (*Glancing at* LOMOV.) He really is dead! My God! Water! Doctor! (*Holds a glass of water to* LOMOV's *lips.*) Take a drink! . . . No, he won't drink . . . . So he's dead and all that . . . . What an unlucky man I am! Why don't I put a bullet through my brain? Why didn't I cut my throat long ago? What am I waiting for? Give me a knife! Give me a gun! (LOMOV *makes a slight movement.*) I believe he's coming round . . . . Do have a drink of water! That's right . . . .

LOMOV: Flashes before my eyes . . . a sort of mist . . . . Where am I?

CHOOBUKOV: You'd better get married as soon as possible and—go to the devil . . . . She consents. (*Joins their hands.*) She consents, and all the rest of it. I give you my blessing, and so forth. Only leave me alone!

LOMOV: Eh? What? (*Getting up.*) Who?

CHOOBUKOV: She consents! Well? Kiss each other and . . . and the devil take you!   185

NATALYIA (*moans*): He's alive . . . . Yes, yes, I consent . . . .

CHOOBUKOV: Come now, kiss each other!

LOMOV: Eh? Who? (*Kisses* NATALYIA.) I am so pleased! . . . Excuse me, what's it all about? Ah! yes, I understand . . . . My heart . . . flashes . . . I'm so happy, Natalyia Stepanovna . . . . (*Kisses her hand.*) My leg's numb . . . .

NATALYIA: I . . . I'm happy too . . . .

CHOOBUKOV: What a load off my back! . . . Ugh!   190

NATALYIA: But . . . all the same, you must admit it now: Tryer is not as good a dog as Flyer.

LOMOV: He's better!

NATALYIA: He's worse!

CHOOBUKOV: There! Family happiness has begun! Bring the champagne!

LOMOV: He's better!   195

NATALYIA: He's worse, worse, worse!

CHOOBUKOV (*trying to shout them down*): Champagne! Bring the champagne!

CURTAIN

- What is Lomov's purpose in coming to visit Choobukov and Natalyia?
- What detail distracts him from this purpose? Who creates the distraction?
- It is possible to divide this play into scenes based upon which characters are onstage. As you look at the scenes of this play, identify which character dominates each exchange. How do specific character traits help define each particular style of dominance?
- How is the tension in the discussion resolved?
- How does Choobukov function in the play? Where does he appear? How does he broker the proposal?

Experiencing Literature through Writing

1. Select a single character in one of the works from this chapter. How has the author made this character seem real? Explain what qualities stand out in this character and how those qualities are significant to the larger story.

   a. What specific details do we learn about the character?

   b. In what context do these details appear?

   c. Are there any apparent contradictions within the character? Identify any, and explain how the author resolves or makes use of these contradictions.

2. The readings in this chapter focus on relationships among people. In many of these relationships, it is clear that the characters within the relationship do not share the same views of that relationship. Describe how one character uses the relationship in this work for self-definition.

3. Characters rarely exist isolated from events. Their characteristics often become more apparent as we see them engaged, in action or with other characters. Find a specific description of a character acting in a specific scene. Explain how specific details of that action reveal the character.

3   Theme

What Does This Text Mean?

Is There One Right Way to Read This Text?

Theme can be seen as central to the experience of literature and film. We want texts to *mean* something. We tend to value depth, complexity, and relevance. We presume that the greatest works of art reward us because they express significant and lasting themes. At some level, each of the elements addressed in the chapters of this book contributes to the shaping of meaning and, for that reason, demands attention. Yet an insistent search for theme can also be viewed as an avoidance of the literary experience. If we translate a poem into a statement, we risk losing the very qualities that made it a poem. If we neatly summarize a story's "message," we may miss out on a range of complex emotions that the story could inspire. If we bring a narrow sense of purpose to our reading, we will fail to engage the work of art on its own terms.

These different perspectives on theme might seem irreconcilable on many counts.

This chapter on "theme" is essential; it's central to the concerns of everything in this book.	This chapter on "theme" is redundant; it's covered in every chapter.
Themes are "in the text" for readers/writers to identify as given.	Themes are defined by readers/writers to make sense of or deepen a text.
A theme is an idea.	A theme is an echo of an idea.
Works of art communicate meaning.	Works of art surpass meaning.

Fortunately, we don't need to reconcile everything in life or in literary study. When we're made conscious of oppositions, the resulting tension can be productive. We can be sensitive to theme without becoming a "theme hunter." We want you to attend to meaning without deadening the immediate sensory or emotional force that literature and film convey. To achieve and maintain such a delicate critical balance, we'll need to think carefully about how we write about theme, what we mean by theme, and what we mean by "meaning."

THEME AND THESIS

It's useful to start thinking about theme by reflecting upon the demands we must satisfy as critics. In an essay, theme suggests "thesis"—a key assertion that guides the entire presentation, an assertion that is woven through the whole. A thesis in an analytical paper should be clearly defined and assertive. It should be a statement that a writer can (and must) back up. This notion of argument is harder to grasp than one might think. It's common for inexperienced writers to arrive at a thesis that is really nothing more than a preview of topics to be discussed in the course of the essay. Consider the following example of what we might call a generic thesis:

> To understand our reaction to the wounded lieutenant in "An Episode of War," we must consider Stephen Crane's management of plot, character, and point of view.

This kind of statement makes no real argumentative claim and therefore doesn't function as a purposeful lead. You could remove the words that identify the object of attention and substitute almost any author and title:

> To understand our reaction to X in "Y," we must consider Z's management of plot, character, and point of view.

A formulaic lead like this is sure to result in an equally formulaic essay that checks off the topics for discussion in a paragraph-by-paragraph fashion without helping anyone see how the paragraphs work together. A critical writer needs to do more than this.

What exactly is our reaction to the wounded lieutenant in Crane's story? Why do we react in that way? How is it that Crane is able to make us respond as we do? Questions like these might lead to a workable, argumentative, and engaging thesis as well as a richer and more coherent sense of the story's meaning. They first of all help us establish a critical issue: Crane presents the lieutenant for the most part from the outside. We see him as others see him.

Only occasionally do we see from the lieutenant's eyes, and even then it usually seems that we're getting a mere report of what he sees. Such observations prepare for an argument, an assertion, a thesis (not a list of points "to discuss"):

> Crane's seemingly objective presentation of the episode actually intensifies our sympathy for the lieutenant, because that objectivity makes us feel the wounded man's helplessness.

The previous sentence, of course, can't stand alone. It needs to be defended and explained. A **thesis**, like a **theme**, can be thought of as a main idea, a motivating idea, or a structuring idea.

Relating theme and thesis in these ways highlights the function of repetition in both art and criticism. A thesis in a critical essay is sustained by transitions that echo the main line. A pattern of key words or subordinate linked assertions helps sustain an argument. Such repetition is also clearly part of how theme plays out in literature and film. If you watch George Lucas's original *Star Wars*, you can't help noticing the rousing score by John Williams that blasts through the opening credits and establishes the tone for the battle between good and evil that lies at the heart of this production. If you listen even casually, you will also notice that each major character in the film has his or her own music to accompany whatever action is going on. Darth Vader's theme is, of course, menacing. The deeply ominous notes accentuate his threatening visual presence. Music guides us with other characters as well. As the rebels fly off to blow up the Death Star, individual pilots may be indistinguishable in their orange suits and helmets, but the music helps us recognize Luke Skywalker and smile in relief when the *Millennium Falcon* swoops in (with its own music) to help knock Darth Vader off his course. The theme music permeates the film with each variation building upon another, adding in the various characters' themes as they enter alliances or conflicts, until the climax or decisive point, which recapitulates the sounds from the opening in a final theater-rattling combination of brass and cymbals.

THEME AND MORAL

Concentrating on theme sometimes leads us to a narrowed sense of what a text might mean. Our experience of a work often feels much larger than the paper that attempts to explain the experience in terms of meaning or message. Perhaps our tendency to isolate, extract, and narrowly restate a single theme from a literary text arises from our familiarity with certain kinds of "easy" works. For example, the simplest children's stories often have a lesson to teach. They may wrap up a message neatly at the end with an explicit moral—a concluding statement that specifies what lesson we are to draw from the narrative. Charles Perrault provides such a structure for his 1697 version of the tale "Little Red Riding Hood." Perrault doesn't want his readers to miss the point, so after narrating the story, he spells out the moral for them.

Charles Perrault (1628–1703)

Little Red Riding Hood (1697)

Once upon a time there was a little village girl, the prettiest that had ever been seen. Her mother doted on her, and her grandmother even more. This good woman made her a little red hood which suited her so well that she was called Little Red Riding Hood wherever she went.

One day, after her mother had baked some biscuits, she said to Little Red Riding Hood: "Go see how your grandmother is feeling, for I have heard that she is sick. Take her some biscuits and this small pot of butter." Little Red Riding Hood departed at once to visit her grandmother, who lived in another village. In passing through a wood she met old neighbor wolf, who had a great desire to eat her. But he did not dare because of some woodcutters who were in the forest. He asked her where she was going. The poor child, who did not know that it is dangerous to stop and listen to a wolf, said to him: "I am going to see my grandmother, and I am bringing some biscuits with a small pot of butter which my mother has sent her."

"Does she live far from here?" asked the wolf.

"Oh, yes!" said Little Red Riding Hood. "You must pass the mill which you can see right over there, and hers is the first house in the village."

"Well, then," said the wolf. "I want to go and see her, too. I'll take this path here, and you take that path there, and we'll see who'll get there first."

The wolf began to run as fast as he could on the path which was shorter, and the little girl took the longer path, and she enjoyed herself by gathering nuts, running after butterflies, and making bouquets of small flowers which she found. It did not take the wolf long to arrive at the grandmother's house. He knocked: Toc, toc.

"Who's there?"

"It's your granddaughter, Little Red Riding Hood," said the wolf, disguising his voice, "I've brought you some biscuits and a little pot of butter which my mother has sent you."

The good grandmother, who was in her bed because she was not feeling well, cried out to him: "Pull the bobbin, and the latch will fall."

The wolf pulled the bobbin, and the door opened. He threw himself upon the good woman and devoured her quicker than a wink, for it had been more than three days since he had last eaten. After that he closed the door and lay down in the grandmother's bed to wait for Little Red Riding Hood, who after awhile came knocking at the door. Toc, toc.

"Who's there?"

When she heard the gruff voice of the wolf, Little Red Riding Hood was scared at first, but, believing that her grandmother had a cold, she responded: "It's your granddaughter, Little Red Riding Hood. I've brought you some biscuits and a little pot of butter which my mother has sent you."

The wolf softened his voice and cried out to her: "Pull the bobbin, and the latch will fall."

Little Red Riding Hood pulled the bobbin, and the door opened. Upon seeing her enter, the wolf hid himself under the bedcovers and said to her: "Put the biscuits and the pot of butter on the bin and come lie down beside me."

Little Red Riding Hood undressed and went to get into bed, where she was quite astonished to see the way her grandmother was dressed in her nightgown. She said to her: "What big arms you have, grandmother!"

"The better to hug you with, my child."

"What big legs you have, grandmother!"

"The better to run with, my child."

"What big ears you have, grandmother!"

"The better to hear you with, my child."

"What big eyes you have, grandmother!"

"The better to see you with, my child."

"What big teeth you have, grandmother!"

"The better to eat you."

And upon saying these words, the wicked wolf threw himself upon Little Red Riding Hood and ate her up.

MORAL
One sees here that young children,
Especially young girls,
Pretty, well brought-up, and Gentle,
Should never listen to anyone who happens by,
And if this occurs, it is not so strange
When the wolf should eat them.
I say the wolf, for all wolves
Are not of the same kind.
There are some with winning ways,
Not loud, nor bitter, or angry,
Who are tame, good-natured, and pleasant
And follow young ladies
Right into their homes, right into their alcoves.
But alas for those who do not know that of all the wolves
the docile ones are those who are most dangerous.

Perrault's moral fits neatly at the end of this familiar tale, and there is some satisfaction at having a tidy reason for a gruesome story of a girl being devoured. The moral justifies the terror: with Perrault's rationale, this story serves as a lesson to any girl who might be seduced by the flattery of a charming young man. But on closer examination, the moral seems to tag on a simpler message than the story itself encourages. Perrault's fable in its entirety suggests a tension between the civility that has been taught this "Pretty, well brought-up, and Gentle" girl and the wolf who is able to use that very sign of class to trick the girl: he speaks politely and engages her in a civil conversation during which he gains the information he needs in order to trap her later. The poor girl is a model of goodness; she goes to visit her sick grandmother, and it is her concern for her grandmother's seemingly worsening condition that leads to her demise. Yet Perrault's moral, in effect, shakes a disapproving finger at her. What wrong does she commit that leads her to such a dismal end? It seems Perrault wants Little Red Riding Hood to be knowing and suspicious as well as innocent and polite. Can a proper young girl possess, within Perrault's view of things, all of these qualities? The moral offers clear advice and a stark warning, but the story itself suggests anxiety over the conflicting signs of goodness and the power of proper manners to hide evil.

None of this is to say that Perrault's explicit message is incongruous with his narrative. He does pick up on elements within the story to draw his conclusion. He does emphasize Little Red Riding Hood's childish innocence and the wily ways of the wolf. But should we go on to impugn all wolves (as Perrault does) for the offense of this particular wolf? Can't there be good, polite wolves (or at least good, polite young men)? Is Perrault suggesting the subversive notion that manners are a dangerous obligation for girls/women and useful tool for boys/men? It seems possible that a good reader of this tale could complicate Perrault's own explicit thematic statement. Couldn't you argue that the theme of the story concerns the unjust moral and social burdens women and girls must bear in a patriarchal society?

The varied interpretive possibilities of "Little Red Riding Hood" suggest that theme doesn't need to be boiled down to a moral even when a moral is offered. When we write about the narratives we read, we should work to be less absolute than Perrault. His moral ends any conversation that we might have about the meanings of the story. One goal of conversation should be to open up ideas and possible interpretations of the story. Finding a moral is satisfying, but it often requires us to overgeneralize about the text in question. It can even be a way to avoid the demands that complex works of literature pose. James Thurber makes some fun of stories with easy morals with his twisted take on the old story.

James Thurber (1894–1961)

The Girl and the Wolf (1939)

One afternoon a big wolf waited in a dark forest for a little girl to come along carrying a basket of food to her grandmother. Finally a little girl did come along and she was carrying a basket of food. "Are you carrying that basket to your grandmother?" asked the wolf. The little girl said yes, she was. So the wolf asked her where her grandmother lived and the little girl told him and he disappeared into the wood.

When the little girl opened the door of her grandmother's house she saw that there was somebody in bed with a nightcap on. She had approached no nearer than twenty-five feet from the bed when she saw that it was not her grandmother but the wolf, for even in a nightcap a wolf does not look any more like your grandmother than the Metro-Goldwyn lion looks like Calvin Coolidge. So the little girl took an automatic out of her basket and shot the wolf dead.

Moral: It is not so easy to fool little girls nowadays as it used to be. ■

Calvin Coolidge, known "Silent Cal," served as thirtieth president of the United States (1923-1929).

Since the founding of the Metro-Goldwyn-Mayer studios in 1924, there have been five different lions used as mascots for the studio. This image shows "Jackie," who was used from 1928 to 1956.

Thurber plays with the conventional story and claims to bring it out of the world of make-believe. We still have a talking wolf prone to developing disguises, but the character of the girl has, comically, changed. This allows Thurber to offer the generalizing moral about "little girls nowadays." The result pokes fun at our tendency to attribute morals to stories; it also teases our conventional notion of Little Red Riding Hood's innocence and passivity as well as the innocence and passivity of any "well-brought up" girl. Thurber's turn against our expectations challenges our tendency to settle easily for morals in the works that we read.

Consider how the following report of a girl-devoured-by-wolf story compares to those of Perrault and Thurber. It doesn't offer a moral so explicitly as either of these, but one could argue the moral remains strongly implied. How does that implied moral work? Does it question the value of a moral, or does it ask us to think about why we construct morals to stories?

Girl Devoured by Wolf

Yesterday, in a nearby village, a wolf which had somehow entered the house ate an old woman and her young granddaughter. The girl's name has been withheld pending notification of her mother, but neighbors report that shortly before her death she was seen wearing a "little red riding hood."

Investigators at the scene of the murders suspect that the wolf entered the old woman's bedroom by pulling at a simple bobbin mechanism at her door. They found traces of the wolf's hair in the bed as well as in a nightcap lying by the side of the bed. A basket containing some biscuits and a small pot of butter, apparently a gift brought by the girl to her grandmother, was overturned and strewn about the room.

Citizens are asked to be on the lookout for a wolf described as having big arms, big legs, big ears, big eyes, and big teeth. Authorities warn children not to talk to any wolves as there has been a rash of incidents in the community in recent months. ■

Experiencing Literature through Theme

Critical writers explore the gray area between a plain statement of meaning, such as a moral, and the more ambiguous reactions that a story inspires. Theme resides in this gray area and cannot be easily extracted from the text. We can think of a literary or filmic theme as an abstract expression made concrete through the carefully patterned fabric of key words, sounds, images, and so on. The content of the expression and the mode of expression must be understood together. For instance, consider the following poem by Marge Piercy.

Marge Piercy (1936–)

A Work of Artifice (1982)

The bonsai tree
in the attractive pot
could have grown eighty feet tall
on the side of a mountain
till split by lightning.   5
But a gardener
carefully pruned it.
It is nine inches high.
Every day as he
whittles back the branches   10
the gardener croons,
It is your nature
to be small and cozy,
domestic and weak;
how lucky, little tree,   15
to have a pot to grow in.
With living creatures
one must begin very early
to dwarf their growth:
the bound feet,   20
the crippled brain,
the hair in curlers,
the hands you
love to touch.

We can all agree that Piercy's poem is "about" the oppression of women, surely an important matter. But the compelling qualities of this poem do not reside in theme so narrowly defined. Consider this: If we register only what the poem is about, if we write about what Piercy writes about, we'll find ourselves as restricted as the bonsai tree; we'll be dealing with abstract ideas and remain one step away from the poem itself. A critical writer who uses the poem to generalize about sexual oppression in our society may fail to account for (or even address) what makes "A Work of Artifice" distinctive. And such a critic will almost certainly rehash familiar ideas in ways that will reduce the power of Piercy's language to the language of summary or statement.

But if we consider how meaning is embodied by the text, we may press forward to a deeper level of appreciation and insight. How does Piercy project and explore a tension between the "natural self" and the artificial, constructed self of our culture? Why does she "whittle" back the lines of the poem (note that the longest line concerns the tree's potential growth)? How does she engage the reader in an increasingly personal and forceful relationship with the bonsai tree? Why does she juxtapose something as foreign and debilitating as "bound feet" with the relatively familiar and seemingly innocuous "hair in curlers"?

Clearly, identifying a message is not necessarily the same thing as writing critically about theme. Mere identification stifles development. Responsive audiences seek to extend analysis. Definition provides one way to elaborate productively upon theme. You could, for example, pause in Piercy's poem over words like *whittles, croons,* and *pruned* in order to consider both what those words denote (what they signify, what they mean literally) and what they connote (what they suggest, what they imply emotionally). You could also pause over the words you use in response to the text. At times, modifying a general word will help you establish a clearer sense of theme. The subject of Piercy's poem, for example, is not simply "oppression." We have previously used the term *sexual oppression,* but we can press harder still on this point of meaning: sexual oppression in this poem is *insidious, subtle, deceptive, manipulative,* and *pervasive.* Oppressive male power finds expression under the guise of *kindness, gentleness, concern.* Ironically, that power is justified as "natural," whereas the entire poem accentuates its "artifice." Such careful thinking upon the meanings of words can enrich your sense of what constitutes theme.

MULTIPLE THEMES IN A SINGLE WORK

Much of what we've discussed in this chapter involves our approach to texts as much as it does the texts themselves. Responsiveness to theme (like any kind of aesthetic responsiveness) requires active engagement with the work. We read for a variety of purposes, and those purposes may well include social or religious instruction. But when we read *exclusively* for a particular kind of instruction, we're not really reading literature—no matter what the quality of the work before us. To put it a slightly different way, a work can become literature only when it is used as literature. Such an active model of reading means that we must be willing to think of theme in the plural. As we suggested earlier, even Perrault's simple tale suggests possibilities that are not contained in the moral. We can underscore important qualities of theme by three statements and three related questions:

1. Themes emerge as problems or questions more often than as specific lessons or morals. How does a work challenge us?
2. Themes tend to be suggestive and open ended. Why does a work matter to us more than a clear summary of its theme?
3. Themes are inevitably a matter of interpretation. Why must we support our reading with evidence from the text?

Some works force us to reflect on such concerns by making us question the validity of common interpretive clues or signs of authority. We tend, for example, to separate literature from news stories because literature is artistically shaped. The events reported by journalists are considered raw accounts driven by reality. But if we give the matter greater thought, we realize that anytime that anyone writes up "facts," some degree of ordering comes into play—usually a good deal more than we like to admit. Stories from the newspaper or television news do more than inform the public; they express and shape values, opinions, and attitudes. They may not be literature, but neither are they merely records of what "really happens." What if we bring a literary sensibility to these everyday materials? We might then be alive to a richer, more complex range of possible meanings.

Experiencing Literature through Theme

Maxine Hong Kingston's "The Wild Man of the Green Swamp" addresses these matters directly. From the very start, Hong Kingston makes us think of the way we select, tell, and understand stories. We are led to question how we know what we know as we read conflicting reports on the Wild Man from eyewitnesses, officials, doctors, ship's officers, journalists, and an interpreter. Behind all of these voices is the narrator, who patches together the reports with no comment on their credibility.

Maxine Hong Kingston (1940–)

The Wild Man of the Green Swamp (1977)

For eight months in 1975, residents on the edge of Green Swamp, Florida, had been reporting to the police that they had seen a Wild Man. When they stepped toward him, he made strange noises as in a foreign language and ran back into the saw grass. At first, authorities said the Wild Man was a mass hallucination. Man-eating animals lived in the swamp, and a human being could hardly find a place to rest without sinking. Perhaps it was some kind of a bear the children had seen.

In October, a game officer saw a man crouched over a small fire, but as he approached, the figure ran away. It couldn't have been a bear because the Wild Man dragged a burlap bag after him. Also, the fire was obviously manmade.

The fish-and-game wardens and the sheriff's deputies entered the swamp with dogs but did not search for long; no one could live in the swamp. The mosquitoes alone would drive him out.

The Wild Man made forays out of the swamp. Farmers encountered him taking fruit and corn from the turkeys. He broke into a house trailer, but the occupant came back, and the Wild Man escaped out a window. The occupant said that a bad smell came off the Wild Man. Usually, the only evidence of him were his abandoned campsites. At one he left the remains of a four-foot-long alligator, of which he had eaten the feet and tail.

In May a posse made an air and land search; the plane signaled down to the hunters on the ground, who circled the Wild Man. A fish-and-game warden "brought him down with a tackle," according to the news. The Wild Man fought, but they took him to jail. He looked Chinese, so they found a Chinese in town to come translate.

The Wild Man talked a lot to the translator. He told him his name. He said he was thirty-nine years old, the father of seven children, who were in Taiwan. To support them, he had shipped out on a Liberian freighter. He had gotten very homesick and asked everyone if he could leave the ship and go home. But the officers would not let him off. They sent messages to China to find out about him. When the ship landed, they took him to the airport and tried to put him on an airplane to some foreign place. Then, he said, the white demons took him to Tampa Hospital, which is for insane people, but he escaped, just walked out and went into the swamp.

The interpreter asked how he lived in the swamp. He said he ate snakes, turtles, armadillos, and alligators. The captors could tell how he lived when they opened up his bag, which was not burlap but a pair of pants with the legs knotted. Inside, he had carried a pot, a piece of sharpened tin, and a small club, which he had made by sticking a railroad spike into a section of aluminum tubing.

The sheriff found the Liberian freighter that the Wild Man had been on. The ship's officers said that they had not tried to stop him from going home. His shipmates had decided that there was something wrong with his mind. They had bought him a plane ticket and arranged his passport to send him back to China. They had driven him to the airport, but there he began screaming and weeping and would not get on the plane. So they had found him a doctor, who sent him to Tampa Hospital.

Now the doctors at the jail gave him medicine for the mosquito bites, which covered his entire body, and medicine for his stomachache. He was getting better, but after he'd been in jail for three days, the U.S. Border Patrol told him they were sending him back. He became hysterical. That night, he fastened his belt to the bars, wrapped it around his neck, and hung himself.

In the newspaper picture he did not look very wild, being led by the posse out of the swamp. He did not look dirty, either. He wore a checkered shirt unbuttoned at the neck, where his white undershirt showed; rounded by men in cowboy hats. His fingers stretching open, his wrists pulling apart to the extent of the handcuffs, he lifted his head, his eyes screwed shut, and cried out.

There was a Wild Man in our slough too, only he was a black man. He wore a shirt and no pants, and some mornings when we walked to school, we saw him asleep under the bridge. The police came and took him away. The newspaper said he was crazy; it said the police had been on the lookout for him for a long time, but we had seen him every day. ∎

Only in the final paragraph of the story do we learn why we've been left with so little guidance as to what to make of all the reports: the narrator is a schoolchild who (like most any child) passes along statements without critically reflecting upon them. We would argue that Hong Kingston uses this narrator to mock the smug, self-satisfied language of established authority; through the child she reveals its judgmental cruelty. For example, the narrator does not think that the Wild Man looks wild in the newspaper pictures yet still calls him the Wild Man because that is the only name used in the media. In other words, the narrator has been taught to reject his or her own instincts and, like most people, doesn't judge on what he or she sees so much as on what he or she is told to see. As a result, a real man becomes a dehumanized "wild man." The narrator is not even mature enough to contest the statements of the authorities when those statements are inconsistent with the narrator's firsthand experience: the narrator sees the second "Wild Man" every day, but the newspaper reported that the police had been looking for this dangerous creature a "long time."

Of course, Hong Kingston doesn't actually tell us all of this. She requires us to go beyond her naïve narrator's understanding. And in going beyond the child, we go beyond the attitudes of the dominant culture depicted in this story. Perhaps one of Hong Kingston's themes is that too many people passively accept too many stories from too many dubious sources. It is not just a child, after all, who reports of a Wild Man in the swamp; the newspapers pick up the story and the name itself from the people who live near the Green Swamp. And it is not a child who presses the Wild Man to suicide; the unsympathetic authorities bear that responsibility. But we can't blame only those authorities, for the child's naïve narration leads us to question our own habits of acceptance. Even though Hong Kingston does not paste a moral at the end of her story, the story may inspire us to ask whether we too often read the world in a childish way when we experience it through the limiting lens of media. This is not *the* theme of the story, but it is *a* theme that the story addresses.

Making Connections

Read the newspaper or watch the evening news, and find one example of a story that focuses on people who are homeless, poor, new immigrants, or "foreigners." How does the presentation encourage a particular interpretation or judgment (its language, its emphasis, its point of view)? Does it imply or even state a moral?

WHEN THE MESSAGE IS UNWANTED

Writers and filmmakers create worlds for us to enter and, for a time, live within. Literary works and films may well ask us to step into unfamiliar territory and see things in context of the artist's vision. To some extent, this involves a willing surrender. We approach works of art receptive to the notion that they may offer us something new, that they may widen our experience or deepen our powers of sympathy and empathy. These are compelling reasons to seek the experience of art. Inevitably and appropriately though, we remember where we entered. We test any new imaginative construction against the ways we've already come to understand the world. We assess the vision, the world, of one artist in relation to our previous experience—including our previous literary experience. We consider our values. Receptivity and openness do not require a total submission to an author's worldview. One's critical intelligence can and should operate along with one's imagination. Although we may discover that the literary work compels us to modify our sense of things, we need not assume that that is the necessary outcome.

Leni Riefenstahl's famous documentary *Triumph of the Will* (1935) serves as a case in point. The film, commissioned by Adolf Hitler, celebrates the glories of Germany's Third Reich and the power of Hitler. Riefenstahl's visual imagination, her sense of structure, her command of the technical dimension of filmmaking all are displayed to grand effect. But what is the world to which we're asked to submit? *Triumph of the Will* opens with gorgeous aerial shots clouds, churches and other grand buildings, city streets unfolding beneath the camera's eye. We also see from our lofty vantage point soldiers marching. An airplane appears alongside us. Interspersed throughout are shots of crowds—not unruly threatening crowds but crowds thrilled by the very things we have seen. The effect is intended to bring the viewer into a world poised at a moment of greatness. Riefenstahl want us to share the excitement—to be one among the many.

From our perspective, critical resistance in this case—not surrender—becomes an essential response. A plane lands, and Adolph Hitler emerges to the adoration of the masses. Riefenstahl makes the grand buildings, the beautiful shots from the sky, the disciplined soldiers, adoring crowds, and sleek aircraft all work to aggrandize the 1934 Nazi Party Congress and, of course, the party's leader. *Triumph of the Will* seeks our assent to National Socialism, to militaristic power, to presumptions of cultural and racial superiority, to far-reaching imperialistic ambitions. The truly extraordinary skill involved in this effort is at the service of a worldview that cost the lives of millions.

The example of *Triumph of the Will* may lead us to a dismal thought about works of art. If we can't trust novels, poems, films, or plays to communicate something good or true, then we should feel no compunction about dismissing them out of hand. No one wants to be manipulated. But we should remember

Director Leni Riefenstahl went to great lengths to create a dramatic impact as she filmed *Triumph of the Will* at the 1934 Nuremberg Nazi Party Rally.

that if we're open to art, no single work stands alone—separate from other works of art and separate from history. Viewed in the context of our complete experience (both life experience and literary experience), Riefenstahl's motives cannot hide. Of course, one could argue that those motives hid well in Germany of 1935 to contribute to a historical nightmare. But those who enthusiastically embraced *Triumph of the Will* were not fully engaged by a work of art; they were eager and ready to accept power and effective expressions of power.

One possible theme of Maxine Hong Kingston's "The Wild Man of the Green Swamp" is worth recalling here: Bring your whole person to the act of reading. The child narrator of her tale can't quite do that and uncritically repeats what the newspapers say even when it's clear that he or she has seen something different. The narrator's childlike puzzlement gives us room to draw out the theme and consider what that theme might mean to us now. In a similar way, our attention to thematic aspects of Perrault's fairy tale allows us to move beyond his moral and to think about the issues that the moral raises for us. How do such stories, for example, make girls/women morally responsible for boys'/men's behavior?

A Note to Student Writers: Discovering What You Want to Say

Many students feel that their own critical writing is disconnected from the imaginative texts they are asked to write about. Misperceptions about theme are sometimes the source of such dissatisfaction. Students sometimes assume that the right answer to an assignment is the key to success; this assumption leads to an emphasis on product, which often amounts to a statement of *what* the work "really" means. But success more likely comes to the student who takes the right *approach* to an assignment; this understanding emphasizes process, which usually involves an exploration of *how* the work achieves meaning.

Good critical writing involves discovery and the rewriting that discovery makes necessary. Interaction with your own writing involves a healthy messiness. We suggest you take notes, ask questions, make lists and then reflect upon your notes, answer your questions, and organize your lists. Be active as a writer before you actually get to the point at which you are "writing the paper." Amid the conflicting demands of a typical course schedule, you might think it unrealistic to do so much in preparation for one paper in one class. But think of this suggestion from another angle: The writer who tries to get to the last thought first (and reduce a literary text to a simple theme) will often get stuck because the literary text doesn't cooperate. So instead of spending time frozen at the keyboard in a futile hope for *the* answer, try spending time testing responses and ideas at the keyboard in a search for answers. You'll find that the more patient route is not necessarily slower and is almost certainly more rewarding.

MODELING CRITICAL ANALYSIS: JAMAICA KINCAID, GIRL

Jamaica Kincaid's "Girl" (p. 16) allows for a fairly simple thematic summary. The story concerns a culture that presses significant limitations upon girls. A girl's life is proscribed by numerous duties and rules. Many are put in the negative: it is as difficult to keep up with all the prohibitions as it is to keep up with demands. But "Girl" is hardly a simple story. Kincaid embodies a cultural mind-set in the concrete attitudes of a particular person. To put it another way, Kincaid registers the heavily layered and burdensome effects of abstract ideas on an individual. Yet the experience of reading "Girl" cannot be captured by identifying a theme of oppression. "Girl" also subtly confronts and defies the very social limitations it depicts.

From the start, Kincaid makes it clear that a girl in the world she presents has little time for anything we might call her "own." On Monday, do this; on Tuesday, do that. Many of these insistent instructions, of course, concern practical matters. The girl must know how to clean, how to cook, how to sew, how to iron, how to tend the vegetable garden, and so on. By putting the whole list in an unbroken stream of a single sentence, Kincaid makes us not only understand but feel the girl's situation. Duties and demands cascade upon her. Even Sundays are no relief, for when the girl is free of active duties, she must be hyperconscious of the things she should not do. The girl apparently bears, on behalf of her sex, an especially heavy moral burden. Seen from the outside through the eyes of one schooled in the culture, a girl can hardly avoid moral condemnation. In relation to behavior between girls and boys, it would seem girls are always to blame. Kincaid's girl will be seen, from the slightest lapse of decorum, as a "slut." And to be seen that way is to be that way. The girl is defined by others before she can define herself.

As powerfully as these social demands press upon the girl, Kincaid also helps us appreciate how girls/women seek to gain on occasion some edge in the grossly imbalanced system within which they must operate. The title directs attention to the girl who is spoken to, not the apparently older woman who speaks. Although we might take this to suggest how thoroughly acculturated one becomes in an unjust social system (women are taught to perpetuate injustices upon women), we have signs that the woman has found ways to gain her own real if limited power. She instructs the girl, for example, in how to "bully a man." She offers warning insight of how a man bullies a girl. She includes, almost casually, information on how to abort an unwanted child in a long list of other more mundane "how-to" items. It would seem that the woman has learned in her own life (probably in part from other older women) how to make decisions separate and secret from the men seemingly in power. And toward the end of her list, the older woman tells the girl "how to spit up in the air if you feel like it." Here we get the first and only sign that the woman knows the girl may *feel* like doing one thing or another that has no relation to the comfort or benefit of the men around her. With it comes the sense that some things can be done purely on feeling if one is astute enough to dodge the consequences.

It's worth finally attending to the two lines in which the girl herself speaks. Neither represents a decisive claim against the demands and judgments made upon her, but both register a real if faint resistance. The girl is not an altogether passive subject. Her first break against the woman's instructions is a complaint: *"but I don't sing benna on Sundays at all and never in Sunday school."* The girl here contests the woman on a point of fairness or of accuracy. She won't wholly accept the way another person sees her. The second is a question: *"but what if the baker won't let me feel the bread?"* In this instance, the girl interjects a concern that the woman's advice isn't covering the real situations she will face or has faced already. The girl, it seems, understands very well practical life difficulties and wants to gain some insight on how to meet those difficulties. If we attend carefully to all the signals Kincaid gives us, we will find that "Girl" is about more than the prohibitions and injustices built into a male-dominated society; it is also about resourceful and (in context) valiant individual responses to such prohibitions and injustices.

Using Theme to Focus Writing and Discussion

- How does this work challenge us?
- What does it ask us to think about?
- As you read the work, what details stand out? Look for words, images, or ideas that seem to fit together, and arrange these details into lists.
- The labels that you develop for these lists could be your initial themes for this work.
- What patterns do you find among the details that you have listed?
- Do any of these patterns seem to conflict with other patterns? For instance, in Perrault's story, we find references to proper deportment, yet the moral warns us against false appearances.
- What significance do you see in the conflict or the congruence of these emerging themes?
- How does your identification of these themes help you see aspects of the text that you did not see before you identified the theme?

Anthology

EXPLORING BOUNDARIES: INTERPRETING THEME

The very nature of art is to press boundaries, to explore areas that remain distant to most people. So it isn't surprising that artists take up the theme of exploring boundaries. The wanderer, the criminal, the political dissident, the lunatic, the scientist, the mystic all have become figures that help us raise the most fundamental questions: What's to be gained by stepping beyond convention? What must be risked? What price was paid? Was it worth it to move beyond the norm? Is moving *outside* the same as moving *beyond*? Where do our deepest responsibilities lie (family, state, religion, self)? Most literary texts make us feel that such questions never lead to a comfortably balanced answer. Yet the resulting discomfort may be essential to the value of the work.

We've included in this anthology works that play variously on the theme of crossing boundaries. It is an ancient theme. The story of Adam and Eve from the book of Genesis is one early and especially famous example. Adam and Eve eat of the tree of knowledge in defiance of their creator's order. This basic desire to have more—to possess knowledge beyond our normal ken—is at the root of many great stories. Christopher Marlowe's *Doctor Faustus* plays upon this profoundly recurrent myth and opens what seem endless possibilities for further reflection. What would we give to achieve knowledge beyond human limits? And if we give our soul for that knowledge, have we ironically sacrificed the very thing that requires and rewards the closest study? Is there knowledge that is appropriately forbidden?

Of course, the theme of crossing boundaries makes no sense if authors don't also give us a powerful sense of what those boundaries might be and how narrowly they are drawn. Linda Pastan's "Ethics" points out that these lines may be artificial; life-and-death decisions simply aren't life-and-death decisions when posed as merely academic exercises for the moral training of disinterested children. However, Elizabeth Bishop's "Casabianca" shows that even an abstract lesson can play out in concrete ways. Her poem invokes the story of Casabianca—a young boy who stayed, and died, upon the deck of a burning ship because he had not been relieved of duty by his father—the admiral. Bishop suggests that not crossing boundaries may, in some cases, be as dangerous as crossing them.

In "The Censors," Luisa Valenzuela establishes her main character within a repressive political environment—an environment that makes us conscious that the slightest transgression can be dangerous. In fact, that environment is constructed so that transgressions become almost impossible. Valenzuela's censor attempts to undermine a system of repression but finds himself trapped within the logic of the system. Carolyn Forché's "The Colonel" immerses us in a similarly repressive world, but here the picture of the most inhumane transgression is seen from the appalled perspective of an outsider. In the face of great cruelty and great power, do we hold to ourselves? Do we "say nothing" at the moment of horrific revelations as the friend signals? How do we then press back against the encroachments the colonel has made upon life and human dignity?

Flannery O'Connor's "A Good Man Is Hard to Find" poises us uncomfortably between a man who accepts no limits and becomes a monster and an old woman who accepts severe limits and becomes a caricature of her society's essentially shallow propriety. The resulting dynamic results in what is for O'Connor a characteristically shocking insight. We are not left with a tidy sense of "good," although we are led to concur that a good man is indeed hard to find. As you read this and other works in this anthology, attend to what happens when one presses toward or crosses a boundary. What meaning do we draw from the experience? What value or violation has taken shape in the work of art?

FICTION

Luisa Valenzuela (1938–)

> Luisa Valenzuela was born in Buenos Aires, Argentina. Her mother was a fiction writer; and while still a child, Valenzuela met some of the most prominent Argentine writers of the time. Rather than attend college, she worked as a journalist and began publishing fiction. After marrying a member of the French merchant marine, Valenzuela moved to Paris, but she returned to Argentina after the marriage ended. She has traveled widely and taught at a number of institutions, and during the 1980s she lived in the United States. Valenzuela's fiction is characterized both by its feminist concerns and by the way in which she weaves fantastic details into an essentially realistic style. In her view, the political oppression of women in society and the personal oppression of women in relationships are intimately connected.

The Censors (1988, trans. David Unger)

Poor Juan! One day they caught him with his guard down before he could even realize that what he had taken as a stroke of luck was really one of fate's dirty tricks. These things happen the minute you're careless, as one often is. Juancito let happiness—a feeling you can't trust—get the better of him when he received from a confidential source Mariana's new address in

Paris and knew that she hadn't forgotten him. Without thinking twice, he sat down at his table and wrote her a letter. *The* letter that now keeps his mind off his job during the day and won't let him sleep at night (what had he scrawled, what had he put on that sheet of paper he sent to Mariana?).

Juan knows there won't be a problem with the letter's contents, that it's irreproachable, harmless. But what about the rest? He knows that they examine, sniff, feel, and read between the lines of each and every letter, and check its tiniest comma and most accidental stain. He knows that all letters pass from hand to hand and go through all sorts of tests in the huge censorship offices and that, in the end, very few continue on their way. Usually it takes months, even years, if there aren't any snags; all this time the freedom, maybe even the life, of both sender and receiver is in jeopardy. And that's why Juan's so troubled: thinking that something might happen to Mariana because of his letters. Of all people, Mariana, who must finally feel safe there where she always dreamt she'd live. But he knows that the *Censor's Secret Command* operates all over the world and cashes in on the discount in air fares; there's nothing to stop them from going as far as that hidden Paris neighborhood, kidnapping Mariana, and returning to their cozy homes, certain of having fulfilled their noble mission.

Well, you've got to beat them to the punch, do what everyone tries to do: sabotage the machinery, throw sand in its gears, get to the bottom of the problem so as to stop it.

This was Juan's sound plan when he, like many others, applied for a censor's job—not because he had a calling or needed a job: no, he applied simply to intercept his own letter, a consoling albeit unoriginal idea. He was hired immediately, for each day more and more censors are needed and no one would bother to check on his references.

Ulterior motives couldn't be overlooked by the *Censorship Division*, but   5
they needn't be too strict with those who applied. They knew how hard it would be for the poor guys to find the letter they wanted and even if they did, what's a letter or two when the new censor would snap up so many others? That's how Juan managed to join the *Post Office's Censorship Division*, with a certain goal in mind.

The building had a festive air on the outside that contrasted with its inner staidness. Little by little, Juan was absorbed by his job, and he felt at peace since he was doing everything he could to get his letter for Mariana. He didn't even worry when, in his first month, he was sent to *Section K* where envelopes are very carefully screened for explosives.

It's true that on the third day, a fellow worker had his right hand blown off by a letter, but the division chief claimed it was sheer negligence on the victim's part. Juan and the other employees were allowed to go back to their work, though feeling less secure. After work, one of them tried to organize a strike to demand higher wages for unhealthy work, but Juan didn't join in; after thinking it over, he reported the man to his superiors and thus got promoted.

You don't form a habit by doing something once, he told himself as he left his boss's office. And when he was transferred to *Section J*, where letters are carefully checked for poison dust, he felt he had climbed a rung in the ladder.

By working hard, he quickly reached *Section E* where the job became more interesting, for he could now read and analyze the letters' contents. Here he could even hope to get hold of his letter, which, judging by the time that had elapsed, had gone through the other sections and was probably floating around in this one.

Soon his work became so absorbing that his noble mission blurred in his mind. Day after day he crossed out whole paragraphs in red ink, pitilessly chucking many letters into the censored basket. These were horrible days when he was shocked by the subtle and conniving ways employed by people to pass on subversive messages; his instincts were so sharp that he found behind a simple "the weather's unsettled" or "prices continue to soar" the wavering hand of someone secretly scheming to overthrow the Government.

His zeal brought him swift promotion. We don't know if this made him happy. Very few letters reached him in *Section B*—only a handful passed the other hurdles—so he read them over and over again, passed them under a magnifying glass, searched for microprint with an electronic microscope, and tuned his sense of smell so that he was beat by the time he made it home. He'd barely manage to warm up his soup, eat some fruit, and fall into bed, satisfied with having done his duty. Only his darling mother worried, but she couldn't get him back on the right track. She'd say, though it wasn't always true: Lola called, she's at the bar with the girls, they miss you, they're waiting for you. Or else she'd leave a bottle of red wine on the table. But Juan wouldn't overdo it: any distraction could make him lose his edge and the perfect censor had to be alert, keen, attentive, and sharp to nab cheats. He had a truly patriotic task, both self-denying and uplifting.

His basket for censored letters became the best fed as well as the most cunning basket in the whole *Censorship Division*. He was about to congratulate himself for having finally discovered his true mission, when his letter to Mariana reached his hands. Naturally, he censored it without regret. And just as naturally, he couldn't stop from executing him the following morning, another victim of his devotion to his work.

- How does Juan's character change over the course of the story?
- What justifies the work of the Censorship Division?
- What boundary does Juan cross?
- What moral, if any, do you think that this story is meant to convey? What evidence leads you to this conclusion?
- What details, if any, in this story are necessary to convey the moral that you have identified?

Flannery O'Connor (1925–1964)

Flannery O'Connor was born in Savannah, Georgia. When she was sixteen, her father died of disseminated lupus, the disease that would later claim her own life. She received her AB in 1945 from Women's College of Georgia (now Georgia College) and her MFA from the State University of Iowa in 1947. At the age of twenty-five she suffered her first attack of lupus, and from then on she lived with her mother. O'Connor died when she was thirty-nine years old. O'Connor is widely regarded as one of the preeminent fiction writers of the twentieth century. Though often violent, her works are essentially religious, in that they express her Catholic vision of the world as a fallen place in need of redemption. Among her works are the novels *Wise Blood* (1952) and *The Violent Bear It Away* (1960) and the story collections *A Good Man Is Hard to Find* (1955) and *Everything That Rises Must Converge* (1965).

A Good Man Is Hard To Find (1953)

The dragon is by the side of the road, watching those who pass. Beware lest he devour you. We go to the Father of Souls, but it is necessary to pass by the dragon.

—St. Cyril of Jerusalem

The grandmother didn't want to go to Florida. She wanted to visit some of her connections in east Tennessee and she was seizing at every chance to change Bailey's mind. Bailey was the son she lived with, her only boy. He was sitting on the edge of his chair at the table, bent over the orange sports section of the *Journal.* "Now look here, Bailey," she said, "see here, read this," and she stood with one hand on her thin hip and the other rattling the newspaper at his bald head. "Here this fellow that calls himself The Misfit is aloose from the Federal Pen and headed toward Florida and you read here what it says he did to these people. Just you read it. I wouldn't take my children in any direction with a criminal like that aloose in it. I couldn't answer to my conscience if I did."

Bailey didn't look up from his reading so she wheeled around then and faced the children's mother, a young woman in slacks, whose face was as broad and innocent as a cabbage and was tied around with a green head-kerchief that had two points on the top like a rabbit's ears. She was sitting on the sofa, feeding the baby his apricots out of a jar. "The children have been to Florida before," the old lady said. "You all ought to take them some-where else for a change so they would see different parts of the world and be broad. They never have been to east Tennessee."

The children's mother didn't seem to hear her but the eight-year-old boy, John Wesley, a stocky child with glasses, said, "If you don't want to go to Florida, why dontcha stay at home?" He and the little girl, June Star, were reading the funny papers on the floor.

"She wouldn't stay at home to be queen for a day," June Star said without raising her yellow head.

"Yes and what would you do if this fellow, The Misfit, caught you?" the grandmother asked.

"I'd smack his face," John Wesley said.

"She wouldn't stay at home for a million bucks," June Star said. "Afraid she'd miss something. She has to go everywhere we go."

"All right, Miss," the grandmother said. "Just remember that the next time you want me to curl your hair."

June Star said her hair was naturally curly.

The next morning the grandmother was the first one in the car, ready to go. She had her big black valise that looked like the head of a hippopotamus in one corner, and underneath it she was hiding a basket with Pitty Sing, the cat, in it. She didn't intend for the cat to be left alone in the house for three days because he would miss her too much and she was afraid he might brush against one of the gas burners and accidentally asphyxiate himself. Her son, Bailey, didn't like to arrive at a motel with a cat.

She sat in the middle of the back seat with John Wesley and June Star on either side of her. Bailey and the children's mother and the baby sat in front and they left Atlanta at eight forty-five with the mileage on the car at 55890. The grandmother wrote this down because she thought it would be interesting to say how many miles they had been when they got back. It took them twenty minutes to reach the outskirts of the city.

The old lady settled herself comfortably, removing her white cotton gloves and putting them up with her purse on the shelf in front of the back window. The children's mother still had on slacks and still had her head tied up in a green kerchief, but the grandmother had on a navy blue straw sailor hat with a bunch of white violets on the brim and a navy blue dress with a small white dot in the print. Her collars and cuffs were white organdy trimmed with lace and at her neck she had pinned a purple spray of cloth violets containing a sachet. In case of an accident, anyone seeing her dead on the highway would know at once that she was a lady.

She said she thought it was going to be a good day for driving, neither too hot nor too cold, and she cautioned Bailey that the speed limit was fifty-five miles an hour and that the patrolmen hid themselves behind billboards and small clumps of trees and sped out after you before you had a chance to slow down. She pointed out interesting details of the scenery: Stone Mountain; the blue granite that in some places came up to both sides of the highway; the brilliant red clay banks slightly streaked with purple; and the various crops that made rows of green lace-work on the ground. The trees were full of silver-white sunlight and the meanest of them sparkled. The children were reading comic magazines and their mother had gone back to sleep.

"Let's go through Georgia fast so we won't have to look at it much," John Wesley said.

"If I were a little boy," said the grandmother, "I wouldn't talk about my native state that way. Tennessee has the mountains and Georgia has the hills." 15

"Tennessee is just a hillbilly dumping ground," John Wesley said, "and Georgia is a lousy state too."

"You said it," June Star said.

"In my time," said the grandmother, folding her thin veined fingers, "children were more respectful of their native states and their parents and everything else. People did right then. Oh look at the cute little pickaninny!" she said and pointed to a Negro child standing in the door of a shack. "Wouldn't that make a picture, now?" she asked and they all turned and looked at the little Negro out of the back window. He waved.

"He didn't have any britches on," June Star said.

"He probably didn't have any," the grandmother explained. "Little niggers in the country don't have things like we do. If I could paint, I'd paint that picture," she said. 20

The children exchanged comic books.

The grandmother offered to hold the baby and the children's mother passed him over the front seat to her. She set him on her knee and bounced him and told him about the things they were passing. She rolled her eyes and screwed up her mouth and stuck her leathery thin face into his smooth bland one. Occasionally he gave her a faraway smile. They passed a large cotton field with five or six graves fenced in the middle of it, like a small island. "Look at the graveyard!" the grandmother said, pointing it out. "That was the old family burying ground. That belonged to the plantation."

"Where's the plantation?" John Wesley asked.

"Gone With the Wind," said the grandmother. "Ha. Ha."

When the children finished all the comic books they had brought, they opened the lunch and ate it. The grandmother ate a peanut butter sandwich and an olive and would not let the children throw the box and the paper napkins out the window. When there was nothing else to do they played a game by choosing a cloud and making the other two guess what shape it suggested. John Wesley took one the shape of a cow and June Star guessed a cow and John Wesley said, no, an automobile, and June Star said he didn't play fair, and they began to slap each other over the grandmother. 25

The grandmother said she would tell them a story if they would keep quiet. When she told a story, she rolled her eyes and waved her head and was very dramatic. She said once when she was a maiden lady she had been courted by a Mr. Edgar Atkins Teagarden from Jasper, Georgia. She said he was a very good-looking man and a gentleman and that he brought her a watermelon every Saturday afternoon with his initials cut in it, E. A. T. Well,

one Saturday, she said, Mr. Teagarden brought the watermelon and there was
nobody at home and he left it on the front porch and returned in his buggy to
Jasper, but she never got the watermelon, she said, because a nigger boy ate it
when he saw the initials, E.A.T.! This story tickled John Wesley's funny bone
and he giggled and giggled but June Star didn't think it was any good. She
said she wouldn't marry a man that just brought her a watermelon on Saturday. The grandmother said she would have done well to marry Mr. Teagarden
because he was a gentleman and had bought Coca-Cola stock when it first
came out and that he had died only a few years ago, a very wealthy man.

They stopped at The Tower for barbecued sandwiches. The Tower was
a part stucco and part wood filling station and dance hall set in a clearing
outside of Timothy. A fat man named Red Sammy Butts ran it and there
were signs stuck here and there on the building and for miles up and down
the highway saying, TRY RED SAMMY'S FAMOUS BARBECUE. NONE
LIKE FAMOUS RED SAMMY'S! RED SAM! THE FAT BOY WITH THE
HAPPY LAUGH. A VETERAN! RED SAMMY'S YOUR MAN!

Red Sammy was lying on the bare ground outside The Tower with his
head under a truck while a gray monkey about a foot high, chained to a
small chinaberry tree, chattered nearby. The monkey sprang back into the
tree and got on the highest limb as soon as he saw the children jump out of
the car and run toward him.

Inside, The Tower was a long dark room with a counter at one end and tables at the other and dancing space in the middle. They all sat down at a board
table next to the nickelodeon and Red Sam's wife, a tall burnt-brown woman
with hair and eyes lighter than her skin, came and took their order. The children's mother put a dime in the machine and played "The Tennessee Waltz,"
and the grandmother said that tune always made her want to dance. She asked
Bailey if he would like to dance but he only glared at her. He didn't have a naturally sunny disposition like she did and trips made him nervous. The grandmother's brown eyes were very bright. She swayed her head from side to side
and pretended she was dancing in her chair. June Star said play something she
could tap to so the children's mother put in another dime and played a fast
number and June Star stepped out onto the dance floor and did her tap routine.

"Ain't she cute?" Red Sam's wife said, leaning over the counter.
"Would you like to come be my little girl?"

"No I certainly wouldn't," June Star said. "I wouldn't live in a broken-
down place like this for a million bucks!" and she ran back to the table.

"Ain't she cute?" the woman repeated, stretching her mouth politely.

"Aren't you ashamed?" hissed the grandmother.

Red Sam came in and told his wife to quit lounging on the counter and
hurry up with these people's order. His khaki trousers reached just to his hip
bones and his stomach hung over them like a sack of meal swaying under his
shirt. He came over and sat down at a table nearby and let out a combination

sigh and yodel. "You can't win," he said. "You can't win," and he wiped his
sweating red face off with a gray handkerchief. "These days you don't know
who to trust," he said. "Ain't that the truth?"

"People are certainly not nice like they used to be," said the grandmother.   35

"Two fellers come in here last week," Red Sammy said, "driving a
Chrysler. It was a old beat-up car but it was a good one and these boys
looked all right to me. Said they worked at the mill and you know I let
them fellers charge the gas they bought? Now why did I do that?"

"Because you're a good man!" the grandmother said at once.

"Yes'm, I suppose so," Red Sam said as if he were struck with this answer.

His wife brought the orders, carrying the five plates all at once without
a tray, two in each hand and one balanced on her arm. "It isn't a soul in
this green world of God's that you can trust," she said. "And I don't count
nobody out of that, not nobody," she repeated, looking at Red Sammy.

"Did you read about that criminal, The Misfit, that's escaped?" asked   40
the grandmother.

"I wouldn't be a bit surprised if he didn't attact this place right here,"
said the woman. "If he hears about it being here, I wouldn't be none surprised to see him. If he hears it's two cent in the cash register, I wouldn't be
a tall surprised if he...."

"That'll do," Red Sam said. "Go bring these people their Co'-Colas,"
and the woman went off to get the rest of the order.

"A good man is hard to find," Red Sammy said. "Everything is getting
terrible. I remember the day you could go off and leave your screen door un-
latched. Not no more."

He and the grandmother discussed better times. The old lady said that
in her opinion Europe was entirely to blame for the way things were now.
She said the way Europe acted you would think we were made of money
and Red Sam said it was no use talking about it, she was exactly right. The
children ran outside into the white sunlight and looked at the monkey in
the lacy chinaberry tree. He was busy catching fleas on himself and biting
each one carefully between his teeth as if it were a delicacy.

They drove off again into the hot afternoon. The grandmother took cat   45
naps and woke up every few minutes with her own snoring. Outside of
Toombsboro she woke up and recalled an old plantation that she had visited
in this neighborhood once when she was a young lady. She said the house
had six white columns across the front and that there was an avenue of oaks
leading up to it and two little wooden trellis arbors on either side in front
where you sat down with your suitor after a stroll in the garden. She recalled
exactly which road to turn off to get to it. She knew that Bailey would not
be willing to lose any time looking at an old house, but the more she talked
about it, the more she wanted to see it once again and find out if the little
twin arbors were still standing. "There was a secret panel in this house," she

said craftily, not telling the truth but wishing that she were, "and the story went that all the family silver was hidden in it when Sherman came through but it was never found...."

"Hey!" John Wesley said. "Let's go see it! We'll find it! We'll poke all the woodwork and find it! Who lives there? Where do you turn off at? Hey Pop, can't we turn off there?"

"We never have seen a house with a secret panel!" June Star shrieked. "Let's go to the house with the secret panel! Hey Pop, can't we go see the house with the secret panel!"

"It's not far from here, I know," the grandmother said. "It won't take over twenty minutes."

Bailey was looking straight ahead. His jaw was as rigid as a horseshoe. "No," he said.

The children began to yell and scream that they wanted to see the house with the secret panel. John Wesley kicked the back of the front seat and June Star hung over her mother's shoulder and whined desperately into her ear that they never had any fun even on their vacation, that they could never do what THEY wanted to do. The baby began to scream and John Wesley kicked the back of the seat so hard that his father could feel the blows in his kidney.

"All right!" he shouted and drew the car to a stop at the side of the road. "Will you all shut up? Will you all just shut up for one second? If you don't shut up, we won't go anywhere."

"It would be very educational for them," the grandmother murmured.

"All right," Bailey said, "but get this: this is the only time we're going to stop for anything like this. This is the one and only time."

"The dirt road that you have to turn down is about a mile back," the grandmother directed. "I marked it when we passed."

"A dirt road," Bailey groaned.

After they had turned around and were headed toward the dirt road, the grandmother recalled other points about the house, the beautiful glass over the front doorway and the candle-lamp in the hall. John Wesley said that the secret panel was probably in the fireplace.

"You can't go inside this house," Bailey said. "You don't know who lives there."

"While you all talk to the people in front, I'll run around behind and get in a window," John Wesley suggested.

"We'll all stay in the car," his mother said.

They turned onto the dirt road and the car raced roughly along in a swirl of pink dust. The grandmother recalled the times when there were no paved roads and thirty miles was a day's journey. The dirt road was hilly and there were sudden washes in it and sharp curves on dangerous embankments. All at once they would be on a hill, looking down over the blue tops of trees for miles around, then the next minute, they would be in a red depression with the dust-coated trees looking down on them.

"This place had better turn up in a minute," Bailey said, "or I'm going to turn around."

The road looked as if no one had traveled on it for months.

"It's not much farther," the grandmother said and just as she said it, a horrible thought came to her. The thought was so embarrassing that she turned red in the face and her eyes dilated and her feet jumped up, upsetting her valise in the corner. The instant the valise moved, the newspaper top she had over the basket under it rose with a snarl and Pitty Sing, the cat, sprang onto Bailey's shoulder.

The children were thrown to the floor and their mother, clutching the baby, was thrown out the door onto the ground; the old lady was thrown into the front seat. The car turned over once and landed right-side-up in a gulch off the side of the road. Bailey remained in the driver's seat with the cat—gray-striped with a broad white face and an orange nose—clinging to his neck like a caterpillar.

As soon as the children saw they could move their arms and legs, they scrambled out of the car, shouting, "We've had an ACCIDENT!" The grandmother was curled up under the dashboard, hoping she was injured so that Bailey's wrath would not come down on her all at once. The horrible thought she had before the accident was that the house she had remembered so vividly was not in Georgia but in Tennessee.

Bailey removed the cat from his neck with both hands and flung it out the window against the side of a pine tree. Then he got out of the car and started looking for the children's mother. She was sitting against the side of the red gutted ditch, holding the screaming baby, but she only had a cut down her face and a broken shoulder. "We've had an ACCIDENT!" the children screamed in a frenzy of delight.

"But nobody's killed," June Star said with disappointment as the grandmother limped out of the car, her hat still pinned to her head but the broken front brim standing up at a jaunty angle and the violet spray hanging off the side. They all sat down in the ditch, except the children, to recover from the shock. They were all shaking.

"Maybe a car will come along," said the children's mother hoarsely.

"I believe I have injured an organ," said the grandmother, pressing her side, but no one answered her. Bailey's teeth were clattering. He had on a yellow sport shirt with bright blue parrots designed in it and his face was as yellow as the shirt. The grandmother decided that she would not mention that the house was in Tennessee.

The road was about ten feet above and they could see only the tops of the trees on the other side of it. Behind the ditch they were sitting in there were more woods, tall and dark and deep. In a few minutes they saw a car

65

70

some distance away on top of a hill, coming slowly as if the occupants were watching them. The grandmother stood up and waved both arms dramatically to attract their attention. The car continued to come on slowly, disappeared around a bend and appeared again, moving even slower, on top of the hill they had gone over. It was a big black battered hearse-like automobile. There were three men in it.

It came to a stop just over them and for some minutes, the driver looked down with a steady expressionless gaze to where they were sitting, and didn't speak. Then he turned his head and muttered something to the other two and they got out. One was a fat boy in black trousers and a red sweat shirt with a silver stallion embossed on the front of it. He moved around on the right side of them and stood staring, his mouth partly open in a kind of loose grin. The other had on khaki pants and a blue striped coat and a gray hat pulled down very low, hiding most of his face. He came around slowly on the left side. Neither spoke.

The driver got out of the car and stood by the side of it, looking down at them. He was an older man than the other two. His hair was just beginning to gray and he wore silver-rimmed spectacles that gave him a scholarly look. He had a long creased face and didn't have on any shirt or undershirt. He had on blue jeans that were too tight for him and was holding a black hat and a gun. The two boys also had guns.

"We've had an ACCIDENT!" the children screamed.

The grandmother had the peculiar feeling that the bespectacled man was someone she knew. His face was as familiar to her as if she had known him all her life but she could not recall who he was. He moved away from the car and began to come down the embankment, placing his feet carefully so that he wouldn't slip. He had on tan and white shoes and no socks, and his ankles were red and thin. "Good afternoon," he said. "I see you all had you a little spill."

"We turned over twice!" said the grandmother.

"Oncet," he corrected. "We seen it happen. Try their car and see will it run, Hiram," he said quietly to the boy with the gray hat.

"What you got that gun for?" John Wesley asked. "Whatcha gonna do with that gun?"

"Lady," the man said to the children's mother, "would you mind calling them children to sit down by you? Children make me nervous. I want all you all to sit down right together there where you're at."

"What are you telling US what to do for?" June Star asked,

Behind them the line of woods gaped like a dark open mouth. "Come here," said their mother.

"Look here now," Bailey said suddenly, "we're in a predicament! We're in …"

The grandmother shrieked. She scrambled to her feet and stood staring. "You're The Misfit!" she said. "I recognized you at once!"

"Yes'm," the man said, smiling slightly as if he were pleased in spite of himself to be known, "but it would have been better for all of you, lady, if you hadn't of reckernized me."

Bailey turned his head sharply and said something to his mother that shocked even the children. The old lady began to cry and The Misfit reddened.

"Lady," he said, "don't you get upset. Sometimes a man says things he   85 don't mean. I don't reckon he meant to talk to you thataway."

"You wouldn't shoot a lady, would you?" the grandmother said and removed a clean handkerchief from her cuff and began to slap at her eyes with it.

The Misfit pointed the toe of his shoe into the ground and made a little hole and then covered it up again. "I would hate to have to," he said.

"Listen," the grandmother almost screamed, "I know you're a good man. You don't look a bit like you have common blood. I know you must come from nice people!"

"Yes mam," he said, "finest people in the world." When he smiled he showed a row of strong white teeth. "God never made a finer woman than my mother and my daddy's heart was pure gold," he said. The boy with the red sweat shirt had come around behind them and was standing with his gun at his hip. The Misfit squatted down on the ground. "Watch them children, Bobby Lee," he said. "You know they make me nervous." He looked at the six of them huddled together in front of him and he seemed to be embarrassed as if he couldn't think of anything to say. "Ain't a cloud in the sky," he remarked, looking up at it. "Don't see no sun but don't see no cloud neither."

"Yes, it's a beautiful day," said the grandmother. "Listen," she said,   90 "you shouldn't call yourself The Misfit because I know you're a good man at heart. I can just look at you and tell."

"Hush!" Bailey yelled. "Hush! Everybody shut up and let me handle this!" He was squatting in the position of a runner about to sprint forward but he didn't move.

"I pre-chate that, lady," The Misfit said and drew a little circle in the ground with the butt of his gun.

"It'll take a half a hour to fix this here car," Hiram called, looking over the raised hood of it.

"Well, first you and Bobby Lee get him and that little boy to step over yonder with you," The Misfit said, pointing to Bailey and John Wesley. "The boys want to ast you something," he said to Bailey. "Would you mind stepping back in them woods there with them?"

"Listen," Bailey began, "we're in a terrible predicament! Nobody rea-   95 lizes what this is," and his voice cracked. His eyes were as blue and intense as the parrots in his shirt and he remained perfectly still.

The grandmother reached up to adjust her hat brim as if she were going to the woods with him but it came off in her hand. She stood staring at it and after a second she let it fall to the ground. Hiram pulled Bailey up by the arm as if he were assisting an old man. John Wesley caught hold of his father's hand and Bobby Lee followed. They went off toward the woods and just as they reached the dark edge, Bailey turned and supporting himself against a gray naked pine trunk, he shouted, "I'll be back in a minute, Mamma, wait on me!"

"Come back this instant!" his mother shrilled but they all disappeared into the woods.

"Bailey Boy!" the grandmother called in a tragic voice but she found she was looking at The Misfit squatting on the ground in front of her. "I just know you're a good man," she said desperately. "You're not a bit common!"

"Nome, I ain't a good man," The Misfit said after a second as if he had considered her statement carefully, "but I ain't the worst in the world neither. My daddy said I was a different breed of dog from my brothers and sisters. 'You know,' Daddy said, 'it's some that can live their whole life out without asking about it and it's others has to know why it is, and this boy is one of the latters. He's going to be into everything!'" He put on his black hat and looked up suddenly and then away deep into the woods as if he were embarrassed again. "I'm sorry I don't have on a shirt before you ladies," he said, hunching his shoulders slightly. "We buried our clothes that we had on when we escaped and we're just making do until we can get better. We borrowed these from some folks we met," he explained.

"That's perfectly all right," the grandmother said. "Maybe Bailey has an extra shirt in his suitcase."

"I'll look and see terrectly," The Misfit said.

"Where are they taking him?" the children's mother screamed.

"Daddy was a card himself," The Misfit said. "You couldn't put anything over on him. He never got in trouble with the Authorities though. Just had the knack of handling them."

"You could be honest too if you'd only try," said the grandmother. "Think how wonderful it would be to settle down and live a comfortable life and not have to think about somebody chasing you all the time."

The Misfit kept scratching in the ground with the butt of his gun as if he were thinking about it. "Yes'm, somebody is always after you," he murmured.

The grandmother noticed how thin his shoulder blades were just behind his hat because she was standing up looking down on him. "Do you ever pray?" she asked.

He shook his head. All she saw was the black hat wiggle between his shoulder blades. "Nome," he said.

There was a pistol shot from the woods, followed closely by another. Then silence. The old lady's head jerked around. She could hear the wind move through the tree tops like a long satisfied insuck of breath. "Bailey Boy!" she called.

"I was a gospel singer for a while," The Misfit said. "I been most everything. Been in the arm service, both land and sea, at home and abroad, been twict married, been an undertaker, been with the railroads, plowed Mother Earth, been in a tornado, seen a man burnt alive oncet," and he looked up at the children's mother and the little girl who were sitting close together, their faces white and their eyes glassy; "I even seen a woman flogged," he said.

"Pray, pray," the grandmother began, "pray, pray...."   110

"I never was a bad boy that I remember of," The Misfit said in an almost dreamy voice, "but somewheres along the line I done something wrong and got sent to the penitentiary. I was buried alive," and he looked up and held her attention to him by a steady stare.

"That's when you should have started to pray," she said. "What did you do to get sent to the penitentiary that first time?"

"Turn to the right, it was a wall," The Misfit said, looking up again at the cloudless sky. "Turn to the left, it was a wall. Look up it was a ceiling, look down it was a floor. I forget what I done, lady. I set there and set there, trying to remember what it was I done and I ain't recalled it to this day. Oncet in a while, I would think it was coming to me, but it never come."

"Maybe they put you in by mistake," the old lady said vaguely.

"Nome," he said. "It wasn't no mistake. They had the papers on me."   115

"You must have stolen something," she said.

The Misfit sneered slightly. "Nobody had nothing I wanted," he said. "It was a head-doctor at the penitentiary said what I had done was kill my daddy but I known that for a lie. My daddy died in nineteen ought nineteen of the epidemic flu and I never had a thing to do with it. He was buried in the Mount Hopewell Baptist churchyard and you can see for yourself."

"If you would pray," the old lady said, "Jesus would help you."

"That's right," The Misfit said.

"Well then, why don't you pray?" she asked trembling with delight   120
suddenly.

"I don't want no hep," he said. "I'm doing all right by myself."

Bobby Lee and Hiram came ambling back from the woods. Bobby Lee was dragging a yellow shirt with bright blue parrots in it.

"Throw me that shirt, Bobby Lee," The Misfit said. The shirt came flying at him and landed on his shoulder and he put it on. The grandmother couldn't name what the shirt reminded her of. "No, lady," The Misfit said while he was buttoning it up, "I found out the crime don't matter. You can do one thing or you can do another, kill a man or take a tire off his car, because sooner or later you're going to forget what it was you done and just be punished for it."

The children's mother had begun to make heaving noises as if she couldn't get her breath. "Lady," he asked, "would you and that little girl like to step off yonder with Bobby Lee and Hiram and join your husband?"

"Yes, thank you," the mother said faintly. Her left arm dangled help-lessly and she was holding the baby, who had gone to sleep, in the other. "Hep that lady up, Hiram," The Misfit said as she struggled to climb out of the ditch, "and Bobby Lee, you hold onto that little girl's hand."

"I don't want to hold hands with him," June Star said. "He reminds me of a pig."

The fat boy blushed and laughed and caught her by the arm and pulled her off into the woods after Hiram and her mother.

Alone with The Misfit, the grandmother found that she had lost her voice. There was not a cloud in the sky nor any sun. There was nothing around her but woods. She wanted to tell him that he must pray. She opened and closed her mouth several times before anything came out. Finally she found herself saying, "Jesus, Jesus," meaning Jesus will help you, but the way she was saying it, it sounded as if she might be cursing.

"Yes'm," The Misfit said as if he agreed. "Jesus thown everything off balance. It was the same case with Him as with me except He hadn't com-mitted any crime and they could prove I had committed one because they had the papers on me. Of course," he said, "they never shown me my pa-pers. That's why I sign myself now. I said long ago, you get your signature and sign everything you do and keep a copy of it. Then you'll know what you done and you can hold up the crime to the punishment and see do they match and in the end you'll have something to prove you ain't been treated right. I call myself The Misfit," he said, "because I can't make what all I done wrong fit what all I gone through in punishment."

There was a piercing scream from the woods, followed closely by a pis-tol report. "Does it seem right to you, lady, that one is punished a heap and another ain't punished at all?"

"Jesus!" the old lady cried. "You've got good blood! I know you wouldn't shoot a lady! I know you come from nice people! Pray! Jesus, you ought not to shoot a lady. I'll give you all the money I've got!"

"Lady," The Misfit said, looking beyond her far into the woods, "there never was a body that give the undertaker a tip."

There were two more pistol reports and the grandmother raised her head like a parched old turkey hen crying for water and called, "Bailey Boy, Bailey Boy!" as if her heart would break.

"Jesus was the only One that ever raised the dead," The Misfit continued, "and He shouldn't have done it. He thown everything off bal-ance. If He did what He said, then it's nothing for you to do but thow away everything and follow Him, and if He didn't, then it's nothing for you to do but enjoy the few minutes you got left the best way you can—by killing somebody or burning down his house or doing some other meanness to him. No pleasure but meanness," he said and his voice had become almost a snarl.

"Maybe He didn't raise the dead," the old lady mumbled, not knowing   135
what she was saying and feeling so dizzy that she sank down in the ditch with her legs twisted under her.

"I wasn't there so I can't say He didn't," The Misfit said. "I wisht I had of been there," he said, hitting the ground with his fist. "It ain't right I wasn't there because if I had of been there I would of known. Listen lady," he said in a high voice, "if I had of been there I would of known and I wouldn't be like I am now." His voice seemed about to crack and the grandmother's head cleared for an instant. She saw the man's face twisted close to her own as if he were going to cry and she murmured, "Why you're one of my babies. You're one of my own children!" She reached out and touched him on the shoulder. The Misfit sprang back as if a snake had bitten him and shot her three times through the chest. Then he put his gun down on the ground and took off his glasses and began to clean them.

Hiram and Bobby Lee returned from the woods and stood over the ditch, looking down at the grandmother who half sat and half lay in a puddle of blood with her legs crossed under her like a child's and her face smiling up at the cloudless sky.

Without his glasses, The Misfit's eyes were red-rimmed and pale and defenseless-looking. "Take her off and thow her where you thown the others," he said, picking up the cat that was rubbing itself against his leg.

"She was a talker, wasn't she?" Bobby Lee said, sliding down the ditch with a yodel.

"She would of been a good woman," The Misfit said, "if it had been   140
somebody there to shoot her every minute of her life."

"Some fun!" Bobby Lee said.

"Shut up, Bobby Lee," The Misfit said. "It's no real pleasure in life."

■ Identify details that seem at first to be irrelevant to the story. What purpose do they serve in the narrative?

■ Identify places later in the story where specific earlier details gain a new meaning.

■ Whose point of view do we get throughout this story?

■ In what ways does O'Connor make each character unsympathetic?

■ How do the various characters relate to one another?

■ How does the assertion "She would of been a good woman" help us identify a theme in this story?

POETRY

John Keats (1795–1821)

La Belle Dame sans Merci: A Ballad (1819, 1820)

1

O what can ail thee, knight at arms,
 Alone and palely loitering?
The sedge has wither'd from the lake,
 And no birds sing.

2

O what can ail thee, knight at arms, 5
 So haggard and so woe-begone?
The squirrel's granary is full,
 And the harvest's done.

3

I see a lily on thy brow
 With anguish moist and fever dew, 10
And on thy cheeks a fading rose
 Fast withereth too.

4

I met a lady in the meads,
 Full beautiful, a fairy's child;
Her hair was long, her foot was light, 15
 And her eyes were wild.

5

I made a garland for her head,
 And bracelets too, and fragrant zone;
She look'd at me as she did love,
 And made sweet moan. 20

6

I set her on my pacing steed,
 And nothing else saw all day long,

For sidelong would she bend, and sing
    A fairy's song.

7

She found me roots of relish sweet,   25
  And honey wild, and manna dew,
And sure in language strange she said—
    I love thee true.

8

She took me to her elfin grot,
  And there she wept, and sigh'd full sore,   30
And there I shut her wild wild eyes
    With kisses four.

9

And there she lullèd me asleep,
  And there I dream'd—Ah! woe betide!
The latest dream I ever dream'd   35
    On the cold hill's side.

10

I saw pale kings, and princes too,
  Pale warriors, death pale were they all;
They cried—"La belle dame sans merci
    Hath thee in thrall!"   40

11

I saw their starv'd lips in the gloam
  With horrid warning gapèd wide,
And I awoke and found me here
    On the cold hill's side.

12

And this is why I sojourn here,   45
  Alone and palely loitering,
Though the sedge is wither'd from the lake,
    And no birds sing.

■ What boundary has the ailing knight crossed?

■ How does the vision in his dream change his view of the maiden?

Edna St. Vincent Millay (1892–1950)

[Women have loved before as I love now] (1931)

Women have loved before as I love now;
At least, in lively chronicles of the past—
Of Irish waters by a Cornish prow
Or Trojan waters by a Spartan mast
Much to their cost invaded—here and there,   5
Hunting the amorous line, skimming the rest,
I find some woman bearing as I bear
Love like a burning city in the breast.
I think however that of all alive
I only in such utter, ancient way   10
Do suffer love; in me alone survive
The unregenerate passions of a day
When treacherous queens, with death upon the tread,
Heedless and willful, took their knights to bed.

■ Compare this poem to those of Yeats (p. 235) and Keats (p. 230). How does the
narrator in this poem set herself in relation to history?

Elizabeth Bishop (1911–1979)

Casabianca (1946)

Love's the boy stood on the burning deck
trying to recite "The boy stood on
the burning deck." Love's the son
      stood stammering elocution
      while the poor ship in flames went down.   5

Love's the obstinate boy, the ship,
even the swimming sailors, who
would like a schoolroom platform, too,
      or an excuse to stay
      on deck. And love's the burning boy.   10

■ "The boy stood on the burning deck" is an 1829 poem that celebrates the
loyalty of a boy who stood on a burning deck because his father, an admiral
who has since become unconscious, told him to stand fast. Bishop's poem

refers to that older poem because so many schoolchildren had been compelled to memorize it in the intervening years. What is the lesson that repetition of the old poem teaches?

- Why might the "swimming sailors" like an excuse to stay on deck?

Ted Hughes (1930–1998)

Lovesong (1972)

He loved her and she loved him.
His kisses sucked out her whole past and future or tried to
He had no other appetite
She bit him she gnawed him she sucked
She wanted him complete inside her   5
Safe and sure forever and ever
Their little cries fluttered into the curtains

Her eyes wanted nothing to get away
Her looks nailed down his hands his wrists his elbows
He gripped her hard so that life   10
Should not drag her from that moment
He wanted all future to cease
He wanted to topple with his arms round her
Off that moment's brink and into nothing
Or everlasting or whatever there was   15

Her embrace was an immense press
To print him into her bones
His smiles were the garrets of a fairy palace
Where the real world would never come
Her smiles were spider bites   20
So he would lie still till she felt hungry
His words were occupying armies
Her laughs were an assassin's attempts
His looks were bullets daggers of revenge
His glances were ghosts in the corner with horrible secrets 25
His whispers were whips and jackboots
Her kisses were lawyers steadily writing
His caresses were the last hooks of a castaway
Her love-tricks were the grinding of locks
And their deep cries crawled over the floors   30
Like an animal dragging a great trap

His promises were the surgeon's gag
Her promises took the top off his skull
She would get a brooch made of it
His vows pulled out all her sinews   35
He showed her how to make a love-knot
Her vows put his eyes in formalin
At the back of her secret drawer
Their screams stuck in the wall

Their heads fell apart into sleep like the two halves   40
Of a lopped melon, but love is hard to stop

In their entwined sleep they exchanged arms and legs
In their dreams their brains took each other hostage

In the morning they wore each other's face

- What images does the poet use to indicate the contentious nature of this love?
- How does the poem progress to the morning when "they wore each other's face"? What is the significance of this exchange?

Carolyn Forché (1950–)

The Colonel (1978)

What you have heard is true. I was in his house. His wife carried a tray of coffee and sugar. His daughter filed her nails, his son went out for the night. There were daily papers, pet dogs, a pistol on the cushion beside him. The moon swung bare on its black cord over the house. On the television was a cop show. It was in English. Broken bottles were embedded in the walls around the house to scoop the kneecaps from a man's legs or cut his hands to lace. On the windows there were gratings like those in liquor stores. We had dinner, rack of lamb, good wine, a gold bell was on the table for calling the maid. The maid brought green mangoes, salt, a type of bread. I was asked how I enjoyed the country. There was a brief commercial in Spanish. His wife took everything away. There was some talk then of how difficult it had become to govern. The parrot said hello on the terrace. The colonel told it to shut up, and pushed himself from the table. My friend said to me with his eyes: say nothing. The colonel returned with a sack used to bring groceries home. He spilled many human ears on the table. They were like dried peach halves. There is no other way to say this. He took one of them in his hands, shook it in our faces, dropped it into a

water glass. It came alive there. I am tired of fooling around he said. As for the
rights of anyone, tell your people they can go fuck themselves. He swept the
ears to the floor with his arm and held the last of his wine in the air. Something
for your poetry, no? he said. Some of the ears on the floor caught this scrap of
his voice. Some of the ears on the floor were pressed to the ground.

- How does the description of the house prepare us for the ears that the colonel
  pours out on the table?
- How does the colonel's question "Something for your poetry, no?" change the
  nature of the description that the remainder of the poem presents?

William Butler Yeats (1865–1939)

Leda and the Swan (1918)

A sudden blow: the great wings beating still
Above the staggering girl, her thighs caressed
By the dark webs, her nape caught in his bill,
He holds her helpless breast upon his breast.

How can those terrified vague fingers push   5
The feathered glory from her loosening thighs?
And how can body, laid in that white rush,
But feel the strange heart beating where it lies?

A shudder in the loins engenders there
The broken wall, the burning roof and tower   10
And Agamemnon dead.
                         Being so caught up,
So mastered by the brute blood of the air,
Did she put on his knowledge with his power
Before the indifferent beak could let her drop?

- The god Zeus, disguised in the form of a swan, raped Leda. One of their
  offspring was Helen, the Greek beauty whose abduction by Paris set off the
  Trojan War. Helen's sister, Clytemnestra, shared her mother's womb, though
  she had a different father. Clytemnestra killed her own husband, Agamemnon,
  when he returned from leading the Greek forces to victory in the Trojan War.
  What are the different boundaries that are broken by this rape (and
  acknowledged in this poem)?

■ How does the poem depict the relation between the rape and subsequent history?

D. H. Lawrence (1885–1930)

Snake (1923)

A snake came to my water-trough
On a hot, hot day, and I in pajamas for the heat,
To drink there.

In the deep, strange-scented shade of the great dark carob-tree
I came down the steps with my pitcher   5
And must wait, must stand and wait, for there he was at the trough before me.

He reached down from a fissure in the earth-wall in the gloom
And trailed his yellow-brown slackness soft-bellied down,
   over the edge of the stone trough
And rested his throat upon the stone bottom,
And where the water had dripped from the tap, in a small clearness,   10
He sipped with his straight mouth,
Softly drank through his straight gums, into his slack long body,
Silently.

Someone was before me at my water-trough,
And I, like a second comer, waiting.   15

He lifted his head from his drinking, as cattle do,
And looked at me vaguely, as drinking cattle do,
And flickered his two-forked tongue from his lips, and mused a moment,
And stooped and drank a little more,
Being earth-brown, earth-golden from the burning bowels of the earth   20
On the day of Sicilian July, with Etna smoking.
The voice of my education said to me
He must be killed,
For in Sicily the black, black snakes are innocent, the gold are venomous.

And voices in me said, If you were a man   25
You would take a stick and break him now, and finish him off.

But must I confess how I liked him,
How glad I was he had come like a guest in quiet, to drink at my water-trough
And depart peaceful, pacified, and thankless,
Into the burning bowels of this earth?   30

Was it cowardice, that I dared not kill him?
Was it perversity, that I longed to talk to him?
Was it humility, to feel so honored?
I felt so honored.

And yet those voices: 35
If you were not afraid, you would kill him!

And truly I was afraid, I was most afraid,
But even so, honored still more
That he should seek my hospitality
From out the dark door of the secret earth.   40

He drank enough
And lifted his head, dreamily, as one who has drunken,
And flickered his tongue like a forked night on the air, so black,
Seeming to lick his lips,
And looked around like a god, unseeing, into the air,   45
And slowly turned his head,
And slowly, very slowly, as if thrice adream,
Proceeded to draw his slow length curving round
And climb again the broken bank of my wall-face.

And as he put his head into that dreadful hole,   50
And as he slowly drew up, snake-easing his shoulders, and entered farther,
A sort of horror, a sort of protest against his withdrawing into that horrid
    black hole,
Deliberately going into the blackness, and slowly drawing himself after,
Overcame me now his back was turned.

I looked round, I put down my pitcher,   55
I picked up a clumsy log
And threw it at the water-trough with a clatter.

I think it did not hit him,
But suddenly that part of him that was left behind convulsed in
    undignified haste,
Writhed like lightning, and was gone   60
Into the black hole, the earth-lipped fissure in the wall-front,
At which, in the intense still noon, I stared with fascination.

And immediately I regretted it.
I thought how paltry, how vulgar, what a mean act!
I despised myself and the voices of my accursed human education.   65

And I thought of the albatross,
And I wished he would come back, my snake.

For he seemed to me again like a king,
Like a king in exile, uncrowned in the underworld,
Now due to be crowned again.   70

And so, I missed my chance with one of the lords
Of life.
And I have something to expiate;
A pettiness.

■ How does the narrator confront his "voice" of his education?

■ What is the source of the horror that he feels as the snake withdraws?

Richard Wilbur (1921–)

A Fable (1987)

Securely sunning in a forest glade,
      A mild, well-meaning snake
Approved the adaptations he had made
        For safety's sake.

     He liked the skin he had—   5
Its mottled camouflage, its look of mail,
And was content that he had thought to add
        A rattling tail.

The tail was not for drumming up a fight;
      No, nothing of the sort.   10
And he would only use his poisoned bite
        As last resort.

     A peasant now drew near,
Collecting wood; the snake, observing this,
Expressed concern by uttering a clear   15
        But civil hiss.

The simple churl, his nerves at once unstrung,
      Mistook the other's tone

And dashed his brains out with a deftly-flung
                    Pre-emptive stone.   20

MORAL
Security, alas, can give
            A threatening impression;
Too much defense-initiative
                    Can prompt aggression.   25

▪ Compare this poem to Lawrence's. How has a similar scenario shifted in this
   version?

▪ How does the moral here indicate meaning beyond the scope of the simple story?

Linda Pastan (1932–)

Ethics (1980)

In ethics class so many years ago
our teacher asked this question every fall:
if there were a fire in a museum
which would you save, a Rembrandt painting
or an old woman who hadn't many   5
years left anyhow? Restless on hard chairs
caring little for pictures or old age
we'd opt one year for life, the next for art
and always half-heartedly. Sometimes
the woman borrowed my grandmother's face   10
leaving her usual kitchen to wander
some drafty, half imagined museum.
One year, feeling clever, I replied
why not let the woman decide herself?
Linda, the teacher would report, eschews   15
the burdens of responsibility.
This fall in a real museum I stand
before a real Rembrandt, old woman,
or nearly so, myself. The colors
within this frame are darker than autumn,   20
darker even than winter—the browns of earth,
though earth's most radiant elements burn
through the canvas. I know now that woman
and painting and season are almost one
and all beyond saving by children.   25

- How has the theoretical question from ethics class changed for the poet?
- How has her answer changed?

DRAMA

Christopher Marlowe (1564–1593)

Christopher Marlowe was born in Canterbury, England. He attended Cambridge University; and while a student there, he apparently undertook a number of missions on behalf of the Protestant queen, Elizabeth. His role as a secret agent (or double agent) remains unclear. In any case, within a year of receiving his MA from Cambridge, two of his plays were produced in London. The remainder of his short life was colorful. He was arrested on a number of occasions for fighting and once on charges of atheism, but was never imprisoned, and he likely continued to act in dangerous political intrigues. He died of knife wounds suffered in a fight in a tavern (recent scholarship suggests that the fight may have been manufactured to cover Marlowe's assassination). Marlowe was unquestionably a great dramatist, and he wrote a number of dramatic and lyric poems in addition to his plays. One of these, the lyric beginning "Come live with me and be my love," is among the best-known poems of the English language, one that has prompted responses from a number of other poets over the centuries.

The Tragical History of the Life and Death of Doctor Faustus (ca. 1593)

CHARACTERS

THE POPE
CARDINAL OF LORRAIN
EMPEROR OF GERMANY
DUKE OF VANHOLT
FAUSTUS
VALDES *and* CORNELIUS, *friends to* FAUSTUS
WAGNER, *servant to* FAUSTUS
CLOWN
ROBIN
RALPH

VINTNER

HORSE-COURSER

KNIGHT

OLD MAN

SCHOLARS, FRIARS, *and* ATTENDANTS

DUCHESS OF VANHOLT

LUCIFER

BELZEBUB

MEPHISTOPHILIS

GOOD ANGEL

EVIL ANGEL

THE SEVEN DEADLY SINS

DEVILS

SPIRITS *in the shape of* ALEXANDER THE GREAT, *of his* PARAMOUR, *and of*
   HELEN OF TROY

CHORUS

(*Enter* CHORUS.)

CHORUS: Not marching now in fields of Thrasimene,
     Where Mars did mate° the Carthaginians;
     Nor sporting in the dalliance of love,
     In courts of kings where state is overturn'd;
     Nor in the pomp of proud audacious deeds,   5
     Intends our Muse to vaunt his heavenly verse:
     Only this, gentlemen,—we must perform
     The form of Faustus' fortunes, good or bad.
     To patient judgments we appeal our plaud°
     And speak for Faustus in his infancy.   10
     Now is he born, his parents base of stock,
     In Germany, within a town call'd Rhodes°
     Of riper years to Wittenberg he went,
     Whereas his kinsmen chiefly brought him up.
     So soon he profits in divinity,   15
     The fruitful plot of scholarism grac'd,°
     That shortly he was grac'd with doctor's name,
     Excelling all whose sweet delight disputes
     In heavenly matters of theology;
     Till swollen with cunning,° of a self-conceit,   20

---

2. **mate:** Confound. But Hannibal was victorious at Lake Trasumennus, B.C. 217. **9. plaud:** For applause.
12. Rhodes: Roda, in the Duchy of Saxe-Altenburg, near Jena. **16. fruitful plot ... grac'd:** The garden of
scholarship being adorned by him. **20. cunning:** Knowledge.

His waxen wings° did mount above his reach,
And, melting, Heavens conspir'd his overthrow;
For, falling to a devilish exercise,
And glutted [more] with learning's golden gifts,
He surfeits upon cursed necromancy.   25
Nothing so sweet as magic is to him,
Which he prefers before his chiefest bliss.
And this the man that in his study sits!

(Exit.)

Scene 1

(Enter FAUSTUS *in his Study.)*

FAUSTUS: Settle my studies, Faustus, and begin
To sound the depth of that thou wilt profess;°
Having commenc'd, be a divine in show.
Yet level° at the end of every art,
And live and die in Aristotle's works.   5
Sweet Analytics,° 'tis thou hast ravish'd me,
Bene disserere est finis logices.
Is to dispute well logic's chiefest end?
Affords this art no greater miracle?
Then read no more, thou hast attain'd the end;   10
A greater subject fitteth Faustus' wit.
Bid ὄν καὶ μὴ ὄν° farewell; Galen° come,
Seeing *Ubi desinit Philosophus, ibi incipit Medicus*°
Be a physician, Faustus, heap up gold,
And be eternis'd for some wondrous cure.   15
Summum bonum medicinæ sanitas,°
"The end of physic is our body's health."
Why, Faustus, hast thou not attain'd that end?
Is not thy common talk sound Aphorisms?°
Are not thy bills° hung up as monuments,   20
Whereby whole cities have escap'd the plague,
And thousand desperate maladies been eas'd?
Yet art thou still but Faustus and a man.
Wouldst thou make men to live eternally,
Or, being dead, raise them to life again?   25

---

21. **His waxen wings:** An allusion to the myth of Icarus, who flew too near the sun. **2. profess:** teach publicly. **4. level:** aim. **6. Analytics:** Logic. **12.** ὄν καὶ μὴ ὄv: The Aristotelian phrase for "being and not being." **12. Galen:** Greek physician whose theories were highly regarded in the Middle Ages. **13. Ubi ... Medicus:** "Where the philosopher leaves off, there the physician begins." **16. Summum ... sanitas:** This and the previous quotation are from Aristotle. **19. Aphorisms:** Medical maxims. **20. bills:** Announcements.

Then this profession were to be esteem'd.
Physic, farewell.—Where is Justinian?
(*Reads.*)
Si una eademque res legatur duobus, alter rem, alter valorem rei, &c.°
A pretty case of paltry legacies!
(*Reads.*)
Exhæreditare filium non potest pater nisi, &c.°   30
Such is the subject of the Institute°
And universal Body of the Law.
His° study fits a mercenary drudge,
Who aims at nothing but external trash;
Too servile and illiberal for me.   35
When all is done, divinity is best;
Jerome's Bible°, Faustus, view it well.
(*Reads.*)
Stipendium peccati mors est. Ha! *Stipendium, &c.*
"The reward of sin is death." That's hard,
(*Reads.*)
Si peccasse negamus, fallimur, et nulla est in nobis veritas.   40
"If we say that we have no sin we deceive ourselves, and there's no
truth in us." Why then, belike we must sin and so consequently die.
Ay, we must die an everlasting death.
What doctrine call you this, *Che sera sera,*
"What will be shall he?" Divinity, adieu!   45
These metaphysics of magicians
And necromantic books are heavenly;
Lines, circles, scenes, letters, and characters,
Ay, these are those that Faustus most desires.
O what a world of profit and delight,   50
Of power, of honour, of omnipotence
Is promis'd to the studious artisan!
All things that move between the quiet poles
Shall be at my command. Emperors and kings
Are but obeyed in their several provinces,   55
Nor can they raise the wind or rend the clouds;
But his dominion that exceeds° in this

---

28. *Si una eademque ... &c.:* "If one and the same thing is bequeathed to two persons, one gets the thing and the other the value of the thing." **30.** *Exhæreditare lium ... &c.:* "A father cannot disinherit the son except," etc. **31. Institute:** Of Justinian, under whom the Roman law was codified. **33. His:** Its. **37. Jerome's Bible:** The Vulgate. **57. exceeds:** Excels.

Stretcheth as far as doth the mind of man.
A sound magician is a mighty god:
Here, Faustus, try thy, brains to gain a deity.   60
Wagner!
(*Enter* WAGNER.)
            Commend me to my dearest friends,
The German Valdes and Cornelius;
Request them earnestly to visit me.
WAG I will, sir.
(*Exit.*)
FAUSTUS: Their conference will be a greater help to me   65
Than all my labours, plod I ne'er so fast.
(*Enter* GOOD ANGEL *and* EVIL ANGEL.)
G. ANG: O Faustus! lay that damned book aside,
And gaze not upon it lest it tempt thy soul,
And heap God's heavy wrath upon thy head.
Read, read the Scriptures: that is blasphemy.   70
E. ANG: Go forward, Faustus, in that famous art,
Wherein all Nature's treasure is contain'd:
Be thou on earth as Jove is in the sky,
Lord and commander of these elements.
(*Exeunt* ANGELS.)
FAUSTUS: How am I glutted with conceit° of this!   75
Shall I make spirits fetch me what I please,
Resolve me of all ambiguities,
Perform what desperate enterprise I will?
I'll have them fly to India for gold,
Ransack the ocean for orient pearl,   80
And search all corners of the new-found world
For pleasant fruits and princely delicates;
I'll have them read me strange philosophy
And tell the secrets of all foreign kings;
I'll have them wall all Germany with brass,   85
And make swift Rhine circle fair Wittenberg;
I'll have them fill the public schools with silk,
Wherewith the students shall be bravely clad;
I'll levy soldiers with the coin they bring,
And chase the Prince of Parma from our land,°   90
And reign sole king of all the provinces;
Yea, stranger engines for the brunt of war

---

75. conceit: Idea. 90. our land: The Netherlands, over which Parma re-established the Spanish dominion.

Than was the fiery keel° at Antwerp's bridge,
I'll make my servile spirits to invent.
Come, German Valdes and Cornelius,   95
And make me blest with your sage conference.
(*Enter* VALDES *and* CORNELIUS.)°
Valdes, sweet Valdes, and Cornelius,
Know that your words have won me at the last
To practise magic and concealed arts:
Yet not your words only, but mine own fantasy,   100
That will receive no object, for my head
But ruminates on necromantic skill.
Philosophy is odious and obscure,
Both law and physic are for petty wits;
Divinity is basest of the three,°   105
Unpleasant, harsh, contemptible, and vile:
'Tis magic, magic, that hath ravish'd me.
Then, gentle friends, aid me in this attempt;
And I that have with concise syllogisms
Gravell'd the pastors of the German church,   110
And made the flow'ring pride of Wittenberg
Swarm to my problems, as the infernal spirits
On sweet Musæus,° when he came to hell,
Will be as cunning as Agrippa was,
Whose shadows made all Europe honour him.   115
VALD: Faustus, these books, thy wit, and our experience
Shall make all nations to canonise us.
As Indian Moors° obey their Spanish lords,
So shall the subjects of every element
Be always serviceable to us three;   120
Like lions shall they guard us when we please;
Like Almain rutters° with their horsemen's staves,
Or Lapland giants, trotting by our sides;
Sometimes like women or unwedded maids,
Shadowing more beauty in their airy brows   125
Than have the white breasts of the queen of love:
From Venice shall they drag huge argosies,

---

93. fiery keel: A ship filled with explosives used to blow up a bridge built by Parma in 1585 at the siege of Antwerp. Valdes and Cornelius: The famous Cornelius Agrippa. German Valdes is not known.
113. Musæus: Cf. Virgil, *Aeneid*, vi. 667. 118. Indian Moors: Americans Indians. 122. Almain rutters: Troopers. Germ. *Reiters*.

And from America the golden fleece
That yearly stuffs old Philip's treasury;
If learned Faustus will be resolute.   130
FAUSTUS: Valdes, as resolute am I in this
   As thou to live; therefore object it not.
CORN: The miracles that magic will perform
   Will make thee vow to study nothing else.
   He that is grounded in astrology,   135
   Enrich'd with tongues, well seen° in minerals,
   Hath all the principles magic doth require.
   Then doubt not, Faustus, but to be renown'd,
   And more frequented for this mystery
   Than heretofore the Delphian Oracle.   140
   The spirits tell me they can dry the sea,
   And fetch the treasure of all foreign wracks,
   Ay, all the wealth that our forefathers hid
   Within the massy entrails of the earth;
   Then tell me, Faustus, what shall we three want?   145
FAUSTUS: Nothing, Cornelius! O this cheers my soul!
   Come show me some demonstrations magical,
   That I may conjure in some lusty grove,
   And have these joys in full possession.
VALD: Then haste thee to some solitary grove   150
   And bear wise Bacon's° and Albanus'° works,
   The Hebrew Psalter and New Testament;
   And whatsoever else is requisite
   We will inform thee ere our conference cease.
CORN: Valdes, first let him know the words of art;   155
   And then, all other ceremonies learn'd,
   Faustus may try his cunning by himself.
VALD: First I'll instruct thee in the rudiments.
   And then wilt thou be perfecter than I.
FAUSTUS: Then come and dine with me, and after meat,   160
   We'll canvass every quiddity° thereof;
   For ere I sleep I'll try what I can do:
   This night I'll conjure though I die therefore.
(*Exeunt.*)

---

136. seen: Versed. **151. Bacon's:** Roger Bacon. **151. Albanus':** Perhaps Pietro d'Abano, a medieval alchemist; perhaps a misprint for Albertus (Magnus), the great schoolman. **161. quiddity:** Fine point.

Scene 2
Before Faustus' House.

(*Enter two* SCHOLARS.)

1 SCHOL: I wonder what's become of Faustus that was wont to make our schools ring with *sic probo?*°

2 SCHOL That shall we know, for see here comes his boy.

(*Enter* WAGNER.)

1 SCHOL: How now, sirrah! Where's thy master?

WAG: God in heaven knows!   5

2 SCHOL: Why, dost not thou know?

WAG: Yes, I know. But that follows not.

1 SCHOL: Go to, sirrah! Leave your jesting, and tell us where he is.

WAG: That follows not necessary by force of argument, that you, being licentiate, should stand upon't: therefore, acknowledge your error and be   10
attentive.

2 SCHOL: Why, didst thou not say thou knew'st?

WAG: Have you any witness on't?

1 SCHOL: Yes, sirrah, I heard you.

WAG: Ask my fellow if I be a thief.   15

2 SCHOL: Well, you will not tell us?

WAG: Yes, sir, I will tell you; yet if you were not dunces, you would never ask me such a question; for is not he *corpus naturale?*° and is not that *mobile?* Then wherefore should you ask me such a question? But that I am by nature phlegmatic, slow to wrath, and prone to lechery (to love,   20
I would say), it were not for you to come within forty foot of the place of execution, although I do not doubt to see you both hang'd the next sessions. Thus having triumph'd over you, I will set my countenance like a precisian,° and begin to speak thus:—Truly, my dear brethren, my master is within at dinner, with Valdes and Cornelius, as this wine,   25
if it could speak, would inform your worships; and so the Lord bless you, preserve you, and keep you, my dear brethren, my dear brethren.

(*Exit.*)

1 SCHOL: Nay, then, I fear he has fallen into that damned Art, for which they two are infamous through the world.

2 SCHOL: Were he a stranger, and not allied to me, yet should I grieve for   30
him. But come, let us go and inform the Rector, and see if he by his grave counsel can reclaim him.

1 SCHOL: O, I fear me nothing can reclaim him.

---

2. *sic probo:* "Thus I prove"—a common formula in scholastic discussions. 18. *corpus naturale:* '*Corpus naturale seu mobile*' (literally, "natural or movable body") was the scholastic expression for the subject matter of Physics. 24. *precisian:* Puritan.

2 SCHOL: Yet let us try what we can do.
(*Exeunt.*)

Scene 3
A Grove.

(*Enter* FAUSTUS *to conjure.*)
FAUSTUS: Now that the gloomy shadow of the earth
    Longing to view Orion's drizzling look,
    Leaps from th' antarctic world unto the sky,
    And dims the welkin with her pitchy breath,
    Faustus, begin thine incantations,   5
    And try if devils will obey thy hest,
    Seeing thou hast pray'd and sacrific'd to them.
    Within this circle is Jehovah's name,
    Forward and backward anagrammatis'd,
    The breviated names of holy saints,   10
    Figures of every adjunct° to the Heavens,
    And characters of signs and erring stars,°
    By which the spirits are enforc'd to rise:
    Then fear not, Faustus, but be resolute,
    And try the uttermost magic can perform.   15
    Sint mihi Dei Acherontis propitii! Valeat numen triplex Jehovae! Ignei,
    aerii, aquatani spiritus, salvete! Orientis princeps Belzebub, inferni ardentis
    monarcha, et Demogorgon, propitiamus vos, ut appareat et surgat Mephi-
    stophilis. Quid tu moraris? Per Jehovam, Gehennam, et consecratum
    aquam quam nunc spargo, signumque crucis quod nunc facio, et per vota   20
    nostra, ipse nunc surgat nobis dicatus Mephistophilis!°
(*Enter* MEPHISTOPHILIS, *a* DEVIL.)
    I charge thee to return and change thy shape;
    Thou art too ugly to attend on me.
    Go, and return an old Franciscan friar;
    That holy shape becomes a devil best.   25
(*Exit* DEVIL.)
    I see there's virtue in my heavenly words;
    Who would not be proficient in this art?

---

11. **every adjunct:** Every star belonging to. 12. **erring stars:** Planets. **16–21.** *Sint mihi … Mephisto-*
philis!: "Be propitious to me, gods of Acheron! May the triple deity of Jehovah prevail! Spirits of fire, air,
water, hail! Belzebub, Prince of the East, monarch of burning hell, and Demogorgon, we propitiate ye, that
Mephistophilis may appear and rise. Why dost thou delay? By Jehovah, Gehenna, and the holy water which
now I sprinkle, and the sign of the cross which now I make, and by our prayer, may Mephistophilis now
summoned by us arise!"

How pliant is this Mephistophilis,
Full of obedience and humility!
Such is the force of magic and my spells.   30
[Now,] Faustus, thou art conjuror laureate,
Thou canst command great Mephistophilis:
Quin regis Mephistophilis fratris imagine.°
(*Re-enter* MEPHISTOPHILIS, *like a Franciscan Friar.*)
MEPH: Now, Faustus, what would'st thou have me do?
FAUSTUS: I charge thee wait upon me whilst I live,   35
To do whatever Faustus shall command,
Be it to make the moon drop from her sphere,
Or the ocean to overwhelm the world.
MEPH: I am a servant to great Lucifer,
And may not follow thee without his leave;   40
No more than he commands must we perform.
FAUSTUS: Did he not charge thee to appear to me?
MEPH: No, I came hither of mine own accord.
FAUSTUS: Did not my conjuring speeches raise thee? Speak:
MEPH: That was the cause, but yet *per accidens*;   45
For when we hear one rack° the name of God,
Abjure the Scriptures and his Saviour Christ,
We fly in hope to get his glorious soul;
Nor will we come, unless he use such means
Whereby he is in danger to be damn'd: 50
Therefore the shortest cut for conjuring
Is stoutly to abjure the Trinity,
And pray devoutly to the Prince of Hell.
FAUSTUS: So Faustus hath
Already done; and holds this principle,   55
There is no chief but only Belzebub,
To whom Faustus doth dedicate himself.
This word "damnation" terrifies not him,
For he confounds hell in Elysium°
His ghost be with the old philosophers!   60
But, leaving these vain trifles of men's souls,
Tell me what is that Lucifer thy lord?
MEPH: Arch-regent and commander of all spirits.
FAUSTUS: Was not that Lucifer an angel once?
MEPH: Yes, Faustus, and most dearly lov'd of God.   65

---

33. *Quin regis ... imagine:* "For indeed thou hast power in the image of thy brother Mephistophilis"
46. rack: Twist in anagrams. 59. he confounds hell in Elysium: Heaven and hell are indifferent to him.

FAUSTUS: How comes it then that he is Prince of devils?

MEPH: O, by aspiring pride and insolence;
 For which God threw him from the face of Heaven.

FAUSTUS: And what are you that you live with Lucifer?

MEPH: Unhappy spirits that fell with Lucifer,   70
 Conspir'd against our God with Lucifer,
 And are for ever damn'd with Lucifer.

FAUSTUS: Where are you damn'd?

MEPH: In hell.

FAUSTUS: How comes it then that thou art out of hell?   75

MEPH: Why this is hell, nor am I out of it.
 Think'st thou that I who saw the face of God,
 And tasted the eternal joys of Heaven,
 Am not tormented with ten thousand hells,
 In being depriv'd of everlasting bliss?   80
 O Faustus! leave these frivolous demands,
 Which strike a terror to my fainting soul.

FAUSTUS: What, is great Mephistophilis so passionate°
 For being depriv'd of the joys of Heaven?
 Learn thou of Faustus manly fortitude,   85
 And scorn those joys thou never shalt possess.
 Go bear these tidings to great Lucifer:
 Seeing Faustus hath incurr'd eternal death
 By desperate thoughts against Jove's deity,
 Say he surrenders up to him his soul,   90
 So he will spare him four and twenty years,
 Letting him live in all voluptuousness;
 Having thee ever to attend on me;
 To give me whatsoever I shall ask,
 To tell me whatsoever I demand,   95
 To slay mine enemies, and aid my friends,
 And always be obedient to my will.
 Go and return to mighty Lucifer,
 And meet me in my study at midnight,
 And then resolve° me of thy master's mind.   100

MEPH: I will, Faustus.

(Exit.)

FAUSTUS: Had I as many souls as there be stars,
 I'd give them all for Mephistophilis.
 By him I'll be great Emperor of the world,

---

83. passionate: Sorrowful. 100. resolve: Inform.

And make a bridge through the moving air,   105
To pass the ocean with a band of men;
I'll join the hills that bind the Afric shore,
And make that [country] continent to Spain,
And both contributory to my crown.
The Emperor shall not live but by my leave,   110
Nor any potentate of Germany.
Now that I have obtain'd what I desire,
I'll live in speculation° of this art
Till Mephistophilis return again.
(*Exit.*)

Scene 4
A Street.

(*Enter* WAGNER *and the* CLOWN.)

WAG: Sirrah, boy, come hither.

CLOWN: How, boy! Swowns, boy! I hope you have seen many boys with
   such pickadevaunts° as I have. Boy, quotha!

WAG: Tell me, sirrah, hast thou any comings in?

CLOWN: Ay, and goings out too. You may see else.   5

WAG: Alas, poor slave! See how poverty jesteth in his nakedness! The villain is bare and out of service, and so hungry that I know he would give
   his soul to the devil for a shoulder of mutton, though it were blood-raw.

CLOWN: How? My soul to the Devil for a shoulder of mutton, though 'twere
   blood-raw! Not so, good friend. By'r Lady, I had need have it well
   roasted and good sauce to it, if I pay so dear.   10

WAG: Well, wilt thou serve me, and I'll make thee go like *Qui mihi discipulus?*°

CLOWN: How, in verse?

WAG: No, sirrah; in beaten silk and stavesacre.°

CLOWN: How, how, Knave's acre!° Ay, I thought that was all the land his   15
   father left him. Do you hear? I would be sorry to rob you of your living.

WAG: Sirrah, I say in stavesacre.

CLOWN: Oho! Oho! Stavesacre! Why, then, belike if I were your man I
   should be full of vermin.

WAG: So thou shalt, whether thou beest with me or no. But, sirrah, leave   20
   your jesting, and bind yourself presently unto me for seven years, or I'll
   turn all the lice about thee into familiars, and they shall tear thee in
   pieces.

---

113. speculation: Study. 3. pickadevaunts: Beards cut to a sharp point (Fr. *pic-á-devant*). 12. *Qui mihi
discipulus:* "Whoever is my disciple," the first words of W. Lily's *"Ad discipulos carmen de moribus"*
(*Ode to His Disciples on Morality*). 14. stavesacre: A kind of larkspur, used for destroying lice.
15. Knave's acre: A mean street in London.

CLOWN: Do you hear, sir? You may save that labour; they are too familiar
with me already. Swowns! they are as bold with my flesh as if they had   25
paid for [their] meat and drink.

WAG: Well, do you hear, sirrah? Hold, take these guilders. (*Gives money.*)

CLOWN: Gridirons! what be they?

WAG: Why, French crowns.

CLOWN: Mass, but for the name of French crowns, a man were as good have   30
as many English counters. And what should I do with these?

WAG: Why, now, sirrah, thou art at an hour's warning, whensoever and
wheresoever the Devil shall fetch thee.

CLOWN: No, no. Here, take your gridirons again.

WAG: Truly I'll none of them.   35

CLOWN: Truly but you shall.

WAG: Bear witness I gave them him.

CLOWN: Bear witness I give them you again.

WAG: Well, I will cause two devils presently to fetch thee away—Baliol and
Belcher.   40

CLOWN: Let your Baliol and your Belcher come here, and I'll knock them,
they were never so knockt since they were devils. Say I should kill one
of them, what would folks say? "Do you see yonder tall fellow in the
round slop°?—he has kill'd the devil." So I should be call'd Kill-devil
all the parish over.   45

(*Enter two* DEVILS: *the* CLOWN *runs up and down crying.*)

WAG: Baliol and Belcher! Spirits, away! (*Exeunt* DEVILS.)

CLOWN: What, are they gone? A vengeance on them, they have vile long
nails! There was a he-devil, and a she-devil! I'll tell you how you shall
know them: all he-devils has horns, and all she-devils has clifts and
cloven feet.   50

WAG: Well, sirrah, follow me.

CLOWN: But, do you hear—if I should serve you, would you teach me to
raise up Banios and Belcheos?

WAG: I will teach thee to turn thyself to anything; to a dog, or a cat, or a
mouse, or a rat, or anything.   55

CLOWN: How! a Christian fellow to a dog or a cat, a mouse or a rat! No,
no, sir. If you turn me into anything, let it be in the likeness of a little
pretty frisky flea, that I may be here and there and everywhere. Oh, I'll
tickle the pretty wenches' plackets; I'll be amongst them, i' faith.

WAG: Well, sirrah, come.   60

CLOWN: But, do you hear, Wagner?

---

44. **round slop:** Short wide breeches.

WAG: How!—Baliol and Belcher!

CLOWN: O Lord! I pray, sir, let Banio and Belcher go sleep.

WAG: Villain—call me Master Wagner, and let thy left eye be diametarily°
    fixt upon my right heel, with *quasi vestigias nostras insistere.*°   65

(Exit.)

CLOWN: God forgive me, he speaks Dutch fustian. Well, I'll follow him, I'll
    serve him, that's flat.

(Exit.)

Scene 5

(Enter FAUSTUS *in his study.)*

FAUSTUS: Now, Faustus, must
    Thou needs be damn'd, and canst thou not be sav'd:
    What boots it then to think of God or Heaven?
    Away with such vain fancies, and despair:
    Despair in God, and trust in Belzebub.   5
    Now go not backward: no, Faustus, be resolute.
    Why waverest thou? O, something soundeth in mine ears
    "Abjure this magic, turn to God again!"
    Ay, and Faustus will turn to God again.
    To God?—He loves thee not—   10
    The God thou serv'st is thine own appetite,
    Wherein is fix'd the love of Belzebub;
    To him I'll build an altar and a church,
    And offer lukewarm blood of new-born babes.

(Enter GOOD ANGEL *and* EVIL ANGEL.*)*

G. ANG: Sweet Faustus, leave that execrable art.   15

FAUSTUS: Contrition, prayer, repentance! What of them?

G. ANG: O, they are means to bring thee unto Heaven.

E. ANG: Rather illusions, fruits of lunacy,
    That makes men foolish that do trust them most.

G. ANG: Sweet Faustus, think of Heaven, and heavenly things.   20

E. ANG: No, Faustus, think of honour and of wealth.

(Exeunt ANGELS.*)*

FAUSTUS: Of wealth!
    Why, the signiory of Emden° shall be mine.
    When Mephistophilis shall stand by me,
    What God can hurt thee, Faustus? Thou art safe;   25
    Cast no more doubts. Come, Mephistophilis,

---

64. diametarily: For *diametrically.* **65. quasi … insistere:** "As if to tread in my tracks." **23. Emden:**
Emden, near the mouth of the river Ems, was an important commercial town in Elizabethan times.

And bring glad tidings from great Lucifer;—
Is't not midnight? Come, Mephistophilis;
Veni, veni, Mephistophile!
(*Enter* MEPHISTOPHILIS.)
Now tell me, what says Lucifer thy lord?   30
MEPH: That I shall wait on Faustus whilst he lives,
   So he will buy my service with his soul.
FAUSTUS: Already Faustus hath hazarded that for thee.
MEPH: But, Faustus, thou must bequeath it solemnly,
   And write a deed of gift with thine own blood,   35
   For that security craves great Lucifer.
   If thou deny it, I will back to hell.
FAUSTUS: Stay, Mephistophilis! and tell me what good
   Will my soul do thy Lord.
MEPH: Enlarge his kingdom.   40
FAUSTUS: Is that the reason why he tempts us thus?
MEPH: *Solamen miseris socios habuisse doloris.*°
FAUSTUS: Why, have you any pain that torture others?
MEPH: As great as have the human souls of men.
   But tell me, Faustus, shall I have thy soul?   45
   And I will be thy slave, and wait on thee,
   And give thee more than thou hast wit to ask.
FAUSTUS: Ay, Mephistophilis, I give it thee.
MEPH: Then Faustus, stab thine arm courageously.
   And bind thy soul that at some certain day   50
   Great Lucifer may claim it as his own;
   And then be thou as great as Lucifer.
FAUSTUS (*Stabbing his arm.*): Lo, Mephistophilis, for love of thee
   I cut mine arm, and with my proper blood
   Assure my soul to be great Lucifer's,   55
   Chief lord and regent of perpetual night!
   View here the blood that trickles from mine arm.
   And let it be propitious for my wish.
MEPH: But, Faustus, thou must
   Write it in manner of a deed of gift.   60
FAUSTUS: Ay, so I will. (*Writes.*) But, Mephistophilis,
   My blood congeals, and I can write no more.

---

42. *Solamen ... doloris:* "Misery loves company."

MEPH: I'll fetch thee fire to dissolve it straight.
(Exit.)
FAUSTUS: What might the staying of my blood portend?
Is it unwilling I should write this bill?   65
Why streams it not that I may write afresh?
Faustus gives to thee his soul. Ah, there it stay'd.
Why should'st thou not? Is not thy soul thine own?
Then write again, *Faustus gives to thee his soul.*
(Re-enter MEPHISTOPHILIS *with a chafer of coals.)*
MEPH: Here's fire. Come, Faustus, set it on.   70
FAUSTUS: So now the blood begins to clear again;
Now will I make an end immediately. *(Writes.)*
MEPH *(Aside.):* O what will not I do to obtain his soul.
FAUSTUS: *Consummatum est:*° this bill is ended,
And Faustus hath bequeath'd his soul to Lucifer—   75
But what is this inscription on mine arm?
Homo, fuge!° Whither should I fly?
If unto God, he'll throw me down to hell.
My senses are deceiv'd; here's nothing writ:—
I see it plain; here in this place is writ   80
Homo, fuge! Yet shall not Faustus fly.
MEPH: I'll fetch him somewhat to delight his mind.
(Exit.)
(Re-enter MEPHISTOPHILIS *with* DEVILS, *giving crowns and rich apparel to*
FAUSTUS, *and dance, and then depart.)*
FAUSTUS: Speak, Mephistophilis, what means this show?
MEPH: Nothing, Faustus, but to delight thy mind withal,
And to show thee what magic can perform.   85
FAUSTUS: But may I raise up spirits when I please?
MEPH: Ay, Faustus, and do greater things than these.
FAUSTUS: Then there's enough for a thousand souls.
Here, Mephistophilis, receive this scroll,
A deed of gift of body and of soul: 90
But yet conditionally that thou perform
All articles prescrib'd between us both.
MEPH: Faustus, I swear by hell and Lucifer
To effect all promises between us made.
FAUSTUS: Then hear me read them: *On these conditions following. First, that*   95
Faustus may be a spirit in form and substance. Secondly, that Mephistophilis

---

74. **Consummatum est:** "It is finished." 77. **Homo, fuge!:** "Man, fly!"

shall be his servant, and at his command. Thirdly, that Mephistophilis shall do
for him and bring him whatsoever [he desires]. Fourthly, that he shall be in his
chamber or house invisible. Lastly, that he shall appear to the said John Faustus,
at all times, in what form or shape soever he pleases. I, John Faustus, of 100
Wittenberg, Doctor, by these presents do give both body and soul to Lucifer,
Prince of the East, and his minister, Mephistophilis; and furthermore grant
unto them, that twenty-four years being expired, the articles above written
inviolate, full power to fetch or carry the said John Faustus, body and soul,
flesh, blood, or goods, into their habitation wheresoever. By me, John Faustus. 105

MEPH: Speak, Faustus, do you deliver this as your deed?
FAUSTUS: Ay, take it, and the Devil give thee good on't.
MEPH: Now, Faustus, ask what thou wilt.
FAUSTUS: First will I question with thee about hell.
        Tell me where is the place that men call hell? 110
MEPH: Under the heavens.
FAUSTUS: Ay, but whereabout?
MEPH: Within the bowels of these elements,
        Where we are tortur'd and remain for ever;
        Hell hath no limits, nor is circumscrib'd 115
        In one self place; for where we are is hell,
        And where hell is there must we ever be:
        And, to conclude, when all the world dissolves,
        And every creature shall be purified,
        All places shall be hell that is not Heaven. 120
FAUSTUS: Come, I think hell's a fable.
MEPH: Ay, think so still, till experience change thy mind.
FAUSTUS: Why, think'st thou then that Faustus shall be damn'd?
MEPH: Ay, of necessity, for here's the scroll
        Wherein thou hast given thy soul to Lucifer. 125
FAUSTUS: Ay, and body too; but what of that?
        Think'st thou that Faustus is so fond° to imagine
        That, after this life, there is any pain?
        Tush; these are trifles, and mere old wives' tales.
MEPH: But, Faustus, I am an instance to prove the contrary, 130
        For I am damned, and am now in hell.
FAUSTUS: How! now in hell!
        Nay, an this be hell, I'll willingly be damn'd here;
        What? walking, disputing, &c.?

127. **fond:** Foolish.

But, leaving off this, let me have a wife,   135
The fairest maid in Germany;
For I am wanton and lascivious,
And cannot live without a wife.
MEPH: How—a wife?
I prithee, Faustus, talk not of a wife.   140
FAUSTUS: Nay, sweet Mephistophilis, fetch me one, for I will have one.
MEPH: Well—thou wilt have one. Sit there till I come:
I'll fetch thee a wife in the Devil's name.
(*Exit.*)
(*Re-enter* MEPHISTOPHILIS *with a* DEVIL *dressed like a woman, with fireworks.*)
MEPH: Tell [me,] Faustus, how dost thou like thy wife?
FAUSTUS: A plague on her for a hot whore!   145
MEPH: Tut, Faustus,
Marriage is but a ceremonial toy;
And if thou lovest me, think no more of it.
I'll cull thee out the fairest courtesans,
And bring them every morning to thy bed;   150
She whom thine eye shall like, thy heart shall have,
Be she as chaste as was Penelope,
As wise as Saba,° or as beautiful
As was bright Lucifer before his fall.
Here, take this book, peruse it thoroughly: 155
(*Gives a book.*)
The iterating° of these lines brings gold;
The framing of this circle on the ground
Brings whirlwinds, tempests, thunder and lightning;
Pronounce this thrice devoutly to thyself,
And men in armour shall appear to thee,   160
Ready to execute what thou desir'st.
FAUSTUS: Thanks, Mephistophilis; yet fain would I have a book wherein
I'might behold all spells and incantations, that I might raise up spirits
when I please.
MEPH: Here they are, in this book. (*Turns to them.*)   165
FAUSTUS: Now would I have a book where I might see all characters and pla-
nets of the heavens, that I might know their motions and dispositions.
MEPH: Here they are too.
(*Turns to them.*)
FAUSTUS: Nay, let me have one book more,—and then I have done,—
wherein I might see all plants, herbs, and trees that grow upon the earth.   170

---

153. Saba: The Queen of Sheba. 156. iterating: Repeating.

MEPH: Here they be.

FAUSTUS: O, thou art deceived.

MEPH: Tut, I warrant thee. *Turns to them.*

(Exeunt.)

Scene 6
The Same

(Enter FAUSTUS *and* MEPHISTOPHILIS.)

FAUSTUS: When I behold the heavens, then I repent,
    And curse thee, wicked Mephistophilis,
    Because thou hast depriv'd me of those joys.

MEPH: Why, Faustus,
    Thinkest thou Heaven is such a glorious thing?   5
    I tell thee 'tis not half so fair as thou,
    Or any man that breathes on earth.

FAUSTUS: How provest thou that?

MEPH: 'Twas made for man, therefore is man more excellent.

FAUSTUS: If it were made for man, 'twas made for me;   10
    I will renounce this magic and repent.

(Enter GOOD ANGEL *and* EVIL ANGEL.)

G. ANG: Faustus, repent; yet God will pity thee.

E. ANG: Thou art a spirit; God cannot pity thee.

FAUSTUS: Who buzzeth in mine ears I am a spirit?
    Be I a devil, yet God may pity me;   15
    Ay, God will pity me if I repent.

E. ANG: Ay, but Faustus never shall repent.

(Exeunt ANGELS.)

FAUSTUS: My heart's so hard'ned I cannot repent.
    Scarce can I name salvation, faith, or heaven,
    But fearful echoes thunder in mine ears   20
    "Faustus, thou art damn'd!" Then swords and knives,
    Poison, gun, halters, and envenom'd steel
    Are laid before me to despatch myself,
    And long ere this I should have slain myself,
    Had not sweet pleasure conquer'd deep despair.   25
    Have I not made blind Homer sing to me
    Of Alexander's love and Œnon's death?
    And hath not he that built the walls of Thebes
    With ravishing sound of his melodious harp,
    Made music with my Mephistophilis?   30
    Why should I die then, or basely despair?
    I am resolv'd: Faustus shall ne'er repent.

Come, Mephistophilis, let us dispute again,
And argue of divine astrology
Tell me, are there many heavens above the moon?   35
Are all celestial bodies but one globe,
As is the substance of this centric earth?
MEPH: As are the elements, such are the spheres
    Mutually folded in each other's orb,
    And, Faustus,   40
    All jointly move upon one axletree
    Whose terminine is term'd the world's wide pole;
    Nor are the names of Saturn, Mars, or Jupiter
    Feign'd, but are erring stars.
FAUSTUS: But tell me, have they all one motion, both *situ et termpore?*°   45
MEPH: All jointly move from east to west in twenty-four hours upon
    the poles of the world; but differ in their motion upon the poles of the
    zodiac.
FAUSTUS: Tush!
    These slender trifles Wagner can decide;   50
    Hath Mephistophilis no greater skill?
    Who knows not the double motion of the planets?
    The first is finish'd in a natural day;
    The second thus: as Saturn in thirty years; Jupiter in twelve; Mars in
    four; the Sun, Venus, and Mercury in a year; the moon in twenty-eight   55
    days. Tush, these are freshmen's suppositions. But tell me, hath every
    sphere a dominion or *intelligentia?*
MEPH: Ay.
FAUSTUS: How many heavens, or spheres, are there?
MEPH: Nine: the Seven planets, the firmament, and the empyreal heaven.   60
FAUSTUS: Well, resolve me in this question: Why have we not conjunc-
    tions, oppositions, aspects, eclipses, all at one time, but in some years
    we have more, in some less?
MEPH: *Per inæqualem motum respecta totius.*°
FAUSTUS: Well, I am answered. Tell me who made the world.   65
MEPH: I will not.
FAUSTUS: Sweet Mephistophilis, tell me.
MEPH: Move me not, for I will not tell thee.
FAUSTUS: Villain, have I not bound thee to tell me anything?
MEPH: Ay, that is not against our kingdom; but this is.   70
    Think thou on hell, Faustus, for thou art damn'd.

---

45. *situ et termpore:* "In direction and in time?" 64. *Per ... totius:* "On account of their unequal motion in
relation to the whole."

FAUSTUS: Think, Faustus, upon God that made the world.
MEPH: Remember this.
FAUSTUS: Ay, go, accursed spirit, to ugly hell.
    'Tis thou hast damn'd distressed Faustus' soul.   75
    Is't not too late?
(*Re-enter* GOOD ANGEL *and* EVIL ANGEL.)
E. ANG: Too late.
G. ANG: Never too late, if Faustus can repent.
E. ANG: If thou repent, devils shall tear thee in pieces.
G. ANG: Repent, and they shall never raze thy skin.   80
(*Exeunt* ANGELS.)
FAUSTUS: Ah, Christ, my Saviour,
    Seek to save distressed Faustus' soul.
(*Enter* LUCIFER, BELZEBUB, *and* MEPHISTOPHILIS.)
LUC: Christ cannot save thy soul, for he is just;
    There's none but I have interest in the same.
FAUSTUS: O, who art thou that look'st so terrible?   85
LUC: I am Lucifer,
    And this is my companion-prince in hell.
FAUSTUS: O Faustus! they are come to fetch away thy soul!
LUC: We come to tell thee thou dost injure us;
    Thou talk'st of Christ contrary to thy promise;   90
    Thou should'st not think of God: think of the Devil,
    And of his dam, too.
FAUSTUS: Nor will I henceforth: pardon me in this,
    And Faustus vows never to look to Heaven,
    Never to name God, or to pray to him,   95
    To burn his Scriptures, slay his ministers,
    And make my spirits pull his churches down.
LUC: Do so, and we will highly gratify thee. Faustus, we are come from hell
    to show thee some pastime. Sit down, and thou shalt see all the Seven
    Deadly Sins appear in their proper shapes.   100
FAUSTUS: That sight will be pleasing unto me, As Paradise was to Adam
    the first day
    Of his creation.
LUC: Talk not of Paradise nor creation, but mark this show: talk of the
    Devil, and nothing else.—Come away!   105
(*Enter the* SEVEN DEADLY SINS.)
    Now, Faustus, examine them of their several names and dispositions.
FAUSTUS: What art thou—the first?
PRIDE: I am Pride. I disdain to have any parents. I am like to Ovid's flea: I
    can creep into every corner of a wench; sometimes, like a periwig, I sit
    upon her brow; or like a fan of feathers, I kiss her lips; indeed I do—what   110

do I not? But, fie, what a scent is here! I'll not speak another word, except the ground were perfum'd, and covered with cloth of arras.

FAUSTUS: What art thou—the second?

COVET: I am Covetousness, begotten of an old churl in an old leathern bag; and might I have my wish I would desire that this house and all the people in it were turn'd to gold, that I might lock you up in my good chest. O, my sweet gold!   115

FAUSTUS: What art thou—the third?

WRATH: I am Wrath. I had neither father nor mother: I leapt out of a lion's mouth when I was scarce half an hour old; and ever since I have run up and down the world with this case° of rapiers wounding myself when I had nobody to fight withal. I was born in hell; and look to it, for some of you shall be my father.   120

FAUSTUS: What art thou—the fourth?

ENVY: I am Envy, begotten of a chimney sweeper and an oyster-wife. I cannot read, and therefore wish all books were burnt. I am lean with seeing others eat. O that there would come a famine through all the world, that all might die, and I live alone! then thou should'st see how fat I would be. But must thou sit and I stand! Come down with a vengeance!   125

FAUSTUS: Away, envious rascal! What art thou—the fifth?   130

GLUT: Who, I, sir? I am Gluttony. My parents are all dead, and the devil a penny they have left me, but a bare pension, and that is thirty meals a day and ten bevers°—a small trifle to suffice nature. O, I come of a royal parentage! My grandfather was a Gammon of Bacon, my grandmother a Hogshead of Claret-wine; my godfathers were these, Peter Pickleherring, and Martin Martlemas-beef.° O, but my godmother, she was a jolly gentlewoman, and well beloved in every good town and city; her name was Mistress Margery Marchbeer. Now, Faustus, thou hast heard all my progeny, wilt thou bid me to supper?   135

FAUSTUS: No, I'll see thee hanged: thou wilt eat up all my victuals.   140

GLUT: Then the Devil choke thee!

FAUSTUS: Choke thyself, glutton! Who art thou—the sixth?

SLOTH: I am Sloth. I was begotten on a sunny bank, where I have lain ever since; and you have done me great injury to bring me from thence: let me be carried thither again by Gluttony and Lechery. I'll not speak another word for a king's ransom.   145

FAUSTUS: What are you, Mistress Minx, the seventh and last?

---

121. case: Pair. 132. bevers: Refreshments between meals. 136. Martin Martlemas-beef: Martlemas or Martinmas was the customary time for hanging up provisions to dry which had been salted for the winter.

LECH: Who, I, sir? I am one that loves an inch of raw mutton better than
    an ell of fried stockfish; and the first letter of my name begins with
    Lechery.   150

LUC: Away to hell, to hell! (*Exeunt the* SINS.)

    —Now, Faustus, how dost thou like this?

FAUSTUS: O, this feeds my soul!

LUC: Tut, Faustus, in hell is all manner of delight.

FAUSTUS: O might I see hell, and return again.   155

    How happy were I then!

LUC: Thou shalt; I will send for thee at midnight.

    In meantime take this book; peruse it throughly,

    And thou shalt turn thyself into what shape thou wilt.

FAUSTUS: Great thanks, mighty Lucifer!   160

    This will I keep as chary as my life.

LUC: Farewell, Faustus, and think on the Devil.

FAUSTUS: Farewell, great Lucifer! Come, Mephistophilis.

(*Exeunt omnes.*)

(*Enter* WAGNER.)

WAG: Learned Faustus,

    To know the secrets of astronomy,   165

    Graven in the book of Jove's high firmament,

    Did mount himself to scale Olympus' top,

    Being seated in a chariot burning bright,

    Drawn by the strength of yoky dragons' necks.

    He now is gone to prove cosmography,   170

    And, as I guess, will first arrive at Rome,

    To see the Pope and manner of his court,

    And take some part of holy Peter's feast,

    That to this day is highly solemnis'd.

(*Exit.*)

Scene 7
The Pope's Privy-Chamber

(*Enter* FAUSTUS *and* MEPHISTOPHILIS.)

FAUSTUS: Having now, my good Mephistophilis,

    Past with delight the stately town of Trier,°

    Environ'd round with airy mountain-tops,

    With walls of flint, and deep entrenched lakes,

    Not to be won by any conquering prince;   5

    From Paris next, coasting the realm of France,

---

2. Trier: Treves.

We saw the river Maine fall into Rhine,
Whose banks are set with groves of fruitful vines;
Then up to Naples, rich Campania,
Whose buildings fair and gorgeous to the eye, 10
The streets straight forth, and pav'd with finest brick,
Quarter the town in four equivalents.
There saw we learned Maro's° golden tomb,
The way he cut, an English mile in length,
Thorough a rock of stone in one night's space; 15
From thence to Venice, Padua, and the rest,
In one of which a sumptuous temple stands,
That threats the stars with her aspiring top,
Thus hitherto has Faustus spent his time:
But tell me, now, what resting-place is this? 20
Hast thou, as erst I did command,
Conducted me within the walls of Rome?
MEPH: Faustus, I have; and because we will not be unprovided, I have taken
    up° his Holiness' privy-chamber for our use.
FAUSTUS: I hope his Holiness will bid us welcome. 25
MEPH: Tut, 'tis no matter, man, we'll be bold with his good cheer.
    And now, my Faustus, that thou may'st perceive
    What Rome containeth to delight thee with,
    Know that this city stands upon seven hills
    That underprop the groundwork of the same. 30
    [Just through the midst runs flowing Tiber's stream,
    With winding banks that cut it in two parts:]
    Over the which four stately bridges lean,
    That make safe passage to each part of Rome:
    Upon the bridge call'd Ponto Angelo 35
    Erected is a castle passing strong,
    Within whose walls such store of ordnance are,
    And double cannons, fram'd of carved brass,
    As match the days within one cómplete year;
    Besides the gates and high pyramides, 40
    Which Julius Cæsar brought from Africa.
FAUSTUS: Now by the kingdoms of infernal rule,
    Of Styx, of Acheron, and the fiery lake
    Of ever-burning Phlegethon, I swear
    That I do long to see the monuments 45

---

13. **Maro's:** Virgil, who was reputed a magician in the Middle Ages, was buried at Naples. **23–24. taken up:** Engaged.

And situation of bright-splendent Rome:
Come therefore, let's away.

MEPH: Nay, Faustus, stay; I know you'd fain see the Pope,
And take some part of holy Peter's feast,
Where thou shalt see a troop of bald-pate friars,   50
Whose *summum bonum* is in belly-cheer.

FAUSTUS: Well, I'm content to compass then some sport,
And by their folly make us merriment.
Then charm me, [Mephistophilis,] that I
May be invisible, to do what I please   55
Unseen of any whilst I stay in Rome.

(MEPHISTOPHILIS *charms him.*)

MEPH: So, Faustus, now
Do what thou wilt, thou shalt not be discern'd.

(*Sound a sennet.*° *Enter the* POPE *and the* CARDINAL *of* LORRAIN *to the banquet,*
with FRIARS *attending.*)

POPE: My Lord of Lorrain, wilt please you draw near?

FAUSTUS: Fall to, and the devil choke you an° you spare!   60

POPE: How now! Who's that which spake?—Friars, look about.

1 FRIAR: Here's nobody, if it like your Holiness.

POPE: My lord, here is a dainty dish was sent me from the Bishop of Milan.

FAUSTUS: I thank you, sir. (*Snatches it.*)

POPE: How now! Who's that which snatch'd the meat from me? Will no   65
man look? My Lord, this dish was sent me from the Cardinal of
Florence.

FAUSTUS: You say true; I'll ha't. (*Snatches it.*)

POPE: What, again! My lord, I'll drink to your Grace.

FAUSTUS: I'll pledge your Grace. (*Snatches the cup.*)   70

C. OF LOR: My lord, it may be some ghost newly crept out of purgatory,
come to beg a pardon of your Holiness.

POPE: It may be so. Friars, prepare a dirge to lay the fury of this ghost. Once
again, my lord, fall to. (*The* POPE *crosseth himself.*)

FAUSTUS: What, are you crossing of yourself? Well, use that trick no more I   75
would advise you.
(*The* POPE *crosses himself again.*)
Well, there's the second time. Aware the third, I give you fair warning.
(*The* POPE *crosses himself again, and* FAUSTUS *hits him a box of the ear; and*
they all run away.)
Come on, Mephistophilis, what shall we do?

°**sennet:** A particular set of notes on the trumpet or cornet, different from a flourish. **60. an:** If.

MEPH: Nay, I know not. We shall be curs'd with bell, book, and candle.

FAUSTUS: How! bell, book, and candle,—candle, book, and bell,   80
Forward and backward to curse Faustus to hell!
Anon you shall hear a hog grunt, a calf bleat, and an ass bray,
Because it is Saint Peter's holiday.

(*Re-enter all the* FRIARS *to sing the Dirge.*)

1 FRIAR: Come, brethren, let's about our business with good devotion.
(*They sing:*)
Cursed be he that stole away his Holiness' meat from the table!   85
Maledicat Dominus!°
Cursed be he that struck his Holiness a blow on the face! *Maledicat
Dominus!*
Cursed be he that took Friar Sandelo a blow on the pate! *Maledicat
Dominus!*   90
Cursed be he that disturbeth our holy dirge! *Maledicat Dominus!*
Cursed be he that took away his Holiness' wine! *Maledicat Dominus!*
Et omnes sancti!° Amen!
(MEPHISTOPHILIS *and* FAUSTUS *beat the* FRIARS, *and fling fireworks among
them, and so exeunt.*)

(*Enter* CHORUS.)

CHORUS: When Faustus had with pleasure ta'en the view
Of rarest things, and royal courts of kings,   95
He stay'd his course, and so returned home;
Where such as bear his absence but with grief,
I mean his friends, and near'st companions,
Did gratulate his safety with kind words,
And in their conference of what befell,   100
Touching his journey through the world and air,
They put forth questions of Astrology,
Which Faustus answer'd with such learned skill,
As they admir'd and wond'red at his wit.
Now is his fame spread forth in every land;   105
Amongst the rest the Emperor is one,
Carolus the Fifth, at whose palace now
Faustus is feasted 'mongst his noblemen.
What there he did in trial of his art,
I leave untold—your eyes shall see perform'd.   110

(*Exit.*)

---

86. *Maledicat Dominus!:* "May the Lord curse him." 93. *Et omnes sancti!:* "And all the saints."

Scene 8
An Inn-yard

(*Enter* ROBIN *the Ostler with a book in his hand.*)

ROBIN: O, this is admirable! here I ha' stolen one of Dr. Faustus' conjuring
books, and i' faith I mean to search some circles for my own use. Now will
I make all the maidens in our parish dance at my pleasure, stark naked before me; and so by that means I shall see more than e'er I felt or saw yet.

(*Enter* RALPH *calling* ROBIN.)

RALPH: Robin, prithee come away; there's a gentleman tarries to have his   5
horse, and he would have his things rubb'd and made clean. He keeps
such a chafing with my mistress about it; and she has sent me to look
thee out. Prithee come away.

ROBIN: Keep out, keep out, or else you are blown up; you are dismemb'red,
Ralph: keep out, for I am about a roaring piece of work.   10

RALPH: Come, what dost thou with that same book? Thou canst not read.

ROBIN: Yes, my master and mistress shall find that I can read, he for his
forehead, she for her private study; she's born to bear with me, or else
my art fails.

RALPH: Why, Robin, what book is that?   15

ROBIN: What book! Why, the most intolerable book for conjuring that e'er
was invented by any brimstone devil.

RALPH: Canst thou conjure with it?

ROBIN: I can do all these things easily with it: first, I can make thee drunk
with ippocras° at any tabern in Europe for nothing; that's one of my   20
conjuring works.

RALPH: Our Master Parson says that's nothing.

ROBIN: True, Ralph; and more, Ralph, if thou hast any mind to Nan Spit,
our kitchenmaid, then turn her and wind her to thy own use as often as
thou wilt, and at midnight.   25

RALPH: O brave Robin, shall I have Nan Spit, and to mine own use? On
that condition I'll feed thy devil with horsebread as long as he lives, of
free cost.

ROBIN: No more, sweet Ralph: let's go and make clean our boots, which lie
foul upon our hands, and then to our conjuring in the Devil's name.   30

(*Exeunt.*)

Scene 9
An Inn

(*Enter* ROBIN *and* RALPH *with a silver goblet.*)

ROBIN: Come, Ralph, did not I tell thee we were for ever made by this

---

20. ippocras: Wine mixed with sugar and spices.

Doctor Faustus' book? *Ecce signum,*° here's a simple purchase° for horse-
keepers; our horses shall eat no hay as long as this lasts.

(Enter the VINTNER.*)*

RALPH: But, Robin, here comes the Vintner.

ROBIN: Hush! I'll gull him supernaturally. Drawer, I hope all is paid: God   5
be with you. Come, Ralph.

VINT: Soft, sir; a word with you. I must yet have a goblet paid from you, ere
you go.

ROBIN: I, a goblet, Ralph; I, a goblet! I scorn you, and you are but a° &c. I,
a goblet! search me.   10

VINT: I mean so, sir, with your favour. *(Searches him.)*

ROBIN: How say you now?

VINT: I must say somewhat to your fellow. You, sir!

RALPH: Me, sir! me, sir! search your fill. *(*VINTNER *searches him.)*

Now, sir, you may be ashamed to burden honest men with a matter of truth.   15

VINT: Well, t' one of you hath this goblet about you.

ROBIN *(Aside.):* You lie, drawer, 'tis afore me.—Sirrah you, I'll teach ye to
impeach honest men; stand by;—I'll scour you for a goblet!—stand
aside you had best, I charge you in the name of Belzebub.

(Aside to RALPH.*)* Look to the goblet, Ralph.   20

VINT: What mean you, sirrah?

ROBIN: I'll tell you what I mean. *(Reads from a book.) Sanctobulorum, Peri-
phrasticon*—Nay, I'll tickle you, Vintner. *(Aside to* RALPH.*)* Look to the
goblet, Ralph. *(Reads.) Polypragmos Belseborams framanto pacostiphos
tostu, Mephistophilis, &c.*   25

(Enter MEPHISTOPHILIS, *sets squibs at their backs, and then exit. They run about.)*

VINT: *O nomine Domini!*° what meanest thou, Robin? Thou hast no goblet.

RALPH: *Peccatum peccatorum!*° Here's thy goblet, good vintner. *(Gives the
goblet to* VINTNER, *who exit.)*

ROBIN: *Misericordia pro nobis!*° What shall I do? Good Devil, forgive me
now, and I'll never rob thy library more.

(Re-enter to them MEPHISTOPHILIS.*)*

MEPH: Monarch of hell, under whose black survey   30
Great potentates do kneel with awful fear,
Upon whose altars thousand souls do lie,
How am I vexed with these villains' charms?
From Constantinople am I hither come
Only for pleasure of these damned slaves.   35

---

2. *Ecce signum:* "Behold the sign." 2. **purchase:** Gain. 9. **you are but a:** The abuse was left to the actor's
inventiveness. 26. *O nomine Domini!:* "In the name of the Lord." 27. *Peccatum peccatorum!:* "Sin of
sins." 28. *Misericordia pro nobis!:* "Mercy on us."

ROBIN: How from Constantinople? You have had a great journey. Will you
 take sixpence in your purse to pay for your supper, and begone?
MEPH: Well, villains, for your presumption, I transform thee into an ape,
 and thee into a dog; and so begone.
(Exit.)
ROBIN: How, into an ape? That's brave! I'll have fine sport with the boys. 40
 I'll get nuts and apples enow.
RALPH: And I must be a dog.
ROBIN: I' faith thy head will never be out of the pottage pot.
(Exeunt.)

Scene 10
The Court of the Emperor

(Enter EMPEROR, FAUSTUS, *and a* KNIGHT *with* ATTENDANTS.*)*
EMP: Master Doctor Faustus, I have heard strange report of thy knowledge
 in the black art, how that none in my empire nor in the whole world
 can compare with thee for the rare effects of magic; they say thou hast
 a familiar spirit, by whom thou canst accomplish what thou list. This,
 therefore, is my request, that thou let me see some proof of thy skill, 5
 that mine eyes may be witnesses to confirm what mine ears have heard
 reported; and here I swear to thee by the honour of mine imperial
 crown, that, whatever thou doest, thou shalt be no ways prejudiced or
 endamaged.
KNIGHT *(Aside.)*: I' faith he looks much like a conjuror. 10
FAUSTUS: My gracious sovereign, though I must confess myself far inferior
 to the report men have published, and nothing answerable° to the hon-
 our of your imperial majesty, yet for that love and duty binds me there-
 unto, I am content to do whatsoever your majesty shall command me.
EMP: Then, Doctor Faustus, mark what I shall say. 15
 As I was sometime solitary set
 Within my closet, sundry thoughts arose
 About the honour of mine ancestors,
 How they had won by prowess such exploits,
 Got such riches, subdued so many kingdoms, 20
 As we that do succeed, or they that shall
 Hereafter possess our throne, shall
 (I fear me) ne'er attain to that degree
 Of high renown and great authority;
 Amongst which kings is Alexander the Great, 25
 Chief spectacle of the world's pre-eminence,

---

12. answerable: Proportionate.

The bright shining of whose glorious acts
Lightens the world with his° reflecting beams,
As, when I heard but motion° made of him,
It grieves my soul I never saw the man.   30
If, therefore, thou by cunning of thine art
Canst raise this man from hollow vaults below,
Where lies entomb'd this famous conqueror,
And bring with him his beauteous paramour,
Both in their right shapes, gesture, and attire   35
They us'd to wear during their time of life,
Thou shalt both satisfy my just desire,
And give me cause to praise thee whilst I live.

FAUSTUS: My gracious lord, I am ready to accomplish your request so far
   forth as by art, and power of my Spirit, I am able to perform.   40

KNIGHT *(Aside.)*: I' faith that's just nothing at all.

FAUSTUS: But, if it like your Grace, it is not in my ability to present before
   your eyes the true substantial bodies of those two deceased princes,
   which long since are consumed to dust.

KNIGHT *(Aside.)*: Ay, marry, Master Doctor, now there's a sign of grace in   45
   you, when you will confess the truth.

FAUSTUS: But such spirits as can lively resemble Alexander and his
   paramour shall appear before your Grace in that manner that they best
   liv'd in, in their most flourishing estate; which I doubt not shall sufficiently content your imperial majesty.   50

EMP: Go to, Master Doctor, let me see them presently.

KNIGHT: Do you hear, Master Doctor? You bring Alexander and his
   paramour before the Emperor!

FAUSTUS: How then, sir?

KNIGHT: I' faith that's as true as Diana turn'd me to a stag!   55

FAUSTUS: No, sir, but when Actæon died, he left the horns for you.
   Mephistophilis, begone.

(Exit MEPHISTOPHILIS.*)*

KNIGHT: Nay, an you go to conjuring, I'll begone.

(Exit.)

FAUSTUS I'll meet with you anon for interrupting me so. Here they are, my
   gracious lord.   60

(Re-enter MEPHISTOPHILIS *and* SPIRITS *in the shape of* ALEXANDER *and his*
   PARAMOUR.*)*

EMP: Master Doctor, I heard this lady while she liv'd had a wart or mole in
   her neck: how shall I know whether it be so or no?

---

28. his: Its. 29. motion: Mention.

FAUSTUS: Your Highness may boldly go and see.

(*Exeunt Spirits.*)

EMP: Sure these are no spirits, but the true substantial bodies of those two deceased princes. 65

FAUSTUS: Will't please your Highness now to send for the Knight that was so pleasant with me here of late?

EMP: One of you call him forth.

(*Exit Attendant.*)

(*Re-enter the* KNIGHT *with a pair of horns on his head.*)

How now, sir Knight! why I had thought thou had'st been a bachelor, but now I see thou hast a wife, that not only gives thee horns, but 70 makes thee wear them. Feel on thy head.

KNIGHT: Thou damned wretch and execrable dog,
Bred in the concave of some monstrous rock,
How darest thou thus abuse a gentleman?
Villain, I say, undo what thou hast done! 75

FAUSTUS: O, not so fast, sir; there's no haste; but, good, are you rememb'red how you crossed me in my conference with the Emperor? I think I have met with you for it.

EMP: Good Master Doctor, at my entreaty release him; he hath done penance sufficient. 80

FAUSTUS: My gracious lord, not so much for the injury he off'red me here in your presence, as to delight you with some mirth, hath Faustus worthily requited this injurious Knight; which, being all I desire, I am content to release him of his horns: and, sir Knight, hereafter speak well of scholars. Mephistophilis, transform him straight. (MEPHISTOPHILIS 85 *removes the horns.*) Now, my good lord, having done my duty I humbly take my leave.

EMP: Farewell, Master Doctor; yet, ere you go,
Expect from me a bounteous reward.

(*Exeunt.*)

Scene 11
A Green; Afterwards, The House of Faustus

(*Enter* FAUSTUS *and* MEPHISTOPHILIS.)

FAUSTUS: Now, Mephistophilis, the restless course
That Time doth run with calm and silent foot,
Short'ning my days and thread of vital life,
Calls for the payment of my latest years;
Therefore, sweet Mephistophilis, let us 5
Make haste to Wittenberg.

MEPH: What, will you go on horseback or on foot?

FAUSTUS: Nay, till I'm past this fair and pleasant green.
   I'll walk on foot.
(*Enter a* HORSE-COURSER).
HORSE-C: I have been all this day seeking one Master Fustian: mass, see   10
   where he is! God save you, Master Doctor!
FAUSTUS: What, horse-Courser! You are well met.
HORSE-C: Do you hear, sir? I have brought you forty dollars for your horse.
FAUSTUS: I cannot sell him so: if thou likest him for fifty, take him.
HORSE-C: Alas, sir, I have no more.—I pray you speak for me.   15
MEPH: I pray you let him have him: he is an honest fellow, and he has a
   great charge, neither wife nor child.
FAUSTUS: Well, come, give me your money. (HORSE-COURSER *gives* FAUSTUS
   the money.) My boy will deliver him to you. But I must tell you one
   thing before you have him; ride him not into the water at any hand.   20
HORSE-C: Why, sir, will he not drink of all waters?
FAUSTUS: O yes, he will drink of all waters, but ride him not into the water:
   ride him over hedge or ditch, or where thou wilt, but not into the water.
HORSE-C: Well, sir.—Now I am made man forever. I'll not leave my horse
   for forty. (*Aside.*) If he had but the quality of hey-ding-ding, hey-ding-   25
   ding, I'd make a brave living on him: he has a buttock as slick as an
   eel. Well, God b' wi'ye, sir, your boy will deliver him me: but hark ye,
   sir; if my horse be sick or ill at ease, if I bring his water to you, you'll
   tell me what it is?
(*Exit* HORSE-COURSER).
FAUSTUS: Away, you villain; what, dost think I am a horse-doctor?   30
   What art thou, Faustus, but a man condemn'd to die?
   Thy fatal time doth draw to final end;
   Despair doth drive distrust unto my thoughts:
   Confound these passions with a quiet sleep:
   Tush, Christ did call the thief upon the cross;   35
   Then rest thee, Faustus, quiet in conceit. (*Sleeps in his chair.*)
(*Re-enter* HORSE-COURSER, *all wet, crying.*)
HORSE-C: Alas, alas! Doctor Fustian, quotha? Mass, Doctor Lopus°was never
   such a doctor. Has given me a purgation has purg'd me of forty dollars;
   I shall never see them more. But yet, like an ass as I was, I would not
   be ruled by him, for he bade me I should ride him into no water. Now   40
   I, thinking my horse had had some rare quality that he would not have
   had me known of, I, like a venturous youth, rid him into the deep
   pond at the town's end. I was no sooner in the middle of the pond, but
   my horse vanish'd away, and I sat upon a bottle of hay, never so near

---

37. Doctor Lopus: Dr. Lopez, physician to Queen Elizabeth, hanged in 1594 on the charge of conspiring to poison the Queen.

drowning in my life. But I'll seek out my Doctor, and have my forty   45
dollars again, or I'll make it the dearest horse!—O, yonder is his snip-
per-snapper.—Do you hear? You hey-pass,° where's your master?

MEPH: Why, sir, what would you? You cannot speak with him.

HORSE-C: But I will speak with him.

MEPH: Why, he's fast asleep. Come some other time.   50

HORSE-C: I'll speak with him now, or I'll break his glass windows about his ears.

MEPH: I tell thee he has not slept this eight nights.

HORSE-C: An he have not slept this eight weeks, I'll speak with him.

MEPH: See where he is, fast asleep.

HORSE-C: Ay, this is he. God save you, Master Doctor! Master Doctor, Mas-   55
ter Doctor Fustian!—Forty dollars, forty dollars for a bottle of hay!

MEPH: Why, thou seest he hears thee not.

HORSE-C So ho, ho!—so, ho, ho! *(Hollas in his ear.)* No, will you not wake?
I'll make you wake ere I go. *(Pulls* FAUSTUS *by the leg, and pulls it away.)*
Alas, I am undone! What shall I do?   60

FAUSTUS: O my leg, my leg! Help, Mephistophilis! call the officers. My leg,
my leg!

MEPH: Come, villain, to the constable.

HORSE-C: O lord, sir, let me go, and I'll give you forty dollars more.

MEPH: Where be they?   65

HORSE-C: I have none about me. Come to my ostry° and I'll give them you.

MEPH: Begone quickly.

*(*HORSE-COURSER *runs away.)*

FAUSTUS: What, is he gone? Farewell he! Faustus has his leg again, and the
horse-courser, I take it, a bottle of hay for his labour. Well, this trick
shall cost him forty dollars more.   70

(Enter WAGNER.*)* How now, Wagner, what's the news with thee?

WAG: Sir, the Duke of Vanholt doth earnestly entreat your company.

FAUSTUS: The Duke of Vanholt! an honourable gentleman, to whom I must
be no niggard of my cunning. Come, Mephistophilis, let's away to him.

(Exeunt.)

Scene 12

The Court of the Duke of Vanholt

(Enter the DUKE *of* VANHOLT, *the* DUCHESS, FAUSTUS, *and* MEPHISTOPHILIS.*)*

DUKE: Believe me, Master Doctor, this merriment hath much pleased me.

FAUSTUS: My gracious lord, I am glad it contents you so well.—But it may
be, madam, you take no delight in this. I have heard that great-bellied

---

47. **hey-pass:** A juggler's term, like "presto, fly!" Here applied to the juggler himself. 66. **ostry:** Inn.

women do long for some dainties or other. What is it, madam? Tell me, and you shall have it.   5

DUCHESS: Thanks, good Master Doctor; and for I see your courteous intent to pleasure me, I will not hide from you the thing my heart desires; and were it now summer, as it is January and the dead time of the winter, I would desire no better meat than a dish of ripe grapes.

FAUSTUS: Alas, madam, that's nothing! Mephistophilis, begone.   10
(*Exit* MEPHISTOPHILIS.)
Were it a greater thing than this, so it would content you, you should have it.

(*Re-enter* MEPHISTOPHILIS *with the grapes.*)
Here they be, madam; wilt please you taste on them?

DUKE: Believe me, Master Doctor, this makes me wonder above the rest, that being in the dead time of winter, and in the month of January,   15
 how you should come by these grapes.

FAUSTUS: If it like your Grace, the year is divided into two circles over the whole world, that, when it is here winter with us, in the contrary circle it is summer with them, as in India, Saba, and farther countries in the East; and by means of a swift spirit that I have, I had them brought   20
hither, as ye see.—How do you like them, madam; be they good?

DUCHESS: Believe me, Master Doctor, they be the best grapes that I e'er tasted in my life before.

FAUSTUS: I am glad they content you so, madam.

DUKE: Come, madam, let us in, where you must well reward this learned   25
man for the great kindness he hath show'd to you.

DUCHESS: And so I will, my lord; and whilst I live, rest beholding for this courtesy.

FAUSTUS: I humbly thank your Grace.

DUKE: Come, Master Doctor, follow us and receive your reward.   30
(*Exeunt.*)

Scene 13
A Room in the House of Faustus

(*Enter* WAGNER, *solus.*)
WAG: I think my master means to die shortly,
        For he hath given to me all his goods;
        And yet, methinks, if that death were near,
        He would not banquet and carouse and swill
        Amongst the students, as even now he doth,   5
        Who are at supper with such belly-cheer
        As Wagner ne'er beheld in all his life.
        See where they come! Belike the feast is ended.
(*Enter* FAUSTUS, *with two or three* SCHOLARS *and* MEPHISTOPHILIS.)

1 SCHOL: Master Doctor Faustus, since our conference about fair ladies,
which was the beautifullest in all the world, we have determined with   10
ourselves that Helen of Greece was the admirablest lady that ever
lived: therefore, Master Doctor, if you will do us that favour, as to let us
see that peerless dame of Greece, whom all the world admires for majesty, we should think ourselves much beholding unto you.
FAUSTUS: Gentlemen,   15
    For that I know your friendship is unfeigned,
    And Faustus' custom is not to deny
    The just requests of those that wish him well,
    You shall behold that peerless dame of Greece,
    No otherways for pomp and majesty   20
    Than when Sir Paris cross'd the seas with her,
    And brought the spoils to rich Dardania.
    Be silent, then, for danger is in words.
(*Music sounds, and* HELEN *passeth over the stage.*)
2 SCHOL: Too simple is my wit to tell her praise,
    Whom all the world admires for majesty.   25
3 SCHOL: No marvel though the angry Greeks pursu'd
    With ten years' war the rape of such a queen,
    Whose heavenly beauty passeth all compare.
1 SCHOL: Since we have seen the pride of Nature's works,
    And only paragon of excellence,   30
    (*Enter an* OLD MAN.) Let us depart; and for this glorious deed
    Happy and blest be Faustus evermore.
FAUSTUS: Gentlemen, farewell—the same I wish to you.
(*Exeunt* SCHOLARS *and* WAGNER.)
OLD MAN: Ah, Doctor Faustus, that I might prevail
    To guide thy steps unto the way of life,   35
    By which sweet path thou may'st attain the goal
    That shall conduct thee to celestial rest!
    Break heart, drop blood, and mingle it with tears,
    Tears falling from repentant heaviness
    Of thy most vile and loathsome filthiness,   40
    The stench whereof corrupts the inward soul
    With such flagitious crimes of heinous sins
    As no commiseration may expel,
    But mercy, Faustus, of thy Saviour sweet,
    Whose blood alone must wash away thy guilt.   45
FAUSTUS: Where art thou, Faustus? Wretch, what hast thou done?
    Damn'd art thou, Faustus, damn'd; despair and die!
    Hell calls for right, and with a roaring voice
    Says "Faustus! come! thine hour is (almost) come!"

And Faustus (now) will come to do thee right.   50
(MEPHISTOPHILIS *gives him a dagger*.)
OLD MAN: Ah stay, good Faustus, stay thy desperate steps!
   I see an angel hovers o'er thy head,
   And, with a vial full of precious grace,
   Offers to pour the same into thy soul:
   Then call for mercy, and avoid despair.   55
FAUSTUS: Ah, my sweet friend, I feel
   Thy words do comfort my distressed soul.
   Leave me a while to ponder on my sins.
OLD MAN: I go, sweet Faustus, but with heavy cheer,
   Fearing the ruin of thy hopeless soul.   60
(*Exit*.)
FAUSTUS: Accursed Faustus, where is mercy now?
   I do repent; and yet I do despair;
   Hell strives with grace for conquest in my breast:
   What shall I do to shun the snares of death?
MEPH: Thou traitor, Faustus, I arrest thy soul   65
   For disobedience to my sovereign lord;
   Revolt, or I'll in piecemeal tear thy flesh.
FAUSTUS: Sweet Mephistophilis, entreat thy lord
   To pardon my unjust presumption,
   And with my blood again I will confirm   70
   My former vow I made to Lucifer.
MEPH: Do it now then quickly, with unfeigned heart,
   Lest danger do attend thy drift.
(FAUSTUS *stabs his arm and writes on a paper with his blood*.)
FAUSTUS: Torment, sweet friend, that base and crooked age,°
   That durst dissuade me from my Lucifer,   75
   With greatest torments that our hell affords.
MEPH: His faith is great, I cannot touch his soul;
   But what I may afflict his body with
   I will attempt, which is but little worth.
FAUSTUS: One thing, good servant, let me crave of thee,   80
   To glut the longing of my heart's desire,—
   That I might have unto my paramour
   That heavenly Helen, which I saw of late,
   Whose sweet embracings may extinguish clean
   These thoughts that do dissuade me from my vow,   85
   And keep mine oath I made to Lucifer.

---

74. base and crooked age: Old Man.

MEPH: Faustus, this or what else thou shalt desire
Shall be perform'd in twinkling of an eye.
(Re-enter HELEN*)*.
FAUSTUS: Was this the face that launch'd a thousand ships,
And burnt the topless° towers of Ilium?   90
Sweet Helen, make me immortal with a kiss.
(Kisses her.)
Her lips suck forth my soul; see where it flies!—
Come, Helen, come, give me my soul again.
Here will I dwell, for Heaven be in these lips,
And all is dross that is not Helena.   95
(Enter OLD MAN*).*
I will be Paris, and for love of thee,
Instead of Troy, shall Wittenberg be sack'd;
And I will combat with weak Menelaus,
And wear thy colours on my plumed crest;
Yea, I will wound Achilles in the heel,   100
And then return to Helen for a kiss.
Oh, thou art fairer than the evening air
Clad in the beauty of a thousand stars;
Brighter art thou than flaming Jupiter
When he appear'd to hapless Semele: 105
More lovely than the monarch of the sky
In wanton Arethusa's azur'd arms:
And none but thou shalt be my paramour.
(Exeunt.)
OLD MAN: Accursed Faustus, miserable man,
That from thy soul exclud'st the grace of Heaven,   110
And fly'st the throne of his tribunal seat!
(Enter DEVILS.*)*
Satan begins to sift me with his pride:
As in this furnace God shall try my faith,
My faith, vile hell, shall triumph over thee.
Ambitious fiends! see how the heavens smiles   115
At your repulse, and laughs your state to scorn!
Hence, hell! for hence I fly unto my God. *Exeunt.*

Scene 14
The Same

(Enter FAUSTUS *with the* SCHOLARS.*)*

---

90. **topless:** Unsurpassed in height.

FAUSTUS: Ah, gentlemen!

1 SCHOL: What ails Faustus?

FAUSTUS: Ah, my sweet chamber-fellow, had I lived with thee, then had I
    lived still! but now I die eternally. Look, comes he not, come he not?

2 SCHOL: What means Faustus?   5

3 SCHOL: Belike he is grown into some sickness by being over solitary.

1 SCHOL: If it be so, we'll have physicians to cure him. 'Tis but a surfeit.
    Never fear, man.

FAUSTUS: A surfeit of deadly sin that hath damn'd both body and soul.

2 SCHOL: Yet, Faustus, look up to Heaven; remember God's mercies are   10
    infinite.

FAUSTUS: But Faustus' offences can never be pardoned: the serpent that
    tempted Eve may be sav'd, but not Faustus. Ah, gentlemen, hear me
    with patience, and tremble not at my speeches! Though my heart pants
    and quivers to remember that I have been a student here these thirty   15
    years, oh, would I had never seen Wittenberg, never read book! And
    what wonders I have done, all Germany can witness, yea, the world; for
    which Faustus hath lost both Germany and the world, yea Heaven it-
    self, Heaven, the seat of God, the throne of the blessed, the kingdom of
    joy; and must remain in hell for ever, hell, ah, hell, for ever! Sweet   20
    friends! what shall become of Faustus being in hell for ever?

3 SCHOL: Yet, Faustus, call on God.

FAUSTUS: On God, whom Faustus hath abjur'd! on God, whom Faustus
    hath blasphemed! Ah, my God, I would weep, but the Devil draws in
    my tears. Gush forth blood instead of tears! Yea, life and soul! Oh, he   25
    stays my tongue! I would lift up my hands, but see, they hold them,
    they hold them!

ALL: Who, Faustus?

FAUSTUS: Lucifer and Mephistophilis. Ah, gentlemen, I gave them my soul
    for my cunning!   30

ALL: God forbid!

FAUSTUS: God forbade it indeed; but Faustus hath done it. For vain pleasure
    of twenty-four years hath Faustus lost eternal joy and felicity. I writ
    them a bill with mine own blood: the date is expired; the time will
    come, and he will fetch me.   35

1 SCHOL: Why did not Faustus tell us of this before, that divines might have
    prayed for thee?

FAUSTUS: Oft have I thought to have done so; but the Devil threat'ned to
    tear me in pieces if I nam'd God; to fetch both body and soul if I once
    gave ear to divinity: and now 't is too late. Gentlemen, away! lest you   40
    perish with me.

2 SCHOL: Oh, what shall we do to save Faustus?

FAUSTUS: Talk not of me, but save yourselves, and depart.

3 SCHOL: God will strengthen me. I will stay with Faustus.

1 SCHOL: Tempt not God, sweet friend; but let us into the next room, and   45
there pray for him.

FAUSTUS: Ay, pray for me, pray for me! and what noise soever ye hear,
come not unto me, for nothing can rescue me.

2 SCHOL: Pray thou, and we will pray that God may have mercy upon thee.

FAUSTUS: Gentlemen, farewell! If I live till morning I'll visit you: if not—   50
Faustus is gone to hell.

ALL: Faustus, farewell!

(*Exeunt* SCHOLARS. *The clock strikes eleven.*)

FAUSTUS: Ah, Faustus,
> Now hast thou but one bare hour to live,
> And then thou must be damn'd perpetually!   55
> Stand still, you ever-moving spheres of Heaven,
> That time may cease, and midnight never come;
> Fair Nature's eye, rise, rise again and make
> Perpetual day; or let this hour be but
> A year, a month, a week, a natural day,   60
> That Faustus may repent and save his soul!
> O *lente, lente, currite noctis equi!*°
> The stars move still,° time runs, the clock will strike,
> The Devil will come, and Faustus must be damn'd.
> O, I'll leap up to my God! Who pulls me down?   65
> See, see where Christ's blood streams in the firmament!
> One drop would save my soul—Half a drop: ah, my Christ!
> Ah, rend not my heart for naming of my Christ!
> Yet will I call on him: O spare me, Lucifer!—
> Where is it now? 'Tis gone; and see where God   70
> Stretcheth out his arm, and bends his ireful brows!
> Mountain and hills come, come and fall on me,
> And hide me from the heavy wrath of God!
> No! no!
> Then will I headlong run into the earth;   75
> Earth gape! O no, it will not harbour me!
> You stars that reign'd at my nativity,
> Whose influence hath allotted death and hell,
> Now draw up Faustus like a foggy mist
> Into the entrails of yon labouring clouds,   80

---

62. O lente … equi!: "Run softly, softly, horses of the night"—Ovid's *Amores*, i. 13. **63. still:** Without
ceasing.

That when they vomit forth into the air,
My limbs may issue from their smoky mouths,
So that my soul may but ascend to Heaven.
(The watch strikes the half hour.)
Ah, half the hour is past! 'Twill all be past anon!
O God!   85
If thou wilt not have mercy on my soul,
Yet for Christ's sake whose blood hath ransom'd me,
Impose some end to my incessant pain;
Let Faustus live in hell a thousand years—
A hundred thousand, and at last be sav'd!   90
O, no end is limited to damned souls!
Why wert thou not a creature wanting soul?
Or why is this immortal that thou hast?
Ah, Pythagoras' metempsychosis! were that true,
This soul should fly from me, and I be chang'd   95
Unto some brutish beast! All beasts are happy,
For, when they die,
Their souls are soon dissolv'd in elements;
But mine must live, still to be plagu'd in hell.
Curst be the parents that engend'red me!   100
No, Faustus: curse thyself: curse Lucifer
That hath depriv'd thee of the joys of Heaven.
(The clock striketh twelve.)
O, it strikes, it strikes! Now, body, turn to air,
Or Lucifer will bear thee quick to hell.
(Thunder and lightning.)
O soul, be chang'd into little water-drops,   105
And fall into the ocean—ne'er be found.
My God! my God! look not so fierce on me!
(Enter DEVILS.)
Adders and serpents, let me breathe awhile!
Ugly hell, gape not! come not, Lucifer!
I'll burn my books!—Ah Mephistophilis!   110
(Exeunt DEVILS with FAUSTUS. Enter CHORUS.)
[CHO.]: Cut is the branch that might have grown full straight,
And burned is Apollo's laurel bough,
That sometimes grew within this learned man,
Faustus is gone; regard his hellish fall,
Whose fiendful fortune may exhort the wise   115
Only to wonder at unlawful things,
Whose deepness doth entice such forward wits
To practise more than heavenly power permits.

(Exit)

> *Terminat hora diem, terminat author opus.*°

- Some characters in this play, rather than being fully developed, represent particular ideas. Identify such characters.
- What are the functions of the Good Angel and the Bad Angel in the play?
- In what ways is Mephistophilis the most admirable character in the play?
- How do the antics of Robin, Ralph, and the Clown relate to the actions of Faustus?
- What does Faustus achieve by selling his soul?
- How do his actions compare to his initial plans?
- How well does Mephistophilis satisfy the requests that Faustus makes?

Experiencing Literature through Theme

1. Select a single work from this chapter. The works have been chosen because they all speak to the general theme "Exploring Boundaries." Identify one other theme that you find within this work. As you make your case that this theme is significant to our understanding of the work, consider the following questions:

   a. How did you arrive at this theme?

   b. Is there a single sentence or detail that reveals this theme? Explain what this detail is and why you consider it to be significant.

   c. Are there repeating words, details, or ideas that lead you to identify this theme? Explain how these fit together.

   d. Which details in the work do not seem to fit into this theme? Explain how they do fit, or show how you can revise your claim about the nature of this theme to accommodate these details.

   e. How does this theme respond to, contrast with, or comment on the theme "Exploring Boundaries"?

2. The works in this chapter fit into the general theme "Exploring Boundaries." This exploration involves pushing boundaries, challenging authority, and questioning the existing order. In your paper, explore the tension between social structures and individual will in one or more of these works. Issues you might consider are the justifications offered for

---

119. **Terminat ...** *opus:* "The hour ends the day, the author ends his work."

challenge (does Marlowe, for instance, justify Faustus in the play?) and our sympathy for the character who is pushing these boundaries.

3. In this chapter, we begin by discussing "Little Red Riding Hood," a story with a clear message. If the message of a work is obvious enough to be summed up in a moral, it may be too obvious to use as the basis for an interesting paper. Look at a work here that has an explicit moral (for instance, Perrault's "Little Red Riding Hood"). Identify one other theme in this work, and explain how it is significant. You might consider how this other theme plays upon or contrasts with the more obvious theme.

4 Point of View

How Do We Know What We Know about What Happened?

We may say that a storyteller *relates* a story to us. That verb helps us think about how any narration of a story not only adds coherence to a series of random events but also gives the audience a relationship to the events, a position in relation to what has happened.

Anyone who has ever experienced some sort of misunderstanding among friends or family members is quite aware of the idea of perspective. Everyone involved has a different version of the events. We spend much time recounting each of our individual perspectives; comparing what we perceived with what someone else saw; searching for the source of the problem within these narratives; and hoping that by unfolding our different narratives, we might bring ourselves back to some semblance of the harmony that existed before the misunderstanding. It is often the person who wasn't there who gets to hear all of the accounts and to judge the merits of the different perspectives. This form of storytelling can be quite tense, and the implications can be far-reaching precisely because everyone involved has some relation to the story. Authors frequently take advantage of the intensity of feeling that comes with a particular point of view: perspective is always part of a narrative.

PERSPECTIVE

Point of view is a term that comes from the study of art and from an interest in making figures on a page seem lifelike. The point of view refers to an actual point or hole that is used to establish the position of objects within a composition. The Dürer woodcut depicts two artists who are using a mechanical method to establish point of view. They have fixed their point to the wall on the right. By stretching a string from that point to the lute that they are about to draw, the artists note where the string passes through the frame of the picture to determine precisely where the object should appear when they swing their white canvas back into the frame.

The artists depicted in the woodcut will make the scene seem real by setting all objects onto the canvas in strict relation to the viewpoint that they have arbitrarily selected. In Western art, the movement to utilize and to codify theories of perspective came during the fifteenth century, when there was a great interest in humanism and the general acknowledgment that human observations tend not to be objective; we notice things that interest us, and we define them not as they actually are but in relation to ourselves.

In a two-dimensional work of art, the sense of depth that perspective gives is an illusion. The artist distorts the objects within the field of vision to make the scene appear just as it would to that single eye "seeing" the picture. The most common "trick" in representing perspective is to make parallel lines converge as they move away from the vantage point. For instance, in the Dürer woodcut, we know that the walls of the room are parallel; the fact that

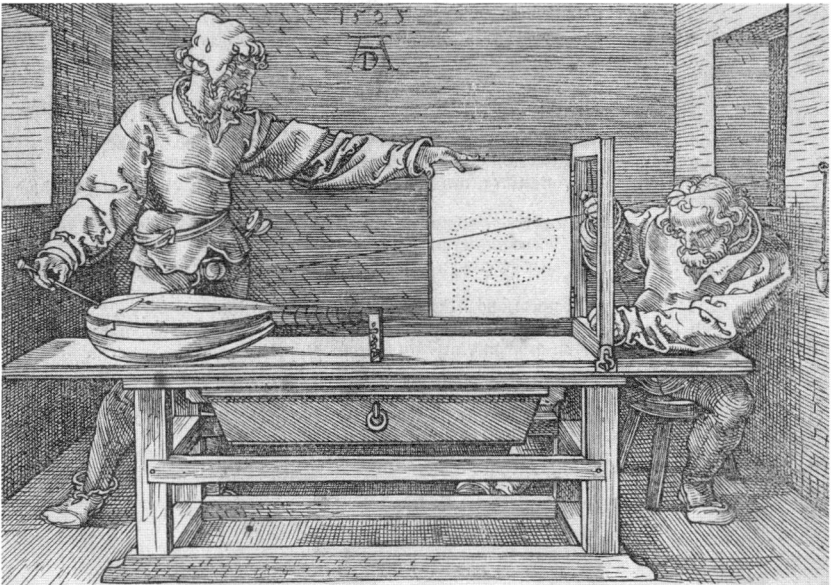

Albrecht Dürer, *Working on Perspective* (1525)

they come together behind our artists is a trick of perspective to indicate increasing distance from our point of view.

Artists of the Renaissance made much more elaborate versions of Dürer's simple exercise. They constructed mathematical models to create the illusion of depth, such as Masaccio creates in *Trinity*. Below, you can see his completed painting with lines drawn in to illustrate Dürer's strings and the distortions that come with perspective. On page 285 is a sketch of the side view (or depth) that is represented by the illusion of perspective in Masaccio's painting, with the strings stretched to their full length.

In the ensuing centuries, the term *point of view* has come to be used much more widely. Often, we hear the term used to mean simply an opinion. But thinking more strictly about the peculiar distortions that come from any specific perspective helps us see narrative issues more clearly. It helps us go beyond the order of events that the narrator has arranged for us and consider how the narrator's interests, personality, motives, and background are an important part of the story.

For example, in the poem that follows, Dorothy Parker writes from the perspective of Penelope, the wife of Odysseus, who waits for twenty years for her husband to return from the Trojan War. Penelope is a literary character from Homer's *Odyssey*; more specifically, we know her from the point of view of her husband, Odysseus, for whom Penelope is symbolic of the stable home

Masaccio, *Trinity* (1427–1428)

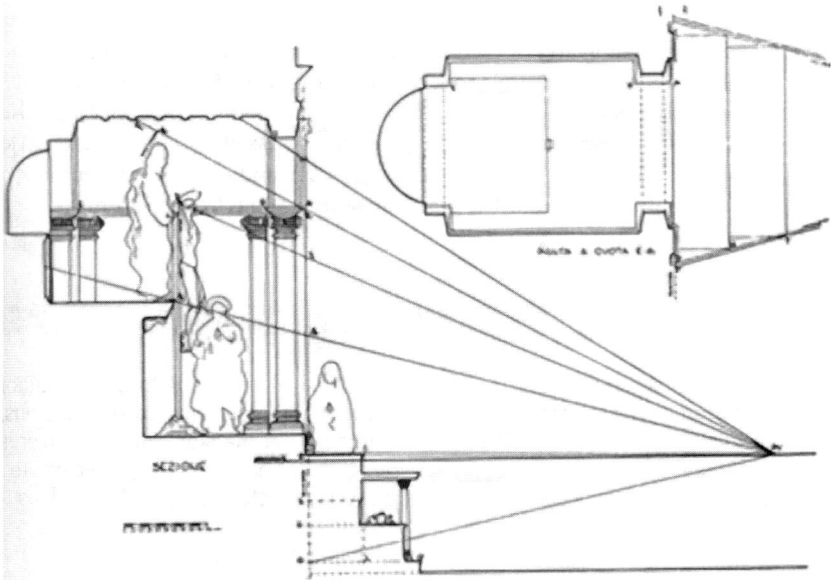

Plan and elevation of Masaccio's *Trinity* according to Piero Sanpaolesi, Brunelleschi

that he longs for throughout his adventures with warriors, gods, and monsters. Even when the story's narrative focuses on her house, Penelope is generally up in her room out of the action. Parker's poem shifts this focus.

Dorothy Parker (1893–1967)

Penelope (1928)

In the pathway of the sun,
In the footsteps of the breeze,
Where the world and sky are one,
    He shall ride the silver seas,
        He shall cut the glittering wave.   5
I shall sit at home, and rock;
Rise, to heed a neighbor's knock;
Brew my tea, and snip my thread;
Bleach the linen for my bed.
        They will call him brave.   10

This poem neatly divides the character of the wandering Odysseus (lines 1–5) from the patience of Penelope (lines 6–9). Penelope echoes the language of the epic poem in her description of her husband's journey. In contrast, her own twenty years of rocking and household chores are much less glamorous, but the final line challenges us to rethink our understanding of the famous story. Parker's poem helps us see Penelope's perspective, but it also points to the fact that the conventions of heroism celebrated in a poem such as the *Odyssey* give little acclaim to the quiet heroism of Penelope, whose endless waiting requires a formidable endurance without the grand adventures that Odysseus enjoys.

A Note to Student Writers: Distinguishing Author from Speaker

You must accurately signal perspective in the narratives you analyze. Although an author of a poem or story may on occasion speak directly from personal feelings and convictions, it is generally best to distinguish the **poet** or **author** from the **speaker**. Although Parker is the author of "Penelope," she is not the speaker. Authors imagine, create, and give life to speakers. Authors use speakers to achieve particular effects. Note that the previous paragraph refers to "Parker's poem" but highlights Penelope as the speaker. In some cases, this distinction is absolutely necessary (an author who relates a story through a cruel and manipulative speaker wouldn't like to be identified as one with the speaker).

THE NARRATIVE EYE

In 1818, Caspar David Friedrich created two paintings that work together as a pair. Their contrasts are pronounced. One uses cool blue colors; the other uses warm oranges. In one, a man stands on top of rugged rocks; in the other, a woman stands amid softer vegetation. But the composition of the two paintings is quite similar. At the center of each, Friedrich gives us the back of a single character: we share something of the characters' point of view. In one picture, we see rocks, mountains, and fog. In the other, we see a brilliant sunrise at daybreak. But we also see the characters who stand before these landscapes. By placing people in the **foreground** of the pictures, Friedrich changes everything. Each landscape is significant because of the character who experiences that landscape and who, therefore, defines it for us. Without the human figures, there would be scant connection between Friedrich's fog and his morning light. And we would not have some important interpretive clues. For example, we would not be prompted to think of how Friedrich defines masculine and feminine in terms of nature.

These paintings remind us again of issues vital both to visual arts and to literary texts in general. The people from whose points of view we are seeing are fictions created by artists. As much as we feel that we are getting the man's

Caspar David Friedrich, *Wanderer above the Sea of Fog* (1818)

Caspar David Friedrich, *Woman in the Morning Light* (1818)

or the woman's **perspective**, that we see from their vantage point, in Friedrich's paintings, we are actually standing behind each of them. Our perspective is the artist's perspective, but the artist makes us feel empathy for these characters in the foreground, and thus we forget that the artist is manipulating our reaction. In addition, it is clear that there is no getting around point of view in a work of art. Even if Friedrich removed the man and the woman from his paintings, we'd still be seeing from a perspective the artist has controlled. So always ask yourself as you read literature: Through whose eyes do I see? How might that point of view influence what I'm seeing and hearing? How does perspective shape my understanding of events?

RELIABLE AND UNRELIABLE NARRATORS

As readers, we must think hard about point of view because it strongly shapes the meaning, authority, and power we draw from fiction. We often cannot understand stories unless we understand how they are told. What is the source of a story? What prompts its telling? How much does the teller know? Can the narrator be trusted? We can begin to respond to such questions by broadly classifying narrative points of view as either third-person or first-person narration.

Third-Person Narrators

In **third-person narration**, the narrator is outside the story and refers to all characters by name or as "he," "she," or "they." An **omniscient narrator** moves freely about in time and space. In many cases, an omniscient narrator may move freely in and out of the minds of the characters. A narrator that breaks into a story to guide the reader's judgment is called an **intrusive narrator**.

At the beginning of A *Christmas Carol*, Charles Dickens employs a narrator who can't quite let the story get going. This narrator digresses upon conventions of language (why do we use "door-nail" to epitomize death?) and conventions in literature (what makes Hamlet's father a remarkable character in Shakespeare's play?) as he strives to convey the simple fact that Scrooge's partner, Marley, is dead.

Charles Dickens (1812–1870)

from ## A Christmas Carol (1843)

Marley was dead: to begin with. There is no doubt whatever about that. The register of his burial was signed by the clergyman, the clerk, the undertaker, and the chief mourner. Scrooge signed it. And Scrooge's name was good upon

'Change, for anything he chose to put his hand to. Old Marley was as dead as a door-nail.

Mind! I don't mean to say that I know, of my own knowledge, what there is particularly dead about a door-nail. I might have been inclined, myself, to regard a coffin-nail as the deadest piece of ironmongery in the trade. But the wisdom of our ancestors is in the simile; and my unhallowed hands shall not disturb it, or the Country's done for. You will therefore permit me to repeat, emphatically, that Marley was as dead as a door-nail.

Scrooge knew he was dead? Of course he did. How could it be otherwise? Scrooge and he were partners for I don't know how many years. Scrooge was his sole executor, his sole administrator, his sole assign, his sole residuary legatee, his sole friend, and sole mourner. And even Scrooge was not so dreadfully cut up by the sad event, but that he was an excellent man of business on the very day of the funeral, and solemnized it with an undoubted bargain.

The mention of Marley's funeral brings me back to the point I started from. There is no doubt that Marley was dead. This must be distinctly understood, or nothing wonderful can come of the story I am going to relate. If we were not perfectly convinced that Hamlet's Father died before the play began, there would be nothing more remarkable in his taking a stroll at night, in an easterly wind, upon his own ramparts, than there would be in any other middle-aged gentleman rashly turning out after dark in a breezy spot—say Saint Paul's Churchyard for instance—literally to astonish his son's weak mind. ■

This intrusive narrator stands outside the action and refers to Scrooge in the third person but is also aware of Scrooge's thoughts (Scrooge is aware of Marley's death but not "dreadfully cut up by the sad event"). This narrator guides the reader's judgment by talking about the convention of ghost stories, pointing out to the reader that the story that follows will fit into that tradition. This narrator establishes a presence as a chatty and personable companion to lead us through a story about a character who is altogether less humane than our guide.

An author who restricts the third-person narration to the consciousness of one or more characters employs a **limited narrator** or **limited omniscient narrator**. An **objective narrator** reports, records, or shows only what could be seen or heard by an outside observer. Authors who use an objective narrator do not comment on the action. Neither do they get inside the minds of any of the characters (at least not directly). Many of Ernest Hemingway's short stories use an objective narrator. An objective narrator is sometimes called an **impersonal narrator**. The following excerpt from Hemingway's "Hills Like White Elephants" serves as a good example of objective or impersonal narration:

The hills across the valley of the Ebro were long and white. On this side there was no shade and no trees and the station was between two lines of rails in the sun. Close against the side of the station there was the warm shadow of the building and a curtain, made of strings of bamboo beads, hung across the open door into the bar, to keep out flies. The American and the girl with him sat at a table in the shade, outside the building. It was very hot and the express from Barcelona would come in forty minutes. It stopped at this junction for two minutes and went on to Madrid. ∎

In this account, in stark contrast to the selection from Dickens, the narrator offers only facts that anyone might observe about this scene. There are no excursions into the peculiarities of the English language or thoughts about the way these characters might think about each other. Especially after reading Dickens, we might say that this narrator has no personality, but the sparse descriptive style that Hemingway uses here has its own peculiarities. What does the narrator notice? The hills, the lack of shade, the string of beads to keep out the flies, and the train schedule. These are all things that any observer might see, but look carefully at another detail. The first character is called "the American." There is not a name, just the nationality. The second character is "the girl"—again no name, and now only a vague indicator of age. How can this objective narrator tell that this is an American rather than someone from somewhere else? Is "girl" the same as "woman"? And what does the narrator fail to describe? The time of day, the relation between these two people, what they are wearing, why they are here. The few details that the narrator has chosen to notice discreetly lends a personality to this impersonal voice and helps us see that even objectivity comes from a particular point of view.

First-Person Narrators

Such particularity is easy to note in some cases. A **first-person narrator** speaks from within the story and can know only what the imagined "I" knows ("I looked back just as he rounded the corner and saw him pick up the wallet"). Just like a jury member who decides how much to value the testimony of an eyewitness, readers of first-person narratives consider evidence of reliability. Ultimately, readers must define where the author stands in relation to the events the author's narrator recounts.

In the Sherlock Holmes stories, Dr. Watson faithfully chronicles the adventures of the detective. His characteristics as Holmes's audience and as the self-conscious recorder of what happens influence what we get to see of Holmes. We see only what Watson sees. He may be on the scene (sometimes performing some duty to help Holmes solve the crime), or he may have to trust the account that Holmes gives him. He acts as an appreciative audience to Holmes's theatrical deductive work, and we have to wonder whether his admiration of Holmes might ever make him change the scene to Holmes's advantage or to interpret events in complimentary ways. Still, all in all, we accept him as a **reliable narrator** within his limits.

An author may, of course, speak directly through a character to register his or her own deepest values. But first-person narrators often express an author's moral perspective indirectly or ironically. For example, the first-person narrator could be a child who reports "facts" without understanding them. Or the first-person narrator could even be a dishonest, self-serving, cruel character. Such narrators are **unreliable narrators**. To further complicate matters, readers must also consider how involved a first-person narrator is in the story. Some first-person narrators are **detached observers** (perhaps Nick Carraway in *The Great Gatsby*); others play the central role in the story they will tell (Huck in *Adventures of Huckleberry Finn*). Sometimes, instead of hearing the polished version of a story that such a narrator might deliver to an audience, we hear it as though it were the narrator's own often rambling, jumbled thoughts, that is, the narrative appears to be a **stream of consciousness** (Bloom in James Joyce's *Ulysses*).

Experiencing Literature through Point of View

In "The Vacation," Wendell Berry describes a video camera as an objective narrative instrument, but he also suggests the limits of such an apparatus.

Wendell Berry (1934–)

The Vacation (1997)

Once there was a man who filmed his vacation.
He went flying down the river in his boat
with his video camera to his eye, making
a moving picture of the moving river
upon which his sleek boat moved swiftly   5
toward the end of his vacation. He showed
his vacation to his camera, which pictured it,
preserving it forever: the river, the trees,
the sky, the light, the bow of his rushing boat
behind which he stood with his camera   10
preserving his vacation even as he was having it

so that after he had had it he would still
have it. It would be there. With a flick
of a switch, there it would be. But he
would not be in it. He would never be in it.   15

This poem is about narration: Berry tells the tale of a man who can see his
vacation only through the point of view of his camera. But this poem about
narration is also narrated. What sort of narrator does Berry use? Berry's
narrator tells a story. The narrator is not a person in the story but does
have access to the thoughts of the man with the camera, as well as to
knowledge that the man does not have and to a future that the man is not anticipating. Berry uses this narrator to judge the man and to comment on the problem of allowing a recording device to substitute for actual experience. Without directly stating so, Berry's narrator suggests that the man pays a price for trying so hard not to lose any of his vacation.

> ### Making Connections
>
> An author uses a variety of techniques to give us a character who seems real and consistent, even in inconsistencies. Character is discussed in Chapter 2. It is important to note that the narrator of a work can be considered another character, but this character may seem to be hidden.

FILM FOCUS AND ANGLES

A film also expresses a narrative voice—a point of view. The building block of any film is the smallest element: the single **frame**. In analyzing the **composition** of a painting or of a single frame, we can learn something about point of view by considering how the characters and all of the other elements are arranged within the frame. The objects in the **foreground** will demand special attention. A foregrounded subject can be further prioritized by **shallow focus**, a technique that brings a specific plane into clear focus and leaves the rest of the picture out of focus.

In this frame from *The Magnificent Ambersons* (1942) on the facing page, the couple in the foreground (Anne Baxter and Tim Holt) commands our attention, and the rest of the room is clearly less important. The shot itself focuses on the couple rather than on anything else in the room. It is clear that there is something else going on, but the shot indicates that whatever this other activity may be, it is not central to this scene. In **deep focus**, objects remain clear as they grow more distant; in deep focus, the cinematographer achieves a greater **depth of field** and forgoes concentration on a specific subject.

In the frame from *Citizen Kane* on page 293, we can see part of the effect that Orson Welles has achieved as the camera pulls away from the window

The Magnificent Ambersons (1942). Objects in the foreground command our attention.

Citizen Kane (1941)

Trapped (1949). The high-angle shot in this scene suggests the power of law enforcement over James Todd.

Nosferatu (1922). The low-angle shot lends the subject power over the viewer.

through which we watch young Kane playing in the snow. As the camera begins to settle on Kane's mother and the other people inside the house, we can still see the window and the young boy whose future is being determined by events inside the house.

The angle from which a picture is taken also contributes to the overall impression we get when we see a scene. A **high-angle shot** (a picture taken from above the subject) may communicate a sweeping feel or may place the viewer in a strong position in relation to the subject.

In the frame from *Trapped* (1949) on the facing page, the high angle of the shot suggests the power that the law enforcement officials hold over James Todd, who is holding his hands in the air. We see the scene from the point of view of the man with the gun in the foreground rather than of Todd. Such an effect can be exaggerated by the degree of the angle (an **extreme high-level shot** or an **aerial view**).

An **eye-level shot** (camera and subject at the same height) generally suggests greater immediacy by putting the viewer right with the subject. A **low-angle shot** (the camera set below the subject) may lend the subject of the picture power over the viewer.

For example, in the frame on the facing page, we look up to the vampire in the film *Nosferatu*. Of course, the degree of the angle is important here as well. In this case, it emphasizes the deformity of the figure. Just as a filmmaker or a painter must choose where to place the camera or where to stand when making a painting, an author must choose where to stand to transfer perceived reality into words. This decision impacts our perception of the entire narrative as we read.

Henry Taylor's poem "After a Movie" uses the cinematic motif to show the point of view of a person who leaves a movie and looks at the world with an eye still used to the dark world of the movie theater. Notice how the person sees real scenes as though they were frames from a film.

Henry Taylor (1942–)

After a Movie (1996)

The last small credits fade
as house lights rise. Dazed in that radiant instant
of transition, you dwindle through the lobby
and out to curbside, pulling on a glove
with the decisive competence   5
of the scarred detective

or his quarry. Scanning
the rainlit street for taxicabs, you visualize,

without looking, your image in the window
of the jeweler's shop, where white hands hover   10
above the string of luminous pearls
on a faceless velvet bust.

Someone across the street
enters a bar, leaving behind a charged vacancy
in which you cut to the dim booth inside,   15
where you are seated, glancing at the door.
You lift an eyebrow, recognizing
the unnamed colleague

who will conspire with you
against whatever the volatile script provides   20
A cab pulls up. You stoop into the dark
and settle toward a version of yourself.
Your profile cruises past the city
on a home-drifting stream

through whose surface, sometimes,   25
you glimpse the life between the streambed and the ripples,
as, when your gestures are your own again,
your fingers lift a cup beyond whose rim
a room bursts into clarity
and light falls on all things.   30

The character in this poem views the world as though he were one of the characters in the film that has just ended: "the scarred detective / or his quarry." He sees the world as if it were carefully arranged for this scene. He is not an actor who knows ahead of time what the "volatile script provides." But he has adopted the consciousness of the fictional character who works within the conventions of film. Instead of just looking across the street, his eyes work like a camera, "Scanning / the rainlit street." In a jeweler's shop window, his own reflection shows in the foreground, but the character sees like a camera through that reflection to focus on the string of pearls. Not until the final lines of the poem is the character able to regain his natural point of view when "a room bursts into clarity / and light falls on all things."

Experiencing Film through Point of View

Alfred Hitchcock dramatizes the problem of limited point of view in *Rear Window* (1954), the story of photographer L. B. Jefferies (Jimmy Stewart), who is confined to his apartment as he recuperates from a broken leg. To pass the time, Jefferies looks out his window into the windows of the apartments that face his, and he sees scenes from the lives of his neighbors. He would seem to be an impartial observer, and he believes that he is detached from the lives that he is observing; these are not people he knows. But as he watches, he becomes involved in the stories that unfold. He becomes a narrator creating his own order from the fragmented scenes that he observes. As the film progresses, Hitchcock suggests that Jefferies may have become more involved in these stories than in his own life.

While looking out over his neighborhood, Jefferies comes to believe that the man in an opposing apartment has killed his wife and somehow disposed of the body. Jefferies's suspicion arises only from odd things that he sees from his window, yet he eventually draws his nurse, Stella (Thelma Ritter), and his girlfriend, Lisa Fremont (Grace Kelly), into his obsession. Jefferies also calls in his friend Doyle (a police detective played by Wendell Corey) to check out the "evidence," but Doyle dismisses Jefferies's theories. The pursuit of the murderer is left to a man who can't get out of his apartment, a beautiful society woman, and a plainspoken practical nurse.

Rear Window is very cleverly scripted, but its pleasures cannot be expressed by a summary of action. Hitchcock establishes in the film's opening

Rear Window (1954)

shot what becomes the film's essential dynamic. The audience looks from an apartment window across to adjacent apartments; the audience, in effect, inhabits the apartment from which the view is shot. After the camera pans over the neighborhood, it turns back to reveal the viewer we have already been linked to (we have seen through his eyes): L. B. Jefferies, broken leg and all. The exchange between looking at and being looked at will underlie everything that follows.

Hitchcock highlights the particularity of point of view in this film by carefully framing individual shots. The border that the camera (and screen) establishes includes the very window frames that Jefferies sees through (both his own windows and his neighbors'). By calling attention to frames, Hitchcock suggests that we always shape what we see. In other words, we construct reality much like we compose a picture; we arrange what we perceive so that it fits together or "adds up" in a way that makes sense to us. Such thoughts lead us to realize that no person's vision is complete; therefore, no person's interpretation of actions can be absolutely trustworthy. Much of the suspense of *Rear Window* arises from the thought that Jefferies may not be seeing all that he needs to see. Perhaps truth requires that he see the very things the frames cut off.

Hitchcock's specific emphasis on window frames keeps us particularly aware that we are not only looking from one apartment but also peering into the private apartments of others. Frames in this respect can be seen as boundaries we are not supposed to cross. For example, that Jefferies is a bit disappointed when the newlywed wife thinks to close the blinds to her bedroom window. If Jefferies is a "Peeping Tom," as his nurse at first claims, we who watch movies (at least this movie) seem no better; we, after all, are eager to see everything he sees across the square. Therefore, the thrill Jefferies and the audience get from discovery is compromised by the knowledge that the thrill does not arise from a praiseworthy pursuit of truth and justice. We all become fascinated by seeing things others would choose to hide from us.

SHIFTING PERSPECTIVES

The medium of film offers a ready alternative to the problem of a limited perspective. Almost every film offers a variety of camera angles to give us a sense that we see what is really happening. When a television network covers a sporting event, it places cameras around the arena to offer some sense of full coverage of the event. When a referee in a football game makes a call, he does so from his unique place on the field, from his observation of that play, and from his memory of what he has observed. He might confer with the other referees to confirm his call; meanwhile, the network will quickly review the play from each of its cameras, and those of us who are watching may feel as though we have a better idea of what really happened than those who have made the official call. There is a sense that the more one sees, the more likely one is to see things "correctly," but every person has a different interpretation of events; the person who hears all the different stories may or may not feel better informed than those who were actually there. The pursuit of "correctness" gives way to an interest in exploring the different approaches made possible by each point of view. Each new view deepens the experience, even if it does not resolve anything.

Just as camera angles alter the way an event is perceived, authors shift the perspective within a narrative to give particular depth to the story. In Stevie Smith's "Not Waving but Drowning," the poem shifts from an objective narrator to the voice of a dead man to those who are watching and back again to the dead man.

Stevie Smith (1902–1971)

Not Waving but Drowning (1957)

Nobody heard him, the dead man,
But still he lay moaning:
I was much further out than you thought
And not waving but drowning.

Poor chap, he always loved larking   5
And now he's dead
It must have been too cold for him his heart gave way,
They said.

Oh, no no no, it was too cold always
(Still the dead one lay moaning)   10
I was much too far out all my life
And not waving but drowning.

A central image of the poem is the difficulty posed by different perspectives: what might have looked like playful waving was actually a cry for help. The tragedy within this image is that the observers, who are aware of the man and his waving, might have offered help, but they were unable to interpret his gesture. As we hear from the man, we learn that there was a much larger communication problem. The observers characterize him as one who enjoys "larking," and even after his death, they assume that the cause of death was cold water. The dead man is still trying to correct their misperception—his "no no no" desperately tries to shake the survivors out of the nearly comical rhythm of the poem and of their confidently wrong explanations. He claims to have been out "too far" all of his life. The image of the drowned man trying to talk with those who get to interpret his life could stand for anyone in any sort of circumstance who has gotten "too far out."

Experiencing Literature through Perspective

In the following poem, Philip Levine confronts issues of perspective at several different levels. He sets his own poem against the context of "famous photographs" that Charles Sheeler took in Dearborn's Ford factories in the late 1920s and early 1930s. The photograph here is an example of Sheeler's style in this series. The machine is a massive presence, but the man who makes this machine work is smaller than most of the machine's pieces. By referring to Sheeler's photographs, Levine situates his own personal narrative and sets up a contrast between the famous "dwarfed" men in the photographs and Mrs. Strempek working with her trowel across the street in a house now "long gone to fire."

Charles Sheeler, *River Rouge Plant Stamping Press* (1927)

Philip Levine (1928–)

Photography 2 (1999)

Across the road from Ford's a Mrs. Strempek
planted tulip bulbs and irises even though

the remnants of winter were still hanging on
in gray speckled mounds. Smoking at all times
she would kneel, bare legged, on the hard ground   5
and half smile when I passed coming or going
as she worked her trowel back and forth for hours
making a little stubborn hole and when that
was done making another.
                              When Charles Sheeler
came to Dearborn to take his famous photographs   10
of the great Rouge plant he caught some workers,
tiny little men, at a distance, dwarfed
under the weight of the tools they thought
they commanded. When they got too close
he left them out of focus, gray lumps with white   15
wild eyes. Mainly he was interested in
the way space got divided or how light
changed nothing.
                        Nowhere does Mrs. Strempek
show up in all the records of that year,
nor do the few pale tulips and irises   20
that bloomed in the yard of her rented house
long gone to fire. For the first time I was
in love that spring and would walk the long mile
from the bus stop knowing it was useless,
at my feet the rutted tracks the trucks made,   25
still half frozen. Ahead the slag heaps
burning at all hours, and the great stacks
blackening the sky, and nothing in between.

Look carefully at the perspectives that Levine offers in his poem. Then,
examine the perspective that Sheeler offers in his photograph. How does
Mrs. Strempek compare to the nameless worker in the photograph? How do
the two narrators (Levine's "I" and Sheeler's photographic point of view)
treat these characters differently? Why does Levine position his own spring
of first love between the images of a smoking woman planting bulbs and the
Ford employees?

In Frank Gaspar's poem "It Is the Nature of the Wing," the narrator
strives to become conscious of multiple perspectives and is fully aware of the
fragmentary nature of each one. Yet the narrator sees every distraction as
potentially enlightening.

Frank X. Gaspar (1946–)

It Is the Nature of the Wing (2004)

The problem is being a fragment trying to live out a whole life.
From this, everything follows. Or the problem is being
fractured and preoccupied with one's own mending, which
lasts as long as you do and comes with its legion of distractions.
Just now, when a lovely-throated motor comes gliding up   5
the street to one driveway or another, I can tell you
there is a certain kind of safety in a fact like that. It is so
solid you can lean on it in your bad hours. It can lift you, too,
from your despair, which is of no consequence, which can
be measured against the dropping flowers of the wisteria,   10
which fall because of their nature and essence, and stain
the redwood planks of the small deck in the back of the house.
That doesn't mean those used-up blossoms feel at home
under everyone's feet or at the mercy of my stiffened broom.
Didn't Plato say it is the nature of the wing to lift what is heavy?   15
He was speaking of love again, I can remember that much, and
then love was a ladder, too, but lifting again, always upward.
Then it is possible to love Plato for his faith, which is so strong
he becomes difficult and obdurate in the late nights. He is
hardly distracted by a passing car. He is fixed on something   20
beautiful, and why not? When I step out onto the porch, there
is nothing shining in the sky. Oh, and the wisteria blooms have
fallen some more and are like a sad carpet. And some small
insects are dancing in the garage's yellow lamp. They don't hear
the little bats squeaking. It's all right. You could even say they   25
look happy, they look joyful. Surely they are beautiful in their
ignorance and danger. See how they hold your head and command
your eye? Looking upward? Looking toward that homely light?

The narrator begins by noticing the unconsciousness of machinery, the
motor (a fragment of the car that is actually moving up the street). He
moves on to grasp at the perspective of wisteria blossoms (which may not
feel at home under our feet), Plato (an attempt to understand the line that
Gaspar uses as his title), and insects by the garage. The narrator simultaneously fails in his quest not to be distracted from the larger questions that
consume him and succeeds by using these seemingly distracting perspectives
to help him look "upward" toward some larger philosophical understanding
of unattainable ideas such as love and faith.

An awareness of perspective helps us as readers see how authors manipulate our attention. Point of view controls the degree of sympathy we may have toward a character; it guides our judgment of the actions of characters; it contributes to our interpretation of the whole work. An awareness of technique gives us a greater appreciation of the craft that goes into the literary production and enriches our conversations about what we are reading.

MODELING CRITICAL ANALYSIS: ROBERT BROWNING, MY LAST DUCHESS

One of the most famous first-person narrators in poetry is the duke who tells the story of his late wife in Robert Browning's "My Last Duchess." The poem takes place in the ducal palace of Ferrara, Italy, during the Renaissance. The duke is speaking admiringly about a painting of his wife (now deceased) that he commissioned the artist "Frà Pandolf" to paint. Through the duke's description of the painting and the manner in which the image was painted, we begin to learn something of the character of this "last Duchess" and of the duke himself. We gradually learn that the duke is speaking to an emissary for the man whose daughter might become the next duchess.

Robert Browning (1812–1889)

My Last Duchess (1842)

FERRARA

That's my last Duchess painted on the wall,
Looking as if she were alive. I call
That piece a wonder, now: Frà Pandolf's hands
Worked busily a day, and there she stands.
Will't please you sit and look at her? I said   5
"Frà Pandolf" by design, for never read
Strangers like you that pictured countenance,
The depth and passion of its earnest glance,
But to myself they turned (since none puts by
The curtain I have drawn for you, but I)   10
And seemed as they would ask me, if they durst,
How such a glance came there; so, not the first
Are you to turn and ask thus. Sir, 'twas not

Her husband's presence only, called that spot
Of joy into the Duchess' cheek: perhaps   15
Frà Pandolf chanced to say "Her mantle laps
Over my Lady's wrist too much," or "Paint
Must never hope to reproduce the faint
Half-flush that dies along her throat": such stuff
Was courtesy, she thought, and cause enough   20
For calling up that spot of joy. She had
A heart—how shall I say?—too soon made glad,
Too easily impressed; she liked whate'er
She looked on, and her looks went everywhere.
Sir, 'twas all one! My favour at her breast,   25
The dropping of the daylight in the West,
The bough of cherries some officious fool
Broke in the orchard for her, the white mule
She rode with round the terrace—all and each
Would draw from her alike the approving speech,   30
Or blush, at least. She thanked men,—good! but thanked
Somehow—I know not how—as if she ranked
My gift of a nine-hundred-years-old name
With anybody's gift. Who'd stoop to blame
This sort of trifling? Even had you skill   35
In speech—which I have not—to make your will
Quite clear to such an one, and say, "Just this
Or that in you disgusts me; here you miss,
Or there exceed the mark"—and if she let
Herself be lessoned so, nor plainly set   40
Her wits to yours, forsooth, and made excuse,
—E'en then would be some stooping, and I choose
Never to stoop. Oh sir, she smiled, no doubt,
Whene'er I passed her; but who passed without
Much the same smile? This grew; I gave commands;   45
Then all smiles stopped together. There she stands
As if alive. Will't please you rise? We'll meet
The company below, then. I repeat,
The Count your master's known munificence
Is ample warrant that no just pretense   50
Of mine for dowry will be disallowed;
Though his fair daughter's self, as I avowed
At starting, is my object. Nay, we'll go
Together down, sir. Notice Neptune, though,
Taming a sea-horse, thought a rarity,   55
Which Claus of Innsbruck cast in bronze for me!

Browning presents the poem as a speech from the duke. That speech is never interrupted by a question or a response. The duke has something to say but has no interest in hearing from someone else. In showing his gallery, the duke offers a self-portrait, perhaps a calculated self-portrait. It's essential to note that the "I" of "My Last Duchess" is emphatically not Robert Browning. Author and speaker must be kept distinct. As the speaker's conversation unfolds, so do his relations with the scene itself. He tells about "my last Duchess" and the artist who rendered her, and in so doing, the duke reveals much about himself. We pick up on his jealousy and his unrestrained frustration at what he perceives to be the lack of respect that his dead wife showed to him. As the duke finishes talking about this painting (in the middle of line 47) and moves on to the next artwork in his collection, we get the poetic equivalent of a widening shot so that we can suddenly see the audience listening to the talking duke. In this revelation, we learn more about the duke's sense of morality. He feels no qualms about having given "commands" that stopped "all smiles" from his wife. Whether he means to warn his future wife of his intolerance for any sort of indiscretion, whether he is simply brutally honest about his past, or whether he is so self-involved as to be unaware of the repugnance of his attitudes and actions, we cannot help feeling that the emissary would be wrong to let the next marriage go forward.

By creating this account from the perspective of the duke, Browning also puts us into the position of the emissary, who is gradually discovering the character of a potential future member of the family. Though we begin by appreciating art and the duke's storytelling, we ultimately realize that the seemingly learned man who is talking about art is, at best, a boor, and, at worst, a murderer without a conscience.

Using Point of View to Focus Writing and Discussion

- Who is speaking? How do we know?
- How does this speaker's position influence our view of events?
- If the narrator is not a character in the action, whose point of view influences our understanding of events?
- What values or limitations impact this narrator's presentation?
- How many, if any, of these limitations did the author intend to include? For instance, we may see limitations such as a view of women's place in society that indicate the author's cultural bias rather than something that the author created as part of a character in the story.
- How do we encounter any other point of view in this narrative?
- What details in the narrative help us understand the speaker?
- What, if anything, can we see that contradicts the account that we hear from our narrator?

Anthology

TRUST AND DOUBT: A MATTER OF POINT OF VIEW

The issue of trust and the problem of doubt are tied very closely to a point of view. Both are involved when diverse perspectives come into contact. When we trust someone else, we are content not to see a situation from our own perspective; in fact, we are willing to be blind to a situation because we believe that we can trust the other person to present a point of view faithfully. When that trust fails, we want to see everything for ourselves.

The conflict between gaining trust and raising doubt propels the story line of many of William Shakespeare's plays. In *Much Ado about Nothing*, the pendulum of trust and doubt swings back and forth as lovers unite and the evil Don John sows seeds of doubt. The spying and the confrontations that ensue balance on the precipice of tragedy without quite falling. In other plays, similar situations have much more tragic results.

The selections in this section illustrate the importance of perspective in shaping the reactions of the characters to a scene and the action itself. Kate Chopin's "The Story of an Hour" shows the tremendous changes that a character undergoes in the span of an hour simply in response to some news. We see a particular sort of conflict in the poems by William Carlos Williams and Erica-Lynn Gambino, as well as in Helane Levine Keating's "My Last Duke," which responds to the Browning poem, when we are given multiple sides of the same story. With the second voice, a more recent poet creates a tension and a relationship that depends upon the first voice but is not evident in the initial narrative.

These added perspectives also lead us to challenge our own capacity as readers. Generally we trust the narratives we hear, but as soon as we hear another version of events, we begin to doubt our confidence in that first version. If one perspective is distorted, how are we to know whether or not all perspectives are similarly flawed? Is there a "true" objective version of events? Would such a version be interesting?

FICTION

Ann Beattie (1947–)

Ann Beattie was born in Washington, D.C. Though a poor student in high school, she earned a BA from American University and an MA from the University of

Connecticut. Her first published works were short stories, which began appearing regularly in the *New Yorker*. Soon thereafter she published her first novel, *Chilly Scenes of Winter*, and she has alternated ever since between the short- and long-fiction formats. Beattie has received considerable critical acclaim for her portraits of characters belonging to her own generation, a generation at once excited and bewildered by the social upheavals of the 1960s. These characters are typically adrift in a world from which any certainty of value or meaning has been removed. Initially described as a "minimalist," a label she never accepted, Beattie has developed over time a more richly descriptive style.

Janus (1986)

The bowl was perfect. Perhaps it was not what you'd select if you faced a shelf of bowls, and not the sort of thing that would inevitably attract a lot of attention at a crafts fair, yet it had real presence. It was as predictably ad-mired as a mutt who has no reason to suspect he might be funny. Just such a dog, in fact, was often brought out (and in) along with the bowl.

Andrea was a real-estate agent, and when she thought that some pro-spective buyers might be dog lovers, she would drop off her dog at the same time she placed the bowl in the house that was up for sale. She would put a dish of water in the kitchen for Mondo, take his squeaking plastic frog out of her purse and drop it on the floor. He would pounce delightedly, just as he did every day at home, batting around his favorite toy. The bowl usually sat on a coffee table, though recently she had displayed it on top of a pine blanket chest and on a lacquered table. It was once placed on a cherry table beneath a Bonnard still life, where it held its own.

Everyone who has purchased a house or who has wanted to sell a house must be familiar with some of the tricks used to convince a buyer that the house is quite special: a fire in the fireplace in early evening; jonquils in a pitcher on the kitchen counter, where no one ordinarily has space to put flowers; perhaps the slight aroma of spring, made by a single drop of scent vaporizing from a lamp bulb.

The wonderful thing about the bowl, Andrea thought, was that it was both subtle and noticeable—a paradox of a bowl. Its glaze was the color of cream and seemed to glow no matter what light it was placed in. There were a few bits of color in it—tiny geometric flashes—and some of these were tinged with flecks of silver. They were as mysterious as cells seen under a microscope; it was difficult not to study them, because they shim-mered, flashing for a split second, and then resumed their shape. Some-thing about the colors and their random placement suggested motion. People who liked country furniture always commented on the bowl, but then it turned out that people who felt comfortable with Biedermeier loved it just as much. But the bowl was not at all ostentatious, or even so

noticeable that anyone would suspect that it had been put in place deliberately. They might notice the height of the ceiling on first entering a
room, and only when their eye moved down from that, or away from the
refraction of sunlight on a pale wall, would they see the bowl. Then they
would go immediately to it and comment. Yet they always faltered when
they tried to say something. Perhaps it was because they were in the
house for a serious reason, not to notice some object.

Once Andrea got a call from a woman who had not put in an offer   5
on a house she had shown her. That bowl, she said—would it be possible
to find out where the owners had bought that beautiful bowl? Andrea pretended that she did not know what the woman was referring to. A bowl,
somewhere in the house? Oh, on a table under the window. Yes, she
would ask, of course. She let a couple of days pass, then called back to say
that the bowl had been a present and the people did not know where it
had been purchased.

When the bowl was not being taken from house to house, it sat on Andrea's coffee table at home. She didn't keep it carefully wrapped (although
she transported it that way, in a box); she kept it on the table, because she
liked to see it. It was large enough so that it didn't seem fragile or particularly vulnerable if anyone sideswiped the table or Mondo blundered into it
at play. She had asked her husband to please not drop his house key in it. It
was meant to be empty.

When her husband first noticed the bowl, he had peered into it and
smiled briefly. He always urged her to buy things she liked. In recent years,
both of them had acquired many things to make up for all the lean years
when they were graduate students, but now that they had been comfortable
for quite a while, the pleasure of new possessions dwindled. Her husband
had pronounced the bowl "pretty," and he had turned away without picking
it up to examine it. He had no more interest in the bowl than she had in
his new Leica.

She was sure that the bowl brought her luck. Bids were often put in
on houses where she had displayed the bowl. Sometimes the owners, who
were always asked to be away or to step outside when the house was
being shown, didn't even know that the bowl had been in their house.
Once—she could not imagine how—she left it behind, and then she was
so afraid that something might have happened to it that she rushed back
to the house and sighed with relief when the woman owner opened the
door. The bowl, Andrea explained—she had purchased a bowl and set it
on the chest for safekeeping while she toured the house with the prospective buyers, and she . . . She felt like rushing past the frowning woman
and seizing her bowl. The owner stepped aside, and it was only when
Andrea ran to the chest that the lady glanced at her a little strangely In
the few seconds before Andrea picked up the bowl, she realized that the

owner must have just seen that it had been perfectly placed, that the sunlight struck the bluer part of it. Her pitcher had been moved to the far side of the chest, and the bowl predominated. All the way home, Andrea wondered how she could have left the bowl behind. It was like leaving a friend at an outing—just walking off. Sometimes there were stories in the paper about families forgetting a child somewhere and driving to the next city. Andrea had only gone a mile down the road before she remembered.

In time, she dreamed of the bowl. Twice, in a waking dream—early in the morning, between sleep and a last nap before rising—she had a clear vision of it. It came into sharp focus and startled her for a moment—the same bowl she looked at every day.

She had a very profitable year selling real estate. Word spread, and   10
she had more clients than she felt comfortable with. She had the foolish thought that if only the bowl were an animate object she could thank it. There were times when she wanted to talk to her husband about the bowl. He was a stockbroker, and sometimes told people that he was fortunate to be married to a woman who had such a fine aesthetic sense and yet could also function in the real world. They were a lot alike, really—they had agreed on that. They were both quiet people—reflective, slow to make value judgments, but almost intractable once they had come to a conclusion. They both liked details, but while ironies attracted her, he was more impatient and dismissive when matters became many sided or unclear. They both knew this, and it was the kind of thing they could talk about when they were alone in the car together, coming home from a party or after a weekend with friends. But she never talked to him about the bowl. When they were at dinner, exchanging their news of the day, or while they lay in bed at night listening to the stereo and murmuring sleepy disconnections, she was often tempted to come right out and say that she thought that the bowl in the living room, the cream-colored bowl, was responsible for her success. But she didn't say it. She couldn't begin to explain it. Sometimes in the morning, she would look at him and feel guilty that she had such a constant secret.

Could it be that she had some deeper connection with the bowl—a relationship of some kind? She corrected her thinking: How could she imagine such a thing, when she was a human being and it was a bowl? It was ridiculous. Just think of how people lived together and loved each other.... But was that always so clear, always a relationship? She was confused by these thoughts, but they remained in her mind. There was something within her now, something real, that she never talked about.

The bowl was a mystery, even to her. It was frustrating, because her involvement with the bowl contained a steady sense of unrequited good fortune; it would have been easier to respond if some sort of demand were made in return. But that only happened in fairy tales. The bowl was just a bowl. She did not believe that for one second. What she believed was that it was something she loved.

In the past, she had sometimes talked to her husband about a new property she was about to buy or sell—confiding some clever strategy she had devised to persuade owners who seemed ready to sell. Now she stopped doing that, for all her strategies involved the bowl. She became more deliberate with the bowl, and more possessive. She put it in houses only when no one was there, and removed it when she left the house. Instead of just moving a pitcher or a dish, she would remove all the other objects from a table. She had to force herself to handle them carefully, because she didn't really care about them. She just wanted them out of sight.

She wondered how the situation would end. As with a lover, there was no exact scenario of how matters would come to a close. Anxiety became the operative force. It would be irrelevant if the lover rushed into someone else's arms, or wrote her a note and departed to another city. The horror was the possibility of the disappearance. That was what mattered.

She would get up at night and look at the bowl. It never occurred to her that she might break it. She washed and dried it without anxiety, and she moved it often, from coffee table to mahogany corner table or wherever, without fearing an accident. It was clear that she would not be the one who would do anything to the bowl. The bowl was only handled by her, set safely on one surface or another; it was not very likely that anyone would break it. A bowl was a poor conductor of electricity: it would not be hit by lightning. Yet the idea of damage persisted. She did not think beyond that—to what her life would be without the bowl. She only continued to fear that some accident would happen. Why not, in a world where people set plants where they did not belong, so that visitors touring a house would be fooled into thinking that dark corners got sunlight—a world full of tricks?

She had first seen the bowl several years earlier, at a crafts fair she had visited half in secret, with her lover. He had urged her to buy the bowl. She didn't *need* any more things, she told him. But she had been drawn to the bowl, and they had lingered near it. Then she went on to the next booth, and he came up behind her, tapping the rim against her shoulder as she ran her fingers over a wood carving. "You're still insisting that I buy that?" she said. "No," he said. "I bought it for you." He had bought her other things before this—things she liked more, at first—the child's ebony-and-turquoise ring that fitted her little finger; the wooden box, long and thin, beautifully dovetailed, that she used to hold paper clips; the soft gray sweater with a pouch pocket. It was his idea that when he could not be there to hold her hand she could hold her own—clasp her hands inside the lone pocket that stretched across the front. But in time she became more attached to the bowl than to any of his other presents. She tried to talk herself out of it. She owned other things that were more striking or valuable. It wasn't an object whose beauty jumped out at you; a lot of people must have passed it by before the two of them saw it that day.

Her lover had said that she was always too slow to know what she really loved. Why continue with her life the way it was? Why be two-faced, he asked her. He had made the first move toward her. When she would not decide in his favor, would not change her life and come to him, he asked her what made her think she could have it both ways. And then he made the last move and left. It was a decision meant to break her will, to shatter her intransigent ideas about honoring previous commitments.

Time passed. Alone in the living room at night, she often looked at the bowl sitting on the table, still and safe, unilluminated. In its way, it was perfect: the world cut in half, deep and smoothly empty. Near the rim, even in dim light, the eye moved toward one small flash of blue, a vanishing point on the horizon.

■ How do we learn about the significance of the bowl? Trace the specific details to their specific position within the story.

■ Who narrates this story? How much does the narrator know? How does this narrator impact our experience of the story? To what extent does the narrator question Andrea's perceptions of the world?

■ What happens in this story? How does the story end? What changes over the course of the narrative?

Kate Chopin (1851–1904)

Kate Chopin was born in St. Louis, Missouri. As a young woman, she developed an interest in the arts and a gift for storytelling that remained with her for the rest of her life. She married and had six children, but her husband died young of a fever. Following this loss, and at the advice of her family physician, Chopin began writing. She is best remembered today for those tales that were groundbreaking in their depictions of married life and sexuality, but it was precisely these elements that were problematic in her own day. The discomfort some readers and editors felt with this aspect of her work came to a head with the publication of her second novel, *The Awakening*. Although the indignation that the book aroused effectively ended Chopin's career, it is now regarded by many as a masterpiece.

The Story of an Hour (1894)

Knowing that Mrs. Mallard was afflicted with a heart trouble, great care was taken to break to her as gently as possible the news of her husband's death.

It was her sister Josephine who told her, in broken sentences, veiled hints that revealed in half concealing. Her husband's friend Richards was there, too, near her. It was he who had been in the newspaper office when intelligence of the railroad disaster was received, with Brently Mallard's name leading the list of "killed." He had only taken the time to assure himself of its truth by a second telegram, and had hastened to forestall any less careful, less tender friend in bearing the sad message.

She did not hear the story as many women have heard the same, with a paralyzed inability to accept its significance. She wept at once, with sudden, wild abandonment, in her sister's arms. When the storm of grief had spent itself she went away to her room alone. She would have no one follow her.

There stood, facing the open window, a comfortable, roomy armchair. Into this she sank, pressed down by a physical exhaustion that haunted her body and seemed to reach into her soul.

She could see in the open square before her house the tops of trees that were all aquiver with the new spring life. The delicious breath of rain was in the air. In the street below a peddler was crying his wares. The notes of a distant song which some one was singing reached her faintly, and countless sparrows were twittering in the eaves.

There were patches of blue sky showing here and there through the clouds that had met and piled one above the other in the west facing her window.

She sat with her head thrown back upon the cushion of the chair, quite motionless, except when a sob came up into her throat and shook her, as a child who has cried itself to sleep continues to sob in its dreams.

She was young, with a fair, calm face, whose lines bespoke repression and even a certain strength. But now there was a dull stare in her eyes, whose gaze was fixed away off yonder on one of those patches of blue sky. It was not a glance of reflection, but rather indicated a suspension of intelligent thought.

There was something coming to her and she was waiting for it, fearfully. What was it? She did not know; it was too subtle and elusive to name. But she felt it, creeping out of the sky, reaching toward her through the sounds, the scents, the color that filled the air.

Now her bosom rose and fell tumultuously. She was beginning to recognize this thing that was approaching to possess her, and she was striving to beat it back with her will—as powerless as her two white slender hands would have been.

When she abandoned herself a little whispered word escaped her slightly parted lips. She said it over and over under her breath: "Free, free, free!" The vacant stare and the look of terror that had followed it went from her eyes. They stayed keen and bright. Her pulses beat fast, and the coursing blood warmed and relaxed every inch of her body.

She did not stop to ask if it were not a monstrous joy that held her. A clear and exalted perception enabled her to dismiss the suggestion as trivial.

She knew that she would weep again when she saw the kind, tender hands folded in death; the face that had never looked save with love upon her, fixed and gray and dead. But she saw beyond that bitter moment a long procession of years to come that would belong to her absolutely. And she opened and spread her arms out to them in welcome.

There would be no one to live for during those coming years; she would live for herself. There would be no powerful will bending her in that blind persistence with which men and women believe they have a right to impose a private will upon a fellow creature. A kind intention or a cruel intention made the act seem no less a crime as she looked upon it in that brief moment of illumination.

And yet she had loved him—sometimes. Often she had not. What did 15 it matter! What could love, the unsolved mystery, count for in face of this possession of self-assertion which she suddenly recognized as the strongest impulse of her being.

"Free! Body and soul free!" she kept whispering.

Josephine was kneeling before the closed door with her lips to the keyhole, imploring for admission. "Louise, open the door! I beg; open the door—you will make yourself ill. What are you doing, Louise? For heaven's sake open the door."

"Go away. I am not making myself ill." No; she was drinking in a very elixir of life through that open window.

Her fancy was running riot along those days ahead of her. Spring days, and summer days, and all sorts of days that would be her own. She breathed a quick prayer that life might be long. It was only yesterday she had thought with a shudder that life might be long.

She arose at length and opened the door to her sister's importunities. 20 There was a feverish triumph in her eyes, and she carried herself unwittingly like a goddess of Victory. She clasped her sister's waist, and together they descended the stairs. Richards stood waiting for them at the bottom.

Some one was opening the front door with a latchkey. It was Brently Mallard who entered, a little travel-stained, composedly carrying his gripsack and umbrella. He had been far from the scene of the accident, and did not even know there had been one. He stood amazed at Josephine's piercing cry; at Richards' quick motion to screen him from the view of his wife.

But Richards was too late.

When the doctors came they said she had died of heart disease—of joy that kills.

- The story ends with a misinterpretation. How has the author prepared us to understand simultaneously how the doctors might arrive at this conclusion and how their conclusion is wrong?
- "There would be no one to live for during those coming years...." How does this sentence contain the dual perspective that is repeatedly presented in this story?
- How do the physical descriptions offered in the story contribute to our understanding of Mrs. Mallard's condition?

Charlotte Perkins Gilman (1860–1935)

Charlotte Perkins Gilman was born in Hartford, Connecticut. Gilman's upbringing and first marriage were far from easy: her father deserted his family and was only in sporadic contact with his daughter, her mother was emotionally distant, and Gilman herself experienced a deep depression after giving birth. This depression, difficult though it was, proved to be a turning point for her. Following her recovery and her subsequent divorce, she began to establish herself as a feminist activist and writer. Gilman wrote in a number of genres, producing poems, political tracts, and novels, but she is best remembered for a semi-autobiographical work of short fiction, "The Yellow Wallpaper," which she published in 1899. Though the techniques for treating depression described in the story are no longer in use, "The Yellow Wallpaper" remains a powerful indictment of the ways in which women can be smothered by relationships.

The Yellow Wallpaper (1892)

It is very seldom that mere ordinary people like John and myself secure ancestral halls for the summer.

A colonial mansion, a hereditary estate, I would say a haunted house and reach the height of romantic felicity—but that would be asking too much of fate!

Still I will proudly declare that there is something queer about it.

Else, why should it be let so cheaply? And why have stood so long untenanted?

John laughs at me, of course, but one expects that in marriage.

John is practical in the extreme. He has no patience with faith, an intense horror of superstition, and he scoffs openly at any talk of things not to be felt and seen and put down in figures.

John is a physician, and *perhaps*—(I would not say it to a living soul, of course, but this is dead paper and a great relief to my mind)— *perhaps* that is one reason I do not get well faster.

You see, he does not believe I am sick!

And what can one do?

If a physician of high standing, and one's own husband, assures friends and relatives that there is really nothing the matter with one but temporary nervous depression—a slight hysterical tendency—what is one to do? 10

My brother is also a physician, and also of high standing, and he says the same thing.

So I take phosphates or phosphites—whichever it is, and tonics, and journeys, and air, and exercise, and am absolutely forbidden to "work" until I am well again.

Personally, I disagree with their ideas.

Personally, I believe that congenial work, with excitement and change, would do me good.

But what is one to do? 15

I did write for a while in spite of them; but it *does* exhaust me a good deal—having to be so sly about it, or else meet with heavy opposition.

I sometimes fancy that in my condition if I had less opposition and more society and stimulus—but John says the very worst thing I can do is to think about my condition, and I confess it always makes me feel bad.

So I will let it alone and talk about the house.

The most beautiful place! It is quite alone, standing well back from the road, quite three miles from the village. It makes me think of English places that you read about, for there are hedges and walls and gates that lock, and lots of separate little houses for the gardeners and people.

There is a *delicious* garden! I never saw such a garden—large and shady, 20 full of box-bordered paths, and lined with long grape-covered arbors with seats under them.

There were greenhouses, too, but they are all broken now.

There was some legal trouble, I believe, something about the heirs and co-heirs; anyhow, the place has been empty for years.

That spoils my ghostliness, I am afraid, but I don't care—there is something strange about the house—I can feel it.

I even said so to John one moonlight evening, but he said what I felt was a *draught*, and shut the window.

I get unreasonably angry with John sometimes. I'm sure I never used to 25 be so sensitive. I think it is due to this nervous condition.

But John says if I feel so, I shall neglect proper self-control; so I take pains to control myself—before him, at least, and that makes me very tired.

I don't like our room a bit. I wanted one downstairs that opened onto the piazza and had roses all over the window, and such pretty old-fashioned chintz hangings! but John would not hear of it.

He said there was only one window and not room for two beds, and no near room for him if he took another.

He is very careful and loving, and hardly lets me stir without special direction.

I have a schedule prescription for each hour in the day; he takes all care from me, and so I feel basely ungrateful not to value it more.

He said we came here solely on my account, that I was to have perfect rest and all the air I could get. "Your exercise depends on your strength, my dear," said he, "and your food somewhat on your appetite; but air you can absorb all the time." So we took the nursery at the top of the house.

It is a big, airy room, the whole floor nearly, with windows that look all ways, and air and sunshine galore. It was nursery first and then playroom and gymnasium, I should judge; for the windows are barred for little children, and there are rings and things in the walls.

The paint and paper look as if a boys' school had used it. It is stripped off—the paper—in great patches all around the head of my bed, about as far as I can reach, and in a great place on the other side of the room low down. I never saw a worse paper in my life.

One of those sprawling flamboyant patterns committing every artistic sin.

It is dull enough to confuse the eye in following, pronounced enough to constantly irritate and provoke study, and when you follow the lame uncertain curves for a little distance they suddenly commit suicide—plunge off at outrageous angles, destroy themselves in unheard of contradictions.

The color is repellant, almost revolting; a smouldering unclean yellow, strangely faded by the slow-turning sunlight.

It is a dull yet lurid orange in some places, a sickly sulphur tint in others.

No wonder the children hated it! I should hate it myself if I had to live in this room long.

There comes John, and I must put this away,—he hates to have me write a word.

We have been here two weeks, and I haven't felt like writing before, since that first day.

I am sitting by the window now, up in this atrocious nursery, and there is nothing to hinder my writing as much as I please, save lack of strength.

John is away all day, and even some nights when his cases are serious.

I am glad my case is not serious!

But these nervous troubles are dreadfully depressing.

John does not know how much I really suffer. He knows there is no *rea-*   45
son to suffer, and that satisfies him.

Of course it is only nervousness. It does weigh on me so not to do my
duty in any way!

I meant to be such a help to John, such a real rest and comfort, and
here I am a comparative burden already!

Nobody would believe what an effort it is to do what little I am able,—
to dress and entertain, and order things.

It is fortunate Mary is so good with the baby. Such a dear baby!

And yet I *cannot* be with him, it makes me so nervous.   50

I suppose John never was nervous in his life. He laughs at me so about
this wallpaper!

At first he meant to repaper the room, but afterward he said that I was
letting it get the better of me, and that nothing was worse for a nervous
patient than to give way to such fancies.

He said that after the wallpaper was changed it would be the heavy
bedstead, and then the barred windows, and then that gate at the head of
the stairs, and so on.

"You know the place is doing you good," he said, "and really, dear, I
don't care to renovate the house just for a three months' rental."

"Then do let us go downstairs," I said, "there are such pretty rooms   55
there."

Then he took me in his arms and called me a blessed little goose, and
said he would go down cellar, if I wished, and have it whitewashed into the
bargain.

But he is right enough about the beds and windows and things.

It is an airy and comfortable room as anyone need wish, and, of course,
I would not be so silly as to make him uncomfortable just for a whim.

I'm really getting quite fond of the big room, all but that horrid paper.

Out of one window I can see the garden, those mysterious deep-shaded   60
arbors, the riotous old-fashioned flowers, and bushes and gnarly trees.

Out of another I get a lovely view of the bay and a little private wharf
belonging to the estate. There is a beautiful shaded lane that runs down there
from the house. I always fancy I see people walking in these numerous paths
and arbors, but John has cautioned me not to give way to fancy in the least.
He says that with my imaginative power and habit of story-making, a nervous
weakness like mine is sure to lead to all manner of excited fancies, and that I
ought to use my will and good sense to check the tendency. So I try.

I think sometimes that if I were only well enough to write a little it
would relieve the press of ideas and rest me.

But I find I get pretty tired when I try.

It is so discouraging not to have any advice and companionship about
my work. When I get really well, John says we will ask Cousin Henry and

Julia down for a long visit; but he says he would as soon put fireworks in my pillow-case as to let me have those stimulating people about now.

I wish I could get well faster.

6

But I must not think about that. This paper looks to me as if it *knew* what a vicious influence it had!

There is a recurrent spot where the pattern lolls like a broken neck and two bulbous eyes stare at you upside down.

I get positively angry with the impertinence of it and the everlasting-ness. Up and down and sideways they crawl, and those absurd, unblinking eyes are everywhere. There is one place where two breadths didn't match, and the eyes go all up and down the line, one a little higher than the other.

I never saw so much expression in an inanimate thing before, and we all know how much expression they have! I used to lie awake as a child and get more entertainment and terror out of blank walls and plain furniture than most children could find in a toy-store.

I remember what a kindly wink the knobs of our big, old bureau used to have, and there was one chair that always seemed like a strong friend.

7

I used to feel that if any of the other things looked too fierce I could always hop into that chair and be safe.

The furniture in this room is no worse than inharmonious, however, for we had to bring it all from downstairs. I suppose when this was used as a playroom they had to take the nursery things out, and no wonder! I never saw such ravages as the children have made here.

The wallpaper, as I said before, is torn off in spots, and it sticketh closer than a brother—they must have had perseverance as well as hatred.

Then the floor is scratched and gouged and splintered, the plaster itself is dug out here and there, and this great heavy bed, which is all we found in the room, looks as if it had been through the wars.

But I don't mind it a bit—only the paper.

7

There comes John's sister. Such a dear girl as she is, and so careful of me! I must not let her find me writing.

She is a perfect and enthusiastic housekeeper, and hopes for no better profession. I verily believe she thinks it is the writing which made me sick!

But I can write when she is out, and see her a long way off from these windows.

There is one that commands the road, a lovely shaded winding road, and one that just looks off over the country. A lovely country, too, full of great elms and velvet meadows.

This wallpaper has a kind of sub-pattern in a different shade, a particu-larly irritating one, for you can only see it in certain lights, and not clearly then.

8

But in the places where it isn't faded and where the sun is just so—I can see a strange, provoking, formless sort of figure, that seems to skulk about behind that silly and conspicuous front design.

There's sister on the stairs!

Well, the Fourth of July is over! The people are all gone, and I am tired out. John thought it might do me good to see a little company, so we just had mother and Nellie and the children down for a week.

Of course I didn't do a thing. Jennie sees to everything now.

But it tired me all the same.   85

John says if I don't pick up faster he shall send me to Weir Mitchell in the fall.

But I don't want to go there at all. I had a friend who was in his hands once, and she says he is just like John and my brother, only more so!

Besides, it is such an undertaking to go so far.

I don't feel as if it was worthwhile to turn my hand over for anything, and I'm getting dreadfully fretful and querulous.

I cry at nothing, and cry most of the time.   90

Of course I don't when John is here, or anybody else, but when I am alone.

And I am alone a good deal just now. John is kept in town very often by serious cases, and Jennie is good and lets me alone when I want her to.

So I walk a little in the garden or down that lovely lane, sit on the porch under the roses, and lie down up here a good deal.

I'm getting really fond of the room in spite of the wallpaper. Perhaps *because* of the wallpaper.

It dwells in my mind so!   95

I lie here on this great immovable bed—it is nailed down, I believe— and follow that pattern about by the hour. It is as good as gymnastics, I assure you. I start, we'll say, at the bottom, down in the corner over there where it has not been touched, and I determine for the thousandth time that I *will* follow that pointless pattern to some sort of a conclusion.

I know a little of the principle of design, and I know this thing was not arranged on any laws of radiation, or alternation, or repetition, or symmetry, or anything else that I ever heard of.

It is repeated, of course, by the breadths, but not otherwise.

Looked at in one way each breadth stands alone, the bloated curves and flourishes—a kind of "debased Romanesque" with *delirium tremens*—go waddling up and down in isolated columns of fatuity.

But, on the other hand, they connect diagonally, and the sprawling out-   100 lines run off in great slanting waves of optic horror, like a lot of wallowing seaweeds in full chase.

The whole thing goes horizontally, too, at least it seems so, and I ex- haust myself in trying to distinguish the order of its going in that direction.

They have used a horizontal breadth for a frieze, and that adds wonder- fully to the confusion.

There is one end of the room where it is almost intact, and there, when the crosslights fade and the low sun shines directly upon it, I can almost fancy radiation after all,—the interminable grotesques seem to form around a common centre and rush off in headlong plunges of equal distraction.

It makes me tired to follow it. I will take a nap, I guess.

I don't know why I should write this.

I don't want to.

I don't feel able.

And I know John would think it absurd. But I *must* say what I feel and think in some way—it is such a relief!

But the effort is getting to be greater than the relief.

Half the time now I am awfully lazy, and lie down ever so much.

John says I mustn't lose my strength, and has me take cod liver oil and lots of tonics and things, to say nothing of ale and wine and rare meat.

Dear John! He loves me very dearly, and hates to have me sick. I tried to have a real earnest reasonable talk with him the other day, and tell him how I wish he would let me go and make a visit to Cousin Henry and Julia.

But he said I wasn't able to go, nor able to stand it after I got there; and I did not make out a very good case for myself, for I was crying before I had finished.

It is getting to be a great effort for me to think straight. Just this nervous weakness I suppose.

And dear John gathered me up in his arms, and just carried me upstairs and laid me on the bed, and sat by me and read to me till it tired my head.

He said I was his darling and his comfort and all he had, and that I must take care of myself for his sake, and keep well.

He says no one but myself can help me out it, that I must use my will and self-control and not let any silly fancies run away with me.

There's one comfort, the baby is well and happy, and does not have to occupy this nursery with the horrid wallpaper.

If we had not used it, that blessed child would have! What a fortunate escape! Why, I wouldn't have a child of mine, an impressionable little thing, live in such a room for worlds.

I never thought of it before, but it is lucky that John kept me here after all, I can stand it so much easier than a baby, you see.

Of course I never mention it to them any more—I am too wise, but I keep watch of it all the same.

There are things in the wallpaper that nobody knows but me, or ever will.

Behind that outside pattern the dim shapes get clearer every day.

It is always the same shape, only very numerous.

And it is like a woman stooping down and creeping about behind that pattern. I don't like it a bit. I wonder—I begin to think—I wish John would take me away from here!   125

It is so hard to talk with John about my case, because he is so wise, and because he loves me so.

But I tried it last night.

It was moonlight. The moon shines in all around just as the sun does.

I hate to see it sometimes, it creeps so slowly, and always comes in by one window or another.

John was asleep and I hated to waken him, so I kept still and watched   130
the moonlight on that undulating wallpaper till I felt creepy.

The faint figure behind seemed to shake the pattern, just as if she wanted to get out.

I got up softly and went to feel and see if the paper *did* move, and when I came back John was awake.

"What is it, little girl?" he said. "Don't go walking about like that— you'll get cold."

I thought it was a good time to talk, so I told him that I really was not gaining here, and that I wished he would take me away.

"Why, darling!" said he, "our lease will be up in three weeks, and I   135
can't see how to leave before.

"The repairs are not done at home, and I cannot possibly leave town just now. Of course if you were in any danger, I could and would, but you really are better, dear, whether you can see it or not. I am a doctor, dear, and I know. You are gaining flesh and color, your appetite is better, I feel really much easier about you."

"I don't weigh a bit more," said I, "nor as much; and my appetite may be better in the evening when you are here but it is worse in the morning when you are away!"

"Bless her little heart!" said he with a big hug, "she shall be as sick as she pleases! But now let's improve the shining hours by going to sleep, and talk about it in the morning!"

"And you won't go away?" I asked gloomily.

"Why, how can I, dear? It is only three weeks more and then we will   140
take a nice little trip of a few days while Jennie is getting the house ready. Really dear you are better!"

"Better in body perhaps—" I began, and stopped short, for he sat up straight and looked at me with such a stern, reproachful look that I could not say another word.

"My darling," said he, "I beg you, for my sake and for our child's sake, as well as for your own, that you will never for one instant let that idea enter your mind! There is nothing so dangerous, so fascinating, to a temperament like yours. It is a false and foolish fancy. Can you trust me as a physician when I tell you so?"

So of course I said no more on that score, and we went to sleep before long. He thought I was asleep first, but I wasn't, and lay there for hours trying to decide whether that front pattern and the back pattern really did move together or separately.

On a pattern like this, by daylight, there is a lack of sequence, a defiance of law, that is a constant irritant to a normal mind.

The color is hideous enough, and unreliable enough, and infuriating enough, but the pattern is torturing.

You think you have mastered it, but just as you get well underway in following, it turns a back-somersault and there you are. It slaps you in the face, knocks you down, and tramples upon you. It is like a bad dream.

The outside pattern is a florid arabesque, reminding one of a fungus. If you can imagine a toadstool in joints, an interminable string of toadstools, budding and sprouting in endless convolutions—why, that is something like it.

That is, sometimes!

There is one marked peculiarity about this paper, a thing nobody seems to notice but myself, and that is that it changes as the light changes.

When the sun shoots in through the east window—I always watch for that first long, straight ray—it changes so quickly that I never can quite believe it.

That is why I watch it always.

By moonlight—the moon shines in all night when there is a moon—I wouldn't know it was the same paper.

At night in any kind of light, in twilight, candlelight, lamplight, and worst of all by moonlight, it becomes bars! The outside pattern I mean, and the woman behind it is as plain as can be.

I didn't realize for a long time what the thing was that showed behind, that dim sub-pattern, but now I am quite sure it is a woman.

By daylight she is subdued, quiet. I fancy it is the pattern that keeps her so still. It is so puzzling. It keeps me quiet by the hour.

I lie down ever so much now. John says it is good for me, and to sleep all I can.

Indeed he started the habit by making me lie down for an hour after each meal.

It is a very bad habit I am convinced, for you see I don't sleep.

And that cultivates deceit, for I don't tell them I'm awake—O, no!

The fact is I am getting a little afraid of John.

He seems very queer sometimes, and even Jennie has an inexplicable look.

It strikes me occasionally, just as a scientific hypothesis,—that perhaps it is the paper!

I have watched John when he did not know I was looking, and come into the room suddenly on the most innocent excuses, and I've caught him several times *looking at the paper!* And Jennie too. I caught Jennie with her hand on it once.

She didn't know I was in the room, and when I asked her in a quiet, a very quiet voice, with the most restrained manner possible, what she was doing with the paper—she turned around as if she had been caught stealing, and looked quite angry—asked me why I should frighten her so!

Then she said that the paper stained everything it touched, that she   165
had found yellow smooches on all my clothes and John's, and she wished we would be more careful!

Did not that sound innocent? But I know she was studying that pattern, and I am determined that nobody shall find it out but myself!

Life is very much more exciting now than it used to be. You see I have something more to expect, to look forward to, to watch. I really do eat better, and am more quiet than I was.

John is so pleased to see me improve! He laughed a little the other day, and said I seemed to be flourishing in spite of my wallpaper.

I turned it off with a laugh. I had no intention of telling him it was *because* of the wallpaper—he would make fun of me. He might even want to take me away.

I don't want to leave now until I have found it out. There is a week   170
more, and I think that will be enough.

I'm feeling ever so much better! I don't sleep much at night, for it is so interesting to watch developments; but I sleep a good deal in the daytime.

In the daytime it is tiresome and perplexing.

There are always new shoots on the fungus, and new shades of yellow all over it. I cannot keep count of them, though I have tried conscientiously.

It is the strangest yellow, that wallpaper! It makes me think of all the yellow things I ever saw—not beautiful ones like buttercups, but old foul, bad yellow things.

But there is something else about that paper—the smell! I noticed it   175
the moment we came into the room, but with so much air and sun it was not bad. Now we have had a week of fog and rain, and whether the windows are open or not, the smell is here.

It creeps all over the house.

I find it hovering in the dining-room, skulking in the parlor, hiding in the hall, lying in wait for me on the stairs.

It gets into my hair.

Even when I go to ride, if I turn my head suddenly and surprise it— there is that smell!

Such a peculiar odor, too! I have spent hours in tying to analyze it, to   180
find what it smelled like.

It is not bad—at first, and very gentle, but quite the subtlest, most enduring odor I ever met.

In this damp weather it is awful, I wake up in the night and find it hanging over me.

It used to disturb me at first. I thought seriously of burning the house—to reach the smell.

But now I am used to it. The only thing I can think of that it is like is the *color* of the paper! A yellow smell.

There is a very funny mark on this wall, low down, near the mopboard. A streak that runs round the room. It goes behind every piece of furniture, except the bed, a long, straight, even *smooch*, as if it had been rubbed over and over.

I wonder how it was done and who did it, and what they did it for. Round and round and round—round and round and round—it makes me dizzy!

I really have discovered something at last.

Through watching so much at night, when it changes so, I have finally found out.

The front pattern *does* move—and no wonder! The woman behind shakes it!

Sometimes I think there are a great many women behind, and sometimes only one, and she crawls around fast, and her crawling shakes it all over.

Then in the very bright spots she keeps still, and in the very shady spots she just takes hold of the bars and shakes them hard.

And she is all the time trying to climb through. But nobody could climb through that pattern—it strangles so; I think that is why it has so many heads.

They get through, and then the pattern strangles them off and turns them upside down, and makes their eyes white!

If those heads were covered or taken off it would not be half so bad.

I think that woman gets out in the daytime!

And I'll tell you why—privately—I've seen her!

I can see her out of every one of my windows!

It is the same woman, I know, for she is always creeping, and most women do not creep by daylight.

I see her in that long shaded lane, creeping up and down. I see her in those dark grape arbors, creeping all around the garden.

I see her on that long road under the trees, creeping along, and when a carriage comes she hides under the blackberry vines.

I don't blame her a bit. It must be very humiliating to be caught creeping by daylight!

I always lock the door when I creep by daylight. I can't do it at night, for I know John would suspect something at once.

And John is so queer now, that I don't want to irritate him. I wish he would take another room! Besides, I don't want anybody to get that woman out at night but myself.

I often wonder if I could see her out of all the windows at once.

But, turn as fast as I can, I can only see out of one at one time.   205

And though I always see her, she *may* be able to creep faster than I can turn!

I have watched her sometimes away off in the open country, creeping as fast as a cloud shadow in a high wind.

If only that top pattern could be gotten off from the under one! I mean to try it, little by little.

I have found out another funny thing, but I shan't tell it this time! It does not do to trust people too much.

There are only two more days to get this paper off, and I believe John is   210
beginning to notice. I don't like the look in his eyes.

And I heard him ask Jennie a lot of professional questions, about me. She had a very good report to give.

She said I slept a good deal in the daytime.

John knows I don't sleep very well at night, for all I'm so quiet!

He asked me all sorts of questions too, and pretended to be very loving and kind.

As if I couldn't see through him!   215

Still, I don't wonder he acts so, sleeping under this paper for three months.

It only interests me, but I feel sure John and Jennie are secretly affected by it.

Hurrah! This is the last day, but it is enough. John to stay in town over night, and won't be out until this evening.

Jennie wanted to sleep with me—the sly thing! But I told her I should undoubtedly rest better for a night all alone.

That was clever, for really I wasn't alone a bit! As soon as it was moon-   220
light and that poor thing began to crawl and shake the pattern, I got up and ran to help her.

I pulled and she shook, I shook and she pulled, and before morning we had peeled off yards of that paper.

A strip about as high as my head and half around the room.

And then when the sun came and that awful pattern began to laugh at me, I declared I would finish it to-day!

We go away to-morrow, and they are moving all my furniture down again to leave things as they were before.

Jennie looked at the wall in amazement, but I told her merrily that I   225
did it out of pure spite at the vicious thing.

She laughed and said she wouldn't mind doing it herself, but I must not get tired.

How she betrayed herself that time!

But I am here, and no person touches this paper but me,—not *alive!*

She tried to get me out of the room—it was too patent! But I said it was so quiet and empty and clean now that I believed I would lie down again and sleep all I could, and not to wake me even for dinner—I would call when I woke.

So now she is gone, and the servants are gone, and the things are gone, and there is nothing left but that great bedstead nailed down, with the canvas mattress we found on it.

We shall sleep downstairs to-night, and take the boat home to-morrow.

I quite enjoy the room, now it is bare again.

How those children did tear about here!

This bedstead is fairly gnawed!

But I must get to work.

I have locked the door and thrown the key down into the front path.

I don't want to go out, and I don't want to have anybody come in, till John comes.

I want to astonish him.

I've got a rope up here that even Jennie did not find. If that woman does get out, and tries to get away, I can tie her!

But I forgot I could not reach far without anything to stand on!

This bed will *not* move!

I tried to lift and push it until I was lame, and then I got so angry I bit off a little piece at one corner—but it hurt my teeth.

Then I peeled off all the paper I could reach standing on the floor. It sticks horribly and the pattern just enjoys it! All those strangled heads and bulbous eyes and waddling fungus growths just shriek with derision!

I am getting angry enough to do something desperate. To jump out of the window would be admirable exercise, but the bars are too strong even to try.

Besides I wouldn't do it. Of course not. I know well enough that a step like that is improper and might be misconstrued.

I don't like to *look* out of the windows even—there are so many of those creeping women, and they creep so fast.

I wonder if they all come out of that wallpaper as I did?

But I am securely fastened now by my well-hidden rope—you don't get *me* out in the road there!

I suppose I shall have to get back behind the pattern when it comes night, and that is hard!

It is so pleasant to be out in this great room and creep around as I please!

I don't want to go outside. I won't, even if Jennie asks me to.

For outside you have to creep on the ground, and everything is green instead of yellow.

But here I can creep smoothly on the floor, and my shoulder just fits in that long smooch around the wall, so I cannot lose my way.

Why, there's John at the door!
It is no use, young man, you can't open it!   255
How he does call and pound!
Now he's crying for an axe.
It would be a shame to break down that beautiful door!
"John dear!" said I in the gentlest voice, "the key is down by the front
steps, under a plantain leaf!"
That silenced him for a few moments.   260
Then he said—very quietly indeed, "Open the door, my darling!"
"I can't," said I. "The key is down by the front door under a plantain leaf!"
And then I said it again, several times, very gently and slowly, and said
it so often that he had to go and see, and he got it of course, and came in.
He stopped short by the door.
"What is the matter?" he cried. "For God's sake, what are you doing!"
I kept on creeping just the same, but I looked at him over my shoulder.   265
"I've got out at last," said I, "in spite of you and Jane. And I've pulled
off most of the paper, so you can't put me back!"
Now why should that man have fainted? But he did, and right across
my path by the wall, so that I had to creep over him every time!

■ In this story, what is the source of all of our information? Why is our awareness
of this source essential to our understanding of the story?

■ What do we learn about the nature of the wallpaper in the room? Why are
these details important? How does this attention on the wallpaper give us
insight into the psychological state of the narrator? Locate specific instances
where her observations about the wallpaper indicate some change in her state
of mind.

■ How does the narrator present her husband? In what ways are our perceptions
of her husband different from what she tells us?

POETRY

Helane Levine Keating (1948–)

My Last Duke (1993)

                    FERRARA
That's my last Duke painted on the wall,
just the way he would limn himself:

cruel mouth, whip raised in his hand
above the white stallion's flank, even the sun
only a backdrop for his ancient radiant splendor.   5
No, I'll ne'er marry again now he's dead
and not a moment too soon. The final time
his threats rose like angry waves
on a churning sea I was certain
he'd slit my thin throat sooner than hear   10
my pleas for forgiveness. And forgiveness
for what? Pleasure in a rose, a mule, the dew?
Merely my waking happy at the sun's generous
outpouring infuriated him. One day he'd curse
the gardener then poor Frà Pandolf   15
and finally every living man, young or old
who passed near enough to hear my breath
until they turned from him, each downcast
and sorrowful, knowing full well the folly
to which his wayward fears had led.   20
Thank heaven he's dead, his green jealous heart
stopped midstream in its awful beating. This meeting
too is at an end; I thank you for your offer
but must indeed refuse your outstretched hand.
For now each day I sing and smile and blush   25
whene'er I choose and even bronze Neptune
has been returned to the sea, his seahorse freed.

- Who is the speaker in this poem?
- To whom is she speaking? What are they discussing? What is her answer to him?
- Which details here appear in the Browning poem? How does each detail change in this retelling?

William Carlos Williams (1883–1963)

This Is Just to Say (1934)

I have eaten
the plums
that were in
the icebox

and which   5
you were probably
saving
for breakfast

Forgive me
they were delicious   10
so sweet
and so cold

- How does Williams divide the poem? Label the content of each stanza.
- What perspective do we get in this poem?
- What sensations does the poem convey?

Erica-Lynn Gambino

This Is Just to Say (1997)

(*for William Carlos Williams*)

I have just
asked you to
get out of my
apartment

even though   5
you never
thought
I would

Forgive me
you were   10
driving
me insane

- How does this poem ask us to re-read the Williams poem?
- Look at each stanza. How does each compare to the Williams stanzas?
- In what ways can this poem stand on its own?

Elizabeth Bishop (1911–1979)

The Fish (1946)

I caught a tremendous fish
and held him beside the boat
half out of water, with my hook
fast in a corner of his mouth.
He didn't fight.   5
He hadn't fought at all.
He hung a grunting weight,
battered and venerable
and homely. Here and there
his brown skin hung in strips   10
like ancient wall-paper,
and its pattern of darker brown
was like wall-paper:
shapes like full-blown roses
stained and lost through age.   15
He was speckled with barnacles,
fine rosettes of lime,
and infested
with tiny white sea-lice,
and underneath two or three   20
rags of green weed hung down.
While his gills were breathing in
the terrible oxygen
—the frightening gills,
fresh and crisp with blood,   25
that can cut so badly—
I thought of the coarse white flesh
packed in like feathers,
the big bones and the little bones,
the dramatic reds and blacks   30
of his shiny entrails,
and the pink swim-bladder
like a big peony.
I looked into his eyes
which were far larger than mine   35
but shallower, and yellowed,
the irises backed and packed
with tarnished tinfoil
seen through the lenses

of old scratched isinglass.   40
They shifted a little, but not
to return my stare.
—It was more like the tipping
of an object toward the light.
I admired his sullen face,   45
the mechanism of his jaw,
and then I saw
that from his lower lip
—if you could call it a lip—
grim, wet, and weapon-like,   50
hung five old pieces of fish-line,
or four and a wire leader
with the swivel still attached,
with all their five big hooks
grown firmly in his mouth.   55
A green line, frayed at the end
where he broke it, two heavier lines,
and a fine black thread
still crimped from the strain and snap
when it broke and he got away.   60
Like medals with their ribbons
frayed and wavering,
a five-haired beard of wisdom
trailing from his aching jaw.
I stared and stared   65
and victory filled up
the little rented boat,
from the pool of bilge
where oil had spread a rainbow
around the rusted engine   70
to the bailer rusted orange,
the sun-cracked thwarts,
the oarlocks on their strings,
the gunnels—until everything
was rainbow, rainbow, rainbow!   75
And I let the fish go.

■ Look at the language that Bishop uses to describe the fish. Where does this
   language begin to persuade the narrator to release the fish?

■ What is the victory that the narrator describes?

■ How does the "little rented boat" compare to the details we learn about the fish?

Edna St. Vincent Millay (1892–1950)

Childhood Is the Kingdom
Where Nobody Dies (1937)

Childhood is not from birth to a certain age and at a certain age
The child is grown, and puts away childish things.
Childhood is the kingdom where nobody dies.
Nobody that matters, that is. Distant relatives of course
Die, whom one never has seen or has seen for an hour,   5
And they gave one candy in a pink-and-green stripéd bag,
   or a jack-knife,
And went away, and cannot really be said to have lived at all.

And cats die. They lie on the floor and lash their tails,
And their reticent fur is suddenly all in motion
With fleas that one never knew were there,   10
Polished and brown, knowing all there is to know,
Trekking off into the living world.
You fetch a shoe-box, but it's much too small, because she won't
   curl up now:
So you find a bigger box, and bury her in the yard, and weep.
But you do not wake up a month from then, two months   15
A year from then, two years, in the middle of the night
And weep, with your knuckles in your mouth, and say Oh, God! Oh, God!
Childhood is the kingdom where nobody dies that matters,
   —mothers and fathers don't die.

And if you have said, "For heaven's sake, must you always
   be kissing a person?"
Or, "I do wish to gracious you'd stop tapping on the window   20
   with your thimble!"
Tomorrow, or even the day after tomorrow if you're busy having fun,
Is plenty of time to say, "I'm sorry, mother."

To be grown up is to sit at the table with people who have died,
   who neither listen nor speak;
Who do not drink their tea, though they always said
Tea was such a comfort.   25

Run down into the cellar and bring up the last jar of raspberries;
   they are not tempted.
Flatter them, ask them what was it they said exactly

That time, to the bishop, or to the overseer, or to Mrs. Mason;
They are not taken in.
Shout at them, get red in the face, rise,   30
Drag them up out of their chairs by their stiff shoulders and
    shake them and yell at them;
They are not startled, they are not even embarrassed; they slide
    back into their chairs.

Your tea is cold now.
You drink it standing up,
And leave the house.   35

■ The perspective of the child is a particularly rich subject for poetry. How does Millay define the difference between the perspective of the child and of the adult?

■ Compare the images that she uses to illustrate this difference.

Charles Simic (1938–)

Prodigy (1999)

I grew up bent over
a chessboard.

I loved the word *endgame*.

All my cousins looked worried.

It was a small house   5
near a Roman graveyard.
Planes and tanks
shook its windowpanes.

A retired professor of astronomy
taught me how to play.   10

That must have been in 1944.

In the set we were using,
the paint had almost chipped off
the black pieces.

The white King was missing   15
and had to be substituted for.

I'm told but do not believe
that that summer I witnessed
men hung from telephone poles.

I remember my mother   20
blindfolding me a lot.
She had a way of tucking my head
suddenly under her overcoat.

In chess, too, the professor told me,
the masters play bindfolded,   25
the great ones on several boards
at the same time.

■ What is it that the narrator fails to see through his "blindfold"?
■ How do we know that he sees differently now than he did then (in 1944)?
■ Why does the narrator describe the ability of grand masters to play chess blindfolded?

John Donne (1572–1631)

The Good-Morrow (published posthumously, 1633)

I wonder, by my troth, what thou and I
    Did, till we loved? were we not weaned till then?
But sucked on country pleasures, childishly?
    Or snorted we in the Seven Sleepers' den?
'Twas so; but this, all pleasures fancies be.   5
If ever any beauty I did see,
Which I desired, and got, twas but a dream of thee.
    And now good-morrow to our waking souls,
        Which watch not one another out of fear,
For love, all love of other sights controls,   10
        And makes one little room an everywhere.
Let sea-discoverers to new worlds have gone,
Let maps to other, worlds on worlds have shown,
Let us possess one world, each hath one, and is one.
    My face in thine eye, thine in mine appears,   15
        And true plain hearts do in the faces rest;

Where can we find two better hemispheres,
    Without sharp north, without declining west?
Whatever dies was not mixed equally,
If our two loves be one, or, thou and I   20
    Love so alike that none do slacken, none can die.

■ How does the poet use images taken from geography to advance his argument
about the love he shares? How does the image expand from "one little room" to
"worlds"?

■ How does he arrive at the argument that ends the poem: "none can die"?

■ Who is meant to believe this argument?

Adrienne Rich (1953–)

Living in Sin (1955)

She had thought the studio would keep itself,
no dust upon the furniture of love.
Half heresy, to wish the taps less vocal,
the panes relieved of grime. A plate of pears,
a piano with a Persian shawl, a cat   5
stalking the picturesque amusing mouse
had risen at his urging.
Not that at five each separate stair would writhe
under the milkman's tramp; that morning light
so coldly would delineate the scraps   10
of last night's cheese and three sepulchral bottles;
that on the kitchen shelf among the saucers
a pair of beetle-eyes would fix her own—
envoy from some black village in the mouldings...
Meanwhile, he, with a yawn,   15
sounded a dozen notes upon the keyboard,
declared it out of tune, shrugged at the mirror,
rubbed at his beard, went out for cigarettes;
while she, jeered by the minor demons,
pulled back the sheets and made the bed and found   20
a towel to dust the table-top,
and let the coffee-pot boil over on the stove.
By evening she was back in love again,
though not so wholly but throughout the night
she woke sometimes to feel the daylight coming   25
like a relentless milkman up the stairs.

■ Look at each of the descriptions of the appearance of the studio. Which descriptors have negative connotations? To what extent does the progress of the poem erase these negative feelings? Can you find any specific place where a negative is replaced by a positive idea?

W. S. Merwin (1927–)

Separation (1963)

Your absence has gone through me
Like thread through a needle.
Everything I do is stitched with its color.

■ What is surprising about the image that Merwin uses to describe separation?
■ How does this image capture the pain of separation at the same time that it affirms the strength of the love that has been separated?

H. D. (1886–1961)

Helen (1924)

All Greece hates
the still eyes in the white face,
the lustre as of olives
where she stands,
and the white hands.   5

All Greece reviles
the wan face when she smiles,
hating it deeper still
when it grows wan and white,
remembering past enchantments   10
and past ills.

Greece sees unmoved,
God's daughter, born of love,
the beauty of cool feet
and slenderest knees,   15
could love indeed the maid,
only if she were laid,
white ash amid funereal cypresses.

■ Helen is traditionally described as the most beautiful woman of all time. Hers is the "face that launched a thousand ships" to fight the Trojan War. What evidence do we get of that beauty in this poem?

Sylvia Plath (1932–1963)

The Applicant (1962)

First, are you our sort of a person?
Do you wear
A glass eye, false teeth or a crutch,
A brace or a hook,
Rubber breasts or a rubber crotch,   5

Stitches to show something's missing? No, no? Then
How can we give you a thing?
Stop crying.
Open your hand.
Empty? Empty. Here is a hand   10

To fill it and willing
To bring teacups and roll away headaches
And do whatever you tell it.
Will you marry it?
It is guaranteed   15

To thumb shut your eyes at the end
And dissolve of sorrow.
We make new stock from the salt.
I notice you are stark naked.
How about this suit—   20

Black and stiff, but not a bad fit.
Will you marry it?
It is waterproof, shatterproof, proof
Against fire and bombs through the roof.
Believe me, they'll bury you in it.   25

Now your head, excuse me, is empty.
I have the ticket for that.
Come here, sweetie, out of the closet.
Well, what do you think of that?
Naked as paper to start   30

But in twenty-five years she'll be silver,
In fifty, gold.
A living doll, everywhere you look.
It can sew, it can cook,
It can talk, talk, talk.   35

It works, there is nothing wrong with it.
You have a hole, it's a poultice.
You have an eye, it's an image.
My boy, it's your last resort.
Will you marry it, marry it, marry it.   40

- To what does the "applicant" refer?
- How are the questions that she poses unusual ones to ask of any applicant?
  How do they represent the sorts of questions that often are asked about
  marriages and the suitability of partners for one another? How is the phrasing
  of these questions jarring?

Sylvia Plath (1932–1963)

Mirror (1963)

I am silver and exact. I have no preconceptions.
Whatever I see I swallow immediately
Just as it is, unmisted by love or dislike.
I am not cruel, only truthful—
The eye of a little god, four-cornered.   5
Most of the time I meditate on the opposite wall.
It is pink, with speckles. I have looked at it so long
I think it is a part of my heart. But it flickers.
Faces and darkness separate us over and over.

Now I am a lake. A woman bends over me,   10
Searching my reaches for what she really is.
Then she turns to those liars, the candles or the moon.
I see her back, and reflect it faithfully.
She rewards me with tears and an agitation of hands.
I am important to her. She comes and goes.   15
Each morning it is her face that replaces the darkness.
In me she has drowned a young girl, and in me an old woman
Rises toward her day after day, like a terrible fish.

- In this poem the speaker is an inanimate object that takes on personal characteristics. Find specific images that describe what a mirror does but that add feeling or personal characteristics to the otherwise unfeeling operation of the mirror.
- Why has Plath divided the poem into two parts? What distinguishes the first from the second? How is the lake distinct from the "silver and exact" mirror of the first stanza?

Robert Morgan (1944–)

Working in the Rain (2000)

My father loved more than anything to
work outside in wet weather. Beginning
at daylight he'd go out in dripping brush
to mow or pull weeds for hog and chickens.
First his shoulders got damp and the drops from   5
his hat ran down his back. When even his
armpits were soaked he came in to dry out
by the fire, make coffee, read a little.
But if the rain continued he'd soon be
restless, and go out to sharpen tools in   10
the shed or carry wood in from the pile,
then open up a puddle to the drain,
working by steps back into the downpour.
I thought he sought the privacy of rain,
the one time no one was likely to be   15
out and he was left to the intimacy
of drops touching every leaf and tree in
the woods and the easy muttering of
drip and runoff, the shine of pools behind
grass dams. He could not resist the long   20
ritual, the companionship and freedom
of falling weather, or even the cold
drenching, the heavy soak and chill of clothes
and sobbing of fingers and sacrifice
of shoes that earned a baking by the fire   25
and washed fatigue after the wandering
and loneliness in the country of rain.

- What specific images help us understand the character of the narrator's father?
- What access do we have to the father's thoughts and feelings?

DRAMA

William Shakespeare (1564–1616)

William Shakespeare, the most renowned poet in the English language, and arguably in any language, was born in Stratford-upon-Avon, England. Although the exact date of Shakespeare's birth is unknown, it is thought to have been on or around April 23. Shakespearean biography is complicated by the fact that there exists relatively little hard information about the author's life. We know for certain that he married Anne Hathaway in 1582 and that the couple's first child, Susanna, was born in 1583. In 1585, the couple had twins, a daughter, Judith, and a son, Hamnet, who died at the age of eleven in 1596. A man of many talents, Shakespeare was active not only as a playwright and actor but also, as part owner of the Globe Theatre, a businessman. He earned a substantial income through his various activities and was able to purchase a large house and much land in Stratford, where he retired several years before his death on April 23, 1616. Shakespeare wrote lyric and narrative poetry in addition to his verse dramas. His best-known lyric poems are the *Sonnets*, widely regarded as containing some of the finest love poetry in the language. His narrative poems include *Venus and Adonis* and *The Rape of Lucrece*. It is as a playwright, though, that William Shakespeare is best remembered.

Much Ado about Nothing (1598)

CHARACTERS

DON PEDRO, *Prince of Arragon*
DON JOHN, *his bastard brother*
CLAUDIO, *young lord of Florence*
BENEDICK, *young lord of Padua*
LEONATO, *Governer of Messina*
ANTONIO, *brother of Leonato*
BALTHASAR, *servant to Don Pedro*
BORACHIO, *follower of Don John*
CONRADE, *follower of Don John*
DOGBERRY, *a constable*
VERGES, *a headborough*
FRIAR FRANCIS
A SEXTON
A BOY
HERO, *daughter of Leonato*
BEATRICE, *niece of Leonato*

MARGARET, *gentlewoman to Hero*
URSULA, *gentlewoman to Hero*
MESSENGERS, WATCH, *and* ATTENDANTS

ACT I

Scene 1

SCENE: *Before* LEONATO'*s house.*

(Enter LEONATO, HERO, *and* BEATRICE, *with a* MESSENGER.*)*
LEONATO: I learn in this letter that Don Peter of Aragon comes this night
  to Messina.
MESSENGER: He is very near by this. He was not three leagues off when I
  left him.
LEONATO: How many gentlemen have you lost in this action?   5
MESSENGER: But few of any sort, and none of name.
LEONATO: A victory is twice itself when the achiever brings home full num-
  bers. I find here that Don Peter hath bestowed much honor on a young
  Florentine called Claudio.
MESSENGER: Much deserved on his part and equally remembered by Don   10
  Pedro. He hath borne himself beyond the promise of his age, doing, in
  the figure of a lamb, the feats of a lion. He hath indeed better bettered
  expectation than you must expect of me to tell you how.
LEONATO: He hath an uncle here in Messina will be very much glad of it.
MESSENGER: I have already delivered him letters, and there appears much 15
  joy in him, even so much that joy could not show itself modest enough
  without a badge of bitterness.
LEONATO: Did he break out into tears?
MESSENGER: In great measure.
LEONATO: A kind overflow of kindness. There are no faces truer than those 20
  that are so washed. How much better is it to weep at joy than to joy at
  weeping!
BEATRICE: I pray you, is Signior Mountanto returned from the wars or no?
MESSENGER: I know none of that name, lady. There was none such in the
  army of any sort.   25
LEONATO: What is he that you ask for, niece?
HERO: My cousin means Signior Benedick of Padua.
MESSENGER: O, he's returned; and as pleasant as ever he was.
BEATRICE: He set up his bills here in Messina and challenged Cupid at the
  flight, and my uncle's Fool, reading the challenge, subscribed for Cupid, 30
  and challenged him at the bird-bolt. I pray you, how many hath he

killed and eaten in these wars? But how many hath he killed? For
indeed I promised to eat all of his killing.

LEONATO: Faith, niece, you tax Signior Benedick too much, but he'll be
meet with you, I doubt it not.   35

MESSENGER: He hath done good service, lady, in these wars.

BEATRICE: You had musty victual, and he hath holp to eat it. He is a very
valiant trencherman; he hath an excellent stomach.

MESSENGER: And a good soldier too, lady.

BEATRICE: And a good soldier to a lady, but what is he to a lord?   40

MESSENGER: A lord to a lord, a man to a man, stuffed with all honorable
virtues.

BEATRICE: It is so, indeed. He is no less than a stuffed man, but for the stuff-
ing—well, we are all mortal.

LEONATO: You must not, sir, mistake my niece. There is a kind of merry war   45
betwixt Signior Benedick and her. They never meet but there's a skir-
mish of wit between them.

BEATRICE: Alas! he gets nothing by that. In our last conflict four of his
five wits went halting off, and now is the whole man governed with
one, so that if he have wit enough to keep himself warm, let him   50
bear it for a difference between himself and his horse, for it is all
the wealth that he hath left, to be known a reasonable creature.
Who is his companion now? He hath every month a new sworn
brother.

MESSENGER: Is't possible?   55

BEATRICE: Very easily possible. He wears his faith but as the fashion of his
hat; it ever changes with the next block.

MESSENGER: I see, lady, the gentleman is not in your books.

BEATRICE: No. An he were, I would burn my study. But, I pray you, who is
his companion? Is there no young squarer now that will make a voyage   60
with him to the devil?

MESSENGER: He is most in the company of the right noble Claudio.

BEATRICE: O Lord, he will hang upon him like a disease! He is sooner
caught than the pestilence, and the taker runs presently mad. God
help the noble Claudio! If he have caught the Benedick, it will cost   65
him a thousand pound ere he be cured.

MESSENGER: I will hold friends with you, lady.

BEATRICE: Do, good friend.

LEONATO: You will never run mad, niece.

BEATRICE: No, not till a hot January.   70

MESSENGER: Don Pedro is approached.

(*Enter* DON PEDRO, DON JOHN, CLAUDIO, BENEDICK, *and* BALTHASAR.)

DON PEDRO: Good Signior Leonato, you are come to meet your trouble?
The fashion of the world is to avoid cost, and you encounter it.

LEONATO: Never came trouble to my house in the likeness of your Grace, for trouble being gone, comfort should remain, but when you depart from me, sorrow abides and happiness takes his leave.   75

DON PEDRO: You embrace your charge too willingly. I think this is your daughter.

LEONATO: Her mother hath many times told me so.

BENEDICK: Were you in doubt, sir, that you asked her?   80

LEONATO: Signior Benedick, no, for then were you a child.

DON PEDRO: You have it full, Benedick. We may guess by this what you are, being a man. Truly, the lady fathers herself.——Be happy, lady; for you are like an honorable father.

BENEDICK: If Signior Leonato be her father, she would not have his head on her shoulders for all Messina, as like him as she is.   85

BEATRICE: I wonder that you will still be talking, Signior Benedick: nobody marks you.

BENEDICK: What, my dear Lady Disdain! Are you yet living?

BEATRICE: Is it possible disdain should die while she hath such meet food to feed it as Signior Benedick? Courtesy itself must convert to disdain, if you come in her presence.   90

BENEDICK: Then is courtesy a turncoat. But it is certain I am loved of all ladies, only you excepted; and I would I could find in my heart that I had not a hard heart, for truly I love none.   95

BEATRICE: A dear happiness to women. They would else have been troubled with a pernicious suitor. I thank God and my cold blood I am of your humour for that. I had rather hear my dog bark at a crow than a man swear he loves me.

BENEDICK: God keep your Ladyship still in that mind, so some gentleman or other shall 'scape a predestinate scratched face.   100

BEATRICE: Scratching could not make it worse, an 'twere such a face as yours were.

BENEDICK: Well, you are a rare parrot-teacher.

BEATRICE: A bird of my tongue is better than a beast of yours.   105

BENEDICK: I would my horse had the speed of your tongue, and so good a continuer. But keep your way, o' God's name, I have done.

BEATRICE: You always end with a jade's trick. I know you of old.

DON PEDRO: That is the sum of all, Leonato. Signior Claudio and Signior Benedick, my dear friend Leonato hath invited you all. I tell him we shall stay here at the least a month; and he heartily prays some occasion may detain us longer. I dare swear he is no hypocrite, but prays from his heart.   110

LEONATO: If you swear, my lord, you shall not be forsworn.

(*To* DON JOHN.)

Let me bid you welcome, my lord, being reconciled to the Prince your brother, I owe you all duty.   115

DON JOHN: I thank you. I am not of many words, but I thank you.

LEONATO: Please it your grace lead on?

DON PEDRO: Your hand, Leonato. We will go together.

(*Exeunt all except* BENEDICK *and* CLAUDIO.)

CLAUDIO: Benedick, didst thou note the daughter of Signior Leonato?

BENEDICK: I noted her not; but I looked on her.   120

CLAUDIO: Is she not a modest young lady?

BENEDICK: Do you question me, as an honest man should do, for my simple true judgment? Or would you have me speak after my custom, as being a professed tyrant to their sex?

CLAUDIO: No, I pray thee, speak in sober judgment.   125

BENEDICK: Why, i' faith, methinks she's too low for a high praise, too brown for a fair praise and too little for a great praise. Only this commendation I can afford her, that were she other than she is, she were unhandsome, and being no other but as she is, I do not like her.

CLAUDIO: Thou thinkest I am in sport. I pray thee tell me truly how thou   130
likest her.

BENEDICK: Would you buy her that you inquire after her?

CLAUDIO: Can the world buy such a jewel?

BENEDICK: Yea, and a case to put it into. But speak you this with a sad brow? Or do you play the flouting jack, to tell us Cupid is a good hare-   135
finder and Vulcan a rare carpenter? Come, in what key shall a man take you, to go in the song?

CLAUDIO: In mine eye she is the sweetest lady that ever I looked on.

BENEDICK: I can see yet without spectacles and I see no such matter. There's her cousin, an she were not possessed with a fury, exceeds her as much   140
in beauty as the first of May doth the last of December. But I hope you have no intent to turn husband, have you?

CLAUDIO: I would scarce trust myself, though I had sworn the contrary, if Hero would be my wife.

BENEDICK: Is't come to this? In faith, hath not the world one man but he   145
will wear his cap with suspicion? Shall I never see a bachelor of three-score again? Go to, i' faith, an thou wilt needs thrust thy neck into a yoke, wear the print of it and sigh away Sundays. Look Don Pedro is returned to seek you.

(*Re-enter* DON PEDRO.)

DON PEDRO: What secret hath held you here, that you followed not to   150
Leonato's?

BENEDICK: I would your grace would constrain me to tell.

DON PEDRO: I charge thee on thy allegiance.

BENEDICK: You hear, Count Claudio, I can be secret as a dumb man, I would have you think so, but on my allegiance—mark you this, on my   155
allegiance—he is in love. With who? Now that is your Grace's part. Mark how short his answer is: With Hero, Leonato's short daughter.

CLAUDIO: If this were so, so were it uttered.

BENEDICK: Like the old tale, my lord: "It is not so, nor 'twas not so, but, indeed, God forbid it should be so." 160

CLAUDIO: If my passion change not shortly, God forbid it should be otherwise.

DON PEDRO: Amen, if you love her, for the lady is very well worthy.

CLAUDIO: You speak this to fetch me in, my lord.

DON PEDRO: By my troth, I speak my thought.

CLAUDIO: And, in faith, my lord, I spoke mine. 165

BENEDICK: And, by my two faiths and troths, my lord, I spoke mine.

CLAUDIO: That I love her, I feel.

DON PEDRO: That she is worthy, I know.

BENEDICK: That I neither feel how she should be loved nor know how she should be worthy is the opinion that fire cannot melt out of me. I will 170 die in it at the stake.

DON PEDRO: Thou wast ever an obstinate heretic in the despite of beauty.

CLAUDIO: And never could maintain his part but in the force of his will.

BENEDICK: That a woman conceived me, I thank her; that she brought me up, I likewise give her most humble thanks. But that I will have a 175 recheat winded in my forehead or hang my bugle in an invisible baldrick, all women shall pardon me. Because I will not do them the wrong to mistrust any, I will do myself the right to trust none. And the fine is, for the which I may go the finer, I will live a bachelor.

DON PEDRO: I shall see thee, ere I die, look pale with love. 180

BENEDICK: With anger, with sickness, or with hunger, my lord, not with love: prove that ever I lose more blood with love than I will get again with drinking, pick out mine eyes with a ballad-maker's pen and hang me up at the door of a brothel-house for the sign of blind Cupid.

DON PEDRO: Well, if ever thou dost fall from this faith, thou wilt prove a 185 notable argument.

BENEDICK: If I do, hang me in a bottle like a cat and shoot at me; and he that hits me, let him be clapped on the shoulder, and called Adam.

DON PEDRO: Well, as time shall try. In time the savage bull doth bear the yoke.

BENEDICK: The savage bull may, but if ever the sensible Benedick bear it, 190 pluck off the bull's horns and set them in my forehead, and let me be vilely painted, and in such great letters as they write "Here is good horse to hire" let them signify under my sign "Here you may see Benedick the married man."

CLAUDIO: If this should ever happen, thou wouldst be horn-mad. 195

DON PEDRO: Nay, if Cupid have not spent all his quiver in Venice, thou wilt quake for this shortly.

BENEDICK: I look for an earthquake too, then.

DON PEDRO: Well, you temporize with the hours. In the meantime, good Signior Benedick, repair to Leonato's. Commend me to him and tell him 200 I will not fail him at supper; for indeed he hath made great preparation.

BENEDICK: I have almost matter enough in me for such an embassage, and
    so I commit you—
CLAUDIO: To the tuition of God: From my house, if I had it—
DON PEDRO: The sixth of July: Your loving friend, Benedick.   205
BENEDICK: Nay, mock not, mock not. The body of your discourse is some-
    time guarded with fragments, and the guards are but slightly basted on
    neither. Ere you flout old ends any further, examine your conscience.
    And so I leave you.
(*Exit.*)
CLAUDIO: My liege, your highness now may do me good.   210
DON PEDRO: My love is thine to teach. Teach it but how,
    And thou shalt see how apt it is to learn
    Any hard lesson that may do thee good.
CLAUDIO: Hath Leonato any son, my lord?
DON PEDRO: No child but Hero; she's his only heir.   215
    Dost thou affect her, Claudio?
CLAUDIO: O, my lord,
    When you went onward on this ended action,
    I look'd upon her with a soldier's eye,
    That liked, but had a rougher task in hand
    Than to drive liking to the name of love.   220
    But now I am return'd and that war thoughts
    Have left their places vacant, in their rooms
    Come thronging soft and delicate desires,
    All prompting me how fair young Hero is,
    Saying I liked her ere I went to wars.   225
DON PEDRO: Thou wilt be like a lover presently
    And tire the hearer with a book of words.
    If thou dost love fair Hero, cherish it,
    And I will break with her and with her father,
    And thou shalt have her. Was't not to this end   230
    That thou began'st to twist so fine a story?
CLAUDIO: How sweetly you do minister to love,
    That know love's grief by his complexion!
    But lest my liking might too sudden seem,
    I would have salved it with a longer treatise.   235
DON PEDRO: What need the bridge much broader than the flood?
    The fairest grant is the necessity.
    Look, what will serve is fit. 'Tis once, thou lovest,
    And I will fit thee with the remedy.
    I know we shall have revelling tonight.   240
    I will assume thy part in some disguise
    And tell fair Hero I am Claudio,

And in her bosom I'll unclasp my heart
And take her hearing prisoner with the force
And strong encounter of my amorous tale.   245
Then after to her father will I break,
And the conclusion is, she shall be thine.
In practise let us put it presently.
(*Exeunt.*)

Scene 2

SCENE: *A room in Leonato's house.*

(*Enter* LEONATO *and* ANTONIO, *meeting.*)

LEONATO: How now, brother, where is my cousin, your son? Hath he
   provided this music?
ANTONIO: He is very busy about it. But, brother, I can tell you strange news
   that you yet dreamt not of.
LEONATO: Are they good?   5
ANTONIO: As the event stamps them, but they have a good cover; they
   show well outward. The Prince and Count Claudio, walking in a thick-
   pleached alley in mine orchard, were thus much overheard by a man of
   mine: the Prince discovered to Claudio that he loved my niece your
   daughter and meant to acknowledge it this night in a dance, and if he   10
   found her accordant, he meant to take the present time by the top and
   instantly break with you of it.
LEONATO: Hath the fellow any wit that told you this?
ANTONIO: A good sharp fellow. I will send for him, and question him yourself.
LEONATO: No, no, we hold it as a dream till it appear itself. But I will   15
   acquaint my daughter withal, that she may be the better prepared for
   an answer, if peradventure this be true. Go you and tell her of it.
(*Enter Attendants.*)
   Cousins, you know what you have to do.—O, I cry you mercy, friend. Go you
   with me and I will use your skill.—Good cousin, have a care this busy time.
(*Exeunt.*)

Scene 3

SCENE: *The same.*

(*Enter* DON JOHN *and* CONRADE.)

CONRADE: What the goodyear, my lord, why are you thus out of measure sad?
DON JOHN: There is no measure in the occasion that breeds. Therefore the
   sadness is without limit.
CONRADE: You should hear reason.
DON JOHN: And when I have heard it, what blessing brings it?   5

CONRADE: If not a present remedy, at least a patient sufferance.

DON JOHN: I wonder that thou, being, as thou sayest thou art, born under Saturn, goest about to apply a moral medicine to a mortifying mischief. I cannot hide what I am. I must be sad when I have cause, and smile at no man's jests; eat when I have stomach, and wait for no man's leisure; sleep when I am drowsy, and tend on no man's business; laugh when I am merry, and claw no man in his humor.   10

CONRADE: Yea, but you must not make the full show of this till you may do it without controlment. You have of late stood out against your brother, and he hath ta'en you newly into his grace, where it is impossible you should take true root but by the fair weather that you make yourself. It is needful that you frame the season for your own harvest.   15

DON JOHN: I had rather be a canker in a hedge than a rose in his grace, and it better fits my blood to be disdained of all than to fashion a carriage to rob love from any. In this, though I cannot be said to be a flattering honest man, it must not be denied but I am a plain-dealing villain. I am trusted with a muzzle and enfranchised with a clog; therefore I have decreed not to sing in my cage. If I had my mouth, I would bite; if I had my liberty, I would do my liking. In the meantime, let me be that I am and seek not to alter me.   20 ... 25

CONRADE: Can you make no use of your discontent?

DON JOHN: I make all use of it, for I use it only. Who comes here?
(Enter BORACHIO.*)* What news, Borachio?

BORACHIO: I came yonder from a great supper: the Prince your brother is royally entertained by Leonato, and I can give you intelligence of an intended marriage.   30

DON JOHN: Will it serve for any model to build mischief on? What is he for a fool that betroths himself to unquietness?

BORACHIO: Marry, it is your brother's right hand.

DON JOHN: Who, the most exquisite Claudio?   35

BORACHIO: Even he.

DON JOHN: A proper squire. And who, and who? Which way looks he?

BORACHIO: Marry, on Hero, the daughter and heir of Leonato.

DON JOHN: A very forward March chick! How came you to this?

BORACHIO: Being entertained for a perfumer, as I was smoking a musty room, comes me the Prince and Claudio, hand in hand, in sad conference. I whipped me behind the arras, and there heard it agreed upon that the Prince should woo Hero for himself, and having obtained her, give her to Count Claudio.   40

DON JOHN: Come, come, let us thither. This may prove food to my displeasure. That young start-up hath all the glory of my overthrow. If I can cross him any way, I bless myself every way. You are both sure, and will assist me?   45

CONRADE: To the death, my lord.

DON JOHN: Let us to the great supper. Their cheer is the greater that I am
   subdued. Would the cook were o' my mind! Shall we go prove what's to   50
   be done?
BORACHIO: We'll wait upon your Lordship.
(Exeunt.)

ACT II

Scene 1

SCENE: *A hall in* LEONATO's *house.*

(Enter LEONATO, ANTONIO, HERO, BEATRICE, *and others.)*
LEONATO: Was not Count John here at supper?
ANTONIO: I saw him not.
BEATRICE: How tartly that gentleman looks! I never can see him but I am
   heartburned an hour after.
HERO: He is of a very melancholy disposition.   5
BEATRICE: He were an excellent man that were made just in the midway
   between him and Benedick. The one is too like an image and says
   nothing, and the other too like my lady's eldest son, evermore tattling.
LEONATO: Then half Signior Benedick's tongue in Count John's mouth, and
   half Count John's melancholy in Signior Benedick's face—   10
BEATRICE: With a good leg and a good foot, uncle, and money enough in
   his purse, such a man would win any woman in the world, if he could
   get her good-will.
LEONATO: By my troth, niece, thou wilt never get thee a husband, if thou
   be so shrewd of thy tongue.   15
ANTONIO: In faith, she's too curst.
BEATRICE: Too curst is more than curst. I shall lessen God's sending that
   way, for it is said "God sends a curst cow short horns," but to a cow too
   curst he sends none.
LEONATO: So, by being too curst, God will send you no horns.   20
BEATRICE: Just, if he send me no husband, for the which blessing I am at
   him upon my knees every morning and evening. Lord, I could not
   endure a husband with a beard on his face. I had rather lie in the woolen!
LEONATO: You may light on a husband that hath no beard.
BEATRICE: What should I do with him? Dress him in my apparel and make   25
   him my waiting gentlewoman? He that hath a beard is more than a
   youth, and he that hath no beard is less than a man; and he that is
   more than a youth is not for me, and he that is less than a man, I am
   not for him. Therefore, I will even take sixpence in earnest of the bear-
   herd, and lead his apes into hell.   30

LEONATO: Well then, go you into hell?

BEATRICE: No, but to the gate; and there will the devil meet me like an old cuckold with horns on his head, and say "Get you to heaven, Beatrice, get you to heaven; here's no place for you maids." So deliver I up my apes and away to Saint Peter for the heavens, he shows me where the bachelors sit, and there live we as merry as the day is long.   35

ANTONIO (*To* HERO.): Well, niece, I trust you will be ruled by your father.

BEATRICE: Yes, faith, it is my cousin's duty to make curtsy and say "Father, as it please you." But yet for all that, cousin, let him be a handsome fellow, or else make another curtsy and say "Father, as it please me."   40

LEONATO: Well, niece, I hope to see you one day fitted with a husband.

BEATRICE: Not till God make men of some other metal than earth. Would it not grieve a woman to be overmastered with a pierce of valiant dust? To make an account of her life to a clod of wayward marl? No, uncle, I'll none. Adam's sons are my brethren, and, truly I hold it a sin to match in my kindred.   45

LEONATO: Daughter, remember what I told you. If the Prince do solicit you in that kind, you know your answer.

BEATRICE: The fault will be in the music, cousin, if you be not wooed in good time. If the Prince be too important, tell him there is measure in everything, and so dance out the answer. For hear me, Hero, wooing, wedding, and repenting is as a Scotch jig, a measure, and a cinquepace. The first suit is hot and hasty, like a Scotch jig, and full as fantastical; the wedding, mannerly modest as a measure, full of state and ancientry; and then comes repentance, and with his bad legs falls into the cinquepace faster and faster till he sink into his grave.   50   55

LEONATO: Cousin, you apprehend passing shrewdly.

BEATRICE: I have a good eye, uncle; I can see a church by daylight.

LEONATO: The revellers are entering, brother: make good room.
(*All put on their masks.*)

(*Enter* DON PEDRO, CLAUDIO, BENEDICK, BALTHASAR, DON JOHN, BORACHIO, MARGARET, URSULA *and others, masked.*)

DON PEDRO: Lady, will you walk a bout with your friend?   60

HERO: So you walk softly, and look sweetly, and say nothing, I am yours for the walk especially when I walk away.

DON PEDRO: With me in your company?

HERO: I may say so when I please.

DON PEDRO: And when please you to say so?   65

HERO: When I like your favor, for God defend the lute should be like the case.

DON PEDRO: My visor is Philemon's roof; within the house is Jove.

HERO: Why, then, your visor should be thatched.

DON PEDRO: Speak low if you speak love.
(*Drawing her aside.*)

BALTHASAR: Well, I would you did like me.   70

MARGARET: So would not I, for your own sake, for I have many ill
    qualities.

BALTHASAR: Which is one?

MARGARET: I say my prayers aloud.

BALTHASAR: I love you the better; the hearers may cry, "Amen."   75

MARGARET: God match me with a good dancer!

BALTHASAR: Amen.

MARGARET: And God keep him out of my sight when the dance is done.
    Answer, clerk.

BALTHASAR: No more words. The clerk is answered.   80

URSULA: I know you well enough. You are Signior Antonio.

ANTONIO: At a word, I am not.

URSULA: I know you by the waggling of your head.

ANTONIO: To tell you true, I counterfeit him.

URSULA: You could never do him so ill-well unless you were the very man.   85
    Here's his dry hand up and down. You are he, you are he.

ANTONIO: At a word, I am not.

URSULA: Come, come, do you think I do not know you by your excellent
    wit? Can virtue hide itself? Go to, mum, you are he. Graces will appear,
    and there's an end.   90

BEATRICE: Will you not tell me who told you so?

BENEDICK: No, you shall pardon me.

BEATRICE: Nor will you not tell me who you are?

BENEDICK: Not now.

BEATRICE: That I was disdainful, and that I had my good wit out of *The*   95
    Hundred Merry Tales! Well, this was Signior Benedick that said so.

BENEDICK: What's he?

BEATRICE: I am sure you know him well enough.

BENEDICK: Not I, believe me.

BEATRICE: Did he never make you laugh?   100

BENEDICK: I pray you, what is he?

BEATRICE: Why, he is the Prince's jester: a very dull fool; only his gift
    is in devising impossible slanders. None but libertines delight in him,
    and the commendation is not in his wit, but in his villany, for he
    both pleases men and angers them, and then they laugh at him and   105
    beat him. I am sure he is in the fleet. I would he had boarded me.

BENEDICK: When I know the gentleman, I'll tell him what you say.

BEATRICE: Do, do. He'll but break a comparison or two on me, which, per-
    adventure not marked or not laughed at, strikes him into melancholy,
    and then there's a partridge wing saved, for the fool will eat no supper   110
    that night. (*Music.*) We must follow the leaders.

BENEDICK: In every good thing.

BEATRICE: Nay, if they lead to any ill, I will leave them at the next turning.
(*Dance. Then exeunt all except* DON JOHN, BORACHIO, *and* CLAUDIO.)
DON JOHN: Sure my brother is amorous on Hero, and hath withdrawn her
    father to break with him about it. The ladies follow her and but one   11
    visor remains.
BORACHIO: And that is Claudio. I know him by his bearing.
DON JOHN: Are not you Signior Benedick?
CLAUDIO: You know me well. I am he.
DON JOHN: Signior, you are very near my brother in his love. He is en-   12
    amoured on Hero. I pray you, dissuade him from her. She is no equal for
    his birth. You may do the part of an honest man in it.
CLAUDIO: How know you he loves her?
DON JOHN: I heard him swear his affection.
BORACHIO: So did I too, and he swore he would marry her tonight.   12
DON JOHN: Come, let us to the banquet.
(*Exeunt* DON JOHN *and* BORACHIO.)
CLAUDIO: Thus answer I in the name of Benedick,
    But hear these ill news with the ears of Claudio.
    'Tis certain so, the Prince wooes for himself.
    Friendship is constant in all other things   13
    Save in the office and affairs of love.
    Therefore all hearts in love use their own tongues.
    Let every eye negotiate for itself
    And trust no agent; for beauty is a witch
    Against whose charms faith melteth into blood.   13
    This is an accident of hourly proof,
    Which I mistrusted not. Farewell therefore, Hero!
(*Re-enter* BENEDICK.)
BENEDICK: Count Claudio?
CLAUDIO: Yea, the same.
BENEDICK: Come, will you go with me?   14
CLAUDIO: Whither?
BENEDICK: Even to the next willow, about your own business, county. What
    fashion will you wear the garland of? About your neck, like an usurer's
    chain? Or under your arm like a lieutenant's scarf? You must wear it
    one way, for the Prince hath got your Hero.   14
CLAUDIO: I wish him joy of her.
BENEDICK: Why, that's spoken like an honest drover: so they sell bullocks.
    But did you think the Prince would have served you thus?
CLAUDIO: I pray you, leave me.
BENEDICK: Ho, now you strike like the blind man. 'Twas the boy that stole   15
    your meat, and you'll beat the post.
CLAUDIO: If it will not be, I'll leave you.
(*Exit.*)

BENEDICK: Alas, poor hurt fowl, now will he creep into sedges. But that my
Lady Beatrice should know me, and not know me! The Prince's fool!
Ha, it may be I go under that title because I am merry. Yea, but so I am   155
apt to do myself wrong. I am not so reputed! It is the base, though bitter, disposition of Beatrice that puts the world into her person and so
gives me out. Well, I'll be revenged as I may.

(Re-enter DON PEDRO.*)*

DON PEDRO: Now, signior, where's the Count? Did you see him?

BENEDICK: Troth, my lord, I have played the part of Lady Fame. I found him   160
here as melancholy as a lodge in a warren. I told him, and I think I told
him true, that your Grace had got the good will of this young lady, and I
offered him my company to a willow tree, either to make him a garland,
as being forsaken, or to bind him up a rod, as being worthy to be whipped.

DON PEDRO: To be whipped? What's his fault?   165

BENEDICK: The flat transgression of a schoolboy who, being overjoyed with
finding a bird's nest, shows it his companion, and he steals it.

DON PEDRO: Wilt thou make a trust a transgression? The transgression is in
the stealer.

BENEDICK: Yet it had not been amiss the rod had been made, and the gar-   170
land too, for the garland he might have worn himself, and the rod he
might have bestowed on you, who, as I take it, have stolen his bird's nest.

DON PEDRO: I will but teach them to sing and restore them to the owner.

BENEDICK: If their singing answer your saying, by my faith, you say honestly.

DON PEDRO: The Lady Beatrice hath a quarrel to you. The gentleman that   175
danced with her told her she is much wronged by you.

BENEDICK: O, she misused me past the endurance of a block! An oak but
with one green leaf on it would have answered her. My very visor
began to assume life and scold with her. She told me, not thinking I
had been myself, that I was the Prince's jester, that I was duller than a   180
great thaw, huddling jest upon jest with such impossible conveyance
upon me that I stood like a man at a mark, with a whole army shooting
at me. She speaks poniards, and every word stabs. If her breath were as
terrible as her terminations, there were no living near her; she would
infect to the North Star. I would not marry her though she were en-   185
dowed with all that Adam bad left him before he transgressed. She
would have made Hercules have turned spit, yea, and have cleft his
club to make the fire, too. Come, talk not of her. You shall find her the
infernal Ate in good apparel. I would to God some scholar would conjure her, for certainly, while she is here, a man may live as quiet in hell   190
as in a sanctuary, and people sin upon purpose, because they would go
thither. So, indeed, all disquiet, horror, and perturbation follows her.

DON PEDRO: Look, here she comes.

(Enter CLAUDIO, BEATRICE, HERO, *and* LEONATO.*)*

BENEDICK: Will your Grace command me any service to the world's end? I will

go on the slightest errand now to the Antipodes that you can devise to   19⁵
send me on. I will fetch you a toothpicker now from the furthest inch of
Asia, bring you the length of Prester John's foot, fetch you a hair off the
great Cham's beard, do you any embassage to the Pigmies, rather than hold
three words' conference with this harpy. You have no employment for me?

DON PEDRO: None, but to desire your good company.   200

BENEDICK: O God, sir, here's a dish I love not! I cannot endure my Lady
Tongue.

(*Exit.*)

DON PEDRO: Come, lady, come, you have lost the heart of Signior Benedick.

BEATRICE: Indeed, my lord, he lent it me awhile, and I gave him use for it,
a double heart for his single one. Marry, once before he won it of me   20⁵
with false dice. Therefore your Grace may well say I have lost it.

DON PEDRO: You have put him down, lady, you have put him down.

BEATRICE: So I would not he should do me, my lord, lest I should prove the
mother of fools. I have brought Count Claudio, whom you sent me to
seek.   21⁰

DON PEDRO: Why, how now, count, wherefore are you sad?

CLAUDIO: Not sad, my lord.

DON PEDRO: How then, sick?

CLAUDIO: Neither, my lord.

BEATRICE: The Count is neither sad, nor sick, nor merry, nor well; but civil   21⁵
count, civil as an orange, and something of that jealous complexion.

DON PEDRO: I' faith, lady, I think your blazon to be true, though, I'll be
sworn, if he be so, his conceit is false.—Here, Claudio, I have wooed in
thy name, and fair Hero is won. I have broke with her father and his
goodwill obtained. Name the day of marriage, and God give thee joy.   22⁰

LEONATO: Count, take of me my daughter, and with her my fortunes. His
Grace hath made the match, and an grace say "Amen" to it.

BEATRICE: Speak, count, 'tis your cue.

CLAUDIO: Silence is the perfectest herald of joy. I were but little happy if I
could say how much.—Lady, as you are mine, I am yours. I give away   22⁵
myself for you and dote upon the exchange.

BEATRICE: Speak, cousin; or, if you cannot, stop his mouth with a kiss and
let not him speak neither.

DON PEDRO: In faith, lady, you have a merry heart.

BEATRICE: Yea, my lord. I thank it, poor fool, it keeps on the windy side of   23⁰
care. My cousin tells him in his ear that he is in her heart.

CLAUDIO: And so she doth, cousin.

BEATRICE: Good Lord for alliance! Thus goes every one to the world but I,
and I am sunburnt. I may sit in a corner and cry "Heigh-ho for a
husband!"   23⁵

DON PEDRO: Lady Beatrice, I will get you one.

BEATRICE: I would rather have one of your father's getting. Hath your
Grace ne'er a brother like you? Your father got excellent husbands, if a
maid could come by them.

DON PEDRO: Will you have me, lady?   240

BEATRICE: No, my lord, unless I might have another for working days? Your
Grace is too costly to wear every day. But I beseech your Grace pardon
me. I was born to speak all mirth and no matter.

DON PEDRO: Your silence most offends me, and to be merry best becomes
you, for, out o' question you were born in a merry hour.   245

BEATRICE: No, sure, my lord, my mother cried, but then there was a star
danced, and under that was I born.—Cousins, God give you joy!

LEONATO: Niece, will you look to those things I told you of?

BEATRICE: I cry you mercy, uncle.—By your Grace's pardon.
(*Exit.*)

DON PEDRO: By my troth, a pleasant-spirited lady.   250

LEONATO: There's little of the melancholy element in her, my lord. She is
never sad but when she sleeps, and not ever sad then, for I have heard
my daughter say she hath often dreamt of unhappiness and waked herself with laughing.

DON PEDRO: She cannot endure to hear tell of a husband.   255

LEONATO: O, by no means. She mocks all her wooers out of suit.

DON PEDRO: She were an excellent wife for Benedict.

LEONATO: O Lord, my lord, if they were but a week married, they would
talk themselves mad.

DON PEDRO: County Claudio, when mean you to go to church?   260

CLAUDIO: Tomorrow, my lord. Time goes on crutches till love have all his
rites.

LEONATO: Not till Monday, my dear son, which is hence a just sevennight,
and a time too brief, too, to have all things answer my mind.

DON PEDRO: Come, you shake the head at so long a breathing, but, I   265
warrant thee, Claudio, the time shall not go dully by us. I will in the
interim undertake one of Hercules' labors, which is, to bring Signior
Benedick and the Lady Beatrice into a mountain of affection, th' one
with th' other. I would fain have it a match, and I doubt not but to
fashion it, if you three will but minister such assistance as I shall give   270
you direction.

LEONATO: My lord, I am for you, though it cost me ten nights' watchings.

CLAUDIO: And I, my lord.

DON PEDRO: And you too, gentle Hero?

HERO: I will do any modest office, my lord, to help my cousin to a good husband.   275

DON PEDRO: And Benedick is not the unhopefullest husband that I know.
Thus far can I praise him: he is of a noble strain, of approved valour,
and confirmed honesty. I will teach you how to humor your cousin that

she shall fall in love with Benedick.—And I, with your two helps, will so practise on Benedick that, in despite of his quick wit and his queasy stomach, he shall fall in love with Beatrice. If we can do this, Cupid is no longer an archer; his glory shall be ours, for we are the only love gods. Go in with me, and I will tell you my drift. 280

(*Exeunt.*)

Scene 2

SCENE: *The same.*

(*Enter* DON JOHN *and* BORACHIO.)

DON JOHN: It is so. The Count Claudio shall marry the daughter of Leonato.

BORACHIO: Yea, my lord, but I can cross it.

DON JOHN: Any bar, any cross, any impediment will be med'cinable to me. I am sick in displeasure to him, and whatsoever comes athwart his affection ranges evenly with mine. How canst thou cross this marriage? 5

BORACHIO: Not honestly, my lord, but so covertly that no dishonesty shall appear in me.

DON JOHN: Show me briefly how.

BORACHIO: I think I told your Lordship a year since, how much I am in the favor of Margaret, the waiting gentlewoman to Hero. 10

DON JOHN: I remember.

BORACHIO: I can, at any unseasonable instant of the night, appoint her to look out at her lady's chamber window.

DON JOHN: What life is in that to be the death of this marriage?

BORACHIO: The poison of that lies in you to temper. Go you to the Prince 15 your brother; spare not to tell him that he hath wronged his honor in marrying the renowned Claudio, whose estimation do you mightily hold up, to a contaminated stale, such a one as Hero.

DON JOHN: What proof shall I make of that?

BORACHIO: Proof enough to misuse the Prince, to vex Claudio, to undo 20 Hero, and kill Leonato. Look you for any other issue?

DON JOHN: Only to despite them I will endeavour any thing.

BORACHIO: Go then; find me a meet hour to draw Don Pedro and the Count Claudio alone. Tell them that you know that Hero loves me; intend a kind of zeal both to the Prince and Claudio, as in love of your 25 brother's honor, who hath made this match, and his friend's reputation, who is thus like to be cozened with the semblance of a maid, that you have discovered thus. They will scarcely believe this without trial. Offer them instances, which shall bear no less likelihood than to see me at her chamber window, hear me call Margaret "Hero," hear Margaret 30 term me "Claudio," and bring them to see this the very night before the intended wedding, for in the meantime I will so fashion the matter that

Hero shall be absent, and there shall appear such seeming truth of
Hero's disloyalty that jealousy shall be called assurance and all the prep-
aration overthrown.   35

DON JOHN: Grow this to what adverse issue it can, I will put it in practise.
Be cunning in the working this, and thy fee is a thousand ducats.

BORACHIO: Be you constant in the accusation, and my cunning shall not
shame me.

DON JOHN: I will presently go learn their day of marriage.   40

(*Exeunt.*)

Scene 3

SCENE: LEONATO'S *orchard.*

(*Enter* BENEDICK.)

BENEDICK: Boy!

(*Enter* BOY.)

BOY: Signior?

BENEDICK: In my chamber window lies a book. Bring it hither to me in the
orchard.

BOY: I am here already, sir.   5

BENEDICK: I know that; but I would have thee hence and here again. (*Exit*
BOY.) I do much wonder that one man, seeing how much another man
is a fool when he dedicates his behaviors to love, will, after he hath
laughed at such shallow follies in others, become the argument of his
own scorn by falling in love—and such a man is Claudio. I have known   10
when there was no music with him but the drum and the fife, and now
had he rather hear the tabor and the pipe; I have known when he would
have walked ten mile a-foot to see a good armour, and now will he lie
ten nights awake carving the fashion of a new doublet. He was wont to
speak plain and to the purpose, like an honest man and a soldier; and   15
now is he turned orthography; his words are a very fantastical banquet,
just so many strange dishes. May I be so converted and see with these
eyes? I cannot tell; I think not. I will not be sworn but love may transform me to an oyster, but I'll take my oath on it, till he have made an
oyster of me, he shall never make me such a fool. One woman is fair, yet   20
I am well; another is wise, yet I am well; another virtuous, yet I am well;
but till all graces be in one woman, one woman shall not come in my
grace. Rich she shall be, that's certain; wise, or I'll none; virtuous, or I'll
never cheapen her; fair, or I'll never look on her; mild, or come not
near me; noble, or not I for an angel; of good discourse, an excellent   25
musician, and her hair shall be of what colour it please God. Ha! The
Prince and Monsieur Love! I will hide me in the arbor.

(*Withdraws.*)

(Enter DON PEDRO, CLAUDIO, *and* LEONATO.*)*

DON PEDRO: Come, shall we hear this music?

CLAUDIO: Yea, my good lord. How still the evening is,
  As hushed on purpose to grace harmony! 30

DON PEDRO: See you where Benedick hath hid himself?

CLAUDIO: O, very well, my lord. The music ended,
  We'll fit the kid-fox with a pennyworth.

(Enter BALTHASAR *with Music.)*

DON PEDRO: Come, Balthasar, we'll hear that song again.

BALTHASAR: O, good my lord, tax not so bad a voice 35
  To slander music any more than once.

DON PEDRO: It is the witness still of excellency
  To put a strange face on his own perfection.
  I pray thee, sing, and let me woo no more.

BALTHASAR: Because you talk of wooing, I will sing, 40
  Since many a wooer doth commence his suit
  To her he thinks not worthy, yet he woos,
  Yet will he swear he loves.

DON PEDRO: Now, pray thee, come;
  Or, if thou wilt hold longer argument,
  Do it in notes. 45

BALTHASAR: Note this before my notes:
  There's not a note of mine that's worth the noting.

DON PEDRO: Why, these are very crotchets that he speaks!
  Note notes, forsooth, and noting.

(Air.)

BENEDICK: Now, divine air! Now is his soul ravished! Is it not strange that
  sheeps' guts should hale souls out of men's bodies? Well, a horn for my 50
  money, when all's done.

(The Song.)

BALTHASAR: Sigh no more, ladies, sigh no more,
           Men were deceivers ever,
           One foot in sea and one on shore,
           To one thing constant never: 55
           Then sigh not so, but let them go,
           And be you blithe and bonny,
           Converting all your sounds of woe
           Into Hey nonny, nonny.

           Sing no more ditties, sing no mo, 60
           Of dumps so dull and heavy.
           The fraud of men was ever so,
           Since summer first was leavy.
           Then sigh not so, but let them go,

And be you blithe and bonny,   65
Converting all sounds of woe
Into Hey, nonny nonny.

DON PEDRO: By my troth, a good song.

BALTHASAR: And an ill singer, my lord.

DON PEDRO: Ha, no, no, faith, thou sing'st well enough for a shift.   70

BENEDICK: An he had been a dog that should have howled thus, they would
have hanged him. And I pray God his bad voice bode no mischief. I
had as lief have heard the night raven, come what plague could have
come after it.

DON PEDRO: Yea, marry, dost thou hear, Balthasar? I pray thee get us some   75
excellent music, for tomorrow night we would have it at the Lady
Hero's chamberwindow.

BALTHASAR: The best I can, my lord.

DON PEDRO: Do so. Farewell.

(*Exit* BALTHASAR.)

Come hither, Leonato. What was it you told me of today, that your niece   80
Beatrice was in love with Signior Benedick?

CLAUDIO: O, ay. Stalk on, stalk on; the fowl sits.—I did never think that
lady would have loved any man.

LEONATO: No, nor I neither; but most wonderful that she should so dote on
Signior Benedick, whom she hath in all outward behaviors seemed ever   85
to abhor.

BENEDICK: Is't possible? Sits the wind in that corner?

LEONATO: By my troth, my lord, I cannot tell what to think of it but
that she loves him with an enraged affection, it is past the infinite
of thought.   90

DON PEDRO: May be she doth but counterfeit.

CLAUDIO: Faith, like enough.

LEONATO: O God! Counterfeit? There was never counterfeit of passion
came so near the life of passion as she discovers it.

DON PEDRO: Why, what effects of passion shows she?   95

CLAUDIO: Bait the hook well; this fish will bite.

LEONATO: What effects, my lord? She will sit you—you heard my daughter
tell you how.

CLAUDIO: She did indeed.

DON PEDRO: How, how pray you? You amaze me. I would have I thought   100
her spirit had been invincible against all assaults of affection.

LEONATO: I would have sworn it had, my lord, especially against Benedick.

BENEDICK: I should think this a gull but that the white-bearded fellow
speaks it. Knavery cannot, sure, hide himself in such reverence.

CLAUDIO: He hath ta'en th' infection. Hold it up.   105

DON PEDRO: Hath she made her affection known to Benedick?

LEONATO: No, and swears she never will. That's her torment.

CLAUDIO: 'Tis true, indeed, so your daughter says. "Shall I," says she, "that have so oft encountered him with scorn, write to him that I love him?"

LEONATO: This says she now when she is beginning to write to him, for she'll be up twenty times a night, and there will she sit in her smock till she have writ a sheet of paper. My daughter tells us all. 110

CLAUDIO: Now you talk of a sheet of paper, I remember a pretty jest your daughter told us of.

LEONATO: O, when she had writ it and was reading it over, she found "Benedick" and "Beatrice" between the sheet? 115

CLAUDIO: That.

LEONATO: O, she tore the letter into a thousand halfpence, railed at herself that she should be so immodest to write to one that she knew would flout her. "I measure him," says she, "by my own spirit, for I should flout him, if he writ to me, yea, though I love him, I should." 120

CLAUDIO: Then down upon her knees she falls, weeps, sobs, beats her heart, tears her hair, prays, curses: "O sweet Benedick, God give me patience!"

LEONATO: She doth indeed, my daughter says so, and the ecstasy hath so much overborne her that my daughter is sometime afeared she will do a desperate outrage to herself. It is very true. 125

DON PEDRO: It were good that Benedick knew of it by some other, if she will not discover it.

CLAUDIO: To what end? He would make but a sport of it and torment the poor lady worse. 130

DON PEDRO: An he should, it were an alms to hang him. She's an excellent sweet lady, and, out of all suspicion, she is virtuous.

CLAUDIO: And she is exceeding wise.

DON PEDRO: In everything but in loving Benedick. 135

LEONATO: O, my lord, wisdom and blood combating in so tender a body, we have ten proofs to one that blood hath the victory. I am sorry for her, as I have just cause, being her uncle and her guardian.

DON PEDRO: I would she had bestowed this dotage on me. I would have daffed all other respects and made her half myself. I pray you, tell Benedick of it, and hear what he will say. 140

LEONATO: Were it good, think you?

CLAUDIO: Hero thinks surely she will die, for she says she will die, if he love her not, and she will die ere she make her love known, and she will die if he woo her, rather than she will bate one breath of her accustomed crossness. 145

DON PEDRO: She doth well. If she should make tender of her love, 'tis very possible he'll scorn it, for the man, as you know all, hath a contemptible spirit.

CLAUDIO: He is a very proper man. 150

DON PEDRO: He hath indeed a good outward happiness.

CLAUDIO: Before God, and in my mind, very wise.

DON PEDRO: He doth indeed show some sparks that are like wit.

CLAUDIO: And I take him to be valiant.

DON PEDRO: As Hector, I assure you, and in the managing of quarrels you   155
may say he is wise, for either he avoids them with great discretion, or
undertakes them with a most Christianlike fear.

LEONATO: If he do fear God, he must necessarily keep peace. If he break the
peace, he ought to enter into a quarrel with fear and trembling.

DON PEDRO: And so will he do, for the man doth fear God, howsoever   160
it seems not in him by some large jests he will make. Well, I am
sorry for your niece. Shall we go seek Benedick and tell him of her
love?

CLAUDIO: Never tell him, my lord, let her wear it out with good counsel.

LEONATO: Nay, that's impossible; she may wear her heart out first.   165

DON PEDRO: Well, we will hear further of it by your daughter. Let it cool
the while. I love Benedick well, and I could wish he would modestly
examine himself to see how much he is unworthy so good a lady.

LEONATO: My lord, will you walk? Dinner is ready.

CLAUDIO: If he do not dote on her upon this, I will never trust my expectation.   170

DON PEDRO: Let there be the same net spread for her, and that must your
daughter and her gentlewomen carry. The sport will be when they hold
one an opinion of another's dotage, and no such matter. That's the
scene that I would see, which will be merely a dumb show. Let us send
her to call him in to dinner.   175

(*Exeunt* DON PEDRO, CLAUDIO, *and* LEONATO.)

BENEDICK (*Coming forward.*): This can be no trick. The conference was
sadly borne; they have the truth of this from Hero; they seem to pity
the lady. It seems her affections have their full bent. Love me? Why, it
must be requited! I hear how I am censured. They say I will bear myself
proudly if I perceive the love come from her. They say too that she will   180
rather die than give any sign of affection. I did never think to marry. I
must not seem proud. Happy are they that hear their detractions and
can put them to mending. They say the lady is fair; 'tis a truth, I can
bear them witness. And virtuous; 'tis so, I cannot reprove it. And wise,
but for loving me; by my troth, it is no addition to her wit, nor no   185
great argument of her folly, for I will be horribly in love with her! I
may chance have some odd quirks and remnants of wit broken on me
because I have railed so long against marriage, but doth not the appetite
alter? A man loves the meat in his youth that he cannot endure in his
age. Shall quips and sentences and these paper bullets of the brain awe   190
a man from the career of his humour? No! The world must be peopled.
When I said I would die a bachelor, I did not think I should live till I

were married. Here comes Beatrice. By this day, she's a fair lady. I do
spy some marks of love in her.

(*Enter* BEATRICE.)

BEATRICE: Against my will, I am sent to bid you come in to dinner. 195

BENEDICK: Fair Beatrice, I thank you for your pains.

BEATRICE: I took no more pains for those thanks than you take pains to
thank me. If it had been painful, I would not have come.

BENEDICK: You take pleasure then in the message?

BEATRICE: Yea, just so much as you may take upon a knife's point and 200
choke a daw withal. You have no stomach, signior. Fare you well.

(*Exit.*)

BENEDICK: Ha! "Against my will I am sent to bid you come in to dinner."
There's a double meaning in that. "I took no more pains for those thanks
than you took pains to thank me." That's as much as to say "Any pains
that I take for you is as easy as thanks." If I do not take pity of her, I am 205
a villain; if I do not love her, I am a Jew. I will go get her picture.

(*Exit.*)

ACT III

Scene 1

SCENE: LEONATO's *garden.*

(*Enter* HERO, MARGARET, *and* URSULA.)

HERO: Good Margaret, run thee to the parlor.
There shalt thou find my cousin Beatrice
Proposing with the Prince and Claudio:
Whisper her ear and tell her I and Ursula
Walk in the orchard, and our whole discourse 5
Is all of her. Say that thou overheardst us,
And bid her steal into the pleached bower
Where honeysuckles ripened by the sun
Forbid the sun to enter, like favourites
Made proud by princes, that advance their pride 10
Against that power that bred it. There will she hide her
To listen our purpose. This is thy office.
Bear thee well in it, and leave us alone.

MARGARET: I'll make her come, I warrant you, presently.

(*Exit.*)

HERO: Now, Ursula, when Beatrice doth come, 15
As we do trace this alley up and down,
Our talk must only be of Benedick.
When I do name him, let it be thy part
To praise him more than ever man did merit.

My talk to thee must be how Benedick   20
Is sick in love with Beatrice. Of this matter
Is little Cupid's crafty arrow made,
That only wounds by hearsay. Now begin,
For look where Beatrice like a lapwing runs
Close by the ground, to hear our conference.   25
(Enter BEATRICE, *behind.)*
URSULA: The pleasant'st angling is to see the fish
Cut with her golden oars the silver stream
And greedily devour the treacherous bait.
So angle we for Beatrice; who even now
Is couched in the woodbine coverture.   30
Fear you not my part of the dialogue.
HERO: Then go we near her, that her ear lose nothing
Of the false sweet bait that we lay for it.—
(Approaching the bower.) No, truly, Ursula, she is too disdainful.
I know her spirits are as coy and wild   35
As haggerds of the rock.
URSULA: But are you sure
That Benedick loves Beatrice so entirely?
HERO: So says the Prince and my new-trothed lord.
URSULA: And did they bid you tell her of it, madam?
HERO: They did entreat me to acquaint her of it,   40
But I persuaded them, if they loved Benedick,
To wish him wrestle with affection
And never to let Beatrice know of it.
URSULA: Why did you so? Doth not the gentleman
Deserve as full as fortunate a bed   45
As ever Beatrice shall couch upon?
HERO: O god of love! I know he doth deserve
As much as may be yielded to a man,
But Nature never framed a woman's heart
Of prouder stuff than that of Beatrice.   50
Disdain and scorn ride sparkling in her eyes,
Misprising what they look on, and her wit
Values itself so highly that to her
All matter else seems weak. She cannot love,
Nor take no shape nor project of affection,   55
She is so self-endeared.
URSULA: Sure, I think so,
And therefore certainly it were not good
She knew his love, lest she make sport at it.
HERO: Why, you speak truth. I never yet saw man,   60
How wise, how noble, young, how rarely featured,

But she would spell him backward. If fair-faced,
She would swear the gentleman should be her sister;
If black, why, Nature, drawing of an antic,
Made a foul blot; if tall, a lance ill-headed;   65
If low, an agate very vilely cut;
If speaking, why, a vane blown with all winds;
If silent, why, a block moved with none.
So turns she every man the wrong side out,
And never gives to truth and virtue that   70
Which simpleness and merit purchaseth.
URSULA: Sure, sure, such carping is not commendable.
HERO: No, not to be so odd and from all fashions
    As Beatrice is cannot be commendable.
    But who dare tell her so? If I should speak,   75
    She would mock me into air; O, she would laugh me
    Out of myself, press me to death with wit.
    Therefore let Benedick, like covered fire,
    Consume away in sighs, waste inwardly.
    It were a better death than die with mocks,   80
    Which is as bad as die with tickling.
URSULA: Yet tell her of it. Hear what she will say.
HERO: No, rather I will go to Benedick
    And counsel him to fight against his passion;
    And truly I'll devise some honest slanders   85
    To stain my cousin with. One doth not know
    How much an ill word may empoison liking.
URSULA: O, do not do your cousin such a wrong!
    She cannot be so much without true judgment,
    Having so swift and excellent a wit   90
    As she is prized to have, as to refuse
    So rare a gentleman as Signior Benedick.
HERO: He is the only man of Italy,
    Always excepted my dear Claudio.
URSULA: I pray you be not angry with me, madam,   95
    Speaking my fancy: Signior Benedick,
    For shape, for bearing, argument, and valour,
    Goes foremost in report through Italy.
HERO: Indeed, he hath an excellent good name.
URSULA: His excellence did earn it ere he had it.   100
    When are you married, madam?
HERO: Why, every day, tomorrow. Come, go in:
    I'll show thee some attires and have thy counsel
    Which is the best to furnish me tomorrow.

URSULA: She's limed, I warrant you. We have caught her, madam.   105
HERO: If it proves so, then loving goes by haps;
    Some Cupid kills with arrows, some with traps.
(*Exeunt* HERO *and* URSULA.)
BEATRICE *(Coming forward.)*:
    What fire is in mine ears? Can this be true?
      Stand I condemned for pride and scorn so much?
    Contempt, farewell, and maiden pride, adieu!   110
      No glory lives behind the back of such.
    And, Benedick, love on; I will requite thee,
      Taming my wild heart to thy loving hand.
    If thou dost love, my kindness shall incite thee
      To bind our loves up in a holy band.   115
    For others say thou dost deserve, and I
    Believe it better than reportingly.
(*Exit.*)

Scene 2

SCENE: *A room in* LEONATO'*s house*

(*Enter* DON PEDRO, CLAUDIO, BENEDICK, *and* LEONATO.)
DON PEDRO: I do but stay till your marriage be consummate, and then go I
    toward Aragon.
CLAUDIO: I'll bring you thither, my lord, if you'll vouchsafe me.
DON PEDRO: Nay, that would be as great a soil in the new gloss of your mar-
    riage as to show a child his new coat and forbid him to wear it. I will   5
    only be bold with Benedick for his company, for from the crown of his
    head to the sole of his foot he is all mirth. He hath twice or thrice cut
    Cupid's bowstring and the little hangman dare not shoot at him. He
    hath a heart as sound as a bell, and his tongue is the clapper, for what
    his heart thinks, his tongue speaks.   10
BENEDICK: Gallants, I am not as I have been.
LEONATO: So say I. Methinks you are sadder.
CLAUDIO: I hope he be in love.
DON PEDRO: Hang him, truant! There's no true drop of blood in him to be
    truly touched with love. If he be sad, he wants money.   15
BENEDICK: I have the toothache.
DON PEDRO: Draw it.
BENEDICK: Hang it!
CLAUDIO: You must hang it first, and draw it afterwards.
DON PEDRO: What, sigh for the toothache?   20
LEONATO: Where is but a humor or a worm.
BENEDICK: Well, everyone can master a grief but he that has it.

CLAUDIO: Yet say I, he is in love.

DON PEDRO: There is no appearance of fancy in him, unless it be a fancy
that he hath to strange disguises, as to be a Dutchman today, a   25
Frenchman tomorrow, or in the shape of two countries at once, as a
German from the waist downward, all slops, and a Spaniard from the
hip upward, no doublet. Unless he have a fancy to this foolery, as it appears he hath, he is no fool for fancy, as you would have it appear he is.

CLAUDIO: If he be not in love with some woman, there is no believing old   30
signs. He brushes his hat o' mornings. What should that bode?

DON PEDRO: Hath any man seen him at the barber's?

CLAUDIO: No, but the barber's man hath been seen with him, and the old
ornament of his cheek hath already stuffed tennis balls.

LEONATO: Indeed, he looks younger than he did, by the loss of a beard.   35

DON PEDRO: Nay, a' rubs himself with civet. Can you smell him out by that?

CLAUDIO: That's as much as to say, the sweet youth's in love.

DON PEDRO: The greatest note of it is his melancholy.

CLAUDIO: And when was he wont to wash his face?

DON PEDRO: Yea, or to paint himself? For the which I hear what they say of   40
him.

CLAUDIO: Nay, but his jesting spirit, which is now crept into a lute string
and now governed by stops—

DON PEDRO: Indeed, that tells a heavy tale for him. Conclude, conclude he
is in love.   45

CLAUDIO: Nay, but I know who loves him.

DON PEDRO: That would I know too. I warrant, one that knows him not.

CLAUDIO: Yes, and his ill conditions; and, in despite of all, dies for him.

DON PEDRO: She shall be buried with her face upwards.

BENEDICK: Yet is this no charm for the toothache.—Old signior, walk aside   50
with me. I have studied eight or nine wise words to speak to you, which
these hobby-horses must not hear.

(*Exeunt* BENEDICK *and* LEONATO.)

DON PEDRO: For my life, to break with him about Beatrice!

CLAUDIO: 'Tis even so. Hero and Margaret have by this played their parts
with Beatrice, and then the two bears will not bite one another when   55
they meet.

(*Enter* DON JOHN.)

DON JOHN: My lord and brother, God save you.

DON PEDRO: Good e'en, brother.

DON JOHN: If your leisure served, I would speak with you.

DON PEDRO: In private?   60

DON JOHN: If it please you. Yet Count Claudio may hear, for what I would
speak of concerns him.

DON PEDRO: What's the matter?

DON JOHN (*To* CLAUDIO.): Means your lordship to be married tomorrow?

DON PEDRO: You know he does. 65

DON JOHN: I know not that, when he knows what I know.

CLAUDIO: If there be any impediment, I pray you discover it.

DON JOHN: You may think I love you not. Let that appear hereafter, and aim better at me by that I now will manifest. For my brother, I think he holds you well, and in dearness of heart hath holp to effect your 70 ensuing marriage—surely suit ill spent and labour ill bestowed.

DON PEDRO: Why, what's the matter?

DON JOHN: I came hither to tell you; and, circumstances shortened, for she has been too long a talking of, the lady is disloyal.

CLAUDIO: Who, Hero? 75

DON PEDRO: Even she: Leonato's Hero, your Hero, every man's Hero.

CLAUDIO: Disloyal?

DON JOHN: The word is too good to paint out her wickedness. I could say she were worse. Think you of a worse title, and I will fit her to it. Wonder not till further warrant. Go but with me tonight, you shall see 80 her chamber window entered, even the night before her wedding day. If you love her then, tomorrow wed her. But it would better fit your honor to change your mind.

CLAUDIO: May this be so?

DON PEDRO: I will not think it. 85

DON JOHN: If you dare not trust that you see, confess not that you know. If you will follow me, I will show you enough, and when you have seen more and heard more, proceed accordingly.

CLAUDIO: If I see any thing tonight why I should not marry her tomorrow in the congregation, where I should wed, there will I shame her. 90

DON PEDRO: And as I wooed for thee to obtain her, I will join with thee to disgrace her.

DON JOHN: I will disparage her no farther till you are my witnesses. Bear it coldly but till midnight, and let the issue show itself.

DON PEDRO: O day untowardly turned! 95

CLAUDIO: O mischief strangely thwarting!

DON JOHN: O plague right well prevented! So will you say when you have seen the sequel.

(*Exeunt.*)

Scene 3

SCENE: *A street.*

(*Enter* DOGBERRY *and* VERGES *with the* WATCH.)

DOGBERRY: Are you good men and true?

VERGES: Yea, or else it were pity but they should suffer salvation, body and soul.

DOGBERRY: Nay, that were a punishment too good for them if they should
    have any allegiance in them, being chosen for the Prince's watch.   5

VERGES: Well, give them their charge, neighbor Dogberry.

DOGBERRY: First, who think you the most desartless man to be constable?

FIRST WATCHMAN: Hugh Otecake, sir, or George Seacole, for they can write
    and read.

DOGBERRY: Come hither, neighbour Seacole. God hath blessed you with a   10
    good name. To be a well-favoured man is the gift of fortune, but to
    write and read comes by nature.

SECOND WATCHMAN: Both which, master constable—

DOGBERRY: You have. I knew it would be your answer. Well, for your favor,
    sir, why, give God thanks, and make no boast of it, and for your writing   15
    and reading, let that appear when there is no need of such vanity. You
    are thought here to be the most senseless and fit man for the constable
    of the watch; therefore bear you the lantern. This is your charge: you
    shall comprehend all vagrom men; you are to bid any man stand, in the
    Prince's name.   20

SECOND WATCHMAN: How if he will not stand?

DOGBERRY: Why, then, take no note of him, but let him go, and presently
    call the rest of the watch together and thank God you are rid of a knave.

VERGES: If he will not stand when he is bidden, he is none of the Prince's
    subjects.   25

DOGBERRY: True, and they are to meddle with none but the Prince's sub-
    jects.—You shall also make no noise in the streets; for, for the watch to
    babble and to talk is most tolerable and not to be endured.

WATCHMAN: We will rather sleep than talk. We know what belongs to a
    watch.   30

DOGBERRY: Why, you speak like an ancient and most quiet watchman, for I
    cannot see how sleeping should offend; only have a care that your bills
    be not stolen. Well, you are to call at all the alehouses and bid those
    that are drunk get them to bed.

WATCHMAN: How if they will not?   35

DOGBERRY: Why then, let them alone till they are sober. If they make you
    not then the better answer, you may say they are not the men you took
    them for.

WATCHMAN: Well, sir.

DOGBERRY: If you meet a thief, you may suspect him, by virtue of your   40
    office, to be no true man, and, for such kind of men, the less you med-
    dle or make with them, why the more is for your honesty.

WATCHMAN: If we know him to be a thief, shall we not lay hands on him?

DOGBERRY: Truly, by your office, you may, but I think they that touch pitch
    will be defiled: the most peaceable way for you, if you do take a thief, is   45
    to let him show himself what he is and steal out of your company.

VERGES: You have been always called a merciful man, partner.

DOGBERRY: Truly, I would not hang a dog by my will, much more a man who hath any honesty in him.

VERGES: If you hear a child cry in the night, you must call to the nurse and bid her still it. 50

WATCHMAN: How if the nurse be asleep and will not hear us?

DOGBERRY: Why, then, depart in peace, and let the child wake her with crying, for the ewe that will not hear her lamb when it baas will never answer a calf when he bleats. 55

VERGES: 'Tis very true.

DOGBERRY: This is the end of the charge. You, constable, are to present the Prince's own person. If you meet the Prince in the night, you may stay him.

VERGES: Nay, by'r lady, that I think he cannot.

DOGBERRY: Five shillings to one on't, with any man that knows the statutes, 60 he may stay him—marry, not without the Prince be willing, for indeed the watch ought to offend no man, and it is an offence to stay a man against his will.

VERGES: By'r lady, I think it be so.

DOGBERRY: Ha, ah ha!—Well, masters, goodnight. An there be any matter 65 of weight chances, call up me. Keep your fellows' counsels and your own, and goodnight. Come, neighbor.

WATCHMAN: Well, masters, we hear our charge. Let us go sit here upon the church bench till two, and then all to bed.

DOGBERRY: One word more, honest neighbors. I pray you watch about 70 Signior Leonato's door, for the wedding being there tomorrow, there is a great coil tonight. Adieu, be vigitant, I beseech you.

(*Exeunt* DOGBERRY *and* VERGES.)

(*Enter* BORACHIO *and* CONRADE.)

BORACHIO: What, Conrade!

WATCHMAN (*Aside.*): Peace, stir not.

BORACHIO: Conrade, I say! 75

CONRADE: Here, man; I am at thy elbow.

BORACHIO: Mass, and my elbow itched, I thought there would a scab follow.

CONRADE: I will owe thee an answer for that. And now forward with thy tale.

BORACHIO: Stand thee close, then, under this pent-house, for it drizzles rain, and I will, like a true drunkard, utter all to thee. 80

WATCHMAN (*Aside.*): Some treason, masters. Yet stand close.

BORACHIO: Therefore know, I have earned of Don John a thousand ducats.

CONRADE: Is it possible that any villany should be so dear?

BORACHIO: Thou shouldst rather ask if it were possible any villany should be so rich. For when rich villains have need of poor ones, poor ones 85 may make what price they will.

CONRADE: I wonder at it.

BORACHIO: That shows thou art unconfirmed. Thou knowest that the
    fashion of a doublet, or a hat, or a cloak, is nothing to a man.

CONRADE: Yes, it is apparel.   90

BORACHIO: I mean the fashion.

CONRADE: Yes, the fashion is the fashion.

BORACHIO: Tush, I may as well say the fool's the fool. But seest thou not
    what a deformed thief this fashion is?

WATCHMAN (*Aside.*): I know that Deformed. He has been a vile thief this   95
    seven year. He goes up and down like a gentleman. I remember his name.

BORACHIO: Didst thou not hear somebody?

CONRADE: No, 'twas the vane on the house.

BORACHIO: Seest thou not, I say, what a deformed thief this fashion is, how
    giddily he turns about all the hot bloods between fourteen and five-   100
    and-thirty, sometimes fashioning them like Pharaoh's soldiers in the
    reechy painting, sometimes like god Bel's priests in the old church win-
    dow, sometimes like the shaven Hercules in the smirched worm-eaten
    tapestry, where his codpiece seems as massy as his club?

CONRADE: All this I see, and I see that the fashion wears out more apparel   105
    than the man. But art not thou thyself giddy with the fashion too, that
    thou hast shifted out of thy tale into telling me of the fashion?

BORACHIO: Not so, neither. But know that I have tonight wooed Margaret,
    the Lady Hero's gentlewoman, by the name of Hero. She leans me out
    at her mistress' chamber window, bids me a thousand times good night.   110
    I tell this tale vilely. I should first tell thee how the Prince, Claudio and
    my master, planted and placed and possessed by my master Don John,
    saw afar off in the orchard this amiable encounter.

CONRADE: And thought they Margaret was Hero?

BORACHIO: Two of them did, the Prince and Claudio, but the devil my master   115
    knew she was Margaret; and partly by his oaths, which first possessed them,
    partly by the dark night, which did deceive them, but chiefly by my villany,
    which did confirm any slander that Don John had made, away went
    Claudio enraged, swore he would meet her as he was appointed, next morn-
    ing at the temple, and there, before the whole congregation, shame her   120
    with what he saw o'er night and send her home again without a husband.

FIRST WATCHMAN: We charge you, in the Prince's name, stand!

SECOND WATCHMAN: Call up the right Master Constable. We have here
    recovered the most dangerous piece of lechery that ever was known in
    the commonwealth.   125

FIRST WATCHMAN: And one Deformed is one of them. I know him; he
    wears a lock.

CONRADE: Masters, masters—

SECOND WATCHMAN: You'll be made bring Deformed forth, I warrant you.

CONRADE: Masters, never speak, we charge you let us obey you to go with us.   130

BORACHIO: We are like to prove a goodly commodity, being taken up of these men's bills.

CONRADE: A commodity in question, I warrant you.—Come, we'll obey you. (*Exeunt.*)

Scene 4

SCENE: HERO's *apartment.*

(*Enter* HERO, MARGARET, *and* URSULA.)

HERO: Good Ursula, wake my cousin Beatrice and desire her to rise.

URSULA: I will, lady.

HERO: And bid her come hither.

URSULA: Well.

(*Exit.*)

MARGARET: Troth, I think your other rabato were better.   5

HERO: No, pray thee, good Meg, I'll wear this.

MARGARET: By my troth, 's not so good, and I warrant your cousin will say so.

HERO: My cousin's a fool, and thou art another. I'll wear none but this.

MARGARET: I like the new tire within excellently, if the hair were a thought browner; and your gown's a most rare fashion, i' faith. I saw the   10 Duchess of Milan's gown that they praise so.

HERO: O, that exceeds, they say.

MARGARET: By my troth, 's but a night-gown in respect of yours—cloth o' gold, and cuts, and laced with silver, set with pearls, down sleeves, side sleeves, and skirts round underborne with a bluish tinsel. But for a fine,   15 quaint, graceful, and excellent fashion, yours is worth ten on 't.

HERO: God give me joy to wear it, for my heart is exceeding heavy.

MARGARET: 'Twill be heavier soon by the weight of a man.

HERO: Fie upon thee! Art not ashamed?

MARGARET: Of what, lady? Of speaking honorably? Is not marriage honor-   20 able in a beggar? Is not your lord honorable without marriage? I think you would have me say "Saving your reverence, a husband." An bad thinking do not wrest true speaking, I'll offend nobody. Is there any harm in "the heavier for a husband"? None, I think, and it be the right husband and the right wife. Otherwise 'tis light, and not heavy. Ask my   25 Lady Beatrice else. Here she comes.

(*Enter* BEATRICE.)

HERO: Good morrow, coz.

BEATRICE: Good morrow, sweet Hero.

HERO: Why, how now? Do you speak in the sick tune?

BEATRICE: I am out of all other tune, methinks.   30

MARGARET: Clap's into "Light o' love." That goes without a burden. Do you sing it, and I'll dance it.

BEATRICE: Ye light o' love, with your heels! Then, if your husband have
 stables enough, you'll see he shall lack no barns.
MARGARET: O, illegitimate construction! I scorn that with my heels. 35
BEATRICE: 'Tis almost five o'clock, cousin. 'Tis time you were ready. By my
 troth, I am exceeding ill. Heigh-ho!
MARGARET: For a hawk, a horse, or a husband?
BEATRICE: For the letter that begins them all, *H.*
MARGARET: Well, and you be not turned Turk, there's no more sailing by 40
 the star.
BEATRICE: What means the fool, trow?
MARGARET: Nothing, I; but God send every one their heart's desire.
HERO: These gloves the Count sent me, they are an excellent perfume.
BEATRICE: I am stuffed, cousin. I cannot smell. 45
MARGARET: A maid, and stuffed! There's goodly catching of cold.
BEATRICE: O, God help me, God help me! How long have you professed
 apprehension?
MARGARET: Even since you left it. Doth not my wit become me rarely?
BEATRICE: It is not seen enough; you should wear it in your cap. By my 50
 troth, I am sick.
MARGARET: Get you some of this distilled *carduus benedictus,* and lay it to
 your heart. It is the only thing for a qualm.
HERO: There thou prick'st her with a thistle.
BEATRICE: *Benedictus!* why *benedictus?* You have some moral in this *benedictus.* 55
MARGARET: Moral? No, by my troth, I have no moral meaning; I meant plain
 holy thistle. You may think perchance that I think you are in love. Nay,
 by'r Lady, I am not such a fool to think what I list, nor I list not to think
 what I can, nor indeed I cannot think, if I would think my heart out of
 thinking, that you are in love or that you will be in love or that you can 60
 be in love. Yet Benedick was such another, and now is he become a
 man. He swore he would never marry, and yet now, in despite of his
 heart, he eats his meat without grudging. And how you may be converted
 I know not, but methinks you look with your eyes as other women do.
BEATRICE: What pace is this that thy tongue keeps? 65
MARGARET: Not a false gallop.
(Re-enter URSULA.*)*
URSULA: Madam, withdraw. the Prince, the Count, Signior Benedick, Don
 John, and all the gallants of the town are come to fetch you to church.
HERO: Help to dress me, good coz, good Meg, good Ursula.
(Exeunt.)

Scene 5
SCENE: *Another room in* LEONATO's *house.*

(Enter LEONATO, *with* DOGBERRY *and* VERGES.*)*

LEONATO: What would you with me, honest neighbor?

DOGBERRY: Marry, sir, I would have some confidence with you that decerns you nearly.

LEONATO: Brief, I pray you, for you see it is a busy time with me.

DOGBERRY: Marry, this it is, sir. 5

VERGES: Yes, in truth it is, sir.

LEONATO: What is it, my good friends?

DOGBERRY: Goodman Verges, sir, speaks a little off the matter: an old man, sir, and his wits are not so blunt as, God help, I would desire they were, but, in faith, honest as the skin between his brows. 10

VERGES: Yes, I thank God I am as honest as any man living that is an old man and no honester than I.

DOGBERRY: Comparisons are odorous: *palabras*, neighbor Verges.

LEONATO: Neighbors, you are tedious.

DOGBERRY: It pleases your Worship to say so, but we are the poor duke's 15 officers. But truly, for mine own part, if I were as tedious as a king, I could find it in my heart to bestow it all of your Worship.

LEONATO: All thy tediousness on me, ah?

DOGBERRY: Yea, an 'twere a thousand pound more than 'tis, for I hear as good exclamation on your Worship as of any man in the city, and 20 though I be but a poor man, I am glad to hear it.

VERGES: And so am I.

LEONATO: I would fain know what you have to say.

VERGES: Marry, sir, our watch tonight, excepting your Worship's presence, ha' ta'en a couple of as arrant knaves as any in Messina. 25

DOGBERRY: A good old man, sir. He will be talking. As they say, "When the age is in, the wit is out." God help us, it is a world to see!—Well said, i' faith, neighbor Verges.—Well, God's a good man. An two men ride of a horse, one must ride behind. An honest soul, i' faith, sir, by my troth he is, as ever broke bread, but God is to be worshipped, all men are not 30 alike, alas, good neighbor!

LEONATO: Indeed, neighbor, he comes too short of you.

DOGBERRY: Gifts that God gives.

LEONATO: I must leave you.

DOGBERRY: One word, sir. Our watch, sir, have indeed comprehended two 35 auspicious persons, and we would have them this morning examined before your Worship.

LEONATO: Take their examination yourself and bring it me. I am now in great haste, as it may appear unto you.

DOGBERRY: It shall be suffigance. 40

LEONATO: Drink some wine ere you go. Fare you well.

(*Enter a* MESSENGER.)

MESSENGER: My lord, they stay for you to give your daughter to her husband.

LEONATO: I'll wait upon them. I am ready.

(*Exeunt* LEONATO *and* MESSENGER.)

DOGBERRY: Go, good partner, go, get you to Francis Seacole. Bid him
  bring his pen and inkhorn to the jail. We are now to examination   45
  these men.

VERGES: And we must do it wisely.

DOGBERRY: We will spare for no wit, I warrant you. Here's that shall drive
  some of them to a noncome. Only get the learned writer to set down
  our excommunication and meet me at the jail.   50

(*Exeunt.*)

ACT IV

Scene 1

SCENE: *A church.*

(*Enter* DON PEDRO, DON JOHN, LEONATO, FRIAR FRANCIS, CLAUDIO, BENEDICK,
HERO, BEATRICE, *and Attendants.*)

LEONATO: Come, Friar Francis, be brief, only to the plain form of marriage,
  and you shall recount their particular duties afterwards.

FRIAR FRANCIS: You come hither, my lord, to marry this lady?

CLAUDIO: No.

LEONATO: To be married to her.—Friar, you come to marry her.   5

FRIAR FRANCIS: Lady, you come hither to be married to this count?

HERO: I do.

FRIAR FRANCIS: If either of you know any inward impediment why you
  should not be conjoined, charge you, on your souls, to utter it.

CLAUDIO: Know you any, Hero?   10

HERO: None, my lord.

FRIAR FRANCIS: Know you any, count?

LEONATO: I dare make his answer, none.

CLAUDIO: O, what men dare do! What men may do! What men daily do,
  not knowing what they do!   15

BENEDICK: How now, interjections? Why, then, some be of laughing, as, ah,
  ha, he!

CLAUDIO: Stand thee by, friar.—Father, by your leave,
  Will you with free and unconstrained soul
  Give me this maid, your daughter?   20

LEONATO: As freely, son, as God did give her me.

CLAUDIO: And what have I to give you back, whose worth
  May counterpoise this rich and precious gift?

DON PEDRO: Nothing, unless you render her again.

CLAUDIO: Sweet prince, you learn me noble thankfulness.—   25

There, Leonato, take her back again.
Give not this rotten orange to your friend.
She's but the sign and semblance of her honor.
Behold how like a maid she blushes here!
O, what authority and show of truth   30
Can cunning sin cover itself withal!
Comes not that blood as modest evidence
To witness simple virtue? Would you not swear,
All you that see her, that she were a maid,
By these exterior shows? But she is none.   35
She knows the heat of a luxurious bed.
Her blush is guiltiness, not modesty.
LEONATO: What do you mean, my lord?
CLAUDIO: Not to be married,
Not to knit my soul to an approved wanton.
LEONATO: Dear my lord, if you, in your own proof   40
Have vanquished the resistance of her youth,
And made defeat of her virginity—
CLAUDIO: I know what you would say: if I have known her,
You will say she did embrace me as a husband,
And so extenuate the 'forehand sin.   45
No, Leonato,
I never tempted her with word too large,
But, as a brother to his sister, showed
Bashful sincerity and comely love.
HERO: And seemed I ever otherwise to you?   50
CLAUDIO: Out on thee, seeming! I will write against it.
You seem to me as Dian in her orb,
As chaste as is the bud ere it be blown.
But you are more intemperate in your blood
Than Venus, or those pampered animals   55
That rage in savage sensuality.
HERO: Is my lord well that he doth speak so wide?
LEONATO: Sweet prince, why speak not you?
DON PEDRO: What should I speak?
I stand dishonoured that have gone about
To link my dear friend to a common stale.   60
LEONATO: Are these things spoken, or do I but dream?
DON JOHN: Sir, they are spoken, and these things are true.
BENEDICK: This looks not like a nuptial.
HERO: True! O God!
CLAUDIO: Leonato, stand I here?   65
Is this the Prince? Is this the Prince's brother?

Is this face Hero's? Are our eyes our own?

LEONATO: All this is so, but what of this, my lord?

CLAUDIO: Let me but move one question to your daughter;
    And, by that fatherly and kindly power   70
    That you have in her, bid her answer truly.

LEONATO: I charge thee do so, as thou art my child.

HERO: O, God defend me, how am I beset!—
    What kind of catechising call you this?

CLAUDIO: To make you answer truly to your name.   75

HERO: Is it not Hero? Who can blot that name
    With any just reproach?

CLAUDIO: Marry, that can Hero!
    Hero itself can blot out Hero's virtue.
    What man was he talked with you yesternight
    Out at your window betwixt twelve and one?   80
    Now, if you are a maid, answer to this.

HERO: I talked with no man at that hour, my lord.

DON PEDRO: Why, then are you no maiden.—Leonato,
    I am sorry you must hear. Upon mine honor,
    Myself, my brother, and this grieved count   85
    Did see her, hear her, at that hour last night
    Talk with a ruffian at her chamber window
    Who hath indeed, most like a liberal villain,
    Confessed the vile encounters they have had
    A thousand times in secret.   90

DON JOHN: Fie, fie, they are not to be named, my lord,
    Not to be spoke of!
    There is not chastity enough in language,
    Without offence, to utter them.—Thus, pretty lady,
    I am sorry for thy much misgovernment.   95

CLAUDIO: O Hero, what a Hero hadst thou been
    If half thy outward graces had been placed
    About thy thoughts and counsels of thy heart!
    But fare thee well, most foul, most fair. Farewell,
    Thou pure impiety and impious purity.   100
    For thee I'll lock up all the gates of love
    And on my eyelids shall conjecture hang,
    To turn all beauty into thoughts of harm,
    And never shall it more be gracious.

LEONATO: Hath no man's dagger here a point for me?   105

(HERO *swoons.*)

BEATRICE: Why, how now, cousin, wherefore sink you down?

DON JOHN: Come, let us go. These things, come thus to light,
  Smother her spirits up.
(*Exeunt* DON PEDRO, DON JOHN, *and* CLAUDIO.)
BENEDICK: How doth the lady?
BEATRICE: Dead, I think.—Help, uncle!—
  Hero, why, Hero! Uncle! Signior Benedick! Friar!   110
LEONATO: O Fate, take not away thy heavy hand!
  Death is the fairest cover for her shame
  That may be wished for.
BEATRICE: How now, cousin Hero?
FRIAR FRANCIS: Have comfort, lady.   115
LEONATO: Dost thou look up?
FRIAR FRANCIS: Yea, wherefore should she not?
LEONATO: Wherefore! Why, doth not every earthly thing
  Cry shame upon her? Could she here deny
  The story that is printed in her blood?—
  Do not live, Hero; do not ope thine eyes,   120
  For, did I think thou wouldst not quickly die,
  Thought I thy spirits were stronger than thy shames,
  Myself would, on the rearward of reproaches,
  Strike at thy life. Grieved I I had but one?
  Chid I for that at frugal Nature's frame?   125
  O, one too much by thee! Why had I one?
  Why ever wast thou lovely in my eyes?
  Why had I not with charitable hand
  Took up a beggar's issue at my gates,
  Who smirched thus and mired with infamy,   130
  I might have said "No part of it is mine;
  This shame derives itself from unknown loins"?
  But mine, and mine I loved, and mine I praised,
  And mine that I was proud on, mine so much
  That I myself was to myself not mine,   135
  Valuing of her—why she, O, she is fall'n
  Into a pit of ink, that the wide sea
  Hath drops too few to wash her clean again,
  And salt too little which may season give
  To her foul tainted flesh!   140
BENEDICK: Sir, sir, be patient.
  For my part, I am so attired in wonder
  I know not what to say.
BEATRICE: O, on my soul, my cousin is belied!
BENEDICK: Lady, were you her bedfellow last night?

BEATRICE: No, truly not; although, until last night   145
   I have this twelvemonth been her bedfellow.
LEONATO: Confirmed, confirmed! O, that is stronger made
   Which was before barred up with ribs of iron!
   Would the two princes lie and Claudio lie,
   Who loved her so that, speaking of her foulness,   150
   Washed it with tears? Hence from her. Let her die!
FRIAR FRANCIS: Hear me a little,
   For I have only been silent so long,
   And given way unto this course of fortune,
   By noting of the lady. I have marked   155
   A thousand blushing apparitions
   To start into her face, a thousand innocent shames
   In angel whiteness beat away those blushes,
   And in her eye there hath appeared a fire
   To burn the errors that these princes hold   160
   Against her maiden truth. Call me a fool,
   Trust not my reading nor my observations,
   Which with experimental seal doth warrant
   The tenor of my book; trust not my age,
   My reverence, calling, nor divinity,   165
   If this sweet lady lie not guiltless here
   Under some biting error.
LEONATO: Friar, it cannot be.
   Thou seest that all the grace that she hath left
   Is that she will not add to her damnation
   A sin of perjury. She not denies it.   170
   Why seek'st thou then to cover with excuse
   That which appears in proper nakedness?
FRIAR FRANCIS: Lady, what man is he you are accused of?
HERO: They know that do accuse me. I know none:
   If I know more of any man alive   175
   Than that which maiden modesty doth warrant,
   Let all my sins lack mercy!—O my father,
   Prove you that any man with me conversed
   At hours unmeet, or that I yesternight
   Maintained the change of words with any creature,   180
   Refuse me, hate me, torture me to death!
FRIAR FRANCIS: There is some strange misprision in the princes.
BENEDICK: Two of them have the very bent of honour,
   And if their wisdoms be misled in this,
   The practice of it lives in John the Bastard,   185
   Whose spirits toil in frame of villainies.

LEONATO: I know not. If they speak but truth of her,
These hands shall tear her. If they wrong her honor,
The proudest of them shall well hear of it.
Time hath not yet so dried this blood of mine,   190
Nor age so eat up my invention,
Nor fortune made such havoc of my means,
Nor my bad life reft me so much of friends,
But they shall find, awaked in such a kind,
Both strength of limb and policy of mind,   195
Ability in means and choice of friends,
To quit me of them throughly.
FRIAR FRANCIS: Pause awhile,
And let my counsel sway you in this case.
Your daughter here the princes left for dead.
Let her awhile be secretly kept in,   200
And publish it that she is dead indeed.
Maintain a mourning ostentation,
And on your family's old monument
Hang mournful epitaphs and do all rites
That appertain unto a burial.   205
LEONATO: What shall become of this? What will this do?
FRIAR FRANCIS: Marry, this well carried shall on her behalf
Change slander to remorse. That is some good.
But not for that dream I on this strange course,
But on this travail look for greater birth.   210
She, dying, as it must so be maintained,
Upon the instant that she was accused,
Shall be lamented, pitied, and excused
Of every hearer. For it so falls out
That what we have we prize not to the worth   215
Whiles we enjoy it, but being lacked and lost,
Why, then we rack the value, then we find
The virtue that possession would not show us
Whiles it was ours. So will it fare with Claudio.
When he shall hear she died upon his words,   220
Th' idea of her life shall sweetly creep
Into his study of imagination,
And every lovely organ of her life
Shall come appareled in more precious habit,
More moving, delicate, and full of life,   225
Into the eye and prospect of his soul,
Than when she lived indeed. Then shall he mourn,
If ever love had interest in his liver,

And wish he had not so accused her,
No, though he thought his accusation true.   230
Let this be so, and doubt not but success
Will fashion the event in better shape
Than I can lay it down in likelihood.
But if all aim but this be leveled false,
The supposition of the lady's death   235
Will quench the wonder of her infamy.
And if it sort not well, you may conceal her,
As best befits her wounded reputation,
In some reclusive and religious life,
Out of all eyes, tongues, minds, and injuries.   240

BENEDICK: Signior Leonato, let the Friar advise you.
And though you know my inwardness and love
Is very much unto the Prince and Claudio,
Yet, by mine honor, I will deal in this
As secretly and justly as your soul   245
Should with your body.

LEONATO: Being that I flow in grief,
The smallest twine may lead me.

FRIAR FRANCIS: 'Tis well consented. Presently away,
For to strange sores strangely they strain the cure.—
Come, lady, die to live: this wedding day   250
Perhaps is but prolonged. Have patience and endure

(*Exeunt all but* BENEDICK *and* BEATRICE.)

BENEDICK: Lady Beatrice, have you wept all this while?

BEATRICE: Yea, and I will weep a while longer.

BENEDICK: I will not desire that.

BEATRICE: You have no reason. I do it freely.   255

BENEDICK: Surely I do believe your fair cousin is wronged.

BEATRICE: Ah, how much might the man deserve of me that would right
her!

BENEDICK: Is there any way to show such friendship?

BEATRICE: A very even way, but no such friend.   260

BENEDICK: May a man do it?

BEATRICE: It is a man's office, but not yours.

BENEDICK: I do love nothing in the world so well as you. Is not that
strange?

BEATRICE: As strange as the thing I know not. It were as possible for me to   265
say I loved nothing so well as you, but believe me not, and yet I lie not,
I confess nothing, nor I deny nothing. I am sorry for my cousin.

BENEDICK: By my sword, Beatrice, thou lovest me!

BEATRICE: Do not swear and eat it.

BENEDICK: I will swear by it that you love me, and I will make him eat it   270
     that says I love not you.
BEATRICE: Will you not eat your word?
BENEDICK: With no sauce that can be devised to it. I protest I love thee.
BEATRICE: Why, then, God forgive me!
BENEDICK: What offence, sweet Beatrice?   275
BEATRICE: You have stayed me in a happy hour: I was about to protest I
     loved you.
BENEDICK: And do it with all thy heart.
BEATRICE: I love you with so much of my heart that none is left to
     protest.   280
BENEDICK: Come, bid me do any thing for thee.
BEATRICE: Kill Claudio.
BENEDICK: Ha! Not for the wide world.
BEATRICE: You kill me to deny it. Farewell.
BENEDICK: Tarry, sweet Beatrice.   285
BEATRICE: I am gone, though I am here. There is no love in you. Nay, I
     pray you, let me go.
BENEDICK: Beatrice—
BEATRICE: In faith, I will go.
BENEDICK: We'll be friends first.   290
BEATRICE: You dare easier be friends with me than fight with mine
     enemy.
BENEDICK: Is Claudio thine enemy?
BEATRICE: Is he not approved in the height a villain, that hath slandered,
     scorned, dishonored my kinswoman? O, that I were a man! What, bear   295
     her in hand until they come to take hands, and then, with public accu-
     sation, uncovered slander, unmitigated rancour—O God, that I were a
     man! I would eat his heart in the marketplace.
BENEDICK: Hear me, Beatrice—
BEATRICE: Talk with a man out at a window! A proper saying.   300
BENEDICK: Nay, but Beatrice—
BEATRICE: Sweet Hero, she is wronged, she is slandered, she is undone.
BENEDICK: Beat—
BEATRICE: Princes and counties! Surely a princely testimony, a goodly
     count, Count Comfect, a sweet gallant, surely! O, that I were a man for   305
     his sake! Or that I had any friend would be a man for my sake! But
     manhood is melted into courtesies, valor into compliment, and men are
     only turned into tongue, and trim ones, too. He is now as valiant as
     Hercules that only tells a lie and swears it. I cannot be a man with
     wishing; therefore I will die a woman with grieving.   310
BENEDICK: Tarry, good Beatrice. By this hand, I love thee.
BEATRICE: Use it for my love some other way than swearing by it.

BENEDICK: Think you in your soul the Count Claudio hath wronged Hero?

BEATRICE: Yea, as sure as I have a thought or a soul.

BENEDICK: Enough, I am engaged. I will challenge him. I will kiss your   315
hand, and so I leave you. By this hand, Claudio shall render me a dear
account. As you hear of me, so think of me. Go, comfort your cousin. I
must say she is dead, and so farewell.

(*Exeunt.*)

Scene 2

SCENE: *A prison.*

(*Enter* DOGBERRY, VERGES, *and* SEXTON, *in gowns; and the* WATCH, *with* CON-
RADE *and* BORACHIO.)

DOGBERRY: Is our whole dissembly appeared?

VERGES: O, a stool and a cushion for the Sexton.

SEXTON: Which be the malefactors?

DOGBERRY: Marry, that am I, and my partner.

VERGES: Nay, that's certain, we have the exhibition to examine.   5

SEXTON: But which are the offenders that are to be examined? Let them
come before Master Constable.

DOGBERRY: Yea, marry, let them come before me. What is your name, friend?

BORACHIO: Borachio.

DOGBERRY: Pray, write down "Borachio."—Yours, sirrah?   10

CONRADE: I am a gentleman, sir, and my name is Conrade.

DOGBERRY: Write down, "Master Gentleman Conrade."— Masters, do you
serve God?

CONRADE & BORACHIO: Yea, sir, we hope.

DOGBERRY: Write down that they hope they serve God; and write God first,   15
for God defend but God should go before such villains!—Masters, it is
proved already that you are little better than false knaves, and it will go
near to be thought so shortly. How answer you for yourselves?

CONRADE: Marry, sir, we say we are none.

DOGBERRY: A marvellous witty fellow, I assure you, but I will go about with   20
him.—Come you hither, sirrah; a word in your ear. Sir, I say to you, it
is thought you are false knaves.

BORACHIO: Sir, I say to you we are none.

DOGBERRY: Well, stand aside.—'Fore God, they are both in a tale. Have you
writ down that they are none?   25

SEXTON: Master constable, you go not the way to examine. You must call
forth the watch that are their accusers.

DOGBERRY: Yea, marry, that's the eftest way.—Let the watch come forth.
Masters, I charge you, in the Prince's name, accuse these men.

FIRST WATCHMAN: This man said, sir, that Don John, the Prince's brother, 30
was a villain.

DOGBERRY: Write down Prince John a villain. Why, this is flat perjury, to
call a prince's brother villain!

BORACHIO: Master constable—

DOGBERRY: Pray thee, fellow, peace: I do not like thy look, I promise thee. 35

SEXTON: What heard you him say else?

SECOND WATCHMAN: Marry, that he had received a thousand ducats of Don
John for accusing the Lady Hero wrongfully.

DOGBERRY: Flat burglary as ever was committed.

VERGES: Yea, by Mass, that it is. 40

SEXTON: What else, fellow?

FIRST WATCHMAN: And that Count Claudio did mean, upon his words, to
disgrace Hero before the whole assembly, and not marry her.

DOGBERRY: O, villain! Thou wilt be condemned into everlasting redemption
for this. 45

SEXTON: What else?

WATCHMAN: This is all.

SEXTON: And this is more, masters, than you can deny. Prince John is this
morning secretly stolen away. Hero was in this manner accused, in this
very manner refused, and upon the grief of this suddenly died.—Master 50
constable, let these men be bound and brought to Leonato's: I will go
before and show him their examination.

(*Exit.*)

DOGBERRY: Come, let them be opinioned.

VERGES: Let them be in the hands—

CONRADE: Off, coxcomb! 55

DOGBERRY: God's my life, where's the Sexton? Let him write down the
Prince's officer "coxcomb." Come, bind them.—Thou naughty varlet!

CONRADE: Away! You are an ass, you are an ass!

DOGBERRY: Dost thou not suspect my place? Dost thou not suspect my
years? O, that he were here to write me down an ass! But masters, 60
remember that I am an ass, though it be not written down, yet forget
not that I am an ass.—No, thou villain, thou art full of piety, as
shall be proved upon thee by good witness. I am a wise fellow and,
which is more, an officer, and, which is more, a householder and,
which is more, as pretty a piece of flesh as any is in Messina, and 65
one that knows the law, go to, and a rich fellow enough, go to, and
a fellow that hath had losses, and one that hath two gowns and
every thing handsome about him.—Bring him away.—O, that I had
been writ down an ass!

(*Exeunt.*)

ACT V

Scene 1

SCENE: *Before* LEONATO's *house.*

(*Enter* LEONATO *and* ANTONIO.)

ANTONIO: If you go on thus, you will kill yourself,
 And 'tis not wisdom thus to second grief
 Against yourself.
LEONATO: I pray thee, cease thy counsel,
 Which falls into mine ears as profitless
 As water in a sieve. Give not me counsel,   5
 Not let no comforter delight mine ear
 But such a one whose wrongs do suit with mine.
 Bring me a father that so loved his child,
 Whose joy of her is overwhelmed like mine,
 And bid him speak of patience.   10
 Measure his woe the length and breadth of mine,
 And let it answer every strain for strain,
 As thus for thus, and such a grief for such,
 In every lineament, branch, shape, and form.
 If such a one will smile and stroke his beard,   15
 Bid sorrow wag, cry "hem" when he should groan,
 Patch grief with proverbs, make misfortune drunk
 With candle-wasters, bring him yet to me,
 And I of him will gather patience.
 But there is no such man. For, brother, men   20
 Can counsel and speak comfort to that grief
 Which they themselves not feel, but tasting it,
 Their counsel turns to passion, which before
 Would give preceptial med'cine to rage,
 Fetter strong madness in a silken thread,   25
 Charm ache with air and agony with words.
 No, no, 'tis all men's office to speak patience
 To those that wring under the load of sorrow,
 But no man's virtue nor sufficiency
 To be so moral when he shall endure   30
 The like himself. Therefore give me no counsel.
 My griefs cry louder than advertisement.
ANTONIO: Therein do men from children nothing differ.
LEONATO: I pray thee, peace. I will be flesh and blood,
 For there was never yet philosopher   35
 That could endure the toothache patiently,

However they have writ the style of gods
And made a push at chance and sufferance.
ANTONIO: Yet bend not all the harm upon yourself.
    Make those that do offend you suffer too.   40
LEONATO: There thou speak'st reason. Nay, I will do so.
    My soul doth tell me Hero is belied,
    And that shall Claudio know; so shall the Prince
    And all of them that thus dishonor her.
ANTONIO: Here comes the Prince and Claudio hastily.   45
(*Enter* DON PEDRO *and* CLAUDIO.)
DON PEDRO: Good e'en, good e'en.
CLAUDIO: Good day to both of you.
LEONATO: Hear you, my lords—
DON PEDRO: We have some haste, Leonato.
LEONATO: Some haste, my lord! Well, fare you well, my lord.
    Are you so hasty now? Well, all is one.
DON PEDRO: Nay, do not quarrel with us, good old man.   50
ANTONIO: If he could right himself with quarreling,
    Some of us would lie low.
CLAUDIO: Who wrongs him?
LEONATO: Marry, thou dost wrong me, thou dissembler, thou.
    Nay, never lay thy hand upon thy sword.
    I fear thee not.   55
CLAUDIO: Marry, beshrew my hand
    If it should give your age such cause of fear.
    In faith, my hand meant nothing to my sword.
LEONATO: Tush, tush, man, never fleer and jest at me.
    I speak not like a dotard nor a fool,
    As under privilege of age to brag   60
    What I have done being young, or what would do
    Were I not old. Know, Claudio, to thy head,
    Thou hast so wronged mine innocent child and me
    That I am forced to lay my reverence by,
    And, with grey hairs and bruise of many days   65
    Do challenge thee to trial of a man.
    I say thou hast belied mine innocent child.
    Thy slander hath gone through and through her heart,
    And she lies buried with her ancestors,
    O, in a tomb where never scandal slept,   70
    Save this of hers, framed by thy villainy.
CLAUDIO: My villainy?
LEONATO: Thine, Claudio, thine, I say.
DON PEDRO: You say not right, old man.

LEONATO: My lord, my lord,
    I'll prove it on his body if he dare,
    Despite his nice fence and his active practice,   75
    His May of youth and bloom of lustihood.
CLAUDIO: Away! I will not have to do with you.
LEONATO: Canst thou so daff me? Thou hast killed my child.
    If thou kill'st me, boy, thou shalt kill a man.
ANTONIO: He shall kill two of us, and men indeed,   80
    But that's no matter. Let him kill one first.
    Win me and wear me! Let him answer me.—
    Come, follow me, boy. Come, sir boy, come, follow me.
    Sir boy, I'll whip you from your foining fence,
    Nay, as I am a gentleman, I will.   85
LEONATO: Brother—
ANTONIO: Content yourself. God knows I loved my niece,
    And she is dead, slandered to death by villains
    That dare as well answer a man indeed
    As I dare take a serpent by the tongue.—   90
    Boys, apes, braggarts, jacks, milksops!
LEONATO: Brother Antony—
ANTONIO: Hold you content. What, man! I know them, yea,
    And what they weigh, even to the utmost scruple—
    Scrambling, outfacing, fashionmonging boys,   95
    That lie and cog and flout, deprave and slander,
    Go anticly show outward hideousness,
    And speak off half a dozen dang'rous words
    How they might hurt their enemies, if they durst,
    And this is all.   100
LEONATO: But, brother Antony—
ANTONIO: Come, 'tis no matter.
    Do not you meddle. Let me deal in this.
DON PEDRO: Gentlemen both, we will not wake your patience.
    My heart is sorry for your daughter's death,   105
    But, on my honor, she was charged with nothing
    But what was true and very full of proof.
LEONATO: My lord, my lord—
DON PEDRO: I will not hear you.
LEONATO: No? Come, brother; away! I will be heard.   110
ANTONIO: And shall, or some of us will smart for it.
(*Exeunt* LEONATO *and* ANTONIO.)
DON PEDRO: See, see, here comes the man we went to seek.
(*Enter* BENEDICK.)
CLAUDIO: Now, signior, what news?

BENEDICK: Good day, my lord.

DON PEDRO: Welcome, signior. You are almost come to part almost a fray.   115

CLAUDIO: We had like to have had our two noses snapped off with two old
    men without teeth.

DON PEDRO: Leonato and his brother. What think'st thou? Had we fought, I
    doubt we should have been too young for them.

BENEDICK: In a false quarrel there is no true valor. I came to seek you both.   120

CLAUDIO: We have been up and down to seek thee, for we are high-proof
    melancholy and would fain have it beaten away. Wilt thou use thy wit?

BENEDICK: It is in my scabbard. Shall I draw it?

DON PEDRO: Dost thou wear thy wit by thy side?

CLAUDIO: Never any did so, though very many have been beside their wit. I   125
    will bid thee draw, as we do the minstrels: draw to pleasure us.

DON PEDRO: As I am an honest man, he looks pale.—Art thou sick, or
    angry?

CLAUDIO: What, courage, man! What though care killed a cat? Thou hast
    mettle enough in thee to kill care.   130

BENEDICK: Sir, I shall meet your wit in the career, and you charge it against
    me. I pray you choose another subject.

CLAUDIO: Nay, then, give him another staff. This last was broke 'cross.

DON PEDRO: By this light, he changes more and more. I think he be angry
    indeed.   135

CLAUDIO: If he be, he knows how to turn his girdle.

BENEDICK: Shall I speak a word in your ear?

CLAUDIO: God bless me from a challenge!

BENEDICK *(Aside to* CLAUDIO.*)*: You are villain. I jest not. I will make it good
    how you dare, with what you dare, and when you dare. Do me right, or   140
    I will protest your cowardice. You have killed a sweet lady, and her
    death shall fall heavy on you. Let me hear from you.

CLAUDIO: Well, I will meet you, so I may have good cheer.

DON PEDRO: What, a feast, a feast?

CLAUDIO: I' faith, I thank him. He hath bid me to a calf's head and a   145
    capon, the which if I do not carve most curiously, say my knife's
    naught. Shall I not find a woodcock too?

BENEDICK: Sir, your wit ambles well; it goes easily.

DON PEDRO: I'll tell thee how Beatrice praised thy wit the other day. I said,
    thou hadst a fine wit: "True," said she, "a fine little one." "No," said I,   150
    "a great wit:" "Right," says she, "a great gross one." "Nay," said I, "a
    good wit:" "Just," said she, "it hurts nobody." "Nay," said I, "the gentle-
    man is wise:" "Certain," said she, "a wise gentleman." "Nay," said I, "he
    hath the tongues:" "That I believe," said she, "for he swore a thing to
    me on Monday night, which he forswore on Tuesday morning; there's a   155
    double tongue; there's two tongues." Thus did she an hour together

transshape thy particular virtues. Yet at last she concluded with a sigh, thou wast the properest man in Italy.

CLAUDIO: For the which she wept heartily and said she cared not.

DON PEDRO: Yea, that she did. But yet for all that, an if she did not hate him deadly, she would love him dearly. The old man's daughter told us all. 160

CLAUDIO: All, all. And, moreover, God saw him when he was hid in the garden.

DON PEDRO: But when shall we set the savage bull's horns on the sensible Benedick's head?

CLAUDIO: Yea, and text underneath: "Here dwells Benedick the married man"? 165

BENEDICK: Fare you well, boy. You know my mind. I will leave you now to your gossip-like humor. You break jests as braggarts do their blades, which God be thanked, hurt not.—My lord, for your many courtesies I thank you. I must discontinue your company. Your brother the Bastard is fled from Messina: you have among you killed a sweet and innocent 170 lady. For my Lord Lackbeard there, he and I shall meet, and till then peace be with him.

(Exit.)

DON PEDRO: He is in earnest.

CLAUDIO: In most profound earnest; and, I'll warrant you, for the love of Beatrice. 175

DON PEDRO: And hath challenged thee?

CLAUDIO: Most sincerely.

DON PEDRO: What a pretty thing man is when he goes in his doublet and hose and leaves off his wit!

CLAUDIO: He is then a giant to an ape; but then is an ape a doctor to such a 180 man.

DON PEDRO: But, soft you, let me be. Pluck up, my heart, and be sad. Did he not say my brother was fled?

(Enter DOGBERRY, VERGES, *and the* WATCH, *with* CONRADE *and* BORACHIO.*)*

DOGBERRY: Come you, sir. If justice cannot tame you, she shall ne'er weigh more reasons in her balance. Nay, an you be a cursing hypocrite once, 185 you must be looked to.

DON PEDRO: How now, two of my brother's men bound! Borachio one!

CLAUDIO: Hearken after their offence, my lord.

DON PEDRO: Officers, what offence have these men done?

DOGBERRY: Marry, sir, they have committed false report; moreover, they 190 have spoken untruths; secondarily, they are slanders; sixth and lastly, they have belied a lady; thirdly, they have verified unjust things; and, to conclude, they are lying knaves.

DON PEDRO: First, I ask thee what they have done; thirdly, I ask thee what's their offence; sixth and lastly, why they are committed; and, to con- 195 clude, what you lay to their charge.

CLAUDIO: Rightly reasoned, and in his own division; and, by my troth,
there's one meaning well suited.

DON PEDRO: Who have you offended, masters, that you are thus bound to
your answer? This learned constable is too cunning to be understood.   200
What's your offense?

BORACHIO: Sweet prince, let me go no farther to mine answer. Do you hear
me, and let this count kill me. I have deceived even your very eyes.
What your wisdoms could not discover, these shallow fools have
brought to light, who in the night overheard me confessing to this man   205
how Don John your brother incensed me to slander the Lady Hero,
how you were brought into the orchard and saw me court Margaret in
Hero's garments, how you disgraced her when you should marry her.
My villainy they have upon record, which I had rather seal with my
death than repeat over to my shame. The lady is dead upon mine and   210
my master's false accusation. And, briefly, I desire nothing but the
reward of a villain.

DON PEDRO: Runs not this speech like iron through your blood?

CLAUDIO: I have drunk poison whiles he uttered it.

DON PEDRO: But did my brother set thee on to this?   215

BORACHIO: Yea, and paid me richly for the practice of it.

DON PEDRO: He is composed and framed of treachery,
And fled he is upon this villainy.

CLAUDIO: Sweet Hero, now thy image doth appear
In the rare semblance that I loved it first.   220

DOGBERRY: Come, bring away the plaintiffs. By this time our sexton hath
reformed Signior Leonato of the matter. And, masters, do not forget to
specify, when time and place shall serve, that I am an ass.

VERGES: Here, here comes master Signior Leonato, and the Sexton too.

(*Reenter* LEONATO *and* ANTONIO, *with the* SEXTON.)

LEONATO: Which is the villain? Let me see his eyes,   225
That, when I note another man like him,
I may avoid him. Which of these is he?

BORACHIO: If you would know your wronger, look on me.

LEONATO: Art thou the slave that with thy breath hast killed
Mine innocent child?   230

BORACHIO: Yea, even I alone.

LEONATO: No, not so, villain; thou beliest thyself:
Here stand a pair of honourable men—
A third is fled—that had a hand in it.—
I thank you, princes, for my daughter's death.
Record it with your high and worthy deeds.   235
'Twas bravely done, if you bethink you of it.

CLAUDIO: I know not how to pray your patience,
　Yet I must speak. Choose your revenge yourself.
　Impose me to what penance your invention
　Can lay upon my sin. Yet sinned I not   240
　But in mistaking.
DON PEDRO:　　　　By my soul, nor I,
　And yet, to satisfy this good old man
　I would bend under any heavy weight
　That he'll enjoin me to.
LEONATO: I cannot bid you bid my daughter live—   245
　That were impossible—but, I pray you both,
　Possess the people in Messina here
　How innocent she died. And if your love
　Can labor ought in sad invention,
　Hang her an epitaph upon her tomb   250
　And sing it to her bones. Sing it tonight.
　Tomorrow morning come you to my house,
　And since you could not be my son-in-law,
　Be yet my nephew. My brother hath a daughter,
　Almost the copy of my child that's dead,   255
　And she alone is heir to both of us.
　Give her the right you should have giv'n her cousin,
　And so dies my revenge.
CLAUDIO:　　　　　　　O, noble sir!
　Your over-kindness doth wring tears from me.
　I do embrace your offer and dispose   260
　For henceforth of poor Claudio.
LEONATO: Tomorrow then I will expect your coming.
　Tonight I take my leave. This naughty man
　Shall face to face be brought to Margaret,
　Who I believe was packed in all this wrong,   265
　Hired to it by your brother.
BORACHIO: No, by my soul, she was not,
　Nor knew not what she did when she spoke to me,
　But always hath been just and virtuous
　In anything that I do know by her.   270
DOGBERRY: Moreover, sir, which indeed is not under white and black, this
　plaintiff here, the offender, did call me ass. I beseech you, let it be
　remembered in his punishment. And also the watch heard them talk of
　one Deformed. They say he wears a key in his ear and a lock hanging
　by it and borrows money in God's name, the which he hath used so   275
　long and never paid that now men grow hardhearted and will lend
　nothing for God's sake. Pray you, examine him upon that point.

LEONATO: I thank thee for thy care and honest pains.

DOGBERRY: Your Worship speaks like a most thankful and reverend youth, and I praise God for you.   280

LEONATO: There's for thy pains.

DOGBERRY: God save the foundation.

LEONATO: Go, I discharge thee of thy prisoner, and I thank thee.

DOGBERRY: I leave an arrant knave with your Worship; which I beseech your Worship to correct yourself, for the example of others. God keep   285 your Worship! I wish your Worship well. God restore you to health. I humbly give you leave to depart, and if a merry meeting may be wished, God prohibit it!—Come, neighbor.

(*Exeunt* DOGBERRY *and* VERGES.)

LEONATO: Until tomorrow morning, lords, farewell.

ANTONIO: Farewell, my lords. We look for you tomorrow.   290

DON PEDRO: We will not fail.

CLAUDIO: Tonight I'll mourn with Hero.

LEONATO (*To the Watch.*):
    Bring you these fellows on.—We'll talk with Margaret, How her ac-
    quaintance grew with this lewd fellow.

(*Exeunt, severally.*)

Scene 2

SCENE: LEONATO's *garden.*

(*Enter* BENEDICK *and* MARGARET, *meeting.*)

BENEDICK: Pray thee, sweet Mistress Margaret, deserve well at my hands by helping me to the speech of Beatrice.

MARGARET: Will you then write me a sonnet in praise of my beauty?

BENEDICK: In so high a style, Margaret, that no man living shall come over it, for in most comely truth, thou deservest it.   5

MARGARET: To have no man come over me? Why, shall I always keep below stairs?

BENEDICK: Thy wit is as quick as the greyhound's mouth; it catches.

MARGARET: And yours as blunt as the fencer's foils, which hit, but hurt not.

BENEDICK: A most manly wit, Margaret; it will not hurt a woman. And so, I   10 pray thee, call Beatrice: I give thee the bucklers.

MARGARET: Give us the swords; we have bucklers of our own.

BENEDICK: If you use them, Margaret, you must put in the pikes with a vice, and they are dangerous weapons for maids.

MARGARET: Well, I will call Beatrice to you, who I think hath legs.   15

BENEDICK: And therefore will come.

(*Exit* MARGARET.)

(Sings.)

> The god of love
> That sits above,
> And knows me, and knows me,
> How pitiful I deserve—   20

I mean in singing. But in loving, Leander the good swimmer, Troilus the first employer of panders, and a whole bookful of these quondam carpetmongers, whose names yet run smoothly in the even road of a blank verse, why, they were never so truly turnedover and over as my poor self in love. Marry, I cannot show it in rhyme; I have tried: I can   25 find out no rhyme to "lady" but "baby,"—an innocent rhyme; for "scorn," "horn,"—a hard rhyme; for "school," "fool,"—a babbling rhyme; very ominous endings. No, I was not born under a rhyming planet, nor I cannot woo in festival terms. *(Enter BEATRICE.)* Sweet Beatrice, wouldst thou come when I called thee?   30

BEATRICE: Yea, signior, and depart when you bid me.

BENEDICK: O, stay but till then!

BEATRICE: "Then" is spoken; fare you well now. And yet, ere I go, let me go with that I came, which is, with knowing what hath passed between you and Claudio.   35

BENEDICK: Only foul words; and thereupon I will kiss thee.

BEATRICE: Foul words is but foul wind, and foul wind is but foul breath, and foul breath is noisome. Therefore I will depart unkissed.

BENEDICK: Thou hast frighted the word out of his right sense, so forcible is thy wit. But I must tell thee plainly, Claudio undergoes my challenge,   40 and either I must shortly hear from him, or I will subscribe him a coward. And I pray thee now, tell me for which of my bad parts didst thou first fall in love with me?

BEATRICE: For them all together, which maintained so politic a state of evil that they will not admit any good part to intermingle with them. But   45 for which of my good parts did you first suffer love for me?

BENEDICK: Suffer love! A good epithet! I do suffer love indeed, for I love thee against my will.

BEATRICE: In spite of your heart, I think. Alas, poor heart, if you spite it for my sake, I will spite it for yours, for I will never love that which my   50 friend hates.

BENEDICK: Thou and I are too wise to woo peaceably.

BEATRICE: It appears not in this confession. There's not one wise man among twenty that will praise himself.

BENEDICK: An old, an old instance, Beatrice, that lived in the lime of good   55 neighbours. If a man do not erect in this age his own tomb ere he dies, he shall live no longer in monument than the bell rings and the widow weeps.

BEATRICE: And how long is that, think you?

BENEDICK: Question: why, an hour in clamour and a quarter in rheum. There-
fore is it most expedient for the wise, if Don Worm, his conscience, find   60
no impediment to the contrary, to be the trumpet of his own virtues, as I
am to myself. So much for praising myself, who, I myself will bear witness,
is praiseworthy. And now tell me, how doth your cousin?
BEATRICE: Very ill.
BENEDICK: And how do you?   65
BEATRICE: Very ill, too.
BENEDICK: Serve God, love me, and mend. There will I leave you too, for
here comes one in haste.
(*Enter* URSULA.)
URSULA: Madam, you must come to your uncle. Yonder's old coil at home.
It is proved my Lady Hero hath been falsely accused, the Prince and   70
Claudio mightily abused, and Don John is the author of all, who is fed
and gone. Will you come presently?
BEATRICE: Will you go hear this news, signior?
BENEDICK: I will live in thy heart, die in thy lap, and be buried in thy
eyes—and, moreover, I will go with thee to thy uncle's.   75
(*Exeunt.*)

Scene 3

SCENE: *A church.*

(*Enter* DON PEDRO, CLAUDIO, *and three or four with tapers.*)
CLAUDIO: Is this the monument of Leonato?
LORD: It is, my lord.
CLAUDIO (*Reading out of a scroll.*):

>   Done to death by slanderous tongues
>   Was the Hero that here lies.
>   Death, in guerdon of her wrongs,   5
>   Gives her fame which never dies.
>   So the life that died with shame
>   Lives in death with glorious fame.
>   Hang thou there upon the tomb
>   Praising her when I am dumb.   10
>   Now, music, sound, and sing your solemn hymn.

(*Song.*)

>   Pardon, goddess of the night,
>   Those that slew thy virgin knight,
>   For the which, with songs of woe,
>   Round about her tomb they go,   15
>   Midnight, assist our moan.
>   Help us to sigh and groan,

Heavily, heavily.
Graves, yawn and yield your dead,
Till death be uttered,   20
Heavily, heavily.

CLAUDIO: Now, unto thy bones, goodnight.
    Yearly will I do this rite.

DON PEDRO: Good morrow, masters. Put your torches out.
    The wolves have preyed; and look, the gentle day   25
    Before the wheels of Phoebus, round about
    Dapples the drowsy east with spots of gray.
    Thanks to you all, and leave us. Fare you well.

CLAUDIO: Good morrow, masters. Each his several way.

DON PEDRO: Come, let us hence, and put on other weeds,   30
    And then to Leonato's we will go.

CLAUDIO: And Hymen now with luckier issue speed's
    Than this for whom we rendered up this woe.

(*Exeunt.*)

Scene 4

SCENE: *A room in* LEONATO's *house.*

(*Enter* LEONATO, ANTONIO, BENEDICK, BEATRICE, MARGARET, URSULA, FRIAR
    FRANCIS, *and* HERO.)

FRIAR FRANCIS: Did I not tell you she was innocent?

LEONATO: So are the Prince and Claudio, who accused her
    Upon the error that you heard debated.
    But Margaret was in some fault for this,
    Although against her will, as it appears   5
    In the true course of all the question.

ANTONIO: Well, I am glad that all things sort so well.

BENEDICK: And so am I, being else by faith enforced
    To call young Claudio to a reckoning for it.

LEONATO: Well, daughter, and you gentlewomen all,   10
    withdraw into a chamber by yourselves,
    And when I send for you, come hither masked.
    (*Exeunt Ladies.*)
    The Prince and Claudio promised by this hour
    To visit me.—You know your office, brother.
    You must be father to your brother's daughter,   15
    And give her to young Claudio.

ANTONIO: Which I will do with confirmed countenance.

BENEDICK: Friar, I must entreat your pains, I think.

FRIAR FRANCIS: To do what, signior?

BENEDICK: To bind me, or undo me, one of them.—   20
    Signior Leonato, truth it is, good signior,
    Your niece regards me with an eye of favor.
LEONATO: That eye my daughter lent her: 'tis most true.
BENEDICK: And I do with an eye of love requite her.
LEONATO: The sight whereof I think you had from me,   25
    From Claudio and the Prince. But what's your will?
BENEDICK: Your answer, sir, is enigmatical.
    But, for my will, my will is your goodwill
    May stand with ours, this day to be conjoined
    In the state of honorable marriage—   30
    In which, good friar, I shall desire your help.
LEONATO: My heart is with your liking.
FRIAR FRANCIS: And my help.
    Here comes the Prince and Claudio.
(*Enter* DON PEDRO *and* CLAUDIO, *and two or three others.*)
DON PEDRO: Good morrow to this fair assembly.
LEONATO: Good morrow, prince; good morrow, Claudio.   35
    We here attend you. Are you yet determined
    Today to marry with my brother's daughter?
CLAUDIO: I'll hold my mind were she an Ethiope.
LEONATO: Call her forth, brother. Here's the Friar ready.
(*Exit* ANTONIO.)
DON PEDRO: Good morrow, Benedick. Why, what's the matter   40
    That you have such a February face,
    So full of frost, of storm and cloudiness?
CLAUDIO: I think he thinks upon the savage bull.
    Tush, fear not, man. We'll tip thy horns with gold,
    And all Europa shall rejoice at thee,   45
    As once Europa did at lusty Jove
    When he would play the noble beast in love.
BENEDICK: Bull Jove, sir, had an amiable low,
    And some such strange bull leapt your father's cow
    And got a calf in that same noble feat   50
    Much like to you, for you have just his bleat.
CLAUDIO: For this I owe you. Here comes other reck'nings.
    (*Re-enter* ANTONIO, *with the Ladies masked.*)
    Which is the lady I must seize upon?
ANTONIO: This same is she, and I do give you her.
CLAUDIO: Why, then, she's mine.—Sweet, let me see your face.   55
LEONATO: No, that you shall not, till you take her hand
    Before this friar and swear to marry her.
CLAUDIO: Give me your hand before this holy friar.
    I am your husband, if you like of me.

HERO: And when I lived, I was your other wife,   60
    (Unmasking.)
    And when you loved, you were my other husband.
CLAUDIO: Another Hero!
HERO: Nothing certainer.
    One Hero died defiled, but I do live,
    And surely as I live, I am a maid.
DON PEDRO: The former Hero! Hero that is dead!   65
LEONATO: She died, my lord, but whiles her slander lived.
FRIAR FRANCIS: All this amazement can I qualify,
    When after that the holy rites are ended,
    I'll tell you largely of fair Hero's death.
    Meantime let wonder seem familiar,   70
    And to the chapel let us presently.
BENEDICK: Soft and fair, friar.—Which is Beatrice?
BEATRICE *(Unmasking.)*: I answer to that name. What is your will?
BENEDICK: Do not you love me?
BEATRICE: Why no, no more than reason.
BENEDICK: Why then, your uncle and the Prince and Claudio   75
    Have been deceived. They swore you did.
BEATRICE: Do not you love me?
BENEDICK: Troth, no no more than reason.
BEATRICE: Why, then my cousin Margaret and Ursula
    Are much deceived, for they did swear you did.
BENEDICK: They swore that you were almost sick for me.   80
BEATRICE: They swore that you were well-nigh dead for me.
BENEDICK: 'Tis no such matter. Then you do not love me?
BEATRICE: No, truly, but in friendly recompense.
LEONATO: Come, cousin, I am sure you love the gentleman.
CLAUDIO: And I'll be sworn upon't that he loves her,   85
    For here's a paper written in his hand,
    A halting sonnet of his own pure brain,
    Fashion'd to Beatrice.
HERO: And here's another,
    Writ in my cousin's hand, stol'n from her pocket,
    Containing her affection unto Benedick.   90
BENEDICK: A miracle! Here's our own hands against our hearts. Come, I
    will have thee, but by this light, I take thee for pity.
BEATRICE: I would not deny you, but, by this good day, I yield upon great
    persuasion, and partly to save your life, for I was told you were in a
    consumption.   95
BENEDICK: Peace! I will stop your mouth.
(Kissing her.)
DON PEDRO: How dost thou, Benedick, the married man?

BENEDICK: I'll tell thee what, prince: a college of wit-crackers cannot flout
me out of my humor. Dost thou think I care for a satire or an epigram?
No. If a man will be beaten with brains, he shall wear nothing hand-   100
some about him. In brief, since I do purpose to marry, I will think nothing to any purpose that the world can say against it, and therefore never
flout at me for what I have said against it. For man is a giddy thing, and
this is my conclusion.—For thy part, Claudio, I did think to have beaten
thee, but in that thou art like to be my kinsman, live unbruised, and   105
love my cousin.

CLAUDIO: I had well hoped thou wouldst have denied Beatrice, that I might
have cudgelled thee out of thy single life, to make thee a double-dealer,
which out of question thou wilt be, if my cousin do not look exceedingly narrowly to thee.   110

BENEDICK: Come, come, we are friends: let's have a dance ere we are
married, that we may lighten our own hearts and our wives' heels.

LEONATO: We'll have dancing afterward.

BENEDICK: First, of my word! Therefore play, music.—Prince, thou art sad.
Get thee a wife, get thee a wife. There is no staff more reverend than   115
one tipped with horn.

(*Enter a* MESSENGER.)

MESSENGER: My lord, your brother John is ta'en in flight,
And brought with armed men back to Messina.

BENEDICK: Think not on him till tomorrow: I'll devise thee brave punish-
ments for him.—Strike up, pipers!   120

(*Dance.*)

(*Exeunt.*)

■ Find the scenes in this play where point of view has an impact on the plot. Look
at instances where characters misunderstand what they see or hear or where
they misreport what they have witnessed. In each instance, establish whose
point of view moves the plot forward (for instance, Dogberry reports X;
therefore, Don Pedro does Y), and explain why that particular point of view
proves problematic.

■ If not for a few "chance" turns of events, this play could easily have been a
tragedy. The misunderstandings here are, by themselves, no more comic than
the misunderstandings that result in Romeo's and Juliet's suicides in another
play by the same author. Where, if ever, does this play shift from this tragic
potential to comedy? What issues are not resolved by the end of the play?

■ Look at the central couples in this play: Beatrice and Benedick, Hero and
Claudio. In what ways is one couple more complex than the other? To
what extent is one couple more important to the action of the play than the
other?

Experiencing Literature through Writing

1. Select a single work from this chapter (or any other). Identify the point of view that guides us through this story. Explain why that point of view is significant to our understanding of the text. As you write, consider the following questions:

   a. What specific details in the work help you determine the point of view in this work?

   b. What details in the work make this point of view particularly interesting? For instance, are there parts of this story that no one else would be able to experience?

   c. How does the author use point of view to influence our sympathies within the story?

   d. Are there details within this work in which point of view does not seem significant? Can you explain how your comments about point of view have some bearing on these details?

2. The reading selections in this chapter are related under the general heading of "Trust and Doubt." In each, the author uses the perspective of a character to tell the story in a particular way. Discuss the manipulation of our sympathies through point of view in one or more of these works. How does the author make us trust (or doubt) the characters through whom we hear each of these stories? How do we get to know the character? How much of that knowledge comes from what the character tells us? How much comes from some other source?

3. The issue of perspective within literary works is tied closely to character, but it also determines how we receive the plot of the story. We make sense of a point of view because we understand the character who is standing in that position, and we make sense of what is happening because of our position in relation to events. Pick one work, and discuss the impact of perspectiove upon our understanding of that work's plot.

5 Setting

Where and When Does This Action Take Place?

Why Does it Make a Difference?

Setting may be thought of in narrow terms as the physical and temporal **background** to a story. In the theater, the word *setting* refers specifically to how items are arranged on a stage. Actors move about the stage in relation to these items. Normally, our attention is focused primarily on the actors. There is nothing wrong about such restrictive ideas of the word when one wants a restricted idea, but this chapter will define **setting** more expansively as the total environment within which narrative actions take place. The characters' general living conditions as well as the time and place in which they live constitute setting.

Such a broad use of the word *setting* also suggests its great importance. Reflect for a moment on an especially powerful event in your life. It's likely that you remember that event not only as an action but as an action grounded in a particular time and place. It would be hard to narrate the action without describing where and when the action unfolded. Or put the case in reverse: Reflect for a moment on a significant place in your life. It's likely that the place will provoke you to feel, to remember, to tell stories. Setting is not merely background—or at least not necessarily only background. Setting can function as part of a literary text's whole effect.

PLACE AND TIME

Place and time function together in our lives as well as in literary texts. We often anticipate the importance of our memories by taking pictures of grand occasions (graduation, birthdays, moving to a new home, and so on). Most of us strive to catch not only people on film but the physical environments closely tied to the people's experience. A common sign of the way we link place and action is displayed every time a vacationer sets out to write a message on a postcard.

The front of the postcard shows an idealized picture of the place where the writer is visiting; the back of the card allows the writer to report on what has happened in that place. The writer may describe what he or she has been doing or might tell about the monuments that are pictured on the front of the card. Even though the results are often banal ("The weather is beautiful; wish you were here"), the linking of action and character with setting makes postcards a pleasure to receive. Skilled authors who can take us fully into another place or time offer far deeper pleasures.

In his famous personal essay "Once More to the Lake," E. B. White shows what it is like to recall old events through the act of revisiting a place. A complex sense of time past, present, and (through the son) future emerges from the description. White registers specific details and makes it clear those details count for something. He writes of how similar the lake (where he had vacationed with his father) still is when he returns years later with his son, but he also comments on the differences that have come about due to progress: "[T]he road under our sneakers was only a two-track road. The middle track was missing, the one with the marks of the hooves and the splotches of dried, flaky manure. There had always been three tracks to choose from in choosing which track to walk in; now the choice was narrowed down to two." The

distinction here between trails carved by horses and trails kept clear by automobiles is subtle, but White uses the difference in the place to help him describe the narrowing options of his own life as he has grown older. The most disconcerting difference for him is the fact that his son has now taken his place, performing his role in the memories that White associates with the lake.

White's setting is hardly mere background; it is an integral part of the meaning that unfolds in the narrative. It exerts a power over the action of the story. The nature of the place is dynamic; it changes over time in ways that chart White's own progress through life. An appeal of setting within fiction is that, as in White's memoir, it brings the past to life—it makes the past meaningful to the present moment.

A Note to Student Writers: Descriptive Summaries

E. B. White is coauthor with Richard Strunk of a classic writing guide still widely used. In *Elements of Style*, Strunk and White emphasize the importance of concrete, specific images to vivid descriptive writing. In the previous passage, White wants to be sure we see the tracks cut in the dirt road, for he knows that if we don't get a very solid feel for the reality of the place, none of the ideas or emotions that have grown from the place will be compelling. Readers need something they can access through touch, sight, or sound.

Critical writers can learn something from this emphasis on the concrete. It's important to establish a very clear sense of a text to be analyzed before jumping into an analysis. We've said that "why" and "how" questions help one think analytically, but it's worth remembering that a simple "what" question often needs to come first. A "what" question won't likely lead you to a thesis, but it may help you clarify your sense of a topic. It's useful to think of summary as a kind of description. And like any good description, summary must build on well-selected and clearly presented details that can be checked against the reader's/viewer's own experience.

Experiencing Literature through Setting

Sometimes, setting makes other elements of narrative (character and action) decidedly secondary; setting can be the primary force of meaning and emotional effect. In "February Evening in New York," Denise Levertov embeds a brief scene involving two characters in the middle of a richly textured impression of a specific place and time. We're forced to read character and incident in context of feelings created by the enormous energy of city life in New York.

Denise Levertov (1923–)

February Evening in New York (1959)

As the stores close, a winter light
  opens air to iris blue,
  glint of frost through the smoke,
  grains of mica, salt of the sidewalk.
As the buildings close, released autonomous   5
  feet pattern the streets
  in hurry and stroll; balloon heads
  drift and dive above them; the bodies
  aren't really there.
As the lights brighten, as the sky darkens,   10
  a woman with crooked heels says to another woman
  while they step along at a fair pace,
  *"You know, I'm telling you, what I love best
  is life. I love life! Even if I ever get
  to be old and wheezy—or limp! You know?*   15
  Limping along?—I'd still ..." Out of hearing.
To the multiple disordered tones
  of gears changing, a dance
  to the compass points, out, four-way river.
  Prospect of sky   20
  wedged into avenues, left at the ends of streets,
  west sky, east sky: more life tonight! A range
  of open time at winter's outskirts.

Notice that unlike many poems we have seen in this book, this poem has no spacing after any of the syntactical or stanzaic breaks in its lines. Everything crowds together as we read, just as the New York sidewalks grow packed as stores close and people are "released." The sentences that begin with "as" also grow progressively longer (four lines, five lines, then seven lines). Impressions pile upon impressions. The importance of setting to this poem is so great that Levertov has the setting reflected in the poem's structure. In the density of this poem's impressions, we're encouraged to read the lines of the "woman with crooked heels" as indicative of a larger encompassing energy that subsumes even the sky that is barely "wedged into avenues" for the viewer who looks to the ends of the streets.

Setting can also take a central function in sections of extended narratives. The following passage is taken from Theodore Dreiser's *Sister Carrie*, a

very long novel published in 1900 and acknowledged for its groundbreaking
realism—a mode of depiction that builds on close, accurate attention to
specific historical and social settings. In this selection, eighteen-year-old
Carrie Meeber has arrived alone in Chicago, and through her eyes we see a
place that is as unfamiliar to us (as a modern audience) as it is to her, a
newcomer to the city. The narrator is telling us about Carrie and about the
Chicago that she sees. This narrator reveals the social pressures that work
upon Carrie through a description of the department store she moves
through. As you read, note the ways in which the setting is essential to our
understanding of Carrie's character.

Theodore Dreiser (1871–1945)

from Sister Carrie (1900)

At that time the department store was in its earliest form of successful
operation, and there were not many. The first three in the United States,
established about 1884, were in Chicago. Carrie was familiar with the names
of several through the advertisements in the "Daily News," and now proceeded to seek them. The words of Mr. McManus had somehow managed to
restore her courage, which had fallen low, and she dared to hope that this
new line would offer her something. Some time she spent in wandering up
and down, thinking to encounter the buildings by chance, so readily is the
mind, bent upon prosecuting a hard but needful errand, eased by that self-
deception which the semblance of search, without the reality, gives. At last
she inquired of a police officer, and was directed to proceed "two blocks up,"
where she would find "The Fair."

The nature of these vast retail combinations, should they ever permanently disappear, will form an interesting chapter in the commercial history
of our nation. Such a flowering out of a modest trade principle the world
had never witnessed up to that time. They were along the line of the most
effective retail organisation, with hundreds of stores coordinated into one
and laid out upon the most imposing and economic basis. They were handsome, bustling, successful affairs, with a host of clerks and a swarm of patrons.
Carrie passed along the busy aisles, much affected by the remarkable displays
of trinkets, dress goods, stationery, and jewelry. Each separate counter was a
show place of dazzling interest and attraction. She could not help feeling the
claim of each trinket and valuable upon her personally, and yet she did not
stop. There was nothing there which she could not have used—nothing
which she did not long to own. The dainty slippers and stockings, the
delicately frilled skirts and petticoats, the laces, ribbons, hair-combs, purses,
all touched her with individual desire, and she felt keenly the fact that not

any of these things were in the range of her purchase. She was a work-seeker, an outcast without employment, one whom the average employee could tell at a glance was poor and in need of a situation.

It must not be thought that any one could have mistaken her for a nervous, sensitive, high-strung nature, cast unduly upon a cold, calculating, and unpoetic world. Such certainly she was not. But women are peculiarly sensitive to their adornment.

Not only did Carrie feel the drag of desire for all which was new and pleasing in apparel for women, but she noticed too, with a touch at the heart, the fine ladies who elbowed and ignored her, brushing past in utter disregard of her presence, themselves eagerly enlisted in the materials which the store contained. Carrie was not familiar with the appearance of her more fortunate sisters of the city. Neither had she before known the nature and appearance of the shop girls with whom she now compared poorly. They were pretty in the main, some even handsome, with an air of independence and indifference which added, in the case of the more favoured, a certain piquancy. Their clothes were neat, in many instances fine, and wherever she encountered the eye of one it was only to recognize in it a keen analysis of her own position—her individual shortcomings of dress and that shadow of manner which she thought must hang about her and make clear to all who and what she was. A flame of envy lighted in her heart. She realised in a dim way how much the city held—wealth, fashion, ease—every adornment for women, and she longed for dress and beauty with a whole heart.

Department store interior, ca. 1900

On the second floor were the managerial offices, to which, after some inquiry, she was now directed. There she found other girls ahead of her, applicants like herself, but with more of that self-satisfied and independent air which experience of the city lends; girls who scrutinised her in a painful manner. After a wait of perhaps three-quarters of an hour, she was called in turn. ■

The place in this instance defines the character. We understand and feel Carrie's insecurity through the environment within which she lives. Her excitement, fear, envy, and ambition, as well as her social status and educational background, all become apparent as things we both know and experience through her engagement with the department store and all it contains.

THE ROLE OF PHYSICAL OBJECTS

Objects can also serve as props to activate the memory and retrieve the past. Well-chosen details can bring alive the social and emotional conditions of a character's environment. In Kazuo Ishiguro's novel *Remains of the Day* (1989), the narrator is Mr. Stevens, a butler whose identity is linked to the prestigious house that he has long served; however, Stevens has had the misfortune to move through his career as the upper class declines both economically and morally. In one scene, while on a journey away from Darlington Hall (the place where he has spent almost all of his adult life), Stevens considers taking a side trip to the English village of Mursden. Because his entire life is bound within a very narrow social world, he assumes that the reader is as fluent in the details of butlery as he is. The fact that we are not so fluent contributes to our understanding of how contained a life Stevens has led. Note the ways in which Ishiguro's butler, addressing the reader directly, evokes a sense of place and time through describing household details.

Kazuo Ishiguro (1954–)

from **Remains of the Day** (1989)

Perhaps "Mursden" will ring a bell for you, as it did for me upon my first spotting it on the road atlas yesterday. In fact, I must say I was tempted to make a slight detour from my planned route just to see the village. Mursden, Somerset, was where the firm of Giffen and Co. was once situated, and it was to Mursden one was required to dispatch one's order for a supply of Giffen's dark candles of polish, "to be flaked, mixed into wax and applied by hand." For some time, Giffen's was undoubtedly the finest silver polish available, and it was only the appearance of new chemical substances on the market shortly before the war that caused the demand for this impressive product to decline.

As I remember, Giffen's appeared at the beginning of the twenties, and I am sure I am not alone in closely associating its emergence with that change of mood within our profession—that change which came to push the polishing of silver to the position of central importance it still by and large maintains today. This shift was, I believe, like so many other major shifts around this period, a generational matter; it was during these years that our generation of butlers "came of age," and figures like Mr. Marshall, in particular, played a crucial part in making silver-polishing so central. This is not to suggest, of course, that the polishing of silver—particularly those items that would appear at table—was not always regarded a serious duty. But it would not be unfair to suggest that many butlers of, say, my father's generation did not consider the matter such a key one, and this is evidenced by the fact that in those days, the butler of a household rarely supervised the polishing of silver directly, being content to leave it to, say, the under-butler's whims, carrying out inspections only intermittently. It was Mr. Marshall, it is generally agreed, who was the first to recognize the full significance of silver—namely, that no other objects in the house were likely to come under such intimate scrutiny from outsiders as was silver during a meal, and as such, it served as a public index of a house's standards. And Mr. Marshall it was who first caused stupefaction amongst ladies and gentlemen visiting Charleville House with displays of silver polished to previously unimagined standards. Very soon, naturally, butlers up and down the country, under pressure from their employers, were focusing their minds on the question of silver-polishing. There quickly sprang up, I recall, various butlers, each claiming to have discovered methods by which they could surpass Mr. Marshall—methods they made a great show of keeping secret, as though they were French chefs guarding their recipes. But I am confident—as I was then—that the sorts of elaborate and mysterious processes performed by someone like Mr. Jack Neighbours had little or no discernible effect on the end result. As far as I was concerned, it was a simple enough matter: one used good polish, and one supervised closely. Giffen's was the polish ordered by all discerning butlers of the time, and if this product was used correctly, one had no fear of one's silver being second best to anybody's.

I am glad to be able to recall numerous occasions when the silver at Darlington Hall had a pleasing impact upon observers. For instance, I recall Lady Astor remarking, not without a certain bitterness, that our silver "was probably unrivalled." I recall also watching Mr. George Bernard Shaw, the renowned playwright, at dinner one evening, examining closely the dessert spoon before him, holding it up to the light and comparing its surface to that of a nearby platter, quite oblivious to the company around him. ∎

The claim that something as mundane as silver polish might be as significant as our narrator suggests would seem preposterous until we see how much this particular product had an impact upon the work that Stevens did. Inspired by an obscure place-name that is familiar to him only from its association with a household product, Stevens tells us much about a time and a social condition that is unfamiliar to us. The idea that butlers might share the social pretensions of their master, the fact that there was competition among household staffs, and the possibility that it might play out in the glow of silver all help put us into another world. That world becomes more grounded in reality through Stevens's reflections upon a specific consumer product.

Making Connections

In Chapter 4, we considered point of view. In this passage from *Remains of the Day*, Ishiguro develops a distinct point of view through the voice of his narrator. He uses Stevens's lengthy reflections on silver polish to create for us a certain view of class and propriety. We see the setting from the perspective of the butler, and we understand that what Stevens reports is controlled by his years of service to the upper class.

This element of setting also contributes to our understanding of the delicate psychological state that Mr. Stevens is in throughout his journey. The imaginative "detour" he takes to Mursden is clearly motivated by his need to find a stable reference point. Stevens's car trip from one part of England to another moves him far from his sense of home. Coming upon a town associated with something he knows well helps him maintain some sense of comfort and confidence in an unfamiliar place. Reflecting so much on this particular commercial product makes him feel that he has in fact been connected to this new, wider world—even if he hasn't *lived* in that world.

Stevens's silver polish is real enough, but it's hardly familiar to us. The fact that we don't know anything about the product contributes to our sense that the world he inhabits is passing. When a product mentioned or shown in a narrative *is* familiar to us, we may grow suspicious: we might dismiss a scene that includes a brand-name item as mere product placement—an advertisement embedded in the work. Although we are often right to be cynical (corporations routinely pay to have their products show up in movies, for example), we should not fail to see how everyday products can be integrated meaningfully into a narrative and may contribute significantly to the way setting functions. Movies illustrate the point nicely. For example, think of the ways familiar items scattered over a tabletop might function in relation to a larger action within a film. In a horror movie, the familiarity might help us identify with the world presented and therefore make impending disasters feel more threatening. In a domestic drama, we might define our relation to characters through the items on the tabletop: a can of Mountain

Dew would say one thing, an open bottle of Jack Daniels another, and a Perrier still another. If a character in a comedy pulls a shiny, late-model Mercedes SUV into a McDonald's drive-thru and orders a Diet Coke, Big Mac, and fries—supersized—we'll pick up a general satiric comment on contemporary American culture. If a character in a detective story parks his 1962 Chevy Impala in front of a Foster's Freeze (a California chain particularly popular in the early days of fast food), we'll be located in a very specific *milieu*—a French word that literally means "center" or "middle" and is used to designate particular social, temporal, and physical surroundings.

Mise-en-scène (another French term) suggests what is quite literally put into the scene. It originally referred to the staging of plays: the arrangement and inclusion of furniture, backdrops, stray items, and props that make up the environment within which characters act. In a similar fashion, film critics use the term *mise-en-scène* to describe what is captured within a shot. The concept applies to any constructed work of art that places objects in a scene. It is useful to remember that details of setting are selected, framed, and foregrounded with a purpose in mind. Objects don't just happen to be part of a setting.

IMAGINARY PLACES

Art is always about bringing imagination to life. So far, we've treated setting in terms of how artists lull us into accepting a setting as real—as identifying it as a place and time we can recognize and relate to. On some occasions, setting functions much differently. In Edgar Allan Poe's "Ulalume—a Ballad," we quickly get lost in both time and space. Even the place-names we have are confusing: "It was hard by the dim lake of Auber, / In the misty mid region of Weir." You can scan a map very closely and not find Auber or Weir. Poe hasn't consulted an atlas, for he doesn't so much want to identify his setting as to use setting to evoke a sensation. Auber and Weir are the names of two landscape painters of the period. Poe is not asking us to accept the reality of these places; he is asking that we associate his poem with feelings we might have in relation to other artistic works. Here, as is often the case in gothic pieces, **atmosphere** (feelings evoked in the reader through setting) prevails over concrete matters of time and space. Poe's setting radically disconnects us from everyday life.

Many other works seek to create through setting an interplay between the real and the fanciful. This problem becomes interesting in the directions that a playwright gives to describe the setting of a play. Unlike fiction, in which the entire setting appears in the text of the story, the play provides only the dialogue. To produce a play, set designers, who follow the instructions the playwright gives in the introduction to the play, will build the actual stages on which the actors will perform. They make the imaginary setting described in the printed play into some realized place. In *The Glass Menagerie* (p. 456), Tennessee Williams describes specific realistic features of the Wingfield apartment, where the play takes place, including a fire escape that is a part of the set. But that detail, which is a rather straightforward instruction for a set designer, is interesting to Williams because it is "*a structure whose name is a touch of accidental poetic truth, for all of these huge buildings are always burning with the slow and implacable fires of human desperation.*" He describes a real object that a stage carpenter might build as he shows that his interest is in the meaning that he finds in that object. He sets the action in a specific, real place, but his explanation is of its symbolic value rather than of its real details. To describe the setting, he insists that this play is set in "*memory and is therefore nonrealistic. Memory takes a lot of poetic license. It omits some details, others are exaggerated, according to the emotional value of the articles it touches, for memory is seated predominantly in the heart. The interior is therefore rather dim and poetic.*" *Dim* is an adjective that is instructive for those who try to translate these directions into a real stage; *poetic* is a bit more problematic and open to a far greater range of possible meanings. This playwright emphasizes the imaginary nature of the real place that is to be created on the stage.

Movies again may serve to illustrate the importance of setting. The level of planning that goes into each frame of film (and every aspect of setting) becomes clear when we look at the storyboards that directors draw long before they begin to shoot a film. Because filming requires so many artists working together, the director will plan out each shot in advance. To tell the story, the director determines where the action will take place and what camera angles will be necessary to track that action. Looking at the storyboards helps us appreciate the tremendous planning and work that often goes into creating everything we see. Initial storyboards quite literally sketch the basic elements of a setting. By the time that we see the final product, the production team has fleshed out that sketch to give it exactly the desired look and feel.

Experiencing Film through Setting

The following sequence includes a detailed sketch from the storyboards and the corresponding shot from two scenes of Jean-Pierre Jeunet's *Amélie* (2001). Jeunet is known to be one of the most conscientious planners in the film business; these sequences demonstrate that planning a film consists

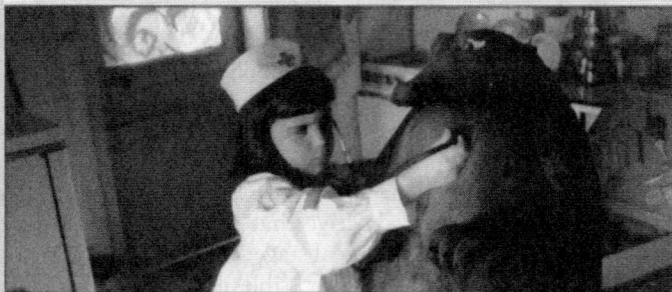

Storyboards and film stills from *Amélie* (2001)

of far more than just writing dialogue. Look at the director's evolving ideas about the angles from which we see the characters. Notice that the director has an idea of how the details of the set should emphasize the action. As you look at the details of each shot, describe the setting. When does the action take place? What sorts of places are these? How do the details that we see here suggest a set of larger details that we cannot see?

Amélie is a film that creates a distinct world that is real in all of its details but does not quite feel like any real world we know. Even in these two shots, one can see something of this effect. The yellow quality of the lighting suggests that the scenes are set in some past time. The serious girl who is examining the stuffed monster is working in an environment that helps emphasize her young professionalism. The woman sits in a bath that is elegant enough to have come out of the latest design catalogue, and the careful arrangement of light and flowers is at odds with her ordinary appearance. Jeunet seems to want us to look at the world with a fresh perspective—to observe subtle beauties that are somehow obscured by their familiarity. The little things that don't quite mesh catch our attention and make us see in unaccustomed ways.

Jeunet's sort of visual playfulness is pressed to a further extreme in *Babe: Pig in the City* (1998). Director George Miller and his team create a city skyline for Babe to look out upon that is a composite of the world's most famous cities. The setting here is a wildly inventive mixture/blending of images that are simultaneously familiar and disorienting. Take a look at

Babe: Pig in the City (1998)

the still from the film, and try to identify as many famous structures as you can. What have the set designers done to make the buildings fit together in this particular cityscape? What sort of effect does this cityscape achieve? To what extent does it seem real? Where does the fantastic aspect begin?

Making Connections

Look back to the Friedrich paintings in Chapter 4 (p. 287). It may seem strange to set this movie still in comparison to famous nineteenth-century paintings, but Miller employs a similar technique in *Babe: Pig in the City*. Setting is felt not only as a place but as a particular character's experience of place. The audience joins in that experience by looking, in effect, over the shoulder of the character. Setting isn't just background.

Why would the filmmakers favor a composite skyline over a real one?

Also consider the effect on the audience of framing the shot with the back of Babe's (the pig's) head looking out at the city. The main character is in the position (along with the audience) of taking it all in.

A Note to Student Writers: Paying Attention to Details

The first step to writing about setting is to notice details. As you read, don't focus just on the action. Look around the characters to see where they are standing, what is in the background, and what objects they are holding as the action goes on around them. Your goal is to freeze the frame of the narrative and to compile lists of the surrounding details. As you develop your thoughts about setting, you must do something with that list. It is never enough just to list, but as you start to discuss a detail or two that you find particularly interesting, you will probably begin to see connections between that detail and other details of the setting. Ask yourself which details are most significant, explain why, and justify your rankings. Notice how these details have been presented, and think about how they contribute to the action that you were focused on before you began to focus closely on setting. When you write about setting, you will quickly discover that the setting is significant precisely because of the insight that it gives you about character or plot or some other element of the story. None of these elements exist in isolation, but the exercise of noticing setting helps a reader pay attention to details of all sorts.

MODELING CRITICAL ANALYSIS: ROBERT BROWNING, MY LAST DUCHESS

Robert Browning's "My Last Duchess" (p. 303) is a **dramatic monologue**— that is, a poem in which a single speaker addresses an audience within a dramatic situation. We can start by thinking here of setting in specifically theatrical terms. To imagine in our mind's eye how Browning sets his stage, we need a chair that is positioned in front of the painting. And of course, we need the painting as well as the drawn curtain to the side of it. We also need some objects of art about the room to indicate the material grandeur of the place and a stairwell that suggests the two are in private quarters above the "company" on the main floor, who likely await news of the negotiation. This need not be a very elaborately set stage, but each item and its placement are important.

Once the scene is set, some interpretive possibilities become clearer. For example, it's possible we can learn something of the power relationship between the duke and the envoy by the position of the chair. Note that the duke seems to orchestrate things throughout. He moves the envoy in position in front of the painting and asks (directs?) him to sit and look carefully. The curtain is normally drawn, so it would seem the duke has a deliberate purpose in placing the envoy before his "last Duchess." Once seated, the duke recounts her story and her fate. She displeased him; she is dead. Once the duchess's story is told, the duke asks the envoy to rise from the chair. He makes his claim on a generous dowry from the prospective duchess's family. He is ready to return to the company. And as he invites (orders?) the envoy to go downstairs with him, he calls attention to a statue that depicts Neptune "Taming a sea-horse." Through that statue, Browning underscores the duke's obsession with control evident from the very start in the way he positioned the chair to direct the envoy's attention.

The specifically dramatic setting of "My Last Duchess" functions as part of the whole action, but it is not the only setting Browning employs. The duke's speech, in effect, also moves us offstage and conjures images of very different places. He recalls the duchess outdoors in an orchard relating to people other than the duke. We see her riding a mule around the terrace. The setting in which the meeting between the duke and envoy occurs grows still colder when contrasted to the vivacity of a life that was not bound by the walls of his house.

Using Setting to Focus Writing and Discussion

- Collect the details that the author offers about the setting. In any constructed world, whether that world is on film or in text, every detail of setting has been created by the artist. Look at the details that we might think of as mundane or insignificant. How do these relate to the rest of the work?
- Where does the author describe the setting? Is it all in one place or dispersed throughout the text?
- Whose voice gives us this setting? In what ways is this fact significant?
- Which does the author describe first, the setting or the character? In what ways does the description of one influence the description of the other?

- To what extent does the setting determine how the characters act or think?
- To what extent is there some contrast, or even conflict, between the characters in the text and the setting that they occupy?
- If there are different settings within the work, how are these differences articulated, and how do the different settings play different roles in the text?
- In what way does the setting help establish a tone in this work?

Anthology

FROM GOTHIC SPACE TO RECOGNIZABLE PLACE: CREATING SETTING

In 1761, Giovanni Piranesi published *Imaginary Prisons*, a book of etchings that depict imaginary interiors of places of torture and confinement. His work as an artist of architecture and as a stage designer is evident in the image that is presented here from that book. This unreal space has depth, texture, and levels of detail that make it seem entirely real. In addition, this place conveys

Giovanni Piranesi, from *Imaginary Prisons* (1761)

a mood: it feels oppressive, confusing, and unpleasant. The vaulted ceilings in the background look much like what we would expect to see in a cathedral, but here the shadows, the network of stairs and bridges, the hanging chains, the projecting beams, and the imposing grillwork make the structure seem more subterranean than soaring. Piranesi's etching provides a useful reminder of the ways in which setting can evoke a mood and suggest a story, even without character or action.

In the selections that follow, you will find some very different created spaces. Some are closely related to the Piranesi etching—vaguely old but without any referent to signal a specific time. These settings often feel dark without necessarily being night. And they can be weird. In Edgar Allan Poe's "The Fall of the House of Usher," you should note how the stones of the ancient house seem woven together with the surrounding damp vegetation. The house's unreality is further emphasized by the narrator's difficulty in distinguishing reality from reflection. Samuel Taylor Coleridge's "Kubla Khan" (written, Coleridge insists, directly from dream imagery) also creates a setting that functions not to ground us in reality but to displace us from the real—to break down familiar ways of knowing and feeling. In these works, atmosphere associated with place is as important as anything that might happen in the narrative.

Also included in this section are stories and poems that depend upon detailed renderings of recognizable places. The poems by Joy Harjo, Gary Soto, and Chitra Banerjee Divakaruni, for example, locate us in specifically defined times and places; such settings relate to the experience of people we might know. The apt detail, the keen eye for specifics makes the ordinary meaningful in works like these. They ground us in the situations of the characters.

Still other works in this group ground us in reality but keep pressing us with the sense that reality is what many people seek to escape or transcend. James Joyce's "Araby" is extremely dense in its particular rendering of a Dublin scene but renders with equal power the narrator's sense of confinement within that setting. Such a tension between mundane and romantic settings also infuses Tennessee Williams's *The Glass Menagerie*. In this play, the gothic seems to have encroached upon real life. The settings in which the characters act become essential to our appreciation of the play.

FICTION

James Joyce (1882–1941)

James Joyce was born in Dublin, Ireland. He was educated by Jesuit priests at Clongowes Wood College before entering the University of Dublin. He graduated in 1902 and moved to Paris but returned to Ireland a year later, where he began his career as a writer. Unfortunately, Dubliners were less than receptive to Joyce's work, so he and his wife, Nora Barnacle, moved to continental Europe. One of the first writers to employ the literary technique stream of consciousness, Joyce is remembered for his collection of short stories, *Dubliners*, as well as his novels, *A Portrait of the Artist as a Young Man*, *Ulysses*, and *Finnegans Wake*. Joyce's public and critical popularity improved as his career progressed, and he received grants from the Royal Literary Fund, the Civil List, and the Society of Authors. He is regarded today as one of the greatest of the modernists, and *Ulysses* as one of the period's undoubted masterpieces.

Araby (1914)

North Richmond Street, being blind, was a quiet street except at the hour when the Christian Brothers' School set the boys free. An uninhabited house of two stories stood at the blind end, detached from its neighbors in a square ground. The other houses of the street, conscious of decent lives within them, gazed at one another with brown imperturbable faces.

   The former tenant of our house, a priest, had died in the back drawing room. Air, musty from having long been enclosed, hung in all the rooms, and the waste room behind the kitchen was littered with old useless papers. Among these I found a few paper-covered books, the pages of which were curled and damp: *The Abbot*, by Walter Scott, *The Devout Communicant*, and *The Memoirs of Vidocq*. I liked the last best because its leaves were yellow. The wild garden behind the house contained a central apple-tree and a few straggling bushes under one of which I found the late tenant's rusty bicycle pump. He had been a very charitable priest; in his will he had left all his money to institutions and the furniture of his house to his sister.

   When the short days of winter came dusk fell before we had well eaten our dinners. When we met in the street the houses had grown somber. The space of sky above us was the color of ever-changing violet and towards it the lamps of the street lifted their feeble lanterns. The cold air stung us and we played till our bodies glowed. Our shouts echoed in the silent street. The career of our play brought us through the dark muddy lanes behind the houses where we ran the gantlet of the rough tribes from the cottages, to the back doors of the dark dripping gardens where odors arose from the ash-pits, to the dark odorous stables where a coachman smoothed and combed the horse or shook music from the buckled harness. When we returned to the street light from the kitchen windows had filled the areas. If my uncle was seen turning the corner we did in the shadow until we had seen him safely housed. Or if Mangan's sister came out on the doorstep to call her brother in to his tea we watched her from our shadow peer up and down the street. We waited to see whether she would remain or go in and, if she remained, we left our shadow and walked up to Mangan's steps resignedly. She was waiting for us, her figure defined by the light from the half-opened door. Her brother always teased her before he obeyed and I stood by the railings looking at her. Her dress swung as she moved her body and the soft rope of her hair tossed from side to side.

Every morning I lay on the floor in the front parlor watching her door. The blind was pulled down within an inch of the sash so that I could not be seen. When she came out on the doorstep my heart leaped. I ran to the hall, seized my books, and followed her. I kept her brown figure always in my eye and, when we came near the point at which our ways diverged, I quickened my pace and passed her. This happened morning after morning. I had never spoken to her, except for a few casual words, and yet her name was like a summons to all my foolish blood.

Her image accompanied me even in places the most hostile to romance. 5
On Saturday evenings when my aunt went marketing I had to go to carry some of the parcels. We walked through the flaring streets, jostled by drunken men and bargaining women, amid the curses of laborers, the shrill litanies of shopboys who stood on guard by the barrels of pigs' cheeks, the nasal chanting of street singers, who sang a *come-all-you* about O'Donovan Rossa, or a ballad about the troubles in our native land. These noises converged in a single sensation of life for me: I imagined that I bore my chalice safely through the throng of foes. Her name sprang to my lips at moments in strange prayers and praises which I myself did not understand. My eyes were often full of tears (I could not tell why) and at times a flood from my heart seemed to pour itself out into my bosom. I thought little of the future. I did not know whether I would ever speak to her or not or, if I spoke to her, how I could tell her of my confused adoration. But my body was like a harp and her words and gestures were like fingers running upon the wires.

One evening I went into the back drawing room in which the priest had died. It was a dark rainy evening and there was no sound in the house. Through one of the broken panes I heard the rain impinge upon the earth, the fine incessant needles of water playing in the sodden beds. Some distant lamp or lighted window gleamed below me. I was thankful that I could see so little. All my senses seemed to desire to veil themselves and, feeling that I was about to slip from them, I pressed the palms of my hands together until they trembled, murmuring: *O love! O love!* many times.

At last she spoke to me. When she addressed the first words to me I was so confused that I did not know what to answer. She asked me was I going to *Araby*. I forget whether I answered yes or no. It would be a splendid bazaar, she said; she would love to go.

"And why can't you?" I asked.

While she spoke she turned a silver bracelet round and round her wrist. She could not go, she said, because there would be a retreat that week in her convent. Her brother and two other boys were fighting for their caps and I was alone at the railings. She held one of the spikes, bowing her head towards me. The light from the lamp opposite our door caught the white curve of her neck, lit up her hair that rested there, and, falling, lit up the hand upon the railing. It fell over one side of her dress and caught the white border of a petticoat, just visible as she stood at ease.

"It's well for you," she said.

"If I go, I said, I will bring you something."

What innumerable follies laid waste my waking and sleeping thoughts after that evening! I wished to annihilate the tedious intervening days. I chafed against the work of school. At night in my bedroom and by day in the classroom her image came between me and the page I strove to read. The syllables of the word *Araby* were called to me through the silence in which my soul luxuriated and cast an Eastern enchantment over me. I asked for leave to go to the bazaar on Saturday night. My aunt was surprised and hoped it was not some Freemason affair. I answered few questions in class. I watched my master's face pass from amiability to sternness; he hoped I was not beginning to idle. I could not call my wandering thoughts together. I had hardly any patience with the serious work of life which, now that it stood between me and my desire, seemed to me child's play, ugly monotonous child's play.

On Saturday morning I reminded my uncle that I wished to go to the bazaar in the evening. He was fussing at the hallstand, looking for the hat-brush, and answered me curtly:

"Yes, boy, I know."

As he was in the hall I could not go into the front parlor and lie at the window. I left the house in bad humor and walked slowly towards the school. The air was pitilessly raw and already my heart misgave me.

When I came home to dinner my uncle had not yet been home. Still it was early. I sat staring at the clock for some time and, when its ticking began to irritate me, I left the room. I mounted the staircase and gained the upper part of the house. The high cold empty gloomy rooms liberated me and I went from room to room singing. From the front window I saw my companions playing below in the street. Their cries reached me weakened and indistinct and, leaning my forehead against the cool glass, I looked over at the dark house where she lived. I may have stood there for an hour, seeing nothing but the brown-clad figure cast by my imagination, touched discreetly by the lamplight at the curved neck, at the hand upon the railings, and at the border below the dress.

When I came downstairs again I found Mrs. Mercer sitting at the fire. She was an old garrulous woman, a pawnbroker's widow, who collected used stamps for some pious purpose. I had to endure the gossip of the tea-table. The meal was prolonged beyond an hour and still my uncle did not come.

Mrs. Mercer stood up to go: she was sorry she couldn't wait any longer, but it was after eight o'clock and she did not like to be out late, as the night air was bad for her. When she had gone I began to walk up and down the room, clenching my fists. My aunt said:

"I'm afraid you may put off your bazaar for this night of Our Lord."

At nine o'clock I heard my uncle's latchkey in the hall door. I heard him talking to himself and heard the hallstand rocking when it had received the weight of his overcoat. I could interpret these signs. When he was midway through his dinner I asked him to give me the money to go to the bazaar. He had forgotten.

"The people are in bed and after their first sleep now," he said. 20

I did not smile. My aunt said to him energetically:

"Can't you give him the money and let him go? You've kept him late enough as it is."

My uncle said he was very sorry he had forgotten. He said he believed in the old saying: *All work and no play makes Jack a dull boy*. He asked me where I was going and, when I had told him a second time he asked me did I know *The Arab's Farewell to His Steed*. When I left the kitchen he was about to recite the opening lines of the piece to my aunt.

I held a florin tightly in my hand as I strode down Buckingham Street towards the station. The sight of the streets thronged with buyers and glaring with gas recalled to me the purpose of my journey. I took my seat in a third-class carriage of a deserted train. After an intolerable delay the train moved out of the station slowly. It crept onward among ruinous houses and over the twinkling river. At Westland Row Station a crowd of people pressed to the carriage doors; but the porters moved them back saying it was a special train for the bazaar. I remained alone in the bare carriage. In a few minutes the train drew up beside an improvised wooden platform. I passed out on to the road and saw by the lighted dial of a clock that it was ten minutes to ten. In front of me was a large building which displayed the magical name.

I could not find any sixpenny entrance and, fearing that the bazaar 25 would be closed, I passed in quickly through a turnstile, handing a shilling to a weary-looking man. I found myself in a big hall girdled at half its height by a gallery. Nearly all the stalls were closed and the greater part of the hall was in darkness. I recognized a silence like that which pervades a church after a service. I walked into the center of the bazaar timidly. A few people were gathered about the stalls which were still open. Before a curtain, over which the words *Café Chantant* were written in colored lamps, two men were counting money on a salver. I listened to the fall of the coins.

Remembering with difficulty why I had come I went over to one of the stalls and examined porcelain vases and flowered tea-sets. At the door of the stall a young lady was talking and laughing with two young gentlemen. I remarked their English accents and listened vaguely to their conversation.

"O, I never said such a thing!"

"O, but you did!"

"O, but I didn't!"

"Didn't she say that?"

"Yes. I heard her."

"O, there's a...fib!"

Observing me the young lady came over and asked me did I wish to buy anything. The tone of her voice was not encouraging; she seemed to have spoken to me out of a sense of duty. I looked humbly at the great jars that stood like Eastern guards at either side of the dark entrance to the stall and murmured:

"No, thank you."

The young lady changed the position of one of the vases and went back to the two young men. They began to talk of the same subject. Once or twice the young lady glanced at me over her shoulder.

I lingered before her stall, though I knew my stay was useless, to make my interest in her wares seem the more real. Then I turned away slowly and walked down the middle of the bazaar. I allowed the two pennies to fall against the sixpence in my pocket. I heard a voice call from one end of the gallery that the light was out. The upper part of the hall was now completely dark.

Gazing into the darkness I saw myself as a creature driven and derided by vanity; and my eyes burned with anguish and anger.

- Discuss the importance of North Richmond Street to this story. How does this setting set up the tension in the story?
- How is Mangan's sister integral to both the plot and the setting of the story?
- How does the narrator's imagined *Araby* compare to the place he actually visits? Give specific details from the text to describe both versions of the place.

Edgar Allan Poe (1809–1849)

Edgar Allan Poe was born in Boston, Massachusetts. He was orphaned before he was three years old and was taken in (although never legally adopted) by the Allan family of Richmond, Virginia. A promising student, Poe attended the University of Virginia, but he gambled himself into debt and was forced to leave the school. Returning to his hometown of Boston, he joined the army, then attended West Point for a time, but was again unable to pay his tuition. He returned to Richmond and worked as a journalist, short story writer, and editor. His personal life was deeply troubled. After the death of his foster mother, he was cut off financially by John Allan (who had accepted young Poe only at the insistence of his childless wife). Poe's marriage to his thirteen-year-old cousin Virginia Clemm ended with her death at the age of twenty-two. Despite an erratic and painfully difficult career, Poe was an important figure in his time. He worked when the young nation was still struggling to find its literary identity; he remains a widely read and influential writer.

The Fall of the House of Usher (1845)

Son cœur est un luth suspendu;
Sitôt qu'on le touche il résonne.

—De Béranger

During the whole of a dull, dark, and soundless day in the autumn of the year, when the clouds hung oppressively low in the heavens, I had been passing alone, on horseback, through a singularly dreary tract of country; and at length found myself, as the shades of the evening drew on, within view of the melancholy House of Usher. I know not how it was—but, with the first glimpse of the building, a sense of insufferable gloom pervaded my spirit. I say insufferable; for the feeling was unrelieved by any of that half-pleasurable, because poetic, sentiment, with which the mind usually received even the sternest natural images of the desolate or terrible. I looked upon the scene before me—upon the mere house, and the simple landscape features of the domain—upon the bleak walls—upon the vacant eyelike windows—upon a few rank sedges—and upon a few white trunks of decayed trees—with an utter depression of soul which I can compare to no earthly sensation more properly than to the after-dream of the reveler upon opium—the bitter lapse into every-day life—the hideous dropping off of the veil. There was an iciness, a sinking, sickening of the heart—an unredeemed dreariness of thought which no goading of the imagination could torture into aught of the sublime. What was it—I paused to think—what was it that so unnerved me in the contemplation of the House of Usher? It was a mystery all insoluble; nor could I grapple with the shadowy fancies that crowded upon me as I pondered. I was forced to fall back upon the unsatisfactory conclusion, that while, beyond doubt, there *are* combinations of very simple natural objects which have the power of thus affecting us, still the analysis of this power lies among considerations beyond our depth. It was possible, I reflected, that a mere different arrangement of the particulars of the scene, of the details of the picture, would be sufficient to modify, or perhaps to annihilate its capacity for sorrowful impression; and acting upon this idea, I reined my horse to the precipitous brink of a black and lurid tarn that lay in unruffled lustre by the dwelling, and gazed down—but with a shudder even more thrilling than before—upon the remodelled and inverted images of the gray sedge, and the ghastly tree-stems, and the vacant and eye-like windows.

Nevertheless, in this mansion of gloom I now proposed to myself a sojourn of some weeks. Its proprietor, Roderick Usher, had been one of my boon companions in boyhood; but many years had elapsed since our last meeting. A letter, however, had lately reached me in a distant part of the country—a letter from him—which, in its wildly importunate nature, had admitted of no other than a personal reply. The MS. gave evidence of nervous agitation. The writer spoke of acute bodily illness—of a mental disorder which oppressed him—and of an earnest desire to see me, as his best and, indeed, his only personal friend, with a view of attempting, by the cheerfulness of my society, some alleviation of his malady. It was the manner in which all this, and much more, was said—it was the apparent *heart* that went with his request—which allowed me no room for hesitation; and I accordingly obeyed forthwith what I still considered a very singular summons.

Although, as boys, we had been even intimate associates, yet I really knew little of my friend. His reserve had been always excessive and habitual. I was aware, however, that his very ancient family had been noted, time out of mind, for a peculiar sensibility of temperament, displaying itself, through long ages, in many works of exalted art, and manifested, of late, in repeated deeds of munificent yet unobtrusive charity, as well as in a passionate devotion to the intricacies, perhaps even more than to the orthodox and easily recognizable beauties, of musical science. I had learned, too, the very remarkable fact, that the stem of the Usher race, all time-honored as it was, had put forth, at no period, any enduring branch; in other words, that the entire family lay in the direct line of descent, and had always, with very trifling and very temporary variation, so lain. It was this deficiency, I considered, while running over in thought the perfect keeping of the character of the premises with the accredited character of the people, and while speculating upon the possible influence which the one, in the long lapse of centuries, might have exercised upon the other—it was this deficiency, perhaps, of collateral issue, and the consequent undeviating transmission, from sire to son, of the patrimony with the name, which had, at length, so identified the two as to merge the original title of the estate in the quaint and equivocal appellation of the "House of Usher"—an appellation which seemed to include, in the minds of the peasantry who used it, both the family and the family mansion.

I have said that the sole effect of my somewhat childish experiment—that of looking down within the tarn—had been to deepen the first singular impression. There can be no doubt that the consciousness of the rapid increase of my superstition—for why should I not so term it?—served mainly to accelerate the increase itself. Such, I have long known, is the paradoxical law of all sentiments having terror as a basis. And it might have been for this reason only, that, when I again uplifted my eyes to the house itself, from its image in the pool, there grew in my mind a strange fancy—a fancy so ridiculous, indeed, that I but mention it to show the vivid force of the

sensations which oppressed me. I had so worked upon my imagination as really to believe that about the whole mansion and domain there hung an atmosphere peculiar to themselves and their immediate vicinity—an
atmosphere which had no affinity with the air of heaven, but which had
reeked up from the decayed trees, and the gray wall, and the silent tarn—a
pestilent and mystic vapor, dull, sluggish, faintly discernible, and leaden-
hued.

Shaking off from my spirit what *must* have been a dream, I scanned   5
more narrowly the real aspect of the building. Its principal feature seemed
to be that of an excessive antiquity. The discoloration of ages had been
great. Minute fungi overspread the whole exterior, hanging in a fine tangled
web-work from the eaves. Yet all this was apart from any extraordinary di-
lapidation. No portion of the masonry had fallen; and there appeared to be
a wild inconsistency between its still perfect adaptation of parts, and the
crumbling condition of the individual stones. In this there was much that
reminded me of the specious totality of old woodwork which has rotted for
long years in some neglected vault, with no disturbance from the breath of
the external air. Beyond this indication of extensive decay, however, the
fabric gave little token of instability. Perhaps the eye of a scrutinizing observer might have discovered a barely perceptible fissure, which, extending
from the roof of the building in front, made its way down the wall in a zigzag
direction, until it became lost in the sullen waters of the tarn.

Noticing these things, I rode over a short causeway to the house. A servant in waiting took my horse, and I entered the Gothic archway of the
hall. A valet, of stealthy step, thence conducted me, in silence, through
many dark and intricate passages in my progress to the *studio* of his master.
Much that I encountered on the way contributed, I know not how, to
heighten the vague sentiments of which I have already spoken. While the
objects around me—while the carvings of the ceilings, the sombre tapestries
of the walls, the ebon blackness of the floors, and the phantasmagoric armo-
rial trophies which rattled as I strode, were but matters to which, or to such
as which, I had been accustomed from my infancy—while I hesitated not to
acknowledge how familiar was all this—I still wondered to find how unfamiliar were the fancies which ordinary images were stirring up. On one of
the staircases, I met the physician of the family. His countenance, I thought,
wore a mingled expression of low cunning and perplexity. He accosted me
with trepidation and passed on. The valet now threw open a door and ushered me into the presence of his master.

The room in which I found myself was very large and lofty. The windows were long, narrow, and pointed, and at so vast a distance from the
black oaken floor as to be altogether inaccessible from within. Feeble
gleams of encrimsoned light made their way through the trellised panes,
and served to render sufficiently distinct the more prominent objects

around; the eye, however, struggled in vain to reach the remoter angles
of the chamber, or the recesses of the vaulted and fretted ceiling. Dark
draperies hung upon the walls. The general furniture was profuse, com-
fortless, antique, and tattered. Many books and musical instruments lay
scattered about, but failed to give any vitality to the scene. I felt that I
breathed an atmosphere of sorrow. An air of stern, deep, and irredeemable gloom hung over and pervaded all.

Upon my entrance, Usher arose from a sofa on which he had been
lying at full length, and greeted me with a vivacious warmth which had
much in it, I at first thought, of an overdone cordiality—of the constrained
effort of the *ennuyé* man of the world. A glance, however, at his countenance, convinced me of his perfect sincerity. We sat down; and for some
moments, while he spoke not, I gazed upon him with a feeling half of pity,
half of awe. Surely, man had never before so terribly altered, in so brief a period, as had Roderick Usher! It was with difficulty that I could bring myself
to admit the identity of the wan being before me with the companion of my
early boyhood. Yet the character of his face had been at all times remarkable. A cadaverousness of complexion; an eye large, liquid, and luminous
beyond comparison; lips somewhat thin and very pallid, but of a surpassingly
beautiful curve; a nose of a delicate Hebrew model, but with a breadth of
nostril unusual in similar formations; a finely molded chin, speaking, in its
want of prominence, of a want of moral energy; hair of a more than web-
like softness and tenuity; these features, with an inordinate expansion above
the regions of the temple, made up altogether a countenance not easily to
be forgotten. And now in the mere exaggeration of the prevailing character
of these features, and of the expression they were wont to convey, lay so
much of change that I doubted to whom I spoke. The now ghastly pallor of
the skin, and the now miraculous luster of the eye, above all things startled
and even awed me. The silken hair, too, had been suffered to grow all un-
heeded, and as, in its wild gossamer texture, it floated rather than fell about
the face, I could not, even with effort, connect its Arabesque expression
with any idea of simple humanity.

In the manner of my friend I was at once struck with an incoherence—
an inconsistency; and I soon found this to arise from a series of feeble and
futile struggles to overcome an habitual trepidancy—an excessive nervous
agitation. For something of this nature I had indeed been prepared, no less
by his letter, than by reminiscences of certain boyish traits, and by conclusions deduced from his peculiar physical conformation and temperament.
His action was alternately vivacious and sullen. His voice varied rapidly
from a tremulous indecision (when the animal spirits seemed utterly in
abeyance) to that species of energetic concision—that abrupt, weighty, un-
hurried, and hollow-sounding enunciation—the leaden, self-balanced and

perfectly modulated guttural utterance, which may be observed in the lost
drunkard, or the irreclaimable eater of opium, during the periods of his most
intense excitement.

It was thus that he spoke of the object of my visit, of his earnest desire   10
to see me, and of the solace he expected me to afford him. He entered, at
some length, into what he conceived to be the nature of his malady. It was,
he said, a constitutional and a family evil, and one for which he despaired
to find a remedy—a mere nervous affection, he immediately added, which
would undoubtedly soon pass off. It displayed itself in a host of unnatural
sensations. Some of these, as he detailed them, interested and bewildered
me; although, perhaps, the terms and the general manner of the narration
had their weight. He suffered much from a morbid acuteness of the senses;
the most insipid food was alone endurable; he could wear only garments of
certain texture; the odors of all flowers were oppressive; his eyes were tortured by even a faint light; and there were but peculiar sounds, and these
from stringed instruments, which did not inspire him with horror.

To an anomalous species of terror I found him a bounden slave. "I shall
perish," said he, "I *must* perish in this deplorable folly. Thus, thus, and not
otherwise, shall I be lost. I dread the events of the future, not in themselves,
but in their results. I shudder at the thought of any, even the most trivial,
incident, which may operate upon this intolerable agitation of soul. I have,
indeed, no abhorrence of danger, except in its absolute effect—in terror. In
this unnerved—in this pitiable condition—I feel that the period will sooner
or later arrive when I must abandon life and reason together, in some struggle with the grim phantasm, FEAR."

I learned, moreover, at intervals, and through broken and equivocal
hints, another singular feature of his mental condition. He was enchained
by certain superstitious impressions in regard to the dwelling which he
tenanted, and whence, for many years, he had never ventured forth—in regard to an influence whose suppositious force was conveyed in terms too
shadowy here to be re-stated—an influence which some peculiarities in the
mere form and substance of his family mansion, had, by dint of long sufferance, he said, obtained over his spirit—an effect which the *physique* of the
gray walls and turrets, and of the dim tarn into which they all looked down,
had, at length, brought about upon the *morale* of his existence.

He admitted, however, although with hesitation, that much of the peculiar gloom which thus afflicted him could be traced to a more natural and
far more palpable origin—to the severe and long-continued illness—indeed
to the evidently approaching dissolution—of a tenderly beloved sister—his
sole companion for long years—his last and only relative on earth. "Her decease," he said, with a bitterness which I can never forget, "would leave
him (him the hopeless and the frail) the last of the ancient race of the

Ushers." While he spoke, the lady Madeline (for so was she called) passed slowly through a remote portion of the apartment, and, without having noticed my presence, disappeared. I regarded her with an utter astonishment not unmingled with dread—and yet I found it impossible to account for such feelings. A sensation of stupor oppressed me, as my eyes followed her retreating steps. When a door, at length, closed upon her, my glance sought instinctively and eagerly the countenance of the brother—but he had buried his face in his hands, and I could only perceive that a far more than ordinary wanness had overspread the emaciated fingers through which trickled many passionate tears.

The disease of the lady Madeline had long baffled the skill of her physicians. A settled apathy, a gradual wasting away of the person, and frequent although transient affections of a partially cataleptical character, were the unusual diagnosis. Hitherto she had steadily borne up against the pressure of her malady, and had not betaken herself finally to bed; but, on the closing in of the evening of my arrival at the house, she succumbed (as her brother told me at night with inexpressible agitation) to the prostrating power of the destroyer; and I learned that the glimpse I had obtained of her person would thus probably be the last I should obtain—that the lady, at least while living, would be seen by me no more.

For several days ensuing, her name was unmentioned by either Usher or myself: and during this period I was busied in earnest endeavors to alleviate the melancholy of my friend. We painted and read together; or I listened, as if in a dream, to the wild improvisations of his speaking guitar. And thus, as a closer and still closer intimacy admitted me more unreservedly into the recesses of his spirit, the more bitterly did I perceive the futility of all attempt at cheering a mind from which darkness, as if an inherent positive quality, poured forth upon all objects of the moral and physical universe, in one unceasing radiation of gloom.

I shall ever bear about me a memory of the many solemn hours I thus spent alone with the master of the House of Usher. Yet I should fail in any attempt to convey an idea of the exact character of the studies, or of the occupations, in which he involved me, or led me the way. An excited and highly distempered ideality threw a sulphureous luster over all. His long improvised dirges will ring forever in my ears. Among other things, I hold painfully in mind a certain singular perversion and amplification of the wild air of the last waltz of Von Weber. From the paintings over which his elaborate fancy brooded, and which grew, touch by touch, into vaguenesses at which I shuddered the more thrillingly, because I shuddered knowing not why;—from these paintings (vivid as their images now are before me) I would in vain endeavor to educe more than a small portion which should lie within the compass of merely written words. By the utter simplicity, by the nakedness of his designs, he arrested and overawed attention. If ever mortal painted an idea, that mortal was Roderick Usher. For me at least—in the circumstances then surrounding me—these arose out of the pure abstractions which the hypochondriac contrived to throw upon his canvas, an intensity of intolerable awe, no shadow of which felt I ever yet in the contemplation of the certainly glowing yet too concrete reveries of Fuseli.

One of the phantasmagoric conceptions of my friend, partaking not so rigidly of the spirit of abstraction, may be shadowed forth, although feebly, in words. A small picture presented the interior of an immensely long and rectangular vault or tunnel, with low walls, smooth, white, and without interruption or device. Certain accessory points of the design served well to convey the idea that this excavation lay at an exceeding depth below the surface of the earth. No outlet was observed in any portion of its vast extent, and no torch, or other artificial source of light was discernible; yet a flood of intense rays rolled throughout, and bathed the whole in a ghastly and inappropriate splendor.

I have just spoken of that morbid condition of the auditory nerve which rendered all music intolerable to the sufferer, with the exception of certain effects of stringed instruments. It was, perhaps, the narrow limits to which he thus confined himself upon the guitar, which gave birth, in great measure, to the fantastic character of his performances. But the fervid *facility* of his *impromptus* could not be so accounted for. They must have been, and were, in the notes, as well as in the words of his wild fantasias (for he not unfrequently accompanied himself with rhymed verbal improvisations), the result of that intense mental collectedness and concentration to which I have previously alluded as observable only in particular moments of the highest artificial excitement. The words of one of these rhapsodies I have easily remembered. I was, perhaps, the more forcibly impressed with it, as he gave it, because in the under or mystic current of its meaning, I fancied that I perceived, and for the first time, a full consciousness on the part of Usher, of the tottering of his lofty reason upon her throne. The verses, which were entitled, "The Haunted Palace," ran very nearly, if not accurately, thus:

I.

In the greenest of our valleys,
   By good angels tenanted,
Once a fair and stately palace—
   Radiant palace—reared its head.
In the monarch Thought's dominion—
   It stood there!
Never seraph spread a pinion
   Over fabric half so fair.

II.

Banners yellow, glorious, golden,
   On its roof did float and flow;
(This—all this—was in the olden
   Time long ago)
And every gentle air that dallied,
   In that sweet day,
Along the ramparts plumed and pallid,
   A winged odor went away.

III.

Wanderers in that happy valley
   Through two luminous windows saw
Spirits moving musically
   To a lute's well tunèd law,
Round about a throne, where sitting
   (Porphyrogene!)
In state his glory well befitting,
   The ruler of the realm was seen.

IV.

And all with pearl and ruby glowing
   Was the fair palace door,
Through which came flowing, flowing, flowing
   And sparkling evermore,
A troop of Echoes whose sweet duty
   Was but to sing,
In voices of surpassing beauty,
   The wit and wisdom of their king.

V.

But evil things, in robes of sorrow,
   Assailed the monarch's high estate;
(Ah, let us mourn, for never morrow
   Shall dawn upon him, desolate!)
And, round about his home, the glory
   That blushed and bloomed
Is but a dim-remembered story
   Of the old time entombed.

VI.

And travelers now within that valley,
   Through the red-litten windows, see

Vast forms that move fantastically
   To a discordant melody;
While, like a rapid ghastly river,
   Through the pale door,
A hideous throng rush out forever,
   And laugh—but smile no more.

I well remember that suggestions arising from this ballad, led us into a train of thought wherein there became manifest an opinion of Usher's which I mention not so much on account of its novelty, (for other men have thought thus,) as on account of the pertinacity with which he maintained it. This opinion, in its general form, was that of the sentience of all vegetable things. But, in his disordered fancy, the idea had assumed a more daring character, and trespassed, under certain conditions, upon the kingdom of inorganization. I lack words to express the full extent, or the earnest *abandon* of his persuasion. The belief, however, was connected (as I have previously hinted) with the gray stones of the home of his forefathers. The conditions of the sentience had been here, he imagined, fulfilled in the method of collocation of these stones—in the order of their arrangement, as well as in that of the many *fungi* which overspread them, and of the decayed trees which stood around—above all, in the long undisturbed endurance of this arrangement, and in its reduplication in the still waters of the tarn. Its evidence—the evidence of the sentience—was to be seen, he said, (and I here started as he spoke,) in the gradual yet certain condensation of an atmosphere of their own about the waters and the walls. The result was discoverable, he added, in that silent, yet importunate and terrible influence which for centuries had molded the destinies of his family, and which made *him* what I now saw him—what he was. Such opinions need no comment, and I will make none.

    Our books—the books which, for years, had formed no small portion of the mental existence of the invalid—were, as might be supposed, in strict keeping with this character of phantasm. We pored together over such works as the Ververt et Chartreuse of Gresset; the Belphegor of Machiavelli; the Heaven and Hell of Swedenborg; the Subterranean Voyage of Nicholas Klimm by Holberg; the Chiromancy of Robert Flud, of Jean D'Indaginé, and of De la Chambre; the Journey into the Blue Distance of Tieck; and the City of the Sun of Campanella. One favorite volume was a small octavo edition of the *Directorium Inquisitorum*, by the Dominican Eymeric de Gironne; and there were passages in Pomponius Mela, about the old African Satyrs and Ægipans, over which Usher would sit dreaming for hours. His chief delight, however, was found in the perusal of an exceedingly rare and curious book in quarto Gothic—the manual of a forgotten church—the *Vigiliae Mortuorum secundum Chorum Ecclesiae Maguntinae.*

20

I could not help thinking of the wild ritual of this work, and of its probable influence upon the hypochondriac, when, one evening, having informed me abruptly that the lady Madeline was no more, he stated his intention of preserving her corpse for a fortnight, (previously to its final interment,) in one of the numerous vaults within the main walls of the building. The worldly reason, however, assigned for this singular proceeding, was one which I did not feel at liberty to dispute. The brother had been led to his resolution (so he told me) by consideration of the unusual character of the malady of the deceased, of certain obtrusive and eager inquiries on the part of her medical men, and of the remote and exposed situation of the burial-ground of the family. I will not deny that when I called to mind the sinister countenance of the person whom I met upon the staircase, on the day of my arrival at the house, I had no desire to oppose what I regarded as at best but a harmless, and by no means an unnatural, precaution.

At the request of Usher, I personally aided him in the arrangements for the temporary entombment. The body having been encoffined, we two alone bore it to its rest. The vault in which we placed it (and which had been so long unopened that our torches, half smothered in its oppressive atmosphere, gave us little opportunity for investigation) was small, damp, and entirely without means of admission for light; lying, at great depth, immediately beneath that portion of the building in which was my own sleeping apartment. It had been used, apparently, in remote feudal times, for the worst purposes of a donjon-keep, and, in later days, as a place of deposit for powder, or some other highly combustible substance, as a portion of its floor, and the whole interior of a long archway through which we reached it, were carefully sheathed with copper. The door, of massive iron, had been, also, similarly protected. Its immense weight caused an unusually sharp grating sound, as it moved upon its hinges.

Having deposited our mournful burden upon tressels within this region of horror, we partially turned aside the yet unscrewed lid of the coffin, and looked upon the face of the tenant. A striking similitude between the brother and sister now first arrested my attention; and Usher, divining, perhaps, my thoughts, murmured out some few words from which I learned that the deceased and himself had been twins, and that sympathies of a scarcely intelligible nature had always existed between them. Our glances, however, rested not long upon the dead—for we could not regard her unawed. The disease which had thus entombed the lady in the maturity of youth, had left, as usual in all maladies of a strictly cataleptical character, the mockery of a faint blush upon the bosom and the face, and that suspiciously lingering smile upon the lip which is so terrible in death. We replaced and screwed down the lid, and, having secured the door of iron, made our way, with toil, into the scarcely less gloomy apartments of the upper portion of the house.

And now, some days of bitter grief having elapsed, an observable change came over the features of the mental disorder of my friend. His ordinary manner had vanished. His ordinary occupations were neglected or forgotten. He roamed from chamber to chamber with hurried, unequal, and objectless step. The pallor of his countenance had assumed, if possible, a more ghastly hue—but the luminousness of his eye had utterly gone out. The once occasional huskiness of his tone was heard no more; and a tremulous quaver, as if of extreme terror, habitually characterized his utterance. There were times, indeed, when I thought his unceasingly agitated mind was laboring with some oppressive secret, to divulge which he struggled for the necessary courage. At times, again, I was obliged to resolve all into the mere inexplicable vagaries of madness, for I beheld him gazing upon vacancy for long hours, in an attitude of the profoundest attention as if listening to some imaginary sound. It was no wonder that his condition terrified— that it infected me. I felt creeping upon me, by slow yet certain degrees, the wild influences of his own fantastic yet impressive superstitions.

It was, especially, upon retiring to bed late in the night of the seventh or eighth day after the placing of the lady Madeline within the donjon, that I experienced the full power of such feelings. Sleep came not near my couch—while the hours waned and waned away. I struggled to reason off the nervousness which had dominion over me. I endeavored to believe that much, if not all of what I felt, was due to the bewildering influence of the gloomy furniture of the room—of the dark and tattered draperies, which, tortured into motion by the breath of a rising tempest, swayed fitfully to and fro upon the walls, and rustled uneasily about the decorations of the bed. But my efforts were fruitless. An irrepressible tremor gradually pervaded my frame; and, at length, there sat upon my very heart an incubus of utterly causeless alarm. Shaking this off with a gasp and a struggle, I uplifted myself upon the pillows, and, peering earnestly within the intense darkness of the chamber, hearkened—I know not why, except that an instinctive spirit prompted me—to certain low and indefinite sounds which came, through the pauses of the storm, at long intervals, I knew not whence. Overpowered by an intense sentiment of horror, unaccountable yet unendurable, I threw on my clothes with haste (for I felt that I should sleep no more during the night), and endeavored to arouse myself from the pitiable condition into which I had fallen, by pacing rapidly to and fro through the apartment.

I had taken but few turns in this manner, when a light step on an adjoining staircase arrested my attention. I presently recognized it as that of Usher. In an instant afterward he rapped, with a gentle touch, at my door, and entered, bearing a lamp. His countenance was, as usual, cadaverously wan—but, moreover, there was a species of mad hilarity in his eyes—an

25

evidently restrained *hysteria* in his whole demeanor. His air appalled me—but anything was preferable to the solitude which I had so long endured, and I even welcomed his presence as a relief.

"And you have not seen it?" he said abruptly, after having stared about him for some moments in silence—"you have not then seen it?—but, stay! you shall." Thus speaking, and having carefully shaded his lamp, he hurried to one of the casements, and threw it freely open to the storm.

The impetuous fury of the entering gust nearly lifted us from our feet. It was, indeed, a tempestuous yet sternly beautiful night, and one wildly singular in its terror and its beauty. A whirlwind had apparently collected its force in our vicinity; for there were frequent and violent alterations in the direction of the wind; and the exceeding density of the clouds (which hung so low as to press upon the turrets of the house) did not prevent our perceiving the life-like velocity with which they flew careering from all points against each other, without passing away into the distance. I say that even their exceeding density did not prevent our perceiving this—yet we had no glimpse of the moon or stars—nor was there any flashing forth of the lightning. But the under surfaces of the huge masses of agitated vapor, as well as all terrestrial objects immediately around us, were glowing in the unnatural light of a faintly luminous and distinctly visible gaseous exhalation which hung about and enshrouded the mansion.

"You must not—you shall not behold this!" said I, shudderingly, to Usher, as I led him, with a gentle violence, from the window to a seat. "These appearances, which bewilder you, are merely electrical phenomena not uncommon—or it may be that they have their ghastly origin in the rank miasma of the tarn. Let us close this casement;—the air is chilling and dangerous to your frame. Here is one of your favorite romances. I will read, and you shall listen;—and so we will pass away this terrible night together."

The antique volume which I had taken up was the "Mad Trist" of Sir Launcelot Canning, but I had called it a favorite of Usher's more in sad jest than in earnest; for, in truth, there is little in its uncouth and unimaginative prolixity which could have had interest for the lofty and spiritual ideality of my friend. It was, however, the only book immediately at hand; and I indulged a vague hope that the excitement which now agitated the hypochondriac, might find relief (for the history of mental disorder is full of similar anomalies) even in the extremeness of the folly which I should read. Could I have judged, indeed, by the wild overstrained air of vivacity with which he hearkened, or apparently hearkened, to the words of the tale, I might well have congratulated myself upon the success of my design.

I had arrived at that well-known portion of the story where Ethelred, the hero of the Trist, having sought in vain for peaceable admission into the dwelling of the hermit, proceeds to make good an entrance by force. Here, it will be remembered, the words of the narrative run thus:

"And Ethelred, who was by nature of a doughty heart, and who was now mighty withal, on account of the powerfulness of the wine which he had drunken, waited no longer to hold parley with the hermit, who, in sooth, was of an obstinate and maliceful turn, but, feeling the rain upon his shoulders, and fearing the rising of the tempest, uplifted his mace outright, and, with blows, made quickly room in the plankings of the door for his gauntleted hand; and now pulling therewith sturdily, he so cracked, and ripped, and tore all asunder, that the noise of the dry and hollow-sounding wood alarumed and reverberated throughout the forest."

At the termination of this sentence I started, and for a moment, paused; for it appeared to me (although I at once concluded that my excited fancy had deceived me)—it appeared to me that, from some very remote portion of the mansion, there came, indistinctly, to my ears, what might have been, in its exact similarity of character, the echo (but a stifled and dull one certainly) of the very cracking and ripping sound which Sir Launcelot had so particularly described. It was, beyond doubt, the coincidence alone which had arrested my attention; for, amid the rattling of the sashes of the casements, and the ordinary commingled noises of the still increasing storm, the sound, in itself, had nothing, surely, which should have interested or disturbed me. I continued the story:

"But the good champion Ethelred, now entering within the door, was sore enraged and amazed to perceive no signal of the maliceful hermit; but, in the stead thereof, a dragon of a scaly and prodigious demeanor, and of a fiery tongue, which sate in guard before a palace of gold, with a floor of silver; and upon the wall there hung a shield of shining brass with this legend enwritten—

> Who entereth herein, a conqueror hath bin;
> Who slayeth the dragon, the shield he shall win;

And Ethelred uplifted his mace, and struck upon the head of the dragon, which fell before him, and gave up his pesty breath, with a shriek so horrid and harsh, and withal so piercing, that Ethelred had fain to close his ears with his hands against the dreadful noise of it, the like whereof was never before heard." 35

Here again I paused abruptly, and now with a feeling of wild amazement—for there could be no doubt whatever that, in this instance, I did actually hear (although from what direction it proceeded I found it impossible to say) a low and apparently distant, but harsh, protracted, and most unusual screaming or grating sound—the exact counterpart of what my fancy had already conjured up for the dragon's unnatural shriek as described by the romancer.

Oppressed, as I certainly was, upon the occurrence of the second and most extraordinary coincidence, by a thousand conflicting sensations, in which wonder and extreme terror were predominant, I still retained sufficient presence of mind to avoid exciting, by any observation, the sensitive nervousness of my companion. I was by no means certain that he had noticed the sounds in question; although, assuredly, a strange alteration had, during the last few minutes, taken place in his demeanor. From a position fronting my own, he had gradually brought round his chair, so as to sit with his face to the door of the chamber; and thus I could but partially perceive his features, although I saw that his lips trembled as if he were murmuring inaudibly. His head had dropped upon his breast—yet I knew that he was not asleep, from the wide and rigid opening of the eye as I caught a glance of it in profile. The motion of his body, too, was at variance with this idea—for he rocked from side to side with a gentle yet constant and uniform sway. Having rapidly taken notice of all this, I resumed the narrative of Sir Launcelot, which thus proceeded:

"And now, the champion, having escaped from the terrible fury of the dragon, bethinking himself of the brazen shield, and of the breaking up of the enchantment which was upon it, removed the carcass from out of the way before him, and approached valorously over the silver pavement of the castle to where the shield was upon the wall; which in sooth tarried not for his full coming, but fell down at his feet upon the silver floor, with a mighty great and terrible ringing sound."

No sooner had these syllables passed my lips, than—as if a shield of brass had indeed, at the moment, fallen heavily upon a floor of silver—I became aware of a distinct, hollow, metallic, and clangorous, yet apparently muffled reverberation. Completely unnerved, I leaped to my feet; but the measured rocking movement of Usher was undisturbed. I rushed to the chair in which he sat. His eyes were bent fixedly before him, and throughout his whole countenance there reigned a stony rigidity. But, as I placed my hand upon his shoulder, there came a strong shudder over his whole person; a sickly smile quivered about his lips; and I saw that he spoke in a low, hurried, and gibbering murmur, as if unconscious of my presence. Bending closely over him, I at length drank in the hideous import of his words.

"Not hear it?—yes, I hear it, and *have* heard it. Long—long—long—many minutes, many hours, many days, have I heard it—yet I dared not—oh, pity me, miserable wretch that I am!—I dared not—I *dared* not speak! *We have put her living in the tomb!* Said I not that my senses were acute? I *now* tell you that I heard her first feeble movements in the hollow coffin. I heard them—many, many days ago—yet I dared not—*I dared not speak!* And now—to-night—Ethelred—ha! ha!—the breaking of the hermit's door, and the death-cry of the dragon, and the clangor of the shield! say, rather, the rending of her coffin, and the grating of the iron hinges of her prison, and her struggles within the coppered archway of the vault! Oh whither shall I fly? Will she not be here anon? Is she not hurrying to upbraid me for my haste? Have I not heard her footstep on the stair? Do I not distinguish that heavy and horrible beating of her heart? *Madman!*" here he sprang furiously to his feet, and shrieked out his syllables, as if in the effort he were giving up his soul—"*Madman! I tell you that she now stands without the door!*"

As if in the superhuman energy of his utterance there had been found the potency of a spell—the huge antique panels to which the speaker pointed, threw slowly back, upon the instant, their ponderous and ebony jaws. It was the work of the rushing gust—but then without those doors there *did* stand the lofty and enshrouded figure of the lady Madeline of Usher. There was blood upon her white robes, and the evidence of some bitter struggle upon every portion of her emaciated frame. For a moment she remained trembling and reeling to and fro upon the threshold, then, with a low moaning cry, fell heavily inward upon the person of her brother, and in her violent and now final death-agonies, bore him to the floor a corpse, and a victim to the terrors he had anticipated.

From that chamber, and from that mansion, I fled aghast. The storm was still abroad in all its wrath as I found myself crossing the old causeway. Suddenly there shot along the path a wild light, and I turned to see whence a gleam so unusual could have issued; for the vast house and its shadows were alone behind me. The radiance was that of the full, setting, and blood-red moon which now shone vividly through that once barely-discernible fissure of which I have before spoken as extending from the roof of the building, in a zigzag direction, to the base. While I gazed, this fissure rapidly widened—there came a fierce breath of the whirlwind—the entire orb of the satellite burst at once upon my sight—my brain reeled as I saw the mighty walls rushing asunder—there was a long tumultuous shouting sound like the voice of a thousand waters—and the deep and dank tarn at my feet closed sullenly and silently over the fragments of the "*House of Usher.*"

- Look at the opening paragraph of the story. How many of the words here describe the physical presence of the place? How many describe the narrator's reaction to that physical presence?

- What do we learn of the narrator's own state of mind? To what extent can we trust his observation and analysis? Give specific examples to support your answer.

- How does the narrator's reading fit into the story? Look closely at these passages. How can we determine where the imaginary stops and the real begins?

POETRY

Samuel Taylor Coleridge (1792–1834)

Kubla Khan: or, a Vision in a Dream (1798)

In Xanadu did Kubla Khan
A stately pleasure-dome decree:
Where Alph, the sacred river, ran
Through caverns measureless to man
    Down to a sunless sea.   5
So twice five miles of fertile ground
With walls and towers were girdled round:
And here were gardens bright with sinuous rills
Where blossomed many an incense-bearing tree;
And there were forests ancient as the hills,   10
Enfolding sunny spots of greenery.

But oh! that deep romantic chasm which slanted
Down the green hill athwart a cedarn cover!
A savage place! as holy and enchanted
As e'er beneath a waning moon was haunted   15
By woman wailing for her demon-lover!
And from this chasm, with ceaseless turmoil seething,
As if this earth in fast thick pants were breathing,
A mighty fountain momently was forced,
Amid whose swift half-intermitted burst   20
Huge fragments vaulted like rebounding hail,
Of chaffy grain beneath the thresher's flail:
And 'mid these dancing rocks at once and ever
It flung up momently the sacred river.
Five miles meandering with a mazy motion   25
Through wood and dale the sacred river ran,
Then reached the caverns measureless to man,
And sank in tumult to a lifeless ocean:
And 'mid this tumult Kubla heard from far
Ancestral voices prophesying war!   30
    The shadow of the dome of pleasure
    Floated midway on the waves;
    Where was heard the mingled measure
    From the fountain and the caves.
It was a miracle of rare device,   35

A sunny pleasure-dome with caves of ice!
    A damsel with a dulcimer
    In a vision once I saw:
    It was an Abyssinian maid,
    And on her dulcimer she played,   40
    Singing of Mount Abora.
    Could I revive within me
    Her symphony and song,
    To such a deep delight 'twould win me,
That with music loud and long,   45
I would build that dome in air,
That sunny dome! those caves of ice!
And all who heard should see them there,
And all should cry, Beware! Beware!
His flashing eyes, his floating hair!   50
Weave a circle round him thrice,
And close your eyes with holy dread,
For he on honey-dew hath fed,
And drunk the milk of Paradise.

■ How does the language in this poem describe the contrast between the "pleasure-dome" and the "caves of ice"?

■ What is the relation between this place and the prophecy?

Edgar Allan Poe (1809–1849)

The Raven (1844)

Once upon a midnight dreary, while I pondered, weak and weary,
Over many a quaint and curious volume of forgotten lore,
While I nodded, nearly napping, suddenly there came a tapping,
As of some one gently rapping, rapping at my chamber door.
"'Tis some visitor," I muttered, "tapping at my chamber door—   5
        Only this, and nothing more."

Ah, distinctly I remember it was in the bleak December,
And each separate dying ember wrought its ghost upon the floor.
Eagerly I wished the morrow;—vainly I had sought to borrow
From my books surcease of sorrow—sorrow for the lost Lenore—   10
For the rare and radiant maiden whom the angels name Lenore—
        Nameless here for evermore.

And the silken sad uncertain rustling of each purple curtain
Thrilled me—filled me with fantastic terrors never felt before;
So that now, to still the beating of my heart, I stood repeating   15
"'Tis some visitor entreating entrance at my chamber door;—
Some late visitor entreating entrance at my chamber door;
                This it is, and nothing more."

Presently my soul grew stronger; hesitating then no longer,
"Sir," said I, "or Madam, truly your forgiveness I implore;   20
But the fact is I was napping, and so gently you came rapping,
And so faintly you came tapping, tapping at my chamber door,
That I scarce was sure I heard you"—here I opened wide the door;—
                Darkness there, and nothing more.

Deep into that darkness peering, long I stood there wondering, fearing, 25
Doubting, dreaming dreams no mortal ever dared to dream before;
But the silence was unbroken, and the darkness gave no token,
And the only word there spoken was the whispered word, "Lenore!"
This I whispered, and an echo murmured back the word, "Lenore!"—
                Merely this, and nothing more.   30

Back into the chamber turning, all my soul within me burning,
Soon I heard again a tapping somewhat louder than before.
"Surely," said I, "surely that is something at my window lattice;
Let me see, then, what thereat is, and this mystery explore—
Let my heart be still a moment and this mystery explore;—   35
              'Tis the wind and nothing more!"

Open here I flung the shutter, when, with many a flirt and flutter,
In there stepped a stately raven of the saintly days of yore;
Not the least obeisance made he; not an instant stopped or stayed he;
But, with mien of lord or lady, perched above my chamber door—   40
Perched upon a bust of Pallas just above my chamber door—
              Perched, and sat, and nothing more.

Then this ebony bird beguiling my sad fancy into smiling,
By the grave and stern decorum of the countenance it wore,
"Though thy crest be shorn and shaven, thou," I said, "art sure no craven, 45
Ghastly grim and ancient raven wandering from the Nightly shore—
Tell me what thy lordly name is on the Night's Plutonian shore!"
              Quoth the raven, "Nevermore."

Much I marvelled this ungainly fowl to hear discourse so plainly,

Though its answer little meaning—little relevancy bore,   50
For we cannot help agreeing that no living human being
Ever yet was blessed with seeing bird above his chamber door—
Bird or beast upon the sculptured bust above his chamber door,
               With such name as "Nevermore."

But the raven, sitting lonely on the placid bust, spoke only   55
That one word, as if his soul in that one word he did outpour.
Nothing farther then he uttered—not a feather then he fluttered—
Till I scarcely more than muttered "Other friends have flown before—
On the morrow *he* will leave me, as my hopes have flown before."
               Then the bird said "Nevermore."   60

Startled at the stillness broken by reply so aptly spoken,
"Doubtless," said I, "what it utters is its only stock and store
Caught from some unhappy master whom unmerciful Disaster
Followed fast and followed faster till his songs one burden bore—
Till the dirges of his Hope that melancholy burden bore   65
               Of 'Never—nevermore.'"

But the raven still beguiling all my sad soul into smiling,
Straight I wheeled a cushioned seat in front of bird and bust and door;
Then, upon the velvet sinking, I betook myself to linking
Fancy unto fancy, thinking what this ominous bird of yore—   70
What this grim, ungainly, ghastly, gaunt, and ominous bird of yore
               Meant in croaking "Nevermore."

This I sat engaged in guessing, but no syllable expressing
To the fowl whose fiery eyes now burned into my bosom's core;
This and more I sat divining, with my head at ease reclining   75
On the cushion's velvet lining that the lamplight gloated o'er,
But whose velvet violet lining with the lamplight gloating o'er,
               She shall press, ah, nevermore!

Then, methought, the air grew denser, perfumed from an unseen censer
Swung by angels whose faint foot-falls tinkled on the tufted floor.   80
"Wretch," I cried, "thy God hath lent thee—by these angels he hath sent thee
Respite—respite and nepenthe from thy memories of Lenore!
Quaff, oh quaff this kind nepenthe and forget this lost Lenore!"
               Quoth the raven, "Nevermore."

"Prophet!" said I, "thing of evil!—prophet still, if bird or devil!—   85
Whether Tempter sent, or whether tempest tossed thee here ashore,

Desolate, yet all undaunted, on this desert land enchanted—
On this home by Horror haunted—tell me truly, I implore—
Is there—*is* there balm in Gilead?—tell me—tell me, I implore!"
                 Quoth the raven, "Nevermore."   90

"Prophet!" said I, "thing of evil—prophet still, if bird or devil!
By that Heaven that bends above us—by that God we both adore—
Tell this soul with sorrow laden if, within the distant Aidenn,
It shall clasp a sainted maiden whom the angels name Lenore—
Clasp a rare and radiant maiden whom the angels name Lenore."   95
                 Quoth the raven, "Nevermore."

"Be that word our sign of parting, bird or fiend!" I shrieked upstarting—
"Get thee back into the tempest and the Night's Plutonian shore!
Leave no black plume as a token of that lie thy soul hath spoken!
Leave my loneliness unbroken!—quit the bust above my door!   100
Take thy beak from out my heart, and take thy form from off my door!"
                 Quoth the raven, "Nevermore."

And the raven, never flitting, still is sitting, still is sitting
On the pallid bust of Pallas just above my chamber door;
And his eyes have all the seeming of a demon's that is dreaming,   105
And the lamp-light o'er him streaming throws his shadow on the floor;
And my soul from out that shadow that lies floating on the floor
                 Shall be lifted—nevermore!

- Locate the specific words in each stanza that describe the setting. How does this setting lend to the tone of the poem?
- What details of this setting seem supernatural? How many of them have a rational explanation?

Christina Rossetti (1830–1894)

Cobwebs (1890)

It is a land with neither night nor day,
    Nor heat nor cold, nor any wind, nor rain,
    Nor hills nor valleys; but one even plain
Stretches thro' long unbroken miles away:
While thro' the sluggish air a twilight grey   5

Broodeth; no moons or seasons wax and wane,
  No ebb and flow are there among the main,
No bud-time no leaf-falling there for aye,
No ripple on the sea, no shifting sand,
    No beat of wings to stir the stagnant space,   10
    No pulse of life thro' all the loveless land:
    And loveless sea; no trace of days before.
      No guarded home, no toil-won restingplace
      No future hope no fear forevermore.

■ Most of the descriptions here are given in the negative. From these
  descriptions, what is this place like?
■ How many of these descriptions offer us a real place? How many describe
  reactions to, or impressions of, the place?

Oscar Wilde (1854–1900)

The Harlot's House (1885)

We caught the tread of dancing feet,
We loitered down the moonlit street,
And stopped beneath the harlot's house.

Inside, above the din and fray,
We heard the loud musicians play   5
The "Treues Liebes Herz" of Strauss.

Like strange mechanical grotesques,
Making fantastic arabesques,
The shadows raced across the blind.

We watched the ghostly dancers spin   10
To sound of horn and violin,
Like black leaves wheeling in the wind.

Like wire-pulled automatons,
Slim silhouetted skeletons
Went sidling through the slow quadrille,   15

Then took each other by the hand,
And danced a stately saraband;

Their laughter echoed thin and shrill.
Sometimes a clockwork puppet pressed
A phantom lover to her breast,   20
Sometimes they seemed to try to sing.

Sometimes a horrible marionette
Came out, and smoked its cigarette
Upon the steps like a live thing.

Then, turning to my love, I said,   25
"The dead are dancing with the dead,
The dust is whirling with the dust."

But she—she heard the violin,
And left my side, and entered in:
Love passed into the house of lust.   30

Then suddenly the tune went false,
The dancers wearied of the waltz,
The shadows ceased to wheel and whirl.

And down the long and silent street,
The dawn, with silver-sandalled feet,   35
Crept like a frightened girl.

■ Compare the setting here with that presented in "Kearney Park" (p. 450)
  and "The *Dumka*" (p. 454). How do they use similar setting elements
  differently?

■ What impact does the title of this poem have upon our understanding of the
  setting? What about the place is real? What is imaginary?

Dudley Randall (1914–2000)

Ballad of Birmingham (1969)

(On the bombing of a church in Birmingham, Alabama, 1963)

"Mother dear, may I go downtown
Instead of out to play,
And march the streets of Birmingham

In a Freedom March today?"
"No, baby, no, you may not go,   5
For the dogs are fierce and wild,
And clubs and hoses, guns and jails
Aren't good for a little child."

"But, mother, I won't be alone.
Other children will go with me,   10
And march the streets of Birmingham
To make our country free."

"No, baby, no you may not go,
For I fear those guns will fire.
But you may go to church instead   15
And sing in the children's choir."

She has combed and brushed her night-dark hair,
And bathed rose petal sweet.
And drawn white gloves on her small brown hands,
And white shoes on her feet.   20

The mother smiled to know her child
Was in the sacred place,
But that smile was the last smile
To come upon her face.

For when she heard the explosion,   25
Her eyes grew wet and wild.
She raced through the streets of Birmingham
Calling for her child.

She clawed through bits of glass and brick,
Then lifted out a shoe.   30
"Oh, here's the shoe my baby wore,
But, baby, where are you?"

- The poem contrasts the perceived dangers of a civil rights march with the safety of a church. How do the events of the poem turn that world upside down?
- What impact does the poem's simple rhyming form have on the story that it tells?

Joy Harjo (1951–)

New Orleans (1983)

This is the south. I look for evidence
of other Creeks, for remnants of voices,
or for tobacco brown bones to come wandering
down Conti Street, Royale, or Decatur.
Near the French Market I see a blue horse   5
caught frozen in stone in the middle of
a square. Brought in by the Spanish on
an endless ocean voyage he became mad
and crazy. They caught him in blue
rock, said   10
        don't talk.

I know it wasn't just a horse
            that went crazy.

Nearby is a shop with ivory and knives.
There are red rocks. The man behind the
counter has no idea that he is inside
magic stones. He should find out before   15
they destroy him. These things
have memory,
        you know.

I have a memory.
           It swims deep in blood.
a delta in the skin. It swims out of Oklahoma,
deep the Mississippi River. It carries my   20
feet to these places: the French Quarter,
stale rooms, the sun behind thick and moist
clouds, and I hear boats hauling themselves up
and down the river.

My spirit comes here to drink.   25
My spirit comes here to drink.
Blood is the undercurrent.

There are voices buried in the Mississippi
mud. There are ancestors and future children
buried beneath the currents stirred up by   30

pleasure boats going up and down.
There are stories here made of memory.

I remember DeSoto. He is buried somewhere in
this river, his bones sunk like the golden
treasure he traveled half the earth to find,   35
came looking for gold cities, for shining streets
of beaten gold to dance on with silk ladies.

He should have stayed home.

          (Creeks knew of him for miles
            before he came into town.   40
             Dreamed of silver blades
              and crosses.)
And knew he was one of the ones who yearned
for something his heart wasn't big enough
to handle.   45
       (And DeSoto thought it was gold.)

The Creeks lived in earth towns,
                not gold,
spun children, not gold.
That's not what DeSoto thought he wanted to see.
The Creeks knew it, and drowned him in
      the Mississippi River   50
          so he wouldn't have to drown himself.

Maybe his body is what I am looking for
as evidence. To know in another way
that my memory is alive.
But he must have got away, somehow,   55
because I have seen New Orleans,
the lace and silk buildings,
trolley cars on beaten silver paths,
graves that rise up out of soft earth in the rain,
shops that sell black mammy dolls   60
holding white babies.

And I know I have seen DeSoto,
          having a drink on Bourbon Street,
    mad and crazy

dancing with a woman as gold   65
as the river bottom.

■ Explain the final lines: "as gold / as the river bottom." How has the poem
  shown us the significance of this gold in New Orleans?

Joy Harjo (1951–)

The Woman Hanging from the Thirteenth Floor Window (1983)

She is the woman hanging from the 13th floor
window. Her hands are pressed white against the
concrete moulding of the tenement building. She
hangs from the 13th floor window in east Chicago,
with a swirl of birds over her head. They could   5
be a halo, or a storm of glass waiting to crush her.

She thinks she will be set free.

The woman hanging from the 13th floor window
on the east side of Chicago is not alone.
She is a woman of children, of the baby, Carlos,   10
and of Margaret, and of Jimmy who is the oldest.
She is her mother's daughter and her father's son.
She is several pieces between the two husbands
she has had. She is all the women of the apartment
building who stand watching her, watching themselves.   15

When she was young she ate wild rice on scraped down
plates in warm wood rooms. It was in the farther
north and she was the baby then. They rocked her.

She sees Lake Michigan lapping at the shores of
herself. It is a dizzy hole of water and the rich   20
live in tall glass houses at the edge of it. In some
places Lake Michigan speaks softly, here, it just sputters
and butts itself against the asphalt. She sees
other buildings just like hers. She sees other
women hanging from many-floored windows   25

counting their lives in the palms of their hands
and in the palms of their children's hands.

She is the woman hanging from the 13th floor window
on the Indian side of town. Her belly is soft from
her children's births, her worn levis swing down below   30
her waist, and then her feet, and then her heart.
She is dangling.

The woman hanging from the 13th floor hears voices.
They come to her in the night when the lights have gone
dim. Sometimes they are little cats mewing and scratching   35
at the door, sometimes they are her grandmother's voice,
and sometimes they are gigantic men of light whispering
to her to get up, to get up, to get up. That's when she wants
to have another child to hold onto in the night, to be able
to fall back into dreams.   40

And the woman hanging from the 13th floor window
hears other voices. Some of them scream out from below
for her to jump, they would push her over. Others cry softly
from the sidewalks, pull their children up like flowers and gather
them into their arms. They would help her, like themselves.   45

But she is the woman hanging from the 13th floor window,
and she knows she is hanging by her own fingers, her
own skin, her own thread of indecision.

She thinks of Carlos, of Margaret, of Jimmy.
She thinks of her father, and of her mother.   50
She thinks of all the women she has been, of all
the men. She thinks of the color of her skin, and
of Chicago streets, and of waterfalls and pines.
She thinks of moonlight nights, and of cool spring storms.
Her mind chatters like neon and northside bars.   55
She thinks of the 4 a.m. lonelinesses that have folded
her up like death, discordant, without logical and
beautiful conclusion. Her teeth break off at the edges.
She would speak.

The woman hangs from the 13th floor window crying for   60
the lost beauty of her own life. She sees the
sun falling west over the grey plane of Chicago.

She thinks she remembers listening to her own life
break loose, as she falls from the 13th floor
window on the east side of Chicago, or as she   65
climbs back up to claim herself again.

■ In what ways is the very specific "13th floor / window" significant to the
poem? What happens in the final stanza?

Gary Soto (1952–)

Braly Street (1977)

Every summer
The asphalt softens
Giving under the edge
Of boot heels and the trucks
That caught radiators   5
Of butterflies.
Bottle caps and glass
Of the '40s and '50s
Hold their breath
Under the black earth   10
Of asphalt and are silent
Like the dead whose mouths
Have eaten dirt and bermuda.
Every summer I come
To this street   15
Where I discovered ants bit,
Matches flare,
And pinto beans unraveled
Into plants; discovered
Aspirin will not cure a dog   20
Whose fur twitches.

It's sixteen years
Since our house
Was bulldozed and my father
Stunned into a coma ...   25
Where it was,
An oasis of chickweed
And foxtails.
Where the almond tree stood

There are wine bottles   30
Whose history
Is a liver. The long caravan
Of my uncle's footprints
Has been paved
With dirt. Where my father   35
Cemented a pond
There is a cavern of red ants
Living on the seeds
The wind brings
And cats that come here   40
To die among
The browning sage.

It's sixteen years
Since bottle collectors
Shoveled around   45
The foundation
And the almond tree
Opened its last fruit
To the summer.
The houses are gone,   50
The Molinas, Morenos,
The Japanese families
Are gone, the Okies gone
Who moved out at night
Under a canopy of   55
Moving stars.

In '57 I sat
On the porch, salting
Slugs that came out
After the rain,   60
While inside my uncle
Weakened with cancer
And the blurred vision
Of his hands
Darkening to earth.   65
In '58 I knelt
Before my father
Whose spine was pulled loose.
Before his face still
Growing a chin of hair,   70
Before the procession

Of stitches behind
His neck, I knelt
And did not understand.

Braly Street is now   75
Tin ventilators
On the warehouses, turning
Our sweat
Towards the yellowing sky;
Acetylene welders   80
Beading manifolds,
Stinging the half-globes
Of retinas. When I come
To where our house was,
I come to weeds   85
And a sewer line tied off
Like an umbilical cord;
To the chinaberry
Not pulled down
And to its rings   90
My father and uncle
Would equal, if alive.

■ Locate instances where the poet describes specific objects as if they had the
lives that he is describing here.

Gary Soto (1952–)

Kearney Park (1985)

True Mexicans or not, let's open our shirts
And dance, a spark of heels
Chipping at the dusty cement. The people
Are shiny like the sea, turning
To the clockwork of *rancheras*,   5
The accordion wheezing, the drum-tap
Of work rising and falling.
Let's dance with our hats in hand.
The sun is behind the trees,
Behind my stutter of awkward steps   10
With a woman who is a brilliant arc of smiles,

An armful of falling water. Her skirt
Opens and closes. My arms
Know no better but to flop
On their own, and we spin, dip   15
And laugh into each other's faces—
Faces that could be famous
On the coffee table of my *abuelita*.
But grandma is here, at the park, with a beer
At her feet, clapping   20
And shouting, "Dance, hijo, dance!"
Laughing, I bend, slide, and throw up
A great cloud of dust,
Until the girl and I are no more.

■ How do the actions of the people in this poem help establish this setting?

Ginger Andrews (1956–)

Rolls-Royce Dreams (1999)

Using salal leaves for money,
my youngest sister and I
paid an older sister
to taxi an abandoned car
in our backyard. Our sister   5
knew how to shift gears,
turn smoothly with a hand signal,
and make perfect screeching stop sounds.

We drove to the beach,
to the market, to Sunday School,   10
past our would-be boyfriends' houses,
to any town, anywhere.
We shopped for expensive clothes everywhere.
Our sister would open our doors
and say, *Meter's runnin' ladies,*   15
but take your time.

We rode all over in that ugly green Hudson
with its broken front windshield, springs poking
through its back seat, blackberry vines growing

through rusted floorboards;   20
with no wheels, no tires, taillights busted,
headlights missing, and gas gauge on empty.

■ How does the final stanza describe a place very different from the one offered
in the first two stanzas? How can we reconcile the two places?

Barbara Ras (1949–)

Childhood (1998)

Driving the last stretch before the home stretch, past the lake,
geese in the road, hard to tell if they're crossing or just now
milling around like consultants in the same old way/new way debates,
probing the air with their long necks to see if it's still penetrable
or if maybe just ahead some future is locked into place   5
like the kind of walls you hit in your childhood, new rules
popping up unexpectedly in a new place—don't say "Hey"
at your aunt's, no sitting on the edge of the bed at your grandmother's.
You wait, feeling the distance you felt as a kid watching from the back seat,
your grandfather's Kaiser, where you went the way you went everywhere,   10
empty-handed. It is the fifties.
You've been told, "Children should be seen
and not heard," but not why, and because you want to please
and because you have nothing to say to your grandparents in front
who may or may not take you to the dairy bar with the huge milk   15
    bottle rising
out of the building, which no one in your family has remarked on so you too
take for granted, you sit quietly, a tidy right angle on the green velveteen
the color of canned pea soup without ham you like
and stretch out a toe to reach the fattish rope slung from side to side
on the back of the front seat, and instead of wondering what it's for,   20
you hope as hard as you can you'll stop at the airport
and get to hang on the diamond chain links of the fence
and if you're lucky watch a plane take off on its scary monster propellers.
But now in another car waiting for geese to waddle to the left
or the right, you think about those upholstered ropes,   25
whether they were there to grab in case of accident or fright
or to stop from swaying too far into the body beside you,
and you wonder whatever happened to them,
whether they went the way of embroidered hankies, candy cigarettes,
gone with the way the moon hits your eye like a big pizza pie,   30

gone with afternoons a five-year-old could walk downtown to the library
alone and back, gone with key skates, three-speed bikes, gone with the days
when children owned the streets.

■ How does the same object, the "upholstered ropes," lead to two different
interpretations of the same setting?

Chitra Banerjee Divakaruni (1957–)

Indian Movie, New Jersey (1990)

Not like the white filmstars, all rib
and gaunt cheekbone, the Indian sex-goddess
smiles plumply from behind a flowery
branch. Below her brief red skirt, her thighs
are satisfying-solid, redeeming   5
as tree trunks. She swings her hips
and the men-viewers whistle. The lover-hero
dances in to a song, his lip-sync
a little off, but no matter, we
know the words already and sing along.   10
It is safe here, the day
golden and cool so no one sweats,
roses on every bush and the Dal Lake
clean again.
            The sex-goddess switches
to thickened English to emphasize   15
a joke. We laugh and clap. Here
we need not be embarrassed by words
dropping like lead pellets into foreign ears.
The flickering movie-light
wipes from our faces years of America, sons   20
who want mohawks and refuse to run
the family store, daughters who date
on the sly.
            When at the end the hero
dies for his friend who also
loves the sex-goddess and now can marry her,   25
we weep, understanding. Even the men
clear their throats to say, "What *qurbani*!
What *dosti*!" After, we mill around
unwilling to leave, exchange greetings

and good news: a new gold chain, a trip 30
to India. We do not speak
of motel raids, canceled permits, stones
thrown through glass windows, daughters and sons
raped by Dotbusters.
                    In this dim foyer
we can pull around us the faint, comforting smell 35
of incense and *pakoras*, can arrange
our children's marriages with hometown boys and girls,
open a franchise, win a million
in the mail. We can retire
in India, a yellow two-storied house 40
with wrought-iron gates, our own
Ambassador car. Or at least
move to a rich white suburb, Summerfield
or Fort Lee, with neighbors that will
talk to us. Here while the film-songs still echo 45
in the corridors and restrooms, we can trust
in movie truths: sacrifice, success, love and luck,
the America that was supposed to be.

■ What place does this poem describe?
■ How does the fantasy world of the movie create a specific community among those who watch it?

B. H. Fairchild (1945–)

The *Dumka* (1998)

His parents would sit alone together
on the blue divan in the small living room
listening to Dvorak's piano quintet.
They would sit there in their old age,
side by side, quite still, backs rigid, hands 5
in their laps, and look straight ahead
at the yellow light of the phonograph
that seemed as distant as a lamplit
window seen across the plains late at night.
They would sit quietly as something dense 10

and radiant swirled around them, something
like the dust storms of the thirties that began

by smearing the sky green with doom
but afterwards drenched the air with an amber
glow and then vanished, leaving profiles   15
of children on pillows and a pale gauze
over mantles and table tops. But it was
the memory of dust that encircled them now
and made them smile faintly and raise
or bow their heads as they spoke about   20

the farm in twilight with piano music
spiraling out across red roads and fields
of maize, bread lines in the city, women
and men lining main street like mannequins
and then the war, the white frame rent house,   25
and the homecoming, the homecoming,
the homecoming, and afterwards, green lawns
and a new piano with its mahogany gleam
like pond ice at dawn, and now alone
in the house in the vanishing neighborhood,   30

the slow mornings of coffee and newspapers
and evenings of music and scattered bits
of talk like leaves suddenly fallen before
one notices the new season. And they would sit
there alone and soon he would reach across   35
and lift her hand as if it were the last unbroken
leaf and he would hold her hand in his hand
for a long time and they would look far off
into the music of their lives as they sat alone
together in the room in the house in Kansas.   40

- How does the poet convey a sense of historic settings?
- Why are the words *alone* and *together* significant in the final lines of the poem?

DRAMA

Tennessee Williams (1911–1983)

Thomas Lanier Williams was born in Columbus, Mississippi, where he spent the first seven years of his life with his mother, his sister Rose, and his maternal grandparents while his father traveled the country as a salesman. His father returned in 1918, and the Williams family moved to St. Louis. The reunion with their gambling, alcoholic father caused great stress on the Williams siblings, and Rose developed serious psychological problems. Williams earned his bachelor's degree from the University of Missouri. He pursued additional studies at the University of Iowa before moving to New Orleans, where he adopted the name Tennessee Williams and established a career as a playwright. His most famous plays, *The Glass Menagerie* (1944) and *A Streetcar Named Desire* (1947), both explore essential human nature. These plays deal with feelings of loneliness, sexual desire, and the need for love and affection. His plays were awarded many honors, including the 1945 New York Drama Critics Circle Award for *The Glass Menagerie*, the 1948 Pulitzer Prize for *A Streetcar Named Desire*, and the 1955 Pulitzer Prize for *Cat on a Hot Tin Roof.*

The Glass Menagerie (1945)

nobody, not even the rain, has such small hands

— e. e. cummings

CHARACTERS

AMANDA WINGFIELD, *the mother. A little woman of great but confused vitality clinging frantically to another time and place. Her characterization must be carefully created, not copied from type. She is not paranoiac, but her life is paranoia. There is much to admire in Amanda, and as much to love and pity as there is to laugh at. Certainly she has endurance and a kind of heroism, and though her foolishness makes her unwittingly cruel at times, there is tenderness in her slight person.*

LAURA WINGFIELD, *her daughter. Amanda, having failed to establish contact with reality, continues to live vitally in her illusions, but Laura's situation is even graver. A childhood illness has left her crippled, one leg slightly shorter than the other, and held in a brace. This defect need not be more than suggested on the stage. Stemming from this, Laura's separation increases till she is like a piece of her own glass collection, too exquisitely fragile to move from the shelf.*

TOM WINGFIELD, *her son. And the narrator of the play. A poet with a job in a warehouse. His nature is not remorseless, but to escape from a trap he has to act without pity.*

JIM O'CONNOR, *the gentleman caller. A nice, ordinary, young man.*

SCENE: *An alley in St. Louis.*

PART I: *Preparation for a Gentleman Caller.*

PART II: *The Gentleman Calls.*

TIME: *Now and the Past.*

Scene 1

SCENE: *The Wingfield apartment is in the rear of the building, one of those vast hive-like conglomerations of cellular living-units that flower as warty growths in overcrowded urban centers of lower middle-class population and are symptomatic of the impulse of this largest and fundamentally enslaved section of American society to avoid fluidity and differentiation and to exist and function as one interfused mass of automatism.*

The apartment faces an alley and is entered by a fire-escape, a structure whose name is a touch of accidental poetic truth, for all of these huge buildings are always burning with the slow and implacable fires of human desperation. The fire-escape is included in the set—that is, the landing of it and steps descending from it.

The scene is memory and is therefore nonrealistic. Memory takes a lot of poetic license. It omits some details; others are exaggerated, according to the emotional value of the articles it touches, for memory is seated predominantly in the heart. The interior is therefore rather dim and poetic.

At the rise of the curtain, the audience is faced with the dark, grim rear wall of the Wingfield tenement. This building, which runs parallel to the footlights, is flanked on both sides by dark, narrow alleys which run into murky canyons of tangled clotheslines, garbage cans, and the sinister latticework of neighboring fire-escapes. It is up and down these side alleys that exterior entrances and exits are made, during the play. At the end of TOM's *opening commentary, the dark tenement wall slowly reveals (by means of a transparency) the interior of the ground floor Wingfield apartment.*

Downstage is the living room, which also serves as a sleeping room for LAURA, *the sofa unfolding to make her bed. Upstage, center, and divided by a wide arch or second proscenium with transparent faded portieres (or second curtain), is the dining room. In an old-fashioned what-not in the living room are seen scores of transparent glass animals. A blown-up photograph of the father hangs on the wall of the living room, facing the audience, to the left of the archway. It is the face of a very handsome young man in a doughboy's First World War cap. He is gallantly smiling, ineluctably smiling, as if to say, "I will be smiling forever."*

The audience hears and sees the opening scene in the dining room through both the transparent fourth wall of the building and the transparent gauze portieres of the dining-room arch. It is during this revealing scene that the fourth wall slowly ascends, out of sight. This transparent exterior wall is not brought down again until the very end of the play, during TOM's *final speech.*

The narrator is an undisguised convention of the play. He takes whatever license with dramatic convention as is convenient to his purposes.

(TOM *enters dressed as a merchant sailor from alley, stage left, and strolls across the front of the stage to the fire-escape. There he stops and lights a cigarette. He addresses the audience.*)

TOM: Yes, I have tricks in my pocket, I have things up my sleeve. But I am the opposite of a stage magician. He gives you illusion that has the appearance of truth. I give you truth in the pleasant disguise of illusion. To begin with, I turn back time. I reverse it to that quaint period, the thirties, when the huge middle class of America was matriculating in a school for the blind. Their eyes had failed them, or they had failed their eyes, and so they were having their fingers pressed forcibly down on the fiery Braille alphabet of a dissolving economy. In Spain there was revolution. Here there was only shouting and confusion. In Spain there was Guernica. Here there were disturbances of labor, sometimes pretty violent, in otherwise peaceful cities such as Chicago, Cleveland, Saint Louis.... This is the social background of the play. *(Music.)*
The play is memory. Being a memory play, it is dimly lighted, it is sentimental, it is not realistic. In memory everything seems to happen to music. That explains the fiddle in the wings. I am the narrator of the play, and also a character in it. The other characters are my mother, Amanda, my sister, Laura, and a gentleman caller who appears in the final scenes. He is the most realistic character in the play, being an emissary from a world of reality that we were somehow set apart from. But since I have a poet's weakness for symbols, I am using this character also as a symbol; he is the long delayed but always expected something that we live for. There is a fifth character in the play who doesn't appear except in this larger-than-life photograph over the mantel. This is our father who left us a long time ago. He was a telephone man who fell in love with long distances; he gave up his job with the telephone company and skipped the light fantastic out of town.... The last we heard of him was a picture post-card from Mazatlán, on the Pacific coast of Mexico, containing a message of two words—"Hello—Good-bye!" and no address. I think the rest of the play will explain itself....

*(*AMANDA*'s voice becomes audible through the portieres.)*
(Legend on screen: "Où sont les neiges.")
(He divides the portieres and enters the upstage area.
AMANDA *and* LAURA *are seated at a drop-leaf table. Eating is indicated by gestures without food or utensils.* AMANDA *faces the audience.*
TOM *and* LAURA *are seated in profile.*
The interior has lit up softly and through the scrim we see AMANDA *and* LAURA *seated at the table in the upstage area.)*
AMANDA *(calling):* Tom?
TOM: Yes, Mother.
AMANDA: We can't say grace until you come to the table!
TOM: Coming, Mother. *(He bows slightly and withdraws, reappearing a few moments later in his place at the table.)*

5

AMANDA *(to her son)*: Honey, don't *push* with your *fingers*. If you have to push with something, the thing to push with is a crust of bread. And chew—chew! Animals have sections in their stomachs which enable them to digest food without mastication, but human beings are supposed to chew their food before they swallow it down. Eat food leisurely, son, and really enjoy it. A well-cooked meal has lots of delicate flavors that have to be held in the mouth for appreciation. So chew your food and give your salivary glands a chance to function!

(TOM deliberately lays his imaginary fork down and pushes his chair back from the table.)

TOM: I haven't enjoyed one bite of this dinner because of your constant directions on how to eat it. It's you that makes me rush through meals with your hawklike attention to every bite I take. Sickening—spoils my appetite—all this discussion of animals' secretion—salivary glands—mastication!

AMANDA *(lightly)*: Temperament like a Metropolitan star! *(He rises and crosses downstage.)* You're not excused from the table.

TOM: I am getting a cigarette.

AMANDA: You smoke too much.   10

(LAURA rises.)

LAURA: I'll bring in the blanc mange.

(He remains standing with his cigarette by the portieres during the following.)

AMANDA *(rising)*: No, sister, no, sister—you be the lady this time and I'll be the darky.

LAURA: I'm already up.

AMANDA: Resume your seat, little sister—I want you to stay fresh and pretty—for gentlemen callers!

LAURA: I'm not expecting any gentlemen callers.   15

AMANDA *(crossing out to kitchenette. Airily)*: Sometimes they come when they are least expected! Why, I remember one Sunday afternoon in Blue Mountain—

(Enters kitchenette.)

TOM: I know what's coming!

LAURA: Yes. But let her tell it.

TOM: Again?

LAURA: She loves to tell it.   20

(AMANDA returns with bowl of dessert.)

AMANDA: One Sunday afternoon in Blue Mountain—your mother received—*seventeen!*—gentlemen callers! Why, sometimes there weren't chairs enough to accommodate them all. We had to send the nigger over to bring in folding chairs from the parish house.

TOM *(remaining at portieres)*: How did you entertain those gentlemen callers?

AMANDA: I understood the art of conversation!

TOM: I bet you could talk.

AMANDA: Girls in those days *knew* how to talk, I can tell you.   25

TOM: Yes?

(Image: AMANDA *as a girl on a porch greeting callers.)*

AMANDA: They knew how to entertain their gentlemen callers. It wasn't enough for a girl to be possessed of a pretty face and a graceful figure—although I wasn't slighted in either respect. She also needed to have a nimble wit and a tongue to meet all occasions.

TOM: What did you talk about?

AMANDA: Things of importance going on in the world! Never anything coarse or common or vulgar.

(She addresses TOM *as though he were seated in the vacant chair at the table though he remains by portieres. He plays this scene as though he held the book.)*

My callers were gentlemen—all! Among my callers were some of the most prominent young planters of the Mississippi Delta—planters and sons of planters!

*(*TOM *motions for music and a spot of light on* AMANDA.

Her eyes lift, her face glows, her voice becomes rich and elegiac.)

(Screen legend: "Où sont les neiges.") There was young Champ Laughlin who later became vice-president of the Delta Planters Bank. Hadley Stevenson who was drowned in Moon Lake and left his widow one hundred and fifty thousand in Government bonds. There were the Cutrere brothers, Wesley and Bates. Bates was one of my bright particular beaux! He got in a quarrel with that wild Wainright boy. They shot it out on the floor of Moon Lake Casino. Bates was shot through the stomach. Died in the ambulance on his way to Memphis. His widow was also well-provided for, came into eight or ten thousand acres, that's all. She married him on the rebound—never loved her—carried my picture on him the night he died! And there was that boy that every girl in the Delta had set her cap for! That beautiful, brilliant young Fitzhugh boy from Green County!

TOM: What did he leave his widow?   30

AMANDA: He never married! Gracious, you talk as though all of my old admirers had turned up their toes to the daisies!

TOM: Isn't this the first you mentioned that still survives?

AMANDA: That Fitzhugh boy went North and made a fortune—came to be known as the Wolf of Wall Street! He had the Midas touch, whatever he touched turned to gold! And I could have been Mrs. Duncan J. Fitzhugh, mind you! But—I picked your *father!*

LAURA *(rising):* Mother, let me clear the table.

AMANDA: No dear, you go in front and study your typewriter chart. Or practice your shorthand a little. Stay fresh and pretty!—It's almost time for   35
our gentlemen callers to start arriving. *(She flounces girlishly toward the*

kitchenette.) How many do you suppose we're going to entertain this
safternoon?
(TOM *throws down the paper and jumps up with a groan.)*
LAURA: *(alone in the dining room)*: I don't believe we're going to receive any,
Mother.
AMANDA *(reappearing, airily)*: What? No one—not one? You must be joking!
(LAURA *nervously echoes her laugh. She slips in a fugitive manner through
the half-open portieres and draws them gently behind her. A shaft of very
clear light is thrown on her face against the faded tapestry of the curtains)*
(Music: *"The Glass Menagerie" under faintly) (Lightly.)* Not one
gentleman caller? It can't be true! There must be a flood, there must
have been a tornado!
LAURA: It isn't a flood, it's not a tornado, Mother. I'm just not popular like
you were in Blue Mountain.... (TOM *utters another groan.* LAURA
glances at him with a faint, apologetic smile. Her voice catching a little.)
Mother's afraid I'm going to be an old maid.
(*The scene dims out with "Glass Menagerie" music.)*

Scene 2

"Laura, Haven't You Ever Liked Some Boy?"
(*On the dark stage the screen is lighted with the image of blue roses.*
Gradually LAURA*'s figure becomes apparent and the screen goes out.*
The music subsides.
LAURA *is seated in the delicate ivory chair at the small clawfoot table.*
*She wears a dress of soft violet material for a kimono—her hair tied back from her
forehead with a ribbon.*
She is washing and polishing her collection of glass.
AMANDA *appears on the fire-escape steps. At the sound of her ascent,* LAURA
*catches her breath, thrusts the bowl of ornaments away, and seats herself
stiffly before the diagram of the typewriter keyboard as though it held her
spellbound. Something has happened to* AMANDA. *It is written in her face
as she climbs to the landing: a look that is grim and hopeless and a little
absurd.*
*She has on one of those cheap or imitation velvety-looking cloth coats with imita-
tion fur collar. Her hat is five or six years old, one of those dreadful cloche
hats that were worn in the late twenties, and she is clasping an enormous
black patent-leather pocketbook with nickel clasp and initials. This is her full-
dress outfit, the one she usually wears to the D.A.R.*
Before entering she looks through the door.
She purses her lips, opens her eyes wide, rolls them upward, and shakes her head.
Then she slowly lets herself in the door. Seeing her mother's expression LAURA
touches her lips with a nervous gesture.)
LAURA: Hello, Mother, I was— (*She makes a nervous gesture toward the chart*

on the wall. AMANDA *leans against the shut door and stares at* LAURA *with a martyred look.)*

AMANDA: Deception? Deception? (*She slowly removes her hat and gloves, continuing the swift suffering stare. She lets the hat and gloves fall on the floor—a bit of acting.*)

LAURA (*shakily*): How was the D.A.R. meeting? (AMANDA *slowly opens her purse and removes a dainty white handkerchief, which she shakes out delicately and delicately touches to her lips and nostrils.*) Didn't you go to the D.A.R. meeting, Mother?

AMANDA (*faintly, almost inaudibly*): —No. —No. (*Then more forcibly.*) I did not have the strength—to go to the D.A.R. In fact, I did not have the courage! I wanted to find a hole in the ground and hide myself in it forever! (*She crosses slowly to the wall and removes the diagram of the typewriter keyboard. She holds it in front of her for a second, staring at it sweetly and sorrowfully—then bites her lips and tears it in two pieces.*)

LAURA (*faintly*): Why did you do that, Mother? (AMANDA *repeats the same procedure with the chart of the Gregg Alphabet.*) Why are you—   5

AMANDA: Why? Why? How old are you, Laura?

LAURA: Mother, you know my age.

AMANDA: I thought that you were an adult; it seems that I was mistaken. (*She crosses slowly to the sofa and sinks down and stares at* LAURA.)

LAURA: Please don't stare at me, Mother.

(AMANDA *closes her eyes and lowers her head. Count ten.*)

AMANDA: What are we going to do, what is going to become of us, what is   10
the future?

Count ten.

LAURA: Has something happened, Mother? (AMANDA *draws a long breath and takes out the handkerchief again. Dabbing process.*) Mother, has—something happened?

AMANDA: I'll be ail right in a minute. I'm just bewildered— (*count five*)— by life....

LAURA: Mother, I wish that you would tell me what's happened.

AMANDA: As you know, I was supposed to be inducted into my office at the D.A.R. this afternoon. (*Image: A swarm of typewriters.*) But I stopped off at Rubicam's Business College to speak to your teachers about your having a cold and ask them what progress they thought you were making down there.

LAURA: Oh....   15

AMANDA: I went to the typing instructor and introduced myself as your mother. She didn't know who you were. Wingfield, she said. We don't have any such student enrolled at the school! I assured her she did, that you had been going to classes since early in January. "I wonder," she said, "if you could be talking about that terribly shy little girl who dropped out of school after only a few days' attendance?" "No," I said,

"Laura, my daughter, has been going to school every day for the past six weeks!" "Excuse me," she said. She took the attendance book out and there was your name, unmistakably printed, and all the dates you were absent until they decided that you had dropped out of school.
I still said, "No, there must have been some mistake! There must have been some mix-up in the records!" And she said, "No—I remember her perfectly now. Her hand shook so that she couldn't hit the right keys! The first time we gave a speed-test, she broke down completely— was sick at the stomach and almost had to be carried into the wash-room! After that morning she never showed up any more. We phoned the house but never got any answer"—while I was working at Famous and Barr, I suppose, demonstrating those—Oh! I felt so weak I could barely keep on my feet. I had to sit down while they got me a glass of water! Fifty dollars' tuition, all of our plans—my hopes and ambitions for you—just gone up the spout, just gone up the spout like that. (LAURA *draws a long breath and gets awkwardly to her feet. She crosses to the Victrola, and winds it up.*) What are you doing?
LAURA: Oh! (*She releases the handle and returns to her seat.*)
AMANDA: Laura, where have you been going when you've gone out pretending that you were going to business college?
LAURA: I've just been going out walking.
AMANDA: That's not true.   20
LAURA: It is. I just went walking.
AMANDA: Walking? Walking? In winter? Deliberately courting pneumonia in that light coat? Where did you walk to, Laura?
LAURA: It was the lesser of two evils, Mother. (*Image: Winter scene in park.*) I couldn't go back up. I—threw up—on the floor!
AMANDA: From half past seven till after five every day you mean to tell me you walked around in the park, because you wanted to make me think that you were still going to Rubicam's Business College?
LAURA: It wasn't as bad as it sounds. I went inside places to get warmed up.   25
AMANDA: Inside where?
LAURA: I went in the art museum and the bird-houses at the Zoo. I visited the penguins every day! Sometimes I did without lunch and went to the movies. Lately I've been spending most of my afternoons in the Jewel-box, that big glass house where they raise the tropical flowers.
AMANDA: You did all this to deceive me, just for the deception? (LAURA *looks down.*) Why?
LAURA: Mother, when you're disappointed, you get that awful suffering look on your face, like the picture of Jesus' mother in the museum!
AMANDA: Hush!   30
LAURA: I couldn't face it.
(*Pause. A whisper of strings.*)
(*Legend: "The Crust of Humility."*)

AMANDA (*hopelessly fingering the huge pocketbook*): So what are we going to do the rest of our lives? Stay home and watch the parades go by? Amuse ourselves with the glass menagerie, darling? Eternally play those worn-out phonograph records your father left as a painful reminder of him? We won't have a business career—we've given that up because it gave us nervous indigestion! (*Laughs wearily.*) What is there left but dependency all our lives? I know so well what becomes of unmarried women who aren't prepared to occupy a position. I've seen such pitiful cases in the South—barely tolerated spinsters living upon the grudging patronage of sister's husband or brother's wife!—stuck away in some little mousetrap of a room—encouraged by one in-law to visit another—little birdlike women without any nest—eating the crust of humility all their life! Is that the future that we've mapped out for ourselves? I swear it's the only alternative I can think of! It isn't a very pleasant alternative, is it? Of course—some girls *do marry*. (LAURA *twists her hands nervously.*) Haven't you ever liked some boy?

LAURA: Yes. I liked one once (*Rises.*) I came across his picture a while ago.

AMANDA (*with some interest*): He gave you his picture?

LAURA: No, it's in the year-book. 35

AMANDA (*disappointed*): Oh—a high-school boy.

(*Screen image:* JIM *as a high-school hero bearing a silver cup.*)

LAURA: Yes. His name was Jim. (LAURA *lifts the heavy annual from the claw-foot table.*) Here he is in *The Pirates of Penzance.*

AMANDA (*absently*): The what?

LAURA: The operetta the senior class put on. He had a wonderful voice and we sat across the aisle from each other Mondays, Wednesdays, and Fridays in the Aud. Here he is with the silver cup for debating! See his grin!

AMANDA (*absently*): He must have had a jolly disposition. 40

LAURA: He used to call me—Blue Roses.

(*Image: Blue roses.*)

AMANDA: Why did he call you such a name as that?

LAURA: When I had that attack of pleurosis—he asked me what was the matter when I came back. I said pleurosis—he thought that I said Blue Roses! So that's what he always called me after that. Whenever he saw me, he'd holler, "Hello, Blue Roses!" I didn't care for the girl that he went out with. Emily Meisenbach. Emily was the best-dressed girl at Soldan. She never struck me, though, as being sincere.... It says in the Personal Section—they're engaged. That's—six years ago! They must be married by now.

AMANDA: Girls that aren't cut out for business careers usually wind up married to some nice man. (*Gets up with a spark of revival.*) Sister, that's what you'll do!

(LAURA *utters a startled, doubtful laugh. She reaches quickly for a piece of glass.*)

LAURA: But, Mother—   45
AMANDA: Yes? (*Crossing to photograph.*)
LAURA (*in a tone of frightened apology*): I'm—crippled!
(*Image: Screen.*)
AMANDA: Nonsense! Laura, I've told you never, never to use that word.
Why, you're not crippled, you just have a little defect—hardly notice-
able, even! When people have some slight disadvantage like that, they
cultivate other things to make up for it—develop charm—and vivaci-
ty—and—*charm*! That's all you have to do! (*She turns again to the pho-
tograph.*) One thing your father had *plenty of*—was *charm*!
(TOM *motions to the fiddle in the wings.*)
(*The scene fades out with music.*)

Scene 3

(*Legend on the screen: "After the Fiasco—"*):
(TOM *speaks from the fire-escape landing.*)
TOM: After the fiasco at Rubicam's Business College, the idea of getting a
gentleman caller for Laura began to play a more important part in
Mother's calculations. It became an obsession, like some archetype of
the universal unconscious, the image of the gentleman caller haunted
our small apartment.... (*Image: Young man at door with flowers.*) An
evening at home rarely passed without some allusion to this image, this
specter, this hope.... Even when he wasn't mentioned, his presence
hung in Mother's preoccupied look and in my sister's frightened, apologetic manner—hung like a sentence passed upon the Wingfields!
Mother was a woman of action as well as words. She began to take logical steps in the planned direction. Late that winter and in the early
spring—realizing that extra money would be needed to properly feather
the nest and plume the bird—she conducted a vigorous campaign on
the telephone, roping in subscribers to one of those magazines for
matrons called *The Home-maker's Companion*, the type of journal that
features the serialized sublimations of ladies of letters who think in
terms of delicate cuplike breasts, slim, tapering waists, rich, creamy
thighs, eyes like wood-smoke in autumn, fingers that soothe and caress
like strains of music, bodies as powerful as Etruscan sculpture.
(*Screen image:* Glamour *magazine cover.*)
(AMANDA *enters with phone on long extension cord. She is spotted in the dim
stage.*)
AMANDA: Ida Scott? This is Amanda Wingfield! We *missed* you at the
D.A.R. last Monday! I said to myself: She's probably suffering with that
sinus condition! How is that sinus condition? Horrors! Heaven have
mercy!—You're a Christian martyr, yes, that's what you are, a Christian

martyr! Well, I just now happened to notice that your subscription to the *Companion*'s about to expire! Yes, it expires with the next issue, honey!—just when that wonderful new serial by Bessie Mae Hopper is getting off to such an exciting start. Oh, honey, it's something that you can't miss! You remember how *Gone with the Wind* took everybody by storm? You simply couldn't go out if you hadn't read it. All everybody *talked* was Scarlett O'Hara. Well, this is a book that critics already compare to *Gone with the Wind*. It's the *Gone with the Wind* of the post-World War generation!—What?—Burning?—Oh, honey, don't let them burn, go take a look in the oven and I'll hold the wire! Heavens—I think she's hung up!

(Dim out.)

(Legend on screen: "You think I'm in love with Continental Shoemakers?")

(Before the stage is lighted, the violent voices of TOM *and* AMANDA *are heard.*
   They are quarreling behind the portieres. In front of them stands LAURA *with*
   clenched hands and panicky expression.
A *clear pool of light on her figure throughout this scene.)*

TOM: What in Christ's name am I—

AMANDA *(shrilly)*: Don't you use that—

TOM: Supposed to do!   5

AMANDA: Expression! Not in my—

TOM: Ohhh!

AMANDA: Presence! Have you gone out of your senses?

TOM: I have, that's true, *driven* out!

AMANDA: What is the matter with you, you—big—big—IDIOT!   10

TOM: Look—I've got *no thing*, no single thing—

AMANDA: Lower your voice!

TOM: In my life here that I can call my own! Everything is—

AMANDA: Stop that shouting!

TOM: Yesterday you confiscated my books! You had the nerve to—   15

AMANDA: I took that horrible novel back to the library—yes! That hideous
   book by that insane Mr. Lawrence. (TOM *laughs wildly.*) I cannot control the output of diseased minds or people who cater to them— (TOM
   laughs still more wildly.) BUT I WON'T ALLOW SUCH FILTH
   BROUGHT INTO MY HOUSE! No, no, no, no, no!

TOM: House, house! Who pays rent on it, who makes a slave of himself to—

AMANDA *(fairly screeching)*: Don't you DARE to—

TOM: No, no, I mustn't say things! *I've* got to just—

AMANDA: Let me tell you—   20

TOM: I don't want to hear any more!

*(He tears the portieres open. The upstage area is lit with a turgid smoky red
   glow.*

AMANDA'*s hair is in metal curlers and she wears a very old bathrobe, much too
   large for her slight figure, a relic of the faithless Mr. Wingfield.*

*An upright typewriter and a wild disarray of manuscripts are on the drop-leaf
  table. The quarrel was probably precipitated by* AMANDA's *interruption of his
  creative labor. A chair lying overthrown on the floor.
Their gesticulating shadows are cast on the ceiling by the fiery glow.)*

AMANDA: You *will* hear more, you—

TOM: No, I won't hear more, I'm going out!

AMANDA: You come right back in—

TOM: Out, out, out! Because I'm—   25

AMANDA: Come back here, Tom Wingfield! I'm not through talking to you!

TOM: Oh, go—

LAURA *(desperately)*: Tom!

AMANDA: You're going to listen, and no more insolence from you! I'm at
  the end of my patience! *(He comes back toward her.)*

TOM: What do you think I'm at? Aren't I supposed to have any patience to   30
  reach the end of, Mother? I know, I know. It seems unimportant to
  you, what I'm *doing*—what *I want* to do—having a little *difference* between them! You don't think that—

AMANDA: I think you've been doing things that you're ashamed of. That's
  why you act like this. I don't believe that you go every night to the
  movies. Nobody goes to the movies night after night. Nobody in their
  right minds goes to the movies as often as you pretend to. People don't
  go to the movies at nearly midnight, and movies don't let out at two
  A.M. Come in stumbling. Muttering to yourself like a maniac! You get
  three hours' sleep and then go to work. Oh, I can picture the way
  you're doing down there. Moping, doping, because you're in no
  condition.

TOM *(wildly)*: No, I'm in no condition!

AMANDA: What right have you got to jeopardize your job? Jeopardize the security of us all? How do you think we'd manage if you were—

TOM: Listen! You think I'm crazy *about* the *warehouse*! *(He bends fiercely toward her slight figure.)* You think I'm in love with the Continental
  Shoemakers? You think I want to spend fifty-five *years* down there in
  that—*celotex interior*! with—*fluorescent*—*tubes*! Look! I'd rather somebody picked up a crowbar and battered out my brains—than go back
  mornings! I *go*! Every time you come in yelling that God damn *"Rise
  and Shine!" "Rise and Shine!"* I say to myself *"How lucky dead* people
  are!"* But I get up. I *go*! For sixty-five dollars a month I give up all that I
  dream of doing and being *ever*! And you say self—*self's* all I ever think
  of. Why, listen, if self is what I thought of, Mother, I'd be where he
  is—! *(Pointing to father's picture.)* As far as the system of transportation
  reaches! *(He starts past her. She grabs his arm.)* Don't grab at me,
  Mother!

AMANDA: Where are you going?   35

TOM: I'm going to the *movies*!

AMANDA: I don't believe that lie!

TOM (*crouching toward her, overtowering her tiny figure. She backs away, gasping*): I'm going to opium dens! Yes, opium dens, dens of vice and criminals' hang-outs, Mother. I've joined the Hogan gang, I'm a hired assassin, I carry a Tommy-gun in a violin case! I run a string of cat-houses in the Valley! They call me Killer, Killer Wingfield, I'm leading a double-life, a simple, honest warehouse worker by day, by night a dynamic *czar* of the *underworld, Mother.* I go to gambling casinos, I spin away fortunes on the roulette table! I wear a patch over one eye and a false mustache, sometimes I put on green whiskers. On those occasions they call me—*El Diablo!* Oh, I could tell you things to make you sleepless! My enemies plan to dynamite this place. They're going to blow us all sky-high some night! I'll be glad, very happy, and so will you! You'll go up, up on a broomstick, over Blue Mountain with seventeen gentlemen callers! You ugly—babbling old—*witch.* (*He goes through a series of violent, clumsy movements, seizing his overcoat, lunging to the door, pulling it fiercely open. The women watch him, aghast. His arm catches in the sleeve of the coat as he struggles to pull it on. For a moment he is pinioned by the bulky garment. With an outraged groan be tears the coat off again, splitting the shoulders of it, and burls it across the room. It strikes against the shelf of Laura's glass collection, there is a tinkle of shattering glass. LAURA cries out as if wounded.*)

(*Music legend: "The Glass Menagerie."*)

LAURA (*shrilly*): My glass!—menagerie. (*She covers her face and turns away.*)

But AMANDA is still stunned and stupefied by the "ugly witch" so that she barely notices this occurrence. Now she recovers her speech.

AMANDA (*in an awful voice*): I won't speak to you—until you apologize! 40

(*She crosses through portieres and draws them together behind her. TOM is left with LAURA. LAURA clings weakly to the mantel with her face averted. TOM stares at her stupidly for a moment. Then he crosses to shelf. Drops awkwardly to his knees to collect the fallen glass, glancing at LAURA as if he would speak but couldn't.*)

(*"The Glass Menagerie" steals in as the scene dims out.*)

Scene 4

(*The interior is dark. Faint light in the alley.*

A deep-voiced bell in a church is tolling the hour of five as the scene commences. TOM appears at the top of the alley. After each solemn boom of the bell in the tower, he shakes a little noise-maker or rattle as if to express the tiny spasm of man in contrast to the sustained power and dignity of the Almighty. This and the unsteadiness of his advance make it evident that he has been drinking.

As he climbs the few steps to the fire-escape landing light steals up inside. LAURA appears in night-dress, observing TOM's empty bed in the front room.

TOM *fishes in his pockets for the door-key, removing a motley assortment of articles in the search, including a perfect shower of movie-ticket stubs and an empty bottle. At last he finds the key, but just as he is about to insert it, it slips from his fingers. He strikes a match and crouches below the door.)*

TOM *(bitterly)*: One crack—and it falls through!

LAURA *opens the door.*

LAURA: Tom! Tom, what are you doing?

TOM: Looking for a door-key.

LAURA: Where have you been all this time?

TOM: I have been to the movies.   5

LAURA: All this time at the movies?

TOM: There was a very long program. There was a Garbo picture and a Mickey Mouse and a travelogue and a newsreel and a preview of coming attractions. And there was an organ solo and a collection for the milk-fund—simultaneously—which ended up in a terrible fight between a fat lady and an usher!

LAURA *(innocently)*: Did you have to stay through everything?

TOM: Of course! And, oh, I forgot! There was a big stage show! The headliner on this stage show was Malvolio the Magician. He performed wonderful tricks, many of them, such as pouring water back and forth between pitchers. First it turned to wine and then it turned to beer and then it turned to whiskey. I know it was whiskey it finally turned into because he needed somebody to come up out of the audience to help him, and I came up—both shows! It was Kentucky Straight Bourbon. A very generous fellow, he gave souvenirs. *(He pulls from his back pocket a shimmering rainbow-colored scarf.)* He gave me this. This is his magic scarf. You can have it, Laura. You wave it over a canary cage and you get a bowl of gold-fish. You wave it over the gold-fish bowl and they fly away canaries…. But the wonderfullest trick of all was the coffin trick. We nailed him into a coffin and he got out of the coffin without removing one nail. *(He has come inside.)* There is a trick that would come in handy for me—get me out of this 2 by 4 situation! *(Flops onto bed and starts removing shoes.)*

LAURA: Tom—Shhh!   10

TOM: What you shushing me for?

LAURA: You'll wake up Mother.

TOM: Goody, goody! Pay 'er back for all those "Rise an' Shines."
(Lies down, groaning.) You know it don't take much intelligence to get yourself into a nailed-up coffin, Laura. But who in hell ever got himself out of one without removing one nail?

(As if in answer, the father's grinning photograph lights up.)

(Scene dims out.)

*(Immediately following: The church bell is heard striking six. At the sixth stroke
the alarm clock goes off in* AMANDA's *room, and after a few moments we
hear her calling: "Rise and Shine! Rise and Shine! Laura, go tell your brother
to rise and shine!")*

TOM *(sitting up slowly)*: I'll rise—but I won't shine.

(The light increases.)

AMANDA: Laura, tell your brother his coffee is ready.   15

LAURA *slips into front room.*

LAURA: Tom! it's nearly seven. Don't make Mother nervous.
   (He stares at her stupidly. Beseechingly.) Tom, speak to Mother this
   morning. Make up with her, apologize, speak to her!

TOM: She won't to me. It's her that started not speaking.

LAURA: If you just say you're sorry she'll start speaking.

TOM: Her not speaking—is that such a tragedy?

LAURA: Please—please!   20

AMANDA *(calling from kitchenette)*: Laura, are you going to do what I asked
   you to do, or do I have to get dressed and go out myself?

LAURA: Going, going—soon as I get on my coat! *(She pulls on a shapeless felt
   hat with nervous, jerky movement, pleadingly glancing at* TOM. *Rushes awkwardly for coat. The coat is one of* AMANDA's, *inaccurately made-over, the
   sleeves too short for* LAURA.*)* Butter and what else?

AMANDA *(entering upstage)*: Just butter. Tell them to charge it.

LAURA: Mother, they make such faces when I do that.

AMANDA: Sticks and stones may break my bones, but the expression on   25
   Mr. Garfinkel's face won't harm us! Tell your brother his coffee is getting
   cold.

LAURA *(at door)*: Do what I asked you, will you, will you, Tom?

(He looks sullenly away.)

AMANDA: Laura, go now or just don't go at all!

LAURA *(rushing out)*: Going—going! *(A second later she cries out.* TOM *springs
   up and crosses to the door.* AMANDA *rushes anxiously in.* TOM *opens the door.)*

TOM: Laura?

LAURA: I'm all right. I slipped, but I'm all right   30

AMANDA *(peering anxiously after her)*: If anyone breaks a leg on those fire-escape steps, the landlord ought to be sued for every cent he possesses!
   (She shuts door. Remembers she isn't speaking and returns to other room.)

(As TOM *enters listlessly for his coffee, she turns her back to him and stands rigidly
   facing the window on the gloomy gray vault of the areaway. Its light on her face
   with its aged but childish features is cruelly sharp, satirical as a Daumier print.)*

(Music under: "Ave Maria.")

*(*TOM *glances sheepishly but sullenly at her averted figure and slumps at the table.
   The coffee is scalding hot; he sips it and gasps and spits it back in the cup.*

At his gasp, AMANDA *catches her breath and half turns. Then catches herself and turns back to window.*)

TOM *blows on his coffee, glancing sidewise at his mother. She clears her throat.* TOM *clears his. He starts to rise. Sinks back down again, scratches his head, clears his throat again.* AMANDA *coughs.* TOM *raises his cup in both hands to blow on it, his eyes staring over the rim of it at his mother for several moments. Then he slowly sets the cup down and awkwardly and hesitantly rises from the chair.*)

TOM (*hoarsely*): Mother. I—I apologize. Mother. (AMANDA *draws a quick, shuddering breath. Her face works grotesquely. She breaks into childlike tears.*) I'm sorry for what I said, for everything that I said, I didn't mean it.

AMANDA (*sobbingly*): My devotion has made me a witch and so I make myself hateful to my children!

TOM: No, you *don't*.

AMANDA: I worry so much, don't sleep, it makes me nervous!   35

TOM (*gently*): I understand that.

AMANDA: I've had to put up a solitary battle all these years. But you're my right-hand bower! Don't fall down, don't fail!

TOM (*gently*): I try, Mother.

AMANDA (*with great enthusiasm*): Try and you will SUCCEED! (*The notion makes her breathless.*) Why, you—you're just *full* of natural endowments! Both of my children—they're *unusual* children! Don't you think I know it? I'm so—*proud*! Happy and—feel I've—so much to be thankful for but—Promise me one thing, son!

TOM: What, Mother?   40

AMANDA: Promise, son, you'll—never be a drunkard!

TOM (*turns to her grinning*): I will never be a drunkard, Mother.

AMANDA: That's what frightened me so, that you'd be drinking! Eat a bowl of Purina!

TOM: Just coffee, Mother.

AMANDA: Shredded wheat biscuit?   45

TOM: No. No, Mother, just coffee.

AMANDA: You can't put in a day's work on an empty stomach. You've got ten minutes—don't gulp! Drinking too-hot liquids makes cancer of the stomach.... Put cream in.

TOM: No, thank you.

AMANDA: To cool it.

TOM: No! No, thank you, I want it black.   50

AMANDA: I know, but it's not good for you. We have to do all that we can to build ourselves up. In these trying times we live in, all that we have to cling to is—each other.... That's why it's so important to—Tom, I—I sent out your sister so I could discuss something with you. If you hadn't spoken I would have spoken to you. (*Sits down.*)

TOM (*gently*): What is it, Mother, that you want to discuss?

AMANDA: Laura!

(TOM *puts his cup down slowly.*)

(*Legend on screen: "Laura."*)

(*Music: "The Glass Menagerie."*)

TOM: —Oh. —Laura ...

AMANDA (*touching his sleeve*): You know how Laura is. So quiet but—still   55
water runs deep! She notices things and I think she—broods about them.
(TOM *looks up.*) A few days ago I came in and she was crying.

TOM: What about?

AMANDA: You.

TOM: Me?

AMANDA: She has an idea that you're not happy here.

TOM: What gave her that idea?   60

AMANDA: What gives her any idea? However, you do act strangely. I—I'm
not criticizing, understand *that*! I know your ambitions do not lie in the
warehouse, that like everybody in the whole wide world—you've had
to—make sacrifices, but—Tom—Tom—life's not easy, it calls for—
Spartan endurance! There's so many things in my heart that I cannot
describe to you! I've never told you but I—*loved* your father....

TOM (*gently*): I know that, Mother.

AMANDA: And you—when I see you taking after his ways! Staying out
late—and—well, you *had* been drinking the night you were in that—
terrifying condition! Laura says that you hate the apartment and that
you go out nights to get away from it! Is that true, Tom?

TOM: No. You say there's so much in your heart that you can't describe to
me. That's true of me, too. There's so much in my heart that I can't describe to *you*! So let's respect each other's—

AMANDA: But, why—*why*, Tom—are you always so *restless*? Where do you   65
go to, nights?

TOM: I—go to the movies.

AMANDA: Why do you go to the movies so much, Tom?

TOM: I go to the movies because—I like adventure. Adventure is something
I don't have much of at work, so I go to the movies.

AMANDA: But, Tom, you go to the movies *entirely too much*!

TOM: I like a lot of adventure.   70

(AMANDA *looks baffled, then hurt. As the familiar inquisition resumes he becomes
hard and impatient again.* AMANDA *slips back into her querulous attitude toward him.*)

(*Image on screen: Sailing vessel with Jolly Roger.*)

AMANDA: Most young men find adventure in their careers.

TOM: Then most young men are not employed in a warehouse.

AMANDA: The world is full of young men employed in warehouses and
offices and factories.

TOM: Do all of them find adventure in their careers?

AMANDA: They do or they do without it! Not everybody has a craze for   75
adventure.

TOM: Man is by instinct a lover, a hunter, a fighter, and none of those
instincts are given much play at the warehouse!

AMANDA: Man is by instinct! Don't quote instinct to me! Instinct is something that people have got away from! It belongs to animals! Christian
adults don't want it!

TOM: What do Christian adults want, then, Mother?

AMANDA: Superior things! Things of the mind and the spirit! Only animals
have to satisfy instincts! Surely your aims are somewhat higher than
theirs! Than monkeys—pigs—

TOM: I reckon they're not.   80

AMANDA: You're joking. However, that isn't what I wanted to discuss.

TOM *(rising)*: I haven't much time.

AMANDA *(pushing his shoulders)*: Sit down.

TOM: You want me to punch in red at the warehouse, Mother?

AMANDA: You have five minutes. I want to talk about Laura.   85

(Legend: "Plans and Provisions.")

TOM: All right! What about Laura?

AMANDA: We have to be making plans and provisions for her. She's older
than you, two years, and nothing has happened. She just drifts along
doing nothing. It frightens me terribly how she just drifts along.

TOM: I guess she's the type that people call home girls.

AMANDA: There's no such type, and if there is, it's a pity! That is unless the
home is hers, with a husband!

TOM: What?   90

AMANDA: Oh, I can see the handwriting on the wall as plain as I see the
nose in front of my face! It's terrifying! More and more you remind me
of your father! He was out all hours without explanation—Then *left!*
Good-bye! And me with the bag to hold. I saw that letter you got from
the Merchant Marine. I know what you're dreaming of. I'm not standing here blindfolded. Very well, then. Then *do* it! But not till there's
somebody to take your place.

TOM: What do you mean?

AMANDA: I mean that as soon as Laura has got somebody to take care of her,
married, a home of her own, independent—why, then you'll be free to
go wherever you please, on land, on sea, whichever way the wind blows!
But until that time you've got to look out for your sister. I don't say me
because I'm old and don't matter! I say for your sister because she's
young and dependent. I put her in business college—a dismal failure!
Frightened her so it made her sick to her stomach. I took her over to
the Young People's League at the church. Another fiasco. She spoke to

nobody, nobody spoke to her. Now all she does is fool with those pieces of glass and play those worn-out records. What kind of a life is that for a girl to lead!

TOM: What can I do about it?

AMANDA: Overcome selfishness! Self, self, self is all that you ever think of!   95

(TOM *springs up and crosses to get his coat. It is ugly and bulky. He pulls on a cap with earmuffs.*) Where is your muffler? Put your wool muffler on! (*He snatches it angrily from the closet and tosses it around his neck and pulls both ends tight.*) Tom! I haven't said what I had in mind to ask you.

TOM: I'm too late to—

AMANDA (*catching his arms—very importunately. Then shyly.*): Down at the warehouse, aren't there some—nice young men?

TOM: No!

AMANDA: There *must* be—*some*.

TOM: Mother—   100

(*Gesture.*)

AMANDA: Find out one that's clean-living—doesn't drink and—ask him out for sister!

TOM: What?

AMANDA: For *sister*! To *meet*! Get *acquainted*!

TOM (*stamping to door*): Oh, my go-osh!

AMANDA: Will you? (*He opens door. Imploringly.*) Will you? (*He starts   105 down.*) Will you? *Will* you, dear?

TOM (*calling back*): YES!

(AMANDA *closes the door hesitantly and with a troubled but faintly hopeful expression.*)

(*Screen image: Glamour magazine cover.*)

Spot AMANDA *at phone.*

AMANDA: Ella Cartwright? This is Amanda Wingfield! How are you, honey? How is that kidney condition? (*Count five.*) Horrors! (*Count five.*) You're a Christian martyr, yes, honey, that's what you are, a Christian martyr! Well, I just happened to notice in my little red book that your subscription to the *Companion* has just run out! I knew that you wouldn't want to miss out on the wonderful serial starting in this new issue. It's by Bessie Mae Hopper, the first thing she's written since *Honeymoon for Three*. Wasn't that a strange and interesting story? Well, this one is even lovelier, I believe. It has a sophisticated society background. It's all about the horsey set on Long Island!

(*Fade out.*)

Scene 5

(*Legend on screen: "Annunciation."*)
(*Fade with music.*)

(It is early dusk of a spring evening. Supper has just been finished in the Wingfield apartment. AMANDA *and* LAURA *in light-colored dresses are removing dishes from the table, in the upstage area, which is shadowy, their movements formalized almost as a dance or ritual, their moving forms as pale and silent as moths.*

TOM, *in white shirt and trousers, rises from the table and crosses toward the fire-escape.)*

AMANDA *(as he passes her):* Son, will you do me a favor?

TOM: What?

AMANDA: Comb your hair! You look so pretty when your hair is combed! *(*TOM *slouches on sofa with evening paper. Enormous caption "Franco Triumphs.")* There is only one respect in which I would like you to emulate your father.

TOM: What respect is that?

AMANDA: The care he always took of his appearance. He never allowed himself to look untidy. *(He throws down the paper and crosses to fire-escape.)* Where are you going?   5

TOM: I'm going out to smoke.

AMANDA: You smoke too much. A pack a day at fifteen cents a pack. How much would that amount to in a month? Thirty times fifteen is how much, Tom? Figure it out and you will be astounded at what you could save. Enough to give you a night-school course in accounting at Washington U! Just think what a wonderful thing that would be for you, son!

*(*TOM *is unmoved by the thought.)*

TOM: I'd rather smoke. *(He steps out on landing, letting the screen door slam.)*

AMANDA *(sharply):* I know! That's the tragedy of it.... *(Alone, she turns to look at her husband's picture.)*

(Dance music: "All the World Is Waiting for the Sunrise!")

TOM *(to the audience):* Across the alley from us was the Paradise Dance Hall. On evenings in spring the windows and doors were open and the music came outdoors. Sometimes the lights were turned out except for a large glass sphere that hung from the ceiling. It would turn slowly about and filter the dusk with delicate rainbow colors. Then the orchestra played a waltz or a tango, something that had a slow and sensuous rhythm. Couples would come outside, to the relative privacy of the alley. You could see them kissing behind ash-pits and telephone poles. This was the compensation for lives that passed like mine, without any change or adventure. Adventure and change were imminent in this year. They were waiting around the corner for all these kids. Suspended in the mist over the Berchtesgaden, caught in the folds of Chamberlain's umbrella— In Spain there was Guernica! But here there was only hot swing music and liquor, dance halls, bars, and movies, and sex that   10 hung in the gloom like a chandelier and flooded the world with brief, deceptive rainbows.... All the world was waiting for bombardments!

(AMANDA *turns from the picture and comes outside.*)

AMANDA (*sighing*): A fire-escape landing's a poor excuse for a porch. (*She spreads a newspaper on a step and sits down, gracefully and demurely as if she were settling into a swing on a Mississippi veranda.*) What are you looking at?

TOM: The moon.

AMANDA: Is there a moon this evening?

TOM: It's rising over Garfinkel's Delicatessen.

AMANDA: So it is! A little silver slipper of a moon. Have you made a wish on it yet? 15

TOM: Um-hum.

AMANDA: What did you wish for?

TOM: That's a secret.

AMANDA: A secret, huh? Well, I won't tell mine either. I will be just as mysterious as you.

TOM: I bet I can guess what yours is. 20

AMANDA: Is my head so transparent?

TOM: You're not a sphinx.

AMANDA: No, I don't have secrets. I'll tell you what I wished for on the moon. Success and happiness for my precious children! I wish for that whenever there's a moon, and when there isn't a moon, I wish for it, too.

TOM: I thought perhaps you wished for a gentleman caller.

AMANDA: Why do you say that? 25

TOM: Don't you remember asking me to fetch one?

AMANDA: I remember suggesting that it would be nice for your sister if you brought home some nice young man from the warehouse. I think I've made that suggestion more than once.

TOM: Yes, you have made it repeatedly.

AMANDA: Well?

TOM: We are going to have one. 30

AMANDA: *What?*

TOM: A gentleman caller!

(*The Annunciation is celebrated with music.*)

AMANDA *rises.*

(*Image on screen: Caller with bouquet.*)

AMANDA: You mean you have asked some nice young man to come over?

TOM: Yep. I've asked him to dinner.

AMANDA: You really did? 35

TOM: I did!

AMANDA: You did, and did he—*accept?*

TOM: He did!

AMANDA: Well, well—well, well! That's—lovely!

TOM: I thought that you would be pleased.   40

AMANDA: It's definite, then?

TOM: Very definite.

AMANDA: Soon?

TOM: Very soon.

AMANDA: For heaven's sake, stop putting on and tell me some things, will you?   45

TOM: What things do you want me to tell you?

AMANDA: Naturally I would like to know when he's *coming*!

TOM: He's coming Tomorrow.

AMANDA: *Tomorrow?*

TOM: Yep. Tomorrow.   50

AMANDA: But, Tom!

TOM: Yes, Mother?

AMANDA: Tomorrow gives me no time!

TOM: Time for what?

AMANDA: Preparations! Why didn't you phone me at once, as soon as you   55
asked him, the minute that he accepted? Then, don't you see, I could
have been getting ready!

TOM: You don't have to make any fuss.

AMANDA: Oh, Tom, Tom, Tom, of course I have to make a fuss! I want
things nice, not sloppy! Not thrown together. I'll certainly have to do
some fast thinking, won't I?

TOM: I don't see why you have to think at all.

AMANDA: You just don't know. We can't have a gentleman caller in a pig-
sty! All my wedding silver has to be polished, the monogrammed table
linen ought to be laundered! The windows have to be washed and fresh
curtains put up. And how about clothes? We have to *wear* something,
don't we?

TOM: Mother, this boy is no one to make a fuss over!   60

AMANDA: Do you realize he's the first young man we've introduced to your
sister? It's terrible, dreadful, disgraceful that poor little sister has never
received a single gentleman caller! Tom, come inside! (*She opens the
screen door.*)

TOM: What for?

AMANDA: I want to ask you some things.

TOM: If you're going to make such a fuss, I'll call it off, I'll tell him not to
come.

AMANDA: You certainly won't do anything of the kind. Nothing offends   65
people worse than broken engagements. It simply means I'll have to
work like a Turk! We won't be brilliant, but we'll pass inspection.
Come on inside. (TOM *follows, groaning.*) Sit down.

TOM: Any particular place you would like me to sit?

AMANDA: Thank heavens I've got that new sofa! I'm also making payments on a floor lamp I'll have sent out! And put the chintz covers on, they'll brighten things up! Of course I'd hoped to have these walls re-papered...What is the young man's name?

TOM: His name is O'Connor.

AMANDA: That, of course, means fish—tomorrow is Friday! I'll have that salmon loaf—with Durkee's dressing! What does he do? He works at the warehouse?

TOM: Of course! How else would I—   70

AMANDA: Tom, he—doesn't drink?

TOM: Why do you ask me that?

AMANDA: Your father *did*!

TOM: Don't get started on that!

AMANDA: He *does* drink, then?   75

TOM: Not that I know of!

AMANDA: Make sure, be certain! The last thing I want for my daughter's a boy who drinks!

TOM: Aren't you being a little premature? Mr. O'Connor has not yet appeared on the scene!

AMANDA: But will tomorrow. To meet your sister, and what do I know about his character? Nothing! Old maids are better off than wives of drunkards!

TOM: Oh, my God!   80

AMANDA: Be still!

TOM (*leaning forward to whisper*): Lots of fellows meet girls whom they don't marry!

AMANDA: Oh, talk sensibly, Tom—and don't be sarcastic! (*She has gotten a hairbrush.*)

TOM: What are you doing?

AMANDA: I'm brushing that cow-lick down! What is this young man's posi-   85
tion at the warehouse?

TOM (*submitting grimly to the brush and the interrogation*): This young man's position is that of a shipping clerk, Mother.

AMANDA: Sounds to me like a fairly responsible job, the sort of a job *you* would be in if you just had more *get-up*. What is his salary? Have you got any idea?

TOM: I would judge it to be approximately eighty-five dollars a month.

AMANDA: Well—not princely, but—

TOM: Twenty more than I make.   90

AMANDA: Yes, how well I know! But for a family man, eighty-five dollars a month is not much more than you can just get by on....

TOM: Yes, but Mr. O'Connor is not a family man.

AMANDA: He might be, mightn't he? Some time in the future?

TOM: I see. Plans and provisions.

AMANDA: You are the only young man that I know of who ignores the fact   95
that the future becomes the present, the present the past, and the past
turns into everlasting regret if you don't plan for it!

TOM: I will think that over and see what I can make of it.

AMANDA: Don't be supercilious with your mother! Tell me some more
about this—what do you call him?

TOM: James D. O'Connor. The D. is for Delaney.

AMANDA: Irish on *both* sides! *Gracious!* And doesn't drink?

TOM: Shall I call him up and ask him right this minute?   100

AMANDA: The only way to find out about those things is to make discreet
inquiries at the proper moment. When I was a girl in Blue Mountain
and it was suspected that a young man drank, the girl whose attentions
he had been receiving, if any girl *was*, would sometimes speak to the
minister of his church, or rather her father would if her father was living, and sort of feel him out on the young man's character. That is the
way such things are discreetly handled to keep a young woman from
making a tragic mistake!

TOM: Then how did you happen to make a tragic mistake?

AMANDA: That innocent look of your father's had everyone fooled! He
smiled—the world was *enchanted!* No girl can do worse than put herself
at the mercy of a handsome appearance! I hope that Mr. O'Connor is
not too good-looking.

TOM: No, he's not too good-looking. He's covered with freckles and hasn't
too much of a nose.

AMANDA: He's not right-down homely, though?   105

TOM: Not right-down homely. Just medium homely, I'd say.

AMANDA: Character's what to look for in a man.

TOM: That's what I've always said, Mother.

AMANDA: You've never said anything of the kind and I suspect you would
never give it a thought.

TOM: Don't be suspicious of me.   110

AMANDA: At least I hope he's the type that's up and coming.

TOM: I think he really goes in for self-improvement.

AMANDA: What reason have you to think so?

TOM: He goes to night school.

AMANDA *(beaming)*: Splendid! What does he do, I mean study?   115

TOM: Radio engineering and public speaking!

AMANDA: Then he has visions of being advanced in the world! Any young
man who studies public speaking is aiming to have an executive job
some day! And radio engineering? A thing for the future! Both of these
facts are very illuminating. Those are the sort of things that a mother

should know concerning any young man who comes to call on her daughter. Seriously or—not.

TOM: One little warning. He doesn't know about Laura. I didn't let on that we had dark ulterior motives. I just said, why don't you come have dinner with us? He said okay and that was the whole conversation.

AMANDA: I bet it was! You're eloquent as an oyster. However, he'll know about Laura when he gets here. When he sees how lovely and sweet and pretty she is, he'll thank his lucky stars he was asked to dinner.

TOM: Mother, you mustn't expect too much of Laura.   120

AMANDA: What do you mean?

TOM: Laura seems all those things to you and me because she's ours and we love her. We don't even notice she's crippled any more.

AMANDA: Don't say crippled! You know that I never allow that word to be used!

TOM: But face facts, Mother. She is and—that's not all—

AMANDA: What do you mean "not all"?   125

TOM: Laura is very different from other girls.

AMANDA: I think the difference is all to her advantage.

TOM: Not quite all—in the eyes of others—strangers—she's terribly shy and lives in a world of her own and those things make her seem a little peculiar to people outside the house.

AMANDA: Don't say peculiar.

TOM: Face the facts. She is.   130

(*The dance-hall music changes to a tango that has a minor and somewhat ominous tone.*)

AMANDA: In what way is she peculiar—may I ask?

TOM (*gently*): She lives in a world of her own—a world of—little glass ornaments, Mother…. (*Gets up.* AMANDA *remains holding brush, looking at him, troubled.*) She plays old phonograph records and—that's about all— (*He glances at himself in the mirror and crosses to door.*)

AMANDA (*sharply*): Where are you going?

TOM: I'm going to the movies. (*Out screen door.*)

AMANDA: Not to the movies, every night to the movies! (*Follows quickly to*   135
screen door.) I don't believe you always go to the movies! (*He is gone.* AMANDA *looks worriedly after him for a moment. Then vitality and optimism return and she turns from the door. Crossing to portieres.*) Laura! Laura! (LAURA *answers from kitchenette.*)

LAURA: Yes, Mother.

AMANDA: Let those dishes go and come in front! (LAURA *appears with dish towel. Gaily.*) Laura, come here and make a wish on the moon!

LAURA (*entering*): Moon—moon?

AMANDA: A little silver slipper of a moon. Look over your left shoulder, Laura, and make a wish! (LAURA *looks faintly puzzled as if called out of*

sleep. AMANDA *seizes her shoulders and turns her at angle by the door.)*
Now! Now, darling, *wish!*

LAURA: What shall I wish for, Mother?   140

AMANDA *(her voice trembling and her eyes suddenly filling with tears):* Happiness! Good Fortune!

(The violin rises and the stage dims out.)

Scene 6

(Image: High-school hero.)

TOM: And so the following evening I brought Jim home to dinner. I had known Jim slightly in high school. In high school Jim was a hero. He had tremendous Irish good nature and vitality with the scrubbed and polished look of white chinaware. He seemed to move in a continual spotlight. He was a star in basketball, captain of the debating club, president of the senior class and the glee club and he sang the male lead in the annual light operas. He was always running or bounding, never just walking. He seemed always at the point of defeating the law of gravity. He was shooting with such velocity through his adolescence that you would logically expect him to arrive at nothing short of the White House by the time he was thirty. But Jim apparently ran into more interference after his graduation from Soldan. His speed had definitely slowed. Six years after he left high school he was holding a job that wasn't much better than mine. *(Image: Clerk.)*

He was the only one at the warehouse with whom I was on friendly terms. I was valuable to him as someone who could remember his former glory, who had seen him win basketball games and the silver cup in debating. He knew of my secret practice of retiring to a cabinet of the washroom to work on poems when business was slack in the warehouse. He called me Shakespeare. And while the other boys in the warehouse regarded me with suspicious hostility, Jim took a humorous attitude toward me. Gradually his attitude affected the others, their hostility wore off, and they also began to smile at me as people smile at an oddly fashioned dog who trots across their paths at some distance.

I knew that Jim and Laura had known each other at Soldan, and I had heard Laura speak admiringly of his voice. I didn't know if Jim remembered her or not. In high school Laura had been as unobtrusive as Jim had been astonishing. If he did remember Laura, it was not as my sister, for when I asked him to dinner, he grinned and said, "You know, Shakespeare, I never thought of you as having folks!"

He was about to discover that I did …

(Light upstage.)

(Legend on screen: "The Accent of a Coming Foot.")

(Friday evening. It is about five o'clock of a late spring evening which comes "scattering poems in the sky."

A delicate lemony light is in the Wingfield apartment.

AMANDA *has worked like a Turk in preparation for the gentleman caller. The results are astonishing. The new floor lamp with its rose-silk shade is in place, a colored paper lantern conceals the broken light fixture in the ceiling, new billowing white curtains are at the windows, chintz covers are on chairs and sofa, a pair of new sofa pillows make their initial appearance.*

Open boxes and tissue paper are scattered on the floor.

LAURA *stands in the middle with lifted arms while* AMANDA *crouches before her, adjusting the hem of the new dress, devout and ritualistic. The dress is colored and designed by memory. The arrangement of* LAURA's *hair is changed; it is softer and more becoming. A fragile, unearthly prettiness has come out in* LAURA: *she is like a piece of translucent glass touched by light, given a momentary radiance, not actual, not lasting.)*

AMANDA *(impatiently)*: Why are you trembling?

LAURA: Mother, you've made me so nervous!

AMANDA: How have I made you nervous?

LAURA: By all this fuss! You make it seem so important!   5

AMANDA: I don't understand you, Laura. You couldn't be satisfied with just sitting home, and yet whenever I try to arrange something for you, you seem to resist it. *(She gets up.)* Now take a look at yourself. No, wait! Wait just a moment—I have an idea!

LAURA: What is it now?

*(*AMANDA *produces two powder puffs which she wraps in handkerchiefs and stuffs in* LAURA's *bosom.)*

LAURA: Mother, what are you doing?

AMANDA: They call them "Gay Deceivers"!

LAURA: I won't wear them!   10

AMANDA: You will!

LAURA: Why should I?

AMANDA: Because, to be painfully honest, your chest is flat.

LAURA: You make it seem like we were setting a trap.

AMANDA: All pretty girls are a trap, a pretty trap, and men expect them to   15
be. *(Legend: "A Pretty Trap.")* Now look at yourself, young lady. This is the prettiest you will ever be! I've got to fix myself now! You're going to be surprised by your mother's appearance! *(She crosses through portieres, humming gaily.)*

*(*LAURA *moves slowly to the long mirror and stares solemnly at herself.*

A wind blows the white curtains inward in a slow, graceful motion and with a faint, sorrowful sighing.)

AMANDA (*off stage*):   It isn't dark enough yet. (*She turns slowly before the mirror with a troubled look.*)

(*Legend on screen: "This Is My Sister: Celebrate Her with Strings!" Music.*)

AMANDA (*laughing, off*):   I'm going to show you something. I'm going to make a spectacular appearance!

LAURA: What is it, Mother?

AMANDA: Possess your soul in patience—you will see! Something I've resurrected from that old trunk! Styles haven't changed so terribly much after all.... (*She parts the portieres.*)   Now just look at your mother! (*She wears a girlish frock of yellowed voile with a blue silk sash. She carries a bunch of jonquils—the legend of her youth is nearly revived. Feverishly.*) This is the dress in which I led the cotillion. Won the cakewalk twice at Sunset Hill, wore one spring to the Governor's ball in Jackson! See how I sashayed around the ballroom, Laura? (*She raises her skirt and does a mincing step around the room.*)   I wore it on Sundays for my gentlemen callers! I had it on the day I met your father—I had malaria fever all that spring. The change of climate from East Tennessee to the Delta—weakened resistance—I had a little temperature all the time—not enough to be serious—just enough to make me restless and giddy! Invitations poured in—parties all over the Delta!—"Stay in bed," said Mother, "you have fever!"—but I just wouldn't.—I took quinine but kept on going, going!—Evenings, dances!—Afternoons, long, long rides! Picnics—lovely!—So lovely, that country in May.—All lacy with dogwood, literally flooded with jonquils!—That was the spring I had the craze for jonquils. Jonquils became an absolute obsession. Mother said, "Honey, there's no more room for jonquils." And still I kept bringing in more jonquils. Whenever, wherever I saw them, I'd say, "Stop! Stop! I see jonquils!" I made the young men help me gather the jonquils! It was a joke, Amanda and her jonquils! Finally there were no more vases to hold them, every available space was filled with jonquils. No vases to hold them? All right, I'll hold them myself! And then I— (*She stops in front of the picture.*) (*Music.*) met your father! Malaria fever and jonquils and then—this—boy.... (*She switches on the rose-colored lamp.*)   I hope they get here before it starts to rain. (*She crosses upstage and places the jonquils in bowl on table.*)   I gave your brother a little extra change so he and Mr. O'Connor could take the service car home.

LAURA (*with altered look*):   What did you say his name was?   20

AMANDA: O'Connor.

LAURA: What is his first name?

AMANDA: I don't remember. Oh, yes, I do. It was—Jim!

(*LAURA sways slightly and catches hold of a chair.*)

(*Legend on screen: "Not Jim!"*)

LAURA (*faintly*): Not—Jim!

AMANDA: Yes, that was it, it was Jim! I've never known a Jim that wasn't nice!   25

(*Music: Ominous.*)

LAURA: Are you sure his name is Jim O'Connor?

AMANDA: Yes. Why?

LAURA: Is he the one that Tom used to know in high school?

AMANDA: He didn't say so. I think he just got to know him at the warehouse.

LAURA: There was a Jim O'Connor we both knew in high school— (*Then,*   30
with effort.) If that is the one that Tom is bringing to dinner—you'll
have to excuse me, I won't come to the table.

AMANDA: What sort of nonsense is this?

LAURA: You asked me once if I'd ever liked a boy. Don't you remember I
showed you this boy's picture?

AMANDA: You mean the boy you showed me in the year-book?

LAURA: Yes, that boy.

AMANDA: Laura, Laura, were you in love with that boy?   35

LAURA: I don't know, Mother. All I know is I couldn't sit at the table if it
was him!

AMANDA: It won't be him! It isn't the least bit likely. But whether it is or
not, you will come to the table. You will not be excused.

LAURA: I'll have to be, Mother.

AMANDA: I don't intend to humor your silliness, Laura. I've had too much
from you and your brother, both! So just sit down and compose yourself
till they come. Tom has forgotten his key so you'll have to let them in,
when they arrive.

LAURA (*panicky*): Oh, Mother—*you* answer the door!   40

AMANDA (*lightly*): I'll be in the kitchen—busy!

LAURA: Oh, Mother, please answer the door, don't make me do it!

AMANDA (*crossing into kitchenette*): I've got to fix the dressing for the
salmon. Fuss, fuss—silliness!—over a gentleman caller!

(*Door swings shut. LAURA is left alone.*)

(*Legend: "Terror!"*)

(*She utters a low moan and turns off the lamp—sits stiffly on the edge of the sofa,
knotting her fingers together.*)

(*Legend on screen: "The Opening of a Door!"*)

(TOM *and* JIM *appear on the fire-escape steps and climb to landing. Hearing their
approach,* LAURA *rises with a panicky gesture. She retreats to the portieres.*
The doorbell. LAURA *catches her breath and touches her throat. Low drums.*)

AMANDA (*calling*): Laura, sweetheart! The door!

(LAURA *stares at it without moving.*)

JIM: I think we just beat the rain.   45

TOM: Uh-huh. (*He rings again, nervously.* JIM *whistles and fishes for a cigarette.*)

AMANDA (*very, very gaily*): Laura, that is your brother and Mr. O'Connor! Will you let them in, darling?

(LAURA *crosses toward kitchenette door.*)

LAURA (*breathlessly*): Mother—you go to the door!

(AMANDA *steps out of kitchenette and stares furiously at* LAURA. *She points imperiously at the door.*)

LAURA: Please, please!

AMANDA (*in a fierce whisper*): What is the matter with you, you silly thing?   50

LAURA (*desperately*): Please, you answer it, *please*!

AMANDA: I told you I wasn't going to humor you, Laura. Why have you chosen this moment to lose your mind?

LAURA: Please, please, please, you go!

AMANDA: You'll have to go to the door because I can't!

LAURA (*despairingly*): I can't either!   55

AMANDA: Why?

LAURA: I'm *sick*!

AMANDA: I'm sick, too—of your nonsense! Why can't you and your brother be normal people? Fantastic whims and behavior! (TOM *gives a long ring.*) Preposterous goings on! Can you give me one reason— (*Calls out lyrically.*) COMING! JUST ONE SECOND!—why should you be afraid to open a door? Now you answer it, Laura!

LAURA: Oh, oh, oh... (*She returns through the portieres. Darts to the Victrola and winds it frantically and turns it on.*)

AMANDA: Laura Wingfield, you march right to that door!   60

LAURA: Yes—yes, Mother!

(*A faraway, scratchy rendition of "Dardanella" softens the air and gives her strength to move through it. She slips to the door and draws it cautiously open.*

TOM *enters with the caller,* JIM O'CONNOR.)

TOM: Laura, this is Jim. Jim, this is my sister, Laura.

JIM (*stepping inside*): I didn't know that Shakespeare had a sister!

LAURA (*retreating stiff and trembling from the door*): How—how do you do?

JIM (*heartily extending his hand*): Okay!   65

(LAURA *touches it hesitantly with hers.*)

JIM: Your hand's *cold*, Laura!

LAURA: Yes, well—I've been playing the Victrola ...

JIM: Must have been playing classical music on it! You ought to play a little hot swing music to warm you up!

LAURA: Excuse me—I haven't finished playing the Victrola ...

(*She turns awkwardly and hurries into the front room. She pauses a second by the Victrola. Then catches her breath and darts through the portieres like a frightened deer.*)

JIM (*grinning*): What was the matter?   70

TOM: Oh—with Laura? Laura is—terribly shy.

JIM: Shy, huh? It's unusual to meet a shy girl nowadays. I don't believe you ever mentioned you had a sister.

TOM: Well, now you know. I have one. Here is the *Post Dispatch*. You want a piece of it?

JIM: Uh-huh.

TOM: What piece? The comics?   75

JIM: Sports! (*Glances at it.*) Ole Dizzy Dean is on his bad behavior.

TOM (*disinterest*): Yeah? (*Lights cigarette and crosses back to fire-escape door.*)

JIM: Where are *you* going?

TOM: I'm going out on the terrace.

JIM (*goes after him*): You know, Shakespeare—I'm going to sell you a bill of   80
goods!

TOM: What goods?

JIM: A course I'm taking.

TOM: Huh?

JIM: In public speaking! You and me, we're not the warehouse type.

TOM: Thanks—that's good news. But what has public speaking got to do   85
with it?

JIM: It fits you for—executive positions!

TOM: Awww.

JIM: I tell you it's done a helluva lot for me.

(*Image: Executive at desk.*)

TOM: In what respect?

JIM: In every! Ask yourself what is the difference between you an' me and   90
men in the office down front? Brains?—No!—Ability?—No! Then
what? Just one little thing—

TOM: What is that one little thing?

JIM: Primarily it amounts to—social poise! Being able to square up to people and hold your own on any social level!

AMANDA (*off stage*): Tom?

TOM: Yes, Mother?

AMANDA: Is that you and Mr. O'Connor?   95

TOM: Yes, Mother.

AMANDA: Well, you just make yourselves comfortable in there.

TOM: Yes, Mother.

AMANDA: Ask Mr. O'Connor if he would like to wash his hands.

JIM: Aw—no—no—thank you—I took care of that at the warehouse. Tom—   10

TOM: Yes?

JIM: Mr. Mendoza was speaking to me about you.

TOM: Favorably?

JIM: What do you think?

TOM: Well—   10

JIM: You're going to be out of a job if you don't wake up.

TOM: I am waking up—

JIM: You show no signs.

TOM: The signs are interior.

(*Image on screen: The sailing vessel with Jolly Roger again.*)

TOM: I'm planning to change. (*He leans over the rail speaking with quiet exhila-*   110
*ration. The incandescent marquees and signs of the first-run movie houses
light his face from across the alley. He looks like a voyager.*) I'm right at the
point of committing myself to a future that doesn't include the warehouse and Mr. Mendoza or even a night-school course in public
speaking.

JIM: What are you gassing about?

TOM: I'm tired of the movies.

JIM: Movies!

TOM: Yes, movies! Look at them— (*A wave toward the marvels of Grand Avenue.*) All of those glamorous people—having adventures—hogging it
all, gobbling the whole thing up! You know what happens? People go
to the *movies* instead of *moving*! Hollywood characters are supposed to
have all the adventures for everybody in America, while everybody in
America sits in a dark room and watches them have them! Yes, until
there's a war. That's when adventure becomes available to the masses!
Everyone's dish, not only Gable's! Then the people in the dark room
come out of the dark room to have some adventures themselves—
Goody, goody—It's our turn now, to go to the South Sea Island—to
make a safari—to be exotic, far-off—But I'm not patient. I don't want
to wait till then. I'm tired of the *movies* and I am *about* to *move*!

JIM (*incredulously*): Move?   115

TOM: Yes.

JIM: When?

TOM: Soon!

JIM: Where? Where?

(*Theme three: Music seems to answer the question, while* TOM *thinks it over. He
searches among his pockets.*)

TOM: I'm starting to boil inside. I know I seem dreamy, but inside—well,   120
I'm boiling! Whenever I pick up a shoe, I shudder a little thinking how
short life is and what I am doing!—Whatever that means. I know it
doesn't mean shoes—except as something to wear on a traveler's feet!
(*Finds paper.*) Look—

JIM: What?

TOM: I'm a member.

JIM (*reading*): The Union of Merchant Seamen.

TOM: I paid my dues this month, instead of the light bill.

JIM: You will regret it when they turn the lights off.   125

TOM: I won't be here.

JIM: How about your mother?

TOM: I'm like my father. The bastard son of a bastard! See how he grins? And he's been absent going on sixteen years!

JIM: You're just talking, you drip. How does your mother feel about it?

TOM: Shhh—Here comes Mother! Mother is not acquainted with my plans!

130

AMANDA (*enters portieres*): Where are you all?

TOM: On the terrace, Mother.

(*They start inside. She advances to them.* TOM *is distinctly shocked at her appearance. Even* JIM *blinks a little. He is making his first contact with girlish Southern vivacity and in spite of the night-school course in public speaking is somewhat thrown off the beam by the unexpected outlay of social charm.*

Certain responses are attempted by JIM *but are swept aside by* AMANDA's *gay laughter and chatter.* TOM *is embarrassed but after the first shock* JIM *reacts very warmly. Grins and chuckles, is altogether won over.*)

(*Image:* AMANDA *as a girl*)

AMANDA (*coyly smiling, shaking her girlish ringlets*): Well, well, well, so this is Mr. O'Connor. Introductions entirely unnecessary. I've heard so much about you from my boy. I finally said to him, Tom—good gracious!— why don't you bring this paragon to supper? I'd like to meet this nice young man at the warehouse!—Instead of just hearing him sing your praises so much! I don't know why my son is so stand-offish—that's not Southern behavior! Let's sit down and—I think we could stand a little more air in here! Tom, leave the door open. I felt a nice fresh breeze a moment ago. Where has it gone? Mmm, so warm already! And not quite summer, even. We're going to burn up when summer really gets started. However, we're having—we're having a very light supper. I think light things are better fo' this time of year. The same as light clothes are. Light clothes an' light food are what warm weather calls fo'. You know our blood gets so thick during th' winter—it takes a while fo' us to *adjust* ou'selves!—when the season changes.... It's come so quick this year. I wasn't prepared. All of a sudden—heavens! Already summer!—I ran to the trunk an' pulled out this light dress— Terribly old! Historical almost! But feels so good—so good an' co-ol, y'know....

TOM: Mother—

AMANDA: Yes, honey?

13!

TOM: How about—supper?

AMANDA: Honey, you go ask Sister if supper is ready! You know that Sister is in full charge of supper! Tell her you hungry boys are waiting for it. (*To* JIM.) Have you met Laura?

JIM: She—

AMANDA: Let you in? Oh, good, you've met already! It's rare for a girl as sweet an' pretty as Laura to be domestic! But Laura is, thank heavens, not only pretty but also very domestic. I'm not at all. I never was a bit. I never could make a thing but angel-food cake. Well, in the South we had so many servants. Gone, gone, gone. All vestiges of gracious living! Gone completely! I wasn't prepared for what the future brought me. All of my gentlemen callers were sons of planters and so of course I assumed that I would be married to one and raise my family on a large piece of land with plenty of servants. But man proposes—and woman accepts the proposal!—To vary that old, old saying a little bit—I married no planter! I married a man who worked for the telephone company!—that gallantly smiling gentleman over there! (*Points to the picture.*) A telephone man who—fell in love with long distance!—Now he travels and I don't even know where!—But what am I going on for about my—tribulations! Tell me yours—I hope you don't have any! Tom?

TOM (*returning*): Yes, Mother?   140

AMANDA: Is supper nearly ready?

TOM: It looks to me like supper is on the table.

AMANDA: Let me look— (*She rises prettily and looks through portieres.*) Oh, lovely—But where is Sister?

TOM: Laura is not feeling well and she says that she thinks she'd better not come to the table.

AMANDA: What?—Nonsense!—Laura? Oh, Laura!   145

LAURA (*off stage, faintly*): Yes, Mother.

AMANDA: You really must come to the table. We won't be seated until you come to the table! Come in, Mr. O'Connor. You sit over there and I'll—Laura? Laura Wingfield! You're keeping us waiting, honey! We can't say grace until you come to the table!

(*The back door is pushed weakly open and LAURA comes in. She is obviously quite faint, her lips trembling, her eyes wide and staring. She moves unsteadily toward the table.*)

(*Legend: "Terror!"*)

(*Outside a summer storm is coming abruptly. The white curtains billow inward at the windows and there is a sorrowful murmur and deep blue dusk.*

LAURA *suddenly stumbles—She catches at a chair with a faint moan.*)

TOM: Laura!

AMANDA: Laura! (*There is a clap of thunder.*) (*Legend: "Ah!"*) (*Despairingly.*) Why, Laura, you *are* sick, darling! Tom, help your sister into the living room, dear! Sit in the living room, Laura—rest on the sofa. Well! (*To the gentleman caller.*) Standing over the hot stove made her ill!—I told her that it was just too warm this evening, but— (TOM *comes back in.* LAURA *is on the sofa.*) Is Laura all right now?

TOM: Yes.   150

AMANDA: What *is* that? Rain? A nice cool rain has come up! (*She gives the gentleman caller a frightened look.*) I think we may—have grace—now ... (TOM *looks at her stupidly.*) Tom, honey—you say grace!

TOM: Oh ... "For these and all thy mercies—" (*They bow their heads,* AMANDA *stealing a nervous glance at* JIM. *In the living room* LAURA, *stretched on the sofa, clenches her hand to her lips, to hold back a shuddering sob.*) God's Holy Name be praised—

(*The scene dims out.*)

Scene 7

A Souvenir

(*Half an hour later. Dinner is just being finished in the upstage area, which is concealed by the drawn portieres.*

As the curtain rises LAURA *is still huddled upon the sofa, her feet drawn under her, her head resting on a pale blue pillow, her eyes wide and mysteriously watchful. The new floor lamp with its shade of rose-colored silk gives a soft, becoming light to her face, bringing out the fragile, unearthly prettiness which usually escapes attention. There is a steady murmur of rain, but it is slackening and stops soon after the scene begins; the air outside becomes pale and luminous as the moon breaks out.*

A moment after the curtain rises, the lights in both rooms flicker and go out.)

JIM: Hey, there, Mr. Light Bulb!

(AMANDA *laughs nervously.*)

(*Legend: "Suspension of a Public Service."*)

AMANDA: Where was Moses when the lights went out? Ha-ha. Do you know the answer to that one, Mr. O'Connor?

JIM: No, Ma'am, what's the answer?

AMANDA: In the dark! (JIM *laughs appreciatively.*) Everybody sit still. I'll light the candles. Isn't it lucky we have them on the table? Where's a match? Which of you gentlemen can provide a match?

JIM: Here.   5

AMANDA: Thank you, sir.

JIM: Not at all, Ma'am!

AMANDA: I guess the fuse has burnt out. Mr. O'Connor, can you tell a burnt-out fuse? I know I can't and Tom is a total loss when it comes to mechanics. (*Sound: Getting up: Voices recede a little to kitchenette.*) Oh, be careful you don't bump into something. We don't want our gentleman caller to break his neck. Now wouldn't that be a fine howdy-do?

JIM: Ha-ha! Where is the fuse-box?

AMANDA: Right here next to the stove. Can you see anything?   10

JIM: Just a minute.

AMANDA: Isn't electricity a mysterious thing? Wasn't it Benjamin Franklin who tied a key to a kite? We live in such a mysterious universe, don't we? Some people say that science clears up all the mysteries for us. In my opinion it only creates more! Have you found it yet?

JIM: No, Ma'am. All these fuses look okay to me.

AMANDA: Tom!

TOM: Yes, Mother?   15

AMANDA: That light bill I gave you several days ago. The one I told you we got the notices about?

TOM: Oh.—Yeah.

(Legend: "Ha!")

AMANDA: You didn't neglect to pay it by any chance?

TOM: Why, I—

AMANDA: Didn't! I might have known it!   20

JIM: Shakespeare probably wrote a poem on that light bill, Mrs. Wingfield.

AMANDA: I might have known better than to trust him with it! There's such a high price for negligence in this world!

JIM: Maybe the poem will win a ten-dollar prize.

AMANDA: We'll just have to spend the remainder of the evening in the nineteenth century, before Mr. Edison made the Mazda lamp!

JIM: Candlelight is my favorite kind of light.   25

AMANDA: That shows you're romantic! But that's no excuse for Tom. Well, we got through dinner. Very considerate of them to let us get through dinner before they plunged us into everlasting darkness, wasn't it, Mr. O'Connor?

JIM: Ha-ha!

AMANDA: Tom, as a penalty for your carelessness you can help me with the dishes.

JIM: Let me give you a hand.

AMANDA: Indeed you will not!   30

JIM: I ought to be good for something.

AMANDA: Good for something? *(Her tone rhapsodic.)* You? Why, Mr. O'Connor, nobody, *nobody's* given me this much entertainment in years—as you have!

JIM: Aw, now, Mrs. Wingfield!

AMANDA: I'm not exaggerating, not one bit! But Sister is all by her lonesome. You go keep her company in the parlor! I'll give you this lovely old candelabrum that used to be on the altar at the church of the Heavenly Rest. It was melted a little out of shape when the church burnt down. Lightning struck it one spring. Gypsy Jones was holding a revival at the time and he intimated that the church was destroyed because the Episcopalians gave card parties.

JIM: Ha-ha.   35

AMANDA: And how about coaxing Sister to drink a little wine? I think it would be good for her! Can you carry both at once?

JIM: Sure. I'm Superman!

AMANDA: Now, Thomas, get into this apron!

(*The door of kitchenette swings closed on* AMANDA'*s gay laughter; the flickering light approaches the portieres.*

LAURA *sits up nervously as he enters. Her speech at first is low and breathless from the almost intolerable strain of being alone with a stranger.*)

(*Legend: "I Don't Suppose You Remember Me at All!"*)

(*In her first speeches in this scene, before* JIM'*s warmth overcomes her paralyzing shyness,* LAURA'*s voice is thin and breathless as though she has run up a steep flight of stairs.*

JIM'*s attitude is gently humorous. In playing this scene it should be stressed that while the incident is apparently unimportant, it is to* LAURA *the climax of her secret life.*)

JIM: Hello, there, Laura.

LAURA (*faintly*): Hello. (*She clears her throat.*) 40

JIM: How are you feeling now? Better?

LAURA: Yes. Yes, thank you.

JIM: This is for you. A little dandelion wine. (*He extends it toward her with extravagant gallantry.*)

LAURA: Thank you.

JIM: Drink it—but don't get drunk! (*He laughs heartily.* LAURA *takes the glass* 45 *uncertainly; laughs shyly.*) Where shall I set the candles?

LAURA: Oh—oh, anywhere ...

JIM: How about here on the floor? Any objections?

LAURA: No.

JIM: I'll spread a newspaper under to catch the drippings. I like to sit on the floor. Mind if I do?

LAURA: Oh, no. 50

JIM: Give me a pillow?

LAURA: What?

JIM: A pillow!

LAURA: Oh ... (*Hands him one quickly.*)

JIM: How about you? Don't you like to sit on the floor? 55

LAURA: Oh—yes.

JIM: Why don't you, then?

LAURA: I—will.

JIM: Take a pillow! (LAURA *does. Sits on the other side of the candelabrum.* JIM *crosses his legs and smiles engagingly at her.*) I can't hardly see you sitting way over there.

LAURA: I can—see you. 60

JIM: I know, but that's not fair, I'm in the limelight. (LAURA *moves her pillow closer.*) Good! Now I can see you! Comfortable?

LAURA: Yes.

JIM: So am I. Comfortable as a cow. Will you have some gum?

LAURA: No, thank you.

JIM: I think that I will indulge, with your permission. (*Musingly unwraps it and holds it up.*) Think of the fortune made by the guy that invented the first piece of chewing gum. Amazing, huh? The Wrigley Building is one of the sights of Chicago.—I saw it summer before last when I went up to the Century of Progress. Did you take in the Century of Progress? 65

LAURA: No, I didn't.

JIM: Well, it was quite a wonderful exposition. What impressed me most was the Hall of Science. Gives you an idea of what the future will be in America, even more wonderful than the present time is! (*Pause. Smiling at her.*) Your brother tells me you're shy. Is that right, Laura?

LAURA: I—don't know.

JIM: I judge you to be an old-fashioned type of girl. Well, I think that's a pretty good type to be. Hope you don't think I'm being too personal— do you?

LAURA (*hastily, out of embarrassment*): I believe I *will* take a piece of gum, if you—don't mind. (*Clearing her throat.*) Mr. O'Connor, have you—kept up with your singing? 70

JIM: Singing? Me?

LAURA: Yes. I remember what a beautiful voice you had.

JIM: When did you hear me sing?

(*Voice offstage in the pause.*)

VOICE (*offstage*):

> O blow, ye winds, high-ho,
> A-roving I will go!
> I'm off to my love
> With a boxing glove—
> Ten thousand miles away!

JIM: You say you've heard me sing? 75

LAURA: Oh, yes! Yes, very often … I—don't suppose you remember me—at all?

JIM (*smiling doubtfully*): You know I have an idea I've seen you before. I had that idea soon as you opened the door. It seemed almost like I was about to remember your name. But the name that I started to call you—wasn't a name! And so I stopped myself before I said it.

LAURA: Wasn't it—Blue Roses?

JIM (*springs up, grinning*): Blue Roses! My gosh, yes—Blue Roses! That's what I had on my tongue when you opened the door! Isn't it funny

what tricks your memory plays? I didn't connect you with the high
school somehow or other. But that's where it was; it was high school. I
didn't even know you were Shakespeare's sister! Gosh, I'm sorry.

LAURA: I didn't expect you to. You—barely knew me!   80

JIM: But we did have a speaking acquaintance, huh?

LAURA: Yes, we—spoke to each other.

JIM: When did you recognize me?

LAURA: Oh, right away!

JIM: Soon as I came in the door?   85

LAURA: When I heard your name I thought it was probably you. I knew
that Tom used to know you a little in high school. So when you came
in the door—Well, then I was—sure.

JIM: Why didn't you *say* something, then?

LAURA *(breathlessly)*: I didn't know what to say, I was—too surprised!

JIM: For goodness' sakes! You know, this sure is funny!

LAURA: Yes! Yes, isn't it, though ...   90

JIM: Didn't we have a class in something together?

LAURA: Yes, we did.

JIM: What class was that?

LAURA: It was—singing—Chorus!

JIM: Aw!   95

LAURA: I sat across the aisle from you in the Aud.

JIM: Aw.

LAURA: Mondays, Wednesdays, and Fridays.

JIM: Now I remember—you always came in late.

LAURA: Yes, it was so hard for me, getting upstairs. I had that brace on my   100
leg—it clumped so loud!

JIM: I never heard any clumping.

LAURA *(wincing in the recollection)*: To me it sounded like—thunder!

JIM: Well, well, well. I never even noticed.

LAURA: And everybody was seated before I came in. I had to walk in front
of all those people. My seat was in the back row. I had to go clumping
all the way up the aisle with everyone watching!

JIM: You shouldn't have been self-conscious.   105

LAURA: I know, but I was. It was always such a relief when the singing started.

JIM: Aw, yes, I've placed you now! I used to call you Blue Roses. How was
it that I got started calling you that?

LAURA: I was out of school a little while with pleurosis. When I came back
you asked me what was the matter. I said I had pleurosis—you thought
I said Blue Roses. That's what you always called me after that!

JIM: I hope you didn't mind.

LAURA: Oh, no—I liked it. You see, I wasn't acquainted with many—   110
people....

JIM: As I remember you sort of stuck by yourself.

LAURA: I—I—never had much luck at—making friends.

JIM: I don't see why you wouldn't.

LAURA: Well, I—started out badly.

JIM: You mean being—   115

LAURA: Yes, it sort of—stood between me—

JIM: You shouldn't have let it!

LAURA: I know, but it did, and—

JIM: You were shy with people!

LAURA: I tried not to be but never could—   120

JIM: Overcome it?

LAURA: No, I—I never could!

JIM: I guess being shy is something you have to work out of kind of
gradually.

LAURA *(sorrowfully)*: Yes—I guess it—

JIM: Takes time!   125

LAURA: Yes—

JIM: People are not so dreadful when you know them. That's what you have
to remember! And everybody has problems, not just you, but practically
everybody has got some problems. You think of yourself as having the
only problems, as being the only one who is disappointed. But just look
around you and you will see lots of people as disappointed as you are.
For instance, I hoped when I was going to high school that I would be
further along at this time, six years later, than I am now—You remember that wonderful write-up I had in *The Torch*?

LAURA: Yes! *(She rises and crosses to table.)*

JIM: It said I was bound to succeed in anything I went into! (LAURA *returns
with the annual.)* Holy Jeez! *The Torch*! *(He accepts it reverently. They
smile across it with mutual wonder.* LAURA *crouches beside him and they
begin to turn through it. Laura's shyness is dissolving in his warmth.)*

LAURA: Here you are in *Pirates of Penzance*!   130

JIM *(wistfully)*: I sang the baritone lead in that operetta.

LAURA *(rapidly)*: So—*beautifully*!

JIM *(protesting)*: Aw—

LAURA: Yes, yes—beautifully—beautifully!

JIM: You heard me?   135

LAURA: All three times!

JIM: No!

LAURA: Yes!

JIM: All three performances?

LAURA *(looking down)*: Yes.   140

JIM: Why?

LAURA: I—wanted to ask you to—autograph my program.

JIM: Why didn't you ask me to?

LAURA: You were always surrounded by your own friends so much that I never had a chance to.

JIM: You should have just—   145

LAURA: Well, I—thought you might think I was—

JIM: Thought I might think you was—what?

LAURA: Oh—

JIM (*with reflective relish*): I was beleaguered by females in those days.

LAURA: You were terribly popular!   150

JIM: Yeah—

LAURA: You had such a—friendly way—

JIM: I was spoiled in high school.

LAURA: Everybody—liked you!

JIM: Including you?   155

LAURA: I—yes, I—I did, too— (*She gently closes the book in her lap.*)

JIM: Well, well, well!—Give me that program, Laura. (*She hands it to him. He signs it with a flourish.*) There you are—better late than never!

LAURA: Oh, I—what a—surprise!

JIM: My signature isn't worth very much right now. But some day— maybe—it will increase in value! Being disappointed is one thing and being discouraged is something else. I am disappointed but I'm not dis- couraged. I'm twenty-three years old. How old are you?

LAURA: I'll be twenty-four in June.   160

JIM: That's not old age.

LAURA: No, but—

JIM: You finished high school?

LAURA (*with difficulty*): I didn't go back.

JIM: You mean you dropped out?   165

LAURA: I made bad grades in my final examinations. (*She rises and replaces the book and the program. Her voice strained.*)
How is—Emily Meisenbach getting along?

JIM: Oh, that kraut-head!

LAURA: Why do you call her that?

JIM: That's what she was.

LAURA: You're not still—going with her?   170

JIM: I never see her.

LAURA: It said in the Personal Section that you were—engaged!

JIM: I know, but I wasn't impressed by that—propaganda!

LAURA: It wasn't—the truth?

JIM: Only in Emily's optimistic opinion!   175

LAURA: Oh—

(*Legend: "What Have You Done since High School?"*)

(JIM *lights a cigarette and leans indolently back on his elbows smiling at* LAURA *with a warmth and charm which light her inwardly with altar candles. She remains by the table and turns in her hands a piece of glass to cover her tumult.*)

JIM (*after several reflective puffs on a cigarette*):   What have you done since high school? (*She seems not to hear him.*) Huh? (LAURA *looks up.*) I said what have you done since high school, Laura?

LAURA: Nothing much.

JIM: You must have been doing something these six long years.

LAURA: Yes.   180

JIM: Well, then, such as what?

LAURA: I took a business course at business college—

JIM: How did that work out?

LAURA: Well, not very—well—I had to drop out, it gave me—indigestion— (JIM *laughs gently.*)

JIM: What are you doing now?   185

LAURA: I don't do anything—much. Oh, please don't think I sit around doing nothing! My glass collection takes up a good deal of my time. Glass is something you have to take good care of.

JIM: What did you say—about glass?

LAURA: Collection I said—I have one— (*She clears her throat and turns away again, acutely shy.*)

JIM (*abruptly*): You know what I judge to be the trouble with you? Inferiority complex! Know what that is? That's what they call it when someone low-rates himself! I understand it because I had it, too. Although my case was not so aggravated as yours seems to be. I had it until I took up public speaking, developed my voice, and learned that I had an aptitude for science. Before that time I never thought of myself as being outstanding in any way whatsoever! Now I've never made a regular study of it, but I have a friend who says I can analyze people better than doctors that make a profession of it. I don't claim that to be necessarily true, but I can sure guess a person's psychology, Laura! (*Takes out his gum.*) Excuse me, Laura. I always take it out when the flavor is gone. I'll use this scrap of paper to wrap it in. I know how it is to get it stuck on a shoe. Yep—that's what I judge to be your principal trouble. A lack of confidence in yourself as a person. You don't have the proper amount of faith in yourself. I'm basing that fact on a number of your remarks and also on certain observations I've made. For instance that clumping you thought was so awful in high school. You say that you even dreaded to walk into class. You see what you did? You dropped out of school, you gave up an education because of a clump, which as far as I know was practically nonexistent! A little physical defect is what you have. Hardly noticeable even! Magnified thousands of times by imagination! You know what my strong advice to you is? Think of yourself as *superior* in some way!

LAURA: In what way would I think? 190

JIM: Why, man alive, Laura! Just look about you a little. What do you see? A world full of common people! All of 'em born and all of 'em going to die! Which of them has one-tenth of your good points! Or mine! Or anyone else's, as for as that goes—Gosh! Everybody excels in some one thing. Some in many! (*Unconsciously glances at himself in the mirror.*) All you've got to do is discover in *what*! Take me, for instance. (*He adjusts his tie at the mirror.*) My interest happened to lie in electrodynamics. I'm taking a course in radio engineering at night school, Laura, on top of a fairly responsible job at the warehouse. I'm taking that course and studying public speaking.

LAURA: Ohhhh.

JIM: Because I believe in the future of television! (*Turning back to her.*) I wish to be ready to go up right along with it. Therefore I'm planning to get in on the ground floor. In fact, I've already made the right connections and all that remains is for the industry itself to get under way! Full steam— (*His eyes are starry.*) Knowledge—Zzzzzp! Money—Zzzzzzp!—Power! That's the cycle democracy is built on! (*His attitude is convincingly dynamic. LAURA stares at him, even her shyness eclipsed in her absolute wonder. He suddenly grins.*) I guess you think I think a lot of myself!

LAURA: No—o-o-o, I—

JIM: Now how about you? Isn't there something you take more interest in than anything else? 195

LAURA: Well, I do—as I said—have my—glass collection—

(*A peal of girlish laughter from the kitchen.*)

JIM: I'm not right sure I know what you're talking about. What kind of glass is it?

LAURA: Little articles of it, they're ornaments mostly! Most of them are little animals made out of glass, the tiniest little animals in the world. Mother calls them a glass menagerie! Here's an example of one, if you'd like to see it! This one is one of the oldest. It's nearly thirteen. (*He stretches out his hand.*) (*Music: "The Glass Menagerie."*) Oh, be careful—if you breathe, it breaks!

JIM: I'd better not take it. I'm pretty clumsy with things.

LAURA: Go on, I trust you with him! (*Places it in his palm.*) There now— 200 you're holding him gently! Hold him over the light, he loves the light! You see how the light shines through him?

JIM: It sure does shine!

LAURA: I shouldn't be partial, but he is my favorite one.

JIM: What kind of thing is this one supposed to be?

LAURA: Haven't you noticed the single horn on his forehead?

JIM: A unicorn, huh? 205

LAURA: Mmm-hmmm!

JIM: Unicorns, aren't they extinct in the modern world?

LAURA: I know!

JIM: Poor little fellow, he must feel sort of lonesome.

LAURA (*smiling*): Well, if he does he doesn't complain about it. He stays on   210
a shelf with some horses that don't have horns and all of them seem to
get along nicely together.

JIM: How do you know?

LAURA (*lightly*): I haven't heard any arguments among them!

JIM (*grinning*): No arguments, huh? Well, that's a pretty good sign! Where
shall I set him?

LAURA: Put him on the table. They all like a change of scenery once in a
while!

JIM (*stretching*): Well, well, well, well—Look how big my shadow is when I   215
stretch!

LAURA: Oh, oh, yes—it stretches across the ceiling!

JIM (*crossing to door*): I think it's stopped raining. (*Opens fire-escape door.*)
Where does the music come from?

LAURA: From the Paradise Dance Hall across the alley.

JIM: How about cutting the rug a little, Miss Wingfield?

LAURA: Oh, I—   220

JIM: Or is your program filled up? Let me have a look at it (*Grasps imaginary
card.*) Why, every dance is taken! I'll have to scratch some out. (*Waltz
music: "La Golondrina."*) Ahhh, a waltz! (*He executes some sweeping
turns by himself then holds his arms toward Laura.*)

LAURA (*breathlessly*): I—can't dance!

JIM: There you go, that inferiority stuff!

LAURA: I've never danced in my life!

JIM: Come on, try!   225

LAURA: Oh, but I'd step on you!

JIM: I'm not made out of glass.

LAURA: How—how—how do we start?

JIM: Just leave it to me. You hold your arms out a little.

LAURA: Like this?   230

JIM: A little bit higher. Right. Now don't tighten up, that's the main thing
about it—relax.

LAURA (*laughing breathlessly*): It's hard not to.

JIM: Okay.

LAURA: I'm afraid you can't budge me.

JIM: What do you bet I can't? (*He swings her into motion.*)   235

LAURA: Goodness, yes, you can!

JIM: Let yourself go, now, Laura, just let yourself go.

LAURA: I'm—

JIM: Come on!

LAURA: Trying. 240

JIM: Not so stiff—Easy does it!

LAURA: I know but I'm—

JIM: Loosen th' backbone! There now, that's a lot better.

LAURA: Am I?

JIM: Lots, lots better! (*He moves her about the room in a clumsy waltz.*) 245

LAURA: Oh, my!

JIM: Ha-ha!

LAURA: Goodness, yes you can!

JIM: Ha-ha-ha! (*They suddenly bump into the table. JIM stops.*) What did we hit on?

LAURA: Table. 250

JIM: Did something fall off it? I think—

LAURA: Yes.

JIM: I hope it wasn't the little glass horse with the horn!

LAURA: Yes.

JIM: Aw, aw, aw. Is it broken? 255

LAURA: Now it is just like all the other horses.

JIM: It's lost its—

LAURA: Horn! It doesn't matter. Maybe it's a blessing in disguise.

JIM: You'll never forgive me. I bet that that was your favorite piece of glass.

LAURA: I don't have favorites much. It's no tragedy, Freckles. Glass breaks 260
so easily. No matter how careful you are. The traffic jars the shelves
and things fall off them.

JIM: Still I'm awfully sorry that I was the cause.

LAURA (*smiling*): I'll just imagine he had an operation. The horn was
removed to make him feel less—freakish! (*They both laugh.*) Now he
will feel more at home with the other horses, the ones that don't have
horns …

JIM: Ha-ha, that's very funny! (*Suddenly serious.*) I'm glad to see that you
have a sense of humor. You know—you're—well—very different! Surprisingly
different from anyone else I know! (*His voice becomes soft and
hesitant with a genuine feeling.*) Do you mind me telling you that?
(LAURA *is abashed beyond speech.*) You make me feel sort of—I don't
know how to put it! I'm usually pretty good at expressing things, but—
This is something that I don't know how to say! (LAURA *touches her
throat and clears it—turns the broken unicorn in her hands.*) (*Even softer.*)
Has anyone ever told you that you were pretty?
(*Pause: Music.*)
(LAURA *looks up slowly, with wonder, and shakes her head.*) Well, you are!
In a very different way from anyone else. And all the nicer because of
the difference, too. (*His voice becomes low and husky.* LAURA *turns away,*

nearly faint with the novelty of her emotions.) I wish that you were my sister. I'd teach you to have some confidence in yourself. The different people are not like other people, but being different is nothing to be ashamed of. Because other people are not such wonderful people. They're one hundred times one thousand. You're one times one! They walk all over the earth. You just stay here. They're common as—weeds, but—you—well, you're—*Blue Roses!*

(*Image on screen: Blue Roses.*)
(*Music changes.*)

LAURA: But blue is wrong for—roses …

JIM: It's right for you—You're—pretty!   265

LAURA: In what respect am I pretty?

JIM: In all respects—believe me! Your eyes—your hair—are pretty! Your hands are pretty! (*He catches hold of her hand.*) You think I'm making this up because I'm invited to dinner and have to be nice. Oh, I could do that! I could put on an act for you, Laura, and say lots of things without being very sincere. But this time I am. I'm talking to you sincerely. I happened to notice you had this inferiority complex that keeps you from feeling comfortable with people. Somebody needs to build your confidence up and make you proud instead of shy and turning away and—blushing—Somebody ought to—ought to—*kiss* you, Laura! (*His hand slips slowly up her arm to her shoulder.*) (*Music swells tumultuously.*) (*He suddenly turns her about and kisses her on the lips. When he releases her* LAURA *sinks on the sofa with a bright, dazed look.* JIM *backs away and fishes in his pocket for a cigarette.*) (*Legend on screen: "Souvenir."*) Stumble-john! (*He lights the cigarette, avoiding her look. There is a peal of girlish laughter from* AMANDA *in the kitchen.* LAURA *slowly raises and opens her hand. It still contains the little broken glass animal. She looks at it with a tender, bewildered expression.*) Stumble-john! I shouldn't have done that—That was way off the beam. You don't smoke, do you? (*She looks up, smiling, not hearing the question. He sits beside her a little gingerly. She looks at him speechlessly—waiting. He coughs decorously and moves a little farther aside as he considers the situation and senses her feelings, dimly, with perturbation. Gently.*) Would you—care for a—mint? (*She doesn't seem to hear him but her look grows brighter even.*) Peppermint—Life Saver? My pocket's a regular drug store—wherever I go … (*He pops a mint in his mouth. Then gulps and decides to make a clean breast of it. He speaks slowly and gingerly.*) Laura, you know, if I had a sister like you, I'd do the same thing as Tom. I'd bring out fellows—introduce her to them. The right type of boys of a type to—appreciate her. Only—well—he made a mistake about me. Maybe I've got no call to be saying this. That may not have been the idea in having me over. But what if it was? There's nothing wrong about that. The only trouble is that in my case—I'm not in a situation to—do the right thing. I can't take down your number and say I'll phone. I can't call up next week and—ask for a date. I thought I had better explain the situation in case you misunderstood it and—hurt your feelings…. (*Pause. Slowly, very slowly,* LAURA's *look changes, her eyes returning slowly from his to the ornament in her palm.*)

(AMANDA *utters another gay laugh in the kitchen.*)

LAURA (*faintly*): You—won't—call again?

JIM: No, Laura, I can't. (*He rises from the sofa.*) As I was just explaining, I've—got strings on me, Laura, I've—been going steady! I go out all the time with a girl named Betty. She's a home-girl like you, and Catholic, and Irish, and in a great many ways we—get along fine. I met her last summer on a moonlight boat trip up the river to Alton, on the *Majestic.* Well—right away from the start it was—love! (*Legend: Love!*) (LAURA *sways slightly forward and grips the arm of the sofa. He fails to notice, now enrapt in his own comfortable being.*) Being in love has made a new man of me! (*Leaning stiffly forward, clutching the arm of the sofa,* LAURA *struggles visibly with her storm. But* JIM *is oblivious, she is a long way off.*) The power of love is really pretty tremendous! Love is something that—changes the whole world, Laura! (*The storm abates a little and* LAURA *leans back. He notices her again.*) It happened that Betty's aunt took sick, she got a wire and had to go to Centralia. So Tom—when he asked me to dinner—I naturally just accepted the invitation, not knowing that you—that he—that I— (*He stops awkwardly.*) Huh—I'm a stumble-john! (*He flops back on the sofa. The holy candles in the altar of* LAURA's *face have been snuffed out! There is a look of almost infinite desolation.* JIM *glances at her uneasily.*) I wish that you would—say something. (*She bites her lip which was trembling and then bravely smiles. She opens her hand again on the broken glass ornament. Then she gently takes his hand and raises it level with her own. She carefully places the unicorn in the palm of his hand, then pushes his fingers closed upon it.*) What are you—doing that for? You want me to have him?—Laura? (*She nods.*) What for?

LAURA: A—souvenir … 270

(*She rises unsteadily and crouches beside the Victrola to wind it up.*)

(*Legend on screen: "Things Have a Way of Turning Out So Badly."*)

(*Or image: "Gentleman caller waving good-bye!—Gaily."*)

(*At this moment* AMANDA *rushes brightly back in the front room. She bears a pitcher of fruit punch in an old-fashioned cut-glass pitcher and a plate of macaroons. The plate has a gold border and poppies painted on it.*)

AMANDA: Well, well, well! Isn't the air delightful after the shower? I've made you children a little liquid refreshment. (*Turns gaily to the gentleman caller.*) Jim, do you know that song about lemonade?

"Lemonade, lemonade
Made in the shade and stirred with a spade—
Good enough for any old maid!"

JIM (*uneasily*): Ha-ha! No—I never heard it

AMANDA: Why, Laura! You look so serious!

JIM: We were having a serious conversation.

AMANDA: Good! Now you're better acquainted!   275

JIM (*uncertainly*): Ha-ha! Yes.

AMANDA: You modern young people are much more serious-minded than
   my generation. I was so gay as a girl!

JIM: You haven't changed, Mrs. Wingfield.

AMANDA: Tonight I'm rejuvenated! The gaiety of the occasion,
   Mr. O'Connor!

(*She tosses her head with a peal of laughter. Spills lemonade.*) Oooo! I'm baptiz-
   ing myself!

JIM: Here—let me—   280

AMANDA (*setting the pitcher down*): There now. I discovered we had some
   maraschino cherries. I dumped them in, juice and all!

JIM: You shouldn't have gone to that trouble, Mrs. Wingfield.

AMANDA: Trouble, trouble? Why it was loads of fun! Didn't you hear me
   cutting up in the kitchen? I bet your ears were burning! I told Tom
   how outdone with him I was for keeping you to himself so long a
   time! He should have brought you over much, much sooner! Well,
   now that you've found your way, I want you to be a very frequent
   caller! Not just occasional but all the time. Oh, we're going to have a
   lot of gay times together! I see them coming! Mmm, just breathe that
   air! So fresh, and the moon's so pretty! I'll skip back out—I know
   where my place is when young folks are having a—serious
   conversation!

JIM: Oh, don't go out, Mrs. Wingfield. The fact of the matter is I've got to
   be going.

AMANDA: Going, now? You're joking! Why, it's only the shank of the even-   285
   ing, Mr. O'Connor!

JIM: Well, you know how it is.

AMANDA: You mean you're a young workingman and have to keep workingmen's hours. We'll let you off early tonight. But only on the condition
   that next time you stay later. What's the best night for you? Isn't
   Saturday night the best night for you workingmen?

JIM: I have a couple of time-clocks to punch, Mrs. Wingfield. One at morning, another one at night!

AMANDA: My, but you *are* ambitious! You work at night, too?

JIM: No, Ma'am, not work but—Betty! (*He crosses deliberately to pick up his   290
   hat. The band at the Paradise Dance Hall goes into a tender waltz.*)

AMANDA: Betty? Betty? Who's—Betty! (*There is an ominous cracking sound in the sky.*)

JIM: Oh, just a girl. The girl I go steady with! (*He smiles charmingly. The sky falls.*)

(*Legend: "The Sky Falls."*)

AMANDA (*a long-drawn exhalation*): Ohhhh ... Is it a serious romance, Mr. O'Connor?

JIM: We're going to be married the second Sunday in June.

AMANDA: Ohhhh—how nice! Tom didn't mention that you were engaged 295
to be married.

JIM: The cat's not out of the bag at the warehouse yet. You know how they are. They call you Romeo and stuff like that. (*He stops at the oval mirror to put on his hat. He carefully shapes the brim and the crown to give a discreetly dashing effect.*) It's been a wonderful evening, Mrs. Wingfield. I guess this is what they mean by Southern hospitality.

AMANDA: It really wasn't anything at all.

JIM: I hope it don't seem like I'm rushing off. But I promised Betty I'd pick her up at the Wabash depot, an' by the time I get my jalopy down there her train'll be in. Some women axe pretty upset if you keep 'em waiting.

AMANDA: Yes, I know—The tyranny of women! (*Extends her hand.*) Goodbye, Mr. O'Connor. I wish you luck—and happiness—and success! All three of them, and so does Laura—Don't you, Laura?

LAURA: Yes! 300

JIM (*taking her hand*): Good-bye, Laura. I'm certainly going to treasure that souvenir. And don't you forget the good advice I gave you. (*Raises his voice to a cheery shout.*) So long, Shakespeare! Thanks again, ladies— Good night!

(*He grins and ducks jauntily out.*

Still bravely grimacing, AMANDA *closes the door on the gentleman caller. Then she turns back to the room with a puzzled expression. She and* LAURA *don't dare to face each other.* LAURA *crouches beside the Victrola to wind it.*)

AMANDA (*faintly*): Things have a way of turning out so badly. I don't believe that I would play the Victrola. Well, well—well—Our gentleman caller was engaged to be married! Tom!

TOM (*from back*): Yes, Mother?

AMANDA: Come in here a minute. I want to tell you something awfully funny.

TOM (*enters with macaroon and a glass of the lemonade*): Has the gentleman 305
caller gotten away already?

AMANDA: The gentleman caller has made an early departure. What a wonderful joke you played on us!

TOM: How do you mean?

AMANDA: You didn't mention that he was engaged to be married.

TOM: Jim? Engaged?

AMANDA: That's what he just informed us.   310

TOM: I'll be jiggered! I didn't know about that.

AMANDA: That seems very peculiar.

TOM: What's peculiar about it?

AMANDA: Didn't you call him your best friend down at the warehouse?

TOM: Tom he is, but how did I know?   315

AMANDA: It seems extremely peculiar that you wouldn't know your best friend was going to be married!

TOM: The warehouse is where I work, not where I know things about people!

AMANDA: You don't know things anywhere! You live in a dream; you manufacture illusions! *(He crosses to door.)* Where are you going?

TOM: I'm going to the movies.

AMANDA: That's right, now that you've had us make such fools of ourselves.   320
The effort, the preparations, all the expense! The new floor lamp, the rug, the clothes for Laura! All for what? To entertain some other girl's fiancé! Go to the movies, go! Don't think about us, a mother deserted, an unmarried sister who's crippled and has no job! Don't let anything interfere with your selfish pleasure! Just go, go, go—to the movies!

TOM: All right, I will! The more you shout about my selfishness to me the quicker I'll go, and I won't go to the movies!

AMANDA: Go, then! Then go to the moon—you selfish dreamer!

(TOM *smashes his glass on the floor. He plunges out on the fire-escape, slamming the door.* LAURA *screams—cut by door.*

Dance-hall music up. TOM *goes to the rail and grips it desperately, lifting his face in the chill white moonlight penetrating the narrow abyss of the alley.)*

(Legend on screen: "And So Good-Bye …")

(TOM's *closing speech is timed with the interior pantomime. The interior scene is played as though viewed through sound-proof glass.* AMANDA *appears to be making a comforting speech to* LAURA *who is huddled upon the sofa. Now that we cannot hear the mother's speech, her silliness is gone and she has dignity and tragic beauty.* LAURA's *dark hair hides her face until at the end of the speech she lifts it to smile at her mother.* AMANDA's *gestures are slow and graceful, almost dancelike, as she comforts the daughter. At the end of her speech she glances a moment at the father's picture—then withdraws through the portieres. At close of* TOM's *speech,* LAURA *blows out the candles, ending the play.)*

TOM: I didn't go to the moon, I went much further—for time is the longest distance between two places—Not long after that I was fired for writing a poem on the lid of a shoe-box. I left Saint Louis. I descended the steps of this fire-escape for a last time and followed, from then on, in my father's footsteps, attempting to find in motion what was lost in space—I traveled around a great deal. The cities swept about me like dead leaves, leaves that were brightly colored but torn away from the branches. I would have stopped, but I was pursued by something. It always came upon me unawares, taking me altogether by surprise. Perhaps it was a familiar bit of music. Perhaps it was only a piece of transparent glass—Perhaps I am walking along a street at night, in some strange city, before I have found companions. I pass the lighted window of a shop where perfume is sold. The window is filled with pieces of colored glass, tiny transparent bottles in delicate colors, like bits of a shattered rainbow. Then all at once my sister touches my shoulder. I turn around and look into her eyes.... Oh, Laura, Laura, I tried to leave you behind me, but I am more faithful than I intended to be! I reach for a cigarette, I cross the street, I run into the movies or a bar, I buy a drink, I speak to the nearest stranger—anything that can blow your candles out! (LAURA *bends over the candles*)—for nowadays the world is lit by lightning! Blow out your candles, Laura—and so good-bye ...

(*She blows the candles out.*)

(*The Scene Dissolves.*)

■ After you have finished reading the play, go back to the description that Williams offers of the setting. How do specific actions in the play take advantage of the setting that he has described? He calls the scene *"memory."* To what extent is the setting unrealistic?

■ How do themes in the play reflect this setting in *"one of those vast hive-like conglomerations of cellular living-units that flower as warty growths in overcrowded urban centers of lower middle-class population"*? What other details in the play help us to understand its setting?

■ Trace the idea of escape as it applies to Tom. What is he trying to escape? How does he escape? To what extent does his escape seem successful?

Experiencing Literature through Writing

1. Select a single work from this chapter (or any other). Identify a significant setting within that work. Explain why that setting is significant to our understanding of the text. As you write, consider the following questions:

   a. What specific details in the work help you recognize the setting?

b. What details in the work make this setting particularly interesting?

c. Are there multiple settings in the work? Does the author develop some contrast among these settings?

d. Are there details within this work that do not seem attached to any setting? How is the setting significant if these details do not seem related to the setting?

2. In the works in this chapter, we get details that help us see some places that seem very real and some that seem much less substantial. Compare two works that allow you to explore this contrast. What makes one seem like a familiar place and the other seem mysterious?

3. Discuss the relation between the details about setting that we get in one work and the point of view that reveals those details to us. For instance, we might get the details through the eyes of a child. How does knowledge of the viewpoint influence our reading of those details? To what extent is our understanding of the setting a function of the point of view?

6

Rhythm, Pace, and Rhyme

How Do Sounds Move?

Usually, when we think of rhythm, we think first of music. It's easy to understand why. We take in and express rhythms physically. We hear; we feel; we dance. Artists and critics together have created a rich technical language to analyze, describe, and appreciate the sensations that music inspires. We can speak of a bass line as what establishes something for all the other players to follow (clumsy dancers sometimes move to a song's melody or tune and disregard the deeper rhythms that melody is built upon). Rhythm is the pulse that undergirds everything; if the pulse grows faint, the entire composition can become vague or listless. If the pulse becomes irregular, the composition can become confusing, disturbing, challenging, annoying, or even comedic.

Many terms rooted in the study of music (*counterpoint/contrapuntal, amplification, cadence, measure, motif*, and so on) carry over easily to literary study—especially to the study of poetry. Poetry has always been music's close relative. And it is certainly true that poets attend strictly to lines (the way every word is sounded in every line and every line is arranged on every page) in a way that doesn't necessarily concern novelists, essayists, filmmakers, or most dramatists. But that said, it's also clear that poets aren't the only artists who care about rhythm. For the pulse that constitutes rhythm isn't something felt only in music and poetry—or experienced exclusively through sound. Even the word *pulse* tells us something: the beating of our hearts is the ultimate rhythmic touchstone. It shouldn't be surprising that a quality so basic to our very existence is accessed as well as expressed in a variety of ways; we hear, see, and feel rhythms.

In this chapter, we consider rhythm in the broadest—and most liberating—sense of the word. We think of rhythm along with related elements of sound, such as the speed or pace of delivery. We also consider distinct qualities of sound, such as rhyme in its various forms, and press further still to address visual and filmic rhythm. Such an approach suggests ways to open up the word *rhythm* and understand more fully how deeply rhythm infuses any kind of writing—not just poetry. This approach also encourages a flexible use of a technical, critical vocabulary without diminishing the precision of that vocabulary. Putting all of these elements in a larger context demonstrates how even the most highly specialized point of focus (for example, the metrical analysis of a poem) relates to vital critical concerns that cross familiar boundaries. We start by crossing a boundary that is often strongly marked: the one that separates sound from sight.

FILMIC RHYTHM

Vladimir Nabokov has said that a good critic reads with his backbone. T. S. Eliot once noted that great art is felt before it is understood. Emily Dickinson was perhaps getting at the same thing when she said that she didn't know how to define "poetry" but knew a poem when she felt it take off the top of her head. These kinds of physical responses register a fine appreciation for rhythm. They also mark what for some people characterizes an essential dimension of the filmgoing experience. We take in the sensory impressions of film at an extraordinarily rapid pace—not too rapidly to process through our backbones but much too fast to immediately sort out intellectually. We know a film has an impact well before we appreciate exactly what that impact involves or how it was achieved. Accounting for the feeling, as noted previously, is the job of the critic. And this process of accounting through discussion and writing can send us back to the film (or other films) more receptive, more alert, and more alive to film's possibilities.

In a film, the illusion of movement is created by running a series of still frames rapidly by a viewer: movies are moving pictures. The component of film beyond the individual **frame** is the **shot**—a single length of film that communicates a continuous action on the screen. This length of film can, of course, be cut at any frame (that is, it can be a brief glimpse or a view that unfolds over many minutes). The joining/splicing (as well as the arranging, organizing) of shots is a function of **editing** (see a more complete discussion in Chapter 9). The relationship among shots (among varying lengths of film/varying lengths of time that pass from one shot to another) creates a rhythmic sense that can convey extraordinary depth of feeling.

It's important here to distinguish pace from rhythm. **Pace** indicates the relative speed of an unfolding action or the variety of actions that unfold within a defined length of time. We might speak of a story or film as fast or slow paced based upon the number of incidents that are packed into our reading or viewing experience. Whereas pace involves relatively simple standards of fast or slow narratives, **filmic rhythm** involves *patterns* of movement, composition, and sound. **Shot analysis** is a means to comprehend how a film (or section of film) communicates meaning and power. In shot analysis, one breaks a film down and assesses the relationship of shot to shot, the rhythms that are created, and the effects of the whole. Although such analysis ultimately involves more than simply measuring the length of each shot, that measurement is important in understanding filmic rhythm.

Experiencing Film through Rhythm

If you've seen the popular film classic *Jaws* (1975), there is a good chance you remember the opening scene very well. That opening demonstrates Steven Spielberg's command of a film's rhythm.

Students off for summer vacations are partying at the beach after dark—and the party is at the sit-around-the-fire, drink-a-little-beer stage. Spielberg opens with a patient shot that slowly pans across the scene and pauses only to center us on one character—a young man who gazes across at a girl. A few brief shots move us back and forth between the boy and the girl who has

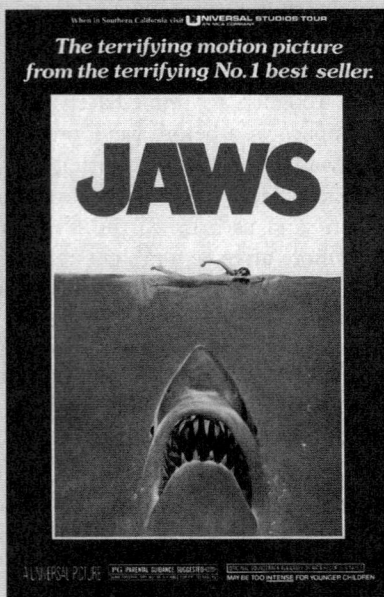

Jaws (1975)

caught his eye. Spielberg continues to cut fairly quickly, but in an evenly spaced way, between shots of the boy and of the girl as they break from the group and run along the beach, undressing as they run. The lines of dialogue, if read separately from the images, convey nothing beyond the most minimal exposition of character and action:

SCENE: *Beach*
CASSIDY: What's your name again?
CHRISSIE: Chrissie!
CASSIDY: Where are we going?
CHRISSIE: Swimming!
CASSIDY: Slow up, slow down! I'm not drunk! Slow down! Wait I'm coming! I'm coming! I'm definitely coming! Wait, slow up! I can swim—just can't walk or dress myself.
CHRISSIE: Come on in the water!
CASSIDY: Take it easy. Take it easy.
CHRISSIE: Oh! God help me! God! Argh! God help!
CASSIDY: I'm coming … I'm coming.
CHRISSIE: It hurts! It hurts! Oh my god! God help me! God please help!

This hardly seems inspired writing, but of course, words alone don't make up the movie. The whole *viewing* experience is terrifying. We see the unfortunate girl get to the water. The boy stumbles, falls on the sand, and goes to sleep. Spielberg again slows the exchange from shot to shot once the boy is out of the action; now the movement builds **tension** as Spielberg moves from a shot of the girl at the surface enjoying the water to a shot of equal length taken beneath from the perspective of the shark hunting for food, to a single brief shot of the boy asleep on the beach. Once the shark attacks, Spielberg holds the shot on the girl at the surface for what seems an excruciatingly long time. He wants to establish her (and our) helplessness in relation to this creature. He does so not by showing the creature itself but by showing what can happen to the people who enter its realm. After the girl is finally pulled under and quiet returns, Spielberg returns to a shot of the boy: silent, unknowing, oblivious to the world and all its dangers. The horror is established in context of the sleepy vacation town and the pleasures of beach life. The opposition finds expression largely through Spielberg's mastery of film's rhythmic possibilities.

POETIC RHYTHM

Shot analysis in film involves closely observing and describing relationships among shots that function thematically and emotionally. It is useful to think of metrical analysis of poetry as in some fundamental way related to shot analysis (or the other way around). A filmmaker arranges and organizes a series of shots into a whole that expresses a pattern of movement—moments of stress and of relief. A poet arranges and organizes a pattern of sounds that reinforce or create meaning, that suggest feeling behind meaning.

In the analysis of poetry, **meter** refers to a regular (therefore discernible) rhythmic pattern of sounds that is charted line by line; in the analysis of film, a pattern of unfolding action is charted shot by shot. At some point, the analogy between analysis of film and the analysis of a poem's meter breaks down (as analogies usually do), but we can think of the poetic foot as the element that most closely corresponds to the frame (in that it is the smallest building block). A poetic **foot** is the combination of one stressed syllable with one or more unstressed syllables that constitutes the recurring rhythmic unit within the larger pattern of a poetic line or of any given stretch of text.

There are five standard units (feet) in English poetry:

- The **iambic** foot (the most common in English poetry) consists of two syllables, the first unstressed and the second stressed (toDAY, but WHY? inSPIRE). Any pattern that moves from unstressed to stressed syllables is sometimes called **rising meter.**

- The **trochaic** foot consists of two syllables, the first stressed and the second unstressed (TRAVel, STANdard). Any pattern that moves from stressed to unstressed syllables is sometimes called **falling meter.**

- The **anapestic** foot consists of three syllables, the first two unstressed and the third stressed (anyMORE).

- The **dactylic** foot consists of three syllables, the first stressed and the last two unstressed (FInally).

- The **spondee**, which consists of two consecutive stressed syllables (HOT DOG, OH MY!), and the **pyrrhic**, which consists of two consecutive unstressed syllables, are considered **variants** (or **substitutions**) of standard feet. That is, a spondee or a pyrrhic can break a prevailing pattern, but spondees and pyrrhics cannot make up a pattern (a line cannot be composed of all stressed syllables or all unstressed syllables, because one quality can be defined only in relation to the other).

A **metric line** of poetry is measured by the number of feet that it comprises. The most common lines are **trimeter** (three feet), **tetrameter** (four feet), **pentameter** (five feet), and **hexameter** (six feet).

If we extend our analogy to film a bit further here, we can think of a metric line of poetry as a shot; for example, a line of **iambic pentameter** (the prevailing rhythm of much English poetry—"oh, GENtle FAUstus, LEAVE this DAMnéd ART"—and a natural speech pattern) could be seen as analogous to a single length of film, a shot. Poetic lines may be organized in still larger patterns by rhyme schemes (arrangements of rhyming words), line length, or more complex metrical forms. These larger patterns are called **stanzas**—a verse paragraph. Lines make up stanzas much as shots in a film can be grouped as scenes. The following examples are common stanzaic forms:

- **couplet** (two lines)
  Early to bed and early to rise
  Makes a man healthy, wealthy, and wise.
- **tercet** (three lines)
  The winged seeds, where they lie cold and low,
  Each like a corpse within its grave, until
  Thine azure sister of the Spring shall blow.
  > —Percy Bysshe Shelley, from "Ode to the West Wind"
- **quatrain** (four lines)
  When the voices of children are heard on the green
  And laughing is heard on the hill,
  My heart is at rest within my breast
  And every thing else is still
  > —William Blake, from "Nurse's Song"

There are, of course, other stanzaic forms, most notably the **octave** (eight lines) and **sestet** (six lines). (See discussion of the sonnet in Chapter 8.)

Experiencing Literature through Rhythm

Rhythm in much poetry in English must be charted by attention to both syllables and stresses. Such attention to the metrical shape of a poem is called **prosody**. To **scan** a line of poetry or any text is to define the rhythmic pattern. Such analysis, or **scansion**, must remain fairly rough (in this book, stressed syllables are shown in all uppercase letters, and unstressed syllables, in all lowercase letters). Syllables are, after all, pronounced with a wide and flexible range of emphases; marking every syllable either stressed (´) or unstressed (˘) cannot register that range with great precision. But judicious metrical analysis can help us describe what rhythms we hear and may deepen our appreciation of the writer's craft. Poets can achieve emphasis through meter; they can make us notice a key word or idea. And as the two following works make clear, a poet may even fuse meter and meaning.

Herman Melville (1819–1891)

The Maldive Shark (1888)

About the Shark, phlegmatical one,
Pale sot of the Maldive sea,
The sleek little pilot-fish, azure and slim,
How alert in attendance be.
From his saw-pit of mouth, from his charnel of maw,   5
They have nothing of harm to dread,
But liquidly glide on his ghastly flank
Or before his Gorgonian head;
Or lurk in the port of serrated teeth
In white triple tiers of glittering gates,   10
And there find a haven when peril's abroad,
An asylum in jaws of the Fates!
They are friends; and friendly they guide him to prey,
Yet never partake of the treat—
Eyes and brains to the dotard lethargic and dull,   15
Pale ravener of horrible meat.

William Blake (1757–1827)

Nurse's Song (1789)

When the voices of children are heard on the green
And laughing is heard on the hill,
My heart is at rest within my breast
And every thing else is still

Then come home my children, the sun is gone down   5
And the dews of the night arise
Come come leave off play, and let us away
Till the morning appears in the skies

No no let us play, for it is yet day
And we cannot go to sleep   10
Besides in the sky, the little birds fly
And the hills are all covered with sheep

"Well well go & play till the light fades away
And then go home to bed

The little ones leaped & shouted & laugh'd   15
And all the hills ecchoed

Read "The Maldive Shark" and "Nurse's Song" aloud several times, and you'll begin to hear a lilting, rather fast meter. It is a rhythm like one you have probably heard before in poems for children or in comic verse. The strongly marked rhythm results from the repeated use of trisyllabic feet. In the first line of "Nurse's Song" anapests prevail:

When the voices of children are heard on the green ...
(when the VOIces of CHILdren are HEARD on the GREEN)

In "The Maldive Shark," the opening line closes with an anapest, and anapests and dactyls generally prevail throughout:

About the Shark, phlegmatical one ...
(aBOUT the SHARK, phlegMATical ONE)

In Blake's poem, the anapests seem clearly appropriate: "Nurse's Song" is (at least on the surface) a song of innocence. The poem centers mainly on the power of children's play and joy to transform the spirit of the speaker. But note how Melville uses rhythms similar to Blake's to create a troubling thematic undercurrent. The trisyllabic feet in "The Maldive Shark" do not function to reinforce themes like innocence, childhood, and peace. The lilting quality of Melville's meter starkly contrasts with images of death and blunt power associated with the shark. The apparent split between form and content suggests that things are not what they seem. A similar, complex mixed signal is evident in the construction of the poem's first sentence. The first *line* seems to announce the shark as subject of the poem (this is a poem "about the shark"), but if we pay attention to the whole sentence, which ends with line 4, we note the focus has shifted the shark isn't even the grammatical subject. The poem actually centers on the "pilot-fish" that swim "about the shark."

The sleek, intelligent, quick, alert, attractive pilot-fish are set before us in the rhythm of the poem; visual images of the heavy, dumb, slow, uncaring, repellent shark move powerfully through this rhythm. The implication of this contrast is that what we sometimes assume to be good or innocent often operates together with what we see as evil or corrupt. In other words, what seems not to go together goes together all too well. The pilot-fish lead the shark to its prey so that they may be safe from its hunger. Melville's play with meter challenges conventional and comfortable notions of morality and order. His poem helps us understand that meter is not mere decoration.

Melville and Blake make meter central to the meaning of these two poems, but meter can be worth attending to even when it is not central to the work. Note, for example, how Stephen Crane's opening sentences from his short story "A Bride Comes to Yellow Sky" rhythmically convey a sense of a train's relentless movement westward (and with the train's movement, the rolling influence of an entire culture):

> The Great Pullman was whirling onward with such dignity of motion that a glance from the window seemed simply to prove that the plains of Texas were pouring eastward. Vast flats of green grass, dull-hued spaces of mesquite and cactus, little groups of frame houses, woods of light and tender trees, all were sweeping into the east, sweeping over the horizon, a precipice. ■

Interpretations of a line's rhythm are subject to debate—as is any kind of interpretation—but a good case could be made here for breaking the last sentence into poetic lines for the sake of directing an oral reading:

Vast flats of green grass,
Dull-hued spaces of mesquite and cactus,
Little groups of frame houses,
Woods of light and tender trees
All were sweeping into the east,
Sweeping over the horizon,
A precipice.

The opening line employs spondees; and trochees, not the more common iambs, prevail in the next three lines. It seems that Crane is both describing and embodying the train's movement along the tracks west. The fourth and fifth lines, though, break that pattern midline. But it's not just a shift to iambs in line 5; rather, in the middle of line 6 and the start of the final line, Crane substitutes pyrrhic feet (the two consecutive unstressed syllables) or perhaps anapests (two unaccented syllables followed by an accented syllable). The effect of the unaccented syllables run together is that his sentence gathers speed as it moves to the precipice. The old West, as we'll come to learn in the story, is falling over that precipice into a more "civilized" (more domesticated, tame) East.

Granted, these changes would fundamentally alter what Crane wrote. Crane didn't arrange his lines as we have. And his story could not reward from beginning to end the attention to rhythmic patterns we've devoted to this sentence. Still, it is worth remembering that Crane was a poet as well as a short story writer and journalist, and it's plain that in this passage he creates effects partly through his attention to both sound and sense. So the altering of the text is not an attempt to make it something it is not; rather, it is a way of revealing what we hear and feel, but imperfectly appreciate. From the perspective of a critical writer, attention to meter in a text may yield fresh insights about how that text achieves meaning and power.

THE RHYTHM OF PAUSES

Scansion can reveal much of a writer's art, but obviously there are rhythmic effects that are not accounted for by marking poetic feet (just as shot analysis alone cannot account for all aspects of a film's rhythm). Artists in various mediums manage pauses of various weights to affect interpretation; much meaning or emotion can be conveyed by pauses (or by the lack of pause). An artist can hold an audience's/reader's attention on a word or image or make the audience/reader wait just a moment before delivering something profound.

Caesura is a pause *within* a line of poetry (sometimes called an **extra-metrical effect** and charted by a double slash [//] between words at the point of pause). A line that comes to a full stop at the end is **end-stopped**. A line that "strides over" into the next line without a pause is **enjambed** (the poet has employed **enjambment**). Although caesura, end stop, and enjambment are terms that apply specifically to the analysis of poetry (how pauses are managed within and between lines), many powerful effects in any piece of writing or film result from the careful management of pauses. A pause at the right time can anticipate a sudden turn; it can allow one to absorb an emotional effect; it can draw attention to what precedes or follows. It can accentuate a rhythmic quality of a text or make us keenly aware of rhythm by breaking the pattern (if something is too regular, we may hardly notice).

Experiencing Literature through Rhythm

Samuel Johnson employs a carefully measured rhythm for thematic purpose. "On the Death of Dr. Robert Levet" is about a man who had a long and well-used life. Levet cut no great figure in terms of what the world values, but Johnson sees Levet's modest accomplishments as deserving real praise. In the context of the hard surrounding world (Johnson casts all humankind as workers in "Hope's delusive mine"), Levet toils faithfully in service to those who seek his help. Death, in Johnson's view, ends that difficult service and brings the aged Levet to his Maker.

Samuel Johnson (1709–1784)

On the Death of Dr. Robert Levet (1783)

Condemn'd to Hope's delusive mine,
   As on we toil from day to day,
By sudden blasts, or slow decline,
   Our social comforts drop away.

Well tried through many a varying year,   5
   See Levet to the grave descend;
Officious, innocent, sincere,
   Of every friendless name the friend.

Yet still he fills affection's eye,
   Obscurely wise and coarsely kind;   10
Nor, letter'd Arrogance, deny
   Thy praise to merit unrefined.

When fainting nature called for aid,
   And hovering death prepared the blow,
His vigorous remedy display'd   15
   The power of art without the show.

In misery's darkest cavern known,
   His useful care was ever nigh,
Where hopeless Anguish pour'd his groan,
   And lonely want retired to die.   20

No summons mock'd by chill delay,
   No petty gain disdained by pride,
The modest wants of every day
   The toil of every day supplied.

His virtues walked their narrow round,   25
   Nor made a pause, nor left a void;
And sure the eternal Master found
   The single talent well employ'd.

The busy day, the peaceful night,
   Unfelt, uncounted, glided by;   30

His frame was firm, his powers were bright,
  Though now his eightieth year was nigh.

Then with no throbbing fiery pain,
  No cold gradations of decay,
Death broke at once the vital chain,   35
  And freed his soul the nearest way.

The feeling in this poem is not narrowly for Levet's death. Indeed, Levet's sudden death is cast as a release. Whatever hardship one faces in this life, Johnson suggests, can be placed in a broader and well-ordered picture. The measured pauses within the lines enforce this sense of balance. Whatever our lot on earth, Johnson seems to say, God has structured a coherent master plan within which we can work. Note the clear midline pauses in lines 3 ("By sudden blasts, // or slow decline"), 10 ("Obscurely wise // and coarsely kind"), 26, 29, and 31. Many other lines convey a much less distinct, but still arguably evident, pause in the middle of the line. Consider, for example, lines 2 ("As on we toil // from day to day"), 14 ("And hovering death // prepared the blow") 16, 20, and 28. When caesuras do not so evenly divide a line in half, they still evenly divide the line, as in line 7 ("Officious, // innocent, // sincere") and 30 ("Unfelt, // uncounted, // glided by"). Johnson's phrasing suggests the steadiness he wishes to maintain in reflecting upon the life and death of his friend.

  We could further note that Johnson maintains this steadiness through his management of the entire stanza. He gives us no metrical surprises, no pronounced breaks from the prevailing iambic tetrameter (a line of four iambic feet). He brings most lines to a full stop or end stop. Every quatrain (poetic paragraph of four lines) closes a complete thought and enforces a pronounced pause. The pace of the poem, the phrases so carefully balanced by caesuras, the structural clarity and consistency—all suggest a poet in command of his message and confident in his faith.

  Ben Jonson feels no such emotional balance or spiritual assurance as he struggles to write about a very different sort of death. "On My First Son" expresses an intensely personal loss. Obviously, one's own seven-year-old child cannot serve as a point of reflection on a life well used and kindly ended—the kind of reflection that prevails in Samuel Johnson's tribute to his old friend Dr. Levet. The intense pain Ben Jonson feels cannot lead him to feel grateful that his son escaped pain by dying young. The grieving father is angry, confused, and hurt. Given such feelings, any measured, balanced, regular rhythm would seem strangely controlled. Not surprisingly, we do not get that steady rhythm.

Ben Jonson (1572–1637)

On My First Son (1616)

Farewell, thou child of my right hand, and joy;
My sin was too much hope of thee, loved boy:
Seven years thou wert lent to me, and I thee pay,
Exacted by thy fate, on the just day.
O could I lose all father now! for why   5
Will man lament the state he should envy,
To have soon 'scaped world's and flesh's rage,
And, if no other misery, yet age?
Rest in soft peace, and asked, say, "Here doth lie
Ben Jonson his best piece of poetry."   10
For whose sake henceforth all his vows be such
As what he loves may never like too much.

Much of Jonson's unresolved emotional torment is conveyed by the sudden, irregularly placed caesuras (the pauses in this poem fall near the beginning or the end of several lines, but not in the middle). It is as if in the first four lines, the speaker makes a tentative, reluctant attempt to say good-bye. This attempt is broken by a rush of feeling that stalls just before the end of the fifth line. At that point, Jonson forces us to rush ahead without stop from the end of line 5 through line 6:

O could I lose all father now! // for why
Will man lament the state he should envy

The enjambment here suggests that emotions cannot be bound by the constraints of line. Again, rhythm relates to sense; it is part of the critic's job to help readers see that relationship.

A Note to Student Writers: Commanding Attention

Clearly, pauses aren't the sole property of poets. Sentences, just like lines of poems, build and release tension in any number of ways. Good writers in any mode want to signal pace and emphasis for their readers. Readers need help sometimes in noticing what is really important. A carefully placed pause, a balanced series, an emphatic turn or break from a prevailing pattern—all can bring a point home. We suggest that you bring this insight into your own writing. You, like any writer, must find ways to make readers concentrate attention on the words that need or demand attention. One way of doing this (as mentioned before in other contexts) is to read your own work aloud periodically as you draft and revise. Reading aloud will help make you conscious of rhythmic effects in works of art and will lead you to appreciate how many of those effects play out in your own prose. We want you, in short, to be alert to how rhythmic effects are deeply part of almost any carefully constructed text—including the texts you construct.

THE RHYTHM OF SOUNDS

The quality of sounds strongly influences the weight and stress we sense that fall on individual words. Sounds also influence the way we speak words in sequence—sounds of individual words influence the rhythm we feel arise from a group of words. And of course, sounds of individual words must be spoken and heard in relation to other words. People do not pronounce words in isolation (such tonelessness is for machines: consider the phonetic, word-by-word correctness of the mechanically generated voices you sometimes hear on phone message systems). We pronounce words in ways that mesh with how those words unfold in a line or a sentence as well as with how they balance, contrast with, or echo each other.

Rhyme serves as an especially powerful means of achieving such balance, contrast, or echo. **Full** or **perfect rhyme** consists of the similarity of sounds in accented vowels and any consonants that follow (*date, fate*). In a **masculine rhyme**, the stress is on the final syllable of the words (*clown, renown*). A **feminine rhyme** is one in which the final two syllables rhyme; the first rhyming syllable is stressed, and the final syllable is unstressed (*buckle, knuckle*). **Assonance** also consists of a similarity in vowel sounds, but the consonants that follow differ (*date, lake*). **Consonance** strikes a similarity in the sounds of the final stressed consonant; the preceding vowel differs (*date, rite*). Words that echo sounds in these ways are sometimes called **slant rhymes** or **off-rhymes**. **Alliteration** refers to the repetition of initial sounds in words (*date, dud*). All of these terms concern sounds, but rhyme generally refers to similar sounds that occur at corresponding places in a line of poetry. Assonance, consonance, and alliteration may be employed at various intervals throughout any given passage of poetry or prose. Rhymes in the middle of a line are called **internal rhymes**; those at the end of a line, **end rhymes**.

Rhyme is so strongly part of the way we voice a word that it sometimes overcomes other rhythmic signals and distorts the way we deliver a line. Think, for example, of the times you feel prompted to pause at the end of a rhymed line of poetry despite the syntactical demand to move forward. Small children will normally pause very heavily after every rhyme, and in a sense that tendency reflects a good impulse even if it is ultimately misguided. Of course, the sounds of words also have much to do with the rhythm and pace of a line. The running together of hard consonants will usually force readers to slow down; one simply can't perfectly pronounce passages full of *p* sounds without pausing and allowing each word to have some space. Other sounds glide together very easily and greatly speed rhythm. Alexander Pope's famous lines from his "Essay on Criticism" illustrate perfectly how slowness and speed can be suggested by sounds:

When Ajax strives some rock's vast weight to throw,
The line too labors, and the words move slow;
Not so when swift Camilla scours the plain,
Flies o'er the unbending corn, and skims along the main.

We also hear sounds differently depending on meaning and context. For example, one might think that the sibilants (*s* sounds) that dominate lines from Alfred, Lord Tennyson's "The Lotus Eaters" (1842) convey softness, easiness, sleepiness:

There is sweet music here that softer falls
Than petals from blown roses on the grass,
Or night-dews on still waters between walls
Of Shadowy granite, in a gleaming pass;
Music that gentlier on the spirit lies,
Than tired eyelids upon tired eyes;
Music that brings sweet sleep down from the blissful skies.

We can use the terms **euphony** (to describe pleasing, soothing sounds) and **cacophony** (to describe harsh, unpleasant sounds), but we do not hear the sounds as soothing purely because of the sounds themselves. There is nothing inherently soothing in the sound of the letter *s* (think of the hissing of a snake). Tennyson's meaning directs us to inflect these particular words with a particular languor. So this section ends with a warning: Avoid arguing a point from sound alone. Be sure that you are attentive to sound in relation to all the other evidence you gather to explain how a given work communicates.

Making Connections

Sound and rhythm can have importance even when they have no apparent meaning. Consider, for example, how music functions in a film or a play. Even when you are absorbed by the action, the rhythmic unfolding of that action may be led by background music you don't consciously notice. Also, consider the way sounds and rhythms can serve as a kind of incantation—that is, sounds can weave a spell. Such atmospheric effects are (as discussed in Chapter 5) very important to gothic works.

Experiencing Literature through Rhythm and Rhyme

As powerful as rhymes can be in the effect of the whole work, they may function in very subtle ways. In the following short poem, you probably will feel upon first reading the matter-of-fact finality of Randall Jarrell's closing line.

Randall Jarrell (1914–1965)

The Death of the Ball Turret Gunner (1945)

From my mother's sleep I fell into the State,
And I hunched in its belly till my wet fur froze.
Six miles from earth, loosed from its dream of life,
I woke to black flak and the nightmare fighters.
When I died they washed me out of the turret with a hose.   5

You might not notice, however, that the feeling is enforced by a rhyme: "hose" rhymes perfectly with "froze." Jarrell's poem does not have the metrical regularity that often leads us to anticipate a rhyme. Nor does the rhyme follow very closely: "froze" ends line 2; "hose" ends line 5. Yet this rather distant rhyme accounts in part for the sudden, forceful finish. The life of the gunner is absolutely over, and so is the poem; the rhyme accentuates the finish of both. It closes off this brief monologue.

Jarrell also employs internal rhymes (rhymes within the line instead of at the end of lines) and consonance to suggest the sensory assault of enemy gunfire that awakens the ball turret gunner to the nightmare of life: "woke to black flak." The sounds communicate experience as well as meaning; confusion and terror mark that experience. The hardness of the sounds in context of the meaning aggressively presses upon us as we read. The example here illustrates **onomatopoeia**—that is, the sounds of the words replicate the meaning they convey.

Making Connections

Rhyme does more than accentuate rhythmic elements; rhyme can be a structuring device—a means to highlight a central meaning or problem (see the discussion of Millay's "I, Being Born a Woman and Distressed" [p. 722]). Robert Frost's "Fire and Ice" (p. 524) is tightly structured around three rhymes (A/B/A/A/B/C/B/C/B). The "A" rhymes set one side of an elemental opposition: fire and the emotion of desire. The "B" rhymes center around a feeling associated with "ice." The "C" rhymes identify that cold feeling: hate.

Frost's word choice (especially at the poem's finish) is also striking. *Suffice* hardly seems the word one would expect in wrapping up a thought about a power great enough to end the world. But the particular quality of hatred that Frost expresses needs to find expression in such a tightly limited, proper little word (for further discussion on word choice, see Chapter 11).

Robert Frost (1874–1963)

Fire and Ice (1923)

Some say the world will end in fire,
Some say in ice.
From what I've tasted of desire
I hold with those who favor fire.
But if it had to perish twice,   5
I think I know enough of hate
To say that for destruction ice
Is also great
And would suffice.

MODELING CRITICAL ANALYSIS:
ROBERT BROWNING, MY LAST DUCHESS

Robert Browning's "My Last Duchess" (p. 303) reads very much like the one-way conversation Browning intends it to be. We hear a man, the duke, *speaking* to another man, the envoy. His delivery might be rather formal in places, but he is a duke after all—one with a "nine-hundred-years-old name." What most readers sense is the naturalness of his style.

Ralph Rader, a literary critic whose reading of this poem has influenced ours, suggests we should not be taken in by the duke's tone. Rader points to something very obvious that few people notice: this poem is written in rhymed couplets throughout. In fact, the rhymes are full or perfect end rhymes; the lines themselves are in iambic pentameter. Something must be amiss: How can we read as speech language that is so clearly crafted? How is it that anyone could read a poem and not notice that it is rhymed so regularly? Not notice that it is so carefully measured rhythmically?

One level of answers to such questions requires attention to Browning's technique. We don't pick up on the rhymes or the accentual/syllabic regularity of lines because Browning hides them. He employs caesuras at various points within the lines; he regularly enjambs lines; and he keeps the structure of his sentences (syntax) out of synch with the arrangement of his poetic lines. For example, notice that the full pause near the end of line 2 comes at the end of a sentence. The line, though, continues briefly after that pause and moves forward without a break into line 3, which then "strides over" into line 4. As a result, any good dramatic reading will not make us *hear* the end rhyme that is there if we *look* (*wall, call*).

So we are led to another question: Why should Browning bother to come up with perfect rhymes and then go to the trouble of making us *not* notice them? The answer, Rader suggests, is that Browning (the poet) wants readers to see how duplicitous the duke (the speaker) is. In other words, the duke only pretends to be casual and spontaneous. He only claims to be a man who has "no skill in speech." A careful reading of the poem—especially to rhythms and rhymes that are at once transparent and hidden—reveals a duke who knows exactly what message he wants to send to the envoy yet also knows not to send that message directly. To put it another way, Browning has built into the poem evidence of how crafty the duke is. And what is the duke's message? Rader argues that the duke wants to make it clear he expects the next wife to know exactly what is expected of her. He also wants everyone involved in the negotiation to know what the consequences of not meeting those expectations will be. Most readers see the duke as unintentionally revealing himself as cruel—indeed murderous. Rader looks to the rhythms and rhymes of Browning's poem to argue that the duke is in full, conscious control of his terrible message.

Using Rhythm, Pace, and Rhyme to Focus Writing and Discussion

- To locate rhythms, we must look at individual words and at sentence structures within the text. What words or sounds are repeated within the text?
- What patterns govern these repetitions?
- What characteristics can we ascribe to the sounds of this text? Are they soothing? Harsh? How do these sounds correspond to the literal meaning of the text?
- Is there some contrast in rhythms? For instance, does the text set up a pattern and then break it? If so, what is the effect?
- What sentence patterns do we find in this work? Does the author use consistently short sentences? Long sentences? Any consistent variety?
- Are there different characters who speak with different rhythms in the text? How are these differences related to the role of the characters in the text?

Anthology

INNOCENCE AND EXPERIENCE: RHYTHM AND MEANING

The poems selected from William Blake's *Songs of Innocence* and *Songs of Experience* provide the keynote for this group of readings. Blake, as pointed out in the discussion of "Nurse's Song" earlier, matches rhythmic features of his poems with the "contrary states of the human soul" he seeks to express. As you read these poems, be sure to think of each as part of a larger fabric of poems. Compare the different rhythmic effects Blake achieves regarding the same subject (the two views of the chimney sweep, the two views of a Holy Thursday) or of paired subjects (the lamb and the tiger). You'll find that any discussion of meaning or theme in these poems requires attention to rhythm and sounds (and perhaps sights too—see Blake's illustration for "A Poison Tree" in chapter 17).

One shouldn't be too quick to simply divide innocence from experience in Blake's poetry. The difference is finally a matter of perspective: there is, after all, profound and terrible experience in poems of innocence (suffering children, repressive authority figures, and so on). The tension between the "contrary states" often exists within a single poem. Such complexity is very much a part of James Baldwin's classic story "Sonny's Blues." Baldwin gives us a narrator who might seem "innocent" in comparison to the brother whose story he tells. But as we get into the story, the word *innocent* grows complex. Does it mean "good" in comparison to the "bad"? Or does Baldwin suggest that the narrator's innocence is a way to mask pain and suffering—to deny feelings? Is it possible that the brother who experiences so much trouble is more innocent in the headlong way he seeks to live through his art? And that art, of course, is music. Baldwin builds his story to a climax that plays out in context of the journey Sonny takes with his band. The narrator says he knows that "not many people ever really hear" music. Only on occasion do sounds touch us powerfully. The narrator also believes that the musician hears, creates, struggles with, and achieves something deeper and more lasting. As you read the story, think of the meaning of the rhythmic dialogue that goes on between Sonny and the bass player at the close of the story.

The ringing of bells that opens Ursula K. Le Guin's "The Ones Who Walk Away from Omelas" sounds the rhythmic equivalent of celebration, of festival, of joy. Le Guin invites readers to take a participatory role in the celebration. Indeed, she wants readers to help create a fantasy world of happiness. But once we've had time to invest some thought and feeling in our ideal of happiness, she turns to a very different sort of description that comes with no bells, no joyous sounds. As you read this story, consider how Le Guin's "contrary states of the human soul" compare to those projected in Blake's poems. And consider too how she meshes the rhythms of her prose with thematic effects, much as Blake's poetry fuses meaning and sound.

In *Topdog/Underdog*, Suzan Lori-Parks gives us a story of two brothers that prompts another comparison. Like James Baldwin's "Sonny's Blues," *Topdog/Underdog* puts specific, individual questions about innocence and experience in context of a rich, painful, and complicated history. These brothers seem condemned to act within and act out a terrible, repetitive dynamic that has been shaped by past collective experience—an enormous haunting national tragedy. The black man named Lincoln who puts on white face to play Lincoln at the local boardwalk comes home to the brother named Booth who wants desperately to be Lincoln (the former king of a shell game who is trying to go straight). If that sounds confusing, it is—sort of. Once you get into the play, you find it develops a powerful logic that moves purposefully to the end. You'll also see how the rhythms of the shell game (rhythms intended to disrupt attention and keep people from seeing accurately) are integrated into the texture of the whole play.

FICTION

James Baldwin (1924–1987)

James Baldwin was born in Harlem, New York. One of nine children, he was profoundly influenced by his father, a preacher and strict, demanding man who was eventually institutionalized for mental illness. Soon after graduating from high school, Baldwin determined to become a professional writer. Discouraged by the racial climate in the United States, he moved to France, where he experienced a creative flowering. Gaining fame as both a novelist and essayist, he was soon recognized as one of the most perceptive observers and critics of America and its racial discontents. Much of his work concerns a search for identity and an attempt to reconcile apparently conflicting elements—black/white, heterosexual/homosexual, American/European. Among his best-known works are the novel *Go Tell It on the Mountain* and the book-length essay *The Fire Next Time.*

Sonny's Blues (1957)

I read about it in the paper, in the subway, on my way to work. I read it, and I couldn't believe it, and I read it again. Then perhaps I just stared at it, at the newsprint spelling out his name, spelling out the story. I stared at it in the swinging lights of the subway car, and in the faces and bodies of the people, and in my own face, trapped in the darkness which roared outside.

It was not to be believed and I kept telling myself that, as I walked from the subway station to the high school. And at the same time I couldn't doubt it. I was scared, scared for Sonny. He became real to me again. A great block of ice got settled in my belly and kept melting there slowly all day long, while I taught my classes algebra. It was a special kind of ice. It kept melting, sending trickles of ice water all up and down my veins, but it never got less. Sometimes it hardened and seemed to expand until I felt my guts were going to come spilling out or that I was going to choke or scream. This would always be at a moment when I was remembering some specific thing Sonny had once said or done.

When he was about as old as the boys in my classes his face had been bright and open, there was a lot of copper in it; and he'd had wonderfully direct brown eyes, and great gentleness and privacy. I wondered what he looked like now. He had been picked up, the evening before, in a raid on an apartment downtown, for peddling and using heroin.

I couldn't believe it: but what I mean by that is that I couldn't find any room for it anywhere inside me. I had kept it outside me for a long time. I hadn't wanted to know. I had had suspicions, but I didn't name them, I kept putting them away. I told myself that Sonny was wild, but he wasn't crazy. And he'd always been a good boy, he hadn't ever turned hard or evil or disrespectful, the way kids can, so quick, so quick, especially in Harlem. I didn't want to believe that I'd ever see my brother going down, coming to nothing, all that light in his face gone out, in the condition I'd already seen so many others. Yet it had happened and here I was, talking about algebra to a lot of boys who might, every one of them for all I knew, be popping off needles every time they went to the head. Maybe it did more for them than algebra could.

I was sure that the first time Sonny had ever had horse, he couldn't have been much older than these boys were now. These boys, now, were living as we'd been living then, they were growing up with a rush and their heads bumped abruptly against the low ceiling of their actual possibilities. They were filled with rage. All they really knew were two darknesses, the darkness of their lives, which was now closing in on them, and the darkness of the movies, which had blinded them to that other darkness, and in which they now, vindictively, dreamed, at once more together than they were at any other time, and more alone.

When the last bell rang, the last class ended, I let out my breath. It seemed I'd been holding it for all that time. My clothes were wet—I may have looked as though I'd been sitting in a steam bath, all dressed up, all afternoon. I sat alone in the classroom a long time. I listened to the boys outside, downstairs, shouting and cursing and laughing. Their laughter struck me for perhaps the first time. It was not the joyous laughter which—God knows why—one associates with children. It was mocking and insular, its intent was to denigrate. It was disenchanted, and in this, also, lay the authority of their curses. Perhaps I was listening to them because I was thinking about my brother and in them I heard my brother. And myself.

One boy was whistling a tune, at once very complicated and very simple, it seemed to be pouring out of him as though he were a bird, and it sounded very cool and moving through all that harsh, bright air, only just holding its own through all those other sounds.

I stood up and walked over to the window and looked down into the courtyard. It was the beginning of the spring and the sap was rising in the boys. A teacher passed through them every now and again, quickly, as though he or she couldn't wait to get out of that courtyard, to get those boys out of their sight and off their minds. I started collecting my stuff. I thought I'd better get home and talk to Isabel.

The courtyard was almost deserted by the time I got downstairs. I saw this boy standing in the shadow of a doorway, looking just like Sonny. I almost called his name. Then I saw that it wasn't Sonny, but somebody we used to know, a boy from around our block. He'd been Sonny's friend. He'd never been mine, having been too young for me, and, anyway, I'd never liked him. And now, even though he was a grown-up man, he still hung around that block, still spent hours on the street corners, was always high and raggy. I used to run into him from time to time and he'd often work around to asking me for a quarter or fifty cents. He always had some real good excuse, too, and I always gave it to him. I don't know why.

But now, abruptly, I hated him. I couldn't stand the way he looked at   10
me, partly like a dog, partly like a cunning child. I wanted to ask him what the hell he was doing in the school courtyard.

He sort of shuffled over to me, and he said, "I see you got the papers. So you already know about it."

"You mean about Sonny? Yes, I already know about it. How come they didn't get you?"

He grinned. It made him repulsive and it also brought to mind what he'd looked like as a kid. "I wasn't there. I stay away from them people."

"Good for you." I offered him a cigarette and I watched him through the smoke. "You come all the way down here just to tell me about Sonny?"

"That's right." He was sort of shaking his head and his eyes looked   15
strange, as though they were about to cross. The bright sun deadened his damp dark brown skin and it made his eyes look yellow and showed up the dirt in his kinked hair. He smelled funky. I moved a little away from him and I said, "Well, thanks. But I already know about it and I got to get home."

"I'll walk you a little ways," he said. We started walking. There were a couple of kids still loitering in the courtyard and one of them said goodnight to me and looked strangely at the boy beside me.

"What're you going to do?" he asked me. "I mean, about Sonny?"

"Look. I haven't seen Sonny for over a year, I'm not sure I'm going to do anything. Anyway, what the hell *can* I do?"

"That's right," he said quickly, "ain't nothing you can do. Can't much help old Sonny no more, I guess."

It was what I was thinking and so it seemed to me he had no right to   20
say it.

"I'm surprised at Sonny, though," he went on—he had a funny way of talking, he looked straight ahead as though he were talking to himself— "I thought Sonny was a smart boy, I thought he was too smart to get hung."

"I guess he thought so too," I said sharply, "and that's how he got hung. And how about you? You're pretty goddamn smart, I bet."

Then he looked directly at me, just for a minute. "I ain't smart," he said. "If I was smart, I'd have reached for a pistol a long time ago."

"Look. Don't tell *me* your sad story, if it was up to me, I'd give you one." Then I felt guilty—guilty, probably, for never having supposed that the poor bastard *had* a story of his own, much less a sad one, and I asked, quickly, "What's going to happen to him now?"

He didn't answer this. He was off by himself some place.

"Funny thing," he said, and from his tone we might have been discussing the quickest way to get to Brooklyn, "when I saw the papers this morning, the first thing I asked myself was if I had anything to do with it. I felt sort of responsible."

I began to listen more carefully. The subway station was on the corner, just before us, and I stopped. He stopped, too. We were in front of a bar and he ducked slightly, peering in, but whoever he was looking for didn't seem to be there. The juke box was blasting away with something black and bouncy and I half watched the barmaid as she danced her way from the juke box to her place behind the bar. And I watched her face as she laughingly responded to something someone said to her, still keeping time to the music. When she smiled one saw the little girl, one sensed the doomed, still-struggling woman beneath the battered face of the semi-whore.

"I never *give* Sonny nothing," the boy said finally, "but a long time ago I come to school high and Sonny asked me how it felt." He paused, I couldn't bear to watch him, I watched the barmaid, and I listened to the music which seemed to be causing the pavement to shake. "I told him it felt great." The music stopped, the barmaid paused and watched the juke box until the music began again. "It did."

All this was carrying me some place I didn't want to go. I certainly didn't want to know how it felt. It filled everything, the people, the houses, the music, the dark, quicksilver barmaid, with menace; and this menace was their reality.

"What's going to happen to him now?" I asked again.

"They'll send him away some place and they'll try to cure him." He shook his head. "Maybe he'll even think he's kicked the habit. Then they'll let him loose"—he gestured, throwing his cigarette into the gutter. "That's all."

"What do you mean, that's *all*?"

But I knew what he meant.

"I *mean*, that's *all*." He turned his head and looked at me, pulling down the corners of his mouth. "Don't you know what I mean?" he asked, softly.

"How the hell *would* I know what you mean?" I almost whispered it, I 35 don't know why.

"That's right," he said to the air, "how would *he* know what I mean?" He turned toward me again, patient and calm, and yet I somehow felt him shaking, shaking as though he were going to fall apart. I felt that ice in my guts again, the dread I'd felt all afternoon; and again I watched the barmaid, moving about the bar, washing glasses, and singing. "Listen. They'll let him out and then it'll just start all over again. That's what I mean."

"You mean—they'll let him out. And then he'll just start working his way back in again. You mean he'll never kick the habit. Is that what you mean?"

"That's right," he said, cheerfully. "*You* see what I mean."

"Tell me," I said at last, "why does he want to die? He must want to die, he's killing himself, why does he want to die?"

He looked at me in surprise. He licked his lips. "He don't want to die. 40 He wants to live. Don't nobody want to die, ever."

Then I wanted to ask him—too many things. He could not have answered, or if he had, I could not have borne the answers. I started walking. "Well, I guess it's none of my business."

"It's going to be rough on old Sonny," he said. We reached the subway station.

"This is your station?" he asked. I nodded. I took one step down. "Damn!" he said, suddenly. I looked up at him. He grinned again. "Damn it if I didn't leave all my money home. You ain't got a dollar on you, have you? Just for a couple of days, is all."

All at once something inside gave and threatened to come pouring out of me. I didn't hate him any more. I felt that in another moment I'd start crying like a child.

"Sure," I said. "Don't sweat." I looked in my wallet and didn't have a 45 dollar, I only had a five. "Here," I said. "That hold you?"

He didn't look at it—he didn't want to look at it. A terrible, closed look came over his face, as though he were keeping the number on the bill a secret from him and me. "Thanks," he said, and now he was dying to see me go. "Don't worry about Sonny. Maybe I'll write him or something."

"Sure," I said. "You do that. So long."

"Be seeing you," he said. I went on down the steps.

And I didn't write Sonny or send him anything for a long time. When I finally did, it was just after my little girl died, and he wrote me back a letter which made me feel like a bastard.

Here's what he said: 50

Dear brother,

You don't know how much I needed to hear from you. I wanted to write you many a time but I dug how much I must have hurt you and so I didn't write. But now I feel like a man who's been trying to climb up out of some deep, real deep and funky hole and just saw the sun up there, outside. I got to get outside.

I can't tell you much about how I got here. I mean I don't know how to tell you. I guess I was afraid of something or I was trying to escape from something and you know I have never been very strong in the head (smile). I'm glad Mama and Daddy are dead and can't see what's happened to their son and I swear if I'd known what I was doing I would never have hurt you so, you and a lot of other fine people who were nice to me and who believed in me.

I don't want you to think it had anything to do with me being a musician. It's more than that. Or maybe less than that. I can't get anything straight in my head down here and I try not to think about what's going to happen to me when I get outside again. Sometime I think I'm going to flip and *never* get outside and sometime I think I'll come straight back. I tell you one thing, though, I'd rather blow my brains out than go through this again. But that's what they all say, so they tell me. If I tell you when I'm coming to New York and if you could meet me, I sure would appreciate it. Give my love to Isabel and the kids and I was sure sorry to hear about little Gracie. I wish I could be like Mama and say the Lord's will be done, but I don't know it seems to me that trouble is the one thing that never does get stopped and I don't know what good it does to blame it on the Lord. But maybe it does some good if you believe it.

Your brother,
Sonny

Then I kept in constant touch with him and I sent him whatever I could and I went to meet him when he came back to New York. When I saw him many things I thought I had forgotten came flooding back to me. This was because I had begun, finally, to wonder about Sonny, about the life that Sonny lived inside. This life, whatever it was, had made him older and thinner and it had deepened the distant stillness in which he had always moved. He looked very unlike my baby brother. Yet, when he smiled, when we shook hands, the baby brother I'd never known looked out from the depths of his private life, like an animal waiting to be coaxed into the light.

"How you been keeping?" he asked me.

"All right. And you?"

"Just fine." He was smiling all over his face. "It's good to see you again."

"It's good to see you."   55

The seven years' difference in our ages lay between us like a chasm: I wondered if these years would ever operate between us as a bridge. I was remembering, and it made it hard to catch my breath, that I had been there when he was born; and I had heard the first words he had ever spoken. When he started to walk, he walked from our mother straight to me. I caught him just before he fell when he took the first steps he ever took in this world.

"How's Isabel?"

"Just fine. She's dying to see you."

"And the boys?"

"They're fine, too. They're anxious to see their uncle."   60

"Oh, come on. You know they don't remember me."

"Are you kidding? Of course they remember you."

He grinned again. We got into a taxi. We had a lot to say to each other, far too much to know how to begin.

As the taxi began to move, I asked, "You still want to go to India?"

He laughed. "You still remember that. Hell, no. This place is Indian   65 enough for me."

"It used to belong to them," I said.

And he laughed again. "They damn sure knew what they were doing when they got rid of it."

Years ago, when he was around fourteen, he'd been all hipped on the idea of going to India. He read books about people sitting on rocks, naked, in all kinds of weather, but mostly bad, naturally, and walking barefoot through hot coals and arriving at wisdom. I used to say that it sounded to me as though they were getting away from wisdom as fast as they could. I think he sort of looked down on me for that.

"Do you mind," he asked, "if we have the driver drive alongside the park? On the west side—I haven't seen the city in so long."

"Of course not," I said. I was afraid that I might sound as though I were   70 humoring him, but I hoped he wouldn't take it that way.

So we drove along, between the green of the park and the stony, lifeless elegance of hotels and apartment buildings, toward the vivid, killing streets of our childhood. These streets hadn't changed, though housing projects jutted up out of them now like rocks in the middle of a boiling sea. Most of the houses in which we had grown up had vanished, as had the stores from which we had stolen, the basements in which we had first tried sex, the rooftops from which we had hurled tin cans and bricks. But houses exactly like the houses of our past yet dominated the landscape, boys exactly like the boys we once had been found themselves smothering in these houses, came down into the streets for light and air and found themselves encircled by disaster. Some escaped the trap, most didn't. Those who got out always left something of themselves behind, as some animals amputate a leg and leave it in the trap. It might be said, perhaps, that I had escaped, after all, I was a school teacher; or that Sonny had, he hadn't lived in Harlem for years. Yet, as the cab moved uptown through streets which seemed, with a rush, to darken with dark people, and as I covertly studied Sonny's face, it came to me that what we both were seeking through our separate cab windows was that part of ourselves which had been left behind. It's always at the hour of trouble and confrontation that the missing member aches.

We hit 110th Street and started rolling up Lenox Avenue. And I'd known this avenue all my life, but it seemed to me again, as it had seemed on the day I'd first heard about Sonny's trouble, filled with a hidden menace which was its very breath of life.

"We almost there," said Sonny.

"Almost." We were both too nervous to say anything more.

We live in a housing project. It hasn't been up long. A few days after it was up it seemed uninhabitably new, now, of course, it's already rundown. It looks like a parody of the good, clean, faceless life—God knows the people who live in it do their best to make it a parody. The beat-looking grass lying around isn't enough to make their lives green, the hedges will never hold out the streets, and they know it. The big windows fool no one, they aren't big enough to make space out of no space. They don't bother with the windows, they watch the TV screen instead. The playground is most popular with the children who don't play at jacks, or skip rope, or roller skate, or swing, and they can be found in it after dark. We moved in partly because it's not too far from where I teach, and partly for the kids; but it's really just like the houses in which Sonny and I grew up. The same things happen, they'll have the same things to remember. The moment Sonny and I started into the house I had the feeling that I was simply bringing him back into the danger he had almost died trying to escape.

Sonny has never been talkative. So I don't know why I was sure he'd be dying to talk to me when supper was over the first night. Everything went fine, the oldest boy remembered him, and the youngest boy liked him, and Sonny had remembered to bring something for each of them; and Isabel, who is really much nicer than I am, more open and giving, had gone to a lot of trouble about dinner and was genuinely glad to see him. And she's always been able to tease Sonny in a way that I haven't. It was nice to see her face so vivid again and to hear her laugh and watch her make Sonny laugh. She wasn't, or, anyway, she didn't seem to be, at all uneasy or embarrassed. She chatted as though there were no subject which had to be avoided and she got Sonny past his first, faint stiffness. And thank God she was there, for I was filled with that icy dread again. Everything I did seemed awkward to me, and everything I said sounded freighted with hidden meaning. I was trying to remember everything I'd heard about dope addiction and I couldn't help watching Sonny for signs. I wasn't doing it out of malice. I was trying to find out something about my brother. I was dying to hear him tell me he was safe.

"Safe!" my father grunted, whenever Mama suggested trying to move to a neighborhood which might be safer for children. "Safe, hell! Ain't no place safe for kids, nor nobody."

He always went on like this, but he wasn't, ever, really as bad as he sounded, not even on weekends, when he got drunk. As a matter of fact, he was always on the lookout for "something a little better," but he died before he found it. He died suddenly, during a drunken weekend in the middle of the war, when Sonny was fifteen. He and Sonny hadn't ever got on too well. And this was partly because Sonny was the apple of his father's eye. It was because he loved Sonny so much and was frightened for him, that he was always fighting with him. It doesn't do any good to fight with Sonny. Sonny just moves back, inside himself, where he can't be reached. But the principal reason that they never hit it off is that they were so much alike. Daddy was big and rough and loud-talking, just the opposite of Sonny, but they both had—that same privacy.

Mama tried to tell me something about this, just after Daddy died. I was home on leave from the army.

This was the last time I ever saw my mother alive. Just the same, this picture gets all mixed up in my mind with pictures I had of her when she was younger. The way I always see her is the way she used to be on a Sunday afternoon, say, when the old folks were talking after the big Sunday dinner. I always see her wearing pale blue. She'd be sitting on the sofa. And my father would be sitting in the easy chair, not far from her. And the living room would be full of church folks and relatives. There they sit, in chairs all around the living room, and the night is creeping up outside, but nobody knows it yet. You can see the darkness growing against the windowpanes and you hear the street noises every now and again, or maybe the jangling beat of a tambourine from one of the churches close by, but it's real quiet in the room. For a moment nobody's talking, but every face looks darkening, like the sky outside. And my mother rocks a little from the waist, and my father's eyes are closed. Everyone is looking at something a child can't see. For a minute they've forgotten the children. Maybe a kid is lying on the rug, half asleep. Maybe somebody's got a kid in his lap and is absentmindedly stroking the kid's head. Maybe there's a kid, quiet and big-eyed, curled up in a big chair in the corner. The silence, the darkness coming, and the darkness in the faces frighten the child obscurely. He hopes that the hand which strokes his forehead will never stop—will never die. He

80

hopes that there will never come a time when the old folks won't be sitting around the living room, talking about where they've come from, and what they've seen, and what's happened to them and their kinfolk.

But something deep and watchful in the child knows that this is bound to end, is already ending. In a moment someone will get up and turn on the light. Then the old folks will remember the children and they won't talk any more that day. And when light fills the room, the child is filled with darkness. He knows that every time this happens he's moved just a little closer to that darkness outside. The darkness outside is what the old folks have been talking about. It's what they've come from. It's what they endure. The child knows that they won't talk any more because if he knows too much about what's happened to *them*, he'll know too much too soon, about what's going to happen to *him*.

The last time I talked to my mother, I remember I was restless. I wanted to get out and see Isabel. We weren't married then and we had a lot to straighten out between us.

There Mama sat, in black, by the window. She was humming an old church song, *Lord, you brought me from a long ways off*. Sonny was out somewhere. Mama kept watching the streets.

"I don't know," she said, "if I'll ever see you again, after you go off from here. But I hope you'll remember the things I tried to teach you."

"Don't talk like that," I said, and smiled. "You'll be here a long time yet."

She smiled, too, but she said nothing. She was quiet for a long time. And I said, "Mama, don't you worry about nothing. I'll be writing all the time, and you be getting the checks...."

"I want to talk to you about your brother," she said, suddenly. "If anything happens to me he ain't going to have nobody to look out for him."

"Mama," I said, "ain't nothing going to happen to you *or* Sonny. Sonny's all right. He's a good boy and he's got good sense."

"It ain't a question of his being a good boy," Mama said, "nor of his having good sense. It ain't only the bad ones, nor yet the dumb ones that gets sucked under." She stopped, looking at me. "Your Daddy once had a brother," she said, and she smiled in a way that made me feel she was in pain. "You didn't never know that, did you?"

"No," I said, "I never knew that," and I watched her face.

"Oh, yes," she said, "your Daddy had a brother." She looked out of the window again. "I know you never saw your Daddy cry. But *I* did—many a time, through all these years."

I asked her, "What happened to his brother? How come nobody's ever talked about him?"

This was the first time I ever saw my mother look old.

"His brother got killed," she said, "when he was just a little younger than you are now. I knew him. He was a fine boy. He was maybe a little full of the devil, but he didn't mean nobody no harm."

Then she stopped and the room was silent, exactly as it had sometimes been on those Sunday afternoons. Mama kept looking out into the streets.

95

"He used to have a job in the mill," she said, "and, like all young folks, he just liked to perform on Saturday nights. Saturday nights, him and your father would drift around to different places, go to dances and things like that, or just sit around with people they knew, and your father's brother would sing, he had a fine voice, and play along with himself on his guitar. Well, this particular Saturday night, him and your father was coming home from some place, and they were both a little drunk and there was a moon that night, it was bright like day. Your father's brother was feeling kind of good, and he was whistling to himself, and he had his guitar slung over his shoulder. They was coming down a hill and beneath them was a road that turned off from the highway. Well, your father's brother, being always kind of frisky, decided to run down this hill, and he did, with that guitar banging and clanging behind him, and he ran across the road, and he was making water behind a tree. And your father was sort of amused at him and he was still coming down the hill, kind of slow. Then he heard a car motor and that same minute his brother stepped from behind the tree, into the road, in the moonlight. And he started to cross the road. And your father started to run down the hill, he says he don't know why. This car was full of white men. They was all drunk, and when they seen your father's brother they let out a great whoop and holler and they aimed the car straight at him. They was having fun, they just wanted to scare him, the way they do sometimes, you know. But they was drunk. And I guess the boy, being drunk, too, and scared, kind of lost his head. By the time he jumped it was too late. Your father says he heard his brother scream when the car rolled over him, and he heard the wood of that guitar when it give, and he heard them strings go flying, and he heard them white men shouting, and the car kept on a-going and it ain't stopped till this day. And, time your father got down the hill, his brother weren't nothing but blood and pulp."

Tears were gleaming on my mother's face. There wasn't anything I could say.

"He never mentioned it," she said, "because I never let him mention it before you children. Your Daddy was like a crazy man that night and for many a night thereafter. He says he never in his life seen anything as dark as that road after the lights of that car had gone away. Weren't nothing, weren't nobody on that road, just your Daddy and his brother and that busted guitar. Oh, yes. Your Daddy never did really get right again. Till the day he died he weren't sure but that every white man he saw was the man that killed his brother."

She stopped and took out her handkerchief and dried her eyes and looked at me.

"I ain't telling you all this," she said, "to make you scared or bitter or to make you hate nobody. I'm telling you this because you got a brother. And the world ain't changed."

I guess I didn't want to believe this. I guess she saw this in my face. She turned away from me, toward the window again, searching those streets.

"But I praise my Redeemer," she said at last, "that He called your Daddy home before me. I ain't saying it to throw no flowers at myself, but, I declare, it keeps me from feeling too cast down to know I helped your father get safely through this world. Your father always acted like he was the roughest, strongest man on earth. And everybody took him to be like that. But if he hadn't had me there—to see his tears!"

She was crying again. Still, I couldn't move. I said, "Lord, Lord, Mama, I didn't know it was like that."

"Oh, honey," she said, "there's a lot that you don't know. But you are going to find out." She stood up from the window and came over to me. "You got to hold on to your brother," she said, "and don't let him fall, no matter what it looks like is happening to him and no matter how evil you gets with him. You going to be evil with him many a time. But don't you forget what I told you, you hear?"

"I won't forget," I said. "Don't you worry, I won't forget. I won't let nothing happen to Sonny."

My mother smiled as though she was amused at something she saw in my face. Then, "You may not be able to stop nothing from happening. But you got to let him know you's *there*."

Two days later I was married, and then I was gone. And I had a lot of things on my mind and I pretty well forgot my promise to Mama until I got shipped home on a special furlough for her funeral.

And, after the funeral, with just Sonny and me alone in the empty kitchen, I tried to find out something about him.

"What do you want to do?" I asked him.

"I'm going to be a musician," he said.

For he had graduated, in the time I had been away, from dancing to the juke box to finding out who was playing what, and what they were doing with it, and he had bought himself a set of drums.

"You mean, you want to be a drummer?" I somehow had the feeling that being a drummer might be all right for other people but not for my brother Sonny.

"I don't think," he said, looking at me very gravely, "that I'll ever be a good drummer. But I think I can play a piano."

I frowned. I'd never played the role of the oldest brother quite so seriously before, had scarcely ever, in fact, *asked* Sonny a damn thing. I sensed myself in the presence of something I didn't really know how to handle, didn't understand. So I made my frown a little deeper as I asked: "What kind of musician do you want to be?"

He grinned. "How many kinds do you think there are?"   115

"Be *serious*," I said.

He laughed, throwing his head back, and then looked at me. "I *am* serious."

"Well, then, for Christ's sake, stop kidding around and answer a serious question. I mean, do you want to be a concert pianist, you want to play classical music and all that, or—or what?" Long before I finished he was laughing again. "For Christ's *sake*, Sonny!"

He sobered, but with difficulty. "I'm sorry. But you sound so—*scared!*" and he was off again.

"Well, you may think it's funny now, baby, but it's not going to be so   120
funny when you have to make your living at it, let me tell you *that*." I was furious because I knew he was laughing at me and I didn't know why.

"No," he said, very sober now, and afraid, perhaps, that he'd hurt me, "I don't want to be a classical pianist. That isn't what interests me. I mean"—he paused, looking hard at me, as though his eyes would help me to understand, and then gestured helplessly, as though perhaps his hand would help—"I mean, I'll have a lot of studying to do, and I'll have to study *everything*, but, I mean, I want to play *with*—jazz musicians." He stopped. "I want to play jazz," he said.

Well, the word had never before sounded as heavy, as real, as it sounded that afternoon in Sonny's mouth. I just looked at him and I was probably frowning a real frown by this time. I simply couldn't see why on earth he'd want to spend his time hanging around nightclubs, clowning around on bandstands, while people pushed each other around a dance floor. It seemed—beneath him, somehow. I had never thought about it before, had never been forced to, but I suppose I had always put jazz musicians in a class with what Daddy called "good-time people."

"Are you *serious*?"

"Hell, *yes*, I'm serious."

He looked more helpless than ever, and annoyed, and deeply hurt.   125

I suggested, helpfully: "You mean—like Louis Armstrong?"

His face closed as though I'd struck him. "No. I'm not talking about none of that old-time, down home crap."

"Well, look, Sonny, I'm sorry, don't get mad. I just don't altogether get it, that's all. Name somebody—you know, a jazz musician you admire."

"Bird."

"Who?"   130

"Bird! Charlie Parker! Don't they teach you nothing in the goddamn army?"

I lit a cigarette. I was surprised and then a little amused to discover that I was trembling. "I've been out of touch," I said. "You'll have to be patient with me. Now. Who's this Parker character?"

"He's just one of the greatest jazz musicians alive," said Sonny, sullenly, his hands in his pockets, his back to me. "Maybe *the* greatest," he added, bitterly, "that's probably why *you* never heard of him."

"All right," I said, "I'm ignorant. I'm sorry. I'll go out and buy all the cat's records right away, all right?"

"It don't," said Sonny, with dignity, "make any difference to me. I don't care what you listen to. Don't do me no favors."

I was beginning to realize that I'd never seen him so upset before. With another part of my mind I was thinking that this would probably turn out to be one of those things kids go through and that I shouldn't make it seem important by pushing it too hard. Still, I didn't think it would do any harm to ask: "Doesn't all this take a lot of time? Can you make a living at it?"

He turned back to me and half leaned, half sat, on the kitchen table. "Everything takes time," he said, "and—well, yes, sure, I can make a living at it. But what I don't seem to be able to make you understand is that it's the only thing I want to do."

"Well, Sonny," I said gently, "you know people can't always do exactly what they *want* to do—"

"*No*, I don't know that," said Sonny, surprising me. "I think people *ought* to do what they want to do, what else are they alive for?"

"You getting to be a big boy," I said desperately, "it's time you started thinking about your future."

"I'm thinking about my future," said Sonny, grimly. "I think about it all the time."

I gave up. I decided, if he didn't change his mind, that we could always talk about it later. "In the meantime," I said, "you got to finish school." We had already decided that he'd have to move in with Isabel and her folks. I knew this wasn't the ideal arrangement because Isabel's folks are inclined to be dicty and they hadn't especially wanted Isabel to marry me. But I didn't know what else to do. "And we have to get you fixed up at Isabel's."

There was a long silence. He moved from the kitchen table to the window. "That's a terrible idea. You know it yourself."

"Do you have a *better* idea?"

He just walked up and down the kitchen for a minute. He was as tall as I was. He had started to shave. I suddenly had the feeling that I didn't know him at all.

He stopped at the kitchen table and picked up my cigarettes. Looking at me with a kind of mocking, amused defiance, he put one between his lips. "You mind?"

"You smoking already?"

He lit the cigarette and nodded, watching me through the smoke. "I just wanted to see if I'd have the courage to smoke in front of you." He grinned and blew a great cloud of smoke to the ceiling. "It was easy." He looked at my face. "Come on, now. I bet you was smoking at my age, tell the truth."

I didn't say anything but the truth was on my face, and he laughed. But now there was something very strained in his laugh. "Sure. And I bet that ain't all you was doing."

He was frightening me a little. "Cut the crap," I said. "We already de-   150
cided that you was going to go and live at Isabel's. Now what's got into you all of a sudden?"

"*You* decided it," he pointed out. "*I* didn't decide nothing." He stopped in front of me, leaning against the stove, arms loosely folded. "Look, brother. I don't want to stay in Harlem no more, I really don't." He was very earnest. He looked at me, then over toward the kitchen window. There was some-thing in his eyes I'd never seen before, some thoughtfulness, some worry all his own. He rubbed the muscle of one arm. "It's time I was getting out of here."

"Where do you want to *go,* Sonny?"

"I want to join the army. Or the navy, I don't care. If I say I'm old enough, they'll believe me."

Then I got mad. It was because I was so scared. "You must be crazy. You goddamn fool, what the hell do you want to go and join the *army* for?"

"I just told you. To get out of Harlem."   155

"Sonny, you haven't even finished *school.* And if you really want to be a musician, how do you expect to study if you're in the *army?*"

He looked at me, trapped, and in anguish. "There's ways. I might be able to work out some kind of deal. Anyway, I'll have the G.I. Bill when I come out."

"*If* you come out." We stared at each other. "Sonny, please. Be reason-able. I know the setup is far from perfect. But we got to do the best we can."

"I ain't learning nothing in school," he said. "Even when I go." He turned away from me and opened the window and threw his cigarette out into the narrow alley. I watched his back. "At least, I ain't learning nothing you'd want me to learn." He slammed the window so hard I thought the glass would fly out, and turned back to me. "And I'm sick of the stink of these garbage cans!"

"Sonny," I said, "I know how you feel. But if you don't finish school   160
now, you're going to be sorry later that you didn't." I grabbed him by the shoulders. "And you only got another year. It ain't so bad. And I'll come back and I swear I'll help you do *whatever* you want to do. Just try to put up with it till I come back. Will you please do that? For me?"

He didn't answer and he wouldn't look at me.

"Sonny. You hear me?"

He pulled away. "I hear you. But you never hear anything *I* say."

I didn't know what to say to that. He looked out of the window and then back at me. "OK," he said, and sighed. "I'll try."

Then I said, trying to cheer him up a little, "They got a piano at Isabel's. You can practice on it."

And as a matter of fact, it did cheer him up for a minute. "That's right," he said to himself. "I forgot that." His face relaxed a little. But the worry, the thoughtfulness, played on it still, the way shadows play on a face which is staring into the fire.

But I thought I'd never hear the end of that piano. At first, Isabel would write me, saying how nice it was that Sonny was so serious about his music and how, as soon as he came in from school, or wherever he had been when he was supposed to be at school, he went straight to that piano and stayed there until suppertime. And, after supper, he went back to that piano and stayed there until everybody went to bed. He was at the piano all day Saturday and all day Sunday. Then he bought a record player and started playing records. He'd play one record over and over again, all day long sometimes, and he'd improvise along with it on the piano. Or he'd play one section of the record, one chord, one change, one progression, then he'd do it on the piano. Then back to the record. Then back to the piano.

Well, I really don't know how they stood it. Isabel finally confessed that it wasn't like living with a person at all, it was like living with sound. And the sound didn't make any sense to her, didn't make any sense to any of them—naturally. They began, in a way, to be afflicted by this presence that was living in their home. It was as though Sonny were some sort of god, or monster. He moved in an atmosphere which wasn't like theirs at all. They fed him and he ate, he washed himself, he walked in and out of their door; he certainly wasn't nasty or unpleasant or rude, Sonny isn't any of those things; but it was as though he were all wrapped up in some cloud, some fire, some vision all his own; and there wasn't any way to reach him.

At the same time, he wasn't really a man yet, he was still a child, and they had to watch out for him in all kinds of ways. They certainly couldn't throw him out. Neither did they dare to make a great scene about that piano because even they dimly sensed, as I sensed, from so many thousands of miles away, that Sonny was at that piano playing for his life.

But he hadn't been going to school. One day a letter came from the school board and Isabel's mother got it—there had, apparently, been other letters but Sonny had torn them up. This day, when Sonny came in, Isabel's mother showed him the letter and asked where he'd been spending his time. And she finally got it out of him that he'd been down in Greenwich Village, with musicians and other characters, in a white girl's apartment. And this scared her and she started to scream at him and what came up, once she began—though she denies it to this day—was what sacrifices they were making to give Sonny a decent home and how little he appreciated it.

Sonny didn't play the piano that day. By evening, Isabel's mother had calmed down but then there was the old man to deal with, and Isabel herself. Isabel says she did her best to be calm but she broke down and started crying. She says she just watched Sonny's face. She could tell, by watching him, what was happening with him. And what was happening was that they penetrated his cloud, they had reached him. Even if their fingers had been a thousand times more gentle than human fingers ever are, he could hardly help feeling that they had stripped him naked and were spitting on that nakedness. For he also had to see that his presence, that music, which was life or death to him, had been torture for them and that they had endured it, not at all for his sake, but only for mine. And Sonny couldn't take that. He can take it a little better today than he could then but he's still not very good at it and, frankly, I don't know anybody who is.

The silence of the next few days must have been louder than the sound of all the music ever played since time began. One morning, before she went to work, Isabel was in his room for something and she suddenly real-ized that all of his records were gone. And she knew for certain that he was gone. And he was. He went as far as the navy would carry him. He finally sent me a postcard from some place in Greece and that was the first I knew that Sonny was still alive. I didn't see him any more until we were both back in New York and the war had long been over.

He was a man by then, of course, but I wasn't willing to see it. He came by the house from time to time, but we fought almost every time we met. I didn't like the way he carried himself, loose and dreamlike all the time, and I didn't like his friends, and his music seemed to be merely an excuse for the life he led. It sounded just that weird and disordered.

Then we had a fight, a pretty awful fight, and I didn't see him for months. By and by I looked him up, where he was living, in a furnished room in the Village, and I tried to make it up. But there were lots of other people in the room and Sonny just lay on his bed, and he wouldn't come downstairs with me, and he treated these other people as though they were his family and I weren't. So I got mad and then he got mad, and then I told him that he might just as well be dead as live the way he was living. Then he stood up and he told me not to worry about him any more in life, that he *was* dead as far as I was concerned. Then he pushed me to the door and the other people looked on as though nothing were happening, and he slammed the door behind me. I stood in the hallway, staring at the door. I heard somebody laugh in the room and then the tears came to my eyes. I started down the steps, whistling to keep from crying, I kept whistling to myself, *You going to need me, baby, one of these cold, rainy days.*

I read about Sonny's trouble in the spring. Little Grace died in the fall. She was a beautiful little girl. But she only lived a little over two years. She died of polio and she suffered. She had a slight fever for a couple of days, but it didn't seem like anything and we just kept her in bed. And we would certainly have called the doctor, but the fever dropped, she seemed to be all right. So we thought it had just been a cold. Then, one day, she was up, playing, Isabel was in the kitchen fixing lunch for the two boys when they'd come in from school, and she heard Grace fall down in the living room. When you have a lot of children you don't always start running when one of them falls, unless they start screaming or something. And, this time, Gracie was quiet. Yet, Isabel says that when she heard that *thump* and then that silence, something happened to her to make her afraid. And she ran to the living room and there was little Grace on the floor, all twisted up, and the reason she hadn't screamed was that she couldn't get her breath. And when she did scream, it was the worst sound, Isabel says, that she'd ever heard in all her life, and she still hears it sometimes in her dreams. Isabel will sometimes wake me up with a low, moaning, strangling sound and I have to be quick to awaken her and hold her to me and where Isabel is weeping against me seems a mortal wound.

I think I may have written Sonny the very day that little Grace was buried. I was sitting in the living room in the dark, by myself, and I suddenly thought of Sonny. My trouble made his real.

One Saturday afternoon, when Sonny had been living with us, or anyway, been in our house, for nearly two weeks, I found myself wandering aimlessly about the living room, drinking from a can of beer, and trying to work up courage to search Sonny's room. He was out, he was usually out whenever I was home, and Isabel had taken the children to see their grandparents. Suddenly I was standing still in front of the living room window, watching Seventh Avenue. The idea of searching Sonny's room made me still. I scarcely dared to admit to myself what I'd be searching for. I didn't know what I'd do if I found it. Or if I didn't.

On the sidewalk across from me, near the entrance to a barbecue joint, some people were holding an old-fashioned revival meeting. The barbecue cook, wearing a dirty white apron, his conked hair reddish and metallic in the pale sun, and a cigarette between his lips, stood in the doorway, watching them. Kids and older people paused in their errands and stood there, along with some older men and a couple of very tough-looking women who watched everything that happened on the avenue, as though they owned it, or were maybe owned by it. Well, they were watching this, too. The revival was being carried on by three sisters in black, and a brother. All they had were their voices and their Bibles and a tambourine. The brother was testify-ing and while he testified two of the sisters stood together, seeming to say, amen, and the third sister walked around with the tambourine outstretched and a couple of people dropped coins into it. Then the brother's testimony ended and the sister who had been taking up the collection dumped the coins into her palm and transferred them to the pocket of her long black robe. Then she raised both hands, striking the tambourine against the air, and then against one hand, and she started to sing. And the two other sisters and the brother joined in.

It was strange, suddenly, to watch, though I had been seeing these meetings all my life. So, of course, had everybody else down there. Yet, they paused and watched and listened and I stood still at the window. "'*Tis the old ship of Zion*," they sang, and the sister with the tambourine kept a steady, jangling beat, "*it has rescued many a thousand!*" Not a soul under the sound of their voices was hearing this song for the first time, not one of them had been rescued. Nor had they seen much in the way of rescue work being done around them. Neither did they especially believe in the holiness of the three sisters and the brother, they knew too much about them, knew where they lived, and how. The woman with the tambourine, whose voice domi-nated the air, whose face was bright with joy, was divided by very little from the woman who stood watching her, a cigarette between her heavy, chapped lips, her hair a cuckoo's nest, her face scarred and swollen from many beat-ings, and her black eyes glittering like coal. Perhaps they both knew this, which was why, when, as rarely, they addressed each other, they addressed each other as Sister. As the singing filled the air the watching, listening faces underwent a change, the eyes focusing on something within; the music seemed to soothe a poison out of them; and time seemed, nearly, to fall away from the sullen, belligerent, battered faces, as though they were fleeing back to their first condition, while dreaming of their last. The barbecue cook half shook his head and smiled, and dropped his cigarette and disap-peared into his joint. A man fumbled in his pockets for change and stood holding it in his hand impatiently, as though he had just remembered a pressing appointment further up the avenue. He looked furious. Then I saw Sonny, standing on the edge of the crowd. He was carrying a wide, flat note-book with a green cover, and it made him look, from where I was standing, almost like a schoolboy. The coppery sun brought out the copper in his skin, he was very faintly smiling, standing very still. Then the singing stopped, the tambourine turned into a collection plate again. The furious man dropped in his coins and vanished, so did a couple of the women, and Sonny dropped some change in the plate, looking directly at the woman with a little smile. He started across the avenue, toward the house. He has a slow, loping walk, something like the way Harlem hipsters walk, only he's imposed on this his own half-beat. I had never really noticed it before.

I stayed at the window, both relieved and apprehensive. As Sonny disappeared from my sight, they began singing again. And they were still singing when his key turned in the lock.

"Hey," he said.

"Hey, yourself. You want some beer?"

"No. Well, maybe." But he came up to the window and stood beside me, looking out. "What a warm voice," he said.

They were singing *If I could only hear my mother pray again!*

"Yes," I said, "and she can sure beat that tambourine."

"But what a terrible song," he said, and laughed. He dropped his notebook on the sofa and disappeared into the kitchen. "Where's Isabel and the kids?"

"I think they went to see their grandparents. You hungry?"

"No." He came back into the living room with his can of beer. "You want to come some place with me tonight?"

I sensed, I don't know how, that I couldn't possibly say no. "Sure. Where?"

He sat down on the sofa and picked up his notebook and started leafing through it. "I'm going to sit in with some fellows in a joint in the Village."

"You mean, you're going to play, tonight?"

"That's right." He took a swallow of his beer and moved back to the window. He gave me a sidelong look. "If you can stand it."

"I'll try," I said.

He smiled to himself and we both watched as the meeting across the way broke up. The three sisters and the brother, heads bowed, were singing *God be with you till we meet again.* The faces around them were very quiet. Then the song ended. The small crowd dispersed. We watched the three women and the lone man walk slowly up the avenue.

"When she was singing before," said Sonny, abruptly, "her voice reminded me for a minute of what heroin feels like sometimes—when it's in your veins. It makes you feel sort of warm and cool at the same time. And distant. And—and sure." He sipped his beer, very deliberately not looking at me. I watched his face. "It makes you feel—in control. Sometimes you've got to have that feeling."

"Do you?" I sat down slowly in the easy chair.

"Sometimes." He went to the sofa and picked up his notebook again. "Some people do."

"In order," I asked, "to play?" And my voice was very ugly, full of contempt and anger.

"Well"—he looked at me with great, troubled eyes, as though, in fact, he hoped his eyes would tell me things he could never otherwise say— "they *think* so. And *if* they think so—!"

"And what do *you* think?" I asked.

He sat on the sofa and put his can of beer on the floor. "I don't know," he said, and I couldn't be sure if he were answering my question or pursuing his thoughts. His face didn't tell me. "It's not so much to *play*. It's to *stand* it, to be able to make it at all. On any level." He frowned and smiled: "In order to keep from shaking to pieces."

"But these friends of yours," I said, "they seem to shake themselves to pieces pretty goddamn fast."

"Maybe." He played with the notebook. And something told me that I should curb my tongue, that Sonny was doing his best to talk, that I should listen. "But of course you only know the ones that've gone to pieces. Some don't—or at least they haven't *yet* and that's just about all *any* of us can say." He paused. "And then there are some who just live, really, in hell, and they know it and they see what's happening and they go right on. I don't know." He sighed, dropped the notebook, folded his arms. "Some guys, you can tell from the way they play, they on something *all* the time. And you can see that, well, it makes something real for them. But of course," he picked up his beer from the floor and sipped it and put the can down again, "they *want* to, too, you've got to see that. Even some of them that say they don't—*some*, not all."

"And what about you?" I asked—I couldn't help it. "What about you? Do *you* want to?"

He stood up and walked to the window and I remained silent for a long time. Then he sighed. "Me," he said. Then: "While I was downstairs before, on my way here, listening to that woman sing, it struck me all of a sudden how much suffering she must have had to go through—to sing like that. It's *repulsive* to think you have to suffer that much."

I said: "But there's no way not to suffer—is there, Sonny?"

"I believe not," he said and smiled, "but that's never stopped anyone from trying. "He looked at me. "Has it?" I realized, with this mocking look, that there stood between us, forever, beyond the power of time or forgiveness, the fact that I had held silence—so long!—when he had needed human speech to help him. He turned back to the window. "No, there's no way not to suffer. But you try all kinds of ways to keep from drowning in it, to keep on top of it, and to make it seem—well, like *you*. Like you did something, all right, and now you're suffering for it. You know?" I said nothing. "Well you know," he said, impatiently, "why *do* people suffer? Maybe it's better to do something to give it a reason, *any* reason."

"But we just agreed," I said, "that there's no way not to suffer. Isn't it better, then, just to—take it?"

"But nobody just takes it," Sonny cried, "that's what I'm telling you! *Everybody* tries not to. You're just hung up on the *way* some people try—it's not *your* way!"

205

The hair on my face began to itch, my face felt wet. "That's not true," I said, "that's not true. I don't give a damn what other people do, I don't even care how they suffer. I just care how *you* suffer." And he looked at me. "Please believe me," I said, "I don't want to see you—die—trying not to suffer."

"I won't," he said flatly, "die trying not to suffer. At least, not any faster than anybody else."

"But there's no need," I said, trying to laugh, "is there? in killing your-self."

I wanted to say more, but I couldn't. I wanted to talk about will power and how life could be—well, beautiful. I wanted to say that it was all within; but was it? or, rather, wasn't that exactly the trouble? And I wanted to promise that I would never fail him again. But it would all have sounded—empty words and lies.

So I made the promise to myself and prayed that I would keep it.

"It's terrible sometimes, inside," he said, "that's what's the trouble. You walk these streets, black and funky and cold, and there's not really a living ass to talk to, and there's nothing shaking, and there's no way of getting it out—that storm inside. You can't talk it and you can't make love with it, and when you finally try to get with it and play it, you realize *nobody's* lis-tening. So *you've* got to listen. You got to find a way to listen."

And then he walked away from the window and sat on the sofa again, as though all the wind had suddenly been knocked out of him. "Sometimes you'll do *anything* to play, even cut your mother's throat." He laughed and looked at me. "Or your brother's." Then he sobered. "Or your own." Then: "Don't worry. I'm all right now and I think I'll *be* all right. But I can't for-get—where I've been. I don't mean just the physical place I've been, I mean where I've *been*. And *what* I've been."

"What have you been, Sonny?" I asked.

He smiled—but sat sideways on the sofa, his elbow resting on the back, his fingers playing with his mouth and chin, not looking at me. "I've been something I didn't recognize, didn't know I could be. Didn't know anybody could be." He stopped, looking inward, looking helplessly young, looking old. "I'm not talking about it now because I feel *guilty* or anything like that—maybe it would be better if I did, I don't know. Anyway, I can't really talk about it. Not to you, not to anybody," and now he turned and faced me. "Sometimes, you know, and it was actually when I was most *out* of the world, I felt that I was in it, that I was *with* it, really, and I could play or I didn't really have to *play*, it just came out of me, it was there. And I don't know how I played, thinking about it now, but I know I did awful things, those times, sometimes, to people. Or it wasn't that I *did* anything to them—it was that they weren't real." He picked up the beer can; it was empty; he rolled it between his palms: "And other times—well, I needed a fix, I needed to find a place to lean, I needed to clear a space to *listen*—and I couldn't find it, and I—went crazy, I did terrible things to *me*, I was terrible *for* me." He began pressing the beer can between his hands, I watched the metal begin to give. It glittered, as he played with it like a knife, and I was afraid he would cut himself, but I said nothing. "Oh well. I can never tell you. I was all by myself at the bottom of something, stinking and sweating and crying and shaking, and I smelled it, you know? *my* stink, and I thought I'd die if I couldn't get away from it and yet, all the same, I knew that everything I was doing was just locking me in with it. And I didn't know," he paused, still flattening the beer can, "I didn't know, I still *don't* know, something kept telling me that maybe it was good to smell your own stink, but I didn't think that *that* was what I'd been trying to do—and—who can stand it?" and he abruptly dropped the ruined beer can, looking at me with a small, still smile, and then rose, walking to the window as though it were the lodestone rock. I watched his face, he watched the avenue. "I couldn't tell you when Mama died—but the reason I wanted to leave Harlem so bad was to get away from drugs. And then, when I ran away, that's what I was running from—really. When I came back, nothing had changed, *I* hadn't changed, I was just—older." And he stopped, drumming with his fingers on the windowpane. The sun had vanished, soon darkness would fall. I watched his face. "It can come again," he said, almost as though speaking to himself. Then he turned to me. "It can come again," he repeated. "I just want you to know that."

"All right," I said, at last. "So it can come again. All right."

He smiled, but the smile was sorrowful. "I had to try to tell you," he said.   220

"Yes," I said. "I understand that."

"You're my brother," he said, looking straight at me, and not smiling at all.

"Yes," I repeated, "yes. I understand that."

He turned back to the window, looking out. "All that hatred down there," he said, "all that hatred and misery and love. It's a wonder it doesn't blow the avenue apart."

We went to the only nightclub on a short, dark street, downtown. We   225
squeezed through the narrow, chattering, jampacked bar to the entrance of the big room, where the bandstand was. And we stood there for a moment, for the lights were very dim in this room and we couldn't see. Then, "Hello, boy," said the voice and an enormous black man, much older than Sonny or myself, erupted out of all that atmospheric lighting and put an arm around Sonny's shoulder. "I been sitting right here," he said, "waiting for you."

He had a big voice, too, and heads in the darkness turned toward us.

Sonny grinned and pulled a little away, and said, "Creole, this is my brother. I told you about him."

Creole shook my hand. "I'm glad to meet you, son," he said, and it was clear that he was glad to meet me *there*, for Sonny's sake. And he smiled, "You got a real musician in *your* family," and he took his arm from Sonny's shoulder and slapped him, lightly, affectionately, with the back of his hand.

"Well. Now I've heard it all," said a voice behind us. This was another musician, and a friend of Sonny's, a coal-black, cheerful-looking man, built close to the ground. He immediately began confiding to me, at the top of his lungs, the most terrible things about Sonny, his teeth gleaming like a lighthouse and his laugh coming up out of him like the beginning of an earthquake. And it turned out that everyone at the bar knew Sonny, or almost everyone; some were musicians, working there, or nearby, or not working, some were simply hangers-on, and some were there to hear Sonny play. I was introduced to all of them and they were all very polite to me. Yet, it was clear that, for them, I was only Sonny's brother. Here, I was in Sonny's world. Or, rather: his kingdom. Here, it was not even a question that his veins bore royal blood.

They were going to play soon and Creole installed me, by myself, at a table in a dark corner. Then I watched them, Creole, and the little black man, and Sonny, and the others, while they horsed around, standing just below the bandstand. The light from the bandstand spilled just a little short of them and, watching them laughing and gesturing and moving about, I had the feeling that they, nevertheless, were being most careful not to step into that circle of light too suddenly; that if they moved into the light too suddenly, without thinking, they would perish in flame. Then, while I watched, one of them, the small black man, moved into the light and crossed the bandstand and started fooling around with his drums. Then— being funny and being, also, extremely ceremonious—Creole took Sonny by the arm and led him to the piano. A woman's voice called Sonny's name and a few hands started clapping. And Sonny, also being funny and being ceremonious, and so touched, I think, that he could have cried, but neither hiding it nor showing it, riding it like a man, grinned, and put both hands to his heart and bowed from the waist.

Creole then went to the bass fiddle and a lean, very bright-skinned brown man jumped up on the bandstand and picked up his horn. So there they were, and the atmosphere on the bandstand and in the room began to change and tighten. Someone stepped up to the microphone and announced them. Then there were all kinds of murmurs. Some people at the bar shushed others. The waitress ran around, frantically getting in the last orders, guys and chicks got closer to each other, and the lights on the bandstand, on the quartet, turned to a kind of indigo. Then they all looked different there. Creole looked about him for the last time, as though he were making certain that all his chickens were in the coop, and then he—jumped and struck the fiddle. And there they were.

All I know about music is that not many people ever really hear it. And even then, on the rare occasions when something opens within, and the music enters, what we mainly hear, or hear corroborated, are personal, private, vanishing evocations. But the man who creates the music is hearing something else, is dealing with the roar rising from the void and imposing order on it as it hits the air. What is evoked in him, then, is of another order, more terrible because it has no words, and triumphant, too, for that same reason. And his triumph, when he triumphs, is ours. I just watched Sonny's face. His face was troubled, he was working hard, but he wasn't with it. And I had the feeling that, in a way, everyone on the bandstand was waiting for him, both waiting for him and pushing him along. But as I began to watch Creole, I realized that it was Creole who held them all back. He had them on a short rein. Up there, keeping the beat with his whole body, wailing on the fiddle, with his eyes half closed, he was listening to everything, but he was listening to Sonny. He was having a dialogue with Sonny. He wanted Sonny to leave the shoreline and strike out for the deep water. He was Sonny's witness that deep water and drowning were not the same thing—he had been there, and he knew. And he wanted Sonny to know. He was waiting for Sonny to do the things on the keys which would let Creole know that Sonny was in the water.

And, while Creole listened, Sonny moved, deep within, exactly like someone in torment. I had never before thought of how awful the relationship must be between the musician and his instrument. He has to fill it, this instrument, with the breath of life, his own. He has to make it do what he wants it to do. And a piano is just a piano. It's made out of so much wood and wires and little hammers and big ones, and ivory. While there's only so much you can do with it, the only way to find this out is to try; to try and make it do everything.

And Sonny hadn't been near a piano for over a year. And he wasn't on much better terms with his life, not the life that stretched before him now. He and the piano stammered, started one way, got scared, stopped; started another way, panicked, marked time, started again; then seemed to have found a direction, panicked again, got stuck. And the face I saw on Sonny I'd never seen before. Everything had been burned out of it, and, at the same time, things usually hidden were being burned in, by the fire and fury of the battle which was occurring in him up there.

Yet, watching Creole's face as they neared the end of the first set, I had the feeling that something had happened, something I hadn't heard. Then they finished, there was scattered applause, and then, without an instant's warning, Creole started into something else, it was almost sardonic, it was *Am I Blue*. And, as though he commanded, Sonny began to play. Something

235

began to happen. And Creole let out the reins. The dry, low, black man said something awful on the drums, Creole answered, and the drums talked back. Then the horn insisted, sweet and high, slightly detached perhaps, and Creole listened, commenting now and then, dry, and driving, beautiful and calm and old. Then they all came together again, and Sonny was part of the family again. I could tell this from his face. He seemed to have found, right there beneath his fingers, a damn brand-new piano. It seemed that he couldn't get over it. Then, for a while, just being happy with Sonny, they seemed to be agreeing with him that brand-new pianos certainly were a gas.

Then Creole stepped forward to remind them that what they were playing was the blues. He hit something in all of them, he hit something in me, myself, and the music tightened and deepened, apprehension began to beat the air. Creole began to tell us what the blues were all about. They were not about anything very new. He and his boys up there were keeping it new, at the risk of ruin, destruction, madness, and death, in order to find new ways to make us listen. For, while the tale of how we suffer, and how we are delighted, and how we may triumph is never new, it always must be heard. There isn't any other tale to tell, it's the only light we've got in all this darkness.

And this tale, according to that face, that body, those strong hands on those strings, has another aspect in every country, and a new depth in every generation. Listen, Creole seemed to be saying, listen. Now these are Sonny's blues. He made the little black man on the drums know it, and the bright, brown man on the horn. Creole wasn't trying any longer to get Sonny in the water. He was wishing him Godspeed. Then he stepped back, very slowly, filling the air with the immense suggestion that Sonny speak for himself.

Then they all gathered around Sonny and Sonny played. Every now and again one of them seemed to say, amen. Sonny's fingers filled the air with life, his life. But that life contained so many others. And Sonny went all the way back, he really began with the spare, flat statement of the opening phrase of the song. Then he began to make it his. It was very beautiful because it wasn't hurried and it was no longer a lament. I seemed to hear with what burning he had made it his, and what burning we had yet to make it ours, how we could cease lamenting. Freedom lurked around us and I understood, at last, that he could help us to be free if we would listen, that he would never be free until we did. Yet, there was no battle in his face now, I heard what he had gone through, and would continue to go through until he came to rest in earth. He had made it his: that long line, of which we knew only Mama and Daddy. And he was giving it back, as everything must be given back, so that, passing through death, it can live forever. I saw my mother's face again, and felt, for the first time, how the stones of the road she had walked on must have bruised her feet. I saw the moonlit road where my father's brother died. And it brought something else back to me, and carried me past it, I saw my little girl again and felt Isabel's tears again, and I felt my own tears begin to rise. And I was yet aware that this was only a moment, that the world waited outside, as hungry as a tiger, and that trouble stretched above us, longer than the sky.

Then it was over. Creole and Sonny let out their breath, both soaking wet, and grinning. There was a lot of applause and some of it was real. In the dark, the girl came by and I asked her to take drinks to the bandstand. There was a long pause, while they talked up there in the indigo light and after awhile I saw the girl put a Scotch and milk on top of the piano for Sonny. He didn't seem to notice it, but just before they started playing again, he sipped from it and looked toward me, and nodded. Then he put it back on top of the piano. For me, then, as they began to play again, it glowed and shook above my brother's head like the very cup of trembling.

- Notice the different sections in this story. Use specific details from each to explain the significance of each different rhythm. For instance, in the opening section, look at the series of short sentences. How do these sentences help set up the story?
- Find the specific places in the story where sounds (or silences) are described. How does Baldwin use a rhythm of language to evoke these sounds?
- There is a clear contrast between the lives of the two brothers here. Which one is innocent? Which is experienced? Use specific details to defend your answers.

Ursula K. Le Guin (1929–)

Ursula Kroeber Le Guin was born in Berkeley, California. As the daughter of an anthropologist, she was frequently exposed to a variety of international and ethnic customs. When she was a child, she particularly enjoyed Norse mythology and Native American tales; these legends later influenced her fantasy and science fiction writings. Le Guin earned her bachelor's degree from Radcliffe College in 1951 and completed her MA one year later at Columbia University. *Rocannon's World* (1966), Le Guin's first published novel, was the beginning of a series of books set on the fictitious planet Hain. As the books grew increasingly popular with audiences, Le Guin was encouraged to write for young adults, and the Earthsea series was created. Le Guin's work has been popular with critics, and her numerous honors and awards include the 1970 International Science Fiction Association's Nebula and Hugo Awards for *The Left Hand of Darkness*, the 1972 National Book Award for Children's Literature for *The Tombs of Atuan*, and the 1995 World Fantasy Convention's Lifetime Achievement Award.

The Ones Who Walk Away from Omelas (1975)

With a clamor of bells that set the swallows soaring, the Festival of Summer
came to the city. Omelas, bright-towered by the sea. The rigging of the
boats in harbor sparkled with flags. In the streets between houses with red
roofs and painted walls, between old moss-grown gardens and under avenues
of trees, past great parks and public buildings, processions moved. Some
were decorous: old people in long stiff robes of mauve and gray, grave master
workmen, quiet, merry women carrying their babies and chatting as they
walked. In other streets the music beat faster, a shimmering of gong and
tambourine, and the people went dancing, the procession was a dance. Children dodged in and out, their high calls rising like the swallows' crossing
flights over the music and the singing. All the processions wound toward
the north side of the city, where on the great water-meadow called the
Green Fields boys and girls, naked in the bright air, with mud-stained feet
and ankles and long, lithe arms, exercised their restive horses before the
race. The horses wore no gear at all but a halter without bit. Their manes
were braided with streamers of silver, gold, and green. They flared their nostrils and pranced and boasted to one another, they were vastly excited, the
horse being the only animal who has adopted our ceremonies as his own.
Far off to the north and west the mountains stood up half encircling Omelas
on her bay. The air of morning was so clear that the snow still crowning the
Eighteen Peaks burned with white-gold fire across the miles of sunlit air,
under the dark blue of the sky. There was just enough wind to make the
banners that marked the racecourse snap and flutter now and then. In the
silence of the broad green meadows one could hear the music winding
through the city streets, farther and nearer and ever approaching, a cheerful
faint sweetness of the air that from time to time trembled and gathered together and broke out into the great joyous clanging of the bells.

Joyous! How is one to tell about joy? How describe the citizens of
Omelas?

They were not simple folk, you see, though they were happy. But we do
not say the words of cheer much any more. All smiles have become archaic.
Given a description such as this one tends to make certain assumptions.
Given a description such as this one tends to look next for the King,
mounted on a splendid stallion and surrounded by his noble knights, or perhaps in a golden litter borne by great-muscled slaves. But there was no king.
They did not use swords, or keep slaves. They were not barbarians. I do not
know the rules and laws of their society, but I suspect that they were singularly few. As they did without monarchy and slavery, so they also got on
without the stock exchange, the advertisement, the secret police, and the
bomb. Yet I repeat that these were not simple folk, not dulcet shepherds,

noble savages, bland utopians. They were not less complex than us. The
trouble is that we have a bad habit, encouraged by pedants and sophisti-
cates, of considering happiness as something rather stupid. Only pain is intellectual, only evil interesting. This is the treason of the artist: a refusal to
admit the banality of evil and the terrible boredom of pain. If you can't lick
'em, join 'em. If it hurts, repeat it. But to praise despair is to condemn delight, to embrace violence is to lose hold of everything else. We have almost
lost hold; we can no longer describe a happy man, nor make any celebration
of joy. How can I tell you about the people of Omelas? They were not naïve
and happy children—though their children were, in fact, happy. They were
mature, intelligent, passionate adults whose lives were not wretched. O miracle! but I wish I could describe it better. I wish I could convince you. Omelas sounds in my words like a city in a fairy tale, long ago and far away,
once upon a time. Perhaps it would be best if you imagined it as your own
fancy bids, assuming it will rise to the occasion, for certainly I cannot suit
you all. For instance, how about technology? I think that there would be no
cars or helicopters in and above the streets; this follows from the fact that
the people of Omelas are happy people. Happiness is based on a just discrimination of what is necessary, what is neither necessary nor destructive,
and what is destructive. In the middle category, however—that of the unnecessary but undestructive, that of comfort, luxury, exuberance, etc.—they
could perfectly well have central heating, subway trains, washing machines,
and all kinds of marvelous devices not yet invented here, floating light-
sources, fuelless power, a cure for the common cold. Or they could have
none of that: it doesn't matter. As you like it. I incline to think that people
from towns up and down the coast have been coming in to Omelas during
the last days before the Festival on very fast little trains and double-decked
trams and that the train station of Omelas is actually the handsomest building in town, though plainer than the magnificent Farmers' Market. But
even granted trains, I fear that Omelas so far strikes some of you as goody-
goody. Smiles, bells, parades, horses, bleh. If so, please add an orgy. If an
orgy would help, don't hesitate. Let us not, however, have temples from
which issue beautiful nude priests and priestesses already half in ecstasy and
ready to copulate with any man or woman, lover or stranger, who desires
union with the deep godhead of the blood, although that was my first idea.
But really it would be better not to have any temples in Omelas—at least,
not manned temples. Religion yes, clergy no. Surely the beautiful nudes can
just wander about, offering themselves like divine soufflés to the hunger of
the needy and the rapture of the flesh. Let them join the processions. Let
tambourines be struck above the copulations, and the glory of desire be proclaimed upon the gongs, and (a not unimportant point) let the offspring of
these delightful rituals be beloved and looked after by all. One thing I know
there is none of in Omelas is guilt. But what else should there be? I thought

at first there were no drugs, but that is puritanical. For those who like it, the faint insistent sweetness of *drooz* may perfume the ways of the city, *drooz* which first brings a great lightness and brilliance to the mind and limbs, and then after some hours a dreamy languor, and wonderful visions at last of the very arcana and inmost secrets of the Universe, as well as exciting the pleasure of sex beyond all belief; and it is not habit-forming. For more modest tastes I think there ought to be beer. What else, what else belongs in the joyous city? The sense of victory, surely, the celebration of courage. But as we did without clergy, let us do without soldiers. The joy built upon successful slaughter is not the right kind of joy; it will not do; it is fearful and it is trivial. A boundless and generous contentment, a magnanimous triumph felt not against some outer enemy but in communion with the finest and fairest in the souls of all men everywhere and the splendor of the world's summer: this is what swells the hearts of the people of Omelas, and the victory they celebrate is that of life. I really don't think many of them need to take *drooz*.

Most of the processions have reached the Green Fields by now. A marvelous smell of cooking goes forth from the red and blue tents of the provisioners. The faces of small children are amiably sticky; in the benign gray beard of a man a couple of crumbs of rich pastry are entangled. The youths and girls have mounted their horses and are beginning to group around the starting line of the course. An old woman, small, fat, and laughing, is passing out flowers from a basket, and tall young men wear her flowers in their shining hair. A child of nine or ten sits at the edge of the crowd, alone, playing on a wooden flute. People pause to listen, and they smile, but they do not speak to him, for he never ceases playing and never sees them, his dark eyes wholly rapt in the sweet, thin magic of the tune.

He finishes, and slowly lowers his hands holding the wooden flute.   5

As if that little private silence were the signal, all at once a trumpet sounds from the pavillion near the starting line: imperious, melancholy, piercing. The horses rear on their slender legs, and some of them neigh in answer. Sober-faced, the young riders stroke the horses' necks and soothe them, whispering, "Quiet, quiet, there my beauty, my hope...." They begin to form in rank along the starting line. The crowds along the racecourse are like a field of grass and flowers in the wind. The Festival of Summer has begun.

Do you believe? Do you accept the festival, the city, the joy? No? Then let me describe one more thing.

In a basement under one of the beautiful public buildings of Omelas, or perhaps in the cellar of one of its spacious private homes, there is a room. It has one locked door, and no window. A little light seeps in dustily between cracks in the boards, secondhand from a cobwebbed window somewhere across the cellar. In one corner of the little room a couple of mops, with stiff, clotted, foul-smelling heads, stand near a rusty bucket. The floor is dirt, a little damp to the touch, as cellar dirt usually is. The room is about three paces long and two wide: a mere broom closet or disused tool room. In the room a child is sitting. It could be a boy or a girl. It looks about six, but actually is nearly ten. It is feeble-minded. Perhaps it was born defective, or perhaps it has become imbecile through fear, malnutrition, and neglect. It picks its nose and occasionally fumbles vaguely with its toes or genitals, as it sits hunched in the corner farthest from the bucket and the two mops. It is afraid of the mops. It finds them horrible. It shuts its eyes, but it knows the mops are still standing there; and the door is locked; and nobody will come. The door is always locked; and nobody ever comes, except that some-times—the child has no understanding of time or interval—sometimes the door rattles terribly and opens, and a person, or several people, are there. One of them may come in and kick the child to make it stand up. The others never come close, but peer in at it with frightened, disgusted eyes. The food bowl and the water jug are hastily filled, the door is locked, the eyes disappear. The people at the door never say anything, but the child, who has not always lived in the tool room, and can remember sunlight and its mother's voice, sometimes speaks. "I will be good," it says. "Please let me out. I will be good!" They never answer. The child used to scream for help at night, and cry a good deal, but now it only makes a kind of whining, "eh-haa, eh-haa," and it speaks less and less often. It is so thin there are no calves to its legs; its belly protrudes; it lives on a half-bowl of corn meal and grease a day. It is naked. Its buttocks and thighs are a mass of festered sores, as it sits in its own excrement continually.

They all know it is there, all the people of Omelas. Some of them have come to see it, others are content merely to know it is there. They all know that it has to be there. Some of them understand why, and some do not, but they all understand that their happiness, the beauty of their city, the tender-ness of their friendships, the health of their children, the wisdom of their scholars, the skill of their makers, even the abundance of their harvest and the kindly weathers of their skies, depend wholly on this child's abominable misery.

This is usually explained to children when they are between eight and twelve, whenever they seem capable of understanding; and most of those who come to see the child are young people, though often enough an adult comes, or comes back, to see the child. No matter how well the matter has been ex-plained to them, these young spectators are always shocked and sickened at the sight. They feel disgust, which they had thought themselves superior to. They feel anger, outrage, impotence, despite all the explanations. They would like to do something for the child. But there is nothing they can do. If the child were brought up into the sunlight out of that vile place, if it were cleaned and fed and comforted, that would be a good thing, indeed; but if it

10

were done, in that day and hour all the prosperity and beauty and delight of Omelas would wither and be destroyed. Those are the terms. To exchange all the goodness and grace of every life in Omelas for that single, small improvement: to throw away the happiness of thousands for the chance of the happiness of one: that would be to let guilt within the walls indeed.

The terms are strict and absolute; there may not even be a kind word spoken to the child.

Often the young people go home in tears, or in a tearless rage, when they have seen the child and faced this terrible paradox. They may brood over it for weeks or years. But as time goes on they begin to realize that even if the child could be released, it would not get much good of its freedom: a little vague pleasure of warmth and food, no doubt, but little more. It is too degraded and imbecile to know any real joy. It has been afraid too long ever to be free of fear. Its habits are too uncouth for it to respond to humane treatment. Indeed, after so long it would probably be wretched without walls about it to protect it, and darkness for its eyes, and its own excrement to sit in. Their tears at the bitter injustice dry when they begin to perceive the terrible justice of reality and to accept it. Yet it is their tears and anger, the trying of their generosity and the acceptance of their helplessness, which are perhaps the true source of the splendor of their lives. Theirs is no vapid, irresponsible happiness. They know that they, like the child, are not free. They know compassion. It is the existence of the child, and their knowledge of its existence, that makes possible the nobility of their architecture, the poignancy of their music, the profundity of their science. It is because of the child that they are so gentle with children. They know that if the wretched one were not there snivelling in the dark, the other one, the flute-player, could make no joyful music as the young riders line up in their beauty for the race in the sunlight of the first morning of summer.

Now do you believe in them? Are they not more credible? But there is one more thing to tell, and this is quite incredible.

At times one of the adolescent girls or boys who go to see the child does not go home to weep or rage, does not, in fact, go home at all. Sometimes also a man or woman much older falls silent for a day or two, and then leaves home. These people go out into the street, and walk down the street alone. They keep walking, and walk straight out of the city of Omelas, through the beautiful gates. They keep walking across the farmlands of Omelas. Each one goes alone, youth or girl, man or woman. Night falls; the traveler must pass down village streets, between the houses with yellow-lit windows, and on out into the darkness of the fields. Each alone, they go west or north, toward the mountains. They go on. They leave Omelas, they walk ahead into the darkness, and they do not come back. The place they go toward is a place even less imaginable to most of us than the city of happiness. I cannot describe it at all. It is possible that it does not exist. But they seem to know where they are going, the ones who walk away from Omelas.

- Look carefully at the description of the procession that opens the story. How does Le Guin establish a distinct rhythm here?
- Look at the third paragraph, where she outlines the rules and ideals of this society. How does the rhythm of the sentences impact the ideas presented by these descriptions?
- The miserable child exists in a very different place from the Festival of Summer. In what ways are language patterns describing the child similar to those used to describe the joy of the general citizenry? Find specific instances surrounding the description of the child that indicate some greater experience than we see in the opening paragraphs of the story.

Susan Minot (1956–)

Susan Minot was born in Manchester, Massachusetts, a northern suburb of Boston. One of seven children, she attended Brown University and then returned home to help care for her father and sister after the death of her mother in a car accident. Several years later she enrolled in the MFA program at Columbia University; she published her first short stories while a student there. Minot's first novel, *Monkeys*, focuses on the way in which the loss of a mother affects a large family very much like her own. Her subsequent short story collection and novels have tended to focus on male–female relationships and on the very different ways in which men and women view those relationships.

Lust (1989)

Leo was from a long time ago, the first one I ever saw nude. In the spring before the Hellmans filled their pool, we'd go down there in the deep end, with baby oil, and like that. I met him the first month away at boarding school. He had a halo from the campus light behind him. I flipped.

Roger was fast. In his illegal car, we drove to the reservoir, the radio blaring, talking fast, fast, fast. He was always going for my zipper. He got kicked out sophomore year.

By the time the band got around to playing "Wild Horses," I had tasted Bruce's tongue. We were clicking in the shadows on the other side of the amplifier, out of Mrs. Donovan's line of vision. It tasted like salt, with my neck bent back, because we had been dancing so hard before.

Tim's line: "I'd like to see you in a bathing suit." I knew it was his line when he said the exact same thing to Annie Hines.

You'd go on walks to get off campus. It was raining like hell, my sweater   5
as sopped as a wet sheep. Tim pinned me to a tree, the woods light brown
and dark brown, a white house half hidden with the lights already on. The
water was as loud as a crowd hissing. He made certain comments about my
forehead, about my cheeks.

We started off sitting at one end of the couch and then our feet were
squished against the armrest and then he went over to turn off the TV and
came back after he had taken off his shirt and then we slid onto the floor
and he got up again to close the door, then came back to me, a body waiting
on the rug.

You'd try to wipe off the table or to do the dishes and Willie would un-
tuck your shirt and get his hands up under in front, standing behind you,
making puffy noises in your ear.

He likes it when I wash my hair. He covers his face with it and if I start
to say something, he goes, "Shush."

For a long time, I had Philip on the brain. The less they noticed you,
the more you got them on the brain.

My parents had no idea. Parents never really know what's going on, es-   1
pecially when you're away at school most of the time. If she met them, my
mother might say, "Oliver seems nice" or "I like that one" without much of
an opinion. If she didn't like them, "He's a funny fellow, isn't he?" or "Johnny's perfectly nice but a drink of water." My father was too shy to talk to
them at all unless they played sports and he'd ask them about that.

The sand was almost cold underneath because the sun was long gone.
Eben piled a mound over my feet, patting around my ankles, the ghostly
surf rumbling behind him in the dark. He was the first person I ever knew
who died, later that summer, in a car crash. I thought about it for a long
time.

"Come here," he says on the porch.
I go over to the hammock and he takes my wrist with two fingers.
"What?"
He kisses my palm then directs my hand to his fly.

Songs went with whichever boy it was. "Sugar Magnolia" was Tim, with the line "Rolling in the rushes / down by the riverside." With "Darkness Darkness," I'd picture Philip with his long hair. Hearing "Under My Thumb" there'd be the smell of Jamie's suede jacket.

We hid in the listening rooms during study hall. With a record cover over the door's window, the teacher on duty couldn't look in. I came out flushed and heady and back at the dorm was surprised how red my lips were in the mirror.

One weekend at Simon's brother's, we stayed inside all day with the shades down, in bed, then went out to Store 24 to get some ice cream. He stood at the magazine rack and read through *MAD* while I got butterscotch sauce, craving something sweet.

I could do some things well. Some things I was good at, like math or painting or even sports, but the second a boy put his arm around me, I forgot about wanting to do anything else, which felt like a relief at first until it became like sinking into a muck.

It was different for a girl.   20

When we were little, the brothers next door tied up our ankles. They held the door of the goat house and wouldn't let us out till we showed them our underpants. Then they'd forget about being after us and when we played whiffle ball, I'd be just as good as they were.

Then it got to be different. Just because you have on a short skirt, they yell from the cars, slowing down for a while, and if you don't look, they screech off and call you a bitch.

"What's the matter with me?" they say, point-blank.
Or else, "Why won't you go out with me? I'm not asking you to get married," about to get mad.
Or it'd be, trying to be reasonable, in a regular voice, "Listen, I just   25
want to have a good time."
So I'd go because I couldn't think of something to say back that wouldn't be obvious, and if you go out with them, you sort of have to do something.

I sat between Mack and Eddie in the front seat of the pickup. They were having a fight about something. I've a feeling about me.

Certain nights you'd feel a certain surrender, maybe if you'd had wine. The surrender would be forgetting yourself and you'd put your nose to his neck and feel like a squirrel, safe, at rest, in a restful dream. But then you'd start to slip from that and the dark would come in and there'd be a cave. You make out the dim shape of the windows and feel yourself become a cave, filled absolutely with air, or with a sadness that wouldn't stop.

Teenage years. You know just what you're doing and don't see the things that start to get in the way.

Lots of boys, but never two at a time. One was plenty to keep you in a state. You'd start to see a boy and something would rush over you like a fast storm cloud and you couldn't possibly think of anyone else. Boys took it differently. Their eyes perked up at any little number that walked by. You'd act like you weren't noticing.

The joke was that the school gave out the pill like aspirin. He didn't ask you anything. I was fifteen. We had a picture of him in assembly, holding up an IUD shaped like a T. Most girls were on the pill, if anything, because they couldn't handle a diaphragm. I kept the dial in my top drawer like my mother and thought of her each time I tipped out the yellow tablets in the morning before chapel.

If they were too shy, I'd be more so. Andrew was nervous. We stayed up with his family album, sharing a pack of Old Golds. Before it got light, we turned on the TV. A man was explaining how to plant seedlings. His mouth jerked to the side in a tic. Andrew thought it was a riot and kept imitating him. I laughed to be polite. When we finally dozed off, he dared to put his arm around me, but that was it.

You wait till they come to you. With half fright, half swagger, they stand one step down. They dare to touch the button on your coat then lose their nerve and quickly drop their hand so you—you'd do anything for them. You touch their cheek.

The girls sit around in the common room and talk about boys, smoking their heads off.

"What are you complaining about?" says Jill to me when we talk about problems.
"Yeah," says Giddy. "You always have a boyfriend."
I look at them and think, As if.

I thought the worst thing anyone could call you was a cock-teaser. So, if you flirted, you had to be prepared to go through with it. Sleeping with someone was perfectly normal once you had done it. You didn't really worry about it. But there were other problems. The problems had to do with something else entirely.

Mack was during the hottest summer ever recorded. We were renting a house on an island with all sorts of other people. No one slept during the heat wave, walking around the house with nothing on which we were used to because of the nude beach. In the living room, Eddie lay on top of a coffee table to cool off. Mack and I, with the bedroom door open for air, sweated and sweated all night.

"I can't take this," he said at three A.M. "I'm going for a swim." He and some guys down the hall went to the beach. The heat put me on edge. I sat on a cracked chest by the open window and smoked and smoked till I felt even worse, waiting for something—I guess for him to get back. 40

One was on a camping trip in Colorado. We zipped our sleeping bags together, the coyotes' hysterical chatter far away. Other couples murmured in other tents. Paul was up before sunrise, starting a fire for breakfast. He wasn't much of a talker in the daytime. At night, his hand leafed about in the hair at my neck.

There'd be times when you overdid it. You'd get carried away. All the next day, you'd be in a total fog, delirious, absent-minded, crossing the street and nearly getting run over.

The more girls a boy has, the better. He has a bright look, having reaped fruits, blooming. He stalks around, sure-shouldered, and you have the feeling he's got more in him, a fatter heart, more stories to tell. For a girl, with each boy it's as though a petal gets plucked each time.

Then you start to get tired. You begin to feel diluted, like watered-down stew.

Oliver came skiing with us. We lolled by the fire after everyone had gone to bed. Each creak you'd think was someone coming downstairs. The silver loop bracelet he gave me had been a present from his girlfriend before. 45

On vacations, we went skiing, or you'd go south if someone invited you. Some people had apartments in New York that their families hardly ever used. Or summer houses, or older sisters. We always managed to find someplace to go.

We made the plan at coffee hour. Simon snuck out and met me at Main Gate after lights-out. We crept to the chapel and spent the night in the balcony. He tasted like onions from a submarine sandwich.

The boys are one of two ways: either they can't sit still or they don't move. In front of the TV, they won't budge. On weekends they play touch football while we sit on the sidelines, picking blades of grass to chew on, and watch. We're always watching them run around. We shiver in the stands, knocking our boots together to keep our toes warm, and they whizz across the ice, chopping their sticks around the puck. When they're in the rink, they refuse to look at you, only eyeing each other beneath low helmets. You cheer for them but they don't look up, even if it's a face-off when nothing's happening, even if they're doing drills before any game has started at all.

Dancing under the pink tent, he bent down and whispered in my ear. We slipped away to the lawn on the other side of the hedge. Much later, as he was leaving the buffet with two plates of eggs and sausage, I saw the grass stains on the knees of his white pants.

Tim's was shaped like a banana, with a graceful curve to it. They're all different. Willie's like a bunch of walnuts when nothing was happening, another's as thin as a thin hot dog. But it's like faces; you're never really surprised.

Still, you're not sure what to expect.

I look into his face and he looks back. I look into his eyes and they look back at mine. Then they look down at my mouth so I look at his mouth, then back to his eyes then, backing up, at his whole face. I think, Who? Who are you? His head tilts to one side.

I say, "Who are you?"

"What do you mean?"

"Nothing."

I look at his eyes again, deeper. Can't tell who he is, what he thinks.

"What?" he says. I look at his mouth.

"I'm just wondering," I say and go wandering across his face. Study the chin line. It's shaped like a persimmon.

"Who are you? What are you thinking?"

He says, "What the hell are you talking about?"

Then they get mad after, when you say enough is enough. After, when it's easier to explain that you don't want to. You wouldn't dream of saying that maybe you weren't really ready to in the first place.

Gentle Eddie. We waded into the sea, the waves round and plowing in, buffalo-headed, slapping our thighs. I put my arms around his freckled shoulders and he held me up, buoyed by the water, and rocked me like a sea shell.

I had no idea whose party it was, the apartment jam-packed, stepping over people in the hallway. The room with the music was practically empty, the bare floor, me in red shoes. This fellow slides onto one knee and takes me around the waist and we rock to jazzy tunes, with my toes pointing heavenward, and waltz and spin and dip to "Smoke Gets in Your Eyes" or "I'll Love You Just for Now." He puts his head to my chest, runs a sweeping hand down my inside thigh and we go loose-limbed and sultry and as smooth as silk and I stamp my red heels and he takes me into a swoon. I never saw him again after that but I thought, I could have loved that one.

You wonder how long you can keep it up. You begin to feel as if you're showing through, like a bathroom window that only lets in gray light, the kind you can't see out of.

They keep coming around. Johnny drives up at Easter vacation from Baltimore and I let him in the kitchen with everyone sound asleep. He has friends waiting in the car.
"What are you crazy? It's pouring out there," I say.
"It's okay," he says. "They understand."
So he gets some long kisses from me, against the refrigerator, before he goes because I hate those girls who push away a boy's face as if she were made out of Ivory soap, as if she's that much greater than he is.

The note on my cubby told me to see the headmaster. I had no idea for what. He had received complaints about my amorous displays on the town green. It was Willie that spring. The headmaster told me he didn't care what I did but that Casey Academy had a reputation to uphold in the town. He lowered his glasses on his nose. "We've got twenty acres of woods on this campus," he said. "If you want to smooch with your boyfriend, there are twenty acres for you to do it out of the public eye. You read me?"

Everybody'd get weekend permissions for different places, then we'd all go to someone's house whose parents were away. Usually there'd be more boys than girls. We raided the liquor closet and smoked pot at the

65

70

kitchen table and you'd never know who would end up where, or with whom. There were always disasters. Ceci got bombed and cracked her head open on the banister and needed stitches. Then there was the time Wendel Blair walked through the picture window at the Lowes' and got slashed to ribbons.

He scared me. In bed, I didn't dare look at him. I lay back with my eyes closed, luxuriating because he knew all sorts of expert angles, his hands never fumbling, going over my whole body, pressing the hair up and off the back of my head, giving an extra hip shove, as if to say *There*. I parted my eyes slightly, keeping the screen of my lashes low because it was too much to look at him, his mouth loose and pink and parted, his eyes looking through my forehead, or kneeling up, looking through my throat. I was ashamed but couldn't look him in the eye.

You wonder about things feeling a little off-kilter. You begin to feel like a piece of pounded veal.

At boarding school, everyone gets depressed. We go in and see the housemother, Mrs. Gunther. She got married when she was eighteen. Mr. Gunther was her high school sweetheart, the only boyfriend she ever had.
"And you knew you wanted to marry him right off?" we ask her.
She smiles and says, "Yes."
"They always want something from you," says Jill, complaining about her boyfriend.
"Yeah," says Giddy. "You always feel like you have to deliver something."
"You do," says Mrs. Gunther. "Babies."

After sex, you curl up like a shrimp, something deep inside you ruined, slammed in a place that sickens at slamming, and slowly you fill up with an overwhelming sadness, an elusive gaping worry. You don't try to explain it, filled with the knowledge that it's nothing after all, everything filling up finally and absolutely with death. After the briskness of loving, loving stops. And you roll over with death stretched out alongside you like a feather boa, or a snake, light as air, and you...you don't even ask for anything or try to say something to him because it's obviously your own damn fault. You haven't been able to—to what? To open your heart. You open your legs but can't, or don't dare anymore, to open your heart.

It starts this way:
You stare into their eyes. They flash like all the stars are out. They look at you seriously, their eyes at a low burn and their hands no matter what

starting off shy and with such a gentle touch that the only thing you can do is take that tenderness and let yourself be swept away. When, with one attentive finger they tuck the hair behind your ear, you—

You do everything they want.

Then comes after. After when they don't look at you. They scratch their balls, stare at the ceiling. Or if they do turn, their gaze is altogether changed. They are surprised. They turn casually to look at you, distracted, and get a mild distracted surprise. You're gone. Their blank look tells you that the girl they were fucking is not there anymore. You seem to have disappeared.

- How does the narrator distinguish among her different encounters here and among specific encounters and comments about encounters in general? Compare the language that she uses in each instance. What language or images are repeated in the different descriptions?

- What constant identity links each of the different encounters that the narrator describes? Find specific examples that work to define this identity.

- What does the narrator learn from her experiences? How does this knowledge contrast with the various instructions that she receives?

POETRY

William Blake (1757–1827)

The Lamb (1789)

Little Lamb, who made thee?
　Dost thou know who made thee?
Gave thee life & bid thee feed,
By the stream & o'er the mead;
Gave thee clothing of delight,　　　　　　　　　　5
Softest clothing wooly bright;
Gave thee such a tender voice,
Making all the vales rejoice!
　Little Lamb who made thee?
　Dost thou know who made thee?　　　　　　　　10

Little Lamb I'll tell thee,
Little Lamb I'll tell thee!

He is callèd by thy name,
For he calls himself a Lamb:
He is meek & he is mild,   15
He became a little child:
I a child & thou a lamb,
We are callèd by his name.
    Little Lamb God bless thee.
    Little Lamb God bless thee.   20

William Blake (1757–1827)

The Chimney Sweeper (Innocence) (1789)

When my mother died I was very young,
And my father sold me while yet my tongue
Could scarcely cry "'weep! 'weep! 'weep! 'weep!"°
So your chimneys I sweep, & in soot I sleep.

There's little Tom Dacre, who cried when his head   5
That curl'd like a lamb's back, was shav'd: so I said.
"Hush Tom! never mind it, for when your head's bare,
You know that the soot cannot spoil your white hair."

And so he was quiet, & that very night,
As Tom was a-sleeping he had such a sight!—   10
That thousands of sweepers Dick, Joe, Ned, & Jack,
Were all of them lock'd up in coffins of black.

And by came an Angel who had a bright key
And he open'd the coffins & set them all free.
Then down a green plain leaping, laughing, they run,   15
And wash in a river, and shine in the Sun.

Then naked & white, all their bags left behind,
They rise upon clouds, and sport in the wind;
And the Angel told Tom, if he'd be a good boy,
He'd have God for his father, & never want joy.   20

---

3. **'weep:** the child's lisping way of uttering his cry through the streets, "sweep, sweep"

And so Tom awoke; and we rose in the dark
And got with our bags & our brushes to work.
Tho' the morning was cold, Tom was happy & warm
So if all do their duty, they need not fear harm.

William Blake (1757–1827)

Holy Thursday (Innocence) (1789)

'Twas on a Holy Thursday, their innocent faces clean
The children walking two & two, in red & blue & green
Grey headed beadles walkd before with wands as white as snow,
Till into the high dome of Pauls they like Thames waters flow.

O what a multitude they seemd, these flowers of London town! 5
Seated in companies they sit with radiance all their own.
The hum of multitudes was there but multitudes of lambs,
Thousands of little boys & girls raising their innocent hands.

Now like a mighty wind they raise to heaven the voice of song,
Or like harmonious thunderings the seats of heaven among. 10
Beneath them sit the agèd men, wise guardians of the poor;
Then cherish pity, lest you drive an angel from your door.

William Blake (1757–1827)

The Tyger (1794)

Tyger! Tyger! burning bright,
In the forests of the night,
What immortal hand or eye
Could frame thy fearful symmetry?

In what distant deeps or skies. 5
Burnt the fire of thine eyes?
On what wings dare he aspire?
What the hand, dare seize the fire?

And what shoulder, & what art,
Could twist the sinews of thy heart? 10

And when thy heart began to beat,
What dread hand? & what dread feet?

What the hammer? what the chain?
In what furnace was thy brain?
What the anvil? what dread grasp   15
Dare its deadly terrors clasp?

When the stars threw down their spears,
And water'd heaven with their tears,
Did he smile his work to see?
Did he who made the Lamb make thee?   20

Tyger! Tyger! burning bright
In the forests of the night,
What immortal hand or eye,
Dare frame thy fearful symmetry?

William Blake (1757–1827)

The Chimney Sweeper (Experience) (1794)

A little black thing among the snow,
Crying "'weep! 'weep!" in notes of woe!
"Where are thy father & mother? say?"
"They are both gone up to the church to pray."

"Because I was happy upon the heath,   5
And smil'd among the winter's snow,
They clothed me in the clothes of death,
And taught me to sing the notes of woe.

"And because I am happy & dance & sing,
They think they have done me no injury,   10
And are gone to praise God & his Priest & King,
Who make up a heaven of our misery."

William Blake (1757–1827)

Holy Thursday (Experience) (1794)

Is this a holy thing to see,
In a rich and fruitful land,

Babes reducd to misery,
Fed with cold and usurous hand?

Is that trembling cry a song?   5
Can it be a song of joy?
And so many children poor?
It is a land of poverty!

And their sun does never shine,
And their fields are bleak & bare,   10
And their ways are fill'd with thorns;
It is eternal winter there.

For where-e'er the sun does shine,
And where-e'er the rain does fall,
Babe can never hunger there,   15
Nor poverty the mind appall.

- Look at the Blake poems as pairs. The first is a poem of innocence. The second is a poem of experience. What differences are there in the rhythms of each pair? Are there any rhythmic consistencies among the experience poems or innocence poems?
- How do their rhythms reflect the different approach to the same subject matter used in these pairs?

Theodore Roethke (1908–1963)

My Papa's Waltz (1940)

The whiskey on your breath
Could make a small boy dizzy;
But I hung on like death:
Such waltzing was not easy.

We romped until the pans   5
Slid from the kitchen shelf;
My mother's countenance
Could not unfrown itself.

The hand that held my wrist
Was battered on one knuckle;   10

At every step you missed
My right ear scraped a buckle.

You beat time on my head
With a palm caked hard by dirt,
Then waltzed me off to bed   15
Still clinging to your shirt.

Theodore Roethke (1908–1963)

The Waking (1958)

I wake to sleep, and take my waking slow.
I feel my fate in what I cannot fear.
I learn by going where I have to go.

We think by feeling. What is there to know?
I hear my being dance from ear to ear.   5
I wake to sleep, and take my waking slow.

Of those so close beside me, which are you?
God bless the Ground! I shall walk softly there,
And learn by going where I have to go.

Light takes the Tree; but who can tell us how?   10
The lowly worm climbs up a winding stair;
I wake to sleep, and take my waking slow.

Great Nature has another thing to do
To you and me; so take the lively air,
And, lovely, learn by going where to go.   15

This shaking keeps me steady. I should know.
What falls away is always. And is near.
I wake to sleep, and take my waking slow.
I learn by going where I have to go.

■ In "My Papa's Waltz," the poet establishes a clear rhythm that lasts throughout the poem. How does this rhythm compare to that established in "The Waking"? How does this different rhythm impact the themes of the two poems?

Langston Hughes (1902–1967)

Dream Boogie (1951)

Good morning, daddy!
Ain't you heard
The boogie-woogie rumble
Of a dream deferred?

Listen closely: 5
You'll hear their feet
Beating out and beating out a —

    You think
    It's a happy beat?

Listen to it closely: 10
Ain't you heard
something underneath
like a —

    What did I say?

Sure,   15
I'm happy!
Take it away!

    Hey, pop!
    Re-bop!
    Mop!   20

    Y-e-a-h!

■ How does Hughes use the rhythm of "boogie-woogie" to drown out the disappointment of "a dream deferred"?

Langston Hughes (1902–1967)

The Negro Speaks of Rivers (1921)

I've known rivers:
I've known rivers ancient as the world and older than the
    flow of human blood in human veins.

My soul has grown deep like the rivers.

I bathed in Euphrates when dawns were young.
I built my hut near the Congo and it lulled me to sleep.   5
I looked upon the Nile and raised the pyramids above it.
I heard the singing of the Mississippi when Abe Lincoln went down to
    New Orleans, and I've seen its muddy bosom turn all golden in the sunset.

I've known rivers:
Ancient, dusky rivers.

My soul has grown deep like the rivers.   10

■ How does the poet use repeated phrases and sentence patterns to develop the idea "My soul has grown deep like the rivers"?

Gwendolyn Brooks (1917–2000)

We Real Cool (1960)

THE POOL PLAYERS.
SEVEN AT THE GOLDEN SHOVEL.

We real cool. We
Left school. We

Lurk late. We
Strike straight. We

Sing sin. We   5
Thin gin. We

Jazz June. We
Die soon.

■ What is the effect of the subject of every sentence (except the first) not being attached to its predicate?
■ Compare "We Real Cool" to "Dream Boogie" (p. 573). How do both poems use their rhythms to imitate the social forces that the poems challenge?

Countee Cullen (1903–1946)

Incident (1925)

Once riding in old Baltimore,
Heart-filled, head-filled with glee,
I saw a Baltimorean
Keep looking straight at me.

Now I was eight and very small,   5
And he was no whit bigger,
And so I smiled, but he poked out
His tongue, and called me, "Nigger."

I saw the whole of Baltimore
From May until December;   10
Of all the things that happened there
That's all that I remember.

■ The poem has the rhythm of a nursery rhyme. How is the rhythm appropriate to
the subject? How does that rhythm contrast with the subject matter presented?

Denise Levertov (1923–1997)

In Mind (1964)

There's in my mind a woman
of innocence, unadorned but

fair-featured and smelling of
apples or grass. She wears

a utopian smock or shift, her hair   5
is light brown and smooth, and she

is kind and very clean without
ostentation—
                  but she has
no imagination.

                  And there's a

turbulent moon-ridden girl   10

or old woman, or both,
dressed in opals and rags, feathers

and torn taffeta,
who knows strange songs—

but she is not kind.   15

■ How are the divisions in this poem important to its meaning?
■ How does the poem distinguish between innocence and experience?

Sharon Olds (1942–)

I Go Back to May 1937 (1997)

I see them standing at the formal gates of their colleges,
I see my father strolling out
under the ochre sandstone arch, the
red tiles glinting like bent
plates of blood behind his head, I   5
see my mother with a few light books at her hip
standing at the pillar made of tiny bricks with the
wrought-iron gate still open behind her, its
sword-tips black in the May air,
they are about to graduate, they are about to get married,   10
they are kids, they are dumb, all they know is they are
innocent, they would never hurt anybody.
I want to go up to them and say Stop,
don't do it—she's the wrong woman,
he's the wrong man, you are going to do things   15
you cannot imagine you would ever do,
you are going to do bad things to children,
you are going to suffer in ways you never heard of,
you are going to want to die. I want to go
up to them there in the late May sunlight and say it,   20
her hungry pretty blank face turning to me,
her pitiful beautiful untouched body,
his arrogant handsome blind face turning to me,

his pitiful beautiful untouched body,
but I don't do it. I want to live. I   25
take them up like the male and female
paper dolls and bang them together
at the hips like chips of flint as if to
strike sparks from them, I say
Do what you are going to do, and I will tell about it.   30

Sharon Olds (1942–)

The Death of Marilyn Monroe (1983)

The ambulance men touched her cold
body, lifted it, heavy as iron,
onto the stretcher, tried to close the
mouth, closed the eyes, tied the
arms to the sides, moved a caught   5
strand of hair, as if it mattered,
saw the shape of her breasts, flattened by
gravity, under the sheet
carried her, as if it were she,
down the steps.   10
These men were never the same. They went out
afterwards, as they always did,
for a drink or two, but they could not meet
each other's eyes.
Their lives took   15
a turn—one had nightmares, strange
pains, impotence, depression. One did not
like his work, his wife looked
different, his kids. Even death
seemed different to him—a place where she   20
would be waiting,
and one found himself standing at night
in the doorway to a room of sleep, listening to a
woman breathing, just an ordinary
woman   25
breathing.

■ In Olds's two poems, what images serve the poet in her descriptions of
innocence and of experience?

■ Look carefully at the long listing sentences that are central to each poem: lines 1–12, 13–19, 19–25 ("I Go Back to May 1937") and lines 1–10 ("The Death of Marilyn Monroe"). What is the impact of these almost breathless lists? Whose experience does each describe?

DRAMA

Suzan-Lori Parks (1964–)

Suzan-Lori Parks was born in Fort Knox, Kentucky. Her father was an army officer, so the family moved frequently. Parks went to high school in Germany, then attended Mount Holyoke College, where she worked with the writer James Baldwin, who encouraged her to write plays. Parks rapidly achieved acclaim for her dramatic works, and her second play received the Obie Award as the best Off Broadway play of 1989. In 2002, she achieved even greater success when her play *Topdog/Underdog* was awarded the Pulitzer Prize in drama. Parks's drama and fiction have been praised for the ways in which they examine African American life and the legacies of slavery and racism.

Topdog/Underdog (2002)

Scene 1

Thursday evening. A seedily furnished rooming house room. A bed, a reclining chair, a small wooden chair, some other stuff but not much else. BOOTH, *a black man in his early 30s, practices his 3-card monte scam on the classic setup: 3 playing cards and the cardboard playing board atop 2 mismatched milk crates. His moves and accompanying patter are. for the most part, studied and awkward.*

BOOTH: Watch me close watch me close now: who-see-thuh-red-card-who-see-thuh-red-card? I-see-thuh-red-card. Thuh-red-card-is-thuh-winner. Pick-thuh-red-card-you-pick-uh-winner. Pick-uh-black-card-you-pick-uh-loser. Theres-thuh-loser, yeah, theres-thuh-black-card, theres-thuh-other-loser-and-theres-thuh-red-card, thuh-winner.
(*Rest.*)
Watch me close watch me close now: 3-Card-throws-thuh-cards-lightning-fast. 3-Card-thats-me-and-Ima-last. Watch-me-throw-cause-here-I-go. One-good-pickll-get-you-in, 2-good-picks-and-you-gone-win. See-thuh-red-card-see-thuh-red-card-who-see-thuh-red-card?
(*Rest.*)

Dont touch my cards, man, just point to thuh one you want. You-pick-that-card-you-pick-a-loser, yeah, that-cards-a-loser. You-pick-that-card-thats-thuh-other-loser. You-pick-that-card-you-pick-a-winner. Follow that card. You gotta chase that card. You-pick-thuh-dark-deuce-thats-a-loser-other-dark-deuces-thuh-other-loser, red-deuce, thuh-deuce-of-heartsll-win-it-all. Follow thuh red card.

(Rest.)

Ima show you thuh cards: 2 black cards but only one heart. Now watch me now. Who-sees-thuh-red-card-who-knows-where-its-at? Go on, man, point to thuh card. Put yr money down cause you aint no clown. No? Ah you had thuh card, but you didnt have thuh heart.

(Rest.)

You wanna bet? 500 dollars? Shoot. You musta been watching 3-Card real close. Ok. Lay the cash in my hand cause 3-Cards thuh man. Thank you, mister. This card you say?

(Rest.)

Wrong! Sucker! Fool! Asshole! Bastard! I bet yr daddy heard how stupid you was and drank himself to death just cause he didnt wanna have nothing to do witchu! I bet yr mama seen you when you was born and she wished she was dead, sucker! Ha Ha Ha! And 3-Card, once again, wins all thuh money!!

(Rest.)

What? Cops looking my way? Fold up thuh game, and walk away. Sneak outa sight. Set up on another corner.

(Rest.)

Yeah.

(Rest.)

(Having won the imaginary loot and dodged the imaginary cops, BOOTH sets up his equipment and starts practicing his scam all over again. LINCOLN comes in quietly. He is a black man in his later 30s. He is dressed in an antique frock coat and wears a top hat and fake beard, that is, he is dressed to look like Abraham Lincoln. He surreptitiously walks into the room to stand right behind BOOTH, who, engrossed in his cards, does not notice LINCOLN right away.)

BOOTH: Watch me close watch me close now: who-see-thuh-red-card-who-see-thuh-red-card? I-see-thuh-red-card. Thuh-red-card-is-thuh-winner. Pick-thuh-red-card-you-pick-uh-winner. Pick-uh-black-card-you-pick-uh-loser. Theres-thuh-loser-yeah-theres-thuh-black-card, theres-thuh-other-loser-and-theres-thuh-red-card, thuh-winner. Don't touch my cards, man, don't—

(Rest.)

Dont do that shit. Dont do that shit. Dont do that shit!

(BOOTH, sensing someone behind him, whirls around, pulling a gun from his pants. While the presence of LINCOLN doesnt surprise him, the Lincoln costume does.)

BOOTH: And woah, man dont *ever* be doing that shit! Who thuh fuck you think you is coming in my shit all spooked out and shit. You pull that one more time I'll shoot you!

LINCOLN: I only had a minute to make the bus.

BOOTH: Bullshit.   5

LINCOLN: Not completely. I mean, its either bull or shit, but not a complete lie so it aint bullshit, right?

(*Rest.*)

Put yr gun away.

BOOTH: Take off the damn hat at least.

(LINCOLN *takes off the stovepipe hat.*)

(BOOTH *puts his gun away.*)

LINCOLN: Its cold out there. This thing kept my head warm.

BOOTH: I dont like you wearing that bullshit, that shit that bull that disguise that getup that motherdisfuckinguise anywhere in the daddy-dick-sticking vicinity of my humble abode.

(LINCOLN *takes off the beard.*)

LINCOLN: Better?   10

BOOTH: Take off the damn coat too. Damn, man. Bad enough you got to wear that shit all day you come up in here wearing it. What my women gonna say?

LINCOLN: What women?

BOOTH: I got a date with Grace tomorrow. Shes in love with me again but she dont know it yet. Aint no man can love her the way I can. She sees you in that getup its gonna reflect bad on me. She coulda seen you coming down the street. Shit. Could be standing outside right now taking her ring off and throwing it on the sidewalk.

(BOOTH *takes a peek out the window.*)

BOOTH: I got her this ring today. Diamond. Well, diamond-esque, but it looks just as good as the real thing. Asked her what size she wore. She say 7 so I go boost a size 6 and a half, right? Show it to her and she loves it and I shove it on her finger and its a tight fit right, so she cant just take it off on a whim, like she did the last one I gave her. Smooth, right?

(BOOTH *takes another peek out the window.*)

LINCOLN: She out there?   15

BOOTH: Nope. Coast is clear.

LINCOLN: You boosted a ring?

BOOTH: Yeah. I thought about spending my inheritance on it but—take off that damn coat, man, you make me nervous standing there looking like a spook, and that damn face paint, take it off. You should take all of it off at work and leave it there.

LINCOLN: I dont bring it home someone might steal it.

BOOTH: At least *take it off* there, then.   20

LINCOLN: Yeah.

(Rest.)

(LINCOLN *takes off the frock coat and applies cold cream, removing the whiteface.*)

LINCOLN: I was riding the bus. Really I only had a minute to make my bus
and I was sitting in the arcade thinking, should I change into my
street clothes or should I make the bus? Nobody was in there today
anyway. Middle of the week middle of winter. Not like on weekends.
Weekends the place is packed. So Im riding the bus home. And this
kid asked me for my autograph. I pretended I didnt hear him at first.
I'd had a long day. But he kept asking. Theyd just done Lincoln in history class and he knew all about him, he'd been to the arcade but, I
dunno, for some reason he was tripping cause there was Honest Abe
right beside him on the bus. I wanted to tell him to go fuck hisself.
But then I got a look at him. A little rich kid. Born on easy street,
you know the type. So I waited until I could tell he really wanted it,
the autograph, and I told him he could have it for 10 bucks. I was
gonna say 5, cause of the Lincoln connection but something in me
made me ask for 10.

BOOTH: But he didnt have a 10. All he had was a penny. So you took the
penny.

LINCOLN: All he had was a 20. So I took the 20 and told him to meet me
on the bus tomorrow and Honest Abe would give him the change.

BOOTH: Shit.   25

LINCOLN: Shit is right.

(Rest.)

BOOTH: Whatd you do with thuh 20?

LINCOLN: Bought drinks at Luckys. A round for everybody. They got a kick
out of the getup.

BOOTH: You shoulda called me down.

LINCOLN: Next time, bro.   30

(Rest.)

You making bookshelves? With the milk crates, you making
bookshelves?

BOOTH: Yeah, big bro, Im making bookshelves.

LINCOLN: Whats the cardboard part for?

BOOTH: Versatility.

LINCOLN: Oh.

BOOTH: I was thinking we dont got no bookshelves we dont got no dining   35
room table so Im making a sorta modular unit you put the books in the
bottom and the table top on top. We can eat and store our books. We
could put the photo album in there.

(BOOTH *gets the raggedy family photo album and puts it in the milk crate.*)

BOOTH: Youd sit there, I'd sit on the edge of the bed. Gathered around the dinner table. Like old times.

LINCOLN: We just gotta get some books but thats great, Booth, thats real great.

BOOTH: Dont be calling me Booth no more, K?

LINCOLN: You changing yr name?

BOOTH: Maybe.   40

LINCOLN

BOOTH

LINCOLN: What to?

BOOTH: Im not ready to reveal it yet.

LINCOLN: You already decided on something?   45

BOOTH: Maybe.

LINCOLN: You gonna call yrself something african? That be cool. Only pick something thats easy to spell and pronounce, man, cause you know, some of them african names, I mean, ok, Im down with the power to the people thing, but, no ones gonna hire you if they cant say yr name. And some of them fellas who got they african names, no one can say they names and they cant say they names neither. I mean, you dont want yr new handle to obstruct yr employment possibilities.

BOOTH

LINCOLN

BOOTH: You bring dinner?   50

LINCOLN: "Shango" would be a good name. The name of the thunder god. If you aint decided already Im just throwing it in the pot. I brought chinese.

BOOTH: Lets try the table out.

LINCOLN: Cool.

(*They both sit at the new table. The food is far away near the door.*)

LINCOLN

BOOTH   55

LINCOLN: I buy it you set it up. Thats the deal. Thats the deal, right?

BOOTH: You like this place?

LINCOLN: Ssallright.

BOOTH: But a little cramped sometimes, right?

LINCOLN: You dont hear me complain. Although that recliner sometimes   60
Booth, man—no Booth, right—man, Im too old to be sleeping in that chair.

BOOTH: Its my place. You dont got a place. Cookie, she threw you out. And you cant seem to get another woman. Yr lucky I let you stay.

LINCOLN: Every Friday you say *mi casa es su casa.*

BOOTH: Every Friday you come home with yr paycheck. Today is Thursday and I tell you brother, its a long way from Friday to Friday. All kinds of

things can happen. All kinds of bad feelings can surface and erupt
while yr little brother waits for you to bring in yr share.
(Rest.)
I got my Thursday head on, Link. Go get the food.
(LINCOLN *doesnt budge.)*
LINCOLN: You dont got no running water in here, man.
BOOTH: So? 65
LINCOLN: You dont got no toilet you dont got no sink.
BOOTH: Bathrooms down the hall.
LINCOLN: You living in thuh Third World, fool! Hey, I'll get thuh food.
(LINCOLN *goes to get the food. He sees a stray card on the floor and examines it
without touching it. He brings the food over, putting it nicely on the table.)*
LINCOLN: You been playing cards?
BOOTH: Yeah. 70
LINCOLN: Solitaire?
BOOTH: Thats right. Im getting pretty good at it.
LINCOLN: Thats soup and thats sauce. I got you the meat and I got me the
skrimps.
BOOTH: I wanted the skrimps.
LINCOLN: You said you wanted the meat. This morning when I left you said 75
you wanted the meat.
(Rest.)
Here man, take the skrimps. No sweat.
*(They eat. Chinese food from styrofoam containers, cans of soda, fortune cook-
ies.* LINCOLN *eats slowly and carefully,* BOOTH *eats ravenously.)*
LINCOLN: Yr getting good at solitaire?
BOOTH: Yeah. How about we play a hand after eating?
LINCOLN: Solitaire?
BOOTH: Poker or rummy or something.
LINCOLN: You know I dont touch thuh cards, man. 80
BOOTH: Just for fun.
LINCOLN: I dont touch thuh cards.
BOOTH: How about for money?
LINCOLN: You dont got no money. All the money you got I bring in here.
BOOTH: I got my inheritance. 85
LINCOLN: Thats like saying you dont got no money cause you aint never
gonna do nothing with it so its like you dont got it.
BOOTH: At least I still got mines. You blew yrs.
LINCOLN
BOOTH
LINCOLN: You like the skrimps? 90
BOOTH: Ssallright.
LINCOLN: Whats yr fortune?

BOOTH: "Waste not want not." Whats yrs?

LINCOLN: "Your luck will change!"

(BOOTH *finishes eating. He turns his back to* LINCOLN *and fiddles around with the cards, keeping them on the bed, just out of* LINCOLNS *sight. He mutters the 3-card patter under his breath. His moves are still clumsy. Every once and a while he darts a look over at* LINCOLN *who does his best to ignore* BOOTH.)

BOOTH: ((((Watch me close watch me close now: who-see-thuh-red-card-   95
who-see-thuh-red-card? I-see-thuh-red-card. Thuh-red-card-is-thuh-
winner. Pick-thuh-red-card-you-pick-uh-winner. Pick-uh-black-card-
and-you-pick-uh-loser. Theres-thuh-loser, yeah, theres-thuh-black-card,
theres-thuh-other-loser-and-theres-thuh-red-card, thuh-winner! Cop C,
Stick, Cop C! Go on—))))

LINCOLN: ((Shit.))

BOOTH: ((((((One-good-pickll-get-you-in, 2-good-picks-and-you-gone-win.
Dont touch my cards, man, just point to thuh one you want. You-pick-
that-card-you-pick-uh-loser, yeah, that-cards-uh-loser. You-pick-that-
card-thats-thuh-other-loser. You-pick-that-card-you-pick-uh-winner.
Follow-that-card. You-gotta-chase-that-card!)))))))

LINCOLN: You wanna hustle 3-card monte, you gotta do it right, you gotta
break it down. Practice it in smaller bits. Yr trying to do the whole
thing at once thats why you keep fucking it up.

BOOTH: Show me.

LINCOLN: No. Im just saying you wanna do it you gotta do it right and   100
if you gonna do it right you gotta work on it in smaller bits,
thatsall.

BOOTH: You and me could team up and do it together. We'd clean up,
Link.

LINCOLN: I'll clean up—bro.

(LINCOLN *cleans up. As he clears the food,* BOOTH *goes back to using the "table" for its original purpose.*)

BOOTH: My new names 3-Card. 3-Card, got it? You wanted to know it so
now you know it. 3-card monte by 3-Card. Call me 3-Card from here
on out.

LINCOLN: 3-Card. Shit.

BOOTH: Im getting everybody to call me 3-Card. Grace likes 3-Card better   105
than Booth. She says 3-Cards got something to it. Anybody not calling
me 3-Card gets a bullet.

LINCOLN: Yr too much, man.

BOOTH: Im making a point.

LINCOLN: Point made, 3-Card. Point made.

(LINCOLN *picks up his guitar. Plays at it.*)

BOOTH: Oh, come on, man, we could make money you and me. Throwing
down the cards. 3-Card and Link: look out! We could clean up you and

me. You would throw the cards and I'd be yr Stickman. The one in the
crowd who looks like just an innocent passerby, who looks like just
another player, like just another customer, but who gots intimate connections with you, the Dealer, the one throwing the cards, the main
man. I'd be the one who brings in the crowd, I'd be the one who makes
them want to put they money down, you do yr moves and I do mines.
You turn yr head and I turn the card—

LINCOLN: It aint as easy as all that. Theres—   110

BOOTH: We could be a team, man. Rake in the money! Sure thered be
some cats out there with fast eyes, some brothers and sisters who would
watch real close and pick the right card, and so thered be some days
when we would lose money, but most of the days we would come out
on top! Pockets bulging, plenty of cash! And the ladies would be thrilling! You could afford to get laid! Grace would be all over me again.

LINCOLN: I thought you said she was all over you.

BOOTH: She is she is. Im seeing her tomorrow but today we gotta solidify
the shit twixt you and me. Big brother Link and little brother Booth—

LINCOLN: 3-Card.

BOOTH: Yeah. Scheming and dreaming. No one throws the cards like you,   115
Link. And with yr moves and my magic, and we get Grace and a girl
for you to round out the posse. We'd be golden, bro! Am I right?

LINCOLN

LINCOLN

BOOTH: Am I right?

LINCOLN: I dont touch thuh cards, 3-Card. I dont touch thuh cards no
more.

LINCOLN   120

BOOTH

LINCOLN

BOOTH

BOOTH: You know what Mom told me when she was packing to leave?
You was at school motherfucker you was at school. You got up that
morning and sat down in yr regular place and read the cereal box
while Dad read the sports section and Mom brought you yr dick
toast and then you got on the damn school bus cause you didnt have
the sense to do nothing else you was so into yr own shit that you
didnt have the sense to feel nothing else going on. I had the sense
to go back cause I was feeling something going on man, I was feeling
something changing. So I—

LINCOLN: Cut school that day like you did almost every day—   125

BOOTH: She was putting her stuff in bags. She had all them nice suitcases
but she was putting her stuff in bags.
    (Rest.)

Packing up her shit. She told me to look out for you. I told her I was the little brother and the big brother should look out after the little brother. She just said it again. That I should look out for you. Yeah. So who gonna look out for me. Not like you care. Here I am interested in an economic opportunity, willing to work hard, willing to take risks and all you can say you shiteating motherfucking pathetic limpdick uncle tom, all you can tell me is how you dont do no more what I be wanting to do. Here I am trying to earn a living and you standing in my way. YOU STANDING IN MY WAY, LINK!

LINCOLN: Im sorry.

BOOTH: Yeah, you sorry all right.

LINCOLN: I cant be hustling no more, bro.

BOOTH: What you do all day aint no hustle?

LINCOLN: Its honest work.

BOOTH: Dressing up like some crackerass white man, some dead president and letting people shoot at you sounds like a hustle to me.

LINCOLN: People know the real deal. When people know the real deal it aint a hustle.

BOOTH: We do the card game people will know the real deal. Sometimes we will win sometimes they will win. They fast they win, we faster we win.

LINCOLN: I aint going back to that, bro. I aint going back.

BOOTH: You play Honest Abe. You aint going back but you going all the way back. Back to way back then when folks was slaves and shit.

LINCOLN: Dont push me.

BOOTH

LINCOLN

BOOTH: You gonna have to leave.

LINCOLN: I'll be gone tomorrow.

BOOTH: Good. Cause this was only supposed to be a temporary arrangement.

LINCOLN: I will be gone tomorrow.

BOOTH: Good.

(BOOTH *sits on his bed.* LINCOLN, *sitting in his easy chair with his guitar, plays and sings.*)

LINCOLN: My dear mother left me, my fathers gone away
My dear mother left me and my fathers gone away
I dont got no money, I dont got no place to stay.

My best girl, she threw me out into the street
My favorite horse, they ground him into meat
Im feeling cold from my head down to my feet

My luck was bad but now it turned to worse

My luck was bad but now it turned to worse
Dont call me up a doctor, just call me up a hearse.
BOOTH: You just made that up?
LINCOLN: I had it in my head for a few days.
BOOTH: Sounds good.
LINCOLN: Thanks.
    (Rest.)
Daddy told me once why we got the names we do.
BOOTH: Yeah?   150
LINCOLN: Yeah.
    (Rest.)
He was drunk when he told me, or maybe I was drunk when he told
me. Anyway he told me, may not be true, but he told me. Why he
named us both. Lincoln and Booth.
BOOTH: How come. How come, man?
LINCOLN: It was his idea of a joke.
(Both men relax back as the lights fade.)

Scene 2

Friday evening. The very next day. BOOTH *comes in looking like he is bundled up
against the cold. He makes sure his brother isnt home, then stands in the middle of
the room. From his big coat sleeves he pulls out one new shoe then another, from
another sleeve come two more shoes. He then slithers out a belt from each sleeve.
He removes his coat. Underneath he wears a very nice new suit. He removes the
jacket and pants revealing another new suit underneath. The suits still have the
price tags on them. He takes two neckties from his pockets and two folded shirts
from the back of his pants. He pulls a magazine from the front of his pants. Hes
clearly had a busy day of shoplifting. He lays one suit out on* LINCOLNS *easy
chair. The other he lays out on his own bed. He goes out into the hall returning
with a folding screen which he sets up between the bed and the recliner creating
2 separate spaces. He takes out a bottle of whiskey and two glasses, setting them
on the two stacked milk crates. He hears footsteps and sits down in the small
wooden chair reading the magazine.* LINCOLN, *dressed in street clothes, comes in.*

LINCOLN: Taaaaadaaaaaaaa!
BOOTH: Lordamighty, Pa, I smells money!
LINCOLN: Sho nuff, Ma. Poppas brung home thuh bacon.
BOOTH: Bringitherebringitherebringithere.
(With a series of very elaborate moves LINCOLN *brings the money over to* BOOTH.*)*
BOOTH: Put it in my hands, Pa!   5
LINCOLN: I want ya tuh smells it first, Ma!
BOOTH: Put it neath my nose then, Pa!

LINCOLN: Take yrself a good long whiff of them greenbacks.
BOOTH: Oh lordamighty Ima faint, Pa! Get me muh med-sin!
(LINCOLN *quickly pours two large glasses of whiskey.*)
LINCOLN: Dont die on me, Ma!   10
BOOTH: Im fading fast, Pa!
LINCOLN: Thinka thuh children, Ma! Thinka thuh farm!
BOOTH: 1-2-3.
(*Both men gulp down their drinks simultaneously.*)
LINCOLN AND BOOTH: AAAAAAAAAAAAAAAAAAAAH!
(*Lots of laughing and slapping on the backs.*)
LINCOLN: Budget it out man budget it out.   15
BOOTH: You in a hurry?
LINCOLN: Yeah. I wanna see how much we got for the week.
BOOTH: You rush in here and dont even look around. Could be a fucking
    A-bomb in the middle of the floor you wouldnt notice. Yr wife,
    Cookie—
LINCOLN: X-wife—
BOOTH: —could be in my bed you wouldnt notice—   20
LINCOLN: She was once—
BOOTH: Look the fuck around please.
(LINCOLN *looks around and sees the new suit on his chair.*)
LINCOLN: Wow.
BOOTH: Its yrs.
LINCOLN: Shit.   25
BOOTH: Got myself one too.
LINCOLN: Boosted?
BOOTH: Yeah, I boosted em. Theys stole from a big-ass department store.
    That store takes in more money in one day than we will in our whole
    life. I stole and I stole generously. I got one for me and I got one for
    you. Shoes belts shirts ties socks in the shoes and everything. Got
    that screen too.
LINCOLN: You all right, man.
BOOTH: Just cause I aint good as you at cards dont mean I cant do nothing. 30
LINCOLN: Lets try em on.
(*They stand in their separate sleeping spaces,* BOOTH *near his bed,* LINCOLN *near
    his recliner, and try on their new clothes.*)
BOOTH: Ima wear mine tonight. Gracell see me in this and *she* gonna ask
    me tuh marry *her.*
    (*Rest.*)
    I got you the blue and I got me the brown. I walked in there and walked
    out and they didnt as much as bat an eye. Thats how smooth lil bro be,
    Link.
LINCOLN: You did good. You did real good, 3-Card.

BOOTH: All in a days work.

LINCOLN: They say the clothes make the man. All day long I wear that   35
getup. But that dont make me who I am. Old black coat not even real
old just fake old. Its got worn spots on the elbows, little raggedy places
thatll break through into holes before the winters out. Shiny strips
around the cuffs and the collar. Dust from the cap guns on the left
shoulder where they shoot him, where they shoot me I should say but
I never feel like they shooting me. The fella who had the gig before I
had it wore the same coat. When I got the job they had the getup
hanging there waiting for me. Said thuh fella before me just took it off
one day and never came back.

(Rest.)

Remember how Dads clothes used to hang in the closet?

BOOTH: Until you took em outside and burned em.

(Rest.)

He had some nice stuff. What he didnt spend on booze he spent on
women. What he didnt spend on them two he spent on clothes. He
had some nice stuff. I would look at his stuff and calculate thuh how
long it would take till I was big enough to fit it. Then you went and
burned it all up.

LINCOLN: I got tired of looking at em without him in em.

(Rest.)

They said thuh fella before me—he took off the getup one day, hung it
up real nice, and never came back. And as they offered me thuh job,
saying of course I would have to wear a little makeup and accept less
than what they would offer a—another guy—

BOOTH: Go on, say it. "White." Theyd pay you less than theyd pay a white
guy.

LINCOLN: I said to myself thats exactly what I would do: wear it out and
then leave it hanging there and not come back. But until then, I would
make a living at it. But it dont make me. Worn suit coat, not even
worn by the fool that Im supposed to be playing, but making fools out
of all those folks who come crowding in for they chance to play at
something great. Fake beard. Top hat. Dont make me into no Lincoln.
I was Lincoln on my own before any of that.

(The men finish dressing. They style and profile.)

BOOTH: Sharp, huh?   40

LINCOLN: Very sharp.

BOOTH: You look sharp too, man. You look like the real you. Most of
the time you walking around all bedraggled and shit. You look good.
Like you used to look back in thuh day when you had Cookie in
love with you and all the women in the world was eating out of yr
hand.

LINCOLN: This is real nice, man. I dont know where Im gonna wear it but its real nice.

BOOTH: Just wear it around. Itll make you feel good and when you feel good yll meet someone nice. Me I aint interested in meeting no one nice, I mean, I only got eyes for Grace. You think she'll go for me in this?

LINCOLN: I think thuh tie you gave me'll go better with what you got on.   45

BOOTH: Yeah?

LINCOLN: Grace likes bright colors dont she? My ties bright, yrs is too subdued.

BOOTH: Yeah. Gimmie yr tie.

LINCOLN: You gonna take back a gift?

BOOTH: I stole the damn thing didnt I? Gimmie yrs! I'll give you mines.   50
(They switch neckties. BOOTH *is pleased.* LINCOLN *is more pleased.)*

LINCOLN: Do thuh budget.

BOOTH: Right. Ok lets see: we got 314 dollars. We put 100 aside for the rent. 100 a week times 4 weeks makes the rent and—

LINCOLN AND BOOTH: —we dont want thuh rent spent.

BOOTH: That leaves 214. We put aside 30 for the electric leaving 184. We put aside 50 for thuh phone leaving 134.

LINCOLN: We dont got a phone.   55

BOOTH: We pay our bill theyll turn it back on.

LINCOLN: We dont need no phone.

BOOTH: How you gonna get a woman if you dont got a phone? Women these days are more cautious, more whaddacallit, more circumspect. You go into a club looking like a fast daddy, you get a filly to give you her numerophono and gone is the days when she just gives you her number and dont ask for yrs.

LINCOLN: Like a woman is gonna call me.

BOOTH: She dont wanna call you she just doing a preliminary survey of the   60
property. Shit, Link, you dont know nothin no more.
(Rest.)
She gives you her number and she asks for yrs. You give her yr number. The phone number of yr home. Thereby telling her 3 things: 1) you got a home, that is, you aint no smooth talking smooth dressing *homeless* joe; 2) that you is in possession of a telephone and a working telephone number which is to say that you got thuh cash and thuh wherewithal to acquire for yr self the worlds most revolutionary communication apparatus and you together enough to pay yr bills!

LINCOLN: Whats 3?

BOOTH: You give her yr number you telling her that its cool to call if she should so please, that is, that you aint got no wife or wife approximation on the premises.

(Rest.)
50 for the phone leaving 134. We put aside 40 for "med-sin."

LINCOLN: The price went up. 2 bucks more a bottle.

BOOTH: We'll put aside 50, then. That covers the bills. We got 84 left. 40
for meals together during the week leaving 44. 30 for me 14 for you. I
got a woman I gotta impress tonight.

LINCOLN: You didnt take out for the phone last week.   65

BOOTH: Last week I was depressed. This week things is looking up. For both
of us.

LINCOLN: Theyre talking about cutbacks at the arcade. I only been there
8 months, so—

BOOTH: Dont sweat it man, we'll find something else.

LINCOLN: Not nothing like this. I like the job. This is sit down, you know,
easy work. I just gotta sit there all day. Folks come in kill phony Honest
Abe with the phony pistol. I can sit there and let my mind travel.

BOOTH: Think of women.   70

LINCOLN: Sometimes.

(Rest.)

All around the whole arcade is buzzing and popping. Thuh whirring of
thuh duckshoot, baseballs smacking the back wall when someone misses
the stack of cans, some woman getting happy cause her fella just won
the ring toss. The Boss playing the barker talking up the fake freaks.
The smell of the ocean and cotton candy and rat shit. And in thuh
middle of all that, I can just sit and let my head go quiet. Make up
songs, make plans. Forget.

(Rest.)

You should come down again.

BOOTH: Once was plenty, but thanks.

(Rest.)

Yr Best Customer, he come in today?

LINCOLN: Oh, yeah, he was there.

BOOTH: He shoot you?

LINCOLN: He shot Honest Abe, yeah.   75

BOOTH: He talk to you?

LINCOLN: In a whisper. Shoots on the left whispers on the right.

BOOTH: Whatd he say this time?

LINCOLN: "Does thuh show stop when no ones watching or does thuh show
go on?"

BOOTH: Hes getting deep.   80

LINCOLN: Yeah.

BOOTH: Whatd he say, that one time? "Yr only yrself—"

LINCOLN: "—when no ones watching," yeah.

BOOTH: Thats deep shit.
 (*Rest.*)
 Hes a brother, right?
LINCOLN: I think so.   85
BOOTH: He know yr a brother?
LINCOLN: I dunno.
BOOTH: Hes a *deep* black brother.
LINCOLN: Yeah. He makes the day interesting.
BOOTH (*Rest.*): Thats a fucked-up job you got.   90
LINCOLN: Its a living.
BOOTH: But you aint living.
LINCOLN: Im alive aint I?
 (*Rest.*)
 One day I was throwing the cards. Next day Lonny died. Somebody
 shot him. I knew I was next, so I quit. I saved my life.
 (*Rest.*)
 The arcade gig is the first lucky break Ive ever had. And Ive actually
 grown to like the work. And now theyre talking about cutting me.
BOOTH: You was lucky with thuh cards.
LINCOLN: Lucky? Aint nothing lucky about cards. Cards aint luck. Cards is   95
 work. Cards is skill. Aint never nothing lucky about cards.
 (*Rest.*)
 I dont wanna lose my job.
BOOTH: Then you gotta jazz up yr act. Elaborate yr moves, you know. You
 was always too stiff with it. You cant just sit there! Maybe, when they
 shoot you, you know, leap up flail yr arms then fall down and wiggle
 around and shit so they gotta shoot you more than once. Blam Blam
 Blam! Blam!
LINCOLN: Help me practice. I'll sit here like I do at work and you be like
 one of the tourists.
BOOTH: No thanks.
LINCOLN: My paychecks on the line, man.
BOOTH: I got a date. Practice on yr own.   10
 (*Rest.*)
 I got a rendezvous with Grace. Shit she so sweet she makes my teeth
 hurt.
 (*Rest.*) Link, uh, howbout slipping me an extra 5 spot. Its the biggest
 night of my life.
LINCOLN
BOOTH
(LINCOLN *gives* BOOTH *a 5er.*)
BOOTH: Thanks.
LINCOLN: No sweat.

BOOTH: Howabout I run through it with you when I get back. Put on yr   105
getup and practice till then.

LINCOLN: Sure.

(BOOTH *leaves.* LINCOLN *stands there alone. He takes off his shoes, giving them a shine. He takes off his socks and his fancy suit, hanging it neatly over the little wooden chair. He takes his getup out of his shopping bag. He puts it on, slowly, like an actor preparing for a great role: frock coat, pants, beard, top hat, necktie. He leaves his feet bare. The top hat has an elastic band which he positions securely underneath his chin. He picks up the white pancake makeup but decides against it. He sits. He pretends to get shot, flings himself on the floor and thrashes around. He gets up, considers giving the new moves another try, but instead pours himself a big glass of whiskey and sits there drinking.*)

Scene 3

Much later that same Friday evening. The recliner is reclined to its maximum horizontal position and LINCOLN *lies there asleep. He wakes with a start. He is horrific, bleary eyed and hungover, in his full Lincoln regalia. He takes a deep breath, realizes where he is and reclines again, going back to sleep.* BOOTH *comes in full of swagger. He slams the door trying to wake his brother who is dead to the world. He opens the door and slams it again. This time* LINCOLN *wakes up, as hungover and horrid as before.* BOOTH *swaggers about, his moves are exaggerated, rooster-like. He walks round and round* LINCOLN *making sure his brother sees him.*

LINCOLN: You hurt yrself?

BOOTH: I had me "an evening to remember."

LINCOLN: You look like you hurt yrself.

BOOTH: Grace Grace Grace. *Grace.* She wants me back. She wants me back so bad she wiped her hand over the past where we wasnt together just so she could say we aint never been apart. She wiped her hand over our breakup. She wiped her hand over her childhood, her teenage years, her first boyfriend, just so she could say that she been mine since the dawn of time.

LINCOLN: Thats great, man.   5

BOOTH: And all the shit I put her through: she wiped it clean. And the women I saw while I was seeing her—

LINCOLN: Wiped clean too?

BOOTH: Mister Clean, Mister, Mister Clean!

LINCOLN: Whered you take her?

BOOTH: We was over at her place. I brought thuh food. Stopped at the best   10
place I could find and stuffed my coat with only the best. We had the music we had the candlelight we had—

LINCOLN: She let you do it?

BOOTH: Course she let me do it.

LINCOLN: She let you do it without a rubber?

BOOTH: —Yeah.

LINCOLN: Bullshit. 15

BOOTH: I put my foot down—and she *melted*. And she was—huh—she was something else. I dont wanna get you jealous, though.

LINCOLN: Go head, I dont mind.

BOOTH (*Rest.*): Well, you know what she looks like.

LINCOLN: She walks on by and the emergency room fills up cause all the guys get whiplash from lookin at her.

BOOTH: Thats right thats right. Well—she comes to the door wearing noth- 20 ing but her little nightie, eats up the food I'd brought like there was no tomorrow and then goes and eats on me.

(*Rest.*)

LINCOLN: Go on.

BOOTH: I dont wanna make you feel bad, man.

LINCOLN: Ssallright. Go on.

BOOTH (*Rest.*): Well, uh, you know what shes like. Wild. Goodlooking. So sweet my teeth hurt.

LINCOLN: A sexmachine. 25

BOOTH: Yeah.

LINCOLN: A hotsy-totsy.

BOOTH: Yeah.

LINCOLN: Amazing Grace.

BOOTH: Amazing Grace! Yeah. Thats right. She let me do her how I wanted. 30 And no rubber.

(*Rest.*)

LINCOLN: Go on.

BOOTH: You dont wanna hear the mushy shit.

LINCOLN: Sure I do.

BOOTH: You hate mushy shit. You always hated thuh mushy shit.

LINCOLN: Ive changed. Go head. You had "an evening to remember," re- 35 member? I was just here alone sitting here. Drinking. Go head. Tell Link thuh stink.

(*Rest.*)

Howd ya do her?

BOOTH: Dogstyle.

LINCOLN: Amazing Grace.

BOOTH: In front of a mirror.

LINCOLN: So you could see her. Her face her breasts her back her ass. Graces got a great ass.

BOOTH: Its all right. 40

LINCOLN: Amazing Grace!

(BOOTH *goes into his bed area and takes off his suit, tossing the clothes on the floor.*)

BOOTH: She said next time Ima have to use a rubber. She let me have my way this time but she said that next time I'd have to put my boots on.

LINCOLN: Im sure you can talk her out of it.

BOOTH: Yeah.

(*Rest.*)

What kind of rubbers you use, I mean, when you was with Cookie.

LINCOLN: We didnt use rubbers. We was married, man.   45

BOOTH: Right. But you had other women on the side. What kind you use when you was with them?

LINCOLN: Magnums.

BOOTH: Thats thuh kind I picked up. For next time. Grace was real strict about it. Magnums.

(*While* BOOTH *sits on his bed fiddling with his box of condoms,* LINCOLN *sits in his chair and resumes drinking.*)

LINCOLN: Theyre for "the larger man."

BOOTH: Right. Right.   50

(LINCOLN *keeps drinking as* BOOTH, *sitting in the privacy of his bedroom, fiddles with the condoms, perhaps trying to put one on.*)

LINCOLN: Thats right.

BOOTH: Graces real different from them fly-by-night gals I was making do with. Shes in school. Making something of herself. Studying cosmetology. You should see what she can do with a womans hair and nails.

LINCOLN: Too bad you aint a woman.

BOOTH: What?

LINCOLN: You could get yrs done for free, I mean.   55

BOOTH: Yeah. She got this way of sitting. Of talking. That. Everything she does is. Shes just so hot.

(*Rest.*)

We was together 2 years. Then we broke up. I had my little employment difficulty and she needed time to think.

LINCOLN: And shes through thinking now.

BOOTH: Thats right.

LINCOLN

BOOTH   60

LINCOLN: Whatcha doing back there?

BOOTH: Resting. That girl wore me out.

LINCOLN: You want some med-sin?

BOOTH: No thanks.

LINCOLN: Come practice my moves with me, then.   65

BOOTH: Lets hit it tomorrow, K?

LINCOLN: I been waiting. I got all dressed up and you said if I waited up—
come on, man, they gonna replace me with a wax dummy.

BOOTH: No shit.

LINCOLN: Thats what theyre talking about. Probably just talk, but—come
on, man, I even lent you 5 bucks.

BOOTH: Im tired.   70

LINCOLN: You didnt get shit tonight.

BOOTH: You jealous, man. You just jail-us.

LINCOLN: You laying over there yr balls blue as my boosted suit. Laying
over there waiting for me to go back to sleep or black out so I wont
hear you rustling thuh pages of yr fuck book.

BOOTH: Fuck you, man.

LINCOLN: I was over there looking for something the other week and theres   75
like 100 fuck books under yr bed and theyre matted together like a bad
fro, bro, cause you spunked in the pages and didnt wipe them off.

BOOTH: Im hot. I need constant sexual release. If I wasnt taking care of myself by myself I would be out there running around on thuh town which
costs cash that I dont have so I would be doing worse: I'd be out there
doing who knows what, shooting people and shit. Out of a need for unresolved sexual release. I'm a hot man. I aint apologizing for it. When
I dont got a woman, I gotta make do. Not like you, Link. When you
dont got a woman you just sit there. Letting yr shit fester. Yr dick, if
it aint falled off yet, is hanging there between yr legs, little whiteface
shriveled-up blank-shooting grub worm. As goes thuh man so goes thuh
mans dick. Thats what I say. Least my shits intact.
(Rest.)
You a limp dick jealous whiteface motherfucker whose wife dumped
him cause he couldnt get it up and she told me so. Came crawling to
me cause she needed a man.
(Rest.)
I gave it to Grace good tonight. So goodnight.

LINCOLN (Rest.): Goodnight.

LINCOLN

BOOTH

LINCOLN   80

BOOTH

LINCOLN

BOOTH

(LINCOLN *sitting in his chair.* BOOTH *lying in bed. Time passes.* BOOTH *peeks out
to see if* LINCOLN *is asleep.* LINCOLN *is watching for him.*)

LINCOLN: You can hustle 3-card monte without me you know.

BOOTH: Im planning to.   85

LINCOLN: I could contact my old crew. You could work with them. Lonny aint around no more but theres the rest of them. Theyre good.

BOOTH: I can get my own crew. I dont need yr crew. Buncha has-beens. I can get my own crew.

LINCOLN: My crews experienced. We usedta pull down a thousand a day. Thats 7 G a week. That was years ago. They probably do twice, 3 times that now.

BOOTH: I got my own connections, thank you.

LINCOLN: Theyd take you on in a heartbeat. With my say. My say still   90
counts with them. They know you from before, when you tried to hang with us but—wernt ready yet. They know you from then, but I'd talk you up. I'd say yr my bro, which they know, and I'd say youd been working the west coast. Little towns. Mexican border. Taking tourists. I'd tell them you got moves like I dreamed of having. Meanwhile youd be working out yr shit right here, right in this room, getting good and getting better every day so when I did do the reintroductions youd have some marketable skills. Youd be passable.

BOOTH: I'd be more than passable, I'd be the be all end all.

LINCOLN: Youd be the be all end all. And youd have my say. If yr interested.

BOOTH: Could do.

LINCOLN: Youd have to get a piece. They all pack pistols, bro.

BOOTH: I *got* a piece.   95

LINCOLN: Youd have to be packing something more substantial than that pop gun, 3-Card. These hustlers is upper echelon hustlers they pack upper echelon heat, not no Saturday night shit, now.

BOOTH: Whata you know of heat? You aint hung with those guys for 6, 7 years. You swore off em. Threw yr heat in thuh river and you "Dont touch thuh cards." I know more about heat than you know about heat.

LINCOLN: Im around guns every day. At the arcade. Theyve all been reworked so they only fire caps but I see guns every day. Lots of guns.

BOOTH: What kinds?

LINCOLN: You been there, you seen them. Shiny deadly metal each with   100
their own deadly personality.

BOOTH: Maybe I *could* visit you over there. I'd boost one of them guns and rework it to make it shoot for real again. What kind you think would best suit my personality?

LINCOLN: You aint stealing nothing from the arcade.

BOOTH: I go in there and steal if I want to go in there and steal I go in there and steal.

LINCOLN: It aint worth it. They dont shoot nothing but blanks.

BOOTH: Yeah, like you. Shooting blanks.   105

(*Rest.*)

(*Rest.*)

You ever wonder if someones gonna come in there with a real gun? A real gun with real slugs? Someone with uh axe tuh grind or something?

LINCOLN: No.

BOOTH: Someone who hates you come in there and guns you down and gets gone before anybody finds out.

LINCOLN: I dont got no enemies.

BOOTH: Yr X.

LINCOLN: Cookie dont hate me.   110

BOOTH: Yr Best Customer? Some miscellaneous stranger?

LINCOLN: I cant be worrying about the actions of miscellaneous strangers.

BOOTH: But there they come day in day out for a chance to shoot Honest Abe.

(*Rest.*)

Who are they mostly?

LINCOLN: I dont really look.

BOOTH: You must see something.   115

LINCOLN: Im supposed to be staring straight ahead. Watching a play, like Abe was.

BOOTH: All day goes by and you never ever take a sneak peek at who be pulling the trigger.

(*Pulled in by his own curiosity,* BOOTH *has come out of his bed area to stand on the dividing line between the two spaces.*)

LINCOLN: Its pretty dark. To keep thuh illusion of thuh whole thing.

(*Rest.*)

But on thuh wall opposite where I sit theres a little electrical box, like a fuse box. Silver metal. Its got uh dent in it like somebody hit it with they fist. Big old dent so everything reflected in it gets reflected upside down. Like yr looking in uh spoon. And thats where I can see em. The assassins.

(*Rest.*)

Not behind me yet but I can hear him coming. Coming in with his gun in hand, thuh gun he already picked out up front when he paid his fare. Coming on in. But not behind me yet. His dress shoes making too much noise on the carpet, the carpets too thin, Boss should get a new one but hes cheap. Not behind me yet. Not behind me yet. Cheap lightbulb just above my head.

(*Rest.*)

And there he is. Standing behind me. Standing in position. Standing upside down. Theres some feet shapes on the floor so he knows just where he oughta stand. So he wont miss. Thuh gun is always cold.

Winter or summer thuh gun is always cold. And when the gun touches
me he can feel that Im warm and he knows Im alive. And if Im alive
then he can shoot me dead. And for a minute, with him hanging back
there behind me, its real. Me looking at him upside down and him
looking at me looking like Lincoln. Then he shoots.
(*Rest.*)
I slump down and close my eyes. And he goes out thuh other way.
More come in. Uh whole day full. Bunches of kids, little good for
nothings, in they school uniforms. Businessmen smelling like two for
one martinis. Tourists in they theme park t-shirts trying to catch it
on film. Housewives with they mouths closed tight, shooting more
than once.
(*Rest.*)
They all get so into it. I do my best for them. And now they talking
bout cutting me, replacing me with uh wax dummy.

BOOTH: You just gotta show yr boss that you can do things a wax dummy
cant do. You too dry with it. You gotta add spicy shit.

LINCOLN: Like what.   120

BOOTH: Like when they shoot you, I dunno, scream or something.

LINCOLN: Scream?

(BOOTH *plays the killer without using his gun.*)

BOOTH: Try it. I'll be the killer. Bang!

LINCOLN: Aaaah!

BOOTH: Thats good.   125

LINCOLN: A wax dummy can scream. They can put a voicebox in it and
make it like its screaming.

BOOTH: You can curse. Try it. Bang!

LINCOLN: Motherfucking cocksucker!

BOOTH: Thats good, man.

LINCOLN: They aint going for that, though.   130

BOOTH: You practice rolling and wiggling on the floor?

LINCOLN: A little.

BOOTH: Lemmie see. Bang!

(LINCOLN *slumps down, falls on the floor and silently wiggles around.*)

BOOTH: You look more like a worm on the sidewalk. Move yr arms. Good.
Now scream or something.

LINCOLN: Aaaah! Aaaaah! Aaaah!   135

BOOTH: A little tougher than that, you sound like yr fucking.

LINCOLN: Aaaaaah!

BOOTH: Hold yr head or something, where I shotcha. Good. And look at
me! I am the assassin! *I am Booth!!* Come on man this is life and death!
Go all out!

(LINCOLN *goes all out!*)

BOOTH: Cool, man thats cool. Thats enough.

LINCOLN: Whatdoyathink? 140

BOOTH: I dunno, man. Something about it. I dunno. It was looking too real or something.

LINCOLN: Goddamn you! They dont want it looking too real. I'd scare the customers. Then I'd be out for sure. Yr trying to get me fired.

BOOTH: Im trying to help. Cross my heart.

LINCOLN: People are funny about they Lincoln shit. Its historical. People like they historical shit in a certain way. They like it to unfold the way they folded it up. Neatly like a book. Not raggedy and bloody and screaming. You trying to get me fired.

(Rest.)

I am uh brother playing Lincoln. Its uh stretch for anyones imagination. And it aint easy for me neither. Every day I put on that shit, I leave my own shit at the door and I put on that shit and I go out there and I make it work. I make it look easy but its hard. That shit is hard. But it works. Cause I work it. And you trying to get me fired.

(Rest.)

I swore off them cards. Took nowhere jobs. Drank. Then Cookie threw me out. What thuh fuck was I gonna do? I seen that "Help Wanted" sign and I went up in there and I looked good in the getup and agreed to the whiteface and they really dug it that me and Honest Abe got the same name.

(Rest.)

Its a sit down job. With benefits. I dont wanna get fired. They wont give me a good reference if I get fired.

BOOTH: Iffen you was tuh get fired, then, well—then you and me could— 14 hustle the cards together. We'd have to support ourselves somehow.

(Rest.)

Just show me how to do the hook part of the card hustle, man. The part where the Dealer looks away but somehow he sees—

LINCOLN: I couldnt remember if I wanted to.

BOOTH: Sure you could.

LINCOLN: No.

(Rest.)

Night, man.

BOOTH: Yeah.

(LINCOLN *stretches out in his recliner.* BOOTH *stands over him waiting for him to get up, to change his mind. But* LINCOLN *is fast asleep.* BOOTH *covers him with a blanket then goes to his bed, turning off the lights as he goes. He quietly rummages underneath his bed for a girlie magazine which, as the lights fade, he reads with great interest.*)

Scene 4

Saturday. Just before dawn. LINCOLN *gets up. Looks around.* BOOTH *is fast asleep, dead to the world.*

LINCOLN: No fucking running water.

(He stumbles around the room looking for something which he finally finds: a plastic cup, which he uses as a urinal. He finishes peeing and finds an out of the way place to stow the cup. He claws at his Lincoln getup, removing it and tearing it in the process. He strips down to his t-shirt and shorts.)

LINCOLN: Hate falling asleep in this damn shit. Shit. Ripped the beard. I can just hear em tomorrow. Busiest day of the week. They looking me over to make sure Im presentable. They got a slew of guys working but Im the only one they look over every day. "Yr beards ripped, pal. Sure, we'll getcha new one but its gonna be coming outa yr pay." Shit. I should quit right then and there. I'd yank off the beard, throw it on the ground and stomp it, then go strangle the fucking boss. Thatd be good. My hands around his neck and his bug eyes bugging out. You been ripping me off since I took this job and now Im gonna have to take it outa yr pay, motherfucker. Shit.

(Rest.)

Sit down job. With benefits.

(Rest.)

Hustling. Shit, I was good. I was great. Hell I was the be all end all. I was throwing cards like throwing cards was made for me. Made for me and me alone. I was the best anyone ever seen. Coast to coast. Everybody said so. And I never lost. Not once. Not one time. Not never. Thats how much them cards was mines. I was the be all end all. I was that good.

(Rest.)

Then you woke up one day and you didnt have the taste for it no more. Like something in you knew—. Like something in you knew it was time to quit. Quit while you was still ahead. Something in you was telling you—. But hells no. Not Link thuh stink. So I went out there and threw one more time. What thuh fuck. And Lonny died.

(Rest.)

Got yrself a good job. And when the arcade lets you go yll get another good job. I dont gotta spend my whole life hustling. Theres more to Link than that. More to me than some cheap hustle. More to life than cheating some idiot out of his paycheck or his life savings.

(Rest.)

Like that joker and his wife from out of town. Always wanted to see the big city. I said you could see the bigger end of the big city with a

little more cash. And if they was fast enough, faster than me, and
here I slowed down my moves I slowed em way down and my Lonny,
my right hand, my Stickman, Lonny could draw a customer in like
nothing else, Lonny could draw a fly from fresh shit, he could draw
Adam outa Eve just with that look he had, Lonny always got folks
playing.
(Rest.)
Somebody shot him. They dont know who. Nobody knows nobody
cares.
(Rest.)
We took that man and his wife for hundreds. No, thousands. We took
them for everything they had and everything they ever wanted to have.
We took a father for the money he was gonna get his kids new bike
with and he cried in the street while we vanished. We took a mothers
welfare check, she pulled a knife on us and we ran. She threw it but her
aim werent shit. People shopping. Greedy. Thinking they could take
me and they got took instead.
(Rest.)
Swore off thuh cards. Something inside me telling me—. But I was
good.

LINCOLN

LINCOLN

*(He sees a packet of cards. He studies them like an alcoholic would study a drink.
Then he reaches for them, delicately picking them up and choosing 3 cards.)*

LINCOLN: Still got my moves. Still got my touch. Still got my chops. Thuh   5
feel of it. And I aint hurting no one, God. Link is just here hustling hisself.
(Rest.)
Lets see whatcha got.

*(He stands over the monte setup. Then he bends over it placing the cards down
and moving them around. Slowly at first, aimlessly, as if hes just making little
ripples in water. But then the game draws him in. Unlike* BOOTH, LINCOLNS
patter and moves are deft, dangerous, electric.)

LINCOLN: (((Lean in close and watch me now: who see thuh black card
who see thuh black card I see thuh black card black cards thuh winner
pick thuh black card thats thuh winner pick thuh red card thats thuh
loser pick thuh other red card thats thuh other loser pick thuh black
card you pick thuh winner. Watch me as I throw thuh cards. Here we
go.)))
(Rest.)
(((Who see thuh black card who see thuh black card? You pick thuh
red card you pick a loser you pick that red card you pick a loser you
pick thuh black card thuh deuce of spades you pick a winner who sees

thuh deuce of spades thuh one who sees it never fades watch me now as
I throw thuh cards. Red losers black winner follow thuh deuce of spades
chase thuh black deuce. Dark deuce will get you thuh win.)))

(*Even though* LINCOLN *speaks softly,* BOOTH *wakes and, unbeknownst to* LINCOLN,
listens intently.)

(*Rest.*)

LINCOLN: ((10 will get you 20, 20 will get you 40.))

(*Rest.*)

((Ima show you thuh cards: 2 red cards but only one spade. Dark winner
in thuh center and thuh red losers on thuh sides. Pick uh red card you
got a loser pick thuh other red card you got a loser pick thuh black card
you got a winner. One good pickll get you in, 2 good picks and you
gone win. Watch me come on watch me now.))

(*Rest.*)

((Who sees thuh winner who knows where its at? You do? You sure? Go
on then, put yr money where yr mouth is. Put yr money down you aint
no clown. No? Ah, you had thuh card but you didnt have thuh heart.))

(*Rest.*)

((Watch me now as I throw thuh cards watch me real close. Ok, man,
you know which card is the deuce of spades? Was you watching Links
lighting fast express? Was you watching Link cause he the best? So you
sure, huh? Point it out first, then place yr bet and Linkll show you yr
winner.))

(*Rest.*)

((500 dollars? You thuh man of thuh hour you thuh man with thuh
power. You musta been watching Link real close. You must be thuh
man who know thuh most. Ok. Lay the cash in my hand cause Link the
man. Thank you, mister. This card you say?))

(*Rest.*)

((Wrong! Ha!))

(*Rest.*)

((Thats thuh show. We gotta go.))

(LINCOLN *puts the cards down. He moves away from the monte setup. He sits on
the edge of his easy chair, but he can't take his eyes off the cards.*)

INTERMISSION

Scene 5

Several days have passed. Its now Wednesday night. BOOTH *is sitting in his brand-new
suit. The monte setup is nowhere in sight. In its place is a table with two nice chairs.
The table is covered with a lovely tablecloth and there are nice plates, silverware,
champagne glasses and candles. All the makings of a very romantic dinner for two.*

*The whole apartment in fact takes its cue from the table. Its been cleaned up consider-
ably. New curtains on the windows, a doily-like object on the recliner.* BOOTH *sits at
the table darting his eyes around, making sure everything is looking good.*

BOOTH: Shit.

*(He notices some of his girlie magazines visible from underneath his bed. He goes
over and nudges them out of sight. He sits back down. He notices that theyre
still visible. He goes over and nudges them some more, kicking at them finally. Then he takes the spread from his bed and pulls it down, hiding them.
He sits back down. He gets up. Checks the champagne on much melted ice.
Checks the food.)*

BOOTH: Foods getting cold, Grace!! Dont worry man, she'll get here, she'll
get here.

*(He sits back down. He goes over to the bed. Checks it for springiness. Smoothes
down the bedspread. Double-checks 2 matching silk dressing gowns, very expensive, marked "His" and "Hers." Lays the dressing gowns across the bed
again. He sits back down. He cant help but notice the visibility of the girlie
magazines again. He goes to the bed, kicks them fiercely, then on his hands
and knees shoves them. Then he begins to get under the bed to push them, but
he remembers his nice clothing and takes off his jacket. After a beat he removes
his pants and, in this half-dressed way, he crawls under the bed to give those
telltale magazines a good and final shove.* LINCOLN *comes in. At first* BOOTH,
*still stripped down to his underwear, thinks its his date. When he realizes its
his brother, he does his best to keep* LINCOLN *from entering the apartment.*
LINCOLN *wears his frock coat and carries the rest of his getup in a plastic bag.)*

LINCOLN: You in the middle of it?

BOOTH: What the hell you doing here?

LINCOLN: If yr in thuh middle of it I can go. Or I can just be real quiet and   5
just—sing a song in my head or something.

BOOTH: The casas off limits to you tonight.

LINCOLN: You know when we lived in that 2-room place with the cement
backyard and the frontyard with nothing but trash in it, Mom and Pops
would do it in the middle of the night and I would always hear them
but I would sing in my head, cause, I dunno, I couldnt bear to listen.

BOOTH: You gotta get out of here.

LINCOLN: I would make up all kinds of songs. Oh, sorry, yr all up in it. No
sweat, bro. No sweat. Hey, Grace, howyadoing?!

BOOTH: She aint here yet, man. Shes running late. And its a good thing too   10
cause I aint all dressed yet. Yr gonna spend thuh night with friends?

LINCOLN: Yeah.

(BOOTH waits for LINCOLN to leave. LINCOLN stands his ground.)

LINCOLN: I lost my job.

BOOTH: Hunh.

LINCOLN: I come in there right on time like I do every day and that motherfucker gives me some song and dance about cutbacks and too many
folks complaining.

BOOTH: Hunh.   15

LINCOLN: Showd me thuh wax dummy—hes buying it right out of a catalog.
   (*Rest.*)
   I walked out still wearing my getup.
   (*Rest.*)
   I could go back in tomorrow. I could tell him I'll take another pay cut.
   Thatll get him to take me back.

BOOTH: Link. Yr free. Dont go crawling back. Yr free at last! Now you can
do anything you want. Yr not tied down by that job. You can—you can
do something else. Something that pays better maybe.

LINCOLN: You mean Hustle.

BOOTH: Maybe. Hey, Graces on her way. You gotta go.

(LINCOLN *flops into his chair.* BOOTH *is waiting for him to move.* LINCOLN *doesnt
   budge.*)

LINCOLN: I'll stay until she gets here. I'll act nice. I wont embarrass you.   20

BOOTH: You gotta go.

LINCOLN: What time she coming?

BOOTH: Shes late. She could be here any second.

LINCOLN: I'll meet her. I met her years ago. I'll meet her again.
   (*Rest.*)
   How late is she?

BOOTH: She was supposed to be here at 8.   25

LINCOLN: Its after 2 A.M. Shes—shes late.
   (*Rest.*)
   Maybe when she comes you could put the blanket over me and I'll just
   pretend like Im not here.
   (*Rest.*)
   I'll wait. And when she comes I'll go. I need to sit down. I been walking
   around all day.

BOOTH

LINCOLN

(BOOTH *goes to his bed and dresses hurriedly.*)

BOOTH: Pretty nice, right? The china thuh silver thuh crystal.

LINCOLN: Its great.   30
   (*Rest.*)
   Boosted?

BOOTH: Yeah.

LINCOLN: Thought you went and spent yr inheritance for a minute, you had
   me going I was thinking shit, Booth—3-Card—that 3-Cards gone and
   spent his inheritance and the gal is—late.

BOOTH: Its boosted. Every bit of it.
   (Rest.)
   Fuck this waiting bullshit.
LINCOLN: She'll be here in a minute. Dont sweat it.
BOOTH: Right.   35
(BOOTH *comes to the table. Sits. Relaxes as best he can.*)
BOOTH: How come I got a hand for boosting and I dont got a hand for
   throwing cards? Its sorta the same thing—you gotta be quick—and
   slick. Maybe yll show me yr moves sometime.
LINCOLN
BOOTH
LINCOLN
BOOTH   40
LINCOLN: Look out the window. When you see Grace coming, I'll go.
BOOTH: Cool. Cause youd jinx it, youd really jinx it. Maybe you being here
   has jinxed it already. Naw. Shes just a little late. You aint jinxed noth-
   ing.
(BOOTH *sits by the window, glancing out, watching for his date.* LINCOLN *sits in
   his recliner. He finds the whiskey bottle, sips from it. He then rummages
   around, finding the raggedy photo album. He looks through it.*)
LINCOLN: There we are at that house. Remember when we moved in?
BOOTH: No.
LINCOLN: You were 2 or 3.   45
BOOTH: I was 4.
LINCOLN: I was 9. We all thought it was the best fucking house in the
   world.
BOOTH: Cement backyard and a frontyard full of trash, yeah, dont be going
   down memory lane man, yll jinx thuh vibe I got going in here. Gracell
   be walking in here and wrinkling up her nose cause you done jinxed up
   thuh joint with yr raggedy recollections.
LINCOLN: We had some great times in that house, bro. Selling lemonade on
   thuh corner, thuh treehouse out back, summers spent lying in thuh
   grass and looking at thuh stars.
BOOTH: We never did none of that shit.   50
LINCOLN: But we had us some good times. That row of nails I got you to
   line up behind Dads car so when he backed out the driveway to
   work—
BOOTH: He came back that night, only time I ever seen his face go red,
   4 flat tires and yelling bout how thuh white man done sabotaged him
   again.
LINCOLN: And neither of us flinched. Neither of us let on that itd been us.
BOOTH: It was at dinner, right? What were we eating?
LINCOLN: Food.   55

BOOTH: We was eating pork chops, mashed potatoes and peas. I remember cause I had to look at them peas real hard to keep from letting on. And I would glance over at you, not really glancing not actually turning my head, but I was looking at you out thuh corner of my eye. I was sure he was gonna find us out and then he woulda whipped us good. But I kept glancing at you and you was cool, man. Like nothing was going on. You was cooooool.

(*Rest.*)

What time is it?

LINCOLN: After 3.

(*Rest.*)

You should call her. Something mighta happened.

BOOTH: No man, Im cool. She'll be here in a minute. Patience is a virtue. She'll be here.

LINCOLN: You look sad.

BOOTH: Nope. Im just, you know, Im just—   60

LINCOLN: Cool.

BOOTH: Yeah. Cool.

(BOOTH *comes over, takes the bottle of whiskey and pours himself a big glassful. He returns to the window looking out and drinking.*)

BOOTH: They give you a severance package, at thuh job?

LINCOLN: A weeks pay.

BOOTH: Great.   65

LINCOLN: I blew it. Spent it all.

BOOTH: On what?

LINCOLN: —. Just spent it.

(*Rest.*)

It felt good, spending it. Felt really good. Like back in thuh day when I was really making money. Throwing thuh cards all day and strutting and rutting all night. Didnt have to take no shit from no fool, didnt have to worry about getting fired in favor of some damn wax dummy. I was thuh shit and they was my fools.

(*Rest.*)

Back in thuh day.

(*Rest.*)

(*Rest.*)

Why you think they left us, man?

BOOTH: Mom and Pops? I dont think about it too much.

LINCOLN: I dont think they liked us.   70

BOOTH: Naw. That aint it.

LINCOLN: I think there was something out there that they liked more than they liked us and for years they was struggling against moving towards that more liked something. Each of them had a special something that they was struggling against. Moms had hers. Pops had his. And they was struggling. We moved out of that nasty apartment into a house. A whole house. It wernt perfect but it was a house and theyd bought it and they brought us there and everything we owned, figuring we could be a family in that house and them things, them two separate things each of them was struggling against, would just leave them be. Them things would see thuh house and be impressed and just leave them be. Would see thuh job Pops had and how he shined his shoes every night before he went to bed, shining them shoes whether they needed it or not, and thuh thing he was struggling against would see all that and just let him be, and thuh thing Moms was struggling against, it would see the food on the table every night and listen to her voice when she'd read to us sometimes, the clean clothes, the buttons sewed on all right and it would just let her be. Just let us all be, just regular people living in a house. That wernt too much to ask.

BOOTH: Least we was grown when they split.

LINCOLN: 16 and 11 aint grown.

BOOTH: 16s grown. Almost. And I was ok cause you were there.   75

(*Rest.*)

Shit man, it aint like they both one day both, together packed all they shit up and left us so they could have fun in thuh sun on some tropical island and you and me would have to grub in thuh dirt forever. They didnt leave together. That makes it different. She left. 2 years go by. Then he left. Like neither of them couldnt handle it no more. She split then he split. Like thuh whole family mortgage bills going to work thing was just too much. And I dont blame them. You dont see me holding down a steady job. Cause its bullshit and I know it. I seen how it cracked them up and I aint going there.

(*Rest.*)

It aint right me trying to make myself into a one woman man just because she wants me like that. One woman rubber-wearing motherfucker. Shit. Not me. She gonna walk in here looking all hot and shit trying to see how much she can get me to sweat, how much she can get me to give her before she gives me mines. Shit.

LINCOLN

BOOTH

LINCOLN: Moms told me I shouldnt never get married.

BOOTH: She told me thuh same thing.

LINCOLN: They gave us each 500 bucks then they cut out.   80

BOOTH: Thats what Im gonna do. Give my kids 500 bucks then cut out.

Thats thuh way to do it.

LINCOLN: You dont got no kids.

BOOTH: Im gonna have kids then Im gonna cut out.

LINCOLN: Leaving each of yr offspring 500 bucks as yr splitting.

BOOTH: Yeah.   85

> (Rest.)

> Just goes to show Mom and Pops had some agreement between them.

LINCOLN: How so.

BOOTH: Theyd stopped talking to eachother. Theyd stopped *screwing* each-other. But they had an agreement. Somewhere in there when it looked like all they had was hate they sat down and did thuh "split" budget.

> (Rest.)

> When Moms splits she gives me 5 hundred-dollar bills rolled up and tied up tight in one of her nylon stockings. She tells me to put it in a safe place, to spend it only in case of an emergency, and not to tell no-body I got it, not even you. 2 years later Pops splits and before he goes—

LINCOLN: He slips me 10 fifties in a clean handkerchief: "Hide this some-wheres good, dont go blowing it, dont tell no one you got it, especially that Booth."

BOOTH: Theyd been scheming together all along. They left separately but they was in agreement. Maybe they arrived at the same place at the same time, maybe they renewed they wedding vows, maybe they got another family.

LINCOLN: Maybe they got 2 new kids. 2 boys. Different than us, though.   90
Better.

BOOTH: Maybe.

(Their glasses are empty. The whiskey bottle is empty too. BOOTH *takes the cham-pagne bottle from the ice tub. He pops the cork and pours drinks for his brother and himself.)*

BOOTH: I didnt mind them leaving cause you was there. Thats why Im hooked on us working together. If we could work together it would be like old times. They split and we got that room downtown. You was done with school and I stopped going. And we had to run around doing odd jobs just to keep the lights on and the heat going and thuh child protection bitch off our backs. It was you and me against thuh world, Link. It could be like that again.

LINCOLN

BOOTH

LINCOLN   95

BOOTH

LINCOLN: Throwing thuh cards aint as easy as it looks.

BOOTH: I aint stupid.

LINCOLN: When you hung with us back then, you was just on thuh side-lines. Thuh perspective from thuh sidelines is thuh perspective of a cus-tomer. There was all kinds of things you didnt know nothing about.

BOOTH: Lonny would entice folks into thuh game as they walked by. Thuh   100
2 folks on either side of ya looked like they was playing but they was
only pretending tuh play. Just tuh generate excitement. You was
moving thuh cards as fast as you could hoping that yr hands would be
faster than yr customers eyes. Sometimes you won sometimes you lost
what else is there to know?

LINCOLN: Thuh customer is actually called the "Mark." You know why?

BOOTH: Cause hes thuh one you got yr eye on. You mark him with yr eye.

LINCOLN

LINCOLN

BOOTH: Im right, right?   105

LINCOLN: Lemmie show you a few moves. If you pick up these yll have a
chance.

BOOTH: Yr playing.

LINCOLN: Get thuh cards and set it up.

BOOTH: No shit.

LINCOLN: Set it up set it up.   110

(In a flash, BOOTH clears away the romantic table setting by gathering it all up in
the tablecloth and tossing it aside. As he does so he reveals the "table" underneath: the 2 stacked monte milk crates and the cardboard playing surface.
LINCOLN lays out the cards. The brothers are ready. LINCOLN begins to teach
BOOTH in earnest.)

LINCOLN: Thuh deuce of spades is thuh card tuh watch.

BOOTH: I work with thuh deuce of hearts. But spades is cool.

LINCOLN: Theres thuh Dealer, thuh Stickman, thuh Sides, thuh Lookout
and thuh Mark. I'll be thuh Dealer.

BOOTH: I'll be thuh Lookout. Lemmie be thuh Lookout, right? I'll keep an
eye for thuh cops. I got my piece in my pants.

LINCOLN: You got it on you right now?   115

BOOTH: I always carry it.

LINCOLN: Even on a date? In yr own home?

BOOTH: You never know, man.
(Rest.)
So Im thuh Lookout.

LINCOLN: Gimmie yr piece.

(BOOTH gives LINCOLN his gun. LINCOLN moves the little wooden chair to face
right in front of the setup. He then puts the gun on the chair.)

LINCOLN: We dont need nobody standing on the corner watching for cops   120
cause there aint none. Thatll be the lookout.

BOOTH: I'll be thuh Stickman, then.

LINCOLN: Stickman knows the game inside out. You aint there yet. But you
will be. You wanna learn good, be my Sideman. Playing along with

the Dealer, moving the Mark to lay his money down. You wanna learn,
 right?
BOOTH: I'll be thuh Side.
LINCOLN: Good.
 (Rest.)
 First thing you learn is what is. Next thing you learn is what aint. You
 dont know what is you dont know what aint, you dont know shit.
BOOTH: Right. 125
LINCOLN
BOOTH
BOOTH: Whatchu looking at?
LINCOLN: Im sizing you up.
BOOTH: Oh yeah?! 130
LINCOLN: Dealer always sizes up thuh crowd.
BOOTH: Im yr Side, Link, Im on yr team, you dont go sizing up yr own
 team. You save looks like that for yr Mark.
LINCOLN: Dealer always sizes up thuh crowd. Everybody out there is part of
 the crowd. His crew is part of the crowd, he himself is part of the
 crowd. Dealer always sizes up thuh crowd.
*(LINCOLN looks BOOTH over some more then looks around at an imaginary
 crowd.)*
BOOTH: Then what then what?
LINCOLN: Dealer dont wanna play. 135
BOOTH: Bullshit man! Come on you promised!
LINCOLN: Thats thuh Dealers attitude. He *acts* like he dont wanna play. He
 holds back and thuh crowd, with their eagerness to see his skill and
 their willingness to take a chance, and their greediness to win his cash,
 the larceny in their hearts, all goad him on and push him to throw his
 cards, although of course the Dealer has been wanting to throw his
 cards all along. Only he dont never show it.
BOOTH: Thats some sneaky shit, Link.
LINCOLN: It sets thuh mood. You wanna have them in yr hand before you
 deal a hand, K?
BOOTH: Cool. —K. 140
LINCOLN: Right.
LINCOLN
BOOTH
BOOTH: You sizing me up again?
LINCOLN: Theres 2 parts to throwing thuh cards. Both parts are fairly com- 145
 plicated. Thuh moves and thuh grooves, thuh talk and thuh walk, thuh
 patter and thuh pitter pat, thuh flap and thuh rap: what yr doing with
 yr mouth and what yr doing with yr hands.

BOOTH: I got thuh words down pretty good.

LINCOLN: You need to work on both.

BOOTH: K.

LINCOLN: A goodlooking walk and a dynamite talk captivates their entire attention. The Mark focuses with 2 organs primarily: his eyes and his ears. Leave one out you lose yr shirt. Captivate both, yr golden.

BOOTH: So them times I seen you lose, them times I seen thuh Mark best   150 you, that was a time when yr hands werent fast enough or yr patter werent right.

LINCOLN: You could say that.

BOOTH: So, there was plenty of times—

(LINCOLN *moves the cards around.*)

LINCOLN: You see what Im doing? Dont look at my hands, man, look at my eyes. Know what is and know what aint.

BOOTH: What is?

LINCOLN: My eyes.   155

BOOTH: What aint?

LINCOLN: My hands. Look at my eyes not my hands. And you standing there thinking how thuh fuck I gonna learn how tuh throw thuh cards if I be looking in his eyes? Look into my eyes and get yr focus. Dont think about learning how tuh throw thuh cards. Dont think about nothing. Just look into my eyes. Get yr focus.

BOOTH: Theyre red.

LINCOLN: Look into my eyes.

BOOTH: You been crying?   160

LINCOLN: Just look into my eyes, fool. Now. Look down at thuh cards. I been moving and moving and moving them around. Ready?

BOOTH: Yeah.

LINCOLN: Ok, Sideman, thuh Marks got his eye on you. Yr gonna show him its easy.

BOOTH: K.

LINCOLN: Pick out thuh deuce of spades. Dont pick it up just point to it.   165

BOOTH: This one, right?

LINCOLN: Dont ask thuh Dealer if yr right, man, point to yr card with confidence.

(BOOTH *points.*)

BOOTH: That one.

   (*Rest.*)

   Flip it over, man.

(LINCOLN *flips over the card. It is in fact the deuce of spades.* BOOTH *struts around gloating like a rooster.* LINCOLN *is mildly crestfallen.*)

BOOTH: Am I right or am I right?! Make room for 3-Card! Here comes thuh champ!

LINCOLN: Cool. Stay focused. Now we gonna add the second element. Listen.   170
Lincoln moves the cards and speaks in a low hypnotic voice.

LINCOLN: Lean in close and watch me now: who see thuh black card who
see thuh black card I see thuh black card black cards thuh winner pick
thuh black card thats thuh winner pick thuh red card thats thuh loser
pick thuh other red card thats thuh other loser pick thuh black card
you pick thuh winner. Watch me as I throw thuh cards. Here we go.
(Rest.)
Who see thuh black card who see thuh black card? You pick thuh red
card you pick a loser you pick that red card you pick a loser you pick
thuh black card thuh deuce of spades you pick a winner who sees thuh
deuce of spades thuh one who sees it never fades watch me now as I
throw thuh cards. Red losers black winner follow thuh deuce of spades
chase thuh black deuce. Dark deuce will get you thuh win. One good
pickll get you in 2 good picks you gone win. 10 will get you 20, 20 will
get you 40.
(Rest.)
Ima show you thuh cards: 2 red cards but only one spade. Dark winner
in thuh center and thuh red losers on thuh sides. Pick uh red card you
got a loser pick thuh other red card you got a loser pick thuh black card
you got a winner. Watch me watch me watch me now.
(Rest.)
Ok, 3-Card, you know which cards thuh deuce of spades?

BOOTH: Yeah.

LINCOLN: You sure? Yeah? You sure you sure or you just think you sure? Oh
you sure you sure huh? Was you watching Links lighting fast express?
Was you watching Link cause he the best? So you sure, huh? Point it
out. Now, place yr bet and Linkll turn over yr card.

BOOTH: What should I bet?

LINCOLN: Dont bet nothing man, we just playing. Slap me 5 and point out   175
thuh deuce.

*(BOOTH slaps LINCOLN 5, then points out a card which LINCOLN flips over. It is
in fact again the deuce of spades.)*

BOOTH: Yeah, baby! 3-Card got thuh moves! You didnt know lil bro had
thuh stuff, huh? Think again, Link, think again.

LINCOLN: You wanna learn or you wanna run yr mouth?

BOOTH: Thought you had fast hands. Wassup? What happened tuh "Links
Lightning Fast Express"? Turned into uh local train looks like tuh me.

LINCOLN: Thats yr whole motherfucking problem. Yr so busy running yr
mouth you aint never gonna learn nothing! You think you something
but you aint shit.

BOOTH: I aint shit, I am *The* Shit. Shit. Wheres thuh dark deuce? Right   180
there! Yes, baby!

LINCOLN: Ok, 3-Card. Cool. Lets switch. Take thuh cards and show me whatcha got. Go on. Dont touch thuh cards too heavy just—its a light touch. Like yr touching Graces skin. Or, whatever, man, just a light touch. Like uh whisper.

BOOTH: Like uh whisper.

(BOOTH *moves the cards around, in an awkward imitation of his brother.*)

LINCOLN: Good.

BOOTH: Yeah. All right. Look into my eyes.

(BOOTHs *speech is loud and his movements are jerky. He is doing worse than when he threw the cards at the top of the play.*)

BOOTH: Watch-me-close-watch-me-close-now: who-see-thuh-black-card- 185
who-see-thuh-black-card? I-see-thuh-black-card. Here-it-is. Thuh-black-card-is-thuh-winner. Pick-thuh-black-card-and-you-pick-uh-winner. Pick-uh-red-card-and-you-pick-uh-loser. Theres-thuh-loser-yeah-theres-thuh-red-card, theres-thuh-other-loser-and-theres-thuh-black-card, thuh-winner. Watch-me-close-watch-me-close-now: 3-Card-throws-thuh-cards-lightning-fast. 3-Card-thats-me-and-Ima-last. Watch-me-throw-cause-here-I-go. See thuh black card? Yeah? Who see I see you see thuh black card?

LINCOLN: Hahahahhahahahahahahah!

(LINCOLN *doubles over laughing.* BOOTH *puts on his coat and pockets his gun.*)

BOOTH: What?

LINCOLN: Nothing, man, nothing.

BOOTH: *What?!*

LINCOLN: Yr just, yr just a little wild with it. You talk like that on thuh 190
street cards or no cards and theyll lock you up, man. Shit. Reminds me of that time when you hung with us and we let you try being thuh Stick cause you wanted to so bad. Thuh hustle was so simple. Remember? I told you that when I put my hand in my left pocket you was to get thuh Mark tuh pick thuh card on that side. You got to thinking something like Links left means my left some dyslexic shit and turned thuh wrong card. There was 800 bucks on the line and you fucked it up.

(*Rest.*)

But it was cool, little bro, cause we made the money back. It worked out cool.

(*Rest.*)

So, yeah, I said a light touch, little bro. Throw thuh cards light. Like uh whisper.

BOOTH: Like Graces skin.

LINCOLN: Like Graces skin.

BOOTH: What time is it?

(LINCOLN *holds up his watch.* BOOTH *takes a look.*)

BOOTH: Bitch. *Bitch!* She said she was gonna show up around 8. 8-a-fucking-clock.

LINCOLN: Maybe she meant 8 A.M.   195

BOOTH: Yeah. She gonna come all up in my place talking bout how she *love* me. How she cant stop *thinking* bout me. Nother mans shit up in her nother mans thing in her nother mans dick on her breath.

LINCOLN: Maybe something happened to her.

BOOTH: Something happened to her all right. She trying to make a chump outa me. I aint her chump. I aint nobodys chump.

LINCOLN: Sit. I'll go to the payphone on the corner. I'll—

BOOTH: Thuh world puts its foot in yr face and you dont move. You tell   200
thuh world tuh keep on stepping. But Im my own man, Link. I aint you.

(BOOTH *goes out, slamming the door behind him.*)

LINCOLN: You got that right.

(*After a moment* LINCOLN *picks up the cards. He moves them around fast, faster, faster.*)

Scene 6

Thursday night. The room looks empty, as if neither brother is home. LINCOLN *comes in. Has high on liquor. He strides in, leaving the door slightly ajar.*

LINCOLN: Taaadaaaa!
(*Rest.*)
(*Rest.*)
Taadaa, motherfucker. Taadaa!
(*Rest.*)
Booth—uh, 3-Card—you here? Nope. Good. Just as well. Ha Ha <u>Ha Ha Ha</u>!

(*He pulls an enormous wad of money from his pocket. He counts it, slowly and luxuriously, arranging and smoothing the bills and sounding the amounts under his breath. He neatly rolls up the money, secures it with a rubber band and puts it back in his pocket. He relaxes in his chair. Then he takes the money out again, counting it all over again, but this time quickly, with the touch of an expert hustler.*)

LINCOLN: You didnt go back, Link, you got back, you got it back you got yr shit back in thuh saddle, man, you got back in business. Walking in Luckys and you seen how they was looking at you? Lucky starts pouring for you when you walk in. And the women. You see how they was look-ing at you? Bought drinks for everybody. Bought drinks for Lucky. Bought drinks for Luckys damn dog. Shit. And thuh women be hanging on me and purring. And I be feeling that old call of thuh wild calling. I got more phone numbers in my pockets between thuh time I walked out that door and thuh time I walked back in than I got in my whole life. Cause my shit is *back*. And back better than it was when it left too. Shoot. Who thuh man? Link. Thats right. Purrrrring all up on me and letting me touch them and promise them shit. 3 of them sweethearts in thuh restroom on my dick all at once and I was *there* my shit was there. And Cookie just went out of my mind which is cool which is very cool. 3 of them. Fighting over it. Shit. Cause they knew I'd been throwing thuh cards. Theyd seen me on thuh corner with thuh old crew or if they aint seed me with they own eyes theyd heard word. Links thuh stink! Theyd heard word and they seed uh sad face on some poor sucker or a tear in thuh eye of some stupid fucking tourist and they figured it was me whod just took thuh suckers last dime, it was me who had all thuh suckers loot. They knew. They knew.

(BOOTH *appears in the room. He was standing behind the screen, unseen all this time. He goes to the door, soundlessly, just stands there.*)

LINCOLN: And they was all in Luckys. Shit. And they was waiting for me to come in from my last throw. Cant take too many fools in one day, its bad luck, Link, so they was all waiting in there for me to come in thuh door and let thuh liquor start flowing and thuh music start going and let thuh boys who dont have thuh balls to get nothing but a regular job and uh weekly paycheck, let them crowd around and get in somehow on thuh excitement, and make way for thuh ladies, so they can run they hands on my clothes and feel thuh magic and imagine thuh man, with plenty to go around, living and breathing underneath.
(Rest.)
They all thought I was down and out! They all thought I was some No-Count HasBeen LostCause motherfucker. But I got my shit back. Thats right. They stepped on me and kept right on stepping. Not no more. Who thuh man?! Goddamnit, who thuh—

(BOOTH *closes the door.*)

LINCOLN

BOOTH   5
(Rest.)
LINCOLN: Another evening to remember, huh?
BOOTH (Rest.): Uh—yeah, man, yeah. Thats right, thats right.
LINCOLN: Had me a memorable evening myself.
BOOTH: I got news.
    (Rest.)
    What you been up to?
LINCOLN: Yr news first.   10
BOOTH: Its good.
LINCOLN: Yeah?
BOOTH: Yeah.

LINCOLN: Go head then.

BOOTH *(Rest.)*: Grace got down on her knees. Down on her knees, man.   15
    Asked *me* tuh marry *her*.

LINCOLN: Shit.

BOOTH: Amazing Grace!

LINCOLN: Lucky you, man.

BOOTH: And guess where she was, I mean, while I was here waiting for her.
    She was over at her house watching tv. I'd told her come over Thursday
    and I got it all wrong and was thinking I said Wednesday and here I
    was sitting waiting my ass off and all she was doing was over at her
    house just watching tv.

LINCOLN: Howboutthat.   20

BOOTH: She wants to get married right away. Shes tired of waiting. Feels
    her clock ticking and shit. Wants to have my baby. But dont look so
    glum man, we gonna have a boy and we gonna name it after you.

LINCOLN: Thats great, man. Thats really great.

BOOTH

LINCOLN

BOOTH: Whats yr news?   25

LINCOLN *(Rest.)*: Nothing.

BOOTH: Mines good news, huh?

LINCOLN: Yeah. Real good news, bro.

BOOTH: Bad news is—well, shes real set on us living together. And she al-
    ways did like this place.
    (Rest.)
    Yr gonna have to leave. Sorry.

LINCOLN: No sweat.   30

BOOTH: This was only a temporary situation anyhow.

LINCOLN: No sweat man. You got a new life opening up for you, no sweat.
    Graces moving in today? I can leave right now.

BOOTH: I dont mean to put you out.

LINCOLN: No sweat. I'll just pack up.

(LINCOLN rummages around finding a suitcase and begins to pack his things.)

BOOTH: Just like that, huh? "No sweat"?! Yesterday you lost yr damn job.   35
    You dont got no cash. You dont got no friends, no nothing, but you
    clearing out just like that and its "no sweat"?!

LINCOLN: Youve been real generous and you and Grace need me gone and
    its time I found my own place.

BOOTH: No sweat.

LINCOLN: No sweat.
    (Rest.)
    K. I'll spill it. I got another job, so getting my own place aint gonna be
    so bad.

BOOTH: You got a new job! Doing what?

LINCOLN: Security guard.   40

BOOTH (*Rest.*): Security guard. Howaboutthat.

(LINCOLN *continues packing the few things he has. He picks up a whiskey bottle.*)

BOOTH: Go head, take thuh med-sin, bro. You gonna need it more than me. I got, you know, I got my love to keep me warm and shit.

LINCOLN: You gonna have to get some kind of work, or are you gonna let Grace support you?

BOOTH: I got plans.

LINCOLN: She might want you now but she wont want you for long if you   45 dont get some kind of job. Shes a smart chick. And she cares about you. But she aint gonna let you treat her like some pack mule while shes out working her ass off and yr laying up in here scheming and dreaming to cover up thuh fact that you dont got no skills.

BOOTH: Grace is very cool with who I am and where Im at, thank you.

LINCOLN: It was just some advice. But, hey, yr doing great just like yr doing.

LINCOLN

BOOTH

LINCOLN   50

BOOTH

BOOTH: When Pops left he didnt take nothing with him. I always thought that was fucked-up.

LINCOLN: He was a drunk. Everything he did was always half regular and half fucked-up.

BOOTH: Whyd he leave his clothes though? Even drunks gotta wear clothes.

LINCOLN: Whyd he leave his clothes whyd he leave us? He was uh drunk,   55 bro. He—whatever, right? I mean, you aint gonna figure it out by think- ing about it. Just call it one of thuh great unsolved mysteries of existence.

BOOTH: Moms had a man on thuh side.

LINCOLN: Yeah? Pops had side shit going on too. More than one. He would take me with him when he went to visit them. Yeah.

(*Rest.*)

Sometimes he'd let me meet the ladies. They was all very nice. Very polite. Most of them real pretty. Sometimes he'd let me watch. Most of thuh time I was just outside on thuh porch or in thuh lobby or in thuh car waiting for him but sometimes he'd let me watch.

BOOTH: What was it like?

LINCOLN: Nothing. It wasnt like nothing. He made it seem like it was this big deal this great thing he was letting me witness but it wasnt like nothing.

(*Rest.*)

One of his ladies liked me, so I would do her after he'd done her. On thuh sly though. He'd be laying there, spent and sleeping and snoring and her and me would be sneaking it.

BOOTH: Shit.   60

LINCOLN: It was alright.

BOOTH

LINCOLN

(LINCOLN *takes his crumpled Abe Lincoln getup from the closet. Isnt sure what to do with it.*)

BOOTH: Im gonna miss you—coming home in that getup. I dont even got a picture of you in it for the album.

LINCOLN: *(Rest.):* Hell, I'll put it on. Get thuh camera get thuh camera.   65

BOOTH: Yeah?

LINCOLN: What thuh fuck, right?

BOOTH: Yeah, what thuh fuck.

(BOOTH *scrambles around the apartment and finds the camera.* LINCOLN *quickly puts on the getup, including 2 thin smears of white pancake makeup, more like war paint than whiteface.*)

LINCOLN: They didnt fire me cause I wasnt no good. They fired me cause they was cutting back. Me getting dismissed didnt have no reflection on my performance. And I was a damn good Honest Abe considering.

BOOTH: Yeah. You look great man, really great. Fix yr hat. Get in thuh   70
light. Smile.

LINCOLN: Lincoln didnt never smile.

BOOTH: Sure he smiled.

LINCOLN: No he didnt, man, you seen thuh pictures of him. In all his pictures he was real serious.

BOOTH: You got a new job, yr having a good day, right?

LINCOLN: Yeah.   75

BOOTH: So smile.

LINCOLN: Snapshots gonna look pretty stupid with me—

(BOOTH *takes a picture.*)

BOOTH: Thisll look great in thuh album.

LINCOLN: Lets take one together, you and me.

BOOTH: No thanks. Save the film for the wedding.   80

LINCOLN: This wasnt a bad job. I just outgrew it. I could put in a word for you down there, maybe when business picks up again theyd hire you.

BOOTH: No thanks. That shit aint for me. I aint into pretending Im someone else all day.

LINCOLN: I was just sitting there in thuh getup. I wasnt pretending nothing.

BOOTH: What was going on in yr head?

LINCOLN: I would make up songs and shit.   85

BOOTH: And think about women.

LINCOLN: Sometimes.

BOOTH: Cookie.

LINCOLN: Sometimes.

620   Chapter 6   Rhythm, Pace, and Rhyme

BOOTH: And how she came over here one night looking for you.   90
LINCOLN: I was at Luckys.
BOOTH: She didnt know that.
LINCOLN: I was drinking.
BOOTH: All she knew was you couldnt get it up. You couldnt get it up with
    her so in her head you was tired of her and had gone out to screw some-
    body new and this time maybe werent never coming back.
    (*Rest.*)
    She had me pour her a drink or 2. I didnt want to. She wanted to get
    back at you by having some fun of her own and when I told her to go out
    and have it, she said she wanted to have her fun right here. With me.
    (*Rest.*)
    And then, just like that, she changed her mind.
    (*Rest.*)
    But she'd hooked me. That bad part of me that I fight down everyday.
    You beat yrs down and it stays there dead but mine keeps coming up for
    another round. And the bad part of me took her clothing off and carried
    her into thuh bed and had her, Link, yr Cookie. It wasnt just thuh bad
    part of me it was all of me, man, I had her. Yr damn wife. Right in that
    bed.
LINCOLN: I used to think about her all thuh time but I dont think about her   95
    no more.
BOOTH: I told her if she dumped you I'd marry her but I changed my mind.
LINCOLN: I dont think about her no more.
BOOTH: You dont go back.
LINCOLN: Nope.
BOOTH: Cause you cant. No matter what you do you cant get back to being   100
    who you was. Best you can do is just pretend to be yr old self.
LINCOLN: Yr outa yr mind.
BOOTH: Least Im still me!
LINCOLN: Least I work. You never did like to work. You better come up
    with some kinda way to bring home the bacon or Gracell drop you like
    a hot rock.
BOOTH: I got plans!
LINCOLN: Yeah, you gonna throw thuh cards, right?   105
BOOTH: Thats right!
LINCOLN: You a double left-handed motherfucker who dont stand a chance
    in all get out out there throwing no cards.
BOOTH: You scared. You scared I got yr shit.
LINCOLN: You aint never gonna do nothing.
BOOTH: You scared you gonna throw and Ima kick yr ass—like yr boss   110
    kicked yr ass like yr wife kicked yr ass—then Ima go out there and do
    thuh cards like you do and Ima be thuh man and you aint gonna be shit.

(*Rest.*)
Ima set it up. And you gonna throw. Or are you scared?
LINCOLN: Im gone.
(LINCOLN *goes to leave.*)
BOOTH: Fuck that!
LINCOLN
BOOTH
LINCOLN: Damn. I didnt know it went so deep for you lil bro. Set up the   115
   cards.
BOOTH: Thought you was gone.
LINCOLN: Set it up.
BOOTH: Ima kick yr ass.
LINCOLN: Set it up!
(BOOTH *hurriedly sets up the milk crates and cardboard top.* LINCOLN *throws the cards.*)
LINCOLN: Lean in close and watch me now: who see thuh black card who   120
   see thuh black card I see thuh black card black cards thuh winner pick
   thuh black card thats thuh winner pick thuh red card thats thuh loser
   pick thuh other red card thats thuh other loser pick thuh black card
   you pick thuh winner. Who see thuh black card who see thuh black
   card? You pick thuh red card you pick a loser you pick that red card you
   pick a loser you pick thuh black card thuh deuce of spades you pick a
   winner who sees thuh deuce of spades thuh one who sees it never fades
   watch me now as I throw thuh cards. Red losers black winner follow
   thuh deuce of spades chase thuh black deuce. Dark deuce will get you
   thuh win. 10 will get you 20, 20 will get you 40. One good pickll get
   you in 2 good picks and you gone win.
   (*Rest.*)
   Ok, man, wheres thuh black deuce?
(BOOTH *points to a card.* LINCOLN *flips it over. It is the deuce of spades.*)
BOOTH: Who thuh man?!
(LINCOLN *turns over the other 2 cards, looking at them confusedly.*)
LINCOLN: Hhhhh.
BOOTH: Who thuh man, Link?! Huh? Who thuh man, Link?!?!
LINCOLN: You thuh man, man.
BOOTH: I got yr shit down.   125
LINCOLN: Right.
BOOTH: "Right"? All you saying is "right"?
   (*Rest.*)
   You was out on the street throwing. Just today. Werent you? You wasnt
   gonna tell me.
LINCOLN: Tell you what?
BOOTH: That you was out throwing.

LINCOLN: I was gonna tell you, sure. Cant go and leave my little bro out   130
thuh loop, can I? Didnt say nothing cause I thought you heard. Did all
right today but Im still rusty, I guess. But hey—yr getting good.

BOOTH: But I'll get out there on thuh street and still fuck up, wont I?

LINCOLN: You seem pretty good, bro.

BOOTH: You gotta do it for real, man.

LINCOLN: I am doing it for real. And yr getting good.

BOOTH: I dunno. It didnt feel real. Kinda felt—well it didnt feel real.   135

LINCOLN: We're missing the essential elements. The crowd, the street, thuh
traffic sounds, all that.

BOOTH: We missing something else too, thuh thing thatll really make it real.

LINCOLN: Whassat, bro?

BOOTH: Thuh cash. Its just bullshit without thuh money. Put some money
down on thuh table then itd be real, then youd do it for real, then I'd
win it for real.
(*Rest.*)
And dont be looking all glum like that. I know you got money. A
whole pocketful. Put it down.

LINCOLN   140

BOOTH

BOOTH: You scared of losing it to thuh man, chump? Put it down, less you
think thuh kid who got two left hands is gonna give you uh left hook.
Put it down, bro, put it down.

(LINCOLN *takes the roll of bills from his pocket and places it on the table.*)

BOOTH: How much you got there?

LINCOLN: 500 bucks.

BOOTH: Cool.   145
(*Rest.*)
Ready?

LINCOLN: Does it feel real?

BOOTH: Yeah. Clean slate. Take it from the top. "One good pickll get you
in 2 good picks and you gone win."
(*Rest.*)
Go head.

LINCOLN: Watch me now:

BOOTH: Woah, man, woah.
(*Rest.*)
You think Ima chump.

LINCOLN: No I dont.   150

BOOTH: You aint going full out.

LINCOLN: I was just getting started.

BOOTH: But when you got good and started you wasnt gonna go full out.
You wasnt gonna go all out. You was gonna do thuh pussy shit, not
thuh real shit.

LINCOLN: I put my money down. Money makes it real.

BOOTH: But not if I dont put no money down tuh match it. 155

LINCOLN: You dont got no money.

BOOTH: I got money!

LINCOLN: You aint worked in years. You dont got shit.

BOOTH: I got money.

LINCOLN: Whatcha been doing, skimming off my weekly paycheck and 160
squirreling it away?

BOOTH: I got money.

(Rest.)

(They stand there sizing eachother up. BOOTH breaks away, going over to his hiding place from which he gets an old nylon stocking with money in the toe, a
knot holding the money secure.)

LINCOLN

BOOTH

BOOTH: You know she was putting her stuff in plastic bags? She was just
putting her stuff in plastic bags not putting but shoving. She was shoving her stuff in plastic bags and I was standing in thuh doorway watching her and she was so busy shoving thuh shit she didnt see me. "I aint
made of money," thats what he always saying. The guy she had on the
side. I would catch them together sometimes. Thuh first time I cut
school I got tired of hanging out so I goes home—figured I could tell
Mom I was sick and cover my ass. Come in thuh house real slow cause
Im sick and moving slow and quiet. He had her bent over. They both
had all they clothes on like they was about to do something like go out
dancing cause they was dressed to thuh 9s but at thuh last minute his
pants had fallen down and her dress had flown up and theyd ended up
doing something else.

(Rest.)

They didnt see me come in, they didnt see me watching them, they
didnt see me going out. That was uh Thursday. Something told me tuh
cut school thuh next Thursday and sure enough—. He was her Thursday man. Every Thursday. Yeah. And Thursday nights she was always
all cleaned up and fresh and smelling nice. Serving up dinner. And
Pops would grab her cause she was all bright and she would look at me,
like she didnt know that I knew but she was asking me not to tell
nohow. She was asking me to—oh who knows.

(Rest.)

She was talking with him one day, her sideman, her Thursday dude, her
backdoor man, she needed some money for something, thered been
some kind of problem some kind of mistake had been made some kind
of mistake that needed cleaning up and she was asking Mr. Thursday
for some money to take care of it. "I aint made of money," he says. He
was putting his foot down. And then there she was 2 months later not

showing yet, maybe she'd got rid of it maybe she hadnt maybe she'd stuffed it along with all her other things in them plastic bags while he waited outside in thuh car with thuh motor running. She musta known I was gonna walk in on her this time cause she had my payoff—my *inheritance*—she had it all ready for me. 500 dollars in a nylon stocking. Huh.

(*He places the stuffed nylon stocking on the table across from* LINCOLNs *money roll.*)

BOOTH: Now its real.   165

LINCOLN: Dont put that down.

BOOTH: Throw thuh cards.

LINCOLN: I dont want to play.

BOOTH: Throw thuh fucking cards, man!!

LINCOLN (*Rest.*):   2 red cards but only one black. Pick thuh black you pick   170
    thuh winner. All thuh cards are face down you point out thuh cards
    and then you move them around. Now watch me now, now watch me
    real close. Put thuh winning deuce down in the center put thuh loser
    reds on either side then you just move thuh cards around. Move them
    slow or move them fast, Links thuh king he gonna last.
    (*Rest.*)
    Wheres thuh deuce of spades?

(BOOTH *chooses a card and chooses correctly.*)

BOOTH: HA!

LINCOLN: One good pickll get you in 2 good picks and you gone win.

BOOTH: I know man I know.

LINCOLN: Im just doing thuh talk.

BOOTH: Throw thuh fucking cards!   175

(*Lincoln throws the cards.*)

LINCOLN: Lean in close and watch me now: who see thuh black card who
    see thuh black card I see thuh black card black cards thuh winner pick
    thuh black card thats thuh winner pick thuh red card thats thuh loser
    pick thuh other red card thats thuh other loser pick thuh black card
    you pick thuh winner. Watch me as I throw thuh cards. Here we go.
    (*Rest.*)
    Ima show you thuh cards: 2 red cards but only one spade. Dark winner
    in thuh center and thuh red losers on thuh sides. Pick uh red card you
    got a loser pick thuh other red card you got a loser pick thuh black card
    you got a winner. Watch me watch me watch me now.
    (*Rest.*)
    Who see thuh black card who see thuh black card? You pick thuh red
    card you pick a loser you pick that red card you pick a loser you pick
    thuh black card thuh deuce of spades you pick a winner who sees thuh
    deuce of spades thuh one who sees it never fades watch me now as I

throw thuh cards. Red losers black winner follow thuh deuce of spades chase thuh black deuce. Dark deuce will get you thuh win.
(*Rest.*)
Ok, 3-Card, you know which cards thuh deuce of spades? This is for real now, man. You pick wrong Im in yr wad and I keep mines.

BOOTH: I pick right I got yr shit.

LINCOLN: Yeah.

BOOTH: Plus I beat you for real.

LINCOLN: Yeah.   180
(*Rest.*)
You think we're really brothers?

BOOTH: Huh?

LINCOLN: I know we *brothers*, but is we really brothers, you know, blood brothers or not, you and me, whatduhyathink?

BOOTH: I think we're brothers.

BOOTH

LINCOLN   185

BOOTH

LINCOLN

BOOTH

LINCOLN

LINCOLN: Go head man, wheres thuh deuce?   190
(*In a flash* BOOTH *points out a card.*)

LINCOLN: You sure?

BOOTH: Im sure!

LINCOLN: Yeah? Dont touch thuh cards, now.

BOOTH: Im sure.
(*The 2 brothers lock eyes.* LINCOLN *turns over the card that* BOOTH *selected and* BOOTH, *in a desperate break of concentration, glances down to see that he has chosen the wrong card.*)

LINCOLN: Deuce of hearts, bro. Im sorry. Thuh deuce of spades was this   195
one.
(*Rest.*)
I guess all this is mines.
(*He slides the money toward himself.*)

LINCOLN: You were almost right. Better luck next time.
(*Rest.*)
Aint yr fault if yr eyes aint fast. And you cant help it if you got 2 left hands, right? Throwing cards aint thuh whole world. You got other shit going for you. You got Grace.

BOOTH: Right.

LINCOLN: Whassamatter?

BOOTH: Mm.

LINCOLN: Whatsup?　　　　　　　　　　　　　　　　　　　　　200

BOOTH: Nothing.

LINCOLN (*Rest.*):　It takes a certain kind of understanding to be able to play this game.

(*Rest.*)

I still got thuh moves, dont I?

BOOTH: Yeah you still got thuh moves.

(LINCOLN *cant help himself. He chuckles.*)

LINCOLN: I aint laughing at you, bro, Im just laughing. Shit there is so much to this game. This game is—there is just so much to it.

(LINCOLN, *still chuckling, flops down in the easy chair. He takes up the nylon stocking and fiddles with the knot.*)

LINCOLN: Woah, she sure did tie this up tight, didnt she?　　　　205

BOOTH: Yeah. I aint opened it since she gived it to me.

LINCOLN: Yr kidding. 500 and you aint never opened it? Shit. Sure is tied tight. She said heres 500 bucks and you didnt undo thuh knot to get a look at the cash? You aint needed to take a peek in all these years? Shit. I woulda opened it right away. Just a little peek.

BOOTH: I been saving it.

(*Rest.*)

Oh, dont open it, man.

LINCOLN: How come?

BOOTH: You won it man, you dont gotta go opening it.　　　　210

LINCOLN: We gotta see whats in it.

BOOTH: We <u>know</u> whats in it. Dont open it.

LINCOLN: You are a chump, bro. There could be millions in here! There could be nothing! I'll open it.

BOOTH: Dont.

LINCOLN　　　　　　　　　　　　　　　　　　　　　　　　215

BOOTH

(*Rest.*)

LINCOLN: Shit this knot aint coming out. I could cut it, but that would spoil the whole effect, wouldnt it? Shit. Sorry. I aint laughing at you Im just laughing. Theres so much about those cards. You think you can learn them just by watching and just by playing but there is more to them cards than that. And—. Tell me something, Mr. 3-Card, she handed you this stocking and she said there was money in it and then she split and you say you didnt open it. Howd you know she was for real?

BOOTH: She was for real.

LINCOLN: How you know? She coulda been jiving you, bro. Jiving you that there really *was* money in this thing. Jiving you big time. Its like thuh cards. And ooooh you certainly was persistent. But you was in such a hurry to learn thuh last move that you didnt bother learning thuh first

one. That was yr mistake. Cause its thuh first move that separates thuh
Player from thuh Played. And thuh first move is to know that there
aint no winning. Taadaaa! It may look like you got a chance but the
only time you pick right is when thuh man lets you. And when its thuh
real deal, when its thuh real fucking deal, bro, and thuh moneys on
thuh line, thats when thuh man wont want you picking right. He will
want you picking wrong so he will make you pick wrong. Wrong wrong
wrong. Ooooh, you thought you was finally happening, didnt you? You
thought yr ship had come in or some shit, huh? Thought you was uh
Player. But I played you, bro.

BOOTH: Fuck you. Fuck you FUCK YOU *FUCK YOU*!!   220
LINCOLN: Whatever, man. Damn this knot is tough. Ima cut it.
(LINCOLN *reaches in his boot, pulling out a knife. He chuckles all the while.*)
LINCOLN: Im not laughing at you, bro, Im just laughing.
(BOOTH *chuckles with him.* LINCOLN *holds the knife high, ready to cut the stocking.*)
LINCOLN: Turn yr head. You may not wanna look.
(BOOTH *turns away slightly. They both continue laughing.* LINCOLN *brings the
knife down to cut the stocking.*)
BOOTH: I popped her.
LINCOLN: Huh?   225
BOOTH: Grace. I popped her. Grace.
(*Rest.*)
Who thuh fuck she think she is doing me like she done? Telling me I
dont got nothing going on. I showed her what I got going on. Popped
her good. Twice. 3 times. Whatever.
(*Rest.*)
She aint dead.
(*Rest.*)
She werent wearing my ring I gived her. Said it was too small. Fuck
that. Said it hurt her. Fuck that. Said she was into bigger things. *Fuck*
that. Shes alive not to worry, she aint going out that easy, shes alive
shes shes—.
LINCOLN: Dead. Shes—
BOOTH: Dead.
LINCOLN: Ima give you back yr stocking, man. Here, bro—
BOOTH: Only so long I can stand that little brother shit. Can only take it so   230
long. Im telling you—
LINCOLN: Take it back, man—
BOOTH: That little bro shit had to go—
LINCOLN: Cool—
BOOTH: Like Booth went—
LINCOLN: Here, 3-Card—   235
BOOTH: That Booth shit is over. 3-Cards thuh man now—

LINCOLN: Ima give you yr stocking back, 3-Card—

BOOTH: Who thuh man now, huh? Who thuh man now?! Think you can
fuck with me, motherfucker think again motherfucker think again!
Think you can take me like Im just some chump some two lefthanded
pussy dickbreath chump who you can take and then go laugh at. Aint
laughing at me you was just laughing bunch uh bullshit and you
know it.

LINCOLN: Here. Take it.

BOOTH: I aint gonna be needing it. Go on. You won it you open it.   240

LINCOLN: No thanks.

BOOTH: Open it open it open it open it. *OPEN IT!!!*
   (Rest.)
   Open it up, bro.

LINCOLN

BOOTH

(LINCOLN *brings the knife down to cut the stocking. In a flash,* BOOTH *grabs*
   LINCOLN *from behind. He pulls his gun and thrusts it into the left side of*
   LINCOLNs *neck. They stop there poised.*)

LINCOLN: Dont.   245

(BOOTH *shoots* LINCOLN. LINCOLN *slumps forward, falling out of his chair and
   onto the floor. He lies there dead.* BOOTH *paces back and forth, like a panther in a cage, holding his gun.*)

BOOTH: Think you can take my shit? My shit. That shit was mines. I kept
it. Saved it. All this while. Through thick and through thin. Through
fucking thick and through fucking thin, motherfucker. And you just
gonna come up in here and mock my shit and call me two lefthanded
talking bout how she coulda been jiving me then go steal from me? My
inheritance. You stole my *inheritance,* man. That aint right. That aint
right and you know it. You had yr own. And you blew it. You *blew it,*
motherfucker! I saved mines and you blew yrs. Thinking you all that
and blew yr shit. And I *saved* mines.
   (Rest.)
   You aint gonna be needing yr fucking money-roll no more, dead motherfucker, so I will pocket it thank you.
   (Rest.)
   Watch me close watch me close now: Ima go out there and make a
   name for myself that dont have nothing to do with you. And 3-Cards
   gonna be in everybodys head and in everybodys mouth like Link was.
   (Rest.)
   Ima take back my inheritance too. It was mines anyhow. Even when
   you stole it from me it was still mines cause she gave it to me. She
   didnt give it to you. And I been saving it all this while.

(*He bends to pick up the money-filled stocking. Then he just crumples. As he sits*

beside LINCOLNS *body, the money-stocking falls away.* BOOTH *holds* LIN-
COLNS *body, hugging him close. He sobs.)*
BOOTH: *AAAAAAAAAAAAAAAAAAAH!*

END OF PLAY

■ Find two specific passages that illustrate the difference in the speech rhythms of Lincoln and Booth. How are these differences significant to our understanding of their characters?

■ Much of the play centers around Booth as he tries to master the patter of the 3-card monte scam. How does this patter relate to the action at various points within the play?

■ Why would Parks name the characters "Lincoln" and "Booth"? Collect details from the play to show the different ways in which these names are appropriate (or terribly inappropriate) to the play's action.

Experiencing Literature through Writing

1. Select a single work from this chapter (or any other). If you are looking at a work of fiction, limit your analysis to one or two paragraphs. Describe the rhythm within that selection. Explain how rhythm is significant to our understanding of the text. As you write, consider the following questions:

   a. What specific words in this passage help you describe the rhythm?

   b. How do the sounds or the length of the words relate to the plot?

   c. Is this rhythm subtle, or is it obvious? In places where it is not obvious, explain why it is significant.

2. The contrast of innocence and experience that we see in this chapter is often reflected in subtle changes within the works. Using a pair of Blake poems or some other example where you see a similar effect, discuss the relation of this contrast between innocence and experience within the rhythm of the passages.

3. As you read these texts (or as you see a film), think about the relation between the rhythm of that work and the plot. What elements of the work convey the rhythm? How does that rhythm reflect what is happening in the work? Find a specific scene to use as the basis for your discussion.

7 Images

How Do We Experience Sensations in a Written Text?

Whenever we set out to describe our experiences to others, we need to do more than recount actions. Life isn't bound merely by "what happens"; the distinct quality of sensory impressions lends substance, particularity, and emotion to events. Things we see, hear, feel, smell, or taste often serve as an index to our most important memories. Sometimes, a physical sensation *is* the memory. Yet it's also true that in the course of any given stretch of time, we can be unconscious of this most elemental truth. We move so quickly through a day that we sometimes don't pause to notice details. It's a common experience, for example, to drive for miles over familiar roads and then think, "Have we already passed Fairview?"

Artists work to make sure we don't pass through Fairview or any other place along the way without observing closely. They register sensory data in ways that make us alert to the physical substance of our experience. In many modest ways we're artists of our own lives. Our vacation pictures, for example, are fascinating to us because they help us pause over details of what we've seen. And they likely trigger memories of a special meal (a local fish caught fresh), a smell (crisp ocean air at daybreak), a sound (gulls squawking over breaking waves), or a touch (wet sand under bare feet). We edit our vacation pictures carefully so that we can more deeply absorb our experience and sensitize ourselves to possibilities that lie ahead in future trips. And we're likely to present our vacation pictures to others from a desire to help them share what we felt, not merely know what we did.

Our reading experience again is not so different from our life experience; the disciplined practice of paying attention to our senses yields much of value in life and art. The novelist Henry James advised that we all try to be someone "upon whom nothing is lost." James's standard may be too high, but all types of experience offer a richness of imagery that must be paused over, not merely "passed through." In this chapter, we'll consider how sensory images serve to intensify literary and, in turn, life experience.

CREATING PICTURES WITH WORDS

It would be hard to overestimate the sheer volume of **visual images** in communication. Ironically, images of color and shape—of things seen—are so pervasive that they sometimes become almost invisible. A too common image may lose all force. A "red rose" or a "blue sky" can descend to the emptiness of advertising clichés like "golden brown french fries." Finding ways to make common descriptors convey an image vividly becomes a challenge that writers sometimes address consciously. Note how William Carlos Williams leads into the following poem by directly telling us that what we see—what we really see—counts for something, however mundane it may be.

William Carlos Williams (1883–1963)

The Red Wheelbarrow (1923)

so much depends
upon

a red wheel
barrow

glazed with rain   5
water

beside the white
chickens.

We are drawn to see the red wheelbarrow here partly because we recognize in the simplicity of these images how much and how often we don't see what is plainly before us. Williams's opening line suggests that the physical act of seeing can become a worthy theme: "so much depends" upon what is before us in the immediate moment. Czeslaw Milosz also asks us to see, absorb, and reflect upon common sights. In "Watering Can" he suggests that images ground us in a concrete reality and help us hold tight against what can be threatening, debilitating abstractions.

Czeslaw Milosz (1911–2004)

Watering Can (Czeslaw Milosz and Robert Hass, trans; 1998)

Of a green color, standing in a shed alongside rakes and spades, it comes alive when it is filled with water from the pond, and an abundant shower pours from its nozzle, in an act, we feel it, of charity towards plants. It is not certain, however, that the watering can would have such a place in our memory, were it not for our training in noticing things. For, after all, we have been trained. Our painters do not often imitate the Dutch, who liked to paint still lifes, and yet photography contributes to our paying attention to detail and the cinema taught us that objects, once they appear on the screen, would participate in the actions of the characters and therefore should be noticed. There are also museums where canvases glorify not only human figures and landscapes but also a multitude of objects. The watering can has thus a good chance of occupying a sizable place in our imagination, and, who knows, perhaps precisely in this, in our clinging to distinctly delineated shapes, does our hope reside, of salvation from the turbulent waters of nothingness and chaos. ■

Milosz suggests that extremely close attention to the physical world that surrounds us is a responsibility no artist can afford to shirk. But what is involved in the powerful production and use of visual images? Why do some images work and others fail to convey anything vivid or substantial? Context is a partial answer to these questions. Artists find ways to frame images so that we focus our attention on them. "A red wheelbarrow" or a "watering can" doesn't automatically make for poetry. But Williams and Milosz make us pay attention. Williams structures his poem in a way that moves us patiently from image to image: "so much depends" not only on the red wheelbarrow but upon the linked clauses that constitute the poem's layered imagery. Milosz employs a common rhetorical strategy: after introducing his modest subject, he grants that it may not seem of much significance. But he quickly turns from that concession to place the watering can in relation to all physical things that we've been trained to notice by painters, filmmakers, photographers, and museum curators.

Milosz's point about attending to detail returns us to specific qualities of the individual image and leads to a yet fuller sense of how images work. It is worth thinking about how we see and communicate a sense of what we see. Digital photography has made us much more aware that a picture emerges from small units of shape and color, whether those units are specks of paint, pixels, or words. Those who sell us digital cameras have taught us that if we pay more to increase our camera's ability to record increasingly minute pixels, the clearer the resolution we can gain in larger and larger reproductions of our image. This paradox—the smaller the area where we are able to focus, the

These digital images illustrate the increasing clarity that comes with dense, numerous, and minute pixels.

Georges Seurat, Port-en-Bessin, *Entrance to the Harbor* (1888). Seurat was influenced by optical color theories that were current in the later nineteenth century. Upon very large canvases, he placed tiny brush strokes or points of color that would blend as they were seen from a distance.

more complete our view of a larger object—drives much of the literature that we read and should help us in our own writing.

Tiny details of shape, size, and color are the raw materials of powerfully realized experiences. In Alice Munro's "How I Met My Husband" (p. 134), the narrator remembers the simple pleasures of bathing in what is for her the grand home of her employers. Those pleasures are linked concretely to images of sight and touch.

The basin and the tub and the toilet were all pink, and there were glass doors with flamingoes painted on them, to shut off the tub. The light had a rosy cast and the mat sank under your feel like snow, except that it was warm. The mirror was three-way. With the mirror all steamed up and the air like a perfume cloud, from things I was allowed to use, I stood up on the side of the tub and admired myself naked, from three directions. ■

The intensity of the narrator's pleasure in her weekly bath is so great that she doesn't want to indulge it too often. An overload of such impressions might risk "making it less wonderful."

Experiencing Literature through Imagery

We can, of course, question our dependence on visual images by considering how people may live intensely without them. In "Courtesy of the Blind," Wislawa Szymborska recognizes how difficult—even problematic—it may sometimes be to communicate what we see in words. Szymborska reflects on the visual images she is accustomed to use in order to connect with readers and to connect readers to the world. She displays a growing awareness of breakdowns between herself and others. In front of an audience of blind readers, she realizes how much of her work depends upon strategies that may often be naïve or misguided.

Wislawa Szymborska (1923–)

The Courtesy of the Blind (Clare Cavanagh and Stanislaw Baranczak, trans; 2006)

A poet reads his lines to the blind.
He hadn't guessed that it would be so hard.
His voice trembles.
His hands shake.

He senses that every sentence   5
is put to the test of darkness.
He must muddle through alone,
without the colors or lights.

A treacherous endeavor
for his poems' stars,   10
dawn, rainbows, clouds, their neon lights, their moon,
for the fish so silvery thus far beneath the water,
and the hawk so high and quiet in the sky.

He reads—since it's too late to stop now—
about the boy in a yellow jacket on a green valley,   15
red roofs that can be counted in the valley,
the restless numbers on soccer players' shirts,
and the naked stranger standing in a half-shut door.

He would like to skip—although it can't be done—
all the saints on that cathedral ceiling,   20
the parting wave from a train,
the microscope lens, the ring casting a glow,
the movie screens, mirrors, the photo albums.

But great is the courtesy of the blind,
great is their forbearance, their largesse.   25

They listen, smile, and applaud.
One of them even comes up
with a book turned wrongside out
asking for an unseen autograph.

In this poem, Szymborska uses an image, such as "all those saints on the cathedral's ceiling," to show how this particular audience has challenged her entire method of communicating. She may have grown too sure that readers had seen something like this cathedral ceiling (or a "green meadow" or a "farewell wave"). Perhaps she feels she has become too dependent upon only one of her five senses. In any case, she suddenly doubts the power of all of the images that she has used as a poet. And yet, by invoking these images in this context, she encourages her sighted audience (like the audience for Williams's "The Red Wheelbarrow") to value the gift of sight—to *choose* to see what sometimes passes unnoticed.

REGISTERING TASTE AND SMELL

It's generally understood that taste and smell powerfully connect us to memories and to specific feelings. In a famous passage from Marcel Proust's *Swann's Way*, the narrator catches a whiff of tea and madeleines (a type of French cookie) and with it reconnects to childhood. The smell acts as a trigger of sorts; it activates a part of the brain that holds not just a memory of past events but a feeling for their reality. Recent research in the physiology of the brain suggests that Proust was on to something. But capturing in words the sense of taste and smell is a difficult task. Certainly, much food and wine criticism struggles against the challenge. We simply don't have the well-tested vocabulary for smell and taste that we have for visual images. And although the senses of taste and smell recall memories vividly, we have a hard time evoking those senses through memory. But in the hands of a skilled writer, the lack of a standard vocabulary can become an opportunity (see the film still from *Sideways* for an example). If images grounded in the senses of taste and smell are less than plentiful, they can also be perhaps fresher.

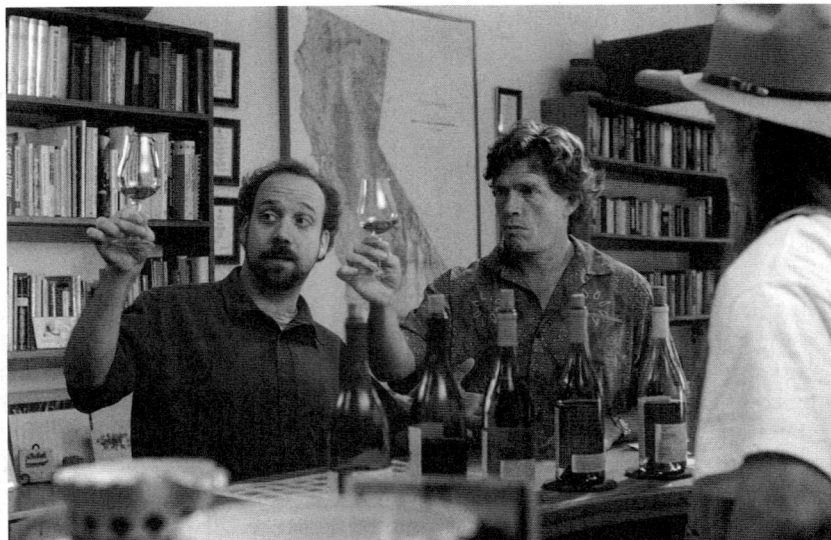

Character Miles Raymond from *Sideways* describes the taste of his wine: "A little citrus. Maybe some strawberry. Mmm. Passion fruit, mmm, and, oh, there's just like the faintest soupçon of like, uh, asparagus, and, there's a, just a flutter of, like a, like a nutty Edam cheese."

Experiencing Literature through Images

Salman Rushdie's account of his love for bread is a contemporary classic of sorts. As you read this reflection on the pleasures of eating and smelling bread, you won't need to think much of plot or character. Concentrate first on his descriptions—on the images he uses to convey his experience of bread. Rushdie was born in India and lives in England; much of his writing describes his native culture to those in the West. In this short essay, we experience the smells and tastes that help Rushdie describe what he sees as an essential difference between the cultures of the East and the West. As you read, pay attention to the different modes of representation Rushdie employs. At the start, Rushdie lists the varieties of unleavened bread that he grew up with in Bombay. Even if we are unfamiliar with these breads, his emphasis on the poetic quality of the names gives us some feeling for the quality of each of these breads that, of course, we cannot access literally through his prose. The "piping hot" phulka is followed by a series of breads that come to life as they are compared with one another in terms of their sweetness or luxury. As you move beyond the first paragraph, notice how comparison continues to function. *Luxury* may not be a term that we immediately associate with bread, but as soon as Rushdie relates "luxury" and bread, we work to make sense of it within the sensual realm. He describes an experience that most of his readers will not have had, so to present his particular situation, he compares his observations to things that might be more familiar to others. As you read, keep track of the way in which Rushdie uses sensory details (comments on texture, temperature, taste) to help us feel the cultural experience he recounts.

Salman Rushdie (1947–)

On Leavened Bread (1996)

There was leavened bread in Bombay, but it was sorry fare: dry, crumbling, tasteless—unleavened bread's paler, unluckier relative. It wasn't "real." Real bread was the chapatti, or phulka, served piping hot; the tandoori nan, and its sweeter Frontier variant, the Peshawari nan; and, for luxury, the reshmi roti, the shirmal, the paratha. Compared with these aristocrats, the leavened white loaves of my childhood seemed to merit the description that Shaw's immortal dustman, Alfred Doolittle, dreamed up for people like himself: they were, in truth, "the undeserving poor."

My first inkling that there might be more to leavened bread than I knew came while I was visiting Karachi, Pakistan, where I learned that a hidden

Nun with bread

order of nuns, in a place known as the Monastery of the Angels, baked a mean loaf. To buy it, you had to get up at dawn—that is, a servant had to get up at dawn—and stand in line outside a small hatch in the monastery's wall. The nun's baking facilities were limited, the daily run was small, and this secret bakery's reputation was high. Only the early bird caught the loaf. The hatch would open, and a nun would hand the bread out to the waiting populace. Loaves were strictly rationed. No bulk buying was permitted. And the price, of course, was high. (All this I knew only by hearsay, for I never got up at such an unearthly hour to see for myself.)

The nun's bread—white, crusty, full of flavor—was a small revelation, but it was also, on account of its unusual provenance, eccentric. It came from beyond the frontiers of the everyday, a mystery trailing an anecdote behind it. It was almost—well, fictional. (Later, it became fictional, when I put the monastery in my novel "Midnight's Children.") Now, in the matter of bread such extraordinariness is not good. You want bread to be a part of daily life. You want it to be ordinary. You want it to be there. You don't want to get up in the middle of the night and wait by a hatch in a wall. So, while the Angels' bread was tasty, it felt like an aberration, a break in the natural order. It didn't really change my mind.

Then, aged thirteen-and-a-half, I flew to England. And suddenly there it was, in every shop window. The White Crusty, the Sliced and Unsliced. The Small Tin, the Large Tin, the Danish Bloomer. The abandoned, plentiful promiscuity of it. The soft pillowy mattressiness of it. The well-sprung boun- ciness of it between your teeth. Hard crust and soft centre: the sensuality of that perfect textural contrast. I was done for. In the whorehouses of the bakeries,

I was serially, gluttonously, irredeemably unfaithful to all those chapatis-next-door waiting for me back home. East was East, but yeast was West.

This, remember, was long before British bread counters were enlivened by the European invasion, long before ciabatta and brioche; this was 1961. But the love affair that began then has never lost its intensity; the new exotic breads have served only to renew the excitement.

I should add that there was a second discovery, almost as thrilling; that is, water. The water back home was dangerous and had to be thoroughly boiled. To be able to drink water from the tap was a privilege indeed. I have never forgotten that when I first arrived in these immeasurably wealthy and powerful lands I found the first proofs of my good fortune in loaf and glass. Since that time, a regime of bread and water has never sounded like a hardship to me. (*The New Yorker*, December 23 and 30, 1996) ■

By the time that Rushdie reaches the fourth paragraph and what he describes as his serial, gluttonous unfaithfulness to his native breads, the essay has built to a climax. It is memorable and often cited, perhaps because of the dense fabric of sensory details Rushdie weaves. This is the sort of text that enters into our real conversations, leading us to talk about our own favorite breads, Indian restaurants, and childhood food memories.

INTERACTION OF THE SENSES

Our senses operate together. A good dinner isn't merely something tasted. It's well presented to the eye. If there is music playing in the background, it's the right music for the meal. Each bite will have a texture as well as a taste and an aroma. Literary works often build on the dense interaction of the senses to fully realize a scene. Think of, for example, how a nineteenth-century novelist describing a London street scene might register sounds and smells, as well as sights, in communicating a sense of busy urban life.

Paradise Lost is an epic poem in which John Milton reimagines the biblical story of Adam and Eve and their loss of Eden. In the brief excerpt that follows, Satan (here, variously called the "Serpent" and the "Evil-one") emerges from the horrors of Hell to encounter the beautiful Eve in the glorious setting of Eden. Milton wants us to appreciate the sensory experience of one who has been cut off from pleasures the unfallen world offers. We are to know Satan as a character largely through what he sees, hears, and feels as well as through our knowledge of what sights, sounds, and textures he has been denied.

In the first ten lines of this passage from *Paradise Lost*, Milton presents a **simile** (a comparison that links two things with *like* or *as*) so that the reader can appreciate what Satan might feel as he moves from Hell into Eden. An **epic simile** (such as the one in the passage) greatly elaborates one side of the comparison; note in the example that the initial "as" is followed by such a long description that we almost lose track of what comparison is being made. This particular epic simile starts off by describing a person who has come to the country from the city. Eventually we return to Satan; it is he who is *like* the stroller presented at such length. Milton uses the simile to humanize Satan; instead of making him unexplainable, Milton creates a Satan whose motivations seem familiarly human. The second selection from *Paradise Lost* moves from the description of the city dweller who walks into the country for fresh air into the mind of Satan; this is how Milton imagines Satan viewing Eve; she embodies beauty in a beautiful world, and Satan's awe at this sight is intensified by its unfamiliarity. He has grown accustomed to the dismal surroundings of Hell. In the third selection, Satan overcomes his momentary lapse into stunned appreciation of beauty and resumes his usual wicked character. Track the sensory details in this passage to determine which are in the simile (after the initial "as") and which appear after the colon that ends the simile. Also note how Milton invokes multiple senses (sight, smell, touch, and sound).

John Milton (1608–1674)

from # Paradise Lost (1667)

As one who long in populous city pent,
Where houses thick and sewers annoy the air,
Forth issuing on a summer's morn, to breathe
Among the pleasant villages and farms
Adjoined, from each thing met conceives delight,   5
The smell of grain, or tedded grass, or kine,
Or dairy, each rural sight, each rural sound;
If chance, with nymph-like step fair virgin pass,
What pleasing seemed, for her now pleases more,
She most, and in her look sums all delight: 10
Such pleasure took the Serpent to behold
This flowery plat, the sweet recess of Eve
Thus early, thus alone: Her heavenly form
Angelic, but more soft and feminine,
Her graceful innocence, her every air   15
Of gesture or least action overawed
His malice, and with rapine sweet bereaved
His fierceness of the fierce intent it brought.

That space the Evil One abstracted stood
From his own evil, and for the time remained   20
Stupidly good, of enmity disarmed,
Of guile, of hate, of envy, of revenge;
But the hot hell that always in him burns,
Though in mid Heaven, soon ended his delight,
And tortures him now more, the more he sees   25
Of pleasure not for him ordained; then soon
Fierce hate he recollects, and all his thoughts
Of mischief, gratulating, thus excites.

In bringing this particular scene to life, Milton makes real the horror of Hell, the glory of Eden, the turpitude of Satan, and the beauty of Eve by calling up an image that is generally familiar, even mundane. In his simile, he borrows the common conceit that cities are like Hell—there are too many people, too much pollution, and bad sewers—and turns it around; in order to imagine Hell, we should imagine a city, because Hell is similar to a city. Satan emerging from Hell is like anyone leaving a city to visit the country and being delighted by everything simply because it is different and fresh. Instead of being some creature from a horror film, this Satan is so happy to be out of Hell that he is like a tourist sightseeing. This passage is filled with detail: "The smell of grain, or tedded grass, or kine [cattle], / Or dairy." In reading this passage, we must decide how to translate this scene into our picture of the Satan character who is about to seduce Eve (and, by extension, all of humanity) into disobeying the will of God. The naïve city person who Milton uses to represent Satan and who is delighted by sights, smells, and sounds of the country is a bit more sophisticated than he appears, and the sensory images in this passage help us understand this character as one shaken out of his usual sense of self and yet able to return quickly to that self. After all, how long are city folk generally excited by the smell of cattle?

Satan's visit to Eden raises a question of large importance for artists of all kinds: What happens when the demands on our senses exceed our ability to process, discriminate, and savor? A rush of sensory data can be exhilarating, as it is momentarily for Satan. When our senses, in effect, overload, we may be forced to take the world in differently and may feel, as a result, a sense of discovery or revelation. A rush of sights, sounds, textures, tastes, and smells can also prompt feelings of confusion and disorientation. The critic Pauline Kael maintained that film was an art form especially equipped to take advantage of the immediacy and multiplicity of sensory experience. In a dark theater, sitting before a giant screen, we're focused intently on complex, rapidly shifting sights and sounds. We don't have either the time or the opportunity to back off and think about what our senses take in at the very moment they are engaged so actively.

Although such qualities are often exploited to no purpose (do we need more explosions and car chases in "action films"?), Kael's observation helps us appreciate the sources of power that a good movie may access. Contrast, for example, Martin Scorsese's lavish re-creation of mid-nineteenth-century

Gangs of New York (2002)

Lost in Translation (2003)

urban life in *Gangs of New York* (2002) with Sophia Coppola's spare, precise, patient, and quietly rendered scenes of loneliness from the hotel bar in *Lost in Translation* (2003). These scenes convey sensory qualities of human life at a given moment: the mud, noise, and movement of the street; the soft and unconnected background noise in the near-empty bar late at night.

Experiencing Literature through Images

Of course, movies have no exclusive right to sensory intensity. Nor do our senses necessarily disconnect from abstract thought or inevitably supplant thought. Richard Wilbur conveys a dense and moving fabric of sight and sound to convey the image of a fire truck careening along a street. The abrupt appearance of the noisy, red, large truck leaves those watching with the raw experience of the truck in the moment it passes but without an opportunity to think about the noise and the vehicle that has interrupted their routine activity. But in this poet's case, the overloading of the senses occasions a philosophical exploration of the relationship between objects, actions, and thoughts.

Richard Wilbur (1921–)

A Fire-Truck (1961)

Right down the shocked street with a siren-blast
That sends all else skittering to the curb,
Redness, brass, ladders and hats hurl past,
    Blurring to sheer verb,

Shift at the corner into uproarious gear   5
And make it around the turn in a squall of traction,
The headlong bell maintaining sure and clear,
    Thought is degraded action!

Beautiful, heavy, unweary, loud, obvious thing!
I stand here purged of nuance, my mind a blank.   10
All I was brooding upon has taken wing,
    And I have you to thank.

As you howl beyond hearing I carry you into my mind,
Ladders and brass and all, there to admire
Your phoenix-red simplicity, enshrined   15
    In that not extinguished fire.

In the first two lines, Wilbur reproduces the impact of a fire truck by announcing its "siren-blast" but also by showing us the effect of this siren on the rest of the "shocked street" where everything is "skittering to the curb." Next, he gives four details that we are allowed to pick out of the blur of the passing truck: "Redness, brass, ladders and hats." Each of the details is something that we might associate with a fire truck, and each of us could easily fill in at least a half dozen other details of fire trucks, but these four words are enough to sketch the image that Wilbur calls up here. As soon as the image is distinct, Wilbur blurs it as it "hurl[s] past," and his narrator changes the concrete image into something else. The nouns that he has just listed blur "to sheer verb," and the fire truck itself, which begins as the representative noun, or the object that we are trying to see in this poem, becomes representative of action.

Wilbur starts with sensory impressions that obliterate intellectual abstractions; ultimately though, he asks that we reflect on the process of obliteration. Nouns describe objects; verbs describe action; and Wilbur uses the fire truck image to examine the problem of thinking itself. In his formulation, action happens; and thought, in an effort to make sense of that blurred fire truck, "*degrade[s] action*." A fire truck is a specific object, but our experience of fire trucks is greater than the things that we see as it rushes past. An integral aspect of our experience of the fire truck is its action: the speed as it roars by and the life-saving actions that it facilitates in emergencies. Therefore, as we think about this specific noun, "fire truck," we are also thinking about a series of verbs as well as the next list of adjectives: "Beautiful, heavy, unweary, loud, obvious." Each applies to the fire truck with its redness and hats, but by taking us into thought, Wilbur has left the realm of sensory experience. The adjectives that apply so well to a fire truck inspire a certain meditation that has very little to do with what the narrator has actually observed; we now begin to think about the nature of beauty, heaviness, weariness, obviousness, and the paradoxical "simplicity" of this fire truck that has inspired the narrator to set this scene and bring us along on the narrator's own inner journey.

Making Connections

In Chapters 12 and 13, we consider how images may become **symbols**; that is, an image may come to represent something other than the specific object that the author names. One might argue that the fire truck in Wilbur's poem or the bread in Rushdie's essay signifies something else. In order to make such an argument, we must show how the author uses specific details in such a way to justify our interpretation. It is also important to remember that images don't need to mean something *else* in order to connect to powerful feelings.

INTERACTION OF WORDS AND PICTURES

As they are used in literary works, images are the building blocks of experience. As words are used to build images, they also help interpret images or make those images achieve meaning or some particular emotional effect. Words contextualize images, just as the body of "A Fire-Truck" organizes and transforms the sensory experience of the fire truck rushing by into a philosophical musing. The further we examine this subject, the clearer it becomes that an image does not stand entirely alone. As Wilbur shows us in his poem, we process the sensory data that we take in. This process involves, among other things, a comparison of one image with others that are familiar to us or that come to us at the same time. Occasionally, it involves conflating senses that we normally take to be separate. Michael Ondaatje dramatizes such combinations in his poem "King Kong Meets Wallace Stevens." The unlikely pairing of the poet Stevens with the movie monster allows Ondaatje to consider his own reactions to the two images.

Michael Ondaatje (1943 –)

King Kong Meets Wallace Stevens (1979)

Take two photographs—
Wallace Stevens and King Kong
(Is it significant that I eat bananas as I write this?)

Stevens is portly, benign, a white brush cut
striped tie. Businessman but   5
for the dark thick hands, the naked brain
the thought in him.

Kong is staggering
lost in New York streets again
a spawn of annoyed cars at his toes.   10
The mind is nowhere.
Fingers are plastic, electric under the skin.
He's at the call of Metro-Goldwyn-Mayer.

Meanwhile W. S. in his suit
is thinking chaos is thinking fences.   15
In his head the seeds of fresh pain
his exorcising,
the bellow of locked blood.

The hands drain from his jacket,
pose in the murder's shadow.   20

The last lines of Ondaatje's poem moves us beyond the mixture of senses or the interaction between sensations and words to what seems the conflation of all senses along with the intellect. How does "locked blood" find expression in a "bellow?" For that matter, how can blood be "locked?" And how can hands "drain" from one's jacket? What would those hands look like? These are difficult images to grasp securely, but if Ondaatje were after something that could be grasped securely, he might not bother to write a poem. As strikingly unusual as these images are, they play upon a fairly familiar notion: the most intense sensations and most subtle thoughts sometimes achieve a kind of fusion.

This conflation of senses is part of what made *American Beauty* (1999) such a moving film for many people. Early in the film, the main character, Lester Burnham (Kevin Spacey), inhabits a home and office environment stripped of any visual distinction. As Lester grows progressively rebellious, colors, textures, feelings, and sounds press upon him. Perhaps by the end of the film, just before his death, Lester could ask: "Have you ever felt a piece of music to be so beautiful that it hurt? Or perhaps even tasted that music?" This cross association—one kind of sensory experience evoking the experience of another kind—is called **synesthesia**. Until recently, synesthesia was

The poet Wallace Stevens

King Kong (1933)

considered a purely fanciful or "poetic" notion; whereas it may be telling to say a color is "loud," surely no one has ever really heard a color. In the past decade, however, advances in brain research have suggested that we can't be so confident in absolute distinctions. Neural activity controlling our sensory responses isn't always neatly compartmentalized in discrete parts of the brain. Some people—especially creative people—do see sounds or feel colors. Those of us not gifted in this way may still discover an inexplicable power or aptness in two senses registered in a single image.

Experiencing Literature through Images

The Japanese **haiku** form of poetry foregrounds its attention to images. Often the poem itself seems to be nothing more than one or two specific images with no attempt to explain how that image is significant. In the following poetic sequence, the poet Yosa Buson offers a series of these short observational poems based upon the four seasons of the year. The third part of the poem, "Autumn," is one of the shorter sections. Buson begins by describing the experience of stepping on a comb—the comb of an absent (some translate "dead") wife. List the details in scenes that make up "Autumn."

What senses does Buson describe? How are the varied feelings connected to the immediate sensual experience of stepping on the comb? What details don't seem part of that immediate experience? How are all details important to Buson's experience of this moment? In the whole sequence, how are details interesting beyond the poet's experience of them?

Yosa Buson (1716–1784)

from Hokku Poems in Four Seasons (Yuki Sawa and Edith M. Shiffert, trans; 1780)

SPRING

The year's first poem done,
with smug self confidence—
a haikai poet.

Daylight longer!
A pheasant has fluttered down   5
onto the bridge.

Yearning for the Past

Lengthening days
Accumulate—farther off
the days of long ago!   10

Slowly passing days,
their echoings are heard
here in Kyoto.

The white elbow
of a priest who is dozing!   15
Dusk in spring.

Into a nobleman
a fox has changed himself—
early evening of spring.

The light of a candle   20
is transferred to another candle—
spring twilight.

A short nap, then
awakening—the spring
day darkened.   25

Who is it for,
the small bed pillow,
twilight in spring?

The big gateway's
massive doors—   30
spring twilight.

Hazy moonlight!
Someone is standing
among the pear trees.

Flowers of the pear—   35
reading a letter by moon light,
a woman.

Springtime rain!
Almost dark, and yet
today still lingers   40

Springtime rain!
Little shells on a small beach,
enough to moisten them.

     SUMMER

In the quietness
of a lull between visitors,   45
the peony flower!

A peony fallen—
on top of one another,
two petals, three petals.

Early summer rain—   50
facing toward the big river,
houses, two of them.

At a Place Called Kaya in Tanba

A summer river
being crossed, how pleasing!   55
Sandals in my hands.

The mountain stonecutter's
chisel is being cooled
in the clear water!

Rainfall on the grasses   60
just after the festival cart
passed by.

To my eyes it is delightful—
the fan of my beloved,
completely white.   65

Hototogisu
over the Heian castle town
flying aslant

In evening wind—
water is slapping against   70
legs of a blue heron.

An old well!
Jumping at a mosquito, a fish's
sound of darkness.

Young bamboo!   75
At Hashimoto, the harlot,
is she still there or not?

After it has fallen
its image still stands—
the peony flower.   80

Ascending the Eastern Slope

Flowering Thorn—
the pathway by my home village
is like this!

Feeling melancholy   85
while climbing the hill,
flowering thorn.

AUTUMN

It goes into me—
the comb of my long gone wife
to step on it in the bedroom.   90

Compared to last year,
this has even more loneliness—
autumn evening.

Being alone
may also even be pleasant—   95
autumn dusk.

Moon in the sky's center,
shabbiness on the village street—
just passing through.

While feeling sad   100
a fishing line being blown
by the autumn wind.

WINTER

I shall go to bed—
New Year's Day is a matter
for tomorrow.   105

Camphor tree roots
silently becoming wet
in a winter shower.

A handsaw
sounding like poverty   110
at midnight in winter.

An old man's love.
while trying to forget it,
a winter rainfall.

In an old pond   115
a straw sandal half sunken—
wet snowfall!

Haiku poetry may be identified by its three-line stanza structure. Each three-line unit in Buson's poem can be read as an independent poem (the stanza that opens "Autumn" is often reprinted alone). In such short poems, there is often a concentrated attention upon a single image with little explanatory material; we access feeling through the quality and intensity of the image and the associations it provokes. Look back over Buson's poem, and notice how many of these three-line units are self-sufficient, yet consider how they work together (just as the seasonal sections work together) to amplify their individual ideas. In what ways does this collection of sensory images create, in the aggregate, a larger commentary? Why does the poet divide his images by seasons? Look, for instance, at the poet's comments about age within each separate season.

A Note to Student Writers: Using Specific Detail

Your writing about literature and film will be most incisive and most immediate when you center your discussion on specific details and when you describe how these details lead you to the larger argumentative context that you provide in your analysis. It is important, though, *not* to get lost in details. Although in the early predraft writing stage you might want to make lengthy lists of various things you notice in a work (key words, recurring images, specific stylistic features, and so on), you'll certainly want to edit, order, and reduce that list as you write the paper. Good critical papers aren't defined by how many things they include; rather, they are characterized by how thoughtfully they select and explain what they include. It is the critic's job to convey some significant *aspect* of our experience of a text. You shouldn't try to "cover" everything so much as seek to register precisely and explain fully what is most relevant to your particular reading. Focus is important. A paper on imagery in *Trifles* will likely wander in several directions without every quite getting anywhere. A paper on images of unfinished work in *Trifles* might lead to real insight.

MODELING CRITICAL ANALYSIS: T. S. ELIOT, THE LOVE SONG OF J. ALFRED PRUFROCK

T. S. Eliot's "The Love Song of J. Alfred Prufrock" echoes the conventions noted earlier that Milton employs to describe Satan's visit to Eden. The city is assumed or presented as a poisonous place of lonely, tired people. It's a place of grit and bad smells. Milton uses escape from the city to intensify Satan's rapt appreciation of the Edenic countryside. Eliot's poem keeps us confined almost entirely in the city. Prufrock never escapes. You'll note that

Eliot's imagery, like Milton's, is vivid and varied. At the start, he uses a simile: "When the evening is spread out against the sky / Like a patient etherized upon a table." He also employs **personification** (that is, he lends human/animal characteristics to an inanimate thing) to express a lingering, languidly moving, dirty quality of the "yellow fog" that hangs about the streets. His narrator's self-description (the bald spot, the clothes) as well as his descriptions of others ("arms that are braceleted and white and bare") offers precisely selected details that register a particular social class and the stifling qualities of that class. This complex and difficult poem has been so well and so widely appreciated largely because of Eliot's ability to make us see, feel, and taste details of place and person; his imagery lends a power to the poem even upon a first reading. Through striking images, Eliot helps us acquire a sense of place, character, and situation essential to our experience of the poem.

T. S. Eliot (1888–1965)

The Love Song of J. Alfred Prufrock (1917)

> S'io credessi che mia risposta fosse
> A persona che mai tornasse al mondo,
> Questa fiamma staria senza più scosse.
> Ma perciocchè giammai di questo fondo
> Non tornó vivo alcun, s'i'odo il vero,
> Senza tema d'infamia ti rispondo.

Let us go then, you and I,
When the evening is spread out against the sky
Like a patient etherized upon a table;
Let us go, through certain half-deserted streets,
The muttering retreats   5
Of restless nights in one-night cheap hotels
And sawdust restaurants with oyster-shells:
Streets that follow like a tedious argument
Of insidious intent
To lead you to an overwhelming question.... .   10
Oh, do not ask, "What is it?"
Let us go and make our visit.

In the room the women come and go
Talking of Michelangelo.

The yellow fog that rubs its back upon the window-panes,   15
The yellow smoke that rubs its muzzle on the window-panes
Licked its tongue into the corners of the evening,
Lingered upon the pools that stand in drains,
Let fall upon its back the soot that falls from chimneys,
Slipped by the terrace, made a sudden leap,   20
And seeing that it was a soft October night,
Curled once about the house, and fell asleep.

And indeed there will be time
For the yellow smoke that slides along the street,
Rubbing its back upon the window-panes;   25
There will be time, there will be time
To prepare a face to meet the faces that you meet;
There will be time to murder and create,
And time for all the works and days of hands
That lift and drop a question on your plate;   30
Time for you and time for me,
And time yet for a hundred indecisions,
And for a hundred visions and revisions,
Before the taking of a toast and tea.

In the room the women come and go   35
Talking of Michelangelo.

And indeed there will be time
To wonder, "Do I dare?" and, "Do I dare?"
Time to turn back and descend the stair,
With a bald spot in the middle of my hair—   40
(They will say: "How his hair is growing thin!")
My morning coat, my collar mounting firmly to the chin,
My necktie rich and modest, but asserted by a simple pin—
(They will say: "But how his arms and legs are thin!")
Do I dare   45
Disturb the universe?
In a minute there is time
For decisions and revisions which a minute will reverse.

For I have known them all already, known them all—
Have known the evenings, mornings, afternoons,   50
I have measured out my life with coffee spoons;
I know the voices dying with a dying fall

Beneath the music from a farther room.
  So how should I presume?

And I have known the eyes already, known them all—   55
The eyes that fix you in a formulated phrase,
And when I am formulated, sprawling on a pin,
When I am pinned and wriggling on the wall,
Then how should I begin
To spit out all the butt-ends of my days and ways?   60
  And how should I presume?

And I have known the arms already, known them all—
Arms that are braceleted and white and bare
(But in the lamplight, downed with light brown hair!)
Is it perfume from a dress   65
That makes me so digress?
Arms that lie along a table, or wrap about a shawl.
    And should I then presume?
    And how should I begin?

                        *   *   *

Shall I say, I have gone at dusk through narrow streets   70
And watched the smoke that rises from the pipes
Of lonely men in shirt-sleeves, leaning out of windows?...

I should have been a pair of ragged claws
Scuttling across the floors of silent seas.

                        *   *   *

And the afternoon, the evening, sleeps so peacefully!   75
Smoothed by long fingers,
Asleep... tired... or it malingers,
Stretched on the floor, here beside you and me.
Should I, after tea and cakes and ices,
Have the strength to force the moment to its crisis?   80
But though I have wept and fasted, wept and prayed,
Though I have seen my head (grown slightly bald) brought in upon a platter,
I am no prophet—and here's no great matter;
I have seen the moment of my greatness flicker,
And I have seen the eternal Footman hold my coat, and snicker,   85
And in short, I was afraid.

And would it have been worth it, after all,
After the cups, the marmalade, the tea,

Among the porcelain, among some talk of you and me,
Would it have been worth while, 90
To have bitten off the matter with a smile,
To have squeezed the universe into a ball
To roll it toward some overwhelming question,
To say: "I am Lazarus, come from the dead,
Come back to tell you all, I shall tell you all"— 95
If one, settling a pillow by her head,
    Should say: "That is not what I meant at all.
    That is not it, at all."

And would it have been worth it, after all,
Would it have been worth while, 100
After the sunsets and the dooryards and the sprinkled streets,
After the novels, after the teacups, after the skirts that trail along the floor—
And this, and so much more?—
It is impossible to say just what I mean!
But as if a magic lantern threw the nerves in patterns on a screen: 105
Would it have been worth while
If one, settling a pillow or throwing off a shawl,
And turning toward the window, should say:
    "That is not it at all,
    That is not what I meant, at all." 110

                 *   *   *

No! I am not Prince Hamlet, nor was meant to be;
Am an attendant lord, one that will do
To swell a progress, start a scene or two,
Advise the prince; no doubt, an easy tool,
Deferential, glad to be of use, 115
Politic, cautious, and meticulous;
Full of high sentence, but a bit obtuse;
At times, indeed, almost ridiculous—
Almost, at times, the Fool.

I grow old… I grow old… 120
I shall wear the bottoms of my trousers rolled.

Shall I part my hair behind? Do I dare to eat a peach?
I shall wear white flannel trousers, and walk upon the beach.
I have heard the mermaids singing, each to each.

I do not think that they will sing to me. 125

I have seen them riding seaward on the waves,
Combing the white hair of the waves blown back
When the wind blows the water white and black.

We have lingered in the chambers of the sea
By sea-girls wreathed with seaweed red and brown   130
Till human voices wake us, and we drown.

Using Images to Focus Writing and Discussion

- Locate significant images within this work. Is there any single image that seems to be especially significant? What details in the text signal this prominence?
- What sense (or senses) does the author use to convey these images?
- How does the author introduce images in this work? Do they come from a particular point of view? Do they come all at once?
- What is the significance of these images to specific characters within the text? How is this significance related to our experience of the text?
- Is there any pattern to the sorts of images that are prominent? For instance, are they generally associated with a single place or time in the text, or are they scattered throughout various places and times?
- How do the images relate to the ideas presented in the text?

Anthology

HOME AND AWAY: PERSONALIZING IMAGES

Images of home and away are common in much literature and film. In simple formulaic works, the contrast between the two is distinct and conventionalized. Home is typically registered through images that are reassuring in their familiarity. Away is suggested by sights that are striking—even disorienting—in their newness. But *newness* and *familiarity* are relative terms. A shady spot under a big tree in the backyard is only an image of home to a person who has a backyard. A grain silo might be strange to a child from New York. A skyscraper is likely an exotic sight to a child from Manhattan, Kansas. But the emotional dynamic is fairly easy to track in popular texts: comfort/excitement; familiar/strange; old/new; family/strangers; sameness/difference; city/country.

Ambitious literary works and films complicate such plain oppositions. In the selections that follow, minutely realized images don't simply fall on one side or the other of a neat divide but become a means to explore, particularize, and discover emotions. Haruki Murakami's "UFO in Kushiro" first appeared in a collection of stories that dealt in various ways with the feelings generated by the catastrophic earthquake that struck Kobe, Japan, in 1995. The first images in this story are filtered through a television set: Komura's wife sits fixated on her couch before the "crumbled banks and hospitals, whole blocks of stories in flames, severed rail lines and expressways." Curiously, images of the home itself are spare and generic. For the wife, and perhaps for us, the most vivid images are secondhand. The relative blankness of the living space itself suggests that home is not simply the place one lives. It is a place one must build in the imagination and the spirit. It is a place one chooses to be as opposed to a place one is. Perhaps Komura doesn't understand that, at least not at first. As you read, consider what is involved in his journey *away* from home—what is lost or found.

Alice Munro reminds us that particular definitions of home are often shaped around notions of gender. The youthful narrator of "Boys and Girls" at first identifies most closely with the outdoor work of her father. In most contexts, we might expect descriptions like the following to evoke feelings of comfortable domesticity:

These days our back porch was piled with baskets of peaches and grapes and pears, bought in town, and onions and tomatoes and cucumbers grown at home, all waiting to be made into jelly and jam and preserves, pickles and chili sauce. In the kitchen there was a fire in the stove all day, jars clinked in boiling water, sometimes a cheesecloth bag was strung on a pole between two chairs, straining blue-black grape pulp for jelly. ∎

But all of these images are set in the context of labor the narrator wants to escape. The mother is a threatening presence, for she pulls the narrator into the "hot dark kitchen" away from the "important" work done outdoors by the father. Eventually, disturbing images from outside profoundly mark a redefined set of associations. Munro's narrator reminds us that no image has a fixed value: people read and interpret actively the things around them.

Robert Frost draws his central image—the bent birches—from the country. The image is resonant of youth and freedom. Yet "Birches" also invokes images of the hard physical "Truth" of nature. Frost's speaker must deliberately conjure against this truth associations that speak to a deep need for a carefully calibrated escape. The speaker wants the sensation of moving toward heaven but doesn't want to *arrive* there. He uses the sight of the bent birches to achieve the desired feeling. Frost, like Munro, helps us see that the power of images resides not merely in physical facts but in the way one processes facts.

The reading, and especially the nonreading, of domestic details runs throughout Susan Glaspell's *Trifles*. The county attorney asks the women to "keep an eye out for anything that might be of use to us." The women do exactly that, but it hardly matters to the men who are in official charge of the investigation. The men see nothing. They are not good detectives (and they wouldn't be good literary critics) because they assume that important things must be big things. And they don't make imaginative connections. They aren't able to appreciate the emotional resonance of details such as the unwashed pans under the sink or the dish towel left on the kitchen table. Glaspell writes these "*signs of incompleted work*" into her stage directions because she wants to communicate something of the quality of the home life lived by Minnie Foster. She wants us to see and appreciate particular images in the way Mrs. Hale and Mrs. Peters do.

The rural home in *Trifles* is an isolated place—a profoundly lonely and disconnected place. Nor does William Blake's "London" offer comfort in the intensity of city life. Note how Blake employs synesthesia in the third stanza: the sound of the soldier's sigh becomes visible: "… the hapless Soldier's sigh / Runs in blood down Palace walls." And the tragedy of his "youthful Harlot" is communicated by the chilling image of how her "curse" (likely a venereal disease) "blasts the new-born Infant's tear." In this image, Blake vividly concentrates the horrors of the new industrial city that erases any notion of home. In "London," as in many works of literature, powerful experiences grow from the writers' ability to make us see, hear, feel, taste, and smell the world that surrounds us.

FICTION

Alice Munro (1931–)

Award-winning short story writer Alice Munro was born in Ontario, Canada. She received her BA from the University of Western Ontario in 1952. Munro was artist-in-residence at the University of Western Ontario from 1974 to 1975 and at the University of British Columbia in 1980. She has received numerous awards for her writing, including the Governor General's Literary Award for *Dance of the Happy Shades* (1969), *Who Do You Think You Are?: Stories* (1978), *The Beggar Maid: Stories of Flo and Rose* (1979), and *The Progress of Love* (1987). Her collection of stories, *Runaway*, was published in October 2004. In 2005, Munro was honored for her lifetime achievement by the National Arts Club, which presented her with the Medal of Honor for Literature.

Boys and Girls (1968)

My father was a fox farmer. That is, he raised silver foxes, in pens; and in the fall and early winter, when their fur was prime, he killed them and skinned them and sold their pelts to the Hudson's Bay Company or the Montreal Fur Traders. These companies supplied us with heroic calendars to hang, one on each side of the kitchen door. Against a background of cold blue sky and black pine forests and treacherous northern rivers, plumed adventurers planted the flags of England or of France; magnificent savages bent their backs to the portage.

For several weeks before Christmas, my father worked after supper in the cellar of our house. The cellar was whitewashed, and lit by a hundred-watt bulb over the worktable. My brother Laird and I sat on the top step and watched. My father removed the pelt inside-out from the body of the fox, which looked surprisingly small, mean and rat-like, deprived of its arrogant weight of fur. The naked, slippery bodies were collected in a sack and buried at the dump. One time the hired man, Henry Bailey, had taken a swipe at me with this sack, saying, "Christmas present!" My mother thought that was not funny. In fact she disliked the whole pelting operation—that was what the killing, skinning, and preparation of the furs was called—and wished it did not have to take place in the house. There was the smell. After the pelt had been stretched inside-out on a long board my father scraped away delicately, removing the little clotted webs of blood vessels, the bubbles of fat; the smell of blood and animal fat, with the strong primitive odour of the fox itself, penetrated all parts of the house. I found it reassuringly seasonal, like the smell of oranges and pine needles.

Henry Bailey suffered from bronchial troubles. He would cough and cough until his narrow face turned scarlet, and his light blue, derisive eyes filled up with tears; then he took the lid off the stove, and, standing well back, shot out a great clot of phlegm—hsss—straight into the heart of the flames. We admired him for his performance and for his ability to make his stomach growl at will, and for his laughter, which was full of high whistlings and gurglings and involved the whole faulty machinery of his chest. It was sometimes hard to tell what he was laughing at, and always possible that it might be us.

After we had been sent to bed we could still smell fox and still hear Henry's laugh, but these things, reminders of the warm, safe, brightly lit downstairs world, seemed lost and diminished, floating on the stale cold air upstairs. We were afraid at night in the winter. We were not afraid of *outside* though this was the time of year when snowdrifts curled around our house like sleeping whales and the wind harassed us all night, coming up from the buried fields, the frozen swamp, with its old bugbear chorus of threats and misery. We were afraid of *inside*, the room where we slept. At this time the upstairs of our house was not finished. A brick chimney went up one wall. In the middle of the floor was a square hole, with a wooden railing around it; that was where the stairs came up. On the other side of the stairwell were the things that nobody had any use for any more—a soldiery roll of linoleum, standing on end, a wicker baby carriage, a fern basket, china jugs and basins with cracks in them, a picture of the Battle of Balaclava, very sad to look at. I had told Laird, as soon as he was old enough to understand such things, that bats and skeletons lived over there; whenever a man escaped from the county jail, twenty miles away, I imagined that he had somehow let himself in the window and was hiding behind the linoleum. But we had rules to keep us safe. When the light was on, we were safe as long as we did not step off the square of worn carpet which defined our bedroom-space; when the light was off no place was safe but the beds themselves. I had to turn out the light kneeling on the end of my bed, and stretching as far as I could to reach the cord.

In the dark we lay on our beds, our narrow life rafts, and fixed our eyes on the faint light coming up the stairwell, and sang songs. Laird sang "Jingle Bells," which he would sing any time, whether it was Christmas or not, and I sang "Danny Boy." I love the sound of my own voice, frail and supplicating, rising in the dark. We could make out the tall frosted shapes of the windows now, gloomy and white. When I came to the part, *When I am dead, as dead I well may be*—a fit of shivering caused not by the cold sheets but by pleasurable emotion almost silenced me. *You'll kneel and say, an Ave there above me*—What was an Ave? Every day I forgot to find out.

Laird went straight from singing to sleep. I could hear his long, satisfied, bubbly breaths. Now for the time that remained to me, the most perfectly private and perhaps the best time of the whole day, I arranged myself tightly under the covers and went on with one of the stories I was telling myself from night to night. These stories were about myself, when I had grown a little older; they took place in a world that was recognizably mine, yet one that presented opportunities for courage, boldness and self-sacrifice, as mine never did. I rescued people from a bombed building (it discouraged me that the real war had gone on so far away from Jubilee). I shot two rabid wolves who were menacing the schoolyard (the teachers cowered terrified at my back). I rode a fine horse spiritedly down the main street of Jubilee, acknowledging the towns-people's gratitude for some yet-to-be-worked-out piece of heroism (nobody ever rode a horse there, except King Billy in the Orangemen's Day parade). There was always riding and shooting in these stories, though I had only been on a horse twice—bareback because we did not own a saddle—and the second time I had slid right around and dropped under the horse's feet; it had stepped placidly

5

over me. I really was learning to shoot, but I could not hit anything yet, not even tin cans on fence posts.

Alive, the foxes inhabited a world my father made for them. It was surrounded by a high guard fence, like a medieval town, with a gate that was padlocked at night. Along the streets of this town were ranged large, sturdy pens. Each of them had a real door that a man could go through, a wooden ramp along the wire, for the foxes to run up and down on, and a kennel—something like a clothes chest with airholes—where they slept and stayed in winter and had their young. There were feeding and watering dishes attached to the wire in such a way that they could be emptied and cleaned from the outside. The dishes were made of old tin cans, and the ramps and kennels of odds and ends of old lumber. Everything was tidy and ingenious; my father was tirelessly inventive and his favourite book in the world was *Robinson Crusoe*. He had fitted a tin drum on a wheelbarrow, for bringing water down to the pens. This was my job in summer, when the foxes had to have water twice a day. Between nine and ten o'clock in the morning, and again after supper, I filled the drum at the pump and trundled it down through the barnyard to the pens, where I parked it, and filled my watering can and went along the streets. Laird came too, with his little cream and green gardening can, filled too full and knocking against his legs and slopping water on his canvas shoes. I had the real watering can, my father's, though I could only carry it three-quarters full.

The foxes all had names, which were printed on a tin plate and hung beside their doors. They were not named when they were born, but when they survived the first year's pelting and were added to the breeding stock. Those my father had named were called names like Prince, Bob, Wally and Betty. Those I had named were called Star or Turk, or Maureen or Diana. Laird named one Maud after a hired girl we had when he was little, one Harold after a boy at school, and one Mexico, he did not say why.

Naming them did not make pets out of them, or anything like it. Nobody but my father ever went into the pens, and he had twice had blood-poisoning from bites. When I was bringing them their water they prowled up and down on the paths they had made inside their pens, barking seldom—they saved that for nighttime, when they might get up a chorus of community frenzy—but always watching me, their eyes burning, clear gold, in their pointed, malevolent faces. They were beautiful for their delicate legs and heavy, aristocratic tails and the bright fur sprinkled on dark down their backs—which gave them their name—but especially for their faces, drawn exquisitely sharp in pure hostility, and their golden eyes.

Besides carrying water I helped my father when he cut the long grass, and the lamb's quarter and flowering money-musk, that grew between the pens. He cut with the scythe and I raked into piles. Then he took a pitchfork and threw fresh-cut grass all over the top of the pens, to keep the foxes cooler and shade their coats, which were browned by too much sun. My father did not talk to me unless it was about the job we were doing. In this he was quite different from my mother, who, if she was feeling cheerful, would tell me all sorts of things—the name of a dog she had had when she was a little girl, the names of boys she had gone out with later on when she was grown up, and what certain dresses of hers had looked like—she could not imagine now what had become of them. Whatever thoughts and stories my father had were private, and I was shy of him and would never ask him questions. Nevertheless I worked willingly under his eyes, and with a feeling of pride. One time a feed salesman came down into the pens to talk to him and my father said, "Like to have you meet my new hired man." I turned away and raked furiously, red in the face with pleasure.

"Could of fooled me," said the salesman. "I thought it was only a girl."

After the grass was cut, it seemed suddenly much later in the year. I walked on stubble in the earlier evening, aware of the reddening skies, the entering silences, of fall. When I wheeled the tank out of the gate and put the padlock on, it was almost dark. One night at this time I saw my mother and father standing talking on the little rise of ground we called the gangway, in front of the barn. My father had just come from the meathouse; he had his stiff bloody apron on, and a pail of cut-up meat in his hand.

It was an odd thing to see my mother down at the barn. She did not often come out of the house unless it was to do something—hang out the wash or dig potatoes in the garden. She looked out of place, with her bare lumpy legs, not touched by the sun, her apron still on and damp across the stomach from the supper dishes. Her hair was tied up in a kerchief, wisps of it falling out. She would tie her hair up like this in the morning, saying she did not have time to do it properly, and it would stay tied up all day. It was true, too; she really did not have time. These days our back porch was piled with baskets of peaches and grapes and pears, bought in town, and onions and tomatoes and cucumbers grown at home, all waiting to be made into jelly and jam and preserves, pickles and chili sauce. In the kitchen there was a fire in the stove all day, jars clinked in boiling water, sometimes a cheesecloth bag was strung on a pole between two chairs, straining blue-black grape pulp for jelly. I was given jobs to do and I would sit at the table peeling peaches that had been soaked in the hot water, or cutting up onions, my eyes smarting and streaming. As soon as I was done I ran out of the house, trying to get out of earshot before my mother thought of what she wanted me to do next. I hated the hot dark kitchen in summer, the green blinds and the flypapers, the same old oilcloth table and wavy mirror and bumpy linoleum. My mother was too tired and preoccupied to talk to me, she had no heart to tell about the Normal School Graduation Dance; sweat trickled over her face and she was always counting under her breath, pointing at jars, dumping cups of sugar. It seemed to me that work in the house was endless, dreary and peculiarly depressing; work done out of doors, and in my father's service, was ritualistically important.

I wheeled the tank up to the barn, where it was kept, and I heard my mother saying, "Wait till Laird gets a little bigger, then you'll have a real help."

What my father said I did not hear. I was pleased by the way he stood listening, politely as he would to a salesman or a stranger, but with an air of wanting to get on with his real work. I felt my mother had no business down here and I wanted him to feel the same way. What did she mean about Laird? He was no help to anybody. Where was he now? Swinging himself sick on the swing, going around in circles, or trying to catch caterpillars. He never once stayed with me till I was finished.

"And then I can use her more in the house," I heard my mother say. She had a dead-quiet, regretful way of talking about me that always made me uneasy. "I just get my back turned and she runs off. It's not like I had a girl in the family at all."

I went and sat on a feedbag in the corner of the barn, not wanting to appear when this conversation was going on. My mother, I felt, was not to be trusted. She was kinder than my father and more easily fooled, but you could not depend on her, and the real reasons for the things she said and did were not to be known. She loved me, and she sat up late at night making a dress of the difficult style I wanted, for me to wear when school started, but she was also my enemy. She was always plotting. She was plotting now to get me to stay in the house more, although she knew I hated it (*because* she knew I hated it) and keep me from working for my father. It seemed to me she would do this simply out of perversity, and to try her power. It did not occur to me that she could be lonely, or jealous. No grown-up could be; they were too fortunate. I sat and kicked my heels monotonously against a feedbag, raising dust, and did not come out till she was gone.

At any rate, I did not expect my father to pay any attention to what she said. Who could imagine Laird doing my work—Laird remembering the padlock and cleaning out the watering-dishes with a leaf on the end of a stick, or even wheeling the tank without it tumbling over? It showed how little my mother knew about the way things really were.

I have forgotten to say what the foxes were fed. My father's bloody apron reminded me. They were fed horsemeat. At this time most farmers still kept horses, and when a horse got too old to work, or broke a leg or got down and would not get up, as they sometimes did, the owner would call my father, and he and Henry went out to the farm in the truck. Usually they shot and butchered the horse there, paying the farmer from five to twelve dollars. If they had already too much meat on hand, they would bring the horse back alive, and keep it for a few days or weeks in our stable, until the meat was needed. After the war the farmers were buying tractors and gradually getting rid of horses altogether, so it sometimes happened that we got a good healthy horse, that there was just no use for any more. If this happened in the winter we might keep the horse in our stable till spring, for we had plenty of hay and if there was a lot of snow—and the plow did not always get our road cleared—it was convenient to be able to go to town with a horse and cutter.

The winter I was eleven years old we had two horses in the stable. We 20 did not know what names they had had before, so we called them Mack and Flora. Mack was an old black workhorse, sooty and indifferent. Flora was a sorrel mare, a driver. We took them both out in the cutter. Mack was slow and easy to handle. Flora was given to fits of violent alarm, veering at cars and even at other horses, but we loved her speed and high-stepping, her general air of gallantry and abandon. On Saturdays we went down to the stable and as soon as we opened the door on its cosy, animal-smelling darkness Flora threw up her head, rolled her eyes, whinnied despairingly and pulled herself through a crisis of nerves on the spot. It was not safe to go into her stall; she would kick.

This winter also I began to hear a great deal more on the theme my mother had sounded when she had been talking in front of the barn. I no longer felt safe. It seemed that in the minds of the people around me there was a steady undercurrent of thought, not to be deflected, on this one subject. The word *girl* had formerly seemed to me innocent and unburdened, like the word *child*; now it appeared that it was no such thing. A girl was not, as I had supposed, simply what I was; it was what I had to become. It was a definition, always touched with emphasis, with reproach and disappointment. Also it was a joke on me. Once Laird and I were fighting, and for the first time ever I had to use all my strength against him; even so, he caught and pinned my arm for a moment, really hurting me. Henry saw this, and laughed, saying, "Oh, that there Laird's gonna show you, one of these days!" Laird was getting a lot bigger. But I was getting bigger too.

My grandmother came to stay with us for a few weeks and I heard other things. "Girls don't slam doors like that." "Girls keep their knees together when they sit down." And worse still, when I asked some questions, "That's none of girls' business." I continued to slam the doors and sit as awkwardly as possible, thinking that by such measures I kept myself free.

When spring came, the horses were let out in the barnyard. Mack stood against the barn wall trying to scratch his neck and haunches, but Flora trotted up and down and reared at the fences, clattering her hooves against the rails. Snow drifts dwindled quickly, revealing the hard grey and brown earth, the familiar rise and fall of the ground, plain and bare after the fantastic landscape of winter. There was a great feeling of opening-out, of release. We just wore rubbers now, over our shoes; our feet felt ridiculously light. One Saturday we went out to the stable and found all the doors open, letting in the unaccustomed sunlight and fresh air. Henry was there, just idling around looking at his collection of calendars which were tacked up behind the stalls in a part of the stable my mother had probably never seen.

"Come to say goodbye to your old friend Mack?" Henry said. "Here, you give him a taste of oats." He poured some oats into Laird's cupped hands and Laird went to feed Mack. Mack's teeth were in bad shape. He ate very slowly, patiently shifting the oats around in his mouth, trying to find a stump of a molar to grind it on. "Poor old Mack," said Henry mournfully. "When a horse's teeth's gone, he's gone. That's about the way."

"Are you going to shoot him today?" I said. Mack and Flora had been in the stable so long I had almost forgotten they were going to be shot.

Henry didn't answer me. Instead he started to sing in a high, trembly, mocking-sorrowful voice, *Oh, there's no more work, for poor Uncle Ned, he's gone where the good darkies go.* Mack's thick, blackish tongue worked diligently at Laird's hand. I went out before the song was ended and sat down on the gangway.

I had never seen them shoot a horse, but I knew where it was done. Last summer Laird and I had come upon a horse's entrails before they were buried. We had thought it was a big black snake, coiled up in the sun. That was around in the field that ran up beside the barn. I thought that if we went inside the barn, and found a wide crack or a knothole to look through, we would be able to see them do it. It was not something I wanted to see; just the same, if a thing really happened, it was better to see it, and know.

My father came down from the house, carrying the gun.

"What are you doing here?" he said.

"Nothing."

"Go on up and play around the house."

He sent Laird out of the stable. I said to Laird, "Do you want to see them shoot Mack?" and without waiting for an answer led him around to the front door of the barn, opened it carefully, and went in. "Be quiet or they'll hear us," I said. We could hear Henry and my father talking in the stable, then the heavy, shuffling steps of Mack being backed out of his stall.

In the loft it was cold and dark. Thin, crisscrossed beams of sunlight fell through the cracks. The hay was low. It was a rolling country, hills and hollows, slipping under our feet. About four feet up was a beam going around the walls. We piled hay up in one corner and I boosted Laird up and hoisted myself. The beam was not very wide; we crept along it with our hands flat on the barn walls. There were plenty of knotholes, and I found one that gave me the view I wanted—a corner of the barnyard, the gate, part of the field. Laird did not have a knothole and began to complain.

I showed him a widened crack between two boards. "Be quiet and wait. If they hear you you'll get us in trouble."

My father came in sight carrying the gun. Henry was leading Mack by   35
the halter. He dropped it and took out his cigarette papers and tobacco; he rolled cigarettes for my father and himself. While this was going on Mack nosed around in the old, dead grass along the fence. Then my father opened the gate and they took Mack through. Henry led Mack away from the path to a patch of ground and they talked together, not loud enough for us to hear. Mack again began searching for a mouthful of fresh grass, which was not to be found. My father walked away in a straight line, and stopped short at a distance which seemed to suit him. Henry was walking away from Mack too, but sideways, still negligently holding on to the halter. My father raised the gun and Mack looked up as if he had noticed something and my father shot him.

Mack did not collapse at once but swayed, lurched sideways and fell, first on his side; then he rolled over on his back and, amazingly, kicked his legs for a few seconds in the air. At this Henry laughed, as if Mack had done a trick for him. Laird, who had drawn a long, groaning breath of surprise when the shot was fired, said out loud, "He's not dead." And it seemed to me it might be true. But his legs stopped, he rolled on his side again, his muscles quivered and sank. The two men walked over and looked at him in a businesslike way; they bent down and examined his forehead where the bullet had gone in, and now I saw his blood on the brown grass.

"Now they just skin him and cut him up," I said. "Let's go." My legs were a little shaky and I jumped gratefully down into the hay. "Now you've seen how they shoot a horse," I said in a congratulatory way, as if I had seen it many times before. "Let's see if any barn cat's had kittens in the hay." Laird jumped. He seemed young and obedient again. Suddenly I remembered how, when he was little, I had brought him into the barn and told him to climb the ladder to the top beam. That was in the spring, too, when the hay was low. I had done it out of a need for excitement, a desire for something to happen so that I could tell about it. He was wearing a little bulky brown and white checked coat, made down from one of mine. He went all the way up, just as I told him, and sat down on the top beam with the hay far below him on one side, and the barn floor and some old machinery on the other. Then I ran screaming to my father, "Laird's up on the top beam!" My father came, my mother came, my father went up the ladder talking very quietly and brought Laird down under his arm, at which my mother leaned against the ladder and began to cry. They said to me, "Why weren't you watching him?" but nobody ever knew the truth. Laird did not know enough to tell. But whenever I saw the brown and white checked coat hanging in the closet, or at the bottom of the rag bag, which was where it ended up, I felt a weight in my stomach, the sadness of unexorcized guilt.

I looked at Laird who did not even remember this, and I did not like the look on his thin, winter-pale face. His expression was not frightened or upset, but remote, concentrating. "Listen," I said, in an unusually bright and friendly voice, "you aren't going to tell, are you?"

"No," he said absently.

"Promise."

"Promise," he said. I grabbed the hand behind his back to make sure he was not crossing his fingers. Even so, he might have a nightmare; it might come out that way. I decided I had better work hard to get all thoughts of what he had seen out of his mind—which, it seemed to me, could not hold very many things at a time. I got some money I had saved and that afternoon we went into Jubilee and saw a show, with Judy Canova, at which we both laughed a great deal. After that I thought it would be all right.

Two weeks later I knew they were going to shoot Flora. I knew from the night before, when I heard my mother ask if the hay was holding out all right, and my father said, "Well, after to-morrow there'll just be the cow, and we should be able to put her out to grass in another week." So I knew it was Flora's turn in the morning.

This time I didn't think of watching it. That was something to see just one time. I had not thought about it very often since, but sometimes when I was busy, working at school, or standing in front of the mirror combing my hair and wondering if I would be pretty when I grew up, the whole scene would flash into my mind: I would see the easy, practised way my father raised the gun, and hear Henry laughing when Mack kicked his legs in the air. I did not have any great feeling of horror and opposition, such as a city child might have had; I was too used to seeing the death of animals as a necessity by which we lived. Yet I felt a little ashamed, and there was a new wariness, a sense of holding-off, in my attitude to my father and his work.

It was a fine day, and we were going around the yard picking up tree branches that had been torn off in winter storms. This was something we had been told to do, and also we wanted to use them to make a teepee. We heard Flora whinny, and then my father's voice and Henry's shouting, and we ran down to the barnyard to see what was going on.

The stable door was open. Henry had just brought Flora out, and she had broken away from him. She was running free in the barnyard, from one end to the other. We climbed up on the fence. It was exciting to see her running, whinnying, going up on her hind legs, prancing and threatening like a horse in a Western movie, an unbroken ranch horse, though she was just an old driver, an old sorrel mare. My father and Henry ran after her and tried to grab the dangling halter. They tried to work her into a corner, and they had almost succeeded when she made a run between them, wild-eyed, and disappeared around the corner of the barn. We heard the rails clatter down as she got over the fence, and Henry yelled, "She's into the field now!"

That meant she was in the long L-shaped field that ran up by the house. If she got around the center, heading towards the lane, the gate was open; the truck had been driven into the field this morning. My father shouted to me, because I was on the other side of the fence, nearest the lane, "Go shut the gate!"

I could run very fast. I ran across the garden, past the tree where our swing was hung, and jumped across a ditch into the lane. There was the open gate. She had not got out, I could not see her up on the road; she must have run to the other end of the field. The gate was heavy. I lifted it out of the gravel and carried it across the roadway. I had it half-way across when she came in sight, galloping straight towards me. There was just time to get the chain on. Laird came scrambling through the ditch to help me.

Instead of shutting the gate, I opened it as wide as I could. I did not make any decision to do this, it was just what I did. Flora never slowed down; she galloped straight past me, and Laird jumped up and down, yelling, "Shut it, shut it!" even after it was too late. My father and Henry appeared in the field a moment too late to see what I had done. They only saw Flora heading for the township road. They would think I had not got there in time.

They did not waste any time asking about it. They went back to the barn and got the gun and the knives they used, and put these in the truck; then they turned the truck around and came bouncing up the field toward us. Laird called to them, "Let me go too, let me go too!" and Henry stopped the truck and they took him in. I shut the gate after they were all gone.

I supposed Laird would tell. I wondered what would happen to me. I   50
had never disobeyed my father before, and I could not understand why I had done it. Flora would not really get away. They would catch up with her in the truck. Or if they did not catch her this morning somebody would see her and telephone us this afternoon or tomorrow. There was no wild country here for her to run to, only farms. What was more, my father had paid for her, we needed the meat to feed the foxes, we needed the foxes to make our living. All I had done was make more work for my father who worked hard enough already. And when my father found out about it he was not going to trust me any more; he would know that I was not entirely on his side. I was on Flora's side, and that made me no use to anybody, not even to her. Just the same, I did not regret it; when she came running at me and I held the gate open, that was the only thing I could do.

I went back to the house, and my mother said, "What's all the commotion?" I told her that Flora had kicked down the fence and got away. "Your poor father," she said, "now he'll have to go chasing over the countryside. Well, there isn't any use planning dinner before one." She put up the ironing board. I wanted to tell her, but thought better of it and went upstairs and sat on my bed.

Lately I had been trying to make my part of the room fancy, spreading the bed with old lace curtains, and fixing myself a dressing-table with some leftovers of cretonne for a skirt. I planned to put up some kind of barricade between my bed and Laird's, to keep my section separate from his. In the sunlight, the lace curtains were just dusty rags. We did not sing at night any more. One night when I was singing Laird said, "You sound silly," and I went right on but the next night I did not start. There was not so much need to anyway, we were no longer afraid. We knew it was just old furniture over there, old jumble and confusion. We did not keep to the rules. I still stayed awake after Laird was asleep and told myself stories, but even in these stories something different was happening, mysterious alterations took place. A story might start off in the old way, with a spectacular danger, a fire or wild animals, and for a while I might rescue people; then things would change around, and instead, somebody would be rescuing me. It might be a boy from our class at school, or even Mr. Campbell, our teacher, who tickled girls under the arms. And at this point the story concerned itself at great length with what I looked like—how long my hair was, and what kind of dress I had on; by the time I had these details worked out the real excitement of the story was lost.

It was later than one o'clock when the truck came back. The tarpaulin was over the back, which meant there was meat in it. My mother had to heat dinner up all over again. Henry and my father had changed from their bloody overalls into ordinary working overalls in the barn, and they washed their arms and necks and faces at the sink, and splashed water on their hair and combed it. Laird lifted his arm to show off a streak of blood. "We shot old Flora," he said, "and cut her up in fifty pieces."

"Well, I don't want to hear about it," my mother said. "And don't come to my table like that."

My family made him go and wash the blood off.

We sat down and my father said grace and Henry pasted his chewing-gum on the end of his fork, the way he always did; when he took it off he would have us admire the pattern. We began to pass the bowls of steaming, overcooked vegetables. Laird looked across the table at me and said proudly, distinctly, "Anyway it was her fault Flora got away."

"What?" my father said.

"She could of shut the gate and she didn't. She just open' it up and Flora run out."

"Is that right?" my father said.

Everybody at the table was looking at me. I nodded, swallowing food 60
with great difficulty. To my shame, tears flooded my eyes.

My father made a curt sound of disgust. "What did you do that for?"

I did not answer. I put down my fork and waited to be sent from the
table, still not looking up.

But this did not happen. For some time nobody said anything, then
Laird said matter-of-factly, "She's crying."

"Never mind," my father said. He spoke with resignation, even good
humour, the words which absolved and dismissed me for good. "She's only a
girl," he said.

I didn't protest that, even in my heart. Maybe it was true. ■ 65

■ What is the significance of foxes within this story? Locate the specific places
where the narrator mentions foxes, and find the places where details about the
foxes influence the characters in the story.

■ How has the rest of the story set us up for the father's final line: "She's only a
girl"?

Haruki Murakami

Haruki Murakami was born in Kyoto, Japan, and now lives in Tokyo. His
collection of stories *After the Quake* from which the following selection is
taken reflects upon the emotional aftershocks of the 1995 Kobe earthquake.
Murakami's works have won many literary prizes, both internationally and in
Japan.

UFO in Kushiro (Jay Rubin, trans; 2002)

Five straight days she spent in front of the television, staring at crumbled
banks and hospitals, whole blocks of stores in flames, severed rail lines and
expressways. She never said a word. Sunk deep in the cushions of the sofa,
her mouth clamped shut, she wouldn't answer when Komura spoke to her.
She wouldn't shake her head or nod. Komura could not be sure the sound
of his voice was even getting through to her.

Komura's wife came from way up north in Yamagata and, as far as he
knew, she had no friends or relatives who could have been hurt in Kobe.
Yet she stayed rooted in front of the television from morning to night. In
his presence, at least, she ate nothing and drank nothing and never went to
the toilet. Aside from an occasional flick of the remote control to change
the channel, she hardly moved a muscle.

Komura would make his own toast and coffee, and head off to work. When he came home in the evening, he'd fix himself a snack with whatever he found in the refrigerator and eat alone. She'd still be glaring at the late news when he dropped off to sleep. A stone wall of silence surrounded her. Komura gave up trying to break through.

When he came home from work that Sunday, the sixth day, his wife had disappeared.

Komura was a salesman at one of the oldest hi-fi-equipment specialty stores in Tokyo's Akihabara "Electronics Town." He handled top-of-the-line stuff and earned a sizeable commission whenever he made a sale. Most of his clients were doctors, wealthy independent businessmen, and rich provincials. He had been doing this for eight years and had a decent income right from the start. The economy was healthy, real-estate prices were rising, and Japan was overflowing with money. People's wallets were bursting with ten thousand-yen bills, and everyone was dying to spend them. The most expensive items were the first to sell out.

Komura was tall and slim and a stylish dresser. He was good with people. In his bachelor days he had dated a lot of women. But after getting married, at twenty-six, he found that his desire for sexual adventures simply and mysteriously vanished. He hadn't slept with any woman but his wife during the five years of their marriage. Not that the opportunity had never presented itself, but he had lost all interest in fleeting affairs and one-night stands. He much preferred to come home early, have a relaxed meal with his wife, talk with her for a while on the sofa, then go to bed and make love. This was everything he wanted.

Komura's friends and colleagues were puzzled by his marriage. Alongside him with his clean, classic good looks, his wife could not have seemed more ordinary. She was short with thick arms, and she had a dull, even stolid appearance. And it wasn't just physical: there was nothing attractive about her personality either. She rarely spoke and always wore a sullen expression.

Still, though he did not quite understand why, Komura always felt his tension dissipate when he and his wife were together under one roof; it was the only time he could truly relax. He slept well with her, undisturbed by the strange dreams that had troubled him in the past. His erections were hard; his sex life was warm. He no longer had to worry about death or venereal disease or the vastness of the universe.

His wife, on the other hand, disliked Tokyo's crowds and longed for Yamagata. She missed her parents and her two elder sisters, and she would go home to see them whenever she felt the need. Her parents operated a successful inn, which kept them financially comfortable. Her father was crazy about his youngest daughter and happily paid her round-trip fares.

Several times, Komura had come home from work to find his wife gone and a note on the kitchen table telling him that she was visiting her parents for a while. He never objected. He just waited for her to come back, and she always did, after a week or ten days, in a good mood.

But the letter his wife left for him when she vanished five days after the earthquake was different: I am never coming back, she had written, then went on to explain, simply but clearly, why she no longer wanted to live with him.

10

The problem is that you never give me anything, she wrote. *Or, to put it more precisely, you have nothing inside you that you can give me. You are good and kind and handsome, but living with you is like living with a chunk of air. It's not entirely your fault, though. There are lots of women who will fall in love with you. But please don't call me. Just get rid of all the stuff I'm leaving behind.*

In fact, she hadn't left much of anything behind. Her clothes, her shoes, her umbrella, her coffee mug, her hair dryer: all were gone. She must have packed them in boxes and shipped them out after he left for work that morning. The only things still in the house that could be called "her stuff" were the bike she used for shopping and a few books. The Beatles and Bill Evans CDs that Komura had been collecting since his bachelor days had also vanished.

The next day, he tried calling his wife's parents in Yamagata. His mother-in-law answered the phone and told him that his wife didn't want to talk to him. She sounded somewhat apologetic. She also told him that they would be sending him the necessary forms soon and that he should put his seal on them and send them back right away.

Komura answered that he might not be able to send them "right away." This was an important matter, and he wanted time to think it over.

"You can think it over all you want, but I know it won't change anything," his mother-in-law said.

15

She was probably right, Komura told himself. No matter how much he thought or waited, things would never be the same. He was sure of that.

Shortly after he had sent the papers back with his seal stamped on them, Komura asked for a week's paid leave. His boss had a general idea of what had been happening, and February was a slow time of the year, so he let Komura go without a fuss. He seemed on the verge of saying something to Komura, but finally said nothing.

Sasaki, a colleague of Komura's, came over to him at lunch and said, "I hear you're taking time off. Are you planning to do something?"

"I don't know," Komura said. "What should I do?"

Sasaki was a bachelor, three years younger than Komura. He had a delicate build and short hair, and he wore round, gold-rimmed glasses. A lot of

20

people thought he talked too much and had a rather arrogant air, but he got along well enough with the easygoing Komura.

"What the hell, as long as you're taking the time off, why not make a nice trip out of it?"

"Not a bad idea," Komura said.

Wiping his glasses with his handkerchief, Sasaki peered at Komura as if looking for some kind of clue.

"Have you ever been to Hokkaido?" he asked.

"Never."

"Would you like to go?"

"Why do you ask?"

Sasaki narrowed his eyes and cleared his throat. "To tell you the truth, I've got a small package I'd like to send to Kushiro, and I'm hoping you'll take it there for me. You'd be doing me a big favor, and I'd be glad to pay for a round-trip ticket. I could cover your hotel in Kushiro, too."

"A small package?"

"Like this," Sasaki said, shaping a four-inch cube with his hands. "Nothing heavy."

"Something to do with work?"

Sasaki shook his head. "Not at all," he said. "Strictly personal. I just don't want it to get knocked around, which is why I can't mail it. I'd like you to deliver it by hand, if possible. I really ought to do it myself, but I haven't got time to fly all the way to Hokkaido."

"Is it something important?"

His closed lips curling slightly, Sasaki nodded. "It's nothing fragile, and there are no 'hazardous materials.' There's no need to worry about it. They're not going to stop you when they X-ray it at the airport. I promise I'm not going to get you in trouble. And it weighs practically nothing. All I'm asking is that you take it along the way you'd take anything else. The only reason I'm not mailing it is I just don't feel like mailing it."

Hokkaido in February would be freezing cold, Komura knew, but cold or hot it was all the same to him.

"So who do I give the package to?"

"My sister. My younger sister. She lives up there."

Komura decided to accept Sasaki's offer. He hadn't thought about how to spend his week off, and making plans now would have been too much trouble. Besides, he had no reason for not wanting to go to Hokkaido. Sasaki called the airline then and there, reserving a ticket to Kushiro. The flight would leave two days later, in the afternoon.

At work the next day, Sasaki handed Komura a box like the ones used for human ashes, only smaller, wrapped in manila paper. Judging from the feel, it was made of wood. As Sasaki had said, it weighed practically nothing. Broad strips of transparent tape went all around the package over the paper. Komura held it in his hands and studied it a few seconds. He gave it a little shake but he couldn't feel or hear anything moving inside.

"My sister will pick you up at the airport. And she'll be arranging a room for you," Sasaki said. "All you have to do is stand outside the gate with the package in your hands where she can see it. Don't worry, the airport's not very big." 40

Komura left home with the box in his suitcase, wrapped in a thick undershirt. The plane was far more crowded than he had expected. Why were all these people going from Tokyo to Kushiro in the middle of winter? he wondered.

The morning paper was full of earthquake reports. He read it from beginning to end on the plane. The number of dead was rising. Many areas were still without water or electricity, and countless people had lost their homes. Each article reported some new tragedy, but to Komura the details seemed oddly lacking in depth. All sounds reached him as far-off, monotonous echos. The only thing he could give any serious thought to was his wife as she retreated ever farther into the distance.

Mechanically he ran his eyes over the earthquake reports, stopped now and then to think about his wife, then went back to the paper. When he grew tired of this, he closed his eyes and napped. And when he woke, he thought about his wife again. Why had she followed the TV earthquake reports with such intensity, from morning to night, without eating or sleeping? What could she have seen in them?

Two young women wearing overcoats of similar design and color approached Komura at the airport. One was fair-skinned and maybe five feet six, with short hair. The area from her nose to her full upper lip was oddly extended in a way that made Komura think of shorthaired ungulates. Her companion was more like five feet one and would have been quite pretty if her nose hadn't been so small. Her long hair fell straight to her shoulders. Her ears were exposed, and there were two moles on her right earlobe which were emphasized by the earrings she wore. Both women looked to be in their mid-twenties. They took Komura to a café in the airport.

"I'm Keiko Sasaki," the taller woman said. "My brother told me how helpful you've been to him. This is my friend Shimao." 45

"Nice to meet you," Komura said.

"Hi," Shimao said.

"My brother tells me your wife recently passed away," Keiko Sasaki said with a respectful expression.

Komura waited a moment before answering, "No, she didn't die."

"I just talked to my brother the day before yesterday. I'm sure he said quite clearly that you'd lost your wife." 50

"I did. She divorced me. But as far as I know she's alive and well."

"That's odd. I couldn't possibly have misheard something so important." She gave him an injured look. Komura put a small amount of sugar in his coffee and gave it a gentle stir before taking a sip. The liquid was thin, with no taste to speak of, more sign than substance. What the hell am I doing here? he wondered.

"Well, I guess I did mishear it. I can't imagine how else to explain the mistake," Keiko Sasaki said, apparently satisfied now. She drew in a deep breath and chewed her lower lip. "Please forgive me. I was very rude."

"Don't worry about it. Either way, she's gone."

Shimao said nothing while Komura and Keiko spoke, but she smiled and kept her eyes on Komura. She seemed to like him. He could tell from her expression and her subtle body language. A brief silence fell over the three of them.

"Anyway, let me give you the important package I brought," Komura said. He unzipped his suitcase and pulled the box out of the folds of the thick ski undershirt he had wrapped it in. The thought struck him then: I was supposed to be holding this when I got off the plane. That's how they were going to recognize me. How did they know who I was?

Keiko Sasaki stretched her hands across the table, her expressionless eyes fixed on the package. After testing its weight, she did as Komura had done and gave it a few shakes by her ear. She flashed him a smile as if to signal that everything was fine, and slipped the box into her oversize shoulder bag.

"I have to make a call," she said. "Do you mind if I excuse myself for a moment?"

"Not at all," Komura said. "Feel free."

Keiko slung the bag over her shoulder and walked off toward a distant phone booth. Komura studied the way she walked. The upper half of her body was still, while everything from the hips down made large, smooth, mechanical movements. He had the strange impression that he was witnessing some moment from the past, shoved with random suddenness into the present.

"Have you been to Hokkaido before?" Shimao asked.

Komura shook his head.

"Yeah, I know. It's a long way to come."

Komura nodded, then turned to survey his surroundings. "Funny," he said, "sitting here like this, it doesn't feel as if I've come all that far."

"Because you flew. Those planes are too damn fast. Your mind can't keep up with your body."

"You may be right."

"Did you want to make such a long trip?"

"I guess so," Komura said.

"Because your wife left?"

He nodded.   70

"No matter how far you travel, you can never get away from yourself," Shimao said.

Komura was staring at the sugar bowl on the table as she spoke, but then he raised his eyes to hers.

"It's true," he said. "No matter how far you travel, you can never get away from yourself. It's like your shadow. It follows you everywhere."

Shimao looked hard at Komura. "I'll bet you loved her, didn't you?"

Komura dodged the question. "You're a friend of Keiko Sasaki's?"   75

"Right. We do stuff together."

"What kind of stuff?"

Instead of answering him, Shimao asked, "Are you hungry?"

"I wonder," Komura said. "I feel kind of hungry and kind of not."

"Let's go and eat something warm, the three of us. It'll help you relax."   80

Shimao drove a small four-wheel-drive Subaru. It had to have way over a hundred thousand miles on it, judging from how battered it was. The rear bumper had a huge dent in it. Keiko Sasaki sat next to Shimao, and Komura had the cramped rear seat to himself. There was nothing particularly wrong with Shimao's driving, but the noise in back was terrible, and the suspension was nearly shot. The automatic transmission slammed into gear whenever it downshifted, and the heater blew hot and cold. Shutting his eyes, Komura felt as if he had been imprisoned in a washing machine.

No snow had been allowed to gather on the streets in Kushiro, but dirty, icy mounds stood at random intervals on both sides of the road. Dense clouds hung low and, although it was not yet sunset, everything was dark and desolate. The wind tore through the city in sharp squeals. There were no pedestrians. Even the traffic lights looked frozen.

"This is one part of Hokkaido that doesn't get much snow," Keiko Sasaki explained in a loud voice, glancing back at Komura. "We're on the coast and the wind is strong, so whatever piles up gets blown away. It's cold, though, *freezing* cold. Sometimes it feels like it's taking your ears off."

"You hear about drunks who freeze to death sleeping on the street," Shimao said.

"Do you get bears around here?" Komura asked.   85

Keiko giggled and turned to Shimao. "Bears, he says."

Shimao gave the same kind of giggle.

"I don't know much about Hokkaido," Komura said by way of explanation.

"I know a good story about bears," Keiko said. "Right, Shimao?"

"A *great* story!" Shimao said.   90

But their talk broke off at that point, and neither of them told the bear story. Komura didn't ask to hear it. Soon they reached their destination, a big noodle shop on the highway. They parked in the lot and went inside. Komura had a beer and a hot bowl of ramen noodles. The place was dirty and empty, and the chairs and tables were rickety, but the ramen was excellent, and when he had finished eating, Komura did, in fact, feel a little more relaxed.

"Tell me, Mr. Komura," Keiko Sasaki said, "do you have something you want to do in Hokkaido? My brother tells me you're going to spend a week here."

Komura thought about it for a moment, but couldn't come up with anything he wanted to do.

"How about a hot spring? Would you like a nice, long soak in a tub? I know a little country place not far from here."

"Not a bad idea," Komura said.

"I'm sure you'd like it. It's really nice. No bears or anything." The two women looked at each other and laughed again. "Do you mind if I ask you about your wife?" Keiko said.

"I don't mind."

"When did she leave?"

"Hmm . . . five days after the earthquake, so that's more than two weeks ago now."

"Did it have something to do with the earthquake?"

Komura shook his head. "Probably not. I don't think so."

"Still, I wonder if things like that aren't connected somehow," Shimao said with a tilt of the head.

"Yeah," Keiko said. "It's just that you can't see how."

"Right," Shimao said. "Stuff like that happens all the time."

"Stuff like what?" Komura asked.

"Like, say, what happened with somebody I know," Keiko said.

"You mean Mr. Saeki?" Shimao asked.

"Exactly," Keiko said. "There's this guy—Saeki. He lives in Kushiro. He's about forty. A hairstylist. His wife saw a UFO last year, in the autumn. She was driving on the edge of town all by herself in the middle of the night and she saw a huge UFO land in a field. *Whoosh!* Like in *Close Encounters.* A week later, she left home. They weren't having any domestic problems or anything. She just disappeared and never came back."

"Into thin air," Shimao said.

"And it was because of the UFO?" Komura asked.

"I don't know why," Keiko said. "She just walked out. No note or anything. She had two kids in elementary school, too. The whole week before she left, all she'd do was tell people about the UFO. You couldn't get her to stop. She'd go on and on about how big and beautiful it was."

She paused to let the story sink in.

"My wife left a note," Komura said. "And we don't have any kids."

"So your situation's a little better than Saeki's," Keiko said.

"Yeah. Kids make a big difference," Shimao said, nodding.   115

"Shimao's father left home when she was seven," Keiko explained with a frown. "Ran off with his wife's younger sister."

"All of a sudden. One day," Shimao said, smiling.

A silence settled over the group.

"Maybe Mr. Saeki's wife didn't run away but was captured by aliens from the UFO," Komura said to smooth things over.

"It's possible," Shimao said with a somber expression. "You hear stories   120 like that all the time."

"You mean like you're-walking-along-the-street-and-a-bear-eats-you kind of thing?" Keiko asked. The two women laughed again.

The three of them left the noodle shop and went to a nearby love hotel. It was on the edge of town, on a street where love hotels alternated with gravestone dealers. The hotel Shimao had chosen was an odd building, constructed to look like a European castle. A triangular red flag flew on its highest tower.

Keiko got the key at the front desk, and the three of them took the elevator to the room. The windows were tiny, compared with the absurdly big bed. Komura hung his down jacket on a hanger and went into the toilet. During the few minutes he was in there, the two women managed to run a bath, dim the lights, check the heat, turn on the television, examine the delivery menus from local restaurants, test the light switches at the head of the bed, and check the contents of the minibar.

"The owners are friends of mine," Keiko said. "I had them get their biggest room ready. It *is* a love hotel, but don't let that bother you. You're not bothered, are you?"

"Not at all," Komura said.   125

"I thought this would make a lot more sense than sticking you in a cramped little room in some cheap business hotel by the station."

"You may be right," Komura said.

"Why don't you take a bath? I filled the tub."

Komura did as he was told. The tub was huge. He felt uneasy soaking in it alone. The couples who came to this hotel probably took baths together.

When he emerged from the bathroom, Komura was surprised to find   130 that Keiko Sasaki had left. Shimao was still there, drinking beer and watching TV.

"Keiko went home," Shimao said. "She wanted me to apologize and tell you that she'll be back tomorrow morning. Do you mind if I stay here a little while and have a beer?"

"Fine," Komura said.

"You're sure it's no problem? Like, you want to be alone or you can't relax if somebody else is around or something?"

Komura insisted it was no problem. Drinking a beer and drying his hair with a towel, he watched TV with Shimao. It was a news special on the Kobe earthquake. The usual images appeared again and again: tilted buildings, buckled streets, old women weeping, confusion and aimless anger. When a commercial came on, Shimao used the remote to switch off the TV.

"Let's talk," she said, "as long as we're here."

"Fine," Komura said.

"Hmm, what should we talk about?"

"In the car, you and Keiko said something about a bear, remember? You said it was a great story."

"Oh yeah," she said, nodding. "The bear story."

"You want to tell it to me?"

"Sure, why not?"

Shimao got a fresh beer from the minibar and filled both their glasses.

"It's a little raunchy," she said. "You don't mind?"

Komura shook his head.

"I mean, some men don't like hearing a woman tell certain kinds of stories."

"I'm not like that."

"It's something that actually happened to me, so it's a little embarrassing."

"I'd like to hear it if you're OK with it."

"I'm OK, if you're OK."

"I'm OK," Komura said.

"Three years ago—back around the time I entered junior college—I was dating this guy. He was a year older than me, a college student. He was the first guy I had sex with. One day the two of us were out hiking—in the mountains way up north."

She took a sip of beer.

"It was fall, and the hills were full of bears. That's the time of year when the bears are getting ready to hibernate, so they're out looking for food and they're really dangerous. Sometimes they attack people. They did an awful job on one hiker just three days before we went out. So somebody gave us a bell to carry—about the same size as a wind-bell. You're supposed to shake it when you walk so the bears know there are people around and won't come out. Bears don't attack people on purpose. I mean, they're pretty much vegetarians. They don't *have* to attack people. What happens is they suddenly bump into people in their territory and they get surprised or angry and they attack out of reflex. So if you walk along ringing your bell, they'll avoid you. Get it?"

"I get it."

"So that's what we were doing, walking along and ringing the bell. We   155
got to this place where there was nobody else around, and all of a sudden he
said he wanted to … do it. I kind of liked the idea, too, so I said OK and
we went into this bushy place off the trail where nobody could see us, and
we spread out a piece of plastic. But I was afraid of the bears. I mean, think
how awful it would be to have some bear attack you from behind and kill
you when you're having sex! I would never want to die that way. Would
you?"

Komura agreed that he would not want to die that way.

"So there we were, shaking the bell with one hand and having sex.
Kept it up from start to finish. *Ding-a-ling! Ding-a-ling!*"

"Which one of you shook the bell?"

"We took turns. We'd trade off when our hands got tired. It was so
weird, shaking this bell the whole time we were doing it! I think about it
sometimes even now, when I'm having sex, and I start laughing."

Komura gave a little laugh, too.   160

Shimao clapped her hands. "Oh, that's wonderful," she said. "You *can*
laugh after all!"

"Of course I can laugh," Komura said, but come to think of it, this
was the first time he had laughed in quite a while. When was the last
time?

"Do you mind if I take a bath, too?" Shimao asked.

"Fine," he said.

While she was bathing, Komura watched a variety show emceed by   165
some comedian with a loud voice. He didn't find it the least bit funny, but
he couldn't tell whether that was the show's fault or his own. He drank a
beer and opened a pack of nuts from the minibar, Shimao stayed in the
bath for a very long time. Finally, she came out wearing nothing but a towel
and sat on the edge of the bed. Dropping the towel, she slid in between the
sheets like a cat and lay there looking straight at Komura.

"When was the last time you did it with your wife?" she asked.

"At the end of December, I think."

"And nothing since?"

"Nothing."

"Not with anybody?"   170

Komura closed his eyes and shook his head.

"You know what *I* think," Shimao said. "You need to lighten up and
learn to enjoy life a little more. I mean, think about it tomorrow there could
be an earthquake; you could be kidnapped by aliens; you could be eaten by a
bear. Nobody knows what's going to happen."

"Nobody knows what's going to happen," Komura echoed.

"*Ding-a-ling*," Shimao said.

After several failed attempts to have sex with Shimao, Komura gave up. This had never happened to him before.

"You must have been thinking about your wife," Shimao said.

"Yup," Komura said, but in fact what he had been thinking about was the earthquake. Images of it had come to him one after another, as if in a slide show, flashing on the screen and fading away. Highways, flames, smoke, piles of rubble, cracks in streets. He couldn't break the chain of silent images.

Shimao pressed her ear against his naked chest.

"These things happen," she said.

"Uh-huh."

"You shouldn't let it bother you."

"I'll try not to," Komura said.

"Men always let it bother them, though."

Komura said nothing.

Shimao played with his nipple.

"You said your wife left a note, didn't you?"

"I did."

"What did it say?"

"That living with me was like living with a chunk of air."

"A chunk of air?" Shimao tilted her head back to look up at Komura. "What does *that* mean?"

"That there's nothing inside me, I guess."

"Is it true?"

"Could be," Komura said. "I'm not sure, though. I may have nothing inside me, but what would *something* be?"

"Yeah, really, come to think of it. What *would* something be? My mother was crazy about salmon skin. She always used to wish there were a kind of salmon made of nothing but skin. So there may be some cases when it's *better* to have nothing inside. Don't you think?"

Komura tried to imagine what a salmon made of nothing but skin would be like. But even supposing there were such a thing, wouldn't the skin itself be the *something* inside? Komura took a deep breath, raising and then lowering Shimao's head on his chest.

"I'll tell you this, though," Shimao said, "I don't know whether you've got nothing or something inside you, but I think you're terrific. I'll bet the world is full of women who would understand you and fall in love with you."

"It said that, too."

"What? Your wife's note?"

"Uh-huh."

"No kidding," Shimao said, lowering her head to Komura's chest again. He felt her earring against his skin like a secret object.

"Come to think of it," Komura said, "what's the *something* inside that box I brought up here?"

"Is it bothering you?"

"It wasn't bothering me before. But now, I don't know, it's starting to."

"Since when?"

"Just now."   205

"All of a sudden?"

"Yeah, once I started thinking about it, all of a sudden."

"I wonder why it's started to bother you now, all of a sudden?"

Komura glared at the ceiling for a minute to think. "I wonder."

They listened to the moaning of the wind. The wind: it came from some-   210
place unknown to Komura, and it blew past to someplace unknown to him.

"I'll tell you why," Shimao said in a low voice. "It's because that box contains the *something* that was inside you. You didn't know that when you carried it here and gave it to Keiko with your own hands. Now, you'll never get it back."

Komura lifted himself from the mattress and looked down at the woman. Tiny nose, moles on the earlobe. In the room's deep silence, his heart beat with a loud, dry sound. His bones cracked as he leaned forward. For one split second, Komura realized that he was on the verge of committing an act of overwhelming violence.

"Just kidding," Shimao said when she saw the look on his face. "I said the first thing that popped into my head. It was a lousy joke. I'm sorry. Try not to let it bother you. I didn't mean to hurt you."

Komura forced himself to calm down and, after a glance around the room, sank his head into his pillow again. He closed his eyes and took a deep breath. The huge bed stretched out around him like a nocturnal sea. He heard the freezing wind. The fierce pounding of his heart shook his bones.

"Are you starting to feel a *little* as if you've come a long way?" Shimao   215
asked.

"Hmm. Now I feel as if I've come a *very* long way," Komura answered honestly.

Shimao traced a complicated design on Komura's chest with her fingertip, as if casting a magic spell.

"But really," she said, "you're just at the beginning." ∎

- Why does Komura leave home? What specific images lead us to understand his situation?
- Locate specific images within the foreground and background of each section of the story. Where do these images appear, and how do they help define the section of the story in which they appear?
- What significance can we ascribe to the box that Komura delivers?

POETRY

William Blake (1757–1827)

London (1794)

I wander thro each chartered street,
Near where the charter'd Thames does flow,
And mark in every face I meet
Marks of weakness, marks of woe.

In every cry of every Man,   5
In every Infant's cry of fear,
In every voice, in every ban,
The mind-forg'd manacles I hear.

How the Chimney-sweeper's cry
Every blackning Church appalls;   10
And the hapless Soldier's sigh
Runs in blood down Palace walls.

But most through midnight streets I hear
How the youthful Harlot's curse
Blasts the new-born Infant's tear,   15
And blights with plagues the Marriage hearse.

■ What are the specific images that Blake "reads" in London's streets? Is the
poet a visitor to the city or a resident?

■ What is the connection that Blake establishes among each of these images and
the conclusions that he draws at the end of each stanza?

William Wordsworth (1770–1850)

London, 1802 (1807)

Milton! thou should'st be living at this hour:
England hath need of thee: she is a fen
Of stagnant waters: altar, sword, and pen,
Fireside, the heroic wealth of hall and bower,

Have forfeited their ancient English dower   5
Of inward happiness. We are selfish men;
Oh! raise us up, return to us again;
And give us manners, virtue, freedom, power.
Thy soul was like a star, and dwelt apart:
Thou hadst a voice whose sound was like the sea: 10
Pure as the naked heavens, majestic, free,
So didst thou travel on life's common way,
In cheerful godliness; and yet thy heart
The lowliest duties on herself did lay.

■ What is the difference between the images that Wordsworth lists in lines 2–4
   and those that appear in lines 9–10? How are these images related to the
   qualities listed in line 8?
■ Why might Milton be helpful?

William Wordsworth (1770–1850)

Composed upon Westminster Bridge, September 3, 1802 (1807)

Earth has not anything to show more fair:
Dull would he be of soul who could pass by
A sight so touching in its majesty:
This City now doth, like a garment, wear
The beauty of the morning; silent, bare,   5
Ships, towers, domes, theatres, and temples lie
Open unto the fields, and to the sky;
All bright and glittering in the smokeless air.
Never did sun more beautifully steep
In his first splendor, valley, rock, or hill;   10
Ne'er saw I, never felt, a calm so deep!
The river glideth at his own sweet will:
Dear God! the very houses seem asleep;
And all that mighty heart is lying still!

■ What gives the city of London its appeal at this hour of the morning?
■ What common quality is shared by the images that Wordsworth celebrates?

William Wordsworth (1770–1850)

The World Is Too Much with Us (1807)

The world is too much with us; late and soon,
Getting and spending, we lay waste our powers;
Little we see in Nature that is ours;
We have given our hearts away, a sordid boon!
This Sea that bares her bosom to the moon;   5
The winds that will be howling at all hours,
And are up-gathered now like sleeping flowers;
For this, for everything, we are out of tune;
It moves us not. —Great God! I'd rather be
A Pagan suckled in a creed outworn;   10
So might I, standing on this pleasant lea,
Have glimpses that would make me less forlorn;
Have sight of Proteus rising from the sea;
Or hear old Triton blow his wreathèd horn.

William Wordsworth (1770–1850)

[I wandered lonely as a cloud] (1807)

I wandered lonely as a cloud
That floats on high o'er vales and hills,
When all at once I saw a crowd,
A host, of golden daffodils,
Beside the lake, beneath the trees,   5
Fluttering and dancing in the breeze.

Continuous as the stars that shine
And twinkle on the milky way,
They stretched in never-ending line
Along the margin of a bay;   10
Ten thousand saw I at a glance,
Tossing their heads in sprightly dance.

The waves beside them danced, but they
Outdid the sparkling waves in glee;
A poet could not but be gay,   15
In such a jocund company;

I gazed—and gazed—but little thought
What wealth the show to me had brought:

For oft, when on my couch I lie
In vacant or in pensive mood,   20
They flash upon that inward eye
Which is the bliss of solitude;
And then my heart with pleasure fills,
And dances with the daffodils.

■ How does the poet seek to use the natural images that he collects?
■ In this poem and the preceding poem, how does the poet describe his relationship with the natural world? Where is he at home?

Emily Dickinson (1830–1886)

[There's a certain Slant of light] (1861)

There's a certain Slant of light,
Winter Afternoons—
That oppresses, like the Heft
Of Cathedral Tunes—

Heavenly Hurt, it gives us—   5
We can find no scar,
But internal difference,
Where the Meanings, are—

None may teach it—Any—
'Tis the Seal Despair—   10
An imperial affliction
Sent us of the Air—

When it comes, the Landscape listens—
Shadows—hold their breath—
When it goes, 'tis like the Distance   15
On the look of Death—

■ How does the poet use the image of a cathedral?
■ How can a landscape listen?

Robert Frost (1874–1963)

Birches (1916)

When I see birches bend to left and right
Across the lines of straighter darker trees,
I like to think some boy's been swinging them.
But swinging doesn't bend them down to stay
As ice-storms do. Often you must have seen them   5
Loaded with ice a sunny winter morning
After a rain. They click upon themselves
As the breeze rises, and turn many-colored
As the stir cracks and crazes their enamel.
Soon the sun's warmth makes them shed crystal shells   10
Shattering and avalanching on the snow-crust—
Such heaps of broken glass to sweep away
You'd think the inner dome of heaven had fallen.
They are dragged to the withered bracken by the load,
And they seem not to break; though once they are bowed   15
So low for long, they never right themselves:
You may see their trunks arching in the woods
Years afterwards, trailing their leaves on the ground
Like girls on hands and knees that throw their hair
Before them over their heads to dry in the sun.   20
But I was going to say when Truth broke in
With all her matter-of-fact about the ice-storm,
I should prefer to have some boy bend them
As he went out and in to fetch the cows—
Some boy too far from town to learn baseball,   25
Whose only play was what he found himself,
Summer or winter, and could play alone.
One by one he subdued his father's trees
By riding them down over and over again
Until he took the stiffness out of them,   30
And not one but hung limp, not one was left
For him to conquer. He learned all there was
To learn about not launching out too soon
And so not carrying the tree away
Clear to the ground. He always kept his poise   35
To the top branches, climbing carefully
With the same pains you use to fill a cup
Up to the brim, and even above the brim.
Then he flung outward, feet first, with a swish,

Kicking his way down through the air to the ground.   40
So was I once myself a swinger of birches.
And so I dream of going back to be.
It's when I'm weary of considerations,
And life is too much like a pathless wood
Where your face burns and tickles with the cobwebs   45
Broken across it, and one eye is weeping
From a twig's having lashed across it open.
I'd like to get away from earth awhile
And then come back to it and begin over.
May no fate willfully misunderstand me   50
And half grant what I wish and snatch me away
Not to return. Earth's the right place for love:
I don't know where it's likely to go better.
I'd like to go by climbing a birch tree,
And climb black branches up a snow-white trunk,   55
Toward heaven, till the tree could bear no more,
But dipped its top and set me down again.
That would be good both going and coming back.
One could do worse than be a swinger of birches.

■ Why does the poet prefer to think that the birches have been bent by some
  boy's swinging?
■ Which images in the poem come from the poet's actual observations? Where
  do others come from?

Robert Frost (1874–1963)

Acquainted with the Night (1928)

I have been one acquainted with the night.
I have walked out in rain—and back in rain.
I have outwalked the furthest city light.

I have looked down the saddest city lane.
I have passed by the watchman on his beat   5
And dropped my eyes, unwilling to explain.

I have stood still and stopped the sound of feet
When far away an interrupted cry
Came over houses from another street,

But not to call me back or say good-by;   10
And further still at an unearthly height
One luminary clock against the sky

Proclaimed the time was neither wrong nor right.
I have been one acquainted with the night.

- How is the poet's distance from home important to the images in this poem?
- What is the significance of the messages that the clock and cry send?

Ezra Pound (1885–1972)

In a Station of the Metro (1913)

The apparition of these faces in the crowd;
Petals on a wet, black bough.

- Why is the title significant? Who is at home in the metro?
- How are the faces connected to petals?

Wallace Stevens (1879–1955)

The Snow Man (1923)

One must have a mind of winter
To regard the frost and the boughs
Of the pine-trees crusted with snow;

And have been cold a long time
To behold the junipers shagged with ice,   5
The spruces rough in the distant glitter

Of the January sun; and not to think
Of any misery in the sound of the wind,
In the sound of a few leaves,

Which is the sound of the land   10
Full of the same wind
That is blowing in the same bare place

For the listener, who listens in the snow,
And, nothing himself, beholds
Nothing that is not there and the nothing that is.   15

- How does each of the images suggest nothingness?
- What does the final stanza say about a listener? What qualities does the poet value?

Wallace Stevens (1879–1955)

Thirteen Ways of Looking at a Blackbird (1923)

I
Among twenty snowy mountains,
The only moving thing
Was the eye of the blackbird.

II
I was of three minds,
Like a tree   5
In which there are three blackbirds.

III
The blackbird whirled in the autumn winds.
It was a small part of the pantomime.

IV
A man and a woman
Are one.   10
A man and a woman and a blackbird
Are one.

V
I do not know which to prefer,
The beauty of inflections
Or the beauty of innuendoes,   15
The blackbird whistling
Or just after.

VI

Icicles filled the long window
With barbaric glass.
The shadow of the blackbird   20
Crossed it, to and fro.
The mood
Traced in the shadow
An indecipherable cause.

VII

O thin men of Haddam,   25
Why do you imagine golden birds?
Do you not see how the blackbird
Walks around the feet
Of the women about you?

VIII

I know noble accents   30
And lucid, inescapable rhythms;
But I know, too,
That the blackbird is involved
In what I know.

IX

When the blackbird flew out of sight,   35
It marked the edge
Of one of many circles.

X

At the sight of blackbirds
Flying in a green light,
Even the bawds of euphony   40
Would cry out sharply.

XI

He rode over Connecticut
In a glass coach.
Once, a fear pierced him,
In that he mistook   45
The shadow of his equipage
For blackbirds.

XII

The river is moving.
The blackbird must be flying.

XIII

It was evening all afternoon.   50
It was snowing
And it was going to snow.
The blackbird sat
In the cedar-limbs.

- What is the difference between the "beauty of inflections" and "the beauty of innuendoes"? How does the blackbird help illustrate this difference?
- How is the thirteenth stanza related to the first?

e. e. cummings (1894–1962)

in Just- (1923)

in Just-
spring   when the world is mud-
luscious the little
lame balloonman

whistles   far   and wee   5

and eddieandbill come
running from marbles and
piracies and it's
spring

when the world is puddle-wonderful   10

the queer
old balloonman whistles
far   and   wee
and bettyandisbel come dancing

from hop-scotch and jump-rope and   15

it's
spring

and
   the
      goat-footed   20

balloonMan   whistles
far
and
wee

- Find specific lines where the rhythm of the words helps establish meaning.
- Where does the poet use images to create meaning out of nonsense words? How do these neologisms work differently than a familiar word would in the same place?

Maya Angelou (1928–)

Harlem Hopscotch (1971)

One foot down, then hop! It's hot.
   Good things for the ones that's got.
Another jump, now to the left.
   Everybody for hisself.

In the air, now both feet down.   5
   Since you black, don't stick around.
Food is gone, the rent is due,
   Curse and cry and then jump two.

All the people out of work,
   Hold for three, then twist and jerk.   10
Cross the line, they count you out,
   That's what hopping's all about.

Both feet flat, the game is done.
They think I lost. I think I won.

- How does the rhythm establish a sense of the setting for this poem and specific images related to that setting?
- How do the final two lines indicate the poet's place within this particular setting?

Richard Wilbur (1921–)

April 5, 1974 (1975)

The air was soft, the ground still cold.
In wet dull pastures where I strolled
Was something I could not believe.
Dead grass appeared to slide and heave,
Though still too frozen-flat to stir,   5
And rocks to twitch, and all to blur.
What was this rippling of the land?
Was matter getting out of hand
And making free with natural law?
I stopped and blinked, and then I saw   10
A fact as eerie as a dream.
There was a subtle flood of stream
Moving upon the face of things.
It came from standing pools and springs
And what of snow was still around;   15
It came of winter's giving ground
So that the freeze was coming out,
As when a set mind, blessed by doubt,
Relaxes into mother-wit.
Flowers, I said, will come of it.   20

■ How does the poet find significance in the "fact as eerie as a dream"?
■ How does the poet interpret the images that he observes? What is his epiphany?

Mary Oliver (1935–)

Spring (1983)

Somewhere
    a black bear
        has just risen from sleep
            and is staring

down the mountain.   5
    All night
        in the brisk and shallow restlessness
            of early spring

I think of her,
  her four black fists   10
    flicking the gravel,
      her tongue

like a red fire
  touching the grass,
    the cold water.   15
      There is only one question:

how to love this world.
  I think of her
    rising
      like a black and leafy ledge   20

to sharpen her claws against
  the silence
    of the trees.
      Whatever else

my life is   25
  with its poems
    and its music
      and its cities,

it is also this dazzling darkness
  coming   30
    down the mountain,
      breathing and tasting;

all day I think of her—
  her white teeth,
    her wordlessness,   35
      her perfect love.

■ How is the central question "how to love this world" relevant to the images that the poet describes? What is the scope of "this world"?

■ In what way is spring important to this image?

Mary Oliver (1935–)

Ghosts (1983)

1

Have you noticed?

2

Where so many millions of powerful bawling beasts
lay down on the earth and died
it's hard to tell now
what's bone, and what merely   5
was once.

The golden eagle, for instance,
has a bit of heaviness in him;
moreover the huge barns
seem ready, sometimes, to ramble off   10
toward deeper grass.

3

1805
near the Bitterroot Mountains:
a man named Lewis kneels down
on the prairie watching   15

a sparrow's nest cleverly concealed in the wild hyssop
and lined with buffalo hair. The chicks,
not more than a day hatched, lean
quietly into the thick wool as if
content, after all,   20
to have left the perfect world and fallen,
helpless and blind,
into the flowered fields and the perils
of this one.

4

In the book of the earth it is written: 25
nothing can die.

In the book of the Sioux it is written:
they have gone away into the earth to hide.
Nothing will coax them out again
but the people dancing.   30

5
Said the old-timers:
the tongue
is the sweetest meat

Passengers shooting from train windows
could hardly miss, they were   35
that many.
Afterward the carcasses
stank unbelievably, and sang with flies, ribboned
with slopes of white fat,
black ropes of blood—hellhunks   40
in the prairie heat.

6
Have you noticed? how the rain
falls soft as the fall
of moccasins. *Have you noticed?*
how the immense circles still,   45
stubbornly, after a hundred years,
mark the grass where the rich droppings
from the roaring bulls
fell to the earth as the herd stood
day after day, moon after moon   50
in their tribal circle, outwaiting
the packs of yellow-eyed wolves that are also
have you noticed? gone now.

7
Once only, and then in a dream,
I watched while, secretly   55
and with the tenderness of any caring woman,
a cow gave birth
to a red calf, tongued him dry and nursed him
in a warm corner
of the clear night   60
in the fragrant grass
in the wild domains
of the prairie spring, and I asked them,
in my dream I knelt down and asked them
to make room for me.   65

- How does each repeated "Have you noticed?" allow the poem to review different sets of images?
- How does the poet use irony in the poem?
- What is the significance of each stanza division?

Derek Walcott (1930 –)

Dry Season (2004)

In the country of the ochre afternoon
it is always still and hot, the dry leaves stirring
infrequently sometimes with the rattling pods
of what they call "women's tongues," in
the afternoon country the far hills are very quiet   5
and heat-hazed, but mostly in the middle
of the country of the afternoon I see the brown heat
of the skin of my first love, so still, so perfect,
so unaltered, and I see how she walked
with her sunburnt hands against the still sea almonds,   10
to a remembered cove, where she stood on the small dock—
that was when I thought we were immortal
and that love would be folded doves and folded oars
and water lapping against eroding stone
in the ochre country of the afternoon.   15

- Trace the different senses that the poet uses throughout the poem. How does each sensation contribute some specific detail that aids the progress of the poem?
- Look at the first line and the last line of the poem. How are the two lines different? How does the difference relate to the comments about immortality that the poet alludes to in line 12?

DRAMA

Susan Glaspell (1882–1948)

Susan Glaspell was born in Davenport, Iowa. She earned her BA from Drake University in Des Moines before beginning her writing career as a reporter for the *Des Moines Daily News* and the *Des Moines Capital*. In addition to her work as a journalist, she published short stories in women's magazines. After a tour of Europe in 1910, Glaspell fell in love with George Cram Cook and began incorporating his socialist ideas into her own writings. Her works began to feature strong female characters who often undergo experiences of self-discovery. In 1915, Glaspell and Cook founded the Provincetown Players, and the group produced many of Glaspell's plays, including *Trifles* (1916), a story of a woman who murders her abusive husband. Glaspell's career flourished during this time, and her play *Alison's House* (1930) was awarded a Pulitzer Prize.

Trifles (1916)

CHARACTERS

GEORGE HENDERSON, *county attorney*
HENRY PETERS, *sheriff*
LEWIS HALE, *a neighboring farmer*
MRS. PETERS
MRS. HALE

SCENE: *The kitchen in the now abandoned farmhouse of John Wright, a gloomy kitchen, and left without having been put in order—unwashed pans under the sink, a loaf of bread outside the bread-box, a dish-towel on the table— other signs of incompleted work. At the rear the outer door opens and the* SHERIFF *comes in followed by the* COUNTY ATTORNEY *and* HALE. *The* SHERIFF *and* HALE *are men in middle life, the* COUNTY ATTORNEY *is a young man; all are much bundled up and go at once to the stove. They are followed by the two women—the* SHERIFF's *wife first; she is a slight wiry woman, a thin nervous face.* MRS. HALE *is larger and would ordinarily be called more comfortable looking, but she is disturbed now and looks fearfully about as she enters. The women have come in slowly, and stand close together near the door.*

COUNTY ATTORNEY *(Rubbing his hands.)* This feels good. Come up to the fire, ladies.

MRS. PETERS *(After taking a step forward.)* I'm not—cold.

SHERIFF *(Unbuttoning his overcoat and stepping away from the stove as if to mark the beginning of official business.)* Now, Mr. Hale, before we move things about, you explain to Mr. Henderson just what you saw when you came here yesterday morning.

COUNTY ATTORNEY: By the way, has anything been moved? Are things just as you left them yesterday?

SHERIFF *(Looking about.)* It's just the same. When it dropped below zero last   5
night I thought I'd better send Frank out this morning to make a fire for
us—no use getting pneumonia with a big case on, but I told him not to
touch anything except the stove—and you know
Frank.

COUNTY ATTORNEY: Somebody should have been left here yesterday.

SHERIFF: Oh—yesterday. When I had to send Frank to Morris Center for
that man who went crazy—I want you to know I had my hands full yesterday. I knew you could get back from Omaha by today and as long as
I went over everything here myself—

COUNTY ATTORNEY: Well, Mr. Hale, tell just what happened when you
came here yesterday morning.

HALE: Harry and I had started to town with a load of potatoes. We came
along the road from my place and as I got here I said, "I'm going to see
if I can't get John Wright to go in with me on a party telephone." I
spoke to Wright about it once before and he put me off, saying folks
talked too much anyway, and all he asked was peace and quiet—I guess
you know about how much he talked himself; but I thought maybe if I
went to the house and talked about it before his wife, though I said to
Harry that I didn't know as what his wife wanted made much difference
to John—

COUNTY ATTORNEY: Let's talk about that later, Mr. Hale. I do want to talk   10
about that, but tell now just what happened when you got to the house.

HALE: I didn't hear or see anything; I knocked at the door, and still it was
all quiet inside. I knew they must be up, it was past eight o'clock. So I
knocked again, and I thought I heard somebody say, "Come in." I
wasn't sure, I'm not sure yet, but I opened the door—this door *(indicating the door by which the two women are still standing)* and there in that
rocker— *(pointing to it)* sat Mrs. Wright.

(They all look at the rocker.)

COUNTY ATTORNEY: What—was she doing?

HALE: She was rockin' back and forth. She had her apron in her hand and
was kind of—pleating it.

COUNTY ATTORNEY: And how did she—look?

HALE: Well, she looked queer.   15

COUNTY ATTORNEY: How do you mean—queer?

HALE: Well, as if she didn't know what she was going to do next. And kind
of done up.

COUNTY ATTORNEY: How did she seem to feel about your coming?

HALE: Why, I don't think she minded—one way or other. She didn't pay
much attention. I said, "How do, Mrs. Wright, it's cold, ain't it?" And
she said, "Is it?"—and went on kind of pleating at her apron. Well, I was
surprised; she didn't ask me to come up to the stove, or to set down, but

just sat there, not even looking at me, so I said, "I want to see John."
And then she—laughed. I guess you would call it a laugh. I thought of
Harry and the team outside, so I said a little sharp: "Can't I see John?"
"No," she says, kind o' dull like. "Ain't he home?" says I. "Yes," says she,
"he's home." "Then why can't I see him?" I asked her, out of patience.
"'Cause he's dead," says she. "*Dead?*" says I. She just nodded her head,
not getting a bit excited, but rockin' back and forth. "Why—where is
he?" says I, not knowing what to say. She just pointed upstairs—like
that (*himself pointing to the room above*). I got up, with the idea of going
up there. I walked from there to here—then I says, "Why, what did he
die of?" "He died of a rope round his neck," says she, and just went on
pleatin' at her apron. Well, I went out and called Harry. I thought I
might—need help. We went upstairs and there he was lyin'—

COUNTY ATTORNEY: I think I'd rather have you go into that upstairs, where   20
you can point it all out. Just go on now with the rest of the story.

HALE: Well, my first thought was to get that rope off. It looked ... (*Stops, his
face twitches*) ... but Harry, he went up to him, and he said, "No, he's
dead all right, and we'd better not touch anything." So we went back
downstairs. She was still sitting that same way. "Has anybody been
notified?" I asked. "No," says she, unconcerned. "Who did this, Mrs.
Wright?" said Harry. He said it business-like—and she stopped pleatin'
of her apron. "I don't know," she says. "You don't *know?*" says Harry.
"No," says she. "Weren't you sleepin' in the bed with him?" says Harry.
"Yes," says she, "but I was on the inside." "Somebody slipped a rope
round his neck and strangled him and you didn't wake up?" says Harry.
"I didn't wake up," she said after him. We must 'a looked as if we didn't
see how that could be, for after a minute she said, "I sleep sound."
Harry was going to ask her more questions but I said maybe we ought to
let her tell her story first to the coroner, or the sheriff, so Harry went
fast as he could to Rivers' place, where there's a telephone.

COUNTY ATTORNEY: And what did Mrs. Wright do when she knew that you
had gone for the coroner?

HALE: She moved from that chair to this one over here (*Pointing to a small
chair in the corner*) and just sat there with her hands held together and
looking down. I got a feeling that I ought to make some conversation,
so I said I had come in to see if John wanted to put in a telephone, and
at that she started to laugh, and then she stopped and looked at me—
scared. (*The* COUNTY ATTORNEY, *who has had his notebook out, makes a
note.*) I dunno, maybe it wasn't scared. I wouldn't like to say it was.
Soon Harry got back, and then Dr. Lloyd came, and you, Mr. Peters,
and so I guess that's all I know that you don't.

COUNTY ATTORNEY (*Looking around.*): I guess we'll go upstairs first—and
then out to the barn and around there. (*To the* SHERIFF.) You're

convinced that there was nothing important here—nothing that would point to any motive.

SHERIFF: Nothing here but kitchen things.   25

(The COUNTY ATTORNEY, *after again looking around the kitchen, opens the door of a cupboard closet. He gets up on a chair and looks on a shelf. Pulls his hand away, sticky.)*

COUNTY ATTORNEY: Here's a nice mess.

(The women draw nearer.)

MRS. PETERS *(To the other woman.)*: Oh, her fruit; it did freeze. *(To the* LAW-YER.*)* She worried about that when it turned so cold. She said the fire'd go out and her jars would break.

SHERIFF: Well, can you beat the woman! Held for murder and worryin' about her preserves.

COUNTY ATTORNEY: I guess before we're through she may have something more serious than preserves to worry about.

HALE: Well, women are used to worrying over trifles.   30

(The two women move a little closer together.)

COUNTY ATTORNEY *(With the gallantry of a young politician.)*: And yet, for all their worries, what would we do without the ladies? *(The women do not unbend. He goes to the sink, takes a dipperful of water from the pail and pouring it into a basin, washes his hands. Starts to wipe them on the roller-towel, turns it for a cleaner place.)* Dirty towels! *(Kicks his foot against the pans under the sink.)* Not much of a housekeeper, would you say, ladies?

MRS. HALE *(Stiffly.)*: There's a great deal of work to be done on a farm.

COUNTY ATTORNEY: To be sure. And yet *(With a little bow to her.)* I know there are some Dickson county farmhouses which do not have such roller towels.

(He gives it a pull to expose its full length again.)

MRS. HALE: Those towels get dirty awful quick. Men's hands aren't always as clean as they might be.

COUNTY ATTORNEY: Ah, loyal to your sex, I see. But you and Mrs. Wright   35
were neighbors. I suppose you were friends, too.

MRS. HALE *(Shaking her head.)*: I've not seen much of her of late years. I've not been in this house—it's more than a year.

COUNTY ATTORNEY: And why was that? You didn't like her?

MRS. HALE: I liked her all well enough. Farmers' wives have their hands full, Mr. Henderson. And then—

COUNTY ATTORNEY: Yes—?

MRS. HALE *(Looking about.)*: It never seemed a very cheerful place.   40

COUNTY ATTORNEY: No—it's not cheerful. I shouldn't say she had the homemaking instinct.

MRS. HALE: Well, I don't know as Wright had, either.

COUNTY ATTORNEY: You mean that they didn't get on very well?

MRS. HALE: No, I don't mean anything. But I don't think a place'd be any cheerfuller for John Wright's being in it.

COUNTY ATTORNEY: I'd like to talk more of that a little later. I want to get 45 the lay of things upstairs now.

(He goes to the left, where three steps lead to a stair door.)

SHERIFF: I suppose anything Mrs. Peters does'll be all right. She was to take in some clothes for her, you know, and a few little things. We left in such a hurry yesterday.

COUNTY ATTORNEY: Yes, but I would like to see what you take, Mrs. Peters, and keep an eye out for anything that might be of use to us.

MRS. PETERS: Yes, Mr. Henderson.

(The women listen to the men's steps on the stairs, then look about the kitchen.)

MRS. HALE: I'd hate to have men coming into my kitchen, snooping around and criticising.

(She arranges the pans under sink which the LAWYER had shoved out of place.)

MRS. PETERS: Of course it's no more than their duty. 50

MRS. HALE: Duty's all right, but I guess that deputy sheriff that came out to make the fire might have got a little of this on. *(Gives the roller towel a pull.)* Wish I'd thought of that sooner. Seems mean to talk about her for not having things slicked up when she had to come away in such a hurry.

MRS. PETERS *(Who has gone to a small table in the left rear corner of the room, and lifted one end of a towel that covers a pan.):* She had bread set.

(Stands still.)

MRS. HALE *(Eyes fixed on a loaf of bread beside the breadbox, which is on a low shelf at the other side of the room. Moves slowly toward it.):* She was going to put this in there. *(Picks up loaf, then abruptly drops it. In a manner of returning to familiar things.)* It' a shame about her fruit. I wonder if it's all gone. *(Gets up on the chair and looks.)* I think there's some here that's all right, Mrs. Peters. Yes—here; *(Holding it toward the window)* this is cherries, too. *(Looking again.)* I declare I believe that's the only one. *(Gets down, bottle in her hand. Goes to the sink and wipes it off on the outside.)* She'll feel awful bad after all her hard work in the hot weather. I remember the afternoon I put up my cherries last summer.

(She puts the bottle on the big kitchen table, center of the room. With a sigh, is about to sit down in the rocking-chair. Before she is seated realizes what chair it is; with a slow look at it, steps back. The chair which she has touched rocks back and forth.)

MRS. PETERS: Well, I must get those things from the front room closet. *(She goes to the door at the right, but after looking into the other room, steps back.)* You coming with me, Mrs. Hale? You could help me carry them.

(They go in the other room; reappear, MRS. PETERS carrying a dress and skirt, MRS. HALE following with a pair of shoes.)

MRS. PETERS: My, it's cold in there.   55
(*She puts the clothes on the big table, and hurries to the stove.*)
MRS. HALE (*Examining the skirt.*): Wright was close. I think maybe that's
   why she kept so much to herself. She didn't even belong to the Ladies Aid. I suppose she felt she couldn't do her part, and then you
   don't enjoy things when you feel shabby. She used to wear pretty
   clothes and be lively, when she was Minnie Foster, one of the town
   girls singing in the choir. But that—oh, that was thirty years ago.
   This all you was to take in?
MRS. PETERS: She said she wanted an apron. Funny thing to want, for there
   isn't much to get you dirty in jail, goodness knows. But I suppose just to
   make her feel more natural. She said they was in the top drawer in this
   cupboard. Yes, here. And then her little shawl that always hung behind
   the door. (*Opens stair door and looks.*) Yes, here it is.
(*Quickly shuts door leading upstairs.*)
MRS. HALE (*Abruptly moving toward her.*): Mrs. Peters?
MRS. PETERS: Yes, Mrs. Hale?
MRS. HALE: Do you think she did it?   60
MRS. PETERS (*In a frightened voice.*): Oh, I don't know.
MRS. HALE: Well, I don't think she did. Asking for an apron and her little
   shawl. Worrying about her fruit.
MRS. PETERS (*Starts to speak, glances up, where footsteps are heard in the room
   above. In a low voice.*): Mr. Peters says it looks bad for her. Mr. Hender-
   son is awful sarcastic in a speech and he'll make fun of her sayin' she
   didn't wake up.
MRS. HALE: Well, I guess John Wright didn't wake when they was slipping
   that rope under his neck.
MRS. PETERS: No, it's strange. It must have been done awful crafty and still.   65
   They say it was such a—funny way to kill a man, rigging it all up like
   that.
MRS. HALE: That's just what Mr. Hale said. There was a gun in the house.
   He says that's what he can't understand.
MRS. PETERS: Mr. Henderson said coming out that what was needed for the
   case was a motive; something to show anger, or—sudden feeling.
MRS. HALE (*Who is standing by the table.*): Well, I don't see any signs of
   anger around here. (*She puts her hand on the dish towel which lies on the
   table, stands looking down at table, one half of which is clean, the other half
   messy.*) It's wiped to here. (*Makes a move as if to finish work, then turns
   and looks at loaf of bread outside the breadbox. Drops towel. In that voice of
   coming back to familiar things.*) Wonder how they are finding things upstairs. I hope she had it a little more red-up up there. You know, it
   seems kind of *sneaking.* Locking her up in town and then coming out
   here and trying to get her own house to turn against her!

MRS. PETERS: But Mrs. Hale, the law is the law.

MRS. HALE: I s'pose 'tis. (*Unbuttoning her coat.*) Better loosen up your things, 70 Mrs. Peters. You won't feel them when you go out.

(MRS. PETERS *takes off her fur tippet, goes to hang it on hook at back of room, stands looking at the under part of the small corner table.*)

MRS. PETERS: She was piecing a quilt.

(*She brings the large sewing basket and they look at the bright pieces.*)

MRS. HALE: It's log cabin pattern. Pretty, isn't it? I wonder if she was goin' to quilt it or just knot it?

(*Footsteps have been heard coming down the stairs. The* SHERIFF *enters followed by* HALE *and the* COUNTY ATTORNEY.)

SHERIFF: They wonder if she was going to quilt it or just knot it!

(*The men laugh, the women look abashed.*)

COUNTY ATTORNEY (*Rubbing his hands over the stove.*): Frank's fire didn't do much up there, did it? Well, let's go out to the barn and get that cleared up.

(*The men go outside.*)

MRS. HALE (*Resentfully.*): I don't know as there's anything so strange, our 75 takin' up our time with little things while we're waiting for them to get the evidence. (*She sits down at the big table smoothing out a block with decision.*) I don't see as it's anything to laugh about.

MRS. PETERS (*Apologetically.*): Of course they've got awful important things on their minds.

(*Pulls up a chair and joins* MRS. HALE *at the table.*)

MRS. HALE (*Examining another block.*): Mrs. Peters, look at this one. Here, this is the one she was working on, and look at the sewing! All the rest of it has been so nice and even. And look at this! It's all over the place! Why, it looks as if she didn't know what she was about!

(*After she has said this they look at each other, then start to glance back at the door. After an instant* MRS. HALE *has pulled at a knot and ripped the sewing.*)

MRS. PETERS: Oh, what are you doing, Mrs. Hale?

MRS. HALE (*Mildly.*): Just pulling out a stitch or two that's not sewed very good. (*Threading a needle.*) Bad sewing always made me fidgety.

MRS. PETERS (*Nervously.*): I don't think we ought to touch things. 80

MRS. HALE: I'll just finish up this end. (*Suddenly stopping and leaning forward.*) Mrs. Peters?

MRS. PETERS: Yes, Mrs. Hale?

MRS. HALE: What do you suppose she was so nervous about?

MRS. PETERS: Oh—I don't know. I don't know as she was nervous. I sometimes sew awful queer when I'm just tired. (*Mrs. Hale starts to say something, looks at Mrs. Peters, then goes on sewing.*) Well I must get these things wrapped up. They may be through sooner than we think. (*Putting apron and other things together.*) I wonder where I can find a piece of paper, and string.

MRS. HALE: In that cupboard, maybe.   85

MRS. PETERS (*Looking in cupboard.*): Why, here's a bird-cage. (*Holds it up.*) Did she have a bird, Mrs. Hale?

MRS. HALE: Why, I don't know whether she did or not—I've not been here for so long. There was a man around last year selling canaries cheap, but I don't know as she took one; maybe she did. She used to sing real pretty herself.

MRS. PETERS (*Glancing around.*): Seems funny to think of a bird here. But she must have had one, or why would she have a cage? I wonder what happened to it.

MRS. HALE: I s'pose maybe the cat got it.

MRS. PETERS: No, she didn't have a cat. She's got that feeling some people   90 have about cats—being afraid of them. My cat got in her room and she was real upset and asked me to take it out.

MRS. HALE: My sister Bessie was like that. Queer, ain't it?

MRS. PETERS (*Examining the cage.*): Why, look at this door. It's broke. One hinge is pulled apart.

MRS. HALE (*Looking too.*): Looks as if someone must have been rough with it.

MRS. PETERS: Why, yes.

(*She brings the cage forward and puts it on the table.*)

MRS. HALE: I wish if they're going to find any evidence they'd be about it. I   95 don't like this place.

MRS. PETERS: But I'm awful glad you came with me, Mrs. Hale. It would be lonesome for me sitting here alone.

MRS. HALE: It would, wouldn't it? (*Dropping her sewing.*) But I tell you what I do wish, Mrs. Peters. I wish I had come over sometimes when *she* was here. I— (*Looking around the room.*) —wish I had.

MRS. PETERS: But of course you were awful busy, Mrs. Hale—your house and your children.

MRS. HALE: I could've come. I stayed away because it weren't cheerful—and that's why I ought to have come. I—I've never liked this place. Maybe because it's down in a hollow and you don't see the road. I dunno what it is, but it's a lonesome place and always was. I wish I had come over to see Minnie Foster sometimes. I can see now—

(*Shakes her head.*)

MRS. PETERS: Well, you mustn't reproach yourself, Mrs. Hale. Somehow we   100 just don't see how it is with other folks until—something comes up.

MRS. HALE: Not having children makes less work—but it makes a quiet house, and Wright out to work all day, and no company when he did come in. Did you know John Wright, Mrs. Peters?

MRS. PETERS: Not to know him; I've seen him in town. They say he was a good man.

MRS. HALE: Yes—good; he didn't drink, and kept his word as well as most, I guess, and paid his debts. But he was a hard man, Mrs. Peters. Just to pass the time of day with him— (*Shivers.*) Like a raw wind that gets to the bone. (*Pauses, her eye falling on the cage.*) I should think she would 'a wanted a bird. But what do you suppose went with it?

MRS. PETERS: I don't know, unless it got sick and died.

(*She reaches over and swings the broken door, swings it again, both women watch it.*)

MRS. HALE: You weren't raised round here, were you? (*Mrs. Peters shakes her head.*) You didn't know—her? 105

MRS. PETERS: Not till they brought her yesterday.

MRS. HALE: She—come to think of it, she was kind of like a bird herself—real sweet and pretty, but kind of timid and—fluttery. How—she—did—change. (*Silence; then as if struck by a happy thought and relieved to get back to everyday things.*) Tell you what, Mrs. Peters, why don't you take the quilt in with you? It might take up her mind.

MRS. PETERS: Why, I think that's a real nice idea, Mrs. Hale. There couldn't possibly be any objection to it, could there? Now, just what would I take? I wonder if her patches are in here—and her things.

(*They look in the sewing basket.*)

MRS. HALE: Here's some red. I expect this has got sewing things in it. (*Brings out a fancy box.*) What a pretty box. Looks like something somebody would give you. Maybe her scissors are in here. (*Opens box. Suddenly puts her hand to her nose.*) Why— (*Mrs. Peters bends nearer, then turns her face away.*) There's something wrapped up in this piece of silk.

MRS. PETERS: Why, this isn't her scissors. 110

MRS. HALE (*Lifting the silk.*): Oh, Mrs. Peters—its—

(MRS. PETERS *bends closer.*)

MRS. PETERS: It's the bird.

MRS. HALE (*Jumping up.*): But, Mrs. Peters—look at it! Its neck! Look at its neck! It's all—other side *to.*

MRS. PETERS: Somebody—wrung—its—neck.

(*Their eyes meet. A look of growing comprehension, of horror. Steps are heard outside.* MRS. HALE *slips box under quilt pieces, and sinks into her chair.* Enter SHERIFF *and* COUNTY ATTORNEY. MRS. PETERS *rises.*)

COUNTY ATTORNEY (*As one turning from serious things to little pleasantries.*): Well, ladies, have you decided whether she was going to quilt it or knot it? 11

MRS. PETERS: We think she was going to—knot it.

COUNTY ATTORNEY: Well, that's interesting, I'm sure. (*Seeing the birdcage.*) Has the bird flown?

MRS. HALE (*Putting more quilt pieces over the box.*): We think the—cat got it.

COUNTY ATTORNEY (*Preoccupied.*): Is there a cat?

(MRS. HALE *glances in a quick covert way at* MRS. PETERS.)

MRS. PETERS: Well, not *now.* They're superstitious, you know. They leave.   120

COUNTY ATTORNEY (*To* SHERIFF PETERS, *continuing an interrupted conversation.*): No sign at all of anyone having come from the outside. Their own rope. Now let's go up again and go over it piece by piece. (*They start upstairs.*) It would have to have been someone who knew just the—

(MRS. PETERS *sits down. The two women sit there not looking at one another, but as if peering into something and at the same time holding back. When they talk now it is in the manner of feeling their way over strange ground, as if afraid of what they are saying, but as if they can not help saying it.*)

MRS. HALE: She liked the bird. She was going to bury it in that pretty box.

MRS. PETERS (*In a whisper.*): When I was a girl—my kitten—there was a boy took a hatchet, and before my eyes—and before I could get there— (*Covers her face an instant.*) If they hadn't held me back I would have— (*Catches herself, looks upstairs where steps are heard, falters weakly*)—hurt him.

MRS. HALE (*With a slow look around her.*): I wonder how it would seem never to have had any children around. (*Pause.*) No, Wright wouldn't like the bird—a thing that sang. She used to sing. He killed that, too.

MRS. PETERS (*Moving uneasily.*): We don't know who killed the bird.   125

MRS. HALE: I knew John Wright.

MRS. PETERS: It was an awful thing was done in this house that night, Mrs. Hale. Killing a man while he slept, slipping a rope around his neck that choked the life out of him.

MRS. HALE: His neck. Choked the life out of him.

(*Her hand goes out and rests on the bird-cage.*)

MRS. PETERS (*With rising voice.*): We don't know who killed him. We don't *know.*

MRS. HALE (*Her own feeling not interrupted.*): If there'd been years and years   130 of nothing, then a bird to sing to you, it would be awful—still, after the bird was still.

MRS. PETERS (*Something within her speaking.*): I know what stillness is. When we homesteaded in Dakota, and my first baby died—after he was two years old, and me with no other then—

MRS. HALE (*Moving.*): How soon do you suppose they'll be through, looking for the evidence?

MRS. PETERS: I know what stillness is. (*Pulling herself back.*) The law has got to punish crime, Mrs. Hale.

MRS. HALE (*Not as if answering that.*): I wish you'd seen Minnie Foster when she wore a white dress with blue ribbons and stood up there in the choir and sang. (*A look around the room.*) Oh, I *wish* I'd come over here once in a while! That was a crime! That was a crime! Who's going to punish that?

MRS. PETERS (*Looking upstairs.*): We mustn't—take on.   135

MRS. HALE: I might have known she needed help! I know how things can be—for women. I tell you, it's queer, Mrs. Peters. We live close to-gether and we live far apart. We all go through the same things—it's all just a different kind of the same thing. (*Brushes her eyes, noticing the bottle of fruit, reaches out for it.*) If I was you I wouldn't tell her her fruit was gone. Tell her it *ain't*. Tell her it's all right. Take this in to prove it to her. She—she may never know whether it was broke or not.

MRS. PETERS (*Takes the bottle, looks about for something to wrap it in; takes pet-ticoat from the clothes brought from the other room, very nervously begins winding this around the bottle. In a false voice.*): My, it's a good thing the men couldn't hear us. Wouldn't they just laugh! Getting all stirred up over a little thing like a—dead canary. As if that could have anything to do with—with—wouldn't they *laugh*!

(*The men are heard coming down stairs.*)

MRS. HALE (*Under her breath.*): Maybe they would—maybe they wouldn't.

COUNTY ATTORNEY: No, Peters, it's all perfectly clear except a reason for doing it. But you know juries when it comes to women. If there was some definite thing. Something to show—something to make a story about—a thing that would connect up with this strange way of doing it—

(*The women's eyes meet for an instant. Enter* HALE *from outer door.*)

HALE: Well, I've got the team around. Pretty cold out there.   140

COUNTY ATTORNEY: I'm going to stay here a while by myself. (*To the* SHER-IFF.) You can send Frank out for me, can't you? I want to go over every-thing. I'm not satisfied that we can't do better.

SHERIFF: Do you want to see what Mrs. Peters is going to take in?

(*The* LAWYER *goes to the table, picks up the apron, laughs.*)

COUNTY ATTORNEY: Oh, I guess they're not very dangerous things the ladies have picked out. (*Moves a few things about, disturbing the quilt pieces which cover the box. Steps back.*) No, Mrs. Peters doesn't need supervis-ing. For that matter, a sheriff's wife is married to the law. Ever think of it that way, Mrs. Peters?

MRS. PETERS: Not—just that way.

SHERIFF (*Chuckling.*): Married to the law. (*Moves toward the other room.*) I just want you to come in here a minute, George. We ought to take a look at these windows.   141

COUNTY ATTORNEY (*Scoffingly.*): Oh, windows!

SHERIFF: We'll be right out, Mr. Hale.

(HALE *goes outside. The* SHERIFF *follows the* COUNTY ATTORNEY *into the*

other room. Then MRS. HALE *rises, hands tight together, looking intensely at*
MRS. PETERS, *whose eyes make a slow turn, finally meeting* MRS. HALE'S. *A*
moment MRS. HALE *holds her, then her own eyes point the way to where*
the box is concealed. Suddenly MRS. PETERS *throws back quilt pieces and tries*
to put the box in the handbag she is carrying. It is too big. She opens box,
starts to take bird out, cannot touch it, goes to pieces, stands there helpless.
Sound of a knob turning in the other room. Mrs. Hale snatches the box and
puts it in the pocket of her big coat. Enter COUNTY ATTORNEY *and*
SHERIFF.)

COUNTY ATTORNEY *(Facetiously.):* Well, Henry, at least we found out that
she was not going to quilt it. She was going to—what is it you call it,
ladies?

MRS. HALE *(Her hand against her pocket.):* We call it—knot it,
Mr. Henderson.

(CURTAIN)

■ How do the women and men see details differently in this play? Give specific
details, and explain why this difference is significant to our understanding of
the play.

■ How does the bird function as an image in this play? How is it presented in the
script, and how does it relate to any themes in the story?

Experiencing Literature through Writing

1. Select a single image from one of the works in this chapter (or any
other). Explain how the author conveys this image and how it is
significant within the work. As you write, consider the following
questions:

   a. What details work together to create this image? Discuss the use of
   any senses that contribute to the effect.

   b. What makes this image stand out among any others that might be in
   the same text?

   c. What is the significance of this particular image? Is this significance
   easy to see? Sometimes the more obscure significances are worth our
   attention.

2. Often we are most aware of our senses when we leave familiar surroundings. The reading selections relate to being "home and away."

Discuss the ways in which a particular work uses a single image to signal the disjunction that comes from entering into an unfamiliar environment.

3. When we consider images, those images are often an aspect of our surroundings. Find a specific image in a text that you can discuss as separate from its setting. Explain why it is interesting to consider the image independently of its context.

8 Coherence

Is There a Pattern Here?

How Does This Fit Together?

In "real life," things are not neatly ordered. Anyone who has ever tried to organize a desk or a computer's desktop knows that maintaining order requires constant vigilance. Personal messages, advertisements, and interesting articles come to us in a random fashion. As receivers of these messages, we must develop some strategy to keep the avalanche of information from becoming incoherent noise that prevents us from doing the work that information is supposed to be facilitating. On desktops, we create folders to group similar items. Some people design very simple and transparent organizational plans. Others set up elaborate structures of networked folders that have an internal logic so complex that no one besides the organizer would ever recognize it. There must be method, though, in even the maddest systems.

In Nick Hornby's novel *High Fidelity* (1995), the main character, Rob Fleming, an avid thirty-something collector of vinyl records, deals with the emotional turmoil in his life by imposing order on something he can control. When his girlfriend leaves him, he turns to his record collection.

Nick Hornby (1957–)

from **High Fidelity** (1995)

Tuesday night I reorganize my record collection; I often do this at periods of emotional stress. There are some people who would find this a pretty dull way

High Fidelity (2000). In the film adaptation of the novel, John Cusack plays Rob Fleming, who reorganizes his record collection as his life falls apart.

to spend an evening, but I'm not one of them. This is my life, and it's nice to be able to wade in, immerse your arms in it, touch it.

When Laura was here I had the records arranged alphabetically; before that I had them filed in chronological order, beginning with Robert Johnson, and ending with, I don't know, Wham!, or somebody African, or whatever else I was listening to when Laura and I met. Tonight, though, I fancy something different, so I try to remember the order I bought them in: that way I hope to write my own autobiography, without having to do anything like pick up a pen. I pull the records off the shelves, put them in piles all over the sitting room floor, look for *Revolver*, and go on from there; and when I've finished, I'm flushed with a sense of self, because this, after all, is who I am. I like being able to see how I got from Deep Purple to Howlin' Wolf in twenty-five moves; I am no longer pained by the memory of listening to "Sexual Healing" all the way through a period of enforced celibacy, or embarrassed by the reminder of forming a rock club at school, so that I and my fellow fifth-formers could get together and talk about Ziggy Stardust and *Tommy*.

But what I really like is the feeling of security I get from my new filing system; I have a couple of thousand records, and you have to be me—or, at the very least, a doctor of Flemingology—to know how to find any of them. If I want to play, say *Blue* by Joni Mitchell, I have to remember that I bought it for someone in the autumn of 1983, and thought better of giving it to her, for reasons I don't really want to go into. Well, you don't know any of that, so you're knackered, really aren't you? You'd have to ask me to dig it out for you, and for some reason I find this enormously comforting. ■

Fleming's love of—or need for—order shows itself at other important times in his life. Later, as he considers dating someone new, he muses over the proper arrangement of a mixed tape.

> I spent hours putting that cassette together. To me, making a tape is like writing a letter—there's a lot of erasing and rethinking and starting again, and I wanted it to be a good one, because … to be honest, because I hadn't met anyone as promising as Laura since I'd started the DJ-ing, and meeting promising women was partly what the DJ-ing was supposed to be about. A good compilation tape, like breaking up, is hard to do. You've got to kick off with a corker, to hold that attention (I started with "Got to Get You off My Mind," but then realized that she might not get any further than track one, side one if I delivered what she wanted straightaway, so I buried it in the middle of side two), and then you've got to up it a notch, or cool it a notch, and you can't have white music and black music together, unless the white music sounds like black music, and you can't have two tracks by the same artist side by side, unless you've done the whole thing in pairs, and … oh, there are loads of rules. ■

Fleming's life is obviously less ordered than his record collection or his meticulously arranged song sets. Fleming is not alone in this novel in devising strategies to maintain order amid chaos; his friends also make lists that neatly arrange life. For our purposes, it's important to note that Hornby uses his characters' obsession with order as the structuring device in his novel; the list making and cataloguing connect the various parts of the story and become a subject of scrutiny within the story. Hornby weaves a dense fabric of systems people employ and prompts his reader to think of how—and how well—those systems function. Most chapters in his novel begin with a new list and some discussion of the standards used to generate that list: the best episode of *Cheers*, best A-side singles of all time, "my desert-island, all-time, top five most memorable split-ups, in chronological order." To the readers these lists are sometimes quite funny but also indicative of how hard it can be to assert control over the events of a life. They function to make the novel thematically coherent. They help us read and make sense of a lengthy narrative.

In this chapter, we'll examine a variety of strategies that writers/filmmakers employ to achieve a forceful, coherent work. We'll also call attention to ways that you, as a critical writer, can learn from these strategies.

DESIGN AND SHAPE

Every literary work or film employs some strategy for how the various pieces fit together. Sometimes the strategy is obvious at a glance. For instance, there is a tradition of creating a poem in the physical shape of the poem's subject; in other words, the lines of the poem illustrate their own subject matter. This is often called **concrete poetry**. Perhaps the most famous of these concrete, or **shape poems**, is George Herbert's "Easter Wings," which actually looks like two pairs of wings.

George Herbert (1593–1633)

Easter Wings (1633)

Lord, Who createdst man in wealth and store,
  Though foolishly he lost the same,
    Decaying more and more,
      Till he became
        Most poore: 5

      With Thee
      O let me rise,
    As larks, harmoniously,
  And sing this day Thy victories:
Then shall the fall further the flight in me.   10

My tender age in sorrow did beginne;
  And still with sicknesses and shame
    Thou didst so punish sinne,
      That I became
        Most thinne.   15

      With Thee
      Let me combine,
    And feel this day Thy victorie;
  For, if I imp my wing on Thine,
Affliction shall advance the flight in me.   20

Writing such a poem requires considerable craftsmanship. The poet must conceive of the poem's arrangement on the page as well as its theme and then find the words and the poetic structure necessary to carry out this plan. Herbert has managed to make the meaning of the lines themselves reflect the appearance of the poem. Where the lines reach their narrowest points, he describes a man who has constricted to become "Most poore" and "Most thinne." As the lines that follow expand, Herbert's idea of resurrection takes flight. Our awareness of the poem's shape helps us see the poem's ideas. It is no accident that the poem looks like wings, and as soon as we see these wings, we can look for corresponding winglike ideas in the poem.

Thomas Hardy's "The Convergence of the Twain" displays a similar correspondence between shape and theme. In each stanza his poem, written in response to the loss of the *Titanic*, suggests the shape of a ship and the shape of the iceberg. Hardy challenges us to meditate on the tragic bringing together of the two. Perhaps the poem's design also forcefully weights each stanza downward; the last line of each rests heavily at the bottom.

Thomas Hardy (1840–1928)

The Convergence of the Twain (1912)

Lines on the Loss of the Titanic

1
In a solitude of the sea
Deep from human vanity,
And the Pride of Life that planned her, stilly couches she.

2
Steel chambers, late the pyres
Of her salamandrine fires,   5
Cold currents third, and turn to rhythmic tidal lyres.

3
Over the mirrors meant
To glass the opulent
The sea-worm crawls—grotesque, slimed, dumb, indifferent.

4
Jewels in joy designed   10
To ravish the sensuous mind
Lie lightless, all their sparkles bleared and black and blind.

5
Dim moon-eyed fishes near
Gaze at the gilded gear
And query: "What does this vaingloriousness down here?"   15

6
Well: while was fashioning
This creature of cleaving wing,
The Immanent Will that stirs and urges everything

7

Prepared a sinister mate
For her—so gaily great—   20
A Shape of Ice, for the time far and dissociate.

8

And as the smart ship grew
In stature, grace, and hue,
In shadowy silent distance grew the Iceberg too.

9

Alien they seemed to be: 25
No mortal eye could see
The intimate welding of their later history,

10

Or sign that they were bent
By paths coincident
On being anon twin halves of one august event,   30

11

Till the Spinner of the Years
Said "Now!" And each one hears,
And consummation comes, and jars two hemispheres.

Such play with form and content provides an excellent exercise for a poet. For a reader, the design provides a concrete representation of an abstract idea. The shape provides a clear idea about what focus the poet feels is important. If we have trouble reading poems like "Easter Wings" or "The Convergence of the Twain," we can consult the shape to test interpretations we develop as we read.

TRADITIONAL STRUCTURES

Just as our awareness of the shape of the previous poems helps us read those poems for complementary details and themes, an awareness of traditional literary structures will help us understand how works hold together.

Extended narratives may build upon large units that help readers pause over and process complex actions. For example, a chapter in a novel (often both numbered and titled) offers readers a chance to break from the story and reflect back on what has unfolded, as well as project ahead to what may occur.

Short story writers may insert more subtle graphic signals. Note how Haruki Murakami's "UFO in Kushiro" (p. 671) employs a simple and common visual cue: changes of scene (from home to workplace and so on) are marked by an extra space between lines. In "A Rose for Emily" (p. 1513), William Faulkner employs a more emphatic signal. His story is divided into five numbered parts. The division by five in this case underscores the development of the story from initial exposition (establishment of place and character) through steps in Emily's life that lead to the ultimate revelation and resolution.

Faulkner's five-part short story might remind us of the division of a full-length play into five acts. The acts in a play can serve multiple functions. They often serve to help an audience appreciate the building and release of tension, as noted in Chapter 1, but the acts also function to allow physical changes in the set. Murakami can move us from Komura's home to Komura's workplace instantly; the extra space is all he offers us in preparation for the shift. But a dramatist must think in terms of **staging** such movements—of how the actors and the stage properties will interact within the physical constraints of the stage, of what needs to be moved on or off the stage as well as how quickly the necessary changes can be made. Dramatists can choose, of course, to keep sets very plain and put trust in an audience's imagination, but that is a choice.

Very short works, particularly short poems, often build upon highly specific and elaborate traditions. The **sonnet** is a fourteen-line poetic structure that has been a proving ground for poets for centuries. Fourteen lines are enough to convey and explore a single coherent idea in some detail, but much discipline is required. Each line must have the same number of syllables (ten), and the final word in each line must follow a specific rhyme scheme that underscores a clearly marked **stanzaic structure;** that is, the rhyme scheme groups lines in regular, definable verse paragraphs. As arbitrary as these defining characteristics might sound, the structure lends itself to a particular kind of tightly logical development and allows for some variation ("defining characteristics" are not "rules"). The sonnet form has proven to be, in the hands of expert poets, dynamic and forceful.

But we should approach sonnets with the main organizational types in mind. A consciousness of basic structuring principles will help us read and understand. The **Italian** or **Petrarchan sonnet** is divided into two parts: the **octave** (eight lines) and the **sestet** (six lines). The pattern of rhyme (see Chapter 6 for more on rhyme) that distinguishes the octave defines two **quatrains** (stanzas of four lines each). The sestet may be marked by various rhyme schemes. The **English** or **Shakespearean sonnet** organizes itself quite differently. Instead of an octave/sestet (eight/six) division, the English sonnet breaks into three quatrains (each with a rhyme scheme of its own) and a **couplet** (a rhymed pair of lines); we have then a twelve (four, four, four)/two division.

The structural differences between these two principal sonnet forms should not obscure the rhetorical or argumentative logic they share—a logic that makes each form coherent. An Italian sonnet raises a problem, asks a question, or establishes a subject in the octave. An English sonnet does the

Petrarchan or Italian Sonnet

Line number	End sound	Form	
1	A	**Quatrain 1:** verse paragraph of 4 lines, followed by	This octave (lines 1–8) establishes complication (problem, issue or question).
2	B		
3	B		
4	A		
5	A	**Quatrain 2:** verse paragraph of 4 lines	
6	B		
7	B		
8	A		

Turn away from/against complication established in octave occurs between lines 8 and 9.

Line number	End sound	Form	
9	C	**Sestet:** final 6 lines	**Resolution:** responds to complication
10	D		
11	E		
12	C		
13	D		
14	E		

Shakespearean Sonnet

Line number	End sound	Form	
1	A	**Quatrain 1:** verse paragraph of 4 lines, followed by	Three quatrains establish the complication (problem, issue, or question).
2	B		
3	A		
4	B		
5	C	**Quatrain 2:** verse paragraph of 4 lines, followed by	Each quatrain typically represents a variation upon or elaboration of the complication.
6	D		
7	C		
8	D		
9	E	**Quatrain 3:** verse paragraph of 4 lines	These quatrains generally employ iambic pentameter and are sometimes called **heroic quatrains.**
10	F		
11	E		
12	F		

Turn away from/against complication established in quatrains occurs between lines 12 and 13.

Line number	End sound	Form	
13	G	**Couplet:** 2 lines rhymed	**Resolution:** responds to complication
14	G		

Sonnet charts

same in the first twelve lines. The sonnet's opening section is often called the **complication**. In an Italian sonnet, the sestet responds to the problem, answers the question, or draws meaning from the subject established in the octave. The couplet in an English sonnet serves this same purpose. This second part of the sonnet's argumentative or rhetorical structure can be called the **resolution** (at least, if the particular poem allows for such a confident word). The brief transition space that gives us pause just between the complication and resolution is called the **turn**. Understanding an Italian sonnet or an English sonnet involves understanding the movement from the problem to the response. The following models represent the common stanzaic structures and signal the underlying argumentative logic of the sonnet (the letters along the left margin represent how the end rhymes are patterned).

Poets have melded aspects of the two main sonnet forms and experimented boldly with many different patterns of rhyme. The Italian sonnet and the English sonnet should not be understood as unbending or exclusive forms but as grids from which poets have worked. It's also useful to appreciate the different effects to which these principal forms lend themselves. Because the Italian sonnet allows space for a rather full response to the complication, it tends to achieve a meditative feel. The English sonnet, on the other hand, will often achieve in the compression of the couplet the effect of surprise, or even shock, as it turns suddenly on the complication. The couplet will also more easily allow a witty, playfully punning resolution.

Experiencing Literature through Form

Although the sonnet has a well-defined form, close reading of some great sonnets quickly reveals that great variety can be realized within the fourteen lines. Knowing the basic forms can be very helpful, partly because variations on a fixed form often signal something meaningful. Sometimes an author can underscore or redefine a message simply by breaking an established pattern. If a poem, for instance, has a steady rhyming pattern, we notice when the author breaks that pattern. Structural variations as well as structural consistency are part of a writer's resources. As you read the following three sonnets, identify patterns of rhyme and trace the argumentative logic those patterns imply. Also consider how the sonnet form in each case becomes part of the poem's meaning. In "Nuns Fret Not," William Wordsworth examines the constrictions of tradition and finds constriction liberating. In "I, Being Born a Woman and Distressed," Edna St. Vincent Millay uses the sonnet to critique gender assumptions that sonnets by males have long perpetuated (see, for example, the selection of love sonnets by William Shakespeare, p. 1084). Note in particular in the octave how the words grouped as A rhymes differ significantly from those of the B rhymes. That difference clarifies the problem or conflict Millay wants to establish. Finally, Robert Frost in "Design" uses the scale and tightness of his sonnet's construction to raise profound questions of scale and design in the universe.

William Wordsworth (1770–1850)

Nuns Fret Not (1807)

Nuns fret not at their convent's narrow room;
And hermits are contented with their cells;
And students with their pensive citadels;
Maids at the wheel, the weaver at his loom,
Sit blithe and happy; bees that soar for bloom,   5
High as the highest Peak of Furness-fells,
Will murmur by the hour in foxglove bells:
In truth the prison, unto which we doom
Ourselves, no prison is: and hence for me,
In sundry moods, 'twas pastime to be bound   10
Within the Sonnet's scanty plot of ground;
Pleased if some Souls (for such there needs must be)
Who have felt the weight of too much liberty,
Should find brief solace there, as I have found.

Edna St. Vincent Millay (1892–1950)

I, Being Born a Woman and Distressed (1932)

I, being born a woman and distressed
By all the needs and notions of my kind,
Am urged by your propinquity to find
Your person fair, and feel a certain zest
To feel your body's weight upon my breast: 5
So subtly is the fume of life designed,
To clarify the pulse and cloud the mind,
And leave me once again undone, possessed.
Think not for this, however, the poor treason
Of my stout blood against my staggering brain,   10
I shall remember you with love, or season
My scorn with pity,—let me make it plain:

I find this frenzy insufficient reason
For conversation when we meet again.

Robert Frost (1874–1963)

Design (1936)

I found a dimpled spider, fat and white,
On a white heal-all, holding up a moth
Like a white piece of rigid satin cloth—
Assorted characters of death and blight
Mixed ready to begin the morning right, 5
Like the ingredients of a witches' broth—
A snow-drop spider, a flower like a froth,
And dead wings carried like a paper kite.

What had that flower to do with being white,
The wayside blue and innocent heal-all? 10
What brought the kindred spider to that height,
Then steered the white moth thither in the night?
What but design of darkness to appall?—
If design govern in a thing so small.

Wordsworth explores the paradox of all structure. Does a confining structure have to be a prison? he asks. Is there some relief in "escaping" from the stress of living (and writing) in a world where one has "too much liberty"? Wordsworth suggests that there is. The sonnet form offers some comfort to the reader as well. We expect to hear rhymes at the end of each line, and they are there. This regularity helps us read. Because we are not "surprised" by the form, we can direct our attention to the content of a sonnet. We know something of the convention that this particular poem is joining, so we can pay closer attention to the use of words and to the poet's skill at placing these words within a predetermined form. We can also compare this particular example of the form to other sonnets that we might have read.

Making Connections

Robert Pinsky's "Lines in Any Order" (p. 4) is a perplexing poem that adopts the form of the sonnet. Explain how thinking of this poem in terms of the sonnet's essential structure helps you make sense of the seeming randomness of the lines. Could you argue that there is a turn before the final two lines? That the final two lines reflect back on the chaos of the first twelve lines?

The sonnet is the poetic form with perhaps the richest history, especially in the English language, but it is hardly the only form. In French verse, the **sestina**, for example, consists of six sestets (six-line stanzas) and three final lines. In this form, the final words in each line of the first sestet are repeated as the final words of each line in each of the next five sestets, but the order changes in each sestet according to a specific pattern. As you can see just from this one obscure example, lists of rules regarding poetic forms as well as the names of the forms can quickly feel intimidating; sometimes, the best approach is to simply attend closely to what a specific poem actually does. Look at each line of the poem. Look for rhyming patterns among the lines. Sometimes, a poem will be written in **blank verse**, a verse form without rhymes but with consistent rhythms, generally iambic pentameter, in each of its lines. Look for structural patterns within the poem. For example, the **villanelle** is certainly a complicated poetic structure. It's unlikely you will read enough villanelles to make memorizing defining characteristics of much value. So rather than review a list of the characteristics of the structure, read the most famous example of the type, "Do Not Go Gentle into That Good Night" by Dylan Thomas. As you look for the pattern here, pay attention to rhyming words, to repetitions, and to the number and groupings of lines.

Dylan Thomas (1914–1953)

Do Not Go Gentle into That Good Night (1952)

Do not go gentle into that good night,
Old age should burn and rave at close of day;
Rage, rage against the dying of the light.

Though wise men at their end know dark is right,
Because their words had forked no lightning they   5
Do not go gentle into that good night,

Good men, the last wave by, crying how bright
Their frail deeds might have danced in a green bay,
Rage, rage against the dying of the light.

Wild men who caught and sang the sun in flight,   10
And learn, too late, they grieved it on its way,
Do not go gentle into that good night,

Grave men, near death, who see with blinding sight
Blind eyes could blaze like meteors and be gay,
Rage, rage against the dying of the light.   15

And you, my father, there on the sad height,
Curse, bless, me now with your fierce tears, I pray.
Do not go gentle into that good night,
Rage, rage against the dying of the light.

If you are interested in writing poetry, this form provides an excellent challenge. The rigorous form requires thirteen words with the first rhyming sound (A) and six words with the second rhyming sound (B). The poet must work quite dexterously with words to convey any idea within such a constricted form. A less than expert poet will expend all creative energy on merely fitting words into the scheme; a less than expert reader will simply identify the scheme. A really accomplished poet will discover in the structure a form that accommodates a particular expression; a really accomplished reader will appreciate that melding of form and content. Thomas has chosen to use a strategy of repetition to fit the structure, but this strategy does more than that. He alternates the line "Rage, rage against the dying of the light" with the line "Do not go gentle into that good night" as the repeated **refrain** at the end of each stanza. Each time we see the same line again, it has acquired new meaning so that the repetition amplifies the original meaning. For instance, the third repetition of the "rage, rage" line takes on an added power because the other two lines speak of blindness. This loss of *sight* (the word that will rhyme with *light*) is an added incentive to "rage."

A Note to Student Writers: Complicating a Thesis

The argumentative logic that we've seen operating at the core of a sonnet is a highly compacted form of a common rhetorical ploy that critical writers often use. At the start of an essay, critical writers may establish an issue, a problem, a question. Then they turn to some striking assertion—a thesis—that responds to the issue/problem/question. The complication/turn/resolution that underlies sonnets is similar to the movement that characterizes introductory paragraphs in many critical essays. Consider the following paragraph from a student paper. Note how the writer quickly establishes a problem (action films are getting tiresome) and turns against the complication (however) in order to respond to the issue raised (action in this case is made meaningful):

In many action films, action overwhelms everything else. Lost amid the crashes, explosions, and shootings is any sense of character, coherence, or even purpose. Do we need movies to show us ever more buildings collapsing, cars colliding, trains overturning? Why do we need to see such extravagant destruction? Do we care anymore? It seems that as special effects get more special, movies get more ordinary. Steven Spielberg's *War of the Worlds* reminds us, however, that the dismal state of big-budget action films can't be blamed altogether on an excess of technical wizardry. Spielberg manages to make the action of his film integral to real and pressing fears. Violent action in this film echoes and comments upon the paranoia that has arisen in our post–9/11 world. ■

The poems that you have just read may provide still other valuable lessons for writers of analytical prose. Critical writers may learn from poets to make their essays coherent by carefully woven patterns of key words or phrases. In essays, transitions from one paragraph to another often serve to explicitly point back to the end of the previous paragraph as they move forward to a new point. Critical writers don't merely want to list insights; they want to show how insights connect and build one upon another. Look back over the section that you have just read in this book. Pay particular attention to the ends and beginnings of paragraphs. Note that the beginning of paragraphs often refers back to some important idea or word expressed in the paragraph just ended. The goal is to help the reader understand how everything fits together.

COHERENCE WITHOUT TRADITIONAL OR FIXED STRUCTURE

Achieving coherence is not merely a matter of poetic shape or form. There is nothing traditional in the form of the following poem by Philip Levine, yet there is clearly some sense of structure—some way the whole poem holds together and achieves force.

Philip Levine (1928–)

The Simple Truth (1995)

I bought a dollar and a half's worth of small red potatoes,
took them home, boiled them in their jackets
and ate them for dinner with a little butter and salt.
Then I walked through the dried fields

on the edge of town. In middle June the light   5
hung on in the dark furrows at my feet,
and in the mountain oaks overhead the birds
were gathering for the night, the jays and mockers
squawking back and forth, the finches still darting
into the dusty light. The woman who sold me   10
the potatoes was from Poland; she was someone
out of my childhood in a pink spangled sweater and sunglasses
praising the perfection of all her fruits and vegetables
at the road-side stand and urging me to taste
even the pale, raw sweet corn trucked all the way,   15
she swore, from New Jersey. "Eat, eat" she said,
"Even if you don't I'll say you did."
                              Some things
you know all your life. They are so simple and true
they must be said without elegance, meter and rhyme,
they must be laid on the table beside the salt shaker,   20
the glass of water, the absence of light gathering
in the shadows of picture frames, they must be
naked and alone, they must stand for themselves.
My friend Henri and I arrived at this together in 1965
before I went away, before he began to kill himself,   25
and the two of us to betray our love. Can you taste
what I'm saying? It is onions or potatoes, a pinch
of simple salt, the wealth of melting butter, it is obvious,
it stays in the back of your throat like a truth
you never uttered because the time was always wrong,   30
it stays there for the rest of your life, unspoken,
made of that dirt we call earth, the metal we call salt,
in a form we have no words for, and you live on it.

This poem is held together by the image of the potatoes. That image begins the poem, and the poet's ruminations about the potatoes take him home, back to the woman who sold them to him, and onto the idea that one might "taste" what he is saying. Notice that the potatoes begin the poem as actual objects that the poet boils, butters, and eats. By the end, the potatoes, with their butter and salt, become an image for an idea that "we have no words for," simple enough to stand, Levine says, outside meter and rhyme. Levine gives us a first stanza full of specific, concrete detail and a second in which those details help him express the more abstract feelings that remain largely unspoken. This progress, in which some specific object inspires a more general observation, is a common structuring device. Levine re-creates the seemingly random thought process that a person goes through, and as we think about the poem this way, we begin to realize how much structure Levine has added in order to render this otherwise anarchic process as a poem, simple in its profundity. Levine's poem reminds us that a simple truth about **free verse** is that "free" doesn't mean artless. The term merely indicates that the poem employs no regular meter or rhyme scheme.

What Levine does in "The Simple Truth" suggests one of the principal ways in which not only poems but stories, novels, plays, and films achieve coherence. Carefully managed **repetition** of a key element, image, or phrase can be extraordinarily valuable. The word **motif** is used sometimes to refer to a recurring element in literature or film. In this sense of the word, a play or novel that opens with a fresh-faced young country boy's decision to move to the city employs a motif; the audience may expect a story of innocence lost because so many stories have opened with just this scene. The word, however, is not used only for something that recurs *across* numerous texts; motif may be applied to an image, word, or action that is repeated *within* a single text. A motif provides structure; it may signal a theme or sustain a mood. This chapter opened with a discussion of how Nick Hornby employs notions of cataloguing as a cohering motif in his novel *High Fidelity*. In any lengthy work, there is a danger that the various parts will become disconnected. Novelists must certainly deal with that danger.°

Even the longest and most complex works may be grounded in a key image or phrase. For example, whiteness (as a blank, as a mystery, as both a kind of innocence and a kind of terrifying emptiness) dominates Herman Melville's *Moby-Dick*. In *Macbeth*, Shakespeare employs the motif of ill-fitting clothes; Macbeth murders the king to become king, but he finds that his new robes are too big for him. The repeated play upon ill-fitting clothes helps us pull together the whole of the action thematically: a person cannot become something greater than he or she is. In Francis Ford Coppola's *Godfather* films, the offhand invocation of

Making Connections

We can think back to Christopher Nolan's *Memento* in context of this discussion of coherence. We discussed that film in Chapter 1, to clarify how artists may ask us to reflect upon the meaning of plot as plot. But without a deliberate "playback" to a scene that just unfolded, without heavy repetition, an audience could easily become as confused as the main character. The main character's life is fragmented by his inability to remember from moment to moment, but our grasp of the film's meaning is strong. Nolan has figured out a way to help us understand a film that is largely about misunderstanding.

°And so, too, must critical writers attend to the dangers of disconnection. By referring back to Hornby here, we're trying to underscore our concern for coherence, but we're also trying to build the chapter as a coherent whole. In this case, we're circling back in order to tie together.

business ("just business"; "we're all businessmen here"; "smart business") in the context of the most brutal actions keeps readers alert to the suffering linked to our culture's competitive ethic of material success.

MODELING CRITICAL ANALYSIS: T. S. ELIOT, THE LOVE SONG OF J. ALFRED PRUFROCK

Especially difficult works of art may seem on the surface to be formless—to defy a reader's search for coherence. It's often true, however, that these difficult works employ a variety of devices to help the audience through. Consider again T. S. Eliot's "The Love Song of J. Alfred Prufrock," first introduced in our discussion of images (p. 653). Many readers find this poem, upon first reading, to be very confusing. Basic questions such as, "Where are we?" "What is happening?" "Who is involved?" become hard to answer. But if we stay alert, we'll find Eliot gives us considerable help.

We are guided through "The Love Song of J. Alfred Prufrock" by a single speaker, one who invites us on a walk through dingy streets and allows us in on thoughts concerning aging, death, failure, cowardice, and so on. We are first centered on a collection of images that make us feel the city's inhospitable environment. It is soon clear that Prufrock is very much a part of the whole environment—of the evening spread against the sky "Like a Patient etherized upon a table," of the lonely city of narrow "half-deserted streets." In fact, Eliot echoes the clinical simile of the city midway through the poem when Prufrock thinks of himself as a mere specimen of others' study: "And when I am formulated, sprawling on a pin, / When I am pinned and, wriggling on the wall." It's clear that the speaker is alien to the world he so timidly encounters. He is even disassociated from his own life.

Repetition functions powerfully to help us grasp the whole of a poem that seems to scorn transitions. We get a series of questions that aren't answered but that collectively make us feel the speaker's inability to take charge or to take risks ("Do I dare?"; "So how should I presume?"; "And how should I begin"; "Shall I part my hair behind?"). We also become aware of Prufrock's painfully self-conscious manner; the line "They will say: 'How his hair is growing thin!'" prepares us for the fear he explicitly registers in line 85, as well as the fear he has that the grandest assertions may meet flat dismissal: "That is not what I meant at all." And consider the following stanza:

> In the room the women come and go
> Talking of Michelangelo.

This stanza appears twice. Although these lines seem to come from nowhere, the repetition cues us in on their place in the whole. Prufrock is a man who hasn't found substance in life. He doesn't find relief from a cold and dreary city in social chat. His disconnection comes through profoundly in relation to women—women whose emptiness makes him intensely aware of his own hollow self. The airy nothingness of the repeated stanza plays out in other clearly painful sexual encounters. The women are mere "eyes" that "fix" him coolly in place or disembodied "arms" that do not caress. It can be of no surprise to us that he thinks it would have been better to be altogether removed from such an empty social life and from the burden of his own humanity: "I should have been a pair of ragged claws / Scuttling across the floors of silent seas."

Using Coherence to Focus Writing and Discussion

- What structuring devices appear in this work?
- How does the physical layout on the page signal this structure? Look first for line-level divisions. In poetry, see how long each line is. Is there some consistent pattern?
- Next, look for sectional divisions. What defines each of the sections? Are all sections of equal length?
- Can you label this structuring device with any of the terms that we have discussed?
- How does this structure help shape the impact of the work?

Anthology

RITUALS AND ROUTINES: STRUCTURING FOR COHERENCE

This chapter asks you to look at the specific structures and stylistic strategies that shape the literary works we read. These structures and strategies are not arbitrary. Writers work to make every choice meaningful. Of course, it's always possible for an author's strategy to backfire. In "To Cole, the Painter Departing for Europe," William Cullen Bryant addresses his friend, a painter of vast American landscapes who is about to leave for an extended stay in Europe. In Bryant's day, the early-nineteenth century, such travel could be seen as a kind of finishing school for artists. Bryant though is worried that such *finishing* goes against Cole's great artistic vision. The American landscape of the time is, after all, larger and wilder than the thoroughly "civilized" or peopled landscapes of Europe. The subject of America, Bryant believes, demands a freshness that breaks from old schools of thought. Yet Bryant chooses to cast his message as a sonnet—a traditional, fixed, and old-world form. Is the form in this case inconsistent with the message? Can he ask his friend to stay true to a more distinctly American and unfettered vision within the formal constraints of a sonnet?

The issues so clearly raised by Bryant's poem help us understand the critical issue that runs throughout this group: in every case, you should observe what holds a work together. But you always need to consider strategy in relation to goals. Authors don't write sonnets merely to write sonnets or repeat in order to repeat. Purpose governs pattern. In what way is a poetic form appropriate, a repetition effective, a design functional? Bryant's poem also helps us understand that the issue of artistic form is hardly separate from the forms that structure our everyday social life.

Phillis Wheatley's "On Being Brought from Africa to America" raises the form/function issue from a different angle. Wheatley was brought to America and sold as a slave at the age of six or seven. We cannot know now the exact circumstances of her earlier childhood, but we do know that "brought" is a strikingly soft word for what must have been the terrible hardship of her kidnapping, the Middle Passage to the New World, and her sale in Boston in 1761. Wheatley became a kind of favored slave—taught to read and write and spared of the hard physical work that her contemporaries endured. Her poem recounts the experience from the perspective of one "saved" by the truth she feels privileged to learn. Appropriately, Wheatley adopts a conventional form (rhymed couplets) and argumentative structure (similar to the sonnet's complication, turn, and resolution). Her final couplet firmly closes the lesson she wants to teach. But as adroit as Wheatley is in presenting her point, we're likely now to respond more powerfully to the way she has been thoroughly schooled in the values of a world that will never acknowledge her full humanity. To put it another way, we may see a profound and tragic irony in her skilled joining of form and message.

Many modern poets selectively repudiate traditional poetic structures; for Lawrence Ferlinghetti and Allen Ginsberg, contemporary life isn't realizable within regular patterns of rhyme, rhythm, or fixed poetic forms. But each of these poets strives to find a way to make coherent expressions of emotions and ideas out of the most chaotic materials. Ferlinghetti's "Constantly Risking Absurdity" displays in its shape the very precariousness he feels as a writer performing for an audience that may be watching mainly for failure. Ginsberg calls upon the spirit of Whitman and the open verse forms he worked with to counterpoint the sterile ordering of a commercialized America. Ferlinghetti and Ginsberg (important voices of what is termed the "beat generation" of poets in the 1950s and 1960s) feel the need to discover new ways to achieve artistic wholeness in an alienating social world.

Stories have their own ways to shape meaning and experience. Charles W. Chesnutt and John Updike put their protagonists in situations that demand choice. The patient establishing of character and social context is crucial to appreciating the weight of that choice. As you read these stories, notice how carefully Chesnutt and Updike set up the crisis. We learn much about the main characters and about the world those characters inhabit. Both characters ultimately act in ways that force them out of the rituals and routines within which they have been accustomed to operate. Each gains dignity from his willingness to take in the situation before him and to act from his own sense of right. These stories have a clearly dramatic quality. We can describe them in structural terms much as we would describe a full-length play or film. At the most basic level, they build tension and then release tension.

Jonathan Safran Foer presents a story that is structured around a quest rather than a choice. An unlikely group composed of three men and a dog find themselves together in a car looking for a past that none of them ever knew and that may no longer exist. The persistently broken English of the narrator reveals the routines of the characters and cultures that meet here, and the story itself does build and release tension with a dramatic quality that is structurally similar to the first two stories.

On the surface, David Ives's *Sure Thing* (a one-act, one-scene play) seems to consistently undercut itself before it establishes anything. Yet Ives manages to create, in miniature, structural elements that roughly correspond to what we expect from a five-act play. Although Ives's single scene is fragmented into many pieces, it keeps trying to complete itself. Bill's initial line, "Excuse me. Is this chair taken?" is an introduction to the whole action. It sets up an encounter that at least has the potential for romantic development. Betty's response in the first encounter, "Yes it is," cuts off that development. Ives has us circle back to the starting point and has the characters try again (something we all wish we could do sometimes). He is interested in the essentially endless possibilities that may unfold from the simplest beginning.

We quickly appreciate some of those possibilities. Once we get past the introduction, we feel action building toward a crisis point and eventually find a resolution. The soft bell stops us (and the characters) at every point in this familiar dramatic structure (introduction/exposition; complication/rising action; climax; falling action; resolution). We keep replaying things until Bill and Betty make it through. The happy ending may well be what we want from this short comedy, but Ives has made it plain that such endings depend on much good luck. We may fantasize about playing a conversation over, about controlling the direction of a given encounter, but we can't just ring a bell and start over. Ives uses interruptions strategically; after the final bell rings, the audience likely feels that *Sure Thing* offers more coherence and structure than we find in our everyday life.

FICTION

Charles W. Chesnutt (1858–1936)

Charles W. Chesnutt was born in Cleveland, Ohio, but his family moved to North Carolina after the end of the Civil War. Both his parents were of mixed race, but however "ambiguous" Chesnutt may have looked, white society had drawn an absolute, albeit thoroughly artificial, "color line" that in theory could not be crossed. As a result, Chesnutt grew up with and felt throughout his life the complicated, contradictory, thoroughly irrational racist culture that surrounded him. His opportunities were particularly limited in the South; after marrying, he decided to relocate to the North, eventually settling in Ohio. While working for a railroad and studying law, Chesnutt also found time to begin writing and in a relatively short time had established himself as a prominent writer of short stories. He published several novels as well, all of them concentrating in one way or another on racial problems in the United States. These novels, including *House Behind the Cedars* and *The Colonel's Dream*, were not financial successes, due in large part to the discomfort white readers in any region felt with Chesnutt's subject matter.

Wife of His Youth (1898)

I

Mr. Ryder was going to give a ball. There were several reasons why this was an opportune time for such an event.

Mr. Ryder might aptly be called the dean of the Blue Veins. The original Blue Veins were a little society of colored persons organized in a certain Northern city shortly after the war. Its purpose was to establish and maintain correct social standards among a people whose social condition presented almost unlimited room for improvement. By accident, combined perhaps with some natural affinity, the society consisted of individuals who were, generally speaking, more white than black. Some envious outsider made the suggestion that no one was eligible for membership who was not white enough to show blue veins. The suggestion was readily adopted by those who were not of the favored few, and since that time the society, though possessing a longer and more pretentious name, had been known far and wide as the "Blue Vein Society," and its members as the "Blue Veins."

The Blue Veins did not allow that any such requirement existed for admission to their circle, but, on the contrary, declared that character and culture were the only things considered; and that if most of their members were light-colored, it was because such persons, as a rule, had had better opportunities to qualify themselves for membership. Opinions differed, too, as to the usefulness of the society. There were those who had been known to assail it violently as a glaring example of the very prejudice from which the colored race had suffered most; and later, when such critics had succeeded in getting on the inside, they had been heard to maintain with zeal and earnestness that the society was a life-boat, an anchor, a bulwark and a shield,—a pillar of cloud by day and of fire by night, to guide their people through the social wilderness. Another alleged prerequisite for Blue Vein membership was that of free birth; and while there was really no such requirement, it is doubtless true that very few of the members would have been unable to meet it if there had been. If there were one or two of the older members who had come up from the South and from slavery, their history presented enough romantic circumstances to rob their servile origin of its grosser aspects.

While there were no such tests of eligibility, it is true that the Blue Veins had their notions on these subjects, and that not all of them were equally liberal in regard to the things they collectively disclaimed. Mr. Ryder was one of the most conservative. Though he had not been among the founders of the society, but had come in some years later, his genius for social leadership was such that he had speedily become its recognized adviser and head, the custodian of its standards, and the preserver of its traditions. He shaped its social policy, was active in providing for its entertainment, and when the interest fell off, as it sometimes did, he fanned the embers until they burst again into a cheerful flame.

There were still other reasons for his popularity. While he was not as white as some of the Blue Veins, his appearance was such as to confer distinction upon them. His features were of a refined type, his hair was almost straight; he was always neatly dressed; his manners were irreproachable, and his morals above suspicion. He had come to Groveland a young man, and obtaining employment in the office of a railroad company as messenger had in time worked himself up to the position of stationery clerk, having charge of the distribution of the office supplies for the whole company. Although the lack of early training had hindered the orderly development of a naturally fine mind, it had not prevented him from doing a great deal of reading or from forming decidedly literary tastes. Poetry was his passion. He could repeat whole pages of the great English poets; and if his pronunciation was sometimes faulty, his eye, his voice, his gestures, would respond to the changing sentiment with a precision that revealed a poetic soul, and disarm criticism. He was economical, and had saved money; he owned and occupied a very comfortable house on a respectable street. His residence was handsomely furnished, containing among other things a good library, especially rich in poetry, a piano, and some choice engravings. He generally shared his house with some young couple, who looked after his wants and were company for him; for Mr. Ryder was a single man. In the early days of his connection with the Blue Veins he had been regarded as quite a catch, and ladies and their mothers had maneuvred with much ingenuity to capture him. Not, however, until Mrs. Molly Dixon visited Groveland had any woman ever made him wish to change his condition to that of a married man.

Mrs. Dixon had come to Groveland from Washington in the spring, and before the summer was over she had won Mr. Ryder's heart. She possessed many attractive qualities. She was much younger than he; in fact, he was old enough to have been her father, though no one knew exactly how old he was. She was whiter than he, and better educated. She had moved in the best colored society of the country, at Washington, and had taught in the schools of that city. Such a superior person had been eagerly welcomed to the Blue Vein Society, and had taken a leading part in its activities. Mr. Ryder had at first been attracted by her charms of person, for she was very good looking and not over twenty-five; then by her refined manners and by the vivacity of her wit. Her husband had been a government clerk, and at his death had left a considerable life insurance. She was visiting friends in Groveland, and, finding the town and the people to her liking, had prolonged her stay indefinitely. She had not seemed displeased at Mr. Ryder's attentions, but on the contrary had given him every proper encouragement; indeed, a younger and less cautious man would long since have spoken. But he had made up his mind, and had only to determine the time when he would ask her to be his wife. He decided to give a ball in her honor, and at some time during the evening of the ball to offer her his heart and hand. He had no special fears about the outcome, but, with a little touch of romance, he wanted the surroundings to be in harmony with his own feelings when he should have received the answer he expected.

Mr. Ryder resolved that this ball should mark an epoch in the social history of Groveland. He knew, of course,—no one could know better,—the entertainments that had taken place in past years, and what must be done to surpass them. His ball must be worthy of the lady in whose honor it was to be given, and must, by the quality of its guests, set an example for the future. He had observed of late a growing liberality, almost a laxity, in social matters, even among members of his own set, and had several times been forced to meet in a social way persons whose complexions and callings in life were hardly up to the standard which he considered proper for the society to maintain. He had a theory of his own.

"I have no race prejudice," he would say, "but we people of mixed blood are ground between the upper and the nether millstone. Our fate lies between absorption by the white race and extinction in the black. The one doesn't want us yet, but may take us in time. The other would welcome us, but it would be for us a backward step. 'With malice towards none, with charity for all,' we must do the best we can for ourselves and those who are to follow us. Self-preservation is the first law of nature."

His ball would serve by its exclusiveness to counteract leveling tenden-cies, and his marriage with Mrs. Dixon would help to further the upward process of absorption he had been wishing and waiting for.

II

The ball was to take place on Friday night. The house had been put in order, the carpets covered with canvas, the halls and stairs decorated with palms and potted plants; and in the afternoon Mr. Ryder sat on his front porch, which the shade of a vine running up over a wire netting made a cool and pleasant lounging-place. He expected to respond to the toast "The Ladies," at the supper, and from a volume of Tennyson—his favorite poet—was fortifying himself with apt quotations. The volume was open at "A Dream of Fair Women." His eyes fell on these lines, and he read them aloud to judge better of their effect:—

> "At length I saw a lady within call.
> Stiller than chisell'd marble, standing there;
> A daughter of the gods, divinely tall, And most divinely fair."

He marked the verse, and turning the page read the stanza beginning,—

> O sweet pale Margaret,
> O rare pale Margaret.

He weighed the passage a moment, and decided that it would not do. Mrs. Dixon was the palest lady he expected at the ball, and she was of a rather ruddy complexion, and of lively disposition and buxom build. So he ran over the leaves until his eye rested on the description of Queen Guinevere:—

> She seem'd a part of joyous Spring:
> A gown of grass-green silk she wore,
> Buckled with golden clasps before;
> A light-green tuft of plumes she bore
> Closed in a golden ring.
> She look'd so lovely, as she sway'd
> The rein with dainty finger-tips,
> A man had given all other bliss,
> And all his worldly worth for this,
> To waste his whole heart in one kiss
> Upon her perfect lips.

As Mr. Ryder murmured these words audibly, with an appreciative thrill, he heard the latch of his gate click, and a light footfall sounding on the steps. He turned his head, and saw a woman standing before the door.

She was a little woman, not five feet tall, and proportioned to her height. Although she stood erect, and looked around her with very bright and restless eyes, she seemed quite old; for her face was crossed and recrossed with a hundred wrinkles, and around the edges of her bonnet could be seen protruding here and there a tuft of short gray wool. She wore a blue calico gown of ancient cut, a little red shawl fastened around her shoulders with an old-fashioned brass brooch, and a large bonnet profusely ornamented with faded red and yellow artificial flowers. And she was very black—so black that her toothless gums, revealed when she opened her mouth to speak, were not red, but blue. She looked like a bit of the old plantation life, summoned up from the past by the wave of a magician's wand, as the poet's fancy had called into being the gracious shapes of which Mr. Ryder had just been reading.

He rose from his chair and came over to where she stood.

"Good-afternoon, madam," he said.

"Good-evenin', suh," she answered, ducking suddenly with a quaint curtsy. Her voice was shrill and piping, but softened somewhat by age. "Is dis yere whar Mistuh Ryduh lib, suh?" she asked, looking around her doubtfully, and glancing into the open windows, through which some of the preparations for the evening were visible.

"Yes," he replied, with an air of kindly patronage, unconsciously flattered by her manner, "I am Mr. Ryder. Did you want to see me?"

"Yas, suh, ef I ain't 'sturbin' of you too much."

"Not at all. Have a seat over here behind the vine, where it is cool. What can I do for you?"

"'Scuse me, suh," she continued, when she had sat down on the edge of a chair, "'scuse me, suh, I's lookin' for my husban'. I heerd you wuz a big man an' had libbed heah a long time, an' I 'lowed you wouldn't min' ef I'd come roun' an' ax you ef you'd eber heerd of a merlatter man by de name er Sam Taylor 'quirin' roun' in de chu'ches ermongs' de people fer his wife 'Liza Jane?"

Mr. Ryder seemed to think for a moment.

"There used to be many such cases right after the war," he said, "but it has been so long that I have forgotten them. There are very few now. But tell me your story, and it may refresh my memory."

She sat back farther in her chair so as to be more comfortable, and folded her withered hands in her lap.

"My name's 'Liza," she began, "'Liza Jane. Wen I wuz young I us'ter b'long ter Marse Bob Smif, down in old Missourn. I wuz bawn down dere. W'en I wuz a gal I wuz married ter a man named Jim. But Jim died, an'

15

20

after dat I married a merlatter man named Sam Taylor. Sam wuz free-bawn, but his mammy and daddy died, an' de w'ite folks 'prenticed him ter my marster fer ter work fer 'im 'tel he wuz growed up. Sam worked in de fiel', an' I wuz de cook. One day Ma'y Ann, ole miss's maid, come rushin' out ter de kitchen, an' says she, 'Liza Jane, ole marse gwine sell yo' Sam down de ribber.'

"'Go way f'm yere,' says I; 'my husban's free!'

"'Don' make no diff 'ence. I heerd ole marse tell ole miss he wuz gwine take yo' Sam 'way wid 'im ter-morrow, fer he needed money, an' he knowed whar he could git a t'ousan' dollars fer Sam an' no questions axed.'

"W'en Sam come home f'm de fiel' dat night, I tole him 'bout ole marse gwine steal 'im, an' Sam run erway. His time wuz mos' up, an' he swo' dat w'en he wuz twenty-one he would come back an' he'p me run erway, er else save up de money ter buy my freedom. An' I know he'd 'a' done it, fer he thought a heap er me, Sam did. But w'en he come back he didn' fin' me, fer I wuzn' dere. Ole marse had heerd dat I warned Sam, so he had me whip' an' sol' down de ribber.

"Den de wah broke out, an' w'en it wuz ober de cullud folks wuz scattered. I went back ter de ole home; but Sam wuzn' dere, an' I couldn' l'arn nuffin' 'bout 'im. But I knowed he'd be'n dere to look fer me an' hadn' foun' me, an' had gone erway ter hunt fer me.

"I's be'n lookin' fer 'im eber sence," she added simply, as though twenty-five years were but a couple of weeks, "an' I knows he's be'n lookin' fer me. Fer he sot a heap er sto' by me, Sam did, an' I know he's be'n huntin' fer me all dese years,—'less'n he's be'n sick er sump'n, so he couldn' work, er out'n his head, so he couldn' 'member his promise. I went back down de ribber, fer I 'lowed he'd gone down dere lookin' fer me. I's be'n ter Noo Orleens, an' Atlanty, an' Charleston, an' Richmon'; an' w'en I'd be'n all ober de Souf I come ter de Norf. Fer I knows I'll fin' 'im some er dese days," she added softly, "er he'll fin' me, an' den we'll bofe be as happy in freedom as we wuz in de ole days befo' de wah." A smile stole over her withered countenance as she paused a moment, and her bright eyes softened into a far-away look.

This was the substance of the old woman's story. She had wandered a little here and there. Mr. Ryder was looking at her curiously when she finished.

"How have you lived all these years?" he asked.

"Cookin', suh. I's a good cook. Does you know anybody w'at needs a good cook, suh? I's stoppin' wid a cullud fam'ly roun' de corner yonder 'tel I kin git a place."

"Do you really expect to find your husband? He may be dead long ago."

She shook her head emphatically. "Oh no, he ain' dead. De signs an' de tokens tells me. I dremp three nights runnin' on'y dis las' week dat I foun' him."

"He may have married another woman. Your slave marriage would not have prevented him, for you never lived with him after the war, and without that your marriage doesn't count."

"Wouldn' make no diff'ence wid Sam. He wouldn' marry no yuther 'ooman 'tel he foun' out 'bout me. I knows it," she added. "Sump'n's be'n tellin' me all dese years dat I's gwine fin' Sam 'fo I dies." 35

"Perhaps he's outgrown you, and climbed up in the world where he wouldn't care to have you find him."

"No, indeed, suh," she replied, "Sam ain' dat kin' er man. He wuz good ter me, Sam wuz, but he wuzn' much good ter nobody e'se, fer he wuz one er de triflin'es' han's on de plantation. I 'spec's ter haf ter suppo't 'im w'en I fin' 'im, fer he nebber would work 'less'n he had ter. But den he wuz free, an' he didn' git no pay fer his work, an' I don' blame 'im much. Mebbe he's done better sence he run erway, but I ain' 'spectin' much."

"You may have passed him on the street a hundred times during the twenty-five years, and not have known him; time works great changes."

She smiled incredulously. "I'd know 'im 'mongs' a hund'ed men. Fer dey wuzn' no yuther merlatter man like my man Sam, an' I couldn' be mistook. I's toted his picture roun' wid me twenty-five years."

"May I see it?" asked Mr. Ryder. "It might help me to remember whether I have seen the original." 40

As she drew a small parcel from her bosom, he saw that it was fastened to a string that went around her neck. Removing several wrappers, she brought to light an old-fashioned daguerreotype in a black case. He looked long and intently at the portrait. It was faded with time, but the features were still distinct, and it was easy to see what manner of man it had represented.

He closed the case, and with a slow movement handed it back to her.

"I don't know of any man in town who goes by that name," he said, "nor have I heard of any one making such inquiries. But if you will leave me your address, I will give the matter some attention, and if I find out anything I will let you know."

She gave him the number of a house in the neighborhood, and went away, after thanking him warmly.

He wrote down the address on the flyleaf of the volume of Tennyson, and, when she had gone, rose to his feet and stood looking after her curiously. As she walked down the street with mincing step, he saw several persons whom she passed turn and look back at her with a smile of kindly amusement. When she had turned the corner, he went upstairs to his bedroom, and stood for a long time before the mirror of his dressing-case, gazing thoughtfully at the reflection of his own face. 45

III

At eight o'clock the ballroom was a blaze of light and the guests had begun to assemble; for there was a literary programme and some routine business of the society to be gone through with before the dancing. A black servant in evening dress waited at the door and directed the guests to the dressing-rooms.

The occasion was long memorable among the colored people of the city; not alone for the dress and display, but for the high average of intelligence and culture that distinguished the gathering as a whole. There were a number of school-teachers, several young doctors, three or four lawyers, some professional singers, an editor, a lieutenant in the United States army spending his furlough in the city, and others in various polite callings; these were colored, though most of them would not have attracted even a casual glance because of any marked difference from white people. Most of the ladies were in evening costume, and dress coats and dancing-pumps were the rule among the men. A band of string music, stationed in an alcove behind a row of palms, played popular airs while the guests were gathering.

The dancing began at half past nine. At eleven o'clock supper was served. Mr. Ryder had left the ballroom some little time before the intermission, but reappeared at the supper-table. The spread was worthy of the occasion, and the guests did full justice to it. When the coffee had been served, the toastmaster, Mr. Solomon Sadler, rapped for order. He made a brief introductory speech, complimenting host and guests, and then presented in their order the toasts of the evening. They were responded to with a very fair display of after-dinner wit.

"The last toast," said the toast-master, when he reached the end of the list, "is one which must appeal to us all. There is no one of us of the sterner sex who is not at some time dependent upon woman,—in infancy for protection, in manhood for companionship, in old age for care and comforting. Our good host has been trying to live alone, but the fair faces I see around me to-night prove that he too is largely dependent upon the gentler sex for most that makes life worth living,—the society and love of friends,—and rumor is at fault if he does not soon yield entire subjection to one of them. Mr. Ryder will now respond to the toast,—The Ladies."

There was a pensive look in Mr. Ryder's eyes as he took the floor and adjusted his eyeglasses. He began by speaking of woman as the gift of Heaven to man, and after some general observations on the relations of the sexes he said: "But perhaps the quality which most distinguishes woman is her fidelity and devotion to those she loves. History is full of examples, but has recorded none more striking than one which only to-day came under my notice."

He then related, simply but effectively, the story told by his visitor of the afternoon. He told it in the same soft dialect, which came readily to his lips, while the company listened attentively and sympathetically. For the story had awakened a responsive thrill in many hearts. There were some present who had seen, and others who had heard their fathers and grandfathers tell, the wrongs and sufferings of this past generation, and all of them still felt, in their darker moments, the shadow hanging over them. Mr. Ryder went on:—

"Such devotion and such confidence are rare even among women. There are many who would have searched a year, some who would have waited five years, a few who might have hoped ten years; but for twenty-five years this woman has retained her affection for and her faith in a man she has not seen or heard of in all that time.

"She came to me to-day in the hope that I might be able to help her find this long-lost husband. And when she was gone I gave my fancy rein, and imagined a case I will put to you.

"Suppose that this husband, soon after his escape, had learned that his wife had been sold away, and that such inquiries as he could make brought no information of her whereabouts. Suppose that he was young, and she much older than he; that he was light, and she was black; that their marriage was a slave marriage, and legally binding only if they chose to make it so after the war. Suppose, too, that he made his way to the North, as some of us have done, and there, where he had larger opportunities, had improved them, and had in the course of all these years grown to be as different from the ignorant boy who ran away from fear of slavery as the day is from the night. Suppose, even, that he had qualified himself, by industry, by thrift, and by study, to win the friendship and be considered worthy the society of such people as these I see around me to-night, gracing my board and filling my heart with gladness; for I am old enough to remember the day when such a gathering would not have been possible in this land. Suppose, too, that, as the years went by, this man's memory of the past grew more and more indistinct, until at last it was rarely, except in his dreams, that any image of this bygone period rose before his mind. And then suppose that accident should bring to his knowledge the fact that the wife of his youth, the wife he had left behind him,—not one who had walked by his side and kept pace with him in his upward struggle, but one upon whom advancing years and a laborious life had set their mark,—was alive and seeking him, but that he was absolutely safe from recognition or discovery, unless he chose to reveal himself. My friends, what would the man do? I will suppose that he was one who loved honor, and tried to deal justly with all men. I will even carry the case further, and suppose that perhaps he had set his heart upon another, whom he had hoped to call his own. What would he do, or rather what ought he to do, in such a crisis of a lifetime?

"It seemed to me that he might hesitate, and I imagined that I was an old friend, a near friend, and that he had come to me for advice; and I argued the case with him. I tried to discuss it impartially. After we had looked upon the matter from every point of view, I said to him, in words that we all know: 55

'This above all: to thine own self be true,
And it must follow, as the night the day,
Thou canst not then be false to any man.'

"Then, finally, I put the question to him, 'Shall you acknowledge her?'"

"And now, ladies and gentlemen, friends and companions, I ask you, what should he have done?"

There was something in Mr. Ryder's voice that stirred the hearts of those who sat around him. It suggested more than mere sympathy with an imaginary situation; it seemed rather in the nature of a personal appeal. It was observed, too, that his look rested more especially upon Mrs. Dixon, with a mingled expression of renunciation and inquiry.

She had listened, with parted lips and streaming eyes. She was the first to speak: "He should have acknowledged her."

"Yes," they all echoed, "he should have acknowledged her."

"My friends and companions," responded Mr. Ryder, "I thank you, one and all. It is the answer I expected, for I knew your hearts."

He turned and walked toward the closed door of an adjoining room, while every eye followed him in wondering curiosity. He came back in a moment, leading by the hand his visitor of the afternoon, who stood startled and trembling at the sudden plunge into this scene of brilliant gayety. She was neatly dressed in gray, and wore the white cap of an elderly woman.

"Ladies and gentlemen," he said, "this is the woman, and I am the man, whose story I have told you. Permit me to introduce to you the wife of my youth." ∎

- Locate and define the divisions within this story. How do they reflect the social divisions that the story describes?
- How does the form of the poetry that he reads constrain Mr. Ryder?
- How does the structure of the story impact our reading of the traditions and social structures that he describes?
- The central event of the ball allows Mr. Ryder to use a public moment to work out his private standards. How does the pressure of public opinion shape his actions and our response to those actions?

John Updike (1932–)

John Updike was born in Shillington, Pennsylvania. He attended Harvard on a scholarship and, while there, edited the *Harvard Lampoon*. Soon after graduating he began writing for *The New Yorker*, the publication that also published his first works of short fiction. In 1957, Updike moved with his family to Ipswich, Massachusetts, where he devoted himself full-time to writing. He has since become one of America's most prominent men of letters, producing novels, short stories, poems, essays, and reviews. He has received several Pulitzer Prizes and National Book Awards, and his novels have achieved great commercial success.

A&P (1961)

In walks these three girls in nothing but bathing suits. I'm in the third checkout slot, with my back to the door, so I don't see them until they're over by the bread. The one that caught my eye first was the one in the plaid green two-piece. She was a chunky kid, with a good tan and a sweet broad soft-looking can with those two crescents of white just under it, where the sun never seems to hit, at the top of the backs of her legs. I stood there with my hand on a box of HiHo crackers trying to remember if I rang it up or not. I ring it up again and the customer starts giving me hell. She's one of these cash-register-watchers, a witch about fifty with rouge on her cheekbones and no eyebrows, and I know it made her day to trip me up. She'd been watching cash registers for fifty years and probably never seen a mistake before.

By the time I got her feathers smoothed and her goodies into a bag— she gives me a little snort in passing, if she'd been born at the right time they would have burned her over in Salem—by the time I get her on her way the girls had circled around the bread and were coming back, without a pushcart, back my way along the counters, in the aisle between the check-outs and the Special bins. They didn't even have shoes on. There was this chunky one, with the two-piece—it was bright green and the seams on the bra were still sharp and her belly was still pretty pale so I guessed she just got it (the suit)—there was this one, with one of those chubby berry-faces, the lips all bunched together under her nose, this one, and a tall one, with black hair that hadn't quite frizzed right, and one of these sunburns right across under the eyes, and a chin that was too long—you know, the kind of girl other girls think is very "striking" and "attractive" but never quite makes it, as they very well know, which is why they like her so much—and then the third one, that wasn't quite so tall. She was the queen. She kind of led them, the other two peeking around and making their shoulders round. She didn't look around, not this queen, she just walked straight on slowly, on these long white prima-donna legs. She came down a little hard on her heels, as if she didn't walk in her bare feet that much, putting down her heels and then letting the weight move along to her toes as if she was test-ing the floor with every step, putting a little deliberate extra action into it. You never know for sure how girls' minds work (do you really think it's a mind in there or just a little buzz like a bee in a glass jar?) but you got the idea she had talked the other two into coming in here with her, and now she was showing them how to do it, walk slow and hold yourself straight.

She had on a kind of dirty-pink—beige maybe, I don't know—bathing suit with a little nubble all over it and, what got me, the straps were down.

They were off her shoulders looped loose around the cool tops of her arms, and I guess as a result the suit had slipped a little on her, so all around the top of the cloth there was this shining rim. If it hadn't been there you wouldn't have known there could have been anything whiter than those shoulders. With the straps pushed off, there was nothing between the top of the suit and the top of her head except just *her*, this clean bare plane of the top of her chest down from the shoulder bones like a dented sheet of metal tilted in the light. I mean, it was more than pretty.

She had sort of oaky hair that the sun and salt had bleached, done up in a bun that was unraveling, and a kind of prim face. Walking into the A & P with your straps down, I suppose it's the only kind of face you *can* have. She held her head so high her neck, coming up out of those white shoulders, looked kind of stretched, but I didn't mind. The longer her neck was, the more of her there was.

She must have felt in the corner of her eye me and over my shoulder Stokesie in the second slot watching, but she didn't tip. Not this queen. She kept her eyes moving across the racks, and stopped, and turned so slow it made my stomach rub the inside of my apron, and buzzed to the other two, who kind of huddled against her for relief, and then they all three of them went up the cat-and-dog-food-breakfast-cereal-macaroni-rice-raisins-season-ings-spreads-spaghetti-soft-drinks-crackers-and-cookies aisle. From the third slot I look straight up this aisle to the meat counter, and I watched them all the way. The fat one with the tan sort of fumbled with the cookies, but on second thought she put the package back. The sheep pushing their carts down the aisle—the girls were walking against the usual traffic (not that we have one-way signs or anything)—were pretty hilarious. You could see them, when Queenie's white shoulders dawned on them, kind of jerk, or hop, or hiccup, but their eyes snapped back to their own baskets and on they pushed. I bet you could set off dynamite in an A & P and the people would by and large keep reaching and checking oatmeal off their lists and mutter-ing "Let me see, there was a third thing, began with A, asparagus, no, ah, yes, applesauce!" or whatever it is they do mutter. But there was no doubt, this jiggled them. A few houseslaves in pin curlers even looked around after pushing their carts past to make sure what they had seen was correct.

You know, it's one thing to have a girl in a bathing suit down on the beach, where what with the glare nobody can look at each other much any-way, and another thing in the cool of the A & P, under the fluorescent lights, against all those stacked packages, with her feet paddling along naked over our checkerboard green-and-cream rubber-tile floor.

"Oh Daddy," Stokesie said beside me. "I feel so faint."

"Darling," I said. "Hold me tight." Stokesie's married, with two babies chalked up on his fuselage already, but as far as I can tell that's the only dif-ference. He's twenty-two, and I was nineteen this April.

"Is it done?" he asks, the responsible married man finding his voice. I forgot to say he thinks he's going to be manager some sunny day, maybe in 1990 when it's called the Great Alexandrov and Petrooshki Tea Company or something.

What he meant was, our town is five miles from a beach, with a big   10
summer colony out on the Point, but we're right in the middle of town, and the women generally put on a shirt or shorts or something before they get out of the car into the street. And anyway these are usually women with six children and varicose veins mapping their legs and nobody, including them, could care less. As I say, we're right in the middle of town, and if you stand at our front doors you can see two banks and the Congregational church and the newspaper store and three real-estate offices and about twenty-seven old freeloaders tearing up Central Street because the sewer broke again. It's not as if we're on the Cape, we're north of Boston and there's people in this town haven't seen the ocean for twenty years.

The girls had reached the meat counter and were asking McMahon something. He pointed, they pointed, and they shuffled out of sight behind a pyramid of Diet Delight peaches. All that was left for us to see was old McMahon patting his mouth and looking after them sizing up their joints. Poor kids, I began to feel sorry for them, they couldn't help it.

Now here comes the sad part of the story, at least my family says it's sad, but I don't think it's so sad myself. The store's pretty empty, it being Thursday afternoon, so there was nothing much to do except lean on the register and wait for the girls to show up again. The whole store was like a pinball machine and I didn't know which tunnel they'd come out of. After a while they come around out of the far aisle, around the light bulbs, records at discount of the Caribbean Six or Tony Martin Sings or some such gunk you wonder they waste the wax on, sixpacks of candy bars, and plastic toys done up in cellophane that fall apart when a kid looks at them anyway. Around they come, Queenie still leading the way, and holding a little gray jar in her hands. Slots Three through Seven are unmanned and I could see her wondering between Stokes and me, but Stokesie with his usual luck draws an old party in baggy gray pants who stumbles up with four giant cans of pineapple juice (what do these bums *do* with all that pineapple juice? I've often asked myself). So the girls come to me. Queenie puts down the jar and I take it into my fingers icy cold. Kingfish Fancy Herring Snacks in Pure Sour Cream: 49¢. Now her hands are empty, not a ring or a bracelet, bare as God made them, and I wonder where the money's coming from. Still with that prim look she lifts a folded dollar bill out of the hollow at the center of her nubbled pink top. The jar went heavy in my hand. Really, I thought that was so cute.

Then everybody's luck begins to run out. Lengel comes in from haggling with a truck full of cabbages on the lot and is about to scuttle into that door marked MANAGER behind which he hides all day when the girls touch his eye. Lengel's pretty dreary, teaches Sunday school and the rest, but he doesn't miss that much. He comes over and says, "Girls, this isn't the beach."

Queenie blushes, though maybe it's just a brush of sunburn I was noticing for the first time, now that she was so close. "My mother asked me to pick up a jar of herring snacks." Her voice kind of startled me, the way voices do when you see the people first, coming out so flat and dumb yet kind of tony, too, the way it ticked over "pick up" and "snacks." All of a sudden I slid right down her voice into the living room. Her father and the other men were standing around in ice-cream coats and bow ties and the women were in sandals picking up herring snacks on toothpicks off a big glass plate and they were all holding drinks the color of water with olives and sprigs of mint in them. When my parents have somebody over they get lemonade and if it's a real racy affair Schlitz in tall glasses with "They'll Do It Every Time" cartoons stenciled on.

"That's all right," Lengel said. "But this isn't the beach." His repeating this struck me as funny, as if it had just occurred to him, and he had been thinking all these years the A & P was a great big dune and he was the head lifeguard. He didn't like my smiling—as I say he doesn't miss much—but he concentrates on giving the girls that sad Sunday-school-superintendent stare.

Queenie's blush is no sunburn now, and the plump one in plaid, that I liked better from the back—a really sweet can—pipes up, "We weren't doing any shopping. We just came in for the one thing."

"That makes no difference," Lengel tells her, and I could see from the way his eyes went that he hadn't noticed she was wearing a two-piece before. "We want you decently dressed when you come in here."

"We *are* decent," Queenie says suddenly, her lower lip pushing, getting sore now that she remembers her place, a place from which the crowd that runs the A & P must look pretty crummy. Fancy Herring Snacks flashed in her very blue eyes.

"Girls, I don't want to argue with you. After this come in here with your shoulders covered. It's our policy." He turns his back. That's policy for you. Policy is what the kingpins want. What the others want is juvenile delinquency.

All this while, the customers had been showing up with their carts but, you know, sheep, seeing a scene, they had all bunched up on Stokesie, who shook open a paper bag as gently as peeling a peach, not wanting to miss a word. I could feel in the silence everybody getting nervous, most of all Lengel, who asks me, "Sammy, have you rung up their purchase?"

I thought and said "No" but it wasn't about that I was thinking. I go through the punches, 4, 9, GROC. TOT—it's more complicated than you think, and after you do it often enough, it begins to make a little song, that you hear words to, in my case "Hello (*bing*) there, you (*gung*) hap-py *pee*-pul (*splat*)!"—the *splat* being the drawer flying out. I uncrease the bill, tenderly as you may imagine, it just having come from between the two smoothest scoops of vanilla I had ever known were there, and pass a half and a penny into her narrow pink palm, and nestle the herrings in a bag and twist its neck and hand it over, all the time thinking.

The girls, and who'd blame them, are in a hurry to get out, so I say "I quit" to Lengel quick enough for them to hear, hoping they'll stop and watch me, their unsuspected hero. They keep right on going, into the electric eye; the door flies open and they flicker across the lot to their car, Queenie and Plaid and Big Tall Goony-Goony (not that as raw material she was so bad), leaving me with Lengel and a kink in his eyebrow.

"Did you say something, Sammy?"

"I said I quit."

"I thought you did."   25

"You didn't have to embarrass them."

"It was they who were embarrassing us."

I started to say something that came out "Fiddle-de-doo." It's a saying of my grandmother's, and I know she would have been pleased.

"I don't think you know what you're saying," Lengel said.

"I know you don't," I said. "But I do." I pull the bow at the back of my   30
apron and start shrugging it off my shoulders. A couple customers that had been heading for my slot begin to knock against each other, like scared pigs in a chute.

Lengel sighs and begins to look very patient and old and gray. He's been a friend of my parents for years. "Sammy, you don't want to do this to your Mom and Dad," he tells me. It's true, I don't. But it seems to me that once you begin a gesture it's fatal not to go through with it. I fold the apron, "Sammy" stitched in red on the pocket, and put it on the counter, and drop the bow tie on top of it. The bow tie is theirs, if you've ever wondered. "You'll feel this for the rest of your life," Lengel says, and I know that's true, too, but remembering how he made the pretty girl blush makes me so scrunchy inside I punch the No Sale tab and the machine whirs "peepul" and the drawer splats out. One advantage to this scene taking place in summer, I can follow this up with a clean exit, there's no fumbling around getting your coat and galoshes, I just saunter into the electric eye in my white shirt that my mother ironed the night before, and the door heaves itself open, and outside the sunshine is skating around on the asphalt.

I look around for my girls, but they're gone, of course. There wasn't anybody but some young married screaming with her children about some candy they didn't get by the door of a powder-blue Falcon station wagon. Looking back in the big windows, over the bags of peat moss and aluminum lawn furniture stacked on the pavement, I could see Lengel in my place in the slot, checking the sheep through. His face was dark gray and his back stiff, as if he'd just had an injection of iron, and my stomach kind of fell as I felt how hard the world was going to be to me hereafter. ■

■ The title of this story refers to a chain of supermarkets on the East Coast of the United States. How do we learn about that setting? How does that setting govern the consciousness of the narrator?

■ Describe the routine that is revealed within this story. To whom is this routine revealed?

■ What tensions do we discover among the characters?

■ Where is the story divided? What is the difference between the two sections of the story?

■ How do they fit together?

■ Compare the final paragraph to the opening paragraph of the story. How do these two paragraphs fit together? How do they both illustrate the same narrative structure?

Jonathan Safran Foer (1977–)

Jonathan Safran Foer was born in Washington, D.C. He attended Princeton University, where he received a number of writing awards. Though he has worked various odd jobs—receptionist, archivist, morgue assistant—his rise to prominence has been remarkably quick, and his short fiction and excerpts from novels have appeared in many of the major U.S. periodicals and journals. His first novel, *Everything Is Illuminated*, appeared in 2002; and his second, *Extremely Loud and Incredibly Close*, centering around the terrorist attacks of 9/11, in 2005. Foer's work employs many of the techniques of literary modernism and post-modernism to examine issues of identity and meaning.

The Very Rigid Search (2001)

My legal name is Alexander Perchov. But all of my many friends dub me Alex, because that is a more flaccid-to-utter version of my legal name. My mother dubs me Alexi-stop-spleening-me!, because I am always spleening her. My father used to dub me Shapka, for the fur hat I would don even in the summer month. He stopped dubbing me that because I ordered him to stop dubbing me that. It sounded boyish to me, and I have always thought of myself as very potent and generative. As for me, I was sired in 1977, the same year as Jonathan Safran Foer, who is the hero of this story. In truth, my life has been very ordinary. I dig American movies. I dig Negroes, particularly Michael Jackson. I dig to disseminate very much currency at famous discothèques in Odessa. Lamborghini Countaches are excellent, and so are cappuccinos. Many girls want to be carnal with me in many good arrangements, notwithstanding the Inebriated Kangaroo, the Gorgky Tickle, and the Unyielding Zoo Keeper. But, nonetheless, it is evident that my life is ordinary. That is why I was so effervescent to go to Lutsk and translate for Jonathan Safran Foer. It would be unordinary.

My mother is a humble woman. She toils at a small café one hour distant from our home. She says to me, "All day I am doing things I do not like. You want to know why? It is for you, Alexi-stop-spleening-me! One day, you will do things for me that you do not like. That is what it means to be a family." What she does not clutch is that I already do things for her that I do not like. I listen to her when she talks, and I resist bewailing about my pygmy allowance. But I do not do these things because we are a family. I do them because they are common decencies. That is an idiom that the hero taught me. I do them because I am not a big fucking asshole. That is another idiom that the hero taught me.

My father toils for a travel agency here in Odessa. It is denominated Heritage Touring. It is for Jewish people, like the hero, who have cravings to leave that ennobled country America, and visit humble towns in Poland and Ukraine. My father's business scores a translator, guide, and driver for the Jews, who try to find places where their families once existed. Jewish people are at intervals having shit between their brains. But Jonathan Safran Foer is not having shit between his brains. He is an ingenious Jew.

Now I will begin the story. My father obtained a telephone call from the American office of Heritage Touring. They required a driver, guide, and translator for a young man who would be in Lutsk at the dawn of the month of July. "Shapka," my father said to me, "what was the language you studied this year at school?" "Do not call me Shapka," I said. "Alex," he said, "what was the language you studied this year at school?" "The language of English," I told him. "Are you good and fine at it?" he asked me. "I am fluid," I told him. "Excellent, Shapka," he said. "Do not call me that," I said. "Excellent, Alex. You must nullify any plans you possess for the first week of the month of July." "I do not possess any plans," I said. "Yes, you do," he said. "Your grandfather and you are going to Lutsk."

Now is a befitting time to mention my grandfather. I will mention him.   5
He has gold teeth, and dubs me Sasha. He toiled for fifty years at many employments, primarily farming, and later machine manipulating. His final employment was at Heritage Touring, where he persevered until several years of yore. But now he is retarded. My grandmother died two years ago of a cancer in her brain, and my grandfather became very melancholy, and also, he says, blind. My father does not believe him, but purchased a seeing-eye bitch for him, nonetheless, because a seeing-eye bitch is not only for blind

people but also for people who pine for the antonym of loneliness—a word I am unable to discover because that page of my very useful thesaurus has vanished. (And I should not have used "purchased" because in truth my father did not purchase her, but only accepted currency to take her from the home for forgotten dogs. Because of this, she is not a real seeing-eye bitch, and is also mentally deranged.) If you're conjecturing what the bitch's name is, it is Sammy Davis, Jr., Jr. She has this name because Sammy Davis, Jr., was my grandfather's beloved singer.

After telephoning me, my father informed my grandfather that he would be the driver of our journey at the dawn of July. If you want to know who would be the guide, the answer is there would be no guide. My father said that a guide was not an indispensable thing, because my grandfather knew a beefy amount from his years at Heritage Touring. But when my grandfather and I roosted in my father's house that night to converse the journey, my grandfather said, "I do not want to do it. I did not become a re-tarded person in order to have to perform shit such as this." "I do not care what you want," my father told him. That was the end of the conversation. In my family, my father has become a world expert at ending conversations. So we made schemes to procure the hero at the Lvov train station, on 2 July, 1999, at 15:00 of the afternoon. From there, we would drive to Lutsk and the neighboring villages. "He is looking for the town his grandfather came from, and someone who salvaged his grandfather from the war," my father said. "He may have low-grade brains. The American office informs me that he telephones them every day and manufactures numerous half-wit-ted queries about eating and the hazard of rapid bowel proceedings." Here I will repeat that the hero is a very ingenious Jew.

My grandfather and I viewed television for several hours after my father reposed. We viewed an American program that had the words in Russian at the bottom of the screen. It was about a Chinaman who was resource-ful with a bazooka. Amid my grandfather and I was a silence you could cut with a scimitar. The only time that either of us spoke was when he ro-tated to me during an advertisement for McDonald's beefburgers and said, "I do not want to drive ten hours to an ugly city to attend to a spoiled American."

It made my girls very mirthless that I should be away for many days. I told them all, "If possible, I would be here with only you forever. But we need currency for famous discothèques, yes? I am doing something I hate for you! This is what it means to be in love." But, in truth, that was not the truth. I was electrified to go.

A few days before the hero was to arrive, I inquired my father if I could go forth to America when I made to graduate from university. "No," he said. "But I want to," I informed him. "I do not care what you want," he said, and that is usually the end of the conversation, but it was not this time. "Why?" I asked. "If you want to know why," he said, unclosing the refrigerator, "it is because your great-grandfather was from Odessa, and your grandfather was from Odessa, and your father, me, was from Odessa, and your boys will be from Odessa." "But what if I want my boys to grow up someplace superior, with superior things, and more things?" I asked. My father excavated three pieces of ice from the refrigerator, closed the refrigerator, and punched me. "Put these on your face," he said, "so you do not look terrible and manufacture disasters in Lvov." This was the end of the conversation.

It was agreed that my grandfather and I would go forth to Lvov at midnight of 1 July. This would present us with fifteen hours. It was agreed that my grandfather would wait with patience in the car at the Lvov train station, while I waited on the tracks for the hero, holding a sign that my father had given me: "Jon-fen!" The drive with my grandfather was not made easier by Sammy Davis, Jr., Jr., whom my grandfather required to bring along. "You are being a fool," my father informed him. "I need her to help me see the road," my grandfather said, pointing his finger at his eyes. "I am blind." "You are not blind, and you are not bringing the bitch. It is not professional for the bitch to go along." "It is either I go with the bitch, or I do not go." My father was in a position. Not like the Latvian Home Stretch, but like amid a rock and a rigid place, which is, in truth, somewhat similar to the Latvian Home Stretch.

Notwithstanding that we had a deranged bitch in the car, the drive was also rigid because the car is so much shit that it would not travel any faster than as fast as I could run, which is sixty kilometres per the hour. Many cars passed us, which made me feel second-rate, especially when the cars were heavy with families, and when they were bicycles. My grandfather and I did not say words pending the drive, which is not abnormal, because we have never said multitudinous words. I made efforts not to spleen him, but did sometimes. For one example, I forgot to examine the map, and we missed our entrance to the superway. "Do not become very spleened," I said, "but I made a miniature error with the map." My grandfather punched the stop pedal, and my face became sociable with the front window. He did not say anything for the major of a minute. "Did I ask you to drive the car?" he asked. "No," I said. "Did I ask you to prepare me breakfast while you roost there?" he asked. "No," I said. "Did I ask you to invent a new kind of wheel?" he asked. "No," I said. "How many things did I ask you to do?" he asked. "Merely one," I said, and I knew that he would yell at me for some durable time, and perhaps even punch me. But he did not. If you want to know what he did, he rotated the car around, and we drove back to where I fashioned the error. Twenty minutes it captured. "If you blunder again," my grandfather said, when we arrived at the location, "I will stop the car and you will get out

10

with a foot in the backside. It will be my foot. It will be your backside. Is this a thing you understand?"

We arrived in Lvov in only eleven hours, but the train station was rigid to find, and we became lost many times. "I hate Lvov," my grandfather said. Lvov is a big, impressive city, but not like Odessa. Odessa is very beautiful, with many famous beaches where girls are lying on their backs and announcing their first-rate bosoms. Lvov is a city like New York City in America. It has very tall buildings, and comprehensive streets, and many cellular phones. I have never witnessed a place fashioned of so much concrete. But Lvov is not very impressive from inside the train station. This is where I loitered for the hero for more than four hours. I was spleened to have to loiter there with nothing to do, without even a hi-fi, and when the hero's train finally arrived, both of my legs were needles and nails from being an upright person for such a duration. I would have roosted, but the floor was very dirty, and I wore my peerless blue-jeans to impress the hero. I did not know what the hero's appearance would be, and he did not know how tall and aristocratic I would appear. This was something we made much repartee about after. He was very nervous, he said. He made shit of a brick. I said to him that I also made shit of a brick, but it was not that I would not recognize him. An American in Ukraine is flaccid to recognize. I made shit of a brick because I desired to show him that I, too, could be an American.

I held the sign with his name and looked into the eyes of every person that walked past. I was trying to select him. The one with the satchel? No. The one with the red hairs? No. When I found the hero, I was very flabbergasted by his appearance. This is an American? I thought. He was severely short. He wore spectacles and had diminutive hairs which rested on his head like a shapka. He did not appear like the Americans I had witnessed in magazines, with yellow hairs and muscles. In truth, he did not look like anything special at all.

He must have witnessed the sign I was holding, because he punched me on the shoulder and said, "Alex?" I told him yes. "You're my translator, right?" I asked him to manufacture brakes, because I could not fathom him. He spoke very rapidly, and in truth I was making a brick wall of shits. "Lesson one. Hello. How are you doing this day?" "What?" "Lesson two. Is not the weather full of delight?" "You're my translator," he said, "yes?" "Yes," I said presenting him my hand. "I am Alexander Perchov. I am your humble translator." "It would not be nice to beat you," he said. "What?" I said. "I said," he said, "it would not be nice to beat you." "Oh yes," I laughed, "it would not be nice to beat you also. I implore you to forgive my speaking of English. I am not so premium with it." "Jonathan Safran Foer," he said, and presented me his hand. "I am Alex," I said. "I know," he said. "Did someone hit you?" He examined at my right eye. "It was nice for my father to beat me," I said. I took his bags from him, and we went forth to the car.

"Your train ride appeased you?" I asked. "Oh, God," he said, "twenty-   15
six hours, fucking unbelievable." This girl Unbelievable must be very majestic, I thought. "You were able to Z Z Z Z Z?" I asked. "What?" "Did
you manufacture any Zs?" "I don't understand." "Repose." "What?" "Did
you repose?" "Oh. No," he said, "didn't repose at all." "And the guards
at the border?" "It was nothing," he said. "I've heard so much about
them, that they would, you know, give me a hard time. But they came in,
checked my passport, and didn't bother me at all." "What?" I asked. "I
had heard it might be a problem, but it wasn't a problem." "You had
heard about them?" "Oh yeah, I was making shit of a brick." In truth, I
was flabbergasted that the hero did not have any tribulations with the border guards. They have an unsavory habit for taking things without asking.
I have also been informed stories of travellers who must present currency
to the guards in order to receive their documents in return. For Americans,
it is best if the guard is in love with America, and wants to overawe the
American by being a premium guard. This kind of guard thinks that he
will encounter the American again one day in America, and that the
American will offer to take him to a Chicago Bulls game, and buy him
blue-jeans and delicate toilet paper. The other kind of guard is also in
love with America, but he will hate the American for being an American.
This is worst. This guard knows he will never go to America or meet the
American again. He will burgle the American, and spleen the American,
only to demonstrate that he can. My father told me this, and I am certain
that it is faithful.

When we arrived at the car, my grandfather was waiting with patience
as my father had ordered him to. He was very patient. He was snoring. He
was snoring with such volume that the hero and I could hear him even
though the windows were elevated. "This is our driver," I said. I observed
distress in the smile of our hero. "Is he O.K.?" he asked. "With certainty," I
said. "But I must tell you, I am very familiar with this driver. He is my grandfather." At this moment, Sammy Davis, Jr., Jr., made herself evident, because she jumped up from the back seat and barked in volumes. "Jesus
Christ!" the hero said with terror, and he moved distant from the car. "Do
not be distressed," I informed him as Sammy Davis, Jr., Jr., punched her
head against the window. "That is only the driver's seeing-eye bitch. She
is deranged," I explained, "but so so playful."

"Grandfather," I said. "Grandfather, he is here." I was able to move my
grandfather from his repose. If you want to know how, I fastened his nose
with my fingers so that he could not breathe. He did not know where he
was. "Anna?" he asked. That was the name of my grandmother.

"No, Grandfather," I said, "it is me. Alex." He was very shamed. I
could perceive this because he rotated his face away from me. "We should
go forth to Lutsk," I suggested, "as Father ordered." "What?" the hero

inquired. "I told him that we should go forth to Lutsk." "Yes, Lutsk. That's where I was told we would go. And from there to Trachimbrod, my grandfather's village." "Correct," I said. "Where's the dog going to be?" the hero inquired. "What?" "Where's...the...dog...going...to...be?" "I do not understand." "I'm afraid of dogs," he said. "I've had some bad experiences with them." I told this to my grandfather, who was still half of himself in repose. "No one is afraid of dogs," he said. "My grandfather informs me that no one is afraid of dogs." The hero moved his shirt up to exhibit me the remains of a wound. "That's from a dog bite," he said. "What is?" "That." "What?" "This thing." "What thing?" "Here. It looks like two intersecting lines." "I don't see it." "Right here," he said, and I said, "Oh yes," although in truth I still could not witness a thing. "So?" "So I'm afraid of dogs." I clutched the situation now. "Sammy Davis, Jr., Jr., must roost in the front with us," I told my grandfather. "Get in the fucking car," he said, having misplaced all of the patience that he had while reposing. "The bitch and the American will share the back seat. It is vast enough for both of them." I did not mention how the back seat was not vast enough for even one of them.

Sammy Davis, Jr., Jr., had made her mouth with blood from masticating her own tail. Next she converted her attention to trying to lick clean the hero's spectacles. "Can you please get this dog away from me," the hero said, making his body into a ball. "Please. I really don't like dogs." "She is only making games with you," I told him when she put her body on top of his and kicked him with her back legs. "It signifies that she likes you." I will now mention that Sammy Davis, Jr., Jr., is very often sociable with her new friends, but I had never witnessed a thing like this. I conjectured that she was in love with the hero. "Are you donning cologne?" I asked. "What?" "Are you donning any cologne?" He rotated his body so that his face was in the seat, away from the bitch. "Maybe a little," he said, defending the back of his head with his hands. "Because she loves cologne. It makes her sexually stimulated." "Great." "She is trying to sex you. This is a good sign. It signifies that she will not bite." "Help!" he said, as Sammy Davis, Jr., Jr., rotated to do a sixty-nine. "He does not like her," I told my grandfather. "Yes, he does," he said.

    I do not think there was a person in the car that was surprised when we became lost amid the Lvov train station and the superway to Lutsk. "I hate Lvov," my grandfather rotated to tell the hero. "What's he saying?" the hero asked me. "He said it will not be long," I told him, which was a befitting lie. "Long until what?" the hero asked. "I hate Lvov, I hate Lutsk, I hate the Jew in the back seat of this car that I hate," my grandfather said. "You are not making this any cinchier," I said. "What?" the hero asked. "He says it will not be long until we get to Lutsk," I said.

It captured five very long hours. If you want to know why, it is because my grandfather is my grandfather first and a driver second. He made us lost often and became on his nerves. I had to translate his anger into useful information for the hero. "Fuck," my grandfather said. "He says if you look at the statues, you can see that some no longer endure. Those are where Communist statues used to be." "Fucking fuck, fuck!" my grandfather shouted. "Oh," I said, "he wants you to know that that building, that building, and that building, are all important." "Why?" the hero inquired. "Fuck!" my grandfather said. "He cannot remember," I said.

"Could you turn on some air-conditioning?" the hero commanded. I was humiliated to the highest degree possible. "This car does not have air-conditioning," I said. "What?" "I am apologetic," I said. "Well, can we roll down the windows? It's really hot in here, and it smells like something died." "Sammy Davis, Jr., Jr., will jump out." "Who?" "The bitch. Her name is Sammy Davis, Jr., Jr." "Is that a joke?" "No, she will truly go forth from the car." "No, his name." "Her name," I rectified him, because I am first-rate with pronouns. "Tell him to Velcro his lips together," my grandfather said. "He says that the bitch was named for his favorite singer, who was Sammy Davis, Jr." "A Jew," the hero said. "What?" "Sammy Davis, Jr., was a Jew." "This is not possible," I said. "A convert. He found the Jewish God or something." I told this to my grandfather. "Sammy Davis, Jr., was not a Jew!" he said, more on his nerves than I would have conjectured. "He was the Negro of the Rat Pack!" "But the American is certain of it." "The Music Man? A Jew?" "He is certain." "Dean Martin, Jr.!" my grandfather hollered to the back seat. "Get up here! Get away from the American!"

It was pending this five-hour car drive from the Lvov train station to Lutsk that the hero explained to me why he came to Ukraine. He excavated several items from his bag. First he exhibited me a photograph. It was yellow and folded and had many pieces of affixative affixing it together. "See this?" he said. "This here is my grandfather." He pointed to a young man, who I am implored to say appeared very much like the hero. "This was taken during the war." "From whom?" "No, not taken like that. The photograph was made." "I understand." "Well, these people he is with are the family that saved him from the Nazis. He escaped the Nazi raid on Trachimbrod. Everyone else was killed. He lost a wife and a baby." "And how will we find this family?" "We're not really looking for the family, so much as this girl in the picture. She would be the only one still alive. If she is still alive." He moved his finger along the face of a girl in the photograph. "I want to see Trachimbrod," the hero said, "to see what it's like, how my grandfather grew up, where I would be now if it weren't for the war." "You would be Ukrainian," I said. "Like me." "I guess." "Only not like me because you would be a farmer in an unimpressive village, and I live in Odessa, which is very much like Miami." "I want to see what it's like now," he said. "I don't think there are any Jews left there, but maybe there are. The shtetls weren't only Jews." "The what?" "Shtetl. It's like a village." "Why don't you merely dub it a village?" "It's a Jewish word, like 'schmuck.'" "What does it mean 'schmuck'?" "A schmuck is someone who does something that you don't agree with." "Teach me another." "'Putz.'" "What does that mean?" "It's like 'schmuck.'" "Teach me another." "'Schmendrik.'" "What does that mean?" "It's also like 'schmuck.'" "Do you know any words that are not like 'schmuck'?" He pondered for a moment. "'Shalom,'" he said, "but that's Hebrew, not Yiddish. The Eskimos have four hundred words for snow, and the Jews have four hundred words for schmuck."

"So we will sightsee the shtetl?" "I figured it would be a good place to begin our search." "Search?" "For Augustine." "Who is Augustine?" "The girl in the photograph." It was very silent for a moment. "And then," I said, "if we find her?" The hero was a pensive person. "I don't know what then. I suppose I'd thank her." "For saving your grandfather." "Yes." "And I am querying, how do you know that her name is Augustine?" "I don't really. On the back, see, here, is written a few words, in my grandfather's writing, I think. It says, 'This is me with Augustine, 1942.'" "Do you think he loved her?" "What?" "Because he remarks only her." "So?" "So perhaps he loved her." "It's funny that you should think that. I've wondered. He was eighteen, and she was, what, about fifteen? He had just lost a wife and daughter when the Nazis raided his town. It seems so improbable that he could have loved her. But isn't there something strange about the picture, the closeness between them, even though they're not looking at each other? The *way* that they aren't looking at each other. It's very powerful, don't you think?" "Yes." "And that we should both think about the possibility of his loving her is also strange." "How did you obtain this photograph?" I asked, holding it to the window. "My grandmother gave it to my mother two years ago, and she said that this was the family that had saved my grandfather from the Nazis." "Why merely two years ago?" "She has her reasons." "What are these reasons?" "I don't know. We couldn't ask her about it." "Why not?" "She held onto the photograph for fifty-five years. If she wanted to tell us anything about it, she would have. I couldn't even tell her I was coming to the Ukraine." "Why is this?" "Her memories of the Ukraine aren't good. Her shtetl is only a few kilometres from Trachimbrod. But all of her family was killed, everyone—mother, father, sisters, grandparents." "Did a Ukrainian save her?" "No, she fled before the war." "It surprises me that no one saved her family." "It shouldn't. The Ukrainians were terrible to the Jews. At the beginning of the war, a lot of Jews wanted to go to the Nazis to be protected from the Ukrainians." "This is not true," I said. "It is." "I cannot believe what you are saying." "Look it up in the history books. Ukrainians were known for being terrible to the Jews. So were the Poles. Listen, I don't mean to offend you. It's got nothing to do with you. We're talking about fifty years ago." "It does not say this in history books," I told the hero. "I don't know what to say, then." "Say that you are mistaken." "I can't." "You must."

"Here are my maps," he said, excavating a few pieces of paper from his bag. He pointed to one that was wet from Sammy Davis, Jr., Jr. Her tongue, I hoped. "This is Trachimbrod. This is Lutsk. This is Kolky. It's an old map. Some of the places we're looking for aren't on new maps. Here," he said, and presented it to me. "You can see where we have to go. This is all I have, these maps and the photograph. It's not much." "I promise you that we will find this Augustine," I said. I could perceive that this made the hero appeased. It also made me appeased. "Grandfather," I said, and I explained everything that the hero had just uttered to me about Augustine, and the maps, and the hero's grandmother. "Augustine," my grandfather said, and pushed Sammy Davis, Jr., Jr., onto me. He scrutinized at the photograph while I fastened the wheel. He put it close to his face, like he wanted to smell it, or touch it with his eyes. "Augustine." "She is the one we are looking for," I said. He moved his head to and fro. "We will find her," he said. "I know," I said. But I did not know, and nor did my grandfather.

When we reached Lutsk, it was already commencing darkness. "Let us eat," my grandfather said. "You are hungry?" I asked the hero, who was again the sexual object of Sammy Davis, Jr., Jr. "Get it off of me," he said. "Are you hungry?" I echoed. "Get the dog away from me, please." I called to her, and, when she did not respond, I punched her in the face. She moved to her side of the back seat, because now she understood what it means to be stupid with the wrong person. "I'm famished," the hero said, lifting his head from amid his knees. "What?" "Yes, I'm hungry." "You are hungry." "Yes." "Then we will eat," I said. "Good," the hero said. "One thing, though." "What?" "You should know …" "Yes?" "I am a vegetarian." "I do not understand." "I don't eat meat." "Why not?" "I just don't." "How can you not eat meat?" "I just don't." "He does not eat meat," I told my grandfather. "Yes, he does," he informed me. "Yes, you do," I likewise informed the hero. "No, I don't." "Why not?" I inquired him again. "I just don't. No meat." "Pork?" "No." "Steak?" "No." "Chickens?" "No." "Do you eat veal?" "Oh, God. Absolutely no veal." "What about sausage?" "No sausage, either." I told my grandfather this, and he presented me a very distressed look. "What is wrong with him?" he asked. "What is wrong with you?" I asked him. "It's just the way I am," he said. "Hamburger?" "No hamburger." "Tongue?" "It's very popular in America to be vegetarian. It's very cool." "What did he say is wrong with him?" my grandfather asked. "It is just the way he is," I said.

"What do you mean he does not eat meat?" the waitress asked, and my grandfather put his head in his hands. "What is wrong with him?" she

25

asked. "It is only the way that he is." "He does not eat any meat at all?" she inquired me. "It is very cool to be like that in America," I told her. "Everyone is that way." "Sausage?" she asked. "No sausage," my grandfather said. "Maybe you could eat some meat," I suggested to the hero, "because they do not have anything that is not meat." "Don't they have potatoes or something?" he asked. "Do you have potatoes?" I asked the waitress. "You only receive a potato with the meat," she said. I told the hero. "Couldn't I just get a plate of potatoes?" "What?" "Couldn't I get two or three potatoes, without meat?" I asked the waitress, and she said she would go to the chef and inquire him. "Ask him if he eats liver," my grandfather said.

The waitress returned and said, "Here is what I have to say. We can make concessions to give him two potatoes, but they are served with a piece of meat on the plate. The chef says that this cannot be negotiated. He will have to eat the meat." When the food arrived, the hero asked for me to remove the meat off his plate. "I'd prefer not to touch it," he said. This spleened me to the maximum. I took the meat off his plate, because I knew that is what my father would have desired me to do, and I did not utter a thing. "We will commence very early in the morning tomorrow," my grandfather said. "Let me inspect at his maps." I asked the hero for the maps. As he was reaching into his side bag, he kicked the table, which made his plate move. One of the potatoes descended to the floor. When it hit the floor it made a sound. *Plomp.* It rolled over, and then was inert. My grandfather and I examined each other. I did not know what to do. "A terrible thing has occurred," my grandfather said. The hero viewed the potato on the floor. It was a dirty floor. It was one of his two potatoes. "This is awful," my grandfather said quietly, and moved his plate to the side. "Awful." He was correct. The waitress returned to our table with the colas we ordered. "Here are …" she began, but then she witnessed the potato on the floor. She put the colas on our table, and walked away with warp speed. The hero was still witnessing the potato on the floor. He did not do anything. We remained silent, and witnessing the potato. Then my grandfather inserted his fork in the potato, picked it up from the floor, and put it on his plate. He cut it into four pieces, and gave one to Sammy Davis, Jr., Jr., under the table, one to me, and one to the hero. He cut off a piece from his piece, and ate it. Then he looked at me. I did not want to, but I knew that I had to. To say that it was not delicious would be an overstatement. Then we looked at the hero. He looked at the floor, and then at his plate. He cut off a piece from his piece, and looked at it. He ate it and smiled at us. "Welcome to Ukraine," my grandfather said to him, and punched me on the back, which was a thing I relished very much. Then my grandfather started laughing. Then I started laughing. Then the hero started laughing. We laughed for a long time. Each of us was manufacturing tears at his eyes. It was not until much in the posterior that I understood that each of us was laughing for a different reason, for our own reason, and that not one of those reasons had a thing to do with the potato. As for Sammy Davis, Jr., Jr., she did not eat her piece of the potato.

The hero and I spoke very much at dinner, mostly about America. "Tell me about things that you have in America," I said. "What do you want to know about?" "You have many good schools for accounting in America, yes?" "I guess, I don't really know. I could find out for you when I get back." "Thank you," I said, because now I had a connection in America, and was not alone. "What do you study?" I asked. "This and that." "What does it mean this and that?" "I don't know, just what it sounds like, some of this, and some of that." "Why do you not inform me?" "Writing, things like that." "It is a good career?" "What?" "Writing." "If you're good at it, I suppose." "Why do you want to write?" "I don't know. I used to think it was what I was born to do." "That is how I feel about accounting." "You're lucky. I don't feel that way anymore." "Now what do you feel like you were born to do?" "I don't know. Maybe writing. But it sounds terrible to say it. Cheap." "It sounds nor terrible nor cheap." "I want to express myself." "The same is faithful for me." "I'm looking for my voice." "It is in your mouth." "The other voice. The voice that can't be spoken." "I understand this." "I want to do something I'm not ashamed of," he said. "Something you are proud of, yes?" "Not even. I just don't want to be ashamed." "If I may partake in a different theme: How much currency would an accountant receive in America?" "I'm not sure. A lot, I imagine, if he or she is good." "She!" "Or he." "Are there Negro accountants?" "There are African-American accountants. You don't want to use that word, though, Alex." "And homosexual accountants?" "There are homosexual everythings. There are homosexual garbage men." "How much currency would a Negro homosexual accountant receive?" "You shouldn't use that word." "Which word?" "The one before homosexual." "What?" "The N-word. Well, it's not *the* N-word, but—" "Negro?" "Shhh!" "I dig Negroes." "You really shouldn't say that." "But I dig them all the way. They are premium people." "It's that word, though. You shouldn't say the N-word." "Negro?" "Please." "What's wrong with Negroes?" "Shhh!" "How much does a cup of coffee cost in America?" "Oh, it depends. Maybe one dollar." "One dollar! This is like giving it for free! In Ukraine one cup of coffee is five dollars!" "Oh, well, I didn't mention cappuccinos. They can be as much as five or six dollars." "Cappuccinos," I said, elevating my hands above my head, "there is no maximum! What about the girls in America?" "What about them?" "They are very informal with their vaginas, yes?" "You hear about girls like that, but nobody I know has ever met one of them." "Are you carnal very often?" "Are you?" "I inquired you. Are you?" "Are you?" "I inquired headmost. Are you?" "Not really." "What do you intend by 'not really'?" "I'm not a priest, but I'm not

John Holmes, either." "I know of this John Holmes." I lifted my hands to my sides. "With the premium penis." "That's the one," he said, and laughed. I made him laugh with my funny. "In Ukraine, everyone has a penis like that." He laughed again. "Even the women?" he asked. "You made a funny?" I asked. "Yes," he said. So I laughed. "Do you think the women in Ukraine are first-rate?" "I haven't seen many since I've been here." "Do you have women like this in America?" "There's at least one of everything in America." "Do you have many motorcycles in America?" "Of course." "And fax machines?" "Yes, but they're very 'passé'." "What does it mean 'passé'?" "They're out of date. Paper is so tedious." "Tedious?" "It makes you fatigued." "I understand what you are telling me, and I harmonize. I would not ever use paper. It makes me a sleeping person. Do most young people have impressive cars in America? Lotus Esprit V8 twin turbos? DeLorean DMC-12s?" "I certainly don't. I have a piece-of-shit Honda." "It is brown?" "No, it's an expression." "How can your car be an expression?" "I have a car that is like a piece of shit. You know, it stinks like shit, and looks shitty." "And if you are a good accountant, you could buy an impressive car?" "Absolutely." "What kind of wife would a good accountant have?" "Who knows?" "Would she have rigid tits?" "I couldn't say for sure." "Probably, although?" "I guess." "I dig this. I dig rigid tits." "But there are also accountants who have ugly wives. That's just the way it works." "If John Holmes was a first-rate accountant, he could have any woman he would like for his wife, yes?" "Probably." "My penis is very big." "O.K."

After dinner, we drove back to the hotel. It was an unimpressive hotel. When we unclosed the door to the hero's room, I could perceive that he was distressed. "It's fine," he said, because he could perceive that I could perceive that he was distressed. "Really, it's just for sleeping." "You do not have hotels like this in America!" I made a funny. "No," he said, and he was laughing. We were like friends. "Make sure you secure the door," I told him. "I do not want to make you a petrified person, but there are many dangerous people who want to take things without asking from Americans, and also kidnap them. Good night." The hero laughed again, but he laughed because he did not know that I was very serious.

"Come on Sammy Davis, Jr., Jr.," my grandfather called to the bitch, but she would not leave the hero's door. "Come on!" he bellowed, but she would not dislodge. I tried to sing to her, which she relishes, especially when I sing "Billie Jean Is Not My Lover," by Michael Jackson. But Sammy Davis, Jr., Jr., only pushed her head against the door to the hero's room. I knocked on the door, and the hero had a toothbrush in his mouth. "Sammy Davis, Jr., Jr., will manufacture Zs with you this evening," I told him, although I knew that it would not be successful. "No," he said, and that was all. "She will not depart from your door," I told him. "Then let her sleep in the hall." "But she is compassionate," I said. "Listen," the hero said. "If she needs to sleep in the room, I'll be happy to sleep in the hall. But if I'm in the room, I'm alone in the room." "Perhaps you could both sleep in the hall," I suggested.

After we left the hero and the bitch to repose—hero in room, bitch in hall—my grandfather and I went downstairs to the hotel bar for drinks of vodka. It was my grandfather's notion. In truth, I was a petite amount terrified of being alone with him. "He is a good boy," my grandfather said. I could not perceive if he was inquiring me, or tutoring me. "He seems good," I said. "We should try inflexibly to help him." "We should," I said. "I would like very much to find Augustine," he said. "So would I." That was all the talking for the night. We had three vodkas each and watched the weather report on the television at the bar, and then we went up to our room. "I will repose on the bed, and you will repose on the floor," my grandfather said. "Of course," I said. We had spent the day thinking what the hero's grandfather did during the war. That night—my grandfather on the bed, me on the floor—there was a new question: what did *my* grandfather do during the war?

The alarm made a noise at six of the morning. "Go get the Jew," my grandfather said. "I will loiter downstairs." "Breakfast?" I asked. "Oh," he said, "let us descend to the restaurant and eat breakfast. Then you will get the Jew." "What about his breakfast?" "They will not have anything without meat, so we should not make him an uncomfortable person." "You are smart," I told him. When we roosted at the restaurant my grandfather said, "Eat very much. It will be a long day, and who could be certain when we will eat next?" For this reason we ordered three breakfasts for the two of us, and ate very much sausage, which is a delicious food. "Get the Jew," my grandfather said, when we had finished. "I will loiter with patience in the car."

I am certain that the hero was not reposing, because before I could punch for the second time he unclosed the door. He was already in clothing. "Listen," he said, "what do you say we have a little breakfast?" "What?" "Breakfast," he said, putting his hands on his stomach. "No," I said, "I think it is superior if we commence the search. We want to search as much as possible while light still exists." "But it's only six-thirty." "Yes, but it will not be six-thirty forever. Look," I said, and pointed to my watch, which is a Rolex from Bulgaria, "it is already six-thirty-one. We are misplacing time." "Maybe a little something?" he said. "What?" "I'm really hungry." "This cannot be negotiated. I think it is best—" "We have a minute, or two. What's that on your breath?" "You will have one cappuccino in the restaurant downstairs, and that will be the end of the conversation." "What do you mean that's the end—" I put my fingers on my lips. This signified "SHUT UP!"

"Back for more breakfast?" the waitress asked. "She says good morning, would you like a cappuccino?" "Oh," he said. "Tell her yes. And maybe some bread, or something." "He is an American," I said. "I know," she said. "I can see." "But he does not eat meat, so just give him a cappuccino." "What are you telling her?" "I told her not to make it too watery." "Good. I hate it when it's watery." "So just one cappuccino will be adequate," I told the waitress, who was a very beautiful girl with the most breasts I had ever seen. "Would you like to go to a famous discothèque with me tonight?" I added. "Will you bring the American?" she asked. This spleened me. "He is a Jew," I said, and I know that I should not have uttered that, but I was beginning to feel very awful about myself. The problem is that I felt more awful after uttering it. "Oh," she said. "I have never seen a Jew before. Can I see his horns?" I told her to attend to her own affairs and merely bring a cappuccino for the Jew and two more orders of sausage for the bitch, because who could be certain when she would eat again.

"How do we get there?" my grandfather inquired me when the hero and I entered the car. "I do not know," I said. "Inquire Jon-fen," he ordered, so I did. "I don't know," he said. "He does not know." "What do you mean he does not know? We are in the car. We are primed to go forth on our journey. How can he not know?" His voice was now with volume, and it frightened Sammy Davis, Jr., Jr., making her bark. "What do you mean you do not know?" "I told you everything I know. I thought one of you was supposed to be a certified Heritage guide." My grandfather punched the car's horn, and it made a sound: *Honk.* "My grandfather is certified!" I informed him, which was faithful, although he was certified to operate an automobile, not find lost history. *Honk.* "Please!" I said at my grandfather. "Please! You are making this impossible!" *Honk. Bark.* "Shut up," he said, "and shut the Jew up!" *Bark.* "You're sure he's certified?" "Of course," I said. *Honk.* "I would not deceive." *Bark.* "Do something," I told my grandfather. *Honk.* "Not that!" I said with volume.

My grandfather drove us to a petrol store that we had passed on the way to the hotel the night yore. A man came to the window. "Yes?" the man asked. "We are looking for Trachimbrod," my grandfather said. "We do not have any," the man said. "It is a place. We are trying to find it." The man turned to a group of men standing in front of the store. "Do we have anything called 'trachimbrod'?" They all elevated their shoulders, and continued to talk to themselves. "Apologies," he said, "we do not have any." "Present me the map," I said to the hero. He investigated his bag. "It's gone. I think Sammy Davis, Jr., Jr., ate it." "Impossible!" I said, although I knew that it was possible. I told the hero to mention the petrol man some of the other names of towns, and perhaps one would sound informal. "Kolky," the hero said, "Kivertsi, Sokeretchy …" "Yes, yes," the man said, "I have heard of these towns." "And you could direct us to them?" I asked.

"Of course. They are very proximal. Maybe thirty kilometres distant. No more. Merely travel north on the superway, and then east through the farm lands." "Here," the hero said. He was holding a package of Marlboro cigarettes at the petrol man. "What the hell is he doing?" my grandfather inquired. "What the hell is he doing?" the petrol man inquired. "What the hell are you doing?" I inquired. "For his help," he said. "I read in a guidebook that it's hard to get Marlboro cigarettes here, and that you should bring several packs with you wherever you go, and give them as tips." "What is a tip?" "It's something you give someone in exchange for help." "You are informed that you will be paying for this trip with currency, yes?" "No, not like that," he said, "tips are for small things, like directions." "He does not eat meat," my grandfather told the petrol man.

It was already seven-ten when we were driving again. I must confess that it was a beautiful day, with much light of the sun. "It is beautiful, yes?" I said to the hero. "What?" "The day. It is a beautiful day." "Yes," he said. "It's absolutely beautiful." This made me proud, and I told my grandfather, and he smiled. "Inform him about Odessa," my grandfather said. "Inform him how beautiful it is there." "In Odessa," I said to the hero, "it is more beautiful than even this. You have never witnessed a thing similar to it." "Inform him," my grandfather said, "that Odessa is the most wonderful place to become in love, and also to make a family." "Do you think this is true?" I inquired. "Of course," he said. "I know that it is true." So I informed the hero. "Odessa," I said, "is the most wonderful place to become in love, and also to make a family." "Have you ever fallen in love?" he inquired me, which seemed like such a queer inquiry, so I returned it to him. "Have you?" "I don't know," he said. "Nor I," I said. "I don't think so," he said. "I do not think so, either." "I've been close to love." "Yes." "Really close, like almost there." "Almost." "But never, I don't think." "No." "Maybe I should go to Odessa," he said. "I could fall in love." We both laughed. "Have you ever had a girlfriend?" I asked the hero. "Have you?" "I am inquiring you." "I sort of have," he said. "What do you signify with 'sort of'?" "Nothing formal, really. Not a girlfriend girlfriend, really. I've dated, I guess. I don't want to be formal." "It is the same state of affairs with me," I said. "I also do not want to be formal. I do not want to be handcuffed to only one girl." "Exactly," he said. "I mean, I've fooled around with girls." "Of course," I said. "Blow jobs." "Yes, of course." "But once you get a girlfriend, well, you know." "I know very well."

"Can I view Augustine again?" I asked the hero. He presented me the photograph. I observed it while he observed the beautiful day. Augustine had short hairs. They did not arrive at her shoulders. They were thin hairs. I did not need to touch them to be certain. "Look at those fields," the hero said, with his finger outside of the car. "They're so green." "Tell him that the land is premium for farming." "My grandfather desires me to tell you that the land is very premium for farming." "Look at those people working in the fields," the hero said. "Some of those women must be sixty, or even seventy." I inquired my grandfather about this. "It is not so unusual," he said. "In the fields, you toil until you are not able to toil. My father died in the fields." "Did your mother work in the fields?" "She was working with him when he died." "What is he saying?" the hero inquired, which prohibited my grandfather from continuing. It was the first occasion that I had ever heard my grandfather speak of his parents, and I wanted to know very much more of them. What did they do during the war? Who did they save? But I felt that it was a common decency for me to be silent on the matter. He would speak when he needed to speak. So I did what the hero and bitch did, which was look out the window. I do not know how much time tumbled, but a lot of time tumbled. "It would be reasonable to inquire someone how to get to Trachimbrod," my grandfather said. "I do not think that we are more than ten kilometres distant." "This seems reasonable," I said, because I did not know what to say. "Of course it seems reasonable," he said. "It is reasonable."

We moved the car to the side of the road. "Go inquire someone," my grandfather said. "And bring the Jew with you." "Come," I informed the hero. "Where?" I pointed at a herd of men in the field who were smoking. "You want me to go with you?" "Of course," I said, because I desired the hero to feel that he was included in every aspect of the voyage. But, in truth, I was also afraid of the men in the field. I had never talked to people like that, poor farming people, and, similar to most people from Odessa, I speak a fusion of Russian and Ukrainian, and they spoke only Ukrainian, and people who speak only Ukrainian sometimes hate people who speak a fusion of Russian and Ukrainian, because very often people who speak a fusion of Russian and Ukrainian think they are superior to people who speak only Ukrainian. We think this because we *are* superior, but that is for another story. I commanded the hero not to speak, because at times people who speak Ukrainian who hate people who speak a fusion of Russian and Ukrainian also hate people who speak English. It is for the selfsame reason that I brought Sammy Davis, Jr., Jr., with us. "Why?" the hero inquired. "Why what?" "Why can't I talk?" "It distresses some people greatly to hear English. We will have a more flaccid time procuring assistance if you keep your lips together." "What?" "Shut up."

"I have never heard of it," said one of the men, with his cigarette at the side of his mouth. "Nor have I," said another, and they exhibited their backs. "Thank you," I said. I rotated my head to inform the hero that they did not know. "Maybe you've seen this woman," the hero said, taking out the photograph of Augustine. "Put that back," I said. "What are you intending here?" one of the men inquired, and cast his cigarette to the ground. "What did he say?" the hero asked. "We are searching for the town Trachimbrod," I informed them, and I could perceive that I was not selling like hotcakes. "I told you, there is no place Trachimbrod." "So stop bothering us," one of the other men said. "Do you want a Marlboro cigarette?" I proposed, because I could not design anything else. "Get out of here," one of the men said. "Go back to Kiev." "I am from Odessa," I said, and this made them laugh with very much violence. "Then go back to Odessa." "Can they help us?" the hero inquired. "Do they know anything?" "Come," I said, and we walked back to the car. I was humbled to the maximum. "Come on, Sammy Davis, Jr., Jr.!" But she would not come, even though the smoking men harassed her. There was merely one option remaining: "Billy Jean is not my lover. She's just a girl, who claims that I am the one." The maximum of humbling was made maximumer.

"What in hell were you doing uttering English!" I said. "I commanded you not to speak English! You understanded me, yes?" "Yes." "Then why did you speak English?" "I don't know." "You don't know! Did I ask you to prepare breakfast?" "What?" "Did I ask you to invent a new kind of wheel?" "I don't—" "I asked you to do merely one thing, and you made a disaster of it!" "I just thought it would be helpful." "But it was not helpful. You contaminated everything!" "Sorry, I just thought, the picture—" "I will do the thinking. You will do the silence." "I'm sorry." "I am the one who is sorry! I am sorry that I brought you with me on this journey!"

I was very shamed by the manner of how the men spoke to me, and I did not want to inform my grandfather of what occurred, because I knew that it would shame him also. But when we returned to the car, I realized that I did not have to inform him a thing. If you want to know why, it is because I first had to move him from his repose. "Grandfather," I said, touching his arm. "Grandfather." "Anna?" "No, Grandfather. It is me, Sasha." "I was dreaming," he said. "They did not know where Trachimbrod is." "Well, enter the car," he said. "We will persevere to drive, and search for another person to inquire."

We ferreted many other people to inquire, but in truth, every person regarded us in the same manner. "Go away," an old man uttered. "Why now?" a woman in a yellow dress inquired. Not one of them knew where Trachimbrod was, and not one of them had ever heard of it, but all of them became spleened or silent when I inquired. We persevered to drive, now unto subordinate roads, lacking any markings. The houses were less proximal to one another, and it was an abnormal thing to see anyone at all. "I have lived here my whole life," one old man said, without amputating himself from his seat under a tree, "and I can inform you that there is no place called Trachimbrod." Another old man, who was escorting a cow across the dirt road, said, "You should stop searching now. I can promise you that you will not find anything." I did not tell this to the hero. Perhaps this is because I am a good person. Perhaps it is because I am a bad one. I told him that each person told us to drive more, and that if we drove more we would discover some person who knew where Trachimbrod was. We would drive until we found Trachimbrod, and drive until we found Augustine. So we drove more, because we were severely lost, and because we did not know what else to do.

It was already the center of the day. "What are we going to do?" my grandfather inquired me. "We have been driving for six hours, and we are no more proximal than six hours yore." "This is a very rigid situation," I said. We persevered to drive. We drove more, farther and farther in the same circles. The car became fixed in the ground many times, and the hero and I had to get out to impel it. "It's not easy," the hero said. "No, it is not," I yielded. "But I guess we should keep driving. Don't you think? If that's what people have been telling us to do?" We drove beyond many of the towns that the hero named to the petrol man. Kolky. Sokeretchy. Kivertsi. But there were approximately no people anywhere, and, when there was a person, the person could not help us. "Go away." "There is no Trachimbrod here." "You are lost." It was seeming as if we were in the wrong country, or the wrong century, or as if Trachimbrod had disappeared, and so had the memory of it.

We drove more, and then drove more. We followed roads that we had already followed, we witnessed parts of the land that we had already witnessed. We drove in circles, and both my grandfather and I were desiring that the hero was not aware of this. I remembered when I was a boy and my father would punch me, and after he would say, "It does not hurt. It does not hurt." And the more he would utter it, the more it was faithful. I believed him, in some measure because he was my father, and in some measure because I, too, did not want it to hurt. This is how I felt with the hero as we persevered to drive. It was as if I were uttering to him, "We will find her. We will find her." I was deceiving him, and I am certain that he desired to be deceived.

"There," my grandfather said, as darkness was verging, and pointed his finger at a person roosting on the steps of a very diminutive house. It was the first person that we had viewed in many minutes. He arrested the car. "Go." Because I did not know what else to say, I said, "O.K." I said to the hero, "Come!" There was no rejoinder. "Come," I said, and rotated. The hero was manufacturing Zs, and so was Sammy Davis, Jr., Jr. There is no necessity for me to move them from repose, I said to my brain. I took with me the photograph of Augustine, and was very circumspect not to disturb them as I closed the car's door.

The house was white wood that was falling off of itself. As I walked more proximal, I could perceive that it was a woman roosting on the steps. She was very aged, and peeling the skin off of corn. "Leniency," I said, while I was still a petite amount distant. I said this so that I would not make her a terrified person. "I have a query for you." She was donning a white shirt and a white dress, but they were covered with dirt and places where liquids had dried. I could perceive that she was a very poor woman. All of the people in the small towns are very poor, but she was more poor. This was clear-cut because of how svelte she was, and how broken all of her belongings were.

She smiled as I became proximal to her, and I could see that she did not have any teeth. Her hairs were white, her skin had brown marks, and her eyes were blue. She was not so much of a woman, and what I signify here is that she was very petite, and appeared as if she could be obliterated with one finger. "Leniency," I said, "I do not want to pester you—" "How could anything pester me on such a beautiful evening?" "Yes, it is beautiful." "Where are you from?" she asked. This shamed me. I rotated over in my head what to manufacture. "Odessa." She put down one piece of corn and picked up another. "I have never been to Odessa," she said, and moved hairs that were in front of her face to behind her ear. It was not until this moment that I perceived how her hairs were as long as her. "You must go there," I said. "I know. I know I must. I am sure there are many things that I must do." "And many things that you must not do also." I was trying to make her a sedate person, and I accomplished. She laughed. "You are a sweet boy." "Have you ever heard of a town dubbed Trachimbrod?" I inquired. "I was informed that someone proximal to here would know of it." She put her corn on her lap. "What?" "I do not want to pester you, but have you ever heard of a town dubbed Trachimbrod?" "No," she said, picking up her corn and removing its skin. "I have never heard of that." "I am sorry to have confiscated your time," I said. "Have a good day." She presented me with a sad smile.

I commenced to perambulate away, but I felt so awful. What would I inform the hero when he was no longer manufacturing Zs? What would I inform my grandfather? For how long could we fail until we surrendered? Darkness was near, and I felt as if all the weight was residing on me. There are only so many times that you can utter "It does not hurt" before that begins to hurt even more than the hurt. Not-truths hung in front of me like fruit. Which could I pick for the hero? Which could I pick for my grandfather? Which for myself? Then I remembered that I had the photograph of Augustine, and, although I do not know what it was that coerced me to do it, I rotated back around and exhibited the photograph to the woman. "Have you ever witnessed anyone in this photograph?"

She examined it for several moments. "No."

I do not know why, but I inquired again. "Have you ever witnessed anyone in this photograph?"

50

"No," she said again, although this second no did not seem like a parrot, but like a different variety of "no."

"Have you ever witnessed anyone in this photograph?" I inquired, and this time I held it very proximal to her face.

"No," she said again, and this seemed like a third variety of "no."

I put the photograph in her hands. "Have you ever witnessed anyone in the photograph?"

"No," she said, but in her "no" I was certain that I could hear, Please persevere. Inquire me again.

So I did. "Have you ever witnessed anyone in the photograph?"

She moved her thumbs over the faces, as if she were attempting to erase them. "No."

"Have you ever witnessed anyone in the photograph?"

"No," she said, and she put the photograph on her lap.

"Have you ever witnessed anyone in the photograph?" I inquired.

"No," she said, still examining it, but only from the angles of her eyes.

"Have you ever witnessed anyone in the photograph?"

"No."

"Have you ever witnessed anyone in the photograph?"

"No," she said. "No."

I saw a tear descend to her white dress.

"Have you ever witnessed anyone in the photograph?" I inquired, and I felt cruel, I felt like an awful person, but I was certain that I was performing the right thing.

"No," she said, "I have not. They all look like strangers."

Darkness was amid us. I perilled everything. "Has anyone in this photograph ever witnessed you?"

"I have been waiting for you for so long."

I pointed to the car. "We are searching for Trachimbrod."

"Oh," she said, and she released a river of tears. "You are here. I am it." ∎

■ Who is telling this story? How do we learn about Alexander Perchov's character?

■ How does he structure his narrative?

■ Look closely at his sentence structure in one or two sentences. How does he arrive at his particular convoluted style?

■ Identify two or three phrases that he misuses. How does his use of English make us aware of the language structures that govern this story?

■ Identify instances in which the narrator describes cultural differences between himself and the American. How does point of view contribute to our interpretation of these differences?

POETRY

William Cullen Bryant (1794–1878)

To Cole, the Painter, Departing for Europe (1829)

Thine eyes shall see the light of distant skies;
   Yet, COLE! thy heart shall bear to Europe's strand
   A living image of our own bright land,
Such as upon thy glorious canvas lies;
Lone lakes—savannas where the bison roves—   5
   Rocks rich with summer garlands—solemn streams—
   Skies, where the desert eagle wheels and screams—
Spring bloom and autumn blaze of boundless groves.
Fair scenes shall greet thee where thou goest—fair,
   But different—everywhere the trace of men,   10
   Paths, homes, graves, ruins, from the lowest glen
To where life shrinks from the fierce Alpine air.
   Gaze on them, till the tears shall dim thy sight,
   But keep that earlier, wilder image bright.

- Identify the elements of the strict sonnet form that the poet uses here.
- How does that adherence to form contrast with the poet's instruction to the painter? In what ways does the poet use the structure to deliver his message?

Joe Kane (1952–)

The Boy Who Nearly Won the Texaco Art Competition (2005)

he took a large sheet
of white paper and on this
he made the world an african world
of flat topped trees and dried grasses
and he painted an elephant in the middle   5
and a lion with a big mane and several giraffes
stood over the elephant and some small animals to fill
in the gaps he worked all day had a bath this was saturday

on sunday he put six jackals
in the world and a great big snake   10
and buzzards in the sky and tickbirds
on the elephants back he drew down blue
from the sky to make a river and got the elephants
legs all wet and smudged and one of the jackals got drowned
he put red flowers in the front of the picture and daffodils in the bottom   15
   corners
and his dog major chewing a bone and mrs murphys two cats tom and jerry
and milo the milkman with a cigarette in the corner of his mouth
and his merville dairy float pulled by his wonder horse trigger
that would walk when he said click click and the holy family
in the top right corner with the donkey and cow   20
and sheep and baby jesus and got the 40A bus
on monday morning in to abbey street to hand
it in and the man on the door said
thats a sure winner

■ What governs the organization of the boy's composition?
■ What is the relation between that picture and the descriptions of his own
  world that begin in line 15? What is the impact of no stanza break between
  lines 14 and 15?

Elizabeth Bishop (1911–1979)

Manners for a Child of 1918 (1965)

My grandfather said to me
as we sat on the wagon seat,
"Be sure to remember to always
speak to everyone you meet."

We met a stranger on foot.   5
My grandfather's whip tapped his hat.
"Good day, sir. Good day. A fine day."
And I said it and bowed where I sat.

Then we overtook a boy we knew
with his big pet crow on his shoulder.   10
"Always offer everyone a ride;
don't forget that when you get older,"

my grandfather said. So Willy
climbed up with us, but the crow
gave a "Caw!" and flew off. I was worried.   15
How would he know where to go?

But he flew a little way at a time
from fence post to fence post, ahead;
and when Willy whistled he answered.
"A fine bird," my grandfather said,   20

"and he's well brought up. See, he answers
nicely when he's spoken to.
Man or beast, that's good manners.
Be sure that you both always do."

When automobiles went by,   25
the dust hid the people's faces,
but we shouted "Good day! Good day!
Fine day!" at the top of our voices.

When we came to Hustler Hill,
he said that the mare was tired,   30
so we all got down and walked,
as our good manners required.

■ How is the seventh stanza ("When automobiles ...") like the other stanzas of
the poem? How is it a departure from them?
■ What does the poet suggest here about the difference between contemporary
culture and that of 1918?

Phillis Wheatley (1753–1784)

On Being Brought from Africa to America (1773)

'Twas mercy brought me from my Pagan land,
Taught my benighted soul to understand
That there's a God, that there's a Saviour too:
Once I redemption neither sought nor knew.
Some view our sable race with scornful eye,   5
"Their colour is a diabolic die."

Remember, Christians, Negros, black as Cain,
May be refin'd and join th'angelic train.

- How does the title of the poem help us interpret specific words within the poem?
- Because we are reading this poem more than two centuries after it was written, how might our interpretation of the author's conversion differ from the sentiments that she expresses here?

Robert Frost (1874–1963)

The Road Not Taken (1916)

Two roads diverged in a yellow wood,
And sorry I could not travel both
And be one traveler, long I stood
And looked down one as far as I could
To where it bent in the undergrowth;   5

Then took the other, as just as fair,
And having perhaps the better claim,
Because it was grassy and wanted wear;
Though as for that the passing there
Had worn them really about the same,   10

And both that morning equally lay
In leaves no step had trodden black.
Oh, I kept the first for another day!
Yet knowing how way leads on to way,
I doubted if I should ever come back.   15

I shall be telling this with a sigh
Somewhere ages and ages hence:
Two roads diverged in a wood, and I—
I took the one less traveled by,
And that has made all the difference.   20

- What details does the poet offer to contrast the two paths? In what ways are they alike?
- How does the final stanza lend coherence to the poet's dilemma as he makes his choice?

Thomas Lux (1948–)

The Swimming Pool (1986)

All around the apt. swimming pool
the boys stare at the girls
and the girls look everywhere but the opposite
or down or up. It is
as it was a thousand years ago: the fat   5
boy has it hardest, he
takes the sneers,
prefers the winter so he can wear
his heavy pants and sweater.
Today, he's here with the others.   10
Better they are cruel to him in his presence
than out. Of the five here now (three boys,
two girls) one is fat, three cruel,
and one, a girl, wavers to the side,
all the world tearing at her.   15
As yet she has no breasts
(her friend does) and were it not
for the forlorn fat boy whom she joins
in taunting, she could not bear her terror,
which is the terror   20
of being him. Does it make her happy
that she has no need, right now, of ingratiation,
of acting fool to salve
her loneliness? She doesn't seem
so happy. She is like   25
the lower middle class, that fatal group
handed crumbs so they can drop a few
down lower, to the poor, so they won't kill
the rich. All around
the apt. swimming pool   30
there is what's everywhere: forsakenness
and fear, a disdain for those beneath us
rather than a rage
against the ones above: the exploiters,
the oblivious and unabashedly cruel.   35

- How does the poet use the image of the swimming pool to represent a
  particular social order?
- Why does he claim, "It is / as it was a thousand years ago"?

Lawrence Ferlinghetti (1919–)

Constantly risking absurdity (1958)

Constantly risking absurdity
                        and death
        whenever he performs
                    above the heads
                                of his audience   5
        the poet like an acrobat
                    climbs on rime
                        to a high wire of his own making
and balancing on eyebeams
                        above a sea of faces   10
            paces his way
                        to the other side of day
performing entrechats
                    and sleight-of-foot tricks
and other high theatrics   15
                        and all without mistaking
        any thing
                    for what it may not be
    For he's the super realist
                        who must perforce perceive   20
        taut truth
                    before the taking of each stance or step
in his supposed advance
                        toward that still higher perch
where Beauty stands and waits   25
                    with gravity
                            to start her death-defying leap
    And he
            a little charleychaplin man
                        who may or may not catch   30
            her fair eternal form
                        spreadeagled in the empty air
            of existence

■ According to the poem, how do poets take risks?

■ What specific images does the poet use to connect the act of writing poetry to
  the performance of an acrobat? How does this specific analogy help elaborate
  the meaning of the poem's title?

Allen Ginsberg (1926–1997)

Supermarket in California (1956)

What thoughts I have of you tonight, Walt Whitman, for I walked down
  the sidestreets under the trees with a headache self-conscious looking at
  the full moon.
In my hungry fatigue, and shopping for images, I went into the neon fruit
  supermarket, dreaming of your enumerations!
What peaches and what penumbras! Whole families shopping at night!
  Aisles full of husbands! Wives in the avocados, babies in the tomatoes—
  and you, Garcia Lorca, what were you doing down by the watermelons?

I saw you, Walt Whitman, childless, lonely old grubber, poking among the
  meats in the refrigerator and eyeing the grocery boys.
I heard you asking questions of each: Who killed the pork chops? What   5
  price bananas? Are you my Angel?
I wandered in and out of the brilliant stacks of cans following you, and
  followed in my imagination by the store detective.
We strode down the open corridors together in our solitary fancy tasting
  artichokes, possessing every frozen delicacy, and never passing the cashier.

Where are we going, Walt Whitman? The doors close in an hour. Which way
  does your beard point tonight?
(I touch your book and dream of our odyssey in the supermarket and feel
  absurd.)
Will we walk all night through solitary streets? The trees add shade to shade, 10
  lights out in the houses, we'll both be lonely.
Will we stroll dreaming of the lost America of love past blue automobiles in
  driveways, home to our silent cottage?
Ah, dear father, graybeard, lonely old courage-teacher, what America did
  you have when Charon quit poling his ferry and you got out on a smoking bank and stood watching the boat disappear on the black waters of
  Lethe?

Berkeley 1955

- How does the phrase "shopping for images" explain the poet's problem in this
  poem?
- How might the world that the poet describes here be different from the one
  that Whitman, who got out of Charon's ferry in 1892, described in his poetry?
  How do these differences influence the poet's sense of what are appropriate
  images for American poetry?

Richard Wilbur (1921–)

A Sketch (1975)

Into the lower right
Square of the window frame
There came
       with scalloped flight

A goldfinch, lit upon
The dead branch of a pine,   5
Shining,
       and then was gone,

Tossed in a double arc
Upward into the thatched
And cross-hatched
       pine-needle dark.

Briefly, as fresh drafts stirred   10
The tree, he dulled and gleamed
And seemed
       more coal than bird,

Then, dodging down, returned
In a new light, his perch
A birch—   15
       twig, where he burned

In the sun's broadside ray,
Some seed pinched in his bill.
Yet still
       he did not stay,

But into a leaf-choken pane,
Changeful as even in heaven,   20
Even
       in Saturn's reign,
Tunneled away and hid.
And then? But I cannot well
Tell
       you all that he did.

It was like glancing at rough   25
Sketches tacked on a wall,
And all
      so less than enough

Of gold on beaten wing,
I could not choose that one
Be done   30
      as the finished thing.

■ How does the idea of "glancing at rough / Sketches tacked on a wall" relate to the poet's observation of the goldfinch?

■ How do the first two lines relate to the closing lines?

Miller Williams (1930–)

Thinking about Bill, Dead of AIDS (1989)

We did not know the first thing about
how blood surrenders to even the smallest threat
when old allergies turn inside out,

the body rescinding all its normal orders
to all defenders of flesh, betraying the head,   5
pulling its guards back from all its borders.

Thinking of friends afraid to shake your hand,
we think of your hand shaking, your mouth set,
your eyes drained of any reprimand.

Loving, we kissed you, partly to persuade   10
both you and us, seeing what eyes had said,
that we were loving and we were not afraid.

If we had had more, we would have given more.
As it was we stood next to your bed,
stopping, though, to set our smiles at the door.   15

Not because we were less sure at the last.
Only because, not knowing anything yet,
we didn't know what look would hurt you least.

■ In the fourth stanza, how does the poet describe the kisses? How do this stanza and the final sentence of the poem comment on the social conventions that govern personal interactions?

DRAMA

David Ives (1951–)

Playwright David Ives was born and raised in Chicago. He attended Northwestern University and Yale University School of Drama. Ives is primarily known for his one-act plays. His works include *All in the Timing: Fourteen Plays* (1995), *Mere Mortals: Six One-Act Comedies* (1998), *Lives of the Saints: Seven One-Act Plays* (2000), and *Time Flies and Other Short Plays* (2001). In 1995, he was awarded a Guggenheim Fellowship in playwriting.

Sure Thing (1988)

CHARACTERS

BILL *and* BETTY, *both in their late twenties*
SCENE: *A café table, with a couple of chairs*

(BETTY, *reading at the table. An empty chair oppoite her.* BILL *enters.*)
BILL: Excuse me. Is this chair taken?
BETTY: Excuse me?
BILL: Is this taken?
BETTY: Yes it is.
BILL: Oh. Sorry.   5
BETTY: Sure thing. (*A bell rings softly.*)
BILL: Excuse me. Is this chair taken?
BETTY: Excuse me?
BILL: Is this taken?
BETTY: No, but I'm expecting somebody in a minute.   10
BILL: Oh. Thanks anyway.
BILL: Oh. Thanks anyway.
BETTY: Sure thing. (*A bell rings softly.*)
BILL: Excuse me. Is this chair taken?
BETTY: No, but I'm expecting somebody very shortly.   15
BILL: Would you mind if I sit here till he or she or it comes?
BETTY (*glances at her watch.*): They seem to be pretty late....

BILL: You never know who you might be turning down.

BETTY: Sorry. Nice try, though.

BILL: Sure thing. *(Bell.)* Is this seat taken?   20

BETTY: No it's not.

BILL: Would you mind if I sit here?

BETTY: Yes I would.

BILL: Oh. *(Bell.)* Is this chair taken?

BETTY: No it's not.   25

BILL: Would you mind if I sit here?

BETTY: No. Go ahead.

BILL: Thanks. *(He sits. She continues reading.)* Everyplace else seems to be taken.

BETTY: Mm-hm.

BILL: Great place.   30

BETTY: Mm-hm.

BILL: What's the book?

BETTY: I just wanted to read in quiet, if you don't mind.

BILL: No. Sure thing. *(Bell.)*

BILL: Everyplace else seems to be taken.   35

BETTY: Mm-hm.

BILL: Great place for reading.

BETTY: Yes, I like it.

BILL: What's the book?

BETTY: *The Sound and the Fury*   40

BILL: Oh. Hemingway. *(Bell.)* What's the book?

BETTY: *The Sound and the Fury*

BILL: Oh. Faulkner.

BETTY: Have you read it?

BILL: Not … actually. I've sure read *about* … it, though. It's supposed to   45
be great.

BETTY: It is great.

BILL: I hear it's great. *(Small pause.)* Waiter? *(Bell.)* What's the book?

BETTY: *The Sound and the Fury*

BILL: Oh. Faulkner.

BETTY: Have you read it?   50

BILL: I'm a Mets fan, myself. *(Bell.)*

BETTY: Have you read it?

BILL: Yeah, I read it in college.

BETTY: Where was college?

BILL: I went to Oral Roberts University. *(Bell.)*   55

BETTY: Where was college?

BILL: I was lying. I never really went to college. I just like to party.
(Bell.)

BETTY: Where was college?

BILL: Harvard.

BETTY: Do you like Faulkner? 60

BILL: I love Faulkner. I spent a whole winter reading him once.

BETTY: I've just started.

BILL: I was so excited after ten pages that I went out and bought everything else he wrote. One of the greatest reading experiences of my life. I mean, all that incredible psychological understanding. Page after page of gorgeous prose. His profound grasp of the mystery of time and human existence. The smells of the earth…What do you think?

BETTY: I think it's pretty boring. *(Bell.)*

BILL: What's the book? 65

BETTY: *The Sound and the Fury*

BILL: Oh! Faulkner!

BETTY: Do you like Faulkner?

BILL: I love Faulkner.

BETTY: He's incredible. 70

BILL: I spent a whole winter reading him once.

BETTY: I was so excited after ten pages that I went out and bought everything else he wrote.

BILL: All that incredible psychological understanding.

BETTY: And the prose is so gorgeous.

BILL: And the way he's grasped the mystery of time— 75

BETTY: —and human existence. I can't believe I've waited this long to read him.

BILL: You never know. You might not have liked him before.

BETTY: That's true.

BILL: You might not have been ready for him. You have to hit these things at the right moment or it's no good.

BETTY: That's happening to me. 80

BILL: It's all in the timing. *(Small pause.)* My name's Bill, by the way.

BETTY: I'm Betty.

BILL: Hi.

BETTY: Hi. *(Small pause.)*

BILL: Yes I thought reading Faulkner was…a great experience. 85

BETTY: Yes. *(Small pause.)*

BILL: *The Sound and the Fury*… *(Another small pause.)*

BETTY: Well. Onwards and upwards. *(She goes back to her book.)*

BILL: Waiter—? *(Bell.)* You have to hit these things at the right moment or it's no good.

BETTY: That's happened to me. 90

BILL: It's all in the timing. My name's Bill, by the way.

BETTY: I'm Betty.

BILL: Hi.

BETTY: Hi.

BILL: Do you come in here a lot?   95

BETTY: Actually I'm just in town for two days from Pakistan.

BILL: Oh. Pakistan. *(Bell.)* My name's Bill, by the way.

BETTY: I'm Betty.

BILL: Hi.

BETTY: Hi.   100

BILL: Do you come here a lot?

BETTY: Every once in a while. Do you?

BILL: Not much anymore. Not as much as I used to. Before my nervous
breakdown. *(Bell.)* Do you come in here a lot?

BETTY: Why are you asking?

BILL: Just interested.   105

BETTY: Are you really interested, or do you just want to pick me up?

BILL: No, I'm really interested.

BETTY: Why would you be interested in whether I come in here a lot?

BILL: Just … getting acquainted.

BETTY: Maybe you're only interested for the sake of making small talk long   110
enough to ask me back to your place to listen to some music, or because
you've just rented some great tape for your VCR, or because you've got
some terrific unknown Django Reinhardt record, only all you'll really
want to do is fuck—which you won't do very well—after which you'll
go into the bathroom and pee very loudly, then pad into the kitchen
and get yourself a beer from the refrigerator without asking me whether
I'd like anything, and then you'll proceed to lie back down beside me
and confess that you've got a girlfriend named Stephanie who's away at
medical school in Belgium for a year, and that you've been involved
with her—*off and on*—in what you'll call a very "intricate" relationship, for about *seven YEARS*. None of which *interests* me, mister!

BILL: Okay. *(Bell.)* Do you come in here a lot?

BETTY: Every other day, I think.

BILL: I come in here quite a lot and I don't remember seeing you.

BETTY: I guess we must be on different schedules.

BILL: Missed connections.   115

BETTY: Yes. Different time zones.

BILL: Amazing how you can live right next door to somebody in this town
and never even know it.

BETTY: I know.

BILL: City life.

BETTY: It's crazy.   120

BILL: We probably pass each other in the street every day. Right in front of
this place, probably.

BETTY: Yep.

BILL *(Looks around.)*: Well,the waiters here sure seem to be in some different time zone. I can't seem to locate one anywhere...Waiter! *(He looks
back.)* So what do you— *(He sees that she's gone back to her book.)*

BETTY: I beg pardon?

BILL: Nothing. Sorry. *(Bell.)*   12⁵

BETTY: I guess we must be on different schedules.

BILL: Missed connections.

BETTY: Yes. Different time zones.

BILL: Amazing how you can live right next door to somebody in this town
and never even know it.

BETTY: I know.   13C

BILL: City life.

BETTY: It's crazy.

BILL: You weren't waiting for somebody when I came in, were you?

BETTY: Actually, I was.

BILL: Oh. Boyfriend?   13⁵

BETTY: Sort of.

BILL: What's a sort-of boyfriend?

BETTY: My husband.

BILL: Ah-ha. *(Bell.)* You weren't waiting for somebody when I came in,
were you?

BETTY: Actually I was.   14C

BILL: Oh. Boyfriend?

BETTY: Sort of.

BILL: What's a sort-of boyfriend?

BETTY: We were meeting here to break up.

BILL: Mm-hm...*(Bell.)* What's a sort-of boyfriend?   14⁵

BETTY: My lover. Here she comes right now! *(Bell.)*

BILL: You weren't waiting for somebody when I came in, were you?

BETTY: No, just reading.

BILL: Sort of a sad occupation for a Friday night, isn't it? Reading here, all
by yourself?

BETTY: Do you think so?   15⁰

BILL: Well sure. I mean, what's a good-looking woman like you doing out
alone on a Friday night?

BETTY: Trying to keep away from lines like that.

BILL: No, listen— *(Bell.)* You weren't waiting for somebody when I came
in, were you?

BETTY: No, just reading.

BILL: Sort of a sad occupation for a Friday night, isn't it? Reading here all   15⁵
by yourself?

BETTY: I guess it is, in a way.

BILL: What's a good-looking woman like you doing out alone on a Friday
night anyway? No offense, but...

BETTY: I'm out alone on a Friday night for the first time in a very long
time.

BILL: Oh.

BETTY: You see, I just recently ended a relationship.   160

BILL: Oh.

BETTY: Of rather long standing.

BILL: I'm sorry. (*Small pause.*) Well listen, since reading by yourself *is* such
a sad occupation for a Friday night, would you like to go elsewhere?

BETTY: No...

BILL: Do something else?   165

BETTY: No thanks.

BILL: I was headed out to the movies in a while anyway.

BETTY: I don't think so.

BILL: Big chance to let Faulkner catch his breath. All those long sentences
get him pretty tired.

BETTY: Thanks anyway.   170

BILL: Okay.

BETTY: I appreciate the invitation.

BILL: Sure thing. (*Bell.*) You weren't waiting for somebody when I came in,
were you?

BETTY: No, just reading.

BILL: Sort of a sad occupation for a Friday night, isn't it? Reading here all   175
by yourself?

BETTY: I guess I was trying to think of it as existentially romantic. You
know—cappuccino, great literature, rainy night...

BILL: That only works in Paris. We *could* hop the late plane to Paris. Get
on a Concorde. Find a café...

BETTY: I'm a little short on plane fare tonight.

BILL: Darn it, so am I.

BETTY: To tell you the truth, I was headed to the movies after I finished   180
this section. Would you like to come along? Since you can't locate a
waiter?

BILL: That's a very nice offer, but...

BETTY: Uh-huh. Girlfriend?

BILL: Two, actually. One of them's pregnant, and Stephanie— (*Bell.*)

BETTY: Girlfriend?

BILL: No, I don't have a girlfriend. Not if you mean the castrating bitch I   185
dumped last night. (*Bell.*)

BETTY: Girlfriend?

BILL: Sort of. Sort of.

BETTY: What's a sort-of girlfriend?

BILL: My mother. *(Bell.)* I just ended a relationship, actually.

BETTY: Oh.

BILL: Of rather long standing.

BETTY: I'm sorry to hear it.

BILL: This is my first night out alone in a long time. I feel a little bit at sea, to tell you the truth.

BETTY: So you didn't stop to talk because you're a Moonie, or you have some weird political affiliation—?

BILL: Nope. Straight-down-the-ticket Republican. *(Bell.)* Straight-down-the-ticket Democrat. *(Bell.)* Can I tell you something about politics? *(Bell.)* I like to think of myself as a citizen of the universe. *(Bell.)* I'm unaffiliated.

BETTY: That's a relief. So am I.

BILL: I vote my beliefs.

BETTY: Labels are not important.

BILL: Labels are not important, exactly. Like me, for example. I mean, what does it matter if I had a two-point at— *(Bell.)* —three-point at *(Bell.)* —four-point at college, or if I did come from Pittsburgh— *(Bell.)* —Cleveland— *(Bell.)* —Westchester County?

BETTY: Sure.

BILL: I believe that a man is what he is. *(Bell.)* A person is what he is. *(Bell.)* A person is…what they are.

BETTY: I think so too.

BILL: So what if I admire Trotsky? *(Bell.)* So what if I once had a total-body liposuction? *(Bell.)* So what if I don't have a penis? *(Bell.)* So what if I once spent a year in the Peace Corps? I was acting on my convictions.

BETTY: Sure.

BILL: You can't just hang a sign on a person.

BETTY: Absolutely. I'll bet you're a Scorpio. *(Many bells ring.)* Listen, I was headed to the movies after I finished this section. Would you like to come along?

BILL: That sounds like fun. What's playing?

BETTY: A couple of the really early Woody Allen movies.

BILL: Oh.

BETTY: Don't you like Woody Allen?

BILL: Sure. I like Woody Allen.

BETTY: But you're not crazy about Woody Allen.

BILL: Those early ones kind of get on my nerves.

BETTY: Uh-huh. *(Bell.)*

BILL: Y'know I was headed to the— *(simultaneously.)*

BETTY: I was thinking about—

BILL: I'm sorry.

BETTY: No, go ahead.

BILL: I was going to say that I was headed to the movies in a little while, and...

BETTY: So was I.   220

BILL: The Woody Allen festival?

BETTY: Just up the street.

BILL: Do you like the early ones?

BETTY: I think anybody who doesn't ought to be run off the planet.

BILL: How many times have you seen *Bananas*?   225

BETTY: Eight times.

BILL: Twelve. So are you still interested? *(Long pause.)*

BETTY: Do you like Entenmann's crumb cake ...?

BILL: Last night I went out at two in the morning to get one. *(Small pause.)* Did you have an Etch-a-Sketch as a child?

BETTY: Yes! And do you like Brussels sprouts? *(Small pause.)*   230

BILL: I think they're gross.

BETTY: They *are* gross!

BILL: Do you still believe in marriage in spite of current sentiments against it?

BETTY: Yes.

BILL: And children?   235

BETTY: Three of them.

BILL: Two girls and a boy.

BETTY: Harvard, Vassar, and Brown.

BILL: And will you love me?

BETTY: Yes.   240

BILL: And cherish me forever?

BETTY: Yes.

BILL: Do you still want to go to the movies?

BETTY: Sure thing.

BILL AND BETTY *(together.)*: *Waiter!*   245

(Blackout.)

■ What is the recurring structural device in this play? What defines the beginning and the end of each scene? How does the plot move forward by using this device?

■ How does this structure contribute to our understanding of the two characters? As they redo their scenes, to what extent do they remain true to their identities in previous scenes?

■ What do the characters resolve by the end of the play?

■ How does the play's structure help reveal the social constructs that govern interpersonal behavior?

Experiencing Literature through Writing

1. Select a single work from this chapter (or any other). Look for structural elements that hold the work together, and explain how these structuring devices influence our understanding of the work. As you write, consider the following questions:

   a. What are the components of each element? For instance, you may say that every line in a poem has x number of syllables.

   b. What pattern emerges among these elements?

   c. Is there any part of the work that violates the pattern you have found? How can you explain this departure?

2. The works in this chapter fit into the general theme "rituals and routines." Often, that which is routine becomes invisible. In order to see the routine, we need some sort of outside perspective. Using one or more of the selected works, discuss the extent to which the outsider in the work disrupts the routine that structures the lives of the people that the work is observing.

3. Looking for structures can be fairly formulaic. A work either is or is not a sonnet. Every work in this book has some sort of structure that we can label. A number of those structures derive from efforts to escape other structures. Find a work that seems to be resisting traditional structural labels, and explore how that structural effort contributes to the final impact of the work.

9 Interruption

Where Did That Come From?

Why Is This Here?

The previous chapter details literary structures and conventions that create a sense of coherence within a crafted text. One of the great attractions of ... Cut the transition. Let's move on to the subject of this chapter: interruption.

Although we do as much as we can to separate our lives into distinct, coherent units (and books into tidy chapters), those divisions inevitably disintegrate. Perhaps the most ubiquitous interruptions in our current culture are the cell phone ring tones that blast out of someone else's purse or pocket during class or at some quiet moment in the middle of a movie. These interruptions break the trance that the undisturbed moment held. But in some respects they are more normal than the perfect silence they violate: How much time in any given week do we spend quietly sitting in a lecture hall or movie theater? Interruptions compel us to be aware of how unusual settled composure is. In this respect, interruption and coherence are closely related. Without order, an interruption is insignificant. Without interruption, we'd hardly appreciate order. In this chapter, we'll look at specific interruptions and interruptive techniques that writers use to create an impact or suggest a theme.

INTERRUPTING THE FICTIONAL FRAME

The technique of interruption sometimes allows an author to signal a self-conscious attitude toward narrative. The popular children's film *The Princess*

Bride (1987) begins with a grandfather (Peter Falk) reading a story to his grandson. As the story (in the book) begins, the movie leaves the child's bedroom and follows the "fictional" story. At points, the grandfather's voice interrupts the narrative of the fantasy "book" world, and the film returns to the child's bedroom until we plunge again into the world of the book. The abrupt shifts remind us of the fragile nature of the imaginary world we are entering. The grandson resists entering the book world at the outset of the film, but as the story goes on, he doesn't want anything to interrupt the story. By watching this child, we see something of our own role as an audience. We choose to embrace the fiction of this story just as the skeptical grandson does. The gap between reading a story and being in the story allows the director to play more than usual with the conventions of the fantasy world. There is a sense that the film is allowed to laugh at these conventions even as it employs them. Calling dangerous and fearful creatures "Rodents of Unusual Size," for instance, has a certain literariness; it is a bookish name that might not sound right without the interrupting frame that shows us that this is a story coming out of a book.

There is a long and distinguished history of strategic breaks in fictional narratives. In *Oedipus the King* (p. 67), Sophocles employs a **chorus** to interrupt, interpret, and even take part in the play's action. This group of

The Princess Bride (1987). Fred Savage and Peter Falk in the "real world," where Falk reads the fairy tale to his grandson.

The Princess Bride (1987). Mel Smith, André the Giant, and Mandy Patinkin in the fantasy world of the fairy tale.

voices begins and ends scenes in the play. They analyze Oedipus's actions. They act like a community in response to this king. They ask him questions; they announce the arrival of characters onstage; they react to the developments within the play. We can think of the chorus as the first audience for what occurs onstage; in that capacity, they help shape our (the second audience's) reactions. If the chorus were removed, we would be without an important interpretive guide. If the choral lines were given to specific characters (or even new characters) within the play, we would be forced to assess different questions of perspective. How did she know that? Why did he tell us that? Of course, some choral lines might seem simply inappropriate coming from the mouth of an actual character. The chorus provides an interruption that guides our response without undermining our investment in the reality of the main action. *The Princess Bride* lets us see two worlds simultaneously; how does the use of the chorus in *Oedipus the King* achieve a similar effect?

Experiencing Literature through Interruption

In dramatic presentations, characters may actually intrude into the action and change our consciousness of the action. In texts that we read, another common form of interruption is the footnote. Traditionally reserved for academic works, a footnote indicates a piece of information that helps support the text but is not quite important enough to include in that text. The simplest use of a footnote is to document a source of a statement, but footnotes become much more compelling when they present pieces of information that are too interesting to be excluded but not quite relevant enough to fit into the main text. These are the extra facts that the scholar has discovered and can't bear to leave out entirely. They give a certain personality to the larger work. Some fiction writers pick up on this effect and use it for their creative purposes.

In *The Hitchhiker's Guide to the Galaxy*, Douglas Adams constructs a wildly inventive novel in the form of a travelogue. Adams uses footnotes to offer "factual" background on the unfolding fictional story. In this case, the facts are meant to be entries from the fictional handbook of this comic novel. This guide supposedly contains entries on all significant facts within the galaxy, and the pride of the novel is that a writer is doing research to help update the guide. The novel makes a distinction between the casual style of the guide and the more formal entries that are contained in an imaginary reference work that exists only in the world of the novel, the *Encyclopedia Galactica*. Adams's novel might be classified as a sort of science fiction, comic, social commentary. The plot is rather episodic. The characters are wacky aliens who exhibit familiar social types. Here is an excerpt from Chapter 4 introducing the character of Zaphod Beeblebrox, along with its accompanying footnote.

Douglas Adams (1952– 2001)

from The Hitchhiker's Guide to the Galaxy (1980)

But it was not in any way a coincidence that today, the day of culmination of the project, the great day of unveiling, the day that the Heart of Gold was finally to be introduced to a marveling Galaxy, was also a great day of culmination for Zaphod Beeblebrox. It was for the sake of this day that he had first decided to run for the presidency, a decision that had sent shock waves of astonishment throughout the Imperial Galaxy. Zaphod Beeblebrox? *President?* Not *the* Zaphod Beeblebrox? Not *the* President? Many had seen it as clinching proof that the whole of known creation had finally gone bananas.

Zaphod grinned and gave the boat an extra kick of speed.

Zaphod Beeblebrox, adventurer, ex-hippie, good-timer (crook? quite possibly), manic self-publicist, terribly bad at personal relationships, often thought to be completely out to lunch.

President?

No one had gone bananas, not in that way at least.

Only six people in the entire Galaxy understood the principle on which the Galaxy was governed, and they knew that once Zaphod Beeblebrox had announced his intention to run as President it was more or less a fait accompli: he was ideal presidency fodder.*

What they completely failed to understand was why Zaphod was doing it.

*President: full title President of the Imperial Galactic Government.

The term *Imperial* is kept though it is now an anachronism. The hereditary Emperor is nearly dead and has been for many centuries. In the last moments of his dying coma he was locked in a stasis field which keeps him in a state of perpetual unchangingness. All his heirs are now long dead, and this means that without any drastic political upheaval, power has simply and effectively moved a rung or two down the ladder, and is now seen to be vested in a body that used to act simply as advisers to the Emperor—an elected governmental assembly headed by a President elected by that assembly. In fact it vests in no such place.

The President in particular is very much a figurehead—he wields no real power whatsoever. He is apparently chosen by the government, but the qualities he is required to display are not those of leadership but those of finely judged outrage. For this reason the President is always a controversial choice, always an infuriating but fascinating character. His job is not to wield power but to draw attention away from it. On those criteria Zaphod Beeblebrox is one of the most successful Presidents the Galaxy has ever had—he has already spent two of his ten presidential years in prison for fraud. Very very few people realize that the President and the Government have virtually no power at all, and of these few people only six know whence ultimate political power is wielded. Most of the others secretly believe that the ultimate decision-making process is handled by a computer. They couldn't be more wrong. ∎

Note that this footnote gives a feeling of authority to the fictional world of the text. It creates the illusion that this world has layers of experience from which the book is drawing. This footnote, added to the casual narration of the story itself, suggests a history that has passed since the narrative was written. It also suggests that there are different narratives available about this single story; the footnoted narrative is a bit more academic, perhaps even a bit more "objective," than the version in the main body of the text. This particular interruption gives the illusion that a different consciousness is available to understand the events being narrated, that there is a strand of thought and conversation about these events other than the single strand recounted in the main narrative.

Making Connections

Interruptions like the ones we've just discussed raise questions of perspective—specifically, of reliability or the lack of reliability. The interruption of a footnote gives us a presence from outside the story that can comment upon, judge, or add to the main action. But do we necessarily trust the footnote more than the story? And if we do, why should we? Do you think the footnote (with its academic or scholarly associations) seems a stronger, surer guide than a chorus? Or do you find it easier to trust the chorus? What do you look for to indicate how much you should trust the "outside" voice? What might indicate that the footnote is no more the author's voice than any other part of the text?

STRUCTURAL INTERRUPTIONS

In the previous examples, a primary effect of the interruption was to enhance the audience's awareness of its own role within the action. The chorus, for example, models an audience that is more involved in the action than any actual audience. Interruption, though, can do more than create audience awareness. It can draw our attention to important moments. For example, look at the following poem by William Butler Yeats.

William Butler Yeats (1865–1939)

The Folly of Being Comforted (1902)

One that is ever kind said yesterday:
"Your well-belovèd's hair has threads of grey,
And little shadows come about her eyes;
Time can but make it easier to be wise
Though now it seems impossible, and so   5
All that you need is patience."
                              Heart cries, "No,
I have not a crumb of comfort, not a grain.
Time can but make her beauty over again:
Because of that great nobleness of hers   10
The fire that stirs about her, when she stirs,
Burns but more clearly. O she had not these ways
When all the wild Summer was in her gaze."
O heart! O heart! if she'd but turn her head,
You'd know the folly of being comforted.   15

You don't even need to read the words to notice that line 7 looks different from the rest of the poem; it is markedly shorter than any of the others. When we look closely at the poetic structure of the poem, we see that this line should be part of line 6; "No" rhymes with "so," and the poem is made up of a series of rhyming couplets. But this break reflects a real break within the action the poem recounts. The first part of the poem is an offer of comfort, but at line 7, the poet rejects that comfort. The comforting thought is interrupted, just as the line is interrupted, with Heart's cry. There is a certain passionate violence to this interruption. The broken line shows us that Heart has lost patience listening to the kind words. The break in the pattern of the poem illustrates the passion of the heart that refuses all rational words of comfort.

Look for a similar division within Mary Oliver's "Bone Poem." The poem begins with a focus on the "litter" from owl meals as it "Sinks into the wet leaves" (line 4). At line 5, the poem begins to change as "time sits with her slow spoon." Within the next three lines (5–8), we move forward through "light years" so that the poet speaks of a singular "*we*"; from this distance, distinct beings are reduced to the primal substances that make up all living things.

Mary Oliver (1935–)

Bone Poem (1979)

The litter under the tree
Where the owl eats—shrapnel

Of rat bones, gull debris—
Sinks into the wet leaves

Where time sits with her slow spoon, 5
Where *we* becomes singular, and a quickening

From light years away
Saves and maintains. O holy

Protein, o hallowed lime,
O precious clay! 10

Tossed under the tree
The cracked bones

Of the owl's most recent feast
Lean like shipwreck, starting

The long fall back to the center— 15
The seepage, the flowing,

The equity: sooner or later
In the shimmering leaves

The rat will learn to fly, the owl
Will be devoured. 20

The interruption occurs in the middle of line 8. One sentence ends, and suddenly, "O holy" crowds into the line. The exclamation continues for two more lines (9–10) ("O holy Protein, o hallowed lime, / O precious clay!"), proclaiming the substances that are the essence of this more distant point of view. After this outburst, the poem returns to the specific debris from "the owl's most recent feast" as these bones start their "long fall back to the center" (line 15) and to their elemental nature. Here the interruption is a central outburst, almost a big bang after which the poem returns to the form, subject, and philosophical musings that it had before the interruption.

Experiencing Film through Interruption

Interruptions often cause us, as the audience of the work, to reexamine our relation to the work that we are viewing. Think about the following example.

Many performing arts venues want to quiet the electronic noises that often interrupt performances. One strategy has been to create a loud ring tone just as the show is about to get under way. This fake interruption (followed by an announcement about turning off all phones) makes people in the audience uncomfortable. First, we are ready to glare at the offender. Then, we realize that we have been drawn into a fiction. This ring tone is not real, but our own real phone has the potential to be just as disruptive. As audience members, we participate in the performance, even if our part in the performance is simply our silence. In fact, this created "interruption" illustrates an aspect of the complex relation that we have to fiction itself. Although people tend to ignore an announcement they have heard many times before (such as the emergency information that flight attendants recite before a plane takes off), they react to this fictional interruption differently. They are prompted to think about the way they relate to the fiction.

Film has been particularly adept at playing with the relations between the fictional world on the screen and the world outside that screen—between reel life and real life. Which of these worlds is the interruption? Are we challenged to question what we take as real by such films as Woody Allen's *The Purple Rose of Cairo?* In the 1984 film, a movie hero steps out of the screen and into the life of a lonely woman watching the picture. That break leads us (like the woman, we are moviegoers) to reflect on our desire to stay in the fictional world that is on the screen. Gary Ross's *Pleasantville* (1998) reverses the ploy; two contemporary characters are thrust into a 1950s black-and-white TV world. This abrupt interruption of a contemporary suburban family drama eventually leads us to rethink our problems as well as our nostalgia for a "better time" that we like to believe really existed. Films can also break our narrative expectations and thereby make us more sensitive to those expectations. The multiple plots of *Pulp Fiction* (1994) and their seemingly random order disrupt our sense of how a film should tell a story, but the apparent disorder actually evolves into its own coherence. When we see

Pulp Fiction (1994). This film still shows Vega, played by John Travolta, in the closing scene of the film. The audience sees him alive and happy *after* seeing him killed.

Vincent Vega (John Travolta) strolling casually offscreen at the end of the film in his UC Santa Cruz Banana Slugs T-shirt, we feel a kind of lightness even though we know Vincent is soon to die humiliatingly while sitting on the toilet. Or perhaps it's more accurate to say we know he has already died in an earlier scene in the movie. The action that unfolds on the screen doesn't mesh with our sense of normal time or linear development of a story. Is director Quentin Tarantino teasing us about our needs for a happy ending or for the artifice of the many happy endings we've seen in movies? Or is he demonstrating that movies have the power to transcend real pain; maybe that, for Tarantino, is their special gift. The sort of disruption that operates so effectively in *Pulp Fiction*, and in a film such as *Run Lola Run* (1999), challenges our notions of what filmed stories can be.

JUXTAPOSITION

Juxtaposition is the rhetorical technique of putting two (or more) things next to each other; the resulting contrast or similarity makes us see both objects differently than we saw them when each stood by itself. A simple exercise in juxtaposition uses two colored fabrics. When two colors are placed next to each other, the juxtaposition will bring out qualities in both colors that are not evident when the colors sit separately. For instance, it might be difficult to determine whether a particular fabric is black or navy blue. By setting the fabric in question next to a fabric that you know to be black, it becomes easier to judge. Neither color has changed, but slight differences become apparent with the comparison. In works of art, juxtapositions are often more strongly marked; radical contrasts break or interrupt our customary ways of interpreting the world. The pairing of objects that initially appear unrelated forces us to search for connections amid obvious differences.

Juxtaposition is especially effective in photography. Margaret Bourke-White's photograph of a bread line of real people (African Americans) standing in front of a fictional white family in the propaganda poster delivers a clear message. The contrast between the real and the imaginary here is stark. The seriousness of the people standing in line makes a mockery of the claim on the billboard. The jubilant white family enjoying a comfortable life above seems to bear no real relation to the American lives being led by the people in line below. "There's no way like the American Way" takes on a different meaning from the billboard's intent because of Bourke-White's juxtaposition. In the photograph, we see an irony of race and class in American society. The sign insists that the country has the "World's Highest Standard of Living," but the real people in this scene have no access to the material goods that the family in the poster behind them are celebrating.

Margaret Bourke-White, *At the Time of the Louisville Flood* (1937)

As we use this photograph to illustrate the idea of juxtaposition, it is important to acknowledge that there is no necessary relation between the particular people standing in line and the billboard that happens to be behind them. As soon as we look at Bourke-White's composition, the convergence of real people and propaganda takes on meaning. **Synchronicity** refers to events that coincide in time and appear to be related but have no discoverable causal connection. In this instance, the people and the poster illustrate tensions within American society more clearly than any extended exploration of race and class in our culture. This moment that Bourke-White has captured symbolizes larger social problems. We should notice the sophistication necessary to read the ironic juxtaposition that appears here. Unless we are aware of the discrepancy between white and black culture and unless we can read the markers of wealth and poverty, we cannot appreciate the synchronicity that Bourke-White has captured. When we compared two fabrics to discover which one was blue, we had a particular standard that we were trying to test; the comparison was useful because we knew what we were looking for. When we come to this photograph, we bring a set of cultural standards that help us see the meanings that Bourke-White presents.

Making Connections

Irony can be considered a strategy of interruption because it works by introducing the unexpected. In general, irony arises from a gap between expectation and actuality, intention and realization, appearance and truth. Because irony depends upon suggestion rather than explicit statement, it requires that a viewer or reader be alert to small signals. It is by nature complex and subject to subtle shading and **ambiguity** (uncertainty or multiplicity of meaning, suggestive qualities of expression, contradictory implications). Critics often specify distinct types of irony. **Dramatic irony** refers to a gap between what a character knows and what an audience understands; a character who doesn't appreciate the significance of the words he or she speaks conveys a dramatic irony. The audience is, in effect, alerted to meanings that the author wants to communicate from outside the character's consciousness. A character who deliberately plays upon the difference between words and meaning expresses **verbal irony**; such a character might deliberately understate a problem to emphasize its gravity or overstate a problem to highlight its triviality. Bourke-White's photograph illustrates what is often called **contextual** or **situational irony** — an irony that arises from coincidence or circumstances.

Experiencing Literature through Juxtaposition

In "Tattoo," Ted Kooser uses juxtaposition to examine the tattoo that he sees on the arm of a man at a yard sale. But instead of describing just the tattoo, Kooser describes the context in which he sees the mark. He reads the tattoo as a signal of an identity that seems out of place in the mundane domestic world of a yard sale.

Ted Kooser (1939–)

Tattoo (2005)

What once was meant to be a statement—
a dripping dagger held in the fist
of a shuddering heart—is now just a bruise
on a bony old shoulder, the spot
where vanity once punched him hard   5
 and the ache lingered on. He looks like
someone you had to reckon with,
strong as a stallion, fast and ornery,
but on this chilly morning, as he walks
between the tables at a yard sale   10
 with the sleeves of his tight black T-shirt
rolled up to show us who he was,
he is only another old man, picking up
broken tools and putting them back,
his heart gone soft and blue with stories.   15

Compare the scene that Kooser presents here with Bourke-White's photograph. In the photograph, we see a scene that captures disturbing inequities within American culture. What does Kooser capture in the tattoo that he sees at this yard sale? Think, too, about the process of conveying this juxtaposition. Bourke-White presents only the image. What commentary does Kooser add to the image that he sees? Look at the specific words and phrases he uses so that we will see the juxtaposition as he sees it.

MONTAGE

In elementary school, you may have been asked to do a montage—that is, to paste a collection of images onto a single sheet of paper. The images might at first glance seem altogether random, but randomness wasn't the point of the assignment. The idea was to create an effect or underscore a theme through juxtaposed images. **Montage** (echoing a French verb meaning "to assemble") is a useful word in the study of both film and literature.

In film criticism, montage refers to a style of editing that uses sudden juxtapositions of images, surprising cuts, and radical shifts in perspective. This technique differs greatly from what has been called the "classic Hollywood" or "invisible" style of editing—a style that seeks to achieve naturalistic effects. The montage style is essentially interruptive; it shakes viewers from a settled attention to narrative and character and forces them to experience film as film. It deliberately breaks the illusion we often seek in films of observing actions as they actually happen.

Literary critics have borrowed the word *montage* to describe dramatic juxtapositions of images or scenes or even narrative voices. A novelist might, for example, break a narrative by inserting actual advertising jingles, headlines, even news stories from the historical time of the narrative to contextualize the fictional action. A fictional or dramatic montage might also be constructed from a collection of short stories/skits or character sketches— almost snapshots of life. Sandra Cisneros's *The House on Mango Street* does just that. A poet might give us a series of images, as does Wallace Stevens in "Thirteen Ways of Looking at a Blackbird" (p. 691), and not require us to connect the images thematically. Stevens wrote, for example, that his famous poem aimed at communicating a series of "sensations."

Experiencing Film through Juxtaposition

Filmmaker Michael Moore is a master of juxtaposition, a gift that has earned him both an Oscar and harsh criticism. In his first film, the documentary *Roger and Me* (1989), Moore argues that corporations have a responsibility to the communities in which they work, not just to their shareholders.

This film traces the actions of General Motors in Flint, Michigan, where the company had recently shut down manufacturing plants and moved production to countries where labor was cheaper. Films and dramatic productions can, of course, add sound as yet another element in the mix: what we see clashes with what we hear. In the devastating final scene, Moore shows General Motors chairman Roger Smith, the "Roger" of the film's title, delivering a banal Christmas address to GM workers, talking about compassion, and quoting Charles Dickens, as "an expert on Christmas" while a choir sings in the background. Moore cuts away from the film footage of the speech to show a laid-off GM worker and her family in Flint being evicted from their home on Christmas Eve. On the sound track, Smith continues to drone on about caring for others while we watch the eviction officer setting the family's Christmas tree and presents out by the curb. As Moore has edited this scene, Smith's words seem empty, self-serving, and hypocritical. By juxtaposing the bland unreality of Smith's speech and the harsh suffering of the evicted family, Moore uses the scene as the culmination of the

A publicity shot for *Roger and Me* dramatizes director Michael Moore's techniques in the film. Moore dresses as a common man who identifies with the hard times suffered in Flint, Michigan, when General Motors closed production facilities there.

Moore juxtaposes news photos, such as this shot of General Motors chairman Roger Smith meeting with President Ronald Reagan, with Smith's on-camera refusal to meet with Moore to talk about laid-off workers in Flint.

argument he is making in his film that Smith, who serves as a symbol of corporate America, is responsible for both the content of this speech and for the corporate actions that impact American workers. The images and words set in such marked contrast make Moore's argument.

In this context, the juxtaposition echoes the work of Bourke-White. Because editing is so apparent in Moore's work, some critics argue that his "documentary" distorts the truth. His editorial techniques, they claim, create a fictional version of reality that suits his political purpose. Try to use the same critique to challenge Bourke-White's image. This photograph suggests that the people standing in line have some actual relation to the poster. Are they deliberately contradicting its image? Is the poster there to mock them? Is the single image more or less manipulative than film? However we respond to such questions, it is clear that we are responding to a crafted work of art.

A Note to Student Writers: Making Comparisons Relevant

Observing juxtaposition as an effective strategy in these crafted texts can help us in our own writing. A common writing assignment will ask students to "compare and contrast" two subjects (books, characters, settings, poems, films, and so on). This technique casts a wide net in the hope that students might find something of value in the comparisons. By juxtaposing, we gain a clearer sense of the issues/elements under analysis. The technique, however, brings with it potential problems.

All writers must be careful to measure and evaluate the demands any form of interruption makes on a reader. In Ted Kooser's "Tattoo," juxtaposition is used to imply or suggest a thought or feeling. Kooser never tells us that the man at the yard sale was foolish to get a tattoo in his earlier life or that the man has now settled down into some sort of domesticity or that his former ferociousness has faded. It is up to us to draw conclusions from the juxtaposition of the yard sale scene and the tattoo's image. The suggestive power of the poem is part of its beauty. An analytical paper that stays at the level of suggestion and implication won't likely be read so favorably. Critical papers usually need to be more explicit about the purpose and the point of the comparison. In a similar way, an abrupt turn in a poem, story, play, or movie might serve as an effective interruption. It might jar us into paying attention or shake us out of our standard way of seeing things. But a strong interruption in a critical essay might be taken as incoherence, or just plain sloppiness. Writers must understand that readers don't come to every text with the same set of expectations and demands.

Compare/contrast assignments are challenging largely because they require you to bring together what might seem dissimilar things. The very nature of the task carries a risk of confusing the reader (what does A have to do with B?; does a discussion of B merely interrupt the discussion of A?). In writing a compare/contrast paper, you are required to bring together ideas whether or not an author has already done that for you. In this sort of paper, the comparison is entirely yours. You must, therefore, justify your approach. It's not enough in a compare/contrast paper to simply note similarities and differences and trust the reader to make sense of how everything adds up. You need to think about how the process of setting two texts alongside each other allows you to see something you might otherwise miss.

As a writer, it is helpful to imagine a nagging voice at your ear, constantly asking, "So what?" about everything that you write down. Your answer to that question is the beginning of your analysis. That answer will structure your paper. Until you answer that question, you have only made observations about the materials you are studying. And after you answer that question the first time, you should continue to ask it of every point of comparison or contrast. The more insistent you can be in challenging your own material, the more effective your analysis will be.

There is yet another lesson about compare/contrast papers to be learned from Michael Moore's film: an organizational lesson. Moore keeps the policies of Roger Smith parallel to the poverty in Flint, Michigan. His attempts to talk with Roger Smith are part of the discussions that he carries on with the unemployed people of Flint. When he talks with the managers at GM, he talks about the responsibility of the corporation to the workers it employs and to the surrounding community. He does not devote half the film to poverty and then switch to a discussion of GM policies. The two strands of the discussion are consistently integrated. By the time we reach the climactic final scenes in the film, Moore has prepared us as viewers to see the connections between Smith's words and the evicted family. Whether or not we agree with Moore's argument, we can see that it is a powerful rhetorical strategy and one that you can adopt for your own purposes.

MODELING CRITICAL ANALYSIS: T. S. ELIOT, THE LOVE SONG OF J. ALFRED PRUFROCK

As we return to Eliot's "Prufrock" (p. 653), we see how much this poem is marked by interruptions of various sorts. The stanzas are irregular. There are rhymed couplets that might be described as a chorus ("In the room the women come and go / Talking of Michelangelo"). Stanzas are divided sometimes with simply a blank line (see for instance, the division between lines 12 and 13); other times there are sectional markers dividing them (between lines 69 and 70, 74 and 75, 110 and 111). Within the stanzas, ellipses, or three successive dots (lines 10, 72, 77, and 120); dashes (lines 83, 95, 102, and 103); and parentheses (lines 41, 44, and 64) interrupt the narrative. Often, it seems the speaker is interrupted before he can complete an idea. In this poem the sheer volume of the interruption is staggering. It is useful to go through and mark each interruption, but in our analysis, we will concentrate on just a few and explain why we find those particular interruptions significant to our growing understanding of this complex poem.

The poem begins with a command, "Let us go," and throughout the first stanza, we see that command three times (lines 1, 4, and 12). The narrator describes the scenes where he means to be going, but by line 10, we feel the tension between that impulse to move forward and the voice that signals inertia. The interruption at line 10 is a series of three dots. The poem's first sentence has finally ended, and the three dots indicate a pause. At the end of this sentence, the narrator compares the streets he describes to a form of intellectual inquiry ("like a tedious argument / Of insidious intent / To lead you to an overwhelming question"). As the speaker interrupts his rambling simile about "half-deserted streets," we begin to see the irony within this voice: in spite of the "Let us go" that begins the sentence, this tendency to lapse into intense scrutiny is precisely what keeps the speaker from going anywhere. We hear that conflict in line 11, a line that interrupts the abstraction of the "overwhelming question" by getting back to the desire to go: "Oh, do not ask, 'What is it?' / Let us go and make our visit.'" Suddenly, we have two sentences in two lines. There are no images to wade through here. This rhymed couplet reacts against the wandering construction of the first ten lines of the poem. This interruption sounds like a different voice from the one that offers elaborate descriptions, not of any destination, but of the circuitous route that they must take as they go. So, the interruption here moves us out of the first stanza as it shows us that there are opposing impulses leading us through the poem.

Lines 13 and 14 offer another interruption: "In the room the women come and go / Talking of Michelangelo." We are suddenly off the street. These women and their room appear out of nowhere. What can we do with these two lines? As noted in the discussion of coherence in the previous chapter, it's helpful to note that they are repeated in lines 35 and 36. When a song has a chorus, a soloist might sing the verse and invite the audience to join in at the chorus. The chorus is usually short and simple enough that everyone can join in at the appropriate moment. In a song it functions to anchor us rhythmically, emotionally, and thematically. But what does Michelangelo have to do with Prufrock's visit? This chorus suggests that the talk about Michelangelo may be rather empty even though it is intimidating to someone who is not part of the women's social circle. The women belong to a place where Prufrock might like to be, but a place he cannot quite bring himself to go. The lines function to interrupt and disconcert Prufrock—the confident chorus in contrast to his tentative indecision. At the same time, they lend some coherence to the poetic form. The repeated interruption offers something familiar within a poem that appears at first to be nothing but interruptions. And as mentioned at the start of the chapter, if there were no structure, there would be nothing to interrupt.

Using Interruption to Focus Writing and Discussion

■ An interruption suggests that there should be some established order to interrupt. What is that order? How is it established in this particular work?

- Is there some interruption of the stasis within the text? For instance, is action interrupted by inaction; inaction interrupted by action; action interrupted by another action; a thought interrupted by action; a thought interrupted by another thought? Is there some interruption of the movement of the text itself? Does a poem suddenly stop rhyming, or is the rhythm thrown off; does a narrator become incoherent; does the style of the section change? Is there something that is simply surprising and difficult to account for? What is the interruption?

- Identify the moment that the interruption occurs in the text. Try to isolate the moment as specifically as possible. Is there a single sentence, phrase, or word that embodies the interruption?

- How is this word (or series of words) somehow different from the words around it? What makes it stand out? Is there some graphic method of representing the difference? What does the author do to announce this interruption? What makes you notice this interruption?

- What are we supposed to do with the interruption? Does the author give us any clues? Does the author offer any analysis of the moment? If so, describe how the author tells us this interruption is important.

- Is there a return to the original order that was interrupted? Or is there some new order? Has all order been lost? Has the text simply gone on to something else? Is there some pattern of interruptions?

- Why is this interruption interesting? Looking at an increasing number of different interruptions, you may begin to see patterns in their significance. How does this specific interruption fit into the patterns of interruptions that we have studied within this chapter?

- What is the purpose of the interruptions? What happens in the text that could not happen without the interruption?

- Locate specific juxtapositions that the interruptions in the text make available to us.

  - What images, ideas, characters, or situations have been paired in this particular text?
  - How is it that the audience gains access to each image?
  - How does one add meaning to the other?
  - In what ways do the two images work differently?
  - How does the author compel the audience to look at the two together?

- How does the comparison of the world of the text before and after the interruption offer insight into the routine that has been interrupted? How much of this insight is available to characters within the text, and how much is available to those who are reading the text?

Anthology

FRAMING, MAPPING, AND EXPLORATION: PLACING INTERRUPTION

Laura Riding's brief poem "The Map of Places" questions assurances. People make maps (and plans and dreams), but the spirit of exploration depends upon a deeply felt sense that we have no maps to guide us with certainty. Maps of places, Riding notes at the outset, are subject to change. The paper they are printed on tears. There is somehow another level of reality that exists securely whether it is charted or not. That insight is interrupted, and the second stanza turns abruptly to a distinct sense of a modern condition "now" we *seem* to have things covered—firmly fixed. But Riding leaves us with a sense that this condition is a debilitating illusion. Some mystery seems essential to our humanity.

The readings in this group map places and map experience. The authors move us to consider how we frame (contain, order, represent) both physical and emotional space. Yet the authors (like Riding) interrupt the effort. The frame of reference breaks, and we're back to the sense that life must remain exploratory. Perhaps Joseph Conrad's "The Secret Sharer" would seem an exception. After all, his young captain learns to take charge decisively, to assert control within his sphere of action. But he is quite self-conscious about this process of maturation; he comes to impose an understanding on his situation. He creates through his choices a sense of self that will serve him well in a career at sea. He is, in a profound way, a self-made man. And all the strenuous self-reflection is prompted by a sudden interruption in routine. The captain's hiding of his secret sharer makes maintaining composure difficult. If a life and a career were not at stake, one could narrate the hiding, the narrow escapes, and the awkward contrivances (think of how confused the poor steward is by the captain's seemingly capricious orders) as a bit of slapstick comedy.

Jorge Luis Borges might be considered a master of interruptive strategies. "The Garden of Forking Paths" is interrupted even before it gets started. Borges opens his story with what seems a scholarly note that abruptly introduces the fragment to follow. Here the announcement of "missing pages" serves to remind us of what we don't know—or what stories can and cannot tell us. The fragment itself contains references to other bits of fragmentary information that must be put together—mapped out—in order to be read. This story takes us on many turns through its own garden of forking paths. As you read, think of how Borges has made you aware of the reader/seeker role you take every time you engage with a constructed work of art.

Shakespeare's *Hamlet* also starts with an interruption (the ghost breaking the stillness of a night watch) and ends with what we might consider the ultimate interruption—sudden death. For our purposes though, it's the interruption in the middle of the play that demands particular attention. Roughly halfway through, Shakespeare gives us a play within the play. That is, he has his hero commission a dramatic piece that he hopes will reveal the guilt of the king. That piece has its effects on us, too, for it influences our understanding of the action that is unfolding in the larger play. And Shakespeare seems to delight in peeling back layers of fiction within his dramatic world, for he has Hamlet interrupt the play within the play in order to comment on the action. Ophelia aptly remarks, "You are as good as a chorus, my lord." And in this scene that is very much the role Hamlet plays. But Hamlet's commentary is not the only interruption. His strategy works so well that the king stands and exits when the action proves too close to the truth of his crime. The evening's entertainment is brought to an abrupt end. Hamlet has framed a play in order to confirm a truth. Shakespeare has, of course, framed that play by a still larger one.

FICTION

Jorge Luis Borges (1899–1986)

Jorge Luis Borges was born in Buenos Aires, Argentina. Because his paternal grandmother was English, Borges was fluent in both English and Spanish from an early age. His frail health prevented him from having what might be considered a normal childhood, but he compensated by spending much of his time reading in his father's well-stocked library. These childhood preoccupations with language and learning are also central themes in the mature Borges's poetry and fiction. Borges's fiction has received the most international acclaim, in part because of the relatively larger audience for fiction and because it loses less in translation than does poetry, but he was also one of the preeminent modern poets in Spanish. Particularly influential are Borges's many meta-fictions, short stories in which the boundaries between art and life, reality and fantasy, writer and work, are blurred or eliminated.

The Garden of Forking Paths (Andrew Hurley, trans;
1941)

For Victoria Ocampo

On page 242 of *The History of the World War*, Liddell Hart tells us that an Allied offensive against the Serre-Montauban line (to be mounted by thirteen

British divisions backed by one thousand four hundred artillery pieces) had been planned for July 24, 1916, but had to be put off until the morning of the twenty-ninth. Torrential rains (notes Capt. Liddell Hart) were the cause of that delay—a delay that entailed no great consequences, as it turns out. The statement which follows—dictated, reread, and signed by Dr. Yu Tsun, former professor of English in the *Hochschule* at Tsingtao—throws unexpected light on the case. The two first pages of the statement are missing.

…and I hung up the receiver. Immediately afterward, I recognised the voice that had answered in German. It was that of Capt. Richard Madden. Madden's presence in Viktor Runeberg's flat meant the end of our efforts and (though this seemed to me quite secondary, or *should have seemed*) our lives as well. It meant that Runeberg had been arrested, or murdered. Before the sun set on that day, I would face the same fate. Madden was implacable—or rather, he was obliged to be implacable. An Irishman at the orders of the English, a man accused of a certain lack of zealousness, perhaps even treason, how could he fail to embrace and give thanks for this miraculous favour—the discovery, capture, perhaps death, of two agents of the German Empire? I went upstairs to my room; absurdly, I locked the door, and then I threw myself, on my back, onto my narrow iron bed. Outside the window were the usual rooftops and the overcast six o'clock sun. I found it incredible that this day, lacking all omens and premonitions, should be the day of my implacable death. Despite my deceased father, despite my having been a child in a symmetrical garden in Hai Feng—was I, now, about to die? Then I reflected that all things happen to *oneself*, and happen precisely, precisely *now*. Century follows century, yet events occur only *in the present*; countless men in the air, on the land and sea, yet everything that truly happens, happens *to me*.… The almost unbearable memory of Madden's horsey face demolished those mental ramblings. In the midst of my hatred and my terror (now I don't mind talking about terror—now that I have foiled Richard Madden, now that my neck hungers for the rope), it occurred to me that that brawling and undoubtedly happy warrior did not suspect that I possessed the Secret—the name of the exact location of the new British artillery park on the Ancre. A bird furrowed the grey sky, and I blindly translated it into an aeroplane, and that aeroplane into many (in the French sky), annihilating the artillery park with vertical bombs. If only my throat, before a bullet crushed it, could cry out that name so that it might be heard in Germany.… But my human voice was so terribly inadequate. How was I to make it reach the Leader's ear—the ear of that sick and hateful man who knew nothing of Runeberg and me save that we were in Staffordshire, and who was vainly awaiting word from us in his arid office in Berlin, poring infinitely through the newspapers?…*I must flee*, I said aloud. I sat up noiselessly, in needless but perfect silence, as though Madden were already just outside my door.

Something—perhaps the mere show of proving that my resources were non-existent—made me go through my pockets. I found what I knew I would find: the American watch, the nickel-plated chain and quadrangular coin, the key ring with the compromising and useless keys to Runeberg's flat, the notebook, a letter I resolved to destroy at once (and never did), the false passport, one crown, two shillings, and a few odd pence, the red-and-blue pencil, the handkerchief, the revolver with its single bullet. Absurdly, I picked it up and hefted it, to give myself courage. I vaguely reflected that a pistol shot can be heard at a considerable distance. In ten minutes, my plan was ripe. The telephone book gave me the name of the only person able to communicate the information: he lived in a suburb of Fenton, less than a half hour away by train.

I am a coward. I can say that, now that I have carried out a plan whose dangerousness and daring no man will deny. I know that it was a terrible thing to do. I did not do it for Germany. What do I care for a barbaric country that has forced me to the ignominy of spying? Furthermore, I know of a man of England—a modest man—who in my view is no less a genius than Goethe. I spoke with him for no more than an hour, but for one hour he was Goethe.... No—I did it because I sensed that the Leader looked down on the people of my race—the countless ancestors whose blood flows through my veins. I wanted to prove to him that a yellow man could save his armies. And I had to escape from Madden. His hands, his voice, could beat upon my door at any moment. I silently dressed, said good-bye to myself in the mirror, made my way downstairs, looked up and down the quiet street, and set off. The train station was not far from my flat, but I thought it better to take a cab. I argued that I ran less chance of being recognised that way; the fact is, I felt I was visible and vulnerable—infinitely vulnerable—in the deserted street. I recall that I told the driver to stop a little ways from the main entrance to the station. I got down from the cab with willed and almost painful slowness. I would be going to the village of Ashgrove, but I bought a ticket for a station farther down the line. The train was to leave at eight-fifty, scant minutes away. I had to hurry; the next train would not be until nine-thirty. There was almost no one on the platform. I walked through the cars; I recall a few workmen, a woman dressed in mourning weeds, a young man fervently reading Tracitus' *Annals*, and a cheerful-looking wounded soldier. The train pulled out at last. A man I recognised ran, vainly, out to the end of the platform; it was Capt. Richard Madden. Shattered, trembling, I huddled on the other end of the seat, far from the feared window.

From that shattered state I passed into a state of almost abject cheerfulness. I told myself that my duel had begun, and that in dodging my adversary's thrust—even by forty minutes, even thanks to the slightest smile from fate—the first round had gone to me. I argued that this small win prefigured total victory. I argued that the win was not really even so small, since without the precious hour that the trains had given me, I'd be in gaol, or dead. I argued (no less sophistically) that my cowardly cheerfulness proved that I was a man capable of following this adventure through to its successful end. From that weakness I drew strength that was never to abandon me. I foresee that mankind will resign itself more and more fully every day to more and more horrendous undertakings; soon there will be nothing but warriors and brigands. I give them this piece of advice: *He who is to perform a horrendous act should imagine to himself that it is already done, should impose upon himself a future as irrevocable as the past.* That is what I did, while my eyes—the eyes of a man already dead—registered the flow of that day perhaps to be my last, and the spreading of the night. The train ran sweetly, gently, through woods of ash trees. It stopped virtually in the middle of the countryside. No one called out the name of the station. "Ashgrove?" I asked some boys on the platform. "Ashgrove," they said, nodding. I got off the train.

A lamp illuminated the platform, but the boy's faces remained within the area of shadow. "Are you going to Dr. Stephen Albert's house?" one queried. Without waiting for an answer, another of them said: "The house is a far way, but you'll not get lost if you follow that road there to the left, and turn left at every crossing." I tossed them a coin (my last), went down some stone steps, and started down the solitary road. It ran ever so slightly downhill and was of elemental dirt. Branches tangled overhead, and the low round moon seemed to walk along beside me.

For one instant, I feared that Richard Madden had somehow seen through my desperate plan, but I soon realized that that was impossible. The boy's advice to turn always to the left reminded me that that was the common way of discovering the central lawn of a certain type of maze. I am something of a *connoisseur* of mazes: not for nothing am I the great-grandson of that Ts'ui Pen who was governor of Yunan province and who renounced all temporal power in order to write a novel containing more characters than the *Hung Lu Meng* and construct a labyrinth in which all men would lose their way. Ts'ui Pen devoted thirteen years to those disparate labours, but the hand of a foreigner murdered him and his novel made no sense and no one ever found the labyrinth. It was under English trees that I meditated on that lost labyrinth: I pictured it perfect and inviolate on the secret summit of a mountain; I pictured its outlines blurred by rice paddies, or underwater; I pictured it as infinite—a labyrinth not of octagonal pavillions and paths that turn back upon themselves, but of rivers and provinces and kingdoms.... I imagined a labyrinth of labyrinths, a maze of mazes, a twisting, turning, ever-widening labyrinth that contained both past and future and somehow implied the stars. Absorbed in those illusory imaginings, I forgot that I was a pursued man; I felt myself, for an indefinite while, the abstract perceiver of the world. The vague, living countryside, the moon, the remains of the day did their work in me; so did the gently downward road, which forestalled all possibility of weariness. The evening was near, yet infinite.

5

The road dropped and forked as it cut through the now-formless meadows. A keen and vaguely syllabic song, blurred by leaves and distance, came and went on the gentle gusts of breeze. I was struck by the thought that a man may be the enemy of other men, the enemy of other men's other moments, yet not be the enemy of a country—of fireflies, words, gardens, watercourses, zephyrs. It was amidst such thoughts that I came to a high rusty gate. Through the iron bars I made out a drive lined with poplars, and a gazebo of some kind. Suddenly, I realised two things—the first trivial, the second almost incredible: the music I had heard was coming from that gazebo, or pavillion, and the music was Chinese. That was why unconsciously I had fully given myself over to it. I do not recall whether there was a bell or whether I had to clap my hands to make my arrival known.

The sputtering of the music continued, but from the rear of the intimate house, a lantern was making its way toward me—a lantern crosshatched and sometimes blotted out altogether by the trees, a paper lantern the shape of a drum and the colour of the moon. It was carried by a tall man. I could not see his face because the light blinded me. He opened the gate and slowly spoke to me in my own language.

"I see that the compassionate Hsi P'eng has undertaken to remedy my solitude. You will no doubt wish to see the garden?"

I recognised the name of one of our consuls, but I could only disconcertedly repeat, "The garden?"

"The garden of forking paths."

Something stirred in my memory, and I spoke with incomprehensible assurance.

"The garden of my ancestor Ts'ui Pen."

"Your ancestor? Your illustrious ancestor? Please—come in."

The dew-drenched path meandered like the paths of my childhood. We came to a library of Western and Oriental books. I recognised, bound in yellow silk, several handwritten volumes of the Lost Encyclopedia compiled by the third emperor of the Luminous Dynasty but never printed. The disk on the gramophone revolved near a bronze phoenix. I also recall a vase of *famille rose* and another, earlier by several hundred years, of that blue colour our artificers copied from the potters of ancient Persia....

Stephen Albert, with a smile, regarded me. He was, as I have said, quite tall, with sharp features, grey eyes, and a grey beard. There was something priestlike about him, somehow, but something sailorlike as well; later he told me he had been a missionary in Tientsin "before aspiring to be a Sinologist."

We sat down, I on a long low divan, he with his back to the window and a tall circular clock. I figured that my pursuer, Richard Madden, could not possibly arrive for at least an hour. My irrevocable decision could wait.

"An amazing life, Ts'ui Pen's," Stephen Albert said. "Governor of the province in which he had been born, a man learned in astronomy, astrology, and the unwearying interpretation of canonical books, a chess player, a renowned poet and calligrapher—he abandoned it all in order to compose a book and a labyrinth. He renounced the pleasures of oppression, justice, the populous marriage bed, banquets, and even erudition in order to sequester himself for thirteen years in the Pavillion of Limpid Solitude. Upon his death, his heirs found nothing but chaotic manuscripts. The family, as you perhaps are aware, were about to deliver them to the fire, but his counsellor—a Taoist or Buddhist monk—insisted upon publishing them."

"To this day," I replied, "we who are descended from Ts'ui Pen execrate that monk. It was senseless to publish those manuscripts. The book is a contradictory jumble of irresolute drafts. I once examined it myself; in the third chapter the hero dies, yet in the fourth he is alive again. As for Ts'ui Pen's other labor, his Labyrinth…"

"Here is the Labyrinth," Albert said, gesturing towards a tall lacquered writing cabinet.   20

"An ivory labyrinth!" I exclaimed. "A very small sort of labyrinth…"

"A labyrinth of symbols," he corrected me. "An invisible labyrinth of time. I, an English barbarian, have somehow been chosen to unveil the diaphanous mystery. Now, more than a hundred years after the fact, the precise details are irrecoverable, but it is not difficult to surmise what happened. Ts'ui Pen must at one point have remarked, 'I shall retire to write a book,' and at another point, 'I shall retire to construct a labyrinth.' Everyone pictured two projects; it occurred to no one that book and labyrinth were one and the same. The Pavillion of Limpid Solitude was erected in the centre of a garden that was, perhaps, most intricately laid out; that fact might well have suggested a physical labyrinth. Ts'ui Pen died; no one in all the wide lands that had been his could find the labyrinth. The novel's confusion—confusedness, I mean, of course—suggested to me that it was that labyrinth. Two circumstances lent me the final solution of the problem—one, the curious legend that Ts'ui Pen had intended to construct a labyrinth which was truly infinite, and two, a fragment of a letter I discovered."

Albert stood. His back was turned to me for several moments; he opened a drawer in the black-and-gold writing cabinet. He turned back with a paper that had once been crimson but was now pink and delicate and rectangular. It was written in Ts'ui Pen's renowned calligraphy. Eagerly yet uncomprehendingly I read the words that a man of my own lineage had written with painstaking brushstrokes: *I leave to several futures (not to all) my garden of forking paths.* I wordlessly handed the paper back to Albert. He continued:

"Before unearthing this letter, I had wondered how a book could be infinite. The only way I could surmise was that it be a cyclical, or circular, volume, a volume whose last page would be identical to the first, so that one might go on indefinitely. I also recalled that night at the centre of the *1001 Nights*, when the queen Scheherazade (through some magical distractedness on the part of the copyist) begins to retell, verbatim, the story of the

1001 Nights, with the risk of returning once again to the night on which
she is telling it—and so on, *ad infinitum*. I also pictured to myself a platonic,
hereditary sort of work, passed down from father to son, in which each new
individual would add a chapter or with reverent care correct his elders'
pages. These imaginings amused and distracted me, but none of them
seemed to correspond even remotely to Ts'ui Pen's contradictory chapters.
As I was floundering about in the mire of these perplexities, I was sent from
Oxford the document you have just examined. I paused, as you may well
imagine, at the sentence 'I leave to several futures (not to all) my garden of
forking paths.' Almost instantly, I saw it—the garden of forking paths was
the chaotic novel; the phrase 'several futures (not all)' suggested to me the
image of a forking in *time*, rather than in space. A full rereading of the
book confirmed my theory. In all fictions, each time a man meets diverse
alternatives, he chooses one and eliminates the others; in the work of the
virtually impossible-to-disentangle Ts'ui Pen, the character chooses—simultaneously—all of them. *He creates*, thereby, 'several futures,' several *times*,
which themselves proliferate and fork. That is the explanation for the novel's contradictions. Fang, let us say, has a secret; a stranger knocks at his
door; Fang decides to kill him. Naturally, there are various possible out-
comes—Fang can kill the intruder, the intruder can kill Fang, they can both
live, they can both be killed, and so on. In Ts'ui Pen's novel, *all* the out-
comes in fact occur; each is the starting point for further bifurcations. Once
in a while, the paths of that labyrinth converge: for example, you come to
this house, but in one of the possible pasts you are my enemy, in another
my friend. If you can bear my incorrigible pronunciation, we shall read a
few pages."

His face, in the vivid circle of the lamp, was undoubtedly that of an old
man, though with something indomitable and even immortal about it. He
read with slow precision two versions of a single epic chapter. In the first,
an army marches off to battle through a mountain wilderness; the horror of
the rocks and darkness inspires in them a disdain for life, and they go on
to an easy victory. In the second, the same army passes through a palace in
which a ball is being held; the brilliant battle seems to them a continuation
of the *fête*, and they win it easily.

I listened with honourable veneration to those ancient fictions, which
were themselves perhaps not as remarkable as the fact that a man of my
blood had invented them and a man of a distant empire was restoring them
to me on an island in the West in the course of a desperate mission. I recall
the final words, repeated in each version like some secret commandment:
"Thus the heroes fought, their admirable hearts calm, their swords violent,
they themselves resigned to killing and to dying."

From that moment on, I felt all about me and within my obscure body
an invisible, intangible pullulation—not that of the divergent, parallel, and

finally coalescing armies, but an agitation more inaccessible, more inward than that, yet one those armies somehow prefigured. Albert went on:

"I do not believe that your venerable ancestor played at idle variations. I cannot think it probable that he would sacrifice thirteen years to the infinite performance of a rhetorical exercise. In your country, the novel is a subordinate genre; at that time it was a genre beneath contempt. Ts'ui Pen was a novelist of genius, but he was also a man of letters, and surely would not have considered himself a mere novelist. The testimony of his contemporaries proclaims his metaphysical, mystical leanings—and his life is their fullest confirmation. Philosophical debate consumes a good part of his novel. I know that of all problems, none disturbed him, none gnawed at him like the unfathomable problem of time. How strange, then, that that problem should be the *only* one that does not figure in the pages of his *Garden*. He never even uses the word. How do you explain that wilful omission?"

I proposed several solutions—all unsatisfactory. We discussed them; finally, Stephen Albert said:

"In a riddle whose answer is chess, what is the only word that must not be used?"   30

I thought for a moment.

"The word 'chess,'" I replied.

"Exactly," Albert said. "*The Garden of Forking Paths* is a huge riddle, or parable, whose subject is time; that secret purpose forbids Ts'ui Pen the merest mention of its name. To *always* omit one word, to employ awkward metaphors and obvious circumlocutions, is perhaps the most emphatic way of calling attention to that word. It is, at any rate, the tortuous path chosen by the devious Ts'ui Pen at each and every one of the turnings of his inexhaustible novel. I have compared hundreds of manuscripts, I have corrected the errors introduced through the negligence of copyists, I have reached a hypothesis for the plan of that chaos, I have reestablished, or believe I've reestablished, its fundamental order—I have translated the entire work; and I know that not once does the word 'time' appear. The explanation is obvious: *The Garden of Forking Paths* is an incomplete, but not false, image of the universe as conceived by Ts'ui Pen. Unlike Newton and Schopenhauer, your ancestor did not believe in a uniform and absolute time; he believed in an infinite series of times, a growing, dizzying web of divergent, covergent, and parallel times. That fabric of times that approach one another, fork, are snipped off, or are simply unknown for centuries, contains *all* possibilities. In most of those times, we do not exist; in some, you exist but I do not; in others, I do and you do not; in others still, we both do. In this one, which the favouring hand of chance has dealt me, you have come to my home; in another, when you come through my garden you find me dead; in another, I say these same words, but I am an error, a ghost."

"In all," I said, not without a tremble, "I am grateful for, and I venerate, your re-creation of the garden of Ts'ui Pen."

"Not in all," he whispered with a smile. "Time forks, perpetually, into countless futures. In one of them, I am your enemy."

I felt again that pullulation I have mentioned. I sensed that the dew-drenched garden that surrounded the house was saturated, infinitely, with invisible persons. Those persons were Albert and myself—secret, busily at work, multiform—in other dimensions of time. I raised my eyes and the gossamer nightmare faded. In the yellow-and-black garden there was but a single man—but that man was as mighty as a statue, and that man was coming down the path, and he was Capt. Richard Madden.

"The future is with us," I replied, "but I am your friend. May I look at the letter again?"

Albert rose once again. He stood tall as he opened the drawer of the tall writing cabinet; he turned his back to me for a moment. I had cocked the revolver. With utmost care, I fired. Albert fell without a groan, without a sound, on the instant. I swear that he died instantly—one clap of thunder.

The rest is unreal, insignificant. Madden burst into the room and arrested me. I have been sentenced to hang. I have most abhorrently triumphed: I have communicated to Berlin the secret name of the city to be attacked. Yesterday it was bombed—I read about it in the same newspapers that posed to all of England the enigma of the murder of the eminent Sinologist Stephen Albert by a stranger, Yu Tsun. The leader solved the riddle. He knew that my problem was how to report (over the deafening noise of the war) the name of the city named Albert, and that the only way I could find was murdering a person of that name. He does not know (no one can know) my endless contrition, and my weariness.

- Locate the various ways in which this story is interrupted, beginning by noticing that we begin on "page 242" of a particular history and "The two first pages of the statement [that we are about to read] are missing." How can we recover any coherent narrative from these interruptions?
- What are the different labyrinths that the narrator encounters in the story? How can a book be a labyrinth?
- How does the espionage story here relate to the solution that the narrator discovers of "The Garden of Forking Paths"?

Joseph Conrad (1857–1924)

Joseph Conrad was born in Russian-occupied Poland. He became a sailor for the British Merchant Service, and it was this career that led him to become a

British citizen. Life as a sailor was difficult, but it provided him with much of the raw material he was to refine and develop in his literary production. Though he struggled as a writer at first, Conrad eventually achieved both commercial and critical success. His best-known work, *Heart of Darkness*, which draws upon the author's own experiences in central Africa, focuses on the ways in which European colonists are tormented and perverted by their own drives to dominate and exploit. His work as a whole is remarkable for the attention it brings to both societal structures and to the working of the individual mind under stress.

The Secret Sharer (1910)

I

On my right hand there were lines of fishing stakes resembling a mysterious system of half-submerged bamboo fences, incomprehensible in its division of the domain of tropical fishes, and crazy of aspect as if abandoned forever by some nomad tribe of fishermen now gone to the other end of the ocean; for there was no sign of human habitation as far as the eye could reach. To the left a group of barren islets, suggesting ruins of stone walls, towers, and block-houses, had its foundations set in a blue sea that itself looked solid, so still and stable did it lie below my feet; even the track of light from the westering sun shone smoothly, without that animated glitter which tells of an imperceptible ripple. And when I turned my head to take a parting glance at the tug which had just left us anchored outside the bar, I saw the straight line of the flat shore joined to the stable sea, edge to edge, with a perfect and unmarked closeness, in one leveled floor half brown, half blue under the enormous dome of the sky. Corresponding in their insignificance to the islets of the sea, two small clumps of trees, one on each side of the only fault in the impeccable joint, marked the mouth of the river Meinam we had just left on the first preparatory stage of our homeward journey; and, far back on the inland level, a larger and loftier mass, the grove surrounding the great Paknam pagoda, was the only thing on which the eye could rest from the vain task of exploring the monotonous sweep of the horizon. Here and there gleams as of a few scattered pieces of silver marked the windings of the great river; and on the nearest of them, just within the bar, the tug steaming right into the land became lost to my sight, hull and funnel and masts, as though the impassive earth had swallowed her up without an effort, without a tremor. My eye followed the light cloud of her smoke, now here, now there, above the plain, according to the devious curves of the stream, but always fainter and farther away, till I lost it at last behind the miter-shaped hill of the great pagoda. And then I was left alone with my ship, anchored at the head of the Gulf of Siam. She floated at the starting point of a long journey, very still in an immense stillness, the shadows of her spars flung far to the eastward by the setting sun. At that moment I was alone on her decks. There was not a sound in her—and around us nothing moved, nothing lived, not a canoe on the water, not a bird in the air, not a cloud in the sky. In this breathless pause at the threshold of a long passage we seemed to be measuring our fitness for a long and arduous enterprise, the appointed task of both our existences to be carried out, far from all human eyes, with only sky and sea for spectators and for judges.

There must have been some glare in the air to interfere with one's sight, because it was only just before the sun left us that my roaming eyes made out beyond the highest ridges of the principal islet of the group something which did away with the solemnity of perfect solitude. The tide of darkness flowed on swiftly; and with tropical suddenness a swarm of stars came out above the shadowy earth, while I lingered yet, my hand resting lightly on my ship's rail as if on the shoulder of a trusted friend. But, with all that multitude of celestial bodies staring down at one, the comfort of quiet communion with her was gone for good. And there were also disturbing sounds by this time—voices, footsteps forward; the steward flitted along the main-deck, a busily ministering spirit; a hand bell tinkled urgently under the poop deck....

I found my two officers waiting for me near the supper table, in the lighted cuddy. We sat down at once, and as I helped the chief mate, I said:

"Are you aware that there is a ship anchored inside the islands? I saw her mastheads above the ridge as the sun went down."

He raised sharply his simple face, overcharged by a terrible growth of whisker, and emitted his usual ejaculations: "Bless my soul, sir! You don't say so!"

My second mate was a round-cheeked, silent young man, grave beyond his years, I thought; but as our eyes happened to meet I detected a slight quiver on his lips. I looked down at once. It was not my part to encourage sneering on board my ship. It must be said, too, that I knew very little of my officers. In consequence of certain events of no particular significance, except to myself, I had been appointed to the command only a fortnight before. Neither did I know much of the hands forward. All these people had been together for eighteen months or so, and my position was that of the only stranger on board. I mention this because it has some bearing on what is to follow. But what I felt most was my being a stranger to the ship; and if all the truth must be told, I was somewhat of a stranger to myself. The youngest man on board (barring the second mate), and untried as yet by a position of the fullest responsibility, I was willing to take the adequacy of the others for granted. They had simply to be equal to their tasks; but I wondered how far I should turn out faithful to that ideal conception of one's own personality every man sets up for himself secretly.

Meantime the chief mate, with an almost visible effect of collaboration on the part of his round eyes and frightful whiskers, was trying to evolve a theory of the anchored ship. His dominant trait was to take all things into earnest consideration. He was of a painstaking turn of mind. As he used to say, he "liked to account to himself" for practically everything that came in his way, down to a miserable scorpion he had found in his cabin a week before. The why and the wherefore of that scorpion—how it got on board and came to select his room rather than the pantry (which was a dark place and more what a scorpion would be partial to), and how on earth it managed to drown itself in the inkwell of his writing desk—had exercised him infinitely. The ship within the islands was much more easily accounted for; and just as we were about to rise from table he made his pronouncement. She was, he doubted not, a ship from home lately arrived. Probably she drew too much water to cross the bar except at the top of spring tides. Therefore she went into that natural harbor to wait for a few days in preference to remaining in an open roadstead.

"That's so," confirmed the second mate, suddenly, in his slightly hoarse voice. "She draws over twenty feet. She's the Liverpool ship Sephora with a cargo of coal. Hundred and twenty-three days from Cardiff."

We looked at him in surprise.

"The tugboat skipper told me when he came on board for your letters, sir," explained the young man. "He expects to take her up the river the day after tomorrow." <!-- 10 -->

After thus overwhelming us with the extent of his information he slipped out of the cabin. The mate observed regretfully that he "could not account for that young fellow's whims." What prevented him telling us all about it at once, he wanted to know.

I detained him as he was making a move. For the last two days the crew had had plenty of hard work, and the night before they had very little sleep. I felt painfully that I—a stranger—was doing something unusual when I directed him to let all hands turn in without setting an anchor watch. I proposed to keep on deck myself till one o'clock or thereabouts. I would get the second mate to relieve me at that hour.

"He will turn out the cook and the steward at four," I concluded, "and then give you a call. Of course at the slightest sign of any sort of wind we'll have the hands up and make a start at once."

He concealed his astonishment. "Very well, sir." Outside the cuddy he put his head in the second mate's door to inform him of my unheard-of caprice to take a five hours' anchor watch on myself. I heard the other raise his voice incredulously——"What? The Captain himself?" Then a few more murmurs, a door closed, then another. A few moments later I went on deck.

My strangeness, which had made me sleepless, had prompted that unconventional arrangement, as if I had expected in those solitary hours of the night to get on terms with the ship of which I knew nothing, manned by men of whom I knew very little more. Fast alongside a wharf, littered like any ship in port with a tangle of unrelated things, invaded <!-- 15 -->

by unrelated shore people, I had hardly seen her yet properly. Now, as she lay cleared for sea, the stretch of her main-deck seemed to me very fine under the stars. Very fine, very roomy for her size, and very inviting. I descended the poop and paced the waist, my mind picturing to myself the coming passage through the Malay Archipelago, down the Indian Ocean, and up the Atlantic. All its phases were familiar enough to me, every characteristic, all the alternatives which were likely to face me on the high seas—everything!...except the novel responsibility of command. But I took heart from the reasonable thought that the ship was like other ships, the men like other men, and that the sea was not likely to keep any special surprises expressly for my discomfiture.

Arrived at that comforting conclusion, I bethought myself of a cigar and went below to get it. All was still down there. Everybody at the after end of the ship was sleeping profoundly. I came out again on the quarter-deck, agreeably at ease in my sleeping suit on that warm breathless night, barefooted, a glowing cigar in my teeth, and, going forward, I was met by the profound silence of the fore end of the ship. Only as I passed the door of the forecastle, I heard a deep, quiet, trustful sigh of some sleeper inside. And suddenly I rejoiced in the great security of the sea as compared with the unrest of the land, in my choice of that untempted life presenting no disquieting problems, invested with an elementary moral beauty by the absolute straightforwardness of its appeal and by the singleness of its purpose.

The riding light in the forerigging burned with a clear, untroubled, as if symbolic, flame, confident and bright in the mysterious shades of the night. Passing on my way aft along the other side of the ship, I observed that the rope side ladder, put over, no doubt, for the master of the tug when he came to fetch away our letters, had not been hauled in as it should have been. I became annoyed at this, for exactitude in some small matters is the very soul of discipline. Then I reflected that I had myself peremptorily dismissed my officers from duty, and by my own act had prevented the anchor watch being formally set and things properly attended to. I asked myself whether it was wise ever to interfere with the established routine of duties even from the kindest of motives. My action might have made me appear eccentric. Goodness only knew how that absurdly whiskered mate would "account" for my conduct, and what the whole ship thought of that informality of their new captain. I was vexed with myself.

Not from compunction certainly, but, as it were mechanically, I proceeded to get the ladder in myself. Now a side ladder of that sort is a light affair and comes in easily, yet my vigorous tug, which should have brought it flying on board, merely recoiled upon my body in a totally unexpected jerk. What the devil!...I was so astounded by the immovableness of that ladder that I remained stockstill, trying to account for it to myself like that imbecile mate of mine. In the end, of course, I put my head over the rail.

The side of the ship made an opaque belt of shadow on the darkling glassy shimmer of the sea. But I saw at once something elongated and pale floating very close to the ladder. Before I could form a guess a faint flash of phosphorescent light, which seemed to issue suddenly from the naked body of a man, flickered in the sleeping water with the elusive, silent play of summer lightning in a night sky. With a gasp I saw revealed to my stare a pair of feet, the long legs, a broad livid back immersed right up to the neck in a greenish cadaverous glow. One hand, awash, clutched the bottom rung of the ladder. He was complete but for the head. A headless corpse! The cigar dropped out of my gaping mouth with a tiny plop and a short hiss quite audible in the absolute stillness of all things under heaven. At that I suppose he raised up his face, a dimly pale oval in the shadow of the ship's side. But even then I could only barely make out down there the shape of his black-haired head. However, it was enough for the horrid, frost-bound sensation which had gripped me about the chest to pass off. The moment of vain exclamations was past, too. I only climbed on the spare spar and leaned over the rail as far as I could, to bring my eyes nearer to that mystery floating alongside.

As he hung by the ladder, like a resting swimmer, the sea lightning played about his limbs at every stir; and he appeared in it ghastly, silvery, fishlike. He remained as mute as a fish, too. He made no motion to get out of the water, either. It was inconceivable that he should not attempt to come on board, and strangely troubling to suspect that perhaps he did not want to. And my first words were prompted by just that troubled incertitude. 20

"What's the matter?" I asked in my ordinary tone, speaking down to the face upturned exactly under mine.

"Cramp," it answered, no louder. Then slightly anxious, "I say, no need to call anyone."

"I was not going to," I said.

"Are you alone on deck?"

"Yes." 25

I had somehow the impression that he was on the point of letting go the ladder to swim away beyond my ken—mysterious as he came. But, for the moment, this being appearing as if he had risen from the bottom of the sea (it was certainly the nearest land to the ship) wanted only to know the time. I told him. And he, down there, tentatively:

"I suppose your captain's turned in?"

"I am sure he isn't," I said.

He seemed to struggle with himself, for I heard something like the low, bitter murmur of doubt. "What's the good?" His next words came out with a hesitating effort.

"Look here, my man. Could you call him out quietly?" 30

I thought the time had come to declare myself.

"I am the captain."

I heard a "By Jove!" whispered at the level of the water. The phosphorescence flashed in the swirl of the water all about his limbs, his other hand seized the ladder.

"My name's Leggatt."

The voice was calm and resolute. A good voice. The self-possession of that man had somehow induced a corresponding state in myself. It was very quietly that I remarked:

"You must be a good swimmer."

"Yes. I've been in the water practically since nine o'clock. The question for me now is whether I am to let go this ladder and go on swimming till I sink from exhaustion, or—to come on board here."

I felt this was no mere formula of desperate speech, but a real alternative in the view of a strong soul. I should have gathered from this that he was young; indeed, it is only the young who are ever confronted by such clear issues. But at the time it was pure intuition on my part. A mysterious communication was established already between us two—in the face of that silent, darkened tropical sea. I was young, too; young enough to make no comment. The man in the water began suddenly to climb up the ladder, and I hastened away from the rail to fetch some clothes.

Before entering the cabin I stood still, listening in the lobby at the foot of the stairs. A faint snore came through the closed door of the chief mate's room. The second mate's door was on the hook, but the darkness in there was absolutely soundless. He, too, was young and could sleep like a stone. Remained the steward, but he was not likely to wake up before he was called. I got a sleeping suit out of my room and, coming back on deck, saw the naked man from the sea sitting on the main hatch, glimmering white in the darkness, his elbows on his knees and his head in his hands. In a moment he had concealed his damp body in a sleeping suit of the same gray-stripe pattern as the one I was wearing and followed me like my double on the poop. Together we moved right aft, barefooted, silent.

"What is it?" I asked in a deadened voice, taking the lighted lamp out of the binnacle, and raising it to his face.

"An ugly business."

He had rather regular features; a good mouth; light eyes under somewhat heavy, dark eyebrows; a smooth, square forehead; no growth on his cheeks; a small, brown mustache, and a well-shaped, round chin. His expression was concentrated, meditative, under the inspecting light of the lamp I held up to his face; such as a man thinking hard in solitude might wear. My sleeping suit was just right for his size. A well-knit young fellow of twenty-five at most. He caught his lower lip with the edge of white, even teeth.

"Yes," I said, replacing the lamp in the binnacle. The warm, heavy tropical night closed upon his head again.

"There's a ship over there," he murmured.

"Yes, I know. The Sephora. Did you know of us?"   45

"Hadn't the slightest idea. I am the mate of her———" He paused and corrected himself. "I should say I *was*."

"Aha! Something wrong?"

"Yes. Very wrong indeed. I've killed a man."

"What do you mean? Just now?"

"No, on the passage. Weeks ago. Thirty-nine south. When I say a   50
man—"

"Fit of temper," I suggested, confidently.

The shadowy, dark head, like mine, seemed to nod imperceptibly above the ghostly gray of my sleeping suit. It was, in the night, as though I had been faced by my own reflection in the depths of a somber and immense mirror.

"A pretty thing to have to own up to for a Conway boy," murmured my double, distinctly.

"You're a Conway boy?"

"I am," he said, as if startled. Then, slowly... "Perhaps you too———"   55

It was so; but being a couple of years older I had left before he joined. After a quick interchange of dates a silence fell; and I thought suddenly of my absurd mate with his terrific whiskers and the "Bless my soul—you don't say so" type of intellect. My double gave me an inkling of his thoughts by saying: "My father's a parson in Norfolk. Do you see me before a judge and jury on that charge? For myself I can't see the necessity. There are fellows that an angel from heaven———And I am not that. He was one of those creatures that are just simmering all the time with a silly sort of wickedness. Miserable devils that have no business to live at all. He wouldn't do his duty and wouldn't let anybody else do theirs. But what's the good of talking! You know well enough the sort of ill-conditioned snarling cur———"

He appealed to me as if our experiences had been as identical as our clothes. And I knew well enough the pestiferous danger of such a character where there are no means of legal repression. And I knew well enough also that my double there was no homicidal ruffian. I did not think of asking him for details, and he told me the story roughly in brusque, disconnected sentences. I needed no more. I saw it all going on as though I were myself inside that other sleeping suit.

"It happened while we were setting a reefed foresail, at dusk. Reefed foresail! You understand the sort of weather. The only sail we had left to keep the ship running; so you may guess what it had been like for days. Anxious sort of job, that. He gave me some of his cursed insolence at the sheet. I tell you I was overdone with this terrific weather that seemed to have no end to it. Terrific, I tell you—and a deep ship. I believe the fellow himself was half crazed with funk. It was no time for gentlemanly reproof, so I turned round and felled him like an ox. He up and at me. We closed just as an awful sea made for the ship. All hands saw it coming and took to the rigging, but I had him by the throat, and went on shaking him like a rat, the men above us yelling, 'Look out! look out!' Then a crash as if the sky had fallen on my head. They say that for over ten minutes hardly anything was to be seen of the ship—just the three masts and a bit of the forecastle head and of the poop all awash driving along in a smother of foam. It was a miracle that they found us, jammed together behind the forebitts. It's clear that I meant business, because I was holding him by the throat still when they picked us up. He was black in the face. It was too much for them. It seems they rushed us aft together, gripped as we were, screaming 'Murder!' like a lot of lunatics, and broke into the cuddy. And the ship running for her life, touch and go all the time, any minute her last in a sea fit to turn your hair gray only a-looking at it. I understand that the skipper, too, started raving like the rest of them. The man had been deprived of sleep for more than a week, and to have this sprung on him at the height of a furious gale nearly drove him out of his mind. I wonder they didn't fling me overboard after getting the carcass of their precious shipmate out of my fingers. They had rather a job to separate us, I've been told. A sufficiently fierce story to make an old judge and a respectable jury sit up a bit. The first thing I heard when I came to myself was the maddening howling of that endless gale, and on that the voice of the old man. He was hanging on to my bunk, staring into my face out of his sou'wester.

"'Mr. Leggatt, you have killed a man. You can act no longer as chief mate of this ship.'"

His care to subdue his voice made it sound monotonous. He rested a hand on the end of the skylight to steady himself with, and all that time did not stir a limb, so far as I could see. "Nice little tale for a quiet tea party," he concluded in the same tone.

One of my hands, too, rested on the end of the skylight; neither did I stir a limb, so far as I knew. We stood less than a foot from each other. It occurred to me that if old "Bless my soul—you don't say so" were to put his head up the companion and catch sight of us, he would think he was seeing double, or imagine himself come upon a scene of weird witchcraft; the strange captain having a quiet confabulation by the wheel with his own gray ghost. I became very much concerned to prevent anything of the sort. I heard the other's soothing undertone.

"My father's a parson in Norfolk," it said. Evidently he had forgotten he had told me this important fact before. Truly a nice little tale.

"You had better slip down into my stateroom now," I said, moving off stealthily. My double followed my movements; our bare feet made no sound; I let him in, closed the door with care, and, after giving a call to the second mate, returned on deck for my relief.

"Not much sign of any wind yet," I remarked when he approached.

"No, sir. Not much," he assented, sleepily, in his hoarse voice, with just   65
enough deference, no more, and barely suppressing a yawn.

"Well, that's all you have to look out for. You have got your orders."

"Yes, sir."

I paced a turn or two on the poop and saw him take up his position face forward with his elbow in the ratlines of the mizzen rigging before I went below. The mate's faint snoring was still going on peacefully. The cuddy lamp was burning over the table on which stood a vase with flowers, a polite attention from the ship's provision merchant—the last flowers we should see for the next three months at the very least. Two bunches of bananas hung from the beam symmetrically, one on each side of the rudder casing. Everything was as before in the ship—except that two of her captain's sleeping suits were simultaneously in use, one motionless in the cuddy, the other keeping very still in the captain's stateroom.

It must be explained here that my cabin had the form of the capital letter L, the door being within the angle and opening into the short part of the letter. A couch was to the left, the bed place to the right; my writing desk and the chronometers' table faced the door. But anyone opening it, unless he stepped right inside, had no view of what I call the long (or vertical) part of the letter. It contained some lockers surmounted by a bookcase; and a few clothes, a thick jacket or two, caps, oilskin coat, and such like, hung on hooks. There was at the bottom of that part a door opening into my bathroom, which could be entered also directly from the saloon. But that way was never used.

The mysterious arrival had discovered the advantage of this particular   70
shape. Entering my room, lighted strongly by a big bulkhead lamp swung on gimbals above my writing desk, I did not see him anywhere till he stepped out quietly from behind the coats hung in the recessed part.

"I heard somebody moving about, and went in there at once," he whispered.

I, too, spoke under my breath.

"Nobody is likely to come in here without knocking and getting permission."

He nodded. His face was thin and the sunburn faded, as though he had been ill. And no wonder. He had been, I heard presently, kept under arrest in his cabin for nearly seven weeks. But there was nothing sickly in his eyes or in his expression. He was not a bit like me, really; yet, as we stood leaning over my bed place, whispering side by side, with our dark heads together and our backs to the door, anybody bold enough to open it stealthily would have been treated to the uncanny sight of a double captain busy talking in whispers with his other self.

"But all this doesn't tell me how you came to hang on to our side ladder," I inquired, in the hardly audible murmurs we used, after he had told
me something more of the proceedings on board the Sephora once the bad
weather was over.

"When we sighted Java Head I had had time to think all those matters
out several times over. I had six weeks of doing nothing else, and with only
an hour or so every evening for a tramp on the quarter-deck."

He whispered, his arms folded on the side of my bed place, staring
through the open port. And I could imagine perfectly the manner of this
thinking out—a stubborn if not a steadfast operation; something of which I
should have been perfectly incapable.

"I reckoned it would be dark before we closed with the land," he
continued, so low that I had to strain my hearing near as we were to each
other, shoulder touching shoulder almost. "So I asked to speak to the old
man. He always seemed very sick when he came to see me—as if he could
not look me in the face. You know, that foresail saved the ship. She was too
deep to have run long under bare poles. And it was I that managed to set it
for him. Anyway, he came. When I had him in my cabin—he stood by the
door looking at me as if I had the halter round my neck already—I asked
him right away to leave my cabin door unlocked at night while the ship was
going through Sunda Straits. There would be the Java coast within two or
three miles, off Angier Point. I wanted nothing more. I've had a prize for
swimming my second year in the Conway."

"I can believe it," I breathed out.

"God only knows why they locked me in every night. To see some of
their faces you'd have thought they were afraid I'd go about at night strangling people. Am I a murdering brute? Do I look it? By Jove! If I had been
he wouldn't have trusted himself like that into my room. You'll say I might
have chucked him aside and bolted out, there and then—it was dark already. Well, no. And for the same reason I wouldn't think of trying to
smash the door. There would have been a rush to stop me at the noise, and
I did not mean to get into a confounded scrimmage. Somebody else might
have got killed—for I would not have broken out only to get chucked back,
and I did not want any more of that work. He refused, looking more sick
than ever. He was afraid of the men, and also of that old second mate of his
who had been sailing with him for years—a gray-headed old humbug; and
his steward, too, had been with him devil knows how long—seventeen years
or more—a dogmatic sort of loafer who hated me like poison, just because I
was the chief mate. No chief mate ever made more than one voyage in the
Sephora, you know. Those two old chaps ran the ship. Devil only knows
what the skipper wasn't afraid of (all his nerve went to pieces altogether in
that hellish spell of bad weather we had)—of what the law would do to
him—of his wife, perhaps. Oh, yes! she's on board. Though I don't think

she would have meddled. She would have been only too glad to have me out of the ship in any way. The 'brand of Cain' business, don't you see. That's all right. I was ready enough to go off wandering on the face of the earth—and that was price enough to pay for an Abel of that sort. Anyhow, he wouldn't listen to me. 'This thing must take its course. I represent the law here.' He was shaking like a leaf. 'So you won't?' 'No!' 'Then I hope you will be able to sleep on that,' I said, and turned my back on him. 'I wonder that you can,' cries he, and locks the door.

"Well after that, I couldn't. Not very well. That was three weeks ago. We have had a slow passage through the Java Sea; drifted about Carimata for ten days. When we anchored here they thought, I suppose, it was all right. The nearest land (and that's five miles) is the ship's destination; the consul would soon set about catching me; and there would have been no ob-ject in bolting to these islets there. I don't suppose there's a drop of water on them. I don't know how it was, but tonight that steward, after bringing me my supper, went out to let me eat it, and left the door unlocked. And I ate it—all there was, too. After I had finished I strolled out on the quarter-deck. I don't know that I meant to do anything. A breath of fresh air was all I wanted, I believe. Then a sudden temptation came over me. I kicked off my slippers and was in the water before I had made up my mind fairly. Somebody heard the splash and they raised an awful hullabaloo. 'He's gone! Lower the boats! He's committed suicide! No, he's swimming.' Certainly I was swimming. It's not so easy for a swimmer like me to commit suicide by drowning. I landed on the nearest islet before the boat left the ship's side. I heard them pulling about in the dark, hailing, and so on, but after a bit they gave up. Everything quieted down and the anchorage became still as death. I sat down on a stone and began to think. I felt certain they would start searching for me at daylight. There was no place to hide on those stony things—and if there had been, what would have been the good? But now I was clear of that ship, I was not going back. So after a while I took off all my clothes, tied them up in a bundle with a stone inside, and dropped them in the deep water on the outer side of that islet. That was suicide enough for me. Let them think what they liked, but I didn't mean to drown myself. I meant to swim till I sank—but that's not the same thing. I struck out for another of these little islands, and it was from that one that I first saw your riding light. Something to swim for. I went on easily, and on the way I came upon a flat rock a foot or two above water. In the daytime, I dare say, you might make it out with a glass from your poop. I scrambled up on it and rested myself for a bit. Then I made another start. That last spell must have been over a mile."

His whisper was getting fainter and fainter, and all the time he stared straight out through the porthole, in which there was not even a star to be seen. I had not interrupted him. There was something that made comment impossible in his narrative, or perhaps in himself; a sort of feeling, a quality, which I can't find a name for. And when he ceased, all I found was a futile whisper: "So you swam for our light?"

"Yes—straight for it. It was something to swim for. I couldn't see any stars low down because the coast was in the way, and I couldn't see the land, either. The water was like glass. One might have been swimming in a confounded thousand-feet deep cistern with no place for scrambling out anywhere; but what I didn't like was the notion of swimming round and round like a crazed bullock before I gave out; and as I didn't mean to go back...No. Do you see me being hauled back, stark naked, off one of these little islands by the scruff of the neck and fighting like a wild beast? Somebody would have got killed for certain, and I did not want any of that. So I went on. Then your ladder——"

"Why didn't you hail the ship?" I asked, a little louder.

He touched my shoulder lightly. Lazy footsteps came right over our heads and stopped. The second mate had crossed from the other side of the poop and might have been hanging over the rail for all we knew.

"He couldn't hear us talking—could he?" My double breathed into my very ear, anxiously.

His anxiety was an answer, a sufficient answer, to the question I had put to him. An answer containing all the difficulty of that situation. I closed the porthole quietly, to make sure. A louder word might have been overheard.

"Who's that?" he whispered then.

"My second mate. But I don't know much more of the fellow than you do."

And I told him a little about myself. I had been appointed to take charge while I least expected anything of the sort, not quite a fortnight ago. I didn't know either the ship or the people. Hadn't had the time in port to look about me or size anybody up. And as to the crew, all they knew was that I was appointed to take the ship home. For the rest, I was almost as much of a stranger on board as himself, I said. And at the moment I felt it most acutely. I felt that it would take very little to make me a suspect person in the eyes of the ship's company.

He had turned about meantime; and we, the two strangers in the ship, faced each other in identical attitudes.

"Your ladder——" he murmured, after a silence. "Who'd have thought of finding a ladder hanging over at night in a ship anchored out here! I felt just then a very unpleasant faintness. After the life I've been leading for nine weeks, anybody would have got out of condition. I wasn't capable of swimming round as far as your rudder chains. And, lo and behold! there was a ladder to get hold of. After I gripped it I said to myself, 'What's the good?' When I saw a man's head looking over I thought I would swim away presently and leave him shouting—in whatever language it was. I didn't mind being looked at. I—I liked it. And then you speaking to me so quietly—as if you had expected me—made me hold on a little longer. It had been a confounded lonely time—I don't mean while swimming. I was glad to talk a little to somebody that didn't belong to the Sephora. As to asking for the captain, that was a mere impulse. It could have been no use, with all the ship knowing about me and the other people pretty certain to be round here in the morning. I don't know—I wanted to be seen, to talk with somebody, before I went on. I don't know what I would have said.... 'Fine night, isn't it?' or something of the sort."

"Do you think they will be round here presently?" I asked with some incredulity.

"Quite likely," he said, faintly.

He looked extremely haggard all of a sudden. His head rolled on his shoulders.   95

"H'm. We shall see then. Meantime get into that bed," I whispered. "Want help? There."

It was a rather high bed place with a set of drawers underneath. This amazing swimmer really needed the lift I gave him by seizing his leg. He tumbled in, rolled over on his back, and flung one arm across his eyes. And then, with his face nearly hidden, he must have looked exactly as I used to look in that bed. I gazed upon my other self for a while before drawing across carefully the two green serge curtains which ran on a brass rod. I thought for a moment of pinning them together for greater safety, but I sat down on the couch, and once there I felt unwilling to rise and hunt for a pin. I would do it in a moment. I was extremely tired, in a peculiarly intimate way, by the strain of stealthiness, by the effort of whispering and the general secrecy of this excitement. It was three o'clock by now and I had been on my feet since nine, but I was not sleepy; I could not have gone to sleep. I sat there, fagged out, looking at the curtains, trying to clear my mind of the confused sensation of being in two places at once, and greatly bothered by an exasperating knocking in my head. It was a relief to discover suddenly that it was not in my head at all, but on the outside of the door. Before I could collect myself the words "Come in" were out of my mouth, and the steward entered with a tray, bringing in my morning coffee. I had slept, after all, and I was so frightened that I shouted, "This way! I am here, steward," as though he had been miles away. He put down the tray on the table next the couch and only then said, very quietly, "I can see you are here, sir." I felt him give me a keen look, but I dared not meet his eyes just then. He must have wondered why I had drawn the curtains of my bed before going to sleep on the couch. He went out, hooking the door open as usual.

I heard the crew washing decks above me. I knew I would have been told at once if there had been any wind. Calm, I thought, and I was doubly vexed. Indeed, I felt dual more than ever. The steward reappeared suddenly in the doorway. I jumped up from the couch so quickly that he gave a start.

"What do you want here?"

"Close your port, sir—they are washing decks."   10

"It is closed," I said, reddening.

"Very well, sir." But he did not move from the doorway and returned my stare in an extraordinary, equivocal manner for a time. Then his eyes wavered, all his expression changed, and in a voice unusually gentle, almost coaxingly:

"May I come in to take the empty cup away, sir?"

"Of course!" I turned my back on him while he popped in and out. Then I unhooked and closed the door and even pushed the bolt. This sort of thing could not go on very long. The cabin was as hot as an oven, too. I took a peep at my double, and discovered that he had not moved, his arm was still over his eyes; but his chest heaved; his hair was wet; his chin glistened with perspiration. I reached over him and opened the port.

"I must show myself on deck," I reflected.   1C

Of course, theoretically, I could do what I liked, with no one to say nay to me within the whole circle of the horizon; but to lock my cabin door and take the key away I did not dare. Directly I put my head out of the companion I saw the group of my two officers, the second mate barefooted, the chief mate in long India-rubber boots, near the break of the poop, and the steward halfway down the poop ladder talking to them eagerly. He happened to catch sight of me and dived, the second ran down on the main-deck shouting some order or other, and the chief mate came to meet me, touching his cap.

There was a sort of curiosity in his eye that I did not like. I don't know whether the steward had told them that I was "queer" only, or downright drunk, but I know the man meant to have a good look at me. I watched him coming with a smile which, as he got into point-blank range, took effect and froze his very whiskers. I did not give him time to open his lips.

"Square the yards by lifts and braces before the hands go to breakfast."

It was the first particular order I had given on board that ship; and I stayed on deck to see it executed, too. I had felt the need of asserting myself without loss of time. That sneering young cub got taken down a peg or two on that occasion, and I also seized the opportunity of having a good look at the face of every foremast man as they filed past me to go to the after braces. At breakfast time, eating nothing myself, I presided with such frigid dignity that the two mates were only too glad to escape from the cabin as soon as decency permitted; and all the time the dual working of my mind distracted me almost to the point of insanity. I was constantly watching myself, my secret self, as dependent on my actions as my own personality, sleeping in that bed, behind that door which faced me as I sat at the head of the table. It was very much like being mad, only it was worse because one was aware of it.

I had to shake him for a solid minute, but when at last he opened his eyes it was in the full possession of his senses, with an inquiring look. 110

"All's well so far," I whispered. "Now you must vanish into the bathroom."

He did so, as noiseless as a ghost, and then I rang for the steward, and facing him boldly, directed him to tidy up my stateroom while I was having my bath—"and be quick about it." As my tone admitted of no excuses, he said, "Yes, sir," and ran off to fetch his dustpan and brushes. I took a bath and did most of my dressing, splashing, and whistling softly for the steward's edification, while the secret sharer of my life stood drawn up bolt upright in that little space, his face looking very sunken in daylight, his eyelids lowered under the stern, dark line of his eyebrows drawn together by a slight frown.

When I left him there to go back to my room the steward was finishing dusting. I sent for the mate and engaged him in some insignificant conversation. It was, as it were, trifling with the terrific character of his whiskers; but my object was to give him an opportunity for a good look at my cabin. And then I could at last shut, with a clear conscience, the door of my stateroom and get my double back into the recessed part. There was nothing else for it. He had to sit still on a small folding stool, half smothered by the heavy coats hanging there. We listened to the steward going into the bathroom out of the saloon, filling the water bottles there, scrubbing the bath, setting things to rights, whisk, bang, clatter—out again into the saloon—turn the key—click. Such was my scheme for keeping my second self invisible. Nothing better could be contrived under the circumstances. And there we sat; I at my writing desk ready to appear busy with some papers, he behind me out of sight of the door. It would not have been prudent to talk in daytime; and I could not have stood the excitement of that queer sense of whispering to myself. Now and then, glancing over my shoulder, I saw him far back there, sitting rigidly on the low stool, his bare feet close together, his arms folded, his head hanging on his breast—and perfectly still. Anybody would have taken him for me.

I was fascinated by it myself. Every moment I had to glance over my shoulder. I was looking at him when a voice outside the door said:

"Beg pardon, sir." 115

"Well!…" I kept my eyes on him, and so when the voice outside the door announced, "There's a ship's boat coming our way, sir," I saw him give a start—the first movement he had made for hours. But he did not raise his bowed head.

"All right. Get the ladder over."

I hesitated. Should I whisper something to him? But what? His immobility seemed to have been never disturbed. What could I tell him he did
not know already?... Finally I went on deck.

II

The skipper of the Sephora had a thin red whisker all round his face,
and the sort of complexion that goes with hair of that color; also the particular, rather smeary shade of blue in the eyes. He was not exactly a showy figure; his shoulders were high, his stature but middling—one leg slightly more
bandy than the other. He shook hands, looking vaguely around. A spiritless
tenacity was his main characteristic, I judged. I behaved with a politeness
which seemed to disconcert him. Perhaps he was shy. He mumbled to me as
if he were ashamed of what he was saying; gave his name (it was something
like Archbold—but at this distance of years I hardly am sure), his ship's
name, and a few other particulars of that sort, in the manner of a criminal
making a reluctant and doleful confession. He had had terrible weather on
the passage out—terrible—terrible—wife aboard, too.

By this time we were seated in the cabin and the steward brought in a
tray with a bottle and glasses. "Thanks! No." Never took liquor. Would
have some water, though. He drank two tumblerfuls. Terrible thirsty work.
Ever since daylight had been exploring the islands round his ship.

"What was that for—fun?" I asked, with an appearance of polite
interest.

"No!" He sighed. "Painful duty."

As he persisted in his mumbling and I wanted my double to hear every
word, I hit upon the notion of informing him that I regretted to say I was
hard of hearing.

"Such a young man, too!" he nodded, keeping his smeary blue, unintel-
ligent eyes fastened upon me. "What was the cause of it—some disease?" he
inquired, without the least sympathy and as if he thought that, if so, I'd got
no more than I deserved.

"Yes; disease," I admitted in a cheerful tone which seemed to shock
him. But my point was gained, because he had to raise his voice to give me
his tale. It is not worth while to record his version. It was just over two
months since all this had happened, and he had thought so much about it
that he seemed completely muddled as to its bearings, but still immensely
impressed.

"What would you think of such a thing happening on board your own
ship? I've had the Sephora for these fifteen years. I am a well-known
shipmaster."

He was densely distressed—and perhaps I should have sympathized
with him if I had been able to detach my mental vision from the unsuspected sharer of my cabin as though he were my second self. There he was

on the other side of the bulkhead, four or five feet from us, no more, as we sat in the saloon. I looked politely at Captain Archbold (if that was his name), but it was the other I saw, in a gray sleeping suit, seated on a low stool, his bare feet close together, his arms folded, and every word said between us falling into the ears of his dark head bowed on his chest.

"I have been at sea now, man and boy, for seven-and-thirty years, and I've never heard of such a thing happening in an English ship. And that it should be my ship. Wife on board, too."

I was hardly listening to him.

"Don't you think," I said, "that the heavy sea which, you told me, came aboard just then might have killed the man? I have seen the sheer weight of a sea kill a man very neatly, by simply breaking his neck."   130

"Good God!" he uttered, impressively, fixing his smeary blue eyes on me. "The sea! No man killed by the sea ever looked like that." He seemed positively scandalized at my suggestion. And as I gazed at him certainly not prepared for anything original on his part, he advanced his head close to mine and thrust his tongue out at me so suddenly that I couldn't help starting back.

After scoring over my calmness in this graphic way he nodded wisely. If I had seen the sight, he assured me, I would never forget it as long as I lived. The weather was too bad to give the corpse a proper sea burial. So next day at dawn they took it up on the poop, covering its face with a bit of bunting; he read a short prayer, and then, just as it was, in its oilskins and long boots, they launched it amongst those mountainous seas that seemed ready every moment to swallow up the ship herself and the terrified lives on board of her.

"That reefed foresail saved you," I threw in.

"Under God—it did," he exclaimed fervently. "It was by a special mercy, I firmly believe, that it stood some of those hurricane squalls."

"It was the setting of that sail which——" I began.   135

"God's own hand in it," he interrupted me. "Nothing less could have done it. I don't mind telling you that I hardly dared give the order. It seemed impossible that we could touch anything without losing it, and then our last hope would have been gone."

The terror of that gale was on him yet. I let him go on for a bit, then said, casually—as if returning to a minor subject:

"You were very anxious to give up your mate to the shore people, I believe?"

He was. To the law. His obscure tenacity on that point had in it something incomprehensible and a little awful; something, as it were, mystical, quite apart from his anxiety that he should not be suspected of "countenancing any doings of that sort." Seven-and-thirty virtuous years at sea, of which over twenty of immaculate command, and the last fifteen in the Sephora, seemed to have laid him under some pitiless obligation.

"And you know," he went on, groping shame-facedly amongst his feel- 14
ings, "I did not engage that young fellow. His people had some interest with
my owners. I was in a way forced to take him on. He looked very smart,
very gentlemanly, and all that. But do you know—I never liked him, somehow. I am a plain man. You see, he wasn't exactly the sort for the chief
mate of a ship like the Sephora."

I had become so connected in thoughts and impressions with the secret
sharer of my cabin that I felt as if I, personally, were being given to understand that I, too, was not the sort that would have done for the chief mate
of a ship like the Sephora. I had no doubt of it in my mind.

"Not at all the style of man. You understand," he insisted, superfluously,
looking hard at me.

I smiled urbanely. He seemed at a loss for a while.

"I suppose I must report a suicide."

"Beg pardon?" 14

"Suicide! That's what I'll have to write to my owners directly I get in."

"Unless you manage to recover him before tomorrow," I assented, dis-
passionately.... "I mean, alive."

He mumbled something which I really did not catch, and I turned my
ear to him in a puzzled manner. He fairly bawled:

"The land—I say, the mainland is at least seven miles off my anchorage."

"About that." 1

My lack of excitement, of curiosity, of surprise, of any sort of pronounced interest, began to arouse his distrust. But except for the felicitous
pretense of deafness I had not tried to pretend anything. I had felt utterly
incapable of playing the part of ignorance properly, and therefore was
afraid to try. It is also certain that he had brought some ready-made suspicions with him, and that he viewed my politeness as a strange and unnatural phenomenon. And yet how else could I have received him? Not
heartily! That was impossible for psychological reasons, which I need not
state here. My only object was to keep off his inquiries. Surlily? Yes, but
surliness might have provoked a point-blank question. From its novelty
to him and from its nature, punctilious courtesy was the manner best calculated to restrain the man. But there was the danger of his breaking
through my defense bluntly. I could not, I think, have met him by a direct lie, also for psychological (not moral) reasons. If he had only known
how afraid I was of his putting my feeling of identity with the other to
the test! But, strangely enough—(I thought of it only afterwards)—I
believe that he was not a little disconcerted by the reverse side of that
weird situation, by something in me that reminded him of the man he
was seeking—suggested a mysterious similitude to the young fellow he had
distrusted and disliked from the first.

However that might have been, the silence was not very prolonged. He took another oblique step.

"I reckon I had no more than a two-mile pull to your ship. Not a bit more."

"And quite enough, too, in this awful heat," I said.

Another pause full of mistrust followed. Necessity, they say, is mother of invention, but fear, too, is not barren of ingenious suggestions. And I was afraid he would ask me point-blank for news of my other self.   155

"Nice little saloon, isn't it?" I remarked, as if noticing for the first time the way his eyes roamed from one closed door to the other. "And very well fitted out, too. Here, for instance," I continued, reaching over the back of my seat negligently and flinging the door open, "is my bathroom."

He made an eager movement, but hardly gave it a glance. I got up, shut the door of the bathroom, and invited him to have a look round, as if I were very proud of my accommodation. He had to rise and be shown round, but he went through the business without any raptures whatever.

"And now we'll have a look at my stateroom," I declared, in a voice as loud as I dared to make it, crossing the cabin to the starboard side with purposely heavy steps.

He followed me in and gazed around. My intelligent double had vanished. I played my part.

"Very convenient—isn't it?"   160

"Very nice. Very comf…" He didn't finish and went out brusquely as if to escape from some unrighteous wiles of mine. But it was not to be. I had been too frightened not to feel vengeful; I felt I had him on the run, and I meant to keep him on the run. My polite insistence must have had something menacing in it, because he gave in suddenly. And I did not let him off a single item; mate's room, pantry, storerooms, the very sail locker which was also under the poop—he had to look into them all. When at last I showed him out on the quarter-deck he drew a long, spiritless sigh, and mumbled dismally that he must really be going back to his ship now. I desired my mate, who had joined us, to see to the captain's boat.

The man of whiskers gave a blast on the whistle which he used to wear hanging round his neck, and yelled, "Sephora's away!" My double down there in my cabin must have heard, and certainly could not feel more relieved than I. Four fellows came running out from somewhere forward and went over the side, while my own men, appearing on deck too, lined the rail. I escorted my visitor to the gangway ceremoniously, and nearly overdid it. He was a tenacious beast. On the very ladder he lingered, and in that unique, guiltily conscientious manner of sticking to the point:

"I say… you… you don't think that——"

I covered his voice loudly:

"Certainly not…. I am delighted. Good-by."   165

I had an idea of what he meant to say, and just saved myself by the privilege of defective hearing. He was too shaken generally to insist, but my mate, close witness of that parting, looked mystified and his face took on a thoughtful cast. As I did not want to appear as if I wished to avoid all communication with my officers, he had the opportunity to address me.

"Seems a very nice man. His boat's crew told our chaps a very extraordinary story, if what I am told by the steward is true. I suppose you had it from the captain, sir?"

"Yes. I had a story from the captain."

"A very horrible affair—isn't it, sir?"

"It is."

"Beats all these tales we hear about murders in Yankee ships."

"I don't think it beats them. I don't think it resembles them in the least."

"Bless my soul—you don't say so! But of course I've no acquaintance whatever with American ships, not I, so I couldn't go against your knowledge. It's horrible enough for me.... But the queerest part is that those fellows seemed to have some idea the man was hidden aboard here. They had really. Did you ever hear of such a thing?"

"Preposterous—isn't it?"

We were walking to and fro athwart the quarter-deck. No one of the crew forward could be seen (the day was Sunday), and the mate pursued:

"There was some little dispute about it. Our chaps took offense. 'As if we would harbor a thing like that,' they said. 'Wouldn't you like to look for him in our coal-hole?' Quite a tiff. But they made it up in the end. I suppose he did drown himself. Don't you, sir?"

"I don't suppose anything."

"You have no doubt in the matter, sir?"

"None whatever."

I left him suddenly. I felt I was producing a bad impression, but with my double down there it was most trying to be on deck. And it was almost as trying to be below. Altogether a nerve-trying situation. But on the whole I felt less torn in two when I was with him. There was no one in the whole ship whom I dared take into my confidence. Since the hands had got to know his story, it would have been impossible to pass him off for anyone else, and an accidental discovery was to be dreaded now more than ever....

The steward being engaged in laying the table for dinner, we could talk only with our eyes when I first went down. Later in the afternoon we had a cautious try at whispering. The Sunday quietness of the ship was against us; the stillness of air and water around her was against us; the elements, the men were against us—everything was against us in our secret partnership; time itself—for this could not go on forever. The very trust in Providence was, I suppose, denied to his guilt. Shall I confess that this thought cast me down very much? And as to the chapter of accidents which counts for so much in the book of success, I could only hope that it was closed. For what favorable accident could be expected?

"Did you hear everything?" were my first words as soon as we took up our position side by side, leaning over my bed place.

He had. And the proof of it was his earnest whisper, "The man told you he hardly dared to give the order."

I understood the reference to be to that saving foresail.

"Yes. He was afraid of it being lost in the setting."   185

"I assure you he never gave the order. He may think he did, but he never gave it. He stood there with me on the break of the poop after the main topsail blew away, and whimpered about our last hope—positively whimpered about it and nothing else—and the night coming on! To hear one's skipper go on like that in such weather was enough to drive any fellow out of his mind. It worked me up into a sort of desperation. I just took it into my own hands and went away from him, boiling, and——But what's the use telling you? *You* know!…Do you think that if I had not been pretty fierce with them I should have got the men to do anything? Not I! The bo's'n perhaps? Perhaps! It wasn't a heavy sea—it was a sea gone mad! I suppose the end of the world will be something like that; and a man may have the heart to see it coming once and be done with it—but to have to face it day after day——I don't blame anybody. I was precious little better than the rest. Only—I was an officer of that old coal wagon, anyhow——"

"I quite understand," I conveyed that sincere assurance into his ear. He was out of breath with whispering; I could hear him pant slightly. It was all very simple. The same strung-up force which had given twenty-four men a chance, at least, for their lives, had, in a sort of recoil, crushed an unworthy mutinous existence.

But I had no leisure to weigh the merits of the matter—footsteps in the saloon, a heavy knock. "There's enough wind to get under way with, sir." Here was the call of a new claim upon my thoughts and even upon my feelings.

"Turn the hands up," I cried through the door. "I'll be on deck directly."

I was going out to make the acquaintance of my ship. Before I left the   190
cabin our eyes met—the eyes of the only two strangers on board. I pointed to the recessed part where the little campstool awaited him and laid my finger on my lips. He made a gesture—somewhat vague—a little mysterious, accompanied by a faint smile, as if of regret.

This is not the place to enlarge upon the sensations of a man who feels for the first time a ship move under his feet to his own independent word. In my case they were not unalloyed. I was not wholly alone with my command; for there was that stranger in my cabin. Or rather, I was not completely and wholly with her. Part of me was absent. That mental feeling of being in two places at once affected me physically as if the mood of secrecy had penetrated my very soul. Before an hour had elapsed since the ship had begun to move, having occasion to ask the mate (he stood by my side) to take a compass bearing of the pagoda, I caught myself reaching up to his ear in whispers. I say I caught myself, but enough had escaped to startle the man. I can't describe it otherwise than by saying that he shied. A grave, preoccupied manner, as though he were in possession of some perplexing intelligence, did not leave him henceforth. A little later I moved away from the rail to look at the compass with such a stealthy gait that the helmsman noticed it—and I could not help noticing the unusual roundness of his eyes. These are trifling instances, though it's to no commander's advantage to be suspected of ludicrous eccentricities. But I was also more seriously affected. There are to a seaman certain words, gestures, that should in given conditions come as naturally, as instinctively as the winking of a menaced eye. A certain order should spring on to his lips without thinking; a certain sign should get itself made, so to speak, without reflection. But all unconscious alertness had abandoned me. I had to make an effort of will to recall myself back (from the cabin) to the conditions of the moment. I felt that I was appearing an irresolute commander to those people who were watching me more or less critically.

And, besides, there were the scares. On the second day out, for instance, coming off the deck in the afternoon (I had straw slippers on my bare feet) I stopped at the open pantry door and spoke to the steward. He was doing something there with his back to me. At the sound of my voice he nearly jumped out of his skin, as the saying is, and incidentally broke a cup.

"What on earth's the matter with you?" I asked, astonished.

He was extremely confused. "Beg your pardon, sir. I made sure you were in your cabin."

"You see I wasn't."

"No, sir. I could have sworn I had heard you moving in there not a moment ago. It's most extraordinary...very sorry, sir."

I passed on with an inward shudder. I was so identified with my secret double that I did not even mention the fact in those scanty, fearful whispers we exchanged. I suppose he had made some slight noise of some kind or other. It would have been miraculous if he hadn't at one time or another. And yet, haggard as he appeared, he looked always perfectly self-controlled, more than calm—almost invulnerable. On my suggestion he remained almost entirely in the bathroom, which, upon the whole, was the safest place. There could be really no shadow of an excuse for anyone ever wanting to go in there, once the steward had done with it. It was a very tiny place. Sometimes he reclined on the floor, his legs bent, his head sustained on one elbow. At others I would find him on the campstool, sitting in his gray sleeping suit and with his cropped dark hair like a patient, unmoved convict. At night I would smuggle him into my bed place, and we would whisper together, with the regular footfalls of the officer of the watch passing and repassing over our heads. It was an infinitely miserable time. It was lucky that some tins of fine preserves were stowed in a locker in my stateroom; hard bread I could always get hold of; and so he lived on stewed chicken, PATE DE FOIE GRAS, asparagus, cooked oysters, sardines—on all sorts of abominable sham delicacies out of tins. My early-morning coffee he always drank; and it was all I dared do for him in that respect.

Every day there was the horrible maneuvering to go through so that my room and then the bathroom should be done in the usual way. I came to hate the sight of the steward, to abhor the voice of that harmless man. I felt that it was he who would bring on the disaster of discovery. It hung like a sword over our heads.

The fourth day out, I think (we were then working down the east side of the Gulf of Siam, tack for tack, in light winds and smooth water)—the fourth day, I say, of this miserable juggling with the unavoidable, as we sat at our evening meal, that man, whose slightest movement I dreaded, after putting down the dishes ran up on deck busily. This could not be dangerous. Presently he came down again; and then it appeared that he had remembered a coat of mine which I had thrown over a rail to dry after having been wetted in a shower which had passed over the ship in the afternoon. Sitting stolidly at the head of the table I became terrified at the sight of the garment on his arm. Of course he made for my door. There was no time to lose.

"Steward," I thundered. My nerves were so shaken that I could not govern my voice and conceal my agitation. This was the sort of thing that made my terrifically whiskered mate tap his forehead with his forefinger. I had detected him using that gesture while talking on deck with a confidential air to the carpenter. It was too far to hear a word, but I had no doubt that this pantomime could only refer to the strange new captain. 200

"Yes, sir," the pale-faced steward turned resignedly to me. It was this maddening course of being shouted at, checked without rhyme or reason, arbitrarily chased out of my cabin, suddenly called into it, sent flying out of his pantry on incomprehensible errands, that accounted for the growing wretchedness of his expression.

"Where are you going with that coat?"

"To your room, sir."

"Is there another shower coming?"

"I'm sure I don't know, sir. Shall I go up again and see, sir?" 205

"No! never mind."

My object was attained, as of course my other self in there would have heard everything that passed. During this interlude my two officers never raised their eyes off their respective plates; but the lip of that confounded cub, the second mate, quivered visibly.

I expected the steward to hook my coat on and come out at once. He was very slow about it; but I dominated my nervousness sufficiently not to shout after him. Suddenly I became aware (it could be heard plainly enough) that the fellow for some reason or other was opening the door of the bathroom. It was the end. The place was literally not big enough to swing a cat in. My voice died in my throat and I went stony all over. I expected to hear a yell of surprise and terror, and made a movement, but had not the strength to get on my legs. Everything remained still. Had my second self taken the poor wretch by the throat? I don't know what I could have done next moment if I had not seen the steward come out of my room, close the door, and then stand quietly by the sideboard.

"Saved," I thought. "But, no! Lost! Gone! He was gone!"

I laid my knife and fork down and leaned back in my chair. My head swam. After a while, when sufficiently recovered to speak in a steady voice, I instructed my mate to put the ship round at eight o'clock himself.

"I won't come on deck," I went on. "I think I'll turn in, and unless the wind shifts I don't want to be disturbed before midnight. I feel a bit seedy."

"You did look middling bad a little while ago," the chief mate remarked without showing any great concern.

They both went out, and I stared at the steward clearing the table. There was nothing to be read on that wretched man's face. But why did he avoid my eyes, I asked myself. Then I thought I should like to hear the sound of his voice.

"Steward!"

"Sir!" Startled as usual.

"Where did you hang up that coat?"

"In the bathroom, sir." The usual anxious tone. "It's not quite dry yet, sir."

For some time longer I sat in the cuddy. Had my double vanished as he had come? But of his coming there was an explanation, whereas his disappearance would be inexplicable.... I went slowly into my dark room, shut the door, lighted the lamp, and for a time dared not turn round. When at last I did I saw him standing bolt-upright in the narrow recessed part. It would not be true to say I had a shock, but an irresistible doubt of his bodily existence flitted through my mind. Can it be, I asked myself, that he is not visible to other eyes than mine? It was like being haunted. Motionless, with a grave face, he raised his hands slightly at me in a gesture which meant clearly, "Heavens! What a narrow escape!" Narrow indeed. I think I had come creeping quietly as near insanity as any man who has not actually gone over the border. That gesture restrained me, so to speak.

The mate with the terrific whiskers was now putting the ship on the other tack. In the moment of profound silence which follows upon the hands going to their stations I heard on the poop his raised voice: "Hard alee!" and the distant shout of the order repeated on the main-deck. The sails, in that light breeze, made but a faint fluttering noise. It ceased. The ship was coming round slowly: I held my breath in the renewed stillness of expectation; one wouldn't have thought that there was a single living soul on her decks. A sudden brisk shout, "Mainsail haul!" broke the spell, and in the noisy cries and rush overhead of the men running away with the main brace we two, down in my cabin, came together in our usual position by the bed place.

He did not wait for my question. "I heard him fumbling here and just managed to squat myself down in the bath," he whispered to me. "The fellow only opened the door and put his arm in to hang the coat up. All the same——" 220

"I never thought of that," I whispered back, even more appalled than before at the closeness of the shave, and marveling at that something unyielding in his character which was carrying him through so finely. There was no agitation in his whisper. Whoever was being driven distracted, it was not he. He was sane. And the proof of his sanity was continued when he took up the whispering again.

"It would never do for me to come to life again."

It was something that a ghost might have said. But what he was alluding to was his old captain's reluctant admission of the theory of suicide. It would obviously serve his turn—if I had understood at all the view which seemed to govern the unalterable purpose of his action.

"You must maroon me as soon as ever you can get amongst these islands off the Cambodge shore," he went on.

"Maroon you! We are not living in a boy's adventure tale," I protested. 225 His scornful whispering took me up.

"We aren't indeed! There's nothing of a boy's tale in this. But there's nothing else for it. I want no more. You don't suppose I am afraid of what can be done to me? Prison or gallows or whatever they may please. But you don't see me coming back to explain such things to an old fellow in a wig and twelve respectable tradesmen, do you? What can they know whether I am guilty or not—or of WHAT I am guilty, either? That's my affair. What does the Bible say? 'Driven off the face of the earth.' Very well, I am off the face of the earth now. As I came at night so I shall go."

"Impossible!" I murmured. "You can't."

"Can't?...Not naked like a soul on the Day of Judgment. I shall freeze on to this sleeping suit. The Last Day is not yet—and...you have understood thoroughly. Didn't you?"

I felt suddenly ashamed of myself. I may say truly that I understood—
and my hesitation in letting that man swim away from my ship's side had
been a mere sham sentiment, a sort of cowardice.

"It can't be done now till next night," I breathed out. "The ship is on
the off-shore tack and the wind may fail us."

"As long as I know that you understand," he whispered. "But of course
you do. It's a great satisfaction to have got somebody to understand. You
seem to have been there on purpose." And in the same whisper, as if we
two whenever we talked had to say things to each other which were not fit
for the world to hear, he added, "It's very wonderful."

We remained side by side talking in our secret way—but sometimes silent or just exchanging a whispered word or two at long intervals. And as
usual he stared through the port. A breath of wind came now and again
into our faces. The ship might have been moored in dock, so gently and on
an even keel she slipped through the water, that did not murmur even at
our passage, shadowy and silent like a phantom sea.

At midnight I went on deck, and to my mate's great surprise put the ship
round on the other tack. His terrible whiskers flitted round me in silent criticism. I certainly should not have done it if it had been only a question of getting out of that sleepy gulf as quickly as possible. I believe he told the second
mate, who relieved him, that it was a great want of judgment. The other only
yawned. That intolerable cub shuffled about so sleepily and lolled against the
rails in such a slack, improper fashion that I came down on him sharply.

"Aren't you properly awake yet?"

"Yes, sir! I am awake."

"Well, then, be good enough to hold yourself as if you were. And keep
a lookout. If there's any current we'll be closing with some islands before
daylight."

The east side of the gulf is fringed with islands, some solitary, others in
groups. On the blue background of the high coast they seem to float on silvery patches of calm water, arid and gray, or dark green and rounded like
clumps of evergreen bushes, with the larger ones, a mile or two long, showing the outlines of ridges, ribs of gray rock under the dark mantle of matted
leafage. Unknown to trade, to travel, almost to geography, the manner of
life they harbor is an unsolved secret. There must be villages—settlements
of fishermen at least—on the largest of them, and some communication with
the world is probably kept up by native craft. But all that forenoon, as we
headed for them, fanned along by the faintest of breezes, I saw no sign of
man or canoe in the field of the telescope I kept on pointing at the scattered
group.

At noon I gave no orders for a change of course, and the mate's whiskers became much concerned and seemed to be offering themselves unduly
to my notice. At last I said:

"I am going to stand right in. Quite in—as far as I can take her."

The stare of extreme surprise imparted an air of ferocity also to his eyes,   240
and he looked truly terrific for a moment.

"We're not doing well in the middle of the gulf," I continued, casually.
"I am going to look for the land breezes tonight."

"Bless my soul! Do you mean, sir, in the dark amongst the lot of all
them islands and reefs and shoals?"

"Well—if there are any regular land breezes at all on this coast one
must get close inshore to find them, mustn't one?"

"Bless my soul!" he exclaimed again under his breath. All that afternoon he wore a dreamy, contemplative appearance which in him was a
mark of perplexity. After dinner I went into my stateroom as if I meant to
take some rest. There we two bent our dark heads over a half-unrolled chart
lying on my bed.

"There," I said. "It's got to be Koh-ring. I've been looking at it ever   245
since sunrise. It has got two hills and a low point. It must be inhabited. And
on the coast opposite there is what looks like the mouth of a biggish river—
with some towns, no doubt, not far up. It's the best chance for you that I
can see."

"Anything. Koh-ring let it be."

He looked thoughtfully at the chart as if surveying chances and distances from a lofty height—and following with his eyes his own figure wandering on the blank land of Cochin-China, and then passing off that piece
of paper clean out of sight into uncharted regions. And it was as if the ship
had two captains to plan her course for her. I had been so worried and restless running up and down that I had not had the patience to dress that day.
I had remained in my sleeping suit, with straw slippers and a soft floppy hat.
The closeness of the heat in the gulf had been most oppressive, and the
crew were used to seeing me wandering in that airy attire.

"She will clear the south point as she heads now," I whispered into his
ear. "Goodness only knows when, though, but certainly after dark. I'll edge
her in to half a mile, as far as I may be able to judge in the dark—"

"Be careful," he murmured, warningly—and I realized suddenly that all
my future, the only future for which I was fit, would perhaps go irretrievably
to pieces in any mishap to my first command.

I could not stop a moment longer in the room. I motioned him to get   250
out of sight and made my way on the poop. That unplayful cub had the
watch. I walked up and down for a while thinking things out, then beckoned him over.

"Send a couple of hands to open the two quarter-deck ports," I said,
mildly.

He actually had the impudence, or else so forgot himself in his wonder
at such an incomprehensible order, as to repeat:

"Open the quarter-deck ports! What for, sir?"

"The only reason you need concern yourself about is because I tell you to do so. Have them open wide and fastened properly."

He reddened and went off, but I believe made some jeering remark to the carpenter as to the sensible practice of ventilating a ship's quarter-deck. I know he popped into the mate's cabin to impart the fact to him because the whiskers came on deck, as it were by chance, and stole glances at me from below—for signs of lunacy or drunkenness, I suppose.

A little before supper, feeling more restless than ever, I rejoined, for a moment, my second self. And to find him sitting so quietly was surprising, like something against nature, inhuman.

I developed my plan in a hurried whisper.

"I shall stand in as close as I dare and then put her round. I will presently find means to smuggle you out of here into the sail locker, which communicates with the lobby. But there is an opening, a sort of square for hauling the sails out, which gives straight on the quarter-deck and which is never closed in fine weather, so as to give air to the sails. When the ship's way is deadened in stays and all the hands are aft at the main braces you will have a clear road to slip out and get overboard through the open quarter-deck port. I've had them both fastened up. Use a rope's end to lower yourself into the water so as to avoid a splash—you know. It could be heard and cause some beastly complication."

He kept silent for a while, then whispered, "I understand."

"I won't be there to see you go," I began with an effort. "The rest... I only hope I have understood, too."

"You have. From first to last"—and for the first time there seemed to be a faltering, something strained in his whisper. He caught hold of my arm, but the ringing of the supper bell made me start. He didn't though; he only released his grip.

After supper I didn't come below again till well past eight o'clock. The faint, steady breeze was loaded with dew; and the wet, darkened sails held all there was of propelling power in it. The night, clear and starry, sparkled darkly, and the opaque, lightless patches shifting slowly against the low stars were the drifting islets. On the port bow there was a big one more distant and shadowily imposing by the great space of sky it eclipsed.

On opening the door I had a back view of my very own self looking at a chart. He had come out of the recess and was standing near the table.

"Quite dark enough," I whispered.

He stepped back and leaned against my bed with a level, quiet glance. I sat on the couch. We had nothing to say to each other. Over our heads the officer of the watch moved here and there. Then I heard him move quickly. I knew what that meant. He was making for the companion; and presently his voice was outside my door.

"We are drawing in pretty fast, sir. Land looks rather close."

"Very well," I answered. "I am coming on deck directly."

I waited till he was gone out of the cuddy, then rose. My double moved too. The time had come to exchange our last whispers, for neither of us was ever to hear each other's natural voice.

"Look here!" I opened a drawer and took out three sovereigns. "Take this anyhow. I've got six and I'd give you the lot, only I must keep a little money to buy some fruit and vegetables for the crew from native boats as we go through Sunda Straits."

He shook his head.   270

"Take it," I urged him, whispering desperately. "No one can tell what——"

He smiled and slapped meaningly the only pocket of the sleeping jacket. It was not safe, certainly. But I produced a large old silk handkerchief of mine, and tying the three pieces of gold in a corner, pressed it on him. He was touched, I supposed, because he took it at last and tied it quickly round his waist under the jacket, on his bare skin.

Our eyes met; several seconds elapsed, till, our glances still mingled, I extended my hand and turned the lamp out. Then I passed through the cuddy, leaving the door of my room wide open.... "Steward!"

He was still lingering in the pantry in the greatness of his zeal, giving a rub-up to a plated cruet stand the last thing before going to bed. Being careful not to wake up the mate, whose room was opposite, I spoke in an undertone.

He looked round anxiously. "Sir!"   275

"Can you get me a little hot water from the galley?"

"I am afraid, sir, the galley fire's been out for some time now."

"Go and see."

He flew up the stairs.

"Now," I whispered, loudly, into the saloon—too loudly, perhaps, but   280
I was afraid I couldn't make a sound. He was by my side in an instant—the double captain slipped past the stairs—through a tiny dark passage...a sliding door. We were in the sail locker, scrambling on our knees over the sails. A sudden thought struck me. I saw myself wandering barefooted, bareheaded, the sun beating on my dark poll. I snatched off my floppy hat and tried hurriedly in the dark to ram it on my other self. He dodged and fended off silently. I wonder what he thought had come to me before he understood and suddenly desisted. Our hands met gropingly, lingered united in a steady, motionless clasp for a second.... No word was breathed by either of us when they separated.

I was standing quietly by the pantry door when the steward returned.

"Sorry, sir. Kettle barely warm. Shall I light the spirit lamp?"

"Never mind."

I came out on deck slowly. It was now a matter of conscience to shave the land as close as possible—for now he must go overboard whenever the ship was put in stays. Must! There could be no going back for him. After a moment I walked over to leeward and my heart flew into my mouth at the nearness of the land on the bow. Under any other circumstances I would not have held on a minute longer. The second mate had followed me anxiously.

I looked on till I felt I could command my voice.

"She will weather," I said then in a quiet tone.

"Are you going to try that, sir?" he stammered out incredulously.

I took no notice of him and raised my tone just enough to be heard by the helmsman.

"Keep her good full."

"Good full, sir."

The wind fanned my cheek, the sails slept, the world was silent. The strain of watching the dark loom of the land grow bigger and denser was too much for me. I had shut my eyes—because the ship must go closer. She must! The stillness was intolerable. Were we standing still?

When I opened my eyes the second view started my heart with a thump. The black southern hill of Koh-ring seemed to hang right over the ship like a towering fragment of everlasting night. On that enormous mass of blackness there was not a gleam to be seen, not a sound to be heard. It was gliding irresistibly towards us and yet seemed already within reach of the hand. I saw the vague figures of the watch grouped in the waist, gazing in awed silence.

"Are you going on, sir?" inquired an unsteady voice at my elbow.

I ignored it. I had to go on.

"Keep her full. Don't check her way. That won't do now," I said warningly.

"I can't see the sails very well," the helmsman answered me, in strange, quavering tones.

Was she close enough? Already she was, I won't say in the shadow of the land, but in the very blackness of it, already swallowed up as it were, gone too close to be recalled, gone from me altogether.

"Give the mate a call," I said to the young man who stood at my elbow as still as death. "And turn all hands up."

My tone had a borrowed loudness reverberated from the height of the land. Several voices cried out together: "We are all on deck, sir."

Then stillness again, with the great shadow gliding closer, towering higher, without a light, without a sound. Such a hush had fallen on the ship that she might have been a bark of the dead floating in slowly under the very gate of Erebus.

"My God! Where are we?"

It was the mate moaning at my elbow. He was thunderstruck, and as it were deprived of the moral support of his whiskers. He clapped his hands and absolutely cried out, "Lost!"

"Be quiet," I said, sternly.

He lowered his tone, but I saw the shadowy gesture of his despair. "What are we doing here?"

"Looking for the land wind."   305

He made as if to tear his hair, and addressed me recklessly.

"She will never get out. You have done it, sir. I knew it'd end in something like this. She will never weather, and you are too close now to stay. She'll drift ashore before she's round. O my God!"

I caught his arm as he was raising it to batter his poor devoted head, and shook it violently.

"She's ashore already," he wailed, trying to tear himself away.

"Is she?…Keep good full there!"   310

"Good full, sir," cried the helmsman in a frightened, thin, childlike voice.

I hadn't let go the mate's arm and went on shaking it. "Ready about, do you hear? You go forward"—shake—"and stop there"—shake—"and hold your noise"—shake—"and see these head-sheets properly overhauled"—shake, shake—shake.

And all the time I dared not look towards the land lest my heart should fail me. I released my grip at last and he ran forward as if fleeing for dear life.

I wondered what my double there in the sail locker thought of this commotion. He was able to hear everything—and perhaps he was able to understand why, on my conscience, it had to be thus close—no less. My first order "Hard alee!" re-echoed ominously under the towering shadow of Koh-ring as if I had shouted in a mountain gorge. And then I watched the land intently. In that smooth water and light wind it was impossible to feel the ship coming-to. No! I could not feel her. And my second self was making now ready to ship out and lower himself overboard. Perhaps he was gone already…?

The great black mass brooding over our very mastheads began to pivot   315
away from the ship's side silently. And now I forgot the secret stranger ready to depart, and remembered only that I was a total stranger to the ship. I did not know her. Would she do it? How was she to be handled?

I swung the mainyard and waited helplessly. She was perhaps stopped, and her very fate hung in the balance, with the black mass of Koh-ring like the gate of the everlasting night towering over her taffrail. What would she do now? Had she way on her yet? I stepped to the side swiftly, and on the shadowy water I could see nothing except a faint phosphorescent flash revealing the glassy smoothness of the sleeping surface. It was impossible to tell—and I had not learned yet the feel of my ship. Was she moving? What I needed was something easily seen, a piece of paper, which I could throw overboard and watch. I had nothing on me. To run down for it I didn't dare. There was no time. All at once my strained, yearning stare distinguished a white object floating within a yard of the ship's side. White on the black water. A phosphorescent flash passed under it. What was that thing?...I recognized my own floppy hat. It must have fallen off his head... and he didn't bother. Now I had what I wanted—the saving mark for my eyes. But I hardly thought of my other self, now gone from the ship, to be hidden forever from all friendly faces, to be a fugitive and a vagabond on the earth, with no brand of the curse on his sane forehead to stay a slaying hand...too proud to explain.

And I watched the hat—the expression of my sudden pity for his mere flesh. It had been meant to save his homeless head from the dangers of the sun. And now—behold—it was saving the ship, by serving me for a mark to help out the ignorance of my strangeness. Ha! It was drifting forward, warning me just in time that the ship had gathered sternaway.

"Shift the helm," I said in a low voice to the seaman standing still like a statue.

The man's eyes glistened wildly in the binnacle light as he jumped round to the other side and spun round the wheel.

I walked to the break of the poop. On the over-shadowed deck all hands stood by the forebraces waiting for my order. The stars ahead seemed to be gliding from right to left. And all was so still in the world that I heard the quiet remark, "She's round," passed in a tone of intense relief between two seamen.

"Let go and haul."

The foreyards ran round with a great noise, amidst cheery cries. And now the frightful whiskers made themselves heard giving various orders. Already the ship was drawing ahead. And I was alone with her. Nothing! no one in the world should stand now between us, throwing a shadow on the way of silent knowledge and mute affection, the perfect communion of a seaman with his first command.

Walking to the taffrail, I was in time to make out, on the very edge of a darkness thrown by a towering black mass like the very gateway of Erebus—yes, I was in time to catch an evanescent glimpse of my white hat left behind to mark the spot where the secret sharer of my cabin and of my thoughts, as though he were my second self, had lowered himself into the water to take his punishment: a free man, a proud swimmer striking out for a new destiny.

■ The story begins with a series of interruptions. List the interruptions that the narrator describes, and explain how each of these helps us understand some established order that has been broken as this story begins.

- How does his juxtaposition with Leggatt help the narrator explore and establish his own position on the ship? Look at specific connections that the two establish. How is the narrator more closely connected to Leggatt than he is to the captain of the other ship?
- Discuss the function of the hat at the end of the story. How does the narrator describe the help that it offers him? Why is it significant that an item he gave to help Leggatt ends up helping the narrator?

Eudora Welty (1909–2001)

Eudora Welty was born and raised in Jackson, Mississippi. Her experiences in the Deep South served as a backdrop for her writings. After completing her primary and secondary education in Jackson, she studied at Mississippi State College for Women from 1925 to 1927. She then transferred to the University of Wisconsin, where she earned her BA in 1929. Upon her father's insistence, she attended the Columbia University Graduate School of Business in New York City from 1930 to 1931. After her father's death in 1931, Welty returned to Jackson, where she spent the remainder of her life. During the Great Depression Welty traveled Mississippi as a photographer and publicity agent for the Works Progress Administration. Inspired by the people she met, Welty began writing short stories about the lives of ordinary people, and her first published piece, "Death of a Traveling Salesman," appeared in the literary magazine *Manuscript* in 1936. Her 1972 publication, *The Optimist's Daughter*, was awarded the Pulitzer Prize; and in 1980 she received the National Medal for Literature for *The Collected Stories of Eudora Welty*.

A Worn Path (1941)

It was December—a bright frozen day in the early morning. Far out in the country there was an old Negro woman with her head tied in a red rag, coming along a path through the pinewoods. Her name was Phoenix Jackson. She was very old and small and she walked slowly in the dark pine shadows, moving a little from side to side in her steps, with the balanced heaviness and lightness of a pendulum in a grandfather clock. She carried a thin, small cane made from an umbrella, and with this she kept tapping the frozen earth in front of her. This made a grave and persistent noise in the still air, that seemed meditative like the chirping of a solitary little bird.

She wore a dark striped dress reaching down to her shoe tops, and an equally long apron of bleached sugar sacks, with a full pocket: all neat and tidy, but every time she took a step she might have fallen over her shoelaces, which dragged from her unlaced shoes. She looked straight ahead.

Her eyes were blue with age. Her skin had a pattern all its own of number-less branching wrinkles and as though a whole little tree stood in the middle of her forehead, but a golden color ran underneath, and the two knobs of her cheeks were illumined by a yellow burning under the dark. Under the red rag her hair came down on her neck in the frailest of ringlets, still black, and with an odor like copper.

Now and then there was a quivering in the thicket. Old Phoenix said, "Out of my way, all you foxes, owls, beetles, jack rabbits, coons and wild animals! ... Keep out from under these feet, little bob-whites.... Keep the big wild hogs out of my path. Don't let none of those come running my direction. I got a long way." Under her small black-freckled hand her cane, limber as a buggy whip, would switch at the brush as if to rouse up any hiding things.

On she went. The woods were deep and still. The sun made the pine needles almost too bright to look at, up where the wind rocked. The cones dropped as light as feathers. Down in the hollow was the mourning dove—it was not too late for him.

The path ran up a hill. "Seem like there is chains about my feet, time I get this far," she said, in the voice of argument old people keep to use with themselves. "Something always take a hold of me on this hill—pleads I should stay."

After she got to the top she turned and gave a full, severe look behind her where she had come. "Up through pines," she said at length. "Now down through oaks."

Her eyes opened their widest, and she started down gently. But before she got to the bottom of the hill a bush caught her dress.

Her fingers were busy and intent, but her skirts were full and long, so that before she could pull them free in one place they were caught in an-other. It was not possible to allow the dress to tear. "I in the thorny bush," she said. "Thorns, you doing your appointed work. Never want to let folks pass, no sir. Old eyes thought you was a pretty little *green* bush."

Finally, trembling all over, she stood free, and after a moment dared to stoop for her cane.

"Sun so high!" she cried, leaning back and looking, while the thick tears went over her eyes. "The time getting all gone here."

At the foot of this hill was a place where a log was laid across the creek. "Now comes the trial," said Phoenix.

Putting her right foot out, she mounted the log and shut her eyes. Lift-ing her skirt, leveling her cane fiercely before her, like a festival figure in some parade, she began to march across. Then she opened her eyes and she was safe on the other side.

"I wasn't as old as I thought," she said.

But she sat down to rest. She spread her skirts on the bank around her and folded her hands over her knees. Up above her was a tree in a pearly cloud of mistletoe. She did not dare to close her eyes, and when a little boy brought her a plate with a slice of marble-cake on it she spoke to him. "That would be acceptable," she said. But when she went to take it there was just her own hand in the air.

So she left that tree, and had to go through a barbed-wire fence. There she had to creep and crawl, spreading her knees and stretching her fingers like a baby trying to climb the steps. But she talked loudly to herself: she could not let her dress be torn now, so late in the day, and she could not pay for having her arm or her leg sawed off if she got caught fast where she was.

At last she was safe through the fence and risen up out in the clearing. Big dead trees, like black men with one arm, were standing in the purple stalks of the withered cotton field. There sat a buzzard.

"Who you watching?"

In the furrow she made her way along.

"Glad this not the season for bulls," she said, looking sideways, "and the good Lord made his snakes to curl up and sleep in the winter. A pleasure I don't see no two-headed snake coming around that tree, where it come once. It took a while to get by him, back in the summer."

She passed through the old cotton and went into a field of dead corn. It whispered and shook and was taller than her head. "Through the maze now," she said, for there was no path.

Then there was something tall, black, and skinny there, moving before her.

At first she took it for a man. It could have been a man dancing in the field. But she stood still and listened, and it did not make a sound. It was as silent as a ghost.

"Ghost," she said sharply, "who be you the ghost of? For I have heard of nary death close by."

But there was no answer—only the ragged dancing in the wind.

She shut her eyes, reached out her hand, and touched a sleeve. She found a coat and inside that an emptiness, cold as ice.

"You scarecrow," she said. Her face lighted. "I ought to be shut up for good," she said with laughter. "My senses is gone. I too old. I the oldest people I ever know. Dance, old scarecrow," she said, "while I dancing with you."

She kicked her foot over the furrow, and with mouth drawn down, shook her head once or twice in a little strutting way. Some husks blew down and whirled in streamers about her skirts.

Then she went on, parting her way from side to side with the cane, through the whispering field. At last she came to the end, to a wagon track where the silver grass blew between the red ruts. The quail were walking around like pullets, seeming all dainty and unseen.

"Walk pretty," she said. "This is the easy place. This the easy going."

She followed the track, swaying through the quiet bare fields, through the little strings of trees silver in their dead leaves, past cabins silver from weather, with the doors and windows boarded shut, all like old women under a spell sitting there. "I walking in their sleep," she said, nodding her head vigorously.

In a ravine she went where a spring was silently flowing through a hollow log. Old Phoenix bent and drank. "Sweet-gum makes the water sweet," she said, and drank more. "Nobody know who made this well, for it was here when I was born."

The track crossed a swampy part where the moss hung as white as lace from every limb. "Sleep on, alligators, and blow your bubbles." Then the track went into the road.

Deep, deep the road went down between the high green-colored banks. Overhead the live-oaks met, and it was as dark as a cave.

A black dog with a lolling tongue came up out of the weeds by the ditch. She was meditating, and not ready, and when he came at her she only hit him a little with her cane. Over she went in the ditch, like a little puff of milkweed.

Down there, her senses drifted away. A dream visited her, and she reached her hand up, but nothing reached down and gave her a pull. So she lay there and presently went to talking. "Old woman," she said to herself, "that black dog come up out of the weeds to stall you off, and now there he sitting on his fine tail, smiling at you."

A white man finally came along and found her—a hunter, a young man, with his dog on a chain.

"Well, Granny!" he laughed. "What are you doing there?"

"Lying on my back like a June-bug waiting to be turned over, mister," she said, reaching up her hand.

He lifted her up, gave her a swing in the air, and set her down. "Anything broken, Granny?"

"No sir, them old dead weeds is springy enough," said Phoenix, when she had got her breath. "I thank you for your trouble."

"Where do you live, Granny?" he asked, while the two dogs were growling at each other.

"Away back yonder, sir, behind the ridge. You can't even see it from here."

"On your way home?"

"No sir, I going to town."

"Why, that's too far! That's as far as I walk when I come out myself, and I get something for my trouble." He patted the stuffed bag he carried, and there hung down a little closed claw. It was one of the bob-whites, with its beak hooked bitterly to show it was dead. "Now you go on home, Granny!"

"I bound to go to town, mister," said Phoenix. "The time come around."

He gave another laugh, filling the whole landscape. "I know you old colored people! Wouldn't miss going to town to see Santa Claus!"

But something held old Phoenix very still. The deep lines in her face went into a fierce and different radiation. Without warning, she had seen with her own eyes a flashing nickel fall out of the man's pocket onto the ground.

"How old are you, Granny?" he was saying.   50

"There is no telling, mister," she said, "no telling."

Then she gave a little cry and clapped her hands and said, "Git on away from here, dog! Look! Look at that dog!" She laughed as if in admiration. "He ain't scared of nobody. He a big black dog." She whispered, "Sic him!"

"Watch me get rid of that cur," said the man. "Sic him, Pete! Sic him!"

Phoenix heard the dogs fighting, and heard the man running and throwing sticks. She even heard a gunshot. But she was slowly bending forward by that time, further and further forward, the lid stretched down over her eyes, as if she were doing this in her sleep. Her chin was lowered almost to her knees. The yellow palm of her hand came out from the fold of her apron. Her fingers slid down and along the ground under the piece of money with the grace and care they would have in lifting an egg from under a setting hen. Then she slowly straightened up, she stood erect, and the nickel was in her apron pocket. A bird flew by. Her lips moved. "God watching me the whole time. I come to stealing."

The man came back, and his own dog panted about them. "Well, I   55
scared him off that time," he said, and then he laughed and lifted his gun and pointed it at Phoenix.

She stood straight and faced him.

"Doesn't the gun scare you?" he said, still pointing it.

"No, sir, I seen plenty go off closer by, in my day, and for less than what I done," she said, holding utterly still.

He smiled, and shouldered the gun. "Well, Granny," he said, "you must be a hundred years old, and scared of nothing. I'd give you a dime if I had any money with me. But you take my advice and stay home, and nothing will happen to you."

"I bound to go on my way, mister," said Phoenix. She inclined her   60
head in the red rag. Then they went in different directions, but she could hear the gun shooting again and again over the hill.

She walked on. The shadows hung from the oak trees to the road like curtains. Then she smelled wood-smoke, and smelled the river, and she saw a steeple and the cabins on their steep steps. Dozens of little black children whirled around her. There ahead was Natchez shining. Bells were ringing. She walked on.

In the paved city it was Christmas time. There were red and green electric lights strung and crisscrossed everywhere, and all turned on in the daytime. Old Phoenix would have been lost if she had not distrusted her eyesight and depended on her feet to know where to take her.

She paused quietly on the sidewalk where people were passing by. A lady came along in the crowd, carrying an armful of red-, green- and silver-wrapped presents; she gave off perfume like the red roses in hot summer, and Phoenix stopped her.

"Please, missy, will you lace up my shoe?" She held up her foot.

"What do you want, Grandma?" 6

"See my shoe," said Phoenix. "Do all right for out in the country, but wouldn't look right to go in a big building."

"Stand still then, Grandma," said the lady. She put her packages down on the sidewalk beside her and laced and tied both shoes tightly.

"Can't lace 'em with a cane," said Phoenix. "Thank you, missy. I doesn't mind asking a nice lady to tie up my shoe, when I gets out on the street."

Moving slowly and from side to side, she went into the big building, and into a tower of steps, where she walked up and around and around until her feet knew to stop.

She entered a door, and there she saw nailed up on the wall the document that had been stamped with the gold seal and framed in the gold frame, which matched the dream that was hung up in her head. 7

"Here I be," she said. There was a fixed and ceremonial stiffness over her body.

"A charity case, I suppose," said an attendant who sat at the desk before her.

But Phoenix only looked above her head. There was sweat on her face, the wrinkles in her face shone like a bright net.

"Speak up, Grandma," the woman said. "What's your name? We must have your history, you know. Have you been here before? What seems to be the trouble with you?"

Old Phoenix only gave a twitch to her face as if a fly were bothering her. 7

"Are you deaf?" cried the attendant.

But then the nurse came in.

"Oh, that's just old Aunt Phoenix," she said. "She doesn't come for herself—she has a little grandson. She makes these trips just as regular as clockwork. She lives away back off the Old Natchez Trace." She bent down. "Well, Aunt Phoenix, why don't you just take a seat? We won't keep you standing after your long trip." She pointed.

The old woman sat down, bolt upright in the chair.

"Now, how is the boy?" asked the nurse.

Old Phoenix did not speak. 8

"I said, how is the boy?"

But Phoenix only waited and stared straight ahead, her face very solemn and withdrawn into rigidity.

"Is his throat any better?" asked the nurse. "Aunt Phoenix, don't you hear me? Is your grandson's throat any better since the last time you came for the medicine?"

With her hands on her knees, the old woman waited, silent, erect and motionless, just as if she were in armor.   85

"You mustn't take up our time this way, Aunt Phoenix," the nurse said. "Tell us quickly about your grandson, and get it over. He isn't dead, is he?"

At last there came a flicker and then a flame of comprehension across her face, and she spoke.

"My grandson. It was my memory had left me. There I sat and forgot why I made my long trip."

"Forgot?" The nurse frowned. "After you came so far?"

Then Phoenix was like an old woman begging a dignified forgiveness   90
for waking up frightened in the night. "I never did go to school, I was too old at the Surrender," she said in a soft voice. "I'm an old woman without an education. It was my memory fail me. My little grandson, he is just the same, and I forgot it in the coming."

"Throat never heals, does it?" said the nurse, speaking in a loud, sure voice to old Phoenix. By now she had a card with something written on it, a little list. "Yes. Swallowed lye. When was it?—January—two-three years ago—"

Phoenix spoke unasked now. "No, missy, he not dead, he just the same. Every little while his throat begin to close up again, and he not able to swallow. He not get his breath. He not able to help himself. So the time come around, and I go on another trip for the soothing medicine."

"All right. The doctor said as long as you came to get it, you could have it," said the nurse. "But it's an obstinate case."

"My little grandson, he sit up there in the house all wrapped up, waiting by himself," Phoenix went on. "We is the only two left in the world. He suffer and it don't seem to put him back at all. He got a sweet look. He going to last. He wear a little patch quilt and peep out holding his mouth open like a little bird. I remembers so plain now. I not going to forget him again, no, the whole enduring time. I could tell him from all the others in creation."

"All right." The nurse was trying to hush her now. She brought her a   95
bottle of medicine. "Charity," she said, making a check mark in a book.

Old Phoenix held the bottle close to her eyes, and then carefully put it into her pocket.

"I thank you," she said.

"It's Christmas time, Grandma," said the attendant. "Could I give you a few pennies out of my purse?"

"Five pennies is a nickel," said Phoenix stiffly.

"Here's a nickel," said the attendant.

Phoenix rose carefully and held out her hand. She received the nickel and then fished the other nickel out of her pocket and laid it beside the new one. She stared at her palm closely, with her head on one side.

Then she gave a tap with her cane on the floor.

"This is what come to me to do," she said. "I going to the store and buy my child a little windmill they sells, made out of paper. He going to find it hard to believe there such a thing in the world. I'll march myself back where he waiting, holding it straight up in this hand."

She lifted her free hand, gave a little nod, turned around, and walked out of the doctor's office. Then her slow step began on the stairs, going down.

- Both this story's tone and its action feel very much like a children's fairy tale. It is the story of an old woman whom other people treat in much the same way that they might treat a child. Find specific details in the story that are similar to those in a fairy tale, and explore the ends to which they are used here.

- How does the idea of mapping apply to Phoenix Jackson's trip into town? How does she determine the direction in which she walks and the direction in which she chooses to act? How does she respond to the various small incidents that interrupt her as she makes her way through this story?

Raymond Carver (1938–1988)

Raymond Carver was born in Clatskanie, Oregon. Carver grew up among loggers, mechanics, waitresses, and factory workers, and he memorialized these people in his fiction. After high school, Carver earned an AB degree from Humboldt State College (now California State University) in 1963 and an MFA from the University of Iowa in 1966. Carver used fiction and poetry to portray the lives of average Americans, and his works often explore themes of love, dissolving relationships, and financial and emotional hardships. His stories are often bleak and ambiguous, and his characters must find comfort and satisfaction in life's everyday occurrences. Carver's honors included the 1970 National Endowment for the Arts Discovery Award for Poetry, a 1977 National Book Award nomination for *Will You Please Be Quiet, Please?*, and Pulitzer Prize nominations for *Cathedral* (1985) and *Where I'm Calling From: New and Selected Stories* (1988).

Cathedral (1983)

This blind man, an old friend of my wife's, he was on his way to spend the night. His wife had died. So he was visiting the dead wife's relatives in Connecticut. He called my wife from his in-laws'. Arrangements were made. He would come by train, a five-hour trip, and my wife would meet him at the station. She hadn't seen him since she worked for him one summer in Seattle ten years ago. But she and the blind man had kept in touch. They made tapes and mailed them back and forth. I wasn't enthusiastic about his visit. He was no one I knew. And his being blind bothered me. My idea of blindness came from the movies. In the movies, the blind moved slowly and never laughed. Sometimes they were led by seeing eye dogs. A blind man in my house was not something I looked forward to.

That summer in Seattle she had needed a job. She didn't have any money. The man she was going to marry at the end of the summer was in officers' training school. He didn't have any money, either. But she was in love with the guy, and he was in love with her, etc. She'd seen something in the paper: HELP WANTED—*Reading to Blind Man*, and a telephone number. She phoned and went over, was hired on the spot. She'd worked with this blind man all summer. She read stuff to him, case studies, reports, that sort of thing. She helped him organize his little office in the county social-service department. They'd become good friends, my wife and the blind man. How do I know these things? She told me. And she told me something else. On her last day in the office, the blind man asked if he could touch her face. She agreed to this. She told me he touched his fingers to every part of her face, her nose—even her neck! She never forgot it. She even tried to write a poem about it. She was always trying to write a poem. She wrote a poem or two every year, usually after something really important had happened to her.

When we first started going out together, she showed me the poem. In the poem, she recalled his fingers and the way they had moved around over her face. In the poem, she talked about what she had felt at the time, about what went through her mind when the blind man touched her nose and lips. I can remember I didn't think much of the poem. Of course, I didn't tell her that. Maybe I just don't understand poetry. I admit it's not the first thing I reach for when I pick up something to read.

Anyway, this man who'd first enjoyed her favors, the officer-to-be, he'd been her childhood sweetheart. So okay. I'm saying that at the end of the summer she let the blind man run his hands over her face, said goodbye to him, married her childhood etc., who was now a commissioned officer, and she moved away from Seattle. But they'd kept in touch, she and the blind man. She made the first contact after a year or so. She called him up one night from an Air Force base in Alabama. She wanted to talk. They talked.

He asked her to send a tape and tell him about her life. She did this. She sent the tape. On the tape, she told the blind man about her husband and about their life together in the military. She told the blind man she loved her husband but she didn't like it where they lived and she didn't like it that he was part of the military-industrial thing. She told the blind man she'd written a poem and he was in it. She told him that she was writing a poem about what it was like to be an Air Force officer's wife. The poem wasn't finished yet. She was still writing it. The blind man made a tape. He sent her the tape. She made a tape. This went on for years. My wife's officer was posted to one base and then another. She sent tapes from Moody AFB, McGuire, McConnell, and finally Travis, near Sacramento, where one night she got to feeling lonely and cut off from people she kept losing in that moving-around life. She got to feeling she couldn't go it another step. She went in and swallowed all the pills and capsules in the medicine chest and washed them down with a bottle of gin. Then she got into a hot bath and passed out.

But instead of dying, she got sick. She threw up. Her officer—why should he have a name? he was the childhood sweetheart, and what more does he want?—came home from somewhere, found her, and called the ambulance. In time, she put it all on a tape and sent the tape to the blind man. Over the years, she put all kinds of stuff on tapes and sent the tapes off lickety-split. Next to writing a poem every year, I think it was her chief means of recreation. On one tape, she told the blind man she'd decided to live away from her officer for a time. On another tape, she told him about her divorce. She and I began going out, and of course she told her blind man about it. She told him everything, or so it seemed to me. Once she asked me if I'd like to hear the latest tape from the blind man. This was a year ago. I was on the tape, she said. So I said okay, I'd listen to it. I got us drinks and we settled down in the living room. We made ready to listen. First she inserted the tape into the player and adjusted a couple of dials. Then she pushed a lever. The tape squeaked and someone began to talk in this loud voice. She lowered the volume. After a few minutes of harmless chitchat, I heard my own name in the mouth of this stranger, this blind man I didn't even know! And then this: "From all you've said about him, I can only conclude—" But we were interrupted, a knock at the door, something, and we didn't ever get back to the tape. Maybe it was just as well. I'd heard all I wanted to.

Now this same blind man was coming to sleep in my house.

"Maybe I could take him bowling," I said to my wife. She was at the draining board doing scalloped potatoes. She put down the knife she was using and turned around.

"If you love me," she said, "you can do this for me. If you don't love me, okay. But if you had a friend, any friend, and the friend came to visit, I'd make him feel comfortable." She wiped her hands with the dish towel.

"I don't have any blind friends," I said.

"You don't have *any* friends," she said. "Period. Besides," she said, "god-   10
damn it, his wife's just died! Don't you understand that? The man's lost his
wife!"

I didn't answer. She'd told me a little about the blind man's wife. Her
name was Beulah. Beulah! That's a name for a colored woman.

"Was his wife a Negro?" I asked.

"Are you crazy?" my wife said. "Have you just flipped or something?"
She picked up a potato. I saw it hit the floor, then roll under the stove.
"What's wrong with you?" she said. "Are you drunk?"

"I'm just asking," I said.

Right then my wife filled me in with more detail than I cared to know.   15
I made a drink and sat at the kitchen table to listen. Pieces of the story
began to fall into place.

Beulah had gone to work for the blind man the summer after my wife
had stopped working for him. Pretty soon Beulah and the blind man had
themselves a church wedding. It was a little wedding—who'd want to go to
such a wedding in the first place?—just the two of them, plus the minister
and the minister's wife. But it was a church wedding just the same. It was
what Beulah had wanted, he'd said. But even then Beulah must have been
carrying the cancer in her glands. After they had been inseparable for eight
years—my wife's word, *inseparable*—Beulah's health went into a rapid decline. She died in a Seattle hospital room, the blind man sitting beside the
bed and holding on to her hand. They'd married, lived and worked together,
slept together—had sex, sure—and then the blind man had to bury her. All
this without his having ever seen what the goddamned woman looked like.
It was beyond my understanding. Hearing this, I felt sorry for the blind man
for a little bit. And then I found myself thinking what a pitiful life this
woman must have led. Imagine a woman who could never see herself as she
was seen in the eyes of her loved one. A woman who could go on day after
day and never receive the smallest compliment from her beloved. A woman
whose husband could never read the expression on her face, be it misery or
something better. Someone who could wear makeup or not—what difference to him? She could, if she wanted, wear green eye-shadow around one
eye, a straight pin in her nostril, yellow slacks, and purple shoes, no matter.
And then to slip off into death, the blind man's hand on her hand, his
blind eyes streaming tears—I'm imagining now—her last thought maybe
this: that he never even knew what she looked like, and she on an express
to the grave. Robert was left with a small insurance policy and a half of a
twenty-peso Mexican coin. The other half of the coin went into the box
with her. Pathetic.

So when the time rolled around, my wife went to the depot to pick him
up. With nothing to do but wait—sure, I blamed him for that—I was having

a drink and watching the TV when I heard the car pull into the drive. I got up from the sofa with my drink and went to the window to have a look.

I saw my wife laughing as she parked the car. I saw her get out of the car and shut the door. She was still wearing a smile. Just amazing. She went around to the other side of the car to where the blind man was already starting to get out. This blind man, feature this, he was wearing a full beard! A beard on a blind man! Too much, I say. The blind man reached into the backseat and dragged out a suitcase. My wife took his arm, shut the car door, and, talking all the way, moved him down the drive and then up the steps to the front porch. I turned off the TV. I finished my drink, rinsed the glass, dried my hands. Then I went to the door.

My wife said, "I want you to meet Robert. Robert, this is my husband. I've told you all about him." She was beaming. She had this blind man by his coat sleeve.

The blind man let go of his suitcase and up came his hand.

I took it. He squeezed hard, held my hand, and then he let it go.

"I feel like we've already met," he boomed.

"Likewise," I said. I didn't know what else to say. Then I said, "Welcome. I've heard a lot about you." We began to move then, a little group, from the porch into the living room, my wife guiding him by the arm. The blind man was carrying his suitcase in his other hand. My wife said things like, "To your left here, Robert. That's right. Now watch it, there's a chair. That's it. Sit down right here. This is the sofa. We just bought this sofa two weeks ago."

I started to say something about the old sofa. I'd liked that old sofa. But I didn't say anything. Then I wanted to say something else, small-talk, about the scenic ride along the Hudson. How going *to* New York, you should sit on the right-hand side of the train, and coming *from* New York, the left-hand side.

"Did you have a good train ride?" I said. "Which side of the train did you sit on, by the way?"

"What a question, which side!" my wife said. "What's it matter which side?" she said.

"I just asked," I said.

"Right side," the blind man said. "I hadn't been on a train in nearly forty years. Not since I was a kid. With my folks. That's been a long time. I'd nearly forgotten the sensation. I have winter in my beard now," he said. "So I've been told, anyway. Do I look distinguished, my dear?" the blind man said to my wife.

"You look distinguished, Robert," she said. "Robert," she said. "Robert, it's just so good to see you."

My wife finally took her eyes off the blind man and looked at me. I had the feeling she didn't like what she saw. I shrugged.

I've never met, or personally known, anyone who was blind. This blind man was late forties, a heavy-set, balding man with stooped shoulders, as if he carried a great weight there. He wore brown slacks, brown shoes, a light-brown shirt, a tie, a sports coat. Spiffy. He also had this full beard. But he didn't use a cane and he didn't wear dark glasses. I'd always thought dark glasses were a must for the blind. Fact was, I wished he had a pair. At first glance, his eyes looked like anyone else's eyes. But if you looked close, there was something different about them. Too much white in the iris, for one thing, and the pupils seemed to move around in the sockets without his knowing it or being able to stop it. Creepy. As I stared at his face, I saw the left pupil turn in toward his nose while the other made an effort to keep in one place. But it was only an effort, for that eye was on the roam without his knowing it or wanting it to be.

I said, "Let me get you a drink. What's your pleasure? We have a little of everything. It's one of our pastimes."

"Bub, I'm a Scotch man myself," he said fast enough in this big voice.

"Right," I said. Bub! "Sure you are. I knew it."

He let his fingers touch his suitcase, which was sitting alongside the   35
sofa. He was taking his bearings. I didn't blame him for that.

"I'll move that up to your room," my wife said.

"No, that's fine," the blind man said loudly. "It can go up when I go up."

"A little water with the Scotch?" I said.

"Very little," he said.

"I knew it," I said.   40

He said, "Just a tad. The Irish actor, Barry Fitzgerald? I'm like that fellow. When I drink water, Fitzgerald said, I drink water. When I drink whiskey, I drink whiskey." My wife laughed. The blind man brought his hand up under his beard. He lifted his beard slowly and let it drop.

I did the drinks, three big glasses of Scotch with a splash of water in each. Then we made ourselves comfortable and talked about Robert's travels. First the long flight from the West Coast to Connecticut, we covered that. Then from Connecticut up here by train. We had another drink concerning that leg of the trip.

I remembered having read somewhere that the blind didn't smoke because, as speculation had it, they couldn't see the smoke they exhaled. I thought I knew that much and that much only about blind people. But this blind man smoked his cigarette down to the nubbin and then lit another one. This blind man filled his ashtray and my wife emptied it.

When we sat down at the table for dinner, we had another drink. My wife heaped Robert's plate with cube steak, scalloped potatoes, green beans. I buttered him up two slices of bread. I said, "Here's bread and butter for you." I swallowed some of my drink. "Now let us pray," I said, and the blind man lowered his head. My wife looked at me, her mouth agape. "Pray the phone won't ring and the food doesn't get cold," I said.

We dug in. We ate everything there was to eat on the table. We ate like there was no tomorrow. We didn't talk. We ate. We scarfed. We grazed that table. We were into serious eating. The blind man had right away located his foods, he knew just where everything was on his plate. I watched with admiration as he used his knife and fork on the meat. He'd cut two pieces of meat, fork the meat into his mouth, and then go all out for the scalloped potatoes, the beans next, and then he'd tear off a hunk of buttered bread and eat that. He'd follow this up with a big drink of milk. It didn't seem to bother him to use his fingers once in a while, either.

We finished everything, including half a strawberry pie. For a few moments, we sat as if stunned. Sweat beaded on our faces. Finally, we got up from the table and left the dirty plates. We didn't look back. We took ourselves into the living room and sank into our places again. Robert and my wife sat on the sofa. I took the big chair. We had us two or three more drinks while they talked about the major things that had come to pass for them in the past ten years. For the most part, I just listened. Now and then I joined in. I didn't want him to think I'd left the room, and I didn't want her to think I was feeling left out. They talked of things that had happened to them—to them!—these past ten years. I waited in vain to hear my name on my wife's sweet lips: "And then my dear husband came into my life"— something like that. But I heard nothing of the sort. More talk of Robert. Robert had done a little of everything, it seemed, a regular blind jack-of-all-trades. But most recently he and his wife had had an Amway distributorship, from which, I gathered, they'd earned their living, such as it was. The blind man was also a ham radio operator. He talked in his loud voice about conversations he'd had with fellow operators in Guam, in the Philippines, in Alaska, and even in Tahiti. He said he'd have a lot of friends there if he ever wanted to go visit those places. From time to time, he'd turn his blind face toward me, put his hand under his beard, ask me something. How long had I been in my present position? (Three years.) Did I like my work? (I didn't.) Was I going to stay with it? (What were the options?) Finally, when I thought he was beginning to run down, I got up and turned on the TV.

My wife looked at me with irritation. She was heading toward a boil. Then she looked at the blind man and said, "Robert, do you have a TV?"

The blind man said, "My dear, I have two TVs. I have a color set and a black-and-white thing, an old relic. It's funny, but if I turn the TV on, and I'm always turning it on, I turn on the color set. It's funny, don't you think?"

I didn't know what to say to that. I had absolutely nothing to say to that. No opinion. So I watched the news program and tried to listen to what the announcer was saying.

"This is a color TV," the blind man said. "Don't ask me how, but I can   50
tell."

"We traded up a while ago," I said.

The blind man had another taste of his drink. He lifted his beard, sniffed it, and let it fall. He leaned forward on the sofa. He positioned his ashtray on the coffee table, then put the lighter to his cigarette. He leaned back on the sofa and crossed his legs at the ankles.

My wife covered her mouth, and then she yawned. She stretched. She said, "I think I'll go upstairs and put on my robe. I think I'll change into something else. Robert, you make yourself comfortable," she said.

"I'm comfortable," the blind man said.

"I want you to feel comfortable in this house," she said.   55

"I am comfortable," the blind man said.

After she'd left the room, he and I listened to the weather report and then to the sports roundup. By that time, she'd been gone so long I didn't know if she was going to come back. I thought she might have gone to bed. I wished she'd come back downstairs. I didn't want to be left alone with a blind man. I asked him if he wanted another drink, and he said sure. Then I asked if he wanted to smoke some dope with me. I said I'd just rolled a number. I hadn't, but I planned to do so in about two shakes.

"I'll try some with you," he said.

"Damn right," I said. "That's the stuff."

I got our drinks and sat down on the sofa with him. Then I rolled us   60
two fat numbers. I lit one and passed it. I brought it to his fingers. He took it and inhaled.

"Hold it as long as you can," I said. I could tell he didn't know the first thing.

My wife came back downstairs wearing her pink robe and her pink slippers.

"What do I smell?" she said.

"We thought we'd have us some cannabis," I said.

My wife gave me a savage look. Then she looked at the blind man and   65
said, "Robert, I didn't know you smoked."

He said, "I do now, my dear. There's a first time for everything. But I don't feel anything yet."

"This stuff is pretty mellow," I said. "This stuff is mild. It's dope you can reason with," I said. "It doesn't mess you up."

"Not much it doesn't, bub," he said, and laughed.

My wife sat on the sofa between the blind man and me. I passed her the number. She took it and toked and then passed it back to me. "Which way is this going?" she said. Then she said, "I shouldn't be smoking this. I can hardly keep my eyes open as it is. That dinner did me in. I shouldn't have eaten so much."

"It was the strawberry pie," the blind man said. "That's what did it," he said, and he laughed his big laugh. Then he shook his head.

"There's more strawberry pie," I said.

"Do you want some more, Robert?" my wife said.

"Maybe in a little while," he said.

We gave our attention to the TV. My wife yawned again. She said, "Your bed is made up when you feel like going to bed, Robert. I know you must have had a long day. When you're ready to go to bed, say so." She pulled his arm. "Robert?"

He came to and said, "I've had a real nice time. This beats tapes, doesn't it?"

I said, "Coming at you," and I put the number between his fingers. He inhaled, held the smoke, and then let it go. It was like he'd been doing it since he was nine years old.

"Thanks, bub," he said. "But I think this is all for me. I think I'm beginning to feel it," he said. He held the burning roach out for my wife.

"Same here," she said. "Ditto. Me, too." She took the roach and passed it to me. "I may just sit here for a while between you two guys with my eyes closed. But don't let me bother you, okay? Either one of you. If it bothers you, say so. Otherwise, I may just sit here with my eyes closed until you're ready to go to bed," she said. "Your bed's made up, Robert, when you're ready. It's right next to our room at the top of the stairs. We'll show you up when you're ready. You wake me up now, you guys, if I fall asleep." She said that and then she closed her eyes and went to sleep.

The news program ended. I got up and changed the channel. I sat back down on the sofa. I wished my wife hadn't pooped out. Her head lay across the back of the sofa, her mouth open. She'd turned so that her robe slipped away from her legs, exposing a juicy thigh. I reached to draw her robe back over her, and it was then that I glanced at the blind man. What the hell! I flipped the robe open again.

"You say when you want some strawberry pie," I said.

"I will," he said.

I said, "Are you tired? Do you want me to take you up to your bed? Are you ready to hit the hay?"

"Not yet," he said. "No, I'll stay up with you, bub. If that's all right. I'll stay up until you're ready to turn in. We haven't had a chance to talk. Know what I mean? I feel like me and her monopolized the evening." He lifted his beard and he let it fall. He picked up his cigarettes and his lighter.

"That's all right," I said. Then I said, "I'm glad for the company."

And I guess I was. Every night I smoked dope and stayed up as long as I could before I fell asleep. My wife and I hardly ever went to bed at the same time. When I did go to sleep, I had these dreams. Sometimes I'd wake up from one of them, my heart going crazy.

Something about the church and the Middle Ages was on the TV. Not your run-of-the-mill TV fare. I wanted to watch something else. I turned to the other channels. But there was nothing on them, either. So I turned back to the first channel and apologized.

"Bub, it's all right," the blind man said. "It's fine with me. Whatever you want to watch is okay. I'm always learning something. Learning never ends. It won't hurt me to learn something tonight. I got ears," he said.

We didn't say anything for a time. He was leaning forward with his head turned at me, his right ear aimed in the direction of the set. Very disconcerting. Now and then his eyelids drooped and then they snapped open again. Now and then he put his fingers into his beard and tugged, like he was thinking about something he was hearing on the television.

On the screen, a group of men wearing cowls was being set upon and tormented by men dressed in skeleton costumes and men dressed as devils. The men dressed as devils wore devil masks, horns, and long tails. This pageant was part of a procession. The Englishman who was narrating the thing said it took place in Spain once a year. I tried to explain to the blind man what was happening.

"Skeletons," he said. "I know about skeletons," he said, and nodded.   90

The TV showed this one cathedral. Then there was a long, slow look at another one. Finally, the picture switched to the famous one in Paris, with its flying buttresses and its spires reaching up to the clouds. The camera pulled away to show the whole of the cathedral rising above the skyline.

There were times when the Englishman who was telling the thing would shut up, would simply let the camera move around the cathedrals. Or else the camera would tour the countryside, men in fields walking behind oxen. I waited as long as I could. Then I felt I had to say something. I said, "They're showing the outside of this cathedral now. Gargoyles. Little statues carved to look like monsters. Now I guess they're in Italy. Yeah, they're in Italy. There's paintings on the walls of this one church."

"Are those fresco paintings, bub?" he asked, and he sipped from his drink.

I reached for my glass. But it was empty. I tried to remember what I could remember. "You're asking me are those frescoes?" I said. "That's a good question. I don't know."

The camera moved to a cathedral outside Lisbon. The differences in   95
the Portuguese cathedral compared with the French and Italian were not that great. But they were there. Mostly the interior stuff. Then something occurred to me, and I said, "Something has occurred to me. Do you have any idea what a cathedral is? What they look like, that is? Do you follow

me? If somebody says cathedral to you, do you have any notion what they're talking about? Do you know the difference between that and a Baptist church, say?"

He let the smoke dribble from his mouth. "I know they took hundreds of workers fifty or a hundred years to build," he said. "I just heard the man say that, of course. I know generations of the same families worked on a cathedral. I heard him say that, too. The men who began their life's work on them, they never lived to see the completion of their work. In that wise, bub, they're no different from the rest of us, right?" He laughed. Then his eyelids drooped again. His head nodded. He seemed to be snoozing. Maybe he was imagining himself in Portugal. The TV was showing another cathedral now. This one was in Germany. The Englishman's voice droned on. "Cathedrals," the blind man said. He sat up and rolled his head back and forth. "If you want the truth, bub, that's about all I know. What I just said. What I heard him say. But maybe you could describe one to me? I wish you'd do it. I'd like that. If you want to know, I really don't have a good idea."

I stared hard at the shot of the cathedral on the TV. How could I even begin to describe it? But say my life depended on it. Say my life was being threatened by an insane guy who said I had to do it or else.

I stared some more at the cathedral before the picture flipped off into the countryside. There was no use. I turned to the blind man and said, "To begin with, they're very tall." I was looking around the room for clues. "They reach way up. Up and up. Toward the sky. They're so big, some of them, they have to have these supports. To help hold them up, so to speak. These supports are called buttresses. They remind me of viaducts, for some reason. But maybe you don't know viaducts, either? Sometimes the cathedrals have devils and such carved into the front. Sometimes lords and ladies. Don't ask me why this is," I said.

He was nodding. The whole upper part of his body seemed to be moving back and forth.

"I'm not doing so good, am I?" I said.

He stopped nodding and leaned forward on the edge of the sofa. As he listened to me, he was running his fingers through his beard. I wasn't getting through to him, I could see that. But he waited for me to go on just the same. He nodded, like he was trying to encourage me. I tried to think what else to say. "They're really big," I said. "They're massive. They're built of stone. Marble, too, sometimes. In those olden days, when they built cathedrals, men wanted to be close to God. In those olden days, God was an important part of everyone's life. You could tell this from their cathedral-building. I'm sorry," I said, "but it looks like that's the best I can do for you. I'm just no good at it."

"That's all right, bub," the blind man said. "Hey, listen. I hope you don't mind my asking you. Can I ask you something? Let me ask you a simple question, yes or no. I'm just curious and there's no offense. You're my host. But let me ask if you are in any way religious? You don't mind my asking?"

I shook my head. He couldn't see that, though. A wink is the same as a nod to a blind man. "I guess I don't believe in it. In anything. Sometimes it's hard. You know what I'm saying?"

"Sure, I do," he said.

"Right," I said.   105

The Englishman was still holding forth. My wife sighed in her sleep. She drew a long breath and went on with her sleeping.

"You'll have to forgive me," I said. "But I can't tell you what a cathedral looks like. It just isn't in me to do it. I can't do any more than I've done."

The blind man sat very still, his head down, as he listened to me.

I said, "The truth is, cathedrals don't mean anything special to me. Nothing. Cathedrals. They're something to look at on late-night TV. That's all they are."

It was then that the blind man cleared his throat. He brought some-   110
thing up. He took a handkerchief from his back pocket. Then he said, "I get it, bub. It's okay. It happens. Don't worry about it," he said. "Hey, listen to me. Will you do me a favor? I got an idea. Why don't you find us some heavy paper? And a pen. We'll do something. We'll draw one together. Get us a pen and some heavy paper. Go on, bub, get the stuff," he said.

So I went upstairs. My legs felt like they didn't have any strength in them. They felt like they did after I'd done some running. In my wife's room, I looked around. I found some ballpoints in a little basket on her table. And then I tried to think where to look for the kind of paper he was talking about.

Downstairs, in the kitchen, I found a shopping bag with onion skins in the bottom of the bag. I emptied the bag and shook it. I brought it into the living room and sat down with it near his legs. I moved some things, smoothed the wrinkles from the bag, spread it out on the coffee table.

The blind man got down from the sofa and sat next to me on the carpet.

He ran his fingers over the paper. He went up and down the sides of the paper. The edges, even the edges. He fingered the corners.

"All right," he said. "All right, let's do her."   115

He found my hand, the hand with the pen. He closed his hand over my hand. "Go ahead, bub, draw," he said. "Draw. You'll see. I'll follow along with you. It'll be okay. Just begin now like I'm telling you. You'll see. Draw," the blind man said.

So I began. First I drew a box that looked like a house. It could have been the house I lived in. Then I put a roof on it. At either end of the roof, I drew spires. Crazy.

"Swell," he said. "Terrific. You're doing fine," he said. "Never thought anything like this could happen in your lifetime, did you, bub? Well, it's a strange life, we all know that. Go on now. Keep it up."

I put in windows with arches. I drew flying buttresses. I hung great doors. I couldn't stop. The TV station went off the air. I put down the pen and closed and opened my fingers. The blind man felt around over the paper. He moved the tips of his fingers over the paper, all over what I had drawn, and he nodded.

"Doing fine," the blind man said.

I took up the pen again, and he found my hand. I kept at it. I'm no artist. But I kept drawing just the same.

My wife opened up her eyes and gazed at us. She sat up on the sofa, her robe hanging open. She said, "What are you doing? Tell me, I want to know."

I didn't answer her.

The blind man said, "We're drawing a cathedral. Me and him are working on it. Press hard," he said to me. "That's right. That's good," he said. "Sure. You got it, bub, I can tell. You didn't think you could. But you can, can't you? You're cooking with gas now. You know what I'm saying? We're going to really have us something here in a minute. How's the old arm?" he said. "Put some people in there now. What's a cathedral without people?"

My wife said, "What's going on? Robert, what are you doing? What's going on?"

"It's all right," he said to her. "Close your eyes now," the blind man said to me.

I did it. I closed them just like he said.

"Are they closed?" he said. "Don't fudge."

"They're closed," I said.

"Keep them that way," he said. He said, "Don't stop now. Draw."

So we kept on with it. His fingers rode my fingers as my hand went over the paper. It was like nothing else in my life up to now.

Then he said, "I think that's it. I think you got it," he said. "Take a look. What do you think?"

But I had my eyes closed. I thought I'd keep them that way for a little longer. I thought it was something I ought to do.

"Well?" he said. "Are you looking?"

My eyes were still closed. I was in my house. I knew that. But I didn't feel like I was inside anything.

"It's really something," I said.

■ What events interrupt each of the scenes? Where does each of these interruptions originate? How does each of these interruptions lead to an exploration of the issues that the narrator is thinking about?

- Trace references to blindness throughout the story. If we think about the story in terms of mapping and exploration, what exploration takes place? What sort of map do we have by the end of the story?
- How does the final scene, where the narrator is drawing with Robert, resolve some of the questions that the narrator has been pondering throughout the story?

POETRY

Elizabeth Bishop (1911–1979)

Brazil, January, 1502 (1955)

embroidered nature…tapestried landscape.
                        —*Landscape into Art*, Sir Kenneth Clark

Januaries, Nature greets our eyes
exactly as she must have greeted theirs:
every square inch filling in with foliage—
big leaves, little leaves, and giant leaves,
blue, blue-green, and olive,   5
with occasional lighter veins and edges,
or a satin underleaf turned over;
monster ferns
in silver-gray relief,
and flowers, too, like giant water lilies   10
up in the air—up, rather, in the leaves—
purple, yellow, two yellows, pink,
rust red and greenish white;
solid but airy; fresh as if just finished
and taken off the frame.   15

A blue-white sky, a simple web,
backing for feathery detail:
brief arcs, a pale-green broken wheel,
a few palms, swarthy, squat, but delicate;
and perching there in profile, beaks agape,   20
the big symbolic birds keep quiet,
each showing only half his puffed and padded,
pure colored or spotted breast.

Still in the foreground there is Sin:
five sooty dragons near some massy rocks.   25
The rocks are worked with lichens, gray moonbursts
splattered and overlapping,
threatened from underneath by moss
in lovely hell-green flames,
attacked above   30
by scaling—ladder vines, oblique and neat,
'one leaf yes and one leaf no' (in Portuguese).
The lizards scarcely breathe; all eyes
are on the smaller, female one, back-to,
her wicked tail straight up and over,   35
red as a red-hot wire.

- How does the poem shift at line 24?
- When the Portuguese conquistadors landed in Brazil in 1502, how was their experience of the country similar to and different from that of a contemporary tourist?

Louise Bogan (1897–1970)

Cartography (1938)

As you lay in sleep
I saw the chart
Of artery and vein
Running from your heart,

Plain as the strength   5
Marked upon the leaf
Along the length,
Mortal and brief,

Of your gaunt hand.
I saw it clear: 10
The wiry brand
Of the life we bear

Mapped like the great
Rivers that rise

Beyond our fate   15
And distant from our eyes.

- How does the poem shift at line 10?
- When the poet thinks of the medical chart as a sort of map, explain how the "Rivers" in line 14 fit into that analogy.

Sharon Olds (1942–)

Topography (1987)

After we flew across the country we
got into bed, laid our bodies
delicately together, like maps laid
face to face, East to West, my
San Francisco against your New York, your   5
Fire Island against my Sonoma, my
New Orleans deep in your Texas, your Idaho
bright on my Great Lakes, my Kansas
burning against your Kansas your Kansas
burning against my Kansas, your Eastern   10
Standard Time pressing into my
Pacific Time, my Mountain Time
beating against your Central Time, your
sun rising swiftly from the right my
sun rising swiftly from the left your   15
moon rising slowly from the left my
moon rising slowly from the right until
all four bodies of the sky
burn above us, sealing us together,
all our cities twin cities,   20
all our states united, one
nation, indivisible, with liberty and justice for all

- How does the poet use enjambment throughout this poem?
- What are the specific juxtapositions that the poet makes in the poem? Explain how the two images together (such as San Francisco and New York) bring out specific aspects of the other.

Langston Hughes (1902–1967)

Theme for English B (1949)

The instructor said,

> Go home and write
> a page tonight.
> And let that page come out of you—
> Then, it will be true.   5

I wonder if it's that simple?
I am twenty-two, colored, born in Winston-Salem.
I went to school there, then Durham, then here
to this college on the hill above Harlem.
I am the only colored student in my class.   10
The steps from the hill lead down into Harlem,
through a park, then I cross St. Nicholas,
Eighth Avenue, Seventh, and I come to the Y,
the Harlem Branch Y, where I take the elevator
up to my room, sit down, and write this page: 15

It's not easy to know what is true for you or me
at twenty-two, my age. But I guess I'm what
I feel and see and hear, Harlem, I hear you:
hear you, hear me—we two—you, me, talk on this page.
(I hear New York, too.) Me—who?   20
Well, I like to eat, sleep, drink, and be in love.
I like to work, read, learn, and understand life.
I like a pipe for a Christmas present,

or records—Bessie, bop, or Bach.
I guess being colored doesn't make me *not* like   25
the same things other folks like who are other races.
So will my page be colored that I write?
Being me, it will not be white.
But it will be
a part of you, instructor.   30
You are white—
yet a part of me, as I am part of you.
That's American.
Sometimes perhaps you don't want to be a part of me.
Nor do I often want to be a part of you.   35
But we are, that's true!
As I learn from you,

I guess you learn from me—
although you're older—and white—
and somewhat more free.   40
This is my page for English B.

■ How does the poet map his own identity in this poem? Where does he claim
that his identity intersects that of his instructor? Locate the specific places
where he juxtaposes these two identities. How important is race within the
identities he describes?

Laura Riding (1901–1968)

The Map of Places (1927)

The map of places passes.
The reality of paper tears.
Land and water where they are
Are only where they were
When words read *here* and *here*   5
Before ships happened there.

Now on naked names feet stand,
No geographies in the hand.
And paper reads anciently,
And ships at sea   10
Turn round and round.
All is known, all is found.
Death meets death everywhere.
Holes in maps look through to nowhere.

■ Explain the distinction that the poet makes between "When words read *here*
and *here* / Before ships happened there."
■ What is the difference that the second stanza describes? What does it mean
that "Holes in maps look through to nowhere"?

Richard Wilbur (1921–)

Worlds (1987)

For Alexander there was no Far East,
Because he thought the Asian continent

India ended. Free Cathay at least
Did not contribute to his discontent.

But Newton, who had grasped all space, was more   5
Serene. To him it seemed that he'd but played
With several shells and pebbles on the shore
Of that profundity he had not made.

Swiss Einstein with his relativity—
Most secure of all. God does not play dice   10
With the cosmos and its activity.
Religionless equations won't suffice.

■ Alexander the Great (356–332 BC) is considered one of the greatest military
leaders. He conquered most of the world that was known to the ancient
Greeks. Isaac Newton (1643–1727) was an English scientist whose innovations
in calculus and astronomy continue to influence thinkers in those disciplines.
Albert Einstein (1879–1955) was a physicist who authored the general theory
of relativity. What are the three worldviews that the poet sets together here?
How does the poet mark the progression from one to the next of these
historical figures?

Samuel Taylor Coleridge (1772–1834)

The Rime of the Ancient Mariner (1798, revised 1817)

An ancient Mariner meeteth
three gallants bidden to a
wedding feast, and detain-
eth one.

PART I

It is an ancient Mariner,
And he stoppeth one of three.
"By thy long beard and glittering eye,
Now wherefore stopp'st thou me?

The Bridegroom's doors are opened wide,   5
And I am next of kin;
The guests are met, the feast is set:
May'st hear the merry din."

The Wedding-Guest is
spell-bound by the eye of
the old seafaring man, and
constrained to hear his tale.

He holds him with his skinny hand,
"There was a ship," quoth he.   10
"Hold off! unhand me, grey-beard loon!"
Eftsoons his hand dropt he.

He holds him with his glittering eye—
The Wedding-Guest stood still,
And listens like a three years' child: 15
The Mariner hath his will.

The Wedding-Guest sat on a stone:
He cannot choose but hear;
And thus spake on that ancient man,
The bright-eyed Mariner.   20

"The ship was cheer'd, the harbour clear'd,
Merrily did we drop
Below the kirk, below the hill,
Below the lighthouse top.

The Mariner tells how the
ship sailed southward with
a good wind and fair
weather, till it reached the
Line.

The Sun came up upon the left,   25
Out of the sea came he!
And he shone bright, and on the right
Went down into the sea.

Higher and higher every day,
Till over the mast at noon——"   30
The Wedding-Guest here beat his breast,
For he heard the loud bassoon.

The Wedding-Guest hear-
eth the bridal music; but the
Mariner continueth his tale.

The bride hath paced into the hall,
Red as a rose is she;
Nodding their heads before her goes   35
The merry minstrelsy.

The Wedding-Guest he beat his breast,
Yet he cannot choose but hear;
And thus spake on that ancient man,
The bright-eyed Mariner.   40

The ship driven by a storm
toward the South Pole.

"And now the Storm-blast came, and he
Was tyrannous and strong:
He struck with his o'ertaking wings,
And chased us south along.

With sloping masts and dipping prow,   45
As who pursued with yell and blow
Still treads the shadow of his foe,
And forward bends his head,

The ship drove fast, loud roar'd the blast,
The southward aye we fled.   50

And now there came both mist and snow,
And it grew wondrous cold:
And ice, mast-high, came floating by,
As green as emerald.

The land of ice, and of
fearful sounds, where no
living thing was to be seen.

And through the drifts the snowy clifts   55
Did send a dismal sheen:
Nor shapes of men nor beasts we ken—
The ice was all between.

The ice was here, the ice was there,
The ice was all around: 60
It crack'd and growl'd, and roar'd and howl'd,
Like noises in a swound!

Till a great sea-bird, called
the Albatross, came
through the snow-fog, and
was received with great joy
and hospitality.

At length did cross an Albatross,
Thorough the fog it came;
As if it had been a Christian soul,   65
We hail'd it in God's name.

It ate the food it ne'er had eat,
And round and round it flew.
The ice did split with a thunder-fit;
The helmsman steer'd us through!   70

And lo! the Albatross pro-
veth a bird of good omen,
and followeth the ship as it
returned northward through
fog and floating ice.

And a good south wind sprung up behind;
The Albatross did follow,
And every day, for food or play,
Came to the mariners' hollo!

In mist or cloud, on mast or shroud,   75
It perch'd for vespers nine;
Whiles all the night, through fog-smoke white,
Glimmer'd the white moonshine."

The ancient Mariner inhos-
pitably killeth the pious
bird of good omen.

"God save thee, ancient Mariner!
From the fiends, that plague thee thus!—   80
Why look'st thou so?"—"With my crossbow
I shot the Albatross."

PART II

"The Sun now rose upon the right:
Out of the sea came he,
Still hid in mist, and on the left   85
Went down into the sea.

And the good south wind still blew behind,
But no sweet bird did follow,
Nor any day for food or play
Came to the mariners' hollo!   90

His shipmates cry out
against the ancient Mariner
for killing the bird of good
luck.

And I had done an hellish thing,
And it would work 'em woe:
For all averr'd, I had kill'd the bird
That made the breeze to blow.
Ah wretch! said they, the bird to slay,   95
That made the breeze to blow!

But when the fog cleared
off, they justify the same,
and thus make themselves
accomplices in the crime.

Nor dim nor red, like God's own head,
The glorious Sun uprist:
Then all averr'd, I had kill'd the bird
That brought the fog an mist.   100
'Twas right, said they, such birds to slay,
That bring the fog and mist.

The fair breeze continues;
the ship enters the Pacific
Ocean, and sails northward,
even till it reaches the Line.

The fair breeze blew, the white foam flew,
The furrow follow'd free;
We were the first that ever burst   105
Into that silent sea.

The ship hath been sud-
denly becalmed.

Down dropt the breeze, the sails dropt down,
'Twas sad as sad could be;
And we did speak only to break
The silence of the sea!   110

All in a hot and copper sky,
The bloody Sun, at noon,
Right up above the mast did stand,
No bigger than the Moon.

Day after day, day after day,   115
We stuck, nor breath nor motion;

As idle as a painted ship
Upon a painted ocean.

And the Albatross begins to
be avenged.

Water, water, everywhere,
And all the boards did shrink;   120
Water, water, everywhere,
Nor any drop to drink.

The very deep did rot: O Christ!
That ever this should be!
Yea, slimy things did crawl with legs   125
Upon the slimy sea.

About, about, in reel and rout
The death-fires danced at night;
The water, like a witch's oils,
Burnt green, and blue, and white.   130

A Spirit had followed them;
one of the invisible inhabitants of this planet, neither
departed souls nor angels;
concerning whom the
learned Jew, Josephus, and
the Platonic Constantino-
politan, Michael Psellus,
may be consulted. They are
very numerous, and there is
no climate or element
without one or more.

And some in dreams assurèd were
Of the Spirit that plagued us so;
Nine fathom deep he had followed us
From the land of mist and snow.

And every tongue, through utter drought,   135
Was wither'd at the root;
We could not speak, no more than if
We had been choked with soot.

The shipmates, in their sore
distress, would fain throw
the whole guilt on the
ancient Mariner: in sign
whereof they hang the dead
sea-bird round his neck.

Ah! well a-day! what evil looks
Had I from old and young!   140
Instead of the cross, the Albatross
About my neck was hung."

PART III
"There passed a weary time. Each throat
Was parch'd, and glazed each eye.

The ancient Mariner be-
holdeth a sign in the element afar off.

A weary time! a weary time!   145
How glazed each weary eye!
When looking westward, I beheld
A something in the sky.

At first it seem'd a little speck,
And then it seem'd a mist;   150

It moved and moved, and took at last
A certain shape, I wist.

A speck, a mist, a shape, I wist!
And still it near'd and near'd:
As if it dodged a water-sprite,   155
It plunged, and tack'd, and veer'd.

At its nearer approach, it
seemeth him to be a ship;
and at a dear ransom he
freeth his speech from the
bonds of thirst.

With throats unslaked, with black lips baked,
We could nor laugh nor wail;
Through utter drought all dumb we stood!
I bit my arm, I suck'd the blood!   160
And cried, A sail! a sail!

A flash of joy;

With throats unslaked, with black lips baked,
Agape they heard me call:
Gramercy! they for joy did grin,
And all at once their breath drew in,   165
As they were drinking all.

And horror follows. For can
it be a ship that comes
onward without wind or
tide?

See! see! (I cried) she tacks no more!
Hither to work us weal—
Without a breeze, without a tide,
She steadies with upright keel!   170

The western wave was all aflame,
The day was wellnigh done!
Almost upon the western wave
Rested the broad, bright Sun;
When that strange shape drove suddenly   175
Betwixt us and the Sun.

It seemeth him but the
skeleton of a ship.

And straight the Sun was fleck'd with bars
(Heaven's Mother send us grace!),
As if through a dungeon-grate he peer'd
With broad and burning face.   180

Alas! (thought I,and my heart beat loud)
How fast she nears and nears!
Are those her sails that glance in the Sun,
Like restless gossameres?

And its ribs are seen as bars on the face of the setting Sun. The Spectre-Woman and her Death-mate, and no other on board the skeleton ship. Like vessel, like crew!

Are those her ribs through which the Sun   185
Did peer, as through a grate?
And is that Woman all her crew?
Is that a Death? and are there two?
Is Death that Woman's mate?

Her lips were red, her looks were free,   190
Her locks were yellow as gold:
Her skin was as white as leprosy,
The Nightmare Life-in-Death was she,
Who thicks man's blood with cold.

Death and Life-in-Death have diced for the ship's crew, and she (the latter) winneth the ancient Mariner.

The naked hulk alongside came,   195
And the twain were casting dice;
'The game is done! I've won! I've won!'
Quoth she, and whistles thrice.

No twilight within the courts of the Sun.

The Sun's rim dips; the stars rush out:
At one stride comes the dark;   200
With far-heard whisper, o'er the sea,
Off shot the spectre-bark.

We listen'd and look'd sideways up!
Fear at my heart, as at a cup,
My life-blood seem'd to sip!   205
The stars were dim, and thick the night,
The steersman's face by his lamp gleam'd white;
From the sails the dew did drip—

At the rising of the Moon,

Till clomb above the eastern bar
The hornèd Moon, with one bright star   210
Within the nether tip.

One after another,

One after one, by the star-dogg'd Moon,
Too quick for groan or sigh,
Each turn'd his face with a ghastly pang,
And cursed me with his eye.   215

His shipmates drop down dead.

Four times fifty living men
(And I heard nor sigh nor groan),
With heavy thump, a lifeless lump,
They dropp'd down one by one.

But Life-in-Death begins her work on the ancient Mariner.

The souls did from their bodies fly—   220
They fled to bliss or woe!

And every soul, it pass'd me by
Like the whizz of my crossbow!"

PART IV

"I fear thee, ancient Mariner!
I fear thy skinny hand!   225
And thou art long, and lank, and brown,
As is the ribb'd sea-sand.

I fear thee and thy glittering eye,
And thy skinny hand so brown."—

"Fear not, fear not, thou Wedding-Guest!   230
This body dropt not down.

Alone, alone, all, all alone,
Alone on a wide, wide sea!
And never a saint took pity on
My soul in agony.   235

The many men, so beautiful!
And they all dead did lie:
And a thousand thousand slimy things
Lived on; and so did I.

I look'd upon the rotting sea,   240
And drew my eyes away;
I look'd upon the rotting deck,
And there the dead men lay.

I look'd to heaven, and tried to pray;
But or ever a prayer had gusht,   245
A wicked whisper came, and made
My heart as dry as dust.

I closed my lids, and kept them close,
And the balls like pulses beat;
For the sky and the sea, and the sea and the sky, 250
Lay like a load on my weary eye,
And the dead were at my feet.

The cold sweat melted from their limbs,
Nor rot nor reek did they:

The look with which they look'd on me 255
Had never pass'd away.

An orphan's curse would drag to hell
A spirit from on high;
But oh! more horrible than that
Is the curse in a dead man's eye! 260
Seven days, seven nights, I saw that curse,
And yet I could not die.

In his loneliness and fixed-
ness he yearneth towards
the journeying Moon, and
the stars that still sojourn,
yet still move onward; and
everywhere the blue sky
belongs to them, and is
their appointed rest and
their native country and
their own natural homes,
which they enter unan-
nounced, as lords that are
certainly expected, and yet
there is a silent joy at their
arrival.

By the light of the Moon he
beholdeth God's creatures
of the great calm.

The moving Moon went up the sky,
And nowhere did abide;
Softly she was going up, 265
And a star or two beside—

Her beams bemock'd the sultry main,
Like April hoar-frost spread;
But where the ship's huge shadow lay,
The charmèd water burnt alway 270
A still and awful red.

Beyond the shadow of the ship,
I watch'd the water-snakes:
They moved in tracks of shining white,
And when they rear'd, the elfish light 275
Fell off in hoary flakes.

Within the shadow of the ship
I watch'd their rich attire:
Blue, glossy green, and velvet black,
They coil'd and swam; and every track 280
Was a flash of golden fire.

Their beauty and their
happiness.

O happy living things! no tongue
Their beauty might declare:
A spring of love gush'd from my heart,

He blesseth them in his
heart.

And I bless'd them unaware: 285

The spell begins to break.

The selfsame moment I could pray;
And from my neck so free
The Albatross fell off, and sank
Like lead into the sea."

PART V

"O sleep! it is a gentle thing,   290
Beloved from pole to pole!
To Mary Queen the praise be given!
She sent the gentle sleep from Heaven,
That slid into my soul.

By grace of the holy
Mother, the ancient Mariner
is refreshed with rain.

The silly buckets on the deck,   295
That had so long remain'd,
I dreamt that they were fill'd with dew;
And when I awoke, it rain'd.

My lips were wet, my throat was cold,
My garments all were dank;   300
Sure I had drunken in my dreams,
And still my body drank.

I moved, and could not feel my limbs:
I was so light—almost
I thought that I had died in sleep,   305
And was a blessèd ghost.

He heareth sounds and
seeth strange sights and
commotions in the sky and
the element.

And soon I heard a roaring wind:
It did not come anear;
But with its sound it shook the sails,
That were so thin and sere.   310

The upper air burst into life;
And a hundred fire-flags sheen;
To and fro they were hurried about!
And to and fro, and in and out,
The wan stars danced between.   315

And the coming wind did roar more loud,
And the sails did sigh like sedge;
And the rain pour'd down from one black cloud;
The Moon was at its edge.

The thick black cloud was cleft, and still   320
The Moon was at its side;
Like waters shot from some high crag,
The lightning fell with never a jag,
A river steep and wide.

The bodies of the ship's crew are inspirited, and the ship moves on;

The loud wind never reach'd the ship, 325
Yet now the ship moved on!
Beneath the lightning and the Moon
The dead men gave a groan.

They groan'd, they stirr'd, they all uprose,
Nor spake, nor moved their eyes; 330
It had been strange, even in a dream,
To have seen those dead men rise.

The helmsman steer'd, the ship moved on;
Yet never a breeze up-blew;
The mariners all 'gan work the ropes, 335
Where they were wont to do;
They raised their limbs like lifeless tools—
We were a ghastly crew.

The body of my brother's son
Stood by me, knee to knee: 340
The body and I pull'd at one rope,
But he said naught to me."

But not by the souls of the men, nor by demons of earth or middle air, but by a blessed troop of angelic spirits, sent down by the invocation of the guardian saint.

"I fear thee, ancient Mariner!"
"Be calm, thou Wedding-Guest:
'Twas not those souls that fled in pain, 345
Which to their corses came again,
But a troop of spirits blest:

For when it dawn'd—they dropp'd their arms,
And cluster'd round the mast;
Sweet sounds rose slowly through their mouths, 350
And from their bodies pass'd.

Around, around, flew each sweet sound,
Then darted to the Sun;
Slowly the sounds came back again,
Now mix'd, now one by one. 355

Sometimes a-dropping from the sky
I heard the skylark sing;
Sometimes all little birds that are,
How they seem'd to fill the sea and air
With their sweet jargoning! 360

And now 'twas like all instruments,
Now like a lonely flute;
And now it is an angel's song,
That makes the Heavens be mute.

It ceased; yet still the sails made on   365
A pleasant noise till noon,
A noise like of a hidden brook
In the leafy month of June,
That to the sleeping woods all night
Singeth a quiet tune.   370

Till noon we quietly sail'd on,
Yet never a breeze did breathe:
Slowly and smoothly went the ship,
Moved onward from beneath.

The lonesome Spirit from the South Pole carries on the ship as far as the Line, in obedience to the angelic troop, but still requireth vengeance.

Under the keel nine fathom deep,   375
From the land of mist and snow,
The Spirit slid: and it was he
That made the ship to go.
The sails at noon left off their tune,
And the ship stood still also.   380

The Sun, right up above the mast,
Had fix'd her to the ocean:
But in a minute she 'gan stir,
With a short uneasy motion—
Backwards and forwards half her length   385
With a short uneasy motion.

Then like a pawing horse let go,
She made a sudden bound:
It flung the blood into my head,
And I fell down in a swound.   390

The Polar Spirit's fellow-demons, the invisible inhabitants of the element, take part in his wrong; and two of them relate, one to the other, that penance long and heavy for the ancient Mariner hath been accorded to the Polar Spirit, who returneth southward.

How long in that same fit I lay,
I have not to declare;
But ere my living life return'd,
I heard, and in my soul discern'd
Two voices in the air.   395

'Is it he?' quoth one, 'is this the man?
By Him who died on cross,

With his cruel bow he laid full low
The harmless Albatross.

The Spirit who bideth by himself   400
In the land of mist and snow,
He loved the bird that loved the man
Who shot him with his bow.'

The other was a softer voice,
As soft as honey-dew: 405
Quoth he, 'The man hath penance done,
And penance more will do.'"

PART VI

The Mariner hath been cast into a trance; for the angelic power causeth the vessel to drive northward faster than human life could endure.

First Voice: "'But tell me, tell me! speak again,
Thy soft response renewing—
What makes that ship drive on so fast?   410
What is the Ocean doing?'

Second Voice: 'Still as a slave before his lord,
The Ocean hath no blast;
His great bright eye most silently
Up to the Moon is cast—   415

If he may know which way to go;
For she guides him smooth or grim.
See, brother, see! now graciously
She looketh down on him.'

First Voice: 'But why drives on that ship so fast,   420
Without or wave or wind?'

Second Voice: 'The air is cut away before,
And closes from behind.

Fly, brother, fly! more high, more high!
Or we shall be belated: 425
For slow and slow that ship will go,
When the Mariner's trance is abated.'

The supernatural motion is retarded; the Mariner awakes, and his penance begins anew.

I woke, and we were sailing on
As in a gentle weather:
'Twas night, calm night, the Moon was high;   43
The dead men stood together.

All stood together on the deck,
For a charnel-dungeon fitter:
All fix'd on me their stony eyes,
That in the Moon did glitter.   435

The pang, the curse, with which they died,
Had never pass'd away:
I could not draw my eyes from theirs,
Nor turn them up to pray.

The curse is finally expiated.

And now this spell was snapt: once more   440
I viewed the ocean green,
And look'd far forth, yet little saw
Of what had else been seen—

Like one that on a lonesome road
Doth walk in fear and dread,   445
And having once turn'd round, walks on,
And turns no more his head;
Because he knows a frightful fiend
Doth close behind him tread.

But soon there breathed a wind on me,   450
Nor sound nor motion made:
Its path was not upon the sea,
In ripple or in shade.

It raised my hair, it fann'd my cheek
Like a meadow-gale of spring—   455
It mingled strangely with my fears,
Yet it felt like a welcoming.

Swiftly, swiftly flew the ship,
Yet she sail'd softly too:
Sweetly, sweetly blew the breeze—   460
On me alone it blew.

And the ancient Mariner beholdeth his native country.

O dream of joy! is this indeed
The lighthouse top I see?
Is this the hill? is this the kirk?
Is this mine own countree?   465

We drifted o'er the harbour-bar,
And I with sobs did pray—

O let me be awake, my God!
Or let me sleep alway.

The harbour-bay was clear as glass,   470
So smoothly it was strewn!
And on the bay the moonlight lay,
And the shadow of the Moon.

The rock shone bright, the kirk no less
That stands above the rock: 475
The moonlight steep'd in silentness
The steady weathercock.

The angelic spirits leave the dead bodies,

And the bay was white with silent light
Till rising from the same,
Full many shapes, that shadows were,   480
In crimson colours came.

And appear in their own forms of light.

A little distance from the prow
Those crimson shadows were:
I turn'd my eyes upon the deck—
O Christ! what saw I there!   485

Each corse lay flat, lifeless and flat,
And, by the holy rood!
A man all light, a seraph-man,
On every corse there stood.

This seraph-band, each waved his hand: 490
It was a heavenly sight!
They stood as signals to the land,
Each one a lovely light;

This seraph-band, each waved his hand,
No voice did they impart—   495
No voice; but O, the silence sank
Like music on my heart.

But soon I heard the dash of oars,
I heard the Pilot's cheer;
My head was turn'd perforce away,   500
And I saw a boat appear.

The Pilot and the Pilot's boy,
I heard them coming fast:
Dear Lord in Heaven! it was a joy
The dead men could not blast.   505

I saw a third—I heard his voice:
It is the Hermit good!
He singeth loud his godly hymns
That he makes in the wood.
He'll shrieve my soul, he'll wash away   510
The Albatross's blood."

The Hermit of the Wood,

PART VII
"This Hermit good lives in that wood
Which slopes down to the sea.
How loudly his sweet voice he rears!
He loves to talk with marineres   515
That come from a far countree.

He kneels at morn, and noon, and eve—
He hath a cushion plump:
It is the moss that wholly hides
The rotted old oak-stump.   520

The skiff-boat near'd: I heard them talk,
'Why, this is strange, I trow!
Where are those lights so many and fair,
That signal made but now?'

Approacheth the ship with
wonder.

'Strange, by my faith!' the Hermit said—   525
'And they answer'd not our cheer!
The planks looked warp'd! and see those sails,
How thin they are and sere!
I never saw aught like to them,
Unless perchance it were   530

Brown skeletons of leaves that lag
My forest-brook along;
When the ivy-tod is heavy with snow,
And the owlet whoops to the wolf below,
That eats the she-wolf's young.'   535

'Dear Lord! it hath a fiendish look—
(The Pilot made reply)
I am a-fear'd'—'Push on, push on!'
Said the Hermit cheerily.

The boat came closer to the ship,　　　　　　540
But I nor spake nor stirr'd;
The boat came close beneath the ship,
And straight a sound was heard.

The ship suddenly sinketh.

Under the water it rumbled on,
Still louder and more dread:　　　　　　　545
It reach'd the ship, it split the bay;
The ship went down like lead.

The ancient Mariner is
saved in the Pilot's boat.

Stunn'd by that loud and dreadful sound,
Which sky and ocean smote,
Like one that hath been seven days drown'd　550
My body lay afloat;
But swift as dreams, myself I found
Within the Pilot's boat.

Upon the whirl, where sank the ship,
The boat spun round and round;　　　　　555
And all was still, save that the hill
Was telling of the sound.

I moved my lips—the Pilot shriek'd
And fell down in a fit;
The holy Hermit raised his eyes,　　　　　560
And pray'd where he did sit.

I took the oars: the Pilot's boy,
Who now doth crazy go,
Laugh'd loud and long, and all the while
His eyes went to and fro.　　　　　　　565
'Ha! ha!' quoth he, 'full plain I see
The Devil knows how to row.'

And now, all in my own countree,
I stood on the firm land!
The Hermit stepp'd forth from the boat,　570
And scarcely he could stand.

The ancient Mariner earnestly entreateth the Hermit to shrieve him; and the penance of life falls on him.

'O shrieve me, shrieve me, holy man!'
The Hermit cross'd his brow.
'Say quick,' quoth he, 'I bid thee say—
What manner of man art thou?'   575

Forthwith this frame of mine was wrench'd
With a woful agony,
Which forced me to begin my tale;
And then it left me free.

And ever and anon throughout his future life an agony constraineth him to travel from land to land;

Since then, at an uncertain hour,   580
That agony returns:
And till my ghastly tale is told,
This heart within me burns.

I pass, like night, from land to land;
I have strange power of speech;   585
That moment that his face I see,
I know the man that must hear me:
To him my tale I teach.

What loud uproar bursts from that door!
The wedding-guests are there: 590
But in the garden-bower the bride
And bride-maids singing are:
And hark the little vesper bell,
Which biddeth me to prayer!

O Wedding-Guest! this soul hath been   595
Alone on a wide, wide sea:
So lonely 'twas, that God Himself
Scarce seemèd there to be.

O sweeter than the marriage-feast,
'Tis sweeter far to me,   600
To walk together to the kirk
With a goodly company!—

To walk together to the kirk,
And all together pray,
While each to his great Father bends,   605
Old men, and babes, and loving friends,
And youths and maidens gay!

And to teach, by his own example, love and reverence to all things that God made and loveth.

Farewell, farewell! but this I tell
To thee, thou Wedding-Guest!
He prayeth well, who loveth well
Both man and bird and beast.   610

He prayeth best, who loveth best
All things both great and small;
For the dear God who loveth us,
He made and loveth all."   615

The Mariner, whose eye is bright,
Whose beard with age is hoar,
Is gone: and now the Wedding-Guest
Turn'd from the bridegroom's door.

He went like one that hath been stunn'd,   620
And is of sense forlorn:
A sadder and a wiser man
He rose the morrow morn.

■ The poem establishes a number of clear patterns that the poet uses throughout, including rhyme, stanzas, and sections. Identify these structural devices.

■ How does the poem depend upon interruptions to move the plot forward? Look also at the way in which the poet's own explanation of the poem in the margins interrupts our reading. How does such interruption also help us as readers by breaking up the poem's rhythm?

Alfred, Lord Tennyson (1809–1892)

Ulysses (1833)

It little profits that an idle king,
By this still hearth, among these barren crags,
Matched with an agèd wife, I mete and dole
Unequal laws unto a savage race,
That hoard, and sleep, and feed, and know not me.   5

I cannot rest from travel; I will drink
Life to the lees. All times I have enjoyed
Greatly, have suffered greatly, both with those
That loved me, and alone; on shore, and when
Through scudding drifts the rainy Hyades   10

Vexed the dim sea. I am become a name;
For always roaming with a hungry heart
Much have I seen and known—cities of men
And manners, climates, councils, governments,
Myself not least, but honored of them all—   15
And drunk delight of battle with my peers,
Far on the ringing plains of windy Troy.
I am a part of all that I have met;
Yet all experience is an arch wherethrough
Gleams that untraveled world, whose margin fades   20
For ever and for ever when I move.
How dull it is to pause, to make an end,
To rust unburnished, not to shine in use!
As though to breathe were life. Life piled on life
Were all too little, and of one to me   25
Little remains; but every hour is saved
From that eternal silence, something more,
A bringer of new things; and vile it were
For some three suns to store and hoard myself,
And this gray spirit yearning in desire   30
To follow knowledge like a sinking star,
Beyond the utmost bound of human thought.

This is my son, mine own Telemachus,
To whom I leave the scepter and the isle—
Well-loved of me, discerning to fulfill   35
This labor, by slow prudence to make mild
A rugged people, and through soft degrees
Subdue them to the useful and the good.
Most blameless is he, centered in the sphere
Of common duties, decent not to fail   40
In offices of tenderness, and pay
Meet adoration to my household gods,
When I am gone. He works his work, I mine.

There lies the port; the vessel puffs her sail:
There gloom the dark, broad seas. My mariners,   45
Souls that have toiled, and wrought, and thought with me—
That ever with a frolic welcome took
The thunder and the sunshine, and opposed
Free hearts, free foreheads—you and I are old;
Old age hath yet his honor and his toil.   50
Death closes all; but something ere the end,
Some work of noble note, may yet be done,

Not unbecoming men that strove with Gods.
The lights begin to twinkle from the rocks;
The long day wanes; the slow moon climbs; the deep   55
Moans round with many voices. Come, my friends,
'Tis not too late to seek a newer world.
Push off, and sitting well in order smite
The sounding furrows; for my purpose holds
To sail beyond the sunset, and the baths   60
Of all the western stars, until I die.
It may be that the gulfs will wash us down;
It may be we shall touch the Happy Isles,
And see the great Achilles, whom we knew.
Though much is taken, much abides; and though   65
We are not now that strength which in old days
Moved earth and heaven, that which we are, we are:
One equal temper of heroic hearts,
Made weak by time and fate, but strong in will
To strive, to seek, to find, and not to yield.   70

■ Ulysses (the Roman name for Odysseus) is most famous for the great trial that he endured in order to return from the Trojan War to his home, his wife, and his son. The story generally ends with his homecoming. How do the opening lines describe his discontent?

■ How does this poem juxtapose the disposition of Ulysses with that of his son Telemachus?

Emily Dickinson (1830–1886)

[The Brain—is wider than the Sky—] (ca. 1862)

The Brain—is wider than the Sky—
For—put them side by side—
The one the other will contain
With ease—and you—beside—

The Brain is deeper than the sea—   5
For—hold them—Blue to Blue—
The one the other will absorb—
As Sponges—Buckets—do—

The Brain is just the weight of God—
For—Heft them—Pound for Pound—   10

And they will differ—if they do—
As Syllable from Sound—

Emily Dickinson (1830–1886)

[I never saw a Moor—] (ca. 1865)

I never saw a Moor—
I never saw the Sea—
Yet know I how the Heather looks
And what a Billow be.

I never spoke with God   5
Nor visited in Heaven—
Yet certain am I of the spot
As if the Checks were given—

Emily Dickinson (1830–1886)

[Tell all the Truth but tell it slant—] (ca. 1868)

Tell all the Truth but tell it slant—
Success in Circuit lies
Too bright for our infirm Delight
The Truth's superb surprise

As Lightning to the Children eased   5
With explanation kind
The Truth must dazzle gradually
Or every man be blind—

Emily Dickinson (1830–1886)

[To make a prairie it takes a clover and one bee]

(ca. 1861)

To make a prairie it takes a clover and one bee,
One clover, and a bee,
And revery.
The revery alone will do,
If bees are few.   5

- How does attention to a single geographic feature lead to a larger meditation in each of these poems?
- Every one of these poems uses dashes. How do these dashes function both to interrupt the flow of the poem and to contribute to the meaning?

John Donne (1572–1631)

The Sun Rising (ca. 1633)

Busy old fool, unruly sun,
   Why dost thou thus,
Through windows, and through curtains, call on us?
Must to thy motions lovers' seasons run?
   Saucy pedantic wretch, go chide   5
   Late schoolboys, and sour prentices,
Go tell court-huntsmen that the king will ride,
   Call country ants to harvest offices;
Love, all alike, no season knows, nor clime,
Nor hours, days, months, which are the rags of time.   10

   Thy beams, so reverend and strong
   Why shouldst thou think?
I could eclipse and cloud them with a wink,
But that I would not lose her sight so long:
   If her eyes have not blinded thine,   15
   Look, and tomorrow late, tell me
Whether both the Indias of spice and mine
   Be where thou left'st them, or lie here with me.
Ask for those kings whom thou saw'st yesterday,
And thou shalt hear, all here in one bed lay.   20

   She is all states, and all princes I,
   Nothing else is.
Princes do but play us; compared to this,
All honor's mimic, all wealth alchemy.
   Thou, sun, art half as happy as we,   25
   In that the world's contracted thus;
Thine age asks ease, and since thy duties be
   To warm the world, that's done in warming us.
Shine here to us, and thou art every where;
This bed thy center is, these walls thy sphere.   30

- The first two stanzas employ the conceit that the poet is talking with the sun. How does the third stanza break from the order established in the first two stanzas?
- Compare Donne's use of the sun to Dickinson's use of natural images in her poems.

John Donne (1572–1631)

A Valediction: Forbidding Mourning (1611)

As virtuous men pass mildly away,
   And whisper to their souls to go,
While some of their sad friends do say,
   The breath goes now, and some say, no:

So let us melt, and make no noise,   5
   No tear-floods, nor sigh-tempests move;
'Twere profanation of our joys
   To tell the laity our love.

Moving of th' earth brings harms and fears,
   Men reckon what it did and meant,   10
But trepidation of the spheres,
   Though greater far, is innocent.

Dull sublunary lovers' love
   (Whose soul is sense) cannot admit
Absence, because it doth remove   15
   Those things which elemented it.

But we by a love so much refined,
   That ourselves know not what it is,
Inter-assurèd of the mind,
   Care less, eyes, lips, and hands to miss.   20

Our two souls therefore, which are one,
   Though I must go, endure not yet
A breach, but an expansion,
   Like gold to airy thinness beat.

If they be two, they are two so   25
   As stiff twin compasses are two;
Thy soul the fixed foot, makes no show
   To move, but doth, if th' other do.

And though it in the center sit,
   Yet when the other far doth roam,   30
It leans, and hearkens after it,
   And grows erect, as that comes home.

Such wilt thou be to me, who must
   Like th' other foot, obliquely run;
Thy firmness makes my circle just,   35
   And makes me end, where I begun.

■ The "twin compasses" that the poet refers to are the tool that we use to draw circles rather than the tool that we use to find the direction north. Locate the specific details that he uses to make the analogy between the compasses and "our love."

■ How does this image resolve the tension of the first half of the poem?

DRAMA

William Shakespeare (1564–1616)

See page 340 for a full biographical note on William Shakespeare.

Hamlet (ca. 1600, edited by Cyrus Hoy)

CHARACTERS

CLAUDIUS, *King of Denmark*
HAMLET, *son to the late, and nephew to the present king*
POLONIUS, *Lord Chamberlain*
HORATIO, *friend to Hamlet*
LAERTES, *son to Polonius*

VOLTEMAND ⎫
CORNELIUS ⎪
ROSENCRANTZ ⎪
GUILDENSTERN ⎬ *courtiers*
OSRIC ⎪
A GENTLEMAN ⎭
A PRIEST
MARCELLUS ⎫ *officers*
BERNARDO ⎭
FRANCISCO, *a soldier*
REYNALDO, *servant to Polonius*

PLAYERS

TWO CLOWNS, *grave-diggers*

FORTINBRAS, *Prince of Norway*

A NORWEGIAN CAPTAIN

ENGLISH AMBASSADORS

GERTRUDE, *Queen of Denmark, and mother of Hamlet*

OPHELIA, *daughter to Polonius*

GHOST OF HAMLET'S FATHER

LORDS, LADIES, OFFICERS, SOLDIERS, SAILORS, MESSENGERS, *and* ATTENDANTS

SCENE: *Denmark.*

ACT I

Scene 1

(*Enter* BERNARDO *and* FRANCISCO, *two sentinels.*)

BERNARDO: Who's there?

FRANCISCO: Nay, answer me. Stand, and unfold yourself.

BERNARDO: Long live the king!

FRANCISCO: Bernardo?

BERNARDO: He.   5

FRANCISCO: You come most carefully upon your hour.

BERNARDO: 'Tis now struck twelve. Get thee to bed, Francisco.

FRANCISCO: For this relief much thanks. 'Tis bitter cold,
    And I am sick at heart.

BERNARDO: Have you had quiet guard?   10

FRANCISCO: Not a mouse stirring.

BERNARDO: Well, good night.
    If you do meet Horatio and Marcellus,
    The rivals° of my watch, bid them make haste.

(*Enter* HORATIO *and* MARCELLUS.)

FRANCISCO: I think I hear them. Stand, ho! Who is there?

HORATIO: Friends to this ground.   15

MARCELLUS: And liegemen to the Dane.°

FRANCISCO: Give you good night.

MARCELLUS: O, farewell, honest soldier!
    Who hath relieved you?

FRANCISCO: Bernardo hath my place
    Give you good night.

(*Exit* FRANCISCO.)

MARCELLUS: Holla, Bernardo!

BERNARDO: Say—
    What, is Horatio there?

---

13. rivals: partners 15. Dane: King of Denmark

HORATIO: A piece of him.
BERNARDO: Welcome, Horatio. Welcome, good Marcellus.   20
HORATIO: What, has this thing appeared again to-night?
BERNARDO: I have seen nothing.
MARCELLUS: Horatio says 'tis but our fantasy,
    And will not let belief take hold of him
    Touching this dreaded sight twice seen of us.   25
    Therefore I have entreated him along
    With us to watch the minutes of this night,
    That if again this apparition come,
    He may approve° our eyes and speak to it.
HORATIO: Tush, tush, 'twill not appear.   30
BERNARDO: Sit down awhile,
    And let us once again assail your ears,
    That are so fortified against our story,
    What we have two nights seen.
HORATIO: Well, sit we down,
    And let us hear Bernardo speak of this.
BERNARDO: Last night of all,   35
    When yond same star that's westward from the pole°
    Had made his course t' illume that part of heaven
    Where now it burns, Marcellus and myself,
    The bell then beating one—
(Enter GHOST.)
MARCELLUS: Peace, break thee off. Look where it comes again.   40
BERNARDO: In the same figure like the king that's dead.
MARCELLUS: Thou art a scholar; speak to it, Horatio.
BERNARDO: Looks 'a not like the king? Mark it, Horatio.
HORATIO: Most like. It harrows° me with fear and wonder.
BERNARDO: It would be spoke to.   45
MARCELLUS: Question it, Horatio.
HORATIO: What art thou that usurp'st this time of night
    Together with that fair and warlike form
    In which the majesty of buried Denmark°
    Did sometimes° march? By heaven I charge thee, speak.
MARCELLUS: It is offended.   50
BERNARDO: See, it stalks away.
HORATIO: Stay. Speak, speak. I charge thee, speak.
(Exit GHOST.)
MARCELLUS: 'Tis gone and will not answer.

---

29. **approve:** confirm 36. **pole:** polestar 44. **harrows:** afflicts, distresses 48. **buried Denmark:** the buried
King of Denmark 49. **sometimes:** formerly

BERNARDO: How now, Horatio! You tremble and look pale.
Is not this something more than fantasy?
What think you on't?   55
HORATIO: Before my God, I might not this believe
Without the sensible° and true avouch
Of mine own eyes.
MARCELLUS: Is it not like the king?
HORATIO: As thou art to thyself.
Such was the very armour he had on   60
When he the ambitious Norway° combated.
So frowned he once when, in an angry parle,°
He smote the sledded Polacks° on the ice.
'Tis strange.
MARCELLUS: Thus twice before, and jump° at this dead hour,   65
With martial stalk hath he gone by our watch.
HORATIO: In what particular thought to work I know not,
But in the gross° and scope of mine opinion,
This bodes some strange eruption to our state.
MARCELLUS: Good now, sit down, and tell me he that knows,   70
Why this same strict and most observant watch
So nightly toils° the subject° of the land,
And why such daily cast of brazen cannon
And foreign mart° for implements of war;
Why such impress° of shipwrights, whose sore task   75
Does not divide the Sunday from the week.
What might be toward° that this sweaty haste
Doth make the night joint-laborer with the day?
Who is't that can inform me?
HORATIO: That can I.
At least, the whisper goes so. Our last king,   80
Whose image even but now appeared to us,
Was as you know by Fortinbras of Norway,
Thereto pricked on by a most emulate° pride,
Dared to the combat; in which our valiant Hamlet
(For so this side of our known world esteemed him)   85
Did slay this Fortinbras; who by a sealed compact
Well ratified by law and heraldry,°
Did forfeit, with his life, all those his lands

---

57. **sensible:** confirmed by one of the senses **61. Norway:** King of Norway **62. parle:** parley **63. sledded
Polacks:** the Poles mounted on sleds or sledges **65. jump:** just, exactly **68. gross and scope:** general
drift **72. toils:** causes to toil **72. subject:** people **74. mart:** traffic, bargaining **75. impress:** conscription
77. toward: imminent, impending **83. emulate:** ambitious **87. heraldry:** the law of arms, regulating
tournaments and state combats

Which he stood seized° of, to the conqueror;
Against the which a moiety competent°   90
Was gagèd° by our king; which had returned
To the inheritance of Fortinbras,
Had he been vanquisher; as, by the same comart°
And carriage° of the article designed,
His fell to Hamlet. Now, sir, young Fortinbras,   95
Of unimprovèd° mettle hot and full,
Hath in the skirts of Norway here and there
Sharked up° a list of lawless resolutes
For food and diet to some enterprise
That hath a stomach° in't; which is no other,   100
As it doth well appear unto our state,
But to recover of us by strong hand
And terms compulsatory, those foresaid lands
So by his father lost; and this, I take it,
Is the main motive of our preparations,   105
The source of this our watch, and the chief head°
Of this post-haste and romage° in the land.
BERNARDO: I think it be no other but e'en so.
     Well may it sort° that this portentous figure
     Comes armèd through our watch; so like the king   110
     That was and is the question of these wars.
HORATIO: A mote° it is to trouble the mind's eye.
     In the most high and palmy° state of Rome,
     A little ere the mightiest Julius fell,
     The graves stood tenantless and the sheeted° dead   115
     Did squeak and gibber in the Roman streets;
     As stars with trains of fire, and dews of blood,
     Disasters° in the sun; and the moist star,°
     Upon whose influence Neptune's empire stands,
     Was sick almost to doomsday with eclipse.   120
     And even the like precurse° of feared events,
     As harbingers° preceding still° the fates
     And prologue to the omen° coming on,
     Have heaven and earth together demonstrated

---

89. seized: possessed 90. moiety competent: sufficient portion 91. gagèd: pledged 93. comart: bargain
94. carriage: import 96. unimprovèd: unrestrained 98. Sharked up: picked up indiscriminately
100. stomach: spice of adventure 106. head: fountainhead 107. romage: turmoil 109. sort: be in
accordance 112. mote: particle of dust 113. palmy: flourishing 115. sheeted: in shrouds 118. Disasters:
ominous signs; 118. moist star: the moon 121. precurse: heralding, foreshadowing 122. harbingers:
forerunners; 122. still: ever 123. omen: ominous event

Unto our climatures° and countrymen.   125
(Enter GHOST.*)*
But soft, behold, lo where it comes again!
I'll cross it° though it blast me.—Stay, illusion.
*(*GHOST *spreads his arms.)*
If thou hast any sound or use of voice,
Speak to me.
If there be any good thing to be done,   130
That may to thee do ease, and grace to me,
Speak to me.
If thou art privy to thy country's fate,
Which happily° foreknowing may avoid,
O, speak!   135
Or if thou hast uphoarded in thy life
Extorted treasure in the womb of earth,
For which, they say, you spirits oft walk in death,
(The cock crows.)
Speak of it. Stay, and speak. Stop it, Marcellus.
MARCELLUS: Shall I strike at it with my partisan?°   140
HORATIO: Do, if it will not stand.
BERNARDO: 'Tis here.
HORATIO: 'Tis here!
(Exit GHOST.*)*
MARCELLUS: 'Tis gone!
    We do it wrong, being so majestical,
    To offer it the show of violence;
    For it is as the air, invulnerable,   145
    And our vain blows malicious mockery.
BERNARDO: It was about to speak when the cock crew.
HORATIO: And then it started like a guilty thing
    Upon a fearful summons. I have heard
    The cock, that is the trumpet to the morn,   150
    Doth with his lofty and shrill-sounding throat
    Awake the god of day and at his warning,
    Whether in sea or fire, in earth or air,
    Th' extravagant° and erring° spirit hies
    To his confine; and of the truth herein   155
    This present object made probation.°
MARCELLUS: It faded on the crowing of the cock.
    Some say that ever 'gainst° that season comes

---

125. **climatures:** regions 127. **cross it:** cross its path 134. **happily:** haply, perchance 140. **partisan:** pike
154. **extravagant:** straying, vagrant; 154. **erring:** wandering 156. **probation:** proof **'gainst:** just before

Wherein our Saviour's birth is celebrated,
The bird of dawning singeth all night long,   160
And then, they say, no spirit dare stir abroad.
The nights are wholesome, then no planets strike,°
No fairy takes,° nor witch hath power to charm,
So hallowed and so gracious is that time.
HORATIO: So have I heard and do in part believe it.   165
But look, the morn in russet mantle clad
Walks o'er the dew of yon high eastward hill.
Break we our watch up, and by my advice
Let us impart what we have seen to-night
Unto young Hamlet, for, upon my life   170
This spirit, dumb to us, will speak to him.
Do you consent we shall acquaint him with it,
As needful in our loves, fitting our duty?
MARCELLUS: Let's do't, I pray, and I this morning know
Where we shall find him most convenient.   175
(Exeunt.)

Scene 2

(Flourish. Enter CLAUDIUS, KING OF DENMARK, GERTRUDE THE QUEEN,
COUNCILLORS, *[including]* POLONIUS *and his son* LAERTES, HAMLET, *cum aliis*°
[including VOLTEMAND *and* CORNELIUS.*])*
KING: Though yet of Hamlet our dear brother's death
The memory be green, and that it us befitted
To bear our hearts in grief, and our whole kingdom
To be contracted in one brow of woe,
Yet so far hath discretion fought with nature   5
That we with wisest sorrow think on him,
Together with remembrance of ourselves.
Therefore our sometime sister, now our queen,
Th' imperial jointress° to this warlike state,
Have we, as 'twere with a defeated joy,   10
With an auspicious and a dropping eye,
With mirth in funeral and with dirge in marriage,
In equal scale weighing delight and dole,
Taken to wife; nor have we herein barred°
Your better wisdoms, which have freely gone   15
With this affair along. For all, our thanks.

---

162. **strike:** blast, destroy by malign influence 163. **takes:** bewitches II. 2, **stage direction: cum aliis:**
with others 9. **jointress:** a widow who holds a jointure or life interest in an estate 14. **barred:** excluded

Now follows that you know young Fortinbras,
Holding a weak supposal of our worth,
Or thinking by our late dear brother's death
Our state to be disjoint and out of frame,   20
Colleaguèd° with this dream of his advantage,
He hath not failed to pester us with message
Importing the surrender of those lands
Lost by his father, with all bands of law,
To our most valiant brother. So much for him.   25
Now for ourself, and for this time of meeting,
Thus much the business is: we have here writ
To Norway, uncle of young Fortinbras—
Who, impotent and bedrid, scarcely hears
Of this his nephew's purpose—to suppress   30
His further gait° herein, in that the levies,
The lists, and full proportions° are all made
Out of his subject; and we here dispatch
You, good Cornelius, and you, Voltemand,
For bearers of this greeting to old Norway,   35
Giving to you no further personal power
To business with the king, more than the scope
Of these delated° articles allow.
Farewell, and let your haste commend your duty.

CORNELIUS: ⎫
VOLTEMAND: ⎬ In that and all things will we show our duty.   40

KING: We doubt it nothing, heartily farewell.
    (*Exeunt* VOLTEMAND *and* CORNELIUS.)
    And now, Laertes, what's the news with you?
    You told us of some suit. What is't, Laertes?
    You cannot speak of reason to the Dane°
    And lose your voice.° What wouldst thou beg, Laertes,   45
    That shall not be my offer, not thy asking?
    The head is not more native° to the heart,
    The hand more instrumental° to the mouth,
    Than is the throne of Denmark to thy father.
    What wouldst thou have, Laertes?   50

LAERTES: My dread lord,
    Your leave and favour to return to France,
    From whence, though willingly, I came to Denmark

---

21. **Colleaguèd:** united 31. **gait:** proceeding 32. **proportions:** forces or supplies for war 38. **delated:**
expressly stated 44. **Dane:** King of Denmark 45. **lose your voice:** speak in vain 47. **native:** joined by nature
48. **instrumental:** serviceable

To show my duty in your coronation,
Yet now I must confess, that duty done,
My thoughts and wishes bend again toward France,   55
And bow them to your gracious leave and pardon.°
KING: Have you your father's leave? What says Polonius?
POLONIUS: He hath, my lord, wrung from me my slow leave
    By laborsome petition, and at last
    Upon his will I sealed my hard° consent.   60
    I do beseech you give him leave to go.
KING: Take thy fair hour, Laertes. Time be thine,
    And thy best graces spend it at thy will.
    But now, my cousin° Hamlet, and my son—
HAMLET: (Aside.): A little more than kin,° and less than kind.°   65
KING: How is it that the clouds still hang on you?
HAMLET: Not so, my lord. I am too much in the sun.
QUEEN: Good Hamlet, cast thy nighted color off,
    And let thine eye look like a friend on Denmark.
    Do not for ever with thy vailèd° lids   70
    Seek for thy noble father in the dust.
    Thou know'st 'tis common—all that lives must die,
    Passing through nature to eternity.
HAMLET: Ay, madam, it is common.
QUEEN: If it be,
    Why seems it so particular° with thee?   75
HAMLET: Seems, madam? Nay, it is. I know not 'seems.'
    'Tis not alone my inky cloak, good mother,
    Nor customary suits of solemn black,
    Nor windy suspiration of forced breath,
    No, nor the fruitful river in the eye,   80
    Nor the dejected haviour of the visage,
    Together with all forms, moods, shapes of grief,
    That can denote me truly. These indeed seem,
    For they are actions that a man might play,
    But I have that within which passeth show—   85
    These but the trappings and the suits of woe.
KING: 'Tis sweet and commendable in your nature, Hamlet,
    To give these mourning duties to your father,
    But you must know your father lost a father,

---

56. **pardon:** indulgence 60. **hard:** reluctant 64. **cousin:** kinsman of any kind except parent, child, brother, or sister 65. **kin:** related as nephew; 65. **kind:** (1) affectionate (2) natural, lawful 70. **vailèd:** lowered 75. **particular:** personal, individual

That father lost, lost his, and the survivor bound   90
In filial obligation for some term
To do obsequious° sorrow. But to persever°
In obstinate condolement is a course
Of impious stubbornness. 'Tis unmanly grief.
It shows a will most incorrect to heaven,   95
A heart unfortified, a mind impatient,
An understanding simple and unschooled.
For what we know must be, and is as common
As any the most vulgar thing to sense,
Why should we in our peevish opposition   100
Take it to heart? Fie, 'tis a fault to heaven,
A fault against the dead, a fault to nature,
To reason most absurd, whose common theme
Is death of fathers, and who still hath cried,
From the first corse° till he that died to-day,   105
'This must be so.' We pray you throw to earth
This unprevailing woe, and think of us
As of a father, for let the world take note
You are the most immediate to our throne,
And with no less nobility of love   110
Than that which dearest father bears his son
Do I impart toward you. For your intent
In going back to school in Wittenberg,
It is most retrograde° to our desire,
And we beseech you, bend you to remain   115
Here in the cheer and comfort of our eye,
Our chiefest courtier, cousin, and our son.
QUEEN: Let not thy mother lose her prayers, Hamlet.
    I pray thee stay with us, go not to Wittenberg.
HAMLET: I shall in all my best obey you, madam.   120
KING: Why, 'tis a loving and a fair reply.
    Be as ourself in Denmark. Madam, come.
    This gentle and unforced accord of Hamlet
    Sits smiling to my heart, in grace whereof,
    No jocund health that Denmark drinks to-day   125
    But the great cannon to the clouds shall tell,
    And the king's rouse° the heaven shall bruit° again,

---

92. obsequious: dutiful in performing funeral obsequies or manifesting regard for the dead; 92. persever: persevere 105. corse: corpse 114. retrograde: contrary 127. rouse: full draught of liquor; 127. bruit: echo

Respeaking earthly thunder. Come away.
(*Flourish. Exeunt all but* HAMLET.)
HAMLET: O, that this too too sallied° flesh would melt,
    Thaw and resolve itself into a dew,   13∎
    Or that the Everlasting had not fixed
    His canon° 'gainst self-slaughter. O God, God,
    How weary, stale, flat, and unprofitable
    Seem to me all the uses of this world!
    Fie on't, ah, fie, 'tis an unweeded garden   13∎
    That grows to seed. Things rank and gross in nature
    Possess it merely.° That it should come to this,
    But two months dead, nay, not so much, not two.
    So excellent a king, that was to this
    Hyperion° to a satyr, so loving to my mother,   14∎
    That he might not beteem° the winds of heaven
    Visit her face too roughly. Heaven and earth,
    Must I remember? Why, she would hang on him
    As if increase of appetite had grown
    By what it fed on, and yet, within a month—   14∎
    Let me not think on't. Frailty, thy name is woman—
    A little month, or ere those shoes were old
    With which she followed my poor father's body
    Like Niobe,° all tears, why she—
    O God, a beast that wants° discourse of reason°   15∎
    Would have mourned longer—married with my uncle,
    My father's brother, but no more like my father
    Than I to Hercules. Within a month,
    Ere yet the salt of most unrighteous tears
    Had left the flushing in her gallèd° eyes,   15∎
    She married. O, most wicked speed, to post
    With such dexterity to incestuous sheets!
    It is not, nor it cannot come to good.
    But break my heart, for I must hold my tongue.
(*Enter* HORATIO, MARCELLUS, *and* BERNARDO.)
HORATIO: Hail to your lordship!   16∎
HAMLET: I am glad to see you well.
    Horatio—or I do forget myself.

---

129. **sallied:** sullied. 132. **canon:** law 137. **merely:** entirely 140. **Hyperion:** the sun god 141. **beteem:** allowed 149. **Niobe:** wife of Amphion, King of Thebes, she boasted of having more children than Leto and was punished when her seven sons and seven daughters were slain by Apollo and Artemis, children of Leto; in her grief she was changed by Zeus into a stone, which continually dropped tears 150. **wants:** lacks; 150. **discourse of reason:** the reasoning faculty 155. **gallèd:** sore from rubbing or chafing

HORATIO: The same, my lord, and your poor servant ever.

HAMLET: Sir, my good friend, I'll change° that name with you.
And what make° you from Wittenberg, Horatio?
Marcellus?   165

MARCELLUS: My good lord!

HAMLET: I am very glad to see you. *(To* BERNARDO.*)* Good even, sir.—
But what, in faith, make you from Wittenberg?

HORATIO: A truant disposition, good my lord.

HAMLET: I would not hear your enemy say so,   170
Nor shall you do my ear that violence
To make it truster of your own report
Against yourself. I know you are no truant.
But what is your affair in Elsinore?
We'll teach you to drink deep ere you depart.   175

HORATIO: My lord, I came to see your father's funeral.

HAMLET: I prithee, do not mock me, fellow-student,
I think it was to see my mother's wedding.

HORATIO: Indeed, my lord, it followed hard upon.

HAMLET: Thrift, thrift, Horatio. The funeral baked meats   180
Did coldly furnish forth the marriage tables.
Would I had met my dearest° foe in heaven
Or ever I had seen that day, Horatio!
My father—methinks I see my father.

HORATIO: Where, my lord?   185

HAMLET: In my mind's eye, Horatio.

HORATIO: I saw him once, 'a was a goodly king.

HAMLET: 'A was a man, take him for all in all,
I shall not look upon his like again.

HORATIO: My lord, I think I saw him yesternight.

HAMLET: Saw who?   190

HORATIO: My lord, the king your father.

HAMLET: The king my father?

HORATIO: Season° your admiration for a° while
With an attent ear, till I may deliver
Upon the witness of these gentlemen
This marvel to you.   195

HAMLET: For God's love, let me hear!

HORATIO: Two nights together had these gentlemen,
Marcellus and Bernardo, on their watch

---

163. **change:** exchange 164. **make:** do 182. **dearest:** direst 192. **Season:** temper, moderate;
192. **admiration:** wonder, astonishment

In the dead waste and middle of the night
Been thus encountered. A figure like your father,
Armed at point exactly,° cap-a-pe,°   200
Appears before them, and with solemn march
Goes slow and stately by them. Thrice he walked
By their oppressed and fear-surprisèd eyes
Within his truncheon's° length, whilst they, distilled
Almost to jelly with the act of fear,   205
Stand dumb and speak not to him. This to me
In dreadful secrecy impart they did,
And I with them the third night kept the watch,
Where, as they had delivered, both in time,
Form of the thing, each word made true and good,   210
The apparition comes. I knew your father.
These hands are not more like.
HAMLET: But where was this?
MARCELLUS: My lord, upon the platform where we watch.
HAMLET: Did you not speak to it?
HORATIO: My lord, I did,
But answer made it none. Yet once methought   215
It lifted up it° head and did address
Itself to motion, like as it would speak;
But even then the morning cock crew loud,
And at the sound it shrunk in haste away
And vanished from our sight.   220
HAMLET: 'Tis very strange.
HORATIO: As I do live, my honoured lord, 'tis true,
And we did think it writ down in our duty
To let you know of it.
HAMLET: Indeed, sirs, but
This troubles me. Hold you the watch to-night?
ALL: We do, my lord.   225
HAMLET: Armed, say you?
ALL: Armed, my lord.
HAMLET: From top to toe?
ALL: My lord, from head to foot.
HAMLET: Then saw you not his face.
HORATIO: O yes, my lord, he wore his beaver° up.
HAMLET: What, looked he frowningly?

---

200. at point exactly: in every particular; **200. cap-a-pe:** from head to foot **204. truncheon:** military
leader's baton **216. it:** its **228. beaver:** the part of the helmet that was drawn down to cover the face

HORATIO: A countenance more in sorrow than in anger.   230
HAMLET: Pale or red?
HORATIO: Nay, very pale.
HAMLET: And fixed his eyes upon you?
HORATIO: Most constantly.
HAMLET: I would I had been there.
HORATIO: It would have much amazed you.
HAMLET: Very like.
    Stayed it long?   235
HORATIO: While one with moderate haste might tell° a hundred.
BOTH: Longer, longer.
HORATIO: Not when I saw't.
HAMLET: His beard was grizzled,° no?
HORATIO: It was as I have seen it in his life,
    A sable° silvered.
HAMLET: I will watch to-night.
    Perchance 'twill walk again.   240
HORATIO: I warr'nt it will.
HAMLET: If it assume my noble father's person,
    I'll speak to it though hell itself should gape
    And bid me hold my peace. I pray you all,
    If you have hitherto concealed this sight,
    Let it be tenable° in your silence still,   245
    And whatsomever° else shall hap to-night,
    Give it an understanding but no tongue.
    I will requite your loves. So fare you well.
    Upon the platform 'twixt eleven and twelve
    I'll visit you.   250
ALL: Our duty to your honor.
HAMLET: Your loves, as mine to you. Farewell.
    (Exeunt all but HAMLET.*)*
    My father's spirit in arms? All is not well.
    I doubt° some foul play. Would the night were come!
    Till then sit still, my soul. Foul deeds will rise,
    Though all the earth o'erwhelm them, to men's eyes.   255
(Exit.)

Scene 3

(Enter LAERTES *and* OPHELIA *his sister.)*

---

235. tell: count 237. grizzled: grayish 239. sable silvered: black mixed with white 245. tenable: retained
246. whatsomever: whatsover 253. doubt: suspect

LAERTES: My necessaries are embarked. Farewell.
    And, sister, as the winds give benefit
    And convoy is assistant, do not sleep,
    But let me hear from you.
OPHELIA: Do you doubt that?
LAERTES: For Hamlet, and the trifling of his favor,   5
    Hold it a fashion° and a toy in blood°,
    A violet in the youth of primy° nature,
    Forward, not permanent, sweet, not lasting,
    The perfume and suppliance of a minute,
    No more.   10
OPHELIA: No more but so?
LAERTES: Think it no more.
    For nature crescent° does not grow alone
    In thews° and bulk, but as this temple° waxes
    The inward service of the mind and soul
    Grows wide withal. Perhaps he loves you now,
    And now no soil nor cautel° doth besmirch   15
    The virtue of his will,° but you must fear,
    His greatness weighed,° his will is not his own,
    For he himself is subject to his birth.
    He may not, as unvalued persons° do,
    Carve for himself,° for on his choice depends   20
    The safety and health of this whole state,
    And therefore must his choice be circumscribed
    Unto the voice and yielding° of that body
    Whereof he is the head. Then if he says he loves you,
    It fits your wisdom so far to believe it   25
    As he in his particular act and place
    May give his saying deed, which is no further
    Than the main voice of Denmark goes withal.
    Then weigh what loss your honor may sustain
    If with too credent° ear you list his songs,   30
    Or lose your heart, or your chaste treasure open
    To his unmastered importunity.
    Fear it, Ophelia, fear it, my dear sister,
    And keep you in the rear of your affection,°
    Out of the shot and danger of desire.   35

---

6. **fashion:** the creation of a season only; 6. **toy in blood:** passing fancy 7. **primy:** of the springtime
11. **crescent:** growing 12. **thews:** sinews, strength; 12. **this temple:** the body 15. **cautel:** deceit 16. **will:**
desire 17. **greatness weighed:** high position considered 19. **unvalued persons:** persons of no social
importance 20. **Carve for himself:** act according to his own inclination 23. **yielding:** assent 30. **credent:**
trusting 34. **affection:** feeling

The chariest maid is prodigal enough
If she unmask her beauty to the moon.
Virtue itself scapes not calumnious strokes.
The canker° galls° the infants of the spring
Too oft before their buttons° be disclosed,   40
And in the morn and liquid dew of youth
Contagious blastments° are most imminent.
Be wary then; best safety lies in fear.
Youth to itself rebels, though none else near.

OPHELIA: I shall the effect of this good lesson keep   45
    As watchman to my heart. But, good my brother,
    Do not as some ungracious pastors do,
    Show me the steep and thorny way to heaven,
    Whiles like a puffed and reckless libertine
    Himself the primrose path of dalliance treads   50
    And recks° not his own rede.°

LAERTES: O, fear me not.
    (*Enter* POLONIUS.)
    I stay too long. But here my father comes.
    A double blessing is a double grace;
    Occasion smiles upon a second leave.

POLONIUS: Yet here, Laertes? Aboard, aboard, for shame!   55
    The wind sits in the shoulder of your sail,
    And you are stayed for. There, my blessing with thee,
    And these few precepts in thy memory
    Look thou character.° Give thy thoughts no tongue,
    Nor any unproportioned° thought his act.   60
    Be thou familiar, but by no means vulgar.°
    Those friends thou hast, and their adoption tried,
    Grapple them to thy soul with hoops of steel,
    But do not dull thy palm with entertainment
    Of each new-hatched, unfledged courage.° Beware   65
    Of entrance to a quarrel, but being in,
    Bear't that th' opposèd may beware of thee.
    Give every man thy ear, but few thy voice;
    Take each man's censure, but reserve thy judgement.
    Costly thy habit as thy purse can buy,   70
    But not expressed in fancy; rich not gaudy,

---

39. canker: canker-worm (which feeds on roses); **39. galls:** injures **40. buttons:** buds **42. blastments:**
blights **51. recks:** regards; **59. rede:** counsel **60. character:** engrave **60. unproportioned:** inordinate
61. vulgar: common **65. courage:** young blood, man of spirit

For the apparel oft proclaims the man,
And they in France of the best rank and station
Are of a most select and generous chief° in that.
Neither a borrower nor a lender be,   75
For loan oft loses both itself and friend,
And borrowing dulls th' edge of husbandry.°
This above all, to thine own self be true,
And it must follow as the night the day
Thou canst not then be false to any man.   80
Farewell. My blessing season° this in thee!
LAERTES: Most humbly do I take my leave, my lord.
POLONIUS: The time invites you. Go, your servants tend.°
LAERTES: Farewell, Ophelia, and remember well
What I have said to you.   85
OPHELIA: 'Tis in my memory locked,
And you yourself shall keep the key of it.
LAERTES: Farewell.
(*Exit* LAERTES.)
POLONIUS: What is 't, Ophelia, he hath said to you?
OPHELIA: So please you, something touching the Lord Hamlet.
POLONIUS: Marry,° well bethought.   90
'Tis told me he hath very oft of late
Given private time to you, and you yourself
Have of your audience been most free and bounteous.
If it be so—as so 'tis put on me,
And that in way of caution—I must tell you,   95
You do not understand yourself so clearly
As it behooves my daughter and your honor.
What is between you? Give me up the truth.
OPHELIA: He hath, my lord, of late made many tenders°
Of his affection to me.   100
POLONIUS: Affection? Pooh! You speak like a green girl,
Unsifted° in such perilous circumstance.
Do you believe his tenders, as you call them?
OPHELIA: I do not know, my lord, what I should think.
POLONIUS: Marry, I will teach you. Think yourself a baby   105
That you have ta'en these tenders for true pay
Which are not sterling. Tender yourself more dearly,

---

74. **chief:** eminence 77. **husbandry:** thriftiness 81. **season:** ripen 83. **tend:** attend, wait 90. **Marry:** by Mary 99. **tenders:** offers 102. **Unsifted:** untried

Or (not to crack the wind of the poor phrase,
Running it thus) you'll tender me a fool.
OPHELIA: My lord, he hath importuned me with love   110
In honorable fashion.
POLONIUS: Ay, fashion you may call it. Go to, go to.
OPHELIA: And hath given countenance to his speech, my lord,
With almost all the holy vows of heaven.
POLONIUS: Ay, springes° to catch woodcocks. I do know,   115
When the blood burns, how prodigal the soul
Lends the tongue vows. These blazes, daughter,
Giving more light than heat, extinct in both
Even in their promise, as it is a-making,
You must not take for fire. From this time   120
Be something scanter of your maiden presence.
Set your entreatments° at a higher rate
Than a command to parle. For Lord Hamlet,
Believe so much in him that he is young,
And with a larger tether may he walk   125
Than may be given you. In few, Ophelia,
Do not believe his vows, for they are brokers,°
Not of that dye which their investments° show,
But mere implorators° of unholy suits,
Breathing like sanctified and pious bawds,   130
The better to beguile. This is for all:
I would not, in plain terms, from this time forth
Have you so slander any moment leisure
As to give words or talk with the Lord Hamlet.
Look to't, I charge you. Come your ways.   135
OPHELIA: I shall obey, my lord.
(*Exeunt.*)

Scene 4

(*Enter* HAMLET, HORATIO, *and* MARCELLUS.)
HAMLET: The air bites shrewdly; it is very cold.
HORATIO: It is a nipping and an eager° air.
HAMLET: What hour now?
HORATIO: I think it lacks of twelve.
MARCELLUS: No, it is struck.

---

115. springes: snares 122. entreatments: military negotiations for surrender 127. brokers: go-betweens
128. investments: clothes 129. implorators: solicitors I.iv.2. eager: sharp

HORATIO: Indeed? I heard it not. It then draws near the season 5
    Wherein the spirit held his wont to walk.
    (*A flourish of trumpets, and two pieces go off.*)
    What does this mean, my lord?
HAMLET: The king doth wake to-night and takes his rouse,
    Keeps wassail,° and the swagg'ring up-spring° reels,
    And as he drains his draughts of Rhenish down, 10
    The kettledrum and trumpet thus bray out
    The triumph of his pledge.
HORATIO: Is it a custom?
HAMLET: Ay, marry, is't,
    But to my mind, though I am native here
    And to the manner born, it is a custom 15
    More honored in the breach than the observance.
    This heavy-headed revel east and west
    Makes us traduced and taxed° of other nations.
    They clepe° us drunkards, and with swinish phrase
    Soil our addition,° and indeed it takes 20
    From our achievements, though performed at height,
    The pith and marrow of our attribute.°
    So oft it chances in particular men,
    That for some vicious mole of nature in them,
    As, in their birth, wherein they are not guilty 25
    (Since nature cannot choose his° origin),
    By the o'ergrowth of some complexion,°
    Oft breaking down the pales and forts of reason,
    Or by some habit that too much o'er-leavens°
    The form of plausive° manners—that these men, 30
    Carrying, I say, the stamp of one defect,
    Being nature's livery° or fortune's star,°
    His virtues else, be they as pure as grace,
    As infinite as man may undergo,
    Shall in the general censure take corruption 35
    From that particular fault. The dram of evil
    Doth all the noble substance often doubt°
    To his° own scandal.
(*Enter* GHOST.)

---

9. wassail: carousal; 9. up-spring: a German dance 18. taxed of: censured by 19. clepe: call 20. addition: title added to a man's name to denote his rank 22. attribute: reputation 27. his: its 28. complexion: one of the four temperaments (sanguine, melancholy, choleric, and phlegmatic) 29. o'er-leavens: works change throughout 30. plausive: pleasing 32. livery: badge; 32. star: a person's fortune, rank, or destiny, viewed as determined by the stars 37. doubt: put out, obliterate 38. his: its

HORATIO: Look, my lord, it comes.
HAMLET: Angels and ministers of grace defend us!
    Be thou a spirit of health or goblin damned,   40
    Bring with thee airs from heaven or blasts from hell,
    Be thy intents wicked or charitable,
    Thou com'st in such a questionable shape
    That I will speak to thee. I'll call thee Hamlet,
    King, father, royal Dane. O, answer me!   45
    Let me not burst in ignorance, but tell
    Why thy canonized° bones, hearsèd° in death,
    Have burst their cerements; why the sepulchre
    Wherein we saw thee quietly interred,
    Hath oped his ponderous and marble jaws   50
    To cast thee up again. What may this mean
    That thou, dead corse, again in complete steel
    Revisits thus the glimpses of the moon,
    Making night hideous, and we fools of nature
    So horridly to shake our disposition   55
    With thoughts beyond the reaches of our souls?
    Say, why is this? wherefore? What should we do?
(GHOST *beckons.*)
HORATIO: It beckons you to go away with it,
    As if it some impartment° did desire
    To you alone.   60
MARCELLUS: Look, with what courteous action
    It waves you to a more removèd ground.
    But do not go with it.
HORATIO: No, by no means.
HAMLET: It will not speak; then I will follow it.
HORATIO: Do not, my lord.
HAMLET: Why, what should be the fear?
    I do not set my life at a pin's fee,   65
    And for my soul, what can it do to that,
    Being a thing immortal as itself?
    It waves me forth again. I'll follow it.
HORATIO: What if it tempt you toward the flood, my lord,
    Or to the dreadful summit of the cliff   70
    That beetles° o'er his base into the sea,
    And there assume some other horrible form,

---

47. canonized: buried according to the church's rule; 47. hearsèd: coffined, buried 59. impartment: communication 71. beetles: juts out

Which might deprive your sovereignty° of reason
And draw you into madness? Think of it.
The very place puts toys° of desperation,   75
Without more motive, into every brain
That looks so many fathoms to the sea
And hears it roar beneath.
HAMLET: It waves me still.
Go on. I'll follow thee.
MARCELLUS: You shall not go, my lord.   80
HAMLET: Hold off your hands.
HORATIO: Be ruled; You shall not go.
HAMLET: My fate cries out,
And makes each petty artere° in this body
As hardy as the Nemean lion's° nerve.
Still am I called. Unhand me, gentlemen.
By heaven, I'll make a ghost of him that lets° me.   85
I say, away—Go on. I'll follow thee.
(*Exeunt* GHOST *and* HAMLET.)
HORATIO: He waxes desperate with imagination.
MARCELLUS: Let's follow. 'Tis not fit thus to obey him.
HORATIO: Have after. To what issue will this come?
MARCELLUS: Something is rotten in the state of Denmark.   90
HORATIO: Heaven will direct it.
MARCELLUS: Nay, let's follow him.
(*Exeunt.*)

Scene 5

(*Enter* GHOST *and* HAMLET.)
HAMLET: Whither wilt thou lead me? Speak. I'll go no further.
GHOST: Mark me.
HAMLET: I will.
GHOST: My hour is almost come
When I to sulph'rous and tormenting flames
Must render up myself.
HAMLET: Alas, poor ghost!
GHOST: Pity me not, but lend thy serious hearing   5
To what I shall unfold.
HAMLET: Speak. I am bound to hear.
GHOST: So art thou to revenge, when thou shalt hear.

---

73. **sovereignty of reason:** state of being ruled by reason 75. **toys:** fancies, impules 82. **artere:** artery
83. **Nemean lion:** slain by Hercules in the performance of one of his twelve labors 85. **lets:** hinders

HAMLET: What?

GHOST: I am thy father's spirit,

    Doomed for a certain term to walk the night,   10

    And for the day confined to fast in fires,

    Till the foul crimes done in my days of nature

    Are burnt and purged away. But that I am forbid

    To tell the secrets of my prison house,

    I could a tale unfold whose lightest word   15

    Would harrow up thy soul, freeze thy young blood,

    Make thy two eyes like stars start from their spheres,

    Thy knotted and combinèd locks to part,

    And each particular hair to stand an° end,

    Like quills upon the fretful porpentine.°   20

    But this eternal blazon° must not be

    To ears of flesh and blood. List, list, O, list!

    If thou didst ever thy dear father love—

HAMLET: O God!

GHOST: Revenge his foul and most unnatural murder.   25

HAMLET: Murder!

GHOST: Murder most foul, as in the best it is,

    But this most foul, strange, and unnatural.

HAMLET: Haste me to know't, that I, with wings as swift

    As meditation or the thoughts of love,   30

    May sweep to my revenge.

GHOST: I find thee apt,

    And duller shouldst thou be than the fat weed

    That roots itself in ease on Lethe° wharf,

    Wouldst thou not stir in this. Now, Hamlet, hear.

    'Tis given out that, sleeping in my orchard,   35

    A serpent stung me. So the whole ear of Denmark

    Is by a forgèd process° of my death

    Rankly abused. But know, thou noble youth,

    The serpent that did sting thy father's life

    Now wears his crown.   40

HAMLET: O my prophetic soul!

    My uncle!

GHOST: Ay, that incestuous, that adulterate beast,

    With witchcraft of his wits, with traitorous gifts—

    O wicked wit and gifts that have the power

I.v.19. an: on 20. porpentine: porcupine 21. eternal blazon: proclamation of the secrets of eternity
33. Lethe: the river in Hades that brings forgetfulness 37. process: account

So to seduce!—won to his shameful lust   45
The will of my most seeming virtuous queen.
O Hamlet, what a falling off was there,
From me, whose love was of that dignity
That it went hand in hand even with the vow
I made to her in marriage, and to decline   50
Upon a wretch whose natural gifts were poor
To those of mine!
But virtue, as it never will be moved,
Though lewdness court it in a shape of heaven,
So lust, though to a radiant angel linked,   55
Will sate itself in a celestial bed
And prey on garbage.
But soft, methinks I scent the morning air.
Brief let me be. Sleeping within my orchard,
My custom always of the afternoon,   60
Upon my secure° hour thy uncle stole,
With juice of cursed hebona° in a vial,
And in the porches of my ears did pour
The leperous distilment, whose effect
Holds such an enmity with blood of man   65
That swift as quicksilver it courses through
The natural gates and alleys of the body,
And with a sudden vigor it doth posset°
And curd, like eager° droppings into milk,
The thin and wholesome blood. So did it mine,   70
And a most instant tetter° barked° about
Most lazar-like with vile and loathsome crust
All my smooth body.
Thus was I sleeping by a brother's hand
Of life, of crown, of queen, at once dispatched,   75
Cut off even in the blossoms of my sin,
Unhouseled,° disappointed,° unaneled,°
No reck'ning made, but sent to my account
With all my imperfections on my head.
O, horrible! O, horrible! most horrible!   80
If thou hast nature in thee, bear it not,
Let not the royal bed of Denmark be

---

61. **secure:** free from suspicion 62. **hebona:** an imaginary poison, associated with henbane 68. **posset:** curdle 69. **eager:** acid 71. **tetter:** a skin eruption; 71. **barked:** covered as with bark 77. **Unhouseled:** without having received the sacrament; 77. **disappointed:** unprepared; 77. **unaneled:** without extreme unction

A couch for luxury° and damnèd incest.
But howsomever thou pursues this act,
Taint not thy mind, nor let thy soul contrive   85
Against thy mother aught. Leave her to heaven,
And to those thorns that in her bosom lodge
To prick and sting her. Fare thee well at once.
The glowworm shows the matin° to be near,
And gins to pale his uneffectual fire.   90
Adieu, adieu, adieu. Remember me.
(*Exit.*)
HAMLET: O all you host of heaven! O earth! What else?
And shall I couple hell? O, fie! Hold, hold, my heart,
And you, my sinews, grow not instant old,
But bear me stiffly up. Remember thee?   95
Ay, thou poor ghost, whiles memory holds a seat
In this distracted globe.° Remember thee?
Yea, from the table° of my memory
I'll wipe away all trivial fond° records,
All saws° of books, all forms,° all pressures° past   100
That youth and observation copied there,
And thy commandment all alone shall live
Within the book and volume of my brain,
Unmixed with baser matter. Yes, by heaven!
O most pernicious woman!   105
O villain, villain, smiling, damnèd villain!
My tables—meet it is I set it down
That one may smile, and smile, and be a villain
At least I am sure it may be so in Denmark.
(*Writing.*)
So, uncle, there you are. Now to my word: 110
It is 'Adieu, adieu! Remember me,'
I have sworn't.
(*Enter* HORATIO *and* MARCELLUS.)
HORATIO: My lord, my lord!
MARCELLUS: Lord Hamlet!
HORATIO: Heavens secure him!
HAMLET: So be it!
MARCELLUS: Illo, ho, ho,° my lord!   115
HAMLET: Hillo, ho, ho, boy! Come, bird, come.

83. **luxury:** lust 89. **matin:** morning 97. **globe:** head 98. **table:** writing tablet, memorandum book 99. **fond:** foolish 100. **saws:** sayings; 100. **forms:** concepts; 115. **pressures:** impressions 115. **Illo, ho, ho:** cry of the falconer to summon his hawk

MARCELLUS: How is't, my noble lord?

HORATIO: What news, my lord?

HAMLET: O, wonderful!

HORATIO: Good my lord, tell it.

HAMLET: No, you will reveal it.

HORATIO: Not I, my lord, by heaven.   120

MARCELLUS: Nor I, my lord.

HAMLET: How say you then, would heart of man once think it?
    But you'll be secret?

BOTH: Ay, by heaven, my lord.

HAMLET: There's never a villain dwelling in all Denmark
    But he's an arrant knave.

HORATIO: There needs no ghost, my lord, come from the grave   125
    To tell us this.

HAMLET: Why, right, you are in the right,
    And so without more circumstance at all
    I hold it fit that we shake hands and part,
    You, as your business and desire shall point you,
    For every man has business and desire   130
    Such as it is, and for my own poor part,
    I will go pray.

HORATIO: These are but wild and whirling words, my lord.

HAMLET: I am sorry they offend you, heartily;
    Yes, faith, heartily.   135

HORATIO: There's no offence, my lord.

HAMLET: Yes, by Saint Patrick,° but there is, Horatio,
    And much offence too. Touching this vision here,
    It is an honest ghost, that let me tell you
    For your desire to know what is between us,
    O'ermaster't as you may. And now, good friends,   140
    As you are friends, scholars, and soldiers,
    Give me one poor request.

HORATIO: What is't, my lord? We will.

HAMLET: Never make known what you have seen to-night.

BOTH: My lord, we will not.   145

HAMLET: Nay, but swear't.

HORATIO: In faith,
    My lord, not I.

MARCELLUS: Nor I, my lord, in faith.

---

136. **Saint Patrick:** associated, in the late middle ages, with purgatory, whence the ghost has presumably come

HAMLET: Upon my sword.

MARCELLUS: We have sworn, my lord, already.

HAMLET: Indeed, upon my sword, indeed.

(GHOST *cries under the stage.*)

GHOST: Swear.

HAMLET: Ha, ha, boy, say'st thou so? Art thou there, truepenny?°
  Come on. You hear this fellow in the cellarage.   150
  Consent to swear.

HORATIO: Propose the oath, my lord.

HAMLET: Never to speak of this that you have seen,
  Swear by my sword.

GHOST (*Beneath.*): Swear.

HAMLET: Hic et ubique?° Then we'll shift our ground.   155
  Come hither, gentlemen,
  And lay your hands again upon my sword.
  Swear by my sword
  Never to speak of this that you have heard.

GHOST (*Beneath.*): Swear by his sword.   160

HAMLET: Well said, old mole! Canst work i' th' earth so fast?
  A worthy pioneer!° Once more remove, good friends.

HORATIO: O day and night, but this is wondrous strange!

HAMLET: And therefore as a stranger give it welcome.
  There are more things in heaven and earth, Horatio,   165
  Than are dreamt of in your philosophy.
  But come.
  Here as before, never, so help you mercy,
  How strange or odd some'er I bear myself
  (As I perchance hereafter shall think meet   170
  To put an antic° disposition on),
  That you, at such times, seeing me, never shall,
  With arms encumbered° thus, or this head-shake,
  Or by pronouncing of some doubtful phrase,
  As 'Well, well, we know,' or 'We could, and if we would'   175
  Or 'If we list to speak,' or 'There be, and if they might'
  Or such ambiguous giving out, to note
  That you know aught of me—this do swear,
  So grace and mercy at your most need help you.

GHOST (*Beneath.*): Swear.   180

---

149. **truepenny:** honest fellow 155. **Hic et ubique:** here and everywhere 162. **pioneer:** miner 171. **antic:**
mad 173. **encumbered:** folded

HAMLET: Rest, rest, perturbèd spirit! So, gentlemen,
       With all my love I do commend me to you,
       And what so poor a man as Hamlet is
       May do t' express his love and friending to you,
       God willing, shall not lack. Let us go in together,   18!
       And still your fingers on your lips, I pray.
       The time is out of joint. O cursèd spite
       That ever I was born to set it right!
       Nay, come, let's go together.
(Exeunt.)

ACT II

Scene 1

(Enter old POLONIUS *with his man* REYNALDO.*)*
POLONIUS: Give him this money and these notes. Reynaldo.
REYNALDO: I will, my lord.
POLONIUS: You shall do marvellous wisely, good Reynaldo,
       Before you visit him, to make inquire
       Of his behavior.   5
REYNALDO: My lord, I did intend it.
POLONIUS: Marry, well said, very well said. Look you, sir,
       Enquire me first what Danskers° are in Paris,
       And how, and who, what means,° and where they keep,
       What company, at what expense; and finding
       By this encompassment° and drift of question   10
       That they do know my son, come you more nearer
       Than your particular demands will touch it.
       Take you as 'twere some distant knowledge of him,
       As thus, 'I know his father and his friends,
       And in part him,' do you mark this, Reynaldo?   15
REYNALDO: Ay, very well, my lord.
POLONIUS: 'And in part him, but,' you may say, 'not well,
       But if 't be he I mean, he's very wild,
       Addicted so and so.' And there put on him
       What forgeries° you please; marry, none so rank   20
       As may dishonour him. Take heed of that.
       But, sir, such wanton, wild, and usual slips
       As are companions noted and most known
       To youth and liberty.°

II.i.7. **Danskers:** Danes **8. means:** wealth **10. encompassment:** talking round the matter **20. forgeries:** invented wrongdoings **24. liberty:** license

REYNALDO: As gaming, my lord?

POLONIUS: Ay, or drinking, fencing, swearing, quarrelling,   25
    Drabbing°—you may go so far.

REYNALDO: My lord, that would dishonour him.

POLONIUS: Faith, no, as you may season° it in the charge.
    You must not put another scandal on him,
    That he is open to incontinency.   30
    That's not my meaning. But breathe his faults so quaintly°
    That they may seem the taints of liberty,
    The flash and outbreak of a fiery mind,
    A savageness in unreclaimèd° blood,
    Of general assault.°   35

REYNALDO: But, my good lord—

POLONIUS: Wherefore should you do this?

REYNALDO: Ay, my lord,
    I would know that.

POLONIUS: Marry, sir, here's my drift,
    And I believe it is a fetch° of warrant.
    You laying these slight sullies on my son,
    As 'twere a thing a little soiled i' th' working,   40
    Mark you,
    Your party in converse, him you would sound,
    Having ever seen in the prenominate° crimes
    The youth you breathe of guilty, be assured
    He closes° with you in this consequence,°   45
    'Good sir', or so, or 'friend', or 'gentleman',
    According to the phrase or the addition°
    Of man and country.

REYNALDO: Very good, my lord.

POLONIUS: And then, sir, does 'a this—'a does—What was I about to say?
    By the mass, I was about to say something.   50
    Where did I leave?

REYNALDO: At 'closes in the consequence.'

POLONIUS: At 'closes in the consequence'—ay, marry,
    He closes thus: 'I know the gentleman.
    I saw him yesterday, or th' other day,   55
    Or then, or then, with such, or such, and as you say,
    There was 'a gaming, there o'ertook in 's rouse;

---

26. Drabbing: whoring 28. season: moderate 31. quaintly: delicately 34. unreclaimèd: untamed
35. Of general assault: assailing all 38. fetch of warrant: allowable device 43. prenominate: before-
named 45. closes: agrees; 45. in this consequence: as follows 47. addition: title

There falling out at tennis', or perchance
'I saw him enter such a house of sale',
Videlicet,° a brothel, or so forth.   60
See you, now—
Your bait of falsehood takes this carp of truth,
And thus do we of wisdom and of reach,°
With windlasses° and with assays of bias,°
By indirections find directions out;   65
So by my former lecture and advice
Shall you my son. You have me, have you not?
REYNALDO: My lord, I have.
POLONIUS: God bye ye;° fare ye well.
REYNALDO: Good my lord.
POLONIUS: Observe his inclination in yourself.   70
REYNALDO: I shall, my lord.
POLONIUS: And let him ply his music.
REYNALDO: Well, my lord.
POLONIUS: Farewell.
(*Exit* REYNALDO.)
(*Enter* OPHELIA.)
                              How now, Ophelia! what's the matter?
OPHELIA: O my lord, my lord, I have been so affrighted!
POLONIUS: With what, i' th' name of God?   75
OPHELIA: My lord, as I was sewing in my closet,°
     Lord Hamlet, with his doublet all unbraced,°
     No hat upon his head, his stockings fouled,
     Ungartered, and down-gyvèd° to his ankle,
     Pale as his shirt, his knees knocking each other,   80
     And with a look so piteous in purport
     As if he had been loosèd out of hell
     To speak of horrors—he comes before me.
POLONIUS: Mad for thy love?
OPHELIA: My lord, I do not know,
     But truly I do fear it.   85
POLONIUS: What said he?
OPHELIA: He took me by the wrist, and held me hard,
     Then goes he to the length of all his arm,
     And with his other hand thus o'er his brow,

---

60. **Videlicet:** namely 63. **reach:** ability 64. **windlasses:** roundabout approaches; 64. **assays of bias:**
indirect attempts 68. **God buy ye:** God be with you 76. **closet:** private room 77. **unbraced:** unlaced
79. **down-gyvèd:** hanging down, like gyves or fetters on a prisoner's ankles

He falls to such perusal of my face
As 'a would draw it. Long stayed he so.   90
At last, a little shaking of mine arm
And thrice his head thus waving up and down,
He raised a sigh so piteous and profound
As it did seem to shatter all his bulk
And end his being. That done, he lets me go,   95
And with his head over his shoulder turned,
He seemed to find his way without his eyes,
For out adoors he went without their helps,
And to the last bended their light on me.
POLONIUS: Come, go with me. I will go seek the king.   100
This is the very ecstasy° of love,
Whose violent property fordoes° itself,
And leads the will to desperate undertakings
As oft as any passion under heaven
That does afflict our natures. I am sorry.   105
What, have you given him any hard words of late?
OPHELIA: No, my good lord, but as you did command
I did repel his letters, and denied
His access to me.
POLONIUS: That hath made him mad.
I am sorry that with better heed and judgement   110
I had not quoted° him. I feared he did but trifle,
And meant to wrack° thee; but beshrew my jealousy.
By heaven, it is as proper to° our age
To cast beyond ourselves in our opinions
As it is common for the younger sort   115
To lack discretion. Come, go we to the king.
This must be known, which being kept close,° might move°
More grief to hide than hate to utter love.
Come.
(Exeunt.)

Scene 2

(Flourish. Enter KING *and* QUEEN, ROSENCRANTZ, *and* GUILDENSTERN *[and*
ATTENDANTS*].)*
KING: Welcome, dear Rosencrantz and Guildenstern.
Moreover that we much did long to see you,

---

101. ecstasy: madness **102. fordoes:** destroys **111. quoted:** observed **112. wrack:** ruin **113. proper to:**
characteristic of **117. close:** secret; **117. move:** cause

The need we have to use you did provoke
Our hasty sending. Something have you heard
Of Hamlet's transformation—so call it, 5
Sith° nor th' exterior nor the inward man
Resembles that it was. What it should be,
More than his father's death, that thus hath put him
So much from th' understanding of himself,
I cannot dream of. I entreat you both 10
That, being of so young days brought up with him,
And sith so neighboured to his youth and havior,
That you vouchsafe your rest here in our court
Some little time, so by your companies
To draw him on to pleasures, and to gather 15
So much as from occasion you may glean,
Whether aught to us unknown afflicts him thus,
That opened,° lies within our remedy.
QUEEN: Good gentlemen, he hath much talked of you,
And sure I am two men there is not living 20
To whom he more adheres. If it will please you
To show us so much gentry° and good will
As to expend your time with us awhile
For the supply and profit of our hope,
Your visitation shall receive such thanks 25
As fits a king's remembrance.
ROSENCRANTZ: Both your majesties
Might, by the sovereign power you have of us,
Put your dread pleasures more into command
Than to entreaty.
GUILDENSTERN: But we both obey,
And here give up ourselves in the full bent 30
To lay our service freely at your feet,
To be commanded.
KING: Thanks, Rosencrantz and gentle Guildenstern.
QUEEN: Thanks, Guildenstern and gentle Rosencrantz.
And I beseech you instantly to visit 35
My too much changed son. Go, some of you,
And bring these gentlemen where Hamlet is.
GUILDENSTERN: Heavens make our presence and our practices
Pleasant and helpful to him!

II.ii.6. Sith: since 18. opened: disclosed 22. gentry: courtesy

QUEEN: Ay, amen!
(Exeunt ROSENCRANTZ *and* GUILDENSTERN *with some* ATTENDANTS.*)*
(Enter POLONIUS.*)*
POLONIUS: Th' ambassadors from Norway, my good lord,   40
    Are joyfully returned.
KING: Thou still° hast been the father of good news.
POLONIUS: Have I, my lord? I assure my good liege,
    I hold my duty as I hold my soul,
    Both to my God and to my gracious king;   45
    And I do think—or else this brain of mine
    Hunts not the trail of policy so sure
    As it hath used to do—that I have found
    The very cause of Hamlet's lunacy.
KING: O, speak of that, that do I long to hear.   50
POLONIUS: Give first admittance to th' ambassadors.
    My news shall be the fruit to that great feast.
KING: Thyself do grace to them, and bring them in.
(Exit POLONIUS.*)*
    He tells me, my dear Gertrude, he hath found
    The head and source of all your son's distemper.   55
QUEEN: I doubt° it is no other but the main,
    His father's death and our o'erhasty marriage.
KING: Well, we shall sift him.
(Enter AMBASSADORS *[*VOLTEMAND *and* CORNELIUS*], with* POLONIUS.*)*
    Welcome, my good friends,
    Say, Voltemand, what from our brother Norway?   60
VOLTEMAND: Most fair return of greetings and desires.
    Upon our first, he sent out to suppress
    His nephew's levies, which to him appeared
    To be a preparation 'gainst the Polack,°
    But better looked into, he truly found   65
    It was against your highness, whereat grieved,
    That so his sickness, age, and impotence
    Was falsely borne in hand,° sends out arrests
    On Fortinbras, which he in brief obeys,
    Receives rebuke from Norway, and in fine,°   70
    Makes vow before his uncle never more
    To give th' assay° of arms against your majesty.

---

42. still: ever **56. doubt:** suspect **64. the Polack:** the Polish nation **68. borne in hand:** deceived **70. in fine:** in the end **72. assay:** trial

Whereon old Norway, overcome with joy,
Gives him three score thousand crowns in annual fee,
And his commission to employ those soldiers,   75
So levied as before, against the Polack,
With an entreaty, herein further shown, (*Gives a paper.*)
That it might please you to give quiet pass
Through your dominions for this enterprise,
On such regards° of safety and allowance   80
As therein are set down.

KING: It likes us well,
And at our more considered time we'll read,
Answer, and think upon this business.
Meantime we thank you for your well-took labor.
Go to your rest; at night we'll feast together.   85
Most welcome home!

(*Exeunt* AMBASSADORS.)

POLONIUS: This business is well ended.
My liege and madam, to expostulate
What majesty should be, what duty is,
Why day is day, night night, and time is time,
Were nothing but to waste night, day and time.   90
Therefore, since brevity is the soul of wit,°
And tediousness the limbs and outward flourishes,
I will be brief. Your noble son is mad.
Mad call I it, for to define true madness,
What is't but to be nothing else but mad?   95
But let that go.

QUEEN: More matter° with less art.

POLONIUS: Madam, I swear I use no art at all.
That he is mad, 'tis true: 'tis true 'tis pity.
And pity 'tis 'tis true. A foolish figure,
But farewell it, for I will use no art.   100
Mad let us grant him, then, and now remains
That we find out the cause of this effect,
Or rather say the cause of this defect,
For this effect defective comes by cause.
Thus it remains, and the remainder thus.   105
Perpend.°
I have a daughter—have while she is mine—
Who in her duty and obedience, mark,

---

80. **regards:** considerations 91. **wit:** understanding 96. **matter:** meaning, sense 106. **Perpend:** consider

Hath given me this. Now gather, and surmise. *(Reads.)*
'Tothe celestial, and my soul's idol, the most beautified Ophelia'—   110
That's an ill phrase, a vile phrase, 'beautified' is a vile phrase. But you
shall hear. Thus: *(Reads.)*
'In her excellent white bosom, these, etc.'
QUEEN: Came this from Hamlet to her?
POLONIUS: Good madam, stay awhile. I will be faithful.   115
(Reads letter.)
> 'Doubt thou the stars are fire,
> Doubt that the sun doth move;
> Doubt truth to be a liar;
> But never doubt I love.
'O dear Ophelia, I am ill at these numbers.° I have not art to reckon   120
my groans, but that I love thee best, O most best, believe it. Adieu.
> 'Thine evermore, most dear lady, whilst
> this machine° is to him, Hamlet.'
This in obedience hath my daughter shown me,
And more above, hath his solicitings,   125
As they fell out by time, by means and place,
All given to mine ear.
KING: But how hath she
Received his love?
POLONIUS: What do you think of me?
KING: As of a man faithful and honourable.
POLONIUS: I would fain prove so. But what might you think,   130
When I had seen this hot love on the wing,
(As I perceived it, I must tell you that,
Before my daughter told me), what might you,
Or my dear majesty your queen here, think,
If I had played° the desk or table-book,   135
Or given my heart a winking, mute and dumb,
Or looked upon this love with idle sight,
What might you think? No, I went round° to work,
And my young mistress thus I did bespeak:
'Lord Hamlet is a prince out of thy star.   140
This must not be'. and then I prescripts gave her,
That she should lock herself from his resort,
Admit no messengers, receive no tokens.
Which done, she took the fruits of my advice;

---

120. numbers: verses 123. machine: body 135. played...table-book: acted as silent go-between
138. round: directly

And he repelled, a short tale to make, 145
Fell into a sadness, then into a fast,
Thence to a watch,° thence into a weakness,
Thence to a lightness,° and, by this declension,
Into the madness wherein now he raves,
And all we mourn for. 150
KING: Do you think 'tis this?
QUEEN: It may be, very like.
POLONIUS: Hath there been such a time—I would fain know that—
That I have positively said ''Tis so,'
When it proved otherwise?
KING: Not that I know.
POLONIUS (*Pointing to his head and shoulder.*): Take this from this, if this be 155
otherwise:
If circumstances lead me, I will find
Where truth is hid, though it were hid indeed
Within the centre.°
KING: How may we try it further?
POLONIUS: You know, sometimes he walks four hours together
Here in the lobby. 160
QUEEN: So he does, indeed.
POLONIUS: At such a time I'll loose my daughter to him.
Be you and I behind an arras then.
Mark the encounter. If he love her not,
And be not from his reason fall'n thereon,
Let me be no assistant for a state, 165
But keep a farm and carters.
KING: We will try it.
(*Enter* HAMLET *reading on a book.*)
QUEEN: But look where sadly the poor wretch comes reading.
POLONIUS: Away, I do beseech you both away,
I'll board° him presently°.
(*Exeunt king and queen with attendants.*)
O, give me leave.
How does my good Lord Hamlet? 170
HAMLET: Well, God-a-mercy.
POLONIUS: Do you know me, my lord?
HAMLET: Excellent well, you are a fishmonger.
POLONIUS: Not I, my lord.

---

147. watch: sleeplessness 148. lightness: lightheadedness 158. centre: centre of the earth and of the Ptlolemaic universe 169. board: accost; 169. presently: immediately

HAMLET: Then I would you were so honest a man.   175

POLONIUS: Honest, my lord?

HAMLET: Ay, sir, to be honest as this world goes, is to be one man picked out of ten thousand.

POLONIUS: That's very true, my lord.

HAMLET: For if the sun breed maggots in a dead dog, being a good kissing   180
carrion—Have you a daughter?

POLONIUS: I have, my lord.

HAMLET: Let her not walk i' th' sun. Conception is a blessing, but as your daughter may conceive—friend, look to 't.

POLONIUS *(Aside.)*: How say you by that? Still harping on my daughter. Yet   185
he knew me not at first. 'A said I was a fishmonger. 'A is far gone. And truly in my youth I suffered much extremity for love, very near this. I'll speak to him again.—What do you read, my lord?

HAMLET: Words, words, words.

POLONIUS: What is the matter, my lord?   190

HAMLET: Between who?

POLONIUS: I mean the matter that you read, my lord.

HAMLET: Slanders, sir; for the satirical rogue says here that old men have grey beards, that their faces are wrinkled, their eyes purging thick amber and plum-tree gum, and that they have a plentiful lack of wit,   195
together with most weak hams—all which, sir, though I most power-fully and potently believe, yet I hold it not honesty to have it thus set down, for yourself, sir, shall grow old as I am, if like a crab you could go backward.

POLONIUS *(Aside.)*: Though this be madness, yet there is method in 't.—   200
Will you walk out of the air, my lord?

HAMLET: Into my grave?

POLONIUS *(Aside.)*: Indeed, that's out of the air. How pregnant° sometimes his replies are! a happiness° that often madness hits on, which reason and sanity could not so prosperously be delivered of. I will leave him,   205
and suddenly contrive the means of meeting between him and my daughter.—My lord, I will take my leave of you.

HAMLET: You cannot take from me anything that I will not more willingly part withal—except my life, except my life, except my life.

(Enter GUILDENSTERN *and* ROSENCRANTZ.*)*

POLONIUS: Fare you well, my lord.   210

HAMLET: These tedious old fools!

POLONIUS: You go to seek the Lord Hamlet. There he is.

ROSENCRANTZ   *(To* POLONIUS.*)*: *God save you, sir!*

(Exit POLONIUS.*)*

---

203. pregnant: full of meaning 204. happiness: aptness

GUILDENSTERN: My honored lord!

ROSENCRANTZ: My most dear lord! 215

HAMLET: My excellent good friends! How dost thou, Guildenstern?
Ah, Rosencrantz! Good lads, how do ye both?

ROSENCRANTZ: As the indifferent° children of the earth.

GUILDENSTERN: Happy in that we are not over-happy;
On Fortune's cap we are not the very button.° 220

HAMLET: Nor the soles of her shoe?

ROSENCRANTZ: Neither, my lord.

HAMLET: Then you live about her waist, or in the middle of her favors?

GUILDENSTERN: Faith, her privates we.

HAMLET: In the secret parts of Fortune? O, most true, she is a strumpet. 225
What news?

ROSENCRANTZ: None, my lord, but that the world's grown honest.

HAMLET: Then is doomsday near. But your news is not true. Let me question more in particular. What have you, my good friends, deserved at
the hands of Fortune, that she sends you to prison hither? 230

GUILDENSTERN: Prison, my lord!

HAMLET: Denmark's a prison.

ROSENCRANTZ: Then is the world one.

HAMLET: A goodly one, in which there are many confines, wards, and dun-
geons, Denmark being one o' th' worst. 235

ROSENCRANTZ: We think not so, my lord.

HAMLET: Why then 'tis none to you; for there is nothing either good or
bad, but thinking makes it so. To me it is a prison.

ROSENCRANTZ: Why then your ambition makes it one. 'Tis too narrow for
your mind. 240

HAMLET: O God, I could be bounded in a nutshell and count myself a king
of infinite space, were it not that I have bad dreams.

GUILDENSTERN: Which dreams indeed are ambition; for the very substance
of the ambitious is merely the shadow of a dream.

HAMLET: A dream itself is but a shadow. 245

ROSENCRANTZ: Truly, and I hold ambition of so airy and light a quality that
it is but a shadow's shadow.

HAMLET: Then are our beggars bodies, and, our monarchs and outstretched
heroes the beggars' shadows. Shall we to th' court? for, by my fay,° I
cannot reason. 250

BOTH: We'll wait upon you.

---

218. indifferent: average 220. button: knob on the top of the cap 249. fay: faith

HAMLET: No such matter. I will not sort you with° the rest of my servants;
for to speak to you like an honest man, I am most dreadfully attended.
But in the beaten way of friendship, what make you at Elsinore?

ROSENCRANTZ: To visit you, my lord; no other occasion.   255

HAMLET: Beggar that I am, I am ever poor in thanks, but I thank you; and
sure, dear friends, my thanks are too dear a halfpenny. Were you not
sent for? Is it your own inclining? Is it a free visitation? Come, come,
deal justly with me. Come, come, nay speak.

GUILDENSTERN: What should we say, my lord?   260

HAMLET: Anything but to the purpose. You were sent for, and there is a
kind of confession in your looks, which your modesties have not craft
enough to color. I know the good king and queen have sent for you.

ROSENCRANTZ: To what end, my lord?

HAMLET: That you must teach me. But let me conjure you by the rights of   265
our fellowship, by the consonancy of our youth, by the obligation of our
ever-preserved love, and by what more dear a better proposer can
charge you withal be even and direct with me whether you were sent
for or no.

ROSENCRANTZ *(Aside to* GUILDENSTERN.*)*: What say you?   270

HAMLET *(Aside.)*: Nay, then, I have an eye of you.—If you love me, hold
not off.

GUILDENSTERN: My lord, we were sent for.

HAMLET: I will tell you why; so shall my anticipation prevent° your discovery,° and your secrecy to the king and queen moult no feather. I have   275
of late—but wherefore I know not—lost all my mirth, forgone all custom of exercises; and indeed it goes so heavily with my disposition, that
this goodly frame the earth seems to me a sterile promontory, this most
excellent canopy the air, look you, this brave o'er-hanging firmament,
this majestical roof fretted° with golden fire, why it appeareth nothing   280
to me but a foul and pestilent congregation of vapors. What a piece of
work is a man, how noble in reason, how infinite in faculties, in form
and moving, how express and admirable in action, how like an angel
in apprehension, how like a god: the beauty of the world, the paragon
of animals. And yet to me, what is this quintessence of dust? Man   285
delights not me, nor woman neither, though by your smiling you seem
to say so.

ROSENCRANTZ: My lord, there was no such stuff in my thoughts.

HAMLET: Why did ye laugh, then, when I said 'Man delights not me'?

---

252. **sort you with:** put you in the same class with 274. **prevent:** forestall 275. **discovery:** disclosure
280. **fretted:** decorated with fretwork

ROSENCRANTZ: To think, my lord, if you delight not in man, what lenten°   290
  entertainment the players shall receive from you. We coted° them on
  the way, and hither are they coming to offer you service.

HAMLET: He that plays the king shall be welcome—his majesty shall have
  tribute on me; the adventurous knight shall use his foil and target;° the
  lover shall not sigh gratis; the humorous° man shall end his part in   295
  peace; the clown shall make those laugh whose lungs are tickle o' th'
  sere;° and the lady shall say her mind freely, or the blank verse shall
  halt° for 't. What players are they?

ROSENCRANTZ: Even those you were wont to take such delight in, the trage-
  dians of the city.   300

HAMLET: How chances it they travel? Their residence, both in reputation
  and profit, was better both ways.

ROSENCRANTZ: I think their inhibition° comes by the means of the late
  innovation.°

HAMLET: Do they hold the same estimation they did when I was in the city?   305
  Are they so followed?

ROSENCRANTZ: No, indeed, are they not.

HAMLET: How comes it? Do they grow rusty?

ROSENCRANTZ: Nay, their endeavour keeps in the wonted pace; but there is,
  sir, an eyrie° of children, little eyases,° that cry out on the top of ques-   310
  tion,° and are most tyrannically clapped for 't. These are now the fashion, and so berattle the common stages° (so they call them) that many
  wearing rapiers are afraid of goose quills° and dare scarce come thither.

HAMLET: What, are they children? Who maintains 'em? How are they
  escoted?° Will they pursue the quality° no longer than they can sing?°   315
  Will they not say afterwards, if they should grow themselves to common players (as it is most like, if their means are no better), their writers
  do them wrong to make them exclaim against their own succession?

ROSENCRANTZ: 'Faith, there has been much to do on both sides; and the
  nation holds it no sin to tarre° them to controversy. There was for a   320
  while no money bid for argument,° unless the poet and the player went
  to cuffs in the question.

---

290. lenten: scanty 291. coted: passed 294. foil and target: spear and shield 295. humorous man: the actor who plays the eccentric character dominated by one of the four humors 296-297. tickle o' th' sere: easily set off (**sere** is that part of a gunlock which keeps the hammer at full or half cock) 298. halt: limp 303. inhibition: prohibition of plays by authority 304. innovation: meaning uncertain 310. eyrie: nest; 310. eyases: nestling hawks (here, the boys in the children's companies training as actors) 310-311. on the top of question: louder than all others on matter of dispute 312. common stages: public theaters of the 312. common players: organized in companies composed mainly of adult actors 313. goose quills: pens (of the satiric dramatists writing for the private theaters) 314. escoted: maintained 315. pursue the quality: continue in the profession of acting 315. sing: i.e., until their voices change 320. tarre: incite 321. argument: plot of a play

HAMLET: Is't possible?

GUILDENSTERN: O, there has been much throwing about of brains.

HAMLET: Do the boys carry it away?   325

ROSENCRANTZ: Ay, that they do, my lord, Hercules and his load° too.

HAMLET: It is not very strange, for my uncle is King of Denmark, and those
that would make mouths° at him while my father lived give twenty,
forty, fifty, a hundred ducats apiece for his picture in little.° 'Sblood,
there is something in this more than natural, if philosophy could find   330
it out.

(*A flourish.*)

GUILDENSTERN: There are the players.

HAMLET: Gentlemen, you are welcome to Elsinore. Your hands. Come then
th' appurtenance° of welcome is fashion and ceremony. Let me comply-
with you in this garb, lest my extent° to the players, which I tell you   335
must show fairly outwards, should more appear like entertainment than
yours. You are welcome. But my uncle-father and aunt-mother are
deceived.

GUILDENSTERN: In what, my dear lord?

HAMLET: I am but mad north-north-west; when the wind is southerly I   340
know a hawk° from a handsaw.°

(*Enter* POLONIUS.)

POLONIUS: Well be with you, gentlemen.

HAMLET: Hark you, Guildenstern—and you too—at each ear a hearer. That
great baby you see there is not yet out of his swaddling clouts.

ROSENCRANTZ: Happily° he is the second time come to them, for they say   345
an old man is twice a child.

HAMLET: I will prophesy he comes to tell me of the players. Mark it.—You
say right, sir, a Monday morning, 'twas then indeed.

POLONIUS: My lord, I have news to tell you.

HAMLET: My lord, I have news to tell you. When Roscius° was an actor in   350
Rome—

POLONIUS: The actors are come hither, my lord.

HAMLET: Buzz, buzz.

POLONIUS: Upon my honor—

HAMLET: Then came each actor on his ass—   355

---

326. **load:** i.e., the world (the sign of the Globe theater represented Hercules bearing the world on his
shoulders) 328. **mouths:** grimaces 329. **in little:** in miniature 334. **appurtenance:** adjuncts 335. **extent:**
welcome 341. **hawk:** mattock or pickaxe (also called "hack," here used with a play on *hawk* as a bird)
341. **handsaw:** a saw managed with one hand (here used with a play on some corrupt form of *hernshaw*,
"heron") 345. **Happily:** perhaps 350. **Roscius:** the greatest of Roman comic actors, though regarded by the
Elizabethans as a tragic one

POLONIUS: The best actors in the world, either for tragedy, comedy, history, pastoral, pastoral-comical, historical-pastoral, tragical-historical, tragical-comical-historical-pastoral, scene individable,° or poem unlimited.° Seneca° cannot be too heavy nor Plautus° too light. For the law of writ and the liberty,° these are the only men.   360

HAMLET: O Jephthah,° judge of Israel, what a treasure hadst thou!

POLONIUS: What a treasure had he, my lord?

HAMLET: Why—

      'One fair daughter, and no more,
      The which he loved passing well.'   365

POLONIUS *(Aside.):* Still on my daughter.

HAMLET: Am I not i' th' right, old Jephthah?

POLONIUS: If you call me Jephthah, my lord, I have a daughter that I love passing well.

HAMLET: Nay, that follows not.   370

POLONIUS: What follows then, my lord?

HAMLET: Why—

      'As by lot, God wot,'
      and then, you know,
      'It came to pass, as most like it was.'   375

The first row° of the pious chanson will show you more, for look where my abridgement comes.

(Enter the PLAYERS.*)*

You are welcome, masters; welcome, all.—I am glad to see thee well.—Welcome, good friends. O, old friend! Why thy face is valanced° since I saw thee last. Come'st thou to beard me in Denmark?—What, my   380
young lady° and mistress? By'r lady, your ladyship is nearer to heaven than when I saw you last by the altitude of a chopine.° Pray God, your voice, like a piece of uncurrent gold, be not cracked within the ring.°—Masters, you are all welcome. We'll e'en to't like French falconers, fly at any thing we see. We'll have a speech straight.° Come give us a taste   385
of your quality, come a passionate speech.

1 PLAYER: What speech, my good lord?

---

358. **scene individable:** i.e., a play that observes the unities of time and place 358. **poem unlimited:** a play that does not observe the unities 359. **Seneca:** Roman writer of tragedies 359. **Plautus:** Roman comic dramatist 360. **law of writ and the liberty:** i.e., plays according to strict classical rules, and those that ignored the unities of time and place 361. **Jephthah:** was compelled to sacrifice a beloved daughter (Judges 2). Hamlet quotes from a contemporary ballad titled *Jephthah, Judge of Israel.* 376. **row:** stanza 379. **valanced:** bearded 381. **young lady:** i.e., the boy who plays female roles 382. **chopine:** a shoe with high cork heel and sole 383. **cracked within the ring:** a coin cracked within the circle surrounding the head of the sovereign was no longer legal tender and so *uncurrent* 385. **straight:** immediately

HAMLET: I heard thee speak me a speech once, but it was never acted, or if
it was, not above once, for the play, I remember, pleased not the million; 'twas caviary° to the general.° But it was—as I received it, and   390
others whose judgements in such matters cried in the top of mine—an
excellent play, well digested° in the scenes, set down with as much
modesty as cunning. I remember one said there were no sallets° in the
lines to make the matter savory, nor no matter in the phrase that might
indict the author of affectation, but called it an honest method, as   395
wholesome as sweet, and by very much more handsome than fine.° One
speech in't I chiefly loved. 'Twas Æneas' tale to Dido and thereabout of
it especially when he speaks of Priam's slaughter. If it live in your memory, begin at this line—let me see, let me see:
> 'The rugged Pyrrhus, like th' Hyrcanian beast'—°   400
'tis not so;—it begins with Pyrrhus—
> 'The rugged Pyrrhus, he whose sable arms,
> Black as his purpose, did the night resemble
> When he lay couchèd in the ominous horse,°
> Hath now this dread and black complexion smeared   405
> With heraldry more dismal; head to foot
> Now is he total gules,° horridly tricked°
> With blood of fathers, mothers, daughters, sons,
> Baked and impasted with the parching streets,
> That lend a tyrannous and a damnèd light   410
> To their lord's murder. Roasted in wrath and fire,
> And thus o'er-sizèd° with coagulate° gore,
> With eyes like carbuncles, the hellish Pyrrhus
>> Old grandsire Priam seeks.'
So, proceed you.   415

POLONIUS: Fore God, my lord, well spoken, with good accent and good
discretion.

1 PLAYER: 'Anon he finds him
> Striking too short at Greeks. His antique sword,
> Rebellious to his arm, lies where it falls,
> Repugnant° to command. Unequal matched,   420
> Pyrrhus at Priam drives, in rage strikes wide.
> But with the whiff and wind of his fell° sword
> Th' unnervèd father falls. Then senseless Ilium,

---

390. **caviary:** caviare; 390. **general:** multitude 392. **digested:** arranged 393. **sallets:** salads, highly
seasoned passages 396. **more handsome than fine:** admirable rather than appealing by mere cleverness
400. **Hyrcanian beast:** tiger 404. **horse:** i.e., the Trojan horse 407. **gules:** heraldic term for red
407. **tricked:** delineated 412. **o'er-sizèd:** covered as with size; 412. **coagulate:** clotted 421. **Repugnant:**
refractory 423. **fell:** fierce, cruel

Seeming to feel this blow, with flaming top   425
Stoops to his base, and with a hideous crash
Takes prisoner Pyrrhus' ear. For, lo! his sword,
Which was declining on the milky head
Of reverend Priam, seemed i' th' air to stick.
So as a painted tyrant Pyrrhus stood,   430
And like a neutral to his will and matter,
Did nothing.
But as we often see, against° some storm,
A silence in the heavens, the rack° stand still,
The bold winds speechless, and the orb below   435
As hush as death, anon the dreadful thunder
Doth rend the region;° so, after Pyrrhus' pause,
A rousèd vengeance sets him new awork,
And never did the Cyclops'° hammers fall
On Mars's armor, forged for proof° eterne   440
With less remorse than Pyrrhus' bleeding sword
Now falls on Priam.
Out, out, thou strumpet, Fortune! All you gods,
In general synod take away her power,
Break all the spokes and fellies° from her wheel,   445
And bowl the round nave° down the hill of heaven
As low as to the fiends.'
POLONIUS: This is too long.
HAMLET: It shall to the barber's with your beard.—Prithee, say on. He's for
a jig, or a tale of bawdry, or he sleeps. Say on, come to Hecuba.   450
1 PLAYER: 'But who, ah woe! had seen the mobled° queen—'
HAMLET: 'The mobled queen'?
POLONIUS: That's good.
1 PLAYER: 'Run barefoot up and down, threat'ning the flames
With bisson rheum;° a clout upon that head   455
Where late the diadem stood, and for a robe,
About her lank and all o'er-teemèd° loins,
A blanket, in the alarm of fear caught up—
Who this had seen, with tongue in venom steeped,
'Gainst Fortune's state° would treason have pronounced.   460
But if the gods themselves did see her then,
When she saw Pyrrhus make malicious sport

---

433. **against:** just before 434. **rack:** mass of cloud 437. **region:** air 439. **Cyclops:** giant workmen who made armor in the smithy of Vulcan 440. **proof eterne:** to be forever impenetrable 445. **fellies:** the curved pieces forming the rim of a wheel 446. **nave:** hub of a wheel 451. **mobled:** muffled 455. **bisson rheum:** blinding tears 457. **o'er-teemed:** exhausted by many births 460. **state:** government

In mincing with his sword her husband's limbs,
The instant burst of clamor that she made,
Unless things mortal move them not at all,   465
Would have made milch° the burning eyes of heaven,
And passion in the gods.'

POLONIUS: Look whe'r he has not turned his color, and has tears in's eyes.
Prithee no more.

HAMLET: 'Tis well. I'll have thee speak out the rest of this soon.—Good my   470
lord, will you see the players well bestowed? Do you hear, let them be
well used, for they are the abstract° and brief chronicles of the time;
after your death you were better have a bad epitaph than their ill report
while you live.

POLONIUS: My lord, I will use them according to their desert.   475

HAMLET: God's bodkin,° man, much better. Use every man after his desert,
and who shall 'scape whipping? Use them after your own honor and
dignity. The less they deserve, the more merit is in your bounty. Take
them in.

POLONIUS: Come, sirs.   480

HAMLET: Follow him, friends. We'll hear a play tomorrow. (*Aside to* 1 PLAYER.)
Dost thou hear me, old friend, can you play the 'Murder of Gonzago'?

1 PLAYER: Ay, my lord.

HAMLET: We'll ha't tomorrow night. You could for a need study a speech of
some dozen or sixteen lines which I would set down and insert in't,   485
could you not?

1 PLAYER: Ay, my lord.

HAMLET: Very well. Follow that lord, and look you mock him not.
(*Exeunt* POLONIUS *and* PLAYERS.)
My good friends, I'll leave you till night. You are welcome to Elsinore.

ROSENCRANTZ: Good my lord!   490
(*Exeunt* ROSENCRANTZ *and* GUILDENSTERN.)

HAMLET: Ay, so God by to you. Now I am alone.
O, what a rogue and peasant slave am I!
Is it not monstrous that this player here,
But in a fiction, in a dream of passion,
Could force his soul so to his own conceit°   495
That from her working all his visage wanned;
Tears in his eyes, distraction in his aspect,
A broken voice, and his whole function suiting
With forms to his conceit? And all for nothing,

---

466. milch: moist, tearful (lit., milk-giving) 472. abstract: summary account 476. God's bodkin: by God's
dear body 495. conceit: imagination

For Hecuba! 500
What's Hecuba to him or he to Hecuba,
That he should weep for her? What would he do
Had he the motive and the cue for passion
That I have? He would drown the stage with tears,
And cleave the general° ear with horrid speech, 505
Make mad the guilty, and appal the free,
Confound the ignorant, and amaze indeed
The very faculties of eyes and ears.
Yet I,
A dull and muddy-mettled° rascal, peak° 510
Like John-a-dreams, unpregnant° of my cause,
And can say nothing; no, not for a king
Upon whose property and most dear life
A damned defeat was made. Am I a coward?
Who calls me villain, breaks my pate across, 515
Plucks off my beard and blows it in my face,
Tweaks me by the nose, gives me the lie i' th' throat
As deep as to the lungs? Who does me this?
Ha, 'swounds, I should take it; for it cannot be
But I am pigeon-livered and lack gall 520
To make oppression bitter, or ere this
I should 'a fatted all the region kites°
With this slave's offal. Bloody, bawdy villain!
Remorseless, treacherous, lecherous, kindless° villain!
Why, what an ass am I! This is most brave, 525
That I, the son of a dear father murdered,
Prompted to my revenge by heaven and hell,
Must like a whore unpack my heart with words,
And fall a-cursing like a very drab,
A scullion!° Fie upon 't! foh! 530
About, my brains! Hum—I have heard
That guilty creatures sitting at a play,
Have by the very cunning of the scene
Been struck so to the soul that presently°
They have proclaimed their malefactions: 535
For murder, though it have no tongue, will speak
With most miraculous organ. I'll have these players

---

505. general: public **510. muddy-mettled:** dull-spirited; **510. peak:** mope **511. unpregnant:** not
quickened to action **522. region kites:** kites of the air **524. kindless:** unnatural **530. scullion:** kitchen
wench **534. presently:** immediately

Play something like the murder of my father
Before mine uncle. I'll observe his looks.
I'll tent° him to the quick. If 'a do blench,°   540
I know my course. The spirit that I have seen
May be the devil, and the devil hath power
T' assume a pleasing shape, yea, and perhaps
Out of my weakness and my melancholy,
As he is very potent with such spirits,   545
Abuses° me to damn me. I'll have grounds
More relative° than this. The play's the thing
Wherein I'll catch the conscience of the king.
(Exit.)

ACT III

Scene 1

(Enter KING, QUEEN, POLONIUS, OPHELIA, ROSENCRANTZ, GUILDENSTERN,
LORDS.*)*

KING: And can you by no drift of conference
   Get from him why he puts on this confusion,
   Grating so harshly all his days of quiet
   With turbulent and dangerous lunacy?
ROSENCRANTZ: He does confess he feels himself distracted,   5
   But from what cause 'a will by no means speak.
GUILDENSTERN: Nor do we find him forward° to be sounded,
   But with a crafty madness keeps aloof
   When we would bring him on to some confession
   Of his true state.   10
QUEEN: Did he receive you well?
ROSENCRANTZ: Most like a gentleman.
GUILDENSTERN: But with much forcing of his disposition.
ROSENCRANTZ: Niggard of question, but of our demands
   Most free in his reply.
QUEEN: Did you assay° him
   To any pastime?   15
ROSENCRANTZ: Madam, it so fell out that certain players
   We o'er-raught° on the way. Of these we told him,
   And there did seem in him a kind of joy

---

540. **tent:** probe; 540. **blench:** flinch 546. **Abuses:** deludes 547. **relative:** relevant III.i.7. **forward:** willing
14. **assay:** try to win 17. **o'erraught:** overtook

To hear of it. They are here about the court,
And as I think, they have already order   20
This night to play before him.
POLONIUS: 'Tis most true,
And he beseeched me to entreat your majesties
To hear and see the matter.
KING: With all my heart, and it doth much content me
To hear him so inclined.   25
Good gentlemen, give him a further edge,°
And drive his purpose into these delights.
ROSENCRANTZ: We shall, my lord.
(*Exeunt* ROSENCRANTZ *and* GUILDENSTERN.)
KING: Sweet Gertrude, leave us too;
For we have closely° sent for Hamlet hither,
That he, as 'twere by accident, may here   30
Affront° Ophelia.
Her father and myself (lawful espials)°
We'll so bestow ourselves that, seeing unseen,
We may of their encounter frankly judge,
And gather by him, as he is behaved,   35
If 't be th' affliction of his love or no
That thus he suffers for.
QUEEN: I shall obey you.—
And for your part, Ophelia, I do wish
That your good beauties be the happy cause
Of Hamlet's wildness. So shall I hope your virtues   40
Will bring him to his wonted way again,
To both your honors.
OPHELIA: Madam, I wish it may.
(*Exit* QUEEN *with* LORDS.)
POLONIUS: Ophelia, walk you here.—Gracious, so please you,
We will bestow ourselves.— (To OPHELIA.) Read on this book,
That show of such an exercise° may color°   45
Your loneliness.—We are oft to blame in this,
'Tis too much proved, that with devotion's visage
And pious action we do sugar o'er
The devil himself.
KING (*Aside.*):   O, 'tis too true.
How smart a lash that speech doth give my conscience!   50

---

26. **give him a further edge:** sharpen his inclination **29. closely:** privately **31. Affront:** meet face to face
32. espials: spies **45. exercise:** act of devotion; **45. color:** give an appearance of naturalness to

The harlot's cheek, beautied with plast'ring art,
Is not more ugly to° the thing that helps it
Then is my deed to my most painted word.
O heavy burden!
POLONIUS: I hear him coming. Let's withdraw, my lord.   55
(*Exeunt* KING *and* POLONIUS.)
(*Enter* HAMLET.)
HAMLET: To be, or not to be, that is the question:
    Whether 'tis nobler in the mind to suffer
    The slings and arrows of outrageous fortune,
    Or to take arms against a sea of troubles,
    And by opposing end them. To die, to sleep—   60
    No more; and by a sleep to say we end
    The heartache, and the thousand natural shocks
    That flesh is heir to: 'tis a consummation
    Devoutly to be wished. To die, to sleep—
    To sleep, perchance to dream, ay there's the rub;°   65
    For in that sleep of death what dreams may come
    When we have shuffled off this mortal coil°
    Must give us pause. There's the respect
    That makes calamity of so long life:
    For who would bear the whips and scorns of time,   70
    Th' oppressor's wrong, the proud man's contumely,
    The pangs of despised love, the law's delay,
    The insolence of office, and the spurns
    That patient merit of th' unworthy takes,
    When he himself might his quietus° make   75
    With a bare bodkin?° Who would fardels° bear,
    To grunt and sweat under a weary life,
    But that the dread of something after death,
    The undiscovered country, from whose bourn°
    No traveller returns, puzzles the will,   80
    And makes us rather bear those ills we have
    Than fly to others that we know not of?
    Thus conscience does make cowards of us all,
    And thus the native hue of resolution
    Is sicklied o'er with the pale cast of thought,   85
    And enterprises of great pitch° and moment
    With this regard° their currents turn awry

---

52. **to:** compared to 65. **rub:** obstacle (lit., obstruction encountered by bowler's ball) 67. **coil:** bustle, turmoil
75. **quietus:** settlement 76. **bodkin:** dagger; 76. **fardels:** burdens 79. **bourn:** realm 86. **pitch:** height
87. **regard:** consideration

And lose the name of action. Soft you now,
The fair Ophelia.—Nymph, in thy orisons°
Be all my sins remembered.   90
OPHELIA: Good my lord,
How does your honor for this many a day?
HAMLET: I humbly thank you, well.
OPHELIA: My lord, I have remembrances of yours
That I have longed long to re-deliver.
I pray you now receive them.   95
HAMLET: No, not I,
I never gave you aught.
OPHELIA: My honored lord, you know right well you did,
And with them words of so sweet breath composed
As made the things more rich. Their perfume lost,
Take these again, for to the noble mind   100
Rich gifts wax poor when givers prove unkind.
There, my lord.
HAMLET: Ha, ha! are you honest?°
OPHELIA: My lord?
HAMLET: Are you fair?   105
OPHELIA: What means your lordship?
HAMLET: That if you be honest and fair, your honesty should admit no dis-
course to your beauty.
OPHELIA: Could beauty, my lord, have better commerce than with honesty?
HAMLET: Ay, truly, for the power of beauty will sooner transform honesty   110
from what it is to a bawd than the force of honesty can translate beauty
into his likeness. This was sometime a paradox, but now the time gives
it proof. I did love you once.
OPHELIA: Indeed, my lord, you made me believe so.
HAMLET: You should not have believed me, for virtue cannot so inoculate°   115
our old stock but we shall relish of it. I loved you not.
OPHELIA: I was the more deceived.
HAMLET: Get thee to a nunnery. Why wouldst thou be a breeder of sinners?
I am myself indifferent° honest, but yet I could accuse me of such
things that it were better my mother had not borne me: I am very   120
proud, revengeful, ambitious, with more offences at my beck than I
have thoughts to put them in, imagination to give them shape, or time
to act them in. What should such fellows as I do crawling between

---

89. orisons: prayers **103. honest:** chaste **115. inoculate:** graft **119. indifferent honest:** moderately
respectable

earth and heaven? We are arrant knaves all; believe none of us. Go thy
ways to a nunnery. Where's your father?   125

OPHELIA: At home, my lord.

HAMLET: Let the doors be shut upon him, that he may play the fool nowhere but in's own house. Farewell.

OPHELIA: O, help him, you sweet heavens!

HAMLET: If thou dost marry, I'll give thee this plague for thy dowry: be thou   130
as chaste as ice, as pure as snow, thou shalt not escape calumny. Get
thee to a nunnery, farewell. Or if thou wilt needs marry, marry a fool,
for wise men know well enough what monsters you make of them. To a
nunnery, go, and quickly too. Farewell.

OPHELIA: Heavenly powers, restore him!   135

HAMLET: I have heard of your paintings well enough. God hath given you
one face, and you make yourselves another. You jig and amble, and you
lisp; you nickname God's creatures, and make your wantonness your ignorance.° Go to, I'll no more on't, it hath made me mad. I say we will
have no moe° marriage. Those that are married already, all but one,   140
shall live. The rest shall keep as they are. To a nunnery, go.

(Exit.)

OPHELIA: O, what a noble mind is here o'erthrown!
The courtier's, soldier's, scholar's, eye, tongue, sword,
Th' expectancy° and rose of the fair state,
The glass° of fashion and the mould of form,   145
Th' observed of all observers, quite quite down!
And I of ladies most deject and wretched,
That sucked the honey of his musiced vows,
Now see that noble and most sovereign reason
Like sweet bells jangled, out of time and harsh;   150
That unmatched form and feature of blown° youth
Blasted with ecstasy.° O, woe is me
T' have seen what I have seen, see what I see!

(Enter KING *and* POLONIUS.*)*

KING: Love? His affections° do not that way tend,
Nor what he spake, though it lacked form a little,   155
Was not like madness. There's something in his soul,
O'er which his melancholy sits on brood,
And I do doubt° the hatch and the disclose
Will be some danger; which for to prevent,

138–139. **make your wantonness your ignorance:** excuse your wanton behavior with the plea that you
don't know any better 140. **moe:** more 144. **expectancy:** hope 145. **glass:** mirror 151. **blown:** blooming
152. **ecstasy:** madness 154. **affections:** emotions 158. **doubt:** fear

I have in quick determination 160
Thus set it down: he shall with speed to England
For the demand of our neglected tribute.
Haply the seas and countries different,
With variable objects, shall expel
This something-settled matter in his heart 165
Whereon his brains still beating puts him thus
From fashion of himself. What think you on't?
POLONIUS: It shall do well. But yet do I believe
The origin and commencement of his grief
Sprung from neglected love.—How now, Ophelia? 170
You need not tell us what Lord Hamlet said;
We heard it all.—My lord, do as you please,
But if you hold it fit, after the play
Let his queen-mother all alone entreat him
To show his grief. Let her be round° with him, 175
And I'll be placed, so please you, in the ear
Of all their conference. If she find him not,
To England send him; or confine him where
Your wisdom best shall think.
KING: It shall be so.
Madness in great ones must not unwatched go. 180
(*Exeunt.*)

Scene 2

(*Enter* HAMLET *and three of the* PLAYERS.)
HAMLET: Speak the speech, I pray you, as I pronounced it to you, trippingly
on the tongue; but if you mouth it as many of our players do, I had as
lief the town-crier spoke my lines. Nor do not saw the air too much
with your hand thus, but use all gently, for in the very torrent, tempest,
and as I may say, whirlwind of your passion, you must acquire and beget 5
a temperance that may give it smoothness. O, it offends me to the soul
to hear a robustious periwig-pated fellow tear a passion to tatters, to
very rags, to split the ears of the groundlings,° who for the most part are
capable of nothing but inexplicable dumb shows and noise. I would
have such a fellow whipped for o'erdoing Termagant.° It out-Herods 10
Herod.° Pray you avoid it.
1 PLAYER: I warrant your honour.

---

175. round: plain-spoken III.ii.8. **groundlings**: spectators who paid least and stood on the ground
10. Termagant: thought to be a Saracen deity, and represented in medieval mystery plays as a violent and
ranting personage **11. Herod**: represented in the mystery plays as a blustering tyrant

HAMLET: Be not too tame neither, but let your own discretion be your
    tutor. Suit the action to the word, the word to the action, with this spe-
    cial observance, that you o'erstep not the modesty of nature; for any   15
    thing so o'erdone is from the purpose of playing, whose end both at the
    first, and now, was and is, to hold as 'twere the mirror up to nature, to
    show virtue her own feature, scorn her own image, and the very age
    and body of the time his form and pressure. Now this overdone, or
    come tardy off, though it make the unskilful laugh, cannot but make   20
    the judicious grieve, the censure° of the which one must in your allow-
    ance o'erweigh a whole theatre of others. O, there be players that I
    have seen play—and heard others praise, and that highly—not to speak
    it profanely, that neither having th' accent of Christians, nor the gait
    of Christian, pagan, nor man, have so strutted and bellowed that I have   25
    thought some of nature's journeymen had made men, and not made
    them well, they imitated humanity so abominably.

1 PLAYER: I hope we have reformed that indifferently° with us.

HAMLET: O, reform it altogether. And let those that play your clowns speak
    no more than is set down for them, for there be of them that will them-   30
    selves laugh, to set on some quantity of barren spectators to laugh too,
    though in the meantime some necessary question of the play be then to
    be considered. That's villanous, and shows a most pitiful ambition in
    the fool that uses it. Go, make you ready.

(Exeunt PLAYERS.*)*

(Enter POLONIUS, GUILDENSTERN, *and* ROSENCRANTZ.*)*

    How now, my lord? Will the king hear this piece of work?   35

POLONIUS: And the queen too, and that presently.

HAMLET: Bid the players make haste. *(Exit* POLONIUS.*)* Will you two help to
    hasten them?

ROSENCRANTZ: Ay, my lord.

(Exeunt they two.)

HAMLET: What, ho! Horatio!   40

(Enter HORATIO.*)*

HORATIO: Here, sweet lord, at your service.

HAMLET: Horatio, thou art e'en as just a man
    As e'er my conversation coped° withal.

HORATIO: O my dear lord!

HAMLET: Nay, do not think I flatter,
    For what advancement may I hope from thee,   45
    That no revenue hast but thy good spirits
    To feed and clothe thee? Why should the poor be flattered?

---

21. **censure:** judgment, opinion 28. **indifferently:** fairly well 43. **coped:** encountered

No, let the candied tongue lick absurd pomp,
And crook the pregnant° hinges of the knee
Where thrift° may follow fawning. Dost thou hear?   50
Since my dear soul was mistress of her choice
And could of men distinguish her election,°
S'hath sealed thee for herself, for thou hast been
As one in suff'ring all that suffers nothing,
A man that Fortune's buffets and rewards   55
Hast ta'en with equal thanks; and blest are those
Whose blood and judgment are so well co-meddled°
That they are not a pipe for Fortune's finger
To sound what stop she please. Give me that man
That is not passion's slave, and I will wear him   60
In my heart's core, ay, in my heart of heart,
As I do thee. Something too much of this.
There is a play to-night before the king.
One scene of it comes near the circumstance
Which I have told thee of my father's death.   65
I prithee, when thou seest that act afoot,
Even with the very comment of thy soul°
Observe my uncle. If his occulted° guilt
Do not itself unkennel° in one speech,
It is a damnèd ghost that we have seen,   70
And my imaginations are as foul
As Vulcan's stithy.° Give him heedful note,
For I mine eyes will rivet to his face,
And after we will both our judgements join
In censure° of his seeming.   75
HORATIO: Well, my lord.
    If 'a steal aught the whilst this play is playing,
    And 'scape detecting, I will pay the theft.
(Enter Trumpets and Kettledrums, KING, QUEEN, POLONIUS, OPHELIA, [ROSEN-
    CRANTZ, GUILDENSTERN, and other LORDS attendant].)
HAMLET: They are coming to the play. I must be idle.°
    Get you a place.
KING: How fares our cousin Hamlet?   80
HAMLET: Excellent, i' faith, of the chameleon's dish.° I eat the air, promise-
    crammed. You cannot feed capons so.

---

49. **pregnant:** ready 50. **thrift:** profit 52. **election:** choice 57. **co-meddled:** mingled 67. **the very
comment of thy soul:** with a keenness of observation that penetrates to the very being 68. **occulted:**
hidden 69. **unkennel:** reveal 72. **stithy:** forge 75. **censure:** opinion 78. **idle:** crazy 81. **chameleon's dish:**
the air, on which the chameleon was supposed to feed

KING: I have nothing with this answer, Hamlet. These words are not mine.

HAMLET: No, nor mine now. *(To* POLONIUS.*)* My lord, you played once i' th'
university, you say?   85

POLONIUS: That did I, my lord; and was accounted a good actor.

HAMLET: What did you enact?

POLONIUS: I did enact Julius Caesar. I was killed i' th' Capitol; Brutus killed
me.

HAMLET: It was a brute part of him to kill so capital a calf there. Be the   90
players ready?

ROSENCRANTZ: Ay, my lord, they stay upon your patience.

QUEEN: Come hither, my dear Hamlet, sit by me.

HAMLET: No, good mother, here's metal more attractive.

POLONIUS *(To the* KING.*)*: O, ho! do you mark that?   95

HAMLET: Lady, shall I lie in your lap?

(Lying down at OPHELIA*'s feet.)*

OPHELIA: No, my lord.

HAMLET: I mean, my head upon your lap?

OPHELIA: Ay, my lord.

HAMLET: Do you think I meant country matters?   100

OPHELIA: I think nothing, my lord.

HAMLET: That's a fair thought to lie between maids' legs.

OPHELIA: What is, my lord?

HAMLET: Nothing.

OPHELIA: You are merry, my lord.   105

HAMLET: Who, I?

OPHELIA: Ay, my lord.

HAMLET: O God, your only jig-maker! What should a man do but be merry?
For look you how cheerfully my mother looks, and my father died within's two hours.   110

OPHELIA: Nay, 'tis twice two months, my lord.

HAMLET: So long? Nay then, let the devil wear black, for I'll have a suit of
sables. O heavens! die two months ago, and not forgotten yet? Then
there's hope a great man's memory may outlive his life half a year, but,
by'r lady 'a must build churches then, or else shall 'a suffer not thinking   115
on, with the hobby-horse,° whose epitaph is
'For O, for O, the hobby-horse is forgot!'

(The trumpets sound. Dumb Show follows.)

(Enter a KING *and a* QUEEN *[very lovingly];* the QUEEN *embracing him and he*

---

115. **hobby-horse:** the figure of a horse fastened round the waist of a morris dancer. Puritan efforts to
suppress the country sports in which the hobby-horse figured led to a popular ballad lamenting the fact that
"the hobby-horse is forgot"

her. She kneels, and makes show of protestation unto him. He takes her up, and declines his head upon her neck. He lies him down upon a bank of flowers; she, seeing him asleep, leaves him. Anon comes in another man, takes off his crown, kisses it, pours poison in the sleeper's ears, and leaves him. The QUEEN *returns, finds the* KING *dead, makes passionate action. The* POISONER *with some three or four come in again, seem to condole with her. The dead body is carried away. The* POISONER *woos the* QUEEN *with gifts; she seems harsh awhile, but in the end accepts love.)*

(Exeunt.)

OPHELIA: What means this, my lord?

HAMLET: Marry, this is miching mallecho;° it means mischief.

OPHELIA: Belike this show imports the argument of the play. 120

(Enter PROLOGUE.*)*

HAMLET: We shall know by this fellow. The players cannot keep counsel; they'll tell all.

OPHELIA: Will 'a tell us what this show meant?

HAMLET: Ay, or any show that you will show him. Be not you ashamed to show, he'll not shame to tell you what it means. 125

OPHELIA: You are naught,° you are naught. I'll mark the play.

PROLOGUE: For us, and for our tragedy,
　　Here stooping to your clemency,
　　We beg your hearing patiently.

(Exit.)

HAMLET: Is this a prologue, or the posy° of a ring? 130

OPHELIA: 'Tis brief, my lord.

HAMLET: As woman's love.

(Enter the PLAYER KING *and* QUEEN.*)*

PLAYER KING: Full thirty times hath Phoebus' cart° gone round
　　Neptune's salt wash and Tellus' orbèd ground,°
　　And thirty dozen moons with borrowed sheen 135
　　About the world have times twelve thirties been,
　　Since love our hearts and Hymen° did our hands
　　Unite comutual in most sacred bands.

PLAYER QUEEN: So many journeys may the sun and moon
　　Make us again count o'er ere love be done! 140
　　But woe is me, you are so sick of late,
　　So far from cheer and from your former state,
　　That I distrust° you. Yet though I distrust,

---

119. **miching mallecho:** skulking or crafty crime 126. **naught:** naughty, lewd 130. **posy:** brief motto engraved on a ring 133. **Phoebus' cart:** the sun's chariot 134. **Tellus' orbed ground:** the earth (Tellus was the Roman goddess of the earth) 137. **Hymen:** god of marriage 143. **distrust:** fear for

Discomfort you, my lord, it nothing must.
For women's fear and love hold quantity,°   145
In neither aught, or in extremity.
Now what my love is proof hath made you know,
And as my love is sized,° my fear is so.
Where love is great, the littlest doubts are fear;
Where little fears grow great, great love grows there.   150
PLAYER KING: Faith, I must leave thee, love, and shortly too;
    My operant° powers their functions leave to do.
    And thou shalt live in this fair world behind,
    Honored, beloved; and haply one as kind
    For husband shalt thou—   155
PLAYER QUEEN: O, confound the rest!
    Such love must needs be treason in my breast.
    In second husband let me be accurst!
    None wed the second but who killed the first.
HAMLET: That's wormwood.
PLAYER QUEEN: The instances° that second marriage move   160
    Are base respects of thrift, but none of love.
    A second time I kill my husband dead,
    When second husband kisses me in bed.
PLAYER KING: I do believe you think what now you speak,
    But what we do determine oft we break.   165
    Purpose is but the slave to memory,
    Of violent birth, but poor validity;°
    Which now, like fruit unripe, sticks on the tree,
    But fall unshaken when they mellow be.
    Most necessary 'tis that we forget   170
    To pay ourselves what to ourselves is debt.
    What to ourselves in passion we propose,
    The passion ending, doth the purpose lose.
    The violence of either grief or joy
    Their own enactures° with themselves destroy.   175
    Where joy most revels, grief doth most lament;
    Grief joys, joy grieves, on slender accident.
    This world is not for aye,° nor 'tis not strange
    That even our loves should with our fortunes change;
    For 'tis a question left us yet to prove,   180

---

145. **hold quantity:** are proportional, weigh alike 148. **as my love is sized:** according to the greatness of my love 152. **operant:** vital 160. **instances:** motives 167. **validity:** endurance 175. **enactures:** enactments 178. **aye:** ever

Whether love lead fortune, or else fortune love.
The great man down, you mark his favorite flies;
The poor advanced makes friends of enemies;
And hitherto doth love on fortune tend,
For who not needs shall never lack a friend, 185
And who in want a hollow friend doth try,
Directly seasons him° his enemy.
But orderly to end where I begun,
Our wills and fates do so contrary run
That our devices still are overthrown; 190
Our thoughts are ours, their ends none of our own.
So think thou wilt no second husband wed,
But die thy thoughts when thy first lord is dead.

PLAYER QUEEN: Nor earth to me give food, nor heaven light,
Sport and repose lock from me day and night. 195
To desperation turn my trust and hope,
An anchor's° cheer in prison be my scope,
Each opposite that blanks the face of joy
Meet what I would have well, and it destroy,
Both here and hence pursue me lasting strife, 200
If once a widow, ever I be wife!

HAMLET: If she should break it now!

PLAYER KING: 'Tis deeply sworn. Sweet, leave me here awhile.
My spirits grow dull, and fain I would beguile
The tedious day with sleep. 205

(Sleeps.)

PLAYER QUEEN: Sleep rock thy brain.
And never come mischance between us twain!

(Exit.)

HAMLET: Madam, how like you this play?

QUEEN: The lady doth protest too much, methinks.

HAMLET: O, but she'll keep her word.

KING: Have you heard the argument? Is there no offence in't? 210

HAMLET: No, no, they do but jest, poison in jest; no offence i' th' world.

KING: What do you call the play?

HAMLET: 'The Mouse-trap.' Marry, how? Tropically. This play is the image
of a murder done in Vienna. Gonzago is the duke's name; his wife, Bap-
tista. You shall see anon. 'Tis a knavish piece of work, but what of that? 215
Your majesty, and we that have free souls, it touches us not. Let the
galled jade° winch, our withers are unwrung.

---

187. seasons him: ripens him into 197. anchor's: anchorite's 217. galled jade: sorebacked horse

(*Enter* LUCIANUS.)
     This is one Lucianus, nephew to the king.
OPHELIA: You are as good as a chorus, my lord.
HAMLET: I could interpret between you and your love, if I could see the   220
     puppets dallying.
OPHELIA: You are keen, my lord, you are keen.
HAMLET: It would cost you a groaning to take off mine edge.
OPHELIA: Still better, and worse.
HAMLET: So you mis-take your husbands.—Begin, murderer. Leave thy dam-   225
     nable faces and begin. Come, the croaking raven doth bellow for
     revenge.
LUCIANUS: Thoughts black, hands apt, drugs fit, and time agreeing,
     Confederate season, else no creature seeing.
     Thou mixture rank, of midnight weeds collected,   230
     With Hecate's° ban thrice blasted°, thrice infected,
     Thy natural magic and dire property
     On wholesome life usurp immediately.
(*Pours the poison in his ears.*)
HAMLET: 'A poisons him i' th' garden for his estate. His name's Gonzago.
     The story is extant, and written in very choice Italian. You shall see   235
     anon how the murderer gets the love of Gonzago's wife.
OPHELIA: The king rises.
HAMLET: What, frighted with false fire?
QUEEN: How fares my lord?
POLONIUS: Give o'er the play.   240
KING: Give me some light. Away!
POLONIUS: Lights, lights, lights!
(*Exeunt all but* HAMLET *and* HORATIO.)
HAMLET: Why, let the strucken deer go weep,
     The hart ungallèd play.
     For some must watch, while some must sleep;   245
     Thus runs the world away.
     Would not this, sir, and a forest of feathers°—if the rest of my fortunes
     turn Turk with me—with two Provincial roses° on my razed° shoes, get
     me a fellowship in a cry° of players?
HORATIO: Half a share.   250
HAMLET: A whole one, I.
     For thou dost know, O Damon dear,
     This realm dismantled was

---

231. **Hecate:** goddess of witchcraft;   231. **blasted:** fallen under a blight 247. **feathers:** plumes for actors'
costumes 248. **Provincial roses:** i.e., Provençal roses. Ribbon rosettes resembling these French roses were
used to decorate shoes 248. **razed:** with ornamental slashing 249. **cry:** company

Of Jove himself, and now reigns here
A very, very—pajock.° 255
HORATIO: You might have rhymed.
HAMLET: O good Horatio, I'll take the ghost's word for a thousand pound.
Didst perceive?
HORATIO: Very well, my lord.
HAMLET: Upon the talk of the poisoning. 260
HORATIO: I did very well note him.
HAMLET: Ah, ha! Come, some music. Come, the recorders.
For if the king like not the comedy,°
Why then, belike, he likes it not, perdy.
Come, some music. 265

(*Enter* ROSENCRANTZ *and* GUILDENSTERN.)

GUILDENSTERN: Good my lord, vouchsafe me a word with you.
HAMLET: Sir, a whole history.
GUILDENSTERN: The king, sir—
HAMLET: Ay, sir what of him?
GUILDENSTERN: Is in his retirement marvellous distempered. 270
HAMLET: With drink, sir?
GUILDENSTERN: No, my lord, with choler.°
HAMLET: Your wisdom should show itself more richer to signify this to the
doctor, for for me to put him to his purgation would perhaps plunge
him into more choler. 275
GUILDENSTERN: Good my lord, put your discourse into some frame, and
start not so wildly from my affair.
HAMLET: I am tame, sir. Pronounce.
GUILDENSTERN: The queen, your mother, in most great affliction of spirit,
hath sent me to you. 280
HAMLET: You are welcome.
GUILDENSTERN: Nay, good my lord, this courtesy is not of the right breed. If
it shall please you to make me a wholesome° answer, I will do your
mother's commandment. If not, your pardon and my return shall be the
end of my business. 285
HAMLET: Sir, I cannot.
GUILDENSTERN: What, my lord?
HAMLET: Make you a wholesome answer; my wit's diseased. But, sir, such
answer as I can make, you shall command, or rather, as you say, my
mother. Therefore no more, but to the matter. My mother, you say— 290

---

255. **pajock:** presumably a variant form of "patch-cock," a despicable person. 263. **For if…comedy:** a
seeming parody of *The Spanish Tragedy*, 4.1.197-98 ("And if the world like not this tragedy, / Hard is the
hap of old Hieronimo"), where another revenger's dramatic entertainment is referred to 272. **choler:** one of
the four bodily humors, an excess of which gave rise to anger 283. **wholesome:** reasonable

ROSENCRANTZ: Then thus she says: your behaviour hath struck her into amazement and admiration.

HAMLET: O wonderful son, that can so stonish a mother! But is there no se-quel at the heels of this mother's admiration?° Impart.

ROSENCRANTZ: She desires to speak with you in her closet ere you go to bed.   295

HAMLET: We shall obey, were she ten times our mother. Have you any fur-ther trade with us?

ROSENCRANTZ: My lord, you once did love me.

HAMLET: And do still, by these pickers and stealers.°   300

ROSENCRANTZ: Good my lord, what is your cause of distemper? You do surely bar the door upon your own liberty, if you deny your griefs to your friend.

HAMLET: Sir, I lack advancement.

ROSENCRANTZ: How can that be, when you have the voice of the king him-self for your succession in Denmark?   305

HAMLET: Ay, sir, but 'While the grass grows'°—the proverb is something musty.

(Enter the PLAYERS *with recorders.)*

O, the recorders! Let me see one. To withdraw° with you—why do you go about to recover the wind of me, as if you would drive me into a toil?°   310

GUILDENSTERN: O, my lord, if my duty be too bold, my love is too unmannerly.

HAMLET: I do not well understand that. Will you play upon this pipe?

GUILDENSTERN: My lord, I cannot.   315

HAMLET: I pray you.

GUILDENSTERN: Believe me, I cannot.

HAMLET: I beseech you.

GUILDENSTERN: I know no touch of it, my lord.

HAMLET: It is easy as lying. Govern these ventages° with your fingers and thumb, give it breath with your mouth, and it will discourse most elo-quent music. Look you, these are the stops.   320

GUILDENSTERN: But these cannot I command to any utt'rance of harmony. I have not the skill.

HAMLET: Why look you now, how unworthy a thing you make of me! You would play upon me, you would seem to know my stops, you would pluck out the heart of my mystery, you would sound me from my lowest note to the top of my compass; and there is music, excellent voice, in   325

---

this little organ, yet cannot you make it speak. 'Sblood, do you think I
am easier to be played on than a pipe? Call me what instrument you   330
will, though you can fret° me, you cannot play upon me.

(Enter POLONIUS.*)*

God bless you, sir!

POLONIUS: My lord, the queen would speak with you, and presently.

HAMLET: Do you see yonder cloud that's almost in shape of a camel?

POLONIUS: By th' mass and 'tis, like a camel indeed.   335

HAMLET: Methinks it is like a weasel.

POLONIUS: It is backed like a weasel.

HAMLET: Or like a whale.

POLONIUS: Very like a whale.

HAMLET: Then I will come to my mother by and by. *(Aside.)* They fool me   340
to the top of my bent.—I will come by and by.

POLONIUS: I will say so.

(Exit POLONIUS.*)*

HAMLET: 'By and by' is easily said. Leave me, friends.

(Exeunt all but HAMLET.*)*

'Tis now the very witching time of night,
When churchyards yawn and hell itself breathes out   345
Contagion to this world. Now could I drink hot blood,
And do such bitter business as the day
Would quake to look on. Soft, now to my mother.
O heart, lose not thy nature; let not ever
The soul of Nero° enter this firm bosom.   350
Let me be cruel, not unnatural;
I will speak daggers to her, but use none.
My tongue and soul in this be hypocrites:
How in my words somedever° she be shent°,
To give them seals never my soul consent!   355

(Exit.)

Scene 3

(Enter KING, ROSENCRANTZ, *and* GUILDENSTERN.*)*

KING: I like him not, nor stands it safe with us
To let his madness range. Therefore prepare you.
I your commission will forthwith dispatch,
And he to England shall along with you.
The terms of our estate° may not endure   5

---

331. fret: (1) a stop on the fingerboard of a guitar (2) annoy **350. Nero:** Roman emperor who murdered his
mother **354. somever:** soever; **354. shent:** reproved, abused **III.iii.5. terms of our estate:** conditions
required for our rule as king

Hazard so near's as doth hourly grow
Out of his brows.°
GUILDENSTERN: We will ourselves provide,
 Most holy and religious fear it is
 To keep those many many bodies safe   10
 That live and feed upon your majesty.
ROSENCRANTZ: The single and peculiar° life is bound
 With all the strength and armor of the mind
 To keep itself from noyance,° but much more
 That spirit upon whose weal depends and rests   15
 The lives of many. The cess° of majesty
 Dies not alone, but like a gulf doth draw
 What's near it with it. It is a massy wheel
 Fixed on the summit of the highest mount,
 To whose huge spokes ten thousand lesser things   20
 Are mortised° and adjoined, which when it falls,
 Each small annexment, petty consequence,
 Attends the boist'rous ruin. Never alone
 Did the king sigh, but with a general groan.
KING: Arm you, I pray you, to this speedy voyage,   25
 For we will fetters put about this fear,
 Which now goes too free-footed.
ROSENCRANTZ: We will haste us.
(*Exeunt Gentlemen* ROSENCRANTZ *and* GUILDENSTERN.)
(*Enter* POLONIUS.)
POLONIUS: My lord, he's going to his mother's closet.
 Behind the arras I'll convey myself
 To hear the process. I'll warrant she'll tax him home,   30
 And as you said, and wisely was it said,
 'Tis meet that some more audience than a mother,
 Since nature makes them partial, should o'erhear
 The speech of vantage.° Fare you well, my liege.
 I'll call upon you ere you go to bed,   35
 And tell you what I know.
KING: Thanks, dear my lord.
 (*Exit* POLONIUS.)
 O, my offence is rank, it smells to heaven;
 It hath the primal eldest curse upon't,
 A brother's murder. Pray can I not,

---

7. **brows:** threatening looks that suggest the dangerous plots Hamlet's brain is hatching **12. peculiar:**
private **14. noyance:** harm **16. cess:** cessation, extinction **21. mortised:** jointed (as with mortise and
tenon) **34. of vantage:** (1) in addition; (2) from a convenient place for listening

Though inclination be as sharp as will.° 40
My stronger guilt defeats my strong intent,
And like a man to double business bound,
I stand in pause where I shall first begin,
And both neglect. What if this cursèd hand
Were thicker than itself with brother's blood, 45
Is there not rain enough in the sweet heavens
To wash it white as snow? Whereto serves mercy
But to confront the visage of offence?
And what's in prayer but this twofold force,
To be forestallèd ere we come to fall, 50
Or pardoned being down? Then I'll look up.
My fault is past. But, O, what form of prayer
Can serve my turn? 'Forgive me my foul murder'?
That cannot be, since I am still possessed
Of those effects for which I did the murder— 55
My crown, mine own ambition, and my queen.
May one be pardoned and retain th' offence?
In the corrupted currents of this world
Offence's gilded hand may shove by justice,
And oft 'tis seen the wicked prize itself 60
Buys out the law. But 'tis not so above
There is no shuffling:° there the action° lies
In his true nature, and we ourselves compelled,
Even to the teeth and forehead of our faults,
To give in evidence. What then? What rests? 65
Try what repentance can. What can it not?
Yet what can it when one can not repent?
O wretched state! O bosom black as death!
O limèd° soul, that struggling to be free
Art more engaged! Help, angels! Make assay.° 70
Bow, stubborn knees, and heart with strings of steel,
Be soft as sinews of the new-born babe.
All may be well.

(*He kneels.*)

(*Enter* HAMLET.)

HAMLET: Now might I do it pat, now 'a is a-praying,
And now I'll do't—and so 'a goes to heaven, 75
And so am I revenged. That would be scanned.

---

40. will: carnal desire **62. shuffling:** doubledealing **62. action:** legal action **69. limèd:** soul caught by sin as the bird by lime **70. assay:** an effort

A villain kills my father, and for that,
I, his sole son, do this same villain send
To heaven.
Why, this is hire and salary, not revenge.   80
'A took my father grossly,° full of bread,
With all his crimes broad blown, as flush as May;°
And how his audit stands who knows save heaven?
But in our circumstance° and course of thought°
'Tis heavy with him; and am I then revenged   85
To take him in the purging of his soul,
When he is fit and seasoned for his passage?
No.
Up, sword, and know thou a more horrid hent.°
When he is drunk asleep, or in his rage,   90
Or in th' incestuous pleasure of his bed,
At game a-swearing, or about some act
That has no relish of salvation in't—
Then trip him, that his heels may kick at heaven,
And that his soul may be as damned and black   95
As hell, whereto it goes. My mother stays.
This physic but prolongs thy sickly days.
(*Exit.*)
KING (*Rising.*): My words fly up, my thoughts remain below.
     Words without thoughts never to heaven go.
(*Exit.*)

Scene 4

(*Enter* QUEEN GERTRUDE *and* POLONIUS.)
POLONIUS: 'A will come straight. Look you lay home to him.
     Tell him his pranks have been too broad to bear with,
     And that your grace hath screened and stood between
     Much heat and him. I'll silence me even here.
     Pray you be round.°   5
QUEEN: I'll warrant you. Fear me not.
     Withdraw, I hear him coming.
(POLONIUS *goes behind the arras.*)
(*Enter* HAMLET.)
HAMLET: Now, mother, what's the matter?

---

81. grossly: unprepared spiritually 82. as flush as May: in full flower 84. in our circumstance: considering all evidence; 84. course: beaten way, habit 89. hent: occasion, opportunity III.iv.5.: Following Polonius's "Pray you be round"

QUEEN: Hamlet, thou hast thy father much offended.

HAMLET: Mother, you have my father much offended.

QUEEN: Come, come, you answer with an idle tongue. 10

HAMLET: Go, go, you question with a wicked tongue.

QUEEN: Why, how, now, Hamlet?

HAMLET: What's the matter now?

QUEEN: Have you forgot me?

HAMLET: No, by the rood,° not so:
    You are the queen, your husband's brother's wife,
    And would it were not so, you are my mother. 15

QUEEN: Nay, then I'll set those to you that can speak.

HAMLET: Come, come, and sit you down. You shall not budge.
    You go not till I set you up a glass
    Where you may see the inmost part of you.

QUEEN: What will thou do? Thou wilt not murder me? 20
    Help, ho!

POLONIUS (*Behind.*): What, ho! help!

HAMLET (*Draws.*): How now! a rat?
    Dead for a ducat, dead!

(*Thrusts his sword through the arras and kills* POLONIUS.)

POLONIUS (*Behind.*): O, I am slain! 25

QUEEN: O me, what hast thou done?

HAMLET: Nay, I know not.
    Is it the king?

QUEEN: O, what a rash and bloody deed is this!

HAMLET: A bloody deed? Almost as bad, good mother,
    As kill a king and marry with his brother. 30

QUEEN: As kill a king?

HAMLET: Ay, lady, it was my word.
    (*Lifts up the arras and sees the body of* POLONIUS.)
    Thou wretched, rash, intruding fool, farewell!
    I took thee for thy better. Take thy fortune.
    Thou find'st to be too busy is some danger.—
    Leave wringing of your hands. Peace, sit you down 35
    And let me wring your heart, for so I shall
    If it be made of penetrable stuff,
    If damnèd custom have not brazed° it so
    That it be proof° and bulwark against sense.

QUEEN: What have I done that thou dar'st wag thy tongue 40
    In noise so rude against me?

---

13. rood: cross **38. brazed:** plated it as with brass **39. proof:** impenetrable, as of armor

HAMLET: Such an act
        That blurs the grace and blush of modesty,
        Calls virtue hypocrite, takes off the rose
        From the fair forehead of an innocent love,
        And sets a blister there, makes marriage-vows   45
        As false as dicers' oaths. O, such a deed
        As from the body of contraction° plucks
        The very soul, and sweet religion makes
        A rhapsody of words. Heaven's face does glow
        O'er this solidity and compound mass°   50
        With heated visage, as against the doom—°
        Is thought-sick at the act.
QUEEN: Ay me, what act,
        That roars so loud, and thunders in the index?°
HAMLET: Look here, upon this picture and on this.
        The counterfeit presentment° of two brothers.   55
        See what a grace was seated on this brow:
        Hyperion's curls, the front° of Jove himself,
        An eye like Mars, to threaten and command,
        A station° like the herald Mercury
        New lighted on a heaven-kissing hill—   60
        A combination and a form indeed
        Where every god did seem to set his seal
        To give the world assurance of a man.
        This was your husband. Look you now what follows.
        Here is your husband, like a mildewed ear   65
        Blasting his wholesome brother. Have you eyes?
        Could you on this fair mountain leave to feed,
        And batten° on this moor? Ha! have you eyes?
        You cannot call it love, for at your age
        The heyday° in the blood is tame, it's humble,   70
        And waits upon the judgement, and what judgement
        Would step from this to this? Sense° sure you have,
        Else could you not have motion, but sure that sense
        Is apoplexed, for madness would not err
        Nor sense to ecstasy° was ne'er so thralled   75
        But it reserved some quantity of choice
        To serve in such a difference. What devil was't

---

47. contraction: the contract of marriage 50. this solidity and compound mass: the earth, as compounded of the four elements 51. doom: Judgment Day 53. index: table of contents; thus, indication of what is to follow 55. counterfeit presentment: portrait 57. front: forehead 59. station: bearing figure 68. batten: feed like an animal 70. heyday: ardor 72. Sense: the senses collectively, which according to Aristotelian tradition are found in all creatures that have the power of locomotion 75. ecstasy: madness

That thus hath cozened you at hoodman-blind?°
Eyes without feeling, feeling without sight,
Ears without hands or eyes, smelling sans° all,   80
Or but a sickly part of one true sense
Could not so mope.° O shame! where is thy blush?
Rebellious hell,
If thou canst mutine in a matron's bones,
To flaming youth let virtue be as wax   85
And melt in her own fire. Proclaim no shame
When the compulsive ardor gives the charge,
Since frost itself as actively doth burn,
And reason pandars will.°
QUEEN: O Hamlet, speak no more!
Thou turn'st mine eyes into my very soul,   90
And there I see such black and grainèd spots°
As will not leave their tinct.°
HAMLET: Nay, but to live
In the rank sweat of an enseamèd° bed,
Stewed in corruption, honeying and making love
Over the nasty sty—   95
QUEEN: O, speak to me no more!
These words like daggers enter in mine ears.
No more, sweet Hamlet.
HAMLET: A murderer and a villain,
A slave that is not twentieth part the tithe
Of your precedent lord, a vice° of kings,
A cutpurse of the empire and the rule,   100
That from a shelf the precious diadem stole
And put it in his pocket—
QUEEN: No more.
(*Enter* GHOST.)
HAMLET: A king of shreds and patches—
Save me and hover o'er me with your wings,   105
You heavenly guards! What would your gracious figure?
QUEEN: Alas, he's mad.
HAMLET: Do you not come your tardy son to chide,
That lapsed in time and passion lets go by
Th' important acting of your dread command?   110
O, say!

---

78. **hoodman-blind:** blindman's bluff 80. **sans:** without 82. **mope:** act without full use of one's wits
89. **will:** desire 91. **grainèd spots:** indelible stains 92. **tinct:** color 93. **enseamèd:** greasy 99. **vice:** a
character in the morality plays, presented often as a buffoon (here, a caricature)

GHOST: Do not forget. This visitation
    Is but to whet thy almost blunted purpose.
    But look, amazement on thy mother sits.
    O, step between her and her fighting soul!   115
    Conceit° in weakest bodies strongest works.
    Speak to her, Hamlet.
HAMLET: How is it with you, lady?
QUEEN: Alas, how is't with you,
    That you do bend your eye on vacancy,
    And with th' incorporal air do hold discourse?   120
    Forth at your eyes your spirits wildly peep,
    And as the sleeping soldiers in th' alarm,
    Your bedded hair like life in excrements°
    Start up and stand an° end. O gentle son,
    Upon the heat and flame of thy distemper   125
    Sprinkle cool patience. Whereon do you look?
HAMLET: On him, on him! Look you how pale he glares.
    His form and cause conjoined, preaching to stones,
    Would make them capable.°—Do not look upon me,
    Lest with this piteous action you convert   130
    My stern effects. Then what I have to do
    Will want° true color—tears perchance for blood.
QUEEN: To whom do you speak this?
HAMLET: Do you see nothing there?
QUEEN: Nothing at all, yet all that is I see.   135
HAMLET: Nor did you nothing hear?
QUEEN: No, nothing but ourselves.
HAMLET: Why, look you there. Look, how it steals away.
    My father, in his habit as he lived!
    Look where he goes even now out at the portal.   140
(*Exit* GHOST.)
QUEEN: This is the very coinage of your brain.
    This bodiless creation ecstasy
    Is very cunning in.
HAMLET: My pulse as yours doth temperately keep time,
    And makes us healthful music. It is not madness   145
    That I have uttered. Bring me to the test,
    And I the matter will re-word, which madness
    Would gambol° from. Mother, for love of grace,

---

116. Conceit: imagination 123. excrements: nails, hair (whatever grows out of the body) 124. an: on
129. capable: able to respond 132. want: lack 148. gambol: leap or start, as a shying horse

Lay not that flattering unction° to your soul,
That not your trespass but my madness speaks.   150
It will but skin and film the ulcerous place
Whiles rank corruption, mining° all within,
Infects unseen. Confess yourself to heaven,
Repent what's past, avoid what is to come,
And do not spread the compost on the weeds,   155
To make them ranker. Forgive me this my virtue,
For in the fatness° of these pursy° times
Virtue itself of vice must pardon beg,
Yea, curb and woo for leave to do him good.
QUEEN: O Hamlet, thou hast cleft my heart in twain.   160
HAMLET: O, throw away the worser part of it,
And live the purer with the other half.
Good night—but go not to my uncle's bed.
Assume a virtue, if you have it not.
That monster custom, who all sense doth eat,°   165
Of habits devil,° is angel yet in this,
That to the use of actions fair and good
He likewise gives a frock or livery
That aptly is put on. Refrain to-night,
And that shall lend a kind of easiness   170
To the next abstinence; the next more easy;
For use almost can change the stamp of nature,
And either curb the devil, or throw him out
With wondrous potency. Once more, good night,
And when you are desirous to be blest,   175
I'll blessing beg of you. For this same lord,
I do repent; but heaven hath pleased it so,
To punish me with this, and this with me,
That I must be their scourge and minister.
I will bestow him and will answer well   180
The death I gave him. So, again, good night.
I must be cruel only to be kind.
This° bad begins and worse remains behind.°
One word more, good lady.

---

149. **unction:** ointment; hence, soothing notion 152. **mining:** undermining 157. **fatness:** grossness, slackness; 157. **pursy:** corpulent 165. **who all sense doth eat:** who consumes all human sense, both bodily and spiritual 166. **Of habits devil:** being a devil in, or in respect of, habits (with a play on "habits," as meaning both settled practices and garments, whereby devilish practices contrast with "actions fair and good," line 167, and devilish garments contrast with the "frock or livery" of line 168, which custom in its angelic aspect provides) 183. **This:** i.e., the death of Polonius (cf. line 24); 183. **remains behind:** is yet to come

QUEEN: What shall I do?

HAMLET: Not this, by no means, that I bid you do: 185
    Let the bloat king tempt you again to bed,
    Pinch wanton on your cheek, call you his mouse,
    And let him, for a pair of reechy° kisses,
    Or paddling in your neck with his damned fingers,
    Make you to ravel all this matter out,   190
    That I essentially° am not in madness,
    But mad in craft. 'Twere good you let him know,
    For who that's but a queen, fair, sober, wise,
    Would from a paddock,° from a bat, a gib°,
    Such dear concernings hide? Who would so do?   195
    No, in despite of sense and secrecy,
    Unpeg° the basket on the house's top,
    Let the birds fly, and like the famous ape,
    To try conclusions, in the basket creep
    And break your own neck down.   200

QUEEN: Be thou assured, if words be made of breath
    And breath of life, I have no life to breathe
    What thou hast said to me.

HAMLET: I must to England; you know that?

QUEEN: Alack,
    I had forgot. 'Tis so concluded on.   205

HAMLET: There's letters sealed, and my two school-fellows,
    Whom I will trust as I will adders fanged,
    They bear the mandate; they must sweep my way
    And marshal me to knavery. Let it work,
    For 'tis the sport to have the engineer   210
    Hoist with his own petar;° and 't shall go hard
    But I will delve one yard below their mines
    And blow them at the moon. O, 'tis most sweet
    When in one line two crafts directly meet.
    This man shall set me packing.   215
    I'll lug the guts into the neighbour room.
    Mother, good night indeed.° This counsellor
    Is now most still, most secret and most grave,

---

188. reechy: dirty 191. essentially: in fact 194. paddock: toad; 194. gib: tom-cat 197. Unpeg the basket
. . . neck down: the story is lost (in it, apparently, the ape carries a cage of birds to the top of a house,
releases them by accident, and, surprised at their flight, imagines he can imitate it by first creeping into the
basket and then leaping out. The moral of the story, for the queen, is not to expose herself to destruction by
making public what good sense decrees should be kept secret.) 211. petar: a bomb or charge for blowing in
gates 217. indeed: in earnest

Who was in life a foolish prating knave.
Come sir, to draw toward an end with you.   220
Good night, mother.
(*Exit* HAMLET *tugging in* POLONIUS.)

ACT IV

Scene 1

(*Enter* KING [*to the*] QUEEN, *with* ROSENCRANTZ *and* GUILDENSTERN.)°
KING: There's matter in these sighs, these profound heaves,
        You must translate,° 'tis fit we understand them.
        Where is your son?
QUEEN: Bestow this place on us a little while.
(*Exeunt* ROSENCRANTZ *and* GUILDENSTERN.)
        Ah, mine own lord, what have I seen to-night!   5
KING: What, Gertrude, how does Hamlet?
QUEEN: Mad as the sea and wind when both contend
        Which is the mightier. In his lawless fit,
        Behind the arras hearing something stir,
        Whips out his rapier, cries 'A rat, a rat!'   10
        And in this brainish apprehension° kills
        The unseen good old man.
KING: O heavy deed!
        It had been so with us had we been there.
        His liberty is full of threats to all—
        To you yourself, to us, to every one.   15
        Alas, how shall this bloody deed be answered?
        It will be laid to us, whose providence
        Should have kept short, restrained, and out of haunt,°
        This mad young man. But so much was our love,
        We would not understand what was most fit,   20
        But like the owner of a foul disease,
        To keep it from divulging, let it feed
        Even on the pith of life. Where is he gone?
QUEEN: To draw apart the body he hath killed,
        O'er whom his very madness, like some ore   25
        Among a mineral° of metals base,
        Shows itself pure: 'a weeps for what is done.

IV.i, **stage direction:** The action is continuous with that of the preceding scene. The Queen does not leave
the stage. **2. translate:** explain **11. brainish apprehension:** frenzied delusion **18. out of haunt:** away
from society **26. mineral:** mine

KING: O Gertrude, come away!
   The sun no sooner shall the mountains touch
   But we will ship him hence, and this vile deed   30
   We must with all our majesty and skill,
   Both countenance and excuse. Ho, Guildenstern!
(*Enter* ROSENCRANTZ *and* GUILDENSTERN.)
   Friends both, go join you with some further aid.
   Hamlet in madness hath Polonius slain,
   And from his mother's closet hath he dragged him.   35
   Go seek him out; speak fair, and bring the body
   Into the chapel. I pray you haste in this.
(*Exeunt* ROSENCRANTZ *and* GUILDENSTERN.)
   Come, Gertrude, we'll call up our wisest friends
   And let them know both what we mean to do
   And what's untimely done; so haply slander—   40
   Whose whisper o'er the world's diameter,
   As level as° the cannon to his blank°,
   Transports his poisoned shot—may miss our name,
   And hit the woundless air. O, come away!
   My soul is full of discord and dismay.   45
(*Exeunt.*)

Scene 2

(*Enter* HAMLET.)
HAMLET: Safely stowed.—But soft, what noise? who calls on Hamlet? O,
   here they come.
(*Enter* ROSENCRANTZ, GUILDENSTERN, *and* OTHERS.)
ROSENCRANTZ: What have you done, my lord, with the dead body?
HAMLET: Compounded it with dust, whereto 'tis kin.
ROSENCRANTZ: Tell us where 'tis, that we may take it thence   5
   And bear it to the chapel.
HAMLET: Do not believe it.
ROSENCRANTZ: Believe what?
HAMLET: That I can keep your counsel and not mine own. Besides, to be
   demanded of a sponge—what replication° should be made by the son of   10
   a king?
ROSENCRANTZ: Take you me for a sponge, my lord?
HAMLET: Ay, sir, that soaks up the king's countenance, his rewards, his
   authorities. But such officers do the king best service in the end. He

---

42. **As level as:** sure of aim; 42. **blank:** target **IV.2.10. replication:** reply

keeps them, like an apple in the corner of his jaw, first mouthed to be   15
last swallowed. When he needs what you have gleaned, it is but squeezing you and, sponge, you shall be dry again.

ROSENCRANTZ: I understand you not, my lord.

HAMLET: I am glad of it. A knavish speech sleeps in a foolish ear.

ROSENCRANTZ: My lord, you must tell us where the body is, and go with us   20
to the king.

HAMLET: The body is with the king, but the king is not with the body. The
king is a thing—

GUILDENSTERN: A thing, my lord!

HAMLET: Of nothing. Bring me to him. Hide fox, and all after.°   25

(*Exeunt.*)

Scene 3

(*Enter* KING, *and two or three.*)

KING: I have sent to seek him, and to find the body.
How dangerous is it that this man goes loose!
Yet must not we put the strong law on him.
He's loved of the distracted multitude,
Who like not in their judgement but their eyes,   5
And where 'tis so, th' offender's scourge is weighed,
But never the offence. To bear all smooth and even,
This sudden sending him away must seem
Deliberate pause.° Diseases desperate grown
By desperate appliance are relieved,   10
Or not at all.

(*Enter* ROSENCRANTZ, GUILDENSTERN, *and all the rest.*)
                    How now! what hath befall'n?

ROSENCRANTZ: Where the dead body is bestowed, my lord,
We cannot get from him.

KING: But where is he?

ROSENCRANTZ: Without, my lord; guarded, to know your pleasure.

KING: Bring him before us.   15

ROSENCRANTZ: Ho! bring in the lord.

(*They enter with* HAMLET.)

KING: Now, Hamlet, where's Polonius?

HAMLET: At supper.

KING: At supper? Where?

HAMLET: Not where he eats, but where 'a is eaten. A certain convocation
of politic worms are e'en at him. Your worm is your only emperor for   20

---

25. Hide fox, and all after: presumably a cry in some game such as hide-and-seek. The words, which do
not occur in *Q2*, may be an actor's addition **IV.iii.9. Deliberate pause:** carefully considered

diet. We fat all creatures else to fat us, and we fat ourselves for maggots. Your fat king and your lean beggar is but variable service—two dishes, but to one table. That's the end.

KING: Alas, alas!

HAMLET: A man may fish with the worm that hath eat of a king, and eat of   25
the fish that hath fed of that worm.

KING: What dost thou mean by this?

HAMLET: Nothing but to show you how a king may go a progress° through the guts of a beggar.

KING: Where is Polonius?   30

HAMLET: In heaven. Send thither to see. If your messenger find him not there, seek him i' th' other place yourself. But if, indeed, you find him not within this month, you shall nose him as you go up the stairs into the lobby.

KING (*To* ATTENDANTS.): Go seek him there.   35

HAMLET: 'A will stay till you come.

(*Exeunt* ATTENDANTS.)

KING: Hamlet, this deed, for thine especial safety—
Which we do tender,° as we dearly grieve
For that which thou hast done—must send thee hence
With fiery quickness. Therefore prepare thyself.   40
The bark is ready, and the wind at help,
Th' associates tend, and everything is bent
For England.

HAMLET: For England?

KING: Ay, Hamlet.

HAMLET: Good.

KING: So is it, if thou knew'st our purposes.

HAMLET: I see a cherub° that sees them. But come, for England! Farewell,   45
dear mother.

KING: Thy loving father, Hamlet.

HAMLET: My mother. Father and mother is man and wife, man and wife is one flesh. So, my mother. Come, for England.

(*Exit.*)

KING: Follow him at foot: tempt him with speed aboard.   50
Delay it not: I'll have him hence to-night.
Away! for every thing is sealed and done
That else leans on th' affair. Pray you make haste.

(*Exeunt all but the* KING.)

And, England, if my love thou hold'st at aught—

---

28. progress: the state journey of a ruler 38. tender: value 45. cherub: one of the cherubim, the watchmen or sentinels of heaven, and thus endowed with the keenest vision

As my great power thereof may give thee sense,   55
Since yet thy cicatrice° looks raw and red
After the Danish sword, and thy free awe
Pays homage to us—thou mayst not coldly set°
Our sovereign process,° which imports at full
By letters congruing to° that effect   60
The present death of Hamlet. Do it, England.
For like the hectic° in my blood he rages,
And thou must cure me. Till I know 'tis done,
Howe'er my haps,° my joys were ne'er begun.
(Exit.)

Scene 4

(Enter FORTINBRAS *with his* ARMY *over the stage.)*
FORTINBRAS: Go, captain, from me greet the Danish king.
    Tell him that by his license Fortinbras
    Craves the conveyance° of a promised march
    Over his kingdom. You know the rendezvous.
    If that his majesty would aught with us,   5
    We shall express our duty in his eye,°
    And let him know so.
CAPTAIN: I will do't, my lord.
FORTINBRAS: Go softly on.
(Exeunt all but the CAPTAIN.*)*
(Enter HAMLET, ROSENCRANTZ, GUILDENSTERN, *and* OTHERS.*)*
HAMLET: Good sir, whose powers are these?
CAPTAIN: They are of Norway, sir.
HAMLET: How purposed, sir, I pray you?   10
CAPTAIN: Against some part of Poland.
HAMLET: Who commands them, sir?
CAPTAIN: The nephew to old Norway, Fortinbras.
HAMLET: Goes it against the main° of Poland, sir,   15
    Or for some frontier?
CAPTAIN: Truly to speak, and with no addition,°
    We go to gain a little patch of ground
    That hath in it no profit but the name.
    To pay° five ducats, five, I would not farm it;   20

---

56. **cicatrice:** scar, used here of memory of a defeat 58. **coldly set:** regard with indifference 59. **process:** mandate 60. **congruing to:** in accordance with 62. **hectic:** consumptive fever 64. **haps:** fortunes IV.iv.3. **conveyance:** conduct 6. **eye:** presence 15. **main:** chief part 17. **addition:** exaggeration 20. **To pay:** i.e., for a yearly rental

Nor will it yield to Norway or the Pole
A ranker rate° should it be sold in fee.

HAMLET: Why, then the Polack never will defend it.

CAPTAIN: Yes, it is already garrisoned.

HAMLET: Two thousand souls and twenty thousand ducats   25
Will not debate the question of this straw.
This is th' imposthume° of much wealth and peace,
That inward breaks, and shows no cause without
Why the man dies. I humbly thank you, sir.

CAPTAIN: God buy you, sir.   30

(Exit.)

ROSENCRANTZ: Will 't please you go, my lord?

HAMLET: I'll be with you straight. Go a little before.

(Exeunt all but HAMLET.)

How all occasions do inform° against me,
And spur my dull revenge! What is a man,
If his chief good and market° of his time
Be but to sleep and feed? A beast, no more.   35
Sure he that made us with such large discourse,°
Looking before and after, gave us not
That capability and godlike reason
To fust° in us unused. Now, whether it be
Bestial oblivion, or some craven scruple   40
Of thinking too precisely on th' event—
A thought which, quartered, hath but one part wisdom
And ever three parts coward—I do not know
Why yet I live to say 'This thing's to do',
Sith I have cause, and will, and strength, and means,   45
To do 't. Examples gross as earth exhort me:
Witness this army of such mass and charge,
Led by a delicate and tender prince,
Whose spirit, with divine ambition puffed,
Makes mouths at° the invisible event,   50
Exposing what is mortal and unsure
To all that fortune, death, and danger dare,
Even for an eggshell. Rightly to be great°

---

22. a ranker rate: a greater price; sold in fee sold with absolute and perpetual possession
27. imposthume: abscess 32. inform: take shape 34. market: profit 36. discourse: power of reasoning
39. fust: grow musty 50. Makes mouths at: makes scornful faces at, derides 53. Rightly to be great...
honor's at the stake: i.e., to be rightly great is *not* to refuse to act ("stir") in a dispute ("argument")
because the grounds are insufficient, but to be moved to action even in trivial circumstances where a
question of honor is involved

Is not to stir without great argument,
But greatly to find quarrel in a straw   55
When honor's at the stake. How stand I then,
That have a father killed, a mother stained,
Excitements of my reason and my blood,
And let all sleep, while to my shame I see
The imminent death of twenty thousand men   60
That for a fantasy and trick of fame
Go to their graves like beds, fight for a plot
Whereon the numbers cannot try the cause,°
Which is not tomb enough and continent°
To hide the slain? O, from this time forth,   65
My thoughts be bloody, or be nothing worth!
(Exit.)

Scene 5

(Enter HORATIO, QUEEN GERTRUDE, *and a* GENTLEMAN.*)*
QUEEN: I will not speak with her.
GENTLEMAN: She is importunate, indeed distract.
    Her mood will needs be pitied.
QUEEN: What would she have?
GENTLEMAN: She speaks much of her father, says she hears
    There's tricks i' th' world, and hems, and beats her heart,   5
    Spurns enviously at straws,° speaks things in doubt
    That carry but half sense. Her speech is nothing,°
    Yet the unshaped use° of it doth move
    The hearers to collection;° they aim° at it,
    And botch the words up fit to their own thoughts,   10
    Which, as her winks and nods and gestures yield them,
    Indeed would make one think there might be thought,
    Though nothing sure,° yet much unhappily.
HORATIO: 'Twere good she were spoken with, for she may strew
    Dangerous conjectures in ill-breeding minds.   15
QUEEN: Let her come in. *(Exit Gentleman.)*
    (Aside.) To my sick soul, as sin's true nature is,
    Each toy° seems prologue to some great amiss.
    So full of artless jealousy° is guilt,
    It spills° itself in fearing to be spilt.   20
(Enter OPHELIA *[distracted].)*

---

63. **try the cause:** settle by combat 64. **continent:** receptacle IV.v.6. **Spurns enviously at straws:** takes exception, spitefully, to trifles 7. **nothing:** nonsense 8. **unshaped use:** disordered manner 9. **collection:** attempts at shaping meaning; 9. **aim:** guess 13. **sure:** certain 18. **toy:** trifle 19. **artless jealousy:** ill-concealed suspicion 20. **spills:** destroys

OPHELIA: Where is the beauteous majesty of Denmark?
QUEEN: How now, Ophelia!
OPHELIA *(She sings.)*: How should I your true love know
                    From another one?
                    By his cockle hat° and staff,   25
                    And his sandal shoon.°
QUEEN: Alas, sweet lady, what imports this song?
OPHELIA: Say you? Nay, pray you mark. *(Song.)*
                    He is dead and gone, lady,
                    He is dead and gone;   30
                    At his head a grass-green turf,
                    At his heels a stone.
                    O, ho!
QUEEN: Nay, but Ophelia—
OPHELIA: Pray you mark.
(Sings.)
    White his shroud as the mountain snow—   35
(Enter KING.)
QUEEN: Alas, look here, my lord.
OPHELIA *(Song.)*: Larded° all with sweet flowers;
    Which bewept to the grave did not go
                    With true-love showers.
KING: How do you, pretty lady?   40
OPHELIA: Well, good dild you!° They say the owl was a baker's daughter.° Lord,
    we know what we are, but know not what we may be. God be at your table!
KING: Conceit upon her father.°
OPHELIA: Pray let's have no words of this, but when they ask you what it
    means, say you this: 45
    (Song.)
                    To-morrow is Saint Valentine's day,
    All in the morning betime,°
    And I a maid at your window,
    To be your Valentine.
    Then up he rose, and donned his clo'es,   50
    And dupped° the chamber-door,
    Let in the maid, that out a maid
                    Never departed more.

---

25. **cockle hat:** hat bearing a cockle shell,worn by a pilgrim who had been to the shrine of St. James of Compostella, in Spain 26. **shoon:** shoes 37. **Larded:** garnished, strewn 41. **good dild you:** God yield (requite) you 41. **They say the owl was a baker's daughter:** allusion to a folktale in which a baker's daughter was transformed into an owl because of her ungenerous behavior (giving short measure) when Christ asked for bread in the baker's shop 43. **Conceit upon her father:** i.e., obsessed with her father's death 47. **betime:** early 51. **dupped:** opened

KING: Pretty Ophelia—

OPHELIA: Indeed, without an oath, I'll make an end on't: 55
>   (*Sings.*)
>> By Gis° and by Saint Charity,
>> Alack, and fie for shame!
>> Young men will do't, if they come to't;
>> By cock,° they are to blame.
>> Quoth she 'Before you tumbled me,   60
>> You promised me to wed.'
>> He answers:
>> 'So would I a' done, by yonder sun,
>> An thou hadst not come to my bed.'

KING: How long hath she been thus?   65

OPHELIA: I hope all will be well. We must be patient, but I cannot choose
>   but weep, to think they would lay him i' th' cold ground. My brother
>   shall know of it, and so I thank you for your good counsel. Come, my
>   coach! Good night, ladies, good night. Sweet ladies, good night, good
>   night.   70

(*Exit.*)

KING: Follow her close; give her good watch, I pray you.
>   (*Exeunt* HORATIO *and* GENTLEMEN.)
>   O, this is the poison of deep grief; it springs
>   All from her father's death, and now behold!
>   O Gertrude, Gertrude,
>   When sorrows come, they come not single spies,   75
>   But in battalions: first, her father slain;
>   Next, your son gone, and he most violent author
>   Of his own just remove;° the people muddied°,
>   Thick and unwholesome in their thoughts and whispers
>   For good Polonius' death; and we have done but greenly°   80
>   In hugger-mugger° to inter him; poor Ophelia
>   Divided from herself and her fair judgement,
>   Without the which we are pictures, or mere beasts;
>   Last, and as much containing as all these,
>   Her brother is in secret come from France,   85
>   Feeds on his wonder, keeps himself in clouds,°
>   And wants° not buzzers to infect his ear
>   With pestilent speeches of his father's death.
>   Wherein necessity, of matter beggared,°

---

56. Gis: Jesus 59. cock: corruption of God 78. remove: banishment, departure 78. muddied: stirred up and confused 80. greenly: without judgment 81. hugger-mugger: secrecy and disorder 86. in clouds: i.e., of suspicion and rumor 87. wants: lacks 89. of matter beggared: lacking facts

Will nothing stick° our person to arraign   90
In ear and ear, O my dear Gertrude, this,
Like to a murd'ring piece,° in many places
Gives me superfluous death. Attend, *(A noise within.)*
(Enter a MESSENGER.*)*
Where are my Switzers?° Let them guard the door.
What is the matter?   95
MESSENGER: Save yourself, my lord.
The ocean, overpeering of his list,°
Eats not the flats with more impiteous haste
Then young Laertes, in a riotous head,°
O'erbears your officers. The rabble call him lord,
And as the world were now but to begin,   100
Antiquity forgot, custom not known,
The ratifiers and props of every word,
They cry 'Choose we, Laertes shall be king'.
Caps, hands, and tongues, applaud it to the clouds,
'Laertes shall be king, Laertes king!'   105
QUEEN: How cheerfully on the false trail they cry!
(A noise within.)
O, this is counter,° you false Danish dogs!
KING: The doors are broke.
(Enter LAERTES *with* OTHERS.*)*
LAERTES: Where is this king?—Sirs, stand you all without.
ALL: No, let's come in.   110
LAERTES: I pray you give me leave.
ALL: We will, we will.
(Exeunt his followers.)
LAERTES: I thank you. Keep the door.—O thou vile king,
Give me my father!
QUEEN: Calmly, good Laertes,
LAERTES: That drop of blood that's calm proclaims me bastard,
Cries cuckold to my father, brands the harlot   115
Even here between the chaste unsmirchèd brow
Of my true mother.
KING: What is the cause, Laertes,
That thy rebellion looks so giant-like?
Let him go, Gertrude. Do not fear° our person.
There's such divinity doth hedge a king   120

---

90. **nothing stick:** in no way hesitate 92. **murd'ring piece:** cannon loaded with shot meant to scatter
94. **Switzers:** Swiss bodyguard 96. **list:** boundary 98. **riotous head:** turbulent mob 107. **counter:** hunting
backward on the trail 119. **fear:** fear for

That treason can but peep to what it would,
Acts little of his will. Tell me, Laertes.
Why thou art thus incensed. Let him go, Gertrude.
Speak, man.

LAERTES: Where is my father?   12?

KING: Dead.

QUEEN: But not by him.

KING: Let him demand his fill.

LAERTES: How came he dead? I'll not be juggled with.
  To hell allegiance, vows to the blackest devil,
  Conscience and grace to the profoundest pit!
  I dare damnation. To this point I stand,   13#
  That both the worlds I give to negligence,
  Let come what comes, only I'll be revenged
  Most throughly° for my father.

KING: Who shall stay you?

LAERTES: My will, not all the world's.
  And for my means, I'll husband them so well   13?
  They shall go far with little.

KING: Good Laertes,
  If you desire to know the certainty
  Of your dear father, is't writ in your revenge
  That, swoopstake,° you will draw both friend and foe,
  Winner and loser?   14#

LAERTES: None but his enemies.

KING: Will you know them, then?

LAERTES: To his good friends thus wide I'll ope my arms,
  And like the kind life-rend'ring pelican,°
  Repast them with my blood.

KING: Why, now you speak
  Like a good child and a true gentleman.   14?
  That I am guiltless of your father's death,
  And am most sensibly in grief for it,
  It shall as level° to your judgement 'pear
  As day does to your eye.

(A noise within: 'Let her come in.')

LAERTES: How now! what noise is that?   15#

(Enter OPHELIA.)

  O heat, dry up my brains! tears seven times salt

---

133. **throughly:** thoroughly 139. **swoopstake:** sweepstake, taking all the stakes on the gambling table
143. **pelican:** supposed to feed her young with her own blood 148. **level:** plain

Burn out the sense and virtue° of mine eye!
By heaven, thy madness shall be paid with weight
Till our scale turn the beam. O rose of May,
Dear maid, kind sister, sweet Ophelia!   155
O heavens! is't possible a young maid's wits
Should be as mortal as an old man's life?
Nature is fine° in love, and where 'tis fine
It sends some precious instance of itself
After the thing it loves.   160

OPHELIA *(Song.)*:
             They bore him barefac'd on the bier;
             Hey non nonny, nonny, hey nonny;
             And in his grave rain'd many a tear—
             Fare you well, my dove!

LAERTES: Hadst thou thy wits, and didst persuade revenge,   165
It could not move thus.

OPHELIA: You must sing 'A-down, a-down,' and you 'Call him a-down-a.' O,
how the wheel° becomes it! It is the false stew ard, that stole his master's daughter.

LAERTES: This nothing's more than matter.   170

OPHELIA: There's rosemary,° that's for remembrance. Pray you, love, remember. And there is pansies, that's for thoughts.

LAERTES: A document in madness, thoughts and remembrance fitted.

OPHELIA: There's fennel for you, and columbines.There's rue for you, and
here's some for me. We may call it herb of grace a Sundays. O, you   175
must wear your rue with a difference. There's a daisy. I would give you
some violets, but they with ered all when my father died. They say'a
made a good end, *(Sings.)*
For bonny sweet Robin is all my joy.

LAERTES: Thought and affliction, passion, hell itself,   180
She turns to favor and to prettiness.

OPHELIA *(Song.)*: And will 'a not come again?
And will 'a not come again?

---

152. **virtue:** power 158. **fine:** refined to purity 168. **wheel:** burden, refrain 171. **rosemary:** Harold Jenkins,
in his Arden edition of *Hamlet* (London and New York, 1982) 536–542, suggests that Ophelia gives rosemary
(emblematic of remembrance) and pansies (of thoughts) to Laertes; that she gives fennel and columbines
(both signifying marital infidelity) to the queen; she gives rue (for repentance) to the king (keeping some for
herself as a sign of her sorrow, but noting that the king is to wear his rue with a **difference**, an heraldic
term designating a mark for distinguishing one branch of a family from another in a coat-of-arms). The daisy,
an emblem of love's victims, is given to the king as substitute for the absent Hamlet, whose absence he has
caused. The king would also be given the violets (emblems of faithfulness, associated both with Ophelia's
love for Hamlet, and Polonius's service to the state, both now lost) were these still available. Each gift of
flowers represents a symbolic reproach to the recipient

No, no, he is dead:
Go to thy death-bed: 185
He never will come again.
His beard was as white as snow,
        All flaxen was his poll:°
        He is gone, he is gone,
        And we cast away moan: 190
        God ha' mercy on his soul!
        And of all Christian souls, I pray God. God buy you.
(Exit.)
LAERTES: Do you see this, O God?
KING: Laertes, I must commune with your grief,
    Or you deny me right. Go but apart,   195
    Make choice of whom your wisest friends you will,
    And they shall hear and judge 'twixt you and me.
    If by direct or by collateral hand
    They find us touched, we will our kingdom give,
    Our crown, our life, and all that we call ours,   200
    To you in satisfaction; but if not,
    Be you content to lend your patience to us,
    And we shall jointly labour with your soul
    To give it due content.
LAERTES: Let this be so.
    His means of death, his obscure funeral—   205
    No trophy, sword, nor hatchment,° o'er his bones,
    No noble rite nor formal ostentation—
    Cry to be heard, as 'twere from heaven to earth,
    That I must call't in question.
KING: So you shall;
    And where th' offence is let the great axe fall.   210
    I pray you go with me.
(Exeunt.)

Scene 6

(Enter HORATIO *and* Others.)
HORATIO: What are they that would speak with me?
GENTLEMAN: Sea-faring men, sir. They say they have letters for you.
HORATIO: Let them come in. *(Exit* GENTLEMAN.)
    I do not know from what part of the world

---

188. **poll:** head 206. **hatchment:** coat of arms

I should be greeted, if not from Lord Hamlet.   5
(Enter SAILORS.*)*

SAILOR: God bless you, sir.

HORATIO: Let him bless thee too.

SAILOR: 'A shall sir, an't please him. There's a letter for you, sir—it comes
 from th' ambassador that was bound for England—if your name be
 Horatio, as I am let to know it is.   10

HORATIO *(Reads.)*: 'Horatio, when thou shalt have overlooked this, give
 these fellows some means to the king. They have letters for him. Ere we
 were two days old at sea, a pirate of very warlike appointment gave us
 chase. Finding ourselves too slow of sail, we put on a compelled valor,
 and in the grapple I boarded them. On the instant they got clear of our   15
 ship, so I alone became their prisoner. They have dealt with me like
 thieves of mercy, but they knew what they did; I am to do a good turn
 for them. Let the king have the letters I have sent, and repair thou to
 me with as much speed as thou wouldest fly death. I have words to
 speak in thine ear will make thee dumb; yet are they much too light for   20
 the bore° of the matter. These good fellows will bring thee where I am.
 Rosencrantz and Guildenstern hold their course for England. Of them I
 have much to tell thee. Farewell.

        'He that thou knowest thine, Hamlet.'

Come, I will give you way for these your letters,
And do't the speedier that you may direct me   25
To him from whom you brought them.

(Exeunt.)

Scene 7

(Enter KING *and* LAERTES.*)*

KING: Now must your conscience my acquittance seal,
 And you must put me in your heart for friend,
 Sith you have heard, and with a knowing ear,
 That he which hath your noble father slain
 Pursued my life.   5

LAERTES: It well appears. But tell me
 Why you proceeded not against these feats,
 So criminal and so capital° in nature,
 As by your safety, wisdom, all things else,
 You mainly were stirred up.

IV.vi.21. **bore:** literally, caliber of a gun; hence, size, importance IV.vii.7. **capital:** punishable by death

KING: O, for two special reasons,
   Which may to you, perhaps, seem much unsinewed,°   10
   But yet to me th' are strong. The queen his mother
   Lives almost by his looks, and for myself—
   My virtue or my plague, be it either which—
   She's so conjunctive° to my life and soul
   That, as the star moves not but in his sphere,   15
   I could not but by her. The other motive,
   Why to a public count° I might not go,
   Is the great love the general gender° bear him,
   Who, dipping all his faults in their affection,
   Work, like the spring that turneth wood to stone,   20
   Convert his gyves° to graces; so that my arrows,
   Too slightly timbered for so loud a wind,
   Would have reverted to my bow again,
   And not where I had aimed them.
LAERTES: And so have I a noble father lost,   25
   A sister driven into desp'rate terms,
   Whose worth, if praises may go back again,
   Stood challenger on mount of all the age
   For her perfections. But my revenge will come.
KING: Break not your sleeps for that. You must not think   30
   That we are made of stuff so flat and dull
   That we can let our beard be shook with danger,
   And think it pastime. You shortly shall hear more.
   I loved your father, and we love our self,
   And that, I hope, will teach you to imagine—   35
(Enter a MESSENGER *with letters.)*
MESSENGER: These to your majesty; this to the queen.
KING: From Hamlet! Who brought them?
MESSENGER: Sailors, my lord, they say. I saw them not.
   They were given me by Claudio; he received them
   Of him that brought them.   40
KING: Laertes, you shall hear them.—
   Leave us. (*Exit* MESSENGER.)
   (*Reads.*) 'High and mighty, you shall know I am set naked on your king-
   dom. To-morrow shall I beg leave to see your kingly eyes, when I shall,
   first asking your pardon, thereunto recount the occasion of my sudden
   and more strange return.   45

---

10. unsinewed: weak **14. conjunctive:** closely joined **17. count:** reckoning **18. general gender:** common people **21. gyves:** fetters

Hamlet.'
What should this mean? Are all the rest come back?
Or is it some abuse, and no such thing?
LAERTES: Know you the hand?
KING: 'Tis Hamlet's character. 'Naked!'   50
And in a postscript here, he says 'alone.'
Can you devise° me?
LAERTES: I am lost in it, my lord. But let him come.
It warms the very sickness in my heart
That I shall live and tell him to his teeth   55
'Thus didst thou.'
KING: If it be so, Laertes—
As how should it be so, how otherwise?—
Will you be ruled by me?
LAERTES: Ay, my lord,
So you will not o'errule me to a peace.
KING: To thine own peace. If he be now returned,   60
As checking at° his voyage, and that he means
No more to undertake it, I will work him
To an exploit now ripe in my device,
Under the which he shall not choose but fall;
And for his death no wind of blame shall breathe   65
But even his mother shall uncharge the practice°
And call it accident.
LAERTES: My lord, I will be ruled;
The rather if you could devise it so
That I might be the organ.°
KING: It falls right.
You have been talked of since your travel much,   70
And that in Hamlet's hearing, for a quality
Wherein they say you shine. Your sum of parts
Did not together pluck such envy from him
As did that one, and that, in my regard,
Of the unworthiest siege.°   75
LAERTES: What part is that, my lord?
KING: A very riband in the cap of youth,
Yet needful too, for youth no less becomes
The light and careless livery that it wears

---

52. devise: explain to **61. checking at:** turning aside from (like a falcon turning from its quarry for other prey) **66. uncharge the practice:** regard the deed as free from villainy **69. organ:** instrument **75. siege:** rank

Than settled age his sables and his weeds,°
Importing health and graveness. Two months since   80
Here was a gentleman of Normandy.
I have seen myself, and served against, the French,
And they can well on horseback, but this gallant
Had witchcraft in't. He grew unto his seat,
And to such wondrous doing brought his horse,   85
As had he been incorpsed° and demi-natured°
With the brave beast. So far he topped° my thought
That I, in forgery° of shapes and tricks,
Come short of what he did.

LAERTES: A Norman was't?

KING: A Norman.   90

LAERTES: Upon my life, Lamord.

KING: The very same.

LAERTES: I know him well. He is the brooch indeed
    And gem of all the nation.

KING: He made confession of you,
    And gave you such a masterly report   95
    For art and exercise in your defence,
    And for your rapier most especial,
    That he cried out 'twould be a sight indeed
    If one could match you. The scrimers° of their nation,
    He swore had neither motion, guard, nor eye,   100
    If you opposed them. Sir, this report of his
    Did Hamlet so envenom with his envy
    That he could nothing do but wish and beg
    Your sudden coming o'er, to play with you.
    Now out of this—   105

LAERTES: What out of this, my lord?

KING: Laertes, was your father dear to you?
    Or are you like the painting of a sorrow,
    A face without a heart?

LAERTES: Why ask you this?

KING: Not that I think you did not love your father,
    But that I know love is begun by time,   110
    And that I see, in passages° of proof,
    Time qualifies° the spark and fire of it.

---

79. **weeds:** garments 86. **incorpsed:** made one body 86. **demi-natured:** like a centaur, half man half horse 87. **topped:** excelled 88. **forgery:** invention 99. **scrimers:** fencers (French *escrimeurs*) 111. **passages of proof:** incidents of experience 112. **qualifies:** weakens

There lives within the very flame of love
A kind of wick or snuff that will abate it,
And nothing is at a like goodness still,   115
For goodness, growing to a plurisy,°
Dies in his own too much. That we would do,
We should do when we would; for this 'would' changes,
And hath abatements and delays as many
As there are tongues, are hands, are accidents,   120
And then this 'should' is like a spendthrift's sigh,
That hurts by easing. But to the quick° of th' ulcer—
Hamlet comes back; what would you undertake
To show yourself in deed your father's son
More than in words?   125
LAERTES: To cut his throat i' th' church.
KING: No place, indeed, should murder sanctuarize;°
      Revenge should have no bounds. But good Laertes,
      Will you do this, keep close within your chamber;
      Hamlet returned shall know you are come home;
      We'll put on those shall praise your excellence,   130
      And set a double varnish on the fame
      The Frenchman gave you, bring you in fine together,
      And wager on your heads. He, being remiss,°
      Most generous, and free from all contriving,
      Will not peruse° the foils, so that with ease,   135
      Or with a little shuffling, you may choose
      A sword unbated,° and in a pass of practice°
      Requite him for your father.
LAERTES: I will do't,
      And for that purpose I'll anoint my sword.
      I bought an unction of a mountebank   140
      So mortal that but dip a knife in it,
      Where it draws blood no cataplasm° so rare,
      Collected from all simples° that have virtue
      Under the moon, can save the thing from death
      That is but scratched withal. I'll touch my point   145
      With this contagion, that if I gall him slightly,
      It may be death.

---

116. **plurisy:** excess 122. **quick:** sensitive flesh 126. **sanctuarize:** give sanctuary to 133. **remiss:** careless
135. **peruse:** inspect 137. **unbated:** not blunted; 137. **pass of practice:** treacherous thrust 142. **cata-plasm:** poultice 143. **simples:** medicinal herbs

KING: Let's further think of this,
      Weigh what convenience both of time and means
      May fit us to our shape.° If this should fail,
      And that our drift° look through our bad performance,   150
      'Twere better not assayed. Therefore this project
      Should have a back or second° that might hold
      If this should blast in proof.° Soft! let me see.
      We'll make a solemn wager on your cunnings—
      I ha't.   155
      When in your motion° you are hot and dry—
      As make your bouts more violent to that end—
      And that he calls for drink, I'll have preferred° him
      A chalice for the nonce,° whereon but sipping,
      If he by chance escape your venomed stuck,°   160
      Our purpose may hold there.—But stay, what noise?
(*Enter* QUEEN.)
QUEEN: One woe doth tread upon another's heel,
      So fast they follow. Your sister's drowned, Laertes.
LAERTES: Drowned! O, where?
QUEEN: There is a willow grows askant° the brook   165
      That shows his hoar° leaves in the glassy stream.
      Therewith fantastic garlands did she make
      Of crowflowers, nettles, daisies, and long purples
      That liberal° shepherds give a grosser name,
      But our cold° maids do dead men's fingers call them.   170
      There on the pendent boughs her crownet° weeds
      Clamb'ring to hang, an envious° sliver broke,
      When down her weedy trophies and herself
      Fell in the weeping brook. Her clothes spread wide,
      And mermaid-like awhile they bore her up,   175
      Which time she chanted snatches of old lauds,°
      As one incapable of° her own distress,
      Or like a creature native and indued°
      Unto that element. But long it could not be
      Till that her garments, heavy with their drink,   180
      Pulled the poor wretch from her melodious lay
      To muddy death.
LAERTES: Alas, then, she is drowned?

---

149. **shape:** plan 150. **drift:** scheme 152. **back or second:** something in support 153. **blast in proof:** burst
during trial (like a faulty cannon) 156. **motion:** exertion 158. **preferred:** offered to 159. **nonce:** occasion
160. **stuck:** thrust 165. **askant:** alongside 166. **hoar:** gray 169. **liberal:** free-spoken, licentious 170. **cold:**
chaste 171. **crownet:** coronet 172. **envious:** malicious 176. **lauds:** hymns 177. **incapable of:** insensible to
178. **indued:** endowed

QUEEN: Drowned, drowned.

LAERTES: Too much of water hast thou, poor Ophelia,
    And therefore I forbid my tears; but yet   185
    It is our trick; nature her custom holds,
    Let shame say what it will. When these are gone,
    The woman° will be out. Adieu, my lord.
    I have a speech o' fire that fain would blaze
    But that this folly drowns it.   190

(Exit.)

KING: Let's follow, Gertrude.
    How much I had to do to calm his rage!
    Now fear I this will give it start again;
    Therefore let's follow.

(Exeunt.)

ACT V

Scene 1

(Enter two CLOWNS.°*)*

CLOWN: Is she to be buried in Christian burial when she wilfully seeks her
    own salvation?

OTHER: I tell thee she is, therefore make her grave straight. The crowner°
    hath sat on her, and finds it Christian burial.

CLOWN: How can that be, unless she drowned herself in her own defence?   5

OTHER: Why, 'tis found so.

CLOWN: It must be "se offendendo',° it cannot be else. For here lies the
    point: if I drown myself wittingly, it argues an act, and an act hath
    three branches—it is to act, to do, and to perform; argal,° she drowned
    herself wittingly.   10

OTHER: Nay, but hear you, Goodman Delver.

CLOWN: Give me leave. Here lies the water; good. Here stands the man;
    good. If the man go to this water and drown himself, it is, will he, nill
    he, he goes—mark you that. But if the water come to him and drown
    him, he drowns not himself. Argal, he that is not guilty of his own   15
    death shortens not his own life.

OTHER: But is this law?

CLOWN: Ay, marry, is't; crowner's quest° law.

OTHER: Will you ha' the truth on 't? If this had not been a gentlewoman,
    she should have been buried out o' Christian burial.   20

---

188. woman: unmanly part of nature V.i, stage directions. clowns: rustics 3. crowner: coroner 7. se
offendendo: the Clown's blunder for "se defendendo": ("in self-defense") 9. argal: therefore (corrupt form
of *ergo*) 18. quest: inquest

CLOWN: Why, there thou say'st. And the more pity that great folk should
     have count'nance in this world to drown or hang themselves more than
     their even-Christen.° Come, my spade. There is no ancient gentlemen
     but gard'ners, ditchers, and grave-makers. They hold up Adam's
     profession.   25
OTHER: Was he a gentleman?
CLOWN: 'A was the first that ever bore arms.
OTHER: Why, he had none.
CLOWN: What, art a heathen? How dost thou understand the Scripture?
     The Scripture says Adam digged. Could he dig without arms? I'll put   30
     another question to thee. If thou answerest me not to the purpose, con-
     fess thyself—
OTHER: Go to.
CLOWN: What is he that builds stronger than either the mason, the ship-
     wright, or the carpenter?   35
OTHER: The gallows-maker for that frame outlives a thousand tenants.
CLOWN: I like thy wit well, in good faith. The gallows does well. But how
     does it well? It does well to those that do ill. Now thou dost ill to say
     the gallows is built stronger than the church. Argal, the gallows may do
     well to thee. To't again, come.   40
OTHER: 'Who builds stronger than a mason, a shipwright, or a carpenter?'
CLOWN: Ay tell me that, and unyoke.°
OTHER: Marry, now I can tell.
CLOWN: To't.
OTHER: Mass, I cannot tell.   45
(*Enter* HAMLET *and* HORATIO *afar off.*)
CLOWN: Cudgel thy brains no more about it, for your dull ass will not
     mend his pace with beating. And when you are asked this question
     next, say 'a grave-maker.' The houses he makes lasts till doomsday. Go,
     get thee in, and fetch me a stoup° of liquor. (*Exit* OTHER CLOWN.)
     (HAMLET *and* HORATIO *come forward as* CLOWN *digs and sings.*)
     (*Song.*)
     In youth, when I did love, did love,   50
     Methought it was very sweet,
     To contract-O-the time, for-a-my behove,°
     O, methought, there-a-was nothing-a-meet.
HAMLET: Has this fellow no feeling of his business, that 'a sings at
     gravemaking?   55

---

23. **even-Christen:** fellow Christian 42. **tell me that, and unyoke:** answer the question and then you
can relax 49. **stoup:** tankard 52. **behove:** benefit The repeated *a* and *o* may represent the Clown's vocal
embellishments, but more probably they represent his grunting as he takes breath in the course of his
digging

HORATIO: Custom hath made it in him a property of easiness.°

HAMLET: 'Tis e'en so. The hand of little employment hath the daintier sense.

CLOWN *(Song.)*: But age, with his stealing steps,
Hath clawed me in his clutch,   60
And hath shipped me into the land,
As if I had never been such.

(Throws up a skull.)

HAMLET: That skull had a tongue in it, and could sing once. How the knave jowls° it to the ground, as if 'twere Cain's jawbone, that did the first murder! This might be the pate of a politician, which this ass now   65
o'erreaches; one that would circumvent° God, might it not?

HORATIO: It might, my lord.

HAMLET: Or of a courtier, which could say 'Good morrow, sweet lord! How dost thou, sweet lord?' This might be my Lord Such-a-one, that praised my Lord Such-a-one's horse, when 'a went to beg it, might it not?   70

HORANTIO: Ay, my lord.

HAMLET: Why, e'en so, and now my Lady Worm's, chopless,° and knock'd about the mazzard° with a sexton's spade. Here's fine revolution, an we had the trick to see't. Did these bones cost no more the breeding but to play at loggats° with them? Mine ache to think on't.   75

CLOWN *(Song.)*: A pick-axe and a spade, a spade,
For and a shrouding sheet:
O, a pit of clay for to be made
For such a guest is meet.

(Throws up another skull.)

HAMLET: There's another. Why may not that be the skull of a lawyer?   80
Where be his quiddities° now, his quillets,° his cases, his tenures, and his tricks? Why does he suffer this mad knave now to knock him about the sconce with a dirty shovel, and will not tell him of his action of battery? Hum! This fellow might be in's time a great buyer of land, with his statutes, his recognizances,° his fines, his double vouchers, his   85
recoveries.° Is this the fine of his fines, and the recovery of his recoveries, to have his fine pate full of fine dirt? Will his vouchers vouch him no more of his purchases, and double ones too, than the length and breadth of a pair of indentures?° The very conveyances° of his lands

---

56. a property of easiness: a habit that comes easily to him 64. jowls: hurls 66. circumvent: cheat
72. chopless: with lower jaw missing 73. mazzard: head 75. loggats: small logs of wood for throwing at a mark 81. quiddities: subtle distinctions 81. quillets: quibbles 85. recognizances: legal bonds, defining debts; vouchers persons vouched or called on to warrant a title 86. recoveries: legal processes to break an entail 89. pair of indentures: deed or legal agreement in duplicate 89. conveyances: deeds by which property is transferred

will scarcely lie in this box, and must th' inheritor himself have no $\quad$ 90
more, ha?

HORATIO: Not a jot more, my lord.

HAMLET: Is not parchment made of sheepskins?

HORANTIO: Ay, my lord, and of calves' skins too.

HAMLET: They are sheep and calves which seek out assurance in that. I will $\quad$ 95
speak to this fellow. Whose grave's this, sirrah?

CLOWN: Mine, sir. *(Sings.)* O, a pit of clay for to be made—

HAMLET: I think it be thine indeed, for thou liest in't.

CLOWN: You lie out on't, sir, and therefore 'tis not yours. For my part, I do
not lie in't, yet it is mine. $\quad$ 100

HAMLET: Thou dost lie in't, to be in't and say it is thine. 'Tis for the dead,
not for the quick; therefore thou liest.

CLOWN: 'Tis a quick lie, sir; 'twill away again from me to you.

HAMLET: What man dost thou dig it for?

CLOWN: For no man, sir. $\quad$ 105

HAMLET: What woman, then?

CLOWN: For none neither.

HAMLET: Who is to be buried in't?

CLOWN: One that was a woman, sir; but, rest her soul, she's dead.

HAMLET: How absolute° the knave is! We must speak by the card,° or $\quad$ 110
equivocation will undo us. By the Lord, Horatio, this three years I have
took note of it, the age is grown so picked° that the toe of the peasant
comes so near the heel of the courtier, he galls his kibe.° How long hast
thou been a grave-maker?

CLOWN: Of all the day i' th' year, I came to't that day that our last King $\quad$ 115
Hamlet overcame Fortinbras.

HAMLET: How long is that since?

CLOWN: Cannot you tell that? Every fool can tell that. It was that very day
that young Hamlet was born—he that is mad, and sent into England.

HAMLET: Ay, marry, why was he sent into England? $\quad$ 120

CLOWN: Why, because 'a was mad. 'A shall recover his wits there; or, if a do
not, 'tis no great matter there.

HAMLET: Why?

CLOWN: 'Twill not be seen in him there. There the men are as mad as he.

HAMLET: How came he mad? $\quad$ 125

CLOWN: Very strangely, they say.

HAMLET: How strangely?

CLOWN: Faith, e'en with losing his wits.

---

110. **absolute:** positive 110. **card:** card on which the points of the mariner's compass are marked (i.e.,
absolutely to the point) 112. **picked:** fastidious 113. **kibe:** chilblain

HAMLET: Upon what ground?

CLOWN: Why, here in Denmark. I have been sexton here, man and boy,   130
thirty years.

HAMLET: How long will a man lie i' th' earth ere he rot?

CLOWN: Faith, if 'a be not rotten before 'a die—as we have many pocky°
corses now-a-days that will scarce hold the laying in—'a will last you
some eight year or nine year. A tanner will last you nine year.   135

HAMLET: Why he more than another?

CLOWN: Why, sir, his hide is so tanned with his trade that 'a will keep out
water a great while and your water is a sore decayer of your whoreson
dead body. Here's a skull now hath lain you i' th' earth three and twenty
years.   140

HAMLET: Whose was it?

CLOWN: A whoreson mad fellow's it was. Whose do you think it was?

HAMLET: Nay, I know not.

CLOWN: A pestilence on him for a mad rogue! 'a poured a flagon of Rhenish°
on my head once. This same skull, sir, was, sir, Yorick's skull, the king's   145
jester.

HAMLET *(Takes the skull.)*: This?

CLOWN: E'en That.

HAMLET: Alas, poor Yorick! I knew him, Horatio—a fellow of infinite jest,
of most excellent fancy. He hath bore me on his back a thousand times,   150
and now how abhorred in my imagination it is! My gorge rises at it.
Here hung those lips that I have kissed I know not how oft. Where be
your gibes now, your gambols, your songs, your flashes of merriment
that were wont to set the table on a roar? Not one now to mock your
own grinning? Quite chop-fall'n? Now get you to my lady's chamber,   155
and tell her, let her paint an inch thick, to this favour she must come.
Make her laugh at that. Prithee, Horatio, tell me one thing.

HORATIO: What's that, my lord?

HAMLET: Dost thou think Alexander looked o' this fashion i' th' earth?

HORATIO: E'en so.   160

HAMLET: And smelt so? Pah!

(Throws down the skull.)

HORATIO: E'en so, my lord.

HAMLET: To what base uses we may return, Horatio! Why may not imagination trace the noble dust of Alexander till 'a find it stopping a bung-
hole?   165

HORATIO: 'Twere to consider too curiously° to consider so.

---

133. pocky: infected with pox (syphilis) **144. Rhenish:** Rhine wine **166. too curiously:** over ingeniously

HAMLET: No, faith, not a jot, but to follow him thither with modesty
  enough, and likelihood to lead it. Alexander died, Alexander was
  buried, Alexander returneth to dust; the dust is earth; of earth we make
  loam; and why of that loam whereto he was converted might they not   170
  stop a beer-barrel?
> Imperious Caesar, dead and turned to clay,
> Might stop a hole to keep the wind away.
> O, that that earth which kept the world in awe
> Should patch a wall t'expel the winter's flaw!°   175
> But soft, but soft awhile! Here comes the king,
> The queen, the courtiers.

(*Enter* KING, QUEEN, LAERTES, *and the Corse [with a Doctor of Divinity as*
  PRIEST *and* LORDS *attendant].*)
> Who is this they follow?
> And with such maimèd rites? This doth betoken
> The corse they follow did with desperate hand
> Fordo° it° own life. 'Twas of some estate.   180
> Couch we awhile and mark.

(*Retires with* HORATIO.)

LAERTES: What ceremony else?

HAMLET: That is Laertes, a very noble youth. Mark.

LAERTES: What ceremony else?

DOCTOR: Her obsequies have been as far enlarged   185
  As we have warranty. Her death was doubtful,
  And but that great command o'ersways the order,
  She should in ground unsanctified been lodged
  Till the last trumpet. For charitable prayers,
  Shards,° flints and pebbles should be thrown on her.   190
  Yet here she is allowed her virgin crants,°
  Her maiden strewments and the bringing home
  Of bell and burial.

LAERTES: Must there no more be done?

DOCTOR: No more be done.
  We should profane the service of the dead   195
  To sing a requiem and such rest to her
  As to peace-parted souls.

LAERTES: Lay her i' th' earth,
  And from her fair and unpolluted flesh
  May violets spring! I tell thee, churlish priest,

---

175. **flaw:** gust 180. **Fordo:** destroy; 180. **it:** its 190. **Shards:** bits of broken pottery 191. **crants:** garland

A minist'ring angel shall my sister be   200
When thou liest howling.
HAMLET: What, the fair Ophelia!
QUEEN: Sweets to the sweet. Farewell!
(*Scatters flowers.*)
I hoped thou shouldst have been my Hamlet's wife.
I thought thy bride-bed to have decked, sweet maid,
And not have strewed thy grave.   205
LAERTES: O treble woe
Fall ten times treble on that cursèd head,
Whose wicked deed thy most ingenious° sense
Deprived thee of! Hold off the earth awhile,
Till I have caught her once more in mine arms.
(*Leaps into the grave.*)
Now pile your dust upon the quick and dead,   210
Till of this flat a mountain you have made
T' o'er-top old Pelion° or the skyish head
Of blue Olympus.
HAMLET (*Coming forward.*): What is he whose grief
Bears such an emphasis,° whose phrase of sorrow   215
Conjures the wand'ring stars, and makes them stand
Like wonder-wounded hearers? This is I,
Hamlet the Dane.
(LAERTES *climbs out of the grave.*)
LAERTES: The devil take thy soul!
(*Grappling with him.*)
HAMLET: Thou pray'st not well.
I prithee take thy fingers from my throat,   220
For though I am not splenitive° and rash,
Yet have I in me something dangerous,
Which let thy wisdom fear. Hold off thy hand.
KING: Pluck them asunder.
QUEEN: Hamlet! Hamlet!   225
ALL: Gentlemen!
HORATIO: Good my lord, be quiet.
(*The Attendants part them.*)
HAMLET: Why, I will fight with him upon this theme
Until my eyelids will no longer wag.

---

207. **most ingenious:** of quickest apprehension 212. **Pelion:** a mountain in Thessaly, like Olympus and Ossa (the allusion is to the war in which the Titans fought the gods and, in their attempt to scale heaven, heaped Ossa and Olympus on Pelion, or Pelion and Ossa on Olympus) 215. **such an emphasis:** so vehement an expression or display 221. **splenitive:** fiery-tempered (from the spleen, seat of anger)

QUEEN: O my son, what theme?   230

HAMLET: I loved Ophelia. Forty thousand brothers
    Could not with all their quantity of love
    Make up my sum. What wilt thou do for her?

KING: O, he is mad, Laertes.

QUEEN: For love of God, forbear him.   235

HAMLET: 'Swounds, show me what thou't do.
    Woo't° weep, woo't fight, woo't fast, woo't tear thyself,
    Woo't drink up eisel,° eat a crocodile?
    I'll do't. Dost come here to whine?
    To outface me with leaping in her grave?   240
    Be buried quick with her, and so will I,
    And if thou prate of mountains, let them throw
    Millions of acres on us, till our ground,
    Singeing his pate against the burning zone,
    Make Ossa like a wart! Nay, an thou'lt mouth,   245
    I'll rant as well as thou.

QUEEN: This is mere madness;
    And thus awhile the fit will work on him.
    Anon, as patient as the female dove
    When that her golden couplets° are disclosed,
    His silence will sit drooping.   250

HAMLET: Hear you, sir.
    What is the reason that you use me thus?
    I loved you ever. But it is no matter.
    Let Hercules himself do what he may,
    The cat will mew, and dog will have his day.

KING: I pray thee, good Horatio, wait upon him.   255

(*Exit* HAMLET *and* HORATIO.)

    (*To* LAERTES.) Strengthen your patience in our last night's speech.
    We'll put the matter to the present push.—
    Good Gertrude, set some watch over your son.—
    This grave shall have a living monument.
    An hour of quiet shortly shall we see;   260
    Till then in patience our proceeding be.

(*Exeunt.*)

Scene 2

(*Enter* HAMLET *and* HORATIO.)

HAMLET: So much for this, sir; now shall you see the other.
    You do remember all the circumstance?

---

237. **Woo't:** wilt (thou) 238. **eisel:** vinegar 249. **couplets:** newly hatched pair

HORATIO: Remember it, my lord!

HAMLET: Sir, in my heart there was a kind of fighting
     That would not let me sleep. Methought I lay   5
     Worse than the mutines° in the bilboes.° Rashly,
     And praised be rashness for it—let us know,
     Our indiscretion sometime serves us well,
     When our deep plots do pall;° and that should learn us
     There's a divinity that shapes our ends,   10
     Rough-hew them how we will—

HORATIO: That is most certain.

HAMLET: Up from my cabin,
     My sea-gown scarfed about me, in the dark
     Groped I to find out them, had my desire,
     Fingered° their packet, and in fine withdrew   15
     To mine own room again, making so bold,
     My fears forgetting manners, to unseal
     Their grand commission; where I found, Horatio—
     Ah, royal knavery!—an exact command,
     Larded° with many several sorts of reasons   20
     Importing Denmark's health and England's too,
     With, ho! such bugs and goblins° in my life,
     That on the supervise,° no leisure bated°,
     No, not to stay° the grinding of the axe,
     My head should be struck off.   25

HORATIO: Is't possible?

HAMLET: Here's the commission; read it at more leisure.
     But will thou hear me how I did proceed?

HORATIO: I beseech you.

HAMLET: Being thus benetted round with villainies,
     Or° I could make a prologue to my brains,   30
     They had begun the play. I sat me down,
     Devised a new commission, wrote it fair.
     I once did hold it, as our statists° do,
     A baseness to write fair, and laboured much
     How to forget that learning; but sir, now   35
     It did me yeoman's service. Wilt thou know
     Th' effect of what I wrote?

HORATIO: Ay, good my lord.

V.ii.6. **mutines:** mutineers **6. bilboes:** fetters **9. pall:** fail **15. Fingered:** filched **20. Larded:** garnished
22. bugs and goblins: imaginary horrors (here, horrendous crimes attributed to Hamlet, and represented as
dangers should he be allowed to live) **23. supervise:** perusal **23. bated:** deducted, allowed **24. stay:** await
30. Or: ere **33. statists:** statesmen

HAMLET: An earnest conjuration from the king,
    As England was his faithful tributary,
    As love between them like the palm might flourish,   40
    As peace should still her wheaten garland wear
    And stand a comma° 'tween their amities,
    And many such like as's of great charge,°
    That on the view and knowing of these contents,
    Without debatement further more or less,   45
    He should the bearers put to sudden death,
    Not shriving-time allowed.
HORATIO: How was this sealed?
HAMLET: Why, even in that was heaven ordinant,°
    I had my father's signet in my pursue,
    Which was the model of that Danish seal,   50
    Folded the writ up the form of th' other,
    Subscribed° it, gave't th' impression, placed it safely,
    The changeling never known. Now the next day
    Was our sea-fight, and what to this was sequent
    Thou knowest already.   55
HORATIO: So Guildenstern and Rosencrantz go to't.
HAMLET: Why, man, they did make love to this employment.
    They are not near my conscience; their defeat
    Does by their own insinuation° grow.
    'Tis dangerous when the baser nature comes   60
    Between the pass° and fell° incensèd points
    Of mighty opposites.
HORATIO: Why, what a king is this!
HAMLET: Does it not, think thee, stand me now upon—°
    He that hath killed my king and whored my mother,
    Popped in between th' election° and my hopes,   65
    Thrown out his angle° for my proper° life,
    And with such coz'nage—is't not perfect conscience,
    To quit° him with this arm? And is't not to be damned
    To let this canker of our nature come
    In further evil?   70
HORATIO: It must be shortly known to him from England
    What is the issue of the business there.

---

42. comma: a connective that also acknowledges separateness 43. charge: (1) importance (2) burden (the double meaning fits the play that makes "as's" into "asses") 48. ordinant: guiding 52. Subscribed: signed 59. insinuation: intrusion 61. pass: thrust 61. fell: fierce 63. Does it not...stand me now upon: is it not incumbent upon me 65. election: i.e., to the kingship. Denmark being an elective monarchy 66. angle: fishing line; 66. proper: own 68. quit: repay

HAMLET: It will be short; the interim is mine.
    And a man's life's no more than to say 'one.'
    But I am very sorry, good Horatio,   75
    That to Laertes I forgot myself;
    For by the image of my cause I see
    The portraiture of his. I'll court his favours.
    But sure the bravery° of his grief did put me
    Into a tow'ring passion.   80
HORATIO: Peace; who comes here?
(*Enter* OSRIC, *a courtier.*)
OSRIC: Your lordship is right welcome back to Denmark.
HAMLET: I humbly thank you, sir. (*Aside to* HORATIO.) Dost know this water-
    fly?
HORATIO (*Aside to* HAMLET.): No, my good lord.
HAMLET (*Aside to* HORATIO.): Thy state is the more gracious, for 'tis a vice   85
    to know him. He hath much land, and fertile. Let a beast be lord of
    beasts, and his crib shall stand at the king's mess.° 'Tis a chough,° but
    as I say, spacious in the possession of dirt.
OSRIC: Sweet lord, if your lordship were at leisure, I should impart a thing
    to you from his majesty.   90
HAMLET: I will receive it, sir, with all diligence of spirit. Put your bonnet to
    his right use. 'Tis for the head.
OSRIC: I thank you lordship, it is very hot.
HAMLET: No, believe me, 'tis very cold; the wind is northerly.
OSRIC: It is indifferent° cold, my lord, indeed.   95
HAMLET: But yet methinks it is very sultry and hot for my complexion.°
OSRIC: Exceedingly, my lord; it is very sultry, as 'twere—I can not tell how.
    My lord, his majesty bade me signify to you that 'a has laid a great
    wager on your head. Sir, this is the matter—
HAMLET: I beseech you, remember.   100
(HAMLET *moves him to put on his hat.*)
OSRIC: Nay, good my lord; for my ease, in good faith. Sir, here is newly
    come to court Laertes; believe me, an absolute gentleman, full of most
    excellent differences,° of very soft society and great showing.° Indeed,
    to speak feelingly of him, he is the card° or calendar of gentry, for you
    shall find in him the continent° of what part a gentleman would see.   105
HAMLET: Sir, his definement° suffers, no perdition in you, though I know to
    divide him inventorially° would dozy° th' arithmetic of memory, and

---

79. **bravery**: ostentatious display 87. **mess**: table 87. **chough**: jackdaw; thus, a chatterer 95. **indifferent**:
somewhat 96. **complexion**: temperament 103. **differences**: distinguishing qualities 103. **great showing**:
distinguished appearance 104. **card**: map 105. **continent**: all-containing embodiment 106. **definement**:
definition 107. **divide him inventorially**: classify him in detail 107. **dozy**: dizzy

yet but yaw° neither in respect of his quick sail. But in the verity of extolment, I take him to be a soul of great article,° and his infusion° of such dearth° and rareness as, to make true diction of him, his semblable° is his mirror, and who else would trace° him, his umbrage,° nothing more. 11▮

OSRIC: Your lordship speaks most infallibly of him.

HAMLET: The concernancy,° sir? Why do we wrap the gentleman in our more rawer breath? 11▮

OSRIC: Sir?

HORATIO: It's not possible to understand in another tongue? You will to't,° sir, really.

HAMLET: What imports the nomination° of this gentleman?

OSRIC: Of Laertes? 12▮

HORATIO (*Aside.*): His purse is empty already. All's golden words are spent.

HAMLET: Of him, sir.

OSRIC: I know you are not ignorant—

HAMLET: I would you did, sir; yet, in faith, if you did, it would not much approve° me. Well, sir. 12▮

OSRIC: You are not ignorant of what excellence Laertes is—

HAMLET: I dare not confess that, lest I should compare° with him in excellence; but to know a man well were to know himself.

OSRIC: I mean, sir, for his weapon; but in the imputation laid on him by them in his meed,° he's unfellowed.° 13▮

HAMLET: What's his weapon?

OSRIC: Rapier and dagger.

HAMLET: That's two of his weapons—but well.

OSRIC: The king, sir, hath wagered with him six Barbary horses, against the which he has impawned,° as I take it, six French rapiers and poniards, with their assigns,° as girdle, hangers, and so. Three of the carriages,° in faith, are very dear to fancy, very responsive to the hilts, most delicate carriages, and of very liberal conceit.° 13▮

HAMLET: What call you the carriages?

HORATIO (*Aside to* HAMLET.): I knew you must be edified by the margent° ere you had done. 14▮

OSRIC: The carriages, sir, are the hangers.

---

108. **yaw:** hold to a course unsteadily, like a ship that steers wild 109. **article:** scope, importance
109. **infusion:** essence 110. **dearth:** scarcity 110-111. **semblable:** likeness 111. **trace:** (1) draw, (2) follow
111. **umbrage:** shadow 114. **concernancy:** import, relevance 117. **to't:** i.e., to get an understanding
119. **nomination:** mention 125. **approve:** commend 127. **compare:** compete 130. **meed:** pay 130. **unfellowed:** unequaled 135. **impawned:** staked 136. **assigns:** appendages 136. **carriages:** an affected word for hangers, i.e., straps from which the weapon was hung 138. **liberal conceit:** elaborate design
140. **margent:** margin (where explanatory notes were printed)

HAMLET: The phrase would be more germane to the matter if we could
 carry cannon by our sides. I would it might be hangers till then. But
 on! Six Barbary horses against six French swords, their assigns, and   145
 three liberal conceited carriages; that's the French bet against the Danish. Why is this all impawned, as you call it?
OSRIC: The king, sir, hath laid, sir, that in a dozen passes between yourself
 and him he shall not exceed you three hits;° he hath laid on twelve for
 nine,° and it would come to immediate trial if your lordship would   150
 vouchsafe the answer.
HAMLET: How if I answer no?
OSRIC: I mean, my lord, the opposition of your person in trial.
HAMLET: Sir, I will walk here in the hall. If it please his majesty, it is the
 breathing time° of day with me. Let the foils be brought, the gentleman   155
 willing, and the king hold his purpose; I will win for him an° I can. If
 not, I will gain nothing but my shame and the odd hits.
OSRIC: Shall I deliver you so?
HAMLET: To this effect, sir, after what flourish your nature will.
OSRIC: I commend my duty to your lordship.   160
HAMLET: Yours. (*Exit* OSRIC.) He does well to commend it himself; there
 are no tongues else for's turn.
HORATIO: This lapwing° runs away with the shell on his head.
HAMLET: 'A did comply,° sir, with his dug,° before 'a sucked it. Thus has he,
 and many more of the same bevy° that I know the drossy° age dotes on,   165
 only got the tune of the time; and out of an habit of encounter,° a kind
 of yesty collection° which carries them through and through the most
 fanned and winnowed° opinions; and do but blow them to their trial,
 the bubbles are out.
(*Enter a* LORD.)
LORD: My lord, his majesty commended him to you by young Osric, who   170
 brings back to him that you attend him in the hall. He sends to know if
 your pleasure hold to play with Laertes, or that you will take longer
 time.

148-149. in a dozen passes...he shall not exceed you three hits: the odds the King proposes seem to
be that in a match of twelve bouts, Hamlet will win at least five. Laertes would need to win by at least eight
to four 149-150. he hath laid on twelve for nine: "he" apparently is Laertes, who has seemingly raised
the odds against himself by wagering that out of twelve bouts he will win nine 155. breathing time: time
for taking exercise 156. an: if 163. lapwing: a bird reputedly so precocious as to run as soon as hatched
164. comply: observe the formalities of courtesy 164. dug: mother's nipple 165. bevy: a covey of quails or
lapwings 165. drossy: frivolous 166. encounter: manner of address or accosting 167. yesty collection: a
frothy and superficial patchwork of terms from the conversation of others 168. winnowed: tested, freed
from inferior elements

HAMLET: I am constant to my purposes: they follow the king's pleasure. If his fitness° speaks, mine is ready; now or whensoever, provided I be so able as now. 175

LORD: The king and queen and all are coming down.

HAMLET: In happy time.

LORD: The queen desires you to use some gentle entertainment to Laertes before you fall to play. 180

HAMLET: She well instructs me.

(*Exit* LORD.)

HORATIO: You will lose, my lord.

HAMLET: I do not think so. Since he went into France, I have been in continual practice. I shall win at the odds. But thou wouldst not think how ill all's here about my heart. But it is no matter. 185

HORATIO: Nay, good my lord—

HAMLET: It is but foolery, but it is such a kind of gaingiving° as would perhaps trouble a woman.

HORATIO: If your mind dislike any thing, obey it. I will forestall their repair hither, and say you are not fit. 190

HAMLET: Not a whit, we defy augury. There is a special providence in the fall of a sparrow. If it be now, 'tis not to come; if it be not to come, it will be now; if it be not now, yet it will come. The readiness is all. Since no man of aught he leaves knows, what is't to leave betimes? Let be.

(*A table prepared. Enter trumpets, drums, and* OFFICERS *with cushions;* KING, QUEEN, OSRIC, *and all the* STATE, *with foils, daggers, and* LAERTES.)

KING: Come, Hamlet, come, and take this hand from me. 195

(*The* KING *puts* LAERTES' *hand into* HAMLET'S.)

HAMLET: Give me your pardon, sir. I have done you wrong,
But pardon 't as you are a gentleman.
This presence knows, and you must needs have heard,
How I am punished with a sore distraction.
What I have done 200
That might your nature, honour, and exception,
Roughly awake, I here proclaim was madness.
Was 't Hamlet wronged Laertes? Never Hamlet.
If Hamlet from himself be ta'en away,
And when he's not himself does wrong Laertes, 205
Then Hamlet does it not. Hamlet denies it.
Who does it then? His madness. If 't be so,
Hamlet is of the faction that is wronged;
His madness is poor Hamlet's enemy.

---

175. fitness: convenience, inclination 187. gaingiving: misgiving

Sir, in this audience,   210
Let my disclaiming from a purposed evil
Free me so far in your most generous thoughts
That I have shot mine arrow o'er the house,
And hurt my brother.
LAERTES: I am satisfied in nature,
Whose motive in this case should stir me most   215
To my revenge. But in my terms of honor
I stand aloof, and will no reconcilement
Till by some elder masters of known honor,
I have a voice and precedent° of peace
To keep my name ungored. But till that time   220
I do receive your offered love like love,
And will not wrong it.
HAMLET: I embrace if freely,
And will this brother's wager frankly play.
Give us the foils.°
LAERTES: Come, one for me.
HAMLET: I'll be your foil, Laertes. In mine ignorance   225
Your skill shall, like a star i' th' darkest night,
Stick fiery off indeed.
LAERTES: You mock me, sir.
HAMLET: No, by this hand.
KING: Give them the foils, young Osric. Cousin Hamlet,
You know the wager?   230
HAMLET: Very well, my lord;
Your Grace has laid the odds o'th' weaker side.
KING: I do not fear it, I have seen you both;
But since he is bettered,° we have therefore odds.
LAERTES: This is too heavy; let me see another.
HAMLET: This likes me well. These foils have all a length?°   235
(*They prepare to play.*)
OSRIC: Ay, my good lord.
KING: Set me the stoups of wine upon that table.
If Hamlet give the first or second hit,
Or quit in answer° of the third exchange,
Let all the battlements their ordnance fire.   240
The king shall drink to Hamlet's better breath,

---

219. **voice and precedent:** authoritative statement justified by precedent 224. **foil:** (1) setting for gem
(2) weapon 233. **bettered:** perfected through training 235. **have all a length:** are all of the same length
239. **quit in answer:** literally, give as good as he gets (i.e., if the third bout is a draw)

And in the cup an union° shall he throw,
Richer than that which four successive kings
In Denmark's crown have worn. Give me the cups,
And let the kettle to the trumpet speak,   24⁵
The trumpet to the cannoneer without,
The cannons to the heavens, the heaven to earth,
'Now the king drinks to Hamlet.' Come begin—
(Trumpets the while.)
And you, the judges, bear a wary eye.
HAMLET: Come on, sir.   25⁰
LAERTES: Come, my lord.
(They play.)
HAMLET: One.
LAERTES: No.
HAMLET: Judgment.   25⁶
OSRIC: A hit, a very palpable hit.
(Drums, trumpets, and shot. Flourish; a piece goes off.)
LAERTES: Well, again.
KING: Stay, give me drink. Hamlet, this pearl is thine.
    Here's to thy health. Give him the cup.
HAMLET: I'll play this bout first; set it by awhile.   25⁵
    Come.
    (They play.)
    Another hit; what say you?
LAERTES: I do confess't.
KING: Our son shall win.
QUEEN: He's fat,° and scant of breath.
    Here, Hamlet, take my napkin, rub thy brows.   26⁰
    The queen carouses to thy fortune, Hamlet.
HAMLET: Good madam!
KING: Gertrude, do not drink.
QUEEN: I will, my lord; I pray you pardon me.
KING *(Aside.)*: It is the poisoned cup; it is too late.   26⁵
HAMLET: I dare not drink yet, madam; by and by.
QUEEN: Come, let me wipe thy face.
LAERTES: My lord, I'll hit him now.
KING: I do not think't.
LAERTES *(Aside.)*: And yet it is almost against my conscience.

---

242. union: pearl 259. fat: out of training

HAMLET: Come, for the third, Laertes. You but dally.   270
    I pray you pass with your best violence;
    I am afeard you make a wanton of me.°
LAERTES: Say you so? come on.
(*They play.*)
OSRIC: Nothing, neither way.
LAERTES: Have at you now!   275
(LAERTES *wounds* HAMLET; *then, in scuffling, they change rapiers.*)
KING: Part them. They are incensed.
HAMLET: Nay, come again.
(HAMLET *wounds* LAERTES. *The* QUEEN *falls.*)
OSRIC: Look to the queen there, ho!
HORATIO: They bleed on both sides. How is it, my lord?
OSRIC: How is't Laertes?   280
LAERTES: Why, as a woodcock to mine own springe,° Osric.
    I am justly killed with mine own treachery.
HAMLET: How does the queen?
KING: She swoons to see them bleed.
QUEEN: No, no, the drink, the drink! O my dear Hamlet!
    The drink, the drink! I am poisoned.   285
(*Dies.*)
HAMLET: O villany! Ho! let the door be locked.
    Treachery! Seek it out.
(LAERTES *falls. Exit* OSRIC.)
LAERTES: It is here, Hamlet. Hamlet, thou art slain;
    No med'cine in the world can do thee good.
    In thee there is not half an hour's life.   290
    The treacherous instrument is in thy hand,
    Unbated° and envenomed. The foul practice
    Hath turned itself on me. Lo, here I lie,
    Never to rise again. Thy mother's poisoned.
    I can no more. The king, the king's to blame.   295
HAMLET: The point envenomed too!
    Then, venom, to thy work.
(*Wounds the* KING.)
ALL: Treason! treason!
KING: O, yet defend me, friends. I am but hurt.
HAMLET: Here, thou incestuous, murd'rous, damnèd Dane,   300
    Drink off this potion. Is thy union here?

---

272. **make a wanton of me:** trifle with me 281. **springe:** trap 292. **Unbated:** unblunted; practice plot

Follow my mother.

(KING *dies.*)

LAERTES: He is justly served.
 It is a poison tempered by himself.
 Exchange forgiveness with me, noble Hamlet.
 Mine and my father's death come not upon thee,   305
 Nor thine on me!

(*Dies.*)

HAMLET: Heaven make thee free of it! I follow thee.
 I am dead, Horatio. Wretched queen, adieu!
 You that look pale and tremble at this chance,
 That are but mutes or audience to this act,   310
 Had I but time, as this fell° sergeant° Death
 Is strict in his arrest, O, I could tell you—
 But let it be. Horatio, I am dead:
 Thou livest; report me and my cause aright
 To the unsatisfied.   315

HORATIO: Never believe it:
 I am more an antique Roman than a Dane.
 Here's yet some liquor left.

HAMLET: As th'art a man,
 Give me the cup. Let go. By heaven, I'll ha't.
 O God, Horatio, what a wounded name,
 Things standing thus unknown, shall live behind me! 320
 If thou didst ever hold me in thy heart,
 Absent thee from felicity awhile,
 And in this harsh world draw thy breath in pain,
 To tell my story.

 (*A march afar off.*)

 What warlike noise is this?   325

(*Enter* OSRIC.)

OSRIC: Young Fortinbras, with conquest come from Poland,
 To th' ambassadors of England gives
 This warlike volley.

HAMLET: O, I die, Horatio!
 The potent poison quite o'er-crows° my spirit.
 I cannot live to hear the news from England,   330
 But I do prophesy th' election lights
 On Fortinbras. He has my dying voice.°

---

311. **fell**: cruel; 311. **sergeant**: an officer whose duty is to summon persons to appear before a court
329. **o'er-crows**: triumphs over 332. **voice**: vote

So tell him, with th' occurrents, more and less,°
Which have solicited°—the rest is silence.
(Dies.)
HORATIO: Now cracks a noble heart. Good night, sweet prince,   335
    And flights of angels sing thee to thy rest!
    (March within.)
    Why does the drum come hither?
(Enter FORTINBRAS, *with the* AMBASSADORS *[and with drum, colors, and*
    ATTENDANTS*].)*
FORTINBRAS: Where is this sight?
HORATIO: What is it you would see?
    If aught of woe or wonder, cease your search.
FORTINBRAS: This quarry° cries on havoc. O proud Death,   340
    What feast is toward° in thine eternal cell
    That thou so many princes at a shot
    So bloodily hast struck?
AMBASSADORS: The sight is dismal;
    And our affairs from England come too late.
    The ears are senseless that should give us hearing   345
    To tell him his commandment is fulfilled,
    That Rosencrantz and Guildenstern are dead.
    Where should we have our thanks?
HORATIO: Not from his mouth,
    Had it th' ability of life to thank you.
    He never gave commandment for their death.   350
    But since, so jump° upon this bloody question,
    You from the Polack wars, and you from England,
    Are here arrived, give order that these bodies
    High on a stage be placèd to the view,
    And let me speak to th' yet unknowing world   355
    How these things came about. So shall you hear
    Of carnal, bloody, and unnatural acts;
    Of accidental judgements, casual slaughters;
    Of deaths put on° by cunning and forced cause°;
    And, in this upshot, purposes mistook   360
    Fall'n on th' inventors' heads. All this can I
    Truly deliver.

---

333. more and less: great and small 334. solicited: incited, prompted 340. quarry: pile of dead
341. toward: impending 351. jump: exactly 359. put on: instigated 359. forced cause: by reason of
compulsion

FORTINBRAS: Let us haste to hear it.
And call the noblest to the audience.
For me, with sorrow I embrace my fortune.
I have some rights of memory in this kingdom,   365
Which now to claim my vantage doth invite me.
HORATIO: Of that I shall have also cause to speak,
And from his mouth whose voice will draw on more.
But let this same be presently performed,
Even while men's minds are wild, lest more mischance   370
On plots and errors happen.
FORTINBRAS: Let four captains
Bear Hamlet like a soldier to the stage,
For he was likely, had he been put on,°
To have proved most royal; and for his passage°
The soldier's music and the rite of war   375
Speak loudly for him.
Take up the bodies. Such a sight as this
Becomes the field, but here shows much amiss.
Go, bid the soldiers shoot.

■ Like Oedipus, Hamlet is a character who is trying to figure out how to act in the face of an apparent murder. The story works as a detective story. It works as a ghost story. Hamlet is simultaneously trying to map out his own position within the court and convince others to act in a manner that might work to his benefit. Find and trace a specific example of such manipulation. Pick a specific character, describe Hamlet's relation to that character, and trace how Hamlet appeals to, reasons with, and manipulates that particular character.

■ Hamlet's interior struggles mark and influence his ability and inability to act within the play. Look at a specific soliloquy. In this speech, to what extent is Hamlet exploring his own character or some moral quandary? How does this speech to no one in the play interrupt or redirect the action of the play? Compare the function of this speech within the play to that of a chorus.

■ By the time that all of the major characters lie dead at the end of the play, we tend to sympathize with Hamlet. Pick one of the other characters who lies there with him, and trace a line of reasoning that justifies his or her actions throughout the play.

---

373. **put on:** set to perform in office 374. **passage:** death

Experiencing Literature through Writing

1. Select a single work from this chapter (or any other). Locate a specific interruption within the text. Give details to indicate how it is apparent that this is an interruption. As you write, consider the following questions:

   a. What is it that has been interrupted? Is it the structure of the text? Is it some event within the text? Is it some idea within the text?

   b. What is the nature of the interruption? Is there any other similar moment within the text? How is this moment different from others within the text?

   c. What is the impact of the interruption? How does the text change after the interruption? How much of this change is obvious to characters within the text? How much is an impact upon those who are reading the text?

   d. Why is the interruption significant? How does attention to this interruption offer either some avenue to interpret the text or insight into the ways in which this text functions?

2. This collection of works shares a common concern with the idea of "framing, mapping, and exploration." As you think about the works in the collection, discuss the sorts of exploration that the text presents. What tools do the texts offer for their explorations? How does the idea of creating a map of some exterior space allow introspection?

3. Filmic juxtaposition sets images (and scenes) next to one another in order to create a powerful emotional impact. Find a specific instance in one work where the author creates a set of juxtaposed images to create such an impact. Explain how the author sets up this impact and constructs the text to control our reaction in some specific way.

10 Tone

Did I Hear That Right?

A tone is simply a sound—a sound that by duration, pitch, or volume achieves a certain quality. The tones we notice most contrast sharply with what we usually hear: "When my mother uses that tone, all trouble stops" or "Don't use that tone with me, young man." When we discuss tone, we refer to the way that a person delivers a message rather than just the message itself. This delivery includes the quality of voice and the choice of words; it tells us about the deliverer's attitude toward the message, and it has an impact upon how we hear the message.

The visual arts also use the quality of tone to describe the impact that an artist creates. The blinking light on the photocopy machine tells us that the machine is low on toner, the pigment used to create the range of black and gray that makes up the images on our page. In black-and-white photography, the photographer might replace the black with the rich brown of sepia to give the print an older appearance. Attention to such toning elements does not change the document that we are photocopying or the scene in the photograph, but it has a marked impact upon the printed images that we see. The photocopy made without enough toner will look quite light, whereas the original sepia photograph, although new, looks as if it came from another time. The tone determines how we receive these visual images just as a tone of voice influences our understanding of the words that we hear.

HEARING RIGHT

Hearing right can make all the difference. The same words delivered with a different tone of voice can have very different meanings. Consider the following poem:

Margaret Atwood (1939–)

you fit into me (1971)

> You fit into me
> like a hook into an eye
> A fish hook
> An open eye

The first words, "you fit into me," make us think that the poem is a love poem. Working through the simile, we imagine the hook and eye that are used as clothing fasteners, but the last two lines shock us out of this reading with the violent image of a fishhook piercing an eyeball. That change in the final lines suggests a severe bitterness about the relation between the narrator and the "you" in the poem. It is no mistake that we read the first lines as almost loving, yet we must abruptly rethink that immediate response. We realize in the final lines that what we read as a shift in tone is really a shift in our understanding of that tone. The narrator has been bitter throughout the poem; we simply do not realize it until we get to the third line.

We usually pick up on conversational signals instantly, but when words are written down, it is sometimes difficult to "hear" clearly. How can you tell that someone is being reverent rather than ironic? One clue is our knowledge of that person. The same sort of knowledge is useful when we read, though more challenging to attain. We learn about certain authors, so we know what to expect from them. This knowledge often makes us better readers. As you get to know authors, your ability to hear their tone improves. But in the Atwood poem, the poet might be taking advantage of what a reader doesn't know about her attitudes toward the difficult complexity of relationships. **Irony** requires us to hold up two possible meanings simultaneously—the narrator could be expressing a great love or could be expressing great revulsion—and to pick one of those readings. Setting up the first interpretation by playing to our investment in the idea of romantic love makes the second (real) interpretation so much more stinging and darkly humorous. Atwood presses toward **sarcasm**—an extreme and aggressive form of **verbal irony** in which the thing *said* and the thing *meant* stand in stark opposition. When we discuss tone in a text, we generally refer to complex forms of expression that do not announce their intentions clearly. A **sincere** tone, for instance, may accurately describe a particular work but would rarely generate much discussion. Sincerity may be taken as the other extreme of sarcasm, for a sincere expression matches word and meaning. When we discuss tone, we usually refer to the distortions that influence how we hear words and how we learn to interpret those words.

What if you have never read the works of a particular author? How can you hear the tone of someone whose work is new to you? Remember that even in conversation, you are aware of the context in which something has been said. A commonplace saying like "Have a nice day" could be either sarcastic or sincere, but in most cases it is unlikely we would have trouble hearing the difference. When someone says that this is the best time he or she has ever had, you have clues surrounding you about whether or not that person seems to be having a good time. Is the person enthusiastic? Do things really appear to be going well? Those clues help you figure out what meaning to take from the words.

Experiencing Literature through Tone

Dorothy Parker, whom you should never trust to deliver a toneless poem, uses the conventions of love poetry to talk about the "perfect rose" that she has received.

Dorothy Parker (1893–1967)

One Perfect Rose (1926)

A single flower he sent me, since we met.
   All tenderly his messenger he chose;
Deep-hearted, pure, with scented dew still wet—
   One perfect rose.

I knew the language of the floweret;   5
   "My fragile leaves," it said, "his heart enclose."
Love long has taken for his amulet
   One perfect rose.

Why is it no one ever sent me yet
   One perfect limousine, do you suppose?   10
Ah no, it's always just my luck to get
   One perfect rose.

Look closely at her word choice that shows how she suggests the tone of conventional love poetry in her first two stanzas. Which word changes the tone of this entire poem? How does this shift change the meaning of all of the lines that have come before it? By the end of the poem, we're ready to go back and read everything differently. Like Atwood, Parker turns against the conventions of romantic love. But her turn doesn't communicate quite the same painful edginess.

Next, look at another of Parker's poems. What common ideas do you associate with the title "Thought for a Sunshiny Morning"?

Dorothy Parker (1893–1967)

Thought for a Sunshiny Morning (1936)

It costs me never a stab nor squirm
To tread by chance upon a worm.
"Aha, my little dear," I say,
"Your clan will pay me back one day."

Notice that having read another poem by Parker does not spoil this second poem. In fact, our experience with the two poems helps us form a preliminary feeling for Parker's distinctive voice. We do have some idea of the sort of thing that we might expect, but here the tone begins with a title that contrasts sharply with the subject of death. The simple rhyme scheme and rhythmic pattern also contribute to the almost cheerful fatalism of Parker's poetic voice. With these two examples, how might you begin to define Parker's tone?

The tone in John Donne's poem "The Flea" is altogether different, but understanding the tone remains an essential key to unlocking the poem. Donne also holds up multiple meanings; he dismisses serious issues of virtue by asking whether a flea has stolen his lover's virginity by sucking first his blood and then hers. Even as Donne delights in turning the metaphor inside out, he hardly seems to be mocking virtue or his beloved. We might say he maintains a playfully sincere tone in this poem.

John Donne (1572–1631)

The Flea (1633)

Mark but this flea, and mark in this,
How little that which thou deniest me is;
It suck'd me first, and now sucks thee,

And in this flea our two bloods mingled be.
Thou know'st that this cannot be said   5
A sin, nor shame, nor loss of maidenhead;
    Yet this enjoys before it woo,
    And pamper'd swells with one blood made of two;
    And this, alas! is more than we would do.

O stay, three lives in one flea spare,   10
Where we almost, yea, more than married are.
This flea is you and I, and this
Our marriage bed, and marriage temple is.
Though parents grudge, and you, we're met,
And cloister'd in these living walls of jet.   15
    Though use make you apt to kill me,
    Let not to that self-murder added be,
    And sacrilege, three sins in killing three.

Cruel and sudden, hast thou since
Purpled thy nail in blood of innocence?   20
Wherein could this flea guilty be,
Except in that drop which it suck'd from thee?
Yet thou triumph'st, and say'st that thou
Find'st not thyself nor me the weaker now.
    'Tis true; then learn how false fears be;   25
    Just so much honour, when thou yield'st to me,
    Will waste, as this flea's death took life from thee.

As we make our way through this poem, Donne's language of virtue constantly must compete with the fact that his subject is really the flea that she kills. Her nail "Purpled" in the "blood of innocence" gives the event an inappropriately lofty language. Until we realize that his single goal here is to break down her virtue, this language may make the poem itself appear much more lofty than it is. Donne wants the flea, now dead even though it had swallowed her blood, to symbolize the meaninglessness of conventions that enforce virginity.

MIXING AND BALANCING OPPOSING TONES

Ted Kooser writes a poem in which he captures the idiosyncratic tone of a person who might be anyone's "Aunt Belle" remarking on a terrible tragedy.

The name of the person gives us a sense of the chattiness and random connections that often accompany such relations where there are shared memories and understandings that help maintain a sense of family. As you read this "letter," note how the tone shifts abruptly as a core story haltingly unfolds. In what ways is this uneven tone appropriate? What details from Aunt Belle's correspondence define this tone for you? Is this poem ultimately about a tragic event or about a character? Perhaps it is about a specific character's response to tragedy.

Ted Kooser (1939–)

A Letter from Aunt Belle (2004)

You couldn't have heard about it there—
I'll send the clippings later on.

The afternoon that the neighbors' stove exploded—
how it reminded me of … Sarah's garden wedding!
Do you remember? It was beautiful.   5

As I was watering those slips
I promised you—the violets—
there was an awful thud, and Samson's wall
puffed up and blew the windows out.
It turned some pictures in the living room,   10
and that lovely vase you children gave to me
Christmas of '56 fell down, but I can glue it.

That Franklin boy you knew in school—
the one who got that girl in trouble—
ran in the Samson's house, but she was dead;   15
the blast collapsed her lungs, poor thing.
She always made me think of you,
but on the stretcher with her hair pinned up
and one old sandal off, she looked as old
as poor old me.   20
                         I have to go—
I've baked a little coffee cake
for Mr. Samson and the boys.

The violet slips are ready—
                         Write.

Identify the clues that help you recognize the tone of this letter: the questions, the promises of future correspondence, the references to an old neighbor, the assumption of authority over the reader, the neighborliness, the chattiness, the gossipy delivery of the tragic news. All of these details teach us to know the character who is writing and help us interpret her words. Notice how this tone nearly hides the most significant news the letter has to communicate. Buried inside the offer of violet slips and memories of Sarah's garden wedding is the death of a wife and mother. But the chatty delivery of this news doesn't lessen the poem's impact. It actually deepens our sense of the speaker; it helps us know her better than she knows herself. Aunt Belle may revert to conversational niceties, but she is struck by this death: "she looked as old / as poor old me." And she does what she can to alleviate the grief of "Mr. Samson and the boys." The poem offers a full account of her old-fashioned neighborliness: she gossips, but she also feels a responsibility to those who live around her.

Experiencing Literature through Tone

Like all considerations of tone, humor requires some understanding of the context in which the performance occurs. Much humor involves an upsetting of traditional, recognizable, and well-understood structures. To recognize that a structure has been upset, one must be fairly familiar with the original. In order to appreciate irreverence, one needs some experience with reverence. In some ways, irreverence may be the more complex attitude, at least in terms of interpretation. In the following passage from *Mules and Men*, Zora Neale Hurston sets us down in the middle of a conversation about the nature of religious controversy in a small town. The main character, Charlie, creates a story that conflates several familiar stories from the New Testament. In order to appreciate Charlie's story (and to laugh with the others around this particular table), one has to know the originals. The religious teachings of Jesus sometimes depend upon a clear literalness; other times they are metaphors. When Jesus says, "Upon this rock, I will build my church," it is generally understood that he is playing with the derivation of Peter's name—he will build a church upon the bedrock, the faith that Peter (*petra*, "rock") has professed. In other biblical incidents, the Christian tradition emphasizes the literalness of Jesus' miraculous work—he was able to feed thousands of people with only five loaves of bread, and he turned water into wine. This particular story finds its humor by having Charlie take everything literally.

Zora Neale Hurston (1891–1960)

from **Mules and Men** (1935)

As the prayer ended the bell of Macedonia, the Baptist church, began to ring.

"Prayer meetin 'night at Macedony," George Thomas said.

"It's too bad that it must be two churches in Eatonville," I commented. "De town's too little. Everybody ought to go to one."

"It's too bad, Zora, and you know better. Fack is, de Christian churches nowhere don't stick together," this from Charlie.

Everybody agreed that this was true. So Charlie went on. "Look at all de kind of denominations we got. But de people can't help dat cause de church wasn't built on no solid foundation to start wid."

"Oh yes, it twas!" Johnnie Mae disputed him. "It was built on solid rock. Didn't Jesus say 'On dis rock Ah build my church?'"

"Yeah," chimed in Antie Hoyt. "And de song says 'On Christ solid rock I stand' and 'Rock of Ages.'"

Charlie was calm and patient. "Yeah, he built it on a rock, but it wasn't solid. It was a pieced-up rock and that's how come de church split up now. Here's de very way it was:

Christ was walkin' long one day wid all his disciples and he said, 'We're goin' for a walk today. Everybody pick up a rock and come along.' So everybody got their selves a nice big rock 'ceptin' Peter. He was lazy so he picked up a li'l bit of a pebble and dropped it in his side pocket and come along.

Well, they walked all day long and de other 'leven disciples changed them rocks from one arm to de other but they kept on totin' 'em. Long towards sundown they come 'long by de Sea of Galilee and Jesus tole 'em, 'Well, le's fish awhile. Cast in yo' nets right here.' They done like he tole ,em and caught a great big mess of fish. Then they cooked 'em and Christ said, 'Now, all y'all bring up yo' rocks.' So they all brought they rocks and Christ turned 'em into bread and they all had a plenty to eat wid they fish exceptin' Peter. He couldn't hardly make a moufful offa de li'l bread he had and he didn't like dat a bit.

Two or three days after dat Christ went out doors and looked up at de sky and says, 'Well, we're goin' for an other walk today. Everybody git yo'self a rock and come along.'

They all picked up a rock apiece and was ready to go. All but Peter. He went and tore down half a mountain. It was so big he couldn't move it wid his hands. He had to take a pinch-bar to move it. All day long Christ walked and talked to his disciples and Peter sweated and strained wid dat rock of his'n.

Way long in de evenin' Christ went up under a great big ole tree and set down and called all of his disciples around 'im and said, 'Now everybody bring up yo' rocks.'

So everybody brought theirs but Peter. Peter was about mile down de road punchin' dat half a mountain he was bringin'. So Christ waited till he got dere. He looked at de rocks dat de other 'leven disciples had, den he seen dis great big mountain dat Peter had and so he got up and walked over to it and put one foot up on it and said, "Why Peter, dis is a fine rock you got here! It's a noble rock! And Peter, on dis rock Ab'm gointer build my church.'

Peter says, 'Naw you ain't neither. You won't build no church house on dis rock. You gointer turn dis rock into bread.'

Christ knowed dat Peter meant dat thing so he turnt de hillside into bread and dat mountain is de bread he fed de 5,000 wid. Den he took dem 'leven other rocks and glued 'em together and built his church on it.

And that's how come de Christian churches is split up into so many different kinds cause it's built on pieced-up rock." ▪

Making Connections

Consider how the tonal clash between different kinds of language and representation function in other works you've read or films you've seen. Shakespeare, for example, is known for mixing the formal and the informal, the "high" and the "low." What specific instances in either *Much Ado about Nothing* (p. 340) or *Hamlet* (p. 896) strike you as especially meaningful? Or consider another dramatic example, *Topdog/Updog* (p. 578) by Suzan-Lori Parks. In that play, one character enacts in a cheap boardwalk show a major event in U.S. history that has been recounted solemnly in standard textbooks. Does Parks use the tone of the boardwalk show against that of the history book in order to comment on the attitude we usually take toward the national tragedy of President Lincoln's assassination? Does she seek to make us rethink the kind of importance we typically grant it?

The humorous tone of Hurston's story is also created out of the informal retelling of what are taken as sacred texts. Such mixing of **colloquial** (spoken) with consciously literary (written) styles is a common way to refresh or challenge language that has grown distant in its formality. Charlie may not have a strong command of the King James Bible (an early seventeenth-century translation that has been called "the noblest monument of English prose"), but he cannot be accused of being a passive reader. We might ask, How does Hurston want us to see Charlie? Do we come away from this comic dialogue with a sense of his foolishness or an appreciation for his wit?

IRONY AND INTROSPECTION

There is something appealing about the fact that opposites can coexist. Peter and his disjointed united church present an explanation of one such coexistence. In the following poem, Margaret Atwood builds upon the legend of the Sirens, the beautiful bird-women whose songs are so alluring that they cause sailors to crash upon the rocks. In this poem, Atwood chooses to imagine that beautiful music from the singer's perspective. That shift again leads to a dramatically different tone.

Margaret Atwood (1939–)

Siren Song (1976)

This is the one song everyone
would like to learn: the song
that is irresistible:
the song that forces men
to leap overboard in squadrons   5
even though they see the beached skulls
the song nobody knows
because anyone who has heard it
is dead, and the others can't remember
Shall I tell you the secret   10
and if I do, will you get me
out of this bird suit?
I don't enjoy it here
squatting on this island
looking picturesque and mythical   15
with these two feathery maniacs,
I don't enjoy singing
this trio, fatal and valuable.
I will tell the secret to you,
to you, only to you.   20
Come closer. This song
is a cry for help: Help me!
Only you, only you can,
you are unique

At last. Alas   25
it is a boring song
but it works every time.

The song that the sailor considers worth risking his life for is "boring" to the woman who is singing it. This irony is based on perceptions, on the different points of view; the two individuals represented in the story perceive the details in the story completely differently. Suddenly, what we may have heard as beautiful (an appeal to strength and uniqueness)sounds disturbing and illusive.

Often tonal shifts signal ironic gaps between the passionate beliefs of a character and the quite different judgments of the narrator or author. In Chinua Achebe's "Dead Men's Path," for instance, Michael Obi's conviction that the old needs to be replaced by the modern must be assessed in light of the quiet assurance of the narrative (and of the village priest) that old ways must be respected. As you read, note how the story sets up Obi, and note the specific instances in the narrative where Obi's confident convictions seem foolish rather than insightful.

Chinua Achebe (1930–)

Dead Men's Path (1972)

Michael Obi's hopes were fulfilled much earlier than he had expected. He was appointed headmaster of Ndume Central School in January 1949. It had always been an unprogressive school, so the Mission authorities decided to send a young and energetic man to run it. Obi accepted this responsibility with enthusiasm. He had many wonderful ideas and this was an opportunity to put them into practice. He had had sound secondary school education which designated him a "pivotal teacher" in the official records and set him apart from the other headmasters in the mission field. He was outspoken in his condemnation of the narrow views of these older and often less-educated ones.

"We shall make a good job of it, shan't we?" he asked his young wife when they first heard the joyful news of his promotion.

"We shall do our best," she replied. "We shall have such beautiful gardens and everything will be just *modern* and delightful ..." In their two years of married life she had become completely infected by his passion for "modern methods" and his denigration of "these old and superannuated people in the teaching field who would be better employed as traders in the Onitsha market." She began to see herself already as the admired wife of the young headmaster, the queen of the school.

The wives of the other teachers would envy her position. She would set the fashion in everything ... Then, suddenly, it occurred to her that there might not be other wives. Wavering between hope and fear, she asked her husband, looking anxiously at him.

"All our colleagues are young and unmarried," he said with enthusiasm   5
which for once she did not share. "Which is a good thing," he continued.

"Why?"

"Why? They will give all their time and energy to the school."

Nancy was downcast. For a few minutes she became skeptical about the new school; but it was only for a few minutes. Her little personal misfortune could not blind her to her husband's happy prospects. She looked at him as he sat folded up in a chair. He was stoop-shouldered and looked frail. But he sometimes surprised people with sudden bursts of physical energy. In his present posture, however, all his bodily strength seemed to have retired behind his deep-set eyes, giving them an extraordinary power of penetration. He was only twenty-six, but looked thirty or more. On the whole, he was not unhandsome.

"A penny for your thoughts, Mike," said Nancy after a while, imitating the woman's magazine she read.

"I was thinking what a grand opportunity we've got at last to show these   10
people how a school should be run." Ndume School was backward in every sense of the word. Mr. Obi put his whole life into the work, and his wife hers too. He had two aims. A high standard of teaching was insisted upon, and the school compound was to be turned into a place of beauty. Nancy's dream-gardens came to life with the coming of the rains, and blossomed. Beautiful hibiscus and allamanda hedges in brilliant red and yellow marked out the carefully tended school compound from the rank neighborhood bushes.

One evening as Obi was admiring his work he was scandalized to see an old woman from the village hobble right across the compound, through a marigold flower-bed and the hedges. On going up there he found faint signs of an almost disused path from the village across the school compound to the bush on the other side.

"It amazes me," said Obi to one of his teachers who had been three years in the school, "that you people allowed the villagers to make use of this footpath. It is simply incredible." He shook his head.

"The path," said the teacher apologetically, "appears to be very important to them. Although it is hardly used, it connects the village shrine with their place of burial."

"And what has that got to do with the school"? asked the headmaster.

"Well, I don't know," replied the other with a shrug of the shoulders. "But I remember there was a big row some time ago when we attempted to close it."

"That was some time ago. But it will not be used now," said Obi as he walked away. "What will the Government Education Officer think of this when he comes to inspect the school next week? The villagers might, for all I know, decide to use the schoolroom for a pagan ritual during the inspection."

Heavy sticks were planted closely across the path at the two places where it entered and left the school premises. These were further strengthened with barbed wire.

Three days later the village priest of Ani called on the headmaster. He was an old man and walked with a slight stoop. He carried a stout walking-stick which he usually tapped on the floor, by way of emphasis, each time he made a new point in his argument.

"I have heard," he said after the usual exchange of cordialities, "that our ancestral footpath has recently been closed ... "

"Yes," replied Mr. Obi. "We cannot allow people to make a highway of our school compound."

"Look here, my son," said the priest bringing down his walking-stick, "this path was here before you were born and before your father was born. The whole life of this village depends on it. Our dead relatives depart by it and our ancestors visit us by it. But most important, it is the path of children coming in to be born ... "

Mr. Obi listened with a satisfied smile on his face.

"The whole purpose of our school," he said finally, "is to eradicate just such beliefs as that. Dead men do not require footpaths. The whole idea is just fantastic. Our duty is to teach your children to laugh at such ideas."

"What you say may be true," replied the priest, "but we follow the practices of our fathers. If you re-open the path we shall have nothing to quarrel about. What I always say is: let the hawk perch and let the eagle perch." He rose to go.

"I am sorry," said the young headmaster. "But the school compound cannot be a thoroughfare. It is against our regulations. I would suggest your constructing another path, skirting our premises. We can even get our boys to help in building it. I don't suppose the ancestors will find the little detour too burdensome."

"I have no more words to say," said the old priest, already outside.

Two days later a young woman in the village died in childbed. A diviner was immediately consulted and he prescribed heavy sacrifices to propitiate ancestors insulted by the fence.

Obi woke up next morning among the ruins of his work. The beautiful hedges were torn up not just near the path but right round the school, the

flowers trampled to death and one of the school buildings pulled down …
That day, the white Supervisor came to inspect the school and wrote a nasty
report on the state of the premises but more seriously about the "tribal-war
situation developing between the school and the village, arising in part from
the misguided zeal of the new headmaster." ∎

Authors often want us to understand more about a situation than their
characters can grasp. In this sense, we sometimes need to hear things
differently, pick up different tones, than do key characters. This gap between a character's understanding and our own is called **dramatic irony**.
When Achebe's narrator speaks of Obi, for example, the narrator and the
reader see the irony, but Obi does not. Atwood's Siren's wisdom is something that no sailor will be able to appreciate, for the sailor is lured to
destruction before wisdom can be appreciated. When Hurston presents the
story of Peter's rock, the critique is of a church in which the speakers
participate. The same technique, though, applies well to **introspection**—a
personal willingness to take in and reflect upon ideas that may seem to
conflict but at some level make sense together. A **paradox** exists when some
truth is embodied in what on the surface seems a contradiction. Czeslaw
Milosz's poem "If There Is No God" contemplates the responsibilities that
come with a godless universe. How would such a "fact" change the nature of
existence?

Czeslaw Milosz (1911–2004)

If There Is No God (*Translated from the Polish by the author and*
Robert Haas, 2004)

If there is no God,
Not everything is permitted to man.
He is still his brother's keeper
And he is not permitted to sadden his brother
By saying there is no God.   5

Milosz suggests that the religious responsibilities of the atheist would actually increase "If there is no God." Recognizing paradox often seems to result
from introspection and to result in an introspective tone. How is Milosz's
tone here different from the religious inquiry in Hurston's story or
the tender affection that Kooser offers in his poem? Do you feel that Milosz
speaks more directly through his speaker? Is the effect more sincere and less
ironic?

When you write critically about a literary text or film, it's important that you be very clear about signaling your own understanding of tonal shifts or of ironic gaps between author and character. Your reader, of course, will understand that a character, a speaker, and an author may possess distinct voices, but if you do not keep the distinctions clear, your *own* understanding may be called into question. Therefore, build into your text explicit explanations. For example, there is an enormous difference between the following two summary remarks regarding the eleventh paragraph in "Dead Men's Path":

1. Mr. Obi is assigned to work in a school stuck in a primitive past. He brings a very high educational standard as well as a love of beauty to the backward village.

2. Mr. Obi can only view the school as backward and in great need of rigorous teaching. He also wants to transform the school compound into a place that meets his preconceived idea of beauty.

The first summary registers Mr. Obi's thoughts without suggesting that any other thoughts might be important in the story. It doesn't suggest a coming transition to any other perspective. In short, it fails to catch anything distinctive about the tone of the paragraph from Achebe's story.

The second makes it clear that judgmental words such as *backward, rigorous, transform,* and *beautiful* all belong to a particular character. It will allow the writer to move easily to distinctly different perspectives (those of the narrator and the village chief). It prepares us to "hear" a different tone than Obi himself can appreciate.

MODELING CRITICAL ANALYSIS: JOEL COEN AND ETHAN COEN, O BROTHER, WHERE ART THOU?

On its surface, *O Brother, Where Art Thou?* (2000) might appear to offer an accurate re-creation of Depression-era Mississippi. Every image from the film, especially the tin of Dapper Dan pomade, looks as though it came directly out of that era, and the sound track transformed obscure folk music from the time and region into a popular album. This movie serves as a useful example in the discussion of tone because, in spite of the film's careful re-creation of historical detail, the audience does not judge the film as it might judge a historical epic. If a film purports to present a true story, we expect it to be faithful to that story; we will challenge such a film when it chooses to depart into fiction. But the opening sequence in *O Brother, Where Art Thou?* sets a tone that frees us from a narrow demand for historical accuracy. A chain gang in striped prison garb opens the film, singing and keeping time with their picks and hammers. The film next shifts to three prisoners, chained together, escaping from the gang. Hampered by their chains, they trip over one another as a traditional version of the folk classic "Big Rock Candy Mountain" tells of a hobo heading toward an imaginary land with cigarette trees and lemonade springs. The music and the carefully choreographed movement of the characters tilt the film more toward the comic than historic mode.

The episodic story stars George Clooney as Ulysses Everett McGill, a hero with a powerful "gift of gab" and an extraordinary attention to his slicked-back hair through all of his adventures. His convoluted language, with its slight grammatical slips, period idioms ("You two are just dumber than a bag of hammers"), and foolishly pretentious vocabulary are hardly what we expect to hear in an argument between escaped prisoners:

> Pete, the personal rancor reflected in that remark I don't intend to dignify with comment. But I would like to address your general attitude of hopeless negativism. Consider the lilies of the goddamn field or … hell! Take at look at Delmar here as your paradigm of hope.

McGill's tireless analytical bent displays a limited self-consciousness that straddles the past in the historical character he inhabits and our present. For instance, he claims that he deserves to be the leader of the group

Margaret Bourke-White, *Guard with a shotgun over his shoulder overseeing men working in a ditch while on chain gang, Hood's Chapel, Georgia* (1937)

O Brother, Where Art Thou? (2000)

because, unlike his fellow travelers, he has a "capacity for abstract thought." He is a walking encyclopedia of information completely useless to someone in his particular circumstances. In answer to a question about the physical description of the devil, he answers, "Well, there are all manner of lesser imps and demons, Pete, but the great Satan hisself is red and scaly with a bifurcated tail, and he carries a hay fork." This out-of-place encyclopedic knowledge can help us hear a tone in a film that announces in the credits that it is "based upon *The Odyssey* by Homer."

Like McGill, the film itself offers choice tidbits of knowledge that seem randomly delivered. Some links to the *Odyssey* are clear enough: John Goodman plays a one-eyed Bible salesman who resembles a Cyclops; three women Sirens doing laundry and singing a lullaby lure the travelers from their journey. Other connections to Homer's epic are far more obscure. But the often-wild mixture of parts is what constitutes the tone of the whole. There is something serious about this comedy. *O Brother, Where Art Thou?* juxtaposes shots that borrow images from the socially conscious photography of Walker Evans, Dorothea Lange, and Margaret Bourke-White with slapstick comedy. In what ways does the scene from *O Brother, Where Art Thou?* differ from the historical photo? What details help you identify the tone in the film still?

The film offers a rather subtle reading of the *Odyssey*, but in their publicity for the movie, the Coen brothers claimed that they never read the original. This self-deprecation makes them seem like students who write book reports for class without doing the reading; it also disguises, through the disarmingly dim characters of McGill and his companions, a thorough knowledge of the epic as well as a detailed rendering of American history, American cinema, and American music. *O Brother, Where Art Thou?* ultimately comments on weighty matters of race, class, progress, and religion. From the early scenes, the Coen brothers establish a tone that guides us to insights none of their characters could ever realize. That is, we hear what the characters say but understand that Ethan and Joel Coen want to say a good deal more to us.

Using Tone to Focus Writing and Discussion

- How does the author set the tone? Is there some lens that teaches us, as readers, how to read what follows? Remember that tone can come out of many of the other literary elements that we have discussed, including setting, character, point of view, and rhythm.

- Does the author reveal the tone immediately? Or does the piece depend upon our discovery of that tone later in the work?

- What is the prevailing effect in this work? Is the tone light or dark? Earnest or mocking? Straightforward or sarcastic? Outraged or enraptured? These are only a few possibilities, but they offer a good starting point for our definition of the tone that we find within any specific work.

- Is there a specific character who speaks or a specific occasion that might give us some clue about the mood of this particular work?

- What role does the tone play in this particular work? Is the tone transparent—is it something that we don't really notice as we read—or is the tone visible? Is it integral to the story?

- Does the tone change over the course of the text? For instance, there might be two different characters who approach a scene differently. The contrast between their tones might be an important barometer into meaning within the work.

- How can a discussion of tone benefit our analysis of this particular work? For instance, contrasts in tone can serve as a topic of discussion, and it may also be fruitful to discuss works that share particular tonal elements.

Anthology

CAUGHT BETWEEN LAUGHTER AND TEARS: CONSIDERING TONE IN ANALYSIS

O Brother, Where Art Thou? sets the tone for our discussion of the often-delicate balance between laughter and tears. The film addresses in a consistently comic vein weighty and even tragic matters. The Coen brothers depict a largely rural community contemplating the impact of industrialization, a region beset by racial tension, a political system subject to systematic abuse. All ends happily, and there are many laughs along the journey, but the action involves racial injustice, abysmal poverty, political corruption, and two barely thwarted lynchings. The tension between laughter and tears is evident throughout. If we cannot "hear" right, we'll dismiss the film as a confused mess. If we tune in, we'll appreciate how O Brother, Where Art Thou? challenges and complicates simple formulations about a region—indeed, about a nation's history and culture in relation to that region.

In "Bartleby, the Scrivener," Herman Melville creates a narrator of "prudence" and "method"—"an eminently *safe* man" who relates the story of a man of a very different sort. The narrator has to contend with a group of clerks and scriveners (law copyists) who are hardly so practical in matters of everyday business. Bartleby, though, is the one who thoroughly disrupts the routine of the office. His refrain, "I would prefer not to," raises issues of choice and individual desire that have been unthinkable to the narrator. Bartleby's persistent refusal to produce work seems to call into question the very nature of work. We might laugh at the comic collision between the narrator and his employee, but at the same time we share some of the narrator's discomfort. Most of us, after all, accept the "reality" of the emptiest abstractions. How would we live, Melville asks, if we did not?

Katherine Mansfield's "A Dill Pickle" shows us a man and a woman who have gone in different directions for six years but are briefly reunited in this story. As we listen to their conversation, we realize that the two remember their past together in very different ways. To the woman, it may have been the high point in a life that has turned tragic; to the man, it was a memorable episode that inspired him to begin the quests that have occupied him in the intervening years. But as we listen, we should listen carefully to the author's tone. Do we want the two to get back together? Might this woman who seems so sad be better off without this man who seems so comfortable?

Billy Collins takes as inspiration Art Blakey's jazz rendition of a simple children's song. What Blakey does in Collins's mind is draw out as obvious something we typically overlook. The playful repetition of the song, the tone of excited merriment, covers up a sad story of those poor, blind, frightened, and finally, tail-less mice. Blakey and then Collins after him prompt us to bring tone into a closer relation to action. In so doing, they make us wonder what other instances of avoidance we habitually practice—what other false notes we hit.

W. H. Auden may seem to announce suffering as his subject in "Musée des Beaux Arts," but that is not quite right. His subject is the understanding great painters had for suffering. Like those painters, Auden makes suffering in his poem a small part of a much larger fabric. Mundane life goes on somehow parallel and largely oblivious to tragedy. Icarus occupies only a small piece of a wide canvas. And without a carefully cultivated, deliberate plainness of tone,

Auden could hardly make his point. Much of life as most people experience it is made up of small pleasures and discomforts. Assertions to the contrary are, Auden feels, romantic and self-absorbed. The grand Icarus, falling to his death because he flew too near the sun, is reduced to an almost comical image of "white legs" disappearing into the vast ocean.

Christopher Durang and Wendy Wasserstein take up a grand and ancient tragedy and play it out in the most playful contemporary terms. The satiric tone emerges from the many rapid references to the most ephemeral aspects of popular culture that are overlaid upon the basic outline of the original myth: Medea's wrath at being abandoned by her husband leads her to murder her husband's new wife and her own children. In this version, Durang and Wasserstein replace the emotion that Euripides evokes in the classical version of the play with a self-consciousness of theatrical conventions and a chorus that breaks into familiar, light theatrical songs. This is another instance in which recognition of the tone is imperative; otherwise, the play might look like an incoherent mess. Remember that the playwrights are changing one of the great tragedies into comedy.

FICTION

Katherine Mansfield (1888–1923)

Katherine Mansfield was born Kathleen Mansfield Beauchamp in New Zealand. Mansfield's family was financially comfortable, and as a result, she attended college abroad. As a student at London's Queen's College, Mansfield studied the cello and served as head editor of *Queen's College Magazine*. After college, she briefly lived in New Zealand but ultimately returned to London. After engaging in several romantic relationships, Mansfield became pregnant but suffered a miscarriage. Using writing as a therapeutic method of expressing her grief over her lost child, Mansfield penned several short stories. She began publishing stories in the literary magazine *New Age*, and her first short story collection, *In a German Pension*, was published in 1911. Mansfield included feminist ideals in her stream-of-consciousness writings and helped further the then-blossoming women's rights movement. She also used her work as a return to a peaceful, prewar past, and her stories about her childhood in New Zealand became some of Mansfield's most popular works.

A Dill Pickle (1920)

And then, after six years, she saw him again. He was seated at one of those little bamboo tables decorated with a Japanese vase of paper daffodils. There was a tall plate of fruit in front of him, and very carefully, in a way she recognized immediately as his "special" way, he was peeling an orange.

He must have felt that shock of recognition in her for he looked up and met her eyes. Incredible! He didn't know her! She smiled; he frowned. She came towards him. He closed his eyes an instant, but opening them his face lit up as though he had struck a match in a dark room. He laid down the orange and pushed back his chair, and she took her little warm hand out of her muff and gave it to him.

"Vera!" he exclaimed. "How strange. Really, for a moment I didn't know you. Won't you sit down? You've had lunch? Won't you have some coffee?"

She hesitated, but of course she meant to.

"Yes, I'd like some coffee." And she sat down opposite him.   5

"You've changed. You've changed very much," he said, staring at her with that eager, lighted look. "You look so well. I've never seen you look so well before."

"Really?" She raised her veil and unbuttoned her high fur collar. "I don't feel very well. I can't bear this weather, you know."

"Ah, no. You hate the cold ..."

"Loathe it." She shuddered. "And the worst of it is that the older one grows ..."

He interrupted her. "Excuse me," and tapped on the table for the wait-   10
ress. "Please bring some coffee and cream." To her: "You are sure you won't eat anything? Some fruit, perhaps. The fruit here is very good."

"No, thanks. Nothing."

"Then that's settled." And smiling just a hint too broadly he took up the orange again. "You were saying—the older one grows—"

"The colder," she laughed. But she was thinking how well she remembered that trick of his—the trick of interrupting her—and of how it used to exasperate her six years ago. She used to feel then as though he, quite suddenly, in the middle of what she was saying, put his hand over her lips, turned from her, attended to something different, and then took his hand away, and with just the same slightly too broad smile, gave her his attention again.... Now we are ready. That is settled.

"The colder!" He echoed her words, laughing too. "Ah, ah. You still say the same things. And there is another thing about you that is not changed at all—your beautiful voice—your beautiful way of speaking." Now he was very grave; he leaned towards her, and she smelled the warm, stinging scent of the orange peel. "You have only to say one word and I would know your voice among all other voices. I don't know what it is—I've often wondered—that makes your voice such a—haunting memory.... Do you remember that first afternoon we spent together at Kew Gardens? You were so surprised because I did not know the names of any flowers. I am still just as ignorant for all your telling me. But whenever it is very fine and warm, and I see some bright colours—it's awfully strange—I hear your voice saying: 'Geranium,marigold, and verbena.' And I feel those three words are all I recall of some forgotten, heavenly language.... You remember that afternoon?"

"Oh, yes, very well." She drew a long, soft breath, as though the paper   15
daffodils between them were almost too sweet to bear. Yet, what had remained in her mind of that particular afternoon was an absurd scene over the tea table. A great many people taking tea in a Chinese pagoda, and he behaving like a maniac about the wasps—waving them away, flapping at them with his straw hat, serious and infuriated out of all proportion to the occasion. How delighted the sniggering tea drinkers had been. And how she had suffered.

But now, as he spoke, that memory faded. His was the truer. Yes, it had been a wonderful afternoon, full of geranium and marigold and verbena, and —warm sunshine. Her thoughts lingered over the last two words as though she sang them.

In the warmth, as it were, another memory unfolded. She saw herself sitting on a lawn. He lay beside her, and suddenly, after a long silence, he rolled over and put his head in her lap.

"I wish," he said, in a low, troubled voice, "I wish that I had taken poison and were about to die—here now!"

At that moment a little girl in a white dress, holding a long, dripping water lily, dodged from behind a bush, stared at them, and dodged back again. But he did not see. She leaned over him.

"Ah, why do you say that? I could not say that."   20

But he gave a kind of soft moan, and taking her hand he held it to his cheek.

"Because I know I am going to love you too much—far too much. And I shall suffer so terribly, Vera, because you never, never will love me."

He was certainly far better looking now than he had been then. He had lost all that dreamy vagueness and indecision. Now he had the air of a man who has found his place in life, and fills it with a confidence and an assurance which was, to say the least, impressive. He must have made money, too. His clothes were admirable, and at that moment he pulled a Russian cigarette case out of his pocket.

"Won't you smoke?"

"Yes, I will." She hovered over them. "They look very good."   25

"I think they are. I get them made for me by a little man in St. James's Street. I don't smoke very much. I'm not like you—but when I do, they must be delicious, very fresh cigarettes. Smoking isn't a habit with me; it's a luxury—like perfume. Are you still so fond of perfumes? Ah, when I was in Russia ... "

She broke in: "You've really been to Russia?"

"Oh, yes. I was there for over a year. Have you forgotten how we used to talk of going there?"

"No, I've not forgotten."

He gave a strange half laugh and leaned back in his chair. "Isn't it curious. I have really carried out all those journeys that we planned. Yes, I have been to all those places that we talked of, and stayed in them long enough to—as you used to say, 'air oneself' in them. In fact, I have spent the last three years of my life travelling all the time. Spain, Corsica, Siberia, Russia, Egypt. The only country left is China, and I mean to go there, too, when the war is over."

As he spoke, so lightly, tapping the end of his cigarette against the ashtray, she felt the strange beast that had slumbered so long within her bosom stir, stretch itself, yawn, prick up its ears, and suddenly bound to its feet, and fix its longing, hungry stare upon those far away places. But all she said was, smiling gently: "How I envy you."

He accepted that. "It has been," he said, "very wonderful—especially Russia. Russia was all that we had imagined, and far, far more. I even spent some days on a river boat on the Volga. Do you remember that boatman's song that you used to play?"

"Yes." It began to play in her mind as she spoke.

"Do you ever play it now?"

"No, I've no piano."

He was amazed at that. "But what has become of your beautiful piano?"

She made a little grimace. "Sold. Ages ago."

"But you were so fond of music," he wondered.

"I've no time for it now," said she.

He let it go at that. "That river life," he went on, "is something quite special. After a day or two you cannot realize that you have ever known another. And it is not necessary to know the language—the life of the boat creates a bond between you and the people that's more than sufficient. You eat with them, pass the day with them, and in the evening there is that endless singing."

She shivered, hearing the boatman's song break out again loud and tragic, and seeing the boat floating on the darkening river with melancholy trees on either side.... "Yes, I should like that," said she, stroking her muff.

"You'd like almost everything about Russian life," he said warmly. "It's so informal, so impulsive, so free without question. And then the peasants are so splendid. They are such human beings—yes, that is it. Even the man who drives your carriage has—has some real part in what is happening. I remember the evening a party of us, two friends of mine and the wife of one of them, went for a picnic by the Black Sea. We took supper and champagne and ate and drank on the grass. And while we were eating the coachman came up. 'Have a dill pickle,' he said. He wanted to share with us. That seemed to me so right, so—you know what I mean?"

And she seemed at that moment to be sitting on the grass beside the mysteriously Black Sea, black as velvet, and rippling against the banks in silent, velvet waves. She saw the carriage drawn up to one side of the road, and the little group on the grass, their faces and hands white in the moonlight. She saw the pale dress of the woman outspread and her folded parasol, lying on the grass like a huge pearl crochet hook. Apart from them, with his supper in a cloth on his knees, sat the coachman. "Have a dill pickle," said he, and although she was not certain what a dill pickle was, she saw the greenish glass jar with a red chili like a parrot's beak glimmering through. She sucked in her cheeks; the dill pickle was terribly sour....

"Yes, I know perfectly what you mean," she said.

In the pause that followed they looked at each other. In the past when 45
they had looked at each other like that they had felt such a boundless understanding between them that their souls had, as it were, put their arms round each other and dropped into the same sea, content to be drowned, like mournful lovers. But now, the surprising thing was that it was he who held back. He who said:

"What a marvellous listener you are. When you look at me with those wild eyes I feel that I could tell you things that I would never breathe to another human being."

Was there just a hint of mockery in his voice or was it her fancy? She could not be sure.

"Before I met you," he said, "I had never spoken of myself to anybody. How well I remember one night, the night that I brought you the little Christmas tree, telling you all about my childhood. And of how I was so miserable that I ran away and lived under a cart in our yard for two days without being discovered. And you listened, and your eyes shone, and I felt that you had even made the little Christmas tree listen too, as in a fairy story."

But of that evening she had remembered a little pot of caviare. It had cost seven and sixpence. He could not get over it. Think of it—a tiny jar like that costing seven and sixpence. While she ate it he watched her, delighted and shocked.

"No, really, that is eating money. You could not get seven shillings into 50
a little pot that size. Only think of the profit they must make...." And he had begun some immensely complicated calculations.... But now good-bye to the caviare. The Christmas tree was on the table, and the little boy lay under the cart with his head pillowed on the yard dog.

"The dog was called Bosun," she cried delightedly.

But he did not follow. "Which dog? Had you a dog? I don't remember a dog at all."

"No, no. I meant the yard dog when you were a little boy." He laughed and snapped the cigarette case to.

"Was he? Do you know I had forgotten that. It seems such ages ago. I cannot believe that it is only six years. After I had recognized you today—I had to take such a leap—I had to take a leap over my whole life to get back to that time. I was such a kid then." He drummed on the table. "I've often thought how I must have bored you. And now I understand so perfectly why you wrote to me as you did—although at the time that letter nearly finished my life. I found it again the other day, and I couldn't help laughing as I read it. It was so clever—such a true picture of me." He glanced up. "You're not going?"

She had buttoned her collar again and drawn down her veil.

"Yes, I am afraid I must," she said, and managed a smile. Now she knew that he had been mocking.

"Ah, no, please," he pleaded. "Don't go just for a moment," and he caught up one of her gloves from the table and clutched at it as if that would hold her. "I see so few people to talk to nowadays, that I have turned into a sort of barbarian," he said. "Have I said something to hurt you?"

"Not a bit," she lied. But as she watched him draw her glove through his fingers, gently, gently, her anger really did die down, and besides, at the moment he looked more like himself of six years ago....

"What I really wanted then," he said softly, "was to be a sort of carpet—to make myself into a sort of carpet for you to walk on so that you need not be hurt by the sharp stones and mud that you hated so. It was nothing more positive than that—nothing more selfish. Only I did desire, eventually, to turn into a magic carpet and carry you away to all those lands you longed to see."

As he spoke she lifted her head as though she drank something; the strange beast in her bosom began to purr ...

"I felt that you were more lonely than anybody else in the world," he went on, "and yet, perhaps, that you were the only person in the world who was really, truly alive. Born out of your time," he murmured, stroking the glove, "fated."

Ah, God! What had she done! How had she dared to throw away her happiness like this. This was the only man who had ever understood her. Was it too late? Could it be too late? *She* was that glove that he held in his fingers....

"And then the fact that you had no friends and never had made friends with people. How I understood that, for neither had I. Is it just the same now?"

"Yes," she breathed. "Just the same. I am as alone as ever."

"So am I," he laughed gently, "just the same."

Suddenly with a quick gesture he handed her back the glove and scraped his chair on the floor. "But what seemed to me so mysterious then is perfectly plain to me now. And to you, too, of course.... It simply was that we were such egoists, so self-engrossed, so wrapped up in ourselves that we hadn't a corner in our hearts for anybody else. Do you know," he cried, naive and hearty, and dreadfully like another side of that old self again, "I began studying a Mind System when I was in Russia, and I found that we were not peculiar at all. It's quite a well-known form of ..."

She had gone. He sat there, thunder-struck, astounded beyond words.... And then he asked the waitress for his bill.

"But the cream has not been touched," he said. "Please do not charge me for it."

- What has happened in the six years since Vera last saw the man she meets again in this story?
- Is the dill pickle an object in the present or in the past? Why is it significant?
- When Vera says that his memory is truer, what does she mean? How do their memories of the same time differ?
- How can we determine whether or not there is "just a hint of mockery in his voice"?
- At the end of the story he claims "that we were such egoists." How does this statement remain relevant to the narrative of the current time?

Herman Melville (1819–1891)

Herman Melville was born in New York City. As a young man he worked as a sailor in the South Seas, and his experiences there became the material for his first two prose books, *Typee: A Peep at Polynesian Life* and *Omoo*, both of which sold well and established Melville as a writer. The relative commercial failure of his later books, including his most ambitious books, *Moby-Dick* and *Pierre*, led him to abandon writing as a viable profession. He worked as a customs inspector to earn a living and wrote poetry and short fiction in his spare time. Among his collections of poetry are *Battle-Pieces and Aspects of the War* (1866) and *Clarel: A Poem and Pilgrimage in the Holy Land* (1876). His classic short novel *Billy Budd* appeared posthumously.

Bartleby, the Scrivener (1853)

A STORY OF WALL STREET

I am a rather elderly man. The nature of my avocations for the last thirty years has brought me into more than ordinary contact with what would seem an interesting and somewhat singular set of men of whom as yet nothing that I know of has ever been written—I mean the law-copyists or scriveners. I have known very many of them, professionally and privately, and if I pleased could relate diverse histories at which good-natured gentlemen might smile and sentimental souls might weep. But I waive the biographies of all other scriveners for a few passages in the life of Bartleby, who was a scrivener the strangest I ever saw or heard of. While of other law-copyists I might write the complete life, of Bartleby nothing of that sort can be done. I believe that no materials exist for a full and satisfactory biography of this man. It is an irreparable loss to literature. Bartleby was one of those beings of whom nothing is ascertainable except from the original sources, and in his case those are very small. What my own astonished eyes saw of Bartleby, *that* is all I know of him except, indeed, one vague report which will appear in the sequel.

Ere introducing the scrivener as he first appeared to me, it is fit I make some mention of myself, my employees, my business, my chambers, and general surroundings, because some such description is indispensable to an adequate understanding of the chief character about to be presented. Imprimis: I am a man who from his youth upwards has been filled with a profound conviction that the easiest way of life is the best. Hence, though I belong to a profession proverbially energetic and nervous, even to turbulence at times, yet nothing of that sort have I ever suffered to invade my peace. I am one of those unambitious lawyers who never addresses a jury or in any way draws down public applause, but in the cool tranquility of a snug retreat do a snug business among rich men's bonds and mortgages and title-deeds. All who know me consider me an eminently *safe* man. The late John Jacob Astor, a personage little given to poetic enthusiasm, had no hesitation in pronouncing my first grand point to be prudence; my next, method. I do not speak it in vanity but simply record the fact that I was not unemployed in my profession by the late John Jacob Astor, a name which, I admit, I love to repeat, for it hath a rounded and orbicular sound to it and rings like unto bullion. I will freely add that I was not insensible to the late John Jacob Astor's good opinion.

Sometime prior to the period at which this little history begins, my avocations had been largely increased. The good old office now extinct in the State of New York of a Master in Chancery had been conferred upon me. It was not a very arduous office but very pleasantly remunerative. I seldom lose my temper; much more seldom indulge in dangerous indignation at wrongs and outrages; but I must be permitted to be rash here and declare that I consider the sudden and violent abrogation of the office of Master in Chancery by the new Constitution as a ——premature act, inasmuch as I had counted upon a life-lease of the profits, whereas I only received those of a few short years. But this is by the way.

My chambers were upstairs at No. — Wall Street. At one end they looked upon the white wall of the interior of a spacious skylight shaft penetrating the building from top to bottom. This view might have been considered rather tame than otherwise, deficient in what landscape painters call "life." But if so, the view from the other end of my chambers offered at least a contrast, if nothing more. In that direction my windows commanded an unobstructed view of a lofty brick wall, black by age and everlasting shade, which wall required no spy-glass to bring out its lurking beauties, but for the benefit of all near-sighted spectators was pushed up to within ten feet of my window-panes. Owing to the great height of the surrounding buildings, and my chambers being on the second floor, the interval between this wall and mine not a little resembled a huge square cistern.

At the period just preceding the advent of Bartleby, I had two persons   5
as copyists in my employment and a promising lad as an office boy. First, Turkey; second, Nippers; third, Ginger Nut. These may seem names the like of which are not usually found in the Directory. In truth they were nicknames mutually conferred upon each other by my three clerks, and were deemed expressive of their respective persons or characters. Turkey was a short, pursy Englishman of about my own age, that is, somewhere not far from sixty. In the morning, one might say, his face was of a fine florid hue, but after twelve o'clock, meridian—his dinner hour—it blazed like a grate full of Christmas coals, and continued blazing—but as it were with a gradual wane—till 6 o'clock P.M. or thereabouts, after which I saw no more of the proprietor of the face, which gaining its meridian with the sun, seemed to set with it, to rise, culminate, and decline the following day, with the like regularity and undiminished glory. There are many singular coincidences I have known in the course of my life, not the least among which was the fact that exactly when Turkey displayed his fullest beams from his red and radiant countenance, just then, too, at the critical moment began the daily period when I considered his business capacities as seriously disturbed for the remainder of the twenty-four hours. Not that he was absolutely idle or averse to business then; far from it. The difficulty was, he was apt to be altogether too energetic. There was a strange, inflamed, flurried, flighty recklessness of activity about him. He would be incautious in dipping his pen into his inkstand. All his blots upon my documents were dropped there after twelve o'clock, meridian. Indeed not only would he be reckless and sadly given to making blots in the afternoon, but some days he went further and was rather noisy. At such times, too, his face flamed with augmented blazonry, as if cannel coal had been heaped on anthracite. He made an unpleasant racket with his chair; spilled his sand-box; in mending his pens, impatiently split them all to pieces, and threw them on the floor in a sudden passion; stood up and leaned over his table, boxing his papers about in a most indecorous manner, very sad to behold in an elderly man like him.

Nevertheless, as he was in many ways a most valuable person to me, and all the time before twelve o'clock, meridian, was the quickest, steadiest creature too, accomplishing a great deal of work in a style not easy to be matched— for these reasons, I was willing to overlook his eccentricities, though indeed occasionally I remonstrated with him. I did this very gently, however, be- cause though the civilest, nay, the blandest and most reverential of men in the morning, yet in the afternoon he was disposed upon provocation to be slightly rash with his tongue, in fact insolent. Now valuing his morning ser- vices as I did, and resolved not to lose them; yet at the same time made un- comfortable by his inflamed ways after twelve o'clock; and being a man of peace, unwilling by my admonitions to call forth unseemly retorts from him, I took upon me one Saturday noon (he was always worse on Saturdays) to hint to him very kindly that perhaps now that he was growing old, it might be well to abridge his labors; in short, he need not come to my chambers after twelve o'clock but, dinner over, had best go home to his lodgings and rest himself till tea-time. But no; he insisted upon his afternoon devotions. His countenance became intolerably fervid as he oratorically assured me— gesticulating with a long ruler at the other end of the room—that if his ser- vices in the morning were useful, how indispensable, then, in the afternoon?

"With submission, sir," said Turkey on this occasion. "I consider myself your right-hand man. In the morning I but marshal and deploy my columns, but in the afternoon I put myself at their head and gallantly charge the foe, thus!"—and he made a violent thrust with the ruler.

"But the blots, Turkey," intimated I.

"True, —but, with submission, sir, behold these hairs! I am getting old. Surely, sir, a blot or two of a warm afternoon is not to be severely urged against gray hairs. Old age—even if it blot the page—is honorable. With submission, sir, we *both* are getting old."

This appeal to my fellow-feeling was hardly to be resisted. At all events, I saw that go he would not. So I made up my mind to let him stay, resolving nevertheless to see to it that during the afternoon he had to do with my less important papers.

Nippers, the second on my list, was a whiskered, sallow, and upon the whole rather piratical-looking young man of about five and twenty. I always deemed him the victim of two evil powers—ambition and indigestion. The ambition was evinced by a certain impatience of the duties of a mere copy- ist, an unwarrantable usurpation of strictly professional affairs such as the original drawing up of legal documents. The indigestion seemed betokened in an occasional nervous testiness and grinning irritability causing the teeth to audibly grind together over mistakes committed in copying; unnecessary maledictions hissed rather than spoken in the heat of business; and espe- cially by a continual discontent with the height of the table where he worked. Though of a very ingenious mechanical turn, Nippers could never get this table to suit him. He put chips under it, blocks of various sorts, bits of pasteboard, and at last went so far as to attempt an exquisite adjustment by final pieces of folded blotting-paper. But no invention would answer. If for the sake of easing his back he brought the table lid at a sharp angle well up towards his chin, and wrote there like a man using the steep roof of a Dutch house for his desk, then he declared that it stopped the circulation in his arms. If now he lowered the table to his waistbands and stooped over it in writing, then there was a sore aching in his back. In short, the truth of the matter was Nippers knew not what he wanted. Or if he wanted anything, it was to be rid of a scrivener's table altogether. Among the manifestations of his diseased ambition was a fondness he had for receiving visits from certain ambiguous-looking fellows in seedy coats, whom he called his clients. Indeed I was aware that not only was he at times considerable of a ward-politician, but he occasionally did a little business at the Justices' courts and was not unknown on the steps of the Tombs. I have good reason to believe however that one individual who called upon him at my chambers and who with a grand air he insisted was his client was no other than a dun, and the alleged title-deed, a bill. But with all his failings, and the annoyances he caused me, Nippers, like his compatriot Turkey, was a very useful man to me; wrote a neat, swift hand; and, when he chose, was not deficient in a gentlemanly sort of deportment. Added to this, he always dressed in a gentlemanly sort of way, and so incidentally reflected credit upon my chambers. Whereas with respect to Turkey, I had much ado to keep him from being a reproach to me. His clothes were apt to look oily and smell of eating-houses. He wore his pantaloons very loose and baggy in the summer. His coats were execrable, his hat not to be handled. But while the hat was a thing of indifference to me inasmuch as his natural civility and deference as a dependent Englishman always led him to doff it the moment he entered the room, yet his coat was another matter. Concerning his coats, I reasoned with him, but with no effect. The truth was I suppose that a man with so small an income could not afford to sport such a lustrous face and a lustrous coat at one and the same time. As Nippers once observed, Turkey's money went chiefly for red ink. One winter day I presented Turkey with a highly respectable looking coat of my own, a padded gray coat of a most comfortable warmth and which buttoned straight up from the knee to the neck. I thought Turkey would appreciate the favor and abate his rashness and obstreperousness of afternoons. But no. I verily believe that buttoning himself up in so downy and blanket-like a coat had a pernicious effect upon him, upon the same principle that too much oats are bad for horses. In fact, precisely as a rash, restive horse is said to feel his oats, so Turkey felt his coat. It made him insolent. He was a man whom prosperity harmed.

Though concerning the self-indulgent habits of Turkey I had my own private surmises, yet touching Nippers I was well persuaded that whatever might be his faults in other respects, he was at least a temperate young man. But indeed, nature herself seemed to have been his vintner and at his birth charged him so thoroughly with an irritable, brandy-like disposition that all subsequent potations were needless. When I consider how amid the stillness of my chambers Nippers would sometimes impatiently rise from his seat and stooping over his table spread his arms wide apart, seize the whole desk, and move it, and jerk it, with a grim, grinding motion on the floor, as if the table were a perverse voluntary agent intent on thwarting and vexing him, I plainly perceive that for Nippers, brandy and water were altogether superfluous.

It was fortunate for me that, owing to its peculiar cause—indigestion— the irritability and consequent nervousness of Nippers were mainly observable in the morning, while in the afternoon he was comparatively mild. So that Turkey's paroxysms only coming on about twelve o'clock, I never had to do with their eccentricities at one time. Their fits relieved each other like guards. When Nippers's was on, Turkey's was off, and vice versa. This was a good natural arrangement under the circumstances.

Ginger Nut, the third on my list, was a lad some twelve years old. His father was a carman, ambitious of seeing his son on the bench instead of a cart before he died. So he sent him to my office as student at law, errand boy, and cleaner and sweeper, at the rate of one dollar a week. He had a little desk to himself but he did not use it much. Upon inspection, the drawer exhibited a great array of the shells of various sorts of nuts. Indeed, to this quick-witted youth the whole noble science of the law was contained in a nutshell. Not the least among the employments of Ginger Nut, as well as one which he discharged with the most alacrity, was his duty as cake and apple purveyor for Turkey and Nippers. Copying law papers being proverbially a dry, husky sort of business, my two scriveners were fain to moisten their mouths very often with Spitzenbergs to be had at the numerous stalls nigh the Custom House and Post Office. Also, they sent Ginger Nut very frequently for that peculiar cake—small, flat, round, and very spicy—after which he had been named by them. Of a cold morning when business was but dull, Turkey would gobble up scores of these cakes as if they were mere wafers—indeed they sell them at the rate of six or eight for a penny— the scrape of his pen blending with the crunching of the crisp particles in his mouth. Of all the fiery afternoon blunders and flurried rashnesses of Turkey was his once moistening a ginger cake between his lips and clapping it on to a mortgage for a seal. I came within an ace of dismissing him then. But he mollified me by making an oriental bow and saying—

"With submission, sir, it was generous of me to find you in stationery on my own account."

Now my original business—that of a conveyancer and title hunter, and drawer-up of recondite documents of all sorts—was considerably increased by receiving the master's office. There was now great work for scriveners. Not only must I push the clerks already with me, but I must have additional help.

In answer to my advertisement, a motionless young man one morning stood upon my office threshold, the door being open, for it was summer. I can see that figure now—pallidly neat, pitiably respectable, incurably forlorn! It was Bartleby.

After a few words touching his qualifications I engaged him, glad to have among my corps of copyists a man of so singularly sedate an aspect, which I thought might operate beneficially upon the flighty temper of Turkey and the fiery one of Nippers.

I should have stated before that ground glass folding doors divided my premises into two parts, one of which was occupied by my scriveners, the other by myself. According to my humor I threw open these doors, or closed them. I resolved to assign Bartleby a corner by the folding doors, but on my side of them so as to have this quiet man within easy call in case any trifling thing was to be done. I placed his desk close up to a small side window in that part of the room, a window which originally had afforded a lateral view of certain grimy backyards and bricks, but which owing to subsequent erections commanded at present no view at all, though it gave some light. Within three feet of the panes was a wall, and the light came down from far above between two lofty buildings as from a very small opening in a dome. Still further to a satisfactory arrangement, I procured a high green folding screen which might entirely isolate Bartleby from my sight though not remove him from my voice. And thus, in a manner privacy and society were conjoined.

At first Bartleby did an extraordinary quantity of writing. As if long famishing for something to copy, he seemed to gorge himself on my documents. There was no pause for digestion. He ran a day and night line, copying by sunlight and by candlelight. I should have been quite delighted with his application had he been cheerfully industrious. But he wrote on silently, palely, mechanically.

It is of course an indispensable part of a scrivener's business to verify the   20
accuracy of his copy, word by word. Where there are two or more scriveners in an office, they assist each other in this examination, one reading from the copy, the other holding the original. It is a very dull, wearisome, and lethargic affair. I can readily imagine that to some sanguine temperaments it would be altogether intolerable. For example, I cannot credit that the mettlesome poet Byron would have contentedly sat down with Bartleby to examine a law document of, say, five hundred pages closely written in a crimpy hand.

Now and then in the haste of business, it had been my habit to assist in comparing some brief document myself, calling Turkey or Nippers for this purpose. One object I had in placing Bartleby so handy to me behind the screen was to avail myself of his services on such trivial occasions. It was on the third day, I think, of his being with me, and before any necessity had arisen for having his own writing examined, that being much hurried to complete a small affair I had in hand, I abruptly called to Bartleby. In my haste and natural expectancy of instant compliance, I sat with my head bent over the original on my desk and my right hand sideways and somewhat nervously extended with the copy, so that immediately upon emerging from his retreat Bartleby might snatch it and proceed to business without the least delay.

In this very attitude did I sit when I called to him, rapidly stating what it was I wanted him to do—namely, to examine a small paper with me. Imagine my surprise, nay my consternation, when without moving from his privacy Bartleby in a singularly mild, firm voice replied, "I would prefer not to."

I sat awhile in perfect silence, rallying my stunned faculties. Immediately it occurred to me that my ears had deceived me, or Bartleby had entirely misunderstood my meaning. I repeated my request in the clearest tone I could assume. But in quite as clear a one came the previous reply, "I would prefer not to."

"Prefer not to," echoed I, rising in high excitement and crossing the room with a stride, "What do you mean? Are you moonstruck? I want you to help me compare this sheet here—take it," and I thrust it towards him.

"I would prefer not to," said he.

I looked at him steadfastly. His face was leanly composed, his gray eye dimly calm. Not a wrinkle of agitation rippled him. Had there been the least uneasiness, anger, impatience or impertinence in his manner, in other words had there been anything ordinarily human about him, doubtless I should have violently dismissed him from the premises. But as it was, I should have as soon thought of turning my pale plaster-of-paris bust of Cicero out of doors. I stood gazing at him awhile as he went on with his own writing, and then reseated myself at my desk. This is very strange, thought I. What had one best do? But my business hurried me. I concluded to forget the matter for the present, reserving it for my future leisure. So calling Nippers from the other room, the paper was speedily examined.

A few days after this Bartleby concluded four lengthy documents, being quadruplicates of a week's testimony taken before me in my High Court of Chancery. It became necessary to examine them. It was an important suit and great accuracy was imperative. Having all things arranged I called Turkey, Nippers and Ginger Nut from the next room, meaning to place the four copies in the hands of my four clerks while I should read from the original. Accordingly Turkey, Nippers and Ginger Nut had taken their seats in a row, each with his document in hand, when I called to Bartleby to join this interesting group.

"Bartleby! quick, I am waiting."

I heard a slow scrape of his chair legs on the unscraped floor, and soon he appeared standing at the entrance of his hermitage.

"What is wanted?" said he mildly.   30

"The copies, the copies," said I hurriedly. "We are going to examine them. There"—and I held towards him the fourth quadruplicate.

"I would prefer not to," he said, and gently disappeared behind the screen.

For a few moments I was turned into a pillar of salt standing at the head of my seated column of clerks. Recovering myself, I advanced towards the screen and demanded the reason for such extraordinary conduct.

"*Why* do you refuse?"

"I would prefer not to."   35

With any other man I should have flown outright into a dreadful passion, scorned all further words, and thrust him ignominiously from my presence. But there was something about Bartleby that not only strangely disarmed me, but in a wonderful manner touched and disconcerted me. I began to reason with him.

"These are your own copies we are about to examine. It is labor saving to you, because one examination will answer for your four papers. It is common usage. Every copyist is bound to help examine his copy. Is it not so? Will you not speak? Answer!"

"I prefer not to," he replied in a flute-like tone. It seemed to me that while I had been addressing him, he carefully revolved every statement that I made, fully comprehended the meaning, could not gainsay the irresistible conclusion, but at the same time some paramount consideration prevailed with him to reply as he did.

"You are decided, then, not to comply with my request—a request made according to common usage and common sense?"

He briefly gave me to understand that on that point my judgment was sound. Yes: his decision was irreversible.   40

It is not seldom the case that when a man is browbeaten in some unprecedented and violently unreasonable way he begins to stagger in his own plainest faith. He begins, as it were, vaguely to surmise that wonderful as it may be, all the justice and all the reason is on the other side. Accordingly, if any disinterested persons are present he turns to them for some reinforcement for his own faltering mind.

"Turkey," said I, "what do you think of this? Am I not right?"

"With submission, sir," said Turkey with his blandest tone, "I think that you are."

"Nippers," said I, "what do *you* think of it?"

"I think I should kick him out of the office."   45

(The reader of nice perceptions will here perceive that, it being morning, Turkey's answer is couched in polite and tranquil terms, but Nippers replies in ill-tempered ones. Or, to repeat a previous sentence, Nippers's ugly mood was on duty, and Turkey's off.)

"Ginger Nut," said I, willing to enlist the smallest suffrage in my behalf, "what do *you* think of it?"

"I think, sir, he's a little *loony*," replied Ginger Nut, with a grin.

"You hear what they say," said I, turning towards the screen, "come forth and do your duty."

But he vouchsafed no reply. I pondered a moment in sore perplexity. But once more business hurried me. I determined again to postpone the consideration of this dilemma to my future leisure. With a little trouble we made out to examine the papers without Bartleby, though at every page or two, Turkey deferentially dropped his opinion that this proceeding was quite out of the common, while Nippers, twitching in his chair with a dyspeptic nervousness, ground out between his set teeth occasional hissing maledictions against the stubborn oaf behind the screen. And for his (Nippers's) part, this was the first and the last time he would do another man's business without pay.

Meanwhile Bartleby sat in his hermitage, oblivious to everything but his own peculiar business there.

Some days passed, the scrivener being employed upon another lengthy work. His late remarkable conduct led me to regard his way narrowly. I observed that he never went to dinner, indeed that he never went anywhere. As yet I had never of my personal knowledge known him to be outside of my office. He was a perpetual sentry in the corner. At about eleven o'clock though, in the morning, I noticed that Ginger Nut would advance toward the opening in Bartleby's screen as if silently beckoned thither by a gesture invisible to me where I sat. That boy would then leave the office jingling a few pence and reappear with a handful of ginger nuts which he delivered in the hermitage, receiving two of the cakes for his trouble.

He lives then on ginger nuts, thought I; never eats a dinner, properly speaking; he must be a vegetarian then, but no, he never eats even vegetables, he eats nothing but ginger nuts. My mind then ran on in reveries concerning the probable effects upon the human constitution of living entirely on ginger nuts. Ginger nuts are so called because they contain ginger as one of their peculiar constituents, and the final flavoring one. Now what was ginger? A hot, spicy thing. Was Bartleby hot and spicy? Not at all. Ginger, then, had no effect upon Bartleby. Probably he preferred it should have none.

Nothing so aggravates an earnest person as a passive resistance. If the individual so resisted be of a not inhumane temper, and the resisting one perfectly harmless in his passivity, then in the better moods of the former, he will endeavor charitably to construe to his imagination what proves impossible to be solved by his judgment. Even so for the most part I regarded Bartleby and his ways. Poor fellow! thought I, he means no mischief; it is plain he intends no insolence; his aspect sufficiently evinces that his eccentricities are involuntary. He is useful to me. I can get along with him. If I turn him away, the chances are he will fall in with some less indulgent employer, and then he will be rudely treated and perhaps driven forth miserably to starve. Yes. Here I can cheaply purchase a delicious self-approval. To befriend Bartleby, to humor him in his strange wilfulness, will cost me little or nothing, while I lay up in my soul what will eventually prove a sweet morsel for my conscience. But this mood was not invariable with me. The passiveness of Bartleby sometimes irritated me. I felt strangely goaded on to encounter him in new opposition, to elicit some angry spark from him answerable to my own. But indeed I might as well have essayed to strike fire with my knuckles against a bit of Windsor soap. But one afternoon the evil impulse in me mastered me, and the following little scene ensued:

"Bartleby," said I, "when those papers are all copied I will compare them with you."   55

"I would prefer not to."

"How? Surely you do not mean to persist in that mulish vagary?"

No answer.

I threw open the folding doors nearby, and turning upon Turkey and Nippers, exclaimed in an excited manner—

"He says, a second time, he won't examine his papers. What do you   60
think of it, Turkey?"

It was afternoon, be it remembered. Turkey sat glowing like a brass boiler, his bald head steaming, his hands reeling among his blotted papers.

"Think of it?" roared Turkey, "I think I'll just step behind his screen and black his eyes for him!"

So saying, Turkey rose to his feet and threw his arms into a pugilistic position. He was hurrying away to make good his promise when I detained him, alarmed at the effect of incautiously rousing Turkey's combativeness after dinner.

"Sit down, Turkey," said I, "and hear what Nippers has to say. What do you think of it, Nippers? Would I not be justified in immediately dismissing Bartleby?"

"Excuse me, that is for you to decide, sir. I think his conduct quite unusual, and indeed unjust as regards Turkey and myself. But it may only be a passing whim."   65

"Ah," exclaimed I, "you have strangely changed your mind then—you speak very gently of him now."

"All beer," cried Turkey, "gentleness is effects of beer—Nippers and I dined together today. You see how gentle *I* am, sir. Shall I go and black his eyes?"

"You refer to Bartleby, I suppose. No, not today, Turkey," I replied, "pray, put up your fists."

I closed the doors, and again advanced towards Bartleby. I felt additional incentives tempting me to my fate. I burned to be rebelled against again. I remembered that Bartleby never left the office.

"Bartleby," said I, "Ginger Nut is away; just step round to the post office, won't you? (it was but a three minutes walk) and see if there is anything for me."

"I would prefer not to."

"You *will* not?"

"I *prefer* not."

I staggered to my desk and sat there in a deep study. My blind inveteracy returned. Was there any other thing in which I could procure myself to be ignominiously repulsed by this lean, penniless wight?—my hired clerk? What added thing is there, perfectly reasonable, that he will be sure to refuse to do?

"Bartleby!"

No answer.

"Bartleby," in a louder tone.

No answer.

"Bartleby," I roared.

Like a very ghost, agreeably to the laws of magical invocation, at the third summons he appeared at the entrance of his hermitage.

"Go to the next room, and tell Nippers to come to me."

"I prefer not to," he respectfully and slowly said, and mildly disappeared.

"Very good, Bartleby," said I, in a quiet sort of serenely severe self-possessed tone, intimating the unalterable purpose of some terrible retribution very close at hand. At the moment I half intended something of the kind. But upon the whole, as it was drawing towards my dinner hour, I thought it best to put on my hat and walk home for the day, suffering much from perplexity and distress of mind.

Shall I acknowledge it? The conclusion of this whole business was that it soon became a fixed fact of my chambers that a pale young scrivener by the name of Bartleby had a desk there; that he copied for me at the usual rate of four cents a folio (one hundred words); but he was permanently exempt from examining the work done by him, that duty being transferred to Turkey and Nippers, one of compliment doubtless to their superior acuteness; moreover, said Bartleby was never on any account to be dispatched on the most trivial errand of any sort, and that even if entreated to take upon him such a matter, it was generally understood that he would prefer not to—in other words, that he would refuse point-blank.

As days passed on, I became considerably reconciled to Bartleby. His steadiness, his freedom from all dissipation, his incessant industry (except when he chose to throw himself into a standing revery behind his screen), his great stillness, his unalterableness of demeanor under all circumstances, made him a valuable acquisition. One prime thing was this—*he was always there*—first in the morning, continually through the day, and the last at night. I had a singular confidence in his honesty. I felt my most precious papers perfectly safe in his hands. Sometimes to be sure I could not for the very soul of me avoid falling into sudden spasmodic passions with him. For it was exceeding difficult to bear in mind all the time those strange peculiarities, privileges, and unheard of exemptions forming the tacit stipulations on Bartleby's part under which he remained in my office. Now and then in the eagerness of dispatching pressing business, I would inadvertently summon Bartleby, in a short rapid tone, to put his finger, say, on the incipient tie of a bit of red tape with which I was about compressing some papers. Of course, from behind the screen the usual answer, "I prefer not to," was sure to come, and then how could a human creature with the common infirmities of our nature, refrain from bitterly exclaiming upon such perverseness—such unreasonableness? However, every added repulse of this sort which I received only tended to lessen the probability of my repeating the inadvertence.

Here it must be said that according to the custom of most legal gentlemen occupying chambers in densely populated law buildings, there were several keys to my door. One was kept by a woman residing in the attic, which person weekly scrubbed and daily swept and dusted my apartments. Another was kept by Turkey for convenience sake. The third I sometimes carried in my own pocket. The fourth I knew not who had.

Now one Sunday morning I happened to go to Trinity Church to hear a celebrated preacher, and finding myself rather early on the ground I thought I would walk round to my chambers for a while. Luckily I had my key with me, but upon applying it to the lock, I found it resisted by something inserted from the inside. Quite surprised, I called out, when to my consternation a key was turned from within, and thrusting his lean visage at me and holding the door ajar, the apparition of Bartleby appeared, in his shirt sleeves, and otherwise in a strangely tattered dishabille, saying quietly that he was sorry but he was deeply engaged just then and—preferred not admitting me at present. In a brief word or two, he moreover added that perhaps I had better walk round the block two or three times, and by that time he would probably have concluded his affairs.

Now, the utterly unsurmised appearance of Bartleby tenanting my law-chambers of a Sunday morning with his cadaverously gentlemanly nonchalance, yet withal firm and self-possessed, had such a strange effect upon me that incontinently I slunk away from my own door and did as desired. But not without sundry twinges of impotent rebellion against the mild effrontery of this unaccountable scrivener. Indeed it was his wonderful mildness chiefly which not only disarmed me but unmanned me, as it were. For I consider that one, for the time, is a sort of unmanned when he tranquilly permits his hired clerk to dictate to him and order him away from his own premises. Furthermore, I was full of uneasiness as to what Bartleby could possibly be doing in my office in his shirt sleeves and in an otherwise dismantled condition of a Sunday morning. Was anything amiss going on? Nay, that was out of the question. It was not to be thought of for a moment that Bartleby was an immoral person. But what could he be doing there?—copying? Nay again, whatever might be his eccentricities, Bartleby was an eminently decorous person. He would be the last man to sit down to his desk in any state approaching to nudity. Besides, it was Sunday, and there was something about Bartleby that forbade the supposition that he would by any secular occupation violate the proprieties of the day.

Nevertheless, my mind was not pacified; and full of a restless curiosity, at last I returned to the door. Without hindrance I inserted my key, opened it, and entered. Bartleby was not to be seen. I looked round anxiously, peeped behind his screen, but it was very plain that he was gone. Upon more closely examining the place, I surmised that for an indefinite period Bartleby must have ate, dressed, and slept in my office, and that too without plate, mirror, or bed. The cushioned seat of a rickety old sofa in one corner bore the faint impress of a lean, reclining form. Rolled away under his desk I found a blanket; under the empty grate, a blacking box and brush; on a chair, a tin basin with soap and a ragged towel; in a newspaper a few crumbs of ginger nuts and a morsel of cheese. Yes, thought I, it is evident enough that Bartleby has been making his home here, keeping bachelor's hall all by himself. Immediately then the thought came sweeping across me, what miserable friendlessness and loneliness are here revealed! His poverty is great; but his solitude, how horrible! Think of it. Of a Sunday, Wall Street is deserted as Petra, and every night of every day it is an emptiness. This building too which of weekdays hums with industry and life at nightfall echoes with sheer vacancy, and all through Sunday is forlorn. And here Bartleby makes his home, sole spectator of a solitude which he has seen all populous—a sort of innocent and transformed Marius brooding among the ruins of Carthage!

For the first time in my life a feeling of overpowering stinging melancholy seized me. Before I had never experienced aught but a not unpleasing sadness. The bond of a common humanity now drew me irresistibly to gloom. A fraternal melancholy! For both I and Bartleby were sons of Adam. I remembered the bright silks and sparkling faces I had seen that day in gala trim, swan-like sailing down the Mississippi of Broadway; and I contrasted them with the pallid copyist, and thought to myself, Ah, happiness courts the light, so we deem the world is gay; but misery hides aloof, so we deem that misery there is none. These sad fancyings—chimeras doubtless of a sick and silly brain—led on to other and more special thoughts concerning the eccentricities of Bartleby. Presentiments of strange discoveries hovered round me. The scrivener's pale form appeared to me laid out, among uncaring strangers, in its shivering winding sheet.

Suddenly I was attracted by Bartleby's closed desk, the key in open sight left in the lock.

I mean no mischief, seek the gratification of no heartless curiosity, thought I; besides, the desk is mine, and its contents too, so I will make bold to look within. Everything was methodically arranged, the papers smoothly placed. The pigeon holes were deep, and removing the files of documents, I groped into their recesses. Presently I felt something there and dragged it out. It was an old bandanna handkerchief, heavy and knotted. I opened it, and saw it was a savings bank. I now recalled all the quiet mysteries which I had noted in the man. I remembered that he never spoke but to answer; that though at intervals he had considerable time to himself, yet I had never seen him reading—no, not even a newspaper; that for long periods he would stand looking out, at his pale window behind the screen, upon the dead brick wall; I was quite sure he never visited any refectory or eating house, while his pale face clearly indicated that he never drank beer like Turkey, or tea and coffee even, like other men; that he never went anywhere in particular that I could learn, never went out for a walk, unless indeed that was the case at present; that he had declined telling who he was or whence he came or whether he had any relatives in the world; that though so thin and pale, he never complained of ill health. And more than all, I remembered a certain unconscious air of pallid—how shall I call it?—of pallid haughtiness, say, or rather an austere reserve about him, which had positively awed me into my tame compliance with his eccentricities when I had feared to ask him to do the slightest incidental thing for me, even though I might know from his long-continued motionlessness that behind his screen he must be standing in one of those dead-wall reveries of his.

Revolving all these things, and coupling them with the recently discovered fact that he made my office his constant abiding place and home, and not forgetful of his morbid moodiness; revolving all these things, a prudential feeling began to steal over me. My first emotions had been those of pure melancholy and sincerest pity; but just in proportion as the forlornness of Bartleby grew and grew to my imagination, did that same melancholy merge into fear, that pity into repulsion. So true it is, and so terrible too, that up to a certain point the thought or sight of misery enlists our best affections; but in certain special cases, beyond that point it does not. They err who would assert that invariably this is owing to the inherent selfishness of the human heart. It rather proceeds from a certain hopelessness of remedying excessive and organic ill. To a sensitive being, pity is not seldom pain. And when at last it is perceived that such pity cannot lead to effectual succor, common sense bids the soul be rid of it. What I saw that morning persuaded me that the scrivener was the victim of innate and incurable disorder. I might give alms to his body, but his body did not pain him; it was his soul that suffered, and his soul I could not reach.

I did not accomplish the purpose of going to Trinity Church that morning. Somehow, the things I had seen disqualified me for the time from church-going. I walked homeward, thinking what I would do with Bartleby. Finally I resolved upon this:—I would put certain calm questions to him the next morning, touching his history, &c., and if he declined to answer them openly and unreservedly (and I supposed he would prefer not), then to give him a twenty dollar bill over and above whatever I might owe him, and tell him his services were no longer required; but that if in any other way I could assist him, I would be happy to do so, especially if he desired to return to his native place, wherever that might be, I would willingly help to defray the expenses. Moreover, if after reaching home he found himself at any time in want of aid, a letter from him would be sure of a reply. The next morning came.

"Bartleby," said I, gently calling to him behind his screen.

No reply.

"Bartleby," said I, in a still gentler tone, "come here; I am not going to ask you to do anything you would prefer not to do—I simply wish to speak to you."

Upon this he noiselessly slid into view.

"Will you tell me, Bartleby, where you were born?"

"I would prefer not to."

"Will you tell me *anything* about yourself?"

"I would prefer not to."

"But what reasonable objection can you have to speak to me? I feel friendly towards you."

He did not look at me while I spoke, but kept his glance fixed upon my bust of Cicero, which as I then sat was directly behind me, some six inches above my head.

"What is your answer, Bartleby?" said I, after waiting a considerable time for a reply, during which his countenance remained immovable, only there was the faintest conceivable tremor of the white attenuated mouth.

"At present I prefer to give no answer," he said, and retired into his hermitage.

It was rather weak in me I confess, but his manner on this occasion nettled me. Not only did there seem to lurk in it a certain disdain, but his perverseness seemed ungrateful, considering the undeniable good usage and indulgence he had received from me.

Again I sat ruminating what I should do. Mortified as I was at his behavior, and resolved as I had been to dismiss him when I entered my office, nevertheless I strangely felt something superstitious knocking at my heart, and forbidding me to carry out my purpose, and denouncing me for a villain if I dared to breathe one bitter word against this forlornest of mankind. At last, familiarly drawing my chair behind his screen, I sat down and said:

"Bartleby, never mind then about revealing your history; but let me entreat you, as a friend, to comply as far as may be with the usages of this office. Say now you will help to examine papers tomorrow or next day: in short, say now that in a day or two you will begin to be a little reasonable:—say so, Bartleby."

"At present I would prefer not to be a little reasonable," was his mildly cadaverous reply.

Just then the folding doors opened, and Nippers approached. He seemed suffering from an unusually bad night's rest, induced by severer indigestion than common. He overheard those final words of Bartleby.   110

"Prefer not, eh?" gritted Nippers—"I'd prefer him, if I were you, sir," addressing me—"I'd prefer him; I'd give him preferences, the stubborn mule! What is it, sir, pray, that he prefers not to do now?"

Bartleby moved not a limb.

"Mr. Nippers," said I, "I'd prefer that you would withdraw for the present."

Somehow, of late I had got into the way of involuntarily using this word "prefer" upon all sorts of not exactly suitable occasions. And I trembled to think that my contact with the scrivener had already and seriously affected me in a mental way. And what further and deeper aberration might it not yet produce? This apprehension had not been without efficacy in determining me to summary means.

As Nippers, looking very sour and sulky, was departing, Turkey blandly   115 and deferentially approached.

"With submission, sir," said he, "yesterday I was thinking about Bartleby here, and I think that if he would but prefer to take a quart of good ale every day, it would do much towards mending him and enabling him to assist in examining his papers."

"So you have got the word too," said I, slightly excited.

"With submission, what word, sir?" asked Turkey, respectfully crowding himself into the contracted space behind the screen, and by so doing making me jostle the scrivener. "What word, sir?"

"I would prefer to be left alone here," said Bartleby, as if offended at being mobbed in his privacy.

"That's the word, Turkey," said I—"that's it."   120

"Oh, prefer? oh yes—queer word. I never use it myself. But, sir, as I was saying, if he would but prefer—"

"Turkey," interrupted I, "you will please withdraw."

"Oh certainly, sir, if you prefer that I should."

As he opened the folding door to retire, Nippers at his desk caught a glimpse of me and asked whether I would prefer to have a certain paper copied on blue paper or white. He did not in the least roguishly accent the word prefer. It was plain that it involuntarily rolled from his tongue. I thought to

myself, surely I must get rid of a demented man who already has in some degree turned the tongues if not the heads of myself and clerks. But I thought
it prudent not to break the dismission at once.

The next day I noticed that Bartleby did nothing but stand at his window in his dead-wall revery. Upon my asking him why he did not write, he
said that he had decided upon doing no more writing.

"Why, how now? what next?" exclaimed I, "do no more writing?"

"No more."

"And what is the reason?"

"Do you not see the reason for yourself?" he indifferently replied.

I looked steadfastly at him, and perceived that his eyes looked dull and
glazed. Instantly it occurred to me that his unexampled diligence in copying
by his dim window for the first few weeks of his stay with me might have
temporarily impaired his vision.

I was touched. I said something in condolence with him. I hinted that
of course he did wisely in abstaining from writing for a while, and urged him
to embrace that opportunity of taking wholesome exercise in the open air.
This, however, he did not do. A few days after this, my other clerks being
absent, and being in a great hurry to dispatch certain letters by the mail, I
thought that, having nothing else earthly to do, Bartleby would surely be
less inflexible than usual and carry these letters to the post office. But he
blankly declined. So, much to my inconvenience, I went myself.

Still added days went by. Whether Bartleby's eyes improved or not, I
could not say. To all appearance, I thought they did. But when I asked him
if they did, he vouchsafed no answer. At all events, he would do no copying.
At last, in reply to my urgings, he informed me that he had permanently
given up copying.

"What!" exclaimed I; "suppose your eyes should get entirely well—better
than ever before—would you not copy then?"

"I have given up copying," he answered, and slid aside.

He remained as ever, a fixture in my chamber. Nay—if that were possible—he became still more of a fixture than before. What was to be done?
He would do nothing in the office: why should he stay there? In plain fact,
he had now become a millstone to me, not only useless as a necklace but af-
flictive to bear. Yet I was sorry for him. I speak less than truth when I say
that on his own account, he occasioned me uneasiness. If he would but
have named a single relative or friend, I would instantly have written and
urged their taking the poor fellow away to some convenient retreat. But he
seemed alone, absolutely alone in the universe. A bit of wreck in the mid-
Atlantic. At length, necessities connected with my business tyrannized over
all other considerations. Decently as I could, I told Bartleby that in six days'
time he must unconditionally leave the office. I warned him to take measures, in the interval, for procuring some other abode. I offered to assist him

in this endeavor, if he himself would but take the first step towards a removal. "And when you finally quit me, Bartleby," added I, "I shall see that you go not away entirely unprovided. Six days from this hour, remember."

At the expiration of that period I peeped behind the screen, and lo! Bartleby was there.

I buttoned up my coat, balanced myself, advanced slowly towards him, touched his shoulder, and said, "The time has come; you must quit this place; I am sorry for you; here is money; but you must go."

"I would prefer not," he replied, with his back still towards me.

"You must."

He remained silent.   140

Now I had an unbounded confidence in this man's common honesty. He had frequently restored to me six pences and shillings carelessly dropped upon the floor, for I am apt to be very reckless in such shirt-button affairs. The proceeding then which followed will not be deemed extraordinary.

"Bartleby," said I, "I owe you twelve dollars on account; here are thirty-two; the odd twenty are yours. Will you take it?" and I handed the bills towards him.

But he made no motion.

"I will leave them here then," putting them under a weight on the table. Then taking my hat and cane and going to the door I tranquilly turned and added, "After you have removed your things from these offices, Bartleby, you will of course lock the door—since every one is now gone for the day but you—and if you please, slip your key underneath the mat so that I may have it in the morning. I shall not see you again, so good-bye to you. If hereafter in your new place of abode I can be of any service to you, do not fail to advise me by letter. Good-bye, Bartleby, and fare you well."

But he answered not a word; like the last column of some ruined tem-   145
ple, he remained standing mute and solitary in the middle of the otherwise deserted room.

As I walked home in a pensive mood, my vanity got the better of my pity. I could not but highly plume myself on my masterly management in getting rid of Bartleby. Masterly I call it, and such it must appear to any dispassionate thinker. The beauty of my procedure seemed to consist in its perfect quietness. There was no vulgar bullying, no bravado of any sort, no choleric hectoring and striding to and fro across the apartment, jerking out vehement commands for Bartleby to bundle himself off with his beggarly traps. Nothing of the kind. Without loudly bidding Bartleby depart—as an inferior genius might have done—I assumed the ground that depart he must, and upon the assumption built all I had to say. The more I thought over my procedure, the more I was charmed with it. Nevertheless, next morning, upon awakening, I had my doubts—I had somehow slept off the fumes of vanity. One of the coolest and wisest hours a man has is just after he awakes in the morning. My procedure seemed as sagacious as ever—but only in theory. How it would prove in practice—there was the rub. It was truly a beautiful thought to have assumed Bartleby's departure; but after all, that assumption was simply my own, and none of Bartleby's. The great point was not whether I had assumed that he would quit me, but whether he would prefer so to do. He was more a man of preferences than assumptions.

After breakfast, I walked downtown, arguing the probabilities pro and con. One moment I thought it would prove a miserable failure, and Bartleby would be found all alive at my office as usual; the next moment it seemed certain that I should see his chair empty. And so I kept veering about. At the corner of Broadway and Canal Street, I saw quite an excited group of people standing in earnest conversation.

"I'll take odds he doesn't," said a voice as I passed.

"Doesn't go?—done!" said I, "put up your money."

I was instinctively putting my hand in my pocket to produce my own, when I remembered that this was an election day. The words I had overheard bore no reference to Bartleby, but to the success or nonsuccess of some candidate for the mayoralty. In my intent frame of mind, I had, as it were, imagined that all Broadway shared in my excitement and were debating the same question with me. I passed on, very thankful that the uproar of the street screened my momentary absentmindedness.

As I had intended, I was earlier than usual at my office door. I stood listening for a moment. All was still. He must be gone. I tried the knob. The door was locked. Yes, my procedure had worked to a charm; he indeed must be vanished. Yet a certain melancholy mixed with this: I was almost sorry for my brilliant success. I was fumbling under the door mat for the key which Bartleby was to have left there for me when accidentally my knee knocked against a panel, producing a summoning sound, and in response a voice came to me from within—"Not yet; I am occupied."

It was Bartleby.

I was thunderstruck. For an instant I stood like the man who, pipe in mouth, was killed one cloudless afternoon long ago in Virginia, by summer lightning; at his own warm open window he was killed, and remained leaning out there upon the dreamy afternoon till someone touched him, when he fell.

"Not gone!" I murmured at last. But again obeying that wondrous ascendancy which the inscrutable scrivener had over me, and from which ascendancy, for all my chafing, I could not completely escape, I slowly went downstairs and out into the street, and while walking round the block, considered what I should next do in this unheard of perplexity. Turn the man out by an actual thrusting I could not; to drive him away by calling him hard names would not do; calling in the police was an unpleasant idea; and yet, permit him to enjoy his cadaverous triumph over me?—this too I could not think of. What was to be done? or if nothing could be done, was there anything further that I could assume in the matter? Yes, as before I had prospectively assumed that Bartleby would depart, so now I might retrospectively assume that departed he was. In the legitimate carrying out of this assumption, I might enter my office in a great hurry, and pretending not to see Bartleby at all, walk straight against him as if he were air. Such a proceeding would in a singular degree have the appearance of a home-thrust. It was hardly possible that Bartleby could withstand such an application of the doctrine of assumptions. But upon second thoughts the success of the plan seemed rather dubious. I resolved to argue the matter over with him again.

"Bartleby," said I, entering the office with a quietly severe expression, "I am seriously displeased. I am pained, Bartleby. I had thought better of you. I had imagined you of such a gentlemanly organization that in my delicate dilemma a slight hint would suffice—in short, an assumption. But it appears I am deceived. Why," I added, unaffectedly starting, "you have not even touched that money yet," pointing to it just where I had left it the evening previous.   155

He answered nothing.

"Will you, or will you not, quit me?" I now demanded in a sudden passion, advancing close to him.

"I would prefer not to quit you," he replied, gently emphasizing the not.

"What earthly right have you to stay here? Do you pay any rent? Do you pay my taxes? Or is this property yours?"

He answered nothing.   160

"Are you ready to go on and write now? Are your eyes recovered? Could you copy a small paper for me this morning? or help examine a few lines? or step round to the post office? In a word, will you do anything at all to give a coloring to your refusal to depart the premises?"

He silently retired into his hermitage.

I was now in such a state of nervous resentment that I thought it but prudent to check myself at present from further demonstrations. Bartleby and I were alone. I remembered the tragedy of the unfortunate Adams and the still more unfortunate Colt in the solitary office of the latter; and how poor Colt, being dreadfully incensed by Adams, and imprudently permitting himself to get wildly excited, was at unawares hurried into his fatal act—an act which certainly no man could possibly deplore more than the actor himself. Often it had occurred to me in my ponderings upon the subject that had that altercation taken place in the public street, or at a private residence, it would not have terminated as it did. It was the circumstance of being alone in a solitary office, upstairs, of a building entirely unhallowed by humanizing domestic associations—an uncarpeted office, doubtless, of a dusty haggard sort of appearance—this it must have been which greatly helped to enhance the irritable desperation of the hapless Colt.

But when this old Adam of resentment rose in me and tempted me concerning Bartleby, I grappled him and threw him. How? Why, simply by recalling the divine injunction: "A new commandment give I unto you, that ye love one another." Yes, this it was that saved me. Aside from higher considerations, charity often operates as a vastly wise and prudent principle—a great safeguard to its possessor. Men have committed murder for jealousy's sake, and anger's sake, and hatred's sake, and selfishness' sake, and spiritual pride's sake; but no man that ever I heard of ever committed a diabolical murder for sweet charity's sake. Mere self-interest, then, if no better motive can be enlisted, should, especially with high-tempered men, prompt all beings to charity and philanthropy. At any rate, upon the occasion in question, I strove to drown my exasperated feelings towards the scrivener by benevolently construing his conduct. Poor fellow, poor fellow! thought I, he don't mean anything; and besides, he has seen hard times, and ought to be indulged.

I endeavored also immediately to occupy myself, and at the same time to comfort my despondency. I tried to fancy that in the course of the morning, at such time as might prove agreeable to him, Bartleby of his own free accord would emerge from his hermitage and take up some decided line of march in the direction of the door. But no. Half-past twelve o'clock came; Turkey began to glow in the face, overturn his inkstand, and become generally obstreperous; Nippers abated down into quietude and courtesy; Ginger Nut munched his noon apple; and Bartleby remained standing at his window in one of his profoundest dead-wall reveries. Will it be credited? Ought I to acknowledge it? That afternoon I left the office without saying one further word to him.

Some days now passed, during which at leisure intervals I looked a little into "Edwards on the Will," and "Priestly on Necessity." Under the circumstances, those books induced a salutary feeling. Gradually I slid into the persuasion that these troubles of mine touching the scrivener had been all predestinated from eternity, and Bartleby was billeted upon me for some mysterious purpose of an all-wise Providence which it was not for a mere mortal like me to fathom. Yes, Bartleby, stay there behind your screen, thought I; I shall persecute you no more; you are harmless and noiseless as any of these old chairs; in short, I never feel so private as when I know you are here. At least I see it, I feel it; I penetrate to the predestinated purpose of my life. I am content. Others may have loftier parts to enact; but my mission in this world, Bartleby, is to furnish you with office-room for such period as you may see fit to remain.

I believe that this wise and blessed frame of mind would have continued with me had it not been for the unsolicited and uncharitable remarks obtruded upon me by my professional friends who visited the rooms. But thus it often is, that the constant friction of illiberal minds wears out at last the best resolves of the more generous. Though to be sure, when I reflected upon it, it was not strange that people entering my office should be struck by the peculiar aspect of the unaccountable Bartleby, and so be tempted to throw out some sinister observations concerning him. Sometimes an attorney having business with me, and calling at my office, and finding no one but the scrivener there, would undertake to obtain some sort of precise information from him touching my whereabouts; but without heeding his idle talk, Bartleby would remain standing immovable in the middle of the room. So after contemplating him in that position for a time, the attorney would depart, no wiser than he came.

Also, when a reference was going on, and the room full of lawyers and witnesses and business was driving fast, some deeply occupied legal gentleman present seeing Bartleby wholly unemployed would request him to run round to his (the legal gentleman's) office and fetch some papers for him. Thereupon, Bartleby would tranquilly decline, and remain idle as before. Then the lawyer would give a great stare and turn to me. And what could I say? At last I was made aware that all through the circle of my professional acquaintance, a whisper of wonder was running round having reference to the strange creature I kept at my office. This worried me very much. And as the idea came upon me of his possibly turning out a long-lived man, and keep occupying my chambers, and denying my authority, and perplexing my visitors, and scandalizing my professional reputation, and casting a general gloom over the premises, keeping soul and body together to the last upon his savings (for doubtless he spent but half a dime a day), and in the end perhaps outliving me, and claiming possession of my office by right of his perpetual occupancy: as all these dark anticipations crowded upon me more and more, and my friends continually intruded their relentless remarks upon the apparition in my room, a great change was wrought in me. I resolved to gather all my faculties together, and forever rid me of this intolerable incubus.

Ere revolving any complicated project, however, adapted to this end, I first simply suggested to Bartleby the propriety of his permanent departure. In a calm and serious tone, I commended the idea to his careful and mature consideration. But having taken three days to meditate upon it, he apprised me that his original determination remained the same, in short, that he still preferred to abide with me.

What shall I do? I now said to myself, buttoning up my coat to the last button. What shall I do? what ought I do? what does conscience say I should do with this man, or rather ghost? Rid myself of him, I must; go, he shall. But how? You will not thrust him, the poor, pale, passive mortal—you will not thrust such a helpless creature out of your door? you will not dishonor yourself by such cruelty? No, I will not, I cannot do that. Rather would I let him live and die here, and then mason up his remains in the wall. What then will you do? For all your coaxing, he will not budge. Bribes he leaves

170

under your own paperweight on your table; in short, it is quite plain that he prefers to cling to you.

Then something severe, something unusual must be done. What! surely you will not have him collared by a constable, and commit his innocent pallor to the common jail? And upon what ground could you procure such a thing to be done?—a vagrant, is he? What! he a vagrant, a wanderer, who refuses to budge? It is because he will not be a vagrant, then, that you seek to count him as a vagrant. That is too absurd. No visible means of support: there I have him. Wrong again: for indubitably he does support himself, and that is the only unanswerable proof that any man can show of his possessing the means so to do. No more then. Since he will not quit me, I must quit him. I will change my offices; I will move elsewhere, and give him fair notice that if I find him on my new premises I will then proceed against him as a common trespasser.

Acting accordingly, next day I thus addressed him: "I find these chambers too far from the City Hall; the air is unwholesome. In a word, I propose to remove my offices next week, and shall no longer require your services. I tell you this now, in order that you may seek another place."

He made no reply, and nothing more was said.

On the appointed day I engaged carts and men, proceeded to my chambers, and having but little furniture, everything was removed in a few hours. Throughout, the scrivener remained standing behind the screen, which I directed to be removed the last thing. It was withdrawn, and being folded up like a huge folio, left him the motionless occupant of a naked room. I stood in the entry watching him a moment, while something from within me upbraided me.

I re-entered, with my hand in my pocket—and—and my heart in my mouth.

"Good-bye, Bartleby; I am going—good-bye, and God some way bless you; and take that," slipping something in his hand. But it dropped upon the floor, and then—strange to say—I tore myself from him whom I had so longed to be rid of.

Established in my new quarters, for a day or two I kept the door locked, and started at every footfall in the passages. When I returned to my rooms after any little absence, I would pause at the threshold for an instant, and attentively listen ere applying my key. But these fears were needless. Bartleby never came nigh me.

I thought all was going well, when a perturbed looking stranger visited me inquiring whether I was the person who had recently occupied rooms at No. — Wall Street. Full of forebodings, I replied that I was.

"Then sir," said the stranger, who proved a lawyer, "you are responsible for the man you left there. He refuses to do any copying; he refuses to do anything; he says he prefers not to; and he refuses to quit the premises."

"I am very sorry, sir," said I, with assumed tranquility, but an inward 180
tremor, "but, really, the man you allude to is nothing to me—he is no relation or apprentice of mine, that you should hold me responsible for him."

"In mercy's name, who is he?"

"I certainly cannot inform you. I know nothing about him. Formerly I
employed him as a copyist, but he has done nothing for me now for some
time past."

"I shall settle him then—good morning, sir."

Several days passed, and I heard nothing more; and though I often felt
a charitable prompting to call at the place and see poor Bartleby, yet a certain squeamishness of I know not what withheld me.

All is over with him by this time, thought I at last, when through an- 185
other week no further intelligence reached me. But coming to my room the
day after, I found several persons waiting at my door in a high state of nervous excitement.

"That's the man—here he comes," cried the foremost one, whom I
recognized as the lawyer who had previously called upon me alone.

"You must take him away, sir, at once," cried a portly person among
them, advancing upon me, and whom I knew to be the landlord of No. —
Wall Street. "These gentlemen, my tenants, cannot stand it any longer;
Mr. B——" pointing to the lawyer, "has turned him out of his room, and he
now persists in haunting the building generally, sitting upon the banisters of
the stairs by day, and sleeping in the entry by night. Everybody is concerned;
clients are leaving the offices; some fears are entertained of a mob; something you must do, and that without delay."

Aghast at this torrent, I fell back before it, and would fain have locked
myself in my new quarters. In vain I persisted that Bartleby was nothing to
me—no more than to anyone else. In vain—I was the last person known to
have anything to do with him, and they held me to the terrible account.
Fearful then of being exposed in the papers (as one person present obscurely
threatened), I considered the matter, and at length said that if the lawyer
would give me a confidential interview with the scrivener, in his (the lawyer's)
own room, I would that afternoon strive my best to rid them of the nuisance
they complained of.

Going upstairs to my old haunt, there was Bartleby silently sitting upon
the banister at the landing.

"What are you doing here, Bartleby?" said I. 190

"Sitting upon the banister," he mildly replied.

I motioned him into the lawyer's room, who then left us.

"Bartleby," said I, "are you aware that you are the cause of great tribula-
tion to me, by persisting in occupying the entry after being dismissed from
the office?"

No answer.

"Now one of two things must take place. Either you must do something or something must be done to you. Now what sort of business would you like to engage in? Would you like to re-engage in copying for someone?"

"No; I would prefer not to make any change."

"Would you like a clerkship in a dry-goods store?"

"There is too much confinement about that. No, I would not like a clerkship; but I am not particular."

"Too much confinement," I cried, "why you keep yourself confined all the time!"

"I would prefer not to take a clerkship," he rejoined, as if to settle that little item at once.

"How would a bar-tender's business suit you? There is no trying of the eyesight in that."

"I would not like it at all; though, as I said before, I am not particular."

His unwonted wordiness inspirited me. I returned to the charge.

"Well then, would you like to travel through the country collecting bills for the merchants? That would improve your health."

"No, I would prefer to be doing something else."

"How then would going as a companion to Europe, to entertain some young gentleman with your conversation—how would that suit you?"

"Not at all. It does not strike me that there is anything definite about that. I like to be stationary. But I am not particular."

"Stationary you shall be then," I cried, now losing all patience, and for the first time in all my exasperating connection with him fairly flying into a passion. "If you do not go away from these premises before night, I shall feel bound—indeed I am bound—to—to—to quit the premises myself !" I rather absurdly concluded, knowing not with what possible threat to try to frighten his immobility into compliance. Despairing of all further efforts, I was pre-cipitately leaving him, when a final thought occurred to me—one which had not been wholly unindulged before.

"Bartleby," said I, in the kindest tone I could assume under such excit-ing circumstances, "will you go home with me now—not to my office, but my dwelling—and remain there till we can conclude upon some convenient arrangement for you at our leisure? Come, let us start now, right away."

"No: at present I would prefer not to make any change at all."

I answered nothing, but effectually dodging everyone by the suddenness and rapidity of my flight, rushed from the building, ran up Wall Street to-wards Broadway, and jumping into the first omnibus was soon removed from pursuit. As soon as tranquility returned I distinctly perceived that I had now done all that I possibly could, both in respect to the demands of the land-lord and his tenants, and with regard to my own desire and sense of duty, to benefit Bartleby and shield him from rude persecution. I now strove to be entirely carefree and quiescent; and my conscience justified me in the attempt though indeed it was not so successful as I could have wished. So fearful was I of being again hunted out by the incensed landlord and his exasperated tenants that, surrendering my business to Nippers, for a few days I drove about the upper part of the town and through the suburbs in my rockaway; crossed over to Jersey City and Hoboken, and paid fugitive visits to Manhattanville and Astoria. In fact I almost lived in my rockaway for the time.

When again I entered my office, lo, a note from the landlord lay upon the desk. I opened it with trembling hands. It informed me that the writer had sent to the police and had Bartleby removed to the Tombs as a vagrant. Moreover, since I knew more about him than anyone else, he wished me to appear at that place and make a suitable statement of the facts. These tidings had a conflicting effect upon me. At first I was indignant, but at last almost approved. The landlord's energetic, summary disposition had led him to adopt a procedure which I do not think I would have decided upon myself; and yet as a last resort, under such peculiar circumstances, it seemed the only plan.

As I afterwards learned, the poor scrivener, when told that he must be conducted to the Tombs, offered not the slightest obstacle, but in his pale unmoving way, silently acquiesced.

Some of the compassionate and curious bystanders joined the party; and headed by one of the constables arm in arm with Bartleby, the silent procession filed its way through all the noise, and heat, and joy of the roaring thoroughfares at noon.

The same day I received the note I went to the Tombs or, to speak more properly, the Halls of Justice. Seeking the right officer, I stated the purpose of my call, and was informed that the individual I described was indeed within. I then assured the functionary that Bartleby was a perfectly honest man, and greatly to be compassionated, however unaccountably eccentric. I narrated all I knew, and closed by suggesting the idea of letting him remain in as indulgent confinement as possible till something less harsh might be done—though indeed I hardly knew what. At all events, if nothing else could be decided upon, the alms-house must receive him. I then begged to have an interview. 215

Being under no disgraceful charge, and quite serene and harmless in all his ways, they had permitted him freely to wander about the prison, and especially in the inclosed grass-platted yards thereof. And so I found him there, standing all alone in the quietest of the yards, his face towards a high wall, while all around, from the narrow slits of the jail windows, I thought I saw peering out upon him the eyes of murderers and thieves.

"Bartleby!"

"I know you," he said, without looking around—"and I want nothing to say to you."

"It was not I that brought you here, Bartleby," said I, keenly pained at his implied suspicion. "And to you, this should not be so vile a place. Nothing reproachful attaches to you by being here. And see, it is not so sad a place as one might think. Look, there is the sky, and here is the grass."

"I know where I am," he replied, but would say nothing more, and so I left him.

As I entered the corridor again, a broad meat-like man in an apron accosted me, and jerking his thumb over his shoulder said—"Is that your friend?"

"Yes."

"Does he want to starve? If he does, let him live on the prison fare, that's all."

"Who are you?" asked I, not knowing what to make of such an unofficially speaking person in such a place.

"I am the grub-man. Such gentlemen as have friends here, hire me to provide them with something good to eat."

"Is this so?" said I, turning to the turnkey.

He said it was.

"Well, then," said I, slipping some silver into the grub-man's hands (for so they called him), "I want you to give particular attention to my friend there; let him have the best dinner you can get. And you must be as polite to him as possible."

"Introduce me, will you?" said the grub-man, looking at me with an expression which seemed to say he was all impatience for an opportunity to give a specimen of his breeding.

Thinking it would prove of benefit to the scrivener, I acquiesced, and asking the grub-man his name, went up with him to Bartleby.

"Bartleby, this is a friend; you will find him very useful to you."

"Your sarvant, sir, your sarvant," said the grub-man making a low salutation behind his apron. "Hope you find it pleasant here, sir—spacious grounds—cool apartments, sir—hope you'll stay with us some time—try to make it agreeable. What will you have for dinner today?"

"I prefer not to dine today," said Bartleby, turning away. "It would disagree with me; I am unused to dinners." So saying he slowly moved to the other side of the enclosure, and took up a position fronting the dead wall.

"How's this?" said the grub-man, addressing me with a stare of astonishment. "He's odd, ain't he?"

"I think he is a little deranged," said I, sadly.

"Deranged? deranged is it? Well now, upon my word, I thought that friend of yourn was a gentleman forger; they are always pale and genteel-like, them forgers. I can't help pity 'em—can't help it, sir. Did you know Monroe Edwards?" he added touchingly, and paused. Then, laying his hand pityingly on my shoulder, sighed, "he died of consumption at Sing-Sing. So you weren't acquainted with Monroe?"

"No, I was never socially acquainted with any forgers. But I cannot stop longer. Look to my friend yonder. You will not lose by it. I will see you again."

Some few days after this, I again obtained admission to the Tombs, and went through the corridors in quest of Bartleby, but without finding him.

"I saw him coming from his cell not long ago," said a turnkey, "maybe he's gone to loiter in the yards."

So I went in that direction.   240

"Are you looking for the silent man?" said another turnkey passing me. "Yonder he lies—sleeping in the yard there. 'Tis not twenty minutes since I saw him lie down."

The yard was entirely quiet. It was not accessible to the common prisoners. The surrounding walls, of amazing thickness, kept off all sound behind them. The Egyptian character of the masonry weighed upon me with its gloom. But a soft imprisoned turf grew under foot. The heart of the eternal pyramids, it seemed, wherein, by some strange magic, through the clefts, grass-seed dropped by birds had sprung.

Strangely huddled at the base of the wall, his knees drawn up, and lying on his side, his head touching the cold stones, I saw the wasted Bartleby. But nothing stirred. I paused; then went close up to him; stooped over, and saw that his dim eyes were open; otherwise he seemed profoundly sleeping. Something prompted me to touch him. I felt his hand, when a tingling shiver ran up my arm and down my spine to my feet.

The round face of the grub-man peered upon me now. "His dinner is ready. Won't he dine today, either? Or does he live without dining?"

"Lives without dining," said I, and closed the eyes.   245

"Eh! —He's asleep, ain't he?"

"With kings and counselors," murmured I.

There would seem little need for proceeding further in this history. Imagination will readily supply the meager recital of poor Bartleby's interment. But ere parting with the reader, let me say that if this little narrative has sufficiently interested him to awaken curiosity as to who Bartleby was, and what manner of life he led prior to the present narrator's making his acquaintance, I can only reply that in such curiosity I fully share, but am wholly unable to gratify it. Yet here I hardly know whether I should divulge one little item of rumor which came to my ear a few months after the scrivener's decease. Upon what basis it rested, I could never ascertain; and hence how true it is I cannot now tell. But inasmuch as this vague report has not been without a certain strange suggestive interest to me, however sad, it may prove the same with some others; and so I will briefly mention it. The report was this: that Bartleby had been a subordinate clerk in the Dead Letter Office at Washington, from which he had been suddenly removed by a change in the administration. When I think over this rumor, I cannot adequately express the emotions which seize me. Dead letters! does it not sound like dead men? Conceive a man by nature and misfortune prone to a pallid hopelessness, can any business seem more fitted to heighten it than that of continually handling these dead letters and assorting them for the flames? For by the cart-load they are annually burned. Sometimes from out the folded paper the pale clerk takes a ring—the finger it was meant for, perhaps, moulders in the grave; a bank note sent in swiftest charity—he whom it would relieve, nor eats nor hungers any more; pardon for those who died despairing; hope for those who died unhoping; good tidings for those who died stifled by unrelieved calamities. On errands of life, these letters speed to death.

Ah, Bartleby! Ah, humanity!

- What does Bartleby actually do over the course of this story?
- How do his words "I would prefer not to" change in meaning as the story progresses?
- How could we characterize the narrator? How is the narrator's business and life impacted by Bartleby's refusal to act?
- Notice that some sections of this story contain narrative exchanges between the narrator and other characters. Other sections contain longer paragraphs. What happens in these paragraphs? How do they move the story forward?
- If we think about the relative importance of Bartleby within the narrator's establishment, how does the narrator account for Bartleby's impact?
- What is the significance of this statement at the end of the story: "Ah, Bartleby! Ah, humanity!"?

POETRY

Billy Collins (1941–)

I Chop Some Parsley While Listening to Art Blakey's Version of "Three Blind Mice" (1998)

And I start wondering how they came to be blind.
If it was congenital, they could be brothers and sister,
and I think of the poor mother
brooding over her sightless young triplets.

Or was it a common accident, all three caught   5
in a searing explosion, a firework perhaps?
If not,
if each came to his or her blindness separately,

how did they ever manage to find one another?
Would it not be difficult for a blind mouse   10
to locate even one fellow mouse with vision
let alone two other blind ones?

And how, in their tiny darkness,
could they possibly have run after a farmer's wife
or anyone else's wife for that matter?   15
Not to mention why.

Just so she could cut off their tails
with a carving knife, is the cynic's answer,
but the thought of them without eyes
and now without tails to trail through the moist grass   20

or slip around the corner of a baseboard
has the cynic who always lounges within me
up off his couch and at the window
trying to hide the rising softness that he feels.

By now I am on to dicing an onion   25
which might account for the wet stinging
in my own eyes, though Freddie Hubbard's
mournful trumpet on "Blue Moon,"

which happens to be the next cut,
cannot be said to be making matters any better.   30

■ Art Blakey is a jazz drummer, and the poem refers to a specific jazz album in
which "Blue Moon" is the song directly after "Three Blind Mice." How
important is this information to your understanding of the poem?

■ Which questions that the poet asks about the familiar Mother Goose story
seem like reasonable questions? How do these questions make us think about
the nursery rhyme differently? How are they at odds with the tone of the
nursery rhyme?

W. H. Auden (1907–1973)

Musée des Beaux Arts (1938)

About suffering they were never wrong,
The Old Masters: how well they understood
Its human position; how it takes place
While someone else is eating or opening a window or just walking dully
    along;
How, when the aged are reverently, passionately waiting   5
For the miraculous birth, there always must be
Children who did not specially want it to happen, skating
On a pond at the edge of the wood:
They never forgot
That even the dreadful martyrdom must run its course   10
Anyhow in a corner, some untidy spot
Where the dogs go on with their doggy life and the torturer's horse
Scratches its innocent behind on a tree.

In Brueghel's *Icarus*, for instance: how everything turns away
Quite leisurely from the disaster; the plowman may   15
Have heard the splash, the forsaken cry,
But for him it was not an important failure; the sun shone
As it had to on the white legs disappearing into the green
Water; and the expensive delicate ship that must have seen
Something amazing, a boy falling out of the sky,   20
Had somewhere to get to and sailed calmly on.

- The poem responds to specific paintings that the poet observes in the Musée des Beaux Arts. How does the poet contrast the reverent and passionate waiting of the aged with the actions of characters such as dogs and horses?
- Explain the significance of the final line in which the ship "Had somewhere to get to and sailed calmly on." How does the contrast between the tragedy of Icarus and this ship's business intensify the tragedy?

Elizabeth Bishop (1911–1979)

One Art (1976)

The art of losing isn't hard to master;
so many things seem filled with the intent
to be lost that their loss is no disaster.

Lose something every day. Accept the fluster
of lost door keys, the hour badly spent.   5
The art of losing isn't hard to master.

Then practice losing farther, losing faster:
places, and names, and where it was you meant
to travel. None of these will bring disaster.

I lost my mother's watch. And look! my last, or   10
next-to-last, of three loved houses went.
The art of losing isn't hard to master.

I lost two cities, lovely ones. And, vaster,
some realms I owned, two rivers, a continent.
I miss them, but it wasn't a disaster.   15

—Even losing you (the joking voice, a gesture
I love) I shan't have lied. It's evident
the art of losing's not too hard to master
though it may look like (*Write* it!) like disaster.

■ How does the poet make a joke out of the tragic here? How do we practice
losing? How can we master such an art? Which losses here might be funny?
Where does the poem indicate that the losses are more difficult? How do the
tone and structure of the poem change with these losses?

Quincy Troupe (1939–)

Untitled (1991)

in brussels, eye sat in the grand place cafe & heard
duke's place, played after salsa
between the old majestic architecture, jazz bouncing off
all that gilded gold history snoring complacently there
flowers all over the ground, up inside the sound   5
the old white band jamming the music
tight & heavy, like some food
pushin pedal to the metal
getting all the way down
under the scaffolding surrounding   10
l'hotel de ville, chattanooga choochoo

choo chooing all the way home, upside walls, under gold eagles
& a gold vaulting girl, naked on a rooftop holding a flag over
her head, like skip rope, surrounded by all manner
of saints & gold madmen, riding emblazoned stallions   15
snorting like crazed demons at their nostrils
the music swirling like a dancing bear
a beautiful girl, flowers in her hair

the air woven with lilting voices in this grand place of parapets
& crowns, jewels & golden torches streaming   20
like a horse's mane, antiquity riding through in a wheel carriage
here, through gargoyles & gothic towers rocketing swordfish lanced crosses
pointing up at a God threatening rain
& it is stunning at this moment when raised beer steins cheer
the music on, hot & heavy, still humming & cooking   25
basic african-american rhythms alive here
in this ancient grand place of europe
this confluence point of nations & cultures
jumping off place for beer & cuisines
fused with music, poetry & stone   30
here in this blinding, beautiful square
sunlit now as the golden eye of God shoots through
flowers all over the cobbled ground, up in the music
the air brightly cool as light after jeweled rain

■ Notice the discussions of architectural elements in this poem. Which words
  describe the place where these "events" take place?
■ Think about the culture represented by the place and the culture represented by
  the music. Find images that emphasize contrasts between these two cultures.
■ How does Troupe weave his descriptions of music into this place?
■ Look at the images in the final lines: "raindrops" and "broken mirrors";
  "parentheses" and "bat wings curved." How are these two forms of
  interruption different from one another? How do they break up (and bring
  together) the music and architecture described in the poem?

Sherman Alexie (1966–)

Defending Walt Whitman (1996)

Basketball is like this for young Indian boys, all arms and legs
and serious stomach muscles. Every body is brown!

These are the twentieth-century warriors who will never kill,
although a few sat quietly in the deserts of Kuwait,
waiting for orders to do something, do something.   5

God, there is nothing as beautiful as a jump shot
on a reservation summer basketball court
where the ball is moist with sweat
and makes a sound when it swishes through the net
that causes Walt Whitman to weep because it is so perfect.   10

There are veterans of foreign wars here,
whose bodies are still dominated
by collarbones and knees, whose bodies still respond
in the ways that bodies are supposed to respond when we are young.
Every body is brown! Look there, that boy can run   15
up and down this court forever. He can leap for a rebound
with his back arched like a salmon, all meat and bone
synchronized, magnetic, as if the court were a river,
as if the rim were a dam, as if the air were a ladder
leading the Indian boy toward home.   20

Some of the Indian boys still wear their military haircuts
while a few have let their hair grow back.
It will never be the same as it was before!
One Indian boy has never cut his hair, not once, and he braids it
into wild patterns that do not measure anything.   25
He is just a boy with too much time on his hands.
Look at him. He wants to play this game in bare feet.

God, the sun is so bright! There is no place like this.
Walt Whitman stretches his calf muscles
on the sidelines. He has the next game.   30
His huge beard is ridiculous on the reservation.
Some body throws a crazy pass and Walt Whitman catches it
        with quick hands.
He brings the ball close to his nose
        and breathes in all of its smells: leather, brown skin, sweat,
        black hair,
burning oil, twisted ankle, long drink of warm water,   35
gunpowder, pine tree. Walt Whitman squeezes the ball tightly.
He wants to run. He hardly has the patience to wait for his turn.
"What's the score?" he asks. He asks, "What's the score?"

Basketball is like this for Walt Whitman. He watches these Indian boys
as if they were the last bodies on earth. Every body is brown!   40
Walt Whitman shakes because he believes in God.
Walt Whitman dreams of the Indian boy who will defend him,
trapping him in the corner, all flailing arms and legs
and legendary stomach muscles. Walt Whitman shakes
because he believes in God. Walt Whitman dreams   45
of the first jumpshot he will take, the ball arcing clumsily
from his fingers, striking the rim so hard that it sparks.
Walt Whitman shakes because he believes in God.
Walt Whitman closes his eyes. He is a small man and his beard
is ludicrous on the reservation, absolutely insane.   50
His beard makes the Indian boys laugh righteously. His beard
     frightens
the smallest Indian boys. His beard tickles the skin
of the Indian boys who dribble past him. His beard, his beard!

God, there is beauty in every body. Walt Whitman stands
at center court while the Indian boys run from basket to basket.   55
Walt Whitman cannot tell the difference between
offense and defense. He does not care if he touches the ball.
Half of the Indian boys wear T-shirts damp with sweat
and the other half are barebacked, skin slick and shiny.
There is no place like this. Walt Whitman smiles.   60
Walt Whitman shakes. This game belongs to him.

■ See the biographical entry on the poet Walt Whitman (see page 1773) and
  his poems on pages 1308 and 1617. How does Alexie indicate the time and place
  where this story takes place? Why are these details important to this narrative?

■ Look at the repeated line "Walt Whitman shakes because he believes in God."
  This must have some significance because Alexie repeats it. At the end of the
  poem, the sentence is shorter: "Walt Whitman shakes." What has happened in
  the poem to make Alexie shorten this sentence? What concept of a belief in
  God do we get from this poem?

Ted Kooser (1939–)

A Hairnet with Stars (1980)

I ate at the counter.
The waitress was wearing
a hairnet with stars,

pale blue stars
over the white clouds   5
of her hair, a woman
still lovely at sixty
or older, full breasted
and proud, her hands
strong and sensual,   10
smoothing the apron
over her belly.
I sighed and she turned
to me smiling.
"Mustard?" she asked.   15

■ How are stars significant to this poem?

■ How is the question "Mustard?" an intrusion into the world that the poem is describing and the tone that the poet presents here?

Yusef Komunyakaa (1947–)

A Break from the Bush (1988)

The South China Sea
drives in another herd.
The volleyball's a punching bag:
Clem's already lost a tooth
& Johnny's left eye is swollen shut.   5
Frozen airlifted steaks burn
on a wire grill, & miles away
machine guns can be heard.
Pretending we're somewhere else,
we play harder.   10
Lee Otis, the point man,
high on Buddha grass,
buries himself up to his neck
in sand. "Can you see me now?
In this spot they gonna build   15
a Hilton. Invest in Paradise.
Bang, bozos! You're dead."
Frenchie's cassette player
unravels Hendrix's "Purple Haze."
Snake, 17, from Daytona,   20
sits at the water's edge,

the ash on his cigarette
pointing to the ground
like a crooked finger. CJ,
who in three days will trip   25
a fragmentation mine,
runs after the ball
into the whitecaps,
laughing.

■ The scene here describes American soldiers in Vietnam. What details help us
recognize them as Americans during this particular conflict?

■ Look at the details in this poem that indicate that the soldiers are conscious of
their own soldiering. What do they say about their own situation? What is their
opinion of the war that they are fighting?

Lisel Mueller (1924–)

Not Only the Eskimos (1996)

Not only the Eskimos
We have only one noun
but as many different kinds:

the grainy snow of the Puritans
and snow of soft, fat flakes,   5

guerrilla snow, which comes in the night
and changes the world by morning,

rabbinical snow, a permanent skullcap
on the highest mountains,

snow that blows in like the Lone Ranger,   10
riding hard from out of the West,

surreal snow in the Dakotas,
when you can't find your house, your street,
though you are not in a dream
or a science-fiction movie,   15
!snow that tastes good to the sun

when it licks black tree limbs,
leaving us only one white stripe,
a replica of a skunk,

unbelievable snows: 20
the blizzard that strikes on the tenth of April,
the false snow before Indian summer,
the Big Snow on Mozart's birthday,
when Chicago became the Elysian Fields
and strangers spoke to each other,   25

paper snow, cut and taped,
to the inside of grade-school windows,

in an old tale, the snow
that covers a nest of strawberries,
small hearts, ripe and sweet,   30
the special snow that goes with Christmas,
whether it falls or not,

the Russian snow we remember
along with the warmth and smell of furs,
though we have never traveled   35
to Russia or worn furs,

Villon's snows of yesteryear,
lost with ladies gone out like matches,
the snow in Joyce's "The Dead,"
the silent, secret snow   40
in a story by Conrad Aiken,
which is the snow of first love,

the snowfall between the child
and the spacewoman on TV,

snow as idea of whiteness,   45
as in snowdrop, snow goose, snowball bush,

the snow that puts stars in your hair,
and your hair, which has turned to snow,

the snow Elinor Wylie walked in
in velvet shoes,   50
the snow before her foot prints

and the snow after,

the snow in the back of our heads,
whiter than white, which has to do
with childhood again each year.   55

- When the poet describes the "Russian snow," she acknowledges that she can understand and appreciate this type of snow without having any experience in Russia. How does this claim seem reasonable? How can we apply the same claim to other descriptions that we get in the poem?
- The poem might be described as a list of literary uses of the versatile image of snow. How does this list of images function as its own statement? Where does the poet go beyond repeating what others have said about snow?

DRAMA

Christopher Durang (1949–)

An award-winning playwright and actor on stage and screen, Christopher Durang was born in New Jersey. He received his BA from Harvard in 1972 and his MFA from Yale in 1974. He has been cochair of the playwriting program at Juilliard since 1994. Some of Durang's plays include *The Actor's Nightmare*, *Sister Mary Ignatius Explains It All for You* (Obie Award; Off Broadway run 1981–1983), *Beyond Therapy*, and *Betty's Summer Vacation*. Durang has appeared in the films *The Secret of My Success*, *The Butcher's Wife*, and *Housesitter*, among others.

Wendy Wasserstein (1950–2006)

Wendy Wasserstein was born in Brooklyn, New York. She earned a BA from Mount Holyoke College, an MA from City University of New York, and an MFA from Yale University. In addition to her work as a playwright, she taught at Columbia University and New York University and occasionally wrote for television. Among her plays are *Happy Birthday*, *Montpelier Pizz-zazz*, *Uncommon Women and Others*, and *The Heidi Chronicles*. Her plays typically offer serious yet wry observations of the experiences of contemporary women, particularly in regard to relationships.

Medea (1994)

CHARACTERS

MEDEA, *an angry Woman*
THE CHORUS, *the chorus*
JASON, *Medea's husband*
MESSENGER
ANGEL

(The actress who is to play MEDEA *comes out and makes the following introduction.)*
ACTRESS: Hello. I am she who will be Medea. That is, I shall play the heroine from that famous Greek tragedy by Euripides for you.
  I attended a first-rate School of Dramatic Arts. At this wonderful
school, I had classical training, which means we start at the very beginning, a very good place to start. Greek tragedy. How many of you in the   5
audience have ever acted in Greek tragedy? How many of your lives are
Greek tragedy? Is Olympia Dukakis here this evening?
  As an actress who studied the classics, one of the first things you learn
in drama school is that there are more roles for men than for women.
This is a wonderful thing to learn because it is true of the real world as   10
well. Except for *Thelma and Louise*. At drama school, in order to com-
pensate for this problem, the women every year got to act in either
The Trojan Women or *The House of Bernarda Alba*. This prepared us
for bit parts on *Designing Women* and *Little House on the Prairie*.
Although these shows are canceled now, and we have nothing to do.   15
Tonight, we would like to present to you a selection from one of the
most famous Greek tragedies ever written, *The Trojan Women*. Our
scene is directed by Michael Cacoyannis and choreographed by June
Taylor. And now, translated from the Greek by George Stephano-
poulous, here is a scene from this terrifying tragedy. *(Names the cast*   20
members.) ——, —— and —— will play the Chorus. —— and ——
will play the men. *(Dramatically.)* And I, ——, will play Medea. *(The*
actress playing MEDEA *exits with purpose and panache. Enter the three*
actresses who play THE CHORUS. *They are dressed in togas. Most of the time*
they speak in unison. Sometimes they speak solo lines. In the style of   25
the piece, they are over-dramatic and over-wrought. But most of the time
they should act their lines as if they are the words from genuine Greek trage-
dy, full of intonation and emotional feeling. Don't send them up or wink at
the audience. Let the juxtaposition of Greek tragedy acting style and the
sometimes silly lines be what creates the humor.)   30
CHORUS *(in unison.)*: So pitiful, so pitiful
  your shame and lamentation.

No more shall I move the shifting pace
of the shuttle at the looms of Ida.

CHORUS MEMBER #3 (echoes.): Looms of Ida.   35

CHORUS: Can you not, Queen Hecuba, stop this Bacchanal before her light
feet whirl her away into the Argive camp?

CHORUS MEMBER #3 (echoes.): Argive camp.

CHORUS (in unison.): O woe, o woe, o woe,
We are so upset we speak in unison,   40
So pitiful, so wretched, so doomed,
Women who run with wolves
Women who love too much,
Whitewater rapids, how did she turn $1000 into $100,000?
O woe, o woe, o woe.   45
Here she comes now.
Wooga, wooga, wooga.

(Enter MEDEA in a dramatic, bloodred toga. She is in high, excessive grief and
fury.)

MEDEA: Come, flame of the sky,
Pierce through my head!
What do I, Medea, gain from living any longer?   50
Oh I hate living! I want
to end my life, leave it behind, and die.

CHORUS (in unison; chanted seriously.): But tell us how you're really feeling.

MEDEA: My husband Jason—the Argonaut—has left me for another
woman. Debbie.   55

CHORUS (in unison.): Dreaded Debbie, dreaded Debbie.
Debutante from hell.

MEDEA: She is the daughter of King Creon, who owns a diner on Fifty-Fifth
Street and Jamaica Avenue. Fie on her! And the House of Creon! And
the four brothers of the Acropolis.   60
I am banished from my husband's bed, and from the country. A bad predicament all around. But I am skilled in poison. Today three of my enemies I will strike down dead: Debbie and Debbie's father and my
husband.

CHORUS (in unison.): Speaking of your husband, here he comes.   65

(Enter JASON, dressed in a toga but also with an armored breastplate and wearing
a soldier's helmet with a nice little red adornment on top. Sort of like a costume from either Ben Hur or Cleopatra. He perhaps is not in the grand
style, but sounds more normal and conversational.)

JASON: Hello, Medea.

MEDEA: Hello, Jason.

JASON: I hear you've been banished to China.

MEDEA (suddenly Noel Coward brittle.): Very large, China.

JASON: And Japan?   70

MEDEA: Very small, Japan. And Debbie?

JASON: She's very striking.

MEDEA: Some women should be struck regularly like gongs.

JASON: Medea, even though thou art banished by Creon to foreign shores,
the two innocent children of our loins, Lyle and Erik, should remain   75
with me. I will enroll them at the Dalton School. And there they will
flourish as citizens of Corinth under the watchful eye of Zeus and his
lovely and talented wife Hera.

MEDEA: Fine, walk on me some more! I was born unlucky and a woman.

CHORUS (*in unison.*):   Men are from Mars, women are from Venus.   80

JASON: Well, whatever. I call the gods to witness that I have done my
bestto help you and the children.

MEDEA: Go! You have spent too long out here. You are consumed with
craving for your newly-won bride, Debbie. Go, enjoy Debbie! (*Jason
shrugs, exits.*) O woe, o woe. I am in pain for I know what I must do.   85
Debbie, kill for sure.

CHORUS (*in unison.*):   Debbie's done, ding dong, Debbie's done.
Done deal, Debbie dead.
Dopey Debbie, Debbie dead.

MEDEA: But also my sons. Never shall their father see them again. I shall   90
kill my children. (*Ferociously, to the* CHORUS.) How do you like that????

CHORUS (*in unison.*):   Aaaaaaagghghghghghghgghhhhh!
O smart women, foolish choices.
Stop the insanity! Stop the insanity!
You can eat one slice of cheese, or sixteen baked potatoes!   95
Make up your mind.

MEDEA: Why is there so little *Trojan Women* in this, and so much of me?

CHORUS (*in unison.*):   We don't know *The Trojan Women* as well as we
know *Medea.*
(*Spoken, not sung.*)
Medea, we just met a girl named Medea,   100
And suddenly that name
Will never be the same.

MEDEA: Bring my children hither.

CHORUS (*in unison.*):   O miserable mother, to destroy your own increase,
murder the babes of your body. The number you have reached is not in   105
service at this time, Call 777-FILM.

MEDEA (*in a boiling fury.*):   I want to kill my children. I want to sleep with
my brother. I want to pluck out the eyes of my father. I want to blow
up the Parthenon. I need a creative outlet for all this anger. (*Enter the*
MESSENGER, *carrying a head. He kneels before* MEDEA.)   110

MESSENGER: I am a messenger. Caesar is dead.

CHORUS *(in unison.)*: Caesar is dead. How interesting. Who is Caesar?

MESSENGER: I am sorry. Wrong message. *(Reads from piece of paper.)* Lady Teazle wishes you to know that Lady Windermere and Lady Bracknell are inviting you and Lady The-Scottish-Play to tea with her cousin 115 Ernest, if he's not visiting Mr. Bunbury.

MEDEA: Mr. Bunbury? I do not need a messenger. I need a deus ex machina. *(Elaborate music. Enter an ANGEL with great big wings. Descending from the ceiling or revealed on a balcony. Or dragging a stepladder that he stands on. Very dramatic whatever he does.)* 120

ANGEL: O Medea, O Medea.

　　I am a deus ex machina.

　　In a bigger production, I would come down from the sky in an angel's outfit, but just use your imagination. Theatre is greatly about imagination, is it not. 125

　　I am an angel.

　　　I I I I I I I, yi yi yi.

　　　I I I I am the Bird of Greek Tragedy.

　　Do not kill your children. Do not sleep with your brother. Rein in your rage, and thank Zeus. I come with glad tidings. Debbie is no more a 130 threat. She's been cast in a series. She has a running part on *Home Improvements.*

CHORUS *(in unison.)*: Home Improvements.

ANGEL: Jason will return to you. He sees the error of his ways. He has been lobotomized. 135

CHORUS *(in unison.)*: O fortunate woman, to whom Zeus has awarded a docile husband.

MEDEA: O, deus ex machina, o angel:

　　O Hecuba, oh, looms of Ida.

CHORUS *(in unison.)*: Ida Ida Ida Ida. 140

MEDEA: I am eternally grateful to you.

CHORUS *(in unison.)*: The things we thought would happen do not happen. The unexpected, God makes possible.

　　(Spoken, not sung.)

　　The camptown races sing a song,Do da, do da. 145

CHORUS AND MEDEA *(switch to singing now.)*: Medea's happy the whole day long.

　　Oh the do da day!

　　Things will be just fine.

　　Things will be just great. 150

　　No need to kill her children now,

　　Oh the do da...

　　(big musical coda:)

Oh the do da,
Zeus and Buddha,
They're as nice as   155
Dionysus,
Oh the do da
Work it through da
Oh the do da, do da, do da Day!
(MEDEA *and the* CHORUS *and the* ANGEL *strike a happy and triumphant pose.*)

- Compare this play to *Oedipus the King* (p. 67). What conventions do you see used here that Sophocles also used?
- Give specific details that make it clear that this play is not a tragedy.
- This is a play filled with references to literature and to popular culture. How do these references function within the play? How do they help us understand the characters? How do the references establish a tone?
- Discuss the function of the chorus in this play. How is the tone of the chorus distinct from that of Medea?
- How does the traditional story of Medea fit into this play?

Experiencing Literature through Writing

1. Identify a prevailing attitude in the work that you are discussing. How does the recognition of this tone help us recognize interesting aspects of this text?

   a. What details reveal this attitude to you?

   b. Is this attitude connected to a single character or to multiple characters?

   c. Does the author share the same attitude as the characters in the text?

2. The selections included here present situations in which a character might either laugh or cry. Understanding the tone of the work often informs us about how we should react. Looking closely at a particular work in this selection, identify the words within the work that provide a breaking point. Explain how that specific passage tells us which way to take the work; how do we know from that selection whether we should laugh or cry?

3. Using a specific work from this chapter (or another), discuss the role of tone in developing coherence within the work. How is tone a structuring device that the author uses to hold the work together? Show how particular details throughout the work reinforce the tone (or shift the tone).

11 Word Choice

Why This Word and Not Another?

If you have ever stood in front of a display of Valentine's Day greeting cards, you have faced the difficulty of translating true sentiment into language. When you walk into that card shop, you are motivated by the desire to express a real emotion to a person you care about. But as you look through all of the cards for sale, you discover that you are standing with other customers who are all buying the same cards to express the same emotions to their own significant others. You might feel frustrated at this point because as clever as any single card might be, it fails to capture a sincere, powerful, individual emotion. If you sit down and try to write your own poetry, you may feel a similar futility: all the variations of "Roses are red, violets are blue" have already been written by someone else, and original and inspiring verses of your own are elusive.

In this chapter, we ask you, as a reader, to consider how authors make words count, how they communicate distinct emotions and ideas with words that may seem in other contexts common. Remember that every word you read is the result of a choice. The author has decided to use a specific word instead of any other that has a similar meaning. By following authors through some of their choices (and the context within which the choices are made), we can see how attention to language can lead us to the sort of critical analysis that we have been describing throughout this book. We will also look at two important language resources—dictionaries and thesauruses—and suggest ways in which these tools can deepen our conversations about the literature we read.

PRECISION AND PLAYFULNESS

Desiderius Erasmus, a sixteenth-century humanist whose many interests included developing methods for instruction in language and writing, recommended that writers have at their disposal a plentiful supply of words. In his colloquy on copiousness (abundance), *De Duplici Copia Verborum et Rerum* (1512), he encourages writers to invent different ways of saying the same thing. Such an exercise stimulates a writer's creativity; also, as his examples show, each variation creates a slightly different meaning. Erasmus chose to begin with the banal sentence "Your letter pleased me very much"; he then wrote 150 variations. Before you read any further, try this exercise yourself. Generate at least five variations of Erasmus's core sentence. Then, having begun, examine this selection of Erasmus's variations, translated from his original Latin. The first examples are largely technical:

Using synonyms.
> Your epistle gladdened me wonderfully.

Variations of sentence construction.
> It is impossible to say how gladdened I was by your writing.

Changing verbs.
> I got incredible pleasure from your letter.
> Your writing brought me no mean joy.
> Your writing filled me with joy.
> Your letter moved me with singular pleasure.

Using the verb "to be."
> Your letter was in many ways most pleasing to me.
> Your letter was as pleasurable as could be.
> Your letter was an unspeakable pleasure to us.
> Your letter was an incredible happiness.

Change to the negative.
> Nothing in my life more pleasing than your letter has befallen me.
> I never took so much pleasure in anything as in your very lovely letter.

Put into the form of a question.
> What in life could have been more pleasing than your letter?

If we stay in the simple mode of reading for meaning, Erasmus's sentences quickly grow monotonous. But if we read to appreciate subtle differences in tone, we can appreciate Erasmus's artistry. It is especially useful to read aloud to capture the glorious absurdity of the exercise, especially as Erasmus moves on to literary **tropes** (see Chapter 13) and his mundane phrase begins to take on literary airs and resemble the very worst poetry:

> The banquet of your writing refreshed us with most delightful dishes.
> Your kind epistle far surpassed all carob and Attic honey and sugar, nectar, and ambrosia of the gods.
> As long as the boar loves the mountain ridges, as long as fish the stream, I will recall the sweetness of your letter.
> What clover is to bees, what willow boughs are to goats, what honey is to the bear, your letter is to me.
> No luxuries titillate the palate more agreeably than what you wrote titillates my mind.

These effusions are but a sampling of the examples that Erasmus offers, but they are enough to show that even though these sentences reproduce the initial thought, the later sentences are certainly not the same as the first. The basic idea may be the same, but the specific method of expression greatly changes the nature of that expression. In these final examples, Erasmus is writing poetically about a situation that simply does not deserve the poetic treatment that he gives it. No sober writer would use any of these expressions to thank a correspondent for a letter, but the exercise demonstrates the author's facility with words as well as his judgment about which words are most appropriate for a given situation.

In fact, Erasmus wrote about this systematic approach to invention in order to instruct schoolchildren to develop their writing skills. The technique was widely used in English schools in the sixteenth century, so it is likely that Shakespeare, for instance, would have encountered this sort of school exercise in his youth. The fundamental aim of Erasmus's exercise is to make writers conscious of word choice, or **diction**. It raises an interesting question for writers of literature: Does a work of art require special diction, **poetic diction**? In the eighteenth century some poets, perhaps too well trained by exercises like the one above, maintained that the language of poetry was *necessarily not* the language of common life. At its most extreme, this led to what seem now some comic choices: a school of fish, for example, could become a "finny tribe"; or a flock of sheep, a "fleecy tribe." William Wordsworth, Samuel Taylor Coleridge, and other poets of the early nineteenth century insisted that absolute distinctions between poetic language and everyday language were unnecessary. Although we now allow literary artists a wide range of words to choose from, no one will ever settle on a simple standard for appropriate diction. Writers must always contend with questions of what is the best word for a particular situation: the best word may or may not be a common one.

A consciousness of levels of formality is certainly essential. A **colloquial expression** may register a speaker's everyday conversation and help us relate to that speaker. But a deliberate move to literary language might be necessary to emphasize an emotional or thematic shift. The quality of specific choices can never be divorced from context. For example, a **euphemism** (a deliberately indirect mode of expression) could be comic ("afflicted by vapors" instead of "suffering from gas"); dignified (a "lasting sleep" instead of a "death"); or morally problematic ("collateral damage" instead of "civilians killed").

Experiencing Film and Literature through Diction

The film *Moulin Rouge* (2001) explores the problem of living in a world where various forms of cultural production have already anticipated all emotions any of us could ever feel. As is true of most works we discuss, this film could fit in just about any section of this book. The story is set in a stylized version of late nineteenth-century Paris and borrows many narrative elements from popular opera, even from ancient mythology. The sets create a fictional version of the cityscape that is indebted to a tradition of artistic representations of Paris at least as much as it is inspired by actual Parisian settings. The rich texture of the entire film, especially the gaudy colors and elaborate sets, alludes to an entire history of movie musicals, perhaps the least realistic of film types, as characters express their emotions with staged outbursts of song. The film particularly salutes India's Bollywood films, world cinema's most vibrant musicals.

But the problems raised by word choice itself are especially prominent in *Moulin Rouge*'s musical numbers; characters sing familiar late twentieth-century pop music with all the familiar words in nineteenth-century settings. For instance, the "original" song "Elephant Love Medley" weaves a musical conversation out of pop hits from the last half-century. The young poet Christian (Ewan McGregor) believes that his emotions are truly original, and he seeks to find a language to voice these emotions. But whenever he bursts into song, we hear words that we already know. To tell the kind-hearted prostitute Satine (Nicole Kidman) that he loves her, he begins with a sentence that has become clichéd through decades of abuse as, among other things, a song title and a movie title "Love is a many splendored thing." Then he begins his potpourri of musical quotations with Joe Cocker and Jennifer Warnes's "Love lifts us up where we belong." He quotes the Beatles, "All you need is love." Throughout the medley, Satine counters his quotation from idealist love songs with her own from more cynical songs about the same subject.

This medley and the film as a whole undercut Christian's youthful enthusiasm by showing us that his "unique" artistic output, as well as his personal emotion, falls into a long tradition. He might feel something that is new to him, but when he tries to express that new feeling, he has to depend on words that have been used repeatedly by others before him—words or expressions that are used lazily or imprecisely and that often become **clichés**. But buried in the cliché may well be a sincere desire to communicate something fresh and (for the speaker) new. The director/writer Baz Luhrman manages to have us both share in Christian's enthusiasm for his love and reflect upon the language all of us use to register and communicate love.

CHRISTIAN: Love is a many splendored thing
    Love lifts us up where we belong
    All you need is love
SATINE: Please don't start that again
CHRISTIAN: All you need is love
SATINE: A girl has got to eat
CHRISTIAN: All you need is love
SATINE: She'll end up on the street
CHRISTIAN: All you need is love
SATINE: Love is just a game

Moulin Rouge (2001)

CHRISTIAN: I was made for loving you baby
    You were made for loving me
SATINE: The only way of loving me baby
    Is to pay a lovely fee
CHRISTIAN: Just one night
    Give me just one night
SATINE: There's no way
    'Cause you can't pay
CHRISTIAN: In the name of love
    One night in the name of love
SATINE: You crazy fool
    I won't give in to you
CHRISTIAN: Don't leave me this way
    I can't survive without your sweet love
    Oh baby don't leave me this way
SATINE: You think that people would have enough of silly love songs
CHRISTIAN: I look around me and I see it isn't so, oh no
SATINE: Some people wanna fill the world with silly love songs
CHRISTIAN: Well what's wrong with that
    I'd like to know
    Cause here I go again
CHRISTIAN: Love lifts us up where we belong
    Where the eagles fly
    On a mountain high
SATINE: Love makes us act like we are fools
    Throw our lives away
    For one happy day
CHRISTIAN: We can be heroes
    Just for one day
SATINE: You, you will be mean
CHRISTIAN: No I won't
SATINE: And I, I'll drink all the time
CHRISTIAN: We should be lovers
SATINE: We can't do that
CHRISTIAN: We should be lovers
    And that's a fact
SATINE: No nothing would keep us together
CHRISTIAN: We could steal time
CHRISTIAN & SATINE: Just for one day
    We can be heroes
    Forever and ever

We can be heroes
Forever and ever
We can be heroes
CHRISTIAN: Just because I, and I will always love you
SATINE: I only can't help
CHRISTIAN & SATINE: Loving You
SATINE: How wonderful life is now
CHRISTIAN & SATINE: You're in the world

Luhrman has done something remarkable in this patched-together song. Although all of his word choices are culled from familiar sources, they feel altogether original in this rousing musical number. The words aren't original if we think of them only as words, but in the setting Luhrman has created, we hear them as fresh and alive. We're convinced that Christian does indeed love Satine, even though we know his passion (from a larger perspective) is hardly as unique as he thinks it is.

Making Connections

The Making Connections features in this book act as interruptions of the main text. But at some level, the intent is to connect (connect to ideas in other chapters, to experiences you may have beyond the classroom, to the writing process). Here, we interrupt to suggest that before you read these poems, you should recall the specific elements of the **sonnet** form that we discussed in Chapter 8. Take note of structural features, track the rhyme, and sum up the argument (the complication and the resolution). Notice that Shakespeare sets up a general principle in the first four lines (quatrain). The next two quatrains apply this general principle to the specific instance that he is describing. And the final couplet offers a conclusion and a way for the young man addressed in the sonnet to rectify the "problem" that the poem has just described.

BEYOND SUMMARY

Variation upon a common theme—the challenge of making distinctive and individual feelings that are universal—is also a central concern in Shakespeare's sonnet sequence. In the brief selection that follows, you'll note considerable thematic overlap from poem to poem. But the sequence doesn't stall; each poem offers a distinct experience for the reader.

William Shakespeare (1564–1616)

Sonnet 1 (1609)

From fairest creatures we desire increase,
That thereby beauty's rose might never die,
But as the riper should by time decease,
His tender heir might bear his memory:
But thou, contracted to thine own bright eyes,   5
Feed'st thy light's flame with self-substantial fuel,
Making a famine where abundance lies,
Thyself thy foe, to thy sweet self too cruel.
Thou that art now the world's fresh ornament
And only herald to the gaudy spring,   10
Within thine own bud buriest thy content
And, tender churl, makest waste in niggarding.
   Pity the world, or else this glutton be,
   To eat the world's due, by the grave and thee.

The poet admires the beauty he sees in the young man he addresses and argues that this youth has a responsibility to procreate. But this simple message is less interesting than the strategies that the poet uses to make his argument; Shakespeare surprises us with the word choices that he makes. In the first quatrain (lines 1–4), the poet speaks of a general desire for immortality, yet he never uses that word. We desire the "fairest creatures," he says, to "increase" (1). Notably, he avoids any of the words that we might think to use in summarizing this poem: *reproduction, procreation, fatherhood, children,* or any other simple variation of that idea. Instead, he talks about a "tender heir" (4) of "beauty's rose" (2) that "might bear his memory" (4), implying that when we see beauty (in something like a rose), we wish that that beauty might endure. In the second quatrain (lines 5–8), the poet shifts to a condemnation of the youth: "thou, contracted to thine own bright eyes" (5). Instead of sharing his beauty, this subject is self-absorbed, and the poet claims that this inward tendency defies the natural order and creates "a famine where abundance lies" (7). What is this famine? It seems a lack of beauty in the world, worsened by the knowledge that, without an heir, the young man's beauty will vanish. And the final lines of the poem emphasize this waste. The youth should be "herald to the gaudy spring" (10). He should be father to a whole field but instead remains a solitary flower. The poet tells him that as a flower, "[thou] buriest thy content" within "thine own bud" (11) instead of sharing with the passing wildlife, thereby preventing the propagation of other flowers. The act of propagation, as depicted in these lines, appears quite passive. By the end of the third quatrain (lines 9–12), the young man is denigrated as a "churl" who paradoxically "makest waste in niggarding" (12). How can saving (or hoarding) be a wasteful activity? In the final couplet (lines 13–14), "beauty's rose" has become a "glutton" (13) consuming "the world's due" (14), killing off potential fields of flowers through his selfishness and knowing that he must eventually die. As is often the case in the sonnet form, the final couplet affects our reading of the previous twelve lines. The **hyperbole** in these final lines (that is, the deliberate exaggeration or overstatement) marks a stark contrast to the apparent restraint at the beginning. Through the poet's choice of words and images, feelings escalate through the sonnet as the narrator becomes more aggressive in pursuit of connections to the flower image.

Let's go back to our initial summary of the poem: "The poet admires the beauty he sees in the young man he addresses and argues that this youth has a responsibility to procreate." Although this summary may accurately recount the general subject of the poem, it fails to capture the poem's impact because the poem is not a generalization but a series of precise words. Yes, the poem is a plea for this young man to sow his seed, but until we look closely at the words that the poet uses to make this plea, we cannot see the images, the twists of meaning, the logical games that the poet plays; in short, we have not begun any analysis. Of course, this process should go beyond what we present here. What can we say about the tone of this particular narrative? As we look at more sonnets, do we develop some sense of a consistent character narrating these individual units? How do differences between similar sonnets alter our readings?

Now, compare your findings from the first sonnet to the second sonnet in Shakespeare's sequence. How different is your summary of this sonnet from that of the first? Does Shakespeare use the same pattern here? Where are the differences? Does his use of clothing as an image (instead of harvests) change the nature of the case that he makes? How directly are the elements of clothing related to his demand? How does this image develop throughout the sonnet?

Sonnet 2 (1609)

When forty winters shall beseige thy brow,
And dig deep trenches in thy beauty's field,
Thy youth's proud livery, so gazed on now,
Will be a tatter'd weed, of small worth held:
Then being ask'd where all thy beauty lies,   5
Where all the treasure of thy lusty days,
To say, within thine own deep-sunken eyes,
Were an all-eating shame and thriftless praise.

How much more praise deserved thy beauty's use,
If thou couldst answer "This fair child of mine   10
Shall sum my count and make my old excuse,"
Proving his beauty by succession thine!
    This were to be new made when thou art old,
    And see thy blood warm when thou feel'st it cold.

As you move through the following sonnets, you will find that reading for a simple summary is no longer necessary. Shakespeare's first twenty sonnets form a sequence that is rather similar to the Erasmian exercise. Instead of reading for their general meaning—as they all convey essentially the same message—you should be reading for the specific words Shakespeare uses to conjure ideas and images about love. Look for any words or combinations of words that are repeated among the sonnets. Look for the juxtaposition of words that might not seem to fit together—for instance, can "Nature" really have such attributes as "thriftiness"?

Sonnet 3 (1609)

Look in thy glass, and tell the face thou viewest
Now is the time that face should form another;
Whose fresh repair if now thou not renewest,
Thou dost beguile the world, unbless some mother.
For where is she so fair whose unear'd womb   5
Disdains the tillage of thy husbandry?
Or who is he so fond will be the tomb
Of his self-love, to stop posterity?
Thou art thy mother's glass, and she in thee
Calls back the lovely April of her prime: 10
So thou through windows of thine age shall see
Despite of wrinkles this thy golden time.
    But if thou live, remember'd not to be,
    Die single, and thine image dies with thee.

Sonnet 7 (1609)

Lo! in the orient when the gracious light
Lifts up his burning head, each under eye
Doth homage to his new-appearing sight,
Serving with looks his sacred majesty;
And having climb'd the steep-up heavenly hill,   5

Resembling strong youth in his middle age,
Yet mortal looks adore his beauty still,
Attending on his golden pilgrimage;
But when from highmost pitch, with weary car,
Like feeble age, he reeleth from the day, 10
The eyes, 'fore duteous, now converted are
From his low tract and look another way:
   So thou, thyself out-going in thy noon,
   Unlook'd on diest, unless thou get a son.

Sonnet 8 (1609)

Music to hear, why hear'st thou music sadly?
Sweets with sweets war not, joy delights in joy.
Why lov'st thou that which thou receiv'st not gladly,
Or else receiv'st with pleasure thine annoy?
If the true concord of well-tuned sounds, 5
By unions married, do offend thine ear,
They do but sweetly chide thee, who confounds
In singleness the parts that thou shouldst bear.
Mark how one string, sweet husband to another,
Strikes each in each by mutual ordering, 10
Resembling sire and child and happy mother
Who all in one, one pleasing note do sing:
   Whose speechless song, being many, seeming one,
   Sings this to thee: 'thou single wilt prove none.'

Sonnet 9 (1609)

Is it for fear to wet a widow's eye
That thou consum'st thyself in single life?
Ah! if thou issueless shalt hap to die,
The world will wail thee, like a makeless wife;
The world will be thy widow and still weep 5
That thou no form of thee hast left behind,
When every private widow well may keep
By children's eyes her husband's shape in mind.
Look, what an unthrift in the world doth spend
Shifts but his place, for still the world enjoys it; 10
But beauty's waste hath in the world an end,

And kept unus'd, the user so destroys it.
  No love toward others in that bosom sits
  That on himself such murd'rous shame commits.

Sonnet 18 (1609)

Shall I compare thee to a summer's day?
Thou art more lovely and more temperate:
Rough winds do shake the darling buds of May,
And summer's lease hath all too short a date:
Sometime too hot the eye of heaven shines,   5
And often is his gold complexion dimm'd;
And every fair from fair sometime declines,
By chance or nature's changing course untrimm'd;
But thy eternal summer shall not fade
Nor lose possession of that fair thou owest;   10
Nor shall Death brag thou wander'st in his shade,
When in eternal lines to time thou growest:
  So long as men can breathe or eyes can see,
  So long lives this and this gives life to thee.

As you read these sonnets in sequence, you may recognize sonnets that you
have read before. Sonnet 18, for example, is often the first of Shakespeare's
sonnets that students read. How does reading a familiar sonnet in the context
of the other sonnets lend it additional meaning? Does the sonnet itself seem
different when it appears with the others?

A Note to Student Writers: On the Paraphrase

To summarize is to convey in your own words an essential idea from a source. To paraphrase is to *restate* the original source in a fairly detailed way. Anytime we paraphrase, we are making choices about the words that we use. However closely we attend to the piece we paraphrase, we inevitably change it in our restatement. As we saw previously in Erasmus's exercise, subtle changes emerge with each variation we choose. Often, the difference is not immediately apparent, but if we paraphrase our own paraphrase, we will begin to see how specific words in different combinations create different meanings. Look back at one of Shakespeare's sonnets, and write three distinct paraphrases of it. By generating multiple paraphrases of the poem, you should begin to clarify your own understanding of that poem. At the same time, you will realize that a poem cannot be reduced to a paraphrase.

DEFINITION AND USAGE

Shakespeare's talent for variation shouldn't lead you to think that variation in and of itself is a virtue. To grant yourself a wider vocabulary, you can turn to a thesaurus, but the choices it offers aren't necessarily helpful. As you begin to look through the entries under *love*, for instance, you will find a list similar to this one:

> fondness, liking, inclination, desire, regard, admiration, affection, tenderness, heart, attachment, yearning, gallantry, passion, flame, devotion, infatuation, adoration, idolatry, benevolence

None of these words precisely replaces the word *love*. Some of them won't do at all for expressing the particular kind of love you want to communicate. But to an inexpert user, a thesaurus might give the false impression that it is appropriate to substitute any one of these words for another. The results of such a misunderstanding can be amusing or bewildering. A bad choice makes it instantly clear: subtleties matter. The poet Billy Collins suggests that we find unnatural groupings in a thesaurus. As you read, follow the images Collins creates to describe the project of clustering synonyms.

Billy Collins (1941–)

Thesaurus (1995)

It could be the name of a prehistoric beast
that roamed the Paleozoic earth, rising up
on its hind legs to show off its large vocabulary,
or some lover in a myth who is metamorphosed into a book.

It means treasury, but it is just a place   5
where words congregate with their relatives,
a big park where hundreds of family reunions
are always being held,
house, home, abode, dwelling, lodgings, and *digs,*
all sharing the same picnic basket and thermos;   10
hairy, hirsute, woolly, furry, fleecy, and *shaggy*
all running a sack race or throwing horseshoes,
inert, static, motionless, fixed and *immobile*
standing and kneeling in rows for a group photograph.

Here father is next to sire and brother close   15
to sibling, separated only by fine shades of meaning.

And every group has its odd cousin, the one
who traveled the farthest to be here:
astereognosis, *polydipsia*, or some eleven
syllable, unpronounceable substitute for the word *tool*.   20
Even their own relatives have to squint at their name tags.

I can see my own copy up on a high shelf.
I rarely open it, because I know there is no
such thing as a synonym and because I get nervous
around people who always assemble with their own kind,   25
forming clubs and nailing signs to closed front doors
while others huddle alone in the dark streets.

I would rather see words out on their own, away
from their families and the warehouse of Roget,
wandering the world where they sometimes fall   30
in love with a completely different word.
Surely, you have seen pairs of them standing forever
next to each other on the same line inside a poem,
a small chapel where weddings like these,
between perfect strangers, can take place.

Collins appreciates the "warehouse" that Roget has created in the thesaurus, but it is a tool that he keeps high on a shelf, he tells us. Collins learns more when he finds words that appear in unexpected and perhaps unusual pairings. As Collins demonstrates, a synonym never really means the *same* thing as another word. Each word has its own meaning; as similar as it may be to another, it is not identical.

A thesaurus tries to generalize; it gives us groupings of words that have approximately the same meaning. A dictionary, on the other hand, makes distinctions among words. Although a dictionary's definitions generally begin with synonyms, the best dictionaries then clarify and justify these definitions with examples or elaboration. The *Oxford English Dictionary* (*OED*), for example, will list a series of quotations using the specified word and show how that word has been used differently at different times. Such a project shows that deriving a precise definition for an abstract term can be a difficult process. Here are only a few excerpts from the *OED* definitions of *love* that begin to show that words can never be pinned down:

1. That disposition or state of feeling with regard to a person which (arising from recognition of attractive qualities, from instincts

of natural relationship, or from sympathy) manifests itself in solici-
tude for the welfare of the object, and usually also in delight in his or
her presence and desire for his or her approval; warm affection, attachment. Const. *of, for, to, towards.*

2. In religious use, applied in an eminent sense to the paternal benevolence and affection of God towards His children, to the affectionate
devotion due to God from His creatures, and to the affection of one
created being to another so far as it is prompted by the sense of their
common relationship to God. (Cf. CHARITY 1.) Theologians distinguish the *love of complacency*, which implies approval of qualities in
the object, and the *love of benevolence*, which is bestowed irrespective
of the character of the object.

3. Strong predilection, liking or fondness *for*, or devotion *to* (something).
Const. *of, for, to* (arch.), *unto. to give, bear love to*: to be devoted or
addicted to.

4. a. That feeling of attachment which is based upon difference of sex;
the affection which subsists between lover and sweetheart and is
the normal basis of marriage. *for love* (*in love*): by reason of love
(often placed in opposition to pecuniary considerations); also in
weakened sense; *love at first sight*: the action or state of falling in
love with someone whom one has never previously seen; *love's
young dream*: the relationship of young lovers; the object of someone's love, a man regarded as the perfect lover.

Perusing the entries for a specific word, comparing the entries in different
dictionaries, and thinking about the relation between definitions and specific
uses of a word can serve as the subject of extended discussions. The complete
entry on *love* from the *OED* is a record of a scholarly conversation about
the meaning of this very familiar word; the editors assemble a collection of
specific instances in which the word *love* has been used in order to show how
definitions evolve over time.

The entry on *love* from the *OED* aims to register far more than the
literal meaning of the word, or its **denotation**. Such a definition would be
impossibly narrow. Note how much of what is quoted from the *OED* concerns a wide range of associations suggested by the word. A grasp of a word's
connotations (what it suggests beyond the most literal level) is essential to
our understanding. Oftentimes, it's useful to use a dictionary to look up a
word that you already know, for a dictionary may help you catch shadings
that could easily be missed. In the same way, a thesaurus is not just a tool to
find a different word but a means to reflect upon a widened range of possible
associations.

Experiencing Literature through Word Choice

Our understanding of words, our own use of language comes not from our knowledge of words in isolation but from our familiarity with their use. In the following poem, Robert Sward enacts a frustration to express what he feels as true in the face of an overbearing tradition of words and the conventions of poetry. His wife in this poem complains that the words that he writes are a different enterprise than "attending to me." To some extent, she is right. The need to choose the precise words turns attention from her to, as the title notes, the dictionary. Yet, although the impersonal definitions in the dictionary make the words that the poet uses mechanical, his own acknowledgment of this challenge helps reclaim those words. He admits to his words' shortcomings but embraces them as his best and only tools. As he plays with words at the end of the poem, he makes them his own and makes them (one would imagine) meaningful to Gloria.

Robert Sward (1933–)

For Gloria on Her 60th Birthday, or Looking for Love in Merriam-Webster (1991)

"Beautiful, splendid, magnificent,
delightful, charming, appealing,"
    says the dictionary.
And that's how I start… But I hear her say,
"Make it less glorious and more Gloria."   5

Imperious, composed, skeptical, serene,
lustrous, irreverent,
she's marked by glory, she attracts glory
"Glory," I say, "Glory, Glory."

"Is there a hallelujah in there?"   10
she asks, when I read her lines one and two.
"Not yet," I say, looking up from my books.
She protests, "Writing a poem isn't the same

"As *really* attending to me." "But it's for
your birthday," I say. Pouting,   15
playfully cross, "That's the price you pay
when your love's a poet."

She has chestnut-colored hair,
old fashioned Clara Bow lips,
moist brown eyes...   20
              arms outstretched, head thrown back
she glides toward me and into her seventh decade.

Her name means "to adore,"
"to rejoice, to be jubilant,
to magnify and honor as in worship, to give or ascribe glory—"   25
    my love, O Gloria, I do, I do.

The literate self-consciousness that we see in this poem differs from the
more common *Moulin Rouge* dilemma of borrowing the words of others to
express our own feelings. We pick out the words that we believe have
come closest to what we think; perhaps these words even shape our
thoughts.

CRITICALLY REFLECTING ON WORDS

Writers sometimes refine their sense of "right words" by noting what makes
for imprecise or ineffective choices. Choosing words deliberately for their
wrongness makes for a satiric game. In the annual Bulwer-Lytton contest,
writers take a perverse pleasure in competing to compose the worst opening
line for an imaginary novel. The contest often favors entries that rely upon
overly melodramatic diction. But before we present samples of those entries,
we'll insert a brief observation on bad writing from *The Turkey City Lexicon*.
These phrases come from a science fiction writers' workshop in which writers
gather and read one another's work, seeking to improve their own writing
through mutually constructive criticism. What follows are common problems
identified so that they can be avoided.

Lewis Shiner (1950–)

from The Turkey City Lexicon: A Primer for Science Fiction Workshops (1990)

Gingerbread: Useless ornament in prose, such as fancy sesquipedalian
    Latinate words where short clear English ones will do. Novice authors

sometimes use "gingerbread" in the hope of disguising faults and conveying an air of refinement. (Attr. Damon Knight)

Not Simultaneous: The mis-use of the present participle is a common structural sentence-fault for beginning writers. "Putting his key in the door, he leapt up the stairs and got his revolver out of the bureau." Alas, our hero couldn't do this even if his arms were forty feet long. This fault shades into "Ing Disease," the tendency to pepper sentences with words ending in "-ing," a grammatical construction which tends to confuse the proper sequence of events. (Attr. Damon Knight)

Pushbutton Words: Words used to evoke a cheap emotional response without engaging the intellect or the critical faculties. Commonly found in story titles, they include such bits of bogus lyricism as "star," "dance," "dream," "song," "tears" and "poet," clichés calculated to render the SF audience misty-eyed and tender-hearted.

Roget's Disease: The ludicrous overuse of far-fetched adjectives, piled into a festering, fungal, tenebrous, troglodytic, ichorous, leprous, synonymic heap. (Attr. John W. Campbell)

With descriptions from the lexicon in mind, look at the following prize-winning examples of overwrought, hyperventilated prose (often called "purple prose") from the Bulwer-Lytton contest. Explain why judges might deem each entry worthy a prize for badness. Which insights from the *Turkey City Lexicon* best apply to each?

Bulwer-Lytton Contest Winners

On reflection, Angela perceived that her relationship with Tom had always been rocky, not quite a roller-coaster ride but more like when the toilet-paper roll gets a little squashed so it hangs crooked and every time you pull some off you can hear the rest going bumpity-bumpity in its holder until you go nuts and push it back into shape, a degree of annoyance that Angela had now almost attained.

— Rephah Berg, Oakland CA (2002)

Sultry it was and humid, but no whisper of air caused the plump, laden spears of golden grain to nod their burdened heads as they unheedingly awaited the cyclic rape of their gleaming treasure, while overhead the burning orb of luminescence ascended its ever-upward path toward a sweltering celestial apex, for although it is not in Kansas that our story takes place, it looks godawful like it.

— Judy Frazier, Lathrop, Missouri (1991)

The bone-chilling scream split the warm summer night in two, the first half being before the scream when it was fairly balmy and calm and pleasant for those who hadn't heard the scream at all, but not calm or balmy or even very nice for those who did hear the scream, discounting the little period of time during the actual scream itself when your ears might have been hearing it but your brain wasn't reacting yet to let you know.

> — Patricia E. Presutti, Lewiston, New York (1986)

Dolores breezed along the surface of her life like a flat stone forever skipping across smooth water, rippling reality sporadically but oblivious to it consistently, until she finally lost momentum, sank, and due to an overdose of fluoride as a child which caused her to lie forever on the floor of her life as useless as an appendix and as lonely as a five-hundred-pound barbell in a steroid-free fitness center.

> — Linda Vernon, Newark, California (1990)

Now at the penultimate point of the current chapter in the tome that you, dear reader, currently peruse, it's time to turn attention to a film that has much to add to our discussion of diction.

MODELING CRITICAL ANALYSIS: JOEL COEN AND ETHAN COEN, O BROTHER, WHERE ART THOU?

The film O Brother, Where Art Thou? is a loose retelling of the Odyssey set in the Depression era. In Homer's epic, Athena, the goddess of wisdom, protects Odysseus; whenever he gets into trouble, he is able to come up with some quick turn of phrase that puts him at the advantage over his adversaries. In this film, Ulysses Everett McGill fills the Odysseus role. He is full of big words, but these words are never quite as wise as he thinks they are, and more often than not, they get him into deeper trouble. For example, when McGill finally first sees his "Penelope"—the wife Penny (Holly Hunter) he has sought to return to—the meeting hardly begins well. Penny has told her seven children (all girls) that their father was run over by a train, a more respectable end she thinks than the reality (McGill is a convicted con artist and petty thief who was serving hard time on the chain gang before his escape). Penny has grown tired of waiting for McGill and has agreed to marry Vernon T. Waldrip (Ray McKinnon); indeed, the marriage is set for the next day. The Coen brothers set up the romantic struggle in broadly comic terms. Vernon T. Waldrip, as the name might suggest, is hardly a dashing adventurer. He is, however, a man with "prospects"; indeed, he is (as we hear from Penny and the older children) "bona fide." These descriptors aptly capture the whole of Vernon's limited attractions. There is no romance in the relationship between Penny and Vernon, but Vernon offers stability and a kind of social legitimacy that McGill has failed to provide.

The initial contest between the men is contained by words of law and possession, not the sorts of words that suggest caring or passion. McGill says that as the "paterfamilias" he is "put in a difficult position vis-à-vis my progeny." *Paterfamilias* is a Latin word for "father" or "master of the house." In Roman society, the term had specific legal meaning: it designated an independent man in charge of a family's holdings. McGill's use of "vis-à-vis" (literally, "face-to-face," but suggesting here "in relation to") continues the dispute in comically legalistic terms. In this context, the words "husband," "wife," and "fiancé" are about social arrangements. Even the word "Daddy" gets swallowed up in matters of legal status: McGill might be "Daddy" today, but "Uncle Vernon" will be "Daddy" tomorrow if the marriage comes off as planned. McGill will then no longer be a "husband" but "just a drifter, a no good drifter."

But there are real emotions barely covered by the silly, Latinate, and inappropriate language of law and property. The Coen brothers make sure we know that Ulysses Everett McGill feels passionately for his Penny. That passion shows partly in the desperate way he attacks her: "you lying, unconstant succubus." The "unconstant" may be less than correct ("inconstant" is the word he wants), and "succubus" is typical of his verbal overreaching. But the words do suggest anger and the hurt that generates anger. More significantly, in the middle of all the foolish talk (and silly diction), Ulysses speaks a line that lends real dignity to his quest: "I've traveled many a weary mile to be back with my wife." The plainness of this statement and apt fit between the character's education, his situation, and his dreams remind us that something is at stake in this comic odyssey. Here, the simple language stands out because so much of the surrounding language is not simple. The Coen brothers shift the level of their hero's diction to help us hear what really lies behind all the fancy expressions. Such moves from a high to a low register (or the other way around) are often used to lend power to words that might, in other contexts, be overlooked.

Using Word Choice to Focus Writing and Discussion

- To examine a selection's word choice, begin by summarizing. As you put the ideas into your own words, which of the author's words seem unusual or are words that you would not have chosen?

- Are there any cases in which the author uses a word in a way different from the conventional definition of the word? When you think about word choice, it is useful to keep a dictionary at hand. There are often multiple definitions of words. Check to see whether an author is using an older or less common definition of a word.

- If there are different characters in the text, do they choose their words differently? Point to specific examples of such differences. Can you tell from their words which characters are speaking?
- How do specific words in the passage convey a tone or attitude about the subject matter? Often, attention to words will help us make our arguments about other elements in the text.
- How are words placed next to one another? Find specific instances where the combination of words makes us notice the words.
- Does the author break grammatical conventions? If so, what is the impact of this break?

Anthology

ROMANTIC LOVE: EXPRESSING THE EXACT EMOTION

Anyone who writes or speaks on any subject needs to be attentive to words. "Close enough" doesn't count when we want to say exactly what we mean or feel. We have noted in this chapter how love as a theme and a subject poses special difficulties for the artist. It seems sometimes too large a subject for any words, no matter how well chosen. Sometimes, it seems too vague a word as well. The title of Raymond Carver's story "What We Talk about When We Talk about Love" suggests that when love is the subject, different people in the same conversation may be talking about very different things. Carver's story responds to that problem. He makes the issues raised by one word the subject of the whole piece. He asks us to test out various ways of thinking about love—about the values we attach to love. We move through an intense if seemingly random set of discussions that cover a great deal without resolving much. Whatever it is that we do talk about when we talk about love seems enormously complex.

Carver's story is probably not like any love story you've ever read, but many love stories cover familiar territory. That can be a problem if the writer stays at a level of cliché. But artists find ways to make even the oldest feelings new. Poets oftentimes achieve power in focus—in precision. We hear about a shared intimacy; even though we are outside it, we get to eavesdrop on the Brownings and sense some particular quality of what they feel. We might hear of enduring love or of betrayed love, or love that somehow gets lost, as in

Denise Levertov's poems on marriage and divorce. You'll find that most of the short love poems in the following collection aren't finally concerned with discovering a new story about love or a new angle on love. Our conversation about these poems turns to the poet's creativity in finding some powerfully original way to capture an emotion that is at some level familiar. Language becomes a way to refresh feelings that can easily grow stale. We read this poetry for the words and the images that the poet has chosen. The sonnets by Henry Howard and Thomas Wyatt illustrate this mode of reading. Line by line, each poet says the same thing, yet each uses different words. We read for the subtle shadings that these different words evoke. We arrive at two overlapping yet distinct experiences of the texts. We can begin to analyze by isolating and examining the word choices that writers make. In Henrik Ibsen's *A Doll's House*, such choices comprise much of the action in the play as we watch Nora choose what to tell her husband, what to tell her friends, and by these language choices how to define her own marital position.

FICTION

Raymond Carver (1938–1988)

For a full biographical note on Raymond Carver, see page 854.

What We Talk about When We Talk about Love (1981)

My friend Mel McGinnis was talking. Mel McGinnis is a cardiologist, and sometimes that gives him the right.

The four of us were sitting around his kitchen table drinking gin. Sunlight filled the kitchen from the big window behind the sink. There were Mel and me and his second wife, Teresa—Terri, we called her—and my wife, Laura. We lived in Albuquerque then. But we were all from somewhere else.

There was an ice bucket on the table. The gin and the tonic water kept going around, and we somehow got on the subject of love. Mel thought real love was nothing less than spiritual love. He said he'd spent five years in a seminary before quitting to go to medical school. He said he still looked back on those years in the seminary as the most important years in his life.

Terri said the man she lived with before she lived with Mel loved her so much he tried to kill her. Then Terri said, "He beat me up one night. He dragged me around the living room by my ankles. He kept saying, 'I love you, I love you, you bitch.' He went on dragging me around the living room. My head kept knocking on things." Terri looked around the table. "What do you do with love like that?"

She was a bone-thin woman with a pretty face, dark eyes, and brown   5
hair that hung down her back. She liked necklaces made of turquoise, and long pendant earrings.

"My God, don't be silly. That's not love, and you know it," Mel said. "I don't know what you'd call it, but I sure know you wouldn't call it love."

"Say what you want to, but I know it was," Terri said. "It may sound crazy to you, but it's true just the same. People are different, Mel. Sure, sometimes he may have acted crazy. Okay. But he loved me. In his own way maybe, but he loved me. There was love there, Mel. Don't say there wasn't."

Mel let out his breath. He held his glass and turned to Laura and me. "The man threatened to kill me," Mel said. He finished his drink and reached for the gin bottle. "Terri's a romantic. Terri's of the kick-me-so-I'll-know-you-love-me school. Terri, hon, don't look that way." Mel reached across the table and touched Terri's cheek with his fingers. He grinned at her.

"Now he wants to make up," Terri said.

"Make up what?" Mel said. "What is there to make up? I know what I   10
know. That's all."

"How'd we get started on this subject, anyway?" Terri said. She raised her glass and drank from it. "Mel always has love on his mind," she said. "Don't you, honey?" She smiled. And I thought that was the last of it.

"I just wouldn't call Ed's behavior love. That's all I'm saying, honey," Mel said. "What about you guys?" Mel said to Laura and me. "Does that sound like love to you?"

"I'm the wrong person to ask," I said. "I didn't even know the man. I've only heard his name mentioned in passing. I wouldn't know. You'd have to know the particulars. But I think what you're saying is that love is an absolute."

Mel said, "The kind of love I'm talking about is. The kind of love I'm talking about, you don't try to kill people."

Laura said, "I don't know anything about Ed, or anything about the sit-   15
uation. But who can judge anyone else's situation?"

I touched the back of Laura's hand. She gave me a quick smile. I picked up Laura's hand. It was warm, the nails polished, perfectly manicured. I encircled the broad wrist with my fingers, and I held her.

"When I left, he drank rat poison," Terri said. She clasped her arms with her hands. "They took him to the hospital in Santa Fe. That's where we lived then, about ten miles out. They saved his life. But his gums went crazy from it. I mean they pulled away from his teeth. After that, his teeth stood out like fangs. My God," Terri said. She waited a minute, then let go of her arms and picked up her glass.

"What people won't do!" Laura said.

"He's out of the action now," Mel said. "He's dead."

Mel handed me the saucer of limes. I took a section, squeezed it over my drink, and stirred the ice cubes with my finger.

"It gets worse," Terri said. "He shot himself in the mouth. But he bungled that too. Poor Ed," she said. Terri shook her head.

"Poor Ed nothing," Mel said. "He was dangerous."

Mel was forty-five years old. He was tall and rangy with curly soft hair. His face and arms were brown from the tennis he played. When he was sober, his gestures, all his movements, were precise, very careful.

"He did love me though, Mel. Grant me that," Terri said. "That's all I'm asking. He didn't love me the way you love me. I'm not saying that. But he loved me. You can grant me that, can't you?"

"What do you mean, he bungled it?" I said.

Laura leaned forward with her glass. She put her elbows on the table and held her glass in both hands. She glanced from Mel to Terri and waited with a look of bewilderment on her open face, as if amazed that such things happened to people you were friendly with.

"How'd he bungle it when he killed himself?" I said.

"I'll tell you what happened," Mel said. "He took this twenty-two pistol he'd bought to threaten Terri and me with. Oh, I'm serious, the man was always threatening. You should have seen the way we lived in those days. Like fugitives. I even bought a gun myself. Can you believe it? A guy like me? But I did. I bought one for self-defense and carried it in the glove compartment. Sometimes I'd have to leave the apartment in the middle of the night. To go to the hospital, you know? Terri and I weren't married then, and my first wife had the house and kids, the dog, everything, and Terri and I were living in this apartment here. Sometimes, as I say, I'd get a call in the middle of the night and have to go in to the hospital at two or three in the morning. It'd be dark out there in the parking lot, and I'd break into a sweat before I could even get to my car. I never knew if he was going to come up out of the shrubbery or from behind a car and start shooting. I mean, the man was crazy. He was capable of wiring a bomb, anything. He used to call my service at all hours and say he needed to talk to the doctor, and when I'd return the call, he'd say, 'Son of a bitch, your days are numbered.' Little things like that. It was scary, I'm telling you."

"I still feel sorry for him," Terri said.

"It sounds like a nightmare," Laura said. "But what exactly happened after he shot himself?"

Laura is a legal secretary. We'd met in a professional capacity. Before we knew it, it was a courtship. She's thirty-five, three years younger than I am. In addition to being in love, we like each other and enjoy one another's company. She's easy to be with.

"What happened?" Laura said.

Mel said, "He shot himself in the mouth in his room. Someone heard the shot and told the manager. They came in with a passkey, saw what had happened, and called an ambulance. I happened to be there when they brought him in, alive but past recall. The man lived for three days. His head swelled up to twice the size of a normal head. I'd never seen anything like it, and I hope I never do again. Terri wanted to go in and sit with him when she found out about it. We had a fight over it. I didn't think she should see him like that. I didn't think she should see him, and I still don't."

"Who won the fight?" Laura said.

"I was in the room with him when he died," Terri said. "He never   35
came up out of it. But I sat with him. He didn't have anyone else."

"He was dangerous," Mel said. "If you call that love, you can have it."

"It was love," Terri said. "Sure, it's abnormal in most people's eyes. But he was willing to die for it. He did die for it."

"I sure as hell wouldn't call it love," Mel said. "I mean, no one knows what he did it for. I've seen a lot of suicides, and I couldn't say anyone ever knew what they did it for."

Mel put his hands behind his neck and tilted his chair back. "I'm not interested in that kind of love," he said. "If that's love, you can have it."

Terri said, "We were afraid. Mel even made a will out and wrote to his   40
brother in California who used to be a Green Beret. Mel told him who to look for if something happened to him."

Terri drank from her glass. She said, "But Mel's right—we lived like fugitives. We were afraid. Mel was, weren't you, honey? I even called the police at one point, but they were no help. They said they couldn't do anything until Ed actually did something. Isn't that a laugh?" Terri said.

She poured the last of the gin into her glass and waggled the bottle. Mel got up from the table and went to the cupboard. He took down another bottle.

"Well, Nick and I know what love is," Laura said. "For us, I mean," Laura said. She bumped my knee with her knee. "You're supposed to say something now," Laura said, and turned her smile on me.

For an answer, I took Laura's hand and raised it to my lips. I made a big production out of kissing her hand. Everyone was amused.

"We're lucky," I said.   45

"You guys," Terri said. "Stop that now. You're making me sick. You're still on the honeymoon, for God's sake. You're still gaga, for crying out loud. Just wait. How long have you been together now? How long has it been? A year? Longer than a year?"

"Going on a year and a half," Laura said, flushed and smiling.

"Oh, now," Terri said. "Wait awhile."

She held her drink and gazed at Laura.

"I'm only kidding," Terri said.

Mel opened the gin and went around the table with the bottle.

"Here, you guys," he said. "Let's have a toast. I want to propose a toast. A toast to love. To true love," Mel said.

We touched glasses.

"To love," we said.

Outside in the backyard, one of the dogs began to bark. The leaves of the aspen that leaned past the window ticked against the glass. The afternoon sun was like a presence in this room, the spacious light of ease and generosity. We could have been anywhere, somewhere enchanted. We raised our glasses again and grinned at each other like children who had agreed on something forbidden.

"I'll tell you what real love is," Mel said. "I mean, I'll give you a good example. And then you can draw your own conclusions." He poured more gin into his glass. He added an ice cube and a sliver of lime. We waited and sipped our drinks. Laura and I touched knees again. I put a hand on her warm thigh and left it there.

"What do any of us really know about love?" Mel said. "It seems to me we're just beginners at love. We say we love each other and we do, I don't doubt it. I love Terri and Terri loves me, and you guys love each other too. You know the kind of love I'm talking about now. Physical love, that impulse that drives you to someone special, as well as love of the other person's being, his or her essence, as it were. Carnal love and, well, call it sentimental love, the day-to-day caring about the other person. But sometimes I have a hard time accounting for the fact that I must have loved my first wife too. But I did, I know I did. So I suppose I am like Terri in that regard. Terri and Ed." He thought about it and then he went on. "There was a time when I thought I loved my first wife more than life itself. But now I hate her guts. I do. How do you explain that? What happened to that love? What happened to it, is what I'd like to know. I wish someone could tell me. Then there's Ed. Okay, we're back to Ed. He loves Terri so much he tries to kill her and he winds up killing himself." Mel stopped talking and swallowed from his glass. "You guys have been together eighteen months and you love each other. It shows all over you. You glow with it. But you both loved other people before you met each other. You've both been married before, just like us. And you probably loved other people before that too, even. Terri and I have been together five years, been married for four.

And the terrible thing, the terrible thing is, but the good thing too, the saving grace, you might say, is that if something happened to one of us—excuse me for saying this—but if something happened to one of us tomorrow, I think the other one, the other person, would grieve for a while, you know, but then the surviving party would go out and love again, have someone else soon enough. All this, all of this love we're talking about, it would just be a memory. Maybe not even a memory. Am I wrong? Am I way off base? Because I want you to set me straight if you think I'm wrong. I want to know. I mean, I don't know anything, and I'm the first one to admit it."

"Mel, for God's sake," Terri said. She reached out and took hold of his wrist. "Are you getting drunk? Honey? Are you drunk?"

"Honey, I'm just talking," Mel said. "All right? I don't have to be drunk to say what I think. I mean, we're all just talking, right?" Mel said. He fixed his eyes on her.

"Sweetie, I'm not criticizing," Terri said.   60

She picked up her glass.

"I'm not on call today," Mel said. "Let me remind you of that. I am not on call," he said.

"Mel, we love you," Laura said.

Mel looked at Laura. He looked at her as if he could not place her, as if she was not the woman she was.

"Love you too, Laura," Mel said. "And you, Nick, love you too. You   65
know something?" Mel said. "You guys are our pals," Mel said.

He picked up his glass.

Mel said, "I was going to tell you about something. I mean, I was going to prove a point. You see, this happened a few months ago, but it's still going on right now, and it ought to make us feel ashamed when we talk like we know what we're talking about when we talk about love."

"Come on now," Terri said. "Don't talk like you're drunk if you're not drunk."

"Just shut up for once in your life," Mel said very quietly. "Will you do me a favor and do that for a minute? So as I was saying, there's this old couple who had this car wreck out on the interstate. A kid hit them and they were all torn to shit and nobody was giving them much chance to pull through."

Terri looked at us and then back at Mel. She seemed anxious, or maybe   70
that's too strong a word.

Mel was handing the bottle around the table.

"I was on call that night," Mel said. "It was May or maybe it was June. Terri and I had just sat down to dinner when the hospital called. There'd been this thing out on the interstate. Drunk kid, teenager, plowed his dad's pickup into this camper with this old couple in it. They were up in their mid-seventies, that couple. The kid—eighteen, nineteen, something—he was DOA. Taken the steering wheel through his sternum. The old couple, they were alive, you understand. I mean, just barely. But they had everything. Multiple fractures, internal injuries, hemorrhaging, contusions, lacerations, the works, and they each of them had themselves concussions. They were in a bad way, believe me. And, of course, their age was two strikes against them. I'd say she was worse off than he was. Ruptured spleen along with everything else. Both kneecaps broken. But they'd been wearing their seatbelts and, God knows, that's what saved them for the time being."

"Folks, this is an advertisement for the National Safety Council," Terri said. "This is your spokesman, Dr. Melvin R. McGinnis, talking." Terri laughed. "Mel," she said, "sometimes you're just too much. But I love you, hon," she said.

"Honey, I love you," Mel said.

He leaned across the table. Terri met him halfway. They kissed.

"Terri's right," Mel said as he settled himself again. "Get those seatbelts on. But seriously, they were in some shape, those oldsters. By the time I got down there, the kid was dead, as I said. He was off in a corner, laid out on a gurney. I took one look at the old couple and told the ER nurse to get me a neurologist and an orthopedic man and a couple of surgeons down there right away."

He drank from his glass. "I'll try to keep this short," he said. "So we took the two of them up to the OR and worked like fuck on them most of the night. They had these incredible reserves, those two. You see that once in a while. So we did everything that could be done, and toward morning we're giving them a fifty-fifty chance, maybe less than that for her. So here they are, still alive the next morning. So, okay, we move them into the ICU, which is where they both kept plugging away at it for two weeks, hitting it better and better on all the scopes. So we transfer them out to their own room."

Mel stopped talking. "Here," he said, "let's drink this cheapo gin the hell up. Then we're going to dinner, right? Terri and I know a new place. That's where we'll go, to this new place we know about. But we're not going until we finish up this cut-rate, lousy gin."

Terri said, "We haven't actually eaten there yet. But it looks good. From the outside, you know."

"I like food," Mel said. "If I had it to do all over again, I'd be a chef, you know? Right, Terri?" Mel said.

He laughed. He fingered the ice in his glass.

"Terri knows," he said. "Terri can tell you. But let me say this. If I could come back again in a different life, a different time and all, you know what? I'd like to come back as a knight. You were pretty safe wearing all that armor. It was all right being a knight until gunpowder and muskets and pistols came along."

"Mel would like to ride a horse and carry a lance," Terri said.

"Carry a woman's scarf with you everywhere," Laura said.

"Or just a woman," Mel said.   85

"Shame on you," Laura said.

Terri said, "Suppose you came back as a serf. The serfs didn't have it so good in those days," Terri said.

"The serfs never had it good," Mel said. "But I guess even the knights were vessels to someone. Isn't that the way it worked? But then everyone is always a vessel to someone. Isn't that right? Terri? But what I liked about knights, besides their ladies, was that they had that suit of armor, you know, and they couldn't get hurt very easy. No cars in those days, you know? No drunk teenagers to tear into your ass."

"Vassals," Terri said.

"What?" Mel said.   90

"Vassals," Terri said. "They were called vassals, not vessels."

"Vassals, vessels," Mel said, "what the fuck's the difference? You knew what I meant anyway. All right," Mel said. "So I'm not educated. I learned my stuff. I'm a heart surgeon, sure, but I'm just a mechanic. I go in and I fuck around and I fix things. Shit," Mel said.

"Modesty doesn't become you," Terri said.

"He's just a humble sawbones," I said. "But sometimes they suffocated in all that armor, Mel. They'd even have heart attacks if it got too hot and they were too tired and worn out. I read somewhere that they'd fall off their horses and not be able to get up because they were too tired to stand with all that armor on them. They got trampled by their own horses sometimes."

"That's terrible," Mel said. "That's a terrible thing, Nicky. I guess   95
they'd just lay there and wait until somebody came along and made a shish kebab out of them."

"Some other vessel," Terri said.

"That's right," Mel said. "Some vassal would come along and spear the bastard in the name of love. Or whatever the fuck it was they fought over in those days."

"Same things we fight over these days," Terri said.

Laura said, "Nothing's changed."

The color was still high in Laura's cheeks. Her eyes were bright. She   100
brought her glass to her lips.

Mel poured himself another drink. He looked at the label closely as if studying a long row of numbers. Then he slowly put the bottle down on the table and slowly reached for the tonic water.

"What about the old couple?" Laura said. "You didn't finish that story you started."

Laura was having a hard time lighting her cigarette. Her matches kept going out.

The sunshine inside the room was different now, changing, getting thinner. But the leaves outside the window were still shimmering, and I stared at the pattern they made on the panes and on the Formica counter. They weren't the same patterns, of course.

"What about the old couple?" I said.

"Older but wiser," Terri said.

Mel stared at her.

Terri said, "Go on with your story, hon. I was only kidding. Then what happened?"

"Terri, sometimes," Mel said.

"Please, Mel," Terri said. "Don't always be so serious, sweetie. Can't you take a joke?"

"Where's the joke?" Mel said.

He held his glass and gazed steadily at his wife.

"What happened?" Laura said.

Mel fastened his eyes on Laura. He said, "Laura, if I didn't have Terri and if I didn't love her so much, and if Nick wasn't my best friend, I'd fall in love with you. I'd carry you off, honey," he said.

"Tell your story," Terri said. "Then we'll go to that new place, okay?"

"Okay," Mel said. "Where was I?" he said. He stared at the table and then he began again.

"I dropped in to see each of them every day, sometimes twice a day if I was up doing other calls anyway. Casts and bandages, head to foot, the both of them. You know, you've seen it in the movies. That's just the way they looked, just like in the movies. Little eye-holes and nose-holes and mouth-holes. And she had to have her legs slung up on top of it. Well, the husband was very depressed for the longest while. Even after he found out that his wife was going to pull through, he was still very depressed. Not about the accident, though. I mean, the accident was one thing, but it wasn't everything. I'd get up to his mouth-hole, you know, and he'd say no, it wasn't the accident exactly but it was because he couldn't see her through his eye-holes. He said that was what was making him feel so bad. Can you imagine? I'm telling you, the man's heart was breaking because he couldn't turn his goddamn head and *see* his goddamn wife."

Mel looked around the table and shook his head at what he was going to say.

"I mean, it was killing the old fart just because he couldn't *look* at the fucking woman."

We all looked at Mel.

"Do you see what I'm saying?" he said.

Maybe we were a little drunk by then. I know it was hard keeping things in focus. The light was draining out of the room, going back through the window where it had come from. Yet nobody made a move to get up from the table to turn on the overhead light.

"Listen," Mel said. "Let's finish this fucking gin. There's about enough left here for one shooter all around. Then let's go eat. Let's go to the new place."

"He's depressed," Terri said. "Mel, why don't you take a pill?"

Mel shook his head. "I've taken everything there is."   125

"We all need a pill now and then," I said.

"Some people are born needing them," Terri said.

She was using her finger to rub at something on the table. Then she stopped rubbing.

"I think I want to call my kids," Mel said. "Is that all right with everybody? I'll call my kids," he said.

Terri said, "What if Marjorie answers the phone? You guys, you've   130
heard us on the subject of Marjorie? Honey, you know you don't want to talk to Marjorie. It'll make you feel even worse."

"I don't want to talk to Marjorie," Mel said. "But I want to talk to my kids."

"There isn't a day goes by that Mel doesn't say he wishes she'd get married again. Or else die," Terri said. "For one thing," Terri said, "she's bankrupting us. Mel says it's just to spite him that she won't get married again. She has a boyfriend who lives with her and the kids, so Mel is supporting the boyfriend too."

"She's allergic to bees," Mel said. "If I'm not praying she'll get married again, I'm praying she'll get herself stung to death by a swarm of fucking bees."

"Shame on you," Laura said.

"Bzzzzzzz," Mel said, turning his fingers into bees and buzzing them at   135
Terri's throat. Then he let his hands drop all the way to his sides.

"She's vicious," Mel said. "Sometimes I think I'll go up there dressed like a beekeeper. You know, that hat that's like a helmet with the plate that comes down over your face, the big gloves, and the padded coat? I'll knock on the door and let loose a hive of bees in the house. But first I'd make sure the kids were out, of course."

He crossed one leg over the other. It seemed to take him a lot of time to do it. Then he put both feet on the floor and leaned forward, elbows on the table, his chin cupped in his hands.

"Maybe I won't call the kids, after all. Maybe it isn't such a hot idea. Maybe we'll just go eat. How does that sound?"

"Sounds fine to me," I said. "Eat or not eat. Or keep drinking. I could head right on out into the sunset."

"What does that mean, honey?" Laura said.

"It just means what I said," I said. "It means I could just keep going. That's all it means."

"I could eat something myself," Laura said. "I don't think I've ever been so hungry in my life. Is there something to nibble on?"

"I'll put out some cheese and crackers," Terri said.

But Terri just sat there. She did not get up to get anything.

Mel turned his glass over. He spilled it out on the table.

"Gin's gone," Mel said.

Terri said, "Now what?"

I could hear my heart beating. I could hear everyone's heart. I could hear the human noise we sat there making, not one of us moving, not even when the room went dark.

- There are four characters involved in this conversation. Characterize the distinctive ways in which each of these characters speaks.
- The major subject of this conversation is a definition of love. What are the different definitions that we hear in this exchange?
- How do we learn about the relationships among these characters from unspoken signals?

Edith Wharton (1862–1937)

Edith Wharton was born Edith Jones in New York City. Her family was relatively wealthy but, due to declining economic fortunes, moved to Europe when she was four years old. The following six years gave the future author a wide experience of travel and a grounding in European culture and languages. Though the Jones family returned to the United States, Wharton never lost her fascination with Europe, and after her marriage to Edward Wharton she maintained an apartment in Paris, where she and her husband spent several months each year. Shortly after her divorce from Edward, she moved permanently to Europe. Wharton was one of the most prominent writers of her generation and produced important works of travel writing and fiction. In 1921, she was awarded the Pulitzer Prize for her best-known novel, *The Age of Innocence*.

Roman Fever (1934)

From the table at which they had been lunching two American ladies of ripe but well-cared-for middle age moved across the lofty terrace of the

Roman restaurant and, leaning on its parapet, looked first at each other, and then down on the outspread glories of the Palatine and the Forum, with the same expression of vague but benevolent approval.

As they leaned there a girlish voice echoed up gaily from the stairs leading to the court below. "Well, come along, then," it cried, not to them but to an invisible companion, "and let's leave the young things to their knitting"; and a voice as fresh laughed back: "Oh, look here, Babs, not actually *knitting*—" "Well, I mean figuratively," rejoined the first. "After all, we haven't left our poor parents much else to do...." and at that point the turn of the stairs engulfed the dialogue.

The two ladies looked at each other again, this time with a tinge of smiling embarrassment, and the smaller and paler one shook her head and colored slightly.

"Barbara!" she murmured, sending an unheard rebuke after the mocking voice in the stairway.

The other lady, who was fuller, and higher in color, with a small determined nose supported by vigorous black eyebrows, gave a good-humored laugh. "That's what our daughters think of us!"

Her companion replied by a deprecating gesture. "Not of us individually. We must remember that. It's just the collective modern idea of Mothers. And you see—" Half-guiltily she drew from her handsomely mounted black handbag a twist of crimson silk run through by two fine knitting needles. "One never knows," she murmured. "The new system has certainly given us a good deal of time to kill; and sometimes I get tired just looking—even at this." Her gesture was now addressed to the stupendous scene at their feet.

The dark lady laughed again, and they both relapsed upon the view, contemplating it in silence, with a sort of diffused serenity which might have been borrowed from the spring effulgence of the Roman skies. The luncheon hour was long past, and the two had their end of the vast terrace to themselves. At its opposite extremity a few groups, detained by a lingering look at the outspread city, were gathering up guidebooks and fumbling for tips. The last of them scattered, and the two ladies were alone on the air-washed height.

"Well, I don't see why we shouldn't just stay here," said Mrs. Slade, the lady of the high color and energetic brows. Two derelict basket chairs stood near, and she pushed them into the angle of the parapet, and settled herself in one, her gaze upon the Palatine. "After all, it's still the most beautiful view in the world."

"It always will be, to me," assented her friend Mrs. Ansley, with so slight a stress on the "me" that Mrs. Slade, though she noticed it, wondered if it were not merely accidental, like the random underlinings of old-fashioned letter writers.

5

"Grace Ansley was always old-fashioned," she thought; and added aloud, with a retrospective smile: "It's a view we've both been familiar with for a good many years. When we first met here we were younger than our girls are now. You remember?"

"Oh, yes, I remember," murmured Mrs. Ansley, with the same undefinable stress. "There's that headwaiter wondering," she interpolated. She was evidently far less sure than her companion of herself and of her rights in the world.

"I'll cure him of wondering," said Mrs. Slade, stretching her hand toward a bag as discreetly opulent-looking as Mrs. Ansley's. Signing to the headwaiter, she explained that she and her friend were old lovers of Rome, and would like to spend the end of the afternoon looking down on the view—that is, if it did not disturb the service? The headwaiter, bowing over her gratuity, assured her that the ladies were most welcome, and would be still more so if they would condescend to remain for dinner. A full-moon night, they would remember....

Mrs. Slade's black brows drew together, as though references to the moon were out of place and even unwelcome. But she smiled away her frown as the headwaiter retreated. "Well, why not? We might do worse. There's no knowing, I suppose, when the girls will be back. Do you even know back from *where*? I don't!"

Mrs. Ansley again colored slightly. "I think those young Italian aviators we met at the Embassy invited them to fly to Tarquinia for tea. I suppose they'll want to wait and fly back by moonlight."

"Moonlight—moonlight! What a part it still plays. Do you suppose they're as sentimental as we were?"

"I've come to the conclusion that I don't in the least know what they are," said Mrs. Ansley. "And perhaps we didn't know much more about each other."

"No; perhaps we didn't."

Her friend gave her a shy glance. "I never should have supposed you were sentimental, Alida."

"Well, perhaps I wasn't." Mrs. Slade drew her lids together in retrospect; and for a few moments the two ladies, who had been intimate since childhood, reflected how little they knew each other. Each one, of course, had a label ready to attach to the other's name; Mrs. Delphin Slade, for instance, would have told herself, or anyone who asked her, that Mrs. Horace Ansley, twenty-five years ago, had been exquisitely lovely—no, you wouldn't believe it, would you?...though, of course, still charming, distinguished.... Well, as a girl she had been exquisite; far more beautiful than her daughter Barbara, though certainly Babs, according to the new standards at any rate, was more effective—had more *edge*, as they say. Funny where she got it, with those two nullities as parents. Yes; Horace Ansley was—well, just the duplicate of his wife. Museum specimens of old New York. Good-looking, irreproachable, exemplary. Mrs. Slade and Mrs. Ansley had lived opposite each other—actually as well as figuratively—for years. When the drawing-room curtains in No. 20 East 73rd Street were renewed, No. 23, across the way, was always aware of it. And of all the movings, buyings, travels, anniversaries, illnesses—the tame chronicle of an estimable pair. Little of it escaped Mrs. Slade. But she had grown bored with it by the time her husband made his big *coup* in Wall Street, and when they bought in upper Park Avenue had already begun to think: "I'd rather live opposite a speakeasy for a change; at least one might see it raided." The idea of seeing Grace raided was so amusing that (before the move) she launched it at a woman's lunch. It made a hit, and went the rounds—she sometimes wondered if it had crossed the street, and reached Mrs. Ansley. She hoped not, but didn't much mind. Those were the days when respectability was at a discount, and it did the irreproachable no harm to laugh at them a little.

A few years later, and not many months apart, both ladies lost their husbands. There was an appropriate exchange of wreaths and condolences, and a brief renewal of intimacy in the half-shadow of their mourning; and now, after another interval, they had run across each other in Rome, at the same hotel, each of them the modest appendage of a salient daughter. The similarity of their lot had again drawn them together, lending itself to mild jokes, and the mutual confession that, if in old days it must have been tiring to "keep up" with daughters, it was now, at times, a little dull not to.

No doubt, Mrs. Slade reflected, she felt her unemployment more than poor Grace ever would. It was a big drop from being the wife of Delphin Slade to being his widow. She had always regarded herself (with a certain conjugal pride) as his equal in social gifts, as contributing her full share to the making of the exceptional couple they were: but the difference after his death was irremediable. As the wife of the famous corporation lawyer, always with an international case or two on hand, every day brought its exciting and unexpected obligation: the impromptu entertaining of eminent colleagues from abroad, the hurried dashes on legal business to London, Paris or Rome, where the entertaining was so handsomely reciprocated; the amusement of hearing in her wake: "What, that handsome woman with the good clothes and the eyes is Mrs. Slade—*the* Slade's wife? Really? Generally the wives of celebrities are such frumps."

Yes; being *the* Slade's widow was a dullish business after that. In living up to such a husband all her faculties had been engaged; now she had only her daughter to live up to, for the son who seemed to have inherited his father's gifts had died suddenly in boyhood. She had fought through that agony because her husband was there, to be helped and to help; now, after the father's death, the thought of the boy had become unbearable. There was nothing left but to mother her daughter; and dear Jenny was such a perfect daughter that she needed no excessive mothering. "Now with Babs Ansley I don't know that I *should* be so quiet," Mrs. Slade sometimes

20

half-enviously reflected; but Jenny, who was younger than her brilliant friend, was that rare accident, an extremely pretty girl who somehow made youth and prettiness seem as safe as their absence. It was all perplexing—and to Mrs. Slade a little boring. She wished that Jenny would fall in love—with the wrong man, even; that she might have to be watched, out-maneuvered, rescued. And instead, it was Jenny who watched her mother, kept her out of drafts, made sure that she had taken her tonic....

Mrs. Ansley was much less articulate than her friend, and her mental portrait of Mrs. Slade was slighter, and drawn with fainter touches. "Alida Slade's awfully brilliant; but not as brilliant as she thinks," would have summed it up; though she would have added, for the enlightenment of strangers, that Mrs. Slade had been an extremely dashing girl; much more so than her daughter, who was pretty, of course, and clever in a way, but had none of her mother's—well, "vividness," someone had once called it. Mrs. Ansley would take up current words like this, and cite them in quotation marks, as unheard-of audacities. No; Jenny was not like her mother. Sometimes Mrs. Ansley thought Alida Slade was disappointed; on the whole she had had a sad life. Full of failures and mistakes; Mrs. Ansley had always been rather sorry for her....

So these two ladies visualized each other, each through the wrong end of her little telescope.

II.

For a long time they continued to sit side by side without speaking. It seemed as though, to both, there was a relief in laying down their some-what futile activities in the presence of the vast Memento Mori which faced them. Mrs. Slade sat quite still, her eyes fixed on the golden slope of the Palace of the Caesars, and after a while Mrs. Ansley ceased to fidget with her bag, and she too sank into meditation. Like many intimate friends, the two ladies had never before had occasion to be silent together, and Mrs. Ansley was slightly embarrassed by what seemed, after so many years, a new stage in their intimacy, and one with which she did not yet know how to deal.

Suddenly the air was full of that deep clangor of bells which period-ically covers Rome with a roof of silver. Mrs. Slade glanced at her wrist-watch. "Five o'clock already," she said, as though surprised.

Mrs. Ansley suggested interrogatively: "There's bridge at the Embassy at five." For a long time Mrs. Slade did not answer. She appeared to be lost in contemplation, and Mrs. Ansley thought the remark had escaped her. But after a while she said, as if speaking out of a dream: "Bridge, did you say? Not unless you want to.... But I don't think I will, you know."

"Oh, no," Mrs. Ansley hastened to assure her. "I don't care to at all. It's so lovely here; and so full of old memories, as you say." She settled herself in her chair, and almost furtively drew forth her knitting. Mrs. Slade took sideway note of this activity, but her own beautifully caredfor hands remained motionless on her knee.

"I was just thinking," she said slowly, "what different things Rome stands for to each generation of travelers. To our grandmothers, Roman fever; to our mothers, sentimental dangers—how we used to be guarded! — to our daughters, no more dangers than the middle of Main Street. They don't know it—but how much they're missing!" The long golden light was beginning to pale, and Mrs. Ansley lifted her knitting a little closer to her eyes. "Yes; how we were guarded!"

"I always used to think," Mrs. Slade continued, "that our mothers had a   30
much more difficult job than our grandmothers. When Roman fever stalked the streets it must have been comparatively easy to gather in the girls at the danger hour; but when you and I were young, with such beauty calling us, and the spice of disobedience thrown in, and no worse risk than catching cold during the cool hour after sunset, the mothers used to be put to it to keep us in—didn't they?"

She turned again toward Mrs. Ansley, but the latter had reached a delicate point in her knitting. "One, two, three—slip two; yes, they must have been," she assented, without looking up. Mrs. Slade's eyes rested on her with a deepened attention. "She can knit—in the face of *this*! How like her...."

Mrs. Slade leaned back, brooding, her eyes ranging from the ruins which faced her to the long green hollow of the Forum, the fading glow of the church fronts beyond it, and the outlying immensity of the Colosseum. Suddenly she thought: "It's all very well to say that our girls have done away with sentiment and moonlight. But if Babs Ansley isn't out to catch that young aviator—the one who's a Marchese—then I don't know anything. And Jenny has no chance beside her. I know that too. I wonder if that's why Grace Ansley likes the two girls to go everywhere together? My poor Jenny as a foil—!" Mrs. Slade gave a hardly audible laugh, and at the sound Mrs. Ansley dropped her knitting.

"Yes—?"

"I—oh, nothing. I was only thinking how your Babs carries everything before her. That Campolieri boy is one of the best matches in Rome. Don't look so innocent, my dear—you know he is. And I was wondering, ever so respectfully, you understand...wondering how two such exemplary characters as you and Horace had managed to produce anything quite so dynamic." Mrs. Slade laughed again, with a touch of asperity.

Mrs. Ansley's hands lay inert across her needles. She looked straight   35
out at the great accumulated wreckage of passion and splendor at her feet. But her small profile was almost expressionless. At length she said: "I think you overrate Babs, my dear."

Mrs. Slade's tone grew easier. "No; I don't. I appreciate her. And perhaps envy you. Oh, my girl's perfect; if I were a chronic invalid I'd—well, I think I'd rather be in Jenny's hands. There must be times...but there! I always wanted a brilliant daughter...and never quite understood why I got an angel instead."

Mrs. Ansley echoed her laugh in a faint murmur. "Babs is an angel too."

"Of course—of course! But she's got rainbow wings. Well, they're wandering by the sea with their young men; and here we sit...and it all brings back the past a little too acutely."

Mrs. Ansley had resumed her knitting. One might almost have imagined (if one had known her less well, Mrs. Slade reflected) that, for her also, too many memories rose from the lengthening shadows of those august ruins. But no; she was simply absorbed in her work. What was there for her to worry about? She knew that Babs would almost certainly come back engaged to the extremely eligible Campolieri. "And she'll sell the New York house, and settle down near them in Rome, and never be in their way...she's much too tactful. But she'll have an excellent cook, and just the right people in for bridge and cocktails...and a perfectly peaceful old age among her grandchildren."

Mrs. Slade broke off this prophetic flight with a recoil of self-disgust. There was no one of whom she had less right to think unkindly than of Grace Ansley. Would she never cure herself of envying her? Perhaps she had begun too long ago.

She stood up and leaned against the parapet, filling her troubled eyes with the tranquilizing magic of the hour. But instead of tranquilizing her the sight seemed to increase her exasperation. Her gaze turned toward the Colosseum. Already its golden flank was drowned in purple shadow, and above it the sky curved crystal clear, without light or color. It was the moment when afternoon and evening hang balanced in mid-heaven.

Mrs. Slade turned back and laid her hand on her friend's arm. The gesture was so abrupt that Mrs. Ansley looked up, startled.

"The sun's set. You're not afraid, my dear?"

"Afraid—?"

"Of Roman fever or pneumonia? I remember how ill you were that winter. As a girl you had a very delicate throat, hadn't you?"

"Oh, we're all right up here. Down below, in the Forum, it does get deathly cold, all of a sudden...but not here."

"Ah, of course you know because you had to be so careful." Mrs. Slade turned back to the parapet. She thought: "I must make one more effort not to hate her." Aloud she said: "Whenever I look at the Forum from up here, I remember that story about a great-aunt of yours, wasn't she? A dreadfully wicked great-aunt?"

"Oh, yes; great-aunt Harriet. The one who was supposed to have sent her young sister out to the Forum after sunset to gather a nightblooming flower for her album. All our great-aunts and grandmothers used to have albums of dried flowers."

Mrs. Slade nodded. "But she really sent her because they were in love with the same man—"

"Well, that was the family tradition. They said Aunt Harriet confessed 50 it years afterward. At any rate, the poor little sister caught the fever and died. Mother used to frighten us with the story when we were children."

"And you frightened *me* with it, that winter when you and I were here as girls. The winter I was engaged to Delphin."

Mrs. Ansley gave a faint laugh. "Oh, did I? Really frightened you? I don't believe you're easily frightened."

"Not often; but I was then. I was easily frightened because I was too happy. I wonder if you know what that means?"

"I—yes ..." Mrs. Ansley faltered.

"Well, I suppose that was why the story of your wicked aunt made such 55 an impression on me. And I thought: 'There's no more Roman fever, but the Forum is deathly cold after sunset—especially after a hot day. And the Colosseum's even colder and damper.'"

"The Colosseum—?"

"Yes. It wasn't easy to get in, after the gates were locked for the night. Far from easy. Still, in those days it could be managed; it *was* managed, often. Lovers met there who couldn't meet elsewhere. You knew that?"

"I—I dare say. I don't remember."

"You don't remember? You don't remember going to visit some ruins or other one evening, just after dark, and catching a bad chill? You were supposed to have gone to see the moon rise. People always said that expedition was what caused your illness."

There was a moment's silence; then Mrs. Ansley rejoined: "Did they? It 60 was all so long ago."

"Yes. And you got well again—so it didn't matter. But I suppose it struck your friends—the reason given for your illness, I mean—because everybody knew you were so prudent on account of your throat, and your mother took such care of you.... You *had* been out late sightseeing, hadn't you, that night?"

"Perhaps I had. The most prudent girls aren't always prudent. What made you think of it now?"

Mrs. Slade seemed to have no answer ready. But after a moment she broke out: "Because I simply can't bear it any longer—!"

Mrs. Ansley lifted her head quickly. Her eyes were wide and very pale. "Can't bear what?"

"Why—your not knowing that I've always known why you went." 65

"Why I went—?"

"Yes. You think I'm bluffing, don't you? Well, you went to meet the man I was engaged to—and I can repeat every word of the letter that took you there."

While Mrs. Slade spoke Mrs. Ansley had risen unsteadily to her feet. Her bag, her knitting and gloves, slid in a panic-stricken heap to the ground. She looked at Mrs. Slade as though she were looking at a ghost.

"No, no—don't," she faltered out.

"Why not? Listen, if you don't believe me. 'My one darling, things can't go on like this. I must see you alone. Come to the Colosseum immediately after dark tomorrow. There will be somebody to let you in. No one whom you need fear will suspect'—but perhaps you've forgotten what the letter said?"

Mrs. Ansley met the challenge with an unexpected composure. Steadying herself against the chair she looked at her friend, and replied: "No; I know it by heart too."

"And the signature? 'Only *your* D.S.' Was that it? I'm right, am I? That was the letter that took you out that evening after dark?"

Mrs. Ansley was still looking at her. It seemed to Mrs. Slade that a slow struggle was going on behind the voluntarily controlled mask of her small quiet face. "I shouldn't have thought she had herself so well in hand," Mrs. Slade reflected, almost resentfully. But at this moment Mrs. Ansley spoke. "I don't know how you knew. I burnt that letter at once."

"Yes; you would, naturally—you're so prudent!" The sneer was open now. "And if you burnt the letter you're wondering how on earth I know what was in it. That's it, isn't it?"

Mrs. Slade waited, but Mrs. Ansley did not speak.

"Well, my dear, I know what was in that letter because I wrote it!"

"You wrote it?"

"Yes."

The two women stood for a minute staring at each other in the last golden light. Then Mrs. Ansley dropped back into her chair. "Oh," she murmured, and covered her face with her hands.

Mrs. Slade waited nervously for another word or movement. None came, and at length she broke out: "I horrify you."

Mrs. Ansley's hands dropped to her knee. The face they uncovered was streaked with tears. "I wasn't thinking of you. I was thinking—it was the only letter I ever had from him!"

"And I wrote it. Yes; I wrote it! But I was the girl he was engaged to. Did you happen to remember that?"

Mrs. Ansley's head drooped again. "I'm not trying to excuse myself...I remembered...."

"And still you went?"

"Still I went."

Mrs. Slade stood looking down on the small bowed figure at her side. The flame of her wrath had already sunk, and she wondered why she had ever thought there would be any satisfaction in inflicting so purposeless a wound on her friend. But she had to justify herself.

"You do understand? I'd found out—and I hated you, hated you. I knew you were in love with Delphin—and I was afraid; afraid of you, of your quiet ways, your sweetness... your... well, I wanted you out of the way, that's all. Just for a few weeks; just till I was sure of him. So in a blind fury I wrote that letter... I don't know why I'm telling you now."

"I suppose," said Mrs. Ansley slowly, "it's because you've always gone on hating me."

"Perhaps. Or because I wanted to get the whole thing off my mind." She paused. "I'm glad you destroyed the letter. Of course I never thought you'd die."

Mrs. Ansley relapsed into silence, and Mrs. Slade, leaning above her, was conscious of a strange sense of isolation, of being cut off from the warm current of human communion. "You think me a monster!"   90

"I don't know.... It was the only letter I had, and you say he didn't write it?"

"Ah, how you care for him still!"

"I cared for that memory," said Mrs. Ansley.

Mrs. Slade continued to look down on her. She seemed physically reduced by the blow—as if, when she got up, the wind might scatter her like a puff of dust. Mrs. Slade's jealousy suddenly leapt up again at the sight. All these years the woman had been living on that letter. How she must have loved him, to treasure the mere memory of its ashes! The letter of the man her friend was engaged to. Wasn't it she who was the monster?

"You tried your best to get him away from me, didn't you? But you failed; and I kept him. That's all."   95

"Yes. That's all."

"I wish now I hadn't told you. I'd no idea you'd feel about it as you do; I thought you'd be amused. It all happened so long ago, as you say; and you must do me the justice to remember that I had no reason to think you'd ever taken it seriously. How could I, when you were married to Horace Ansley two months afterward? As soon as you could get out of bed your mother rushed you off to Florence and married you. People were rather surprised— they wondered at its being done so quickly; but I thought I knew. I had an idea you did it out of *pique*—to be able to say you'd got ahead of Delphin and me. Girls have such silly reasons for doing the most serious things. And your marrying so soon convinced me that you'd never really cared."

"Yes. I suppose it would," Mrs. Ansley assented.

The clear heaven overhead was emptied of all its gold. Dusk spread over it, abruptly darkening the Seven Hills. Here and there lights began to twinkle through the foliage at their feet. Steps were coming and going on the deserted terrace—waiters looking out of the doorway at the head of the stairs, then reappearing with trays and napkins and flasks of wine. Tables were moved, chairs straightened. A feeble string of electric lights flickered out. Some vases of faded flowers were carried away, and brought back replenished. A stout lady in a dust coat suddenly appeared, asking in broken Italian if anyone had seen the elastic band which held together her tattered Baedeker. She poked with her stick under the table at which she had lunched, the waiters assisting.

The corner where Mrs. Slade and Mrs. Ansley sat was still shadowy and deserted. For a long time neither of them spoke. At length Mrs. Slade began again: "I suppose I did it as a sort of joke—"

"A joke?"

"Well, girls are ferocious sometimes, you know. Girls in love especially. And I remember laughing to myself all that evening at the idea that you were waiting around there in the dark, dodging out of sight, listening for every sound, trying to get in—Of course I was upset when I heard you were so ill afterward."

Mrs. Ansley had not moved for a long time. But now she turned slowly toward her companion. "But I didn't wait. He'd arranged everything. He was there. We were let in at once," she said.

Mrs. Slade sprang up from her leaning position. "Delphin there? They let you in?—Ah, now you're lying!" she burst out with violence.

Mrs. Ansley's voice grew clearer, and full of surprise. "But of course he was there. Naturally he came—"

"Came? How did he know he'd find you there? You must be raving!"

Mrs. Ansley hesitated, as though reflecting. "But I answered the letter. I told him I'd be there. So he came."

Mrs. Slade flung her hands up to her face. "Oh, God—you answered! I never thought of your answering...."

"It's odd you never thought of it, if you wrote the letter."

"Yes. I was blind with rage."

Mrs. Ansley rose, and drew her fur scarf about her. "It is cold here. We'd better go...I'm sorry for you," she said, as she clasped the fur about her throat.

The unexpected words sent a pang through Mrs. Slade. "Yes; we'd better go." She gathered up her bag and cloak. "I don't know why you should be sorry for me," she muttered.

Mrs. Ansley stood looking away from her toward the dusky secret mass of the Colosseum. "Well—because I didn't have to wait that night."

Mrs. Slade gave an unquiet laugh. "Yes; I was beaten there. But I oughtn't to begrudge it to you, I suppose. At the end of all these years. After all, I had everything; I had him for twenty-five years. And you had nothing but that one letter that he didn't write."

Mrs. Ansley was again silent. At length she turned toward the door of the terrace. She took a step, and turned back, facing her companion.

"I had Barbara," she said, and began to move ahead of Mrs. Slade toward the stairway.

■ Characterize the relationship between Mrs. Slade and Mrs. Ansley. Who dominates the conversation between the two women? How do the final words of the story change our understanding of what has come before?

■ How does the current atmosphere relate to the historical atmosphere that the two women review? How do children appear within the narrative?

■ Look carefully at the descriptions of the setting, including descriptions of the built environment as well as those of the light and weather. How do these descriptions relate to the development of the narrative?

POETRY

Anonymous

My Love in Her Attire

My Love in her attire doth show her wit,
It doth so well become her:
For every season she hath dressings fit,
For Winter, Spring, and Summer.
No beauty she doth miss   5
When all her robes are on;
But Beauty's self she is
When all her robes are gone.

■ Look at the words that are capitalized. How is this capitalization significant? How does it impact the meaning of the poem?

■ What is the difference between the two beauties that the poet describes in the final four lines?

John Donne (1572–1631)

Elegy 19: To His Mistress Going to Bed (1635)

Come, Madam, come, all rest my powers defy,
Until I labour, I in labour lie.

The foe oft-times having the foe in sight,
Is tired with standing though he never fight.
Off with that girdle, like heaven's zone glistering,   5
But a far fairer world encompassing.
Unpin that spangled breastplate which you wear,
That th' eyes of busy fools may be stopped there.
Unlace yourself, for that harmonious chime
Tells me from you, that now 'tis your bed time.   10
Off with that happy busk, which I envy,
That still can be, and still can stand so nigh.
Your gown going off, such beauteous state reveals,
As when from flowery meads th' hill's shadow steals.
Off with that wiry coronet and show   15
The hairy diadem which on you doth grow;
Now off with those shoes, and then safely tread
In this love's hallowed temple, this soft bed.
In such white robes heaven's angels used to be
Received by men; thou angel bring'st with thee   20
A heaven like Mahomet's paradise; and though
Ill spirits walk in white, we easily know
By this these angels from an evil sprite,
Those set our hairs, but these our flesh upright.
    Licence my roving hands, and let them go   25
Before, behind, between, above, below.
O my America, my new found land,
My kingdom, safeliest when with one man manned,
My mine of precious stones, my empery,
How blessed am I in this discovering thee!   30
To enter in these bonds, is to be free;
Then, where my hand is set, my seal shall be.
    Full nakedness, all joys are due to thee.
As souls unbodied, bodies unclothed must be,
To taste whole joys. Gems which you women use   35
Are like Atalanta's balls, cast in men's views,
That when a fool's eye lighteth on a gem,
His earthly soul may covet theirs, not them.
Like pictures, or like books' gay coverings made
For laymen, are all women thus arrayed;   40
Themselves are mystic books, which only we
(Whom their imputed grace will dignify)
Must see revealed. Then since that I may know,
As liberally, as to a midwife, show
Thyself: cast all, yea, this white linen hence,   45
Here is no penance, much less innocence.

To teach thee, I am naked first; why then
What needst thou have more covering than a man?

- Note the various strategies that the poet employs to describe his desires in this poem. For instance, what is the poetic strategy that makes sense of his exclamation, "O my America"?
- Compare the wordplay in this seduction with that used in the previous poem.

John Fletcher (1579–1625)

[Take, oh take those lips away] (1639)

Take, oh take those lips away,
That so sweetly were forsworn,
And those eyes, the break of day,
Lights that do mislead the morn:
But my kisses bring again,   5
Seals of love, but sealed in vain.
Hide, oh hide those hills of snow,
Which thy frozen bosom bears,
On whose tops the pinks that grow
Are yet of those that April wears.   10
But first set my poor heart free,
Bound in those icy chains by thee.

- How is the opening command in this poem at odds with the poem's intent? What specific words help us see this contrast?

Anonymous

Western Wind (ca. 1500)

Western wind, when wilt thou blow,
The small rain down can rain?
Christ, if my love were in my arms,
And I in my bed again!

- What meaning might we find in the fact that the poet addresses "Western wind"?

■ How can we interpret the question that the poet asks in the first two lines? How is this question related to the desire that the poet expresses in the final two lines?

Henry Howard, Earl of Surrey (1517–1547)

[Love that doth reign and live within my thought] (1557)

Love that doth reign and live within my thought
And built his seat within my captive breast,
Clad in the arms wherein with me he fought,
Oft in my face he doth his banner rest.
But she that taught me love and suffer pain,   5
My doubtful hope and eke my hot desire
With shamefast look to shadow and refrain,
Her smiling grace converteth straight to ire.
And coward Love then to the heart apace
Taketh his flight, where he doth lurk and plain   10
His purpose lost, and dare not show his face.
For my lord's guilt thus faultless bide I pain;
Yet from my lord shall not my foot remove:
Sweet is the death that taketh end by love.

Thomas Wyatt (1503–1642)

[The long love that in my heart doth harbor]
(1810)

The long love that in my heart doth harbor
And in mine heart doth keep his residence,
Into my face presseth with bold pretence
And therein campeth, spreading his banner.
She that me learneth to love and suffer   5
And will that my trust and lust's negligence
Be reined by reason, shame, and reverence,
With his hardiness taketh displeasure.
Wherewithal unto the heart's forest he fleeth,
Leaving his enterprise with pain and cry,   10
And there him hideth and not appeareth.
What may I do when my master feareth

But in the field with him to live and die?
For good is the life ending faithfully.

- Compare Howard's poem to Wyatt's poem. How closely related are the two structures?
- Find specific instances where their parallel lines express a similar idea in different words. In what way does this slight difference lead to a difference in the idea that the poem is expressing?

e. e. cummings (1894–1962)

Spring is like a perhaps hand (1925)

Spring is like a perhaps hand
(which comes carefully
out of Nowhere)arranging
a window,into which people look(while
people stare   5
arranging and changing placing
carefully there a strange
thing and a known thing here)and

changing everything carefully

spring is like a perhaps   10
Hand in a window
(carefully to

and fro moving New and
Old things,while
people stare carefully   15
moving a perhaps
fraction of flower here placing
an inch of air there)and

without breaking anything.

- Look at the word *perhaps* as it is used throughout the poem. How is the poet's use of the word unusual? What meaning does the poet achieve with this unusual usage pattern?

e. e. cummings (1894–1962)

since feeling is first (1926)

since feeling is first
who pays any attention
to the syntax of things
will never wholly kiss you;

wholly to be a fool   5
while Spring is in the world

my blood approves,
and kisses are a better fate
than wisdom
lady i swear by all flowers. Don't cry   10
—the best gesture of my brain is less than
your eyelids' flutter which says

we are for each other: then
laugh, leaning back in my arms
for life's not a paragraph   15

And death i think is no parenthesis

- How does the poet use the language of syntax to describe feelings?
- In the two cummings poems, how does the poet develop some similar ideas about spring?

Emily Dickinson (1830–1886)

[Wild Nights—Wild Nights!] (ca. 1861)

Wild Nights—Wild Nights!
Were I with thee
Wild Nights should be
Our luxury!

Futile—the Winds—   5
To a Heart in port—
Done with the Compass—
Done with the Chart!

Rowing in Eden—
Ah, the Sea!   10
Might I but moor—Tonight—
In Thee!

■ How are compass and chart relevant to a discussion of the "Heart"? What
  other images in the poem develop this idea?
■ How does the rhythm of the poem illustrate the notion of "Wild Nights"?

Galway Kinnell (1927–)

Shelley (2004)

When I was twenty the one true
free spirit I had heard of was Shelley,
Shelley, who wrote tracts advocating
atheism, free love, the emancipation
of women, the abolition of wealth and class,   5
and poems on the bliss of romantic love,
Shelley, who, I learned later, perhaps
almost too late, remarried Harriet,
then pregnant with their second child,
and a few months later ran off with Mary,   10
already pregnant herself, bringing
with them Mary's stepsister Claire,
who very likely also became his lover,

and in this malaise à trois, which Shelley
had imagined would be "a paradise of exiles,"   15
they lived, along with the spectre of Harriet,
who drowned herself in the Serpentine,
and of Mary's half sister Fanny,
who killed herself, maybe for unrequited
love of Shelley, and with the spirits   20
of adored but often neglected
children conceived incidentally
in the pursuit of Eros—Harriet's
Ianthe and Charles, denied to Shelley
and consigned to foster parents; Mary's   25
Clara, dead at one; her Willmouse,
Shelley's favorite, dead at three; Elena,

the baby in Naples, almost surely
Shelley's own, whom he "adopted"
and then left behind, dead at one and a half;   30
Allegra, Claire's daughter by Byron,
whom Byron sent off to the convent
at Bagnacavallo at four, dead at five—

and in those days, before I knew
any of this, I thought I followed Shelley,   35
who thought he was following radiant desire.

- Compare this poem to the biography of the poet Shelley on page 1769. How does the tone of this poem differ from that of the biography?
- What is the significance of the word *thought* in the final two lines of the poem?

Robert Burns (1759–1796)

A Red, Red Rose (1794)

O, my Love's like a red, red rose,
That's newly sprung in June:
O my Love's like the melodie,
That's sweetly play'd in tune.

As fair art thou, my bonnie lass,   5
So deep in love am I;
And I will love thee still, my dear,
Till a' the seas gang dry.

Till a' the seas gang dry, my dear,
And the rocks melt wi' the sun;   10
And I will love thee still, my dear,
While the sands o' life shall run.

And fare-thee-weel, my only Love!
And fare-thee-weel, a while!
And I will come again, my Love,   15
Tho' 'twere ten thousand mile.

- The poet writes his English in order to replicate the sounds of Scottish speech. What impact does this dialect have on the tone of the poem?

- How does the poetic structure of this poem contribute to a tone that is distinct from that of the previous poem? How does this difference account for our interpretation of the poem?

Edna St. Vincent Millay (1892–1950)

What Lips My Lips Have Kissed (1923)

What lips my lips have kissed, and where, and why,
I have forgotten, and what arms have lain
Under my head till morning; but the rain
Is full of ghosts tonight, that tap and sigh
Upon the glass and listen for reply,   5
And in my heart there stirs a quiet pain
For unremembered lads that not again
Will turn to me at midnight with a cry.
Thus in the winter stands the lonely tree,
Nor knows what birds have vanished one by one,   10
Yet knows its boughs more silent than before:
I cannot say what loves have come and gone,
I only know that summer sang in me
A little while, that in me sings no more.

- What are the "ghosts" that the poet detects? How else does she describe them in the poem?
- Look at the line breaks throughout the poem. Where does the poet break up sentences in unexpected places? How do these breaks contribute to the impact of the poem?

Denise Levertov (1923–)

The Ache of Marriage (1966)

The ache of marriage:

thigh and tongue, beloved,
are heavy with it,
it throbs in the teeth

We look for communion   5
and are turned away, beloved,
each and each

It is leviathan and we
in its belly
looking for joy, some joy   10
not to be known outside it

two by two in the ark of
the ache of it.

Denise Levertov (1923–)

Divorcing (1975)

One garland
of flowers, leaves, thorns
was twined round our two necks.
Drawn tight, it could choke us,
yet we loved its scratchy grace,   5
our fragrant yoke.

We were Siamese twins.
Our blood's not sure
if it can circulate,
now we are cut apart.   10
Something in each of us is waiting
to see if we can survive,
severed.

■ In both poems, the poet sets out words (*communion, leviathan, ark, garland,*
and *Siamese twins*) as points of exploration. Compare the use of this strategy
in the two poems. Where do we see similar sentiments in the different poems?

Christopher Marlowe (1564–1593)

The Passionate Shepherd to His Love (1599?)

Come live with me and be my love,
And we will all the pleasures prove
That valleys, groves, hills, and fields,
Woods, or steepy mountain yields.

And we will sit upon the rocks,   5
Seeing the shepherds feed their flocks

By shallow rivers, to whose falls
Melodious birds sing madrigals.

And I will make thee beds of roses
And a thousand fragrant posies,   10
A cap of flowers and a kirtle
Embroidered all with leaves of myrtle;

A gown made of the finest wool
Which from our pretty lambs we pull;
Fair-linèd slippers for the cold,   15
With buckles of the purest gold;

A belt of straw and ivy buds,
With coral clasps and amber studs.
And if these pleasures may thee move,
Come live with me and be my love.   20
The shepherds' swains shall dance and sing
For thy delight each May morning.
If these delights thy mind may move,
Then live with me and be my love.

Sir Walter Ralegh (1554–1618)

The Nymph's Reply to the Shepherd (1600)

If all the world and love were young,
And truth in every shepherd's tongue,
These pretty pleasures might me move
To live with thee and be thy love.

Time drives the flocks from field to fold,   5
When rivers rage and rocks grow cold;
And Philomel becometh dumb;
The rest complains of cares to come.

The flowers do fade, and wanton fields
To wayward winter reckoning yields: 10
A honey tongue, a heart of gall,
Is fancy's spring, but sorrow's fall.

Thy gowns, thy shoes, thy beds of roses,
Thy cap, thy kirtle, and thy posies

Soon break, soon wither, soon forgotten,   15
In folly ripe, in reason rotten.

Thy belt of straw and ivy buds,
Thy coral clasps and amber studs,
All these in me no means can move
To come to thee and be thy love.   20

But could youth last, and love still breed,
Had joys no date, nor age no need,
Then these delights my mind might move
To live with thee and be thy love.

- How does Ralegh use Marlowe's words to change the point of view in "The Nymph's Reply to the Shepherd"?
- How do the two poems, with their contrasting approach to nature and their pastoral setting, represent different approaches to love and to poetry itself? Begin by contrasting the tone and themes of the two poems.

Andrew Marvell (1621–1678)

To His Coy Mistress (1681)

Had we but world enough and time,
This coyness, lady, were no crime.
We would sit down and think which way
To walk, and pass our long love's day.
Thou by the Indian Ganges' side   5
Should'st rubies find; I by the tide
Of Humber would complain. I would
Love you ten years before the Flood,
And you should, if you please, refuse
Till the conversion of the Jews.   10
My vegetable love should grow
Vaster than empires, and more slow.
An hundred years should go to praise
Thine eyes, and on thy forehead gaze,
Two hundred to adore each breast,   15
But thirty thousand to the rest.
An age at least to every part,
And the last age should show your heart.
For, lady, you deserve this state,
Nor would I love at lower rate.   20

But at my back I always hear
Time's wingèd chariot hurrying near,
And yonder all before us lie
Deserts of vast eternity.
Thy beauty shall no more be found,   25
Nor in thy marble vault shall sound
My echoing song; then worms shall try
That long preserved virginity,
And your quaint honor turn to dust,
And into ashes all my lust.   30
The grave's a fine and private place,
But none, I think, do there embrace.
    Now therefore, while the youthful hue
Sits on thy skin like morning dew
And while thy willing soul transpires   35
At every pore with instant fires,
Now let us sport us while we may;
And now, like amorous birds of prey,
Rather at once our time devour
Than languish in his slow-chapped power.   40
Let us roll all our strength and all
Our sweetness up into one ball
And tear our pleasures with rough strife
Thorough the iron gates of life.
Thus, though we cannot make our sun   45
Stand still, yet we will make him run.

■ Look at the pace of this poem and at specific words that indicate the passage
  of time. How does the pace shift from the beginning to the end of the poem?
■ How do images within the poem reflect this quickening pace?

Elizabeth Barrett Browning (1806–1861)

[How do I love thee? Let me count the ways.]

(1850)

How do I love thee? Let me count the ways.
I love thee to the depth and breadth and height
My soul can reach, when feeling out of sight
For the ends of Being and ideal Grace.
I love thee to the level of everyday's   5

Most quiet need, by sun and candle-light.
I love thee freely, as men strive for Right.
I love thee purely, as they turn from Praise.
I love thee with the passion put to use
In my old griefs, and with my childhood's faith.   10
I love thee with a love I seemed to lose
With my lost saints,—I love thee with the breath,
Smiles, tears, of all my life!—and, if God choose,
I shall but love thee better after death.

Elizabeth Barrett Browning (1806–1861)

[When our two souls stand up] (1897)

When our two souls stand up erect and strong,
Face to face, silent, drawing nigh and nigher,
Until the lengthening wings break into fire
At either curvèd point,—what bitter wrong
Can the earth do us, that we should not long   5
Be here contented? Think. In mounting higher,
The angels would press on us and aspire
To drop some golden orb of perfect song
Into our deep, dear silence. Let us stay
Rather on earth, Belovèd,—where the unfit   10
Contrarious moods of men recoil away
And isolate pure spirits, and permit
A place to stand and love in for a day,
With darkness and the death-hour rounding it.

■ In both poems, look at the poetic structure. How does this structure contribute
   to the impact of the poem?
■ How do the otherworldly images of "lost saints" and "pure spirits" contribute
   to the argument in these two poems? Describe how each poem reaches a
   different conclusion to that argument.

Robert Browning (1812–1886)

Meeting at Night (1845)

The gray sea and the long black land;
And the yellow half-moon large and low;

And the startled little waves that leap
In fiery ringlets from their sleep,
As I gain the cove with pushing prow,   5
And quench its speed i' the slushy sand.

Then a mile of warm sea-scented beach;
Three fields to cross till a farm appears;
A tap at the pane, the quick sharp scratch
And blue spurt of a lighted match,   10
And a voice less loud, thro' its joys and fears,
Than the two hearts beating each to each!

Robert Browning (1812–1886)

Parting at Morning (1845)

Round the cape of a sudden came the sea,
And the sun look'd over the mountain's rim:
And straight was a path of gold for him,
And the need of a world of men for me.

■ Narrate the action that the poet describes in these two poems. Identify the specific verbs that the poet uses. How does the poet indicate action without verbs?

DRAMA

Henrik Ibsen (1828–1906)

Henrik Ibsen was born in Skien, Norway, to wealthy parents; however, young Henrik grew up in poverty after his father's business failed. Determined to achieve his own success, Ibsen moved to Christiania, where he attempted to further his education at the local university. Denied admission, he instead focused on writing and found a job as an assistant stage manager at the Norwegian Theatre. During the next fifty-six years, Ibsen published thirty-two plays, including satire, drama, and comedy, and poetry. As a writer, he is known for his realistic character portrayals, his social and political consciousness, and his psychological depth. He is considered to be one of the greatest contributors to both Norwegian and world literature.

A Doll's House (1879)

CHARACTERS

TORVALD HELMER, *a lawyer*
NORA, *his wife*
DR. RANK
MRS. LINDE
NILS KROGSTAD, *also a lawyer*
THE HELMERS' THREE SMALL CHILDREN
ANNE-MARIE, *their nurse*
HELEN, *the maid*
A PORTER

SCENE: *The action takes place in the Helmers' apartment.*

ACT I

(*A comfortably and tastefully, but not expensively furnished room. Backstage right a door leads out to the hall; backstage left, another door to* HELMER'S *study. Between these two doors stands a piano. In the middle of the left-hand wall is a door, with a window downstage of it. near the window, a round table with armchairs and a small sofa. In the right-hand wall, slightly upstage, is a door; downstage of this, against the same wall, a stove lined with porcelain tiles, with a couple of armchairs and a rocking-chair in front of it. Between the stove and the side door is a small table. Engravings on the wall. a what-not with china and other bric-a-brac; a small bookcase with leather-bound books. A carpet on the floor; a fire in the stove. A winter's day.*

A bell rings in the hall outside. After a moment, we hear the front door being opened. NORA *enters the room, humming contentedly to herself. She is wearing outdoor clothes and carrying a lot of parcels, which she puts down on the table right. Ahe leaves the door to the hall open; through it, we can see a* PORTER *carrying a Christmas tree and a basket. He gives these to the* MAID, *who has opened the door for them.*)

NORA: Hide that Christmas tree away, Helen. The children mustn't see it
    before I've decorated it this evening. (*to the* PORTER, *taking out her
    purse.*) How much—?

PORTER: A shilling.

NORA: Here's half a crown. No, keep it.

(*The* PORTER *touches his cap and goes.* NORA *closes the door. She continues to laugh happily to herself as she removes her coat, etc. She takes from her pocket a bag containing macaroons and eats a couple. Then she tiptoes across and listens at her husband's door.*)

NORA: Yes, he's here. (*Starts humming again as she goes over to the table, right.*)

HELMER (*from his room.*): Is that my skylark twittering out there?   5

NORA (*opening some of the parcels.*): It is!

HELMER: Is that my squirrel rustling?

NORA: Yes!

HELMER: When did my squirrel come home?

NORA: Just now. (*Pops the bag of macaroons in her pocket and wipes her*   10
mouth.) Come out here, Torvald, and see what I've bought.

HELMER: You mustn't disturb me! (*Short pause, then he opens the door and looks in, his pen in his hand.*) Bought, did you say? All that? Has my little squanderbird been overspending again?

NORA: Oh, Torvald, surely we can let ourselves go a little this year! It's the first Christmas we don't have to scrape.

HELMER: Well, you know, we can't afford to be extravagant.

NORA: Oh yes, Torvald, we can be a little extravagant now. Can't we? Just a tiny bit? You've got a big salary now, and you're going to make lots and lots of money.

HELMER: Next year, yes. But my new salary doesn't start till April.   15

NORA: Pooh; we can borrow till then.

HELMER: Nora! (*Goes over to her and takes her playfully by the ear.*) What a little spendthrift you are! Suppose I were to borrow fifty pounds today, and you spent it all over Christmas, and then on New Year's Eve a tile fell off a roof on to my head—

NORA (*puts her hand over his mouth.*): Oh, Torvald! Don't say such dreadful things!

HELMER: Yes, but suppose something like that did happen? What then?

NORA: If anything as frightful as that happened, it wouldn't make much dif-   20
ference whether I was in debt or not.

HELMER: But what about the people I'd borrowed from?

NORA: Them? Who cares about them? They're strangers.

HELMER: Oh, Nora, Nora, how like a woman! No, but seriously, Nora, you know how I feel about this. No debts! Never borrow! A home that is founded on debts can never be a place of freedom and beauty. We two have stuck it out bravely up to now; and we shall continue to do so for the short time we still have to.

NORA (*goes over toward the stove.*): Very well, Torvald. As you say.

HELMER (*follows her.*): Now, now! My little songbird mustn't droop her   25
wings. What's this? Is little squirrel sulking? (*Takes out his purse.*) Nora; guess what I've got here!

NORA (*turns quickly.*): Money!

HELMER: Look. (*Hands her some banknotes.*) I know how these small expenses crop up at Christmas.

NORA (*counts them.*): One—two—three—four. Oh, thank you, Torvald, thank you! I should be able to manage with this.

HELMER: You'll have to.

NORA: Yes, yes, of course I will. But come over here, I want to show you ev-   30
erything I've bought. And so cheaply! Look, here are new clothes for Ivar—and a sword. And a horse and a trumpet for Bob. And a doll and a cradle for Emmy—they're nothing much, but she'll pull them apart in a few days. And some bits of material and handkerchiefs for the maids. Old Anne-Marie ought to have had something better, really.

HELMER: And what's in that parcel?

NORA (*cries.*): No, Torvald, you mustn't see that before this evening!

HELMER: Very well. But now, tell me, you little spendthrift, what do you want for Christmas?

NORA: Me? Oh, pooh, I don't want anything.

HELMER: Oh, yes, you do. Now tell me, what, within reason, would you   35
most like?

NORA: No, I really don't know. Oh, yes—Torvald—!

HELMER: Well?

NORA (*plays with his coat-buttons, not looking at him.*): If you really want to give me something, you could—you could—

HELMER: Come on, out with it.

NORA (*quickly.*): You could give me money, Torvald. Only as much as you   40
feel you can afford; then later I'll buy something with it.

HELMER: But, Nora—

NORA: Oh yes, Torvald dear, please! Please! Then I'll wrap up the notes in pretty gold paper and hang them on the Christmas tree. Wouldn't that be fun?

HELMER: What's the name of that little bird that can never keep any money?

NORA: Yes, yes, squanderbird; I know. But let's do as I say, Torvald; then I'll have time to think about what I need most. Isn't that the best way? Mm?

HELMER (*smiles.*): To be sure it would be, if you could keep what I gave you   45
and really buy yourself something with it. But you'll spend it on all sorts of useless things for the house, and then I'll have to put my hand in my pocket again.

NORA: Oh, but Torvald—

HELMER: You can't deny it, Nora dear. (*Puts his arm round her waist.*) The squanderbird's a pretty little creature, but she gets through an awful lot of money. It's incredible what an expensive pet she is for a man to keep.

NORA: For shame! How can you say such a thing? I save every penny I can.

HELMER (*laughs.*): That's quite true. Every penny you can. But you can't.

NORA (*hums and smiles, quietly gleeful.*): Hm. If you only knew how many 50
expenses we larks and squirrels have, Torvald.

HELMER: You're a funny little creature. Just like your father used to be. Always on the look-out for some way to get money, but as soon as you have any it just runs through your fingers, and you never know where it's gone. Well, I suppose I must take you as you are. It's in your blood. Yes, yes, yes, these things are hereditary. Nora.

NORA: Oh, I wish I'd inherited more of Papa's qualities.

HELMER: And I wouldn't wish my darling little songbird to be any different from what she is. By the way, that reminds me. You look awfully—how shall I put it?—awfully guilty today.

NORA: Do I—

HELMER: Yes, you do. Look me in the eyes. 55

NORA (*looks at him.*): Well?

HELMER (*wags his finger.*): Has my little sweet-tooth been indulging herself in town today, by any chance?

NORA: No, how can you think of such a thing?

HELMER: Not a tiny little digression into a pastry shop?

NORA: No, Torvald, I promise— 60

HELMER: Not just a wee jam tart?

NORA: Certainly not.

HELMER: Not a little nibble at a macaroon?

NORA: No, Torvald—I promise you, honestly—

HELMER: There, there. I was only joking. 65

NORA (*goes over to the table, right.*): You know I could never act against your wishes.

HELMER: Of course not. And you've given me your word— (*Goes over to her.*) Well, my beloved Nora, you keep your little Christmas secrets to yourself. They'll be revealed this evening, I've no doubt, once the Christmas tree has been lit.

NORA: Have you remembered to invite Dr. Rank?

HELMER: No. But there's no need; he knows he'll be dining with us. Anyway, I'll ask him when he comes this morning. I've ordered some good wine. Oh, Nora, you can't imagine how I'm looking forward to this evening.

NORA: So am I, And, Torvald, how the children will love it! 70

HELMER: Yes, it's a wonderful thing to know that one's position is assured and that one has an ample income. Don't you agree? It's good to know that, isn't it?

NORA: Yes, it's almost like a miracle.

HELMER: Do you remember last Christmas? For three whole weeks you shut yourself away every evening to make flowers for the Christmas tree, and all those other things you were going to surprise us with. Ugh, it was the most boring time I've ever had in my life.

NORA: I didn't find it boring.

HELMER (*smiles.*): But it all came to nothing in the end, didn't it?   75

NORA: Oh, are you going to bring that up again? How could I help the cat getting in and tearing everything to bits?

HELMER: No, my poor little Nora, of course you couldn't. You simply wanted to make us happy, and that's all that matters. But it's good that those hard times are past.

NORA: Yes, it's wonderful.

HELMER: I don't have to sit by myself and be bored. And you don't have to tire your pretty eyes and your delicate little hands—

NORA (*claps her hands.*): No, Torvald, that's true, isn't it—I don't have to   80
any longer? Oh, it's really all just like a miracle. (*Takes his arm.*) Now.
I'm going to tell you what I thought we might do, Torvald. As soon as Christmas is over— (*A bell rings in the hall.*) Oh, there's the doorbell. (*Tidies up one or two things in the room.*) Someone's coming. What a bore.

HELMER: I'm not at home to any visitors. Remember!

MAID (*in the doorway.*): A lady's called, madam. A stranger.

NORA: Well, ask her to come in.

MAID: And the doctor's here too, sir.

HELMER: Has he gone to my room?   85

MAID: Yes, sir.

(HELMER *goes into his room. The* MAID *shows in* MRS. LINDE, *who is dressed in travelling clothes, and closes the door.*)

MRS. LINDE (*shyly and a little hesitantly.*): Good evening, Nora.

NORA (*uncertainly.*): Good evening—

MRS. LINDE: I don't suppose you recognize me.

NORA: No, I'm afraid I—Yes, wait a minute—surely— (*Exclaims.*) Why,   90
Christine! Is it really you?

MRS. LINDE: Yes, it's me.

NORA: Christine! And I didn't recognize you! But how could I—? (*More quietly.*) How you've changed, Christine!

MRS. LINDE: Yes, I know. It's been nine years—nearly ten—

NORA: Is it so long? Yes, it must be. Oh, these last eight years have been such a happy time for me! So you've come to town! All that way in winter! How brave of you!

MRS. LINDE: I arrived by the steamer this morning.   95

NORA: Yes, of course—to enjoy yourself over Christmas. Oh, how splendid! We'll have to celebrate! But take off your coat. You're not cold, are you? (*Helps her off with it.*) There! Now let's sit down here by the stove and be comfortable. No, you take the armchair. I'll sit here in the rocking-chair. (*Clasps* MRS. LINDE's *hands.*) Yes, now you look like your old self. It was just at first that—you've got a little paler, though, Christine. And perhaps a bit thinner.

MRS. LINDE: And older, Nora. Much, much older.

NORA: Yes, perhaps a little older. Just a tiny bit. Not much. (*Checks herself suddenly and says earnestly.*) Oh, but how thoughtless of me to sit here and chatter away like this! Dear, sweet Christine, can you forgive me?

MRS. LINDE: What do you mean, Nora?

NORA (*quietly.*): Poor Christine, you've become a widow.   100

MRS. LINDE: Yes. Three years ago.

NORA: I know, I know—I read it in the papers. Oh, Christine, I meant to write to you so often, honestly. But I always put it off, and something else always cropped up.

MRS. LINDE: I understand, Nora dear.

NORA: No, Christine, it was beastly of me. Oh, my poor darling, what you've gone through! And he didn't leave you anything?

MRS. LINDE: No.   105

NORA: No children, either?

MRS. LINDE: No.

NORA: Nothing at all, then?

MRS. LINDE: Not even a feeling of loss or sorrow.

NORA (*looks incredulously at her.*): But, Christine, how is that possible?   110

MRS. LINDE (*smiles sadly and strokes* NORA's *hair.*): Oh, these things happen, Nora.

NORA: All alone. How dreadful that must be for you. I've three lovely children. I'm afraid you can't see them now, because they're out with nanny. But you must tell me everything—

MRS. LINDE: No, no, no. I want to hear about you.

NORA: No, you start. I'm not going to be selfish today. I'm just going to think about you. Oh, but there's one thing I *must* tell you. Have you heard of the wonderful luck we've just had?

MRS. LINDE: No. What?   115

NORA: Would you believe it—my husband's just been made manager of the bank!

MRS. LINDE: Your husband? Oh, how lucky—!

NORA: Yes, isn't it? Being a lawyer is so uncertain, you know, especially if one isn't prepared to touch any case that isn't—well—quite nice. And of course Torvald's been very firm about that—and I'm absolutely with him. Oh, you can imagine how happy we are! He's joining the bank in the New Year, and he'll be getting a big salary, and lots of percentages too. From now on we'll be able to live quite differently—we'll be able to do whatever we want. Oh, Christine, it's such a relief! I feel so

happy! Well, I mean, it's lovely to have heaps of money and not to
have to worry about anything. Don't you think?

MRS. LINDE: It must be lovely to have enough to cover one's needs, anyway.

NORA: Not just our needs! We're going to have heaps and heaps of money! 120

MRS. LINDE (*smiles.*): Nora, Nora, haven't you grown up yet? When we were
at school you were a terrible little spendthrift.

NORA (*laughs quietly.*): Yes, Torvald still says that. (*Wags her finger.*) But
"Nora, Nora" isn't as silly as you think. Oh, we've been in no position
for me to waste money. We've both had to work.

MRS. LINDE: You too?

NORA: Yes, little things—fancy work, crocheting, embroidery and so forth.
(*Casually.*) And other things too. I suppose you know Torvald left the
Ministry when we got married? There were no prospects for promotion
in his department, and of course he needed more money. But the first
year he overworked himself quite dreadfully. He had to take on all sorts
of extra jobs, and worked day and night. But it was too much for him,
and he became frightfully ill. The doctors said he'd have to go to a
warmer climate.

MRS. LINDE: Yes, you spent a whole year in Italy, didn't you? 125

NORA: Yes. It wasn't easy for me to get away, you know. I'd just had Ivar.
But of course we had to do it. Oh, it was a marvelous trip! And it saved
Torvald's life. But it cost an awful lot of money, Christine.

MRS. LINDE: I can imagine.

NORA: Two hundred and fifty pounds. That's a lot of money, you know.

MRS. LINDE: How lucky you had it.

NORA: Well, actually, we got it from my father. 130

MRS. LINDE: Oh, I see. Didn't he die just about that time?

NORA: Yes, Christine, just about then. Wasn't it dreadful, I couldn't go and
look after him. I was expecting little Ivar any day. And then I had my
poor Torvald to care for—we really didn't think he'd live. Dear, kind
Papa! I never saw him again, Christine. Oh, it's the saddest thing that's
happened to me since I got married.

MRS. LINDE: I know you were very fond of him. But you went to Italy—?

NORA: Yes. Well, we had the money, you see, and the doctors said we
mustn't delay. So we went the month after Papa died.

MRS. LINDE: And your husband came back completely cured? 135

NORA: Fit as a fiddle!

MRS. LINDE: But—the doctor?

NORA: How do you mean?

MRS. LINDE: I thought the maid said that the gentleman who arrived with
me was the doctor.

NORA: Oh yes, that's Doctor Rank, but he doesn't come because anyone's 140
ill. He's our best friend, and he looks us up at least once every day. No,

Torvald hasn't had a moment's illness since we went away. And the children are fit and healthy and so am I. (*Jumps up and claps her hands.*) Oh God, oh God, Christine, isn't it a wonderful thing to be alive and happy! Oh, but how beastly of me! I'm only talking about myself. (*Sits on a footstool and rests her arms on* MRS. LINDE's *knee.*) Oh, please don't be angry with me! Tell me, is it really true you didn't love your husband? Why did you marry him, then?

MRS. LINDE: Well, my mother was still alive; and she was helpless and bed-ridden. And I had my two little brothers to take care of. I didn't feel I could say no.

NORA: Yes, well, perhaps you're right. He was rich then, was he?

MRS. LINDE: Quite comfortably off, I believe. But his business was unsound, you see, Nora. When he died it went bankrupt, and there was nothing left.

NORA: What did you do?

MRS. LINDE: Well, I had to try to make ends meet somehow, so I started a   145
little shop, and a little school, and anything else I could turn my hand to. These last three years have been just one endless slog for me, with-out a moment's rest. But now it's over, Nora. My poor dear mother doesn't need me any more; she's passed away. And the boys don't need me either; they've got jobs now and can look after themselves.

NORA: How relieved you must feel—

MRS. LINDE: No, Nora. Just unspeakably empty. No one to live for any more. (*Gets up restlessly.*) That's why I couldn't bear to stay out there any longer, cut off from the world. I thought it'd be easier to find some work here that will exercise and occupy my mind. If only I could get a regular job—office work of some kind—

NORA: Oh but, Christine, that's dreadfully exhausting; and you look practi-cally finished already. It'd be much better for you if you could go away somewhere.

MRS. LINDE (*goes over to the window.*): I have no Papa to pay for my holi-days, Nora.

NORA (*gets up.*): Oh, please don't be angry with me.   150

MRS. LINDE: My dear Nora, it's I who should ask you not to be angry. That's the worst thing about this kind of situation—it makes one so bitter. One has no one to work for; and yet one has to be continually sponging for jobs. One has to live; and so one becomes completely egocentric. When you told me about this luck you've just had with Torvald's new job—can you imagine?—I was happy not so much on your account, as on my own.

NORA: How do you mean? Oh, I understand. You mean Torvald might be able to do something for you?

MRS. LINDE: Yes, I was thinking that.

NORA: He will too, Christine. Just you leave it to me. I'll lead up to it so delicately, so delicately; I'll get him in the right mood. Oh, Christine, I do so want to help you.

MRS. LINDE: It's sweet of you to bother so much about me. Nora. Especially since you know so little of the worries and hardships of life. 155

NORA: You say I know little of—?

MRS. LINDE (smiles.): Well, good heavens—those bits of fancy work of yours—well, really—! You're a child, Nora.

NORA (tosses her head and walks across the room.): You shouldn't say that so patronizingly.

MRS. LINDE: Oh?

NORA: You're like the rest. You all think I'm incapable of getting down to 160 anything serious—

MRS. LINDE: My dear—

NORA: You think I've never had any worries like the rest of you.

MRS. LINDE: Nora dear, you've just told me about all your difficulties—

NORA: Pooh—that! (Quietly.) I haven't told you about the big thing.

MRS. LINDE: What big thing? What do you mean? 165

NORA: You patronize me, Christine; but you shouldn't. You're proud that you've worked so long and so hard for your mother.

MRS. LINDE: I don't patronize anyone, Nora. But you're right—I am both proud and happy that I was able to make my mother's last months on earth comparatively easy.

NORA: And you're also proud at what you've done for your brothers.

MRS. LINDE: I think I have a right to be.

NORA: I think so too. But let me tell you something, Christine. I too have 170 done something to be proud and happy about.

MRS. LINDE: I don't doubt it. But—how do you mean?

NORA: Speak quietly! Suppose Torvald should hear! He mustn't, at any price—no one must know, Christine—no one but you.

MRS. LINDE: But what is this?

NORA: Come over here. (Pulls her down on to the sofa beside her.) Yes, Christine—I too have done something to be happy and proud about. It was I who saved Torvald's life.

MRS. LINDE: Saved his—? How did you save it? 175

NORA: I told you about our trip to Italy. Torvald couldn't have lived if he hadn't managed to get down there—

MRS. LINDE: Yes, well—your father provided the money—

NORA (smiles.): So Torvald and everyone else thinks. But—

MRS. LINDE: Yes?

NORA: Papa didn't give us a penny. It was I who found the money. 180

MRS. LINDE: You? All of it?

NORA: Two hundred and fifty pounds. What do you say to that?

MRS. LINDE: But Nora, how could you? Did you win a lottery or something?

NORA *(scornfully.)*: Lottery? *(Sniffs.)* What would there be to be proud of in that?

MRS. LINDE: But where did you get it from, then? 185

NORA *(hums and smiles secretively.)*: Hm; tra-la-la-la!

MRS. LINDE: You couldn't have borrowed it.

NORA: Oh? Why not?

MRS. LINDE: Well, a wife can't borrow money without her husband's consent.

NORA *(tosses her head.)*: Ah, but when a wife has a little business sense, and 190 knows how to be clever—

MRS. LINDE: But Nora, I simply don't understand—

NORA: You don't have to. No one has said I borrowed the money. I could have got it in some other way. *(Throws herself back on the sofa.)* I could have got it from an admirer. When a girl's as pretty as I am—

MRS. LINDE: Nora, you're crazy!

NORA: You're dying of curiosity now, aren't you, Christine?

MRS. LINDE: Nora, dear, you haven't done anything foolish? 195

NORA *(sits up again.)*: Is it foolish to save one's husband's life?

MRS. LINDE: I think it's foolish if without his knowledge you—

NORA: But the whole point was that he mustn't know! Great heavens, don't you see? He hadn't to know how dangerously ill he was. I was the one they told that his life was in danger and that only going to a warm climate could save him. Do you suppose I didn't try to think of other ways of getting him down there? I told him how wonderful it would be for me to go abroad like other young wives: I cried and prayed; I asked him to remember my condition, and said he ought to be nice and tender to me; and then I suggested he might quite easily borrow the money. But then he got almost angry with me, Christine. He said I was frivolous, and that it was his duty as a husband not to pander to my moods and caprices—I think that's what he called them. Well, well, I thought, you've got to be saved somehow. And then I thought of a way—

MRS. LINDE: But didn't your husband find out from your father that the money hadn't come from him?

NORA: No, never. Papa died just then. I'd thought of letting him into the 200 plot and asking him not to tell. But since he was so ill—! And as things turned out, it didn't become necessary.

MRS. LINDE: And you've never told your husband about this?

NORA: For heaven's sake, no! What an idea! He's frightfully strict about such matters. And besides—he's so proud of being a *man*—it'd be so painful and humiliating for him to know that he owed anything to me. It'd completely wreck our relationship. This life we have built together would no longer exist.

MRS. LINDE: Will you never tell him?

NORA (*thoughtfully, half-smiling.*): Yes—some time, perhaps. Years from now, when I'm no longer pretty. You mustn't laugh! I mean of course, when Torvald no longer loves me as he does now; when it no longer amuses him to see me dance and dress up and play the fool for him. Then it might be useful to have something up my sleeve. (*Breaks off.*) Stupid, stupid, stupid! That time will never come. Well, what do you think of my big secret, Christine? I'm not completely useless, am I? Mind you, all this has caused me a frightful lot of worry. It hasn't been easy for me to meet my obligations punctually. In case you don't know, in the world of business there are things called quarterly instalments and interest, and they're a terrible problem to cope with. So I've had to scrape a little here and save a little there as best I can. I haven't been able to save much on the housekeeping money, because Torvald likes to live well, and I couldn't let the children go short of clothes—I couldn't take anything out of what he gives me for them. The poor little angels!

MRS. LINDE: So you've had to stint yourself, my poor Nora?   205

NORA: Of course. Well, after all, it was my problem. Whenever Torvald gave me money to buy myself new clothes, I never used more than half of it; and I always bought what was cheapest and plainest. Thank heaven anything suits me, so that Torvald's never noticed. But it made me a bit sad sometimes, because it's lovely to wear pretty clothes. Don't you think?

MRS. LINDE: Indeed it is.

NORA: And then I've found one or two other sources of income. Last winter I managed to get a lot of copying to do. So I shut myself away and wrote every evening, late into the night. Oh, I often got so tired. But it was great fun, though, sitting there working and earning money. It was almost like being a man.

MRS. LINDE: But how much have you managed to pay off like this?

NORA: Well, I can't say exactly. It's awfully difficult to keep an exact check   21C
on these kind of transactions. I only know I've paid everything I've managed to scrape together. Sometimes I really didn't know where to turn. (*Smiles.*) Then I'd sit here and imagine some rich old gentleman had fallen in love with me—

MRS. LINDE: What! What gentleman?

NORA: Silly! And that now he'd died and when they opened his will it said in big letters: "Everything I possess is to be paid forthwith to my beloved Mrs. Nora Helmer in cash."

MRS. LINDE: But, Nora dear, who was this gentleman?

NORA: Great heavens, don't you understand? There wasn't any old gentleman; he was just something I used to dream up as I sat here evening after evening wondering how on earth I could raise the money. But what does it matter? The old bore can stay imaginary as far as I'm concerned, because now I don't have to worry any longer! (*Jumps up.*)

Oh, Christine, isn't it wonderful! I don't have to worry any more! No
more troubles! I can play all day with the children, I can fill the house
with pretty things, just the way Torvald likes. And, Christine, it'll soon
be spring, and the air'll be fresh and the skies blue,—and then perhaps
we'll be able to take a little trip somewhere. I shall be able to see the sun
again. Oh, yes, yes, it's a wonderful thing to be alive and happy!

(The bell rings in the hall.)

MRS. LINDE *(gets up.):* You've a visitor. Perhaps I'd better go.　　　215

NORA: No, stay. It won't be for me. It's someone for Torvald—

MAID *(in the doorway.):* Excuse me, madam, a gentleman's called who says
he wants to speak to the master. But I didn't know—seeing as the doctor's with him—

NORA: Who is this gentleman?

KROGSTAD *(in the doorway.):* It's me, Mrs. Helmer.

(MRS. LINDE starts, composes herself and turns away to the window.)

NORA *(takes a step towards him and whispers tensely.):* You? What is it? What　　220
do you want to talk to my husband about?

KROGSTAD: Business—you might call it. I hold a minor post in the bank,
and I hear your husband is to become our new chief—

NORA: Oh—then it isn't—?

KROGSTAD: Pure business, Mrs. Helmer. Nothing more.

NORA: Well, you'll find him in his study.

*(Nods indifferently as she closes the hall door behind him. Then she walks across
the room and sees to the stove.)*

MRS. LINDE: Nora, who was that man?　　　225

NORA: A lawyer called Krogstad.

MRS. LINDE: It was him, then.

NORA: Do you know that man?

MRS. LINDE: I used to know him—some years ago. He was a solicitor's clerk
in our town, for a while.

NORA: Yes, of course, so he was.　　　230

MRS. LINDE: How he's changed!

NORA: He was very unhappily married, I believe.

MRS. LINDE: Is he a widower now?

NORA: Yes, with a lot of children. Ah, now it's alight.

(She closes the door of the stove and moves the rocking-chair a little to one side.)

MRS. LINDE: He does—various things now, I hear?　　　235

NORA: Does he? It's quite possible—I really don't know. But don't let's talk
about business. It's so boring.

(DR. RANK enters from HELMER's study.)

RANK *(still in the doorway.):* No, no, my dear chap, don't see me out. I'll go
and have a word with your wife. *(Closes the door and notices MRS. LINDE.)*
Oh, I beg your pardon. I seem to be *de trop* here too.

NORA: Not in the least. *(Introduces them.)* Dr. Rank. Mrs. Linde.

RANK: Ah! A name I have often heard in this house. I believe I passed you on the stairs as I came up.

MRS. LINDE: Yes. Stairs tire me; I have to take them slowly. 240

RANK: Oh, have you hurt yourself?

MRS. LINDE: No, I'm just a little run down.

RANK: Ah, is that all? Then I take it you've come to town to cure yourself by a round of parties?

MRS. LINDE: I have come here to find work.

RANK: Is that an approved remedy for being run down? 245

MRS. LINDE: One has to live, Doctor.

RANK: Yes, people do seem to regard it as a necessity.

NORA: Oh, really, Dr. Rank. I bet you want to stay alive.

RANK: You bet I do. However miserable I sometimes feel, I still want to go on being tortured for as long as possible. It's the same with all my patients; and with people who are morally sick, too. There's a moral cripple in with Helmer at this very moment—

MRS. LINDE *(softly.)*: Oh! 250

NORA: Whom do you mean?

RANK: Oh, a lawyer fellow called Krogstad—you wouldn't know him. He's crippled all right; morally twisted. But even he started off by announcing, as though it were a matter of enormous importance, that he had to live.

NORA: Oh? What did he want to talk to Torvald about?

RANK: I haven't the faintest idea. All I heard was something about the bank.

NORA: I didn't know that Krog—that this man Krogstad had any connection with the bank. 255

RANK: Yes, he's got some kind of job down there. *(to MRS. LINDE.)* I wonder if in your part of the world you too have a species of human being that spends its time fussing around trying to smell out moral corruption? And when they find a case they give him some nice, comfortable position so that they can keep a good watch on him. The healthy ones just have to lump it.

MRS. LINDE: But surely it's the sick who need care most?

RANK *(shrugs his shoulders.)*: Well, there we have it. It's that attitude that's turning human society into a hospital.

(NORA, lost in her own thoughts, laughs half to herself and claps her hands.)

RANK: Why are you laughing? Do you really know what society is?

NORA: What do I care about society? I think it's a bore. I was laughing at something else—something frightfully funny. Tell me, Dr. Rank—will everyone who works at the bank come under Torvald now? 260

RANK: Do you find that particularly funny?

NORA (*smiles and hums.*): Never mind! Never you mind! (*Walks around the room.*) Yes, I find it very amusing to think that we—I mean, Torvald—has obtained so much influence over so many people. (*Takes the paper bag from her pocket.*) Dr. Rank, would you like a small macaroon?

RANK: Macaroons! I say! I thought they were forbidden here.

NORA: Yes, well, these are some Christine gave me.

MRS. LINDE: What? I—? 265

NORA: All right, all right, don't get frightened. You weren't to know Torvald had forbidden them. He's afraid they'll ruin my teeth. But, dash it—for once—! Don't you agree, Dr. Rank? Here! (*Pops a macaroon into his mouth.*) You too, Christine. And I'll have one too. Just a little one. Two at the most. (*Begins to walk round again.*) Yes, now I feel really, really happy. Now there's just one thing in the world I'd really love to do.

RANK: Oh? And what is that?

NORA: Just something I'd love to say to Torvald.

RANK: Well, why don't you say it?

NORA: No, I daren't. It's too dreadful. 270

MRS. LINDE: Dreadful?

RANK: Well, then, you'd better not. But you can say it to us. What is it you'd so love to say to Torvald?

NORA: I've the most extraordinary longing to say: "Bloody hell!"

RANK: Are you mad?

MRS. LINDE: My dear Nora—! 275

RANK: Say it. Here he is.

NORA (*hiding the bag of macaroons.*): Ssh! Ssh!

(HELMER, *with his overcoat on his arm and his hat in his hand, enters from his study.*)

NORA (*goes to meet him.*): Well, Torvald dear, did you get rid of him?

HELMER: Yes, he's just gone.

NORA: May I introduce you—? This is Christine. She's just arrived in town. 280

HELMER: Christine—? Forgive me, but I don't think—

NORA: Mrs. Linde, Torvald dear. Christine Linde.

HELMER: Ah. A childhood friend of my wife's, I presume?

MRS. LINDE: Yes, we knew each other in earlier days.

NORA: And imagine, now she's traveled all this way to talk to you. 285

HELMER: Oh?

MRS. LINDE: Well, I didn't really—

NORA: You see, Christine's frightfully good at office work, and she's mad to come under some really clever man who can teach her even more than she knows already—

HELMER: Very sensible, madam.

NORA: So when she heard you'd become head of the bank—it was in her   290
local paper—she came here as quickly as she could and—Torvald, you
will, won't you? Do a little something to help Christine? For my sake?

HELMER: Well, that shouldn't be impossible. You are a widow, I take it,
Mrs. Linde?

MRS. LINDE: Yes.

HELMER: And you have experience of office work?

MRS. LINDE: Yes, quite a bit.

HELMER: Well then, it's quite likely I may be able to find some job for   295
you—

NORA (*claps her hands.*): You see, you see!

HELMER: You've come at a lucky moment, Mrs. Linde.

MRS. LINDE: Oh, how can I ever thank you—?

HELMER: There's absolutely no need. (*Puts on his overcoat.*) But now I'm
afraid I must ask you to excuse me—

RANK: Wait. I'll come with you.   300

(*He gets his fur coat from the hall and warms it at the stove.*)

NORA: Don't be long, Torvald dear.

HELMER: I'll only be an hour.

NORA: Are you going too, Christine?

MRS. LINDE (*puts on her outdoor clothes.*): Yes, I must start to look round for
a room.

HELMER: Then perhaps we can walk part of the way together.   305

NORA (*helps her.*): It's such a nuisance we're so cramped here—I'm afraid
we can't offer to—

MRS. LINDE: Oh, I wouldn't dream of it. Goodbye, Nora dear, and thanks
for everything.

NORA: *Au revoir.* You'll be coming back this evening, of course. And you
too, Dr. Rank. What? If you're well enough? Of course you'll be well
enough. Wrap up warmly, though.

(*They go out, talking, into the hall. Children's voices are heard from the
stairs.*)

NORA: Here they are! Here they are!

(*She runs out and opens the door, Anne-Marie, the* NURSE, *enters with the*
CHILDREN.)

NORA: Come in, come in! (*Stoops down and kisses them.*) Oh, my sweet dar-   310
lings—! Look at them, Christine! Aren't they beautiful?

RANK: Don't stand here chattering in this draught!

HELMER: Come, Mrs. Linde. This is for mothers only.

(DR. RANK, HELMER, *and* MRS. LINDE *go down the stairs. The* NURSE *brings the*
CHILDREN *into the room.* NORA *follows, and closes the door to the hall.*)

NORA: How well you look! What red cheeks you've got! Like apples and
roses! (*The* CHILDREN *answer her inaudibly as she talks to them.*) Have

you had fun? That's splendid. You gave Emmy and Bob a ride on the sledge? What, both together? I say! What a clever boy you are, Ivar! Oh, let me hold her for a moment, Anne-Marie! My sweet little baby doll! (*Takes the smallest* CHILD *from the* NURSE *and dances with her.*) Yes, yes, Mummy will dance with Bob too. What? Have you been throwing snowballs? Oh, I wish I'd been there! No, don't—I'll undress them my-self, Anne-Marie. No, please let me; it's such fun. Go inside and warm yourself; you look frozen. There's some hot coffee on the stove. (*The* NURSE *goes into the room on the left.* NORA *takes off the* CHILDREN's *outdoor clothes and throws them anywhere while they all chatter simultaneously.*) What? A big dog ran after you? But he didn't bite you? No, dogs don't bite lovely little baby dolls. Leave those parcels alone, Ivar. What's in them? Ah, wouldn't you like to know! No, no; it's nothing nice. Come on, let's play a game. What shall we play? Hide and seek. Yes, let's play hide and seek. Bob shall hide first. You want me to? All right, let me hide first.

(NORA *and the* CHILDREN *play around the room, and in the adjacent room to the left, laughing and shouting. At length* NORA *hides under the table. The* CHILDREN *rush in, look, but cannot find her. Then they hear her half-stifled laughter, run to the table, lift up the cloth and see her. Great excitement. She crawls out as though to frighten them. Further excitement. Meanwhile, there has been a knock on the door leading from the hall, but no one has noticed it. Now the door is half-opened and* KROGSTAD *enters. He waits for a moment; the game continues.*)

KROGSTAD: Excuse me, Mrs. Helmer—

NORA (*turns with a stifled cry and half jumps up.*): Oh! What do you want?   315

KROGSTAD: I beg your pardon; the front door was ajar. Someone must have forgotten to close it.

NORA (*gets up.*): My husband is not at home, Mr. Krogstad.

KROGSTAD: I know.

NORA: Well, what do you want here, then?

KROGSTAD: A word with you.   320

NORA: With—? (*to the* CHILDREN, *quietly.*) Go inside to Anne-Marie. What? No, the strange gentleman won't do anything to hurt Mummy. When he's gone we'll start playing again.

(*She takes the* CHILDREN *into the room on the left and closes the door behind them.*)

NORA (*uneasy, tense.*): You want to speak to me?

KROGSTAD: Yes.

NORA: Today? But it's not the first of the month yet.

KROGSTAD: No, it is Christmas Eve. Whether or not you have a merry   325
Christmas depends on you.

NORA: What do you want? I can't give you anything today—

KROGSTAD: We won't talk about that for the present. There's something else. You have a moment to spare?

NORA: Oh, yes. Yes, I suppose so; though—

KROGSTAD: Good. I was sitting in the cafe down below and I saw your husband cross the street—

NORA: Yes.   330

KROGSTAD: With a lady.

NORA: Well?

KROGSTAD: Might I be so bold as to ask: was not that lady a Mrs. Linde?

NORA: Yes.

KROGSTAD: Recently arrived in town?   335

NORA: Yes, today.

KROGSTAD: She is a good friend of yours, is she not?

NORA: Yes, she is. But I don't see—

KROGSTAD: I used to know her too once.

NORA: I know.   340

KROGSTAD: Oh? You've discovered that. Yes, I thought you would. Well then, may I ask you a straight question: is Mrs. Linde to be employed at the bank?

NORA: How dare you presume to cross-examine me, Mr. Krogstad? You, one of my husband's employees? But since you ask, you shall have an answer. Yes, Mrs. Linde is to be employed by the bank. And I arranged it, Mr. Krogstad. Now you know.

KROGSTAD: I guessed right, then.

NORA (*walks up and down the room.*): Oh, one has a little influence, you know. Just because one's a woman it doesn't necessarily mean that— When one is in a humble position, Mr. Krogstad, one should think twice before offending someone who—hm—

KROGSTAD: —who has influence?   345

NORA: Precisely.

KROGSTAD (*changes his tone.*): Mrs. Helmer, will you have the kindness to use your influence on my behalf?

NORA: What? What do you mean?

KROGSTAD: Will you be so good as to see that I keep my humble position at the bank?

NORA: What do you mean? Who is thinking of removing you from your   350
position?

KROGSTAD: Oh, you don't need to play the innocent with me. I realize it can't be very pleasant for your friend to risk bumping into me; and now I also realize whom I have to thank for being hounded out like this.

NORA: But I assure you—

KROGSTAD: Look, let's not beat about the bush. There's still time, and I'd advise you to use your influence to stop it.

NORA: But, Mr. Krogstad, I have no influence!

KROGSTAD: Oh? I thought you just said— 355

NORA: But I didn't mean it like that! I? How on earth could you imagine that I would have any influence over my husband?

KROGSTAD: Oh, I've known your husband since we were students together. I imagine he has his weaknesses like other married men.

NORA: If you speak impertinently of my husband, I shall show you the door.

KROGSTAD: You're a bold woman, Mrs. Helmer.

NORA: I'm not afraid of you any longer. Once the New Year is in, I'll soon 360
be rid of you.

KROGSTAD (*more controlled.*): Now listen to me, Mrs. Helmer. If I'm forced to, I shall fight for my little job at the bank as I would fight for my life.

NORA: So it sounds.

KROGSTAD: It isn't just the money; that's the last thing I care about. There's something else—well, you might as well know. It's like this, you see. You know of course, as everyone else does, that some years ago I committed an indiscretion.

NORA: I think I did hear something—

KROGSTAD: It never came into court; but from that day, every opening was 365
barred to me. So I turned my hand to the kind of business you know about. I had to do something; and I don't think I was one of the worst. But now I want to give up all that. My sons are growing up; for their sake, I must try to regain what respectability I can. This job in the bank was the first step on the ladder. And now your husband wants to kick me off that ladder back into the dirt.

NORA: But my dear Mr. Krogstad, it simply isn't in my power to help you.

KROGSTAD: You say that because you don't want to help me. But I have the means to make you.

NORA: You don't mean you'd tell my husband that I owe you money?

KROGSTAD: And if I did?

NORA: That'd be a filthy trick! (*Almost in tears.*) This secret that is my pride 370
and my joy—that he should hear about it in such a filthy, beastly way—hear about it from you! It'd involve me in the most dreadful unpleasantness—

KROGSTAD: Only—unpleasantness?

NORA (*vehemently.*): All right, do it! You'll be the one who'll suffer. It'll show my husband the kind of man you are, and then you'll never keep your job.

KROGSTAD: I asked you whether it was merely domestic unpleasantness you were afraid of.

NORA: If my husband hears about it, he will of course immediately pay you whatever is owing. And then we shall have nothing more to do with you.

KROGSTAD (*takes a step closer.*): Listen, Mrs. Helmer. Either you've a bad   375
memory or else you know very little about financial transactions. I had
better enlighten you.

NORA: What do you mean?

KROGSTAD: When your husband was ill, you came to me to borrow two hundred and fifty pounds.

NORA: I didn't know anyone else.

KROGSTAD: I promised to find that sum for you—

NORA: And you did find it.   380

KROGSTAD: I promised to find that sum for you on certain conditions. You
were so worried about your husband's illness and so keen to get the
money to take him abroad that I don't think you bothered much about
the details. So it won't be out of place if I refresh your memory. Well—
I promised to get you the money in exchange for an I.O.U., which I
drew up.

NORA: Yes, and which I signed.

KROGSTAD: Exactly. But then I added a few lines naming your father as security for the debt. This paragraph was to be signed by your father.

NORA: Was to be? He did sign it.

KROGSTAD: I left the date blank for your father to fill in when he signed this   385
paper. You remember, Mrs. Helmer?

NORA: Yes, I think so—

KROGSTAD: Then I gave you back this I.O.U. for you to post to your father.
Is that not correct?

NORA: Yes.

KROGSTAD: And of course you posted it at once; for within five or six days
you brought it along to me with your father's signature on it. Whereupon I handed you the money.

NORA: Yes, well. Haven't I repaid the instalments as agreed?   390

KROGSTAD: Mm—yes, more or less. But to return to what we were speaking
about—that was a difficult time for you just then, wasn't it, Mrs. Helmer?

NORA: Yes, it was.

KROGSTAD: Your father was very ill, if I am not mistaken.

NORA: He was dying.

KROGSTAD: He did in fact die shortly afterwards?   395

NORA: Yes.

KROGSTAD: Tell me, Mrs. Helmer, do you by any chance remember the date
of your father's death? The day of the month, I mean.

NORA: Papa died on the twenty-ninth of September.

KROGSTAD: Quite correct; I took the trouble to confirm it. And that leaves
me with a curious little problem— (*Takes out a paper.*) —which I simply cannot solve.

NORA: Problem? I don't see—   400

KROGSTAD: The problem, Mrs. Helmer, is that your father signed this paper
three days after his death.

NORA: What? I don't understand—

KROGSTAD: Your father died on the twenty-ninth of September. But look at
this. Here your father has dated his signature the second of October.
Isn't that a curious little problem, Mrs. Helmer? (*Nora is silent.*) Can
you suggest any explanation? (*She remains silent.*) And there's another
curious thing. The words "second of October" and the year are written
in a hand which is not your father's, but which I seem to know. Well,
there's a simple explanation to that. Your father could have forgotten
to write in the date when he signed, and someone else could have
added it before the news came of his death. There's nothing criminal
about that. It's the signature itself I'm wondering about. It *is* genuine, I
suppose, Mrs. Helmer? It was your father who wrote his name here?

NORA (*after a short silence, throws back her head and looks defiantly at him.*):
No, it was not. It was I who wrote Papa's name there.

KROGSTAD: Look, Mrs. Helmer, do you realize this is a dangerous admission?   405

NORA: Why? You'll get your money.

KROGSTAD: May I ask you a question? Why didn't you send this paper to
your father?

NORA: I couldn't. Papa was very ill. If I'd asked him to sign this, I'd have had
to tell him what the money was for. But I couldn't have told him in his
condition that my husband's life was in danger. I couldn't have done that!

KROGSTAD: Then you would have been wiser to have given up your idea of
a holiday.

NORA: But I couldn't! It was to save my husband's life. I couldn't put it off.   410

KROGSTAD: But didn't it occur to you that you were being dishonest towards
me?

NORA: I couldn't bother about that. I didn't care about you. I hated you because of all the beastly difficulties you'd put in my way when you knew
how dangerously ill my husband was.

KROGSTAD: Mrs. Helmer, you evidently don't appreciate exactly what you
have done. But I can assure you that it is no bigger nor worse a crime
then the one I once committed, and thereby ruined my whole social
position.

NORA: You? Do you expect me to believe that you would have taken a risk
like that to save your wife's life?

KROGSTAD: The law does not concern itself with motives.   415

NORA: Then the law must be very stupid.

KROGSTAD: Stupid or not, if I show this paper to the police, you will be
judged according to it.

NORA: I don't believe that. Hasn't a daughter the right to shield her father from worry and anxiety when he's old and dying? Hasn't a wife the right to save her husband's life? I don't know much about the law, but there must be something somewhere that says that such things are allowed. You ought to know about that, you're meant to be a lawyer, aren't you? You can't be a very good lawyer, Mr. Krogstad.

KROGSTAD: Possibly not. But business, the kind of business we two have been transacting—I think you'll admit I understand something about that? Good. Do as you please. But I tell you this. If I get thrown into the gutter for a second time, I shall take you with me.

(*He bows and goes out through the hall.*)

NORA (*stands for a moment in thought, then tosses her head.*): What nonsense!   420
He's trying to frighten me! I'm not that stupid. (*Busies herself gathering together the children's clothes; then she suddenly stops.*) But—? No, it's impossible. I did it for love, didn't I?

THE CHILDREN (*in the doorway, left.*): Mummy, the strange gentleman's gone out into the street.

NORA: Yes, yes, I know. But don't talk to anyone about the strange gentleman. You hear? Not even to Daddy.

CHILDREN: No, Mummy. Will you play with us again now?

NORA: No, no. Not now.

CHILDREN: Oh but, Mummy, you promised!   425

NORA: I know, but I can't just now. Go back to the nursery. I've got a lot to do. Go away, my darlings, go away. (*She pushes them gently into the other room, and closes the door behind them. She sits on the sofa, takes up her embroidery, stitches for a few moments, but soon stops.*) No! (*Throws the embroidery aside, gets up, goes to the door leading to the hall and calls.*) Helen! Bring in the Christmas tree! (*She goes to the table on the left and opens the drawer in it; then pauses again.*) No, but it's utterly impossible!

MAID (*enters with the tree.*): Where shall I put it, madam?

NORA: There, in the middle of the room.

MAID: Will you be wanting anything else?

NORA: No, thank you. I have everything I need.   430

(*The MAID puts down the tree and goes out.*)

NORA (*busy decorating the tree.*): Now—candles here—and flowers here. That loathsome man! Nonsense, nonsense, there's nothing to be frightened about. The Christmas tree must be beautiful. I'll do everything that you like, Torvald. I'll sing for you, dance for you—

(HELMER, *with a bundle of papers under his arm, enters.*)

NORA: Oh—are you back already?

HELMER: Yes. Has anyone been here?

NORA: Here? No.

HELMER: That's strange. I saw Krogstad come out of the front door.   435

NORA: Did you? Oh yes, that's quite right—Krogstad was here for a few
minutes.

HELMER: Nora, I can tell from your face, he's been here and asked you to
put in a good word for him.

NORA: Yes.

HELMER: And you were to pretend you were doing it of your own accord?
You weren't going to tell me he'd been here? He asked you to do that
too, didn't he?

NORA: Yes, Torvald. But—   440

HELMER: Nora, Nora! And you were ready to enter into such a conspiracy?
Talking to a man like that, and making him promises—and then, on
top of it all, to tell me an untruth!

NORA: An untruth?

HELMER: Didn't you say no one had been here? (*Wags his finger.*) My little
songbird must never do that again. A songbird must have a clean beak
to sing with; otherwise she'll start twittering out of tune. (*Puts his arm
around her waist.*) Isn't that the way we want things? Yes, of course it is.
(*Lets go of her.*) So let's hear no more about that. (*Sits down in front of
the stove.*) Ah, how cosy and peaceful it is here. (*Glances for a few
moments at his papers.*)

NORA (*busy with the tree, after a short silence.*): Torvald.

HELMER: Yes.   445

NORA: I'm terribly looking forward to that fancy dress ball at the Stenborgs
on Boxing Day.

HELMER: And I'm terribly curious to see what you're going to surprise me with.

NORA: Oh, it's so maddening.

HELMER: What is?

NORA: I can't think of anything to wear. It all seems so stupid and   450
meaningless.

HELMER: So my little Nora's come to that conclusion, has she?

NORA (*behind his chair, resting her arms on its back.*): Are you very busy,
Torvald?

HELMER: Oh—

NORA: What are those papers?

HELMER: Just something to do with the bank.   455

NORA: Already?

HELMER: I persuaded the trustees to give me authority to make certain immediate changes in the staff and organization. I want to have everything straight by the New Year.

NORA: Then that's why this poor man Krogstad—

HELMER: Hm.

NORA (*still leaning over his chair, slowly strokes the back of his head.*): If you hadn't   460
been so busy, I was going to ask you an enormous favour, Torvald.

HELMER: Well, tell me. What was it to be?

NORA: You know I trust your taste more than anyone's. I'm so anxious to look really beautiful at the fancy dress ball. Torvald, couldn't you help me to decide what I shall go as, and what kind of costume I ought to wear?

HELMER: Aha! So little Miss Independent's in trouble and needs a man to rescue her, does she?

NORA: Yes, Torvald. I can't get anywhere without your help.

HELMER: Well, well, I'll give the matter thought. We'll find something. 465

NORA: Oh, how kind of you! (*Goes back to the tree. Pause.*) How pretty these red flowers look! But, tell me is it so dreadful, this thing that Krogstad's done?

HELMER: He forged someone else's name. Have you any idea what that means?

NORA: Mightn't he have been forced to do it by some emergency?

HELMER: He probably just didn't think—that's what usually happens. I'm not so heartless as to condemn a man for an isolated action.

NORA: No, Torvald, of course not! 470

HELMER: Men often succeed in re-establishing themselves if they admit their crime and take their punishment.

NORA: Punishment?

HELMER: But Krogstad didn't do that. He chose to try and trick his way out of it; and that's what has morally destroyed him.

NORA: You think that would—?

HELMER: Just think how a man with that load on his conscience must al- 475
ways be lying and cheating and dissembling; how he must wear a mask even in the presence of those who are dearest to him, even his own wife and children! Yes, the children. That's the worst danger, Nora.

NORA: Why?

HELMER: Because an atmosphere of lies contaminates and poisons every corner of the home. Every breath that the children draw in such a house contains the germs of evil.

NORA (*comes closer behind him.*): Do you really believe that?

HELMER: Oh, my dear, I've come across it so often in my work at the bar. Nearly all young criminals are the children of mothers who are constitutional liars.

NORA: Why do you say mothers? 480

HELMER: It's usually the mother; though of course the father can have the same influence. Every lawyer knows that only too well. And yet this fellow Krogstad has been sitting at home all these years poisoning his children with his lies and pretences. That's why I say that, morally speaking, he is dead. (*Stretches out his hands toward her.*) So my pretty little Nora must promise me not to plead his case. Your hand on it.

Come, come, what's this? Give me your hand. There. That's settled, now. I assure you it'd be quite impossible for me to work in the same building as him. I literally feel physically ill in the presence of a man like that.

NORA (*draws her hand from his and goes over to the other side of the Christmas tree.*): How hot it is in here! And I've so much to do.

HELMER (*gets up and gathers his papers.*): Yes, and I must try to get some of this read before dinner. I'll think about your costume too. And I may even have something up my sleeve to hang in gold paper on the Christmas tree. (*Lays his hand on her head.*) My precious little songbird!

(*He goes into his study and closes the door.*)

NORA (*softly, after a pause.*): It's nonsense. It must be. It's impossible. It *must* be impossible!

NURSE (*in the doorway, left.*): The children are asking if they can come in   485
to Mummy.

NORA: No, no, no; don't let them in! You stay with them, Anne-Marie.

NURSE: Very good, madam. (*Closes the door.*)

NORA (*pale with fear.*): Corrupt my little children—! Poison my home! (*Short pause. She throws back her head.*) It isn't true! It *couldn't* be true!

ACT II

(*The same room. In the corner by the piano the Christmas tree stands, stripped and disheveled, its candles burned to their sockets. NORA's outdoor clothes lie on the sofa. She is alone in the room, walking restlessly to and fro. At length she stops by the sofa and picks up her coat.*)

NORA (*drops the coat again.*): There's someone coming! (*Goes to the door and listens.*) No, it's no one. Of course—no one'll come today, it's Christmas Day. Nor tomorrow. But perhaps—! (*Opens the door and looks out.*) No. Nothing in the letter-box. Quite empty. (*Walks across the room.*) Silly, silly. Of course he won't do anything. It couldn't happen. It isn't possible. Why, I've three small children.

(*The NURSE, carrying a large cardboard box, enters from the room on the left.*)

NURSE: I found those fancy dress clothes at last, madam.

NORA: Thank you. Put them on the table.

NURSE (*does so.*): They're all rumpled up.

NORA: Oh, I wish I could tear them into a million pieces!   5

NURSE: Why, madam! They'll be all right. Just a little patience.

NORA: Yes, of course. I'll go and get Mrs. Linde to help me.

NURSE: What, out again? In this dreadful weather? You'll catch a chill, madam.

NORA: Well, that wouldn't be the worst. How are the children?

NURSE: Playing with their Christmas presents, poor little dears. But—   10

NORA: Are they still asking to see me?

NURSE: They're so used to having their Mummy with them.

NORA: Yes, but, Anne-Marie, from now on I shan't be able to spend so much time with them.

NURSE: Well, children get used to anything in time.

NORA: Do you think so? Do you think they'd forget their mother if she went away from them—for ever? 15

NURSE: Mercy's sake, madam! For ever!

NORA: Tell me, Anne-Marie—I've so often wondered. How could you bear to give your child away—to strangers?

NURSE: But I had to when I came to nurse my little Miss Nora.

NORA: Do you mean you wanted to?

NURSE: When I had the chance of such a good job? A poor girl what's got into trouble can't afford to pick and choose. That good-for-nothing didn't lift a finger. 20

NORA: But your daughter must have completely forgotten you.

NURSE: Oh no, indeed she hasn't. She's written to me twice, once when she got confirmed and then again when she got married.

NORA (hugs her.): Dear old Anne-Marie, you were a good mother to me.

NURSE: Poor little Miss Nora, you never had any mother but me.

NORA: And if my little ones had no one else, I know you would—no, silly, silly, silly! (Opens the cardboard box.) Go back to them, Anne-Marie. Now I must—Tomorrow you'll see how pretty I shall look. 25

NURSE: Why, there'll be no one at the ball as beautiful as my Miss Nora. (She goes into the room, left.)

NORA (begins to unpack the clothes from the box, but soon throws them down again.): Oh, if only I dared go out! If I could be sure no one would come and nothing would happen while I was away! Stupid, stupid! No one will come. I just mustn't think about it. Brush this muff. Pretty gloves, pretty gloves! Don't think about it, don't think about it! One, two, three, four, five, six—(Cries.) Ah—they're coming—! (She begins to run towards the door, but stops uncertainly. MRS. LINDE enters from the hall, where she has been taking off her outdoor clothes.)

NORA: Oh, it's you, Christine. There's no one else out there, is there? Oh, I'm so glad you've come.

MRS LINDE: I hear you were at my room asking for me.

NORA: Yes, I just happened to be passing. I want to ask you to help me with something. Let's sit down here on the sofa. Look at this. There's going to be a fancy dress ball tomorrow night upstairs at Consul Stenborg's, and Torvald wants me to go as a Neapolitan fisher-girl and dance the tarantella. I learned it on Capri. 30

MRS. LINDE: I say, are you going to give a performance?

NORA: Yes, Torvald says I should. Look, here's the dress. Torvald had it made for me in Italy; but now it's all so torn, I don't know—

MRS. LINDE: Oh, we'll soon put that right; the stitching's just come away. Needle and thread? Ah, here we are.

NORA: You're being awfully sweet.

MRS. LINDE (sews.): So you're going to dress up tomorrow, Nora? I must pop over for a moment to see how you look. Oh, but I've completely forgotten to thank you for that nice evening yesterday.

NORA (gets up and walks across the room.): Oh, I didn't think it was as nice as usual. You ought to have come to town a little earlier, Christine…. Yes, Torvald understands how to make a home look attractive.

MRS. LINDE: I'm sure you do, too. You're not your father's daughter for nothing. But tell me. Is Dr. Rank always in such low spirits as he was yesterday?

NORA: No, last night it was very noticeable. But he's got a terrible disease; he's got spinal tuberculosis, poor man. His father was a frightful creature who kept mistresses and so on. As a result Dr. Rank has been sickly ever since he was a child—you understand—

MRS. LINDE (puts down her sewing.): But, my dear Nora, how on earth did you get to know about such things?

NORA (walks about the room.): Oh, don't be silly, Christine—when one has three children, one comes into contact with women who—well, who know about medical matters, and they tell one a thing or two.

MRS. LINDE (sews again; a short silence.): Does Dr. Rank visit you every day?

NORA: Yes, every day. He's Torvald's oldest friend, and a good friend to me too. Dr. Rank's almost one of the family.

MRS. LINDE: But, tell me—is he quite sincere? I mean, doesn't he rather say the sort of thing he thinks people want to hear?

NORA: No, quite the contrary. What gave you that idea?

MRS. LINDE: When you introduced me to him yesterday, he said he'd often heard my name mentioned here. But later I noticed your husband had no idea who I was. So how could Dr. Rank—?

NORA: Yes, that's quite right, Christine. You see, Torvald's so hopelessly in love with me that he wants to have me all to himself—those were his very words. When we were first married, he got quite jealous if I as much as mentioned any of my old friends back home. So naturally, I stopped talking about them. But I often chat with Dr. Rank about that kind of thing. He enjoys it, you see.

MRS. LINDE: Now listen, Nora. In many ways you're still a child; I'm a bit older than you and have a little more experience of the world. There's something I want to say to you. You ought to give up this business with Dr. Rank.

NORA: What business?

MRS. LINDE: Well, everything. Last night you were speaking about this rich admirer of yours who was going to give you money—

NORA: Yes, and who doesn't exist—unfortunately. But what's that got to do with—? 50

MRS. LINDE: Is Dr. Rank rich?

NORA: Yes.

MRS. LINDE: And he has no dependents?

NORA: No, no one. But—

MRS. LINDE: And he comes here to see you every day? 55

NORA: Yes, I've told you.

MRS. LINDE: But how dare a man of his education be so forward?

NORA: What on earth are you talking about?

MRS. LINDE: Oh, stop pretending, Nora. Do you think I haven't guessed who it was who lent you that two hundred pounds?

NORA: Are you out of your mind? How could you imagine such a thing? A 60 friend, someone who comes here every day! Why, that'd be an impossible situation!

MRS. LINDE: Then it really wasn't him?

NORA: No, of course not. I've never for a moment dreamed of—anyway, he hadn't any money to lend then. He didn't come into that till later.

MRS. LINDE: Well, I think that was a lucky thing for you, Nora dear.

NORA: No, I could never have dreamed of asking Dr. Rank—though I'm sure that if I ever did ask him—

MRS. LINDE: But of course you won't. 65

NORA: Of course not. I can't imagine that it should ever become necessary. But I'm perfectly sure that if I did speak to Dr. Rank—

MRS. LINDE: Behind your husband's back?

NORA: I've got to get out of this other business; and *that's* been going on behind his back. I've *got* to get out of it.

MRS. LINDE: Yes, well, that's what I told you yesterday. But—

NORA *(walking up and down.)*: It's much easier for a man to arrange these 70 things than a woman—

MRS. LINDE: One's own husband, yes.

NORA: Oh, bosh. *(Stops walking.)*: When you've completely repaid a debt, you get your I.O.U. back, don't you?

MRS. LINDE: Yes, of course.

NORA: And you can tear it into a thousand pieces and burn the filthy, beastly thing!

MRS. LINDE *(looks hard at her, puts down her sewing and gets up slowly.)*: Nora, 75 you're hiding something from me.

NORA: Can you see that?

MRS. LINDE: Something has happened since yesterday morning. Nora, what is it?

NORA (*goes toward her.*): Christine! (*Listens.*) Ssh! There's Torvald. Would you mind going into the nursery for a few minutes? Torvald can't bear to see sewing around. Anne-Marie'll help you.

MRS. LINDE (*gathers some of her things together.*): Very well. But I shan't leave this house until we've talked this matter out.

(*She goes into the nursery, left. As she does so,* HELMER *enters from the hall.*)

NORA (*runs to meet him.*): Oh, Torvald dear, I've been so longing for you to come back!   80

HELMER: Was that the dressmaker?

NORA: No, it was Christine. She's helping me mend my costume. I'm going to look rather splendid in that.

HELMER: Yes, that was quite a bright idea of mine, wasn't it?

NORA: Wonderful! But wasn't it nice of me to give in to you?

HELMER (*takes her chin in his hand.*): Nice—to give in to your husband? All   85
right, little silly, I know you didn't mean it like that. But I won't disturb you. I expect you'll be wanting to try it on.

NORA: Are you going to work now?

HELMER: Yes. (*Shows her a bundle of papers.*) Look at these. I've been down to the bank—(*Turns to go into his study.*)

NORA: Torvald.

HELMER (*stops.*): Yes.

NORA: If little squirrel asked you really prettily to grant her a wish—   90

HELMER: Well?

NORA: Would you grant it to her?

HELMER: First I should naturally have to know what it was.

NORA: Squirrel would do lots of pretty tricks for you if you granted her wish.

HELMER: Out with it, then.   95

NORA: Your little skylark would sing in every room—

HELMER: My little skylark does that already.

NORA: I'd turn myself into a little fairy and dance for you in the moonlight, Torvald.

HELMER: Nora, it isn't that business you were talking about this morning?

NORA (*comes closer.*): Yes, Torvald—oh, please! I beg of you!   100

HELMER: Have you really the nerve to bring that up again?

NORA: Yes, Torvald, yes, you must do as I ask! You must let Krogstad keep his place at the bank!

HELMER: My dear Nora, his is the job I'm giving to Mrs. Linde.

NORA: Yes, that's terribly sweet of you. But you can get rid of one of the other clerks instead of Krogstad.

HELMER: Really, you're being incredibly obstinate. Just because you thought-   105
lessly promised to put in a word for him, you expect me to—

NORA: No, it isn't that, Helmer. It's for your own sake. That man writes for
the most beastly newspapers—you said so yourself. He could do you tremendous harm. I'm so dreadfully frightened of him—

HELMER: Oh, I understand. Memories of the past. That's what's frightening
you.

NORA: What do you mean?

HELMER: You're thinking of your father, aren't you?

NORA: Yes, yes. Of course. Just think what those dreadful men wrote in the   110
papers about Papa! The most frightful slanders. I really believe it would
have lost him his job if the Ministry hadn't sent you down to investigate, and you hadn't been so kind and helpful to him.

HELMER: But my dear little Nora, there's a considerable difference between
your father and me. Your father was not a man of unassailable reputation. But I am; and I hope to remain so all my life.

NORA: But no one knows what spiteful people may not dig up. We could be
so peaceful and happy now, Torvald—we could be free from every
worry—you and I and the children. Oh, please Torvald, please—!

HELMER: The very fact of your pleading his cause makes it impossible for
me to keep him. Everyone at the bank already knows that I intend to
dismiss Krogstad. If the rumor got about that the new manager had
allowed his wife to persuade him to change his mind—

NORA: Well, what then?

HELMER: Oh, nothing, nothing. As long as my little Miss Obstinate gets her   115
way—! Do you expect me to make a laughing-stock of myself before my
entire staff—give people the idea that I am open to outside influence?
Believe me, I'd soon feel the consequences! Besides—there's something
else that makes it impossible for Krogstad to remain in the bank while I
am its manager.

NORA: What is that?

HELMER: I might conceivably have allowed myself to ignore his moral
obloquies—

NORA: Yes, Torvald, surely?

HELMER: And I hear he's quite efficient at his job. But we—well, we were
schoolfriends. It was one of those friendships that one enters into over-
hastily and so often comes to regret later in life. I might as well confess
the truth. We—well, we're on Christian name terms. And the tactless
idiot makes no attempt to conceal it when other people are present. On
the contrary, he thinks it gives him the right to be familiar with me.
He shows off the whole time, with "Torvald this," and "Torvald that."
I can tell you, I find it damned annoying. If he stayed, he'd make my
position intolerable.

NORA: Torvald, you can't mean this seriously. 120

HELMER: Oh? And why not?

NORA: But it's so petty.

HELMER: What did you say? Petty? You think *I* am petty?

NORA: No, Torvald dear, of course you're not. That's just why—

HELMER: Don't quibble! You call my motives petty. Then I must be petty 125
too. Petty! I see. Well, I've had enough of this. *(Goes to the door and calls into the hall.)* Helen!

NORA: What are you going to do?

HELMER *(searching among his papers.)*: I'm going to settle this matter once and for all. *(The* MAID *enters.)* Take this letter downstairs at once. Find a messenger and see that he delivers it. Immediately! The address is on the envelope. Here's the money.

MAID: Very good, sir. *(Goes out with the letter.)*

HELMER *(putting his papers in order.)*: There now, little Miss Obstinate.

NORA *(tensely.)*: Torvald—what was in that letter? 130

HELMER: Krogstad's dismissal.

NORA: Call her back, Torvald! There's still time. Oh, Torvald, call her back! Do it for my sake—for your own sake—for the children! Do you hear me, Torvald? Please do it! You don't realize what this may do to us all!

HELMER: Too late.

NORA: Yes. Too late.

HELMER: My dear Nora, I forgive you this anxiety. Though it is a bit of an 135
insult to me. Oh, but it is! Isn't it an insult to imply that I should be frightened by the vindictiveness of a depraved hack journalist? But I forgive you, because it so charmingly testifies to the love you bear me. *(Takes her in his arms.)* Which is as it should be, my own dearest Nora. Let what will happen, happen. When the real crisis comes, you will not find me lacking in strength or courage. I am man enough to bear the burden for us both.

NORA *(fearfully.)*: What do you mean?

HELMER: The whole burden, I say—

NORA *(calmly.)*: I shall never let you do that.

HELMER: Very well. We shall share it, Nora—as man and wife. And that is as it should be. *(Caresses her.)* Are you happy now? There, there, there; don't look at me with those frightened little eyes. You're simply imagining things. You go ahead now and do your tarantella, and get some practice on that tambourine. I'll sit in my study and close the door. Then I won't hear anything, and you can make all the noise you want. *(Turns in the doorway.)* When Dr. Rank comes, tell him where to find me. *(He nods to her, goes into his room with his papers and closes the door.)*

NORA *(desperate with anxiety, stands as though transfixed, and whispers.)*: He 140
said he'd do it. He will do it. He will do it, and nothing'll stop him. No,

never that. I'd rather anything. There must be some escape—! Some
way out—! (*The bell rings in the hall.*) Dr. Rank—! Anything but that!
Anything, I don't care—!

(*She passes her hand across her face, composes herself, walks across and opens the
door to the hall.* DR. RANK *is standing there, hanging up his fur coat. During
the following scene it begins to grow dark.*)

NORA: Good evening, Dr. Rank. I recognized your ring. But you mustn't go
in to Torvald yet. I think he's busy.

RANK: And—you?

NORA (*as he enters the room and she closes the door behind him.*): Oh, you
know very well I've always time to talk to you.

RANK: Thank you. I shall avail myself of that privilege as long as I can.

NORA: What do you mean by that? As long as you *can?*

RANK: Yes. Does that frighten you?

NORA: Well, it's rather a curious expression. Is something going to happen?

RANK: Something I've been expecting to happen for a long time. But I
didn't think it would happen quite so soon.

NORA (*seizes his arm.*): What is it? Dr. Rank, you must tell me!

RANK (*sits down by the stove.*): I'm on the way out. And there's nothing to
be done about it.

NORA (*sighs with relief.*): Oh, it's you—?

RANK: Who else? No, it's no good lying to oneself. I am the most
wretched of all my patients, Mrs. Helmer. These last few days I've
been going through the books of this poor body of mine, and I find
I am bankrupt. Within a month I may be rotting up there in the
churchyard.

NORA: Ugh, what a nasty way to talk!

RANK: The facts aren't exactly nice. But the worst is that there's so much
else that's nasty to come first. I've only one more test to make. When
that's done I'll have a pretty accurate idea of when the final disintegra-
tion is likely to begin. I want to ask you a favor. Helmer's a sensitive
chap, and I know how he hates anything ugly. I don't want him to visit
me when I'm in hospital—

NORA: Oh but, Dr. Rank—

RANK: I don't want him there. On any pretext. I shan't have him allowed in.
As soon as I know the worst, I'll send you my visiting card with a black
cross on it, and then you'll know that the final filthy process has begun.

NORA: Really, you're being quite impossible this evening. And I did hope
you'd be in a good mood.

RANK: With death on my hands? And all this to atone for someone else's
sin? Is there justice in that? And in every single family, in one way or
another, the same merciless law of retribution is at work—

NORA (*holds her hands to her ears.*): Nonsense! Cheer up! Laugh!

RANK: Yes, you're right. Laughter's all the damned thing's fit for. My poor   160
innocent spine must pay for the fun my father had as a gay young
lieutenant.

NORA (*at the table, left.*): You mean he was too fond of asparagus and *foie gras?*

RANK: Yes; and truffles too.

NORA: Yes, of course, truffles, yes. And oysters too, I suppose?

RANK: Yes, oysters, oysters. Of course.

NORA: And all that port and champagne to wash them down. It's too sad   165
that all those lovely things should affect one's spine.

RANK: Especially a poor spine that never got any pleasure out of them.

NORA: Oh yes, that's the saddest thing of all.

RANK (*looks searchingly at her.*): Hm—

NORA (*after a moment.*): Why did you smile?

RANK: No, it was you who laughed.   170

NORA: No, it was you who smiled, Dr. Rank!

RANK (*gets up.*): You're a worse little rogue than I thought.

NORA: Oh, I'm full of stupid tricks today.

RANK: So it seems.

NORA (*puts both her hands on his shoulders.*): Dear, dear Dr. Rank, you   175
mustn't die and leave Torvald and me.

RANK: Oh, you'll soon get over it. Once one is gone, one is soon forgotten.

NORA (*looks at him anxiously.*): Do you believe that?

RANK: One finds replacements, and then—

NORA: Who will find a replacement?

RANK: You and Helmer both will, when I am gone. You seem to have made   180
a start already, haven't you? What was this Mrs. Linde doing here yesterday evening?

NORA: Aha! But surely you can't be jealous of poor Christine?

RANK: Indeed I am. She will be my successor in this house. When I have
moved on, this lady will—

NORA: Ssh—don't speak so loud! She's in there!

RANK: Today again? You see!

NORA: She's only come to mend my dress. Good heavens, how unreasonable   185
you are! (*Sits on the sofa.*) Be nice now, Dr. Rank. Tomorrow you'll see
how beautifully I shall dance; and you must imagine that I'm doing it
just for you. And for Torvald, of course; obviously. (*Takes some things
out of the box.*) Dr. Rank, sit down here and I'll show you something.

RANK (*sits.*): What's this?

NORA: Look here! Look!

RANK: Silk stockings!

NORA: Flesh-coloured. Aren't they beautiful? It's very dark in here now, of
course, but tomorrow—! No, no, no; only the soles. Oh well, I suppose
you can look a bit higher if you want to.

RANK: Hm— 190

NORA: Why are you looking so critical? Don't you think they'll fit me?

RANK: I can't really give you a qualified opinion on that.

NORA *(looks at him for a moment.)*: Shame on you! *(Flicks him on the ear with the stockings.)* Take that. *(Puts them back in the box.)*

RANK: What other wonders are to be revealed to me?

NORA: I shan't show you anything else. You're being naughty. 195

(She hums a little and looks among the things in the box.)

RANK *(after a short silence.)*: When I sit here like this being so intimate with you, I can't think—I cannot imagine what would have become of me if I had never entered this house.

NORA *(smiles.)*: Yes, I think you enjoy being with us, don't you?

RANK *(more quietly, looking into the middle distance.)*: And now to have to leave it all—

NORA: Nonsense. You're not leaving us.

RANK *(as before.)*: And not to be able to leave even the most wretched 200 token of gratitude behind; hardly even a passing sense of loss; only an empty place, to be filled by the next comer.

NORA: Suppose I were to ask you to—? No—

RANK: To do what?

NORA: To give me proof of your friendship—

RANK: Yes, yes?

NORA: No, I mean—to do me a very great service— 205

RANK: Would you really for once grant me that happiness?

NORA: But you've no idea what it is.

RANK: Very well, tell me, then.

NORA: No, but, Dr. Rank, I can't. It's far too much—I want your help and advice, and I want you to do something for me.

RANK: The more the better. I've no idea what it can be. But tell me. You 210 do trust me, don't you?

NORA: Oh, yes, more than anyone. You're my best and truest friend. Otherwise I couldn't tell you. Well then, Dr. Rank—there's something you must help me to prevent. You know how much Torvald loves me—he'd never hesitate for an instant to lay down his life for me—

RANK *(leans over toward her.)*: Nora—do you think he is the only one—?

NORA *(with a slight start.)*: What do you mean?

RANK: Who would gladly lay down his life for you?

NORA *(sadly.)*: Oh, I see. 215

RANK: I swore to myself I would let you know that before I go. I shall never have a better opportunity.... Well, Nora, now you know that. And now you also know that you can trust me as you can trust nobody else.

NORA *(rises; calmly and quietly.)*: Let me pass, please.

RANK *(makes room for her but remains seated.)*: Nora—

NORA (*in the doorway to the hall.*): Helen, bring the lamp. (*Goes over to the stove.*) Oh, dear Dr. Rank, this was really horrid of you.

RANK (*gets up.*): That I have loved you as deeply as anyone else has? Was   220
that horrid of me?

NORA: No—but that you should go and tell me. That was quite unnecessary—

RANK: What do you mean? Did you know, then—?

(*The* MAID *enters with the lamp, puts it on the table and goes out.*)

RANK: Nora—Mrs. Helmer—I am asking you, did you know this?

NORA: Oh, what do I know, what did I know, what didn't I know—I really can't say. How could you be so stupid, Dr. Rank? Everything was so nice.

RANK: Well, at any rate now you know that I am ready to serve you, body   225
and soul. So—please continue.

NORA (*looks at him.*): After this?

RANK: Please tell me what it is.

NORA: I can't possibly tell you now.

RANK: Yes, yes! You mustn't punish me like this. Let me be allowed to do what I can for you.

NORA: You can't do anything for me now. Anyway, I don't need any help. It   230
was only my imagination—you'll see. Yes, really. Honestly. (*Sits in the rocking chair, looks at him and smiles.*) Well, upon my word you *are* a fine gentleman, Dr. Rank. Aren't you ashamed of yourself, now that the lamp's been lit?

RANK: Frankly, no. But perhaps I ought to say—*adieu?*

NORA: Of course not. You will naturally continue to visit us as before. You know quite well how Torvald depends on your company.

RANK: Yes, but you?

NORA: Oh, I always think it's enormous fun having you here.

RANK: That was what misled me. You're a riddle to me, you know. I'd often   235
felt you'd just as soon be with me as with Helmer.

NORA: Well, you see, there are some people whom one loves, and others whom it's almost more fun to be with.

RANK: Oh yes, there's some truth in that.

NORA: When I was at home, of course I loved Papa best. But I always used to think it was terribly amusing to go down and talk to the servants; because they never told me what I ought to do; and they were such fun to listen to.

RANK: I see. So I've taken their place?

NORA (*jumps up and runs over to him.*): Oh, dear sweet Dr. Rank, I didn't   240
mean that at all. But I'm sure you understand—I feel the same about Torvald as I did about Papa.

MAID (*enters from the hall.*): Excuse me, madam. (*Whispers to her and hands her a visiting card.*)

NORA *(glances at the card.)*: Oh! *(Puts it quickly in her pocket.)*

RANK: Anything wrong?

NORA: No, no, nothing at all. It's just something that—it's my new dress.

RANK: What? But your costume is lying over there.   24

NORA: Oh—that, yes—but there's another—I ordered it specially—Torvald mustn't know—

RANK: Ah, so that's your big secret?

NORA: Yes, yes. Go in and talk to him—he's in his study—keep him talking for a bit—

RANK: Don't worry. He won't get away from me. *(Goes into* HELMER'*s study.)*

NORA *(to the* MAID.*)*: Is he waiting in the kitchen?   25

MAID: Yes, madam, he came up the back way—

NORA: But didn't you tell him I had a visitor?

MAID: Yes, but he wouldn't go.

NORA: Wouldn't go?

MAID: No, madam, not until he'd spoken with you.   25

NORA: Very well, show him in; but quietly. Helen, you mustn't tell anyone about this. It's a surprise for my husband.

MAID: Very good, madam. I understand. *(Goes.)*

NORA: It's happening. It's happening after all. No, no, no, it can't happen, it mustn't happen.

(She walks across and bolts the door of HELMER'*s study. The* MAID *opens the door from the hall to admit* KROGSTAD, *and closes it behind him. He is wearing an overcoat, heavy boots and a fur cap.)*

NORA *(goes toward him.)*: Speak quietly. My husband's at home.

KROGSTAD: Let him hear.   26

NORA: What do you want from me?

KROGSTAD: Information.

NORA: Hurry up, then. What is it?

KROGSTAD: I suppose you know I've been given the sack.

NORA: I couldn't stop it, Mr. Krogstad. I did my best for you, but it didn't   26
help.

KROGSTAD: Does your husband love you so little? He knows what I can do to you, and yet he dares to—

NORA: Surely you don't imagine I told him?

KROGSTAD: No, I didn't really think you had. It wouldn't have been like my old friend Torvald Helmer to show that much courage—

NORA: Mr. Krogstad, I'll trouble you to speak respectfully of my husband.

KROGSTAD: Don't worry, I'll show him all the respect he deserves. But since   27
you're so anxious to keep this matter hushed up, I presume you're better informed than you were yesterday of the gravity of what you've done?

NORA: I've learned more than you could ever teach me.

KROGSTAD: Yes, a bad lawyer like me—

NORA: What do you want from me?

KROGSTAD: I just wanted to see how things were with you, Mrs. Helmer.
  I've been thinking about you all day. Even duns and hack journalists
  have hearts, you know.

NORA: Show some heart, then. Think of my little children.   275

KROGSTAD: Have you and your husband thought of mine? Well, let's forget
  that. I just wanted to tell you, you don't need to take this business too
  seriously. I'm not going to take any action for the present.

NORA: Oh, no—you won't, will you? I knew it.

KROGSTAD: It can all be settled quite amicably. There's no need for it to become public. We'll keep it among the three of us.

NORA: My husband must never know about this.

KROGSTAD: How can you stop him? Can you pay the balance of what you   280
  owe me?

NORA: Not immediately.

KROGSTAD: Have you any means of raising the money during the next few
  days?

NORA: None that I would care to use.

KROGSTAD: Well, it wouldn't have helped anyway. However much money
  you offered me now I wouldn't give you back that paper.

NORA: What are you going to do with it?   285

KROGSTAD: Just keep it. No one else need ever hear about it. So in case you
  were thinking of doing anything desperate—

NORA: I am.

KROGSTAD: Such as running away—

NORA: I am.

KROGSTAD: Or anything more desperate—   290

NORA: How did you know?

KROGSTAD: —just give up the idea.

NORA: How did you know?

KROGSTAD: Most of us think of that at first. I did. But I hadn't the
  courage—

NORA (*dully.*): Neither have I.   295

KROGSTAD (*relieved.*): It's true, isn't it? You haven't the courage either?

NORA: No. I haven't. I haven't.

KROGSTAD: It'd be a stupid thing to do anyway. Once the first little domestic explosion is over.... I've got a letter in my pocket here addressed to
  your husband—

NORA: Telling him everything?

KROGSTAD: As delicately as possibly.   300

NORA (*quickly.*): He must never see that letter. Tear it up. I'll find the
  money somehow—

KROGSTAD: I'm sorry, Mrs. Helmer, I thought I'd explained—

NORA: Oh, I don't mean the money I owe you. Let me know how much you want from my husband, and I'll find it for you.

KROGSTAD: I'm not asking your husband for money.

NORA: What do you want, then?   305

KROGSTAD: I'll tell you. I want to get on my feet again, Mrs. Helmer. I want to get to the top. And your husband's going to help me. For eighteen months now my record's been clean. I've been in hard straits all that time; I was content to fight my way back inch by inch. Now I've been chucked back into the mud, and I'm not going to be satisfied with just getting back my job. I'm going to get to the top, I tell you. I'm going to get back into the bank, and it's going to be higher up. Your husband's going to create a new job for me—

NORA: He'll never do that!

KROGSTAD: Oh, yes he will. I know him. He won't dare to risk a scandal. And once I'm in there with him, you'll see! Within a year I'll be his right-hand man. It'll be Nils Krogstad who'll be running that bank, not Torvald Helmer!

NORA: That will never happen.

KROGSTAD: Are you thinking of—?   31C

NORA: Now I *have* the courage.

KROGSTAD: Oh, you can't frighten me. A pampered little pretty like you—

NORA: You'll see! You'll see!

KROGSTAD: Under the ice? Down in the cold, black water? And then, in the spring to float up again, ugly, unrecognizable, hairless—?

NORA: You can't frighten me.   31!

KROGSTAD: And you can't frighten me. People don't do such things, Mrs. Helmer. And anyway, what'd be the use? I've got him in my pocket.

NORA: But afterwards? When I'm no longer—?

KROGSTAD: Have you forgotten that then your reputation will be in my hands? (*She looks at him speechlessly.*) Well, I've warned you. Don't do anything silly. When Helmer's read my letter, he'll get in touch with me. And remember, it's your husband who's forced me to act like this. And for that I'll never forgive him. Goodbye, Mrs. Helmer.

(*He goes out through the hall.*)

NORA (*runs to the hall door, opens it a few inches and listens.*): He's going. He's not going to give him the letter. Oh, no, no, it couldn't possibly happen. (*Opens the door a little wider.*) What's he doing? Standing outside the front door. He's not going downstairs. Is he changing his mind? Yes, he—!

(*A letter falls into the letter-box.* KROGSTAD's *footsteps die away down the stairs.*)

NORA (*with a stifled cry, runs across the room toward the table by the sofa. A pause.*): In the letter-box. (*Steals timidly over toward the hall door.*) There it is! Oh, Torvald, Torvald! Now we're lost!   32♦

MRS. LINDE (*enters from the nursery with* NORA's *costume.*): Well, I've done the best I can. Shall we see how it looks—?

NORA (*whispers hoarsely.*): Christine, come here.

MRS. LINDE (*throws the dress on the sofa.*): What's wrong with you? You look as though you'd seen a ghost!

NORA: Come here. Do you see that letter? There—look—through the glass of the letter-box.

MRS. LINDE: Yes, yes, I see it.   325

NORA: That letter's from Krogstad—

MRS. LINDE: Nora! It was Krogstad who lent you the money!

NORA: Yes. And now Torvald's going to discover everything.

MRS. LINDE: Oh, believe me, Nora, it'll be best for you both.

NORA: You don't know what's happened. I've committed a forgery—   330

MRS. LINDE: But, for heaven's sake—!

NORA: Christine, all I want is for you to be my witness.

MRS. LINDE: What do you mean? Witness what?

NORA: If I should go out of my mind—and it might easily happen—

MRS. LINDE: Nora!   335

NORA: Or if anything else should happen to me—so that I wasn't here any longer—

MRS. LINDE: Nora, Nora, you don't know what you're saying!

NORA: If anyone should try to take the blame, and say it was all his fault—you understand—?

MRS. LINDE: Yes, yes—but how can you think—?

NORA: Then you must testify that it isn't true, Christine. I'm not mad—I   340
know exactly what I'm saying—and I'm telling you, no one else knows anything about this. I did it entirely on my own. Remember that.

MRS. LINDE: All right. But I simply don't understand—

NORA: Oh, how could you understand? A miracle—is—about to happen.

MRS. LINDE: Miracle?

NORA: Yes. A miracle. But it's so frightening, Christine. It *mustn't* happen, not for anything in the world.

MRS. LINDE: I'll go over and talk to Krogstad.   345

NORA: Don't go near him. He'll only do something to hurt you.

MRS. LINDE: Once upon a time he'd have done anything for my sake.

NORA: He?

MRS. LINDE: Where does he live?

NORA: Oh, how should I know—? Oh yes, wait a moment—! (*Feels in her*   350
pocket.) Here's his card. But the letter, the letter—!

HELMER (*from his study, knocks on the door.*): Nora!

NORA (*cries in alarm.*): What is it?

HELMER: Now, now, don't get alarmed. We're not coming in, you've closed the door. Are you trying on your costume?

NORA: Yes, yes—I'm trying on my costume. I'm going to look so pretty for you, Torvald.

MRS. LINDE (*who has been reading the card.*): Why, he lives just round the corner.   355

NORA: Yes; but it's no use. There's nothing to be done now. The letter's lying there in the box.

MRS. LINDE: And your husband has the key?

NORA: Yes, he always keeps it.

MRS. LINDE: Krogstad must ask him to send the letter back unread. He must find some excuse—

NORA: But Torvald always opens the box at just about this time—   360

MRS. LINDE: You must stop him. Go in and keep him talking. I'll be back as quickly as I can.

(*She hurries out through the hall.*)

NORA (*goes over to* HELMER's *door, opens it and peeps in.*): Torvald!

HELMER (*offstage.*): Well, may a man enter his own drawing room again? Come on, Rank, now we'll see what— (*In the doorway.*) But what's this?

NORA: What, Torvald dear?

HELMER: Rank's been preparing me for some great transformation scene.   365

RANK (*in the doorway.*): So I understood. But I seem to have been mistaken.

NORA: Yes, no one's to be allowed to see me before tomorrow night.

HELMER: But, my dear Nora, you look quite worn out. Have you been practising too hard?

NORA: No, I haven't practised at all yet.

HELMER: Well, you must.   370

NORA: Yes, Torvald, I must, I know. But I can't get anywhere without your help. I've completely forgotten everything.

HELMER: Oh, we'll soon put that to rights.

NORA: Yes, help me, Torvald. Promise me you will? Oh, I'm so nervous. All those people—! You must forget everything except me this evening. You mustn't think of business—I won't even let you touch a pen. Promise me, Torvald?

HELMER: I promise. This evening I shall think of nothing but you—my poor, helpless little darling. Oh, there's just one thing I must see to—(*Goes toward the hall door.*)

NORA: What do you want out there?   375

HELMER: I'm only going to see if any letters have come.

NORA: No, Torvald, no!

HELMER: Why, what's the matter?

NORA: Torvald, I beg you. There's nothing there.

HELMER: Well, I'll just make sure.   380

(*He moves toward the door.* NORA *runs to the piano and plays the first bars of the tarantella.*)

HELMER (*at the door, turns.*): Aha!

NORA: I can't dance tomorrow if I don't practise with you now.

HELMER (*goes over to her.*): Are you really so frightened, Nora dear?

NORA: Yes, terribly frightened. Let me start practising now, at once—we've still time before dinner. Oh, do sit down and play for me, Torvald dear. Correct me, lead me, the way you always do.

HELMER: Very well, my dear, if you wish it.   385

(*He sits down at the piano.* NORA *seizes the tambourine and a long multi-coloured shawl from the cardboard box, wraps the latter hastily around her, then takes a quick leap into the center of the room.*)

NORA: Play for me! I want to dance!

(HELMER *plays and* NORA *dances.* DR. RANK *stands behind* HELMER *at the piano and watches her.*)

HELMER (*as he plays.*): Slower, slower!

NORA: I can't!

HELMER: Not so violently, Nora.

NORA: I must!   390

HELMER (*stops playing.*): No, no, this won't do at all.

NORA (*laughs and swings her tambourine.*): Isn't that what I told you?

RANK: Let me play for her.

HELMER (*gets up.*): Yes, would you? Then it'll be easier for me to show her.

(RANK *sits down at the piano and plays.* NORA *dances more and more wildly.* HELMER *has stationed himself by the stove and tries repeatedly to correct her, but she seems not to hear him. Her hair works loose and falls over her shoulders; she ignores it and continues to dance.* MRS. LINDE *enters.*)

MRS. LINDE (*stands in the doorway as though tongue-tied.*): Ah—!   395

NORA (*as she dances.*): Christine, we're having such fun!

HELMER: But, Nora darling, you're dancing as if your life depended on it.

NORA: It does.

HELMER: Rank, stop it! This is sheer lunacy. Stop it, I say!

(RANK *ceases playing.* NORA *suddenly stops dancing.*)

HELMER (*goes over to her.*): I'd never have believed it. You've forgotten ev-   400
erything I taught you.

NORA (*throws away the tambourine.*): You see!

HELMER: I'll have to show you every step.

NORA: You see how much I need you! You must show me every step of the way. Right to the end of the dance. Promise me you will, Torvald?

HELMER: Never fear. I will.

NORA: You musn't think about anything but me—today or tomorrow. Don't   405
open any letters—don't even open the letter-box—

HELMER: Aha, you're still worried about that fellow—

NORA: Oh, yes, yes, him too.

HELMER: Nora, I can tell from the way you're behaving, there's a letter from him already there.

NORA: I don't know. I think so. But you mustn't read it now. I don't want anything ugly to come between us till it's all over.

RANK *(quietly, to* HELMER.*)*: Better give her her way.   41⟨

HELMER *(puts his arm around her.)*: My child shall have her way. But tomorrow night, when your dance is over—

NORA: Then you will be free.

MAID *(appears in the doorway, right.)*: Dinner is served, madam.

NORA: Put out some champagne, Helen.

MAID: Very good, madam. *(Goes.)*   41⟨

HELMER: I say! What's this, a banquet?

NORA: We'll drink champagne until dawn! *(Calls.)* And, Helen! Put out some macaroons! Lots of macaroons—for once!

HELMER *(takes her hands in his.)*: Now, now, now. Don't get so excited. Where's my little songbird, the one I know?

NORA: All right. Go and sit down—and you too, Dr. Rank. I'll be with you in a minute. Christine, you must help me put my hair up.

RANK *(quietly, as they go.)*: There's nothing wrong, is there? I mean, she isn't—er—expecting—?   42

HELMER: Good heavens no, my dear chap. She just gets scared like a child sometimes—I told you before—

(They go out right.)

NORA: Well?

MRS. LINDE: He's left town.

NORA: I saw it from your face.

MRS. LINDE: He'll be back tomorrow evening. I left a note for him.   42

NORA: You needn't have bothered. You can't stop anything now. Anyway, it's wonderful really, in a way—sitting here and waiting for the miracle to happen.

MRS. LINDE: Waiting for what?

NORA: Oh, you wouldn't understand. Go in and join them. I'll be with you in a moment.

(MRS. LINDE goes into the dining-room.)

NORA *(stands for a moment as though collecting herself. Then she looks at her watch.)*: Five o'clock. Seven hours till midnight. Then another twenty-four hours till midnight tomorrow. And then the tarantella will be finished. Twenty-four and seven? Thirty-one hours to live.

HELMER *(appears in the doorway, right.)*: What's happened to my little songbird?   43

NORA *(runs to him with her arms wide.)*: Your songbird is here!

ACT III

(The same room. The table which was formerly by the sofa has been moved into the centre of the room; the chairs surround it as before. The door to the hall stands

open. Dance music can be heard from the floor above. MRS. LINDE *is seated at the table, absent-mindedly glancing through a book. She is trying to read, but seems unable to keep her mind on it. More than once she turns and listens anxiously toward the front door.)*

MRS LINDE *(looks at her watch.)*: Not here yet. There's not much time left. Please God he hasn't—! *(Listens again.)* Ah, here he is. *(Goes out into the hall and cautiously opens the front door. Footsteps can be heard softly ascending the stairs. She whispers.)* Come in. There's no one here.

KROGSTAD *(in the doorway.)*: I found a note from you at my lodgings. What does this mean?

MRS. LINDE: I must speak with you.

KROGSTAND: Oh? And must our conversation take place in this house?

MRS. LINDE: We couldn't meet at my place; my room has no separate   5
entrance. Come in. We're quite alone. The maid's asleep, and the Helmers are at the dance upstairs.

KROGSTAD *(comes into the room.)*: Well, well! So the Helmers are dancing this evening? Are they indeed?

MRS. LINDE: Yes, why not?

KROGSTAND: True enough. Why not?

MRS. LINDE: Well, Krogstad. You and I must have a talk together.

KROGSTAND: Have we two anything further to discuss?   10

MRS. LINDE: We have a great deal to discuss.

KROGSTAND: I wasn't aware of it.

MRS. LINDE: That's because you've never really understood me.

KROGSTAND: Was there anything to understand? It's the old story, isn't it— a woman chucking a man because something better turns up?

MRS. LINDE: Do you really think I'm so utterly heartless? You think it was   15
easy for me to give you up?

KROGSTAND: Wasn't it?

MRS. LINDE: Oh, Nils, did you really believe that?

KROGSTAND: Then why did you write to me the way you did?

MRS. LINDE: I had to. Since I had to break with you, I thought it my duty to destroy all the feelings you had for me.

KROGSTAD *(clenches his fists.)*: So that was it. And you did this for money!   20

MRS. LINDE: You mustn't forget I had a helpless mother to take care of, and two little brothers. We couldn't wait for you, Nils. It would have been so long before you'd had enough to support us.

KROGSTAND: Maybe. But you had no right to cast me off for someone else.

MRS. LINDE: Perhaps not. I've often asked myself that.

KROGSTAD *(more quietly.)*: When I lost you, it was just as though all solid ground had been swept from under my feet. Look at me. Now I am a shipwrecked man, clinging to a spar.

MRS. LINDE: Help may be near at hand.   25

KROGSTAND: It was near. But then you came, and stood between it and me.

MRS. LINDE: I didn't know, Nils. No one told me till today that this job I'd found was yours.

KROGSTAND: I believe you, since you say so. But now you know, won't you give it up?

MRS. LINDE: No—because it wouldn't help you even if I did.

KROGSTAND: Wouldn't it? I'd do it all the same.   30

MRS. LINDE: I've learned to look at things practically. Life and poverty have taught me that.

KROGSTAND: And life has taught me to distrust fine words.

MRS. LINDE: Then it's taught you a useful lesson. But surely you still believe in actions?

KROGSTAND: What do you mean?

MRS. LINDE: You said you were like a shipwrecked man clinging to a spar.   35

KROGSTAND: I have good reason to say it.

MRS. LINDE: I'm in the same position as you. No one to care about, no one to care for.

KROGSTAND: You made your own choice.

MRS. LINDE: I had no choice—then.

KROGSTAND: Well?   40

MRS. LINDE: Nils, suppose we two shipwrecked souls could join hands?

KROGSTAND: What are you saying?

MRS. LINDE: Castaways have a better chance of survival together than on their own.

KROGSTAND: Christine!

MRS. LINDE: Why do you suppose I came to this town?   45

KROGSTAND: You mean—you came because of me?

MRS. LINDE: I must work if I'm to find life worth living. I've always worked, for as long as I can remember; it's been the greatest joy of my life—my only joy. But now I'm alone in the world, and I feel so dreadfully lost and empty. There's no joy in working just for oneself. Oh, Nils, give me something—someone—to work for.

KROGSTAND: I don't believe all that. You're just being hysterical and romantic. You want to find an excuse for self-sacrifice.

MRS. LINDE: Have you ever known me to be hysterical?

KROGSTAND: You mean you really—? Is it possible? Tell me—you know all   50
about my past?

MRS. LINDE: Yes.

KROGSTAND: And you know what people think of me here?

MRS. LINDE: You said just now that with me you might have become a different person.

KROGSTAND: I know I could have.

MRS. LINDE: Could it still happen?   55

KROGSTAND: Christine—do you really mean this? Yes—you do—I see it in your face. Have you really the courage—?

MRS. LINDE: I need someone to be a mother to; and your children need a mother. And you and I need each other. I believe in you, Nils. I am afraid of nothing—with you.

KROGSTAD *(clasps her hands.)*: Thank you, Christine—thank you! Now I shall make the world believe in me as you do! Oh—but I'd forgotten—

MRS. LINDE *(listens.)*: Ssh! The tarantella! Go quickly, go!

KROGSTAND: Why? What is it?   60

MRS. LINDE: You hear that dance? As soon as it's finished, they'll be coming down.

KROGSTAND: All right, I'll go. It's no good, Christine. I'd forgotten—you don't know what I've just done to the Helmers.

MRS. LINDE: Yes, Nils. I know.

KROGSTAND: And yet you'd still have the courage to—?

MRS. LINDE: I know what despair can drive a man like you to.   65

KROGSTAND: Oh, if only I could undo this!

MRS. LINDE: You can. Your letter is still lying in the box.

KROGSTAND: Are you sure?

MRS. LINDE: Quite sure. But—

KROGSTAD *(looks searchingly.)*: Is that why you're doing this? You want to   70
save your friend at any price? Tell me the truth. Is that the reason?

MRS. LINDE: Nils, a woman who has sold herself once for the sake of others doesn't make the same mistake again.

KROGSTAND: I shall demand my letter back.

MRS. LINDE: No, no.

KROGSTAND: Of course I shall. I shall stay here till Helmer comes down. I'll tell him he must give me back my letter—I'll say it was only to do with my dismissal, and that I don't want him to read it—

MRS. LINDE: No, Nils, you mustn't ask for that letter back.   75

KROGSTAND: But—tell me—wasn't that the real reason you asked me to come here?

MRS. LINDE: Yes—at first, when I was frightened. But a day has passed since then, and in that time I've seen incredible things happen in this house. Helmer must know the truth. This unhappy secret of Nora's must be revealed. They must come to a full understanding; there must be an end of all these shiftings and evasions.

KROGSTAND: Very well. If you're prepared to risk it. But one thing I can do—and at once—

MRS. LINDE *(listens.)*: Hurry! Go, go! The dance is over. We aren't safe here another moment.

KROGSTAND: I'll wait for you downstairs.   80

MRS. LINDE: Yes, do. You can see me home.

KROGSTAND: I've never been so happy in my life before!

(*He goes through the front door. The door leading from the room into the hall remains open.*)

MRS. LINDE (*tidies the room a little and gets her hat and coat.*): What a change! Oh, what a change! Someone to work for—to live for! A home to bring joy into! I won't let this chance of happiness slip through my fingers. Oh, why don't they come? (*Listens.*) Ah, here they are. I must get my coat on.

(*She takes her hat and coat.* HELMER's *and* NORA's *voices become audible outside. A key is turned in the lock and* HELMER *leads* NORA *almost forcibly into the hall. She is dressed in an Italian costume with a large black shawl. He is in evening dress, with a black cloak.*)

NORA (*still in the doorway, resisting him.*): No, no, no—not in here! I want to go back upstairs. I don't want to leave so early.

HELMER: But my dearest Nora—   85

NORA: Oh, please, Torvald, please! Just another hour!

HELMER: Not another minute, Nora, my sweet. You know what we agreed. Come along, now. Into the drawing-room. You'll catch cold if you stay out here.

(*He leads her, despite her efforts to resist him, gently into the room.*)

MRS. LINDE: Good evening.

NORA: Christine!

HELMER: Oh, hullo, Mrs. Linde. You still here?   90

MRS. LINDE: Please forgive me. I did so want to see Nora in her costume.

NORA: Have you been sitting here waiting for me?

MRS. LINDE: Yes, I got here too late, I'm afraid. You'd already gone up. And I felt I really couldn't go back home without seeing you.

HELMER (*takes off* NORA's *shawl.*): Well, take a good look at her. She's worth looking at, don't you think? Isn't she beautiful, Mrs. Linde?

MRS. LINDE: Oh, yes, indeed—   95

HELMER: Isn't she unbelievably beautiful? Everyone at the party said so. But dreadfully stubborn she is, bless her pretty little heart. What's to be done about that? Would you believe it, I practically had to use force to get her away!

NORA: Oh, Torvald, you're going to regret not letting me stay—just half an hour longer.

HELMER: Hear that, Mrs. Linde? She dances her tarantella—makes a roaring success—and very well deserved—though possibly a trifle too realistic—more so than was aesthetically necessary, strictly speaking. But never mind that. Main thing is—she had a success—roaring success. Was I going to let her stay on after that and spoil the impression? No, thank you. I took my beautiful little Capri signorina—my capricious little Capricienne, what?—under my arm—a swift round of the ballroom, a curtsey to the company, and, as they say in novels, the beautiful apparition disappeared! An exit should always be dramatic, Mrs. Linde. But unfortunately that's just what I can't get Nora to realize. I say, it's hot in here. (*Throws his cloak on a chair and opens the door to his study.*) What's this? It's dark in here. Ah, yes, of course—excuse me. (*Goes in and lights a couple of candles.*)

NORA (*whispers swiftly, breathlessly.*): Well?

MRS. LINDE (*quietly.*): I've spoken to him.   100

NORA: Yes?

MRS. LINDE: Nora—you must tell your husband everything.

NORA (*dully.*): I knew it.

MRS. LINDE: You've nothing to fear from Krogstad. But you must tell him.

NORA: I shan't tell him anything.   105

MRS. LINDE: Then the letter will.

NORA: Thank you, Christine. Now I know what I must do. Ssh!

HELMER (*returns.*): Well, Mrs. Linde, finished admiring her?

MRS. LINDE: Yes. Now I must say good night.

HELMER: Oh, already? Does this knitting belong to you?   110

MRS. LINDE (*takes it.*): Thank you, yes. I nearly forgot it.

HELMER: You knit, then?

MRS. LINDE: Why, yes.

HELMER: Know what? You ought to take up embroidery.

MRS. LINDE: Oh? Why?   115

HELMER: It's much prettier. Watch me, now. You hold the embroidery in your left hand, like this, and then you take the needle in your right hand and go in and out in a slow, easy movement—like this. I am right, aren't I?

MRS. LINDE: Yes, I'm sure—

HELMER: But knitting, now—that's an ugly business—can't help it. Look— arms all huddled up—great clumsy needles going up and down—makes you look like a damned Chinaman. I say, that really was a magnificent champagne they served us.

MRS. LINDE: Well, good night, Nora. And stop being stubborn. Remember!

HELMER: Quite right, Mrs. Linde!   120

MRS. LINDE: Good night, Mr. Helmer.

HELMER (*accompanies her to the door.*): Good night, good night! I hope you'll manage to get home all right? I'd gladly—but you haven't far to go, have you? Good night, good night. (*She goes. He closes the door behind her and returns.*) Well, we've got rid of her at last. Dreadful bore that woman is!

NORA: Aren't you very tired, Torvald?

HELMER: No, not in the least.

NORA: Aren't you sleepy?   125

HELMER: Not a bit. On the contrary, I feel extraordinarily exhilarated. But what about you? Yes, you look very sleepy and tired.

NORA: Yes, I am very tired. Soon I shall sleep.

HELMER: You see, you see! How right I was not to let you stay longer!

NORA: Oh, you're always right, whatever you do.

HELMER (*kisses her on the forehead.*): Now my little songbird's talking just   13(
like a real big human being. I say, did you notice how cheerful Rank was this evening?

NORA: Oh? Was he? I didn't have a chance to speak with him.

HELMER: I hardly did. But I haven't seen him in such a jolly mood for ages. (*Looks at her for a moment, then comes closer.*) I say, it's nice to get back to one's home again, and be all alone with you. Upon my word, you're a distractingly beautiful young woman.

NORA: Don't look at me like that, Torvald!

HELMER: What, not look at my most treasured possession? At all this wonderful beauty that's mine, mine alone, all mine.

NORA (*goes round to the other side of the table.*): You mustn't talk to me like   13
that tonight.

HELMER (*follows her.*): You've still the tarantella in your blood, I see. And that makes you even more desirable. Listen! Now the other guests are beginning to go. (*More quietly.*) Nora—soon the whole house will be absolutely quiet.

NORA: Yes, I hope so.

HELMER: Yes, my beloved Nora, of course you do! Do you know—when I'm out with you among other people like we were tonight, do you know why I say so little to you, why I keep so aloof from you, and just throw you an occasional glance? Do you know why I do that? It's because I pretend to myself that you're my secret mistress, my clandestine little sweetheart, and that nobody knows there's anything at all between us.

NORA: Oh, yes, yes, yes—I know you never think of anything but me.

HELMER: And then when we're about to go, and I wrap the shawl round   14
your lovely young shoulders, over this wonderful curve of your neck— Then I pretend to myself that you are my young bride, that we've just come from the wedding, that I'm taking you to my house for the first time—that, for the first time, I am alone with you—quite alone with you, as you stand there young and trembling and beautiful. All evening I've had no eyes for anyone but you. When I saw you dance the tarantella, like a huntress, a temptress, my blood grew hot, I couldn't stand it any longer! That was why I seized you and dragged you down here with me—

NORA: Leave me, Torvald! Get away from me! I don't want all this.

HELMER: What? Now, Nora, you're joking with me. Don't want, don't want—? Aren't I your husband—?

(*There is a knock on the front door.*)

NORA (*starts.*): What was that?

HELMER (*goes toward the hall.*): Who is it?

RANK (*outside.*): It's me. May I come in for a moment?   145

HELMER (*quietly, annoyed.*): Oh, what does he want now? (*Calls.*) Wait a moment. (*Walks over and opens the door.*) Well! Nice of you not to go by without looking in.

RANK: I thought I heard your voice, so I felt I had to say goodbye. (*His eyes travel swiftly around the room.*) Ah, yes—these dear rooms, how well I know them. What a happy, peaceful home you two have.

HELMER: You seemed to be having a pretty happy time yourself upstairs.

RANK: Indeed I did. Why not? Why shouldn't one make the most of this world? As much as one can, and for as long as one can. The wine was excellent—

HELMER: Especially the champagne.   150

RANK: You noticed that too? It's almost incredible how much I managed to get down.

NORA: Torvald drank a lot of champagne too, this evening.

RANK: Oh?

NORA: Yes. It always makes him merry afterwards.

RANK: Well, why shouldn't a man have a merry evening after a well-spent   155
day?

HELMER: Well-spent? Oh, I don't know that I can claim that.

RANK (*slaps him across the back.*): I can, though, my dear fellow!

NORA: Yes, of course, Dr. Rank—you've been carrying out a scientific experiment today, haven't you?

RANK: Exactly.

HELMER: Scientific experiment! Those are big words for my little Nora to use!   160

NORA: And may I congratulate you on the finding?

RANK: You may indeed.

NORA: It was good, then?

RANK: The best possible finding—both for the doctor and the patient. Certainty.

NORA (*quickly.*): Certainty?   165

RANK: Absolute certainty. So aren't I entitled to have a merry evening after that?

NORA: Yes, Dr. Rank. You were quite right to.

HELMER: I agree. Provided you don't have to regret it tomorrow.

RANK: Well, you never get anything in this life without paying for it.

NORA: Dr. Rank—you like masquerades, don't you?   170

RANK: Yes, if the disguises are sufficiently amusing.

NORA: Tell me. What shall we two wear at the next masquerade?

HELMER: You little gadabout! Are you thinking about the next one already?

RANK: We two? Yes, I'll tell you. You must go as the Spirit of Happiness—

HELMER: You try to think of a costume that'll convey that.   175

RANK: Your wife need only appear as her normal, everyday self—

HELMER: Quite right! Well said! But what are you going to be? Have you decided that?

RANK: Yes, my dear friend. I have decided that.

HELMER: Well?

RANK: At the next masquerade, I shall be invisible.   180

HELMER: Well, that's a funny idea.

RANK: There's a big, black hat—haven't you heard of the invisible hat? Once it's over your head, no one can see you any more.

HELMER (*represses a smile.*): Ah yes, of course.

RANK: But I'm forgetting what I came for. Helmer, give me a cigar. One of your black Havanas.

HELMER: With the greatest pleasure. (*Offers him the box.*)   18?

RANK (*takes one and cuts off the tip.*): Thank you.

NORA (*strikes a match.*): Let me give you a light.

RANK: Thank you. (*She holds out the match for him. He lights his cigar.*) And now—goodbye.

HELMER: Goodbye, my dear chap, goodbye.

NORA: Sleep well, Dr. Rank.   19?

RANK: Thank you for that kind wish.

NORA: Wish me the same.

RANK: You? Very well—since you ask. Sleep well. And thank you for the light. (*He nods to them both and goes.*)

HELMER (*quietly.*): He's been drinking too much.

NORA (*abstractedly.*): Perhaps.   19?

(HELMER *takes his bunch of keys from his pocket and goes out into the hall.*)

NORA: Torvald, what do you want out there?

HELMER: I must empty the letter-box. It's absolutely full. There'll be no room for the newspapers in the morning.

NORA: Are you going to work tonight?

HELMER: You know very well I'm not. Hullo, what's this? Someone's been at the lock.

NORA: At the lock—?   20?

HELMER: Yes, I'm sure of it. Who on earth—? Surely not one of the maids? Here's a broken hairpin. Nora, it's yours—

NORA (*quickly.*): Then it must have been the children.

HELMER: Well, you'll have to break them of that habit. Hm, hm. Ah, that's done it. (*Takes out the contents of the box and calls into the kitchen.*)

Helen! Helen! Put out the light on the staircase. (*Comes back into the drawing room with the letters in his hand and closes the door to the hall.*) Look at this! You see how they've piled up? (*Glances through them.*) What on earth's this?

NORA (*at the window.*): The letter! Oh, no, Torvald, no!

HELMER: Two visiting cards—from Rank.   205

NORA: From Dr. Rank?

HELMER (*looks at them.*): Peter Rank, M.D. They were on top. He must have dropped them in as he left.

NORA: Has he written anything on them?

HELMER: There's a black cross above his name. Look. Rather gruesome, isn't it? It looks just as though he was announcing his death.

NORA: He is.   210

HELMER: What? Do you know something? Has he told you anything?

NORA: Yes. When these cards come, it means he's said goodbye to us. He wants to shut himself up in his house and die.

HELMER: Ah, poor fellow. I knew I wouldn't be seeing him for much longer. But so soon—! And now he's going to slink away and hide like a wounded beast.

NORA: When the time comes, it's best to go silently. Don't you think so, Torvald?

HELMER (*walks up and down.*): He was so much a part of our life. I can't re-   215
alize that he's gone. His suffering and loneliness seemed to provide a kind of dark background to the happy sunlight of our marriage. Well, perhaps it's best this way. For him, anyway. (*Stops walking.*) And perhaps for us too, Nora. Now we have only each other. (*Embraces her.*) Oh, my beloved wife—I feel as though I could never hold you close enough. Do you know, Nora, often I wish some terrible danger might threaten you, so that I could offer my life and my blood, everything, for your sake.

NORA (*tears herself loose and says in a clear, firm voice.*): Read your letters now, Torvald.

HELMER: No, no. Not tonight. Tonight I want to be with you, my darling wife—

NORA: When your friend is about to die—?

HELMER: You're right. This news has upset us both. An ugliness has come between us; thoughts of death and dissolution. We must try to forget them. Until then—you go to your room; I shall go to mine.

NORA (*throws her arms round his neck.*): Good night, Torvald! Good night!   220

HELMER (*kisses her on the forehead.*): Good night, my darling little songbird. Sleep well, Nora. I'll go and read my letters.

(*He goes into the study with the letters in his hand, and closes the door.*)

NORA (*wild-eyed, fumbles around, seizes* HELMER'*s cloak, throws it round herself and whispers quickly, hoarsely.*): Never see him again. Never. Never.

Never. *(Throws the shawl over her head.)* Never see the children again.
Them too. Never. Never. Oh—the icy black water! Oh—that bottom-
less—that—! Oh, if only it were all over! Now he's got it—he's reading
it. Oh, no, no! Goodbye, Torvald! Goodbye, my darlings!

(She turns to run into the hall. As she does so, HELMER *throws open his door and
stands there with an open letter in his hand.)*

HELMER: Nora!

NORA *(shrieks.)*: Ah—!

HELMER: What is this? Do you know what is in this letter?   22

NORA: Yes, I know. Let me go! Let me go!

HELMER *(holds her back.)*: Go? Where?

NORA *(tries to tear herself loose.)*: You mustn't try to save me, Torvald!

HELMER *(staggers back.)*: Is it true? Is it true, what he writes? Oh, my God!
No, no—it's impossible, it can't be true!

NORA: It *is* true. I've loved you more than anything else in the world.   23

HELMER: Oh, don't try to make silly excuses.

NORA *(takes a step toward him.)*: Torvald—

HELMER: Wretched woman! What have you done?

NORA: Let me go! You're not going to suffer for my sake. I won't let you!

HELMER: Stop being theatrical. *(Locks the front door.)* You're going to stay   23
here and explain yourself. Do you understand what you've done? Answer me! Do you understand?

NORA *(looks unflinchingly at him and, her expression growing colder, says.)*:
Yes. Now I am beginning to understand.

HELMER *(walking round the room.)*: Oh, what a dreadful awakening! For
eight whole years—she who was my joy and my pride—a hypocrite, a
liar—worse, worse—a criminal! Oh, the hideousness of it! Shame on
you, shame!

(NORA is silent and stares unblinkingly at him.)

HELMER *(stops in front of her.)*: I ought to have guessed that something of
this sort would happen. I should have foreseen it. All your father's recklessness and instability—be quiet!—I repeat, all your father's recklessness and instability he has handed on to you. No religion, no morals,
no sense of duty! Oh, how I have been punished for closing my eyes to
his faults! I did it for your sake. And now you reward me like this.

NORA: Yes. Like this.

HELMER: Now you have destroyed all my happiness. You have ruined my   24
whole future. Oh, it's too dreadful to contemplate! I am in the power of
a man who is completely without scruples. He can do what he likes
with me, demand what he pleases, order me to do anything—I dare not
disobey him. I am condemned to humiliation and ruin simply for the
weakness of a woman.

NORA: When I am gone from this world, you will be free.

HELMER: Oh, don't be melodramatic. Your father was always ready with that kind of remark. How would it help me if you were "gone from this world," as you put it? It wouldn't assist me in the slightest. He can still make all the facts public; and if he does, I may quite easily be suspected of having been an accomplice in your crime. People may think that I was behind it—that it was I who encouraged you! And for all this I have to thank you, you whom I have carried on my hands through all the years of our marriage! Now do you realize what you've done to me?

NORA (*coldly calm.*): Yes.

HELMER: It's so unbelievable I can hardly credit it. But we must try to find some way out. Take off that shawl. Take it off, I say! I must try to buy him off somehow. This thing must be hushed up at any price. As regards our relationship—we must appear to be living together just as before. Only *appear*, of course. You will therefore continue to reside here. That is understood. But the children shall be taken out of your hands. I dare no longer entrust them to you. Oh, to have to say this to the woman I once loved so dearly—and whom I still—! Well, all that must be finished. Henceforth there can be no question of happiness; we must merely strive to save what shreds and tatters—(*The front door bell rings.* HELMER *starts.*) What can that be? At this hour? Surely not—? He wouldn't—? Hide yourself, Nora. Say you're ill.

(NORA *does not move.* HELMER *goes to the door of the room and opens it. The* MAID *is standing half-dressed in the hall.*)

MAID: A letter for madam.   245

HELMER: Give it me. (*Seizes the letter and shuts the door.*) Yes, it's from him. You're not having it. I'll read this myself.

NORA: Read it.

HELMER (*by the lamp.*): I hardly dare to. This may mean the end for us both. No. I must know. (*Tears open the letter hastily; reads a few lines; looks at a piece of paper which is enclosed with it; utters a cry of joy.*) Nora! (*She looks at him questioningly.*) Nora! No—I must read it once more. Yes, yes, it's true! I am saved! Nora, I am saved!

NORA: What about me?

HELMER: You too, of course. We're both saved, you and I. Look! He's   250
returning your I.O.U. He writes that he is sorry for what has happened—a happy accident has changed his life—oh, what does it matter what he writes? We are saved, Nora! No one can harm you now. Oh, Nora, Nora—no, first let me destroy this filthy thing. Let me see—! (*Glances at the I.O.U.*) No, I don't want to look at it. I shall merely regard the whole business as a dream. (*He tears the I.O.U. and both letters into pieces, throws them into the stove and watches them burn.*) There. Now they're destroyed. He wrote that ever since

Christmas Eve you've been—oh, these must have been three dreadful days for you, Nora.

NORA: Yes. It's been a hard fight.

HELMER: It must have been terrible—seeing no way out except—no, we'll forget the whole sordid business. We'll just be happy and go on telling ourselves over and over again: "It's over! It's over!" Listen to me, Nora. You don't seem to realize. It's over! Why are you looking so pale? Ah, my poor little Nora, I understand. You can't believe that I have forgiven you. But I have, Nora. I swear it to you. I have forgiven you everything. I know that what you did you did for your love of me.

NORA: That is true.

HELMER: You have loved me as a wife should love her husband. It was simply that in your inexperience you chose the wrong means. But do you think I love you any the less because you don't know how to act on your own initiative? No, no. Just lean on me. I shall counsel you. I shall guide you. I would not be a true man if your feminine helplessness did not make you doubly attractive in my eyes. You mustn't mind the hard words I said to you in those first dreadful moments when my whole world seemed to be tumbling about my ears. I have forgiven you, Nora. I swear it to you; I have forgiven you.

NORA: Thank you for your forgiveness.   25

(*She goes out through the door, right.*)

HELMER: No, don't go—(*Looks in.*) What are you doing there?

NORA (*offstage.*): Taking off my fancy dress.

HELMER (*by the open door.*): Yes, do that. Try to calm yourself and get your balance again, my frightened little songbird. Don't be afraid. I have broad wings to shield you. (*Begins to walk around near the door.*) How lovely and peaceful this little home of ours is, Nora. You are safe here; I shall watch over you like a hunted dove which I have snatched unharmed from the claws of the falcon. Your wildly beating little heart shall find peace with me. It will happen, Nora; it will take time, but it will happen, believe me. Tomorrow all this will seem quite different. Soon everything will be as it was before. I shall no longer need to remind you that I have forgiven you; your own heart will tell you that it is true. Do you really think I could ever bring myself to disown you, or even to reproach you? Ah, Nora, you don't understand what goes on in a husband's heart. There is something indescribably wonderful and satisfying for a husband in knowing that he has forgiven his wife—forgiven her unreservedly, from the bottom of his heart. It means that she has become his property in a double sense; he has, as it were, brought her into the world anew; she is now not only his wife but also his child. From now on that is what you shall be to me, my poor, helpless, bewildered little creature. Never be frightened of anything again, Nora. Just open your heart to me. I shall be both your will and your conscience. What's this? Not in bed? Have you changed?

NORA *(in her everyday dress.)*: Yes, Torvald. I've changed.

HELMER: But why now—so late—?   260

NORA: I shall not sleep tonight.

HELMER: But, my dear Nora—

NORA *(looks at her watch.)*: It isn't that late. Sit down here, Torvald. You and I have a lot to talk about.

(She sits down on one side of the table.)

HELMER: Nora, what does this mean? You look quite drawn—

NORA: Sit down. It's going to take a long time. I've a lot to say to you.   265

HELMER *(sits down on the other side of the table.)*: You alarm me, Nora. I don't understand you.

NORA: No, that's just it. You don't understand me. And I've never understood you—until this evening. No, don't interrupt me. Just listen to what I have to say. You and I have got to face facts, Torvald.

HELMER: What do you mean by that?

NORA *(after a short silence.)*: Doesn't anything strike you about the way we're sitting here?

HELMER: What?   270

NORA: We've been married for eight years. Does it occur to you that this is the first time that we two, you and I, man and wife, have ever had a serious talk together?

HELMER: Serious? What do you mean, serious?

NORA: In eight whole years—no, longer—ever since we first met—we have never exchanged a serious word on a serious subject.

HELMER: Did you expect me to drag you into all my worries—worries you couldn't possibly have helped me with?

NORA: I'm not talking about worries. I'm simply saying that we have never   275
sat down seriously to try to get to the bottom of anything.

HELMER: But, my dear Nora, what on earth has that got to do with you?

NORA: That's just the point. You have never understood me. A great wrong has been done to me, Torvald. First by Papa, and then by you.

HELMER: What? But we two have loved you more than anyone in the world!

NORA *(shakes her head.)*: You have never loved me. You just thought it was fun to be in love with me.

HELMER: Nora, what kind of a way is this to talk?   280

NORA: It's the truth, Torvald. When I lived with Papa, he used to tell me what he thought about everything, so that I never had any opinions but his. And if I did have any of my own, I kept them quiet, because he wouldn't have liked them. He called me his little doll, and he played with me just the way I played with my dolls. Then I came here to live in your house—

HELMER: What kind of a way is that to describe our marriage?

NORA (*undisturbed.*): I mean, then I passed from Papa's hands into yours. You arranged everything the way you wanted it, so that I simply took over your taste in everything—or pretended I did—I don't really know—I think it was a little of both—first one and then the other. Now I look back on it, it's as if I've been living here like a pauper, from hand to mouth. I performed tricks for you, and you gave me food and drink. But that was how you wanted it. You and Papa have done me a great wrong. It's your fault that I have done nothing with my life.

HELMER: Nora, how can you be so unreasonable and ungrateful? Haven't you been happy here?

NORA: No; never. I used to think I was; but I haven't ever been happy.   28!

HELMER: Not—not happy?

NORA: No. I've just had fun. You've always been very kind to me. But our home has never been anything but a playroom. I've been your doll-wife, just as I used to be Papa's doll-child. And the children have been my dolls. I used to think it was fun when you came in and played with me, just as they think it's fun when I go in and play games with them. That's all our marriage has been, Torvald.

HELMER: There may be a little truth in what you say, though you exaggerate and romanticize. But from now on it'll be different. Playtime is over. Now the time has come for education.

NORA: Whose education? Mine or the children's?

HELMER: Both yours and the children's, my dearest Nora.   29!

NORA: Oh, Torvald, you're not the man to educate me into being the right wife for you.

HELMER: How can you say that?

NORA: And what about me? Am I fit to educate the children?

HELMER: Nora!

NORA: Didn't you say yourself a few minutes ago that you dare not leave   29!
them in my charge?

HELMER: In a moment of excitement. Surely you don't think I meant it seriously?

NORA: Yes. You were perfectly right. I'm not fitted to educate them. There's something else I must do first. I must educate myself. And you can't help me with that. It's something I must do by myself. That's why I'm leaving you.

HELMER (*jumps up.*): What did you say?

NORA: I must stand on my own feet if I am to find out the truth about my-self and about life. So I can't go on living here with you any longer.

HELMER: Nora, Nora!   30!

NORA: I'm leaving you now, at once. Christine will put me up for tonight—

HELMER: You're out of your mind! You can't do this! I forbid you!

NORA: It's no use your trying to forbid me any more. I shall take with me nothing but what is mine. I don't want anything from you, now or ever.

HELMER: What kind of madness is this?

NORA: Tomorrow I shall go home—I mean, to where I was born. It'll be easiest for me to find some kind of a job there.   305

HELMER: But you're blind! You've no experience of the world—

NORA: I must try to get some, Torvald.

HELMER: But to leave your home, your husband, your children! Have you thought what people will say?

NORA: I can't help that. I only know that I must do this.

HELMER: But this is monstrous! Can you neglect your most sacred duties?   310

NORA: What do you call my most sacred duties?

HELMER: Do I have to tell you? Your duties towards your husband, and your children.

NORA: I have another duty which is equally sacred.

HELMER: You have not. What on earth could that be?

NORA: My duty towards myself.   315

HELMER: First and foremost you are a wife and a mother.

NORA: I don't believe that any longer. I believe that I am first and foremost a human being, like you—or anyway, that I must try to become one. I know most people think as you do, Torvald, and I know there's something of the sort to be found in books. But I'm no longer prepared to accept what people say and what's written in books. I must think things out for myself, and try to find my own answer.

HELMER: Do you need to ask where your duty lies in your own home? Haven't you an infallible guide in such matters—your religion?

NORA: Oh, Torvald, I don't really know what religion means.

HELMER: What are you saying?   320

NORA: I only know what Pastor Hansen told me when I went to confirmation. He explained that religion meant this and that. When I get away from all this and can think things out on my own, that's one of the questions I want to look into. I want to find out whether what Pastor Hansen said was right—or anyway, whether it is right for me.

HELMER: But it's unheard of for so young a woman to behave like this! If religion cannot guide you, let me at least appeal to your conscience. I presume you have some moral feelings left? Or—perhaps you haven't? Well, answer me.

NORA: Oh, Torvald, that isn't an easy question to answer. I simply don't know. I don't know where I am in these matters. I only know that these things mean something quite different to me from what they do to you. I've learned now that certain laws are different from what I'd imagined them to be; but I can't accept that such laws can be right. Has a woman really not the right to spare her dying father pain, or save her husband's life? I can't believe that.

HELMER: You're talking like a child. You don't understand how society works.

NORA: No, I don't. But now I intend to learn. I must try to satisfy myself which is right, society or I.

HELMER: Nora, you're ill; you're feverish. I almost believe you're out of your mind.

NORA: I've never felt so sane and sure in my life.

HELMER: You feel sure that it is right to leave your husband and your children?

NORA: Yes. I do.

HELMER: Then there is only one possible explanation.

NORA: What?

HELMER: That you don't love me any longer.

NORA: No, that's exactly it.

HELMER: Nora! How can you say this to me?

NORA: Oh, Torvald, it hurts me terribly to have to say it, because you've always been so kind to me. But I can't help it. I don't love you any longer.

HELMER (*controlling his emotions with difficulty.*): And you feel quite sure about this too?

NORA: Yes, absolutely sure. That's why I can't go on living here any longer.

HELMER: Can you also explain why I have lost your love?

NORA: Yes, I can. It happened this evening, when the miracle failed to happen. It was then that I realized you weren't the man I'd thought you to be.

HELMER: Explain more clearly. I don't understand you.

NORA: I've waited so patiently, for eight whole years—well, good heavens, I'm not such a fool as to suppose that miracles occur every day. Then this dreadful thing happened to me, and then I *knew*: "Now the miracle will take place!" When Krogstad's letter was lying out there, it never occurred to me for a moment that you would let that man trample over you. I *knew* that you would say to him: "Publish the facts to the world." And when he had done this—

HELMER: Yes, what then? When I'd exposed my wife's name to shame and scandal—

NORA: Then I was certain that you would step forward and take all the blame on yourself, and say: "I am the one who is guilty!"

HELMER: Nora!

NORA: You're thinking I wouldn't have accepted such a sacrifice from you? No, of course I wouldn't! But what would my word have counted for against yours? That was the miracle I was hoping for, and dreading. And it was to prevent it happening that I wanted to end my life.

HELMER: Nora, I would gladly work for you night and day, and endure sorrow and hardship for your sake. But no man can be expected to sacrifice his honor, even for the person he loves.

NORA: Millions of women have done it.

HELMER: Oh, you think and talk like a stupid child.

NORA: That may be. But you neither think nor talk like the man I could share my life with. Once you'd got over your fright—and you weren't frightened of what might threaten me, but only of what threatened you—once the danger was past, then as far as you were concerned it was exactly as though nothing had happened. I was your little songbird just as before—your doll whom henceforth you would take particular care to protect from the world because she was so weak and fragile. (*Gets up.*) Torvald, in that moment I realized that for eight years I had been living here with a complete stranger, and had borne him three children—! Oh, I can't bear to think of it! I could tear myself to pieces!

HELMER (*sadly.*): I see it, I see it. A gulf has indeed opened between us. Oh, but Nora—couldn't it be bridged?   350

NORA: As I am now, I am no wife for you.

HELMER: I have the strength to change.

NORA: Perhaps—if your doll is taken from you.

HELMER: But to be parted—to be parted from you! No, no, Nora, I can't conceive of it happening!

NORA (*goes into the room, right.*): All the more necessary that it should happen.   355

(*She comes back with her outdoor things and a small traveling-bag, which she puts down on a chair by the table.*)

HELMER: Nora, Nora, not now! Wait till tomorrow!

NORA (*puts on her coat.*): I can't spend the night in a strange man's house.

HELMER: But can't we live here as brother and sister, then—?

NORA (*fastens her hat.*): You know quite well it wouldn't last. (*Puts on her shawl.*) Goodbye, Torvald. I don't want to see the children. I know they're in better hands than mine. As I am now, I can be nothing to them.

HELMER: But some time, Nora—some time—?   360

NORA: How can I tell? I've no idea what will happen to me.

HELMER: But you are my wife, both as you are and as you will be.

NORA: Listen, Torvald. When a wife leaves her husband's house, as I'm doing now, I'm told that according to the law he is freed of any obligations towards her. In any case, I release you from any such obligations. You mustn't feel bound to me in any way, however small, just as I shall not feel bound to you. We must both be quite free. Here is your ring back. Give me mine.

HELMER: That too?

NORA: That too. 365

HELMER: Here it is.

NORA: Good. Well, now it's over. I'll leave the keys here. The servants know about everything to do with the house—much better than I do. Tomorrow, when I have left town, Christine will come to pack the things I brought here from home. I'll have them sent on after me.

HELMER: This is the end then! Nora, will you never think of me any more?

NORA: Yes, of course. I shall often think of you and the children and this house.

HELMER: May I write to you, Nora? 370

NORA: No. Never. You mustn't do that.

HELMER: But at least you must let me send you—

NORA: Nothing. Nothing.

HELMER: But if you should need help—?

NORA: I tell you, no. I don't accept things from strangers. 375

HELMER: Nora—can I never be anything but a stranger to you?

NORA (*picks up her bag.*): Oh, Torvald! Then the miracle of miracles would have to happen.

HELMER: The miracle of miracles?

NORA: You and I would both have to change so much that—oh, Torvald, I don't believe in miracles any longer.

HELMER: But I want to believe in them. Tell me. We should have to change 380 so much that—?

NORA: That life together between us two could become a marriage. Goodbye.

(*She goes out through the hall.*)

HELMER (*sinks down on a chair by the door and buries his face in his hands.*): Nora! Nora! (*Looks round and gets up.*) Empty! She's gone! (*A hope strikes him.*) The miracle of miracles—?

(*The street door is slammed shut downstairs.*)

■ How does Nora choose what to say to her husband and what to keep hidden?

■ How does a definition of "wife" emerge from the interactions between Nora and Mrs. Linde? In what ways is this definition important to the action within the play?

■ Trace references to possessions and ownership within the play. How are these references significant to the progress of the play? How are they related to the title of the play?

Experiencing Literature through Writing

1. Looking closely at a specific word, choose a word or a grouping of words that seems to be significant within this particular presentation. In your discussion, explain what it is about this language choice that makes this particular work distinctive. As you write, consider the following questions:

    a. How does this word usage adhere to or depart from conventional usage? Use a dictionary to help you answer the question.

    b. How does this word usage set a style for the rest of this particular text?

    c. How is this word usage significant to our understanding of the larger text?

2. In this set of readings, there are several pairs of poems in which the same author discusses contrasting ideas (Levertov's marriage and divorce, Browning's night and morning). These works develop explicit contrasts, and similar effects are apparent within Wharton's short story. Using either one of these pairs or some other contrasting elements of a work, discuss how the specific words in the contrasting pair differ. What is the impact of that difference?

3. Using one or more works in this chapter (or in another chapter), explore the tension between an author's attempt to convey some original emotion and the impact of certain words that convention dictates should be used when discussing that emotion. In this exploration, think about the constraints that language places upon the attempt to create a life out of words.

12 Allegory

Is This Supposed to Mean Something Else, Too?

Consider for a moment the concept of "duty." You could look the word up in a dictionary, although you probably don't feel the need. Duty seems a familiar if rather dry notion. We tend to think politely of duty as a good thing. Duty compels us to act in ways we're "supposed" to act. It's what guides us to make tough choices or prompts us to serve others, even when such service is inconvenient or dangerous. But if we think long enough, our simplest responses may begin to seem inadequate. Duty can't be touched, weighed, or counted; it can only be held in our minds. Duty is an abstraction that may call forth a wide range of associations. What distinguishes "duty" in a positive sense from other abstractions that register overlapping and disturbing qualities (narrow devotion, slavish obligation, external compulsion, societal demand)? Even assuming we are able to stay clear of such ambiguity, how can we write about duty in a way that is positive, educational, and interesting? How can we foreground the idea of duty and make that idea clear without resorting to a straightforward (and most likely ineffective and/or reductive) lecture or sermon? How can we make something so vague and intangible come alive?

Allegory is a means to convey meaning. In allegory, abstract notions are embodied and given life by concrete characters and actions. Usually, there is a lesson set out for us to grasp. For example, imagine a story in which a violent character named "Anger" attacks a gentle character named "Love." Anger soon expends every ounce of energy and crashes down exhausted and alone, whereas Love (nursed by two friends, Patience and Duty) recovers quickly from the assault. We know there is a lesson being taught, and we are not likely to mistake the main points: Love (the character and the quality) is stronger than Anger (the character and the quality). Duty and Patience serve Love but cannot help Anger.

Although this type of story is premised in the belief that lessons can be taught in compelling and entertaining ways, we have all suffered through a television special, an earnest song, or a textbook reading exercise (like the one just given) whose good intentions far surpass its aesthetic qualities. Contrived lessons about caring for the environment and being kind to others who are different from us tend to be the greatest offenders in our current culture; such themes are important, but importance alone doesn't make for a great poem, film, or play. Fortunately, on occasion an artist is able to break through with a remarkable image or with a story that achieves a working (and often dynamic) balance between the moral and the action. This sort of achievement is one that we can easily appreciate, perhaps because we have so much experience with less successful examples.

LEARNING THROUGH LIKENESS

We sometimes forget that the literary experience can be socially and morally instructive. Works driven by an explicit teaching purpose are called **didactic works**. One of the clearest examples of a transparently didactic allegorical tale is Gertrude Crampton's *Tootle* (1945), a children's picture book that remains in print and tells the story of a little train who must learn that it is wrong to go off the tracks. When Tootle wanders out into a delightful meadow, his teacher conspires with the inhabitants of Lower Trainswitch to make him think that life off the established track is filled with red flags. Crampton describes Tootle's submission to discipline.

> There were red flags waving from the buttercups, in the daisies, under the trees, near the bluebirds' nest, and even one behind the rain barrel. And, of course, Tootle had to stop for each one, for a locomotive must always Stop for a Red Flag Waving.
>
> "Red flags," muttered Tootle, "This meadow is full of red flags. How can I have any fun?
>
> "Whenever I start, I have to stop. Why did I think this meadow was such a fine place? Why don't I ever see a green flag?"
>
> Just as the tears were ready to slide out of his boiler, Tootle happened to look back over his coal car. On the tracks stood Bill, and in his hand was a big green flag. "Oh!" said Tootle.
>
> He puffed up to Bill and stopped.
>
> "This is the place for me," said Tootle. "There is nothing but red flags for locomotives that get off their tracks."

Gertrude Crampton, *Tootle* (1945)

"Hurray!" shouted the people of Lower Trainswitch, and jumped from their hiding places. "Hurray for Tootle the Flyer!" ■

Through characters like Tootle's teacher, Bill, and the jubilant townspeople, the story insists that only by following social regulations can a train—or, in other words, an unruly child—feel truly free. But the coercive nature of Tootle's training and the narrator's voice give this lesson book a somewhat hollow ring. As mature readers, we tend to be unruly, like the young Tootle. We don't want the message to be spelled out in too heavy a fashion. We might ask if it really was all right for Bill and the townspeople to trick Tootle. Wouldn't Tootle have enjoyed the meadow if they had not placed all the red flags about? Doesn't it seem a little small-minded of them to hide and watch him suffer and then shout happily when Tootle "learns his lesson"? But Gertrude Crampton tries to discourage such questions. She wants us to stay on the tracks and learn what she teaches.

Allegories constructed to force us down a single track can quickly grow tiresome. Fortunately, allegories need not be so controlling. In some ways, we can think of an allegory as an extended or elaborate **simile**. A simile explicitly associates (through the words *like* or *as*) an abstraction with a concrete image: for example, love is like a red rose. Such comparisons are directive, of course, but similes can provoke complex responses to likeness and difference. Love, like a red rose, is beautiful in bloom—full, richly layered, deeply fragrant. But rosebushes do have thorns. Red roses in particular wither quickly. The simile initiates not just a simple thought but a range of thoughts.

If we strip away all the directional signals from Tootle, we are left with a core simile such as the following: social conventions are like railroad tracks. Left at that elemental level, we're encouraged to play more freely with the comparison than Crampton might wish. Social customs and rules may, like tracks, keep us moving toward something. These tracks (when we stay on them properly) help us avoid collisions with others. Tracks allow us to move faster. But we can also be "stuck" on the tracks. We can be "railroaded." We may complain of someone who has a "one-track mind." And tracks are fixed, whereas customs and rules are varied, changeable, and open. Tracks are something we are either on or off. People may engage with customs and rules actively—even playfully. A simile such as "social conventions are like railroad tracks" might lead us to think from many different perspectives. An allegory could well be built on such a simile that would extend or complicate the possibilities—not just shut them down.

Some critics prefer to think of allegory as an extended **metaphor**. In a metaphor, the explicit connection (*like* or *as*) is dropped. Love is not merely like a red rose, it *is* a red rose. Social conventions *are* tracks we are all placed on. The qualities of one thing are fused (not merely paralleled) with the other. Simile invites comparison; it calls attention to sometimes surprising likenesses and asks that we test out or seek the meaning of the aligned parts. Metaphor presses boldly toward some elemental correspondence. It is perhaps more suggestive (less directive) than simile. For this reason, we'll have more to say about metaphor in Chapter 13. Here it's sufficient to say that allegory involves an extended parallel between concrete characters, things, and actions on one side and abstract meanings on the other.

A Note to Student Writers: Using Analogies in Arguments

A simile involves a comparison between what might seem unlike things; a simile leaves it to the reader to tease out the meaning or effect. An **analogy** also involves a comparison. But in an analogy, the comparison depends upon likeness and is intended to serve a point—to build a logically forceful argument. Students are often warned not to build arguments from perceived similarities: "Don't argue from analogy" or "That's a false analogy." Although it is certainly true that you're not likely to successfully sustain an argument based on likeness through an entire paper, it is possible to illustrate a point or develop part of an argument through a carefully thought out analogy. For instance, Oliver Wendell Holmes, while Chief Justice of the Supreme Court, argued that the right to free speech must be limited when the speech in question is like someone shouting "Fire!" in a crowded theater.

Because many writers have, along with Holmes, used analogy effectively in analytical and argumentative essays, it seems plain wrong to require students to avoid analogies altogether. But it's not wrong to warn students to construct (or evaluate) an analogy with care. When you use (or read) an analogy, consider the following: First, are the two things that are put together really similar? Second, is the similarity *relevant* to the point made? Third, is there some difference between the two things that undermines the point? Use these questions to test a specific application of Holmes's analogy.

Experiencing Literature through Allegory

Crampton's train is part of a tradition of stories in which the actors are not human; Tootle is a **personification** of an unruly child. This train acts exactly like a child, but the story and the pictures are engaging precisely because a train is *not* a child: we see a familiar world altered. Even children who don't want to accept Crampton's lesson might smile at the thought of a train sitting in a schoolroom. In this sort of story, anthropomorphic animals often present models of appropriate and inappropriate human behavior. The most famous may be the many ingenious animals that Aesop created to personify human dilemmas.

Aesop (620 BC–564 BC)

The Crow and the Pitcher (ca. 300 BC)

A Thirsty Crow found a Pitcher with some water in it, but so little was there that, try as she might, she could not reach it with her beak, and it seemed as though she would die of thirst within sight of the remedy. At last she hit upon a clever plan. She began dropping pebbles into the Pitcher, and with each pebble the water rose a little higher until at last it reached the brim, and the knowing bird was enabled to quench her thirst.

Moral: *Necessity is the mother of invention.* ■

In Aesop's **fable**, the crow is hardly developed as a character. It is important that she be a crow primarily so that she cannot have hands to pick up the pitcher. Her only attributes in this short paragraph are her ingenuity and her thirst. In illustrations of this tale, the crow looks like a crow. Unlike the story of Tootle, the fable of the crow and the pitcher seems like it could be true. The pithy moral conjoined to the image of the crow using pebbles to quench her thirst has a remarkable staying power.

Part of that power arises from the fit between concrete images and intangible qualities. Aesop helps us picture necessity, invention, and resourcefulness (all qualities difficult to describe). The thirsty crow stands for all forms of necessity; the pebble trick signifies all forms of invention. Readers take it from there. We're not bound by the moral to limit "necessity" to thirst. As soon as we understand the situation of the crow, we see how this instance could be illustrated by many other similar situations (even though few seem to be able to do it as economically as Aesop's tale). His fable is very clear, yet it's not restrictive.

Perhaps still less restrictive is the miniature allegory of Eden that Emily Dickinson offers us about the everyday beauties of life we may miss through inattention.

THE CROW & THE · PITCHER ·

HoW the cunning old Crow got his drink
When 'twas low in the pitcher, just think!
Don't say that he spilled it!
With pebbles he filled it,
Till the water rose up to the brink.

· USE · YOUR · WITS ·

THE · EAGLE · AND · THE · CROW :

THE Eagle flew off with a lamb;
Then the Crow thought to lift an old ram,
In his eaglish conceit,
The wool tangled. his feet,
And the shepherd laid hold of the sham.

: BEWARE · OF · OVERRATING · YOUR · OWN · POWERS :

Walter Crane, *Illustration for Aesop's "The Crow and the Pitcher"*

Emily Dickinson (1830–1886)

[Eden is that old-fashioned House] (ca. 1861)

Eden is that old-fashioned House
We dwell in every day

Without suspecting our abode
Until we drive away.

How fair on looking back, the Day   5
We sauntered from the Door—
Unconscious our returning,
But discover it no more.

Eden is established at the outset as our familiar home—a place we live in yet
do not recognize. Only in losing home, it seems, do we appreciate it. Yet
with the insight is loss, for the insight cannot bring us back to the original
state of perfection. As you read this poem, ask yourself: Why are "House,"
"Day," and "Door" capitalized? How closely allegorical is Dickinson's logic?
That is, does the parallel between Eden and the House hold through the
whole poem?

EMBODYING TIMELESS QUALITIES

Most of us recognize the blindfolded figure of Justice holding a set of scales in
one hand and a sword in the other. We have learned that the blindfold helps

Engraving of Statue of Justice holding the scales

Dosso Dossi, *Allegory of Fortune* (ca. 1530)

her be impartial so that she will weigh the two sides in a dispute evenhand-edly, without bias, and her sword will render that verdict. When she makes her decision, the figure suggests, her verdict will be fair and will help contribute to the civility of our society. We are familiar with the image largely because it is repeated in various forms at courthouses throughout the country.

The allegorical figure of Fortune may be a bit less familiar, but the explanation of the objects in the image is clear enough. The female Fortune holds a cornucopia representing the bounty that she offers, but she sits upon a bubble (easily burst) to indicate the fleeting nature of her gifts. The man with her is Chance, whose lottery tickets offer little more than the dream of owning that cornucopia.

These images deal with qualities we often consider universal or timeless. Justice is not thought of as a construction of a particular culture; we typically assume it's a transcendent value that all must seek. Chance is a condition that operates far above any individual level. If we doubt the eternal quality of such notions, the figures of Justice and Fortune may start to look a bit tacky and outdated. The poet Billy Collins observes that the contemporary literary scene is largely devoid of allegorical figures. As he introduces each figure, he calls up familiar images from a tradition in which these figures played much more prominent roles. He then observes that it is only the plainest things—bare of any explicit meaning—that we choose to invoke.

Billy Collins (1941–)

The Death of Allegory (1999)

I am wondering what become of all those tall abstractions
that used to pose, robed and statuesque, in paintings
and parade about on the pages of the Renaissance
displaying their capital letters like license plates.

Truth cantering on a powerful horse,   5
Chastity, eyes downcast, fluttering with veils.
Each one was marble come to life, a thought in a coat,
Courtesy bowing with one hand always extended,

Villainy sharpening an instrument behind a wall,
Reason with her crown and Constancy alert behind a helm,   10
They are all retired now, consigned to a Florida for tropes.
Justice is there standing by an open refrigerator.

Valor lies in bed listening to the rain.
Even Death has nothing to do but mend his cloak and hood,
and all their props are locked away in a warehouse,   15
hourglasses, globes, blindfolds and shackles.

Even if you called them back, there are no places left
for them to go, no Garden of Mirth or Bower of Bliss.
The Valley of Forgiveness is lined with condominiums
and chainsaws are howling in the Forest of Despair.   20

Here on the table near the window is a vase of peonies
and next to it black binoculars and a money clip,
exactly the kind of thing we now prefer,
objects that sit quietly on a line in lower case,

themselves and nothing more, a wheelbarrow,   25
an empty mailbox, a razor blade resting in a glass ashtray.
As for the others, the great ideas on horseback
and the long-haired virtues in embroidered gowns,

it looks as though they have traveled down
that road you see on the final page of storybooks,   30
the one that winds up a green hillside and disappears
into an unseen valley where everyone must be fast asleep.

Collins speaks longingly of a time when artists engaged with big ideas and compares that to a current time when allegorical figures are much less meaningful, when artists concentrate on the details of everyday life. The ideas that have replaced such "tall abstractions" as Truth and Chastity are the "lowercase objects" that populate this poem. Although it seems true that contemporary artists resist grand generalities and abstractions, Collins's observation says much about allegory in any age. Much of the inclination to use allegory, even in the older times that Collins celebrates, begins with the sense that big ideas are a thing of the past. The statue that adorns the Department of Justice was not a product of ancient Greece or Rome but was made deliberately to invoke those times. Its form suggests the links between the modern courthouse and classical civilization. The statue depicts an ancient ideal of justice and gives us more faith in the system than we might gain from a statue of a modern lawyer. Allegory has long exploited this sense of an idealized past. When Edmund Spenser wrote the *Faerie Queene* in 1596, he constructed a deliberately artificial and antique language in which to present his allegories. Just as the statue of Justice hearkens to an earlier iconography, Spenser, like many of the artists in the Renaissance, gave his own work an appearance of being older than it really was to lend seriousness to his project. So even in the sixteenth century, Spenser's allegory seemed like a literary style from the past.

Making Connections

Reread Czeslaw Milosz's "Watering Can" (p. 632) and William Carlos Williams's "The Red Wheelbarrow" (p. 631) in light of Billy Collins's remarks on the decline of allegory. Explore the differences among the ideas presented by these three poets. How does Collins's lament about the decline of allegory relate to Milosz and Williams and their insistence on "things"? How would you defend Milosz and Williams against a charge that they diminish poetry's grand potential?

READING ALLEGORY

Static allegorical figures like the ones pictured on pages 1200–1201 and like the ones Collins refers to strike some people as rather cold. They are, after all, forever frozen in a moment that captures a specific meaning. For example, in Dosso Dossi's painting, Fortune sits perpetually on her bubble. The idea is that the bubble is always on the verge of breaking, yet in the image itself the bubble will never burst. As soon as we make a story out of the image that is presented in the painting, the balance may be broken. The bubble could burst. And if it did, we'd have a particular, dynamic situation—not simply a fixed universal message.

Plato uses the image of a dark cave as an instructional device so that the students of Socrates (the primary speaker in Plato's dialogues) can understand his distinction between the physical, observable world and some greater reality unavailable to ordinary human perception. This allegorical world contains some slight action as figures pass in front of the light and cast shadows and as a figure moves from the cave to the sunlight and back again; but for the most part, Plato's world can be viewed much as one views the allegorical paintings. Plato is after a general and stable truth. All of the details of the allegory are there to help us understand an idea, not as the setting for a story. We use the constructed cave world to see Plato's abstract point. We can keep coming back to Plato's allegory to grasp the larger reality of those imprisoned in any cave of ignorance.

Plato (428 BC−348 BC)

The Allegory of the Cave (from Book VII of *The Republic*)

(ca. 360 BC)

[SOCRATES is speaking with GLAUCON.]

SOCRATES: And now, I said, let me show in a figure how far our nature is enlightened or unenlightened: —Behold! human beings living in a underground den, which has a mouth open towards the light and reaching all along the den; here they have been from their childhood, and have their legs and necks chained so that they cannot move, and can only see before them, being prevented by the chains from turning round their heads. Above and behind them a fire is blazing at a distance, and between the fire and the prisoners there is a raised way; and you will see, if you look, a low wall built along the way, like the screen which marionette players have in front of them, over which they show the puppets.

GLAUCON: I see.

SOCRATES: And do you see, I said, men passing along the wall carrying all sorts of vessels, and statues and figures of animals made of wood and stone and various materials, which appear over the wall? Some of them are talking, others silent.

GLAUCON: You have shown me a strange image, and they are strange prisoners.

SOCRATES: Like ourselves, I replied; and they see only their own shadows, or   5
the shadows of one another, which the fire throws on the opposite wall of the cave?

GLAUCON: True, he said; how could they see anything but the shadows if they were never allowed to move their heads?

SOCRATES: And of the objects which are being carried in like manner they would only see the shadows?

GLAUCON: Yes, he said.

SOCRATES: And if they were able to converse with one another, would they not suppose that they were naming what was actually before them?

GLAUCON: Very true.   10

SOCRATES: And suppose further that the prison had an echo which came from the other side, would they not be sure to fancy when one of the passers-by spoke that the voice which they heard came from the passing shadow?

GLAUCON: No question, he replied.

SOCRATES: To them, I said, the truth would be literally nothing but the shadows of the images.

GLAUCON: That is certain.

SOCRATES: And now look again, and see what will naturally follow if the   15
prisoners are released and disabused of their error. At first, when any of them is liberated and compelled suddenly to stand up and turn his neck round and walk and look towards the light, he will suffer sharp pains; the glare will distress him, and he will be unable to see the realities of which in his former state he had seen the shadows; and then conceive some one saying to him, that what he saw before was an illusion, but that now, when he is approaching nearer to being and his eye is turned towards more real existence, he has a clearer vision, —what will be his reply? And you may further imagine that his instructor is pointing to the objects as they pass and requiring him to name them, —will he not be perplexed? Will he not fancy that the shadows which he formerly saw are truer than the objects which are now shown to him?

GLAUCON: Far truer.

SOCRATES: And if he is compelled to look straight at the light, will he not have a pain in his eyes which will make him turn away to take refuge in the objects of vision which he can see, and which he will conceive to be in reality clearer than the things which are now being shown to him?

GLAUCON: True, he said.

SOCRATES: And suppose once more, that he is reluctantly dragged up a steep and rugged ascent, and held fast until he's forced into the presence of the sun himself, is he not likely to be pained and irritated? When he approaches the light his eyes will be dazzled, and he will not be able to see anything at all of what are now called realities.

GLAUCON: Not all in a moment, he said.   20

SOCRATES: He will require to grow accustomed to the sight of the upper world. And first he will see the shadows best, next the reflections of men and other objects in the water, and then the objects themselves; then he will gaze upon the light of the moon and the stars and the spangled heaven; and he will see the sky and the stars by night better than the sun or the light of the sun by day?

GLAUCON: Certainly.

SOCRATES: Last of all he will be able to see the sun, and not mere reflections of him in the water, but he will see him in his own proper place, and not in another; and he will contemplate him as he is.

GLAUCON: Certainly.

SOCRATES: He will then proceed to argue that this is he who gives the sea-   25
son and the years, and is the guardian of all that is in the visible world, and in a certain way the cause of all things which he and his fellows have been accustomed to behold?

GLAUCON: Clearly, he said, he would first see the sun and then reason about him.

SOCRATES: And when he remembered his old habitation, and the wisdom of the den and his fellow-prisoners, do you not suppose that he would fe-licitate himself on the change, and pity them?

GLAUCON: Certainly, he would.

SOCRATES: And if they were in the habit of conferring honours among themselves on those who were quickest to observe the passing shadows and to remark which of them went before, and which followed after, and which were together; and who were therefore best able to draw con-clusions as to the future, do you think that he would care for such hon-ours and glories, or envy the possessors of them? Would he not say with Homer, "Better to be the poor servant of a poor master, and to endure anything, rather than think as they do and live after their manner?"

GLAUCON: Yes, he said, I think that he would rather suffer anything than   30
entertain these false notions and live in this miserable manner.

SOCRATES: Imagine once more, I said, such a one coming suddenly out of the sun to be replaced in his old situation; would he not be certain to have his eyes full of darkness?

GLAUCON: To be sure, he said.

SOCRATES: And if there were a contest, and he had to compete in measuring the shadows with the prisoners who had never moved out of the den, while his sight was still weak, and before his eyes had become steady (and the time which would be needed to acquire this new habit of sight might be very considerable), would he not be ridiculous? Men would say of him that up he went and down he came without his eyes; and that it was better not even to think of ascending; and if any one tried to loose another and lead him up to the light, let them only catch the offender, and they would put him to death.

GLAUCON: No question, he said.

SOCRATES: This entire allegory, I said, you may now append, dear Glaucon, 35
to the previous argument; the prison-house is the world of sight, the
light of the fire is the sun, and you will not misapprehend me if you interpret the journey upwards to be the ascent of the soul into the intellectual world according to my poor belief, which, at your desire, I have
expressed whether rightly or wrongly God knows. But, whether true or
false, my opinion is that in the world of knowledge the idea of good
appears last of all, and is seen only with an effort; and, when seen, is
also inferred to be the universal author of all things beautiful and right,
parent of light and of the lord of light in this visible world, and the immediate source of reason and truth in the intellectual; and that this is
the power upon which he who would act rationally, either in public or
private life, must have his eye fixed.

You'll note that in this dialogue, Socrates does most of the talking; he controls
the responses of Glaucon, his student. Plato presents all so that Glaucon (and
the readers of the dialogue) will arrive at the desired insight. But it's rare that a
narrative can keep such a tight control over materials so complex.

Experiencing Film through Allegory

In the film *The Matrix* (1999), Andy and Larry Wachowski create a film
version of Plato's allegory. By turning the allegory into action, the Wachowskis must test the limits of the scenario that Plato has created. An advantage
of pushing beyond the static quality of Plato's allegorical world is that further
development reveals problems that Glaucon had not noted. In moving from
Plato's largely descriptive "story" into the plot of a mainstream movie, the
tension that emerges occurs between the nearly invisible characters who
control the puppets in Plato's cave and those who have seen the light. Plato
describes the difficulty of convincing prisoners with such limited life experience that there was anything that they might want to escape. The screen-
writers, though, begin to ask questions that the original allegory does not
attempt to answer. For instance, Why are these people being held prisoner?
What sort of evil force would be responsible for such cruelty? How could
anyone ever escape from this enslavement? Would escape be desirable given
the paucity of the real world that remains?

The Matrix's plot concerns the difficulty of conveying the message of the
light to the prisoners. Neo (Keanu Reeves) must battle against these prison
keepers as well as against his own perception of which world is reality. The
life that he has experienced before his awakening is, like the cave, merely a
shadow that has been presented to him by the machines in order to keep him

The Matrix (1999)

in captivity. In opening up Plato's allegory, the Wachowskis also stumble upon ironies they seem unable to solve (or perhaps do not even recognize). For example, it is often not noticed amid all the expertly choreographed action that Neo kills the sorts of people he is supposed to be liberating. The

Making Connections

The language of war often makes use of the allegory. War posters have traditionally pictured figures such as Liberty, Truth, or Justice (almost always female) in order to represent the cause for which soldiers are fighting. The opponent is typically presented as some sort of animal or menacing threat. Examine contemporary military recruiting ads (posters and print ads, but also short narratives played in movie theaters before the trailers or during televised sports events), and analyze how allegories are used today. Explain how the allegory is designed to address a particular context.

guards and police gunned down in the final scene are shadows projected by the prison keepers, but these shadows are connected to the mental activity of real people wired into the matrix by the masters. Their death in the projected world leads to their physical death in the world not seen. So, are these unconscious victims mere collateral damage? Are we to assume that some shadows are more equal than others? Does Neo (or anyone else in his group) stop to think of the difference between the puppets/ humans and the puppet masters/ machines? It seems that the highly controlled sorts of meaning that Crampton had sought through allegory aren't achieved by many provocative works. Sometimes, allegory becomes most interesting when it breaks down and allows the reader/viewer to participate strongly in the creation of meaning.

MODELING CRITICAL ANALYSIS: JOÃO GUIMARÃES ROSA, THE THIRD BANK OF THE RIVER

"The Third Bank of River" by João Guimarães Rosa defies easy interpretation. If we think of it as a realistic story, it becomes confusing. The general tone seems fairly straightforward, and there is nothing startling in the first few paragraphs, but the story's action quickly grows impossible. This father leaves his family and lives silently for many years on a little boat just beyond the old home. How could he survive? The narrator tells us that he has been taking food to the father, but that hardly seems a satisfactory answer. No one could live on such a boat subject to the elements in complete silence and survive for so long. We can't answer many other simple questions about this story: Why doesn't someone go bring the father in? Why doesn't the father ever seem delirious? How is it that the family grows accustomed to such a strange situation? The fact that we cannot easily respond to these questions suggests that they are the wrong kinds of questions. Guimarães Rosa may well be writing about something very real, but this is not a realistic story.

João Guimarães Rosa (1908–1967)

The Third Bank of the River (Willian L. Grossman, trans; 1967)

My father was a dutiful, orderly, straightforward man. And according to several reliable people of whom I inquired, he had had these qualities since adolescence or even childhood. By my own recollection, he was neither jollier nor more melancholy than the other men we knew. Maybe a little quieter. It was Mother, not Father, who ruled the house. She scolded us daily—my sister, my brother, and me. But it happened one day that Father ordered a boat.

He was very serious about it. It was to be made specially for him, of mimosa wood. It was to be sturdy enough to last twenty or thirty years and just large enough for one person. Mother carried on plenty about it. Was her husband going to become a fisherman all of a sudden? Or a hunter? Father said nothing. Our house was less than a mile from the river, which around there was deep, quiet, and so wide you couldn't see across it.

I can never forget the day the rowboat was delivered. Father showed no joy or other emotion. He just put on his hat as he always did and said good-by to us. He took along no food or bundle of any sort. We expected Mother to rant and rave, but she didn't. She looked very pale and bit her lip, but all she said was: "If you go away, stay away. Don't ever come back!"

Father made no reply. He looked gently at me and motioned me to walk along with him. I feared Mother's wrath, yet I eagerly obeyed. We headed toward the river together. I felt bold and exhilarated, so much so that I said: "Father, will you take me with you in your boat?"

He just looked at me, gave me his blessing, and by a gesture, told me to 5 go back. I made as if to do so but, when his back was turned, I ducked behind some bushes to watch him. Father got into the boat and rowed away. Its shadow slid across the water like a crocodile, long and quiet.

Father did not come back. Nor did he go anywhere, really. He just rowed and floated across and around, out there in the river. Everyone was appalled. What had never happened, what could not possibly happen, was happening. Our relatives, neighbors, and friends came over to discuss the phenomenon.

Mother was ashamed. She said little and conducted herself with great composure. As a consequence, almost everyone thought (though no one said it) that Father had gone insane. A few, however, suggested that Father might be fulfilling a promise he had made to God or to a saint, or that he might have some horrible disease, maybe leprosy, and that he left for the sake of the family, at the same time wishing to remain fairly near them.

Travelers along the river and people living near the bank on one side or the other reported that Father never put foot on land, by day or night. He just moved about on the river, solitary, aimless, like a derelict. Mother and our relatives agreed that the food which he had doubtless hidden in the boat would soon give out and that then he would either leave the river and travel off somewhere (which would be at least a little more respectable) or he would repent and come home.

How far from the truth they were! Father had a secret source of provisions: me. Every day I stole food and brought it to him. The first night after he left, we all lit fires on the shore and prayed and called to him. I was deeply distressed and felt a need to do something more. The following day I went down to the river with a loaf of corn bread, a bunch of bananas, and some bricks of raw brown sugar. I waited impatiently a long, long hour. Then I saw the boat, far off, alone, gliding almost imperceptibly on the smoothness of the river. Father was sitting in the bottom of the boat. He saw me but he did not row toward me or make any gesture. I showed him the food and then I placed it in a hollow rock on the river bank; it was safe there from animals, rain, and dew. I did this day after day, on and on and on. Later I learned, to my surprise, that Mother knew what I was doing and left food around where I could easily steal it. She had a lot of feelings she didn't show.

Mother sent for her brother to come and help on the farm and in business matters. She had the schoolteacher come and tutor us children at home because of the time we had lost. One day, at her request, the priest put on his vestments, went down to the shore, and tried to exorcise the devils that had got into my father. He shouted that Father had a duty to cease his unholy obstinacy. Another day she arranged to have two soldiers come and try to frighten him. All to no avail. My father went by in the distance, sometimes so far away he could barely be seen. He never replied to anyone and no one ever got close to him. When some newspapermen came in a launch to take his picture, Father headed his boat to the other side of the river and into the marshes, which he knew like the palm of his hand but in which other people quickly got lost. There in his private maze, which extended for miles, with heavy foliage overhead and rushes on all sides, he was safe.

We had to get accustomed to the idea of Father's being out on the river. We had to but we couldn't, we never could. I think I was the only one who understood to some degree what our father wanted and what he did not want. The thing I could not understand at all was how he stood the hardship. Day and night, in sun and rain, in heat and in the terrible midyear cold spells, with his old hat on his head and very little other clothing, week after week, month after month, year after year, unheedful of the waste and emptiness in which his life was slipping by. He never set foot on earth or grass, on isle or mainland shore. No doubt he sometimes tied up the boat at a secret place, perhaps at the tip of some island, to get a little sleep. He never lit a fire or even struck a match and he had no flashlight. He took only a small part of the food that I left in the hollow rock—not enough, it seemed to me, for survival. What could his state of health have been? How about the continual drain on his energy, pulling and pushing the oars to control the boat? And how did he survive the annual floods, when the river rose and swept along with it all sorts of dangerous objects—branches of trees, dead bodies of animals—that might suddenly crash against his little boat?

He never talked to a living soul. And we never talked about him. We just thought. No, we could never put our father out of mind. If for a short time we seemed to, it was just a lull from which we would be sharply awakened by the realization of his frightening situation.

My sister got married, but Mother didn't want a wedding party. It would have been a sad affair, for we thought of him every time we ate some especially tasty food. Just as we thought of him in our cozy beds on a cold, stormy night—out there, alone and unprotected, trying to bail out the boat with only his hands and a gourd. Now and then someone would say that I was getting to look more and more like my father. But I knew that by then his hair and beard must have been shaggy and his nails long. I pictured him thin and sickly, black with hair and sunburn, and almost naked despite the articles of clothing I occasionally left for him.

He didn't seem to care about us at all. But I felt affection and respect for him, and, whenever they praised me because I had done something good, I said: "My father taught me to act that way."

It wasn't exactly accurate but it was a truthful sort of lie. As I said, Father didn't seem to care about us. But then why did he stay around there? Why didn't he go up the river or down the river, beyond the possibility of seeing us or being seen by us? He alone knew the answer.

My sister had a baby boy. She insisted on showing Father his grandson. One beautiful day we all went down to the riverbank, my sister in her white wedding dress, and she lifted the baby high. Her husband held a parasol above them. We shouted to Father and waited. He did not appear. My sister cried; we all cried in each other's arms.

My sister and her husband moved far away. My brother went to live in a city. Times changed, with their usual imperceptible rapidity. Mother finally moved too; she was old and went to live with her daughter. I remained behind, a leftover. I could never think of marrying. I just stayed there with the impedimenta of my life. Father, wandering alone and forlorn on the river, needed me. I knew he needed me, although he never even told me why he was doing it. When I put the question to people bluntly and insistently, all they told me was that they heard that Father had explained it to the man who made the boat. But now this man was dead and nobody knew or remembered anything. There was just some foolish talk, when the rains were especially severe and persistent, that my father was wise like Noah and had the boat built in anticipation of a new flood; I dimly remember people saying this. In any case, I would not condemn my father for what he was doing. My hair was beginning to turn gray.

I have only sad things to say. What bad had I done, what was my great guilt? My father always away and his absence always with me. And the river, always the river, perpetually renewing itself. The river, always. I was beginning to suffer from old age, in which life is just a sort of lingering. I had attacks of illness and of anxiety. I had a nagging rheumatism. And he? Why, why was he doing it? He must have been suffering terribly. He was so old. One day, in his failing strength, he might let the boat capsize; or he might let the current carry it downstream, on and on, until it plunged over the waterfall to the boiling turmoil below. It pressed upon my heart. He was out there and I was forever robbed of my peace. I am guilty of I know not what, and my pain is an open wound inside me. Perhaps I would know—if things were different. I began to guess what was wrong.

Out with it! Had I gone crazy? No, in our house that word was never spoken, never through all the years. No one called anybody crazy, for nobody is crazy. Or maybe everybody. All I did was go there and wave a handkerchief so he would be more likely to see me. I was in complete command of myself. I waited. Finally he appeared in the distance, there, then over there, a vague shape sitting in the back of the boat. I called to him several times. And I said what I was so eager to say, to state formally and under oath. I said it as loud as I could:

"Father, you have been out there long enough. You are old. . . . Come   20
back, you don't have to do it anymore. . . . Come back and I'll go instead. Right now, if you want. Any time. I'll get into the boat. I'll take your place."

And when I had said this my heart beat more firmly.

He heard me. He stood up. He maneuvered with his oars and headed the boat toward me. He had accepted my offer. And suddenly I trembled, down deep. For he had raised his arm and waved—the first time in so many, so many years. And I couldn't. . . In terror, my hair on end, I ran, I fled madly. For he seemed to come from another world. And I'm begging forgiveness, begging, begging.

I experienced the dreadful sense of cold that comes from deadly fear, and I became ill. Nobody ever saw or heard about him again. Am I a man, after such a failure? I am what never should have been. I am what must be silent. I know it is too late. I must stay in the deserts and unmarked plains of my life, and I fear I shall shorten it. But when death comes I want them to take me and put me in a little boat in this perpetual water between the long shores; and I, down the river, lost in the river, inside the river. . . the river. . . ■

What happens if we try to read this story as an allegory? It's worth noticing that the father is "very serious" about the boat. It is made to carry one person and one person only. When it is delivered, the father shows no emotion. He simply says "good-by" to the family and heads off to the river. The son wants to go with him, but the father sends him back and moves off silently, alone. Is it possible that Guimarães Rosa's story allegorizes death and the process of grief? If we think in such terms, we may be prepared to answer new questions: How is it that the father doesn't "come back" or "go anywhere"? How can he be so present and so absent? The boat carries only one because only one dies; others left behind must deal with the death. The father is no longer a physical presence in the life of his family, but his death has not ended a relationship that transcends the physical. The son, in particular, struggles with his own identity in the father's absence. He works hard to keep the father alive in memory.

Such a reading begins to open possibilities, but it doesn't suddenly snap everything into place. It seems that Guimarães Rosa's story has allegorical elements but never sustains a clear and consistent parallel between the concrete and the abstract. We're invited to consider alternative readings. Perhaps rather than death, Guimarães Rosa's allegory concerns more generally disconnection and loneliness in families. Or perhaps the emphasis needs to shift to the narrator, to the son. How do we read this story if we think of it as the struggles of a young man to grow up? Is separation from the father a crucial part of that maturation? Has the narrator been unable to accept the distance his father has established in their relationship? Understanding how allegory works helps us enter the world of this story and respond to it powerfully.

Using Allegory to Focus Writing and Discussion

- What makes you think that it is appropriate to read this work allegorically? Find specific signals that the author gives to allow you to explore allegorical interpretations.
- Describe the tone of the work. How does the tone of the surface narrative lead us to allegorical interpretations?
- If we can offer sufficient proof that there is some justification in the text for an allegorical interpretation, we can go on to the next questions.
- Set up an interpretive table to explain the significance of specific characters within the work. To develop this chart, identify the character by name, the idea that this character represents, and your justification (from the text itself) that allows you to make this connection.
- What is the advantage of reading the text allegorically? How does this interpretation offer insight that is not available by reading the surface narrative "straight"?
- Why is it useful for the author to approach this particular subject indirectly?

Anthology

THE QUEST FOR TRUTH: READING ALLEGORY

In Chapter 1, we noted how some texts narrow the notion of truth to an accurate account of what happened. And we also explored how such a seemingly limited goal sometimes opens up unanswerable questions. Some modern detective stories don't so much solve a problem as help us understand the dimensions of a problem. In a way, all writing sets us on a quest. Words commit us to follow through on ideas, and often we're led places we never thought to go. Allegory might be thought of as a deliberate search strategy—a thought experiment. What happens if we set in motion a character in a specific situation who stands in for some abstract idea? What happens if we have Love fight with Anger? Who will win, and what will it mean to win? Of course, we might also think of allegory as the mechanism that we employ once we've thought through our desired meaning. But we'd still need to test the elements and decide how the parts fit in order to register that desired meaning. Whether working to discover a truth or working to embody one we've already discovered, we're on a quest when we commit ourselves to allegory.

Readers of an allegory, of course, embark on the same quest. We might feel guided by some key signals. But it's hard to extend a simile or a metaphor in narrative form and keep things simple. Nathaniel Hawthorne sends young Goodman Brown out into the dark forest away from his wife, Faith. That Goodman Brown loses Faith seems clear, but the terms of the allegory don't force us to share Brown's interpretation of his own experience. On his quest, has he arrived at a terrible truth about human depravity? Or has he merely bounced from a naïve innocence to an equally naïve cynicism? To present it from the author's perspective, is Hawthorne interested primarily in sin or in the effects of thinking about sin? We need to read carefully and consider such questions for ourselves because Hawthorne doesn't guide us as forcefully as the author of *Tootle*.

Plato suggests something important about the nature of allegory when he casts his work in the form of a dialogue. We test out, apply, question, and discuss the parallels that allegories put in motion. We don't want to just "get" the message but to explore and evaluate the message. We want to find out if it can help us understand something of our world. We want it to help us on our quest. Collins suggests in his poem "The Death of Allegory" that allegory is about big ideas, often ideas written in an initial capital letter (Truth, not truth). In order to consider his claim, it is useful to look back at some of the older pieces that carry these capitalized qualities. In the *Faerie Queene*, Spenser creates a land of knights and faeries to talk about religion and sixteenth-century English politics; the principles of good and evil remain relatively straightforward. The Red Cross Knight who opens the story in the brief excerpt included in this anthology is literally on a quest for truth: he is looking for Una, the princess who represents the true church, but he keeps getting confused by her counterfeit. The allegorical form is equally appropriate for John Donne to ponder both religious truths and secular love.

Jane Martin's *Beauty* explores how the quest can go wrong if it's founded upon false assumptions. Her characters come to an insight they would have never thought they were looking for. That insight is delivered as a punch line to a joke. But there is a serious dimension to Martin's comic quest. Her commentary is finally not only on the desires of her two characters but a broader confusion that afflicts the culture. As you read, ask yourself, What do these characters stand for? How does their foolishness comment on common misunderstandings?

FICTION

Nathaniel Hawthorne (1804–1864)

Nathaniel Hawthorne was born in Salem, Massachusetts. His childhood was marred by the tragic death of his father, and Hawthorne, his mother, and his siblings moved to Maine to reside with relatives. Hawthorne attended Bowdoin College in Maine and graduated in 1825. After graduation, Hawthorne returned to Salem, where he spent twelve years as a literary apprentice. In 1836, he moved to Boston, where he and his sister began writing children's books. He continued to publish short stories but took various jobs, including weigher and surveyor, to support himself. After marrying in 1842, Hawthorne moved to Concord, where he associated with the transcendentalists Henry David Thoreau, Ralph Waldo Emerson, and Louisa May Alcott; after only three years, the Hawthorne family returned to Salem. In 1850, he published the now classic novel *The Scarlet Letter*. Like most of his previous writings, Hawthorne's second novel explored the themes of sin, guilt, and forgiveness through the use of symbolism.

Young Goodman Brown (1835)

Young Goodman Brown came forth at sunset into the street at Salem village; but put his head back, after crossing the threshold, to exchange a parting kiss with his young wife. And Faith, as the wife was aptly named, thrust her own pretty head into the street, letting the wind play with the pink ribbons of her cap while she called to Goodman Brown.

"Dearest heart," whispered she, softly and rather sadly, when her lips were close to his ear, "prithee put off your journey until sunrise and sleep in your own bed tonight. A lone woman is troubled with such dreams and such thoughts that she's afeared of herself sometimes. Pray tarry with me this night, dear husband, of all nights in the year."

"My love and my Faith," replied young Goodman Brown, "of all nights in the year, this one night must I tarry away from thee. My journey, as thou callest it, forth and back again, must needs be done 'twixt now and sunrise.

What, my sweet, pretty wife, dost thou doubt me already, and we but three months married?"

"Then God bless you!" said Faith, with the pink ribbons; "and may you find all well when you come back."

"Amen!" cried Goodman Brown, "Say thy prayers, dear Faith, and go to bed at dusk, and no harm will come to thee."   5

So they parted; and the young man pursued his way until, being about to turn the corner by the meeting-house, he looked back and saw the head of Faith still peeping after him with a melancholy air, in spite of her pink ribbons.

"Poor little Faith!" thought he, for his heart smote him. "What a wretch am I to leave her on such an errand! She talks of dreams, too. Methought as she spoke there was trouble in her face, as if a dream had warned her what work is to be done tonight. But no, no; 't would kill her to think it. Well, she's a blessed angel on earth; and after this one night I'll cling to her skirts and follow her to heaven."

With this excellent resolve for the future, Goodman Brown felt himself justified in making more haste on his present evil purpose. He had taken a dreary road, darkened by all the gloomiest trees of the forest, which barely stood aside to let the narrow path creep through, and closed immediately behind. It was all as lonely as could be; and there is this peculiarity in such a solitude, that the traveler knows not who may be concealed by the innumerable trunks and the thick boughs overhead; so that with lonely footsteps he may yet be passing through an unseen multitude.

"There may be a devilish Indian behind every tree," said Goodman Brown to himself; and he glanced fearfully behind him as he added, "What if the devil himself should be at my very elbow!"

His head being turned back, he passed a crook of the road, and, looking forward again, beheld the figure of a man, in grave and decent attire, seated at the foot of an old tree. He arose at Goodman Brown's approach and walked onward side by side with him.   10

"You are late, Goodman Brown," said he. "The clock of the Old South was striking as I came through Boston, and that is full fifteen minutes agone."

"Faith kept me back a while," replied the young man, with a tremor in his voice, caused by the sudden appearance of his companion, though not wholly unexpected.

It was now deep dusk in the forest, and deepest in that part of it where these two were journeying. As nearly as could be discerned, the second traveler was about fifty years old, apparently in the same rank of life as Goodman Brown, and bearing a considerable resemblance to him, though perhaps more in expression than features. Still they might have been taken for father and son. And yet, though the elder person was as simply clad as the younger, and as simple in manner too, he had an indescribable air of one who knew the world, and who would not have felt abashed at the governor's dinner table or in King William's court, were it possible that his affairs should call him thither. But the only thing about him that could be fixed upon as remarkable was his staff, which bore the likeness of a great black snake, so curiously wrought that it might almost be seen to twist and wriggle itself like a living serpent. This, of course, must have been an ocular deception, assisted by the uncertain light.

"Come, Goodman Brown," cried his fellow-traveler, "this is a dull pace for the beginning of a journey. Take my staff, if you are so soon weary."

"Friend," said the other, exchanging his slow pace for a full stop, "having kept covenant by meeting thee here, it is my purpose now to return whence I came. I have scruples touching the matter thou wot'st of."

"Sayest thou so?" replied he of the serpent, smiling apart. "Let us walk on, nevertheless, reasoning as we go; and if I convince thee not thou shalt turn back. We are but a little way in the forest yet."

"Too far! too far!" exclaimed the goodman, unconsciously resuming his walk. "My father never went into the woods on such an errand, nor his father before him. We have been a race of honest men and good Christians since the days of the martyrs; and shall I be the first of the name of Brown that ever took this path and kept"—

"Such company, thou wouldst say," observed the elder person, interpreting his pause. "Well said, Goodman Brown! I have been as well acquainted with your family as with ever a one among the Puritans; and that's no trifle to say. I helped your grandfather, the constable, when he lashed the Quaker woman so smartly through the streets of Salem; and it was I that brought your father a pitch-pine knot, kindled at my own hearth, to set fire to an Indian village, in King Philip's war. They were my good friends, both; and many a pleasant walk have we had along this path, and returned merrily after midnight. I would fain be friends with you for their sake."

"If it be as thou sayest," replied Goodman Brown, "I marvel they never spoke of these matters; or, verily, I marvel not, seeing that the least rumor of the sort would have driven them from New England. We are a people of prayer, and good works to boot, and abide no such wickedness."

"Wickedness or not," said the traveler with the twisted staff, "I have a very general acquaintance here in New England. The deacons of many a church have drunk the communion wine with me; the selectmen of divers towns make me their chairman; and a majority of the Great and General Court are firm supporters of my interest. The governor and I, too—But these are state secrets."

"Can this be so?" cried Goodman Brown, with a stare of amazement at his undisturbed companion. "Howbeit, I have nothing to do with the governor and council; they have their own ways, and are no rule for a simple husbandman like me. But, were I to go on with thee, how should I meet the eye of that good old man, our minister, at Salem village? Oh, his voice would make me tremble both Sabbath day and lecture day."

Thus far the elder traveler had listened with due gravity; but now burst into a fit of irrepressible mirth, shaking himself so violently that his snake-like staff actually seemed to wriggle in sympathy.

"Ha! ha! ha!" shouted he again and again; then composing himself, "Well, go on, Goodman Brown, go on; but, prithee, don't kill me with laughing."

"Well, then, to end the matter at once," said Goodman Brown, considerably nettled, "there is my wife, Faith. It would break her dear little heart; and I'd rather break my own."

"Nay, if that be the case," answered the other, "e'en go thy ways, Goodman Brown. I would not for twenty old women like the one hobbling before us that Faith should come to any harm."

As he spoke he pointed his staff at a female figure on the path, in whom Goodman Brown recognized a very pious and exemplary dame, who had taught him his catechism in youth, and was still his moral and spiritual adviser, jointly with the minister and Deacon Gookin.

"A marvel, truly that Goody Cloyse should be so far in the wilderness at nightfall," said he. "But with your leave, friend, I shall take a cut through the woods until we have left this Christian woman behind. Being a stranger to you, she might ask whom I was consorting with and whither I was going."

"Be it so," said his fellow-traveler. "Betake you to the woods, and let me keep the path."

Accordingly the young man turned aside, but took care to watch his companion, who advanced softly along the road until he had come within a staff's length of the old dame. She, meanwhile, was making the best of her way, with singular speed for so aged a woman, and mumbling some indistinct words—a prayer, doubtless—as she went. The traveler put forth his staff and touched her withered neck with what seemed the serpent's tail.

"The devil!" screamed the pious old lady.

"Then Goody Cloyse knows her old friend?" observed the traveler, confronting her and leaning on his writhing stick.

"Ah, forsooth, and is it your worship indeed?" cried the good dame. "Yea, truly is it, and in the very image of my old gossip, Goodman Brown, the grandfather of the silly fellow that now is. But—would your worship believe it?—my broomstick hath strangely disappeared, stolen, as I suspect, by that unhanged witch, Goody Cory, and that, too, when I was all anointed with the juice of smallage, and cinquefoil, and wolfsbane"—

"Mingled with fine wheat and the fat of a newborn babe," said the shape of old Goodman Brown.

"Ah, your worship knows the recipe," cried the old lady, cackling aloud. "So, as I was saying, being all ready for the meeting, and no horse to ride on, I made up my mind to foot it; for they tell me there is a nice young man to be taken into communion tonight. But now your good worship will lend me your arm, and we shall be there in a twinkling."

"That can hardly be," answered her friend. "I may not spare you my arm, Goody Cloyse; but here is my staff, if you will." 35

So saying, he threw it down at her feet, where, perhaps, it assumed life, being one of the rods which its owner had formerly lent to the Egyptian magi. Of this fact, however, Goodman Brown could not take cognizance. He had cast up his eyes in astonishment, and, looking down again, beheld neither Goody Cloyse nor the serpentine staff, but his fellow-traveler alone, who waited for him as calmly as if nothing had happened.

"That old woman taught me my catechism," said the young man; and there was a world of meaning in this simple comment.

They continued to walk onward, while the elder traveler exhorted his companion to make good speed and persevere in the path, discoursing so aptly that his arguments seemed rather to spring up in the bosom of his auditor than to be suggested by himself. As they went, he plucked a branch of maple to serve for a walking stick, and began to strip it of the twigs and little boughs, which were wet with evening dew. The moment his fingers touched them they became strangely withered and dried up as with a week's sunshine. Thus the pair proceeded, at a good free pace, until suddenly, in a gloomy hollow of the road, Goodman Brown sat himself down on the stump of a tree and refused to go any farther.

"Friend," he said, stubbornly, "my mind is made up. Not another step will I budge on this errand. What if a wretched old woman do choose to go to the devil when I thought she was going to heaven: is that any reason why I should quit my dear Faith and go after her?"

"You will think better of this by and by," said his acquaintance, composedly. "Sit here and rest yourself a while; and when you feel like moving again, there is my staff to help you along." 40

Without more words, he threw his companion the maple stick, and was as speedily out of sight as if he had vanished into the deepening gloom. The young man sat a few moments by the roadside, applauding himself greatly, and thinking with how clear a conscience he should meet the minister in his morning walk, nor shrink from the eye of good old Deacon Gookin. And what calm sleep would be his that very night, which was to have been spent so wickedly, but so purely and sweetly now, in the arms of Faith! Amidst these pleasant and praiseworthy meditations, Goodman Brown heard the tramp of horses along the road, and deemed it advisable to conceal himself within the verge of the forest, conscious of the guilty purpose that had brought him thither, though now so happily turned from it.

On came the hoof tramps and the voices of the riders, two grave old voices, conversing soberly as they drew near. These mingled sounds appeared to pass along the road, within a few yards of the young man's hiding-place; but, owing doubtless to the depth of the gloom at that particular spot, neither the travelers nor their steeds were visible. Though their figures brushed the small boughs by the wayside, it could not be seen that they intercepted, even for a moment, the faint gleam from the strip of bright sky athwart which they must have passed. Goodman Brown alternately crouched and stood on tiptoe, pulling aside the branches and thrusting forth his head as far as he durst without discerning so much as a shadow. It vexed him the more, because he could have sworn, were such a thing possible, that he recognized the voices of the minister and Deacon Gookin, jogging along quietly, as they were wont to do, when bound to some ordination or ecclesiastical council. While yet within hearing, one of the riders stopped to pluck a switch,

"Of the two, reverend sir," said the voice like the deacon's, "I had rather miss an ordination dinner than tonight's meeting. They tell me that some of our community are to be here from Falmouth and beyond, and others from Connecticut and Rhode Island, besides several of the Indian powwows, who, after their fashion, know almost as much deviltry as the best of us. Moreover, there is a goodly young woman to be taken into communion."

"Mighty well, Deacon Gookin!" replied the solemn old tones of the minister. "Spur up, or we shall be late. Nothing can be done, you know, until I get on the ground."

The hoofs clattered again; and the voices, talking so strangely in the empty air, passed on through the forest, where no church had ever been gathered or solitary Christian prayed. Whither, then, could these holy men be journeying so deep into the heathen wilderness? Young Goodman Brown caught hold of a tree for support, being ready to sink down on the ground, faint and overburdened with the heavy sickness of his heart. He looked up to the sky, doubting whether there really was a heaven above him. Yet there was the blue arch, and the stars brightening in it. 45

"With heaven above and Faith below, I will yet stand firm against the devil!" cried Goodman Brown.

While he still gazed upward into the deep arch of the firmament and had lifted his hands to pray, a cloud, though no wind was stirring, hurried across the zenith and hid the brightening stars. The blue sky was still visible, except directly overhead, where this black mass of cloud was sweeping swiftly northward. Aloft in the air, as if from the depths of the cloud, came a confused and doubtful sound of voices. Once the listener fancied that he could distinguish the accents of townspeople of his own, men and women, both pious and ungodly, many of whom he had met at the communion table, and had seen others rioting at the tavern. The next moment, so indistinct were the sounds, he doubted whether he had heard aught but the murmur of the old forest, whispering without a wind. Then came a stronger swell of those familiar tones, heard daily in the sunshine at Salem village, but never until now from a cloud of night. There was one voice, of a young woman, uttering lamentations, yet with an uncertain sorrow, and entreating for some favor, which, perhaps, it would grieve her to obtain; and all the unseen multitude, both saints and sinners, seemed to encourage her onward.

"Faith!" shouted Goodman Brown, in a voice of agony and desperation; and the echoes of the forest mocked him, crying, "Faith! Faith!" as if bewildered wretches were seeking her all through the wilderness.

The cry of grief, rage, and terror was yet piercing the night, when the unhappy husband held his breath for a response. There was a scream, drowned immediately in a louder murmur of voices, fading into far-off laughter, as the dark cloud swept away, leaving the clear and silent sky above Goodman Brown. But something fluttered lightly down through the air and caught on the branch of a tree. The young man seized it, and beheld a pink ribbon.

"My Faith is gone!" cried he after one stupefied moment. "There is no good on earth; and sin is but a name. Come, devil; for to thee is this world given."

And, maddened with despair, so that he laughed loud and long, did Goodman Brown grasp his staff and set forth again, at such a rate that he seemed to fly along the forest path rather than to walk or run. The road grew wilder and drearier and more faintly traced, and vanished at length, leaving him in the heart of the dark wilderness, still rushing onward with the instinct that guides mortal man to evil. The whole forest was peopled with frightful sounds—the creaking of the trees, the howling of wild beasts, and the yell of Indians; while sometimes the wind tolled like a distant church bell, and sometimes gave a broad roar around the traveler, as if all Nature were laughing him to scorn. But he was himself the chief horror of the scene, and shrank not from its other horrors.

"Ha! ha! ha!" roared Goodman Brown when the wind laughed at him. "Let us hear which will laugh loudest. Think not to frighten me with your deviltry. Come witch, come wizard, come Indian powwow, come devil himself, and here comes Goodman Brown. You may as well fear him as he fear you."

In truth, all through the haunted forest there could be nothing more frightful than the figure of Goodman Brown. On he flew among the black pines, brandishing his staff with frenzied gestures, now giving vent to an inspiration of horrid blasphemy, and now shouting forth such laughter as set all the echoes of the forest laughing like demons around him. The fiend in his own shape is less hideous than when he rages in the breast of man. Thus sped the demoniac on his course, until, quivering among the trees, he saw a red light before him, as when the felled trunks and branches of a clearing have been set on fire, and throw up their lurid blaze against the sky, at the hour of midnight. He paused, in a lull of the tempest that had driven him onward, and heard the swell of what seemed a hymn, rolling solemnly from a distance with the weight of many voices. He knew the tune; it was a familiar one in the choir of the village meeting-house. The verse died heavily away. and was lengthened by a chorus, not of human voices, but of all the sounds of the benighted wilderness pealing in awful harmony together. Goodman Brown cried out, and his cry was lost to his own ear by its unison with the cry of the desert.

In the interval of silence he stole forward until the light glared full upon his eyes. At one extremity of an open space, hemmed in by the dark wall of the forest, arose a rock, bearing some rude, natural resemblance either to an altar or a pulpit, and surrounded by four blazing pines, their tops aflame, their stems untouched, like candles at an evening meeting. The mass of foliage that had overgrown the summit of the rock was all on fire, blazing high into the night and fitfully illuminating the whole field. Each pendent twig and leafy festoon was in a blaze. As the red light arose and fell, a numerous congregation alternately shone forth, then disappeared in shadow, and again grew, as it were, out of the darkness, peopling the heart of the solitary woods at once.

"A grave and dark-clad company," quoth Goodman Brown.   55

In truth they were such. Among them, quivering to and fro between gloom and splendor, appeared faces that would be seen next day at the council board of the province, and others which, Sabbath after Sabbath, looked devoutly heavenward, and benignantly over the crowded pews, from the holiest pulpits in the land. Some affirm that the lady of the governor was there. At least there were high dames well known to her, and wives of honored husbands, and widows, a great multitude, and ancient maidens, all of excellent repute, and fair young girls, who trembled lest their mothers should espy them. Either the sudden gleams of light flashing over the obscure field bedazzled Goodman Brown, or he recognized a score of the church members of Salem village famous for their especial sanctity. Good old Deacon Gookin had arrived, and waited at the skirts of that venerable saint, his revered pastor. But, irreverently consorting with these grave, reputable, and pious people, these elders of the church, these chaste dames and dewy virgins, there were men of dissolute lives and women of spotted fame, wretches given over to all mean and filthy vice, and suspected even of horrid crimes. It was strange to see that the good shrank not from the wicked, nor were the sinners abashed by the saints. Scattered also among their pale-faced enemies were the Indian priests, or powwows, who had often scared their native forest with more hideous incantations than any known to English witchcraft.

"But where is Faith?" thought Goodman Brown; and, as hope came into his heart, he trembled.

Another verse of the hymn arose, a slow and mournful strain, such as the pious love, but joined to words which expressed all that our nature can conceive of sin, and darkly hinted at far more. Unfathomable to mere mortals is the lore of fiends. Verse after verse was sung; and still the chorus of the desert swelled between like the deepest tone of a mighty organ; and with the final peal of that dreadful anthem there came a sound, as if the roaring wind, the rushing streams, the howling beasts, and every other voice of the unconcerted wilderness were mingling and according with the voice of guilty man in homage to the prince of all. The four blazing pines threw up a loftier flame, and obscurely discovered shapes and visages of horror on the smoke wreaths above the impious assembly. At the same moment the fire on the rock shot redly forth and formed a glowing arch above its base, where now appeared a figure. With reverence be it spoken, the figure bore no slight similitude, both in garb and manner, to some grave divine of the New England churches.

"Bring forth the converts!" cried a voice that echoed through the field and rolled into the forest.

At the word, Goodman Brown stepped forth from the shadow of the trees and approached the congregation, with whom he felt a loathful brotherhood by the sympathy of all that was wicked in his heart. He could have well-nigh sworn that the shape of his own dead father beckoned him to advance, looking downward from a smoke wreath, while a woman, with dim features of despair, threw out her hand to warn him back. Was it his mother? But he had no power to retreat one step, nor to resist, even in thought, when the minister and good old Deacon Gookin seized his arms and led him to the blazing rock. Thither came also the slender form of a veiled female, led between Goody Cloyse, that pious teacher of the catechism, and Martha Carrier, who had received the devil's promise to be queen of hell. A rampant hag was she. And there stood the proselytes beneath the canopy of fire.

"Welcome, my children," said the dark figure, "to the communion of your race. Ye have found thus young your nature and your destiny. My children, look behind you!"

They turned; and flashing forth, as it were, in a sheet of flame, the fiend worshipers were seen; the smile of welcome gleamed darkly on every visage.

"There," resumed the sable form, "are all whom ye have reverenced from youth. Ye deemed them holier than yourselves and shrank from your own sin, contrasting it with their lives of righteousness and prayerful aspirations heavenward. Yet here are they all in my worshiping assembly. This night it shall be granted you to know their secret deeds: how hoary-bearded elders of the church have whispered wanton words to the young maids of their households; how many a woman, eager for widows' weeds, has given her husband a drink at bedtime and let him sleep his last sleep in her bosom; how beardless youths have made haste to inherit their fathers' wealth; and how fair damsels—blush not, sweet ones—have dug little graves in the garden, and bidden me, the sole guest, to an infant's funeral. By the sympathy of your human hearts for sin ye shall scent out all the places—whether in church, bedchamber, street, field, or forest—where crime has been committed, and shall exult to behold the whole earth one stain of guilt, one mighty blood spot. Far more than this. It shall be yours to penetrate, in every bosom, the deep mystery of sin, the fountain of all wicked arts, and which inexhaustibly supplies more evil impulses than human power—than my power at its utmost—can make manifest in deeds. And now, my children, look upon each other."

They did so; and, by the blaze of the hell-kindled torches, the wretched man beheld his Faith, and the wife her husband, trembling before that unhallowed altar.

"Lo, there ye stand, my children," said the figure, in a deep and solemn   65
tone, almost sad with its despairing awfulness, as if his once angelic nature could yet mourn for our miserable race, "Depending upon one another's hearts, ye had still hoped that virtue were not all a dream. Now are ye undeceived. Evil is the nature of mankind. Evil must be your only happiness. Welcome again, my children, to the communion of your race."

"Welcome," repeated the fiend worshipers; in one cry of despair and triumph.

And there they stood, the only pair, as it seemed, who were yet hesitating on the verge of wickedness in this dark world. A basin was hollowed, naturally, in the rock. Did it contain water, reddened by the lurid light? or was it blood? or, perchance, a liquid flame? Herein did the shape of evil dip his hand and prepare to lay the mark of baptism upon their foreheads, that they might be partakers of the mystery of sin, more conscious of the secret guilt of others, both in deed and thought, than they could now be of their own. The husband cast one look at his pale wife, and Faith at him. What polluted wretches would the next glance show them to each other, shuddering alike at what they disclosed and what they saw!

"Faith! Faith!" cried the husband, "look up to heaven, and resist the wicked one."

Whether Faith obeyed he knew not. Hardly had he spoken when he found himself amid calm night and solitude, listening to a roar of the wind which died heavily away through the forest. He staggered against the rock, and felt it chill and damp; while a hanging twig, that had been all on fire, besprinkled his cheek with the coldest dew.

The next morning young Goodman Brown came slowly into the street   70
of Salem village, staring around him like a bewildered man. The good old minister was taking a walk along the graveyard to get an appetite for

breakfast and meditate his sermon, and bestowed a blessing, as he passed, on Goodman Brown. He shrank from the venerable saint as if to avoid an anathema. Old Deacon Gookin was at domestic worship, and the holy words of his prayer were heard through the open window. "What God doth the wizard pray to?" quoth Goodman Brown. Goody Cloyse, that excellent old Christian, stood in the early sunshine at her own lattice, catechizing a little girl who had brought her a pint of morning's milk. Goodman Brown snatched away the child as from the grasp of the fiend himself. Turning the corner by the meeting-house, he spied the head of Faith, with the pink ribbons, gazing anxiously forth, and bursting into such joy at sight of him that she skipped along the street and almost kissed her husband before the whole village. But Goodman Brown looked sternly and sadly into her face, and passed on without a greeting.

Had Goodman Brown fallen asleep in the forest and only dreamed a wild dream of a witch-meeting?

Be it so if you will; but, alas! it was a dream of evil omen for young Goodman Brown. A stern, a sad, a darkly meditative, a distrustful, if not a desperate man did he become from the night of that fearful dream. On the Sabbath day, when the congregation were singing a holy psalm, he could not listen because an anthem of sin rushed loudly upon his ear and drowned all the blessed strain. When the minister spoke from the pulpit with power and fervid eloquence, and, with his hand on the open Bible, of the sacred truths of our religion, and of saintlike lives and triumphant deaths, and of future bliss or misery unutterable, then did Goodman Brown turn pale, dreading lest the roof should thunder down upon the gray blasphemer and his hearers. Often, awaking suddenly at midnight, he shrank from the bosom of Faith; and at morning or eventide, when the family knelt down at prayer, he scowled and muttered to himself, and gazed sternly at his wife, and turned away. And when he had lived long, and was borne to his grave a hoary corpse, followed by Faith, an aged woman, and children and grandchildren, a goodly procession, besides neighbors not a few, they carved no hopeful verse upon his tombstone, for his dying hour was gloom.

- What is the significance of Goodman Brown's wife?
- Why does Goodman Brown go out into the woods?
- Look carefully at the details Hawthorne presents about Brown's guide. How do these details give us insight into Brown's character?
- What does Brown see in the woods?
- What happens once Brown comes home? How does his experience influence the rest of his life?
- What is Hawthorne's message in this text?

POETRY

Lewis Carroll (1832–1898)

Jabberwocky (1871)

'Twas brillig, and the slithy toves
    Did gyre and gimble in the wabe:
All mimsy were the borogoves,
    And the mome raths outgrabe.

"Beware the Jabberwock, my son!   5
    The jaws that bite, the claws that catch!
Beware the Jubjub bird, and shun
    The frumious Bandersnatch!"

He took his vorpal sword in hand;
    Long time the manxome foe he sought—   10
So rested he by the Tumtum tree
    And stood awhile in thought.

And, as in uffish thought he stood,
    The Jabberwock, with eyes of flame,
Came whiffling through the tulgey wood,   15
    And burbled as it came!

One, two! One, two! And through and through
    The vorpal blade went snicker-snack!
He left it dead, and with its head
    He went galumphing back.   20

"And hast thou slain the Jabberwock?
    Come to my arms, my beamish boy!
O frabjous day! Callooh, Callay!"
    He chortled in his joy.

'Twas brillig, and the slithy toves   25
    Did gyre and gimble in the wabe:
All mimsy were the borogoves,
    And the mome raths outgrabe.

■ How would you define such nonsense words as *vorpal, manxome,* and *beamish*?

Sir John Tenniel's illustration of "The Jabberwocky."

■ How does the context of the poem provide hints for reading such words? How does the formulaic quest story that we see represented in this poem help us understand the content of each stanza? How does the language make us read the quest differently than we might read it otherwise?

Edmund Spenser (1552–1599)

from # The Faerie Queene (1596)

Canto I.
The Patron of true Holinesse,
Foule Errour doth defeat:
Hypocrisie him to entrappe;
Doth to his home entreate.

1

A Gentle Knight was pricking on the plaine,
Ycladd in mightie armes and silver shielde,
Wherein old dints of deepe wounds did remaine,
The cruell markes of many a bloudy fielde;
Yet armes till that time did he never wield: 5

His angry steede did chide his foming bitt,
As much disdayning to the curbe to yield:
Full jolly knight he seemd, and faire did sitt,
As one for knightly giusts and fierce encounters fitt.

2

But on his brest a bloudie Crosse he bore,   10
The deare remembrance of his dying Lord,
For whose sweete sake that glorious badge he wore,
And dead as living ever him ador'd:
Upon his shield the like was also scor'd,
For soveraine hope, which in his helpe he had: 15
Right faithfull true he was in deede and word,
But of his cheere did seeme too solemne sad;
Yet nothing did he dread, but ever was ydrad.

3

Upon a great aduenture he was bond,
That greatest Gloriana to him gave,   20
That greatest Glorious Queene of Faerie lond,
To winne him worship, and her grace to have,
Which of all earthly things he most did crave;
And ever as he rode, his hart did earne
To prove his puissance in battell brave   25
Upon his foe, and his new force to learne;
Upon his foe, a Dragon horrible and stearne.

4

A lovely Ladie rode him faire beside,
Upon a lowly Asse more white then snow,
Yet she much whiter, but the same did hide   30
Under a vele, that wimpled was full low,
And over all a blacke stole she did throw,
As one that inly mournd: so was she sad,
And heavie sat upon her palfrey slow:
Seemed in heart some hidden care she had,   35
And by her in a line a milke white lambe she lad.

5

So pure an innocent, as that same lambe,
She was in life and every vertuous lore,
And by descent from Royall lynage came
Of ancient Kings and Queens, that had of yore   40

Their scepters stretcht from East to Westerne shore,
And all the world in their subjection held;
Till that infernall feend with foule uprore
Forwasted all their land, and them expeld:
Whom to avenge, she had this Knight from far compeld.   45

6

Behind her farre away a Dwarfe did lag,
That lasie seemd in being ever last,
Or wearied with bearing of her bag
Of needments at his backe. Thus as they past,
The day with cloudes was suddeine overcast,   50
And angry *Jove* an hideous storme of raine
Did poure into his Lemans lap so fast,
That every wight to shrowd it did constrain,
And this faire couple eke to shroud themselves were fain.

7

Enforst to seeke some covert nigh at hand,   55
A shadie grove not far away they spide,
That promist ayde the tempest to withstand:
Whose loftie trees yclad with sommers pride,
Did spred so broad, that heavens light did hide,
Not perceable with power of any starre: 60
And all within were pathes and alleies wide,
With footing worne, and leading inward farre:
Faire harbour that them seemes; so in they entred arre.

8

And foorth they passe, with pleasure forward led,
Joying to heare the birdes sweete harmony,   65
Which therein shrouded from the tempest dred,
Seemd in their song to scorne the cruell sky.
Much can they prayse the trees so straight and hy,
The sayling Pine, the Cedar proud and tall,
The vine-prop Elme, the Poplar neuer dry,   70
The builder Oake, sole king of forrests all,
The Aspine good for staves, the Cypresse funerall.

■ These stanzas set the stage for a story about the Red Cross Knight and his
quest. The language here, like Carroll's, is artificially constructed. One of

Walter Crane's illustration from **Faerie Queene** (1894–1897)

Albrecht Dürer, *The Knight, Death and the Devil* (1514)

Spenser's goals was to make the poetry itself seem older than it was. Find specific words describing the knight that indicate something about his character and about the ideals that he represents. What is his quest?

■ What indications do we get in the seventh and eighth stanzas that this group of travelers might find trouble in the "shadie grove" that they have entered?

Richard Corbett (1582–1635)

The Fairies Farewell (1615)

Farewell, rewards and fairies,
    Good housewives now may say,
For now foul sluts in dairies
    Do fare as well as they.
And though they sweep their hearths no less   5
    Than maids were wont to do,
Yet who of late for cleanness
    Finds sixpence in her shoe?
Lament, lament, old Abbeys,
    The Fairies' lost command!   10
They did but change Priests' babies,
    But some have changed your land.
And all your children, sprung from thence,

Are now grown Puritans,
Who live as Changelings ever since   15
    For love of your demains.

At morning and at evening both
    You merry were and glad,
So little care of sleep or sloth
    These pretty ladies had;   20
When Tom came home from labour,
    Or Cis to milking rose,
Then merrily went their tabor,
    And nimbly went their toes.

Witness those rings and roundelays   25
    Of theirs, which yet remain,
Were footed in Queen Mary's days
    On many a grassy plain;
But since of late, Elizabeth,
    And later, James came in,   30
They never danced on any heath
    As when the time hath been.

By which we note the Fairies
    Were of the old Profession.
Their songs were Ave Marys,   35
    Their dances were Procession.
But now, alas, they all are dead;
    Or gone beyond the seas;
Or farther for Religion fled;
    Or else they take their ease.   40

A tell-tale in their company
    They never could endure!
And whoso kept not secretly
    Their mirth, was punished, sure;
It was a just and Christian deed   45
    To pinch such black and blue.
Oh how the commonwealth doth want
    Such Justices as you!
Now they have left our quarters,
    A register they have,   50
Who can preserve their charters,
    A man both wise and grave;

A hundred of their merry pranks
  By one that I could name
Are kept in store; con twenty thanks   55
  To William for the same.

To William Chourne of Staffordshire
  Give land and praises due,
Who every meal can mend your cheer
  With tales both old and true;   60
To William all give audience,
  And pray ye for his noddle,
Fo all the fairies' evidence
  Were lost, if that were addle.

- When England became a Protestant nation in the sixteenth century, Roman Catholic practices were outlawed. The abbeys where nuns had been cloistered were destroyed. "Ave Maria" prayers were banned. For a brief time, in the reign of Queen Mary, these practices were restored, but under Queen Elizabeth and King James, the abolition of the old religious traditions was complete. How does the poem react to these religious changes?

- What images does the poet use to represent the old ways?

Robert Browning (1812–1889)

Porphyria's Lover (1842)

The rain set early in to-night,
  The sullen wind was soon awake,
It tore the elm-tops down for spite,
  And did its worst to vex the lake:
  I listened with heart fit to break.   5
When glided in Porphyria; straight
  She shut the cold out and the storm,
And kneeled and made the cheerless grate
  Blaze up, and all the cottage warm;
  Which done, she rose, and from her form   10
Withdrew the dripping cloak and shawl,
  And laid her soiled gloves by, untied
Her hat and let the damp hair fall,
  And, last, she sat down by my side
  And called me. When no voice replied,   15

She put my arm about her waist,
    And made her smooth white shoulder bare,
And all her yellow hair displaced,
    And, stooping, made my cheek lie there,
    And spread, o'er all, her yellow hair,   20
Murmuring how she loved me—she
    Too weak, for all her heart's endeavour,
To set its struggling passion free
    From pride, and vainer ties dissever,
    And give herself to me for ever.   25
But passion sometimes would prevail,
    Nor could to-night's gay feast restrain
A sudden thought of one so pale
    For love of her, and all in vain:
    So, she was come through wind and rain.   30
Be sure I looked up at her eyes
    Happy and proud; at last I knew
Porphyria worshipped me; surprise
    Made my heart swell, and still it grew
    While I debated what to do.   35
That moment she was mine, mine, fair,
    Perfectly pure and good: I found
A thing to do, and all her hair
    In one long yellow string I wound
    Three times her little throat around,   40
And strangled her. No pain felt she;
    I am quite sure she felt no pain.
As a shut bud that holds a bee,
    I warily oped her lids: again
    Laughed the blue eyes without a stain.   45
And I untightened next the tress
    About her neck; her cheek once more
Blushed bright beneath my burning kiss:
    I propped her head up as before,
    Only, this time my shoulder bore   50
Her head, which droops upon it still:
    The smiling rosy little head,
So glad it has its utmost will,
    That all it scorned at once is fled,
    And I, its love, am gained instead!   55
Porphyria's love: she guessed not how
    Her darling one wish would be heard.
And thus we sit together now,

And all night long we have not stirred,
And yet God has not said a word   60

■ Compare Porphyria's treatment of the narrator in the first half of the poem to
the narrator's treatment of Porphyria at the end of the poem. What significance
might these parallels have?

■ How might this story be interpreted as an allegory about the nature of love?
How might you challenge such an allegorical reading?

John Donne (1572–1631)

Batter My Heart, Three-Personed God (1610)

Batter my heart, three-personed God; for you
As yet but knock, breathe, shine, and seek to mend;
That I may rise and stand, o'erthrow me, and bend
Your force to break, blow, burn, and make me new.
I, like an usurped town, to another due,   5
Labor to admit you, but oh, to no end;
Reason, your viceroy in me, me should defend,
But is captived, and proves weak or untrue.
Yet dearly I love you and would be lovèd fain,
But am betrothed unto your enemy;   10
Divorce me, untie or break that knot again,
Take me to you, imprison me, for I,
Except you enthrall me, never shall be free, unless
Nor ever chaste, except you ravish me.

■ How does the image of "an usurped town" illustrate the poet's relation to God?
In what ways is this an unusual way to describe reverence?

■ What paradoxes does the poet raise in this poem?

John Donne (1572–1631)

The Canonization (1635)

For God's sake, hold your tongue, and let me love!
  Or chide my palsy or my gout,
My five gray hairs or ruined fortune flout;

With wealth your state, your mind with arts improve,
   Take you a course, get you a place,   5
    Observe his honor or his grace,
Or the king's real or his stamped face
   Contemplate; what you will, approve,
   So you will let me love.

Alas, alas, who's injured by my love?   10
   What merchant ships have my sighs drowned?
Who says my tears have overflowed his ground?
   When did my colds a forward spring remove?
    When did the heats which my veins fill
    Add one more to the plaguy bill?   15
Soldiers find wars, and lawyers find out still
   Litigious men which quarrels move,
   Though she and I do love.

Call us what you will, we are made such by love.
   Call her one, me another fly;   20
We are tapers too, and at our own cost die;
   And we in us find the eagle and the dove;
    The phoenix riddle hath more wit
    By us; we two, being one, are it.
So to one neutral thing both sexes fit.   25
   We die and rise the same, and prove
   Mysterious by this love.

We can die by it, if not live by love,
   And if unfit for tombs and hearse
Our legend be, it will be fit for verse;   30
   And if no piece of chronicle we prove, history
    We'll build in sonnets pretty rooms:
    As well a well-wrought urn becomes
The greatest ashes as half-acre tombs,
   And by these hymns all shall approve confirm   35
   Us canonized for love,

And thus invoke us: "You whom reverend love
   Made one another's hermitage,
You to whom love was peace, that now is rage,
   Who did the whole world's soul contract, and drove   40
    Into the glasses of your eyes
    (So made such mirrors and such spies

That they did all to you epitomize)
  Countries, towns, courts: beg from above
  A pattern of your love!"   45

■ Canonization refers to the official acknowledgment by the Roman Catholic
  Church that a person should be revered as a saint. In order for a person to earn
  such recognition, there should be some proof that miracles can be attributed to
  the person. In what way is the subject in this poem unlikely to qualify for
  sainthood? How does the poem itself acknowledge and then refute this
  argument?

John Donne (1572–1631)

Death Be Not Proud (1611)

Death, be not proud, though some have callèd thee
Mighty and dreadful, for thou art not so;
For those whom thou think'st thou dost overthrow
Die not, poor Death, nor yet canst thou kill me.
From rest and sleep, which but thy pictures be,   5
Much pleasure—then, from thee much more must flow;
And soonest our best men with thee do go,
Rest of their bones and soul's delivery.
Thou art slave to Fate, Chance, kings, and desperate men,
And dost with Poison, War, and Sickness dwell;   10
And poppy or charms can make us sleep as well,
And better than thy stroke. Why swell'st thou then?
One short sleep passed, we wake eternally,
And death shall be no more; Death, thou shalt die.

■ How is Death a "slave to Fate, Chance, kings, and desperate men"?
■ By what standard might the poet claim, "Death, thou shalt die"?

Emily Dickinson (1830–1886)

[Because I could not stop for Death—] (ca. 1863)

Because I could not stop for Death—
He kindly stopped for me—

The Carriage held but just Ourselves—
And Immortality.

We slowly drove—He knew no haste   5
And I had put away
My labor and my leisure too,
For His Civility—

We passed the School, where Children strove
At Recess—in the Ring—   10
We passed the Fields of Gazing Grain—
We passed the Setting Sun—

Or rather—He passed Us—
The Dews drew quivering and chill—
For only Gossamer, my Gown—   15
My Tippet—only Tulle—

We paused before a House that seemed
A Swelling of the Ground—
The Roof was scarcely visible—
The Cornice—in the Ground—   20

Since then—'tis Centuries—and yet
Feels shorter than the Day
I first surmised the Horses' Heads
Were toward Eternity—

- Explain how the carriage might hold both Death and Immortality.
- In the second stanza, why has the poet "put away / My labor and my leisure too"?
- Compare the tone of this poem to the tone of Donne's "Death Be Not Proud."

Gerard Manley Hopkins (1844–1889)

Pied Beauty (1877)

Glory be to God for dappled things—
        For skies of couple-color as a brinded cow;
                For rose-moles all in stipple upon trout that swim;
Fresh-firecoal chestnut-falls; finches' wings;
        Landscape plotted and pieced—fold, fallow and plow;   5
                And all trades, their gear and tackle and trim.

All things counter, original, spare, strange;
      Whatever is fickle, freckled (who knows how?)
        With swift, slow; sweet, sour; adazzle, dim;
He fathers-forth whose beauty is past change: 10
           Praise him.

Gerard Manley Hopkins (1844–1889)

The Windhover (1877)

To Christ Our Lord

I caught this morning morning's minion, king-
      dom of daylight's dauphin, dapple-dawn-drawn Falcon, in his riding
      Of the rolling level underneath him steady air, and striding
High there, how he rung upon the rein of a wimpling wing
In his ecstasy! then off, off forth on swing,   5
      As a skate's heel sweeps smooth on a bow-bend: the hurl and gliding
      Rebuffed the big wind. My heart in hiding
Stirred for a bird,—the achieve of, the mastery of the thing!

Brute beauty and valor and act, oh, air, pride, plume, here
      Buckle! AND the fire that breaks from thee then, a billion   10
Times told lovelier, more dangerous, O my chevalier!
      No wonder of it: shéer plód, makes plow down sillion
Shine, and blue-bleak embers, ah my dear,
      Fall, gall themselves, and gash gold-vermilion.

- How does the poet use consonance and alliteration throughout the poems? How do these sounds contribute to or distract from each poem's reverent attitude?
- There are many sentences or sections of sentences (for example, "the achieve of, the mastery of the thing!") in both poems that do not appear to be coherent. How is such tortured syntax appropriate to the religious context of both poems?

Ogden Nash (1902–1971)

Kind of an Ode to Duty (1935)

O Duty,
Why hast thou not the visage of a sweetie or a cutie?
Why displayest thou the countenance of the kind of conscientious
  organizing spinster

That the minute you see her you are aginster?
Why glitter thy spectacles so ominously?   5
Why art thou clad so abominously?
Why are thou so different from Venus
And why do thou and I have so few interests mutually in common
    between us?
Why art thou fifty per cent martyr
And fifty-one per cent Tartar?   10
Why is it thy unfortunate wont
To try to attract people by calling on them either to leave undone the
    deeds they like, or to do the deeds they don't?
Why art thou so like an April postmortem
Or something that died in the ortumn?
Above all, why dost thou continue to hound me?   15
Why art thou always albatrossly hanging around me?
Thou so ubiquitous,
And I so iniquitous,
I seem to be the one person in the world thou art perpetually
    preaching at who or to who;
Whatever looks like fun, there art thou standing between me and it,   20
    calling "you-hoo."
O Duty, Duty!
How noble a man should I be hadst thou the visage of a sweetie or a cutie!
Wert thou but houri instead of hag
Then would my halo indeed be in the bag!
But as it is thou art so much forbiddinger than a Wodehouse hero's   25
    forbiddingest aunt
That in the words of the poet, When Duty whispers low, "Thou must,"
    this erstwhile youth replies, "I just can't."

■ In spite of the poem's tone, what images of duty here seem to be descriptions
  that might be appropriate in any context?

■ What does the poet achieve by portraying Duty as an allegorical figure? Locate
  specific instances where Duty takes on these characteristics.

Amiri Baraka (1934–)

In Memory of Radio (1961)

Who has ever stopped to think of the divinity of Lamont Cranston?
(Only Jack Kerouac, that I know of: & me.

The rest of you probably had on WCBS and Kate Smith,
Or something equally unattractive.)

What can I say?   5
It is better to have loved and lost
Than to put linoleum in your living rooms?

Am I a sage or something?
Mandrake's hypnotic gesture of the week?
(Remember, I do not have the healing powers of Oral Roberts...   10
I cannot, like F. J. Sheen, tell you how to get saved & rich!
I cannot even order you to the gaschamber satori like Hitler or Gody
    Knight.

& Love is an evil word.
Turn it backwards/see, see what I mean?
An evol word. & besides   15
who understands it?
I certainly wouldn't like to go out on that kind of limb.

Saturday mornings we listened to the *Red Lantern* & his undersea folk.
At 11, *Let's Pretend*
& we did   20
& I, the poet, still do, Thank God!

What was it he used to say (after the transformation when he was safe
& invisible & the unbelievers couldn't throw stones?) "Heh, heh, heh,
Who knows what evil lurks in the hearts of men? The Shadow knows."

O, yes he does   25
O, yes he does.
An evil word it is,
This Love.

■ How does the poet contrast the lives of normal listeners with the sorts of
  stories that they heard on their radios?

■ Like Spenser's poem, this poem is recalling an early time when storytelling
  took a different form. In this case, the poet in 1961 is recalling the radio
  programs that dominated his childhood. How does the poet suggest that this
  particular medium worked in a different way from the storytelling that
  replaced it?

Anne Carson (1950–)

TV Men: Lazarus (2000)
DIRECTOR OF PHOTOGRAPHY: VOICEOVER

Yes I admit a degree of unease about my
motives in making
this documentary.
Mere prurience of a kind that is all too common nowadays   5
in public catastrophes. I was listening

to a peace negotiator for the Balkans talk
about his vocation
on the radio the other day.
"We drove down through this wasteland and I didn't know   10
much about the area but I was

fascinated by the horrors of it. I had never
seen a thing like this.
I videotaped it.
Then sent a 13-page memo to the UN with my suggestions."   15
This person was a member

of the International Rescue Committee,
not a man of TV.
But you can see
how the pull is irresistible. The pull to handle horrors   20
and to have a theory of them.

But now I see my assistant producer waving her arms
at me to get
on with the script.
The name Lazarus is an abbreviated form of Hebrew 'El'azar,   25
meaning "God has helped."

I have long been interested in those whom God has helped.
It seems often to be the case,
e.g. with saints or martyrs,
that God helps them to far more suffering than they would have   30
without God's help. But then you get

someone like Lazarus, a man of no
particular importance,

on whom God bestows
the ultimate benevolence, without explanation, then abandons   35
him again to his nonentity.

We are left wondering, *Why Lazarus?*
My theory is
God wants us to wonder this.
After all, if there were some quality that Lazarus possessed,   40
some criterion of excellence

by which he was chosen to be called
back
from death,
then we would all start competing to achieve this.   45
But if

God's gift is simply random, well
for one thing
it makes a
more interesting TV show. God's choice can be seen emerging   50
from the dark side of reason

like a new planet. No use being historical
about this planet,
it is just an imitation.
As Lazarus is an imitation of Christ. As TV is an imitation of   55
Lazarus. As you and I are an imitation of

TV. Already you notice that
although I am merely
a director of photography,
I have grasped certain fundamental notions first advanced by Plato,   60
e.g. that our reality is just a TV set

inside a TV set inside a TV set, with nobody watching
but Sokrates,
who changed
the channel in 399 B.C. But my bond with Lazarus goes deeper, indeed   65
nausea overtakes me when faced with

the prospect of something simply beginning all over again.
Each time I have to
raise my slate and say

"Take 12!" or "Take 13!" and then "Take 14!"   70
I cannot restrain a shudder.

Repetition is horrible. Poor Lazarus cannot have known
he was an
imitation Christ,
but who can doubt he realized, soon after being ripped out of his   75
warm little bed in the ground,

his own epoch of repetition just beginning.
Lazarus Take 2!
Poor drop.
As a bit of salt falls back down the funnel. Or maybe my pity   80
is misplaced. Some people think Lazarus lucky,

like Samuel Beckett who calls him "Happy Larry" or Rilke
who speaks of
that moment in a game
when "the pure too-little flips over into the empty too-much."   85
Well I am now explaining why my documentary

focuses entirely on this moment, the flip-over moment.
Before and after
don't interest me.
You won't be seeing any clips from home videos of Lazarus   90
in short pants racing his sisters up a hill.

No footage of Mary and Martha side by side on the sofa
discussing how they manage
at home
with a dead one sitting down to dinner. No panel of experts   95
debating who was really the victim here.

Our sequence begins and ends with that moment of complete
innocence
and sport—
when Lazarus licks the first drop of afterlife off the nipple   100
of his own old death.

I put tiny microphones all over the ground
to pick up
the magic

of the vermin in his ten fingers and I stand back to wait   105
for the miracle.

- The New Testament book of John recounts the miracle of Jesus restoring Lazarus to life. How does the idea of television help the poet explain the mysterious and seemingly random actions of God?
- How is the notion of a miracle at odds with the director of photography who says, "Take 12!"?

DRAMA

Jane Martin (unknown)

No one, aside from Jane Martin, and perhaps a few close confidants, knows who Jane Martin really is. She (if the playwright in question is in fact a woman, which seems likely) has been called "America's best-known, unknown playwright" and is the author of such plays as *Anton in Show Business*, *Audition*, and *Beauty*.

Beauty (2000)

CHARACTERS

CARLA
BETHANY

SCENE: *An apartment. Minimalist set. A young woman,* CARLA, *on the phone.*

CARLA: In love with me? You're in love with me? Could you describe your-self again? Uh-huh. Uh-huh. And you spoke to me? (*A knock at the door.*) Listen, I always hate to interrupt a marriage proposal, but... could you possibly hold that thought? (*Puts phone down and goes to door.* BETHANY, *the same age as* CARLA *and a friend, is there. She carries the sort of Mideastern lamp we know of from Aladdin.*)

BETHANY: Thank God you were home. I mean, you're not going to believe this!

CARLA: Somebody on the phone. (*Goes back to it.*)

BETHANY: I mean, I just had a beach urge, so I told them at work my uncle was dying...

CARLA (*motions to* BETHANY *for quiet.*): And you were the one in the leather 5
    jacket with the tattoo? What was the tattoo? (CARLA *again asks*
    BETHANY, *who is gesturing wildly that she should hang up, to cool it.*) Look,
    a screaming eagle from shoulder to shoulder, maybe. There were a lot of
    people in the bar.
BETHANY (*gesturing and mouthing.*): I have to get back to work.
CARLA (*on phone.*): See, the thing is, I'm probably not going to marry some-
    one I can't remember... particularly when I don't drink. Sorry. Sorry.
    Sorry. (*She hangs up.*) Madness.
BETHANY: So I ran out to the beach...
CARLA: This was some guy I never met who apparently offered me a beer...
BETHANY: ...low tide and this... (*The lamp.*)... was just sitting there, lying 10
    there...
CARLA: ...and he tracks me down...
BETHANY: ...on the beach, and I lift this lid thing...
CARLA: ...and seriously proposes marriage.
BETHANY: ...and a genie comes out.
CARLA: I mean, that's twice in a... what? 15
BETHANY: A genie comes out of this thing.
CARLA: A genie?
BETHANY: I'm not kidding, the whole Disney kind of thing, swirling smoke,
    and then this twenty-foot-high, see-through guy in like an Arabian outfit.
CARLA: Very funny.
BETHANY: Yes, funny, but twenty feet high! I look up and down the beach, 20
    I'm alone. I don't have my pepper spray or my hand alarm. You know
    me, when I'm petrified I joke. I say his voice is too high for Robin Wil-
    liams, and he says he's a castrati. Naturally. Who else would I meet?
CARLA: What's a castrati?
BETHANY: You know... (*The appropriate gesture.*)
CARLA: Bethany, dear one, I have three modeling calls. I am meeting Ralph
    Lauren!
BETHANY: Okay, good. Ralph Lauren. Look, I am not kidding!
CARLA: You're not kidding what?! 25
BETHANY: There is a genie in this thingamajig.
CARLA: Uh-huh. I'll be back around eight.
BETHANY: And he offered me *wishes!*
CARLA: Is this some elaborate practical joke because it's my birthday?
BETHANY: No, happy birthday, but I'm like crazed because I'm on this 30
    deserted beach with a twenty-foot-high, see-through genie, so like sar-
    castically... you know how I need a new car... I said fine, gimme
    25,000 dollars...
CARLA: On the beach with the genie?
BETHANY: Yeah, right, exactly, and it rains down out of the sky.

CARLA: Oh sure.

BETHANY *(pulling a wad out of her purse.)*: Count it, those are thousands. I lost one in the surf.

(CARLA sees the top bill. Looks at BETHANY, who nods encouragement. CARLA thumbs through them.)

CARLA: These look real.   35

BETHANY: Yeah.

CARLA: And they rained down out of the sky?

BETHANY: Yeah.

CARLA: You've been really strange lately, are you dealing?

BETHANY: Dealing what, I've even given up chocolate.   40

CARLA: Let me see the genie.

BETHANY: Wait, wait.

CARLA: Bethany, I don't have time to screw around. Let me see the genie or let me go on my appointments.

BETHANY: Wait! So I pick up the money... see, there's sand on the money ... and I'm like nuts so I say, you know, "Okay, look, ummm, big guy, my uncle is in the hospital"... because as you know when I said to the people at work my uncle was dying, I was on one level telling the truth although it had nothing to do with the beach, but he was in Intensive Care after the accident, and that's on my mind, so I say, okay, Genie, heal my uncle... which is like impossible given he was hit by two trucks, and the genie says, "Yes, Master"... like they're supposed to say, and he goes into this like kind of whirlwind, kicking up sand and stuff, and I'm like, "Oh my God!" and the air clears, and he bows, you know, and says, "It is done, Master," and I say, "Okay, whatever-you-are, I'm calling on my cell phone," and I get it out and I get this doctor who is like dumbstruck who says my uncle came to, walked out of Intensive Care and left the hospital! I'm not kidding, Carla.

CARLA: On your mother's grave?   45

BETHANY: On my mother's grave.

(They look at each other.)

CARLA: Let me see the genie.

BETHANY: No, no, look, that's the whole thing... I was just, like, reacting, you know, responding, and that's already two wishes... although I'm really pleased about my uncle, the $25,000 thing, I could have asked for $10 million, and there is only one wish left.

CARLA: So ask for $10 million.

BETHANY: I don't think so. I don't think so. I mean, I gotta focus in here.   50
Do you have a sparkling water?

CARLA: No. Bethany, I'm missing Ralph Lauren now. Very possibly my one chance to go from catalogue model to the very, very big time, so, if you are joking, stop joking.

BETHANY: Not joking. See, see, the thing is, I know what I want. In my guts. Yes. Underneath my entire bitch of a life is this unspoken, ferocious, all-consuming urge...

CARLA (*trying to get her to move this along.*): Ferocious, all-consuming urge...

BETHANY: I want to be like you.

CARLA: Me?   55

BETHANY: Yes.

CARLA: Half the time you don't even like me.

BETHANY: Jealous. The ogre of jealousy.

CARLA: You're the one with the $40,000 job straight out of school. You're the one who has published short stories. I'm the one hanging on by her fingernails in modeling. The one who has creeps calling her on the phone. The one who had to have a nose job.

BETHANY: I want to be beautiful.   60

CARLA: You are beautiful.

BETHANY: Carla, I'm not beautiful.

CARLA: You have charm. You have personality. You know perfectly well you're pretty.

BETHANY: "Pretty," see, that's it. Pretty is the minor leagues of beautiful. Pretty is what people discover about you after they know you. Beautiful is what knocks them out across the room. Pretty, you get called a couple of times a year; *beautiful* is twenty-four hours a day.

CARLA: Yeah? So?   65

BETHANY: So?! We're talking *beauty* here. Don't say "So?" Beauty is the real deal. You are the center of any moment of your life. People stare. Men flock. I've seen you get offered discounts on makeup for no reason. Parents treat beautiful children better. Studies show your income goes up. You can have sex anytime you want it. Men have to know me. That takes up to a year. I'm continually horny.

CARLA: Bethany, I don't even like sex. I can't have a conversation without men coming on to me. I have no privacy. I get hassled on the street. They start pressuring me from the beginning. Half the time, it never occurs to them to start with a conversation. Smart guys like you. You've had three long-term relationships, and you're only twenty-three. I haven't had one. The good guys, the smart guys are scared to death of me. I'm surrounded by male bimbos who think a preposition is when you go to school away from home. I have no woman friends except you. I don't even want to talk about this!

BETHANY: I knew you'd say something like this. See, you're "in the club" so you can say this. It's the way beauty functions as an elite. You're trying to keep it all for yourself.

CARLA: I'm trying to tell you it's no picnic.

BETHANY: But it's what everybody wants. It's the nasty secret at large in the   70
world. It's the unspoken tidal desire in every room and on every street.
It's the unspoken, the soundless whisper... millions upon millions of
people longing hopelessly and forever to stop being whatever they are
and be beautiful, but the difference between those ardent multitudes
and me is that I have a goddamn genie and one more wish!

CARLA: Well, it's not what I want. This is me, Carla. I have never read a
whole book. Page six, I can't remember page four. The last thing I read
was *The Complete Idiot's Guide to WordPerfect.* I leave dinner parties
right after the dessert because I'm out of conversation. You know the
dumb blond joke about the application where it says, "Sign here," she
put Sagittarius? I've done that. Only beautiful guys approach me, and
that's because they want to borrow my eye shadow. I barely exist outside a mirror! You don't want to be me.

BETHANY: None of you tell the truth. That's why you have no friends. We
can all see you're just trying to make us feel better because we aren't in
your league. This only proves to me it should be my third wish. Money
can only buy things. Beauty makes you the center of the universe.
(BETHANY *picks up the lamp.*)

CARLA: Don't do it. Bethany, don't wish it! I am telling you you'll regret it.
(BETHANY *lifts the lid. There is a tremendous crash, and the lights go out.
Then they flicker and come back up, revealing* BETHANY *and* CARLA *on the
floor where they have been thrown by the explosion. We don't realize it at
first, but they have exchanged places.*)

CARLA/BETHANY: Oh God.

BETHANY/CARLA: Oh God.   75

CARLA/BETHANY: Am I bleeding? Am I dying?

BETHANY/CARLA: I'm so dizzy. You're not bleeding.

CARLA/BETHANY: Neither are you.

BETHANY/CARLA: I feel so weird.

CARLA/BETHANY: Me too. I feel... (*Looking at her hands.*) Oh, my God, I'm   80
wearing your jewelry. I'm wearing your nail polish.

BETHANY/CARLA: I know I'm over here, but I can see myself over there.

CARLA/BETHANY: I'm wearing your dress. I have your legs!!

BETHANY/CARLA: These aren't my shoes. I can't meet Ralph Lauren wearing
these shoes!

CARLA/BETHANY: I wanted to be beautiful, but I didn't want to be you.

BETHANY/CARLA: Thanks a lot!!   85

CARLA/BETHANY: I've got to go. I want to pick someone out and get laid.

BETHANY/CARLA: You can't just walk out of here in my body!

CARLA/BETHANY: Wait a minute. Wait a minute. What's eleven eighteenths
of 1,726?

BETHANY/CARLA: Why?

CARLA/BETHANY: I'm a public accountant. I want to know if you have my   90
   brain.
BETHANY/CARLA: One hundred thirty-two and a half.
CARLA/BETHANY: You have my brain.
BETHANY/CARLA: What shade of Rubenstein lipstick does Cindy Crawford
   wear with teal blue?
CARLA/BETHANY: Raging Storm.
BETHANY/CARLA: You have my brain. You poor bastard.   95
CARLA/BETHANY: I don't care. Don't you see?
BETHANY/CARLA: See what?
CARLA/BETHANY: We both have the one thing, the one and only thing
   everybody wants.
BETHANY/CARLA: What is that?
CARLA/BETHANY: It's better than beauty for me; it's better than brains for   10C
   you.
BETHANY/CARLA: What? What?!
CARLA/BETHANY: Different problems.
(*Blackout.*)

- How does the genie in this story call upon our knowledge of genies in other stories?
- Describe the differences between the two main characters.
- How does the story combine the supernatural with the mundane?
- What are the allegorical elements within this story? How significant are they to your understanding of the story?
- What message does the story send with the final change?

Experiencing Literature through Writing

1. Identify the allegorical elements within a particular text. As you make your claim that this text functions allegorically, you must justify your argument that it is appropriate to find allegory in the text. As you write, consider the following questions:

   a. What signals has the author given to justify an allegorical reading?

   b. How does the surface narrative lend itself to allegorical interpretations?

   c. What tensions do you find between the surface narrative and the allegorical reading?

   d. How does this allegory allow an approach to a social, political, or cultural issue that might not be possible with a less subtle approach?

2. The readings gathered here are grouped under the broad category of "The Quest for Truth." The idea of truth with a capital T signals an ideal that we assume is impossible to achieve. Allegory here is useful because the enterprise itself is fantastic. Discuss the element of the fantastic as it appears in one (or more) of these works. What details give the work a fantastic feel? How do these elements support (or undermine) the allegorical or didactic elements of the work?

3. The inclination to find a clear meaning or message in a text sometimes blinds us to other significant aspects of that text. In this discussion, argue against the impulse to make these texts allegorical. Explain how a reading of the surface narrative allows an interesting insight into this text that an allegorical reading might ignore.

13 Symbolism

How Do I Know When an Event or an Image Is Supposed to Stand for Something Else?

One of the easiest questions to ever appear in an exam for a driver's license is the following:

When you come to a stop sign at an intersection, you should

    A. slow down and proceed with caution

    B. continue only if the intersection is clear

    C. pass stopped cars on the left

    D. stop

We'll assume that all of you (whether you drive or not) would answer "D." A stop sign means stop, a meaning we can all agree upon. But how exactly do a few marks (letters), a shape (an octagon), and a color (red) so uniformly make the point? The answer is pretty simple (even if the implications of that answer are more complicated): We have collectively agreed within our time and place to use these marks, this shape, and that color to signal "stop." The choice was not "natural" in the sense that only these marks, this shape, and that color would do. But we as members of a particular society made the choice and live with it so easily that it seems natural. A stop sign is not ambiguous or unknown to us. A local traffic court judge wouldn't accept alternative interpretations from a ticketed driver.

Literature and film also employ some easy-to-read signs. In monster movies from the 1950s and early 1960s, the monster would die in the final scene, the closing credits would announce "The End," and then a question mark would emerge from the darkened screen. Every person in the theater knew that the terrifying creature that had lurked beneath the dark waters of the lake didn't actually die, even though the characters in the film thought so. All in the audience realized that "The End...?" meant "sort of the end": leave the theater, but take your scary feelings home with you because the monster is still "out there." Although this sign prompts a bit more open interpretation than a stop sign does, it still severely limits likely responses. In both literature and life, we are trained to read and interpret the most common signs in particular ways by experience. The simplest signs express a remarkably narrow range of meanings.

What happens, though, when one thing suggests possible meanings without being specific about any particular single meaning? How can we read and interpret a sign when we are not taught by established custom exactly how to read it? Or when the function of the sign is *not* to communicate a specific, limited meaning (a prohibition, an order, a direction)? What happens when a sign provokes conflicting responses? The backslash across the hand signaling stop shown here builds in a contradiction that forces us to read, interpret, and argue by giving us something we are not accustomed to see.

The slash could be read to cancel out the hand signal. It suggests "don't stop," but it's not clear what it is exactly that we're not supposed to stop. We might consider many possibilities: If we see this sign carried by a protester in

front of a police station, we might think it means "don't listen to authority" or "don't stop defying rules"; if we see the same sign inside a nightclub, we might think it means "don't stop dancing" or "don't stop having fun." In any case, we'll need to consider this sign and consciously interpret it rather than just accept it.

At some point we need a new word. The stop sign that speaks so clearly at the corner of an intersection becomes a bit less clear when the extra graphics are added, and it begins to move from sign to **symbol**. In the broadest sense, all words are symbols, or words that stand in for something else. But it's useful to define symbol as something (an object, a word, an image) that is used to suggest a range of associations or feelings. Symbols prompt reflection and inquiry; they don't (like signs) point us to a highly defined action or message. Symbols are oftentimes highly personal—not controlled by an established public understanding. Symbols force us to grapple with meanings that are suggestive, resonant, and subtly nuanced. This can lead to uncomfortable territory for some readers. One of the most frustrating experiences many people have with complex literary works and films arises from the sense that one thing means something else, yet that "something else" can hardly be identified, captured, or named. To a person who wants things clear-cut, a discussion of symbols can seem like an imposition: a "reading into" a text rather than a "reading of" a text.

But we cannot dismiss the power of symbols because we sometimes find them hard to read. And we need not be helpless before them. Writers don't want symbols to obscure meaning. They want to use symbols to reach new meaning. If we trust the signals writers provide and don't expect only highly defined messages, we'll find that symbols don't present any special problems. Our efforts to understand and articulate how symbols emerge and take on meaning can be profoundly rewarding. In this chapter, we'll consider how we can be released from explicit and easily identified directions and still develop grounded, persuasive readings.

FIGURATIVE LANGUAGE

Figurative language is, broadly defined, any language that is used in ways that deviate from standard significance, order, or meaning. Such language may lend freshness or strength to expression. It may also extend or complicate the meaning of a word or expression. Figurative language, then, moves us from signs to symbols.

Figurative language is often divided into two types. A **rhetorical figure** uses a word or words in an unusual context or sequence but does not radically change the customary meaning of the word or words. For example, an **apostrophe** refers to the speaker's direct address to an absent person or to some abstract idea or spirit; although we don't usually speak to someone or something that is not physically present, the words themselves may be familiar.

Of greater importance for our purposes is the second type of figurative language. A **trope** (sometimes called a **figure of thought**) differs from a rhetorical figure in that it moves us to a changed or significantly extended meaning of a word or words. **Personification** is an example of a trope; to personify is to cast an abstract concept or inanimate material as a living thing endowed with human qualities. When the wrestler-turned-movie star "The Rock" chose his stage name, he used a trope—he sought to personify qualities of strength, indestructibility, hardness. The name may come to take on broader meanings depending on the roles he plays (indicating solidity, steadiness, and so on). **Similes** and **metaphors** are also tropes. As we noted in Chapter 12, such figures of thought move us into the realm of allegory and symbol.

The roots of the word *trope* are from Greek: "to turn" or "a turning." Tropes use words to *turn* someone from conventional understanding; they test the elasticity of language. A writer might help us see that "stop" does not need to be fixed in meaning by the function of an octagonal red sign. This "turning" though is different from arbitrarily redefining a word. If we were all to invent our own definitions for words, our language would fail. We depend upon some common understanding in order to communicate. An effectively employed trope will bring new meaning from old. The old or the familiar will give us, along with our understanding of the surrounding situation, an interpretive lead. We know, for example, that the red sign usually means "stop your car." We know that the backslash cancels the primary message. When we see the backslash laid over the stop sign, we look for clues that might help us understand what it is we need to go forward with, what it is we should not stop.

What we're suggesting is that readers not "hunt" for symbols as an archeologist hunts for evidence of a buried civilization. Symbols arise out of the suggestive turns an artist employs (whether consciously or not). An effective "turn" moves *from* something familiar (established, conventional) *to* something fresh. Such turns are part of what brings symbols to the surface for us to see, feel, and reflect upon. So, to find symbols, don't dig for what is covered. Start by paying close attention to the signals a text provides.

Experiencing Literature through Symbols

Words, things, and images do not become symbols in isolation. Symbols are defined by and emerge from what surrounds them. In her poem "Home Movies," Mary Jo Salter reviews the images in her family's home movies to find scenes that have meaning to her now. She rejects the most common scenes and signs: "Christmases" and "birthday candles." The same holiday rituals repeated year after year have lost meaning to her over the years. Her father's attempt to create richer symbolism through photography also fails to achieve any lasting effect. It is finally "the stoneware mixing bowl" that the speaker still has in her own kitchen that emerges with symbolic force. The bowl moves her because it connects her current life to a rare moment of childhood happiness with her mother. In this poem, the ordinary object takes on meaning that it did not have before the poet reviewed the home movies. As she says, this object has meaning only for her in this particular context. And the poem shares that private symbol with us. The mixing bowl is symbolic of any ordinary object that might have meaning to us because of its connection to our peculiar interactions with it.

Mary Jo Salter (1954–)

Home Movies: A Sort of Ode (1999)

Because it hadn't seemed enough,
after a while, to catalogue
more Christmases, the three-layer cakes
ablaze with birthday candles, the blizzard
Billy took a shovel to,   5
Phil's lawnmower tour of the yard,
the tree forts, the shoot-'em-ups
between the boys in new string ties
and cowboy hats and holsters,
or Mother sticking a bow as big   10
as Mouseketeer ears in my hair,

my father sometimes turned the gaze
of his camera to subjects more
artistic or universal:
long closeups of a rose's face;   15
a real-time sunset (nearly an hour);

what surely were some brilliant autumn
leaves before their colors faded
to dry beige on the aging film;
a great deal of pacing, at the zoo,   20
by polar bears and tigers caged,
he seemed to say, like him.

What happened between him and her
is another story. And just as well
we have no movie of it, only   25
some unforgiving scowls she gave
through terrifying, ticking silence
when he must have asked her (no
sound track) for a smile.
Still, what I keep yearning for   30
isn't those generic cherry
blossoms at their peak, or the brave
daffodil after a snowfall,

it's the re-run surprise
of the unshuttered, prefab blanks   35
of windows at the back of the house,
and how the lines of aluminum
siding are scribbled on with meaning
only for us who lived there;
it's the pair of elephant bookends   40
I'd forgotten, with the upraised trunks
like handles, and the books they meant
to carry in one block to a future
that scattered all of us.

And look: it's the stoneware mixing bowl   45
figured with hand-holding dancers
handed down so many years
ago to my own kitchen, still
valueless, unbroken. Here
she's happy, teaching us to dye   50
the Easter eggs in it, a Grecian
urn of sorts near which—a foster
child of silence and slow time
myself—I smile because she does
and patiently await my turn.   55

Making Connections

Making Connections

The symbolic importance of Salter's mixing bowl is signaled by how she calls attention to it at the start of the final stanza and how, in that stanza, she elevates this "valueless" object by referring to another well-known poem, John Keats's "Ode On a Grecian Urn" (p. 1524). Keats addresses the urn as a "foster-child of silence and slow time." For Keats, the urn captures in its design something eternal—a feeling of a moment that is fleeting in life but maintained forever in art. By asking us to think of Keats's poem, Salter encourages us to consider how Keats's symbolic use of the urn relates to her mixing bowl. For further attention to the effect of such references, see Chapter 15.

There isn't, of course, anything inherently symbolic about a mixing bowl. Salter looks for an object that can capture something essential about her relationship with her mother. She tells us that what she is "yearning for" isn't the "generic cherry / blossoms." It's something captured in a few assorted things; then, in the last stanza, she lights upon the mixing bowl. The speaker's moment of recognition ("And look: it's the stoneware mixing bowl") becomes our moment of recognition. We're alerted to see this object as full of significance.

RECOGNIZING SYMBOLS

As we noted previously, an object is not a symbol until it is used as a symbol. Salter treats a mixing bowl in a way that makes us think of memory, mothers and daughters, family tensions. Her treatment is so persuasive that we may now look at a mixing bowl and think of Salter's mother, Easter eggs, and even other literary texts. We need to always consider how the surrounding words support a symbolic (rather than a literal) reading. The following pages contain images with apples in various symbol contexts. Consider how the apple's use in each image supports a different symbolic reading of the apple.

Now, think for a moment of an orange, a fruit whose symbolic use is rather less common than the apple's. What comes to mind? First responses are likely to be to the thing itself: color, weight, shape, smell, and taste. We think in terms of concrete images. We don't necessarily go beyond those images. As we pointed out in Chapter 7, we don't always need or want to go beyond those images. You'll note that Gary Soto's "Oranges" registers physical characteristics of the fruit. You will also be encouraged to think of the oranges as symbols. How does Soto persuade us to move from one kind of understanding to another? Compare his first mention of a cold twelve-year-old, "weighted down / With two oranges" (lines 3–4), with his glorious "I peeled my orange" (line 51) near the end of the poem. He only mentions "orange" three times,

What does an apple symbolize?

Churchman's Cigarettes

Gravity

What does an apple symbolize?

yet our sense of how we interpret oranges changes considerably. What has happened to give the orange symbolic meaning?

Gary Soto (1952–)

Oranges (1995)

The first time I walked
With a girl, I was twelve,
Cold, and weighted down
With two oranges in my jacket.
December. Frost cracking   5
Beneath my steps, my breath
Before me, then gone,
As I walked toward
Her house, the one whose
Porch light burned yellow   10
Night and day, in any weather.
A dog barked at me, until
She came out pulling
At her gloves, face bright
With rouge. I smiled,   15
Touched her shoulder, and led
Her down the street, across
A used car lot and a line
Of newly planted trees,
Until we were breathing   20
Before a drugstore. We
Entered, the tiny bell
Bringing a saleslady
Down a narrow aisle of goods.
I turned to the candies   25
Tiered like bleachers,
And asked what she wanted—
Light in her eyes, a smile
Starting at the corners
Of her mouth. I fingered   30
A nickel in my pocket,
And when she lifted a chocolate
That cost a dime,
I didn't say anything.
I took the nickel from   35

My pocket, then an orange,
And set them quietly on
The counter. When I looked up,
The lady's eyes met mine,
And held them, knowing   40
Very well what it was all
About.

Outside,
A few cars hissing past,
Fog hanging like old   45
Coats between the trees.
I took my girl's hand
In mine for two blocks,
Then released it to let
Her unwrap the chocolate.   50
I peeled my orange
That was so bright against
The gray of December
That, from some distance,
Someone might have thought   55
I was making a fire in my hands.

By the time Soto gives us his most precise physical description of the orange (near the end of the poem), the orange has grown symbolically rich. His desire to impress this girl is so intense that he has persuaded the woman behind the counter in the drugstore to enter into his world. She has accepted his orange as sufficient payment for the candy bar that the girl wants; the saleslady understands that he has only half as much money as he needs to buy this candy bar and that to admit his poverty here will destroy him. He persuades the saleslady to abandon the conventional sign—one candy bar is equivalent to one dime—and to accept his substitution of an orange for the missing nickel. This story describes the triumph of the poet's act of symbolism. He presents his symbol powerfully enough that someone outside his consciousness agrees to accept that symbol. In the final scene, he revels in his triumph, consuming an orange that means so much more than it meant at the beginning of the poem.

ALLEGORY AND SYMBOL

Allegory, as discussed in Chapter 12, develops a parallel between the concrete and the abstract that is generally sustained throughout a narrative. In allegory, we observe two levels of meaning that play out in a fairly consistent manner as actions unfold. The Red Cross Knight in Edmund Spenser's *The Faerie Queene* meets a variety of challenges, but he remains always on a quest for truth (p. 1228). Every narrated encounter teaches us something about the difficulties goodness faces in a fallen world. The fabric of the whole work helps us interpret each action; our reading is conditioned by the entire created structure. The elements of a straightforward allegory can be likened to signs—signs that most readers interpret in similar ways. Just as driving experience teaches us to respond to a variety of road signs confidently and coherently, literary experience teaches us to sort out and read the many signs that make up an allegory.

Of course, no literary text is as reductive as a stop sign. And some texts are more reductive than others. But it's fair to say that symbols ask us to move between the concrete and the abstract rather more flexibly than allegory does. Because a symbol is not conditioned by parallels sustained and consistently reinforced over the course of an entire narrative, we have more room to speculate.

- Allegory *tends* to direct readers to a level of meaning that is *relatively* defined, uniform, and instructional (didactic).
- Symbols *generally encourage* readers to reflect upon meaning that is *relatively* luminous, multiple, and abstract.

You might note we've left these distinctions a little blurry ("allegory *tends*," "symbols *generally encourage*," and "*relatively*"). Some interpretive challenges as well as interpretive pleasures occur in the gray areas.

Experiencing Literature through Symbolism

We mentioned in Chapter 12 that even though Nathaniel Hawthorne's "Young Goodman Brown" can be considered an allegory, it can't be easily reduced to any single lesson. In fact, some critics have insisted that Hawthorne is essentially a symbolist, for there is no consistent parallel carried throughout the story that clarifies every element and guides us through to a moral. These critics point out that although Goodman Brown himself seems to read things with great certainty, we have little reason to accept his interpretation. Did he lose "his faith" or cruelly reject a loving wife? Did he encounter and ultimately recoil from pure evil, or did he fail to contend with moral complexity? Did he grow bitter because he could not accept wickedness or because he could not tolerate truth? Was he innocent before his journey or merely naïve? Is he experienced after the journey, or is he still naïve?

Hawthorne himself said he worked in the shadowy areas of the human spirit. And we can get some sense of the shadow land we will enter in the first few paragraphs of his story. The very first begins to signal the symbolic undercurrent of the whole:

> Young Goodman Brown came forth at sunset into the street at Salem village; but put his head back, after crossing the threshold, to exchange a

parting kiss with his young wife. And Faith, as the wife was aptly named, thrust her own pretty head into the street, letting the wind play with the pink ribbons of her cap while she called to Goodman Brown. ■

Note that the wife is not only named "Faith" but that Hawthorne calls attention to the name for us. And in the introductory paragraphs to follow, we find "my love and my Faith," "dear Faith," and "poor little Faith." The pink ribbons may not seem important immediately but are soon noted twice more. Note how subtly Hawthorne moves from something as tangible as a doorway to multiple abstractions suggested by the doorway. When Goodman Brown steps out the door, he crosses a "threshold." Faith stays in the house. But note how they kiss: Goodman Brown moves back near the door, and Faith moves her head forward across the threshold into the street. As the story develops, we sense the importance of these two spaces: one kind of space (the home with Faith) is protected, enclosed, small, known, safe; the other (the street and beyond into the forest) is wild, open, large, mysterious, dangerous.

If we are to insist on allegory, we might maintain that the protected space inside the door is pure. We might argue that Hawthorne has a lesson to teach and uses the doorway as one piece of an allegory: don't cross the threshold (that is, don't seek knowledge you are not supposed to have). But as the story develops, it seems there are other, more open possibilities. Perhaps this purity is only an illusion. Perhaps reality, not wild wickedness, lies across the threshold. However we interpret it, the doorway/threshold seems to suggest a critical point that once passed cannot be regained. The threshold may be a psychological one, or a moral one, and/or an experiential one.

Note that when we think of a doorway/threshold as a symbol, we don't give it some random meaning nor do we identify a single meaning. Although our response to a symbol isn't as conditioned as our response to a stop sign, interpretation still depends upon linguistic, cultural, interpretive cues. We have many here to work with. We can start with plain meanings. A doorway, after all, does mark boundaries; it leads from one place to another. We commonly speak both literally and figuratively of "walking out," "coming in," or "crossing over." Within the story, Hawthorne **foregrounds** (calls attention to) the doorway by word choice (*threshold*), by the doorway's place in the narrative (the crossing marks the start of a journey), and by Faith's appeals at the threshold (don't leave this house tonight). Given what happens after Goodman Brown steps out, we are encouraged to consider what doorways/thresholds we all must cross in life. We could argue that crossing the threshold doesn't set up a lesson for us; rather, it leads to a revelation about Brown's character: Young Goodman Brown cannot handle truth or complexity. The doorway symbolizes a passage from the comfortable innocence of youth. We all must cross thresholds—real and symbolic. We need to think about how we process the experience of crossing thresholds.

As mentioned previously, critical writers offer *a contribution* to an ongoing conversation about a text; a contribution isn't a "solution," a "proof," or a "last word." But we cannot contribute to a discussion without engaging others who are involved in the discussion. Solid contributions depend upon attention to textual evidence and to relevant scholarship. Writing about a symbol is ultimately no different from writing about any element. We must always think about evidence, about how we account for/explain an interpretation, and about how we draw out the significance of an interpretation. Analysis involves "taking apart" in order to see how parts "fit together."

An attraction of reading for symbols is thinking that there is a reason for the otherwise inexplicable. Once we begin to find symbols in literary works, it is easy to jump to symbolic interpretations. We like to think that an author is exercising a higher power and that every object must be there for some symbolic reason. But power, beauty, and significance don't depend upon cleverly making one thing seem to be something else. A "deep reading" is not necessarily a reading that centers on symbols. So don't abandon all of the other literary elements for the sake of symbols. Remember that it is not enough to assert that an object symbolizes something; such a claim is an argument that we must back up by providing evidence in the literature and by showing how such symbolism helps us understand/experience the whole text. It may be useful to hold yourself to a higher standard whenever you claim to see symbols. Keep some basic questions in mind:

- What in the work encourages you to think beyond the concrete?
- Why is it important to appreciate a particular image as symbolic?
- How are words or images used in ways that "turn" us from straightforward meanings?

MODELING CRITICAL ANALYSIS: JOÃO GUIMARÃES ROSA, THE THIRD BANK OF THE RIVER

In Chapter 12, we present an allegorical reading of João Guimarães Rosa's "The Third Bank of the River." Guimarães Rosa's narrative teases us to consider how each part along the way means something about a process, perhaps a process of grieving or of separation. The son may stand in for all children who lose parents or, even more broadly, all children who need to grow into their own selves, separate from parents. The father's "going out" on the river may be an abandonment that is both essential and inevitable. Perhaps we're to consider how a son registers the death of a father, how he contends with the loss or tries to deny the full meaning of the loss.

But our testing out did not and perhaps could not confidently identify a parallel sustained throughout the narrative between the concrete and the abstract. By loosening us from the control exercised by the kind of point-to-point correspondences we find in a work such as *The Faerie Queene*, Guimarães Rosa casts us into the realm of symbol. We're encouraged to play out multiple possibilities. And we're not forced to consider those possibilities as a set of "either-or" propositions. In other words, the river in Guimarães Rosa's story can suggest a widely resonant and textured set of meanings. We may think of how the experience of death unfolds for those left behind and may reflect more generally upon themes of abandonment. We may also consider how Guimarães Rosa projects feelings of loneliness (as a feeling, as a necessary fact of human existence?). It's not that Guimarães Rosa's tale can mean anything we want it to mean but that elements in it are laid out in ways that prompt a disciplined, yet open-ended meditation upon profound abstractions.

Using Symbolism to Focus Writing and Discussion

- What makes you think that this object is a symbol?
- What clues does the author give us that we should look at this object symbolically?
- How can we justify the meaning that we ascribe to this symbol?
- What alternative meanings might this symbol have? Does it make sense to entertain these alternative meanings simultaneously? Why might it be appropriate to abandon these alternative meanings?
- What nuances does this particular symbol give to the meaning that we identify here? What does the author gain by using a symbol rather than stating the idea directly?
- For whom does this symbol have meaning? Is it necessary to be part of some particular group or to have some specific experience in order for this symbol to have significance?
- How does our attention to this detail as a symbol enhance our understanding of the text?

Anthology

BUILDING AND UNDOING COMMUNITY: TAKING PART IN SYMBOLISM

Most people feel a deep desire to establish a sense of community. It's a desire that can easily be frustrated by the conditions of modern life. Sometimes we move too fast to know our neighbors. It is often difficult to hold on to customs. Even families find themselves widely scattered. These difficulties don't make community irrelevant; in fact, they heighten our sense of its importance.

Symbols must be read as part of a system of meaning. That system may encompass references to history, culture, or other works of literature. Sometimes, authors develop symbolic systems that cross from one work to another. The two García Márquez stories we've included in these selections are among the most commonly anthologized of his works; rarely are both published together. This is unfortunate, for García Márquez clearly signals an important pairing. Both stories are subtitled "A Tale for Children," take up a common theme, and foreground an arresting central symbol announced by the main titles "A Very Old Man with Enormous Wings" and "The Handsomest Drowned Man in the World." Either alone offers a rewarding reading experience, but together these stories powerfully explore how people may use or not use symbols to build community.

"A Very Old Man with Enormous Wings" presents us at the outset with something quite extraordinary. Yes, the old man is rather dirty and sick, but he is a man with wings, a man who flies, an amazing being who drops into a very ordinary and unpleasant little town. What could we make of such a creation? Most of us could make a great deal, but the townspeople in the story suffer from a fatal lack of faith, imagination, and generosity. At the end of the story, the town is the same ugly place it was at the beginning. If a living winged man can't inspire people to anything noble, what transformative force can a drowned man washed up on the shore possess? Obviously, no force—unless people find their own way to create a viable, ennobling, and shared symbol. That is exactly what the people of the village do; they create a powerful symbol out of the drowned man and transform their surroundings.

Jhumpa Lahiri, like García Márquez, helps us think about symbols by explicitly raising questions of interpretation: How do characters within a text read objects as symbols? In "This Blessed House" religious symbols become points of reference that help us center on the personal dynamics between the newly married couple. Sanjeev (the husband) reads these items as signs that can function meaningfully only within a Christian belief system. Because neither he nor Twinkle (his wife) is a Christian, Sanjeev considers it silly and undignified to attend much to statues of Jesus, crosses, or any such thing. But Twinkle enthusiastically searches for and showcases every item. For her, these objects connect her to something about the house, about the human community that it has sheltered. These items make her house special; they give it character. They even "bless" the house—not in any particular Christian way but in a way that allows her to feel a personal ownership that the more literal-minded Sanjeev cannot understand.

The contrasting interpretations here remind us of an important point about symbolism: The religious items take on symbolic meaning for Twinkle because she places them in the context of her life, her needs. She interprets them within a large fabric of meaning that encompasses the cultural mix in which she has learned to live through experience. Sanjeev strongly resists the notion of making the objects anything other than objects. He is threatened by the significance Twinkle lends them. He feels uneasy embracing things he sees as new and confusing. But perhaps even he must eventually consider these items as personally significant symbols, albeit symbols of something radically different. He seems at the end to see these artifacts as symbols of disconnection: differences between himself and his wife, between how he sees himself and how others see him, between the power he felt he possessed and the power he actually has. As readers of the story, we can comprehend both perspectives. Lahiri manages to complicate the point of view within the story so that we may appreciate how the same objects take on fundamentally opposed symbolic meanings.

The poems in this anthology contain many symbols to embody themes of community and disconnection. Some of the symbols are fairly traditional. The sea in Matthew Arnold's "Dover Beach" is something to look upon and describe. But it sets up an ever-widening set of thoughts on time, suffering, and faith. And tides do change. Arnold finds that the "Sea of Faith," once full upon the shore, has drawn back. Without the fullness of that faith, the speaker feels compelled to seek comfort in the love of an individual. Any wider sense of human interaction seems dangerous and threatening. In "The Wild Swans at Coole," William Butler Yeats adopts a somewhat less obvious symbol to communicate a related mood. He watches the "nine and fifty swans" that swim upon the waters of a lake within the grounds of Coole Park, a country estate of a friend whom Yeats often visited. The swans are wild and beautiful. They represent for Yeats something of the place they inhabit but also of an entire social world that he loves. The precarious state of that world is registered through the unpredictability of the swans' movement. Will they someday be gone? Will this world survive? Note in this poem how the word *still* helps reinforce symbolic qualities of the swans. *Still* can mean "placid" or "quiet" (for example, "in the still of the night"). It can also suggest continuity over time ("do you still feel that way?"). The swans at Coole Park encompass both senses of that word. By such repetition, Yeats helps us grasp the force of his central symbol.

Arthur Miller's *Death of a Salesman* helps us understand how symbols may be woven into even the most solidly textured realistic narratives. The Loman family's concerns are ordinary: aging, trouble at work, changes in the neighborhood, relationships, money. None of the characters strike us as especially eloquent or deeply self-aware. We're watching people whom we may recognize and perhaps identify with—people who struggle with common problems and nagging dissatisfactions. We're not dealing with heroes or grand events, or moments of personal transformation. We can read/view and concentrate on how the characters relate to one another, how their dreams and frustrations undermine notions of family and community. But as grounded as we may be on such everyday matters, it is clear that many people respond to Miller's play as symbolic of something larger. The characters for the most part have no understanding of how their stories play into something larger, but mainly through Biff we become aware of Miller's desire to make their fate represent something about the common culture. *Death of a Salesman* meditates on notions of success and failure, more particularly on the material markers of success and failure that make dreams problematic. For many, the life as well as death of Willy Loman symbolizes the essentially reductive and life-denying effects of the American Dream as many have come to envision it.

FICTION

Gabriel García Márquez (1928–)

Gabriel García Márquez was born in Aracataca, Colombia. He attended the Universidad Nacional de Colombia from 1947 to 1948 and Universidad de Cartagena from 1948 to 1949. He worked as a reporter for newspapers in Colombia, France, England, Venezuela, and Cuba. García Márquez often combines his journalistic skills with elements of fantasy. The mixture results in what many English-speaking critics have called "magical realism," but García Márquez has himself resisted that term. He believes that the poverty, instability, and violence of much modern life defy conventional realistic treatment. García Márquez has expressed a special affinity for William Faulkner among North American writers. A prolific and flexible writer, García Márquez has published novellas, novels, short story collections, plays, screenplays, film scripts, children's books, essays, and journalistic pieces. His novel *One Hundred Years of Solitude* has gained popularity with critics around the world. The Chilean poet Pablo Neruda called it "the greatest revelation in the Spanish language since the *Don Quixote* of Cervantes." García Márquez's other award-winning works include *Love in the Time of Cholera*. In 1982, García Márquez received the Nobel Prize in literature.

A Very Old Man with Enormous Wings: A Tale for Children (1955)

Translated by Gregory Rabassa

On the third day of rain they had killed so many crabs inside the house that Pelayo had to cross his drenched courtyard and throw them into the sea, because the newborn child had a temperature all night and they thought it was due to the stench. The world had been sad since Tuesday. Sea and sky were a single ash-gray thing and the sands of the beach, which on March nights glimmered like powdered light, had become a stew of mud and rotten shellfish. The light was so weak at noon that when Pelayo was coming back to the house after throwing away the crabs, it was hard for him to see what it was that was moving and groaning in the rear of the courtyard. He had to go very close to see that it was an old man, a very old man, lying face down in the mud, who, in spite of his tremendous efforts, couldn't get up, impeded by his enormous wings.

Frightened by that nightmare, Pelayo ran to get Elisenda, his wife, who was putting compresses on the sick child, and he took her to the rear of the courtyard. They both looked at the fallen body with mute stupor. He was dressed like a ragpicker. There were only a few faded hairs left on his bald skull and very few teeth in his mouth, and his pitiful condition of a drenched great-grandfather had taken away any sense of grandeur he might have had. His huge buzzard wings, dirty and half-plucked, were forever entangled in the mud. They looked at him so long and so closely that Pelayo and Elisenda very soon overcame their surprise and in the end found him familiar. Then they dared speak to him, and he answered in an incomprehensible dialect with a strong sailor's voice. That was how they skipped over the inconvenience of the wings and quite intelligently concluded that he was a lonely castaway from some foreign ship wrecked by the storm. And yet, they called in a neighbor woman who knew everything about life and death to see him, and all she needed was one look to show them their mistake.

"He's an angel," she told them. "He must have been coming for the child, but the poor fellow is so old that the rain knocked him down."

On the following day everyone knew that a flesh-and-blood angel was held captive in Pelayo's house. Against the judgment of the wise neighbor woman, for whom angels in those times were the fugitive survivors of a celestial conspiracy, they did not have the heart to club him to death. Pelayo watched over him all afternoon from the kitchen, armed with his bailiff's club, and before going to bed he dragged him out of the mud and locked him up with the hens in the wire chicken coop. In the middle of the night, when the rain stopped, Pelayo and Elisenda were still killing crabs. A short time afterward the child woke up without a fever and with a desire to eat. Then they felt magnanimous and decided to put the angel on a raft with fresh water and provisions for three days and leave him to his fate on the high seas. But when they went out into the courtyard with the first light of dawn, they found the whole neighborhood in front of the chicken coop having fun with the angel, without the slightest reverence, tossing him things to eat through the openings in the wire as if he weren't a supernatural creature but a circus animal.

Father Gonzaga arrived before seven o'clock, alarmed at the strange   5
news. By that time onlookers less frivolous than those at dawn had already
arrived and they were making all kinds of conjectures concerning the captive's future. The simplest among them thought that he should be named
mayor of the world. Others of sterner mind felt that he should be promoted
to the rank of five-star general in order to win all wars. Some visionaries
hoped that he could be put to stud in order to implant on earth a race of
winged wise men who could take charge of the universe. But Father Gonzaga, before becoming a priest, had been a robust woodcutter. Standing by
the wire, he reviewed his catechism in an instant and asked them to open
the door so that he could take a close look at that pitiful man who looked
more like a huge decrepit hen among the fascinated chickens. He was lying
in a corner drying his open wings in the sunlight among the fruit peels and
breakfast leftovers that the early risers had thrown him. Alien to the imper-
tinences of the world, he only lifted his antiquarian eyes and murmured
something in his dialect when Father Gonzaga went into the chicken coop
and said good morning to him in Latin. The parish priest had his first suspicion of an impostor when he saw that he did not understand the language
of God or know how to greet His ministers. Then he noticed that seen close
up he was much too human: he had an unbearable smell of the outdoors,
the back side of his wings were strewn with parasites and his main feathers
had been mistreated by terrestrial winds, and nothing about him measured
up to the proud dignity of angels. Then he came out of the chicken coop
and in a brief sermon warned the curious against the risks of being ingenu-
ous. He reminded them that the devil had the bad habit of making use of
carnival tricks in order to confuse the unwary. He argued that if wings were
not the essential element in determining the difference between a hawk and
an airplane, they were even less so in the recognition of angels. Nevertheless, he promised to write a letter to his bishop so that the latter would write
to his primate so that the latter would write to the Supreme Pontiff in order
to get the final verdict from the highest courts.

His prudence fell on sterile hearts. The news of the captive angel spread
with such rapidity that after a few hours the courtyard had the bustle of a
marketplace and they had to call in troops with fixed bayonets to disperse
the mob that was about to knock the house down. Elisenda, her spine all
twisted from sweeping up so much marketplace trash, then got the idea of
fencing in the yard and charging five cents admission to see the angel.

The curious came from far away. A traveling carnival arrived with a flying acrobat who buzzed over the crowd several times, but no one paid any
attention to him because his wings were not those of an angel but, rather,
those of a sidereal bat. The most unfortunate invalids on earth came in
search of health: a poor woman who since childhood had been counting her
heartbeats and had run out of numbers; a Portuguese man who couldn't

sleep because the noise of the stars disturbed him; a sleepwalker who got up at night to undo the things he had done while awake; and many others with less serious ailments. In the midst of that shipwreck disorder that made the earth tremble, Pelayo and Elisenda were happy with fatigue, for in less than a week they had crammed their rooms with money and the line of pilgrims waiting their turn to enter still reached beyond the horizon.

The angel was the only one who took no part in his own act. He spent his time trying to get comfortable in his borrowed nest, befuddled by the hellish heat of the oil lamps and sacramental candles that had been placed along the wire. At first they tried to make him eat some mothballs, which, according to the wisdom of the wise neighbor woman, were the food prescribed for angels. But he turned them down, just as he turned down the papal lunches that the penitents brought him, and they never found out whether it was because he was an angel or because he was an old man that in the end ate nothing but eggplant mush. His only supernatural virtue seemed to be patience. Especially during the first days, when the hens pecked at him, searching for the stellar parasites that proliferated in his wings, and the cripples pulled out feathers to touch their defective parts with, and even the most merciful threw stones at him, trying to get him to rise so they could see him standing. The only time they succeeded in arousing him was when they burned his side with an iron for branding steers, for he had been motionless for so many hours that they thought he was dead. He awoke with a start, ranting in his hermetic language and with tears in his eyes, and he flapped his wings a couple of times, which brought on a whirlwind of chicken dung and lunar dust and a gale of panic that did not seem to be of this world. Although many thought that his reaction had been one not of rage but of pain, from then on they were careful not to annoy him, because the majority understood that his passivity was not that of a hero taking his ease but that of a cataclysm in repose.

Father Gonzaga held back the crowd's frivolity with formulas of maidservant inspiration while awaiting the arrival of a final judgment on the nature of the captive. But the mail from Rome showed no sense of urgency. They spent their time finding out if the prisoner had a navel, if his dialect had any connection with Aramaic, how many times he could fit on the head of a pin, or whether he wasn't just a Norwegian with wings. Those meager letters might have come and gone until the end of time if a providential event had not put an end to the priest's tribulations.

It so happened that during those days, among so many other carnival attractions, there arrived in town the traveling show of the woman who had been changed into a spider for having disobeyed her parents. The admission to see her was not only less than the admission to see the angel, but people were permitted to ask her all manner of questions about her absurd state and to examine her up and down so that no one would ever doubt the truth of her horror. She was a frightful tarantula the size of a ram and with the head of a sad maiden. What was most heart-rending, however, was not her outlandish shape but the sincere affliction with which she recounted the details of her misfortune. While still practically a child she had sneaked out of her parents' house to go to a dance, and while she was coming back through the woods after having danced all night without permission, a fearful thunderclap rent the sky in two and through the crack came the lightning bolt of brimstone that changed her into a spider. Her only nourishment came from the meatballs that charitable souls chose to toss into her mouth. A spectacle like that, full of so much human truth and with such a fearful lesson, was bound to defeat without even trying that of a haughty angel who scarcely deigned to look at mortals. Besides, the few miracles attributed to the angel showed a certain mental disorder, like the blind man who didn't recover his sight but grew three new teeth, or the paralytic who didn't get to walk but almost won the lottery, and the leper whose sores sprouted sunflowers. Those consolation miracles, which were more like mocking fun, had already ruined the angel's reputation when the woman who had been changed into a spider finally crushed him completely. That was how Father Gonzaga was cured forever of his insomnia and Pelayo's courtyard went back to being as empty as during the time it had rained for three days and crabs walked through the bedrooms.

The owners of the house had no reason to lament. With the money they saved they built a two-story mansion with balconies and gardens and high netting so that crabs wouldn't get in during the winter, and with iron bars on the windows so that angels wouldn't get in. Pelayo also set up a rabbit warren close to town and gave up his job as bailiff for good, and Elisenda bought some satin pumps with high heels and many dresses of iridescent silk, the kind worn on Sunday by the most desirable women in those times. The chicken coop was the only thing that didn't receive any attention. If they washed it down with Creolin and burned tears of myrrh inside it every so often, it was not in homage to the angel but to drive away the dungheap stench that still hung everywhere like a ghost and was turning the new house into an old one. At first, when the child learned to walk, they were careful that he not get too close to the chicken coop. But then they began to lose their fears and got used to the smell, and before the child got his second teeth he'd gone inside the chicken coop to play, where the wires were falling apart. The angel was no less standoffish with him than with other mortals, but he tolerated the most ingenious infamies with the patience of a dog who had no illusions. They both came down with chicken pox at the same time. The doctor who took care of the child couldn't resist the temptation to listen to the angel's heart, and he found so much whistling in the heart and so many sounds in his kidneys that it seemed impossible for him to be alive. What surprised him most, however, was the logic of his wings.

They seemed so natural on that completely human organism that he couldn't understand why other men didn't have them too.

When the child began school it had been some time since the sun and rain had caused the collapse of the chicken coop. The angel went dragging himself about here and there like a stray dying man. They would drive him out of the bedroom with a broom and a moment later find him in the kitchen. He seemed to be in so many places at the same time that they grew to think that he'd been duplicated, that he was reproducing himself all through the house, and the exasperated and unhinged Elisenda shouted that it was awful living in that hell full of angels. He could scarcely eat and his antiquarian eyes had also become so foggy that he went about bumping into posts. All he had left were the bare cannulae of his last feathers. Pelayo threw a blanket over him and extended him the charity of letting him sleep in the shed, and only then did they notice that he had a temperature at night, and was delirious with the tongue twisters of an old Norwegian. That was one of the few times they became alarmed, for they thought he was going to die and not even the wise neighbor woman had been able to tell them what to do with dead angels.

And yet he not only survived his worst winter, but seemed improved with the first sunny days. He remained motionless for several days in the farthest corner of the courtyard, where no one would see him, and at the beginning of December some large, stiff feathers began to grow on his wings, the feathers of a scarecrow, which looked more like another misfortune of decrepitude. But he must have known the reason for those changes, for he was quite careful that no one should notice them, that no one should hear the sea chanteys that he sometimes sang under the stars. One morning Elisenda was cutting some bunches of onions for lunch when a wind that seemed to come from the high seas blew into the kitchen. Then she went to the window and caught the angel in his first attempts at flight. They were so clumsy that his fingernails opened a furrow in the vegetable patch and he was on the point of knocking the shed down with the ungainly flapping that slipped on the light and couldn't get a grip on the air. But he did manage to gain altitude. Elisenda let out a sigh of relief, for herself and for him, when she saw him pass over the last houses, holding himself up in some way with the risky flapping of a senile vulture. She kept watching him even when she was through cutting the onions and she kept on watching until it was no longer possible for her to see him, because then he was no longer an annoyance in her life but an imaginary dot on the horizon of the sea.

■ This story is subtitled "A Tale for Children." In what specific instances in the story does this subtitle seem appropriate? In what instances does it seem to be something else?

- Father Gonzaga attempts to place the mysterious "old man" into the symbolic systems with which he is familiar. Find the specific passages where he draws his conclusions, trace his reasoning, and discuss its limits.

- When the "very old man" flies away, why does Elisenda "let out a sigh of relief"? How has the "very old man" impacted the life that she had established with Pelayo?

- How does García Márquez depict the community that revives the "very old man"? Locate specific details to describe his attitude toward this group.

Gabriel García Márquez (1928–)

The Handsomest Drowned Man in the World: A Tale for Children (Gregory Rabassa, trans; 1968)

The first children who saw the dark and slinky bulge approaching through the sea let themselves think it was an enemy ship. Then they saw it had no flags or masts and they thought it was a whale. But when it was washed up on the beach, they removed the clumps of seaweed, the jellyfish tentacles, and the remains of fish and flotsam, and only then did they see that it was a drowned man.

They had been playing with him all afternoon, burying him in the sand and digging him up again, when someone chanced to see them and spread the alarm in the village. The men who carried him to the nearest house noticed that he weighed more than any dead man they had ever known, almost as much as a horse, and they said to each other that maybe he'd been floating too long and the water had got into his bones. When they laid him on the floor they said he'd been taller than all other men because there was barely enough room for him in the house, but they thought that maybe the ability to keep on growing after death was part of the nature of certain drowned men. He had the smell of the sea about him and only his shape gave one to suppose that it was the corpse of a human being, because the skin was covered with a crust of mud and scales.

They did not even have to clean off his face to know that the dead man was a stranger. The village was made up of only twenty-odd wooden houses that had stone courtyards with no flowers and which were spread about on the end of a desertlike cape. There was so little land that mothers always went about with the fear that the wind would carry off their children and the few dead that the years had caused among them had to be thrown off the cliffs. But the sea was calm and bountiful and all the men fit into seven boats. So when they found the drowned man they simply had to look at one another to see that they were all there.

That night they did not go out to work at sea. While the men went to find out if anyone was missing in neighboring villages, the women stayed behind to care for the drowned man. They took the mud off with grass swabs, they removed the underwater stones entangled in his hair, and they scraped the crust off with tools used for scaling fish. As they were doing that they noticed that the vegetation on him came from faraway oceans and deep water and that his clothes were in tatters, as if he had sailed through labyrinths of coral. They noticed too that he bore his death with pride, for he did not have the lonely look of other drowned men who came out of the sea or that haggard, needy look of men who drowned in rivers. But only when they finished cleaning him off did they become aware of the kind of man he was and it left them breathless. Not only was he the tallest, strongest, most virile, and best built man they had ever seen, but even though they were looking at him there was no room for him in their imagination.

They could not find a bed in the village large enough to lay him on nor was there a table solid enough to use for his wake. The tallest men's holiday pants would not fit him, not the fattest ones' Sunday shirts, nor the shoes of the one with the biggest feet. Fascinated by his huge size and his beauty, the women then decided to make him some pants from a large piece of sail and a shirt from some bridal brabant linen so that he could continue through his death with dignity. As they sewed, sitting in a circle and gazing at the corpse between stitches, it seemed to them that the wind had never been so steady nor the sea so restless as on that night and they supposed that the change had something to do with the dead man. They thought that if that magnificent man had lived in the village, his house would have had the widest doors, the highest ceiling, and the strongest floor, his bedstead would have been made from a midship frame held together by iron bolts, and his wife would have been the happiest woman. They thought that he would have had so much authority that he could have drawn fish out of the sea simply by calling their names and that he would have put so much work into his land that springs would have burst forth from among the rocks so that he would have been able to plant flowers on the cliffs. They secretly compared him to their own men, thinking that for all their lives theirs were incapable of doing what he could do in one night, and they ended up dismissing them deep in their hearts as the weakest, meanest, and most useless creatures on earth. They were wandering through that maze of fantasy when the oldest woman, who as the oldest had looked upon the drowned man with more compassion than passion, sighed:

"He has the face of someone called Esteban."

It was true. Most of them had only to take another look at him to see that he could not have any other name. The more stubborn among them, who were the youngest, still lived for a few hours with the illusion that when they put his clothes on and he lay among the flowers in patent leather shoes his name might be Lautaro. But it was a vain illusion. There had not been enough canvas, the poorly cut and worse sewn pants were too tight, and the hidden strength of his heart popped the buttons on his shirt. After midnight the whistling of the wind died down and the sea fell into its Wednesday drowsiness. The silence put an end to any last doubts: he was Esteban. The women who had dressed him, who had combed his hair, had cut his nails and shaved him were unable to hold back a shudder of pity when they had to resign themselves to his being dragged along the ground. It was then that they understood how unhappy he must have been with that huge body since it bothered him even after death. They could see him in life, condemned to going through doors sideways, cracking his head on crossbeams, remaining on his feet during visits, not knowing what to do with his soft, pink, sea lion hands while the lady of the house looked for her most resistant chair and begged him, frightened to death, sit here, Esteban, please, and he, leaning against the wall, smiling, don't bother, ma'am, I'm fine where I am, his heels raw and his back roasted from having done the same thing so many times whenever he paid a visit, don't bother, ma'am, I'm fine where I am, just to avoid the embarrassment of breaking up the chair, and never knowing perhaps that the ones who said don't go, Esteban, at least wait till the coffee's ready, were the ones who later on would whisper the big boob finally left, how nice, the handsome fool has gone. That was what the women were thinking beside the body a little before dawn. Later, when they covered his face with a handkerchief so that the light would not bother him, he looked so forever dead, so defenseless, so much like their men that the first furrows of tears opened in their hearts. It was one of the younger ones who began the weeping. The others, coming to, went from sighs to wails, and the more they sobbed the more they felt like weeping, because the drowned man was becoming all the more Esteban for them, and so they wept so much, for he was the most destitute, most peaceful, and most obliging man on earth, poor Esteban. So when the men returned with the news that the drowned man was not from the neighboring villages either, the women felt an opening of jubilation in the midst of their tears.

"Praise the Lord," they sighed, "he's ours!"

The men thought the fuss was only womanish frivolity. Fatigued because of the difficult nighttime inquiries, all they wanted was to get rid of the bother of the newcomer once and for all before the sun grew strong on that arid, windless day. They improvised a litter with the remains of foremasts and gaffs, tying it together with rigging so that it would bear the weight of the body until they reached the cliffs. They wanted to tie the anchor from a cargo ship to him so that he would sink easily into the deepest waves, where fish are blind and divers die of nostalgia, and bad currents would not bring him back to shore, as had happened with other bodies. But the more they hurried, the more the women thought of ways to waste time.

They walked about like startled hens, pecking with the sea charms on their breasts, some interfering on one side to put a scapular of the good wind on the drowned man, some on the other side to put a wrist compass on him, and after a great deal of *get away from there, woman, stay out of the way, look, you almost made me fall on top of the dead man*, the men began to feel mistrust in their livers and started grumbling about why so many main-altar decorations for a stranger, because no matter how many nails and holy-water jars he had on him, the sharks would chew him all the same, but the women kept piling on their junk relics, running back and forth, stumbling, while they released in sighs what they did not in tears, so that the men finally exploded with *since when has there ever been such a fuss over a drifting corpse, a drowned nobody, a piece of cold Wednesday meat*. One of the women, mortified by so much lack of care, then removed the handkerchief from the dead man's face and the men were left breathless too.

He was Esteban. It was not necessary to repeat it for them to recognize him. If they had been told Sir Walter Raleigh, even they might have been impressed with his gringo accent, the macaw on his shoulder, his cannibal-killing blunderbuss, but there could be only one Esteban in the world and there he was, stretched out like a sperm whale, shoeless, wearing the pants of an undersized child, and with those stony nails that had to be cut with a knife. They only had to take the handkerchief off his face to see that he was ashamed, that it was not his fault that he was so big or so heavy or so hand-some, and if he had known that this was going to happen, he would have looked for a more discreet place to drown in, seriously, I even would have tied the anchor off a galleon around my neck and staggered off a cliff like someone who doesn't like things in order not to be upsetting people now with this Wednesday dead body, as you people say, in order not to be bothering anyone with this filthy piece of cold meat that doesn't have anything to do with me. There was so much truth in his manner that even the most mistrustful men, the ones who felt the bitterness of endless nights at sea fearing that their women would tire of dreaming about them and begin to dream of drowned men, even they and others who were harder still shuddered in the marrow of their bones at Esteban's sincerity.

That was how they came to hold the most splendid funeral they could conceive of for an abandoned drowned man. Some women who had gone to get flowers in the neighboring villages returned with other women who could not believe what they had been told, and those women went back for more flowers when they saw the dead man, and they brought more and more until there were so many flowers and so many people that it was hard to walk about. At the final moment it pained them to return him to the waters as an orphan and they chose a father and mother from among the best people, and aunts and uncles and cousins, so that through him all the inhabitants of the village became kinsmen. Some sailors who heard the

weeping from a distance went off course and people heard of one who had
himself tied to the mainmast, remembering ancient fables about sirens.
While they fought for the privilege of carrying him on their shoulders along
the steep escarpment by the cliffs, men and women became aware for the
first time of the desolation of their streets, the dryness of their courtyards,
the narrowness of their dreams as they faced the splendor and beauty of
their drowned man. They let him go without an anchor so that he could
come back if he wished and whenever he wished, and they all held their
breath for the fraction of centuries the body took to fall into the abyss.
They did not need to look at one another to realize that they were no
longer all present, that they would never be. But they also knew that everything would be different from then on, that their houses would have wider
doors, higher ceilings, and stronger floors so that Esteban's memory could go
everywhere without bumping into beams and so that no one in the future
would dare whisper the big boob finally died, too bad, the handsome fool
has finally died, because they were going to paint their house fronts gay colors to make Esteban's memory eternal and they were going to break their
backs digging for springs among the stones and planting flowers on the cliffs
so that in future years at dawn the passengers on great liners would awaken,
suffocated by the smell of gardens on the high seas, and the captain would
have to come down from the bridge in his dress uniform, with his astrolabe,
his pole star, and his row of war medals and, pointing to the promontory of
roses on the horizon, he would say in fourteen languages, look there, where
the wind is so peaceful now that it's gone to sleep beneath the beds, over
there, where the sun's so bright that the sunflowers don't know which way
to turn, yes, over there, that's Esteban's village.

- How do the elements of this story echo those found in "A Very Old Man with
  Enormous Wings"?
- How does the community's reaction to this outsider differ from that of the "very
  old man"? Look, for instance, at the issue of tracing the provenance of the
  body, of naming it, displaying it, and claiming ownership of it. Look also at the
  significance of the funeral.

Jhumpa Lahiri (1967–)

Jhumpa Lahiri was born in London, England. Lahiri, the daughter of Bengali
parents, grew up in Rhode Island but made many family visits to Calcutta, India.
She received her BA from Barnard College and an MA and PhD from Boston
University. Lahiri currently lives in New York City. Lahiri's debut story collection,
Interpreter of Maladies (1999), was a critical success and received the O. Henry

Award in 1999 and the Pulitzer Prize in fiction in 2000. In 1999, Lahiri was named one of the twenty best young fiction writers in America by the *New Yorker*. Her novel, *The Namesake*, was published in 2003.

This Blessed House (1999)

They discovered the first one in a cupboard above the stove, beside an unopened bottle of malt vinegar.

"Guess what I found." Twinkle walked into the living room, lined from end to end with taped-up packing boxes, waving the vinegar in one hand and a white porcelain effigy of Christ, roughly the same size as the vinegar bottle, in the other.

Sanjeev looked up. He was kneeling on the floor, marking, with ripped bits of a Post-it, patches on the baseboard that needed to be retouched with paint. "Throw it away."

"Which?"

"Both."

"But I can cook something with the vinegar. It's brand-new."

"You've never cooked anything with vinegar."

"I'll look something up. In one of those books we got for our wedding."

Sanjeev turned back to the baseboard, to replace a Post-it scrap that had fallen to the floor. "Check the expiration. And at the very least get rid of that idiotic statue."

"But it could be worth something. Who knows?" She turned it upside down, then stroked, with her index finger, the minuscule frozen folds of its robes. "It's pretty."

"We're not Christian," Sanjeev said. Lately he had begun noticing the need to state the obvious to Twinkle. The day before he had to tell her that if she dragged her end of the bureau instead of lifting it, the parquet floor would scratch.

She shrugged. "No, we're not Christian. We're good little Hindus." She planted a kiss on top of Christ's head, then placed the statue on top of the fireplace mantel, which needed, Sanjeev observed, to be dusted.

By the end of the week the mantel had still not been dusted; it had, however, come to serve as the display shelf for a sizable collection of Christian paraphernalia. There was a 3-D postcard of Saint Francis done in four colors, which Twinkle had found taped to the back of the medicine cabinet, and a wooden cross key chain, which Sanjeev had stepped on with bare feet as he was installing extra shelving in Twinkle's study. There was a framed paint-by-number of the three wise men, against a black velvet background, tucked in the linen closet. There was also a tile trivet depicting a blond, unbearded Jesus, delivering a sermon on a mountaintop, left in one of the drawers of the built-in china cabinet in the dining room.

"Do you think the previous owners were born-agains?" asked Twinkle, making room the next day for a small plastic snow-filled dome containing a miniature Nativity scene, found behind the pipes of the kitchen sink.

Sanjeev was organizing his engineering texts from MIT in alphabetical order on a bookshelf, though it had been several years since he had needed to consult any of them. After graduating, he moved from Boston to Connecticut, to work for a firm near Hartford, and he had recently learned that he was being considered for the position of vice president. At thirty-three he had a secretary of his own and a dozen people working under his supervision who gladly supplied him with any information he needed. Still, the presence of his college books in the room reminded him of a time in his life he recalled with fondness, when he would walk each evening across the Mass. Avenue bridge to order Mughlai chicken with spinach from his favorite Indian restaurant on the other side of the Charles, and return to his dorm to write out clean copies of his problem sets.

"Or perhaps it's an attempt to convert people," Twinkle mused.

"Clearly the scheme has succeeded in your case."

She disregarded him, shaking the little plastic dome so that the snow swirled over the manger.

He studied the items on the mantel. It puzzled him that each was in its own way so silly. Clearly they lacked a sense of sacredness. He was further puzzled that Twinkle, who normally displayed good taste, was so charmed. These objects meant something to Twinkle, but they meant nothing to him. They irritated him. "We should call the Realtor. Tell him there's all this nonsense left behind. Tell him to take it away."

"Oh, Sanj." Twinkle groaned. "Please. I would feel terrible throwing them away. Obviously they were important to the people who used to live here. It would feel, I don't know, sacrilegious or something."

"If they're so precious, then why are they hidden all over the house? Why didn't they take them with them?

"There must be others," Twinkle said. Her eyes roamed the bare off-white walls of the room, as if there were other things concealed behind the plaster. "What else do you think we'll find?"

But as they unpacked their boxes and hung up their winter clothes and the silk paintings of elephant processions bought on their honeymoon in Jaipur, Twinkle, much to her dismay, could not find a thing. Nearly a week had passed before they discovered, one Saturday afternoon, a larger-than-life-sized watercolor poster of Christ, weeping translucent tears the size of peanut shells and sporting a crown of thorns, rolled up behind a radiator in the guest bedroom. Sanjeev had mistaken it for a window shade.

"Oh, we must, we simply must put it up. It's too spectacular." Twinkle lit a cigarette and began to smoke it with relish, waving it around Sanjeev's head as if it were a conductor's baton as Mahler's Fifth Symphony roared from the stereo downstairs.

"Now, look. I will tolerate, for now, your little biblical menagerie in   25
the living room. But I refuse to have this," he said, flicking at one of the
painted peanut-tears, "displayed in our home."

Twinkle stared at him, placidly exhaling, the smoke emerging in two
thin blue streams from her nostrils. She rolled up the poster slowly, securing it
with one of the elastic bands she always wore around her wrist for tying back
her thick, unruly hair, streaked here and there with henna. "I'm going to put
it in my study," she informed him. "That way you don't have to look at it."

"What about the housewarming? They'll want to see all the rooms. I've
invited people from the office."

She rolled her eyes. Sanjeev noted that the symphony, now in its third
movement, had reached a crescendo, for it pulsed with the telltale clashing
of cymbals.

"I'll put it behind the door," she offered. "That way, when they peek
in, they won't see. Happy?"

He stood watching her as she left the room, with her poster and her   30
cigarette; a few ashes had fallen to the floor where she'd been standing. He
bent down, pinched them between his fingers, and deposited them in his
cupped palm. The tender fourth movement, the *adagietto*, began. During
breakfast, Sanjeev had read in the liner notes that Mahler had proposed to
his wife by sending her the manuscript of this portion of the score. Although there were elements of tragedy and struggle in the Fifth Symphony,
he had read, it was principally music of love and happiness.

He heard the toilet flush. "By the way," Twinkle hollered, "if you want
to impress people, I wouldn't play this music. It's putting me to sleep."

Sanjeev went to the bathroom to throw away the ashes. The cigarette
butt still bobbed in the toilet bowl, but the tank was refilling, so he had to
wait a moment before he could flush it again. In the mirror of the medicine
cabinet he inspected his long eyelashes—like a girl's, Twinkle liked to
tease. Though he was of average build, his cheeks had a plumpness to them;
this, along with the eyelashes, detracted, he feared, from what he hoped was
a distinguished profile. He was of average height as well, and had wished
ever since he had stopped growing that he were just one inch taller. For this
reason it irritated him when Twinkle insisted on wearing high heels, as she
had done the other night when they ate dinner in Manhattan. This was the
first weekend after they'd moved into the house; by then the mantel had already filled up considerably, and they had bickered about it in the car on
the way down. But then Twinkle had drunk four glasses of whiskey in a
nameless bar in Alphabet City, and forgot all about it. She dragged him to a
tiny bookshop on St. Mark's Place, where she browsed for nearly an hour,
and when they left she insisted that they dance a tango on the sidewalk in
front of strangers.

Afterward, she tottered on his arm, rising faintly over his line of vision,
in a pair of suede three-inch leopard-print pumps. In this manner they

walked the endless blocks back to a parking garage on Washington Square, for Sanjeev had heard far too many stories about the terrible things that happened to cars in Manhattan. "But I do nothing all day except sit at my desk," she fretted when they were driving home, after he had mentioned that her shoes looked uncomfortable and suggested that perhaps she should not wear them. "I can't exactly wear heels when I'm typing." Though he abandoned the argument, he knew for a fact that she didn't spend all day at her desk; just that afternoon, when he got back from a run, he found her inexplicably in bed, reading. When he asked why she was in bed in the middle of the day she told him she was bored. He had wanted to say to her then, You could unpack some boxes. You could sweep the attic. You could retouch the paint on the bathroom windowsill, and after you do it you could warn me so that I don't put my watch on it. They didn't bother her, these scattered, unsettled matters. She seemed content with whatever clothes she found at the front of the closet, with whatever magazine was lying around, with whatever song was on the radio—content yet curious. And now all of her curiosity centered around discovering the next treasure.

A few days later when Sanjeev returned from the office, he found Twinkle on the telephone, smoking and talking to one of her girlfriends in California even though it was before five o'clock and the long-distance rates were at their peak. "Highly devout people," she was saying, pausing every now and then to exhale. "Each day is like a treasure hunt. I'm serious. This you won't believe. The switch plates in the bedrooms were decorated with scenes from the Bible. You know, Noah's Ark and all that. Three bedrooms, but one is my study. Sanjeev went to the hardware store right away and replaced them, can you imagine, he replaced every single one."

Now it was the friend's turn to talk. Twinkle nodded, slouched on the   35
floor in front of the fridge, wearing black stirrup pants and a yellow chenille sweater, groping for her lighter. Sanjeev could smell something aromatic on the stove, and he picked his way carefully across the extra-long phone cord tangled on the Mexican terra-cotta tiles. He opened the lid of a pot with some sort of reddish brown sauce dripping over the sides, boiling furiously.

"It's a stew made with fish. I put the vinegar in it," she said to him, interrupting her friend, crossing her fingers. "Sorry, you were saying?" She was like that, excited and delighted by little things, crossing her fingers before any remotely unpredictable event, like tasting a new flavor of ice cream, or dropping a letter in a mailbox. It was a quality he did not understand. It made him feel stupid, as if the world contained hidden wonders he could not anticipate, or see. He looked at her face, which, it occurred to him, had not grown out of its girlhood, the eyes untroubled, the pleasing features unfirm, as if they still had to settle into some sort of permanent expression. Nicknamed after a nursery rhyme, she had yet to shed a childhood endearment. Now, in the second month of their marriage, certain things nettled him—the way she sometimes spat a little when she spoke, or left her undergarments after removing them at night at the foot of their bed rather than depositing them in the laundry hamper.

They had met only four months before. Her parents, who lived in California, and his, who still lived in Calcutta, were old friends, and across continents they had arranged the occasion at which Twinkle and Sanjeev were introduced—a sixteenth birthday party for a daughter in their circle—when Sanjeev was in Palo Alto on business. At the restaurant they were seated side by side at a round table with a revolving platter of spareribs and egg rolls and chicken wings, which, they concurred, all tasted the same. They had concurred too on their adolescent but still persistent fondness for Wodehouse novels, and their dislike for the sitar, and later Twinkle confessed that she was charmed by the way Sanjeev had dutifully refilled her teacup during their conversation.

And so the phone calls began, and grew longer, and then the visits, first he to Stanford, then she to Connecticut, after which Sanjeev would save in an ashtray left on the balcony the crushed cigarettes she had smoked during the weekend—saved them, that is, until the next time she came to visit him, and then he vacuumed the apartment, washed the sheets, even dusted the plant leaves in her honor. She was twenty-seven and recently abandoned, he had gathered, by an American who had tried and failed to be an actor; Sanjeev was lonely, with an excessively generous income for a single man, and had never been in love. At the urging of their matchmakers, they married in India, amid hundreds of well-wishers whom he barely remembered from his childhood, in incessant August rains, under a red and orange tent strung with Christmas tree lights on Mandeville Road.

"Did you sweep the attic?" he asked Twinkle later as she was folding paper napkins and wedging them by their plates. The attic was the only part of the house they had not yet given an initial cleaning.

"Not yet. I will, I promise. I hope this tastes good," she said, planting   40
the steaming pot on top of the Jesus trivet. There was a loaf of Italian bread in a little basket, and iceberg lettuce and grated carrots tossed with bottled dressing and croutons, and glasses of red wine. She was not terribly ambitious in the kitchen. She bought preroasted chickens from the supermarket and served them with potato salad prepared who knew when, sold in little plastic containers. Indian food, she complained, was a bother; she detested chopping garlic, and peeling ginger, and could not operate a blender, and so it was Sanjeev who, on weekends, seasoned mustard oil with cinnamon sticks and cloves in order to produce a proper curry.

He had to admit, though, that whatever it was that she had cooked today, it was unusually tasty, attractive even, with bright white cubes of fish, and flecks of parsley, and fresh tomatoes gleaming in the dark brown-red broth.

"How did you make it?"

"I made it up."

"What did you do?"

"I just put some things into the pot and added the malt vinegar at the 45
end."

"How much vinegar?"

She shrugged, ripping off some bread and plunging it into her bowl.

"What do you mean you don't know? You should write it down. What
if you need to make it again, for a party or something?"

"I'll remember," she said. She covered the bread basket with a dish-
towel that had, he suddenly noticed, the Ten Commandments printed on it.
She flashed him a smile, giving his knee a little squeeze under the table.
"Face it. This house is blessed."

The housewarming party was scheduled for the last Saturday in October, 50
and they had invited about thirty people. All were Sanjeev's acquaintances,
people from the office, and a number of Indian couples in the Connecticut
area, many of whom he barely knew, but who had regularly invited him, in
his bachelor days, to supper on Saturdays. He often wondered why they included him in their circle. He had little in common with any of them, but
he always attended their gatherings, to eat spiced chickpeas and shrimp cut-
lets, and gossip and discuss politics, for he seldom had other plans. So far,
no one had met Twinkle; back when they were still dating, Sanjeev didn't
want to waste their brief weekends together with people he associated with
being alone. Other than Sanjeev and an ex-boyfriend who she believed
worked in a pottery studio in Brookfield, she knew no one in the state of
Connecticut. She was completing her master's thesis at Stanford, a study of
an Irish poet whom Sanjeev had never heard of.

Sanjeev had found the house on his own before leaving for the wedding,
for a good price, in a neighborhood with a fine school system. He was impressed by the elegant curved staircase with its wrought-iron banister, and the
dark wooden wainscoting, and the solarium overlooking rhododendron bushes,
and the solid brass 22, which also happened to be the date of his birth, nailed
impressively to the vaguely Tudor facade. There were two working fireplaces, a
two-car garage, and an attic suitable for converting into extra bedrooms if, the
Realtor mentioned, the need should arise. By then Sanjeev had already made
up his mind, was determined that he and Twinkle should live there together,
forever, and so he had not bothered to notice the switch plates covered with
biblical stickers, or the transparent decal of the Virgin on the half shell,
as Twinkle liked to call it, adhered to the window in the master bedroom.
When, after moving in, he tried to scrape it off, he scratched the glass.

The weekend before the party they were raking the lawn when he heard
Twinkle shriek. He ran to her, clutching his rake, worried that she had

discovered a dead animal, or a snake. A brisk October breeze stung the tops of his ears as his sneakers crunched over brown and yellow leaves. When he reached her, she had collapsed on the grass, dissolved in nearly silent laughter. Behind an overgrown forsythia bush was a plaster Virgin Mary as tall as their waists, with a blue painted hood draped over her head in the manner of an Indian bride. Twinkle grabbed the hem of her T-shirt and began wiping away the dirt staining the statue's brow.

"I suppose you want to put her by the foot of our bed," Sanjeev said.

She looked at him, astonished. Her belly was exposed, and he saw that there were goose bumps around her navel. "What do you think? Of course we can't put this in our bedroom."

"We can't?" 55

"No, silly Sanj. This is meant for outside. For the lawn."

"Oh God, no. Twinkle, no."

"But we must. It would be bad luck not to."

"All the neighbors will see. They'll think we're insane."

"Why, for having a statue of the Virgin Mary on our lawn? Every other 60 person in this neighborhood has a statue of Mary on the lawn. We'll fit right in."

"We're not Christian."

"So you keep reminding me." She spat onto the tip of her finger and started to rub intently at a particularly stubborn stain on Mary's chin. "Do you think this is dirt, or some kind of fungus?"

He was getting nowhere with her, with this woman whom he had known for only four months and whom he had married, this woman with whom he now shared his life. He thought with a flicker of regret of the snapshots his mother used to send him from Calcutta, of prospective brides who could sing and sew and season lentils without consulting a cookbook. Sanjeev had considered these women, had even ranked them in order of preference, but then he had met Twinkle. "Twinkle, I can't have the people I work with see this statue on my lawn."

"They can't fire you for being a believer. It would be discrimination."

"That's not the point." 65

"Why does it matter to you so much what other people think?"

"Twinkle, please." He was tired. He let his weight rest against his rake as she began dragging the statue toward an oval bed of myrtle, beside the lamppost that flanked the brick pathway. "Look, Sanj. She's so lovely."

He returned to his pile of leaves and began to deposit them by handfuls into a plastic garbage bag. Over his head the blue sky was cloudless. One tree on the lawn was still full of leaves, red and orange, like the tent in which he had married Twinkle.

He did not know if he loved her. He said he did when she had first asked him, one afternoon in Palo Alto as they sat side by side in a darkened, nearly empty movie theater. Before the film, one of her favorites, some-thing in German that he found extremely depressing, she had pressed the tip of her nose to his so that he could feel the flutter of her mascara-coated eyelashes. That afternoon he had replied, yes, he loved her, and she was delighted, and fed him a piece of popcorn, letting her finger linger an in-stant between his lips, as if it were his reward for coming up with the right answer.

Though she did not say it herself, he assumed then that she loved him too, but now he was no longer sure. In truth, Sanjeev did not know what love was, only what he thought it was not. It was not, he had decided, re-turning to an empty carpeted condominium each night, and using only the top fork in his cutlery drawer, and turning away politely at those weekend dinner parties when the other men eventually put their arms around the waists of their wives and girlfriends, leaning over every now and again to kiss their shoulders or necks. It was not sending away for classical music CDs by mail, working his way methodically through the major composers that the catalogue recommended, and always sending his payments in on time. In the months before meeting Twinkle, Sanjeev had begun to realize this. "You have enough money in the bank to raise three families," his mother reminded him when they spoke at the start of each month on the phone. "You need a wife to look after and love." Now he had one, a pretty one, from a suitably high caste, who would soon have a master's degree. What was there not to love?

That evening Sanjeev poured himself a gin and tonic, drank it and most of another during one segment of the news, and then approached Twinkle, who was taking a bubble bath, for she announced that her limbs ached from raking the lawn, something she had never done before. He didn't knock. She had applied a bright blue mask to her face, was smoking and sipping some bourbon with ice and leafing through a fat paperback book whose pages had buckled and turned gray from the water. He glanced at the cover; the only thing written on it was the word "Sonnets" in dark red letters. He took a breath, and then he informed her very calmly that after finishing his drink he was going to put on his shoes and go outside and remove the Virgin from the front lawn.

"Where are you going to put it?" she asked him dreamily, her eyes closed. One of her legs emerged, unfolding gracefully, from the layer of suds. She flexed and pointed her toes.

"For now I am going to put it in the garage. Then tomorrow morning on my way to work I am going to take it to the dump."

"Don't you dare." She stood up, letting the book fall into the water, bubbles dripping down her thighs. "I hate you," she informed him, her eyes narrowing at the word "hate." She reached for her bathrobe, tied it tightly about her waist, and padded down the winding staircase, leaving sloppy wet

70

footprints along the parquet floor. When she reached the foyer, Sanjeev said, "Are you planning on leaving the house that way?" He felt a throbbing in his temples, and his voice revealed an unfamiliar snarl when he spoke.

"Who cares? Who cares what way I leave this house?" 75

"Where are you planning on going at this hour?"

"You can't throw away that statue. I won't let you." Her mask, now dry, had assumed an ashen quality; and water from her hair dripped onto the caked contours of her face.

"Yes I can. I will."

"No," Twinkle said, her voice suddenly small. "This is our house. We own it together. The statue is a part of our property." She had begun to shiver. A small pool of bathwater had collected around her ankles. He went to shut a window, fearing that she would catch cold. Then he noticed that some of the water dripping down her hard blue face was tears.

"Oh God, Twinkle, please, I didn't mean it." He had never seen her 80 cry before, had never seen such sadness in her eyes. She didn't turn away or try to stop the tears; instead she looked strangely at peace. For a moment she closed her lids, pale and unprotected compared to the blue that caked the rest of her face. Sanjeev felt ill, as if he had eaten either too much or too little.

She went to him, placing her damp toweled arms about his neck, sobbing into his chest, soaking his shirt. The mask flaked onto his shoulders.

In the end they settled on a compromise: the statue would be placed in a recess at the side of the house, so that it wasn't obvious to passersby, but was still clearly visible to all who came.

The menu for the party was fairly simple: there would be a case of champagne, and samosas from an Indian restaurant in Hartford, and big trays of rice with chicken and almonds and orange peels, which Sanjeev had spent the greater part of the morning and afternoon preparing. He had never entertained on such a large scale before and, worried that there would not be enough to drink, ran out at one point to buy another case of champagne just in case. For this reason he burned one of the rice trays and had to start it over again. Twinkle swept the floors and volunteered to pick up the samosas; she had an appointment for a manicure and a pedicure in that direction, anyway. Sanjeev had planned to ask if she would consider clearing the menagerie off the mantel, if only for the party, but she left while he was in the shower. She was gone for a good three hours, and so it was Sanjeev who did the rest of the cleaning. By five-thirty the entire house sparkled, with scented candles that Twinkle had picked up in Hartford illuminating the items on the mantel, and slender stalks of burning incense planted into the soil of potted plants. Each time he passed the mantel he winced, dreading the raised eyebrows of his guests as they viewed the flickering ceramic saints, the salt and pepper shakers designed to resemble Mary and Joseph. Still, they would be impressed, he hoped, by the lovely bay windows, the shining parquet floors, the impressive winding staircase, the wooden wainscoting, as they sipped champagne and dipped samosas in chutney.

Douglas, one of the new consultants at the firm, and his girlfriend Nora were the first to arrive. Both were tall and blond, wearing matching wire-rimmed glasses and long black overcoats. Nora wore a black hat full of sharp thin feathers that corresponded to the sharp thin angles of her face. Her left hand was joined with Douglas's. In her right hand was a bottle of cognac with a red ribbon wrapped around its neck, which she gave to Twinkle.

"Great lawn, Sanjeev," Douglas remarked. "We've got to get that rake   85
out ourselves, sweetie. And this must be…"

"My wife. Tanima."

"Call me Twinkle."

"What an unusual name," Nora remarked.

Twinkle shrugged. "Not really. There's an actress in Bombay named Dimple Kapadia. She even has a sister named Simple."

Douglas and Nora raised their eyebrows simultaneously, nodding slowly,   90
as if to let the absurdity of the names settle in. "Pleased to meet you, Twinkle."

"Help yourself to champagne. There's gallons."

"I hope you don't mind my asking," Douglas said, "but I noticed the statue outside, and are you guys Christian? I thought you were Indian."

"There are Christians in India," Sanjeev replied, "but we're not."

"I love your outfit," Nora told Twinkle.

"And I adore your hat. Would you like the grand tour?"   95

The bell rang again, and again and again. Within minutes, it seemed, the house had filled with bodies and conversations and unfamiliar fragrances. The women wore heels and sheer stockings, and short black dresses made of crepe and chiffon. They handed their wraps and coats to Sanjeev, who draped them carefully on hangers in the spacious coat closet, though Twinkle told people to throw their things on the ottomans in the solarium. Some of the Indian women wore their finest saris, made with gold filigree that draped in elegant pleats over their shoulders. The men wore jackets and ties and citrus-scented aftershaves. As people filtered from one room to the next, presents piled onto the long cherry-wood table that ran from one end of the downstairs hall to the other.

It bewildered Sanjeev that it was for him, and his house, and his wife, that they had all gone to so much care. The only other time in his life that something similar had happened was his wedding day, but somehow this was different, for these were not his family, but people who knew him only casually, and in a sense owed him nothing. Everyone congratulated him. Lester, another coworker, predicted that Sanjeev would be promoted to vice president in two months maximum. People devoured the samosas, and dutifully admired the freshly painted ceilings and walls, the hanging plants, the bay windows, the silk paintings from Jaipur. But most of all they admired Twinkle, and her brocaded *salwar-kameez*, which was the shade of a persimmon with a low scoop in the back, and the little string of white rose petals she had coiled cleverly around her head, and the pearl choker with a sapphire at its center that adorned her throat. Over hectic jazz records, played under Twinkle's supervision, they laughed at her anecdotes and observations, forming a widening circle around her, while Sanjeev replenished the samosas that he kept warming evenly in the oven, and getting ice for people's drinks, and opening more bottles of champagne with some difficulty, and explaining for the fortieth time that he wasn't Christian. It was Twinkle who led them in separate groups up and down the winding stairs, to gaze at the back lawn, to peer down the cellar steps. "Your friends adore the poster in my study," she mentioned to him triumphantly, placing her hand on the small of his back as they, at one point, brushed past each other.

Sanjeev went to the kitchen, which was empty, and ate a piece of chicken out of the tray on the counter with his fingers because he thought no one was looking. He ate a second piece, then washed it down with a gulp of gin straight from the bottle.

"Great house. Great rice." Sunil, an anesthesiologist, walked in, spooning food from his paper plate into his mouth. "Do you have more champagne?"

"Your wife's wow," added Prabal, following behind. He was an unmarried professor of physics at Yale. For a moment Sanjeev stared at him blankly, then blushed; once at a dinner party Prabal had pronounced that Sophia Loren was wow, as was Audrey Hepburn. "Does she have a sister?"

Sunil picked a raisin out of the rice tray. "Is her last name Little Star?"

The two men laughed and started eating more rice from the tray, plowing through it with their plastic spoons. Sanjeev went down to the cellar for more liquor. For a few minutes he paused on the steps, in the damp, cool silence, hugging the second crate of champagne to his chest as the party drifted above the rafters. Then he set the reinforcements on the dining table.

"Yes, everything, we found them all in the house, in the most unusual places," he heard Twinkle saying in the living room. "In fact we keep finding them."

"No!"

"Yes! Every day is like a treasure hunt. It's too good. God only knows what else we'll find, no pun intended."

That was what started it. As if by some unspoken pact, the whole party joined forces and began combing through each of the rooms, opening closets on their own, peering under chairs and cushions, feeling behind curtains, removing books from bookcases. Groups scampered, giggling and swaying, up and down the winding staircase.

"We've never explored the attic," Twinkle announced suddenly, and so everybody followed.

"How do we get up there?"

"There's a ladder in the hallway, somewhere in the ceiling."

Wearily Sanjeev followed at the back of the crowd, to point out the location of the ladder, but Twinkle had already found it on her own. "Eureka!" she hollered.

Douglas pulled the chain that released the steps. His face was flushed and he was wearing Nora's feather hat on his head. One by one the guests disappeared, men helping women as they placed their strappy high heels on the narrow slats of the ladder, the Indian women wrapping the free ends of their expensive saris into their waistbands. The men followed behind, all quickly disappearing, until Sanjeev alone remained at the top of the winding staircase. Footsteps thundered over his head. He had no desire to join them. He wondered if the ceiling would collapse, imagined, for a split second, the sight of all the tumbling drunk perfumed bodies crashing, tangled, around him. He heard a shriek, and then rising, spreading waves of laughter in discordant tones. Something fell, something else shattered. He could hear them babbling about a trunk. They seemed to be struggling to get it open, banging feverishly on its surface.

He thought perhaps Twinkle would call for his assistance, but he was not summoned. He looked about the hallway and to the landing below, at the champagne glasses and half-eaten samosas and napkins smeared with lipstick abandoned in every corner, on every available surface. Then he noticed that Twinkle, in her haste, had discarded her shoes altogether, for they lay by the foot of the ladder, black patent-leather mules with heels like golf tees, open toes, and slightly soiled silk labels on the instep where her soles had rested. He placed them in the doorway of the master bedroom so that no one would trip when they descended.

He heard something creaking open slowly. The strident voices had subsided to an even murmur. It occurred to Sanjeev that he had the house all to himself. The music had ended and he could hear, if he concentrated, the hum of the refrigerator, and the rustle of the last leaves on the trees outside, and the tapping of their branches against the windowpanes. With one flick of his hand he could snap the ladder back on its spring into the ceiling, and they would have no way of getting down unless he were to pull the chain and let them. He thought of all the things he could do, undisturbed. He could sweep Twinkle's menagerie into a garbage bag and get in the car and drive it all to the dump, and tear down the poster of weeping Jesus, and take a hammer to the Virgin Mary while he was at it. Then he would return to the empty house; he could easily

110

clear up the cups and plates in an hour's time, and pour himself a gin and
tonic, and eat a plate of warmed rice and listen to his new Bach CD
while reading the liner notes so as to understand it properly. He nudged
the ladder slightly, but it was sturdily planted against the floor. Budging it
would require some effort.

"My God, I need a cigarette," Twinkle exclaimed from above.

Sanjeev felt knots forming at the back of his neck. He felt dizzy. He
needed to lie down. He walked toward the bedroom, but stopped short when
he saw Twinkle's shoes facing him in the doorway. He thought of her slipping them on her feet. But instead of feeling irritated, as he had ever since
they'd moved into the house together, he felt a pang of anticipation at the
thought of her rushing unsteadily down the winding staircase in them,
scratching the floor a bit in her path. The pang intensified as he thought of
her rushing to the bathroom to brighten her lipstick, and eventually rushing
to get people their coats, and finally rushing to the cherry-wood table when
the last guest had left, to begin opening their housewarming presents. It was
the same pang he used to feel before they were married, when he would
hang up the phone after one of their conversations, or when he would drive
back from the airport, wondering which ascending plane in the sky was hers.

"Sanj, you won't believe this."

She emerged with her back to him, her hands over her head, the tops
of her bare shoulder blades perspiring, supporting something still hidden
from view.

"You got it, Twinkle?" someone asked.

"Yes, you can let go."

Now he saw that her hands were wrapped around it: a solid silver bust
of Christ, the head easily three times the size of his own. It had a patrician
bump on its nose, magnificent curly hair that rested atop a pronounced col-
larbone, and a broad forehead that reflected in miniature the walls and
doors and lampshades around them. Its expression was confident, as if assured of its devotees, the unyielding lips sensuous and full. It was also sporting Nora's feather hat. As Twinkle descended, Sanjeev put his hands around
her waist to balance her, and he relieved her of the bust when she had
reached the ground. It weighed a good thirty pounds. The others began lowering themselves slowly, exhausted from the hunt. Some trickled downstairs
in search of a fresh drink.

She took a breath, raised her eyebrows, crossed her fingers. "Would you
mind terribly if we displayed it on the mantel? Just for tonight? I know you
hate it."

He did hate it. He hated its immensity, and its flawless, polished surface, and its undeniable value. He hated that it was in his house, and that
he owned it. Unlike the other things they'd found, this contained dignity,
solemnity, beauty even. But to his surprise these qualities made him hate

it all the more. Most of all he hated it because he knew that Twinkle loved it.

"I'll keep it in my study from tomorrow," Twinkle added. "I promise."

She would never put it in her study, he knew. For the rest of their days together she would keep it on the center of the mantel, flanked on either side by the rest of the menagerie. Each time they had guests Twinkle would explain how she had found it, and they would admire her as they listened. He gazed at the crushed rose petals in her hair, at the pearl and sapphire choker at her throat, at the sparkly crimson polish on her toes. He decided these were among the things that made Prabal think she was wow. His head ached from gin and his arms ached from the weight of the statue. He said, "I put your shoes in the bedroom."

"Thanks. But my feet are killing me." Twinkle gave his elbow a little   125
squeeze and headed for the living room.

Sanjeev pressed the massive silver face to his ribs, careful not to let the feather hat slip, and followed her.

■ Look at the description of the Christian symbols that appear throughout the house. How do they emerge? How do their intended meanings differ from the meanings given to them by Sanjeev and Twinkle?

■ How do Sanjeev and Twinkle define their own identity in relation to one another, to the cultural community with which they identify, and to the communities in which they live and work?

■ How do details about their work on the house symbolize their developing sense of community?

Shirley Jackson (1919–1965)

Shirley Jackson was born in San Francisco, where she spent her childhood. A tomboy, Jackson preferred playing with her brother to pursuing the ladylike interests of her mother. Her rebellious behavior continued through her teenage years. After moving to New York with her family, Jackson chose writing as a career and became politically active—taboo actions that infuriated her mother. After marrying Stanley Edgar Hyman, Jackson moved to Vermont, where she juggled writing and caring for her growing family. Over the course of her literary career, she published novels, plays, children's books, and humorous sketches, but she is best known for her short story "The Lottery." Shortly after the debut of "The Lottery," Jackson published her first novel, *The Road through the Wall*, another examination of a community's psyche. Fifteen more of her literary works were published before her death.

The Lottery (1948)

The morning of June 27th was clear and sunny, with the fresh warmth of a full-summer day; the flowers were blossoming profusely and the grass was richly green. The people of the village began to gather in the square, between the post office and the bank, around ten o'clock; in some towns there were so many people that the lottery took two days and had to be started on June 26th, but in this village, where there were only about three hundred people, the whole lottery took less than two hours, so it could begin at ten o'clock in the morning and still be through in time to allow the villagers to get home for noon dinner.

The children assembled first, of course. School was recently over for the summer, and the feeling of liberty sat uneasily on most of them; they tended to gather together quietly for a while before they broke into boisterous play, and their talk was still of the classroom and the teacher, of books and reprimands. Bobby Martin had already stuffed his pockets full of stones, and the other boys soon followed his example, selecting the smoothest and roundest stones; Bobby and Harry Jones and Dickie Delacroix—the villagers pronounced this name "Dellacroy"—eventually made a great pile of stones in one corner of the square and guarded it against the raids of the other boys. The girls stood aside, talking among themselves, looking over their shoulders at the boys, and the very small children rolled in the dust or clung to the hands of their older brothers or sisters.

Soon the men began to gather, surveying their own children, speaking of planting and rain, tractors and taxes. They stood together, away from the pile of stones in the corner, and their jokes were quiet and they smiled rather than laughed. The women, wearing faded house dresses and sweaters, came shortly after their menfolk. They greeted one another and exchanged bits of gossip as they went to join their husbands. Soon the women, standing by their husbands, began to call to their children, and the children came reluctantly, having to be called four or five times. Bobby Martin ducked under his mother's grasping hand and ran, laughing, back to the pile of stones. His father spoke up sharply, and Bobby came quickly and took his place between his father and his oldest brother.

The lottery was conducted—as were the square dances, the teenage club, the Halloween program—by Mr. Summers, who had time and energy to devote to civic activities. He was a round-faced, jovial man, and he ran the coal business, and people were sorry for him, because he had no children and his wife was a scold. When he arrived in the square, carrying the black wooden box, there was a murmur of conversation among the villagers, and he waved and called, "Little late today, folks." The postmaster, Mr. Graves, followed him, carrying a three-legged stool, and the stool was put in the center of the square ands Mr. Summers set the black box down on it. The villagers kept their distance, leaving a space between themselves and the stool and when Mr. Summers said, "Some of you fellows want to give me a hand?" there was a hesitation before two men, Mr. Martin and his oldest son, Baxter, came forward to hold the box steady on the stool while Mr. Summers stirred up the papers inside it.

The original paraphernalia for the lottery had been lost long ago, and the black box now resting on the stool had been put into use even before Old Man Warner, the oldest man in town, was born. Mr. Summers spoke frequently to the villagers about making a new box, but no one liked to upset even as much tradition as was represented by the black box. There was a story that the present box had been made with some pieces of the box that had preceded it, the one that had been constructed when the first people settled down to make a village here. Every year, after the lottery, Mr. Summers began talking again about a new box, but every year the subject was allowed to fade off without anything's being done. The black box grew shabbier each year; by now it was no longer completely black but splintered badly along one side to show the original wood color, and in some places faded or stained.

Mr. Martin and his oldest son, Baxter, held the black box securely on the stool until Mr. Summers had stirred the papers thoroughly with his hand. Because so much of the ritual had been forgotten or discarded, Mr. Summers had been successful in having slips of paper substituted for the chips of wood that had been used for generations. Chips of wood, Mr. Summers had argued, had been all very well when the village was tiny, but now that the population was more than three hundred and likely to keep on growing, it was necessary to use something that would fit more easily into the black box. The night before the lottery, Mr. Summers and Mr. Graves made up the slips of paper and put them in the box, and it was then taken to the safe of Mr. Summers's coal company and locked up until Mr. Summers was ready to take it to the square next morning. The rest of the year, the box was put away, sometimes one place, sometimes another; it had spent one year in Mr. Graves's barn and another year underfoot in the post office, and sometimes it was set on a shelf in the Martin grocery and left there.

There was a great deal of fussing to be done before Mr. Summers declared the lottery open. There were the lists to make up—of heads of families, heads of households in each family, members of each household in each family. There was the proper swearing-in of Mr. Summers by the postmaster, as the official of the lottery; at one time, some people remembered, there had been a recital of some sort, performed by the official of the lottery, a perfunctory, tuneless chant that had been rattled off duly each year; some people believed that the official of the lottery used to stand just so when he said or sang it, others believed that he was supposed to walk among the

5

people, but years and years ago this part of the ritual had been allowed to lapse. There had been, also, a ritual salute, which the official of the lottery had had to use in addressing each person who came up to draw from the box, but this also had changed with time, until now it was felt necessary only for the official to speak to each person approaching. Mr. Summers was very good at all this; in his clean white shirt and blue jeans, with one hand resting carelessly on the black box, he seemed very proper and important as he talked interminably to Mr. Graves and the Martins.

Just as Mr. Summers finally left off talking and turned to the assembled villagers, Mrs. Hutchinson came hurriedly along the path to the square, her sweater thrown over her shoulders, and slid into place in the back of the crowd. "Clean forgot what day it was," she said to Mrs. Delacroix, who stood next to her, and they both laughed softly. "Thought my old man was out back stacking wood," Mrs. Hutchinson went on, "and then I looked out the window and the kids were gone, and then I remembered it was the twenty-seventh and came a running." She dried her hands on her apron, and Mrs. Delacroix said, "You're in time, though. They're still talking away up there."

Mrs. Hutchinson craned her neck to see through the crowd and found her husband and children standing near the front. She tapped Mrs. Delacroix on the arm as a farewell and began to make her way through the crowd. The people separated good-humoredly to let her through; two or three people said, in voices just loud enough to be heard across the crowd, "Here comes your Missus, Hutchinson," and "Bill, she made it after all." Mrs. Hutchinson reached her husband, and Mr. Summers, who had been waiting, said cheerfully, "Thought we were going to have to get on without you, Tessie." Mrs. Hutchinson said, grinning, "Wouldn't have me leave m'dishes in the sink, now, would you, Joe?" and soft laughter ran through the crowd as the people stirred back into position after Mrs. Hutchinson's arrival.

"Well, now," Mr. Summers said soberly, "guess we better get started, get this over with, so's we can go back to work. Anybody ain't here?" 10

"Dunbar," several people said. "Dunbar, Dunbar."

Mr. Summers consulted his list. "Clyde Dunbar," he said. "That's right. He's broke his leg, hasn't he? Who's drawing for him?"

"Me, I guess," a woman said, and Mr. Summers turned to look at her. "Wife draws for her husband," Mr. Summers said. "Don't you have a grown boy to do it for you, Janey?" Although Mr. Summers and everyone else in the village knew the answer perfectly well, it was the business of the official of the lottery to ask such questions formally. Mr. Summers waited with an expression of polite interest while Mrs. Dunbar answered.

"Horace's not but sixteen yet," Mrs. Dunbar said regretfully. "Guess I gotta fill in for the old man this year."

"Right," Mr. Summers said. He made a note on the list he was holding.   15
Then he asked, "Watson boy drawing this year?"

A tall boy in the crowd raised his hand. "Here," he said. "I'm drawing
for m'mother and me." He blinked his eyes nervously and ducked his head
as several voices in the crowd said things like "Good fellow, Jack," and
"Glad to see your mother's got a man to do it."

"Well," Mr. Summers said, "guess that's everyone. Old Man Warner
make it?"

"Here," a voice said, and Mr. Summers nodded.

A sudden hush fell on the crowd as Mr. Summers cleared his throat and
looked at the list. "All ready?" he called. "Now, I'll read the names—heads
of families first—and the men come up and take a paper out of the box.
Keep the paper folded in your hand without looking at it until everyone has
had a turn. Everything clear?"

The people had done it so many times that they only half listened to   20
the directions; most of them were quiet, wetting their lips, not looking
around. Then Mr. Summers raised one hand high and said, "Adams." A
man disengaged himself from the crowd and came forward. "Hi, Steve,"
Mr. Summers said, and Mr. Adams said, "Hi, Joe." They grinned at one
another humorlessly and nervously. Then Mr. Adams reached into the
black box and took out a folded paper. He held it firmly by one corner as
he turned and went hastily back to his place in the crowd, where he
stood a little apart from his family, not looking down at his hand.

"Allen," Mr. Summers said. "Anderson…Bentham."

"Seems like there's no time at all between lotteries any more," Mrs. Delacroix said to Mrs. Graves in the back row. "Seems like we got through with
the last one only last week."

"Time sure goes fast," Mrs. Graves said.

"Clark…Delacroix."

"There goes my old man," Mrs. Delacroix said. She held her breath   25
while her husband went forward.

"Dunbar," Mr. Summers said, and Mrs. Dunbar went steadily to the box
while one of the women said, "Go on, Janey," and another said, "There she
goes."

"We're next," Mrs. Graves said. She watched while Mr. Graves came
around from the side of the box, greeted Mr. Summers gravely, and selected
a slip of paper from the box. By now, all through the crowd there were men
holding the small folded papers in their large hands, turning them over and
over nervously. Mrs. Dunbar and her two sons stood together, Mrs. Dunbar
holding the slip of paper.

"Harburt…Hutchinson."

"Get up there, Bill," Mrs. Hutchinson said, and the people near her
laughed.

"Jones." 30

"They do say," Mr. Adams said to Old Man Warner, who stood next to him, "that over in the north village they're talking of giving up the lottery."

Old Man Warner snorted. "Pack of crazy fools," he said. "Listening to the young folks, nothing's good enough for *them*. Next thing you know, they'll be wanting to go back to living in caves, nobody work any more, live *that* way for a while. Used to be a saying about 'Lottery in June, corn be heavy soon.' First thing you know, we'd all be eating stewed chickweed and acorns. There's *always* been a lottery," he added petulantly. "Bad enough to see young Joe Summers up there joking with everybody."

"Some places have already quit lotteries," Mrs. Adams said.

"Nothing but trouble in *that*," Old Man Warner said stoutly. "Pack of young fools."

"Martin." And Bobby Martin watched his father go forward. 35

"Overdyke...Percy."

"I wish they'd hurry," Mrs. Dunbar said to her older son. "I wish they'd hurry."

"They're almost through," her son said.

"You get ready to run tell Dad," Mrs. Dunbar said.

Mr. Summers called his own name and then stepped forward precisely 40 and selected a slip from the box. Then he called, "Warner."

"Seventy-seventh year I been in the lottery," Old Man Warner said as he went through the crowd. "Seventy-seventh time."

"Watson." The tall boy came awkwardly through the crowd. Someone said, "Don't be nervous, Jack," and Mr. Summers said, "Take your time, son."

"Zanini."

After that, there was a long pause, a breathless pause, until Mr. Summers, holding his slip of paper in the air, said, "All right, fellows." For a minute, no one moved, and then all the slips of paper were opened. Suddenly, all the women began to speak at once, saying, "Who is it?" "Who's got it?" "Is it the Dunbars?" "Is it the Watsons?" Then the voices began to say, "It's Hutchinson. It's Bill." "Bill Hutchinson's got it."

"Go tell your father," Mrs. Dunbar said to her older son. 45

People began to look around to see the Hutchinsons. Bill Hutchinson was standing quiet, staring down at the paper in his hand. Suddenly, Tessie Hutchinson shouted to Mr. Summers. "You didn't give him time enough to take any paper he wanted. I saw you. It wasn't fair."

"Be a good sport, Tessie," Mrs. Delacroix called, and Mrs. Graves said, "All of us took the same chance."

"Shut up, Tessie," Bill Hutchinson said.

"Well, everyone," Mr. Summers said, "that was done pretty fast, and now we've got to be hurrying a little more to get done in time." He consulted his next list. "Bill," he said, "you draw for the Hutchinson family. You got any other households in the Hutchinsons?"

"There's Don and Eva," Mrs. Hutchinson yelled. "Make *them* take their   50
chance!"

"Daughters draw with their husband's families, Tessie," Mr. Summers said gently. "You know that as well as anyone else."

"It wasn't *fair*," Tessie said.

"I guess not, Joe," Bill Hutchinson said regretfully. "My daughter draws with her husband's family, that's only fair. And I've got no other family except the kids."

"Then, as far as drawing for families is concerned, it's you," Mr. Summers said in explanation, "and as far as drawing for households is concerned that's you, too. Right?"

"Right," Bill Hutchinson said.   55

"How many kids, Bill?" Mr. Summers asked formally.

"Three," Bill Hutchinson said. "There's Bill, Jr., and Nancy, and little Dave. And Tessie and me."

"All right, then," Mr. Summers said. "Harry, you got their tickets back?"

Mr. Graves nodded and held up the slips of paper. "Put them in the box, then," Mr. Summers directed. "Take Bill's and put it in."

"I think we ought to start over," Mrs. Hutchinson said, as quietly as she   60
could. "I tell you it wasn't *fair*. You didn't give him time enough to choose. *Everybody* saw that."

Mr. Graves had selected the five slips and put them in the box, and he dropped all the papers but those onto the ground, where the breeze caught them and lifted them off.

"Listen, everybody," Mrs. Hutchinson was saying to the people around her.

"Ready, Bill?" Mr. Summers asked, and Bill Hutchinson, with one quick glance around at his wife and children, nodded.

"Remember," Mr. Summers said, "take the slips and keep them folded until each person has taken one. Harry, you help little Dave." Mr. Graves took the hand of the little boy, who came willingly with him up to the box. "Take a paper out of the box, Davy," Mr. Summers said. Davy put his hand into the box and laughed. "Take just *one* paper," Mr. Summers said. "Harry, you hold it for him." Mr. Graves took the child's hand and removed the folded paper from the tight fist and held it while little Dave stood next to him and looked up at him wonderingly.

"Nancy next," Mr. Summers said. Nancy was twelve, and her school   65
friends breathed heavily as she went forward, switching her skirt, and took a slip daintily from the box. "Bill, Jr.," Mr. Summers said, and Billy, his face

red and his feet over-large, nearly knocked the box over as he got a paper out. "Tessie," Mr. Summers said. She hesitated for a minute, looking around defiantly, and then set her lips and went up to the box. She snatched a paper out and held it behind her.

"Bill," Mr. Summers said, and Bill Hutchinson reached into the box and felt around, bringing his hand out at last with the slip of paper in it.

The crowd was quiet. A girl whispered, "I hope it's not Nancy," and the sound of the whisper reached the edges of the crowd.

"It's not the way it used to be," Old Man Warner said clearly. "People ain't the way they used to be."

"All right," Mr. Summers said. "Open the papers. Harry, you open little Dave's."

Mr. Graves opened the slip of paper and there was a general sigh 70 through the crowd as he held it up and everyone could see that it was blank. Nancy and Bill, Jr., opened theirs at the same time, and both beamed and laughed, turning around to the crowd and holding their slips of paper above their heads.

"Tessie," Mr. Summers said. There was a pause, and then Mr. Summers looked at Bill Hutchinson, and Bill unfolded his paper and showed it. It was blank.

"It's Tessie," Mr. Summers said, and his voice was hushed. "Show us her paper, Bill."

Bill Hutchinson went over to his wife and forced the slip of paper out of her hand. It had a black spot on it, the black spot Mr. Summers had made the night before with the heavy pencil in the coal-company office. Bill Hutchinson held it up, and there was a stir in the crowd.

"All right, folks," Mr. Summers said. "Let's finish quickly."

Although the villagers had forgotten the ritual and lost the original 75 black box, they still remembered to use stones. The pile of stones the boys had made earlier was ready; there were stones on the ground with the blowing scraps of paper that had come out of the box. Mrs. Delacroix selected a stone so large she had to pick it up with both hands and turned to Mrs. Dunbar. "Come on," she said. "Hurry up."

Mrs. Dunbar had small stones in both hands, and she said, gasping for breath, "I can't run at all. You'll have to go ahead and I'll catch up with you."

The children had stones already, and someone gave little Davy Hutchinson a few pebbles.

Tessie Hutchinson was in the center of a cleared space by now, and she held her hands out desperately as the villagers moved in on her. "It isn't fair," she said. A stone hit her on the side of the head.

Old Man Warner was saying, "Come on, come on, everyone." Steve Adams was in front of the crowd of villagers, with Mrs. Graves beside him.

"It isn't fair, it isn't right," Mrs. Hutchinson screamed, and then they were upon her.

- What binds this community together?
- Identify specific instances in the story when the narrative describes details of the community ritual that have been forgotten by the village. Are these forgotten elements symbolic? Explain why or why not. How do these symbols that function (or fail to function) within the story help us interpret the story itself symbolically?

POETRY

Matthew Arnold (1822–1888)

Dover Beach (1867)

The sea is calm tonight.
The tide is full, the moon lies fair
Upon the straits;—on the French coast the light
Gleams and is gone; the cliffs of England stand,
Glimmering and vast, out in the tranquil bay.   5
Come to the window, sweet is the night-air!
Only, from the long line of spray
Where the sea meets the moon-blanched land,
Listen! you hear the grating roar
Of pebbles which the waves draw back, and fling,   10
At their return, up the high strand,
Begin, and cease, and then again begin,
With tremulous cadence slow, and bring
The eternal note of sadness in.

Sophocles long ago   15
Heard it on the Aegean, and it brought
Into his mind the turbid ebb and flow
Of human misery; we
Find also in the sound a thought,
Hearing it by this distant northern sea.   20

The Sea of Faith
Was once, too, at the full, and round earth's shore
Lay like the folds of a bright girdle furled.
But now I only hear
Its melancholy, long, withdrawing roar,   25
Retreating, to the breath
Of the night-wind, down the vast edges drear
And naked shingles of the world.

Ah, love, let us be true
To one another! for the world, which seems   30
To lie before us like a land of dreams,
So various, so beautiful, so new,
Hath really neither joy, nor love, nor light,
Nor certitude, nor peace, nor help for pain;
And we are here as on a darkling plain   35
Swept with confused alarms of struggle and flight,
Where ignorant armies clash by night.

■ How can we reconcile the poet's claim that the world "Hath really neither joy,
nor love, nor light" with the earlier suggestion that the waves carry "The
eternal note of sadness"? Why does the poet simultaneously find meaning in
the natural world (reading the world as a symbol) and acknowledge that that
meaning is not really there?

Jimmy Santiago Baca (1952–)

Green Chile (1989)

I prefer red chile over my eggs
and potatoes for breakfast.
Red chile *ristras* decorate my door,
dry on my roof, and hang from eaves.
They lend open-air vegetable stands   5
historical grandeur, and gently swing
with an air of festive welcome.
I can hear them talking in the wind,
haggard, yellowing, crisp, rasping
tongues of old men, licking the breeze.   10

But grandmother loves green chile.
When I visit her,
she holds the green chile pepper
in her wrinkled hands.
Ah, voluptuous, masculine,   15
an air of authority and youth simmers
from its swan-neck stem, tapering to a flowery
collar, fermenting resinous spice.
A well-dressed gentleman at the door
my grandmother takes sensuously in her hand,   20
rubbing its firm glossed sides,
caressing the oily rubbery serpent,
with mouth-watering fulfillment,
fondling its curves with gentle fingers.
Its bearing magnificent and taut   25
as flanks of a tiger in mid-leap,

she thrusts her blade into
and cuts it open, with lust
on her hot mouth, sweating over the stove,
bandanna round her forehead,   30
mysterious passion on her face
and she serves me green chile con carne
between soft warm leaves of corn tortillas,
with beans and rice—her sacrifice
to her little prince.   35
I slurp from my plate
with last bit of tortilla, my mouth burns
and I hiss and drink a tall glass of cold water.

All over New Mexico, sunburned men and women
drive rickety trucks stuffed with gunny-sacks   40
of green chile, from Belen, Veguita, Willard, Estancia,
San Antonio y Socorro, from fields
to roadside stands, you see them roasting green chile
in screen-sided homemade barrels, and for a dollar a bag,
we relive this old, beautiful ritual again and again.   45

■ What form does the green chile take when the poet's grandmother begins to
work with it? How is this form important to the ritual that the poet describes?
How does the ritual extend beyond the poet's family?

e. e. cummings (1894–1962)

[anyone lived in a pretty how town] (1940)

anyone lived in a pretty how town
(with up so floating many bells down)
spring summer autumn winter
he sang his didn't he danced his did.

Women and men (both little and small)   5
cared for anyone not at all
they sowed their isn't they reaped their same
sun moon stars rain

children guessed (but only a few
and down they forgot as up they grew   10
autumn winter spring summer)
that noone loved him more by more

when by now and tree by leaf
she laughed his joy she cried his grief
bird by snow and stir by still   15
anyone's any was all to her

someones married their everyones
laughed their cryings and did their dance
(sleep wake hope and then) they
said their nevers they slept their dream   20

stars rain sun moon
(and only the snow can begin to explain
how children are apt to forget to remember
with up so floating many bells down)

one day anyone died i guess   25
(and noone stooped to kiss his face)
busy folk buried them side by side
little by little and was by was

all by all and deep by deep
and more by more they dream their sleep   30
noone and anyone earth by april
wish by spirit and if by yes.

Women and men (both dong and ding)
summer autumn winter spring
reaped their sowing and went their came   35
sun moon stars rain

■ How does the poet use the pronouns "anyone" and "noone" symbolically? How
  does each word refer simultaneously to an individual and to a collective experience?
■ What are possible meanings of the line "(and noone stooped to kiss his face)"?

Emily Dickinson (1830–1886)

[The Soul selects her own Society—] (ca. 1862)

The Soul selects her own Society—
Then—shuts the Door—
To her divine Majority—
Present no more—

Unmoved—she notes the Chariots—pausing—   5
At her low Gate—
Unmoved—an Emperor be kneeling
Upon her Mat—

I've known her—from an ample nation—
Choose One—   10
Then—close the Valves of her attention—
Like Stone—

■ Explain the significance of the kneeling Emperor and "Valves of her attention"
  closed "Like Stone." How does the poem connect these two images?

Seamus Heaney (1939–)

Valediction (1966)

Lady with the frilled blouse
And simple tartan skirt,
Since you left the house
Its emptiness has hurt
All thought. In your presence   5

Time rode easy, anchored
On a smile; but absence
Rocked love's balance, unmoored
The days. They buck and bound
Across the calendar,   10
Pitched from the quiet sound
Of your flower-tender
Voice. Need breaks on my strand;
You've gone, I am at sea.
Until you resume command,   15
Self is in mutiny.

■ What is the prevailing image in the poem? How is this image particularly apt
for representing the problem that begins the poem? Explain how "mutiny" fits
into this image.

Peter Meinke (1932–)

Sunday at the Apple Market (1977)

Apple-smell everywhere!
Haralson   McIntosh   Fireside   Rome
old ciderpresses weathering in the shed
old ladders tilting at empty branches
boxes and bins of apples by the cartload   5
yellow and green and red
piled crazy in the storehouse barn
miraculous profusion, the crowd
around the testing table laughing rolling
the cool applechunks in their mouths   10
dogs barking at children in the appletrees
couples holding hands, so many people
out in the country carrying bushels
and baskets and bags and boxes of apples
to their cars, the smell of apples   15
making us for one Sunday afternoon free
and happy as people must have been meant to be.

■ How do the images fit together into a coherent scene? How does that setting
convey a particular tone?

■ Look at the various photos of apples on pages 1249 and 1250. Which image (if
any) fits with this poem? Explain your answer.

Sharon Olds (1942–)

The Possessive (1980)

My daughter—as if I
owned her—that girl with the
hair wispy as a frayed bellpull
has been to the barber, that knife grinder,
and had the edge of her hair sharpened.   5
Each strand now cuts
both ways. The blade of new bangs
hangs over her red-brown eyes
like carbon steel.
All the little   10
spliced ropes are sliced. The curtain of
dark paper-cuts veils the face that
started from next to nothing in my body—
My body. My daughter. I'll have to find
another word. In her bright helmet   15
she looks at me as if across a
great distance. Distant fires can be
glimpsed in the resin lights of her eyes:
the watch fires of an enemy, a while before
the war starts.   20

■ Why does the poet say, "I'll have to find / another word"?
■ Trace the progression of images describing the daughter's hair that lead finally
  to "the watch fires of an enemy." Why does the poet invoke images of
  impending war?

Alice Walker (1944–)

Women (1981)

They were women then
My mama's generation
Husky of voice—Stout of
Step
With fists as well as   5
Hands
How they battered down
Doors
And ironed

Starched white   10
Shirts
How they led
Armies
Head dragged Generals
Across mined   15
Fields
Booby-trapped
Ditches
To discover books
Desks   20
A place for us
How they knew what we
Must know
Without knowing a page
Of it   25
Themselves.

■ What does the poet suggest when she asserts that these women had "fists as
   well as / Hands"?
■ How does the war imagery in this poem lead to a different conclusion from that
   of "The Possessive"?

Walt Whitman (1819–1892)

There Was a Child Went Forth (1855)

There was a child went forth every day,
And the first object he looked upon, that object he became,
And that object became part of him for the day or a certain part of the day,
Or for many years or stretching cycles of years.

The early lilacs became part of this child,   5
And grass and white and red morning-glories, and white and red clover,
   and the song of the phoebe-bird,
And the Third-month lambs and the sow's pink-faint litter, and the mare's
   foal and the cow's calf,
And the noisy brood of the barnyard or by the mire of the pond-side,
And the fish suspending themselves so curiously below there, and the beau-
   tiful curious liquid,
And the water-plants with their graceful flat heads, all became part of him.   10

The field-sprouts of Fourth-month and Fifth-month became part of him,
Winter-grain sprouts and those of the light-yellow corn, and the esculent
    roots of the garden,
And the apple-trees covered with blossoms and the fruit afterward, and
    wood-berries, and the commonest weeds by the road,
And the old drunkard staggering home from the outside of the tavern
    whence he had lately risen,
And the schoolmistress that passed on her way to the school,   15
And the friendly boys that passed, and the quarrelsome boys,
And the tidy and fresh-cheeked girls, and the barefoot negro boy and girl,
And all the changes of city and country wherever he went.

His own parents, he that had fathered him and she that had conceived him
    in her womb and birthed him,
They gave this child more of themselves than that,   20

They gave him afterward every day, they became part of him.
The mother at home quietly placing the dishes on the supper-table,
The mother with mild words, clean her cap and gown, a wholesome odor
    falling off her person and clothes as she walks by,
The father, strong, self-sufficient, manly, mean, angered, unjust,
The blow, the quick word, the tight bargain, the crafty lure,   25
The family usages, the language, the company, the furniture, the yearning
    and swelling heart,
Affection that will not be gainsayed, the sense of what is real, the thought if
    after all it should prove unreal,
The doubts of day-time and the doubts of night-time, the curious whether
    and how,
Whether that which appears so is so, or is it all flashes and specks?
Men and women crowding fast in the streets, if they are not flashes and   30
    specks what are they?
The streets themselves and the facades of houses, and goods in the windows,
Vehicles, teams, the heavy-planked wharves, the huge crossing at the ferries,
The village on the highland seen from afar at sunset, the river between,
Shadows, aureola and mist, the light falling on roofs and gables of white or
    brown two miles off,
The schooner near by sleepily dropping down the tide, the little boat slack-   35
    towed astern,
The hurrying tumbling waves, quick-broken crests, slapping,
The strata of colored clouds, the long bar of maroon-tint away solitary by it-
    self, the spread of purity it lies motionless in,
The horizon's edge, the flying sea-crow, the fragrance of salt marsh and
    shore mud,

These became part of that child who went forth every day, and who now
goes, and will always go forth every day.

- How does the poet indicate how an object "became part of him for the day"?
- What image of community emerges from the variety of objects that the child
  encounters in this poem?

William Carlos Williams (1883–1963)

At the Ball Game (1923)

The crowd at the ball game
is moved uniformly

by a spirit of uselessness
which delights them—

all the exciting detail   5
of the chase

and the escape, the error
the flash of genius—

all to no end save beauty
the eternal—   10

So in detail they, the crowd,
are beautiful

for this
to be warned against

saluted and defied—   15
It is alive, venomous

it smiles grimly
its words cut—

The flashy female with her
mother, gets it—   20

The Jew gets it straight—it
is deadly, terrifying—

It is the Inquisition, the
Revolution

It is beauty itself   25
that lives

day by day in them
idly—

This is
the power of their faces   30

It is summer, it is the solstice
the crowd is

cheering, the crowd is laughing
in detail

permanently, seriously   35
without thought

- How can the crowd be "the Inquisition" or "the / Revolution"? What is it that "The flashy female" and "The Jew" get? What is the significance of the final line?
- Compare the tone of this poem to that of Whitman's poem.

William Butler Yeats (1865–1939)

The Wild Swans at Coole (1919)

The trees are in their autumn beauty,
The woodland paths are dry,
Under the October twilight the water
Mirrors a still sky;
Upon the brimming water among the stones   5
Are nine and fifty swans.

The nineteenth Autumn has come upon me
Since I first made my count;

I saw, before I had well finished,
All suddenly mount   10
And scatter wheeling in great broken rings
Upon their clamorous wings.

I have looked upon those brilliant creatures,
And now my heart is sore.
All's changed since I, hearing at twilight,   15
The first time on this shore,
The bell-beat of their wings above my head,
Trod with a lighter tread.

Unwearied still, lover by lover,
They paddle in the cold,   20
Companionable streams or climb the air;
Their hearts have not grown old;
Passion or conquest, wander where they will,
Attend upon them still.

But now they drift on the still water   25
Mysterious, beautiful;
Among what rushes will they build,
By what lake's edge or pool
Delight men's eyes, when I awake some day
To find they have flown away?   30

- How do the swans make the poet's heart sore?
- What is symbolized by their flying away?
- What is the relation between the swans and the human community?

Elizabeth Bishop (1911–1979)

Pink Dog (1979)

[Rio de Janeiro]

The sun is blazing and the sky is blue.
Umbrellas clothe the beach in every hue.
Naked, you trot across the avenue.

Oh, never have I seen a dog so bare!
Naked and pink, without a single hair... 5
Startled, the passersby draw back and stare.

Of course they're mortally afraid of rabies.
You are not mad; you have a case of scabies
but look intelligent. Where are your babies?

(A nursing mother, by those hanging teats.) 10
In what slum have you hidden them, poor bitch,
while you go begging, living by your wits?

Didn't you know? It's been in all the papers,
to solve this problem, how they deal with beggars?
They take and throw them in the tidal rivers. 15

Yes, idiots, paralytics, parasites
go bobbing in the ebbing sewage, nights
out in the suburbs, where there are no lights.

If they do this to anyone who begs,
drugged, drunk, or sober, with or without legs, 20
what would they do to sick, four-legged dogs?

In the cafés and on the sidewalk corners
the joke is going round that all the beggars
who can afford them now wear life preservers.

In your condition you would not be able 25
even to float, much less to dog-paddle.
Now look, the practical, the sensible

solution is to wear a fantasía.
Tonight you simply can't afford to be a-
n eyesore...But no one will ever see a 30

dog in máscara this time of year.
Ash Wednesday'll come but Carnival is here.
What sambas can you dance? What will you wear?

They say that Carnival's degenerating
— radios, Americans, or something, 35
have ruined it completely. They're just talking.

Carnival is always wonderful!
A depilated dog would not look well.
Dress up! Dress up and dance at Carnival!

■ What is the relation between this "pink dog" and the beggars of Rio de
Janeiro?
■ How does the idea of dressing up relate to the social problems (and the
solutions) addressed in the poem?

Emma Lazarus (1849–1887)

The New Colossus (1883)

Not like the brazen giant of Greek fame
With conquering limbs astride from land to land;
Here at our sea-washed, sunset gates shall stand
A mighty woman with a torch, whose flame
Is the imprisoned lightning, and her name   5
Mother of Exiles. From her beacon-hand
Glows world-wide welcome; her mild eyes command
The air-bridged harbor that twin cities frame,
"Keep, ancient lands, your storied pomp!" cries she
With silent lips. "Give me your tired, your poor,   10
Your huddled masses yearning to breathe free,
The wretched refuse of your teeming shore,
Send these, the homeless, tempest-tossed to me,
I lift my lamp beside the golden door!"

■ This is the poem that is inscribed on the base of the Statue of Liberty. How
does the poem give meaning to the statue? To what extent is this poem
important to the symbol of the statue as you are familiar with it?

DRAMA

Arthur Miller (1915–2005)

Arthur Miller was born in New York City. He is widely recognized as one of the
preeminent twentieth-century American playwrights. Miller began playwriting

while at the University of Michigan and had early critical success—winning the university's prestigious Avery Hopwood Award for his plays in both 1936 and 1937. He received his AB in 1938. Some of Miller's best-known plays include *All My Sons* (1947), *Death of a Salesman* (1949), and *The Crucible* (1953). In 1999, *Death of a Salesman* received a Tony Award for Best Revival.

Death of a Salesman: Certain Private Conversations in Two Acts and a Requiem

(1949)

CHARACTERS

WILLY LOMAN

THE WOMAN

LINDA, *his wife*

HOWARD WAGNER

BIFF
HAPPY } *his sons*

JENNY

STANLEY

UNCLE BEN

MISS FORSYTHE

CHARLEY

LETTA

BERNARD

TIME AND SCENE: *The action takes place in* WILLY LOMAN'*s house and yard and in various places he visits in the New York and Boston of today.*

Throughout the play, in the stage directions, left and right mean stage left and stage right.

ACT I

A melody is heard, played upon a flute. It is small and fine, telling of grass and trees and the horizon. The curtain rises.

Before us is the SALESMAN'*s house. We are aware of towering, angular shapes behind it, surrounding it on all sides. Only the blue light of the sky falls upon the house and forestage; the surrounding area shows an angry glow of orange. As more light appears, we see a solid vault of apartment houses around the small, fragile-seeming home. An air of the dream clings to the place, a dream rising out of reality. The kitchen at center seems actual enough, for there is a kitchen table with three chairs, and a refrigerator. But no other fixtures are seen. At the back of the kitchen there is a draped entrance, which leads to the living room. To the right of the kitchen, on a level raised two feet, is a bedroom* furnished only with a brass bedstead and a straight chair. On a shelf over the bed a silver athletic trophy stands. A window opens onto the apartment house at the side.

Behind the kitchen, on a level raised six and a half feet, is the boys' bedroom, at present barely visible. Two beds are dimly seen, and at the back of the room a dormer window. (This bedroom is above the unseen living room.) At the left a stairway curves up to it from the kitchen.

The entire setting is wholly or, in some places, partially transparent. The roofline of the house is one-dimensional; under and over it we see the apartment buildings. Before the house lies an apron, curving beyond the forestage into the orchestra. This forward area serves as the back yard as well as the locale of all WILLY's imaginings and of his city scenes. Whenever the action is in the present the actors observe the imaginary wall-lines, entering the house only through the door at the left. But in the scenes of the past these boundaries are broken, and characters enter or leave a room by stepping "through" a wall onto the forestage.

From the right, WILLY LOMAN, the SALESMAN, enters, carrying two large sample cases. The flute plays on. He hears but is not aware of it. He is past sixty years of age, dressed quietly. Even as he crosses the stage to the doorway of the house, his exhaustion is apparent. He unlocks the door, comes into the kitchen, and thankfully lets his burden down, feeling the soreness of his palms. A word-sigh escapes his lips — it might be "Oh, boy, oh, boy." He closes the door, then carries his cases out into the living room, through the draped kitchen doorway.

LINDA, his wife, has stirred in her bed at the right. She gets out and puts on a robe, listening. Most often jovial, she has developed an iron repression of her exceptions to WILLY's behavior — she more than loves him, she admires him, as though his mercurial nature, his temper, his massive dreams and little cruelties, served her only as sharp reminders of the turbulent longings within him, longings which she shares but lacks the temperament to utter and follow to their end.

LINDA (hearing WILLY outside the bedroom, calls with some trepidation.): Willy!

WILLY: It's all right. I came back.

LINDA: Why? What happened? (Slight pause.) Did something happen, Willy?

WILLY: No, nothing happened.

LINDA: You didn't smash the car, did you?   5

WILLY (with casual irritation.): I said nothing happened. Didn't you hear me?

LINDA: Don't you feel well?

WILLY: I am tired to the death. (The flute has faded away. He sits on the bed beside her, a little numb.) I couldn't make it. I just couldn't make it, Linda.

LINDA (very carefully, delicately.): Where were you all day? You look terrible.

WILLY: I got as far as a little above Yonkers. I stopped for a cup of coffee.   10
Maybe it was the coffee.

LINDA: What?

WILLY *(after a pause.)*: I suddenly couldn't drive any more. The car kept going onto the shoulder, y'know?

LINDA *(helpfully.)*: Oh. Maybe it was the steering again. I don't think Angelo knows the Studebaker.

WILLY: No, it's me, it's me. Suddenly I realize I'm goin' sixty miles an hour and I don't remember the last five minutes. I'm—I can't seem to—keep my mind to it.

LINDA: Maybe it's your glasses. You never went for your new glasses.   15

WILLY: No, I see everything. I came back ten miles an hour. It took me nearly four hours from Yonkers.

LINDA *(resigned.)*: Well, you'll just have to take a rest, Willy, you can't continue this way.

WILLY: I just got back from Florida.

LINDA: But you didn't rest your mind. Your mind is overactive, and the mind is what counts, dear.

WILLY: I'll start out in the morning. Maybe I'll feel better in the morning.   20
(She is taking off his shoes.) These goddam arch supports are killing me.

LINDA: Take an aspirin. Should I get you an aspirin? It'll soothe you.

WILLY *(with wonder.)*: I was driving along, you understand? And I was fine. I was even observing the scenery. You can imagine, me looking at scenery, on the road every week of my life. But it's so beautiful up there, Linda, the trees are so thick, and the sun is warm. I opened the windshield and just let the warm air bathe over me. And then all of a sudden I'm goin' off the road! I'm tellin' ya, I absolutely forgot I was driving. If I'd've gone the other way over the white line I might've killed somebody. So I went on again—and five minutes later I'm dreamin' again, and I nearly—*(He presses two fingers against his eyes.)* I have such thoughts, I have such strange thoughts.

LINDA: Willy, dear. Talk to them again. There's no reason why you can't work in New York.

WILLY: They don't need me in New York. I'm the New England man. I'm vital in New England.

LINDA: But you're sixty years old. They can't expect you to keep traveling   25
every week.

WILLY: I'll have to send a wire to Portland. I'm supposed to see Brown and Morrison tomorrow morning at ten o'clock to show the line. Goddammit, I could sell them! *(He starts putting on his jacket.)*

LINDA *(taking the jacket from him.)*: Why don't you go down to the place tomorrow and tell Howard you've simply got to work in New York? You're too accommodating, dear.

WILLY: If old man Wagner was alive I'd a been in charge of New York now! That man was a prince, he was a masterful man. But that boy of his,

that Howard, he don't appreciate. When I went north the first time,
the Wagner Company didn't know where New England was!

LINDA: Why don't you tell those things to Howard, dear?

WILLY (*encouraged.*): I will, I definitely will. Is there any cheese? 30

LINDA: I'll make you a sandwich.

WILLY: No, go to sleep. I'll take some milk. I'll be up right away. The boys
in?

LINDA: They're sleeping. Happy took Biff on a date tonight.

WILLY (*interested.*): That so?

LINDA: It was so nice to see them shaving together, one behind the other, 35
in the bathroom. And going out together. You notice? The whole
house smells of shaving lotion.

WILLY: Figure it out. Work a lifetime to pay off a house. You finally own it,
and there's nobody to live in it.

LINDA: Well, dear, life is a casting off. It's always that way.

WILLY: No, no, some people—some people accomplish something. Did Biff
say anything after I went this morning?

LINDA: You shouldn't have criticized him, Willy, especially after he just got
off the train. You mustn't lose your temper with him.

WILLY: When the hell did I lose my temper? I simply asked him if he was 40
making any money. Is that a criticism?

LINDA: But, dear, how could he make any money?

WILLY (*worried and angered.*): There's such an undercurrent in him. He
became a moody man. Did he apologize when I left this morning?

LINDA: He was crestfallen, Willy. You know how he admires you. I think if
he finds himself, then you'll both be happier and not fight any more.

WILLY: How can he find himself on a farm? Is that a life? A farmhand? In
the beginning, when he was young, I thought, well, a young man, it's
good for him to tramp around, take a lot of different jobs. But it's more
than ten years now and he has yet to make thirty-five dollars a week!

LINDA: He's finding himself, Willy. 45

WILLY: Not finding yourself at the age of thirty-four is a disgrace!

LINDA: Shh!

WILLY: The trouble is he's lazy, goddammit!

LINDA: Willy, please!

WILLY: Biff is a lazy bum! 50

LINDA: They're sleeping. Get something to eat. Go on down.

WILLY: Why did he come home? I would like to know what brought him
home.

LINDA: I don't know. I think he's still lost, Willy. I think he's very lost.

WILLY: Biff Loman is lost. In the greatest country in the world a young man
with such—personal attractiveness, gets lost. And such a hard worker.
There's one thing about Biff—he's not lazy.

LINDA: Never.   55

WILLY (*with pity and resolve.*): I'll see him in the morning; I'll have a nice talk with him. I'll get him a job selling. He could be big in no time. My God! Remember how they used to follow him around in high school? When he smiled at one of them their faces lit up. When he walked down the street…(*He loses himself in reminiscences.*)

LINDA (*trying to bring him out of it.*): Willy, dear, I got a new kind of American-type cheese today. It's whipped.

WILLY: Why do you get American when I like Swiss?

LINDA: I just thought you'd like a change—

WILLY: I don't want a change! I want Swiss cheese. Why am I always being   60
contradicted?

LINDA (*with a covering laugh.*): I thought it would be a surprise.

WILLY: Why don't you open a window in here, for God's sake?

LINDA (*with infinite patience.*): They're all open, dear.

WILLY: The way they boxed us in here. Bricks and windows, windows and bricks.

LINDA: We should've bought the land next door.   65

WILLY: The street is lined with cars. There's not a breath of fresh air in the neighborhood. The grass don't grow any more, you can't raise a carrot in the back yard. They should've had a law against apartment houses. Remember those two beautiful elm trees out there? When I and Biff hung the swing between them?

LINDA: Yeah, like being a million miles from the city.

WILLY: They should've arrested the builder for cutting those down. They massacred the neighborhood. (*Lost.*) More and more I think of those days, Linda. This time of year it was lilac and wisteria. And then the peonies would come out, and the daffodils. What fragrance in this room!

LINDA: Well, after all, people had to move somewhere.

WILLY: No, there's more people now.   70

LINDA: I don't think there's more people. I think—

WILLY: There's more people! That's what's ruining this country! Population is getting out of control. The competition is maddening! Smell the stink from that apartment house! And another on the other side… How can they whip cheese?

(*On* WILLY's *last line,* BIFF *and* HAPPY *raise themselves up in their beds, listening.*)

LINDA: Go down, try it. And be quiet.

WILLY (*turning to* LINDA, *guiltily.*): You're not worried about me, are you, sweetheart?

BIFF: What's the matter?   75

HAPPY: Listen!

LINDA: You've got too much on the ball to worry about.

WILLY: You're my foundation and my support, Linda.

LINDA: Just try to relax, dear. You make mountains out of molehills.

WILLY: I won't fight with him any more. If he wants to go back to Texas, let 80
him go.

LINDA: He'll find his way.

WILLY: Sure. Certain men just don't get started till later in life. Like
Thomas Edison, I think. Or B. F. Goodrich. One of them was deaf.
(He starts for the bedroom doorway.) I'll put my money on Biff.

LINDA: And Willy—if it's warm Sunday we'll drive in the country. And
we'll open the windshield, and take lunch.

WILLY: No, the windshields don't open on the new cars.

LINDA: But you opened it today. 85

WILLY: Me? I didn't. *(He stops.)* Now isn't that peculiar! Isn't that remarkable—

(He breaks off in amazement and fright as the flute is heard distantly.)

LINDA: What, darling?

WILLY: That is the most remarkable thing.

LINDA: What, dear?

WILLY: I was thinking of the Chevvy. *(Slight pause.)* Nineteen twenty-eight 90
...when I had that red Chevvy—*(Breaks off.)* That funny? I coulda
sworn I was driving that Chevvy today.

LINDA: Well, that's nothing. Something must've reminded you.

WILLY: Remarkable. Ts. Remember those days? The way Biff used to simon-
ize that car? The dealer refused to believe there was eighty thousand
miles on it. *(He shakes his head.)* Heh! *(To* LINDA.*)* Close your eyes, I'll
be right up. *(He walks out of the bedroom.)*

HAPPY *(to* BIFF.*)*: Jesus, maybe he smashed up the car again!

LINDA *(calling after* WILLY.*)*: Be careful on the stairs, dear! The cheese is on
the middle shelf! *(She turns, goes over to the bed, takes his jacket, and goes
out of the bedroom.)*

(Light has risen on the boys' room. Unseen, WILLY *is heard talking to himself,
"Eighty thousand miles," and a little laugh.* BIFF *gets out of bed, comes
downstage a bit, and stands attentively.* BIFF *is two years older than his
brother* HAPPY, *well built, but in these days bears a worn air and seems less
self-assured. He has succeeded less, and his dreams are stronger and less acceptable than* HAPPY'S. HAPPY *is tall, powerfully made. Sexuality is like a
visible color on him, or a scent that many women have discovered. He, like
his brother, is lost, but in a different way, for he has never allowed himself
to turn his face toward defeat and is thus more confused and hard-skinned,
although seemingly more content.)*

HAPPY *(getting out of bed.)*: He's going to get his license taken away if he 95
keeps that up. I'm getting nervous about him, y'know, Biff?

BIFF: His eyes are going.

HAPPY: No, I've driven with him. He sees all right. He just doesn't keep his mind on it. I drove into the city with him last week. He stops at a green light and then it turns red and he goes. *(He laughs.)*:

BIFF: Maybe he's color-blind.

HAPPY: Pop? Why he's got the finest eye for color in the business. You know that.

BIFF *(sitting down on his bed.)*: I'm going to sleep.   100

HAPPY: You're not still sour on Dad, are you, Biff?

BIFF: He's all right, I guess.

WILLY *(underneath them, in the living room.)*: Yes, sir, eighty thousand miles— eighty-two thousand!

BIFF: You smoking?

HAPPY *(holding out a pack of cigarettes.)*: Want one?   105

BIFF *(taking a cigarette.)*: I can never sleep when I smell it.

WILLY: What a simonizing job, heh!

HAPPY *(with deep sentiment.)*: Funny, Biff, y'know? Us sleeping in here again? The old beds. *(He pats his bed affectionately.)* All the talk that went across those two beds, huh? Our whole lives.

BIFF: Yeah. Lotta dreams and plans.

HAPPY *(with a deep and masculine laugh.)*: About five hundred women would   110 like to know what was said in this room.

(They share a soft laugh.)

BIFF: Remember that big Betsy something—what the hell was her name— over on Bushwick Avenue?

HAPPY *(combing his hair.)*: With the collie dog!

BIFF: That's the one. I got you in there, remember?

HAPPY: Yeah, that was my first time—I think. Boy, there was a pig! *(They laugh, almost crudely.)* You taught me everything I know about women. Don't forget that.

BIFF: I bet you forgot how bashful you used to be. Especially with girls.   115

HAPPY: Oh, I still am, Biff.

BIFF: Oh, go on.

HAPPY: I just control it, that's all. I think I got less bashful and you got more so. What happened, Biff? Where's the old humor, the old confidence? *(He shakes BIFF's knee. BIFF gets up and moves restlessly about the room.)* What's the matter?

BIFF: Why does Dad mock me all the time?

HAPPY: He's not mocking you, he—   120

BIFF: Everything I say there's a twist of mockery on his face. I can't get near him.

HAPPY: He just wants you to make good, that's all. I wanted to talk to you about Dad for a long time, Biff. Something's—happening to him. He—talks to himself.

BIFF: I noticed that this morning. But he always mumbled.

HAPPY: But not so noticeable. It got so embarrassing I sent him to Florida. And you know something? Most of the time he's talking to you.

BIFF: What's he say about me? 125

HAPPY: I can't make it out.

BIFF: What's he say about me?

HAPPY: I think the fact that you're not settled, that you're still kind of up in the air...

BIFF: There's one or two other things depressing him, Happy.

HAPPY: What do you mean? 130

BIFF: Never mind. Just don't lay it all to me.

HAPPY: But I think if you just got started—I mean—is there any future for you out there?

BIFF: I tell ya, Hap, I don't know what the future is. I don't know—what I'm supposed to want.

HAPPY: What do you mean?

BIFF: Well, I spent six or seven years after high school trying to work myself 135 up. Shipping clerk, salesman, business of one kind or another. And it's a measly manner of existence. To get on that subway on the hot mornings in summer. To devote your whole life to keeping stock, or making phone calls, or selling or buying. To suffer fifty weeks of the year for the sake of a two-week vacation, when all you really desire is to be outdoors, with your shirt off. And always to have to get ahead of the next fella. And still—that's how you build a future.

HAPPY: Well, you really enjoy it on a farm? Are you content out there?

BIFF (*with rising agitation.*): Hap, I've had twenty or thirty different kinds of jobs since I left home before the war, and it always turns out the same. I just realized it lately. In Nebraska when I herded cattle, and the Dakotas, and Arizona, and now in Texas. It's why I came home now, I guess, because I realized it. This farm I work on, it's spring there now, see? And they've got about fifteen new colts. There's nothing more inspiring or—beautiful than the sight of a mare and a new colt. And it's cool there now, see? Texas is cool now, and it's spring. And whenever spring comes to where I am, I suddenly get the feeling, my God, I'm not gettin' anywhere! What the hell am I doing, playing around with horses, twenty-eight dollars a week! I'm thirty-four years old, I oughta be makin' my future. That's when I come running home. And now, I get here, and I don't know what to do with myself. (*After a pause.*) I've always made a point of not wasting my life, and every time I come back here I know that all I've done is to waste my life.

HAPPY: You're a poet, you know that, Biff? You're a—you're an idealist!

BIFF: No, I'm mixed up very bad. Maybe I oughta get married. Maybe I oughta get stuck into something. Maybe that's my trouble. I'm like a

boy. I'm not married, I'm not in business, I just—I'm like a boy. Are
you content, Hap? You're a success, aren't you? Are you content?

HAPPY: Hell, no! 140

BIFF: Why? You're making money, aren't you?

HAPPY (*moving about with energy, expressiveness.*): All I can do now is wait
for the merchandise manager to die. And suppose I get to be merchandise manager? He's a good friend of mine, and he just built a terrific estate on Long Island. And he lived there about two months and sold it,
and now he's building another one. He can't enjoy it once it's finished.
And I know that's just what I would do. I don't know what the hell I'm
workin' for. Sometimes I sit in my apartment—all alone. And I think
of the rent I'm paying. And it's crazy. But then, it's what I always
wanted. My own apartment, a car, and plenty of women. And still, goddammit, I'm lonely.

BIFF (*with enthusiasm.*): Listen, why don't you come out West with me?

HAPPY: You and I, heh?

BIFF: Sure, maybe we could buy a ranch. Raise cattle, use our muscles. Men 145
built like we are should be working out in the open.

HAPPY (*avidly.*): The Loman Brothers, heh?

BIFF (*with vast affection.*): Sure, we'd be known all over the counties!

HAPPY (*enthralled.*): That's what I dream about, Biff. Sometimes I want to
just rip my clothes off in the middle of the store and outbox that goddam merchandise manager. I mean I can outbox, outrun, and outlift
anybody in that store, and I have to take orders from those common,
petty sons-of-bitches till I can't stand it any more.

BIFF: I'm tellin' you, kid, if you were with me I'd be happy out there.

HAPPY (*enthused.*): See, Biff, everybody around me is so false that I'm con- 150
stantly lowering my ideals…

BIFF: Baby, together we'd stand up for one another, we'd have someone to
trust.

HAPPY: If I were around you—

BIFF: Hap, the trouble is we weren't brought up to grub for money. I don't
know how to do it.

HAPPY: Neither can I!

BIFF: Then let's go! 155

HAPPY: The only thing is—what can you make out there?

BIFF: But look at your friend. Builds an estate and then hasn't the peace of
mind to live in it.

HAPPY: Yeah, but when he walks into the store the waves part in front of
him. That's fifty-two thousand dollars a year coming through the
revolving door, and I got more in my pinky finger than he's got in his
head.

BIFF: Yeah, but you just said—

HAPPY: I gotta show some of those pompous, self-important executives over   160
there that Hap Loman can make the grade. I want to walk into the
store the way he walks in. Then I'll go with you, Biff. We'll be together
yet, I swear. But take those two we had tonight. Now weren't they gorgeous creatures?

BIFF: Yeah, yeah, most gorgeous I've had in years.

HAPPY: I get that any time I want, Biff. Whenever I feel disgusted. The only
trouble is, it gets like bowling or something. I just keep knockin' them
over and it doesn't mean anything. You still run around a lot?

BIFF: Naa. I'd like to find a girl—steady, somebody with substance.

HAPPY: That's what I long for.

BIFF: Go on! You'd never come home.   165

HAPPY: I would! Somebody with character, with resistance! Like Mom,
y'know? You're gonna call me a bastard when I tell you this. That girl
Charlotte I was with tonight is engaged to be married in five weeks.

(He tries on his new hat.)

BIFF: No kiddin'!

HAPPY: Sure, the guy's in line for the vice-presidency of the store. I don't
know what gets into me, maybe I just have an overdeveloped sense of
competition or something, but I went and ruined her, and furthermore I
can't get rid of her. And he's the third executive I've done that to. Isn't
that a crummy characteristic? And to top it all, I go to their weddings!
(Indignantly, but laughing.) Like I'm not supposed to take bribes. Manu-
facturers offer me a hundred-dollar bill now and then to throw an order
their way. You know how honest I am, but it's like this girl, see. I hate
myself for it. Because I don't want the girl, and, still, I take it and—I
love it!

BIFF: Let's go to sleep.

HAPPY: I guess we didn't settle anything, heh?   170

BIFF: I just got one idea that I think I'm going to try.

HAPPY: What's that?

BIFF: Remember Bill Oliver?

HAPPY: Sure, Oliver is very big now. You want to work for him again?

BIFF: No, but when I quit he said something to me. He put his arm on   175
my shoulder, and he said, "Biff, if you ever need anything, come
to me."

HAPPY: I remember that. That sounds good.

BIFF: I think I'll go to see him. If I could get ten thousand or even seven or
eight thousand dollars I could buy a beautiful ranch.

HAPPY: I bet he'd back you. 'Cause he thought highly of you, Biff, I mean,
they all do. You're well liked, Biff. That's why I say to come back here,
and we both have the apartment. And I'm tellin' you, Biff, any babe
you want…

BIFF: No, with a ranch I could do the work I like and still be something. I just wonder though. I wonder if Oliver still thinks I stole that carton of basketballs.

HAPPY: Oh, he probably forgot that long ago. It's almost ten years. You're too sensitive. Anyway, he didn't really fire you.   180

BIFF: Well, I think he was going to. I think that's why I quit. I was never sure whether he knew or not. I know he thought the world of me, though. I was the only one he'd let lock up the place.

WILLY (*below.*): You gonna wash the engine, Biff?

HAPPY: Shh!

(BIFF *looks at* HAPPY, *who is gazing down, listening.* WILLY *is mumbling in the parlor.*)

HAPPY: You hear that?

(*They listen.* WILLY *laughs warmly.*)

BIFF (*growing angry.*): Doesn't he know Mom can hear that?   185

WILLY: Don't get your sweater dirty, Biff!

(*A look of pain crosses* BIFF's *face.*)

HAPPY: Isn't that terrible? Don't leave again, will you? You'll find a job here. You gotta stick around. I don't know what to do about him, it's getting embarrassing.

WILLY: What a simonizing job!

BIFF: Mom's hearing that!

WILLY: No kiddin', Biff, you got a date? Wonderful!   190

HAPPY: Go on to sleep. But talk to him in the morning, will you?

BIFF (*reluctantly getting into bed.*): With her in the house. Brother!

HAPPY (*getting into bed.*): I wish you'd have a good talk with him.

(*The light on their room begins to fade.*)

BIFF (*to himself in bed.*): That selfish, stupid…

HAPPY: Sh…Sleep, Biff.   195

(*Their light is out. Well before they have finished speaking,* WILLY's *form is dimly seen below in the darkened kitchen. He opens the refrigerator, searches in there, and takes out a bottle of milk. The apartment houses are fading out, and the entire house and surroundings become covered with leaves. Music insinuates itself as the leaves appear.*)

WILLY: Just wanna be careful with those girls, Biff, that's all. Don't make any promises. No promises of any kind. Because a girl, y'know, they always believe what you tell 'em, and you're very young, Biff, you're too young to be talking seriously to girls.

(*Light rises on the kitchen.* WILLY, *talking, shuts the refrigerator door and comes downstage to the kitchen table. He pours milk into a glass. He is totally immersed in himself, smiling faintly.*)

WILLY: Too young entirely, Biff. You want to watch your schooling first. Then when you're all set, there'll be plenty of girls for a boy like you.

(He smiles broadly at a kitchen chair.) That so? The girls pay for you? *(He laughs.)* Boy, you must really be makin' a hit.

(WILLY is gradually addressing—physically—a point offstage, speaking through the wall of the kitchen, and his voice has been rising in volume to that of a normal conversation.)

WILLY: I been wondering why you polish the car so careful. Ha! Don't leave the hubcaps, boys. Get the chamois to the hubcaps. Happy, use newspaper on the windows, it's the easiest thing. Show him how to do it, Biff! You see, Happy? Pad it up, use it like a pad. That's it, that's it, good work. You're doin' all right, Hap. *(He pauses, then nods in approbation for a few seconds, then looks upward.)* Biff, first thing we gotta do when we get time is clip that big branch over the house. Afraid it's gonna fall in a storm and hit the roof. Tell you what. We get a rope and sling her around, and then we climb up there with a couple of saws and take her down. Soon as you finish the car, boys, I wanna see ya. I got a surprise for you, boys.

BIFF *(offstage.)*: Whatta ya got, Dad?

WILLY: No, you finish first. Never leave a job till you're finished—remember that. *(Looking toward the "big trees.")* Biff, up in Albany I saw a beautiful hammock. I think I'll buy it next trip, and we'll hang it right between those two elms. Wouldn't that be something? Just swingin' there under those branches. Boy, that would be... 200

(Young BIFF and Young HAPPY appear from the direction WILLY was addressing. HAPPY carries rags and a pail of water. BIFF, wearing a sweater with a block "S," carries a football.)

BIFF *(pointing in the direction of the car offstage.)*: How's that, Pop, professional?

WILLY: Terrific. Terrific job, boys. Good work, Biff.

HAPPY: Where's the surprise, Pop?

WILLY: In the back seat of the car.

HAPPY: Boy! *(He runs off.)* 205

BIFF: What is it, Dad? Tell me, what'd you buy?

WILLY *(laughing, cuffs him.)*: Never mind, something I want you to have.

BIFF *(turns and starts off.)*: What is it, Hap?

HAPPY *(offstage.)*: It's a punching bag!

BIFF: Oh, Pop! 210

WILLY: It's got Gene Tunney's° signature on it!

(HAPPY runs onstage with a punching bag.)

BIFF: Gee, how'd you know we wanted a punching bag?

°**Gene Tunney's:** James Joseph ("Gene") Tunney (1897–1978)—American boxer, world heavyweight champion from his defeat of Jack Dempsey in 1926 until his retirement in 1928.

WILLY: Well, it's the finest thing for the timing.

HAPPY *(lies down on his back and pedals with his feet.)*: I'm losing weight, you notice, Pop?

WILLY *(to HAPPY.)*: Jumping rope is good too.   215

BIFF: Did you see the new football I got?

WILLY *(examining the ball.)*: Where'd you get a new ball?

BIFF: The coach told me to practice my passing.

WILLY: That so? And he gave you the ball, heh?

BIFF: Well, I borrowed it from the locker room. *(He laughs confidentially.)*   220

WILLY *(laughing with him at the theft.)*: I want you to return that.

HAPPY: I told you he wouldn't like it!

BIFF *(angrily.)*: Well, I'm bringing it back!

WILLY *(stopping the incipient argument, to HAPPY.)*: Sure, he's gotta practice with a regulation ball, doesn't he? *(To BIFF.)* Coach'll probably congratulate you on your initiative!

BIFF: Oh, he keeps congratulating my initiative all the time, Pop.   225

WILLY: That's because he likes you. If somebody else took that ball there'd be an uproar. So what's the report, boys, what's the report?

BIFF: Where'd you go this time, Dad? Gee we were lonesome for you.

WILLY *(pleased, puts an arm around each boy and they come down to the apron.)*: Lonesome, heh?

BIFF: Missed you every minute.

WILLY: Don't say? Tell you a secret, boys. Don't breathe it to a soul. Some-   230
day I'll have my own business, and I'll never have to leave home any more.

HAPPY: Like Uncle Charley, heh?

WILLY: Bigger than Uncle Charley! Because Charley is not—liked. He's liked, but he's not—well liked.

BIFF: Where'd you go this time, Dad?

WILLY: Well, I got on the road, and I went north to Providence. Met the Mayor.

BIFF: The Mayor of Providence!   235

WILLY: He was sitting in the hotel lobby.

BIFF: What'd he say?

WILLY: He said, "Morning!" And I said, "You've got a fine city here, Mayor." And then he had coffee with me. And then I went to Waterbury. Waterbury is a fine city. Big clock city, the famous Waterbury clock. Sold a nice bill there. And then Boston—Boston is the cradle of the Revolution. A fine city. And a couple of other towns in Mass., and on to Portland and Bangor and straight home!

BIFF: Gee, I'd love to go with you sometime, Dad.

WILLY: Soon as summer comes.   240

HAPPY: Promise?

WILLY: You and Hap and I, and I'll show you all the towns. America is full of beautiful towns and fine, upstanding people. And they know me, boys, they know me up and down New England. The finest people. And when I bring you fellas up, there'll be open sesame for all of us, 'cause one thing, boys: I have friends. I can park my car in any street in New England, and the cops protect it like their own. This summer, heh?

BIFF AND HAPPY (*together.*): Yeah! You bet!

WILLY: We'll take our bathing suits.

HAPPY: We'll carry your bags, Pop! 245

WILLY: Oh, won't that be something! Me comin' into the Boston store with you boys carryin' my bags. What a sensation!

(BIFF *is prancing around, practicing passing the ball.*)

WILLY: You nervous, Biff, about the game?

BIFF: Not if you're gonna be there.

WILLY: What do they say about you in school, now that they made you captain?

HAPPY: There's a crowd of girls behind him everytime the classes change. 250

BIFF (*taking* WILLY's *hand.*): This Saturday, Pop, this Saturday—just for you, I'm going to break through for a touchdown.

HAPPY: You're supposed to pass.

BIFF: I'm takin' one play for Pop. You watch me, Pop, and when I take off my helmet, that means I'm breakin' out. Then you watch me crash through that line!

WILLY (*kisses* BIFF.): Oh, wait'll I tell this in Boston!

(BERNARD *enters in knickers. He is younger than* BIFF, *earnest and loyal, a worried boy.*)

BERNARD: Biff, where are you? You're supposed to study with me today. 255

WILLY: Hey, looka Bernard. What're you lookin' so anemic about, Bernard?

BERNARD: He's gotta study, Uncle Willy. He's got Regents next week.

HAPPY (*tauntingly, spinning* BERNARD *around.*): Let's box, Bernard!

BERNARD: Biff! (*He gets away from* HAPPY.) Listen, Biff, I heard Mr. Birnbaum say that if you don't start studyin' math he's gonna flunk you, and you won't graduate. I heard him!

WILLY: You better study with him, Biff. Go ahead now. 260

BERNARD: I heard him!

BIFF: Oh, Pop, you didn't see my sneakers! (*He holds up a foot for* WILLY *to look at.*)

WILLY: Hey, that's a beautiful job of printing!

BERNARD (*wiping his glasses.*): Just because he printed University of Virginia on his sneakers doesn't mean they've got to graduate him, Uncle Willy!

WILLY (*angrily.*): What're you talking about? With scholarships to three universities they're gonna flunk him? 265

BERNARD: But I heard Mr. Birnbaum say—

WILLY: Don't be a pest, Bernard! *(To his boys.)* What an anemic!

BERNARD: Okay, I'm waiting for you in my house, Biff.

(BERNARD goes off. THE LOMANS laugh.)

WILLY: Bernard is not well liked, is he?

BIFF: He's liked, but he's not well liked.   270

HAPPY: That's right, Pop.

WILLY: That's just what I mean. Bernard can get the best marks in school,
y'understand, but when he gets out in the business world, y'understand,
you are going to be five times ahead of him. That's why I thank
Almighty God you're both built like Adonises. Because the man who
makes an appearance in the business world, the man who creates personal interest, is the man who gets ahead. Be liked and you will never
want. You take me, for instance. I never have to wait in line to see a
buyer. "Willy Loman is here!" That's all they have to know, and I go
right through.

BIFF: Did you knock them dead, Pop?

WILLY: Knocked 'em cold in Providence, slaughtered 'em in Boston.

HAPPY *(on his back, pedaling again.)*: I'm losing weight, you notice, Pop?   275

(LINDA enters, as of old, a ribbon in her hair, carrying a basket of washing.)

LINDA *(with youthful energy.)*: Hello, dear!

WILLY: Sweetheart!

LINDA: How'd the Chevvy run?

WILLY: Chevrolet, Linda, is the greatest car ever built. *(To the boys.)* Since
when do you let your mother carry wash up the stairs?

BIFF: Grab hold there, boy!   280

HAPPY: Where to, Mom?

LINDA: Hang them up on the line. And you better go down to your friends,
Biff. The cellar is full of boys. They don't know what to do with
themselves.

BIFF: Ah, when Pop comes home they can wait!

WILLY *(laughs appreciatively.)*: You better go down and tell them what to do,
Biff.

BIFF: I think I'll have them sweep out the furnace room.   285

WILLY: Good work, Biff.

BIFF *(goes through wall-line of kitchen to doorway at back and calls down.)*:
Fellas! Everybody sweep out the furnace room! I'll be right down!

VOICES: All right! Okay, Biff.

BIFF: George and Sam and Frank, come out back! We're hangin' up the
wash! Come on, Hap, on the double! *(He and HAPPY carry out the basket.)*

LINDA: The way they obey him!   290

WILLY: Well, that's training, the training. I'm tellin' you, I was sellin'
thousands and thousands, but I had to come home.

LINDA: Oh, the whole block'll be at that game. Did you sell anything?

WILLY: I did five hundred gross in Providence and seven hundred gross in Boston.

LINDA: No! Wait a minute, I've got a pencil. (*She pulls pencil and paper out of her apron pocket.*) That makes your commission... Two hundred— my God! Two hundred and twelve dollars!

WILLY: Well, I didn't figure it yet, but...   295

LINDA: How much did you do?

WILLY: Well, I—I did—about a hundred and eighty gross in Providence. Well, no—it came to—roughly two hundred gross on the whole trip.

LINDA (*without hesitation.*): Two hundred gross. That's... (*She figures.*)

WILLY: The trouble was that three of the stores were half closed for inventory in Boston. Otherwise I woulda broke records.

LINDA: Well, it makes seventy dollars and some pennies. That's very good.   300

WILLY: What do we owe?

LINDA: Well, on the first there's sixteen dollars on the refrigerator—

WILLY: Why sixteen?

LINDA: Well, the fan belt broke, so it was a dollar eighty.

WILLY: But it's brand new.   305

LINDA: Well, the man said that's the way it is. Till they work themselves in, y'know.

(*They move through the wall-line into the kitchen.*)

WILLY: I hope we didn't get stuck on that machine.

LINDA: They got the biggest ads of any of them!

WILLY: I know, it's a fine machine. What else?

LINDA: Well, there's nine-sixty for the washing machine. And for the vac-   310
uum cleaner there's three and a half due on the fifteenth. Then the roof, you got twenty-one dollars remaining.

WILLY: It don't leak, does it?

LINDA: No, they did a wonderful job. Then you owe Frank for the carburetor.

WILLY: I'm not going to pay that man! That goddam Chevrolet, they ought to prohibit the manufacture of that car!

LINDA: Well, you owe him three and a half. And odds and ends, comes to around a hundred and twenty dollars by the fifteenth.

WILLY: A hundred and twenty dollars! My God, if business don't pick up I   315
don't know what I'm gonna do!

LINDA: Well, next week you'll do better.

WILLY: Oh, I'll knock them dead next week. I'll go to Hartford. I'm very well liked in Hartford. You know, the trouble is, Linda, people don't seem to take to me.

(*They move onto the forestage.*)

LINDA: Oh, don't be foolish.

WILLY: I know it when I walk in. They seem to laugh at me.

LINDA: Why? Why would they laugh at you? Don't talk that way, Willy.   320

(WILLY *moves to the edge of the stage.* LINDA *goes into the kitchen and starts to darn stockings.*)

WILLY: I don't know the reason for it, but they just pass me by. I'm not noticed.

LINDA: But you're doing wonderful, dear. You're making seventy to a hundred dollars a week.

WILLY: But I gotta be at it ten, twelve hours a day. Other men—I don't know—they do it easier. I don't know why—I can't stop myself—I talk too much. A man oughta come in with a few words. One thing about Charley. He's a man of few words, and they respect him.

LINDA: You don't talk too much, you're just lively.

WILLY (*smiling.*): Well, I figure, what the hell, life is short, a couple of jokes.   325
(*To himself.*) I joke too much! (*The smile goes.*)

LINDA: Why? You're—

WILLY: I'm fat. I'm very—foolish to look at, Linda. I didn't tell you, but Christmas time I happened to be calling on F. H. Stewarts, and a salesman I know, as I was going in to see the buyer, I heard him say something about—walrus. And I—I cracked him right across the face. I won't take that. I simply will not take that. But they do laugh at me. I know that.

LINDA: Darling...

WILLY: I gotta overcome it. I know I gotta overcome it. I'm not dressing to advantage, maybe.

LINDA: Willy, darling, you're the handsomest man in the world—   330

WILLY: Oh, no, Linda.

LINDA: To me you are. (*Slight pause.*) The handsomest.

(*From the darkness is heard the laughter of a woman.* WILLY *doesn't turn to it, but it continues through* LINDA's *lines.*)

LINDA: And the boys, Willy. Few men are idolized by their children the way you are.

(*Music is heard as behind a scrim, to the left of the house,* THE WOMAN, *dimly seen, is dressing.*)

WILLY (*with great feeling.*): You're the best there is, Linda, you're a pal, you know that? On the road—on the road I want to grab you sometimes and just kiss the life outa you.

(*The laughter is loud now, and he moves into a brightening area at the left, where* THE WOMAN *has come from behind the scrim and is standing, putting on her hat, looking into a "mirror" and laughing.*)

WILLY: 'Cause I get so lonely—especially when business is bad and there's   335
nobody to talk to. I get the feeling that I'll never sell anything again, that I won't make a living for you, or a business, a business for the boys.

(*He talks through* THE WOMAN's *subsiding laughter;* THE WOMAN *primps at the "mirror."*) There's so much I want to make for—

THE WOMAN: Me? You didn't make me, Willy. I picked you.

WILLY (*pleased.*): You picked me?

THE WOMAN (*who is quite proper-looking,* WILLY's *age.*): I did. I've been sitting at that desk watching all the salesmen go by, day in, day out. But you've got such a sense of humor, and we do have such a good time together, don't we?

WILLY: Sure, sure. (*He takes her in his arms.*) Why do you have to go now?

THE WOMAN: It's two o'clock...   340

WILLY: No, come on in! (*He pulls her.*)

THE WOMAN: ...my sisters'll be scandalized. When'll you be back?

WILLY: Oh, two weeks about. Will you come up again?

THE WOMAN: Sure thing. You do make me laugh. It's good for me. (*She squeezes his arm, kisses him.*) And I think you're a wonderful man.

WILLY: You picked me, heh?   345

THE WOMAN: Sure. Because you're so sweet. And such a kidder.

WILLY: Well, I'll see you next time I'm in Boston.

THE WOMAN: I'll put you right through to the buyers.

WILLY (*slapping her bottom.*): Right. Well, bottoms up!

THE WOMAN (*slaps him gently and laughs.*): You just kill me, Willy. (*He suddenly grabs her and kisses her roughly.*) You kill me. And thanks for the stockings. I love a lot of stockings. Well, good night.   350

WILLY: Good night. And keep your pores open!

THE WOMAN: Oh, Willy!

(THE WOMAN *bursts out laughing, and* LINDA's *laughter blends in.* THE WOMAN *disappears into the dark. Now the area at the kitchen table brightens.* LINDA *is sitting where she was at the kitchen table, but now is mending a pair of silk stockings.*)

LINDA: You are, Willy. The handsomest man. You've got no reason to feel that—

WILLY (*coming out of* THE WOMAN's *dimming area and going over to* LINDA.): I'll make it all up to you, Linda, I'll—

LINDA: There's nothing to make up, dear. You're doing fine, better than—   355

WILLY (*noticing her mending.*): What's that?

LINDA: Just mending my stockings. They're so expensive—

WILLY (*angrily, taking them from her.*): I won't have you mending stockings in this house! Now throw them out!

(LINDA *puts the stockings in her pocket.*)

BERNARD (*entering on the run.*): Where is he? If he doesn't study!

WILLY (*moving to the forestage, with great agitation.*): You'll give him the answers!   360

BERNARD: I do, but I can't on a Regents! That's a state exam! They're liable
  to arrest me!

WILLY: Where is he? I'll whip him, I'll whip him!

LINDA: And he'd better give back that football, Willy, it's not nice.

WILLY: Biff! Where is he? Why is he taking everything?

LINDA: He's too tough with the girls, Willy. All the mothers are afraid of him!   365

WILLY: I'll whip him!

BERNARD: He's driving the car without a license!

(THE WOMAN's *laugh is heard.*)

WILLY: Shut up!

LINDA: All the mothers—

WILLY: Shut up!   370

BERNARD (*backing quietly away and out.*): Mr. Birnbaum says he's stuck up.

WILLY: Get outa here!

BERNARD: If he doesn't buckle down he'll flunk math! (*He goes off.*)

LINDA: He's right, Willy, you've gotta—

WILLY (*exploding at her.*): There's nothing the matter with him! You want   375
  him to be a worm like Bernard? He's got spirit, personality...

(As he speaks, LINDA, *almost in tears, exits into the living room.* WILLY *is alone
  in the kitchen, wilting and staring. The leaves are gone. It is night again, and
  the apartment houses look down from behind.*)

WILLY: Loaded with it. Loaded! What is he stealing? He's giving it back,
  isn't he? Why is he stealing? What did I tell him? I never in my life
  told him anything but decent things.

(HAPPY *in pajamas has come down the stairs;* WILLY *suddenly becomes aware of*
  HAPPY's *presence.*)

HAPPY: Let's go now, come on.

WILLY (*sitting down at the kitchen table.*): Huh! Why did she have to wax the
  floors herself? Everytime she waxes the floors she keels over. She knows
  that!

HAPPY: Shh! Take it easy. What brought you back tonight?

WILLY: I got an awful scare. Nearly hit a kid in Yonkers. God! Why didn't I   380
  go to Alaska with my brother Ben that time! Ben! That man was a genius, that man was success incarnate! What a mistake! He begged me
  to go.

HAPPY: Well, there's no use in—

WILLY: You guys! There was a man started with the clothes on his back and
  ended up with diamond mines!

HAPPY: Boy, someday I'd like to know how he did it.

WILLY: What's the mystery? The man knew what he wanted and went out
  and got it! Walked into a jungle, and comes out, the age of twenty-one,
  and he's rich! The world is an oyster, but you don't crack it open on a
  mattress!

HAPPY: Pop, I told you I'm gonna retire you for life. 385

WILLY: You'll retire me for life on seventy goddam dollars a week? And your women and your car and your apartment, and you'll retire me for life! Christ's sake, I couldn't get past Yonkers today! Where are you guys, where are you? The woods are burning! I can't drive a car!

(CHARLEY *has appeared in the doorway. He is a large man, slow of speech, laconic, immovable. In all he says, despite what he says, there is pity, and now, trepidation. He has a robe over his pajamas, slippers on his feet. He enters the kitchen.*)

CHARLEY: Everything all right?

HAPPY: Yeah, Charley, everything's...

WILLY: What's the matter?

CHARLEY: I heard some noise. I thought something happened. Can't we do 390 something about the walls? You sneeze in here, and in my house hats blow off.

HAPPY: Let's go to bed, Dad. Come on.

(CHARLEY *signals to* HAPPY *to go.*)

WILLY: You go ahead, I'm not tired at the moment.

HAPPY (*to* WILLY.): Take it easy, huh? (*He exits.*)

WILLY: What're you doin' up?

CHARLEY (*sitting down at the kitchen table opposite* WILLY.): Couldn't sleep 395 good. I had a heartburn.

WILLY: Well, you don't know how to eat.

CHARLEY: I eat with my mouth.

WILLY: No, you're ignorant. You gotta know about vitamins and things like that.

CHARLEY: Come on, let's shoot. Tire you out a little.

WILLY (*hesitantly.*): All right. You got cards? 400

CHARLEY (*taking a deck from his pocket.*): Yeah, I got them. Someplace. What is it with those vitamins?

WILLY (*dealing.*): They build up your bones. Chemistry.

CHARLEY: Yeah, but there's no bones in a heartburn.

WILLY: What are you talkin' about? Do you know the first thing about it?

CHARLEY: Don't get insulted. 405

WILLY: Don't talk about something you don't know anything about.

(*They are playing. Pause.*)

CHARLEY: What're you doin' home?

WILLY: A little trouble with the car.

CHARLEY: Oh. (*Pause.*) I'd like to take a trip to California.

WILLY: Don't say. 410

CHARLEY: You want a job?

WILLY: I got a job, I told you that. (*After a slight pause.*) What the hell are you offering me a job for?

CHARLEY: Don't get insulted.

WILLY: Don't insult me.

CHARLEY: I don't see no sense in it. You don't have to go on this way.   415

WILLY: I got a good job. (*Slight pause.*) What do you keep comin' in here for?

CHARLEY: You want me to go?

WILLY (*after a pause, withering.*): I can't understand it. He's going back to Texas again. What the hell is that?

CHARLEY: Let him go.

WILLY: I got nothin' to give him, Charley, I'm clean, I'm clean.   420

CHARLEY: He won't starve. None a them starve. Forget about him.

WILLY: Then what have I got to remember?

CHARLEY: You take it too hard. To hell with it. When a deposit bottle is broken you don't get your nickel back.

WILLY: That's easy enough for you to say.

CHARLEY: That ain't easy for me to say.   425

WILLY: Did you see the ceiling I put up in the living room?

CHARLEY: Yeah, that's a piece of work. To put up a ceiling is a mystery to me. How do you do it?

WILLY: What's the difference?

CHARLEY: Well, talk about it.

WILLY: You gonna put up a ceiling?   430

CHARLEY: How could I put up a ceiling?

WILLY: Then what the hell are you bothering me for?

CHARLEY: You're insulted again.

WILLY: A man who can't handle tools is not a man. You're disgusting.

CHARLEY: Don't call me disgusting, Willy.   435

(UNCLE BEN, *carrying a valise and an umbrella, enters the forestage from around the right corner of the house. He is a stolid man, in his sixties, with a mustache and an authoritative air. He is utterly certain of his destiny, and there is an aura of far places about him. He enters exactly as* WILLY *speaks.*)

WILLY: I'm getting awfully tired, Ben.

(BEN's *music is heard.* BEN *looks around at everything.*)

CHARLEY: Good, keep playing; you'll sleep better. Did you call me Ben?

(BEN *looks at his watch.*)

WILLY: That's funny. For a second there you reminded me of my brother Ben.

BEN: I have only a few minutes. (*He strolls, inspecting the place.* WILLY *and* CHARLEY *continue playing.*)

CHARLEY: You never heard from him again, heh? Since that time?   440

WILLY: Didn't Linda tell you? Couple of weeks ago we got a letter from his wife in Africa. He died.

CHARLEY: That so.

BEN (*chuckling.*): So this is Brooklyn, eh?

CHARLEY: Maybe you're in for some of his money.

WILLY: Naa, he had seven sons. There's just one opportunity I had with that man... 445

BEN: I must make a train, William. There are several properties I'm looking at in Alaska.

WILLY: Sure, sure! If I'd gone with him to Alaska that time, everything would've been totally different.

CHARLEY: Go on, you'd froze to death up there.

WILLY: What're you talking about?

BEN: Opportunity is tremendous in Alaska, William. Surprised you're not up there. 450

WILLY: Sure, tremendous.

CHARLEY: Heh?

WILLY: There was the only man I ever met who knew the answers.

CHARLEY: Who?

BEN: How are you all? 455

WILLY (*taking a pot, smiling.*): Fine, fine.

CHARLEY: Pretty sharp tonight.

BEN: Is Mother living with you?

WILLY: No, she died a long time ago.

CHARLEY: Who? 460

BEN: That's too bad. Fine specimen of a lady, Mother.

WILLY (*to* CHARLEY.): Heh?

BEN: I'd hoped to see the old girl.

CHARLEY: Who died?

BEN: Heard anything from Father, have you? 465

WILLY (*unnerved.*): What do you mean, who died?

CHARLEY (*taking a pot.*): What're you talkin' about?

BEN (*looking at his watch.*): William, it's half-past eight!

WILLY (*as though to dispel his confusion he angrily stops* CHARLEY's *hand.*): That's my build!

CHARLEY: I put the ace— 470

WILLY: If you don't know how to play the game I'm not gonna throw my money away on you!

CHARLEY (*rising.*): It was my ace, for God's sake!

WILLY: I'm through, I'm through!

BEN: When did Mother die?

WILLY: Long ago. Since the beginning you never knew how to play cards. 475

CHARLEY (*picks up the cards and goes to the door.*): All right! Next time I'll bring a deck with five aces.

WILLY: I don't play that kind of game!

CHARLEY (*turning to him.*): You should be ashamed of yourself!

WILLY: Yeah?

CHARLEY: Yeah! (*He goes out.*)   480

WILLY (*slamming the door after him.*): Ignoramus!

BEN (*as* WILLY *comes toward him through the wall-line of the kitchen.*): So you're William.

WILLY (*shaking* BEN's *hand.*): Ben! I've been waiting for you so long! What's the answer? How did you do it?

BEN: Oh, there's a story in that.

(LINDA *enters the forestage, as of old, carrying the wash basket.*)

LINDA: Is this Ben?   485

BEN (*gallantly.*): How do you do, my dear.

LINDA: Where've you been all these years? Willy's always wondered why you—

WILLY (*pulling* BEN *away from her impatiently.*): Where is Dad? Didn't you follow him? How did you get started?

BEN: Well, I don't know how much you remember.

WILLY: Well, I was just a baby, of course, only three or four years old—   490

BEN: Three years and eleven months.

WILLY: What a memory, Ben!

BEN: I have many enterprises, William, and I have never kept books.

WILLY: I remember I was sitting under the wagon in—was it Nebraska?

BEN: It was South Dakota, and I gave you a bunch of wild flowers.   495

WILLY: I remember you walking away down some open road.

BEN (*laughing.*): I was going to find Father in Alaska.

WILLY: Where is he?

BEN: At that age I had a very faulty view of geography, William. I discovered after a few days that I was heading due south, so instead of Alaska, I ended up in Africa.

LINDA: Africa!   500

WILLY: The Gold Coast!

BEN: Principally, diamond mines.

LINDA: Diamond mines!

BEN: Yes, my dear. But I've only a few minutes—

WILLY: No! Boys! Boys! (*Young* BIFF *and* HAPPY *appear.*) Listen to this. This   505
is your Uncle Ben, a great man! Tell my boys, Ben!

BEN: Why, boys, when I was seventeen I walked into the jungle, and when I was twenty-one I walked out. (*He laughs.*) And by God I was rich.

WILLY (*to the boys.*): You see what I been talking about? The greatest things can happen!

BEN (*glancing at his watch.*): I have an appointment in Ketchikan Tuesday week.

WILLY: No, Ben! Please tell about Dad. I want my boys to hear. I want them to know the kind of stock they spring from. All I remember is a man with a big beard, and I was in Mamma's lap, sitting around a fire, and some kind of high music.

BEN: His flute. He played the flute.   510

WILLY: Sure, the flute, that's right!

(New music is heard, a high, rollicking tune.)

BEN: Father was a very great and a very wild-hearted man. We would start in Boston, and he'd toss the whole family into the wagon, and then he'd drive the team right across the country; through Ohio, and Indiana, Michigan, Illinois, and all the Western states. And we'd stop in the towns and sell the flutes that he'd made on the way. Great inventor, Father. With one gadget he made more in a week than a man like you could make in a lifetime.

WILLY: That's just the way I'm bringing them up, Ben—rugged, well liked, all-around.

BEN: Yeah? *(To BIFF.)* Hit that, boy—hard as you can. *(He pounds his stomach.)*

BIFF: Oh, no, sir!   515

BEN *(taking boxing stance.)*: Come on, get to me! *(He laughs.)*

WILLY: Go to it, Biff! Go ahead, show him!

BIFF: Okay! *(He cocks his fist and starts in.)*

LINDA *(to WILLY.)*: Why must he fight, dear?

BEN *(sparring with BIFF.)*: Good boy! Good boy!   520

WILLY: How's that, Ben, heh?

HAPPY: Give him the left, Biff!

LINDA: Why are you fighting?

BEN: Good boy! *(Suddenly comes in, trips BIFF, and stands over him, the point of his umbrella poised over BIFF's eye.)*

LINDA: Look out, Biff!   525

BIFF: Gee!

BEN *(patting BIFF's knee.)*: Never fight fair with a stranger, boy. You'll never get out of the jungle that way. *(Taking LINDA's hand and bowing.)* It was an honor and a pleasure to meet you, Linda.

LINDA *(withdrawing her hand coldly, frightened.)*: Have a nice—trip.

BEN *(to WILLY.)*: And good luck with your—what do you do?

WILLY: Selling.   530

BEN: Yes. Well...*(He raises his hand in farewell to all.)*

WILLY: No, Ben, I don't want you to think...*(He takes BEN's arm to show him.)* It's Brooklyn, I know, but we hunt too.

BEN: Really, now.

WILLY: Oh, sure, there's snakes and rabbits and—that's why I moved out here. Why, Biff can fell any one of these trees in no time! Boys! Go right over to where they're building the apartment house and get some sand. We're gonna rebuild the entire front stoop right now! Watch this, Ben!

BIFF: Yes, sir! On the double, Hap!   535

HAPPY (*as he and* BIFF *run off.*): I lost weight, Pop, you notice?

(CHARLEY *enters in knickers, even before the boys are gone.*)

CHARLEY: Listen, if they steal any more from that building the watchman'll put the cops on them!

LINDA (*to* WILLY.): Don't let Biff…

(BEN *laughs lustily.*)

WILLY: You shoulda seen the lumber they brought home last week. At least a dozen six-by-tens worth all kinds of money.

CHARLEY: Listen, if that watchman—   540

WILLY: I gave them hell, understand. But I got a couple of fearless characters there.

CHARLEY: Willy, the jails are full of fearless characters.

BEN (*clapping* WILLY *on the back, with a laugh at* CHARLEY.): And the stock exchange, friend!

WILLY (*joining in* BEN'*s laughter.*): Where are the rest of your pants?

CHARLEY: My wife bought them.   545

WILLY: Now all you need is a golf club and you can go upstairs and go to sleep. (*To* BEN.) Great athlete! Between him and his son Bernard they can't hammer a nail!

BERNARD (*rushing in.*): The watchman's chasing Biff!

WILLY (*angrily.*): Shut up! He's not stealing anything!

LINDA (*alarmed, hurrying off left.*): Where is he? Biff, dear! (*She exits.*)

WILLY (*moving toward the left, away from* BEN.): There's nothing wrong.   550
What's the matter with you?

BEN: Nervy boy. Good!

WILLY (*laughing.*): Oh, nerves of iron, that Biff!

CHARLEY: Don't know what it is. My New England man comes back and he's bleedin', they murdered him up there.

WILLY: It's contacts, Charley, I got important contacts!

CHARLEY (*sarcastically.*): Glad to hear it, Willy. Come in later, we'll shoot a   555
little casino. I'll take some of your Portland money. (*He laughs at* WILLY *and exits.*)

WILLY (*turning to* BEN.): Business is bad, it's murderous. But not for me, of course.

BEN: I'll stop by on my way back to Africa.

WILLY (*longingly.*): Can't you stay a few days? You're just what I need, Ben, because I—I have a fine position here, but I—well, Dad left when I was such a baby and I never had a chance to talk to him and I still feel—kind of temporary about myself.

BEN: I'll be late for my train.

(*They are at opposite ends of the stage.*)

WILLY: Ben, my boys—can't we talk? They'd go into the jaws of hell for me, see, but I— 560

BEN: William, you're being first-rate with your boys. Outstanding, manly chaps!

WILLY (*hanging on to his words.*): Oh, Ben, that's good to hear! Because some times I'm afraid that I'm not teaching them the right kind of—Ben, how should I teach them?

BEN (*giving great weight to each word, and with a certain vicious audacity.*): William, when I walked into the jungle, I was seventeen. When I walked out I was twenty-one. And, by God, I was rich! (*He goes off into darkness around the right corner of the house.*)

WILLY: …was rich! That's just the spirit I want to imbue them with! To walk into a jungle! I was right! I was right! I was right!

(BEN *is gone, but* WILLY *is still speaking to him as* LINDA, *in nightgown and robe, enters the kitchen, glances around for* WILLY, *then goes to the door of the house, looks out and sees him. Comes down to his left. He looks at her.*)

LINDA: Willy, dear? Willy? 565

WILLY: I was right!

LINDA: Did you have some cheese? (*He can't answer.*) It's very late, darling. Come to bed, heh?

WILLY (*looking straight up.*): Gotta break your neck to see a star in this yard.

LINDA: You coming in?

WILLY: What ever happened to that diamond watch fob? Remember? When Ben came from Africa that time? Didn't he give me a watch fob with a diamond in it? 570

LINDA: You pawned it, dear. Twelve, thirteen years ago. For Biff's radio correspondence course.

WILLY: Gee, that was a beautiful thing. I'll take a walk.

LINDA: But you're in your slippers.

WILLY (*starting to go around the house at the left.*): I was right! I was! (*Half to* LINDA, *as he goes, shaking his head.*) What a man! There was a man worth talking to. I was right!

LINDA (*calling after* WILLY.): But in your slippers, Willy! 575

(WILLY *is almost gone when* BIFF, *in his pajamas, comes down the stairs and enters the kitchen.*)

BIFF: What is he doing out there?

LINDA: Sh!

BIFF: God Almighty, Mom, how long has he been doing this?

LINDA: Don't, he'll hear you.

BIFF: What the hell is the matter with him? 580

LINDA: It'll pass by morning.

BIFF: Shouldn't we do anything?

LINDA: Oh, my dear, you should do a lot of things, but there's nothing to do, so go to sleep.

(HAPPY *comes down the stairs and sits on the steps.*)

HAPPY: I never heard him so loud, Mom.

LINDA: Well, come around more often; you'll hear him. (*She sits down at the table and mends the lining of* WILLY'*s jacket.*)   585

BIFF: Why didn't you ever write me about this, Mom?

LINDA: How would I write to you? For over three months you had no address.

BIFF: I was on the move. But you know I thought of you all the time. You know that, don't you, pal?

LINDA: I know, dear, I know. But he likes to have a letter. Just to know that there's still a possibility for better things.

BIFF: He's not like this all the time, is he?   590

LINDA: It's when you come home he's always the worst.

BIFF: When I come home?

LINDA: When you write you're coming, he's all smiles, and talks about the future, and—he's just wonderful. And then the closer you seem to come, the more shaky he gets, and then, by the time you get here, he's arguing, and he seems angry at you. I think it's just that maybe he can't bring himself to—to open up to you. Why are you so hateful to each other? Why is that?

BIFF (*evasively.*): I'm not hateful, Mom.

LINDA: But you no sooner come in the door than you're fighting!   595

BIFF: I don't know why. I mean to change. I'm tryin', Mom, you understand?

LINDA: Are you home to stay now?

BIFF: I don't know. I want to look around, see what's doin'.

LINDA: Biff, you can't look around all your life, can you?

BIFF: I just can't take hold, Mom. I can't take hold of some kind of a life.   600

LINDA: Biff, a man is not a bird, to come and go with the springtime.

BIFF: Your hair…(*He touches her hair.*) Your hair got so gray.

LINDA: Oh, it's been gray since you were in high school. I just stopped dyeing it, that's all.

BIFF: Dye it again, will ya? I don't want my pal looking old. (*He smiles.*)

LINDA: You're such a boy! You think you can go away for a year and…   605
You've got to get it into your head now that one day you'll knock on this door and there'll be strange people here—

BIFF: What are you talking about? You're not even sixty, Mom.

LINDA: But what about your father?

BIFF (*lamely.*): Well, I meant him too.

HAPPY: He admires Pop.

LINDA: Biff, dear, if you don't have any feeling for him, then you can't have   610
any feeling for me.

BIFF: Sure I can, Mom.

LINDA: No. You can't just come to see me, because I love him. (*With a
threat, but only a threat, of tears.*) He's the dearest man in the world to
me, and I won't have anyone making him feel unwanted and low and
blue. You've got to make up your mind now, darling, there's no leeway
any more. Either he's your father and you pay him that respect, or else
you're not to come here. I know he's not easy to get along with—nobody knows that better than me—but...

WILLY (*from the left, with a laugh.*): Hey, hey, Biffo!

BIFF (*starting to go out after* WILLY.): What the hell is the matter with him?
(HAPPY *stops him.*)

LINDA: Don't—don't go near him!   615

BIFF: Stop making excuses for him! He always, always wiped the floor with
you. Never had an ounce of respect for you.

HAPPY: He's always had respect for—

BIFF: What the hell do you know about it?

HAPPY (*surlily.*): Just don't call him crazy!

BIFF: He's got no character—Charley wouldn't do this. Not in his own   620
house—spewing out that vomit from his mind.

HAPPY: Charley never had to cope with what he's got to.

BIFF: People are worse off than Willy Loman. Believe me, I've seen them!

LINDA: Then make Charley your father, Biff. You can't do that, can you? I
don't say he's a great man. Willy Loman never made a lot of money.
His name was never in the paper. He's not the finest character that
ever lived. But he's a human being, and a terrible thing is happening to
him. So attention must be paid. He's not to be allowed to fall into his
grave like an old dog. Attention, attention must be finally paid to such
a person. You called him crazy—

BIFF: I didn't mean—

LINDA: No, a lot of people think he's lost his—balance. But you don't   625
have to be very smart to know what his trouble is. The man is
exhausted.

HAPPY: Sure!

LINDA: A small man can be just as exhausted as a great man. He works
for a company thirty-six years this March, opens up unheard-of terri-
tories to their trademark, and now in his old age they take his salary
away.

HAPPY (*indignantly.*): I didn't know that, Mom.

LINDA: You never asked, my dear! Now that you get your spending money
someplace else you don't trouble your mind with him.

HAPPY: But I gave you money last—   630

LINDA: Christmas time, fifty dollars! To fix the hot water it cost ninety-seven fifty! For five weeks he's been on straight commission, like a beginner, an unknown!

BIFF: Those ungrateful bastards!

LINDA: Are they any worse than his sons? When he brought them business, when he was young, they were glad to see him. But now his old friends, the old buyers that loved him so and always found some order to hand him in a pinch—they're all dead, retired. He used to be able to make six, seven calls a day in Boston. Now he takes his valises out of the car and puts them back and takes them out again and he's exhausted. Instead of walking he talks now. He drives seven hundred miles, and when he gets there no one knows him any more, no one welcomes him. And what goes through a man's mind, driving seven hundred miles home without having earned a cent? Why shouldn't he talk to himself? Why? When he has to go to Charley and borrow fifty dollars a week and pretend to me that it's his pay? How long can that go on? How long? You see what I'm sitting here and waiting for? And you tell me he has no character? The man who never worked a day but for your benefit? When does he get the medal for that? Is this his reward—to turn around at the age of sixty-three and find his sons, who he loved better than his life, one a philandering bum—

HAPPY: Mom!

LINDA: That's all you are, my baby! (*To* BIFF.) And you! What happened to the love you had for him? You were such pals! How you used to talk to him on the phone every night! How lonely he was till he could come home to you!

BIFF: All right, Mom. I'll live here in my room, and I'll get a job. I'll keep away from him, that's all.

LINDA: No, Biff. You can't stay here and fight all the time.

BIFF: He threw me out of this house, remember that.

LINDA: Why did he do that? I never knew why.

BIFF: Because I know he's a fake and he doesn't like anybody around who knows!

LINDA: Why a fake? In what way? What do you mean?

BIFF: Just don't lay it all at my feet. It's between me and him—that's all I have to say. I'll chip in from now on. He'll settle for half my pay check. He'll be all right. I'm going to bed. (*He starts for the stairs.*)

LINDA: He won't be all right.

BIFF (*turning on the stairs, furiously.*): I hate this city and I'll stay here. Now what do you want?

LINDA: He's dying, Biff.

(HAPPY *turns quickly to her, shocked.*)

635

640

645

BIFF *(after a pause.)*: Why is he dying?

LINDA: He's been trying to kill himself.

BIFF *(with great horror.)*: How?

LINDA: I live from day to day.

BIFF: What're you talking about?   650

LINDA: Remember I wrote you that he smashed up the car again? In February?

BIFF: Well?

LINDA: The insurance inspector came. He said that they have evidence. That all these accidents in the last year—weren't—weren't—accidents.

HAPPY: How can they tell that? That's a lie.

LINDA: It seems there's a woman... *(She takes a breath as—)*   655

BIFF *(sharply but contained.)*: What woman?

LINDA *(simultaneously.)*: ...and this woman...

LINDA: What?

BIFF: Nothing. Go ahead.

LINDA: What did you say?   660

BIFF: Nothing. I just said what woman?

HAPPY: What about her?

LINDA: Well, it seems she was walking down the road and saw his car. She says that he wasn't driving fast at all, and that he didn't skid. She says he came to that little bridge, and then deliberately smashed into the railing, and it was only the shallowness of the water that saved him.

BIFF: Oh, no, he probably just fell asleep again.

LINDA: I don't think he fell asleep.   665

BIFF: Why not?

LINDA: Last month... *(With great difficulty.)* Oh, boys, it's so hard to say a thing like this! He's just a big stupid man to you, but I tell you there's more good in him than in many other people. *(She chokes, wipes her eyes.)* I was looking for a fuse. The lights blew out, and I went down the cellar. And behind the fuse box—it happened to fall out—was a length of rubber pipe—just short.

HAPPY: No kidding?

LINDA: There's a little attachment on the end of it. I knew right away. And sure enough, on the bottom of the water heater there's a new little nipple on the gas pipe.

HAPPY *(angrily.)*: That—jerk.   670

BIFF: Did you have it taken off?

LINDA: I'm—I'm ashamed to. How can I mention it to him? Every day I go down and take away that little rubber pipe. But, when he comes home, I put it back where it was. How can I insult him that way? I don't know what to do. I live from day to day, boys. I tell you, I know every thought in his mind. It sounds so old-fashioned and silly, but I tell you he put his whole life into you and you've turned your backs on him. *(She is bent over in the chair, weeping, her face in her hands.)* Biff, I swear to God! Biff, his life is in your hands!

HAPPY *(to BIFF.)*: How do you like that damned fool!

BIFF *(kissing her.)*: All right, pal, all right. It's all settled now. I've been remiss. I know that, Mom, but now I'll stay, and I swear to you, I'll apply myself. *(Kneeling in front of her, in a fever of self-reproach.)* It's just—you see, Mom, I don't fit in business. Not that I won't try. I'll try, and I'll make good.

HAPPY: Sure you will. The trouble with you in business was you never tried to please people.   675

BIFF: I know, I—

HAPPY: Like when you worked for Harrison's. Bob Harrison said you were tops, and then you go and do some damn fool thing like whistling whole songs in the elevator like a comedian.

BIFF *(against HAPPY.)*: So what? I like to whistle sometimes.

HAPPY: You don't raise a guy to a responsible job who whistles in the elevator!

LINDA: Well, don't argue about it now.   680

HAPPY: Like when you'd go off and swim in the middle of the day instead of taking the line around.

BIFF *(his resentment rising.)*: Well, don't you run off? You take off sometimes, don't you? On a nice summer day?

HAPPY: Yeah, but I cover myself!

LINDA: Boys!

HAPPY: If I'm going to take a fade the boss can call any number where I'm supposed to be and they'll swear to him that I just left. I'll tell you something that I hate to say, Biff, but in the business world some of them think you're crazy.   685

BIFF *(angered.)*: Screw the business world!

HAPPY: All right, screw it! Great, but cover yourself!

LINDA: Hap, Hap!

BIFF: I don't care what they think! They've laughed at Dad for years, and you know why? Because we don't belong in this nut-house of a city! We should be mixing cement on some open plain, or—or carpenters. A carpenter is allowed to whistle!

(WILLY walks in from the entrance of the house, at left.)

WILLY: Even your grandfather was better than a carpenter. *(Pause. They watch him.)* You never grew up. Bernard does not whistle in the elevator, I assure you.   690

BIFF *(as though to laugh WILLY out of it.)*: Yeah, but you do, Pop.

WILLY: I never in my life whistled in an elevator! And who in the business world thinks I'm crazy?

BIFF: I didn't mean it like that, Pop. Now don't make a whole thing out of it, will ya?

WILLY: Go back to the West! Be a carpenter, a cowboy, enjoy yourself!

LINDA: Willy, he was just saying—   695

WILLY: I heard what he said!

HAPPY (*trying to quiet* WILLY.): Hey, Pop, come on now...

WILLY (*continuing over* HAPPY's *line.*): They laugh at me, heh? Go to Filene's, go to the Hub, go to Slattery's, Boston. Call out the name Willy Loman and see what happens! Big shot!

BIFF: All right, Pop.

WILLY: Big!   700

BIFF: All right!

WILLY: Why do you always insult me?

BIFF: I didn't say a word. (*To* LINDA.) Did I say a word?

LINDA: He didn't say anything, Willy.

WILLY (*going to the doorway of the living room.*): All right, good night, good   705
night.

LINDA: Willy, dear, he just decided...

WILLY (*to* BIFF.): If you get tired hanging around tomorrow, paint the ceiling I put up in the living room.

BIFF: I'm leaving early tomorrow.

HAPPY: He's going to see Bill Oliver, Pop.

WILLY (*interestedly.*): Oliver? For what?   710

BIFF (*with reserve, but trying, trying.*): He always said he'd stake me. I'd like to go into business, so maybe I can take him up on it.

LINDA: Isn't that wonderful?

WILLY: Don't interrupt. What's wonderful about it? There's fifty men in the City of New York who'd stake him. (*To* BIFF.) Sporting goods?

BIFF: I guess so. I know something about it and—

WILLY: He knows something about it! You know sporting goods better than   715
Spalding, for God's sake! How much is he giving you?

BIFF: I don't know, I didn't even see him yet, but—

WILLY: Then what're you talkin' about?

BIFF (*getting angry.*): Well, all I said was I'm gonna see him, that's all!

WILLY (*turning away.*): Ah, you're counting your chickens again.

BIFF (*starting left for the stairs.*): Oh, Jesus, I'm going to sleep!   720

WILLY (*calling after him.*): Don't curse in this house!

BIFF (*turning.*): Since when did you get so clean!

HAPPY (*trying to stop them.*): Wait a...

WILLY: Don't use that language to me! I won't have it!

HAPPY (*grabbing* BIFF, *shouts.*): Wait a minute! I got an idea. I got a feasible   725
idea. Come here, BIFF, let's talk this over now, let's talk some sense
here. When I was down in Florida last time, I thought of a great idea to

sell sporting goods. It just came back to me. You and I, Biff—we have a line, the Loman Line. We train a couple of weeks, and put on a couple of exhibitions, see?

WILLY: That's an idea!

HAPPY: Wait! We form two basketball teams, see? Two water-polo teams. We play each other. It's a million dollars' worth of publicity. Two brothers, see? The Loman Brothers. Displays in the Royal Palms—all the hotels. And banners over the ring and the basketball court: "Loman Brothers." Baby, we could sell sporting goods!

WILLY: That is a one-million-dollar idea.

LINDA: Marvelous!

BIFF: I'm in great shape as far as that's concerned.   730

HAPPY: And the beauty of it is, Biff, it wouldn't be like a business. We'd be out playin' ball again...

BIFF *(enthused.)*: Yeah, that's...

WILLY: Million-dollar...

HAPPY: And you wouldn't get fed up with it, Biff. It'd be the family again. There'd be the old honor, and comradeship, and if you wanted to go off for a swim or somethin'—well, you'd do it! Without some smart cooky gettin' up ahead of you!

WILLY: Lick the world! You guys together could absolutely lick the civilized   735
world.

BIFF: I'll see Oliver tomorrow. Hap, if we could work that out...

LINDA: Maybe things are beginning to—

WILLY *(wildly enthused, to* LINDA.*)*: Stop interrupting! *(To* BIFF.*)* But don't wear sport jacket and slacks when you see Oliver.

BIFF: No, I'll—

WILLY: A business suit, and talk as little as possible, and don't crack any jokes.   740

BIFF: He did like me. Always liked me.

LINDA: He loved you!

WILLY *(to* LINDA.*)*: Will you stop! *(To* BIFF.*)* Walk in very serious. You are not applying for a boy's job. Money is to pass. Be quiet, fine, and serious. Everybody likes a kidder, but nobody lends him money.

HAPPY: I'll try to get some myself, Biff. I'm sure I can.

WILLY: I can see great things for you, kids, I think your troubles are over.   745
But remember, start big and you'll end big. Ask for fifteen. How much you gonna ask for?

BIFF: Gee, I don't know—

WILLY: And don't say "Gee." "Gee" is a boy's word. A man walking in for fifteen thousand dollars does not say "Gee!"

BIFF: Ten, I think, would be top though.

WILLY: Don't be so modest. You always started too low. Walk in with a big laugh. Don't look worried. Start off with a couple of your good stories to lighten things up. It's not what you say, it's how you say it—because personality always wins the day.

LINDA: Oliver always thought the highest of him—   750

WILLY: Will you let me talk?

BIFF: Don't yell at her, Pop, will ya?

WILLY (*angrily.*): I was talking, wasn't I!

BIFF: I don't like you yelling at her all the time, and I'm tellin' you, that's all.

WILLY: What're you, takin' over this house?   755

LINDA: Willy—

WILLY (*turning on her.*): Don't take his side all the time, goddammit!

BIFF (*furiously.*): Stop yelling at her!

WILLY (*suddenly pulling on his cheek, beaten down, guilt ridden.*): Give my best to Bill Oliver—he may remember me. (*He exits through the living room doorway.*)

LINDA (*her voice subdued.*): What'd you have to start that for? (BIFF *turns*   760
away.) You see how sweet he was as soon as you talked hopefully? (*She goes over to* BIFF.) Come up and say good night to him. Don't let him go to bed that way.

HAPPY: Come on, Biff, let's buck him up.

LINDA: Please, dear. Just say good night. It takes so little to make him happy. Come. (*She goes through the living room doorway, calling upstairs from within the living room.*) Your pajamas are hanging in the bathroom. Willy!

HAPPY (*looking toward where* LINDA *went out.*): What a woman! They broke the mold when they made her. You know that, Biff?

BIFF: He's off salary. My God, working on commission!

HAPPY: Well, let's face it he's no hot-shot selling man. Except that some-   765
times, you have to admit, he's a sweet personality.

BIFF (*deciding.*): Lend me ten bucks, will ya? I want to buy some new ties.

HAPPY: I'll take you to a place I know. Beautiful stuff. Wear one of my striped shirts tomorrow.

BIFF: She got gray. Mom got awful old. Gee, I'm gonna go in to Oliver to-morrow and knock him for a—

HAPPY: Come on up. Tell that to Dad. Let's give him a whirl. Come on.

BIFF (*steamed up.*): You know, with ten thousand bucks, boy!   770

HAPPY (*as they go into the living room.*): That's the talk, Biff, that's the first time I've heard the old confidence out of you! (*From within the living room, fading off.*) You're gonna live with me, kid, and any babe you want you just say the word...

(*The last lines are hardly heard. They are mounting the stairs to their parents' bedroom.*)

LINDA (*entering her bedroom and addressing* WILLY, *who is in the bathroom. She is straightening the bed for him.*): Can you do anything about the shower? It drips.

WILLY (*from the bathroom.*): All of a sudden everything falls to pieces! God-dam plumbing, oughta be sued, those people. I hardly finished putting it in and the thing…

(*His words rumble off.*)

LINDA: I'm just wondering if Oliver will remember him. You think he might?

WILLY (*coming out of the bathroom in his pajamas.*): Remember him? What's   775
the matter with you, you crazy? If he'd've stayed with Oliver he'd be on top by now! Wait'll Oliver gets a look at him. You don't know the average caliber any more. The average young man today—(*he is getting into bed.*)—is got a caliber of zero. Greatest thing in the world for him was to bum around.

(BIFF *and* HAPPY *enter the bedroom. Slight pause.*)

WILLY (*stops short, looking at* BIFF.): Glad to hear it, boy.

HAPPY: He wanted to say good night to you, sport.

WILLY (*to* BIFF.): Yeah. Knock him dead, boy. What'd you want to tell me?

BIFF: Just take it easy, Pop. Good night. (*He turns to go.*)

WILLY (*unable to resist.*): And if anything falls off the desk while you're talk-   780
ing to him—like a package or something—don't you pick it up. They have office boys for that.

LINDA: I'll make a big breakfast—

WILLY: Will you let me finish? (*To* BIFF.) Tell him you were in the business in the West. Not farm work.

BIFF: All right, Dad.

LINDA: I think everything—

WILLY (*going right through her speech.*): And don't undersell yourself. No less   785
than fifteen thousand dollars.

BIFF (*unable to bear him.*): Okay. Good night, Mom. (*He starts moving.*)

WILLY: Because you got a greatness in you, Biff, remember that. You got all kinds a greatness…(*He lies back, exhausted.* BIFF *walks out.*)

LINDA (*calling after* BIFF.): Sleep well, darling!

HAPPY: I'm gonna get married, Mom. I wanted to tell you.

LINDA: Go to sleep, dear.   790

HAPPY (*going.*): I just wanted to tell you.

WILLY: Keep up the good work. (HAPPY *exits.*) God…remember that Ebbets Field game? The championship of the city?

LINDA: Just rest. Should I sing to you?

WILLY: Yeah. Sing to me. (LINDA *hums a soft lullaby.*) When that team came out—he was the tallest, remember?

LINDA: Oh, yes. And in gold.   795

(BIFF *enters the darkened kitchen, takes a cigarette, and leaves the house. He comes downstage into a golden pool of light. He smokes, staring at the night.*)

WILLY: Like a young god. Hercules—something like that. And the sun, the sun all around him. Remember how he waved to me? Right up from the field, with the representatives of three colleges standing by? And the buyers I brought, and the cheers when he came out—Loman, Loman, Loman! God Almighty, he'll be great yet. A star like that, magnificent, can never really fade away!

(*The light on* WILLY *is fading. The gas heater begins to glow through the kitchen wall, near the stairs, a blue flame beneath red coils.*)

LINDA (*timidly.*): Willy, dear, what has he got against you?

WILLY: I'm so tired. Don't talk any more.

(BIFF *slowly returns to the kitchen. He stops, stares toward the heater.*)

LINDA: Will you ask Howard to let you work in New York?

WILLY: First thing in the morning. Everything'll be all right.   800

(BIFF *reaches behind the heater and draws out a length of rubber tubing. He is horrified and turns his head toward* WILLY's *room, still dimly lit, from which the strains of* LINDA's *desperate but monotonous humming rise.*)

WILLY (*staring through the window into the moonlight.*): Gee, look at the moon moving between the buildings!

(BIFF *wraps the tubing around his hand and quickly goes up the stairs.*)

CURTAIN.

ACT II

Music is heard, gay and bright. The curtain rises as the music fades away. WILLY, *in shirt sleeves, is sitting at the kitchen table, sipping coffee, his hat in his lap.* LINDA *is filling his cup when she can.*

WILLY: Wonderful coffee. Meal in itself.

LINDA: Can I make you some eggs?

WILLY: No. Take a breath.

LINDA: You look so rested, dear.

WILLY: I slept like a dead one. First time in months. Imagine, sleeping till   5
ten on a Tuesday morning. Boys left nice and early, heh?

LINDA: They were out of here by eight o'clock.

WILLY: Good work!

LINDA: It was so thrilling to see them leaving together. I can't get over the shaving lotion in this house.

WILLY (*smiling.*): Mmm—

LINDA: Biff was very changed this morning. His whole attitude seemed to   10
be hopeful. He couldn't wait to get downtown to see Oliver.

WILLY: He's heading for a change. There's no question, there simply are certain men that take longer to get—solidified. How did he dress?

LINDA: His blue suit. He's so handsome in that suit. He could be a—anything in that suit!

(WILLY *gets up from the table.* LINDA *holds his jacket for him.*)

WILLY: There's no question, no question at all. Gee, on the way home tonight I'd like to buy some seeds.

LINDA (*laughing.*): That'd be wonderful. But not enough sun gets back
   there. Nothing'll grow any more.

WILLY: You wait, kid, before it's all over we're gonna get a little place out in   15
   the country, and I'll raise some vegetables, a couple of chickens…

LINDA: You'll do it yet, dear.

(WILLY *walks out of his jacket.* LINDA *follows him.*)

WILLY: And they'll get married, and come for a weekend. I'd build a little
   guest house. 'Cause I got so many fine tools, all I'd need would be a little lumber and some peace of mind.

LINDA (*joyfully.*): I sewed the lining…

WILLY: I could build two guest houses, so they'd both come. Did he decide
   how much he's going to ask Oliver for?

LINDA (*getting him into the jacket.*): He didn't mention it, but I imagine ten   20
   or fifteen thousand. You going to talk to Howard today?

WILLY: Yeah. I'll put it to him straight and simple. He'll just have to take
   me off the road.

LINDA: And Willy, don't forget to ask for a little advance, because we've
   got the insurance premium. It's the grace period now.

WILLY: That's a hundred…?

LINDA: A hundred and eight, sixty-eight. Because we're a little short again.

WILLY: Why are we short?   25

LINDA: Well, you had the motor job on the car…

WILLY: That goddam Studebaker!

LINDA: And you got one more payment on the refrigerator…

WILLY: But it just broke again!

LINDA: Well, it's old, dear.   30

WILLY: I told you we should've bought a well-advertised machine. Charley
   bought a General Electric and it's twenty years old and it's still good,
   that son-of-a-bitch.

LINDA: But, Willy—

WILLY: Whoever heard of a Hastings refrigerator? Once in my life I would like
   to own something outright before it's broken! I'm always in a race with
   the junkyard! I just finished paying for the car and it's on its last legs. The
   refrigerator consumes belts like a goddam maniac. They time those things.
   They time them so when you finally paid for them, they're used up.

LINDA (*buttoning up his jacket as he unbuttons it.*): All told, about two hundred dollars would carry us, dear. But that includes the last payment on
   the mortgage. After this payment, Willy, the house belongs to us.

WILLY: It's twenty-five years!   35

LINDA: Biff was nine years old when we bought it.

WILLY: Well, that's a great thing. To weather a twenty-five year mortgage is—

LINDA: It's an accomplishment.

WILLY: All the cement, the lumber, the reconstruction I put in this house!
   There ain't a crack to be found in it any more.

LINDA: Well, it served its purpose. 40

WILLY: What purpose? Some stranger'll come along, move in, and that's that. If only Biff would take this house, and raise a family... (*He starts to go.*) Good-by, I'm late.

LINDA (*suddenly remembering.*): Oh, I forgot! You're supposed to meet them for dinner.

WILLY: Me?

LINDA: At Frank's Chop House on Forty-eighth near Sixth Avenue.

WILLY: Is that so! How about you? 45

LINDA: No, just the three of you. They're gonna blow you to a big meal!

WILLY: Don't say! Who thought of that?

LINDA: Biff came to me this morning, Willy, and he said, "Tell Dad, we want to blow him to a big meal." Be there six o'clock. You and your two boys are going to have dinner.

WILLY: Gee whiz! That's really somethin'. I'm gonna knock Howard for a loop, kid. I'll get an advance, and I'll come home with a New York job. Goddammit, now I'm gonna do it!

LINDA: Oh, that's the spirit, Willy! 50

WILLY: I will never get behind a wheel the rest of my life!

LINDA: It's changing, Willy, I can feel it changing!

WILLY: Beyond a question. G'by, I'm late. (*He starts to go again.*)

LINDA (*calling after him as she runs to the kitchen table for a handkerchief.*): You got your glasses?

WILLY (*feels for them, then comes back in.*): Yeah, yeah, got my glasses. 55

LINDA (*giving him the handkerchief.*): And a handkerchief.

WILLY: Yeah, handkerchief.

LINDA: And your saccharine?

WILLY: Yeah, my saccharine.

LINDA: Be careful on the subway stairs. 60

(*She kisses him, and a silk stocking is seen hanging from her hand.* WILLY *notices it.*)

WILLY: Will you stop mending stockings? At least while I'm in the house. It gets me nervous. I can't tell you. Please.

(LINDA *hides the stocking in her hand as she follows* WILLY *across the forestage in front of the house.*)

LINDA: Remember, Frank's Chop House.

WILLY (*passing the apron.*): Maybe beets would grow out there.

LINDA (*laughing.*): But you tried so many times.

WILLY: Yeah. Well, don't work hard today. (*He disappears around the right corner of the house.*) 65

LINDA: Be careful!

(*As* WILLY *vanishes,* LINDA *waves to him. Suddenly the phone rings. She runs across the stage and into the kitchen and lifts it.*)

LINDA: Hello? Oh, Biff! I'm so glad you called, I just... Yes, sure, I just told him. Yes, he'll be there for dinner at six o'clock, I didn't forget. Listen,

I was just dying to tell you. You know that little rubber pipe I told you about? That he connected to the gas heater? I finally decided to go down the cellar this morning and take it away and destroy it. But it's gone! Imagine? He took it away himself, it isn't there! (*She listens.*) When? Oh, then you took it. Oh—nothing, it's just that I'd hoped he'd taken it away himself. Oh, I'm not worried, darling, because this morning he left in such high spirits, it was like the old days! I'm not afraid any more. Did Mr. Oliver see you?... Well, you wait there then. And make a nice impression on him, darling. Just don't perspire too much before you see him. And have a nice time with Dad. He may have big news too!... That's right, a New York job. And be sweet to him tonight, dear. Be loving to him. Because he's only a little boat looking for a harbor. (*She is trembling with sorrow and joy.*) Oh, that's wonderful, Biff, you'll save his life. Thanks, darling. Just put your arm around him when he comes into the restaurant. Give him a smile. That's the boy... Good-by, dear.... You got your comb?... That's fine. Good-by, Biff dear.

(*In the middle of her speech,* HOWARD WAGNER, *thirty-six, wheels in a small typewriter table on which is a wire-recording machine and proceeds to plug it in. This is on the left forestage. Light slowly fades on* LINDA *as it rises on* HOWARD. HOWARD *is intent on threading the machine and only glances over his shoulder as* WILLY *appears.*)

WILLY: Pst! Pst!

HOWARD: Hello, Willy, come in.

WILLY: Like to have a little talk with you, Howard.   70

HOWARD: Sorry to keep you waiting. I'll be with you in a minute.

WILLY: What's that, Howard?

HOWARD: Didn't you ever see one of these? Wire recorder.

WILLY: Oh. Can we talk a minute?

HOWARD: Records things. Just got delivery yesterday. Been driving me crazy,   75
   the most terrific machine I ever saw in my life. I was up all night with it.

WILLY: What do you do with it?

HOWARD: I bought it for dictation, but you can do anything with it. Listen
   to this. I had it home last night. Listen to what I picked up. The first
   one is my daughter. Get this. (*He flicks the switch and "Roll out the Barrel" is heard being whistled.*) Listen to that kid whistle.

WILLY: That is lifelike, isn't it?

HOWARD: Seven years old. Get that tone.

WILLY: Ts, ts. Like to ask a little favor if you...   80

(*The whistling breaks off, and the voice of* HOWARD's DAUGHTER *is heard.*)

HIS DAUGHTER: "Now you, Daddy."

HOWARD: She's crazy for me! (*Again the same song is whistled.*) That's me!
   Ha! (*He winks.*)

WILLY: You're very good!

(The whistling breaks off again. The machine runs silent for a moment.)

HOWARD: Sh! Get this now, this is my son.

HIS SON: "The capital of Alabama is Montgomery; the capital of Arizona is [85]
Phoenix; the capital of Arkansas is Little Rock; the capital of California
is Sacramento…"

(And on, and on.)

HOWARD *(holding up five fingers.)*: Five years old, Willy!

WILLY: He'll make an announcer some day!

HIS SON *(continuing.)*: "The capital…"

HOWARD: Get that—alphabetical order! *(The machine breaks off suddenly.)*
Wait a minute. The maid kicked the plug out.

WILLY: It certainly is a— [90]

HOWARD: Sh, for God's sake!

HIS SON: "It's nine o'clock, Bulova watch time. So I have to go to sleep."

WILLY: That really is—

HOWARD: Wait a minute! The next is my wife.

(They wait.)

HOWARD'S VOICE: "Go on, say something." *(Pause.)* "Well, you gonna talk?" [95]

HIS WIFE: "I can't think of anything."

HOWARD'S VOICE: "Well, talk—it's turning."

HIS WIFE *(shyly, beaten.)*: "Hello." *(Silence.)* "Oh, Howard, I can't talk into
this…"

HOWARD *(snapping the machine off.)*: That was my wife.

WILLY: That is a wonderful machine. Can we— [10]

HOWARD: I tell you, Willy, I'm gonna take my camera, and my bandsaw,
and all my hobbies, and out they go. This is the most fascinating relaxa-
tion I ever found.

WILLY: I think I'll get one myself.

HOWARD: Sure, they're only a hundred and a half. You can't do without
it. Supposing you wanna hear Jack Benny, see? But you can't be at
home at that hour. So you tell the maid to turn the radio on when
Jack Benny comes on, and this automatically goes on with the
radio…

WILLY: And when you come home you…

HOWARD: You can come home twelve o'clock, one o'clock, any time you [10]
like, and you get yourself a Coke and sit yourself down, throw the
switch, and there's Jack Benny's program in the middle of the
night!

WILLY: I'm definitely going to get one. Because lots of time I'm on the road,
and I think to myself, what I must be missing on the radio!

HOWARD: Don't you have a radio in the car?

WILLY: Well, yeah, but who ever thinks of turning it on?

HOWARD: Say, aren't you supposed to be in Boston?

WILLY: That's what I want to talk to you about, Howard. You got a minute?   110
(*He draws a chair in from the wing.*)

HOWARD: What happened? What're you doing here?

WILLY: Well…

HOWARD: You didn't crack up again, did you?

WILLY: Oh, no. No…

HOWARD: Geez, you had me worried there for a minute. What's the trouble?   115

WILLY: Well, to tell you the truth, Howard, I've come to the decision that
    I'd rather not travel any more.

HOWARD: Not travel! Well, what'll you do?

WILLY: Remember, Christmas time, when you had the party here? You said
    you'd try to think of some spot for me here in town.

HOWARD: With us?

WILLY: Well, sure.   120

HOWARD: Oh, yeah, yeah. I remember. Well, I couldn't think of anything
    for you, Willy.

WILLY: I tell ya, Howard. The kids are all grown up, y'know. I don't need
    much any more. If I could take home—well, sixty-five dollars a week, I
    could swing it.

HOWARD: Yeah, but Willy, see I—

WILLY: I tell ya why, Howard. Speaking frankly and between the two of us,
    y'know—I'm just a little tired.

HOWARD: Oh, I could understand that, Willy. But you're a road man, Willy,   125
    and we do a road business. We've only got a half-dozen salesmen on the
    floor here.

WILLY: God knows, Howard, I never asked a favor of any man. But I was
    with the firm when your father used to carry you in here in his arms.

HOWARD: I know that, Willy, but—

WILLY: Your father came to me the day you were born and asked me what I
    thought of the name of Howard, may he rest in peace.

HOWARD: I appreciate that, Willy, but there just is no spot here for you. If I
    had a spot I'd slam you right in, but I just don't have a single, solitary spot.
(*He looks for his lighter.* WILLY *has picked it up and gives it to him. Pause.*)

WILLY (*with increasing anger.*): Howard, all I need to set my table is fifty dol-   130
    lars a week.

HOWARD: But where am I going to put you, kid?

WILLY: Look, it isn't a question of whether I can sell merchandise, is it?

HOWARD: No, but it's a business, kid, and everybody's gotta pull his own
    weight.

WILLY (*desperately.*): Just let me tell you a story, Howard—

HOWARD: 'Cause you gotta admit, business is business.   135

WILLY (*angrily.*): Business is definitely business, but just listen for a minute.
    You don't understand this. When I was a boy—eighteen, nineteen—I

was already on the road. And there was a question in my mind as to whether selling had a future for me. Because in those days I had a yearning to go to Alaska. See, there were three gold strikes in one month in Alaska, and I felt like going out. Just for the ride, you might say.

HOWARD (*barely interested.*): Don't say.

WILLY: Oh, yeah, my father lived many years in Alaska. He was an adventurous man. We've got quite a little streak of self-reliance in our family. I thought I'd go out with my older brother and try to locate him, and maybe settle in the North with the old man. And I was almost decided to go, when I met a salesman in the Parker House. His name was Dave Singleman. And he was eighty-four years old, and he'd drummed merchandise in thirty-one states. And old Dave, he'd go up to his room, y'understand, put on his green velvet slippers—I'll never forget—and pick up his phone and call the buyers, and without ever leaving his room, at the age of eighty-four, he made his living. And when I saw that, I realized that selling was the greatest career a man could want. 'Cause what could be more satisfying than to be able to go, at the age of eighty-four, into twenty or thirty different cities, and pick up a phone, and be remembered and loved and helped by so many different people? Do you know? when he died—and by the way he died the death of a salesman, in his green velvet slippers in the smoker of the New York, New Haven and Hartford, going into Boston—when he died, hundreds of salesmen and buyers were at his funeral. Things were sad on a lotta trains for months after that. (*He stands up.* HOWARD *has not looked at him.*) In those days there was personality in it, Howard. There was respect, and comradeship, and gratitude in it. Today, it's all cut and dried, and there's no chance for bringing friendship to bear—or personality. You see what I mean? They don't know me any more.

HOWARD (*moving away, to the right.*): That's just the thing, Willy.

WILLY: If I had forty dollars a week—that's all I'd need. Forty dollars, Howard.

HOWARD: Kid, I can't take blood from a stone, I—

WILLY (*desperation is on him now.*): Howard, the year Al Smith was nominated, your father came to me and—

HOWARD (*starting to go off.*): I've got to see some people, kid.

WILLY (*stopping him.*): I'm talking about your father! There were promises made across this desk! You mustn't tell me you've got people to see—I put thirty-four years into this firm, Howard, and now I can't pay my insurance! You can't eat the orange and throw the peel away—a man is not a piece of fruit! (*After a pause.*) Now pay attention. Your father—in 1928 I had a big year. I averaged a hundred and seventy dollars a week in commissions.

HOWARD (*impatiently.*): Now, Willy, you never averaged—   145

WILLY (*banging his hand on the desk.*): I averaged a hundred and seventy dollars a week in the year of 1928! And your father came to me—or rather, I was in the office here—it was right over this desk—and he put his hand on my shoulder—

HOWARD (*getting up.*): You'll have to excuse me, Willy, I gotta see some people. Pull yourself together. (*Going out.*) I'll be back in a little while.

(*On* HOWARD's *exit, the light on his chair grows very bright and strange.*)

WILLY : Pull myself together! What the hell did I say to him? My God, I was yelling at him! How could I! (WILLY *breaks off, staring at the light, which occupies the chair, animating it. He approaches this chair, standing across the desk from it.*) Frank, Frank, don't you remember what you told me that time? How you put your hand on my shoulder, and Frank... (*He leans on the desk and as he speaks the dead man's name he accidentally switches on the recorder, and instantly—*)

HOWARD's SON: "...of New York is Albany. The capital of Ohio is Cincinnati, the capital of Rhode Island is..." (*The recitation continues.*)

WILLY (*leaping away with fright, shouting.*): Ha! Howard! Howard! Howard!   150

HOWARD (*rushing in.*): What happened?

WILLY (*pointing at the machine, which continues nasally, childishly, with the capital cities.*): Shut it off! Shut it off!

HOWARD (*pulling the plug out.*): Look, Willy...

WILLY (*pressing his hands to his eyes.*): I gotta get myself some coffee. I'll get some coffee...

(WILLY *starts to walk out.* HOWARD *stops him.*)

HOWARD (*rolling up the cord.*): Willy, look...   155

WILLY: I'll go to Boston.

HOWARD: Willy, you can't go to Boston for us.

WILLY: Why can't I go?

HOWARD: I don't want you to represent us. I've been meaning to tell you for a long time now.

WILLY: Howard, are you firing me?   160

HOWARD: I think you need a good long rest, Willy.

WILLY: Howard—

HOWARD: And when you feel better, come back, and we'll see if we can work something out.

WILLY: But I gotta earn money, Howard. I'm in no position—

HOWARD: Where are your sons? Why don't your sons give you a hand?   165

WILLY: They're working on a very big deal.

HOWARD: This is no time for false pride, Willy. You go to your sons and tell them that you're tired. You've got two great boys, haven't you?

WILLY: Oh, no question, no question, but in the meantime...

HOWARD: Then that's that, heh?

WILLY: All right, I'll go to Boston tomorrow.   17

HOWARD: No, no.

WILLY: I can't throw myself on my sons. I'm not a cripple!

HOWARD: Look, kid, I'm busy this morning.

WILLY (*grasping* HOWARD's *arm.*): Howard, you've got to let me go to Boston!

HOWARD (*hard, keeping himself under control.*): I've got a line of people to see   17
    this morning. Sit down, take five minutes, and pull yourself together,
    and then go home, will ya? I need the office, Willy. (*He starts to go,
    turns, remembering the recorder, starts to push off the table holding the re-
    corder.*) Oh, yeah. Whenever you can this week, stop by and drop off
    the samples. You'll feel better, Willy, and then come back and we'll
    talk. Pull yourself together, kid, there's people outside.

(HOWARD *exits, pushing the table off left.* WILLY *stares into space, exhausted.*
    Now the music is heard—BEN's *music*—*first distantly, then closer, closer.*
    As WILLY *speaks,* BEN *enters from the right. He carries valise and umbrella.*)

WILLY: Oh, Ben, how did you do it? What is the answer? Did you wind up
    the Alaska deal already?

BEN: Doesn't take much time if you know what you're doing. Just a short
    business trip. Boarding ship in an hour. Wanted to say good-by.

WILLY: Ben, I've got to talk to you.

BEN (*glancing at his watch.*): Haven't the time, William.

WILLY (*crossing the apron to* BEN.): Ben, nothing's working out. I don't know   18
    what to do.

BEN: Now, look here, William. I've bought timberland in Alaska and I
    need a man to look after things for me.

WILLY: God, timberland! Me and my boys in those grand outdoors!

BEN: You've a new continent at your doorstep, William. Get out of these
    cities, they're full of talk and time payments and courts of law. Screw
    on your fists and you can fight for a fortune up there.

WILLY: Yes, yes! Linda! Linda!

(LINDA *enters as of old, with the wash.*)

LINDA: Oh, you're back?   18

BEN: I haven't much time.

WILLY: No, wait! Linda, he's got a proposition for me in Alaska.

LINDA: But you've got— (*To* BEN.) He's got a beautiful job here.

WILLY: But in Alaska, kid, I could—

LINDA: You're doing well enough, Willy!   19

BEN (*to* LINDA.): Enough for what, my dear?

LINDA (*frightened of* BEN *and angry at him.*): Don't say those things to him!
    Enough to be happy right here, right now. (*To* WILLY, *while* BEN *laughs.*)
    Why must everybody conquer the world? You're well liked, and the
    boys love you, and someday—(*to* BEN)—why, old man Wagner told
    him just the other day that if he keeps it up he'll be a member of the
    firm, didn't he, Willy?

WILLY: Sure, sure. I am building something with this firm, Ben, and if a man is building something he must be on the right track, mustn't he?

BEN: What are you building? Lay your hand on it. Where is it?

WILLY (*hesitantly.*): That's true, Linda, there's nothing.   195

LINDA: Why? (*To* BEN.) There's a man eighty-four years old—

WILLY: That's right, Ben, that's right. When I look at that man I say, what is there to worry about?

BEN: Bah!

WILLY: It's true, Ben. All he has to do is go into any city, pick up the phone, and he's making his living and you know why?

BEN (*picking up his valise.*): I've got to go.   200

WILLY (*holding* BEN *back.*): Look at this boy!

(BIFF, *in his high school sweater, enters carrying suitcase.* HAPPY *carries* BIFF's *shoulder guards, gold helmet, and football pants.*)

WILLY: Without a penny to his name, three great universities are begging for him, and from there the sky's the limit, because it's not what you do, Ben. It's who you know and the smile on your face! It's contacts, Ben, contacts! The whole wealth of Alaska passes over the lunch table at the Commodore Hotel, and that's the wonder, the wonder of this country, that a man can end with diamonds here on the basis of being liked! (*He turns to* BIFF.) And that's why when you get out on that field today it's important. Because thousands of people will be rooting for you and loving you. (*To* BEN, *who has again begun to leave.*) And Ben! when he walks into a business office his name will sound out like a bell and all the doors will open to him! I've seen it, Ben, I've seen it a thousand times! You can't feel it with your hand like timber, but it's there!

BEN: Good-by, William.

WILLY: Ben, am I right? Don't you think I'm right? I value your advice.

BEN: There's a new continent at your doorstep, William. You could walk   205
out rich. Rich. (*He is gone.*)

WILLY: We'll do it here, Ben! You hear me? We're gonna do it here!

(*Young* BERNARD *rushes in. The gay music of the boys is heard.*)

BERNARD: Oh, gee, I was afraid you left already!

WILLY: Why? What time is it?

BERNARD: It's half-past one!

WILLY: Well, come on, everybody! Ebbets Field° next stop! Where's the   210
pennants?

(*He rushes through the wall-line of the kitchen and out into the living room.*)

LINDA (*to* BIFF.): Did you pack fresh underwear?

BIFF (*who has been limbering up.*): I want to go!

°**Ebbets Field:** The home park of the Brooklyn Dodgers.

BERNARD: Biff, I'm carrying your helmet, ain't I?

HAPPY: No, I'm carrying the helmet.

BERNARD: Oh, Biff, you promised me.   21?

HAPPY: I'm carrying the helmet.

BERNARD: How am I going to get in the locker room?

LINDA: Let him carry the shoulder guards. (*She puts her coat and hat on in the kitchen.*)

BERNARD: Can I, Biff? 'Cause I told everybody I'm going to be in the locker room.

HAPPY: In Ebbets Field it's the clubhouse.   22(

BERNARD: I meant the clubhouse. Biff!

HAPPY: Biff!

BIFF (*grandly, after a slight pause.*): Let him carry the shoulder guards.

HAPPY (*as he gives* BERNARD *the shoulder guards.*): Stay close to us now.

(WILLY *rushes in with the pennants.*)

WILLY (*handing them out.*): Everybody wave when Biff comes out on the   22?
field. (HAPPY *and* BERNARD *run off.*) You set now, boy?

(*The music has died away.*)

BIFF: Ready to go, Pop. Every muscle is ready.

WILLY (*at the edge of the apron.*): You realize what this means?

BIFF: That's right, Pop.

WILLY (*feeling* BIFF'*s muscles.*): You're comin' home this afternoon captain of
the All-Scholastic Championship Team of the City of New York.

BIFF: I got it, Pop. And remember, pal, when I take off my helmet, that   23(
touchdown is for you.

WILLY: Let's go! (*He is starting out, with his arm around* BIFF, *when* CHARLEY
enters, as of old, in knickers.) I got no room for you, Charley.

CHARLEY: Room? For what?

WILLY: In the car.

CHARLEY: You goin' for a ride? I wanted to shoot some casino.

WILLY (*furiously.*): Casino! (*Incredulously.*) Don't you realize what today is?   23?

LINDA: Oh, he knows, Willy. He's just kidding you.

WILLY: That's nothing to kid about!

CHARLEY: No, Linda, what's goin' on?

LINDA: He's playing in Ebbets Field.

CHARLEY: Baseball in this weather?   24(

WILLY: Don't talk to him. Come on, come on! (*He is pushing them out.*)

CHARLEY: Wait a minute, didn't you hear the news?

WILLY: What?

CHARLEY: Don't you listen to the radio? Ebbets Field just blew up.

WILLY: You go to hell! (CHARLEY *laughs. Pushing them out.*) Come on, come   245
on! We're late.

CHARLEY (*as they go.*): Knock a homer, Biff, knock a homer!

WILLY (*the last to leave, turning to* CHARLEY.): I don't think that was funny, Charley. This is the greatest day of his life.

CHARLEY: Willy, when are you going to grow up?

WILLY: Yeah, heh? When this game is over, Charley, you'll be laughing out of the other side of your face. They'll be calling him another Red Grange° Twenty-five thousand a year.

CHARLEY (*kidding.*): Is that so?   250

WILLY: Yeah, that's so.

CHARLEY: Well, then, I'm sorry, Willy. But tell me something.

WILLY: What?

CHARLEY: Who is Red Grange?

WILLY: Put up your hands. Goddam you, put up your hands!   255

(CHARLEY, *chuckling, shakes his head and walks away, around the left corner of the stage.* WILLY *follows him. The music rises to a mocking frenzy.*)

WILLY: Who the hell do you think you are, better than everybody else? You don't know everything, you big, ignorant, stupid...Put up your hands!

(*Light rises, on the right side of the forestage, on a small table in the reception room of* CHARLEY's *office. Traffic sounds are heard.* BERNARD, *now mature, sits whistling to himself. A pair of tennis rackets and an overnight bag are on the floor beside him.*)

WILLY (*offstage.*): What are you walking away for? Don't walk away! If you're going to say something say it to my face! I know you laugh at me behind my back. You'll laugh out of the other side of your goddam face after this game. Touchdown! Touchdown! Eighty thousand people! Touchdown! Right between the goal posts.

(BERNARD *is a quiet, earnest, but self-assured young man.* WILLY's *voice is coming from right upstage now.* BERNARD *lowers his feet off the table and listens.* JENNY, *his father's secretary, enters.*)

JENNY (*distressed.*): Say, Bernard, will you go out in the hall?

BERNARD: What is that noise? Who is it?

JENNY: Mr. Loman. He just got off the elevator.   260

BERNARD (*getting up.*): Who's he arguing with?

JENNY: Nobody. There's nobody with him. I can't deal with him any more, and your father gets all upset everytime he comes. I've got a lot of typing to do, and your father's waiting to sign it. Will you see him?

WILLY (*entering.*): Touchdown! Touch—(*He sees* JENNY.) Jenny, Jenny, good to see you. How're ya? Workin'? Or still honest?

°**Red Grange:** Harold Edward ("Red") Grange (1903–1991)—American football player. A running back for the New York Yankees football team and the Chicago Bears, Grange was elected to the Football Hall of Fame in 1963.

JENNY: Fine. How've you been feeling?

WILLY: Not much any more, Jenny. Ha, ha! *(He is surprised to see the rackets.)* 265

BERNARD: Hello, Uncle Willy.

WILLY *(almost shocked.):* Bernard! Well, look who's here! *(He comes quickly, guiltily, to Bernard and warmly shakes his hand.)*

BERNARD: How are you? Good to see you.

WILLY: What are you doing here?

BERNARD: Oh, just stopped by to see Pop. Get off my feet till my train leaves. I'm going to Washington in a few minutes. 270

WILLY: Is he in?

BERNARD: Yes, he's in his office with the accountant. Sit down.

WILLY *(sitting down.):* What're you going to do in Washington?

BERNARD: Oh, just a case I've got there, Willy.

WILLY: That so? *(indicating the rackets.)* You going to play tennis there? 275

BERNARD: I'm staying with a friend who's got a court.

WILLY: Don't say. His own tennis court. Must be fine people, I bet.

BERNARD: They are, very nice. Dad tells me Biff's in town.

WILLY *(with a big smile.):* Yeah, Biff's in. Working on a very big deal, Bernard.

BERNARD: What's Biff doing? 280

WILLY: Well, he's been doing very big things in the West. But he decided to establish himself here. Very big. We're having dinner. Did I hear your wife had a boy?

BERNARD: That's right. Our second.

WILLY: Two boys! What do you know!

BERNARD: What kind of a deal has Biff got?

WILLY: Well, Bill Oliver—very big sporting-goods man—he wants Biff very badly. Called him in from the West. Long distance, carte blanche, special deliveries. Your friends have their own private tennis court? 285

BERNARD: You still with the old firm, Willy?

WILLY *(after a pause.):* I'm—I'm overjoyed to see how you made the grade, Bernard, overjoyed. It's an encouraging thing to see a young man really—really—Looks very good for Biff—very—*(He breaks off, then.)* Bernard—*(He is so full of emotion, he breaks off again.)*

BERNARD: What is it, Willy?

WILLY *(small and alone.):* What—what's the secret?

BERNARD: What secret? 290

WILLY: How—how did you? Why didn't he ever catch on?

BERNARD: I wouldn't know that, Willy.

WILLY *(confidentially, desperately.):* You were his friend, his boyhood friend. There's something I don't understand about it. His life ended after that Ebbets Field game. From the age of seventeen nothing good ever happened to him.

BERNARD: He never trained himself for anything.

WILLY: But he did, he did. After high school he took so many correspon-   295
dence courses. Radio mechanics; television; God knows what, and
never made the slightest mark.

BERNARD *(taking off his glasses.)*: Willy, do you want to talk candidly?

WILLY *(rising, faces* BERNARD.*)*: I regard you as a very brilliant man, Bernard.
I value your advice.

BERNARD: Oh, the hell with the advice, Willy. I couldn't advise you.
There's just one thing I've always wanted to ask you. When he was supposed to graduate, and the math teacher flunked him—

WILLY: Oh, that son-of-a-bitch ruined his life.

BERNARD: Yeah, but, Willy, all he had to do was go to summer school and   300
make up that subject.

WILLY: That's right, that's right.

BERNARD: Did you tell him not to go to summer school?

WILLY: Me? I begged him to go. I ordered him to go!

BERNARD: Then why wouldn't he go?

WILLY: Why? Why! Bernard, that question has been trailing me like a ghost   305
for the last fifteen years. He flunked the subject, and laid down and
died like a hammer hit him!

BERNARD: Take it easy, kid.

WILLY: Let me talk to you—I got nobody to talk to. Bernard, Bernard, was
it my fault? Y'see? It keeps going around in my mind, maybe I did something to him. I got nothing to give him.

BERNARD: Don't take it so hard.

WILLY: Why did he lay down? What is the story there? You were his friend!

BERNARD: Willy, I remember, it was June, and our grades came out. And   310
he'd flunked math.

WILLY: That son-of-a-bitch!

BERNARD: No, it wasn't right then. Biff just got very angry, I remember, and
he was ready to enroll in summer school.

WILLY *(surprised.)*: He was?

BERNARD: He wasn't beaten by it at all. But then, Willy, he disappeared
from the block for almost a month. And I got the idea that he'd gone
up to New England to see you. Did he have a talk with you then?

*(*WILLY *stares in silence.)*

BERNARD: Willy?   315

WILLY *(with a strong edge of resentment in his voice.)*: Yeah, he came to Boston. What about it?

BERNARD: Well, just that when he came back—I'll never forget this, it always mystifies me. Because I'd thought so well of Biff, even though
he'd always taken advantage of me. I loved him, Willy, y'know? And
he came back after that month and took his sneakers—remember

those sneakers with "University of Virginia" printed on them? He was so proud of those, wore them every day. And he took them down in the cellar, and burned them up in the furnace. We had a fist fight. It lasted at least half an hour. Just the two of us, punching each other down the cellar, and crying right through it. I've often thought of how strange it was that I knew he'd given up his life. What happened in Boston, Willy?

(WILLY *looks at him as at an intruder.*)

BERNARD: I just bring it up because you asked me.

WILLY (*angrily.*): Nothing. What do you mean, "What happened?" What's that got to do with anything?

BERNARD: Well, don't get sore.   320

WILLY: What are you trying to do, blame it on me? If a boy lays down is that my fault?

BERNARD: Now, Willy, don't get—

WILLY: Well, don't—don't talk to me that way! What does that mean, "What happened?"

(CHARLEY *enters. He is in his vest, and he carries a bottle of bourbon.*)

CHARLEY: Hey, you're going to miss that train. (*He waves the bottle.*)

BERNARD: Yeah, I'm going. (*He takes the bottle.*) Thanks, Pop. (*He picks up*   325
his rackets and bag.) Good-by, Willy, and don't worry about it. You know, "If at first you don't succeed..."

WILLY: Yes, I believe in that.

BERNARD: But sometimes, Willy, it's better for a man just to walk away.

WILLY: Walk away?

BERNARD: That's right.

WILLY: But if you can't walk away?   330

BERNARD (*after a slight pause.*): I guess that's when it's tough. (*Extending his hand.*) Good-by, Willy.

WILLY (*shaking* BERNARD's *hand.*): Good-by, boy.

CHARLEY (*an arm on* BERNARD's *shoulder.*): How do you like this kid? Gonna argue a case in front of the Supreme Court.

BERNARD (*protesting.*): Pop!

WILLY (*genuinely shocked, pained, and happy.*): No! The Supreme Court!   335

BERNARD: I gotta run, 'By, Dad!

CHARLEY: Knock 'em dead, Bernard!

(BERNARD *goes off.*)

WILLY (*as* CHARLEY *takes out his wallet.*): The Supreme Court! And he didn't even mention it!

CHARLEY (*counting out money on the desk.*): He don't have to—he's gonna do it.

WILLY: And you never told him what to do, did you? You never took any in-   340
terest in him.

CHARLEY: My salvation is that I never took any interest in anything. There's some money—fifty dollars. I got an accountant inside.

WILLY: Charley, look…(*With difficulty.*) I got my insurance to pay. If you can manage it—I need a hundred and ten dollars.

(CHARLEY *doesn't reply for a moment; merely stops moving.*)

WILLY: I'd draw it from my bank but Linda would know, and I…

CHARLEY: Sit down, Willy.

WILLY (*moving toward the chair.*): I'm keeping an account of everything, re-   345
member. I'll pay every penny back. (*He sits.*)

CHARLEY: Now listen to me, Willy.

WILLY: I want you to know I appreciate…

CHARLEY (*sitting down on the table.*): Willy, what're you doin'? What the hell is goin' on in your head?

WILLY: Why? I'm simply…

CHARLEY: I offered you a job. You can make fifty dollars a week. And I   350
won't send you on the road.

WILLY: I've got a job.

CHARLEY: Without pay? What kind of a job is a job without pay? (*He rises.*)
Now, look, kid, enough is enough. I'm no genius but I know when I'm being insulted.

WILLY: Insulted!

CHARLEY: Why don't you want to work for me?

WILLY: What's the matter with you? I've got a job.   355

CHARLEY: Then what're you walkin' in here every week for?

WILLY (*getting up.*): Well, if you don't want me to walk in here—

CHARLEY: I am offering you a job.

WILLY: I don't want your goddam job!

CHARLEY: When the hell are you going to grow up?   360

WILLY (*furiously.*): You big ignoramus, if you say that to me again I'll rap you one! I don't care how big you are! (*He's ready to fight.*)
(*Pause.*)

CHARLEY (*kindly, going to him.*): How much do you need, Willy?

WILLY: Charley, I'm strapped. I'm strapped. I don't know what to do. I was just fired.

CHARLEY: Howard fired you?

WILLY: That snotnose. Imagine that? I named him. I named him   365
Howard.

CHARLEY: Willy, when're you gonna realize that them things don't mean anything? You named him Howard, but you can't sell that. The only thing you got in this world is what you can sell. And the funny thing is that you're a salesman, and you don't know that.

WILLY: I've always tried to think otherwise, I guess. I always felt that if a man was impressive, and well liked, that nothing—

CHARLEY: Why must everybody like you? Who liked J. P. Morgan?° Was he impressive? In a Turkish bath he'd look like a butcher. But with his pockets on he was very well liked. Now listen, Willy, I know you don't like me, and nobody can say I'm in love with you, but I'll give you a job because—just for the hell of it, put it that way. Now what do you say?

WILLY: I—I just can't work for you, Charley.

CHARLEY: What're you, jealous of me? 370

WILLY: I can't work for you, that's all, don't ask me why.

CHARLEY (angered, takes out more bills.): You been jealous of me all your life, you damned fool! Here, pay your insurance. (He puts the money in WILLY's hand.)

WILLY: I'm keeping strict accounts.

CHARLEY: I've got some work to do. Take care of yourself. And pay your insurance.

WILLY (moving to the right.): Funny, y'know? After all the highways, and the 375 trains, and the appointments, and the years, you end up worth more dead than alive.

CHARLEY: Willy, nobody's worth nothin' dead. (After a slight pause.) Did you hear what I said?

(WILLY stands still, dreaming.)

CHARLEY: Willy!

WILLY: Apologize to Bernard for me when you see him. I didn't mean to argue with him. He's a fine boy. They're all fine boys, and they'll end up big—all of them. Someday they'll all play tennis together. Wish me luck, Charley. He saw Bill Oliver today.

CHARLEY: Good luck.

WILLY (on the verge of tears.): Charley, you're the only friend I got. Isn't that 380 a remarkable thing? (He goes out.)

CHARLEY: Jesus!

(CHARLEY stares after him a moment and follows. All light blacks out. Suddenly raucous music is heard, and a red glow rises behind the screen at right. STAN-LEY, a young waiter, appears, carrying a table, followed by HAPPY, who is carrying two chairs.)

STANLEY (putting the table down.): That's all right, Mr. Loman, I can handle it myself. (He turns and takes the chairs from HAPPY and places them at the table.)

HAPPY (glancing around.): Oh, this is better.

STANLEY: Sure, in the front there you're in the middle of all kinds a noise. Whenever you got a party, Mr. Loman, you just tell me and I'll put you back here. Y'know, there's a lotta people they don't like it

---

° **J. P. Morgan:** John Pierpont Morgan (1837–1913)—American financier.

private, because when they go out they like to see a lotta action around them because they're sick and tired to stay in the house by theirself. But I know you, you ain't from Hackensack. You know what I mean?

HAPPY *(sitting down.)*: So, how's it coming, Stanley? 385

STANLEY: Ah, it's a dog's life. I only wish during the war they'd a took me in the Army. I coulda been dead by now.

HAPPY: My brother's back, Stanley.

STANLEY: Oh, he come back, heh? From the Far West.

HAPPY: Yeah, big cattle man, my brother, so treat him right. And my father's coming too.

STANLEY: Oh, your father too! 390

HAPPY: You got a couple of nice lobsters?

STANLEY: Hundred per cent, big.

HAPPY: I want them with the claws.

STANLEY: Don't worry, I don't give you no mice. *(HAPPY laughs.)* How about some wine? It'll put a head on the meal.

HAPPY: No. You remember, Stanley, that recipe I brought you from over- 395
seas? With the champagne in it?

STANLEY: Oh, yeah, sure. I still got it tacked up yet in the kitchen. But that'll have to cost a buck apiece anyways.

HAPPY: That's all right.

STANLEY: What'd you, hit a number or somethin'?

HAPPY: No, it's a little celebration. My brother is—I think he pulled off a big deal today. I think we're going into business together.

STANLEY: Great! That's the best for you. Because a family business, you 400
know what I mean?—that's the best.

HAPPY: That's what I think.

STANLEY: 'Cause what's the difference? Somebody steals? It's in the family. Know what I mean? *(Sotto voce.)* Like this bartender here. The boss is goin' crazy what kinda leak he's got in the cash register. You put it in but it don't come out.

HAPPY *(raising his head.)*: Sh!

STANLEY: What?

HAPPY: You notice I wasn't lookin' right or left, was I? 405

STANLEY: No.

HAPPY: And my eyes are closed.

STANLEY: So what's the—

HAPPY: Strudel's comin'.

STANLEY *(catching on, looks around.)*: Ah, no, there's no— 410
(He breaks off as a furred, lavishly dressed GIRL enters and sits at the next table. Both follow her with their eyes.)

STANLEY: Geez, how'd ya know?

HAPPY: I got radar or something. (*Staring directly at her profile.*) Oooooooo
...Stanley.

STANLEY: I think that's for you, Mr. Loman.

HAPPY: Look at that mouth. Oh, God. And the binoculars.

STANLEY: Geez, you got a life, Mr. Loman.   41

HAPPY: Wait on her.

STANLEY (*going to* THE GIRL's *table.*): Would you like a menu, ma'am?

GIRL: I'm expecting someone, but I'd like a—

HAPPY: Why don't you bring her—excuse me, miss, do you mind? I sell champagne, and I'd like you to try my brand. Bring her a champagne, Stanley.

GIRL: That's awfully nice of you.   42

HAPPY: Don't mention it. It's all company money. (*He laughs.*)

GIRL: That's a charming product to be selling, isn't it?

HAPPY: Oh, gets to be like everything else. Selling is selling, y'know.

GIRL: I suppose.

HAPPY: You don't happen to sell, do you?   42

GIRL: No, I don't sell.

HAPPY: Would you object to a compliment from a stranger? You ought to
be on a magazine cover.

GIRL (*looking at him a little archly.*): I have been.

(STANLEY *comes in with a glass of champagne.*)

HAPPY: What'd I say before, Stanley? You see? She's a cover girl.

STANLEY: Oh, I could see, I could see.   43

HAPPY (*to* THE GIRL.): What magazine?

GIRL: Oh, a lot of them. (*She takes the drink.*) Thank you.

HAPPY: You know what they say in France, don't you? "Champagne is the
drink of the complexion"—Hya, Biff!

(BIFF *has entered and sits with* HAPPY.)

BIFF: Hello, kid. Sorry I'm late.

HAPPY: I just got here. Uh, Miss—?   43

GIRL: Forsythe.

HAPPY: Miss Forsythe, this is my brother.

BIFF: Is Dad here?

HAPPY: His name is Biff. You might've heard of him. Great football player.

GIRL: Really? What team?   44

HAPPY: Are you familiar with football?

GIRL: No, I'm afraid I'm not.

HAPPY: Biff is quarterback with the New York Giants.

GIRL: Well, that is nice, isn't it? (*She drinks.*)

HAPPY: Good health.   44

GIRL: I'm happy to meet you.

HAPPY: That's my name. Hap. It's really Harold, but at West Point they
called me Happy.

GIRL *(now really impressed.):* Oh, I see. How do you do? *(She turns her profile.)*

BIFF: Isn't Dad coming?

HAPPY: You want her? 450

BIFF: Oh, I could never make that.

HAPPY: I remember the time that idea would never come into your head. Where's the old confidence, Biff?

BIFF: I just saw Oliver—

HAPPY: Wait a minute. I've got to see that old confidence again. Do you want her? She's on call.

BIFF: Oh, no. *(He turns to look at* THE GIRL.*)* 455

HAPPY: I'm telling you. Watch this. *(Turning to* THE GIRL.*)* Honey? *(She turns to him.)* Are you busy?

GIRL: Well, I am…but I could make a phone call.

HAPPY: Do that, will you, honey? And see if you can get a friend. We'll be here for a while. Biff is one of the greatest football players in the country.

GIRL *(standing up.):* Well, I'm certainly happy to meet you.

HAPPY: Come back soon. 460

GIRL: I'll try.

HAPPY: Don't try, honey, try hard.

*(*THE GIRL *exits.* STANLEY *follows, shaking his head in bewildered admiration.)*

HAPPY: Isn't that a shame now? A beautiful girl like that? That's why I can't get married. There's not a good woman in a thousand. New York is loaded with them, kid!

BIFF: Hap, look—

HAPPY: I told you she was on call! 465

BIFF *(strangely unnerved.):* Cut it out, will ya? I want to say something to you.

HAPPY: Did you see Oliver?

BIFF: I saw him all right. Now look, I want to tell Dad a couple of things and I want you to help me.

HAPPY: What? Is he going to back you?

BIFF: Are you crazy? You're out of your goddam head, you know that? 470

HAPPY: Why? What happened?

BIFF *(breathlessly.):* I did a terrible thing today, Hap. It's been the strangest day I ever went through. I'm all numb, I swear.

HAPPY: You mean he wouldn't see you?

BIFF: Well, I waited six hours for him, see? All day. Kept sending my name in. Even tried to date his secretary so she'd get me to him, but no soap.

HAPPY: Because you're not showin' the old confidence, Biff. He remembered 475 you, didn't he?

BIFF *(stopping* HAPPY *with a gesture.):* Finally, about five o'clock, he comes out. Didn't remember who I was or anything. I felt like such an idiot, Hap.

HAPPY: Did you tell him my Florida idea?

BIFF: He walked away. I saw him for one minute. I got so mad I could've torn the walls down! How the hell did I ever get the idea I was a salesman there? I even believed myself that I'd been a salesman for him! And then he gave me one look and—I realized what a ridiculous lie my whole life has been! We've been talking in a dream for fifteen years. I was a shipping clerk.

HAPPY: What'd you do?

BIFF (*with great tension and wonder.*): Well, he left, see. And the secretary   48
went out. I was all alone in the waiting-room. I don't know what came over me, Hap. The next thing I know I'm in his office—paneled walls, everything. I can't explain it. I—Hap, I took his fountain pen.

HAPPY: Geez, did he catch you?

BIFF: I ran out. I ran down all eleven flights. I ran and ran and ran.

HAPPY: That was an awful dumb—what'd you do that for?

BIFF (*agonized.*): I don't know, I just—wanted to take something, I don't know. You gotta help me, Hap. I'm gonna tell Pop.

HAPPY: You crazy? What for?   48

BIFF: Hap, he's got to understand that I'm not the man somebody lends that kind of money to. He thinks I've been spiting him all these years and it's eating him up.

HAPPY: That's just it. You tell him something nice.

BIFF: I can't.

HAPPY: Say you got a lunch date with Oliver tomorrow.

BIFF: So what do I do tomorrow?   49

HAPPY: You leave the house tomorrow and come back at night and say Oliver is thinking it over. And he thinks it over for a couple of weeks, and gradually it fades away and nobody's the worse.

BIFF: But it'll go on forever!

HAPPY: Dad is never so happy as when he's looking forward to something!

(WILLY *enters.*)

HAPPY: Hello, scout!

WILLY: Gee, I haven't been here in years!   49

(STANLEY *has followed* WILLY *in and sets a chair for him.* STANLEY *starts off but* HAPPY *stops him.*)

HAPPY: Stanley!

(STANLEY *stands by, waiting for an order.*)

BIFF (*going to* WILLY *with guilt, as to an invalid.*): Sit down, Pop. You want a drink?

WILLY: Sure, I don't mind.

BIFF: Let's get a load on.

WILLY: You look worried.   50

BIFF: N-no. (*To* STANLEY.) Scotch all around. Make it doubles.

STANLEY: Doubles, right. *(He goes.)*

WILLY: You had a couple already, didn't you?

BIFF: Just a couple, yeah.

WILLY: Well, what happened, boy? *(Nodding affirmatively, with a smile.)*   505
Everything go all right?

BIFF *(takes a breath, then reaches out and grasps* WILLY's *hand.):* Pal…*(He is
smiling bravely, and* WILLY *is smiling too.)* I had an experience today.

HAPPY: Terrific, Pop.

WILLY: That so? What happened?

BIFF *(high, slightly alcoholic, above the earth.):* I'm going to tell you everything
from first to last. It's been a strange day. *(Silence. He looks around, composes himself as best he can, but his breath keeps breaking the rhythm of his
voice.)* I had to wait quite a while for him, and—

WILLY: Oliver?   510

BIFF: Yeah, Oliver. All day, as a matter of cold fact. And a lot of—
instances—facts, Pop, facts about my life came back to me. Who was
it, Pop? Who ever said I was a salesman with Oliver?

WILLY: Well, you were.

BIFF: No, Dad, I was a shipping clerk.

WILLY: But you were practically—

BIFF *(with determination.):* Dad, I don't know who said it first, but I was   515
never a salesman for Bill Oliver.

WILLY: What're you talking about?

BIFF: Let's hold on to the facts tonight, Pop. We're not going to get anywhere bullin' around. I was a shipping clerk.

WILLY *(angrily.):* All right, now listen to me—

BIFF: Why don't you let me finish?

WILLY: I'm not interested in stories about the past or any crap of that kind   520
because the woods are burning, boys, you understand? There's a big
blaze going on all around. I was fired today.

BIFF *(shocked.):* How could you be?

WILLY: I was fired, and I'm looking for a little good news to tell your mother,
because the woman has waited and the woman has suffered. The gist of
it is that I haven't got a story left in my head, Biff. So don't give me a
lecture about facts and aspects. I am not interested. Now what've you
got to say to me?

(STANLEY enters with three drinks. They wait until he leaves.)

WILLY: Did you see Oliver?

BIFF: Jesus, Dad!

WILLY: You mean you didn't go up there?   525

HAPPY: Sure he went up there.

BIFF: I did. I—saw him. How could they fire you?

WILLY *(on the edge of his chair.):* What kind of a welcome did he give you?

BIFF: He won't even let you work on commission?

WILLY: I'm out! (*Driving.*) So tell me, he gave you a warm welcome?   53

HAPPY: Sure, Pop, sure!

BIFF (*driven.*): Well, it was kind of—

WILLY: I was wondering if he'd remember you. (*To* HAPPY.) Imagine, man doesn't see him for ten, twelve years and gives him that kind of a welcome!

HAPPY: Damn right!

BIFF (*trying to return to the offensive.*): Pop, look—   53

WILLY: You know why he remembered you, don't you? Because you impressed him in those days.

BIFF: Let's talk quietly and get this down to the facts, huh?

WILLY (*as though* BIFF *had been interrupting.*): Well, what happened? It's great news, Biff. Did he take you into his office or'd you talk in the waiting-room?

BIFF: Well, he came in, see, and—

WILLY (*with a big smile.*): What'd he say? Betcha he threw his arm around   54 you.

BIFF: Well, he kinda—

WILLY: He's a fine man. (*To* HAPPY.) Very hard man to see, y'know.

HAPPY (*agreeing.*): Oh, I know.

WILLY (*to* BIFF.): Is that where you had the drinks?

BIFF: Yeah, he gave me a couple of—no, no!   54

HAPPY (*cutting in.*): He told him my Florida idea.

WILLY: Don't interrupt. (*To* BIFF.) How'd he react to the Florida idea?

BIFF: Dad, will you give me a minute to explain?

WILLY: I've been waiting for you to explain since I sat down here! What happened? He took you into his office and what?

BIFF: Well—I talked. And—and he listened, see.   55

WILLY: Famous for the way he listens, y'know. What was his answer?

BIFF: His answer was—(*He breaks off, suddenly angry.*) Dad, you're not letting me tell you what I want to tell you!

WILLY (*accusing, angered.*): You didn't see him, did you?

BIFF: I did see him!

WILLY: What'd you insult him or something? You insulted him, didn't you?   55

BIFF: Listen, will you let me out of it, will you just let me out of it!

HAPPY: What the hell!

WILLY: Tell me what happened!

BIFF (*to* HAPPY.): I can't talk to him!

(*A single trumpet note jars the ear. The light of green leaves stains the house, which holds the air of night and a dream. Young* BERNARD *enters and knocks on the door of the house.*)

YOUNG BERNARD (*frantically.*): Mrs. Loman, Mrs. Loman!   56

HAPPY: Tell him what happened!

BIFF (*to* HAPPY.): Shut up and leave me alone!

WILLY: No, no! You had to go and flunk math!

BIFF: What math? What're you talking about?

YOUNG BERNARD: Mrs. Loman, Mrs. Loman!   565

(LINDA *appears in the house, as of old.*)

WILLY (*wildly.*): Math, math, math!

BIFF: Take it easy, Pop!

YOUNG BERNARD: Mrs. Loman!

WILLY (*furiously.*): If you hadn't flunked you'd've been set by now!

BIFF: Now, look, I'm gonna tell you what happened, and you're going to lis-   570
ten to me.

YOUNG BERNARD: Mrs. Loman!

BIFF: I waited six hours—

HAPPY: What the hell are you saying?

BIFF: I kept sending in my name but he wouldn't see me. So finally he...

(*He continues unheard as light fades low on the restaurant.*)

YOUNG BERNARD: Biff flunked math!   575

LINDA: No!

YOUNG BERNARD: Birnbaum flunked him! They won't graduate him!

LINDA: But they have to. He's gotta go to the university. Where is he? Biff!
Biff!

YOUNG BERNARD: No, he left. He went to Grand Central.

LINDA: Grand—You mean he went to Boston!   580

YOUNG BERNARD: Is Uncle Willy in Boston?

LINDA: Oh, maybe Willy can talk to the teacher. Oh, the poor, poor boy!

(*Light on house area snaps out.*)

BIFF (*at the table, now audible, holding up a gold fountain pen.*): ...so I'm
washed up with Oliver, you understand? Are you listening to me?

WILLY (*at a loss.*): Yeah, sure. If you hadn't flunked—

BIFF: Flunked what? What're you talking about?   585

WILLY: Don't blame everything on me! I didn't flunk math—you did! What
pen?

HAPPY: That was awful dumb, Biff, a pen like that is worth—

WILLY (*seeing the pen for the first time.*): You took Oliver's pen?

BIFF (*weakening.*): Dad, I just explained it to you.

WILLY: You stole Bill Oliver's fountain pen!   590

BIFF: I didn't exactly steal it! That's just what I've been explaining to you!

HAPPY: He had it in his hand and just then Oliver walked in, so he got nervous and stuck it in his pocket!

WILLY: My God, Biff!

BIFF: I never intended to do it, Dad!

OPERATOR'S VOICE: Standish Arms, good evening!   595

WILLY (*shouting.*): I'm not in my room!

BIFF (*frightened.*): Dad, what's the matter? (*He and* HAPPY *stand up.*)

OPERATOR: Ringing Mr. Loman for you!

WILLY: I'm not there, stop it!

BIFF (*horrified, gets down on one knee before* WILLY.): Dad, I'll make good, I'll   600
make good. (WILLY *tries to get to his feet.* BIFF *holds him down.*) Sit down
now.

WILLY: No, you're no good, you're no good for anything.

BIFF: I am, Dad, I'll find something else, you understand? Now don't worry
about anything. (*He holds up* WILLY's *face.*) Talk to me, Dad.

OPERATOR: Mr. Loman does not answer. Shall I page him?

WILLY (*attempting to stand, as though to rush and silence the* OPERATOR.): No,
no, no!

HAPPY: He'll strike something, Pop.   605

WILLY: No, no…

BIFF (*desperately, standing over* WILLY.): Pop, listen! Listen to me! I'm
telling you something good. Oliver talked to his partner about the
Florida idea. You listening? He—he talked to his partner, and he
came to me…I'm going to be all right, you hear? Dad, listen to me,
he said it was just a question of the amount!

WILLY: Then you…got it?

HAPPY: He's gonna be terrific, Pop!

WILLY (*trying to stand.*): Then you got it, haven't you? You got it! You got it!   61

BIFF (*agonized, holds* WILLY *down.*): No, no. Look, Pop. I'm supposed to have
lunch with them tomorrow. I'm just telling you this so you'll know that
I can still make an impression, Pop. And I'll make good somewhere, but
I can't go tomorrow, see?

WILLY: Why not? You simply—

BIFF: But the pen, Pop!

WILLY: You give it to him and tell him it was an oversight!

HAPPY: Sure, have lunch tomorrow!   61

BIFF: I can't say that—

WILLY: You were doing a crossword puzzle and accidentally used his pen!

BIFF: Listen, kid, I took those balls years ago, now I walk in with his fountain pen? That clinches it, don't you see? I can't face him like that! I'll
try elsewhere.

PAGE'S VOICE: Paging Mr. Loman!

WILLY: Don't you want to be anything?   62

BIFF: Pop, how can I go back?

WILLY: You don't want to be anything, is that what's behind it?

BIFF (*now angry at* WILLY *for not crediting his sympathy.*): Don't take it that
way! You think it was easy walking into that office after what I'd done
to him? A team of horses couldn't have dragged me back to Bill Oliver!

WILLY: Then why'd you go?

BIFF: Why did I go? Why did I go? Look at you! Look at what's become of you!   625

(*Off left,* THE WOMAN *laughs.*)

WILLY: Biff, you're going to go to that lunch tomorrow, or—

BIFF: I can't go. I've got no appointment!

HAPPY: Biff, for...!

WILLY: Are you spiting me?

BIFF: Don't take it that way! Goddammit!   630

WILLY (*strikes* BIFF *and falters away from the table.*): You rotten little louse!
Are you spiting me?

THE WOMAN: Someone's at the door, WILLY!

BIFF: I'm no good, can't you see what I am?

HAPPY (*separating them.*): Hey, you're in a restaurant! Now cut it out, both
of you! (THE GIRLS *enter.*) Hello, girls, sit down.

(THE WOMAN *laughs, off left.*)

MISS FORSYTHE: I guess we might as well. This is Letta.   635

THE WOMAN: Willy, are you going to wake up?

BIFF (*ignoring* WILLY.): How're ya, miss, sit down. What do you drink?

MISS FORSYTHE: Letta might not be able to stay long.

LETTA: I gotta get up very early tomorrow. I got jury duty. I'm so excited!
Were you fellows ever on a jury?

BIFF: No, but I been in front of them! (THE GIRLS *laugh.*) This is my father.   640

LETTA: Isn't he cute? Sit down with us, Pop.

HAPPY: Sit him down, Biff!

BIFF (*going to him.*): Come on, slugger, drink us under the table. To hell
with it! Come on, sit down, pal.

(*On* BIFF's *last insistence,* WILLY *is about to sit.*)

THE WOMAN (*now urgently.*): Willy, are you going to answer the door!

(THE WOMAN's *call pulls* WILLY *back. He starts right, befuddled.*)

BIFF: Hey, where are you going?   645

WILLY: Open the door.

BIFF: The door?

WILLY: The washroom...the door...where's the door?

BIFF (*leading* WILLY *to the left.*): Just go straight down.

(WILLY *moves left.*)

THE WOMAN: Willy, Willy, are you going to get up, get up, get up, get up?   650

(WILLY *exits left.*)

LETTA: I think it's sweet you bring your daddy along.

MISS FORSYTHE: Oh, he isn't really your father!

BIFF (*at left, turning to her resentfully.*): Miss Forsythe, you've just seen a
prince walk by. A fine, troubled prince. A hard-working, unappreciated
prince. A pal, you understand? A good companion. Always for his boys.

LETTA: That's so sweet.

HAPPY: Well, girls, what's the program? We're wasting time. Come on, Biff. 65
Gather round. Where would you like to go?

BIFF: Why don't you do something for him?

HAPPY: Me!

BIFF: Don't you give a damn for him, Hap?

HAPPY: What're you talking about? I'm the one who—

BIFF: I sense it, you don't give a good goddam about him. (*He takes the* 66
rolled-up hose from his pocket and puts it on the table in front of HAPPY.)
Look what I found in the cellar, for Christ's sake. How can you bear to
let it go on?

HAPPY: Me? Who goes away? Who runs off and—

BIFF: Yeah, but he doesn't mean anything to you. You could help him—I
can't! Don't you understand what I'm talking about? He's going to kill
himself, don't you know that?

HAPPY: Don't I know it! Me!

BIFF: Hap, help him! Jesus...help him...Help me, help me, I can't bear to
look at his face! (*Ready to weep, he hurries out, up right.*)

HAPPY (*starting after him.*): Where are you going? 66

MISS FORSYTHE: What's he so mad about?

HAPPY: Come on, girls, we'll catch up with him.

MISS FORSYTHE (*as* HAPPY *pushes her out.*): Say, I don't like that temper of his!

HAPPY: He's just a little overstrung, he'll be all right!

WILLY (*off left, as* THE WOMAN *laughs.*): Don't answer! Don't answer! 67

LETTA: Don't you want to tell your father—

HAPPY: No, that's not my father. He's just a guy. Come on, we'll catch Biff,
and, honey, we're going to paint this town! Stanley, where's the check!
Hey, Stanley!

(*They exit.* STANLEY *looks toward left.*)

STANLEY (*calling to* HAPPY *indignantly.*): Mr. Loman! Mr. Loman!

(STANLEY *picks up a chair and follows them off. Knocking is heard off left.*

THE WOMAN *enters, laughing.* WILLY *follows her. She is in a black slip; he is but-*
toning his shirt. Raw, sensuous music accompanies their speech.)

WILLY: Will you stop laughing? Will you stop?

THE WOMAN: Aren't you going to answer the door? He'll wake the whole 67
hotel.

WILLY: I'm not expecting anybody.

THE WOMAN: Whyn't you have another drink, honey, and stop being so
damn self-centered?

WILLY: I'm so lonely.

THE WOMAN: You know you ruined me, Willy? From now on, whenever you
come to the office, I'll see that you go right through to the buyers. No
waiting at my desk any more, Willy. You ruined me.

WILLY: That's nice of you to say that.   680

THE WOMAN: Gee, you are self-centered! Why so sad? You are the saddest
self-centeredest soul I ever did see-saw. *(She laughs. He kisses her.)*
Come on inside, drummer boy. It's silly to be dressing in the middle of
the night. *(As knocking is heard.)* Aren't you going to answer the door?

WILLY: They're knocking on the wrong door.

THE WOMAN: But I felt the knocking. And he heard us talking in here.
Maybe the hotel's on fire!

WILLY *(his terror rising.):* It's a mistake.

THE WOMAN: Then tell him to go away!   685

WILLY: There's nobody there.

THE WOMAN: It's getting on my nerves, Willy. There's somebody standing
out there and it's getting on my nerves!

WILLY *(pushing her away from him.):* All right, stay in the bathroom here,
and don't come out. I think there's a law in Massachusetts about it, so
don't come out. It may be that new room clerk. He looked very mean.
So don't come out. It's a mistake, there's no fire.

*(The knocking is heard again. He takes a few steps away from her, and she
vanishes into the wing. The light follows him, and now he is facing Young
BIFF, who carries a suitcase. BIFF steps toward him. The music is gone.)*

BIFF: Why didn't you answer?

WILLY: Biff! What are you doing in Boston?   690

BIFF: Why didn't you answer? I've been knocking for five minutes, I called
you on the phone—

WILLY: I just heard you. I was in the bathroom and had the door shut. Did
anything happen home?

BIFF: Dad—I let you down.

WILLY: What do you mean?

BIFF: Dad...   695

WILLY: Biffo, what's this about? *(Putting his arm around BIFF.)* Come on,
let's go downstairs and get you a malted.

BIFF: Dad, I flunked math.

WILLY: Not for the term?

BIFF: The term. I haven't got enough credits to graduate.

WILLY: You mean to say Bernard wouldn't give you the answers?   700

BIFF: He did, he tried, but I only got a sixty-one.

WILLY: And they wouldn't give you four points?

BIFF: Birnbaum refused absolutely. I begged him, Pop, but he won't give me
those points. You gotta talk to him before they close the school. Because if he saw the kind of man you are, and you just talked to him in
your way, I'm sure he'd come through for me. The class came right before practice, see, and I didn't go enough. Would you talk to him? He'd
like you, Pop. You know the way you could talk.

WILLY: You're on. We'll drive right back.

BIFF: Oh, Dad, good work! I'm sure he'll change it for you! 70!

WILLY: Go downstairs and tell the clerk I'm checkin' out. Go right down.

BIFF: Yes, Sir! See, the reason he hates me, Pop—one day he was late for class so I got up at the blackboard and imitated him. I crossed my eyes and talked with a lithp.

WILLY (*laughing.*): You did? The kids like it?

BIFF: They nearly died laughing!

WILLY: Yeah? What'd you do? 71|

BIFF: The thquare root of thixthy twee is...(WILLY *bursts out laughing;* BIFF *joins him.*) And in the middle of it he walked in!

(WILLY *laughs and* THE WOMAN *joins in offstage.*)

WILLY (*without hesitating.*): Hurry downstairs and—

BIFF: Somebody in there?

WILLY: No, that was next door.

(THE WOMAN *laughs offstage.*)

BIFF: Somebody got in your bathroom! 71!

WILLY: No, it's the next room, there's a party—

THE WOMAN (*enters, laughing. She lisps this.*): Can I come in? There's something in the bathtub, Willy, and it's moving!

(WILLY *looks at* BIFF, *who is staring open-mouthed and horrified at* THE WOMAN.)

WILLY: Ah—you better go back to your room. They must be finished painting by now. They're painting her room so I let her take a shower here. Go back, go back...(*He pushes her.*)

THE WOMAN (*resisting.*): But I've got to get dressed, Willy, I can't—

WILLY: Get out of here! Go back, go back...(*Suddenly striving for the ordi-* 72| *nary.*) This is Miss Francis, Biff, she's a buyer. They're painting her room. Go back, Miss Francis, go back...

THE WOMAN: But my clothes, I can't go out naked in the hall!

WILLY (*pushing her offstage.*): Get outa here! Go back, go back!

(BIFF *slowly sits down on his suitcase as the argument continues offstage.*)

THE WOMAN: Where's my stockings? You promised me stockings, Willy!

WILLY: I have no stockings here!

THE WOMAN: You had two boxes of size nine sheers for me, and I want them! 72|

WILLY: Here, for God's sake, will you get outa here!

THE WOMAN (*enters holding a box of stockings.*): I just hope there's nobody in the hall. That's all I hope. (*To* BIFF.) Are you football or baseball?

BIFF: Football.

THE WOMAN (*angry, humiliated.*): That's me too. G'night. (*She snatches her clothes from* WILLY, *and walks out.*)

WILLY (*after a pause.*): Well, better get going. I want to get to the school 73| first thing in the morning. Get my suits out of the closet. I'll get my va- lise. (BIFF *doesn't move.*) What's the matter? (BIFF *remains motionless, tears falling.*) She's a buyer. Buys for J. H. Simmons. She lives down the hall—they're painting. You don't imagine—(*He breaks off. After a pause.*) Now listen, pal, she's just a buyer. She sees merchandise in her room and they have to keep it looking just so...(*Pause. Assuming command.*) All right, get my suits. (BIFF *doesn't move.*) Now stop crying and do as I say. I gave you an order. Biff, I gave you an order! Is that what you do when I give you an order? How dare you cry! (*Putting his arm around* BIFF.) Now look, Biff, when you grow up you'll understand about these things. You mustn't—you mustn't overemphasize a thing like this. I'll see Birnbaum first thing in the morning.

BIFF: Never mind.

WILLY (*getting down beside* BIFF.): Never mind! He's going to give you those points. I'll see to it.

BIFF: He wouldn't listen to you.

WILLY: He certainly will listen to me. You need those points for the U. of Virginia.

BIFF: I'm not going there.   735

WILLY: Heh? If I can't get him to change that mark you'll make it up in summer school. You've got all summer to—

BIFF (*his weeping breaking from him.*): Dad...

WILLY (*infected by it.*): Oh, my boy...

BIFF: Dad...

WILLY: She's nothing to me, Biff. I was lonely, I was terribly lonely.   740

BIFF: You—you gave her Mama's stockings! (*His tears break through and he rises to go.*)

WILLY (*grabbing for* BIFF.): I gave you an order!

BIFF: Don't touch me, you—liar!

WILLY: Apologize for that!

BIFF: You fake! You phony little fake! You fake! (*Overcome, he turns quickly* 745 *and weeping fully goes out with his suitcase.* WILLY *is left on the floor on his knees.*)

WILLY: I gave you an order! Biff, come back here or I'll beat you! Come back here! I'll whip you!

(STANLEY *comes quickly in from the right and stands in front of* WILLY.)

WILLY (*shouts at* STANLEY.): I gave you an order...

STANLEY: Hey, let's pick it up, pick it up, Mr. Loman. (*He helps* WILLY *to his feet.*) Your boys left with the chippies. They said they'll see you home.

(*A second waiter watches some distance away.*)

WILLY: But we were supposed to have dinner together.

(*Music is heard,* WILLY's *theme.*)

STANLEY: Can you make it?   750

WILLY: I'll—sure, I can make it. (*Suddenly concerned about his clothes.*) Do I—I look all right?

STANLEY: Sure, you look all right. (*He flicks a speck off* WILLY's *lapel.*)

WILLY: Here—here's a dollar.

STANLEY: Oh, your son paid me. It's all right.

WILLY (*putting it in* STANLEY's *hand.*): No, take it. You're a good boy. 755

STANLEY: Oh, no, you don't have to…

WILLY: Here—here's some more, I don't need it any more. (*After a slight pause.*) Tell me—is there a seed store in the neighborhood?

STANLEY: Seeds? You mean like to plant?

(*As* WILLY *turns,* STANLEY *slips the money back into his jacket pocket.*)

WILLY: Yes. Carrots, peas…

STANLEY: Well, there's hardware stores on Sixth Avenue, but it may be too 760
late now.

WILLY (*anxiously.*): Oh, I'd better hurry. I've got to get some seeds. (*He starts off to the right.*) I've got to get some seeds, right away. Nothing's planted. I don't have a thing in the ground.

(WILLY *hurries out as the light goes down.* STANLEY *moves over to the right after him, watches him off. The other waiter has been staring at* WILLY.)

STANLEY (*to the waiter.*): Well, whatta you looking at?

(*The waiter picks up the chairs and moves off right.* STANLEY *takes the table and follows him. The light fades on this area. There is a long pause, the sound of the flute coming over. The light gradually rises on the kitchen, which is empty.* HAPPY *appears at the door of the house, followed by* BIFF. HAPPY *is carrying a large bunch of long-stemmed roses. He enters the kitchen, looks around for* LINDA. *Not seeing her, he turns to* BIFF, *who is just outside the house door, and makes a gesture with his hands, indicating "Not here, I guess." He looks into the living room and freezes. Inside,* LINDA, *unseen, is seated,* WILLY's *coat on her lap. She rises ominously and quietly and moves toward* HAPPY, *who backs up into the kitchen, afraid.*)

HAPPY: Hey, what're you doing up? (LINDA *says nothing but moves toward him implacably.*) Where's Pop? (*He keeps backing to the right, and now* LINDA *is in full view in the doorway to the living room.*) Is he sleeping?

LINDA: Where were you?

HAPPY (*trying to laugh it off.*): We met two girls, Mom, very fine types. Here, 765
we brought you some flowers. (*Offering them to her.*) Put them in your room, Ma.

(*She knocks them to the floor at* BIFF's *feet. He has now come inside and closed the door behind him. She stares at* BIFF, *silent.*)

HAPPY: Now what'd you do that for? Mom, I want you to have some flowers—

LINDA (*cutting* HAPPY *off, violently to* BIFF.): Don't you care whether he lives or dies?

HAPPY (*going to the stairs.*): Come upstairs, Biff.

BIFF (*with a flare of disgust, to* HAPPY.): Go away from me! (*To* LINDA.) What do you mean, lives or dies? Nobody's dying around here, pal.

LINDA: Get out of my sight! Get out of here!   770

BIFF: I wanna see the boss.

LINDA: You're not going near him!

BIFF: Where is he? (*He moves into the living room and* LINDA *follows.*)

LINDA (*shouting after* BIFF.): You invite him for dinner. He looks forward to it all day—(BIFF *appears in his parents' bedroom, looks around, and exits*)—and then you desert him there. There's no stranger you'd do that to!

HAPPY: Why? He had a swell time with us. Listen, when I—(LINDA *comes*   775 *back into the kitchen.*)—desert him I hope I don't outlive the day!

LINDA: Get out of here!

HAPPY: Now look, Mom....

LINDA: Did you have to go to women tonight? You and your lousy rotten whores!

(BIFF *re-enters the kitchen.*)

HAPPY: Mom, all we did was follow Biff around trying to cheer him up! (*To* BIFF.) Boy, what a night you gave me!

LINDA: Get out of here, both of you, and don't come back! I don't want you   780 tormenting him any more. Go on now, get your things together! (*To* BIFF.) You can sleep in his apartment. (*She starts to pick up the flowers and stops herself.*) Pick up this stuff, I'm not your maid any more. Pick it up, you bum, you!

(HAPPY *turns his back to her in refusal.* BIFF *slowly moves over and gets down on his knees, picking up the flowers.*)

LINDA: You're a pair of animals! Not one, not another living soul would have had the cruelty to walk out on that man in a restaurant!

BIFF (*not looking at her.*): Is that what he said?

LINDA: He didn't have to say anything. He was so humiliated he nearly limped when he came in.

HAPPY: But, Mom he had a great time with us—

BIFF (*cutting him off violently.*): Shut up!   785

(*Without another word,* HAPPY *goes upstairs.*)

LINDA: You! You didn't even go in to see if he was all right!

BIFF (*still on the floor in front of* LINDA, *the flowers in his hand; with self-loathing.*): No. Didn't. Didn't do a damned thing. How do you like that, heh? Left him babbling in a toilet.

LINDA: You louse. You...

BIFF: Now you hit it on the nose! (*He gets up, throws the flowers in the waste-basket.*) The scum of the earth, and you're looking at him!

LINDA: Get out of here!   790

BIFF: I gotta talk to the boss, Mom. Where is he?

LINDA: You're not going near him. Get out of this house!

BIFF (*with absolute assurance, determination.*): No. We're gonna have an abrupt conversation, him and me.

LINDA: You're not talking to him!

(*Hammering is heard from outside the house, off right.* BIFF *turns toward the noise.*)

LINDA (*suddenly pleading.*): Will you please leave him alone? 79

BIFF: What's he doing out there?

LINDA: He's planting the garden!

BIFF (*quietly.*): Now? Oh, my God!

(BIFF *moves outside,* LINDA *following. The light dies down on them and comes up on the center of the apron as* WILLY *walks into it. He is carrying a flashlight, a hoe and a handful of seed packets. He raps the top of the hoe sharply to fix it firmly, and then moves to the left, measuring off the distance with his foot. He holds the flashlight to look at the seed packets, reading off the instructions. He is in the blue of night.*)

WILLY: Carrots…quarter-inch apart. Rows…one-foot rows. (*He measures it off.*) One foot. (*He puts down a package and measures off.*) Beets. (*He puts down another package and measures again.*) Lettuce. (*He reads the package, puts it down.*) One foot—(*He breaks off as* BEN *appears at the right and moves slowly down to him.*) What a proposition, ts, ts. Terrific, terrific. 'Cause she's suffered, Ben, the woman has suffered. You understand me? A man can't go out the way he came in, Ben, a man has got to add up to something. You can't, you can't—(BEN *moves toward him as though to interrupt.*) You gotta consider, now. Don't answer so quick. Remember, it's a guaranteed twenty-thousand-dollar proposition. Now look, Ben, I want you to go through the ins and outs of this thing with me. I've got nobody to talk to, Ben, and the woman has suffered, you hear me?

BEN (*standing still, considering.*): What's the proposition? 80

WILLY: It's twenty thousand dollars on the barrelhead. Guaranteed, gilt-edged, you understand?

BEN: You don't want to make a fool of yourself. They might not honor the policy.

WILLY: How can they dare refuse? Didn't I work like a coolie to meet every premium on the nose? And now they don't pay off? Impossible!

BEN: It's called a cowardly thing, William.

WILLY: Why? Does it take more guts to stand here the rest of my life ringing 80 up a zero?

BEN (*yielding.*): That's a point, William. (*He moves, thinking, turns.*) And twenty thousand—that *is* something one can feel with the hand, it is there.

WILLY (*now assured, with rising power.*): Oh, Ben, that's the whole beauty of it! I see it like a diamond, shining in the dark, hard and rough, that I can pick up and touch in my hand. Not like—like an appointment! This would not be another damned-fool appointment, Ben, and it changes all the aspects. Because he thinks I'm nothing, see, and so he spites me. But the funeral—(*Straightening up.*) Ben, that funeral will be massive! They'll come from Maine, Massachusetts, Vermont, New Hampshire! All the old-timers with the strange license plates—that boy will be thunder-struck, Ben, because he never realized—I am known! Rhode Island, New York, New Jersey—I am known, Ben, and he'll see it with his eyes once and for all. He'll see what I am, Ben! He's in for a shock, that boy!

BEN (*coming down to the edge of the garden.*): He'll call you a coward.

WILLY (*suddenly fearful.*): No, that would be terrible.

BEN: Yes. And a damned fool.   810

WILLY: No, no, he mustn't, I won't have that! (*He is broken and desperate.*)

BEN: He'll hate you, William.

(*The gay music of the boys is heard.*)

WILLY: Oh, Ben, how do we get back to all the great times? Used to be so full of light, and comradeship, the sleigh-riding in winter, and the ruddiness on his cheeks. And always some kind of good news coming up, always something nice coming up ahead. And never even let me carry the valises in the house, and simonizing, simonizing that little red car! Why, why can't I give him something and not have him hate me?

BEN: Let me think about it. (*He glances at his watch.*) I still have a little time. Remarkable proposition, but you've got to be sure you're not making a fool of yourself.

(BEN *drifts off upstage and goes out of sight.* BIFF *comes down from the left.*)

WILLY (*suddenly conscious of* BIFF, *turns and looks up at him, then begins picking*   815
up the packages of seeds in confusion.): Where the hell is that seed? (*Indignantly.*) You can't see nothing out here! They boxed in the whole goddam neighborhood!

BIFF: There are people all around here. Don't you realize that?

WILLY: I'm busy. Don't bother me.

BIFF (*taking the hoe from* WILLY.): I'm saying good-by to you, Pop. (WILLY *looks at him, silent, unable to move.*) I'm not coming back any more.

WILLY: You're not going to see Oliver tomorrow?

BIFF: I've got no appointment, Dad.   820

WILLY: He put his arm around you, and you've got no appointment?

BIFF: Pop, get this now, will you? Everytime I've left it's been a fight that sent me out of here. Today I realized something about myself and I tried to explain it to you and I—I think I'm just not smart enough to make any sense out of it for you. To hell with whose fault it is or anything like that. (*He takes* WILLY's *arm.*) Let's just wrap it up, heh? Come on in, we'll tell Mom. (*He gently tries to pull* WILLY *to the left.*)

WILLY (*frozen, immobile, with guilt in his voice.*): No, I don't want to see her.

BIFF: Come on! (*He pulls again, and* WILLY *tries to pull away.*)

WILLY (*highly nervous.*): No, no, I don't want to see her.   82?

BIFF (*tries to look into* WILLY's *face, as if to find the answer there.*): Why don't you want to see her?

WILLY (*more harshly now.*): Don't bother me, will you?

BIFF: What do you mean, you don't want to see her? You don't want them calling you yellow, do you? This isn't your fault; it's me, I'm a bum. Now come inside! (WILLY *strains to get away.*) Did you hear what I said to you?

(WILLY *pulls away and quickly goes by himself into the house.* BIFF *follows.*)

LINDA (*to* WILLY.): Did you plant, dear?

BIFF (*at the door, to* LINDA.): All right, we had it out. I'm going and I'm not   83? writing any more.

LINDA (*going to* WILLY *in the kitchen.*): I think that's the best way, dear. 'Cause there's no use drawing it out, you'll just never get along.

(WILLY *doesn't respond.*)

BIFF: People ask where I am and what I'm doing, you don't know, and you don't care. That way it'll be off your mind and you can start brightening up again. All right? That clears it, doesn't it? (WILLY *is silent, and* BIFF *goes to him.*) You gonna wish me luck, scout? (*He extends his hand.*) What do you say?

LINDA: Shake his hand, Willy.

WILLY (*turning to her, seething with hurt.*): There's no necessity to mention the pen at all, y'know.

BIFF (*gently.*): I've got no appointment, Dad.   83

WILLY (*erupting fiercely.*): He put his arm around...?

BIFF: Dad, you're never going to see what I am, so what's the use of arguing? If I strike oil I'll send you a check. Meantime forget I'm alive.

WILLY (*to* LINDA.): Spite, see?

BIFF: Shake hands, Dad.

WILLY: Not my hand.   84

BIFF: I was hoping not to go this way.

WILLY: Well, this is the way you're going. Good-by.

(BIFF *looks at him a moment, then turns sharply and goes to the stairs.*)

WILLY (*stops him with.*): May you rot in hell if you leave this house!

BIFF (*turning.*): Exactly what is it that you want from me?

WILLY: I want you to know, on the train, in the mountains, in the valleys,   84 wherever you go, that you cut down your life for spite!

BIFF: No, no.

WILLY: Spite, spite, is the word of your undoing! And when you're down and out, remember what did it. When you're rotting somewhere beside the railroad tracks, remember, and don't you dare blame it on me!

BIFF: I'm not blaming it on you!

WILLY: I won't take the rap for this, you hear?

(HAPPY *comes down the stairs and stands on the bottom step, watching.*)

BIFF: That's just what I'm telling you!   850

WILLY (*sinking into a chair at the table, with full accusation.*): You're trying to put a knife in me—don't think I don't know what you're doing!

BIFF: All right, phony! Then let's lay it on the line. (*He whips the rubber tube out of his pocket and puts it on the table.*)

HAPPY: You crazy—

LINDA: Biff! (*She moves to grab the hose, but* BIFF *holds it down with his hand.*)

BIFF: Leave it there! Don't move it!   855

WILLY (*not looking at it.*): What is that?

BIFF: You know goddam well what that is.

WILLY (*caged, wanting to escape.*): I never saw that.

BIFF: You saw it. The mice didn't bring it into the cellar! What is this supposed to do, make a hero out of you? This supposed to make me sorry for you?

WILLY: Never heard of it.   860

BIFF: There'll be no pity for you, you hear it? No pity!

WILLY (*to* LINDA.): You hear the spite!

BIFF: No, you're going to hear the truth—what you are and what I am!

LINDA: Stop it!

WILLY: Spite!   865

HAPPY (*coming down toward* BIFF.): You cut it now!

BIFF (*to* HAPPY.): The man don't know who we are! The man is gonna know! (*To* WILLY.) We never told the truth for ten minutes in this house!

HAPPY: We always told the truth!

BIFF (*turning on him.*): You big blow, are you the assistant buyer? You're one of the two assistants to the assistant, aren't you?

HAPPY: Well, I'm practically   870

BIFF: You're practically full of it! We all are! And I'm through with it. (*To* WILLY.) Now hear this, Willy, this is me.

WILLY: I know you!

BIFF: You know why I had no address for three months? I stole a suit in Kansas City and I was in jail. (*To* LINDA, *who is sobbing.*) Stop crying. I'm through with it.

(LINDA *turns away from them, her hands covering her face.*)

WILLY: I suppose that's my fault!

BIFF: I stole myself out of every good job since high school!   875

WILLY: And whose fault is that?

BIFF: And I never got anywhere because you blew me so full of hot air I could never stand taking orders from anybody! That's whose fault it is!

WILLY: I hear that!

LINDA: Don't, Biff!

BIFF: It's goddam time you heard that! I had to be boss big shot in two weeks, and I'm through with it! 880

WILLY: Then hang yourself! For spite, hang yourself!

BIFF: No! Nobody's hanging himself, Willy! I ran down eleven flights with a pen in my hand today. And suddenly I stopped, you hear me? And in the middle of that office building, do you hear this? I stopped in the middle of that building and I saw—the sky. I saw the things that I love in this world. The work and the food and time to sit and smoke. And I looked at the pen and said to myself, what the hell am I grabbing this for? Why am I trying to become what I don't want to be? What am I doing in an office, making a contemptuous, begging fool of myself, when all I want is out there, waiting for me the minute I say I know who I am! Why can't I say that, Willy? (*He tries to make* WILLY *face him, but* WILLY *pulls away and moves to the left.*)

WILLY (*with hatred, threateningly.*): The door of your life is wide open!

BIFF: Pop! I'm a dime a dozen, and so are you!

WILLY (*turning on him now in an uncontrolled outburst.*): I am not a dime a dozen! I am Willy Loman, and you are Biff Loman! 885

(BIFF *starts for* WILLY, *but is blocked by* HAPPY. *In his fury,* BIFF *seems on the verge of attacking his father.*)

BIFF: I am not a leader of men, Willy, and neither are you. You were never anything but a hard-working drummer who landed in the ash can like all the rest of them! I'm one dollar an hour, Willy! I tried seven states and couldn't raise it. A buck an hour! Do you gather my meaning? I'm not bringing home any prizes any more, and you're going to stop waiting for me to bring them home!

WILLY (*directly to* BIFF.): You vengeful, spiteful mutt!

(BIFF *breaks from* HAPPY. WILLY, *in fright, starts up the stairs.* BIFF *grabs him.*)

BIFF (*at the peak of his fury.*): Pop, I'm nothing! I'm nothing, Pop. Can't you understand that? There's no spite in it any more. I'm just what I am, that's all.

(BIFF's *fury has spent itself, and he breaks down, sobbing, holding on to* WILLY, *who dumbly fumbles for* BIFF's *face.*)

WILLY (*astonished.*): What're you doing? What're you doing? (*To* LINDA.) Why is he crying?

BIFF (*crying, broken.*): Will you let me go, for Christ's sake? Will you take that phony dream and burn it before something happens? (*Struggling to contain himself, he pulls away and moves to the stairs.*) I'll go in the 890 morning. Put him—put him to bed. (*Exhausted,* BIFF *moves up the stairs to his room.*)

WILLY (*after a long pause, astonished, elevated.*): Isn't that remarkable? Biff—he likes me!

LINDA: He loves you, Willy!

HAPPY (*deeply moved.*): Always did, Pop.

WILLY: Oh, Biff! (*Staring wildly.*) He cried! Cried to me! (*He is choking with his love, and now cries out his promise.*) That boy—that boy is going to be magnificent!

(BEN *appears in the light just outside the kitchen.*)

BEN: Yes, outstanding, with twenty thousand behind him.   895

LINDA (*sensing the racing of his mind, fearfully, carefully.*): Now come to bed, Willy. It's all settled now.

WILLY (*finding it difficult not to rush out of the house.*): Yes, we'll sleep. Come on. Go to sleep, Hap.

BEN: And it does take a great kind of man to crack the jungle.

(*In accents of dread,* BEN's *idyllic music starts up.*)

HAPPY (*his arm around* LINDA.): I'm getting married, Pop, don't forget it. I'm changing everything. I'm gonna run that department before the year is up. You'll see, Mom. (*He kisses her.*)

BEN: The jungle is dark but full of diamonds, Willy.   900

(WILLY *turns, moves, listening to* BEN.)

LINDA: Be good. You're both good boys, just act that way, that's all.

HAPPY: 'Night, Pop. (*He goes upstairs.*)

LINDA (*to* WILLY.): Come, dear.

BEN (*with greater force.*): One must go in to fetch a diamond out.

WILLY (*to* LINDA, *as he moves slowly along the edge of the kitchen, toward the*   905
door.): I just want to get settled down, Linda. Let me sit alone for a little.

LINDA (*almost uttering her fear.*): I want you upstairs.

WILLY (*taking her in his arms.*): In a few minutes, Linda. I couldn't sleep right now. Go on, you look awful tired. (*He kisses her.*)

BEN: Not like an appointment at all. A diamond is rough and hard to the touch.

WILLY: Go on now. I'll be right up.

LINDA: I think this is the only way, Willy.   910

WILLY: Sure, it's the best thing.

BEN: Best thing!

WILLY: The only way. Everything is gonna be—go on, kid, get to bed. You look so tired.

LINDA: Come right up.

WILLY: Two minutes.   915

(LINDA *goes into the living room, then reappears in her bedroom.* WILLY *moves just outside the kitchen door.*)

WILLY: Loves me. (*Wonderingly.*) Always loved me. Isn't that a remarkable thing? Ben, he'll worship me for it!

BEN (*with promise.*): It's dark there, but full of diamonds.

WILLY: Can you imagine that magnificence with twenty thousand dollars in his pocket?

LINDA (*calling from her room.*): Willy! Come up!

WILLY (*calling from the kitchen.*): Yes! Yes! Coming! It's very smart, you realize that, don't you, sweetheart? Even Ben sees it. I gotta go, baby. By! By! (*Going over to Ben, almost dancing.*) Imagine? When the mail comes he'll be ahead of Bernard again! 920

BEN: A perfect proposition all around.

WILLY: Did you see how he cried to me? Oh, if I could kiss him, Ben!

BEN: Time, William, time!

WILLY: Oh, Ben, I always knew one way or another we were gonna make it, Biff and I!

BEN (*looking at his watch.*): The boat. We'll be late. (*He moves slowly off into the darkness.*) 925

WILLY (*elegiacally, turning to the house.*): Now when you kick off, boy, I want a seventy-yard boot, and get right down the field under the ball, and when you hit, hit low and hit hard, because it's important, boy. (*He swings around and faces the audience.*) There's all kinds of important people in the stands, and the first thing you know... (*Suddenly realizing he is alone.*) Ben! Ben, where do I...? (*He makes a sudden movement of search.*) Ben, how do I...?

LINDA (*calling.*): Willy, you coming up?

WILLY (*uttering a gasp of fear, whirling about as if to quiet her.*): Sh! (*He turns around as if to find his way; sounds, faces, voices, seem to be swarming in upon him and he flicks at them, crying.*) Sh! Sh! (*Suddenly music, faint and high, stops him. It rises in intensity, almost to an unbearable scream. He goes up and down on his toes, and rushes off around the house.*) Shhh!

LINDA: Willy?

(*There is no answer.* LINDA *waits.* BIFF *gets up off his bed. He is still in his clothes.* HAPPY *sits up.* BIFF *stands listening.*)

LINDA (*with real fear.*): Willy, answer me! Willy! 930

(*There is the sound of a car starting and moving away at full speed.*)

LINDA: No!

BIFF (*rushing down the stairs.*): Pop!

(*As the car speeds off, the music crashes down in a frenzy of sound, which becomes the soft pulsation of a single cello string.* BIFF *slowly returns to his bedroom. He and* HAPPY *gravely don their jackets.* LINDA *slowly walks out of her room. The music has developed into a dead march. The leaves of day are appearing over everything.* CHARLEY *and* BERNARD, *somberly dressed, appear and knock on the kitchen door.* BIFF *and* HAPPY *slowly descend the stairs to*

the kitchen as CHARLEY *and* BERNARD *enter. All stop a moment when*
LINDA, *in clothes of mourning, bearing a little bunch of roses, comes through
the draped doorway into the kitchen. She goes to* CHARLEY *and takes his arm.
Now all move toward the audience, through the wall-line of the kitchen. At
the limit of the apron,* LINDA *lays down the flowers, kneels, and sits back on
her heels. All stare down at the grave.)*

REQUIEM

CHARLEY: It's getting dark, Linda.

(LINDA *doesn't react. She stares at the grave.)*

BIFF: How about it, Mom? Better get some rest, heh? They'll be closing the
gate soon.

(LINDA *makes no move. Pause.)*

HAPPY *(deeply angered.):* He had no right to do that! There was no necessity
for it. We would've helped him.

CHARLEY *(grunting.):* Hmmm.

BIFF: Come along, Mom.

LINDA: Why didn't anybody come?   5

CHARLEY: It was a very nice funeral.

LINDA: But where are all the people he knew? Maybe they blame him.

CHARLEY: Naa. It's a rough world, Linda. They wouldn't blame him.

LINDA: I can't understand it. At this time especially. First time in thirty-five
years we were just about free and clear. He only needed a little salary.
He was even finished with the dentist.

CHARLEY: No man only needs a little salary.   10

LINDA: I can't understand it.

BIFF: There were a lot of nice days. When he'd come home from a trip; or
on Sundays, making the stoop; finishing the cellar; putting on the new
porch; when he built the extra bathroom; and put up the garage. You
know something, Charley, there's more of him in that front stoop than
in all the sales he ever made.

CHARLEY: Yeah. He was a happy man with a batch of cement.

LINDA: He was so wonderful with his hands.

BIFF: He had the wrong dreams. All, all, wrong.   15

HAPPY *(almost ready to fight* BIFF.*):* Don't say that!

BIFF: He never knew who he was.

CHARLEY *(stopping* HAPPY's *movement and reply. To* BIFF.*):* Nobody dast
blame this man. You don't understand: Willy was a salesman. And for a
salesman, there is no rock bottom to the life. He don't put a bolt to a
nut, he don't tell you the law or give you medicine. He's a man out
there in the blue, riding on a smile and a shoeshine. And when they
start not smiling back—that's an earthquake. And then you get yourself
a couple of spots on your hat, and you're finished. Nobody dast blame

this man. A salesman is got to dream, boy. It comes with the territory.

BIFF: Charley, the man didn't know who he was.

HAPPY (*infuriated.*): Don't say that! 20

BIFF: Why don't you come with me, Happy?

HAPPY: I'm not licked that easily. I'm staying right in this city, and I'm gonna beat this racket! (*He looks at* BIFF, *his chin set.*) The Loman Brothers!

BIFF: I know who I am, kid.

HAPPY: All right, boy. I'm gonna show you and everybody else that Willy Loman did not die in vain. He had a good dream. It's the only dream you can have—to come out number-one man. He fought it out here, and this is where I'm gonna win it for him.

BIFF (*with a hopeless glance at* HAPPY, *bends toward his mother.*): Let's go, 25 Mom.

LINDA: I'll be with you in a minute. Go on, Charley. (*He hesitates.*) I want to, just for a minute. I never had a chance to say good-by.

(CHARLEY *moves away, followed by* HAPPY. BIFF *remains a slight distance up and left of* LINDA. *She sits there, summoning herself. The flute begins, not far away, playing behind her speech.*)

LINDA: Forgive me, dear. I can't cry. I don't know what it is, but I can't cry. I don't understand it. Why did you ever do that? Help me, Willy, I can't cry. It seems to me that you're just on another trip. I keep expecting you. Willy, dear, I can't cry. Why did you do it? I search and search and I search, and I can't understand it, Willy. I made the last payment on the house today. Today, dear. And there'll be nobody home. (*A sob rises in her throat.*) We're free and clear. (*Sobbing more fully, released.*) We're free. (BIFF *comes slowly toward her.*): We're free...We're free...

(BIFF *lifts her to her feet and moves out up right with her in his arms.* LINDA *sobs quietly.* BERNARD *and* CHARLEY *come together and follow them, followed by* HAPPY. *Only the music of the flute is left on the darkening stage as over the house the hard towers of the apartment buildings rise into sharp focus, and—*)

THE CURTAIN FALLS

- Biff claims that his father had "the wrong dreams." What are these dreams, and how are they presented in the play? How does the play demonstrate them to be wrong?

- How are Willy's dreams different from those of Linda, Biff, and Happy?

- Some readers suggest that Willy Loman symbolizes American strengths and weaknesses. What details in the play support this broad reading of the character? How does such a reading expand our understanding of the play? What individual details might we lose if we focus only on the symbolic nature of Willy's character?

Experiencing Literature through Writing

1. Locate a single symbol within a specific work. Describe how attention to this symbol is appropriate and lends insight into the larger work. As you write, consider the following questions:

   a. How can you justify your claim that this particular detail is symbolic? Explain how this detail relates to other specific details within the text.

   b. Are there strong alternative readings of this symbol? What would be the implications of this alternative?

   c. How is attention to this symbol important to the text as a whole?

2. How is the subject of community particularly suited to symbolic representations? Using one (or more) specific works for detail, explain how the issues that pertain to groups of people within a community become clearer when presented symbolically.

14 Context

What Outside Information Do We Really Need to Know to Understand the Text?

It's often claimed that great art transcends the specific context within which it is produced: great works are timeless. That common assertion seems credible enough when we think of Greek drama, or *Othello*, or *Don Quixote*. But as durable as such masterpieces have proven to be, it seems far too simple to cite abstract "universals" like *anger, love, jealousy,* and *idealism* as the source of our continued appreciation. It's more accurate to say that great art prompts fresh, varied, powerful, new, and concrete experiences of fundamental human concerns. A play like *Othello* (with its themes of jealousy and envy as well as its racial subtext) hasn't so much transcended our time as it has *absorbed* our time and remained powerful. Issues of race, for example, can't ultimately mean the same thing for twenty-first-century Americans that they meant for the Elizabethan audience. When our literary experiences bridge the cultural gap between then and now, the literature enables us to enlarge our sense of who we are and of the world that surrounds us.

Good reading involves sustaining a healthy tension. On the one hand, we don't want to disregard a text's origins. We want to understand the history and culture of the author. On the other hand, we cannot—and should not—avoid experiencing art in terms of who we are now. We cannot avoid bringing new knowledge to old texts. In this chapter, we'll consider how our contemporary situation affects our experience of art as well as how knowledge of a work's historical context can deepen that experience.

HOW DOES NEW KNOWLEDGE INFLUENCE OUR EXPERIENCE OF OLD TEXTS?

In writing about the action that takes place in a literary text, it's customary to use the present tense. Shakespeare wrote *Othello* early in the seventeenth century, but Othello kills Desdemona every time we read the play. This is a small stylistic convention, but it's a convention that suggests something important. *A literary text comes alive as we experience it; the action is always present.* Othello the play and Othello the character aren't frozen in place by the words on the page. If we keep this in mind, we can understand how it is that our *Othello* isn't necessarily the same *Othello* that someone in Victorian England might have experienced. And of course, texts that Victorians produced aren't necessarily read today as they were when they first appeared.

Over a century and a half ago, Alfred, Lord Tennyson read a newspaper account of a confused and disastrous cavalry charge of British soldiers in the Crimean War. He was inspired to commemorate that event. Tennyson's poetic intent was to valorize his country's military men. They served, followed orders, and died valiantly in a cause. Tennyson's key themes were loyalty, courage, discipline, patriotism. He wrote from a conviction of his country's goodness and the legitimacy of its imperialistic endeavors. The poem was a great success in some ways, exactly the sort of poem a poet laureate (the official poet of the state) was expected to produce. Since its appearance, many a schoolchild both in Great Britain and the United States has stood before a class and dutifully recited "The Charge of the Light Brigade." Despite the poem's popularity, there has always been a ripple of uneasiness among some readers about the tone of unqualified military zeal it endorses. The light brigade, after all, charged forward to death on botched orders in service of an uncertain cause. That ripple grew to waves in England after World War I and in the United States during the Vietnam War. Tennyson's poem today hardly works as a lofty tribute; we're more likely to respond to themes of waste, futility, and patriotic vanity—themes that Tennyson himself didn't intend to strike. The words of the poem haven't changed, but the surrounding cultural/historical **context** has changed.

Alfred, Lord Tennyson (1809–1892)

The Charge of the Light Brigade (1854)

1

Half a league, half a league,
Half a league onward,

All in the valley of Death
   Rode the six hundred.
"Forward the Light Brigade!
Charge for the guns!" he said.   5
Into the valley of Death
   Rode the six hundred.

         2
"Forward, the Light Brigade!"
Was there a man dismayed?   10
Not though the soldier knew
   Someone had blundered.
Theirs not to make reply,
Theirs not to reason why,
Theirs but to do and die.   15
Into the valley of Death
   Rode the six hundred.

         3
Cannon to right of them,
Cannon to left of them,
Cannon in front of them   20
   Volleyed and thundered;
Stormed at with shot and shell,
Boldly they rode and well,
Into the jaws of Death,
Into the mouth of hell   25
   Rode the six hundred.

         4
Flashed all their sabers bare,
Flashed as they turned in air
Sab'ring the gunners there,
Charging an army, while   30
   All the world wondered.
Plunged in the battery smoke
Right through the line they broke;
Cossack and Russian
Reeled from the saber stroke   35
   Shattered and sundered.
Then they rode back, but not,
   Not the six hundred.

                5
Cannon to right of them,
Cannon to left of them,   40
Cannon behind them
   Volleyed and thundered;
Stormed at with shot and shell,
While horse and hero fell.
They that had fought so well   45
Came through the jaws of Death,
Back from the mouth of hell,
All that was left of them,
   Left of six hundred.

                6
When can their glory fade?   50
O the wild charge they made!
   All the world wondered.
Honor the charge they made!
Honor the Light Brigade,
   Noble six hundred!   55

Tennyson invokes a number of abstractions he could expect to be taken as
"universals": nobility, bravery, self-sacrifice, and honor. He writes with a
confident assumption that those abstractions will long endure: "All the
world" is caught in rapt admiration of the brigade's martial virtues. The
closing stanza asks the question, "When can their glory fade?" which implies
an answer: not for a long, long time, not for as long as we honor courage and
steadfast loyalty to a cause.

   Of course, Tennyson could not envision the human costs of World
War I. Nor could he be expected to imagine wars in Vietnam or Iraq from
the perspective of a U.S. citizen. But these wars are part of our political,
moral, and historical identity. Lines like "Theirs not to reason why, /
Theirs but to do and die" strike most of us as disturbing and even
dangerous. It's worth noting that we commonly misquote these lines in a
way that diminishes the discomfort they have come to produce. One may
hear the phrase repeated as "theirs but to do *or* die." It may seem a small
matter, but *or* serves to soften Tennyson's point and perhaps helps sustain
his romantic notions of war. If we charge forward boldly enough, we may
die but we may instead accomplish something and still live (do and *not*
die). Tennyson writing in 1856 seemed so secure in his ideals of duty that a
perfect willingness to "do *and* die" only underscored for him the nobility of
the act.

Perhaps the quickest way to imagine a modern counterpoint to Tennyson's vision is to recall any one of several notable American films about the war in Vietnam. For example, Francis Ford Coppola's *Apocalypse Now* (1979) depicts commitment to the cause as a kind of insanity, or perhaps even more accurately Coppola depicts zealous military commitment as a cause of insanity. *Apocalypse Now* is based on Joseph Conrad's novel *Heart of Darkness*, which chronicles the effects of imperialism in the Congo at the end of the nineteenth century. Both *Heart of Darkness* and *Apocalypse Now* strip away the sorts of abstract notions that Tennyson calls on for inspiration. Coppola uses the grand sweep of the film screen to suggest the enormity of destruction, cruelty, and death. He undercuts rather than invokes patriotic themes.

Making Connections

Varied elements of any work of art will work together to achieve an effect. How does the rhythm and pace of "The Charge of the Light Brigade" complement the theme? How do the rhymes work to mark Tennyson's perspective on the event? Does Tennyson's technical command make the poem compelling, or does it merely exaggerate themes many modern readers find problematic (see Chapters 3 and 6)?

Apocalypse Now (1979)

HOW IS KNOWLEDGE "OUTSIDE" THE TEXT HELPFUL?

Some poems, of course, manage to generalize on matters of the human condition in ways that hold up, or promise to hold up, very well. As much as we warn you against easy notions of "universals," we don't want to dismiss what has long been a motivating belief in the enduring power of art. Czeslaw Milosz in "A Song on the End of the World" relies upon simple images to invoke a sense of the universal. In Milosz's poem, nature provides a constant: bees approach the flower, porpoises jump, sparrows play. Human activity runs a familiar course: fishermen mend nets, women walk in fields, a "drunkard grows sleepy." Although Milosz employs concrete images of nature and everyday life, he has in the body of the poem deliberately avoided the sorts of specifics that allow us to "locate" the action in any narrow way; we are not tied to any particular time and place.

Czeslaw Milosz (1911–2004)

A Song on the End of the World (1944)

On the day the world ends
A bee circles a clover,
A fisherman mends a glimmering net.
Happy porpoises jump in the sea,
By the rainspout young sparrows are playing   5
And the snake is gold-skinned as it should always be.

On the day the world ends
Women walk through the fields under the umbrellas,
A drunkard grows sleepy at the edge of a lawn,
Vegetable peddlers shout in the street   10
And a yellow-sailed boat comes nearer the island,
The voice of a violin lasts in the air
And leads into a starry night.

And those who expected lightning and thunder
Are disappointed.   15
And those who expected signs and archangels' trumps
Do not believe it is happening now.
As long as the sun and the moon are above,
As long as the bumblebee visits a rose,
As long as rosy infants are born   20
No one believes it is happening now.

Only a white-haired old man, who would be a prophet
Yet is not a prophet, for he's much too busy,
Repeats while he binds his tomatoes:
There will be no other end of the world,   25
There will be no other end of the world.

Warsaw, 1944

Now ask yourself, what is the last line of this poem? One answer seems obvious: "There will be no other end of the world." But another possible answer lies just below that line: "*Warsaw, 1944.*" Milosz included that identifying place and date in the text of the poem as it appears in his collected poems. If taken as part of the poem, it stands as a resonant and dramatic close that influences how we absorb the lines that precede it. Poland was sacrificed to the Germans by the rest of the world in hopes that Hitler's ambitions would find a limit. Those ambitions, of course, knew no limits, and the cost to Poland, particularly Polish Jews, was staggering. By 1944, the disaster had unfolded for all to see who were willing to look and not flinch. Only the most deliberately resistant could refuse to acknowledge the end of the world that was "happening."

Milosz has achieved in this poem a balanced tension that he seeks in so many of his poems: The desire to find something real and eternal is set against a recognition of the most profound dishonesty or disconnection; the need to identify what it means to be human is placed in the context of a brutal, inhuman history. He wants us to engage the **universal** and the **particular**, the **abstract** and the **concrete**. If we don't know anything of Milosz's life, of the history he has experienced—if we erase "*Warsaw, 1944*" from the end of his poem, we still have a beautiful poem. But with that historical marker, we're prompted to think not only of Poland's tragic history but also of how the poem applies to the various large-scale traumas that have unfolded within our own history. We can add new particulars to give the abstractions life. The best readers will respond with curiosity about Milosz's closing signal and a willingness to follow it by learning more of the author, his poetry, and the history he grapples with. Those readers will also consider how Milosz speaks from this rich context to our condition now.

Experiencing Literature in Context

The following biographical sketch of Milosz touches only lightly on major events of a long and full life, but even the barest knowledge of such events will influence responses to Milosz's poetry.

CZESLAW MILOSZ BIOGRAPHY

Czeslaw Milosz (1911–2004) was born in Wilno, Lithuania, which was then controlled by czarist Russia. At the outbreak of World War I, his father was drafted as an engineer by the czar's army, and the family spent the war years traveling throughout Russia and Siberia. After the Russian Revolution in 1917, the family returned to the village of his birth. Milosz published his first poems in 1930, the year after he graduated from high school.

In 1935, he began to work for Polish Radio. During the first days of World War II, he was sent to the front as a radio operator. In January 1940, he returned to Wilno and was caught there when Soviet tanks entered the city. In July, he escaped across Soviet lines into Poland and spent most of the war working for underground presses in Nazi-occupied Warsaw.

After the war, Milosz came to the United States as a diplomat for the new government of the People's Republic of Poland. In 1950, he was transferred to Paris, where he requested and was granted asylum the following year. He spent the next decade writing in Paris. Among the most famous of his works during this period is *The Captive Mind* (1953), in which Milosz writes about "the vulnerability of the twentieth-century mind to seduction by sociopolitical doctrines and its readiness to accept totalitarian terror for the sake of a hypothetical future." In 1960, he accepted a post at the University of California, Berkeley. He was awarded the Nobel Prize in literature in 1981. That year, he returned to Poland for the first time since his exile in 1951 and met with solidarity leader Lech Walesa. Shortly thereafter, Polish presses published Milosz's poetry, making it possible for Poles to read their celebrated national poet for the first time. Milosz's wife, Janka, died in 1986 after a ten-year battle with Alzheimer's disease. His second wife, Carol, died in 2002.

Now as you read the next Milosz poem, you are prepared in subtle yet profound ways to experience more in the act of reading. His reflection in "Christopher Robin" on much-loved characters from a famous children's book, for example, can hardly be seen as mere playfulness once we know something of what Milosz had lived through.

Czeslaw Milosz (1911–2004)

Christopher Robin (1998)

In April of 1996 the international press carried the news of the death, at age seventy-five, of Christopher Robin Milne, immortalized in a book by his father, A.A. Milne, Winnie-the-Pooh, as Christopher Robin.

I must think suddenly of matters too difficult for a bear of little brain. I have never asked myself what lies beyond the place where we live, I and Rabbit, Piglet and Eeyore, with our friend Christopher Robin. That is, we continued to live here, and nothing changed, and I just ate my little something. Only Christopher Robin left for a moment.

Owl says that immediately beyond our garden Time begins, and that it is an awfully deep well. If you fall in it, you go down and down, very quickly, and no one knows what happens to you next. I was a bit worried about Christopher Robin falling in, but he came back and then I asked him about the well. "Old Bear," he answered. "I was in it and I was falling and I wore trousers down to the ground, I had a gray beard, then I died. It was probably just a dream, it was quite unreal. The only real thing was you, old bear, and our shared fun. Now I won't go anywhere, even if I'm called for an afternoon snack." ■

What do you make of Christopher Robin's remark to Pooh that falling into "Time" is "quite unreal"? Is Milosz suggesting that "real" life is full of delusions? Could he be commenting instead (or in addition) on how strenuously some people escape living actively and responsibly? Do you think the world of "Time" is real for Milosz?

DO WE NEED TO KNOW *EVERYTHING* IN ORDER TO UNDERSTAND?

Poems like "The Charge of the Light Brigade," "A Song on the End of the World," and "Christopher Robin" help us consider questions about what knowledge we need to bring to texts as well as what knowledge we unavoidably bring to texts. These poems also help us respond to a problem some people have with reading serious literature or seeing ambitious plays and films: serious work (the complaint goes) demands "too much" knowledge. We believe that it's a rare text that asks "too much" of a reader. The charge of "too much" builds on a mistaken and unrealistic notion of "understanding." Understanding or not understanding is rarely an either-or proposition. In reading or viewing a challenging text, we commonly gain some understanding as we read and seek more as we write, re-read, and re-see. It's also normal to *not* understand some things at the same time we respond powerfully to others. Dismissing the task as too hard from the outset presumes that reading is something we do in a straight line and that when we get to the end of the line, our reading is over; once the pages are turned, we're done. This misleading notion of reading presumes that the only good reading is a "complete" reading. But denying the centrality of process cuts us off from the chance to discover what the text may offer. It forces us to think of one final understanding that we must get in order to validate our effort. It dismisses the renewed and deepened pleasure we can experience in successive readings. It also prevents us from acquiring the "knowledge" that we sometimes complain we don't possess. So, what we don't know about European history shouldn't stop us from reading Milosz and coming to a valuable understanding of his work; and reading Milosz will help us learn a great deal about European history.

It might seem odd to move from Milosz's poem to a one-liner in a Woody Allen story, but jokes illustrate nicely how we can sometimes "understand" quite a bit without "knowing" much. In "Mr. Big," a comic detective piece, Allen presents a scene in which a glamorous woman clings to a tough, "hard-boiled" detective named Kaiser Lupowitz and pleads, "Just don't get ontological, not now. I couldn't bear it if you were ontological with me." Even with the minimal context we've supplied, it's possible you

"Just don't get ontological, not now. I couldn't bear it if you were ontological with me."

find the line funny. We can use it as a caption to the photograph from *The Maltese Falcon* (1941) to mimic the joke's working dynamic.

If the photograph has absolutely no resonance for you (you've *never* seen Humphrey Bogart play a detective, *never* read Raymond Chandler or Dashiell Hammett, *never* read or seen other works of this type), the line will fall flat. Although some slight knowledge is absolutely necessary, extensive knowledge really isn't required to "get" the joke. You need to know only enough to sense, for example, that most tough guys in detective stories aren't named "Kaiser Lupowitz." More important, you need to know enough to recognize that the word *ontological* doesn't fit the character type of the speaker. You don't even need to know what *ontological* means as long as you recognize that it doesn't sound tough, sexy, or colloquial. So we can have one kind of **understanding** (the word *sounds* funny) without another kind of understanding (the definition of the word). In this case, the former kind of understanding is far more important than the latter. *Ontological* pertains to a philosophical theory of reality that presumes universal and essential characteristics of all existence. Knowing that, we think, doesn't make the joke much funnier.

We're not suggesting that knowing things isn't important, but we do make the following claims:

- We often *do* know more than we realize.
- We don't need to know *everything* in order to *understand many things* very well.
- We acquire new knowledge by encountering things we don't know.

Experiencing Art in Context

Look carefully at the painting *Young Man at His Window*. The painting evokes in most people a sense of loneliness. The young man, back turned to us, stands by himself in a room and looks out on almost empty streets. Everything darkens from the window inward; the young man seems boxed in. The railing and the window frame separate the young man from the world outside. That outside world also seems contained. The large buildings across from his room close in the street on all sides. Only a small bit of sky shows at the top of the picture. The city is all around. And yet people are almost entirely absent. Only one woman is visible on the streets below the young man's window, and she is a distant figure. The young man seems tired, disconnected, and alone.

This interpretation may be argued from the painting itself. What is within the frame can inspire a thoughtful response—a valuable level of understanding. But we don't need to stop at that level. Caillebotte was not only a painter but also a collector and a scholar. He knew Caspar David Friedrich's *Wanderer above the Sea of Fog* (p. 287) very well. Friedrich's painting spoke to the Byronic spirit of his day. That is, it captured a feeling for the powerful man depicted by the Romantic poet Byron, who sought to move beyond the limits set by society. It placed a grand figure on a mountaintop aggressively confronting the vastness of nature itself. One could argue that Caillebotte echoes Friedrich's painting. He has his figure stand—like the wanderer—with his back to us as he looks over the world before him. But Caillebotte's figure strikes a less confident pose. A visible shrug seems much different than the posture of the one who just strode to the top of a mountain. The city, not nature, spreads out in front of Caillebotte's young man. In fact, nature has nearly been squeezed out of the picture. If we see Caillebotte's painting as a conscious revision of (and commentary on) Friedrich's well-known work, our response to *Young Man at His Window* will become more richly textured although not necessarily more correct or even necessarily different in the main points. The theme of "loneliness" now might

Making Connections

Artists who choose to deal with historically distant subjects may find ways to build the necessary context into their work. In "Shelley," for example, the contemporary poet Galway Kinnell provides information that allows readers who may know nothing of the title subject to understand the essential point he wants to make (p. 1125). The poem is for the most part a brief and wrenching summary of key events in Shelley's domestic life (suicides of lovers, deaths of children). That summary is framed by two different perspectives: one of youthful idolatry and the other of painful disengagement. Kinnell includes a great deal in relatively few lines that allows readers to understand his poem without having read previously about Shelley's life. To what extent does reading Kinnell's poem prompt you to learn more? Do you think it likely that reading a more sympathetic biography would influence your experience of Kinnell's "Shelley"?

Gustave Caillebotte, *Young Man at His Window* (1875)

be seen more sharply as a condition of urban life. Caillebotte may well be commenting on a broad-scale cultural change: As an earlier generation "conquered" nature, the new generation has become progressively disconnected from life as it deals with the consequences of that conquering. There's no space for Caillebotte's young man to move, no opportunities for a heroic gesture.

WHAT IF SUBSTANTIAL OUTSIDE KNOWLEDGE IS ESSENTIAL?

What happens to a literary text that gets heavily caught up in historical particulars? Can an audience's shifting interests and changed knowledge base make a great work into an irrelevant or hopelessly opaque work? These are questions that we need to consider even if we can't finally answer them. Some texts do require us to work, and it's reasonable that we ask if the effort is worth it. Herman Melville's "The House-Top," like "A Song on the End of the World," makes a date important to the reading of the poem. Melville provides the date up front with a subheading that fleshes out the setting (on a "house-top" at night). But for most readers, the date marks nothing specific that easily comes to mind. And the setting hardly helps upon first reading. Our guess is that you'll find it impossible to get a grip on the following poem without some background that lies outside most readers' knowledge base. Still, we'll present the poem here without preparation. Read it to the end, even though you'll likely feel lost. Then return to the poem once you've read the background information following the poem.

Herman Melville (1819–1891)

The House-Top (1866)

A Night Piece.
(July, 1863)

No sleep. The sultriness pervades the air
And binds the brain—a dense oppression,
As tawny tigers feel in matter shades,

Vexing their blood and making apt for ravage.
Beneath the stars the roofy desert spreads   5
Vacant as Libya. All is hushed near by.
Yet fitfully from the far breaks a mixed surf
Of muffled sound, the Atheist roar of riot.
Yonder, where parching Sirius set in drought,
Balefully glares red Arson—there—and there.   10
The Town is taken by its rats—ship-rats
And rats of the wharves. All civil charms
And priestly spells which late held hearts in awe—
Fear-bound, subjected to a better sway
Than sway of self; these like a dream dissolve,   15
And man rebounds whole aeons back in nature.
Hail to the low dull rumble, dull and dead,
And ponderous drag that shakes the wall.
Wise Draco comes, deep in the midnight roll
Of black artillery; he comes, though late;   20
In code corroborating Calvin's creed
And cynic tyrannies of honest kings;
He comes, nor parlies; and the Town, redeemed,
Gives thanks devout; nor, being thankful, heeds
The grimy slur on the Republic's faith implied,   25
Which holds that Man is naturally good,
And—more—is Nature's Roman, never to be scourged.

In "The House-Top," Melville is casting a very specific event in broad philosophical and theological terms. He's placing a contemporary situation in relation to distant historical periods in order to universalize the poem; he raises fundamental questions about law, power, and human nature. The problem is that almost all readers today are at a loss concerning either the specific or the general as it plays out in this poem. Melville was a voracious reader, and the knowledge he draws on can be baffling—even off-putting. To make things more difficult, the event that inspired him to write is not one that gets much space in most general history textbooks. Is this poem, then, dead as a piece of literature? If not, what must we do to rescue it or, as a scholar might say, preserve it as literature?

The questions we've asked are the sorts of questions you'll ultimately have to answer for yourself, but we think that "The House-Top" is absolutely worth the demands it makes, that even the slightest historical gloss makes the poem not only accessible but urgently alive. July 1863 is the date of the draft riots that occurred in New York City. Hundreds of young men (mostly poor young men because the wealthy could choose to buy their way out of the draft) rebelled at the prospect of forced service in the Union cause. The city's blacks were blamed for these men's situation. If it were not for the North's abhorrence of slavery, there would be no Civil War. At least that was the feeling of the moment. The angry crowds moved through the city at night and turned much of their frenzied energy on those they blamed. They burned a black church and a black orphanage: people suffered, people died. Melville, who lived in New York, was appalled. For him, the fact of slavery made the Civil War a moral necessity for the North. That citizens would attack helpless people in defiance of that cause was a profound mark of human depravity. The rioters, then, are the "rats" that have taken the town. The personified "red Arson" glares from flames seen, and the "Atheist roar" can be heard from the house-top. The town is overtaken by an evil that is no longer controlled by "civil charms" (laws) or "priestly spells" (religious beliefs) that had earlier worked effectively through the power of fear.

This endorsement of fear as a means to control helps us understand the darkness of Melville's vision and the depth of his anger. Laws and beliefs at least forced people to obey something outside their own selfish nature (the "sway of self"). Draco, the harsh lawgiver, marches to reassert order, but Melville's Draco is not the severe and cruel figure of common understanding; he is "wise," for he understands Calvin's insight: Humans are by nature bad. The town's citizens are "redeemed," but that word must be seen as loaded with irony. They are thankful for being saved from themselves, yet they do not acknowledge the underlying (and unpleasant) message (the "grimy slur") about their foolish belief in the natural goodness of humankind. A Roman citizen was not subject to the punishment of whipping; Americans, Melville suggests, like to think of themselves as Nature's Roman citizen. But in fact, they deserved, needed, and received a whipping from authorities who came to reclaim the city.

If the previous summary serves to replace the poem, then the poem is indeed dead. But we'd suggest you take the information we have supplied and read the poem over several times. Melville's images, his word choice, his allusions, his close engagement with a powerful moment in his own history and his willingness to imagine what that moment means in larger terms operate together to create a powerful and unsettling vision of society and law. Our summary informs but doesn't encourage the kind of experience available in a work of art. And though the context we've supplied may seem substantial, it is not hard to acquire. Professional scholars will often provide useful glosses that accompany modern editions of older works. And standard reference books along with useful websites allow us to quickly access information about names we don't recognize, events we hadn't learned in class, ideas we hadn't encountered in our earlier reading.

A Note to Student Writers: Using Electronic and Printed Sources for Research

The birth of the World Wide Web has changed strategies for doing background research, but it's important to understand the limits of the Web. Although you can find much useful information online, an enormous amount of irrelevant, erroneous, and distracting information also waits there. A Google search of "Draco" yields more than thirty-four thousand entries; far more of those address Draco Malfoy, a villain in the Harry Potter series, than the Roman man of law in Melville's allusion. "Wise Draco" gets us quickly to the poem itself, but that is no help. "Cynic" yields more than a million hits. "Calvin's creed" leads to discussions of Calvinism (a promising start), but a closer look reveals that the first discussion in the list of possibilities comes from a very specific political interest group. Of course, by the time you are reading this book, any search you undertake will differ. But you'll face the same sorts of traps and bad leads we found. Wikipedia has become a favorite online source for many college students; it's a site that offers an alternative to traditional methods of prioritizing and disseminating information. All readers of Wikipedia are allowed to participate as editors. This openness enables the site to draw upon the knowledge of millions of people, but it also creates a much larger pool for errors to creep into the database. The problems shouldn't keep you from the Web but should remind you that reference *books* still have value.

One source a student of literature should know is the *Oxford English Dictionary* (commonly referred to as the *OED*). As discussed in Chapter 11, the *OED* provides not just definitions but histories of words. At the simplest level, it helps us through the confusion over words that may arise with change: "berries" can be "rude" in Milton's work because *rude* in the seventeenth century could mean "unripe." But the *OED* can provoke us to explore fundamental interpretive matters. Hamlet's charge to Ophelia, "Get thee to a nunnery!" seems straightforward enough, but the *OED* tells us that *nunnery* in Shakespeare's day could also refer to a house of prostitution. Does Shakespeare want us to set the two meanings in opposition? Does he want us to understand Hamlet's command as cruelly sarcastic? What might we learn from the *OED* about Melville's use of the "cynic" to modify the "tyrannies" that are expressed by "honest kings"?

As you might imagine, the *OED* is a huge, multivolume work. Your library, however, may have the *OED* in electronic form. This makes it possible to quickly cross-reference words. It also allows you to search the *OED* for quotations (every entry has examples of a word's use over time). Obviously, if you are concerned only with the contemporary meaning and usage of a word, consult one of the many current desk dictionaries now available.

Specialized handbooks, encyclopedias, dictionaries, and "companions" provide brief, informative discussions of plots, authors, characters, critical terms, and aesthetic movements. One widely used series that offers much biographical, textual, and historical background is published by the Oxford University Press: *The Oxford Companion to English Literature*, *The Oxford Companion to American Literature*, *The Oxford Companion to the Theatre*, *The Oxford Companion to Film* (*to Art, to the Bible*, and so on) are particularly useful to students of literature and film. Although the book you are reading offers much information on critical terms, other reference works are still worth noting: *The Princeton Encyclopedia of Poetry and Poetics*; M. H. Abrams's *A Glossary of Literary Terms*; Ira Konigsberg's *The Complete Film Dictionary*. There are also substantial, sophisticated works that provide much information helpful to critical writers who desire a broad grasp of intellectual context: *The Encyclopedia of Philosophy* and *A Dictionary of the History of Ideas* are both likely to be part of your college's reference library.

The range, variety, and accessibility of such works make even poems as densely packed as Melville's "The House-Top" quite approachable. So we hope that you read ambitiously and without fear of what you don't know; we also hope that you'll read with confidence about what you do know and what you can learn.

MODELING CRITICAL ANALYSIS: JOÃO GUIMARÃES ROSA, THE THIRD BANK OF THE RIVER

In Chapters 12 and 13, we considered how João Guimarães Rosa's "The Third Bank of the River" provokes allegorical or symbolic readings. The title itself demands that we move beyond the limits of a realistic story. What would a "third bank of a river" be, after all? We might try to imagine a sharp bend in a river that makes from some perspectives a sort of third bank, but such a literal approach would surely seem strained. Given the story we read, it seems clear Guimarães Rosa asks us to consider some new dimension to what we ordinarily consider the real. So far, we have taken on the challenge without addressing any matters of Guimarães Rosa's life or language.

It's likely that you haven't read Guimarães Rosa before. He is greatly admired and the author of a novel many critics consider to be one of the great works of the twentieth century, *Grande Sertão: Veredes (The Devil to Pay in the Backlands)*. But Guimarães Rosa writes in Portuguese, not a language as widely translated for English readers as, say, Spanish or French. Some of his books are also quite demanding—even for those who are native speakers of Portuguese. Fortunately, "The Third Bank of the River" doesn't require any special context for a deeply rewarding reading in English. But that hardly means that context is irrelevant. Consider how any of the following background might help you return to "The Third Bank of the River" with an openness to new interpretive possibilities.

Guimarães Rosa has been considered by some a regional writer; to the extent this is true, his region is Minas Gerais—a state in Brazil's interior notable for its mining and its agriculture. He was trained and practiced as a medical doctor in Minas Gerais. Some of his stories catch the flavor of local idioms and legends he may have heard from patients. But *regionalist* is far too narrow a word to describe his ambition or achievement. Guimarães Rosa possessed a lifelong fascination with languages; he spoke six well and read several other languages. He was a diplomat (stationed for some years in Colombia). And he was an avid reader of world literatures. His stories are not tied to regional traditions either in subject matter or in technique.

In 1958, at the age of fifty, Guimarães Rosa suffered a life-threatening heart attack. The collection in which "The Third Bank of the River" appeared, *Primeiros Estórias*, was published four years later. These were not "first stories" in the usual sense, but they were the first stories Guimarães Rosa wrote and published after the heart attack. The stories in this collection, according to one critic, involve a profound change that "implies the crossing of a threshold." In this respect, "The Third Bank of the River" seems typical—even central. In fact, the English translation of *Primeiros Estórias* is *The Third Bank of the River and Other Stories*. In an index to the first edition of the stories, Guimarães Rosa signaled themes of change, transition, and transcendence in what we might call a set of hieroglyphics for every story. The hieroglyphic line for "The Third Bank of the River" ends with a symbol of infinity. The entire line appears as follows:

VI – A TERCEIRA MARGEM DO RIO ....

Does knowledge of Guimarães Rosa's medical training, his heart attack, the general themes of the stories in the collection that followed that heart attack, the title of the collection in which the story first appeared, and the hieroglyph pictured contribute to your understanding of "The Third Bank of the River"? Does any of this contextual material enrich or change your reading? Does it merely reinforce an original impression? How is this knowledge relevant or irrelevant to your reading experience?

Using Context to Focus Writing and Discussion

- What outside knowledge do you have in addition to the knowledge the text itself offers? How is any piece of this information relevant to the text that you are reading? For instance, we might know when the author lived. If the author wrote a work of fiction set in some historical event that the author experienced, how would that knowledge influence our reading of the fictional text? If the author wrote a work of fiction set in a different time, how would our knowledge of the author's life help us read this work of fiction?

- What specific connections can you draw between the literary work and its context? Why are these connections interesting? (Just finding connections isn't enough to make them interesting.)

- How does your understanding of the text change as you learn historical or biographical facts that relate to its production?

- How influential is the context in guiding your reading of the text? For instance, were you aware of or asking questions about the author's life and times as you were reading the text?

- How does the work change as you read it in different contexts? For instance, how do you read a poem that was written to raise spirits about a war that is long over?

- Make a list of abstract words that appear in more than one text in this anthology (such as *courage, hero, great*). Explain how these words take on different meanings depending upon the context the writer supplies or assumes.

- How are readers encouraged to—or discouraged from—generalizing the meaning of a particular work? In other words, how closely are we tied to the specific war or battle that is the subject of the work? Is there any work in which the specific historical circumstances are unimportant?

- Which works demand the most contextual knowledge? Are any unreadable without substantial background information? What kinds of information do you need to achieve understanding? Conversely, what kinds of information seem nonessential to your understanding?

Anthology

LANGUAGE AND WAR: CONSIDERING CONTEXT IN ANALYSIS

War inevitably forces us to measure abstractions against human lives. Tennyson's notions of loyalty and bravery haven't, for most readers, measured up very well to the specific action he commemorates in "The Charge of the Light Brigade." Still, the notions aren't discarded. Every person who considers the subject of war is left to measure again: What is the value? What are the prospects? What is the likely cost?

    World War I (1914–1918) lent those questions—in the wake of an unfolding disaster—great urgency. The scale and speed of the devastation forced an entire generation of writers to question the words that justified or valorized the event. In a review article ("The Big One," *The New Yorker*, August 23, 2004), Adam Gopnik writes powerfully of the raw facts: "The scale and suddenness of the killing that began that summer still has the power to amaze us. The war began on August 4th. By August 29th, there were two hundred and sixty thousand French dead." And of course, this was only the first month in what was to be a long fight. The fierce trench warfare along the Western Front came to symbolize for many the brutal futility of the whole endeavor. Gopnik continues: "On one day during the Battle of the Somme, in the summer of 1916, more than fifty thousand British troops died walking directly into German fire, without advancing the front by a single foot. In fact, the entire front, which cost the lives of more than three million human beings, moved scarcely five miles in three years." It's no wonder that the rhythmic pounding of Tennyson's charge struck post–World War I writers as obscenely upbeat.

Most of the works in this anthology are poised around World War I. The poems by Henry Newbolt and Edgar Guest serve to support the war effort in the most confident tones. The poems of Wilfred Owen, Siegfried Sassoon, e. e. cummings, and Herbert Read, as well as much of Hemingway's early fiction, take on an especially hard edge in response. These works weren't only opposing the war but were contesting a whole way of speaking about war. They were trying to offer a picture and feeling of immediate experience that would blow away any inspiring abstractions. It's important in reading this material to keep in mind the facts that Gopnik provides and the language Newbolt and Guest employ. Context, both historical and literary, is essential to a full reading of these postwar works.

Herbert Read's "The Execution of Cornelius Vane" may be an especially provocative text for today's reader. Cornelius is glad to shoot away his own finger if it can take him out of the action. And if that is not enough, he will run. The fact that others, his fellow soldiers, do die doesn't affect the way Cornelius makes choices. He never sees his own participation as significant. In a war where millions can die over a stretch of land that scarcely moves over a period of three years, who can blame him? Still, Read refuses to make his protagonist heroic in opposition to the war. Cornelius never considers his desertion a statement. He merely wants to survive, to feel the warmth of the sun and hear birds sing. In this way, Cornelius is hardly unusual. Many soldiers in World War I were executed by their own side for desertion. Such severity was felt a necessity, for how else could men facing such conditions be held in line? Read's poem can be interpreted as a response to the ideals of heroism and loyalty that Tennyson had expressed. Nearly a century has passed since "The Execution of Cornelius Vane" first appeared, and we need now to ask ourselves how we measure bravery and responsibility against an assertion of individual worth.

Other works in this anthology address other wars, but similar themes recur. In every case we need to learn what we can of the occasion for the text and at the same time consider how our own history is relevant to reading. The tension between old and new, between ideal and real, or between abstract and concrete plays out in Melville's "A Utilitarian View of the Monitor's Fight." The *Monitor* was an ironclad in the Union navy. It battled the Confederacy's ironclad, the *Merrimac*, in 1862. This battle signaled for Melville a profound change in the nature of warfare. There could be no pretense to pomp or romantic heroism in such a mechanized struggle. "Warriors" in this poem become mere "operatives." Units of energy, "caloric," are calculated in the management of the battle; the quality of passion, the *heroic*, can't be so measured. Yet the battle was intense, and the demands on the men greater than those exacted by earlier wars. Melville seems to register a faint regret that something ennobling has been lost while at the same time recognizes that that loss is appropriate. The harsh mechanization of war ultimately helps reveal war's truer nature. To see war clearly for what it is, is to see that war is less grand than peace.

Siegfried Sassoon's "Repression of War Experience" and Hemingway's "Soldier's Home" both remind us that wars don't end simply because the fighting stops. Those who battle accrue memories and feelings that cannot be simply set aside. Tim O'Brien's "The Things They Carried" provides a densely textured record of war experience. He, along with Anne Sexton, suggests that the feelings behind a notion like courage are more complicated than Tennyson ever suggested. So complicated, in fact, that war's effects can hardly be understood only by those who have fought; Tillie Olsen's "I Stand Here Ironing" might seem hardly to fit within this group of works, but the first-person narrator registers how her personal, domestic struggles can be appreciated only in context of a larger historical backdrop. Economic troubles and war abroad come home in particular ways. Gina Shaffer's *War Spelled Backwards* is a play that employs a twilight zone-like twist to juxtapose our current situation in Iraq against our past experience in Vietnam.

FICTION

Ernest Hemingway (1899–1961)

Ernest Hemingway was born in Oak Park, Illinois. His novels and short stories have become staples of American literature courses today, but Hemingway also experienced great popular and critical acclaim during his lifetime. His fantastic hunting and sporting adventures not only served as material for his writings but also were avidly followed by the media. Similarly, his service as an ambulance driver in Italy during World War I and his work as a war correspondent in Europe and Asia during the Greco-Turkish War, the Spanish Civil War, and World War II influenced his literature while simultaneously placing him in the p⋅blic limelight. The "Hemingway Hero" is typically a strong, self-sufficient, quiet male character less afraid of physical death than a listless earthly existence. Hemingway's seventh novel, *The Old Man and the Sea*, was awarded the 1953 Pulitzer Prize, and in 1954 he received the Nobel Prize in literature. Despite his great success, Hemingway suffered emotionally and committed suicide in 1961.

Soldier's Home (1925)

Krebs went to the war from a Methodist college in Kansas. There is a picture which shows him among his fraternity brothers, all of them wearing exactly the same height and style collar. He enlisted in the Marines in 1917 and did not return to the United States until the second division returned from the Rhine in the summer of 1919.

There is a picture which shows him on the Rhine with two German girls and another corporal. Krebs and the corporal look too big for their uniforms. The German girls are not beautiful. The Rhine does not show in the picture.

By the time Krebs returned to his home town in Oklahoma the greeting of heroes was over. He came back much too late. The men from the town who had been drafted had all been welcomed elaborately on their return. There had been a great deal of hysteria. Now the reaction had set in. People seemed to think it was rather ridiculous for Krebs to be getting back so late, years after the war was over.

At first Krebs, who had been at Belleau Wood, Soissons, the Champagne, St. Mihiel, and in the Argonne did not want to talk about the war at all. Later he felt the need to talk but no one wanted to hear about it. His town had heard too many atrocity stories to be thrilled by actualities. Krebs found that to be listened to at all he had to lie, and after he had done this twice he, too, had a reaction against the war and against talking about it. A distaste for everything that had happened to him in the war set in because of the lies he had told. All of the times that had been able to make him feel cool and clear inside himself when he thought of them; the times so long back when he had done the one thing, the only thing for a man to do, easily and naturally, when he might have done something else, now lost their cool, valuable quality and then were lost themselves.

His lies were quite unimportant lies and consisted in attributing to himself things other men had seen, done, or heard of, and stating as facts certain apocryphal incidents familiar to all soldiers. Even his lies were not sensational at the pool room. His acquaintances, who had heard detailed accounts of German women found chained to machine guns in the Argonne forest and who could not comprehend, or were barred by their patriotism

5

from interest in, any German machine gunners who were not chained, were not thrilled by his stories.

Krebs acquired the nausea in regard to experience that is the result of untruth or exaggeration, and when he occasionally met another man who had really been a soldier and they talked a few minutes in the dressing room at a dance he fell into the easy pose of the old soldier among other soldiers: that he had been badly, sickeningly frightened all the time. In this way he lost everything.

During this time, it was late summer, he was sleeping late in bed, getting up to walk down town to the library to get a book, eating lunch at home, reading on the front porch until he became bored, and then walking down through the town to spend the hottest hours of the day in the cool dark of the pool room. He loved to play pool.

In the evening he practiced on his clarinet, strolled down town, read, and went to bed. He was still a hero to his two young sisters. His mother would have given him breakfast in bed if he had wanted it. She often came in when he was in bed and asked him to tell her about the war, but her attention always wandered. His father was noncommittal.

Before Krebs went away to the war he had never been allowed to drive the family motor car. His father was in the real estate business and always wanted the car to be at his command when he required it to take clients out into the country to show them a piece of farm property. The car always stood outside the First National Bank building where his father had an office on the second floor. Now, after the war, it was still the same car.

Nothing was changed in the town except that the young girls had grown up. But they lived in such a complicated world of already defined alliances and shifting feuds that Krebs did not feel the energy or the courage to break into it. He liked to look at them, though. There were so many good-looking young girls. Most of them had their hair cut short. When he went away only little girls wore their hair like that or girls that were fast. They all wore sweaters and shirt waists with round Dutch collars. It was a pattern. He liked to look at them from the front porch as they walked on the other side of the street. He liked to watch them walking under the shade of the trees. He liked the round Dutch collars above their sweaters. He liked their silk stockings and flat shoes. He liked their bobbed hair and the way they walked.

When he was in town their appeal to him was not very strong. He did not like them when he saw them in the Greek's ice cream parlor. He did not want them themselves really. They were too complicated. There was something else. Vaguely he wanted a girl but he did not want to have to work to get her. He would have liked to have a girl but he did not want to have to spend a long time getting her. He did not want to get into the intrigue and the politics. He did not want to have to do any courting. He did not want to tell any more lies. It wasn't worth it.

He did not want any consequences. He did not want any consequences ever again. He wanted to live along without consequences. Besides he did not really need a girl. The army had taught him that. It was all right to pose as though you had to have a girl. Nearly everybody did that. But it wasn't true. You did not need a girl. That was the funny thing. First a fellow boasted how girls mean nothing to him, that he never thought of them, that they could not touch him. Then a fellow boasted that he could not get along without girls, that he had to have them all the time, that he could not go to sleep without them.

That was all a lie. It was all a lie both ways. You did not need a girl unless you thought about them. He learned that in the army. Then sooner or later you always got one. When you were really ripe for a girl you always got one. You did not have to think about it. Sooner or later it would come. He had learned that in the army.

Now he would have liked a girl if she had come to him and not wanted to talk. But here at home it was all too complicated. He knew he could never get through it all again. It was not worth the trouble. That was the thing about French girls and German girls. There was not all this talking. You couldn't talk much and you did not need to talk. It was simple and you were friends. He thought about France and then he began to think about Germany. On the whole he had liked Germany better. He did not want to leave Germany. He did not want to come home. Still, he had come home. He sat on the front porch.

He liked the girls that were walking along the other side of the street. He liked the look of them much better than the French girls or the German girls. But the world they were in was not the world he was in. He would like to have one of them. But it was not worth it. They were such a nice pattern. He liked the pattern. It was exciting. But he would not go through all the talking. He did not want one badly enough. He liked to look at them all, though. It was not worth it. Not now when things were getting good again.

He sat there on the porch reading a book on the war. It was a history and he was reading about all the engagements he had been in. It was the most interesting reading he had ever done. He wished there were more maps. He looked forward with a good feeling to reading all the really good histories when they would come out with good detail maps. Now he was really learning about the war. He had been a good soldier. That made a difference.

One morning after he had been home about a month his mother came into his bedroom and sat on the bed. She smoothed her apron.

"I had a talk with your father last night, Harold," she said, "and he is willing for you to take the car out in the evenings."

"Yeah?" said Krebs, who was not fully awake. "Take the car out? Yeah?"

15

"Yes. Your father has felt for some time that you should be able to take the car out in the evenings whenever you wished but we only talked it over last night."

"I'll bet you made him," Krebs said.

"No. It was your father's suggestion that we talk the matter over."

"Yeah. I'll bet you made him," Krebs sat up in bed.

"Will you come down to breakfast, Harold?" his mother said.

"As soon as I get my clothes on," Krebs said.

His mother went out of the room and he could hear her frying something downstairs while he washed, shaved, and dressed to go down into the dining-room for breakfast. While he was eating breakfast his sister brought in the mail.

"Well, Hare," she said. "You old sleepyhead. What do you ever get up for?"

Krebs looked at her. He liked her. She was his best sister.

"Have you got the paper?" he asked.

She handed him the Kansas City *Star* and he shucked off its brown wrapper and opened it to the sporting page. He folded the *Star* open and propped it against the water pitcher with his cereal dish to steady it, so he could read while he ate.

"Harold," his mother stood in the kitchen doorway, "Harold, please don't muss up the paper. Your father can't read his *Star* if it's been mussed."

"I won't muss it," Krebs said.

His sister sat down at the table and watched him while he read.

"We're playing indoor over at school this afternoon," she said. "I'm going to pitch."

"Good," said Krebs. "How's the old wing?"

"I can pitch better than lots of the boys. I tell them all you taught me. The other girls aren't much good."

"Yeah?" said Krebs.

"I tell them all you're my beau. Aren't you my beau, Hare?"

"You bet."

"Couldn't your brother really be your beau just because he's your brother?"

"I don't know."

"Sure you know. Couldn't you be my beau, Hare, if I was old enough and if you wanted to?"

"Sure. You're my girl now."

"Am I really your girl?"

"Sure."

"Do you love me?"

"Uh, huh."

"Will you love me always?"

"Sure."

"Will you come over and watch me play indoor?"   50

"Maybe."

"Aw, Hare, you don't love me. If you loved me, you'd want to come over and watch me play indoor."

Krebs's mother came into the dining-room from the kitchen. She carried a plate with two fried eggs and some crisp bacon on it and a plate of buckwheat cakes.

"You run along, Helen," she said. "I want to talk to Harold."

She put the eggs and bacon down in front of him and brought in a jug   55
of maple syrup for the buckwheat cakes. Then she sat down across the table from Krebs.

"I wish you'd put down the paper a minute, Harold," she said.

Krebs took down the paper and folded it.

"Have you decided what you are going to do yet, Harold?" his mother said, taking off her glasses.

"No," said Krebs.

"Don't you think it's about time?" His mother did not say this in a   60
mean way. She seemed worried.

"I hadn't thought about it," Krebs said.

"God has some work for everyone to do," his mother said. "There can be no idle hands in His Kingdom."

"I'm not in His Kingdom," Krebs said.

"We are all of us in His Kingdom."

Krebs felt embarrassed and resentful as always.   65

"I've worried about you so much, Harold," his mother went on. "I know the temptations you must have been exposed to. I know how weak men are. I know what your own dear grandfather, my own father, told us about the Civil War and I have prayed for you. I pray for you all day long, Harold."

Krebs looked at the bacon fat hardening on his plate.

"Your father is worried, too," his mother went on. "He thinks you have lost your ambition, that you haven't got a definite aim in life. Charley Simmons, who is just your age, has a good job and is going to be married. The boys are all settling down; they're all determined to get somewhere; you can see that boys like Charley Simmons are on their way to being really a credit to the community."

Krebs said nothing.

"Don't look that way, Harold," his mother said. "You know we love   70
you and I want to tell you for your own good how matters stand. Your father does not want to hamper your freedom. He thinks you should be allowed to drive the car. If you want to take some of the nice girls out riding with you, we are only too pleased. We want you to enjoy yourself. But you are going to have to settle down to work, Harold. Your father doesn't care what you start in at. All work is honorable as he says. But you've got to make a start

at something. He asked me to speak to you this morning and then you can stop in and see him at his office."

"Is that all?" Krebs said.

"Yes. Don't you love your mother, dear boy?"

"No," Krebs said.

His mother looked at him across the table. Her eyes were shiny. She started crying.

"I don't love anybody," Krebs said.

It wasn't any good. He couldn't tell her, he couldn't make her see it. It was silly to have said it. He had only hurt her. He went over and took hold of her arm. She was crying with her head in her hands.

"I didn't mean it," he said. "I was just angry at something. I didn't mean I didn't love you."

His mother went on crying. Krebs put his arm on her shoulder.

"Can't you believe me, mother?"

His mother shook her head.

"Please, please, mother. Please believe me."

"All right," his mother said chokily. She looked up at him. "I believe you, Harold."

Krebs kissed her hair. She put her face up to him.

"I'm your mother," she said. "I held you next to my heart when you were a tiny baby."

Krebs felt sick and vaguely nauseated.

"I know, Mummy," he said. "I'll try and be a good boy for you."

"Would you kneel and pray with me, Harold?" his mother asked.

They knelt down beside the dining-room table and Krebs's mother prayed.

"Now, you pray, Harold," she said.

"I can't," Krebs said.

"Try, Harold."

"I can't."

"Do you want me to pray for you?"

"Yes."

So his mother prayed for him and then they stood up and Krebs kissed his mother and went out of the house. He had tried so to keep his life from being complicated. Still, none of it had touched him. He had felt sorry for his mother and she had made him lie. He would go to Kansas City and get a job and she would feel all right about it. There would be one more scene maybe before he got away. He would not go down to his father's office. He would miss that one. He wanted his life to go smoothly. It had just gotten going that way. Well, that was all over now, anyway. He would go over to the schoolyard and watch Helen play indoor baseball.

- Discuss the significance of specific details that the story presents about World War I.
- At the end of the sixth paragraph the narrator tells us, "In this way he lost everything." What details illustrate what Krebs has lost, and how has he lost it?
- How does the internal experience of Krebs that we see in the beginning of the story relate to the conversation that we hear in the second half? How is this contrast significant?

Tim O'Brien (1946–)

Tim O'Brien was born in Worthington, Minnesota. In 1968, after he earned his degree in political science, summa cum laude, at McAlester College in St. Paul, he was drafted into the army during the Vietnam War. Though he had been an active protester of the war and considered escaping to Canada, he feared losing connection with his family and home and agreed to join the Fifth Battalion, Forty-sixth Infantry, for a year and a half. After gaining a Purple Heart for his service, he began studying for his PhD in government at Harvard University while practicing his technical skills as a writer for the *Washington Post*. In 1978, he published *Going after Cacciato*, a combination of real and invented events from his life, which earned the National Book Award. After this publication, several of his stories appeared in magazines and were soon adapted into the highly successful book *The Things They Carried* (1990).

The Things They Carried (1990)

First Lieutenant Jimmy Cross carried letters from a girl named Martha, a junior at Mount Sebastian College in New Jersey. They were not love letters, but Lieutenant Cross was hoping, so he kept them folded in plastic at the bottom of his rucksack. In the late afternoon, after a day's march, he would dig his foxhole, wash his hands under a canteen, unwrap the letters, hold them with the tips of his fingers, and spend the last hour of light pretending. He would imagine romantic camping trips into the White Mountains in New Hampshire. He would sometimes taste the envelope flaps, knowing her tongue had been there. More than anything, he wanted Martha to love him as he loved her, but the letters were mostly chatty, elusive on the matter of love. She was a virgin, he was almost sure. She was an English major at Mount Sebastian, and she wrote beautifully about her professors and roommates and midterm exams, about her respect for Chaucer and her great affection for Virginia Woolf. She often quoted lines of poetry; she never mentioned the war, except to say, Jimmy, take care of yourself. The letters weighed ten ounces. They were signed "Love, Martha," but Lieutenant Cross understood that "Love" was only a way of signing and did not mean what he sometimes pretended it meant. At dusk, he would carefully return the letters to his rucksack. Slowly, a bit distracted, he would get up and move among his men, checking the perimeter, then at full dark he would return to his hole and watch the night and wonder if Martha was a virgin.

The things they carried were largely determined by necessity. Among the necessities or near necessities were P-38 can openers, pocket knives, heat tabs, wrist watches, dog tags, mosquito repellent, chewing gum, candy, cigarettes, salt tablets, packets of Kool-Aid, lighters, matches, sewing kits, Military Payment Certificates, C rations, and two or three canteens of water. Together, these items weighed between fifteen and twenty pounds, depending upon a man's habits or rate of metabolism. Henry Dobbins, who was a big man, carried extra rations; he was especially fond of canned peaches in heavy syrup over pound cake. Dave Jensen, who practiced field hygiene, carried a toothbrush, dental floss, and several hotel-size bars of soap he'd stolen on R&R in Sydney, Australia. Ted Lavender, who was scared, carried tranquilizers until he was shot in the head outside the village of Than Khe in mid-April. By necessity, and because it was SOP°, they all carried steel helmets that weighed five pounds including the liner and camouflage cover. They carried the standard fatigue jackets and trousers. Very few carried underwear. On their feet they carried jungle boots—2.1 pounds—and Dave Jensen carried three pairs of socks and a can of Dr. Scholl's foot powder as a precaution against trench foot. Until he was shot, Ted Lavender carried six or seven ounces of premium dope, which for him was a necessity. Mitchell Sanders, the RTO°, carried condoms. Norman Bowker carried a diary. Rat Kiley carried comic books. Kiowa, a devout Baptist, carried an illustrated New Testament that had been presented to him by his father, who taught Sunday school in Oklahoma City, Oklahoma. As a hedge against bad times, however, Kiowa also carried his grandmother's distrust of the white man, his grandfather's old hunting hatchet. Necessity dictated. Because the land was mined and booby-trapped, it was SOP for each man to carry a steel-centered, nylon-covered flak jacket, which weighed 6.7 pounds, but which on hot days seemed much heavier. Because you could die so quickly, each man carried at least one large compress bandage, usually in the helmet band for easy access. Because the nights were cold, and because the monsoons were wet, each carried a green plastic poncho that could be used as a raincoat or ground sheet or makeshift tent.

°**SOP:** Standard operating procedure. °**RTO:** Radio telephone operator.

With its quilted liner, the poncho weighed almost two pounds, but it was worth every ounce. In April, for instance, when Ted Lavender was shot, they used his poncho to wrap him up, then to carry him across the paddy, then to lift him into the chopper that took him away.

They were called legs or grunts.

To carry something was to "hump" it, as when Lieutenant Jimmy Cross humped his love for Martha up the hills and through the swamps. In its intransitive form, "to hump" meant "to walk," or "to march," but it implied burdens far beyond the intransitive.

Almost everyone humped photographs. In his wallet, Lieutenant   5
Cross carried two photographs of Martha. The first was a Kodachrome snapshot signed "Love," though he knew better. She stood against a brick wall. Her eyes were gray and neutral, her lips slightly open as she stared straight-on at the camera. At night, sometimes, Lieutenant Cross wondered who had taken the picture, because he knew she had boyfriends, because he loved her so much, and because he could see the shadow of the picture taker spreading out against the brick wall. The second photograph had been clipped from the 1968 Mount Sebastian yearbook. It was an action shot—women's volleyball—and Martha was bent horizontal to the floor, reaching, the palms of her hands in sharp focus, the tongue taut, the expression frank and competitive. There was no visible sweat. She wore white gym shorts. Her legs, he thought, were almost certainly the legs of a virgin, dry and without hair, the left knee cocked and carrying her entire weight, which was just over one hundred pounds. Lieutenant Cross remembered touching that left knee. A dark theater, he remembered, and the movie was *Bonnie and Clyde*, and Martha wore a tweed skirt, and during the final scene, when he touched her knee, she turned and looked at him in a sad, sober way that made him pull his hand back, but he would always remember the feel of the tweed skirt and the knee beneath it and the sound of the gunfire that killed Bonnie and Clyde, how embarrassing it was, how slow and oppressive. He remembered kissing her good night at the dorm door. Right then, he thought, he should've done something brave. He should've carried her up the stairs to her room and tied her to the bed and touched that left knee all night long. He should've risked it. Whenever he looked at the photographs, he thought of new things he should've done.

What they carried was partly a function of rank, partly of field specialty.

As a first lieutenant and platoon leader, Jimmy Cross carried a compass, maps, code books, binoculars, and a .45-caliber pistol that weighed 2.9 pounds fully loaded. He carried a strobe light and the responsibility for the lives of his men.

As an RTO, Mitchell Sanders carried the PRC-25 radio, a killer, twenty-six pounds with its battery.

As a medic, Rat Kiley carried a canvas satchel filled with morphine and plasma and malaria tablets and surgical tape and comic books and all the things a medic must carry, including M&M's for especially bad wounds, for a total weight of nearly twenty pounds.

As a big man, therefore a machine gunner, Henry Dobbins carried the M-60, which weighed twenty-three pounds unloaded, but which was almost always loaded. In addition, Dobbins carried between ten and fifteen pounds of ammunition draped in belts across his chest and shoulders.

As PFCs or Spec 4s, most of them were common grunts and carried the standard M-16 gas-operated assault rifle. The weapon weighed 7.5 pounds unloaded, 8.2 pounds with its full twenty-round magazine. Depending on numerous factors, such as topography and psychology, the riflemen carried anywhere from twelve to twenty magazines, usually in cloth bandoliers, adding on another 8.4 pounds at minimum, fourteen pounds at maximum. When it was available, they also carried M-16 maintenance gear—rods and steel brushes and swabs and tubes of LSA oil—all of which weighed about a pound. Among the grunts, some carried the M-79 grenade launcher, 5.9 pounds unloaded, a reasonably light weapon except for the ammunition, which was heavy. A single round weighed ten ounces. The typical load was twenty-five rounds. But Ted Lavender, who was scared, carried thirty-four rounds when he was shot and killed outside Than Khe, and he went down under an exceptional burden, more than twenty pounds of ammunition, plus the flak jacket and helmet and rations and water and toilet paper and tranquilizers and all the rest, plus the unweighed fear. He was dead weight. There was no twitching or flopping. Kiowa, who saw it happen, said it was like watching a rock fall, or a big sandbag or something—just boom, then down—not like the movies where the dead guy rolls around and does fancy spins and goes ass over teakettle—not like that, Kiowa said, the poor bastard just flat-fuck fell. Boom. Down. Nothing else. It was a bright morning in mid-April. Lieutenant Cross felt the pain. He blamed himself. They stripped off Lavender's canteens and ammo, all the heavy things, and Rat Kiley said the obvious, the guy's dead, and Mitchell Sanders used his radio to report one U.S. KIA and to request a chopper. Then they wrapped Lavender in his poncho. They carried him out to a dry paddy, established security, and sat smoking the dead man's dope until the chopper came. Lieutenant Cross kept to himself. He pictured Martha's smooth young face, thinking he loved her more than anything, more than his men, and now Ted Lavender was dead because he loved her so much and could not stop thinking about her. When the dust-off arrived, they carried Lavender aboard. Afterward they burned Than Khe. They marched until dusk, then dug their holes, and that night Kiowa kept explaining how you had to be there, how fast it was, how the poor guy just dropped like so much concrete. Boom-down, he said. Like cement.

In addition to the three standard weapons—the M-60, M-16, and M-79—they carried whatever presented itself, or whatever seemed appropriate as a means of killing or staying alive. They carried catch-as-catch-can. At various times, in various situations, they carried M-14s and CAR-15s and Swedish Ks and grease guns and captured AK-47s and Chi-Coms and RPGs and Simonov carbines and black-market Uzis and .38-caliber Smith & Wesson handguns and 66 mm LAWs and shotguns and silencers and blackjacks and bayonets and C-4 plastic explosives. Lee Strunk carried a slingshot; a weapon of last resort, he called it. Mitchell Sanders carried brass knuckles. Kiowa carried his grandfather's feathered hatchet. Every third or fourth man carried a Claymore antipersonnel mine—3.5 pounds with its firing device. They all carried fragmentation grenades—fourteen ounces each. They all carried at least one M-18 colored smoke grenade—twenty-four ounces. Some carried CS or tear-gas grenades. Some carried white-phosphorus grenades. They carried all they could bear, and then some, including a silent awe for the terrible power of the things they carried.

In the first week of April, before Lavender died, Lieutenant Jimmy Cross received a good-luck charm from Martha. It was a simple pebble, an ounce at most. Smooth to the touch, it was a milky-white color with flecks of orange and violet, oval-shaped, like a miniature egg. In the accompanying letter, Martha wrote that she had found the pebble on the Jersey shoreline, precisely where the land touched water at high tide, where things came together but also separated. It was this separate-but-together quality, she wrote, that had inspired her to pick up the pebble and to carry it in her breast pocket for several days, where it seemed weightless, and then to send it through the mail, by air, as a token of her truest feelings for him. Lieutenant Cross found this romantic. But he wondered what her truest feelings were, exactly, and what she meant by separate-but-together. He wondered how the tides and waves had come into play on that afternoon along the Jersey shoreline when Martha saw the pebble and bent down to rescue it from geology. He imagined bare feet. Martha was a poet, with the poet's sensibilities, and her feet would be brown and bare, the toenails unpainted, the eyes chilly and somber like the ocean in March, and though it was painful, he wondered who had been with her that afternoon. He imagined a pair of shadows moving along the strip of sand where things came together but also separated. It was phantom jealousy, he knew, but he couldn't help himself. He loved her so much. On the march, through the hot days of early April, he carried the pebble in his mouth, turning it with his tongue, tasting

sea salts and moisture. His mind wandered. He had difficulty keeping his attention on the war. On occasion he would yell at his men to spread out the
column, to keep their eyes open, but then he would slip away into daydreams, just pretending, walking barefoot along the Jersey shore, with Martha, carrying nothing. He would feel himself rising. Sun and waves and
gentle winds, all love and lightness.

What they carried varied by mission.

When a mission took them to the mountains, they carried mosquito
netting, machetes, canvas tarps, and extra bug juice.

If a mission seemed especially hazardous, or if it involved a place they
knew to be bad, they carried everything they could. In certain heavily
mined AOs°, where the land was dense with Toe Poppers and Bouncing
Betties, they took turns humping a twenty-eight-pound mine detector. With
its headphones and big sensing plate, the equipment was a stress on the
lower back and shoulders, awkward to handle, often useless because of the
shrapnel in the earth, but they carried it anyway, partly for safety, partly for
the illusion of safety.

On ambush, or other night missions, they carried peculiar little odds
and ends. Kiowa always took along his New Testament and a pair of moccasins for silence. Dave Jensen carried night-sight vitamins high in carotin.
Lee Strunk carried his slingshot; ammo, he claimed, would never be a problem. Rat Kiley carried brandy and M&M's. Until he was shot, Ted Lavender
carried the starlight scope, which weighed 6.3 pounds with its aluminum
carrying case. Henry Dobbins carried his girlfriend's panty-hose wrapped
around his neck as a comforter. They all carried ghosts. When dark came,
they would move out single file across the meadows and paddies to their ambush coordinates, where they would quietly set up the Claymores and lie
down and spend the night waiting.

Other missions were more complicated and required special equipment.
In mid-April, it was their mission to search out and destroy the elaborate
tunnel complexes in the Than Khe area south of Chu Lai. To blow the tunnels, they carried one-pound blocks of pentrite high explosives, four blocks
to a man, sixty-eight pounds in all. They carried wiring, detonators, and
battery-powered clackers. Dave Jensen carried earplugs. Most often, before
blowing the tunnels, they were ordered by higher command to search them,
which was considered bad news, but by and large they just shrugged and carried out orders. Because he was a big man, Henry Dobbins was excused from
tunnel duty. The others would draw numbers. Before Lavender died there

°**AOs:** Areas of operation.

were seventeen men in the platoon, and whoever drew the number seventeen would strip off his gear and crawl in head first with a flashlight and Lieutenant Cross's .45-caliber pistol. The rest of them would fan out as security. They would sit down or kneel, not facing the hole, listening to the ground beneath them, imagining cobwebs and ghosts, whatever was down there—the tunnel walls squeezing in—how the flashlight seemed impossibly heavy in the hand and how it was tunnel vision in the very strictest sense, compression in all ways, even time, and how you had to wiggle in—ass and elbows—a swallowed-up feeling—and how you found yourself worrying about odd things—will your flashlight go dead? Do rats carry rabies? If you screamed, how far would the sound carry? Would your buddies hear it? Would they have the courage to drag you out? In some respects, though not many, the waiting was worse than the tunnel itself. Imagination was a killer.

On April 16, when Lee Strunk drew the number seventeen, he laughed and muttered something and went down quickly. The morning was hot and very still. Not good, Kiowa said. He looked at the tunnel opening, then out across a dry paddy toward the village of Than Khe. Nothing moved. No clouds or birds or people. As they waited, the men smoked and drank Kool-Aid, not talking much, feeling sympathy for Lee Strunk but also feeling the luck of the draw. You win some, you lose some, said Mitchell Sanders, and sometimes you settle for a rain check. It was a tired line and no one laughed.

Henry Dobbins ate a tropical chocolate bar. Ted Lavender popped a tranquilizer and went off to pee.   20

After five minutes, Lieutenant Jimmy Cross moved to the tunnel, leaned down, and examined the darkness. Trouble, he thought—a cave-in maybe. And then suddenly, without willing it, he was thinking about Martha. The stresses and fractures, the quick collapse, the two of them buried alive under all that weight. Dense, crushing love. Kneeling, watching the hole, he tried to concentrate on Lee Strunk and the war, all the dangers, but his love was too much for him, he felt paralyzed, he wanted to sleep inside her lungs and breathe her blood and be smothered. He wanted her to be a virgin and not a virgin, all at once. He wanted to know her. Intimate secrets—why poetry? Why so sad? Why that grayness in her eyes? Why so alone? Not lonely, just alone—riding her bike across campus or sitting off by herself in the cafeteria. Even dancing, she danced alone—and it was the aloneness that filled him with love. He remembered telling her that one evening. How she nodded and looked away. And how, later, when he kissed her, she received the kiss without returning it, her eyes wide open, not afraid, not a virgin's eyes, just flat and uninvolved.

Lieutenant Cross gazed at the tunnel. But he was not there. He was buried with Martha under the white sand at the Jersey shore. They were

pressed together, and the pebble in his mouth was her tongue. He was smiling. Vaguely, he was aware of how quiet the day was, the sullen paddies, yet
he could not bring himself to worry about matters of security. He was beyond that. He was just a kid at war, in love. He was twenty-two years old.
He couldn't help it.

A few moments later Lee Strunk crawled out of the tunnel. He came up
grinning, filthy but alive. Lieutenant Cross nodded and closed his eyes while
the others clapped Strunk on the back and made jokes about rising from the
dead. Worms, Rat Kiley said. Right out of the grave. Fuckin' zombie.

The men laughed. They all felt great relief.

Spook City, said Mitchell Sanders.

Lee Strunk made a funny ghost sound, a kind of moaning, yet very
happy, and right then, when Strunk made that high happy moaning sound,
when he went *Ahhooooo,* right then Ted Lavender was shot in the head on
his way back from peeing. He lay with his mouth open. The teeth were broken. There was a swollen black bruise under his left eye. The cheekbone
was gone. Oh shit, Rat Kiley said, the guy's dead. The guy's dead, he kept
saying, which seemed profound—the guy's dead. I mean really.

The things they carried were determined to some extent by superstition.
Lieutenant Cross carried his good-luck pebble. Dave Jensen carried a
rabbit's foot. Norman Bowker, otherwise a very gentle person, carried a
thumb that had been presented to him as a gift by Mitchell Sanders. The
thumb was dark brown, rubbery to the touch, and weighed four ounces at
most. It had been cut from a VC corpse, a boy of fifteen or sixteen. They'd
found him at the bottom of an irrigation ditch, badly burned, flies in his
mouth and eyes. The boy wore black shorts and sandals. At the time of his
death he had been carrying a pouch of rice, a rifle, and three magazines of
ammunition.

You want my opinion, Mitchell Sanders said, there's a definite moral
here.

He put his hand on the dead boy's wrist. He was quiet for a time, as if
counting a pulse, then he patted the stomach, almost affectionately, and
used Kiowa's hunting hatchet to remove the thumb.

Henry Dobbins asked what the moral was.

Moral?

You know. *Moral.*

Sanders wrapped the thumb in toilet paper and handed it across to Norman Bowker. There was no blood. Smiling, he kicked the boy's head,
watched the flies scatter, and said, It's like with that old TV show—Paladin.
Have gun, will travel.

Henry Dobbins thought about it.

Yeah, well, he finally said. I don't see no moral.

There it *is*, man.

Fuck off.

They carried USO stationery and pencils and pens. They carried Sterno, safety pins, trip flares, signal flares, spools of wire, razor blades, chewing tobacco, liberated joss sticks and statuettes of the smiling Buddha, candles, grease pencils, *The Stars and Stripes*, fingernail clippers, Psy Ops leaflets, bush hats, bolos, and much more. Twice a week, when the resupply choppers came in, they carried hot chow in green Mermite cans and large canvas bags filled with iced beer and soda pop. They carried plastic water containers, each with a two-gallon capacity. Mitchell Sanders carried a set of starched tiger fatigues for special occasions. Henry Dobbins carried Black Flag insecticide. Dave Jensen carried empty sandbags that could be filled at night for added protection. Lee Strunk carried tanning lotion. Some things they carried in common. Taking turns, they carried the big PRC77 scrambler radio, which weighed thirty pounds with its battery. They shared the weight of memory. They took up what others could no longer bear. Often, they carried each other, the wounded or weak. They carried infections. They carried chess sets, basketballs, Vietnamese-English dictionaries, insignia of rank, Bronze Stars and Purple Hearts, plastic cards imprinted with the Code of Conduct. They carried diseases, among them malaria and dysentery. They carried lice and ringworm and leeches and paddy algae and various rots and molds. They carried the land itself—Vietnam, the place, the soil—a powdery orange-red dust that covered their boots and fatigues and faces. They carried the sky. The whole atmosphere, they carried it, the humidity, the monsoons, the stink of fungus and decay, all of it, they carried gravity. They moved like mules. By daylight they took sniper fire, at night they were mortared, but it was not battle, it was just the endless march, village to village, without purpose, nothing won or lost. They marched for the sake of the march. They plodded along slowly, dumbly, leaning forward against the heat, unthinking, all blood and bone, simple grunts, soldiering with their legs, toiling up the hills and down into the paddies and across the rivers and up again and down, just humping, one step and then the next and then another, but no volition, no will, because it was automatic, it was anatomy, and the war was entirely a matter of posture and carriage, the hump was everything, a kind of inertia, a kind of emptiness, a dullness of desire and intellect and conscience and hope and human sensibility. Their principles were in their feet. Their calculations were biological. They had no sense of strategy or mission. They searched the villages without knowing what to look for, not caring, kicking over jars of rice, frisking children and old men, blowing tunnels, sometimes setting fires and sometimes not, then forming up and moving on to the next village, then other villages, where it would always be the same. They carried their own lives. The pressures were enormous. In the heat of early afternoon, they would remove their helmets and flak jackets, walking bare, which was dangerous but which helped ease the strain. They would often discard things along the route of march. Purely for comfort, they would throw away rations, blow their Claymores and grenades, no matter, because by nightfall the resupply choppers would arrive with more of the same, then a day or two later still more, fresh watermelons and crates of ammunition and sunglasses and woolen sweaters—the resources were stunning—sparklers for the Fourth of July, colored eggs for Easter. It was the great American war chest—the fruits of science, the smokestacks, the canneries, the arsenals at Hartford, the Minnesota forests, the machine shops, the vast fields of corn and wheat—they carried like freight trains; they carried it on their backs and shoulders—and for all the ambiguities of Vietnam, all the mysteries and unknowns, there was at least the single abiding certainty that they would never be at a loss for things to carry.

After the chopper took Lavender away, Lieutenant Jimmy Cross led his men into the village of Than Khe. They burned everything. They shot chickens and dogs, they trashed the village well, they called in artillery and watched the wreckage, then they marched for several hours through the hot afternoon, and then at dusk, while Kiowa explained how Lavender died, Lieutenant Cross found himself trembling.

He tried not to cry. With his entrenching tool, which weighed five pounds, he began digging a hole in the earth.

He felt shame. He hated himself. He had loved Martha more than his men, and as a consequence Lavender was now dead, and this was something he would have to carry like a stone in his stomach for the rest of the war.

All he could do was dig. He used his entrenching tool like an ax, slashing, feeling both love and hate, and then later, when it was full dark, he sat at the bottom of his foxhole and wept. It went on for a long while. In part, he was grieving for Ted Lavender, but mostly it was for Martha, and for himself, because she belonged to another world, which was not quite real, and because she was a junior at Mount Sebastian College in New Jersey, a poet and a virgin and uninvolved, and because he realized she did not love him and never would.

Like cement, Kiowa whispered in the dark. I swear to God—boom-down. Not a word.

I've heard this, said Norman Bowker.

A pisser, you know? Still zipping himself up. Zapped while zipping.

All right, fine. That's enough.

Yeah, but you had to see it, the guy just—

I *heard*, man. Cement. So why not shut the fuck *up*?

Kiowa shook his head sadly and glanced over at the hole where Lieutenant Jimmy Cross sat watching the night. The air was thick and wet. A warm, dense fog had settled over the paddies and there was the stillness that precedes rain.

After a time Kiowa sighed.   50

One thing for sure, he said. The Lieutenant's in some deep hurt. I mean that crying jag—the way he was carrying on—it wasn't fake or anything, it was real heavy-duty hurt. The man cares.

Sure, Norman Bowker said.

Say what you want, the man does care.

We all got problems.

Not Lavender.   55

No, I guess not, Bowker said. Do me a favor, though.

Shut up?

That's a smart Indian. Shut up.

Shrugging, Kiowa pulled off his boots. He wanted to say more, just to lighten up his sleep, but instead he opened his New Testament and arranged it beneath his head as a pillow. The fog made things seem hollow and unattached. He tried not to think about Ted Lavender, but then he was thinking how fast it was, no drama, down and dead, and how it was hard to feel anything except surprise. It seemed un-Christian. He wished he could find some great sadness, or even anger, but the emotion wasn't there and he couldn't make it happen. Mostly he felt pleased to be alive. He liked the smell of the New Testament under his cheek, the leather and ink and paper and glue, whatever the chemicals were. He liked hearing the sounds of night. Even his fatigue, it felt fine, the stiff muscles and the prickly awareness of his own body, a floating feeling. He enjoyed not being dead. Lying there, Kiowa admired Lieutenant Jimmy Cross's capacity for grief. He wanted to share the man's pain, he wanted to care as Jimmy Cross cared. And yet when he closed his eyes, all he could think was Boom-down, and all he could feel was the pleasure of having his boots off and the fog curling in around him and the damp soil and the Bible smells and the plush comfort of night.

After a moment Norman Bowker sat up in the dark.   60

What the hell, he said. You want to talk, *talk*. Tell it to me.

Forget it.

No, man, go on. One thing I hate, it's a silent Indian.

For the most part they carried themselves with poise, a kind of dignity. Now and then, however, there were times of panic, when they squealed or wanted to squeal but couldn't, when they twitched and made moaning sounds and covered their heads and said Dear Jesus and flopped around on the earth and fired their weapons blindly and cringed and sobbed and begged for the noise to stop and went wild and made stupid promises to themselves and to God and to their mothers and fathers, hoping not to die. In different ways, it happened to all of them. Afterward, when the firing ended, they would blink and peek up. They would touch their bodies, feeling shame, then quickly hiding it. They would force themselves to stand. As if in slow motion, frame by frame, the world would take on the old logic—absolute silence, then the wind, then sunlight, then voices. It was the burden of being alive. Awkwardly, the men would reassemble themselves, first in private, then in groups, becoming soldiers again. They would repair the leaks in their eyes. They would check for casualties, call in dust-offs, light cigarettes, try to smile, clear their throats and spit and begin cleaning their weapons. After a time someone would shake his head and say, No lie, I almost shit my pants, and someone else would laugh, which meant it was bad, yes, but the guy had obviously not shit his pants, it wasn't that bad, and in any case nobody would ever do such a thing and then go ahead and talk about it. They would squint into the dense, oppressive sunlight. For a few moments, perhaps, they would fall silent, lighting a joint and tracking its passage from man to man, inhaling, holding in the humiliation. Scary stuff, one of them might say. But then someone else would grin or flick his eyebrows and say, Roger-dodger, almost cut me a new asshole, *almost.*

There were numerous such poses. Some carried themselves with a sort of wistful resignation, others with pride or stiff soldierly discipline or good humor or macho zeal. They were afraid of dying but they were even more afraid to show it.

They found jokes to tell.

They used a hard vocabulary to contain the terrible softness. *Greased,* they'd say. *Offed, lit up°, zapped while zipping°* It wasn't cruelty, just stage presence. They were actors and the war came at them in 3-D. When someone died, it wasn't quite dying, because in a curious way it seemed scripted, and because they had their lines mostly memorized, irony mixed with tragedy, and because they called it by other names, as if to encyst and destroy the reality of death itself. They kicked corpses. They cut off thumbs. They talked grunt lingo. They told stories about Ted Lavender's supply of tranquilizers, how the poor guy didn't feel a thing, how incredibly tranquil he was.

There's a moral here, said Mitchell Sanders.

They were waiting for Lavender's chopper, smoking the dead man's dope.

The moral's pretty obvious, Sanders said, and winked. Stay away from drugs. No joke, they'll ruin your day every time.

Cute, said Henry Dobbins.

Mind-blower, get it? Talk about wiggy—nothing left, just blood and brains.

They made themselves laugh.

°**Offed, lit up:** Killed. °**zapped while zipping:** Killed while urinating.

There it is, they'd say, over and over, as if the repetition itself were an act of poise, a balance between crazy and almost crazy, knowing without going. There it is, which meant be cool, let it ride, because oh yeah, man, you can't change what can't be changed, there it is, there it absolutely and positively and fucking well *is*.

They were tough.   75

They carried all the emotional baggage of men who might die. Grief, terror, love, longing—these were intangibles, but the intangibles had their own mass and specific gravity, they had tangible weight. They carried shameful memories. They carried the common secret of cowardice barely restrained, the instinct to run or freeze or hide, and in many respects this was the heaviest burden of all, for it could never be put down, it required perfect balance and perfect posture. They carried their reputations. They carried the soldier's greatest fear, which was the fear of blushing. Men killed, and died, because they were embarrassed not to. It was what had brought them to the war in the first place, nothing positive, no dreams of glory or honor, just to avoid the blush of dishonor. They died so as not to die of embarrassment. They crawled into tunnels and walked point and advanced under fire. Each morning, despite the unknowns, they made their legs move. They endured. They kept humping. They did not submit to the obvious alternative, which was simply to close the eyes and fall. So easy, really. Go limp and tumble to the ground and let the muscles unwind and not speak and not budge until your buddies picked you up and lifted you into the chopper that would roar and dip its nose and carry you off to the world. A mere matter of falling, yet no one ever fell. It was not courage, exactly; the object was not valor. Rather, they were too frightened to be cowards.

By and large they carried these things inside, maintaining the masks of composure. They sneered at sick call. They spoke bitterly about guys who had found release by shooting off their own toes or fingers. Pussies, they'd say. Candyasses. It was fierce, mocking talk, with only a trace of envy or awe, but even so, the image played itself out behind their eyes.

They imagined the muzzle against flesh. They imagined the quick, sweet pain, then the evacuation to Japan, then a hospital with warm beds and cute geisha nurses.

They dreamed of freedom birds.

At night, on guard, staring into the dark, they were carried away by   80
jumbo jets. They felt the rush of takeoff. *Gone!* they yelled. And then velocity, wings and engines, a smiling stewardess—but it was more than a plane, it was a real bird, a big sleek silver bird with feathers and talons and high screeching. They were flying. The weights fell off, there was nothing to bear. They laughed and held on tight, feeling the cold slap of wind and altitude, soaring, thinking *It's over, I'm gone!*—they were naked, they were light and free—it was all lightness, bright and fast and buoyant,

light as light, a helium buzz in the brain, a giddy bubbling in the lungs as they were taken up over the clouds and the war, beyond duty, beyond gravity and mortification and global entanglements—*Sin loi!* they yelled, *I'm sorry, motherfuckers, but I'm out of it, I'm goofed, I'm on a space cruise, I'm gone!*—and it was a restful, disencumbered sensation, just riding the light waves, sailing that big silver freedom bird over the mountains and oceans, over America, over the farms and great sleeping cities and cemeteries and highways and the golden arches of McDonald's. It was flight, a kind of fleeing, a kind of falling, falling thing weighed exactly nothing. *Gone!* they screamed, *I'm sorry but I'm gone!* And so at night, not quite dreaming, they gave themselves over to lightness, they were carried, they were purely borne.

On the morning after Ted Lavender died, First Lieutenant Jimmy Cross crouched at the bottom of his foxhole and burned Martha's letters. Then he burned the two photographs. There was a steady rain falling, which made it difficult, but he used heat tabs and Sterno to build a small fire, screening it with his body, holding the photographs over the tight blue flame with the tips of his fingers.

He realized it was only a gesture. Stupid, he thought. Sentimental, too, but mostly just stupid.

Lavender was dead. You couldn't burn the blame.

Besides, the letters were in his head. And even now, without photographs, Lieutenant Cross could see Martha playing volleyball in her white gym shorts and yellow T-shirt. He could see her moving in the rain.

When the fire died out, Lieutenant Cross pulled his poncho over his shoulders and ate breakfast from a can.

There was no great mystery, he decided.

In those burned letters Martha had never mentioned the war, except to say, Jimmy, take care of yourself. She wasn't involved. She signed the letters "Love," but it wasn't love, and all the fine lines and technicalities did not matter.

The morning came up wet and blurry. Everything seemed part of everything else, the fog and Martha and the deepening rain.

It was a war, after all.

Half smiling, Lieutenant Jimmy Cross took out his maps. He shook his head hard, as if to clear it, then bent forward and began planning the day's march. In ten minutes, or maybe twenty, he would rouse the men and they would pack up and head west, where the maps showed the country to be green and inviting. They would do what they had always done. The rain might add some weight, but otherwise it would be one more day layered upon all the other days.

He was realistic about it. There was that new hardness in his stomach.
No more fantasies, he told himself.

Henceforth, when he thought about Martha, it would be only to think
that she belonged elsewhere. He would shut down the daydreams. This was
not Mount Sebastian, it was another world, where there were no pretty
poems or midterm exams, a place where men died because of carelessness
and gross stupidity. Kiowa was right. Boom-down, and you were dead, never
partly dead.

Briefly, in the rain, Lieutenant Cross saw Martha's gray eyes gazing
back at him.

He understood.   95

It was very sad, he thought. The things men carried inside. The things
men did or felt they had to do.

He almost nodded at her, but didn't.

Instead he went back to his maps. He was now determined to perform
his duties firmly and without negligence. It wouldn't help Lavender, he
knew that, but from this point on he would comport himself as a soldier.
He would dispose of his good-luck pebble. Swallow it, maybe, or use Lee
Strunk's slingshot, or just drop it along the trail. On the march he would
impose strict field discipline. He would be careful to send out flank security,
to prevent straggling or bunching up, to keep his troops moving at the
proper pace and at the proper interval. He would insist on clean weapons.
He would confiscate the remainder of Lavender's dope. Later in the day,
perhaps, he would call the men together and speak to them plainly. He
would accept the blame for what had happened to Ted Lavender. He would
be a man about it. He would look them in the eyes, keeping his chin level,
and he would issue the new SOPs in a calm, impersonal tone of voice, an
officer's voice, leaving no room for argument or discussion. Commencing
immediately, he'd tell them, they would no longer abandon equipment
along the route of march. They would police up their acts. They would get
their shit together, and keep it together, and maintain it neatly and in good
working order.

He would not tolerate laxity. He would show strength, distancing
himself.

Among the men there would be grumbling, of course, and maybe worse,   100
because their days would seem longer and their loads heavier, but Lieutenant Cross reminded himself that his obligation was not to be loved but to
lead. He would dispense with love; it was not now a factor. And if anyone
quarreled or complained, he would simply tighten his lips and arrange his
shoulders in the correct command posture. He might give a curt little nod.
Or he might not. He might just shrug and say Carry on, then they would
saddle up and form into a column and move out toward the villages west of
Than Khe.

- Explain how the narrator uses specific objects to reveal details about the experience of war. How does the narrative emerge from these details? Trace the details that lead us to understand that Ted Lavender died and the circumstances of his death. How is perspective important to our understanding of this event?

Tillie Olsen (1912–)

Tillie Olsen was born in Omaha, Nebraska. She and her parents, Russian Jewish immigrants, were active in local socialist politics. After high school, Olsen worked odd jobs and was arrested twice for political protests. After moving to San Francisco and marrying, she worked as a waitress and secretary and cared for her four children, abandoning the writing she had been doing up until that time. Olsen resumed writing in 1956 when she began studying at Stanford University and San Francisco University. Olsen's works portray the lives of working-class Americans whose dreams often are not realized because of lack of educational and financial resources. Olsen is the recipient of awards for both her writing and her social activism, including a Guggenheim Fellowship, a literature award from the American Academy and National Institute of Arts and Letters, and the Unitarian Women's Federation Ministry to Women Award. San Francisco, where Olsen still resides, celebrates Tillie Olsen Day on May 18.

I Stand Here Ironing (1961)

I stand here ironing, and what you asked me moves tormented back and forth with the iron.

"I wish you would manage the time to come and talk with me about your daughter. I'm sure you can help me understand her. She's a youngster who needs help and whom I'm deeply interested in helping."

"Who needs help." . . . Even if I came, what good would it do? You think because I am her mother I have a key, or that in some way you could use me as a key? She has lived for nineteen years. There is all that life that has happened outside of me, beyond me.

And when is there time to remember, to sift, to weigh, to estimate, to total? I will start and there will be an interruption and I will have to gather it all together again. Or I will become engulfed with all I did or did not do, with what should have been and what cannot be helped.

She was a beautiful baby. The first and only one of our five that was beautiful at birth. You do not guess how new and uneasy her tenancy in her now-loveliness. You did not know her all those years she was thought homely, or see her poring over her baby pictures, making me tell her over and over how beautiful she had been—and would be, I would tell her—and was now, to the seeing eye. But the seeing eyes were few or nonexistent. Including mine.

I nursed her. They feel that's important nowadays. I nursed all the children, but with her, with all the fierce rigidity of first motherhood, I did like the books then said. Though her cries battered me to trembling and my breasts ached with swollenness, I waited till the clock decreed.

Why do I put that first? I do not even know if it matters, or if it explains anything.

She was a beautiful baby. She blew shining bubbles of sound. She loved motion, loved light, loved color and music and textures. She would lie on the floor in her blue overalls patting the surface so hard in ecstasy her hands and feet would blur. She was a miracle to me, but when she was eight months old I had to leave her daytimes with the woman downstairs to whom she was no miracle at all, for I worked or looked for work and for Emily's father, who "could no longer endure" (he wrote in his good-bye note) "sharing want with us."

I was nineteen. It was the pre-relief, pre-WPA° world of the depression. I would start running as soon as I got off the streetcar, running up the stairs, the place smelling sour, and awake or asleep to startle awake, when she saw me she would break into a clogged weeping that could not be comforted, a weeping I can hear yet.

After a while I found a job hashing at night so I could be with her days,   10
and it was better. But it came to where I had to bring her to his family and leave her.

It took a long time to raise the money for her fare back. Then she got chicken pox and I had to wait longer. When she finally came, I hardly knew her, walking quick and nervous like her father, looking like her father, thin, and dressed in a shoddy red that yellowed her skin and glared at the pockmarks. All the baby loveliness gone.

She was two. Old enough for nursery school they said, and I did not know then what I know now—the fatigue of the long day, and the lacerations of group life in the kinds of nurseries that are only parking places for children.

Except that it would have made no difference if I had known. It was the only place there was. It was the only way we could be together, the only way I could hold a job.

°**WPA:** The Works Progress Administration, created in 1935 as part of President Franklin D. Roosevelt's New Deal program. The purpose of the WPA (renamed the Works Projects Administration in 1939) was to provide jobs for the unemployed during the Great Depression.

And even without knowing, I knew. I knew the teacher that was evil because all these years it has curdled into my memory, the little boy hunched in the corner, her rasp, "why aren't you outside, because Alvin hits you? that's no reason, go out, scaredy." I knew Emily hated it even if she did not clutch and implore "don't go Mommy" like the other children, mornings.

She always had a reason why we should stay home. Momma, you look sick. Momma, I feel sick. Momma, the teachers aren't there today, they're sick. Momma, we can't go, there was a fire there last night. Momma, it's a holiday today, no school, they told me.

But never a direct protest, never rebellion. I think of our others in their three-, four-year-oldness—the explosions, the tempers, the denunciations, the demands—and I feel suddenly ill. I put the iron down. What in me demanded that goodness in her? And what was the cost, the cost to her of such goodness?

The old man living in the back once said in his gentle way: "You should smile at Emily more when you look at her." What *was* in my face when I looked at her? I loved her. There were all the acts of love.

It was only with the others I remembered what he said, and it was the face of joy, and not of care or tightness or worry I turned to them—too late for Emily. She does not smile easily, let alone almost always as her brothers and sisters do. Her face is closed and sombre, but when she wants, how fluid. You must have seen it in her pantomimes, you spoke of her rare gift for comedy on the stage that rouses laughter out of the audience so dear they applaud and applaud and do not want to let her go.

Where does it come from, that comedy? There was none of it in her when she came back to me that second time, after I had had to send her away again. She had a new daddy now to learn to love, and I think perhaps it was a better time.

Except when we left her alone nights, telling ourselves she was old enough.

"Can't you go some other time, Mommy, like tomorrow?" she would ask. "Will it be just a little while you'll be gone? Do you promise?"

The time we came back, the front door open, the clock on the floor in the hall. She rigid awake. "It wasn't just a little while. I didn't cry. Three times I called you, just three times, and then I ran downstairs to open the door so you could come faster. The clock talked loud. I threw it away, it scared me what it talked."

She said the clock talked loud again that night I went to the hospital to have Susan. She was delirious with the fever that comes before red measles, but she was fully conscious all the week I was gone and the week after we were home when she could not come near the new baby or me.

She did not get well. She stayed skeleton thin, not wanting to eat, and night after night she had nightmares. She would call for me, and I would rouse from exhaustion to sleepily call back: "You're all right, darling, go to sleep, it's just a dream," and if she still called, in a sterner voice, "now go to sleep, Emily, there's nothing to hurt you." Twice, only twice, when I had to get up for Susan anyhow, I went in to sit with her.

Now when it is too late (as if she would let me hold and comfort her   25 like I do the others) I get up and go to her at once at her moan or restless stirring. "Are you awake, Emily? Can I get you something?" And the answer is always the same: "No, I'm all right, go back to sleep, Mother."

They persuaded me at the clinic to send her away to a convalescent home in the country where "she can have the kind of food and care you can't manage for her, and you'll be free to concentrate on the new baby." They still send children to that place. I see pictures on the society page of sleek young women planning affairs to raise money for it, or dancing at the affairs, or decorating Easter eggs or filling Christmas stockings for the children.

They never have a picture of the children so I do not know if the girls still wear those gigantic red bows and the ravaged looks on the every other Sunday when parents can come to visit "unless otherwise notified"—as we were notified the first six weeks.

Oh it is a handsome place, green lawns and tall trees and fluted flower beds. High up on the balconies of each cottage the children stand, the girls in their red bows and white dresses, the boys in white suits and giant red ties. The parents stand below shrieking up to be heard, and the children shriek down to be heard, and between them the invisible wall: "Not to Be Contaminated by Parental Germs or Physical Affection."

There was a tiny girl who always stood hand in hand with Emily. Her parents never came. One visit she was gone. "They moved her to Rose Cottage," Emily shouted in explanation. "They don't like you to love anybody here."

She wrote once a week, the labored writing of a seven-year-old. "I am   30 fine. How is the baby. If I write my leter nicly I will have a star. Love." There never was a star. We wrote every other day, letters she could never hold or keep but only hear read—once. "We simply do not have room for children to keep any personal possessions," they patiently explained when we pieced one Sunday's shrieking together to plead how much it would mean to Emily, who loved so to keep things, to be allowed to keep her letters and cards.

Each visit she looked frailer. "She isn't eating," they told us.

(They had runny eggs for breakfast or mush with lumps, Emily said later, I'd hold it in my mouth and not swallow. Nothing ever tasted good, just when they had chicken.)

It took us eight months to get her released home, and only the fact that she gained back so little of her seven lost pounds convinced the social worker.

I used to try to hold and love her after she came back, but her body would stay stiff, and after a while she'd push away. She ate little. Food sickened her, and I think much of life too. Oh she had physical lightness and brightness, twinkling by on skates, bouncing like a ball up and down up and down over the jump rope, skimming over the hill; but these were momentary.

She fretted about her appearance, thin and dark and foreign-looking at a time when every little girl was supposed to look or thought she should look a chubby blonde replica of Shirley Temple. The doorbell sometimes rang for her, but no one seemed to come and play in the house or be a best friend. Maybe because we moved so much.

There was a boy she loved painfully through two school semesters. Months later she told me how she had taken pennies from my purse to buy him candy. "Licorice was his favorite and I brought him some every day, but he still liked Jennifer better'n me. Why, Mommy?" The kind of question for which there is no answer.

School was a worry to her. She was not glib or quick in a world where glibness and quickness were easily confused with ability to learn. To her overworked and exasperated teachers she was an overconscientious "slow learner" who kept trying to catch up and was absent entirely too often.

I let her be absent, though sometimes the illness was imaginary. How different from my now-strictness about attendance with the others. I wasn't working. We had a new baby, I was home anyhow. Sometimes, after Susan grew old enough, I would keep her home from school, too, to have them all together.

Mostly Emily had asthma, and her breathing, harsh and labored, would fill the house with a curiously tranquil sound. I would bring the two old dresser mirrors and her boxes of collections to her bed. She would select beads and single earrings, bottle tops and shells, dried flowers and pebbles, old postcards and scraps, all sorts of oddments; then she and Susan would play Kingdom, setting up landscapes and furniture, peopling them with action.

Those were the only times of peaceful companionship between her and Susan. I have edged away from it, that poisonous feeling between them, that terrible balancing of hurts and needs I had to do between the two, and did so badly, those earlier years.

Oh there are conflicts between the others too, each one human, needing, demanding, hurting, taking—but only between Emily and Susan, no, Emily toward Susan that corroding resentment. It seems so obvious on the surface, yet it is not obvious. Susan, the second child, Susan, golden- and curly-haired and chubby, quick and articulate and assured, everything in appearance and manner Emily was not; Susan, not able to resist Emily's precious things, losing or sometimes clumsily breaking them; Susan telling jokes and riddles to company for applause while Emily sat silent (to say to me later: that was *my* riddle, Mother, I told it to Susan); Susan, who for all the five years' difference in age was just a year behind Emily in developing physically.

I am glad for that slow physical development that widened the difference between her and her contemporaries, though she suffered over it. She was too vulnerable for that terrible world of youthful competition, of preening and parading, of constant measuring of yourself against every other, of envy, "If I had that copper hair," "If I had that skin. . . ." She tormented herself enough about not looking like the others, there was enough of the unsureness, the having to be conscious of words before you speak, the constant caring—what are they thinking of me? without having it all magnified by the merciless physical drives.

Ronnie is calling. He is wet and I change him. It is rare there is such a cry now. That time of motherhood is almost behind me when the ear is not one's own but must always be racked and listening for the child cry, the child call. We sit for a while and I hold him, looking out over the city spread in charcoal with its soft aisles of light. "*Shoogily*," he breathes and curls closer. I carry him back to bed, asleep. *Shoogily*. A funny word, a family word, inherited from Emily, invented by her to say: *comfort*.

In this and other ways she leaves her seal, I say aloud. And startle at my saying it. What do I mean? What did I start to gather together, to try and make coherent? I was at the terrible, growing years. War years. I do not remember them well. I was working, there were four smaller ones now, there was not time for her. She had to help be a mother, and housekeeper, and shopper. She had to set her seal. Mornings of crisis and near hysteria trying to get lunches packed, hair combed, coats and shoes found, everyone to school or Child Care on time, the baby ready for transportation. And always the paper scribbled on by a smaller one, the book looked at by Susan then mislaid, the homework not done. Running out to that huge school where she was one, she was lost, she was a drop; suffering over the unpreparedness, stammering and unsure in her classes.

There was so little time left at night after the kids were bedded down.   45
She would struggle over books, always eating (it was in those years she developed her enormous appetite that is legendary in our family) and I would be ironing, or preparing food for the next day, or writing V-mail° to Bill, or

---

°**V-mail:** Mail sent to or from members of the armed forces during World War II. Letters were reduced onto microfilm and enlarged and printed out at their destination.

tending the baby. Sometimes, to make me laugh, or out of her despair, she would imitate happenings or types at school.

I think I said once: "Why don't you do something like this in the school amateur show?" One morning she phoned me at work, hardly understandable through the weeping: "Mother, I did it. I won, I won; they gave me first prize; they clapped and clapped and wouldn't let me go."

Now suddenly she was Somebody, and as imprisoned in her difference as she had been in anonymity.

She began to be asked to perform at other high schools, even in colleges, then at city and statewide affairs. The first one we went to, I only recognized her that first moment when thin, shy, she almost drowned herself into the curtains. Then: Was this Emily? The control, the command, the convulsing and deadly clowning, the spell, then the roaring, stamping audience, unwilling to let this rare and precious laughter out of their lives.

Afterwards: You ought to do something about her with a gift like that—but without money or knowing how, what does one do? We have left it all to her, and the gift has as often eddied inside, clogged and clotted, as been used and growing.

She is coming. She runs up the stairs two at a time with her light graceful step, and I know she is happy tonight. Whatever it was that occasioned your call did not happen today.

"Aren't you ever going to finish the ironing, Mother? Whistler painted his mother in a rocker. I'd have to paint mine standing over an ironing board." This is one of her communicative nights and she tells me everything and nothing as she fixes herself a plate of food out of the icebox.

She is so lovely. Why did you want me to come in at all? Why were you concerned? She will find her way.

She starts up the stairs to bed. "Don't get me up with the rest in the morning." "But I thought you were having midterms." "Oh, those," she comes back in, kisses me, and says quite lightly, "in a couple of years when we'll all be atom-dead they won't matter a bit."

She has said it before. She *believes* it. But because I have been dredging the past, and all that compounds a human being is so heavy and meaningful in me, I cannot endure it tonight.

I will never total it all. I will never come in to say: She was a child seldom smiled at. Her father left me before she was a year old. I had to work her first six years when there was work, or I sent her home and to his relatives. There were years she had care she hated. She was dark and thin and foreign-looking in a world where the prestige went to blondeness and curly hair and dimples, she was slow where glibness was prized. She was a child of anxious, not proud, love. We were poor and could not afford for her the soil of easy growth. I was a young mother, I was a distracted mother. There were other children pushing up, demanding. Her

younger sister seemed all that she was not. There were years she did not
want me to touch her. She kept too much in herself, her life was such she
had to keep too much in herself. My wisdom came too late. She has
much to her and probably little will come of it. She is a child of her age,
of depression, of war, of fear.

Let her be. So all that is in her will not bloom—but in how many does
it? There is still enough left to live by. Only help her to know—help make
it so there is cause for her to know—that she is more than this dress on the
ironing board, helpless before the iron.

- What details in this story relate to the war that is in the background? How has
  the war impacted the characters, and how appropriate is it to continue to
  calculate the impact of the war on those characters' lives in the present action
  of the story? What do we learn in this story about the nature of life during
  World War II?
- What language does the narrator use to describe her own action in the story?
  How is this language related to the conditions in which she lived?

POETRY

Herman Melville (1819–1891)

A Utilitarian View of the Monitor's Fight

(1866)

Plain be the phrase, yet apt the verse,
   More ponderous than nimble;
For since grimed War here laid aside
His painted pomp, 'twould ill befit
     Overmuch to ply   5
   The rhyme's barbaric symbol.

Hail to victory without the gaud
   Of glory; zeal that needs no fans
Of banners; plain mechanic power
Plied cogently in War now placed—   10
     Where War belongs—
   Among the trades and artisans.

Yet this was battle, and intense—
   Beyond the strife of fleets heroic;
Deadlier, closer, calm 'mid storm;   15
No passion; all went on by crank.
      Pivot, and screw,
   And calculations of caloric.

Needless to dwell; the story's known.
   The ringing of those plates on plates   20
Still ringeth round the world—
The clangor of the blacksmiths' fray.
     The anvil-din
   Resounds this message from the Fates:

War shall yet be, and to the end;   25
   But war-paint shows the streaks of weather;
War yet shall be, but the warriors
Are now but operatives; War's made
     Less grand than Peace,
   And a singe runs through lace and feather.   30

■ The poem describes the Civil War confrontation between the *Monitor* and the *Merrimac*, two ironclad fighting ships. The novelty of a confrontation between these war machines inspired much discussion about the changing nature of war.

■ How does the poet suggest that the nature of "grimed War" has changed? How do these ships signify this change? What remains the same?

Herbert Read (1893–1968)

The Execution of Cornelius Vane (1919)

*Le combat spirituel est aussi brutal que la
bataille d'hommes; mais la vision de la
justice est le plaisir de Dieu seul.*

                              —Arthur Rimbaud

Arraign'd before his worldly gods
He would have said:
"I, Cornelius Vane,

A fly in the sticky web of life,
Shot away my right index finger.   5

I was alone, on sentry, in the chill twilight after dawn,
And the act cost me a bloody sweat.
Otherwise the cost was trivial—they had no evidence.
And I lied to the wooden fools who tried me.
When I returned from hospital   10
They made me a company cook:
I peel potatoes and other men fight."

For nearly a year Cornelius peeled potatoes
And his life was full of serenity.
Then the enemy broke our line   15
And their hosts spread over the plains
Like unleash'd beads.
Every man was taken—
Shoemakers, storemen, grooms—
And arms were given them   20
That they might stem the oncoming host.

Cornelius held out his fingerless hand
And remarked that he couldn't shoot.
"But you can stab," the sergeant said,
So he fell in with the rest, and, a little group,   25
They marched away towards the enemy.

After an hour they halted for a rest.
They were already in the fringe of the fight:
Desultory shells fell about them,
And past them retreating gunteams   30
Galloped in haste.
But they must go on.

Wounded stragglers came down the road,
Haggard and limping
Their arms and equipment tossed away.   35
Cornelius Vane saw them, and his heart was beating wildly,
For he must go on.

At the next halt
He went aside to piss,
And whilst away a black shell   40

Burst near him:
Hot metal shrieked past his face;
Bricks and earth descended like hail,
And the acrid stench of explosive filled his nostrils.

Cornelius pitched his body to the ground   45
And crouched in trembling fear.
Another shell came singing overhead,
Nowhere near.

But Cornelius sprang to his feet, his pale face set.
He willed nothing, saw nothing, only before him   50
Were the free open fields:
To the fields he ran.

He was still running when he began to perceive
The tranquillity of the fields
And the battle distant.   55
Away in the north-east were men marching on a road;
Behind were the smoke-puffs of shrapnel,
And in the west the sun declining
In a sky of limpid gold.

When night came finally   60
He had reached a wood.
In the thickness of the trees
The cold wind was excluded,
And here he slept a few hours.

In the early dawn   65
The chill mist and heavy dew
Pierced his bones and wakened him.
There was no sound of battle to be heard.
In the open fields again
The sun shone sickly through the mist   70
And the dew was icy to the feet.
So Cornelius ran about in that white night,
The sun's wan glare his only guide.

Coming to a canal
He ran up and down like a dog   75
Deliberating where to cross.

One way he saw a bridge
Loom vaguely, but approaching
He heard voices and turned about.
He went far the other way,   80
But growing tired before he found a crossing,
Plunged into the icy water and swam.
The water gripped with agony;
His clothes sucked the heavy water,
And as he ran again   85
Water oozed and squelched from his boots
His coat dripped and his teeth chattered.

He came to a farm.
Approaching cautiously, he found it deserted.
Within he discarded his sopping uniform, dried himself and donned   90
Mufti he found in a cupboard.
Dark mouldy bread and bottled cider he also found
And was refreshed.
Whilst he was eating,
Suddenly,   95
Machine-guns opened fire not far away,
And their harsh throbbing
Darkened his soul with fear.

The sun was more golden now,
And as he went—   100
Always going west—
The mist grew thin.

About noon,
As he skirted the length of a wood
The warmth had triumphed and the spring day was beautiful.   105
Cornelius perceived with a new joy
Pale anemones and violets of the wood,
And wished that he might ever
Exist in the perception of these woodland flowers
And the shafts of yellow light that pierced   110
The green dusk.

Two days later
He entered a village and was arrested.
He was hungry, and the peace of the fields
Dissipated the terror that had been the strength of his will.   115

He was charged with desertion
And eventually tried by court-martial.

The evidence was heavy against him,
And he was mute in his own defence.
A dumb anger and a despair   120
Filled his soul.

He was found guilty.
Sentence: To suffer death by being shot.

The sentence duly confirmed,
One morning at dawn they led him forth.   125
He saw a party of his own regiment,
With rifles, looking very sad.
The morning was bright, and as they tied
The cloth over his eyes, he said to the assembly:
"What wrong have I done that I should leave these: 130
The bright sun rising
And the birds that sing?"

- Although it was a capital offense, it was not uncommon during World War I for soldiers to shoot off their own fingers in order to avoid some of the horrors of war. What does Vane avoid? Is his sentence just?
- What comment does the poem make about the obligation of a soldier in a war?

Stephen Crane (1871–1900)

There Was a Crimson Clash of War (1895)

There was crimson clash of war.
Lands turned black and bare;
Women wept;
Babes ran, wondering.
There came one who understood not these things.   5
He said, "Why is this?"
Whereupon a million strove to answer him.
There was such intricate clamour of tongues,
That still the reason was not.

- Explain the final two lines of the poem.
- Why does the poet use the perspective of an outsider to question the rationale for war?

e. e. cummings (1894–1962)

[i sing of Olaf glad and big] (1931)

i sing of Olaf glad and big
whose warmest heart recoiled at war:
a conscientious object-or

his wellbeloved colonel(trig
westpointer most succinctly bred)   5
took erring Olaf soon in hand;
but—though an host of overjoyed
noncoms(first knocking on the head
him)do through icy waters roll
that helplessness which others stroke   10
with brushes recently employed
anent this muddy toiletbowl,
while kindred intellects evoke
allegiance per blunt instruments—
Olaf(being to all intents   15
a corpse and wanting any rag
upon what God unto him gave)
responds,without getting annoyed
"I will not kiss your fucking flag"

straightway the silver bird looked grave   20
(departing hurriedly to shave)

but—though all kinds of officers
(a yearning nation's blueeyed pride)
their passive prey did kick and curse
until for wear their clarion   25
voices and boots were much the worse,
and egged the firstclassprivates on
his rectum wickedly to tease
by means of skilfully applied
bayonets roasted hot with heat—   30

Olaf(upon what were once knees)
does almost ceaselessly repeat
"there is some shit I will not eat"

our president,being of which
assertions duly notified   35
threw the yellowsonofabitch
into a dungeon, where he died

Christ(of His mercy infinite)
i pray to see;and Olaf, too

preponderatingly because   40
unless statistics lie he was
more brave than me:more blond than you.

- Who becomes the enemy in this poem? What details in the poem make their actions seem reprehensible?
- What heroic qualities does Olaf demonstrate?

Richard Eberhart (1904–2005)

The Fury of Aerial Bombardment (1945)

You would think the fury of aerial bombardment
Would rouse God to relent; the infinite spaces
Are still silent. He looks on shock-pried faces.
History, even, does not know what is meant.

You would feel that after so many centuries   5
God would give man to repent; yet he can kill
As Cain could, but with multitudinous will,
No farther advanced than in his ancient furies.

Was man made stupid to see his own stupidity?
Is God by definition indifferent, beyond us all?   10
Is the eternal truth man's fighting soul
Wherein the Beast ravens in its own avidity?

Of Van Wettering I speak, and Averill,
Names on a list, whose faces I do not recall

But they are gone to early death, who late in school   15
Distinguished the belt feed lever from the belt holding pawl.

- The "belt feed lever" and the "belt holding pawl" are parts of a machine gun. How does this poem describe the mechanical efficiency of modern warfare?
- How is this particular meditation distinct from Melville's comments (p. 1442) on a similar theme?

Edgar A. Guest (1881–1959)

The Things That Make a Soldier Great (1918)

The things that make a soldier great
and send him out to die,
To face the flaming cannon's mouth
nor ever question why,
Are lilacs by a little porch,   5
the row of tulips red,
The peonies and pansies, too,
the old petunia bed,
The grass plot where his children play,
the roses on the wall: 10
'Tis these that make a soldier great.
He's fighting for them all.

'Tis not the pomp and pride of kings
that make a soldier brave;
'Tis not allegiance to the flag   15
that over him may wave;
For soldiers never fight so well
on land or on the foam
As when behind the cause they see
the little place called home.   20
Endanger but that humble street
whereon his children run,
You make a soldier of the man
who never bore a gun.

What is it through the battle smoke   25
the valiant soldier sees?

The little garden far away,
the budding apple trees,
The little patch of ground back there,
the children at their play,   30
Perhaps a tiny mound behind
the simple church of gray.
The golden thread of courage
isn't linked to castle dome
But to the spot, where'er it be—   35
the humblest spot called home.

And now the lilacs bud again
and all is lovely there
And homesick soldiers far away
know spring is in the air;   40
The tulips come to bloom again,
the grass once more is green,
And every man can see the spot
where all his joys have been.
He sees his children smile at him,   45
he hears the bugle call,
And only death can stop him now—
he's fighting for them all.

■ Mark the ways in which this poem presents the dilemma of war in a different
  light than the previous poems.
■ To what extent does it answer the challenge posed by Crane (p. 1446)? How
  does it fit into Eberhart's vision of war (p. 1448)?

Sir Henry Newbolt (1862–1938)

Vitai Lampada (1897)

There's a breathless hush in the Close to-night—
Ten to make and the match to win—
A bumping pitch and a blinding light,
An hour to play and the last man in.
And it's not for the sake of a ribboned coat,   5

Or the selfish hope of a season's fame,
But his Captain's hand on his shoulder smote
"Play up! play up! and play the game!"

The sand of the desert is sodden red,—
Red with the wreck of a square that broke;—   10
The Gatling's jammed and the colonel dead,
And the regiment blind with dust and smoke.
The river of death has brimmed his banks,
And England's far, and Honour a name,
But the voice of schoolboy rallies the ranks,   15
"Play up! play up! and play the game!"

This is the word that year by year
While in her place the School is set
Every one of her sons must hear,
And none that hears it dare forget.   20
This they all with a joyful mind
Bear through life like a torch in flame,
And falling fling to the host behind—
"Play up! play up! and play the game!"

■ How are the contexts for the cries "Play up!" different? Why is it appropriate to juxtapose them here?
■ What is the impact of this repeated refrain? How does this poem fit among the other poems that are gathered here?

Wilfred Owen (1893–1918)

Anthem for Doomed Youth (1917)

What passing-bells for these who die as cattle?
Only the monstrous anger of the guns.
Only the stuttering rifles' rapid rattle
Can patter out their hasty orisons.
No mockeries now for them; no prayers nor bells,   5
Nor any voice of mourning save the choirs,—
The shrill, demented choirs of wailing shells;

And bugles calling for them from sad shires.
What candles may be held to speed them all?
Not in the hands of boys, but in their eyes   10
Shall shine the holy glimmers of good-byes.
The pallor of girls' brows shall be their pall;
Their flowers the tenderness of patient minds,
And each slow dusk of drawing-down of blinds.

Wilfred Owen (1893–1918)

Dulce et Decorum Est (1920)

Bent double, like old beggars under sacks,
Knock-kneed, coughing like hags, we cursed through sludge,
Till on the haunting flares we turned our backs,
And towards our distant rest began to trudge.
Men marched asleep. Many had lost their boots,   5
But limped on, blood-shod. All went lame, all blind;
Drunk with fatigue; deaf even to the hoots
Of gas-shells dropping softly behind.

Gas! GAS! Quick, boys!—An ecstasy of fumbling,
Fitting the clumsy helmets just in time,   10
But someone still was yelling out and stumbling
And flound'ring like a man in fire or lime.—
Dim through the misty panes and thick green light,
As under a green sea, I saw him drowning.
In all my dreams before my helpless sight   15
He plunges at me, guttering, choking, drowning.
If in some smothering dreams, you too could pace
Behind the wagon that we flung him in,
And watch the white eyes writhing in his face,
His hanging face, like a devil's sick of sin,   20
If you could hear, at every jolt, the blood
Come gargling from the froth-corrupted lungs
Bitter as the cud
Of vile, incurable sores on innocent tongues,—
My friend, you would not tell with such high zest   25
To children ardent for some desperate glory,
The old lie: *Dulce et decorum est*
Pro patria mori.

- Owen died as a soldier in World War I. How does this context add to the impact of the poem that calls the old Latin phrase "Sweet and honorable it is to die for one's country" a lie?
- What impact does the poet achieve by adopting a Latin phrase or "Anthem" for the titles of his poems? How do Owen's poems build upon the tradition that we see in Newbolt's poem?

Carl Sandburg (1878–1967)

Grass (1918)

Pile the bodies high at Austerlitz and Waterloo.
Shovel them under and let me work—
          I am the grass; I cover all.

And pile them high at Gettysburg
And pile them high at Ypres and Verdun.   5
Shovel them under and let me work.
Two years, ten years, and passengers ask the conductor:
          What place is this?
          Where are we now?

          I am the grass.   10
          Let me work.

- What is the work that the grass is doing?
- What is the significance of the questions that the passengers ask the conductor?

Siegfried Sassoon (1886–1967)

The Rear-Guard (1918)

(Hindenburg Line, April 1917)

Groping along the tunnel, step by step,
He winked his prying torch with patching glare
From side to side, and sniffed the unwholesome air.

Tins, boxes, bottles, shapes too vague to know;
A mirror smashed, the mattress from a bed;   5

And he, exploring fifty feet below
The rosy gloom of battle overhead.

Tripping, he grabbed the wall; saw some one lie
Humped at his feet, half-hidden by a rug,
And stooped to give the sleeper's arm a tug.   10
"I'm looking for headquarters." No reply.
"God blast your neck!" (For days he'd had no sleep.)

"Get up and guide me through this stinking place."
Savage, he kicked a soft, unanswering heap,
And flashed his beam across the livid face   15
Terribly glaring up, whose eyes yet wore
Agony dying hard ten days before;
And fists of fingers clutched a blackening wound.

Alone he staggered on until he found
Dawn's ghost that filtered down a shafted stair   20
To the dazed, muttering creatures underground
Who hear the boom of shells in muffled sound.
At last, with sweat of horror in his hair,
He climbed through darkness to the twilight air,
Unloading hell behind him step by step.   25

Siegfried Sassoon (1886–1967)

Repression of War Experience (1918)

Now light the candles; one; two; there's a moth;
What silly beggars they are to blunder in
And scorch their wings with glory, liquid flame—
No, no, not that,—it's bad to think of war,
When thoughts you've gagged all day come back to scare you;   5
And it's been proved that soldiers don't go mad
Unless they lose control of ugly thoughts
That drive them out to jabber among the trees.

Now light your pipe; look, what a steady hand.
Draw a deep breath; stop thinking; count fifteen,   10
And you're as right as rain . . .
                        Why won't it rain? . . .

I wish there'd be a thunder-storm to-night,
With bucketsful of water to sluice the dark,
And make the roses hang their dripping heads.
Books; what a jolly company they are,   15
Standing so quiet and patient on their shelves,
Dressed in dim brown, and black, and white, and green,
And every kind of colour. Which will you read?
Come on; O *do* read something; they're so wise.
I tell you all the wisdom of the world   20
Is waiting for you on those shelves; and yet
You sit and gnaw your nails, and let your pipe out,
And listen to the silence: on the ceiling
There's one big, dizzy moth that bumps and flutters;
And in the breathless air outside the house   25
The garden waits for something that delays.
There must be crowds of ghosts among the trees,—
Not people killed in battle,—they're in France,—
Slow, natural deaths,—old men with ugly souls,
Who wore their bodies out with nasty sins.   30
                    *   *   *
You're quiet and peaceful, summering safe at home;
You'd never think there was a bloody war on! . . .
O yes, you would . . . why, you can hear the guns.
Hark! Thud, thud, thud,—quite soft . . . they never cease—
Those whispering guns—O Christ, I want to go out   35
And screech at them to stop—I'm going crazy;
I'm going stark, staring mad because of the guns.

■ These two poems describe the experience of war from the perspective of the
soldier. How does the "Repression of War Experience" change the context
from that in "The Rear-Guard"? In this new context, what must the protagonist
fight? Compare the images that the poet uses to evoke horror in the first poem
to those that appear in the second.

Anne Sexton (1928–1974)

Courage (1975)

It is in the small things we see it.
The child's first step,

as awesome as an earthquake.
The first time you rode a bike,
wallowing up the sidewalk.   5
The first spanking when your heart
went on a journey all alone.
When they called you crybaby
or poor or fatty or crazy
and made you into an alien,   10
you drank their acid
and concealed it.

Later,
if you faced the death of bombs and bullets
you did not do it with a banner,   15
you did it with only a hat to
cover your heart.
You did not fondle the weakness inside you
though it was there.
Your courage was a small coal   20
that you kept swallowing.
If your buddy saved you
and died himself in so doing,
then his courage was not courage,
it was love; love as simple as shaving soap.   25

Later,
if you have endured a great despair,
then you did it alone,
getting a transfusion from the fire,
picking the scabs off your heart,   30
then wringing it out like a sock.
Next, my kinsman, you powdered your sorrow,
you gave it a back rub
and then you covered it with a blanket
and after it had slept a while   35
it woke to the wings of the roses
and was transformed.

Later,
when you face old age and its natural conclusion
your courage will still be shown in the little ways,   40
each spring will be a sword you'll sharpen,

those you love will live in a fever of love,
and you'll bargain with the calendar
and at the last moment
when death opens the back door   45
you'll put on your carpet slippers
and stride out.

■ How do the four different contexts present different interpretations of the word
  courage? What do they each have in common? Is any one of the types of
  courage more courageous than the others? Explain how the poem supports your
  claim.

■ In the second stanza, the soldier's "buddy" demonstrates love rather than
  courage. Who makes this distinction?

Alice Moore Dunbar-Nelson (1875–1935)

I Sit and Sew (1920)

I sit and sew—a useless task it seems,
My hands grown tired, my head weighed down with dreams—
The panoply of war, the martial tred of men
Grim-faced, stern-eyed, gazing beyond the ken
Of lesser souls, whose eyes have not seen Death   5
Nor learned to hold their lives but as a breath—
But—I must sit and sew.

I sit and sew—my heart aches with desire—
That pageant terrible, that fiercely pouring fire
On wasted fields, and writhing grotesque things   10
Once men. My soul in pity flings
Appealing cries, yearning only to go
There in that holocaust of hell, those fields of woe—
But—I must sit and sew.

The little useless seam, the idle patch;   15
Why dream I here beneath my homely thatch,
When there they lie in sodden mud and rain,
Pitifully calling me, the quick ones and the slain?
You need me, Christ! It is no roseate dream
That beckons me—this pretty futile seam,   20
It stifles me—God, must I sit and sew?

- Look at the specific words the poet uses to give value to experience. Why does the narrator describe the seam as "little" and "useless"?
- How does this perspective relate to that described in "Courage"?

Yusef Komunyakaa (1947–)

Facing It (1988)

My black face fades,
hiding inside the black granite.
I said I wouldn't,
dammit: No tears.
I'm stone. I'm flesh.   5
My clouded reflection eyes me
like a bird of prey, the profile of night
slanted against morning. I turn
this way—the stone lets me go.
I turn that way—I'm inside   10
the Vietnam Veterans Memorial
again, depending on the light
to make a difference.
I go down the 58,022 names,
half-expecting to find   15
my own in letters like smoke.
I touch the name Andrew Johnson;
I see the booby trap's white flash.
Names shimmer on a woman's blouse
but when she walks away   20
the names stay on the wall.
Brushstrokes flash, a red bird's
wings cutting across my stare.

The sky. A plane in the sky.
A white vet's image floats   25
closer to me, then his pale eyes
look through mine. I'm a window.
He's lost his right arm
inside the stone. In the black mirror
a woman's trying to erase names: 30
No, she's brushing a boy's hair.

- The Vietnam Veterans Memorial in Washington, D.C., has a polished black granite wall on which the names of those who died in the war are carved. How does this poem offer descriptions of both the physical appearance of this monument and of the ways in which its appearance inspires memory of the dead?
- How does the poet describe the different interactions that the visitors have with the names on the wall?

Judith Ortiz Cofer (1952–)

The Changeling (1993)

As a young girl
vying for my father's attention,
I invented a game that made him look up
from his reading and shake his head
as if both baffled and amused.   5

In my brother's closet, I'd change
into his dungarees—the rough material
molding me into boy shape; hide
my long hair under an army helmet
he'd been given by Father, and emerge   10
transformed into the legendary Ché
of grown-up talk.

Strutting around the room,
I'd tell of life in the mountains,
of carnage and rivers of blood,   15
and of manly feasts with rum and music
to celebrate victories *para la libertad.*
He would listen with a smile
to my tales of battles and brotherhood
until Mother called us to dinner.   20

She was not amused
by my transformations, sternly forbidding me
from sitting down with them as a man.
She'd order me back to the dark cubicle
that smelled of adventure, to shed   25
my costume, to braid my hair furiously
with blind hands, and to return invisible,

as myself,
to the real world of her kitchen.

■ Like "Facing It" (p. 1458), this poem deals with characters for whom war is at
some distance. How does this poem distinguish between the "legendary" and
"the real world"?

■ How are the "tales of battles and brotherhood" that the narrator relates
colored by the image we get of this narrator?

Mary Jo Salter (1954–)

Welcome to Hiroshima (1984)

is what you first see, stepping off the train:
a billboard brought to you in living English
by Toshiba Electric. While a channel
silent in the TV of the brain

projects those flickering re-runs of a cloud   5
that brims its risen columnful like beer
and, spilling over, hangs its foamy head,
you feel a thirst for history: what year

it started to be safe to breathe the air,
and when to drink the blood and scum afloat   10
on the Ohta River. But no, the water's clear,
they pour it for your morning cup of tea

in one of the countless sunny coffee shops
whose plastic dioramas advertise
mutations of cuisine behind the glass: 15
a pancake sandwich; a pizza someone tops

with a maraschino cherry. Passing by
the Peace Park's floral hypocenter (where
how bravely, or with what mistaken cheer,
humanity erased its own erasure),   20

you enter the memorial museum
and through more glass are served, as on a dish
of blistered grass, three mannequins. Like gloves
a mother clips to coatsleeves, strings of flesh

hang from their fingertips; or as if tied   25
to recall a duty for us, *Reverence*
the dead whose mourners too shall soon be dead,
but all commemoration's swallowed up

in questions of bad taste, how re-created
horror mocks the grim original,   30
and thinking at last *They should have left it all*
you stop. This is the wristwatch of a child.

Jammed on the moment's impact, resolute
to communicate some message, although mute,
it gestures with its hands at eight-fifteen   35
and eight-fifteen and eight-fifteen again

while tables of statistics on the wall
update the news by calling on a roll
of tape, death gummed on death, and in the case
adjacent, an exhibit under glass   40

is glass itself: a shard the bomb slammed in
a woman's arm at eight-fifteen, but some
three decades on—as if to make it plain
hope's only as renewable as pain,

and as if all the unsung   45
debasements of the past may one day come
rising to the surface once again—
worked its filthy way out like a tongue.

■ On August 6, 1945, the United States dropped the first atomic bomb on Hiroshima, Japan. This poem describes the actual place where the bomb was dropped. How has the place changed? How has the memory of that bombing been preserved?

■ According to this poem, how has "humanity erased its own erasure"?

Wislawa Szymborska (1923–)

The End and the Beginning (1993)

After each war
somebody has to clear up

put things in order
by itself it won't happen.

Somebody's got to push   5
rubble to the highway shoulder
making way
for the carts filled up with corpses.

Someone might trudge
through muck and ashes,   10
sofa springs,
splintered glass
and blood-soaked rugs.

Somebody has to haul
beams for propping a wall,   15
another put glass in a window
and hang the door on hinges.

This is not photogenic
and takes years.

All the cameras have left already   20
for another war.

Bridges are needed
also new railroad stations.
Tatters turn into sleeves
for rolling up.   25

Somebody, broom in hand,
still recalls how it was.
Someone whose head was not
torn away listens nodding.
But nearby already   30
begin to bustle those
who'll need persuasion.

Somebody still at times
digs up from under the bushes
some rusty quibble   35
to add it to burning refuse.

Those who knew
what this was all about

must yield to those
who know little   40
or less than little
essentially nothing.

In the grass that has covered
effects in causes
somebody must recline,   45
a stalk of rye in the teeth,
ogling the clouds.

■ What point of view does this poem take? How do we respond to the fact that
"Those who knew / what this was all about / must yield to those / who know
little / or less than little / essentially nothing"?

■ Compare the claim that "somebody must recline . . . ogling the clouds" with the
criticisms in "Welcome to Hiroshima" about the refiguring of the scene of the
first atomic bombing?

Wislawa Szymborska (1923–)

Monologue of a Dog Ensnared in History (2002)

There are dogs and dogs. I was among the chosen.
I had good papers and wolf's blood in my veins.
I lived upon the heights inhaling the odors of views:
meadows in sunlight, spruces after rain,
and clumps of earth beneath the snow.   5

I had a decent home and people on call.
I was fed, washed, groomed,
and taken for lovely strolls.
Respectfully, though, and *comme il faut*.
They all knew full well whose dog I was.   10

Any lousy mutt can have a master.
Take care, though—beware comparisons.
My master was a breed apart.
He had a splendid herd that trailed his every step
and fixed their eyes on him in fearful awe.   15

For me they always had smiles,
with envy poorly hidden.

Since only I had the right
to greet him with nimble leaps,
Only I could say goodbye by worrying his trousers with my teeth   20
Only I was permitted
to receive scratching and stroking
with my head laid in his lap.
Only I could feign sleep
while he bent over me to whisper something.   25

He raged at others often, loudly.
He snarled, barked,
raced from wall to wall.
I suspect he liked only me
and nobody else, ever.   30

I also had responsibilities: waiting, trusting.
Since he would turn up briefly and then vanish.
What kept him down there in the lowlands, I don't know.
I guessed, though, it must be pressing business,
at least as pressing   35
as my battle with the cats
and everything that moves for no good reason.

There's fate and fate. Mine changed abruptly.
One spring came
and he wasn't there.   40
All hell broke loose at home.
Suitcases, chests, trunks crammed into cars.
The wheels squealed tearing downhill
and fell silent round the bend.

On the terrace scraps and tatters flamed,   45
yellow shirts, armbands with black emblems,
and lots and lots of battered cartons
with banners tumbling out.

I was adrift in this whirlwind,
more amazed than peeved.   50
I felt unfriendly glances on my fur.
As if I were a dog without a master,
some pushy stray
chased downstairs with a broom.

Someone tore my silver-trimmed collar off,   55
someone kicked my bowl, empty for days.
Then someone else, driving away,
leaned out from the car
and shot me twice.

He couldn't even shoot straight,   60
since I died for a long time, in pain,
to the buzz of impertinent flies.
I, the dog of my master.

■ How does the life of the master resemble the life of the narrating dog? How
can we understand elements of this master's life even though the dog may not
be aware of them?

Adrienne Rich (1929–)

For the Record (1983)

The clouds and the stars didn't wage this war
the brooks gave no information
if the mountain spewed stones of fire into the river
it was not taking sides
the raindrop faintly swaying under the leaf   5
had no political opinions

and if here or there a house
filled with backed-up raw sewage
or poisoned those who lived there
with slow fumes, over years   10
the houses were not at war
nor did the tinned-up buildings

intend to refuse shelter
to homeless old women and roaming children
they had no policy to keep them roaming   15
or dying, no, the cities were not the problem
the bridges were non-partisan
the freeways burned, but not with hatred

Even the miles of barbed-wire
stretched around crouching temporary huts   20

designed to keep the unwanted
at a safe distance, out of sight
even the boards that had to absorb
year upon year, so many human sounds

so many depths of vomit, tears   25
slow-soaking blood
had not offered themselves for this
The trees didn't volunteer to be cut into boards
nor the thorns for tearing flesh
Look around at all of it   30

and ask whose signature
is stamped on the orders, traced
in the corner of the building plans
Ask where the illiterate, big-bellied
women were, the drunks and crazies,   35
the ones you fear most of all: ask where you were.

■ In the final stanza, the poet asks "whose signature / is stamped on the orders."
How does the poem treat the subject of agency? Look at the specific words that
the poet uses to describe violence and suffering and the words that excuse
raindrops, freeways, and thorns from responsibility. How do these juxtapositions help give power to the final line of the poem?

DRAMA

Gina Victoria Shaffer (1960–)

Gina Victoria Shaffer was born in Miami and worked as a newspaper reporter
before receiving a PhD in English at the University of California, Irvine. She is
now a member of the UCLA Writing Programs faculty. As a playwright, Shaffer
has authored several works that have been staged Off Broadway and in theaters
throughout Southern California. They include *Out of Her Time, If Memory Serves,
Dreaming of Barbie, Splitting Ends,* and *You're Not Hamlet.*

War Spelled Backwards (2006)

CHARACTERS

TIME AND SCENE: *All four characters are U.S. Army soldiers.*

RANDALL ALAN WILKINS, *20s*
ROBERT ANTHONY WALLACE, *20s to 40s, speaks with Southern inflection*
MARTINEZ, *20s*
ARNIE, *20s*

TIME AND SCENE: *The desert about 25 miles west of Baghdad during a sandstorm on April 12, 2004.*
SONGS: *I suggest playing "Deja Vu (All Over Again)" by John Fogerty after the play ends.*

(Sitting next to their truck in the desert west of Baghdad at 1 A.M., three U.S. Army soldiers are stranded during a sandstorm. ARNIE *and* MARTINEZ *are sipping wine from a flask.* RANDY *is communicating with the command base via radio.)*
RANDY: This is Echo 4 Whiskey calling Delta. Do you read? Over. This is Echo 4 Whiskey calling Delta. Do you copy? Over. We're still stuck, sir. The truck won't budge. Wind's coming at us at 35 mph. Over.
ARNIE: That's good booze. Gimme some more of that. Where'd you get it, Martinez?
MARTINEZ *(hands it off to* ARNIE.): Traded it for a pack of Marlboros at that little shack in Falluja. I heard about this Iraqi wine. They make it themselves. Didn't know it was going to be this strong.
ARNIE: How long before this fuckin' sand stops blowing? And it's fuckin' red, too.
(Offers flask to RANDY, *who waves it off.)*
RANDY *(speaking into radio mike.)*: We've got rations for two more days, sir. 5
Over. *(Pause.)* Negative, sir. We haven't slept for three days. Over. *(Pause.)* We'll do that, lieutenant. Roger. Copy that. Out.
ARNIE: Man, this is as good as that Hawaiian weed JJ brought with him. Superfine wine. I close my eyes and I see my hometown . . . New Orleans, Ninth Ward. . . . music . . . and my mama's cooking . . . gumbo and cornbread. Mmmm! You seein' your hometown, Martinez?
MARTINEZ *(shrugging.)*: I'm from Pico Rivera, dog.
ARNIE: Hey, Corporal, what's the word?
RANDY *(after putting radio down.)*: Lt. Jaffey told me it could be at least another day before the repair unit gets here. We're stuck.
MARTINEZ: Just our luck to get stuck with a shitty truck in the middle of a 10 sandstorm. Dammit!
(The sound of wind grows louder.)
ARNIE: I'm not going to be able to keep my eyes open any longer. I'm wasted. Later, guys . . . *(*ARNIE *goes to sleep.)*
MARTINEZ: You got this watch, Randy? I'm going down, too, dog . . .
*(*MARTINEZ *drifts off to sleep.)*

RANDY: I got us covered, bro. Can't sleep anyways. This wind . . . (*Stands up. Pause. Wind, then noise.*) Hear that? Shit. Something's . . . Somebody's out there.

(*There is silence. Then the wind picks up again.* RANDY *hears a voice to his left call out the name "*FRENCHY!*" He turns to his left. The same voice calls out the name "*DOC!*" from his right side.* RANDY *turns to the right. The wind grows even louder as* RANDY *sees a man in green combat uniform emerge from the swirling sand.*)

WALLACE: Daryl!

RANDY (*giving the Iraqi command for "Stop," pronounced "kiff."*): Qif!   15

WALLACE: That's no way to greet your superior, soldier.

RANDY: Sorry, sir. (RANDY *salutes.*)

WALLACE (*Circling him and sizing him up.*): Thought I was one of them gooks, did ya? Don't even recognize one of your own. Now do I look like a gook to you? Is my skin yellow? Eyes slanted?

RANDY: Gook, sir? I don't . . .

WALLACE: You're trained to smell the difference before you even see my   20 eyes. What kind of mama's boys are they drafting these days?

RANDY: Drafting? I wasn't—

WALLACE: Can't you even recognize a superior officer at close range? Captain Wallace, Headquarters Company, First Battalion, Second Brigade, Fourth Infantry Division.

RANDY (*puts rifle down and snaps to.*): Sincere apology, Captain.

WALLACE: Am I close to the river, soldier?

RANDY: No river around here, sir.   25

WALLACE: No river around here? Have you guys been smoking the local dope or what?

RANDY: No, sir. It's wine, sir.

WALLACE: Got some left for me?

RANDY: Sir, no, sir . . . sorry, sir.

WALLACE: Must have been strong shit to knock 'em both down like that.   30

RANDY: It's homemade Iraqi wine, sir.

WALLACE: Iraqi wine? Where'd you get that?

RANDY: Martinez says he picked it up in Falluja.

WALLACE: Where?

RANDY: Falluja.   35

WALLACE: Ain't no Falluja in 'Nam, soldier.

RANDY: Sir, that's the name of the place. Falluja. Just west of Baghdad.

WALLACE: Baghdad? Man, my head is really messed up. I was supposed to get across the river to meet up with Doc and Frenchy. You seen them anywhere?

RANDY: Don't recognize those names, Captain.

WALLACE: Where the fuck am I?   40

RANDY: We're about 25 miles west of Baghdad.

WALLACE: Last thing I remember, we were on patrol near Khe Sanh. All of
a sudden, Charlie comes at us in the dark. Firing like all hell broke
loose. Darryl was kneeling in the jungle next to me. Somebody yelled,
"Incoming!" Next thing I know, his guts are spilling all over me. Next
thing I feel . . . I feel . . . Something warm. Something burning in my
chest. I touch it. It's tore open. Gawd. It hurts like a sonofabitch. I
taste blood in my mouth. Warm. Salty. I pass out.

RANDY: Sir, are you talking about Vietnam?

WALLACE: Ain't you heard a goddam thing I've said?

RANDY: Sir, this is Iraq. We're in the desert, sir.   45

WALLACE (*Looking around.*): God dammit, boy. First thing you got right tonight. This ain't the jungle. Where the hell is everybody? Darryl?
Frenchy? Doc? Where the hell are you?

RANDY: Don't know those names, Captain. I'm with the First Battalion,
68th Armored Regiment, Third Brigade, Fourth Infantry Division.

WALLACE: What'd they do? Ship us out to fight gooks here in the middle of
the desert?

RANDY: Gooks—that's what you call the Vietnamese, right?

WALLACE: And what the hell do you call them?   50

RANDY: We're not saving the Vietnamese any more, sir. We're liberating
the Iraqis now.

WALLACE: Iraqis? What the fuck's happening to me?

RANDY: Captain, I think you're wounded, sir. Your chest—

WALLACE: Charlie's done some wicked shit to my mind.

RANDY: Sir, let me help you clean that wound.   55

(WALLACE *picks up* RANDY'*s rifle, running his hand along the barrel.*)

WALLACE: That's a fine-looking rifle you've got there.

RANDY: You're wounded, Captain.

(WALLACE *suddenly points the rifle at* RANDY.)

WALLACE: Don't fucking touch me. You're a gook, ain't you? With a mask
on. Disguised as an American. I know it. I want you to take the mask
off. Take it off or I'll shoot.

RANDY: Please, Captain. Please don't shoot, sir.

WALLACE: Take it off. I want to see your gook face. The one behind the mask.   60

RANDY: I'm not.

WALLACE: You're not what?

RANDY: I'm not a gook, Captain. I'm an American soldier. Just like you.

WALLACE: Where'd you do your training?

RANDY: Fort Hood, sir. Joined the Army the day after 9-11.   65

WALLACE: Nine eleven. What's that code for, boy?

RANDY: September 11, 2001, sir.

(WALLACE *slowly lowers the rifle and puts it down.*)

WALLACE: Two thousand and one?

RANDY: I joined the day after the towers came down. I wanted to protect my country, sir. That's why they sent me here. To Iraq. Been swallowing sand ever since, sir.

WALLACE: Soldier, what day is it today?   70

RANDY: 4-12-2004, sir.

WALLACE: Something's wrong with your numbers. (*Looks at his watch.*) It's 0100 hours, 4-12-1968. (*Pause.*) I'm looking for the river, soldier. You got to get me 'cross the river. You got to get me 'cross that river!

RANDY: Sir, there's no rivers around here. Not for miles.

WALLACE: What's your name, soldier?

RANDY: Randall Alan Wilkins, sir. I go by Randy.   75

WALLACE: My initials are R.A.W. Robert Anthony Wallace. They call me Raw.

RANDY: Those are my initials, too.

WALLACE: They are! Know what raw spells backwards, Randy?

RANDY: War.

WALLACE: War spelled backwards is r-a-w, raw, soldier. Our mamas named 80
us right. Ass backwards to war. Glorious thing, ain't it soldier?

RANDY: What, sir?

WALLACE: To fight for your country.

RANDY: Sir, yes, sir.

WALLACE: To take a bullet for your country.

RANDY: Sir, Yes, Sir.   85

WALLACE: To die for your country. Am I right? Am I right, soldier?

RANDY: Yes . . . Yes, sir.

WALLACE: Don't shit me, soldier. You don't want to die for your country. Not over here. Not this way, not here. You're waiting to get your ass shipped back home on the next rotation. I could see it in your eyes when you pointed your rifle at me. Am I right?

RANDY: Yes, sir. I thought I was here to protect my country. But that's not what we're doing. I'm just fighting for my buddies. We're just trying to stay alive. I don't want to get shot. I don't want to die here. Not for this. Not here. (*Pause.*) The wind's died down.

(WALLACE *retreats slowly back to the red desert sands.*)

WALLACE (*heading offstage.*): I got to catch up with Daryl and Doc and 90
Frenchy. Got to get to the other side of the river.
Doc . . . Frenchy . . . Daryl . . .

(*Suddenly, the sound of gunfire erupts and mayhem breaks loose.* ARNIE *and*
MARTINEZ *awaken suddenly from their sleep as* RANDY *signals them to take
defensive positions.*)

RANDY: Arnie! Martinez! We're taking fire . . . we're taking fire!

ARNIE: Where the hell is it coming from?

RANDY: I don't know. Dammit, Martinez. Get down!

MARTINEZ: We got no targets. What do we do?

RANDY: I'll check it out.   95

MARTINEZ: I'll go with you.

RANDY: No, stay down. Hold your positions 'til I come back.

(*Rifle in hand,* RANDY *moves toward the gunfire as* MARTINEZ *and* ARNIE *nervously scan the swirling sand. Intermittent gunfire surrounds them.*)

MARTINEZ: Shit!!! They're all around us.

ARNIE: In the middle of all this motherfuckin' sand?

MARTINEZ: I can't see . . . I can't see anything out there.   100

ARNIE: Goddam sand!

MARTINEZ: Where's Randy?

ARNIE: We can't shoot until we know where he is.

MARTINEZ: We've got nobody backing us up, Arnie. We're gonna die out here.

ARNIE: Shut up, Martinez. I'm backing up your ass.   105

MARTINEZ: I was supposed to be home six months ago. I'm not here. I'm not here.

ARNIE: God dammit, Martinez. Pull yourself together.

(RANDY *returns, his chest wet with blood.*)

RANDY (*Staggering.*): I shot somebody. Saw him go down.

MARTINEZ: You're hit . . . you're hit. (RANDY *crumples to the ground as* MARTINEZ *goes to him.*) Arnie, radio for a medic.

ARNIE (*Picks up the radio, calls for assistance, rifle poised.*): This is Echo   110
2 Poppa. We're taking fire. Small-arms fire all around us, sir. And we've got a man down, Sergeant. Chest wound. Request immediate medivac and air support. Over. Copy that. Out.

MARTINEZ (*Checking* RANDY's *chest wound.*): It's not that bad, man. You'll be OK. Ya with me?

(*With* RANDY *lying between his buddies,* MARTINEZ *cradles his torso while* ARNIE *grabs his hand, forming a tableau.*)

RANDY: Got to get across the river.

MARTINEZ: Work with me, Randy. You're gonna be OK.

RANDY: Got to get to the other side.

MARTINEZ: I'll get you there. Stick with me, man. Just hang on.   115

RANDY: Glorious thing, ain't it soldier?

MARTINEZ: Yeah, man.

RANDY: To fight for your country.

MARTINEZ: Hang with me, bro.

RANDY: To take a bullet for your country. To die for your country.   120

MARTINEZ: Not over here. Not this way. Not here.

■ What language in the play illustrates the juxtaposition between the contemporary soldier and the soldier from the past?

■ What other differences do we observe besides those that are related to the fact that these are soldiers fighting in different wars? How significant are the similarities in their conditions?

Experiencing Literature through Writing

1. Select a single work from this chapter (or any other). Determine what contextual information is available to you. In this book, for instance, we give you the year in which the work was written, and we supply you with biographical information about the author. As you write, consider the following questions:

    a. Once you have collected this information, how does it help you read this specific text? You will probably need some more contextual knowledge. For instance, in this chapter the works are related by the general theme of war. It is important to know what war, if any, was going on at the time that the work was written. It would also be useful to have some basic details about that particular war: When was it fought? What were the results? What was at issue in the war? Who was impacted?

    b. Which of the issues that you know about this war (or event) are evident in this particular text? How can you demonstrate that they are important to the text?

    c. Remember that the text might also supply you with contextual information. What do you learn about this war from the text? How reliable is this information?

    d. Which details in the text take on added significance when you think about this particular context?

2. Consider context as you compare two texts within this chapter's anthology. How does one particular text take on added meaning in relation to some other text that meets one of the following criteria:

    a. It was written at the same time.

    b. It deals with the same historical moment but was written at a different time.

c. It deals with the same theme but was written within a different context.

As you compare the texts, point to specific details that seem similar in at least some way. How does the context in which the texts were written relate to these details? How do the different contexts help you explain some significant aspects of these details?

15 Allusions

In Order to Understand This Text, Is There Something Else That I Am Supposed to Have Read?

In personal conversations, we speak in passing about some event or person with only a reference to a name or a quick description of some part of the event. "Remember the story about your uncle Art, who went out to the desert to look for silver and came back with a pile of worthless rocks?" This brief reference works upon the assumption that those participating in the conversation are familiar with the events in question and interpret them similarly. We might shorten the reference considerably. For instance, as a warning to someone about to set off on some ill-conceived adventure: "Remember Uncle Art." Instead of retelling the story, we refer to a story that we have told (probably many times) before. The longer people are together and the more experiences they share, the less they need to engage in the complexities of linguistic exchange. They develop a shorthand of brief phrases—code words, if you will—looks and signs that convey meanings available only to those who have shared the same experiences. And these words and phrases need not be reductive. The smallest remark can trigger layered memories that convey emotions, beliefs, and values. Writers develop their own shorthand to thicken the texture of their works. They know their readers come to any new piece with some previous literary experience. They may invoke that experience through a brief reference to a passage or scene from another work—through an **allusion**.

CREATING COMMUNITY

An old joke tells of prisoners who had been together in the same cell block for many years. A new convict assigned to the cell block found their conversation bewildering. "Fifty-three!" called a large bald fellow, and the rest burst into riotous laughter. An ancient sailor with a blurred blue anchor tattooed on his arm hollered, "One hundred twenty-six!" Again the rest of the block dissolved in laughs. When he had a chance, the newcomer spoke privately with a white-haired old-timer. The old man explained that they had one joke book in the cell block. No one remembered where it came from, but the jokes in it never failed. The men in this cell had been telling them to one another for decades, yet each joke still struck all of them as much as it had the first time they had heard it. Over the years, they came to know the book so well that they didn't have to deliver the entire joke anymore. A guy would read the first line, and everyone would start laughing; no one needed to make it to the punch line. Now, they had reached the point that they just read out page numbers as their evening's entertainment. Emboldened, the new convict studied the ragged book. After about a week of listening evening after evening to the numbers called and the laughter in response, the new guy hollered, "Twenty-seven!" All the laughter stopped. The old-timer turned to him, "Some guys can just tell them better than others."

Within this joke, we see two important aspects of allusion. First, an allusion is brief. Instead of retelling an entire story, the speaker relies on the common knowledge of the audience in order to convey a complex idea that otherwise would have taken a long narrative or full explanation. Second, an allusion may depend on, create, or limit a sense of community. Within the cell block, a long-established community defines its membership by a person's knowledge and command of a special language. Access to this community isn't easy. The new convict, for example, lacks the common experience that allows him to join. He studies the book but perhaps needs to observe and internalize the small gestures that will allow him both to hear and tell "jokes" in the cell block. Or perhaps he must be a recognized figure in the community to use their private language.

This power of allusion to exclude as well as include might make us wary of highly allusive works. Allusions do sometimes seem to be a way for authors to show off, especially to any of us who feel left outside the conversation that is going on. We might ask why an author needs to display knowledge, especially if the story can do without it. But mere display is rarely the point or the purpose of an allusion. When an author alludes to another work, that author is invoking some quality of the work to enrich the new text. The allusion isn't something merely to recognize; it is something to absorb and appreciate as an integral part of a whole.

Consider, for example, the famous opening sentence of J. D. Salinger's *The Catcher in the Rye*: "If you really want to hear about it, the first thing you'll probably want to know is where I was born, and what my lousy childhood was like, and how my parents were occupied and all before they had me, and all that David Copperfield kind of crap, but I don't feel like going into it, if you want to know the truth." The allusion here is to Charles Dickens's massive autobiographical novel; the first chapter is titled "I am Born." By having Holden Caulfield refer so dismissively to this classic, Salinger achieves a good deal. We know immediately that the narrator doesn't accept conventional judgments. He's not interested in what other people consider "classic." He has his own opinions to register. We also understand that Holden's story will be a focused one. He's not working on a broad canvas, as Dickens did. And if he is not to start where Dickens started, it's likely he won't end where Dickens ended (happily for David—with marriage, children, and professional success). The allusion catches a kind of attitude or tone that helps establish Holden's character.

As we read further in *The Catcher in the Rye*, the allusion to *David Copperfield* makes still more sense. We learn that Holden has been kicked out of Pencey Prep, his elite boarding school. He is failing four of his five courses, mostly because he finds those courses boring and irrelevant. For Holden, Pencey Prep is all about a sterile process of socialization. It's about attitude and gesture with no substance. Pencey people read Dickens because they are supposed to read Dickens; any real engagement with novels (or with history, or with any subject) won't happen in Pencey Prep courses. We can also imagine that the success David Copperfield wins in Dickens's novel would bother Holden because he sees success as built on dishonesty. When his history teacher, Mr. Spencer, echoes a common bit of wisdom about life as a game, Holden thinks to himself: "Game, my ass. Some game. If you get on the side where all the hotshots are, then it's a game, all right—I'll admit that. But if you get on the other side, where there

Making Connections

Salinger's allusion to *David Copperfield* also works because of the place that novel had in the curriculum of college and college prep classes at the time that *The Catcher in the Rye* was set and written (the late 1940s and early 1950s). Salinger needed to invoke a book that was often assigned (not the same as often read) in a certain sort of class at a certain sort of school. He is alluding to the book not only for its content but for its status as a cultural commodity. If you were to recast Salinger's novel in the context of a current college prep course, it's likely you'd pick a different book—a book you feel is assigned today out of habit. As we note in Chapter 17, standards of quality or relevance do change over time. What might be a good substitute for *David Copperfield* if you were to revise that first sentence for a reader today?

aren't any hot-shots, then what's a game about it? Nothing. No game."
The kind of Victorian earnestness that Dickens affirms in *David Copperfield*
has become for Holden a thoroughgoing "phoniness" that he cannot
tolerate. Salinger's allusion defines a community of outsiders who will
follow Holden through the narrative.

Experiencing Literature through Allusions

In "My Weariness of Epic Proportions," the poet Charles Simic's first sentence assumes that his reader is familiar with Achilles. Classical mythology
has been included in Western education for centuries; authors frequently use
allusions to the most famous, widely read works of a given culture (such as
those by Homer, Shakespeare, Dante, and Cervantes) without any explanation. But Simic's opening allusion doesn't assume we must all accept the
classics for what they have often been taken to represent. Homer celebrates
the exploits of Achilles and sets up most of the warriors who died in the
Trojan War as remarkable individuals worthy of heroic status. So Simic's
allusive opening is rather jarring.

Charles Simic (1938–)

My Weariness of Epic Proportions (1982)

I like it when
Achilles
Gets killed
And even his buddy Patroclus—
And that hothead Hector—   5
And the whole Greek and Trojan
Jeunesse dorée
Are more or less
Expertly slaughtered
So there's finally   10
Peace and quiet
(The gods having momentarily
Shut up)
One can hear
A bird sing   15
And a daughter ask her mother

Whether she can go to the well
And of course she can
By that lovely little path
That winds through   20
The olive orchard

We don't normally like it when the heroes of a story are "Expertly slaughtered." Simic's poem puts itself in opposition to our usual reading experience from the very start: his speaker likes it when Achilles, Patroclus, Hector, and the whole mass of Greek and Trojan soldiers die in battle. Anyone who has read *The Iliad* can quickly grasp Simic's perspective: peace and quiet are indeed refreshing after widespread carnage—however heroic we might have taken that violence to be. Simic conveys through allusion at the start of the first stanza the overwhelming exhaustion that comes from reading *The Iliad*— an epic poem full of descriptions of relentless destruction. Simic's second stanza turns to very different matters: descriptions of simple, peaceful, ordinary events that don't belong to the world of *The Iliad*. Yet even as Simic claims to be weary of "epic proportions," the proportions and scale of the epic help reaffirm the value of the everyday, peaceful existence he champions. He intensifies our sense of the latter qualities by setting them against the action of Homer's epic.

REVISITING AND RENEWAL

The previous example clarifies another aspect of allusion. The allusion not only can work to enrich a new piece but can encourage us to rethink a past literary experience. Simic's poem challenges us to consider what it means to read Homer in ways that many people have read Homer. He may make us more sensitive to suffering and less enamored of heroic deeds when we return to *The Iliad*. In this way, allusions can be critical and generative of new readings.

   In "Up Home Where I Come From," the poet Dick Barnes presents an account of a hawk that a trapper caught accidentally. The first nineteen lines describe the hawk and its wild dignity. At line 19, Barnes offers an allusion. The allusion affects the meaning of Barnes's poem profoundly. It changes our understanding of what comes before and after it. This allusion also challenges us to think freshly about the source text. In other words, the allusion doesn't just use an older story; it challenges our conventional understanding of the older story.

Dick Barnes (1933–2000)

Up Home Where I Come From (2005)

Roy Smith ran traps for furs
but a hawk got caught in one of them

spreading its wings, there in the trap
turning its sharp beak toward him

as he came to get it out, its glaring eyes so deep   5
they seemed to open onto another world in there

and steady: thus the hawk in time past
came to be an image of aristocracy.

One leg hung by a tendon; with his sharp pocketknife
Roy cut it off and left it lay   10

but brought the hawk home
to feed it til it got well.

There in his basement, in a hutch built for rabbits,
it glared at us with its unfathomable eyes,

accepted the dead meat he brought it, even hamburger,   15
unquenched. That wildness

is what we can know of dignity.
We aspire to it ourselves but seldom—

seldom. Nailed to the tree
Jesus must have been as still as that,   20

as wild. And I'd say
that was the right way to be, there.

Later it got well and he let it go,
our hearts leapt up when we saw it

living somehow in the wild with its one leg: 25
in its life we felt forgiven.

Probably it learned to pin its prey to the ground
and eat there, running that risk.

Risen, that was one thing Jesus did too:
showed he was alive and could still eat.   30

Barnes expects his reader to have at least an elementary knowledge of the
Christian story that tells of Jesus being nailed to a cross, dying, and being
resurrected to continue his ministry. In this poem, though, the allusion is
something of a surprise. The poet concentrates on the wildness of the hawk
and its dignity even in captivity. Comparing that wounded hawk to Jesus
creates a particular poetic experience in which the familiar story changes.
The poet asks us to use the image of Jesus on a cross and to make his dignity
akin to the wildness that we see in this injured hawk. With this allusion, we
ask how that dignified, wounded hawk compares to the crucified figure of
Jesus on a cross that adorns so many Christian churches. The hawk is so
powerfully established in particular detail that the allusion midway through
the poem challenges any comfortable interpretation of the religious story.
What happens when we place the Jesus commonly depicted eating in
Leonardo da Vinci's *The Last Supper* against the one-legged hawk that has

Leonardo da Vinci, *The Last Supper* (1496–1498)

learned to pin its prey to the ground? Barnes's allusion develops a complex image of both figures. When the poet ends by saying that Jesus "showed he was alive and could still eat," the comparison might seem to reduce the religious narrative to a story of simple survival. But the hawk's resilience in the face of the accidental trapping, its ability to reclaim its life and to adjust to the unwanted changes offers a powerful natural lesson to the poet that echoes the story of Jesus. It is not the same story, but the poet shows us how the incident gives him insight into the more familiar religious narrative.

Barnes includes one more subtle allusion toward the end of the poem when the trapper lets the hawk go: "our hearts leapt up when we saw it." This seems to recall William Wordsworth's "My Heart Leaps Up."

William Wordsworth (1770–1850)

My Heart Leaps Up (1807)

My heart leaps up when I behold
    A rainbow in the sky:
So was it when my life began;
So is it now I am a man;
So be it when I shall grow old,   5
    Or let me die!
The Child is father of the Man;
And I could wish my days to be
Bound each to each by natural piety.

The natural piety that Wordsworth seeks here is a deep responsiveness to the power of natural things. Life for him isn't life without the intensity gained through that responsiveness. Is Barnes using Wordsworth to help us interpret the quality of "forgiveness" that he refers to in line 26? How does this forgiveness relate to the New Testament story to which Barnes alludes?

Experiencing Film through Allusions

Legend has it that Quentin Tarantino trained to be a film director by working as a clerk in a video store where he immersed himself in countless old films. It is a plausible legend. As a director, Tarantino has created a fresh new film style that builds heavily upon allusions to old films and yet refuses to use the structures of the films to which he alludes. His films make so many references to other movies that each of his films has inspired hundreds of web pages that document what goes on in every frame. But it's not just film geeks who are interested in Tarantino's work. *Pulp Fiction* (1994) in particular stands as a powerfully innovative and influential film. Understanding that film requires more than close attention to how many allusions Tarantino employs (a mere accounting of allusions)—it requires careful thought about how allusions may function. Consider, for example, the scene in which Mia insists that her escort, Vincent, join her in a dance contest. If John Travolta were not cast as Vincent, this scene might simply function to define the sort of playfully charged relationship that seems to be unfolding. But because John Travolta *is* cast as Vincent, viewers over the age of thirty will almost surely recognize an allusion and respond to the whole scene with that allusion in mind.

In the early 1990s, before *Pulp Fiction* was released, John Travolta was best known for having been a movie star in the 1970s. When he, as Vincent

John Travolta and Karen Lynn Gorney in
Saturday Night Fever (1977)

John Travolta and Uma Thurman in *Pulp Fiction*
(1994)

Vega in *Pulp Fiction*, comes out on the dance floor with Mia Wallace (Uma Thurman), much of the original audience could not help remembering a younger, skinnier Travolta dancing in *Saturday Night Fever*—a tremendous hit in 1977. The reference does not necessarily change the meaning of the scene itself, but it deepens our reaction. We see the character in *Pulp Fiction* about to begin dancing, but we also see a familiar actor regaining his status as a movie star and commenting upon his past and potential within a notoriously fickle industry. These allusions to the old film and to the characters he used to play create a tension within us as we ask whether this older Travolta can go out and dance the way he used to. Which character are we responding to in this movie? The conflicted thoughts that we have about John Travolta, a public figure who has a life in our own experiences outside this particular film, bring us into an active engagement with the story.

There is clearly a way in which such allusions remind us of the fictionality of the entire enterprise; in this case, art refers us back to art, not to life. Is *Pulp Fiction* really about two hit men in Los Angeles? Or is it about the pleasure we've experienced watching movies about all sorts of things that would be very unpleasant in real life? *Pulp Fiction* is violent—brutally violent—profane and oftentimes deliberately over the top, but viewers generally respond to all with a sense of exuberance. Tarantino's playful self-consciousness (his sense that in a movie anything can happen) comes through in the way he fractures the sequence of events

Making Connections

Christopher Durang and Wendy Wasserstein's *Medea* (p. 1071) is thick with allusions to popular culture, even if its central allusion is to a Greek tragedy. Here, as in *Pulp Fiction*, we might wonder if the most ephemeral and specific allusions will quickly date the work and make it unwatchable in the near future. Will anyone respond to allusions to television shows from the past (*Designing Women, Little House on the Prairie, Home Improvement*), to political side stories and names of the day (Whitewater, Olympia Dukakis, George Stephanopoulos), or to self-help manuals and new age obsessions ("Women who run with wolves / Women who love too much")? Some of the allusions speak to a very narrow audience. But if we think about how the allusions function, we could argue that their fleeting relevance is part of the point. Subsumed by such matters are real emotions and tragedies. In addition to that rather serious point, it's possible that allusions to popular culture will take on a different quality with the passing of time. What seems at one point an immediate commentary on a characteristic of the lives we live becomes a kind of nostalgic gesture or even a fun game of trivial pursuit. As noted in Chapter 14, even if the words of a text do not change, the way those words are read can change dramatically. And as noted in Chapter 3, there are different kinds of meaning.

so that Vincent Vega can stroll away coolly in the final scene after an earlier scene of his dismal death. The tendency to make transparent through allusion the unreality of art is characteristic of works we've come to label "postmodern." The implications of **postmodernism** aren't necessarily light or purely comic; they are more characteristic of the **absurd** (that is, characteristic of a vision that sees meaning drained from life). Postmodernism blurs distinctions between the real and imagined. It suggests that in our commodified world—a world where everything becomes a product for sale and consumption—the reality of most people is a reality created by popular fictions (television, advertising, personality magazines, and so on). Perhaps allusions in works like *Pulp Fiction* center so heavily on pop culture because some people have come to feel that pop culture is what dominates our experience of the world.

IDENTIFYING AND RESPONDING TO ALLUSIONS

An allusion works only if we catch it, so we've attended mainly to fairly clear examples in this chapter. But once we know about allusions, we might become anxious as readers. Are we passing over important things because we don't share the author's aesthetic experience? Although most allusions are hardly hidden, they sometimes do restrict access to a text. The uninitiated, those who don't have particular experiences, like the new convict (p. 1475), are not allowed to share in the communal experience. The problem is compounded by the fact that many highly allusive texts arose out of societies that are far more homogeneous than any that exist today. John Milton could take it for granted that anyone who read his *Paradise Lost* in seventeenth-century England had a thorough knowledge of the Bible and could appreciate some subtleties of religious controversy. But far more people are exposed to *Paradise Lost* today than the narrow group of the educated elite that first appreciated its significance. And today's readers are hardly in the know about the theological concerns that occupy Milton. There are many such examples. James Joyce wrote as though his readers knew the details of the Catholic liturgy, the streets of Dublin, Irish music, and Irish politics. These texts are challenging for anyone, but readers who are not Irish might find portions particularly obscure.

These problems lead us to a practical reflection. It is important to remember that literary texts and films are rich works of art. Allusions may be *one* element in a complex system of meaning; in other words, you don't necessarily fail to read a work well because you've missed some allusions. And even when allusion is a main element, you need not catch every allusion (nor are you likely to catch every allusion) in any single reading/viewing. One simple bit of advice is to read confidently and take the time to appreciate what you do catch (as opposed to anxious concerns over what you don't). Patience, in this case, is a virtue. The more you read, the more receptive you'll be to allusion. And although that may sound discouraging in the short term, it really should not be. The literary experience can be a lifelong experience. A sense of new discovery is part of what keeps the experience alive over time. So read and view boldly. Trust that you'll find much that is rewarding and will keep finding more as you experience more.

There are, however, some shortcuts you should be aware of and use. In many cases, modern editions of older works point out important allusions for us. These, as well as printed guides and web sources, can help lead us through the thickest of allusive texts. For example, more than one modern paperback edition of Dickens's *Great Expectations* identifies the following allusion for us. Pip, the narrator, is reflecting on the startling news that the person who "made him a gentleman" is himself no gentleman. The criminal Magwitch, now returned illegally to England, has set up Pip's expectations. Pip remarks on the feeling of being chased down: "The imaginary student pursued by the misshapen creature he had impiously made, was not more wretched than I, pursued by the creature who had made me, and recoiling from him with a stronger repulsion, the more he admired me and the fonder he was of me." In this line, we're told in notes of varying length that Pip compares himself to Victor Frankenstein pursued by the monster he has created.

Those who know Mary Shelley's novel might notice that Pip revises the roles between Victor and his monster. Pip doesn't claim the role of creator: he is himself the product of the creature and is pursued not out of a desire for revenge but from admiration, even love. This variation on the Frankenstein/ monster theme adds layers of complexity to Pip's character and situation. Pip seems still morally confused at this point. He hasn't quite realized that he is the monster, nor has he fully appreciated the admiration and fondness Magwitch has for him—however inconvenient those feelings may be. Yet Pip's self-confessed repulsion does anticipate the mature and responsible insight he ultimately must attain.

Our example of allusion and its explanation are meant to suggest, first, that you do not need to resign yourself to missing allusions: help is available. But we also suggest that identifying allusions isn't ultimately the most important aspect of reading. This chapter has not concentrated on finding allusions (identifying, listing, and so on); our efforts are to show how allusions work and what purposes they serve. We have explored ways to approach, analyze, and understand allusions. Responding to an allusion is a far more substantial matter than merely finding or identifying one. Our poor convict from the joke early in this chapter did not understand the difference.

A Note to Student Writers: Reference versus Allusion

Allusions are generally thought of as a tool for the creative writer to use and for the critical writer to avoid. That is not altogether bad advice. Allusions are suggestive more than directive. They invite the reader to draw upon experience from other texts but don't spell out fully what the reader should do with that experience. Dickens teases us into thinking about how the *Frankenstein* allusion works. He doesn't explain. Critical writers are, though, expected to explain. A brief allusion in an analytical essay to another critic or to a work of literature might well be seen as inappropriately showing off. Rather than richly suggestive, such an allusion might seem superficial. It's usually important to thoroughly integrate references—to lead into them and to follow them out. Never "plug in" a source or simply "drop" a reference in order to meet a quota. Critical writers need to show why a reference appears in the text; readers need to grasp where that reference comes from and how it applies. An overly allusive style in a critic can quickly become mannered and exclusive. That is, such a critic implies there is a little club of experienced readers who will understand and a larger group of outsiders who need not bother.

Although the previous information stands as good advice and useful commentary, nothing about writing is ever simple or absolute. As mentioned before, critical writing takes place in the context of an ongoing conversation. Critical writers seek to contribute to the conversation. On occasion, you may feel the conversation is so well established for your audience that you can refer very briefly to a key critic or to an important line or scene in a well-known literary text. Just be sure that any quick reference you make has a clear function in the context of your larger discussion and that it draws from something your audience will recognize and apply easily. Also be sure that you do not assume a very brief reference will carry more weight than it can sustain; a well-placed allusion might highlight a point or signal your place in a community of writers, but it won't make an argument. Ultimately, to allude or not to allude is not the question; it is better to ask whether and how an allusion will work for a particular audience at a specific point in an essay.

MODELING CRITICAL ANALYSIS: TOM STOPPARD, THE FIFTEEN MINUTE HAMLET

We normally think of allusions as short elements existing within texts; we don't think of them as constituting a whole text, as they do in Tom Stoppard's *The Fifteen Minute Hamlet*. In the play, we get nothing but allusions—in this case, exact words lifted from Shakespeare and strung together to make what seems a brief highlight film of famous moments from this most famous of plays. Beginning with the title, Stoppard assumes we are familiar with William Shakespeare's *Hamlet*—so familiar that we'll enjoy the radical cutting and splicing that he has done. But also beginning with the title, we might ask how much we have to know about the real *Hamlet* to appreciate the fifteen-minute version.

Tom Stoppard (1937–)

The Fifteen Minute Hamlet (1976)

CHARACTERS

MARCELLUS, BERNARDO, LAERTES, HORATIO (*Scenes 1, 3, and encore*)
FRANCISCO, OSRIC, FORTINBRAS, GRAVEDIGGER, GHOST, HORATIO (*Scene 1*)
OPHELIA
GERTRUDE
HAMLET
SHAKESPEARE, CLAUDIUS, POLONIUS

TIME AND SCENE: *The action takes place at a shortened version of Elsinore Castle.*

Scene 1

A castle battlement. Thunder and wind. Two guards, BERNARDO/MARCELLUS *and* FRANCISCO/HORATIO, *enter.*
BERNARDO/MARCELLUS: Who's there?
FRANCISCO/HORATIO: Nay, answer me.
BERNARDO/MARCELLUS: Long live the King. Get thee to bed.
FRANCISCO/HORATIO: For this relief, much thanks.
BERNARDO/MARCELLUS: What, has this thing appeared again tonight?   5
FRANCISCO/HORATIO: Peace, break thee off: look where it comes again. *(He points off left.)*
BERNARDO/MARCELLUS: Looks it not like the King?
FRANCISCO/HORATIO: By heaven, I charge thee, speak!
BERNARDO/MARCELLUS *(He points and looks left.):* 'Tis here.
FRANCISCO/HORATIO *(He points and looks centre.):* 'Tis there.   10
BERNARDO/MARCELLUS *(He looks right.):* 'Tis gone.
FRANCISCO/HORATIO: But look, the morn in russet mantle clad
    Walks o'er the dew of yon high eastern hill.
BERNARDO/MARCELLUS: Let us impart what we have seen tonight
    Unto young Hamlet.   15
(They exit.)

Scene 2

A room of state within the castle. A flourish of trumpets as CLAUDIUS *and* GER-TRUDE *enter.*
CLAUDIUS: Though yet of Hamlet our dear brother's death
    The memory be green
(HAMLET enters.)

our sometime sister, now our Queen,
Have we taken to wife.
But now, my cousin Hamlet, and my son— 5
HAMLET: A little more than kin, and less than kind.
  (CLAUDIUS *and* GERTRUDE *exit.*)
  O that this too too solid flesh would melt!
  That it should come to this—but two months dead!
  So loving to my mother: Frailty, thy name is woman!
  Married with mine uncle, my father's brother. 10
  The funeral baked meats did coldly furnish forth
  The marriage tables.
(HORATIO *rushes on.*)
HORATIO: My lord, I think I saw him yesternight—
  The King, your father—upon the platform where we watched.
HAMLET: 'Tis very strange. 15
HORATIO: Armed, my lord—
  A countenance more in sorrow than in anger.
HAMLET: My father's spirit in arms? All is not well.
  Would the night were come!
(HAMLET *and* HORATIO *exit to the parapet.*)

Scene 3

The castle battlements at night. There is the noise of carousing, cannon, fire-works. HORATIO *and* HAMLET *appear on the parapet.*
HAMLET: The King doth wake tonight and takes his rouse.
  Though I am native here and to the manner born,
  It is a custom more honoured in the breach
  Than in the observance.
  (*There is the sound of wind.*)
HORATIO: Look, my lord, it comes. (*He points.*) 5
(*The* GHOST *enters.*)
HAMLET: Angels and ministers of grace defend us!
  Something is rotten in the state of Denmark!
  Alas, poor ghost.
GHOST: I am thy father's spirit.
  Revenge his foul and most unnatural murder. 10
HAMLET: Murder?
GHOST: The serpent that did sting thy father's life
  Now wears his crown.
HAMLET: O my prophetic soul! Mine uncle?
(*The* GHOST *exits.*)
(*To* HORATIO.) There are more things in heaven and earth 15
  Than are dreamt of in your philosophy.

(HORATIO *exits.*)
Hereafer I shall think meet
To put an antic disposition on.
The time is out of joint. O cursed spite
That ever I was born to set it right!   20
(HAMLET *exits.*)

Scene 4

*A room within the castle. There is a flourish of trumpets, leading into flute and
harpsichord music.* POLONIUS *enters and immediately* OPHELIA *rushes on.*
POLONIUS: How now, Ophelia, what's the matter?
OPHELIA: My lord, as I was sewing in my chamber, Lord Hamlet with his
    doublet all unbraced, no hat upon his head, pale as his shirt, his
    knees knocking each other, and with a look so piteous, he comes be-
    fore me.   5
POLONIUS: Mad for thy love?
    I have found the very cause of Hamlet's lunacy.
    (HAMLET *enters as* OPHELIA *exits.*)
    Look where sadly the poor wretch comes reading.
    What do you read, my lord?
HAMLET: Words, words, words.   10
POLONIUS: Though this be madness, yet there is method in it.
HAMLET: I am but mad north northwest: when the wind is southerly! I
    know a hawk from a handsaw.
POLONIUS: The actors are come hither, my lord. (*He goes.*)
HAMLET: We'll hear a play tomorrow.   15
    I have heard that guilty creatures sitting at a play
    Have by the very cunning of the scene
    Been struck so to the soul that presently
    They have proclaimed their malefactions.
    I'll have these players play something   20
    Like the murder of my father before mine uncle.
    If he but blench, I know my course,
    The play's the thing
    Wherein I'll catch the conscience of the King.
    (*Pause.*)
    To be, or not to be (*He puts a dagger to his heart.*)   25
    (CLAUDIUS *and* OPHELIA *enter.*)
    that is the question.
OPHELIA: My lord—
HAMLET: Get thee to a nunnery!
(OPHELIA *and* HAMLET *exit.*)

CLAUDIUS: Love? His affections do not that way tend
    There's something in his soul   30
    O'er which his melancholy sits on brood.
    He shall with speed to England.
(CLAUDIUS *exits.*)

Scene 5

A hall within the castle. A flourish of trumpets heralds the entrance of HAMLET
and OPHELIA, MARCELLUS *and* HORATIO *who are joking together,* CLAUDIUS *and*
GERTRUDE.
  HAMLET *(to imaginary players.)*: Speak the speech, I pray you, as I pro-
    nounced it to you; trippingly on the tongue. Hold, as t'were, the mirror
    up to nature.
(Everyone sits to watch imaginary play. Masque music is heard.)
    (to GERTRUDE.) Madam, how like you the play?
GERTRUDE: The lady doth protest too much, methinks.   5
HAMLET: He poisons him in the garden for his estate. You shall see
    anon how the murderer gets the love of Gonzago's wife.
    (CLAUDIUS rises.)
    The King rises!
    (Music stops, hubbub noise starts.)
    What, frighted with false fire?
    (CLAUDIUS exits; re-enters at side as POLONIUS.)
ALL: Give o'er the play.   10
HAMLET: Lights! Lights! Lights! I'll take the ghost's word for a thousand
    pounds!
(Exeunt all except POLONIUS.)
POLONIUS *(standing at side.)*: He's going to his mother's closet. Behind the
    arras I'll convey myself to hear the process.

Scene 6

The QUEEN'*s apartment.* POLONIUS *slips behind the arras as it is raised. Lute
music is heard.* HAMLET *and* GERTRUDE *enter.*
HAMLET: Now, Mother, what's the matter?
GERTRUDE: Hamlet, thou hast thy father much offended.
HAMLET: Mother, you have my father much offended. *(He holds her.)*
GERTRUDE: What wilt thou do? Thou wilt not murder me? Help! Help! Ho!
POLONIUS *(behind arras.)*: Help!   5
HAMLET: How now? A rat? *(He stabs POLONIUS.)* Dead for a ducat, dead!
GERTRUDE: O me, what has thou done?
HAMLET: Nay, I know not.
GERTRUDE: Alas, he's mad.

HAMLET: I must be cruel only to be kind. Good night, Mother.   10
(HAMLET *exits dragging* POLONIUS. GERTRUDE *exits, sobbing. The arras is dropped.*)

Scene 7

Another room in the castle. Flourish of trumpets as CLAUDIUS *and* HAMLET
enter.
CLAUDIUS: Now, Hamlet, where's Polonius?
HAMLET: At supper.
CLAUDIUS: Hamlet, this deed must send thee hence.
    Therefore prepare thyself,
    Everything is bent for England.   5
    (HAMLET *exits.*)
    And England, if my love thou holds't at aught,
    Thou mayst not coldly set our sov'reign process,
    The present death of Hamlet. Do it, England!
(CLAUDIUS *exits.*)

Interlude

At sea. Sea music. HAMLET *enters on parapet, swaying as if on a ship's bridge.
Sea music ends.* HAMLET *exits.*

Scene 8

Yet another room in the castle. Flourish of trumpets as CLAUDIUS *and* LAERTES
enter.
LAERTES: Where is my father?
CLAUDIUS: Dead.
(OPHELIA *enters in mad trance, singing. Lute music is heard.*)
OPHELIA: They bore him barefaced on the bier,
    Hey nonny nonny, hey nonny.
    And on his grave rained many a tear . . .   5
LAERTES: O heat dry up my brains—O kind Sister,
    (OPHELIA *falls to ground.*)
    Had'st thou thy wits, and did'st persuade revenge
    It could not move thus.
CLAUDIUS: And where the offence is, let the great axe fall.
(CLAUDIUS *and* LAERTES *exit. Gravestone rises to hide* OPHELIA. *Bell tolls four times.*)

Scene 9

A churchyard. A GRAVEDIGGER *and* HAMLET *enter.*
HAMLET: Ere we were two days old at sea, a pirate of very warlike appoint-
    ment gave us chase. In the grapple I boarded them. On the instant they
    got clear of our ship; so I alone became their prisoner. They have dealt
    with me like thieves of mercy.

GRAVEDIGGER: What is he that builds stronger than either the mason, the   5
   shipwright or the carpenter?

HAMLET: A gravemaker. The houses he makes will last till Doomsday.
   (GRAVEDIGGER *gives skull to* HAMLET.)
   Whose was it?

GRAVEDIGGER: This same skull, Sir, was Yorick's skull, the King's jester.

HAMLET: Alas, poor Yorick. (*He returns skull to* GRAVEDIGGER.)   10
   But soft—that is Laertes. (*He withdraws to side.*)
(LAERTES *enters.*)

LAERTES: What ceremony else?
   Lay her in the earth,
   And from her fair and unpolluted flesh
   May violets spring. I tell thee, churlish priest,   15
   (CLAUDIUS *and* GERTRUDE *enter.*)
   A ministering angel shall my sister be
   When thou liest howling.

HAMLET (*offstage.*): What, the fair Ophelia?

LAERTES: O treble woe. Hold off the earth awhile,
   Till I have caught her once more in my arms.   20

HAMLET (*re-entering acting area.*):
   What is he whose grief bears such an emphasis?
   This is I, Hamlet the Dane!

LAERTES: The devil take thy soul.
(*They grapple.*)

HAMLET: Away thy hand!   25
(CLAUDIUS *and* GERTRUDE *pull them apart.*)

CLAUDIUS AND GERTRUDE: Hamlet! Hamlet! (*speaking together.*)

HAMLET: I loved Ophelia. What wilt thou do for her?

GERTRUDE: O he is mad, Laertes!
(CLAUDIUS, GERTRUDE *and* LAERTES *exit.*)

HAMLET: The cat will mew, and dog will have his day!
(*He exits. Gravestone is dropped.*)

Scene 10

A Hall in the castle. A flourish of trumpets as HAMLET *enters.*

HAMLET: There's a divinity that shapes our ends, rough hew them how
   we will. But thou would'st not think how ill all's here about my
   heart. But 'tis no matter. We defy augury. There is a special providence in the fall of a sparrow. If it be now, 'tis not to come; If it be
   not to come, it will be now; it if be not now yet it will come. The   5
   readiness is all.

(LAERTES *enters with* OSRIC *bearing swords followed by* CLAUDIUS *and* GERTRUDE *with goblets.*)

Come on, Sir!

LAERTES: Come, my lord.

(*Fanfare of trumpets.* LAERTES *and* HAMLET *draw swords and duel.*)

HAMLET: One.

LAERTES: No.   10

HAMLET: Judgement?

OSRIC: A hit, a very palpable hit.

CLAUDIUS: Stay, give me a drink.

    Hamlet, this pearl is thine, here's to thy health.

(*He drops pearl in goblet.*) Give him the cup.   15

GERTRUDE: The Queen carouses to thy fortune, Hamlet.

(GERTRUDE *takes the cup.*)

CLAUDIUS: Gertrude, do not drink!

GERTRUDE: I will, my lord. (*She drinks.*)

LAERTES: My lord, I'll hit him now.

    Have at you, now!   20

(HAMLET *and* LAERTES *grapple and fight.*)

CLAUDIUS: Part them, they are incensed.

    They bleed on both sides.

(OSRIC *and* CLAUDIUS *part them.* OSRIC *exits.*)

LAERTES: I am justly killed by my own treachery. (*He falls.*)

GERTRUDE: The drink, the drink! I am poisoned! (*She dies.*)

HAMLET: Treachery! Seek it out.   25

(FORTINBRAS *enters.*)

LAERTES: It is here, Hamlet. Hamlet thou art slain.

    Lo, here I lie, never to rise again.

    The King, the King's to blame.

HAMLET: The point envenomed too?

    Then venom to thy work. (*He kills* CLAUDIUS.)   30

LAERTES: Exchange forgiveness with me, noble Ha … m … (*He dies.*)

HAMLET: I follow thee.

    I cannot live to hear the news from England.

    The rest is silence. (*He dies.*)

FORTINBRAS: Goodnight sweet prince,   35

    And flights of angels sing thee to thy rest.

    (*He turns to face away from audience.*)

    Go, bid the soldiers shoot.

    (*Four shots heard from off stage. All stand, bow once and exit.*)

END

The Encore

A stagehand enters with a placard bearing the legend "Encore." He parades across the stage and exits. A flourish of trumpets. CLAUDIUS *and* GERTRUDE *enter.*

CLAUDIUS: Our sometime sister, now our Queen,

   (HAMLET *enters.*)

   have we taken to wife.

HAMLET: That it should come to this!

(CLAUDIUS *and* GERTRUDE *exit. Sound of wind.* HORATIO *enters.*)

HORATIO: My lord. I saw him yesternight—

   The King, your father.   5

HAMLET: Angels and ministers of grace defend us! (*He exits, running,*

   through rest of speech.) Something is rotten in the state of Denmark.

(GHOST *enters above.*)

GHOST: I am thy father's spirit.

   The serpent that did sting thy father's life.

(HAMLET *enters above.*)

   Now wears his crown.   10

HAMLET: O my prophetic soul!

   Hereafter I shall think meet

   To put an antic disposition on.

(*They exit. Short flourish of trumpets. Enter* POLONIUS *below, running.*)

POLONIUS: Look where sadly the poor wretch comes.

(POLONIUS *exits, running.* HAMLET *enters.*)

HAMLET: I have heard that guilty creatures sitting at a play   15

   Have by the very cunning of the scene been struck.

   (*Enter* CLAUDIUS, GERTRUDE, OPHELIA, MARCELLUS *and* HORATIO *joking.*

   All sit to watch imaginary play.)

   If he but blench, I know my course.

   (*Masque music.* CLAUDIUS *rises.*)

   The King rises!

ALL: Give o'er the play!

(*Exeunt* ALL *except* GERTRUDE *and* HAMLET.)

HAMLET: I'll take the ghost's word for a thousand pounds.   20

   (POLONIUS *enters, goes behind arras. Short flourish of trumpets.*)

   Mother, you have my father much offended.

GERTRUDE: Help!

POLONIUS: Help, Ho!

HAMLET (*He stabs* POLONIUS.): Dead for a ducat, dead!

   (POLONIUS *falls dead off stage.* GERTRUDE *and* HAMLET *exit. Short flourish*

   of trumpets. CLAUDIUS *enters followed by* HAMLET.)

CLAUDIUS: Hamlet, this deed must send thee hence.   25

   (HAMLET *exits.*)

Do it, England.

(CLAUDIUS *exits.* OPHELIA *enters and falls to the ground. Gravestone rises to hide her. Bell tolls twice.* GRAVEDIGGER *and* HAMLET *enter.*)

HAMLET: A pirate gave us chase. I alone became their prisoner. (*He takes skull from* GRAVEDIGGER.) Alas poor Yorick—but soft (*He returns skull to* GRAVEDIGGER.)—This is I, Hamlet the Dane!

(GRAVEDIGGER *exits.* LAERTES *enters.*)

LAERTES: The devil take thy soul!   30

(*They grapple, then break. Enter* OSRIC *between them with swords. They draw. Enter* CLAUDIUS *and* GERTRUDE *with goblets.*)

HAMLET: Come on, Sir!

(LAERTES *and* HAMLET *fight.*

Pause.)

OSRIC: A hit, a very palpable hit

CLAUDIUS: Give him the cup. Gertrude, do not drink!

GERTRUDE: I am poisoned? (*She dies.*)

LAERTES: Hamlet, thou art slain? (*He dies.*)   35

HAMLET: Then venom to thy work! (*He kills* CLAUDIUS.)

The rest is silence. (*He dies.*)

(*Two shots off stage.*)

END

Shakespeare's play is longer than fifteen minutes—about four hours longer! It is, in fact, the longest of Shakespeare's works. Efforts to trim the play into a manageable stage production or movie always ignite controversy among the Shakespearean purists. How could anyone be so brazen as to trim anything from this masterpiece? Yet trimming is what has happened routinely in productions of the last few centuries. Stoppard takes the task of trimming to a whole new level. He boldly reduces every aspect of the play but still maintains the basic elements of the tragic plot. What are we to make of what is left? We have a series of familiar quotes strung together. It's almost as if Stoppard has lifted the yellowed-over lines from his old class text and made those lines his play.

One thing that is clearly lost is any sense of character development. Hamlet's most famous soliloquy becomes simply "To be, or not to be / that is the question" before he is interrupted by Ophelia. His speech has been replaced by its first line. The rhetorical term **synecdoche** describes a situation in which the whole is represented by just a part. For instance, when a ship's captain orders, "All hands on deck," he does not want just the hands; he wants the entire sailor even though it may be primarily the hands that will do the work. Similarly, in this version of the play, the opening line stands in for the entire soliloquy; the wide familiarity with the whole makes this work—sort of. Obviously, mere recognition of the speech doesn't equal the impact of the whole in a conventional production. Just as the audience gears up for the famous speech, the speech is over, and Hamlet has moved on to his next famous line, "Get thee to a nunnery!" The tragic plot remains true to the original, but by the elimination of any attempt to develop character or motive in the play, the impact becomes comic. We laugh at this Hamlet, who doesn't bother to ponder about anything, not because he says or does anything that is funny but because the juxtaposition of what little he says here and what we know he should really have said is so jarring.

There may be a more subtle allusion to something not directly expressed in Stoppard's play. A longstanding critical argument concerns Hamlet's hesitation: Why does he delay in acting upon the command of his father's ghost? Stoppard may be teasing those who obsess too much about this matter. If things move quickly, after all, we have an altogether different main character and an altogether different play. Hamlet is meditative, conflicted, a sensitive man in an insensitive world. When we rocket through the main points toward the general destruction at the end, we no longer have Hamlet, play or character, even though the lines are all taken directly from the original.

Using Allusions to Focus Discussion and Writing

- A particular challenge with allusions is figuring out whether or not there is any reason to research them. Can we tell whether a name within a work, for instance, is just an author's arbitrary invention or whether it refers to some other character in another work? Don't overdo your attention to allusions. When you see them, or when your professor or your footnotes point them out to you, try to establish how your attention to this allusion can help you engage with your analysis of this text.

- What is the specific reference?

- How can we tell that this is a reference to another text, to a historical event, or to some existence outside the text?

- How does the author introduce the allusion? How is it incorporated within this text? For instance, is the allusion something that the fictional characters in the story are conscious of, or is it introduced by a third-person narrator?

- How does the author interpret the allusion? How does the text ask us to read this outside event?

- How does the allusion impact our understanding of or engagement in the present text? For instance, does it shape the text itself?

Anthology

THE MYTH OF CHEATING DEATH: KEEPING LITERATURE ALIVE WITH ALLUSION

Mythology is one of the most common sources of literary allusion. The subjects are familiar, and the myths themselves cover territory that holds perennial interest: questions about sources of life, the origins of war or love, and explorations of death. In this anthology, the selections address different versions of stories in which characters cheat death (or at least try). The classical allusion that runs through many of these works is the story of Orpheus, the musician whose ability was so remarkable that he charmed the goddess of the underworld, Persephone, into allowing him to bring his beloved Eurydice back to the world of the living. (Persephone, by the way, has her own story of cheating death.) In mythic tales, there is frequently a simple catch that complicates any good fortune. For Orpheus, the catch is that he cannot look back at Eurydice until he has returned to the land of the living. This simple stricture might seem a minor one, but it carries great weight. A little glance can result in a harsh punishment.

As you read the different responses to the Orpheus story, work to develop your understanding of how allusions work and what purpose they serve. A number of the poems are retellings of the myth. The poet imagines, for instance, that moment when Orpheus looks back. The poet imagines a scenario in which looking back seems only natural. In such a retelling, where is the allusion? To what extent does the poet depend upon the reader's knowledge of the story to supplement what actually appears in the poem? Are any of the poems complete without such background information? In H. D.'s "Eurydice," we get the story from the perspective of the woman who has been taken back to the underworld because of her husband's glance. She wants to know why he looked; it doesn't seem a mistake born of simple love. In Czeslaw Milosz's "Orpheus and Eurydice," the poet uses the myth to make sense of his own personal story where the much older man has lost his younger wife. In this poem, the classical gods seem to play unfairly with even contemporary humanity.

Joyce Carol Oates's "Where Are You Going, Where Have You Been?" alludes at the outset to Bob Dylan. Oates has said that she was particularly mindful of Dylan's ballad "It's All Over Now, Baby Blue." This may be a case of an allusion wrapped in an allusion. The final verse of Dylan's song begins "Leave your stepping stones behind, something calls for you. / Forget the dead you've left, they will not follow you." Arnold Friend does call Connie out of her house. Connie, like Eurydice, may also be called to leave the dead behind.

But she seems to have nowhere safe to go. The many allusions to the short-lived stuff of popular culture (the phrases, songs, gestures, and clothes) trap not only the mysterious and ominous Arnold Friend but also Connie, along with all her friends and family. It is a chilling story partly because Connie seems to have no choice to move toward life.

Mary Zimmerman's *Metamorphoses* takes a number of myths from Ovid and weaves them into a single, coherent narrative. Like Tarantino's *Pulp Fiction*, the final work is original and very much her own; think about the place of the classical influence within the dramatic structure. How important is originality here? How does the play expect that its audience will fill in gaps in the narrative? It may be interesting to remember that Sophocles in his *Oedipus the King* (p. 67) does not give us all of the information we need to know his character. Sophocles writes for an audience that already knows the character of Oedipus. His version of that dramatic tale leaves out details of the story—the story of the sphinx is not told in the play—but includes enough to create the particular dramatic effect. To what extent does Zimmerman's play (or any of the works included in this anthology) give us elements of the familiar story with the expectation that we already know enough of these stories to fill in the remaining details ourselves?

FICTION

Joyce Carol Oates (1938–)

Joyce Carol Oates was born in Lockport, New York. She began writing when she was a child and submitted a novel to a publisher when she was only fifteen. She earned her BA from Syracuse University and her MA from the University of Wisconsin, then embarked on a career as a writer. Although she is best known for her fiction, Oates has also written essays, plays, and poetry and has dealt with a wide variety of subjects, from race relations to boxing. She has been a prolific writer, producing an average of two books per year, and a respected one. She has received the National Book Award and several O. Henry Awards.

Where Are You Going, Where Have You Been? (1970)

For Bob Dylan

Her name was Connie. She was fifteen and she had a quick nervous giggling habit of craning her neck to glance into mirrors, or checking other people's faces to make sure her own was all right. Her mother, who noticed everything and knew everything and who hadn't much reason any longer to look at her own face, always scolded Connie about it. "Stop gawking at yourself, who are you? You think you're so pretty?" she would say. Connie would raise her eyebrows at these familiar complaints and look right through her mother, into a shadowy vision of herself as she was right at that moment: she knew she was pretty and that was everything. Her mother had been pretty once too, if you could believe those old snapshots in the album, but now her looks were gone and that was why she was always after Connie.

"Why don't you keep your room clean like your sister? How've you got your hair fixed—what the hell stinks? Hair spray? You don't see your sister using that junk."

Her sister June was twenty-four and still lived at home. She was a secretary in the high school Connie attended, and if that wasn't bad enough—with her in the same building—she was so plain and chunky and steady that Connie had to hear her praised all the time by her mother and her mother's sisters. June did this, June did that, she saved money and helped clean the house and cooked and Connie couldn't do a thing, her mind was all filled with trashy daydreams. Their father was away at work most of the time and when he came home he wanted supper and he read the newspaper at supper and after supper he went to bed. He didn't bother talking much to them, but around his bent head Connie's mother kept picking at her until Connie wished her mother was dead and she herself was dead and it was all over. "She makes me want to throw up sometimes," she complained to her friends. She had a high, breathless, amused voice which made everything she said sound a little forced, whether it was sincere or not.

There was one good thing: June went places with girl friends of hers, girls who were just as plain and steady as she, and so when Connie wanted to do that her mother had no objections. The father of Connie's best girl friend drove the girls the three miles to town and left them off at a shopping plaza, so that they could walk through the stores or go to a movie, and when he came to pick them up again at eleven he never bothered to ask what they had done.

They must have been familiar sights, walking around that shopping plaza in their shorts and flat ballerina slippers that always scuffed the sidewalk, with charm bracelets jingling on their thin wrists; they would lean together to whisper and laugh secretly if someone passed by who amused or interested them. Connie had long dark blond hair that drew anyone's eye to it, and she wore part of it pulled up on her head and puffed out and the rest of it she let fall down her back. She wore a pull-over jersey blouse that looked one way when she was at home and another way when she was away from home. Everything about her had two sides to it, one for home and one for anywhere that was not home: her walk that could be childlike

5

and bobbing, or languid enough to make anyone think she was hearing music in her head, her mouth which was pale and smirking most of the time, but bright and pink on these evenings out, her laugh which was cynical and drawling at home—"Ha, ha, very funny"—but high-pitched and nervous anywhere else like the jingling of the charms on her bracelet.

Sometimes they did go shopping or to a movie, but sometimes they went across the highway, ducking fast across the busy road, to a drive-in restaurant where older kids hung out. The restaurant was shaped like a big bottle, though squatter than a real bottle, and on its cap was a revolving figure of a grinning boy who held a hamburger aloft. One night in mid-summer they ran across, breathless with daring, and right away someone leaned out a car window and invited them over, but it was just a boy from high school they didn't like. It made them feel good to be able to ignore him. They went up through the maze of parked and cruising cars to the bright-lit, fly-infested restaurant, their faces pleased and expectant as if they were entering a sacred building that loomed out of the night to give them what haven and what blessing they yearned for. They sat at the counter and crossed their legs at the ankles, their thin shoulders rigid with excitement, and listened to the music that made everything so good: the music was always in the background like music at a church service, it was something to depend upon.

A boy named Eddie came in to talk with them. He sat backwards on his stool, turning himself jerkily around in semi-circles and then stopping and turning again, and after a while he asked Connie if she would like something to eat. She said she did and so she tapped her friend's arm on her way out—her friend pulled her face up into a brave droll look—and Connie said she would meet her at eleven, across the way. "I just hate to leave her like that," Connie said earnestly, but the boy said that she wouldn't be alone for long. So they went out to his car and on the way Connie couldn't help but let her eyes wander over the windshields and faces all around her, her face gleaming with a joy that had nothing to do with Eddie or even this place; it might have been the music. She drew her shoulders up and sucked in her breath with the pure pleasure of being alive, and just at that moment she happened to glance at a face just a few feet from hers. It was a boy with shaggy black hair, in a convertible jalopy painted gold. He stared at her and then his lips widened into a grin. Connie slit her eyes at him and turned away, but she couldn't help glancing back and there he was still watching her. He wagged a finger and laughed and said, "Gonna get you, baby," and Connie turned away again without Eddie noticing anything.

She spent three hours with him, at the restaurant where they ate hamburgers and drank Cokes in wax cups that were always sweating, and then down an alley a mile or so away, and when he left her off at five to eleven only the movie house was still open at the plaza. Her girl friend was there, talking with a boy. When Connie came up the two girls smiled at each other and Connie said, "How was the movie?" and the girl said, "*You* should know." They rode off with the girl's father, sleepy and pleased, and Connie couldn't help but look at the darkened shopping plaza with its big empty parking lot and its signs that were faded and ghostly now, and over at the drive-in restaurant where cars were still circling tirelessly. She couldn't hear the music at this distance.

Next morning June asked her how the movie was and Connie said, "So-so."

She and that girl and occasionally another girl went out several times a week that way, and the rest of the time Connie spent around the house—it was summer vacation—getting in her mother's way and thinking, dreaming, about the boys she met. But all the boys fell back and dissolved into a single face that was not even a face, but an idea, a feeling, mixed up with the urgent insistent pounding of the music and the humid night air of July. Connie's mother kept dragging her back to the daylight by finding things for her to do or saying, suddenly, "What's this about the Pettinger girl?"

And Connie would say nervously, "Oh, her. That dope." She always drew thick clear lines between herself and such girls, and her mother was simple and kindly enough to believe her. Her mother was so simple, Connie thought, that it was maybe cruel to fool her so much. Her mother went scuffling around the house in old bedroom slippers and complained over the telephone to one sister about the other, then the other called up and the two of them complained about the third one. If June's name was mentioned her mother's tone was approving, and if Connie's name was mentioned it was disapproving. This did not really mean she disliked Connie and actually Connie thought that her mother preferred her to June because she was prettier, but the two of them kept up a pretense of exasperation, a sense that they were tugging and struggling over something of little value to either of them. Sometimes, over coffee, they were almost friends, but something would come up—some vexation that was like a fly buzzing suddenly around their heads—and their faces went hard with contempt.

One Sunday Connie got up at eleven—none of them bothered with church—and washed her hair so that it could dry all day long, in the sun. Her parents and sister were going to a barbecue at an aunt's house and Connie said no, she wasn't interested, rolling her eyes to let her mother know just what she thought of it. "Stay home alone then," her mother said sharply. Connie sat out back in a lawn chair and watched them drive away, her father quiet and bald, hunched around so that he could back the car out, her mother with a look that was still angry and not at all softened through the windshield, and in the back seat poor old June all dressed up as if she didn't know what a barbecue was, with all the running yelling kids and the flies. Connie sat with her eyes closed in the sun, dreaming and dazed with the

10

warmth about her as if this were a kind of love, the caresses of love, and her mind slipped over onto thoughts of the boy she had been with the night before and how nice he had been, how sweet it always was, not the way someone like June would suppose but sweet, gentle, the way it was in movies and promised in songs; and when she opened her eyes she hardly knew where she was, the back yard ran off into weeds and a fence-line of trees and behind it the sky was perfectly blue and still. The asbestos "ranch house" that was now three years old startled her—it looked small. She shook her head as if to get awake.

It was too hot. She went inside the house and turned on the radio to drown out the quiet. She sat on the edge of her bed, barefoot, and listened for an hour and a half to a program called XYZ Sunday Jamboree, record after record of hard, fast, shrieking songs she sang along with, interspersed by exclamations from "Bobby King": "An' look here you girls at Napoleon's—Son and Charley want you to pay real close attention to this song coming up!"

And Connie paid close attention herself, bathed in a glow of slow-pulsed joy that seemed to rise mysteriously out of the music itself and lay languidly about the airless little room, breathed in and breathed out with each gentle rise and fall of her chest.

After a while she heard a car coming up the drive. She sat up at once, startled because it couldn't be her father so soon. The gravel kept crunching all the way in from the road—the driveway was long—and Connie ran to the window. It was a car she didn't know. It was an open jalopy, painted a bright gold that caught the sunlight opaquely. Her heart began to pound and her fingers snatched at her hair, checking it, and she whispered "Christ. Christ," wondering how bad she looked. The car came to a stop at the side door and the horn sounded four short taps as if this were a signal Connie knew.

She went into the kitchen and approached the door slowly, then hung out the screen door, her bare toes curling down off the step. There were two boys in the car and now she recognized the driver: he had shaggy, shabby black hair that looked crazy as a wig and he was grinning at her.

"I ain't late, am I?" he said.

"Who the hell do you think you are?" Connie said.

"Toldja I'd be out, didn't I?"

"I don't even know who you are."

She spoke sullenly, careful to show no interest or pleasure, and he spoke in a fast, bright monotone. Connie looked past him to the other boy, taking her time. He had fair brown hair, with a lock that fell onto his forehead. His sideburns gave him a fierce, embarrassed look, but so far he hadn't even bothered to glance at her. Both boys wore sunglasses. The driver's glasses were metallic and mirrored everything in miniature.

"You wanta come for a ride?" he said.

Connie smirked and let her hair fall loose over one shoulder.

"Don'tcha like my car? New paint job," he said. "Hey."

"What?"   25

"You're cute"

She pretended to fidget, chasing flies away from the door.

"Don'tcha believe me, or what?" he said.

"Look, I don't even know who you are," Connie said in disgust.

"Hey, Ellie's got a radio, see. Mine's broke down." He lifted his friend's   30
arm and showed her the little transistor the boy was holding, and now
Connie began to hear the music. It was the same program that was playing
inside the house.

"Bobby King?" she said.

"I listen to him all the time. I think he's great."

"He's kind of great," Connie said reluctantly.

"Listen, that guy's *great*. He knows where the action is."

Connie blushed a little, because the glasses made it impossible for her   35
to see just what this boy was looking at. She couldn't decide if she liked
him or if he was just a jerk, and so she dawdled in the doorway and wouldn't
come down or go back inside. She said, "What's all that stuff painted on
your car?"

"Can'tcha read it?" He opened the door very carefully, as if he was
afraid it might fall off. He slid out just as carefully, planting his feet firmly
on the ground, the tiny metallic world in his glasses slowing down like gela-
tine hardening and in the midst of it Connie's bright green blouse. "This
here is my name, to begin with," he said. ARNOLD FRIEND was written
in tarlike black letters on the side, with a drawing of a round grinning face
that reminded Connie of a pumpkin, execpt it wore sunglasses. "I wanta introduce myself, I'm Arnold Friend and that's my real name and I'm gonna
be your friend, honey, and inside the car's Ellie Oscar, he's kinda shy." Ellie
brought his transistor radio up to his shoulder and balanced it there. "Now
these numbers are a secret code, honey," Arnold Friend explained. He read
off the numbers 33, 19, 17 and raised his eyebrows at her to see what she
thought of that, but she didn't think much of it. The left rear fender had
been smashed and around it was written, on the gleaming gold background,
DONE BY CRAZY WOMAN DRIVER. Connie had to laugh at that.
Arnold Friend was pleased at her laughter and looked up at her. "Around
the other side's a lot more—you wanta come and see them?"

"No."

"Why not?"

"Why should I?"

"Don'tcha wanta see what's on the car? Don'tcha wanta go for a ride?"   40

"I don't know."

"Why not?"

"I got things to do."

"Like what?"

"Things."

He laughed as if she had said something funny. He slapped his thighs. He was standing in a strange way, leaning back against the car as if he were balancing himself. He wasn't tall, only an inch or so taller than she would be if she came down to him. Connie liked the way he was dressed, which was the way all of them dressed: tight faded jeans stuffed into black, scuffed boots, a belt that pulled his waist in and showed how lean he was, and a white pull-over shirt that was a little soiled and showed the hard small muscles of his arms and shoulders. He looked as if he probably did hard work, lifting and carrying things. Even his neck looked muscular. And his face was a familiar face, somehow: the jaw and chin and cheeks slightly darkened, because he hadn't shaved for a day or two, and the nose long and hawk-like, sniffing as if she were a treat he was going to gobble up and it was all a joke.

"Connie, you ain't telling the truth. This is your day set aside for a ride with me and you know it," he said, still laughing. The way he straightened and recovered from his fit of laughing showed that it had been all fake.

"How do you know what my name is?" she said suspiciously.

"It's Connie."

"Maybe and maybe not."

"I know my Connie," he said, wagging his finger. Now she remembered him even better, back at the restaurant, and her cheeks warmed at the thought of how she sucked in her breath just at the moment she passed him—how she must have looked to him. And he had remembered her. "Ellie and I come out here especially for you," he said. "Ellie can sit in back. How about it?"

"Where?"

"Where what?"

"Where're we going?"

He looked at her. He took off the sunglasses and she saw how pale the skin around his eyes was, like holes that were not in shadow but instead in light. His eyes were chips of broken glass that catch the light in an amiable way. He smiled. It was as if the idea of going for a ride somewhere, to some place, was a new idea to him.

"Just for a ride, Connie sweetheart."

"I never said my name was Connie," she said.

"But I know what it is. I know your name and all about you, lots of things," Arnold Friend said. He had not moved yet but stood still leaning back against the side of his jalopy. "I took a special interest in you, such a pretty girl, and found out all about you like I know your parents and sister are gone somewheres and I know where and how long they're going to be gone, and I know who you were with last night, and your best girl friend's name is Betty. Right?"

He spoke in a simple lilting voice, exactly as if he were reciting the words to a song. His smile assured her that everything was fine. In the car Ellie turned up the volume on his radio and did not bother to look around at them.

"Ellie can sit in the back seat," Arnold Friend said. He indicated his   60
friend with a casual jerk of his chin, as if Ellie did not count and she should not bother with him.

"How'd you find out all that stuff?" Connie said.

"Listen: Betty Schultz and Tony Fitch and Jimmy Pettinger and Nancy Pettinger," he said, in a chant. "Raymond Stanley and Bob Hutter—"

"Do you know all those kids?"

"I know everybody."

"Look, you're kidding. You're not from around here."   65

"Sure."

"But—how come we never saw you before?"

"Sure you saw me before," he said. He looked down at his boots, as if he were a little offended. "You just don't remember."

"I guess I'd remember you," Connie said.

"Yeah?" He looked up at this, beaming. He was pleased. He began to   70
mark time with the music from Ellie's radio, tapping his fists lightly together. Connie looked away from his smile to the car, which was painted so bright it almost hurt her eyes to look at it. She looked at that name, ARNOLD FRIEND. And up at the front fender was an expression that was familiar—MAN THE FLYING SAUCERS. It was an expression kids had used the year before, but didn't use this year. She looked at it for a while as if the words meant something to her that she did not yet know.

"What're you thinking about? Huh?" Arnold Friend demanded. "Not worried about your hair blowing around in the car, are you?"

"No."

"Think I maybe can't drive good?"

"How do I know?"

"You're a hard girl to handle. How come?" he said. "Don't you know   75
I'm your friend? Didn't you see me put my sign in the air when you walked by?"

"What sign?"

"My sign." And he drew an X in the air, leaning out toward her. They were maybe ten feet apart. After his hand fell back to his side the X was still in the air, almost visible. Connie let the screen door close and stood perfectly still inside it, listening to the music from her radio and the boy's blend together. She stared at Arnold Friend. He stood there so stiffly relaxed, pretending to be relaxed, with one hand idly on the door handle as if he were keeping himself up that way and had no intention of ever moving again. She recognized most things about him, the tight jeans that showed his thighs and buttocks and the greasy leather boots and the tight shirt, and even that slippery friendly smile of his, that sleepy dreamy smile that all the boys used to get across ideas they didn't want to put into words. She recognized all this and also the singsong way he talked, slightly mocking, kidding, but serious and a little melancholy, and she recognized the way he tapped one fist against the other in homage to the perpetual music behind him. But all these things did not come together.

She said suddenly, "Hey, how old are you?"

His smile faded. She could see then that he wasn't a kid, he was much older—thirty, maybe more. At this knowledge her heart began to pound faster.

"That's a crazy thing to ask, Can'tcha see I'm your own age?"

"Like hell you are."

"Or maybe a coupla years older, I'm eighteen."

"Eighteen?" she said doubtfully.

He grinned to reassure her and lines appeared at the corners of his mouth. His teeth were big and white. He grinned so broadly his eyes became slits and she saw how thick the lashes were, thick and black as if painted with a black tarlike material. Then he seemed to become embarrassed, abruptly, and looked over his shoulder at Ellie. "*Him*, he's crazy," he said. "Ain't he a riot, he's a nut, a real character." Ellie was still listening to the music. His sunglasses told nothing about what he was thinking. He wore a bright orange shirt unbuttoned halfway to show his chest, which was a pale, bluish chest and not muscular like Arnold Friend's. His shirt collar was turned up all around and the very tips of the collar pointed out past his chin as if they were protecting him. He was pressing the transistor radio up against his ear and sat there in a kind of daze, right in the sun.

"He's kinda strange," Connie said.

"Hey, she says you're kinda strange! Kinda strange!" Arnold Friend cried. He pounded on the car to get Ellie's attention. Ellie turned for the first time and Connie saw with shock that he wasn't a kid either—he had a fair, hairless face, cheeks reddened slightly as if the veins grew too close to the surface of his skin, the face of a forty-year-old baby. Connie felt a wave of dizziness rise in her at this sight and she stared at him as if waiting for something to change the shock of the moment, make it all right again. Ellie's lips kept shaping words, mumbling along with the words blasting in his ear.

"Maybe you two better go away," Connie said faintly.

"What? How come?" Arnold Friend cried. "We come out here to take you for a ride. It's Sunday." He had the voice of the man on the radio now.

It was same voice, Connie thought. "Don'tcha know it's Sunday all day and honey, no matter who you were with last night today you're with Arnold Friend and don't you forget it!—Maybe you better step out here," he said, and this last was in a different voice. It was a little flatter, as if the heat was finally getting to him.

"No. I got things to do."

"Hey."   90

"You two better leave."

"We ain't leaving until you come with us."

"Like hell I am—"

"Connie, don't fool around with me. I mean, I mean, don't fool *around*," he said, shaking his head. He laughed incredulously. He placed his sunglasses on top of his head, carefully, as if he were indeed wearing a wig, and brought the stems down behind his ears. Connie stared at him, another wave of dizziness and fear rising in her so that for a moment he wasn't even in focus but was just a blur, standing there against his gold car, and she had the idea that he had driven up the driveway all right but had come from nowhere before that and belonged nowhere and that everything about him and even about the music that was so familiar to her was only half real.

"If my father comes and sees you—"   95

"He ain't coming. He's at a barbecue."

"How do you know that?"

"Aunt Tillie's. Right now they're—uh—they're drinking. Sitting around," he said vaguely, squinting as if he were staring all the way to town and over to Aunt Tillie's backyard. Then the vision seemed to get clear and he nodded energetically. "Yeah. Sitting around. There's your sister in a blue dress, huh? And high heels, the poor sad bitch—nothing like you sweetheart. And your mother's helping some fat woman with the corn, they're cleaning the corn—husking the corn—"

"What fat woman?" Connie cried.

"How do I know what fat woman. I don't know every goddam fat   100
woman in the world!" Arnold Friend laughed.

"Oh, that's Mrs. Hornby. . . . Who invited her?" Connie said. She felt a little light-headed. Her breath was coming quickly.

"She's too fat. I don't like them fat. I like them the way you are, honey," he said, smiling sleepily at her. They stared at each other for a while, through the screen door. He said softly, "Now what you're going to do is this: you're going to come out that door. You're going to sit up front with me and Ellie's going to sit in the back, the hell with Ellie, right? This isn't Ellie's date. You're my date. I'm your lover, honey."

"What? You're crazy—"

"Yes, I'm your lover. You don't know what that is but you will," he said. "I know that too. I know all about you. But look: it's real nice and you couldn't ask for nobody better than me, or more polite. I always keep my word. I'll tell you how it is, I'm always nice at first, the first time. I'll hold you so tight you won't think you have to try to get away or pretend anything because you'll know you can't. And I'll come inside you where it's all secret and you'll give in to me and you'll love me—"

"Shut up! You're crazy!" Connie said. She backed away from the door. She put her hands against her ears as if she'd heard something terrible, something not meant for her. "People don't talk like that, you're crazy," she muttered. Her heart was almost too big now for her chest and its pumping made sweat break out all over her. She looked out to see Arnold Friend pause and then take a step toward the porch lurching. He almost fell. But, like a clever drunken man, he managed to catch his balance. He wobbled in his high boots and grabbed hold of one of the porch posts.

"Honey?" he said. "You still listening?"

"Get the hell out of here!"

"Be nice, honey. Listen."

"I'm going to call the police—"

He wobbled again and out of the side of his mouth came a fast spat curse, an aside not meant for her to hear. But even this "Christ!" sounded forced. Then he began to smile again. She watched this smile come, awkward as if he were smiling from inside a mask. His whole face was a mask, she thought wildly, tanned down onto his throat but then running out as if he had plastered makeup on his face but had forgotten about his throat.

"Honey—? Listen, here's how it is. I always tell the truth and I promise you this: I ain't coming in that house after you."

"You better not! I'm going to call the police if you—if you don't—"

"Honey," he said, talking right through her voice, "honey, I'm not coming in there but you are coming out here. You know why?"

She was panting. The kitchen looked like a place she had never seen before, some room she had run inside but which wasn't good enough, wasn't going to help her. The kitchen window had never had a curtain, after three years, and there were dishes in the sink for her to do—probably—and if you ran your hand across the table you'd probably feel something sticky there.

"You listening, honey? Hey?"

"—going to call the police—"

"Soon as you touch the phone I don't need to keep my promise and can come inside. You won't want that."

She rushed forward and tried to lock the door. Her fingers were shaking. "But why lock it," Arnold Friend said gently, talking right into her face. "It's just a screen door. It's just nothing." One of his boots was at a strange angle, as if his foot wasn't in it. It pointed out to the left, bent at the ankle. "I mean, anybody can break through a screen door and glass and wood and iron or anything else if he needs to, anybody at all and specially Arnold Friend. If the place got lit up with a fire honey you'd come running out into my arms, right into my arms and safe at home—like you knew I was your lover and'd stopped fooling around. I don't mind a nice shy girl but I don't like no fooling around." Part of those words were spoken with a slight rhythmic lilt, and Connie somehow recognized them—the echo of a song from last year, about a girl rushing into her boy friend's arms and coming home again—

Connie stood barefoot on the linoleum floor, staring at him. "What do you want?" she whispered.

"I want you," he said.   120

"What?"

"Seen you that night and thought, that's the one, yes sir. I never needed to look any more."

"But my father's coming back. He's coming to get me. I had to wash my hair first—" She spoke in a dry, rapid voice, hardly raising it for him to hear.

"No, your daddy is not coming and yes, you had to wash your hair and you washed it for me. It's nice and shining and all for me, I thank you, sweetheart," he said with a mock bow, but again he almost lost his balance. He had to bend and adjust his boots. Evidently his feet did not go all the way down; the boots must have been stuffed with something so that he would seem taller. Connie stared out at him and behind him Ellie in the car, who seemed to be looking off toward Connie's right, into nothing. This Ellie said, pulling the words out of the air one after another as if he were just discovering them, "You want me to pull out the phone?"

"Shut your mouth and keep it shut," Arnold Friend said, his face red   125
from bending over or maybe from embarrassment because Connie had seen his boots. "This ain't none of your business."

"What—what are you doing? What do you want?" Connie said. "If I call the police they'll get you, they'll arrest you—"

"Promise was not to come in unless you touch that phone, and I'll keep that promise," he said. He resumed his erect position and tried to force his shoulders back. He sounded like a hero in a movie, declaring something important. He spoke too loudly and it was as if he were speaking to someone behind Connie. "I ain't made plans for coming in that house where I don't belong but just for you to come out to me, the way you should. Don't you know who I am?"

"You're crazy," she whispered. She backed away from the door but did not want to go into another part of the house, as if this would give him permission to come through the door. "What do you. . . . You're crazy, you . . . "

"Huh? What're you saying, honey?"

Her eyes darted everywhere in the kitchen. She could not remember   130
what it was, this room.

"This is how it is, honey: you come out and we'll drive away, have a nice ride. But if you don't come out we're gonna wait till your people come home and then they're all going to get it."

"You want that telephone pulled out?" Ellie said. He held the radio away from his ear and grimaced, as if without the radio the air was too much for him.

"I toldja shut up, Ellie," Arnold Friend said, "you're deaf, get a hearing aid, right? Fix yourself up. This little girl's no trouble and's gonna be nice to me, so Ellie keep to yourself, this ain't your date—right? Don't hem in on me. Don't hog. Don't crush. Don't bird dog. Don't trail me," he said in a rapid meaningless voice, as if he were running through all the expressions he'd learned but was no longer sure which one of them was in style, then rushing on to new ones, making them up with his eyes closed, "Don't crawl under my fence, don't squeeze in my chipmunk hole, don't sniff my glue, suck my popsicle, keep your own greasy fingers on yourself!" He shaded his eyes and peered in at Connie, who was backed against the kitchen table. "Don't mind him honey he's just a creep. He's a dope. Right? I'm the boy for you and like I said you come out here nice like a lady and give me your hand, and nobody else gets hurt, I mean, your nice old bald-headed daddy and your mummy and your sister in her high heels. Because listen: why bring them in this?"

"Leave me alone," Connie whispered.

"Hey, you know that old woman down the road, the one with the chickens and stuff—you know her?"

"She's dead!"

"Dead? What? You know her?" Arnold Friend said.

"She's dead—"

"Don't you like her?"

"She's dead—she's—she isn't here any more—"

"But don't you like her, I mean, you got something against her? Some grudge or something?" Then his voice dipped as if he were conscious of a rudeness. He touched the sunglasses perched on top of his head as if to make sure they were still there. "Now you be a good girl."

"What are you going to do?"

"Just two things, or maybe three," Arnold Friend said. "But I promise it won't last long and you'll like me that way you get to like people you're close to. You will. It's all over for you here, so come on out. You don't want your people in any trouble, do you?"

She turned and bumped against a chair or something, hurting her leg, but she ran into the back room and picked up the telephone. Something roared in her ear, a tiny roaring, and she was so sick with fear that she could do nothing but listen to it—the telephone was clammy and very heavy and her fingers groped down to the dial but were too weak to touch it. She began to scream into the phone, into the roaring. She cried out, she cried for her mother, she felt her breath start jerking back and forth in her lungs as if it were something Arnold Friend were stabbing her with again and again with no tenderness. A noisy sorrowful wailing rose all about her and she was locked inside it the way she was locked inside the house.

After a while she could hear again. She was sitting on the floor with 145 herwet back against the wall.

Arnold Friend was saying from the door, "That's a good girl. Put the phone back."

She kicked the phone away from her.

"No, honey. Pick it up. Put it back right."

She picked it up and put it back. The dial tone stopped.

"That's a good girl. Now you come outside." 150

She was hollow with what had been fear, but what was now just an emptiness. All that screaming had blasted it out of her. She sat, one leg cramped under her, and deep inside her brain was something like a pinpoint of light that kept going and would not let her relax. She thought, I'm not going to see my mother again. She thought, I'm not going to sleep in my bed again. Her bright green blouse was all wet.

Arnold Friend said, in a gentle-loud voice that was like a stage voice, "The place where you came from ain't there any more, and where you had in mind to go is cancelled out. This place you are now—inside your daddy's house—is nothing but a cardboard box I can knock down any time. You know that and always did know it. You hear me?"

She thought, I have got to think. I have to know what to do.

"We'll go out to a nice field, out in the country here where it smells so nice and it's sunny," Arnold Friend said. "I'll have my arms around you so you won't need to try to get away and I'll show you what love is like, what it does. The hell with this house! It looks solid all right," he said. He ran a fingernail down the screen and the noise did not make Connie shiver, as it would have the day before. "Now put your hand on your heart, honey. Feel that? That feels solid too but we know better, be nice to me, be sweet like you can because what else is there for a girl like you but to be sweet and pretty and give in?—and get away before her people come back?"

She felt her pounding heart. Her hand seemed to enclose it. She 155 thought for the first time in her life that it was nothing that was hers, that belonged to her, but just a pounding, living thing inside this body that wasn't really hers either.

"You don't want them to get hurt," Arnold Friend went on. "Now get up, honey. Get up all by yourself."

She stood.

"Now turn this way. That's right. Come over here to me—Ellie, put that away, didn't I tell you? You dope. You miserable creepy dope," Arnold Friend said. His words were not angry but only part of an incantation. The incantation was kindly. "Now come out through the kitchen to me honey and let's see a smile, try it, you're a brave sweet little girl and now they're eating corn and hotdogs cooked to bursting over an outdoor fire, and they don't know one thing about you and never did and honey you're better than them because not a one of them would have done this for you."

Connie felt the linoleum under her feet; it was cool. She brushed her hair back out of her eyes. Arnold Friend let go of the post tentatively and opened his arms for her, his elbows pointing in toward each other and his wrists limp, to show that this was an embarrassed embrace and a little mocking, he didn't want to make her self-conscious.

She put out her hand against the screen. She watched herself push the door slowly open as if she were safe back somewhere in the other doorway, watching this body and this head of long hair moving out into the sunlight where Arnold Friend waited.

"My sweet little blue-eyed girl," he said, in a half-sung sigh that had nothing to do with her brown eyes but was taken up just the same by the vast sunlit reaches of the land behind him and on all sides of him, so much land that Connie had never seen before and did not recognize except to know that she was going to it.

- What details convey the character of Arnold Friend? How does this particular character echo and develop the evil characters that we have seen in such places as *Doctor Faustus* (p. 240) and "Young Goodman Brown" (p. 1216)?
- When Arnold Friend claims that "these numbers are a secret code," he cites "33, 19, 17." If you read Judges 19:17 in the Bible, you will find a story that anticipates the title, plot, and structure of this story. How does such an influence shape our reading of this text?
- Oates dedicates this story to Bob Dylan and recounts that she was listening to his song "It's All Over Now, Baby Blue." Track down an audio recording of this song. How do any elements (including the structure) of this story reflect specific lines or specific feelings evoked by the song?
- In the mid-1960s in Tucson, Arizona, Charles Schmid, a five-foot-three, twenty-three-year-old who stuffed three or four inches of rags and cans into his boots to make himself look taller, was arrested for the murder of three teenage girls whom he picked up at Johnie's Drive-in. The similarities to the short story go on. How is it possible to analyze this story as an independent work of literature when so many of its components come from other sources?

William Faulkner (1897–1962)

William Faulkner was born in New Albany, Mississippi. A high school dropout, Faulkner was rejected by the U.S. Army because of his small size. He joined the

Royal Canadian Air Force and then the Royal Air Force but did not see action in World War I. Returning to Mississippi after the war, Faulkner took classes at the University of Mississippi but did not complete his degree. After brief periods living in New York, New Orleans, and Europe, Faulkner moved back to Mississippi, where he found inspiration for his first great work, *The Sound and the Fury* (1929). It was followed by critical successes such as *As I Lay Dying, Light in August,* and *Absalom, Absalom!* His many awards include the Nobel Prize in literature in 1949, the National Book Award for Collected Stories in 1951, and two Pulitzer Prizes.

A Rose for Emily (1931)

1

When Miss Emily Grierson died, our whole town went to her funeral: the men through a sort of respectful affection for a fallen monument, the women mostly out of curiosity to see the inside of her house, which no one save an old manservant—a combined gardener and cook—had seen in at least ten years.

It was a big, squarish frame house that had once been white, decorated with cupolas and spires and scrolled balconies in the heavily lightsome style of the seventies, set on what had once been our most select street. But garages and cotton gins had encroached and obliterated even the august names of that neighborhood; only Miss Emily's house was left, lifting its stubborn and coquettish decay above the cotton wagons and the gasoline pumps—an eyesore among eyesores. And now Miss Emily had gone to join the representatives of those august names where they lay in the cedar-bemused cemetery among the ranked and anonymous graves of Union and Confederate soldiers who fell at the battle of Jefferson.

Alive, Miss Emily had been a tradition, a duty, and a care; a sort of hereditary obligation upon the town, dating from that day in 1894 when Colonel Sartoris, the mayor—he who fathered the edict that no Negro woman should appear on the streets without an apron—remitted her taxes, the dispensation dating from the death of her father on into perpetuity. Not that Miss Emily would have accepted charity. Colonel Sartoris invented an involved tale to the effect that Miss Emily's father had loaned money to the town, which the town, as a matter of business, preferred this way of repaying. Only a man of Colonel Sartoris' generation and thought could have invented it, and only a woman could have believed it.

When the next generation, with its more modern ideas, became mayors and aldermen, this arrangement created some little dissatisfaction. On the first of the year they mailed her a tax notice. February came, and there was no reply. They wrote her a formal letter, asking her to call at the sheriff's office at her convenience. A week later the mayor wrote her himself, offering to call or to send his car for her, and received in reply a note on paper of an archaic shape, in a thin, flowing calligraphy in faded ink, to the effect that she no longer went out at all. The tax notice was also enclosed, without comment.

They called a special meeting of the Board of Aldermen. A deputation waited upon her, knocked at the door through which no visitor had passed since she ceased giving china-painting lessons eight or ten years earlier. They were admitted by the old Negro into a dim hall from which a stairway mounted into still more shadow. It smelled of dust and disuse—a close, dank smell. The Negro led them into the parlor. It was furnished in heavy, leather-covered furniture. When the Negro opened the blinds of one window, they could see that the leather was cracked; and when they sat down, a faint dust rose sluggishly about their thighs, spinning with slow motes in the single sun-ray. On a tarnished gilt easel before the fireplace stood a crayon portrait of Miss Emily's father.

They rose when she entered—a small, fat woman in black, with a thin gold chain descending to her waist and vanishing into her belt, leaning on an ebony cane with a tarnished gold head. Her skeleton was small and spare; perhaps that was why what would have been merely plumpness in another was obesity in her. She looked bloated, like a body long submerged in motionless water, and of that pallid hue. Her eyes, lost in the fatty ridges of her face, looked like two small pieces of coal pressed into a lump of dough as they moved from one face to another while the visitors stated their errand.

She did not ask them to sit. She just stood in the door and listened quietly until the spokesman came to a stumbling halt. Then they could hear the invisible watch ticking at the end of the gold chain.

Her voice was dry and cold. "I have no taxes in Jefferson. Colonel Sartoris explained it to me. Perhaps one of you can gain access to the city records and satisfy yourselves."

"But we have. We are the city authorities, Miss Emily. Didn't you get a notice from the sheriff, signed by him?"

"I received a paper, yes," Miss Emily said. "Perhaps he considers himself the sheriff . . . I have no taxes in Jefferson."

"But there is nothing on the books to show that, you see. We must go by the—"

"See Colonel Sartoris. I have no taxes in Jefferson."

"But, Miss Emily—"

"See Colonel Sartoris." (Colonel Sartoris had been dead almost ten years.) "I have no taxes in Jefferson. Tobe!" The Negro appeared. "Show these gentlemen out."

2

So she vanquished them, horse and foot, just as she had vanquished their fathers thirty years before about the smell. That was two years after her father's death and a short time after her sweetheart—the one we believed would marry her—had deserted her. After her father's death she went out very little; after her sweetheart went away, people hardly saw her at all. A few of the ladies had the temerity to call, but were not received, and the only sign of life about the place was the Negro man—a young man then—going in and out with a market basket.

"Just as if a man—any man—could keep a kitchen properly," the ladies said; so they were not surprised when the smell developed. It was another link between the gross, teeming world and the high and mighty Griersons.

A neighbor, a woman, complained to the mayor, Judge Stevens, eighty years old.

"But what will you have me do about it, madam?" he said.

"Why, send her word to stop it," the woman said. "Isn't there a law?"

"I'm sure that won't be necessary," Judge Stevens said. "It's probably   20
just a snake or a rat that nigger of hers killed in the yard. I'll speak to him about it."

The next day he received two more complaints, one from a man who came in diffident deprecation. "We really must do something about it, Judge. I'd be the last one in the world to bother Miss Emily, but we've got to do something." That night the Board of Aldermen met—three graybeards and one younger man, a member of the rising generation.

"It's simple enough," he said. "Send her word to have her place cleaned up. Give her a certain time to do it in, and if she don't . . . "

"Dammit, sir," Judge Stevens said, "will you accuse a lady to her face of smelling bad?"

So the next night, after midnight, four men crossed Miss Emily's lawn and slunk about the house like burglars, sniffing along the base of the brickwork and at the cellar openings while one of them performed a regular sowing motion with his hand out of a sack slung from his shoulder. They broke open the cellar door and sprinkled lime there, and in all the outbuildings. As they recrossed the lawn, a window that had been dark was lighted and Miss Emily sat in it, the light behind her, and her upright torso motionless as that of an idol. They crept quietly across the lawn and into the shadow of the locusts that lined the street. After a week or two the smell went away.

That was when people had begun to feel really sorry for her. People in   25
our town, remembering how old lady Wyatt, her great-aunt, had gone completely crazy at last, believed that the Griersons held themselves a little too high for what they really were. None of the young men were quite good enough for Miss Emily and such. We had long thought of them as a tableau: Miss Emily a slender figure in white in the background, her father a spraddled silhouette in the foreground, his back to her and clutching a horsewhip, the two of them framed by the back-flung front door. So when she got to be thirty and was still single, we were not pleased exactly, but vindicated;

even with insanity in the family she wouldn't have turned down all of her chances if they had really materialized.

When her father died, it got about that the house was all that was left to her; and in a way, people were glad. At last they could pity Miss Emily. Being left alone, and a pauper, she had become humanized. Now she too would know the old thrill and the old despair of a penny more or less.

The day after his death all the ladies prepared to call at the house and offer condolence and aid, as is our custom. Miss Emily met them at the door, dressed as usual and with no trace of grief on her face. She told them that her father was not dead. She did that for three days, with the ministers calling on her, and the doctors, trying to persuade her to let them dispose of the body. Just as they were about to resort to law and force, she broke down, and they buried her father quickly.

We did not say she was crazy then. We believed she had to do that. We remembered all the young men her father had driven away, and we knew that with nothing left, she would have to cling to that which had robbed her, as people will.

3

She was sick for a long time. When we saw her again, her hair was cut short, making her look like a girl, with a vague resemblance to those angels in colored church windows—sort of tragic and serene.

The town had just let the contracts for paving the sidewalks, and in the summer after her father's death they began to work. The construction company came with niggers and mules and machinery, and a foreman named Homer Barron, a Yankee—a big, dark, ready man, with a big voice and eyes lighter than his face. The little boys would follow in groups to hear him cuss the niggers, and the niggers singing in time to the rise and fall of picks. Pretty soon he knew everybody in town. Whenever you heard a lot of laughing anywhere about the square, Homer Barron would be in the center of the group. Presently we began to see him and Miss Emily on Sunday afternoons driving in the yellow-wheeled buggy and the matched team of bays from the livery stable.

At first we were glad that Miss Emily would have an interest, because the ladies all said, "Of course a Grierson would not think seriously of a Northerner, a day laborer." But there were still others, older people, who said that even grief could not cause a real lady to forget *noblesse oblige*—without calling it *noblesse oblige*. They just said, "Poor Emily. Her kinsfolk should come to her." She had some kin in Alabama; but years ago her father had fallen out with them over the estate of old lady Wyatt, the crazy woman, and there was no communication between the two families. They had not even been represented at the funeral.

And as soon as the old people said, "Poor Emily," the whispering began. "Do you suppose it's really so?" they said to one another. "Of course it is. What else could . . ." This behind their hands; rustling of craned silk and satin behind jalousies closed upon the sun of Sunday afternoon as the thin, swift clop-clop-clop of the matched team passed: "Poor Emily."

She carried her head high enough—even when we believed that she was fallen. It was as if she demanded more than ever the recognition of her dignity as the last Grierson; as if it had wanted that touch of earthiness to reaffirm her imperviousness. Like when she bought the rat poison, the arsenic. That was over a year after they had begun to say "Poor Emily," and while the two female cousins were visiting her.

"I want some poison," she said to the druggist. She was over thirty then, still a slight woman, though thinner than usual, with cold, haughty black eyes in a face the flesh of which was strained across the temples and about the eye-sockets as you imagine a lighthouse-keeper's face ought to look. "I want some poison," she said.

"Yes, Miss Emily. What kind? For rats and such? I'd recom—"   35

"I want the best you have. I don't care what kind."

The druggist named several. "They'll kill anything up to an elephant. But what you want is—"

"Arsenic," Miss Emily said. "Is that a good one?"

"Is . . . arsenic? Yes, ma'am. But what you want—"

"I want arsenic."   40

The druggist looked down at her. She looked back at him, erect, her face like a strained flag. "Why, of course," the druggist said. "If that's what you want. But the law requires you to tell what you are going to use it for."

Miss Emily just stared at him, her head tilted back in order to look him eye for eye, until he looked away and went and got the arsenic and wrapped it up. The Negro delivery boy brought her the package; the druggist didn't come back. When she opened the package at home there was written on the box, under the skull and bones: "For rats."

4

So the next day we all said, "She will kill herself"; and we said it would be the best thing. When she had first begun to be seen with Homer Barron, we had said, "She will marry him." Then we said, "She will persuade him yet," because Homer himself had remarked—he liked men, and it was known that he drank with the younger men in the Elks' Club—that he was not a marrying man. Later we said, "Poor Emily," behind the jalousies as they passed on Sunday afternoon in the glittering buggy, Miss Emily with her head high and Homer Barron with his hat cocked and a cigar in his teeth, reins and whip in a yellow glove.

Then some of the ladies began to say that it was a disgrace to the town and a bad example to the young people. The men did not want to interfere, but at last the ladies forced the Baptist minister—Miss Emily's people were

Episcopal—to call upon her. He would never divulge what happened during that interview, but he refused to go back again. The next Sunday they again drove about the streets, and the following day the minister's wife wrote to Miss Emily's relations in Alabama.

So she had blood-kin under her roof again and we sat back to watch developments. At first nothing happened. Then we were sure that they were to be married. We learned that Miss Emily had been to the jeweler's and ordered a man's toilet set in silver, with the letters H. B. on each piece. Two days later we learned that she had bought a complete outfit of men's clothing, including a nightshirt, and we said, "They are married." We were really glad. We were glad because the two female cousins were even more Grierson than Miss Emily had ever been.

So we were not surprised when Homer Barron—the streets had been finished some time since—was gone. We were a little disappointed that there was not a public blowing-off, but we believed that he had gone on to prepare for Miss Emily's coming, or to give her a chance to get rid of the cousins. (By that time it was a cabal, and we were all Miss Emily's allies to help circumvent the cousins.) Sure enough, after another week they departed. And, as we had expected all along, within three days Homer Barron was back in town. A neighbor saw the Negro man admit him at the kitchen door at dusk one evening.

And that was the last we saw of Homer Barron. And of Miss Emily for some time. The Negro man went in and out with the market basket, but the front door remained closed. Now and then we would see her at a window for a moment, as the men did that night when they sprinkled the lime, but for almost six months she did not appear on the streets. Then we knew that this was to be expected too; as if that quality of her father which had thwarted her woman's life so many times had been too virulent and too furious to die.

When we next saw Miss Emily, she had grown fat and her hair was turning gray. During the next few years it grew grayer and grayer until it attained an even pepper-and-salt iron-gray, when it ceased turning. Up to the day of her death at seventy-four it was still that vigorous iron-gray, like the hair of an active man.

From that time on her front door remained closed, save for a period of six or seven years, when she was about forty, during which she gave lessons in china-painting. She fitted up a studio in one of the downstairs rooms, where the daughters and grand-daughters of Colonel Sartoris' contemporaries were sent to her with the same regularity and in the same spirit that they were sent to church on Sundays with a twenty-five-cent piece for the collection plate. Meanwhile her taxes had been remitted.

Then the newer generation became the backbone and the spirit of the town, and the painting pupils grew up and fell away and did not send their children to her with boxes of color and tedious brushes and pictures cut from the ladies' magazines. The front door closed upon the last one and remained closed for good. When the town got free postal delivery, Miss Emily alone refused to let them fasten the metal numbers above her door and attach a mailbox to it. She would not listen to them.

Daily, monthly, yearly we watched the Negro grow grayer and more stooped, going in and out with the market basket. Each December we sent her a tax notice, which would be returned by the post office a week later, unclaimed. Now and then we would see her in one of the downstairs windows—she had evidently shut up the top floor of the house—like the carven torso of an idol in a niche, looking or not looking at us, we could never tell which. Thus she passed from generation to generation—dear, inescapable, impervious, tranquil, and perverse.

And so she died. Fell ill in the house filled with dust and shadows, with only a doddering Negro man to wait on her. We did not even know she was sick; we had long since given up trying to get information from the Negro. He talked to no one, probably not even to her, for his voice had grown harsh and rusty, as if from disuse.

She died in one of the downstairs rooms, in a heavy walnut bed with a curtain, her gray head propped on a pillow yellow and moldy with age and lack of sunlight.

5

The Negro met the first of the ladies at the front door and let them in, with their hushed, sibilant voices and their quick, curious glances, and then he disappeared. He walked right through the house and out the back and was not seen again.

The two female cousins came at once. They held the funeral on the second day, with the town coming to look at Miss Emily beneath a mass of bought flowers, with the crayon face of her father musing profoundly above the bier and the ladies sibilant and macabre; and the very old men—some in their brushed Confederate uniforms—on the porch and the lawn, talking of Miss Emily as if she had been a contemporary of theirs, believing that they had danced with her and courted her perhaps, confusing time with its mathematical progression, as the old do, to whom all the past is not a diminishing road but, instead, a huge meadow which no winter ever quite touches, divided from them now by the narrow bottle-neck of the most recent decade of years.

Already we knew that there was one room in that region above stairs which no one had seen in forty years, and which would have to be forced. They waited until Miss Emily was decently in the ground before they opened it.

The violence of breaking down the door seemed to fill this room with pervading dust. A thin, acrid pall as of the tomb seemed to lie everywhere upon this room decked and furnished as for a bridal: upon the valance curtains of faded rose color, upon the rose-shaded lights, upon the dressing table, upon the delicate array of crystal and the man's toilet things backed with tarnished silver, silver so tarnished that the monogram was obscured. Among them lay a collar and tie, as if they had just been removed, which, lifted, left upon the surface a pale crescent in the dust. Upon a chair hung the suit, carefully folded; beneath it the two mute shoes and the discarded socks.

The man himself lay in the bed.

For a long while we just stood there, looking down at the profound and fleshless grin. The body had apparently once lain in the attitude of an embrace, but now the long sleep that outlasts love, that conquers even the grimace of love, had cuckolded him. What was left of him, rotted beneath what was left of the nightshirt, had become inextricable from the bed in which he lay; and upon him and upon the pillow beside him lay that even coating of the patient and biding dust.

Then we noticed that in the second pillow was the indentation of a head. One of us lifted something from it, and leaning forward, that faint and invisible dust dry and acrid in the nostrils, we saw a long strand of iron-gray hair.

■ Find details in the story that describe the setting and the social situation of the characters in the story. What is Emily Grierson's social class and regional affiliation? Describe Homer Barron and "the Negro" according to the same criteria. How are these details significant within the story? How do they influence the actions of the townspeople?

■ How might we construct an allegorical reading of this story? What details in the story justify such a reading? Which specific historical allusions in the story are important to such a reading?

POETRY

Percy Bysshe Shelley (1792–1822)

Ozymandias (1818)

I met a traveler from an antique land
Who said: Two vast and trunkless legs of stone
Stand in the desert. Near them, on the sand,
Half sunk, a shattered visage lies, whose frown,
And wrinkled lip, and sneer of cold command,   5

Tell that its sculptor well those passions read
Which yet survive, stamped on these lifeless things,
The hand that mocked them, and the heart that fed;
And on the pedestal these words appear:
"My name is Ozymandias, king of kings: 10
Look on my works, ye Mighty, and despair!"
Nothing beside remains. Round the decay
Of that colossal wreck, boundless and bare
The lone and level sands stretch far away.

■ How does "mocked" function within the narrative?
■ How does the poem juxtapose the inscription on the pedestal with its current context?
■ How does this poem illustrate the myth of cheating death?

Sharon McCartney (1959–)

After the Chuck Jones Tribute on Teletoon
(2002)

Swan-diving off the crewcut mesas of Monument Valley
in an Icarus contraption of fluff and paste, roadrunner
bull's-eyed far below, coyote can't help it—it's an addiction,
a disease, beyond his control. He's resigned to pain,
the blacksmith's anvil stuka-ing his skull, the Sisyphean boulder   5
snowballing down each time he shoulders it upward,
his crabbed frame of bones and hide steamrollered, accordion-
folded or simply incinerated. *Hope is the thing with feathers,*
he grumbles but he can't get Prometheus out of his craw;
his scrawny belly cringes under the eagle's talons, cold avian   10
claws on his abdomen. He paws the packed earth of the river
gorge, fear and sorrow a garment he can't shed, a raiment,
his scratchy winter coat. What else is there to do in the desert?
Experience tells him he can't win and yet he persists.
Who can predict the actions of the Gods? The chances   15
are slim but statistics mean nothing to the one who succeeds.
He splashes a false horizon on sandstone, sets the sun
precariously low, dots the vanishing point, steps three paces
back with his Picasso beret and palette, thumb up to correct
the perspective, and plummets off the predictable cliff.   20

■ The poet describes the actions of the cartoon characters Coyote and Roadrunner in terms of characters in classical mythology. How are such allusions appropriate? How do they impact our understanding of the cartoon actions?

Robert Duncan (1919–1988)

Persephone (1939)

> *"We have passed the great Trauma.*
> *These wounds disclose our loss."*

memory: farfields of morning,
     maimd winter, wheel and hoofhammerd weeds,
bare patches of earth. We heard rumor of the rape
among the women who wait at the wells with dry urns,
talk among leaves and among the old men   5
who sift tin cans and seashells searching for driftwood
to make fires on cold hearthstones. Stone hearts
and arteries hardend to stone.
        This sound of our mourning, wailing of reeds,
comes over the ice and the grey wastes of water.   10
We listen: it shrieks thru the ruins of cities,
whistles in shellholes
and freezes like ether in our lungs.

Shades falling under the oakshadow . . . shade upon shade
intent with their sorrow. The lust of such sorrow   15
listless, moving over the leafmold,
footmolded and hoofmolded, spoors of past violence.
From such clay our roots writhe, sucking the life
from corpsemold and footclay
and mold of the skull rooting.   20

Spore-spotted Onan, baldheaded, trickling with seed,
moved among us, or troops of swift women
    pursuing the leopard
passd. The quiet unbroken, dark beneath dark
branches spotted with light; or a flute in the morning   25
made truce, awakening the leaves like birds.
We shot green from the bark to flute music,
moving out from the trunk in a dream.

The sun was like gold on my body,
roots in the cold dark below me and arms   30
from the slender trunk showerd in gold light and shadows,
fingers green seeking the sun.

Lost, lost such peace, and Persephone lost.
Last dream brought silence,
silent thread of death-threatening dream.   35

We remember in symbols such violence:
the splintering of rock, the shock of the trauma,
in which she was taken from us. Shade
falls under the shadow . . . shade upon shade.
Spotted with bonewhite, splinter of driftwood,   40
the bark wet with terror, no sleep,
only waiting. Only we wait, our wounds barely heald
for the counterattack before sunrise.

- In the myth, Hades, the god of the underworld, opens up the earth and abducts the young Persephone, who has been out gathering flowers. Her mother, Demeter, the goddess of the harvest, is so distraught at her daughter's disappearance that the earth began to die. Zeus strikes a bargain with his brother Hades that Persephone can return to her mother for part of the year (beginning in the spring), but she must live in the underworld for part of the year (fall and winter). During the time that she spends with her husband, her mother continues to make the earth barren.
- Look at the line "We remember in symbols." What are some of the remembered symbols that are used in the poem?
- What are some explanations for what Persephone symbolizes in the poem?

Sylvia Plath (1932–1963)

Two Sisters of Persephone (1956)

Two girls there are: within the house
One sits; the other, without.
Daylong a duet of shade and light
Plays between these.

In her dark wainscoted room   5
The first works problems on

A mathematical machine.
Dry ticks mark time

As she calculates each sum.
At this barren enterprise   10
Rat-shrewd go her squint eyes,
Root-pale her meager frame.

Bronzed as earth, the second lies,
Hearing ticks blown gold
Like pollen on bright air. Lulled   15
Near a bed of poppies,

She sees how their red silk flare
Of petaled blood
Burns open to the sun's blade.
On that green altar   20

Freely become sun's bride, the latter
Grows quick with seed.
Grass-couched in her labor's pride,
She bears a king. Turned bitter

And sallow as any lemon,   25
The other, wry virgin to the last,
Goes graveward with flesh laid waste,
Worm-husbanded, yet no woman.

- What are the contrasting characteristics of these two sisters? Which option does the poem validate?
- How are these two sisters related to the plight of Persephone?

John Keats (1795–1821)

Ode on a Grecian Urn (1819)

I

Thou still unravish'd bride of quietness,
    Thou foster-child of silence and slow time,
Sylvan historian, who canst thus express

A flowery tale more sweetly than our rhyme:
What leaf-fring'd legend haunts about thy shape   5
    Of deities or mortals, or of both,
        In Tempe or the dales of Arcady?
What men or gods are these? What maidens loth?
    What mad pursuit? What struggle to escape?
        What pipes and timbrels? What wild ecstasy?   10

II
Heard melodies are sweet, but those unheard
    Are sweeter; therefore, ye soft pipes, play on;
Not to the sensual ear, but, more endear'd,
    Pipe to the spirit ditties of no tone:
Fair youth, beneath the trees, thou canst not leave   15
    Thy song, nor ever can those trees be bare;
        Bold lover, never, never canst thou kiss,
Though winning near the goal—yet, do not grieve;
    She cannot fade, though thou hast not thy bliss,
        For ever wilt thou love, and she be fair!   20

III
Ah, happy, happy boughs! that cannot shed
    Your leaves, nor ever bid the spring adieu;
And, happy melodist, unwearièd,
    For ever piping songs for ever new;
More happy love! more happy, happy love!   25
    For ever warm and still to be enjoy'd,
        For ever panting, and for ever young;
All breathing human passion far above,
    That leaves a heart high-sorrowful and cloy'd,
        A burning forehead, and a parching tongue.   30

IV
Who are these coming to the sacrifice?
    To what green altar, O mysterious priest,
Lead'st thou that heifer lowing at the skies,
    And all her silken flanks with garlands drest?
What little town by river or sea shore,   35
    Or mountain-built with peaceful citadel,
        Is emptied of this folk, this pious morn?
And, little town, thy streets for evermore
    Will silent be; and not a soul to tell
        Why thou art desolate, can e'er return.   40

V

O Attic shape! Fair attitude! with brede
    Of marble men and maidens overwrought,
With forest branches and the trodden weed;
    Thou, silent form, dost tease us out of thought
As doth eternity: Cold Pastoral!   45
    When old age shall this generation waste,
        Thou shalt remain, in midst of other woe
Than ours, a friend to man, to whom thou say'st,
    "Beauty is truth, truth beauty,"—that is all
        Ye know on earth, and all ye need to know.   50

■ Why does the poet describe the scene as "Cold Pastoral"?

■ How does the poem discuss the complications of reading allusions? What
understanding is the poet able to achieve even without answering such
questions as, "What men or gods are these?"

John Keats (1795–1821)

[When I have fears that I may cease to be] (1818)

When I have fears that I may cease to be
    Before my pen has gleaned my teeming brain,
Before high-piléd books, in charactery,
    Hold like rich garners the full-ripened grain;
When I behold, upon the night's starred face,   5
    Huge cloudy symbols of a high romance,
And think that I may never live to trace
    Their shadows, with the magic hand of chance;
And when I feel, fair creature of an hour,
    That I shall never look upon thee more,   10
Never have relish in the faery power
    Of unreflecting love—then on the shore
Of the wide world I stand alone, and think
Till love and fame to nothingness do sink.

■ How does the poet reflect upon the problem of mortality?

■ How is the question here related to that raised in "Ode on a Grecian Urn"?

John Keats (1795–1821)

On First Looking into Chapman's Homer (1816)

Much have I traveled in the realms of gold,
    And many goodly states and kingdoms seen;
    Round many western islands have I been
Which bards in fealty to Apollo hold.
Oft of one wide expanse had I been told   5
    That deep-browed Homer ruled as his demesne,
    Yet did I never breathe its pure serene
Till I heard Chapman speak out loud and bold.
Then felt I like some watcher of the skies
    When a new planet swims into his ken;   10
Or like stout Cortez when with eagle eyes
    He started at the Pacific—and all his men
Looked at each other with a wild surmise—
    Silent, upon a peak in Darien.

■ Contrast the reaction to this version of Homer to the scene on the urn. How does the poet assert the value of Chapman's translation of Homer?

■ What is the significance of the silence that the poet describes in the final line?

Amy Clampitt (1920–1994)

The Dakota (1983)

Grief for a generation—all
the lonely people
gone, the riffraff
out there now mainly pigeons—
steps from its limousine   5
and lights a taper
inside the brownstone catacomb
of the Dakota. Pick up
the wedding rice, take out
the face left over from   10
the funeral nobody came to,
bring flowers, leave them woven
with the lugubrious ironwork
of the Dakota. Grief

is original, but it   15
repeats itself: there is nothing
more original it can do.

■ How is the allegorical figure of Grief presented in this poem?
■ How can we resolve the apparent contradiction in the final lines of the poem?

Alfred, Lord Tennyson (1809–1892)

The Lady of Shalott (1842)

PART I

On either side the river lie
Long fields of barley and of rye,
That clothe the wold and meet the sky;
And through the field the road runs by
    To many-tower'd Camelot;   5
And up and down the people go,
Gazing where the lilies blow
Round an island there below,
    The island of Shalott.

Willows whiten, aspens quiver,   10
Little breezes dusk and shiver
Through' the wave that runs for ever
By the island in the river
    Flowing down to Camelot.
Four gray walls, and four gray towers,   15
Overlook a space of flowers,
And the silent isle imbowers
    The Lady of Shalott.

By the margin, willow-veiled,
Slide the heavy barges trailed   20
By slow horses; and unhailed
The shallop flitteth silken-sailed
    Skimming down to Camelot:
But who hath seen her wave her hand?
Or at the casement seen her stand?   25
Or is she known in all the land,
    The Lady of Shalott?

Only reapers, reaping early
In among the bearded barley,
Hear a song that echoes cheerly   30
From the river winding clearly,
     Down to towered Camelot:
And by the moon the reaper weary,
Piling sheaves in uplands airy,
Listening, whispers "'Tis the fairy   35
     Lady of Shalott."

     PART II
There she weaves by night and day
A magic web with colours gay.
She has heard a whisper say,
A curse is on her if she stay   40
     To look down to Camelot.
She knows not what the curse may be,
And so she weaveth steadily,
And little other care hath she,
     The Lady of Shalott.   45

And moving through a mirror clear
That hangs before her all the year,
Shadows of the world appear.
There she sees the highway near
     Winding down to Camelot: 50
There the river eddy whirls,
And there the surly village-churls,
And the red cloaks of market girls,
     Pass onward from Shalott.

Sometimes a troop of damsels glad,   55
An abbot on an ambling pad,
Sometimes a curly shepherd-lad,
Or long-haired page in crimson clad,
     Goes by to towered Camelot;
And sometimes through the mirror blue   60
The knights come riding two and two:
She hath no loyal knight and true,
     The Lady of Shalott.

But in her web she still delights
To weave the mirror's magic sights,   65
For often through the silent nights

A funeral, with plumes and lights
        And music, went to Camelot:
Or when the moon was overhead,
Came two young lovers lately wed;
"I am half sick of shadows," said
The Lady of Shalott.

                PART III
A bow-shot from her bower-eaves,
He rode between the barley-sheaves,
The sun came dazzling through the leaves,
And flamed upon the brazen greaves
        Of bold Sir Lancelot.
A red-cross knight for ever kneeled
To a lady in his shield,
That sparkled on the yellow field,
        Beside remote Shalott.

The gemmy bridle glittered free,
Like to some branch of stars we see
Hung in the golden Galaxy.
The bridle bells rang merrily
        As he rode down to Camelot:
And from his blazoned baldric slung
A mighty silver bugle hung,
And as he rode his armour rung,
        Beside remote Shalott.

All in the blue unclouded weather
Thick-jewelled shone the saddle-leather,
The helmet and the helmet-feather
Burned like one burning flame together,
        As he rode down to Camelot.
As often through the purple night,
Below the starry clusters bright,
Some bearded meteor, trailing light,
        Moves over still Shalott.

His broad clear brow in sunlight glowed;
On burnished hooves his war-horse trode;
From underneath his helmet flowed
His coal-black curls as on he rode,
        As he rode down to Camelot.

70

75

80

85

90

95

100

From the bank and from the river   105
He flashed into the crystal mirror,
"Tirra lirra," by the river
  Sang Sir Lancelot.

She left the web, she left the loom,
She made three paces through the room,   110
She saw the water-lily bloom,
She saw the helmet and the plume,
  She looked down to Camelot.
Out flew the web and floated wide;
The mirror cracked from side to side;   115
"The curse is come upon me!" cried
  The Lady of Shalott.

    PART IV
In the stormy east-wind straining,
The pale yellow woods were waning,
The broad stream in his banks complaining,   120
Heavily the low sky raining
  Over towered Camelot;
Down she came and found a boat
Beneath a willow left afloat,
And round about the prow she wrote   125
  The Lady of Shalott.

And down the river's dim expanse—
Like some bold seër in a trance,
Seeing all his own mischance—
With a glassy countenance   130
  Did she look to Camelot.
And at the closing of the day
She loosed the chain, and down she lay;
The broad stream bore her far away,
  The Lady of Shalott.   135

Lying, robed in snowy white
That loosely flew to left and right—
The leaves upon her falling light—
Thro' the noises of the night
  She floated down to Camelot: 140
And as the boat-head wound along
The willowy hills and fields among,

They heard her singing her last song,
    The Lady of Shalott.

Heard a carol, mournful, holy,   145
Chanted loudly, chanted lowly,
Till her blood was frozen slowly,
And her eyes were darkened wholly,
    Turned to towered Camelot.
For ere she reached upon the tide   150
The first house by the water-side,
Singing in her song she died,
    The Lady of Shalott.

Under tower and balcony,
By garden-wall and gallery,   155
A gleaming shape she floated by,
Dead-pale between the houses high,
    Silent into Camelot.
Out upon the wharfs they came,
Knight and burgher, lord and dame,   160
And round the prow they read her name,
    The Lady of Shalott.

Who is this? and what is here?
And in the lighted palace near
Died the sound of royal cheer,   165
And they crossed themselves for fear,
    All the knights at Camelot:
But Lancelot mused a little space;
He said, "She has a lovely face;
God in His mercy lend her grace,   170
    The Lady of Shalott."

- Camelot is the legendary home of King Arthur. Lancelot was among the noblest of Arthur's knights, but his relationship with Arthur was tempered by the fact that Lancelot loved Arthur's wife, Guinevere. Much of the story of Lancelot shows the man's great effort to replace his love for this woman with his love for God. How does this story relate to the poem?

- How does the structure of each stanza contribute to the impact of the poem? Compare that common structure to "She left the web, she left the loom, / She made three paces through the room." In what way, if any, is there some interruption here?

- What is the mirror in the poem?

William Butler Yeats (1865–1939)

Sailing to Byzantium (1927)

I

That is no country for old men. The young
In one another's arms, birds in the trees
—Those dying generations—at their song,
The salmon-falls, the mackerel-crowded seas,
Fish, flesh, or fowl, commend all summer long   5
Whatever is begotten, born, and dies.
Caught in that sensual music all neglect
Monuments of unaging intellect.

II

An aged man is but a paltry thing,
A tattered coat upon a stick, unless   10
Soul clap its hands and sing, and louder sing
For every tatter in its mortal dress,
Nor is there singing school but studying
Monuments of its own magnificence;
And therefore I have sailed the seas and come   15
To the holy city of Byzantium.

III

O sages standing in God's holy fire
As in the gold mosaic of a wall,
Come from the holy fire, perne in a gyre,
And be the singing-masters of my soul.   20
Consume my heart away; sick with desire
And fastened to a dying animal
It knows not what it is; and gather me
Into the artifice of eternity.

IV

Once out of nature I shall never take   25
My bodily form from any natural thing,
But such a form as Grecian goldsmiths make
Of hammered gold and gold enameling
To keep a drowsy Emperor awake;
Or set upon a golden bough to sing   30
To lords and ladies of Byzantium
Of what is past, or passing, or to come.

- What efforts does the poet describe to deny the fact that "That is no country for old men"?
- Look carefully at the grammatical construction of the final stanza. Explain the significance of the last line: "Of what is past, or passing, or to come." How does this relate to the first line of the stanza?

Czeslaw Milosz (1911–2004)

Orpheus and Eurydice (2004)

Standing on flagstones of the sidewalk at the entrance to Hades
Orpheus hunched in a gust of wind
That tore at his coat, rolled past in waves of fog,
Tossed the leaves of the trees. The headlights of cars
Flared and dimmed in each succeeding wave.   5

He stopped at the glass-paneled door, uncertain
Whether he was strong enough for that ultimate trial.

He remembered her words: "You are a good man."
He did not quite believe it. Lyric poets
Usually have—as he knew—cold hearts.   10
It is like a medical condition. Perfection in art
Is given in exchange for such an affliction.

Only her love warmed him, humanized him.
When he was with her, he thought differently about himself.
He could not fail her now, when she was dead.   15

He pushed open the door and found himself walking in a labyrinth,
Corridors, elevators. The livid light was not light but the dark of the earth.
Electronic dogs passed him noiselessly.
He descended many floors, a hundred, three hundred, down.

He was cold, aware that he was Nowhere.   20
Under thousands of frozen centuries,
On an ashy trace where generations had moldered,
In a kingdom that seemed to have no bottom and no end.

Thronging shadows surrounded him.
He recognized some of the faces.   25
He felt the rhythm of his blood.

He felt strongly his life with its guilt
And he was afraid to meet those to whom he had done harm.
But they had lost the ability to remember
And gave him only a glance, indifferent to all that.   30

For his defense he had a nine-stringed lyre.
He carried in it the music of the earth, against the abyss
That buries all of sound in silence.
He submitted the music, yielded
To the dictation of a song, listening with rapt attention,   35
Became, like his lyre, its instrument.

Thus he arrived at the palace of the rulers of that land.
Persephone, in her garden of withered pear and apple trees,
Black, with naked branches and verrucose twigs,
Listened from the funereal amethyst of her throne.   40

He sang the brightness of mornings and green rivers,
He sang of smoking water in the rose-colored daybreaks,
Of colors: cinnabar, carmine, burnt sienna, blue,
Of the delight of swimming in the sea under marble cliffs,
Of feasting on a terrace above the tumult of a fishing port,   45
Of the tastes of wine, olive oil, almonds, mustard, salt.
Of the flight of the swallow, the falcon,
Of a dignified flock of pelicans above a bay,
Of the scent of an armful of lilacs in summer rain,
Of his having composed his words always against death   50
And of having made no rhyme in praise of nothingness.

I don't know—said the goddess—whether you loved her or not.
Yet you have come here to rescue her.
She will be returned to you. But there are conditions:
You are not permitted to speak to her, or on the journey back   55
To turn your head, even once, to assure yourself that she is behind you.

And so Hermes brought forth Eurydice.
Her face no longer hers, utterly gray,
Her eyelids lowered beneath the shade of her lashes.
She stepped rigidly, directed by the hand   60
Of her guide. Orpheus wanted so much
To call her name, to wake her from that sleep.
But he refrained, for he had accepted the conditions.
And so they set out. He first, and then, not right away,
The slap of the god's sandals and the light patter   65

Of her feet fettered by her robe, as if by a shroud.
A steep climbing path phosphorized
Out of darkness like the walls of a tunnel.
He would stop and listen. But then
They stopped too, and the echo faded.   70
And when he began to walk the double tapping commenced again.
Sometimes it seemed closer, sometimes more distant.
Under his faith a doubt sprang up
And entwined him like cold bindweed.
Unable to weep, he wept at the loss   75
Of the human hope for the resurrection of the dead,
Because he was, now, like every other mortal.
His lyre was silent, yet he dreamed, defenseless.
He knew he must have faith and he could not have faith.
And so he would persist for a very long time,   80
Counting his steps in, a half-wakeful torpor.

Day was breaking. Shapes of rock loomed up
Under the luminous eye of the exit from underground.
It happened as he expected. He turned his head
And behind him on the path was no one.   85

Sun. And sky. And in the sky white clouds.
Only now everything cried to him: Eurydice!
How will I live without you, my consoling one!
But there was a fragrant scent of herbs, the low humming of bees,
And he fell asleep with his cheek on the sun-warmed earth.   90

■ Trace the different sensory images throughout the poem.
■ How does the poet modernize the descent into the underworld?
■ How does the narrator justify the turning of the head?

Rainer Maria Rilke (1875–1926)

Orpheus, Eurydice, Hermes (1908)

That was the deep uncanny mine of souls.
Like veins of silver ore, they silently
moved through its massive darkness. Blood welled up
among the roots, on its way to the world of men,

and in the dark it looked as hard as stone.   5
Nothing else was red.

There were cliffs there,
and forests made of mist. There were bridges
spanning the void, and that great gray blind lake
which hung above its distant bottom   10
like the sky on a rainy day above a landscape.
And through the gentle, unresisting meadows
one pale path unrolled like a strip of cotton.

Down this path they were coming.

In front, the slender man in the blue cloak—   15
mute, impatient, looking straight ahead.
In large, greedy, unchewed bites his walk
devoured the path; his hands hung at his sides,
tight and heavy, out of the failing folds,
no longer conscious of the delicate lyre   20
which had grown into his left arm, like a slip
of roses grafted onto an olive tree.
His senses felt as though they were split in two:
his sight would race ahead of him like a dog,
stop, come back, then rushing off again   25
would stand, impatient, at the path's next turn,—
but his hearing, like an odor, stayed behind.
Sometimes it seemed to him as though it reached
back to the footsteps of those other two
who were to follow him, up the long path home.   30
But then, once more, it was just his own steps' echo,
or the wind inside his cloak, that made the sound.
He said to himself, they had to be behind him;
said it aloud and heard it fade away.
They had to be behind him, but their steps   35
were ominously soft. If only he could
turn around, just once (but looking back
would ruin this entire work, so near
completion), then he could not fail to see them,
those other two, who followed him so softly: 40

The god of speed and distant messages,
a traveler's hood above his shining eyes,

his slender staff held out in front of him,
and little wings fluttering at his ankles;
and on his left arm, barely touching it: she.   45

A woman so loved that from one lyre there came
more lament than from all lamenting women;
that a whole world of lament arose, in which
all nature reappeared: forest and valley,
road and village, field and stream and animal;   50
and that around this lament-world, even as
around the other earth, a sun revolved
and a silent star-filled heaven, a lament-
heaven, with its own, disfigured stars—:
So greatly was she loved.   55

But now she walked beside the graceful god,
her steps constricted by the trailing graveclothes,
uncertain, gentle, and without impatience.
She was deep within herself, like a woman heavy
with child, and did not see the man in front   60
or the path ascending steeply into life.
Deep within herself. Being dead
filled her beyond fulfillment, Like a fruit
suffused with its own mystery and sweetness,
she was filled with her vast death, which was so new,   65
she could not understand that it had happened.

She had come into a new virginity
and was untouchable; her sex had closed
like a young flower at nightfall, and her hands
had grown so unused to marriage that the god's   70
infinitely gentle touch of guidance
hurt her, like an undesired kiss.

She was no longer that woman with blue eyes
who once had echoed through the poet's songs,
no longer the wide couch's scent and island,   75
and that man's property no longer.

She was already loosened like long hair,
poured out like fallen rain,
shared like a limitless supply.

She was already root,   80
And when, abruptly,
the god put out his hand to stop her, saying,
with sorrow in his voice: He has turned around—,
she could not understand, and softly answered
Who?   85

Far away,
dark before the shining exit-gates,
someone or other stood, whose features were
unrecognizable. He stood and saw
how, on the strip of road among the meadows,   90
with a mournful look, the god of messages
silently turned to follow the small figure
already walking back along the path,
her steps constricted by the trailing graveclothes,
uncertain, gentle, and without impatience   95

- How does the poet use perspective in telling this story? For example, how does point of view explain the final words, "without impatience"?
- Orpheus's lyre "had grown into his left arm, like a slip / of roses grafted onto an olive tree," and Eurydice "was already root." How are these images significant to the poem?

Jorie Graham (1950–)

Orpheus and Eurydice (1998)

Up ahead, I know, he felt it stirring in himself already, the glance, the
   darting thing in the pile of rocks,

already in him, there, shiny in the rubble, hissing Did you want to remain
   completely unharmed?—

the point-of-view darting in him, shiny head in the ash-heap,

hissing Once upon a time, and then Turn now darling give me that look,

that perfect shot, give me that place where I'm erased . . .   5

The thing, he must have wondered, could it be put to rest, there, in the
   glance,

could it lie back down into the dustyness, giving its outline up?

When we turn to them—limbs, fields, expanses of dust called meadow
and avenue—

will they be freed then to slip back in?

Because you see he could not be married to it anymore, this field with   10
minutes in it

called woman, its presence in him the thing called

future—could not be married to it anymore, expanse tugging his mind
out into it,

tugging the wanting-to-finish out.

What he dreamed of was this road (as he walked on it), this dustyness,
but without their steps on it, their prints, without
song—   15

What she dreamed, as she watched him turning with the bend in
the road (can you understand this?)—what she dreamed

was of disappearing into the seen

not of disappearing, lord, into the real—

And yes she could feel it in him already, up ahead, that wanting-to-turn-   20
and-cast-the-outline-over-her

by his glance,

sealing the edges down,

saying I know you from somewhere darling, don't I,
saying You're the kind of woman who etcetera—

(Now the cypress are swaying) (Now the lake in the distance) (Now the   25
view-from-above, the aerial attack of *do you remember?*)—

now the glance reaching her shoreline wanting only to be recalled, now
the glance reaching her shoreline wanting only to be taken in,

(somewhere the castle above the river)

(somewhere you holding this piece of paper)

(what will you do next?) (—feel it beginning?)

now she's raising her eyes, as if pulled from above,   30

now she's looking back into it, into the poison the beginning,

giving herself to it, looking back into the eyes,

feeling the dry soft grass beneath her feet for the first time now the mind

looking into that which sets the _____ in motion and seeing in there

a doorway open nothing on either side   35
(a slight wind now around them, three notes from up the hill)

through which morning creeps and the first true notes—

For they were deep in the earth and what is possible swiftly took hold.

- The poem focuses on the moment when Orpheus glances back at Eurydice. In what ways does the poet examine this single instance? How does the poet present perspective in the poem?
- How is it appropriate to describe this glance as both "hissing Once upon a time" and "what is possible"?

H. D. (1886–1961)

Eurydice (1916)

I
So you have swept me back,
I who have walked with the live souls
above the earth,
I who have slept among the live flowers
at last;   5

so for your arrogance
and your ruthlessness
I am swept back
where dead lichens drip
dead cinders upon moss of ash;   10

so for your arrogance
I am broken at last,
I who had lived unconscious,
who was almost forgot;

if you had let me wait   15
I had grown from listlessness into peace,
if you had let me rest with the dead,
I had forgot you
and the past.

                    II
Here only flame upon flame   20
and black among the red sparks,
streaks of black and light
grown colorless

why did you turn back,
that hell should be reinhabited   25
of myself thus
swept into nothingness?

why did you turn back,
why did you glance back?
why did you hesitate for that moment?   30
why did you bend your face
caught with the flame of the upper earth,
above my face?

what was it that crossed my face
with the light from yours   35
and your glance?
what was it you saw in my face?
the light of your own face,
the fire of your own presence?

what had my face to offer   40
but reflex of the earth,

hyacinth colour
caught from the raw fissure in the rock
where the light struck,
and the colour of azure crocuses,   45
and the bright surface of gold crocuses
and of the wind-flower,
swift in its veins as lightning
and as white.

III
Saffron from the fringe of the earth,   50
wild saffron that has bent
over the sharp edge of earth,
all the flowers that cut through the earth,
all, all the flowers are lost;

everything is lost,   55
everything is crossed with black,
black upon black
and worse than black,
this colourless light.

IV
Fringe upon fringe   60
of blue crocuses,
crocuses, walled against blue of themselves,
blue of that upper earth.
blue of the depth upon depth of flowers,
lost;   65
flowers, if I could have taken once my breath of them,
enough of them,
more than earth,
even than of the upper earth,
had passed with me   70
beneath the earth;

If I could have caught up from the earth,
the whole of the flowers of the earth,
if once I could have breathed into myself
the very golden crocuses   75
and the red
and the very golden hearts of the first saffron,
the whole of the golden mass,

the whole of the great fragrance,
I could have dared the loss.   80

                        V
So for your arrogance
and your ruthlessness
I have lost the earth
and the flowers of the earth,
and the live souls above the earth,   85
and you who passed across the light
and reached
ruthless;

you who have your own light,
who are to yourself a presence,   90
who need no presence;

yet for all your arrogance
and your glance,
I tell you this:

such loss is no loss,   95
such terror, such coils and strands and pitfalls
of blackness
such terror
is no loss;

hell is no worse than your earth   100
above the earth,
hell is no worse,
no, nor your flowers
nor your veins of light
nor your presence,   105
a loss;
my hell is no worse than yours
though you pass among the flowers and speak
with the spirits above the earth.

                        VI
Against the black   110
I have more fervour
than you in all the splendour of that place,
against the blackness

and the stark grey
I have more light;   115

and the flowers,
if I should tell you,
you would turn from your own fit paths
toward hell,
turn again and glance back   120
and I would sink into a place even more terrible than this

               VII
At least I have the flowers of myself,
and my thoughts, no god
can take that;
I have the fervour of myself for a presence   125
and my own spirit for light;

and my spirit with its loss
knows this;
though small against the black,
small against the formless rocks,   130
hell must break before I am lost;

before I am lost,
hell must open like a red rose
for the dead to pass.

■ How does the poem use colors to symbolize the perspective of Eurydice? What
  is her attitude toward Orpheus? Why does she say "I am broken at last"?
■ What are the different definitions of hell that the poem offers?

Adrienne Rich (1929–)

I Dream I'm the Death of Orpheus (1968)

I am walking rapidly through striations of light and dark thrown under an
    arcade.

I am a woman in the prime of life, with certain powers,
and those powers severely limited
by authorities whose faces I rarely see.

I am a woman in the prime of life   5
driving her dead poet in a black Rolls-Royce
through a landscape of twilight and thorns.
A woman with a certain mission
which if obeyed to the letter will leave her intact.
A woman with the nerves of a panther   10
a woman with contacts among Hell's Angels
a woman feeling the fullness of her powers
at the precise moment when she must not use them
a woman sworn to lucidity
who sees through the mayhem, the smoky fires   15
of those underground streets
her dead poet learning to walk backward against the wind
on the wrong side of the mirror.

- In what ways is the dead poet on the "wrong side of the mirror"?
- How does the narrator's voice contrast with that of "Death"? How does her
  "certain mission" relate to the Orpheus and Eurydice story?

Robert Pinsky (1940–)

Keyboard (2003)

A disembodied piano. The headphones allow
The one who touches the keys a solitude
Inside his music; shout and he may not turn:

Image of the soul that thinks to turn from the world.
Serpent-scaled Apollo skins the naïve musician   5
Alive: then Marsyas was sensitive enough

To feel the world in a touch. In Africa
The raiders with machetes to cut off hands
Might make the victim choose, "long sleeve or short."

Shahid Ali says it happened to Kashmiri weavers,   10
To kill the art. There are only so many stories.
The Loss. The Chosen. And even before The Journey,

The Turning: the fruit from any tree, the door
To any chamber, but this one—and the greedy soul,
Blade of the lathe. The Red Army smashed pianos,   15

But once they caught an S.S. man who could play.
They sat him at the piano and pulled their fingers
Across their throats to explain that they would kill him

When he stopped playing, and so for sixteen hours
They drank and raped while the Nazi fingered the keys.   20
The great Song of the World. When he collapsed

Sobbing at the instrument they stroked his head
And blew his brains out. Cold-blooded Orpheus turns
Again to his keyboard to improvise a plaint:

Her little cries of pleasure, blah-blah, the place   25
Behind her ear, lilacs in rain, a sus chord,
A phrase like a moonlit moth in tentative flight,

O lost Eurydice, blah-blah. His archaic head
Kept singing after the body was torn away:
Body, old long companion, supporter—the mist   30

Of oranges, la-la-la, the smell of almonds,
The taste of olives, her woollen skirt. The great old
Poet said, What should we wear for the reading—necktie?

Or better no necktie, turtleneck? The head
Afloat turns toward Apollo to sing and Apollo,   35
The cool-eyed rainbow lizard, plies the keys.

■ How does the poem justify its final symbol of Apollo, the god of music, as a
"cool-eyed rainbow lizard"? What relations does it draw between music and
death?

DRAMA

Mary Zimmerman (1960–)

Mary Zimmerman was born in Lincoln, Nebraska. Her parents were college
professors. She dreamed of becoming an actress and eventually chose a path
that would combine the theatrical and the academic. She received her BA, MA,

and PhD from Northwestern University, where she has taught since. In 1998, she received a MacArthur Fellowship, commonly referred to as a "genius grant," and in 2004 she received an Obie Award for her play *Metamorphoses*. Throughout her career she has been fascinated by fairy tales and myths and by the possibility of adapting them to a modern setting.

Metamorphoses (2002)

A NOTE ON THE STAGING

TIME AND SCENE: *The stage is entirely occupied by a square or rectangular pool of water, of varying depth, bordered on all four sides by a wooden deck approximately three feet wide. Hanging above the pool is a large crystal chandelier. Upstage, there is a large painting of the sky, above which gods and goddesses might appear. Also upstage is a tall double door, with steps leading to it from the deck. Ideally, there should be six entrances to the playing area: one on each of the deck's four corners, one through the doors, and one between the doors and sky. Additionally, there is a platform for the actors behind the sky, with its own entrance and exit. The set has sat well in both thrust and proscenium theaters, but it is essential that the audience look down at the playing space in such a way that the entire surface of the water is visible.*

All scenes take place in and around the pool, with shifts between stories, scenes, and settings indicated by nothing more than a shift in light or merely a shift in the actors' orientation or perhaps a music cue. Although there is a great deal of narration in the play, it should not be taken as a substitute for action or a superfluous description of action: The staging should rarely be a literal embodiment of the text; rather, it should provide images that amplify the text, lend it poetic resonance, or, even, sometimes contradict it.

CHARACTERS

WOMAN BY THE WATER
SCIENTIST
ZEUS
THREE LAUNDRESSES
MIDAS and HIS DAUGHTER
SILENUS
BACCHUS
CEYX
ALCYONE
HERMES
APHRODITE
ERYSICHTHON AND HIS MOTHER

ORPHEUS
EURYDICE
VERTUMNUS
POMONA
CINYRAS
MYRRHA
NURSEMAID
PHAETON
THERAPIST
EROS
PSYCHE
Q AND A
BAUCIS
PHILEMON

In addition, there are several important narrators, servants, sailors, other gods and goddesses, denizens of the Underworld, spirits, and so forth.

(A WOMAN *is kneeling by the side of the pool, looking at her own reflection. She looks up and addresses the audience.)*

WOMAN: Bodies, I have in mind, and how they can change to assume
    new shapes—I ask the help of the gods, who know the trick:
    change me, and let me glimpse the secret and speak,
    better than I know how, of the world's birthing,
    and the creation of all things, from the first to the very latest.   5

(The SCIENTIST *enters, wearing a lab coat and shaking a jar of water and sand. As she speaks she walks forward, sets the jar down, and the elements separate.)*

SCIENTIST: Before there was water and dry land, or even heaven and earth,
    nature was all the same: what we call "chaos,"
    with neither sun to shed its light, nor moon to wax
    and wane, nor earth hung in its atmosphere of air.
    If there was land and sea, there was no discernible shoreline,   10
    no way to walk on the one, or swim or sail in the other.
    There was neither reason nor order, until at last, a god sparked,
    *(*ZEUS *appears above the sky. He lights a cigarette.)*
    glowed, then shone like a beam of light to define earth and the heavens
    and separate water from hard ground.

WOMAN: Once these distinctions were made and matter began to behave,   15
    the sky displayed its array of stars in their constellations—
    (The lights of the chandelier begin to glow.)
    a twinkling template of order. The sea upon which they shone quick-
    ened with fish, and the woods and meadows with game,
    and the air with twittering birds. Each order of creature
    settling into itself.   20

ZEUS: A paradise, it would seem, except one thing was lacking: words.
WOMAN: And so
(MIDAS *enters through the doors.*)
WOMAN: man was born. He was born that he might
(MIDAS *comes forward and steps into the water.*)
WOMAN: talk.
ZEUS: Some say the god perfected the world,   25
    creating of his divine substance the race of humans;
SCIENTIST: others maintain that we come from the natural order of things.
(*Two* LAUNDRESSES *enter with a dreamy air, carrying a basket of laundry.*)
WOMAN: But one way or another, people came—erect, standing tall,
    with our faces set not to gaze down at the dirt beneath our feet,
    but upward toward the sky in pride or, perhaps, nostalgia.

MIDAS

(ZEUS *and the* WOMAN *depart. The* SCIENTIST *takes off her lab coat and joins the*
B. LAUNDRESSES. *The trio settles. Two of the women dip linens into the pool*
while the FIRST C. LAUNDRESS *lounges.*)
FIRST LAUNDRESS: What would you do with all the money in the world?
SECOND LAUNDRESS: What a question.
FIRST LAUNDRESS: I know what I'd do. (*Pause.*) Do you want to know what
    I'd do?
SECOND LAUNDRESS: No.   5
FIRST LAUNDRESS: I'd never do laundry again.
SECOND LAUNDRESS: That's it. That's the big dream?
FIRST LAUNDRESS: Among other things.
SECOND LAUNDRESS: Do you want to hear a little story?
FIRST LAUNDRESS: About rich people?   10
SECOND LAUNDRESS: Yes.
FIRST LAUNDRESS: Always!
SECOND LAUNDRESS: There was a certain king, named Midas. Net worth:
    one hundred billion.
(*As* MIDAS *begins to speak, his young* DAUGHTER *comes out, bouncing a red ball.*)
MIDAS: Now, I'm not a greedy man, but it is an accepted fact—a proven   15
    fact—that money is a good thing. A thing to be longed for, a *necessary*
    thing. And my god, I have a lot of it! It wasn't always this way with
    me—the boats, the houses by the sea, the summer cottages and the win-
    ter palaces, the exotic furnishings, the soft clothes, the food and—
(*To his* DAUGHTER.)
    Honey, can you stop that now? Be still now. Daddy's talking.   20
(*She stops, momentarily.* MIDAS *turns back to the audience.*)
    Excuse me. The outrageous food and two-hundred-year-old wine. No, it
    wasn't always like this. I came up from poor and I worked hard all my

life. Still do, mind you. My father was a minor manufacturer in (*he can't remember*) ... somewhere ... in ... somewhere. But I was born with a head for business and it's always been as though everything I touched has turned to gold. Not literally, of course—wouldn't that be something? Turned a profit, I meant. And— 25

(*Again to his* DAUGHTER.)

Sweetheart, Daddy asked you: Be still. Take it inside.

(*She retreats but shortly reenters, jumping rope.*)

You see this pool? It cost a pretty penny, I can tell you. But all it takes is hard work. Plain and simple. And those who haven't got it in them, well, what can anyone do? They just haven't got it. 30

(*To his* DAUGHTER.)

Be still! You're driving me nuts already!—

(*To the audience.*)

But you know, I never forget that I do it all for my (*he can't remember*) ... let's see, all for my ... it's all for the, uh ... for the, um ... the *family*. Yes, that's what it's all for. Family is the most important thing, isn't it? One's own family, I mean—not anyone else's for god's sake. When I get home at midnight seven days a week, in the moments before sleep, I realize that ... um ... I realize ... what was I—? Oh yes, that the family is what really matters. 35

(*A* SERVANT *enters.*)

SERVANT: Sir—? 40

MIDAS: Yes, what is it?

(SILENUS *enters, drunk, vine leaves in his hair, wearing a leopard-skin skirt and holding a wine bottle in a brown paper bag and some chips.*)

SERVANT: This man's been making trouble in the town. We believe he is a vagrant, sir, of the worst, most drunken kind.

SILENUS: Hello, King!

SERVANT: What should we do? 45

SILENUS: Nice place!

SERVANT: Execute him?

MIDAS: No need, no need. In my day, I've certainly been three sheets to the wind.

SILENUS: Three sheets to the—? What—? What the hell are you talking about, King? I'm all rummed up! 50

MIDAS: Why even last week at the feast for—

SILENUS: Let me tell you something. You know what?

MIDAS: No, what?

SILENUS: Let me tell you— 55

MIDAS: Yes?

SILENUS: Let me tell you something.

MIDAS: Yes, all right.

SILENUS: I've been all over the world.

(*He settles into the pool, beside* MIDAS.)

MIDAS: Oh, have you?   60

SILENUS: Yes. I—I'm lost now. But I have been—all over the place.

MIDAS: Mmm. How nice for you.

SILENUS: You listening? Well, let me tell you there is a country beyond this
  one, where ... uh ...

MIDAS: How very fascinating. Well, if you will excuse me—   65

SILENUS: No., Listen. I strayed from the crowd, and I'm lost now, but there
  is a country—

MIDAS: Asia?

SILENUS: Further.

MIDAS: Africa?   70

SILENUS: No. Further. Over the ocean. I've been there.

MIDAS: Oh?

SILENUS: King, I tell ya, it's like a dream, a dream. I. Am. Telling. You.
  That in this place the people ... they see each other. And in this
  place they live without desire of any kind and so time? There is no   75
  time—just the blue sky above and the pretty moon at night and they
  got the meadows under their feet with the yellow flowers and—

MIDAS: Well, thank you, this has been most entertaining, but—

SILENUS: And the people live forever.

MIDAS: What?   80

(MIDAS'S DAUGHTER *begins to skip rope.*)

SILENUS: They live forever. They never die.

MIDAS: What is it, some herb they have, some ...

SILENUS: Oh, no. No no no.

MIDAS: Something in the air? Something we could distill? I have shipping
  fleets you know to bring it—   85

SILENUS: No, no. It's—

MIDAS: Yes?

SILENUS: Is that your daughter?

MIDAS: What? Yes. (*To her.*) Go on, get out of here! Be still for once in
  your life! (*To him.*) Go on, go on.   90

(*She retreats for good.*)

SILENUS: You're rich indeed.

MIDAS: Go on. Is it an animal? Even better if it's an animal, we could breed them
  here. My god, the millions! Don't worry, young man, you'll get your cut—

SILENUS: No. Nope. No.

MIDAS: It's not an animal? What is it? What is this secret to eternal life?   95

SILENUS (*pointing to his own head*): It's here.

MIDAS: Some formula, you have it? The formula?

SILENUS: No, no. It's here *(pointing to* MIDAS*'s head)*.

MIDAS: What?

SILENUS: And here *(pointing to* MIDAS*'s heart)*.   100

MIDAS: Oh, that. The "inner life." What uselessness. All right then. Off you
go. You may sleep in the cabana.

SILENUS: Thank you. *(He falls drunkenly, facedown in the water.)*

MIDAS: Oh for god's sake, turn him over. Someone turn him over before he
drowns.   105

(The SERVANT, *with distaste, goes into the pool and turns* SILENUS *over with his
foot.)*

SECOND LAUNDRESS: Night fell, but when the rosy-fingered dawn came back
again—

BACCHUS *(entering drunkenly above, behind the sky)*: Midas?

MIDAS: Good lord! Who's there?

BACCHUS: It's Bacchus. I hear you have a follower of mine.   110

MIDAS: A follower?

BACCHUS: Yes, Silenus. He wandered from our group as we passed close to
town and I hear he is with you.

MIDAS: Oh, the fellow in the cabana? Yes, take him, he's all yours.

*(*SILENUS *rises and exits.)*

BACCHUS *(lachrymose)*: I'm grateful that you didn't turn him away, Midas,   115
that you took care of him and saw that he didn't drown in his condition. And I'd like to present you with a gift.

MIDAS: A gift?

BACCHUS: Some ability. A minor miracle. Something to do at parties?

MIDAS: Anything?   120

*(*SILENUS *appears above the clouds with* BACCHUS.*)*

BACCHUS: Anything at all.

MIDAS: You promise?

BACCHUS: Yes, of course.

MIDAS: Then grant me that everything I touch, everything I put my hand
to, will turn to solid gold.   125

(Long pause.)

BACCHUS: That's a really, really bad idea.

MIDAS: What do you mean it's a bad idea? It's a brilliant idea!

BACCHUS: Think about it, Midas.

MIDAS: No, you think about it! You gave your oath. We had a deal for god's
sake. Now follow through!   130

BACCHUS: All right then.

*(*BACCHUS *and* SILENUS *exit.)*

SECOND LAUNDRESS: And from that moment on, everything he touched
turned to solid gold.

MIDAS: Wait a minute, wait a minute, let me think where to begin...

(MIDAS *reaches into the water, picks up a large seashell. It is gold. He becomes giddy. He places the shell on his chair and then begins to walk around the deck. From now on, each of his steps is accompanied by the ring of little finger cymbals, perhaps played by one of the* LAUNDRESSES.)

SECOND LAUNDRESS: He went out walking and with every step, the gravel under his feet turned to golden nuggets. Delighted, he put his hand to branches of trees and to flowers and he had gold branches and flowers. All day long he experimented, almost insane with happiness, that the whole of the world could become his personal treasure. Late at night, he stumbled back into the courtyard, laden with precious gold.   140

MIDAS'S DAUGHTER (*entering and running toward him*): Papa!

MIDAS: NO!

(*It's too late. She jumps into his arms and turns to gold.* BACCHUS *re-enters.*)

Take it away. (*Pause.*) Bacchus, (*pause*) take it away.

BACCHUS: I can't.

MIDAS: Yes you can. You must. Take it away now.   145

BACCHUS: I'm sorry.

MIDAS: No, take it away, now!

BACCHUS: There is one way, Midas.

MIDAS: What? What is it?

BACCHUS: Walk as far as the ends of the earth. Look for a pool of water   150
that reflects the stars at night. Wash your hands in it and there is a
chance that everything will be restored.

(MIDAS *slowly walks away, his steps accompanied by the ringing cymbals. He reaches behind the desk and picks up his* DAUGHTER's *jump-rope. It has turned to gold.*)

SECOND LAUNDRESS: Was that too sad for you?

THIRD LAUNDRESS: A little.   155

SECOND LAUNDRESS: All right then, here's another.

ALCYONE AND CEYX

(*Music. Transition. The* SECOND LAUNDRESS *becomes the* NARRATOR *of the following story.* ALCYONE *and* CEYX *enter variously.*)

NARRATOR: There once was a king named Ceyx who had as his queen Alcyone, daughter of Aeolus, master of the winds. These two adored each other and lived in a monotony of happiness. But nothing in this world is safe.

ALCYONE: It isn't true.   5

CEYX: It is.

NARRATOR: One day Alcyone had heard that Ceyx had ordered his ship to be made ready for a sea voyage, to visit a far-off oracle.

ALCYONE: How can you leave me alone? I'll pine in your absence.
Overland, it's a long and arduous trip, but I'd still prefer that   10

to a voyage by sea—which I fear, for my father's winds are wild and
    savage.
You think as his son-in-law you may get some special treatment.
    Not so!
Once they've escaped my father's cave, those winds are wild
and beyond anyone's control. As a girl I watched them come home
exhausted and spent, and I learned to fear them then.   15
Now I am petrified, surely—
NARRATOR: she said,
ALCYONE: if you die my life is over
    and I shall be cursed with every reluctant breath I draw.
CEYX: My love, I hate to choose between my journey and you
    but how can I live this way? Stranded on shore, afraid,   20
    domesticated, diminished, a kind of lap dog?
ALCYONE: Take me with you at least, and we'll meet the storms together,
    which I fear much less than to be left a widow.
CEYX: In two months' time, I'll be back.
ALCYONE: No. I fear you won't. I know you won't.   25
CEYX: In two months' time. For that short time, you can be brave
    and endure the trial of waiting.
NARRATOR: She was hardly consoled, but she saw she could not hold out any
    longer
    in the face of his resolve. She allowed herself to be soothed
    and consented to his going.   30
    (Music begins and continues through the next long sequence. SAILORS *enter
        with oars.)*
    There were no more details left to be checked,
    no last-minute changes to make, and the men, arranged on their
        benches,
    were ready to row and go. He boarded and gave the sign.
    And then he turned to wave at her.
    She waved at him while the ribbon of black water widened between   35
        the ship
    and shore. She gazed at him until he was no longer distinguishable
    but still she could see the ship. And she narrowed her eyes to the horizon
    and watched it as it receded to a smaller and smaller object. And then
    the whole hull was gone, and only the sails remained,
    and then they, too, disappeared.   40
    She gazed still at the empty and desolate blue
    and then went to her empty bedroom to lie on the huge
    and vacant bed and give herself over to weeping.
CEYX: The vessel cleared the harbor and caught the freshening wind,
    which set the rigging to singing and slapping against the spars.   45

I ordered the rowers to ship their oars and the sailors
to set the yards and make sail. Our ship ran before the wind.
We made satisfactory progress all that day and had reached
a point of no return, with as much blue water astern
as remained ahead.   50
NARRATOR: But as the sun was sinking in the West, the water,
    everywhere blue until now, began to be flecked
    with the whitecapped waves sailors dislike.
    (*Enter* POSEIDON *and his* HENCHMAN.)
    The weather was worse with every moment
    for the winds were on the loose.   55
(*The storm begins.* POSEIDON *and his* HENCHMAN *attack* CEYX, *the boat, the*
    SAILORS.)
CEYX: Reef the sails! Bail the water! Secure the spars!
NARRATOR: But Poseidon and his Henchman had arrived. The rest
    was one enormous green catastrophe.
(*The storm escalates. The chandelier flashes as though it were lightning or as if it
    were a lamp shorting out. The men wrestle in the pool.*)
CEYX: He thinks in an oddly abstracted way that the waves are lions
    crazed with hunters' wounds, or that the ship   60
    is a besieged town attacked by a horde of madmen.
HENCHMAN AND CEYX: One would think that the heavens were crazed with
        lust
CEYX: to join the turbulent sea
HENCHMAN AND CEYX: which returned their bizarre passion
    and tried to rise up and embrace the air.   65
NARRATOR: The men have lost their belief in their captain, their courage,
        their nautical skill, and even their will to live as they wait for the
        end. One weeps
    and groans aloud. Another, no braver, is silent, dumbstruck.
    One calls on the gods for mercy. Another curses his fate.
    And one says one word,   70
CEYX: Alcyone,
NARRATOR: again and again,
CEYX: Alcyone, my treasure, Alcyone.
NARRATOR: And this is the end of the world.
(APHRODITE *enters above the sky.*)
CEYX: O gods, hear my modest prayer: that my body may wash ashore at her   75
    feet where she may with gentle hands prepare it to be buried.
(CEYX *sinks below the water.*)
NARRATOR: Nothing left but the slow parade led by Hermes to the Under-
        world.
(*Music ends. Everyone but* ALCYONE *exits.* ALCYONE *stirs in her sleep and begins*

to count, covering her eyes, like a child who counts to a certain number, hoping that when she reaches it her wish will be granted.)

ALCYONE: One two three four, fifteen sixteen seventeen eighteen, ninety-eight ninety-nine, one hundred . . .   80

(She uncovers her eyes and looks toward the horizon, then covers her eyes and begins again. APHRODITE *enters and watches from the sky. She summons* IRIS *to watch.)*

One two three four, fifteen sixteen seventeen eighteen, ninety-eight ninety-nine, one hundred . . .

(She uncovers her eyes and looks toward the horizon. She then begins again and continues under the following lines.)

APHRODITE: Look at her, Iris, she's moved her vigil down to the shore and now she's sleeping there.

ALCYONE: . . . ninety-eight, ninety-nine, one hundred. Ceyx? Come home. I'm   85
nearer now, I'm sleeping on the shore. It's not so far until you see me.

(She begins to count again, quietly.)

APHRODITE: This can't go on forever. Go to the house of Sleep and ask him to arrange a nighttime visitation, a dream that might show our Alcyone the sorry truth.

*(*IRIS *departs.* ALCYONE *falls asleep in the shallow waters of the pool. A* SECOND NARRATOR *appears. As he speaks,* SLEEP *enters, wrapped in a black velvet blanket, with eyeshades.* APHRODITE *slowly drops white letter Z's from the sky.)*

SECOND NARRATOR: Far off in remotest Campania, beyond where the Cim-   90
merians live in their gloomy caves, is a deeper and even darker grotto, the home of Sleep. In this place the sun never can, even at midday, penetrate with the faintest beams. In that cloudy twilight no rooster dares disturb the silence with his rude crowing, no dog or nervous goose gives voice to challenge the passing   95
stranger. Not even branches sigh in occasional passing breezes, but an almost total silence fills the air.

*(*SLEEP *snores.* IRIS *creeps in, wearing an illuminated rainbow-colored skirt and carrying an alarm clock.)*

At the heart of an almost painted stillness, in a huge, darkened chamber, the god himself relaxes, drifting in languor. Around him the fragments of ill-assorted   100
dreams hover over the floor in grand profusion like leaves the trees have let go to float through the currents of air and fall in their gorgeous billows below.

IRIS: Hello?

SECOND NARRATOR: Into this strange and breathless place, Iris the rainbow   105
intrudes.

IRIS: O Somnolent One? Somnolent One? Wake up!

SLEEP: Wha—?

IRIS: Mildest of all the gods, soother of souls, and healer of wearied and
  pain-wracked bodies and minds—   110

SLEEP: Iris! Let me rest a moment.

(He sleeps a bit. Wakes up.)
  Iris! What do you want?

IRIS: Devise, if you can, some form to resemble King Ceyx
  and send it down in a dream to his wife, the Queen Alcyone.
  Let her know the news of the wreck of his ship and the death   115
  of the husband she loves so well. Sleep *(she yawns)* do this for us—
  can you?
  *(She yawns and falls asleep with him for a moment, but luckily her alarm
  goes off, startling them both. She runs away.)*
  Farewell!

SLEEP *(calling.)*: Morpheus! Mor-phe-us! Come and change your shape to
  that of King Ceyx. Go to his wife and tell her *(yawning)*   120
  . . . tell her he is dead.
  (MORPHEUS enters as CEYX. SLEEP sees him.)
  That's good. That's very good. Now go!

(SLEEP stumbles away. CEYX, shrouded, approaches ALCYONE. She stirs.)

ALCYONE: Sir, you seem like a seafaring man, can you tell me,
  Where is my husband, Ceyx? Have you seen him on the sea? When is
  he coming home? His ship is strong and unmistakable.   125
  Have you seen him? *(Pause.)* Sir?

CEYX *(dropping his shroud)*:
  Do you not know me? Has death undone me so?

ALCYONE: No!

CEYX: Look at me, I charge you—look at me.

ALCYONE: No! I won't. I won't!   130

CEYX: Look at me, and know your husband's ghost.
  Your prayers have done no good,
  for I am gone, beyond all help or hope forever.

ALCYONE: Go away!

CEYX: I am not some bearer of tales, but the man himself   135
  to whom it happened. Look at me, my little bird.

ALCYONE: I told you. I knew it would happen and I begged you
  not to go. I knew the day you sailed I had lost you forever.
  The ship, my hopes, and my life grew smaller
  all at the same time. You should have allowed me to come—   140

CEYX: Little bird—

ALCYONE: This is no good, no good—that I should be living
  and you be elsewhere or nowhere? I'm drowning now

in the air, I'm wrecked here on the land
where the currents are just as cold and cruel.   145
CEYX: Get up from your bed and put on your mourning clothes.
(*He begins to go.*)
ALCYONE: Wait for me! Come back! Where are you going?
Wait and I'll go with you
as wives are supposed to go with their husbands.
(*But he is gone.*)
(*Calling*) Lucina! Lucina! Give me your lantern.   150
(*LUCINA enters and gives her lantern to ALCYONE, who searches the pool
with it, stumbling and frantic.*)
Ceyx! Come back! Where are you?
Come back! He was here, Where is he? Where is he?
LUCINA: All that night she searched along the shore for her drowned,
dreamed husband. But she found nothing, not even footprints,only
wave after wave of black water. When morning came   155
(*Music begins.*)
she narrowed her eyes to the horizon, and remembered
how she had looked on that other day.
(*HERMES enters carrying CEYX and places him in the water.*)
                                                 She remembered
his last kiss, the way he turned to the ship, could not bear it,
and turned again to her.
ALCYONE: What is that out there? Oh, it is a man. Alas, poor sailor, for   160
your wife and . . .
(*She sees that it is CEYX. Music ends.*)
LUCINA: The gods are not altogether unkind. Some prayers are answered.
ALCYONE: Ceyx, is this how you return to me?
LUCINA: She began to run to him; but as she ran, crying, a strange thing
happened.   165
(*ALCYONE moves slowly toward CEYX, transforming. The sound of waves and sea-
birds crying comes up.*)
By the time she reached him, she was a bird.
She tried to kiss him with her bill, and by some trick
of the ocean's heaving, it seemed that his head reached up to hers
in response. You ask, How could he have felt her kiss?
APHRODITE: But better ask, How could the gods not have felt it?   170
Seen this, and not had compassion?
LUCINA: For the dead body was changing, restored to life,
and renewed as another seabird.
Together they still fly, just over the water's surface,
and mate and rear their young, and for seven days each winter   175

Alcyone broods on her nest that floats on the gentled water—
for Aeolus, her father, then keeps the winds short reined
and every year gives seven days of calm upon the ocean—
the days we call the halcyon days.

ERYSICHTHON

(*Music. Transition. Singers come out, and, as they mop or dry the deck, they sing the following song.*)

   Would, oh would, I were a kingfisher
   That flies with the halcyons
   Along the breaking waves, with a fearless heart,
   That noble bird, that holy bird,
   The deep blue of the ocean.   5
   (*A new* NARRATOR *arrives.*)

NARRATOR: When you see a miracle like that, how can you deny the existence of the gods? Believe it or not, there are some that do. There was a man called Erysichthon, who scorned the gods and declined to sacrifice on their altars or do them honor. Nothing was sacred to him—he only looked for the usefulness of things. One day he found himself in a   10
grove sacred to Ceres.

ERYSICHTHON: Cut it down.

NARRATOR: Sir, that tree is centuries old—

ERYSICHTHON: We need the wood, cut it down.

NARRATOR: Sir, this is a sacred grove; and this tree is beloved by Ceres,   15
(CERES *enters above the sky and watches.*)

ERYSICHTHON: It's only a tree that the goddess likes, but say it was the goddess herself, I'd cut it down just the same.

NARRATOR: Sir, please—

ERYSICHTHON (*shoving him away*): Get off me, you pious son of a bitch!

NARRATOR: And he tore the tree down.   20
(*Enormous sound of the tree falling.*)

SPIRIT OF THE TREE (*offstage*): Sir.

ERYSICHTHON: Who's that?

SPIRIT OF THE TREE: I am the tree itself speaking. My pangs of death are eased by one thing.

ERYSICHTHON: And what might that be?   25

SPIRIT OF THE TREE: That you will never get away with this.

ERYSICHTHON: Oh, now I'm really frightened.

(*He laughs and goes home to sleep.*)

NARRATOR: But the goddess Ceres heard the cry of her tree, and her mind immediately began to move upon torments that she might inflict.

CERES: Oread!   30

OREAD (*a handmaid, entering.*): Yes?

CERES: There is a place in far-off Scythia. Nothing grows there, no wheat, no grass, no trees. There you will find, huddling together, Cold, Fear, and gaunt Hunger. Tell Hunger I command her to visit this brute and establish a home for herself in his belly. I give him to her as a toy.   35

OREAD: I will.

CERES: I would go myself, but it is forbidden for Hunger and me ever to meet.

(OREAD *exits.*)

NARRATOR: Oread flew off to the Caucasus, a bleak and nightmarish region. There, in a field of stones, crouched Hunger,   40

(HUNGER *crawls up onto the deck.*)

pulling from between the rocks, with her teeth and filthy fingernails, some tiny bits of moss. Her hair hung down in lank and matted locks. Her eyes were sunken and circled, her lips were slack and cracked. The vaults of her ribs stuck out, as did every bone in her body. One could count the knobs of her spine.   45

OREAD (*entering*): Hunger?

(HUNGER *turns to face her, and* OREAD *is struck with sudden, terrible hunger pains.*)

OREAD: Ceres commands—or rather permits you—

HUNGER: Yes?

OREAD (*backing up, starving, as* HUNGER *crawls toward her*): To go to—

HUNGER: Yes?   50

OREAD: To go to Erysichthon and . . . and never to leave him until he is finished.
(*Runs off.*)

HUNGER: Gladly.

NARRATOR: Hunger crawled through the air to the house of the victim. As she flew overhead, fields withered and men starved. The birds scattered from her path, too weak to fly. It is night when she arrives at Erysichthon's home and curdles through the halls until she finds him sleeping in his room. She wraps cadaverous arms around him in an embrace as strong as love, but quite the opposite of love. She breathes her spirit into his spirit. And he begins to dream.   60

ERYSICHTHON (*with* HUNGER *clinging to his back*): Pastries, cheese, grapes . . .

NARRATOR: He wakes.

ERYSICHTHON: Bring me something to eat! Anything! I'm starving!

(ERYSICHTHON *dashes into the pool, attempting to consume it.* HUNGER *clings to his back.*)

NARRATOR: But he can't wait to be served. He begins to eat everything in sight: meal after meal after meal after meal. But he can't shake this hunger.   65

ERYSICHTHON: More! I need more! More to eat!

NARRATOR: Baked shrimp and marshmallows, salami and ice cream, liver and doughnuts, everything in every possible combination. Even as he eats he is planning other menus and complaining of his hunger. As the ocean ingests the water from the rivers of the world but still is never filled and remains thirsty and guzzles more and more forever, so he calls out for more. 70

ERYSICHTHON: It isn't enough. It isn't enough!

NARRATOR: His gorging empties the larder and storerooms, the warehouses and barns of the city. His hunger is unabated. What is left to sell? 75

ERYSICHTHON: Mother?

MOTHER (*entering*): My son?

ERYSICHTHON: Come with me.

(ERYSICHTHON'S MOTHER, *delighted, goes to fetch her purse and hat. The* BUYER *enters with an oar, eating an apple.*)

NARRATOR: Now this part is true, though you may not believe it: His hunger led him to sell his poor, his darling mother. 80

BUYER: She doesn't look so strong.

ERYSICHTHON: She is, she is. We've had her forever.

BUYER: I can't give you much . . .

ERYSICHTHON: Just give—just whatever—just give it to me— 85

BUYER: All right then.

(*Tosses him a coin.*)

NARRATOR: With the few coins he received, he ran home to eat. Riding in a boat behind her new master, Erysichthon's mother leaned over the hull and prayed to someone she once knew.

MOTHER: Poseidon, if you remember me, come and save me now. 90

(POSEIDON *swims toward* ERYSICHTHON'S MOTHER.)

NARRATOR: From the briny deep, Poseidon heard her prayer, pulled her into the water, and changed her back into the little girl who used to play along his shores. The salty water licked the years away, until she emerged: the one who gave him praise in childhood, shouting as she ran among the waves. This is the kind of sweet, unbidden praise the gods adore and do not forget. 95

(*The* BUYER *notices the* MOTHER *is gone and sees the little girl on shore.*)

BUYER: Hey! Hey you, little girl! Listen up! Where is the old woman who was here a moment ago? Did she dive overboard and swim up to shore?

MOTHER (*now a child*): Sir, I swear by the god of the sea that no one except myself has come to this shore. I swear it! 100

NARRATOR: To this day, at every hour, somewhere in the world, you can still catch a glimpse of that child playing by the shore.

(*The* MOTHER *exits with* POSEIDON, *and the* BUYER *leaves as well.*)

But let us return to our king. It was not enough. The money she earned for him was not enough for his needs. The emptiness within him was unappeasable. You've seen such men yourself, I'm sure. 105

ERYSICHTHON: I need more! I must have more!
NARRATOR: The godless are always hungry.
ERYSICHTHON: MORE!
NARRATOR: Always yelling at waitresses.
ERYSICHTHON: I WANT MORE!   110
NARRATOR: There can be only one end to such a man.
(CERES *comes toward* ERYSICHTHON *with a silver tray holding a plate, a large fork and knife, and a rosebud in a vase. She sets it down on the deck.*)
NARRATOR: He will destroy himself.
(ERYSICHTHON *goes to the tray, takes off his shoe, places his own foot on the plate, and raises the knife and fork.*)
CERES: Bon appétit.

ORPHEUS AND EURYDICE
(*Music. Transition. We may see glimpses of various myths:* PANDORA *and her box,* ATALANTA *and the golden apple.*)
NARRATOR: You've heard of Orpheus, the greatest musician of all time, and his bride Eurydice? His was the unluckiest of wedding days.
(*The sound of wedding bells. The chandelier is fully illuminated.* ORPHEUS *and* EURYDICE *move toward each other with* ATTENDANTS*. But, as she approaches,* EURYDICE *steps on a snake. We hear a loud hissing, and the joyful wedding bells become funereal. The scene changes to one of mourning, as the dead* EURYDICE *is carried away by* HERMES*. A new* NARRATOR *enters with a music stand and steps into the pool.*)
NARRATOR ONE: Orpheus and Eurydice: Number One: Ovid, A.D. 8.
(*As he speaks, the Underworld materializes around him. We see* PERSEPHONE *and* HADES; THE FATES, *snipping their threads;* A SISYPHEAN CHARACTER; *and various other* DENIZENS *of the Underworld.*)
Orpheus, the widower bridegroom, mourned her
in the upper world but his grief was limitless.   5
Inconsolable, desperate, he left the warmth
and sweetness of our air, he dared to descend
to the River Styx and crossed it to the Underworld.
(*Music begins.*)
Through that dim domain, with all
its shimmering, buried ghosts, he passed,   10
until he arrived at its melancholy heart
and found its king, lying with Persephone.
He knelt before them, drowning in his grief.
(ORPHEUS *kneels in a shower of water pouring down from above.*)
ORPHEUS: I don't know what power love has down here,
but I have heard that he has some, for he brought you two together.   15
If that is true—that passion moved you once—then listen to me:
I've tried to master this grief and I can't.

I understand we all come here in the end.
My bride Eurydice will soon enough be your citizen
in the ripeness of her years. I am asking for a loan,   20
not a gift. If you deny me, one thing is certain:
I want you to keep me here as well.
(*The shower of water and the music end.*)

NARRATOR ONE: As Orpheus spoke, the pale phantoms began to weep. Tantalus was no longer thirsty, and Sisyphus sat on his rock to listen.

HADES: Orpheus, turn around. (*Calling*) Eurydice.   25
(EURYDICE *enters.*)

Your song has moved us, Orpheus, and you may have her on one condition. As you ascend and leave this place, she will not walk beside you;
but she will be following. You must not, until you pass our gates, turn
around to look at her. If you look at her before you reach the sunlight,
she is ours. Forever.   30

ORPHEUS: I understand.

HADES: Hermes will accompany you. Remember, hesitation or doubt and
our gift must be returned. A simple enough condition?

NARRATOR ONE: It ought to have been. The singer led the way,
ascending the sloping path through the murk.   35
(ORPHEUS *walks on the deck, followed at a little distance by* EURYDICE, *who
is limping from the snake bite.* HERMES *follows her.*)
A long way they traveled, almost all the way.
But you know what happened: Concerned for her,
or not quite believing that it wasn't a cruel delusion,
a dream, or a mirage, he turned.
(ORPHEUS *turns around; as he does,* HERMES *lifts* EURYDICE *and pulls her away
as she and* ORPHEUS *reach for each other.*)

EURYDICE: Farewell.   40

NARRATOR ONE: That was his last sight of her. But he saw it again and again.
(ORPHEUS, EURYDICE, *and* HERMES *reassemble in their original positions. They
walk forward, Orpheus turns around; as he does,* HERMES *lifts* EURYDICE
and pulls her away as she and ORPHEUS *reach for each other.*)

EURYDICE: Farewell.

NARRATOR ONE: Is this story a story of love and how it always goes away?
(ORPHEUS, EURYDICE, *and* HERMES *continue to repeat their action. Each time,*
EURYDICE *is a little closer to* ORPHEUS *when he turns.*)

EURYDICE: Farewell.

NARRATOR ONE: Is this a story of how time can move only in one direction?   45
(*The action repeats.*)

EURYDICE: Farewell.

(*The action repeats.*)

NARRATOR ONE: Is this story a story of an artist, and the loss that comes
from sudden self-consciousness or impatience?

(The action repeats.)

EURYDICE: Farewell.

*(*NARRATOR ONE *exits as* NARRATOR TWO *enters and places her music stand in the water. During the following,* ORPHEUS, EURYDICE, *and* HERMES *walk slowly and continually around the periphery of the pool.)*

NARRATOR TWO: Orpheus and Eurydice: Number Two. Rainer Maria Rilke. 50
   A.D. 1908.

ORPHEUS: He said to himself, they had to be behind him;
   said it aloud and heard it fade away.
   They had to be behind him, but their steps
   were ominously soft. If only he could   55
   turn around, just once.

NARRATOR TWO: But looking back would ruin this entire work, so near
   completion.

ORPHEUS: Then he could not fail to see them,
   those other two, who followed him so softly: 60

HERMES: The god of speed and distant messages,
   a golden crown above his shining eyes,
   his slender staff held out in front of him,
   and little wings fluttering at his ankles;
   and on his left arm, barely touching it: *she.*   65

NARRATOR TWO: A woman so loved that from one lyre there came
   more lament than from all lamenting women;
   that a whole world of lament arose, in which
   all nature reappeared: forest and valley,
   road and village, field and stream and animal;   70
   and that around this lament-world, even as
   around the other earth, a sun revolved
   and a silent star-filled heaven, a lament-
   heaven, with its own disfigured stars—:
   So greatly was she loved.   75

EURYDICE: But now she walked behind the graceful god,
   her steps constricted by the trailing graveclothes,

NARRATOR TWO: uncertain, gentle, and without impatience.

EURYDICE: She was deep within herself, like a woman heavy
   with child, and did not see the man in front   80
   or the path ascending steeply into life.
   Deep within herself. Being dead
   filled her beyond fulfillment. Like a fruit
   suffused with its own mystery and sweetness,
   she was filled with her vast death, which was so new,   85
   she could not understand that it had happened.

HERMES: She had come into a new virginity
   and was untouchable; her sex had closed

like a young flower at nightfall, and her hands
had grown so unused to things that the god's 90
infinitely gentle touch of guidance
hurt her, like an undesired kiss.

NARRATOR TWO: She was no longer that woman with brown eyes
who once had echoed through the poet's songs,
no longer the wide couch's scent and island, 95
and that man's property no longer.

EURYDICE: She was already loosened like long hair,
poured out like fallen rain,
shared like a limitless supply.

(ORPHEUS *slowly turns to look at her*.)

NARRATOR TWO: And when, abruptly, 100
the god put out his hand to stop her, saying,
with sorrow in his voice:

HERMES: He has turned around—

NARRATOR TWO: she could not understand, and softly answered,

EURYDICE: Who? 105

(*She looks at* HERMES, *who then looks at* ORPHEUS. *Then she looks at*
ORPHEUS.)

Far away,
dark before the shining exit-gates,
someone or other stood, whose features were
unrecognizable.

(*She looks back to* HERMES, *and then slowly turns and walks away, back to the
Underworld*.)

ORPHEUS: He stood and saw how, on the strip of road among the meadows,
with a mournful look, the god of messages 110
silently turned to follow the small figure
already walking back along the path,
her steps constricted by the trailing graveclothes,

NARRATOR TWO: uncertain, gentle, and without impatience.

**POMONA AND VERTUMNUS
(WITH NARCISSUS INTERLUDE)**

(*Music. Everyone leaves the stage. In the silence that follows, two performers
enter. One begins to mop the deck; the other [*NARCISSUS*] moves to strike the
music stand from the water. But as he starts to exit, he catches sight of his reflection in the pool. It arrests him. He leans down to it. He becomes still.
The other performer finishes mopping and notices the stillness of her companion. She tries to move him, but he is paralyzed. She looks offstage impatiently.
A third performer enters, carrying a potted narcissus. He hands the plant to
the first performer. In one motion, he lifts the second performer, and the first*

*performer fills the newly empty position with the plant. Everyone leaves, the
third performer carrying the second, still-frozen performer. A new* NARRATOR
enters.)

NARRATOR: There lived at one time a wood nymph named Pomona

(POMONA *enters, skipping and swinging a basket of flowers. She skips around the
      periphery of the pool throughout the following.)*

      whose skill in the care of plants and trees has never been equaled. She
      hardly noticed the rivers and forests but loved the fields and orchards.
      These were her passion, her life. She didn't disdain Aphrodite as much
      as ignore her. She kept aloof from any suitor.   5

(VERTUMNUS *enters with his suitcase full of his disguises.)*

      There was however, one suitor, the god of springtime, Vertumnus. He was

VERTUMNUS: in love

NARRATOR: with her—more than all the rest.

VERTUMNUS: He adored her.

(*Throughout the following,* VERTUMNUS *quickly takes on his various disguises, to
      little or no effect on the skipping* POMONA.)

NARRATOR: In the manner of the shyer gods he used to disguise himself,   10
      would put on the clothes of a farmhand, wear a straw hat and a working
      man's shirt, and stick hay stalks behind his ears, to look like some story-
      book yokel.

VERTUMNUS: Howdy!

NARRATOR: When that produced nothing, he thought he might hold in his   15
      hand a pruner, trying to look like a field hand who tends the grapes in
      their arbors. After the complete failure of that, he came with a ladder,
      to seem as though he were bound for some nearby orchard to gather
      apples. With wigs, costume, and makeup, he once tricked himself out as
      a soldier, romantically returned from foreign wars. Another time, he set   20
      himself up as an ordinary fisherman fishing in her path on the chance
      she might pass by. He waited from dawn to dusk, passing from boredom
      to terror and back again.

VERTUMNUS: The point was just to be near her,

NARRATOR: stand there and gaze at her beauty,   25

VERTUMNUS: and maybe to wish her good morning

NARRATOR: or

VERTUMNUS: good afternoon

NARRATOR: or

VERTUMNUS: good evening   30

NARRATOR: before he plodded on by.

VERTUMNUS: I live for these trivial moments!

NARRATOR: One day he put on an old woman's dress and a wig and wan-
      dered through the green, green hills until he saw his beloved standing
      in the lavender.   35

(VERTUMNUS *walks along with a cane, as an old woman, admiring the orchard.*
      He approaches POMONA, *who has finally stopped skipping.*)
VERTUMNUS: Lovely, truly lovely. But you, miss, are lovelier still.
(*He dares to kiss her on the cheek, then points out vine and tree.*)
      Just look at that, would you? And think how that tree and vine com-
      plement each other, complete each other. Separate they aren't much,
      but together, they're splendid. There's a lesson in that, my dear, one
      that you might consider. The way you've been keeping to yourself is   40
      no good, it's a sad violation of nature, as well as a waste. A lover is
      what you need to make you complete as a woman. You'd have many
      choices, I think. As many as Helen. But there is one in particular I'd
      recommend: Vertumnus. I know him as well as I know myself, and I
      warrant, I guarantee, that his eyes are for you alone. Consider that   45
      he's young, attractive, healthy, and strong. Your tastes, too, are the
      same, for he likes trees and gardens almost as much as you. Besides,
      he's fun and takes on various disguises—it's a game he likes to play.
      Believe me, you may take these words that I speak as if they were
      coming from his own mouth.   50
NARRATOR: None of this was working.
VERTUMNUS: Listen, aren't you afraid of offending Aphrodite? Don't you
      know the story?
POMONA: What story?
VERTUMNUS: The story of Cinyras, his daughter Myrrha, and Aphrodite?   55
(*The characters enter as they are named.* MYRRHA *carries a bunch of red flowers*
      and a fan that is red on one side, white on the other. APHRODITE *is smoking*
      a cigarette.)
POMONA: No.
NARRATOR: And he began to tell her.

MYRRHA

VERTUMNUS: Part One: The Mistake.
      There was a girl like you named Myrrha, and she too ignored Aphrodite.
      She wouldn't fall in love. There were suitors everywhere, but she was
      blind to them. Finally, Aphrodite had had enough, and seized her with
      a passion.   5
(APHRODITE *literally seizes* MYRRHA; *the flowers fall into the pool and scatter.*)
POMONA: So?
VERTUMNUS: It was a passion for her father.
POMONA: That isn't true.
VERTUMNUS: It is.
APHRODITE (*in* MYRRHA's *ear*):   You can shut yourself in a room, bolt the   10
      door,
      but love will come through the window.

Draw the curtains, lock the casement,
but love will seep through the walls.
Never think, never think that you can be safe from love.
NARRATOR: She struggled hard against her passion.   15
MYRRHA: O gods, I pray you, keep off this wickedness,
make me a daughter to my parents.
Even to think what I am thinking is a crime—
or is it a crime? Who would condemn
such love as crime? The animals, I've seen,   20
will do as they desire. A ram goes to the ewe
that he has sired; and birds will make a nest
with those the nest once held. How happy
they are to be so free!
                    But we have laws.
Yet there are countries, I have heard,   25
with no such laws, where in the dark,
the bonds of love, already strong, might
be made perfect.
              Why do I keep thinking
of such things? Leave me alone! He is the best of men—
the best of *fathers*. If I were not his daughter   30
then I might lie with Cinyras—
but I am his daughter. You have been
virtuous in body, Myrrha; now be so in mind.
(*She struggles free of* APHRODITE *and crouches in a corner of the pool.*)
CINYRAS: Myrrha?
MYRRHA: Father?   35
CINYRAS: Why are you crying?
MYRRHA: It's nothing. Nothing.
CINYRAS: Why should a girl like you be sad? There are suitors at our door
    every day, yet you keep refusing them, and weeping in the corners of
    the house. Is there someone special you are hiding?   40
MYRRHA: No.
CINYRAS: What are you waiting for?
MYRRHA: Nothing.
CINYRAS: None of them pleases you?
MYRRHA: No.   45
CINYRAS: What sort of husband would you like?
MYRRHA: One like you.
CINYRAS: May you always be such a good, sweet girl.
APHRODITE (*to the audience while* MYRRHA, *in her dreams, encounters her father*):
    Midnight came, and sleep crept in the palace
    to fold men in his arms. But Myrrha could not sleep.   50

Tangled in a dream of her father she tossed
all night long, caught between her shame and her desire;
like a tree once wounded by the woodman's ax,
that leans first one way in the wind, then another,
hesitates, but always falls.   55

VERTUMNUS: Part Two: The Solution.
(*A noose appears.* MYRRHA *starts to move toward it. Her* NURSEMAID *enters and sees.*)
NURSEMAID: Myrrha, what are you doing? My child, what are you doing?
MYRRHA: Nurse, leave me alone!
NURSEMAID: What is it? I'll help you, whatever it is. The old are not alto-
    gether helpless.
Has someone bewitched you? Spells may be broken.   60
Or have you crossed some god? Still you may look to appease
by sacrifices and prayers even the heavens' anger.
What else can it be? Your mother and father are well—
(MYRRHA *sighs.*)
I know. It is love. It must be love. But I can help you.
Whatever it is, whatever you want, I swear by the gods to help you.   65
Only tell me. Your father will never know—
MYRRHA: Go away!
NURSEMAID: But why—?
MYRRHA: Go away or stop it! Stop asking why I grieve.
    It's a crime, the thing you're trying to learn, a crime!   70
VERTUMNUS: This went on and on. But the old nurse would not give up.
MYRRHA: O Mother, Mother, happy in your husband!
NURSEMAID: What does your mother have to do wi—? Oh, child. Whisper
    in my ear, and tell me I am wrong.
(MYRRHA *whispers.*) I swore to help you and now I must. (*They embrace.*)   75
    Tomorrow your mother leaves for the Feast of Ceres. She'll be gone
    nine days. Your father will drink. He will be likely—as any man can
    be—to listen to my suggestion
    (*The scene slides away from* MYRRHA *and toward* CINYRAS *without break.*)
    that a pretty girl adores you, loves you, and wants to visit
    your bedroom. Can she?   80
CINYRAS: She's attractive?
NURSEMAID: Yes, and young.
CINYRAS: How young?
NURSEMAID: Your daughter's age.
CINYRAS: All right then.   85
NURSEMAID: There's only one condition. She's very shy and is afraid
    for you to see her.
CINYRAS: How charming.

(The NURSEMAID *removes her headscarf and blindfolds* CINYRAS.*)*

VERTUMNUS: Part Three: The Corridor.

APHRODITE: In the small hours of the night, when all was still in the palace, 90
when the moon had fled from the sky and the stars were concealing
themselves in a shroud of cloud, she set out for her father's apartment.
She stumbled, recognized this as an omen, but nevertheless turned
down the hallway.

(An owl screeches.)

She continued down the corridor, clutching her nurse's arm for support. 95
The hall is apparently endless, but then—too soon—they arrive at the
door.

NURSEMAID: Your girl is here.

VERTUMNUS: Part Four: Unnameable.

*(*CINYRAS *wades slowly toward* MYRRHA. *He touches her, lifts her. They lie down,
kiss, and are submerged in the water.* MYRRHA *pulls away and leaves him.)*

APHRODITE: Full of her father, the girl slips out of the room; guilty but 100
shameless.

MYRRHA: There's nothing to fear or to hope for now.

APHRODITE: The next night, she returns.

MYRRHA: Because twice is no worse than once.

(The father and daughter encounter each other again. MYRRHA *departs.)*

APHRODITE: And the third night she's back again.

(They encounter each other again.)

CINYRAS: Let me see you. 105

MYRRHA: No.

CINYRAS: I want to see you.

MYRRHA: No.

CINYRAS: Let me see you.

MYRRHA: No! 110

*(He pulls off his blindfold. He sees her for a long moment. Then, with a cry,
he lunges toward her and tries to drown her. Finally, she escapes. He runs
off.)*

NURSEMAID: She escaped into darkness, out of the room, the house, the
city, into remote
and exotic lands, even as far as the Arab wilderness.

(Music begins.)

MYRRHA: O Gods, I pray you, change me; make me something else;
transform me entirely;
let me step out of my own heart.

VERTUMNUS: Someone must have heard her prayer—for she did change. 115

APHRODITE: Some say she changed into a tree;

NURSEMAID: some say she gave birth to a boy called Adonis;

NARRATOR: others contend that she dissolved into tears.

APHRODITE: And this last was not a mere expression, some rhetorical turn
or poetic and hyperbolic trope, but simply the unadorned,   12C
terrible truth. She stepped into a shimmering stream and
began to dissolve: Her body melted.
(Music rises as MYRRHA *melts into the pool and vanishes. Music ends.)*
VERTUMNUS *(to* POMONA*):* And then she was gone.
NARRATOR: This story got Vertumnus nowhere.
POMONA *(to* VERTUMNUS*):* Why are you wearing that ridiculous wig?   12E
VERTUMNUS: I don't know. I thought—
POMONA: Take it off. *(He does.)* And take off that idiotic dress.
VERTUMNUS: I'm embarrassed—
POMONA: Take it off.
NARRATOR: When at last the god revealed himself just as he was, much to   13C
his surprise, he had no need of words. Little Pomona was happy with
what she saw, unadorned and undisguised. Soon enough, the vine was
clinging to the tree.

PHAETON

(Music. Transition. The stage is cleared. PHAETON *enters, wearing sunglasses
and carrying a yellow rubber raft. He tests the water with his toe, then launches
his raft and goes to lie on it. The* THERAPIST *enters with her notepad and sits in a
chair on the deck of the pool. Music ends. Throughout the following,* PHAETON
floats on his yellow raft. He does not exactly hear the THERAPIST *when she speaks
to the audience, or perhaps he just isn't paying attention.)*
THERAPIST: Go on.
PHAETON: Well, my parents were separated when I was really little. Before I
was even born. It was a sort of a one-night sort of thing—except it was
in the day, in a meadow, where my mother went to watch my father
pass by every day. Anyway, I always knew who he was, and I would see   5
him pass by every day—of course—who doesn't? But I never knew him,
and he wasn't really around. I mean, not *around* around.
THERAPIST: Where better might we find a more precise illustration of the
dangers of premature initiation than in this ancient tale of alternating
parental indulgence and neglect?   10
PHAETON: I went to an expensive school and there were a lot of boys
there who were, you know, sons of the rich and famous. And one day
we're all on the playground and this one kid, Epaphus, he goes to me,
"So Phaeton blah blah who's your father, what does he do? Blah blah
blah." So I tell him my father's the sun and he says, "Tell me an-   15
other," and I say, "He's the sun, he's Phoebus Apollo." And he just
basically trampled me, just basically beat the shit out of me. Like I
was lying.

THERAPIST: Neither his own opinion of himself, nor the regard for him or
   lack of it in his peers, obviates the father's primitive role as initiating   20
   priest for the younger being. Now, it cannot be contested that the absence of this figure is, for the son, an almost irredeemable loss.

PHAETON: So I go home and I say, Mom this happened, you know at school.
   And she gets all upset, crying and everything, because she still loves him
   and it's an insult to her as well. And I'm like, well, if it's true how come   25
   there's no proof of it? It's unfair to us, you know, that there's no proof.
   And she gets more upset and she says: "Hear me, my child. In all his
   glory, your father looks down upon us. By his splendor, I swear that you
   are his truly begotten son. That fiery orb you see crossing the sky each
   day whose heat enlivens and enables the world and orders our days and   30
   nights is indeed your sire. Believe me, my darling!" Blah, blah, blah.

THERAPIST: When he matures beyond the customary Eden of the mother
   breast, the child seeks to individuate beyond its enfolding gate and
   turns to the new symbols of the paternal realm, thus beginning his spiritual passage from one sphere to the next.   35

(At this point PHAETON's *father,* APOLLO, *enters upstage, carrying a music stand.*
   Throughout the rest of the scene he sings "Un' Aura Amorosa" from Cosi
   Fan Tutti, *in Italian, softly, under the entire text. Occasionally, when*
   PHAETON *quotes him in his narrative,* APOLLO *echoes his son in English, all*
   the while never departing from the melody of the song but sliding seamlessly
   between the Italian lyrics and the English text. PHAETON *pauses only slightly*
   between APOLLO's *English phrases. He neither sees his father nor acknowl-*
   edges his presence.)

PHAETON: So she tells me to go over to the valley where my dad goes to
   work every morning and just ask him to set things straight. To, you
   know, "do right by me." So I set out and it's hot and it's dusty and it's a
   long way—across Ethiopia. And I hitch part of the time and part of the
   time I walk and finally, *finally,* I get there. And the hill is steep.   40

THERAPIST: But this passage is never easy.

PHAETON: At the door are my dad's secretaries, the days and the hours and
   the century, but they recognize me and they say go on in. And there he
   is all shining and golden, and I can't even look at him he's so bright.
   And you know what he says to me? He says, "My son, you are   45
   welcome."

APOLLO *(singing underneath):* My son, you are welcome . . .

PHAETON: "Speak, Phaeton, to your father."

APOLLO: *Speak, Phaeton, to your father.*

PHAETON: I cannot even tell you what this was to me. So I tell him every-   50
   thing, you know, I just spill my guts. He listens to me and he says, "Let
   me grant you a favor,

APOLLO: *Let me grant you a favor...*

PHAETON: whatever you ask shall be yours."

APOLLO: *Whate'er you ask, shall be yours.* 55

PHAETON: And he swears to it.

THERAPIST: The conventional exordium of the initiate from latent to realized potential is inevitably accompanied by a radical realignment of his emotional relationship with the imago of parental authority.

PHAETON: Now, there's only one thing I want, I mean it's obvious, right? I 60 say, "Give me the keys to your car." *Immediately,* he starts backpedaling, saying it's his job

APOLLO: *It's my job...*

PHAETON: and no one else can do it,

APOLLO: *You can't do it.* 65

PHAETON: and that up in the sky there are the bull and the lion and the scorpion

APOLLO: *There's a scorpion.*

PHAETON: to get me, and I say, "Give me the keys to your car. I want to drive it myself across the sky. It's my turn. You promised. I want to 70 light the world today."

THERAPIST: The father, or his substitute, must be assured, before he transfers the symbols of adult vocation, that the son no longer is operating from infantile complexes—complexes that might dangerously redirect his new task through the unconscious promptings of self-aggrandizement, 75 personal preference, or even resentment.

PHAETON: Where have you been all my life, Dad? It's my turn. Hand it over! So he hands over the reins, but he won't stop giving advice. You know, like "Don't fly too high,

APOLLO: *Don't fly too high...* 80

PHAETON: nor too low, stay in the tracks, go slantwise."

APOLLO: *Go slantwise...*

PHAETON: On and on. But I didn't listen.

THERAPIST: Myths are the earliest forms of science.

PHAETON: It was over before it began. It was chaos, okay? Out of control, as 85 if no one was driving. You know, my knees were weak, I was blind from all the light. I set the earth on fire. And I fell. And it just destroyed me—you know, I was just completely and utterly destroyed. O-V-E-R. Over.

(APOLLO's *song ends.* PHAETON *rises abruptly and leaves the stage.* APOLLO *exits.*)

THERAPIST: It has been said that the myth is a public dream, dreams are pri- 90 vate myths. Unfortunately we give our mythic side scant attention these days. As a result, a great deal escapes us and we no longer understand our own actions. So it remains important and salutary to speak not only

of the rational and easily understood, but also of enigmatic things: the irrational and the ambiguous. To speak both privately and publicly.   95

EROS AND PSYCHE

(*Music. Transition. A raft, covered in red fabric, and bound with gold rope, is
placed in the water.* Q *and* A *enter and sit on diagonally opposite corners of the
deck. The doors open and* EROS *enters. He is winged, naked, blindfolded, and carrying a golden arrow. Throughout the following he will come forward and lie
down to sleep on the raft in the water.*)

Q: Who is this?

A: This is Eros, god of love.

Q: Why does he have wings?

A: So he can move quickly from body to body.

Q: Why is he naked?   5

A: To make us transparent.

Q: To make us what?

A: Transparent in our love. Foolish to others. Exposed.

Q: Why is he blind?

A: He is always pictured blind, but he really isn't.   10

Q: Because in love we are so ignorant and so compulsive?

A: There's that.

Q: What else?

A: He is blind to show how he takes away our ordinary vision, our mistaken
   vision, that depends on the appearance of things.   15

(EROS *lies down on the raft to sleep. Throughout the following,* PSYCHE *enters,
   carrying a candelabra. She makes her way down the stairs and along the
   deck, very slowly and quietly.*)

Q: Who's this coming down the stairs?

A: Her name is Psyche.

Q: Psyche? Her name is Psyche?

A: Yes.

Q: What's she doing here?   20

A: She's married to the god, but she's never seen him.

Q: Why is that?

A: He forbids it.

Q: How did they meet?

A: Psyche was so beautiful, the goddess Aphrodite hated her. She sent her   25
   son to punish her, but he fell in love instead.

Q: Does she know that he is a god?

A: No. She suspects he is a monster.

(PSYCHE *is startled by something. She looks over her shoulder, then continues
   along the deck.*)

Q: Have they had sex already?

A: Oh yes. 30
Q: And how was that?
A: It was good.
Q: Then why does she suspect he is a monster?
A: Her jealous sisters told her so.
(PSYCHE *is startled again. Then she continues.*)
Q: And she listened to them? 35
A: Unfortunately, yes.
Q: So now she's coming to see him as he sleeps?
A: Yes.
Q: To make certain.
A: Yes. 40
Q: With her eyes.
A: Yes. She's very young. It happens all the time.
Q: She doesn't trust what she has felt herself?
A: Not with the radical trust we need.
(PSYCHE *steps into the pool. She moves slowly, so as not to make noise. She approaches the sleeping* EROS *and holds the candelabra over him, looking. This happens in silence.*)
Q: What does the word "Psyche" mean? 45
A: In Greek it means "the soul."
(*Wax from the candles falls on* EROS. *He wakes suddenly and turns abruptly toward* PSYCHE. *They stare at each other a long moment. Then, in one motion, she extinguishes the candelabra in the water. She and* EROS *begin to separate under the following.*)
Q: What's going to happen to her now?
A: She's going to suffer.
Q: And?
A: She's going to suffer. 50
Q: And?
A: She's going to suffer.
Q: What does she have to do?
A: She is given horrible and lonely tasks by Aphrodite.
Q: Such as? 55
A: Sorting thousands of little seeds one from the other.
Q: How did she manage?
A: Some little insects help her.
Q: Like in fairy tales?
A: Like in all the fairy tales. 60
Q: What else?
(PSYCHE *sinks into the water.*)
A: She had to go down to the Underworld, fetch various things.

Q: Wasn't she afraid?

A: She was petrified, but she did it all the same.

Q: Wasn't it hopeless?   65

A: It was hopeless, but she did it all the same.

Q: What did Love do in the meantime?

A: He healed his little wound. It hurt him so much when she looked at him like that. The wax from the candle fell on him and burnt him.

Q: How does it end?   70

A: She finishes her tasks and Zeus declares enough's enough.

Q: He overrides Love's mother?

(EROS *and* PSYCHE *look at each other. They begin to move toward each other.*)

A: Yes. And further, he gives Psyche a special potion and she becomes immortal. Then he declares that their marriage will last forever.

Q: Does it?   75

A: Of course.

Q: So it has a happy ending?

A: It has a very happy ending.

(EROS *and* PSYCHE *approach the raft and sit on it together.*)

Q: Almost none of these stories have completely happy endings.

A: This is different.   80

Q: Why is that?

(PSYCHE *and* EROS *kiss. And kiss again.*)

A: It's just inevitable. The soul wanders in the dark, until it finds love. And so, wherever our love goes, there we find our soul.

Q: It always happens?

A: If we're lucky. And if we let ourselves be blind.   85

Q: Instead of watching out?

A: Instead of always watching out.

(*Silence.*)

PSYCHE (*turning out to the audience*): If you will indulge us, we have one more tale to tell: a coda, if you will.

BAUCIS AND PHILEMON

(*Music. Transition. The raft and candelabra are struck.*)

NARRATOR ONE: It happened that one night, Zeus, the lord of the heavens, and Hermes, his son, came down to earth to see what people were really like. They disguised themselves as two old beggars, stinking and poor, ragged and filthy. They knocked on a thousand doors.

(ZEUS *knocks on the surface of the deck. Both adopt supplicating poses.*)

ZEUS: Hello, do you have any spare—?   5

OFFSTAGE VOICE: Get out of here! Get the hell out of here! I work hard for my money!

NARRATOR ONE: And a thousand doors were slammed on them.

(*They knock on the deck, and a* WOMAN *opens the door.*)

HERMES: Hello, we're tired, we live on the Street, and we hoped that you
 might—   10

WOMAN AT THE DOOR: I'm sorry, I'm . . . um . . . soooo sorry. Sorry.

(*She slams the door shut.*)

NARRATOR ONE: At last they came to a little hut on the outskirts of town.

HERMES: Why bother knocking here? We've knocked on houses of all kinds,
 the homes of people with plenty to spare. Whoever lives here obviously
 has nothing.   15

ZEUS: Let's give it a try all the same. We've come all this way.

(*He knocks.*)

HERMES: This is hopeless. Let's just go ho—

BAUCIS (*entering*): Poor strangers! Philemon, there are guests at our door!

ZEUS: Hello. We are strangers to these parts. We've lost our way and—

PHILEMON (*entering*): Baucis, why are you standing there! We must bring   20
 our guests inside.

ZEUS: Do you know us?

PHILEMON: Of course.

HERMES: You do?

PHILEMON: Yes—   25

HERMES: Then who are we?

PHILEMON: Why, you are children of God. Come in, come in.

(*At this point, the narrative divides among several members of the company. They
 enter and exit variously, carrying illuminated candles in wooden bowls, which
 stand in for all the items they will mention. They hand these bowls to* BAUCIS
 and PHILEMON, *or place them in the water themselves. The scene is active:
 The entire surface of the water becomes the "table" being set with illuminated
 candles.*)

NARRATOR TWO: The two immortals, satisfied that their disguises had not
 been seen through, entered the house, lowering their heads to fit
 through the door.   30

BAUCIS: No, don't sit on the floor! Sit on chairs, as quality people do.

NARRATOR THREE: Philemon ran to get another chair.

NARRATOR FOUR: And Baucis fetched two pieces of cloth to pad them so
 the strangers might rest easy.

NARRATOR FIVE: She stirred the coals in the hearth and fanned the fire to   35
 cook them a meal.

NARRATOR ONE: Philemon set out the embroidered cloth that they saved for
 feast days.

NARRATOR TWO: Baucis saw that one of the legs of the chair was short and
 she propped it up with a shard of a pot.   40

NARRATOR THREE: Philemon set out a plate of olives, green ones and black, and a saucer of cherry plums.

NARRATOR FOUR: Then there was cabbage and some roasted eggs . . .

NARRATOR FIVE: For dessert there were nuts, figs, dates, and plums.

NARRATOR ONE: And a basket of ripe apples.   45

NARRATOR TWO: Remember how apples smell?

(*A pause. Everyone inhales and remembers. Then they continue.*)

NARRATOR ONE: At last, with a show of modest pride, they brought out a bit of honeycomb for sweetness.

NARRATOR TWO: Philemon poured wine from a bottle, but as he filled the glasses of the guests, he saw that the bottle remained full.   50

ALL NARRATORS: And then they knew.

(NARRATORS *exit.*)

BAUCIS: Oh, mercy! Mercy!

(*She runs with her husband to kneel in front of the gods.*)

PHILEMON: You are divine and we've served you such a simple meal. Baucis, go and kill the goose!

ZEUS: Let it live. We are gods and we thank you. You've done enough,   55
more than your nasty neighbors thought to do.

(*The original* NARRATOR *of the scene enters with three other members of the company, all carrying bowls of candles. As she speaks, they come forward, kneel in the water, and set the bowls floating. There is music under the next line of* NARRATOR ONE.)

NARRATOR ONE: Suddenly, everything was changing. The poor little house, their simple cottage, was becoming grander and grander,
a glittering marble-columned temple. The straw and reeds
of the thatched roof metamorphosed into gold, and gates   60
with elaborate carvings sprang up, as ground gave way
to marble paving stones.

HERMES: Old man, old woman, ask of us what you will. We shall grant whatever request you make of us.

(BAUCIS *and* PHILEMON *whisper to each other.*)

BAUCIS: Having spent all our lives together, we ask that you allow us to die   65
at the same moment.

PHILEMON: I'd hate to see my wife's grave, or have her weep at mine.

NARRATOR TWO: The gods granted their wish. Arrived at a very old age together, the two stood at what had been their modest doorway and now
was a grandiose facade.   70

ZEUS: And Baucis noticed her husband was beginning to put forth leaves, and he saw that she, too, was producing leaves and bark. They were turning into trees. They stood there, held each other, and called, before the bark closed over their mouths,

PHILEMON AND BAUCIS: Farewell.   75
NARRATOR ONE: Walking down the street at night, when you're all alone,
    you can still hear, stirring in the intermingled branches of the trees
    above, the ardent prayer of Baucis and Philemon. They whisper:
ALL: Let me die the moment my love dies.
NARRATOR ONE: They whisper: 80
ALL: Let me not outlive my own capacity to love.
NARRATOR ONE: They whisper:
ALL: Let me die still loving, and so, never die.
(MIDAS *enters, clutching the stiff, gold jump-rope. Each of his steps is accompanied
    by the ring of little finger cymbals. He stops on the edge of the deck, kneels,
    and drops the rope in the water. He washes his face. He reaches into the water
    and retrieves the jump-rope, now restored to its original state. He looks toward
    the doors, which open to reveal his* DAUGHTER, *also restored to life. They
    move toward each other in the pool. She tries two times to embrace him, but he
    starts away, frightened. The third time, she succeeds. They kneel together in
    the water. The members of the company all blow out the floating candles.*)

- What devices does the play use to create coherent connections among the
  different myths that are presented here?
- In the "Orpheus and Eurydice" section, there are two narrators who have a
  conversation about how to interpret this story. How does their conversation
  guide our reading of the story? How does it compare to the choruses that we
  have seen in *Oedipus the King* and in *Medea*?
- What does the play achieve by presenting two different versions of the "Orpheus
  and Eurydice" story? Why does the play include specific references to the
  sources for these stories when it does not do the same for the other stories that
  it relates? Compare the presentation of Rilke's poem here to the poem itself
  (p. 1536). How does this reference shape our experience of this particular story?

Experiencing Literature through Writing

1. Choose a pair of texts that have some specific, stated connection. One
   may allude to the other, or both may allude to a common text. Identify
   the common element in the two texts. As you write, consider the
   following questions:

   a. How important is that element in both of the texts? Does it hold
      the same place in both of the narratives?

b. To what extent does each text treat the material in the allusion in the same manner as the original text? What sorts of changes do you see?

c. How does the material in the allusion become more interesting within this new context?

d. How does the "new" text become richer because of this particular allusion?

e. How does the allusion add to our understanding of both of the texts involved in this shared element?

2. The texts here have a common theme: "The Myth of Cheating Death." How does the strategy of allusion serve the authors as they attempt to tackle a subject as perplexing as death? By appealing to an established myth, an author can, among other possibilities, make the experience of a single individual representative of a culture or make sense of individual experience by calling upon the collective experience that is represented in such myths. Look for examples in which the texts use allusions for each of these purposes. Explain how the particular texts illustrate each of these strategies and how this particular example fits into the myth.

3. It may be appropriate to treat the theme of death by thinking about the element of interruption. Death may seem to be more than an interruption, but often death intrudes on lives as an interruption, a reminder of mortality; everyone who is still living has in some way "cheated death." As you look at the readings in this section, discuss specific instances in which the texts treat the impact of some intruding death upon the worlds that these texts create. How does death interrupt in this specific instance? What is its impact? How does this interruption create the given work? Where do other texts also intrude upon these narratives?

16 Genre

How Do Our Expectations Impact Our Literary Experience?

How Are Those Expectations Formed?

If you've grown up in the United States, it's likely you think of an avocado as a salad vegetable or salad fruit. If you've grown up in Brazil, it's likely you think of the avocado as a dessert fruit. Neither way of classifying arises from what an avocado "really" is; nor are categories like "appetizers," "salads," "main courses," "desserts"—even "fruits" and "vegetables"—universally fixed. Custom and use guide our understanding. In the United States, we see avocados sliced over lettuce and added to sandwiches with onions and tomatoes; avocados are served before or with the main meal. We don't think of ordering an avocado milk shake for a snack or enjoying a frothy avocado mousse after dinner. But in Brazil, an avocado is customarily prepared as a sweet, as a dessert; avocados come after the meal or altogether separate from it.

Of course, there is nothing wrong with either way of looking at the avocado—that is, as long as the way of looking allows you to enjoy avocados. If you've grown to love them in a salad, try them with arugula or watercress. If you've grown accustomed to thinking of them as dessert, feel free to make an avocado cake. But in either case, it's good to know that the avocado doesn't have to be one type of food or the other; if you are locked into a single way of using an avocado, you'll probably find variations distasteful or strange. If you are an adventurous diner, you might want to try both American and Brazilian ways of preparing an avocado, or you might thoroughly rethink the categories or even discard categories altogether in order to consider the avocado purely as an avocado.

A work of art, like an avocado, can be put into a category according to custom and use. A work of art, also like an avocado, can be moved from one group to another. And the groups themselves may be redefined or discarded. Determinations of kind or type along with decisions about what individual items belong to those types are variable; they are not absolute, not unchanging. With literature and film, we often find ourselves adjusting the basis upon which distinctions of kind are made. This ever-shifting way of defining a category and of what belongs in a category is what makes the concept of genre such a tricky subject.

WHAT IS GENRE?

Genre is defined most broadly as a literary/artistic type or kind; it suggests the grouping of individual works into larger categories. That grouping can be made in various ways. Genres are commonly defined by reference to fairly basic **expectations** an audience brings to a work. Some of the most basic expectations have long been observed: a **tragedy** ends in death; a **comedy** ends in marriage. To expand upon that distinction slightly, we expect tragedies to concern grand failures—a powerful sense of lost promise is crucial. We expect comedies to offer some sense of fulfillment, albeit oftentimes of a small sort. Characters in comedies overcome misunderstandings and limitations to achieve their fair share of happiness.

There are, of course, different kinds of comedies and tragedies. There are additional terms that register more specific expectations. A **farce** (a form of **low comedy**) sustains no tension that arises from complexities of character. Consequently, a farce builds upon silly actions that require only superficial resolution (there may be situational complexities in farce, but not emotional ones). The pleasure of watching *Seinfeld* depends largely on how cleverly episode after episode adds up to nothing. In contrast to such light entertainments, **high comedy** delivers the emotional substance of complex people. For example, the lovers in Shakespeare's *Much Ado about Nothing* (p. 340) face great obstacles created by ill will, anger, pride, and jealousy. They also suffer for the mistakes they make. And partly because of this capacity to suffer, they can appreciate the happiness they finally achieve.

Although it is important to know the key terms commonly used to identify elements of a genre, it is more important to understand how identifying those elements helps us appreciate an individual text. A good critic must do more than merely name genres or provide information *about* genres.

Shakespeare's foolish busybody Polonius from *Hamlet* takes the naming approach, and it leads him to a long and ultimately pointless list: "tragedy, comedy, history, pastoral, pastoral-comical, historical pastoral, tragical-historical, tragical-comical-historical-pastoral." Polonius does not understand that a genre is something to explore and test, not merely to label and list. The study of genre demands that we reflect upon categories we identify and name. We must consider what we have been taught to expect from a particular kind of work and ask ourselves what those expectations signify. We must understand the following aspects of genre:

- Creative works of art precede the critical discussion of those works as representative of a type or kind. Aristotle wouldn't have written about tragedy as a genre if he had not viewed many plays that he felt shared essential characteristics. (We wouldn't consider an avocado a salad fruit if we had not grown up eating avocados in salads.)

- Defining a genre does not fix the characteristics of a genre permanently in place. Aristotle was a brilliant critic, but his description of tragedy should not be taken as a set of rules all tragedies must follow. (Even if you think of avocados only as a salad fruit, there remain many inventive ways to use avocados in a great variety of salads.)

- If it doesn't help you to think of a particular work existing within a particular genre, don't hesitate to move that work into another genre, redefine the genre, or dismiss the notion of genre. (If you are tired of avocados in salads, try an avocado dessert, make an avocado main dish, or just eat the avocado plain.)

CONVENTIONS

Elements that have become familiar through our reading/viewing experience are called **conventions** (**formula** is a related although somewhat stricter word). Without conventions, there can be no genre. Our recognition of conventions becomes the basis upon which we construct a sense of genre. Often conventions emerge in elements of plot. In teen horror films (like *Halloween* or *Nightmare on Elm Street*), our viewing experience leads us to expect a crazed killer to attack the young couple who have sneaked off to make out. In courtroom dramas (like *A Few Good Men*), we learn to expect an explosive confrontation between a defense lawyer and a difficult witness that will reveal the truth that has been hidden. In romantic comedies (like *My Best Friend's Wedding* or *Pride and Prejudice*), we learn to expect the leading male and female characters to stumble over a series of misunderstandings before they discover that they are meant for each other. We often take satisfaction in such familiar genre stories because they at some level provide reassurance. They confirm unspoken beliefs or underscore common wisdom: young couples shouldn't sneak around to make out, false accusations will not be sustained in our courts, or true love always finds a way.

Conventions, of course, don't take shape only in elements of a story line. Anything our reading/viewing experience has taught us to expect as essential to a type can trigger our identification of a genre. A dark and stormy night serves as a conventional setting for certain types of gothic fiction. A character sporting a straggly mustache and a black hat instantly signals a threat in the world of the western. A pairing of unlike personalities in a shared endeavor becomes the basis for dozens of buddy films. And the mood or tone of reflective sadness over the death of a promising youth marks the conventional tone and subject of the elegy. We begin to respond to many individual works in context of a body of expectations we have acquired in our past reading and viewing.

Experiencing Literature through Genre

Ghost stories often begin by establishing a tension between rational skepticism and unexplained, disturbing occurrences. The initial tension acknowledges our resistance to tales of the supernatural in order to lure us in. Readers are, in effect, moved from their mundane lives into fictional worlds where anything can happen. Consider how quickly Mrs. J. H. Riddell (a nineteenth-century writer of supernatural tales) invokes basic generic conventions in the opening paragraphs of one of her many ghost stories. We are introduced to a no-nonsense narrator and his more vulnerable family. As you read, think of how this opening relates to familiar elements in ghost stories you may have heard or of horror films you have seen.

Mrs. J. H. Riddell (1832–1906)

from Nut Bush Farm (1882)

When I entered upon the tenancy of Nut Bush Farm almost the first piece of news which met me, in the shape of a whispered rumour, was that "something" had been seen in the "long field."

Pressed closely as to what he meant, my informant reluctantly stated that the "something" took the "form of a man," and that the wood and the path leading thereto from Whittleby were supposed to be haunted.

Now, all this annoyed me exceedingly. I do not know when I was more put out than by this intelligence. It is unnecessary to say I did not believe in ghosts or anything of that kind, but my wife being a very nervous, impressionable woman, and our only child a delicate weakling, in the habit of crying himself into fits if left alone at night without a candle, I really felt at my wits' end to imagine what I should do if a story of this sort reached their ears. ■

This narrator represents a kind of commonsense approach to the world, but he does not seem at the outset a very sympathetic figure. We're hardly surprised or disappointed to see this narrator shaken progressively from his confident faith in the material reality of everyday life. We expect and want ghost stories to shake up the most hardheaded skeptics. That is what ghost stories do. Significantly, by the end of this tale, we have the same tension we had at the start. But now it is the narrator who is shaken and the people who surround him who are the skeptics. We're now able to align ourselves with the narrator against all those sensible fools who refuse to accept a reality that lies outside the ordinary. Note how the essential dynamic has been repeated and yet revised in the closing lines from "Nut Bush Farm."

My brother took Nut Bush Farm off my hands. He says the place never was haunted—that I never saw Mr. Hascot except in my own imagination—that the whole thing originated in a poor state of health and a too credulous disposition!
    I leave the reader to judge between us. ■

We may well finish our reading of "Nut Bush Farm" still thinking of ghosts as existing only in stories, but the generic elements evident in the passage are clearly intended to help us accept *in the reading of the story* an alternative belief.

DISRUPTIONS

Genres depend upon our recognition of familiar features. But it would be a mistake to assume a genre piece never veers from the expected. Genres aren't absolutely fixed or altogether predictable. A deviation from an established convention—a surprise that results from breaking an expectation—is called a **disruption**. The familiar element is revised or even reversed. A disruption can be thought of as a specific kind of interruption (see Chapter 9)—one that serves to challenge thematic implications of a genre. Disruptions in a genre piece may call into question the beliefs that lie behind the conventions. If the sexually eager young couple we think is doomed in a horror movie turn out to have a good (and safe) time together, maybe we shouldn't worry so much about young couples sneaking off; if the defense lawyer in a courtroom drama can't break through what we see as a tissue of lies, maybe our legal system doesn't work as well as we like to think; if the "right couple" in what appeared to be a conventional romantic comedy turns out to be very wrong together, maybe our notions of "true love" need to be rethought. While conventions reassure, disruptions challenge and upset. Mixing familiar conventions that do not normally appear together is a common mode of disruption.

Experiencing Literature through Genre

A famous example of generic mixing occurs in Shakespeare's *Macbeth*. Just after the king has been assassinated, just as Macbeth and Lady Macbeth begin to feel the terrible weight of what they have done, a foulmouthed, drunken Porter arrives at the castle and seeks entrance. He knocks at the gate. He speaks (to himself, Macduff, the audience, and anyone who will listen from within the castle walls) about subjects that hardly seem fitting in context of the grand tragedy that has begun to unfold. He punctuates his rambling, bawdy soliloquy with continued knocking at the gate. As you read the following dialogue, keep in mind that it is placed just after the murder of the king and just before the general discovery of the murder. Some of the grandest and most intense lines in the play bracket the lowly dialogue we've reprinted here. For example, just before the entrance of the Porter, Macbeth reflects upon his act.

To know my deed, 'twere best not know myself.
(*Knock*)
Wake Duncan with thy knocking! I would thou couldst.

And shortly after the Porter's final line, we have Macduff's announcement upon finding the King slain:

Confusion now hath made his masterpiece:
Most sacrilegious murder hath broke ope
The Lord's anointed temple and stole thence
The life of th' building!

In the middle of such lines the Porter's speech might seem out of place.

William Shakespeare (1564–1616)

from **Macbeth** (1607)

ACT II

Scene 3
The court within the castle.
(Enter a PORTER.*)*
(Knocking within.)
PORTER: Here's a knocking, indeed! If a man were Porter of Hell Gate, he
should have old turning the key. *(Knocking.)* Knock, knock, knock.
Who's there, i'th'name of Belzebub?—Here's a farmer, that hang'd himself on th'expectation of plenty: come in, time-pleaser; have napkins
enow about you; here you'll sweat for't. *(Knocking.)* Knock, knock.
Who's there, i'th'other devil's name?—Faith, here's an equivocator,
that could swear in both the scales against either scale; who committed
treason enough for God's sake, yet could not equivocate to heaven: O!
come in, equivocator. *(Knocking.)* Knock, knock, knock. Who's
there?—Faith, here's an English tailor come hither for stealing out of a
French hose: come in, tailor; here you may roast your goose.
(Knocking.) Knock, knock. Never at quiet! What are you?—But this
place is too cold for Hell. I'll devil-porter it no further: I had thought to
have let in some of all professions, that go the primrose way to
th'everlasting bonfire. *(Knocking.)* Anon, anon: I pray you, remember
the Porter.
(Opens the gate.)
(Enter MACDUFF *and* LENOX.*)*
MACD.: Was it so late, friend, ere you went to bed,
    That you do lie so late?
PORT.: Faith, Sir, we were carousing till the second cock;
    and drink, Sir, is a great provoker of three things.
MACD.: What three things does drink especially provoke?
PORT.: Marry, Sir, nose-painting, sleep, and urine. Lechery, Sir, it provokes, and unprovokes: it provokes the desire, but it takes away the
performance. Therefore, much drink may be said to be an equivocator
with lechery: it makes him, and it mars him; it sets him on, and it
takes him off; it persuades him, and disheartens him; makes him stand
to, and not stand to: in conclusion, equivocates him in a sleep, and,
giving him the lie, leaves him.
MACD.: I believe, drink gave thee the lie last night.

The Porter alludes in his speech to serious matters (the Jesuits tried for political conspiracies against the crown were considered by Protestants to be "equivo-cators") but immediately turns such serious matters to bawdy jokes on how drink makes him both sexually aroused and sexually incapable. The low comic tone clashes greatly with the tragic weight and dignity of the surrounding text.

Some critics call this kind of mixing **comic relief**, but that term hardly fits this instance. In this case, Shakespeare is clarifying and intensifying—not undercutting—the tragedy of *Macbeth*. The knocking-at-the-gate scene provokes at most uncomfortable laughter; the wrongness of the deed has thrown everything out of synch. The Porter's incessant pounding at the gate intensifies the horror of what has occurred within the gates. Macbeth's treasonous and brutal act has undermined the stability and integrity of his world. The breakdown of generic categories through the mixing of the high and the low complements the moral breakdown that results from the murder.

DISPLACEMENT AND PARODY

A **displacement** of one genre for another or a complete **blending** of genres extends mixing to its furthest limit. Joss Whedon's television series *Buffy the Vampire Slayer* places conventional high school coming-of-age stories in con-text of the horror genre. Comedy blends with terror; the mundane ("does this boy/girl like me?") blends with the cosmic ("the end of the world is upon us").

The demon here (in the lower left corner of the publicity poster) is dressed and posed very much like a conven-tional song-and-dance man, but he has a demon's face and does pose a threat that seems out of place amid the stars and clouds of this musical package.

We come to understand that the comic is at times horrific or that the mundane can feel cosmic (a breakup in a serious relationship may indeed seem like the end of the world). Once Whedon establishes the ongoing generic blend, he can overlay still more generic elements as he wishes in individual episodes. A particularly striking instance is the musical episode "Once More, with Feeling" (2001). In that episode, a particularly inventive singing demon gains power over residents of Sunnydale (the town's name, of course, is part of the generic fusion). People burst into song and dance, very much in the fashion of standard Broadway musicals. The catch is that they must sing the feelings that best remain private. Eventually, they burst not just into song but into flames. The lightness of a conventional musical takes a bitter and genuinely dangerous edge. The various genres merge as something new and provocative.

Perhaps the most radical disruption involves mockery; the very elements that had been established as meaningful in a genre become the subject of ridicule. Such sustained comic imitation of a serious work is called **parody**. Although parody is sometimes thought to mark the death of a genre, it's perhaps more accurate and useful to consider it a form of revision. If the genre were really dead, the parody wouldn't be funny and wouldn't serve any purpose. Why laugh at something that no one cares about? Occasionally, critics will use the term **self-parody**. Whereas a parody is a controlled work of satire, a purposeful diminishment of a work or works taken by some as serious, a self-parody is an unintentional revelation of empty and tired formulas. Self-parody results from a genre writer/director who fails to infuse conventions with meaning or life; the result of such a failure is often that we laugh at the conventions rather than respond to them in ways that we are "supposed" to respond. Think of a spy film, for example, that tries very hard to be sexy and suspenseful but turns out to be so clichéd that it becomes funny. Or a horror movie that guarantees everyone scares and frights but delivers its "shockers" so lamely that the audience responds only with laughter.

Making Connections

An allusion calls to mind ideas or associations that a reader has acquired from previous reading experience (see Chapter 15). A writer's purposeful use of genre also demands prior experience from the reader. It might seem, then, that a heavily allusive text is essentially the same as a genre work. Although there may be overlap, it is useful to make a distinction. An allusion casts the reader back to a particular text or type of texts at a particular place in a text. There may be many allusions in a single work, and those allusions might be drawn from various texts. Each allusion demands particular consideration in the context of its specific occurrence. Genre works ask us to think in more general terms of patterns, types, or kinds. That is, we're asked to think of how shared features work similarly in different texts.

Mark Twain's "Ode to Stephen Dowling Bots, Dec'd" shows that it is possible to parody a type of work that has already diminished itself by numerous uninspired formulaic pieces. Twain is motivated not so much by the badness of a kind of work but by the widespread acceptance of that bad work. He suggests that our culture produces and praises a ponderous and polite literature that needs to be seen for what it is—fake, empty, cliché ridden, and dishonest. It's worth noting that the conventions of an **ode** have in the last century become less conventions of form and more conventions of mood and subject. That is, odes were once structured in three parts that reflected their origins as public poems, performed by a chorus that moved in one direction as it delivered the first part (the **strophe**), the opposite direction as it voiced the second part (the **antistrophe**), and stood still as it came to the final section (the **epode**). Now we may think of odes as substantial poems of a meditative cast. They normally sustain a tone of dignity, high seriousness, and calm dispassion in dealing with a public matter. These conventions, although broadly defined, may be considered a basis for thinking of the ode in terms of genre. But Twain wants to explode what he sees as stifling conventions of propriety that keep people distant from real feelings. In his parody, he calls attention to our low expectations by meeting them only too well.

Mark Twain (1835–1910)

Ode to Stephen Dowling Bots, Dec'd (from
Adventures of Huckleberry Finn, 1884)

And did young Stephen sicken,
    And did young Stephen die?
And did the sad hearts thicken,
    And did the mourners cry?

No; such was not the fate of   5
    Young Stephen Dowling Bots;
Though sad hearts round him thickened,
    'Twas not from sickness' shots.

No whooping-cough did rack his frame,
    Nor measles drear, with spots;   10
Not these impaired the sacred name
    Of Stephen Dowling Bots.

Despised love struck not with woe
    That head of curly knots,
Not stomach troubles laid him low;   15
    Young Stephen Dowling Bots.

O no. Then list with tearful eye,
    Whilst I his fate do tell.
His soul did from this cold world fly,
    By falling down a well.   20

They got him out and emptied him;
    Alas it was too late;
His spirit was gone for to sport aloft
    In the realms of the good and the great.

After reading Twain's parody, we're likely to be very careful about the ways we speak or write about death in formal or public occasions. The last thing we'll want to do is trust too much in the most common of generic expressions. In this case, the conventions have been so overused that the poem loses any authentic relationship to the individual supposedly being honored.

GENRE AND POPULAR CULTURE

When we think hard about genre, we learn about the culture that produces the genre. Conventions embody values, wishes, and fears. For example, until the late 1960s the western was among the most clearly established film genres and a popular genre of fiction as well. Many children growing up in the United States of the 1950s had thoroughly internalized the western's conventions. Television stories, dime novels, Saturday matinees had laid down the guidelines. Boys especially learned to recognize and employ all the necessary elements.

    American children of this generation had no difficulty recognizing a western. Although they had no critical consciousness of genre, their expectations were easily put into play. When they saw the quiet stranger ride into town, they knew much of what was to follow. The stranger would befriend a weak person. He would stand tall against a threatening bad guy (usually a braggart). He would resist "gunplay," but after many provocations he would enter and win a shoot-out. Then a grateful town would watch him ride off into the sunset. In various forms, all had seen that story many times. Good and bad were black and white. Good guys didn't want to fight, yet they always won the fights they entered—at least the fight that really counted, the decisive shoot-out at the climax. Civilization, peace, and stability were at stake at the

Very young boys who grew up in the 1950s learned to mimic the gestures of their western heroes.

Note that the conventional signs of the western are placed amid more generalized military symbols.

opening of the film and were accomplished facts by the end. Of course, the real world of the 1950s was not so simple. No period of history is ever simple. But the highly conventionalized westerns of that time may have signaled a desire for clarity or perhaps a denial of complexity.

Experiencing Film through Genre

Popular movies provide especially clear illustrations of how genres take shape and change to reflect the mood of the times. Film and television are, after all, the most widely shared forms of artistic expression in our culture. We sit with others to watch a movie; we see and hear how others respond as we respond. We come to build a shared knowledge of scenes, characters, images, and plots that we bring to and add to each movie we see. We can all readily identify a wealth of types: screwball comedies, combat films, horror films, musicals, gangster movies, buddy movies, and so on. Thinking about three western movies from three different periods can help us see how—and to what end—conventions take shape and are disrupted as social and political attitudes shift.

Shane (1953) has been called the "perfect" western, and to the extent that it embodies key elements of the classic western, it may well be. Based on a 1949 novel of the same title by Jack Schaefer, Shane evokes a myth of growth and opportunity that had a powerful hold on the United States just after World War II. The country had come out of the Depression and a war. Men were coming back to start careers. Women were sometimes forced to leave careers to make room for those men. Tract homes were laid down; marriages made; children born; schools built. It's this cultural context that gives rise to Shane. The main action of Shane deals with the threat to the Starrett family and resolves itself in the defense of that family. Joe (Van Heflin), Marian (Jean Arthur), and their son (Brandon De Wilde) are the idealized ancestors of people going to the movies in 1953. Those moviegoers appreciated the conventions that both tested and rewarded the Starretts' hard work, honesty, determination, and decency. They felt that they had inherited the world that Shane and the Starretts had labored and fought to secure.

By the mid- to late 1960s, the western's myth of progress seemed too accepting of conventional roles and rules and too optimistic about what violence could achieve. Shane had been one of the most popular films of its day, but by 1970 straightforward westerns had nearly disappeared. In fact, one of the biggest box-office hits of 1974 was Blazing Saddles—a western made to ridicule westerns. In this film, director Mel Brooks shrewdly plays a fairly common strategy: when a genre becomes overworked or out of touch, it

Shane (1953)

is ripe for satire. The values that once gave it force become subject to dismissal. In *Blazing Saddles*, the western's conventions are wildly disrupted. The main result is a kind of low humor: cowboys noisily fart around the campfire after eating beans; the barmaid (Madeline Kahn) enjoys decidedly phallic sausages at dinner with the new sheriff (Cleavon Little). In the more serious parts of the general fun, Brooks pokes holes in racial and gender assumptions built into conventional westerns: a crooked politician (Harvey Korman) appoints an African American man sheriff because he knows that the racist townspeople won't accept the rule of law from a man they consider inferior. By mocking most everything that was presented seriously in *Shane*, *Blazing Saddles* signaled a new perspective on earlier notions of social progress. A popular genre, along with the beliefs that the genre supported, seemed almost laughed out of existence.

The western, however, was too much a part of the general culture to die out completely. Even if people could no longer accept conventions of the western uncritically, they could still be trusted to recognize those conventions and the values they once encoded. In *Unforgiven* (1992), director Clint Eastwood found ways to use the audience's knowledge of genre in serious and unsettling ways. Working from a screenplay by David Webb Peoples, Eastwood creates a film that subtly disrupts the conventional western point by point. *Unforgiven* makes us reflect upon the significance of the

Unforgiven (1992)

expectations shaped by classic westerns like *Shane*. William Munny (played by Eastwood)—a man of notorious temper and character—has been "reformed" by the love of a woman. This seems to begin where Shane wanted to end, but *Unforgiven* opens with Munny digging his wife's grave. Although Munny had become a hardworking family man, he finds the farm and the children offer little satisfaction. To make matters worse, Munny's pigs have "the fever." As he labors to separate those infected from the few that remain healthy, Munny is literally dragged through the mud and excrement. Conventionalized scenes of work in *Shane* had idealized the healthiness and productivity of hard work.

Munny soon receives an offer to join in the contract killing of two cowboys who "cut up a woman." So, like Shane, he finds himself returning to his violent past; unlike Shane, however, Munny returns to type at the beginning, not the end, of the story. Even though Munny at first says the cowboys "deserve" killing, it quickly becomes clear that "deserve has nothing to do with it" (a point made explicit at the end).

A Note to Student Writers: Moving beyond Formulaic Writing

Genres aren't identifiable only in stories, poems, films, and plays. Academic essays also develop generic characteristics. Although it is important to understand that conventions of form, tone, argument, and presentation do operate in critical essays of various types, far too often academic genres are reduced to one overly simple and severely limited formula: "five-paragraph essay." This formula is sometimes presented (or understood) as a fixed model. Students are taught that they *must* introduce a topic and assert a thesis in the first paragraph, follow the thesis with three supporting points (a paragraph for each point), and conclude in a final paragraph. More generous, but still cramped, lessons allow for a slight expansion of the same basic model (that is, students are allowed an additional paragraph or two in the body for more supporting points). If we understand the teaching of such models as intended to communicate very basic ideas about structure (that papers should have a beginning, middle, and end), there is little harm done. But it is very important to realize that not all "good writing" about any subject can be neatly contained by an inflexible organizational formula.

Perhaps the biggest problem with working from any set model is that such a practice makes the formula the primary point. In other words, the structure doesn't allow for ideas to grow. It imposes limits upon any complex thoughts we may discover or hope to explore. A careful reading of almost any good essay will reveal that one point need not be contained by one paragraph, that there is no "right" number of paragraphs. Writers don't "fill in" a preset number of paragraphs; they develop paragraphs as their ideas unfold and as the argument demands. We suggest that you remember that academic genres, like literary genres, are multiple and are subject to change. Most important, remember that genres function to shape and express meaning, not to box meaning in.

MODELING CRITICAL ANALYSIS: TOM STOPPARD, THE FIFTEEN MINUTE HAMLET

Tom Stoppard's *The Fifteen Minute Hamlet* (p. 1487) presents much of the action of the original play: the ghost of Hamlet's father comes and asks for revenge; Hamlet rebukes his mother; Hamlet kills Polonius; Claudius sends him away; Ophelia goes mad, dies, and is buried; Laertes mourns. Laertes strikes Hamlet with a poison-tipped foil; Hamlet cuts Laertes with the same; Gertrude drinks unknowingly from a poisoned cup; Hamlet stabs Claudius. All die. Fortinbras arrives and acknowledges Hamlet's nobility. Surely all that death adds up to tragedy—or surely not. Stoppard's radical cutting disrupts any sense of tragedy. Aristotle defined tragedy as an imitation of a profound action that an audience could identify with and through that identification achieve a kind of release, what Aristotle termed **catharsis**. Stoppard keeps a distance from reality; he imitates only a play. We're conscious from the start of gaps in character development as his version of *Hamlet* rockets forward. Because we're not given any reason to care about the characters, we cannot react emotionally to their fates. In fact, we have no reason to think of these characters as having any existence off the stage. The artifice of it all is made especially apparent by the fact that in this fifteen-minute version, everyone dies twice—once in the main body of the play and once in the still more radically abbreviated encore.

By racing through Shakespeare's *Hamlet* and grabbing tiny bits of memorable lines and key scenes, Stoppard asks us to consider what constitutes the play and the genre. We know this is not *Hamlet*, yet we recognize much of *Hamlet* in it. Whatever made that play a tragedy gets left out. What is left in it moves us to a very different genre. Imagine how this play would be performed. The speed would lend it many of the characteristics of a slapstick comedy or farce (a physical comedy): characters in *The Fifteen Minute Hamlet* charge about, rush onstage and offstage, deliver lines without context, fall down dead, get up, and fall down dead again before getting up once more to welcome the cheers of the audience. The audience at a well-produced staging of *The Fifteen Minute Hamlet* will be laughing throughout.

Stoppard may also be asking us to reflect back seriously on Shakespeare's play and on the way we may diminish tragedies. It's possible his reduction serves as a comment on a common resistance to really experiencing literature. Do we engage great works of art directly or look for shortcuts (study guides, for example) that allow us to display knowledge (on tests or in social situations) about great works? Do we too often substitute secondhand representations of literature in place of literature itself? Do we learn "about" literature, or do we read and respond? Stoppard reminds us that a plot summary cannot communicate the experience that we have when we watch or read *Hamlet*; the work is a complex organism that deserves study because of the careful balance that it achieves among all literary elements. And if we've read it only for what happens, we've written our own fifteen-minute version without knowing it. If that were the case, the laugh would be on us.

Using Genre to Focus Writing and Discussion

To write about any genre, we must establish the characteristics that define it. Remember that in most cases, the label of type of genre comes after the creation of the text. The generic label is a critical tool that we can use to group similar works together, and it is quite appropriate to consider a single work in multiple generic categories.

- To define the genre, first consider which specific works we have grouped together. What common elements do these works share? What is the rationale for this particular grouping?

- How important are these particular elements to understanding each work?

- How do we understand each of the works better because we have grouped them in this manner?

- To what extent is our definition of this genre something that the works themselves are conscious of? How can you demonstrate this consciousness? For instance, are there allusions to other works within the genre or discussions of conventions within the work itself or disruptions of the generic conventions within the work?

- What aspects of the work does our attention to genre keep us from considering?

- What other genres might we use to group any of the works that we have gathered here?

- Considerations of genre are often fairly clear in the field of film. Think of a recent film that you think belongs to a well-established genre. What would you call the genre? What elements are repeated? What expectations are invoked? Does this film disrupt any conventions? How would you describe the disruption? What is the effect of both the conventions and the disruptions?

Anthology

HONORING THE DEAD AND DIGNIFYING DEATH: TRACING GENRE

People seek ways to register an appropriate seriousness about the subject of death—a respectful seriousness that validates not only the life of the person who died but life in general. Works of art that address the passing of an individual are often highly conventionalized (the word *passing* itself acknowledges a convention of "high" diction). There are words, gestures, routines, and rituals that we use to give public shape to our feelings. In the seventeenth century, John Milton could draw upon a rich poetic tradition to lament the loss of his college friend Edward King. Milton's poem "Lycidas" works within the genre of the elegy, more specifically the **pastoral** elegy. King becomes Lycidas, a young shepherd who had been "nursed upon the self-same hill" as the speaker of the poem. That shepherd's life was one of music, poetry, and ardent love of surrounding nature. Milton's poem is an acknowledged masterpiece of its type, but it may seem silly to a reader today who is totally unfamiliar with that type. After all, neither Milton nor King was a shepherd. And real shepherds hardly have the time, comfort, or inclination to play "rural ditties" and tame "rough satyrs" with the melodious tones of the flute. Perhaps even more notably, Milton's sadness for his friend becomes secondary to his feeling for other, more generalized losses. How do we move from a tribute to a young man who has died to a subject such as the corruption of the clergy?

The generic conventions Milton worked within were intended to lend both dignity and distance to the life of the individual who had died. The pastoral elegy deliberately invoked "antique" words and settings—a kind of mythic past that no one (now or in Milton's time) would take as real. Milton sought to universalize his friend, to make his life transcend the specific conditions of everyday matters; death itself was for Milton a much bigger subject than the death of a particular person. We've lost touch with the specific conditions of the pastoral elegy (although we can certainly learn them and respond to "Lycidas" if we give it a chance). But we still have our own conventions for dealing with death and making meaning of it. And we need to both employ and occasionally disrupt those conventions if we are to communicate fully regarding a subject of such profound importance.

In the following anthology you'll find works that accept, disrupt, or dismiss elegiac conventions our culture has used to honor individuals who have died as well as to reflect upon death and loss. We've used the word *elegy* in a broadly descriptive way. Poetic conventions, after all, need not be exclusively invoked by poems. It's common to refer to novels, plays, or films as elegies or as expressing an elegiac mood. In this usage, death itself may be subordinate to a broader sense of loss, a lament for a quality of life that has passed. As you read and reflect upon each work, think of how the work functions in relation to established conventions.

Langston Hughes's "Night Funeral in Harlem" conveys a delicate mixture of emotional involvement and philosophical detachment. Hughes acknowledges poetic as well as social conventions, but he can't employ those conventions uncritically. His central question is a cuttingly direct one: How can such a poor young man have a funeral of any substance? The young man whom Hughes reflects upon is exactly the sort of young man many people dismiss in death as well as life. He is young, black, and poor; he has no "important" friends to extend him favors. The insurance man will help out in a small way only because he does not have to come up with a settlement (the subject's insurance had just lapsed).

But the young man has lived and has touched his immediate community. His friends (conscious of their own mortality) collect enough for some flowers. And his girlfriend has enough to pay the preacher. In context of the friends' own limited resources, these gestures are profoundly generous. The people who knew the young man—not the fine cars, or flowers, or preacher—make the funeral "grand." Perhaps the last gift to the young man, however, is the poem itself. It notices and records the grandness. In writing an elegy, Hughes is formally recognizing the human reality of this nameless young man and of those who loved him. He is laying claim for the worth and dignity of his subject.

Hughes's poem reminds us that death may be the occasion that prompts an expression, but it need not be the subject of the expression. In "Happy Endings" Margaret Atwood suggests that death is hardly the best subject for an author. Her playfully serious story both recognizes conventions and suggests we dispense with most of them. She observes that the end of any story, if we follow it far enough, is death; that truth seems to leave Atwood with little to say. So why not, she asks, accept the ending and concentrate on the motivations that lie behind the infinitely variable actions that unfold on the way to that end? Questions that focus on "how" and "why" to her mind will defy the restrictions of any formula. Katherine Anne Porter's story "The Jilting of Granny Weatherall" ends as Atwood suggests all stories end. It's likely that Atwood would be pleased though that Porter has Granny Weatherall's death intensify those difficult passages that compose the middle portions of life. Death, in fact, is cast as a final jilting that encompasses all the cheats and injustices felt over the main character's eighty years of living. In their very different ways, Hughes, Atwood, and Porter try to turn attention back from the occasion of death to the concerns of life.

Sophocles' *Antigone* is a play in which all action grows from honoring/dishonoring the dead. The action of *Antigone* occurs after that of *Oedipus the King* (p. 67). Eteocles and Polyneices had ruled Thebes jointly after the abdication of their father, Oedipus, but their partnership did not last. Polyneices, after being expelled by Eteocles, returns to Thebes to regain his throne. The brothers kill each other in battle, and the next king, Creon, chooses to bury only Eteocles with proper ceremony; Polyneices' body is to be left exposed to the elements. Antigone, their sister, refuses to accept Creon's judgment. Her death results, and that death serves to register the depth of her own commitment and dignity.

FICTION

Katherine Anne Porter (1890–1980)

Katherine Anne Porter was born Callie Russell Porter in Indian Creek, Texas. Her mother died when Porter was two, and she, her siblings, and her father moved to Kyle, Texas, where they lived with Porter's paternal grandmother, Catherine Anne Skaggs Porter. Porter later lived with various relatives before marrying her first husband in 1906. Their marriage was unhappy, and Porter eventually divorced her husband. Her personal life would continue to be marked by unfulfilling relationships, and she married and divorced four times. She began her writing career as a reporter, and her travels to war-torn Mexico inspired her first and second creative publications, the short stories "Maria Conception" (1922) and "The Martyr" (1923). Porter continued to travel and write and published nearly two dozen works of fiction and nonfiction. Her 1965 publication *The Collected Stories of Katherine Anne Porter* received both the National Book Award and Pulitzer Prize in 1966.

The Jilting of Granny Weatherall (1930)

She flicked her wrist neatly out of Doctor Harry's pudgy careful fingers and pulled the sheet up to her chin. The brat ought to be in knee breeches. Doctoring around the country with spectacles on his nose! "Get along now, take your schoolbooks and go. There's nothing wrong with me."

Doctor Harry spread a warm paw like a cushion on her forehead where the forked green vein danced and made her eyelids twitch. "Now, now, be a good girl, and we'll have you up in no time."

"That's no way to speak to a woman nearly eighty years old just because she's down. I'd have you respect your elders, young man."

"Well, Missy, excuse me." Doctor Harry patted her cheek. "But I've got to warn you, haven't I? You're a marvel, but you must be careful or you're going to be good and sorry."

"Don't tell me what I'm going to be. I'm on my feet now, morally speaking. It's Cornelia. I had to go to bed to get rid of her." 5

Her bones felt loose, and floated around in her skin, and Doctor Harry floated like a balloon around the foot of the bed. He floated and pulled down his waist-coat and swung his glasses on a cord. "Well, stay where you are, it certainly can't hurt you."

"Get along and doctor your sick," said Granny Weatherall. "Leave a well woman alone. I'll call for you when I want you. . . . Where were you forty years ago when I pulled through milk-leg and double pneumonia? You weren't even born. Don't let Cornelia lead you on," she shouted, because Doctor Harry appeared to float up to the ceiling and out. "I pay my own bills, and I don't throw my money away on nonsense!"

She meant to wave good-by, but it was too much trouble. Her eyes closed of themselves, it was like a dark curtain drawn around the bed. The pillow rose and floated under her, pleasant as a hammock in a light wind. She listened to the leaves rustling outside the window. No, somebody was swishing newspapers: no, Cornelia and Doctor Harry were whispering together. She leaped broad awake, thinking they whispered in her ear.

"She was never like this, *never* like this!" "Well, what can we expect?" "Yes, eighty years old. . . ."

Well, and what if she was? She still had ears. It was like Cornelia to whisper around doors. She always kept things secret in such a public way. She was always being tactful and kind. Cornelia was dutiful; that was the trouble with her. Dutiful and good: "So good and dutiful," said Granny, "that I'd like to spank her." She saw herself spanking Cornelia and making a fine job of it.

"What'd you say, Mother?"

Granny felt her face tying up in hard knots.

"Can't a body think, I'd like to know?"

"I thought you might want something."

"I do. I want a lot of things. First off, go away and don't whisper."

She lay and drowsed, hoping in her sleep that the children would keep out and let her rest a minute. It had been a long day. Not that she was tired. It was always pleasant to snatch a minute now and then. There was always so much to be done, let me see: tomorrow.

Tomorrow was far away and there was nothing to trouble about. Things were finished somehow when the time came; thank God there was always a little margin over for peace: then a person could spread out the plan of life and tuck in the edges orderly. It was good to have everything clean and folded away, with the hair brushes and tonic bottles sitting straight on the white embroidered linen: the day started without fuss and the pantry shelves laid out with rows of jelly glasses and brown jugs and white stone-china jars with blue whirligigs and words painted on them: coffee, tea, sugar, ginger, cinnamon, allspice: and the bronze clock with the lion on top nicely dusted off. The dust that lion could collect in twenty-four hours! The box in the attic with all those letters tied up, well, she'd have to go through that tomorrow. All those letters—George's letters and John's letters and her letters to them both—lying around for the children to find afterwards made her uneasy. Yes, that would be tomorrow's business. No use to let them know how silly she had been once.

While she was rummaging around she found death in her mind and it felt clammy and unfamiliar. She had spent so much time preparing for

death there was no need for bringing it up again. Let it take care of itself
now. When she was sixty she had felt very old, finished, and went around
making farewell trips to see her children and grandchildren, with a secret in
her mind: This is the very last of your mother, children! Then she made her
will and came down with a long fever. That was all just a notion like a lot
of other things, but it was lucky too, for she had once and for all got over
the idea of dying for a long time. Now she couldn't be worried. She hoped
she had better sense now. Her father had lived to be one hundred and two
years old and had drunk a noggin of strong hot toddy on his last birthday.
He told the reporters it was his daily habit, and he owed his long life to
that. He had made quite a scandal and was very pleased about it. She believed she'd just plague Cornelia a little.

"Cornelia! Cornelia!" No footsteps, but a sudden hand on her cheek.
"Bless you, where have you been?"

"Here, Mother."   20

"Well, Cornelia, I want a noggin of hot toddy."

"Are you cold, darling?"

"I'm chilly, Cornelia. Lying in bed stops the circulation. I must have
told you that a thousand times."

Well, she could just hear Cornelia telling her husband that Mother was
getting a little childish and they'd have to humor her. The thing that most
annoyed her was that Cornelia thought she was deaf, dumb, and blind. Little hasty glances and tiny gestures tossed around her and over her head
saying, "Don't cross her, let her have her way, she's eighty years old," and
she sitting there as if she lived in a thin glass cage. Sometimes Granny almost made up her mind to pack up and move back to her own house where
nobody could remind her every minute that she was old. Wait, wait, Cornelia, till your own children whisper behind your back!

In her day she had kept a better house and had got more work done.   25
She wasn't too old yet for Lydia to be driving eighty miles for advice when
one of the children jumped the track, and Jimmy still dropped in and talked
things over: "Now, Mammy, you've a good business head, I want to know
what you think of this? . . . " Old. Cornelia couldn't change the furniture
around without asking. Little things, little things! They had been so sweet
when they were little. Granny wished the old days were back again with the
children young and everything to be done over. It had been a hard pull, but
not too much for her. When she thought of all the food she had cooked,
and all the clothes she had cut and sewed, and all the gardens she had
made—well, the children showed it. There they were, made out of her, and
they couldn't get away from that. Sometimes she wanted to see John again
and point to them and say, Well, I didn't do so badly, did I? But that would
have to wait. That was for tomorrow. She used to think of him as a man,
but now all the children were older than their father, and he would be a

child beside her if she saw him now. It seemed strange and there was something wrong in the idea. Why, he couldn't possibly recognize her. She had fenced in a hundred acres once, digging the post holes herself and clamping the wires with just a negro boy to help. That changed a woman. John would be looking for a young woman with the peaked Spanish comb in her hair and the painted fan. Digging post holes changed a woman. Riding country roads in the winter when women had their babies was another thing: sitting up nights with sick horses and sick negroes and sick children and hardly ever losing one. John, I hardly ever lost one of them! John would see that in a minute, that would be something he could understand, she wouldn't have to explain anything!

It made her feel like rolling up her sleeves and putting the whole place to rights again. No matter if Cornelia was determined to be everywhere at once, there were a great many things left undone on this place. She would start tomorrow and do them. It was good to be strong enough for everything, even if all you made melted and changed and slipped under your hands, so that by the time you finished you almost forgot what you were working for. What was it I set out to do? she asked herself intently, but she could not remember. A fog rose over the valley, she saw it marching across the creek swallowing the trees and moving up the hill like an army of ghosts. Soon it would be at the near edge of the orchard, and then it was time to go in and light the lamps. Come in, children, don't stay out in the night air.

Lighting the lamps had been beautiful. The children huddled up to her and breathed like little calves waiting at the bars in the twilight. Their eyes followed the match and watched the flame rise and settle in a blue curve, then they moved away from her. The lamp was lit, they didn't have to be scared and hang on to mother any more. Never, never, never more. God, for all my life I thank Thee. Without Thee, my God, I could never have done it. Hail, Mary, full of grace.

I want you to pick all the fruit this year and see that nothing is wasted. There's always someone who can use it. Don't let good things rot for want of using. You waste life when you waste good food. Don't let things get lost. It's bitter to lose things. Now, don't let me get to thinking, not when I am tired and taking a little nap before supper....

The pillow rose about her shoulders and pressed against her heart and the memory was being squeezed out of it: oh, push down the pillow, somebody: it would smother her if she tried to hold it. Such a fresh breeze blowing and such a green day with no threats in it. But he had not come, just the same. What does a woman do when she has put on the white veil and set out the white cake for a man and he doesn't come? She tried to remember. No, I swear he never harmed me but in that. He never harmed me but in that ... and what if he did? There was the day, the day, but a whirl of dark smoke rose and covered it, crept up and over into the bright field where everything was planted so carefully in orderly rows. That was hell, she knew hell when she saw it. For sixty years she had prayed against remembering him and against losing her soul in the deep pit of hell, and now the two things were mingled in one and the thought of him was a smoky cloud from hell that moved and crept in her head when she had just got rid of Doctor Harry and was trying to rest a minute. Wounded vanity, Ellen, said a sharp voice in the top of her mind. Don't let your wounded vanity get the upper hand of you. Plenty of girls get jilted. You were jilted, weren't you? Then stand up to it. Her eyelids wavered and let in streamers of blue-gray light like tissue paper over her eyes. She must get up and pull the shades down or she'd never sleep. She was in bed again and the shades were not down. How could that happen? Better turn over, hide from the light, sleeping in the light gave you nightmares. "Mother, how do you feel now?" and a stinging wetness on her forehead. But I don't like having my face washed in cold water!

Hapsy? George? Lydia? Jimmy? No, Cornelia, and her features were 30 swollen and full of little puddles. "They're coming, darling, they'll all be here soon." Go wash your face, child, you look funny.

Instead of obeying, Cornelia knelt down and put her head on the pillow. She seemed to be talking but there was no sound. "Well, are you tongue-tied? Whose birthday is it? Are you going to give a party?"

Cornelia's mouth moved urgently in strange shapes. "Don't do that, you bother me, daughter."

"O, no, Mother. Oh, no. . . ."

Nonsense. It was strange about children. They disputed your every word. "No what, Cornelia?"

"Here's Doctor Harry." 35

"I won't see that boy again. He just left five minutes ago."

"That was this morning, Mother. It's night now. Here's the nurse."

"This is Doctor Harry, Mrs. Weatherall. I never saw you look so young and happy!"

"Ah, I'll never be young again—but I'd be happy if they'd let me lie in peace and get rested."

She thought she spoke up loudly, but no one answered. A warm weight 40 on her forehead, a warm bracelet on her wrist, and a breeze went on whispering, trying to tell her something. A shuffle of leaves in the everlasting hand of God. He blew on them and they danced and rattled. "Mother, don't mind, we're going to give you a little hypodermic." "Look here, daughter, how do ants get in this bed? I saw sugar ants yesterday." Did you send for Hapsy too?

It was Hapsy she really wanted. She had to go a long way back through a great many rooms to find Hapsy standing with a baby on her arm. She seemed to herself to be Hapsy also, and the baby on Hapsy's arm was Hapsy and himself and herself, all at once, and there was no surprise in the meeting. Then Hapsy melted from within and turned flimsy as gray gauze and the baby was a gauzy shadow, and Hapsy came up close and said. "I thought you'd never come," and looked at her very searchingly and said, "You haven't changed a bit!" They leaned forward to kiss, when Cornelia began whispering from a long way off, "Oh, is there anything you want to tell me? Is there anything I can do for you?"

Yes, she had changed her mind after sixty years and she would like to see George. I want you to find George. Find him and be sure to tell him I forgot him. I want him to know I had my husband just the same and my children and my house like any other woman. A good house too and a good husband that I loved and fine children out of him. Better than I hoped for even. Tell him I was given back everything he took away and more. Oh, no, oh, God, no, there was something else besides the house and the man and the children. Oh, surely they were not all? What was it? Something not given back. . . . Her breath crowded down under her ribs and grew into a monstrous frightening shape with cutting edges; it bored up into her head, and the agony was un-believable: Yes, John, get the Doctor now, no more talk, my time has come.

When this one was born it should be the last. The last. It should have been born first, for it was the one she had truly wanted. Everything came in good time. Nothing left out, left over. She was strong, in three days she would be as well as ever. Better. A woman needed milk in her to have her full health.

"Mother, do you hear me?"

"I've been telling you—"

"Mother, Father Connolly's here."

"I went to Holy Communion last week. Tell him I'm not so sinful as all that."

"Father just wants to speak to you."

He could speak as much as he pleased. It was like him to drop in and in-quire about her soul as if it were a teething baby, and then stay on for a cup of tea and a round of cards and gossip. He always had a funny story of some sort, usually about an Irishman who made his little mistakes and confessed them, and the point lay in some absurd thing he would blurt out in the con-fessional showing his struggles between native piety and original sin. Granny felt easy about her soul. Cornelia, where are your manners? Give Father Con-nolly a chair. She had her secret comfortable understanding with a few favor-ite saints who cleared a straight road to God for her. All as surely signed and sealed as the papers for the new Forty Acres. Forever . . . heirs and assigns forever. Since the day the wedding cake was not cut, but thrown out and wasted. The whole bottom dropped out of the world, and there she was blind and sweating with nothing under her feet and the walls falling away. His hand had caught her under the breast, she had not fallen, there was the freshly polished floor with the green rug on it, just as before. He had cursed like a sailor's parrot and said, "I'll kill him for you." Don't lay a hand on him, for my sake leave something to God. "Now, Ellen, you must believe what I tell you. . . ."

So there was nothing, nothing to worry about any more, except some-   50
times in the night one of the children screamed in a nightmare, and they both hustled out shaking and hunting for the matches and calling, "There, wait a minute, here we are!" John, get the doctor now, Hapsy's time has come. But there was Hapsy standing by the bed in a white cap. "Cornelia, tell Hapsy to take off her cap. I can't see her plain."

Her eyes opened very wide and the room stood out like a picture she had seen somewhere. Dark colors with the shadows rising towards the ceiling in long angles. The tall black dresser gleamed with nothing on it but John's picture, enlarged from a little one, with John's eyes very black when they should have been blue. You never saw him, so how do you know how he looked? But the man insisted the copy was perfect, it was very rich and handsome. For a picture, yes, but it's not my husband. The table by the bed had a linen cover and a candle and a crucifix. The light was blue from Cornelia's silk lampshades. No sort of light at all, just frippery. You had to live forty years with kerosene lamps to appreciate honest electricity. She felt very strong and she saw Doctor Harry with a rosy nimbus around him.

"You look like a saint, Doctor Harry, and I vow that's as near as you'll ever come to it."

"She's saying something."

"I heard you, Cornelia. What's all this carrying-on?"

"Father Connolly's saying—"   55

Cornelia's voice staggered and bumped like a cart in a bad road. It rounded corners and turned back again and arrived nowhere. Granny stepped up in the cart very lightly and reached for the reins, but a man sat beside her and she knew him by his hands, driving the cart. She did not look in his face, for she knew without seeing, but looked instead down the road where the trees leaned over and bowed to each other and a thousand birds were singing a Mass. She felt like singing too, but she put her hand in the bosom of her dress and pulled out a rosary and Father Connolly murmured Latin in a very solemn voice and tickled her feet. My God, will you stop that nonsense? I'm a married woman. What if he did run away and leave me to face the priest by myself? I found another a whole world better. I wouldn't have exchanged my husband for anybody except St. Michael himself, and you may tell him that for me with a thank you in the bargain.

Light flashed on her closed eyelids, and a deep roaring shook her. Cornelia, is that lightning? I hear thunder. There's going to be a storm. Close all the windows. Call the children in. . . . "Mother, here we are, all of us." "Is that you, Hapsy?" "Oh, no, I'm Lydia. We drove as fast as we could." Their faces drifted above her, drifted away. The rosary fell out of her hands and Lydia put it back. Jimmy tried to help, their hands fumbled together, and Granny closed two fingers around Jimmy's thumb. Beads wouldn't do, it must be something alive. She was so amazed her thoughts ran round and round. So, my dear Lord, this is my death and I wasn't even thinking about it. My children have come to see me die. But I can't, it's not time. Oh, I always hated surprises. I wanted to give Cornelia the amethyst set—Cornelia, you're to have the amethyst set, but Hapsy's to wear it when she wants, and, Doctor Harry, do shut up. Nobody sent for you. Oh, my dear Lord, do wait a minute. I meant to do something about the Forty Acres, Jimmy doesn't need it and Lydia will later on, with that worthless husband of hers. I meant to finish the altar cloth and send six bottles of wine to Sister Borgia for her dyspepsia. I want to send six bottles of wine to Sister Borgia, Father Connolly, now don't let me forget.

Cornelia's voice made short turns and tilted over and crashed. "Oh, Mother, oh, Mother, oh, Mother...."

"I'm not going, Cornelia. I'm taken by surprise. I can't go."

You'll see Hapsy again. What about her? "I thought you'd never come." Granny made a long journey outward, looking for Hapsy. What if I don't find her? What then? Her heart sank down and down, there was no bottom to death, she couldn't come to the end of it. The blue light from Cornelia's lampshade drew into a tiny point in the center of her brain, it flickered and winked like an eye, quietly it fluttered and dwindled. Granny lay curled down within herself, amazed and watchful, staring at the point of light that was herself; her body was now only a deeper mass of shadow in an endless darkness and this darkness would curl around the light and swallow it up. God, give a sign!

For the second time there was no sign. Again no bridegroom and the priest in the house. She could not remember any other sorrow because this grief wiped them all away. Oh, no, there's nothing more cruel than this—I'll never forgive it. She stretched herself with a deep breath and blew out the light.

- How does this story present the specter of death? Look at specific instances where Granny Weatherall uses other events in her life to explain what is happening as she dies.
- In what ways does she cheat death?
- How might we describe this story as part of a genre of stories about death? As you read the other works in this section, consider what techniques used in this story we see in other works.
- How do the other characters in the story relate to Granny Weatherall? How does she relate to them?

Margaret Atwood (1939–)

The most prominent Canadian writer of her generation, Margaret Atwood was born in Ottawa. She began her literary career as a poet and then moved into other genres. Over the course of her career she has become an important cultural spokesperson, focusing in particular on feminist concerns. In addition to writing in almost every genre, she is a painter and illustrator. Atwood focuses often in her poetry on images of violence, and critics have commented on the impersonality of her early poetry, while noting the relative openness of her more recent work. It is not as a poet, however, that she is best known, but as the author of such best-selling novels as *The Handmaid's Tale*, which was made into a motion picture, and *Cat's Cradle*.

Happy Endings (1992)

John and Mary meet.
>What happens next?
>If you want a happy ending, try A.

A. John and Mary fall in love and get married. They both have worthwhile and remunerative jobs which they find stimulating and challenging. They buy a charming house. Real estate values go up. Eventually, when they can afford live-in help, they have two children, to whom they are devoted. The children turn out well. John and Mary have a stimulating and challenging sex life and worthwhile friends. They go on fun vacations together. They retire. They both have hobbies which they find stimulating and challenging. Eventually they die. This is the end of the story.

B. Mary falls in love with John but John doesn't fall in love with Mary. He   5
merely uses her body for selfish pleasure and ego gratification of a tepid kind. He comes to her apartment twice a week and she cooks him dinner, you'll notice that he doesn't even consider her worth the price of a dinner out, and after he's eaten the dinner he fucks her and after that he falls asleep, while she does the dishes so he won't think she's untidy, having all those dirty dishes lying around, and puts on fresh lipstick so she'll look good when he wakes up, but when he wakes up he doesn't even notice, he puts on his socks and his shorts and his pants and his shirt and his tie and his shoes, the reverse order from the one in which he took them off. He doesn't take off Mary's clothes, she takes them off herself, she acts as if she's dying for it every time, not because she likes sex exactly, she doesn't, but she wants John to think she does because if they do it often enough surely he'll get used to her, he'll come

to depend on her and they will get married, but John goes out the door with hardly so much as a good-night and three days later he turns up at six o'clock and they do the whole thing over again.

Mary gets run-down. Crying is bad for your face, everyone knows that and so does Mary but she can't stop. People at work notice. Her friends tell her John is a rat, a pig, a dog, he isn't good enough for her, but she can't believe it. Inside John, she thinks, is another John, who is much nicer. This other John will emerge like a butterfly from a cocoon, a Jack from a box, a pit from a prune, if the first John is only squeezed enough.

One evening John complains about the food. He has never complained about the food before. Mary is hurt.

Her friends tell her they've seen him in a restaurant with another woman, whose name is Madge. It's not even Madge that finally gets to Mary: it's the restaurant. John has never taken Mary to a restaurant. Mary collects all the sleeping pills and aspirins she can find, and takes them and a half a bottle of sherry. You can see what kind of a woman she is by the fact that it's not even whiskey. She leaves a note for John. She hopes he'll discover her and get her to the hospital in time and repent and then they can get married, but this fails to happen and she dies.

John marries Madge and everything continues as in A.

C. John, who is an older man, falls in love with Mary, and Mary, who is only twenty-two, feels sorry for him because he's worried about his hair falling out. She sleeps with him even though she's not in love with him. She met him at work. She's in love with someone called James, who is twenty-two also and not yet ready to settle down.

John on the contrary settled down long ago: this is what is bothering him. John has a steady, respectable job and is getting ahead in his field, but Mary isn't impressed by him, she's impressed by James, who has a motorcycle and a fabulous record collection. But James is often away on his motorcycle, being free. Freedom isn't the same for girls, so in the meantime Mary spends Thursday evenings with John. Thursdays are the only days John can get away.

John is married to a woman called Madge and they have two children, a charming house which they bought just before the real estate values went up, and hobbies which they find stimulating and challenging, when they have the time. John tells Mary how important she is to him, but of course he can't leave his wife because a commitment is a commitment. He goes on about this more than is necessary and Mary finds it boring, but older men can keep it up longer so on the whole she has a fairly good time.

One day James breezes in on his motorcycle with some top-grade California hybrid and James and Mary get higher than you'd believe possible and they climb into bed. Everything becomes very underwater, but along comes John, who has a key to Mary's apartment. He finds them stoned and entwined. He's hardly in any position to be jealous, considering Madge, but nevertheless he's overcome with despair. Finally he's middle-aged, in two years he'll be bald as an egg and he can't stand it. He purchases a handgun, saying he needs it for target practice—this is the thin part of the plot, but it can be dealt with later—and shoots the two of them and himself.

Madge, after a suitable period of mourning, marries an understanding man called Fred and everything continues as in A, but under different names.

D. Fred and Madge have no problems. They get along exceptionally well   15
and are good at working out any little difficulties that may arise. But their charming house is by the seashore and one day a giant tidal wave approaches. Real estate values go down. The rest of the story is about what caused the tidal wave and how they escape from it. They do, though thousands drown, but Fred and Madge are virtuous and lucky. Finally on high ground they clasp each other, wet and dripping and grateful, and continue as in A.

E. Yes, but Fred has a bad heart. The rest of the story is about how kind and understanding they both are until Fred dies. Then Madge devotes herself to charity work until the end of A. If you like, it can be "Madge," "cancer," "guilty and confused," and "bird watching."

F. If you think this is all too bourgeois, make John a revolutionary and Mary a counterespionage agent and see how far that gets you. Remember, this is Canada. You'll still end up with A, though in between you may get a lustful brawling saga of passionate involvement, a chronicle of our times, sort of.

You'll have to face it, the endings are the same however you slice it. Don't be deluded by any other endings, they're all fake, either deliberately fake, with malicious intent to deceive, or just motivated by excessive optimism if not by downright sentimentality.

The only authentic ending is the one provided here:
John and Mary die. John and Mary die. John and Mary die.   20

So much for endings. Beginnings are always more fun. True connoisseurs, however, are known to favor the stretch in between, since it's the hardest to do anything with.

That's about all that can be said for plots, which anyway are just one thing after another, a what and a what and a what. Now try How and Why.

- This short story makes us think about the genre of stories, especially the conventions of endings. How could we label each of the endings that the author gives here? Define the elements that characterize each of these genres.
- What, if anything, happens in this story? Where do we see coherent action in spite of the sectional breaks?
- How do the final three paragraphs fit into the rest of this story? To what extent do these remarks shape our understanding of the previous six sections? To what extent is it true that this is a story without "the stretch in between" the beginning and the ending?

POETRY

John Milton (1608–1674)

Lycidas (1638)

A lament for a friend drowned in his passage from Chester on the Irish Seas, 1637.

Yet once more, O ye laurels, and once more
Ye myrtles brown, with ivy never seer,
I come to pluck your Berries harsh and crude,
And with forced fingers rude
Shatter your leaves before the mellowing year.   5
Bitter constraint and sad occasion dear
Compels me to disturb your season due;
For Lycidas is dead, dead ere his prime,
Young Lycidas, and hath not left his peer:
Who would not sing for Lycidas? He knew   10
Himself to sing, and build the lofty rhyme.
He must not float upon his watery bier
Unwept, and welter to the parching wind,
Without the meed of some melodious tear.
   Begin, then, sisters of the sacred well,   15
That from beneath the seat of Jove doth spring;
Begin, and somewhat loudly sweep the string.
Hence with denial vain and coy excuse,
So may some gentle Muse
With lucky words favour my destined urn,   20
And as he passes turn,

And bid fair peace be to my sable shroud.
For we were nursed upon the self-same hill,
Fed the same flock; by fountain, shade, and rill.
Together both, ere the high lawns appeared   25
Under the opening eyelids of the morn,
We drove afield, and both together heard
What time the grey-fly winds her sultry horn,
Battening our flocks with the fresh dews of night
Oft till the star that rose, at evening, bright   30
Toward heaven's descent had sloped his westering wheel.
Meanwhile the rural ditties were not mute,
Tempered to the oaten flute,
Rough satyrs danced, and fauns with cloven heel,
From the glad sound would not be absent long,   35
And old Damætas lov'd to hear our song.
    But oh the heavy change, now thou art gone,
Now thou art gone, and never must return!
Thee shepherd, thee the woods, and desert caves,
With wild thyme and the gadding vine o'ergrown,   40
And all their echoes mourn.
The willows, and the hazel copses green,
Shall now no more be seen,
Fanning their joyous leaves to thy soft lays.
As killing as the canker to the rose,   45
Or taint-worm to the weanling herds that graze,
Or frost to flowers that their gay wardrobe wear
When first the white-thorn blows:
Such, Lycidas, thy loss to shepherd's ear.
    Where were ye nymphs when the remorseless deep   50
Closed o'er the head of your loved Lycidas?
For neither were ye playing on the steep,
Where your old bards, the famous Druids, lie,
Nor on the shaggy top of Mona high,
Nor yet where Deva spreads her wizard stream: 55
Ay me, I fondly dream!
Had ye been there ... for what could that have done?
What could the Muse herself that Orpheus bore,
The Muse herself for her enchanting son
Whom universal nature did lament,   60
When by the rout that made the hideous roar,
His gory visage down the stream was sent,
Down the swift Hebrus to the Lesbian shore.
    Alas! What boots it with uncessant care

To tend the homely slighted shepherd's trade,   65
And strictly meditate the thankless Muse;
Were it not better done as others use,
To sport with Amaryllis in the shade,
Or with the tangles of Neæra's hair?
Fame is the spur that the clear spirit doth raise   70
(That last infirmity of noble mind)
To scorn delights, and live laborious days;
But the fair guerdon when we hope to find,
And think to burst out into sudden blaze,
Comes the blind Fury with th'abhorrèd shears,   75
And slits the thin-spun life. 'But not the praise,'
Phoebus replied, and touched my trembling ears:
'Fame is no plant that grows on mortal soil,
Nor in the glistering foil
Set off to the world, nor in broad rumor lies,   80
But lives and spreads aloft by those pure eyes,
And perfect witnes of all-judging Jove;
As he pronounces lastly on each deed,
Of so much fame in Heaven expect thy meed.'
    O fountain Arethuse, and thou honoured flood,   85
Smooth-sliding Mincius, crown'd with vocal reeds,
That strain I heard was of a higher mood;
But now my oat proceeds,
And listens to the herald of the sea
That came in Neptune's plea,   90
He asked the waves, and asked the fellon winds,
What hard mishap hath doomed this gentle swain,
And questioned every gust of rugged wings
That blows from off each beakèd promontory:
They knew not of his story,   95
And sage Hippotades their answer brings,
That not a blast was from his dungeon strayed,
The air was calm, and on the level brine
Sleek Panope with all her sisters played.
It was that fatal and perfidious bark,   100
Built in the eclipse and rigged with curses dark,
That sunk so low that sacred head of thine.
    Next Camus, reverend sire, went footing slow,
His mantle hairy, and his bonnet sedge,
Inwrought with figures dim, and on the edge   105
Like to that sanguine flower inscribed with woe.
'Ah! Who hath reft,' quoth he, 'my dearest pledge?"

Last came, and last did go,
The pilot of the Galilean lake,
Two massy keys he bore of metals twain, 110
(The golden opes, the Iron shuts amain)
He shook his mitered locks, and stern bespake,
'How well could I have spared for thee, young swain,
Enough of such as for their bellies' sake,
Creep and intrude, and climb into the fold! 115
Of other care they little reckoning make
Than how to scramble at the shearer's feast,
And shove away the worthy bidden guest;
Blind mouths! that scarce themselves know how to hold
A sheep-hook, or have learned aught else the least 120
That to the faithful Herdman's art belongs!
What recks it them? What need they? They are sped;
And when they list, their lean and flashy songs
Grate on their scrannel pipes of wretched straw,
The hungry sheep look up, and are not fed, 125
But swollen with wind and the rank mist they draw
Rot inwardly, and foul contagion spread;
Besides what the grim wolf with privy paw
Daily devours apace, and nothing said,
But that two-handed engine at the door 130
Stands ready to smite once, and smite no more.
    Return Alpheus, the dread voice is past
That shrunk thy streams; return Sicilian Muse,
And call the vales, and bid them hither cast
Their bells, and flowrets of a thousand hues. 135
Ye valleys low where the mild whispers use
Of shades and wanton winds and gushing brooks,
On whose fresh lap the swart star sparely looks,
Throw hither all your quaint enamelled eyes,
That on the green turf suck the honied showers, 140
And purple all the ground with vernal flowers.
Bring the rathe primrose that forsaken dies;
The tufted crow-toe, and pale gessamine,
The white pink, and the pansy freaked with jet,
The glowing violet, 145
The musk-rose, and the well-attired woodbine.
With cowslips wan that hang the pensive head,
And every flower that sad embroidery wears:
Bid amaranthus all his beauty shed,
And daffadillies fill their cups with tears, 150

To strew the laureat herse where Lycid lies.
For so to interpose a little ease
Let our frail thoughts dally with false surmise.
Ay me! Whilst thee the shores and sounding seas
Wash far away, where'er thy bones are hurled: 155
Whether beyond the stormy Hebrides,
Where thou perhaps under the whelming tide
Visitst the bottom of the monstrous world;
Or whether thou, to our moist vows denied,
Sleepst by the fable of Bellerus old,   160
Where the great vision of the guarded mount
Looks toward Namancos and Bayona's hold;
Look homeward angel now, and melt with ruth.
And, O ye dolphins, waft the hapless youth.
  Weep no more, woeful shepherds weep no more,   165
For Lycidas your sorrow is not dead,
Sunk though he be beneath the watery floor,
So sinks the day-star in the ocean bed,
And yet anon repairs his drooping head,
And tricks his beams, and with new spangled ore,   170
Flames in the forehead of the morning sky:
So Lycidas sunk low, but mounted high,
Through the dear might of him that walked the waves;
Where other groves, and other streams along,
With nectar pure his oozy locks he laves,   175
And hears the unexpressive nuptial song,
In the blest kingdoms meek of joy and love.
There entertain him all the saints above,
In solemn troops and sweet societies
That sing, and singing in their glory move,   180
And wipe the tears for ever from his eyes.
Now Lycidas, the shepherds weep no more;
Henceforth thou art the genius of the shore,
In thy large recompense, and shalt be good
To all that wander in that perilous flood.   185
  Thus sang the uncouth swain to the oaks and rills;
While the still morn went out with sandals grey,
He touched the tender stops of various quills,
With eager thought warbling his Doric lay:
And now the sun had stretched out all the hills,   190
And now was dropped into the western bay;
At last he rose, and twitched his mantle blew:
Tomorrow to fresh woods, and pastures new.

- Milton begins his elegy for Lycidas with the phrase "Yet once more," acknowledging that this poem is part of a genre, part of a traditional way of honoring the dead. Within this particular elegy, there is much allusion to classical stories concerning death. Among these allusions, what specific details do we learn about the real person who has died? Find specific instances where the poet describes the failure of different entities to provide appropriate recognition of this death.
- The conceit of this poem is that Lycidas was a shepherd and that the poet, his fellow shepherd, is seeking ways to mourn his friend properly. In lines 152–153, after detailing all of the flowers that could decorate the hearse where the dead boy lies, the poet says, "For so to interpose a little ease, / Let our frail thoughts dally with false surmise." What are these imaginings that the poet invents? How do they provide any ease?

Walt Whitman (1819–1892)

When Lilacs Last in the Dooryard Bloom'd
(1900)

1
When lilacs last in the dooryard bloom'd,
And the great star early droop'd in the western sky in the night,
I mourn'd, and yet shall mourn with ever-returning spring.

Ever-returning spring, trinity sure to me you bring,
Lilac blooming perennial and drooping star in the west,   5
And thought of him I love.

2
O powerful western fallen star!
O shades of night—O moody, tearful night!
O great star disappear'd—O the black murk that hides the star!
O cruel hands that hold me powerless—O helpless soul of me!   10
O harsh surrounding cloud that will not free my soul.

3
In the dooryard fronting an old farm-house near the white-wash'd palings,
Stands the lilac-bush tall-growing with heart-shaped leaves of rich green,
With many a pointed blossom rising delicate, with the perfume strong I
    love,

With every leaf a miracle—and from this bush in the dooryard,   15
With delicate-color'd blossoms and heart-shaped leaves of rich green,
A sprig with its flower I break.

4

In the swamp in secluded recesses,
A shy and hidden bird is warbling a song.

Solitary the thrush,   20
The hermit withdrawn to himself, avoiding the settlements,
Sings by himself a song.

Song of the bleeding throat,
Death's outlet song of life, (for well dear brother I know,
If thou wast not granted to sing thou would'st surely die.)   25

5

Over the breast of the spring, the land, amid cities,
Amid lanes and through old woods, where lately the violets peep'd from the
    ground, spotting the gray debris,
Amid the grass in the fields each side of the lanes, passing the endless grass,
Passing the yellow-spear'd wheat, every grain from its shroud in the dark-
    brown fields uprisen,
Passing the apple-tree blows of white and pink in the orchards,   30
Carrying a corpse to where it shall rest in the grave,
Night and day journeys a coffin.

6

Coffin that passes through lanes and streets,
Through day and night with the great cloud darkening the land,
With the pomp of the inloop'd flags with the cities draped in black,   35
With the show of the States themselves as of crape-veil'd women standing,
With processions long and winding and the flambeaus of the night,
With the countless torches lit, with the silent sea of faces and the unbared
    heads,
With the waiting depot, the arriving coffin, and the sombre faces,
With dirges through the night, with the thousand voices rising strong and   40
    solemn,
With all the mournful voices of the dirges pour'd around the coffin,
The dim-lit churches and the shuddering organs—where amid these you
    journey,
With the tolling tolling bells' perpetual clang,
Here, coffin that slowly passes,
I give you my sprig of lilac.   45

7

(Nor for you, for one alone,
Blossoms and branches green to coffins all I bring,
For fresh as the morning, thus would I chant a song for you O sane and
    sacred death.

All over bouquets of roses,
O death, I cover you over with roses and early lilies,   50
But mostly and now the lilac that blooms the first,
Copious I break, I break the sprigs from the bushes,
With loaded arms I come, pouring for you,
For you and the coffins all of you, O death.)

8

O western orb sailing the heaven,   55
Now I know what you must have meant as a month since I walk'd,
As I walk'd in silence the transparent shadowy night,
As I saw you had something to tell as you bent to me night after night,
As you droop'd from the sky low down as if to my side, (while the other
    stars all look'd on,)
As we wander'd together the solemn night, (for something I know not what 60
    kept me from sleep,)
As the night advanced, and I saw on the rim of the west how full you were
    of woe,
As I stood on the rising ground in the breeze in the cool transparent night,
As I watch'd where you pass'd and was lost in the netherward black of the
    night,
As my soul in its trouble dissatisfied sank, as where you sad orb,
Concluded, dropt in the night, and was gone.   65

9

Sing on there in the swamp,
O singer bashful and tender, I hear your notes, I hear your call,
I hear, I come presently, I understand you,
But a moment I linger, for the lustrous star has detain'd me,
The star my departing comrade holds and detains me.   70

10

O how shall I warble myself for the dead one there I loved?
And how shall I deck my song for the large sweet soul that has gone?
And what shall my perfume be for the grave of him I love?
Sea-winds blown from east and west,
Blown from the Eastern sea and blown from the Western sea, till there on 75
    the prairies meeting,

These and with these and the breath of my chant,
I'll perfume the grave of him I love.

11

O what shall I hang on the chamber walls?
And what shall the pictures be that I hang on the walls,
To adorn the burial-house of him I love?   80

Pictures of growing spring and farms and homes,
With the Fourth-month eve at sundown, and the gray smoke lucid and
    bright,
With floods of the yellow gold of the gorgeous, indolent, sinking sun,
    burning, expanding the air,
With the fresh sweet herbage under foot, and the pale green leaves of the
    trees prolific,
In the distance the flowing glaze, the breast of the river, with a wind-dapple   85
    here and there,
With ranging hills on the banks, with many a line against the sky, and
    shadows,
And the city at hand with dwellings so dense, and stacks of chimneys,
And all the scenes of life and the workshops, and the workmen homeward
    returning.

12

Lo, body and soul—this land,
My own Manhattan with spires, and the sparkling and hurrying tides, and   90
    the ships,
The varied and ample land, the South and the North in the light, Ohio's
    shores and flashing Missouri,
And ever the far-spreading prairies cover'd with grass and corn.
Lo, the most excellent sun so calm and haughty,
The violet and purple morn with just-felt breezes,
The gentle soft-born measureless light,   95
The miracle spreading bathing all, the fulfill'd noon,
The coming eve delicious, the welcome night and the stars,
Over my cities shining all, enveloping man and land.

13

Sing on, sing on you gray-brown bird,
Sing from the swamps, the recesses, pour your chant from the bushes,   100
Limitless out of the dusk, out of the cedars and pines.
Sing on dearest brother, warble your reedy song,
Loud human song, with voice of uttermost woe.

O liquid and free and tender!
O wild and loose to my soul—O wondrous singer!   105
You only I hear—yet the star holds me, (but will soon depart,)
Yet the lilac with mastering odor holds me.

                    14
Now while I sat in the day and look'd forth,
In the close of the day with its light and the fields of spring, and the farmers
        preparing their crops,
In the large unconscious scenery of my land with its lakes and forests,   110
In the heavenly aerial beauty, (after the perturb'd winds and the storms,)
Under the arching heavens of the afternoon swift passing, and the voices of
        children and women,
The many-moving sea-tides, and I saw the ships how they sail'd,
And the summer approaching with richness, and the fields all busy with
        labor,
And the infinite separate houses, how they all went on, each with its meals 115
        and minutia of daily usages,
And the streets how their throbbings throbb'd, and the cities pent—lo, then
        and there,
Falling upon them all and among them all, enveloping me with the rest,
Appear'd the cloud, appear'd the long black trail,
And I knew death, its thought, and the sacred knowledge of death.

Then with the knowledge of death as walking one side of me,   120
And the thought of death close-walking the other side of me,
And I in the middle as with companions, and as holding the hands of com-
        panions,
I fled forth to the hiding receiving night that talks not,
Down to the shores of the water, the path by the swamp in the dimness,
To the solemn shadowy cedars and the ghostly pines so still.   125

And the singer so shy to the rest receiv'd me,
The gray-brown bird I know received us comrades three,
And he sang the carol of death, and a verse for him I love.

From deep secluded recesses,
From the fragrant cedars and the ghostly pines so still,   130
Came the carol of the bird.

And the charm of the carol rapt me,
As I held as if by their hands my comrades in the night,
And the voice of my spirit tallied the song of the bird.

Comely lovely and soothing death, 13!
Undulate round the world, serenely arriving, arriving,
In the day, in the night, to all, to each,
Sooner or later delicate death.

Prais'd be the fathomless universe,
For life and joy, and for objects and knowledge curious, 14C
And for love, sweet love—but praise! praise! praise!
For the sure-enwinding arms of cool-enfolding death.

Dark mother always gliding near with soft feet,
Have none chanted for thee a chant of fullest welcome?
Then I chant it for thee, I glorify thee above all, 14!
I bring thee a song that when thou must indeed come, come unfalteringly.

Approach strong deliveress,
When it is so, when thou hast taken them I joyously sing the dead,
Lost in the loving floating ocean of thee,
Laved in the flood of thy bliss O death. 15C

From me to thee glad serenades,
Dances for thee I propose saluting thee, adornments and feastings for thee,
And the sights of the open landscape and the high-spread sky are fitting,
And life and the fields, and the huge and thoughtful night.

The night in silence under many a star,
The ocean shore and the husky whispering wave whose voice I know, 155
And the soul turning to thee O vast well-veil'd death,
And the body gratefully nestling close to thee.

Over the tree-tops I float thee a song,
Over the rising and sinking waves, over the myriad fields and the prairies 160
   wide,
Over the dense-pack'd cities all and the teeming wharves and ways,
I float this carol with joy, with joy to thee O death.

15

To the tally of my soul,
Loud and strong kept up the gray-brown bird,
With pure deliberate notes spreading filling the night. 165
Loud in the pines and cedars dim,
Clear in the freshness moist and the swamp-perfume,

And I with my comrades there in the night.
While my sight that was bound in my eyes unclosed,
As to long panoramas of visions. 170

And I saw askant the armies,
I saw as in noiseless dreams hundred of battle-flags,
Borne through the smoke of the battles and pierced with missiles I saw
    them,
And carried hither and yon through the smoke, and torn and bloody,
And at last but a few shreds left on the staffs, (and all in silence,) 175
And the staffs all splinter'd and broken.

I saw battle-corpses, myriads of them,
And the white skeletons of young men, I saw them,
I saw the debris and debris of all the slain soldiers of the war,
But I saw they were not as was thought, 180
They themselves were fully at rest, they suffer'd not,
The living remain'd and suffer'd, the mother suffer'd,
And the wife and the child and the musing comrade suffer'd,
And the armies that remain'd suffer'd.

16
Passing the visions, passing the night, 185
Passing, unloosing the hold of my comrades' hands,
Passing the song of the hermit bird and the tallying song of my soul,
Victorious song, death's outlet song, yet varying ever-altering song,
As low and wailing, yet clear the notes, rising and falling, flooding the
    night,
Sadly sinking and fainting, as warning and warning, and yet again bursting 190
    with joy,
Covering the earth and filling the spread of the heaven,
As that powerful psalm in the night I heard from recesses,
Passing, I leave thee lilac with heart-shaped leaves,
I leave thee there in the door-yard, blooming, returning with spring.

I cease from my song for thee, 195
From my gaze on thee in the west, fronting the west, communing with thee,
O comrade lustrous with silver face in the night.
Yet each to keep and all, retrievements out of the night,
The song, the wondrous chant of the gray-brown bird,
And the tallying chant, the echo arous'd in my soul, 200
With the lustrous and drooping star with the countenance full of woe,

With the holders holding my hand nearing the call of the bird,
Comrades mine and I in the midst, and their memory ever to keep, for the
    dead I loved so well,
For the sweetest, wisest soul of all my days and lands—and this for his dear
    sake,
Lilac and star and bird twined with the chant of my soul,   20
There in the fragrant pines and the cedars dusk and dim.

- Throughout the poem are images of lilac, star, and bird. Identify moments when
  we see each image, and explain how each works within the poem.
- Where do we see allusions to the Civil War in this poem? How does this
  reference impact our understanding of the poem?
- Whitman's poem about the death of Abraham Lincoln has many structural
  similarities to Milton's "Lycidas." Look for such similarities, and explain how
  these common elements contribute to our understanding of this particular
  poem as well as to our understanding of a genre that commemorates the
  dead.

Gwendolyn Brooks (1917–2000)

De Witt Williams on His Way to Lincoln Cemetery (1987)

He was born in Alabama.
He was bred in Illinois.
He was nothing but a
Plain black boy.

Swing low swing low sweet sweet chariot.   5
Nothing but a plain black boy.

Drive him past the Pool Hall.
Drive him past the Show.
Blind within his casket,
But maybe he will know.   10

Down through Forty-seventh Street:
Underneath the L,
And—Northwest Corner, Prairie,
That he loved so well.

Don't forget the Dance Halls—   15
Warwick and Savoy,
Where he picked his women, where
He drank his liquid joy.

Born in Alabama.
Bred in Illinois.   20
He was nothing but a
Plain black boy.

Swing low swing low sweet sweet chariot.
Nothing but a plain black boy

- How do the images and the narrative in this poem function in ways similar to what we have read in "When Lilacs Last in the Dooryard Bloom'd"?
- The repeated line "Swing low swing low sweet sweet chariot" comes from a well-known African American spiritual. The next line of the hymn is "coming for to carry me home." How does the poet rework that line throughout the poem?

Allen Tate (1899–1979)

Ode to the Confederate Dead (1930)

Row after row with strict impunity
The headstones yield their names to the element,
The wind whirrs without recollection;
In the riven troughs the splayed leaves
Pile up, of nature the casual sacrament   5
To the seasonal eternity of death;
Then driven by the fierce scrutiny
Of heaven to their election in the vast breath,
They sough the rumour of mortality.

Autumn is desolation in the plot   10
Of a thousand acres where these memories grow
From the inexhaustible bodies that are not
Dead, but feed the grass row after rich row.
Think of the autumns that have come and gone!—

Ambitious November with the humors of the year,   15
With a particular zeal for every slab,
Staining the uncomfortable angels that rot
On the slabs, a wing chipped here, an arm there:
The brute curiosity of an angel's stare
Turns you, like them, to stone,   20
Transforms the heaving air
Till plunged to a heavier world below
You shift your sea-space blindly
Heaving, turning like the blind crab.

Dazed by the wind, only the wind   25
The leaves flying, plunge

You know who have waited by the wall
The twilight certainty of an animal,
Those midnight restitutions of the blood
You know—the immitigable pines, the smoky frieze   30
Of the sky, the sudden call: you know the rage,
The cold pool left by the mounting flood,
Of muted Zeno and Parmenides.
You who have waited for the angry resolution
Of those desires that should be yours tomorrow,   35
You know the unimportant shrift of death
And praise the vision
And praise the arrogant circumstance
Of those who fall
Rank upon rank, hurried beyond decision—   40
Here by the sagging gate, stopped by the wall.

Seeing, seeing only the leaves
Flying, plunge and expire

Turn your eyes to the immoderate past,
Turn to the inscrutable infantry rising   45
Demons out of the earth—they will not last.
Stonewall, Stonewall, and the sunken fields of hemp,
Shiloh, Antietam, Malvern Hill, Bull Run.
Lost in that orient of the thick-and-fast
You will curse the setting sun.   50

Cursing only the leaves crying
Like an old man in a storm

You hear the shout, the crazy hemlocks point
With troubled fingers to the silence which
Smothers you, a mummy, in time.   55
                              The hound bitch
Toothless and dying, in a musty cellar
Hears the wind only.
                    Now that the salt of their blood
Stiffens the saltier oblivion of the sea,
Seals the malignant purity of the flood,
What shall we who count our days and bow   60
Our heads with a commemorial woe
In the ribboned coats of grim felicity,
What shall we say of the bones, unclean,
Whose verdurous anonymity will grow?
The ragged arms, the ragged heads and eyes   65
Lost in these acres of the insane green?
The gray lean spiders come, they come and go;
In a tangle of willows without light
The singular screech-owl's tight
Invisible lyric seeds the mind   70
With the furious murmur of their chivalry.

We shall say only the leaves
Flying, plunge and expire

We shall say only the leaves whispering
In the improbable mist of nightfall   75
That flies on multiple wing;
Night is the beginning and the end
And in between the ends of distraction
Waits mute speculation, the patient curse
That stones the eyes, or like the jaguar leaps   80
For his own image in a jungle pool, his victim.
What shall we say who have knowledge
Carried to the heart? Shall we take the act
To the grave? Shall we, more hopeful, set up the grave
In the house? The ravenous grave?   85
                              Leave now
The shut gate and the decomposing wall:
The gentle serpent, green in the mulberry bush,
Riots with his tongue through the hush—
Sentinel of the grave who counts us all!

- How do specific images throughout the poem give sense to the term "ravenous grave" that comes at the end of the poem?
- The title of the poem refers to those in the Confederate army who died during the Civil War. Which specific lines describe these soldiers or the battles in which they fought?
- Notice that the poem was written after World War I. How does this context help us understand the ideas presented in the poem?

Robert Lowell (1917–1977)

For the Union Dead (1964)

"Relinquunt Omnia Servare Rem Publicam."

The old South Boston Aquarium stands
in a Sahara of snow now. Its broken windows are boarded.
The bronze weathervane cod has lost half its scales.
The airy tanks are dry.

Once my nose crawled like a snail on the glass;   5
my hand tingled
to burst the bubbles
drifting from the noses of the cowed, compliant fish.

My hand draws back. I often sigh still
for the dark downward and vegetating kingdom   10
of the fish and reptile. One morning last March,
I pressed against the new barbed and galvanized

fence on the Boston Common. Behind their cage,
yellow dinosaur steamshovels were grunting
as they cropped up tons of mush and grass   15
to gouge their underworld garage.

Parking spaces luxuriate like civic
sandpiles in the heart of Boston.
A girdle of orange, Puritan-pumpkin colored girders
braces the tingling Statehouse,   20

shaking over the excavations, as it faces Colonel Shaw
and his bell-cheeked Negro infantry
on St. Gaudens' shaking Civil War relief,
propped by a plank splint against the garage's earthquake.

Two months after marching through Boston,   25
half the regiment was dead;
at the dedication,
William James could almost hear the bronze Negroes breathe.

Their monument sticks like a fishbone
in the city's throat.   30
Its Colonel is as lean
as a compass-needle.

He has an angry wrenlike vigilance,
a greyhound's gentle tautness;
he seems to wince at pleasure,   35
and suffocate for privacy.

He is out of bounds now. He rejoices in man's lovely,
peculiar power to choose life and die—
when he leads his black soldiers to death,
he cannot bend his back.   40

On a thousand small town New England greens,
the old white churches hold their air
of sparse, sincere rebellion; frayed flags
quilt the graveyards of the Grand Army of the Republic.

The stone statues of the abstract Union Soldier   45
grow slimmer and younger each year—
wasp-waisted, they doze over muskets
and muse through their sideburns . . .

Shaw's father wanted no monument
except the ditch,   50
where his son's body was thrown
and lost with his "niggers."

The ditch is nearer.
There are no statues for the last war here;
on Boylston Street, a commercial photograph   55
shows Hiroshima boiling

over a Mosler Safe, the "Rock of Ages"
that survived the blast. Space is nearer.
When I crouch to my television set,
the drained faces of Negro school-children rise like balloons.   60

Colonel Shaw
is riding on his bubble,
he waits
for the blessed break.

The Aquarium is gone. Everywhere,   65
giant finned cars nose forward like fish;
a savage servility
slides by on grease.

- What is the effect of the poet's description of the end of the old South Boston Aquarium juxtaposed with the narration of the history of Colonel Shaw? How are the two stories connected?
- Why does the poet note that there are no statues in Boston of "the last war"? Which war would this have been? How does Lowell's poem respond to Tate's?
- How is it both surprising and appropriate to describe small-town New England churches as holding an air "of sparse, sincere rebellion"?

John Keats (1795–1821)

Ode to Autumn (1819)

I

Season of mists and mellow fruitfulness,
  Close bosom-friend of the maturing sun;
Conspiring with him how to load and bless
  With fruit the vines that round the thatch-eaves run;
To bend with apples the mossed cottage-trees,   5
  And fill all fruit with ripeness to the core;
    To swell the gourd, and plump the hazel shells
With a sweet kernel; to set budding more,
  And still more, later flowers for the bees,
  Until they think warm days will never cease,   10
    For summer has o'er-brimmed their clammy cells.

II

Who hath not seen thee oft amid thy store?
  Sometimes whoever seeks abroad may find
Thee sitting careless on a granary floor,
  Thy hair soft-lifted by the winnowing wind;   15

Or on a half-reaped furrow sound asleep,
    Drowsed with the fume of poppies, while thy hook
        Spares the next swath and all its twinèd flowers:
And sometimes like a gleaner thou dost keep
    Steady thy laden head across a brook;   20
    Or by a cider-press, with patient look,
        Thou watchest the last oozings hours by hours.

III

Where are the songs of spring? Ay, where are they?
    Think not of them, thou hast thy music too,—
While barred clouds bloom the soft-dying day,   25
    And touch the stubble-plains with rosy hue;
Then in a wailful choir the small gnats mourn
    Among the river sallows, borne aloft
        Or sinking as the light wind lives or dies;
And full-grown lambs loud bleat from hilly bourn;   30
    Hedge-crickets sing; and now with treble soft
    The red-breast whistles from a garden-croft;
        And gathering swallows twitter in the skies.

■ What images does the poet use to define the character of autumn? How do these images (such as the "last oozings") contrast with the images we associate with spring?

■ As you look at other poems in this section, how do autumnal images fit into the genre of works about death?

Anne Bradstreet (1612–1672)

In Memory of My Dear Grandchild, Elizabeth Bradstreet, Who Deceased August 1665, Being a Year and Half Old (1678)

Farewell dear babe, my heart's too much content,
Farewell sweet babe, the pleasure of mine eye,
Farewell fair flower that for a space was lent,
Then ta'en away unto eternity.
Blest babe, why should I once bewail thy fate,   5
Or sigh thy days so soon were terminate,
Sith thou art settled in an everlasting state.

2

By nature trees do rot when they are grown,
And plums and apples thoroughly ripe do fall,
And corn and grass are in their season mown,   10
And time brings down what is both strong and tall.
But plants new set to be eradicate,
And buds new blown to have so short a date,
Is by His hand alone that guides nature and fate.

■ Describe the structure of this poem. How does its subject progress from grief to consolation?

Anne Bradstreet (1612–1672)

Here Followes Some Verses upon the Burning of Our House July 10, 1666 (1667)

In silent night when rest I took,
For sorrow near I did not look,
I wakened was with thund'ring noise
And piteous shrieks of dreadful voice.
That fearful sound of "Fire!" and "Fire!"   5
Let no man know is my desire.
I, starting up, the light did spy,
And to my God my heart did cry
To straighten me in my distress
And not to leave me succourless.   10
Then, coming out, behold a space
The flame consume my dwelling place.
And when I could no longer look,
I blest His name that gave and took,
That laid my goods now in the dust.   15
Yea, so it was, and so 'twas just.
It was His own; it was not mine,
Far be it that I should repine;
He might of all justly bereft
But yet sufficient for us left.   20
When by the ruins oft I past
My sorrowing eyes aside did cast,
And here and there the places spy
Where oft I sat and long did lie:
Here stood that trunk, and there that chest,   25

There lay that store I counted best.
My pleasant things in ashes lie,
And them behold no more shall I.
Under thy roof no guest shall sit,
Nor at thy table eat a bit.   30
No pleasant tale shall e'er be told,
Nor things recounted done of old.
No candle e'er shall shine in thee,
Nor bridegroom's voice e'er heard shall be.
In silence ever shall thou lie,   35
Adieu, Adieu, all's vanity.
Then straight I 'gin my heart to chide,
And did thy wealth on earth abide?
Didst fix thy hope on mold'ring dust?
The arm of flesh didst make they trust?   40
Raise up thy thoughts above the sky
That dunghill mists away may fly.
Thou hast an house on high erect,
Framed by that might Architect,
With glory richly furnished,   45
Stands permanent though this be fled.
His purchased and paid for too
By Him who hath enough to do.
A price so vast as is unknown
Yet by His gift is made thine own;   50
There's wealth enough, I need no more,
Farewell, my pelf, farewell my store.
The world no longer let me love,
My hope and treasure lies above.

■ Compare the narrative of the burning to the poet's discussion of her reaction to
  the fire. How does this poem progress differently from her discussion of her
  grandchild's death?

Chidiock Tichborne (1568–1586)

Elegy Written with His Own Hand in the Tower before His Execution (1586)

My prime of youth is but a frost of cares,
   My feast of joy is but a dish of pain,

My crop of corn is but a field of tares,
    And all my good is but vain hope of gain;
The day is past, and yet I saw no sun,   5
And now I live, and now my life is done.

My tale was heard and yet it was not told,
    My fruit is fallen and yet my leaves are green,
My youth is spent and yet I am not old,
    I saw the world and yet I was not seen;   10
My thread is cut and yet it is not spun,
And now I live, and now my life is done.

I sought my death and found it in my womb,
    I looked for life and saw it was a shade,
I trod the earth and knew it was my tomb,   15
    And now I die, and now I was but made;
My glass is full, and now my glass is run,
And now I live, and now my life is done.

■ The entire poem is constructed of apparent paradoxes. How does the poem
  itself reconcile them?
■ Chidiock Tichborne was a practicing Roman Catholic at a time when the
  religion had become outlawed in England. His offense was conspiring to
  murder Queen Elizabeth. This poem was written to his wife. How does this
  contextual information add to a reading of the poem?

Theodore Roethke (1908–1963)

Elegy for Jane (1953)

My student, thrown by a horse

I remember the neckcurls, limp and damp as tendrils;
And her quick look, a sidelong pickerel smile;
And how, once startled into talk, the light syllables leaped for her,
And she balanced in the delight of her thought,

A wren, happy, tail into the wind,   5
Her song trembling the twigs and small branches.
The shade sang with her;

The leaves, their whispers turned to kissing;
And the mold sang in the bleached valleys under the rose.

Oh, when she was sad, she cast herself down into such a pure depth,   10
Even a father could not find her:
Scraping her cheek against straw;
Stirring the clearest water.

My sparrow, you are not here,
Waiting like a fern, making a spiny shadow.   15
The sides of wet stones cannot console me,
Nor the moss, wound with the last light.

If only I could nudge you from this sleep,
My maimed darling, my skittery pigeon.
Over this damp grave I speak the words of my love: 20
I, with no rights in this matter,
Neither father nor lover.

■ In the final lines, the poet admits that he has "no rights in this matter." How does the poem prove that, in spite of conventions, he does have a right to feel grief? How is the question of propriety here both similar to and different from the question as it arises in so many of the works in this section?

Seamus Heaney (1939–)

Punishment (1975)

I can feel the tug
of the halter at the nape
of her neck, the wind
on her naked front.

It blows her nipples   5
to amber beads,
it shakes the frail rigging
of her ribs.

I can see her drowned
body in the bog,   10
the weighing stone,
the floating rods and boughs.

Under which at first
she was a barked sapling
that is dug up   15
oak-bone, brain-firkin:

her shaved head
like a stubble of black corn,
her blindfold a soiled bandage,
her noose a ring   20

to store
the memories of love.
Little adulteress,
before they punished you

you were flaxen-haired,   25
undernourished, and your
tar-black face was beautiful.
My poor scapegoat,

I almost love you
but would have cast, I know,   30
the stones of silence.
I am the artful voyeur

of your brain's exposed
and darkened combs,
your muscles' webbing   35
and all your numbered bones:

I who have stood dumb
when your betraying sisters,
cauled in tar,
wept by the railings,   40

who would connive
in civilized outrage
yet understand the exact
and tribal, intimate revenge.

■ How has the "little adulteress" died? How do you reconcile the first stanza
with the third?

■ In what way does the poet feel that he is guilty here? In what ways is such a reaction appropriate to record this particular death? To whom does the poem's title refer?

Louise Erdrich (1954–)

Dear John Wayne (1984)

August and the drive-in picture is packed.
We lounge on the hood of the Pontiac
surrounded by the slow-burning spirals they sell
at the window, to vanquish the hordes of mosquitoes.
Nothing works. They break through the smoke screen for blood.   5

Always the lookout spots the Indians first,
spread north to south, barring progress.
The Sioux or some other Plains bunch
in spectacular columns, ICBM missiles,
feathers bristling in the meaningful sunset.   10

The drum breaks. There will be no parlance.
Only the arrows whining, a death-cloud of nerves
swarming down on the settlers
who die beautifully, tumbling like dust weeds
into the history that brought us all here   15
together: this wide screen beneath the sign of the bear.

The sky fills, acres of blue squint and eye
that the crowd cheers. His face moves over us,
a thick cloud of vengeance, pitted
like the land that was once flesh. Each rut,   20
each scar makes a promise: *It is*
not over, this fight, not as long as you resist.

Everything we see belongs to us.

A few laughing Indians fall over the hood
slipping in the hot spilled butter.   25
The eye sees a lot, John, but the heart is so blind.
Death makes us owners of nothing.
He smiles, a horizon of teeth
the credits reel over, and then the white fields

again blowing in the true-to-life dark.   30
The dark films over everything.
We get into the car
scratching our mosquito bites, speechless and small
as people are when the movie is done.
We are back in our skins.   35

How can we help but keep hearing his voice,
the flip side of the sound track, still playing:
Come on, boys, we got them
where we want them, drunk, running.
They'll give us what we want, what we need.   40
Even his disease was the idea of taking everything.
Those cells, burning, doubling, splitting out of their skins.

■ The poem juxtaposes the experience of seeing a particular kind of movie
  at a drive-in with scenes from the types of films in which John Wayne
  starred. Look at the details presented in stanzas 2–5, and identify the
  action-movie genres that are their source. Where do the details seem not to
  fit together?

■ Wayne died of cancer in 1979. How do the final two lines of the poem portray
  this disease and its relation to his life?

Langston Hughes (1902–1967)

Night Funeral in Harlem (1967)

Night funeral
    In Harlem:

    Where did they get
    Them two fine cars?

Insurance man, he did not pay—   5
His insurance lapsed the other day—
Yet they got a satin box
For his head to lay.

    Night funeral
    In Harlem: 10

Who was it sent
That wreath of flowers?

Them flowers came
from that poor boy's friends—
They'll want flowers, too,   15
When they meet their ends.

Night funeral
in Harlem:

Who preached that
Black boy to his grave?   20

Old preacher-man
Preached that boy away—
Charged Five Dollars
His girl friend had to pay.

Night funeral   25
In Harlem:

When it was all over
And the lid shut on his head
and the organ had done played
and the last prayers been said   30
and six pallbearers
Carried him out for dead
And off down Lenox Avenue
That long black hearse done sped,
    The street light   35
    At his corner
    Shined just like a tear—
That boy that they was mournin'
Was so dear, so dear
To them folks that brought the flowers,   40
To that girl who paid the preacher-man—
It was all their tears that made
    That poor boy's
    Funeral grand.

Night funeral   45
In Harlem.

■ The poem uses a pattern of questions and answers to describe the nature of this funeral. From what perspective do we hear this particular narrative? Where is the grief in this poem? How does the grief function differently than in the previous poems?

Emily Dickinson (1830–1886)

[I like a look of Agony] (ca. 1861)

I like a look of Agony,
Because I know it's true—
Men do not sham Convulsion,
Nor simulate, a Throe—

The Eyes glaze once—and that is Death—   5
Impossible to feign
The Beads upon the Forehead
By homely Anguish strung.

Emily Dickinson (1830–1886)

[After great pain, a formal feeling comes—]
(ca. 1863)

After great pain, a formal feeling comes—
The Nerves sit ceremonious, like Tombs—
The stiff Heart questions was it He, that bore,
And Yesterday, or Centuries before?

The Feet, mechanical, go round—   4
Of Ground, or Air, or Ought—
A Wooden way
Regardless grown,
A Quartz contentment, like a stone—

This is the Hour of Lead—   10
Remembered, if outlived,
As Freezing persons, recollect the Snow—
First—Chill—then Stupor—then the letting go—

■ How do both of these poems avoid the "ceremonious" that we see in most of the other poems in this section? On what do they focus instead? How does this focus impact the tone of each of these poems?

Rudyard Kipling (1865–1936)

The Power of the Dog (1909)

There is sorrow enough in the natural way
From men and women to fill our day;
And when we are certain of sorrow in store,
Why do we always arrange for more?
Brothers and Sisters, I bid you beware   5
Of giving your heart to a dog to tear.

Buy a pup and your money will buy
Love unflinching that cannot lie—
Perfect passion and worship fed
By a kick in the ribs or a pat on the head.   10
Nevertheless it is hardly fair
To risk your heart for a dog to tear.

When the fourteen years which Nature permits
Are closing in asthma, or tumour, or fits,
And the vet's unspoken prescription runs   15
To lethal chambers or loaded guns,
Then you will find—it's your own affair—
But ... you've given your heart to a dog to tear.

When the body that lived at your single will,
With its whimper of welcome, is stilled (how still!).   20
When the spirit that answered your every mood
Is gone—wherever it goes—for good,
You will discover how much you care,
And will give your heart to a dog to tear.

We've sorrow enough in the natural way,   25
When it comes to burying Christian clay.
Our loves are not given, but only lent,
At compound interest of cent per cent.
Though it is not always the case, I believe,

That the longer we've kept 'em, the more do we grieve.   30
For, when debts are payable, right or wrong,
A short-time loan is as bad as a long—
So why in—Heaven (before we are there)
Should we give our hearts to a dog to tear?

■ This poem is simultaneously part of the genre of honoring the dead and a
  commentary upon that genre. Is it appropriate to honor a dog in the same forms
  that we honor people? How does the poet pose (and answer) this question
  within this poem?

■ What is the impact of the refrain that appears at the end of each stanza?

John Updike (1932–)

Dog's Death (1969)

She must have been kicked unseen or brushed by a car.
Too young to know much, she was beginning to learn
To use the newspapers spread on the kitchen floor
And to win, wetting there, the words, "Good dog! Good dog!"

We thought her shy malaise was a shot reaction.   5
The autopsy disclosed a rupture in her liver.

As we teased her with play, blood was filling her skin
And her heart was learning to lie down forever.

Monday morning, as the children were noisily fed
And sent to school, she crawled beneath the youngest's bed.   10
We found her twisted and limp but still alive.
In the car to the vet's, on my lap, she tried

To bite my hand and died. I stroked her warm fur
And my wife called in a voice imperious with tears.
Though surrounded by love that would have upheld her,   15
Nevertheless she sank and, stiffening, disappeared.

Back home, we found that in the night her frame,
Drawing near to dissolution, had endured the shame
Of diarrhoea and had dragged across the floor
To a newspaper carelessly left there. *Good dog.*   20

- How does the image in the final line change in meaning from the similar image that is introduced in the opening stanza?
- How does the impact of this poem compare with that of "Lycidas"? To what extent does the poem describe the specific characteristics of this dog? To what extent does it describe the general nature of grief?

DRAMA

Sophocles (497 BC–406 BC)

For a full biographical note on Sophocles, see page 67.

Antigone (ca. 441 BC; trans. Elizabeth Wyckoff)

CHARACTERS

ANTIGONE
ISMENE
CHORUS *of Theban Elders*
CREON
A GUARD
HAEMON
TEIRESIAS
A MESSENGER
EURYDICE

SCENE: *Thebes, before the royal palace.* ANTIGONE *and* ISMENE *emerge from its great central door.*

ANTIGONE: My sister, my Ismene, do you know
    of any suffering from our father sprung
    that Zeus does not achieve for us survivors?
    There's nothing grievous, nothing free from doom,
    not shameful, not dishonored, I've not seen.   5
    Your sufferings and mine.
    And now, what of this edict which they say
    the commander has proclaimed to the whole people?
    Have you heard anything? Or don't you know
    that the foes' trouble comes upon our friends?   10

ISMENE: I've heard no word, Antigone, of our friends.
　　Not sweet nor bitter, since that single moment
　　when we two lost two brothers
　　who died on one day by a double blow.
　　And since the Argive army went away　　　　　　　　15
　　this very night, I have no further news
　　of fortune or disaster for myself.
ANTIGONE: I knew it well, and brought you from the house
　　for just this reason, that you alone may hear.
ISMENE: What is it? Clearly some news has clouded you.　　20
ANTIGONE: It has indeed. Creon will give the one
　　of our two brothers honor in the tomb;
　　the other none.
　　Eteocles, with just entreatment treated,
　　as law provides he has hidden under earth　　　　　　25
　　to have full honor with the dead below.
　　But Polyneices' corpse who died in pain,
　　they say he has proclaimed to the whole town
　　that none may bury him and none bewail,
　　but leave him unwept, untombed, a rich sweet sight　　30
　　for the hungry birds' beholding.
　　Such orders they say the worthy Creon gives
　　to you and me—yes, yes, I say to *me*—
　　and that he's coming to proclaim it clear
　　to those who know it not.　　　　　　　　　　　　35
　　Further: he has the matter so at heart
　　that anyone who dares attempt the act
　　will die by public stoning in the town.
　　So there you have it and you soon will show
　　if you are noble, or fallen from your descent.　　　　40
ISMENE: If things have reached this stage, what can I do,
　　poor sister, that will help to make or mend?
ANTIGONE: Think will you share my labor and my act.
ISMENE: What will you risk? And where is your intent?
ANTIGONE: Will you take up that corpse along with me?　　45
ISMENE: To bury him you mean, when it's forbidden?
ANTIGONE: My brother, and yours, though you may wish he were not.
　　I never shall be found to be his traitor.
ISMENE: O hard of mind! When Creon spoke against it!
ANTIGONE: It's not for him to keep me from my own.　　　　50
ISMENE: Alas. Remember, sister, how our father
　　perished abhorred, ill-famed.

Himself with his own hand, through his own curse
destroyed both eyes.
Remember next his mother and his wife   55
finishing life in the shame of the twisted strings.
And third two brothers on a single day,
poor creatures, murdering, a common doom
each with his arm accomplished on the other.
And now look at the two of us alone.   60
We'll perish terribly if we force law
and try to cross the royal vote and power.
We must remember that we two are women
so not to fight with men.
And that since we are subject to strong power   65
we must hear these orders, or any that may be worse.
So I shall ask of them beneath the earth
forgiveness, for in these things I am forced,
and shall obey the men in power. I know
that wild and futile action makes no sense.   70
ANTIGONE: I wouldn't urge it. And if now you wished
    to act, you wouldn't please me as a partner.
    Be what you want to; but that man shall I
    bury. For me, the doer, death is best.
    Friend shall I lie with him, yes friend with friend,   75
    when I have dared the crime of piety.
    Longer the time in which to please the dead
    than that for those up here.
    There shall I lie forever. You may see fit
    to keep from honor what the gods have honored.   80
ISMENE: I shall do no dishonor. But to act
    against the citizens? I cannot.
ANTIGONE: That's your protection. Now I go, to pile
    the burial-mound for him, my dearest brother.
ISMENE: Oh my poor sister. How I fear for you!   85
ANTIGONE: For me, don't borrow trouble. Clear your fate.
ISMENE: At least give no one warning of this act;
    you keep it hidden, and I'll do the same.
ANTIGONE: Dear God! Denounce me. I shall hate you more
    if silent, not proclaiming this to all.   90
ISMENE: You have a hot mind over chilly things.
ANTIGONE: I know I please those whom I most should please.
ISMENE: If but you can. You crave what can't be done.
ANTIGONE: And so, when strength runs out, I shall give over.

ISMENE: Wrong from the start, to chase what cannot be.   95
ANTIGONE: If that's your saying, I shall hate you first,
 and next the dead will hate you in all justice.
 But let me and my own ill-counselling
 suffer this terror. I shall suffer nothing
 as great as dying with a lack of grace.   100
ISMENE: Go, since you want to. But know this: you go
 senseless indeed, but loved by those who love you.
(ISMENE *returns to the palace;* ANTIGONE *leaves by one of the side entrances.*
 The CHORUS *now enters from the other side.*)
CHORUS: Sun's own radiance, fairest light ever shone on the gates of
  Thebes,
 then did you shine, O golden day's
 eye, coming over Dirce's stream,   105
 on the Man who had come from Argos with all his armor
 running now in headlong fear as you shook his bridle free.
 He was stirred by the dubious quarrel of Polyneices.
 So, screaming shrill,
 like an eagle over the land he flew,   110
 covered with white-snow wing,
 with many weapons,
 with horse-hair crested helms.
 He who had stood above our halls, gaping about our seven gates,
 with that circle of thirsting spears.   115
 Gone, without our blood in his jaws,
 before the torch took hold on our tower-crown.
 Rattle of war at his back; hard the fight for the dragon's foe.
 The boasts of a proud tongue are for Zeus to hate.
 So seeing them streaming on   120
 in insolent clangor of gold,
 he struck with hurling fire him who rushed
 for the high wall's top,
 to cry conquest abroad.
 Swinging, striking the earth he fell   125
 fire in hand, who in mad attack,
 had raged against us with blasts of hate.
 He failed. He failed of his aim.
 For the rest great Ares dealt his blows about,
 first in the war-team.   130
 The captains stationed at seven gates
 fought with seven and left behind
 their brazen arms as an offering
 to Zeus who is turner of battle.

All but those wretches, sons of one man,   135
one mother's sons, who sent their spears
each against each and found the share
of a common death together.
Great-named Victory comes to us
answering Thebes' warrior-joy.   140
Let us forget the wars just done
and visit the shrines of the gods.
All, with night-long dance which Bacchus will lead,
who shakes Thebes' acres.
(CREON *enters from the palace.*)
Now here he comes, the king of the land,   145
Creon, Menoeceus' son,
newly named by the gods' new fate.
What plan that beats about his mind
has made him call this council-session,
sending his summons to all?   150
CREON: My friends, the very gods who shook the state
      with mighty surge have set it straight again.
      So now I sent for you, chosen from all,
      first that I knew you constant in respect
      to Laius' royal power; and again   155
      when Oedipus had set the state to rights,
      and when he perished, you were faithful still
      in mind to the descendants of the dead.
      When they two perished by a double fate,
      on one day struck and striking and defiled   160
      each by his own hand, now it comes that I
      hold all the power and the royal throne
      through close connection with the perished men.
      You cannot learn of any man the soul,
      the mind, and the intent until he shows   165
      his practise of the government and law.
      For I believe that who controls the state
      and does not hold to the best plans of all,
      but locks his tongue up through some kind of fear,
      that he is worst of all who are or were.   170
      And he who counts another greater friend
      than his own fatherland, I put him nowhere.
      So I—may Zeus all-seeing always know it—
      could not keep silent as disaster crept
      upon the town, destroying hope of safety.   175
      Nor could I count the enemy of the land

friend to myself, not I who know so well
that she it is who saves us, sailing straight,
and only so can we have friends at all.
With such good rules shall I enlarge our state.   180
And now I have proclaimed their brother-edict.
In the matter of the sons of Oedipus,
citizens, know: Eteocles who died,
defending this our town with champion spear,
is to be covered in the grave and granted   185
all holy rites we give the noble dead.
But his brother Polyneices whom I name
the exile who came back and sought to burn
his fatherland, the gods who were his kin,
who tried to gorge on blood he shared, and lead   190
the rest of us as slaves—
it is announced that no one in this town
may give him burial or mourn for him.
Leave him unburied, leave his corpse disgraced,
a dinner for the birds and for the dogs.   195
Such is my mind. Never shall I, myself,
honor the wicked and reject the just.
The man who is well-minded to the state
from me in death and life shall have his honor.
CHORUS: This resolution, Creon, is your own,   200
    in the matter of the traitor and the true.
    For you can make such rulings as you will
    about the living and about the dead.
CREON: Now you be sentinels of the decree.
CHORUS: Order some younger man to take this on.   205
CREON: Already there are watchers of the corpse.
CHORUS: What other order would you give us, then?
CREON: Not to take sides with any who disobey.
CHORUS: No fool is fool as far as loving death.
CREON: Death is the price. But often we have known   210
    men to be ruined by the hope of profit.
(*Enter, from the side, a* GUARD.)
GUARD: Lord, I can't claim that I am out of breath
    from rushing here with light and hasty step,
    for I had many haltings in my thought
    making me double back upon my road.   215
    My mind kept saying many things to me:
    "Why go where you will surely pay the price?"
    "Fool, are you halting? And if Creon learns

from someone else, how shall you not be hurt?"
Turning this over, on I dilly-dallied.   220
And so a short trip turns itself to long.
Finally, though, my coming here won out.
If what I say is nothing, still I'll say it.
For I come clutching to one single hope
that I can't suffer what is not my fate.   225
CREON: What is it that brings on this gloom of yours?
GUARD: I want to tell you first about myself.
    I didn't do it, didn't see who did it.
    It isn't right for me to get in trouble.
CREON: Your aim is good. You fence the fact around.   230
    It's clear you have some shocking news to tell.
GUARD: Terrible tidings make for long delays.
CREON: Speak out the story, and then get away.
GUARD: I'll tell you. Someone left the corpse just now,
    burial all accomplished, thirsty dust   235
    strewn on the flesh, the ritual complete.
CREON: What are you saying? What man has dared to do it?
GUARD: I wouldn't know. There were no marks of picks,
    no grubbed-out earth. The ground was dry and hard,
    no trace of wheels. The doer left no sign.   240
    When the first fellow on the day-shift showed us,
    we all were sick with wonder.
    For he was hidden, not inside a tomb,
    light dust upon him, enough to turn the curse,
    no wild beast's track, nor track of any hound   245
    having been near, nor was the body torn.
    We roared bad words about, guard against guard,
    and came to blows. No one was there to stop us.
    Each man had done it, nobody had done it
    so as to prove it on him—we couldn't tell.   250
    We were prepared to hold to red-hot iron,
    to walk through fire, to swear before the gods
    we hadn't done it, hadn't shared the plan,
    when it was plotted or when it was done.
    And last, when all our sleuthing came out nowhere,   255
    one fellow spoke, who made our heads to droop
    low toward the ground. We couldn't disagree.
    We couldn't see a chance of getting off.
    He said we had to tell you all about it.
    We couldn't hide the fact.   260
    So he won out. The lot chose poor old me

to win the prize. So here I am unwilling,
quite sure you people hardly want to see me.
Nobody likes the bringer of bad news.

CHORUS: Lord, while he spoke, my mind kept on debating.   265
Isn't this action possibly a god's?

CREON: Stop now, before you fill me up with rage,
or you'll prove yourself insane as well as old.
Unbearable, your saying that the gods
take any kindly forethought for this corpse.   270
Would it be they had hidden him away,
honoring his good service, his who came
to burn their pillared temples and their wealth,
even their land, and break apart their laws?
Or have you seen them honor wicked men?   275
It isn't so.
No, from the first there were some men in town
who took the edict hard, and growled against me,
who hid the fact that they were rearing back,
not rightly in the yoke, no way my friends.   280
These are the people—oh it's clear to me—
who have bribed these men and brought about the deed.
No current custom among men as bad
as silver currency. This destroys the state;
this drives men from their homes; this wicked teacher   285
drives solid citizens to acts of shame.
It shows men how to practice infamy
and know the deeds of all unholiness.
Every least hireling who helped in this
brought about then the sentence he shall have.   290
But further, as I still revere great Zeus,
understand this, I tell you under oath,
if you don't find the very man whose hands
buried the corpse, bring him for me to see,
not death alone shall be enough for you   295
till living, hanging, you make clear the crime.
For any future grabbings you'll have learned
where to get pay, and that it doesn't pay
to squeeze a profit out of every source.
For you'll have felt that more men come to doom   300
through dirty profits than are kept by them.

GUARD: May I say something? Or just turn and go?

CREON: Aren't you aware your speech is most unwelcome?

GUARD: Does it annoy your hearing or your mind?

CREON: Why are you out to allocate my pain?   305

GUARD: The doer hurts your mind. I hurt your ears.
CREON: You are a quibbling rascal through and through.
GUARD: But anyhow I never did the deed.
CREON: And you the man who sold your mind for money!
GUARD: Oh!   310
    How terrible to guess, and guess at lies!
CREON: Go pretty up your guesswork. If you don't
    show me the doers you will have to say
    that wicked payments work their own revenge.
GUARD: Indeed, I pray he's found, but yes or no,   315
    taken or not as luck may settle it,
    you won't see me returning to this place.
    Saved when I neither hoped nor thought to be,
    I owe the gods a mighty debt of thanks.
(CREON *enters the palace. The* GUARD *leaves by the way he came.*)
CHORUS: Many the wonders but nothing walks stranger than man.   320
    This thing crosses the sea in the winter's storm,
    making his path through the roaring waves.
    And she, the greatest of gods, the earth—
    ageless she is, and unwearied—he wears her away
    as the ploughs go up and down from year to year   325
    and his mules turn up the soil.
    Gay nations of birds he snares and leads,
    wild beast tribes and the salty brood of the sea,
    with the twisted mesh of his nets, this clever man.
    He controls with craft the beasts of the open air,   330
    walkers on hills. The horse with his shaggy mane
    he holds and harnesses, yoked about the neck,
    and the strong bull of the mountain.
    Language, and thought like the wind
    and the feelings that make the town,   335
    he has taught himself, and shelter against the cold,
    refuge from rain. He can always help himself.
    He faces no future helpless. There's only death
    that he cannot find an escape from. He has contrived
    refuge from illnesses once beyond all cure.   340
    Clever beyond all dreams
    the inventive craft that he has
    which may drive him one time or another to well or ill.
    When he honors the laws of the land and the gods' sworn right
    high indeed is his city; but stateless the man   345
    who dares to dwell with dishonor. Not by my fire,
    never to share my thoughts, who does these things.
    (*The* GUARD *enters with* ANTIGONE.)

My mind is split at this awful sight.
I know her. I cannot deny
Antigone is here. 350
Alas, the unhappy girl,
her unhappy father's child.
Oh what is the meaning of this?
It cannot be you that they bring
for breaking the royal law, 355
caught in open shame.

GUARD: This is the woman who has done the deed.
We caught her at the burying. Where's the king?

(CREON *enters.*)

CHORUS: Back from the house again just when he's needed.

CREON: What must I measure up to? What has happened? 360

GUARD: Lord, one should never swear off anything.
Afterthought makes the first resolve a liar.
I could have vowed I wouldn't come back here
after your threats, after the storm I faced.
But joy that comes beyond the wildest hope 365
is bigger than all other pleasure known.
I'm here, though I swore not to be, and bring
this girl. We caught her burying the dead.
This time we didn't need to shake the lots;
mine was the luck, all mine. 370
So now, lord, take her, you, and question her
and prove her as you will. But I am free.
And I deserve full clearance on this charge.

CREON: Explain the circumstance of the arrest.

GUARD: She was burying the man. You have it all. 375

CREON: Is this the truth? And do you grasp its meaning?

GUARD: I saw her burying the very corpse
you had forbidden. Is this adequate?

CREON: How was she caught and taken in the act?

GUARD: It was like this: when we got back again 380
struck with those dreadful threatenings of yours,
we swept away the dust that hid the corpse.
We stripped it back to slimy nakedness.
And then we sat to windward on the hill
so as to dodge the smell. 385
We poked each other up with growling threats
if anyone was careless of his work.
For some time this went on, till it was noon.
The sun was high and hot. Then from the earth
up rose a dusty whirlwind to the sky, 390

filling the plain, smearing the forest-leaves,
clogging the upper air. We shut our eyes,
sat and endured the plague the gods had sent.
So the storm left us after a long time.
We saw the girl. She cried the sharp and shrill   395
cry of a bitter bird which sees the nest
bare where the young birds lay.
So this same girl, seeing the body stripped,
cried with great groanings, cried a dreadful curse
upon the people who had done the deed.   400
Soon in her hands she brought the thirsty dust,
and holding high a pitcher of wrought bronze
she poured the three libations for the dead.
We saw this and surged down. We trapped her fast;
and she was calm. We taxed her with the deeds   405
both past and present. Nothing was denied.
And I was glad, and yet I took it hard.
One's own escape from trouble makes one glad;
but bringing friends to trouble is hard grief.
Still, I care less for all these second thoughts   410
than for the fact that I myself am safe.
CREON: You there, whose head is drooping to the ground,
   do you admit this, or deny you did it?
ANTIGONE: I say I did it and I don't deny it.
CREON (*to the* GUARD): Take yourself off wherever you wish to go   415
   free of a heavy charge.
CREON (*to* ANTIGONE): You—tell me not at length but in a word.
   You knew the order not to do this thing?
ANTIGONE: I knew, of course I knew. The word was plain.
CREON: And still you dared to overstep these laws?   420
ANTIGONE: For me it was not Zeus who made that order.
   Nor did that Justice who lives with the gods below
   mark out such laws to hold among mankind.
   Nor did I think your orders were so strong
   that you, a mortal man, could over-run   425
   the gods' unwritten and unfailing laws.
   Not now, nor yesterday's, they always live,
   and no one knows their origin in time.
   So not through fear of any man's proud spirit
   would I be likely to neglect these laws,   430
   draw on myself the gods' sure punishment.
   I knew that I must die; how could I not?
   even without your warning. If I die
   before my time, I say it is a gain.

Who lives in sorrows many as are mine 435
how shall he not be glad to gain his death?
And so, for me to meet this fate, no grief.
But if I left that corpse, my mother's son,
dead and unburied I'd have cause to grieve
as now I grieve not. 440
And if you think my acts are foolishness
the foolishness may be in a fool's eye.
CHORUS: The girl is bitter. She's her father's child.
She cannot yield to trouble; nor could he.
CREON: These rigid spirits are the first to fall. 445
The strongest iron, hardened in the fire,
most often ends in scraps and shatterings.
Small curbs bring raging horses back to terms.
Slave to his neighbor, who can think of pride?
This girl was expert in her insolence 450
when she broke bounds beyond established law.
Once she had done it, insolence the second,
to boast her doing, and to laugh in it.
I am no man and she the man instead
if she can have this conquest without pain. 455
She is my sister's child, but were she child
of closer kin than any at my hearth,
she and her sister should not so escape
their death and doom. I charge Ismene too.
She shared the planning of this burial. 460
Call her outside. I saw her in the house,
maddened, no longer mistress of herself.
The sly intent betrays itself sometimes
before the secret plotters work their wrong.
I hate it too when someone caught in crime 465
then wants to make it seem a lovely thing.
ANTIGONE: Do you want more than my arrest and death?
CREON: No more than that. For that is all I need.
ANTIGONE: Why are you waiting? Nothing that you say
fits with my thought, I pray it never will. 470
Nor will you ever like to hear my words.
And yet what greater glory could I find
than giving my own brother funeral?
All these would say that they approved my act
did fear not mute them. 475
(A king is fortunate in many ways,
and most, that he can act and speak at will.)

CREON: None of these others see the case this way.
ANTIGONE: They see, and do not say. You have them cowed.
CREON: And you are not ashamed to think alone?   480
ANTIGONE: No, I am not ashamed. When was it shame
    to serve the children of my mother's womb?
CREON: It was not your brother who died against him, then?
ANTIGONE: Full brother, on both sides, my parents' child.
CREON: Your act of grace, in his regard, is crime.   485
ANTIGONE: The corpse below would never say it was.
CREON: When you honor him and the criminal just alike?
ANTIGONE: It was a brother, not a slave, who died.
CREON: Died to destroy this land the other guarded.
ANTIGONE: Death yearns for equal law for all the dead.   490
CREON: Not that the good and bad draw equal shares.
ANTIGONE: Who knows that this is holiness below?
CREON: Never the enemy, even in death, a friend.
ANTIGONE: I cannot share in hatred, but in love.
CREON: Then go down there, if you must love, and love   495
    the dead. No woman rules me while I live.
(ISMENE *is brought from the palace under guard.*)
CHORUS: Look there! Ismene is coming out.
    She loves her sister and mourns,
    with clouded brow and bloodied cheeks,
    tears on her lovely face.   500
CREON: You, lurking like a viper in the house,
    who sucked me dry, I looked the other way
    while twin destruction planned against the throne.
    Now tell me, do you say you shared this deed?
    Or will you swear you didn't even know?   505
ISMENE: I did the deed, if she agrees I did.
    I am accessory and share the blame.
ANTIGONE: Justice will not allow this. You did not
    wish for a part, nor did I give you one.
ISMENE: You are in trouble, and I'm not ashamed   510
    to sail beside you into suffering.
ANTIGONE: Death and the dead, they know whose act it was.
    I cannot love a friend whose love is words.
ISMENE: Sister, I pray, don't fence me out from honor,
    from death with you, and honor done the dead.   515
ANTIGONE: Don't die along with me, nor make your own
    that which you did not do. My death's enough.
ISMENE: When you are gone what life can be my friend?
ANTIGONE: Love Creon. He's your kinsman and your care.

ISMENE: Why hurt me, when it does yourself no good? 520
ANTIGONE: I also suffer, when I laugh at you.
ISMENE: What further service can I do you now?
ANTIGONE: To save yourself. I shall not envy you.
ISMENE: Alas for me. Am I outside your fate?
ANTIGONE: Yes. For you chose to live when I chose death. 525
ISMENE: At least I was not silent. You were warned.
ANTIGONE: Some will have thought you wiser. Some will not.
ISMENE: And yet the blame is equal for us both.
ANTIGONE: Take heart. You live. My life died long ago.
    And that has made me fit to help the dead. 530
CREON: One of these girls has shown her lack of sense
    just now. The other had it from her birth.
ISMENE: Yes, lord. When people fall in deep distress
    their native sense departs, and will not stay.
CREON: You chose your mind's distraction when you chose 535
    to work out wickedness with this wicked girl.
ISMENE: What life is there for me to live without her?
CREON: Don't speak of her. For she is here no more.
ISMENE: But will you kill your own son's promised bride?
CREON: Oh, there are other furrows for his plough. 540
ISMENE: But where the closeness that has bound these two?
CREON: Not for my sons will I choose wicked wives.
ISMENE: Dear Haemon, your father robs you of your rights.
CREON: You and your marriage trouble me too much.
ISMENE: You will take away his bride from your own son? 545
CREON: Yes. Death will help me break this marriage off.
CHORUS: It seems determined that the girl must die.
CREON: You helped determine it. Now, no delay!
    Slaves, take them in. They must be women now.
    No more free running. 550
    Even the bold will fly when they see Death
    drawing in close enough to end their life.
(ANTIGONE *and* ISMENE *are taken inside.*)
CHORUS: Fortunate they whose lives have no taste of pain.
    For those whose house is shaken by the gods
    escape no kind of doom. It extends to all the kin 555
    like the wave that comes when the winds of Thrace
    run over the dark of the sea.
    The black sand of the bottom is brought from the depth;
    the beaten capes sound back with a hollow cry.
    Ancient the sorrow of Labdacus' house, I know. 560
    Dead men's grief comes back, and falls on grief.
    No generation can free the next.

One of the gods will strike. There is no escape.
So now the light goes out
for the house of Oedipus, while the bloody knife   565
cuts the remaining root. Folly and Fury have done this.
What madness of man, O Zeus, can bind your power?
Not sleep can destroy it who ages all,
nor the weariless months the gods have set. Unaged in time
monarch you rule of Olympus' gleaming light.   570
Near time, far future, and the past,
one law controls them all:
any greatness in human life brings doom.
Wandering hope brings help to many men.
But others she tricks from their giddy loves,   575
and her quarry knows nothing until he has walked into flame.
Word of wisdom it was when someone said,
"The bad becomes the good
to him a god would doom."
Only briefly is that one from under doom.   580
(HAEMON *enters from the side.*)
Here is your one surviving son.
Does he come in grief at the fate of his bride,
in pain that he's tricked of his wedding?
CREON: Soon we shall know more than a seer could tell us.
Son, have you heard the vote condemned your bride?   585
And are you here, maddened against your father,
or are we friends, whatever I may do?
HAEMON: My father, I am yours. You keep me straight
with your good judgment, which I shall ever follow.
Nor shall a marriage count for more with me   590
than your kind leading.
CREON: There's my good boy. So should you hold at heart
and stand behind your father all the way.
It is for this men pray they may beget
households of dutiful obedient sons,   595
who share alike in punishing enemies,
and give due honor to their father's friends.
Whoever breeds a child that will not help
what has he sown but trouble for himself,
and for his enemies laughter full and free?   600
Son, do not let your lust mislead your mind,
all for a woman's sake, for well you know
how cold the thing he takes into his arms
who has a wicked woman for his wife.
What deeper wounding than a friend no friend?   605

Oh spit her forth forever, as your foe.
Let the girl marry somebody in Hades.
Since I have caught her in the open act,
the only one in town who disobeyed,
I shall not now proclaim myself a liar,   610
but kill her. Let her sing her song of Zeus
who guards the kindred.
If I allow disorder in my house
I'd surely have to license it abroad.
A man who deals in fairness with his own,   615
he can make manifest justice in the state.
But he who crosses law, or forces it,
or hopes to bring the rulers under him,
shall never have a word of praise from me.
The man the state has put in place must have   620
obedient hearing to his least command
when it is right, and even when it's not.
He who accepts this teaching I can trust,
ruler, or ruled, to function in his place,
to stand his ground even in the storm of spears,   625
a mate to trust in battle at one's side.
There is no greater wrong than disobedience.
This ruins cities, this tears down our homes,
this breaks the battle-front in panic-rout.
If men live decently it is because   630
discipline saves their very lives for them.
So I must guard the men who yield to order,
not let myself be beaten by a woman.
Better, if it must happen, that a man
should overset me.   635
I won't be called weaker than womankind.
CHORUS: We think—unless our age is cheating us—
       that what you say is sensible and right.
HAEMON: Father, the gods have given men good sense,
       the only sure possession that we have.   640
       I couldn't find the words in which to claim
       that there was error in your late remarks.
       Yet someone else might bring some further light.
       Because I am your son I must keep watch
       on all men's doing where it touches you,   645
       their speech, and most of all, their discontents.
       Your presence frightens any common man
       from saying things you would not care to hear.

But in dark corners I have heard them say
how the whole town is grieving for this girl,   650
unjustly doomed, if ever woman was,
to die in shame for glorious action done.
She would not leave her fallen, slaughtered brother
there, as he lay, unburied, for the birds
and hungry dogs to make an end of him.   655
Isn't her real desert a golden prize?
This is the undercover speech in town.
Father, your welfare is my greatest good.
What loveliness in life for any child
outweighs a father's fortune and good fame?   660
And so a father feels his children's faring.
Then, do not have one mind, and one alone
that only your opinion can be right.
Whoever thinks that he alone is wise,
his eloquence, his mind, above the rest,   665
come the unfolding, shows his emptiness.
A man, though wise, should never be ashamed
of learning more, and must unbend his mind.
Have you not seen the trees beside the torrent,
the ones that bend them saving every leaf,   670
while the resistant perish root and branch?
And so the ship that will not slacken sail,
the sheet drawn tight, unyielding, overturns.
She ends the voyage with her keel on top.
No, yield your wrath, allow a change of stand.   675
Young as I am, if I may give advice,
I'd say it would be best if men were born
perfect in wisdom, but that failing this
(which often fails) it can be no dishonor
to learn from others when they speak good sense.   680
CHORUS: Lord, if your son has spoken to the point
   you should take his lesson. He should do the same.
   Both sides have spoken well.
CREON: At my age I'm to school my mind by his?
   This boy instructor is my master, then?   685
HAEMON: I urge no wrong. I'm young, but you should watch
   my actions, not my years, to judge of me.
CREON: A loyal action, to respect disorder?
HAEMON: I wouldn't urge respect for wickedness.
CREON: You don't think she is sick with that disease? 690
HAEMON: Your fellow-citizens maintain she's not.

CREON: Is the town to tell me how I ought to rule?
HAEMON: Now there you speak just like a boy yourself.
CREON: Am I to rule by other mind than mine?
HAEMON: No city is property of a single man.   695
CREON: But custom gives possession to the ruler.
HAEMON: You'd rule a desert beautifully alone.
CREON *(to the* CHORUS*)*: It seems he's firmly on the woman's side.
HAEMON: If you're a woman. It is you I care for.
CREON: Wicked, to try conclusions with your father.   700
HAEMON: When you conclude unjustly, so I must.
CREON: Am I unjust, when I respect my office?
HAEMON: You tread down the gods' due. Respect is gone.
CREON: Your mind is poisoned. Weaker than a woman!
HAEMON: At least you'll never see me yield to shame.   705
CREON: Your whole long argument is but for her.
HAEMON: And you, and me, and for the gods below.
CREON: You shall not marry her while she's alive.
HAEMON: Then she shall die. Her death will bring another.
CREON: Your boldness has made progress. Threats, indeed!   710
HAEMON: No threat, to speak against your empty plan.
CREON: Past due, sharp lessons for your empty brain.
HAEMON: If you weren't father, I should call you mad,
CREON: Don't flatter me with "father," you woman's slave.
HAEMON: You wish to speak but never wish to hear.   715
CREON: You think so? By Olympus, you shall not
    revile me with these tauntings and go free.
    Bring out the hateful creature; she shall die
    full in his sight, close at her bridegroom's side.
HAEMON: Not at my side her death, and you will not   720
    ever lay eyes upon my face again.
    Find other friends to rave with after this.
(HAEMON *leaves, by one of the side entrances.*)
CHORUS: Lord, he has gone with all the speed of rage.
    When such a man is grieved his mind is hard.
CREON: Oh, let him go, plan superhuman action.   725
    In any case the girls shall not escape.
CHORUS: You plan for both the punishment of death?
CREON: Not her who did not do it. You are right.
CHORUS: And what death have you chosen for the other?
CREON: To take her where the foot of man comes not.   730
    There shall I hide her in a hollowed cave
    living, and leave her just so much to eat
    as clears the city from the guilt of death.
    There, if she prays to Death, the only god

of her respect, she may manage not to die.   735
Or she may learn at last and even then
how much too much her labor for the dead.
(CREON *returns to the palace.*)
CHORUS: Love unconquered in fight, love who falls on our havings.
You rest in the bloom of a girl's unwithered face.
You cross the sea, you are known in the wildest lairs.   740
Not the immortal gods can fly,
nor men of a day. Who has you within him is mad.
You twist the minds of the just. Wrong they pursue and are ruined.
You made this quarrel of kindred before us now.
Desire looks clear from the eyes of a lovely bride: 745
power as strong as the founded world.
For there is the goddess at play with whom no man can fight.
(ANTIGONE *is brought from the palace under guard.*)
Now I am carried beyond all bounds.
My tears will not be checked.
I see Antigone depart   750
to the chamber where all men sleep.
ANTIGONE: Men of my fathers' land, you see me go
my last journey. My last sight of the sun,
then never again. Death who brings all to sleep
takes me alive to the shore   755
of the river underground.
Not for me was the marriage-hymn, nor will anyone start the song
at a wedding of mine, Acheron is my mate.
CHORUS: With praise as your portion you go
in fame to the vault of the dead.   760
Untouched by wasting disease,
not paying the price of the sword,
of your own motion you go.
Alone among mortals will you descend
in life to the house of Death.   765
ANTIGONE: Pitiful was the death that stranger died,
our queen once, Tantalus' daughter. The rock
it covered her over, like stubborn ivy it grew.
Still, as she wastes, the rain
and snow companion her.   770
Pouring down from her mourning eyes comes the water that soaks the
    stone.
My own putting to sleep a god has planned like hers.
CHORUS: God's child and god she was.
We are born to death.
Yet even in death you will have your fame,   775

to have gone like a god to your fate,
in living and dying alike.
ANTIGONE: Laughter against me now. In the name of our fathers' gods,
could you not wait till I went? Must affront be thrown in my face?
O city of wealthy men. 780
I call upon Dirce's spring,
I call upon Thebes' grove in the armored plain,
to be my witnesses, how with no friend's mourning,
by what decree I go to the fresh-made prison-tomb.
Alive to the place of corpses, an alien still, 785
never at home with the living nor with the dead.
CHORUS: You went to the furthest verge
of daring, but there you found
the high foundation of justice, and fell.
Perhaps you are paying your father's pain. 790
ANTIGONE: You speak of my darkest thought, my pitiful father's fame,
spread through all the world, and the doom that haunts our house,
the royal house of Thebes.
My mother's marriage-bed.
Destruction where she lay with her husband-son, 795
my father. These are my parents and I their child.
I go to stay with them. My curse is to die unwed.
My brother, you found your fate when you found your bride,
found it for me as well. Dead, you destroy my life.
CHORUS: You showed respect for the dead. 800
So we for you: but power
is not to be thwarted so.
Your self-sufficiency has brought you down.
ANTIGONE: Unwept, no wedding-song, unfriended, now I go
the road laid down for me. 805
No longer shall I see this holy light of the sun.
No friend to bewail my fate.
(CREON *enters from the palace.*)
CREON: When people sing the dirge for their own deaths
ahead of time, nothing will break them off
if they can hope that this will buy delay. 810
Take her away at once, and open up
the tomb I spoke of. Leave her there alone.
There let her choose: death, or a buried life.
No stain of guilt upon us in this case,
but she is exiled from our life on earth. 815
ANTIGONE: O tomb, O marriage-chamber, hollowed out
house that will watch forever, where I go.

To my own people, who are mostly there;
Persephone has taken them to her.
Last of them all, ill-fated past the rest,   820
shall I descend, before my course is run.
Still when I get there I may hope to find
I come as a dear friend to my dear father,
to you, my mother, and my brother too.
All three of you have known my hand in death.   825
I washed your bodies, dressed them for the grave,
poured out the last libation at the tomb.
Last, Polyneices knows the price I pay
for doing final service to his corpse.
And yet the wise will know my choice was right.   830
Had I had children or their father dead,
I'd let them moulder. I should not have chosen
in such a case to cross the state's decree.
What is the law that lies behind these words?
One husband gone, I might have found another,   835
or a child from a new man in first child's place,
but with my parents hid away in death,
no brother, ever, could spring up for me.
Such was the law by which I honored you.
But Creon thought the doing was a crime,   840
a dreadful daring, brother of my heart.
So now he takes and leads me out by force.
No marriage-bed, no marriage-song for me,
and since no wedding, so no child to rear.
I go, without a friend, struck down by fate,   845
live to the hollow chambers of the dead.
What divine justice have I disobeyed?
Why, in my misery, look to the gods for help?
Can I call any of them my ally?
I stand convicted of impiety,   850
the evidence my pious duty done.
Should the gods think that this is righteousness,
in suffering I'll see my error clear.
But if it is the others who are wrong
I wish them no greater punishment than mine.   855
CHORUS: The same tempest of mind
    as ever, controls the girl.
CREON: Therefore her guards shall regret
    the slowness with which they move.
ANTIGONE: That word comes close to death.   860

CREON: You are perfectly right in that.

ANTIGONE: O town of my fathers in Thebes' land,
    O gods of our house.
    I am led away at last.
    Look, leaders of Thebes,   865
    I am last of your royal line.
    Look what I suffer, at whose command,
    because I respected the right.

(ANTIGONE *is led away. The slow procession should begin during the preceding passage.*)

CHORUS: Danaë suffered too.
    She went from the light to the brass-built room,   870
    chamber and tomb together. Like you, poor child,
    she was of great descent, and more, she held and kept
    the seed of the golden rain which was Zeus.
    Fate has terrible power.
    You cannot escape it by wealth or war.   875
    No fort will keep it out, no ships outrun it.
    Remember the angry king,
    son of Dryas, who raged at the god and paid,
    pent in a rock-walled prison. His bursting wrath
    slowly went down. As the terror of madness went,   880
    he learned of his frenzied attack on the god.
    Fool, he had tried to stop
    the dancing women possessed of god,
    the fire of Dionysus, the songs and flutes.
    Where the dark rocks divide   885
    sea from sea in Thrace
    is Salmydessus whose savage god
    beheld the terrible blinding wounds
    dealt to Phineus' sons by their father's wife.
    Dark the eyes that looked to avenge their mother.   890
    Sharp with her shuttle she struck, and blooded her hands.
    Wasting they wept their fate,
    settled when they were born
    to Cleopatra, unhappy queen.
    She was a princess too, of an ancient house,   895
    reared in the cave of the wild north wind, her father.
    Half a goddess but, child, she suffered like you.

(*Enter, from the side* TEIRESIAS, *the blind prophet, led by a boy attendant.*)

TEIRESIAS: Elders of Thebes, we two have come one road,
    two of us looking through one pair of eyes.
    This is the way of walking for the blind.   900

CREON: Teiresias, what news has brought you here?

TEIRESIAS: I'll tell you. You in turn must trust the prophet.

CREON: I've always been attentive to your counsel.

TEIRESIAS: And therefore you have steered this city straight.

CREON: So I can say how helpful you have been.   905

TEIRESIAS: But now you are balanced on a razor's edge.

CREON: What is it? How I shudder at your words!

TEIRESIAS: You'll know, when you hear the signs that I have marked
    I sat where every bird of heaven comes
    in my old place of augury, and heard   910
    bird-cries I'd never known. They screeched about
    goaded by madness, inarticulate.
    I marked that they were tearing one another
    with claws of murder. I could hear the wing-beats.
    I was afraid, so straight away I tried   915
    burnt sacrifice upon the flaming altar.
    No fire caught my offerings. Slimy ooze
    dripped on the ashes, smoked and sputtered there.
    Gall burst its bladder, vanished into vapor;
    the fat dripped from the bones and would not burn.   920
    These are the omens of the rites that failed,
    as my boy here has told me. He's my guide
    as I am guide to others.
    Why has this sickness struck against the state?
    Through your decision.   925
    All of the altars of the town are choked
    with leavings of the dogs and birds; their feast
    was on that fated, fallen Polyneices.
    So the gods will have no offering from us,
    not prayer, nor flame of sacrifice. The birds   930
    will not cry out a sound I can distinguish,
    gorged with the greasy blood of that dead man.
    Think of these things, my son. All men may err
    but error once committed, he's no fool
    nor yet unfortunate, who gives up his stiffness   935
    and cures the trouble he has fallen in.
    Stubbornness and stupidity are twins.
    Yield to the dead. Why goad him where he lies?
    What use to kill the dead a second time?
    I speak for your own good. And I am right.   940
    Learning from a wise counsellor is not pain
    if what he speaks are profitable words.

CREON: Old man, you all, like bowmen at a mark,
    have bent your bows at me. I've had my share
    of seers. I've been an item in your accounts.   945

Make profit, trade in Lydian silver-gold,
pure gold of India; that's your chief desire.
But you will never cover up that corpse.
Not if the very eagles tear their food
from him, and leave it at the throne of Zeus. 950
I wouldn't give him up for burial
in fear of that pollution. For I know
no mortal being can pollute the gods.
O old Teiresias, human beings fall;
the clever ones the furthest, when they plead 955
a shameful case so well in hope of profit.
TEIRESIAS: Alas!
What man can tell me, has he thought at all . . .
CREON: What hackneyed saw is coming from your lips?
TEIRESIAS: How better than all wealth is sound good counsel. 960
CREON: And so is folly worse than anything.
TEIRESIAS: And you're infected with that same disease.
CREON: I'm reluctant to be uncivil to a seer . . .
TEIRESIAS: You're that already. You have said I lie.
CREON: Well, the whole crew of seers are money-mad. 965
TEIRESIAS: And the whole tribe of tyrants grab at gain.
CREON: Do you realize you are talking to a king?
TEIRESIAS: I know. Who helped you save this town you hold?
CREON: You're a wise seer, but you love wickedness.
TEIRESIAS: You'll bring me to speak the unspeakable, very soon. 970
CREON: Well, speak it out. But do not speak for profit.
TEIRESIAS: No, there's no profit in my words for you.
CREON: You'd better realise that you can't deliver
my mind, if you should sell it, to the buyer.
TEIRESIAS: Know well, the sun will not have rolled its course 975
many more days, before you come to give
corpse for these corpses, child of your own loins.
For you've confused the upper and lower worlds.
You sent a life to settle in a tomb;
you keep up here that which belongs below 980
the corpse unburied, robbed of its release.
Not you, nor any god that rules on high
can claim him now.
You rob the nether gods of what is theirs.
So the pursuing horrors lie in wait 985
to track you down. The Furies sent by Hades
and by all gods will even you with your victims.
Now say that I am bribed! At no far time

shall men and women wail within your house.
And all the cities that you fought in war   990
whose sons had burial from wild beasts, or dogs,
or birds that brought the stench of your great wrong
back to each hearth, they move against you now.
A bowman, as you said, I send my shafts,
now you have moved me, straight. You'll feel the wound.   995
Boy, take me home now. Let him spend his rage
on younger men, and learn to calm his tongue,
and keep a better mind than now he does.
(*Exit.*)
CHORUS: Lord, he has gone. Terrible prophecies!
And since the time when I first grew grey hair   1000
his sayings to the city have been true.
CREON: I also know this. And my mind is torn.
To yield is dreadful. But to stand against him.
Dreadful to strike my spirit to destruction.
CHORUS: Now you must come to counsel, and take advice.   1005
CREON: What must I do? Speak, and I shall obey.
CHORUS: Go free the maiden from that rocky house.
Bury the dead who lies in readiness.
CREON: This is your counsel? You would have me yield?
CHORUS: Quick as you can. The gods move very fast   1010
when they bring ruin on misguided men.
CREON: How hard, abandonment of my desire.
But I can fight necessity no more.
CHORUS: Do it yourself. Leave it to no one else.
CREON: I'll go at once. Come, followers, to your work.   1015
You that are here round up the other fellows.
Take axes with you, hurry to that place
that overlooks us.
Now my decision has been overturned
shall I, who bound her, set her free myself.   1020
I've come to fear it's best to hold the laws
of old tradition to the end of life.
(*Exit.*)
CHORUS: God of the many names, Semele's golden child,
child of Olympian thunder, Italy's lord.
Lord of Eleusis, where all men come   1025
to mother Demeter's plain.
Bacchus, who dwells in Thebes,
by Ismenus' running water,
where wild Bacchic women are at home,

on the soil of the dragon seed.   1030
Seen in the glaring flame, high on the double mount,
with the nymphs of Parnassus at play on the hill,
seen by Kastalia's flowing stream.
You come from the ivied heights,
from green Euboea's shore.   1035
In immortal words we cry
your name, lord, who watch the ways,
the many ways of Thebes.
This is your city, honored beyond the rest,
the town of your mother's miracle-death.   1040
Now, as we wrestle our grim disease,
come with healing step from Parnassus' slope
or over the moaning sea.
Leader in dance of the fire-pulsing stars,
overseer of the voices of night,   1045
child of Zeus, be manifest,
with due companionship of Maenad maids
whose cry is but your name.
(*Enter one of those who left with* CREON, *as* MESSENGER.)
MESSENGER: Neighbors of Cadmus, and Amphion's house,
there is no kind of state in human life   1050
which I now dare to envy or to blame.
Luck sets it straight, and luck she overturns
the happy or unhappy day by day.
No prophecy can deal with men's affairs.
Creon was envied once, as I believe,   1055
for having saved this city from its foes
and having got full power in this land.
He steered it well. And he had noble sons.
Now everything is gone.
Yes, when a man has lost all happiness,   1060
he's not alive. Call him a breathing corpse.
Be very rich at home. Live as a king.
But once your joy has gone, though these are left
they are smoke's shadow to lost happiness.
CHORUS: What is the grief of princes that you bring?   1065
MESSENGER: They're dead. The living are responsible.
CHORUS: Who died? Who did the murder? Tell us now.
MESSENGER: Haemon is gone. One of his kin drew blood.
CHORUS: But whose arm struck? His father's or his own?
MESSENGER: He killed himself. His blood is on his father.   1070
CHORUS: Seer, all too true the prophecy you told!

MESSENGER: This is the state of things. Now make your plans.
(Enter, from the palace, EURYDICE.*)*
CHORUS: Eurydice is with us now, I see.
    Creon's poor wife. She may have come by chance.
    She may have heard something about her son.   1075
EURYDICE: I heard your talk as I was coming out
    to greet the goddess Pallas with my prayer.
    And as I moved the bolts that held the door
    I heard of my own sorrow.
    I fell back fainting in my women's arms.   1080
    But say again just what the news you bring.
    I, whom you speak to, have known grief before.
MESSENGER: Dear lady, I was there, and I shall tell,
    leaving out nothing of the true account.
    Why should I make it soft for you with tales   1085
    to prove myself a liar? Truth is right.
    I followed your husband to the plain's far edge,
    where Polyneices' corpse was lying still
    unpitied. The dogs had torn him all apart.
    We prayed the goddess of all journeyings,   1090
    and Pluto, that they turn their wrath to kindness,
    we gave the final purifying bath,
    then burned the poor remains on new-cut boughs,
    and heaped a high mound of his native earth.
    Then turned we to the maiden's rocky bed,   1095
    death's hollow marriage-chamber.
    But, still far off, one of us heard a voice
    in keen lament by that unblest abode.
    He ran and told the master. As Creon came
    he heard confusion crying. He groaned and spoke: 1100
    "Am I a prophet now, and do I tread
    the saddest of all roads I ever trod?
    My son's voice crying! Servants, run up close,
    stand by the tomb and look, push through the crevice
    where we built the pile of rock, right to the entry.   1105
    Find out if that is Haemon's voice I hear
    or if the gods are tricking me indeed."
    We obeyed the order of our mournful master.
    In the far corner of the tomb we saw
    her, hanging by the neck, caught in a noose   1110
    of her own linen veiling.
    Haemon embraced her as she hung, and mourned
    his bride's destruction, dead and gone below,

his father's actions, the unfated marriage.
When Creon saw him, he groaned terribly, 1115
and went toward him, and called him with lament:
"What have you done, what plan have you caught up,
what sort of suffering is killing you?
Come out, my child, I do beseech you, come!"
The boy looked at him with his angry eyes, 1120
spat in his face and spoke no further word.
He drew his sword, but as his father ran,
he missed his aim. Then the unhappy boy,
in anger at himself, leant on the blade.
It entered, half its length, into his side. 1125
While he was conscious he embraced the maiden,
holding her gently. Last, he gasped out blood,
red blood on her white cheek.
Corpse on a corpse he lies. He found his marriage.
Its celebration in the halls of Hades. 1130
So he has made it very clear to men
that to reject good counsel is a crime.
(EURYDICE *returns to the house.*)
CHORUS: What do you make of this? The queen has gone
in silence. We know nothing of her mind.
MESSENGER: I wonder at her, too. But we can hope 1135
that she has gone to mourn her son within
with her own women, not before the town.
She knows discretion. She will do no wrong.
CHORUS: I am not sure. This muteness may portend
as great disaster as a loud lament. 1140
MESSENGER: I will go in and see if some deep plan
hides in her heart's wild pain. You may be right.
There can be heavy danger in mute grief.
(*The* MESSENGER *goes into the house.* CREON *enters with his followers.*
They are carrying HAEMON'*s body on a bier.*)
CHORUS: But look, the king draws near.
His own hand brings 1145
the witness of his crime,
the doom he brought on himself.
CREON: O crimes of my wicked heart,
harshness bringing death.
You see the killer, you see the kin he killed. 1150
My planning was all unblest.
Son, you have died too soon.

Oh, you have gone away
through my fault, not your own.
CHORUS: You have learned justice, though it comes too late.   1155
CREON: Yes, I have learned in sorrow. It was a god who struck,
who has weighted my head with disaster; he drove me to wild
strange ways,
his heavy heel on my joy.
Oh sorrows, sorrows of men.   1160
(Re-enter the MESSENGER, *from a side door of the palace.)*
MESSENGER: Master, you hold one sorrow in your hands
but you have more, stored up inside the house.
CREON: What further suffering can come on me?
MESSENGER: Your wife has died. The dead man's mother in deed,
poor soul, her wounds are fresh.   1165
CREON: Hades, harbor of all,
you have destroyed me now.
Terrible news to hear, horror the tale you tell.
I was dead, and you kill me again.
Boy, did I hear you right?   1170
Did you say the queen was dead,
slaughter on slaughter heaped?
(The central doors of the palace begin to open.)
CHORUS: Now you can see. Concealment is all over.
(The doors are open, and the corpse of EURYDICE *is revealed.)*
CREON: My second sorrow is here. Surely no fate remains
which can strike me again. Just now, I held my son in my arms.   1175
And now I see her dead.
Woe for the mother and son.
MESSENGER: There, by the altar, dying on the sword,
her eyes fell shut. She wept her older son
who died before, and this one. Last of all   1180
she cursed you as the killer of her children.
CREON: I am mad with fear. Will no one strike
and kill me with cutting sword?
Sorrowful, soaked in sorrow to the bone!
MESSENGER: Yes, for she held you guilty in the death   1185
of him before you, and the elder dead.
CREON: How did she die?
MESSENGER: Struck home at her own heart
when she had heard of Haemon's suffering.
CREON: This is my guilt, all mine. I killed you, I say it clear.   1190
Servants, take me away, out of the sight of men.

I who am nothing more than nothing now.
CHORUS: Your plan is good—if any good is left.
    Best to cut short our sorrow.
CREON: Let me go, let me go. May death come quick,   1195
    bringing my final day.
    O let me never see tomorrow's dawn.
CHORUS: That is the future's. We must look to now.
    What will be is in other hands than ours.
CREON: All my desire was in that prayer of mine.   1200
CHORUS: Pray not again. No mortal can escape
    the doom prepared for him.
CREON: Take me away at once, the frantic man who killed
    my son, against my meaning. I cannot rest.
    My life is warped past cure. My fate has struck me down.   1205
(CREON *and his attendants enter the house.*)
CHORUS: Our happiness depends
    on wisdom all the way.
    The gods must have their due.
    Great words by men of pride
    bring greater blows upon them.   1210
    So wisdom comes to the old.

- In this play, we see a battle of wills between Antigone and Creon. Both characters take a difficult stand for something that they feel is right. Both ask for the loyalty of others and finally defy their own family members in taking that stand. For whom is this play tragic? Which character earns our sympathy?

- Trace the loyalties of the chorus throughout the play. To what extent does our own reaction to the characters reflect or diverge from the opinions expressed by the chorus?

- Look carefully at the scene in which Creon confronts Antigone (lines 412–496 and 808–868). In the exchange, Creon accuses Antigone, and as she acknowledges her guilt, she defends the propriety of her actions and turns the blame upon Creon. The scene could be described generically as courtroom drama. Explain how the scene uses such conventions to establish guilt and innocence, to raise questions of morality, and to explore the boundaries of power within the play.

- The conflict between Antigone and Creon centers on the issue of how to treat Polyneices after his death. Antigone defies Creon by sprinkling dust on her brother's body. How do the discussions here of the treatment of the dead reflect similar concerns to those we see in other works in this section?

Experiencing Literature through Writing

1. The works in this anthology help us define a genre of "dignifying death." Use at least three of the works that we have included to construct your own definition of this genre of writing. As you choose the works that you will use, it may be most interesting to look at the works that do not have the most in common.

    a. As you look at the works, try to distinguish techniques that you define as representative of the genre of "dignifying death" from specific allusions to other works. What are specific formal devices that you see repeated in the works in this section? How do authors share a common use of language? How do they construct their poetry in a similar way? How do they structure their plays along similar lines?

    b. How can you explain how two works here that seem quite different actually belong in the same category?

    c. How is your definition of this "genre" useful to your understanding of each of the texts that you have chosen? How does it help you develop your analysis of each?

2. Pick at least one work from this section and one by the same author from another section of the book (Milton, Atwood, Whitman, Updike, Keats, Dickinson, Bradstreet, Roethke, Brooks, Hughes, or Sophocles are all possibilities). Compare these to at least one work by the same author (from elsewhere in the book) in which the author is not "dignifying death." What differences do you see in the construction of the works?

3. Compare the texts in this anthology with those in the anthology titled "Language and War." Compare specific texts to explain whether or not it is appropriate to group all of these works within the same genre. How would you define this genre? Why is inclusion or exclusion from this grouping useful to our understanding of these particular texts?

17 The Production and Reproduction of Texts

How Does Retelling and Revising Impact My Experience of a Text?

How Can Literary Theory Clarify What Constitutes That Experience?

Whatever historical or social changes surround a work of art and however those changes influence our perception of the work, we tend to trust in the stable reality of a physical text. After all, words move from left to right across a page; pages are bound to turn in a fixed order. Film winds from one spool to another; the images pass across the projecting light in a set sequence. Given the arguments and ambiguities that are part of any serious reading, it's nice to think we have in hand a text—a single object—that grounds our study and gives us a common starting point for critical discussion.

But maybe that object isn't as stable as we usually assume. Given the labor William Blake put in to meld word and image onto an elaborately designed page, is it adequate to read just the poems themselves as they are presented in books like the one you are reading now? Charles Dickens first published all of his novels in weekly or monthly serial forms. What happens when the experience of those novels is no longer extended in small parts on a regular basis over a long period of time? Francis Ford Coppola ambitiously re-edited *Apocalypse Now* years after its original release. Which version should command our critical attention now? And is the experience of the film altered by its transmission to DVD and, consequently, from the theater to our living room?

Academic critics and scholars tend to be a fussy group. Some are especially devoted to the presentation of the truest text. But the most sophisticated textual critics understand that the notion of a single "best" text or "pure" text is problematic. Literature isn't merely an *object* of academic study. It's a human activity and experience that cannot be contained or bound within covers. And a literary text isn't created by an individual operating in a vacuum. Nothing stops a powerful producer from cutting a scene a director or screenwriter thought important, or an actor from improvising well beyond an author's stage directions, or a writer from revising an already published poem. These varied creative forces need not lead to crucial critical problems; after all, most people are focused on the actual text they encounter, not an idealized text someone thinks they "should" have. Throughout this book, we've been primarily interested in the literary experience, not the physical objects of literary study.

Yet it's also true that if we are oblivious to textual issues, we may fail to appreciate important aspects of an artist's craft. We may also remain insensitive to complex external forces that contribute to the shaping of a particular work. This chapter emphasizes critical issues concerning the production and reproduction of a text. We'll reflect upon how people have used—revised, abridged, and translated—literary texts and films. We'll explore how those uses matter. And we'll examine the underlying theoretical implications of choices we routinely (and often unconsciously) make as readers.

TEXTS AND TECHNOLOGY

Many people have observed that the development of the personal computer, of the Internet, and of the World Wide Web make our age the "information age." It's often said that what is unfolding now compares in significance to the invention of movable type in the fifteenth century. Gutenberg's printing of the Bible had enormous implications. The ability to produce and distribute texts in great numbers changed notions of literacy and upset established bases of power. In arts, the primacy of spoken or performed works was overtaken by our modern notion of literature, which gave the printed word a privileged place.

In many ways, the computer further emphasizes the printed word. But some things about how words can be arranged and displayed have changed. A book (as we noted previously) makes us turn pages. We read in a linear way, even when authors call into question notions of linear time or sequence. Words in an electronic space allow fresh design possibilities. Writers working in cyberspace are liberated from the physical demands of paper and binding. An electronic manuscript can mix forms of presentation (moving images,

As dramatic as recent developments in textual production may seem, one could argue that there is still nothing new. Many writers who worked decades, even centuries, before the first director's track ever appeared on a DVD have included forewords, prefaces, introductions, afterwords, postscripts, footnotes, and so on that frame the presentation of the main narrative in ways that keep readers conscious of the crafted nature of the text and of the presence of the author within the act of storytelling. In the earliest days of film, images were sped up or run backward to achieve comic effects. As film matured as an art, directors employed styles of editing that made audiences aware of film as film (see Chapter 9). **Split-screen** techniques, for example, may be used to remind viewers that there is never only one thing happening at any one point in time. So, hypertext could be seen as a new technology for the exploration of ideas and techniques about not strictly linear narrative that surfaced long ago.

sound, and so on). Readers may feel liberated as well. The notion of **hypertext** puts the reader/user in a strong position. Hypertext allows readers to access on a computer screen any variety of linked documents instantly, at any time, and in any order. These developments are now apparent in few significant works. The crafting and appreciation of great electronic manuscripts lie in the future. But some writers have begun to shape works that acknowledge new ways of presenting paper texts. It is fairly easy now, for example, to use multiple fonts, introduce color into a text, experiment with formats, or package a paper text with a CD or DVD. Writers have long challenged the idea that a story must be linear. Today, writers hoping to press the challenge further might choose to address the issue of linearity directly in the design of the page.

TEXTUAL FORM AND CONDITIONS OF PRODUCTION

There is a cliché often invoked when a good writer turns out an inferior bit of work: "even Homer nods." This cliché suggests that even a great writer can be sleepily inattentive to a line or a word, can "nod off" at one point or another in the writing process. It's a nice little saying, but it's also misleading. Homer, after all, wasn't a writer—at least not in the way we now think of what it is to be a writer. The great epics of ancient Greece were first delivered orally. No one lined up at the local bookstore to get copies of the next new work by Homer. *The Iliad* and *The Odyssey* as we know them were, of course, eventually written down. And the person (or persons) who did that writing had an extraordinary command of language. But the source materials were worked and reworked, revised, improvised, and elaborated upon over many years of oral performances.

Our current notions of poetry, drama, fiction, and film don't then simply represent different forms of presentation that have always been available. These genres can be traced back to specific technologies and changing social conditions. Before print, poets spoke or sung to audiences. Rhythmic devices and rhyming effects were used both to assist the memory of the performer and to sustain attention of a listener. Early printed poems tended to circulate within a very narrow range of society. Live drama could not have arisen without a complex social structure to support it (if there were no theaters or no paying audience, would there be playwrights?). The novel emerged only when there was large middle-class readership; in fact, up until the early nineteenth century, novels were primarily aimed at women who had the time, the education, and the means necessary for sustaining a new form of entertainment and instruction. As for one of the latest "new forms" of entertainment, many observers of the film business believe that the growing popularity of DVDs and "home theaters" will redefine the moviegoing experience.

Experiencing Literature through Issues of Production

William Blake designed pages as well as wrote poems. The interaction of word and image in his works offers an experience that conventional reprinting with words alone cannot match. One must even consider how and to what extent our interpretation of a given Blake poem may be controlled by the form we have of it. Consider, for example, "A Poison Tree," from *Songs of Experience*.

The tree, in the words of the poem, is a tree of wrath—something that has grown from anger and hatred. It is the product of the speaker's experience. The words deliver a powerful and fairly direct message: be open with your anger, or it will become deadly. But our experience of the whole text is much broader and more subtly nuanced. In Blake's engraving, the fallen "foe" beneath the tree lies with arms open wide. He seems at peace in a sacrificial position. His long hair spreads upon the earth. The broad chest is foregrounded; the lower body melds with the landscape behind. There is an almost sensual quality to the figure; if not for the accompanying poem, the figure could be seen as sleeping. The tree *drawn* on Blake's page seems part of a beautiful landscape. But the poem's title, "A Poison Tree," along with the fairly specific allegorical tree conjured by the words alone, jars against the image of the tree that so gracefully frames the whole composition. Blake had written of innocence and experience as qualities marking the "contrary states of the human soul." Viewing the whole page in this case (text and artwork) suggests he has encompassed that range. To put the point in a different way, the "experience" of the poem's speaker doesn't match Blake's complete vision or our own experience of the whole text. How does Blake's image complicate our sense of his poem?

A POISON TREE.

I was angry with my friend:
I told my wrath, my wrath did end.
I was angry with my foe:
I told it not. my wrath did grow.

And I waterd it in fears,
Night & morning with my tears;
And I sunned it with smiles,
And with soft deceitful wiles.

And it grew both day and night,
Till it bore an apple bright.
And my foe beheld it shine,
And he knew that it was mine.

And into my garden stole.
When the night had veild the pole;
In the morning glad I see:
My foe outstretchd beneath the tree.

AN ORIENTATION TO CONTEMPORARY CRITICAL THEORY

Reading literature can be a challenge, but reading critical analyses of literature can seem impossible to a person unfamiliar with key ideas and assumptions. Not only is it easy to get lost amid the confusing names that signal the different angles critics take in studying literature and film but it can be hard to know what the angle is. What is this critic's point of view? What assumptions does she or he make about the critical task? If you are to tune into conversations that occur in a college environment, you must acquire some understanding of common theoretical approaches to the literary experience.

New Criticism and *Auteur* Theory

We can orient ourselves to much current theory by knowing something about a critical movement that emerged in the middle of the twentieth century and that continues to influence much teaching. The name—**new criticism**—seems odd now, given that it's relatively old in context of recent schools of thought, but new criticism is the name that has stuck. The new critics were **formalists**; they argued that literary texts are the sole material of literary study. Literary criticism is *not* (the argument went) a branch of history, biography, psychology, or sociology, but a distinct discipline that must focus upon the structure, style, and language of a particular work of literary art. The "object itself" (a poem, story, or play) became the point of intense study for a generation of critics and scholars. **Explication** (the unfolding, the close reading, the analysis of the text) became the heart—indeed the end goal—of literary study. The best reading was the reading that accounted most fully for the work's complex features.

We've certainly assumed in this book that close attention to a work of art leads to a measure of exploration and discovery; but however valuable new criticism was as a disciplined method of analysis, it was ultimately narrow and arbitrary. The text, as we've suggested, can be in itself a problematic concept. And literature, like all human activities, is dynamic, changing, and messy. Both the strengths and the limitations of new criticism emerged quite clearly in the context of film studies. **Auteur** theory closely paralleled the new criticism (*auteur* is the French word for "author"). *Auteur* criticism assumed that if films were to be considered "art," they needed to be created by an artist (that is, the director). The focus on the director's management of the whole gave the critic a point of analytical focus. It led to serious and rigorous treatment of a film's structure and style. It worked from a sense that a single controlling creative force was shaping the whole work that unfolded. But *auteur* criticism disregarded the social and economic processes that influenced the making of films. It also could not encompass the essentially collaborative nature of filmmaking.

Deconstruction

The limits of new criticism and *auteur* theory met progressively aggressive challenges beginning in the 1960s. The French philosopher Jacques Derrida, in particular, undermined some of the formalists' most basic assumptions. Derrida pointed out that no word has a fixed or "natural" meaning. He argued that a word takes on meaning only within a complex, arbitrary, and ever-changing structure of words. A word is used to *refer* to something or is *associated* with something; a word must not be mistaken for the thing it stands for and must not be read separate from a system of other words. *Carriage*, for example, can in one text refer to a fancy horse-drawn cart and, in another, to a pushcart for babies. An automobile ad might use the word to suggest a substantial, expensive car. In still other contexts, *carriage* could refer to a loading mechanism for a gun or for the roller on a typewriter. Literary texts exploit (with or without the author's intention) such variable associations. It becomes the job of the critic to unfold a play of possible meanings that reveal multiple, even contrary, messages. For Derrida, to read closely is to deconstruct, not interpret, the text. This line of thinking leads to the notion that literary texts are not great because of their wholeness or consistency (qualities new criticism would emphasize) but because of the irreducibly complex associations that they provoke. **Deconstruction**, then, is not a practice that seeks to make a work coherent or consistent. The deconstructionist would reveal inconsistencies and revel in them.

The American critic J. Hillis Miller attempted to clarify deconstruction's task by calling attention to the following description of Eve in John Milton's *Paradise Lost*:

> She as a veil down to the slender waist
> Her unadorned golden tresses wore
>   Dissheveld, but in wanton ringlets wav'd
> As the vine curls her tendrils, which impli'd
>   Subjection.

Miller notes Eve is at this point in Milton's story a free, yet unfallen part of creation. Her place in nature is defined by her subjection to the authority of Adam and ultimately of God. Her loosely flowing hair is as natural as the growth of the garden that surrounds her. But however much Milton may stress Eve's innocence before the fall, "unadorned golden tresses" and "wanton ringlets" also achieve meaning in the context of a culture that sees a woman's loosely flowing hair as associated with sexuality and sin. It would seem the innocent Eve has already fallen or must necessarily fall by some flaw of her nature. But how can this be in a perfect creation? Even if Milton were to tell us that his description of Eve's hair implies nothing more than "subjection" to God's perfect order ("As the vine curls her tendrils"), should we be convinced by his authority? How can we so limit our understanding of "wanton" or the general luxuriance that dominates Milton's description of nature and of Eve herself? Along these lines, Miller argues that there are associations conveyed by the words in Milton's lines that contradict one another. A rigorous deconstructive reading (unlike the interpretation of a new critic) would expose rather than explain those contradictions. The orthodoxy of Milton's theological system may collapse under such analysis, but from a deconstructionist's perspective *Paradise Lost* is no less a poem for that. The richness of a literary text resides in the very complexity that makes final meaning impossible. To translate this into critical practice, a deconstructionist reading unfolds possible meanings rather than the correct meaning.

As you might imagine, deconstruction became highly controversial. Some people found it liberating. The new critical readings/interpretations that competed with one another for status as conclusive could now be seen as multiple and alternative lines of inquiry. New possibilities were opened and encouraged. Critics became strongly and self-consciously involved in the creative shaping of meaning, because meaning was no longer assumed to be determined by the work of art. But as you might also imagine, many academics found deconstruction profoundly threatening: What do we have left if *meaning* cannot be determined? Did deconstruction send us down a path toward nihilism—the belief in nothing? Many other skeptics also pointed out that deconstruction in practice often led to trivial, self-absorbed, and overcomplicated essays. Still others suggested that deconstruction was merely new jargon for essentially old ideas, many of those ideas very well established.

New Historicism and Other Historically Grounded Approaches

Deconstruction itself no longer stands at the center of critical disputes. It is not so much that matters have been resolved but that the grounds of discussion have shifted. Deconstruction's influence, for example, now shows in ways critics think of the relationship between history and literature. It is nothing new to observe that much can be learned about a given time by reading the literary works of that time. But in past decades literary artists were given a special status as especially accurate mirrors or as particularly perceptive critics of their age. Advocates of **new historicism** don't give a poem or play a privileged place in the materials that make up a given culture. New historicists see systems of meaning as conditional and shifting depending upon the interests the systems represent. In their view, literary artists are both caught in and contribute to the complex formation of ideas about power. From the perspective of a new historicist, a nineteenth-century American writer wouldn't merely take up the "frontier" as a subject but would participate (perhaps unknowingly) in the formation of his culture's attitude toward the frontier. The very notion of "frontier" is, after all, conditioned by assumptions of forward movement and conquest that make sense only to those who move forward and conquer: the western frontier was no frontier for the Native Americans who lived on it.

New historicism hardly had the chance to grow old before some academics began using the term **cultural poetics** (which accents the blurred distinctions between history, culture, and art); others adopted the term **postcolonial criticism** (which highlights a sense of power/authority imposed by one culture/system over another). **Reader-response criticism** stands as yet another variant of new historicism that reflects the influence of deconstruction. As that name implies, reader-response critics shift emphasis from a text to how people read or use a text; the work of art is studied not through its own inherent qualities but through the way readers of a particular time and place react to it. Any of these approaches can be taken from a distinct point of view. **Feminist criticism**, for example, seeks to gain insights largely obscured or bypassed by the men who have until recent decades dominated critical discussions. Feminists join the varieties of new historicists in assuming that a work of art is a product not only of an author but of a specific culture. The "object of study" has shifted from the "text itself" that the new critics identified to a complex set of social/historical/linguistic contexts.

WHY WE STUDY THE TEXTS WE STUDY

Many people read novels by Michael Crichton (*Congo, Jurassic Park,* among many), but relatively few people study them in literature classes. The distinction relates to the idea of the **canon**. The canon refers to those works considered appropriate for literary study. They are the durable works that a culture adopts and uses over time. Canonical works have achieved "classic" status. This seems simple enough: great books find a secure place in the canon; books less than great find a temporary place on a sales chart. But value judgments are never as clear as this. Canonical works may indeed be great, but one must acknowledge that ideas of greatness change. And perhaps more important, one must acknowledge that literary/artistic greatness is usually defined by a very particular group of people: mostly college professors. This means that the interests, ethnicity, education, and class of a particular profession have great influence in determining what belongs or doesn't belong in the canon.

Challenges to the canon have been prepared for by the unhinging effects of contemporary critical theory, but this challenge has been even more strongly motivated by broad social changes. Literary theories relate to, but do not motivate, battles regarding the canon. The fact is that today's student and teaching population is more highly varied in age, ethnicity, gender, and race than ever before. The multicultural population has understandably inspired revisions of long-established course offerings and text selections. In fact, our perspective on entire genres or art forms changes as the surrounding world changes. For example, movies were once thought barely worth critical attention; they were seen as popular entertainments, not works of art. Although movies are still popular entertainment, the best of them claim attention and respect. Entire college courses are devoted to film (the change in name from "movie" to "film" or "cinema" suggests the higher status within the university). Film (and film studies) has been around long enough now that we can speak of certain movies/films as canonical.

Experiencing Literature through Theory

The following two passages are taken from the introduction of two very different (although both very large) anthologies of American literature. The first, *Major Writers of America*, was published in 1962—in the days when the new critics held sway in an institution that was still largely white and male. The second, from *The Heath Anthology of American Literature*, first appeared in 1990 and clearly sounded a challenge to conventional notions of "major" or canonical. The first focuses on concepts of quality that are presumed discernible through rigorous analysis. The second shifts attention to historical context and implies that quality is relative to the interests of the reader. As you read, identify how assumptions that govern the editors' principle of selection are signaled in specific words or phrases. Think too about how the editors define the audience or readership of their textbook. What can you learn about education in the United States or about the place literature takes in that education by reading these passages?

from Major Writers of America (1962)

... while the canon is at long last becoming established, a realization gradually forces itself upon us that, as the age of discovery and of elementary mapping closes, the era of evaluation opens.... [It] is incumbent upon us to make clear which are the few peaks and which the many low-lying hills.... We must vindicate the study of American literature because primarily the matter is literature, and only secondarily because it is American.

> ... The first requirement of the design, therefore, was inevitably that the authors so nominated be represented fully enough to testify to their superiority.° ■

from The Heath Anthology of American Literature (1990)

... a major principle of selection has been to represent as fully as possible the varied cultures of the United States. American cultures sometimes overlap, sometimes differ, sometimes develop separately, sometimes in interactive patterns. To convey this diversity, we have included what is by far the widest sampling of the work of minority and white women writers available in any anthology of American literature. This selection includes material by 109 women of all races, 25 individual Native American authors (as well as 17 texts from tribal origins), 53 African Americans, 13 Hispanics (as well as 12 texts from earlier Spanish originals and two from French) and 9 Asian Americans. We have included significant selections from Jewish, Italian, and other ethnic traditions. ■

These two selections represent radically opposed notions of what literary study involves. It's important that you understand that the arguments behind each position influence the education you now experience. Professors, after all, must decide on which texts to assign. Can you sense where your professors fit into the conversation about inclusion/exclusion (or "quality"/context) carried on by the two anthologies?

A Note to Student Writers: Using Theory to Develop Critical Analysis

Although it is important to reflect upon the theoretical implications that lie behind any paper we write, it is not necessarily good to work consciously from a set theoretical perspective. To think from the start, "now I'm going to write as a deconstructionist," may be putting the cart before the horse. The cognitive activities that writing in response to a complex subject inevitably prompts should not be scripted in advance. It is better to discover you've deconstructed a poem than to insist that deconstructing poetry is your job.

We suggest that you attend closely to the prompt your professor offers and begin to write without thinking too much about critical theory. Once you've worked through an

---

°*Major Writers of America* included substantial selections of twenty-eight writers. Only one (Emily Dickinson) was a woman. Dickinson, however, was in the majority on another count: nineteen of the authors included were, like her, from the northeastern United States.

argument very carefully and prepared an essay for submission, you can ask yourself, What characterizes my approach? What assumptions am I making about literary criticism? How do I look upon matters of interpretation or meaning? To what extent have I treated the text as an object of art? To what extent have I seen meaning as conditioned by things "outside" the text? From what perspective is my argument a strong one? If in answering these questions, you achieve a clearer sense of the theoretical underpinnings of your work, you may be able to revise key points effectively. Theory may prove to enrich your reading and strengthen your analysis. But revision and development that bring theory forward happen after careful drafting. Don't allow theory to interfere with your powerful and immediate experience of a text. Don't allow theory to artificially force your writing in any particular direction. And don't assume that imposing a critical vocabulary will make your paper seem more sophisticated.

ABRIDGING, REVISING, AND REPACKAGING TEXT

For the most part in this book, we've offered "whole" works. But we haven't hesitated to use a fragment from a long novel or poem if we felt that the fragment helped illustrate a point. In relation to the subject of this chapter, it's important to also say that we don't assume that fragments cease to be literature. The passage excerpted from John Milton's *Paradise Lost* (p. 640) no doubt functions fully only in context of the whole poem, yet it reads on its own very well as a short poem. Although we certainly don't want to disregard an author's carefully crafted whole work, it's worth remembering that writers have made or approved abridgments of their own works in various forms (public readings, anthologies, translations, and so on). For that matter, individual readers may well choose to skip a chapter of the most meticulously prepared "critical edition." Such behaviors complicate our sense of what we study when we study literature and film. But these behaviors don't fundamentally change anything that we've addressed in other chapters. Rather than simply dismiss any abridgment as something less than literary, consider how an abridgment functions on its own terms. In other words, understand the limitations of an abridgment, but critically attend to whatever you have before you.

An abridged work normally intends to fairly represent something of the whole from which it is taken. At least, it shouldn't mislead one about the source text. But any substantial change presses a reader to experience a work of art as a new thing. Charles Dickens excerpted sections of his novels for his own dramatic readings. Although he could expect his audience to know the complete novel, the readings inevitably had a strongly focusing effect. From *Oliver Twist*, Dickens selected and strung together passages that told of the murder of Nancy by Bill Sykes. His readings (by all accounts, brilliantly presented) inevitably concentrated attention in such a way as to change the original—or even displace the larger narrative. *Oliver Twist,* for those rapt by Dickens's readings, became an almost unbearably compelling story of a brutal murder. That was hardly the reaction of moviegoers to the musical version that appeared in 1968 (directed by Carol Reed), *Oliver!* Nancy's murder remained an important part of the story, but elaborately staged musical/ dance numbers gave the audience some distance from the most dramatic and melodramatic moments. Roman Polanski recently offered his own film version (*Oliver Twist,* 2005) that stripped away some of Dickens's elaborate side stories and concentrated heavily on a child's terrifying progress through a bitterly hard world. As often happens, an original work of art provides the occasion for variations upon a theme. Even though the new works reward attention to their own merits, it becomes necessary to think of film versions of novels or stage productions of plays as interpretations of a text. What does the director choose to foreground? Why does a casting choice matter? How does the look of a film or stage set (dark/light, elaborate/plain) have an effect on our experience of the film or play?

Oliver Twist has been subject to very different treatments since its publication.

Experiencing Literature through Issues of Production and Reproduction of Texts

No author has been subject to more interpretations than Shakespeare. Despite the rigorous efforts to establish the truest texts of his plays, there has never been a time when the texts were strictly honored in performance. Mark Twain has the bogus "king" from *Adventures of Huckleberry Finn* test out an especially corrupt version of "Hamlet's Immortal Soliloquy!!" on an unlettered audience. Twain's comedy doesn't pretend to say anything about Shakespeare, but it does say something about the breadth and variety of ways Shakespeare has been repackaged for innumerable audiences. In other words, it says something about the way people use literature.

Mark Twain (1835–1910)

from Adventures of Huckleberry Finn (1885)

To be, or not to be; that is the bare bodkin
That makes calamity of so long life;
For who would fardels bear, till Birnam Wood do come to Dunsinane,
But that the fear of something after death
Murders the innocent sleep,   5
Great nature's second course,
And makes us rather sling the arrows of outrageous fortune
Than fly to others that we know not of.
There's the respect must give us pause:
Wake Duncan with thy knocking! I would thou couldst;   10
For who would bear the whips and scorns of time,
The oppressor's wrong, the proud man's contumely,
The law's delay, and the quietus which his pangs might take,
In the dead waste and middle of the night, when churchyards yawn
In customary suits of solemn black,   15
But that the undiscovered country from whose bourne no traveler returns,
Breathes forth contagion on the world,
And thus the native hue of resolution, like the poor cat i' the adage,
Is sicklied o'er with care,
And all the clouds that lowered o'er our housetops,   20
With this regard their currents turn awry,
And lose the name of action.
'Tis a consummation devoutly to be wished. But soft you, the fair Ophelia:
Ope not thy ponderous and marble jaws,
But get thee to a nunnery—go!   25

The king's version manages to mix up sequence and phrasing, misuse words, and interject lines from other sources (most notably *Macbeth*). Twain teases our reverence to texts by making us see how easily and wildly we transform texts over time. For Huck, the king's soliloquy is a privileged discourse that gains its power from being so grandly unlike everyday speech. For educated readers of Twain's novel, the king's speech becomes a kind of game in which one tries to spot all the slips. Inevitably, those readers must think back (perhaps uneasily) on what they do *not* know when an error remains uncaught or is misidentified.

Twain may have left Shakespeare even further behind than Tom Stoppard does in *The Fifteen Minute Hamlet* (p. 1487), but Twain and Stoppard together remind us again that every play or filmed version must always be understood as a distinct interpretation of an original work. In fact, every time we read a text, we necessarily interpret it anew. The text doesn't stay the same over successive readings. This may seem like a strange idea, but just reflect upon your own experience in re-reading a poem or a story. Is the second reading just like the first? To take just one example: Reading a Sherlock Holmes story for the first time throws emphasis on the mystery Doyle conjures. Once we know "whodunit," we return to the story and note qualities of character or perhaps admire the complex storytelling strategies Doyle employs.

TRANSLATIONS, SUBTITLES, AND DUBBING

We don't read or speak Polish, but we've included English translations of several Polish poems in this book (see those by Wislawa Szymborska, pp. 5, 634, 1461, and 1463, and Czeslaw Milosz, pp. 632, 1019, and 1397). For practical purposes, we treat these poems (along with all translated works in this book) as we know them in the English language. Our practice requires an obvious concession: a translation is not the same work as the original. Translation isn't merely a matter of trading one word for another equal word. Those of you who know a language other than English know that there are words and phrases that do not easily translate. Specific idioms may in fact be highly regional. And the sounds of one language will not be easily accommodated by another. Romance languages, for example, employ word endings that facilitate rhyming. An English translator approaching Dante is immediately faced with difficult choices: maintaining rhymes in English requires one to sacrifice much flexibility, yet dismissing rhyme changes a fundamental quality of the original poem's sound and rhythm.

A good translator is not simply one who decodes a text but one who grapples creatively with essential qualities of the text—one who seeks to catch and convey the spirit, sense, and tone of the original. A strong command of both languages (and cultures) is essential. Because we don't know Polish, we must trust the expertise and taste of those who have translated Szymborska and Milosz for us. And we feel the trust is rewarded if it results in a reading like the one we experience in, say, "Monologue of a Dog Ensnared in History" (p. 1463). We are forced to think of this poem to some degree as a new, independent work—one inspired by, but not equivalent to, the original piece. If you possess knowledge of a language other than English, we suggest you seek out original works and translations and read them consecutively. What differences do you notice? How does the translation not only translate but *interpret* the original? Do you feel there are any subtle shifts in emphasis from one text to the other? Are there any points at which you feel that the translation has helped you read the original? Or is there anything in the original that you would want to explain to a reader who knew only the translation? Is there something in the translation that strikes you as effective, yet unwarranted by the original?

Issues of translation take on yet still other dimensions in film, for there we do have visual cues that don't depend on words. For that matter, we have sounds (theme music, background noises like the roar of a crowd, the barking of a dog, the ringing of a bell) not tied to a specific language. Sometimes, these elements are so richly textured and suggestive that we feel we experience the film without even keeping up with the subtitles. Other times, however, we're painfully aware of how much we must be missing. There is a clever scene in Sophia Coppola's *Lost in Translation* (2003) that gets at this difficulty. The protagonist, Bob Harris (an aging actor played by Bill Murray) listens without understanding to lengthy instructions offered in an energetic fashion by the director of a television commercial in the making. Bob turns to his translator, who offers the briefest of orders. The exchange that follows comically underscores a serious theme about human communication that runs through the whole film.

> TRANSLATOR: He want you to turn, look in camera. OK?
> BOB: That's all he said?
> TRANSLATOR: Yes. Turn to camera.
> BOB: Right. Does he want me to turn from the right or from the left?
> (*Another lengthy and animated exchange between the director and the translator leaves* BOB *waiting for an answer.*)
> TRANSLATOR: Right side. With intensity.
> BOB: Is that everything? It seemed he said quite a bit more than that.

Bob is frustrated, for he knows that so many words spoken with such energy in one language cannot be reduced to the few words in the language he understands. He's left groping for something that is surely missing. He's left responding back with the most reductive of phrases: "OK."

Bob's predicament is one many of us have shared in a very specific way while watching a film in a language we do not know. On occasion, after several lengthy lines of spoken dialogue that we cannot follow, we see a scant few words on the screen as subtitles. Like Bob, we believe there must be much we are missing. And it's likely we are right. But we should not give up on foreign films as unwatchable. Once again, we need to remember that we can deal with only what our education and experience allow us to deal with. We don't want to demand of the subtitles something they cannot supply. And in most films, we'll still have a great deal to respond to. In fact, sometimes our deficiencies in language force us to be especially attentive to an actor's physical gestures, expressions, or vocal tones. And we may better appreciate matters of editing, cinematography, or dramatic structure that operate separately from dialogue. If you've ever watched a movie on an airplane flight without purchasing the headphones, you may have had the feeling that much can be learned about the art of film by experiencing a film in silence. So, in dealing with works of art in a foreign language, don't too easily let yourself feel lost in translation.

Watching a dubbed film is another way around language problems. But dubbing presents its own difficulties. We've all seen how the words of one language just don't fit the vocalizations of another language; when the movements of the mouth are out of synch with the sounds we hear, the results are distracting. And there are the poor dubbing jobs in which the physical qualities of a voice simply don't match the physical presence of the person on-screen or voice tones are not matched with the performer's gestures. Dubbing perhaps lends itself best to comedy—oftentimes unintentional comedy. Woody Allen's first full-length film was, in fact, an extended play on bad dubbing. In *What's Up, Tiger Lily?* (1966), Allen simply took a hard-boiled B movie produced in Japan, threw out the original sound track, and imposed his own clumsily dubbed and ridiculous dialogue in English. In some ways, his film made points similar to Twain's appropriation of Hamlet's soliloquy. The ridiculous quality of *What's Up, Tiger Lily?* helps us understand something of the ridiculousness of all inept translations. More important, Allen (like Coppola with *Lost in Translation*) points out the real difficulty of moving from one cultural framework to another.

MODELING CRITICAL ANALYSIS: TOM STOPPARD, THE FIFTEEN MINUTE HAMLET

William Shakespeare's *Hamlet* is a notoriously unstable text. Even though it is considered to be one of the greatest works by one of the greatest writers, no written record of Shakespeare's original work survives. So, what do we mean when we discuss *Hamlet*? There is evidence that a play fitting *Hamlet's* description was performed in about 1601. In 1603, a version of *Hamlet* appeared in print, apparently based upon an actor's memory of the lines.

Some scholars believe that this actor played the minor part of Marcellus, because all of his lines are rendered perfectly, and the text tends to vary considerably from other editions whenever Marcellus is not in the scene. As incomplete and imperfect as this text may be, it can't be dismissed. After all, we have no clearly authoritative alternative. And the 1603 version surely offers insight into the actual production of the play; this is how an original actor experienced *Hamlet*. What the actor from this early production of *Hamlet* thought to record in this first edition may not be a complete text, but it represents what stood out to him—a particular participant from a distant time we seek to recover as best we can.

It's important to remember that the entire process of recording a play in textual form is always problematic. A play is designed to be performed. Unlike a book, a play takes place on a specific stage with a specific set of actors performing to a specific live audience. Even when different productions use the same script (not by any means a given), every performance of the play is different from every other performance simply because it is live theater; actors forget lines or ad lib, the audience laughs in different places, and the weather outside changes the conditions in which this play occurs. Those in charge of a specific production don't necessarily see themselves obligated to the words the author gives them. Would a pared-down version of *Hamlet* command a bigger audience?

Later in 1603 or early in 1604, another version of the play appeared: the second quarto. This one was about twice as long as the previous edition and advertised itself as "according to the true and perfect coppie." If we are to believe this claim, this edition of the text comes from Shakespeare's own copy of the play. This may be a more accurate reflection of what the playwright wrote down, but it may not account for any changes to the play that came about as the play was actually performed. It would be naïve to assume that Shakespeare never revised a play after seeing how it unfolded onstage.

Another version of *Hamlet* appeared in the first complete works of Shakespeare in 1623 the first folio. This script apparently comes from the notes that the playhouse put together (but never used) to prompt actors who forgot their lines in production. It is shorter than the second edition but also includes some material that is not in the longer second edition.

Most modern editions of the play combine material from the second quarto and the first folio; as a result, we usually read a *Hamlet* that is longer than either of these editions. It is striking to realize we have no evidence that this *Hamlet* ever existed in Shakespeare's lifetime. A performance of this "complete" play lasts about four hours, whereas the short first quarto lasts about two. Almost every production of the play edits the version we typically read in some way. Every staged or filmed version of the play must contend with critics who compare text to production and complain that a failure to adhere to the original somehow undermines the integrity of the work. Critics can and should complain, of course, about omissions or revisions that don't make dramatic or thematic sense. In the case of Shakespeare, though, it is problematic to assume that there is a single, true standard to which we can all refer.

Tom Stoppard plays with these critical problems in *The Fifteen Minute Hamlet* by giving us a prologue that catches at bits and pieces of famous lines, a ten-act play that manages to cover essential actions, and then an encore that reduces *Hamlet* further still. Instead of one play in four hours, we have one play performed twice and have what seems a "greatest hits" prologue thrown in for good measure. The effect is a frantic comedy that responds to a long-standing critical problem What is it that makes *Hamlet Hamlet?* Huck Finn listening to "Hamlet's Immortal Soliloquy!!" is satisfied with high-blown phrases that sound grandly important. Theater for Huck is all about posing. He doesn't bother to demand sense. He doesn't even demand plot. Stoppard is asking, What do we demand? Is it plot? Is it the characters? Is it the language? Is it some aura of specialness that is realized in performance? At what point do editorial changes make the play into something different? Something less? In the first quarto, for instance, Hamlet's famous soliloquy begins "to be or not to be, aye there's the point." Is this enough to destroy the play? It is possible that Shakespeare originally wrote the line that way; what does it mean if we say that it doesn't sound Shakespearean?

Using the Production and Reproduction of Texts to Focus Writing and Discussion

As we study texts, we can keep in mind some general lessons from the various schools of criticism:

- What are the specific details of the language and structure of the text? How is our interpretation rooted in these details?

- How can we unlock meanings within a text rather than look for a single definitive reading?

- What are the historical and cultural contexts of this text? How do these contexts lend to our understanding of this text, and how does this text help us understand these contexts?

- What information do we have about the development of this particular text? How is the version that we are reading different from some original version of the text? How are these differences significant or interesting? Who has been responsible for the different versions? Can we trace some genealogy of the evolution of this text?

Experiencing Literature through Writing

1. How do the physical properties of a text shape our interpretation of that text? This is a comparative exercise. Find at least two versions of the same text. Blake's poem "A Poison Tree" (p. 1678), for instance, looks quite different on the page that he prepared and as it appears on a page in this textbook.

   a. Describe the specific differences that you see.

   b. How are these differences significant?

   c. How do they change the nature of the text? Remember that even a reproduction of Blake's page is out of context here—it is not sur-rounded by the rest of the pages that he created, and we have not reproduced the size and quality of the paper that Blake originally selected.

2. How is a particular text part of the culture that developed it? This question is one that works nicely for examining different productions of a particular play. Because each production begins with a script that is fairly stable, each difference within the production becomes material for our discussion. How do these differences help us make specific claims about the culture in which this play was produced? We must remember that every artist who is involved in any production has some individual artistic consciousness, but as we look at productions from different eras, we will identify specific details as representative of that era. The various film images of *Oliver Twist* (p. 1687) that we have included in this chapter offer an example of the sorts of comparisons that we might make within this question.

3. How does a particular cultural reading of a text contradict our close reading of that text? This is a more complex question, but working to explain the apparent contradiction can result in a very rewarding dis-cussion. In this question, we look for an interpretation of the text that we can support with specific details from within the text. Then, we look at the cultural context of the work. For instance, a text that states "all men are created equal" becomes problematic when juxtaposed with the fact that the author was himself the owner of slaves. The goal in this paper is not simply to point out that there is a contradiction. We must explain why that contradiction is interesting. What does it tell us about this text or this culture that this apparent contradiction might be tolerated?

18 An Orientation to Research

Why Should I Use Sources?

How Do I Find Them?

What Material Do I Document?

We have maintained throughout this book that critical writing involves an extension and a deepening of the literary experience. The experience starts with our reading of a literary work or our viewing of a film. But it deepens as we engage with others in conversation. When we come to class, we hear what others have been thinking. We might take some of these ideas in and make them part of our own understanding. We are often prompted to argue and, through argument, more clearly understand our own responses. Perhaps we modify or enlarge our sense of the text or even discover a new set of questions to ask about it. By the end of a good class discussion, our ideas about the work we are studying have become far more complex, far more interesting, and much closer to something that we might want to develop in an essay. The conversation has helped us deepen our literary experience.

When we do research, we are looking for the sort of inspiration and insight that we get from a good class session. With research, though, we have more time to think about our responses. We don't need to respond quickly to participate, as we sometimes do in discussions. In addition, the material that we find will probably be more carefully formulated than anything presented in class; a good article can even model the sort of writing we strive for in our own essays. Still, we don't simply accept the published work of scholars and critics. We modify, contest, enlarge, and apply ideas we come across as readers, just as we do as participants in a discussion. We test reactions of others against our own experience of a work. When we turn to our own writing, we seek to bring the voices of others into the conversation we've joined; we also seek to contribute to that conversation.

WHY WE USE SOURCES

Some people view writing a "critical essay" as completely different from writing a research paper. The critical essay is seen as the analytical response of an individual; the research essay, as a compilation of opinions. This distinction is built on a big mistake. Analysis isn't done in a vacuum. And research involves much more than mere data gathering; it involves a process of active reading and thinking. So, this chapter should be read as an extension of (not a break from) the chapters that precede it.

False divisions between criticism and research lead writers to weak positions in relation to materials they gather. Sometimes we hear students speak of "plugging in" quotations or "sticking in" some facts; we want to use instead "integrating," "relating," and "weaving in." Good critical writers go beyond a mere display of materials; they see and use their research in the context of an argument they themselves shape. A "good" quotation, a "meaningful" summary, a "relevant" fact can only be good, meaningful, or relevant as it relates to a carefully defined point. We need to use sources, not let sources use us. Writers use research to support their points; to put it another way, research serves a purpose the writer has defined. Either way, the writer is in charge.

It's also important to think specifically about what "support" might mean. In some instances, a writer might enlist the support of a critic whose argument "backs up" the new discussion very directly. In such cases, writers essentially invoke the authority of others to confirm their own insights. But more often, writers define a particular aspect of a larger argument and apply that aspect to a specific point they want to make. Note how the following writer uses insights not only of those who write specifically about the paper's main subject—Nathanael West's *The Day of the Locust*—but of the Shakespearean critic A. C. Bradley. The writer carefully leads into and follows each reference so that none of the references feel out of place in relation to the main point of the passage. The writer has integrated, not "plugged in," research. Note also that the references aren't just to words (quotations) but to ideas as well.

> With the riot at the end of the novel, West releases the potential energy and violence of a city (and perhaps a country) full of broken dreamers. The fantasy of Hollywood has been sold to them and it has disappointed. Nasty, ugly, and completely vacuous, Hollywood, with the machinery of

its vast studios, has pushed its self-perpetuating plaster dream onto America. Kingsley Widmer examines the scope of Hollywood's failure as a dream factory and what it means for the double-crossed.[1] No one is more betrayed than one who has been cheated by false dreams. This representation of Hollywood as the purveyor of a bastardized art form that conveys powerfully corrosive effects (it even corrupts dreams!) is central to understanding West's novel. West ultimately sees Hollywood as the cheater, the force that rips off people who live there. In fact, as Lavonne Mueller notes, *The Day of the Locust* "was originally called The Cheated."[2]

When we conceptualize the novel as a story of "the cheated" rather than the story of Tod [the protagonist], *The Day of the Locust* begins to take on truly tragic proportions. The type of tragedy however is not traditional. As defined by A. C. Bradley, the classic Shakespearean form of tragedy "is pre-eminently the story of one person, the 'hero,' or at most of two, the 'hero' and the 'heroine.'"[3] Bradley goes on to note that the actions of this central character are the source of the tragedy. The stories of each of *The Day of the Locust*'s characters are merely minor tragedies in and of themselves, and their actions have little effect on their fates; but through the patching together of a tapestry of circumstance and torment, West begins to create a sense of communal tragedy. Hollywood has seduced an enormous number of suckers with its empty dream, and the losses are measured in numerous lives wasted.

The writer of the passage has woven in ideas of others into a new fabric. Sometimes, such weaving involves a deliberate kind of counterpointing. In the passage, the writer uses Bradley's definition of Shakespearean tragedy to clarify a quite different kind of tragedy apparent in West's novel. Sometimes, the counterpoint is more blunt; one can support one's own idea by repudiating someone else's. Identifying and making explicit a disagreement can sharpen or emphasize a writer's contribution. Note how the writer of the following passage on H. G. Wells's *The Invisible Man* clarifies the interpretation by strongly rejecting another critic:

Alfred Borrello argues that the scientist Griffin represents a "god-man" in Wells's *The Invisible Man*. Borrello sees Griffin as one "dedicated to research for the good of his species but frustrated by the inability of his

---

[1] Kingsley Widmer, <u>Nathanael West</u> (Boston: Twayne, 1982).

[2] David Madden, ed., <u>Nathanael West: The Cheaters and the Cheated: A Collection of Critical Essays</u> (DeLand: Everett/Edwards, 1973).

[3] A. C. Bradley, <u>Shakespearean Tragedy: Lectures on Hamlet, Othello, King Lear, Macbeth</u>, 3rd rpt. (New York: Palgrave, 1992) 7.

fellowman to accept what lies outside of the familiar."[4] This interpretation completely ignores the signals Wells so carefully builds into Griffin's first person narration. Griffin reveals himself as a totally selfish man. He has no feelings for his father, his fiancé, or his friends. His work absorbs him, but not for the good that work may do; in fact, Griffin never once considers the "good of his species" as Borrello contends. On the contrary, it would seem that Griffin's disregard for the species is exactly what leads him to madness, murder, and death.

The main underlying lessons of the previous two examples is first, to always consider how a given piece may help us build our argument; and second, to always weave sources into the newly constructed fabric of ideas.

SHAPING A TOPIC

There is, of course, no sense of effective "weaving into" if there is no plan for the design of a new fabric. It's important, therefore, in the early stages of the writing process to think carefully about what constitutes a topic. In the broadest sense, a topic is a subject. It is what a paper is about, what it addresses, what it concerns. That sounds simple enough. But critical writing is never simple. Writers don't pick topics; they *construct* them. Even in response to a specific assignment, a writer must set a topic's limits and establish a topic's significance. Framing the topic is a crucial step in the research process.

A good topic is first of all a doable one. If the scope is too large at the outset, the sheer weight of available materials will become overwhelming. A writer focuses on an aspect of a work; the entire work is too much. For example, *Hamlet* isn't a topic. A topic that might lead somewhere could be "Hamlet's methods of interrogation and detection." A doable topic must also be concretely grounded; it cannot be a large abstraction that remains detached from any particular evidence in a text. One could examine *Hamlet* closely and analyze specific lines or scenes where he questions and investigates. One could look for critical essays that address ways Hamlet searches for truth or seeks to confirm suspicions and so on.

To create and shape a topic, we suggest that you follow these guidelines:

- Be specific. No critical essay "covers" everything about a text; a good essay merely covers what it has promised to cover.
- Focus first on the main text. A topic cannot be cast as a purely abstract issue or as a large, independent historical event or condition. Keep in

---

[4] Alfred Borello, H.G. Wells: Author in Agony (Carbondale: Southern Illinois UP, 1972).

mind the paradox: the grandest ambitions generally result in the smallest papers, both in quality and in length. Grand ambitions are often a disguise for familiar generalities; they prompt summary and statement. However, a particular, concrete observation on a text (how it works, what it says, why it moves us) can help us develop ideas analytically and argumentatively.

■ Define key terms. Definition provides a way to get at a precise yet full sense of a subject. Your definition will be much more specific than anything that we might find in any dictionary. What might "interrogation" mean in relation to Hamlet's exchanges with Claudius and Gertrude? Exactly how is it that he plays the detective role given that the ghost has offered clear testimony of the murder in the first act?

■ Think of how your topic sets up an argument—a thesis, a contribution to a conversation. Don't settle for writing "about" a topic; press forward to an assertion you need to back up, a point you need to explain.

HOW TO FIND SOURCES

The writer who has a topic in mind and a sense of how to use information to explore the topic is usually the researcher who enjoys looking for sources. The search for sources is a treasure hunt—a chance to browse through libraries, archives, databases, troves of information. But the sheer wealth of available material in even a modest library can make looking intimidating.

You might think you can avoid the library, given the wealth of material available online. But as mentioned in Chapter 14, each online source has its own kinds of limits. In classrooms around the world, students are generating the same sort of writing that you may be now preparing to create. In the past decade or so, students have been able to post their work online. So, too, have many others with some interest in literature and film (fans, casual readers, independent scholars, and so on). Some of this writing may be quite good, but much of it is still in a fairly early stage of the revision process, and some is quite simply not worth attention. When you do your research, try to find writing that is at least a level or two higher than you think that you are able to produce. You want to learn to use materials that offer a more complex thesis than you might have thought of. Look for a work that uses other sources to create a combination of works different from what you would have put together.

Remember too that carefully chosen sources help establish the authority of your own work. Generally, it is best to pick articles or sources that have been published by a reputable press. Because at least a few people who have professional knowledge in the matter have read the material and have acknowledged that it has some value, the publication indicates that the source might be appropriate for your analysis. There is no avoiding it; you do need to use the library. An important trick here is learning to use your library's online catalogue system as well as the best available databases. Catalogue systems will differ, so do take the time to become familiar with how your library has organized the material it contains. But a few general words of advice will likely apply to most. Any online search can begin by author/title searches when you happen to know author and title. But also test out "key word" searches. This requires a little imagination, but you'll find the misses and hits will help you sharpen ways you define your topic as well as ways others categorize broad topics. Most systems build upon the Library of Congress Subject Headings. You'll begin to note those headings as you experiment with your own key words, but you need not rely on guessing. Most online systems have search commands that allow you to check Library of Congress headings. And don't be afraid to ask librarians for help. They will respond to your general questions and needs in terms of the specific systems in operation at your institution.

Armed with call numbers, you'll need to find the physical book itself. Libraries of higher education generally use the Library of Congress cataloguing system to organize their collections. You will find literary studies in the "P" section of the library. As you browse through the shelves, you can see how the organization works. If you look at a call number, it is fairly simple to determine some useful information about the work. Every book has a unique Library of Congress call number. For instance, *The Complete Works of William Shakespeare*, fourth edition, edited by David Bevington, has the LC number PR2754.B4. The "PR" indicates that this is a work of English literature; "2754" falls within the range of PR2199–3195, which contains works from the English Renaissance (1500–1640). The letter after the period indicates the last name of the author or, in this case, the editor of the text. It is not necessary to memorize any of this information, but it may be useful to have an overview of the "P" section (or languages and literature division) of this system, because it will help you navigate the aisles in the book stacks:

P	Language and Literature
P	Linguistics
PA	Classical Philology (Greek and Latin)
PB	Modern European Languages, Celtic Languages
PC	Romance Languages
PD	Old Germanic and Scandinavian Languages
PE	English Language
PF	Dutch, Flemish, and German Languages
PG	Slavic Languages and Literature
PH	Finno-Ugrian, Basque Languages & Literature
PJ–PL	Oriental Languages

PM	American Indian and Artificial Languages
PN	Literature, Literary History and Collections
PQ	Romance Literature
PR	English Literature
PS	American Literature
PT	German Literature
PZ	Children's Literature

As you work with this system, you will find sections of the stacks relevant to your search. Browse through those shelves to find books and journals related to your research. Many journals specialize in literary studies. You can find journals that focus on literature in general, on British literature, American literature, literature from different time periods, and literature by a specific author. If you are searching for an idea and you are writing about Shakespeare, browse through a shelf of *Shakespeare Quarterlies*. As you look through the tables of contents (we have reproduced a sample on the next page), you will see the range of articles that scholars have generated just in a single quarter on the subject of this single playwright.

A number of us use libraries that are not rich in these resources. But all schools subscribe to databases that make this library experience available. Although there is an enormous body of material on the web that does not exist on paper in any library, many published articles in volumes on library shelves can be accessed online. Even students at the richest libraries can do much of their research online. In fact, the table of contents in the previous list comes from one of those databases. The important thing is not whether you find material online or in print but that you've found material that has gone through a serious review process and has been published by a scholarly press or organization.

Once you have gathered some materials for review, you'll need to approach them effectively. Read the writing about the literature with the same attention that you read the primary literature.

- Read for understanding—what does the work mean?
- Remember that the author is going to have some main idea—what is that idea?
- In what ways might that idea inspire controversy?
- Does the author mention any others who might disagree with the argument? (Read one or two of these other authors if possible.)
- Can you apply this argument to anything beyond the work in question? For instance, can you see how the argument might apply to another work that you have been reading this term?
- To what extent does the author introduce factual information into the analysis? Does that information have any bearing on your own topic?

SHAKESPEARE QUARTERLY

Published for the Folger Shakespeare Library
in association with
The George Washington University
by The Johns Hopkins University Press

VOLUME 57	2006	NUMBER 1

Historica Passio: Early Modern Medicine, *King Lear*,
and Editorial Practice   KAARA L. PETERSON   1

"'What is thy body but a swallowing grave . . . ?'":
Desire Underground in *Titus Andronicus*   TINA MOHLER   23

"'Read it in me'": The Author's Will in *Lucrece*   AMY GREENSTADT   45

SHAKESPEARE PERFORMED

Facing History, Facing Now: Deborah Warner's
Julius Caesar at the Barbican Theatre   CAROL CHILLINGTON RUTTER   71

BOOK REVIEWS

Dympna Callaghan, ed. *Romeo and Juliet: Texts and
Contexts*.   IAN FREDERICK MOULTON   86

Willy Maley and Andrew Murphy, eds. *Shakespeare
and Scotland*.   RONALD J. BOLING   88

Ton Hoenselaars, ed. *Shakespeare's History Plays:
Performance, Translation and Adaptation in Britain
and Abroad*.   MANFRED PFISTER   91

Hugh Macrae Richmond. *Shakespeare's Theatre:
A Dictionary of His Stage Context*.   TIFFANY STERN   94

Michele Marrapodi, ed. *Shakespeare, Italy, and Intertexuality*.   SONIA MASSAI   97

Ton Hoenselaars, ed. *Shakespeare and the Language of
Translation*.   JERZY LIMON   100

Kim C. Sturgess. *Shakespeare and the American Nation*.   RICHARD BURT   102

Gabriel Egan. *Shakespeare and Marx*.   DOUGLAS BRUSTER   105

Arthur Freeman and Janet Ing Freeman. *John Payne Collier:
Scholarship and Forgery in the Nineteenth Century*.   BERNICE W. KLIMAN   108

Often, you will not learn any new information from reading a piece of criticism. Instead, you are looking for some new insight, some different way of looking at the work that you have been reading. Many times an article will put a work into a different context that you might not have considered before you began your own writing.

GIVING APPROPRIATE CREDIT: THE ISSUE OF PLAGIARISM

We often value ideas as we value other possessions. Our society considers ownership an important aspect of our relations with things and with other people. We own electronic devices, cars, and houses, and we face anxiety because we would like to own more and don't want anyone to steal what we have. Even the less materialistic like to own the ideas that they have created. If any of us have an idea, no matter how mundane—where to go for dinner, a nice turn of phrase in conversation, a suggestion for some music that we have discovered—we know how annoying it can be to have someone else take the credit for our original thought. Most of us try to give appropriate credit whenever we can. But, as we have been discussing throughout this book, it may be difficult to determine where any idea has been created. We have been thinking about ideas as subjects in the ongoing conversations that we are describing here. Our ideas come from what we read, from what we watch, and from the conversations that we have. With all of these stimuli, it gets increasingly difficult to establish a clear pedigree for every idea that we put to paper. Anyone who writes, though, needs to know when it is necessary to cite sources. Sometimes the rules are pretty obvious.

The poet Neal Bowers was shocked when he read the following poem by David Sumner (Jones).

David Sumner (Jones)

Someone Forgotten (1991)

He is too heavy and careless, my father,
Always leaving me at rest-stops, coffee shops,
Some wide spot in the road. I come out,
Rubbing my hands on my pants or levitating
Two foam cups of coffee, and I can't find him   5
Anywhere, that beat-up Ford gone.

It's the trip itself that blinds him,
black highway like a funeral ribbon
leading to the mesmerizing end,
his hands like Vise Grips on the wheel   10
and following, until he misses me,
steers wide on the graveled shoulders,
and turns around.
This time he's been gone so long
I've settled in here—married, built a house,   15
started a family, stopped waiting to see him
pull into the driveway though the wind
sometimes makes a highway roar high up
in the branches,
and I stop whatever I'm doing and look up.   20

Compare that poem to the following poem that Bowers had written a few
years earlier. Look for the specific similarities. Find the differences. It is
appropriate to evaluate the work here as well—set the differences side by
side—which are the better poetic choices? Can you explain why?

Neal Bowers (1948–)

Ten-Year Elegy (1990)

Careless man, my father,
Always leaving me at rest stops,
Coffee shops, some wide spot in the road.
I come out, rubbing my hands on my pants
Or levitating two foam cups of coffee,   5
And can't find him anywhere,
Those banged-up fenders gone.
It's the trip itself that blinds him,
black highway like a chute
leading to the mesmerizing end,   10
his hands locked dead on the wheel
and following, until he misses me,
steers wide on the graveled shoulders,
turns around.
This time he's been gone so long   15
I've settled in here—married,
built a house, planted trees for shade,
stopped waiting to see him pull into the drive—

though the wind sometimes makes a high-way roar
high up in the branches, and I stop   20
whatever I'm doing and look up.

We should all be able to agree that there is so much similarity between these two poems that it is not possible that one could have been written without the other. The fact that most words are the same, that the different words are synonyms for the words that have been left out, that the line changes don't do much but disrupt the poetry here suggests that it was inappropriate for David Sumner (who sometimes calls himself David Jones) to try to claim credit for this poem. It does not belong to him. The fact that he republished this same poem multiple times, with different titles and similarly superficial changes under different names should help convince us that he is the sort of true plagiarist that all rules against plagiarism were designed to foil. We should be happy to hear that Bowers wrote up his experiences with this plagiarist and exposed him to ridicule. What is wrong with what Jones did? He has taken Bowers's personal remembrance of his father, disfigured the poetry, and published the mangled result under various aliases. Bowers writes about the extent to which this violation has infected even his own reminiscences about his father. The main reason to avoid plagiarism is to avoid this sort of violation.°

A straightforward definition of **plagiarism** is "intellectual theft—the unacknowledged (or inadequately acknowledged) use of the words and/or ideas of another." This leads to a simple moral directive: Do not cheat! But like many simple directives, this one doesn't always address the real issue. Most students have no desire to cheat, yet they remain confused and worried about exactly what professors expect them to document. Something beyond the plain demand that one do his or her own work is clearly needed, for much gray lurks about the edges of the definition just offered.

The writing that you do for your classes is a kind of personal expression. Even though you may feel that it seems more artificial than what you might do naturally, you are turning in this writing so that you can join and contribute to conversations about the texts you've been assigned. Your instructor has a professional obligation to read your work carefully in relation to the work of other students. Such review (and ultimately assessment) takes considerable time and energy. If you do the sort of lifting that Jones has done when you turn in your writing, you are violating the relationship that you have with your instructor; you've pretended to contribute to a conversation but haven't in fact offered your own work. You should be aware of how easy it is to see through such deceptive practices. To anyone who has read student papers for any length of

---

° Neal Bowers, <u>Words for the Taking: The Hunt for a Plagiarist</u> (New York: Norton, 1997).

time, stolen papers in which a few words have been changed from a website or a published source might as well be announced by flashing neon lights.

The best practice for student writers is to acknowledge sources as much as possible within your writing. You will actually be given greater credit for tracing your ideas back to other sources than you will get for simply generating "original" ideas out of thin air. After all, a big part of research is figuring out where ideas have come from, tracing conversations back to their sources, and understanding how the ideas of others can be used to build a new set of ideas.

Experiencing Literature through Considerations of Plagiarism

One intriguing exercise in this sort of tracing game is the subject of Shakespeare. In many of his plays, Shakespeare borrowed material from sources. Most of his stories were stories that had appeared elsewhere. For instance, much of the historical material in his plays about Rome came from Thomas North's translation of Plutarch's *Lives of the Noble Grecians and Romans*. Here is an excerpt from Plutarch that describes Portia, the wife of the Roman senator Brutus. Brutus has been approached about joining in the conspiracy to murder Julius Caesar, and he is considering whether he believes it to be a moral enterprise, but his reflections are all private. Portia complains that because she is his wife, he should share his concerns with her.

Plutarch (ca. 46–127)

from Lives of the Noble Grecians and Romans
(ca. AD 100, trans. Thomas North, 1579)

This Porcia, being addicted to philosophy, a great lover of her husband, and full of an understanding courage, resolved not to inquire into Brutus's secrets before she had made this trial of herself. She turned all her attendants out of her chamber, and taking a little knife, such as they use to cut nails with, she gave herself a deep gash in the thigh; upon which followed a great flow of blood, and soon after, violent pains and a shivering fever, occasioned by the wound. Now when Brutus was extremely anxious and afflicted for her, she, in the height of all her pain, spoke thus to him: "I, Brutus, being the daughter of Cato, was given to you in marriage, not like a concubine, to partake only in the common intercourse of bed and board, but to bear a part in all your good and all your evil fortunes; and for your part, as regards your care for me, I find no reason to complain; but from me, what evidence of my love, what satisfaction can you receive, if I may not share with you in bearing your hidden griefs, nor to be admitted to any of your counsels that require secrecy and trust? I know very well that women seem to be of too weak a nature to be trusted with secrets; but certainly, Brutus, a virtuous birth and education, and the company of the good and honourable, are of some force to the forming our manners; and I can boast that I am the daughter of Cato, and the wife of Brutus, in which two titles though before I put less confidence, yet now I have tried myself, and find that I can bid defiance to pain." Which words having spoken, she showed him her wound, and related to him the trial that she had made of her constancy; at which he being astonished, lifted up his hands to heaven, and begged the assistance of the gods in his enterprise, that he might show himself a husband worthy of such a wife as Porcia. So then he comforted his wife. ■

Shakespeare creates a dramatic scene out of these incidents in his play *Julius Caesar* (Act II, Scene 1). Note how he adds a life to Portia's character by developing details within her conversation. She begins with specific incidents that lead to her complaint. Find the specific sections of her speech that contain the ideas and even the words from the Plutarch selection. Think now about any differences between what David Jones has done in his "rewriting" of the Bowers poem and what Shakespeare has done in his rewriting of North's Plutarch.

William Shakespeare (1564–1616)

from Julius Caesar (1599)

PORTIA: Nor for yours neither. You've ungently, Brutus,
   Stole from my bed: and yesternight, at supper,
   You suddenly arose, and walk'd about,
   Musing and sighing, with your arms across,
   And when I ask'd you what the matter was,
   You stared upon me with ungentle looks;
   I urged you further; then you scratch'd your head,
   And too impatiently stamp'd with your foot;
   Yet I insisted, yet you answer'd not,
   But, with an angry wafture of your hand,
   Gave sign for me to leave you: so I did;
   Fearing to strengthen that impatience
   Which seem'd too much enkindled, and withal

Hoping it was but an effect of humour,
Which sometime hath his hour with every man.
It will not let you eat, nor talk, nor sleep,
And could it work so much upon your shape
As it hath much prevail'd on your condition,
I should not know you, Brutus. Dear my lord,
Make me acquainted with your cause of grief.

BRUTUS: I am not well in health, and that is all.

PORTIA: Brutus is wise, and, were he not in health,
He would embrace the means to come by it.

BRUTUS: Why, so I do. Good Portia, go to bed.

PORTIA: Is Brutus sick? and is it physical
To walk unbraced and suck up the humours
Of the dank morning? What, is Brutus sick,
And will he steal out of his wholesome bed,
To dare the vile contagion of the night
And tempt the rheumy and unpurged air
To add unto his sickness? No, my Brutus;
You have some sick offence within your mind,
Which, by the right and virtue of my place,
I ought to know of: and, upon my knees,
I charm you, by my once-commended beauty,
By all your vows of love and that great vow
Which did incorporate and make us one,
That you unfold to me, yourself, your half,
Why you are heavy, and what men to-night
Have had to resort to you: for here have been
Some six or seven, who did hide their faces
Even from darkness.

BRUTUS: Kneel not, gentle Portia.

PORTIA: I should not need, if you were gentle Brutus.
Within the bond of marriage, tell me, Brutus,
Is it excepted I should know no secrets
That appertain to you? Am I yourself
But, as it were, in sort or limitation,
To keep with you at meals, comfort your bed,
And talk to you sometimes? Dwell I but in the suburbs
Of your good pleasure? If it be no more,
Portia is Brutus' harlot, not his wife.

BRUTUS: You are my true and honourable wife,
As dear to me as are the ruddy drops
That visit my sad heart

PORTIA: If this were true, then should I know this secret.
   I grant I am a woman; but withal
   A woman that Lord Brutus took to wife:
   I grant I am a woman; but withal
   A woman well-reputed, Cato's daughter.
   Think you I am no stronger than my sex,
   Being so father'd and so husbanded?
   Tell me your counsels, I will not disclose 'em:
   I have made strong proof of my constancy,
   Giving myself a voluntary wound
   Here, in the thigh: can I bear that with patience.
   And not my husband's secrets?
BRUTUS: O ye gods,
   Render me worthy of this noble wife!
   (Knocking within.)
   Hark, hark! one knocks: Portia, go in awhile;
   And by and by thy bosom shall partake
   The secrets of my heart.
   All my engagements I will construe to thee,
   All the charactery of my sad brows:
   Leave me with haste.
(Exit PORTIA.*)*

Shakespeare was not writing a paper to be graded for a class; in fact, the *Julius Caesar* that we quote here comes from the text that was published in 1623, about seven years after Shakespeare's death, so we can't hold him responsible for our standards in citation. If this Shakespeare excerpt were a student paper, though, a direct acknowledgment of North's Plutarch would seem essential.

INTEGRATING SOURCES INTO WRITING: WHAT WE DOCUMENT

Accurate and full citation of sources is an essential part of writing in college. To omit or inadequately cite a source in an academic essay would be to undermine much of your own hard-earned authority. Think again of writing as conversation: a person who borrows the ideas of others without offering the slightest nod of recognition to those others will be seen, at best, as careless; at worst, as rude and dishonest. Thoughtful citation of sources should be understood not only as an ethical obligation but as part of the entire essay's effectiveness.

All citations show our general respect for others who might be part of our conversation. First, we acknowledge our debt to someone who has introduced us to some particular idea. Second, we offer a guide to anyone who might follow our thoughts to show them how they might have access to the thoughts that have influenced us. Precision is important here so that we don't frustrate those who follow our lead. Just as we would not like to chase after some source only to find that the author we are reading was careless enough to list the wrong volume, note the wrong page, or misspell the author's name, we must do all that we can to ensure that our own bibliographic entries are accurate. This is a map to the intellectual treasure that you have discovered. Be diligent as you record the directions. You might want to come back sometime as well.

Quotation, Paraphrase, and Summary

It's an easy matter to understand that direct quotations must be written as such and cited: that is, place quotation marks around the quoted material—or set off long passages as block quotes—and note the source (specific forms will be displayed as this chapter progresses). But quotations are not the only things that must be documented: ideas require citation as well. When is an idea really someone else's? If plagiarism is intellectual theft, what constitutes protected intellectual property? How much documentation does a reader expect, want, and need?

We can start by illustrating different kinds of borrowings and the credit each requires or encourages. The following passage is from "*Frankenstein* and Comedy" by Philip Stevick:

Frankenstein, like early Gothic before it, like Kafka after it, and like a multitude of works of various periods, such a Melville's *Bartleby*, makes itself out of dream images told, but not fully elaborated, into rational and sequential art. The result is a narrative vehicle which allows a large measure of self-exposure, terror, pathos, and psychic pain to coexist with much absurdity, apparent ineptitude, silliness, and the risk that the whole enterprise will be brushed aside by the reader as making no claims on his mature scrutiny.°

Now consider the following two passages that were written with Stevick's work in mind:

1. Like the Gothic novels that preceded it, like Kafka that followed it, and like many other works including Melville's *Bartleby*, Mary Shelley's *Frankenstein* builds itself from dream images that never quite get

---

° Philip Stevick, "Frankenstein and Comedy," The Endurance of Frankenstein: Essays on Mary Shelley's Novel, ed. George Levine and U. C. Knoepflmacher (Berkeley: U of California P, 1979) 221-39.

fully expressed in an orderly or consciously controlled story. The rough narrative that results exposes private terrors of the self, psychic pain, and terror along with sheer nonsense and absurdity. It is no wonder that many mature readers are tempted to dismiss *Frankenstein* as unworthy of serious attention.

2. Philip Stevick maintains that *Frankenstein* seems closer to a dream than to a story. Dreams can be painfully self-revealing; but those same dreams can also be downright silly. Gothic novels and Kafka's stories share these wildly mixed qualities with Mary Shelley's work. Narratives such as these are sometimes difficult to take seriously (Stevick 231).

Passage 1 closely paraphrases Stevick—it follows his paragraph from start to finish and never strays far from the words he uses. It is, in fact, almost exactly the same length as the original. Yet the writer of passage 1 makes no mention of Stevick. A citation (a note or parenthetical reference) to Stevick at the close of passage 1 would be a small step in the right direction, but it would still *not* be enough. Such a note would acknowledge that the writer of the passage has used an idea of Stevick, but it would not spell out how heavily Stevick had been used. This first passage is an example of an inappropriate paraphrase; it would be considered plagiarism.

It's useful to make a distinction between two words that are often used as synonyms: **paraphrase** and **summary**. Think of a paraphrase of another writer's text as a superficial revision of that text; the writer of a paraphrase stays close to the logic, language, and length of the original passage (as illustrated in passage 1). In contrast, think of a summary of another's text as a thorough rewriting of that text (a rewriting wholly in your own language) in as brief a form as your purpose will allow. Paraphrase as defined here should *always* be avoided. If you feel you need to stay very close to the words of your source, quote those words exactly and be sure your reader sees it as a quotation. If you do not need to stay close to the words of the original, convey as briefly as possible the essential idea and signal your debt to that idea.

Passage 2 more effectively summarizes Stevick's original paragraph. It remains close to the original, but it is tightly focused. It is not stuck on the particular words and phrases of the original (close paraphrase sometimes suggests that the writer doesn't understand the original well enough to confidently separate from it). Stevick's name also leads off passage 2—a good idea when the summary runs beyond a sentence or two. The parenthetical reference at the end of this passage gives the reader a clear sense of Stevick's contribution. The summary is neatly framed by the first mention of Stevick and the closing parenthetical reference. A reader who came across passage 2 in a critical paper would understand the degree of indebtedness that is expressed.

Distinct Insights and Common Observations

Any full summary or particular use of Stevick's insights must give credit to Stevick. But what happens when one reads Stevick yet uses nothing in particular that would easily be identified as distinctly his? Consider this third passage that only vaguely echoes Stevick:

> 3. *Frankenstein* evokes the disturbing and mixed sensations of dreams: terror, confusion, anxiety. The most absurd images in the novel (or in a dream) must be understood as part of a wider fear.

These two sentences move far away from the original and might not seem to owe Stevick any recognition. Not only is this passage significantly shorter than the original but it is wholly rewritten. Indeed, it doesn't borrow anything from Stevick that a good reader could not get from the novel itself. If this is summary at all, it is the barest sort. In effect, this third passage reduces the distinct contributions of Stevick to a very general, much-discussed level. Many critics before and after Stevick have associated *Frankenstein* with dreams. Why should Stevick get any special credit here for what seems a common insight? The writer has chosen to give him none.

You *must* cite distinct contributions or insights but need not credit observations that many writers have shared in common. But you could move beyond such a grudging attention to rules and consider a more generous policy. Citations, after all, do not merely serve to protect you from charges of plagiarism; citations have a positive purpose as well. Strange as it may seem, academic readers are interested in citations. A note at the end of the third passage would gracefully inform these readers of Stevick's article; it would display the writer's research without diminishing in any way the writer's own contribution. Indeed, if Stevick were found to be an especially significant voice in the conversation about *Frankenstein*, then the writer might want to mention him. This could be done quite easily:

Stevick observes that *Frankenstein* evokes the disturbing and mixed sensations of dreams: terror, confusion, anxiety. The most absurd images in the novel (or in a dream) must be understood as part of a wider fear (Stevick 231).

These options posed by the third example illustrate the fact that rules cannot always suffice; good judgment about what the audience wants, along with a sense of fairness, comes into play when deciding whether to cite a source or not.

Common Knowledge

You do not need to cite material that is **common knowledge**. But there may be some confusion about this deceptively simple rule, for *common knowledge* does not mean "what most people know"; in the context of academic writing, *common knowledge* means "knowledge that the readership could acquire or confirm from any one of several sources." For example, most people do not know that Edith Wharton's *The Age of Innocence* received a Pulitzer Prize in fiction in 1921. But a writer would not need to cite a source for this bit of information. Any academic reader could, if necessary, check for its accuracy without the slightest difficulty; in source after source, the information will be the same: Edith Wharton's *The Age of Innocence* did receive a Pulitzer Prize in fiction in 1921.

As always, sound judgment and good faith must help you through less clear-cut examples. For even seemingly plain facts should be cited when they invite controversy, depend upon interpretation, or are not widely established. A professor might want to know, for example, where a student discovered that the Pulitzer Prize advisory board overrode the recommendations of the nominating jury in awarding William Styron's *The Confessions of Nat Turner* the Pulitzer in 1968. This is not a disputed point, nor is it something that a particular scholar "discovered"; but not many references to Styron's award are this detailed. Such facts are not easily checked and should therefore be documented.

HOW TO CITE

Questions about the form of documentation often cause students more anxiety than the substance of their papers. This is both unfortunate and unnecessary. In literary studies, the Modern Language Association (MLA) has established guidelines for writers of research papers. With a little time and patience you can master the essential forms of citation. The following section displays model forms (based on the *MLA Handbook for Writers of Research Papers*, Sixth Edition) that you can use as checkpoints in preparing a research paper.

Parenthetical References in the Text

Debts are signaled in a text by parenthetical references (not numbered notes).° A sentence in a paper about Tolstoy that uses an idea from Yi-Fu

---

° The traditional format for citations is the footnote. The superscripted numbers, lines at the bottom of the page, and the abbreviated Latin were all part of the indoctrination process to separate true scholars from the mere dabbler. Anyone who could construct a typed manuscript that successfully accommodated a footnote deserved a higher degree. Now that we all use word-processing programs that can easily create elegant footnoting for us, the practice of using a footnote for every citation has been largely abandoned, especially for the types of academic papers that you will be producing. Generally, footnotes are places where an author can include additional informational details that are not essential to the main argument of the paper.

Tuan's *Space and Place* might look like any one of the following:

> Yi-Fu Tuan notes that Tolstoy's sense of space subtly registers "profound political and moral commitments" (57–58).

> Tolstoy's sense of space subtly registers "profound political and moral commitments" (Tuan 57–58).

> Yi-Fu Tuan claims that Tolstoy's sense of space registers deeply felt commitments (57–58).

The information within parentheses at the end of each sentence indicates that a discussion of Tolstoy's sense of space appears on pages 57 and 58 in a book or article by Tuan. Tuan's name does not appear within the parentheses in the first and third examples because the sentence itself makes it clear that Tuan is referred to. Information about Tuan's book will appear in a separate section: a "works cited" list.

The Works Cited List

The Works Cited list starts on a separate page at the end of the essay (such a list must *not* be subdivided by theme or types of research materials). There, under "Tuan, Yi-Fu," the reader will find full bibliographic information on the work cited in the text:

Tuan, Yi Fu. Space and Place: The Perspective of Experience.
   Minneapolis: U of Minnesota P, 1977.

Throughout the list, entries are alphabetized based upon the first word in the entry. The following examples model common bibliographic forms. Note that there is an underlying structure among the entries that refers to books or parts of books. All begin with the name of the author of the piece cited (last name first). All include full titles and complete publishing information. Names of editors or translators are placed after the title and before the publishing information.

A book by a single author

Bonca, Teddi Chichester. Shelley's Mirrors of Love: Narcissism,
   Sacrice, and Sorority. Albany: State U of New York P, 1999.

Moore, Rod Val. Igloo among Palms. Iowa City: U of Iowa P, 1994.

The content and the order here (as in all entry forms) are the important elements. Included are the author's name (last name first), the book's title, the place of publication, the publisher (note that for University Press, the abbreviation UP is standard form), and the year of publication. On the first line, the last name is flush on the left margin, and any subsequent lines are indented five spaces. All citations in MLA format must be double-spaced.

A book by more than one author

Gilbert, Sandra M., and Susan Gubar. <u>The Madwoman in the Attic:
     The Woman Writer and the Nineteenth-Century Literary
     Imagination</u>. New Haven: Yale UP, 1979.

Note here that the second author's name is not in reverse order; there is no need to put her last name first because the listing is not alphabetized under her name. Use a comma between the names.

An article in an edited collection

Glatthaar, Joseph T. "Black Glory: The African-American Role in
     Union Victory." <u>Why the Confederacy Lost</u>. Ed. Gabor S. Boritt.
     Oxford: Oxford UP, 1992. 133-62.

The author's name is listed first, then the title of the article (in quotation marks), followed by the title of the book in which it is collected (italicized or underlined), the editor of the book, the place of publication, publisher, and year of publication. Note that the pages placed at the end of the entry denote where the article begins and ends in the book. The parenthetical reference in the text of the paper itself would specify only the pages relevant to the point being made.

A translated book

Foucault, Michel. <u>Discipline and Punish: The Birth of the Prison</u>.
     Trans. Alan Sheridan. New York: Pantheon, 1977.

Literary texts, editions

Collins, Billy. "Thesaurus." <u>The Literary Experience</u>. Ed. Bruce
     Beiderwell and Jeffrey Wheeler. Boston: Wadsworth, 2008.
     109-92.

Dickens, Charles. <u>Great Expectations</u>. Edited by Edgar Rosenberg.
     New York: Norton, 1999.

Griffin Wolff, Cynthia. Introduction. <u>Ethan Frome</u>. By Edith Wharton.
     New York: Signet, 1986.

Stein, Gertrude. "Three Portraits of Painters." <u>Selected Writings of Gertrude Stein</u>. Ed. Carl Van Vechten. New York: Vintage, 1972. 327-35.

Zimmerman, Mary. "Metamorphoses." <u>The Literary Experience</u>. Ed. Bruce Beiderwell and Jeffrey Wheeler. Boston: Wadsworth, 2008. 1548-80.

Sometimes you will need to cite a periodical article. These entries will differ from entries for books, but the most common forms are not complicated.

An article from an academic journal

Rader, Ralph W. "The Dramatic Monologue and Related Lyric Forms." <u>Critical Inquiry</u> 3 (1976): 131-51.

List the author's name, followed by the title of the article (in quotation marks), the title of the journal (italicized or underlined) in which it appears, the volume number of the journal, the year of publication, and the inclusive pages. Most academic journals paginate continuously throughout a volume. A volume represents the collected issues of single year (usually four issues). The first issue of the year starts on page 1. The second issue starts on the page following the last page of the previous issue, and so on throughout the year. This makes it unnecessary to note which issue the article appears in. But if each issue of a volume begins at page 1, simply cite the volume number as above, then add a period and the issue number:

Tafoya, Eddie. "Born in East L.A.: Cheech as the Chicano Moses." <u>Journal of Popular Culture</u> 26.4 (1993): 123-29.

In your research, it is very likely that you will find this information in a database rather than by looking in an actual journal. It is still essential that you record the information that we have included here, but you must also include information about the database that you have used, including the date that you accessed the information:

Dobson, Hugh. "Mr. Sparkle Meets the Japanese Yakuza: Depictions of Japan in <u>The Simpsons</u>." <u>Journal of Popular Culture</u> 39.1 (2006): 44-68. <u>Project Muse</u>. UCLA Lib., Los Angeles. 15 July 2006 <http://www.muse.jhu.edu>.

A newspaper article

Heffley, Lynne. "L.A. Critics are Crazy for <u>Crazy, Tavern</u>." <u>Los Angeles Times</u> 8 Mar. 1994, valley ed.: F1.

If a specific edition is listed in the masthead, include that after the date (not all editions of the same paper contain the same material). If no edition is listed in the masthead of the paper's first page, place the colon after the date and before the section and page number of the article cited.

An article from a weekly or monthly magazine

Gopnik, Adam. "The Big One: Historians Rethink the War to End All Wars." The New Yorker 23 Aug. 2004: 78–85.

Many magazines and newspapers have their own websites on which they post material that appears in their printed publications. Here is a listing for a short story that appears in this format:

Munro, Alice. "The View from Castle Rock." The New Yorker 29 Aug. 2005. 6 Dec. 2006 <http://www.newyorker.com>.

A review

Appelo, Tim. Rev. of Three Tall Women, by Edward Albee. The Nation 14 Mar. 1994: 355–56.

The review above was not titled. Note the description of the contents in place of the missing title. Of course, if there is a title, use it. If you find the article online, include information about the database that you used to access it:

Ebert, Roger. "Throbbing Pain Overwhelms Pleasures in Basic Instinct 2." Chicago Sun-Times 31 Mar. 2006: NC29. ProQuest. Long Beach City College Lib.,Long Beach. 23 Apr. 2006 <http://www.proquest.umi.com>.

A film

The Purple Rose of Cairo. Dir. Woody Allen. Perf. Jeff Daniels, Danny Aiello, and Mia Farrow. Orion, 1985.

Works Cited

Bonca, Teddi Chichester. Shelley's Mirrors of Love: Narcissism,
    Sacrifice, and Sorority. Albany: State U of New York P, 1999.

Dickens, Charles. Great Expectations. Ed. Edgar Rosenberg. New York:
    Norton, 1999.

Dobson, Hugh. "Mr. Sparkle Meets the Japanese Yakuza: Depictions of
    Japan in The Simpsons." Journal of Popular Culture 39.1
    (2006): 44–68. Project Muse. UCLA Lib., Los Angeles. 15 July
    2006 <http://www.muse.jhu.edu>.

Ebert, Roger. "Throbbing Pain Overwhelms Pleasures in Basic
    Instinct 2." Chicago Sun-Times 31 Mar. 2006: NC29. ProQuest.
    Long Beach City College Lib., Long Beach. 23 Apr. 2006
    <http://www.proquest.umi.com>.

Foucault, Michel. Discipline and Punish: The Birth of the Prison.
    Trans. Alan Sheridan. New York: Pantheon, 1977.

Gilbert, Sandra M., and Susan Gubar. The Madwoman in the Attic: The
    Woman Writer and the Nineteenth-Century Literary Imagination.
    New Haven: Yale UP, 1979.

Gopnik, Adam. "The Big One: Historians Rethink the War to End All
    Wars." The New Yorker 23 Aug. 2004: 78–85.

Munro, Alice. "The View from Castle Rock." The New Yorker 29 Aug.
    2005. 6 Dec. 2006 <http://www.newyorker.com>.

The Purple Rose of Cairo. Dir. Woody Allen. Perf. Jeff Daniels, Danny
    Aiello, and Mia Farrow. Orion, 1985.

Rader, Ralph W. "The Dramatic Monologue and Related Lyric Forms."
    Critical Inquiry 3 (1976): 131–51.

Stein, Gertrude. "Three Portraits of Painters." Selected Writings
    of Gertrude Stein. Ed. Carl Van Vechten. New York: Vintage, 1972.
    327–35.

Tuan, Yi Fu. Space and Place: The Perspective of Experience.
    Minneapolis: U of Minnesota P, 1977.

Zimmerman, Mary. "Metamorphoses." The Literary Experience. Ed.
    Bruce Beiderwell and Jeffrey Wheeler. Boston: Wadsworth, 2008.
    1548–80.

Inevitably, we find works that do not fit into the general categories outlined here. Remember that these citation rules are entirely systematic, that it is possible to figure out the appropriate format even if your specific instance is not covered precisely.

Many databases that you will use in your school's library have a special function that will let you download information about each source in MLA format. This is a useful tool for gathering most of the bibliographic information that you need, but it will not complete the Works Cited page for you. Most databases will leave blank spaces that you need to fill in yourself. You must look closely at each entry to ensure that it conforms to the style that we have described in this section.

Using Research to Focus Writing and Discussion

- What issues are of interest to me as I read this work?
- What ideas have I found in this article?
- How does this article point to a larger critical conversation that I might want to join?
- How have I given credit to every source I have used in this paper (and at the same time, how have I indicated the research that I have done to develop my ideas)?
- Where have I given full and accurate citation of my sources? A writer can join a critical conversation only by acknowledging other participants in the conversation.
- Have I displayed every quotation as a quotation and cited it appropriately? Distinct ideas, contested or little-known facts, and particular insights must also be cited, even if they are cast in the writer's own words. A careless writer might mistake notes from another source as an original thought. Even though this might be an easy mistake to make, it is never acceptable.
- Have I avoided including extended paraphrases? Remember that we are writing our own papers, not summaries of articles. It is important to return again and again to our own point, to show how this outside information is relevant to the current discussion.

Appendix A

STUDENT MODEL ESSAY COLLECTION

Each of the essays on the following pages engages a literary text closely. Each grounds an argument in the evidence the text offers. Each may lead you back to your own reading with a richer sense of how the poem, play, or story works. But our main purpose here is not to supply still more critical commentary on texts. We want you to read these works from the perspective of a practicing (and perhaps inexperienced) critical writer. These essays then are offered as models of thoughtful critical analysis. Although we've stressed the importance of process throughout our book, it seems reasonable to display what product might result. After all, you'll be asked to write critically, and you'll be evaluated on your command of that task.

To learn from these models, you'll need to read carefully and actively. No model can or should provide a simple formula for success. How do these authors establish or define a topic? How do they signal the significance of their approach? How and why do they use the examples that they use? Do they explain carefully? How do they shape and follow an argument? Do you find the argument provocative or convincing? You'll also need to consider how you can achieve some of the qualities evident in these pieces (or how you can surpass any weaknesses you detect). How can you practice and build upon the strategies evident here as you write in response to a literary text?

We begin with the paper on "Harlem" by Langston Hughes by highlighting general organizational and argumentative qualities evident in some fashion in most critical essays. Observe a few very basic features as you read the model essay below:

- The title of the paper serves a purpose; it informs the reader of the broadly drawn subject (in effect, "this paper is about Hughes's 'Harlem'") and hints at the writer's insight regarding the subject (this poem moves from thinking to doing).

- The essay opens with a broad description of an important aspect of the poem and, thereby, establishes a topic.

- The essay moves toward an argument (the third, fourth, and fifth sentences) as the topic is more narrowly defined.

- The first paragraph ends with a thesis. The analysis will have a point to make, an argument to develop.

- The paragraphs that follow include evidence from the text to back up the thesis. Those paragraphs slow down our reading or unfold the text in relation to the thesis.

- The thesis serves as a controlling or leading idea; the writer's notion of how Hughes builds pressure, intensity, or tension can be charted in the first sentence of each paragraph. These sentences also provide a full sense of transition from one point to the next.

In the papers that follow the one on "Harlem," we call attention to more particular features evident in the specific model.

STUDENT MODEL ESSAY
LANGSTON HUGHES, HARLEM

Smith 1

Leslie Smith
Professor Jones
EN 112
September 25, 2006

From Thoughts to Deed in
Hughes's "Harlem"
        Langston Hughes's "Harlem" opens by asking a
big question that generates a number of what may seem
very uncertain responses. The only sentence in the
poem, after all, that does not end with a question mark
begins with a "maybe." But "Harlem" ultimately

Smith 2

moves well beyond uncertainty. The question that ends the poem builds forcefully from the questions that precede it. Indeed, it seems more like a statement that implies a soon-to-be-realized event. In "Harlem," Hughes transforms passive speculation into a feeling of concrete and immediate action.

In the first stanza (or verse paragraph), which responds to the initial question ("What happens to a dream deferred?"), Hughes offers a series of similes as tentative possibilities. All are unpleasant possibilities. The likeness he draws makes us taste and smell frustration. Hughes links an abstract feeling to physical sensations, but the similes keep us aware of the mind's intellectual play. Similes, after all, clearly announce with "like" or "as" comparisons of things we don't usually place side by side; we are asked if a dream might dry up "like" a raisin, ooze "like" a sore, smell "like" spoiled meat, or crystallize "like" old syrup. The very fact that these possibilities are grouped together in one stanza strengthens the sense that they exist as possibilities. The speaker is thinking over feelings associated with deferred dreams; no one of those feelings seems any more likely or powerful than any other.

The collective force of these possibilities taken altogether, however, generates some sense of increasing intensity through sheer repetition. The

four questions that pose themselves in such vivid
physical images of death and decay come to a full stop
at the end of the stanza. It seems that this line of
possibilities must be exhausted, as dry and stuck as
crusted sugar on the top of a syrup bottle.

The thinking process marked by similes and
questions gathers great potential force in the next
two lines; these lines are set off from the rest of the
poem and express the burden of passive speculation.
Again the possible result of deferring dreams is cast
in the form of a simile. And again, there is a
tentative quality to the idea. The "maybe" that
begins the sentence keeps the reader in a state of
uncertainty that seems appropriate for a poem largely
about uncertainty. But here the separation of one
possibility from the others as a group indicates that
this feeling of weight is an inevitable result of the
collected frustration. And for the first time, the
tentative quality is not directly expressed as a
question.

These shifts mark an increasing pressure in this
two-line stanza. The pressure logically anticipates a
breaking point. The first responses concerned taste
and smell, but here the feeling is of sheer heaviness.
At some point, something must happen. By setting off
this simile in its own little stanza, Hughes makes the
reader pause fully over it and sense the burden of
oppression. And by separating this one simile, Hughes

builds a greater sense of focus. No more are we quickly listing a series of possibilities. We are, on the contrary, moving to a point that seems too heavy to bear.

The closing line also ends with a question mark, but clearly we have arrived at something much closer to a flat statement of fact. We sense that this idea carries with it the force of an impending action. Hughes emphasizes the final line first of all by separating it from the rest of the poem. We have moved from the series of the first full stanza to the heaviness of the two-line load, to the focus of a single short line. Furthermore, that line is italicized. Its final word rhymes precisely with the last word of the line that precedes it (the other rhymes in the poem chime in on alternate lines). This nearness and the precision of this rhyme emphasize a kind of abrupt decisiveness.

But perhaps the most dramatic change in mood from tentative thoughts to substantial deeds is marked by a shift from simile to metaphor; in this final line, Hughes drops the "like" that has kept us speculating about possibilities. The final idea is expressed through metaphor. A deferred dream will not result in something "like" an explosion. Rather, it is a bomb that <u>will</u> explode. Hughes ends the poem by suggesting that violent revolution builds from frustration.

STUDENT MODEL ESSAY
SUSAN GLASPELL, TRIFLES

A major theme of Susan Glaspell's *Trifles* can be used to underscore an essential concern of critical writers: small things matter, or to put it another way, the "big picture" may obscure the significance of specifics. The paper that follows attends to small things to demonstrate how Glaspell leads the audience to sympathize with a character who never actually appears on the stage. For example, the writer notes Glaspell's title and explains how that title signals the play's central irony. The writer also pays attention to how the setting (the cold and depressing farmhouse) serves to clue us in on the quality of the lives lived there. So before moving to the first line of dialogue, a case is being made about how Glaspell controls the way we respond to her characters and to the distinct tone of specific words (think, for example, of the attitude behind the District Attorney's reference to Mrs. Peters as a "housekeeper").

Marquez 1

Joseph Marquez
Professor Wheeler
EN 101
October 9, 2006

Glaspell's Control of the Audience's
Sympathy in <u>Trifles</u>
Susan Glaspell's <u>Trifles</u> doesn't take long to get to a point where many murder stories end: the audience knows almost immediately "whodunit." The audience also knows "why" in a general sense (the murdered man was cruel to his wife). The only mystery

Marquez 2

involves the specific motive the District Attorney
needs to discover so that he can aggressively pursue
the case against his suspect, but this mystery
doesn't really move the action forward. This play
is more about character than plot. Ironically,
the audience cares most about a murderer who never
appears onstage, never speaks in her own voice, and
never says a word in her own defense. Glaspell makes
the absent Mrs. Wright the emotional center of the
play.

The title of the play strongly directs the
audience's sympathy. The "trifles" suggest a
profound difference between the men who have power
and the women who have no power. The County Attorney
thinks that trifles are the concern of women. As a
man, he believes he has really important matters
to busy himself with. But as the action unfolds,
we become aware that significance is a matter of
imagination, sympathy, and intelligence. These are
qualities that the male officials or authorities in
this play do not possess.

The County Attorney, for example, is looking for
something big but completely misses many leads. He
abruptly cuts off Hale, the man who found the body,
just as Hale begins to comment upon the relationship
Mr. and Mrs. Wright shared. He also assumes that the
dreary quality of the home (ill kept and gloomy)
reflects directly upon the character of the

"housekeeper," not upon the quality of life she had been forced to live. The Sheriff registers nothing beyond the County Attorney's narrow emotional limits; he merely reinforces the sense that authority either breeds insensitivity or grows from insensitivity.

The women who come along with the County Attorney and the Sheriff supply a clear counterpoint. They are, no less than Mrs. Wright, subject to the condescending attitudes of those in charge. The official investigators find it amusing that Mrs. Hale and Mrs. Peters notice small things when something as important as a murder has happened. They seem to think that attention to small things indicates a woman's inability to deal with big concerns. The audience feels distant from this rude and self-satisfied attitude and sympathizes with the women.

Mrs. Hale and Mrs. Peters are the first characters the audience sides with, but Glaspell employs dramatic irony to extend sympathy to Mrs. Wright. The County Attorney and the Sheriff are totally oblivious to what the audience and the women know about Mrs. Wright's married life. The gloomy farmhouse does not reflect bad housekeeping but a miserable, cramped, and lonely existence. It is clear early on that Mr. Wright has controlled that existence. He doesn't want a phone because he doesn't want human contact. According to Mr. Hale (an apparently sensitive man, but not one in power),

Marquez 4

Wright never cared about what his wife might think or want. Wright doesn't want to talk to his wife any more than he wants to talk to anyone.

For a time, Glaspell keeps the audience a small step ahead of Mrs. Hale and Mrs. Peters. They are in a way also controlled by the men around them. The women do not easily refute the assumptions the men make about their value. Mrs. Peters is, in fact, apologetic about the men's rudeness. She accepts their self-importance on their terms: "Of course they've got awful important things on their minds." Just at this point the audience is once again strongly cued to look for the importance of small things. Mrs. Hale notices the sewing Mrs. Wright had left unfinished and observes that the good stitching abruptly turns ragged. This small detail is evidence that Mrs. Wright became powerfully upset at a particular time. But Mrs. Hale keeps the insight to herself. Significantly, Mrs. Hale resews the bad portions to cover for Mrs. Wright. This act reveals the depth of her sympathy for the accused woman and the contempt she begins to feel for the Sheriff and the County Attorney.

From this point on, the audience participates with Mrs. Hale in her defiance of authority. And the stakes in that defiance grow ever higher, for the motif of the singing and silence brings Mrs. Wright forward as the real victim. Mrs. Hale had already

remembered Mrs. Wright as the youthful Minnie Foster.
Minnie once dressed in "pretty clothes," acted in
a "lively" manner, and sang in the church choir;
but that was thirty years ago (enough time for great
rage to build over the loss of joy). After Mrs. Hale
notices and repairs the ragged sewing, Mrs. Peters
comes across the empty birdcage with the broken door:
"Someone must have been rough with it." Mrs. Hale
pursues her chain of memories: Mrs. Wright "used to
sing real pretty."

All singing is in the past tense. Minnie Foster,
Mrs. Hale tells us, was "like a bird." But the Wright
home is marked by silence. The contrast foreshadows
the dead bird the women discover in Mrs. Wright's
sewing box. Its symbolic meaning is clear; Minnie
Foster was like the singing bird, but John Wright had
silenced her just as he had killed the bird. Mrs.
Wright must have seen her fate in the dead bird and
lashed out in her sense of loss.

All is in place in the closing scene for the
audience to identify with the women's efforts to
protect Mrs. Wright from further injustice. The
audience is aligned in particular with the poised and
able Mrs. Hale. Her final action (snatching the box
from the stunned Mrs. Peters just before the officials
arrive) speaks eloquently of her complete empathy
with Mrs. Wright. By this final point, it is an empathy
the audience shares with her.

STUDENT MODEL ESSAY
ERNEST HEMINGWAY,
HILLS LIKE WHITE ELEPHANTS

The essay that follows responds to Ernest Hemingway's "Hills Like White Elephants." Notice that the author shapes a fairly specific approach to the story: the way Hemingway establishes a perspective on his characters through their response to the environment. This kind of focus is essential; a writer cannot take on everything about any work. But notice, too, that the author does not artificially restrict the topic. Insights about point of view, imagery, symbol, metaphor, and plot all support the thesis. Finally, observe how the author weaves in (and documents) relevant ideas of other critics.

Wright 1

Robin Wright
Professor Beiderwell
EN 110
October 16, 2006

Setting and Character in "Hills Like
White Elephants"
Ernest Hemingway's "Hills Like White
Elephants" conveys in clipped dialogue and spare
descriptions a conflict between an American man and
his girlfriend, Jig. It would seem that the objective
narrator gives the reader only the most impersonal
glimpse at their relationship. Even the specific
issue that generates the conflict, abortion, is only
suggested indirectly. Yet Hemingway strongly guides

the reader's sympathies. He contrasts the perspectives of his two main characters on the surrounding environment in order to define their moral substance.

The story opens with the couple seated in a shaded area at a train station; they stare across a hot, dry land. This is not a comfortable moment for either of them. When Jig states that the barren hills look like white elephants, the American retorts that he has never seen one. His answer is abrupt, and the girl's comment, "No, you wouldn't have," sets off a round of arguments. Something is going on here besides a dispute over the color of the mountain range.

After much frustrating, strained, and indirect discussion, the girl gets up and walks to the end of the station. From there she looks to the opposite side. By the river she sees trees, lush growth, and fields of grain. Her vision stands in sharp contrast to the dried landscape of the hills that were viewed from the other side.

Jig's fresh vision provides perspective on the man's persistent advice: "They just let the air in and then it's all perfectly natural" (726). The man presses Jig to have an abortion without any regard for what she may feel. His selfish manner hurts her more than the advice itself. He simply does not see the

Wright 3

green world that she sees. Nor does he have a clue
as to what Jig feels about the state of their
relationship.

Jig and the reader understand what the American
man misses. Mary Dell Fletcher argues that Jig's
vision of the river Ebro aligns her with the forces of
life:

> The life giving landscape is now
> associated in Jig's mind with ... a
> fruitful life where natural relations
> culminate in new life and spiritual
> fulfillment, not barrenness and
> sterility, as represented by the dry
> hills. (17)

Fletcher may overestimate the importance
Hemingway lends abortion itself; Hemingway seems
more interested in a feeling than he is in the
morality of a specific decision. But the contrasting
attitudes toward abortion do reveal the general
conflict Jig identifies in relation to her lover. One
thing is clear: she feels lonely because she realizes
how remote the man is from her.

By conveying the differing perceptions these
characters have of the landscape, Hemingway helps
the reader see each character fully. Gary Brenner
notes that Hemingway's use of the setting allows
readers to "overhear" the dialogue correctly and

note Jig's "depth of character and [the man's]
shallowness" (198). Once we pick up the cues from
the ways the characters see the world, we become alert
to even the subtlest signs of the man's controlling
tendencies and Jig's more vital being. The following
dialogue illustrates the point:

> "Doesn't it mean anything to you? We
> could get along."

> "Of course it does. But I don't want
> anyone but you. I don't want anyone else. And
> I know it's perfectly simple." (728)

The man first claims that the child means
something but quickly shifts the plural pronoun "we"
to the singular forms "I" and "you" (Smiley 9).
He refuses to accept the implications of Jig's use
of the plural pronoun.

This profound separation is also made plain in
the images Hemingway employs to mark off physical
spaces. The bead curtain in the bar, for example,
forms a barrier between the man (who stays inside)
and Jig (who steps outside and reflects upon the
landscape). The curtain emphasizes the perceptual
differences between Jig and her lover: the image of
the curtain becomes, in effect, a metaphor of all that
divides them in their relationship.

The man's self-absorption is something Jig comes
to understand and accept. She sees things between her

and her lover plainly; there is no reason for her to
talk to a man who cannot listen. The climax of the
story marks her absolute recognition of the state her
relationship has come to: "Would you please please
please please please please please stop talking"
(728). In light of this obvious anger, Jig's terse
words at the story's conclusion must be read as
ironic:

>"Do you feel better?" he asked.
>
>"I feel fine," she said. "There's
>nothing wrong with me. I feel fine." (728)

Obviously, she does not feel "fine," but she
recognizes what is wrong. She has gained insight
about herself and the man who has been her lover and
understands very well that the man will not achieve
any similar insight.

Jig even knows that the man will not understand
the implications of her statement. He will take these
words straight because he wants to believe that
everything is fixed or "fine." The mysterious smile
that precedes Jig's final words indicates her
superior understanding. Perhaps this superior level
of insight explains why it is that only Jig has a name;
her lover is merely "the American." Everything is
broken between these two characters, and only she and
alert readers of Hemingway's story are in on that
knowledge.

Works Cited

Brenner, Gerry. "A Semiotic Inquiry into Hemingway's 'A Simple Inquiry.'" Hemingway's Neglected Short Fiction. Ed. Susan F. Beegel. Ann Arbor: UMI Research P, 1989. 195-205.

Fletcher, Mary Dell. "Hemingway's 'Hills Like White Elephants.'" The Explicator 38 (1980): 16-18.

Hemingway, Ernest. "Hills Like White Elephants." The Complete Short Stories of Ernest Hemingway: The Finca Vigia Edition. New York: Simon, 1987. 211-14.

STUDENT MODEL ESSAY
EDNA ST. VINCENT MILLAY, I, BEING BORN A WOMAN AND DISTRESSED

The love sonnet by Thomas Wyatt that appears on page 1122 raises some interesting issues regarding society's assumptions about gender roles. Wyatt's language is the language of battle. The man enters the fray of sexual warfare and seeks to win the prize of a woman's favor; the woman herself is essentially passive (if the man is the conqueror, the woman must be the conquered). Needless to say, Wyatt's notion of love is not, in the idiom of our own time, "politically correct." But his notions of love and of poetic conventions regarding love certainly have a substantial history.

Sonnet writing was in Wyatt's age a "gentleman's" endeavor. A woman writing (or at least publishing) a love sonnet in the sixteenth century would be a near impossibility. Things did not change much for generations. Given this background, one might understand how a woman writing a love sonnet in the early twentieth century would be conscious of the gender assumptions the form had acquired over time. Such a woman might, for example, write a sonnet that critiques the gender assumptions that sonnets had long perpetuated. The brief essay reprinted here arises from the context of this conversation on the sonnet and socially defined gender roles. The essay specifically addresses Edna St. Vincent Millay's sonnet "I, Being Born a Woman and Distressed."

Note how the writer pays close attention to the function of rhyme and how the rhyme scheme signals an underlying tension in the piece. Note also that the writer doesn't just say that Millay employs a conversational tone but explains how and for what purpose Millay creates a conversational tone. Notice also how the writer uses specific terms aptly (for example, *enjambs*, *turn*, *caesura*, *complication*).

Greene 1

Hunter Greene
Professor Smith
EN 102
October 30, 2006

Millay's Self-Assertive Sonnet

Edna St. Vincent Millay must have read many love sonnets by men and heard many proclamations of love by men. She must have become tired of such romantic expressions. Millay lived in an age when women were still usually portrayed as passive objects of men's desire. "I, Being Born a Woman and Distressed"

Greene 2

suggests that she found these portraits one-sided, presumptuous, and stifling. Millay defies conventional ways of defining courtship roles by writing a sonnet about sexual desires from a woman's frank, self-assured perspective.

Millay raises in the octave what would be in the context of her time a shocking problem: the female speaker admits to experiencing sexual desires that occasionally overpower her rational faculties. Millay enjambs many of her lines to achieve a conversational tone, but the inner war between brain and body is highlighted by an intricate rhyme scheme that is not characteristic of everyday conversation. The "a" rhymes suggest qualities of thought or reason: "kind," "find," "designed," "mind." The "b" rhymes communicate physical, passionate impressions: "distressed," "zest," "breast," "possessed." The caesura before "possessed" (the last word of the octave) emphasizes the speaker's problem: the speaker feels desire but confesses that her desire often leaves her vulnerable.

The turn in this sonnet, however, is decidedly away from possession. The full pause that closes the octave allows the speaker to catch her breath and assert herself against any mistaken ideas the man (the implied audience) may have about her frank admission. The speaker does not regret her feelings but forcefully spells out what the audience should not

Greene 3

think: don't think I have strong feelings still, she
states; don't think I have any pity for anything you
might feel now; don't even think I'm interested in
anything about you. Millay's speaker strongly
dismisses any romantic, soft conventions of love even
as she admits to the power of her own sexual nature.

Conventional poetic ideas of how a woman should
act, or what a woman should feel, have of course been
established and perpetuated by men. Millay's speaker
dismisses male attitudes in general and her former
lover in particular; the split personified by "stout
blood" and "staggering brain" is only one
temporary, internal breakdown. It does not mean that
she will feel anything like enduring love, respect,
or even interest in the future for the object of the
passion.

The complication that loomed so large in the
octave is thus put in perspective in the sestet.
The speaker accepts her passion and will neither
apologize for it nor be forever ruled by it. Men have,
after all, had the liberty of that "love them and
leave them" attitude all along. Millay announces the
final dismissal. She emphasizes the resolution by
telling the man that she will "make it plain."

The final two lines make the message very plain
indeed; in fact, these lines seem very unpoetic:
"I find this frenzy insufficient reason / For
conversation when we meet again" (13-14). Millay

Greene 4

conveys a mundane, spoken quality (the enjambment here is important); the word choice seems cold ("insufficient reason"); and no marked rhythm is discernible. But the matter-of-fact, conversational tone these lines express is in perfect accord with the poem's logic. The speaker acquires control by claiming her feelings and expressing her desires without apology.

Appendix B

COLLECTION OF POET BIOGRAPHIES

Sherman Alexie (1966–)

Sherman Alexie was born in Spokane, Washington, and grew up on the nearby Spokane Indian Reservation. He read voraciously when he was a child, partly in an attempt to escape an unhappy home life, and began to write while attending Washington State University. He has devoted himself to writing since then and has been an extraordinarily productive writer of poetry, short stories, and novels. Alexie has received considerable praise for his writing and is often regarded as a spokesperson for Native Americans, though he rejects this role. Among the awards he has received are a National Endowment for the Arts Poetry Fellowship and the 2001 PEN/Malamud Award from PEN/Faulkner Foundation. His books include the collection of poetry, *I Would Steal Horses* (1992), and *Ten Little Indians: Stories* (2003).

Maya Angelou (1928–)

Maya Angelou was born in St. Louis, Missouri. Her childhood was a difficult one, filled with racism and abuse. She was raped when she was seven years old and did not speak for five years afterward. When she was a young woman, she drifted into prostitution. Angelou transformed her life dramatically, however, when she began working in the theater. She rose to become a civil rights activist and one of the most prominent writers in America. In 1993, she delivered the inaugural poem at President Bill Clinton's first inauguration. Angelou has written in every conceivable genre of literature, including autobiography, poetry, fiction, and journalism. In particular, *I Know Why the Caged Bird Sings* (1969), the first volume of her autobiography, has proven enduringly popular. She has been nominated for a number of the nation's most prestigious literary awards.

Matthew Arnold (1822–1888)

Matthew Arnold, born in Laleham-on-Thames, England, was the son of a clergyman. Arnold attended Oxford University, where he later held the position of professor of poetry. For most of his life he was an inspector of schools, a position that kept him engaged in the educational issues that were central to his thinking. He was successful in a number of genres, but he is best remembered as a poet and critic. Arnold is regarded as an important social commentator and a masterful prose stylist. Critical opinions of his poetry have varied, but there seems little doubt that poems such as "Dover Beach," "To Marguerite," and "The Scholar Gypsy" have an enduring value. In these and other works Arnold expressed the doubts and difficulties of the modern mind.

Margaret Atwood (1939–)

The most prominent Canadian writer of her generation, Margaret Atwood was born in Ottawa. She began her literary career as a poet and then moved into other genres. Over the course of her career she has become an important cultural spokesperson, focusing in particular on feminist concerns. In addition to writing in almost every genre, she is a painter and illustrator. Atwood focuses often in her poetry on images of violence, and critics have commented on the impersonality of her early poetry while noting the relative openness of her more recent work. It is not as a poet, however, that she is best known, but as the author of such best-selling novels as *The Handmaid's Tale,* which was made into a motion picture, and *Cat's Cradle.*

W. H. Auden (1907–1973)

W(ystan) H(ugh) Auden was one of the most technically gifted poets of his age. Born in York, England, he attended Oxford University, where he became the focal point for a group of promising young writers. His first book was published the same year he graduated from Oxford, and he quickly became recognized as the most important British poet of his generation. In 1939, he immigrated to the United States and shortly thereafter became an American citizen. Although poetry was his chief passion, Auden worked in other genres as well, gaining recognition as a critic and dramatist. Auden's critical reputation has fluctuated slightly, both during and after his lifetime, but there is little question that he was one of the most important poets writing in English during the twentieth century.

Jimmy Santiago Baca (1952–)

Abandoned by his parents at the age of five, Jimmy Santiago Baca drifted into a life on the streets that eventually led to a prison term for narcotics possession. While in prison, Santiago Baca not only taught himself to read but began writing and publishing the poetry that would bring him to national prominence. He has received a number of prestigious awards, including the American Book Award, for his poetry and has also published acclaimed short fiction and an autobiography. Of Hispanic and Apache descent, Santiago Baca has often focused in his writing on the experiences of people who are poor or underprivileged, both in the barrio and in prison, and has made ample use of his own experiences of poverty and violence. In his most recent works he has begun to incorporate material that reflects his newer roles of husband, father, and author. In addition to working as a writer, Santiago Baca is a teacher and community activist.

Amiri Baraka (1934–)

Imamu Amiri Baraka was born LeRoi Jones in Newark, New Jersey. He attended Howard University and Rutgers University before entering the U.S. Air Force. He later attended Columbia University, where he became friendly with poets belonging to the Beat Generation. As an African American, Baraka was deeply sympathetic to the civil rights movement, and his politics were to become increasingly radical over the years. In 1965, he became a Black Nationalist, and several years later he changed his name. Readers and critics have been polarized by Baraka's work since the mid-1960s. Whereas some feel that the poet's preoccupation with politics has damaged his art, others feel that his political consciousness is the power that drives his imagination. His books of poetry include *Black Art* (1966), *Reggae or Not!* (1982), and *Transbluency: The Selected Poems of Amiri Baraka/LeRoi Jones (1961–1995).*

Elizabeth Bishop (1911–1979)

Born in Worcester, Massachusetts, Elizabeth Bishop was one of the most important American poets of the post–World War II era. Her father died when she was very young, and her mother was confined to a mental institution, so Bishop lived with sympathetic relatives until she went away to school. She worked for most of her life as a freelance writer and teacher. Bishop published only four slim volumes during her lifetime—*North and South* (1946), *Poems: North and South— A Cold Spring* (1955), *Questions of Travel* (1965), and *Geography III* (1976)—but she was praised by critics and received a number of prestigious awards, including, in 1955, a Pulitzer Prize. Her poems are typically quiet and subtle, but their accessible language and musicality give them a broad appeal.

William Blake (1757–1827)

William Blake was born in London, England. Early on, he demonstrated gifts for language and the visual arts; as an adult he supported himself as a printer and engraver. In addition to having indisputable artistic talents, Blake believed that he had the ability to see spiritual realities—angels, for example—that were hidden from most people. During his lifetime, Blake was better known as a visual artist than a writer, although *Songs of Innocence* and *Songs of Experience,* his two most accessible works, did enjoy some popularity. His longer, more philosophically and politically weighty works, such as *Milton* and *The Marriage of Heaven and Hell,* were more appreciated by succeeding generations than by his contemporaries.

Louise Bogan (1897–1970)

Louise Bogan was born in Livermore Falls, Maine. Her childhood was complicated by economic difficulties and by her mother's erratic behavior. Though she attended college for only one year, Bogan was a gifted, perceptive reader and writer of poetry. She taught on occasion, but she made her living chiefly as a freelance writer and translator. Bogan always had her admirers, but she did not achieve the fame that she might have. She nevertheless received a number of important awards, such as the Harriett Monroe Award in Poetry and the Bollingen Prize, and recent years have seen a renewed interest in her work. Her collections of poetry include *Body of This Death* (1923), *The Sleeping Fury* (1937), and *The Blue Estuaries: Poems 1923–1968* (1968).

Eavan Boland (1944–)

Eavan Boland was born in Dublin, Ireland. Her father was a diplomat, and her mother, a painter. Her father's work necessitated moving the family several times. When Boland was five, they moved to London for six years and then to New York; they returned to Ireland when she was fourteen. She wrote poetry while attending Trinity College in Dublin and published her first book shortly after graduation. She has taught at a number of universities in Ireland and the United States. Boland's reputation developed slowly, and the critical consensus is that she did not find her own voice until she had written several books. She is now regarded, both abroad and at home, as one of the preeminent Irish poets of her generation. Among the many prizes she has received are the Lannan Foundation Award in Poetry and an American Ireland Fund Literary Award. Her books of poetry include *Outside History: Selected Poems, 1980–1990* (1990), *In a Time of Violence* (1994), and *Against Love Poetry* (2001).

Anne Bradstreet (1612?–1672)

Anne Bradstreet was born Anne Dudley in Northampton, England. Her father had a large library, and it was from this collection that the future poet received much of her education. When she was sixteen, she married Simon Bradstreet, and shortly thereafter the couple, together with her parents, immigrated to the American colonies. Despite the hardships of the New World, and despite the fact that she bore eight children, Bradstreet found time to write poetry, some of which was published during her lifetime. Although she was born in England, Bradstreet is commonly considered the first American poet, and a number of poems—among them "A Letter to Her Husband, Absent upon Public Employment," "To My Dear and Loving Husband," and "The Author to Her Book"—are regarded as American classics. In these and other poems she provides a compelling picture of a woman's struggles with faith and doubt and with her role as a woman in Puritan society.

Gwendolyn Brooks (1917–2000)

Gwendolyn Brooks was born in Topeka, Kansas. She began writing poetry at an early age and while still in her teens, received positive feedback from the well-known poets James Weldon Johnson and Langston Hughes. Her identity as an African American was crucial to her work, and throughout her career she was deeply involved in the struggle for racial equality. From a wide-ranging combination of poetic influences, Brooks formed a distinctive style that brought her honors and acclaim. In 1950, while still in her early thirties, she received the Pulitzer Prize in poetry for *Annie Allen*. In the decades that followed she received numerous fellowships and honorary degrees.

Elizabeth Barrett Browning (1806–1861)

Elizabeth Barrett Browning was born at her family's estate south of Durham, England. Largely self-educated, she began writing poetry and reading classical literature at an early age. While in her teens she developed an illness that experts were unable to diagnose and that left her weakened and frail for the rest of her life. Despite her condition, she gradually established herself as one of the preeminent poets of her day. In 1846, she married the considerably younger poet Robert Browning, and they had one child. Elizabeth Barrett Browning died in 1861 in Italy, where she and her husband spent much of their time together. Though she received more fame and critical praise than Robert did during her lifetime, this situation was later reversed—eventually, she became regarded primarily as the wife of a famous poet. Recent decades have seen a renewed appreciation of her lyrical gifts and a new appreciation of her interest in the status of women and in national liberation movements.

Robert Browning (1812–1889)

Born in Camberwell, near London, England, Robert Browning was both an outstanding poet in his own right and the husband of another well-known poet, Elizabeth Barrett Browning. Browning had just begun to establish his reputation as a poet when he met Elizabeth Barrett. The two were married in 1846 and soon moved to Venice, Italy, where they made their home until Elizabeth's death in 1861. Popular acclaim came slowly to Robert Browning, and for much of his career he was less well known than his wife. Although he had published such masterpieces as "My Last Duchess" and "Fra Lippo Lippi" before his return to England, only with the publication of the four volumes of *The Ring and the Book* in 1868 and 1869 did he achieve true success. He is now recognized as one of the greatest English poets and as the greatest writer of dramatic monologues since Shakespeare.

Robert Burns (1759–1796)

Robert Burns was born into a hardworking but poor farming family in southwestern Scotland. Although he attended school whenever circumstances allowed, Burn's early life was marked by hard physical labor. His poetry struck many of his contemporaries as "natural"—that is, as springing from the land, common speech, and immediate feelings. While Burns was largely self-educated, he was hardly uneducated. He developed his poetic voice consciously; his knowledge of Scottish traditions was considerable. Still, Burns enjoyed playing the role of the untutored genius. He had, in fact, extraordinary early success with Scottish intellectuals and landed people, who felt he broke through conventions that had become stifling, though he never fully embraced the high culture that lionized him. As much as he relished attention, he remained sensitive to any hint of condescending praise or presumptions of class. Burns suffered throughout his life from heart trouble and died at the age of thirty-seven.

Lewis Carroll (1832–1898)

Lewis Carroll was born Charles Lutwidge Dodgson in Daresbury, in Cheshire, England. One of eleven children of a clergyman, he initially intended to be ordained a priest of the Church of England but decided against it because of a stutter. He was a gifted mathematician and became a professor in the subject at Oxford. When he began publishing humorous stories and poems, he adopted the pen name Lewis Carroll, the name under which he is internationally famous. His two most famous works, *Alice's Adventures in Wonderland* and *Through the Looking-Glass*, although intended for children, are also read with pleasure by adults and have been translated into numerous languages. He was also the author of books on mathematics and a talented photographer, especially of children.

Anne Carson (1950–)

Anne Carson was born in Toronto, Canada. She studied classics at the University of Toronto and has worked for most of her professional life as a teacher in this field. After living and working in the United States for many years, she returned to Canada in 2002 when she accepted a position at McGill University in Montreal. She has traveled widely, at one point walking across Spain, and this interest in travel is evident in her work. Carson has received considerable critical attention in recent years, particularly for the way in which she mixes and subverts literary genres and conventions. She has received a number of prestigious awards for her work, including a MacArthur Fellowship and the Lannan Award. Her books of poetry (portions of which are often in prose) include *Autobiography of Red: A Novel in Verse*, *Men in the Off Hours* and *The Beauty of the Husband: A Fictional Essay in 29 Tangos*.

Amy Clampitt (1920–1994)

Amy Clampitt was born in New Providence, Iowa, a rural area where she grew up on a farm. She attended Grinnell College in Grinnell, Iowa; Columbia University; and the New School for Social Research in New York City. In the 1940s and 1950s, she floundered as a novelist, working an assortment of jobs to support her writing career; in the 1960s, she began writing poetry. Finally, at the age of sixty-three, Clampitt won critical acclaim with her collection of poetry, *The Kingfisher* (1983). Widespread acclaim followed, and hers is regarded as one of the more spectacular late debuts by a poet. She received a Guggenheim Fellowship in 1982 and a MacArthur Fellowship in 1992, among other awards. Her poetry is remarkable both for its sonic richness and for its precise descriptions of the natural world.

Judith Ortiz Cofer (1952–)

Judith Ortiz Cofer was born in Hormigueros, Puerto Rico. When her father joined the U.S. Navy, the family moved first to New Jersey and then to Georgia. Though Ortiz Cofer's first language was Spanish, she learned English while still a young child, and it is in English that she has written the poetry, fiction, and essays that explore the sense of divided identity she feels as a Puerto Rican living in America. Critics have praised Ortiz Cofer's work both for its sophisticated, sympathetic depiction of Puerto Rican culture and for its stylistic flair. Her books of poetry include *The Latin Deli: Prose & Poetry* (1993), for which she received the Ainsfield Wolf Book Award, and *The Year of Our Revolution: New and Selected Stories and Poems* (1998), which was awarded the Paterson Book Prize.

Samuel Taylor Coleridge (1772–1834)

Samuel Taylor Coleridge, one of the chief figures in English poetry of the Romantic period, was born in Ottery St. Mary in Devonshire, England. He was a precocious child, and by the time he attended Oxford University, he was already writing poetry and reading Greek philosophy in the original language. Coleridge was later active not only as a poet but as a theologian, social philosopher, and literary critic. His life was complicated both by his emotional instability and his opium addiction, but he was nonetheless a productive author. Critical reception to Coleridge during his lifetime was mixed, in part because his contemporaries, including his friends, saw him as a scattered, if brilliant, thinker. His contributions to the various genres in which he wrote are now widely recognized, however. A number of his poems, particularly "Kubla Khan" and "The Rime of the Ancient Mariner," are appreciated for the music of their verse and for their rich symbolism.

Billy Collins (1941–)

Born in New York City, Billy Collins attended Holy Cross College and the University of California, Riverside, before beginning his career as a professor of English. In 1991, his collection *Questions about Angels* received the National Poetry Series prize, bringing him to a wide audience for the first time. Collins is a popular reader of his own work and has appeared on radio and television, in addition to making audio and visual recordings of his work. During 2001, he served as the eleventh Poet Laureate of the United States. Collins's work has enjoyed remarkable popularity with the public, and he is without a doubt the most commercially successful poet of his generation.

Countee Cullen (1903–1946)

Countee Cullen was born in Harlem in New York City and was raised by his grandmother until she died in 1918. Adopted by a prominent clergyman in the neighborhood, he was exposed at an early age to the political and intellectual currents of thought that were so alive in Harlem. Cullen began publishing poetry even before graduating from high school. He completed his graduate education at Harvard University and became a central figure of the period known as the Harlem Renaissance with the publication of his first book of poetry, *Color*. Cullen adopted conventional literary forms to write powerfully and concretely about complexities of race and racism in America. Perhaps a narrow focus on Cullen's formal achievements led some critics to overlook his intensity and anger. In any case, recent years have seen a revival of interest in Cullen's work, after a period of relative obscurity.

e. e. cummings (1894–1962)

Edward Estlin Cummings was born in Cambridge, Massachusetts. He was the son of a professor at Harvard University, the school he himself later attended. *Tulips and Chimneys* (1923) established him as a promising avant-garde poet. The collection that followed, *XLI poems,* solidified his reputation. At the time of his death in 1962, e. e. cummings (he had dropped the conventional use of the upper case as well as his full name) was one of America's most-read poets. The change of his name's appearance suggests a larger matter: even on the page, cummings's poems look experimental, because he played in dramatic ways with punctuation and capitalization (or lack of it). His subjects, on the other hand, were often traditional, and he is especially known for his love poems. Although his reputation has declined in the years since his death, there are those, notably the poet and critic Brad Leithauser, who have argued forcefully for his continuing importance.

Emily Dickinson (1830–1886)

Though she is now regarded as one of the greatest American poets, Emily Dickinson was almost completely unknown during her lifetime. Born in Amherst, Massachusetts, she died in the same town in 1886, having lived for most of her life as a relative recluse in her family's home. Her retiring lifestyle did not prevent her, however, from corresponding regularly with friends or from producing a large and distinctive body of work. It's likely, in fact, that her isolation helped rather than hindered her writing. There's little doubt, certainly, that her lack of involvement in the literary world of her day gave her the freedom to experiment with new techniques, such as the slant rhymes for which she would one day become so famous. Despite a few publications during her life, Dickinson's public career as a poet began only after her death.

John Donne (1572–1631)

John Donne was born in London, England, into a Roman Catholic family during a time when the English Reformation had made it increasingly difficult for Catholics to obtain an education or public employment. When Donne was thirty, he complicated his life still further by eloping with the seventeen-year-old daughter of an influential nobleman. Over the course of many years Donne reassessed his religious allegiances and concluded that he should join the Church of England, eventually going so far as to become a priest in that church. Donne's poetry falls into two distinct phases: The earlier lyrics are witty and worldly, and many deal directly with sex. The later poetry is almost exclusively religious in character, though wit remains a characteristic of Donne's style, and he continues to use sexual imagery. Donne's poetry was undervalued for several centuries after his death, and it was really only in the twentieth century that critics, T. S. Eliot chief among them, began to reevaluate his reputation.

H. D. (1886–1961)

H(ilda) D(oolitle) was born in Bethlehem, Pennsylvania. Her mother's family were members of a mystical Protestant group known as the Unitas Fratrum, and her father was a scientist. She attended Bryn Mawr College with other one-day-to-be-famous poets like Ezra Pound, William Carlos Williams, and Marianne Moore. Pound in particular was to be a great help to H. D.—it was he who abbreviated her name—when she was beginning her poetic career. After graduating from Bryn Mawr, she moved to Europe, where she remained for the rest of her life. Her poetry received considerable praise for its technical brilliance, but the feminist concerns that give much of her work its power really only found a sympathetic audience after her death. Her works include *Sea Garden* (1916), *Hymen* (1921), and *Helen in Egypt* (1961).

Richard Eberhart (1904–2005)

Richard Eberhart was born in Austin, Minnesota, into a well-to-do family that was to be shaken by economic hard times and by the early death of Eberhart's mother. It took time for Eberhart to settle in a career and to find his voice as a poet. He worked as a tutor, served in the U.S. Navy, and became an executive in a furniture company before his growing fame as a poet allowed him to earn a living from freelance writing and teaching. In the course of his long career, Eberhart received many of American poetry's most prestigious awards, including the Pulitzer Prize and the Bollingen Prize. Critics have noted his abiding concern with the central issues and questions of human existence. In particular, he writes powerfully about death in poems such as "For a Lamb" and "The Fury of Aerial Bombardment."

T. S. Eliot (1888–1965)

Born in St. Louis, Missouri, T(homas) S(tearns) Eliot moved first to Boston, where he attended Harvard University, and then (after a time on the European continent) to England, where he lived until his death in 1965. His life was a series of apparent contradictions. Arguably the most influential American poet of the twentieth century, he became a British citizen; a conservative in religion and politics, he produced some of the most revolutionary work of the modern age. Eliot viewed the modern world as fragmented and ruined, and his poetry is in many respects an attempt to recognize this problem and to deal with it in some way. His long poem *The Wasteland* (1922) uses fragments, quotations from older literature, and bits of popular songs to give a sense of the chaos he saw overtaking Europe. The height of Eliot's critical reputation came in the 1940s, when he published his last major work, *The Four Quartets,* and received the Nobel Prize in literature.

Louise Erdrich (1954–)

Louise Erdrich was born in Little Falls, Minnesota. Her mother was Native American, and although Erdrich did not grow up on a reservation, she made frequent trips there to visit relatives. While attending Dartmouth College, she met the writer and anthropologist Michael Dorris, who later became her literary collaborator and husband. The couple later separated, and Dorris committed suicide in 1997. Although she is better known now for her works of fiction, Erdrich began her literary career as a poet. Critics have praised her work for the way in which she uses elements of Native American myths and stories and for what has been called her "magical realism," the realistic depiction of fantastic elements. These elements are present in collections of poetry, such as *Jacklight* (1984) and *Baptism of Fire* (1989), and in the novels *Love Medicine* (1984) and *The Last Report on the Miracles at Little No Horse* (2001).

Lawrence Ferlinghetti (1919–)

Lawrence Ferlinghetti was born in Yonkers, New York. His father died before he was born, and his mother suffered a nervous breakdown a few years later. Ferlinghetti's aunt took him to France for several years, after which the two returned to the United States. When his aunt disappeared, Ferlinghetti stayed on with the wealthy family whose children she had been tutoring. He served in the U.S. Army during World War II, after which he earned his PhD at the Sorbonne in Paris. He then moved to San Francisco, where he developed into a poet and publisher. His opposition to the poetic establishment, coupled with his energetic, colloquial poetic voice, has helped make him an exceptionally popular poet. Among his books are *A Coney Island of the Mind* (1958) and *These Are My Rivers: New and Selected Poems, 1955–1993* (1993).

Carolyn Forché (1950–)

Carolyn Forché was born in Detroit, Michigan. In 1975, when she was only twenty-four, Forché's first collection of poems, *Gathering the Tribes,* was selected for the prestigious Yale Series of Younger Poets. Throughout her career she has combined poetry and politics, and she has been particularly interested in the human rights situation in El Salvador and the rest of Central America. The reaction of critics has often focused on the overtly political nature of Forché's work. Whereas some have felt that her concerns add power and real-life urgency to the poems, others maintain that this power comes at the expense of poetic subtlety. Since her debut, Forché has published two additional collections, *The Country between Us* (1981) and *The Angel of History* (1994).

Robert Frost (1874–1963)

Though born in San Francisco, Frost set most of his poems in New England, where he moved with his mother at the age of eleven. Critical and popular acclaim came slowly to Frost, who taught and farmed to make ends meet while writing on the side. In 1912, however, he moved with his family to England, where he devoted himself full-time to writing. The books he produced during this time—*A Boy's Will* and *North of Boston*—were accepted for publication and sold well, marking the beginning of his poetic career. By the time he died in 1963, Robert Frost was the most popular poet in America. Frost's self-created persona of a wise and kindly old New England grandfather has proven to be misleading for many casual readers. Although Frost was certainly capable of celebrating the rural New England he knew well, many of his best poems were ambiguous or dark, something an increasing number of critics had come to realize before the poet's death.

Allen Ginsberg (1926–1997)

Allen Ginsberg was born in Newark, New Jersey. His childhood was complicated by the emotional instability of his mother, who suffered a series of nervous breakdowns. While attending Columbia University, he became friends with William Burroughs and Jack Kerouac, and the three friends later became the core of what was known as the Beat Generation. As a member of this group Ginsberg became something of a celebrity, a status that was only reinforced by his participation in the cultural upheavals of the 1960s. Ginsberg's work—with its long free-verse lines and its open celebration of homosexuality and drug use—has been controversial, but few would dispute the fact that it radically changed the direction of American poetry. Among his awards are the National Book Award (1974), the Harriet Monroe Poetry Award (1991), and the Medal of Chevalier de l'Ordre des Arts et Lettres (1993).

Jorie Graham (1950–)

Jorie Graham was born in New York City but grew up in Italy and France. Her mother was a sculptor; and her father, a theologian and the head of *Newsweek* magazine's office in Rome. She began writing poetry while attending New York University. In 1983, she married the poet James Galvin, but the two divorced in 2000. She currently serves as the Boylston Professor of Rhetoric and Oratory at Harvard University. Critics have compared Graham with the great modernist poets, especially Wallace Stevens, because of her fascination with the relationship between thought, speech, and reality. She has received numerous awards, including a Pulitzer Prize and the Academy of American Poets Lavan Award. Among her collections of poetry are *Hybrids of Plants and of Ghosts* (1980), *The Dream of the Unified Field: Poems, 1974–1994* (1995), and *Swarm* (2000).

Thomas Hardy (1840–1928)

Thomas Hardy was born in Dorset, England. At the time that Hardy's public career as a poet began in 1898, he had already established a career as England's most prominent novelist. He had always greatly loved poetry, however, and the controversy caused by his views on sexuality and religion in the last novels he wrote led him to seek out other means of expression. *Wessex Poems and Other Verses,* which appeared in 1898, contained what would become some of his best-known poems, including ''Hap'' and ''Neutral Tones.'' His epic, *The Dynasts,* published in three parts between 1904 and 1908, established him as one of the major poets of his time. Hardy died in 1928, and his ashes were buried in the Poets' Corner in Westminster Abbey.

Robert Hayden (1913–1980)

Robert Hayden was born in Detroit, Michigan. His parents separated when he was still quite young, at which point he was adopted by William and Sue Ellen Westerfield Hayden. In 1940, he published his first book of poems, *Heart-Shape in the Dust,* and married Erma Morris. Together with his wife, he converted to the Bahai faith, a religion that stresses the fundamental unity of the world's spiritual traditions and looks forward to a more unified, peaceful society. His most public recognition came in 1976 and again in 1977, when he was named Consultant in Poetry to the Library of Congress, a position now called Poet Laureate of the United States. He died of cancer in 1980.

Joy Harjo (1941–)

Joy Harjo, a member of the Muskogee Creek tribe, was born in Tulsa, Oklahoma. Her father was Creek; and her mother, part French, part Cherokee. Raised in Oklahoma, Harjo pursued many career avenues, such as joining a dance troupe and studying medicine, before deciding to major in poetry at the University of New Mexico. Since graduating from the University of Iowa's Writing Workshop in 1957 with an MFA, Harjo has taught at several colleges and has received such honors as the American Book Award and the Delmore Schwartz Memorial Poetry Award.

Seamus Heaney (1939–)

Seamus Heaney grew up Catholic in predominantly Protestant Northern Ireland. He began writing poetry while at Trinity College in Dublin and quickly established himself as one of the most promising members his generation of Irish poets. He moved south to the Republic of Ireland in 1971, and since 1981 he has divided his time between Dublin and Cambridge, Massachusetts, where he teaches at Harvard University. Heaney's poetry has received widespread acclaim, and it was in particular his collection *Field Work* (1979) that established him as an international figure. Critics have noted his feel for natural landscapes, the obvious pleasure he takes in working with language, and his tremendous technical proficiency. The sometimes violent struggles between Catholics and Protestants that have characterized so much of Irish history occupy an important place in Heaney's work, but he is by no means a narrowly political or partisan poet. In 1995, he received the Nobel Prize in literature.

George Herbert (1593–1633)

George Herbert was born in Montgomery, Wales. He attended Cambridge University, where he began work as a lecturer after his graduation. He was elected to Parliament, but after a long spiritual struggle he decided to forgo a career in public life. In 1629, he married Jane Danvers, with whom he adopted two daughters; and in 1630, he was ordained a priest in the Church of England. *The Temple* (1633), Herbert's only volume of poetry, was popular in the period following his death, but with time critics came to see him as a pious but not terribly exciting poet. The nineteenth century saw a revival of interest in his work, however. Today he is widely acknowledged as one of the great poets in the history of English literature.

Gerard Manley Hopkins (1844–1889)

Gerard Manley Hopkins was born in Stratford, in Essex, England. His family was artistic, literary, and deeply religious, and these influences were to determine the direction of the poet's life. In 1866, while studying at Oxford University, Hopkins converted from the Church of England to Roman Catholicism. Two years later he became a Jesuit priest, and he served the Church until his early death in 1889. Hopkins published only a few poems during his lifetime, so the majority of his contemporaries had no chance to read or respond to his work. One poet who saw nearly everything Hopkins wrote was his friend Robert Bridges, later the poet laureate, who arranged to have Hopkins's poems published in 1918. Twentieth-century readers were impressed both by Hopkins's technical innovations—no other poet in the English language sounds quite like him—and by his descriptions of nature.

Henry Howard, Earl of Surrey (1517–1574)

Henry Howard, Earl of Surrey, was born in Hunsdon, in Hertfordshire, England. Both of his parents came from noble families, and he was raised at the royal court, where he was well liked by Henry VIII. His position, and that of his family, was further strengthened when Anne Boleyn, his first cousin, became Henry VIII's second wife and thereby, the Queen of England. When Henry VIII later had Anne executed, Howard and his family suffered a reversal of political fortunes. He had a long history of behaving violently and erratically, and his political enemies eventually found a pretext on which to have him charged with treason and executed. Although he died before he was thirty and few of his poems were published during his lifetime, Howard played a crucial role in the development of poetry in English.

Langston Hughes (1902–1967)

More than any other poet of the twentieth century, Langston Hughes helped place African American experiences and art forms at the center of American cultural life. Born in Joplin, Missouri, to a family troubled by domestic and economic difficulties, Hughes discovered literature at an early age while on a visit to a public library. By the time he was twenty years old, he had already written one of his best-known poems, "The Negro Speaks of Rivers." Hughes moved to New York City in 1921 to attend Columbia University and soon became involved in the flowering of African American cultural life known as the Harlem Renaissance. Throughout the rest of his life he wrote steadily in a wide variety of genres and garnered both popularity and critical recognition.

Ted Hughes (1930–1998)

Ted Hughes was born in Mytholmroyd, West Yorkshire, a rural town whose harsh natural surroundings would be an important influence on Hughes's imagination. He began writing at an early age, but not until after he had graduated Cambridge University did he begin to take writing and publishing seriously. In 1956, he met and married the American poet Sylvia Plath. The couple had two children together but then separated, and Plath soon committed suicide. This event was to color the public reception of Hughes and his work for the remainder of his life, with many of Plath's readers blaming Hughes for his wife's death. In 1984, Hughes was named Poet Laureate of Great Britain. His most famous works, such as *The Hawk in the Rain* and *Crow,* look to the natural world and its creatures as sources of vitality and unsentimental wisdom.

John Keats (1795–1821)

John Keats was born in London, England. His childhood was relatively happy and secure until he was eight, when his father died of injuries sustained in an accident. His mother soon remarried, but the marriage was unsuccessful, and she died of tuberculosis several years later. Although Keats studied for a while to be a doctor, he had already fallen in love with poetry and eventually gave up the study of medicine. He had relatively few productive years as a writer before he died of tuberculosis in 1821. Although his writing career was cut short, Keats was enormously productive, and he produced some of the most memorable poetry in the English language. In addition, the many letters he wrote to friends and family contain advice on the craft of poetry that has influenced succeeding generations of poets and critics. Among his most famous poems are "On First Looking into Chapman's Homer," "Ode to a Nightingale," and "To Autumn."

Galway Kinnell (1927–)

Galway Kinnell was born in Providence, Rhode Island. He began to seriously write poetry while attending Princeton University, and he initially set out on a career as an academic. He eventually decided against full-time teaching, however. Over the next few decades he held a variety of jobs. He became deeply interested in contemporary social issues and actively opposed the war in Vietnam. One of the most immediately striking aspects of Kinnell's poetry is its emphasis on the physical world, including its less pleasant aspects. The poet's voice has changed considerably over the years. In *The Book of Nightmares* (1971) it has a primitive, incantatory feel, whereas in the later work, *When One Has Lived a Long Time Alone* (1990), for example, it is more ruminative and conversational. Kinnell's work has been widely acclaimed, and his awards include the National Book Award and the Pulitzer Prize.

Rudyard Kipling (1865–1936)

Rudyard Kipling was born in Bombay, India. His parents were involved in the preservation of native Indian art, and Kipling grew up in an atmosphere in which artistic and literary endeavors were encouraged. His first job was as a journalist in India; during this period his poems and short stories first attracted attention in England. He traveled and lived abroad, primarily in the United States, for long periods of time but eventually made England his home, settling in Sussex. Kipling was enormously popular in his lifetime, and the height of his critical reputation came in 1907, when he received the Nobel Prize in literature. His reputation has suffered somewhat since his own time, primarily because he is seen as a proponent of outmoded colonial values. A closer examination of his verse, however, will show that he is more subtle, and perhaps less jingoistic, than his critics have claimed.

Yusef Komunyakaa (1947–)

Yusef Komunyakaa was born in Bogalusa, Louisiana, and the landscape of his native region has provided the backdrop for many of his best poems. After graduating from high school, Komunyakaa served in Vietnam, where he earned a Bronze Star for his work as an editor and reporter. After returning to the United States, he obtained his undergraduate and graduate degrees and began writing and publishing poetry. Critics have noted the skillful way in which Komunyakaa has integrated his personal experience—whether of growing up African American during the time of the civil rights struggle or of his time in Vietnam—into his poetry. He has been greatly influenced by jazz, which he has used both as the subject matter of poems and as the inspiration for the sound textures of his poems. His *Neon Vernacular: New and Selected Poems* received the Pulitzer Prize in 1994.

Ted Kooser (1939–)

Ted Kooser was born in Ames, Iowa. After receiving a degree from Iowa State University, he began teaching high school before switching to a career in insurance. While rising to prominence in the insurance field, Kooser earned his MA at Nebraska State University and began publishing poems. In the 1990s, following a bout with cancer, he left his insurance job to devote himself to writing and to teaching at the college level. Though he maintained a relatively low profile for much of his career, Kooser came to national prominence in 2004, when he was named Poet Laureate of the United States. Kooser's poems are typically brief and imagistic; they prominently feature the landscapes and inhabitants of Nebraska and the other plains states.

D. H. Lawrence (1885–1930)

D(avid) H(erbert) Lawrence was born in Eastwood, in Nottinghamshire, England. Lawrence's home life was complicated by the constant domestic tensions between his parents, and he felt out of place in Eastwood, which was a rough mining town. After attending university, Lawrence began teaching and worked at establishing a literary career. He created a scandal by eloping with Frieda Weekly, the German-born wife of one of his former professors and the person who was to have the profoundest impact on his work. During his lifetime Lawrence was best known as a novelist, although his first published works were in fact poems. Among his works were *Birds, Beasts, and Flowers,* a collection of poems, and the novels *Sons and Lovers* and *Lady Chatterley's Lover.*

Denise Levertov (1923–1997)

Denise Levertov was born in Ilford, in Essex, England. She was educated entirely at home and began writing at a very early age. In 1947, Levertov married an

American writer and moved with him to the United States, where she soon established herself as a part of the American avant-garde. In addition to her work as a college professor, Levertov was active in the antiwar and feminist movements. Levertov received widespread acclaim for her poetry, which focused on issues of social justice and spirituality. Among her honors were the Harriet Monroe Memorial Prize, the Shelley Memorial Award, and the Lannan Award. Her collections of poetry include *The Cold Spring and Other Poems* (1969), *A Door in the Hive* (1989), and *This Great Unknowing: Last Poems* (1999).

Philip Levine (1928–)

Born in Detroit, Michigan, Philip Levine was the child of Russian Jewish immigrants. After earning his BA and MA from Wayne State University, he spent time in the 1950s working at various factories, which opened his eyes to working-class issues. Levine also earned his MFA in 1957 from the University of Iowa as a way to avoid fighting in the Korean War. He has received many awards for his poetry, including the Pulitzer Prize for *The Simple Truth* (1994) and has taught and lectured at various schools in the United States, as well as abroad.

Audre Lorde (1934–1992)

Audre Lorde was born in New York City. She earned her BA from Hunter College and her MA in library science from Columbia University. She then worked for seven years as a librarian before leaving to become poet-in-residence at Tougaloo College. After her marriage in 1962, she had two children, but the marriage ended in divorce in 1970, the same year in which she directly addressed her lesbianism in poetry for the first time. She worked as a teacher, editor, and activist. Lorde identified herself as "a black feminist lesbian mother poet," and the interaction between these different roles was central to her work, which grew more overtly political with the passage of time. She received a number of important awards for her poetry, including an American Book Award from the Before Columbus Foundation, two Lambda Literary Awards, and several grants from the National Endowment for the Arts. Among her collections of poetry are *Coal* (1976), *Our Dead behind Us* (1986), and *The Collected Poems of Audre Lorde* (1997).

Robert Lowell (1917–1977)

Robert Lowell was born in Boston, Massachusetts. He attended Harvard University for two years but transferred to Kenyon University, where he studied with the poet John Crowe Ransom. Lowell was married several times, and, troubled by mental illness and alcoholism, was institutionalized on a number of occasions. He was a conscientious objector during World War II and a prominent opponent of the war in Vietnam. Lowell was without question the most prominent American poet of his generation. His work, which combined the intimately personal with the historical, constantly pushed his stylistic limits. He received a number of important awards, including two Pulitzers and a National Book Award. His collections of poetry include *Lord Weary's Castle* (1946), *For the Union Dead* (1964), and *Near the Ocean* (1967).

Thomas Lux (1946–)

Thomas Lux, born in Northampton, Massachusetts, grew up on a dairy farm. He received his BA from Emerson College and pursued graduate studies at the University of Iowa. He directs the MFA program at Sarah Lawrence College, where he has taught since 1975. Critics have noted Lux's ironic tone and his ability to combine apparently disparate images in startling but illuminating ways. He has received a number of important awards for his work, including the Kingsley Tufts Poetry Award, and has received three grants from the National Endowment for the Arts. Among his collections of poetry are *Half Promised Land* (1986), *The Drowned River: New Poems* (1990), and *New and Selected Poems, 1975–1995* (1997).

Andrew Marvell (1621–1678)

Andrew Marvell was born in Holderness, England. His father was a clergyman in the Church of England. After attending Cambridge University, he traveled for several years on the European continent. There is some question about where his loyalties lay in the English civil war, but he ended up, at least officially, on the side of the Puritans who overthrew the monarchy. Marvell worked as a civil servant and later served in Parliament, managing to avoid any punishment for his political views after the monarchy was restored. Marvell's poetry was not widely circulated during his life; only with the posthumous publication of *Miscellaneous Poems* did his work reach a wide public. Today he is regarded as one of the greatest of the metaphysical poets, and poems such as "The Garden," "An Horatian Ode," and "To His Coy Mistress" are acknowledged as classics.

Edgar Lee Masters (1868–1950)

Edgar Lee Masters was born in Garnett, Kansas, and raised in Illinois. He worked for decades as a lawyer, even as he published plays, political essays, and poetry under a pseudonym. It was the poetry collection *Spoon River Anthology,* published in 1915, that brought Masters to national and international prominence. The free-verse poems in that book, spoken by the deceased citizens of a small midwestern town, were considered revolutionary at the time, both because of the verse style itself and of the frankness with which the poems address issues of morality and sexuality. Masters never achieved another success, in either critical or popular terms, on the level of *Spoon River Anthology,* but he had an enormous influence on the direction of American poetry and helped initiate the literary flowering known as the Chicago Renaissance.

Herman Melville (1819–1891)

See page 1031 for a full biographical note on Herman Melville.

W. S. Merwin (1927–)

W(illiam) S(tanley) Merwin, the son of a Presbyterian minister, was born in New York City. After attending Princeton University, he lived and worked in Europe for several years as a tutor and translator, and translation has continued to be one of his primary occupations. He has lived for many years in Hawaii and has been an active supporter of environmental causes. Merwin has experimented relentlessly with his style, moving from tightly structured poems to looser ones in free verse and, more recently, to an approach that seems to combine the best aspects of his earlier phases. He has received numerous awards, including the Yale Series of Younger Poets prize, the Pulitzer Prize, and the Bollingen Prize. Among his books of poetry are *The Lice* (1967), *The Rain in the Trees* (1988), and *The River Sound* (1999).

Edna St. Vincent Millay (1892–1950)

Edna St. Vincent Millay was born in Rockland, Maine. Although she grew up in relative poverty, Millay was encouraged by her mother in her literary pursuits and was able to attend Vassar College. Her personal life was tumultuous: she was both physically and psychologically frail, and she had numerous affairs, some of which provided material for her poetry. The physical and mental strain were in the end too much, and she died in 1950 of a heart attack. Millay's early poetry was both popular with the public and widely praised by the critics; she had a striking ability to write lyrics that combined emotional directness with formal polish. Her poems conveyed a woman's view of love and sexuality in a way that had not been seen before in poetry in English. Though Millay's popularity began to fade even after her death, recent decades have seen a revival of interest in her work.

Czeslaw Milosz (1911–2004)

See page 1399 for a full biographical note on Czeslaw Milosz.

John Milton (1608–1674)

John Milton was born in London, England. Even when he was a young man, it was obvious that he was phenomenally gifted. In addition to his work as a writer, he was an accomplished musician and was fluent in numerous languages. Nor was he content with a life devoted to the arts. He was intensely political and active in the struggles of his day, both as the writer of political tracts and as a civil servant. His vision was weak throughout his life, and by 1652 he was completely blind, though he did not allow this to stop him writing. Of the many great poems Milton produced, he is best known for his epic *Paradise Lost,* a verse retelling of the biblical story of the Fall of Adam and Eve. Some readers, the poet William Blake, for example, have felt that the devil is the most admirable character in the poem and that Milton's sympathies were, perhaps unconsciously, with Satan. Other critics have argued that such a reading distorts the text.

Robert Morgan (1944–)

Poet and fiction writer Robert Morgan was born in Hendersonville, North Carolina. He began as a math student at University of North Carolina, Chapel Hill, but soon realized that writing was a constant need in his life. He received his MFA from UNC, Greensboro, in 1968 and soon held a teaching position at Salem College and then Cornell University. He also worked as a farmer and housepainter from 1969 to 1971 and as editor of *Epoch* magazine from 1971 to 1975. His awards include National Endowment for the Arts grants, a Guggenheim Fellowship, the North Carolina Award in Literature, and a Southern Book Critics Circle Award. Morgan's work draws on his experience of living in the mountains of North Carolina as a child. His novel *Gap Creek,* a story dealing with the impoverished but dignified lives of an Appalachian family, became a best seller in 2000.

Ogden Nash (1902–1974)

Born into a well-known and well-to-do family in Rye, New York, Ogden Nash attended Harvard University briefly before dropping out and working at a number of different jobs. It was while he was writing advertising copy that Nash's first book, *Hard Lines* (1931), was published. From that time on, Nash's career was a series of successes, including the hit Broadway musical on which he collaborated, *One Touch of Venus* (1943). Nash had a fantastically successful career as a writer of light verse, earning much popular acclaim. His rhymes were inventive and often ridiculous, his meter was deliberately stumbling, and his points were witty and occasionally biting. Today, decades after his death, lines such as "Candy is dandy/ But liquor is quicker" have become standard American aphorisms.

Sharon Olds (1942–)

Sharon Olds was born in San Francisco. She attended first Stanford and then Columbia University, where she received her PhD in 1972. She has worked as a creative writing teacher at New York University and given numerous readings of her poetry. Olds's poems are typically frank, sometimes extreme descriptions of personal situations; she deals directly with issues related to sex and the human body, for example. For this reason she is most often classed as a "confessional" poet. In part because of the accessibility of her subject matter, she has also been an exceptionally popular poet. Her first book, *Satan Says,* was the only one of her collections that was not initially released by a major publishing company.

Mary Oliver (1935–)

Mary Oliver was born in Cleveland, Ohio. She began writing poetry in her teens and was so engaged by the work of the late Edna St. Vincent Millay that she wrote to Millay's sister and received permission to visit the house where the poet had lived. She later stayed at the house and helped edit Millay's papers. Oliver attended Ohio State University and Vassar College, where she earned her BA. She wrote for more than twenty-five years before publishing her first book, since which time she has made her living as a writer and teacher of writing. She has received a number of important awards for her work, including the Christopher Award, the Natural Book Award, and the Pulitzer Prize. Among her collections of poetry are *American Primitive* (1983), *New and Selected Poems* (1992), and *Why I Wake Early* (2004).

Wilfred Owen (1893–1918)

Generally regarded as the best British poet of the World War I, Wilfred Owen was born in Oswestry, in Shropshire, England. Although World War I began in 1914, it was not until September 1915 that Owen returned to England from France, where he had been teaching. He enlisted in the army shortly thereafter; in the summer of 1916, he was sent to join the fighting in France. He was wounded and sent to recuperate in Scotland, where he began to write poetry about his war experiences. He later returned to France, where he died in combat in 1918. Owen received no critical notice during his short life, but that situation changed quickly in the years after his death. Although he wrote relatively little, most critics would agree that his best poems are extraordinarily powerful.

Dorothy Parker (1893–1967)

Born in West End, New Jersey, Dorothy Parker began her writing career at *Vogue* and eventually became a theater and book critic for *Vanity Fair* and *New Yorker*. A founding member of the Algonquin Round Table in New York, a famed literary group that met daily at the Algonquin Hotel, Parker's books of poetry *Enough Rope* (1926) and *Sunset Gun* (1928) won public popularity. She then retired from her formal magazine career to concentrate on her poetry, short stories, and screenplays. Later in her life, she lived in Hollywood, California, with her second husband, actor Alan Campbell, with whom she collaborated on many screenplays.

Linda Pastan (1932–)

Linda Pastan was born in New York City. She temporarily abandoned a promising literary career to start a family but later, with her husband's encouragement, returned to writing. The mother of four children, Pastan has made domestic life a central concern of her poetry. Pastan has been praised by critics for her ability to render that life with both accuracy and compassion. She has received numerous awards, and from 1991 to 1995 she served as the Poet Laureate of Maryland. Among her books of poetry are *The Five Stages of Grief* (1978), *Heroes in Disguise* (1991), and *The Last Uncle: Poems* (2002).

Marge Piercy (1936–)

Marge Piercy was born in Detroit, Michigan, and received degrees from the University of Michigan and Northwestern University. Piercy is a novelist as well as a poet and has alternated poetry and prose throughout her career. In the 1960s, she was active in a variety of radical political causes, but her chief loyalty then and since has been to the feminist movement. Piercy's feminist views have aroused strong reactions among critics; however, Piercy has dismissed the criticisms, and her work remains popular.

Robert Pinsky (1940–)

Robert Pinsky was born in Long Branch, New Jersey. He earned his BA from Rutgers University and his PhD from Stanford University, where he studied with the poet and critic Yvor Winters. He has taught at a number of colleges, including Wellesley College, the University of California, Berkeley, and since 1989, Boston University. From 1997 to 2000, he served as Poet Laureate of the United States. Critics have praised Pinsky for his ability to combine an openness to varied phenomena and experiences with a mastery of traditional poetic forms. He has received a number of important awards, including a Guggenheim Fellowship and the William Carlos Williams Prize. Among his collections of poetry are *An Explanation of America* (1980), *The Want Bone* (1990), and *Jersey Rain* (2000).

Sylvia Plath (1932–1963)

Sylvia Plath's life was short and troubled, but she made an enormous impact on poetry. Born in Boston, Plath showed early promise as a writer. She also suffered from mental instability, however, and within a year of graduating from college she attempted suicide for the first time. She met and married the British poet Ted Hughes, but the marriage ended in 1962. In 1963, she committed suicide. *Ariel,* her most influential collection of poems, was published after her death. Plath is often classed as a "confessional" poet because she, like a number of other writers at the time, wrote an emotionally charged poetry that seemed drawn from intense personal experiences. This label has to some extent obscured Plath's achievement, because readers often try to read the poems as spontaneous confessions rather than as the carefully crafted works they are.

Edgar Allan Poe (1809–1849)

See page 420 for a full biographical note on Edgar Allan Poe.

Ezra Pound (1885–1972)

Ezra Pound was born in Hailey, Idaho. He was a gifted child and started college at the age of sixteen. After completing his education, he relocated to London, where he quickly found himself at the heart of that city's literary life. In the 1930s, he began spending his summers in Italy, and he remained there after the outbreak of World War II. Pound, who had become both increasingly anti-Semitic and critical of capitalism, made a number of broadcasts for the Italian government during the war and was imprisoned after the fall of Italy. He escaped execution for treason only because he was found mentally unfit, and he was committed to St. Elizabeth's Hospital for just over twelve years. Pound was one of the most influential of the modernist poets and thinkers, although critics quarrel over the value of his work. Even his admirers admit that his major work, *The Cantos,* is not a complete success, and even his detractors conceded that the work has passages of great beauty.

Sir Walter Ralegh (1554–1618)

Sir Walter Ralegh was born in Hayes Barton, in Devonshire, England. He established himself early on as a man of action, fighting in several wars before coming to London, where he attached himself to the royal court. There he became a favorite of Queen Elizabeth, but his secret marriage to one of her maids-in-waiting effectively ruined his political future. He tried to prove his worth by returning to war and by making voyages of discovery, but none of this helped. When King James I came to the throne, Ralegh was accused and convicted of treason and locked in the Tower of London. He made use of his time there by working on a massive history of the world until his execution thirteen years later. Today, poems such as "The Lie" and "The Nymph's Reply to the Shepherd" are recognized as classics.

Dudley Randall (1914–2000)

Dudley Randall was born in Washington, D.C. Although he began reading and writing poetry at a young age, he was not able to attend college immediately after graduating from high school, so he worked at a variety of jobs and served time in the army before continuing his education. After receiving his degree, Randall became involved in the cultural life of Detroit, where he was then living. As an African American, he was especially drawn in the 1960s to Boone House, a center of black artistic endeavors in the city. In 1966, Randall founded Broadside Press, which would publish not only his work but also the work of a number of other important African American poets. His first collection of poems, a collaboration with fellow poet Margaret Danner called *Poem Counterpoem,* appeared in 1966, followed two years later by *Cities Burning.* It was the 1971 publication of *More to Remember: Poems of Four Decades,* however, that established Randall's reputation.

Adrienne Rich (1921–)

Born in Baltimore, Maryland, Adrienne Rich is perhaps the most prominent feminist poet writing in English in the latter half of the twentieth century. She received the Yale Series of Younger Poets prize for her first book, *A Change of World,* in 1951, the same year she graduated from Radcliff College. She married in 1952 and over the next eight years had three sons. Rich and her husband separated in 1969, and having already declared herself a radical feminist, she came out as a lesbian in 1976. Rich moved gradually from rhymed, strictly metered poems to free verse, a development that paralleled her increased inclusion of personal material. Among her most influential collections are *Diving into the Wreck* (1973) and *The Dream of a Common Language* (1978).

Rainer Maria Rilke (1875–1926)

Rainer Maria Rilke was born in Prague, which was then part of the Austro-Hungarian Empire. His parents divorced while he was still young, and he was sent to military academies before he eventually moved to Munich and began his career as a writer. The son of a dominating, status-conscious mother who also encouraged his literary ambitions, Rilke was profoundly influenced, personally and artistically, by his relationships with women who served as both muses and teachers and by the friendships he formed with fellow artists. His best-known and most-admired works are the *Duino Elegies* and the *Sonnets to Orpheus,* arguably two of the most influential books of poetry, in any language, of the twentieth century. In these, as in his other works, Rilke meditates on the relationship between art and the world and on the ability of art to transcend suffering and decay.

Edwin Arlington Robinson (1869–1935)

It may be difficult for readers today to imagine the level of Edwin Arlington Robinson's popularity as a poet in his own time. This success did not come overnight, however. Born in Head Tide, Maine, Robinson had already begun to write verse before attending Harvard University. He was unable to interest publishers in his first two volumes of poetry, however, so was forced to publish them himself. His fortunes changed considerably when President Theodore Roosevelt's son gave his father a copy of Robinson's second book, *The Children of the Night*. The president not only enjoyed the book but wrote a review of it himself, and the poet became immediately popular. Robinson received three Pulitzer Prizes during his life.

Theodore Roethke (1908–1963)

Theodore Roethke was born in Saginaw, Michigan. His family owned and ran a greenhouse, and his early exposure to the world of plants and growing things had a profound effect on his poetry. He was emotionally troubled even as a child, and his condition became worse with age, leading to his hospitalization on numerous occasions. His marriage in 1953 and his success as a poet brought him some measure of happiness, but he died of a heart attack in 1963 when he was fifty-five years old. Roethke enjoyed considerable critical success; even those who faulted his first book, *Open House,* for being too derivative, acknowledged his talent. The reception of the works that followed was even more positive, and he received numerous awards, including the Pulitzer Prize for *The Waking* (1954).

Christina Rossetti (1830–1894)

Christina Rossetti was born in London, England. Her father was an emigrant from Italy who became a professor of Italian language and literature. All of the children in her family made substantial contributions to the arts, particularly her brother, Dante Gabriel, one of the most prominent poets of the time. She shared his gift and produced numerous works of poetry and prose during the course of her lifetime. By the time of her death, Christina Rossetti was the most respected female poet in the English-speaking world. Her critical reputation faded some-what after her death, but she remained popular, and the rise of feminist criticism led to a revival of critical interest in her work. She is noted in particular for the lyricism of her work, much of which is concerned with spiritual matters. A number of her poems were made into hymns and continue to be sung today.

Muriel Rukeyser (1913–1980)

Muriel Rukeyser was born in New York City. She attended Vassar College, where she helped found and co-edit a literary magazine. From a very early age she was involved in politics and protest, and the issues in which she took an interest—the Spanish civil war, the civil rights movement, the war in Vietnam—appear frequently in her poetry. In addition to her work as an activist, she was a teacher and translator, and she wrote in genres as varied as screenwriting and children's literature. She received a number of important awards, including the Yale Series of Younger Poets prize, the Levinson Prize for Poetry, and the Shelley Memorial Award. Among her books of poetry are *Theory of Flight* (1935), *Elegies* (1949), and *The Collected Poems of Muriel Rukeyser* (1978).

Mary Jo Salter (1954–)

Mary Jo Salter was born in Grand Rapids, Michigan. She received her BA from Harvard University, where she met her future husband, the poet and novelist Brad Leithauser, and her MA from Cambridge University in England. Salter has traveled widely with her family, spending three years in Japan and briefer periods in France, Italy, and Iceland. Since 1984, she has taught at Mount Holyoke College. In addition to noting her technical proficiency, critics have also praised her eye for detail. She has received a number of important awards, including the Lamont Poetry Prize, the Witter Bynner Foundation Poetry Prize, and the Peter I. B. Lavin Award. Among her collections of poetry are *Henry Purcell in Japan* (1985), *Sunday Skaters* (1994), and *Open Shutters* (2003).

Carl Sandburg (1878–1967)

Carl Sandburg was born in Galesburg, Illinois. His parents were Swedish immigrants, so he grew up speaking both Swedish and English. When he was thirteen years old, he left school to support his family. In his late teens and early twenties he traveled widely, sometimes by stowing away on a freight train. He worked as a journalist while composing the poems that went into his first book. As he became well known, he took the opportunity to devote himself to projects close to his heart, including a collection of American folk songs and a biography of Abraham Lincoln. Sandburg received a number of important awards, including the Levinson Poetry Prize, the Poetry Society of America Gold Medal for Poetry, and the Pulitzer Prize.

Siegfried Sassoon (1886–1967)

Siegfried Sassoon was born in Kent, England. His father, who died when he was nine, was a wealthy businessman of Spanish and Jewish descent; his mother was a member of a prominent English family. Sassoon attended Cambridge University, where he began to publish poetry, but he lost interest in his studies and left after two years. He was wounded in World War I; while recuperating in England, he became convinced that the war should be ended. This did not stop him from returning to combat, however, where he was again wounded and sent home. He was a prominent man of letters—producing poetry, memoirs, and fiction—for the remainder of his life. Though Sassoon lived into his eighties, he is best remembered for the poems he wrote during and immediately after his military.

Anne Sexton (1928–1974)

Anne Sexton was born Anne Gray Harvey in Newton, Massachusetts. She first began to write poetry seriously while in psychotherapy. Many of her poems record her struggles with mental illness and her stays in various institutions. Writing provided an outlet, but neither it nor her increasing fame was able to cure Sexton's mental illness. She committed suicide in 1974. Sexton's work was always controversial and remains so to some degree. Where some critics saw courageous honesty, others saw self-pity and self-indulgence. Despite this controversy, Sexton received some of the most important awards in American Literature, including the Pulitzer Prize in 1966 for *Live or Die* and the Poetry Society of America's Shelley Memorial Award in 1967.

William Shakespeare (1564–1616)

See page 340 for a full biographical note on William Shakespeare.

Percy Bysshe Shelley (1792–1822)

Percy Bysshe Shelley was one of the most colorful figures of his very colorful generation of poets. Expelled from Oxford University for co-authoring a pamphlet titled "A Defense of Atheism," he eloped with his sixteen-year-old cousin, Harriette. The marriage soon bored Shelley, however, and he eloped with Mary Godwin, who, writing as Mary Shelley, was to author the novel *Frankenstein*. The couple moved to Italy, where in 1822, Shelley drowned at the age of twenty-nine. Shelley's poetry was almost universally condemned during his lifetime, much of it being regarded as immoral, incomprehensible, or both. Today it is generally agreed, however, that Shelley was one of the major figures of the Romantic period.

Charles Simic (1938–)

Poet, translator, and prose writer Charles Simic was born in Belgrade, Yugoslavia. Bombings from World War II forced his family to escape their house multiple times. Until he was fifteen, Simic lived in Belgrade, where he was regarded as a sub par student with bad behavior. His family then moved to Paris for a year, where he learned English in school, then moved to Chicago. At this point, with the support of his teachers and other involved students, Simic began to excel in literature, particularly poetry. His poems began to appear in journals when he was twenty-one. His poems have gained recognition for their strange, comedic, and terrifying unraveling of the physical world and history in central Europe. Among his many awards are the 1990 Pulitzer Prize and a "genius grant" from the MacArthur Foundation.

Gary Soto (1952–)

Gary Soto was born in Fresno, California. Soto's parents were both Mexican immigrants, so he grew up speaking Spanish in his home and neighborhood. His experience of poverty while growing up has profoundly influenced both his literary and political pursuits. After teaching college for a number of years, Soto quit to work as a freelance writer. In addition to poetry, he has written fiction and essays, as well as works for children and young adults. Among Soto's collections of poetry are *The Elements of San Joaquin* (1977), *Where Sparrows Work Hard* (1981), and *New and Selected Poems* (1995). His many awards include the Discovery/Nation Award, the Carnegie Medal, and the Tomás Rivera Prize.

Edmund Spenser (1552–1599)

Edmund Spenser was born in London, England. He attended Cambridge University, where he excelled in his studies, then began a career as a private secretary and administrator, primarily in Ireland. In 1591, Queen Elizabeth awarded Spenser an annual sum of fifty pounds as thanks for his epic poem *The Faerie Queene,* which he had dedicated to her. Spenser is universally acknowledged as one of the great writers in the history of English literature. His best-known work is undoubtedly *The Faerie Queene,* but his other work, including "Epithalamion" and "Prothalamion," is highly regarded. His sonnet sequence, *Amoretti*, contains numerous poems that have become both popular and critical favorites, among them "One day I wrote her name upon the sand."

William Stafford (1914–1993)

William Stafford was born in Hutchinson, Kansas. He refused to serve in World War II for religious reasons, and he spent much of the war living in work camps in the western states. He earned his PhD at the University of Iowa and spent the rest of his working life teaching, primarily at Lewis and Clark College in Oregon. Stafford's poetry is most often set in the American West, and his work has been widely acclaimed for its descriptions of the natural world and for its understated power, evident in such poems as "Traveling through the Dark" and "At the Bomb Testing Sight."

Wallace Stevens (1879–1955)

Wallace Stevens was born in Reading, Pennsylvania. After leaving Harvard University, where he had established a reputation for literary talent, Stevens moved to New York City to work as a journalist. He then attended law school, after which he worked for various law firms before entering the insurance business. Stevens's very successful career in business did not mean the end of his writing, however, and he went on to become one of the most important American poets of the twentieth century. Stevens's literary reputation developed only slowly, but this was due less to the pressures of business and family life than to the lack of understanding he initially faced from critics. In later years he received a number of poetry's most important prizes, culminating with the Pulitzer Prize for *Collected Poems* (1955).

Wislawa Szymborska (1923–)

The poet and critic Wislawa Szymborska was born in Prowent-Bnin, Poland. She studied at Jagellonian University from 1945 to 1948 and worked as poetry editor and writer for *Zycie literackie,* a weekly literary journal. By the 1990s, many of her collections were being translated into English, such as *People on a Bridge* (1990), *View with a Grain of Sand* (1995), and *Nonrequired Reading: Prose Pieces* (2002). She received international recognition in 1996 when she was awarded the Nobel Prize in literature. Critics praise her concise language and the irony and wisdom she achieves in addressing the largest subjects. Skeptical of absolutes and simplifications, she confronts them with her knowledge of philosophy, literature, history, and humanity. Her writing has been translated into Arabic, Hebrew, Japanese, and Chinese, among other languages.

Allen Tate (1899–1979)

Allen Tate was born in Winchester, Kentucky. While attending Vanderbilt University, Tate became associated with a number of other writers, including John Crowe Ransom, Donald Davidson, and Robert Penn Warren, known collectively as the "Fugitives," a name derived from *The Fugitive*, a literary magazine that they published. This group was concerned with asserting a Southern literature, and indeed a Southern philosophy of life. Throughout his life Tate remained concerned with the American South: his best-known poem is "Ode to the Confederate Dead," and he wrote a number of biographies of Southern political and military figures. In addition to his other work, he was a prolific and influential literary critic. In 1950, after years of religious struggles, he converted to

Roman Catholicism. By the time of his death he had established himself as one of the most prominent men of letters in the United States.

Alfred, Lord Tennyson (1809–1892)

Alfred Tennyson was born in Somersby, in Lincolnshire, England. His family was large, and his father and most of his siblings were troubled by mental instability. His first book of poems was published when he was only eighteen. While attending university, he formed a deep friendship—probably the closest of his life—with Arthur Hallam, another undergraduate poet. Hallam died unexpectedly in 1833, and the loss, combined with the critical failure of Tennyson's most recent book, was catastrophic for the poet. His next volume, *Poems* (1842), revived his career and drew almost universal praise. For the rest of his life, Tennyson enjoyed a growing audience and critical respect. His popularity was confirmed in 1850 when he published *In Memoriam,* a book of elegies dedicated to Hallam. Soon after, he was made Poet Laureate of Great Britain; and in 1883, he was made a member of the House of Lords.

Dylan Thomas (1914–1953)

Dylan Thomas was born in Swansea, Wales. He began writing poetry at an early age, and some of the poems he composed in his teens are among his best-known work. Thomas quickly became one of the more popular poets of his day; however, he drank heavily and had numerous extramarital affairs, especially during his tours of the United States. Complications related to alcoholism led to his early death in 1953.

Quincy Troupe (1943–)

Quincy Troupe was born in New York City. He briefly attended Grambling College but after suffering racial discrimination dropped out to enlist in the army. While in the army, in the period following a knee injury, Troupe first began to write. After his discharge, he moved to California, where he continues to live and work. In his poetry, academic works, and scripts he has focused on the experience of African Americans, especially on the work of jazz greats such as Miles Davis, John Coltrane, and Thelonius Monk. Among his many books of poetry is *Trans-circularities: New and Selected Poems.* In 2002, he was appointed the first Poet Laureate of California but was soon forced to resign after the discovery that he had falsely claimed to have earned a bachelor's degree from Grambling College.

Derek Walcott (1930–)

Derek Walcott was born on the Island of St. Lucia, in the West Indies. After attending University College of the West Indies, he began a career as a teacher and freelance writer. He has also taught in the United States. He currently divides his time between St. Lucia and Boston, where he teaches at Boston University. Walcott has been widely praised for his technical mastery and for the energy with which his language is charged. His work often deals with the struggles of former colonial peoples to make sense of their divided heritage. He has received many awards, including the New Statesman Award, The Royal Society of Literature Award, and the Nobel Prize in literature. His many volumes of poetry include *Another Life* (1973), *The Fortunate Traveler* (1982), and *Omeros* (1989). He is also a highly regarded playwright and essayist.

Phillis Wheatley (1753–1784)

Phillis Wheatley was born in West Africa. She was captured by slave traders when she was approximately seven years old. Because she was judged to be physically unfit for plantation work, she was sent to Boston, where the Wheatley family purchased her as a domestic servant. The family taught her to read and write, and she soon mastered English, Greek, and Latin. She published her first book by the time she was eighteen, and she met and corresponded with a number of the most prominent figures of her time. After the members of the Wheatley family died, she was left to poverty and obscurity. Her marriage failed to provide security or comfort, and two of her children died. The third died soon after Wheatley's death. Recent years have brought a renewed interest in her work and a better understanding of its merits, as well as a keener appreciation of the complex, difficult society in which she was compelled to live.

Walt Whitman (1819–1892)

Walt Whitman is often regarded as the most "American" of poets, because both his subject matter and his verse style were shaped by his views of his country and its potential. Born on Long Island, New York, Whitman became first a printer, then a teacher, a journalist, and finally an editor. In 1855, he published *Leaves of Grass,* the book of poems that he would revise and add to for the rest of his life. One of the few critics who was enthusiastic about his poems was the famous poet and critic Ralph Waldo Emerson, who wrote to Whitman, predicting he would have a brilliant career. Although Whitman's reputation grew steadily during his own lifetime and after, not until the mid-twentieth century did he became recognized as one of America's greatest poets.

Richard Wilbur (1921–)

Richard Wilbur was born in New York City. He attended Amherst College, where he edited the school's newspaper and contributed poems to its literary magazine. World War II was under way when he graduated from college. Shortly after his marriage in 1942, Wilbur was sent to Europe, where he saw combat in a number of countries. After returning to the United States, he received his master's degree from Harvard University and published his first book, *The Beautiful Changes and Other Poems.* Wilbur has gone on to become one of the most honored poets of his, or any other, generation. He has received the Pulitzer Prize twice, for *Things of This World* (1957) and *New and Collected Poems* (1989); in 1983, he was named the second Poet Laureate of the United States. He is also a noted translator.

Oscar Wilde (1854–1900)

Oscar Wilde was born in Dublin, Ireland. Both of Wilde's parents wrote, and his mother in particular encouraged him in his literary pursuits. He also learned from his mother the importance of making a stand and of drawing attention through flamboyant clothing. A precocious child, Wilde went on to prove himself a gifted student and had established himself as a poet before graduating from Oxford. Wilde was an aesthete, a spokesman for the idea of "art for art's sake." At the same time, however, he was dedicated to a number of radical or progressive causes. His career as a poet, essayist, lecturer, and playwright was cut short when he was tried and imprisoned on charges related to his homosexuality. The scandal ruined him, and he died in Paris in 1900 at a young age. Of his many works, he is best known for his satirical play *The Importance of Being Ernest.*

Miller Williams (1930–)

Poet, editor, and translator Miller Williams was born in Hoxie, Arkansas. He earned his MS in biology and served as an educator before working in sales and private industry, but the poets John Ciardi and Howard Nemerov encouraged him to teach at Louisiana State University. He began teaching there in 1962. Williams received positive reviews and a number of awards for the books he published over the next several decades. However, he first gained popular recognition when President Bill Clinton appointed him to read "Of History and Hope" at his inauguration. Subsequently, Clinton gave him the National Arts Award for his lifetime achievements as a writer. In 1999, Williams published another collection, *Some Jazz a While*, which reaffirmed his prominence as an articulate and intelligent formal poet with a musical ear for language.

William Carlos Williams (1883–1963)

William Carlos Williams was born and died in Rutherford, New Jersey. The sense of attachment to the local and particular that this implies is one of the main ingredients in Williams's poetry. Another important factor was his long career as a physician, which he carried on alongside his literary work and which gave him a keen insight into everyday sufferings and difficulties. Williams's impact on American poetry was revolutionary. He abandoned metrical verse for free verse, which he felt was better able to express American experiences in a distinctively American voice. By the time of his death he had received many of the available literary awards and honors, including the Pulitzer Prize, for *Pictures from Brueghel,* his last volume.

William Wordsworth (1770–1850)

Born in West Cumberland, just north of England's Lake District, William Wordsworth sought to attend to what he saw as common speech and common subjects. He felt poetry needed to turn away from ornamental language and artificial forms. He sought power and inspiration from the natural world. A gifted student, Wordsworth was expected to distinguish himself at Cambridge University, but his interests lay elsewhere—in travel, in radical politics, and above all, in poetry. Although a number of fellow poets appreciated and even idolized him, it took years for him to gain widespread popularity. Since his death in 1850, Wordsworth's reputation has only grown. He is remembered today for poems such as "The World Is Too Much with Us," "Resolution and Independence," and "Lines Composed a Few Miles above Tintern Abbey."

William Butler Yeats (1865–1939)

William Butler Yeats is one of the greatest English-language poets in the history of Ireland, and indeed one of the greatest poets of the twentieth century. Born in Dublin, Ireland, he grew up with a love of art and poetry inherited from his father. Yeats was deeply interested in spirituality and occultism, and this interest informed much of his poetry. His interests were not entirely otherworldly, however; he was involved in the political movement to secure political independence for his country, and after the Republic of Ireland was established, he served as a member of the Irish senate. It is difficult to overestimate Yeats's influence. During his lifetime he was perhaps the most-honored poet in the world, receiving the Nobel Prize in literature in 1923. Even after his death in 1939 his work continued to inspire poets both in Ireland and beyond, with poems such as

"Leda and the Swan" and "The Second Coming" regarded as masterpieces of world literature.

Kevin Young (1970–)

Kevin Young was born in Lincoln, Nebraska. He earned his BA from Harvard University, where he studied with Seamus Heaney, and his MFA from Brown University. His poetry examines issues of race and identity and often does so by incorporating references to, and devices borrowed from, the African American musical traditions of jazz and blues. Young is currently Ruth Lilly Professor of Poetry at Indiana University. Among his collections of poetry are *Jelly Roll: A Blues* and *To Repel Ghosts: The Remix*.

Appendix C

ALTERNATE CONTENTS BY GENRE

FICTION AND PROSE

SCENE, EPISODE, AND PLOT
Stephen Crane, An Episode of War   8
Jamaica Kincaid, Girl   16
Arthur Conan Doyle, A Scandal in Bohemia   20
Don Lee, The Price of Eggs in China   39

CHARACTER
Michael Chabon, from *The Amazing Adventures of Kavalier & Clay*   117
Alice Munro, How I Met My Husband   134
Luigi Pirandello, The Soft Touch of Grass   148
Alice Walker, Everyday Use   152

THEME
Charles Perrault, Little Red Riding Hood   198
James Thurber, The Girl and the Wolf   201
Maxine Hong Kingston, The Wild Man of the Green Swamp   205
Luisa Valenzuela, The Censors   214
Flannery O'Connor, A Good Man Is Hard to Find   217

POINT OF VIEW
Charles Dickens, from *A Christmas Carol*   288
Ernest Hemingway, from *Hills Like White Elephants*   289
Ann Beattie, Janus   306
Kate Chopin, The Story of an Hour   311
Charlotte Perkins Gilman, The Yellow Wallpaper   314

SETTING
Theodore Dreiser, from *Sister Carrie*   403
Kazuo Ishiguro, from *Remains of the Day*   405
James Joyce, Araby   415
Edgar Allan Poe, The Fall of the House of Usher   420

RHYTHM, PACE, and RHYME
James Baldwin, Sonny's Blues   527
Ursula K. Le Guin, The Ones Who Walk Away from Omelas   553
Susan Minot, Lust   559

IMAGES
Salman Rushdie, On Leavened Bread   637
Alice Munro, Boys and Girls   659
Haruki Murakami, UFO in Kushiro   671

COHERENCE
Nick Hornby, from High Fidelity   713
Charles W. Chesnutt, The Wife of His Youth   733
John Updike, A&P   742
Jonathan Safran Foer, The Very Rigid Search   748

INTERRUPTION
Douglas Adams, from The Hitchhiker's Guide to the Galaxy   790
Jorge Luis Borges, The Garden of Forking Paths   806
Joseph Conrad, Secret Sharer   814
Eudora Welty, A Worn Path   847
Raymond Carver, Cathedral   854

TONE
Zora Neale Hurston, from Mules and Men   1013
Chinua Achebe, Dead Men's Path   1016
Katherine Mansfield, A Dill Pickle   1025
Herman Melville, Bartleby, the Scrivener   1031

WORD CHOICE
Lewis Shiner, from The Turkey City Lexicon: A Primer
   for Science Fiction Workshops   1093
Raymond Carver, What We Talk about When We Talk about Love   1098
Edith Wharton, Roman Fever   1108

ALLEGORY
Gertrude Crampton, from Tootle   1195
Aesop, The Crow and the Pitcher   1198
Plato, The Allegory of the Cave   1204
João Guimarães Rosa, The Third Bank of the River   1209
Nathaniel Hawthorne, Young Goodman Brown   1216

SYMBOLISM
Nathaniel Hawthorne, from Young Goodman Brown   1263
Gabriel García Márquez, A Very Old Man with Enormous Wings   1269
Gabriel García Márquez, The Handsomest Drowned Man in the World   1275
Jhumpa Lahiri, This Blessed House   1279
Shirley Jackson, The Lottery   1293

CONTEXT
Ernest Hemingway, Soldier's Home 1412
Tim O'Brien, The Things They Carried 1419
Tillie Olsen, I Stand Here Ironing 1434

ALLUSIONS
Joyce Carol Oates, Where Are You Going, Where Have You Been? 1498
William Faulkner, A Rose for Emily 1512

GENRE
Mrs. J. Riddell, from *Nut Bush Farm* 1585
Katherine Anne Porter, The Jilting of Granny Weatherall 1601
Margaret Atwood, Happy Endings 1609

THE PRODUCTION AND REPRODUCTION OF TEXTS
from *Major Writers of America* 1683
from *Heath Anthology of American Literature* 1684
Mark Twain, from *Huckleberry Finn* 1688
from *Lost in Translation* 1690

AN ORIENTATION TO RESEARCH
Plutarch, from *Lives of the Noble Grecians and Romans* 1706

POETRY

SCENE, EPISODE, AND PLOT
Robert Pinsky, Poem with Lines in Any Order 4
Wislawa Szymborska, ABC 5
Marge Piercy, Unlearning to not speak 15
Emily Dickinson, [A Route of Evanescence] 59
Emily Dickinson, [I like to see it lap the Miles—] 60
E. A. Robinson, Richard Cory 60
Robert Frost, Stopping by Woods on a Snowy Evening 61
William Stafford, Traveling through the Dark 62
Kevin Young, The Set-Up 62
Kevin Young, The Chase 64
Aron Keesbury, On the Robbery Across the Street 65
Muriel Rukeyser, Myth 66

CHARACTER
Rita Dove, Hattie McDaniel Arrives at the Coconut Grove 124
Cathy Song, Picture Bride 127
Robert Hayden, Those Winter Sundays 128
Judith Ortiz Cofer, My Father in the Navy: A Childhood Memory 130

Edgar Lee Masters, Elsa Wertman   160
Edgar Lee Masters, Hamilton Greene   161
Robert Frost, Home Burial   161
Audre Lorde, Now That I Am Forever with Child   165
Eavan Boland, The Pomegranate   165
Sylvia Plath, Daddy   167
Quincy Troupe, Poem for My Father   170
Kitty Tsui, A Chinese Banquet   171
Billy Collins, Lanyard   173
E. A. Robinson, The Mill   174
Liz Rosenberg, 1:53 A.M.   175
Gwendolyn Brooks, Sadie and Maud   176
Seamus Heaney, Mid-Term Break   176
Michael Lassell, How to Watch Your Brother Die   177
Adrienne Rich, Aunt Jennifer's Tigers   180
Gary Soto, Black Hair   181

THEME
Marge Piercy, A Work of Artifice   203
John Keats, La Belle Dame sans Merci: A Ballad   230
Edna St. Vincent Millay, [Women have loved before as I love now]   232
Elizabeth Bishop, Casabianca   232
Ted Hughes, Lovesong   233
Carolyn Forché, The Colonel   234
William Butler Yeats, Leda and the Swan   235
D. H. Lawrence, Snake   236
Richard Wilbur, A Fable   238
Linda Pastan, Ethics   239

POINT OF VIEW
Dorothy Parker, Penelope   285
Wendell Berry, The Vacation   291
Henry Taylor, After a Movie   295
Stevie Smith, Not Waving but Drowning   299
Philip Levine, Photography 2   300
Frank X. Gaspar, It Is the Nature of the Wing   302
Robert Browning, My Last Duchess   303
Helane Levine Keating, My Last Duke   327
William Carlos Williams, This Is Just to Say   328
Erica-Lynn Gambino, This Is Just to Say   329
Elizabeth Bishop, The Fish   330
Edna St. Vincent Millay, Childhood Is the Kingdom Where Nobody Dies   332
Charles Simic, Prodigy   333
John Donne, The Good-Morrow   334
Adrienne Rich, Living in Sin   335
W. S. Merwin, Separation   336
H. D., Helen   336

Sylvia Plath, The Applicant   337
Sylvia Plath, Mirror   338
Robert Morgan, Working in the Rain   339

SETTING
Denise Levertov, February Evening in New York   420
Samuel Taylor Coleridge, Kubla Khan: Or, a Vision in a Dream   436
Edgar Allan Poe, The Raven   437
Christina Rossetti, Cobwebs   440
Oscar Wilde, The Harlot's House   441
Dudley Randall, Ballad of Birmingham   442
Joy Harjo, New Orleans   444
Joy Harjo, The Woman Hanging from the Thirteenth Floor Window   446
Gary Soto, Braly Street   448
Gary Soto, Kearney Park   450
Ginger Andrews, Rolls-Royce Dreams   451
Barbara Ras, Childhood   452
Chitra Banerjee Divakaruni, Indian Movie, New Jersey   453
B. H. Fairchild, The *Dumka*   454

RHYTHM, PACE, and RHYME
Herman Melville, The Maldive Shark   514
William Blake, The Nurse's Song   514
Samuel Johnson, On the Death of Dr. Robert Levet   518
Ben Jonson, On My First Son   520
Alexander Pope, from *An Essay on Criticism*   522
Alfred, Lord Tennyson, The Lotus Eaters   522
Randall Jarrell, The Death of the Ball Turret Gunner   523
Robert Frost, Fire and Ice   524
William Blake, The Chimney Sweeper (Innocence)   568
William Blake, Holy Thursday (Innocence)   569
William Blake, The Tyger   569
William Blake, The Chimney Sweeper (Experience)   570
William Blake, Holy Thursday (Experience)   570
Theodore Roethke, My Papa's Waltz   571
Theodore Roethke, The Waking   572
Langston Hughes, Dream Boogie   573
Langston Hughes, The Negro Speaks of Rivers   573
Gwendolyn Brooks, We Real Cool   574
Countee Cullen, Incident   575
Denise Levertov, In Mind   575
Sharon Olds, I Go Back to May 1937   576
Sharon Olds, The Death of Marilyn Monroe   577

IMAGES
William Carlos Williams, The Red Wheelbarrow   631
Czeslaw Milosz, Watering Can   632

Wislawa Szymborska, Courtesy of the Blind   634
John Milton, from *Paradise Lost*   640
Richard Wilbur, A Fire-Truck   643
Michael Ondaatje, King Kong Meets Wallace Stevens   645
Yosa Buson, Hokku Poems in Four Seasons   648
T. S. Eliot, The Love Song of J. Alfred Prufrock   653
William Blake, London   684
William Wordsworth, London, 1802   684
William Wordsworth, Composed upon Westminster Bridge,
    September, 1802   685
William Wordsworth, The World Is Too Much with Us   686
William Wordsworth, [I wandered lonely as a cloud]   686
Emily Dickinson, [There's a certain Slant of light]   687
Robert Frost, Birches   688
Robert Frost, Acquainted with the Night   689
Ezra Pound, In a Station of the Metro   690
Wallace Stevens, The Snow Man   690
Wallace Stevens, Thirteen Ways of Looking at a Blackbird   691
e. e. cummings, in Just-   693
Maya Angelou, Harlem Hopscotch   694
Richard Wilbur, April 5, 1974   695
Mary Oliver, Spring   695
Mary Oliver, Ghosts   697
Derek Walcott, Dry Season   699

COHERENCE
George Herbert, Easter Wings   716
Thomas Hardy, The Convergence of the Twain   717
William Wordsworth, Nuns Fret Not   722
Edna St. Vincent Millay, I, Being Born a Woman and Distressed   722
Robert Frost, Design   723
Dylan Thomas, Do Not Go Gentle into That Good Night   724
Philip Levine, The Simple Truth   726
William Cullen Bryant, To Cole, the Painter, Departing for Europe   769
Joe Kane, The Boy Who Nearly Won the Texaco Art Competition   769
Elizabeth Bishop, Manners For a Child of 1918   770
Phillis Wheatley, On Being Brought from Africa to America   771
Robert Frost, The Road Not Taken   772
Thomas Lux, The Swimming Pool   773
Lawrence Ferlinghetti, Constantly risking absurdity   774
Allen Ginsberg, Supermarket in California   775
Richard Wilbur, A Sketch   776
Miller Williams, Thinking about Bill, Dead of AIDS   777

INTERRUPTION
William Butler Yeats, The Folly of Being Comforted   792
Mary Oliver, Bone Poem   793

Ted Kooser, Tattoo   798
Elizabeth Bishop, Brazil, January, 1502   867
Louise Bogan, Cartography   868
Sharon Olds, Topography   869
Langston Hughes, Theme for English B   870
Laura Riding, The Map of Places   871
Richard Wilbur, Worlds   871
Samuel Taylor Coleridge, The Rime of the Ancient Mariner   872
Alfred, Lord Tennyson, Ulysses   890
Emily Dickinson, [The Brain—is wider than the Sky—]   892
Emily Dickinson, [I never saw a Moor—]   893
Emily Dickinson, [Tell all the Truth but tell it slant—]   893
Emily Dickinson, [To make a prairie it takes a clover and one bee]   893
John Donne, The Sun Rising   894
John Donne, A Valediction: Forbidding Mourning   895

TONE
Margaret Atwood, you fit into me   1007
Dorothy Parker, One Perfect Rose   1008
Dorothy Parker, Thought for a Sunshiny Morning   1009
John Donne, The Flea   1009
Ted Kooser, A Letter from Aunt Belle   1011
Margaret Atwood, Siren Song   1015
Czeslaw Milosz, If There Is No God   1019
Billy Collins, I Chop Some Parsley While Listening to Art
    Blakey's Version of "Three Blind Mice"   1060
W. H. Auden, Musée des Beaux Arts   1062
Elizabeth Bishop, One Art   1062
Quincy Troupe, Untitled   1063
Sherman Alexie, Defending Walt Whitman   1064
Ted Kooser, A Hairnet with Stars   1066
Yusef Komunyakaa, A Break from the Bush   1067
Lisel Mueller, Not Only the Eskimos   1068

WORD CHOICE
Erasmus, from *De Duplici Copia Verborum et Rerum*   1078
William Shakespeare, From fairest creatures we desire increase   1084
William Shakespeare, When forty winters shall beseige thy brow   1085
William Shakespeare, Look in thy glass, and tell the face thou viewest   1086
William Shakespeare, Lo! in the orient when the gracious light   1086
William Shakespeare, Music to hear, why hear'st thou music sadly?   1087
William Shakespeare, Is it for fear to wet a widow's eye   1087
William Shakespeare, Shall I compare thee to a summer's day?   1088
Billy Collins, Thesaurus   1089
Robert Sward, For Gloria on Her 60th Birthday, or Looking for Love in
    Merriam-Webster   1092
Anonymous, My Love in Her Attire   1119

John Donne, Elegy 19: To His Mistress Going to Bed   1119
John Fletcher, [Take, oh take those lips away]   1121
Anonymous, Western Wind   1121
Henry Howard, Earl of Surrey, [Love, that doth reign within my thought]   1122
Thomas Wyatt, [The long love that in my heart doth harbor]   1122
e. e. cummings, spring is like a perhaps hand   1123
e. e. cummings, since feeling is first   1124
Emily Dickinson, [Wild Nights—Wild Nights!]   1124
Galway Kinnell, Shelley   1125
Robert Burns, A Red, Red Rose   1126
Edna St. Vincent Millay, What Lips My Lips Have Kissed   1127
Denise Levertov, The Ache of Marriage   1127
Denise Levertov, Divorcing   1128
Christopher Marlowe, The Passionate Shepherd to His Love   1128
Sir Walter Ralegh, The Nymph's Reply to the Shepherd   1129
Andrew Marvell, To His Coy Mistress   1130
Elizabeth Barrett Browning, [How do I love thee? Let me count the ways.]   1131
Elizabeth Barrett Browning, [When our two souls stand up]   1132
Robert Browning, Meeting at Night   1132
Robert Browning, Parting at Morning   1133

ALLEGORY
Emily Dickinson, [Eden is that old-fashioned House]   1199
Billy Collins, The Death of Allegory   1202
Lewis Carroll, Jabberwocky   1227
Edmund Spenser, from *The Faerie Queene*   1228
Richard Corbett, The Fairies Farewell   1231
Robert Browning, Porphyria's Lover   1233
John Donne, Batter My Heart, Three-Personed God   1235
John Donne, The Canonization   1235
John Donne, Death, Be Not Proud   1237
Emily Dickinson, [Because I could not stop for Death—]   1237
Gerard Manley Hopkins, Pied Beauty   1238
Gerard Manley Hopkins, The Windhover   1239
Ogden Nash, Kind of an Ode to Duty   1239
Amiri Baraka, In Memory of Radio   1240
Anne Carson, TV Men: Lazarus   1242

SYMBOLISM
Mary Jo Salter, Home Movies: A Sort of Ode   1256
Gary Soto, Oranges   1261
Matthew Arnold, Dover Beach   1301
Jimmy Santiago Baca, Green Chile   1302
e. e. cummings, [anyone lived in a pretty how town]   1304
Emily Dickinson, [The Soul selects her own Society—]   1305

Seamus Heaney, Valediction   1305
Peter Meinke, Sunday at the Apple Market   1306
Sharon Olds, The Possessive   1307
Alice Walker, Women   1307
Walt Whitman, There Was a Child Went Forth   1308
William Carlos Williams, At the Ball Game   1310
William Butler Yeats, The Wild Swans at Coole   1311
Elizabeth Bishop, Pink Dog   1312
Emma Lazarus, The New Colossus   1314

CONTEXT
Alfred, Lord Tennyson, The Charge of the Light Brigade   1393
Czeslaw Milosz, A Song on the End of the World   1397
Czeslaw Milosz, Christopher Robin   1399
Herman Melville, The House-Top   1404
Herman Melville, A Utilitarian View of the Monitor's Fight   1441
Herbert Read, The Execution of Cornelius Vane   1442
Stephen Crane, There Was a Crimson Clash of War   1446
e. e. cummings, [i sing of Olaf glad and big]   1447
Richard Eberhart, The Fury of Aerial Bombardment   1448
Edgar A. Guest, The Things That Make a Soldier Great   1449
Sir Henry Newbolt, Vitai Lampada   1450
Wilfred Owen, Anthem for Doomed Youth   1451
Wilfred Owen, Dulce et Decorum Est   1452
Carl Sandburg, Grass   1453
Siegfried Sassoon, The Rear-Guard   1453
Siegfried Sassoon, Repression of War Experience   1454
Anne Sexton, Courage   1455
Alice Moore Dunbar-Nelson, I Sit and Sew   1457
Yusef Komunyakaa, Facing It   1458
Judith Ortiz Cofer, The Changeling   1459
Mary Jo Salter, Welcome to Hiroshima   1460
Wislawa Szymborska, The End and the Beginning   1461
Wislawa Szymborska, Monologue of a Dog Ensnared in History   1463
Adrienne Rich, For the Record   1465

ALLUSIONS
Charles Simic, My Weariness of Epic Proportions   1477
Dick Barnes, Up Home Where I Come From   1479
William Wordsworth, My Heart Leaps Up   1481
Percy Bysshe Shelley, Ozymandias   1520
Sharon McCartney, After the Chuck Jones Tribute on Teletoon   1521
Robert Duncan, Persephone   1522
Sylvia Plath, Two Sisters of Persephone   1523
John Keats, Ode on a Grecian Urn   1524
John Keats, [When I have fears that I may cease to be]   1526
John Keats, On First Looking into Chapman's Homer   1527

Amy Clampitt, The Dakota   1527
Alfred, Lord Tennyson, The Lady of Shalott   1528
William Butler Yeats, Sailing to Byzantium   1533
Czeslaw Milosz, Orpheus and Eurydice   1534
Rainer Maria Rilke, Orpheus, Eurydice, Hermes   1536
Jorie Graham, Orpheus and Eurydice   1539
H. D., Eurydice   1541
Adrienne Rich, I Dream I'm the Death of Orpheus   1545
Robert Pinsky, Keyboard   1546

GENRE
Mark Twain, Ode to Stephen Dowling Bots, Dec'd   1591
John Milton, Lycidas   1612
Walt Whitman, When Lilacs Last in the Dooryard Bloom'd   1617
Gwendolyn Brooks, De Witt Williams on His Way to Lincoln Cemetery   1624
Allen Tate, Ode to the Confederate Dead   1625
Robert Lowell, For the Union Dead   1628
John Keats, Ode to Autumn   1630
Anne Bradstreet, In Memory of My Dear Grandchild, Elizabeth Bradstreet, Who Deceased August 1665, Being a Year and a Half Old   1631
Anne Bradstreet, Here Followes Some Verses upon the Burning of Our House July 10, 1666   1632
Chidiock Tichborne, Elegy Written with His Own Hand in the Tower before His Execution   1633
Theodore Roethke, Elegy for Jane   1634
Seamus Heaney, Punishment   1635
Louise Erdrich, Dear John Wayne   1637
Langston Hughes, Night Funeral in Harlem   1638
Emily Dickinson, [I like a look of Agony]   1640
Emily Dickinson, [After great pain, a formal feeling comes—]   1640
Rudyard Kipling, The Power of the Dog   1641
John Updike, Dog's Death   1642

AN ORIENTATION TO RESEARCH
David Sumner (Jones), Someone Forgotten   1703
Neal Bowers, Ten-Year Elegy   1704

DRAMA

SCENE, EPISODE, AND PLOT
Sophocles, *Oedipus the King*   67

CHARACTER
Anton Chekhov, The Proposal: A Jest in One Act   182

THEME
Christopher Marlowe, *Doctor Faustus* 240

POINT OF VIEW
William Shakespeare, *Much Ado about Nothing* 340

SETTING
Tennessee Williams, *The Glass Menagerie* 455

RHYTHM, PACE, and RHYME
Suzan-Lori Parks, *Topdog/Underdog* 578

IMAGES
Susan Glaspell, *Trifles* 699

COHERENCE
David Ives, *Sure Thing* 778

INTERRUPTION
William Shakespeare, *Hamlet* 896

TONE
Christopher Durang and **Wendy Wasserstein**, *Medea* 1070

WORD CHOICE
Henrik Ibsen, *A Doll's House* 1133

ALLEGORY
Jane Martin, Beauty 1245

SYMBOLISM
Arthur Miller, *Death of a Salesman* 1314

CONTEXT
Gina Victoria Shaffer, War Spelled Backwards 1466

ALLUSIONS
Tom Stoppard, *The Fifteen Minute Hamlet* 1487
Mary Zimmerman, *Metamorphoses* 1547

GENRE
William Shakespeare, from *Macbeth* 1588
Sophocles, *Antigone* 1643

Glossary

Abstract: Describing an idea, concept, theme, or feeling as opposed to a thing or person. In literary texts, as in analytical essays, abstractions must occasionally be grounded by particular examples. See **concrete.**

Absurd: Characteristic of a vision in which meaning is drained from life. An absurdist work challenges the way we make sense of the world or the way we lend significance to events.

Aerial view: See **high-angle shot.**

Allegory: Serves to convey meaning through a narrative in which abstract notions are embodied and given life by concrete characters and actions. Usually, allegories set forth a lesson. See **didactic work.**

Alliteration: Refers to the repetition of consonant sounds in words. For example, *woke to black flak.*

Allusion: A reference within a text to some other text or bit of knowledge outside the text. Allusion involves the author's play upon what is assumed the reader's literary experience; a brief reference in one work to a passage or scene from another work is an allusion.

Ambiguity: Uncertainty or multiplicity of meaning. Ambiguity involves suggestive qualities of expression as opposed to plainly directive statements. Ambiguity may also arise from statements in a single text that seem on the surface to possess contradictory implications or intents.

Analogy: A comparison used to make a point. An analogy uses the likeness of two things to build a forceful argument. If the comparison seems strained or if it does not apply clearly to the point made, the analogy breaks down.

Anapest: An anapest (anapestic foot) consists of two unaccented syllables followed by one accented syllable.

Antagonist: The character set in opposition to the **protagonist.**

Antistrophe: In classical drama, a part of the choral ode. While singing, the chorus would dance. According to some analysts, for the **strophe,** the chorus would move from left to right; for the antistrophe, they moved from right to left back to the original position. The two movements are identical in meter. See **strophe.**

Apostrophe: Refers to the speaker's direct address to an absent person or to some abstract idea or spirit.

Assonance: Consists of a similarity in vowel sounds, but the final consonants differ: *date/lake*. See **rhyme.**

Atmosphere: Feelings invoked in the reader or viewer through **setting.** Gothic works are said to be heavily atmospheric.

Auteur theory: Closely parallels notions of **new criticism.** *Auteur* theory identifies the director of a film as the creative center (*auteur* is French for "author"). Such a focus on the choices of a single maker gave critics a point of analytical focus. But this focus necessarily disregarded the essentially collaborative nature of filmmaking.

Author: See **poet.**

Background: The physical elements against which characters are set. In Caspar David Friedrich's *Woman in the Morning Light* (p. 287), the rolling hills, spacious fields, and rising sun are the background. Background can also suggest information supplied about a situation or a character from outside the immediate narrative. For example, in *Oedipus the King* (p. 67) the **chorus,** along with Oedipus's opening speech, supply information about the past and Oedipus's current situation that helps us understand the action that unfolds.

Blank verse: Unrhymed verse in a prevailing **iambic pentameter.** Blank verse lends itself to serious subjects of lofty speech.

Blending: The thorough mixture of genres. The *Buffy the Vampire Slayer* episode "Once More, with Feeling" adopts many conventions of a traditional material but also plays out as a horror story; elements of comedy and tragedy unfold together as well in this episode.

Cacophony: A style marked by harsh, grating, hard sounds. Opposite of **euphony.**

Caesura: A pause within a line of poetry. The word may be used to suggest a pause in any text that has built some sense of rhythm. A caesura may suggest a shift in mood, a turn to another subject, a characteristic of common speech, or any number of effects. Oftentimes, a caesura serves to foreground a word, idea, or moment.

Canon: Refers to a body of works deemed (by experts/scholars) as worthy of critical study, as literature or art. Canonical works are seen as those works that a culture adopts and uses over time.

Catharsis: The release of strong emotions (pity and fear) inspired by **tragedy.** Catharsis is presented by Aristotle as purgation or a cleansing. The audience feels the terror associated with a tragic end yet finds in the action an affirmation of values or life.

Character: A person in a literary text/film/dramatic production.

Characterization: The method of creating **character.** Authors may, for example, create character through **dialogue,** description, or narration (revealing character through actions).

Chorus: A form of commentary in dramatic works that helps an audience contextualize, interpret, or judge the action that unfolds. In classical Greek drama, the chorus was sung by a group onstage in a highly formalized fashion.

Cliché: An expression that has been greatly overused and through overuse has lost its original force or meaning.

Climax: The turning point in a narrative. The point to which **tension** builds and at which must be released.

Closed ending: An ending in which all the questions raised in the plot are answered. The reader senses that things have been neatly pulled together in a way that strongly ends the narrative. Detective stories typically are tightly closed.

Colloquial: Casual language that reflects common usage and informal conversation. The language of everyday life.

Comedy: At the simplest level, a work that ends in marriage (and thereby implies happiness, resolution, stability, continuity, and so on). Although comedies offer some sense of fulfillment, that fulfillment may be of a small sort. See **high comedy** and **farce.**

Comic relief: A form of mixing comic elements in the midst of a **tragedy.** Comic relief diminishes tragedy. The term is often misused, for most such mixing of comic with tragic provides no relief. Indeed, a surprising disruption of the comic into a tragic action may well intensify—not diminish—the action.

Common knowledge: *Not* what most people know, *but* what a reader or writer could acquire or confirm from any one of several accessible sources. Most people, for example, don't know the date of George Washington's death. But that date is common knowledge: several people could go to the library or look on the Internet and find the same information.

Complication: A problem, difficulty, or question raised in a literary text. See **sonnet.**

Composition: In film, the arrangement of objects within a frame seen from a particular **point of view;** more broadly, the arrangement of all elements within a single **scene** (lighting, movement, and so on). Composition can also refer to the arrangement of parts in a poem, play, fiction, or essay.

Concrete: Relating to some thing or person that has a physical presence, to something we can touch, see, or hear, to something we know through our senses. See **abstract.**

Concrete poetry: Poetry that is graphically set so that it takes the shape on the page of the thing it describes; in other words, the lines of the poem illustrate their own subject matter. Sometimes called **shape poetry.**

Conflict: That which creates the **tension** that moves a narrative forward to its **climax.** Conflict arises from opposing forces. A character might be set in conflict with another character, or perhaps a social condition, or nature itself. A conflict could even grow from a single character's inner struggle.

Connotation: What a word suggests that lies beyond what a word means in the strictest sense. Connotations may be complex, varied, and subtle, for they arise from a wide range of ever-changing associations. Compare **denotation.**

Consonance: Strikes a similarity in the sounds of the final stressed consonant, but the preceding vowel sounds differ: *date/rite*. See **rhyme.**

Context: Information from outside the text relevant to understanding the text. For example, it is important to know that Tennyson was Poet Laureate of Great Britain when he wrote "The Charge of the Light Brigade" (p. 1393). He wrote, then, in an official position, not to question why the soldiers were asked to fight and die but to celebrate the fact that they did fight and die. The context for our own contemporary reading of this poem has changed dramatically.

Contextual or **situational irony:**   Contextual irony arises from circumstances or from coincidence (for example, a homeless person arrested for vagrancy on the street in front of a governmental housing and urban development office). See **irony.**

Convention: An element that has become familiar through our reading or viewing experience.

Couplet: A verse paragraph made up of two lines. See **stanza.**

Cultural poetics: See **new historicism.**

Dactyl (dactylic foot):   Consists of an accented syllable followed by two unaccented syllables.

Deconstruction: Posited notion that meaning is not fixed within a text but is both created and undone by a complex and ever-changing structure of words. Whereas new criticism sought a "best" or most complete reading of a text, deconstruction sought to revel in inconsistencies.

Deep focus: In film/photography, a technique that allows all objects to remain clear—even those objects distant from the camera. Deep focus creates a sense of density, fullness, and sometimes activity; it does not direct or hold a viewer's attention to a particular place on the screen. See **shallow focus.**

Denotation: The literal meaning of a word. The leading definition of a word one would find in a contemporary dictionary. Compare **connotation.**

Denouement: Often suggests not only action that follows the **climax** but the explanation or resolution of what has happened. Denouement suggests an untying of a knot. See **falling action.**

Depth of field: In film/photography, an extended range of focus. See **deep focus.**

Detached observer: An observer who is not an active participant in the action he or she relates.

Dialogue: Conversation between characters. Authors may through dialogue create the impression that characters reveal themselves in speech directly to the reader.

Diction: Word choice. See **colloquial.**

Didactic work: Literature intended to teach, to instruct readers in points of moral or social significance.

Displacement: The overlaying of one generic mode upon another. See **blending.**

Disruption: A break from what is expected; a deviation from an established **convention.** A familiar element that is revised or even reversed in a text; for example, Clint Eastwood disrupts the conventions of a western when he has his main character ride off not into the sunset but into a dark, rainy night.

Dramatic irony: Dramatic irony signals a distinction between what a character knows and what an audience understands. In other words, dramatic irony arises at moments when the audience knows more than the character or characters that are part of the action. See **irony.**

Dramatic monologue: A work in which a single speaker addresses an audience within a dramatic situation. Robert Browning's "My Last Duchess" (p. 303) is an especially good example of a dramatic monologue.

Dynamic character: Character who changes over the course of a story. The change might be fundamental (the result, for example, of a transformative experience) or might be superficial (the result of new information).

Editing: In film, the selecting, arranging, and organizing of **shots** to create desired effects. More broadly still, editing involves the integration of sound and image.

End rhyme: Rhyme that falls at the end of the poetic line, the most common place for rhyming words.

End stop: A full stop at the end of a poetic line.

English or **Shakespearean sonnet:** A lyric poem of fourteen lines that lends itself to a tightly developed problem/response structure. The English sonnet often repeats the **complication** over the first twelve lines (three **quatrains**) and saves the **resolution** for the final two lines (**couplet**). See **sonnet.**

Enjambment: Literally, a striding over. Enjambment involves the running of one poetic line into the next without pause. A line that strides over is enjambed.

Epic simile: An extended and highly elaborate **simile.** Essentially, an epic simile carries on at length after the word *like* or *as* that introduces it.

Episode: Suggests a single, continuous, and brief action that either stands alone or could be detached from a larger narrative.

Episodic narrative/Episodic novel: An extended fiction made up of a **sequence** of episodes.

Epode: In classical drama, the third part of the ode (after the **strophe** and **antistrophe**), which completed the movement of the chorus with singing in unison at the center of the stage or altar. See **strophe** and **antistrophe.**

Euphemism: A deliberately indirect expression. A euphemism may arise from a sense of delicacy, politeness, or respect. Sometimes, however, a euphemism is employed to avoid truth or responsibility (for example, "collateral damage").

Euphony: A style marked by smooth, pleasing sounds. Opposite of **cacophony.**

Expectations: The result of a reader's previous literary experience. Someone, for example, who has seen many romantic comedies comes to expect the feuding couple to somehow realize at some point that they really can't live without each other. In conventional romantic comedies, the couple will indeed get together at the end—no matter how many misunderstandings they have along the way. In conventional works, expectations are met or satisfied.

Explication: Literally, an unfolding. Explication involves the close reading or analysis of a text. Through explication, one seeks to understand how a work achieves meaning and power, as well as what the meaning is. Explication can be thought of as a kind of slow-motion reading.

Exposition: A type of composition that centers on explanation (as opposed to argumentation, description, or narration). In relation to narrative works, exposition functions to introduce or contextualize the action that will unfold.

Extrametrical: Something that occurs within a **metric line** of poetry, like a pronounced pause, that is not accounted for by simple **scansion.**

Extreme high-level shot: See **high-angle shot.**

Eye-level shot: In film/photography, a **shot** taken from the same height as the subject. Such shots put the viewer on the same level as the subject.

Fable: A short story, usually with an explicit or implicit **moral,** that conveys some general truth through a fictional example. Talking animals are a frequent convention of the fable.

Falling action: The action that follows the **climax.** The action that releases **tension** built into the narrative and moves toward the work's conclusion. See **denouement.**

Falling meter: A **foot** in which the accent falls on the first syllable.

Farce: A form of **comedy** that sustains no **tension** that arises from the emotional complexities of **character.** A farce builds upon silly actions that require only superficial **resolution.** The complexities in farce are situational; complexities do not grow from depth or complexity of character. Chekhov's "The Proposal" (p. 183) is a farce. Television's *Seinfeld* is a good modern example of farce.

Feminine rhyme: A rhyme of two syllables, the second unstressed. Also called a double rhyme. Such rhymes tend to create a light, quick effect.

Feminist criticism: Seeks to gain insights largely obscured or bypassed by the men who have until recent decades dominated critical discussions. Feminists along with **new historicists** assume that a work of art (or a work of criticism for that matter) is a product not only of an author but of a specific culture.

Figurative language: Any language that is used in ways that deviate from standard significance, order, or meaning.

Figure of thought: See **trope.**

Filmic rhythm: Patterns of movement, **composition,** and sound that work together in a film for a particular effect.

First-person narrator: A story told from the perspective of one inside the story; that is to say, the narrator speaks as "I." A first-person narrator may be the **protagonist** of the story, but does not necessarily have that role. Dr. Watson in "A Scandal in Bohemia" (p. 21), for example, reports what he sees and hears of Sherlock Holmes's adventure, but Holmes himself is the protagonist.

Flashback: A return in a narrative to an action that occurred in the past (that is, before the present action of the story).

Flat character: A term used to describe a one-dimensional character. The term is often used negatively, but it is important to remember that characters have to be viewed in relation to how they function in the whole work. See **stock character.**

Foil: A minor character that functions in a narrative to highlight characteristics of more significant and complex characters.

Foot: The combination of one stressed and one or more unstressed syllables that constitutes the recurring rhythmic unit within the larger pattern of a poetic line.

Foreground: In film, that which is in front of the screen, closest to the audience; usually the space where the main action occurs. Foreground also signifies the front of the stage in a dramatic production. More broadly, foreground (used as a verb) may suggest the way an author has highlighted an element for the reader/viewer to note as important.

Foreshadowing: A hint about what will follow—a scene that prepares for action that is to come. In Edgar Allan Poe's "The Fall of the House of Usher" (p. 421), the crack in the foundation that the narrator notices as he first sees the house foreshadows the final collapse of the house.

Formalist: See **new criticism.**

Formula: The strict adherence in all elements of a work to the established **expectations** of readers/viewers. See **convention.**

Fragment: A partial action. An action that suggests something larger left unexplored or unstated. A fragment could be a piece of a whole text, but it could also be an artistic device used to create feelings of mystery, for example, or to comment upon the impossibility of wholeness.

Frame: The smallest element of a film: a single photograph that, strung together with many other photos in **sequence,** creates the illusion of movement. Frame can also suggest the boundary that surrounds the image. In a literary context, frame may also refer to the way a narrative or argument is set up or introduced. For example, Ursula K. Le Guin frames "The Ones Who Walk Away from Omelas" (p. 554) by inviting readers to create their own fantasy paradise. Once readers imagine that perfect world, Le Guin presents the terrible conditions required of such perfection. Conversely, in the film *The Wizard of Oz* the fantasy is framed by the mundane black-and-white world of Kansas.

Free verse: Poetry that is not marked by any regular metrical scheme or pattern of rhyme. Free verse may achieve coherence through repeated images or through purposeful variation of line length.

Full or **perfect rhyme:** Consists of the sameness of sounds in accented vowels and any consonants that follow: *date/fate.* See **rhyme.**

Genre: Literary/artistic type or kind. Genre suggests the grouping of individual works into larger categories. The grouping can be made in various ways. For the sake of convenience, for example, a teacher might treat poems, prose narratives, plays, and films as genres. But it is usually best to define genres on the basis of more particular **expectations** an audience brings to a work.

Haiku: A poetic form borrowed from a Japanese tradition. Haikus contain three unrhymed lines. The brevity serves to intensify emotions that find expression in what is usually a highly specific image.

Hero/heroine: Sometimes considered the same as **protagonist,** but that word more strictly signals the character's function to lead the action. Hero/heroine usually implies a moral prominence (the most admirable or sympathetic character in the narrative, the strongest force for good).

Hexameter: A line of poetry made up of six feet. See **metric line.**

High-angle shot: In film/photography, a **shot** taken from above the subject. A high-angle shot may be used to give the viewer a sense of power over the subject. Think, for example, of seeing a fallen boxer from the perspective of the boxer's opponent. An extreme high-level shot or an aerial view extends the logic of such shots further still by exaggerating the angle between camera above and subject below.

High comedy: Develops from the emotional substance of complex **characters.** Oftentimes, high comedies press toward tragic possibilities that are barely averted. For example, the lovers in Shakespeare's *Much Ado about Nothing* (p. 340) face difficult obstacles created by ill will, anger, pride, and jealousy. They also genuinely suffer for the mistakes they make before achieving happiness at the end.

Hyperbole: Deliberate overstatement, exaggeration.

Hypertext: Allows readers to access on a screen any variety of linked documents instantly, at any time, in any order. Hypertext is not bound to a text laid out on a page.

Iamb: A metrical unit within a poetic line. An iamb consists of two syllables, the first unstressed and the second stressed. The iamb might consist of one word with multiple syllables (aTTEMPT) or multiple words (in LOVE).

Iambic: The most common standard rhythmic unit (**foot**) in English poetry. See **iamb.**

Iambic pentameter: A line consisting of ten syllables marked by prevailing **iambs.**

Identification: The effect of close sympathy and understanding with a character in a literary work. If we identify with a character, we see something of ourselves in the character.

Impersonal narrator: See **objective narrator** or **third-person narration.**

Impressionism: The invocation of an immediate, subjective feeling created by the conditions of a particular moment. An impressionist painter, for example, doesn't paint an idealized object but an object in specific conditions of light (not a church, but a church seen from a certain angle at a particular time of day in specific weather conditions).

Incident: A specific, small action that usually takes place within a more extended narrative.

Internal rhyme: Rhyme that occurs within a poetic line as opposed to the end of the line.

Introspection: A personal willingness to consider and reflect upon ideas that may seem to conflict or that may prove uncomfortable.

Intrusive narrator: A narrator who breaks into the story in order to offer judgment or guidance to the reader or to comment on the unfolding action.

Irony: A literary device that plays upon a gap between appearance and reality. Irony requires us to hold up two possible meanings simultaneously and to appreciate how the implied meaning overrides what seems apparent on the surface. There are many different types of irony. **Contextual irony** arises from circumstances or from coincidence (for example, a homeless person arrested for vagrancy on the street in front of a governmental housing and urban development office). **Dramatic irony** signals a distinction between what a character knows and what an audience understands. In other words, dramatic irony arises at moments when the audience knows more than the character or characters that are part of the action. **Verbal irony** (perhaps the most common ironic mode) suggests a deliberate play upon the difference between what is said and what is meant. **Sarcasm** is an especially blunt and aggressive form of verbal irony.

Italian or **Petrarchan sonnet:** A lyric poem made up of fourteen lines that lends itself to a tightly developed problem/response structure. It builds the **complication** (problem, question) in the first eight lines (**octave**), and the **resolution** (response, answer) is delivered after the **turn** in the final six lines (**sestet**). See **sonnet.**

Juxtaposition: A rhetorical technique of putting two (or more) things next to each other; the resulting contrast or similarity makes us see both objects differently than we saw them when each stood alone.

Limited narrator: See **limited omniscient narrator** and **third-person narration.**

Limited omniscient narrator: A narrator who knows most things but cannot relate selected bits of information or insight. See **third-person narration.**

Line break: The point at which a line of poetry breaks; the end of a line of poetry.

Low-angle shot: In film/photography, a **shot** taken from below the subject. A low-angle shot may be used to place the viewer in a weak position. For example, in the film *Rear Window*, Hitchcock uses a low-angle shot to have us look up at the murderer who is about to attack the wheelchair-bound hero. The viewer is, in effect, put in the wheelchair and feels the threat of the attacker.

Low comedy: A comedy that involves **characters** of little emotional or intellectual substance.

Masculine rhyme: A rhyme in which the rhyming syllable falls on the stressed and final syllable.

Metaphor: A joining of two qualities or things to create new meaning. For example, the phrase "love is a red rose" fuses two essentially unlike things to communicate something about the quality of love. Usually, metaphors build upon one concrete thing (like a rose) and an abstraction (like love). **Similes,** unlike metaphor, signal a comparison as opposed to a fusion (love is *like* a red rose).

Meter: The regular and therefore discernible rhythmic pattern of sounds that can be charted in poetry line by line.

Metric line: A line of poetry measured by the number of feet that compose it. The most common lines are **trimeter** (three feet), **tetrameter** (four feet), **pentameter** (five feet), and **hexameter** (six feet). See **iamb.**

Milieu: A French word that literally means "center" or "middle" and is used to designate particular social, temporal, and physical surroundings.

Mise en scène: A French term that indicates what is put into the scene. Mise en scène originally referred to the staging of plays: the arrangement and inclusion of furniture, backdrops, stray items, and props that make up the environment within which characters act. Film critics use the term to describe what is captured in a shot. The concept applies to any work of art that places objects in a scene. It's important to remember that if an item is in a scene, it's there because the author/director put it there.

Montage: From the French verb "to assemble." In film criticism, refers to a style of editing that uses sudden **juxtapositions** of images, surprising cuts, and radical shifts in **perspective.** Literary critics may use the word to describe dramatic contrasts of images, voices, or **genres.**

Moral: An explicit lesson oftentimes stated at the end of a narrative. An overt message signaled by the **author.** See **didactic work.**

Motif: A recurring element (an image, a key word, a **symbol,** a phrase, and so on) in a work of literature, film, or music. A motif may be analyzed in context of a group of works (that is, as a familiar element repeated in many different texts) or may be seen to operate within a single text.

Multiple plots: The weaving together of two or more plots in a single work; multiple plots suggest complexity or density of experience.

New criticism: A school of criticism that emerged in the middle of the twentieth century and continues to influence much teaching of literature and film. New critics were **formalists:** they argued that literary texts are the sole material of literary study. Literary criticism was seen as a distinct discipline that focused on the structure, style, and language of particular works.

New historicism: Views systems of meaning as conditional and shifting depending upon the interests the system represents. Literary artists are not free of the assumptions of power that are encoded in language. New historicism has also been called **cultural poetics** and **postcolonial criticism.** The former term puts emphasis on the cultural context that produces literary texts; the latter term calls attention to the ways in which language functions within a system of power.

Objective narrator: A narrator who reports from the outside what can be seen but makes no effort to get inside the minds of any character (sometimes called an **impersonal narrator**). See **third-person narration.**

Octave: A **stanza** of eight lines. An octave often constitutes the first part of an **Italian sonnet.** See **sonnet** and **sestet.**

Ode: Once structured in three parts that reflected their origins as public poems, performed by a **chorus** that moved in one direction as it delivered the first part (the strophe), moved in the opposite direction as it voiced the second part (the antistrophe), and stood still as it came to the final section (the epode). Those conventions of form and performance have worn away. Now odes are characterized more by elements of mood and subject; they are substantial poems of a meditative cast—serious and dignified.

Omniscient narrator: A narrator who knows everything about the characters' actions and thoughts. See **third-person narration.**

Open ending: An ending that prompts the reader to think, question, or project beyond the narrative. A reader might wonder after reading an open-ended novel, for example, what will happen to a character or might be left thinking about the implications of an action.

Pace: The relative speed of an unfolding action, presentation, or argument.

Paradox: An expression that seems to contradict itself but that actually realizes something genuine and deeply coherent. Paradox demands that we question common assumptions or understandings. Blake often plays upon paradox in his *Songs of Innocence* and *Songs of Experience* (p. 568–569; 570–571).

Paraphrase: Involves a superficial revision of the original text; the writer of a paraphrase stays close to the logic, length, and language of the original. See **summary.**

Parody: A comic imitation of a serious work or **genre.** Mel Brooks has made a career of making parodies of successful films or film genres (*Robin Hood* becomes *Men in Tights*; *Star Wars* becomes *Space Balls*; classic westerns become *Blazing Saddles*, and so on). **Self-parody** suggests an unintentional revelation of empty and tired formulas. Some critics would argue that Michael Bay's action films have descended into self-parody.

Particular: The specific and concrete illustration/image as opposed to the general and **abstract** idea. Authors often use the particular in order to ground more ambitious ideas and feelings—and make those ideas and feelings vivid and convincing. Note for example, Czeslaw Milosz's "A Song on the End of the World" (p. 1397).

Pastoral: Marked by setting in the quiet countryside amid a gently cultivated nature. Pastorals once had elaborate conventions (shepherds living the simple life upon nature's bounty), but the word has come to signal broader qualities: a peaceful and uncomplicated life away from the city can be called pastoral.

Pentameter: A line of poetry made up of five feet. See **metric line.**

Personification: Projecting animate (human or animal) qualities on an inanimate thing.

Perspective: See **point of view.**

Plagiarism: The inappropriate use of the words or ideas of another writer. Plagiarism is a form of theft. In its most extreme form, plagiarism involves lifting directly from a prior source and passing off the work as original. But inadequately acknowledged **summary** and/or an extended **paraphrase** (as opposed to straight copying) can also be deemed plagiarism and be subject to disciplinary or legal action.

Plot: A meaningful fabric of action. Plot suggests structure (a beginning, middle, and end). It suggests not only *what happened* but also *how what happened was conveyed.*

Poet: The source of the word suggests "maker." Poet can, of course, simply mean one who makes poetry. But oftentimes, the word is used more broadly. It can be important to distinguish the poet or **author** (the maker of any text you read) from the **speaker** or narrator (a voice created by the poet/author).

Poetic diction: The notion that the poetic words are necessarily different from everyday words.

Point of view: Strictly speaking, the point from which one sees. More broadly, point of view signals narrative perspective—the way a story is related. Thinking in terms of point of view involves considering who tells the story as well as how the teller's interests, personality, motives, and background influence what is observed and reported.

Postcolonial criticism: See **new historicism.**

Postmodernism: A highly self-conscious mode of expression that calls attention to the artifice of a work of art—the fictionality of a work of fiction. Postmodernism can be playful, but it also blurs distinctions between real and imagined in ways that challenge our conventional ways of understanding. *Pulp Fiction* has been called a postmodern film. The stories of Borges have also been called postmodern.

Prosody: The study of **meter** and verse.

Protagonist: From the Greek, "the first one to battle." The main or leading **character.** Although the protagonist is usually the **hero** of a story, the terms are not synonymous. See **antagonist.**

Pyrrhic: A foot that consists of two consecutive unstressed syllables; a **variant** or **substitution** of a standard rhythmic unit. That is, a pyrrhic foot may break a pattern, but it cannot be the pattern (a line cannot be made up of only unstressed syllables).

Quatrain: A verse paragraph made up of four lines. See **stanza.**

Reader-response criticism: A variant of **new historicism.** Reader-response critics shift emphasis from a text to how people read/use a text; the work of art is studied not through its own inherent qualities but through the way readers of a particular time and place react to it.

Realism: A mode of depiction that builds on close, accurate attention to specific historical and social conditions. Realism is a constructed illusion; it involves the author's efforts to convince the reader of the reality of a particular vision.

Reflexive plot (also reflexive or **self-conscious narrative**):   A story in which the way a story is constructed becomes the very thing we are forced to think about. For example, the film *Memento* makes questions of narration central to its theme. A self-conscious narrator is aware of the artfulness of the story he or she tells.

Refrain: A phrase, line, or **stanza** that recurs regularly throughout a poem or song.

Reliable narrator: A narrator who offers accurate information and a credible interpretation of action. A narrator who establishes and rewards trust.

Repetition: A means to foreground an image or theme.

Resolution: A satisfying explanation; the part of a **plot** in which problems are addressed. In a long Victorian novel, for example, the resolution might involve a final word on how all the characters turn out (who gets married and has children, who dies miserable and alone, and so on). In a **sonnet,** resolution suggests a response to the **complication** set forth in the first part of the poem.

Rhetorical figure: Uses a word or words in an unusual context or sequence but does not radically change the customary meaning of the word or words. See **trope.**

Rhyme: Consists of the similarity of the last stressed vowel of one word with the last stressed vowel of another. **Full** or **perfect rhyme** consists of the sameness of sounds in accented vowels and any consonants that follow: *date/fate*. **Assonance** also consists of a similarity in vowel sounds, but the final consonants differ: *date/lake*. **Consonance** strikes a similarity in the sounds of the final stressed consonant, but the preceding vowel sounds differ: *date/rite*. Such examples are often called **slant rhymes** or **off-rhymes.**

Riddle poem: A poem that leaves its subject unstated, that invites or requires readers to supply the missing subject. Emily Dickinson's "[A Route of Evanescence]" (p. 59), for example, describes something that it doesn't name: a hummingbird. Part of the fun is guessing the subject from the evidence supplied. See also Dickinson's "[I like to see it lap the Miles—]" (p. 60).

Rising action: The building part of a narrative that establishes, sustains, and intensifies a **conflict.**

Rising meter: A **foot** in which the accent falls on the last syllable.

Round character: A term used to describe characters that possess a complex psychology. A term used in opposition to **flat character.**

Sarcasm: An especially blunt and aggressive form of **verbal irony.** See **irony.**

Scan: To define by close metrical analysis the rhythmic pattern of poetic lines.

Scansion: The metrical analysis of a line of poetry.

Scene: In a dramatic work, may simply indicate the entrance and/or exit of characters from the stage. More broadly understood, a scene is an action within a larger narrative that has some thematic or dramatic function. A scene may be defined by mood, function, or place. It may convey a particular **conflict** that is subordinate to the larger conflict of the entire narrative.

Self-conscious narrative: See **reflexive plot.**

Self-parody: Self-parody suggests an unintentional revelation of empty and tired formulas. See **parody.**

Sequence: A series of actions or a list of points with no necessary logic; sequence alone implies no more than one thing after another.

Sestet: A **stanza** of six lines. A sestet often constitutes the second and final part of an Italian sonnet. See **sonnet.**

Sestina: A highly complicated, fixed poetic form. The sestina consists of six **sestets** (thirty-six lines) and a concluding **tercet** (three lines). The six words that close the first sestet must also appear (not necessarily in the same order) at the ends of the other sestets and then must appear in the final tercet. The **repetition** serves to foreground or develop **themes** and feelings central to the whole.

Setting: The total environment within which narrative actions take place. The characters' living conditions as well as the time and place in which they live constitute setting.

Shallow focus: In film/photography, a technique that brings a specific plane into clear focus and leaves the rest of the picture blurry. A director might use shallow focus to get us to look closely at the face of one character. See **deep focus.**

Shape poem: See **concrete poetry.**

Shot: A single length of film that communicates a continuous action on the screen.

Shot analysis: A means to comprehend how a film communicates meaning and power. In shot analysis, one breaks a film down and assesses the relationship of shot to shot.

Simile: A comparison that links two things with *like* or *as*. Langston Hughes employs a series of similes in "Harlem" (p. xxxvii) to answer the question "what happens to a dream deferred": for example, it may dry up *like* a raisin. See **metaphor.**

Sincere: The antithesis of **irony;** the perfect correspondence between words and intended meaning. But it is important to remember that sincerity in a literary text may be a device used by an author as opposed to a quality the author actually possesses.

Slant rhyme or **off-rhyme:** Rhyme in which the sounds of the final stressed consonant are similar, but the preceding vowel sounds differ: *date/rite*. See **consonance** and **rhyme.**

Sonnet: A lyric poem of fourteen lines that lends itself to a tightly developed problem/response structure. The sonnet's opening section is often called the **complication;** the second part, the **resolution.** The brief transition that gives us pause just between these two parts is called the **turn.** The two most common forms are the **Italian** (or **Petrarchan**) sonnet and **English** (or **Shakespearean**) sonnet. The Italian sonnet builds the complication (problem, question, and so on) in the first eight lines (octave), and the resolution (response, answer, and so on) is delivered after the turn in the final six lines (sestet). The English sonnet often repeats the complication over the first twelve lines (three **quatrains**) and saves the resolution for the final two lines (**couplet**).

Speaker: Distinct from **poet** or **author.** The speaker is the voice created by the poet/author of a text. Robert Browning is the author/poet of "My Last Duchess," but the speaker is the duke (a character Browning has created).

Split-screen: A film-editing technique in which the screen space is split so that two or more film sequences run simultaneously next to each other. One of the more famous of these sequences shows a man and a woman talking on the phone with each other. Although they are in different places, the split screen allows us to see both sides of the conversation.

Spondee or **spondaic foot:**   Consists of two consecutive stressed syllables. A spondee is a **variant** or **substitution** of a standard rhythmic unit. That is, a spondee may break a pattern, but it cannot be the pattern (a line cannot be made up of only stressed syllables).

Staging: The elements that concern the physical production of a dramatic work: lighting, sound effects, costumes, mise-en-scène, and so on.

Stanza: A verse paragraph organized by a pattern of rhyme. The most common forms are the **couplet** (two lines), **tercet** (three lines), and **quatrain** (four lines). See also **octave** and **sestet.**

Stanzaic structure: The shape of a **stanza**, marked and knit together by a pattern of **rhyme.** Sometimes called **rhyme scheme.**

Static character: Character who does not change over the course of a story.

Stock character: Simple or **flat character** that is wholly defined by a familiar type or characteristic (for example, Nelson, the schoolyard bully in *The Simpsons* is a stock character).

Stream of consciousness: Direct access to the thoughts and feelings of a character as those thoughts and feelings unfold.

Strophe: In classical drama, a part of the choral ode. While singing, the chorus would dance. According to some analysts, for the strophe, they would move from left to right; for the **antistrophe**, they would move from right to left back to the original position. The two movements are identical in meter. See **antistrophe.**

Subplot: A secondary plot that runs parallel to the main plot. Subplots complement (reinforce, complicate, and deepen) the main plot. There may be more than one subplot in an extended narrative. See **multiple plots.**

Substitution: A break in the prevailing rhythmic pattern of a poetic line; a **foot** (oftentimes a **spondaic** or **pyrrhic** foot) that interrupts a pattern. Substitutions (also called **variants**) may be used to draw attention to a word or phrase. Substitutions/variants might be used to speed or slow the pace of a line.

Summary: Often used interchangeably with **paraphrase,** but a clear distinction between the two is useful. Paraphrase involves a superficial revision of the original text; the writer of a paraphrase stays close to the logic, length, and language of the original. Summary suggests a thorough rewriting and significant compression of the original. Whereas a summary may be appropriate when the source and the extent of the debt are clearly signaled and cited, an extended paraphrase should always be avoided.

Symbol: A type of **trope** in which an object or image comes to represent something more than or other than the object or image alone.

Synchronicity: Events that coincide in time and appear to be related but have no discoverable causal connection.

Synesthesia: The conflation or cross association of two or more of the five senses. For example, hearing a beautiful piece of music might lead one to feel a particular touch (perhaps a piercing pain or a soft caress).

Synecdoche: A figure of speech in which a part represents the whole (for example, all hands on deck).

Tension: A feeling (suspense, doubt, worry, puzzlement, and so on) that is sustained and released/resolved in a work. These feelings do not need to be the broadly drawn **conflicts** that press forward a narrative; many of Emily Dickinson's short poems, for example, are built upon a tension between highly specific words/images and cosmic associations/suggestions.

Tercet: A verse paragraph made up of three lines. See **stanza.**

Tetrameter: A line of poetry made up of four feet. See **metric line.**

Theme: A recurrent idea or feeling woven through a text. Although themes may be explicit (as in a moral to a **fable**), they are more often suggestive and open ended. See **motif.**

Thesis: An assertion that guides an argument, a main point, or a leading insight. A strong, clearly defined thesis underlies the development of a critical essay.

Third-person narration: A story told from outside; that is, the narrator refers to all characters as "he," "she," or "they." There are varied forms of third-person narration. An **omniscient narrator** knows everything about the characters' actions and thoughts. A **limited omniscient narrator** (as the name would suggest) knows most things but cannot relate selected bits of information or insight. Such a limited narrator might, for example, be able to report on the thoughts of all characters but one. An **objective narrator** (sometimes called an **impersonal narrator**) reports from the outside what can be seen but makes no effort to get inside the minds of any character.

Tragedy: At the simplest level, a work that ends in death. More particularly, tragedy involves a powerful sense of lost promise.

Trimeter: A line of poetry made up of three feet. See **metric line.**

Trochee: (trochaic foot) Consists of two syllables, the first stressed and the second unstressed.

Trope: From the Greek for a "turn" or "turning." Tropes use words to turn from conventional understanding; they significantly alter or enlarge meaning. A trope is also called a **figure of thought** (as opposed to a **rhetorical figure**). **Metaphor, simile,** and **personification** are all tropes. A sarcastic statement (**sarcasm**) is also a trope (if one says, "thanks a lot" in response to an insult, no genuine thanks is intended).

Turn: Suggests a transition space between the **complication** and the **resolution** in a **sonnet.** More broadly, a turn can suggest a sudden movement against a main line of development in any literary work. It also suggests a break from the usual sense of a word or phrase. See **trope.**

Understanding: Grasping a key thought or feeling in a text. Understanding is distinct from knowing. Knowing suggests certainty and completeness (for example, we know Emily Dickinson is an American poet who lived in the nineteenth century). Conversely, one can attain a level of understanding or achieve an insight about an aspect of a text.

Universal: The belief that some ideas transcend historical or social **context** and apply across generations and cultures.

Unreliable narrator: A narrator who provides false leads or misinterprets important actions. Readers are forced to consider how the entire situation (not just what is related) help establish a fair view of what unfolds.

Variant: See **substitution.**

Verbal irony: Perhaps the most common ironic mode; suggests a deliberate play upon the difference between what is said and what is meant. See **irony.**

Villanelle: A fixed and especially complex poetic form. A villanelle consists of nineteen lines. The first fifteen are made up of a series of five **tercets** (rhymed *aba*); a **quatrain** closes the poem (*abaa*). Dylan Thomas's "Do Not Go Gentle into That Good Night" (p. 724) is a famous example.

Visual image: The realization in words of something seen.

Credits

This page constitutes an extension of the copyright page. We have made every effort to trace the ownership of all copyrighted material and to secure permission from copyright holders. In the event of any question arising as to the use of any material, we will be pleased to make the necessary corrections in future printings. Thanks are due to the following authors, publishers, and agents for permission to use the material indicated.

TEXT CREDITS

Chinua Achebe "Dead Man's Path" copyright © 1972, 1973 by Chinua Achebe, from *Girls at War and Other Stories.* Used by permission of Doubleday, a division of Random House, Inc. and Emma Sweeney Agency.

Douglas Adams excerpt from *The Hitchhiker's Guide to the Galaxy* by Douglas Adams. Copyright © 1979 by Douglas Adams. Reprinted by permission of Harmony Books, a division of Random House, Inc.

Sherman Alexie "Defending Walt Whitman" from *The Summer of Black Widows.* Copyright © 1996 by Sherman Alexie. Used by permission of Hanging Loose Press.

Ginger Andrews "Rolls-Royce Dreams" from *An Honest Answer.* Copyright © Ginger Andrews. Reprinted by permission of the author and Story Line Press.

Maya Angelou "Harlem Hopscotch" from *Just Give Me a Cool Drink of Water Before I Die.* Copyright © 1971 by Maya Angelou. Used by permission of Random House, Inc.

Margaret Atwood "Siren Song" from *Selected Poems: 1965–1975 and 1966–1984* by Margaret Atwood. Copyright © 1976, 1990 by Margaret Atwood. Reprinted by permission of Houghton Mifflin Company and Oxford University Press. All rights reserved; "you fit into me" from *Selected Poems: 1965–1975* by Margaret Atwood. Copyright © 1976 by Margaret Atwood. Reprinted by permission of Houghton Mifflin Company. All rights reserved. Permission granted by House of Anansi for "you fit into me" from *Power Politics* by Margaret Atwood; "Happy Endings" from *Good Bones and Simple Murders* by Margaret Atwood. Copyright © 1983, 1992, 1994 by O. W. Toad Ltd., a Nan A. Talese Book. Used by permission of Doubleday, a division of Random House, Inc.

W. H. Auden "Musée des Beaux Arts" from *Collected Poems.* Copyright 1940 and renewed © 1968 by W. H. Auden. Used by permission of Random House, Inc.

Caroline Gassner Levine   Footnotes from William Shakespeare, *Hamlet*, edited by John Gassner. Copyright © the Estate of John Gassner.

Allen Ginsberg   "Supermarket in California" from *Collected Poems: 1947–1980.* Copyright © 1988 Allen Ginsberg.

Jorie Graham   "Orpheus and Eurydice" from *The End of Beauty.* Copyright © 1987 by Jorie Graham. Reprinted by permission of HarperCollins Publishers.

Joy Harjo   "New Orleans" and "The Woman Hanging from the Thirteenth Floor Window" from *She Had Some Horses.* Copyright © 1983, 1997 by Joy Harjo. Appears by permission of the publisher, Thunder's Mouth Press, a Division of Avalon Publishing Group, Inc.

Robert Hayden   "Those Winter Sundays." Copyright © 1966 by Robert Hayden from *Angle of Ascent: New and Selected Poems* by Robert Hayden. Used by permission of Liveright Publishing Corp.

Seamus Heaney   "Valediction" from *Poems 1965–1975* by Seamus Heaney. Copyright © 1980 by Seamus Heaney. Reprinted by permission of Farrar, Straus & Giroux, LLC; "Mid-Term Break" and "Punishment" from *Opened Ground: Selected Poems 1966–1996* by Seamus Heaney. Copyright © 1998 by Seamus Heaney. Reprinted by permission of Farrar, Straus & Giroux, LLC, and Faber & Faber LLC.

Ernest Hemingway   "Soldier's Home" reprinted with the permission of Scribner, an imprint of Simon & Schuster Adult Publishing Group, from *In Our Time* by Ernest Hemingway. Copyright 1926 by Charles Scribner's Sons. Copyright renewed 1953 by Ernest Hemingway. All rights reserved; opening paragraph from "Hills Like White Elephants" reprinted with the permission of Scribner, an imprint of Simon & Schuster Adult Publishing Group, from *Men Without Women* by Ernest Hemingway. Copyright 1927 by Charles Scribner's Sons. Copyright renewed © 1955 by Ernest Hemingway. All rights reserved.

Nick Hornby   excerpt from *High Fidelity.* Copyright © 1995 by Nick Hornby. Used by permission of Riverhead Books, an imprint of Penguin Group (USA), Inc.

Langston Hughes   "Night Funeral in Harlem," "Theme for English B," and "Harlem" copyright © 1994 by The Estate of Langston Hughes. Used by permission of Alfred A. Knopf, a division of Random House, Inc.; "Dream Boogie" and "The Negro Speaks of Rivers" copyright © 1994 by The Estate of Langston Hughes from *The Collected Poems of Langston Hughes.* Used by permission of Alfred A. Knopf, a division of Random House, Inc.

Ted Hughes   "Lovesong" from *Collected Poems.* Copyright © 2003 Estate of Ted Hughes. Published by permission of Farrar, Straus & Giroux, LLC, and Faber & Faber, LLC.

Zora Neale Hurston   pages 27–28 from *Mules and Men.* Copyright © 1935 by Zora Neale Hurston; renewed copyright © 1963 by

John C. Hurston and Joel Hurston. Reprinted by permission of HarperCollins Publishers.

Henrik Ibsen "A Doll's House," translated by Michael Meyer. Copyright © 1966 by Michael Meyer. Reprinted by permission of Harold Ober Associates Inc. For reading only. Dramatic rights reserved. Controlled by Robert Freedman Dramatic Agency, 1501 Broadway, NY, NY 10036.

Kazuo Ishiguro *The Remains of the Day.* Copyright © 1989. Reprinted by permission.

David Ives "Sure Thing" from *All in the Timing.* Copyright © 1989, 1990, 1992 by David Ives. Used by permission of Vintage Books, a division of Random House, Inc.

Shirley Jackson "The Lottery" from *The Lottery and Other Stories.* Copyright 1948, 1949 by Shirley Jackson. Copyright renewed © 1976, 1977 by Laurence Hyman, Barry Hyman, Mrs. Sarah Webster, and Mrs. Joanne Schnurer. Reprinted by permission of Farrar, Straus & Giroux, LLC.

Randall Jarrell "The Death of the Ball Turret Gunner" from *The Complete Poems.* Copyright © 1969, renewed 1997 by Mar von S. Jarrell. Reprinted by permission of Farrar, Straus & Giroux, LLC.

Joe Kane "The Boy Who Nearly Won the Texaco Art Competition," *New York Review of Books,* 2/10/05. Copyright © 2005 Joe Kane. Used with permission.

Helane Levine Keating "My Last Duke." Copyright © 1995 by Helane Levine Keating. Reprinted with the permission of the author.

Aron Keesbury "On the Robbery across the Street," *College English,* January 1998, Vol. 60, No. 1. Copyright © 1998 National Council of Teachers of English. Used with permission.

Jamaica Kincaid "Girl" from *At the Bottom of the River.* Copyright © 1983 by Jamaica Kincaid. Reprinted by permission of Farrar, Straus & Giroux, LLC.

Maxine Hong Kingston "Wild Man of the Green Swamp" from *China Men* by Maxine Hong Kingston. Copyright © 1977, 1978, 1979, 1980 by Maxine Hong Kingston. Used by permission of Alfred A. Knopf, a division of Random House, Inc.

Galway Kinnell "Shelley." Copyright © Galway Kinnell.

Yusef Komunyakaa "A Break from the Bush" from *Neon Vernacular* (Wesleyan University Press, 1993.) Copyright © 1993 by Yusef Komunyakaa. Reprinted by permission of Wesleyan University Press; "Facing It" from *Pleasure Dome* (Wesleyan University Press, 2001). Copyright © 2001 Yusef Komunyakaa. Reprinted by permission of Wesleyan University Press.

Ted Kooser "A Hairnet with Stars" from *Sure Signs: New and Selected Poems.* Copyright © 1980. Reprinted by permission of University of Pittsburgh Press; "Tattoo" from *Delights & Shadows.* Copyright © 2004

Laura Riding "The Map of Places" from *The Poems of Laura Riding*.
Copyright © 1938 Laura Riding.
Ranier Maria Rilke "Orpheus, Eurydice, Hermes" from *The Selected
Poetry of Rainer Maria Rilke*, translated by Stephen Mitchell. Copyright ©
1982 by Stephen Mitchell. Used by permission of Random House, Inc.
Edwin Arlington Robinson "Richard Cory" and "The Mill" reprinted
with the permission of Scribner, an imprint of Simon & Schuster Adult
Publishing Group, from *Collected Poems*. Copyright © 1935 by The
Macmillan Company, copyright renewed 1963.
Theodore Roethke "Elegy for Jane" copyright © 1950 by Theodore
Roethke; "The Waking" copyright © 1953 by Theodore Roethke;
"My Papa's Waltz" copyright © 1942 by Hearst Magazines, Inc. All from
Collected Poems of Theodore Roethke. Used by permission of Doubleday,
a division of Random House, Inc.
João Guimarães Rosa "The Third Bank of the River," translated by
William Grossman. Copyright © 1968. Used by permission of
R. G. Mertin, literary agent for the author.
Liz Rosenberg "1:53 A.M." *The New Yorker*, September 20, 2004.
Copyright © 2004 Liz Rosenberg. Used with permission.
Muriel Rukeyser "Myth" from *Out of Silence*. Copyright © Muriel
Rukeyser. Reprinted by permission of International Creative
Management, Inc.
Salman Rushdie "On Leavened Bread" from *Step across This Line*.
Copyright © 2002 by Salman Rushdie. Used by permission of Random
House, Inc.
Edna St. Vincent Millay "Women have loved before as I love now,"
"Childhood Is the Kingdom Where Nobody Dies," "What Lips My Lips
Have Kissed," and "I, Being Born a Woman and Distressed," from
Collected Poems, published by HarperCollins. Copyright © 1923, 1951 by
Edna St. Vincent Millay and Norma Millay Ellis. All rights reserved.
Reprinted by permission of Elizabeth Barnett, literary executor.
Mary Jo Salter "Welcome to Hiroshima" from *Henry Purcell in Japan*.
Copyright © 1984 by Mary Jo Salter. Reprinted by permission of Alfred A.
Knopf, a division of Random House, Inc.; "Home Movies: A Sort of Ode"
from *A Kiss in Space: Poems by Mary Jo Salter*. Copyright © 1999 by Mary
Jo Salter. Used by permission of Alfred A. Knopf, a division of Random
House, Inc.
Carl Sandburg "Grass" from *Chicago Poems*. Copyright © 1916 by Holt,
Rinehart and Winston, renewed 1944 by Carl Sandburg. Reprinted by
permission of Harcourt, Inc.
Siegfried Sassoon "The Rear Guard" copyright © 1918 E. P. Dutton.
Copyright renewed 1946 by Siegfried Sassoon from *Collected Poems of*

Richard Wilbur "April 5, 1974" and "A Sketch" from *The Mind-Reader*. Copyright © 1975 by Richard Wilbur. Reprinted by permission of Harcourt, Inc.; "A Fable" and "Worlds" from *New and Collected Poems*. Copyright © 1988 by Richard Wilbur. Reprinted by permission of Harcourt, Inc.; "A Fire Truck" from *Advice to a Prophet and Other Poems*. Copyright © 1975 and renewed 2003 by Richard Wilbur, reprinted by permission of Harcourt, Inc.
Miller Williams "Thinking of Bill, Dead of AIDS," from *Living on the Surface: New and Selected Poems*. Copyright © 1989 by Miller Williams. Reprinted by permission of Louisiana State University Press.
Tennessee Williams "The Glass Menagerie." Copyright © 1945 The University of The South. Reprinted by permission of Georges Borchardt, Inc. for the Tennessee Williams Estate.
William Carlos Williams "At the Ball Game," "This Is Just to Say" and "The Red Wheelbarrow" from *Collected Poems: 1909–1939, Volume I* by William Carlos Williams. Copyright © 1938 by New Directions Publishing Corp. Reprinted by permission of New Directions Publishing Corp.
W. B. Yeats "The Folly of Being Comforted," "The Wild Swans at Coole," "Sailing to Byzantium," and "Leda and the Swan" reprinted with the permission of Scribner, an imprint of Simon & Schuster Adult Publishing Group, from *The Collected Works of W. B. Yeats, Volume I: The Poems, Revised*, edited by Richard J. Finneran (New York: Scribner, 1927).
Kevin Young "The Set Up" and "The Chase" from *Black Maria*. Copyright © 2005 by Kevin Young. Used by permission of Alfred A. Knopf, a division of Random House, Inc.
Mary Zimmerman *Metamorphoses*. Evanston: Northwestern University Press, 2002. Copyright © 2002 Mary Zimmerman. Reprinted by permission of Northwest University Press.

IMAGE CREDITS

Chapter 1. 2: top Edouard Boubat/Rapho/H.P.P. **7:** top center, Erich Lessing/Art Resource, NY **14:** top, Summit Entertainment/ The Kobal Collection
Chapter 2. 123: top, Bettman/Corbis **124:** top center, Bettman/Corbis
Chapter 3. 201: center left, Corbis; center right, MGM/The Kobal Collection **209:** bottom center, Mary Evans Picture Library/The Image Works
Chapter 4. 283: bottom, Stapleton Collection/Corbis **284:** bottom center, Erich Lessing/Art Resource, NY **285:** top, Piero Sanpaolesi,

BRUNELLESCHI. Florence, S. Barbera, 1962, figure C, opposite page 52
287: bottom center, Foto Marburg/Art Resource, NY; top center, Photo:
Elke Walford. Bildarchiv Preussischer Kulturbesitz/Art Resource, NY **293:**
bottom, Everett Collection; top, © Jerry Tavin/Everett Collection **294:**
top, Everett Collection; bottom, Prana-Film/The Kobal Collection **297:**
bottom, Bettmann/Corbis **300:** bottom center, © The Lane Collection
Courtesy, Museum of Fine Arts, Boston
Chapter 5. 400: bottom, Lake Country Museum/Corbis **404:** bottom,
Bettmann/Corbis **410:** top, Sketch by Luc Desportes, used with
permission; sketch and film still reproduced with the permission of
Jean-Pierre Jeunet **410:** bottom, Sketch by Luc Desportes, used with
permission; sketch and film still reproduced with the permission of
Jean-Pierre Jeunet **411:** bottom, Universal/The Kobal Collection/
Mill Film
Chapter 6. 510: bottom center, Everett Collection
Chapter 7. 633: top left, Onne van der Wal/Corbis **633:** top right, Onne
van der Wal/Corbis **633:** center, Onne van der Wal/Corbis **633:** bottom
center, The Museum of Modern Art, New York, NY. Digital Image © The
Museum of Modern Art/Licensed by SCALA /Art Resource, NY **636:**
bottom center, Fox Searchlight Pictures/The Kobal Collection/Wallace,
Merie W. **638:** top center, Hulton-Deutsch Collection/Corbis **642:**
bottom, Focus Features/The Kobal Collection/Sato, Yoshio; top, Miramax/
Dimension Films/The Kobal Collection/Tursi, Mario **646:** bottom center,
Photograph by Rollie McKenna. Copyright © 2006 The Estate of Rosalie
Thorne McKenna **647:** top, RKO/The Kobal Collection
Chapter 8. 712: top, Toutchstone/The Kobal Collection/Moseley,
Melissa
Chapter 9. 788: bottom, 20th Century Fox/The Kobal Collection **789:**
top, 20th Century Fox/The Kobal Collection **795:** top, © Miramax/
Everett Collection **796:** bottom, Photo by Margaret Bourke-White//Time
Life Pictures/Getty Images **800:** bottom, Photo by Dirck Halstead//Time
Life Pictures/Getty Images; top, Photo by Taro Yamasaki/Time Life
Pictures/Getty Images
Chapter 10. 1021: bottom center, Photo by Margaret Bourke-White/
Time Life Pictures/Getty Images **1022:** top, copyright © Walt Disney Co./
Courtesy Everett/Everett Collection
Chapter 11. 1081: bottom, 20th Century Fox/The Kobal Collection/
Kirkland, Douglas
Chapter 12. 1196: top center, From TOOTLE by Gertrude Crampton
and Tibor Gergeley, copyright 1945, renewed 1972 by Random House,
Inc. Used by permission of Golden Books, an imprint of Random House
Children's Books, a division of Random House, Inc. **1199:** top, Corbis
1200: bottom center, Bettmann/Corbis **1201:** top center, 89.PA.32, The

J. Paul Getty Museum, Los Angeles **1208:** top center, Corbis Sygma **1228:** top center, Hulton Archive/Getty Images **1231:** top right, Stapleton Collection/Corbis; top left, Trustees, Cecil Higgins Art Gallery, Bedford, England
Chapter 13. 1253: bottom center, Clarita Natoli/moreguefile.com **1259:** top, Bettmann/Corbis; bottom left, Blue Lantern Studio/Corbis; center right, Chris Hellier/Corbis; bottom right, Royalty-Free/Corbis **1260:** bottom left, Bettmann/Corbis; center right, Bettmann/Corbis; bottom right, James Leynes/Corbis; top, John Springer Collection/Corbis
Chapter 14. 1396: bottom, Zoetrope/United Artists/The Kobal Collection **1401:** bottom, Warner Bros/First National/The Kobal Collection **1403:** bottom right, © Private Collection/The Bridgeman Art Library **1409:** center, Hieroglyphic line for "The Third Bank of the River" (A Terceira Margem Do Rio), from João Guimarães Rosa, Primeiras Estórias, Editora Nova Fronteira, Rio de Janeiro, Brazil
Chapter 15. 1480: bottom center, Scala/Art Resource, NY **1482:** center, Bettmann/Corbis; bottom center, Corbis Sygma
Chapter 16. 1589: bottom center, Photo by Kevin Winter/Getty Images **1593:** top left, Bettmann/Corbis; top right, Bettmann/Corbis **1594:** bottom, Paramount/The Kobal Collection **1595:** bottom center, Warner Bros/The Kobal Collection
Chapter 17. 1678: Yale Center for British Art, Paul Mellon Collection, USA/The Bridgeman Art Library **1686:** bottom center, Private Collection/Ken Walsh/The Bridgeman Art Library **1687:** top, John Springer Collection/Corbis; bottom, R.P. Productions/Runteam Ltd/The Kobal Collection/Ferrandis, Guy
Chapter 18. 1704: Shakespeare Quarterly 57:1 (2006). Table of Contents Page. © Folger Shakespeare Library. Reprinted with permission of The Johns Hopkins University Press.

Index of First Lines of Poetry

A disembodied piano. The headphones allow,   1546

A Gentle Knight was pricking on the plaine,   1228

A little black thing among the snow,   570

A poet reads his lines to the blind,   634

A Route of Evanescence,   59

A single flower he sent me, since we met,   1008

A snake came to my water-trough,   236

A sudden blow: the great wings beating still,   235

About suffering they were never wrong,   1062

About the Shark, phlegmatical one,   514

Across the road from Ford's a Mrs. Strempek,   300

After each war,   1461

After great pain, a formal feeling comes—,   1640

After we flew across the country we,   869

All around the apt. swimming pool,   773

All Greece hates,   336

Among twenty snowy mountains,   691

And did young Stephen sicken,   1591

And I start wondering how they came to be blind,   1060

anyone lived in a pretty how town,   1304

Apple-smell everywhere!,   1306

Arraign'd before his worldly gods,   1442

As a young girl,   1459

As one who long in populous city pent,   640

As the stores close, a winter light,   402

As virtuous men pass mildly away,   895

As you lay in sleep,   868

At eight I was brilliant with my body,   181

August and the drive-in picture is packed,   1637

Aunt Jennifer's tigers prance across a screen,   180

Basketball is like this for young Indian boys, all arms and legs,   1064

Batter my heart, three-personed God; for you,   1235

Beautiful, splendid, magnificent,   1092

Because I could not stop for Death—,   1237

Because it hadn't seemed enough,   1256

Bent double, like old beggars under sacks,   1452

Blizzards of paper,   15

Busy old fool, unruly sun,   894

Careless man, my father,   1704

Childhood is not from birth to a certain age and at a certain age,   332

Come live with me and be my love,   1128

Come, Madam, come, all rest my powers defy,   1119

Condemn'd to Hope's delusive
mine,   518
Constantly risking absurdity,   774

Death, be not proud, though some
have callèd thee,   1237
Do not go gentle into that good
night,   724
Driving the last stretch before the
home stretch, past the lake,   452

Earth has not anything to show more
fair,   685
Eden is that old-fashioned
House,   1199
Every summer,   448

Farewell dear babe, my heart's too
much content,   1631
Farewell, rewards and fairies,   1231
Farewell, thou child of my right hand,
and joy,   520
father, it was an honor to be there, in
the dugout,   170
First, are you our sort of a
person?,   337
For Alexander there was no Far
East,   871
For God's sake, hold your tongue, and
let me love!,   1235
From fairest creatures we desire
increase,   1084
From my mother's sleep I fell into the
State,   523

Glory be to God for dappled
things—,   1238
Good morning, daddy!,   573
Grief for a generation—all,   1527
Groping along the tunnel, step by
step,   1453

Had we but world enough and
time,   1130
Half a league, half a league,   1393
Have you noticed?,   697

He is too heavy and careless, my
father,   1703
He loved her and she loved
him,   233
He saw her from the bottom of the
stairs,   161
he took a large sheet,   769
He was born in Alabama,   1624
His parents would sit alone
together,   454
How do I love thee? Let me count the
ways,   1131
How the days went,   165

I am silver and exact. I have no
preconceptions,   338
I am walking rapidly through striations
of light and dark thrown under an
arcade,   1545
I am wondering what become of all
those tall abstractions,   1202
I ate at the counter,   1066
I bought a dollar and a half 's worth of
small red potatoes,   726
I can feel the tug,   1635
I caught a tremendous fish,   330
I caught this morning morning's
minion, king,   1239
I didn't have a rat's chance,   64
I found a dimpled spider, fat and
white,   723
I grew up bent over a
chessboard,   333
I have been one acquainted with the
night,   689
I have eaten,   328
I have just,   329
I like a look of Agony,   1640
I like it when,   1477
I like to see it lap the Miles—,   60
I met a traveler from an antique
land,   1520
I never saw a Moor—,   893
I prefer red chile over my eggs,   1302
I remember the neckcurls, limp and
damp as tendrils,   1634

I sat all morning in the college sick bay, 176
I see them standing at the formal gates of their colleges, 576
i sing of Olaf glad and big, 1447
I sit and sew—a useless task it seems, 1457
I tell them, look. Sure, I was around, 65
I wake to sleep, and take my waking slow, 572
I wander thro each chartered street, 684
I wandered lonely as a cloud, 686
I was a peasant girl from Germany, 160
I was the only child of Frances Harris of Virginia, 161
I wonder, by my troth, what thou and I, 334
I, being born a woman and distressed, 722
I'll never find out now, 5
I've known rivers, 573
If all the world and love were young, 1129
If there is no God, 1019
In a solitude of the sea, 717
in brussels, eye sat in the grand place cafe & heard, 1063
In ethics class so many years ago, 239
in Just-, 693
In silent night when rest I took, 1632
In the country of the ochre afternoon, 699
In the pathway of the sun, 285
In Xanadu did Kubla Khan, 436
Into the lower right, 776
Is it for fear to wet a widow's eye, 1087
Is this a holy thing to see, 570
is what you first see, stepping off the train, 1460
It costs me never a stab nor squirm, 1009

It could be the name of a prehistoric beast, 1089
It is a land with neither night nor day, 440
It is an ancient Mariner, 872
It is in the small things we see it, 1455
It little profits that an idle king, 890
it was not a very formal affair but, 171

Januaries, Nature greets our eyes, 867

Lady with the frilled blouse, 1305
late, in aqua and ermine, gardenias, 124
Let us go then, you and I, 653
Little Lamb, who made thee?, 567
Lo! in the orient when the gracious light, 1086
Long afterward, Oedipus, old and blinded, walked the, 66
Look in thy glass, and tell the face thou viewest, 1086
Lord, Who createdst man in wealth and store, 716
Love that doth reign and live within my thought, 1122
Love's the boy stood on the burning deck, 232

Mark but this flea, and mark in this, 1009
Maud went to college, 176
memory: farfields of morning, 1522
Milton! thou should'st be living at this hour, 684
Mother dear, may I go downtown, 447
Much have I traveled in the realms of gold, 1527
Music to hear, why hear'st thou music sadly?, 1087
My black face fades, 1458
My daughter—as if I, 1307

My father loved more than
    anything to,   339
My grandfather said to me,   770
My heart leaps up when I
    behold,   1481
My Love in her attire doth show
    her wit,   1119
My prime of youth is but a frost of
    cares,   1633

Night funeral,   1638
No sleep. The sultriness pervades
    the air,   1404
Nobody heard him, the dead
    man,   299
Not like the brazen giant of Greek
    fame,   1314
Not like the white filmstars,
    all rib,   453
Not only the Eskimos,   1068
Now light the candles; one; two;
    there's a moth,   1454
Nuns fret not at their convent's
    narrow room,   722

O Duty,   1239
O, my Love's like a red, red
    rose,   1126
O what can ail thee, knight at
    arms,   230
Of a green color, standing in a shed
    alongside rakes and spades, it comes
    alive,   632
On either side the river lie,   1528
On the day the world ends,   1397
Once riding in old Baltimore,   575
Once there was a man who filmed his
    vacation,   291
Once upon a midnight dreary,
    while I pondered, weak and
    weary,   437
One foot down, then hop! It's
    hot,   694
One garland,   1128
One must have a mind of
    winter,   690

One that is ever kind said
    yesterday,   792
Pile the bodies high at Austerlitz and
    Waterloo,   1453
Plain be the phrase, yet apt the
    verse,   1441

Right down the shocked street with a
    siren-blast,   643
Round the cape of a sudden came
    the sea,   1133
Row after row with strict
    impunity,   1625
Roy Smith ran traps for furs,   1479

Season of mists and mellow
    fruitfulness,   1630
Securely sunning in a forest
    glade,   238
Shall I compare thee to a summer's
    day?,   1088
She had thought the studio would
    keep itself,   335
She is the woman hanging from the
    13th floor,   446
She must have been kicked unseen or
    brushed by a car,   1642
She was a year younger,   127
since feeling is first,   1124
Snake oil sales,   62
so much depends,   631
So you have swept me back,   1541
Some say the world will end in
    fire,   524
Somewhere,   695
Sonny said, Then he shouldn't have
    given Molly the two more
    babies,   4
Spring is like a perhaps hand,   1123
Standing on flagstones of the sidewalk
    at the entrance to Hades,   1534
Stiff and immaculate,   130
Sundays too my father got up
    early,   128
Swan-diving off the crewcut mesas of
    Monument Valley,   1521

Take two photographs—,   645

Take, oh take those lips
away,   1121

Tell all the Truth but tell it
slant—,   893

That is no country for old men. The
young,   1533

That was the deep uncanny mine of
souls,   1536

That's my last Duchess painted on the
wall,   303

That's my last Duke painted on the
wall,   327

The ache of marriage,   1127

The air was soft, the ground still
cold,   695

The ambulance men touched her
cold,   577

The apparition of these faces in the
crowd,   690

The art of losing isn't hard to
master,   1062

The bonsai tree,   203

The Brain—is wider than the
Sky—,   892

The clouds and the stars didn't wage
this war,   1465

The crowd at the ball game,   1310

The first time I walked,   1261

The gray sea and the long black
land,   1132

The instructor said,   870

The last small credits fade,   295

The litter under the tree,   793

The long love that in my heart doth
harbor,   1122

The map of places passes,   871

The miller's wife had waited
long,   174

The old South Boston Aquarium
stands,   1628

The only legend I have ever loved
is,   165

The other day I was ricocheting
slowly,   173

The problem is being a fragment trying
to live out a whole life,   302

The rain set early in to-night,   1233

The sea is calm tonight,   1301

The Soul selects her own
Society—,   1305

The South China Sea,   1067

The sun is blazing and the sky is
blue,   1312

The things that make a soldier
great,   1449

The trees are in their autumn
beauty,   1311

The whiskey on your breath,   571

The world is too much with us;
late and soon,   686

The year's first poem done,   648

There are dogs and dogs. I was among
the chosen,   1463

There is sorrow enough in the natural
way,   1641

There is sweet music here that softer
falls,   522

There was a child went forth every
day,   1308

There was crimson clash of
war,   1446

There's a breathless hush in the
Close to-night—,   1450

There's a certain Slant of light,   687

There's a thin film of March snow on
the street—,   175

There's in my mind a woman,   575

They were women then,   1307

Thine eyes shall see the light of
distant skies,   769

This is the one song everyone,   1015

This is the south. I look for
evidence,   444

Thou still unravish'd bride of
quietness,   1524

To make a prairie it takes a clover
and one bee,   893

Traveling through the dark I found a
deer,   62

True Mexicans or not, let's open our
shirts,   450

'Twas brillig, and the slithy
toves,   1227

Twas mercy brought me from my Pagan land, 771

Twas on a Holy Thursday their innocent faces clean, 569

Two girls there are: within the house, 1523

Two roads diverged in a yellow wood, 772

Tyger! Tyger! burning bright, 569

Up ahead, I know, he felt it stirring in himself already, the glance, the, 1539

Using salal leaves for money, 451

We caught the tread of dancing feet, 441

We did not know the first thing about, 777

We real cool. We, 574

Western wind, when wilt thou blow, 1121

What happens to a dream deferred?, xxxvii

What lips my lips have kissed, and where, and why, 1127

What once was meant to be a statement, 798

What passing-bells for these who die as cattle?, 1451

What thoughts I have of you tonight, Walt Whitman, for I walked down, 775

What you have heard is true. I was in his house. His wife carried a tray of coffee, 234

When forty winters shall beseige thy brow, 1085

When I have fears that I may cease to be, 1526

When I see birches bend to left and right, 688

When I was twenty the one true, 1125

When lilacs last in the dooryard bloom'd, 1617

When my mother died I was very young, 568

When our two souls stand up erect and strong, 1132

When the call comes, be calm, 177

When the voices of children are heard on the green, 514

Whenever Richard Cory went down town, 60

Who has ever stopped to think of the divinity of Lamont Cranston?, 1240

Whose woods these are I think I know, 61

Wild Nights—Wild Nights!, 1124

Women have loved before as I love now, 232

Yes I admit a degree of unease about my, 1242

Yet once more, O ye laurels, and once more, 1612

You couldn't have heard about it there—, 1011

You do not do, you do not do, 167

You fit into me, 1007

You would think the fury of aerial bombardment, 1448

Your absence has gone through me, 336

Index of Authors and Titles

Italics indicate a title of a work of art, film, or literature.

1:53 A.M., 175

A&P, 743
ABC, 5
Ache of Marriage, The, 1127
Achebe, Chinua, 1016
  Dead Men's Path, 1016
Acquainted with the Night, 689
Adams, Douglas, 790
  Hitchhiker's Guide to the Galaxy, The, from, 790
Adventures of Huckleberry Finn, from, 1688
Aesop, 1198, 1199
  Crow and the Pitcher, The, 1198
After a Movie, 295
After great pain, a formal feeling comes, 1640
After the Chuck Jones Tribute on Teletoon, 1521
Alexie, Sherman, 1064, 1739
  Defending Walt Whitman, 1064
Allegory of the Cave, The, 1204
Amazing Adventures of Kavalier & Clay, The, from, 117
Andrews, Ginger, 451
  Rolls-Royce Dreams, 451
Angelou, Maya, 694, 1739
  Harlem Hopscotch, 694
Anonymous, 1119, 1121
  Western Wind, 1121
  My Love in Her Attire, 1119
Anthem for Doomed Youth, 1451
Antigone, 20, 67, 68, 1600, 1643
anyone lived in a pretty how town, 1304
Applicant, The, 337
April 5, 1974, 695
Araby, 416

Arnold, Matthew, 1268, 1301, 1740
  Dover Beach, 1301
At the Ball Game, 1310
Atwood, Margaret, 1007, 1015, 1600, 1609, 1740
  Happy Endings, 1609
  Siren Song, 1015
  you fit into me, 1007
Auden, W. H., 1062, 1740
  Musée des Beaux Arts, 1062
Aunt Jennifer's Tigers, 180

Baca, Jimmy Santiago, 1302, 1741
  Green Chile, 1302
Baldwin, James, 526, 527, 578
  Sonny's Blues, 527
Ballad of Birmingham, 442
Baraka, Amiri, 1240, 1741
  In Memory of Radio, 1240
Barnes, Dick, 1478, 1479
  Up Home Where I Come From, 1479
Bartleby, the Scrivener, 1031
Batter My Heart, Three Personed God, 1235
Beattie, Ann, 306
Janus, 307
Beauty, 1245
Because I could not stop for Death—, 1237
Berry, Wendell, 291
  Vacation, The, 291
Birches, 688
Bishop, Elizabeth, 213, 232, 330, 770, 867, 1062, 1312, 1741
  Brazil, January, 1502, 867
  Casabianca, 232
  Fish, The, 330
  Manners for a Child of 1918, 770

One Art,   1062
Pink Dog,   1312
Black Hair,   181
Blake, William,   514, 562, 567, 568,
   569, 570, 684, 1742
   A Poison Tree,   1678
   Chimney Sweeper (Experience),
      The,   570
   Chimney Sweeper (Innocence),
      The,   568
   Holy Thursday (Experience),   570
   Holy Thursday (Innocence),   569
   Lamb, The,   567
   London,   684
   Nurse's Song,   514
   Tyger, The,   569
Bogan, Louise,   868, 1742
   Cartography,   868
Boland, Eavan,   165, 1742
   Pomegranate, The,   165
Bone Poem,   793
Borges, Jorge Luis,   806
   Garden of Forking Paths, The,   806
Bowers, Neale,   1704
   Ten-Year Elegy,   1704
Boy Who Nearly Won the Texaco Art
   Competition, The,   769
Boys and Girls,   660
Bradstreet, Anne,   1631, 1632, 1743
   Here Followes Some Verses upon the
      Burning of Our House July 10,
      1666,   1632
   In Memory of My Dear Grandchild,
      Elizabeth Bradstreet, Who Deceased
      August 1665, Being a Year and a
      Half Old,   1631
Brain—is wider than the Sky—,
   The,   892
Braly Street,   448
Brazil, January, 1502,   867
Break from the Bush, A,   1069
Brooks, Gwendolyn,   176, 574, 1624,
   1743
   De Witt Williams on His Way to
      Lincoln Cemetery,   1624
   Sadie and Maud,   176
   We Real Cool,   574

Browning, Elizabeth Barrett,   1131,
   1132, 1743
   How do I love thee? Let me count the
      ways,   1131
   When our two souls stand up,   1132
Browning, Robert,   303, 412, 524,
   1132, 1133, 1233, 1744
   Meeting at Night,   1132
   My Last Duchess,   303
   Parting at Morning,   1133
   Porphyria's Lover,   1233
Bryant, William Cullen,   730, 769
   To Cole, the Painter, Departing for
      Europe,   769
Bulwer-Lytton Contest Winners,   1094
Burns, Robert,   1126, 1744
   Red, Red Rose, A,   1126
Buson, Yosa,   648
   Hokku Poems in Four Seasons,   648

Canonization, The,   1235
Carroll, Lewis,   1745
   Jabberwocky,   1227
Carson, Anne,   1242, 1745
   TV Men: Lazarus,   1242
Cartography,   868
Carver, Raymond,   854, 1098
   Cathedral,   855
   What We Talk about When We Talk
      about Love,   1098
Casabianca,   232
Cathedral,   855
Censors, The,   214
Chabon, Michael,   117
   Amazing Adventures of Kavalier &
      Clay, The, from,   117
Changeling, The,   1459
Charge of the Light Brigade,
   The,   1393
Chase, The,   64
Chekhov, Anton,   182
   Proposal, The,   182
Chesnutt, Charles W.,   733
   Wife of His Youth, The,   733
Childhood,   452
Childhood Is the Kingdom Where Nobody
   Dies,   332

Chimney Sweeper (Experience),
    The,   568
Chimney Sweeper (Innocence),
    The,   570
Chinese Banquet, A,   171
Chopin, Kate,   306, 311
    Story of an Hour,   312
Christmas Carol, A, from,   288
Christopher Robin,   1399
Clampitt, Amy,   1527, 1745
    Dakota, The,   1527
Cobwebs,   440
Cofer, Judith Ortiz,   130, 1459, 1746
    Changeling, The,   1459
    My Father in the Navy: A Childhood
        Memory,   130
Coleridge, Samuel Taylor,   415, 436,
    872, 1746
    Kubla Khan: or, a Vision in a
        Dream,   436
    Rime of the Ancient Mariner,
        The,   872
Collins, Billy,   173, 1060, 1089, 1202,
    1746
    Death of Allegory, The,   1202
    I Chop Some Parsley While Listening
        to Art Blakey's Version of "Three
        Blind Mice",   1060
    Lanyard,   173
    Thesaurus,   234
Colonel, The,   685
Composed upon Westminster Bridge,
    September, 3, 1802,   685
Conrad, Joseph,   805, 814
    Secret Sharer, The,   815
Constantly risking absurdity,   774
Convergence of the Twain, The,   717
Corbett, Richard,   1231
    Fairies Farewell, The,   1231
Courage,   1455
Courtesy of the Blind,   634
Crampton, Gertrude,   1196
    Tootle, from,   1446
Crane, Stephen,   8, 516, 1446, 1747
    Episode of War, An,   8
    There Was a Crimson Clash of
        War,   1446

Crow and the Pitcher, The,   1198
Cullen, Countee,   575, 1747
    Incident,   575
cummings, e. e.,   456, 693, 1123,
    1124, 1304, 1411, 1447, 1747
    anyone lived in a pretty how
        town,   1304
    in Just-,   693
    I sing of Olaf glad and big,   1447
    since feeling is first,   1124
    Spring is like a perhaps hand,   1123

Daddy,   167
Dakota, The,   1527
De Duplici Copia Verborum et Rerum,
    from,   1278
De Witt Williams on His Way to Lincoln
    Cemetery,   1624
Dead Men's Path,   1016
Dear John Wayne,   1637
Death Be Not Proud,   1237
Death of Allegory, The,   1202
Death of a Salesman,   1315
Death of Marilyn Monroe, The,   577
Death of the Ball Turret Gunner,
    The,   523
Defending Walt Whitman,   1064
Design,   723
Dickens, Charles,   288, 799, 1476
    Christmas Carol, from,   288
Dickinson, Emily,   19, 59, 687, 892,
    893, 1124, 1199, 1237, 1305,
    1640, 1747
    After great pain, a formal feeling
        comes,   1640
    Because I could not stop for
        Death—,   1237
    Brain—is wider than the Sky—,
        The,   892
    Eden is that old-fashioned
        House,   1199
    I like a look of Agony,   1640
    I like to see it lap the Miles—,   60
    I never saw a Moor—,   893
    Route of Evanescence, A,   59
    Soul selects her own Society—
        The,   1305

Tell all the Truth but tell it slant—, 893
There's a certain Slant of light, 687
To make a prairie it takes a clover and one bee, 893
Wild Nights—Wild Nights!, 1124
Dill Pickle, A, 1024
Divakaruni, Chitra Banerjee, 415, 453
Indian Movie, New Jersey, 453
Divorcing, 1128
Do Not Go Gentle into That Good Night, 724
Doctor Faustus, 240
Dog's Death, 1642
Doll's House, A, 1134
Donne, John, 334, 894, 895, 1009, 1119, 1215, 1235, 1237, 1748
Batter My Heart, Three-Personed God, 1235
Canonization, The, 1235
Death Be Not Proud, 1237
Elegy 19: To His Mistress Going to Bed, 1119
Flea, The, 1009
Good-Morrow, The, 334
Sun Rising, The, 894
Valediction: Forbidding Mourning, A, 895
Dove, Rita, 123, 124, 133
Hattie McDaniel Arrives at the Coconut Grove, 124
Dover Beach, 1301
Doyle, Arthur Conan, 12, 20
Scandal in Bohemia, A, 21
Dream Boogie, 573
Dreiser, Theodore, 402, 403
Sister Carrie, from, 403
Dry Season, 699
Dulce et Decorum Est, 1452
Dumka, The, 454
Dunbar-Nelson, Alice Moore, 1457
I Sit and Sew, 1457
Duncan, Robert, 1522
Persephone, 1522
Durang, Christopher, 1025, 1070, 1483
Medea, 1071

Easter Wings, 716
Eberhart, Richard, 1448, 1749
Fury of Aerial Bombardment, The, 1448
Eden is that old-fashioned House, 1199
Elegy for Jane, 1634
Elegy Written with His Own Hand in the Tower before His Execution, 1633
Elegy 19: To His Mistress Going to Bed, 1119
Eliot, T. S., 509, 653, 652, 729, 802, 1748, 1749
Love Song of J. Alfred Prufrock, The, 653
Elsa Wertman, 160
End and the Beginning, The, 1461
Episode of War, An, 8
Erasmus, 1078, 1079, 1088
De Duplici Copia Verborum et Rerum, from, 1078
Erdrich, Louise, 1637, 1749
Dear John Wayne, 1637
Essay on Criticism, An, from, 522
Ethics, 239
Eurydice, 1541
Everyday Use, 153
Execution of Cornelius Vane, The, 1442

Fable, A, 238
Facing It, 1458
Faerie Queene, The, from, 1228
Fairchild, B. H., 454
The Dumka, 454
Fairies Farewell, The, 1231
Fall of the House of Usher, The, 421
Faulkner, William, 719, 1269, 1512
Rose for Emily, A, 1513
February Evening in New York, 402
Ferlinghetti, Lawrence, 731, 774, 1750
Constantly risking absurdity, 774
Fifteen Minute Hamlet, The, 1487
Fire and Ice, 524
Fire-Truck, A, 643
Fish, The, 330
Flea, The, 1009

Fletcher, John,   1121
  Take, oh take those lips away,   1121
Foer, Jonathan Safran,   732, 748,
  749, 751
  Very Rigid Search, The,   748
Folly of Being Comforted, The,   792
Forché, Carolyn,   214, 234, 1750
  Colonel, The,   234
For Gloria on Her 60th Birthday,
  or Looking for Love in
  Merriam-Webster,   1092
For the Record,   1465
For the Union Dead,   1628
From fairest creatures we desire
  increase,   1084
Frost, Robert,   61, 133, 161, 523,
  524, 658, 688, 689, 722, 723,
  772, 1750
  Acquainted with the Night,   689
  Birches,   688
  Design,   723
  Fire and Ice,   524
  Home Burial,   161
  Road Not Taken, The,   772
  Stopping by Woods on a Snowy
    Evening,   61
Fury of Aerial Bombardment,
  The,   1448

Gambino, Erica-Lynn,   306, 329
  This Is Just to Say,   329
García Márquez, Gabriel,   1269, 1275
  Handsomest Drowned Man in the
    World, The,   1275
  Very Old Man with Enormous
    Wings, A,   1269
Garden of Forking Paths, The,   806
Gaspar, Frank X.,   302
  It Is the Nature of the Wing,   302
Ghosts,   697
Gilman, Charlotte Perkins,   314
  Yellow Wallpaper, The,   314
Ginsberg, Allen,   731, 775, 1751
  Supermarket in California,   775
Girl,   16
Girl and the Wolf, The,   201

Glaspell, Susan,   659, 699, 1725,
  1726
  Trifles,   700
Glass Menagerie, The,   456
Good Man Is Hard To Find, A,   217
Good-Morrow, The,   334
Graham, Jorie,   1539, 1751
  Orpheus and Eurydice,   1539
Grass,   1453
Green Chile,   1302
Guest, Edgar A.,   1449
  Things That Make a Soldier
    Great, The,   1449

Hairnet with Stars, A,   1066
Hamilton Greene,   161
Hamlet,   896
Handsomest Drowned Man in the World,
  The,   1275
Happy Endings,   1609
Hardy, Thomas,   717, 1752
  Convergence of the Twain, The,   717
Harjo, Joy,   415, 444, 446, 1752
  Woman Hanging from the Thirteenth
    Floor Window, The,   446
  New Orleans,   444
Harlem,   xxxvii
Harlem Hopscotch,   694
Harlot's House, The,   441
Hattie McDaniel Arrives at the Coconut
  Grove,   124
Hawthorne, Nathaniel,   1215, 1216,
  1263
  Young Goodman Brown,   1216
Hayden, Robert,   128, 1752
  Those Winter Sundays,   128
H. D.,   336, 1541, 1497, 1748
  Eurydice,   1541
  Helen,   336
Heaney, Seamus,   176, 1305, 1635,
  1753, 1775
  Mid-Term Break,   176
  Punishment,   1635
  Valediction,   1305
Helen,   336
Hemingway, Ernest,   289, 290, 1412,
  1730, 1735

Hills Like White Elephants,
   from,   1730
Soldier's Home,   1413
Herbert, George,   716, 1753
   Easter Wings,   716
Here Followes Some Verses upon the
   Burning of Our House July 10,
   1666,   1632
Hills Like White Elephants, from,   1730
Hitchhiker's Guide to the Galaxy, The,
   from,   790
Hokku Poems in Four Seasons,   648
Holy Thursday (Experience),   570
Holy Thursday (Innocence),   569
Home Burial,   161
Home Movies: A Sort of Ode,   1256
Hopkins, Gerard Manley,   1238,
   1239, 1753
   Pied Beauty,   1238
   Windhover, The,   1239
House-Top, The,   1404
How do I love thee? Let me count the
   ways,   1131
How I Met My Husband,   134
How to Watch Your Brother Die,   177
Howard, Henry, Earl of Surrey,   1122,
   1754
   Love, that doth reign within my
   thought,   1122
Hughes, Langston,   573, 870, 1599,
   1638, 1721, 1722, 1743, 1754
   Dream Boogie,   573
   Harlem,   xxxvii
   Negro Speaks of Rivers, The,   573,
   1743
   Night Funeral in Harlem,   1638
   Theme for English B,   870
Hughes, Ted,   233, 1764, 1755
   Lovesong,   233
Hurston, Zora Neale,   1012, 1013
   Mules and Men, from,   1013

I, Being Born a Woman and
   Distressed,   722
I Chop Some Parsley While Listening to
   Art Blakey's Version of "Three
   Blind Mice",   1060

I Dream I'm the Death of
   Orpheus,   1545
I Go Back to May 1937,   576
I like a look of Agony,   1640
I like to see it lap the miles—,   60
I never saw a Moor—,   893
I sing of Olaf glad and big,   1447
I Sit and Sew,   1457
I Stand Here Ironing,   1434
I wandered lonely as a cloud,   686
Ibsen, Henrik,   1098, 1133
   Doll's House, A,   1134
If There Is No God,   1019
In a Station of the Metro,   690
in Just-,   693
In Memory of My Dear Grandchild,
   Elizabeth Bradstreet, Who Deceased
   August 1665, Being a Year and
   Half Old,   1631
In Memory of Radio,   1240
In Mind,   575
Incident,   575
Indian Movie, New Jersey,   453
Is it for fear to wet a widow's
   eye,   1087
Ishiguro, Kazuo,   405
   Remains of the Day, from,   406
It Is the Nature of the Wing,   302
Ives, David,   732, 778
   Sure Thing,   778

Jabberwocky,   1227
Jackson, Shirley,   1293
   Lottery, The,   1294
Janus,   307
Jarrell, Randall,   523
   Death of the Ball Turret Gunner,
   The,   523
Jilting of Granny Weatherall,
   The,   1601
Johnson, Samuel,   517, 518, 519
   On the Death of Dr. Robert
   Levet,   518
Jones, David,   1705, 1707
   Ten-Year Elegy (plagiarized),   1704
Jonson, Ben,   519, 520
   On My First Son,   520

Joyce, James,   291, 415, 1484
  Araby,   416
Julius Caesar, from,   1707

Kane, Joe,   769
  Boy Who Nearly Won the Texaco Art
    Competition, The,   769
Kearney Park,   450
Keating, Helane Levine,   306, 327
  My Last Duke,   327
Keats, John,   230, 1258, 1524, 1526,
    1527, 1630, 1755
  La Belle Dame sans Merci: A
    Ballad,   230
  Ode on a Grecian Urn,   1524
  Ode to Autumn,   1630
  On First Looking into Chapman's
    Homer,   1527
  When I have fears that I may cease
    to be,   1526
Keesbury, Aron,   65
  On the Robbery across the Street,   65
Keyboard,   1546
Kincaid, Jamaica,   16, 131, 211
  Girl,   10
Kind of an Ode to Duty,   1239
King Kong Meets Wallace Stevens,   645
Kingston, Maxine Hong,   205, 210
  Wild Man of the Green Swamp,
    The,   205
Kinnell, Galway,   1125, 1403, 1755
  Shelley,   1125
Kipling, Rudyard,   1641, 1756
  Power of the Dog, The,   1641
Komunyakaa, Yusef,   1067, 1458,
    1756
  Break from the Bush, A,   1067
  Facing It,   1458
Kooser, Ted,   1797, 798, 1010, 1011,
    1066, 1756
  Hairnet with Stars, A,   1066
  Letter from Aunt Belle, A,   1011
  Tattoo,   798
Kubla Khan: or, a Vision in a
    Dream,   436

La Belle Dame sars Merci:
  A Ballad,   230
Lady of Shalott, The,   1528
Lahiri, Jhumpa,   1267, 1279
  This Blessed House,   1280
Lamb, The,   567
Lanyard,   173
Lassell, Michael,   177
  How to Watch Your Brother
    Die,   177
Lawrence, D. H.,   1757
  Snake,   236
Lazarus, Emma,   1314
  New Colossus, The,   1314
Le Guin, Ursula K.,   526, 553, 1778
  Ones Who Walk Away from Omelas,
    The,   554
Leda and the Swan,   235
Lee, Don,   19, 39, 116
  Price of Eggs in China, The,   39
Letter from Aunt Belle, A,   1011
Levertov, Denise,   401, 402, 575,
    1098, 1127, 1128, 1757
  Ache of Marriage, The,   1127
  Divorcing,   1128
  February Evening in New York,   402
  In Mind,   575
Levine, Philip,   300, 726, 1757
  Photography 2.   300
  Simple Truth, The,   726
Little Red Riding Hood,   198
Living in Sin,   335
Lo! in the orient when the gracious
    light,   1086
London,   1086
London, 1802,   684
Long love that in my heart doth harbor,
    the,   1122
Look in thy glass, and tell the face thou
    viewest,   1086
Lorde, Audre,   165, 1758
  Now That I Am Forever with
    Child,   165
Lottery, The,   1294
Lotus Eaters, The,   522

Love Song of J. Alfred Prufrock,
    The, 653
Love that doth reign and live within my
    thought, 1122
Lovesong, 233
Lowell, Robert, 1628, 1758
    For the Union Dead, 1628
Lust, 559
Lux, Thomas, 773, 1758
    Swimming Pool, The, 773
Lycidas, 1612

Macbeth, from, 1588
Maldive Shark, The, 514
Manners for a Child of 1918, 770
Mansfield, Katherine, 1024, 1025
    Dill Pickle, A, 1025
Map of Places, The, 871
Marlowe, Christopher, 213, 240,
    1128
    Passionate Shepherd to His Love,
        The, 1128
    Tragical History of the Life and Death
        of Doctor Faustus, The, 240
Martin, Jane, 1215, 1245
    Beauty, 1245
Marvell, Andrew, 1130, 1759
    To His Coy Mistress, 1130
Masters, Edgar Lee, 133, 160, 1759
    Elsa Wertman, 160
    Hamilton Greene, 161
McCartney, Sharon, 1521
    After the Chuck Jones Tribute on
        Teletoon, 1521
Medea, 1071
Meeting at Night, 1132
Meinke, Peter, 1306
    Sunday at the Apple Market, 1306
Melville, Herman, 514, 728, 1024,
    1031, 1404, 1441, 1759
    Bartleby, the Scrivener, 1031
    House-Top, The, 1404
    Maldive Shark, The, 514
    Utilitarian View of the Monitor's
        Fight, A, 1441
Merwin, W. S., 336, 1760
    Separation, 336

Metamorphoses, 1548
Mid-Term Break, 176
Mill, The, 174
Millay, Edna St. Vincent, 232,
    332, 721, 722, 1127, 1735,
    1736, 1760
    Childhood Is the Kingdom Where
        Nobody Dies, 332
    I, Being Born a Woman and
        Distressed, 722
    What Lips My Lips Have
        Kissed, 1127
    Women have loved before as I love
        now, 232
Miller, Arthur, 1268, 1314
    Death of a Salesman, 1315
Milosz, Czeslaw, 631, 632, 1019,
    1203, 1397, 1399, 1534, 1760
    Christopher Robin, 1399
    If There Is No God, 1019
    Orpheus and Eurydice, 1534
    Song on the End of the World,
        A, 1397
    Watering Can, 632
Milton, John, 639, 640, 1484, 1599,
    1612, 1680, 1685, 1760
    Paradise Lost, from, 640
    Lycidas, 1612
Minot, Susan, 559
    Lust, 559
Mirror, 338
Monologue of a Dog Ensnared in
    History, 1463
Morgan, Robert, 339, 1761
    Working in the Rain, 339
Much Ado about Nothing, 340
Mueller, Lisel, 1068
    Not Only the Eskimos, 1068
Mules and Men, from, 1013
Munro, Alice, 134, 634, 658, 659
    Boys and Girls, 660
    How I Met My Husband, 134
Murakami, Haruki, 658, 671, 719
    UFO in Kushiro, 671
Musée des Beaux Arts, 1062
Music to hear, why hear'st thou music
    sadly?, 1087

*My Father in the Navy: A Childhood
   Memory*,   130
My Heart Leaps Up,   1481
My Last Duchess,   303
My Last Duke,   327
My Love in Her Attire,   1119
My Papa's Waltz,   571
*My Weariness of Epic
   Proportions*,   1477
Myth,   66

Nash, Ogden,   1239, 1761
   Kind of an Ode to Duty,   1239
Negro Speaks of Rivers, The,   573
New Colossus, The,   1314
New Orleans,   444
Newbolt, Sir Henry,   1450
   Vitaï Lampada,   1450
Night Funeral in Harlem,   1638
Not only the Eskimos,   1068
Not Waving but Drowning,   299
*Now That I Am Forever with
   Child*,   165
Nuns Fret Not,   722
Nurse's Song,   514
Nut Bush Farm, from,   1585
*Nymph's Reply to the Shepherd,
   The*,   1129

O'Brien, Tim,   1412, 1419
   Things They Carried, The,   1419
O'Connor, Flannery,   214, 217
   Good Man Is Hard To Find, A,   217
Oates, Joyce Carol,   1497, 1498
   *Where Are You Going, Where Have
      You Been?*,   1498
Ode on a Grecian Urn,   1524
Ode to Autumn,   1630
*Ode to Stephen Dowling Bots,
   Dec'd*,   1591
Ode to the Confederate Dead,   1625
Oedipus the King,   67
Olds, Sharon,   576, 577, 869, 1307,
   1761
   Death of Marilyn Monroe, The,   577
   I Go Back to May 1937,   576

Possessive, The,   1307
Topography,   869
Oliver, Mary,   695, 697, 792, 793,
   1762
   Bone Poem,   793
   Ghosts,   697
   Spring,   695
Olsen, Tillie,   1412, 1434
   I Stand Here Ironing,   1412, 1434
*On Being Brought from Africa to
   America*,   771
*On First Looking into Chapman's
   Homer*,   1527
On Leavened Bread,   637
On My First Son,   520
*On the Death of Dr. Robert
   Levet*,   518
On the Robbery across the Street,   66
Ondaatje, Michael,   645
   *King Kong Meets Wallace
      Stevens*,   645
One Art,   1062
One Perfect Rose,   1008
*Ones Who Walk Away from Omeles,
   The*,   554
Oranges,   1261
*Orpheus and Eurydice
   (Graham)*,   1539
Orpheus and Eurydice (Milosz),   1534
Orpheus, Eurydice, Hermes,   1536
Owen, Wilfred,   1411, 1451, 1452,
   1762
   Anthem for Doomed Youth,   1451
   Dulce et Decorum Est,   1452
Ozymandias,   1520

Paradise Lost, from,   640
Parker, Dorothy,   284, 285, 1008,
   1009, 1762
   One Perfect Rose,   1008
   Penelope,   285
   *Thought for a Sunshiny
      Morning*,   1009
Parks, Suzan-Lori,   578, 1014
   Topdog/Underdog,   578
Parting at Morning,   1133

Passionate Shepherd to His Love,
    The, 1128
Pastan, Linda, 213, 239, 1763
    Ethics, 239
Penelope, 285
Perrault, Charles, 198
    Little Red Riding Hood, 198
Persephone, 1522
Photography 2, 300
Picture Bride, 127
Pied Beauty, 1238
Piercy, Marge, 15, 17, 202, 203, 1763
    Unlearning to not speak, 15
    Work of Artifice, A, 203
Pink Dog, 1312
Pinsky, Robert, 3, 4, 723, 1546, 1763
    Keyboard, 1546
    Poem with Lines in Any Order, 4
Pirandello, Luigi, 148
    Soft Touch of Grass, The, 148
Plath, Sylvia, 134, 167, 337, 338,
    1523, 1755, 1764
    Applicant, The, 337
    Daddy, 167
    Mirror, 338
    Two Sisters of Persephone, 1523
Plato, 1204, 1207, 1208, 1215
    Allegory of the Cave, The, 1204
Plutarch, 1706, 1707, 1709
    On Julius Caesar, 1706
Poe, Edgar Allan, 408, 415, 420,
    437, 1764
    Fall of the House of Usher, The, 421
    Raven, The, 437
Poem for My Father, 170
Poem with Lines in Any Order, 4
Poison Tree, A, 1678
Pomegranate, The, 165
Pope, Alexander, 522
    Essay on Criticism, from, 522
Porphyria's Lover, 1233
Porter, Katherine Anne, 1600
    Jilting of Granny Weatherall,
    The, 1601
Possessive, The, 1307
Pound, Ezra, 690, 1748, 1764

In a Station of the Metro, 690
Power of the Dog, The, 1641
Price of Eggs in China, The, 39
Prodigy, 333
Proposal, The, 182
Punishment, 1635

Ralegh, Sir Walter, 1129, 1764
    Nymph's Reply to the Shepherd,
    The, 1129
Randall, Dudley, 442, 1765
    Ballad of Birmingham, 442
Ras, Barbara, 452
    Childhood, 452
Raven, The, 437
Read, Herbert, 1411, 1422
    Execution of Cornelius Vane,
    The, 1442
Rear-Guard, The, 1453
Red, Red Rose, A, 1126
Red Wheelbarrow, The, 631
Remains of the Day, from, 405
Repression of War Experience, 1454
Rich, Adrienne, 180, 335, 1465,
    1549, 1765
    Aunt Jennifer's Tigers, 180
    For the Record, 1465
    I Dream I'm the Death of
    Orpheus, 1545
    Living in Sin, 335
Richard Cory, 60
Riddell, Mrs. J. H., 1585
    Nut Bush Farm, from, 1585
Riding, Laura, 805, 871
    Map of Places, The, 871
Rilke, Rainer Maria, 1536, 1565,
    1766
    Orpheus, Eurydice, Hermes, 1536
Rime of the Ancient Mariner, The, 872
Road Not Taken, The, 772
Robinson, E. A., 60, 174, 1766
    Mill, The, 174
    Richard Cory, 60
Roethke, Theodore, 571, 572, 1634,
    1766
    Elegy for Jane, 1634

My Papa's Waltz,   571
    Waking, The,   572
Rolls-Royce Dreams,   451
Roman Fever,   1108
Rosa, João Guimarães,   1209, 1265,
    1408
    Third Bank of the River, The,   1209
Rose for Emily, A,   1513
Rosenberg, Liz,   175
    1:53 A.M.,   175
Rossetti, Christina,   440, 1767
    Cobwebs,   440
Route of Evanescence, A,   59
Rukeyser, Muriel,   66, 1767
    Myth,   66
Rushdie, Salman,   637
    On Leavened Bread,   637

Sadie and Maud,   176
Sailing to Byzantium,   1533
Salter, Mary Jo,   1265, 1460, 1767
    Home Movies: A Sort of Ode,   1256
    Welcome to Hiroshima,   1460
Sandburg, Carl,   1453, 1768
    Grass,   1453
Sassoon, Siegfried,   1411, 1412, 1453,
    1454, 1768
    Rear-Guard, The,   1453
    Repression of War Experience,   1454
Scandal in Bohemia, A,   21
Secret Sharer, The,   815
Separation,   336
Set-Up, The,   62
Sexton, Anne,   1412, 1455, 1768
    Courage,   1455
Shaffer, Gina,   1412, 1466
    War Spelled Backwards,   1466
Shakespeare, William,   340, 720, 896,
    1084, 1486, 1588, 1691, 1707,
    1769
    *From fairest creatures we desire
        increase,*   1084
    Hamlet,   896
    *Is it for fear to wet a
        widow's eye,*   1087
    Julius Caesar, from,   1707
    *Lo! in the orient when the gracious
        light,*   1086

    *Look in thy glass, and tell the face thou
        viewest,*   1086
    Macbeth, from,   1588
    Much Ado about Nothing,   340
    *Music to hear, why hear'st thou music
        sadly?,*   1087
    *Shall I compare thee to a summer's
        day?,*   1088
    *When forty winters shall beseige thy
        brow,*   1085
*Shall I compare thee to a summer's
    day?,*   1088
Shelley, Percy Bysshe,   513, 1520,
    1769
    Ozymandias,   1520
Shelley,   1125
Shiner, Lewis,   1093
    *The Turkey City Lexicon: A
        Primer for Science Fiction
        Workshops,*   1769
Simic, Charles,   333, 1477, 1769
    *My Weariness of Epic
        Proportions,*   1477
    Prodigy,   333
Simple Truth, The,   726
since feeling is first,   1124
Siren Song,   1015
Sister Carrie, from,   403
Sketch, A,   776
Smith, Stevie,   299
    Not Waving but Drowning,   299
Snake,   236
Snow Man, The,   690
Soft Touch of Grass, The,   148
Soldier's Home,   1413
Song, Cathy,   126, 127, 133
    Picture Bride,   127
Song on the End of the World, A,   1397
Sonny's Blues,   527
Sophocles,   67, 1498, 1600, 1643
    Antigone,   1643
    Oedipus the King,   67
Soto, Gary,   181, 448, 450, 1261,
    1769
    Black Hair,   181
    Braly Street,   448
    Kearney Park,   450
    Oranges,   1261

Soul selects her own Society, The, 1305

Spenser, Edmund, 1228, 1770

   Faerie Queene, The, from, 1228

Spring, 695

Spring is like a perhaps hand, 1123

Stafford, William, 1770

   Traveling through the Dark, 62

Stevens, Wallace, 1770

   Snow Man, The, 690

   Thirteen Ways of Looking at a Blackbird, 691

Stoppard, Tom, 1487, 1597, 1689, 1691

   Fifteen Minute Hamlet, The, 1487

Stopping by Woods on a Snowy Evening, 61

Story of an Hour, 312

Sun Rising, The, 894

Sunday at the Apple Market, 1306

Supermarket in California, 775

Sure Thing, 778

Sward, Robert, 1092

   For Gloria on Her 60th Birthday, or Looking for Love in Merriam-Webster, 1092

Swimming Pool, The, 773

Szymborska, Wislawa, 1771

   ABC, 5, 634, 1461, 1463, 1689, 1771

   Courtesy of the Blind, The, 634

   End and the Beginning, The, 1461

   Monologue of a Dog Ensnared in History, 1463

Take, oh take those lips away, 1121

Tate, Allen, 1625, 1771

   Ode to the Confederate Dead, 1625

Tattoo, 798

Taylor, Henry, 295

   After a Movie, 295

Tell all the Truth but tell it slant—, 893

Tennyson, Alfred Lord, 522, 890, 1393, 1528, 1771

   Charge of the Light Brigade, The, 1393

Lady of Shalott, The, 1528

Lotus Eaters, The, 522

Ulysses, 890

Ten-Year Elegy, 1704

Ten-Year Elegy (plagiarized), 1704

Theme for English B, 870

There Was a Child Went Forth, 1308

There Was a Crimson Clash of War, 1446

There's a certain Slant of light, 687

Thesaurus, 1089

Things That Make a Soldier Great, The, 1449

Things They Carried, The, 1419

Thinking about Bill, Dead of AIDS, 777

Third Bank of the River, The, 1209

Thirteen Ways of Looking at a Blackbird, 691

This Blessed House, 1280

This Is Just to Say (Gambino), 329

This Is Just to Say (Williams), 328

Thomas, Dylan, 724, 1772

   Do Not Go Gentle into That Good Night, 724

Those Winter Sundays, 128

Thought for a Sunshiny Morning, 1009

Thurber, James, 201

   Girl and the Wolf, The, 201

Tichborne, Chidiock, 1633

   Elegy Written with His Own Hand in the Tower before His Execution, 1633

To Cole, the Painter, Departing for Europe, 769

To His Coy Mistress, 1130

To make a prairie it takes a clover and one bee, 893

Tootle, from, 1197

Topdog/Underdog, 578

Topography, 869

Traveling through the Dark, 62

Trifles, 700

Troupe, Quincy, 170, 1063, 1772

   Poem for My Father, 170

   Untitled, 1063

Tsui, Kitty, 171
  Chinese Banquet, A, 171
Turkey City Lexicon: A Primer for
  Science Fiction Workshops,
  The, 1093
TV Men: Lazarus, 1242
Twain, Mark, 5, 1591, 1688
  Adventures of Huckleberry Finn,
    from, 1688
  Ode to Stephen Dowling Bots,
    Dec'd, 1591
Two Sisters of Persephone, 1523
Tyger, The, 569

UFO in Kushiro, 671
Ulysses, 890
Unlearning to not speak, 15
Untitled, 1063
Up Home Where I Come From, 1479
Updike, John, 732, 742, 1642
  A&P, 743
  Dog's Death, 1642
Utilitarian View of the Monitor's
  Fight, A, 1441

Vacation, The, 291
Valediction, 1305
Valediction: Forbidding
  Mourning, A, 895
Valenzuela, Luisa, 213, 214
  Censors, The, 214
Very Old Man with Enormous
  Wings, A, 1269
Very Rigid Search, The, 748
Vitai Lampada, 1450

Waking, The, 572
Walcott, Derek, 699, 1772
  Dry Season, 699
Walker, Alice, 133, 152, 1307
  Everyday Use, 153
  Women, 1307
War Spelled Backwards, 1466
Wasserstein, Wendy, 1025, 1070,
  1483
  Medea, 1071

Watering Can, 632
We Real Cool, 574
Welcome to Hiroshima, 1460
Welty, Eudora, 847
  Worn Path, A, 847
Western Wind, 1121
Wharton, Edith, 1108, 1713, 1715
  Roman Fever, 1108
What Lips My Lips Have Kissed, 1127
What We Talk about When We Talk
  about Love, 1098
Wheatley, Phillis, 731, 771, 1773
  On Being Brought from Africa to
    America, 771
When forty winters shall beseige thy
  brow, 1085
When I have fears that I may cease to
  be, 1526
When Lilacs Last in the Dooryard
  Bloom'd, 1617
When our two souls stand up, 1132
Where Are You Going, Where Have You
  Been?, 1497
Whitman, Walt, 1038, 1066, 1617,
  1773
  There Was a Child Went
    Forth, 1308
  When Lilacs Last in the Dooryard
    Bloom'd, 1617
Wife of His Youth, 733
Wilbur, Richard, 238, 643, 695, 776,
  871, 1773
  April 5, 1974, 695
  Fable, A, 238
  Fire-Truck, A, 643
  Sketch, A, 776
  Worlds, 871
Wild Man of the Green Swamp,
  The, 205
Wild Nights—Wild Nights!, 1124
Wild Swans at Coole, The, 1311
Wilde, Oscar, 441, 1774
  Harlot's House, The, 441
Williams, Miller, 777, 1774
  Thinking about Bill, Dead of
    AIDS, 777

Williams, Tennessee, 409, 415, 455
   Glass Menagerie, The, 456
Williams, William Carlos, 328, 329,
   631, 1203, 1310, 1748, 1763,
   1774
   At the Ball Game, 1310
   Red Wheelbarrow, The, 631
   This Is Just to Say, 328
Windhover, The, 1239
Woman Hanging from the Thirteenth
   Floor Window, The, 446
Women, 1307
Women have loved before as I love
   now, 232
Wordsworth, William, 684,
   685, 686, 721, 722, 1079,
   1481, 1775
   Composed upon Westminster Bridge,
      September 3, 1802, 685
   I wandered lonely as a cloud, 686
   London, 1802, 684
   My Heart Leaps Up, 1481
   Nuns Fret Not, 722
   World Is Too Much with Us,
      The, 686

Work of Artifice, A, 203
Working in the Rain, 339
World Is Too Much with Us, The, 686
Worlds, 871
Worn Path, A, 847
Wyatt, Thomas, 1098, 1122, 1735
   Long love that in my heart doth
      harbor, the, 1122

Yeats, William Butler, 235, 792,
   1268, 1533, 1775
   Folly of Being Comforted, The, 792
   Leda and the Swan, 235
   Sailing to Byzantium, 1533
   Wild Swans at Coole, The, 1311
Yellow Wallpaper, The, 314
you fit into me, 1007
Young, Kevin, 62, 1775
   Chase, The, 64
   Set-Up, The, 62
Young Goodman Brown, 1216

Zimmerman, Mary, 1498, 1547
   Metamorphoses, 1548